Department of Economic and
Social Affairs

Statistics Division

Département des affaires économiques
et sociales

Division de statistique

Statistical Yearbook
Forty-seventh issue

2000
Data available as of
31 January 2003

Annuaire statistique
Quarante-septième édition

Données disponibles
au 31 janvier 2003

United Nations/Nations Unies • New York, 2003

Note

The designations employed and the presentation of material in this publication do not imply the expression of any opinion whatsoever on the part of the Secretariat of the United Nations concerning the legal status of any country, territory, city or area or of its authorities, or concerning the delimitation of its frontiers or boundaries.

In general, statistics contained in the present publication are those available to the United Nations Secretariat up to January 2003 and refer to 2000/2001 or earlier. They therefore reflect country nomenclature currently in use.

The term "country" as used in this publication also refers, as appropriate, to territories or areas.

The designations "developed" and "developing" are intended for statistical convenience and do not necessarily express a judgement about the stage reached by a particular country or area in the development process.

Symbols of United Nations documents are composed of capital letters combined with figures.

Note

Les appellations employées dans la présente publication et la présentation des données qui y figurent n'impliquent, de la part du Secrétariat de l'Organisation des Nations Unies, aucune prise de position quant au statut juridique des pays, territoires, villes ou zones, ou de leurs autorités, ni quant au tracé de leurs frontières ou limites.

En règle générale, les statistiques contenues dans la présente publication sont celles dont disposait le Secrétariat de l'Organisation des Nations Unies jusqu'à janvier 2003 et portent sur la période finissant en 2001. Elles reflètent donc la nomenclature des pays en vigueur à l'époque.

Le terme "pays", tel qu'il est utilisé ci-après, peut également désigner des territoires ou des zones.

Les appellations "développées" et "en développement" sont employées à des fins exclusivement statistiques et n'expriment pas nécessairement un jugement quant au niveau de développement atteint par tel pays ou telle région.

Les cotes des documents de l'Organisation des Nations Unies se composent de lettres majuscules et de chiffres.

ST/ESA/STAT/SER.S/23

UNITED NATIONS PUBLICATION
Sales No. E/F.02.XVII.1

PUBLICATION DES NATIONS UNIES
Numéro de vente : E/F.02.XVII.1

ISBN 92-1-061202-7
ISSN 0082-8459

Inquiries should be directed to:

SALES SECTION
PUBLISHING DIVISION
UNITED NATIONS
NEW YORK 10017
USA

Adresser toutes demandes de renseignements à la :

SECTION DES VENTES
DIVISION DES PUBLICATIONS
NATIONS UNIES
NEW YORK 10017
ÉTATS-UNIS D'AMÉRIQUE

E-mail: publications@un.org
Internet: http://www.un.org/Pubs

Preface

The present United Nations *Statistical Yearbook* is the forty-seventh issue in a series initiated in 1948. It has been prepared by the Statistics Division of the Department of Economic and Social Affairs, and contains series covering, in general, 1991-2000 or 1992-2001. For the most part the statistics presented are those which were available to the Statistics Division as of 31 January 2003.

The 83 tables of the *Yearbook* are based on data compiled by the Statistics Division from over 35 international and national sources. These sources include the United Nations Statistics Division in the fields of national accounts, industry, energy, transport and international trade, the United Nations Statistics Division and Population Division in the field of demographic statistics, and over 20 offices of the United Nations system and international organizations in other specialized fields.

United Nations agencies and other international, national and specialized organizations which furnished data are listed under "Statistical sources and references" at the end of the *Yearbook*. Acknowledgement is gratefully made for their generous cooperation in continually providing data.

The Statistics Division also publishes the *Monthly Bulletin of Statistics* [26]*, which provides a valuable complement to the *Yearbook* by covering current international economic statistics for most countries and areas of the world and quarterly world and regional aggregates. Subscribers to the print version of the *Monthly Bulletin of Statistics* are provided full on-line access to the Internet version. The *MBS On-Line* allows time-sensitive statistics to reach users much faster than the traditional print publication. For further information see <http://unstats.un.org/unsd/>.

Recognizing the interest in obtaining statistics in machine-readable form for further study and analysis by users, the *Yearbook* has also been published on CD-ROM for IBM-compatible microcomputers, since the thirty-eighth issue. The CD-ROM contains time series data from 1980 to the most recent year available, and includes the historical data of those series not shown in the present print version due to space limitations. Ad hoc or standing orders for the *Yearbook* in print and/or on CD-ROM may be placed with United Nations Publications sales offices in New York and Geneva. A full list of machine- readable products in statistics available from the United Nations Statistics Division may be obtained, upon request, from the Statistics

Préface

La présente édition de l'*Annuaire statistique* des Nations Unies est la quarante-septième d'une série instaurée en 1948. Elle a été préparée par la Division de statistique du Département des affaires économiques et sociales et contient des séries qui portent d'une manière générale sur la période 1991 à 2000 ou 1992 à 2001 et pour lesquelles ont été utilisées les informations dont disposait la Division de statistique au 31 janvier 2003.

Les 83 tableaux de l'*Annuaire* sont établis à partir des données que la Division de statistique a recueillies auprès de plus de 35 sources, internationales et nationales. Ces sources sont: la Division de statistique du Secrétariat de l'Organisation des Nations Unies pour ce qui concerne les comptabilités nationales, les industries manufacturières, l'énergie, les transports et le commerce international, la Division de statistique et la Division de la population du Secrétariat de l'Organisation des Nations Unies pour les statistiques démographiques; et plus de 20 bureaux du système des Nations Unies et d'organisations internationales pour les autres domaines spécialisés.

Les institutions spécialisées des Nations Unies et les autres organisations internationales, nationales et spécialisées qui ont fourni des données sont énumérées dans la section "Sources statistiques et références" figurant à la fin de l'ouvrage. Les auteurs de l'*Annuaire statistique* les remercient de leur généreuse coopération.

La Division de Statistique publie également le *Bulletin Mensuel de Statistiques* [26]*, qui est un complément intéressant à l'*Annuaire Statistique* qui couvre les statistiques économiques courantes sur la plupart des pays et zones du monde et des aggrégats trimestriels, au niveau du monde et des grandes régions. Les abonnés à l'édition imprimée du *Bulletin Mensuel de Statistiques* ont aussi à leur disposition le *Bulletin* en ligne, accessible sur Internet. Grâce à "BMS en ligne" les utilisateurs disposent plus rapidement des données conjonctuelles que par la voie traditionnelle de la publication imprimée. Pour des informations supplémentaires, voir <http://unstats.un.org/unsd/>.

En raison de l'intérêt que suscite la présentation de statistiques sur des supports lisibles en machine et exploitables directement par l'utilisateur, l'*Annuaire* a été publiée sur disque compact (CD/ROM) pour micro-ordinateurs IBM et compatibles depuis la publication de la trente-huitième édition. Le CD-ROM contient des séries chronologiques allant de 1980 à la dernière année pour laquelle on dispose de statistiques, y compris les données historiques qui, faute d'espace suffisant, n'apparaissent pas dans la présente version imprimée de l'*Annuaire*. Les commandes individuelles et les

---

*   Numbers in square brackets in the text refer to numbered entries in the section "Statistical sources and references".

*   Les chiffres entre crochets dans le texte se réfèrent aux entrées numérotées dans la section «Sources statistiques et références».

Division of the United Nations Secretariat, New York or from the Division's Internet home page <http://unstats.un.org/unsd/>.

The *Yearbook* is organized in four parts. The first part, World and Region Summary, presents key world and regional aggregates and totals. In the other three parts, the subject matter is generally presented by countries or areas, with world and regional aggregates shown in some cases only. Parts two, three and four cover, respectively, population and social topics, national economic activity, and international economic relations. The organization of the population and social topics generally follows the arrangement of subject matter in the United Nations *Handbook on Social Indicators* [48]; economic activity is taken up according to the classes of the United Nations International Standard Industrial Classification of All Economic Activities (ISIC) [50]. The tables on international economic relations cover merchandise trade, international tourism (a major factor in international trade in services and balance of payments) and financial transactions including development assistance. Each chapter ends with brief technical notes on statistical sources and methods for the tables it includes. References to sources and related methodological publications are provided at the end of the *Yearbook* in the section "Statistical sources and references".

Annex I provides complete information on country and area nomenclature, and regional and other groupings used in the *Yearbook*. Annex II lists conversion coefficients and factors used in various tables. Symbols and conventions used in the *Yearbook* are shown in the section "Explanatory notes", preceding the Introduction.

A list of tables added to or omitted from the last issue of the *Yearbook* is given in annex III. Tables for which a sufficient amount of new data is not available are not being published in this *Yearbook*. Their titles nevertheless are still listed in the table of contents since it is planned that they will be published in a later issue as new data are compiled by the collecting agency. However, the complete set of tables is retained in the CD-ROM version of the *Yearbook*.

As described more fully in the Introduction below, every attempt has been made to ensure that the series contained in the *Yearbook* are sufficiently comparable to provide a reliable general description of economic and social topics throughout the world. Nevertheless, the reader should carefully consult the footnotes and technical notes for any given table for explanations of general limitations of series presented and specific limitations affecting particular data items; the section "comparability of statistics" should also be consulted. Readers interested in more detailed figures than those shown in the present publication, and in further information on the full range of internationally assembled statistics in specialized fields, should also consult the specialized publications listed in the "Statistical sources and references" at the end of the *Yearbook*.

abonnements à l'*Annuaire statistique* (édition imprimée ou sur CD/ROM) peuvent être adressées aux bureaux de vente des publications des Nations Unies à New York et à Genève ou sur Internet page d'accueil de la Division <http://unstats.un.org/unsd/>.

Le plan de l'*Annuaire* comprend quatre parties. La première partie, "Aperçu mondial et régional", se compose des principaux agrégats et totaux aux niveaux mondial et régional. Les trois autres sont consacrées à la population et aux questions sociales (deuxième partie), à l'activité économique nationale (troisième partie) et aux relations économiques internationales (quatrième partie). L'organisation de la deuxième partie, "Population et questions sociales", suit généralement le plan adopté par l'ONU "*Manuel des indicateurs sociaux*" [48]; dans la troisième partie, l'activité économique est présentée conformément aux catégories adoptées par l'ONU dans la *Classification internationale type, par industrie, de toutes les branches d'activité économique* [50]. Les tableaux de la quatrième partie, consacrée aux relations économiques internationales, portent sur le commerce des marchandises, le tourisme international (élément essentiel du secteur international des services et balance des paiements) et les opérations financières, y compris l'aide au développement. Chaque chapitre termine avec une brève note technique sur les sources et méthodes statistiques utilisées pour les tableaux du chapitre. On trouvera à la fin de l'*Annuaire*, dans la section "Sources statistiques et références", des références aux sources et publications méthodologiques connexes.

L'annexe I donne des renseignements complets sur la nomenclature des pays et des zones et sur la façon dont ceux-ci ont été regroupés pour former les régions et autres entités géographiques utilisées dans l'*Annuaire*; l'annexe II fournit des renseignements sur les coefficients et facteurs de conversion employés dans les différents tableaux. Les divers symboles et conventions utilisés dans l'*Annuaire* sont présentés dans la section "Notes explicatives" qui précède l'introduction.

Une liste des tableaux ajoutés et supprimés depuis la dernière édition de l'*Annuaire* figure à l'annexe III. Les tableaux pour lesquels on ne dispose pas d'une quantité suffisante des données nouvelles, n'ont pas été publiés dans cet *Annuaire*. Comme ils seront repris dans une prochaine édition à mesure que des données nouvelles seront dépouillées par l'office statistique d'origine, ses titres figurent toujours dans la table des matières. Tous les tableaux sont cependant repris dans l'édition publiée sur CD/ROM.

Comme il est précisé ci-après dans l'introduction, aucun effort n'a été épargné afin que les séries figurant dans l'*Annuaire* soient suffisamment comparables pour fournir une description générale fiable de la situation économique et sociale dans le monde entier. Néanmoins, le lecteur devra consulter avec soins les renvois individuels et les notes techniques de chaque tableau pour y trouver l'explication des limites générales imposées aux séries présentées et des limites particulières propres à

Needless to say, much more can be done to improve the *Yearbook*'s scope, coverage, timeliness, design, and technical notes. The process is inevitably an evolutionary one. Comments on the present *Yearbook* and its future evolution are welcome and should be addressed to the Director, United Nations Statistics Division, New York 10017 USA, or via e-mail to statistics@un.org.

certains types de données; aussi le lecteur devra consulter la section "comparabilité des statistiques". Les lecteurs qui souhaitent avoir des chiffres plus détaillés que ceux figurant dans le présent volume ou qui désirent se procurer des renseignements sur la gamme complète des statistiques qui ont été compilées à l'échelon international dans tel ou tel domaine particulier devraient consulter les publications énumérées dans la section "Sources statistiques et références".

Inutile de dire qu'il reste beaucoup à faire pour mettre l'*Annuaire* pleinement à jour en ce qui concerne son champ, sa couverture, sa mise à jour, sa conception générale, et ses notes techniques. Il s'agit là inévitablement d'un processus évolutif. Les observations sur la présente édition de l'*Annuaire* et les modifications suggérées pour l'avenir seront reçues avec intérêt et doivent être adressées au Directeur de la Division de statistique de l'ONU, New York, N.Y. 10017 (États-Unis d'Amérique), ou e-mail à statistics@un.org.

Contents

Table des matières

Part Four
International Economic Relations

Quatrième partie
Relations économiques internationales

# List of tables	# Liste des tableaux

**   Asterisks preceding table names identify tables presented in previous issues of the *Statistical Yearbook* but not contained in the present issue because of insufficient new data. These tables will be updated in future issues of the *Yearbook* when new data become available.

**   Ce symbole indique les tableaux publiés dans les éditions précédentes de l'*Annuaire statistique* mais qui n'ont pas été repris dans la présente édition fautes de données nouvelles suffisantes. Ces tableaux seront actualisés dans les futures livraisons de l'*Annuaire* à mesure que des données nouvelles deviendront disponibles.

Explanatory notes

In general, the statistics presented in the present publication are based on information available to the Statistics Division of the United Nations Secretariat as of 31 January 2003.

Units of measurement

The metric system of weights and measures has been employed throughout the *Statistical Yearbook*. For conversion coefficients and factors, see annex II.

Country notes and nomenclature

As a general rule, the data presented in the *Yearbook* relate to a given country or area within its present de facto boundaries. A complete list of countries and territories is presented in Annex I.

Changes in country names are reflected in Annex I. The most recent name changes that the reader should be aware of are: Serbia and Montenegro, previously listed as Yugoslavia; and Timor-Leste, formerly listed as East Timor.

It should also be noted that unless otherwise indicated, for statistical purposes the data for China exclude those for Hong Kong Special Administrative Region of China, Macao Special Administrative Region of China and Taiwan province of China.

Symbols and conventions used in the tables

A point (.) is used to indicate decimals.

A hyphen (-) between years, e.g., 1994-1995, indicates the full period involved, including the beginning and end years; a slash (/) indicates a financial year, school year or crop year, e.g., 1994/95.

Not applicable or not separately reported	..
Data not available	...
Magnitude zero	-
Less than half of unit employed	0 or 0.0
Provisional or estimated figure	*
United Nations estimate	x
Marked break in series	#

Details and percentages in the tables do not necessarily add to totals because of rounding.

Numbers in square brackets ([ ]) in the text refer to the numbered entries in the section "Statistical sources and references" at the end of the *Yearbook*.

Notes explicatives

En général, les statistiques qui figurent dans la présente publication sont fondées sur les informations dont disposait la Division de statistique du Secrétariat de l'ONU au 31 janvier 2003.

Unités de mesure

Le système métrique de poids et mesures a été utilisé dans tout l'*Annuaire statistique*. On trouvera à l'annexe II les coefficients et facteurs de conversion.

Notes sur les pays et nomenclature

En règle générale, les données renvoient au pays ou zone en question dans ses frontières actuelles effectives. Une liste complete des pays et territoires figure à l'annexe I.

Le lecteur est renvoyé à l'annexe I où il trouvera une liste des changements de désignation. Les changements de nom de pays survenus récemment sont: Serbie-et-Monténégro, apparaissait antérieurement sous le nom de Yougoslavie; et Timor-Leste, apparaissait antérieurement sous le nom de Timor Oriental.

Il convient de noter aussi que sauf indication contraire, les données statistiques relatives à la Chine ne comprennent pas celles qui concernent la région administrative spéciale de Hong Kong, la région administrative spéciale de Macao et la province chinoise de Taiwan.

Signes et conventions employés dans les tableaux:

Les décimales sont précédées d'un point (.).

Un tiret (-) entre des années, par exemple "1994-1995", indique que la période est embrassée dans sa totalité, y compris la première et la dernière année; une barre oblique (/) renvoie à un exercice financier, à une année scolaire ou à une campagne agricole, par exemple "1994/95".

Non applicable ou non communiqué séparément	..
Données non disponibles	...
Néant	-
Valeur inférieure à la moitié de la dernière unité retenue	0 ou 0.0
Chiffre provisoire ou estimatif	*
Estimation des Nations Unies	x
Discontinuité notable dans la série	#

Les chiffres étant arrondis, les totaux ne correspondent pas toujours à la somme exacte des éléments ou pourcentages figurant dans les tableaux.

Les chiffres figurant entre crochets ([ ]) se réfèrent aux entrées numérotées dans la liste des sources et références statistiques à la fin de l'ouvrage.

Introduction

This is the forty-seventh issue of the United Nations *Statistical Yearbook*, prepared by the Statistics Division, Department of Economic and Social Affairs of the United Nations Secretariat. It presents series covering, in general, 1991-2000 or 1992-2001, based on statistics available to the Statistics Division up to 31 January 2003.

The main purpose of the *Statistical Yearbook* is to provide in a single volume a comprehensive compilation of internationally available statistics on social and economic conditions and activities, at world, regional and national levels, covering, whenever possible, a ten-year period.

Most of the statistics presented in the *Yearbook* are extracted from more detailed, specialized publications prepared by the Statistics Division and by many other international statistical services. Thus, while the specialized publications concentrate on monitoring topics and trends in particular social and economic fields, the *Statistical Yearbook* tables provide data for a more comprehensive, overall description of social and economic structures, conditions, changes and activities. The objective has been to collect, systematize and coordinate the most essential components of comparable statistical information which can give a broad and, to the extent feasible, a consistent picture of social and economic processes at world, regional and national levels.

More specifically, the *Statistical Yearbook* provides systematic information on a wide range of social and economic issues which are of concern in the United Nations system and among the governments and peoples of the world. A particular value of the *Yearbook*, but also its greatest challenge, is that these issues are extensively interrelated. Meaningful analysis of these issues requires systematization and coordination of the data across many fields. These issues include:

— General economic growth and related economic conditions;

— The economic situation in developing countries and progress towards the objectives adopted for the United Nations development decades;

— Population and urbanization, and their growth and impact;

— Employment, inflation and wages;

— Energy production and consumption and the development of new energy sources;

— Expansion of trade;

— Supply of food and alleviation of hunger;

— The financial situation of countries and external payments and receipts;

— Education, training and eradication of illiteracy;

— Improvement in general living conditions;

— Pollution and protection of the environment;

Introduction

La présente édition est la quarante-septième de l'*Annuaire statistique* des Nations Unies, établi par la Division de statistique du Département des affaires économiques et sociales du Secrétariat de l'Organisation des Nations Unies. Elle contient des séries de données qui portent d'une manière générale sur les années 1991 à 2000 ou 1992 à 2001, et pour lesquelles ont été utilisées les informations dont disposait la Division de statistique au 31 janvier 2003.

L'*Annuaire statistique* a principalement pour objet de présenter en un seul volume un inventaire complet de statistiques disponibles sur le plan international et concernant la situation et les activités sociales et économiques aux échelons mondial, régional et national, pour une période d'environ dix ans.

Une bonne partie des données qui figurent dans l'*Annuaire* existent sous une forme plus détaillée dans les publications spécialisées établies par la Division de statistique et par bien d'autres services statistiques internationaux. Alors que les publications spécialisées suivent essentiellement l'évolution dans certains domaines socio-économiques précis, l'*Annuaire statistique* présente les données de manière à fournir une description plus globale et exhaustive des structures, conditions, transformations et activités socio-économiques. On a cherché à recueillir, systématiser et coordonner les principaux éléments de renseignements statistiques comparables, de manière à dresser un tableau général et autant que possible cohérent des processus socio-économiques en cours aux échelons mondial, régional et national.

Plus précisément, l'*Annuaire statistique* a pour objet de présenter des renseignements systématiques sur toutes sortes de questions socio-économiques qui sont liées aux préoccupations actuelles du système des Nations Unies ainsi que des gouvernements et des peuples du monde. Le principal avantage de l'*Annuaire* — et aussi la principale difficulté à surmonter — tient à ce que ces questions sont étroitement interdépendantes. Pour en faire une analyse utile, il est essentiel de systématiser et de coordonner les données se rapportant à de nombreux domaines différents. Ces questions sont notamment les suivantes:

— La croissance économique générale et les aspects connexes de l'économie;

— La situation économique dans les pays en développement et les progrès accomplis vers la réalisation des objectifs des décennies des Nations Unies pour le développement;

— La population et l'urbanisation, leur croissance et leur impact;

— L'emploi, l'inflation et les salaires;

— La production et la consommation d'énergie et la mise en valeur des énergies nouvelles;

— L'expansion des échanges;

— Assistance provided to developing countries for social and economic development purposes.

Organization of the *Yearbook*

The contents of the *Statistical Yearbook* are planned to serve a general readership. The *Yearbook* endeavours to provide information for various bodies of the United Nations system as well as for other international organizations, for governments and non-governmental organizations, for national statistical, economic and social policy bodies, for scientific and educational institutions, for libraries and for the public. Data published in the *Statistical Yearbook* are also of interest to companies and enterprises and to agencies engaged in marketing research.

The 83 tables of the *Yearbook* are grouped into four broad parts:

— Part One: World and Region Summary (chapter I, tables 1-7);

— Part Two: Population and Social Statistics (chapters II-V: tables 8-19);

— Part Three: Economic Activity (chapters VI-XV: tables 20-71);

— Part Four: International Economic Relations (chapters XVI-XX: tables 72-83).

These four parts together present data at two levels of aggregation. The more aggregated information shown in Part One provides an overall picture of development at the world and region levels. More specific and detailed information for analysis concerning individual countries or areas is presented in the three following parts. Each of these parts is divided into chapters, by topic, and each chapter ends with a section on "Technical notes", which provides brief descriptions of major statistical concepts, definitions and classifications required for interpretation and analysis of the data. Systematic information on the methodology used for the computation of the figures can be found in the publications on methodology of the United Nations and its agencies, listed in the section "Statistical sources and references" at the end of the *Yearbook*. Additional general information on statistical methodology is provided in the section below on "Comparability of statistics" and in the explanatory notes following the Introduction.

Part One, World and Region Summary, comprises seven tables highlighting the principal trends in the world as well as in each of the regions and in the major economic and social sectors. It contains global totals of important aggregate statistics needed for the analysis of economic growth, the structure of the world economy, major changes in world population and expansion of external merchandise trade. The global totals are, as a rule, subdivided into major geographical areas.

Part Two, Population and Social Statistics, comprises 12 tables which contain more detailed statistical series on population, social conditions and levels of living, for example, illiteracy, health, culture and communication.

— Les approvisionnements alimentaires et la lutte contre la faim;

— La situation financière, les paiements extérieurs et les recettes extérieures;

— L'éducation, la formation et l'élimination de l'analphabétisme;

— L'amélioration des conditions de vie;

— La pollution et la protection de l'environnement;

— L'assistance fournie aux pays en développement à des fins socio-économiques.

Présentation de l'*Annuaire*

Le contenu de l'*Annuaire statistique* a été préparé à l'intention de tous les lecteurs intéressés. Les renseignements fournis devraient pouvoir être utilisés par les divers organismes du système des Nations Unies ainsi que par d'autres organisations internationales, par les gouvernements et les organisations non gouvernementales, par les organismes nationaux de statistique et de politique économique et sociale, par les institutions scientifiques et les établissements d'enseignement, les bibliothèques et les particuliers. Les données publiées dans l'*Annuaire statistique* peuvent également intéresser les sociétés et entreprises, et les organismes spécialisés dans les études de marché.

Les 83 tableaux de l'*Annuaire* sont groupés en quatre parties:

— La première partie: Aperçu mondial et régional (chapitre I, tableaux 1 à 7);

— La deuxième partie: Statistiques démographiques et sociales (chapitres II à V, tableaux 8 à 19);

— La troisième partie: Activité économique (chapitres VI à XV, tableaux 20 à 71);

— La quatrième partie: Relations économiques internationales (chapitres XVI à XX, tableaux 72 à 83).

Ces quatre parties présentent les données à deux niveaux d'agrégation: les valeurs les plus agrégées qui figurent dans la première partie donnent un tableau global du développement à l'échelon mondial et régional, tandis que les trois autres parties contiennent des renseignements plus précis et détaillés qui se prêtent mieux à une analyse par pays ou par zones. Chacune de ces trois parties est divisée en chapitres portant sur des sujets donnés, et chaque chapitre comprend une section intitulée "Notes techniques" où l'on trouve une brève description des principales notions, définitions et classifications statistiques nécessaires pour interpréter et analyser les données. Les méthodes de calcul utilisées sont décrites de façon systématique dans les publications se référant à la méthodologie des Nations Unies et de leurs organismes, énumérées à la fin de l'*Annuaire* dans la section "Sources et références statistiques". Le lecteur trouvera un complément d'informations générales ci-après dans la section intitulée "Comparabilité des statistiques", ainsi que dans les notes explicatives qui suivent l'introduction.

Of the 52 tables in Part Three, Economic Activity, 27 provide data on national accounts, index numbers of industrial production, interest rates, labour force, wages and prices, transport, energy, environment, science and technology and intellectual property; 25 tables provide data on production in the major branches of the economy (using, in general, the International Standard Industrial Classification, ISIC), namely agriculture, hunting, forestry and fishing, and manufacturing. Consumption data are combined with the production data in tables on specific commodities, where feasible.

Part Four, International Economic Relations, comprises 12 tables on international merchandise trade, balance of payments, international tourism, international finance and development assistance.

An index (in English only) is provided at the end of the *Yearbook*.

Annexes and regional groupings of countries or areas

The annexes to the *Statistical Yearbook* and the section "Explanatory notes" preceding the Introduction, provide additional essential information on the *Yearbook*'s contents and presentation of data.

Annex I provides information on countries or areas covered in the *Yearbook* tables and on their grouping into geographical regions. The geographical groupings shown in the *Yearbook* are generally based on continental regions unless otherwise indicated. However, strict consistency in this regard is impossible. A wide range of classifications is used for different purposes in the various international agencies and other sources of statistics for the *Yearbook*. These classifications vary in response to administrative and analytical requirements.

Similarly, there is no common agreement in the United Nations system concerning the terms "developed" and "developing" when referring to the stage of development reached by any given country or area, and its corresponding classification in one or the other grouping. The *Yearbook* thus refers more generally to "developed" or "developing" regions on the basis of conventional practice. Following this practice, "developed regions" comprises Northern America, Europe and the former USSR, Australia, Japan and New Zealand, while all of Africa and the remainder of the Americas, Asia and Oceania comprise the "developing regions". These designations are intended for statistical convenience and do not necessarily express a judgement about the stage reached by a particular country or area in the development process.

Annex II provides detailed information on conversion coefficients and factors used in various tables, and annex III provides listings of tables added and omitted in the present edition of the *Yearbook*.

La première partie, intitulée "Aperçu mondial et régional", comprend sept tableaux présentant les principales tendances dans le monde et dans les régions ainsi que dans les principaux secteurs économiques et sociaux. Elle fournit des chiffres mondiaux pour les principaux agrégats statistiques nécessaires pour analyser la croissance économique, la structure de l'économie mondiale, les principaux changements dans la population mondiale et l'expansion du commerce extérieur de marchandises. En règle générale, les chiffres mondiaux sont ventilés par grandes régions géographiques.

La deuxième partie, intitulée "Statistiques démographiques et sociales", comporte 12 tableaux où figurent des séries plus détaillées concernant la population, les conditions sociales et les niveaux de vie, notamment des données sur l'alphabétisation, la santé, la culture et la communication.

La troisième partie, intitulée "Activité économique", comporte 52 tableaux, 27 qui présentent des statistiques concernant les comptes nationaux, les nombres indices relatifs à la production industrielle, les taux d'intérêt, la population active, les prix et les salaires, le transport, l'énergie, l'environnement, la science et technologie, et la propriété intellectuelle; et 25 qui présentent des données sur la production des principales branches d'activité économique (en utilisant en général la *Classification internationale type, par industrie, de toutes les branches d'activité économique*): agriculture, chasse, sylviculture et pêche, et industries manufacturières. Les tableaux traitant de certains produits de base associent autant que possible les données relatives à la consommation aux valeurs concernant la production.

La quatrième partie, intitulée "Relations économiques internationales", comprend 12 tableaux relatifs au commerce international de marchandises, aux balances des paiements, au tourisme international, aux finances internationales, et à l'aide au développement.

Un index (en anglais seulement) figure à la fin de l'*Annuaire*.

Annexes et groupements régionaux des pays et zones

Les annexes à l'*Annuaire statistique* et la section intitulée "Notes explicatives" qui précède l'introduction, offrent d'importantes informations complémentaires quant à la teneur et à la présentation des données figurant dans le présent ouvrage.

L'annexe I donne des renseignements sur les pays ou zones couverts par les tableaux de l'*Annuaire* et sur leur regroupement en régions géographiques. Sauf indication contraire, les groupements géographiques figurant dans l'*Annuaire* sont généralement fondés sur les régions continentales, mais une présentation absolument systématique est impossible à cet égard car les diverses institutions internationales et autres sources de statistiques employées pour la confection de l'*Annuaire*

Comparability of statistics

One major aim of the *Statistical Yearbook* is to present series which are as nearly comparable across countries as the available statistics permit. Considerable efforts are also made among the international suppliers of data and by the staff of the *Yearbook* to ensure the compatibility of various series by coordinating time periods, base years, prices chosen for valuation and so on. This is indispensable in relating various bodies of data to each other and to facilitate analysis across different sectors. Thus, for example, relating data on economic output to those on employment makes it possible to derive some trends in the field of productivity; relating data on exports and imports to those on national product allows an evaluation of the relative importance of external trade in different countries and reveals changes in the role of trade over time.

In general, the data presented reflect the methodological recommendations of the United Nations Statistical Commission, issued in various United Nations publications, and of other international bodies concerned with statistics. Publications containing these recommendations and guidelines are listed in the section "Statistical sources and references" at the end of the *Yearbook*. Use of international recommendations not only promotes international comparability of the data but also ensures a degree of compatibility regarding the underlying concepts, definitions and classifications relating to different series. However, much work remains to be done in this area and, for this reason, some tables can serve only as a first source of data, which require further adjustment before being used for more in-depth analytical studies. While on the whole, a significant degree of comparability has been achieved in international statistics, there are many limitations, for a variety of reasons.

One common cause of non-comparability of economic data is different valuations of statistical aggregates such as national income, wages and salaries, output of industries and so forth. Conversion of these and similar series originally expressed in national prices into a common currency, for example into United States dollars, through the use of exchange rates, is not always satisfactory owing to frequent wide fluctuations in market rates and differences between official rates and rates which would be indicated by unofficial markets or purchasing power parities. For this reason, data on national income in United States dollars which are published in the *Yearbook* are subject to certain distortions and can be used as only a rough approximation of the relative magnitudes involved.

The use of different kinds of sources for obtaining data is another cause of incomparability. This is true, for example, in the case of employment and unemployment, where data are collected from such non-comparable sources as sample surveys, social insurance statistics and establishment surveys.

emploient, selon l'objet de l'exercice, des classifications fort différentes en réponse à diverses exigences d'ordre administratif ou analytique.

Il n'existe pas non plus dans le système des Nations Unies de définition commune des termes "développé" et "en développement" pour décrire le niveau atteint en la matière par un pays ou une zone donnés ni pour les classifier dans l'un ou l'autre de ces groupes. Ainsi, dans l'*Annuaire*, on s'en remet à l'usage pour qualifier les régions de "développées" ou "en développement". Selon cet usage, les régions développées sont l'Amérique septentrionale, l'Europe et l'ancienne URSS, l'Australie, le Japon et la Nouvelle-Zélande, alors que toute l'Afrique et le reste des Amériques, l'Asie et l'Océanie constituent les régions en développement. Ces appellations sont utilisées pour plus de commodité dans la présentation des statistiques et n'impliquent pas nécessairement un jugement quant au stade de développement auquel est parvenu tel pays ou telle zone.

L'annexe II fournit des renseignements sur les coefficients et facteurs de conversion employés dans les différents tableaux, et l'annexe III contient les listes de tableaux qui ont été ajoutés ou omis dans la présente édition de l'*Annuaire*.

Comparabilité des statistiques

L'*Annuaire statistique* a principalement pour objet de présenter des statistiques aussi comparables d'un pays à l'autre que les données le permettent. Les sources internationales de données et les auteurs de l'*Annuaire* ont réalisés des efforts considérables pour faire en sorte que les diverses séries soient compatibles en harmonisant les périodes de référence, les années de base, les prix utilisés pour les évaluations, etc. Cette démarche est indispensable si l'on veut rapprocher divers ensembles de données pour faciliter l'analyse intersectorielle de l'économie. Ainsi, en liant les données concernant la production à celles de l'emploi, on parvient à dégager certaines tendances dans le domaine de la productivité; de même, en associant les données concernant les exportations et importations aux valeurs du produit national, on obtient une évaluation de l'importance relative des échanges extérieurs dans différents pays et de l'évolution du rôle joué par le commerce.

De façon générale, les données sont présentées selon les recommandations méthodologiques formulées par la Commission de statistique de l'ONU et par les autres organisations internationales qui s'intéressent aux statistiques. Les titres des publications contenant ces recommandations et lignes directrices figurent à la fin de l'ouvrage dans la section intitulée "Sources et références statistiques". Le respect des recommandations internationales tend non seulement à promouvoir la comparabilité des données à l'échelon international, mais elle assure également une certaine comparabilité entre les concepts, les définitions et classifications utilisés. Mais comme il reste encore beaucoup à faire dans ce domaine, les don-

Non-comparability of data may also result from differences in the institutional patterns of countries. Certain variations in social and economic organization and institutions may have an impact on the comparability of the data even if the underlying concepts and definitions are identical.

These and other causes of non-comparability of the data are briefly explained in the technical notes to each chapter.

Statistical sources and reliability and timeliness of data

Statistics and indicators have been compiled mainly from official national and international sources, as these are more authoritative and comprehensive, more generally available as time series and more comparable among countries than other sources. In a few cases, official sources are supplemented by other sources and estimates, where these have been subjected to professional scrutiny and debate and are consistent with other independent sources. The comprehensive international data sources used for most of the tables are presented in the list of "Statistical sources and references" at the end of the *Yearbook*.

Users of international statistics are often concerned about the apparent lack of timeliness in the available data. Unfortunately, most international data are only available with a delay of at least one to three years after the latest year to which they refer. The reasons for the delay are that the data must first be processed by the national statistical services at the country level, then forwarded to the international statistical services and processed again to ensure as much consistency across countries and over time as possible.

nées présentées dans certains tableaux n'ont qu'une valeur indicative et nécessiteront des ajustements plus poussés avant de pouvoir servir à des analyses approfondies. Bien que l'on soit parvenu, dans l'ensemble, à un degré de comparabilité appréciable en matière de statistiques internationales, diverses raisons expliquent que subsistent encore de nombreuses limitations.

Une cause commune de non-comparabilité des données réside dans la diversité des méthodes d'évaluation employées pour comptabiliser des agrégats tels que le revenu national, les salaires et traitements, la production des différentes branches d'activité industrielle, etc. Il n'est pas toujours satisfaisant de ramener la valeur des séries de ce type — exprimée à l'origine en prix nationaux — à une monnaie commune (par exemple le dollar des États-Unis) car les taux de change du marché connaissent fréquemment de fortes fluctuations tandis que les taux officiels ne coïncident pas avec ceux des marchés officieux ni avec les parités réelles de pouvoir d'achat. C'est pourquoi les données relatives au revenu national, qui sont publiées dans l'*Annuaire* en dollars des États-Unis, souffrent de certaines distorsions et ne peuvent servir qu'à donner une idée approximative des ordres de grandeur relatifs.

Le recours à des sources diverses pour la collecte des données est une autre facteur qui limite la comparabilité, en particulier dans les secteurs de l'emploi et du chômage où les statistiques sont obtenues par des moyens aussi peu comparables que les sondages, le dépouillement des registres d'assurances sociales et les enquêtes auprès des entreprises.

Dans certains cas, les données ne sont pas comparables en raison de différences entre les structures institutionnelles des pays. Certaines variations dans l'organisation et les institutions économiques et sociales peuvent affecter la comparabilité des données même si les concepts et définitions sont fondamentalement identiques.

Ces causes de non-comparabilité des données sont parmi celles qui sont brièvement expliquées dans les notes techniques de chaque chapitre.

Origine, fiabilité et actualité des données

Les statistiques et les indicateurs sont fondés essentiellement sur des données provenant de sources officielles nationales et internationales; c'est en effet la meilleure source si l'on veut des données fiables, complètes et comparables et si l'on a besoin de séries chronologiques. Dans quelques cas, les données officielles sont complétées par des informations et des estimations provenant d'autres sources qui ont été examinées par des spécialistes et confirmées par des sources indépendantes. On trouvera à la fin de l'*Annuaire* la liste des "Sources statistiques et références", qui récapitule les sources des données internationales utilisées pour la plupart des tableaux.

Les utilisateurs des statistiques internationales se plaignent souvent du fait que les données disponibles ne sont pas actualisées. Malheureusement, la plupart des données internationales ne sont disponibles qu'avec un délai de deux ou trois ans après la dernière année à laquelle elles se rapportent. S'il en est ainsi, c'est parce que les données sont d'abord traitées par les services statistiques nationaux avant d'être transmises aux services statistiques internationaux, qui les traitent à nouveau pour assurer la plus grande comparabilité possible entre les pays et entre les périodes.

Part One
World and Region Summary

Chapter I
World and region summary (tables 1-7)

This part of the *Statistical Yearbook* presents selected aggregate series on principal economic and social topics for the world as a whole and for the major regions. The topics include population and surface area, agricultural and industrial production, motor vehicles in use, external trade, government financial reserves, and energy production and consumption. More detailed data on individual countries and areas are provided in the subsequent parts of the present *Yearbook*. These comprise Part Two: Population and Social Statistics; Part Three: Economic Activity; and Part Four: International Economic Relations.

Regional totals may contain incomparabilities between series owing to differences in definitions of regions and lack of data for particular regional components. General information on regional groupings is provided in annex I of the *Yearbook*. Supplementary information on regional groupings used in specific series is provided, as necessary, in table footnotes and in the technical notes at the end of chapter I.

Première partie
Aperçu mondial et régional

Chapitre I
Aperçu mondial et régional (tableaux 1 à 7)

Cette partie de l'*Annuaire statistique* présente, pour le monde entier et ses principales subdivisions, un choix d'agrégats ayant trait à des questions économiques et sociales essentielles: population et superficie, production agricole et industrielle, véhicules automobiles en circulation, commerce extérieur, réserves financières publiques, et la production et la consommation d'énergie. Des statistiques plus détaillées pour divers pays ou zones figurent dans les parties ultérieures de l'*Annuaire*, c'est-à-dire dans les deuxième, troisième et quatrième parties intitulées respectivement: population et statistiques sociales, activités économiques et relations économiques internationales.

Les totaux régionaux peuvent présenter des incomparabilités entre les séries en raison de différences dans la définition des régions et de l'absence de données sur tel ou tel élément régional. A l'annexe I de l'*Annuaire*, on trouvera des renseignements généraux sur les groupements régionaux. Des informations complémentaires sur les groupements régionaux pour certaines séries bien précises sont fournies, lorsqu'il y a lieu, dans les notes figurant au bas des tableaux et dans les notes techniques à la fin du chapitre I.

1
Selected series of world statistics
Population, production, transport, external trade and finance
Séries principales de statistiques mondiales
Population, production, transports, commerce extérieur et finances

Series / Séries	Unit or base / Unité ou base	1992	1993	1994	1995	1996	1997	1998	1999	2000	2001
World population [1] **Population mondiale** [1]	million	**5431**	**5513**	**5594**	**5674**	**5755**	**5834**	**5914**	**5992**	**6071**	**6148**

Agriculture, forestry and fishing production • Production agricole, forestière et de la pêche
Index numbers • Indices

Series / Séries	Unit or base / Unité ou base	1992	1993	1994	1995	1996	1997	1998	1999	2000	2001
All commodities Tous produits	1989−91=100	104	104	107	109	114	117	119	123	125	126
Food Produits alimentaires	1989−91=100	104	105	108	110	115	118	120	124	126	127
Crops Cultures	1989−91=100	104	104	107	108	115	117	118	122	124	125
Cereals Céréales	1989−91=100	103	100	103	100	109	111	111	111	110	112
Livestock products Produits de l'élevage	1989−91=100	102	103	106	109	111	114	117	120	122	123

Quantities • Quantités

Series / Séries	Unit or base / Unité ou base	1992	1993	1994	1995	1996	1997	1998	1999	2000	2001
Oil crops Cultures d'huile	million t.	79	80	88	92	93	98	103	109	110	112
Meat Viande	million t.	138	140	144	146	146	151	156	161	161	162
Roundwood Bois rond	million m³	3201	3189	3194	3244	3238	3308	3224	3334	3377	3328
Fish production Production halieutique	million t.	107.8	112.2	120.6	124.4	128.6	130.9	127.5	137.5	141.8	...

Industrial production • Production industrielle
Index numbers [2] • Indices [2]

Series / Séries	Unit or base / Unité ou base	1992	1993	1994	1995	1996	1997	1998	1999	2000	2001
All commodities Tous produits	1995=100	93	93	96	100	103	108	110	114	121	118
Mining Mines	1995=100	95	96	98	100	103	105	105	103	107	107
Manufacturing Manufactures	1995=100	93	92	96	100	103	109	111	115	123	119

Quantities • Quantités

Series / Séries	Unit or base / Unité ou base	1992	1993	1994	1995	1996	1997	1998	1999	2000	2001
Coal Houille	million t.	3528	3453	3580	3731	3795	3827	3704	3470	3439	...
Lignite and brown coal Lignite et charbon brun	million t.	1040	994	963	943	926	916	917	926	844	...
Crude petroleum Pétrole brut	million t.	3007	3036	3063	3096	3151	3246	3285	3212	3329	...
Natural gas Gaz naturel	petajoules pétajoules	80290	81573	83399	85546	89864	89293	91714	92590	84349	...
Pig−iron and ferro−alloys Fonte et ferro−alliages	million t.	492	493	502	503	510	533	526	531	560	...
Fabrics • Tissus Cellulosic and non−cellulosic fibres Cellulosiques et non cellulosiques	million m²	18470	17248	12871	13467	13058	13180	12831	12494	12340	...
Cotton and wool Coton et laines	million m²	66892	67335	64489	69602	63613	68740	66740	67041	71089	...
Leather footwear Chaussures de cuir	million pairs	4325	4080	3832	3754	3694	3654	3609	3560	3575	...
Sulphuric acid Acide sulfurique	million t.	89	81	81	87	88	91	93	97	96	...
Refrigerators Réfrigérateurs	million	54	57	62	64	63	68	66	67	71	...
Washing machines Machines à laver	million	45	49	50	47	49	54	54	55	58	...

1
Selected series of world statistics
Population, production, transport, external trade and finance [*cont.*]
Séries principales de statistiques mondiales
Population, production, transports, commerce extérieur et finances [*suite*]

Series / Séries	Unit or base / Unité ou base	1992	1993	1994	1995	1996	1997	1998	1999	2000	2001
Machine tools · Machines outils											
Drilling and boring machines	thousands										
Perceuses	milliers	93	86	71	75	66	67	54	39	41	...
Lathes	thousands										
Tours	milliers	702	2798	6799	6345	4749	4943	6960	12486	21636	...
Lorries · Camions											
Assembled	thousands										
Assemblés	milliers	599	685	694	678	714	746	669	646	706	...
Produced	thousands										
Fabriqués	milliers	11620	10484	10447	10077	10133	10395	10458	10154	10323	...
Aluminium	thousands t.										
Aluminium	milliers t.	24557	24978	25083	25496	26984	27684	28415	29638	30079	...
Cement											
Ciment	million t.	1216	1280	1353	1422	1467	1516	1522	1579	1613	...
Electricity [3]	billion kWh										
Electricité [3]	milliard kWh	12387	12660	12974	13331	13772	14170	14523	15055	15660	...
Fertilizers [4]											
Engrais [4]	million t.	137.8	132.4	135.0	142.7	147.0	146.5	146.4	145.3	141.9	...
Sugar, raw											
Sucre, brut	million t.	115.4	109.3	108.0	118.6	126.1	126.7	128.2	133.7	135.6	131.8
Woodpulp											
Pâte de bois	million t.	152.1	151.3	162.0	161.7	156.7	162.7	159.9	163.6	171.4	166.3
Sawnwood											
Sciages	million m³	438	431	434	425	424	431	375	383	388	378
Motor vehicles · Véhicules automobiles											
Passenger cars											
Voitures de tourisme	million	33.94	32.09	33.78	33.31	34.22	34.61	33.26	34.07	34.67	...
Commercial vehicles											
Véhicules utilitaires	million	12.29	11.16	11.07	10.76	10.81	11.08	11.10	11.01	11.41	...

Transport · Transports

Motor vehicles in use [5] · Véhicules automobiles en circulation [5]

Series	Unit	1992	1993	1994	1995	1996	1997	1998	1999	2000	2001
Passenger cars	thousands										
Voitures de tourisme	milliers	445742	449990	469303	457763	470587	452101	475450	489982	...	...
Commercial vehicles	thousands										
Véhicules utilitaires	milliers	139575	141023	149548	165368	186867	176943	184862	191891	...	...

External trade · Commerce extérieur

Value · Valeur

Series	Unit	1992	1993	1994	1995	1996	1997	1998	1999	2000	2001
Imports, c.i.f.	billion US$										
Importations c.a.f.	milliard $E.–U.	3797.9	3741.5	4255.4	4939.8	5184.5	5354.7	5295.1	5511.4	6203.6	5981.4
Exports, f.o.b.	billion US$										
Exportations f.o.b.	milliard $E.–U.	3688.2	3707.8	4218.5	4910.0	5114.7	5302.5	5239.0	5421.5	6048.0	5814.6
Quantum: index of exports · Quantum : indice des exportations											
All commodities											
Tous produits	1990=100	110	113	122	134	142	157	167	177	195	196
Manufactures											
Produits manufacturés	1990=100	111	115	130	141	152	172	172	180	206	210
Unit value: index of exports [6] · Valeur unitaire : indice des exportations [6]											
All commodities											
Tous produits	1990=100	100	97	101	109	108	101	94	93	92	88
Manufactures											
Produits manufacturés	1990=100	103	99	101	110	106	98	95	91	88	86
Primary commodities: price indexes [67] · Produits de base : indices des prix [67]											
All commodities											
Tous produits	1980=100	71	65	66	72	76	71	56	63	81	73
Food											
Produits alimentaires	1980=100	87	82	87	92	90	87	80	74	69	69
Non-food: of agricultural origin											
Non alimentaires: d'origine agricole	1980=100	91	84	95	106	98	90	81	73	72	66
Minerals											
Minéraux	1980=100	62	55	53	58	67	62	43	57	87	76

1
Selected series of world statistics
Population, production, transport, external trade and finance [*cont.*]
Séries principales de statistiques mondiales
Population, production, transports, commerce extérieur et finances [*suite*]

Series Séries	Unit or base Unité ou base	1992	1993	1994	1995	1996	1997	1998	1999	2000	2001

Finance • Finances

International reserves minus gold, billion SDR [8] · Réserves internationales moins l'or, milliard de DTS [8]

Series Séries	Unit or base Unité ou base	1992	1993	1994	1995	1996	1997	1998	1999	2000	2001
All countries	billion SDR										
Tous les pays	milliard DTS	720.1	797.8	858.3	988.4	1142.2	1261.3	1244.0	1370.5	1550.8	1703.0
Position in IMF	billion SDR										
Disponibilité au FMI	milliard DTS	33.9	32.8	31.7	36.7	38.0	47.1	60.6	54.8	47.4	56.9
Foreign exchange	billion SDR										
Devises	milliard DTS	673.5	750.4	811.8	932.0	1085.7	1193.7	1163.1	1295.2	1485.0	1626.7
SDR (special drawing rights)	billion SDR										
DTS (droits de tirage spéciaux)	milliard DTS	12.9	14.6	15.8	19.8	18.5	20.5	20.4	18.5	18.5	19.6

Sources:
Databases of the Food and Agriculture Organization of the
United Nations (FAO), Rome; the International Monetary
Fund (IMF), Washington, D.C.; and the United Nations
Statistics Division, New York.

1   Annual data: mid–year estimates.
2   Excluding China and the countries of the former USSR (except
    Russian Federation and Ukraine).
3   Electricity generated by establishments for public or private use.
4   Year beginning 1 July.
5   Source: World Automotive Market Report, Auto and Truck
    International (Illinois).
6   Indexes computed in US dollars.
7   Export price indexes.
8   End of period.

Sources:
Les bases de données de l'Organisation des Nations Unies pour
l'alimentation et l'agriculture (FAO), Rome; du Fonds Monétaire
International (FMI), Washington, D.C.; et de la Division de statistique
de l'Organisation des Nations Unies, New York.

1   Données annuelles : estimations au milieu de l'année.
2   Non compris la Chine et les pays de l'ancienne URSS (sauf
    la Fédération de Russie et Ukraine).
3   L'électricité produite par des entreprises d'utilisation publique
    ou privée.
4   L'année commençant le 1er juillet.
5   Source : "World Automotive Market Report, Auto and Truck
    International" (Illinois).
6   Indice calculé en dollars des Etats–Unis.
7   Indice des prix à l'exportation.
8   Fin de la période.

2
Population, rate of increase, birth and death rates, surface area and density
Population, taux d'accroissement, taux de natalité et taux de mortalité, superficie et densité

Major areas and regions Grandes régions	Mid-year population estimates (millions) Estimations de population au milieu de l'année (millions)							Annual rate of increase Taux d'accroissement annuel %	Birth rate Taux de natalité (0/000)	Death rate Taux de mortalité (0/000)	Surface area (km²) Superficie (km²) (000's)	Density[1] Densité[1]
	1950	1960	1970	1980	1990	1995	2000	1995–2000			2000	2000
World												
Monde	**2 519**	**3 020**	**3 691**	**4 430**	**5 255**	**5 662**	**6 057**	**1.4**	**22**	**9**	**135 641**	**45**
Africa												
Afrique	**221**	**277**	**356**	**467**	**619**	**703**	**794**	**2.4**	**39**	**14**	**30 306**	**26**
Eastern Africa												
Afrique orientale	65	82	108	143	193	219	250	2.7	43	18	6 356	39
Middle Africa												
Afrique centrale	26	32	40	52	71	84	95	2.6	46	16	6 613	14
Northern Africa												
Afrique septentrionale	53	67	86	111	143	159	174	1.9	28	8	8 525	20
Southern Africa												
Afrique méridionale	16	20	26	33	41	46	50	1.6	28	12	2 675	18
Western Africa												
Afrique occidentale	60	76	97	128	171	196	224	2.7	42	15	6 138	36
Northern America[2]												
Amérique septentrionale [2]	**172**	**204**	**232**	**255**	**283**	**298**	**314**	**1.0**	**14**	**8**	**21 517**	**15**
Latin America and Caribbean												
Amérique latine et Caraïbes	**167**	**218**	**285**	**361**	**440**	**480**	**519**	**1.6**	**23**	**6**	**20 533**	**25**
Caribbean												
Caraïbes	17	20	25	29	34	36	38	1.1	21	8	235	162
Central America												
Amérique centrale	37	49	68	90	111	123	135	1.8	26	5	2 480	54
South America												
Amérique du Sud	178	223	286	358	440	483	522	1.6	24	7	17 819	29
Asia[3]												
Asie[3]	**1 399**	**1 700**	**2 142**	**2 631**	**3 164**	**3 423**	**3 672**	**1.4**	**22**	**8**	**31 764**	**116**
Eastern Asia												
Asie orientale	672	792	987	1 178	1 350	1 420	1 481	0.8	16	7	11 762	126
South–central Asia												
Asie central et du Sud	498	621	783	982	1 225	1 353	1 481	1.8	28	9	10 776	137
South–eastern Asia												
Asie du Sud–Est	178	223	286	358	440	483	522	1.6	24	7	4 495	116
Western Asia[3]												
Asie occidentale[3]	50	66	86	113	149	168	188	2.3	29	7	4 731	40
Europe[3]												
Europe[3]	**548**	**605**	**657**	**693**	**722**	**729**	**727**	**0.0**	**10**	**12**	**22 986**	**32**
Eastern Europe												
Europe orientale	220	253	276	295	311	310	304	−0.4	9	13	18 813	16
Northern Europe												
Europe septentrionale	78	82	87	90	92	94	95	0.2	12	11	1 749	54
Southern Europe												
Europe mériodionale	109	118	127	138	143	144	145	0.2	10	10	1 316	110
Western Europe												
Europe occidentale	141	152	166	170	176	181	183	0.2	11	10	1 107	165
Oceania[2]												
Océanie[2]	**12.6**	**15.7**	**19.2**	**22.5**	**26.3**	**28.5**	**30.5**	**1.4**	**18**	**8**	**8 537**	**4**
Australia and New Zealand												
Australie et Nouvelle–Zélande	10.1	12.6	15.4	17.7	20.2	21.7	22.9	1.1	14	7	7 984	3
Melanesia												
Mélanésie	2.1	2.5	3.2	4.1	5.1	5.8	6.5	2.3	33	9	541	12
Micronesia												
Micronésie	0.2	0.2	0.3	0.3	0.4	0.5	0.5	2.2	31	5	3	172
Polynesia												
Polynésie	0.2	0.3	0.4	0.5	0.5	0.6	0.6	1.1	25	5	9	67

2
Population, rate of increase, birth and death rates, surface area and density [*cont.*]
Population, taux d'accroissement, taux de natalité et taux de
mortalité, superficie et densité [*suite*]

Source:
United Nations Division, New York, "Demographic
Yearbook 2000" and the demographic statistics database.

1   Population per square kilometre of surface area. Figures
     are merely the quotients of population divided by surface
     area and are not to be considered as either reflecting
     density in the urban sense or as indicating the supporting
     power of a territory's land and resources.
2   Hawaii, a state of the United States of America, is included
     in Northern America rather than Oceania.
3   The European portion of Turkey is included in Western
     Asia rather than Europe.

Source:
Organisation des Nations Unies, Division de statistique, New York,
"Annuaire démographique 2000" et la base de données pour les
statistiques démographiques.

1   Habitants per kilomètre carré. Il s'agit simplement du quotient
     calculé en divisant la population par la superficie et n'est pas
     considéré comme indiquant la densité au sens urbain du mot ni
     l'effectif de population que les terres et les ressources du
     territoire sont capables de nourrir.
2   Hawaii, un Etat des Etats – Unis d'Amérique, est compris en
     Amérique septentrionale plutôt qu'en Océanie.
3   La partie européenne de la Turquie est comprise en Asie
     Occidentale plutôt qu'en Europe.

3
Index numbers of total agricultural and food production
Indices de la production agricole totale et de la production alimentaire

1989–1991 = 100

Region or area Région ou zone	1992	1993	1994	1995	1996	1997	1998	1999	2000	2001
A. Total agricultural production · Production agricole totale										
World Monde	104	104	107	109	114	117	118	122	123	124
Africa Afrique	103	106	109	110	122	120	124	128	129	130
America, North Amérique du Nord	108	101	114	110	114	118	119	121	123	122
America, South Amérique du Sud	105	106	113	119	121	125	128	136	138	142
Asia Asie	112	117	122	127	133	137	141	146	148	149
Europe Europe	94	91	86	86	88	89	87	88	87	88
Oceania Océanie	105	107	102	109	116	118	122	126	127	129
B. Food production · Production alimentaire										
World Monde	104	105	108	110	115	118	120	124	125	125
Africa Afrique	103	106	110	110	122	120	125	129	130	131
America, North Amérique du Nord	108	101	113	110	114	118	120	122	124	122
America, South Amérique du Sud	106	107	115	122	124	129	131	140	142	147
Asia Asie	112	118	123	128	134	139	143	148	151	151
Europe Europe	94	91	86	86	88	89	87	88	87	88
Oceania Océanie	108	112	107	117	127	128	133	139	139	140

Source:
Food and Agriculture Organization of the United Nations (FAO), Rome, "FAO Production Yearbook 2001" and the FAOSTAT database.

Source:
Organisation des Nations Unies pour l'alimentation et l'agriculture (FAO), Rome, "Annuaire FAO de la production 2001 "et la base de données FAOSTAT.

4
Index numbers of per capita total agricultural and food production
Indices de la production agricole totale et de la production alimentaire par habitant

1989–1991 = 100

Region or area Région ou zone	1992	1993	1994	1995	1996	1997	1998	1999	2000	2001
A. Per capita total agricultural production · Production agricole totale par habitant										
World **Monde**	**100**	**99**	**101**	**101**	**104**	**105**	**105**	**107**	**107**	**106**
Africa Afrique	97	98	98	97	104	101	102	102	101	99
America, North Amérique du Nord	105	97	108	102	105	107	107	108	108	106
America, South Amérique du Sud	102	101	105	110	110	112	112	118	118	120
Asia Asie	106	110	112	115	118	121	122	125	125	124
Europe Europe	93	91	85	85	87	88	86	87	87	87
Oceania Océanie	101	102	96	101	106	106	108	111	110	110
B. Per capita food production · Production alimentaire par habitant										
World **Monde**	**101**	**100**	**102**	**102**	**105**	**106**	**107**	**109**	**108**	**107**
Africa Afrique	98	98	99	97	105	101	102	103	102	100
America, North Amérique du Nord	105	97	108	103	105	107	108	109	109	106
America, South Amérique du Sud	102	102	107	113	112	115	115	121	121	123
Asia Asie	106	110	113	116	119	122	124	127	127	126
Europe Europe	93	91	85	85	87	88	86	87	87	87
Oceania Océanie	105	107	100	108	115	115	118	121	120	120

Source:
Food and Agriculture Organization of the United Nations (FAO), Rome, "FAO Production Yearbook 2001" and the FAOSTAT database.

Source:
Organisation des Nations Unies pour l'alimentation et l'agriculture (FAO), Rome, "Annuaire FAO de la production 2001 "et la base de données FAOSTAT.

5

Index numbers of industrial production: world and regions
Indices de la production industrielle: monde et régions
1995=100

Region and industry [ISIC Rev.3] Région et industrie [CITI Rév.3]	Weight(%) Pond.(%)	1993	1994	1996	1997	1998	1999	2000	2001
World · Monde									
Total industry [CDE]									
Total, industrie [CDE]	**100.0**	**92.7**	**96.4**	**103.1**	**108.2**	**110.0**	**113.1**	**120.7**	**117.7**
Total mining [C]									
Total, industries extractives [C]	**7.4**	**95.6**	**98.1**	**103.3**	**105.0**	**105.1**	**103.0**	**106.7**	**105.9**
Coal									
Houille	0.7	100.6	98.1	100.3	100.9	99.1	100.4	100.8	103.1
Crude petroleum and natural gas									
Pétrole brut et gaz naturel	5.0	95.1	98.2	102.9	104.7	104.1	100.7	105.0	103.3
Metal ores									
Minerais métalliques	0.7	98.2	97.3	107.0	108.9	115.4	115.8	121.5	124.5
Total manufacturing [D]									
Total, industries manufacturières [D]	**82.6**	**92.3**	**96.2**	**103.0**	**108.8**	**110.7**	**114.3**	**122.6**	**119.0**
Food, beverages, tobacco									
Industries alimentaires, boissons, tabac	10.3	95.9	98.3	101.3	102.6	102.8	104.0	105.8	105.6
Textiles									
Textiles	2.4	99.6	101.4	98.9	101.3	97.7	95.8	95.9	90.3
Wearing apparel, leather and footwear									
Articles d'habillement, cuir et chaussures	2.7	104.4	102.5	97.1	95.2	90.9	87.0	84.0	78.8
Wood and wood products									
Bois et articles en bois	1.9	96.2	99.6	100.2	102.3	101.6	103.0	103.5	98.2
Paper, printing, publishing and recorded media									
Papier, imprimerie, édition et supports enregistrés	7.1	96.0	98.4	100.3	104.1	104.7	98.6	107.3	104.1
Chemicals and related products									
Produits chimiques et alliés	14.0	91.7	96.3	103.1	108.7	109.9	113.5	116.9	116.9
Non−metallic mineral products									
Produits minéraux non métalliques	3.4	93.5	97.5	100.9	103.7	101.5	103.5	106.8	103.6
Basic metals									
Métallurgie de base	4.7	91.8	96.5	101.2	107.7	104.6	105.7	111.8	108.0
Fabricated metal products									
Fabrications d'ouvrages en métaux	11.7	88.3	93.8	102.6	106.8	106.8	106.6	112.8	109.0
Office and related electrical products									
Machines de bureau et autres appareils élect.	12.7	82.4	89.2	111.1	126.0	139.3	158.9	192.6	182.4
Transport equipment									
Equipement de transports	8.0	93.5	97.9	102.4	110.9	113.6	118.7	123.8	122.2
Electricity, gas, water [E]									
Electricité, gaz et eau [E]	**10.0**	**94.0**	**96.6**	**103.8**	**105.6**	**107.4**	**110.8**	**114.7**	**115.7**
Developed regions [1] · Régions développées [1]									
Total industry [CDE]									
Total, industrie [CDE]	**100.0**	**93.1**	**96.5**	**102.7**	**107.7**	**110.2**	**113.0**	**120.4**	**117.1**
Total mining [C]									
Total, industries extractives [C]	**4.6**	**95.2**	**98.3**	**102.8**	**103.2**	**102.4**	**100.1**	**102.2**	**102.2**
Coal									
Houille	0.6	103.6	100.0	98.6	98.0	94.6	93.5	91.5	91.5
Crude petroleum and natural gas									
Pétrole brut et gaz naturel	2.7	93.1	98.1	104.0	104.6	102.9	99.3	102.7	103.0
Metal ores									
Minerais métalliques	0.4	103.0	101.1	102.5	103.8	105.0	100.3	101.3	99.1
Total manufacturing [D]									
Total, industries manufacturières [D]	**84.9**	**92.7**	**96.3**	**102.6**	**108.4**	**111.2**	**114.3**	**122.5**	**118.6**
Food, beverages, tobacco									
Industries alimentaires, boissons, tabac	9.5	97.0	99.1	100.6	101.9	102.7	103.8	105.7	105.1
Textiles									
Textiles	1.8	100.4	102.2	97.0	99.4	96.2	92.3	90.8	84.9
Wearing apparel, leather and footwear									
Articles d'habillement, cuir et chaussures	2.4	103.4	102.6	96.4	94.5	89.3	84.8	80.0	75.1
Wood and wood products									
Bois et articles en bois	2.0	95.5	99.4	99.9	102.2	103.3	105.7	106.3	100.6

5
Index numbers of industrial production: world and regions [*cont.*]
Indices de la production industrielle: monde et régions [*suite*]
1995=100

Region and industry [ISIC Rev.3] Région et industrie [CITI Rév.3]	Weight(%) Pond.(%)	1993	1994	1996	1997	1998	1999	2000	2001
Paper, printing, publishing and recorded media Papier, imprimerie, édition et supports enregistrés	8.1	96.5	98.7	100.2	104.1	104.8	97.8	107.1	103.8
Chemicals and related products Produits chimiques et alliés	13.7	92.2	96.5	102.1	107.0	108.6	111.7	114.6	114.4
Non–metallic mineral products Produits minéraux non métalliques	3.2	94.0	98.1	100.0	102.0	101.0	103.0	106.3	102.5
Basic metals Métallurgie de base	4.7	92.9	97.1	99.8	105.1	101.8	101.4	107.5	103.6
Fabricated metal products Fabrications d'ouvrages en métaux	12.7	88.5	93.6	102.5	106.5	108.0	107.4	112.5	108.9
Office and related electrical products Machines de bureau et autres appareils élect.	14.0	83.1	89.4	111.3	126.4	140.2	158.3	191.0	180.5
Transport equipment Equipement de transports	8.7	94.6	98.5	101.8	109.8	114.4	119.2	123.1	121.0
Electricity, gas, water [E] **Electricité, gaz et eau [E]**	**10.5**	**95.3**	**97.2**	**103.3**	**104.0**	**105.5**	**108.2**	**111.5**	**111.6**

Developing countries [2] · Pays en développement [2]

Total industry [CDE] **Total, industrie [CDE]**	**100.0**	**91.3**	**95.7**	**104.8**	**110.3**	**108.9**	**113.5**	**121.5**	**120.0**
Total mining [C] **Total, industries extractives [C]**	**18.3**	**95.9**	**98.0**	**103.9**	**106.7**	**107.9**	**106.0**	**111.3**	**109.7**
Coal Houille	1.2	95.0	94.5	103.3	106.2	107.6	113.2	118.0	124.7
Crude petroleum and natural gas Pétrole brut et gaz naturel	14.3	96.6	98.2	102.0	104.7	104.9	101.9	106.7	103.6
Metal ores Minerais métalliques	1.7	93.5	93.5	111.6	114.1	126.0	131.5	141.9	150.1
Total manufacturing [D] **Total, industries manufacturières [D]**	**73.7**	**90.6**	**95.4**	**104.8**	**110.8**	**108.2**	**114.1**	**123.0**	**120.7**
Food, beverages, tobacco Industries alimentaires, boissons, tabac	13.3	92.8	95.9	103.4	104.5	103.2	104.5	106.3	107.1
Textiles Textiles	4.8	98.3	100.2	101.7	104.4	99.9	101.2	103.7	98.6
Wearing apparel, leather and footwear Articles d'habillement, cuir et chaussures	3.6	107.0	102.2	98.9	97.1	95.2	93.0	94.8	88.9
Wood and wood products Bois et articles bois	1.5	100.3	101.1	102.1	102.9	92.0	88.0	87.9	85.0
Paper, printing, publishing and recorded media Papier, imprimerie, édition et supports enregistrés	3.2	91.0	95.7	102.0	104.8	103.4	106.2	109.3	108.0
Chemicals and related products Produits chimiques et alliés	15.0	90.1	95.2	106.9	114.9	114.7	120.3	125.2	125.7
Non–metallic mineral products Produits minéraux non métalliques	4.2	92.1	95.5	103.7	108.9	103.1	105.1	108.2	106.7
Basic metals Métallurgie de base	4.7	87.0	94.1	106.6	118.1	115.9	122.9	128.7	125.5
Fabricated metal products Fabrications d'ouvrages en métaux	7.9	87.5	95.3	103.7	108.6	98.8	101.9	114.6	110.0
Office and related electrical products Machines de bureau et autres appareils élect.	7.3	77.5	87.6	109.3	123.7	132.9	163.1	204.7	196.6
Transport equipment Equipement de transports	5.2	86.7	93.9	106.3	117.8	108.4	115.4	128.7	129.9
Electricity, gas, water [E] **Electricité, gaz et eau [E]**	**8.0**	**87.2**	**93.5**	**106.5**	**113.7**	**117.7**	**124.3**	**131.3**	**137.2**

Northern America [3] · Amérique septentrionale [3]

Total industry [CDE] **Total, industrie [CDE]**	**100.0**	**90.2**	**95.2**	**104.9**	**113.1**	**120.6**	**128.2**	**138.9**	**133.3**
Total mining [C] **Total, industries extractives [C]**	**6.6**	**97.6**	**99.6**	**101.4**	**103.4**	**101.9**	**97.7**	**101.2**	**101.9**
Coal Houille	0.6	91.6	99.8	102.4	105.7	106.9	104.9	103.7	108.1

5
Index numbers of industrial production: world and regions [*cont.*]
Indices de la production industrielle: monde et régions [*suite*]
1995=100

Region and industry [ISIC Rev.3] Région et industrie [CITI Rév.3]	Weight(%) Pond.(%)	1993	1994	1996	1997	1998	1999	2000	2001
Crude petroleum and natural gas									
Pétrole brut et gaz naturel	4.8	98.5	100.2	101.1	102.8	100.1	94.6	99.2	100.0
Metal ores									
Minerais métalliques	0.6	100.8	98.8	102.8	104.0	105.3	98.4	98.5	93.9
Total manufacturing [D]									
Total, industries manufacturières [D]	**81.6**	**88.9**	**94.6**	**105.4**	**115.3**	**124.5**	**133.8**	**146.1**	**139.3**
Food, beverages, tobacco									
Industries alimentaires, boissons, tabac	8.1	95.0	97.9	99.8	101.2	104.2	104.4	106.1	105.9
Textiles									
Textiles	1.6	95.1	100.1	98.5	99.7	98.8	96.4	92.0	81.0
Wearing apparel, leather and footwear									
Articles d'habillement, cuir et chaussures	2.1	98.5	100.4	98.5	100.5	96.6	96.0	92.2	83.9
Wood and wood products									
Bois et articles bois	2.9	94.1	98.4	102.4	106.6	110.8	115.3	113.0	107.6
Paper, printing, publishing and recorded media									
Papier, imprimerie, édition et supports enregistrés	9.1	98.0	99.6	99.8	105.4	105.3	105.6	106.4	101.2
Chemicals and related products									
Produits chimiques et alliés	14.2	94.1	97.7	102.7	108.4	111.0	112.9	115.3	113.4
Non−metallic mineral products									
Produits minéraux non métalliques	2.0	92.3	97.5	106.1	110.7	116.5	119.7	122.4	119.9
Basic metals									
Métallurgie de base	3.5	91.2	97.8	102.8	107.8	110.6	112.5	114.6	102.9
Fabricated metal products									
Fabrications d'ouvrages en métaux	12.1	83.0	91.9	105.9	113.0	118.3	119.6	123.8	115.5
Office and related electrical products									
Machines de bureau et autres appareils élect.	13.7	72.0	82.3	122.0	153.8	190.5	234.0	299.7	285.7
Transport equipment									
Equipement de transports	9.5	92.0	98.1	100.2	108.6	117.1	125.9	126.0	118.1
Electricity, gas, water [E]									
Electricité, gaz et eau [E]	**11.8**	**95.1**	**96.6**	**103.1**	**103.0**	**104.0**	**106.7**	**110.1**	**109.1**

Latin America and the Caribbean · Amérique latine et Caraïbes

Total industry [CDE]									
Total, industrie [CDE]	**100.0**	**93.9**	**99.6**	**104.9**	**110.9**	**112.2**	**112.1**	**117.5**	**117.4**
Total mining [C]									
Total, industries extractives [C]	**10.2**	**89.3**	**94.6**	**111.3**	**117.9**	**122.2**	**123.1**	**126.2**	**128.2**
Coal									
Houille	0.3	92.8	96.6	107.6	112.3	100.4	109.9	117.5	126.0
Crude petroleum and natural gas									
Pétrole brut et gaz naturel	5.6	89.8	93.8	107.3	113.6	119.3	114.6	113.6	112.9
Metal ores									
Minerais métalliques	2.7	87.7	91.4	113.6	120.6	124.1	137.3	146.3	152.4
Total manufacturing [D]									
Total, industries manufacturières [D]	**81.2**	**95.1**	**100.7**	**104.1**	**110.0**	**110.5**	**109.6**	**115.4**	**114.6**
Food, beverages, tobacco									
Industries alimentaires, boissons, tabac	18.4	94.9	98.0	102.9	105.7	108.0	110.8	111.6	113.4
Textiles									
Textiles	3.3	105.8	108.9	101.1	101.3	94.1	89.6	94.4	87.0
Wearing apparel, leather and footwear									
Articles d'habillement, cuir et chaussures	3.4	108.2	106.4	101.2	101.6	99.4	91.5	96.1	88.5
Wood and wood products									
Bois et articles bois	2.0	103.6	106.9	104.7	114.9	115.5	115.2	118.2	117.2
Paper, printing, publishing and recorded media									
Papier, imprimerie, édition et supports enregistrés	3.7	95.7	99.6	101.6	105.6	107.9	107.7	112.7	109.0
Chemicals and related products									
Produits chimiques et alliés	19.5	93.8	98.8	105.3	111.0	114.3	114.6	118.5	116.8
Non−metallic mineral products									
Produits minéraux non métalliques	4.0	96.2	100.5	105.7	112.8	114.7	110.9	114.2	112.3
Basic metals									
Métallurgie de base	4.1	91.4	98.4	106.3	115.4	116.0	115.3	118.3	117.0
Fabricated metal products									
Fabrications d'ouvrages en métaux	8.8	92.0	104.0	100.7	108.5	105.5	102.8	114.0	114.4

5

Index numbers of industrial production: world and regions [*cont.*]
Indices de la production industrielle: monde et régions [*suite*]
1995=100

Region and industry [ISIC Rev.3] Région et industrie [CITI Rév.3]	Weight(%) Pond.(%)	1993	1994	1996	1997	1998	1999	2000	2001
Office and related electrical products									
Machines de bureau et autres appareils élect.	4.9	85.0	95.5	109.3	116.5	114.2	108.4	120.8	122.1
Transport equipment									
Equipement de transports	5.5	95.1	105.0	107.4	124.1	121.2	118.4	137.2	136.1
Electricity, gas, water [E]									
Electricité, gaz et eau [E]	**8.6**	**88.2**	**95.2**	**105.6**	**111.5**	**115.8**	**121.7**	**126.9**	**131.4**

Asia · Asie

Total industry [CDE]									
Total, industrie [CDE]	**100.0**	**94.3**	**96.4**	**103.2**	**107.2**	**102.5**	**103.7**	**111.1**	**106.8**
Total mining [C]									
Total, industries extractives [C]	**7.9**	**96.1**	**98.2**	**102.3**	**103.2**	**104.3**	**102.2**	**107.4**	**105.4**
Coal									
Houille	0.7	97.0	95.3	102.8	102.6	105.3	110.4	113.6	119.5
Crude petroleum and natural gas									
Pétrole brut et gaz naturel	5.8	97.0	98.8	100.9	102.2	102.4	99.6	105.4	102.0
Metal ores									
Minerais métalliques	0.3	94.9	94.6	113.5	112.0	141.3	141.2	158.0	172.3
Total manufacturing [D]									
Total, industries manufacturières [D]	**82.8**	**94.7**	**96.2**	**103.2**	**107.4**	**101.4**	**102.6**	**110.5**	**105.2**
Food, beverages, tobacco									
Industries alimentaires, boissons, tabac	10.3	95.5	97.9	102.1	101.6	97.9	98.6	100.2	99.0
Textiles									
Textiles	2.8	101.0	100.5	100.6	103.1	96.8	97.3	97.6	92.9
Wearing apparel, leather and footwear									
Articles d'habillement, cuir et chaussures	2.9	110.1	104.6	96.3	90.9	84.3	81.4	76.5	69.5
Wood and wood products									
Bois et articles bois	1.2	105.2	102.7	99.5	95.2	80.8	76.4	74.0	68.0
Paper, printing, publishing and recorded media									
Papier, imprimerie, édition et supports enregistrés	5.7	94.5	96.6	101.7	103.3	100.4	73.4	99.8	98.1
Chemicals and related products									
Produits chimiques et alliés	13.1	90.7	94.9	103.4	108.8	106.0	110.6	113.0	113.1
Non−metallic mineral products									
Produits minéraux non métalliques	3.7	95.0	96.9	101.1	103.1	92.2	93.8	97.6	90.3
Basic metals									
Métallurgie de base	5.9	93.4	95.4	101.4	108.5	99.3	101.9	109.8	106.9
Fabricated metal products									
Fabrications d'ouvrages en métaux	9.0	91.3	94.3	103.4	104.6	92.8	92.7	99.4	91.5
Office and related electrical products									
Machines de bureau et autres appareils élect.	16.4	85.6	90.5	108.2	116.5	115.4	126.4	147.2	133.9
Transport equipment									
Equipement de transports	7.3	99.7	98.2	103.7	112.2	101.9	106.0	110.4	110.9
Electricity, gas, water [E]									
Electricité, gaz et eau [E]	**9.3**	**89.8**	**95.8**	**104.7**	**109.2**	**111.2**	**114.7**	**120.0**	**122.1**

Asia excluding Israel and Japan · Asie à l'exception de l'Israël et du Japon

Total industry [CDE]									
Total, industrie [CDE]	**100.0**	**89.4**	**93.7**	**104.7**	**110.0**	**107.1**	**114.3**	**124.0**	**121.5**
Total mining [C]									
Total, industries extractives [C]	**19.1**	**96.6**	**98.7**	**101.8**	**103.2**	**104.2**	**101.9**	**107.8**	**105.4**
Coal									
Houille	1.8	95.5	94.0	102.8	105.5	109.3	114.4	119.0	125.3
Crude petroleum and natural gas									
Pétrole brut et gaz naturel	15.7	97.0	98.7	100.9	102.2	102.4	99.6	105.4	101.9
Metal ores									
Minerais métalliques	0.7	94.5	94.2	114.4	112.9	143.4	142.9	161.0	176.1
Total manufacturing [D]									
Total, industries manufacturières [D]	**73.2**	**87.9**	**92.5**	**105.1**	**111.2**	**106.6**	**116.2**	**127.0**	**123.5**

5
Index numbers of industrial production: world and regions [*cont.*]
Indices de la production industrielle: monde et régions [*suite*]
1995=100

Region and industry [ISIC Rev.3] Région et industrie [CITI Rév.3]	Weight(%) Pond.(%)	1993	1994	1996	1997	1998	1999	2000	2001
Food, beverages, tobacco Industries alimentaires, boissons, tabac	11.0	90.7	94.0	103.7	103.4	97.9	97.8	100.3	100.1
Textiles Textiles	5.6	95.7	97.4	102.2	105.5	101.5	104.7	106.7	102.0
Wearing apparel, leather and footwear Articles d'habillement, cuir et chaussures	3.7	107.9	100.2	96.9	92.1	89.9	91.0	90.4	84.2
Wood and wood products Bois et articles bois	1.2	99.1	98.6	101.6	100.4	84.8	79.6	78.7	74.3
Paper, printing, publishing and recorded media Papier, imprimerie, édition et supports enregistrés	3.1	87.3	92.6	102.0	104.0	100.0	104.4	105.9	105.9
Chemicals and related products Produits chimiques et alliés	13.6	87.4	92.8	107.6	117.3	115.4	124.2	130.0	131.7
Non−metallic mineral products Produits minéraux non métalliques	4.3	89.9	93.4	101.9	106.8	96.5	100.4	103.1	100.7
Basic metals Métallurgie de base	5.4	85.4	92.7	106.7	119.3	115.8	125.1	131.8	127.5
Fabricated metal products Fabrications d'ouvrages en métaux	7.9	84.8	90.5	105.0	107.8	93.2	100.3	114.0	106.5
Office and related electrical products Machines de bureau et autres appareils élect.	9.0	75.5	85.6	109.2	125.4	136.9	176.6	225.5	215.1
Transport equipment Equipement de transports	5.4	81.8	87.7	105.8	114.7	101.5	113.9	124.4	126.6
Electricity, gas, water [E] **Electricité, gaz et eau [E]**	**7.7**	**86.0**	**92.0**	**107.5**	**115.9**	**119.5**	**127.0**	**135.9**	**142.6**

Europe · Europe

Total industry [CDE] **Total, industrie [CDE]**	**100.0**	**93.8**	**97.2**	**100.7**	**104.2**	**107.8**	**110.0**	**116.1**	**116.2**
Total mining [C] **Total, industries extractives [C]**	**5.1**	**94.0**	**98.0**	**103.2**	**101.9**	**100.5**	**100.8**	**101.7**	**101.3**
Coal Houille	1.1	111.6	102.3	96.8	93.2	83.3	79.9	76.6	73.0
Crude petroleum and natural gas Pétrole brut et gaz naturel	3.1	87.8	96.5	107.1	106.3	105.2	105.5	107.0	107.1
Metal ores Minerais métalliques	0.2	93.1	90.9	102.0	96.2	125.8	124.3	129.7	145.5
Total manufacturing [D] **Total, industries manufacturières [D]**	**85.0**	**93.3**	**97.1**	**100.3**	**104.4**	**108.6**	**110.8**	**117.5**	**117.5**
Food, beverages, tobacco Industries alimentaires, boissons, tabac	10.4	97.7	99.3	100.6	102.4	103.5	105.0	107.5	107.4
Textiles Textiles	2.5	99.7	102.0	96.0	99.5	97.8	93.6	95.1	91.7
Wearing apparel, leather and footwear Articles d'habillement, cuir et chaussures	2.7	102.3	101.8	96.1	94.0	90.6	84.1	81.2	80.7
Wood and wood products Bois et articles bois	1.9	93.4	98.8	97.1	100.4	104.2	107.2	113.0	108.2
Paper, printing, publishing and recorded media Papier, imprimerie, édition et supports enregistrés	7.4	95.6	98.7	99.5	103.7	108.0	111.7	115.2	113.4
Chemicals and related products Produits chimiques et alliés	13.9	90.9	96.2	102.0	107.4	111.0	115.2	120.8	122.5
Non−metallic mineral products Produits minéraux non métalliques	4.2	93.8	98.5	97.5	98.6	100.9	103.5	108.0	107.8
Basic metals Métallurgie de base	4.6	91.2	97.3	98.1	104.4	104.4	102.2	110.2	109.8
Fabricated metal products Fabrications d'ouvrages en métaux	15.5	92.3	94.8	99.2	102.6	106.6	106.1	112.8	114.1
Office and related electrical products Machines de bureau et autres appareils élect.	9.7	89.9	94.7	103.1	109.7	119.1	126.6	145.9	144.1
Transport equipment Equipement de transports	8.1	90.6	97.3	102.7	110.2	120.9	124.8	133.2	135.0
Electricity, gas, water [E] **Electricité, gaz et eau [E]**	**9.8**	**98.1**	**98.0**	**102.9**	**103.4**	**105.1**	**108.0**	**111.6**	**112.8**

5

Index numbers of industrial production: world and regions [*cont.*]
Indices de la production industrielle: monde et régions [*suite*]
1995=100

Region and industry [ISIC Rev.3] Région et industrie [CITI Rév.3]	Weight(%) Pond.(%)	1993	1994	1996	1997	1998	1999	2000	2001
European Union [4] · Union européenne [4]									
Total industry [CDE] **Total, industrie [CDE]**	**100.0**	**92.7**	**96.8**	**100.8**	**104.5**	**108.5**	**110.6**	**116.1**	**115.7**
Total mining [C] **Total, industries extractives [C]**	**3.6**	**94.0**	**98.5**	**102.3**	**100.0**	**99.2**	**99.6**	**97.3**	**94.1**
Coal Houille	0.8	116.4	102.0	94.3	91.1	81.3	77.9	72.0	66.7
Crude petroleum and natural gas Pétrole brut et gaz naturel	2.0	85.9	97.1	107.1	104.3	105.2	105.2	102.2	99.6
Metal ores Minerais métalliques	0.1	108.8	96.5	95.7	90.4	85.7	77.7	73.8	69.9
Total manufacturing [D] **Total, industries manufacturières [D]**	**86.8**	**92.1**	**96.6**	**100.3**	**104.7**	**109.2**	**111.1**	**117.2**	**116.7**
Food, beverages, tobacco Industries alimentaires, boissons, tabac	10.2	97.2	99.2	100.7	103.5	104.5	106.1	108.4	107.7
Textiles Textiles	2.6	98.9	101.6	96.2	100.1	98.7	94.5	95.4	92.1
Wearing apparel, leather and footwear Articles d'habillement, cuir et chaussures	2.8	101.9	101.5	95.3	92.9	89.7	82.7	78.7	77.9
Wood and wood products Bois et articles bois	1.7	91.8	97.8	97.0	100.5	104.2	107.3	112.2	106.7
Paper, printing, publishing and recorded media Papier, imprimerie, édition et supports enregistrés	7.8	96.0	98.9	99.4	103.6	107.6	110.9	113.7	111.7
Chemicals and related products Produits chimiques et alliés	14.1	90.6	96.1	101.6	107.1	111.0	115.0	120.3	121.2
Non–metallic mineral products Produits minéraux non métalliques	4.2	92.0	97.6	97.3	99.4	101.8	104.0	107.0	105.3
Basic metals Métallurgie de base	4.2	89.4	96.9	97.7	103.8	104.8	102.2	108.5	105.8
Fabricated metal products Fabrications d'ouvrages en métaux	16.9	89.2	93.5	100.1	103.5	107.9	107.3	113.3	114.3
Office and related electrical products Machines de bureau et autres appareils élect.	10.3	89.4	94.5	103.1	109.3	118.7	125.4	143.9	141.8
Transport equipment Equipement de transports	8.7	89.4	96.9	102.5	110.2	121.5	125.1	133.3	135.3
Electricity, gas, water [E] **Electricité, gaz et eau [E]**	**9.6**	**97.0**	**97.6**	**104.0**	**104.3**	**106.3**	**109.5**	**112.8**	**114.1**
Oceania · Océanie									
Total industry [CDE] **Total, industrie [CDE]**	**100.0**	**93.8**	**97.2**	**102.5**	**104.2**	**108.1**	**109.6**	**113.8**	**115.6**
Total mining [C] **Total, industries extractives [C]**	**18.3**	**96.2**	**96.2**	**102.6**	**103.4**	**112.3**	**108.9**	**120.9**	**127.0**
Coal Houille	4.2	93.9	94.5	103.1	103.4	108.5	116.6	126.5	134.3
Crude petroleum and natural gas Pétrole brut et gaz naturel	6.0	93.4	91.6	98.9	100.1	107.9	94.9	116.4	119.4
Metal ores Minerais métalliques	6.7	100.0	102.0	106.4	109.9	121.0	121.1	131.4	143.2
Total manufacturing [D] **Total, industries manufacturières [D]**	**69.4**	**93.0**	**97.3**	**102.4**	**104.3**	**107.3**	**110.5**	**113.4**	**114.0**
Food, beverages, tobacco Industries alimentaires, boissons, tabac	15.0	94.9	98.5	103.8	104.9	112.6	117.8	124.3	131.8
Textiles Textiles	1.9	99.5	101.4	95.2	96.0	96.5	97.2	92.6	88.1
Wearing apparel, leather and footwear Articles d'habillement, cuir et chaussures	2.2	99.5	101.4	95.1	95.9	96.3	97.1	92.5	87.9
Wood and wood products Bois et articles bois	2.8	93.2	96.6	101.4	99.3	99.2	97.2	111.2	102.5
Paper, printing, publishing and recorded media Papier, imprimerie, édition et supports enregistrés	7.3	92.5	94.8	102.2	104.8	103.9	103.3	107.7	100.6

5
Index numbers of industrial production: world and regions [*cont.*]
Indices de la production industrielle: monde et régions [*suite*]
1995=100

Region and industry [ISIC Rev.3] Région et industrie [CITI Rév.3]	Weight(%) Pond.(%)	1993	1994	1996	1997	1998	1999	2000	2001
Chemicals and related products									
Produits chimiques et alliés	10.0	91.5	96.4	105.0	107.2	109.0	114.9	114.9	121.1
Non−metallic mineral products									
Produits minéraux non métalliques	3.7	96.3	98.8	94.0	95.3	98.4	108.8	91.1	95.9
Basic metals									
Métallurgie de base	8.5	96.6	101.1	102.6	104.9	105.8	108.2	103.7	104.0
Fabricated metal products									
Fabrications d'ouvrages en métaux	5.6	90.3	96.5	103.3	105.8	108.0	109.4	114.3	113.5
Office and related electrical products									
Machines de bureau et autres appareils élect.	4.8	86.8	93.7	104.0	107.2	110.9	113.2	125.0	122.6
Transport equipment									
Equipement de transports	5.8	86.8	93.8	104.0	107.2	111.1	113.7	125.7	123.1
Electricity, gas, water [E]									
Electricité, gaz et eau [E]	**12.3**	**94.9**	**98.0**	**102.9**	**104.5**	**106.0**	**105.0**	**105.3**	**107.9**

Source:
United Nations Statistics Division, New York, "Industrial Commodity Statistics Yearbook 2000" and the industrial statistics database.

Source :
Organisation des Nations Unies, Division de statistique, New York, "Annuaire de statistiques industrielles par produit 2000" et la base de données pour les statistiques industrielles.

1 Northern America (Canada and the United States), Europe, Australia, Israel, Japan, New Zealand and South Africa.
2 Latin America and the Caribbean, Africa (excluding South Africa), Asia (excluding Israel and Japan), Oceania (excluding Australia and New Zealand).
3 Canada and the United States only.
4 Austria, Belgium, Denmark, Finland, France, Germany, Greece, Ireland, Italy, Luxembourg, Netherlands, Portugal, Spain, Sweden and the United Kingdom.

1 Amérique septentrionale (le Canada et les Etats−Unis), Europe, l'Australie, l'Israël, la Nouvelle−Zélande et l'Afrique du Sud.
2 Amérique latine et Caraïbes, Afrique (non compris l'Afrique du Sud), Asie (non compris l'Israël et le Japon), Océanie (non compris l'Australie et la Nouvelle−Zélande).
3 Le Canada et les Etats−Unis seulement.
4 L'Autriche, la Belgique, le Danemark, la Finlande, la France, l'Allemagne, la Grèce, l'Irlande, l'Italie, le Luxembourg, les Pays−Bas, le Portugal, l'Espagne, la Suède et le Royaume−Uni.

Table 6 follows overleaf

Le tableau 6 est présenté au verso

6
Production, trade and consumption of commercial energy
Thousand metric tons of oil equivalent and kilograms per capita
Production, commerce et consommation d'énergie commerciale
Milliers de tonnes d'équivalent pétrole et kilogrammes par habitant

Regions	Year	Primary energy production – Production d'énergie primaire					Changes in stocks	Imports	Exports
		Total	Solids Solides	Liquids Liquides	Gas Gaz	Electricity Electricité	Variations des stocks	Imports Importations	Exports Exportations
World	1993	8 216 863	2 172 408	3 275 998	1 953 455	815 001	− 29 304	2 951 800	2 878 766
	1994	8 420 157	2 244 559	3 344 629	1 998 558	832 410	34 851	2 964 620	2 900 544
	1995	8 625 341	2 321 720	3 386 198	2 050 512	866 911	15 952	3 030 491	3 016 564
	1996	8 850 528	2 361 410	3 442 999	2 152 096	894 023	1 803	3 210 555	3 149 577
	1997	8 966 415	2 379 338	3 542 876	2 152 762	891 439	25 326	3 340 746	3 298 078
	1998	9 001 683	2 307 393	3 593 221	2 192 847	908 221	53 041	3 381 342	3 393 649
	1999	8 861 452	2 183 749	3 516 092	2 227 619	933 992	− 83 437	3 412 729	3 387 099
Africa	1993	558 844	137 028	341 198	73 567	7 051	− 4 699	50 359	344 599
	1994	560 977	142 655	338 796	71 708	7 819	6 999	54 040	337 384
	1995	591 658	149 984	348 520	84 872	8 283	7 470	56 382	355 754
	1996	617 031	149 546	367 270	91 367	8 849	6 153	60 526	374 700
	1997	651 345	159 164	381 696	101 125	9 360	8 541	67 107	403 764
	1998	651 160	160 945	376 437	103 778	9 999	16 623	69 293	396 969
	1999	650 538	161 018	366 177	113 352	9 992	4 661	74 007	407 605
America, North	1993	2 143 444	525 863	700 728	643 887	272 966	− 27 523	627 707	325 032
	1994	2 245 599	575 970	700 969	682 469	286 190	28 137	660 662	327 040
	1995	2 251 600	573 356	701 196	679 505	297 543	− 10 958	647 355	350 121
	1996	2 267 968	589 982	675 741	700 065	302 180	− 6 899	682 904	363 936
	1997	2 293 700	605 486	694 805	708 769	284 639	− 7 450	733 467	379 340
	1998	2 296 079	613 242	682 352	711 100	289 386	17 923	772 011	389 330
	1999	2 267 554	600 079	647 428	710 436	309 612	− 28 404	791 327	376 794
America, South	1993	365 944	19 676	253 791	54 688	37 789	1 935	64 796	166 839
	1994	393 546	21 417	270 083	62 360	39 686	− 2 338	68 589	182 996
	1995	414 437	22 976	286 372	63 568	41 522	− 600	71 148	201 730
	1996	448 399	24 847	317 384	63 189	42 979	6 372	77 635	221 870
	1997	480 301	28 191	335 730	70 867	45 513	− 658	81 574	249 271
	1998	489 647	30 399	339 838	73 064	46 346	1 128	84 571	249 775
	1999	487 787	29 163	337 637	74 179	46 808	− 4 114	78 349	241 456
Asia	1993	2 721 224	889 481	1 331 653	354 906	145 185	7 584	936 811	1 151 301
	1994	2 843 240	938 840	1 381 249	369 067	154 084	4 256	944 522	1 112 679
	1995	2 965 380	1 003 489	1 393 351	401 469	167 070	10 924	989 503	1 147 965
	1996	3 060 808	1 038 492	1 414 934	433 009	174 373	2 112	1 063 575	1 172 274
	1997	3 110 219	1 030 917	1 459 165	438 949	181 188	23 024	1 129 103	1 224 722
	1998	3 142 978	970 254	1 525 887	455 843	190 994	13 891	1 095 175	1 293 234
	1999	3 024 197	862 590	1 490 994	480 472	190 142	− 41 729	1 122 268	1 289 766
Europe	1993	2 245 656	487 680	613 070	798 338	346 569	− 4 664	1 244 975	793 137
	1994	2 186 180	444 340	619 460	783 416	338 964	122	1 208 614	835 510
	1995	2 195 904	438 397	621 663	789 002	346 842	6 897	1 237 473	847 301
	1996	2 247 356	422 745	633 566	831 033	360 012	− 5 152	1 294 093	901 051
	1997	2 212 156	410 478	637 151	799 408	365 119	− 119	1 296 746	918 519
	1998	2 189 040	376 712	631 708	814 901	365 719	3 108	1 327 679	930 237
	1999	2 201 227	372 938	642 919	813 743	371 626	− 9 685	1 307 533	933 516
Oceania	1993	181 750	112 680	35 559	28 070	5 441	− 1 938	27 151	97 857
	1994	190 614	121 338	34 072	29 537	5 667	− 2 324	28 194	104 934
	1995	206 362	133 519	35 097	32 096	5 650	2 219	28 630	113 693
	1996	208 965	135 798	34 105	33 432	5 630	− 783	31 822	115 747
	1997	218 694	145 102	34 328	33 644	5 621	1 988	32 749	122 462
	1998	232 779	155 842	36 999	34 161	5 777	368	32 613	134 103
	1999	230 148	157 961	30 937	35 438	5 812	− 4 166	39 244	137 963

Source:
United Nations Statistics Division, New York, "Energy Statistics Yearbook 1999" and the energy statistics database.

Source:
Organisation des Nations Unies, Division de statistique, New York, "Annuaire des statistiques de l'énergie 1999" et la base de données pour les statistiques énergétiques.

Bunkers – Soutes			Consumption – Consommation							
Air Avion	Sea Maritime	Unallocated Nondistribué	Per capita Par habitant	Total Totale	Solids Solides	Liquids Liquides	Gas Gaz	Electricity Electricité	Année	Régions
64 478	117 062	317 956	1 376	7 819 705	2 255 900	2 812 872	1 935 932	815 001	1993	*Monde*
67 947	117 696	375 289	1 367	7 888 450	2 274 121	2 817 667	1 964 251	832 410	1994	
70 651	124 114	357 956	1 380	8 070 596	2 328 792	2 832 328	2 042 566	866 911	1995	
73 488	125 577	366 340	1 405	8 344 298	2 407 786	2 894 092	2 148 397	894 023	1996	
77 569	128 318	405 499	1 393	8 372 371	2 394 305	2 923 989	2 162 637	891 439	1997	
79 580	133 250	377 855	1 370	8 345 651	2 329 935	2 942 904	2 164 591	908 221	1998	
83 457	137 864	367 733	1 358	8 381 464	2 237 332	2 972 947	2 237 193	933 992	1999	
1 893	6 195	26 457	328	234 758	103 607	83 663	40 438	7 051	1993	Afrique
2 241	7 288	20 988	327	240 117	107 289	82 738	42 271	7 819	1994	
2 127	7 845	17 558	344	257 286	111 475	87 508	50 020	8 283	1995	
2 333	8 318	17 968	349	268 085	113 189	92 433	53 614	8 849	1996	
2 236	7 525	25 354	343	271 032	116 072	90 415	55 185	9 360	1997	
1 962	7 249	20 211	344	277 439	114 288	98 363	54 790	9 999	1998	
2 282	8 038	14 561	347	287 399	117 871	102 834	56 703	9 992	1999	
17 175	31 704	67 615	5 355	2 357 148	513 155	926 847	644 181	272 966	1993	Amérique du Nord
17 970	31 375	83 471	5 424	2 418 268	508 301	949 595	674 181	286 190	1994	
18 756	33 058	75 151	5 400	2 432 827	510 613	932 731	691 940	297 543	1995	
19 473	31 303	60 858	5 435	2 482 202	534 261	945 876	699 885	302 180	1996	
20 993	27 618	78 138	5 468	2 528 528	566 845	968 495	708 549	284 639	1997	
21 557	27 794	71 776	5 426	2 539 711	575 254	982 558	692 514	289 386	1998	
22 983	31 010	53 171	5 491	2 603 328	574 772	997 289	721 654	309 612	1999	
593	2 910	18 210	791	240 252	17 729	130 381	54 353	37 789	1993	Amérique du Sud
703	2 949	21 404	822	256 420	18 707	135 653	62 374	39 686	1994	
772	3 145	18 431	827	262 107	19 591	137 471	63 523	41 522	1995	
876	3 430	24 112	837	269 374	20 734	142 918	62 743	42 979	1996	
960	3 702	22 496	876	286 104	21 908	148 587	70 097	45 513	1997	
1 131	3 394	25 136	886	293 654	21 822	152 864	72 622	46 346	1998	
894	4 547	30 839	865	292 515	21 214	152 428	72 065	46 808	1999	
14 857	37 343	149 786	687	2 297 164	1 000 302	821 453	330 225	145 185	1993	Asie
16 007	38 182	196 725	713	2 419 914	1 051 133	846 249	368 447	154 084	1994	
17 051	40 676	189 794	739	2 548 473	1 104 953	877 235	399 215	167 070	1995	
17 759	40 364	205 520	767	2 686 355	1 158 628	916 465	436 889	174 373	1996	
18 618	43 533	221 995	763	2 707 430	1 138 848	931 149	456 245	181 188	1997	
17 959	47 462	205 452	739	2 660 155	1 085 687	917 374	466 100	190 994	1998	
16 811	48 387	204 138	721	2 629 092	1 002 780	939 192	496 978	190 142	1999	
27 309	37 660	58 170	3 022	2 579 020	580 063	807 111	845 277	346 569	1993	Europe
28 328	36 446	53 805	2 855	2 440 582	545 306	761 206	795 107	338 964	1994	
29 035	37 908	58 031	2 868	2 454 204	537 461	754 950	814 951	346 842	1995	
29 963	40 685	58 027	2 939	2 516 876	532 629	752 562	871 673	360 012	1996	
31 578	44 515	55 666	2 873	2 458 743	500 406	744 690	848 529	365 119	1997	
33 573	46 065	52 962	2 865	2 450 773	479 909	750 893	854 251	365 719	1998	
36 998	44 523	62 039	2 854	2 441 368	466 543	738 992	864 206	371 626	1999	
2 652	1 251	− 2 282	4 065	111 361	41 044	43 417	21 459	5 441	1993	Océanie
2 698	1 456	− 1 105	4 076	113 149	43 384	42 226	21 872	5 667	1994	
2 910	1 481	− 1 008	4 111	115 697	44 699	42 432	22 917	5 650	1995	
3 084	1 477	− 145	4 220	121 406	48 347	43 837	23 593	5 630	1996	
3 183	1 426	1 850	4 172	120 534	50 227	40 654	24 033	5 621	1997	
3 398	1 286	2 317	4 192	123 919	52 975	40 851	24 315	5 777	1998	
3 489	1 359	2 986	4 269	127 763	54 151	42 212	25 587	5 812	1999	

7
Total exports and imports: index numbers
Quantum and unit value indices and terms of trade (1990 = 100)
Exportations et importations totales: indices
Indices du quantum et de la valeur unitaire et termes de l'échange (1990 = 100)

Regions [1]	1994	1995	1996	1997	1998	1999	2000	2001	Régions [1]
Total									**Total**
Exports: Quantum indices [2]	122	134	142	157	167	175	195	196	**Exp.: Indices du quantum [2]**
Exports: Unit value indices US $ [3]	101	109	108	101	94	93	92	88	**Exp.: Indices de la val. unit. en $ E.−U. [3]**
Imports: Quantum indices [2]	125	136	144	157	165	176	195	195	**Imp.: Indices du quantum [2]**
Imports: Unit value indices US $ [3]	97	105	104	99	93	91	92	89	**Imp.: Indices de la val. unit. en $ E.−U. [3]**
Developed economies [4]									**Economies développées [4]**
Exports: Quantum indices [2]	118	129	136	150	157	165	181	180	**Exp.: Indices du quantum [2]**
Exports: Unit value indices US $ [3]	100	109	107	99	95	92	89	87	**Exp.: Indices de la val. unit. en $ E.−U. [3]**
Imports: Quantum indices [2]	118	129	136	149	161	173	190	186	**Imp.: Indices du quantum [2]**
Imports: Unit value indices US $ [3]	95	103	102	95	90	88	88	86	**Imp.: Indices de la val. unit. en $ E.−U. [3]**
Terms of trade [5]	106	106	105	104	105	105	102	101	**Termes de l'échange [5]**
Africa [6]									**Afrique [6]**
Exports: Quantum indices [2]	107	103	116	139	140	158	200	239	Exp.: Indices du quantum [2]
Exports: Unit value indices US $ [3]	100	114	106	94	80	72	64	52	Exp.: Indices de la val. unit. en $ E.−U. [3]
Imports: Quantum indices [2]	127	150	165	203	216	217	262	303	Imp.: Indices du quantum [2]
Imports: Unit value indices US $ [3]	100	112	100	89	74	68	63	51	Imp.: Indices de la val. unit. en $ E.−U. [3]
Terms of trade [5]	99	102	106	106	107	106	103	101	Termes de l'échange [5]
North America									**Amérique du Nord**
Exports: Quantum indices [2]	127	137	145	160	166	175	189	179	Exp.: Indices du quantum [2]
Exports: Unit value indices US $ [3]	101	107	108	106	102	101	104	102	Exp.: Indices de la val. unit. en $ E.−U. [3]
Imports: Quantum indices [2]	129	137	144	163	180	199	220	214	Imp.: Indices du quantum [2]
Imports: Unit value indices US $ [3]	101	106	106	104	98	99	105	101	Imp.: Indices de la val. unit. en $ E.−U. [3]
Terms of trade [5]	100	101	101	102	103	102	99	101	Termes de l'échange [5]
Asia									**Asie**
Exports: Quantum indices [2]	104	108	109	119	117	120	133	119	Exp.: Indices du quantum [2]
Exports: Unit value indices US $ [3]	132	143	132	123	115	121	127	119	Exp.: Indices de la val. unit. en $ E.−U. [3]
Imports: Quantum indices [2]	123	138	143	146	138	151	169	165	Imp.: Indices du quantum [2]
Imports: Unit value indices US $ [3]	97	105	105	99	87	88	96	90	Imp.: Indices de la val. unit. en $ E.−U. [3]
Terms of trade [5]	137	136	125	124	132	138	132	132	Termes de l'échange [5]
Europe									**Europe**
Exports: Quantum indices [2]	117	131	138	152	162	170	188	191	Exp.: Indices du quantum [2]
Exports: Unit value indices US $ [3]	95	105	103	93	90	86	80	79	Exp.: Indices de la val. unit. en $ E.−U. [3]
Imports: Quantum indices [2]	113	125	131	143	157	167	183	180	Imp.: Indices du quantum [2]
Imports: Unit value indices US $ [3]	92	101	99	90	87	82	79	78	Imp.: Indices de la val. unit. en $ E.−U. [3]
Terms of trade [5]	104	104	104	103	104	104	101	100	Termes de l'échange [5]
EU +									UE +
Exports: Quantum indices [2]	117	132	139	154	164	172	190	194	Exp.: Indices du quantum [2]
Exports: Unit value indices US $ [3]	95	105	103	93	90	85	79	78	Exp.: Indices de la val. unit. en $ E.−U. [3]
Imports: Quantum indices [2]	114	126	132	145	159	169	185	182	Imp.: Indices du quantum [2]
Imports: Unit value indices US $ [3]	92	101	99	90	87	82	79	78	Imp.: Indices de la val. unit. en $ E.−U. [3]
Terms of trade [5]	104	104	104	103	104	104	100	100	Termes de l'échange [5]
EFTA +									AELE +
Exports: Quantum indices [2]	112	118	124	132	135	141	147	152	Exp.: Indices du quantum [2]
Exports: Unit value indices US $ [3]	92	104	104	94	87	88	92	91	Exp.: Indices de la val. unit. en $ E.−U. [3]
Imports: Quantum indices [2]	101	108	112	121	131	137	145	144	Imp.: Indices du quantum [2]
Imports: Unit value indices US $ [3]	94	105	102	91	87	83	78	79	Imp.: Indices de la val. unit. en $ E.−U. [3]
Terms of trade [5]	98	99	102	103	100	107	118	116	Termes de l'échange [5]
Oceania									**Océanie**
Exports: Quantum indices [2]	136	139	155	167	166	174	190	191	Exp.: Indices du quantum [2]
Exports: Unit value indices US $ [3]	89	97	98	94	82	79	82	81	Exp.: Indices de la val. unit. en $ E.−U. [3]
Imports: Quantum indices [2]	121	132	140	148	157	169	176	167	Imp.: Indices du quantum [2]
Imports: Unit value indices US $ [3]	104	110	111	105	95	95	93	88	Imp.: Indices de la val. unit. en $ E.−U. [3]
Terms of trade [5]	85	88	88	89	87	83	87	92	Termes de l'échange [5]
Developing economies [4]									**Economies en développement [4]**
Exports: Quantum indices [2]	135	151	160	180	199	207	239	245	**Exp.: Indices du quantum [2]**
Exports: Unit value indices US $ [3]	103	109	111	105	90	95	100	91	**Exp.: Indices de la val. unit. en $ E.−U. [3]**
Imports: Quantum indices [2]	149	159	171	181	178	183	208	219	**Imp.: Indices du quantum [2]**
Imports: Unit value indices US $ [3][7]	101	113	112	111	102	103	108	99	**Imp.: Indices de la val. unit. en $ E.−U. [3][7]**
Terms of trade [5][7]	102	97	99	95	88	92	93	92	**Termes de l'échange [5][7]**

7
Total exports and imports: index numbers
Quantum and unit value indices and terms of trade (1990 = 100)
Exportations et importations totales: indices
Indices du quantum et de la valeur unitaire et termes de l'échange (1990 = 100)

Regions [1]	1994	1995	1996	1997	1998	1999	2000	2001	Régions [1]
Africa									**Afrique**
Exports: Quantum indices [2]	97	101	121	121	146	146	154	172	Exp.: Indices du quantum [2]
Exports: Unit value indices US $ [3]	88	99	92	91	71	80	87	74	Exp.: Indices de la val. unit. en $ E.−U [3]
Imports: Quantum indices [2]	95	102	112	119	147	154	157	165	Imp.: Indices du quantum [2]
Imports: Unit value indices US $ [3]	98	108	101	96	88	82	80	81	Imp.: Indices de la val. unit. en $ E.−U [3]
Terms of trade [5]	90	91	91	95	81	97	109	92	Termes de l'échange [5]
America									**Amérique**
Exports: Quantum indices [2]	144	152	146	158	171	180	202	228	Exp.: Indices du quantum [2]
Exports: Unit value indices US $ [3]	96	103	120	122	112	114	121	103	Exp.: Indices de la val. unit. en $ E.−U [3]
Imports: Quantum indices [2]	173	152	172	164	185	187	212	226	Imp.: Indices du quantum [2]
Imports: Unit value indices US $ [3]	105	126	125	152	141	134	137	126	Imp.: Indices de la val. unit. en $ E.−U [3]
Terms of trade [5]	92	81	96	80	79	85	89	81	Termes de l'échange [5]
Asia									**Asie**
Exports: Quantum indices [2]	141	161	171	196	216	226	265	265	Exp.: Indices du quantum [2]
Exports: Unit value indices US $ [3]	105	111	111	103	88	92	97	90	Exp.: Indices de la val. unit. en $ E.−U [3]
Imports: Quantum indices [2]	153	171	182	194	180	188	218	228	Imp.: Indices du quantum [2]
Imports: Unit value indices US $ [3]	100	111	111	106	95	99	104	95	Imp.: Indices de la val. unit. en $ E.−U [3]
Terms of trade [5]	105	100	100	97	92	93	93	95	Termes de l'échange [5]
Middle East									**Moyen−Orient**
Exports: Quantum indices [2]	116	118	124	140	162	149	153	157	Exp.: Indices du quantum [2]
Exports: Unit value indices US $ [3]	89	97	106	100	74	101	131	120	Exp.: Indices de la val. unit. en $ E.−U [3]
Imports: Quantum indices [2]	113	125	139	156	162	161	184	172	Imp.: Indices du quantum [2]
Imports: Unit value indices US $ [3]	95	103	104	99	92	90	92	93	Imp.: Indices de la val. unit. en $ E.−U [3]
Terms of trade [5]	93	94	102	101	80	113	143	129	Termes de l'échange [5]
Other Asia									**Autres pays d'Asie**
Exports: Quantum indices [2]	147	172	183	212	230	248	299	298	Exp.: Indices du quantum [2]
Exports: Unit value indices US $ [3]	110	114	112	104	91	91	91	85	Exp.: Indices de la val. unit. en $ E.−U [3]
Imports: Quantum indices [2]	161	180	190	202	182	192	224	238	Imp.: Indices du quantum [2]
Imports: Unit value indices US $ [3]	101	112	112	107	96	101	107	95	Imp.: Indices de la val. unit. en $ E.−U [3]
Terms of trade [5]	109	102	100	97	95	90	85	89	Termes de l'échange [5]
Europe [8]									**Europe [8]**
Exports: Quantum indices [2]	78	83	77	84	90	78	81	81	Exp.: Indices du quantum [2]
Exports: Unit value indices US $ [3]	130	133	144	138	139	150	150	150	Exp.: Indices de la val. unit. en $ E.−U [3]
Imports: Quantum indices [2]	77	91	98	119	124	111	148	153	Imp.: Indices du quantum [2]
Imports: Unit value indices US $ [3]	123	125	124	125	120	126	94	100	Imp.: Indices de la val. unit. en $ E.−U [3]
Terms of trade [5]	77	91	98	119	124	111	148	153	Termes de l'échange [5]

Source:
United Nations Statistics Division, New York, trade statistics database.

Source:
Organisation des Nations Unies, Division de statistique, New York, la base de données pour les statistiques du commerce extérieur.

+   For Member States of this grouping, see Annex I − Other groupings.

+   Pour les Etats membres de ce groupement, voir annexe I − Autres groupements.

1   The regional analysis in this table is in accordance with the groupings of countries or areas specified in table 69.

2   Quantum indices are derived from value data and unit value indices. They are base period weighted.

3   Regional aggregates are current period weighted.

4   This classification is intended for statistical convenience and does not necessarily express a judgement about the stage reached by a particular country in the development process.

5   Unit value index of exports divided by unit value index of imports.

6   Beginning 1 January 1998, data refer to South Africa only. Prior to January 1998, data refer to South African Common Customs Area.

1   L'analyse régionale dans ce tableau est conforme aux groupes des pays ou zones paraissant dans le tableau 69.

2   Les indices du quantum sont calculés à partir des chiffres de la valeur et des indices de valeur unitaire. Ils sont àcoéfficients de pondération correspondant à la périod en base.

3   Les totaux régionaux sont à coéfficients de pondération correspondant à la période en cours.

4   Cette classification est utilisée pour plus de commodité dans la présentation des statistiques et n'implique pas nécessairement un jugement quant au stage de développement auquel est parvenu un pays donné.

5   Indices de la valeur unitaire des exportations divisé par l'indice de la valeur unitaire des importations.

6   A compter de janvier 1998, les données se rapportent qu'à l'Afrique du Sud. Avant janvier 1998, les données se rapportent à l'Union Douanière de l'Afrique

7
Total exports and imports: index numbers
Quantum and unit value indices and terms of trade (1990 = 100)
Exportations et importations totales: indices
Indices du quantum et de la valeur unitaire et termes de l'échange (1990 = 100)

7 Indices, except those for Europe, are based on estimates
prepared by the International Monetary Fund.

8 Beginning 1 January 1992, data refer to the Federal Republic of
Yugoslavia. Prior to that date, data refer to the Socialist Federal
Republic of Yugoslavia.

méridionale.

7 Le calcul des indices, sauf ceux pour l'Europe, sont basés
sur les estimations preparées par le Fonds monétaire
international.

8 A partir de ler janvier 1992 les données se rapportent à la République
fédérative de Yougoslavie. Avant cetta date les données se rapportent à la
République socialiste fédérative de Yougoslavie.

Technical notes, tables 1-7

Table 1: The series of world aggregates on population, production, transport, external trade and finance have been compiled from statistical publications and databases of the United Nations and the specialized agencies and other institutions [1, 6, 7, 8, 9, 15, 22, 23, 24, 25]. These sources should be consulted for details on compilation and coverage.

Table 2 presents estimates of population size, rates of population increase, crude birth and death rates, surface area and population density for the world and regions. Unless otherwise specified, all figures are estimates of the order of magnitude and are subject to a substantial margin of error.

The population estimates and rates presented in this table were prepared by the Population Division of the United Nations Secretariat and published in *World Population Prospects: 2000 Revision* [29].

The average annual percentage rates of population growth were calculated by the Population Division of the United Nations Secretariat, using an exponential rate of increase formula.

Crude birth and crude death rates are expressed in terms of the average annual number of births and deaths respectively, per 1,000 mid-year population. These rates are estimated.

Surface area totals were obtained by summing the figures for the individual countries or areas.

Density is the number of persons in the 2000 total population per square kilometre of total surface area.

The scheme of regionalization used for the purpose of making these estimates is presented in annex I. Although some continental totals are given, and all can be derived, the basic scheme presents eight macro regions that are so drawn as to obtain greater homogeneity in sizes of population, types of demographic circumstances and accuracy of demographic statistics.

Tables 3-4: The index numbers in table 3 refer to agricultural production, which is defined to include both crop and livestock products. Seeds and feed are excluded. The index numbers of food refer to commodities which are considered edible and contain nutrients. Coffee, tea and other inedible commodities are excluded.

The index numbers of total agricultural and food production in table 3 are calculated by the Laspeyres formula with the base year period 1989-1991. The latter is provided in order to diminish the impact of annual fluctuations in agricultural output during base years on the indices for the period. Production quantities of each commodity are weighted by 1989-1991 average national producer prices and summed for each year. The index numbers are based on production data for a calendar year.

Notes techniques, tableaux 1 à 7

Tableau 1: Les séries d'agrégats mondiaux sur la population, la production, les transports, le commerce extérieur et les finances ont été établies à partir de publications statistiques et bases de données des Nations Unies et les institutions spécialisées et autres organismes [1, 6, 7, 8, 9, 15, 22, 23, 24, 25]. On doit se référer à ces sources pour tous renseignements détaillés sur les méthodes de calcul et la portée des statistiques.

Le *Tableau 2* présente les estimations mondiales et régionales de la population, des taux d'accroissement de la population, des taux bruts de natalité et de mortalité, de la superficie et de la densité de population. Sauf indication contraire, tous les chiffres sont des estimations de l'ordre de grandeur et comportent une assez grande marge d'erreur.

Les estimations de la population et tous les taux présentés dans ce tableau ont été établis par la Division de la population du Secrétariat des Nations Unies et publiés dans "*World Population Prospects: 2000 Revision*" [29].

Les pourcentages annuels moyens de l'accroissement de la population ont été calculés par la Division de la population du Secrétariat des Nations Unies, sur la base d'une formule de taux d'accroissement exponentiel.

Les taux bruts de natalité et de mortalité sont exprimés, respectivement, sur la base du nombre annuel moyen de naissances et de décès par tranche de 1.000 habitants au milieu de l'année. Ces taux sont estimatifs.

On a déterminé les superficies totales en additionnant les chiffres correspondant aux différents pays ou régions.

La densité est le nombre de personnes de la population totale de 2000 par kilomètre carré de la superficie totale.

Le schéma de régionalisation utilisé aux fins de l'établissement de ces estimations est présenté dans l'annexe I. Bien que les totaux de certains continents soient donnés et que tous puissent être déterminés, le schéma de base présente huit grandes régions qui sont établies de manière à obtenir une plus grande homogénéité en ce qui concerne l'ampleur des populations, les types de conditions démographiques et la précision des statistiques démographiques.

Tableaux 3-4: Les indices du tableau 3 se rapportent à la production agricole, qui est définie comme comprenant à la fois les produits de l'agriculture et de l'élevage. Les semences et les aliments pour les animaux sont exclus de cette définition. Les indices de la production alimentaire se rapportent aux produits considérés comme

As in the past, the series include a large number of estimates made by FAO in cases where figures are not available from official country sources.

Index numbers for the world and regions are computed in a similar way to the country index numbers except that instead of using different commodity prices for each country group, "international commodity prices" derived from the Gheary-Khamis formula are used for all country groupings. This method assigns a single "price" to each commodity.

The indexes in table 4 are calculated as a ratio between the index numbers of total agricultural and food production in table 3 described above and the corresponding index numbers of population.

For further information on the series presented in these tables, see the FAO *Production Yearbook* [6] and <www.fao.org>.

Table 5: The index numbers of industrial production are classified according to tabulation categories, divisions and combinations of divisions of the International Standard Industrial Classification of All Economic Activities, Revision 3, (ISIC Rev. 3) [50] for mining (category C), manufacturing (category D), and electricity, gas and water (category E).

The indices indicate trends in value added in constant US dollars. The measure of value added used is the national accounts concept, which is defined as gross output less the cost of materials, supplies, fuel and electricity consumed and services received.

Each series is compiled using the Laspeyres formula, that is, the indices are base-weighted arithmetic means. The weight base year is 1995 and value added, generally at factor values, is used in weighting.

For most countries the estimates of value added used as weights are derived from the results of national industrial censuses or similar inquiries relating to 1995. These data, in national currency, are adjusted to the ISIC where necessary and are subsequently converted into US dollars.

Within each of the ISIC categories (tabulation categories, divisions and combinations of divisions) shown in the tables, the indices for the country aggregations (regions or economic groupings) are calculated directly from the country data. The indices for the World, however, are calculated from the aggregated indices for the groupings of developed and developing countries.

China and the countries of the former USSR (except Russian Federation and Ukraine) are excluded from their respective regions.

Table 6: For a description of the series in table 6, see the technical notes to chapter XIII.

comestibles et contenant des éléments nutritifs. Le café, le thé et les produits non comestibles sont exclus.

Les indices de la production agricole et de la production alimentaire présentés au tableau 3 sont calculés selon la formule de Laspeyres avec les années 1989-1991 comme période de référence, cela afin de limiter l'incidence, sur les indices correspondant à la période considérée, des fluctuations annuelles de la production agricole enregistrée pendant les années de référence. Les chiffres de production de chaque produit sont pondérés par les prix nationaux moyens à la production pour la période 1989-1991 et additionnés pour chaque année. Les indices sont fondés sur les données de production de l'année civile. Comme dans le passé, les séries comprennent un grand nombre d'estimations établies par la FAO lorsqu'elle n'avait pu obtenir de chiffres de sources officielles dans les pays eux-mêmes.

Les indices pour le monde et les régions sont calculés de la même façon que les indices par pays, mais au lieu d'appliquer des prix différents aux produits de base pour chaque groupe de pays, on a utilisé des "prix internationaux" établis d'après la formule de Gheary-Khamis pour tous les groupes de pays. Cette méthode attribue un seul "prix" à chaque produit de base.

Les indices du tableau 4 sont calculés comme ratio entre les indices de la production alimentaire et de la production agricole totale du tableau 3 décrits ci-dessus et les indices de population correspondants.

Pour tout renseignement complémentaire sur les séries présentées dans ces tableaux, voir l'*Annuaire FAO de la production* [6] et <www.fao.org>.

Tableau 5: Les indices de la production industrielle sont classés selon les catégories de classement, les divisions ou des combinaisons des divisions de la Classification Internationale type, par industrie, de toutes les branches d'activité économique, Révision 3 (CITI Rev. 3) [50] qui concernent les industries extractives (la catégorie C) et les industries manufacturières (la catégorie D), ainsi que l'électricité, le gaz et l'eau (la catégorie E).

Ces indices représentent les tendances de la valeur ajoutée en dollars constants des Etats-Unis. La mesure utilisée pour la valeur ajoutée correspond à celle qui est appliquée aux fins de la comptabilité nationale, c'est-à-dire égale à la valeur de la production brute diminuée des coûts des matériaux, des fournitures, de la consommation de carburant et d'électricité ainsi que des services reçus.

Chaque série a été établie au moyen de la formule de Laspeyres, ce qui signifie que les indices sont des moyennes arithmétiques affectées de coefficients de pondération. L'année de base de pondération est l'année 1995 et on utilise généralement pour la pondération la valeur ajoutée aux coûts des facteurs.

Table 7: For a description of the series in table 7, see the technical notes to chapter XVI. The composition of the regions is presented in table 74.

Pour la plupart des pays, les estimations de la valeur ajoutée qui sont utilisées comme coefficients de pondération sont tirées des résultats des recensements industriels nationaux ou enquêtes analogues concernant l'année 1995. Ces données, en monnaie nationale, sont ajustées s'il y a lieu aux normes de la CITI et ultérieurement converties en dollars des Etats-Unis.

A l'intérieur de chacune des subdivisions de la CITI (catégories de classement, divisions et combinaisons des divisions) indiquées dans les tableaux, les indices relatifs aux assemblages de pays (régions géographiques ou groupements économiques) sont calculés directement à partir des données des pays. Toutefois, les indices concernant le *Monde* sont calculés à partir des indices agrégés applicables aux groupements de pays développés et de pays en développement.

La Chine et les pays de l'ancienne URSS (sauf la Fédération de Russie et Ukraine) sont exclus de leurs régions respectives.

Tableau 6: On trouvera une description de la série de statistiques du tableau 6 dans les notes techniques du chapitre XIII.

Tableau 7: On trouvera une description de la série de statistiques du tableau 7 dans les notes techniques du chapitre XVI. La composition des régions est présentée au tableau 74.

Part Two
Population and Social Statistics

Chapter II
Population (table 8)
Chapter III
Education and literacy (tables 9 and 10)
Chapter IV
Health and nutrition (tables 11 and 12)
Chapter V
Culture and communication
(tables 13-19)

Part Two of the *Yearbook* presents statistical series on a wide range of population and social topics for all countries or areas of the world for which data have been made available. The topics include population and population growth, surface area and density; education and the illiterate population; AIDS cases; food supply; book production; newspapers and periodicals; cinemas; telephones; and Internet users.

Deuxième partie
Population et statistiques sociales

Chapitre II
Population (tableau 8)
Chapitre III
Instruction et alphabétisation (tableaux 9 et 10)
Chapitre IV
Santé et nutrition (tableaux 11 et 12)
Chapitre V
Culture et communication
(tableaux 13 à 19)

La deuxième partie de l'*Annuaire* présente, pour tous les pays ou zones du monde pour lesquels des données sont disponibles, des séries statistiques intéressant une large gamme de questions démographiques et sociales: population et croissance démographique, superficie et densité; l'instruction et la population analphabète; cas de SIDA; disponibilités alimentaires; production de livres; journaux et périodiques; cinémas; téléphones; et usagers d'Internet.

8
Population by sex, rate of population increase, surface area and density
Population selon le sexe, taux d'accroissement de la population, superficie et densité

Country or area Pays ou zone	Latest census Dernier recensement Date	Both sexes Les deux sexes	Men Hommes	Women Femmes	Mid-year estimates (thousands) Estimations au milieu de l'année (milliers) 1995	2000	Annual rate of increase Taux d'accrois-sement annuel % 1995–00	Surface area (km²) Superficie (km²) 2000	Density Densité 2000[1]
Africa · Afrique									
Algeria[2] Algérie[2]	25 VI 1998	29 100 867	14 698 589	14 402 278	28 060	*30 386	1.6	2 381 741	13
Angola[3] Angola[3]	15 XII 1970	5 646 166	2 943 974	2 702 192	x11 339	x13 134	2.9	1 246 700	11
Benin Bénin	15 II 1992	4 915 555	2 390 336	2 525 219	5 412	*6 169	2.6	112 622	55
Botswana Botswana	11 VIII 2001	*1 693 970	...	...	1 459	*1 653	2.5	581 730	3
Burkina Faso [4] Burkina Faso [4]	10 XII 1996	10 312 609	4 970 882	5 341 727	10 200	x11 535	...	274 000	42
Burundi [4] Burundi [4]	16 VIII 1990	5 139 073	2 473 599	2 665 474	5 982	x6 356	...	27 834	228
Cameroon [4] Cameroun [4]	11 IV 1987	10493655	...	...	13 277	x14 876	...	475 442	31
Cape Verde [4] Cap–Vert [4]	11 VI 2000	*434 812	...	...	386	x427	...	4 033	106
Central African Republic République centrafricaine	8 XII 1988	2 463 616	1 210 734	1 252 882	x3 347	x3 717	2.1	622 984	6
Chad [5] Tchad [5]	8 IV 1993	6 279 931	...	...	x6 735	x7 885	3.2	1 284 000	6
Comoros [6] Comores [6]	15 IX 1991	446 817	221 152	225 665	x609	x706	3.0	2 235	316
Congo Congo	22 XII 1984	1 843 421	...	...	x2 603	x3 018	3.0	342 000	9
Côte d'Ivoire Côte d'Ivoire	1 III 1988	10 815 694	5 527 343	5 288 351	14 230	*16 398	2.8	322 463	51
Dem. Rep. of the Congo Rép. dém du Congo	1 VII 1984	29 916 800	14 543 800	15 373 000	x44 834	x50 948	2.6	2 344 858	22
Djibouti Djibouti	11 XII 1960	81 200	...	...	x545	x632	3.0	23 200	27
Egypt Egypte	19 XI 1996	59 312 914	30 351 390	28 961 524	57 510	*63 976	2.1	1 001 449	64
Equatorial Guinea [7] Guinée équatoriale [7]	4 VII 1983	300 000	144 760	155 240	x399	x457	2.7	28 051	16
Eritrea Erythrée	9 V 1984	2 748 304	1 374 452	1 373 852	x3 189	x3 659	2.8	117 600	31
Ethiopia Ethiopie	11 X 1994	53 477 265	26 910 698	26 566 567	54 649	*63 495	3.0	1 104 300	57
Gabon Gabon	31 VII 1993	1 014 976	501 784	513 192	1 093	*1 206	2.0	267 668	5
Gambia [4] Gambie [4]	13 IV 1993	1 025 867	514 530	511 337	x1 115	*1 393	...	11 295	123
Ghana Ghana	26 III 2000	18 912 079	9 357 382	9 554 697	x17 297	x19 306	2.2	238 533	81
Guinea [8] Guinée [8]	4 II 1983	4 533 240	...	...	x7 332	x8 154	2.1	245 857	33
Guinea–Bissau Guinée–Bissau	1 XII 1991	983 367	476 210	507 157	x1 078	x1 199	2.1	36 125	33
Kenya [4] Kenya [4]	24 VIII 1999	*28 679 000	*14 165 000	*14 514 000	30 522	x30 669	...	580 367	53
Lesotho [4] Lesotho [4]	14 IV 1996	*1 862 275	...	...	x1 869	*2 144	...	30 355	71
Liberia [4] Libéria [4]	1 II 1984	2 101 628	1 063 127	1 038 501	2 760	x2 913	...	111 369	26

8
Population by sex, rate of population increase, surface area and density [*cont.*]
Population selon le sexe, taux d'accroissement de la population,
superficie et densité [*suite*]

Country or area Pays ou zone	Latest census Dernier recensement Date	Both sexes Les deux sexes	Men Hommes	Women Femmes	Mid-year estimates (thousands) Estimations au milieu de l'année (milliers) 1995	2000	Annual rate of increase Taux d'accrois-sement annuel % 1995–00	Surface area (km²) Superficie (km²) 2000	Density Densité 2000[1]
Libyan Arab Jamahiriya Jamahiriya arabe libyenne	11 VIII 1995	4 404 986	2 236 943	2 168 043	x4 755	x5 290	2.1	1 759 540	3
Madagascar Madagascar	1 VIII 1993	12092157	5 991 171	6 100 986	x13 789	x15 970	2.9	587 041	27
Malawi [4] Malawi [4]	1 IX 1998	9 933 868	4 867 563	5 066 305	9 788	x11 308	...	118 484	95
Mali [9] Mali [9]	17 IV 1998	9 790 492	4 847 436	4 943 056	x9 928	x11 351	2.7	1 240 192	9
Mauritania [4] [10] Mauritanie [4] [10]	5 IV 1988	1 864 236	923 175	941 061	2 284	x2 665	...	1 025 520	3
Mauritius Maurice	1 VII 1990	1 056 660	527 760	528 900	1 122	1 186	1.1	2 040	581
Morocco Maroc	2 IX 1994	26 073 717	...	...	26 386	*28 705	1.7	446 550	64
Mozambique [8] Mozambique [8]	1 VIII 1997	15 278 334	7 320 948	7 957 386	15 820	*17 691	2.2	801 590	22
Namibia [4] Namibie [4]	21 X 1991	1 409 920	686 327	723 593	x1 585	*1 817	...	824 292	2
Niger Niger	20 V 1988	7 248 100	3 590 070	3 658 030	x9 109	x10 832	3.5	1 267 000	9
Nigeria [4] Nigéria [4]	26 XI 1991	88 992 220	44 529 608	44 462 612	x99 278	*115 224	...	923 768	125
Reunion [9] Réunion [9]	15 III 1990	597 828	294 256	303 572	x664	x721	1.6	2 510	287
Rwanda Rwanda	15 VIII 1991	7 142 755	...	...	x4 979	x7 609	8.5	26 338	289
St. Helena ex. dep. Sainte–Hélène sans dép.	8 III 1998	5 157	2 612	2 545	5	x6	...	122	52
Ascension Ascension	31 XII 1978	849	608	241	...	...	...	88	...
Tristan da Cunha Tristan da Cunha	31 XII 1988	296	139	157	...	...	...	...	...
Sao Tome and Principe [4] Sao Tomé–et–Principe [4]	4 VIII 1991	116 998	57 837	59 161	127	x138	...	964	143
Senegal Sénégal	27 V 1988	6 896 808	3 353 599	3 543 209	8 347	*9 524	2.6	196 722	48
Seychelles Seychelles	29 VIII 1997	75 876	37 589	38 287	75	*81	1.5	455	178
Sierra Leone [8] Sierra Leone [8]	15 XII 1985	3 515 812	1 746 055	1 769 757	x4 080	x4 405	1.5	71 740	61
Somalia Somalie	15 II 1987	7 114 431	3 741 664	3 372 767	x7 348	x8 778	3.6	637 657	14
South Africa [8] Afrique du Sud [8]	10 X 1996	40 583 573	19 520 887	21 062 686	39 477	*43 686	2.0	1 221 037	36
Sudan Soudan	15 IV 1993	24 940 683	12 518 638	12 422 045	x27 952	x31 095	2.1	2 505 813	12
Swaziland [4] Swaziland [4]	11 V 1997	*965 859	...	...	908	x925	...	17 364	53
Togo Togo	22 XI 1981	2 703 250	...	...	x3 844	x4 527	3.3	56 785	80
Tunisia Tunisie	20 IV 1994	8 785 711	4 439 289	4 346 422	8 958	*9 561	1.3	163 610	58
Uganda Ouganda	12 I 1991	16 671 705	8 185 747	8 485 958	19 263	*22 210	2.8	241 038	92
United Rep. of Tanzania [4] Rép.–Unie de Tanzanie [4]	28 VIII 1988	23 126 310	11 217 723	11 908 587	28 279	x35 119	...	883 749	40
Western Sahara [11] Sahara occidental [11]	31 XII 1970	76 425	43 981	32 444	x213	x252	3.4	266 000	1

8
Population by sex, rate of population increase, surface area and density [*cont.*]
Population selon le sexe, taux d'accroissement de la population,
superficie et densité [*suite*]

Country or area Pays ou zone	Latest census Dernier recensement Date	Both sexes Les deux sexes	Men Hommes	Women Femmes	Mid-year estimates (thousands) Estimations au milieu de l'année (milliers) 1995	2000	Annual rate of increase Taux d'accrois- sement annuel % 1995–00	Surface area (km²) Superficie (km²) 2000	Density Densité 2000[1]
Zambia Zambie	25 X 2000	10 285 631	5 070 891	5 214 740	9 112	*10 723	3.3	752 618	14
Zimbabwe [4] Zimbabwe [4]	18 VIII 1992	10 412 548	5 083 537	5 329 011	11 526	x12 627	...	390 757	32
America, North · Amérique du Nord									
Anguilla [4] Anguilla [4]	9 V 2001	*11 430	*5 628	*5 802	10	x11	...	96	115
Antigua and Barbuda [4] Antigua–et–Barbuda [4]	28 V 2001	*77 426	*37 002	*40 424	68	x65	...	442	147
Aruba [2][4] Aruba [2][4]	6 X 1991	66 687	32 821	33 866	82	x101	...	193	523
Bahamas Bahamas	1 V 2000	*304 913	*147 804	*157 109	279	*303	1.6	13 878	22
Barbados Barbade	2 V 1990	257 082	...	...	264	*267	0.2	430	622
Belize Belize	12 V 2000	240 204	121 278	118 926	216	*250	2.9	22 966	11
Bermuda [2][4][12] Bermudes [2][4][12]	20 V 1991	74 837	...	...	60	x63	...	53	1 189
British Virgin Islands Iles Vierges britanniques	12 V 1991	17 809	...	...	x20	x24	3.6	151	159
Canada [2][8][13] Canada [2][8][13]	14 V 1996	28 846 760	14 170 030	14 676 735	29 354	*30 750	0.9	9 970 610	3
Cayman Islands [2] Iles Caïmanes [2]	15 X 1989	25 355	12 372	12 983	x32	x38	3.4	264	144
Costa Rica [2] Costa Rica [2]	26 VI 2000	*3 810 179	*1 902 614	*1 907 565	3 333	*3 825	2.8	51 100	75
Cuba Cuba	11 IX 1981	9 723 605	4 914 873	4 808 732	10 978	*11 188	0.4	110 861	101
Dominica Dominique	12 V 1991	71 794	35 927	35 867	75	*72	–1.0	751	95
Dominican Republic Rép. dominicaine	24 IX 1993	7 293 390	3 550 797	3 742 593	7 705	*8 518	2.0	48 511	176
El Salvador El Salvador	27 IX 1992	5 118 599	2 485 613	2 632 986	5 669	*6 276	2.0	21 041	298
Greenland [2] Groenland [2]	26 X 1976	49 630	26 856	22 774	56	*56	0.1	2 175 600	–
Grenada [4][14] Grenade [4][14]	12 V 1991	85 123	41 893	43 230	x92	*101	...	344	295
Guadeloupe [2][15] Guadeloupe [2][15]	15 III 1990	387 034	189 187	197 847	x409	x428	0.9	1 705	251
Guatemala [8] Guatemala [8]	17 IV 1994	8 322 051	...	...	9 976	*11 385	2.6	108 889	105
Haiti [2] Haïti [2]	30 VIII 1982	5 053 792	2 448 370	2 605 422	7 180	*7 959	2.1	27 750	287
Honduras [4] Honduras [4]	29 V 1988	4 248 561	2 110 106	2 138 455	5 602	x6 417	...	112 088	57
Jamaica Jamaïque	7 IV 1991	2 314 479	1 134 386	1 180 093	2 503	*2 633	1.0	10 991	240
Martinique [2] Martinique [2]	15 III 1990	359 579	173 878	185 701	x372	x383	0.6	1 102	348
Mexico [2] Mexique [2]	7 II 2000	97 361 711	47 354 386	50 007 325	90 487	*97 015	1.4	1 958 201	50
Montserrat [4] Montserrat [4]	12 V 1991	10 639	5 290	5 349	x10	*5	...	102	52
Netherlands Antilles [4][16] Antilles néerlandaises [4][16]	27 I 1992	189 474	90 707	98 767	202	x215	...	800	269

8

Population by sex, rate of population increase, surface area and density [*cont.*]
Population selon le sexe, taux d'accroissement de la population,
superficie et densité [*suite*]

Country or area Pays ou zone	Latest census Dernier recensement				Mid-year estimates (thousands) Estimations au milieu de l'année (milliers)		Annual rate of increase Taux d'accroissement annuel %	Surface area (km²) Superficie (km²)	Density Densité
	Date	Both sexes Les deux sexes	Men Hommes	Women Femmes	1995	2000	1995–00	2000	2000[1]
Nicaragua[2] Nicaragua[2]	25 IV 1995	4 357 099	2 147 105	2 209 994	4 427	*5 072	2.7	130 000	39
Panama Panama	14 V 2000	2 839 177	1 432 566	1 406 611	2 631	*2 856	1.6	75 517	38
Puerto Rico[2 17] Porto Rico[2 17]	1 IV 1990	3 522 037	1 705 642	1 816 395	3 719	*3 879	0.8	8 875	437
Saint Kitts and Nevis Saint-Kitts-et-Nevis	14 V 2001	*45 841	*22 784	*23 057	44	*40	−1.5	261	155
Saint Lucia Sainte-Lucie	22 V 2001	*156 635	*77 664	*78 971	145	x148	...	539	275
St. Pierre and Miquelon[4] Saint-Pierre et Miquelon[4]	5 III 1990	6 392	...	...	7	x7	...	242	29
St. Vincent and the Grenadines[4 18] St.-Vincent-et-Grenadines[4 18]	12 V 1991	106 499	53 165	53 334	111	x113	...	388	291
Trinidad and Tobago Trinité-et-Tobago	2 V 1990	1 169 572	584 445	585 127	1 260	*1 290	0.5	5 130	251
Turks and Caicos Islands Iles Turques et Caïques	31 V 1990	12 350	6 289	6 061	x14	x17	3.9	430	40
United States[2 19] Etats-Unis[2 19]	1 IV 2000	281 421 906	138 053 563	143 368 343	263 044	x283 230	...	9 629 091	29
United States Virgin Islands[2 17] Iles Vierges américaines[2 17]	1 IV 1990	101 809	49 210	52 599	x114	x121	1.2	347	349
America, South · Amérique du Sud									
Argentina Argentine	15 V 1991	32 615 528	15 937 980	16 677 548	34 768	*37 032	1.3	2 780 400	13
Bolivia[8] Bolivie[8]	5 IX 2001	*8 280 184	*4 130 342	*4 149 842	7 414	*8 329	2.3	1 098 581	8
Brazil[9 20] Brésil[9 20]	1 VIII 2000	169 544 443	*83 423 553	*86 120 890	155 822	*167 724	1.5	8 514 215	20
Chile Chili	22 IV 1992	13 348 401	6 553 254	6 795 147	14 210	*15 211	1.4	756 626	20
Colombia Colombie	24 X 1993	33 109 840	16 296 539	16 813 301	38 542	*42 321	1.9	1 138 914	37
Ecuador[8 21] Equateur[8 21]	25 XI 1990	9 648 189	4 796 412	4 851 777	11 460	*12 646	2.0	283 561	45
Falkland Is. (Malvinas)[22 23] Iles Falkland (Malvinas)[22 23]	24 IV 1996	2 564	1 447	1 117	x2	x2	−	12 173	−
French Guyana[2] Guyane française[2]	08 III 1999	156 790	78 963	77 827	x138	x165	3.6	90 000	2
Guyana[4] Guyana[4]	12 V 1991	701 704	344 928	356 776	x743	*772	...	214 969	4
Paraguay[4 8] Paraguay[4 8]	26 VIII 1992	4 152 588	2 085 905	2 066 683	4 828	x5 496	...	406 752	14
Peru[8 24] Pérou[8 24]	11 VII 1993	22 048 356	10 956 375	11 091 981	23 532	*25 662	1.7	1 285 216	20
Suriname Suriname	1 VII 1980	355 240	...	...	409	*436	1.3	163 265	3
Uruguay[8] Uruguay[8]	22 V 1996	3 163 763	1 532 288	1 631 475	3 218	*3 337	0.7	175 016	19
Venezuela[8 24] Venezuela[8 24]	20 X 1990	18 105 265	9 019 757	9 085 508	21 844	*24 170	2.0	912 050	27
Asia · Asie									
Afghanistan[25] Afghanistan[25]	23 VI 1979	13 051 358	6 712 377	6 338 981	x19 073	x21 765	2.6	652 090	33

8

Population by sex, rate of population increase, surface area and density [*cont.*]
Population selon le sexe, taux d'accroissement de la population,
superficie et densité [*suite*]

Country or area Pays ou zone	Latest census Dernier recensement Date	Both sexes Les deux sexes	Men Hommes	Women Femmes	Mid-year estimates (thousands) Estimations au milieu de l'année (milliers) 1995	2000	Annual rate of increase Taux d'accrois- sement annuel % 1995–00	Surface area (km²) Superficie (km²) 2000	Density Densité 2000[1]
Armenia [9] Arménie [9]	12 I 1989	3 304 776	1 619 308	1 685 468	3 760	*3 803	0.2	29 800	128
Azerbaijan [9] Azerbaïdjan [9]	27 I 1999	*7 953 000	*4 119 000	*3 834 000	7 685	*8 049	0.9	86 600	93
Bahrain Bahreïn	16 XI 1991	508 037	294 346	213 691	578	*691	3.6	694	995
Bangladesh [4] Bangladesh [4]	22 III 2001	123 151 246	*62 735 988	*60 415 258	119 900	x137 439	...	143 998	954
Bhutan Bhoutan	11 XI 1969	1 034 774	...	...	x1 831	x2 085	2.6	47 000	44
Brunei Darussalam [8] Brunéi Darussalam [8]	7 VIII 1991	260 482	137 616	122 866	296	*338	2.7	5 765	59
Cambodia [4 26] Cambodge [4 26]	3 III 1998	*11 437 656	*5 511 408	*5 926 248	9 836	x13 104	...	181 035	72
China [27 28] Chine [27 28]	1 XI 2000	*1 295 330 000	...	...	x1219349	x1 275 133	0.9	9 596 961	133
China, Hong Kong SAR [4 29] Chine, Hong Kong RAS [4 29]	30 VI 2000	*6 780 000	...	...	6 156	*6 797	...	1 075	6 323
China, Macao SAR Chine, Macao RAS	30 IX 2000	*440 000	...	...	409	*438	1.3	18	24 316
Cyprus [30] Chypre [30]	1 X 1992	602 025	299 614	302 411	733	*757	0.7	9 251	82
Georgia [4 9] Géorgie [4 9]	12 I 1989	5 400 841	2 562 040	2 838 801	5 417	x5 262	...	69 700	75
India [31] Inde [31]	01 III 2001	*1 027 015 247	*531 277 078	*495 738 169	921 989	*1 002 142	1.7	3 287 263	305
Indonesia [4] Indonésie [4]	30 VI 2000	203 456 005	101 641 570	101 814 435	x197 622	*210 486	...	1 904 569	111
Iran (Islamic Republic of) [2] Iran (Rép. islamique d') [2]	1 X 1996	60 055 488	30 515 159	29 540 329	59 187	*63 664	1.5	1 648 195	39
Iraq Iraq	17 X 1987	16 335 199	8 395 889	7 939 310	x20 049	x22 946	2.7	438 317	52
Israel [2 4 8 32] Israël [2 4 8 32]	4 XI 1995	5 548 523	2 738 175	2 810 348	5 545	x6 040	...	22 145	273
Japan [33] Japon [33]	1 X 2000	126 920 000	...	...	125 197	*126 867	0.3	377 829	336
Jordan [34 35] Jordanie [34 35]	10 XII 1994	4 139 458	2 160 725	1 978 733	x4 249	x4 913	2.9	89 342	55
Kazakhstan Kazakhstan	26 II 1999	14 953 126	7 201 785	7 751 341	16 066	*14 896	−1.5	2 724 900	5
Korea, Dem. People's Rep. Corée, Rép. pop. dém. de	31 XII 1993	21 213 378	10 329 699	10 883 679	x21 373	x22 268	0.8	120 538	185
Korea, Republic of [8 36] Corée, Rép. de [8 36]	1 XI 1995	44 608 726	22 389 324	22 219 402	45 093	*47 275	0.9	99 268	476
Kuwait Koweït	20 IV 1995	1 575 983	914 324	661 659	1 802	*2 190	3.9	17 818	123
Kyrgyzstan [9] Kirghizistan [9]	24 III 1999	4 822 938	2 380 438	2 442 500	4 555	*4 895	1.4	199 900	24
Lao People's Dem. Rep. [4] Rép. dém. populaire lao [4]	1 III 1985	3 584 803	1 757 115	1 827 688	x4 686	*5 218	...	236 800	22
Lebanon [37 38] Liban [37 38]	15 XI 1970	2 126 325	1 080 015	1 046 310	x3 169	x3 496	2.0	10 400	336
Malaysia Malaisie	5 VII 2000	*22 202 614	*11 212 525	*10 990 089	20 689	*23 266	2.3	329 758	71
Maldives [4] Maldives [4]	25 III 1995	244 814	124 622	120 192	x250	*271	...	298	911

8
Population by sex, rate of population increase, surface area and density [*cont.*]
Population selon le sexe, taux d'accroissement de la population,
superficie et densité [*suite*]

Country or area Pays ou zone	Latest census Dernier recensement				Mid-year estimates (thousands) Estimations au milieu de l'année (milliers)		Annual rate of increase Taux d'accrois-sement annuel %	Surface area (km²) Superficie (km²)	Density Densité
	Date	Both sexes Les deux sexes	Men Hommes	Women Femmes	1995	2000	1995-00	2000	2000[1]
Mongolia Mongolie	5 I 2000	2 373 493	1 177 981	1 195 512	2 299	*2 390	0.8	1 566 500	2
Myanmar [9] Myanmar [9]	31 III 1983	35 307 913	17 518 255	17 789 658	x44 352	x47 749	1.5	676 578	71
Nepal [2] Népal [2]	22 VI 1991	18 491 097	9 220 974	9 270 123	20 341	*22 904	2.4	147 181	156
Occupied Palestinian Territory [39] [40] Territoire palestinien occupé [39] [40]	9 XII 1997	2 601 669	1 322 264	1 279 405	x2 635	x3 191	3.8	6 213	514
Oman Oman	1 XII 1993	2 018 074	1 178 005	840 069	2 131	*2 402	2.4	309 500	8
Pakistan [41] Pakistan [41]	2 III 1998	130 579 571	67 840 137	62 739 434	122 360	*137 500	2.3	796 095	173
Philippines [2] Philippines [2]	1 V 2000	*76 500 000	...	...	70 267	*76 320	1.7	300 000	254
Qatar Qatar	1 III 1997	522 023	342 459	179 564	x512	x565	2.0	11 000	51
Saudi Arabia Arabie saoudite	27 IX 1992	16 948 388	9 479 973	7 468 415	x17 091	x20 346	3.5	2 149 690	9
Singapore [42] Singapour [42]	30 VI 2000	*4 017 700	*2 061 800	*1 955 900	3 526	*4 131	3.2	683	6 049
Sri Lanka Sri Lanka	17 VII 2001	*16 864 544	...	...	18 136	*19 359	1.3	65 610	295
Syrian Arab Republic [43] Rép. arabe syrienne [43]	3 IX 1994	13 782 315	7 048 906	6 733 409	14 153	*16 320	2.8	185 180	88
Tajikistan Tadjikistan	20 I 2000	*6 127 000	*3 082 000	*3 045 000	5 836	*6 170	1.1	143 100	43
Thailand [2] Thaïlande [2]	1 IV 2000	60 617 200	29 850 100	30 767 100	59 401	*62 320	1.0	513 115	121
Timor-Leste Timor-Leste	31 X 1990	747 750	386 939	360 811	x840	x737	-2.6	14 874	50
Turkey Turquie	21 X 1990	56 473 035	28 607 047	27 865 988	60 613	*65 293	1.5	774 815	84
Turkmenistan [4] Turkménistan [4]	10 I 1995	4 483 251	2 225 331	2 257 920	4 509	x4 737	...	488 100	10
United Arab Emirates [4] [44] Emirats arabes unis [4] [44]	11 XII 1995	2 377 453	1 579 743	797 710	2 314	x2 606	...	83 600	31
Uzbekistan [9] Ouzbékistan [9]	12 I 1989	19 810 077	9 784 156	10 025 921	22 690	*24 752	1.7	447 400	55
Viet Nam Viet Nam	01 IV 1999	*76 324 753	*37 519 754	*38 804 999	73 962	*77 686	1.0	331 689	234
Yemen Yémen	16 XII 1994	14 587 807	7 473 540	7 114 267	15 369	*18 295	3.5	527 968	35
Europe · Europe									
Albania [4] Albanie [4]	12 IV 1989	3 182 400	1 638 900	1 543 500	3 609	x3 134	...	28 748	109
Andorra [4] Andorre [4]	11 XI 1954	5 664	...	...	x68	*66	...	468	141
Austria [2] Autriche [2]	15 V 1991	7 795 786	3 753 989	4 041 797	8 047	*8 110	0.2	83 859	97
Belarus [9] Bélarus [9]	16 II 1999	10045237	4 717 621	5 327 616	10 281	*10 002	-0.6	207 600	48
Belgium [2] [4] Belgique [2] [4]	1 III 1991	9 978 681	4 875 982	5 102 699	10 137	x10 249	...	30 528	336
Bosnia and Herzegovina [2] [4] Bosnie-Herzégovine [2] [4]	31 III 1991	4 377 033	2 183 795	2 193 238	4 180	x3 977	...	51 197	78
Bulgaria [4] Bulgarie [4]	4 XII 1992	8 472 724	...	...	8 406	x7 949	...	110 912	72

8
Population by sex, rate of population increase, surface area and density [*cont.*]
Population selon le sexe, taux d'accroissement de la population,
superficie et densité [*suite*]

Country or area Pays ou zone	Latest census Dernier recensement Date	Both sexes Les deux sexes	Men Hommes	Women Femmes	Mid-year estimates (thousands) Estimations au milieu de l'année (milliers) 1995	2000	Annual rate of increase Taux d'accrois- sement annuel % 1995–00	Surface area (km²) Superficie (km²) 2000	Density Densité 2000¹
Channel Islands [4] Iles Anglo–Normandes [4]	10 III 1996	143 831	69 638	74 193	143	x144	...	195	738
Croatia [2] Croatie [2]	11 III 2001	*4 381 000	...	...	4 669	*4 381	−1.3	56 538	77
Czech Republic [2] Rép. tchéque [2]	3 III 1991	10 302 215	4 999 935	5 302 280	10 331	*10 273	−0.1	78 866	130
Denmark [2] [45] Danemark [2] [45]	1 I 1998	5 294 860	2 615 669	2 679 191	5 228	*5 337	0.4	43 094	124
Estonia Estonie	31 III 2000	*1370500	*631 900	*738 600	1 484	*1 369	−1.6	45 100	30
Faeroe Islands [2] Iles Féroé [2]	22 IX 1977	41 969	21 997	19 972	x44	x46	0.9	1 399	33
Finland [2] Finlande [2]	31 XII 1990	4 998 478	2 426 204	2 572 274	5 108	*5 176	0.3	338 145	15
France [46] [47] France [46] [47]	5 III 1990	56 634 299	27 553 788	29 080 511	58 139	*58 892	0.3	551 500	107
Germany [2] [4] [48] Allemagne [2] [4] [48]		...	...	...	81 661	x82 017	...	357 022	230
Fed. Rep. of Germany [2] Rép. féd. d'Allemagne [2]	25 V 1987	61 077 042	29 322 923	31 754 119	...	...	...	248 647	...
German Dem Rep. (former) l'ex–R. d. allemande [2]	31 XII 1981	16 705 635	7 849 112	8 856 523	...	...	...	108 333	...
Gibraltar [49] Gibraltar [49]	14 X 1991	26 703	13 628	13 075	27	x27	...	6	4 500
Greece [50] [51] Grèce [50] [51]	17 III 1991	10 259 900	5 055 408	5 204 492	10 454	*10 008	−0.9	131 957	76
Holy See [52] Saint–Siège [52]	30 IV 1948	890	548	342	x1	*1	...	−	...
Hungary Hongrie	1 I 1990	10 374 823	4 984 904	5 389 919	10 229	*10 024	−0.4	93 032	108
Iceland [2] Islande [2]	1 XII 1970	204 930	103 621	101 309	267	*281	1.0	103 000	3
Ireland Irlande	28 IV 1996	3 626 087	1 800 232	1 825 855	3 601	*3 787	1.0	70 273	54
Isle of Man Ile de Man	14 IV 1996	71 714	34 797	36 917	72	*75	0.8	572	131
Italy [2] Italie [2]	20 X 1991	56 411 290	27 404 812	29 006 478	57 301	*57 762	0.2	301 318	192
Latvia [9] Lettonie [9]	12 I 1989	2 666 567	1 238 806	1 427 761	2 516	*2 432	−0.7	64 600	38
Liechtenstein [4] Liechtenstein [4]	2 XII 1980	25 215	...	...	31	x33	...	160	206
Lithuania [9] Lithuanie [9]	12 I 1989	3 674 802	1 738 953	1 935 849	3 715	*3 696	−0.1	65 200	57
Luxembourg [2] Luxembourg [2]	31 III 1991	384 634	188 570	196 064	410	*436	1.2	2 586	168
Malta [53] [54] Malte [53] [54]	16 XI 1985	345 418	169 832	175 586	371	*391	1.0	316	1 239
Monaco [2] [4] Monaco [2] [4]	23 VII 1990	29 972	14 237	15 735	x32	*33	...	1	33 268
Netherlands [2] [4] [55] Pays–Bas [2] [4] [55]	1 I 1991	15010445	7 419 501	7 590 944	15 459	x15 864	...	41 526	382
Norway [2] Norvège [2]	3 XI 1990	4 247 546	2 099 881	2 147 665	4 359	*4 493	0.6	323 877	14
Poland [56] Pologne [56]	6 XII 1988	37 878 641	18 464 373	19 414 268	38 588	*38 646	−	323 250	120

8
Population by sex, rate of population increase, surface area and density [cont.]
Population selon le sexe, taux d'accroissement de la population,
superficie et densité [suite]

Country or area Pays ou zone	Latest census Dernier recensement Date	Both sexes Les deux sexes	Men Hommes	Women Femmes	Mid-year estimates (thousands) Estimations au milieu de l'année (milliers) 1995	2000	Annual rate of increase Taux d'accrois- sement annuel % 1995-00	Surface area (km²) Superficie (km²) 2000	Density Densité 2000[1]
Portugal [57] Portugal [57]	15 IV 1991	9 862 540	4 754 632	5 107 908	9 916	*10 008	0.2	91 982	109
Republic of Moldova République de Moldova	12 I 1989	4 337 592	2 058 160	2 279 432	4 348	*3 639	−3.6	33 851	108
Romania Roumanie	7 I 1992	22 810 035	11 213 763	11 596 272	22 684	*22 435	−0.2	238 391	94
Russian Federation [4 9] Fédération de Russie [4 9]	12 I 1989	147 021 869	68 713 869	78 308 000	147 774	x145 491	...	17075400	9
San Marino Saint-Marin	30 XI 1976	19 149	9 654	9 495	25	*27	1.5	61	442
Serbia and Montenegro [2] Serbie−et−Monténégro [2]	31 III 1991	10 394 026	5 157 120	5 236 906	10 547	*10 635	0.2	102 173	104
Slovakia [2] Slovaquie [2]	3 III 1991	5 274 335	2 574 061	2 700 274	5 364	*5 400	0.1	49 012	110
Slovenia [2 4] Slovénie [2 4]	31 III 1991	1 965 986	952 611	1 013 375	1 988	x1 988	...	20 256	98
Spain [2 58] Espagne [2 58]	1 III 1991	39 433 942	19 338 083	20 095 859	39 210	*39 466	0.1	505 992	78
Svalbard and Jan Mayen Islands [59] Svalbard et Ile Jan−Mayen [59]	1 XI 1960	3 431	2 545	886	...	...	...	62 422	...
Sweden [2] Suède [2]	1 IX 1990	8 587 353	4 242 351	4 345 002	8 827	*8 872	0.1	449 964	20
Switzerland [2 4] Suisse [2 4]	4 XII 1990	6 873 687	3 390 212	3 483 475	7 041	x7 170	...	41 284	174
TFYR of Macedonia [4] L'ex−R.y. Macédoine [4]	20 VI 1994	1 945 932	974 255	971 677	1 963	x2 034	...	25 713	79
Ukraine [9] Ukraine [9]	12 I 1989	51452034	23745108	27706926	51 728	x49 568	...	603 700	82
United Kingdom [60] Royaume−Uni [60]	21 IV 1991	56352200	...	...	58 606	*59 501	0.3	242 900	245
Oceania · Océanie									
American Samoa [2 17] Samoa américaines [2 17]	1 IV 1990	46 773	24 023	22 750	56	x68	...	199	342
Australia [2] Australie [2]	30 VI 1996	17892423	8 849 224	9 043 199	18 072	*19 157	1.2	7 741 220	2
Cook Islands [61] Iles Cook [61]	1 XII 1996	19 103	9 842	9 261	19	*18	−1.6	236	76
Fiji [4] Fidji [4]	25 VIII 1996	775 077	393 931	381 146	796	x814	...	18 274	45
French Polynesia [4 62] Polynésie française [4 62]	3 IX 1996	219 521	113 830	105 691	216	x233	...	4 000	58
Guam [2 17] Guam [2 17]	1 IV 2000	*154 805	...	...	149	*155	0.7	549	282
Kiribati [4 63] Kiribati [4 63]	7 XI 1995	*77 658	*38 478	*39 180	*78	x83	...	726	114
Marshall Islands [4] Iles Marshall [4]	13 XI 1988	43 380	22 181	21 199	56	x51	...	181	282
Micronesia (Fed. States of) Micronésie (Etats féd. de)	18 IX 1994	105 506	53 923	51 583	105	*119	2.4	702	169
Nauru [4] Nauru [4]	17 IV 1992	9 919	...	...	11	x12	...	21	571
New Caledonia [64] Nouvelle−Calédonie [64]	4 IV 1989	164 173	83 862	80 311	194	*211	1.7	18 575	11
New Zealand [2 65] Nouvelle−Zélande [2 65]	5 III 1996	3 618 303	1 777 464	1 840 839	3 656	*3 831	0.9	270 534	14

8
Population by sex, rate of population increase, surface area and density [cont.]
Population selon le sexe, taux d'accroissement de la population,
superficie et densité [suite]

Country or area Pays ou zone	Latest census Dernier recensement				Mid-year estimates (thousands) Estimations au milieu de l'année (milliers)		Annual rate of increase Taux d'accrois-sement annuel %	Surface area (km²) Superficie (km²)	Density Densité
	Date	Both sexes Les deux sexes	Men Hommes	Women Femmes	1995	2000	1995–00	2000	2000[1]
Niue Nioué	17 VIII 1997	*2 088	*1 053	*1 035	x2	x2	–	260	8
Norfolk Island Ile Norfolk	30 VI 1986	2 367	1 170	1 197	...	...	...	36	...
Northern Mariana Islands Iles Mariannes du Nord	1 IV 1990	43 345	...	...	x58	x73	4.6	464	157
Palau [4] Palaos [4]	9 IX 1995	17 225	9 213	8 012	17	x19	...	459	41
Papua New Guinea [4][66] Papouasie–Nouveau–Guinée [4][66]	9 VII 2000	*5 130 365	*2 661 091	*2 469 274	4 074	x4 809	...	462 840	10
Pitcairn Pitcairn	31 XII 1991	66	...	...	x0	x0	...	5	0
Samoa [4] Samoa [4]	11 V 1991	161 298	...	...	x158	*171	...	2 831	60
Solomon Islands [67] Iles Salomon [67]	23 XI 1986	285 176	147 972	137 204	x377	x447	3.4	28 896	15
Tokelau Tokélaou	11 XII 1991	1 577	...	...	x2	x1	–13.9	12	83
Tonga [4] Tonga [4]	30 XI 1996	97 784	49 615	48 169	98	x99	...	650	152
Tuvalu Tuvalu	17 IX 1991	9 043	4 376	4 667	x9	x10	2.1	26	385
Vanuatu Vanuatu	16 V 1989	142 944	73 674	69 270	x172	x197	2.7	12 189	16
Wallis and Futuna Islands Iles Wallis et Futuna	11 XII 1990	13 705	...	...	x14	x14	–	200	70

Source:
United Nations Statistics Division, New York, "Demographic
Yearbook 2000" and the demographic statistics database.

Source:
Organisation des Nations Unies, Division de statistique, New York,
"Annuaire démographique 2000" et la base de données pour les
statistiques démographiques.

*   Provisional.
x   Estimates for 1995–2000 prepared by the Population Division
    of the United Nations.
1   Population per square kilometre of surface area in 2000. Figures are
    merely the quotients of population divided by surface area and are not
    to be considered either as reflecting density in the urban sense or as
    indicating the supporting power of a territory's land and resources.

2   De jure population.
3   Including the enclave of Cabinda.
4   Rate not computed because of apparent lack of comparability
    between estimates shown for 1995 and 2000.
5   Census results have been adjusted for under–enumeration
    estimated at 1.4 per cent.
6   Census results, excluding Mayotte.
7   Comprising Bioko (which includes Pagalu) and Rio Muni
    (which includes Corisco and Elobeys).
8   Mid–year estimates have been adjusted for under–enumeration.
    Census data have not been adjusted for this under–enumeration.

9   Census results for de jure population.
10 Including nomads, estimated at 224 095.

*   Données provisoires.
x   Estimations pour 1995–2000 établies par la Division de la
    population de l'Organisation des Nations Unies.
1   Nombre d'habitants au kilomètre carré en 2000. Il s'agit
    simplement du quotient du chiffre de la population divisé par
    celui de la superficie: il ne faut pas y voir d'indication de la
    densité au sens urbain du terme ni de l'effectif de population que
    les terres et les ressources du territoire sont capables de nourrir.

2   Population de droit.
3   Y compris l'enclave de Cabinda.
4   On n'a pas calculé le taux parce que les estimations pour 1995 et
    2000 ne paraissent pas comparables.
5   Les résultats du recensement ont été ajustés pour compenser les
    lacunes du dénombrement estimées à 1,4 p. 100.
6   Les résultats du recensement, non compris Mayotte.
7   Comprend Bioko (qui comprend Pagalu) et Rio Muni (qui
    comprend Corisco et Elobeys).
8   Les estimations au milieu de l'année tiennent compte d'un
    ajustement destiné à compenser les lacunes du dénombrement.
    Les données de recensement ne tiennent pas compte de cet
    ajustement.

9   Les résultats du recensement. Population de droit.
10 Y compris les nomades, estimées à 224 095.

8

Population by sex, rate of population increase, surface area and density [cont.]
Population selon le sexe, taux d'accroissement de la population,
superficie et densité [suite]

11 Comprising the Northern Region (former Saguia el Hamra) and Southern Region (former Rio de Oro).	11 Comprend la région septentrionale (ancien Saguia–el–Hamra) et la région méridionale (ancien Rio de Oro).
12 Excluding institutional population.	12 Non compris la population dans les institutions.
13 Because of rounding, totals are not in all cases the sum of the parts.	13 Les chiffres étant arrondis, les totaux ne correspondent pas toujours rigoureusement à la somme des chiffres partiels.
14 Including Carriacou and other dependencies in the Grenadines.	14 Y compris Carriacou et les autres dépendances du groupe des îles Grenadines.
15 Including dependencies: Marie–Galante, la Désirade, les Saintes, Petite–Terre, St. Barthélemy and French part of St. Martin.	15 Y compris les dépendances: Marie–Galante, la Désirade, les Saintes, Petite–Terre, Saint–Barthélemy et la partie française de Saint–Martin.
16 De jure population, comprising Bonaire, Curaçao, Saba, St. Eustatius and Dutch part of St. Martin.	16 Population de droit, comprend Bonaire, Curaçao, Saba, Saint–Eustache et la partie néederlandaise de Saint–Martin.
17 Including armed forces stationed in the area.	17 Y compris les militaires en garnison sur le territoire.
18 Including Bequia and other islands in the Grenadines.	18 Y compris Bequia et des autres îles dans les Grenadines.
19 Excluding armed forces overseas and civilian citizens absent from country for an extended period of time.	19 Non compris les militaires à l'étranger, et les civils hors du pays pendant une période prolongée.
20 Data refer to de facto estimates, including persons in remote areas, military personel outside the country, merchant seamen at sea, civilian seasonal workers outside the country, and other civilians outside the country, and excluding nomads, foreign military, civilian aliens temporarily in the country, transients on ships and Indian jungle population.	20 Les données se rapportent aux évaluations de fait, y compris des personne régions éloignées, au personel militaire en dehors du pays, aux marins mar ouvriers saisonniers civils de couture en dehors du pays, et à d'autres civils pays, et non compris les nomades, les militaires étrangers, les étrangers civ dans le pays, les transiteurs sur des bateaux et les Indiens de la jungle.
21 Excluding nomadic Indian tribes.	21 Non compris les tribus d'Indiens nomades.
22 Excluding dependencies, of which South Georgia (area 3 755 km²) had an estimated population of 499 in 1964 (494 males, 5 females). The other dependencies namely, the South Sandwich group (surface area 337 km²) and a number of smaller islands, are presumed to be uninhabited.	22 Non compris les dépendances, parmi lesquelles figure la Georgie du Sud (3 755 km²) avec une population estimée à 499 personnes en 1964 (494 du sexe masculin et 5 du sexe féminin). Les autres dépendances, c'est–à–dire le groupe des Sandwich de Sud (superficie: 337 km²) et certaines petites–îles, sont présumées inhabitées.
23 A dispute exists between the governments of Argentina and the United Kingdom of Great Britain and Northern Ireland concerning sovereignty over the Falkland Islands (Malvinas).	23 La souveraineté sur les îles Falkland (Malvinas) fait l'objet d'un différend entre le Gouvernement argentin et le Gouvernement du Royaume–Uni de Grande–Bretagne et d'Irlande du Nord.
24 Excluding Indian jungle population.	24 Non compris les Indiens de la jungle.
25 Census results, excluding nomad population.	25 Les résultats du recensement, non compris la population nomade.
26 Excluding foreign diplomatic personnel and their dependants.	26 Non compris le personnel diplomatique étranger et les membres de leur famille les accompagnant.
27 For statistical purposes, the data for China do not include those for the Hong Kong Special Administrative Region (Hong Kong SAR) and Macao special Administrative Region (Macao SAR).	27 Pour la présentation des statistiques, les données pour Chine ne comprend pas la Région Administrative Spéciale de Hong Kong (Hong Kong RAS) et la Région Administrative Spéciale de Macao (Macao RAS).
28 Census figures for China, as given in the communiqué of the State Statistical Bureau releasing the major figures of the census, include the population of Hong Kong and Macao.	28 Les chiffres de recensement de la Chine, qui figure dans le communiqué du Bureau du statistique de l'Etat publiant les principaux chiffres du recensement, comprennent la population de Hong–kong et Macao.
29 After 1996, population is de jure.	29 Après 1996, la population est de droit.
30 Census results, for government controlled areas.	30 Les résultats du recensement, pour les zones contrôlées par le Gouvernement.
31 Including data for the Indian–held part of Jammu and Kashmir, the final status of which has not yet been determined.	31 Y compris les données pour la partie du Jammu et du Cachemire occupée par l'Inde dont le statut définitif n'a pas encore été déterminé.
32 Including data for East Jerusalem and Israeli residents in certain other territories under occupation by Israeli military forces since June 1967.	32 Y compris les données pour Jérusalem–Est et les résidents israéliens dans certains autres territoires occupés depuis juin 1967 pour les forces armées israéliennes.
33 Comprising Hokkaido, Honshu, Shikoku, Kyushu.	33 Comprend Hokkaido, Honshu, Shikoku, Kyushu.
34 Including military and diplomatic personnel and their families abroad, numbering 933 at 1961 census, but excluding foreign military and diplomatic personnel and their families in the country, numbering 389 at 1961 census. Also including registered Palestinian refugees numbering 654 092 and 722 687 at 30 June 1963 and 31 May 1967, respectively.	34 Y compris les militaires et le personnel diplomatique à l'étranger et les members de leur famille les accompagnant, au nombre de 933 personnes au recensement de 1961, mais non compris les militaires et le personnel diplomatique étrangers sur le territoire et les membres de leur famille les accompagnant, au nombre de 389 personnes au recensement de 1961. Y compris également les réfugiés de Palestine immatriculés: 654 092 au 30 juin 1963

8
Population by sex, rate of population increase, surface area and density [*cont.*]
Population selon le sexe, taux d'accroissement de la population,
superficie et densité [*suite*]

et 722 687 au 31 mai 1967.

35   Census results, excluding data for Jordanian territory under occupation since June 1967 by Israeli military forces.

35   Les résultats du recensement, non compris les données pour le territoire jordanien occupé depuis juin 1967 par les forces armées israéliennes.

36   Excluding alien armed forces, civilian aliens employed by armed forces, foreign diplomatic personnel and their dependants and Korean diplomatic personnel and their dependants outside the country.

36   Non compris les militaires étrangers, les civils étrangers employés par les forces armées, le personnel diplomatique étranger et les membres de leur famille les accompagnant et le personnel diplomatique coréen hors du pays et les membres de leur familles les accompagnant.

37   Based on results of sample survey.

38   Excluding Palestinian refugees in camps.

39   The figures were received from the Palestinian Authority and refer to the Palestinian population.

40   Census results exclude an estimate for under−enumeration estimated at 2.4 per cent.

41   Excluding data for Jammu and Kashmir, the final status of which has not yet been determined, Junagardh, Manavadar, Gilgit and Baltistan.

42   Census results, excluding transients afloat and non−locally domiciled military and civilian services personnel and their dependants and visitors.

43   Including Palestinian refugees.

44   Comprising 7 sheikdoms of Abu Dhabi, Dubai, Sharjah, Ajaman, Umm al Qaiwain, Ras al Khaimah and Fujairah, and the area lying within the modified Riyadh line as announced in October 1955.

45   Excluding Faeroe Islands and Greenland.

46   Excluding Overseas Departments, namely French Guiana, Guadeloupe, Martinique and Réunion, shown separately. De jure population, but excluding diplomatic personnel outside the country and including foreign diplomatic personnel not living in embassies or consulates.

47   For 1990 census, excluding military personnel stationed outside the country who do not have a personal residence in France.

48   All data shown pertaining to Germany prior to 3 October 1990 are indicated separately for the Federal Republic of Germany and the former German Democratic Republic based on their respective territories at the time indicated.

49   Excluding armed forces.

50   Census results, include armed forces stationed outside the country, but excluding alien armed forces stationed in the area.

51   Mid−year population excludes armed forces stationed outside the country, but includes alien armed forces stationed in the area.

52   Data refer to the Vatican City State.

53   Including civilian nationals temporarily outside the country.

54   Including Gozo and Comino Islands.

55   Census results, based on compilation of continuous accounting and sample surveys.

56   Excluding civilian aliens within the country, but including civilian nationals temporarily outside the country.

57   Including the Azores and Madeira Islands.

58   Including the Balearic and Canary Islands, and Alhucemas, Ceuta, Chafarinas, Melilla and Penon de Vélez de la Gomera.

59   Inhabited only during the winter season. Census data are for total

37   D'après les résultats d'une enquête par sondage.

38   Non compris les réfugiés de Palestine dans les camps.

39   Les chiffres sont fournis par l'autorité palestinienne et comprennent la population palestinienne.

40   Les résultats du recensement n'ont pas été ajustées pour compenser les lacunes de denombrement, estimées à 2,4 p. 100.

41   Non compris les données pour le Jammu et le Cachemire, dont le statut définitif n'a pas encore été déterminé, le Junagardh, la Manavadar, le Gilgit et le Batistan.

42   Les résultats du recensement, non compris les personnes de passage à bord de navires, les militaires et agents civils non résidents et les membres de leur famille les accompagnant, et les visiteurs.

43   Y compris les réfugiés de Palestine.

44   Comprend les sept cheikhats de Abou Dhabi, Dabai, Ghârdja, Adjmân, Oumm−al−Quiwaïn, Ras al Khaïma et Foudjaïra, ainsi que la zone délimitée par la ligne de Riad modifiée comme il a été annoncé en octobre 1955.

45   Non compris les îles Féroé et le Groenland.

46   Non compris les départements d'outre−mer, c'est−à−dire la Guyane française, la Guadeloupe, la Martinique et la Réunion, qui font l'objet de rubriques distinctes. Population de droit, non compris le personnel diplomatique hors du pays et y compris le personnel diplomatique étranger qui ne vivent pas dans les ambassades ou les consulats.

47   Les données pour le recensement de 1990, non compris les militaires en garnison hors du pays et sans résidence personnelle en France.

48   Toutes les données se rapportant à l'Allemagne avant le 3 octobre 1990 figurent dans deux rubriques séparées basées sur les territoires respectifs de la République fédérale d'Allemagne et l'ancienne République démocratique allemande selon la période indiquée.

49   Non compris les militaires.

50   Les résultats du recensement, y compris les militaires en garnison hors du pays, mais non compris les militaires étrangers en garnison sur le territoire.

51   Les estimations au milieu de l'année non compris les militaires en garnison hors du pays, mais y compris les militaires étrangers en garnison sur le territoire.

52   Les données se rapportent à l'Etat de la Cité du Vatican.

53   Y compris les civils nationaux temporairement hors du pays.

54   Y compris les îles de Gozo et de Comino.

55   Les résultats du recensement, d'après les résultats des dénombrements et enquêtes par sondage continue.

56   Non compris les civils étrangers dans le pays, mais y compris les civils nationaux temporairement hors du pays.

57   Y compris les Açores et Madère.

58   Y compris les Baléares et les Canaries, Al Hoceima, Ceuta, les îles Zaffarines, Melilla et Penon de Vélez de la Gomera.

59   N'est habitée que pendant la saison d'hiver. Les données de

8
Population by sex, rate of population increase, surface area and density [*cont.*]
Population selon le sexe, taux d'accroissement de la population, superficie et densité [*suite*]

population while estimates refer to Norwegian population only. Included also in the de jure population of Norway.

60   Excluding Channel Islands and Isle of Man, shown separately.

61   Excluding Niue, shown separately, which is part of Cook Islands, but because of remoteness is administered separately.

62   Comprising Austral, Gambier, Marquesas, Rapa, Society and Tuamotu Islands.

63   Including Christmas, Fanning, Ocean and Washington Islands.

64   Including the islands of Huon, Chesterfield, Loyalty, Walpole and Belep Archipelago.

65   Including Campbell and Kermadec Islands (population 20 in 1961, surface area 148 km²) as well as Antipodes, Auckland, Bounty, Snares, Solander and Three Kings island, all of which are uninhabited. Excluding diplomatic personnel and armed forces outside the country, the latter numbering 1 936 at 1966 census; also excluding alien armed forces within the country.

66   Comprising eastern part of New Guinea, the Bismarck Archipelago, Bougainville and Buka of Solomon Islands group and about 600 smaller islands.

67   Comprising the Solomon Islands group (except Bougainville and Buka which are included with Papua New Guinea shown separately), Ontong, Java, Rennel and Santa Cruz Islands.

recensement se rapportent à la population totale, mais les estimations ne concernent que la population norvégienne, comprise également dans la population de droit de la Norvège.

60   Non compris les îles Anglo–Normandes et l'île de Man, qui font l'objet de rubriques distinctes.

61   Non compris Nioué, qui fait l'objet d'une rubrique distincte et qui fait partie des îles Cook, mais qui, en raison de son éloignement, est administrée séparément.

62   Comprend les îles Australes, Gambier, Marquises, Rapa, de la Societé et Tuamotou.

63   Y compris les îles Christmas, Fanning, Océan et Washington.

64   Y compris les îles Huon, Chesterfield, Loyauté et Walpole, et l'archipel Belep.

65   Y compris les îles Campbell et Kermadec (20 habitants en 1961, superficie: 148 km²) ainsi que les îles Antipodes, Auckland, Bounty, Snares, Solander et Three Kings, qui sont toutes inhabitées. Non compris les personnel diplomatique et les militaires hors du pays, ces derniers au nombre de 1 936 au recensement de 1966; non compris également les militaires étrangers dans le pays.

66   Comprend l'est de la Nouvelle–Guinée, l'archipel Bismarck, Bougainville et Buka (ces deux dernières du group des Salomon) et environ 600 îlots.

67   Comprend les îles Salomon (à l'exception de Bougainville et de Buka dont la population est comprise dans celle de Papouasie–Nouvelle Guinée qui font l'objet d'une rubrique distincte), ainsi que les îles Ontong, Java, Rennel et Santa Cruz.

Technical notes, table 8

Table 8 is based on detailed data on population and its growth and distribution published in the United Nations *Demographic Yearbook* [22], which also provides a comprehensive description of methods of evaluation and limitations of the data.

Unless otherwise indicated, figures refer to de facto (present-in-area) population for the present territory; surface area estimates include inland waters.

Notes techniques, tableau 8

Le *tableau 8* est fondé sur des données détaillées sur la population, sa croissance et sa distribution, publiées dans l'*Annuaire démographique* des Nations Unies [22], qui offre également une description complète des méthodes d'évaluation et une indication des limites des données.

Sauf indication contraire, les chiffres se rapportent à la population effectivement présente sur le territoire tel qu'il est actuellement défini; les estimations de superficie comprennent les étendues d'eau intérieures.

9
Education at the primary, secondary and tertiary levels
Number of students enrolled and percentage female
Enseignement primaire, secondaire et supérieur
Nombre d'étudiants inscrits et étudiantes feminines en pourcentage

Country or area Pays ou zone	Years Années	Primary education Enseignement primaire		Secondary education Enseignement secondaire		Tertiary education Enseignement supérieur	
		Total	% F	Total	% F	Total	% F
Africa · Afrique							
Algeria	1998	4 778 870	46.65	2 808 675	49.69	456 358[1]	...
Algérie	1999	4 843 313	46.76	2 817 710	50.58	...	...
Angola	1998	1 342 116	45.58	329 544[1]	41.26[1]	8 337	41.08
Angola	1999	* 1 001 963	* 46.43	339 702[1]	43.47[1]	7 845	39.01
Benin	1998	872 217	39.28	213 474	31.36	16 284	20.55
Bénin	1999	932 424	40.18	229 228	31.17	18 753	19.83
Botswana	1998	321 271	49.62	147 525	52.13	5 532	44.03
Botswana	1999	...	...	158 555	52.12	6 332	42.39
Burkina Faso	1998	816 393	40.43	173 205	37.54	...	...
Burkina Faso	1999	852 160	40.82[1]	189 689	38.95	...	...
Burundi	1998	568 700[1]	44.91[1]	73 115[1]	42.97[1]	5 037	29.54
Burundi	1999	* 710 364	* 44.47	...	...	8 655	29.12
Cameroon	1998	2 133 707	44.87	463 561[1]	43.74[1]	66 902	...
Cameroun	1999	2 237 083	45.74	...	...	65 697	14.38
Cape Verde	1998	91 636	49.01	...	...	...	...
Cap–Vert	1999	...	...	...	...	...	...
Central African Rep.	1998	330 000[1]	40.00[1]	...	...	6 229	16.09
Rép. centrafricaine	1999	...	...	...	...	6 323	16.24
Chad	1998	839 932	36.74	123 408	20.69	...	...
Tchad	1999	913 547	37.79	137 269	22.10	5 901	15.00
Comoros	1998	82 789	45.34	28 718	44.33	649	42.68
Comores	1999	93 421	45.00[1]	24 324[1]	44.46[1]	714[1]	41.88[1]
Congo	1998	276 451	48.76	...	...	...	...
Congo	1999	418 707	47.77	...	...	15 629	23.78
Côte d'Ivoire	1998	1 910 820	42.57	586 431[1]	34.63[1]	96 681	26.27
Côte d'Ivoire	1999	1 996 806[1]	42.57[1]	...	...	...	...
Dem. Rep. of the Congo	1998	4 022 411	47.38	1 234 528[1]	34.29[1]	60 341	...
Rép. dém du Congo	1999	...	...	...	...	...	...
Djibouti	1998	38 194	41.17	15 511	41.56	175	50.86
Djibouti	1999	38 106	42.00	14 214	56.13	190[1]	46.84[1]
Egypt	1998	8 086 230[1]	46.69[1]	7 671 031[1]	46.75[1]	2 447 088	...
Egypte	1999	7 947 488[1]	46.91[1]	8 028 170[1]	47.05[1]	...	...
Equatorial Guinea	1998	74 940	44.00	20 422[1]	27.18[1]	...	...
Guinée équatoriale	1999	73 307[1]	44.97[1]	20 809[1]	30.78[1]	1 003	30.31
Eritrea	1998	261 963	45.19	115 393	40.89	3 994	13.52
Erythrée	1999	295 941	44.96	135 209	41.14	4 135	14.32
Ethiopia	1998	4 367 929	38.00	1 859 406	38.20	52 305	18.68
Ethiopie	1999	4 873 683	39.97	579 457	40.53	67 732	21.68
Gabon	1998	265 244	49.66	86 543	46.33	7 473	35.69
Gabon	1999	270 549[1]	49.66[1]	...	...	...	...
Gambia	1998	150 403	45.91	47 106	39.80	...	...
Gambie	1999	138 985	47.42	42 095	42.61	1 169	22.67
Ghana	1998	2 377 444	46.95	1 024 135	43.64	...	...
Ghana	1999	...	...	1 042 521	44.47	44 427	24.78
Guinea	1998	726 561	38.08	171 934[1]	26.02[1]	...	...
Guinée	1999	790 497	39.82	...	...	...	...
Guinea–Bissau	1998	...	...	...	...	...	...
Guinée–Bissau	1999	150 041	40.25	25 736	35.44	463	15.55
Kenya	1998	5 480 689	49.44	1 156 289[1]	47.26[1]	44 411	31.92
Kenya	1999	...	...	...	...	44 411	31.92
Lesotho	1998	369 515	51.79	72 235	58.38	4 046	63.74
Lesotho	1999	364 951	51.67	73 620	57.43	3 524	60.24
Liberia	1998	395 611	42.38	113 878	38.95	...	...
Libéria	1999	465 368	42.00	117 967	40.64	44 107	42.78
Libyan Arab Jamahiriya	1998	821 775	48.50	642 090[1]	51.70[1]	308 474[1]	50.00[1]
Jamah. arabe libyenne	1999	...	...	...	...	290 060	48.62
Madagascar	1998	2 012 416	49.10	346 941[1]	48.90[1]	31 013	45.75
Madagascar	1999	2 208 321	49.00	...	...	32 156	46.21
Malawi	1998	2 102 424[1]	49.71[1]	...	...	3 179	27.56
Malawi	1999	2 087 951	49.53	244 045	37.52	...	...
Mali	1998	958 935	41.00	217 700	34.18	18 662	...
Mali	1999	784 774	41.63	...	...	...	...

9
Education at the primary, secondary and tertiary levels
Number of students enrolled and percentage female [*cont.*]
Enseignement primaire, secondaire et supérieur
Nombre d'étudiants inscrits et étudiantes feminines en pourcentage [*suite*]

Country or area Pays ou zone	Years Années	Primary education Enseignement primaire		Secondary education Enseignement secondaire		Tertiary education Enseignement supérieur	
		Total	% F	Total	% F	Total	% F
Mauritania	1998	346 222	48.39	63 482[1]	42.03[1]	12 912	...
Mauritanie	1999	355 822	48.39	65 606	41.66	...	...
Mauritius	1998	130 505	49.40	101 517	49.63	7 559	46.14
Maurice	1999	133 489	49.39	104 070	48.92	8 256	44.99
Morocco	1998	3 461 940	43.97	1 469 794	43.36	273 183	41.79
Maroc	1999	3 669 605	44.81	1 541 100	43.67	276 375	42.30
Mozambique	1998	1 918 400	42.09	277 421[1]	40.35[1]	...	...
Mozambique	1999	2 108 790	42.77	296 670	40.52	...	...
Namibia	1998	386 647	50.04	110 076	53.48	11 209	53.27
Namibie	1999	383 267	50.10	116 131	52.74	9 561	55.10
Niger	1998	529 806	39.18	104 933	37.97		
Niger	1999	579 486	39.35	106 182[1]	38.69[1]	...	...
Rwanda	1998	1 288 669	49.96	91 219	49.63	5 678	
Rwanda	1999	1 431 657	49.58	129 620	49.11	...	...
Sao Tome and Principe	1998	23 769	48.65	5 347[1]	27.12[1]	...	...
Sao Tomé-et-Principe	1999	...	...	...	...	...	...
Senegal	1998	1 034 065	44.77	237 454	38.89	...	...
Sénégal	1999	1 107 712	46.00	...	...	...	...
Seychelles	1998	9 738	49.20	8 027	48.97	...	...
Seychelles	1999	10 014	49.28	7 788	50.14	...	...
Sierra Leone	1998	...	...	...	...		
Sierra Leone	1999	442 915	48.38	...	...	6 744	45.21
South Africa	1998	* 7 997 945	* 49.19	* 4 244 415	* 53.05	633 918	53.77
Afrique du Sud	1999	7 935 221	49.10	4 238 924	52.64	...	...
Sudan	1998	2 478 309[1]	45.57[1]	...	...	200 538	47.20
Soudan	1999	2 566 503	45.14	979 514	61.71	...	...
Swaziland	1998	212 052	48.66	60 830[1]	50.31[1]	4 880	47.89
Swaziland	1999	213 041	48.65	...	...	4 646	46.97
Togo	1998	953 886	43.08	231 948	28.62	15 028	17.40
Togo	1999	914 919	43.82	259 054[1]	30.56[1]	15 171	16.90
Tunisia	1998	1 442 904	47.38	1 058 877	49.26	157 479[1]	48.31[1]
Tunisie	1999	1 413 795	47.43	1 087 818	49.94	180 044[1]	48.29[1]
Uganda	1998	6 591 429	47.40	465 605[1]	39.16[1]	40 591[1]	34.50[1]
Ouganda	1999	6 559 013	48.23	...	...	55 767	33.85
United Rep. of Tanzania	1998	4 042 568	49.70	...	...	...	...
Rép. Unie de Tanzanie	1999	4 189 816	49.89	247 579	46.10	...	...
Zambia	1998	1 557 257	47.93	290 085	43.12	...	...
Zambie	1999	1 555 707	47.79	186 295	48.15	...	...
Zimbabwe	1998	...	...	...	...	...	...
Zimbabwe	1999	2 460 323	49.13	834 880	46.93	42 775[1]	25.45[1]
America, North · Amerique du Nord							
Anguilla	1998	1 569	50.22	1 012	52.67	...	...
Anguilla	1999	1 539	50.29	1 130	50.80	...	...
Antigua and Barbuda	1998	...	...	...	...	...	...
Antigua-et-Barbuda	1999	13 025	62.03	5 276	71.66	...	...
Aruba	1998	9 096	48.86	6 159	50.72	1 446	53.94
Aruba	1999	9 263	48.60	6 178	50.50	1 578	60.65
Bahamas	1998	33 780	48.44	...	...	...	...
Bahamas	1999	...	...	...	...	...	...
Barbados	1998	24 729	49.05	28 383[1]	49.08[1]	6 915	69.21
Barbade	1999	24 476	48.90	21 016	50.26	12 050	...
Belize	1998	44 180[1]	48.47[1]	22 267[1]	49.84[1]	...	...
Belize	1999	44 788	48.25	23 235	49.15	...	...
British Virgin Islands	1998	2 757	48.97	1 511	46.79	...	...
Iles Vierges britanniques	1999	2 928	50.00	1 556	49.61	...	...
Canada	1998	2 403 709	48.76	2 564 963	48.51	1 192 570	55.65
Canada	1999	2 428 620	48.83	2 511 518	49.08	1 220 651	55.98
Cayman Islands	1998	3 231	46.83	2 151	48.40	...	...
Iles Caïmanes	1999	3 435	49.87	2 342	49.23	...	...
Costa Rica	1998	...	...	...	...	...	...
Costa Rica	1999	552 280	48.11	212 945	51.55	...	...
Cuba	1998	1 074 097[1]	47.82[1]	739 980	50.33	...	...
Cuba	1999	1 045 578	47.74	789 927	49.92	...	...
Dominica	1998	12 044	48.29	7 126	53.16	...	...
Dominique	1999	11 774	48.31	7 429	52.83	...	...

9
Education at the primary, secondary and tertiary levels
Number of students enrolled and percentage female [*cont.*]
Enseignement primaire, secondaire et supérieur
Nombre d'étudiants inscrits et étudiantes feminines en pourcentage [*suite*]

Country or area Pays ou zone	Years Années	Primary education Enseignement primaire		Secondary education Enseignement secondaire		Tertiary education Enseignement supérieur	
		Total	% F	Total	% F	Total	% F
Dominican Republic	1998	1 316 113[1]	48.62[1]	577 924[1]	54.82[1]	...	...
Rép. dominicaine	1999	1 400 605[1]	48.41[1]	724 712[1]	54.61[1]	...	...
El Salvador	1998	925 511	48.45	401 545	49.14	118 491	55.11
El Salvador	1999	...	...	...	...	...	...
Grenada	1998	20 017	48.81	8 274	58.61	...	...
Grenade	1999	15 974	48.38	...	...	...	...
Guatemala	1998	...	...	...	...	...	...
Guatemala	1999	1 825 088	46.12	434 912	45.49	...	...
Haiti	1998	2 023 319	49.73	449 597	44.68	...	...
Haïti	1999	...	...	...	...	...	...
Honduras	1998	...	...	...	...	77 768	...
Honduras	1999	...	...	...	...	...	...
Jamaica	1998	316 290[1]	49.27[1]	231 177[1]	50.26[1]	...	...
Jamaïque	1999	326 846	50.82	228 764	48.75	35 995	65.03
Mexico	1998	14 697 915	48.64	8 721 726	49.95	1 837 884	48.30
Mexique	1999	14 765 603	48.73	9 094 103	50.22	1 962 763	48.72
Montserrat	1998	392	43.88	272	47.06	...	...
Montserrat	1999	330	44.24	284	48.59	...	...
Netherlands Antilles	1998	25 398	48.20	15 426	53.66	2 320	53.19
Antilles néerlandaises	1999	24 911	48.40	14 418	52.40	2 561	55.53
Nicaragua	1998	...	...	...	...	...	...
Nicaragua	1999	830 206	49.36	365 061[1]	53.66[1]	...	...
Panama	1998	...	...	...	...	...	...
Panama	1999	393 030	48.16	230 034	50.78	...	...
St. Kitts and Nevis	1998	...	...	...	...	...	...
Saint–Kitts–et–Nevis	1999	6 922	48.63	4 768	50.46	...	...
Saint Lucia	1998	25 000[1]	47.66[1]	14 323[1]	52.38[1]	3 881	...
Sainte–Lucie	1999	24 999[1]	47.65[1]	14 323[1]	55.53[1]	...	...
St. Vincent and the Grenadines	1998	...	...	...	...	...	...
St. Vincent–Grenadines	1999	19 176	48.30	10 096	53.43	...	...
Trinidad and Tobago	1998	172 204	49.12	115 011	51.59	7 572	57.41
Trinité–et–Tobago	1999	168 532	49.06	111 128	51.75	7 737	59.30
Turks and Caicos Islands	1998	1 822	48.57	1 114	51.08	27	100.00
Iles Turques et Caiques	1999	2 018	47.72	1 089	52.53	...	...
United States	1998	24 937 931	49.47	...	...	13 769 362	52.79
Etats–Unis	1999	24 973 176	48.39	22 593 562	49.00	13 202 880	55.76
America, South • Amerique du Sud							
Argentina	1998	4 821 090	49.25	3 555 848	51.20	1 526 515[1]	58.58[1]
Argentine	1999	4 820 908	49.24	3 722 449	50.96	1 600 882	61.66
Bolivia	1998	1 400 205	48.57	...	...	...	...
Bolivie	1999	1 457 141[1]	48.69[1]	842 937[1]	47.63[1]	252 706[1]	35.00[1]
Brazil	1998	...	...	...	...	2 203 599	54.96
Brésil	1999	21 917 948	47.99	24 982 899	51.81	2 456 961	55.56
Chile	1998	1 831 082	48.28	1 334 239	49.58	406 553	46.08
Chili	1999	1 863 105	48.03	1 396 631	49.69	450 952	47.11
Colombia	1998	5 062 284	49.05	3 549 368	51.85	...	...
Colombie	1999	5 162 260	49.01	3 589 425	51.72	877 944	52.12
Ecuador	1998	1 899 466	49.11	903 569	49.91	...	...
Equateur	1999	1 925 420	49.01	917 245	49.65	...	...
Guyana	1998	107 207	48.98	66 495	49.86	...	...
Guyana	1999	...	...	...	...	...	...
Paraguay	1998	958 734	48.38	367 567	50.45	...	...
Paraguay	1999	956 067	48.27	425 214	50.18	...	...
Peru	1998	4 299 407	48.88	2 212 033	47.89	734 392	25.26
Pérou	1999	4 349 594	49.01	...	...	...	...
Uruguay	1998	365 297	48.63	275 090	56.05	94 219	64.01
Uruguay	1999	366 461	48.59	283 838	52.96	91 175[1]	62.99[1]
Venezuela	1998	3 261 343	48.52	1 439 122	54.13	...	...
Venezuela	1999	3 328 067[1]	48.52[1]	1 522 225[1]	53.42[1]	668 109	58.62
Asia • Asie							
Azerbaijan	1998	691 259	48.68	929 065	48.87	146 099[1]	45.69[1]
Azerbaïdjan	1999	696 823	48.89	945 393	48.89	...	...
Bahrain	1998	76 302	48.72	58 804	50.85	11 048[1]	60.01[1]
Bahreïn	1999	77 720	48.90	65 422	49.95	...	...

9

Education at the primary, secondary and tertiary levels
Number of students enrolled and percentage female [*cont.*]
Enseignement primaire, secondaire et supérieur
Nombre d'étudiants inscrits et étudiantes feminines en pourcentage [*suite*]

Country or area	Years	Primary education Enseignement primaire		Secondary education Enseignement secondaire		Tertiary education Enseignement supérieur	
Pays ou zone	Années	Total	% F	Total	% F	Total	% F
Bangladesh	1998	18 360 574[1]	47.84[1]	8 066 091	50.93	709 224	32.27
Bangladesh	1999	...	...	9 912 318	48.73	726 701	32.31
Bhutan	1998	78 006	45.15	17 374	43.57	...	...
Bhoutan	1999	81 156	45.66	20 123	44.15	1 479[1]	36.44[1]
Brunei Darussalam	1998	45 369	47.13	32 663	50.94	2 917	64.55
Brunéi Darussalam	1999	45 827	47.00	34 426	50.75	3 705	65.91
Cambodia	1998	2 127 878[1]	45.70[1]	316 343	34.38	...	...
Cambodge	1999	2 248 109	45.85	351 431	34.89	22 108	25.09
China	1998	145 027 888	48.05	77 436 268[1]	44.95[1]	6 365 625	...
Chine	1999	141 184 231	47.98	81 487 960[1]	45.28[1]	7 364 111	...
China, Macao SAR	1998	47 064	47.36	31 943	51.33	8 879	44.53
Chine, Macao RAS	1999	47 486	47.40	35 565	50.51	7 471	51.97
Cyprus	1998	64 248	48.40	63 050	49.49	10 842	56.03
Chypre	1999	63 952	48.50	63 677	49.38	10 414	57.09
Georgia	1998	302 488	48.73	442 473	48.71	130 164	51.98
Géorgie	1999	298 352	48.72	467 249	49.26	137 046	49.19
India	1998	134 647 632	44.78	50 994 338	38.25	...	...
Inde	1999	134 815 883	44.17	52 049 548	38.75	...	...
Indonesia	1998	...	...	...	...	...	...
Indonésie	1999	28 201 934[1]	48.33[1]	14 263 912[1]	48.07[1]	...	...
Iran, Islamic Rep. of	1998	...	...	9 181 276	46.85	...	...
Iran, Rép. islamique d'	1999	8 287 537	47.53	9 181 276	46.85	678 652	44.11
Iraq	1998	...	...	...	...	271 508	34.21
Iraq	1999	3 639 362	43.99	1 224 353	37.02	288 670	34.05
Israel	1998	722 293	48.54	569 408	48.52	246 806	57.61
Israël	1999	738 610	48.54	587 663	48.76	255 891	57.30
Japan	1998	7 691 872	48.77	8 958 699	49.12	3 940 756	44.67
Japon	1999	7 528 907	48.76	8 782 114	49.09	3 982 069	44.88
Jordan	1998	706 198	48.84	579 445	49.43	...	...
Jordanie	1999	723 508[1]	48.84[1]	583 535[1]	49.55[1]	142 190	51.41
Kazakhstan	1998	1 248 900	49.18	1 966 471	49.21	323 949	53.38
Kazakhstan	1999	1 208 320	49.26	2 002 880	49.58	370 321	54.03
Korea, Republic of	1998	...	...	...	...	...	...
Corée, République de	1999	3 945 977	47.21	4 176 780	47.92	2 837 880	35.18
Kuwait	1998	139 690	48.77	231 115	49.61	32 320[1]	67.66[1]
Koweït	1999	140 182	48.94	239 997	49.52	...	...
Kyrgyzstan	1998	470 746	48.97	633 356	50.10	131 222	50.77
Kirghizistan	1999	466 250	48.83	...	...	...	...
Lao People's Dem. Rep.	1998	827 664	45.11	240 267	40.30	12 076	32.13
Rép. dém. pop. lao	1999	831 521	45.18	264 586	40.54	14 074	34.02
Lebanon	1998	394 505	47.97	396 027	51.86	113 022	50.30
Liban	1999	384 539	47.94	383 217	51.43	116 014	51.72
Malaysia	1998	2 887 753	48.58	2 153 537	51.22	...	...
Malaisie	1999	3 040 333	48.15	2 176 863	51.00	473 357	49.99
Maldives	1998	* 73 519	* 49.10	* 12 281	* 50.64	...	...
Maldives	1999	74 050	48.89	14 988	51.13	...	...
Mongolia	1998	251 476	50.21	207 295	55.53	65 272	64.93
Mongolie	1999	253 441	50.20	235 099	54.58	74 025	63.83
Myanmar	1998	4 732 947	49.12	2 066 704[1]	49.60[1]	...	...
Myanmar	1999	4 857 955	49.28	...	...	383 833	63.58
Nepal	1998	3 587 665	41.91	1 349 816	38.23	67 911	...
Népal	1999	3 780 314	42.62	1 399 340	39.96	...	...
Occupied Palestinian Terr.	1998	368 321	49.04	444 401	49.56	66 282	45.56
Territoire palestinien occupé	1999	388 162	48.91	477 378	50.12	71 207	46.52
Oman	1998	315 557	47.91	229 031	49.14	...	...
Oman	1999	315 976	47.97	242 533	49.10	...	...
Pakistan	1998	...	...	...	...	...	...
Pakistan	1999	18 365 958	37.29	6 567 978	39.53	...	...
Philippines	1998	12 502 524	48.91	5 117 459	51.28	2 208 635	54.94
Philippines	1999	...	...	...	...	...	...
Qatar	1998	60 989	47.81	44 403	56.44	8 880[1]	71.85[1]
Qatar	1999	...	...	...	...	...	...
Saudi Arabia	1998	2 259 707	47.98	1 773 725	45.94	349 599	56.98
Arabie saoudite	1999	2 285 328	47.96	1 861 755	46.25	404 094	55.93

9
Education at the primary, secondary and tertiary levels
Number of students enrolled and percentage female [cont.]
Enseignement primaire, secondaire et supérieur
Nombre d'étudiants inscrits et étudiantes feminines en pourcentage [suite]

Country or area Pays ou zone	Years Années	Primary education Enseignement primaire		Secondary education Enseignement secondaire		Tertiary education Enseignement supérieur	
		Total	% F	Total	% F	Total	% F
Sri Lanka	1998	1 801 933	48.50	2 135 075[1]	50.83[1]	...	...
Sri Lanka	1999	...	...	...	...	...	...
Syrian Arab Republic	1998	2 738 084	46.84	1 029 769	46.34	94 110[1]	...
Rép. arabe syrienne	1999	...	...	...	...	...	...
Tajikistan	1998	690 306	47.95	772 633	45.60	...	...
Tadjikistan	1999	691 891	47.44	798 701	45.55	79 978	25.16
Thailand	1998	6 120 400	48.26	...	...	1 814 096	53.39
Thaïlande	1999	6 100 647	48.29	5 432 205	50.20	1 900 272	54.11
Turkey	1998	...	...	...	...	953 295	60.90
Turquie	1999	7 850 103[1]	46.74[1]	4 370 320[1]	40.29[1]	1 015 412	39.79
United Arab Emirates	1998	270 486	48.03	201 522	50.11	21 000[1]	...
Emirats arabes unis	1999	273 144	47.86	210 002	50.00	...	...
Viet Nam	1998	10 250 214	47.24	7 445 336	46.45	810 072	42.91
Viet Nam	1999	10 063 025	47.71	7 875 963	46.97	732 187	41.64
Yemen	1998	2 302 787	34.95	1 041 816	26.04	164 166	20.75
Yémen	1999	...	...	...	...	...	...
Europe · Europe							
Albania	1998	...	...	...	...	...	...
Albanie	1999	283 249	48.27	363 689	48.74	40 125	59.86
Austria	1998	388 777	48.47	747 681	47.59	252 893	50.03
Autriche	1999	392 407	48.45	748 659	47.71	261 229	50.96
Belarus	1998	632 127	47.69	1 002 621	49.84	353 108	56.14
Bélarus	1999	599 732	48.36	1 112 547	48.57	377 167	56.10
Belgium	1998	762 734	48.55	1 033 484	50.63	...	...
Belgique	1999	773 742	48.64	1 057 536	51.23	355 748	52.26
Bulgaria	1998	411 726	48.13	699 957	48.22	270 077	59.47
Bulgarie	1999	392 876	48.12	696 073	48.14	261 321	57.27
Croatia	1998	202 999	48.52	426 915	49.64	95 889	52.90
Croatie	1999	199 084	48.55	420 689	49.75	158 810	53.46
Czech Republic	1998	654 511	48.50	928 467	49.87	231 224	49.73
République tchèque	1999	644 956	48.56	957 763	49.27	253 695	49.78
Denmark	1998	371 694	48.65	422 399	50.32	189 970	56.30
Danemark	1999	384 197	48.63	426 149	50.06	189 162	56.91
Estonia	1998	126 671	47.92	115 885	50.08	48 684	57.77
Estonie	1999	123 406	47.90	116 886	49.93	53 613	58.47
Finland	1998	382 746	48.81	479 882	51.02	262 890	53.97
Finlande	1999	388 063	48.78	490 454	51.10	270 185	53.70
France	1998	3 944 227	48.55	5 955 495	48.87	2 012 193	54.43
France	1999	3 884 560	48.58	5 928 745	48.93	2 015 344	54.21
Germany	1998	3 767 460	48.51	...	...	2 087 044	47.40
Allemagne	1999	3 655 859	48.53	8 307 277	48.35	...	...
Gibraltar	1998	2 607	40.58	1 370	47.45	...	...
Gibraltar	1999	2 366[1]	47.97[1]	1 483	48.42	...	...
Greece	1998	645 534	48.44	770 883	48.93	387 859	50.25
Grèce	1999	645 313	48.42	738 744	49.38	422 317	49.98
Holy See	1998	...	...	...	...	9 389	30.08
Saint Siège	1999	...	...	...	...	...	...
Hungary	1998	503 302	48.40	1 006 546	49.28	279 397	54.21
Hongrie	1999	500 946	48.44	1 001 855	49.11	307 071	53.87
Iceland	1998	30 355	48.17	32 480	50.39	8 462	62.16
Islande	1999	31 282	48.31	32 133	50.68	9 667	61.91
Ireland	1998	...	...	...	...	151 137	53.53
Irlande	1999	392 323	48.44	395 562	50.39	160 611	54.11
Italy	1998	2 875 852	48.47	4 450 012	48.61	1 797 241	55.17
Italie	1999	2 836 333	48.62	4 404 321	47.77	1 770 002	55.52
Latvia	1998	141 408	48.33	255 381	49.95	82 042	61.60
Lettonie	1999	134 919	48.45	266 498	49.65	91 237	63.41
Lithuania	1998	219 661	48.45	406 951	49.24	107 419	60.00
Lituanie	1999	218 181	48.68	...	...	121 904	59.96
Luxembourg	1998	31 492	49.23	...	...	2 717	51.67
Luxembourg	1999	32 458	49.16	32 996	50.19	2 437[1]	54.21[1]
Malta	1998	34 914	48.63	36 946	45.90	5 768	51.47
Malte	1999	...	...	...	...	...	...
Monaco	1998	2 022	49.90	2 883	50.92	...	...
Monaco	1999	2 008	48.46	2 929	50.73	...	...

9
Education at the primary, secondary and tertiary levels
Number of students enrolled and percentage female [cont.]
Enseignement primaire, secondaire et supérieur
Nombre d'étudiants inscrits et étudiantes feminines en pourcentage [suite]

Country or area Pays ou zone	Years Années	Primary education Enseignement primaire		Secondary education Enseignement secondaire		Tertiary education Enseignement supérieur	
		Total	% F	Total	% F	Total	% F
Netherlands	1998	1 268 093	48.32	1 364 806	47.78	469 885	49.29
Pays−Bas	1999	1 278 581	48.33	1 379 253	47.88	487 649	49.96
Norway	1998	411 878	48.66	377 640	49.36	187 482	57.40
Norvège	1999	419 805	48.74	371 659	49.37	190 943	58.42
Poland	1998	...	...	...	...	1 399 090	57.02
Pologne	1999	3 398 868[1]	48.05[1]	3 916 560[1]	48.78[1]	1 579 571	57.53
Portugal	1998	815 231	47.73	847 516	50.92	356 790	55.90
Portugal	1999	810 996	47.73	831 193	50.55	373 745	56.51
Romania	1998	1 284 507	48.51	2 218 025	49.34	...	...
Roumanie	1999	1 189 058	48.46	2 225 691	49.37	...	...
Russian Federation	1998	6 138 300	48.59	14 516 500	50.45	6 322 400	55.81
Fédération de Russie	1999	6 138 300	48.59	13 857 896	50.81	7 224 014	55.42
San Marino	1998	...	...	...	...	...	...
Saint−Marin	1999	1 249	48.04	988	47.98	942	57.86
Serbia and Montenegro	1998	417 830	48.56	813 956	49.23	197 410	53.51
Serbie−et−Monténégro	1999	389 314	48.70	784 526	49.38	233 043	53.01
Slovakia	1998	316 601	48.51	674 405	49.51	122 886	51.70
Slovaquie	1999	309 399	48.53	671 670	49.41	135 914	50.39
Slovenia	1998	91 536	48.47	220 033	49.46	79 917[1]	56.04[1]
Slovénie	1999	...	...	...	...	...	...
Spain	1998	2 579 908	48.31	3 299 469	50.33	1 786 778	53.04
Espagne	1999	2 539 995	48.36	3 245 950	50.19	1 828 987	52.94
Sweden	1998	763 028	49.43	963 918	54.78	335 124	57.58
Suède	1999	775 706	49.33	933 669	54.60	346 878	58.22
Switzerland	1998	529 610	48.57	544 433	46.80	156 390	41.71
Suisse	1999	538 372	48.62	549 369	46.96	156 879	42.64
TFYR Macedonia	1998	129 633	48.12	218 666	48.03	35 141	55.09
L'ex−R.y. Macédoine	1999	126 606	48.36	221 961	47.84	40 125	59.86
Ukraine	1998	2 200 098	45.59	* 4 971 154	* 52.60	1 583 354	52.58
Ukraine	1999	...	...	...	...	...	...
United Kingdom	1998	4 661 234	48.83	8 092 272	52.01	2 080 960	53.20
Royaume−Uni	1999	4 631 623	48.80	8 298 776	52.43	2 024 138	53.94
Oceania • Océanie							
Australia	1998	...	...	...	...	...	...
Australie	1999	1 885 341	48.68	2 491 404	48.80	845 636	54.12
Cook Islands	1998	2 711	47.58	1 779	50.48	...	...
Iles Cook	1999	2 594	46.38	1 751	50.03	...	...
Fiji	1998	116 410[1]	48.26[1]	...	...	...	...
Fidji	1999	...	...	...	...	...	...
Marshall Islands	1998	8 209	48.24	5 957	50.46	...	...
Iles Marshall	1999	...	...	...	...	...	...
Micronesia (Fed. States of)	1998	...	...	...	...	1 510	...
Micronésie (Etats féd. de)	1999	...	...	...	...	...	...
Nauru	1998	1 598[1]	50.56[1]	738[1]	51.22[1]	...	...
Nauru	1999	...	...	...	...	...	...
New Zealand	1998	...	...	...	...	167 308	59.01
Nouvelle−Zélande	1999	360 621	48.56	436 901	50.14	167 308	59.01
Niue	1998	282	43.26	282	46.81	...	...
Nioué	1999	268	46.27	268	54.10	...	...
Papua New Guinea	1998	580 623	45.16	132 635	40.09	9 859	35.53
Papouasie−Nvl−Guinée	1999	...	...	...	...	...	...
Samoa	1998	27 439	48.70	21 522	50.01	1 482	45.07
Samoa	1999	27 297	47.65	21 748	49.51	1 871	47.46
Tonga	1998	16 460	46.19	13 661	50.73	...	...
Tonga	1999	16 783	46.43	14 710	50.02	364	54.95
Tuvalu	1998	1 419[1]	45.95[1]	830[1]	44.82[1]	...	...
Tuvalu	1999	...	...	...	...	...	...
Vanuatu	1998	34 479	47.70	7 587	52.56	52	38.46
Vanuatu	1999	37 030	49.74	10 023	43.46	...	...

Source:
United Nations Educational, Scientific and Cultural Organization.
(UNESCO) Institute for Statistics, Montreal, the UNESCO
statistics database.

Source:
L'Institut de statistique de l'Organisation des Nations Unies
pour l'éducation, la science et la culture (UNESCO), Montréal.
la base de données de l'UNESCO.

1   UNESCO estimate.

1   Estimations de l'UNESCO.

10
Illiterate population by sex, aged 15 years and over, estimates and projections
Population analphabète selon le sexe, âgée de 15 ans et plus, estimations et projections

Country or area Pays ou zone	Year Année	Illiterate population (thousands) Population analphabète (milliers)			Percentage of illiterates Pourcentage d'analphabètes		
		Total	M	F	Total	M	F
Africa · Afrique							
Algeria	1995	6 754	2 491	4 265	39.7	29.1	50.5
Algérie	2001	6 538	2 339	4 199	32.2	22.9	41.7
	2003	6 445	2 287	4 158	30.1	21.1	39.1
Benin	1995	1 953	763	1 189	68.4	55.1	80.9
Bénin	2001	2 137	787	1 350	61.4	46.5	75.4
	2003	2 201	794	1 406	59.1	43.8	73.5
Botswana	1995	218	113	105	27.4	30.0	25.0
Botswana	2001	198	107	91	21.9	24.7	19.4
	2003	187	103	84	20.2	23.0	17.6
Burkina Faso	1995	4 255	1 754	2 527	80.2	70.8	89.4
Burkina Faso	2001	4 576	1 844	2 769	75.2	65.1	85.1
	2003	4 757	1 918	2 875	73.4	63.1	83.4
Burundi	1995	1 870	736	1 136	57.8	47.8	66.9
Burundi	2001	1 747	701	1 049	50.8	43.1	58.0
	2003	1 812	741	1 073	48.4	41.5	54.8
Cameroon	1995	2 582	933	1 648	35.1	25.8	44.1
Cameroun	2001	2 402	864	1 535	27.6	20.1	34.9
	2003	2 325	838	1 485	25.4	18.5	32.1
Cape Verde	1995	68	18	50	30.4	19.2	39.1
Cap−Vert	2001	67	18	49	25.1	15.1	33.0
	2003	66	18	48	23.5	14.3	30.8
Central African Republic	1995	1 145	420	724	60.3	46.5	72.7
Rép. centrafricaine	2001	1 118	404	713	51.8	39.2	63.4
	2003	1 090	393	697	48.9	36.8	60.1
Chad	1995	2 379	994	1 386	65.4	56.0	74.3
Tchad	2001	2 425	999	1 426	55.8	47.0	64.2
	2003	2 421	994	1 427	52.5	44.0	60.7
Comoros	1995	151	62	89	45.2	37.6	52.6
Comores	2001	183	76	107	44.0	36.7	51.2
	2003	193	80	113	43.6	36.4	50.7
Congo	1995	363	118	244	25.6	17.3	33.2
Congo	2001	303	95	208	18.2	11.8	24.1
	2003	285	88	197	16.2	10.4	21.6
Côte d'Ivoire	1995	4 487	1 871	2 604	56.4	44.9	68.7
Côte d'Ivoire	2001	4 803	1 966	2 824	50.3	39.7	61.6
	2003	4 877	1 987	2 876	48.3	38.0	59.1
Democratic Republic of the Congo	1995	10 770	3 754	7 013	45.4	32.4	57.7
Rép. dém. du Congo	2001	9 992	3 395	6 591	37.3	25.8	48.2
	2003	9 897	3 340	6 550	34.5	23.8	44.9
Djibouti	1995	123	38	89	41.1	28.8	52.8
Djibouti	2001	126	39	90	34.5	23.9	44.5
	2003	120	37	86	32.1	22.0	41.6
Egypt	1995	18 687	7 025	11 669	48.9	36.5	61.5
Egypte	2001	19 802	7 452	12 363	43.9	32.8	55.2
	2003	20 165	7 606	12 572	42.3	31.7	53.1
Equatorial Guinea	1995	50	12	38	22.2	10.5	32.9
Guinée équatoriale	2001	42	9	33	15.8	7.2	24.0
	2003	40	9	31	14.3	6.7	21.6
Eritrea	1995	872	324	547	48.9	37.0	60.5
Erythrée	2001	929	336	592	43.3	31.8	54.4
	2003	980	351	628	41.4	30.1	52.4
Ethiopia	1995	20 336	8 719	11 676	66.4	57.9	75.0
Ethiopie	2001	21 083	9 036	12 097	59.7	51.9	67.6
	2003	21 214	9 107	12 152	57.2	49.8	64.8
Gambia	1995	455	201	254	69.0	62.3	75.5
Gambie	2001	498	216	282	62.2	55.0	69.1
	2003	505	217	288	59.9	52.5	66.9
Ghana	1995	3 392	1 182	2 209	34.8	24.6	44.7
Ghana	2001	3 208	1 100	2 106	27.3	18.9	35.5
	2003	3 126	1 069	2 055	25.1	17.4	32.7

10
Illiterate population by sex, aged 15 and over,
estimates and projections [*cont.*]
Population analphabète selon le sexe, âgée de 15 ans et plus,
estimations et projections [*suite*]

Country or area Pays ou zone	Year Année	Illiterate population (thousands) Population analphabète (milliers)			Percentage of illiterates Pourcentage d'analphabètes		
		Total	M	F	Total	M	F
Guinea−Bissau	1995	415	155	260	67.5	51.7	82.4
Guinée−Bissau	2001	418	151	267	60.4	44.8	75.3
	2003	418	149	268	57.7	42.2	72.4
Kenya	1995	3 358	1 065	2 301	23.0	14.8	31.1
Kenya	2001	2 976	931	2 052	16.7	10.5	22.7
	2003	2 807	880	1 935	14.9	9.4	20.3
Lesotho	1995	214	168	47	19.1	30.9	8.2
Lesotho	2001	202	164	39	16.1	26.7	6.1
	2003	194	160	35	15.2	25.4	5.5
Liberia	1995	546	192	354	54.7	38.1	71.8
Libéria	2001	808	258	549	45.2	28.7	61.9
	2003	848	265	583	43.0	26.7	59.5
Libyan Arab Jamahiriya	1995	742	195	546	25.5	12.7	39.8
Jamahiriya arabe libyenne	2001	693	163	530	19.2	8.7	30.7
	2003	666	150	515	17.5	7.6	28.1
Madagascar	1995	2 871	1 125	1 741	37.7	29.9	45.2
Madagascar	2001	2 973	1 161	1 809	32.7	25.8	39.4
	2003	3 002	1 172	1 828	31.1	24.5	37.5
Malawi	1995	2 356	734	1 621	44.1	28.4	58.8
Malawi	2001	2 428	762	1 663	39.0	25.0	52.4
	2003	2 434	768	1 663	37.3	23.9	50.2
Mali	1995	4 183	1 782	2 400	78.0	68.3	87.1
Mali	2001	4 627	1 948	2 675	73.6	63.3	83.4
	2003	4 791	2 010	2 778	72.1	61.7	82.0
Mauritania	1995	786	316	469	62.4	51.3	73.0
Mauritanie	2001	909	368	541	59.3	48.9	69.3
	2003	948	385	563	58.3	48.2	68.1
Mauritius	1995	143	55	88	17.7	13.6	21.7
Maurice	2001	133	52	81	15.2	12.0	18.3
	2003	129	51	78	14.4	11.4	17.4
Morocco	1995	9 584	3 593	5 991	56.1	42.4	69.5
Maroc	2001	10 055	3 723	6 332	50.2	37.4	62.8
	2003	10 168	3 756	6 412	48.3	35.9	60.6
Mozambique	1995	5 640	2 033	3 604	61.5	45.4	76.9
Mozambique	2001	5 722	1 991	3 726	54.8	38.8	70.0
	2003	5 657	1 947	3 704	52.2	36.6	67.3
Namibia	1995	192	85	107	21.5	19.8	23.1
Namibie	2001	175	82	93	17.3	16.6	18.1
	2003	168	80	87	16.0	15.6	16.3
Niger	1995	3 958	1 809	2 142	86.5	79.3	93.3
Niger	2001	4 693	2 127	2 556	83.5	75.6	91.1
	2003	4 965	2 243	2 710	82.4	74.2	90.2
Nigeria	1995	23 401	9 104	14 210	43.6	34.0	52.8
Nigéria	2001	22 314	8 617	13 598	34.6	26.7	42.3
	2003	21 823	8 414	13 307	31.9	24.5	39.0
Réunion	1995	69	38	31	14.7	16.8	12.7
Réunion	2001	63	36	27	11.9	13.9	10.0
	2003	61	35	26	11.2	13.1	9.3
Rwanda	1995	1 062	410	651	39.8	31.4	47.8
Rwanda	2001	1 421	558	862	32.0	25.5	38.1
	2003	1 374	543	829	29.6	23.8	35.2
Senegal	1995	3 063	1 290	1 773	67.2	57.2	77.0
Sénégal	2001	3 332	1 382	1 950	61.7	51.9	71.3
	2003	3 425	1 415	2 010	59.8	50.1	69.2
South Africa	1995	4 276	1 981	2 294	16.7	15.8	17.5
Afrique du Sud	2001	4 175	1 938	2 237	14.4	13.7	15.0
	2003	4 055	1 884	2 169	13.6	13.0	14.3

Illiterate population by sex, aged 15 and over,
estimates and projections [*cont.*]
Population analphabète selon le sexe, âgée de 15 ans et plus,
estimations et projections [*suite*]

Country or area Pays ou zone	Year Année	Illiterate population (thousands) Population analphabète (milliers)			Percentage of illiterates Pourcentage d'analphabètes		
		Total	M	F	Total	M	F
Sudan	1995	7 973	2 898	5 075	48.5	35.4	61.4
Soudan	2001	7 871	2 855	5 010	41.2	30.0	52.3
	2003	7 858	2 854	4 997	39.0	28.4	49.5
Swaziland	1995	115	53	62	24.0	22.5	25.3
Swaziland	2001	108	50	58	19.7	18.7	20.6
	2003	103	48	55	18.4	17.4	19.2
Togo	1995	1 045	347	698	49.4	33.4	64.7
Togo	2001	1 082	341	740	41.6	26.6	56.0
	2003	1 077	334	741	39.1	24.6	53.1
Tunisia	1995	2 085	711	1 374	35.3	24.0	46.7
Tunisie	2001	1 896	603	1 293	27.9	17.7	38.1
	2003	1 829	569	1 261	25.8	16.0	35.7
Uganda	1995	3 951	1 349	2 596	38.2	26.4	49.7
Ouganda	2001	3 898	1 322	2 570	32.0	21.9	42.0
	2003	3 896	1 321	2 569	30.2	20.6	39.6
United Rep. of Tanzania	1995	5 140	1 635	3 506	30.8	20.1	41.1
Rép.– Unie de Tanzanie	2001	4 759	1 509	3 250	24.0	15.5	32.1
	2003	4 604	1 463	3 140	21.9	14.2	29.4
Zambia	1995	1 329	442	874	26.7	17.9	34.8
Zambie	2001	1 192	405	776	21.0	14.2	27.3
	2003	1 145	392	743	19.3	13.2	25.2
Zimbabwe	1995	945	314	629	15.3	10.2	20.1
Zimbabwe	2001	754	237	514	10.7	6.7	14.5
	2003	691	213	475	9.3	5.8	12.9
America, North · Amérique du Nord							
Bahamas	1995	10	6	4	5.0	5.9	4.2
Bahamas	2001	10	6	4	4.5	5.4	3.7
	2003	10	6	4	4.4	5.3	3.5
Barbados	1995	1	0	0	0.5	0.4	0.5
Barbade	2001	1	0	0	0.3	0.3	0.3
	2003	1	0	0	0.3	0.3	0.3
Belize	1995	10	5	5	8.4	7.7	9.1
Belize	2001	9	5	5	6.6	6.4	6.7
	2003	9	5	4	5.9	5.9	5.9
Costa Rica	1995	122	62	60	5.2	5.3	5.2
Costa Rica	2001	121	62	59	4.3	4.4	4.2
	2003	120	62	58	4.0	4.1	4.0
Cuba	1995	349	171	177	4.1	4.0	4.2
Cuba	2001	286	137	149	3.2	3.1	3.3
	2003	269	129	141	3.0	2.9	3.1
Dominican Republic	1995	897	452	446	18.3	18.2	18.5
Rép. dominicaine	2001	912	463	449	16.0	16.0	16.0
	2003	910	464	446	15.3	15.4	15.2
El Salvador	1995	856	355	501	24.1	20.9	27.1
El Salvador	2001	863	360	503	20.8	18.1	23.4
	2003	862	360	502	19.9	17.2	22.3
Guatemala	1995	1 922	751	1 171	35.1	27.4	42.7
Guatemala	2001	2 040	773	1 268	30.8	23.4	38.2
	2003	2 080	780	1 301	29.5	22.1	36.8
Haiti	1995	2 372	1 083	1 288	55.3	52.7	57.7
Haïti	2001	2 440	1 118	1 323	49.2	47.1	51.1
	2003	2 462	1 130	1 333	47.1	45.3	48.8
Honduras	1995	894	441	453	28.3	28.0	28.6
Honduras	2001	942	473	470	24.4	24.6	24.3
	2003	954	481	473	23.2	23.5	23.0
Jamaica	1995	249	154	95	15.2	19.4	11.3
Jamaïque	2001	228	145	83	12.7	16.6	9.0
	2003	222	142	79	12.0	15.8	8.3
Martinique	1995	10	5	4	3.5	4.0	2.9
Martinique	2001	7	4	3	2.5	2.9	2.1
	2003	7	4	3	2.3	2.7	1.9

10
Illiterate population by sex, aged 15 and over,
estimates and projections [*cont.*]
Population analphabète selon le sexe, âgée de 15 ans et plus,
estimations et projections [*suite*]

Country or area Pays ou zone	Year Année	Illiterate population (thousands) Population analphabète (milliers)			Percentage of illiterates Pourcentage d'analphabètes		
		Total	M	F	Total	M	F
Mexico	1995	6 187	2 271	3 916	10.5	7.9	13.0
Mexique	2001	5 788	2 143	3 645	8.6	6.5	10.5
	2003	5 644	2 096	3 549	8.0	6.1	9.8
Netherlands Antilles	1995	6	3	3	3.9	3.9	3.9
Antilles néerlandaises	2001	6	3	3	3.4	3.4	3.4
	2003	5	3	3	3.2	3.3	3.2
Nicaragua	1995	862	422	439	35.4	35.5	35.2
Nicaragua	2001	998	493	505	33.2	33.5	32.9
	2003	1 043	516	527	32.5	32.8	32.2
Panama	1995	165	77	88	9.4	8.8	10.1
Panama	2001	159	73	86	7.9	7.3	8.6
	2003	156	72	85	7.5	6.8	8.1
Puerto Rico	1995	200	96	104	7.2	7.3	7.1
Porto Rico	2001	182	89	93	6.0	6.3	5.8
	2003	176	87	89	5.7	6.0	5.5
Trinidad and Tobago	1995	20	6	14	2.3	1.4	3.2
Trinité−et−Tobago	2001	16	5	11	1.6	1.0	2.2
	2003	15	5	10	1.4	0.9	2.0
America, South · Amérique du Sud							
Argentina	1995	906	428	478	3.7	3.6	3.7
Argentine	2001	840	406	434	3.1	3.1	3.1
	2003	820	399	421	2.9	2.9	2.9
Bolivia	1995	790	223	567	17.9	10.4	25.2
Bolivie	2001	723	195	528	14.0	7.7	20.1
	2003	699	186	513	12.8	7.0	18.5
Brazil	1995	16 658	7 922	8 736	15.3	14.9	15.7
Brésil	2001	15 715	7 633	8 082	12.7	12.6	12.8
	2003	15 301	7 488	7 814	11.9	12.0	11.9
Chile	1995	507	234	274	5.1	4.8	5.3
Chili	2001	454	213	241	4.1	3.9	4.3
	2003	436	206	230	3.8	3.7	3.9
Colombia	1995	2 490	1 193	1 296	9.9	9.7	10.0
Colombie	2001	2 345	1 144	1 201	8.1	8.1	8.1
	2003	2 288	1 123	1 165	7.6	7.7	7.5
Ecuador	1995	744	296	448	10.2	8.2	12.3
Equateur	2001	700	281	420	8.2	6.6	9.7
	2003	684	275	409	7.6	6.1	9.1
Guyana	1995	10	3	7	2.1	1.4	2.8
Guyana	2001	8	3	5	1.4	1.0	1.8
	2003	7	2	4	1.2	0.9	1.5
Paraguay	1995	228	93	135	8.1	6.6	9.6
Paraguay	2001	223	94	129	6.5	5.5	7.5
	2003	221	94	127	6.1	5.1	7.0
Peru	1995	1 837	485	1 352	12.2	6.6	17.6
Pérou	2001	1 717	442	1 275	9.8	5.2	14.3
	2003	1 674	428	1 246	9.1	4.8	13.3
Uruguay	1995	70	39	31	2.9	3.4	2.5
Uruguay	2001	60	34	26	2.4	2.8	1.9
	2003	57	33	24	2.2	2.7	1.8
Venezuela	1995	1 271	578	693	9.1	8.3	9.9
Venezuela	2001	1 174	550	624	7.2	6.7	7.6
	2003	1 136	537	599	6.6	6.2	6.9
Asia · Asie							
Armenia	1995	54	11	43	2.0	0.9	3.0
Arménie	2001	44	10	35	1.5	0.7	2.2
	2003	41	9	32	1.4	0.6	2.0
Bahrain	1995	59	26	32	14.8	11.0	20.7
Bahreïn	2001	57	25	32	12.1	8.9	16.8
	2003	54	24	30	10.9	8.1	15.0
Bangladesh	1995	46 003	20 160	25 735	62.9	53.2	73.1
Bangladesh	2001	51 507	22 424	29 007	59.4	50.1	69.2
	2003	53 458	23 227	30 154	58.4	49.2	68.0

10
Illiterate population by sex, aged 15 and over,
estimates and projections [*cont.*]
Population analphabète selon le sexe, âgée de 15 ans et plus,
estimations et projections [*suite*]

Country or area Pays ou zone	Year Année	Illiterate population (thousands) Population analphabète (milliers)			Percentage of illiterates Pourcentage d'analphabètes		
		Total	M	F	Total	M	F
Brunei Darussalam	1995	21	7	14	11.0	6.9	15.5
Brunéi Darussalam	2001	19	7	13	8.4	5.4	11.9
	2003	20	7	13	8.2	5.2	11.5
Cambodia	1995	2 128	591	1 536	35.5	21.3	47.8
Cambodge	2001	2 386	706	1 676	31.3	19.5	41.8
	2003	2 432	733	1 696	29.9	18.9	39.8
China	1995	161 980	46 451	115 540	18.1	10.1	26.4
Chine	2001	138 401	37 125	101 296	14.2	7.5	21.3
	2003	130 678	34 293	96 406	13.0	6.7	19.6
China, Hong Kong SAR	1995	426	96	336	8.5	3.7	13.6
Chine, Hong Kong RAS	2001	380	91	300	6.5	3.1	10.4
	2003	359	88	283	6.0	2.9	9.5
China, Macao SAR	1995	24	6	18	7.7	4.1	11.0
Chine, Macao RAS	2001	21	5	16	5.9	3.1	8.6
	2003	20	5	15	5.5	2.8	8.0
Cyprus	1995	23	5	18	4.2	1.7	6.5
Chypre	2001	17	4	13	2.8	1.2	4.3
	2003	15	3	12	2.4	1.1	3.7
India	1995	280 197	107 689	172 585	46.7	34.8	59.4
Inde	2001	288 000	109 625	178 481	42.0	31.0	53.6
	2003	289 643	109 944	179 801	40.5	29.8	51.7
Indonesia	1995	21 684	6 861	14 763	16.5	10.4	22.3
Indonésie	2001	18 975	5 879	13 045	12.7	7.9	17.4
	2003	18 049	5 560	12 441	11.6	7.2	15.9
Iran (Islamic Rep. of)	1995	11 013	4 136	6 825	30.0	22.0	38.1
Iran (Rép. islamique d')	2001	10 440	3 753	6 654	22.9	16.2	29.8
	2003	10 121	3 584	6 510	20.9	14.5	27.4
Iraq	1995	7 164	2 720	4 444	62.5	46.8	78.6
Iraq	2001	8 352	3 138	5 216	60.3	44.7	76.3
	2003	8 843	3 311	5 534	59.6	44.1	75.6
Israel	1995	255	72	184	6.7	3.9	9.4
Israël	2001	219	62	158	4.9	2.9	6.9
	2003	206	59	148	4.4	2.6	6.2
Jordan	1995	336	91	242	13.5	6.9	20.6
Jordanie	2001	293	76	216	9.7	4.8	14.9
	2003	279	71	206	8.6	4.2	13.4
Kazakhstan	1995	99	24	75	0.8	0.4	1.2
Kazakhstan	2001	69	19	50	0.6	0.3	0.8
	2003	63	18	45	0.5	0.3	0.7
Korea, Republic of	1995	1 056	203	853	3.1	1.2	4.9
Corée, République de	2001	799	154	646	2.1	0.8	3.4
	2003	724	141	583	1.9	0.7	3.0
Kuwait	1995	208	114	87	21.0	18.0	24.3
Koweït	2001	245	134	107	17.6	15.7	19.7
	2003	253	139	111	16.5	15.0	18.3
Lao People's Dem. Rep.	1995	1 040	346	700	39.4	26.7	52.0
Rép. dém. pop. lao	2001	1 070	356	720	34.4	23.2	45.6
	2003	1 080	359	726	32.7	22.0	43.4
Lebanon	1995	350	96	254	16.7	9.6	23.1
Liban	2001	334	90	244	13.5	7.6	19.0
	2003	326	87	240	12.6	6.9	17.8
Malaysia	1995	2 013	689	1 324	15.7	10.7	20.8
Malaisie	2001	1 817	626	1 191	12.1	8.3	16.0
	2003	1 743	603	1 141	11.1	7.7	14.7
Maldives	1995	6	3	3	4.1	3.9	4.3
Maldives	2001	5	3	3	3.0	2.9	3.1
	2003	5	2	2	2.6	2.6	2.7
Mongolia	1995	27	11	17	1.9	1.5	2.2
Mongolie	2001	26	12	14	1.5	1.4	1.7
	2003	25	12	13	1.4	1.3	1.5
Myanmar	1995	4 938	1 677	3 260	17.2	11.8	22.4
Myanmar	2001	4 890	1 752	3 143	15.0	10.9	19.0
	2003	4 870	1 774	3 103	14.4	10.7	18.1

10
Illiterate population by sex, aged 15 and over,
estimates and projections [*cont.*]
Population analphabète selon le sexe, âgée de 15 ans et plus,
estimations et projections [*suite*]

Country or area Pays ou zone	Year Année	Illiterate population (thousands) Population analphabète (milliers)			Percentage of illiterates Pourcentage d'analphabètes		
		Total	M	F	Total	M	F
Nepal	1995	7 690	2 845	4 779	64.0	46.3	81.4
Népal	2001	7 964	2 804	5 115	57.1	39.5	74.8
	2003	8 048	2 794	5 217	54.9	37.4	72.4
Oman	1995	423	168	255	36.3	25.9	49.4
Oman	2001	399	154	245	27.0	19.1	36.5
	2003	388	148	240	24.2	17.0	32.8
Pakistan	1995	43 057	16 995	26 215	60.7	46.5	76.2
Pakistan	2001	47 387	18 154	29 385	56.0	41.8	71.2
	2003	48 674	18 439	30 405	54.3	40.2	69.4
Philippines	1995	2 690	1 280	1 409	6.5	6.2	6.8
Philippines	2001	2 355	1 144	1 210	4.9	4.7	5.0
	2003	2 258	1 105	1 154	4.4	4.3	4.5
Qatar	1995	78	56	21	20.8	21.0	20.1
Qatar	2001	77	56	21	18.3	19.2	16.3
	2003	77	56	21	17.5	18.6	15.0
Saudi Arabia	1995	2 719	1 086	1 695	28.7	20.5	40.7
Arabie saoudite	2001	2 773	1 096	1 730	22.9	16.5	31.8
	2003	2 772	1 094	1 729	21.3	15.4	29.2
Singapore	1995	252	62	190	9.3	4.6	14.0
Singapour	2001	240	59	181	7.5	3.6	11.3
	2003	231	56	175	6.9	3.4	10.4
Sri Lanka	1995	1 239	418	796	9.8	6.3	13.1
Sri Lanka	2001	1 154	398	736	8.1	5.5	10.7
	2003	1 123	390	715	7.7	5.2	10.1
Syrian Arab Republic	1995	2 362	577	1 784	30.1	14.6	45.9
Rép. arabe syrienne	2001	2 467	565	1 898	24.7	11.2	38.4
	2003	2 491	558	1 928	23.1	10.3	36.1
Tajikistan	1995	40	9	31	1.2	0.6	1.8
Tadjikistan	2001	28	7	21	0.7	0.4	1.1
	2003	25	7	18	0.6	0.4	0.9
Thailand	1995	2 469	753	1 724	5.9	3.7	8.1
Thaïlande	2001	2 035	632	1 410	4.3	2.7	5.9
	2003	1 924	597	1 334	4.0	2.5	5.4
Turkey	1995	7 563	1 759	5 804	18.2	8.4	28.1
Turquie	2001	6 879	1 499	5 378	14.5	6.3	22.8
	2003	6 608	1 407	5 200	13.5	5.7	21.4
United Arab Emirates	1995	444	328	116	26.6	27.1	25.3
Emirats arabes unis	2001	462	347	118	23.3	24.8	20.2
	2003	465	352	116	22.2	24.0	18.5
Uzbekistan	1995	147	31	115	1.1	0.5	1.6
Ouzbékistan	2001	124	32	92	0.8	0.4	1.1
	2003	120	32	88	0.7	0.4	1.0
Viet Nam	1995	3 908	1 313	2 565	8.5	5.8	11.0
Viet Nam	2001	3 909	1 441	2 451	7.3	5.5	9.1
	2003	3 923	1 486	2 423	7.0	5.4	8.5
Yemen	1995	4 621	1 400	3 280	59.9	37.9	81.5
Yémen	2001	4 962	1 453	3 561	52.3	31.5	73.1
	2003	5 060	1 469	3 639	49.7	29.5	69.9
Europe · Europe							
Albania	1995	411	114	296	18.8	10.3	27.7
Albanie	2001	326	85	241	14.7	7.5	22.2
	2003	308	78	229	13.5	6.7	20.5
Belarus	1995	34	9	25	0.4	0.3	0.6
Bélarus	2001	28	9	19	0.3	0.2	0.4
	2003	26	9	17	0.3	0.2	0.4
Bulgaria	1995	147	45	102	2.1	1.4	2.9
Bulgarie	2001	101	32	69	1.5	1.0	2.0
	2003	90	28	61	1.4	0.9	1.8
Croatia	1995	87	14	73	2.3	0.8	3.7
Croatie	2001	63	12	51	1.6	0.6	2.6
	2003	56	11	45	1.5	0.6	2.2
Estonia	1995	2	1	1	0.2	0.2	0.2
Estonie	2001	2	1	1	0.2	0.2	0.2
	2003	3	1	1	0.2	0.2	0.2

10
Illiterate population by sex, aged 15 and over,
estimates and projections [*cont.*]
Population analphabète selon le sexe, âgée de 15 ans et plus,
estimations et projections [*suite*]

Country or area Pays ou zone	Year Année	Illiterate population (thousands) Population analphabète (milliers)			Percentage of illiterates Pourcentage d'analphabètes		
		Total	M	F	Total	M	F
Greece	1995	327	79	248	3.8	1.9	5.6
Grèce	2001	248	65	183	2.7	1.5	3.9
	2003	229	61	168	2.5	1.4	3.6
Hungary	1995	65	24	41	0.8	0.6	0.9
Hongrie	2001	55	20	35	0.7	0.5	0.8
	2003	51	19	33	0.6	0.5	0.7
Italy	1995	900	316	584	1.8	1.4	2.3
Italie	2001	748	260	488	1.5	1.1	1.9
	2003	686	238	447	1.4	1.0	1.7
Latvia	1995	4	2	2	0.2	0.2	0.2
Lettonie	2001	4	2	2	0.2	0.2	0.2
	2003	4	2	2	0.2	0.2	0.2
Lithuania	1995	16	5	10	0.5	0.4	0.7
Lituanie	2001	13	5	8	0.4	0.3	0.5
	2003	12	5	7	0.4	0.3	0.4
Malta	1995	28	15	14	9.6	10.2	9.0
Malte	2001	24	13	11	7.7	8.5	7.0
	2003	23	13	10	7.2	8.0	6.4
Poland	1995	96	42	54	0.3	0.3	0.4
Pologne	2001	82	38	45	0.3	0.2	0.3
	2003	79	36	42	0.2	0.2	0.3
Portugal	1995	822	270	551	10.1	7.0	12.9
Portugal	2001	625	200	425	7.5	5.0	9.7
	2003	565	179	386	6.7	4.5	8.8
Republic of Moldova	1995	55	10	45	1.7	0.6	2.6
République de Moldova	2001	35	7	28	1.0	0.4	1.6
	2003	29	6	23	0.9	0.4	1.3
Romania	1995	432	103	330	2.4	1.2	3.6
Roumanie	2001	329	84	245	1.8	0.9	2.6
	2003	300	80	221	1.6	0.9	2.3
Russian Federation	1995	698	178	518	0.6	0.3	0.8
Fédération de Russie	2001	515	156	359	0.4	0.3	0.6
	2003	475	150	325	0.4	0.3	0.5
Slovenia	1995	6	3	4	0.4	0.4	0.4
Slovénie	2001	6	3	3	0.4	0.3	0.4
	2003	6	3	3	0.3	0.3	0.4
Spain	1995	981	286	695	3.0	1.8	4.1
Espagne	2001	779	232	547	2.3	1.4	3.1
	2003	718	215	503	2.1	1.3	2.8
Ukraine	1995	195	51	144	0.5	0.3	0.6
Ukraine	2001	153	45	108	0.4	0.2	0.5
	2003	140	44	97	0.3	0.2	0.4
Oceania · Océanie							
Fiji	1995	44	16	28	9.0	6.5	11.5
Fidji	2001	37	13	24	6.8	4.8	8.8
	2003	36	13	23	6.3	4.5	8.1
Papua New Guinea	1995	987	422	564	39.7	32.4	47.5
Papouasie–Nvl–Guinée	2001	1 046	446	597	35.4	28.9	42.3
	2003	1 053	448	601	34.0	27.7	40.7
Samoa	1995	2	1	1	1.7	1.3	2.1
Samoa	2001	1	1	1	1.3	1.1	1.6
	2003	1	1	1	1.3	1.0	1.5

Source:
United Nations Educational, Scientific and Cultural Organization
(UNESCO) Institute for Statistics, Montreal, estimates and
projections from the July 2002 assessment.

Source:
L'Institut de statistique de l'Organisation des Nations Unies pour
l'éducation, la science et la culture (UNESCO), Montréal,
estimations et projections de l'UNESCO, révisées en juillet 2002.

Technical notes, tables 9 and 10

Detailed data and explanatory notes on education and literacy can be found on the UNESCO Institute for Statistics website <www.uis.unesco.org> and in the *UNESCO Statistical Yearbook* [31]. Brief notes which pertain to the statistical information shown in the tables in this chapter are given below.

Table 9: The definitions and classifications applied by UNESCO are those set out in the *Revised Recommendation concerning the International Standardization of Education Statistics* (1978) and the 1976 and 1997 versions of the *International Standard Classification of Education* (ISCED). Data are presented in Table 9 according to the revised terminology of the ISCED-97.

According to the ISCED, these educational levels are defined as follows:

Primary education (ISCED level 1), of which the main function is to provide the basic elements of education at such establishments as elementary schools or primary schools.

Secondary education (ISCED levels 2 and 3), providing general and/or specialized instruction at middle schools, secondary schools, high schools, teaching training schools and schools of a vocational or technical nature.

Tertiary education (ISCED levels 5, 6 and 7) provided at universities, teachers' colleges, and higher professional schools, which requires, as a minimum condition of admission, the successful completion of secondary education or evidence of the attainment of an equivalent level of knowledge.

The ISCED-97 also introduces a new category or level between upper secondary and tertiary education called post-secondary non-tertiary education (ISCED level 4). Beginning 1997, this level is included in secondary education in Table 9 for those countries footnoted accordingly. It is assumed that the programmes which countries now report separately to UNESCO as post-secondary non-tertiary have also been reported in the past, in either secondary or tertiary education depending on the country. These programmes typically fall into two categories: (a) second cycle programmes at upper secondary and (b) access or foundation programmes for entry to tertiary programmes. Countries with type (a) programmes will typically have reported them in the past as secondary programmes whilst countries with type (b) programmes will more often have reported them as tertiary in the past. Some countries will have both types of programmes.

In general, the statistics shown in Table 9 refer to both public and private education. Since 1994, special needs education is, in principle, included in the statistics reported.

Notes techniques, tableaux 9 et 10

On trouvera des données détaillées et des notes explicatives sur l'instruction et l'alphabétisation sur le site Web de l'Institut de statistique de l'UNESCO <www.uis.unesco.org> et dans l'*Annuaire statistique de l'UNESCO* [31]. Ci-après figurent des notes sommaires, relatives aux principaux éléments d'information statistique figurant dans les tableaux.

Tableau 9: Les définitions et classifications appliquées par l'UNESCO sont tirées de la *Recommandation révisée concernant la normalisation internationale des statistiques de l'éducation* (1978) et des versions de 1976 et de 1997 de la *Classification internationale type de l'éducation* (CITE). La terminologie utilisée dans le tableau 9 est celle de la CITE-1997.

Dans la CITE, les niveaux d'enseignement sont définis comme suit:

Enseignement primaire (niveau 1 de la CITE), dispensé par exemple dans les écoles élémentaires ou les écoles primaires, et dont la fonction principale est de fournir un enseignement de base.

Enseignement secondaire (niveaux 2 et 3 de la CITE), dispensé par exemple dans les écoles moyennes, les écoles secondaires, les lycées, les collèges, les écoles de formation des maîtres et les écoles professionnelles ou techniques.

Enseignement supérieur (niveaux 5, 6 et 7 de la CITE), dispensé par exemple dans les universités, les établissements d'enseignement pédagogique et d'enseignement spécialisé, exigeant comme condition minimale d'admission d'avoir achevé avec succès des études secondaires ou de faire preuve de connaissances équivalentes.

La CITE de 1997 introduit également une catégorie nouvelle, à savoir un niveau intermédiaire entre le deuxième cycle de l'enseignement secondaire et l'enseignement supérieur, appelé "enseignement post secondaire qui n'est pas du supérieur" (niveau 4 de la CITE). À compter de 1997, dans le tableau 9, pour les pays marqués d'une note à cet effet, ce niveau est inclus dans l'enseignement secondaire. On suppose que les programmes que les pays signalent désormais à l'UNESCO comme programmes d'enseignement post secondaire qui n'est pas du supérieur l'étaient par le passé comme programmes d'enseignement soit secondaire soit supérieur selon le pays. Ils relèvent généralement de l'une ou l'autre des deux catégories suivantes: (a) programmes de deuxième cycle du secondaire, et (b) cours de base ou de transition préparant à l'enseignement supérieur. Les pays où ces programmes relèvent du type (a) les auront normalement inclus dans l'enseignement secondaire avant 1997, les pays où ils

Table 10: Data on the illiterate population by sex refer to the population 15 years of age and over. The ability to both read and write, with understanding, a simple sentence on everyday life is used as the criterion of literacy; hence semi-literates (persons who can read but not write) are included with illiterates. Persons for whom literacy is not known are excluded from calculations; consequently the percentage of illiteracy for a given country is based on the number of reported illiterates, divided by the total number of reported literates and illiterates.

The data shown in the table are the estimates and projections of UNESCO from the July 2002 assessment.

relèvent du type (b) les auront souvent inclus dans l'enseignement supérieur. Dans certains pays, il y a des programmes de niveau 4 relevant de l'un et de l'autre type.

En règle générale, les statistiques du tableau 9 portent sur l'enseignement public et privé. Depuis 1994, l'éducation répondant à des besoins spéciaux est en principe incluse dans les statistiques communiquées par les pays.

Tableau 10: Les données sur la population analphabète selon le sexe se réfèrent à la population âgée de 15 ans et plus. On utilise l'aptitude à lire et à écrire, en le comprenant, une phrase simple sur la vie quotidienne comme critère d'alphabétisme; par conséquent, les semi-alphabètes (c'est-à-dire les personnes qui savent lire, mais non écrire) sont assimilés aux analphabètes. Les personnes dont on ne sait pas si elles savent lire ou écrire sont exclues de ces calculs; par conséquent, le pourcentage d'analphabétisme d'un pays donné est fondé sur le nombre d'analphabètes connus divisé par le total des alphabètes et analphabètes connus.

Les données présentées sont les estimations et projections de l'UNESCO, révisées en juillet 2002.

11
HIV/AIDS epidemic: estimates of the number of people living with HIV/AIDS, people newly infected with HIV, AIDS deaths and reported AIDS cases
L'épidemie de VIH/SIDA: Chiffres estimatifs du nombre de personnes vivant avec le VIH/SIDA, nouveaux cas d'infection à VIH, décès dus au SIDA et cas déclarés de SIDA

A. Estimates of the number of people living with HIV/AIDS, people newly infected with HIV, and AIDS deaths in 2002
Chiffres estimatifs du nombre de personnes vivant aves le VIH/SIDA, nouveaux cas d'infection àVIH et décès dus au SIDA en 2002

	Number of cases (millions) – Nombre de cas (millions)		
	Total	Men Hommes	Women Femmes
Number of people living with HIV/AIDS **Nombre de personnes vivant avec le VIH/SIDA**	42.0	...	...
Adults Adultes	38.6	19.4	19.2
Children under 15 years Enfants < 15 ans	3.2	...	...
People newly infected with HIV in 2002 **Nouveaux cas d'infecttion à VIH en 2002**	5.0	...	...
Adults Adultes	4.2	2.2	2.0
Children under 15 years Enfants < 15 ans	0.8	...	...
Aids deaths in 2002 **Décès causés par le SIDA en 2002**	3.1	...	...
Adults Adultes	2.5	1.3	1.2
Children under 15 years Enfants < 15 ans	0.6	...	...

B. Reported AIDS cases to the World Health Organization
Cas de SIDA déclarés à l'Organisation mondiale de la santé

Regions Régions	Total reported cases to 1992 Nombre total de cas déclarés jusqu' au 1992	New cases reported in: / Nombre de cas nouveaux déclarés en:								Cumulative total Nombre total cumulé
		1993	1994	1995	1996	1997	1998	1999	2000	
World **Monde**	859 444	227 617	231 199	257 864	248 851	238 833	239 491	233 396	197 040	2 769 822[1]
Africa Afrique	318 402	84 402	81 477	100 385	93 722	94 413	108 725	107 073	84 675	1 103 957[1]
North America Amérique du Nord	378 994	90 329	82 685	80 568	71 627	63 564	54 689	56 791	50 676	929 923[1]
South America Amérique du Sud	66 971	21 432	24 631	26 416	29 444	28 792	28 206	23 981	17 271	267 146[1]
Asia Asie	5 424	8 000	15 604	23 624	28 496	32 284	32 879	32 805	31 571	213 439[1]
Europe Europe	84 871	22 505	25 751	25 961	24 739	19 228	14 425	12 301	12 336	244 761[1]
Oceania Océanie	4 782	949	1 051	910	823	552	567	445	511	10 596[1]

11 C. Reported AIDS cases • Cas de SIDA déclarés

Country or area Pays ou zone	Cumulative number to 1992[2] Chiffre cumulé jusqu' au 1992[2]	1993	1994	1995	1996	1997	1998	1999	2000	2001
Africa • Afrique										
Algeria Algérie	134	31	53	32	48	39	49	40	58	43
Angola Angola	1014	339	361	427	465	1121	1186	453	1271	...
Benin Bénin	465	277	324	214	503	1030	725	650	769	...
Botswana Botswana	971	876	575	1172	1368	2224	2992	...	...	...
Burkina Faso Burkina Faso	2886	836	1892	1684	1838	2216	2166	2031	1532	1063
Burundi Burundi	6763	799	443	1358	2239	3510	4092	4395	1762	...
Cameroon Cameroun	2229	1385	1761	2766	1485	3950	6843	8756	5700	0
Cape Verde Cap–Vert	93	18	16	24	36	39	43	64	75	
Central African Rep. Rép. centrafricaine	3950	290	50	649	2077	0	...	...	...	...
Chad Tchad	587	1010	1268	1132	1242	2748	2030	1664	1704	1661
Comoros Comores	6	4	3	2	2	3	2	1	4	...
Congo Congo	16174	6473	7773	10223	...	...	...	...		2381
Côte d'Ivoire Côte d'Ivoire	14653	4015	6566	6727	5935	5949	5685	6427	...	...
Dem. Rep. of the Congo Rép. dém. du Congo	23071	4215	2637	8329	11572	9642	5809	9953	9848	
Djibouti Djibouti	309	144	196	231	358	434	111	...	...	...
Egypt Egypte	52	29	22	16	14	25	23	34	44	35
Equatorial Guinea Guinée équatoriale	19	24	16	98	74	111	189	122	222	...
Eritrea Erythrée	369	300	625	727	896	1260	1610	1086	...	...
Ethiopia Ethiopie	4895	5132	6927	3793	832	7631	9416	11964	13347	5872
Gabon Gabon	306	128	204	334	601	559	708	594	794	1238
Gambia Gambie	236	38	53	32	78	74	126	...	...	...
Ghana Ghana	10285	2371	2330	2578	3295	3833	4854	7752	6289	3857
Guinea Guinée	677	328	543	610	922	1005	1648	1069	1646	...
Guinea–Bissau Guinée–Bissau	290	165	254	77	37	217	...	120	...	...
Kenya Kenya	37273	12204	8588	9133	6844	4885	2565	...	...	...
Lesotho Lesotho	191	166	238	341	936	2203	3242	3563	3760	...
Liberia Libéria	19	4	13	11	8	59	114	79	81	52
Libyan Arab Jamah. Jamah. arabe libyenne	15	2	3	2	3	7	33	4	5	...
Madagascar Madagascar	4	6	9	6	1	6	2	0	2	6
Malawi Malawi	26955	4916	4732	5209	5406	3705	1878	1711	...	...
Mali Mali	1313	672	609	454	594	711	620	290	...	...
Mauritania Mauritanie	63	94	56	103	98	...	...	...	...	...

11 C. Reported AIDS cases [*cont.*] • Cas de SIDA déclarés [*suite*]

Country or area Pays ou zone	Cumulative number to 1992[2] Chiffre cumulé jusqu' au 1992[2]	New cases reported in:/ Nombre de cas nouveaux déclarés en:								
		1993	1994	1995	1996	1997	1998	1999	2000	2001
Mauritius Maurice	19	5	6	6	4	6	2	7	8	7
Morocco Maroc	128	44	77	57	66	92	93	165	112	129
Mozambique Mozambique	662	164	534	1380	2086	1661	4376	6361	7800	...
Namibia Namibie	430	355	452	1836	2687	3797	5158	6878	4503	...
Niger Niger	809	453	467	621	652	217	425	940	1014	...
Nigeria Nigéria	1083	719	1114	2829	2980	3815	18490	16188	9715	3661
Réunion Réunion	88	25	23	30	0	0	...	...	...	...
Rwanda Rwanda	9486	1220	0	2072	3847	1350	3948	671	...	...
Sao Tome and Principe Sao Tomé−et−Principe	11	2	1	4	6	11	25	10	19	...
Senegal Sénégal	648	263	534	396	327	225	311	208	...	...
Seychelles Seychelles	1	3	3	6	6	5	5	8	4	...
Sierra Leone Sierra Leone	88	23	22	29	62	67	26	...	...	...
Somalia Somalie	13	...	...	...	...	...	...	...	...	...
South Africa Afrique du Sud	2170	1882	3816	4219	738	...	...	...	...	...
Sudan Soudan	692	191	201	257	221	270	511	517	652	492
Swaziland Swaziland	277	165	120	154	613	1466	733	1259	...	...
Togo Togo	2102	1330	1284	1710	1527	1211	1623	998	262	...
Tunisia Tunisie	172	52	50	65	54	62	44	42	...	...
Uganda Ouganda	36552	4641	4927	2192	3032	1962	1406	1149	...	...
United Rep. of Tanzania Rép. Unie de Tanzanie	60066	13506	6096	4722	8426	10592	8675	8850	11673	...
Zambia Zambie	27907	2894	1963	5950	4552	1676	...	...	...	...
Zimbabwe Zimbabwe	18731	9174	10647	13356	12029	6732	4113	...	...	...
America, North • Amérique du Nord										
Anguilla Anguilla	5	0	0	0	0	0	...	...	...	...
Antigua and Barbuda Antigua−et−Barbuda	31	23	16	7	13	7	2	14		
Aruba Aruba	14	1	0	22	0	0	0	...		...
Bahamas Bahamas	1098	296	317	388	375	387	323	314	...	...
Barbados Barbade	330	88	119	95	130	113	168	133	23	...
Belize Belize	50	29	45	28	38	30	37	90	46	...
Bermuda Bermudes	218	33	44	48	40	14	17	10	...	...
British Virgin Islands Iles Vierges britanniques	8	2	1	3	0	3	1	2	...	...
Canada Canada	9772	1859	1855	1727	1184	793	734	584	644	...
Cayman Islands Iles Caïmanes	15	0	4	0	3	1	2	1	...	...

11 C. Reported AIDS cases [*cont.*] · Cas de SIDA déclarés [*suite*]

Country or area Pays ou zone	Cumulative number to 1992[2] Chiffre cumulé jusqu' au 1992[2]	1993	1994	1995	1996	1997	1998	1999	2000	2001
Costa Rica Costa Rica	452	126	173	214	214	250	281	215	177	...
Cuba Cuba	179	82	102	116	99	129	150	176	247	268
Dominica Dominique	48	15	6	5	14	19	12	15	...	
Dominican Republic Rép. dominicaine	2230	408	433	505	450	427	414	495	438	320
El Salvador El Salvador	432	177	384	383	418	414	352	425	...	
Grenada Grenade	37	21	7	18	18	10	7	...	...	
Guadeloupe Guadeloupe	391	135	104	106	73	0	0	...	...	
Guatemala Guatemala	371	178	110	141	835	649	397	730	519	303
Haiti Haïti	4970	0	0	0	0	3932	0	...	...	
Honduras Honduras	2900	1201	1123	1221	1086	1261	1492	1136	369	...
Jamaica Jamaïque	496	219	335	511	491	609	643	892	903	445
Martinique Martinique	237	44	49	41	42	23	...	...	...	...
Mexico Mexique	12267	5058	4111	4310	4216	3670	4758	4372	4855	4297
Montserrat Montserrat	6	1	0	0	0	0	1	...	...	...
Netherlands Antilles Antilles néerlandaises	123	36	0	76	0	0	0	...	...	
Nicaragua Nicaragua	39	24	38	21	28	20	30	36	36	...
Panama Panama	486	204	289	344	380	463	563	534	263	453
Saint Kitts and Nevis Saint–Kitts–et–Nevis	37	3	7	6	6	3	1	5	...	
Saint Lucia Sainte–Lucie	41	12	13	10	14	15	10	21	...	
St. Vincent and the Grenadines St. Vincent–et–Grenadines	44	8	16	6	28	31	45	51	...	
Trinidad and Tobago Trinité–et–Tobago	1167	280	247	324	323	291	355	397	...	
Turks and Caicos Islands Iles Turques et Caïques	25	14	0	0	0	0	0	...	...	
United States Etats–Unis	340474	79752	72737	69892	61109	50000	43894	46143	42156	...
America, South · Amérique du Sud										
Argentina Argentine	3037	1466	2181	2184	2622	2297	1899	1401	528	...
Bolivia Bolivie	73	23	20	15	8	16	42	34	43	73
Brazil Brésil	51720	16829	18341	20357	22943	23546	24017	20009	15013	3024
Chile Chili	737	246	316	351	427	553	490	541	511	474
Colombia Colombie	3738	740	1361	910	1095	589	...	...	...	...
Ecuador Equateur	267	89	116	70	65	128	186	325	313	...
French Guiana Guyane française	344	52	70	78	62	35	0	...	...	
Guyana Guyana	392	107	105	192	144	115	222	338	248	425
Paraguay Paraguay	79	55	35	50	78	96	27	49	...	...

11 C. Reported AIDS cases [*cont.*] · Cas de SIDA déclarés [*suite*]

Country or area Pays ou zone	Cumulative number to 1992[2] Chiffre cumulé jusqu' au 1992[2]	New cases reported in:/ Nombre de cas nouveaux déclarés en:								
		1993	1994	1995	1996	1997	1998	1999	2000	2001
Peru Pérou	2333	709	840	1090	1177	1078	1031	1009	615	...
Suriname Suriname	134	35	26	20	...	120	112	103	...	...
Uruguay Uruguay	335	103	119	127	156	173	180	172	...	...
Venezuela Venezuela	3782	978	1101	972	667	46	0	...	...	...
Asia · Asie										
Armenia Arménie	3	0	0	0	7	2	2	8	3	4
Azerbaijan Azerbaïdjan	0	0	1	1	2	5	3	8	19	17
Bahrain Bahreïn	10	3	5	10	9	14	11	8	8	4
Bangladesh Bangladesh	1	0	0	6	0	3	0	...	...	...
Bhutan Bhoutan	0	...	...	...	...	1	1	1	...	...
Brunei Darussalam Brunéi Darussalam	2	1	2	4	2	2	0	2	3	0
Cambodia Cambodge	906	1	14	91	300	572	1494	2556	3684	...
China Chine	13	23	29	52	38	126	136	230	233	231
China, Hong Kong SAR Chine, Hong Kong RAS	74	19	37	45	70	64	63	61	67	24
China, Macao SAR Chine, Macao RAS	4	2	2	0	1	2	4	2	4	0
Cyprus Chypre	34	7	11	5	18	10	6	13	24	9
Georgia Géorgie	9	0	2	3	2	6	2	7	14	11
India Inde	242	252	523	1091	888	2108	1148	...	...	...
Indonesia Indonésie	35	17	15	20	31	34	75	57	166	185
Iran, Islamic Rep. of Iran, Rép. islamique d'	60	32	19	16	27	40	21	27	67	60
Iraq Iraq	13	21	37	16	15	2	4	0	...	...
Israel Israël	209	47	32	45	67	45	36	137	50	82
Japan Japon	180	86	136	169	234	250	231	300	327	155
Jordan Jordanie	28	8	6	2	4	12	11	3	14	7
Kazakhstan Kazakhstan	0	1	0	3	3	8	9	1	0	0
Korea, Dem.People's Rep. Corée, Rép. pop. dém. de	0	0	0	0	0	0	...	...	...	...
Korea, Republic of Corée, République de	10	6	11	14	22	33	35	34	32	...
Kuwait Koweït	8	2	5	4	5	2	19	4	12	5
Kyrgyzstan Kirghizistan	0	0	0	0	0	0	0	0	0	1
Lao People's Dem. Rep. Rép. dém. populaire lao	1	5	4	4	16	48	27	18	27	27
Lebanon Liban	42	22	12	18	5	8	37	32	19	21
Malaysia Malaisie	155	71	105	233	347	568	875	1200	1168	482

11 C. Reported AIDS cases [*cont.*] • Cas de SIDA déclarés [*suite*]

Country or area Pays ou zone	Cumulative number to 1992[2] Chiffre cumulé jusqu' au 1992[2]	New cases reported in:/ Nombre de cas nouveaux déclarés en:								
		1993	1994	1995	1996	1997	1998	1999	2000	2001
Maldives										
Maldives	1	1	1	4	1	2	0	0	1	0
Mongolia										
Mongolie	0	0	0	0	0	0	0	1	0	1
Myanmar										
Myanmar	47	142	286	618	890	554	231	802	816	668
Occupied Palestinian Terr.										
Terr. palestinien occupé	12	1	3	3	1	9	3	1	...	...
Oman										
Oman	156	38	60	41	27	43	28	36	32	23
Pakistan										
Pakistan	64	16	9	19	20	19	23	17	15	8
Philippines										
Philippines	104	36	56	52	52	23	42	77	42	24
Qatar										
Qatar	80	8	8	6	2	4	3	9	3	2
Saudi Arabia										
Arabie saoudite	50	12	38	37	100	112	39	24	24	...
Singapore										
Singapour	53	22	48	56	92	88	125	140	143	59
Sri Lanka										
Sri Lanka	22	11	14	11	11	9	15	12	14	13
Syrian Arab Republic										
Rép. arabe syrienne	23	3	4	6	9	8	8	7	7	12
Tajikistan										
Tadjikistan	0	0	0	0	0	0	0	0	0	0
Thailand										
Thaïlande	2676	6949	13923	20686	24709	26713	27128	26003	23352	9345
Turkey										
Turquie	89	29	34	34	37	38	29	28	46	27
Turkmenistan										
Turkménistan	1	0	0	0	0	0	...	...	...	...
United Arab Emirates										
Emirats arabes unis	12	1	2	1	2	1	1	2	...	...
Uzbekistan										
Ouzbékistan	1	1	0	0	2	1	2	1	3	0
Viet Nam										
Viet Nam	0	106	118	201	390	688	953	970	1164	742
Yemen										
Yémen	4	4	3	11	60	40	34	...	...	...
Europe • Europe										
Albania										
Albanie	0	0	2	5	1	2	1	0	4	0
Austria										
Autriche	889	210	188	214	142	130	111	89	84	74
Belarus										
Bélarus	7	2	1	3	0	2	4	7	0	5
Belgium										
Belgique	1299	224	236	237	219	135	164	97	105	162
Bosnia & Herzegovina										
Bosnie – Herzégovine	1	2	3	4	3	5	4	6	2	6
Bulgaria										
Bulgarie	18	6	10	1	10	8	3	11	16	14
Croatia										
Croatie	50	10	17	15	18	17	12	16	19	7
Czech Republic										
République tchèque	32	15	12	13	19	20	8	16	14	6
Denmark										
Danemark	1119	236	249	228	161	108	71	73	61	76
Estonia										
Estonie	1	1	1	4	7	3	4	2	3	2
Finland										
Finlande	119	24	46	37	25	17	20	10	16	18

11 C. Reported AIDS cases [*cont.*] • Cas de SIDA déclarés [*suite*]

Country or area Pays ou zone	Cumulative number to 1992[2] Chiffre cumulé jusqu' au 1992[2]	New cases reported in:/ Nombre de cas nouveaux déclarés en:								
		1993	1994	1995	1996	1997	1998	1999	2000	2001
France France	22850	5582	5797	5482	4836	2832	2099	1784	1771	1690
Germany Allemagne	8427	1843	1858	1778	1628	1414	939	575	1433	920
Greece Grèce	693	160	123	310	214	239	146	137	143	96
Hungary Hongrie	111	35	23	31	45	32	35	38	27	20
Iceland Islande	25	6	4	3	3	2	2	5	1	1
Ireland Irlande	307	74	62	53	78	30	41	41	21	12
Italy Italie	14817	4532	5440	6062	5376	3782	2483	2200	1904	1836
Latvia Lettonie	4	3	2	0	8	3	11	17	24	42
Lithuania Lituanie	4	0	2	1	3	3	8	7	8	8
Luxembourg Luxembourg	57	20	13	15	12	10	10	5	10	4
Malta Malte	26	3	5	3	4	2	4	1	3	0
Monaco Monaco	17	7	9	4	2	1	0	0	0	0
Netherlands Pays–Bas	2476	435	461	469	449	343	288	234	192	94
Norway Norvège	312	64	74	67	56	34	39	28	38	27
Poland Pologne	125	42	94	120	96	117	132	113	109	168
Portugal Portugal	1214	465	610	693	897	893	874	1010	1123	931
Republic of Moldova République de Moldova	2	2	0	2	1	10	4	5	4	9
Romania Roumanie	2407	477	525	643	600	654	678	492	490	192
Russian Federation Fédération de Russie	108	21	27	39	57	13	94	39	50	0
San Marino Saint–Marin	0	0	0	0	4	4	4	2	1	0
Serbia and Montenegro Serbie–et–Monténégro	261	54	101	99	92	56	114	57	66	22
Slovakia Slovaquie	4	1	3	2	0	5	3	2	4	5
Slovenia Slovénie	24	7	6	15	9	1	14	8	7	5
Spain Espagne	16520	5472	7056	6750	6929	6054	4222	3427	2847	2942
Sweden Suède	771	176	181	198	156	77	63	74	54	21
Switzerland Suisse	2863	672	711	736	543	565	423	262	257	175
TFYR of Macedonia L'ex–R.y. Macédonie	6	5	8	3	1	1	3	5	5	6
Ukraine Ukraine	12	10	10	37	159	193	287	580	648	361
United Kingdom Royaume–Uni	6883	1601	1770	1571	1854	1378	963	790	737	824
Oceania • Océanie										
American Samoa Samoa américaines	0	0	0	0	0	0	0	0	1	...
Australia Australie	4217	844	954	805	658	371	301	181	212	27
Cook Islands Iles Cook	0	0	0	0	0	0	0	0	0	0

11 C. Reported AIDS cases [*cont.*] • Cas de SIDA déclarés [*suite*]

Country or area Pays ou zone	Cumulative number to 1992[2] Chiffre cumulé jusqu' au 1992[2]	New cases reported in:/ Nombre de cas nouveaux déclarés en:								
		1993	1994	1995	1996	1997	1998	1999	2000	2001
Fiji Fidji	5	1	2	0	0	0	0	4	3	0
French Polynesia Polynésie française	55	5	1	4	2	2	2	1	0	0
Guam Guam	14	5	11	2	10	5	7	8	2	9
Kiribati Kiribati	2	0	0	0	2	2	4	5	2	1
Marshall Islands Iles Marshall	2	0	0	...	0	...	0	0	0	0
Micronesia, Federated States of Micronésie, Etats fédérés de	2	0	0	0	0	0	0	1	0	1
New Caledonia Nouvelle − Calédonie	33	10	9	5	2	9	3	4	5	0
New Zealand Nouvelle − Zélande	375	70	44	49	76	43	29	33	27	...
Niue Nioué	0	0	0	0	0	0	0	0	0	0
Northern Mariana Islands Iles Mariannes du Nord	0	0	0	0	0	0	5	2	3	...
Palau Palaos	0	...	...	0	0	0	0	0	0	0
Papua New Guinea Papouasie − Nvl − Guinée	74	12	26	44	69	120	220	207	259	132
Samoa Samoa	1	0	2	1	2	0	0	0	0	0
Solomon Islands Iles Salomon	0	...	...	...	...	...	...	0	0	0
Tokelau Tokélaou	0	...	...	...	...	...	...	0	0	0
Tonga Tonga	2	1	2	0	2	0	1	1	0	...
Wallis and Futuna Islands Iles Wallis − et − Futuna	0	1	...	...	...	0	0	0	0	...

Source:
Joint United Nations Programme on HIV/AIDS (UNAIDS) and
World Health Organization (WHO), Geneva, "Aids epidemic
update: December 2002" and the UNAIDS/WHO HIV/AIDS
database.

1 Total includes AIDS cases with unreported year of diagnosis.

2 Cumulative number of cases reported from 1979 to 1992.
   Excludes cases for which the year of diagnosis is unknown.

Source:
Programme commun des Nations Unies sur le VIH/SIDA (ONUSIDA)
et l'Organisation mondiale de la santé (OMS), Genève, "Le point sur
l'épidémie de SIDA: décembre 2002" et la base de données sur le VIH
et le SIDA de l'ONUSIDA/OMS.

1 Y compris les cas de SIDA pour lesquels l'année de diagnostic n'a pas
   été précisée.
2 Chiffre cumulé du nombre total de cas de SIDA déclarés entre 1979
   et 1992. Non compris les cas de SIDA pour lesquels l'année de diagnostic
   n'a pas été précisée.

12
Food supply
Calories, protein and fat: per capita per day
Disponibilités alimentaires
Calories, protéine et lipides : par habitant, par jour

Country or area	Calories (number) Calories (nombre)			Protein (grams) Protéine (grammes)			Fat (grams) Lipides (grammes)		
Pays ou zone	1986−88	1988−90	1998−00	1986−88	1988−90	1998−00	1986−88	1988−90	1998−00
World **Monde**	**2 677.6**	**2 702.5**	**2 799.0**	**71.0**	**71.6**	**75.4**	**65.7**	**67.5**	**74.2**
Africa · Afrique									
Algeria Algérie	2 777.1	2 879.6	2 955.7	75.3	77.4	82.3	60.5	70.1	68.7
Angola Angola	1 770.0	1 741.6	1 893.8	44.8	42.9	40.1	43.1	45.6	37.9
Benin Bénin	2 052.4	2 232.3	2 568.9	51.3	54.1	59.8	41.1	42.2	45.4
Botswana Botswana	2 363.2	2 352.7	2 242.0	71.3	72.9	69.0	53.7	59.8	57.8
Burkina Faso Burkina Faso	2 174.2	2 228.3	2 316.4	65.3	65.8	68.3	46.7	46.8	49.8
Burundi Burundi	1 960.6	1 862.2	1 615.3	61.2	56.7	46.4	14.7	13.9	10.4
Cameroon Cameroun	2 144.4	2 101.3	2 272.2	51.7	51.0	55.7	45.1	45.4	46.3
Cape Verde Cap−Vert	2 973.0	2 991.8	3 280.8	75.6	73.9	74.6	70.2	72.5	99.2
Central African Rep. Rép. centrafricaine	1 864.2	1 870.6	1 951.9	37.2	38.3	42.7	61.4	62.5	60.6
Chad Tchad	1 666.7	1 710.5	2 176.5	49.3	49.9	67.0	39.4	40.9	66.5
Comoros Comores	1 813.8	1 839.4	1 765.9	39.4	42.3	42.0	36.2	37.0	39.6
Congo Congo	2 293.8	2 192.8	2 166.3	46.6	44.9	44.0	52.7	49.6	49.8
Côte d'Ivoire Côte d'Ivoire	2 580.4	2 490.3	2 592.9	53.8	52.7	52.2	48.2	48.1	54.5
Dem. Rep. of the Congo Rép. dém. du Congo	2 211.5	2 199.8	1 591.8	35.3	34.7	25.9	33.1	33.8	24.8
Djibouti Djibouti	1 934.6	1 914.1	2 051.8	49.1	49.0	45.8	45.4	42.4	60.3
Egypt Egypte	3 097.9	3 133.5	3 322.4	81.2	82.6	92.5	62.7	60.3	57.4
Eritrea Erythrée	...	...	1 706.2	...	...	54.6	...	...	24.4
Ethiopia Ethiopie	...	...	1 877.4	...	...	55.0	...	...	19.8
Ethiopia including Eritrea Ethiopie y compris Erythrée	1 735.4	1 705.9	...	50.2	49.3	...	25.0	24.7	...
Gabon Gabon	2 507.8	2 464.8	2 548.7	75.4	70.4	73.9	45.3	48.8	61.4
Gambia Gambie	2 480.9	2 436.8	2 401.4	54.1	52.7	53.6	51.3	52.6	77.1
Ghana Ghana	1 978.8	1 944.4	2 647.4	44.3	43.7	54.6	38.7	37.9	39.2
Guinea Guinée	1 938.4	1 953.7	2 234.5	44.7	45.5	47.5	39.8	39.2	53.0
Guinea−Bissau Guinée−Bissau	2 420.9	2 399.3	2 313.3	48.7	48.4	45.7	63.2	58.4	57.7
Kenya Kenya	2 040.9	1 946.3	1 955.9	55.3	52.9	50.9	41.7	43.6	46.7
Lesotho Lesotho	2 228.0	2 237.7	2 296.1	63.5	63.9	64.0	36.1	34.8	31.8
Liberia Libéria	2 497.8	2 397.8	2 143.5	48.0	44.7	39.0	48.7	41.3	59.6
Libyan Arab Jamahirya Jamah. arabe libyenne	3 325.6	3 277.3	3 301.9	82.1	82.5	86.9	103.9	107.5	103.4
Madagascar Madagascar	2 221.8	2 133.9	2 005.3	53.2	50.8	47.0	31.4	31.2	30.0
Malawi Malawi	2 014.3	1 962.2	2 155.9	57.6	54.7	53.7	30.7	27.4	27.9

12
Food supply
Calories, protein and fat: per capita per day [*cont.*]
Disponibilités alimentaires
Calories, protéine et lipides : par habitant, par jour [*suite*]

Country or area	Calories (number) Calories (nombre)			Protein (grams) Protéine (grammes)			Fat (grams) Lipides (grammes)		
Pays ou zone	1986−88	1988−90	1998−00	1986−88	1988−90	1998−00	1986−88	1988−90	1998−00
Mali									
Mali	2 277.7	2 328.7	2 395.0	64.0	64.6	67.6	46.2	51.0	47.9
Mauritania									
Mauritanie	2 524.5	2 568.7	2 656.6	79.3	80.3	74.5	64.8	63.6	66.5
Mauritius									
Maurice	2 761.2	2 800.8	2 969.7	64.0	67.4	76.6	70.3	69.9	85.7
Morocco									
Maroc	3 020.0	3 050.9	3 005.9	82.1	84.5	80.9	59.2	59.6	58.9
Mozambique									
Mozambique	1 783.8	1 808.1	1 914.1	32.8	32.7	38.0	37.3	38.5	32.5
Namibia									
Namibie	2 241.0	2 184.4	2 596.8	63.8	61.7	66.8	37.2	36.5	37.3
Niger									
Niger	2 048.7	2 098.1	2 096.9	56.5	56.9	57.8	30.3	30.5	34.7
Nigeria									
Nigéria	2 199.0	2 301.8	2 840.3	51.6	54.6	64.6	54.6	55.5	68.9
Rwanda									
Rwanda	2 080.1	1 987.1	2 022.0	50.7	46.7	47.2	16.4	15.7	22.1
Sao Tome and Principe									
Sao Tomé−et−Principe	2 002.6	2 244.7	2 291.7	44.0	50.3	45.8	77.8	86.5	70.8
Senegal									
Sénégal	2 224.4	2 211.9	2 256.6	69.5	68.8	64.2	53.5	48.4	67.5
Seychelles									
Seychelles	2 296.3	2 344.9	2 415.9	66.2	68.2	76.7	47.4	52.4	77.2
Sierra Leone									
Sierra Leone	1 973.1	1 940.4	1 977.7	41.6	41.0	44.1	59.8	56.4	47.5
Somalia									
Somalie	1 944.3	1 838.5	1 601.6	62.8	60.4	49.6	68.2	66.1	55.3
South Africa									
Afrique du Sud	2 855.4	2 863.9	2 880.9	74.3	75.2	74.2	70.4	68.9	72.5
Sudan									
Soudan	2 170.6	2 156.9	2 357.5	64.0	65.5	75.0	64.4	60.0	73.8
Swaziland									
Swaziland	2 568.8	2 589.6	2 568.2	64.5	64.0	65.1	46.0	50.7	53.8
Togo									
Togo	2 078.4	2 315.8	2 370.1	49.7	54.4	54.0	36.8	45.7	43.5
Tunisia									
Tunisie	3 097.0	3 141.9	3 361.9	84.8	84.4	91.4	82.6	85.9	100.0
Uganda									
Ouganda	2 166.3	2 306.7	2 330.1	49.0	54.0	53.9	24.7	27.9	31.9
United Rep. of Tanzania									
Rép. Unie de Tanzanie	2 172.0	2 146.1	1 916.1	54.1	53.9	46.5	31.4	31.5	30.9
Zambia									
Zambie	2 036.8	2 027.2	1 897.5	52.6	51.4	47.4	29.8	30.4	28.7
Zimbabwe									
Zimbabwe	2 127.4	2 137.1	2 110.2	53.0	53.9	49.8	48.3	50.9	52.7
America, North · Amérique du Nord									
Antigua and Barbuda									
Antigua et Barbuda	2 328.1	2 431.1	2 388.3	82.8	83.7	81.0	92.4	97.8	89.6
Bahamas									
Bahamas	2 770.5	2 785.9	2 486.2	83.0	83.1	76.6	95.0	93.3	75.0
Barbados									
Barbade	3 166.5	3 190.8	3 025.2	95.7	98.0	85.5	103.8	109.3	97.8
Belize									
Belize	2 552.4	2 569.3	2 874.6	68.0	68.1	66.2	74.4	70.7	69.8
Bermuda									
Bermudes	3 062.6	2 917.9	3 035.8	107.7	104.2	90.3	128.9	126.6	122.7
Canada									
Canada	3 053.6	2 997.1	3 165.9	95.6	94.9	102.6	129.9	128.3	127.2
Costa Rica									
Costa Rica	2 711.0	2 743.5	2 782.1	64.3	66.6	69.6	66.9	67.8	72.0
Cuba									
Cuba	3 063.6	3 064.4	2 557.3	72.3	70.8	58.6	82.0	83.0	47.8
Dominica									
Dominique	2 893.9	2 997.2	2 980.1	72.5	75.5	86.9	78.6	82.9	80.4

12
Food supply
Calories, protein and fat: per capita per day [*cont.*]
　　Disponibilités alimentaires
　　Calories, protéine et lipides : par habitant, par jour [*suite*]

Country or area Pays ou zone	Calories (number) Calories (nombre)			Protein (grams) Protéine (grammes)			Fat (grams) Lipides (grammes)		
	1986−88	1988−90	1998−00	1986−88	1988−90	1998−00	1986−88	1988−90	1998−00
Dominican Republic 　Rép. dominicaine	2 325.2	2 273.5	2 308.5	50.3	50.6	49.8	57.4	63.2	80.4
El Salvador 　El Salvador	2 335.1	2 402.0	2 454.4	55.1	57.7	60.0	52.5	54.3	56.1
Grenada 　Grenade	2 530.1	2 638.8	2 754.7	70.9	70.6	72.6	87.9	89.0	97.7
Guatemala 　Guatemala	2 390.1	2 426.9	2 164.6	61.7	62.4	55.7	41.9	44.1	45.4
Haiti 　Haïti	1 856.4	1 767.4	2 036.5	48.2	44.9	45.7	32.6	28.5	42.3
Honduras 　Honduras	2 218.6	2 298.4	2 392.4	52.1	54.4	58.9	56.6	57.7	66.0
Jamaica 　Jamaïque	2 581.7	2 558.1	2 679.6	66.9	64.4	68.2	67.5	65.2	77.1
Mexico 　Mexique	3 109.9	3 102.7	3 145.5	82.2	80.9	87.2	84.5	81.3	88.2
Netherlands Antilles 　Antilles néerlandaises	2 572.6	2 525.9	2 574.2	82.3	81.0	81.6	91.5	84.1	96.3
Nicaragua 　Nicaragua	2 335.0	2 260.4	2 237.6	57.5	56.3	58.2	43.7	43.5	47.5
Panama 　Panama	2 398.6	2 296.2	2 406.6	61.3	59.0	64.8	68.7	63.6	74.7
Saint Kitts and Nevis 　Saint−Kitts−et−Nevis	2 546.5	2 606.0	2 678.4	67.5	70.3	72.4	86.9	85.6	81.7
Saint Lucia 　Sainte−Lucie	2 566.9	2 630.1	2 829.6	75.4	79.1	84.8	61.1	60.2	69.9
St. Vincent and the Grenadines 　St. Vincent−et−Grenadines	2 465.5	2 401.9	2 569.2	60.3	60.4	67.3	65.4	68.4	77.8
Trinidad and Tobago 　Trinité−et−Tobago	2 927.4	2 711.8	2 721.0	73.5	63.6	63.3	79.3	71.8	76.3
United States 　Etats−Unis	3 405.7	3 451.7	3 738.7	105.8	106.9	113.9	139.3	139.0	147.9
America, South · Amérique du Sud									
Argentina 　Argentine	3 067.3	2 964.7	3 180.7	98.9	94.9	102.5	108.3	103.7	117.8
Bolivia 　Bolivie	2 122.4	2 130.9	2 211.1	54.9	54.4	57.5	47.9	49.8	52.9
Brazil 　Brésil	2 746.4	2 766.3	2 956.8	66.8	67.0	78.7	73.9	78.5	86.9
Chile 　Chili	2 498.2	2 499.8	2 845.3	66.4	68.5	77.8	55.9	59.4	84.0
Colombia 　Colombie	2 309.9	2 376.9	2 568.1	50.3	52.9	59.9	52.1	54.7	65.4
Ecuador 　Equateur	2 457.3	2 521.7	2 676.2	50.2	51.4	55.8	74.9	80.1	88.8
Guyana 　Guyana	2 479.2	2 391.8	2 553.8	56.7	57.1	72.5	32.5	28.2	50.0
Paraguay 　Paraguay	2 550.1	2 498.7	2 544.1	68.7	68.6	73.1	66.2	67.7	84.6
Peru 　Pérou	2 290.9	2 143.3	2 598.1	57.3	52.7	64.8	50.5	44.6	48.7
Suriname 　Suriname	2 436.5	2 426.8	2 626.4	60.0	61.3	62.3	47.6	45.6	67.1
Uruguay 　Uruguay	2 600.6	2 541.7	2 852.7	80.6	78.2	88.8	90.5	88.8	96.9
Venezuela 　Venezuela	2 612.3	2 509.3	2 277.5	64.5	60.9	60.1	78.8	75.1	59.4
Asia · Asic									
Afghanistan 　Afghanistan	2 092.4	2 004.3	1 626.0	57.8	56.2	49.4	37.1	39.7	32.2
Armenia 　Arménie	...	...	2 038.8	...	...	58.9	...	...	37.9
Azerbaijan 　Azerbaïdjan	...	...	2 327.6	...	...	69.1	...	...	37.0

12
Food supply
Calories, protein and fat: per capita per day [*cont.*]
Disponibilités alimentaires
Calories, protéine et lipides : par habitant, par jour [*suite*]

Country or area Pays ou zone	Calories (number) Calories (nombre)			Protein (grams) Protéine (grammes)			Fat (grams) Lipides (grammes)		
	1986–88	1988–90	1998–00	1986–88	1988–90	1998–00	1986–88	1988–90	1998–00
Bangladesh Bangladesh	2 051.9	2 059.5	2 100.7	43.9	44.3	45.1	18.8	18.7	21.4
Brunei Darussalam Brunéi Darussalam	2 814.0	2 807.6	2 797.2	82.8	82.3	77.5	71.7	76.5	73.3
Cambodia Cambodge	1 782.5	1 807.4	1 988.8	42.6	43.1	46.9	19.3	20.7	30.6
China Chine	2 618.5	2 653.0	3 031.7	62.7	64.0	84.0	44.8	49.3	80.7
China, Hong Kong SAR Chine, Hong Kong RAS	3 196.6	3 276.6	3 096.8	93.6	93.2	99.5	122.9	138.4	130.7
China, Macao SAR Chine, Macao RAS	2 565.5	2 657.0	2 560.2	72.0	73.5	68.3	97.0	104.5	111.8
Cyprus Chypre	3 003.1	3 010.7	3 230.9	90.4	94.5	103.1	126.1	124.0	128.9
Georgia Géorgie	...	...	2 443.4	...	...	69.8	...	...	45.2
India Inde	2 252.3	2 316.6	2 425.4	55.5	56.6	57.8	38.2	40.7	47.2
Indonesia Indonésie	2 505.1	2 606.3	2 904.4	54.6	57.2	63.8	46.3	49.8	55.5
Iran (Islamic Republic of) Iran (Rép. islamique d')	2 776.0	2 814.2	2 910.4	73.0	74.1	77.4	59.7	60.0	60.1
Iraq Iraq	3 502.1	3 430.3	2 147.8	89.3	87.8	50.5	80.5	78.8	52.1
Israel Israël	3 407.4	3 392.5	3 566.4	109.8	111.1	116.2	122.2	121.6	126.6
Japan Japon	2 811.9	2 834.0	2 758.9	93.0	94.6	91.5	77.5	79.1	81.9
Jordan Jordanie	2 746.2	2 790.9	2 715.4	75.7	74.3	72.8	72.3	69.5	80.3
Kazakhstan Kazakhstan	...	...	2 720.2	...	...	86.8	...	...	65.9
Korea, Dem. People's Rep. Corée, Rép. pop. dém. de	2 559.6	2 580.1	2 172.3	81.6	82.6	60.7	44.5	46.7	33.2
Korea, Republic of Corée, République de	3 048.9	3 068.3	3 063.5	83.7	84.7	87.1	50.1	54.9	73.5
Kuwait Koweït	3 043.9	2 802.4	3 127.7	90.7	82.8	97.2	100.2	94.9	96.9
Kyrgyzstan Kirghizistan	...	...	2 824.1	...	...	91.8	...	...	53.0
Lao People's Democratic Rep. Rép. dém. populaire lao	2 046.3	2 079.1	2 243.4	49.5	49.9	56.2	21.7	22.3	28.1
Lebanon Liban	3 041.9	3 129.0	3 162.0	78.2	77.0	83.7	91.3	97.1	96.7
Malaysia Malaisie	2 609.9	2 691.0	2 925.0	58.8	60.9	75.7	87.9	94.1	87.5
Maldives Maldives	2 257.1	2 331.0	2 578.2	85.5	82.7	112.9	40.7	46.3	65.1
Mongolia Mongolie	2 279.0	2 247.3	2 015.0	74.8	73.9	76.6	75.7	76.7	78.0
Myanmar Myanmar	2 729.9	2 647.6	2 822.5	69.9	66.6	72.6	46.8	42.7	45.1
Nepal Népal	2 195.6	2 425.1	2 379.8	57.1	62.4	61.0	29.1	32.1	34.4
Pakistan Pakistan	2 196.7	2 294.3	2 457.8	53.1	56.6	63.0	52.2	55.9	64.7
Philippines Philippines	2 194.4	2 294.8	2 359.4	51.2	54.3	54.9	34.8	39.4	47.4
Saudi Arabia Arabie saoudite	2 659.5	2 758.2	2 836.8	75.3	77.0	78.1	82.0	82.0	80.2
Sri Lanka Sri Lanka	2 312.1	2 246.8	2 359.9	48.9	47.8	53.4	43.7	43.9	44.8
Syrian Arab Republic Rép. arabe syrienne	2 946.1	2 835.7	3 052.3	78.4	74.0	74.3	82.6	80.4	103.3
Tajikistan Tadjikistan	...	...	1 790.4	...	...	46.7	...	...	33.7

12
Food supply
Calories, protein and fat: per capita per day [*cont.*]
Disponibilités alimentaires
Calories, protéine et lipides : par habitant, par jour [*suite*]

Country or area Pays ou zone	Calories (number) Calories (nombre)			Protein (grams) Protéine (grammes)			Fat (grams) Lipides (grammes)		
	1986−88	1988−90	1998−00	1986−88	1988−90	1998−00	1986−88	1988−90	1998−00
Thailand Thaïlande	2 263.4	2 254.0	2 477.4	50.6	50.3	55.3	40.5	43.6	50.2
Turkey Turquie	3 482.0	3 532.9	3 390.8	101.8	101.2	97.8	89.0	93.4	87.7
Turkmenistan Turkménistan	...	...	2 724.1	...	...	77.5	...	...	70.9
United Arab Emirates Emirats arabes unis	3 030.4	3 043.1	3 175.7	96.7	95.4	99.8	94.2	92.7	100.8
Uzbekistan Ouzbékistan	...	...	2 374.5	...	...	68.0	...	...	65.5
Viet Nam Viet Nam	2 235.9	2 206.9	2 537.0	50.4	50.2	60.4	26.2	26.9	39.1
Yemen Yémen	2 141.8	2 130.5	2 044.1	59.4	60.0	56.5	37.1	36.6	39.4
Europe • Europe									
Albania Albanie	2 653.1	2 649.4	2 747.6	78.7	79.9	92.4	60.3	63.1	82.9
Austria Autriche	3 411.3	3 454.0	3 730.8	97.8	100.0	109.7	152.5	153.3	161.4
Belarus Bélarus	...	...	3 051.5	...	...	90.8	...	...	98.2
Belgium−Luxembourg Belgique−Luxembourg	3 475.4	3 530.2	3 654.6	102.5	102.8	103.6	154.5	157.3	159.0
Bosnia and Herzegovina Bosnie−Herzégovine	...	...	2 816.4	...	...	76.2	...	...	54.0
Bulgaria Bulgarie	3 696.9	3 643.3	2 638.1	110.3	111.3	82.6	121.9	121.7	93.1
Croatia Croatie	...	...	2 479.5	...	...	63.6	...	...	74.8
Czech Republic République tchèque	...	...	3 170.2	...	...	92.2	...	...	115.9
Czechoslovakia (former) Tchécoslovaquie (anc.)	3 521.9	3 616.7	...	104.2	106.7	...	134.1	137.4	...
Denmark Danemark	3 204.3	3 203.6	3 402.5	101.7	101.8	107.1	130.4	134.4	135.5
Estonia Estonie	...	...	3 252.6	...	...	99.2	...	...	100.1
Finland Finlande	3 001.6	3 158.6	3 192.4	95.5	99.8	103.2	125.2	127.1	126.3
France France	3 524.3	3 547.2	3 581.3	115.7	116.0	116.5	159.1	162.6	165.0
Germany Allemagne	3 484.1	3 426.5	3 413.5	101.4	100.3	95.2	141.1	141.6	148.5
Greece Grèce	3 467.3	3 571.5	3 679.0	108.0	111.3	118.5	137.0	140.2	151.5
Hungary Hongrie	3 678.0	3 714.5	3 421.2	105.5	104.4	91.1	149.7	153.0	136.4
Iceland Islande	3 205.2	3 105.5	3 266.9	123.9	114.4	123.5	130.6	124.6	133.7
Ireland Irlande	3 633.9	3 624.9	3 625.1	117.7	115.6	112.6	142.5	139.3	135.8
Italy Italie	3 526.9	3 564.9	3 636.5	107.7	109.2	113.5	146.4	149.3	152.7
Latvia Lettonie	...	...	2 881.9	...	...	78.3	...	...	87.5
Lithuania Lituanie	...	...	3 009.1	...	...	93.5	...	...	82.3
Malta Malte	3 146.4	3 252.5	3 502.3	95.7	99.4	113.3	110.6	112.6	112.9
Netherlands Pays−Bas	3 125.2	3 239.0	3 242.6	94.8	95.8	106.2	133.0	138.7	140.9
Norway Norvège	3 223.1	3 15...	3 385.4	100.4	97.7	104.5	135.4	129.1	137.3
Poland Pologne	3 464.9	3 443.2	3 365.2	105.3	103.9	99.3	116.9	115.5	113.6

12
Food supply
Calories, protein and fat: per capita per day [*cont.*]
Disponibilités alimentaires
Calories, protéine et lipides : par habitant, par jour [*suite*]

Country or area	Calories (number) Calories (nombre)			Protein (grams) Protéine (grammes)			Fat (grams) Lipides (grammes)		
Pays ou zone	1986–88	1988–90	1998–00	1986–88	1988–90	1998–00	1986–88	1988–90	1998–00
Portugal Portugal	3 241.9	3 358.9	3 669.9	95.1	99.3	117.9	102.0	113.6	132.6
Republic of Moldova République de Moldova	...	...	2 734.4	...	...	63.4	...	...	55.7
Romania Roumanie	2 950.8	2 979.4	3 277.5	91.7	90.9	101.0	88.6	90.0	89.5
Russian Federation Fédération de Russie	...	...	2 895.4	...	...	87.1	...	...	76.9
Serbia and Montenegro Serbie–et–Monténégro	...	...	2 746.0	...	...	82.6	...	...	116.3
Slovakia Slovaquie	...	...	3 100.5	...	...	80.1	...	...	120.9
Slovenia Slovénie	...	...	3 074.7	...	...	103.2	...	...	109.6
Spain Espagne	3 141.4	3 222.8	3 349.1	100.5	103.2	110.8	129.5	135.8	150.9
Sweden Suède	2 939.0	2 969.8	3 103.8	95.0	95.8	101.4	123.2	123.2	126.0
Switzerland Suisse	3 354.7	3 341.3	3 288.4	95.0	94.3	91.0	153.4	151.9	146.0
TFYR of Macedonia L'ex–R.y. Macédoine	...	...	2 957.8	...	...	71.7	...	...	78.6
Ukraine Ukraine	...	...	2 826.7	...	...	79.6	...	...	73.3
United Kingdom Royaume–Uni	3 212.3	3 214.2	3 326.1	92.4	92.5	98.3	137.3	135.6	142.0
Yugoslavia, SFR Yougoslavie, Rfs	3 668.0	3 648.4	...	103.0	103.4	...	117.3	116.3	...
USSR (former) URSS (anc.)	3 382.9	3 367.6	...	106.3	106.4	...	102.8	105.6	...
Oceania · Océanie									
Australia Australie	3 157.2	3 205.8	3 141.7	108.9	109.6	106.5	125.8	129.3	133.8
Fiji Fidji	2 602.4	2 598.6	2 826.4	64.5	66.8	73.9	87.8	95.5	99.3
French Polynesia Polynésie française	2 814.7	2 834.2	2 853.7	82.1	83.6	94.2	102.1	101.6	112.7
Kiribati Kiribati	2 499.4	2 530.9	2 932.0	62.2	63.1	71.0	90.3	90.7	106.6
New Caledonia Nouvelle–Calédonie	2 852.8	2 817.7	2 761.9	77.7	76.6	79.8	105.1	99.1	109.5
New Zealand Nouvelle–Zélande	3 146.2	3 159.1	3 237.5	96.1	95.5	103.6	125.3	128.3	120.6
Papua New Guinea Papouasie–Nvl–Guinée	2 217.8	2 217.6	2 176.7	48.1	47.6	45.5	42.1	42.6	43.7
Solomon Islands Iles Salomon	2 250.5	2 090.9	2 267.3	57.3	53.5	56.0	47.3	45.8	44.5
Vanuatu Vanuatu	2 687.1	2 558.3	2 584.1	61.9	58.2	60.8	100.7	100.4	91.7

Source:
Food and Agriculture Organization of the United Nations (FAO), Rome,
FAOSTAT Nutrition database.

Source:
Organisation des Nations Unies pour l'alimentation et l'agriculture
(FAO), Rome, les données alimentaires de FAOSTAT.

Technical notes, tables 11 and 12

Table 11: Data on acquired immunodeficiency syndrome (AIDS) have been compiled and estimated by the Joint United Nations Programme on HIV/AIDS (UNAIDS) and the World Health Organization (WHO). UNAIDS is composed of the United Nations Children's Fund, the United Nations Development Programme, the United Nations Population Fund, the United Nations International Drug Control Programme, the United Nations Educational, Scientific and Cultural Organization, the World Health Organization and the World Bank. Data are published in the *AIDS epidemic update* [34] and UNAID'S Web site <www.unaids.org>.

Table 12: Estimates on food supply are published by the Food and Agriculture Organization of the United Nations in *Food Balance Sheets* [5] and on its Web site <www.fao.org>, in which the data give estimates of total and per caput food supplies per day available for human consumption during the reference period in terms of quantity and, by applying appropriate food composition factors for all primary and processed products, also in terms of caloric value and protein and fat content. Calorie supplies are reported in kilocalories. The traditional unit of calories is being retained for the time being until the proposed kilojoule gains wider acceptance and understanding (1 calorie = 4.19 kilojoules). Per caput supplies in terms of product weight are derived from the total supplies available for human consumption (i.e. Food) by dividing the quantities of Food by the total population actually partaking of the food supplies during the reference period, i.e. the present in-area (de facto) population within the present geographical boundaries of the country. In other words, nationals living abroad during the reference period are excluded, but foreigners living in the country are included. Adjustments are made wherever possible for part-time presence or absence, such as temporary migrants, tourists and refugees supported by special schemes (if it has not been possible to allow for the amounts provided by such schemes under imports). In almost all cases, the population figures used are the mid-year estimates published by the United Nations Population Division.

Per caput supply figures shown in the commodity balances therefore represent only the average supply available for the population as a whole and do not necessarily indicate what is actually consumed by individuals. Even if they are taken as an approximation of per caput consumption, it is important to bear in mind that there could be considerable variation in consumption between individuals.

Notes techniques, tableaux 11 et 12

Tableau 11: Les données sur le syndrome d'immunodéficience acquise (SIDA) ont été compilées et estimées par le Programme commun des Nations Unies sur le VIH/SIDA (ONUSIDA) et l'Organisation mondiale de la santé (OMS). L'ONUSIDA se compose du Fonds des Nations Unies pour l'enfance, du Programme des Nations Unies pour le développement, du Fonds des Nations Unies pour la population, du Programme des Nations Unies pour le contrôle international des drogues, de l'Organisation des Nations pour l'éducation, la science et la culture, de l'Organisation mondiale de la santé et de la Banque mondiale. Les données sont publiées dans "*AIDS epidemic update*" [34] et sur le site Web de l'ONUSIDA <www.unaids.org>.

Tableau 12: Les estimations sur les disponibilités alimentaires sont publiées par l'Organisation des Nations Unies pour l'alimentation et l'agriculture dans les *Bilans alimentaires* [5] et sur le site Web <www.fao.org> où les données donnent des estimations des disponibilités alimentaires totales et par habitant par jour pour la consommation humaine durant la période de référence, en quantité, en calories, en protéines et en lipides. Les calories sont exprimées en kilocalories. L'unité traditionnelle pour les calories n'est pas utilisée pour l'instant jusqu'à ce que le kilojoule soit plus largement accepté (1 calorie = 4,19 kilojoules). Les disponibilités par habitant exprimées en poids du produit sont calculées à partir des disponibilités totales pour la consommation humaine (c'est-à-dire "Alimentation humaine") en divisant ce chiffre par la population totale qui a effectivement eu accès aux approvisionnements alimentaires durant la période de référence, c'est-à-dire par la population présente (de facto) dans les limites géographiques actuelles du pays. En d'autres termes, les ressortissants du pays vivant à l'étranger durant la période de référence sont exclus, mais les étrangers vivant dans le pays sont inclus. Des ajustements ont été opérés chaque fois que possible pour tenir compte des présences ou des absences de durée limitée, comme dans le cas des imigrants/émigrants temporaires, des touristes et des réfugiés bénéficiant de programmes alimentaires spéciaux (s'il n'a pas été possible de tenir compte des vivres fournis à ce titre à travers les importations). Dans la plupart des cas, les données démographiques utilisés sont les estimations au milieu de l'année publiées par la Division de la population des Nations Unies.

Les disponibilités alimentaires par habitant figurant dans les bilans ne représentent donc que les disponibilités moyennes pour l'ensemble de la population et n'indiquent pas nécessairement la consommation effective des individus. Même si elles sont considérées comme une estimation approximative de la consommation par habitant, il importe de ne pas oublier que la consommation peut varier beaucoup selon les individus.

13
Book production: number of titles by UDC classes
Production de livres : nombre de titres classés d'après la CDU

Country or area Pays ou zone	Year Année	Total	Gener- alities Géné- ralités	Philo- sophy Philo- sophie	Reli- gion	Social sciences Sciences sociales	Philo- logy Philo- logie	Pure sciences Sciences pures	Applied sciences Sciences appl.	Arts Arts	Litera- ture Litté- rature	Geogr./ History Géogr./ histoire
Africa · Afrique												
Algeria	1994	323	22	21	9	97	4	42	14	10	72	32
Algérie	1996[1]	670	39	21	112	96	34	71	157	30	77	33
	1999	133	...	4	2	57	1	11	46	2	10	0
Angola	1985	47	...	...	...	1	...	...	...	...	46	...
Angola	1995	22	...	...	...	...	...	...	...	...	22	...
Benin	1992[1 2]	647	10	4	...	534	7	12	77	...	...	3
Bénin	1994[2]	84	5	...	1	22	6	6	37	1	5	1
	1998	9	...	...	2	...	...	...	1	...	5	1
Botswana [2]	1980	97	...	...	...	67	...	6	19	2	...	3
Botswana [2]	1991	158	8	...	...	125	1	10	11	...	...	3
Burkina Faso	1995[2]	17	1	...	...	3	...	...	...	1	11	1
Burkina Faso	1996[1 2]	12	1	...	...	1	...	...	1	...	9	...
	1997	5	...	...	...	...	...	...	...	1	4	...
Cameroon												
Cameroun	1999	52	...	...	...	52	...	...	...	...	...	...
Dem. Rep. of the Congo	1992[2]	64	...	1	30	27	...	...	5	...	...	1
Rép. dém. du Congo	1996	112	...	...	40	46	...	1	10	1	12	2
Egypt	1996	1 917	85	53	205	186	315	180	282	63	442	106
Egypte	1997	2 507	246	79	481	285	260	224	203	128	460	141
	1998	1 410	96	18	200	126	215	219	150	44	256	86
Eritrea												
Erythrée	1993	106	...	...	...	37	33	29	7	...	...	...
Ethiopia	1990[2 5]	385	32	1	15	179	11	24	71	9	32	11
Ethiopie	1991[2 5]	240	36	...	23	66	11	8	44	3	31	18
	1999	444	40	...	63	203	8	6	77	8	18	21
Gambia	1994	21	...	...	4	5	4	6	1	...	...	1
Gambie	1996[3]	14	...	...	...	10	...	...	2	...	...	2
	1998	10	...	...	...	6	...	1	1	1	1	...
Ghana	1980	209	10	4	52	65	3	5	27	2	35	6
Ghana	1992	28	...	1	6	7	3	...	5	2	4	...
	1998	7	...	...	...	3	2	1	1	...	...	...
Kenya	1990	348	2	...	115	47	56	26	41	12	23	26
Kenya	1991[1]	239	7	...	84	48	26	13	34	1	19	7
	1994[1 2]	300	3	3	76	73	41	19	41	13	12	14
Libyan Arab Jamahiriya												
Jamahiriya arabe libyenne	1994	26	...	2	2	2	1	2	5	...	11	1
Madagascar	1995	131	3	3	32	44	2	2	13	4	19	9
Madagascar	1996	119	1	3	25	22	2	4	36	6	18	2
	1997	108	7	...	26	36	...	2	21	5	8	3
Malawi	1994	243	10	...	41	92	11	11	40	10	24	4
Malawi	1995	182	10	...	44	81	5	5	18	5	14	...
	1996[12 20 22]	120	...	...	1	76	14	10	5	3	...	8
Mali	1984[5]	160	...	...	...	98	19	17	23	...	...	3
Mali	1995[1 2]	14	1	...	...	1	...	...	1	...	11	...
	1998	33	23	...	...	...	...	...	5	...	5	...
Mauritius	1995	64	4	1	3	20	6	1	4	2	18	5
Maurice	1996	80	1	4	4	14	4	1	6	6	32	8
	1998	55	10	...	5	12	6	...	2	2	5	13
Morocco	1997	1 339	37	28	82	549	15	67	175	142	141	103
Maroc	1998	894	41	9	90	377	21	16	75	21	150	94
	1999	386	25	3	34	151	5	1	33	12	75	47
Namibia												
Namibie	1990	106	7	...	2	57	...	2	18	2	14	4
Niger [2]												
Niger [2]	1991	5	...	...	...	...	...	...	...	...	5	...
Nigeria	1992	1 562	55	14	142	733	104	71	196	30	148	69
Nigéria	1994	1 008	11	7	121	458	53	72	114	37	60	75
	1995	1 314	18	36	203	530	91	80	116	52	133	55
Reunion	1980	99	...	...	5	23	...	12	16	10	24	9
Réunion	1985	73	1	...	6	15	2	2	12	4	18	13
	1992	69	1	...	...	20	...	4	5	12	14	13
South Africa	1993	4 751	123	35	584	1 080	332	345	938	173	966	175
Afrique du Sud	1994	4 574	116	40	491	1 034	315	363	911	189	907	208
	1995	5 418	136	33	516	1 262	566	330	1 002	156	1 227	190

13
Book production: number of titles by UDC classes [cont.]
Production de livres : nombre de titres classés d'après la CDU [suite]

Country or area Pays ou zone	Year Année	Total	Gener- alities Géné- ralités	Philo- sophy Philo- sophie	Reli- gion	Social sciences Sciences sociales	Philo- logy Philo- logie	Pure sciences Sciences pures	Applied sciences Sciences appl.	Arts Arts	Litera- ture Litté- rature	Geogr./ History Géogr./ histoire
Togo Togo	1998	5	...	...	1	1	1	...	1	...	...	1
Tunisia	1995[1]	563	8	25	7	132	23	9	19	24	166	150
Tunisie	1996[20]	720	24	18	14	138	6	4	38	23	338	111
	1999	1 260	13	13	41	200	...	119	103	39	656	76
Uganda	1992	162	4	2	...	77	...	...	78	...	...	1
Ouganda	1993[17]	314	...	...	4	10	43	35	14	...	4	11
	1996[1 20 24]	288	...	...	7	...	45	41	7	...	4	9
United Republic of Tanzania	1980	512	31	4	94	151	17	50	86	57	22	...
Rép.-Unie de Tanzanie	1984[2]	363	17	1	41	195	6	7	77	4	9	6
	1990[2]	172	...	1	18	45	2	7	40	3	47	9
Zimbabwe	1985	544	5	2	15	132	141	58	89	16	66	20
Zimbabwe	1990	349	6	...	14	153	22	16	70	7	56	5
	1992	232	6	...	15	107	15	3	48	7	24	7
America, North · Amérique du Nord												
Belize Belize	1996	107	...	...	7	39	4	16	15	14	5	7
Canada	1997	21 669	654	533	648	8 386	683	1 040	3 429	1 207	3 491	1 598
Canada	1998	20 848	553	527	660	7 756	646	1 041	3 266	1 199	3 616	1 584
	1999	22 941	594	516	740	8 182	620	1 101	3 634	1 402	4 248	1 904
Costa Rica	1995[1 20 24]	1 034	36	22	26	307	25	51	150	14	186	58
Costa Rica	1997	949	23	8	46	495	14	39	88	27	166	43
	1998	1 464	60	23	49	656	20	66	253	40	221	76
Cuba	1997	785	44	16	13	170	35	30	96	35	279	67
Cuba	1998	796	59	32	10	209	15	24	61	38	306	42
	1999	952	75	11	6	253	15	43	73	34	380	62
Dominican Republic Rép. dominicaine	1997[15]	1 013	...	...	...	112	...	...	...	...	553	348
El Salvador	1996	103	...	...	...	27	...	6	...	42	25	3
El Salvador	1998	663	...	...	5	125	1	4	458	5	59	6
Haiti Haïti	1995	340	...	...	...	...	...	...	...	...	...	...
Honduras Honduras	1999	26	...	...	...	13	1	...	...	...	12	...
Mexico	1996[1]	6 183	423	690	425	1 894	291	172	1 093	374	419	402
Mexique	1998	6 952	473	725	475	2 059	341	256	1 241	478	468	436
United States [9]	1994	51 863	2 208	1 741	2 730	11 072	700	3 021	8 384	3 146	8 836	4 704
Etats-Unis [9]	1995	62 039	2 751	2 068	3 324	12 840	732	3 323	9 891	4 238	11 537	5 657
	1996	68 175	3 027	2 333	3 803	14 225	898	3 725	10 762	4 245	13 221	6 583
America, South · Amérique du Sud												
Argentina	1996[1 20]	9 850	339	818	541	2 529	111	111	900	490	2 520	525
Argentine	1997	10 590	419	846	634	3 021	124	194	1 049	638	3 044	621
	1998	11 991	357	953	656	3 428	138	271	1 409	821	3 210	748
Brazil	1996	18 883	1 566	1 739	2 192	4 964	1 138	360	2 064	922	3 158	780
Brésil	1997	22 071	2 097	1 997	3 738	5 780	1 702	328	2 195	919	2 582	733
	1998	21 689	1 113	2 162	4 003	5 562	649	644	2 264	636	3 524	1 132
Chile	1992	1 820	13	59	127	587	34	58	183	43	548	168
Chili	1995	2 469	18	59	158	707	33	71	261	80	860	222
	1999	1 443	3	44	112	394	31	30	125	43	538	123
Colombia	1984	15 041	1 078	239	352	2 784	290	1 098	6 067	997	1 501	635
Colombie	1991[1]	1 481	141	28	88	570	43	40	243	52	216	60
	1997	5 302	616	261	236	1 830	132	230	717	212	884	184
Ecuador	1994[2]	11	...	...	...	...	1	...	...	1	9	...
Equateur	1995[2]	12	...	...	...	...	1	...	...	...	11	...
	1999	1 050	20	17	30	513	11	33	134	38	195	59
Guyana	1994[2 12]	33	...	...	...	5	9	10	9	...	...	...
Guyana	1996[2]	42	3	...	2	23	...	1	1	3	4	5
	1997	25	3	...	2	13	...	2	1	1	1	2
Paraguay Paraguay	1993	152	11	2	4	71	6	4	14	2	28	10
Peru	1996	612	44	24	25	266	13	27	66	11	97	39
Pérou	1997	1 416	30	26	92	702	25	47	134	42	224	94
	1998	1 942	42	26	85	862	200	173	107	63	273	111
Suriname [2] Suriname [2]	1996	47	18	1	16	6	2	...	2	...	1	1

13
Book production: number of titles by UDC classes [*cont.*]
Production de livres : nombre de titres classés d'après la CDU [*suite*]

Country or area Pays ou zone	Year Année	Total	Gener- alities Géné- ralités	Philo- sophy Philo- sophie	Reli- gion	Social sciences Sciences sociales	Philo- logy Philo- logie	Pure sciences Sciences pures	Applied sciences Sciences appl.	Arts Arts	Litera- ture Litté- rature	Geogr./ History Géogr./ histoire
Uruguay	1996	934	22	33	33	264	9	29	201	77	193	73
Uruguay	1997	1 191	26	42	40	311	9	42	250	95	281	95
	1999	674	16	19	7	194	6	5	153	28	181	65
Venezuela [2]	1995	4 225	229	217	186	1 106	85	187	1 032	243	636	304
Venezuela [2]	1996	3 468	87	210	188	955	81	136	608	274	682	247
	1997	3 851	166	155	203	1 082	57	230	719	294	701	244
Asia · Asie												
Afghanistan	1980	273	40	3	5	126	13	26	35	3	4	18
Afghanistan	1990	2 795	165	25	170	1 045	30	125	680	95	200	260
Armenia	1997	387	3	9	25	134	17	7	26	17	113	36
Arménie	1998	535	15	18	6	167	16	17	56	20	182	38
	1999	516	20	23	25	131	12	21	32	27	188	37
Azerbaijan	1996	542	12	10	25	167	21	17	44	9	209	28
Azerbaïdjan	1997	496	4	7	13	112	13	15	24	17	235	56
	1998	444	9	6	7	107	8	20	26	15	196	50
Bahrain	1996[2]	40	6	...	...	7	...	...	1	...	14	12
Bahreïn	1998	92	3	...	10	15	1	...	8	4	39	12
Brunei Darussalam	1990[1 13]	25	2	...	...	13	2	...	...	...	8	...
Brunéi Darussalam	1992[12]	45	4	3	7	24	2	2	1	1	...	1
	1998	38	...	1	10	7	6	6	6	...	...	2
China [6 23]	1990[1]	73 923	2 588	1 206	./.	36 231	2 403	3 087	12 196	5 727	7 756	2 729
Chine [6 23]	1993	92 972	3 098	1 222	./.	48 796	2 724	3 248	15 311	5 560	9 488	3 525
	1994	100 951	3 013	1 156	./.	55 380	3 175	3 673	15 783	5 350	9 735	3 686
China, Macao SAR	1996	67	2	...	...	44	3	...	2	13	2	1
Chine, Macao RAS	1999	340	5	1	11	93	...	6	31	53	91	49
Cyprus	1997	918	15	8	40	370	85	20	165	96	72	47
Chypre	1998	927	19	7	43	362	97	17	168	97	71	46
	1999	931	21	10	32	381	87	20	154	94	80	52
Georgia	1995	1 104	574	17	17	81	23	36	67	10	216	63
Géorgie	1996[2]	581	4	17	18	124	38	49	74	16	190	51
	1999	697	476	14	17	84	14	16	7	4	65	0
India	1996	11 903	505	354	764	2 504	256	593	1 314	298	4 423	892
Inde	1997	12 006	359	411	927	2 474	220	465	876	252	4 979	1 043
	1998	14 085	406	408	1 150	3 350	275	570	760	573	5 294	1 299
Indonesia	1997	1 902	78	42	226	523	141	170	402	56	176	88
Indonésie	1998	537	13	9	17	117	12	145	69	72	5	78
	1999	121	17	...	...	88	...	...	16	...	...	...
Iran, Islamic Rep. of	1997	10 410	392	541	3 112	953	944	1 388	1 499	531	431	619
Iran, Rép. islamique d'	1998	12 020	299	565	3 617	1 325	1 307	1 437	1 790	566	291	823
	1999	14 783	612	706	4 504	1 319	1 486	1 844	2 426	733	247	906
Israel	1985	2 214	25	40	173	230	50	79	71	44	718	234
Israël	1992[7]	2 310	22	53	182	263	92	101	85	31	638	173
	1998	1 969	43	71	130	439	59	221	181	30	630	165
Japan [1]	1985[7]	45 430	1 529	1 608	679	10 708	2 493	2 709	7 349	5 698	10 506	2 151
Japon [1]	1992[2]	35 496	539	1 539	638	8 529	917	1 142	6 276	5 532	8 525	1 859
	1996[2]	56 221	1 149	1 791	1 078	12 770	1 402	1 363	12 155	10 046	11 924	2 543
Jordan	1995	465	15	9	74	106	10	19	26	22	128	56
Jordanie	1996	511	25	8	60	122	16	39	45	21	116	59
Kazakhstan	1995	1 115	65	12	17	339	50	44	197	31	291	69
Kazakhstan	1996	1 226	53	22	23	464	44	58	202	39	253	68
	1999	1 223	52	13	21	579	40	89	173	18	166	72
Korea, Republic of	1994	34 204	579	640	1 844	6 584	2 371	2 025	3 856	6 315	8 885	1 105
Corée, République de	1995	35 864	1 854	947	2 146	4 300	4 421	2 692	4 422	6 614	6 958	1 510
	1996[1 2 20]	30 487	303	678	1 605	3 201	1 384	359	3 513	6 543	4 164	716
Kuwait	1997	460	11	16	61	169	32	55	33	28	21	34
Koweït	1998	295	36	6	45	74	8	8	36	6	38	38
	1999	219*	36	13	31	71	1	8	9	5	19	26
Kyrgyzstan	1995	407	16	3	6	177	17	15	58	4	97	14
Kirghizistan	1996	351	11	5	3	176	16	19	25	8	73	15
	1998	420	...	2	15	157	26	13	92	9	93	13
Lao People's Dem. Rep.	1991[1]	58	...	...	1	31	2	...	2	1	20	1
Rép. dém. pop. lao	1992[12]	64	...	...	1	7	11	...	6	...	36	3
	1995[2]	88	...	...	2	41	6	6	9	2	15	7
Lebanon	1997	516	54	10	256	131	...	...	12	1	47	5
Liban	1998	289	183	5	...	41	5	2	19	1	26	7

13
Book production: number of titles by UDC classes [*cont.*]
Production de livres : nombre de titres classés d'après la CDU [*suite*]

Country or area Pays ou zone	Year Année	Total	Gener- alities Géné- ralités	Philo- sophy Philo- sophie	Reli- gion	Social sciences Sciences sociales	Philo- logy Philo- logie	Pure sciences Sciences pures	Applied sciences Sciences appl.	Arts Arts	Litera- ture Litté- rature	Geogr./ History Géogr./ histoire
Malaysia	1996	5 843	73	36	606	1 088	1 043	685	538	221	1 259	294
Malaisie	1998	5 816	100	55	721	751	803	467	443	133	2 160	183
	1999	5 084	157	59	547	1 058	662	526	614	222	998	241
Mongolia	1986	889	...	...	...	467	6	16	181	41	178	...
Mongolie	1990	717	49	...	...	300	2	45	103	...	218	...
	1992[2]	285	26	12	5	36	6	17	20	9	135	19
Myanmar	1992[6]	3 785	11	78	720	18	./.	66	26	1 274	1 584[10]	8
Myanmar	1993[6]	3 660	...	73	713	26	./.	82	22	1 171	1 551[10]	22
	1999	227	106	...	1	76	20	16	1	1	4	2
Occupied Palestinian Terr.	1996[2]	114	3	2	8	47	3	12	21	...	10	8
Terr. palestinien occupé	1998	2	...	...	...	...	...	...	...	...	...	2
Oman	1996[2]	7	...	...	4	...	...	...	1	...	1	1
Oman	1998	136	18	2	24	15	3	27	...	4	34	9
	1999	12	...	1	5	...	...	...	1	5	...	...
Philippines	1997	546	26	11	36	212	18	38	63	15	103	24
Philippines	1998	958	88	22	40	329	41	37	130	17	208	46
	1999	1 380	63	15	41	631	79	53	117	79	227	75
Qatar [1]	1994	371	23	6	26	149	15	60	41	4	11	36
Qatar [1]	1995	419	21	5	70	84	36	120	40	5	16	22
	1996[3]	209	9	3	26	88	7	19	27	6	12	12
Saudi Arabia	1980	218	3	...	67	27	2	1	11	4	61	31
Arabie saoudite	1996[2]	3 900	209	154	1 042	620	250	404	363	128	421	309
	1997	3 780	300	60	850	310	180	270	440	132	710	528
Sri Lanka	1996	4 115	338	29	28	2 505	139	55	390	33	483	115
Sri Lanka	1998	2 822	328	71	312	639	127	76	192	124	809	144
	1999	4 655	426	368	533	1 384	169	68	347	103	1 110	147
Syrian Arab Republic	1980[2]	95	...	4	...	22	...	4	1	3	34	4
Rép. arabe syrienne	1992[1]	598	144	24	62	79	13	1	89	25	112	49
Tajikistan	1996[2]	132	...	5	...	18	11	14	19	9	27	12
Tadjikistan	1997	150	...	...	...	61	9	9	21	8	42	...
	1998	9	...	...	...	7	...	...	...	...	2	...
Thailand	1991	7 676	429	198	273	2 415	260	539	2 271	411	477	403
Thaïlande	1992	7 626	413	189	302	2 341	234	591	2 235	443	457	421
	1996	8 142	464	202	275	2 456	259	617	2 371	407	644	447
Turkey	1997	5 109	109	126	513	1 557	141	110	1 003	190	927	433
Turquie	1998	9 313	182	369	669	2 585	205	255	938	255	3 014	841
	1999	2 920	45	139	255	649	82	68	285	91	1 096	210
Turkmenistan	1992	565	47	5	6	147	21	72	74	18	136	39
Turkménistan	1994[2]	450	1	5	7	150	23	46	60	20	121	17
United Arab Emirates	1990[4]	281	6	3	37	16	86	104	17	...	...	12
Emirats arabes unis	1992	302	10	3	46	20	85	99	9	3	...	27
	1993[4]	293	...	3	68	2	83	99	9	2	...	27
Uzbekistan	1993[6]	1 340	./.	118	./.	54	71	./.	136	./.	605	./.
Ouzbékistan	1995	1 200	18	20	20	414	60	60	213	11	316	68
	1996	1 003	8	7	22	367	44	42	158	10	277	68
Viet Nam [6]	1991	3 429	./.	./.	./.	444	./.	./.	395	./.	979	./.
Viet Nam [6]	1992	4 707	./.	./.	./.	683	./.	./.	603	./.	1 024	./.
	1993	5 581	./.	./.	./.	647	./.	./.	646	./.	1 502	./.
Europe • Europe												
Albania	1980	948	21	2	...	211	63	103	223	46	237	42
Albanie	1985	939	9	6	...	189	75	159	281	42	139	39
	1991	381	12	...	4	28	35	74	127	20	63	18
Andorra	1994[1]	57	...	...	...	24	...	3	4	5	15	6
Andorre	1998	104	19	...	...	39	6	5	4	11	12	8
	1999	173	5	...	1	45	4	...	17	47	27	27
Austria [8]	1994	7 987	229	246	284	2 758	229	847	703	922	1 181	588
Autriche [8]	1995	8 222	406	255	239	2 948	239	657	738	929	1 208	603
	1996	8 056	243	289	289	2 851	209[14]	651	682	963	1 188	691
Belarus	1996	3 809	214	84	153	930	146	182	776	100	1 127	97
Bélarus	1997	5 331	206	167	199	1 304	189	265	1 092	118	1 640	151
	1998	6 073	206	193	139	1 970	235	316	1 380	188	1 236	210
Belgium [16]	1985	8 327	169	240	480	1 235	291	343	1 153	890	2 807	719
Belgique [16]	1990	12 157	303	285	458	2 530	335	461	1 886	1 074	3 673	1 152
	1991	13 913	300	311	686	2 847	478	817	2 228	1 325	3 696	1 225
Bulgaria	1997	3 773	132	224	116	777	118	145	478	113	1 520	150
Bulgarie	1998	4 863	183	208	152	1 039	161	159	722	176	1 819	244
	1999	4 971	170	235	205	1 029	159	211	715	178	1 803	266

13
Book production: number of titles by UDC classes [cont.]
Production de livres : nombre de titres classés d'après la CDU [suite]

Country or area Pays ou zone	Year Année	Total	Gener- alities Géné- ralités	Philo- sophy Philo- sophie	Reli- gion	Social sciences Sciences sociales	Philo- logy Philo- logie	Pure sciences Sciences pures	Applied sciences Sciences appl.	Arts Arts	Litera- ture Litté- rature	Geogr./ History Géogr./ histoire
Croatia	1997	3 015	63	108	235	773	70	98	421	153	936	158
Croatie	1998	3 265	75	126	262	858	73	116	639	170	818	128
	1999	2 309	78	83	209	655	5	106	398	110	554	111
Czech Republic	1997	11 519	187	443	425	1 972	367	1 138	1 413	788	3 807	979
République tchèque	1998	11 738	263	383	406	2 223	359	1 081	1 655	719	3 581	1 068
	1999	12 551	358	387	363	2 440	396	1 277	1 771	781	3 708	1 070
Denmark	1997	13 450	356	595	307	2 642	356	916	3 216	923	2 850	1 289
Danemark	1998	13 175	264	485	306	2 757	366	959	2 987	756	3 055	1 240
	1999	14 455	306	642	381	2 914	338	1 090	3 228	864	3 369	1 323
Estonia	1997	3 317	229	108	109	820	...	273	416	236	990	136
Estonie	1998	3 090	226	99	90	774	...	285	362	177	925	152
	1999	3 265	122	86	99	718	...	274	519	186	1 082	179
Finland	1997	12 717	316	248	313	3 176	316	1 183	3 554	792	1 851	968
Finlande	1998	12 887	253	221	319	2 986	355	1 148	3 188	746	1 945	1 726
	1999	13 173	294	238	318	3 068	364	1 169	3 252	760	2 144	1 566
France	1997	45 453	1 068	2 051	1 514	7 738	1 033	1 889	5 822	4 132	14 663	5 543
France	1998	47 916	1 765	2 138	1 562	7 031	1 082	2 052	6 178	4 399	15 695	6 014
	1999	39 083	5 226	...	1 214	8 810	313	...	2 791	1 316	12 013	7 400
Germany	1996	71 515	6 287	3 580	3 718	16 210	...	2 756	10 550	5 921	12 798[10]	9 695
Allemagne	1997	77 889	...	...	...	...	...	...	...	...	...	...
	1998	78 042	...	...	...	...	...	...	...	...	...	...
Greece	1995	4 134[1]	152	98	204	613	190	254	287	284	1 598	454
Grèce	1996	4 225[1]	166	83	242	659	131	363	300	282	1 595	404
	1997	4 067	139	119	208	596	156	239	318	296	1 568	428
Holy See [19]	1992[1]	205	5	37	117	31	7	...	...	...	...	8
Saint-Siège [19]	1995	298	...	48	198	42	1	...	...	2	...	7
	1996	228	...	38	105	78	2	...	...	...	5	
Hungary	1997	9 343	320	393	361	1 395	684	614	1 390	482	2 663	1 041
Hongrie	1998	11 306	196	454	615	1 456	541	787	1 832	670	3 642	1 113
	1999	10 352	290	378	593	1 121	602	854	1 609	565	3 338	1 002
Iceland	1996	1 527	29	30	43	354	124	114	168	107	414	144
Islande	1997	1 652	23	26	49	435	149	121	192	105	403	149
	1998	1 796	44	27	46	476	150	140	192	138	444	139
Italy	1997	36 217	700	2 175	2 444	6 893	772	1 036	4 271	4 258	8 644	5 024
Italie	1998	30 835	1 030	1 804	2 346	5 577	628	909	3 433	3 518	7 457	4 133
	1999	32 365	603	2 075	2 338	6 446	608	1 110	3 537	3 353	7 826	4 469
Latvia	1996[20]	1 965	91	63	87	414	67	54	166	87	364	65
Lettonie	1998[20]	2 093	102	114	113	740	86	81	282	81	381	113
	1999	2 178	104	131	104	627	158	102	343	87	385	137
Lithuania	1997	3 827	303	104	168	768	217	282	566	180	1 064	175
Lituanie	1998	4 109	335	123	138	783	258	346	546	218	1 172	190
	1999	4 097	301	126	153	794	309	320	509	215	1 151	219
Luxembourg	1992	586	44	9	10	240	2	9	61	108	48	55
Luxembourg	1993	640	19	...	11	292	5	7	85	118	46	57
	1994	681	64	13	15	246	2	19	49	118	67	88
Malta	1993	417	8	11	80	163	18	4	16	29	41	47
Malte	1995	404	4	6	78	159	8	4	13	28	47	57
	1998	237	5	3	40	65	10	...	6	11	46	51
Monaco	1998	29	4	1	3	8	...	1	...	10	1	1
Monaco	1999	72	14	1	10	14	...	11	1	18	1	2
	2000	70	7	...	5	16	...	3	10	21	2	6
Netherlands [1]	1991	16 017	84	612	823	1 615	307	351	2 581	880	3 082	1 278
Pays-Bas [1]	1992	15 997	71	628	833	1 701	233	358	2 502	874	3 251	1 393
	1993	34 067	70	710	788	1 883	334	215	2 310	2 826	2 950	1 364
Norway	1997[78]	6 220	141	172	192	1 084	120	266	613	322	2 656	654
Norvège	1998	5 068	152	141	221	858	96	170	597	355	2 146	332
	1999	4 985	162	141	242	814	69	143	556	315	2 130	413
Poland	1997	15 996	231	417	1 078	3 147	623	1 371	2 951	844	3 798	1 536
Pologne	1998	16 462	621	496	944	3 081	621	1 319	2 670	803	4 311	1 596
	1999	19 192	676	589	1 274	3 829	823	1 545	3 304	1 045	4 176	1 931
Portugal	1996	7 868	312	178	233	1 207	17	190	506	260	4 554	411
Portugal	1997	8 331	324	160	295	2 255	23	157	852	268	3 503	494
	1998	2 186	...	...	...	...	...	...	...	145	2 041	...
Republic of Moldova	1997	1 097	53	12	23	281	75	103	242	21	224	63
République de Moldova	1998	1 196	67	27	38	267	21	94	250	45	313	74
	1999	1 166	181	23	22	320	44	76	215	25	177	83

13
Book production: number of titles by UDC classes [*cont.*]
Production de livres : nombre de titres classés d'après la CDU [*suite*]

Country or area Pays ou zone	Year Année	Total	Gener-alities Géné-ralités	Philo-sophy Philo-sophie	Reli-gion	Social sciences Sciences sociales	Philo-logy Philo-logie	Pure sciences Sciences pures	Applied sciences Sciences appl.	Arts Arts	Litera-ture Litté-rature	Geogr./ History Géogr./ histoire
Romania	1997	6 471	728	246	386	886	383	867	1 617	96	931	331
Roumanie	1998	6 231	1 398	149	233	902	352	759	1 907	125	57	349
	1999	7 874	925	207	357	943	24	761	1 629	134	2 466[23]	428
Russian Federation	1994	30 390	2 860	896	957	5 965	995	2 644	6 849	704	7 176	1 344
Fédération de Russie	1995	33 623	2 968	1 038	854	7 719	988	2 790	6 783	685	7 704	2 094
	1996	36 237	3 362	1 275	984	8 801	1 171	2 869	7 003	664	8 493	1 615
Serbia and Montenegro	1994	2 799	117	62	48	908	4	76	409	165	846	164
Serbie-et-Monténégro	1995	3 531	121	54	75	1 023	3	151	624	225	975	280
	1996	5 367	206	102	136	1 515	6	234	791	302	1 613	462
Slovakia	1997	2 064	39	64	111	515	61	188	439	84	428	135
Slovaquie	1998	4 386	107	177	291	1 045	204	418	852	175	901	216
	1999	3 153	69	123	264	681	97	254	684	117	711	153
Slovenia	1997	3 647	83	135	124	706	115	333	624	460	761	306
Slovénie	1998	3 722	85	159	147	672	121	320	654	521	770	273
	1999	3 450	78	163	157	740	...	242	671	137	929	333
Spain	1997	48 713	1 409	1 807	1 807	9 147	2 119	3 196	7 561	4 063	13 004	4 600
Espagne	1998	55 774	1 381	2 314	2 032	9 884	2 164	3 318	8 352	4 717	16 455	5 157
	1999	59 174	1 446	2 455	1 962	10 899	2 064	3 245	8 800	5 032	18 145	5 126
Sweden	1996	13 496	396	328	502	2 685	464	900	3 285	850	2 876	1 210
Suède	1997	13 220	367	351	498	2 562	474	975	3 222	794	2 901	1 076
	1998	12 547	323	364	373	2 480	400	826	2 986	821	2 974	1 000
Switzerland	1997	16 241	315	803	835	4 165	269	1 656	3 564	1 695	2 077	862
Suisse	1998	13 816	212	620	748	3 516	203	1 491	3 138	1 442	1 730	716
	1999	18 273	336	825	1 101	4 885	306	1 761	3 862	1 881	2 379	937
TFYR of Macedonia	1997	791	36	10	25	347	15	29	25	47	197	60
L'ex-R.y. Macédoine	1998	738	39	17	9	325	19	26	36	40	197	30
	1999	733	29	7	8	345	25	27	46	47	174	25
Ukraine	1997	7 362	260	213	364	2 455	398	382	1 669	164	1 166	291
Ukraine	1998	7 065	298	173	218	3 231	187	241	1 225	114	1 034	344
	1999	6 282	198	121	186	2 960	137	213	1 086	100	1 011	270
United Kingdom	1996	107 263	2 082	3 548	5 003	23 889	3 563	9 417	16 616	9 431	21 686	12 028
Royaume-Uni	1997	106 444	2 047	3 357	4 968	24 009	3 213	8 973	16 761	9 898	21 222	11 996
	1998	110 965	2 143	3 570	5 199	24 714	4 274	8 902	17 106	10 520	22 104	12 433
Oceania · Océanie												
Australia	1985	10 251	427	82	363	3 623	447	609	2 016	946	842	896
Australie	1989[16]	10 723	353	135	333	3 997	277	627	1 753	966	1 205	1 077
	1994[16]	10 835	218	151	246	4 453	157	511	1 730	700	1 812	857
Fiji	1980	110	3	...	...	4	31	19	26	11	...	16
Fidji	1994[18]	401	...	...	...	22	21	40	39	2	...	21
New Zealand	1997	5 088	173	64	104	1 989	429	381	830	380	433	305
Nouvelle-Zélande	1998	5 204	132	58	140	2 034	382	362	771	380	540	405
	1999	5 405	182	50	119	2 173	401	400	798	357	535	390
Papua New Guinea Papouasie-Nvl-Guinée	1991	122	8	...	19	64	1	6	16	4	...	4

Source:
United Nations Educational, Scientific and Cultural Organization (UNESCO) Institute for Statistics, Montreal, the UNESCO statistics database.

1   Not including pamphlets.
2   First editions only.
3   Data refer to school textbooks and government publications only.
4   Data refer to school textbooks only.
5   Data refer to school textbooks, government publications and university theses only.
6   Works indicated by the symbol ./. are distributed without specification among other classes for which a figure is shown.

7   Not including government publications.
8   Not including school textbooks or yearbooks.
9   Not including pamphlets, school textbooks, government publications and university theses but including juvenile titles for which a class breakdown is not available.

10   Data on philology are included with those on literature.

Source:
L'Institut de statistique de l'Organisation des Nations Unies pour l'éducation, la science et la culture (UNESCO), Montréal, la base de données de l'UNESCO.

1   Non compris les brochures.
2   Premières éditions seulement.
3   Les données se réfèrent aux manuels scolaires et aux publications officielles seulement.
4   Les données se réfèrent aux manuels scolaires seulement.
5   Les données se réfèrent aux manuels scolaires, aux publications officielles et aux thèses universitaires seulement.
6   Les ouvrages représentés par le symbole ./. sont distribués sans spécification entre les autres catégories pour lesquelles un chiffre est donné.

7   Non compris les publications officielles.
8   Non compris les manuels scolaires ou les annuaires.
9   Non compris les brochures, les manuels scolaires, les publications officielles et les thèses universitaires mais y compris les livres pour jeunes pour lesquels repartition par catégories n'est pas disponible.

10   Les données relatives à la philologie sont comprises avec

13
Book production: number of titles by UDC classes [*cont.*]
Production de livres : nombre de titres classés d'après la CDU [*suite*]

11   Including reprints.
12   Data refer to school textbooks and children's books only.

13   Data refer to school textbooks, children's books and government publications only.
14   Includes history of literature and literary criticism.
15   Partial data.
16   The figures do not represent the total book production, but only those actually received in the National Library.

17   Government publications are included in the total but are not reported in the subject areas.
18   Data refer only to books published by the Ministry of Education and the government printing department.

19   Refers to the Vatican City State.
20   School textbooks and children's books are included in the total but are not distributed among the other subject areas.
21   Includes books on trade, communication, transport and tourism.

22   Children's books are included in the total but are not distributed among the other groups.
23   Including children's books.
24   The difference between the total and the sum of the subject areas is the result of data not being reported in the subject breakdown.
25   Including Eritrea.

celles de la littérature.
11   Y compris les réimpressions.
12   Les données se réfèrent aux manuels scolaires et aux livres pour enfants saulement.
13   Les données se réfèrent aux manuels scolaires, aux livres pour enfants et aux publications officielles seulement.
14   Y compris la histoire de la littérature et la critique littéraire.
15   Données partielles.
16   Les chiffres ne représentent pas la totalité de l'édition des livres mais seulement le nombre de titres enregistrés à la Bibliothèque Nationale.
17   Les publications officielles sont inclues dans le total mais elles ne sont pas reparties selon les catégories.
18   Les données se réfèrent seulement aux livres publiés par le Ministére de l'Education et le départment des publications du gouvernement.
19   Concerne la Cité du Vatican.
20   Les manuels scolaires et les livres pour enfants sont inclus dans le total mais ils ne sont pas repartis selon les catégories.
21   Y compris les ouvrages relatifs au commerce, à la communication, au transport, et au tourisme.
22   Les livres pour enfants sont inclus dans le total mais ils ne sont pas repartis selon les catégories.
23   Y compris des livres pour enfants.
24   La différence entre le total et la répartition des catégories est dû au fait que les données n'ont pas été rapportées par catégorie.
25   Y compris Erythrée.

14
Daily newspapers
Journaux quotidiens

Country or area	Number of titles Nombre de titres				Total average circulation (thousands) Diffusion moyenne (en milliers)				Circulation per 1000 inhabitants Diffusion pour 1000 habitants			
Pays ou zone	1997	1998	1999	2000	1997	1998	1999	2000	1997	1998	1999	2000
Africa • Afrique												
Algeria Algérie	18	24	...	...	761[1]	796[1]	...	...	25.9	27.2	...	...
Benin Bénin	...	...	13	...	...	...	33[1]	...	...	...	5.3	...
Burundi Burundi	1	1	...	...	* 15	* 15	...	...	* 2.4	* 2.4	...	...
Chad Tchad	2	2	...	...	* 2	* 2	...	...	* 0.2	* 0.2	...	...
Egypt Egypte	14	15	16		2 100	2 332	2 080	...	32.4	35.6	31.2	...
Ethiopia Ethiopie	2	2	...	...	23	23	...	...	0.4	0.4	...	...
Mauritius Maurice	8	6	6	5	88[1]	* 82[1]	116[1]	138[1]	77.7	* 71.7	100.7	118.8
Morocco Maroc	21	22	22	23	657[1]	715[1]	728[1]	846[1]	24.4	24.8	24.8	28.3
Mozambique Mozambique	12	12	...	...	43[1]	43[1]	...	...	2.3	2.5	...	...
Senegal Sénégal	4	5	...	...	...	...	...	...	...	...	...	...
Togo Togo	...	...	1	1	...	...	10[1]	10[1]	...	...	2.3	2.2
Tunisia Tunisie	...	...	...	7	...	...	...	180[1]	...	...	...	19.0
America, North • Amérique du Nord												
Bermuda Bermudes	...	...	1	1			15	15	...	...	...	...
Costa Rica Costa Rica	8	8	8	8	...	...	...	...	...	...	...	...
Dominican Republic République dominicaine	10	10	10	9	...	...	230	230	...	...	27.9	27.5
El Salvador El Salvador	4	4	...	...	219[1]	171[1]	...	...	37.1	28.3	...	...
Mexico Mexique	...	...	300	311	...	...	9 332	9 251	...	...	95.9	93.6
America, South • Amérique du Sud												
Bolivia Bolivie	27	29	...	...	...	...	...	...	...	...	...	...
Brazil Brésil	400	372	...	...	6 892	7 163	...	...	42.1	43.1	...	...
Ecuador Equateur	11	11	36	36	569	529	1 220	1 220	47.7	43.5	98.3	96.5
Guyana Guyana	...	...	2	2	...	...	57[1]	57[1]	...	...	74.9	74.6
Suriname Suriname	2	2	...	...	29[1]	28[1]	...	...	69.2	67.7	...	...
Asia • Asie												
Armenia Arménie	8	7	7	8	...	...	31	19	...	...	8.2	5.0
China, Macao SAR Chine, Macao RAS	...	...	10	10	...	...	158	167	...	...	358.2	376.5
Cyprus Chypre	8	7	8	8	76	79	86	87	99.6	102.6	110.7	111.0
Georgia Géorgie	...	...	30	35	...	...	43	26	...	...	8.2	4.9
India Inde	5	5	...	...	46 452[3]	59 023[3]	...	...	48.1	60.5	...	...
Indonesia Indonésie	81	172	...	...	4 975	4 713	...	...	24.5	22.8	...	...
Jordan Jordanie	8	8	5	5	350[1]	352[1]	...	...	57.1	75.4	...	...
Kyrgyzstan Kirghizistan	...	...	3	3	...	...	...	...	...	...	...	...

14
Daily newspapers [*cont.*]
Journaux quotidiens [*suite*]

Country or area Pays ou zone	Number of titles Nombre de titres				Total average circulation (thousands) Diffusion moyenne (en milliers)				Circulation per 1000 inhabitants Diffusion pour 1000 habitants			
	1997	1998	1999	2000	1997	1998	1999	2000	1997	1998	1999	2000
Mongolia Mongolie	...	3	5	5	...	...	...	...	...	...	...	...
Myanmar Myanmar	4	4	...	...	420[1]	400[1]	...	...	9.6	8.6	...	...
Oman Oman	5	5	...	...	...	...	...	...	...	...	...	...
Pakistan Pakistan	359	...	352	...	3 915	...	5 559	...	27.2	...	40.4	...
Turkey Turquie	980	960	560	542	...	...	...	...	...	...	...	...
Turkmenistan Turkménistan	...	...	2	2	...	...	26	32	...	...	5.7	6.7
Europe • Europe												
Andorra Andorre	...	...	2	2								
Austria Autriche	17	17	...	...	...	...	...	...	...	...	...	...
Belarus Bélarus	19	20	...	...	1 437[1]	1 559[1]	...	...	138.8	151.9	...	...
Bulgaria Bulgarie	...	...	52	...	...	...	936	...	...	...	116.4	...
Croatia Croatie	...	...	14	14	...	...	...	...	...	...	...	...
Czech Republic République tchèque	99	103	104	103	...	...	...	...	...	...	...	...
Denmark Danemark	37	36	33	33	1 615	1 613	1 558	1 507	307.3	305.1	293.7	283.3
Estonia Estonie	15	16	17	16	...	...	...	...	...	...	...	...
Finland Finlande	56	56	56	55	2 336	2 343	2 331[2]	2 304[2]	454.4	454.6	451.4	445.5
Germany Allemagne	402	398	...	...	25 200	25 000	...	...	307.1	304.8	...	...
Gibraltar Gibraltar	1	1	...	...	6	6	...	...	234.2	...	...	...
Greece Grèce	...	207	...	...	...	...	...	...	...	...	...	...
Hungary Hongrie	33	33	...	...	4 660[1]	4 688[1]	...	...	458.9	465.5	...	...
Iceland Islande	4	3	3	...	100[1]	...	93	...	365.6	...	335.7	...
Latvia Lettonie	...	...	27	26	...	...	354	327[2]	...	...	145.4	135.1
Lithuania Lituanie	23	23	29	22	113[1]	123[1]	126[1]	108[1]	30.6	33.1	33.9	29.3
Malta Malte	5	4	...	...	...	...	...	...	...	...	...	...
Norway Norvège	82	81	82	81	2 598	2 592	2 591	2 545	591.0	585.4	582.4	569.5
Poland Pologne	55	52	46	42	4 194[1]	4 168[1]	3 870[1]	3 928[1]	108.4	107.9	100.2	101.7
Portugal Portugal	31	...	...	...	316[1]	...	...	...	32.0	...	...	...
Republic of Moldova République de Moldova	5	6	6	6	480[1]	660[1]	...	...	109.7	153.0	...	...
Romania Roumanie	74	95	139	* 145	...	...	...	...	...	...	...	...
San Marino Saint-Marin	3	3	...	...	2[1]	2	...	...	70.4	...	...	...
Slovakia Slovaquie	21	19	24	16	1 324[1]	939[1]	851[1]	705[1]	246.4	174.2	157.8	130.6
Slovenia Slovénie	5	5	5	5	343[1]	340[1]	341[1]	335[1]	171.9	170.5	171.3	168.5
Spain Espagne	...	...	84	87	...	...	4 191	4 003	...	...	105.1	100.3

14
Daily newspapers [*cont.*]
Journaux quotidiens [*suite*]

Country or area Pays ou zone	Number of titles Nombre de titres				Total average circulation (thousands) Diffusion moyenne (en milliers)				Circulation per 1000 inhabitants Diffusion pour 1000 habitants			
	1997	1998	1999	2000	1997	1998	1999	2000	1997	1998	1999	2000
Sweden Suède	94	94	94	90	3 881	3 820	3 750	3 627	438.2	431.3	423.7	410.2
Switzerland Suisse	78	74	81	...	2 680	2 620	2 676	...	369.6	365.5	373.2	...
TFYR of Macedonia L'ex–R.y. de Macédoine	4	4	5	6	88	106	109	108	44.2	52.7	53.9	53.3
Ukraine Ukraine	53	41	67	61	3 495[1]	5 059[1]	6 107[1]	8 683[1]	68.4	100.2	122.1	175.2
Occania • Océanie												
New Zealand Nouvelle–Zélande	28	28	28	28	821	786	1 382	1 369	218.4	211.5	368.8	362.4

Source:
United Nations Educational, Scientific and Cultural Organization
(UNESCO) Institute for Statistics, Montreal, the UNESCO
statistics database.

1   Total copies printed.
2   Data do not include non–members of the Finnish Newspaper
     Association.
3   Includes tri–weeklies and bi–weeklies.

Source:
L'Institut de statistique de l'Organisation des Nations Unies pour
l'éducation, la science et la culture (UNESCO), Montréal, la base
de données de l'UNESCO.

1 Nombre d'exemplaires imprimés.
2 Les données ne comprennent pas celles qui ne sont pas membres de
  l'Association de journaux finlandais.
3 Y compris les journaux paraissant deux ou tois fois par semaine.

15
Non-daily newspapers and periodicals
Journaux non quotidiens et périodiques

Country or area Pays ou zone	Non-daily newspapers Journaux non quotidiens				Periodicals Périodiques			
			Circulation Diffusion				Circulation Diffusion	
	Year [§] Année [§]	Number Nombre	Total (000)	Per 1000 inhabitants Pour 1000 habitants	Year [§] Année [§]	Number Nombre	Total (000)	Per 1000 inhabitants Pour 1000 habitants
Africa · Afrique								
Algeria	1997	64	1 266	43		...	...	...
Algérie	1998	82	909	31	1998	106	...	...
Benin	1996	4	* 66	* 12		...	...	...
Bénin	1999	2	44	7	1999	62	110	18
Botswana	1995	5	79	53		...	...	...
Botswana	1996	3	51	33		...	...	...
Burkina Faso								
Burkina Faso	1995	9	42	4		...	...	...
Burundi	1997	5	8	1		...	...	...
Burundi	1998	5	8	1		...	...	...
Cameroon								
Cameroun	1996	7	152	11		...	...	...
Cape Verde	1995	6	21	55		...	...	...
Cap–Vert	1996	4	* 20	* 51		...	...	...
Central African Republic	1995	1	2	1		...	...	...
Rép. centrafricaine	1996	7	13	4		...	...	...
Chad	1997	14	...	...	1997	35		
Tchad	1998	10	...	...	1998	32		
Comoros								
Comores	1995	1	0	0		...	...	...
Congo								
Congo	1995	15	38	15		...	...	...
Côte d'Ivoire	1995	13	235	17		...	...	...
Côte d'Ivoire	1996	15	251	18		...	...	...
Djibouti								
Djibouti	1995	1	1	1		...	...	...
Egypt	1998	47	1 448	22	1998	237	2 223	34
Egypte	1999	45	1 371	21	1999	235	2 773	42
Ethiopia	1997	85	338	6	1999	15	40	1
Ethiopie	1998	78	402	7	2000	15	40	1
Gambia								
Gambie	1996	4	* 6	* 5				
Guinea								
Guinée	1996	1	20	3		...	...	...
Kenya	1995	7	484	18		...	...	...
Kenya	1996	7	524	19		...	...	...
Lesotho								
Lesotho	1996	7	74	37		...	...	...
Madagascar								
Madagascar	1995	31	* 90	* 7		...	...	...
Malawi								
Malawi	1996	4	* 120	* 12		...	...	...
Mauritius	1999	31	125	108	1999	43	43	37
Maurice	2000	33	150	129	2000	64	65	56
Morocco	1999	581	3 724	127	1999	586	4 329	148
Maroc	2000	507[1]	4 108	137	2000	364	4 956	166
Mozambique	1997	40	206	11	1997	32	83	5
Mozambique	1998	40	206	12	1998	32	83	5
Namibia								
Namibie	1996	2	16	10		...	...	...
Niger	1995	5	15	2		...	...	...
Niger	1996	5	14	1		...	...	...
Rwanda	1999	13	11	2		...	...	...
Rwanda	2000	8	13	2		...	...	...
Saint Helena	1996	1	2	246		...	...	...
Sainte Hélène	1998	1	...	...	1998	4	...	...
Senegal	1995	6	37	4				
Sénégal	1997	139	...	...	1995	9	...	...

15
Non–daily newspapers and periodicals [*cont.*]
Journaux non quotidiens et périodiques [*suite*]

Country or area Pays ou zone	Non–daily newspapers Journaux non quotidiens				Periodicals Périodiques			
			Circulation Diffusion				Circulation Diffusion	
	Year[§] Année[§]	Number Nombre	Total (000)	Per 1000 inhabitants Pour 1000 habitants	Year[§] Année[§]	Number Nombre	Total (000)	Per 1000 inhabitants Pour 1000 habitants
Seychelles	1995	3	7	93		...	...	...
Seychelles	1996	3	7	92		...	...	...
Somalia						...	...	...
Somalie	1996	2	...	...		...	...	...
South Africa	1996	48	1 110	29		...	...	...
Afrique du Sud	1997	48	1 287	33		...	...	...
Sudan	1997	11	5 644	204	1997	54	68	2
Soudan	1998	11	5 644	189	1998	54	68	2
Togo	1999	41	4 032	919	1999	23	2 256	514
Togo	2000	52	5 184	1 145	2000	24	2 496	551
Tunisia	1996	25	900	99	1996	166	1 751	193
Tunisie	2000	29	940	99	2000	182	525	55
Uganda	1995	4	74	4		...	...	...
Ouganda	1996	4	67	3		...	...	...
America, North · Amérique du Nord								
Antigua and Barbuda								
Antigua–et–Barbuda	1996	4	...	...		...	...	...
Belize								
Belize	1996	6	80	363		...	...	...
Bermuda	1999	3	...	...				
Bermudes	2000	3	...	...	1995	13	169	2 729
British Virgin Islands								
Iles Vierges brit.	1996	2	4	182		...	...	...
Canada								
Canada	1996	* 1 071	* 21 235	* 709		...	...	...
Costa Rica	1999	24	...	...	1999	142	...	...
Costa Rico	2000	27	...	...	2000	306	...	...
Cuba	1996	24	456	41	1995	12	218	20
Cuba	2000	31	923	82	1996	14	385	35
Dominica								
Dominique	1996	1	5	64		...	...	...
Dominican Republic	1999	8	215	26	1999	180	...	...
République dominicaine	2000	8	215	26	2000	188	...	...
El Salvador	1995	6	48	8		...	...	...
El Salvador	1996	6	52	9		...	...	...
Grenada	1995	4	13	136	1995	4	90	975
Grenade	1996	4	14	151	1996	4	90	971
Mexico	1999	27	805	8	1999	296	19 592	201
Mexique	2000	26	614	6	2000	278	20 362	206
Montserrat	1997	1	1	93		...	...	...
Montserrat	1998	1	...	...		...	...	...
Saint Kitts and Nevis								
Saint Kitts–et–Nevis	1996	2	10	239		...	...	...
Saint Lucia	1995	5	34	236		...	...	...
Sainte Lucie	1996	5	34	233		...	...	...
Saint Pierre and Miquelon								
Saint–Pierre et Miquelon	1996	1	2	293				
Saint Vincent and the Grenadines	1995	6	34	305	1995	6	...	...
Saint–Vincent–et–les Grenadines	1996	6	34	302	1996	6	...	...
Trinidad and Tobago								
Trinité–et–Tobago	1996	5	* 150	* 118		...	...	...
Turks and Caicos Islands								
Iles Turques et Caïques	1996	1	5	344		...	...	...
United States								
Etats–Unis	1995	* 9 728	* 70 000	* 262		...	...	...
America, South · Amérique du Sud								
Argentina	1997	...	2 041	57	1999	119	5 748	157
Argentine	1998	...	1 933	54	2000	113	4 936	133

15
Non-daily newspapers and periodicals [*cont.*]
Journaux non quotidiens et périodiques [*suite*]

	Non-daily newspapers Journaux non quotidiens				Periodicals Périodiques			
			Circulation Diffusion				Circulation Diffusion	
Country or area Pays ou zone	Year[§] Année[§]	Number Nombre	Total (000)	Per 1000 inhabitants Pour 1000 habitants	Year[§] Année[§]	Number Nombre	Total (000)	Per 1000 inhabitants Pour 1000 habitants
Bolivia	1997	10	8 626	1 110	...	...	...	...
Bolivie	1998	10	7 884	991	...	...	...	...
Brazil	1997	892	...	...	...	...	...	...
Brésil	1998	1 251	...	...	...	...	...	...
Chile	1995	68	...	...	...	...	...	...
Chili	1996	63	...	...	...	...	...	...
Colombia	1996	5[3]	65	2	...	...	...	...
Colombie	1997	5[3]	71	2	...	...	...	...
Ecuador	1997	34	150	13	1999	27	1 086	88
Equateur	1998	45	175	14	2000	27	1 086	86
Falkland Islands (Malvinas)	1999	1	...	...	...	...	...	...
Iles Falkland (Malvinas)	2000	1	...	...	...	...	...	...
Guyana	1999	4	48	63	1999	24	131	173
Guyana	2000	4	48	63	2000	24	131	172
Peru								
Pérou	1998	7	...	...	1998	43	...	...
Suriname	1997	9	65	157	1997	4	4	8
Suriname	1998	9	63	153	1998	8	8	20
Uruguay	1995	76	...	...	1995	607	...	...
Uruguay	1996	62	...	...	1996	601	...	...
Asia · Asie								
Armenia	1999	95	168	44	1998	75	220	58
Arménie	2000	83	283	75	2000	41	114	30
Azerbaijan	1995	238	...	...	1997	34	57	7
Azerbaïdjan	1996	251	...	...	1998	38	50	6
Bangladesh								
Bangladesh	1997	...	...	...	1997	274	30 216	246
Bhutan								
Bhoutan	1996	1	11	6	...	...	...	...
Brunei Darussalam								
Brunéi Darussalam	1996	1	45	149	...	...	...	...
China ††								
Chine ††	1995	1 049[2]	125 512	103	...	...	...	...
China, Hong Kong SAR	1995	8	...	...	...	...	...	...
Chine, Hong-Kong RAS	1996	11	...	...	...	...	...	...
China, Macao SAR	1999	8	24	54	1999	169	...	...
Chine, Macao RAS	2000	7	20	44	2000	188	...	...
Cyprus	1999	33	188	242	1999	45	360	463
Chypre	2000	38	200	255	2000	50	372	475
Georgia					1999	122	331	63
Georgie	1999	122	331	63	2000	149	4 780	908
India	1997	36 661	59 256	61	...	...	...	...
Inde	1998	38 607	67 826	69	...	...	...	...
Indonesia	1997	90	4 711[4]	23	1997	114	4 390	22
Indonésie	1998	433	7 838	38	1998	266	4 156	20
Iran, Islamic Rep. of								
Iran, Rép. islamique d'	1999	843	152 534	2 203	1996	721	5 559	88
Japan	1996	6	...	...	1995	3 116	...	...
Japon	1997	6	...	...	1996	3 257	...	...
Jordan	1999	17	...	...	1997	256	144	23
Jordanie	2000	20	...	...	1998	270	148	32
Korea, Rep. of	1995	4	...	...	1995	9 570	...	...
Corée, Rép. dé	1996	4	...	...	1996	7 800	...	...
Kuwait	1995	57	...	...	...	...	...	...
Koweït	1996	78	...	...	...	...	...	...
Kyrgyzstan	1999	164	425	88	1999	33	95	20
Kirghizistan	2000	181	329	67	2000	36	170	35
Lebanon								
Liban	2000	7	9 340	2 671	2000	49	7 038	2 013
Malaysia	1996	44	1 424	69	...	...	...	...
Malaisie	1997	3	312	15	...	...	...	...

15
Non–daily newspapers and periodicals [cont.]
Journaux non quotidiens et périodiques [suite]

Country or area Pays ou zone	Year § Année §	Number Nombre	Total (000)	Per 1000 inhabitants Pour 1000 habitants	Year § Année §	Number Nombre	Total (000)	Per 1000 inhabitants Pour 1000 habitants
	Non–daily newspapers Journaux non quotidiens		Circulation Diffusion		Periodicals Périodiques		Circulation Diffusion	
Mongolia	1999	...	...	...	1999	27	177	70
Mongolie	2000	...	...		2000	38	85	33
Myanmar					1997	54	4 483	102
Myanmar	1998	...	...	...	1998	38	3 397	73
Nepal	1997	2 144	...	...	1997	2 312	...	...
Népal	1998	2 288	...	...	1998	2 463	...	...
Occupied Palestinian Territory	1999	10	1 617	526	1999	57	2 244	730
Territoire palestinien occupé	2000	13	2 058	645	2000	62	1 854	581
Oman	1995	23	...	...	1997	29	...	...
Oman	1996	23	...	...	1998	29	...	...
Pakistan	1997	681	...	...				
Pakistan	1999	560	1 782	13	1999	559	1 713	12
Philippines	1995	243	153	2		...	...	
Philippines	1997	47	199	3		...	...	
Qatar	1995	* 1	* 7	* 12		...	...	
Qatar	1996	* 1	* 7	* 13		...	...	
Saudi Arabia	1999	2	47 608	2 423		...	...	
Arabie saoudite	2000	2	52 683	2 589		...	...	
Singapore	1996	2				...	...	
Singapour	1997	2	68	20		...	...	
Sri Lanka	1996	40	2 665	147		...	...	
Sri Lanka	1997	29	1 320	72		...	...	
Syrian Arab Republic	1995	5	55	4		...	...	
Rép. arabe syrienne	1996	5	57	4		...	...	...
Tajikistan	1995	92	399	69	1995	17	34	6
Tadjikistan	1996	73	153	26	1996	11	131	22
Thailand	1995	280	1 850	32		...	...	
Thaïlande	1996	320	2 550	43		...	...	
Turkey	1999	610	...	...	1999	1 572	...	...
Turquie	2000	688	...	...	2000	1 635	...	...
Turkmenistan	1999	23	294	63	1999	20	36	8
Turkmenistan	2000	22	338	71	2000	20	47	10
Uzbekistan	1995	338	1 507	67	1995	76	754	34
Ouzbékistan	1996	350	1 404	61	1996	81	684	30
Viet Nam	1995	184	2 910	39	1995	285	2 305	31
Viet Nam	1996	214	4 023	54	1996	338	2 710	36
Europe · Europe								
Andorra					1999	38	...	...
Andorre	2000	...	...	...	2000	39	...	...
Austria	1997	125	...	...	1997	2 637	...	...
Autriche	1998	155	...	...	1998	2 685	...	...
Belarus	1997	539	7 823	756	1997	302	1 647	159
Bélarus	1998	560	8 973	875	1998	318	1 687	164
Bosnia and Herzegovina Bosnie–et–Herzégovine	1996	...	...	...	1996	70	18	5
Bulgaria	1996	864⁵	5 765	682	1996	760	1 717	203
Bulgarie	1999	527	2 644	329	1999	619	1 247	155
Croatia	1999	234	...	...	1999	1 827	...	...
Croatie	2000	229	...	...	2000	2 003	...	...
Czech Republic	1999	675	...	...	1999	2 277	...	...
République tchèque	2000	712	...	...	2000	2 437	...	...
Denmark	1999	10	1 482	279	1999	127	...	...
Danemark	2000	10	1 415	266	2000	117	...	...
Estonia	1999	88	...	...	1999	930	1 972	1 398
Estonie	2000	93	...	...	2000	956	2 144	1 539
Finland	1999	151⁶	942	182	1999	5 777	...	...
Finlande	2000	149⁶	924	179	2000	5 711	...	...
France France	1995	278	1 714	30		...	...	...
Germany	1997	26	2 043	25		...	...	...
Allemagne	1998	33	6 500	79		...	...	...

15
Non-daily newspapers and periodicals [*cont.*]
Journaux non quotidiens et périodiques [*suite*]

Country or area Pays ou zone	Non-daily newspapers Journaux non quotidiens				Periodicals Périodiques			
			Circulation Diffusion				Circulation Diffusion	
	Year [§] Année [§]	Number Nombre	Total (000)	Per 1000 inhabitants Pour 1000 habitants	Year [§] Année [§]	Number Nombre	Total (000)	Per 1000 inhabitants Pour 1000 habitants
Gibraltar	1998	3	...	...		...	...	...
Gibraltar	1999	2	...	...		...	...	...
Holy See	1999	...	...	...	1999	2	...	...
Saint–Siège	2000	...	...	...	2000	2	...	...
Hungary	1996	79	5 824	571	1995	642	8 822	863
Hongrie	1997	121	5 209	513	1996	520	9 867	968
Iceland	1998	68	...	...	1998	880	...	...
Islande	1999	22	57	206	1999	* 938	...	...
Ireland	1996	77	1 561	430		...	...	...
Irlande	1997	61	916	250		...	...	...
Italy								
Italie	1995	274	2 132	37		...	...	...
Latvia	1999	208	1 751	719	1999	262	1 391	571
Lettonie	2000	201	1 754	725	2000	325	1 856	767
Liechtenstein								
Liechtenstein	1996	1	14	449		...		
Lithuania	1999	...	...	...	1999	720	...	
Lituanie	2000	...	...	...	2000	753		
Luxembourg	1996	5	70	170				
Luxembourg	1997	1	10	24		...	...	...
Malta	1997	11	...	...	1997	502	...	...
Malte	1998	11	...	...	1998	523	...	...
Monaco	1995	5	50	1 572	1995	5	50	1 572
Monaco	1996	5	50	1 554	1996	5	50	1 554
Netherlands	1996	63[3]	590	38		...	...	...
Pays–Bas	1997	58[3]	564	36		...	...	...
Norway	1999	74[8]	374	84		...	...	...
Norvège	2000	70	367	82		...	...	...
Poland	1999	28	722	19	1999	5 518	65 997	1 709
Pologne	2000	24	583	15	2000	5 468	67 820	1 757
Portugal	1997	248	1 473	149	1996	727	8 692	882
Portugal	1999	557	3 282	328	1999	1 065	15 762	1 577
Republic of Moldova	1999	177	933	217	1999	88	238	55
République de Moldova	2000	170	915	213	2000	99	258	60
Romania	1999	315	...	...	1999	1 589	...	...
Roumanie	2000	320	...	...	2000	1 608	...	...
Russian Federation	1995	4 809	103 542	699	1995	2 471	299 271	2 021
Fédération de Russie	1996	4 596	98 558	666	1996	2 751	387 832	2 623
San Marino	1997	8	12	470	1997	15	9	352
Saint–Marin	1998	8	...	...	1998	17	...	...
Serbia and Montenegro	1995	573	3 781	358	1995	590	...	...
Serbie–et–Monténégro	1996	602	3 934	371	1996	620	...	...
Slovakia	1999	445	4 201	779	1999	821	10 196	1 890
Slovaquie	2000	435	2 651	491	2000	1 014	13 823	2 560
Slovenia	1999	221	...	...	1999	1 304	...	...
Slovénie	2000	200	...	...	2000	1 278	...	...
Spain	1997	10[9]	4 971	125		...	...	...
Espagne	1999	11	5 371	135		...	...	...
Sweden	1999	70	370	42	1999	374	21 632	2 444
Suède	2000	71	382	43	2000	389	22 112	2 501
Switzerland	1998	119	1 144	160				
Suisse	1999	120	1 190	166		...	...	...
TFYR of Macedonia	1999	29	102	50				
L'ex–R.y. Macédoine	2000	33	121	59	2000	116	3 465	1 704
Ukraine	1999	2 572	36 106	722	1999	1 374	5 090	102
Ukraine	2000	2 606	38 985	786	2000	1 245	3 988	80
United Kingdom	1996	478[3]	6 220	106		...	...	...
Royaume–Uni	1997	462[3]	5 840	100		...	...	...
Oceania · Océanie								
American Samoa								
Samoa américaines	1996	1	3	48		...	...	...

15
Non-daily newspapers and periodicals [*cont.*]
Journaux non quotidiens et périodiques [*suite*]

| Country or area
Pays ou zone | Non-daily newspapers
Journaux non quotidiens | | | | Periodicals
Périodiques | | | |
| | | | Circulation
Diffusion | | | | Circulation
Diffusion | |
	Year [§] Année [§]	Number Nombre	Total (000)	Per 1000 inhabitants Pour 1000 habitants	Year [§] Année [§]	Number Nombre	Total (000)	Per 1000 inhabitants Pour 1000 habitants
Australia	1996	98	383	21		...	...	...
Australie	1997	96	370	20		...	...	...
Cook Islands	1995	1	1	53		...	...	...
Iles Cook	1996	1	1	53		...	...	...
Marshall Islands								
Iles Marshall	1996	1	10	177		...	...	...
New Zealand	1997	...	...	...	1997	164	4 524	1 203
Nouvelle-Zélande	1998	...	...	...	1998	188	5 500	1 480
Niue								
Nioué	1996	1	* 2	* 941				
Norfolk Island								
Ile Norfolk	1996	1	...	...		...	...	...
Solomon Islands								
Iles Salomon	1996	3	9	23		...	...	...
Tuvalu								
Tuvalu	1996	1	0	28		...	...	...
Vanuatu								
Vanuatu	1996	2	4	23		...	...	...

Source:
United Nations Educational, Scientific and Cultural
Organization (UNESCO) Institute for Statistics, Montreal,
the UNESCO statistics database.

[§] Data prior to 1997 may not be comparable to data
   for later years due to UNESCO's use of
   different sources.

1 Data do not include non-dailies issued 2 or 3 times a week.

2 Data on non-dailies include daily newspapers.

3 Data refer to regional/local non-dailies only.

4 Includes Sunday issues.
5 Data include regional editions.
6 Data do not include non-members of the Finnish Newspaper
   Association (non members: 13 non-dailies in 1999 and 9 in
   2000).
7 Data refer to newspapers published 1 to 3 times a week.

8 Data do not include Sunday issues
9 Data refer to weekly newspapers only.

Source:
L'Institut de statistique de l'Organisation des Nations Unies pour
l'éducation, la science et la culture (UNESCO), Montréal, la base
de données de l'UNESCO.

[§] Les données antérieures à 1997 peuvent n'être pas comparables
   à celles des années suivantes, l'UNESCO ayant utilisé des
   sources différentes.

1 Les données n'incluent pas les parutions non-quotidiennes publiées
   2 à 3 fois par semaine.
2 Les données relatives aux journaux non-quotidiens comprennent les
   journaux quotidiens.
3 Les données se réfèrent aux journaux non-quotidiens régionaux/
   locaux seulement.
4 Inclut les parutions du dimanche.
5 Les données comprennent les éditions régionales.
6 Les données n'incluent pas les non-membres de l'Association
   finnoise de journaux (non-membres: 13 parutions non-
   quotidiennes en 1999 et 9 en 2000).
7 Les données concernent les journaux paraissant 1 à 3 fois par
   semaine.
8 Les données n'incluent pas les parutions du dimanche.
9 Les données ne concernent que les journaux hebdomadaires.

16
Cinemas: number, seating capacity and annual attendance
Cinémas: nombre d'établissements, nombre de sièges, et fréquentation annuelle

Country or area Pays ou zone	Year Année	Number Nombre	Seating capacity Sièges		Annual attendance Fréquentation annuelle	
			Thousands Milliers	Per 1000 Pour 1000	Millions	Per capita Pour habitant
Africa • Afrique						
Algeria	1985	216	110.0	5.0	20.5	0.90
Algérie	1996	136	...	...	0.6	0.02
	1997	136	...	...	0.6	0.02
Benin	1993	23¹	9.4	1.9	0.7	0.10
Bénin	1996	3	2.5	0.5	0.3	0.06
	1997	3	2.5	0.4	0.3	0.05
Burkina Faso	1986	23	24.0	3.0	6.2	0.80
Burkina Faso	1996	35	55.0	5.1	4.7	0.44
	1997	35	55.0	5.0	4.9	0.45
Cameroon	1985	197¹	39.8	4.0	...	...
Cameroun	1990	230¹	38.9	3.4	...	...
	1991	232¹	39.9	3.4	...	...
Congo	1994	28¹	11.2	4.5	...	...
Congo	1995	30¹	4.4	1.7	...	...
Côte d'Ivoire	1992	60	70.0	5.6	7.9	0.60
Côte d'Ivoire	1993	60	70.0	5.5	7.3	0.60
Egypt	1991	149	126.0	2.2	16.5	0.30
Egypte	1994	138	106.0	1.7	12.9	0.20
	1996	122	96.1	1.5	10.6	0.17
Guinea	1985	29	61.2	12.3	2.6	0.50
Guinée	1990	88	46.4	8.1	4.4	0.80
	1991	80	41.0	6.8	3.9	0.60
Kenya	1993	42¹	7.0	0.3	5.8	0.20
Kenya	1998	20	6.6	0.2	0.6	0.02
	1999	20	6.6	0.2	0.9	0.03
Libyan Arab Jamahiriya	1998	27	14.4	2.8	2.5	0.50
Jamah. arabe libyenne	1999	27	14.4	2.8	2.9	0.56
Madagascar	1990	20	...	...	0.7	0.10
Madagascar	1991	11	...	...	0.4	0.00
Mauritius	1993	16	14.0	12.8	0.7	0.70
Maurice	1998	25	13.0	11.4	1.3	1.09
	1999	32	16.0	13.9	1.3	1.15
Morocco	1995	185	131.0	5.0	17.3	0.67
Maroc	1996	183	130.0	4.9	16.3	0.62
	1997	175	124.0	4.6	14.3	0.53
Rwanda	1980	10	3.1	0.6	0.3	0.10
Rwanda	1985	34	9.3	1.5	...	...
	1990	4	1.9	0.3	...	...
United Rep. of Tanzania	1986	31	16.4	0.7	4.2	0.20
Rép.–Unie de Tanzanie	1990	28	12.4	0.5	1.9	* 0.10
	1991	28	12.4	0.5	1.9	* 0.10
Zimbabwe	1991	24	12.2	1.2	1.8	0.20
Zimbabwe	1998	22	...	...	* 1.5	* 0.12
	1999	22	...	...	* 1.2	* 0.10
America, North • Amérique du Nord						
Barbados	1990	3	...	...	0.0	0.00
Barbade	1991	4	...	...	0.0	0.00
Bermuda	1998	4	...	...	...	...
Bermudes	1999	4	...	...	...	...
Canada	1996	...	...	...	92.0	3.07
Canada	1997	685	588.9	19.5	99.1	3.27
	1998	692	646.7	21.4	112.8	3.73
Costa Rica	1985	105	...	...	0.2	* 0.10
Costa Rica	1994	38	...	...	1.5	0.40
	1995	39	...	...	1.7	0.48
Cuba	1993	903¹	187.9	17.3	23.8	2.20
Cuba	1996	944	193.3	17.5	10.8	0.98
	1997	782	172.5	15.6	9.2	0.84

16
Cinemas: number, seating capacity and annual attendance [*cont.*]
Cinémas: nombre d'établissements, nombre de sièges et fréquentation annuelle [*suite*]

Country or area Pays ou zone	Year Année	Number Nombre	Seating capacity Sièges Thousands Milliers	Per 1000 Pour 1000	Annual attendance Fréquentation annuelle Millions	Per capita Pour habitant
El Salvador El Salvador	1995	33	...	...	...	...
Mexico	1997	1 842	...	...	95.0	1.01
Mexique	1998	2 313	627.3	6.5	112.6	1.18
	1999	2 320	624.1	6.4	120.0	1.23
Nicaragua	1998	6	1 800.0	0.4	0.7	0.15
Nicaragua	1999	10	2 700.0	0.5	1.2	0.24
United States	1998	...	...	...	1 390.0	5.01
Etats – Unis	1999	...	...	...	1 465.0	5.22
	2000	15 559	...	...	1 421.0	5.02

America, South · Amérique du Sud

Country or area Pays ou zone	Year Année	Number Nombre	Seating capacity Sièges Thousands Milliers	Per 1000 Pour 1000	Annual attendance Fréquentation annuelle Millions	Per capita Pour habitant
Argentina	1996	523	...	...	21.5	0.61
Argentine	1997	635	...	...	26.6	0.74
	1998	780	...	...	32.5	0.90
Bolivia	1997	72	...	...	1.2	0.15
Bolivie	1998	27	...	...	1.6	0.20
	1999	27	...	...	1.4	0.18
Brazil	1998	1 300	...	...	70.0	0.42
Brésil	1999	1 400	...	...	70.0	0.42
	2000	1 525	...	...	80.0	0.47
Chile	1992	* 133	* 75.9	* 5.5	8.0	* 0.60
Chili	1998	198	...	...	6.8	0.46
Colombia	1998	258	...	...	18.4	0.45
Colombie	1999	277	43.0	1.0	...	...
Ecuador	1986	118	110.0	11.8	11.1	1.20
Equateur	1990	161	77.6	7.6	7.8	0.80
	1991	134	75.3	7.2	6.8	0.60
Peru	1996	124	...	...	...	...
Pérou	1997	116	...	...	...	...
	1998	148	...	...	6.5	0.26
Suriname	1996	1	0.8	1.9	0.2	0.37
Suriname	1997	1	0.8	1.9	0.1	0.25
Venezuela	1996	220	1 387.0	62.2	6.2	0.28
Venezuela	1997	241	1 394.7	61.2	6.4	0.28
	1998	284	...	...	14.2	0.61

Asia · Asie

Country or area Pays ou zone	Year Année	Number Nombre	Seating capacity Sièges Thousands Milliers	Per 1000 Pour 1000	Annual attendance Fréquentation annuelle Millions	Per capita Pour habitant
Armenia	1993	577[1]	118.5	33.1	...	...
Arménie	1994	599[1]	124.9	34.9	...	...
	1995	599[1]	124.9	34.9	...	...
Azerbaijan	1997	234	37.6	4.9	0.2	0.03
Azerbaïdjan	1998	225	37.1	4.7	0.2	0.02
	1999	222	34.8	4.4	0.2	0.02
Bahrain	1980	6	4.0	11.5	...	...
Bahreïn	1985	6	4.0	9.7	1.1	2.60
	1989	6	3.2	6.7	0.6	1.30
China	1995	...	...	...	130.0	0.11
Chine	1996	...	...	...	140.0	0.11
	1998	...	...	...	...	...
China, Hong Kong SAR	1991	166	...	...	...	...
Chine, Hong Kong RAS	1994	186	99.9	16.4	35.0	5.70
	1995	184	94.8	15.2	28.0	4.50
China, Macao SAR	1998	...	5.0	11.5	0.2	0.41
Chine, Macao RAS	1999	...	5.0	11.4	0.2	0.35
Cyprus	1997	29	8.0	10.5	0.9	1.22
Chypre	1998	26	9.3	12.1	1.0	1.31
	1999	28	9.6	12.4	0.8	1.08
Georgia	1993	290[1]	106.8	19.9	30.4	5.70
Géorgie	1996	97	22.8	4.4	20.5	3.95
	1997	97	22.8	4.5	18.7	3.65
India	1996	21 848	...	...	3 380.0	3.56
Inde	1997	21 801	...	...	3 580.0	3.71
	1998	...	...	...	2 860.0	2.93

16
Cinemas: number, seating capacity and annual attendance [*cont.*]
Cinémas: nombre d'établissements, nombre de sièges et fréquentation annuelle [*suite*]

Country or area Pays ou zone	Year Année	Number Nombre	Seating capacity Sièges		Annual attendance Fréquentation annuelle	
			Thousands Milliers	Per 1000 Pour 1000	Millions	Per capita Pour habitant
Indonesia	1995	...	...	...	170.0	0.86
Indonésie	1996	1 009	674.4	3.4	180.0	0.90
	1997	1 009	674.4	3.3	190.0	0.93
Iran (Islamic Rep. of)	1993	277	171.4	2.9	29.0	0.50
Iran (Rép. islamique de)	1994	294	197.0	3.2	56.0	0.90
	1995	287	173.0	2.8	26.0	0.42
Iraq	1996	144	...	...	...	...
Iraq	1997	144	...	...	...	...
Israel	1992	241	71.1	14.2	...	...
Israël	1993	256	63.9	12.3	...	...
	1994	266	62.5	11.6	10.0	1.90
Japan	1997	1 884	...	...	140.7	1.12
Japon	1998	1 993	...	...	153.1	1.21
	1999	2 221	...	...	145.0	1.14
Jordan	1989	61	94.0	20.9	1.0	0.20
Jordanie	1992	35	...	...	0.2	0.00
	1993	35	...	...	0.2	0.00
Kazakhstan	1995	1 580	346.7	21.0	6.2	0.38
Kazakhstan	1996	1 720	...	...	3.4	0.21
	1997	1 129	...	...	1.0	0.06
Korea, Republic of	1997	241	...	...	47.5	1.04
Corée, République de	1998	507	182.0	4.0	50.2	1.09
	1999	588	195.0	4.2	54.7	1.18
Kuwait	1992	14	...	...	0.4	0.20
Kowëit	1993	7	...	...	0.7	0.40
	1994	6	...	...	0.8	0.50
Kyrgyzstan	1997	305	80.8	17.5	0.4	0.09
Kirghizistan	1998	296	...	...	0.4	0.09
	1999	293	...	...	0.3	0.07
Lao People's Dem. Rep.	1990	31[1]	6.6	1.6	1.4	0.30
Rép. dém. pop. lao	1991	31[1]	6.6	1.5	1.0	0.20
Lebanon	1997	25	35.6	11.3	35.6	11.31
Liban	1998	...	38.9	11.5	10.9	3.22
	1999	...	38.9	11.3	10.9	3.16
Malaysia	1997	106	37.6	1.8	16.1	0.77
Malaisie	1998	162	...	...	0.3	0.01
	1999	...	...	...	0.3	0.02
Mongolia	1980	520	...	...	15.3	9.20
Mongolie	1985	562	...	...	19.1	10.00
	1989	581	...	...	20.1	9.30
Myanmar	1991	163	127.2	3.1	...	...
Myanmar	1992	162	125.3	3.0	...	...
	1993	163	126.0	3.0	...	...
Oman	1996	2	902.0	0.4	0.3	0.11
Oman	1997	2	902.0	0.4	0.3	0.11
Pakistan	1997	652	...	...	9.7	0.07
Pakistan	1998	574	...	...	...	...
	1999	574	...	...	...	...
Qatar	1980	4	4.0	17.4	1.2	5.20
Qatar	1989	4	4.0	8.6	0.3	0.60
Singapore	1995	80	...	...	18.1	5.46
Singapour	1996	...	...	...	17.0	5.04
	1997	...	...	...	17.0	4.96
Sri Lanka	1985	318	201.0	12.5	36.5	2.30
Sri Lanka	1992	255	142.0	8.2	29.2	1.70
	1993	259	143.0	8.1	27.2	1.50
Syrian Arab Republic	1989	77	40.0	3.3	7.0	0.60
Rép. arabe syrienne	1992	56	24.8	1.9	4.0	0.30
	1993	55	23.8	1.8	3.9	0.30
Tajikistan	1993	916[1]	200.2	35.8	12.7	2.30
Tadjikistan	1994	514[1]	108.0	19.1	2.5	0.40
	1995	172	39.0	6.8	0.4	0.07

16

Cinemas: number, seating capacity and annual attendance [*cont.*]

Cinémas: nombre d'établissements, nombre de sièges et fréquentation annuelle [*suite*]

Country or area Pays ou zone	Year Année	Number Nombre	Seating capacity Sièges		Annual attendance Fréquentation annuelle	
			Thousands Milliers	Per 1000 Pour 1000	Millions	Per capita Pour habitant
Turkey	1996	300	115.0	1.8	9.5	0.15
Turquie	1997	344	118.0	1.9	11.3	0.18
	1998	...	...	...	31.5	0.49
Uzbekistan	1992	3 357	669.2	31.4	64.2	3.00
Ouzbékistan	1993	2 777	609.3	28.0	29.0	1.30
Viet Nam	1980	1 107[1]	...	...	288.9	5.40
Viet Nam	1985	1 394[1]	...	...	345.8	5.80
	1988	1 451[1]	...	...	240.0	3.80
Europe · Europe						
Austria	1997	441	73.2	9.0	13.7	1.69
Autriche	1998	...	...	...	15.2	1.88
	1999	...	...	...	15.0	1.86
Belarus	1993	4 168	744.3	71.8	29.5	2.80
Bélarus	1994	3 900	712.9	68.6	18.7	1.80
	1995	3 780	700.1	67.4	12.5	1.20
Belgium	1997	438	...	...	22.1	2.18
Belgique	1998	463	...	...	25.4	2.49
	1999	463	...	...	21.9	2.14
Bulgaria	1996	403	99.0	11.7	3.7	0.44
Bulgarie	1998	205	94.0	11.6	3.2	0.39
	1999	191	83.0	10.3	1.9	0.24
Croatia	1997	146	53.0	11.8	3.2	0.72
Croatie	1998	147	52.0	11.2	2.7	0.59
	1999	141	52.0	11.2	2.3	0.49
Czech Republic	1997	851	300.0	29.1	9.8	0.95
République tchèque	1998	832	290.0	28.2	9.2	0.90
	1999	823	292.0	28.4	8.4	0.81
Denmark	1997	321	51.0	9.7	10.8	2.06
Danemark	1998	167	50.6	9.6	11.0	2.08
	1999	169	52.0	9.8	10.9	2.06
Estonia	1997	200	...	...	1.0	0.66
Estonie	1998	...	...	...	1.1	0.74
	1999	...	...	...	0.9	0.62
Finland	1997	321	55.5	10.8	5.9	1.15
Finlande	1998	232	55.8	10.8	6.4	1.24
	1999	...	...	...	7.0	1.36
France	1997	3 331	942.0	16.1	148.1	2.53
France	1998	2 150	990.0	16.8	170.1	2.89
	1999	...	...	...	155.4	2.63
Germany	1997	4 182	772.0	9.4	143.1	1.74
Allemagne	1998	4 491	801.0	9.8	148.9	1.81
	1999	4 712	835.0	10.2	149.0	1.82
Gibraltar						
Gibraltar	1980	4	2.3	80.7	0.2	6.70
Greece	1997	...	...	...	11.6	1.10
Grèce	1998	...	...	...	12.4	1.17
	1999	...	...	...	13.0	1.23
Hungary	1997	652	121.0	11.9	16.6	1.63
Hongrie	1998	628	121.0	12.0	14.6	1.45
	1999	..	...	...	13.4	1.34
Iceland	1997	32	10.0	36.6	1.5	5.41
Islande	1998	45	9.0	32.8	1.5	5.51
	1999	46	9.0	32.5	1.5	5.53
Ireland	1997	...	...	...	11.5	3.14
Irlande	1998	...	...	...	12.4	3.33
	1999	...	...	...	12.4	3.30
Italy	1997	...	...	...	102.8	1.79
Italie	1998	4 603	...	...	119.6	2.08
	1999	...	...	...	104.9	1.82
Latvia	1997	118	23.0	9.3	1.3	0.52
Lettonie	1998	117	24.1	9.8	1.4	0.58
	1999	115	26.1	10.7	1.4	0.56

16
Cinemas: number, seating capacity and annual attendance [cont.]
Cinémas: nombre d'établissements, nombre de sièges et fréquentation annuelle [suite]

Country or area Pays ou zone	Year Année	Number Nombre	Seating capacity Sièges		Annual attendance Fréquentation annuelle	
			Thousands Milliers	Per 1000 Pour 1000	Millions	Per capita Pour habitant
Lithuania	1997	124	28.2	7.6	0.5	0.14
Lituanie	1998	113	26.8	7.2	1.6	0.42
	1999	105	26.1	7.1	1.8	0.48
Luxembourg	1997	26	5.3	12.7	1.2	2.84
Luxembourg	1998	21	4.5	10.5	1.4	3.32
	1999	21	4.5	10.4	1.3	3.05
Malta	1990	10	7.0	19.8	0.3	0.70
Malte	1991	10	7.0	19.6	0.3	0.70
	1992	10	7.0	19.3	0.3	0.80
Monaco	1980	3	1.4	52.7	0.1	3.80
Monaco	1990	4	1.6	53.4	0.1	3.70
Netherlands	1997	444	88.8	5.7	18.9	1.21
Pays−Bas	1998	461	...	...	20.1	1.28
	1999	465	...	...	18.6	1.18
Norway	1997	631	90.1	20.5	10.9	2.49
Norvège	1998	604	88.0	19.9	11.5	2.60
	1999	605	89.0	20.0	11.4	2.55
Poland	1997	686	200.0	5.2	24.3	0.63
Pologne	1998	686	201.0	5.2	20.3	0.53
	1999	695	211.0	5.5	27.5	0.71
Portugal	1997	595	97.1	9.8	* 13.5	1.37
Portugal	1998	516	180.0	18.0	14.8	1.49
	1999	537	143.0	14.3	* 15.2	* 1.52
Republic of Moldova	1997	50	23.0	5.3	0.2	0.05
République de Moldova	1998	48	28.8	6.7	0.2	0.04
	1999	48	28.8	6.7	0.1	0.02
Romania	1997	469	149.0	6.6	9.5	0.42
Roumanie	1998	330	110.0	4.9	6.8	0.30
	1999	331	129.0	5.7	4.2	0.19
Russian Federation	1997	1 746	778.9	5.3	16.2	0.11
Fédération de Russie	1998	1 568	691.0	4.7	20.2	0.14
	1999	1 416	613.0	4.2	19.1	0.13
San Marino	1995	2	1.8	72.3	0.1	2.05
Saint−Marin	1996	3	1.8	70.6	0.1	2.69
	1997	3	1.9	74.4	0.1	2.97
Serbia and Montenegro	1997	195	80.0	7.5	5.4	0.50
Serbie−et−Monténégro	1998	164	70.0	6.6	5.3	0.50
	1999	165	70.5	6.7	3.9	0.37
Slovakia	1997	296	83.6	15.6	4.0	0.75
Slovaquie	1998	296	83.5	15.5	4.1	0.76
	1999	335	95.3	17.7	3.0	0.56
Slovenia	1997	91	27.0	13.5	2.5	1.25
Slovénie	1998	90	26.0	13.0	2.6	1.29
	1999	85	24.0	12.1	2.0	0.99
Spain	1997	2 530	...	...	101.4	2.56
Espagne	1998	3 025	...	...	112.1	2.81
	1999	3 354	...	...	131.3	3.29
Sweden	1997	1 164	435.0	49.1	15.2	1.72
Suède	1998	839	198.9	22.5	15.8	1.79
	1999	1 167	...	...	15.8	1.79
Switzerland	1997	502	110.9	15.3	15.6	2.14
Suisse	1998	499	191.0	26.6	15.9	2.22
	1999	384	230.8	32.2	15.4	2.15
TFYR of Macedonia	1997	37	10.0	5.0	0.5	0.23
L'ex−R.Y. Macédoine	1998	23	9.0	4.5	0.6	0.28
	1999	30	12.0	5.9	0.5	0.24
Ukraine	1997	10 768	2 477.0	48.5	7.3	0.14
Ukraine	1998	9 040	2 088.1	41.4	5.3	0.11
	1999	7 795	1 837.4	36.7	5.1	0.10
United Kingdom	1997	...	...	...	139.3	2.38
Royaume−Uni	1998	...	...	...	135.4	2.29
	1999	...	...	...	139.5	2.35

16
Cinemas: number, seating capacity and annual attendance [*cont.*]
Cinémas: nombre d'établissements, nombre de sièges et fréquentation annuelle [*suite*]

Country or area Pays ou zone	Year Année	Number Nombre	Seating capacity Sièges		Annual attendance Fréquentation annuelle	
			Thousands Milliers	Per 1000 Pour 1000	Millions	Per capita Pour habitant
Oceania · Océanie						
Australia	1996	1 251	356.0	19.6	74.0	4.08
Australie	1997	1 422	387.0	21.1	76.0	4.15
	1998	...	...	...	80.0	4.27
New Zealand	1997	285	...	...	16.5	4.40
Nouvelle-Zélande	1998	290	...	...	16.3	4.38
	1999	315	...	...	16.8	4.47

Source:
United Nations Educational, Scientific and Cultural Organization (UNESCO) Institute for Statistics, Montreal, the UNESCO statistics database.

1   Including non-commercial units.

Source:
L'Institut de statistiques de l'Organisation des Nations Unies pour l'éducation, la science et la culture (UNESCO), Montréal, la base de données de l'UNESCO.

1   Y compris des établissements non commerciaux.

17

Cellular mobile telephone subscribers
Number

Abonnés au téléphone mobile
Nombre

Country or area Pays ou zone	1994	1995	1996	1997	1998	1999	2000	2001
Albania Albanie	0	0	2 300	3 300	5 600	11 008	29 791	392 650
Algeria Algérie	1 348	4 691	11 700	17 400	18 000	72 000	86 000	100 000
American Samoa Samoa américaines	1 200	2 000	2 500	2 550	2 650	2 377	...	...
Andorra Andorre	784	2 825	5 488	8 618	14 117	20 600	23 543	...
Angola Angola	1 824	1 994	3 298	7 052	9 820	24 000	25 806	86 500
Anguilla Anguilla	0	160	359	707	787	* 1 475	2 163	1 773
Antigua and Barbuda Antigua-et-Barbuda	...	...	1 300 [1]	* 1 400 [1]	*1 500 [1]	8 500 [1]	22 000 [1]	25 000 [2]
Argentina [3] Argentine [3]	241 163	340 743	568 000	1 588 000	2 530 000	4 434 000	6 049 963	6 974 939
Armenia Arménie	0	0	300	5 000	7 831	8 161	17 486	25 504
Aruba Aruba	...	1 718	3 000	3 402	5 380	12 000	15 000	53 000
Australia [4] Australie [4]	1 220 000	2 242 000	3 990 000	4 578 000	4 918 000	6 315 000	8 562 000	11 132 000
Austria Autriche	278 199	383 535	598 708	1 159 700	2 292 900	4 250 393	6 252 830	6 650 291
Azerbaijan Azerbaïdjan	500	6 000	17 000	40 000	65 000	370 000	430 000	621 000
Bahamas Bahamas	...	4 100	4 948	6 152	8 072	15 911	31 524	60 555
Bahrain Bahreïn	17 616	27 600	40 080	58 543	92 063	133 468	205 727	299 587
Bangladesh [4] Bangladesh [4]	1 104	2 500	4 000 [5]	26 000 [5]	75 000	149 000	279 000	520 000 [5]
Barbados [1] Barbade [1]	2 967	4 614	6 283	8 013	12 000	20 309	28 467	53 111
Belarus Bélarus	1 724	5 897	6 548	8 167	12 155	23 457	49 353	138 029
Belgium Belgique	128 071	235 258	478 172	974 494	1 756 287	3 186 602	5 335 851	7 690 000
Belize [1] Belize [1]	832	1 547	2 184	2 544	3 535	6 591	16 812	39 155
Benin Bénin	0	1 050	2 707	4 295	6 286	7 269	55 476	125 000 [5]
Bermuda Bermudes	5 127 [1]	6 324 [1]	7 980 [1]	* 10 276 [1]	12 572 [1]	...	...	13 333 [2]
Bolivia Bolivie	4 056	7 229	33 400	118 433	239 272	420 344	582 620	779 917
Bosnia and Herzegovina Bosnie-Herzégovine	0	0	1 500	9 000	25 181	52 607	93 386	233 534
Botswana [1] Botswana [1]	0	0	0	0	15 190	92 000	200 000	316 000

17

Cellular mobile telephone subscribers
Number *[cont.]*
Abonnés au téléphone mobile
Nombre *[suite]*

Country or area Pays ou zone	1994	1995	1996	1997	1998	1999	2000	2001
Brazil Brésil	574 009	1 285 533	2 498 154	4 550 000	7 368 218	15 032 698	23 188 171	28 745 769
British Virgin Islands [1] Iles Vierges britanniques [1]	...	...	1 200	...	...	...	...	...
Brunei Darussalam Brunéi Darussalam	15 623	35 881	43 524	45 000	49 129	66 000	95 000	137 000
Bulgaria Bulgarie	6 500	20 920	26 588	70 000	127 000	350 000	738 000	1 550 000
Burkina Faso Burkina Faso	0	0	525	1 503	2 730	5 036	25 245	75 000 [6]
Burundi Burundi	378	564	561	619	620	800	16 320	30 687 [5]
Cambodia Cambodge	10 239	14 100	23 098	33 556	61 345	89 117	130 547	223 458
Cameroon Cameroun	1 600	2 800	3 500	4 200	5 000	6 000	148 000	310 000 [7]
Canada Canada	1 865 779	2 589 780	3 497 779	4 265 778	5 365 459	6 911 038	8 751 338	10 862 000
Cape Verde Cap-Vert	0	0	0	20	1 020	8 068	19 729	31 507
Cayman Islands [1] Iles Caïmanes [1]	1 813	2 534	...	4 109	5 170	8 410	10 700	17 000
Central African Rep. Rép. centrafricaine	0	44	1 071	1 370	1 633	4 162	4 967	11 000
Chad Tchad	0	0	0	0	0	0	5 500	22 000
Chile Chili	115 691	197 314	319 474	409 740	964 248	2 260 687	3 401 525	5 271 565
China Chine	1 568 000	3 629 000	6 853 000	13 233 000	23 863 000	43 296 000	85 260 000	144 820 000
China, Hong Kong SAR [1] Chine, Hong Kong RAS [1]	484 823	798 373	1 361 861	2 229 862	3 174 369	4 275 048	5 447 346	5 776 360
China, Macao SAR Chine, Macao RAS	21 445	35 881	44 788	50 624	82 114	118 101	141 052	194 475
Colombia Colombie	86 805	274 590	522 857	1 264 763	1 800 229	1 966 535	2 256 801	3 265 261
Congo Congo	0	0	1 000	...	3 390	5 000	70 000	150 000
Cook Islands Iles Cook	0 [1]	0 [1]	182 [8]	196 [1]	285 [1]	506 [1]	552 [1]	942 [2]
Costa Rica Costa Rica	6 985	18 750	46 531	64 387	108 770	138 178	205 275	311 329
Côte d'Ivoire Côte d'Ivoire	0	0	13 549	36 000	91 212	257 134	472 952	728 545
Croatia Croatie	21 664	33 688	64 943	120 420	182 500	295 000	1 033 000	* 1 755 000
Cuba Cuba	1 152	1 939	2 427	2 994	4 056	5 136	6 536	8 579
Cyprus Chypre	22 938	44 453	70 781	91 968	116 429	151 649	218 324	314 355

17

Cellular mobile telephone subscribers
Number *[cont.]*
Abonnés au téléphone mobile
Nombre *[suite]*

Country or area Pays ou zone	1994	1995	1996	1997	1998	1999	2000	2001
Czech Republic République tchèque	30 429	48 900	200 315	526 339	965 476	1 944 553	4 346 009	6 947 151
Dem. Rep. of the Congo Rép. dém. du Congo	...	8 500	7 200 [5]	8 900 [5]	10 000 [5]	12 000 [5]	15 000 [5]	150 000 [5]
Denmark Danemark	503 500	822 264	1 316 592	1 444 016	1 931 101	2 628 585	3 363 552	3 960 165
Djibouti Djibouti	0	0	110	203	220	280	230	3 000
Dominica [1] Dominique [1]	0	0	461	* 556	650	* 800	* 1 200	...
Dominican Republic Rép. dominicaine	20 990	55 979	82 547	141 592	209 384	424 434	705 431	1 270 082
Ecuador Equateur	18 920	54 380	59 779	126 505	242 812	383 185	482 213	859 152
Egypt [4] Egypte [4]	7 371	7 368	7 369	65 378	90 786	480 974	1 359 900	2 793 800
El Salvador El Salvador	4 868	13 475	23 270	40 163	137 114	511 365	743 628	857 782
Equatorial Guinea Guinée équatoriale	0	0	61	300	297	600	5 000	15 000
Estonia Estonie	13 774	30 452	69 500	144 200	247 000	387 000	557 000	651 200
Ethiopia [4] Ethiopie [4]	0	0	0	0	0	6 740	17 757	27 500
Faeroe Islands Iles Féroé	1 960	2 558	3 265	4 701	6 516	10 761	16 971	...
Fiji Fidji	1 100	2 200	3 700	5 200	8 000	23 380	55 057	80 933
Finland Finlande	675 565	1 039 126	1 502 003	2 162 574	2 845 985	3 273 433	3 728 625	4 175 587
France France	883 000	1 302 496	2 462 700	5 817 300	11 210 100	21 433 500	29 052 360	35 922 270
French Guiana Guyane française	0	0	0	0	4 000	18 000	39 830	75 320
French Polynesia Polynésie française	0	1 150	2 719	5 427	11 060	21 929	39 900	67 300
Gabon Gabon	2 581	4 000	6 800	9 500	9 694	8 891	120 000	258 087
Gambia [1] Gambie [1]	812	1 442	3 096	4 734	5 048	5 307	* 5 600	55 085
Georgia Géorgie	0	150	2 300	30 000	60 000	133 243	194 741	301 327
Germany Allemagne	2 490 500	3 725 000	5 512 000	8 276 000	13 913 000	23 446 000	48 202 000	56 245 000
Ghana Ghana	3 336	6 200	12 766	21 866	41 753	70 026	130 045	193 773
Gibraltar Gibraltar	0	660	1 002	1 620	2 445	3 648	5 558	0
Greece Grèce	153 000	273 000	532 000	937 700	2 047 000	3 904 000	5 932 000	7 962 000

17

Cellular mobile telephone subscribers
Number *[cont.]*
Abonnés au téléphone mobile
Nombre *[suite]*

Country or area Pays ou zone	1994	1995	1996	1997	1998	1999	2000	2001
Greenland Groenland	964	2 052	4 122	6 481	8 899	13 521	15 977	16 747
Grenada Grenade	350	400	570	976	1 410	2 012	4 300	6 414
Guadeloupe Guadeloupe	0	0	...	...	14 227	88 080	169 840	292 520
Guam Guam	4 098	4 965	5 803	5 673	*12 837	20 000	27 200	32 600
Guatemala Guatemala	10 462	29 999	43 421	64 194	111 445	337 800	843 091	1 134 007
Guinea Guinée	812	950	950	2 868	21 567	25 182	42 112	55 670
Guyana Guyana	1 251	1 243	1 200	1 400	1 454	2 815	39 830	75 320
Haiti Haïti	0	0	0	0	10 000	25 000	55 000	91 500
Honduras Honduras	0	0	2 311	14 427	34 896	78 588	155 271	237 629
Hungary Hongrie	143 000	265 000	473 100	705 786	1 070 154	1 628 153	3 076 279	4 967 430
Iceland Islande	21 845	30 883	46 805	65 368	104 280	172 614	214 896	248 131
India [1] Inde [1]	0	76 680	327 967	881 839	1 195 400	1 884 311	3 577 095	6 431 520
Indonesia Indonésie	78 024	210 643	562 517	916 173	1 065 820	2 220 969	3 669 327	6 520 947
Iran (Islamic Rep. of) [9] Iran (Rép. islamique d') [9]	9 200	15 902	59 967	238 942	389 974	490 478	962 595	2 087 353
Ireland [1] Irlande [1]	88 000	158 000	288 600	545 000	946 000	1 677 000	2 461 000	2 970 000
Israel Israël	133 425	445 456	1 047 582	1 672 442	2 147 000	2 880 000	4 400 000	5 900 000
Italy Italie	2 240 000	3 923 000	6 422 000	11 737 904	20 489 000	30 296 000	42 246 000	51 246 000
Jamaica [1] Jamaïque [1]	26 106	45 138	54 640	65 995	78 624	144 388	366 952	*635 000
Japan [1,10] Japon [1,10]	4 331 369	11 712 137	26 906 511	38 253 893	47 307 592	56 845 594	66 784 374	74 819 158
Jordan Jordanie	1 446	12 400	16 100	45 037 [5]	82 429	118 417	388 949	866 000
Kazakhstan Kazakhstan	400	4 600	9 798	11 202	29 700	49 500	197 300	582 000
Kenya Kenya	1 990 [4]	2 279 [4]	2 826 [4]	6 767 [4]	10 756 [4]	23 757 [4]	127 404 [2]	600 000 [4]
Kiribati Kiribati	0	0	0	0	22	200	395	498
Korea, Republic of Corée, République de	960 258	1 641 293	3 180 989	6 878 786	14 018 612	23 442 724	26 816 398	29 045 596
Kuwait Koweït	85 195	117 609	151 063	210 000	250 000	300 000	476 000	877 920

17

Cellular mobile telephone subscribers
Number [cont.]
Abonnés au téléphone mobile
Nombre [suite]

Country or area Pays ou zone	1994	1995	1996	1997	1998	1999	2000	2001
Kyrgyzstan Kirghizistan	0	0	0	0	1 350	2 574	9 000	27 000
Lao People's Dem. Rep. Rép. dém. pop. lao	625	1 539	3 790	4 915	6 453	12 078	12 681	29 545
Latvia Lettonie	8 364	15 003	28 500	77 100	167 460	274 344	401 272	656 835
Lebanon [5] Liban [5]	0	120 000	198 000	373 900	505 300	627 000	743 000	800 000
Lesotho [1] Lesotho [1]	0	0	1 262	3 500	9 831	12 000	21 600	57 000
Liberia Libéria	0	0	0	0	0	0	1 500	2 000
Libyan Arab Jamah. Jamah. arabe libyenne	0	0	0	10 000 [5]	20 000	30 000	40 000	50 000
Liechtenstein Liechtenstein	...	...	...	...	7 500	9 500	14 743	15 500
Lithuania [11] Lituanie [11]	4 512	14 795	50 973	165 337	267 615	332 000	524 000	932 000
Luxembourg Luxembourg	12 895	26 838	45 000	67 208	130 500	209 190	303 274	409 064
Madagascar Madagascar	300	1 300	2 300	4 100	12 784	35 752	63 094	147 500
Malawi Malawi	0	382	3 700	7 000	10 500	22 500	49 000	55 730
Malaysia Malaisie	571 720	1 005 066	1 520 320	2 000 000	2 200 000	2 990 000	4 960 800	7 477 000
Maldives Maldives	0	0	20	1 290	1 600	2 926	7 638	18 894
Mali Mali	0	0	1 187	2 842	4 473	6 387	10 398	45 340
Malta Malte	7 500	10 791	12 500	17 691	22 531	37 541	114 444	239 416
Marshall Islands Iles Marshall	280	264	365	466	345	443	447	489
Martinique Martinique	0	0	...	15 000	55 000	102 000	162 080	286 120
Mauritania Mauritanie	0	0	0	0	0	0	7 133	112 463
Mauritius Maurice	5 706	11 735	20 843	42 515	60 448	102 119	180 000	272 416
Mexico Mexique	569 251	688 513	1 021 900	1 740 814	3 349 475	7 731 635	14 077 880	21 757 000
Monaco Monaco	2 559	3 005	5 400	7 200	11 474	16 000	17 028	19 600
Mongolia Mongolie	0	0	900	2 000	9 032	34 562	154 600	195 000
Montserrat Montserrat	71	84	250	325	250	300	489	...
Morocco Maroc	13 794	29 511	42 942	74 472	116 645	369 174	2 342 000	4 771 739

17

Cellular mobile telephone subscribers
Number *[cont.]*
Abonnés au téléphone mobile
Nombre *[suite]*

Country or area Pays ou zone	1994	1995	1996	1997	1998	1999	2000	2001
Mozambique Mozambique	0	0	0	2 500	6 725	12 243	51 065	152 652
Myanmar Myanmar	1 920	2 766	7 260	8 492	8 516	11 389	13 397	13 780
Namibia [3] Namibie [3]	0	3 500	6 644	12 500	19 500	30 000	82 000	100 000
Nauru [5] Nauru [5]	450	500	600	750	850	1 000	1 200	1 500
Nepal [12] Népal [12]	0	0	0	0	0	5 500	10 226	17 286 [2]
Netherlands Pays-Bas	321 000	539 000	1 016 000	1 717 000	3 351 000	6 745 460	10 755 000	12 352 000
Netherlands Antilles Antilles néerlandaises	8 486	11 698	13 977	* 14 500	16 000	...	...	...
New Caledonia Nouvelle-Calédonie	0	825	2 060	5 198	13 040	25 450	49 948	67 917
New Zealand Nouvelle-Zélande	239 200 [1]	365 000 [1]	492 800 [1]	566 200 [1]	790 000 [1]	1 395 000 [1]	1 542 000 [4]	2 288 000 [4]
Nicaragua Nicaragua	2 183	4 400	5 100	7 560	18 310	44 229	90 294	154 526
Niger Niger	0	0	0	98	1 349	2 192	2 056	2 126
Nigeria Nigéria	12 800	13 000	14 000	15 000	20 000	25 000	30 000	* 400 000
Niue Nioué	0	0	0	...	...	380	410	400
Northern Mariana Islands Iles Mariannes du Nord	765	1 200	...	...	...	2 905	3 000 [13]	...
Norway Norvège	588 478	981 305	1 261 445	1 676 763	2 106 414	2 744 793	3 367 763	3 689 246
Occupied Palestinian Terr. [14] Terr. palestinien occupé [14]	0	20 000	25 000	40 000	100 000	117 000	175 941	300 000
Oman Oman	6 751	8 052	12 934	59 822	103 032	124 119	164 348	324 540
Pakistan [4] Pakistan [4]	24 662	40 964	68 038	135 027	206 908	278 830	349 460	812 000
Panama Panama	0	0	7 000	18 542	85 883	232 888	410 401	475 354
Papua New Guinea Papouasie-Nvl-Guinée	0	0	2 285	3 857	5 558	7 059	8 560	10 700
Paraguay Paraguay	7 660	15 807	32 860	84 240	231 520	435 611	820 810	1 150 000
Peru Pérou	52 200	73 543	200 972	421 814	742 642	1 013 314	1 273 857	1 545 000
Philippines Philippines	171 903	493 862	959 024	1 343 620	1 733 652	2 849 980	6 454 359	11 700 000
Poland Pologne	38 942	75 000	216 900	812 200	1 928 042	3 956 500	6 747 000	10 004 661
Portugal Portugal	173 508	340 845	663 651	1 506 958	3 074 633	4 671 458	6 664 951	7 977 537

17

Cellular mobile telephone subscribers
Number *[cont.]*
Abonnés au téléphone mobile
Nombre *[suite]*

Country or area Pays ou zone	1994	1995	1996	1997	1998	1999	2000	2001
Puerto Rico [15] Porto Rico [15]	175 000	287 000	329 000	367 000	580 000	813 800	926 448	1 211 111
Qatar Qatar	11 533	18 469	28 772	43 476	65 756	84 365	120 856	178 789
Republic of Moldova République de Moldova	0	14	920	2 200	7 000	18 000	139 000	225 000
Réunion Réunion	0	5 500	14 000	26 700	50 300	111 000	276 100	421 100
Romania Roumanie	2 775	9 068	17 000	201 000	643 000	1 355 500	2 499 000	3 845 116
Russian Federation Fédération de Russie	27 744	88 526	223 002	484 883	747 160	1 370 630	3 263 200	7 750 499
Rwanda Rwanda	0	0	0	0	5 000	11 000	39 000	65 000
Saint Kitts and Nevis [1] Saint-Kitts-et-Nevis [1]	...	...	300	205	440	700	1 200	* 2 100
Saint Lucia * [1] Sainte-Lucie * [1]	524	1 000	1 400	1 600	1 900	2 300	2 500	2 700
St. Vincent-Grenadines [1] St. Vincent-Grenadines [1]	* 150	* 215	* 280	346	750	1 420	2 361	7 492
Samoa Samoa	0	0	0	766 [16]	1 480	2 432	3 053	3 175
San Marino Saint-Marin	1 900	2 340	2 279	2 350	4 980	9 580	14 503	15 854
Saudi Arabia Arabie saoudite	15 959	16 008	190 736	332 068	627 321	836 628	1 375 881	2 528 640
Senegal Sénégal	98	122	1 412	6 942	27 487	87 879	250 251	301 811
Serbia and Montenegro * Serbie-et-Monténégro *	0	0	14 800	87 000	240 000	605 697	1 303 609	1 997 809
Seychelles Seychelles	0 [1]	50 [1]	1 043 [1]	2 247 [1]	5 190 [1]	16 316 [1]	25 961 [1]	44 116 [2]
Sierra Leone Sierra Leone	0	0	0	0	0	0	11 940	26 895
Singapore [1] Singapour [1]	235 630	306 000	431 010	848 600	1 094 700	1 630 800	2 747 400	2 991 600
Slovakia Slovaquie	5 946	12 315	28 658	200 140	473 173	664 072	1 109 888	2 147 331
Slovenia Slovénie	16 332	27 301	41 205	93 611	161 606	631 411	1 215 601	1 470 085
Solomon Islands [1] Iles Salomon [1]	144	230	337	658	702	1 093	1 151	967
South Africa [1] Afrique du Sud [1]	340 000	535 000	953 000	1 836 000	3 337 000	5 188 000	8 339 000	10 789 000
Spain Espagne	411 930	944 955	2 997 645	4 337 696	6 437 444	15 003 708	24 265 059	29 655 729
Sri Lanka Sri Lanka	29 182	51 316	71 029	114 888	174 202	256 655	430 202	667 662
Sudan Soudan	0	0	2 200	3 800	8 600	13 000	23 000	103 846

17

Cellular mobile telephone subscribers
Number *[cont.]*
Abonnés au téléphone mobile
Nombre *[suite]*

Country or area Pays ou zone	1994	1995	1996	1997	1998	1999	2000	2001
Suriname Suriname	1 382	1 687	2 416	2 258	6 007	17 500	41 048	87 000
Swaziland [1] Swaziland [1]	0	0	0	0	4 700	14 000	33 000	55 000
Sweden Suède	1 381 000	2 008 000	2 492 000	3 169 000	4 109 000	5 165 000	6 369 000	7 042 000
Switzerland Suisse	332 165	447 167	662 713	1 044 379	1 698 565	3 057 509	4 638 519	5 275 791
Syrian Arab Republic Rép. arabe syrienne	0	0	0	0	0	4 000	30 000	200 000
Tajikistan Tadjikistan	0	0	102	320	420	625	1 160	1 630
Thailand [3] Thaïlande [3]	737 283	1 297 826	1 844 627	2 203 905	1 976 957	2 339 401	3 056 000	7 550 000
TFYR of Macedonia L'ex-R.y. Macédoine	0	0	1 058	12 362	30 087	48 733	115 748	223 275
Togo Togo	0	0	0	2 995	7 500	17 000	50 000	120 000
Tonga [5] Tonga [5]	0	300	302	120	130	140	180	236
Trinidad and Tobago Trinité-et-Tobago	2 599 [1]	6 353 [1]	9 534 [1]	17 140 [1]	26 307 [1]	38 659 [1]	161 860 [1]	256 106 [2]
Tunisia Tunisie	2 709	3 185	5 439	7 656	38 973	55 258	119 075	389 208
Turkey Turquie	174 779	437 130	806 339	1 609 809	3 506 127	8 121 517	16 133 405	19 572 897
Turkmenistan Turkménistan	0	0	0	2 500	3 000	4 000	7 500	8 173
Uganda [4] Ouganda [4]	0	1 747	4 000	5 000	30 000	56 358	188 568	276 034
Ukraine Ukraine	5 000	14 000	30 000	57 200	115 500	216 567	818 524	2 224 600
United Arab Emirates Emirats arabes unis	91 488	128 968	193 834	309 373	493 278	832 267	1 428 115	1 909 303
United Kingdom [1] Royaume-Uni [1]	3 940 000	5 735 785	7 248 355	8 841 000	14 878 000	27 185 000	43 452 000	46 282 000
United Rep. of Tanzania Rép.-Unie de Tanzanie	371	3 500	9 038	20 200	37 940	50 950	180 200	426 964
United States Etats-Unis	24 134 421	33 785 661	44 042 992	55 312 293	69 209 321	86 047 003	109 478 031	128 374 512
United States Virgin Is. * Iles Vierges américaines *	...	...	...	16 000	25 000	30 000	35 000	41 000
Uruguay Uruguay	6 825	39 904	78 601	99 235	151 341	319 131	410 787	519 991
Uzbekistan Ouzbékistan	902	3 731	9 510	17 232	26 826	40 389	53 128	62 756
Vanuatu Vanuatu	64	121	154	207	220	300	365	350
Venezuela Venezuela	319 000	403 800	581 700	1 071 900	2 009 757	3 784 735	5 447 172	6 489 907

17

Cellular mobile telephone subscribers
Number *[cont.]*
Abonnés au téléphone mobile
Nombre *[suite]*

Country or area Pays ou zone	1994	1995	1996	1997	1998	1999	2000	2001
Viet Nam Viet Nam	12 500	23 500	68 910	160 457	222 700	328 671	788 559	1 251 195
Yemen Yémen	8 191	8 250	8 810	12 245	16 146	27 677	32 000	152 000
Zambia [1] Zambie [1]	0 [17]	1 547 [17]	2 721 [17]	4 550 [17]	8 260	28 190	98 853	121 200
Zimbabwe [4] Zimbabwe [4]	0	0	0	5 734	19 000	174 000	309 000	328 669

Source:
International Telecommunication Union (ITU), Geneva, "Yearbook of Statistics, Telecommunication Services, Chronological Time Series 1991-2000" and the ITU database

Source:
Union internationale des télécommunications (UIT), Genève, "Yearbook of Statistics, Telecommunication Services, Chronological Time Series 1991-2000" et la base de données de l'UIT.

1   Data refer to fiscal years beginning 1 April.

2   As of 31 December.
3   Data refer to fiscal years ending 30 September.

4   Data refer to fiscal years ending 30 June.
5   ITU estimate.
6   Including Celtel subscribers.
7   September.
8   Year ending November 1997.
9   Data refer to fiscal years beginning 22 March.

10   Including PHS.
11   Not including radiotelephone connections of "Altaj" System.
12   Data refer to fiscal years ending 15 July.

13   As of 31 March 2000.
14   Users use Israel cellular network.
15   Data refer to the Puerto Rico Telephone Authority.
16   As of 10 February 1998.
17   Zamtel (Zambian Telecommunications Company Limited) only.

1   Les données se réfèrent aux exercices budgétaires commençant le 1er avril.
2   Dès le 31 décembre.
3   Les données se réfèrent aux exercices budgétaires finissant le 30 septembre.
4   Les données se réfèrent aux exercices budgétaires finissant le 30 juin.
5   Estimation de l'UIT.
6   Y compris les abonnés au Celtel.
7   Septembre.
8   Année s'achevant en novembre 1997.
9   Les données se réfèrent aux exercices budgétaires commençant le 22 mars.
10   Y compris "PHS"
11   Non compris les connections radio-téléphonique du système d'Altaj.
12   Les données se réfèrent aux exercices budgétaires finissant le 15 juillet.
13   Dès le 31 mars 2000.
14   Les abonnés utilisent le réseau israélien de téléphonie mobile.
15   Les données se réfèrent à "Puerto Rico Telephone Authority".
16   Dès le 10 février 1998.
17   Zamtel seulement.

18

Telephones
Main telephone lines in operation and per 100 inhabitants

Téléphones
Nombre de lignes téléphoniques en service et pour 100 habitants

Country or area Pays ou zone	Number (thousands) Nombre (en milliers)					Per 100 inhabitants Pour 100 habitants				
	1997	1998	1999	2000	2001	1997	1998	1999	2000	2001
Afghanistan Afghanistan	* 29	* 29	* 29	* 29	29	0.1	0.1	0.1	0.1	0.1
Albania Albanie	87	116	140	153	197	2.3	3.1	3.7	3.9	5.0
Algeria Algérie	1 400	1 477	1 600	1 761	1 880	4.8	5.0	5.3	5.8	6.1
American Samoa Samoa américaines	13	14	14	* 14	*15	24.5	24.6	24.8	25.0	25.2
Andorra Andorre	32	33	34	34	*35	43.1	43.9	44.7	43.9	43.8
Angola Angola	62[1]	65[1]	67[1]	70[1]	80[1]	0.5	0.5	0.5	0.5	0.6
Anguilla Anguilla	5	6	6[2]	6	6	67.8	68.9	71.1	74.5	74.9
Antigua and Barbuda Antigua-et-Barbuda	31[3]	34[3]	37[3]	38[3]	37[4]	43.9[3]	46.8[3]	48.9[3]	50.0[3]	48.1[4]
Argentina [5] Argentine [5]	6 852	7 323	7 357	7 894	8 108	19.7	20.9	20.7	22.0	22.4
Armenia Arménie	568	557	544	533	531	15.0	14.7	14.3	14.0	14.0
Aruba Aruba	33	35	37	* 38	37	36.7	37.3	37.2	37.2	35.0
Australia [6] Australie [6]	9 498	9 540	9 760	10 350	10 485	51.1	50.9	51.5	54.0	54.1
Austria Autriche	3 969[7]	3 997[7]	3 862[7]	3 833[7]	3 810[7,8]	49.2	49.1	47.2	47.2	46.8[8]
Azerbaijan Azerbaïdjan	658	680	730	801	866	8.6	8.9	9.5	10.4	11.1
Bahamas Bahamas	98	106	111	114	123	34.0	35.8	36.9	37.5	40.0
Bahrain Bahreïn	152	158	165	171	174	25.8	26.1	26.7	26.9	26.7
Bangladesh [6] Bangladesh [6]	368	413	433	472	565	0.3	0.3	0.3	0.4	0.4
Barbados [3] Barbade [3]	108	113	115	* 124	129	40.8	42.4	43.0	46.3	48.1
Belarus Bélarus	2 313	2 490	2 638	2 752	2 862	22.9	24.8	26.3	27.6	28.8
Belgium Belgique	4 964[7]	5 056[7]	5 215[7]	5 302[7]	5 133[7]	48.7	49.5	50.9	51.7	49.8
Belize [3] Belize [3]	31	32	36	36	35	13.8	14.3	15.4	14.9	14.3
Benin Bénin	36	38	44	52	59	0.7	0.7	0.7	0.9	0.9
Bermuda Bermudes	52[3]	54[3]	55[3]	56[3]	56[4]	81.0[3]	84.0[3]	85.7[3]	87.0[3]	86.9[4]
Bhutan Bhoutan	6	10	12	14	18	1.0	1.6	1.8	2.1	2.5
Bolivia Bolivie	385	452	503	511	524	5.0	5.7	6.2	6.2	6.3

18

Telephones
Main telephone lines in operation and per 100 inhabitants *[cont.]*

Téléphones
Nombre de lignes téléphoniques en service et pour 100 habitants *[suite]*

Country or area Pays ou zone	Number (thousands) Nombre (en milliers)					Per 100 inhabitants Pour 100 habitants				
	1997	1998	1999	2000	2001	1997	1998	1999	2000	2001
Bosnia and Herzegovina Bosnie-Herzégovine	303	333	368	409[7]	453[7]	8.0	9.1	9.6	10.3	11.1
Botswana [3] Botswana [3]	86	102	124	136	143	5.6	6.5	7.7	8.3	8.5
Brazil Brésil	17 039[9]	19 987[9]	24 985[9]	30 926[9]	37 431[9]	10.7	12.1	14.9	18.2	21.8
British Virgin Islands [3] Iles Vierges britanniques [3]	* 10	* 10	* 10	* 10	*11	53.0	52.9	52.9	52.8	50.9
Brunei Darussalam Brunéi Darussalam	77	78	79	* 81	*88	25.0	24.7	24.6	24.3	25.9
Bulgaria Bulgarie	2 681	2 758	2 833	2 882	2 914	32.3	33.1	34.2	35.4	35.9
Burkina Faso Burkina Faso	36	41	47	53	58	0.3	0.4	0.4	0.5	0.5
Burundi Burundi	16	18	19	* 20	*20	0.3	0.3	0.3	0.3	0.3
Cambodia Cambodge	20[10]	24[10]	28[10]	31[10]	33[10]	0.2	0.2	0.2	0.2	0.3
Cameroon Cameroun	75	94	95	* 95	*101	0.5	0.7	0.6	0.6	0.7
Canada Canada	18 660	19 294	20 051	20 803	20 278	64.2	65.8	67.9	69.9	67.6
Cape Verde Cap-Vert	33	40	47	55	62	8.2	9.6	10.9	12.6	14.3
Cayman Islands [3] Iles Caïmanes [3]	19	28	32	35	38	52.0	72.1	78.8	82.1	84.9
Central African Rep. Rép. centrafricaine	10	10	10	9	9	0.3	0.3	0.3	0.3	0.2
Chad Tchad	7	9	10	10[2]	11[2]	0.1	0.1	0.1	0.1	0.1
Chile Chili	2 693	3 047	3 109	3 387	3 581	18.4	20.6	20.7	22.3	23.3
China Chine	70 310	87 421	108 716	144 829	180 368	5.6	7.0	8.6	11.2	13.7
China, Hong Kong SAR [3] Chine, Hong Kong RAS [3]	3 647	3 729	3 869	3 926	3 898	56.2	57.0	58.6	58.9	58.0
China, Macao SAR Chine, Macao RAS	170	174	178	177	176	40.2	40.4	40.8	40.2	39.4
Colombia Colombie	5 395	6 367	6 665	7 193	*7 372	13.5	15.6	16.0	17.0	17.2
Comoros Comores	6	6	7	7	9	0.8	1.0	1.0	1.0	1.2
Congo Congo	22[2]	22[2]	22[2]	22[2]	22	0.8	0.8	0.8	0.8	0.7
Cook Islands Iles Cook	5[3]	5[3]	5[3]	6[3]	6[4]	26.9[3]	27.5[3]	28.0[3]	29.3[3]	29.5[4]
Costa Rica Costa Rica	685	742	803	899	945	18.9	19.3	20.4	22.3	23.0
Côte d'Ivoire Côte d'Ivoire	142	170	219	264	294	1.0	1.2	1.5	1.8	1.8

18

Telephones
Main telephone lines in operation and per 100 inhabitants *[cont.]*

Téléphones
Nombre de lignes téléphoniques en service et pour 100 habitants *[suite]*

Country or area Pays ou zone	Number (thousands) Nombre (en milliers)					Per 100 inhabitants Pour 100 habitants				
	1997	1998	1999	2000	2001	1997	1998	1999	2000	2001
Croatia Croatie	1 488	1 558	1 634	1 721	*1 700	33.2	34.8	36.5	38.5	36.5
Cuba Cuba	371	388	434	489	574	3.4	3.5	3.9	4.4	5.1
Cyprus Chypre	386[11]	405[11]	424[11]	440[11]	435[11]	59.5	61.4	63.4	64.8	63.1
Czech Republic République tchèque	3 280	3 741	3 806	3 872	3 861	31.8	36.3	37.0	37.7	37.8
Dem. Rep. of the Congo Rép. dém. du Congo	* 21	* 20	* 20	* 20	*20	0.0	0.0	0.0	0.0	0.0
Denmark Danemark	3 341[7]	3 496[7]	3 638[7]	3 809[7]	3 865[7]	63.3	66.0	68.5	71.5	72.2
Djibouti Djibouti	8	8	9	10	10	1.4	1.3	1.4	1.5	1.5
Dominica [3] Dominique [3]	* 19	20	21	* 23	23[12]	25.6	26.5	27.9	29.4	29.9[12]
Dominican Republic Rép. dominicaine	704	772	827	894	955	8.8	9.5	9.9	10.5	11.0
Ecuador Equateur	900	991	1 130	1 224	1 336	7.5	8.1	9.1	9.7	10.4
Egypt [6] Egypte [6]	3 453	3 972	4 686	5 484	6 688	5.7	6.5	7.5	8.6	10.4
El Salvador El Salvador	360	387	495	625	650	6.1	6.4	8.1	10.0	10.2
Equatorial Guinea Guinée équatoriale	* 4	* 6	* 6	* 6	*7	0.9	1.3	1.3	1.4	1.5
Eritrea Erythrée	22	24	27	31	31	0.6	0.7	0.8	0.8	0.8
Estonia Estonie	469	499	515	523	506	32.1	34.4	35.7	36.3	35.4
Ethiopia [6] Ethiopie [6]	157	164	194	232	284	0.3	0.3	0.3	0.4	0.4
Faeroe Islands Iles Féroé	24	24	25	25	...	53.8	54.4	55.7	55.5	...
Falkland Is. (Malvinas) [3] Iles Falkland (Malvinas) [3]	2	2	2	2	2	87.0	93.2	96.1	98.6	99.0
Fiji Fidji	72	77	82	* 86	92	9.2	9.7	10.2	10.7	11.2
Finland Finlande	2 861[13]	2 841[13]	2 850[13]	2 848[13]	2 845[13,14]	55.6	55.1	55.2	55.0	54.8[14]
France France	33 700[7]	34 099[7]	33 888[7]	33 987[7]	34 033[7]	57.9	58.4	57.8	57.7	57.4
French Guiana Guyane française	47	46	49	50[2]	51[2]	29.2	27.7	28.3	27.6	26.8
French Polynesia Polynésie française	52	53	52	52[2]	53	23.5	23.5	22.8	22.1	22.3
Gabon Gabon	37	39	38	39	37	3.3	3.3	3.2	3.2	3.0
Gambia [3] Gambie [3]	25[15]	26[15]	29[15]	* 33[15]	35[15]	2.1	2.1	2.3	2.6	2.6

18

Telephones
Main telephone lines in operation and per 100 inhabitants *[cont.]*

Téléphones
Nombre de lignes téléphoniques en service et pour 100 habitants *[suite]*

Country or area Pays ou zone	Number (thousands) Nombre (en milliers)					Per 100 inhabitants Pour 100 habitants				
	1997	1998	1999	2000	2001	1997	1998	1999	2000	2001
Georgia Géorgie	617	629	672	758	868	11.3	12.2	13.0	15.1	17.4
Germany Allemagne	45 200[7,16]	46 530[7]	48 210[7]	50 220[7]	52 280[7]	55.1	56.7	58.7	61.1	63.4
Ghana Ghana	106	133	159	237	242	0.6	0.7	0.8	1.2	1.2
Greece Grèce	5 431	5 536	5 611	5 659	5 608[17]	51.6	52.2	52.8	53.6	52.9
Greenland Groenland	23	25	26	26	26	41.7	44.6	45.7	46.8	46.7
Grenada Grenade	27	27	29	31	33	29.0	29.8	31.5	33.2	32.8
Guadeloupe Guadeloupe	180[2]	197	201	205	210[2]	41.2	44.5	47.6	44.9	45.7
Guam Guam	71	75	78	74	80	48.1	50.0	50.9	48.0	50.9
Guatemala Guatemala	430	517	611	678	756	4.1	4.8	5.5	6.0	6.5
Guinea Guinée	20	15	21	24	25	0.3	0.2	0.3	0.3	0.3
Guinea-Bissau Guinée-Bissau	8	8	6	11	12	0.7	0.7	0.5	0.9	1.0
Guyana Guyana	55	60	64	* 68	80	6.5	7.1	7.5	7.9	9.2
Haiti Haïti	60[2]	65[2]	70[2]	73[2]	80[2]	0.8	0.8	0.9	0.9	1.0
Honduras Honduras	234	249	279	299	311	3.8	4.0	4.4	4.6	4.8
Hungary Hongrie	3 095	3 423	3 726	3 798	3 742	30.4	33.6	37.1	38.0	37.5
Iceland Islande	168[7]	178[7]	189[7]	192[7]	191[7]	61.4	64.8	67.7	68.3	66.4
India[3] Inde[3]	17 802	21 594	26 511	32 436	38 536	1.9	2.2	2.7	3.2	3.8
Indonesia Indonésie	4 982	5 572	6 080	6 663	7 219	2.5	2.7	3.0	3.2	3.5
Iran (Islamic Rep. of)[18] Iran (Rép. islamique d')[18]	6 503	7 355	8 371	9 486	10 897	10.7	11.9	13.3	14.9	16.9
Iraq[6] Iraq[6]	651	650	* 675	* 675	675	3.1	3.0	3.0	2.9	2.9
Ireland[3] Irlande[3]	1 558[7]	1 633[7]	1 737[7]	1 832[7]	1 860[7]	42.6	44.1	46.4	48.4	48.5
Israel Israël	2 675	2 807	2 878	2 974	3 033	45.3	46.9	47.2	47.4	46.6
Italy Italie	25 698[7]	25 986[7]	26 502[7]	27 153[7]	27 353[7,8]	44.8	45.3	46.2	47.4	47.2[8]
Jamaica[3] Jamaïque[3]	416	463	487	512	*532	16.5	18.3	19.1	19.8	20.5
Japan[3] Japon[3]	65 735[19]	67 488[19]	70 530[19]	74 344[19]	74 567[19]	52.1	53.4	55.7	58.6	58.6

18

Telephones
Main telephone lines in operation and per 100 inhabitants *[cont.]*

Téléphones
Nombre de lignes téléphoniques en service et pour 100 habitants *[suite]*

Country or area Pays ou zone	Number (thousands) Nombre (en milliers)					Per 100 inhabitants Pour 100 habitants				
	1997	1998	1999	2000	2001	1997	1998	1999	2000	2001
Jordan Jordanie	404	511	565	614	668	8.8	10.7	11.5	12.2	12.9
Kazakhstan Kazakhstan	1 805	1 775	1 760	1 834	1 940	11.0	10.9	10.8	11.3	12.1
Kenya [6] Kenya [6]	272	288	305	321	326 [20]	1.0	1.0	1.1	1.1	1.0 [20]
Kiribati Kiribati	2	3	3	3 [2]	4	3.1	3.4	3.7	4.0	4.2
Korea, Dem. P. R. Corée, R. p. dém. de	* 500	* 500	* 500	* 500	*500	2.2	2.2	2.2	2.2	2.1
Korea, Republic of Corée, République de	20 422 [13]	20 089 [13]	20 518 [13]	21 932 [13]	22 725 [13]	45.3	44.2	44.9	47.7	48.6
Kuwait Koweït	412	427	456	467	472	20.8	21.1	21.6	21.3	20.8
Kyrgyzstan Kirghizistan	351	368	371	376	388	7.6	7.8	7.6	7.7	7.8
Lao People's Dem. Rep. Rép. dém. pop. lao	25	28	35	41	53	0.5	0.6	0.7	0.8	1.0
Latvia Lettonie	740	742	732	735	722	29.8	30.2	30.0	30.3	30.7
Lebanon Liban	562	620	650 [2]	682 [2]	741	17.9	19.4	20.1	20.7	22.1
Lesotho [3] Lesotho [3]	20	21	* 22	* 22	*22	1.0	1.0	1.0	1.0	1.0
Liberia Libéria	6	* 7	* 7	* 7	7	0.2	0.2	0.2	0.2	0.2
Libyan Arab Jamah. Jamah. arabe libyenne	400	500	* 550	* 605	610	7.2	9.1	10.1	10.8	10.9
Liechtenstein Liechtenstein	20	20	20	20	20	63.1	61.7	61.0	61.1	60.0
Lithuania Lituanie	1 054 [15]	1 113 [15]	1 153 [15]	1 188 [15]	1 152 [15]	28.5	30.1	31.2	32.2	31.3
Luxembourg Luxembourg	280 [21]	293 [21]	311 [21]	331 [21]	347 [21]	66.5	68.7	71.9	75.5	78.0
Madagascar Madagascar	43	47	50	55	58	0.3	0.3	0.3	0.4	0.4
Malawi Malawi	37	37	41	45	54	0.4	0.4	0.4	0.4	0.5
Malaysia Malaisie	4 223	4 384	4 431	4 634	4 710	19.5	20.2	20.3	19.9	19.8
Maldives Maldives	18	20	22	24	27	7.1	7.7	8.4	9.1	9.9
Mali Mali	24	27	34	39	50	0.3	0.3	0.3	0.4	0.5
Malta Malte	187	192	198	204	208	49.3	49.9	51.2	52.4	53.0
Marshall Islands Iles Marshall	3	4	4	4	4	6.9	7.5	7.6	7.6	7.7
Martinique Martinique	170	172	172	172 [2]	172 [2]	43.8	44.3	45.1	43.4	43.0

18

Telephones
Main telephone lines in operation and per 100 inhabitants *[cont.]*
Téléphones
Nombre de lignes téléphoniques en service et pour 100 habitants *[suite]*

Country or area Pays ou zone	Number (thousands) Nombre (en milliers)					Per 100 inhabitants Pour 100 habitants				
	1997	1998	1999	2000	2001	1997	1998	1999	2000	2001
Mauritania Mauritanie	13	15	17	19	25	0.6	0.6	0.7	0.7	1.0
Mauritius Maurice	223	245	257	281	307	19.5	21.2	21.9	23.5	25.7
Mayotte Mayotte	9	12	10	10	*10	7.6	9.5	7.3	7.2	7.0
Mexico Mexique	9 254[22]	9 927[22]	10 927[22]	12 332[22]	13 773[22]	9.7	10.4	11.2	12.5	13.7
Micronesia (Fed. States) Micronésie (Etats féd. de)	8	9	10[2]	10[2]	10	7.7	8.2	8.7	8.4	8.7
Monaco Monaco	31	30	30	30	30	99.7	95.9	94.0	93.6	92.1
Mongolia Mongolie	87	103	103	118	124	3.8	4.5	4.4	5.0	5.2
Montserrat Montserrat	4	* 3	* 3	3	...	62.2	95.7	74.3	70.3	...
Morocco Maroc	1 301	1 393	1 471	1 425	1 191	4.7	5.0	5.3	5.0	4.1
Mozambique Mozambique	66	75	78	86	89	0.4	0.5	0.5	0.5	0.5
Myanmar Myanmar	214	229	249	271	295	0.5	0.5	0.6	0.6	0.6
Namibia [5] Namibie [5]	100	106	108	110	117	6.1	6.3	6.2	6.2	6.4
Nauru Nauru	2	2	2[2]	2[2]	2	14.5	15.0	15.5	15.7	16.0
Nepal Népal	140[23]	208[23]	253[23]	267[23]	298[4]	0.7[23]	1.0[23]	1.2[23]	1.2[23]	1.3[4]
Netherlands Pays-Bas	8 860[7]	9 337[7]	9 613[7]	9 889[7]	10 003[7]	56.6	59.2	60.6	61.9	62.1
Netherlands Antilles Antilles néerlandaises	* 77	* 78	* 79	* 80	*81	36.5	36.7	36.8	37.2	37.2
New Caledonia Nouvelle-Calédonie	47	49	51	51	51	23.6	24.0	24.1	23.8	23.1
New Zealand Nouvelle-Zélande	1 776[3]	1 809[3]	1 833[3]	1 831[6]	1 823[6]	47.9	48.5	48.9	48.5	47.7
Nicaragua Nicaragua	123	141	150	159	154	2.8	3.0	3.0	3.1	2.9
Niger Niger	16	18	19[2]	20	22	0.2	0.2	0.2	0.2	0.2
Nigeria Nigéria	400	407	* 450	497	541	0.4	0.4	0.4	0.4	0.5
Niue Nioué	1[2]	1[2]	1[2]	1[2]	1	37.0	42.0	49.8	54.5	54.1
Northern Mariana Islands Iles Mariannes du Nord	21	21	21	21	...	41.3	40.4	39.5	39.6	...
Norway Norvège	2 735	2 935	3 176	3 302	3 262	61.9	66.0	70.9	73.6	72.0
Occupied Palestinian Terr. Terr. palestinien occupé	111	167	222	272	292	4.0	5.8	7.4	8.6	8.9

18

Telephones
Main telephone lines in operation and per 100 inhabitants *[cont.]*

Téléphones
Nombre de lignes téléphoniques en service et pour 100 habitants *[suite]*

Country or area Pays ou zone	Number (thousands) Nombre (en milliers)					Per 100 inhabitants Pour 100 habitants				
	1997	1998	1999	2000	2001	1997	1998	1999	2000	2001
Oman Oman	201	220	220	225	235	8.6	9.2	9.0	8.9	9.0
Pakistan [6] Pakistan [6]	2 558	2 756	2 986	3 053	3 381	2.0	2.1	2.2	2.2	2.3
Panama Panama	366	419	462	429	376	13.4	15.1	16.4	15.1	13.0
Papua New Guinea Papouasie-Nvl-Guinée	54	57	60	65	62	1.2	1.2	1.2	1.3	1.2
Paraguay Paraguay	218	261	268	300	289 [24]	4.3	5.0	5.0	5.5	5.1
Peru Pérou	1 646	1 555	1 688	1 717	2 022	6.8	6.3	6.7	6.7	7.8
Philippines Philippines	2 078 [2]	2 492 [13]	2 892 [13]	3 061	3 315	2.9	3.4	3.9	4.0	4.2
Poland Pologne	7 510 [7]	8 812 [7]	10 175 [7]	10 946 [7]	11 400 [7]	19.4	22.8	26.3	28.3	29.5
Portugal Portugal	4 002 [7]	4 117 [7]	4 230 [7]	4 314 [7]	4 378 [7]	40.2	41.3	42.3	43.0	42.5
Puerto Rico Porto Rico	1 257 [25,26]	1 262 [25,26]	1 295 [25,26]	1 332 [25,26]	1 330 [25,26]	33.8	33.7	34.3	35.0	34.6
Qatar Qatar	142	151	155	160	167	24.9	26.0	26.3	26.8	27.5
Republic of Moldova République de Moldova	627	657	555	584	639	14.4	15.0	12.7	13.3	14.6
Réunion Réunion	236	243	268	280 [2]	300 [2]	35.1	35.6	38.0	40.1	41.0
Romania Roumanie	3 398	3 599	3 740	3 899	4 116	15.1	16.0	16.7	17.4	18.4
Russian Federation Fédération de Russie	28 250	29 246	30 949	32 070	35 700	19.2	19.9	21.0	21.8	24.3
Rwanda Rwanda	12	11	13	18	22	0.2	0.2	0.2	0.2	0.3
Saint Helena Sainte-Hélène	2 [3]	2 [3]	2 [3]	2 [3]	2 [4]	31.1 [3]	31.9 [3]	32.4 [3]	32.9 [3]	33.5 [4]
Saint Kitts and Nevis [3] Saint-Kitts-et-Nevis [3]	17	18	20	* 22	*23	39.4	41.7	45.0	48.6	49.1
Saint Lucia [3] Sainte-Lucie [3]	37	40	44	* 49	50	25.1	26.9	29.2	31.5	31.7
St. Vincent-Grenadines [3] St. Vincent-Grenadines [3]	20	21	24	25	26	18.4	18.8	20.9	22.0	22.7
Samoa Samoa	8	8	9 [2]	9 [2]	11	4.9	4.9	4.9	4.8	6.4
San Marino Saint-Marin	18	19	20	20	21	70.2	77.3	76.0	75.2	75.9
Sao Tome and Principe Sao Tomé-et-Principe	4	4	5	5	5	3.1	3.1	3.2	3.1	3.6
Saudi Arabia Arabie saoudite	1 877	2 167	2 706	2 965	3 233	9.6	10.7	13.0	13.7	14.5
Senegal Sénégal	116	140	166	206	237	1.3	1.6	1.8	2.2	2.5

18

Telephones
Main telephone lines in operation and per 100 inhabitants *[cont.]*

Téléphones
Nombre de lignes téléphoniques en service et pour 100 habitants *[suite]*

Country or area Pays ou zone	Number (thousands) Nombre (en milliers)					Per 100 inhabitants Pour 100 habitants				
	1997	1998	1999	2000	2001	1997	1998	1999	2000	2001
Serbia and Montenegro Serbie-et-Monténégro	2 182	2 319	2 281	2 406	2 444	20.6	21.8	21.4	22.6	22.9
Seychelles Seychelles	18[3]	19[3]	20[3]	19[3]	21[4]	23.1[3]	23.8[3]	24.4[3]	23.5[3]	26.1[4]
Sierra Leone Sierra Leone	17	17	18	19	23	0.4	0.4	0.4	0.4	0.5
Singapore [3] Singapour [3]	1 685	1 778	1 877	1 947	1 948	44.4	45.3	47.5	48.5	47.1
Slovakia Slovaquie	1 392	1 539	1 655	1 698	1 556	25.8	28.5	30.7	31.4	28.9
Slovenia Slovénie	710	723	758	785	802	35.8	36.3	38.1	39.5	40.2
Solomon Islands [3] Iles Salomon [3]	8[27]	8[27]	8[27]	8[27]	7[27]	2.0	2.0	2.0	1.8	1.7
Somalia Somalie	* 15	* 20	* 35	* 35	*35	0.2	0.2	0.4	0.4	0.4
South Africa [3] Afrique du Sud [3]	4 645	5 075	5 493	4 962	4 924	11.3	12.1	12.8	11.4	11.1
Spain Espagne	15 854	16 289	16 480	17 104	17 531	40.3	41.4	41.0	42.6	43.4
Sri Lanka Sri Lanka	342	524	672	767	829	1.9	2.9	3.7	4.1	4.4
Sudan Soudan	113	162	251	387	453	0.4	0.6	0.9	1.2	1.4
Suriname Suriname	64	67	71	75	77	15.5	15.8	16.5	17.4	17.6
Swaziland [3] Swaziland [3]	25	29	31	32	*32	2.7	3.1	3.2	3.2	3.1
Sweden Suède	6 254[7]	6 389[7]	6 519[7]	6 621[7]	6 585[7]	70.7	72.2	73.6	74.6	73.9
Switzerland Suisse	4 688[7]	4 884[7]	5 066[7]	5 235[7]	5 383[7,8]	66.0	68.4	70.6	72.6	74.3[8]
Syrian Arab Republic Rép. arabe syrienne	1 313	1 477	1 600	1 675	1 710	8.7	9.5	9.9	10.4	10.3
Tajikistan Tadjikistan	226	221	213	219	223	3.8	3.7	3.5	3.6	3.6
Thailand [5] Thaïlande [5]	4 827	5 038	5 216	5 591	6 042	8.2	8.5	8.7	9.2	9.9
TFYR of Macedonia L'ex-R.y. Macédoine	408	439	471	507	539	20.5	21.9	23.4	25.1	26.4
Togo Togo	25	31	38	43	48	0.6	0.7	0.9	0.9	1.0
Tonga Tonga	7	9	9	10[2]	11	7.5	8.7	9.3	9.8	10.9
Trinidad and Tobago Trinité-et-Tobago	243[3]	264[3]	279[3]	305[3]	312[4]	19.1[3]	20.6[3]	21.6[3]	23.6[3]	24.0[4]
Tunisia Tunisie	654	752	850	955	1 056	7.1	8.1	9.0	10.0	10.9
Turkey Turquie	15 744	16 960	18 054	18 395	18 904	25.2	26.7	28.1	28.2	28.5

18

Telephones
Main telephone lines in operation and per 100 inhabitants *[cont.]*

Téléphones
Nombre de lignes téléphoniques en service et pour 100 habitants *[suite]*

Country or area Pays ou zone	Number (thousands) Nombre (en milliers)					Per 100 inhabitants Pour 100 habitants				
	1997	1998	1999	2000	2001	1997	1998	1999	2000	2001
Turkmenistan Turkménistan	354	354	359	364	388	8.0	8.2	8.2	8.2	8.0
Turks and Caicos Islands Iles Turques et Caïques	* 4	* 5	* 5	* 6	...	28.7	30.5	32.5	34.3	...
Tuvalu Tuvalu	1	1	1	* 1	1	4.9	5.5	5.5	5.6	6.5
Uganda [6] Ouganda [6]	54	57	57[28]	62	56	0.3	0.3	0.3	0.3	0.2
Ukraine Ukraine	9 410	9 698	10 074	10 417	10 670	18.5	19.1	19.9	20.7	21.2
United Arab Emirates Emirats arabes unis	835	915	975	1 020	1 053	35.1	38.9	40.7	34.7	34.0
United Kingdom [3] Royaume-Uni [3]	31 879[7]	32 829[7]	34 021[7]	35 027[7]	35 290[7,12]	54.0	55.4	57.2	58.6	58.7[12]
United Rep. of Tanzania Rép.-Unie de Tanzanie	105	122	150	174	148	0.4	0.4	0.5	0.5	0.4
United States Etats-Unis	172 452	179 822	183 521	187 002	*190 000	63.6	65.5	66.0	66.5	66.7
United States Virgin Is. Iles Vierges américaines	62	65	67	68	*69	58.0	60.3	62.3	62.9	63.5
Uruguay Uruguay	761	824	897	929	951	23.5	25.0	27.1	27.8	28.3
Uzbekistan Ouzbékistan	1 541	1 537	1 599	1 655	1 663	6.5	6.4	6.6	6.7	6.7
Vanuatu Vanuatu	5	5	* 6	7	7	2.7	2.8	3.0	3.4	3.4
Venezuela Venezuela	2 804	2 592	2 551	2 536	2 693	12.2	11.2	10.8	10.5	10.9
Viet Nam Viet Nam	1 333	1 744	2 106	2 543	3 050	1.7	2.3	2.7	3.2	3.8
Yemen Yémen	220	250	284	347	423	1.3	1.5	1.6	1.9	2.2
Zambia [3] Zambie [3]	77	78	83	83	86	0.8	0.8	0.8	0.8	0.8
Zimbabwe [6] Zimbabwe [6]	212	237	239	* 249	254	1.9	2.1	2.1	2.2	2.2

Source:
International Telecommunication Union (ITU), Geneva, "Yearbook of Statistics, Telecommunication Services, Chronological Time Series 1991-2000" and the ITU database.

Source:
Union internationale des télécommunications (UIT), Genève, "Yearbook of Statistics, Telecommunication Services, Chronological Time Series 1991-2000" et la base de données de l'UIT.

1 Data refer to Angola Telecom.
2 ITU estimate.
3 Data refer to fiscal years beginning 1 April.

4 As of 31 December.
5 Data refer to fiscal years ending 30 September.

6 Data refer to fiscal years ending 30 June.

1 Les données se réfèrent à "Angola Telecom".
2 Estimation de l'UIT.
3 Les données se réfèrent aux exercices budgétaires commençant le 1er avril.
4 Dès le 31 décembre.
5 Les données se réfèrent aux exercices budgétaires finissant le 30 septembre.
6 Les données se réfèrent aux exercices budgétaires finissant le 30 juin.

18

Telephones
Main telephone lines in operation and per 100 inhabitants *[cont.]*

Téléphones
Nombre de lignes téléphoniques en service et pour 100 habitants *[suite]*

7 Including ISDN channels.	7 RNIS inclu.
8 September.	8 Septembre.
9 Conventional telephony terminals in service.	9 Terminaux de téléphonie conventionnelle en service.
10 WLL lines included.	10 Y compris les lignes "WLL".
11 Excluding 8,960 main lines in the occupied areas.	11 Non compris 8 960 lignes principales dans les territoires occupés.
12 As of December.	12 Dès décembre.
13 Telephone subscribers (Finland: from 1996 the basis for the compilation of the statistics changed).	13 Abonnés au téléphone. (Finland : à compter de 1996, la base de calcul des statistiques à changé).
14 June.	14 Juin.
15 Excluding public call offices.	15 Cabines publiques exclues.
16 Only Deutsche Telekom AG.	16 Deutsche Telekom AG seulement.
17 Decrease was due to switching of users to ISDN and mobile services.	17 La diminution tient au fait que les usagers sont passés au RNIS et aux téléphones portables.
18 Data refer to fiscal years beginning 22 March.	18 Les données se réfèrent aux exercices budgétaires commençant le 22 mars.
19 Main lines with ISDN channels.	19 Lignes principales inclu RNIS.
20 November.	20 Novembre.
21 Including digital lines.	21 Y compris lignes digitales.
22 Lines in service.	22 Lignes en service.
23 Data refer to fiscal years ending 15 July.	23 Les données se réfèrent aux exercices budgétaires finissant le 15 juillet.
24 Decrease in lines available in the public sector.	24 Diminution des lignes disponibles dans la secteur publique.
25 Switched access lines.	25 Lignes d'accès déviées.
26 Data refer to the Puerto Rico Telephone Authority.	26 Les données se réfèrent à "Puerto Rico Telephone Authority".
27 Billable lines.	27 Lignes payables.
28 Including data from MTN.	28 Y compris les données du "MTN".

19

Internet users
Estimated number

Usagers d'Internet
Nombre estimatif

Country or area Pays ou zone	1994	1995	1996	1997	1998	1999	2000	2001
Albania Albanie	...	350	1 000	1 500	2 000	2 500	3 500	10 000
Algeria Algérie	100	500	500	3 000	6 000	60 000	150 000	200 000
Andorra Andorre	...	...	1 000	2 000	4 500	5 000	7 000	...
Angola Angola	...	...	100	750	2 500	10 000	15 000	20 000
Anguilla Anguilla	...	80	...	...	...	...	2 500	3 000
Antigua and Barbuda [1] Antigua-et-Barbuda [1]	...	1 500	2 000	2 500	3 000	4 000	5 000	7 000
Argentina [2] Argentine [2]	15 000	30 000	50 000	100 000	300 000	1 200 000	2 600 000	3 650 000
Armenia Arménie	300	1 700	3 000	3 500	4 000	30 000	50 000	70 000
Aruba Aruba	...	...	2 300		...	4 000	14 000	24 000
Australia [3] Australie [3]	400 000	500 000	600 000	1 600 000	4 200 000	5 600 000	6 600 000	7 200 000
Austria Autriche	110 000 [4]	150 000 [4]	550 000	760 000	1 230 000	1 840 000	2 700 000	3 150 000
Azerbaijan Azerbaïdjan	110	160	500	2 000	3 000	8 000	12 000	25 000
Bahamas Bahamas	...	2 700	5 000	3 967	6 908	11 307	13 130	16 923
Bahrain Bahreïn	...	2 000	5 000	10 000	20 000	30 000	40 000	132 330
Bangladesh [3] Bangladesh [3]	...	...	...	1 000	5 000	50 000	100 000	250 000
Barbados [1] Barbade [1]	...	20	1 000	2 000	5 000	6 000	10 000	15 000
Belarus Bélarus	50	300	3 000	5 000	7 500	50 000	182 350	422 165
Belgium Belgique	70 000	100 000	300 000	500 000	800 000	1 400 000	3 000 000	3 200 000
Belize [1] Belize [1]	...	100	2 000	3 000	5 000	10 000	15 000	18 000
Benin Bénin	...	...	100	1 500	3 000	10 000	15 000	25 000
Bermuda [1] Bermudes [1]	...	4 200	10 000	15 000	20 000	25 000	27 000	30 000
Bhutan Bhoutan	...	...	...	...	...	750	2 250	3 000
Bolivia Bolivie	...	5 000	15 000	35 000	50 000	80 000	120 000	180 000
Bosnia and Herzegovina Bosnie-Herzégovine	...	...	500	2 000	5 000	7 000	40 000	45 000
Botswana [1] Botswana [1]	...	1 000	2 500	5 000	10 000	19 000	25 000	50 000

19

Internet users
Estimated number *[cont.]*
   Usagers d'Internet
   Nombre estimatif *[suite]*

Country or area Pays ou zone	1994	1995	1996	1997	1998	1999	2000	2001
Brazil [4] Brésil [4]	60 000	170 000	740 000	1 310 000	2 500 000	3 500 000	5 000 000	8 000 000
Brunei Darussalam Brunéi Darussalam	...	3 000	10 000	15 000	20 000	25 000	30 000	35 000
Bulgaria Bulgarie	1 650	10 000	60 000	100 000	150 000	234 600	430 000	605 000
Burkina Faso Burkina Faso	...	...	100	2 000	5 000	7 000	9 000	19 000
Burundi Burundi	0	0	50	500	1 000	2 500	5 000	6 000
Cambodia Cambodge	...	...	...	700	2 000	4 000	6 000	10 000
Cameroon Cameroun	...	...	...	1 000	2 000	20 000	40 000	45 000
Canada Canada	690 000 [4]	1 220 000 [4]	2 000 000 [4]	4 500 000 [4]	7 500 000 [4]	11 000 000 [4]	12 971 000	14 000 000
Cape Verde Cap-Vert	...	...	...	1 000	2 000	5 000	8 000	12 000
Cayman Islands [1] Iles Caïmanes [1]	0	1 300	...	...	...	...	...	...
Central African Rep. Rép. centrafricaine	...	...	200	500	1 000	1 500	2 000	3 000
Chad Tchad	...	...	...	50	335	1 000	3 000	4 000
Chile Chili	20 000	50 000	100 000	156 875	250 000	625 000	2 537 308	3 102 200
China Chine	14 000	60 000	160 000	400 000	2 100 000	8 900 000	22 500 000	33 700 000
China, Hong Kong SAR [1] Chine, Hong Kong RAS [1]	170 000 [4]	200 000 [4]	300 000 [4]	675 000 [4]	947 000 [4]	1 400 000 [4]	1 855 200	2 601 300
China, Macao SAR Chine, Macao RAS	150	1 153	3 037	10 000	30 000	40 000	60 000	101 000
Colombia Colombie	38 371	68 560	122 500	208 000	433 000	664 000	878 000	1 154 000
Comoros Comores	...	...	...	0	200	800	1 500	2 500
Congo Congo	...	...	100	100	100	500	800	1 000
Cook Islands Iles Cook	...	220 [1]	1 000 [5]	1 200 [1]	...	2 300 [1]	2 750 [1]	3 200 [1]
Costa Rica Costa Rica	9 500	14 500	30 000	60 000	100 000	150 000	228 000	384 000
Côte d'Ivoire Côte d'Ivoire	...	30	1 300	3 000	10 000	20 000	40 000	70 000
Croatia Croatie	12 500	24 000	40 000	80 000	150 000	200 000	250 000	...
Cuba Cuba	...	10	3 500	7 500	25 000	34 800	60 000	120 000
Cyprus Chypre	800	3 000	5 000	33 000	68 000	88 000	120 000	150 000

19

Internet users
Estimated number *[cont.]*
Usagers d'Internet
Nombre estimatif *[suite]*

Country or area Pays ou zone	1994	1995	1996	1997	1998	1999	2000	2001
Czech Republic République tchèque	130 000	150 000	200 000	300 000	400 000	700 000	1 000 000	1 500 000
Dem. Rep. of the Congo Rép. dém. du Congo	...	...	50	100	200	500	3 000	6 000
Denmark Danemark	70 000 [4]	200 000 [4]	300 000 [4]	600 000 [4]	1 200 000 [4]	1 626 000	2 090 000	2 300 000 [4]
Djibouti Djibouti	...	100	200	550	650	750	1 400	3 300
Dominica [1] Dominique [1]	...	377	800	...	2 000	2 000	6 000	9 000
Dominican Republic Rép. dominicaine	...	1 400	6 200	12 000	20 000	96 000	159 000	186 000 [6]
Ecuador Equateur	3 900	5 000	10 000	13 000	15 000	100 000	180 000	333 000
Egypt [3] Egypte [3]	4 000	20 000	40 000	60 000	100 000	200 000	450 000	600 000
El Salvador El Salvador	...	...	5 000	15 000	25 000	50 000	70 000	100 000
Equatorial Guinea Guinée équatoriale	...	...	...	200	470	500	700	900
Eritrea Erythrée	0	0	0	300	300	900	5 000	15 000
Estonia Estonie	17 000	40 000	50 000	80 000	150 000	200 000	391 600	429 656
Ethiopia [3] Ethiopie [3]	...	10	1 000	3 000	6 000	8 000	10 000	25 000
Faeroe Islands Iles Féroé	...	...	500	1 000	2 000	3 000	...	...
Falkland Is. (Malvinas) [1] Iles Falkland (Malvinas) [1]	0	0	...	100	...	1 600	1 700	1 900
Fiji Fidji	60	70	500	1 750	5 000	7 500	12 000	15 000
Finland Finlande	250 000	710 000	860 000	1 000 000	1 311 000	1 667 000	1 927 000	2 235 320 [7]
France France	520 000 [4]	950 000 [4]	1 504 000	2 485 000	3 704 000	5 370 000	8 460 000	15 653 000
French Guiana Guyane française	...	...	500	1 000	1 500	2 000	2 700	3 200
French Polynesia Polynésie française	...	...	200	480	3 000	8 000	15 000	20 000
Gabon Gabon	...	...	0	550	2 000	3 000	15 000	17 000
Gambia [1] Gambie [1]	...	100	400	600	2 500	9 000	12 000	18 000
Georgia Géorgie	...	600	2 000	3 000	5 000	20 000	23 000	46 500
Germany Allemagne	750 000	1 500 000	2 500 000	5 500 000	8 100 000	17 100 000	24 800 000	30 800 000
Ghana Ghana	...	60	1 000	5 000	6 000	20 000	30 000	40 520

19

Internet users
Estimated number *[cont.]*
Usagers d'Internet
Nombre estimatif *[suite]*

Country or area Pays ou zone	1994	1995	1996	1997	1998	1999	2000	2001
Gibraltar Gibraltar	...	...	...	765	1 201	1 707	5 530	...
Greece Grèce	40 000	80 000	150 000	200 000	350 000	750 000	1 000 000	1 400 000
Greenland Groenland	36	30	1 000	4 434	8 187	12 102	17 841	20 000
Grenada Grenade	0	0	300	1 000	1 500	2 500	4 113	5 200
Guadeloupe Guadeloupe	...	...	100	1 000	2 000	7 000	14 000	20 000
Guam Guam	500	960	1 842	3 536	6 787	13 028	25 007	48 000
Guatemala Guatemala	...	300	2 000	10 000	50 000	65 000	80 000	200 000
Guinea Guinée	10	50	150	300	500	5 000	8 000	15 000
Guinea-Bissau Guinée-Bissau	...	...	...	200	300	1 500	3 000	4 000
Guyana Guyana	...	...	500	1 000	2 000	28 000	52 000	95 000
Haiti Haïti	...	...	600	...	2 000	6 000	20 000	30 000
Honduras Honduras	...	2 055	2 500	10 000	18 000	35 000	55 000	90 000
Hungary Hongrie	50 000	70 000	100 000	200 000	400 000	600 000	715 000	1 480 000
Iceland Islande	18 000	30 000	40 000	75 000	100 000	150 000	168 000	172 000
India [1] Inde [1]	10 000	250 000	450 000	700 000	1 400 000	2 800 000	5 500 000	7 000 000
Indonesia Indonésie	2 000	50 000	110 000	384 000	510 000	900 000	2 000 000	4 000 000
Iran (Islamic Rep. of) [8] Iran (Rép. islamique d') [8]	250	2 600	10 000	30 000	65 000	250 000	625 000	1 005 000
Ireland [1] Irlande [1]	20 000 [4]	40 000 [4]	80 000 [4]	150 000 [4]	300 000 [4]	410 000	679 000	895 000
Israel Israël	30 000	50 000	120 000	250 000	600 000	800 000	1 270 000	1 800 000
Italy Italie	110 000	300 000	585 000	1 300 000	2 600 000	8 200 000	13 200 000	15 600 000
Jamaica [1] Jamaïque [1]	900	2 700	14 700	20 000	50 000	60 000	80 000	100 000
Japan [1] Japon [1]	1 000 000	2 000 000	5 500 000	11 550 000	16 940 000	27 060 000	38 000 000	48 900 000
Jordan Jordanie	...	1 000	2 000	27 354	60 816	120 000	127 317	234 000
Kazakhstan Kazakhstan	84	1 800	5 000	10 000	20 000	70 000	100 000	150 000
Kenya [3] Kenya [3]	...	200	2 500	10 000	15 000	35 000	200 000	500 000

19

Internet users
Estimated number *[cont.]*
Usagers d'Internet
Nombre estimatif *[suite]*

Country or area Pays ou zone	1994	1995	1996	1997	1998	1999	2000	2001
Kiribati Kiribati	...	...	...	...	500	1 000	1 500	2 000
Korea, Republic of Corée, République de	138 000	366 000	731 000	1 634 000	3 103 000	10 860 000	19 040 000	24 380 000
Kuwait Koweït	2 600	3 500	15 000	40 000	60 000	100 000	150 000	200 000
Kyrgyzstan Kirghizistan	...	...	...	...	3 500	10 000	51 600	150 600
Lao People's Dem. Rep. Rép. dém. pop. lao	...	...	...	...	500	2 000	6 000	10 000
Latvia Lettonie	...	...	20 000	50 000	80 000	105 000	150 000	170 000
Lebanon Liban	...	2 500	5 000	45 000	100 000	200 000	300 000	420 000
Lesotho [1] Lesotho [1]	...	...	50	100	200	1 000	4 000	5 000
Liberia Libéria	...	...	...	100	100	300	500	1 000
Libyan Arab Jamah. Jamah. arabe libyenne	...	...	...	...	...	7 000	10 000	20 000
Liechtenstein Liechtenstein	...	...	...	...	...	...	...	8 000
Lithuania Lituanie	...	...	10 000	35 000	70 000	103 000	225 000	250 000
Luxembourg Luxembourg	2 000 [4]	6 500 [4]	23 000 [4]	30 000 [4]	50 000 [4]	75 000 [4]	100 000 [4]	160 000
Madagascar Madagascar	...	...	500	2 000	9 000	25 000	30 000	35 000
Malawi Malawi	...	...	...	500	2 000	10 000	15 000	20 000
Malaysia Malaisie	20 000 [4]	30 000 [4]	180 000	500 000	1 500 000	2 800 000	4 000 000	6 500 000
Maldives Maldives	0	0	575	800	1 500	3 000	6 000	10 000
Mali Mali	...	...	200	1 000	2 000	6 277	18 804	30 000
Malta Malte	...	850	4 000	15 000	25 000	30 000	51 000	99 000
Marshall Islands Iles Marshall	0	0	19	...	...	500	800	900
Martinique Martinique	...	...	...	...	2 000	5 000	30 000	40 000
Mauritania Mauritanie	...	...	...	100	1 000	3 000	5 000	7 000
Mauritius Maurice	...	...	2 100	5 500	30 000	55 000	87 000	158 000
Mexico Mexique	39 000	94 000	187 000	595 700	1 222 379	1 822 198	2 712 375	3 635 600
Micronesia (Fed. States) Micronésie (Etats féd. de)	...	...	300	616	2 000	3 000	4 000	5 000

19

Internet users
Estimated number *[cont.]*
Usagers d'Internet
Nombre estimatif *[suite]*

Country or area Pays ou zone	1994	1995	1996	1997	1998	1999	2000	2001
Monaco Monaco	...	...	...	...	...	...	13 500	15 000
Mongolia Mongolie	...	200	415	2 600	3 400	12 000	30 000	40 000
Morocco Maroc	...	1 000	1 552	6 000	40 000	50 000	200 000	400 000
Mozambique Mozambique	...	...	500	2 000	3 500	10 000	20 000	30 000
Myanmar Myanmar	...	...	...	...	...	500	7 000	10 000
Namibia [2] Namibie [2]	...	100	150	1 000	5 000	6 000	30 000	45 000
Nepal Népal	0 [9]	200 [9]	1 000 [9]	5 000 [9]	15 000 [9]	35 000 [9]	50 000 [9]	60 000 [10]
Netherlands Pays-Bas	500 000	1 000 000	1 500 000	2 200 000	3 500 000	6 200 000	7 000 000	7 900 000
Netherlands Antilles Antilles néerlandaises	...	...	500	...	...	2 000	...	...
New Caledonia Nouvelle-Calédonie	...	10	500	2 000	4 000	12 000	20 000	24 900
New Zealand Nouvelle-Zélande	115 000 [1]	180 000 [1]	300 000 [1]	550 000 [1]	750 000 [1]	1 113 000 [1]	1 515 000 [3]	1 762 000 [3]
Nicaragua Nicaragua	600	1 400	4 000	10 000	15 000	25 000	50 000	75 000
Niger Niger	...	...	100	200	300	3 000	4 000	12 000
Nigeria Nigéria	...	...	10 000	20 000	30 000	50 000	80 000	115 000
Niue Nioué	...	...	...	...	...	300	500	600
Norway Norvège	180 000 [4]	280 000 [4]	800 000 [4]	1 300 000 [4]	1 600 000 [4]	1 800 000	1 950 000	2 100 000
Occupied Palestinian Terr. Terr. palestinien occupé	...	...	...	...	...	...	35 000	60 000
Oman Oman	...	...	...	10 000	20 000	50 000	90 000	120 000
Pakistan [3] Pakistan [3]	...	160	4 000	37 800	61 900	80 000	300 000	500 000
Panama Panama	200	1 500	6 000	15 000	30 000	45 000	90 000	120 000
Papua New Guinea Papouasie-Nvl-Guinée	...	...	100	5 000	12 000	35 000	45 000	50 000
Paraguay Paraguay	...	...	1 000	5 000	10 000	20 000	40 000	60 000
Peru Pérou	2 000	8 000	60 000	100 000	300 000	500 000	800 000	2 000 000
Philippines Philippines	4 000	20 000	40 000	100 000	823 000	1 090 000	1 540 000	2 000 000
Poland Pologne	150 000	250 000	500 000	800 000	1 581 000	2 100 000	2 800 000	3 800 000

19

Internet users
Estimated number *[cont.]*
Usagers d'Internet
Nombre estimatif *[suite]*

Country or area Pays ou zone	1994	1995	1996	1997	1998	1999	2000	2001
Portugal Portugal	72 000 [4]	150 000 [4]	300 000 [4]	500 000 [4]	1 000 000 [4]	1 500 000 [4]	2 500 000	2 900 000
Puerto Rico Porto Rico	1 000	5 000	10 000	50 000	100 000	200 000	400 000	600 000
Qatar Qatar	...	1 000	5 000	17 000	20 000	24 000	30 000	40 000
Republic of Moldova République de Moldova	36	150	200	1 200	11 000	25 000	52 600	60 000
Réunion [11] Réunion [11]	...	...	...	...	9 000	10 000	130 000	150 000
Romania Roumanie	6 000	17 000	50 000	100 000	500 000	600 000	800 000	1 000 000
Russian Federation Fédération de Russie	80 000	220 000	400 000	700 000	1 200 000	1 500 000	3 100 000	4 300 000
Rwanda Rwanda	...	...	50	100	800	5 000	5 000	20 000
Saint Helena Sainte-Hélène	...	...	...	...	79 [1]	300 [1]	300 [1]	400 [10]
Saint Kitts and Nevis [1] Saint-Kitts-et-Nevis [1]	...	...	850	1 000	1 500	2 000	2 700	3 600
Saint Lucia [1] Sainte-Lucie [1]	...	450	1 000	1 500	2 000	3 000	8 000	13 000
St. Vincent-Grenadines [1] St. Vincent-Grenadines [1]	...	139	522	1 000	2 000	3 000	3 500	5 500
Samoa Samoa	...	...	...	300	400	500	1 000	3 000
San Marino Saint-Marin	...	350	370	370	370	11 360	13 150	13 850
Sao Tome and Principe Sao Tomé-et-Principe	...	...	...	...	400	500	6 500	9 000
Saudi Arabia Arabie saoudite	...	2 000	5 000	10 000	20 000	100 000	200 000	300 000
Senegal Sénégal	...	60	1 000	2 500	7 500	30 000	40 000	100 000
Serbia and Montenegro Serbie-et-Monténégro	...	...	20 000	50 000	65 000	80 000	400 000	600 000
Seychelles Seychelles	...	...	500 [1]	1 000 [1]	2 000 [1]	5 000 [1]	6 000 [1,4]	9 000 [10]
Sierra Leone Sierra Leone	0	0	100	200	600	2 000	5 000	7 000
Singapore [1] Singapour [1]	40 000	100 000	300 000	500 000	750 000	950 000	1 300 000	1 700 000
Slovakia Slovaquie	17 000	28 000	50 000 [4]	100 000 [4]	144 539	292 359	507 029	674 039
Slovenia Slovénie	21 000	57 000	100 000	150 000	200 000	250 000	300 000	600 000
Solomon Islands [1] Iles Salomon [1]	...	90	1 000	1 500	2 000	2 000	2 000	2 000
Somalia Somalie	...	0	0	0	100	200	500	1 000

19

Internet users
Estimated number *[cont.]*
Usagers d'Internet
Nombre estimatif *[suite]*

Country or area Pays ou zone	1994	1995	1996	1997	1998	1999	2000	2001
South Africa [1] Afrique du Sud [1]	100 000	280 000	355 000	700 000	1 266 000	1 820 000	2 400 000	2 890 000
Spain Espagne	110 000	150 000	526 000	1 110 000	1 733 000	2 830 000	5 486 000	7 388 000
Sri Lanka Sri Lanka	500	1 000	10 000	30 000	55 000	65 000	121 500	150 000
Sudan Soudan	0	0	0	700	2 000	5 000	30 000	56 000
Suriname Suriname	...	500	1 000	4 494	7 587	8 715	11 709	14 520
Swaziland [1] Swaziland [1]	...	10	500	900	1 000	5 000	10 000	14 000
Sweden Suède	300 000	450 000	800 000	2 100 000	2 961 000	3 666 000	4 048 000	4 600 000
Switzerland Suisse	190 000	250 000	322 000	548 000	939 000	1 473 000	2 096 000	2 224 000
Syrian Arab Republic Rép. arabe syrienne	0	0	0	5 000	10 000	20 000	30 000	60 000
Tajikistan Tadjikistan	...	...	...	...	...	2 000	3 000	3 200
Thailand [2] Thaïlande [2]	30 000	55 000	135 000	375 000	500 000	1 300 000	2 300 000	3 536 001
TFYR of Macedonia L'ex-R.y. Macédoine	...	800	1 500	10 000	20 000	30 000	50 000	70 000
Togo Togo	0	0	500	10 000	15 000	30 000	100 000	150 000
Tonga Tonga	...	120	160	500	750	1 000	2 400	2 800
Trinidad and Tobago Trinité-et-Tobago	...	2 000 [1]	5 000 [1]	15 000 [1]	35 000 [1]	75 000 [1]	100 000 [1]	120 000 [10]
Tunisia Tunisie	650	1 000	2 500	4 000	10 000	150 000	250 000	400 000
Turkey Turquie	30 000	50 000	120 000	300 000	450 000	1 500 000	2 000 000	2 500 000
Turkmenistan Turkménistan	...	...	...	...	...	2 000	6 000	8 000
Tuvalu Tuvalu	...	...	...	...	...	...	500	1 000
Uganda [3] Ouganda [3]	...	600	1 000	2 300	15 000	25 000	40 000	60 000
Ukraine Ukraine	7 000	22 000	50 000	100 000	150 000	200 000	350 000	600 000
United Arab Emirates Emirats arabes unis	...	2 503 [1] [2]	9 669	90 000	200 000	458 000	765 000	976 000
United Kingdom [1] Royaume-Uni [1]	600 000 [4]	1 100 000 [4]	2 400 000 [4]	4 310 000 [4]	8 000 000 [4]	12 500 000 [4]	15 800 000	19 800 000
United Rep. of Tanzania Rép.-Unie de Tanzanie	...	...	500	2 500	3 000	25 000	40 000	100 000
United States Etats-Unis	13 000 000	25 000 000	45 000 000	60 000 000	84 587 000	102 000 000	124 000 000	142 823 000

19

Internet users
Estimated number *[cont.]*
Usagers d'Internet
Nombre estimatif *[suite]*

Country or area Pays ou zone	1994	1995	1996	1997	1998	1999	2000	2001
United States Virgin Is. Iles Vierges américaines	1 000	3 000	5 000	7 500	10 000	12 000	15 000	17 000
Uruguay Uruguay	2 000	10 000	60 000	110 000	230 000	330 000	370 000	400 000
Uzbekistan Ouzbékistan	...	350	1 000	2 500	5 000	7 500	120 000	150 000
Vanuatu Vanuatu	...	...	100	250	500	1 000	4 000	5 500
Venezuela Venezuela	12 000	27 000	56 000	90 000	322 244	680 000	820 022	1 152 502
Viet Nam Viet Nam	...	...	100	3 000	10 000	100 000	200 000	1 009 544
Yemen Yémen	...	...	100	2 500	4 000	10 000	15 000	17 000
Zambia [1] Zambie [1]	600	800	850	900	3 000	15 000	20 000	25 000
Zimbabwe [3,4] Zimbabwe [3,4]	200	900	2 000	4 000	10 000	20 000	50 000	100 000

Source:
International Telecommunication Union (ITU), Geneva, "Yearbook of Statistics, Telecommunication Services, Chronological Time Series 1991-2000" and the ITU database.

Source:
Union internationale des télécommunications (UIT), Genève, "Yearbook of Statistics, Telecommunication Services, Chronological Time Series 1991-2000" et la base de données de l'UIT.

1   Data refer to fiscal years beginning 1 April.

2   Data refer to fiscal years ending 30 September.

3   Data refer to fiscal years ending 30 June.
4   ITU estimate.
5   Year ending November 1997.
6   As of 30 September.
7   June.
8   Data refer to fiscal years beginning 22 March.

9   Data refer to fiscal years ending 15 July.

10   As of 31 December.
11   France Télécom only.
12   Internet dial-up customers.

1   Les données se réfèrent aux exercices budgétaires commençant le 1er avril.
2   Les données se réfèrent aux exercices budgétaires finissant le 30 septembre.
3   Les données se réfèrent aux exercices budgétaires finissant le 30 juin.
4   Estimation de l'UIT.
5   Année s'achevant en novembre 1997.
6   Dès le 30 septembre.
7   Juin.
8   Les données se réfèrent aux exercices budgétaires commençant le 22 mars.
9   Les données se réfèrent aux exercices budgétaires finissant le 15 juillet.
10   Dès le 31 décembre.
11   France Télécom seulement.
12   Clients accédant à l'Internet par numérotation.

Technical notes, tables 13-19

Tables 13-16: The data on books, newspapers, periodicals and cinemas have been compiled from the UNESCO Institute for Statistics database (see <www.uis.unesco.org>) and from earlier editions of the UNESCO *Statistical Yearbook* [31].

Table 13: Data on books by subject groups cover printed books and pamphlets and, unless otherwise stated, refer to first editions and re-editions as well as to reprints that do not require a new ISBN. The grouping by subject follows the Universal Decimal Classification (UDC).

Table 14: For the purposes of this table, a daily general interest newspaper is defined as a publication devoted primarily to recording general news. It is considered to be "daily" if it appears at least four times a week. It should be noted that data prior to 1997 may not be comparable to data for later years due to UNESCO's use of different sources.

Table 15: For the purposes of this table, a non-daily general interest newspaper is defined as a publication which is devoted primarily to recording general news and which is published three times a week or less. Under the category of periodicals are included publications of periodical issue, other than newspapers, containing information of a general or of a specialized nature. It should be noted that data prior to 1997 may not be comparable to data for later years due to UNESCO's use of different sources.

Table 16: The data refer to fixed cinemas and mobile units regularly used for commercial exhibition of long films of 1,600 metres and over. The term fixed cinema used in this table refers to establishments possessing their own equipment and includes indoor cinemas (those with a permanent fixed roof over most of the seating accommodation), outdoor cinemas and drive-ins (establishments designed to enable the audience to watch a film while seated in their automobile). Mobile units are defined as projection units equipped and used to serve more than one site.

The capacity of fixed cinemas refers to the number of seats in indoor and outdoor cinemas plus the number of places for automobiles, multiplied by a factor of 4 in the case of drive-ins.

Cinema attendance is calculated from the number of tickets sold during a given year.

As a rule, figures refer only to commercial establishments but in the case of mobile units, it is possible that the figures for some countries may also include non-commercial units.

The statistics included in *Tables 17-19* were obtained from the statistics database (see <www.itu.int>)

Notes techniques, tableaux 13 à 19

Tableaux 13 à 16: Les données concernant les livres, les journaux, les périodiques et les cinémas proviennent de la base de données de l'Institut de statistique de l'UNESCO (voir <www.uis.unesco.org>) et des éditions précédentes de l'*Annuaire statistique* de l'UNESCO [31].

Tableau 13: Les données concernant la production de livres par groupes de sujets se rapportent aux livres et brochures imprimés, sauf indication contraire, aux premières éditions et aux rééditions, ainsi qu'aux réimpressions qui ne nécessitent pas un nouveau numéro de ISBN. Les sujets sont groupés selon la Classification décimale universelle (CDU).

Tableau 14: Dans ce tableau, par "journal quotidien d'information générale", on entend une publication qui a essentiellement pour objet de rendre compte des événements courants. Il est considéré comme "quotidien" s'il paraît au moins quatre fois par semaine. Les données antérieures à 1997 peuvent n'être pas comparables à celles des années suivantes, l'UNESCO ayant utilisé des sources différentes.

Tableau 15: Aux fins de ce tableau, par "journal non quotidien d'information générale", on entend une publication qui a essentiellement pour objet de rendre compte des événements courants et qui est publié trois fois par semaine ou moins. La catégorie périodique comprend les publications périodiques autres que les journaux, contenant des informations de caractère général ou spécialisé. Les données antérieures à 1997 peuvent n'être pas comparables à celles des années suivantes, l'UNESCO ayant utilisé des sources différentes.

Tableau 16: Les données concernent les établissements fixes et les cinémas itinérants d'exploitation commerciale de films d'une longueur de 1600 mètres et plus. Le terme établissement fixe désigne tout établissement doté de son propre équipement; il englobe les salles fermées (c'est-à-dire celles où un toit fixe recouvre la plupart des places assises), les cinémas de plein air et les cinémas pour automobilistes ou drive-ins (conçus pour permettre aux spectateurs d'assister à la projection sans quitter leur voiture). Les cinémas itinérants sont définis comme groupes mobiles de projection équipés de manière à pouvoir être utilisés dans des lieux différents.

La capacité des cinémas fixes se réfère au nombre de sièges dans les salles fermées et les cinémas de plein air, plus le nombre de places d'automobiles multiplié par le facteur 4 dans le cas des drive-ins.

La fréquentation des cinémas est calculée sur la base du nombre de billets vendus au cours d'une année donnée.

and the *Yearbook of Statistics, Telecommunication Services* [18] of the International Telecommunication Union.

Table 17: The number of mobile cellular telephone subscribers refers to users of portable telephones subscribing to an automatic public mobile telephone service using cellular technology which provides access to the Public Switched Telephone Network (PSTN).

Table 18: This table shows the number of main lines in operation and the main lines in operation per 100 inhabitants for the years indicated. Main telephone lines refer to the telephone lines connecting a customer's equipment to the Public Switched Telephone Network (PSTN) and which have a dedicated port on a telephone exchange. Note that in most countries, main lines also include public telephones. Main telephone lines per 100 inhabitants is calculated by dividing the number of main lines by the population and multiplying by 100.

Table 19: Internet user data is based on reported estimates, derivations based on reported Internet Access Provider subscriber counts, or calculated by multiplying the number of hosts by an estimated multiplier. However, comparisons of user data are misleading because there is no standard definition of frequency (e.g., daily, weekly, monthly) or services used (e.g., e-mail, World Wide Web).

En général, les statistiques présentées ne concernent que les établissements commerciaux: toutefois, dans le cas des cinémas itinérants, il se peut que les données relatives à certains pays tiennent compte aussi des établissements non-commerciaux.

Les données présentées dans les *Tableaux 17 à 19* proviennent de la base de données (voir <www.itu.int>) et *l'Annuaire statistique, Services de télécommunications* [18] de l'Union internationale des télécommunications.

Tableau 17: Les abonnés mobiles désignent les utilisateurs de téléphones portatifs abonnés à un service automatique public de téléphones mobiles ayant accès au Réseau de téléphone public connecté (RTPC).

Tableau 18: Ce tableau indique le nombre de lignes principales en service et les lignes principales en service pour 100 habitants pour les années indiquées. Les lignes principales sont des lignes téléphoniques qui relient l'équipement terminal de l'abonné au Réseau de téléphone public connecté (RTPC) et qui possèdent un accès individualisé aux équipements d'un central téléphonique. Pour la plupart des pays, le nombre de lignes principales en service indiqué comprend également les lignes publiques. Le nombre de lignes principales pour 100 habitants se calcule en divisant le nombre de lignes principales par la population et en multipliant par 100.

Tableau 19: Les chiffres relatifs aux usagers d'Internet sont basés sur les estimations communiquées, calculés à partir des chiffres issus de dénombrements d'abonnés aux services de fournisseurs d'accès, ou obtenus en multipliant le nombre d'hôtes par un facteur estimatif. Mais les comparaisons de chiffres relatifs aux usagers prêtent à confusion, car il n'existe pas de définition normalisée de la fréquence (quotidienne, hebdomadaire, mensuelle) ni des services utilisés (courrier électronique, Web).

Part Three
Economic Activity

Chapter VI
National accounts and industrial production (tables 20-26)
Chapter VII
Financial statistics (tables 27 and 28)
Chapter VIII
Labour force (tables 29 and 30)
Chapter IX
Wages and prices (tables 31-33)
Chapter X
Agriculture, forestry and fishing (tables 34-40)
Chapter XI
Manufacturing (tables 41-58)
Chapter XII
Transport (tables 59-63)
Chapter XIII
Energy (tables 64 and 65)
Chapter XIV
Environment (tables 66-68)
Chapter XV
Science and technology, intellectual property (tables 69-71)

Part Three of the *Yearbook* presents statistical series on production and consumption for a wide range of economic activities, and other basic series on major economic topics, for all countries or areas of the world for which data are available. Included are basic tables on national accounts, finance, labour force, wages and prices, a wide range of agricultural, mined and manufactured commodities, transport, energy, environment, research and development personnel and expenditure, and intellectual property.

International economic topics such as external trade are covered in Part Four.

Troisième partie
Activité économique

Chapitre VI
Comptabilités nationales et production industrielle (tableaux 20 à 26)
Chapitre VII
Statistiques financières (tableaux 27 et 29)
Chapitre VIII
Main-d'oeuvre (tableaux 29 et 30)
Chapitre IX
Salaires et prix (tableaux 31 à 33)
Chapitre X
Agriculture, forêts et pêche (tableaux 34 à 40)
Chapitre XI
Industries manufacturières (tableaux 41 à 58)
Chapitre XII
Transports (tableaux 59 à 63)
Chapitre XIII
Energie (tableaux 64 et 65)
Chapitre XIV
Environnement (tableaux 66 à 68)
Chapitre XV
Science et technologie, propriété intellectuelle (tableaux 69 à 71)

La troisième partie de l'*Annuaire* présente, pour une large gamme d'activités économiques, des séries statistiques sur la production et la consommation, et, pour tous les pays ou zones du monde pour lesquels des données sont disponibles, d'autres séries fondamentales ayant trait à des questions économiques importantes. Y figurent des tableaux de base consacrés à la comptabilité nationale, aux finances, à la main-d'oeuvre, aux salaires et aux prix, à un large éventail de produits agricoles, miniers et manufacturés, aux transports, à l'énergie, à l'environnement, au personnel employé à des travaux de recherche et développement, et dépenses de recherche et développement, et à la propriété intellectuelle.

Les questions économiques internationales comme le commerce extérieur sont traitées dans la quatrième partie.

20
Gross domestic product and gross domestic product per capita
In millions of US dollars [1] at current and constant 1990 prices; per capita US dollars;
real rates of growth
Produit intérieur brut et produit intérieur brut par habitant
En millions de dollars E.–U. [1] aux prix courants et constants de 1990; par habitant en dollars E.–U.;
taux de l'accroissement réels

Country or area Pays ou zone	1992	1993	1994	1995	1996	1997	1998	1999	2000
World Monde									
At current prices	24869856	24590778	26444576	29319975	30066874	29948970	29860066	30870153	31700950
Per capita	4591	4472	4740	5182	5240	5148	5064	5167	5238
At constant prices	23738813	23991318	24640142	25315856	26127519	27058591	27711141	28560657	29734237
Growth rates	1.4	1.1	2.7	2.7	3.2	3.6	2.4	3.1	4.1
Afghanistan [2] Afghanistan [2]									
At current prices	4 519	4 030	3 630	3 460	3 687	4 175	4 394	3 851	2 169
Per capita	290	239	201	181	186	205	212	182	100
At constant prices	4 519	4 030	3 909	3 726	3 970	4 497	4 732	4 147	2 336
Growth rates	−12.5	−10.8	−3.0	−4.7	6.6	13.3	5.2	−12.4	−43.7
Albania Albanie									
At current prices	676	1 228	1 949	2 479	2 689	2 294	3 058	3 676	3 752
Per capita	206	378	606	778	850	730	975	1 174	1 197
At constant prices	1 450	1 589	1 721	1 950	2 128	1 978	2 136	2 291	2 470
Growth rates	−7.2	9.6	8.3	13.3	9.1	−7.0	8.0	7.3	7.8
Algeria Algérie									
At current prices	49 217	50 962	42 426	42 017	46 845	47 869	47 347	44 959	50 363
Per capita	1 893	1 919	1 565	1 519	1 662	1 667	1 620	1 511	1 663
At constant prices	62 128	60 763	60 052	62 333	64 702	65 413	68 748	71 929	73 674
Growth rates	1.6	−2.2	−1.2	3.8	3.8	1.1	5.1	4.6	2.4
Andorra Andorre									
At current prices	887	775	825	1 003	1 098	1 059	1 160	1 242	1 208
Per capita	15 248	12 624	12 729	14 701	15 327	14 098	14 749	15 102	14 054
At constant prices	779	810	873	942	1 012	1 102	1 203	1 308	1 433
Growth rates	5.8	4.1	7.7	8.0	7.5	8.9	9.1	8.7	9.6
Angola Angola									
At current prices	13 995	10 142	10 437	4 994	6 617	7 629	6 455	6 408	7 751
Per capita	1 368	957	951	440	566	633	521	502	590
At constant prices	9 727	7 394	7 493	8 359	9 326	9 861	10 491	10 625	10 849
Growth rates	−5.8	−24.0	1.3	11.6	11.6	5.7	6.4	1.3	2.1
Anguilla Anguilla									
At current prices	61	66	74	75	79	89	94	105	108
Per capita	6 734	7 120	7 719	7 575	7 767	8 457	8 743	9 453	9 430
At constant prices	57	62	67	65	67	74	77	83	85
Growth rates	7.3	7.4	8.2	−2.1	2.5	10.8	3.8	8.5	2.1
Antigua and Barbuda Antigua−et−Barbuda									
At current prices	424	457	500	494	540	581	620	651	662
Per capita	6 710	7 204	7 865	7 737	8 442	9 047	9 623	10 073	10 204
At constant prices	406	426	453	430	456	482	505	530	544
Growth rates	0.8	5.1	6.2	−5.0	6.1	5.6	4.9	4.9	2.5
Argentina Argentine									
At current prices	228 779	236 755	257 696	258 097	272 242	293 006	299 098	283 665	284 346
Per capita	6 845	6 990	7 509	7 423	7 730	8 214	8 280	7 755	7 678
At constant prices	172 284	183 055	193 738	188 226	198 628	214 739	223 007	215 457	213 758
Growth rates	10.3	6.3	5.8	−2.8	5.5	8.1	3.9	−3.4	−0.8
Armenia Arménie									
At current prices	324	468	648	1 287	1 597	1 639	1 892	1 845	1 915
Per capita	89	127	174	342	423	433	499	487	506
At constant prices	7 763	7 080	7 463	7 977	8 448	8 727	9 364	9 673	10 252
Growth rates	−41.8	−8.8	5.4	6.9	5.9	3.3	7.3	3.3	6.0
Australia Australie									
At current prices	312 640	303 612	344 615	372 732	414 666	416 534	371 643	405 956	388 462
Per capita	17 993	17 239	19 313	20 625	22 666	22 501	19 848	21 442	20 298
At constant prices	322 420	334 959	348 930	363 638	377 006	393 787	414 535	432 234	440 586
Growth rates	3.7	3.9	4.2	4.2	3.7	4.5	5.3	4.3	1.9
Austria Autriche									
At current prices	190 116	185 651	199 277	235 156	231 422	205 753	211 130	209 516	188 725
Per capita	24 187	23 402	24 917	29 225	28 654	25 435	26 097	25 913	23 357
At constant prices	170 914	171 626	176 097	178 956	182 538	185 447	191 977	197 365	203 206
Growth rates	2.3	0.4	2.6	1.6	2.0	1.6	3.5	2.8	3.0

20

Gross domestic product and gross domestic product per capita
In millions of US dollars [1] at current and constant 1990 prices; per capita US dollars;
real rates of growth [cont.]

Produit intérieur brut et produit intérieur brut par habitant
En millions de dollars E.−U. [1] aux prix courants et constants de 1990; par habitant en dollars E.−U.;
taux de l'accroissement réels [suite]

Country or area Pays ou zone	1992	1993	1994	1995	1996	1997	1998	1999	2000
Azerbaijan Azerbaïdjan									
At current prices	445	1 571	1 193	2 417	3 177	3 962	4 446	4 581	5 267
Per capita	60	210	157	315	409	505	562	574	655
At constant prices	16 918	13 010	10 453	9 218	9 333	9 875	10 859	11 664	12 934
Growth rates	−22.6	−23.1	−19.7	−11.8	1.3	5.8	10.0	7.4	10.9
Bahamas Bahamas									
At current prices	2 857	2 854	3 053	3 069	3 277	3 451	3 670	3 994	4 304
Per capita	10 731	10 488	10 989	10 840	11 383	11 806	12 383	13 300	14 147
At constant prices	2 779	2 722	2 775	2 805	2 923	3 019	3 110	3 296	3 463
Growth rates	−5.8	−2.1	2.0	1.1	4.2	3.3	3.0	6.0	5.1
Bahrain Bahrein									
At current prices	4 433	4 648	4 861	5 054	5 361	5 578	5 433	5 878	6 348
Per capita	8 468	8 600	8 728	8 824	9 125	9 274	8 839	9 369	9 923
At constant prices	4 515	4 888	5 004	5 112	5 270	5 433	5 693	5 605	5 840
Growth rates	7.8	8.3	2.4	2.2	3.1	3.1	4.8	−1.6	4.2
Bangladesh Bangladesh									
At current prices	32 187	34 223	37 929	41 294	43 236	45 607	46 838	48 301	49 752
Per capita	279	290	314	334	342	353	355	359	362
At constant prices	34 693	36 110	37 889	39 640	41 776	43 960	46 100	48 841	52 070
Growth rates	4.6	4.1	4.9	4.6	5.4	5.2	4.9	5.9	6.6
Barbados Barbados									
At current prices	1 588	1 654	1 743	1 871	1 997	2 206	2 374	2 485	2 600
Per capita	6 125	6 353	6 663	7 126	7 576	8 337	8 937	9 323	9 721
At constant prices	1 546	1 570	1 629	1 673	1 741	1 787	1 872	1 927	1 986
Growth rates	−6.2	1.5	3.8	2.7	4.1	2.6	4.8	2.9	3.1
Belarus Bélarus									
At current prices	4 785	6 719	5 915	10 538	14 500	14 098	15 222	12 163	10 408
Per capita	464	651	572	1 020	1 406	1 370	1 484	1 190	1 022
At constant prices	57 931	53 551	47 294	42 353	43 529	48 501	52 596	54 410	57 620
Growth rates	−9.6	−7.6	−11.7	−10.4	2.8	11.4	8.4	3.4	5.9
Belgium Belgique									
At current prices	227 334	215 935	233 673	276 856	269 915	245 195	251 020	250 939	228 798
Per capita	22 655	21 443	23 125	27 312	26 552	24 060	24 578	24 524	22 323
At constant prices	205 382	202 360	207 931	213 306	215 856	223 561	228 583	235 485	244 971
Growth rates	1.6	−1.5	2.8	2.6	1.2	3.6	2.2	3.0	4.0
Belize Belize									
At current prices	468	530	552	587	604	616	629	689	757
Per capita	2 427	2 707	2 770	2 888	2 912	2 905	2 904	3 109	3 345
At constant prices	441	469	481	501	509	526	539	572	615
Growth rates	6.0	6.4	2.5	4.1	1.6	3.4	2.4	6.1	7.5
Benin Bénin									
At current prices	2 105	2 074	1 487	2 065	2 156	2 123	2 246	2 299	2 189
Per capita	423	403	279	376	381	366	377	376	349
At constant prices	2 015	2 079	2 146	2 281	2 395	2 491	2 590	2 719	2 884
Growth rates	4.2	3.2	3.2	6.3	5.0	4.0	4.0	5.0	6.1
Bermuda Bermudes									
At current prices	1 720	1 864	1 914	2 083	2 194	2 330	2 457	2 624	2 774
Per capita	28 785	30 988	31 611	34 177	35 763	37 732	39 531	41 946	44 060
At constant prices	1 592	1 665	1 677	1 794	1 846	1 914	1 944	2 008	2 066
Growth rates	−4.1	4.6	0.7	6.9	2.9	3.7	1.5	3.3	2.9
Bhutan Bhoutan									
At current prices	245	236	274	310	333	394	396	444	483
Per capita	140	133	152	169	178	205	201	219	232
At constant prices	308	327	347	373	393	422	450	483	510
Growth rates	4.5	6.1	6.4	7.4	5.2	7.6	6.4	7.4	5.7
Bolivia Bolivie									
At current prices	5 644	5 735	5 974	6 715	7 397	7 926	8 434	8 304	8 290
Per capita	819	812	825	906	974	1 020	1 060	1 020	995
At constant prices	5 133	5 352	5 602	5 864	6 120	6 423	6 759	6 788	6 949
Growth rates	1.6	4.3	4.7	4.7	4.4	5.0	5.2	0.4	2.4
Bosnia & Herzegovina Bosnie−Herzégovine									
At current prices	1 387	1 231	1 096	2 043	2 293	3 786	4 254	4 528	4 270
Per capita	351	331	311	597	669	1 074	1 155	1 177	1 074

20
Gross domestic product and gross domestic product per capita
In millions of US dollars [1] at current and constant 1990 prices; per capita US dollars;
real rates of growth [cont.]
Produit intérieur brut et produit intérieur brut par habitant
En millions de dollars E.−U. [1] aux prix courants et constants de 1990; par habitant en dollars E.−U.;
taux de l'accroissement réels [suite]

Country or area Pays ou zone	1992	1993	1994	1995	1996	1997	1998	1999	2000
At constant prices	8 513	6 214	6 618	8 802	13 203	17 164	20 597	22 657	21 342
Growth rates	−26.1	−27.0	6.5	33.0	50.0	30.0	20.0	10.0	−5.8
Botswana Botswana									
At current prices	3 970	3 763	4 113	4 423	4 273	4 859	4 771	4 654	4 971
Per capita	3 018	2 781	2 960	3 110	2 941	3 283	3 172	3 053	3 225
At constant prices	4 067	4 059	4 223	4 359	4 601	4 859	5 250	5 467	5 909
Growth rates	6.3	−0.2	4.0	3.2	5.5	5.6	8.1	4.1	8.1
Brazil Brésil									
At current prices	390 789	438 515	546 501	704 518	775 319	808 146	787 742	531 135	593 779
Per capita	2 559	2 829	3 475	4 418	4 795	4 931	4 743	3 157	3 484
At constant prices	467 508	490 726	519 303	541 234	555 418	575 686	575 049	579 621	605 491
Growth rates	−0.6	5.0	5.8	4.2	2.6	3.6	−0.1	0.8	4.5
British Virgin Islands Iles Vierges britanniques									
At current prices	345	364	431	479	511	574	612	654	683
Per capita	18 638	19 045	21 811	23 477	24 278	26 459	27 394	28 452	28 897
At constant prices	313	324	342	360	368	390	395	406	424
Growth rates	2.5	3.5	5.7	5.0	2.3	5.9	1.3	3.0	4.4
Brunei Darussalam Brunéi Darussalam									
At current prices	4 030	4 075	4 377	4 986	5 450	5 422	4 846	4 833	5 038
Per capita	14 821	14 579	15 249	16 935	18 074	17 579	15 376	15 020	15 345
At constant prices	3 695	3 713	3 781	3 856	4 034	4 155	4 240	4 219	4 367
Growth rates	−1.1	0.5	1.8	2.0	4.6	3.0	2.0	−0.5	3.5
Bulgaria Bulgarie									
At current prices	8 604	10 833	9 708	13 106	9 830	10 141	12 257	12 403	11 988
Per capita	1 000	1 268	1 145	1 559	1 181	1 232	1 507	1 543	1 508
At constant prices	17 894	17 630	17 950	18 463	16 592	15 424	15 969	16 368	17 314
Growth rates	−7.3	−1.5	1.8	2.9	−10.1	−7.0	3.5	2.5	5.8
Burkina Faso Burkina Faso									
At current prices	3 070	2 939	1 887	2 390	2 583	2 424	2 626	2 628	2 356
Per capita	323	301	188	233	246	226	239	234	204
At constant prices	3 221	3 196	3 234	3 363	3 564	3 733	3 963	4 111	4 365
Growth rates	2.5	−0.8	1.2	4.0	6.0	4.8	6.2	3.7	6.2
Burundi Burundi									
At current prices	1 087	977	1 071	1 000	902	960	887	803	787
Per capita	186	164	178	165	147	156	143	128	124
At constant prices	1 231	1 145	1 110	1 032	943	946	989	1 036	1 026
Growth rates	1.8	−7.0	−3.1	−7.0	−8.6	0.4	4.5	4.7	−0.9
Cambodia Cambodge									
At current prices	2 228	2 265	2 439	3 081	3 176	3 109	2 816	3 059	3 104
Per capita	216	212	221	270	271	257	227	240	237
At constant prices	1 854	1 930	2 006	2 139	2 257	2 340	2 383	2 547	2 685
Growth rates	7.0	4.1	3.9	6.7	5.5	3.7	1.8	6.9	5.4
Cameroon Cameroun									
At current prices	13 904	12 269	6 762	8 945	9 370	9 201	9 736	9 984	9 307
Per capita	1 132	973	522	674	689	661	684	686	626
At constant prices	13 352	13 153	12 726	13 122	13 774	14 476	15 200	15 869	16 532
Growth rates	−3.1	−1.5	−3.2	3.1	5.0	5.1	5.0	4.4	4.2
Canada Canada									
At current prices	571 862	556 547	557 271	583 146	605 985	629 249	607 524	646 285	700 572
Per capita	20 136	19 373	19 186	19 866	20 436	21 016	20 103	21 195	22 778
At constant prices	569 845	582 960	610 525	627 251	636 844	664 797	686 747	718 289	751 934
Growth rates	0.9	2.3	4.7	2.7	1.5	4.4	3.3	4.6	4.7
Cape Verde Cap−Vert									
At current prices	358	362	409	491	496	509	543	584	555
Per capita	1 007	994	1 099	1 289	1 275	1 278	1 331	1 400	1 299
At constant prices	322	345	369	397	407	434	469	507	541
Growth rates	3.0	7.3	6.9	7.5	2.6	6.6	8.0	8.0	6.8
Cayman Islands Iles Caïmanes									
At current prices	825	894	971	1 019	1 075	1 173	1 237	1 321	1 396
Per capita	28 925	30 140	31 497	31 853	32 387	34 058	34 659	35 745	36 517

20

Gross domestic product and gross domestic product per capita
In millions of US dollars [1] at current and constant 1990 prices; per capita US dollars;
real rates of growth [cont.]

Produit intérieur brut et produit intérieur brut par habitant
En millions de dollars E.–U. [1] aux prix courants et constants de 1990; par habitant en dollars E.–U.;
taux de l'accroissement réels [suite]

Country or area Pays ou zone	1992	1993	1994	1995	1996	1997	1998	1999	2000
At constant prices	713	720	723	720	721	724	735	760	782
Growth rates	−0.6	0.9	0.5	−0.5	0.2	0.5	1.5	3.3	2.9
Central African Rep. Rép. centrafricaine									
At current prices	1 339	1 213	797	1 065	1 000	929	979	979	896
Per capita	432	381	244	318	292	265	274	268	241
At constant prices	1 207	1 211	1 270	1 346	1 303	1 377	1 444	1 488	1 515
Growth rates	−6.4	0.3	4.9	6.0	−3.2	5.7	4.8	3.1	1.8
Chad Tchad									
At current prices	1 325	1 030	830	1 006	1 060	994	1 091	974	882
Per capita	215	162	127	149	153	139	147	128	112
At constant prices	1 434	1 206	1 292	1 325	1 352	1 393	1 477	1 460	1 456
Growth rates	8.0	−15.9	7.1	2.6	2.0	3.0	6.0	−1.1	−0.3
Chile Chili									
At current prices	41 882	44 474	50 920	65 215	69 218	76 000	73 499	68 108	71 015
Per capita	3 092	3 229	3 639	4 589	4 800	5 197	4 958	4 535	4 669
At constant prices	36 759	39 327	41 572	45 990	49 378	53 051	55 133	54 503	57 435
Growth rates	12.3	7.0	5.7	10.6	7.4	7.4	3.9	−1.1	5.4
China Chine									
At current prices	469 003	598 765	541 734	700 606	821 854	903 449	964 533	995 738	1 084 892
Per capita	403	510	457	585	679	740	783	801	866
At constant prices	477 621	542 098	610 404	674 497	739 249	804 301	867 037	928 596	1 002 884
Growth rates	14.2	13.5	12.6	10.5	9.6	8.8	7.8	7.1	8.0
China, Hong Kong SAR Chine, Hong Kong RAS									
At current prices	100 512	115 822	130 580	139 006	153 845	170 706	162 589	158 254	162 643
Per capita	17 116	19 383	21 446	22 385	24 270	26 363	24 587	23 470	23 709
At constant prices	83 346	88 457	93 235	96 865	101 212	106 244	100 624	103 669	114 527
Growth rates	6.3	6.1	5.4	3.9	4.5	5.0	−5.3	3.0	10.5
Colombia Colombie									
At current prices	51 411	59 241	79 936	92 503	97 147	106 671	98 843	84 865	81 280
Per capita	1 413	1 597	2 114	2 400	2 474	2 668	2 429	2 050	1 930
At constant prices	49 782	52 463	55 514	58 402	59 602	61 647	61 991	59 479	61 153
Growth rates	4.0	5.4	5.8	5.2	2.1	3.4	0.6	−4.1	2.8
Comoros Comores									
At current prices	266	264	186	215	213	194	197	193	175
Per capita	477	459	314	352	340	299	296	281	248
At constant prices	250	254	249	243	247	245	242	244	242
Growth rates	−1.7	1.8	−2.2	−2.3	1.7	−1.1	−1.1	1.0	−1.1
Congo Congo									
At current prices	2 933	2 684	1 769	2 116	2 526	2 285	1 944	2 244	3 034
Per capita	1 236	1 096	701	813	942	827	683	766	1 005
At constant prices	2 941	2 912	2 752	2 862	3 043	2 959	3 067	3 017	3 243
Growth rates	2.6	−1.0	−5.5	4.0	6.3	−2.7	3.6	−1.6	7.5
Cook Islands Iles Cook									
At current prices	72	81	96	102	102	95	78	82	78
Per capita	3 872	4 302	5 074	5 365	5 367	4 962	4 047	4 230	3 975
At constant prices	73	75	78	75	75	73	70	74	82
Growth rates	6.0	3.9	3.9	−4.4	−0.2	−2.8	−3.2	5.8	9.8
Costa Rica Costa Rica									
At current prices	8 574	9 638	10 558	11 716	11 844	12 829	14 094	15 796	15 948
Per capita	2 642	2 878	3 058	3 297	3 243	3 423	3 669	4 016	3 964
At constant prices	8 097	8 697	9 109	9 466	9 550	10 083	10 929	11 828	12 092
Growth rates	9.2	7.4	4.7	3.9	0.9	5.6	8.4	8.2	2.2
Côte d'Ivoire Côte d'Ivoire									
At current prices	12 033	11 153	8 314	11 105	12 075	11 571	12 336	12 666	10 693
Per capita	902	814	592	772	820	769	803	808	668
At constant prices	11 825	11 778	12 031	12 879	13 748	14 567	15 222	15 883	15 470
Growth rates	−0.6	−0.4	2.1	7.1	6.7	6.0	4.5	4.3	−2.6
Croatia Croatie									
At current prices	10 241	10 903	14 583	18 811	19 872	20 294	21 628	20 063	19 031
Per capita	2 244	2 375	3 160	4 060	4 278	4 363	4 648	4 312	4 089
At constant prices	17 263	15 877	16 809	17 976	19 035	20 327	20 840	20 767	21 534
Growth rates	−11.7	−8.0	5.9	6.9	5.9	6.8	2.5	−0.4	3.7
Cuba Cuba									
At current prices	14 905	15 095	19 198	21 737	22 815	22 952	23 901	24 639	26 698

20
Gross domestic product and gross domestic product per capita
In millions of US dollars [1] at current and constant 1990 prices; per capita US dollars;
real rates of growth [cont.]
Produit intérieur brut et produit intérieur brut par habitant
En millions de dollars E.–U. [1] aux prix courants et constants de 1990; par habitant en dollars E.–U.;
taux de l'accroissement réels [suite]

Country or area Pays ou zone	1992	1993	1994	1995	1996	1997	1998	1999	2000
Per capita	1 382	1 391	1 760	1 983	2 071	2 074	2 150	2 208	2 384
At constant prices	15 513	13 205	13 299	13 626	14 694	15 060	15 248	16 199	17 111
Growth rates	−11.6	−14.9	0.7	2.5	7.8	2.5	1.2	6.2	5.6
Cyprus Chypre									
At current prices	6 902	6 584	7 414	8 856	8 923	8 505	9 066	9 226	8 803
Per capita	9 796	9 164	10 131	11 907	11 836	11 152	11 772	11 872	11 231
At constant prices	6 145	6 188	6 547	6 911	7 043	7 219	7 580	7 921	8 325
Growth rates	9.4	0.7	5.8	5.6	1.9	2.5	5.0	4.5	5.1
Czech Republic République tchèque									
At current prices	29 901	34 998	41 090	52 035	57 726	52 997	56 908	54 595	50 766
Per capita	2 898	3 389	3 977	5 037	5 591	5 138	5 525	5 308	4 942
At constant prices	30 671	30 690	31 372	33 234	34 661	34 396	33 984	33 852	34 848
Growth rates	−0.5	0.1	2.2	5.9	4.3	−0.8	−1.2	−0.4	2.9
Dem. Rep. of the Congo Rép. dém. du Congo									
At current prices	8 204	10 708	5 721	5 542	5 492	5 686	5 542	5 749	6 585
Per capita	205	256	132	124	119	120	115	116	129
At constant prices	7 666	6 629	6 372	6 417	6 475	6 060	5 848	4 971	4 260
Growth rates	−10.5	−13.5	−3.9	0.7	0.9	−6.4	−3.5	−15.0	−14.3
Denmark Danemark									
At current prices	147 092	138 828	151 829	180 237	182 953	169 026	172 428	173 961	160 351
Per capita	28 452	26 758	29 154	34 476	34 862	32 086	32 612	32 793	30 141
At constant prices	135 671	135 669	143 085	147 024	150 727	155 203	159 033	162 707	167 626
Growth rates	0.6	0.0	5.5	2.8	2.5	3.0	2.5	2.3	3.0
Djibouti Djibouti									
At current prices	482	482	511	510	496	491	498	519	535
Per capita	913	907	953	935	887	850	833	841	847
At constant prices	468	491	479	506	480	502	502	509	522
Growth rates	5.9	4.8	−2.4	5.6	−5.1	4.6	−0.2	1.5	2.6
Dominica Dominica									
At current prices	192	200	215	219	236	245	259	268	268
Per capita	2 696	2 821	3 035	3 090	3 335	3 463	3 670	3 790	3 803
At constant prices	175	178	182	185	190	194	199	203	203
Growth rates	2.7	1.9	2.1	1.6	3.1	2.0	2.8	1.6	0.2
Dominican Republic Rép. dominicaine									
At current prices	11 189	12 680	13 612	15 418	16 915	19 139	20 116	22 025	24 970
Per capita	1 531	1 705	1 799	2 003	2 160	2 403	2 483	2 674	2 982
At constant prices	10 146	10 719	11 139	11 647	12 613	13 649	14 672	15 964	17 004
Growth rates	10.2	5.6	3.9	4.6	8.3	8.2	7.5	8.8	6.5
Ecuador Equateur									
At current prices	12 656	14 304	16 606	17 939	19 040	19 769	19 723	13 689	13 759
Per capita	1 178	1 303	1 480	1 565	1 627	1 656	1 620	1 103	1 088
At constant prices	11 622	11 858	12 371	12 661	12 911	13 348	13 403	12 428	12 670
Growth rates	3.6	2.0	4.3	2.3	2.0	3.4	0.4	−7.3	1.9
Egypt Egypte									
At current prices	40 999	45 938	50 615	59 168	65 907	74 036	80 979	87 174	91 962
Per capita	700	769	832	954	1 044	1 151	1 236	1 307	1 355
At constant prices	57 078	59 978	62 346	65 187	68 523	72 155	76 327	80 900	85 785
Growth rates	0.5	5.1	3.9	4.6	5.1	5.3	5.8	6.0	6.0
El Salvador El Salvador									
At current prices	5 961	6 936	8 105	9 496	10 310	11 127	12 002	12 463	13 205
Per capita	1 121	1 277	1 460	1 675	1 780	1 882	1 989	2 025	2 103
At constant prices	5 935	6 372	6 758	7 190	7 312	7 623	7 909	8 174	8 338
Growth rates	7.5	7.4	6.0	6.4	1.7	4.2	3.8	3.4	2.0
Equatorial Guinea Guinée équatoriale									
At current prices	179	181	118	178	302	606	780	1 120	1 200
Per capita	485	477	303	445	735	1 440	1 803	2 521	2 628
At constant prices	178	189	199	228	294	503	614	868	1 015
Growth rates	10.7	6.3	5.1	14.3	29.1	71.2	22.0	41.4	16.9
Eritrea Erythrée									
At current prices	715	504	619	629	670	702	676	702	737
Per capita	227	160	196	197	207	212	198	199	202
At constant prices	968	943	1 036	1 066	1 138	1 227	1 264	1 302	1 289
Growth rates	...	−2.5	9.8	2.9	6.8	7.9	3.0	3.0	−1.0

20
Gross domestic product and gross domestic product per capita
In millions of US dollars [1] at current and constant 1990 prices; per capita US dollars;
real rates of growth [*cont.*]
Produit intérieur brut et produit intérieur brut par habitant
En millions de dollars E.−U. [1] aux prix courants et constants de 1990; par habitant en dollars E.−U.;
taux de l'accroissement réels [*suite*]

Country or area Pays ou zone	1992	1993	1994	1995	1996	1997	1998	1999	2000
Estonia Estonie									
At current prices	1 100	1 634	2 278	3 550	4 358	4 634	5 210	5 130	4 973
Per capita	710	1 070	1 514	2 393	2 977	3 206	3 649	3 637	3 569
At constant prices	8 686	7 947	7 788	8 122	8 440	9 336	9 776	9 667	10 289
Growth rates	−21.2	−8.5	−2.0	4.3	3.9	10.6	4.7	−1.1	6.4
Ethiopia Ethiopie									
At current prices	7 419	5 354	5 184	5 502	5 973	6 180	6 329	6 200	6 385
Per capita	147	103	96	99	105	106	106	101	102
At constant prices	7 500	8 397	8 530	9 056	10 017	10 535	10 478	11 139	11 640
Growth rates	0.0	12.0	1.6	6.2	10.6	5.2	−0.5	6.3	4.5
Fiji Fidji									
At current prices	1 533	1 637	1 826	1 990	2 114	2 119	1 587	1 861	1 653
Per capita	2 077	2 189	2 408	2 592	2 719	2 694	1 995	2 313	2 031
At constant prices	1 352	1 375	1 445	1 481	1 527	1 514	1 536	1 638	1 591
Growth rates	3.9	1.7	5.1	2.5	3.1	−0.9	1.5	6.6	−2.8
Finland Finlande									
At current prices	108 702	86 237	99 992	129 290	127 540	122 420	129 025	128 363	120 904
Per capita	21 592	17 040	19 661	25 312	24 880	23 811	25 036	24 859	23 377
At constant prices	123 976	122 552	127 399	132 252	137 555	146 210	154 010	160 254	169 208
Growth rates	−3.3	−1.1	4.0	3.8	4.0	6.3	5.3	4.1	5.6
France France									
At current prices	1 346 104	1 276 044	1 350 800	1 553 131	1 554 360	1 406 120	1 451 954	1 438 440	1 294 245
Per capita	23 484	22 151	23 338	26 714	26 625	23 994	24 686	24 370	21 848
At constant prices	1 246 323	1 235 266	1 260 787	1 281 844	1 295 981	1 320 662	1 365 582	1 405 411	1 448 960
Growth rates	1.5	−0.9	2.1	1.7	1.1	1.9	3.4	2.9	3.1
French Guiana Guyane française									
At current prices	1 507	1 411	1 482	1 675	1 672	1 500	1 518	1 488	1 316
Per capita	12 001	10 881	11 077	12 110	11 678	10 106	9 870	9 341	7 988
At constant prices	1 448	1 406	1 492	1 516	1 540	1 565	1 590	1 616	1 642
Growth rates	8.0	−2.9	6.1	1.6	1.6	1.6	1.6	1.6	1.6
French Polynesia Polynésie française									
At current prices	3 265	3 479	3 741	4 111	4 123	3 703	3 753	3 703	3 297
Per capita	16 059	16 794	17 735	19 150	18 877	16 668	16 617	16 129	14 131
At constant prices	3 160	3 263	3 682	3 597	3 656	3 698	3 737	3 836	3 938
Growth rates	3.8	3.3	12.8	−2.3	1.6	1.1	1.1	2.7	2.7
Gabon Gabon									
At current prices	5 593	5 406	4 191	4 959	5 630	5 341	4 666	4 504	4 906
Per capita	5 642	5 300	3 995	4 599	5 081	4 693	3 994	3 756	3 988
At constant prices	5 572	5 792	6 005	6 304	6 556	6 851	6 995	6 596	6 515
Growth rates	−3.2	4.0	3.7	5.0	4.0	4.5	2.1	−5.7	−1.2
Gambia Gambie									
At current prices	346	355	363	367	390	394	418	416	405
Per capita	345	342	337	330	338	331	340	328	311
At constant prices	353	376	391	377	397	400	440	458	484
Growth rates	0.4	6.6	3.8	−3.4	5.3	0.8	9.9	4.2	5.6
Georgia Géorgie									
At current prices	716	2 247	1 639	2 841	3 046	3 575	3 627	2 798	3 014
Per capita	132	415	305	531	571	673	685	530	573
At constant prices	9 766	6 905	6 188	6 348	7 048	7 707	7 800	8 003	8 110
Growth rates	−44.9	−29.3	−10.4	2.6	11.0	9.4	1.2	2.6	1.3
Germany Allemagne									
At current prices	2 020 392	1 956 870	2 091 666	2 458 277	2 383 351	2 110 965	2 144 484	2 103 391	1 866 131
Per capita	25 122	24 186	25 718	30 103	29 108	25 746	26 143	25 643	22 753
At constant prices	1 775 409	1 756 123	1 797 334	1 828 394	1 842 402	1 868 082	1 904 624	1 939 846	1 998 109
Growth rates	2.2	−1.1	2.3	1.7	0.8	1.4	2.0	1.8	3.0
Ghana Ghana									
At current prices	6 884	5 966	5 441	6 458	6 926	6 884	7 474	7 493	4 838
Per capita	430	363	322	373	391	380	404	397	251

20
Gross domestic product and gross domestic product per capita
In millions of US dollars [1] at current and constant 1990 prices; per capita US dollars;
real rates of growth [cont.]
Produit intérieur brut et produit intérieur brut par habitant
En millions de dollars E.–U. [1] aux prix courants et constants de 1990; par habitant en dollars E.–U.;
taux de l'accroissement réels [suite]

Country or area Pays ou zone	1992	1993	1994	1995	1996	1997	1998	1999	2000
At constant prices	6 812	7 148	7 382	7 679	8 032	8 441	8 825	9 311	9 657
Growth rates	3.9	4.9	3.3	4.0	4.6	5.1	4.6	5.5	3.7
Greece Grèce									
At current prices	99 814	93 453	100 147	117 564	124 361	121 339	121 958	125 599	113 319
Per capita	9 711	9 037	9 628	11 246	11 845	11 516	11 542	11 859	10 680
At constant prices	87 286	85 858	87 614	89 460	91 569	94 900	98 092	101 451	105 824
Growth rates	0.7	−1.6	2.0	2.1	2.4	3.6	3.4	3.4	4.3
Grenada Grenade									
At current prices	251	250	263	276	295	315	351	378	411
Per capita	2 750	2 731	2 859	2 999	3 188	3 397	3 771	4 056	4 391
At constant prices	232	229	236	244	251	261	280	301	321
Growth rates	1.1	−1.2	3.3	3.1	2.9	4.2	7.3	7.5	6.4
Guadeloupe Guadeloupe									
At current prices	3 395	3 461	3 946	4 439	4 575	4 453	4 697	4 645	4 146
Per capita	8 498	8 595	9 726	10 854	11 089	10 697	11 177	10 953	9 691
At constant prices	2 460	2 639	2 835	2 711	2 828	3 089	3 217	3 237	3 258
Growth rates	7.3	7.3	7.4	−4.3	4.3	9.2	4.1	0.6	0.6
Guatemala Guatemala									
At current prices	10 441	11 400	12 983	14 656	15 783	17 797	19 008	18 149	18 885
Per capita	1 133	1 205	1 336	1 469	1 541	1 692	1 760	1 637	1 659
At constant prices	8 314	8 640	8 989	9 434	9 712	10 129	10 612	10 986	11 349
Growth rates	4.8	3.9	4.0	5.0	2.9	4.3	4.8	3.5	3.3
Guinea Guinée									
At current prices	2 958	3 218	3 434	3 729	3 959	3 895	3 782	3 635	3 235
Per capita	448	469	483	509	526	505	480	453	397
At constant prices	2 979	3 119	3 243	3 386	3 542	3 714	3 880	4 025	4 098
Growth rates	3.0	4.7	4.0	4.4	4.6	4.8	4.5	3.7	1.8
Guinea−Bissau Guinée−Bissau									
At current prices	222	235	226	245	265	290	311	324	334
Per capita	223	229	215	227	241	258	271	276	279
At constant prices	247	254	271	283	297	313	225	243	266
Growth rates	2.8	2.7	6.9	4.4	5.0	5.4	−28.1	7.8	9.3
Guyana Guyana									
At current prices	374	467	545	622	706	749	725	647	643
Per capita	510	634	738	837	945	999	961	854	846
At constant prices	453	490	534	558	602	640	631	643	638
Growth rates	7.8	8.2	9.0	4.6	7.9	6.3	−1.3	1.8	−0.7
Haiti Haïti									
At current prices	1 532	1 551	2 057	2 334	2 722	3 097	3 522	3 922	3 515
Per capita	214	213	278	310	356	399	446	489	432
At constant prices	2 275	2 220	2 036	2 126	2 183	2 214	2 282	2 334	2 354
Growth rates	−13.2	−2.4	−8.3	4.4	2.7	1.4	3.1	2.3	0.9
Holy See [3] Saint−Siège [3]									
At current prices	17	14	14	15	17	16	16	16	15
Per capita	21 630	17 409	17 930	19 148	21 482	20 306	20 809	20 528	18 653
At constant prices	16	16	16	16	16	17	17	17	17
Growth rates	−0.3	−1.0	2.4	2.7	0.6	1.4	1.1	0.9	2.5
Honduras Honduras									
At current prices	3 419	3 505	3 432	3 959	4 080	4 716	5 262	5 424	5 898
Per capita	662	659	627	704	706	794	863	867	919
At constant prices	3 324	3 531	3 485	3 628	3 761	3 949	4 063	3 987	4 185
Growth rates	5.6	6.2	−1.3	4.1	3.7	5.0	2.9	−1.9	5.0
Hungary Hongrie									
At current prices	37 604	38 958	41 896	44 669	45 163	45 724	47 049	48 044	46 337
Per capita	3 650	3 791	4 088	4 373	4 440	4 516	4 671	4 795	4 649
At constant prices	30 842	30 664	31 568	32 038	32 467	33 952	35 601	37 095	39 008
Growth rates	−3.1	−0.6	2.9	1.5	1.3	4.6	4.9	4.2	5.2
Iceland Islande									
At current prices	6 958	6 095	6 274	6 977	7 278	7 392	8 164	8 618	8 569
Per capita	26 771	23 226	23 684	26 095	26 968	27 145	29 714	31 105	30 681
At constant prices	6 158	6 194	6 471	6 480	6 814	7 126	7 505	7 800	8 188
Growth rates	−3.3	0.6	4.5	0.1	5.2	4.6	5.3	3.9	5.0
India Inde									
At current prices	288 649	281 773	322 808	366 364	386 138	419 252	426 152	449 954	479 780

20

Gross domestic product and gross domestic product per capita
In millions of US dollars [1] at current and constant 1990 prices; per capita US dollars;
real rates of growth [cont.]

Produit intérieur brut et produit intérieur brut par habitant
En millions de dollars E.-U. [1]   aux prix courants et constants de 1990; par habitant en dollars E.-U.;
taux de l'accroissement réels [suite]

Country or area Pays ou zone	1992	1993	1994	1995	1996	1997	1998	1999	2000
Per capita	329	315	354	395	409	437	436	453	476
At constant prices	343 273	360 282	387 636	417 405	447 593	467 500	495 578	528 999	560 762
Growth rates	5.4	5.0	7.6	7.7	7.2	4.4	6.0	6.7	6.0
Indonesia Indonésie									
At current prices	139 116	158 007	176 892	202 131	227 370	215 749	95 445	141 306	153 256
Per capita	738	824	909	1 023	1 134	1 060	462	675	723
At constant prices	133 642	143 336	154 143	166 814	179 856	188 309	163 590	164 973	172 844
Growth rates	7.2	7.3	7.5	8.2	7.8	4.7	−13.1	0.8	4.8
Iran (Islamic Rep. of) [4] Iran (Rép. islamique d') [4]									
At current prices	965 418	75 273	72 047	98 707	136 618	160 346	180 998	243 231	329 880
Per capita	15 766	1 206	1 134	1 527	2 077	2 395	2 657	3 513	4 690
At constant prices	601 471	594 979	602 501	638 678	676 579	694 957	720 731	742 743	787 828
Growth rates	6.1	−1.1	1.3	6.0	5.9	2.7	3.7	3.1	6.1
Iraq [2] Iraq [2]									
At current prices	64 511	45 141	45 536	43 713	44 630	55 787	64 155	69 288	76 909
Per capita	3 522	2 390	2 339	2 180	2 165	2 634	2 950	3 102	3 352
At constant prices	29 144	20 393	20 572	19 748	20 162	25 203	28 983	31 302	34 745
Growth rates	14.8	−30.0	0.9	−4.0	2.1	25.0	15.0	8.0	11.0
Ireland Irlande									
At current prices	53 646	50 283	54 775	66 538	73 157	80 014	86 476	94 850	95 329
Per capita	15 179	14 147	15 302	18 437	20 084	21 740	23 237	25 207	25 066
At constant prices	49 826	51 167	54 112	59 513	64 127	71 073	77 192	85 567	95 376
Growth rates	3.3	2.7	5.8	10.0	7.8	10.8	8.6	10.8	11.5
Israel Israël									
At current prices	72 298	72 477	81 740	94 780	103 377	107 151	106 582	107 024	117 915
Per capita	14 993	14 491	15 777	17 718	18 784	18 979	18 442	18 110	19 521
At constant prices	65 777	68 247	73 230	78 271	82 036	84 482	86 741	89 088	95 158
Growth rates	7.5	3.8	7.3	6.9	4.8	3.0	2.7	2.7	6.8
Italy Italie									
At current prices	1 231 411	993 394	1 025 400	1 097 208	1 232 885	1 166 795	1 196 662	1 180 977	1 073 121
Per capita	21 630	17 409	17 930	19 148	21 482	20 306	20 809	20 528	18 653
At constant prices	1 126 265	1 116 311	1 140 953	1 174 313	1 187 150	1 211 205	1 232 934	1 252 573	1 288 494
Growth rates	0.8	−0.9	2.2	2.9	1.1	2.0	1.8	1.6	2.9
Jamaica Jamaïque									
At current prices	3 418	4 403	4 399	5 305	5 974	6 857	7 042	7 083	7 216
Per capita	1 420	1 813	1 795	2 146	2 397	2 728	2 779	2 773	2 801
At constant prices	4 378	4 452	4 501	4 535	4 478	4 387	4 364	4 347	4 381
Growth rates	1.6	1.7	1.1	0.7	−1.3	−2.0	−0.5	−0.4	0.8
Japan Japon									
At current prices	3 802 420	4 375 259	4 812 110	5 291 746	4 695 779	4 313 231	3 940 519	4 493 473	4 765 291
Per capita	30 574	35 073	38 462	42 175	37 319	34 184	31 148	35 432	37 494
At constant prices	3 176 387	3 189 693	3 221 476	3 272 046	3 385 579	3 446 534	3 408 630	3 431 443	3 512 466
Growth rates	0.9	0.4	1.0	1.6	3.5	1.8	−1.1	0.7	2.4
Jordan Jordanie									
At current prices	5 203	5 569	6 078	6 512	6 645	6 976	7 306	7 403	7 647
Per capita	1 431	1 445	1 496	1 533	1 507	1 535	1 566	1 547	1 556
At constant prices	4 752	5 017	5 444	5 767	5 800	5 877	5 817	5 893	6 122
Growth rates	16.1	5.6	8.5	5.9	0.6	1.3	−1.0	1.3	3.9
Kazakhstan Kazakhstan									
At current prices	6 303	11 722	11 916	16 640	21 035	22 166	22 135	16 871	18 264
Per capita	375	700	714	1 002	1 273	1 348	1 354	1 038	1 129
At constant prices	60 581	55 007	48 076	44 134	44 355	45 109	44 252	45 446	49 900
Growth rates	−5.3	−9.2	−12.6	−8.2	0.5	1.7	−1.9	2.7	9.8
Kenya Kenya									
At current prices	7 951	5 520	7 024	9 047	9 257	10 614	11 465	10 649	10 477
Per capita	317	213	264	331	330	370	390	355	342
At constant prices	8 587	8 617	8 844	9 234	9 616	9 817	9 975	10 104	10 078
Growth rates	−0.8	0.4	2.6	4.4	4.1	2.1	1.6	1.3	−0.3
Kiribati Kiribati									
At current prices	34	33	40	46	50	48	45	51	44
Per capita	459	441	520	596	633	606	564	51	531
At constant prices	30	30	32	34	35	36	39	41	40
Growth rates	−1.6	0.8	7.2	6.5	2.6	2.3	8.3	6.1	−3.8

20

Gross domestic product and gross domestic product per capita
In millions of US dollars [1] at current and constant 1990 prices; per capita US dollars;
real rates of growth [cont.]

Produit intérieur brut et produit intérieur brut par habitant
En millions de dollars E.−U. [1] aux prix courants et constants de 1990; par habitant en dollars E.−U.;
taux de l'accroissement réels [suite]

Country or area Pays ou zone	1992	1993	1994	1995	1996	1997	1998	1999	2000
Korea, Dem. P. R. Corée, R.p. dém.									
At current prices	13 921	11 745	9 387	5 244	10 588	10 088	10 040	9 992	12 016
Per capita	677	563	444	245	490	463	457	452	540
At constant prices	14 716	14 098	13 844	13 208	12 719	11 854	11 724	12 450	12 612
Growth rates	−7.7	−4.2	−1.8	−4.6	−3.7	−6.8	−1.1	6.2	1.3
Korea, Republic of Corée, République de									
At current prices	314 737	345 716	402 525	489 256	520 203	476 486	317 079	406 071	457 220
Per capita	7 201	7 833	9 035	10 884	11 474	10 426	6 884	8 751	9 782
At constant prices	290 936	306 913	332 233	361 867	386 294	405 651	378 516	419 750	456 728
Growth rates	5.4	5.5	8.3	8.9	6.8	5.0	−6.7	10.9	8.8
Kuwait Koweït									
At current prices	19 869	23 957	24 859	26 554	31 085	30 368	25 617	30 015	38 042
Per capita	9 957	12 816	14 141	15 705	18 525	17 754	14 437	16 244	19 871
At constant prices	21 142	28 328	30 718	31 050	34 140	33 109	28 805	33 167	34 162
Growth rates	87.3	34.0	8.4	1.1	10.0	−3.0	−13.0	15.1	3.0
Kyrgyzstan Kirghizistan									
At current prices	767	993	1 109	1 492	1 827	1 767	1 640	1 250	1 304
Per capita	172	221	245	327	395	377	344	258	265
At constant prices	10 287	8 697	6 950	6 573	7 039	7 737	7 901	8 190	8 603
Growth rates	−13.8	−15.5	−20.1	−5.4	7.1	9.9	2.1	3.7	5.0
Lao People's Dem. Rep. Rép. dém. pop. lao									
At current prices	1 180	1 328	1 544	1 764	1 874	1 747	1 286	1 451	1 711
Per capita	271	298	338	376	390	355	255	281	324
At constant prices	964	1 020	1 103	1 181	1 262	1 349	1 403	1 505	1 593
Growth rates	7.0	5.8	8.1	7.0	6.9	6.9	4.0	7.3	5.8
Latvia Lettonie									
At current prices	1 364	2 172	3 649	4 453	5 137	5 638	6 086	6 660	7 144
Per capita	519	839	1 431	1 770	2 064	2 285	2 483	2 734	2 952
At constant prices	10 943	9 316	9 376	9 300	9 611	10 438	10 843	10 960	11 681
Growth rates	−34.9	−14.9	0.6	−0.8	3.3	8.6	3.9	1.1	6.6
Lebanon [2] Liban [2]									
At current prices	5 465	7 537	8 923	10 965	12 819	14 289	15 525	16 796	16 740
Per capita	1 904	2 536	2 902	3 461	3 946	4 306	4 594	4 886	4 788
At constant prices	4 063	4 348	4 696	5 001	5 201	5 383	5 544	5 766	5 766
Growth rates	4.5	7.0	8.0	6.5	4.0	3.5	3.0	4.0	0.0
Lesotho Lesotho									
At current prices	827	818	837	933	940	1 023	877	923	911
Per capita	471	456	457	499	493	527	444	460	448
At constant prices	680	704	728	760	835	903	861	886	908
Growth rates	5.3	3.5	3.4	4.4	10.0	8.2	−4.6	2.8	2.5
Liberia [2] Libéria [2]									
At current prices	852	852	562	562	573	651	668	698	719
Per capita	416	425	281	275	266	282	267	258	247
At constant prices	852	852	562	562	573	651	668	698	730
Growth rates	−14.6	0.0	−34.1	0.0	2.0	13.5	2.7	4.6	4.5
Libyan Arab Jamah. Jamah. arabe libyenne									
At current prices	32 047	22 600	22 049	22 540	23 203	22 511	26 574	25 206	29 979
Per capita	7 141	4 941	4 729	4 740	4 781	4 543	5 248	4 871	5 667
At constant prices	28 379	27 074	26 478	26 055	26 367	26 710	25 909	26 427	27 220
Growth rates	−4.2	−4.6	−2.2	−1.6	1.2	1.3	−3.0	2.0	3.0
Liechtenstein Liechtenstein									
At current prices	1 035	1 010	1 120	1 325	1 287	1 125	1 165	1 164	1 090
Per capita	34 964	33 701	36 930	43 165	41 417	35 727	36 561	36 075	33 394
At constant prices	962	961	970	981	993	1 020	1 056	1 085	1 131
Growth rates	0.2	−0.1	1.0	1.2	1.2	2.8	3.5	2.8	4.2
Lithuania Lituanie									
At current prices	1 921	2 668	4 250	6 026	7 892	9 585	10 747	10 664	11 232
Per capita	514	715	1 142	1 622	2 127	2 586	2 901	2 881	3 039
At constant prices	14 955	12 528	11 305	11 676	12 227	13 116	13 787	13 250	13 686
Growth rates	−21.3	−16.2	−9.8	3.3	4.7	7.3	5.1	−3.9	3.3
Luxembourg Luxembourg									
At current prices	13 359	13 573	15 319	18 090	18 169	17 623	18 865	19 655	18 946
Per capita	34 065	34 105	37 930	44 155	43 745	41 881	44 269	45 555	43 372

20

Gross domestic product and gross domestic product per capita
In millions of US dollars [1] at current and constant 1990 prices; per capita US dollars;
real rates of growth [*cont.*]
Produit intérieur brut et produit intérieur brut par habitant
En millions de dollars E.−U. [1] aux prix courants et constants de 1990; par habitant en dollars E.−U.;
taux de l'accroissement réels [*suite*]

Country or area Pays ou zone	1992	1993	1994	1995	1996	1997	1998	1999	2000
At constant prices	12 246	13 313	13 872	14 397	14 813	15 888	16 685	17 937	19 287
Growth rates	4.5	8.7	4.2	3.8	2.9	7.3	5.0	7.5	7.5
Madagascar Madagascar									
At current prices	2 996	3 366	2 972	3 155	3 987	3 546	3 741	3 715	3 969
Per capita	237	259	222	229	281	242	248	239	249
At constant prices	2 920	2 981	2 979	3 030	3 095	3 209	3 336	3 491	3 659
Growth rates	1.2	2.1	−0.1	1.7	2.1	3.7	3.9	4.7	4.8
Malawi Malawi									
At current prices	1 858	2 014	1 182	1 493	2 321	2 527	1 687	1 816	1 596
Per capita	190	205	119	149	227	242	157	165	141
At constant prices	1 814	1 989	2 301	2 630	2 917	3 063	3 164	3 299	3 373
Growth rates	−8.9	9.6	15.7	14.3	10.9	5.0	3.3	4.3	2.3
Malaysia Malaisie									
At current prices	59 152	66 895	74 482	88 833	100 850	100 169	72 175	79 037	89 659
Per capita	3 161	3 494	3 804	4 438	4 929	4 791	3 380	3 627	4 035
At constant prices	52 512	57 708	63 024	69 219	76 143	81 718	75 698	80 300	77 403
Growth rates	8.9	9.9	9.2	9.8	10.0	7.3	−7.4	6.1	−3.6
Maldives Maldives									
At current prices	284	321	356	401	449	506	544	581	578
Per capita	1 239	1 361	1 465	1 600	1 740	1 903	1 987	2 058	1 985
At constant prices	247	262	279	299	326	362	391	424	448
Growth rates	6.3	6.2	6.6	7.2	8.8	11.2	7.9	8.5	5.6
Mali Mali									
At current prices	2 786	2 590	1 813	2 310	2 669	2 535	2 716	2 801	2 609
Per capita	302	274	187	233	262	242	253	254	230
At constant prices	2 747	2 633	2 738	2 903	3 196	3 403	3 597	3 786	3 960
Growth rates	9.7	−4.2	4.0	6.1	10.1	6.5	5.7	5.3	4.6
Malta Malte									
At current prices	2 743	2 459	2 722	3 245	3 333	3 338	3 507	3 627	3 536
Per capita	7 468	6 629	7 267	8 588	8 754	8 706	9 091	9 348	9 069
At constant prices	2 572	2 687	2 839	3 019	3 140	3 292	3 403	3 542	3 711
Growth rates	4.7	4.5	5.7	6.3	4.0	4.9	3.4	4.1	4.8
Marshall Islands Iles Marshall									
At current prices	80	87	95	105	97	92	95	97	98
Per capita	1 733	1 869	2 006	2 205	2 006	1 880	1 914	1 920	1 925
At constant prices	69	72	70	76	64	58	60	60	60
Growth rates	0.0	4.1	−3.8	9.8	−15.9	−9.4	2.5	0.8	−0.9
Martinique Martinique									
At current prices	4 173	4 055	4 273	4 838	4 863	4 377	4 617	4 566	4 076
Per capita	11 408	11 016	11 545	12 996	12 986	11 621	12 183	11 979	10 631
At constant prices	3 463	3 520	3 577	3 635	3 695	3 755	3 910	3 935	3 961
Growth rates	1.6	1.6	1.6	1.6	1.6	1.6	4.1	0.6	0.6
Mauritania Mauritanie									
At current prices	1 146	894	903	971	985	959	830	808	789
Per capita	547	416	408	427	420	396	332	313	296
At constant prices	1 127	1 162	1 193	1 248	1 295	1 342	1 382	1 439	1 510
Growth rates	3.8	3.1	2.7	4.6	3.7	3.6	3.0	4.1	5.0
Mauritius Maurice									
At current prices	3 256	3 273	3 584	4 057	4 398	4 190	4 163	4 263	4 514
Per capita	3 018	3 000	3 249	3 640	3 910	3 695	3 642	3 700	3 886
At constant prices	2 886	3 047	3 167	3 315	3 508	3 712	3 929	4 058	4 274
Growth rates	6.2	5.6	3.9	4.7	5.8	5.8	5.9	3.3	5.3
Mexico Mexique									
At current prices	363 609	403 193	420 773	286 166	332 337	400 870	421 008	479 453	573 924
Per capita	4 209	4 583	4 698	3 140	3 585	4 252	4 394	4 925	5 805
At constant prices	283 737	289 272	302 044	283 417	298 022	318 204	334 211	346 760	370 762
Growth rates	3.6	2.0	4.4	−6.2	5.2	6.8	5.0	3.8	6.9
Micronesia (Fed. States of) Micron (Etats fédérés de)									
At current prices	187	208	211	224	258	222	224	230	237
Per capita	1 877	2 031	2 013	2 083	2 333	1 952	1 918	1 922	1 934
At constant prices	176	190	188	194	190	182	181	182	186
Growth rates	5.2	8.1	−1.2	3.5	−2.3	−3.9	−0.6	0.2	2.5
Monaco Monaco									
At current prices	721	688	733	848	855	778	809	807	730

20
Gross domestic product and gross domestic product per capita
In millions of US dollars [1] at current and constant 1990 prices; per capita US dollars;
real rates of growth [*cont.*]
Produit intérieur brut et produit intérieur brut par habitant
En millions de dollars E.-U. [1]   aux prix courants et constants de 1990; par habitant en dollars E.-U.;
taux de l'accroissement réels [*suite*]

Country or area Pays ou zone	1992	1993	1994	1995	1996	1997	1998	1999	2000
Per capita	23 484	22 151	23 338	26 714	26 625	23 994	24 686	24 370	21 848
At constant prices	667	666	684	700	713	731	761	788	817
Growth rates	2.2	−0.2	2.7	2.4	1.8	2.6	4.1	3.6	3.7
Mongolia Mongolie									
At current prices	1 111	614	686	1 235	1 203	1 071	992	924	990
Per capita	481	262	288	512	493	435	399	368	391
At constant prices	1 994	1 934	1 979	2 104	2 155	2 240	2 319	2 393	2 419
Growth rates	−9.5	−3.0	2.3	6.3	2.4	4.0	3.5	3.2	1.1
Montserrat Montserrat									
At current prices	59	62	64	60	49	41	37	35	34
Per capita	5 372	5 626	5 882	5 885	5 315	5 274	6 120	7 459	8 942
At constant prices	55	56	56	52	41	33	29	26	24
Growth rates	2.6	2.5	0.9	−7.6	−21.4	−20.0	−10.1	−12.6	−6.7
Morocco Maroc									
At current prices	28 451	26 802	30 352	32 985	36 673	33 414	35 667	34 998	32 906
Per capita	1 109	1 024	1 137	1 212	1 322	1 182	1 239	1 193	1 101
At constant prices	26 505	26 237	28 954	27 050	30 328	29 678	31 699	31 478	31 569
Growth rates	−4.0	−1.0	10.4	−6.6	12.1	−2.1	6.8	−0.7	0.3
Mozambique Mozambique									
At current prices	1 946	2 004	2 137	2 220	2 807	3 408	3 597	3 731	3 570
Per capita	134	132	136	136	167	198	205	208	195
At constant prices	1 303	1 392	1 489	1 538	1 642	1 827	2 047	2 231	2 278
Growth rates	−8.6	6.8	7.0	3.3	6.8	11.3	12.1	9.0	2.1
Myanmar [2] Myanmar [2]									
At current prices	21 599	22 904	24 617	26 327	28 023	29 607	31 073	32 854	34 647
Per capita	514	535	565	594	622	647	669	697	726
At constant prices	21 599	22 904	24 617	26 327	28 023	29 607	31 073	32 854	34 647
Growth rates	9.7	6.0	7.5	6.9	6.4	5.7	5.0	5.7	5.5
Namibia Namibie									
At current prices	3 058	2 847	3 253	3 503	3 492	3 645	3 411	3 475	3 479
Per capita	2 084	1 888	2 103	2 211	2 153	2 200	2 017	2 015	1 981
At constant prices	2 938	2 888	3 099	3 227	3 330	3 480	3 596	3 751	3 896
Growth rates	7.1	−1.7	7.3	4.1	3.2	4.5	3.3	4.3	3.9
Nauru Nauru									
At current prices	46	41	42	41	41	37	32	34	31
Per capita	4 604	3 973	3 984	3 767	3 710	3 284	2 767	2 830	2 533
At constant prices	46	42	39	36	34	31	31	30	29
Growth rates	−7.3	−7.3	−7.3	−7.3	−7.3	−7.3	−1.9	−1.9	−1.9
Nepal Népal									
At current prices	3 499	3 528	4 034	4 224	4 391	4 836	4 495	4 973	5 295
Per capita	184	181	202	207	210	225	205	221	230
At constant prices	3 899	4 049	4 382	4 534	4 776	5 017	5 165	5 368	5 691
Growth rates	4.1	3.8	8.2	3.5	5.3	5.0	3.0	3.9	6.0
Netherlands Pays−Bas									
At current prices	334 409	325 311	348 553	414 801	411 827	376 900	393 471	398 096	369 531
Per capita	22 063	21 317	22 689	26 832	26 483	24 104	25 034	25 207	23 294
At constant prices	306 872	309 599	317 626	326 982	336 915	349 848	365 066	378 609	391 737
Growth rates	1.7	0.9	2.6	2.9	3.0	3.8	4.3	3.7	3.5
Netherlands Antilles Antilles néerlandaises									
At current prices	1 998	2 129	2 288	2 360	2 471	2 504	2 530	2 515	2 581
Per capita	10 297	10 759	11 347	11 518	11 902	11 933	11 950	11 783	11 988
At constant prices	1 895	1 982	2 091	2 097	2 124	2 086	2 069	2 009	1 963
Growth rates	3.2	4.6	5.5	0.3	1.3	−1.8	−0.8	−2.9	−2.3
New Caledonia Nouvelle−Calédonie									
At current prices	2 924	3 070	3 039	3 628	3 607	3 291	3 159	3 057	2 670
Per capita	16 299	16 695	16 120	18 792	18 254	16 290	15 299	14 497	12 401
At constant prices	2 655	2 673	2 743	2 905	2 919	2 978	2 882	2 908	2 935
Growth rates	1.0	0.7	2.6	5.9	0.5	2.0	−3.2	0.9	0.9
New Zealand Nouvelle−Zélande									
At current prices	40 431	44 043	51 776	60 818	66 612	65 875	54 152	56 018	50 781
Per capita	11 716	12 569	14 558	16 874	18 269	17 886	14 572	14 948	13 441
At constant prices	43 588	46 340	48 832	50 677	52 019	53 022	53 038	55 374	56 493
Growth rates	1.2	6.3	5.4	3.8	2.7	1.9	0.0	4.4	2.0

20

Gross domestic product and gross domestic product per capita
In millions of US dollars [1] at current and constant 1990 prices; per capita US dollars;
real rates of growth [cont.]
Produit intérieur brut et produit intérieur brut par habitant
En millions de dollars E.−U. [1] aux prix courants et constants de 1990; par habitant en dollars E.−U.;
taux de l'accroissement réels [suite]

Country or area Pays ou zone	1992	1993	1994	1995	1996	1997	1998	1999	2000
Nicaragua Nicaragua									
At current prices	1 793	1 913	1 930	1 836	1 921	1 969	2 068	2 213	2 423
Per capita	443	458	449	415	422	421	430	448	478
At constant prices	2 157	2 149	2 221	2 316	2 427	2 551	2 655	2 850	3 006
Growth rates	0.4	−0.4	3.3	4.3	4.8	5.1	4.1	7.4	5.5
Niger Niger									
At current prices	2 420	2 244	1 580	1 901	2 009	1 865	2 099	2 039	1 845
Per capita	294	264	179	209	213	191	208	195	170
At constant prices	2 401	2 436	2 534	2 600	2 689	2 763	3 051	3 033	2 991
Growth rates	−6.5	1.4	4.0	2.6	3.4	2.8	10.4	−0.6	−1.4
Nigeria [2] Nigéria [2]									
At current prices	31 784	31 791	41 568	66 759	95 370	99 271	95 834	25 792	27 808
Per capita	349	339	431	672	934	946	888	233	244
At constant prices	34 952	35 871	36 230	37 169	39 547	40 758	41 535	41 998	43 500
Growth rates	2.9	2.6	1.0	2.6	6.4	3.1	1.9	1.1	3.6
Norway Norvège									
At current prices	126 307	116 111	122 926	146 602	157 615	154 971	147 755	153 536	161 769
Per capita	29 465	26 934	28 356	33 631	35 963	35 176	33 370	34 511	36 198
At constant prices	122 940	126 302	133 239	138 365	145 140	151 953	155 636	157 301	160 875
Growth rates	3.3	2.7	5.5	3.8	4.9	4.7	2.4	1.1	2.3
Oman Oman									
At current prices	12 453	12 494	12 918	13 802	15 277	15 839	14 086	15 713	19 826
Per capita	6 446	6 229	6 212	6 409	6 856	6 877	5 921	6 395	7 811
At constant prices	13 445	14 270	14 818	15 533	15 984	16 971	17 429	17 260	18 283
Growth rates	8.5	6.1	3.8	4.8	2.9	6.2	2.7	−1.0	5.9
Pakistan Pakistan									
At current prices	53 389	55 804	61 333	67 321	67 624	65 440	65 380	64 799	64 721
Per capita	463	473	508	544	533	502	488	471	458
At constant prices	51 581	53 508	56 164	58 886	59 483	61 000	63 233	66 036	68 240
Growth rates	1.3	3.7	5.0	4.8	1.0	2.6	3.7	4.4	3.3
Palau Palaos									
At current prices	76	76	84	95	108	113	117	114	118
Per capita	4 795	4 659	4 987	5 552	6 166	6 306	6 390	6 048	6 163
At constant prices	68	70	75	83	91	93	95	90	91
Growth rates	1.5	2.0	7.3	10.9	10.4	2.3	2.0	−5.4	1.1
Panama Panama									
At current prices	6 641	7 253	7 734	7 906	8 151	8 658	9 345	9 637	10 019
Per capita	2 666	2 858	2 992	3 005	3 045	3 180	3 377	3 427	3 508
At constant prices	6 290	6 634	6 823	6 942	7 152	7 472	7 781	8 031	8 228
Growth rates	8.2	5.5	2.9	1.8	3.0	4.5	4.1	3.2	2.5
Papua New Guinea Papouasie−Nvl−Guinée									
At current prices	4 378	4 976	5 321	4 601	5 217	4 912	3 792	3 416	3 417
Per capita	1 105	1 224	1 275	1 075	1 190	1 094	825	727	710
At constant prices	4 017	4 748	5 030	4 863	5 239	5 035	4 845	5 212	5 253
Growth rates	13.9	18.2	5.9	−3.3	7.7	−3.9	−3.8	7.6	0.8
Paraguay Paraguay									
At current prices	6 446	6 875	7 854	9 016	9 629	9 612	8 596	7 741	7 722
Per capita	1 445	1 501	1 670	1 867	1 943	1 889	1 646	1 445	1 405
At constant prices	5 492	5 719	5 896	6 173	6 252	6 413	6 387	6 419	6 396
Growth rates	1.8	4.1	3.1	4.7	1.3	2.6	−0.4	0.5	−0.4
Peru Pérou									
At current prices	36 083	34 834	44 910	53 636	55 813	59 033	56 830	51 641	53 512
Per capita	1 614	1 532	1 942	2 279	2 331	2 423	2 292	2 047	2 085
At constant prices	29 971	31 399	35 425	38 466	39 425	42 084	41 860	42 258	43 579
Growth rates	−0.4	4.8	12.8	8.6	2.5	6.7	−0.5	0.9	3.1
Philippines Philippines									
At current prices	52 976	54 368	64 085	74 120	82 847	82 344	65 171	76 157	74 732
Per capita	829	831	958	1 085	1 187	1 155	896	1 027	988
At constant prices	44 204	45 140	47 120	49 325	52 208	54 915	54 599	56 453	58 716
Growth rates	0.3	2.1	4.4	4.7	5.8	5.2	−0.6	3.4	4.0
Poland Pologne									
At current prices	84 354	85 995	99 063	127 054	143 847	144 040	159 280	155 054	157 596
Per capita	2 199	2 236	2 571	3 292	3 724	3 727	4 122	4 014	4 082

20
Gross domestic product and gross domestic product per capita
In millions of US dollars [1] at current and constant 1990 prices; per capita US dollars;
real rates of growth [cont.]
Produit intérieur brut et produit intérieur brut par habitant
En millions de dollars E.–U. [1] aux prix courants et constants de 1990; par habitant en dollars E.–U.;
taux de l'accroissement réels [suite]

Country or area Pays ou zone	1992	1993	1994	1995	1996	1997	1998	1999	2000
At constant prices	56 218	58 319	61 365	65 675	69 634	74 388	77 991	81 149	84 436
Growth rates	2.5	3.7	5.2	7.0	6.0	6.8	4.8	4.1	4.1
Portugal Portugal									
At current prices	97 685	86 260	90 508	107 217	112 418	106 698	112 787	115 292	106 193
Per capita	9 882	8 721	9 140	10 812	11 318	10 721	11 308	11 534	10 603
At constant prices	74 980	74 148	75 809	77 970	80 765	83 732	86 755	89 365	92 326
Growth rates	2.5	−1.1	2.2	2.9	3.6	3.7	3.6	3.0	3.3
Puerto Rico Porto Rico									
At current prices	36 923	39 691	42 647	45 341	48 187	54 133	60 039	63 150	66 821
Per capita	10 258	10 910	11 596	12 196	12 824	14 255	15 646	16 291	17 069
At constant prices	35 330	36 808	38 482	39 374	41 296	43 986	47 253	49 237	50 763
Growth rates	4.6	4.2	4.5	2.3	4.9	6.5	7.4	4.2	3.1
Qatar Qatar									
At current prices	7 646	7 157	7 374	8 138	9 059	11 298	10 255	12 393	16 454
Per capita	15 946	14 586	14 711	15 896	17 328	21 164	18 825	22 314	29 100
At constant prices	8 011	7 964	8 151	8 391	8 795	10 909	11 827	12 204	14 035
Growth rates	9.7	−0.6	2.3	2.9	4.8	24.0	8.4	3.2	15.0
Republic of Moldova République de Moldova									
At current prices	463	500	1 109	1 441	1 693	1 929	1 698	1 172	1 285
Per capita	106	115	255	332	391	446	394	272	299
At constant prices	15 330	10 884	7 519	7 415	6 979	7 094	6 630	6 407	6 531
Growth rates	−17.5	−29.0	−30.9	−1.4	−5.9	1.6	−6.5	−3.4	1.9
Réunion Réunion									
At current prices	6 382	5 953	6 352	7 420	7 564	6 929	7 172	7 184	6 494
Per capita	10 180	9 314	9 752	11 183	11 198	10 082	10 263	10 116	9 005
At constant prices	5 475	5 711	5 839	5 998	6 169	6 360	6 553	6 750	6 952
Growth rates	3.5	4.3	2.3	2.7	2.9	3.1	3.0	3.0	3.0
Romania Roumanie									
At current prices	19 578	26 361	30 073	35 478	35 315	35 286	41 491	34 027	36 692
Per capita	849	1 150	1 319	1 564	1 562	1 565	1 843	1 514	1 635
At constant prices	30 382	30 847	32 060	34 348	35 704	33 543	31 725	30 705	31 196
Growth rates	−8.8	1.5	3.9	7.1	3.9	−6.1	−5.4	−3.2	1.6
Russian Federation Fédération de Russie									
At current prices	85 572	172 951	278 784	337 890	419 006	428 464	282 440	193 225	251 106
Per capita	575	1 163	1 878	2 281	2 835	2 908	1 924	1 322	1 726
At constant prices	785 663	717 310	626 209	600 535	580 416	585 639	556 943	574 765	622 471
Growth rates	−14.5	−8.7	−12.7	−4.1	−3.4	0.9	−4.9	3.2	8.3
Rwanda Rwanda									
At current prices	1 630	1 579	610	1 038	1 135	1 505	1 635	1 538	1 421
Per capita	272	289	120	209	217	262	255	217	187
At constant prices	2 410	2 211	1 101	1 480	1 714	1 933	2 117	2 240	2 373
Growth rates	5.9	−8.3	−50.2	34.4	15.8	12.8	9.5	5.8	6.0
Saint Kitts and Nevis Saint–Kitts–et–Nevis									
At current prices	182	198	222	231	246	275	287	305	329
Per capita	4 429	4 874	5 497	5 766	6 195	6 986	7 353	7 861	8 539
At constant prices	168	177	186	193	204	219	222	230	247
Growth rates	3.1	5.4	5.4	3.5	5.9	7.3	1.0	3.7	7.5
Saint Lucia Sainte–Lucie									
At current prices	497	498	519	554	571	575	619	675	700
Per capita	3 686	3 646	3 756	3 968	4 046	4 022	4 287	4 621	4 735
At constant prices	447	452	460	468	474	477	492	509	513
Growth rates	7.4	1.1	1.8	1.7	1.4	0.6	3.1	3.5	0.7
St. Vincent–Grenadines St. Vincent–Grenadines									
At current prices	233	239	243	264	279	294	318	330	342
Per capita	2 174	2 207	2 232	2 406	2 524	2 644	2 842	2 929	3 021
At constant prices	214	218	212	230	232	239	253	264	269
Growth rates	7.9	1.8	−3.0	8.5	1.1	3.0	5.8	4.1	2.1
Samoa Samoa									
At current prices	165	167	189	193	217	236	221	238	225
Per capita	1 033	1 050	1 189	1 220	1 372	1 492	1 395	1 505	1 419
At constant prices	192	196	189	201	216	218	226	238	240
Growth rates	−2.3	2.4	−3.7	6.4	7.3	1.0	3.4	5.3	1.0
San Marino Saint–Marin									
At current prices	514	420	440	476	542	519	539	538	495

20
Gross domestic product and gross domestic product per capita
In millions of US dollars [1] at current and constant 1990 prices; per capita US dollars;
real rates of growth [cont.]
Produit intérieur brut et produit intérieur brut par habitant
En millions de dollars E.–U. [1]   aux prix courants et constants de 1990; par habitant en dollars E.–U.;
taux de l'accroissement réels [suite]

Country or area Pays ou zone	1992	1993	1994	1995	1996	1997	1998	1999	2000
Per capita	21 630	17 409	17 930	19 148	21 482	20 306	20 809	20 528	18 653
At constant prices	470	472	489	510	522	539	555	570	594
Growth rates	2.0	0.4	3.6	4.2	2.3	3.2	3.0	2.8	4.1
Sao Tome and Principe Sao Tomé–et–Principe									
At current prices	45	48	50	45	45	44	41	47	46
Per capita	381	393	401	362	350	337	307	347	336
At constant prices	59	59	61	62	63	63	65	67	69
Growth rates	0.7	1.1	2.2	2.0	1.5	1.0	2.5	2.5	3.0
Saudi Arabia Arabie saoudite									
At current prices	123 204	118 516	120 167	127 811	141 322	146 494	128 377	139 383	169 064
Per capita	7 646	7 235	7 201	7 478	8 023	8 033	6 782	7 095	8 309
At constant prices	118 112	117 360	117 963	118 515	120 167	123 378	125 318	125 819	131 458
Growth rates	2.8	−0.6	0.5	0.5	1.4	2.7	1.6	0.4	4.5
Senegal Sénégal									
At current prices	6 027	5 431	3 642	4 476	4 653	4 377	4 666	4 798	4 413
Per capita	782	688	450	539	547	502	521	522	468
At constant prices	5 802	5 673	5 836	6 136	6 454	6 780	7 163	7 526	7 936
Growth rates	2.2	−2.2	2.9	5.2	5.2	5.0	5.6	5.1	5.5
Serbia and Montenegro Serbie–et–Monténégro									
At current prices	19 885	14 006	14 743	25 722	16 064	19 839	20 742	18 348	11 545
Per capita	1 925	1 345	1 405	2 439	1 519	1 874	1 960	1 736	1 094
At constant prices	19 240	13 322	13 660	14 494	15 345	16 476	16 887	13 295	14 227
Growth rates	−27.9	−30.8	2.5	6.1	5.9	7.4	2.5	−21.3	7.0
Seychelles Seychelles									
At current prices	434	474	486	508	503	566	582	591	585
Per capita	6 042	6 493	6 559	6 748	6 586	7 311	7 417	7 439	7 272
At constant prices	406	431	428	425	433	532	544	528	534
Growth rates	7.2	6.2	−0.8	−0.6	1.9	22.8	2.3	−3.0	1.2
Sierra Leone Sierra Leone									
At current prices	655	823	927	941	950	832	662	658	624
Per capita	160	201	227	231	232	202	158	154	142
At constant prices	533	500	501	487	475	443	444	392	407
Growth rates	−13.6	−6.2	0.2	−2.8	−2.5	−6.6	0.1	−11.6	3.8
Singapore Singapour									
At current prices	49 067	57 668	69 824	83 089	90 920	94 442	82 137	83 843	92 254
Per capita	15 423	17 614	20 704	23 904	25 364	25 543	21 557	21 397	22 959
At constant prices	41 842	47 153	52 539	56 749	61 074	66 283	66 320	70 206	77 152
Growth rates	4.2	12.7	11.4	8.0	7.6	8.5	0.1	5.9	9.9
Slovakia Slovaquie									
At current prices	11 757	12 694	14 548	18 377	19 772	20 409	21 308	19 712	19 272
Per capita	2 217	2 383	2 721	3 426	3 678	3 791	3 953	3 654	3 570
At constant prices	12 364	12 599	13 219	14 109	14 984	15 914	16 566	16 881	17 254
Growth rates	−6.6	1.9	4.9	6.7	6.2	6.2	4.1	1.9	2.2
Slovenia Slovénie									
At current prices	12 523	12 673	14 386	18 744	18 878	18 206	19 585	20 072	18 124
Per capita	6 429	6 449	7 267	9 419	9 461	9 120	9 822	10 083	9 118
At constant prices	14 653	15 268	16 138	16 917	17 515	18 313	19 008	19 997	20 920
Growth rates	−6.4	4.2	5.7	4.8	3.5	4.6	3.8	5.2	4.6
Solomon Islands Iles Salomon									
At current prices	209	245	282	322	355	376	319	346	267
Per capita	614	696	774	854	911	932	763	801	598
At constant prices	190	195	205	219	226	224	219	221	191
Growth rates	10.7	2.4	5.1	6.7	3.5	−1.0	−2.2	1.0	−13.8
Somalia Somalie									
At current prices	583	996	1 125	1 122	1 260	1 482	1 926	2 013	1 899
Per capita	81	138	155	153	167	191	238	239	216
At constant prices	866	866	684	684	711	692	709	724	743
Growth rates	−12.0	0.0	−21.0	0.0	3.9	−2.7	2.5	2.1	2.6
South Africa Afrique du Sud									
At current prices	130 514	130 406	135 778	151 113	143 732	148 814	133 767	131 409	127 928
Per capita	3 449	3 381	3 454	3 775	3 527	3 590	3 175	3 074	2 954
At constant prices	108 504	109 842	113 395	116 928	121 964	125 192	126 146	128 819	133 147
Growth rates	−2.1	1.2	3.2	3.1	4.3	2.6	0.8	2.1	3.4

20

Gross domestic product and gross domestic product per capita
In millions of US dollars [1] at current and constant 1990 prices; per capita US dollars;
real rates of growth [cont.]

Produit intérieur brut et produit intérieur brut par habitant
En millions de dollars E.−U. [1] aux prix courants et constants de 1990; par habitant en dollars E.−U.;
taux de l'accroissement réels [suite]

Country or area Pays ou zone	1992	1993	1994	1995	1996	1997	1998	1999	2000
Spain Espagne									
At current prices	602 646	499 975	505 048	584 187	609 853	561 545	588 002	602 457	560 887
Per capita	15 248	12 624	12 729	14 701	15 327	14 098	14 749	15 102	14 054
At constant prices	528 779	522 626	534 391	548 909	562 287	584 437	609 670	634 187	665 414
Growth rates	0.7	−1.2	2.3	2.7	2.4	3.9	4.3	4.0	4.9
Sri Lanka Sri Lanka									
At current prices	9 623	10 341	11 720	12 924	13 957	15 104	15 692	15 585	16 168
Per capita	551	585	656	716	766	821	845	831	854
At constant prices	8 682	9 282	9 807	10 349	10 738	11 430	11 972	12 487	13 230
Growth rates	4.4	6.9	5.6	5.5	3.8	6.4	4.7	4.3	6.0
Sudan Soudan									
At current prices	7 058	8 881	12 783	12 514	8 259	10 642	10 092	9 569	10 992
Per capita	271	333	468	448	289	365	339	315	353
At constant prices	37 255	38 282	40 338	42 478	43 739	46 670	49 003	51 946	55 682
Growth rates	4.4	2.8	5.4	5.3	3.0	6.7	5.0	6.0	7.2
Suriname [2] Suriname [2]									
At current prices	1 126	981	457	475	684	692	893	702	661
Per capita	2 779	2 413	1 122	1 162	1 665	1 678	2 159	1 690	1 584
At constant prices	1 195	1 196	1 074	1 118	1 261	1 271	1 263	1 163	1 082
Growth rates	−2.6	0.1	−10.2	4.0	12.9	0.8	−0.6	−7.9	−7.0
Swaziland Swaziland									
At current prices	981	1 027	1 146	1 364	1 323	1 435	1 347	1 376	1 394
Per capita	1 228	1 268	1 395	1 634	1 552	1 648	1 513	1 514	1 507
At constant prices	892	924	955	991	1 030	1 069	1 104	1 142	1 167
Growth rates	1.2	3.5	3.4	3.8	3.9	3.8	3.2	3.5	2.2
Sweden Suède									
At current prices	255 009	192 415	206 890	240 187	261 910	238 877	239 671	242 622	229 032
Per capita	29 386	22 022	23 540	27 211	29 595	26 965	27 059	27 414	25 903
At constant prices	231 578	227 324	236 683	245 418	248 064	253 199	262 271	274 099	283 993
Growth rates	−1.7	−1.8	4.1	3.7	1.1	2.1	3.6	4.5	3.6
Switzerland Suisse									
At current prices	243 464	236 731	261 362	307 263	295 979	255 887	262 095	258 674	239 449
Per capita	34 964	33 701	36 930	43 165	41 417	35 727	36 561	36 075	33 394
At constant prices	226 300	225 210	226 409	227 551	228 276	232 207	237 627	241 276	248 453
Growth rates	−0.1	−0.5	0.5	0.5	0.3	1.7	2.3	1.5	3.0
Syrian Arab Republic [2] Rép. arabe syrienne [2]									
At current prices	31 297	32 918	35 437	37 475	40 226	41 227	44 360	43 475	43 749
Per capita	2 383	2 440	2 558	2 635	2 756	2 752	2 885	2 755	2 702
At constant prices	29 268	30 783	33 139	35 045	37 618	38 554	41 484	40 656	40 912
Growth rates	13.5	5.2	7.7	5.8	7.3	2.5	7.6	−2.0	0.6
Tajikistan Tadjikistan									
At current prices	2 613	683	729	568	1 044	922	1 320	1 087	870
Per capita	474	122	129	99	179	156	221	180	143
At constant prices	6 791	5 684	4 473	3 919	3 264	3 320	3 496	3 625	3 925
Growth rates	−32.3	−16.3	−21.3	−12.4	−16.7	1.7	5.3	3.7	8.3
Thailand Thaïlande									
At current prices	111 456	125 199	144 493	168 279	182 413	151 135	111 908	122 056	122 167
Per capita	1 978	2 192	2 495	2 865	3 063	2 504	1 829	1 968	1 945
At constant prices	100 195	108 577	118 277	129 303	136 912	134 933	120 399	125 481	130 948
Growth rates	8.1	8.4	8.9	9.3	5.9	−1.4	−10.8	4.2	4.4
TFYR of Macedonia L'ex−R.y. Macédoine									
At current prices	2 317	2 544	3 384	4 475	4 413	3 699	3 504	3 432	3 338
Per capita	1 199	1 310	1 734	2 279	2 232	1 857	1 745	1 697	1 641
At constant prices	3 919	3 627	3 563	3 523	3 565	3 616	3 728	3 824	3 989
Growth rates	−6.6	−7.5	−1.8	−1.1	1.2	1.4	3.1	2.6	4.3
Togo Togo									
At current prices	1 676	1 244	982	1 307	1 450	1 400	1 511	1 500	1 385
Per capita	466	339	262	340	366	342	356	342	306
At constant prices	1 526	1 317	1 532	1 666	1 733	1 816	1 925	1 966	1 956
Growth rates	−3.7	−13.7	16.3	8.8	4.0	4.8	6.0	2.1	−0.5
Tonga Tonga									
At current prices	137	143	161	173	185	182	161	154	145
Per capita	1 424	1 484	1 657	1 774	1 894	1 861	1 639	1 556	1 460

20
Gross domestic product and gross domestic product per capita
In millions of US dollars [1] at current and constant 1990 prices; per capita US dollars;
real rates of growth [cont.]
Produit intérieur brut et produit intérieur brut par habitant
En millions de dollars E.-U. [1] aux prix courants et constants de 1990; par habitant en dollars E.-U.;
taux de l'accroissement réels [suite]

Country or area Pays ou zone	1992	1993	1994	1995	1996	1997	1998	1999	2000
At constant prices	122	127	133	150	144	142	143	146	155
Growth rates	0.3	3.7	5.0	12.5	−3.7	−1.4	0.1	2.2	6.2
Trinidad and Tobago Trinité−et−Tobago									
At current prices	5 440	4 577	4 947	5 329	5 760	5 859	6 319	6 867	8 075
Per capita	4 410	3 680	3 946	4 221	4 535	4 588	4 925	5 329	6 239
At constant prices	5 118	5 044	5 224	5 430	5 645	5 841	6 167	6 604	6 921
Growth rates	−1.6	−1.5	3.6	4.0	3.9	3.5	5.6	7.1	4.8
Tunisia Tunisie									
At current prices	15 497	14 608	15 633	18 030	19 587	18 897	19 830	20 799	19 463
Per capita	1 825	1 688	1 775	2 016	2 161	2 061	2 140	2 222	2 058
At constant prices	13 793	14 095	14 543	14 894	15 951	16 819	17 618	18 687	19 568
Growth rates	7.8	2.2	3.2	2.4	7.1	5.4	4.8	6.1	4.7
Turkey Turquie									
At current prices	159 095	180 422	130 652	169 319	181 465	189 878	200 307	184 858	199 902
Per capita	2 729	3 039	2 162	2 753	2 901	2 985	3 098	2 815	2 998
At constant prices	161 174	174 136	164 635	176 476	188 838	203 053	209 333	198 826	213 141
Growth rates	6.0	8.0	−5.5	7.2	7.0	7.5	3.1	−5.0	7.2
Turkmenistan Turkménistan									
At current prices	4 145	5 725	4 539	5 879	2 380	2 681	2 862	3 269	4 423
Per capita	1 069	1 435	1 107	1 396	551	606	631	705	934
At constant prices	9 244	9 382	7 759	7 201	7 683	6 807	7 148	8 291	10 364
Growth rates	−15.0	1.5	−17.3	−7.2	6.7	−11.4	5.0	16.0	25.0
Tuvalu Tuvalu									
At current prices	11	10	11	12	13	14	14	16	15
Per capita	1 180	1 040	1 223	1 240	1 383	1 420	1 399	1 556	1 491
At constant prices	10	11	12	11	12	13	15	15	16
Growth rates	2.8	4.1	10.3	−5.0	10.3	3.5	14.9	6.1	3.0
Uganda Ouganda									
At current prices	3 252	3 361	5 286	6 184	6 267	6 676	6 691	6 277	5 997
Per capita	177	177	271	308	303	313	305	278	257
At constant prices	4 124	4 415	4 892	5 364	5 662	5 965	6 394	6 712	7 045
Growth rates	4.6	7.1	10.8	9.6	5.6	5.3	7.2	5.0	5.0
Ukraine Ukraine									
At current prices	20 970	32 713	36 755	37 009	44 559	50 152	41 883	31 483	31 693
Per capita	404	631	710	718	870	986	830	629	639
At constant prices	206 327	176 983	136 394	119 821	107 787	104 566	102 533	102 174	108 096
Growth rates	−9.9	−14.2	−22.9	−12.2	−10.0	−3.0	−1.9	−0.3	5.8
United Arab Emirates Emirats arabes unis									
At current prices	34 977	35 305	37 797	42 280	47 403	48 745	45 899	49 775	53 309
Per capita	16 166	15 828	16 482	17 974	19 687	19 815	18 288	19 457	20 457
At constant prices	34 789	34 497	35 256	37 760	41 688	42 500	39 513	40 501	42 688
Growth rates	2.8	−0.8	2.2	7.1	10.4	1.9	−7.0	2.5	5.4
United Kingdom Royaume−Uni									
At current prices	1 072 098	963 361	1 042 699	1 134 941	1 189 179	1 327 798	1 423 934	1 458 230	1 429 384
Per capita	18 490	16 553	17 852	19 366	20 227	22 518	24 083	24 600	24 058
At constant prices	978 147	1 002 524	1 049 229	1 079 645	1 107 973	1 146 144	1 180 418	1 205 513	1 242 199
Growth rates	0.2	2.5	4.7	2.9	2.6	3.4	3.0	2.1	3.0
United Rep. of Tanzania Rép.−Unie de Tanzanie									
At current prices	3 798	3 465	3 576	4 166	5 150	6 099	6 646	6 847	7 365
Per capita	136	120	120	135	162	187	199	200	210
At constant prices	4 131	4 303	4 434	4 592	4 785	4 943	5 190	5 467	5 725
Growth rates	3.5	4.2	3.0	3.6	4.2	3.3	5.0	5.3	4.7
United States Etats−Unis									
At current prices	6 261 800	6 582 900	6 993 300	7 338 400	7 751 100	8 256 500	8 720 200	9 206 900	9 810 200
Per capita	24 067	25 031	26 305	27 306	28 532	30 066	31 418	32 831	34 637
At constant prices	5 897 558	6 055 163	6 302 023	6 472 153	6 705 518	7 005 384	7 307 807	7 608 378	7 926 059
Growth rates	3.1	2.7	4.1	2.7	3.6	4.5	4.3	4.1	4.2
Uruguay Uruguay									
At current prices	12 878	15 002	17 475	19 298	20 516	21 704	22 371	20 913	20 053
Per capita	4 090	4 730	5 470	5 996	6 329	6 647	6 801	6 312	6 009
At constant prices	7 530	7 720	8 289	8 163	8 605	9 048	9 460	9 175	9 080
Growth rates	−2.9	2.5	7.4	−1.5	5.4	5.1	4.5	−3.0	−1.0
Uzbekistan Ouzbékistan									
At current prices	2 298	5 497	6 514	10 169	13 954	15 525	14 988	17 081	13 501

20
Gross domestic product and gross domestic product per capita
In millions of US dollars [1] at current and constant 1990 prices; per capita US dollars;
real rates of growth [cont.]
Produit intérieur brut et produit intérieur brut par habitant
En millions de dollars E.−U. [1] aux prix courants et constants de 1990; par habitant en dollars E.−U.;
taux de l'accroissement réels [suite]

Country or area Pays ou zone	1992	1993	1994	1995	1996	1997	1998	1999	2000
Per capita	107	251	292	446	601	656	622	698	543
At constant prices	43 072	42 082	39 893	39 534	40 206	42 297	44 158	46 101	48 130
Growth rates	−11.1	−2.3	−5.2	−0.9	1.7	5.2	4.4	4.4	4.4
Vanuatu Vanuatu									
At current prices	190	196	214	243	253	254	232	229	224
Per capita	1 202	1 202	1 281	1 412	1 427	1 399	1 240	1 193	1 140
At constant prices	170	178	182	191	196	200	205	201	206
Growth rates	−0.7	4.5	2.5	4.7	2.6	2.4	2.1	−2.0	2.5
Venezuela Venezuela									
At current prices	60 423	60 048	58 418	77 389	70 538	88 704	95 849	103 311	121 258
Per capita	2 955	2 871	2 733	3 543	3 162	3 894	4 124	4 358	5 017
At constant prices	56 558	56 714	55 381	57 570	57 456	61 117	61 221	57 495	59 355
Growth rates	6.1	0.3	−2.3	4.0	−0.2	6.4	0.2	−6.1	3.2
Viet Nam Viet Nam									
At current prices	9 867	13 181	16 281	20 736	24 658	26 844	27 210	28 684	31 349
Per capita	143	188	227	285	333	358	358	372	401
At constant prices	7 450	8 052	8 764	9 600	10 496	11 352	12 006	12 579	13 429
Growth rates	8.6	8.1	8.8	9.5	9.3	8.2	5.8	4.8	6.8
Yemen Yémen									
At current prices	15 991	19 844	25 512	12 514	7 821	6 875	6 250	7 274	8 532
Per capita	1 249	1 471	1 797	840	502	423	369	413	465
At constant prices	13 954	14 522	14 836	16 447	17 416	18 824	19 747	20 586	21 367
Growth rates	4.9	4.1	2.2	10.9	5.9	8.1	4.9	4.2	3.8
Zambia Zambie									
At current prices	3 308	3 273	3 348	3 470	3 312	3 956	3 384	3 518	3 504
Per capita	388	374	373	376	350	408	340	345	336
At constant prices	3 676	3 926	3 788	3 701	3 942	4 072	3 994	4 090	4 217
Growth rates	−1.7	6.8	−3.5	−2.3	6.5	3.3	−1.9	2.4	3.1
Zimbabwe Zimbabwe									
At current prices	6 746	6 553	6 889	7 111	8 474	8 428	5 732	5 613	7 229
Per capita	626	595	613	620	724	706	471	453	572
At constant prices	8 417	8 506	9 113	9 062	9 848	10 216	10 469	10 475	10 031
Growth rates	−9.0	1.1	7.1	−0.6	8.7	3.7	2.5	0.1	−4.2

Source:
United Nations Statistics Division, New York, the
national accounts database.

Source:
Organisation des Nations Unies, Division de statistique, New York,
la base de données sur les comptes nationaux.

1   The conversion rates used to translate national currency
data into United States dollars are the period averages of
market exchange rates (MERs) for members of the
International Monetary Fund (IMF). These rates, which are
published in the *International Financial Statistics*, are
communicated to the IMF by national central banks and
consist of three types of rates:

    a) Market rates, determined largely by market
      forces;
    b) Official rates, determined by government
      authorities;
    c) Principal rates, for countries maintaining
      multiple exchange rate arrangements.

1   Les taux de conversion utilisés pour exprimer les données
nationales en dollars des États−Unis sont, pour les membres du
Fonds monétaire international (FMI), les moyennes pour la
période considérée des taux de change du marché. Ces derniers,
qui sont publiés dans "Statistiques financières internationales,"
sont communiqués au FMI par les banques centrales nationales
et reposent sur trois types de taux :

    a) Taux du marché, déterminés surtout par les facteurs du marché;

    b) Taux officiels, déterminés par les pouvoirs publics;

    c) Taux principaux, pour les pays pratiquant différents
      arrangements en matière de taux de change.

20
Gross domestic product: total and per capita
In US dollars (millions) [1] at current and constant 1990 prices; per capita US dollars;
real rates of growth [*cont.*]

Produit intérieur brut : total et par habitant
En dollars E.–U. (millions) [1] aux prix courants et constants de 1990; par habitant en dollars E.–U.;
taux de l'accroissement réels [*suite*]

Market rates always take priority and official rates are
used only when a free market rate is not available.

For non–members of the IMF, averages of the United Nations
operational rates, used for accounting purposes in UN
transactions with member countries, are applied. These are
based on official, commercial and/or tourist rates of
exchange.

It should be noted that there are practical constraints in
the use of MERs for conversion purposes, particularly in the
case of countries with multiple exchange rates, those coping
with inordinate levels of inflation or experiencing
misalignments caused by market fluctuations, the use of
which may result in excessive fluctuations or distortions in
the dollar income levels of a number of countries. Caution
is therefore urged when making inter–country comparisons of
incomes as expressed in US dollars.

2   For Afghanistan, Iraq, Lebanon, Liberia, Myanmar, Nigeria, Suriname
and Syrian Arab Republic, price–adjusted rates of exchange (PARE)
were used due to large distortions in the levels of per capita
GDP with the use of IMF market exchange rates.

3   Data refer to the Vatican City State.

4   Weighted rates of exchange were used for the period 1987 – 1992.

On donne toujours la priorité aux taux du marché, n'utilisant
les taux officiels que lorsqu'il n'y a pas de taux du marché libre.

Pour les pays qui ne sont pas membres du FMI, on utilise des
moyennes des taux de change opérationnels de l'ONU (qui servent
à des fins comptables, pour les opérations de l'ONU avec les
les pays qui en sont membres). Ces taux reposent sur les taux
de change officiels, les taux du commerce et/ou les taux
touristiques.

Il est à noter qu'on se heurte à des difficultés pratiques
en utilisant les taux de change du marché pour convertir
les données en monnaie nationale, surtout dans le cas des
pays qui pratiquent plusieurs taux de change et de ceux qui
connaissent des taux d'inflation exceptionnels ou des
décalages provenant des fluctuations du marché; on risque en
les utilisant d'aboutir à des fluctuations excessives ou à des
distorsions du revenu en dollars de certains pays. Les
comparaisons de revenu entre pays sont donc sujettes à
caution lorsqu'on se fonde sur le revenu en dollars des
États–Unis.

2   Pour l'Afghanistan, l'Iraq, le Liban, le Libéria, le Myanmar, le
Nigéria, le Suriname et le République arabe syrienne on a utilisé
des taux de change corrigés des prix, car les taux de change du
marché publiés par le FMI induisent des distorsions importantes
dans les montants du produit intérieur brut par habitant.

3   Les données se rapportent à l'Etat de la Cité du Vatican.

4   Pour la période 1987 à 1992, on a utilisé des taux de change
pondérés.

21
Expenditure on gross domestic product in current prices
Percentage distribution
Dépenses imputées au produit intérieur brut aux prix courants
Répartition en pourcentage

Country or area Pays ou zone	Year Année	GDP in current prices (Million nat. cur.) PIB aux prix courants (Mil. monnaie nat.)	% of GDP − en % du PIB					
			Govt. final consumption expenditure Consom. finale des admin. publiques	Household final consumption expenditure Consom. finale des ménages	Changes in inventories Variation des stocks	Gross fixed capital formation Formation brute de capital fixe	Exports of goods and services Exportations de biens et services	Imports of goods and services Importations de biens et services
Albania	1987	17 246	9.6	62.5	−4.0	31.9	−0.1[1]	...
Albanie	1988	17 001	9.5	63.3	−2.6	31.9	−2.0[1]	...
	1989	18 674	8.8	61.0	0.4	31.3	−1.5[1]	...
Algeria	1998	2 810 124	17.9	55.3	0.9	25.9	23.2	23.3
Algérie	1999	3 215 126	16.9	51.9	1.1	24.6	28.6	23.0
	2000	4 078 676	13.7	42.0	0.4	21.3	42.9	20.3
Angola	1988	239 640	32.9	45.5	0.0	14.6	32.8	25.8
Angola	1989	278 866	28.9	48.2	0.9	11.2	33.8	23.1
	1990	308 062	28.5	44.7	0.6	11.1	38.9	23.8
Anguilla	1999	283	15.0	86.5	...	43.8	68.5	113.5
Anguilla	2000	292	20.2	86.6	...	43.5	64.4	114.7
	2001	298	21.5	71.5	...	30.9	67.4	91.3
Antigua and Barbuda	1984	468	18.5	69.8	...	23.6	73.7	85.6
Antigua−et−Barbuda	1985	541	18.3	71.5	...	28.0	75.7	93.5
	1986	642	18.9	69.7	...	36.1	75.2	99.9
Argentina [2]	1998	298 948[3]	12.5	69.1	...	19.9[5]	10.4	12.9
Argentine [2]	1999	283 523[3]	13.7	70.1	...	18.0[5]	9.8	11.5
	2000	284 204[3]	13.8	69.3	...	16.2[5]	10.9	11.5
Armenia [2]	1998	955 400[3]	11.1	100.1[4]	2.9	16.2	19.0	52.8
Arménie [2]	1999	987 400[3]	11.9	96.4[4]	1.9	16.4	20.8	49.8
	2000	1 033 300[3]	12.0	95.4[4]	1.5	17.7	23.4	52.5
Aruba [2]	1996	2 459	18.7	49.3	0.5	26.3	94.4	89.2
Aruba [2]	1997	2 745	22.0	47.4	0.8	24.7	91.9	86.8
	1998	2 923	19.8	49.3	1.3	25.2	91.8	87.4
Australia [2 6]	1998	591 592	18.3	60.0	0.9	23.3	18.9	21.4
Australie [2 6]	1999	629 212	18.8	59.6	0.3	23.7	20.0	22.3
	2000	670 029	18.7	60.1	0.1	21.1	22.9	22.7
Austria [2]	1998	189 937[3]	19.6	57.1[4]	0.7[7]	23.6	43.5	44.1
Autriche [2]	1999	196 658[3]	19.7	57.1[4]	0.8[7]	23.3	45.6	46.4
	2000	204 843[3]	19.4	57.0[4]	0.5[7]	23.7	50.1	51.1
Azerbaijan [2]	1999	18 875 400[3]	15.6	75.8[4]	−2.0	28.5	28.0	41.9
Azerbaïdjan [2]	2000	23 590 500[3]	15.2	64.4[4]	−2.5	23.1	40.2	38.4
	2001	26 619 800[3]	12.3	60.6[4]	−0.3	21.2	42.4	37.6
Bahamas [2]	1993	2 854[3]	14.3	69.6	1.2	18.4	53.2	51.6
Bahamas [2]	1994	3 053[3]	16.7	67.3	1.0	20.1	51.4	53.5
	1995	3 069[3]	15.8	67.7	0.5	22.7	54.7	59.3
Bahrain	1998	2 325	20.8	57.1	7.4	14.0	64.6	63.9
Bahreïn	1999	2 489	20.8	55.4	−4.8	13.6	77.2	62.2
	2000	2 996	17.6	47.1	−2.6	13.5	88.1	63.7
Bangladesh [2 6]	1997	2 001 766[3]	4.7	77.9	...	21.6	13.3	18.3
Bangladesh [2 6]	1998	2 196 972[3]	4.6	77.7	...	22.2	13.2	18.7
	1999	2 370 856[3]	4.6	77.5	...	23.0	14.0	19.2
Barbados	1998	4 747	20.7	63.0	0.2	18.2	53.1	55.2
Barbade	1999	4 970	20.7	65.9	0.6	18.8	50.8	56.8
	2000	5 201	20.8	66.5	0.1	18.1	50.6	56.1
Belarus [2]	1998	702 161 100[8]	19.9	57.8[4]	0.8	25.9	59.1	63.9
Bélarus [2]	1999	3 026 063 700[8]	19.5	58.6[4]	−2.6	26.3	59.2	61.6
	2000	9 133 800	19.5	56.9[4]	0.2	25.2	69.2	72.4
Belgium [2]	1998	225 873	21.1	54.3[4]	−0.2	20.6	75.1	71.0
Belgique [2]	1999	235 538	21.2	53.8[4]	−0.1	20.9	75.6	71.3
	2000	248 338	21.2	54.1[4]	0.4	21.1	86.3	83.0
Belize [2]	1998	1 258	17.4	67.3	3.1	21.3	52.9	62.1
Belize [2]	1999	1 377	17.1	65.1	3.0	26.5	51.3	63.2
	2000	1 514	15.3	68.4	3.2	31.0	48.8	66.7
Benin	1989	479 200	13.0	81.4	−0.6	12.5	18.3	24.5
Bénin	1990	502 300	13.2	80.4	0.8	13.4	20.4	28.2
	1991	535 500	12.0	82.6	0.9	13.6	22.0	31.1

21
Expenditure on gross domestic product in current prices
Percentage distribution *[cont.]*
Dépenses imputées au produit intérieur brut aux prix courants
Répartition en pourcentage *[suite]*

Country or area Pays ou zone	Year Année	GDP in current prices (Million nat. cur.) PIB aux prix courants (Mil. monnaie nat.)	Govt. final consumption expenditure Consom. finale des admin. publiques	Household final consumption expenditure Consom. finale des ménages	Changes in inventories Variation des stocks	Gross fixed capital formation Formation brute de capital fixe	Exports of goods and services Exportations de biens et services	Imports of goods and services Importations de biens et services
Bermuda [2] [9] Bermudes [2] [9]	1998	3 053	10.6	60.8[4]	0.6[7]	19.3	47.4	38.7
	1999	3 272	10.8	61.2[4]	0.6[7]	19.4	47.0	39.0
	2000	3 397	10.8	61.2[4]	0.6[7]	19.4	47.0	39.0
Bhutan Bhoutan	1998	16 337	20.2	57.1	0.3	37.9	31.5	47.0
	1999	19 123	22.3	52.6	0.6	42.5	29.9	47.9
	2000	21 698	20.4	52.2	0.2	43.5	29.8	46.1
Bolivia [2] Bolivie [2]	1998	46 471	14.3	74.8	0.5	23.4	19.9	32.9
	1999	48 268	14.6	77.1	−1.1	19.4	17.2	27.1
	2000	51 261	14.3	76.2	0.0	18.2	18.8	27.4
Botswana [2] [10] Botswana [2] [10]	1998	20 163	27.0	30.4[4]	4.4	25.6	56.5	44.0
	1999	21 524	30.6	32.2[4]	7.7	29.1	46.7	46.3
	2000	25 363	29.7	30.8[4]	−8.4	26.6	60.4	39.1
Brazil [2] Brésil [2]	1998	914 188	19.1	61.9	1.4	19.7	7.4	9.6
	1999	963 869	19.3	62.0	1.2	19.1	10.4	11.9
	2000	1 086 700	19.3	60.6	2.3	19.4	10.8	12.4
British Virgin Islands Iles Vierges brit.	1987	117	17.3	73.7	2.3	36.9	95.5	125.7
	1988	131	20.1	68.9	2.7	34.3	107.6	133.5
	1989	156	20.7	64.9	2.6	31.6	104.8	124.6
Brunei Darussalam Brunéi Darussalam	1982	9 126	10.0	5.5	0.0	12.4	89.3	17.2
	1983	8 124	11.4	9.5	0.0	9.9	88.3	19.0
	1984	8 069	31.1	−5.6	0.0	6.5	84.5	16.5
Bulgaria [2] Bulgarie [2]	1998	21 577 020[3]	15.1	72.9[4][11]	3.6[7]	13.2	48.0	50.9
	1999	22 776 444[3]	15.9	74.8[4][11]	3.1[7]	15.9	44.1	51.9
	2000	25 453 649[3]	17.7	72.2[4][11]	0.4[7]	16.2	58.5	64.1
Burkina Faso Burkina Faso	1991	811 676	14.7	76.2	1.4	21.8	11.4	25.4
	1992	812 590	14.4	76.2	−0.2	21.3	9.7	21.4
	1993	832 349	14.4	77.2	0.8	20.4	9.7	22.5
Burundi Burundi	1990	196 656	19.5	83.0	−0.6	16.4	8.0	26.2
	1991	211 898	17.0	83.9	−0.5	18.1	10.0	28.5
	1992	226 384	15.6	82.9	0.4	21.1	9.0	29.0
Cambodia Cambodge	1998	10 543 430[3]	5.6	88.9	−0.9	12.9	36.8	46.2
	1999	11 646 360[3]	6.2	87.0	1.6	15.3	37.2	51.6
	2000	11 922 980[3]	6.7	86.4	−1.3	15.5	48.4	54.8
Cameroon [2] [6] Cameroun [2] [6]	1996	4 793 080	79.8[12]	...	−0.2	13.1	24.7	17.4
	1997	5 370 580	82.0[12]	...	0.1	12.8	24.0	19.0
	1998	5 744 000	82.9[12]	...	−0.1	13.5	24.0	20.4
Canada [2] Canada [2]	1998	901 239[3]	19.6	57.8[4]	0.6	20.2	41.7	39.9
	1999	960 206[3]	19.0	57.0[4]	0.4	20.2	43.4	40.1
	2000	1 040 426[3]	18.5	55.7[4]	0.7	20.1	45.9	40.9
Cape Verde Cap−Vert	1993	29 078	23.3	83.5	−1.0	40.0	18.0	63.8
	1994	33 497	21.6	83.0	0.7	43.7	18.4	67.3
	1995	37 705	22.8	86.3	2.0	38.8	16.6	66.5
Cayman Islands Iles Caïmanes	1989	474[3]	14.1	65.0	...	23.2	60.1	68.8
	1990	590[3]	14.2	62.5	...	21.4	64.1	58.5
	1991	616[3]	15.1	62.5	...	21.8	58.9	52.8
Central African Rep. Rép. centrafricaine	1985	388 545	15.1	79.1	3.0	12.4	22.0	31.6
	1986	388 647	15.6	82.1	−0.1	12.9	18.2	28.6
	1987	360 942	17.5	80.6	−0.2	12.9	17.8	28.6
Chad Tchad	1992	350 632	17.6	75.6	...	8.7	17.6	19.5
	1993	291 691	24.1	83.1	...	7.7	19.9	34.8
	1994	460 851	12.8	56.0	...	9.8	22.7	1.3
Chile Chili	1998	33 630 367	11.2	65.5	1.4	26.0	26.7	30.9
	1999	34 422 796	12.0	64.1	0.2	21.9	29.0	27.2
	2000	37 774 743	12.2	63.3	1.1	22.3	31.8	30.8
China [2] Chine [2]	1997	7 489 430	11.6	46.5	4.4	33.6	22.9	19.1
	1998	7 985 330	11.9	46.2	2.8	35.3	21.5	17.7
	1999	8 242 970	12.5	47.8	1.2	35.8	21.9	19.2
China, Hong Kong SAR Chine, Hong Kong RAS	1998	1 259 306	9.4	60.5[4]	−1.2	30.3	129.3	128.2
	1999	1 227 658	9.9	59.8[4]	−0.9	25.8	133.4	128.0
	2000	1 267 175	9.6	58.1[4]	1.3	26.3	150.0	145.3

21
Expenditure on gross domestic product in current prices
Percentage distribution *[cont.]*
Dépenses imputées au produit intérieur brut aux prix courants
Répartition en pourcentage *[suite]*

Country or area Pays ou zone	Year Année	GDP in current prices (Million nat. cur.) PIB aux prix courants (Mil. monnaie nat.)	% of GDP — en % du PIB					
			Govt. final consumption expenditure Consom. finale des admin. publiques	Household final consumption expenditure Consom. finale des ménages	Changes in inventories Variation des stocks	Gross fixed capital formation Formation brute de capital fixe	Exports of goods and services Exportations de biens et services	Imports of goods and services Importations de biens et services
Colombia [2] Colombie [2]	1998	140 953 206	20.6	65.7[4]	0.8[7]	18.8	15.1	21.0
	1999	149 042 204	23.1	64.4[4]	−0.6[7]	13.2	18.6	18.6
	2000	169 703 948	...	...	...	...	21.3	19.8
Comoros Comores	1989	63 397	27.6	77.8	4.6	14.4	14.9	39.3
	1990	66 370	25.7	79.7	8.0	12.2	11.7	37.3
	1991	69 248	25.3	80.9	4.0	12.3	15.5	38.0
Congo Congo	1987	690 523	20.6	56.6[4]	−1.1	20.9	41.7	38.6
	1988	658 964	21.1	60.1[4]	−1.0	19.6	40.6	40.4
	1989	773 524	18.7	52.8	−0.5	16.4	47.6	35.0
Costa Rica [2] Costa Rica [2]	1998	3 625 330	13.0	69.3	0.1	20.4	47.4	50.1
	1999	4 512 763	12.5	64.6	−0.8	18.0	51.6	45.9
	2000	4 915 089	13.3	67.8	−0.8	17.4	48.1	45.8
Côte d'Ivoire Côte d'Ivoire	1994	4 616 000	18.1	60.4[4]	2.2	10.2	39.6	30.5
	1995	5 543 000	16.9	64.1[4]	1.9	12.2	37.0	32.1
	1996	6 177 000	16.0	65.1[4]	−4.1	13.7	41.0	31.7
Croatia [2] Croatie [2]	1999	142 700	27.8	57.1	0.3	23.1	40.6	48.9
	2000	157 511	26.5	57.2	1.0	21.0	45.0	50.6
	2001	168 972	24.1	58.2	1.9	21.9	46.7	52.8
Cuba Cuba	1998	23 901[3]	23.6	71.6	−2.3	10.2	15.2	18.0
	1999	25 504[3]	23.5	70.9	−1.6	10.4	16.0	18.7
	2000	27 635[3]	23.1	68.9	−1.0	10.8	15.7	18.2
Cyprus Chypre	1997	4 371[3]	18.8	66.0	0.8	19.0	47.1	52.0
	1998	4 695[3]	19.3	67.5	1.5	19.2	43.5	51.1
	1999	5 009[3]	17.5	66.1	1.2	18.2	44.6	48.6
Czech Republic [2] République tchèque [2]	1998	1 837 060	18.9	52.4[4]	1.2[7]	29.0	58.6	60.0
	1999	1 887 325	19.7	53.9[4]	−0.1[7]	27.9	60.9	62.3
	2000	1 959 479	19.6	54.4[4]	1.4[7]	28.3	71.4	75.2
Dem. Rep. of the Congo Rép. dém. du Congo	1987	326 946	22.4	77.1	5.3	20.3	63.2	88.2
	1988	622 822	37.2	...	3.7	19.0	81.0	...
	1989	2 146 811	14.4	...	3.2	13.4	46.5	...
Denmark [2] Danemark [2]	1999	1 213 595	25.9	49.2[4]	−0.1[7]	20.3	37.9	33.1
	2000	1 296 137	25.1	47.3[4]	0.0[7]	21.6	43.8	37.9
	2001	1 352 069	25.4	46.9[4]	0.4[7]	20.5	45.2	38.3
Djibouti Djibouti	1996	88 233	33.6	64.6	−0.9	19.3	40.3	56.8
	1997	87 289	34.7	59.3	0.2	21.4	42.2	57.8
	1998	88 461	29.0	67.3	0.2	23.2	43.4	63.0
Dominica Dominique	1989	423	20.5	71.5	1.5	38.8	41.0	73.4
	1990	452	20.3	64.1	1.1	39.7	50.1	75.3
	1991	479	20.0	71.4	1.1	40.2	46.4	79.1
Dominican Republic [2] Rép. dominicaine [2]	1994	179 130	4.6	76.8	3.4	17.9	37.4	40.2
	1995	209 646	4.3	78.6	3.3	16.1	34.5	36.7
	1996	232 993	4.7	81.4	3.6	17.3	18.1	25.1
Ecuador Equateur	1998	107 421 048	11.7	70.4	3.7	21.0	25.3	32.0
	1999	161 350 379	10.4	65.5	−1.9	14.8	37.1	25.8
	2000	340 021 704	9.5	62.1	0.6	16.2	42.4	30.8
Egypt [6] Egypte [6]	1989	87 741	11.0	71.7	5.5	25.6	22.0	35.8
	1990	110 143	10.0	76.3	−0.6	22.4	28.1	36.2
	1991	136 190	8.9	80.8	0.1	17.9	29.5	37.2
El Salvador El Salvador	1998	105 074	9.7	85.0	0.9	16.7	24.8	37.1
	1999	109 115	10.0	85.8	0.2	16.3	24.8	37.2
	2000	115 610	10.2	88.0	0.0	17.0	27.6	42.7
Equatorial Guinea Guinée équatoriale	1989	42 256	22.2	54.3	0.0	19.6	40.4	36.6
	1990	44 349	15.3	53.2	−3.1	34.6	59.7	59.7
	1991	46 429	14.4	75.9	−2.3	18.4	28.4	34.7
Estonia [2] Estonie [2]	1999	76 327[3]	23.4	58.2[4]	−0.4[7]	24.9	77.2	82.1
	2000	85 436[3]	21.8	58.4[4]	1.3[7]	23.4	95.4	100.4
	2001	95 275[3]	20.7	57.2[4]	1.3[7]	25.4	91.8	95.9
Ethiopia [13] Ethiopie [13]	1997	41 465	10.9	79.2	...	19.1	16.2	23.3
	1998	44 896	14.2	78.4	...	19.0	16.2	26.4
	1999	48 949	16.0	81.4	...	20.8	14.5	30.2

21
Expenditure on gross domestic product in current prices
Percentage distribution *[cont.]*
Dépenses imputées au produit intérieur brut aux prix courants
Répartition en pourcentage *[suite]*

Country or area Pays ou zone	Year Année	GDP in current prices (Million nat. cur.) PIB aux prix courants (Mil. monnaie nat.)	% of GDP – en % du PIB Govt. final consumption expenditure Consom. finale des admin. publiques	Household final consumption expenditure Consom. finale des ménages	Changes in inventories Variation des stocks	Gross fixed capital formation Formation brute de capital fixe	Exports of goods and services Exportations de biens et services	Imports of goods and services Importations de biens et services
Fiji	1998	3 154[3]	18.0	67.3	1.3	12.7	58.2	60.8
Fidji	1999	3 665[3]	16.5	58.5	1.1	12.7	60.3	63.7
	2000	3 518[3]	17.8	62.4	1.1	9.9	60.2	64.5
Finland [2]	1999	120 485[3]	21.7	50.7[4]	−0.1	18.9	37.8	29.4
Finlande [2]	2000	131 229[3]	20.6	49.5[4]	0.7	19.3	42.9	33.6
	2001	135 057[3]	21.2	50.0[4]	0.3	19.8	40.4	31.6
France [2]	1998	1 305 851	23.4	54.8[4]	0.6[7]	18.4	26.1	23.5
France [2]	1999	1 350 159	23.4	54.7[4]	0.4[7]	19.1	26.1	23.6
	2000	1 404 775	23.3	54.8[4]	0.9[7]	19.7	28.7	27.2
French Guyana	1990	6 526	35.0	64.4	−0.2	47.8	67.3	114.3
Guyane française	1991	7 404	34.4	60.1	1.5	40.5	81.1	117.6
	1992	7 976	34.2	58.9	1.5	30.8	65.4	90.8
French Polynesia	1991	305 211	39.3	63.9	−0.2	18.4	9.3	30.7
Polynésie française	1992	314 265	47.8	63.9	0.0	16.7	8.3	27.4
	1993	329 266	38.3	61.5	−0.2	16.2	10.5	26.4
Gabon	1986	1 201 100	25.3	46.8	...	45.2[5]	39.6	57.0
Gabon	1987	1 020 600	23.7	48.6	...	26.7[5]	41.3	40.3
	1988	1 013 600	21.8	48.1	...	36.2[5]	37.3	43.4
Gambia [6]	1991	2 920	13.0	83.7	...	...	45.3	60.1
Gambie [6]	1992	3 078	13.2	81.2	...	...	45.2	61.9
	1993	3 243	15.1	78.1	...	...	36.6	56.9
Georgia [2]	1999	5 666[3]	10.3	84.0	1.2	18.1	19.1	38.1
Georgie [2]	2000	5 971[3]	8.5	85.0	1.3	15.8	23.3	40.1
	2001	6 506[3]	8.6	79.5	1.2	17.6	22.1	38.1
Germany [2]	1999	1 974 300	19.2	58.2[4]	0.2[7]	21.6	29.7	28.9
Allemagne [2]	2000	2 025 500	19.0	58.4[4]	0.6[7]	21.6	33.7	33.3
	2001	2 063 000	19.1	59.0[4]	−0.3[7]	20.3	35.0	33.1
Ghana	1994	5 205 200	13.7	73.7	1.4	22.6	22.5	33.9
Ghana	1995	7 752 600	12.1	76.2	−1.1	21.1	24.5	32.8
	1996	11 339 200	12.0	76.1	0.9	20.6	24.9	34.5
Greece [2]	1998	105 773	15.3	71.7[4]	0.2	21.1	19.8	28.2
Grèce [2]	1999	112 660	15.2	70.7[4]	−0.3	21.7	20.6	27.9
	2000	121 516	15.5	69.8[4]	0.0	22.6	25.0	32.9
Grenada	1990	541	20.5	64.9	3.1	38.9	44.4	71.8
Grenade	1991	567	18.8	69.2	3.7	40.0	45.4	77.1
	1992	578	19.9	66.5	2.1	32.4	38.6	59.4
Guadeloupe	1990	15 201	30.8	92.8	1.1	33.9	4.9	63.5
Guadeloupe	1991	16 415	31.0	87.3	1.0	33.0	6.1	58.4
	1992	17 972	29.3	84.1	1.3	27.8	4.5	47.0
Guatemala	1996	95 479	5.1	87.0	−0.6	13.3	17.8	22.6
Guatemala	1997	107 943	4.9	86.9	−1.0	14.8	17.9	23.6
	1998	121 548	6.2	86.6	−0.2	15.7	17.9	26.2
Guinea−Bissau	1990	510 094	11.4	100.9	0.9	13.8	12.0	39.0
Guinée−Bissau	1991	854 985	12.6	100.6	0.9	10.4	13.4	38.0
	1992	1 530 010	10.7	111.1	0.0	26.5[2]	8.2	56.5
Guyana	1999	123 665	24.2	43.8	...	36.8[5]	−10.1[1]	...
Guyana	2000	130 013	27.5	49.9	...	38.5[5]	...	...
	2001	133 544	18.5	59.9	...	38.5[5]	...	...
Haiti [14]	1997	51 578	103.1[12]	...	...	12.5	11.5	27.1
Haïti [14]	1998	59 055	102.5[12]	...	...	12.9	13.2	28.6
	1999	66 425	101.8[12]	...	...	13.1	13.3	28.2
Honduras	1998	70 438	10.1	67.0	2.7	28.2	46.1	54.1
Honduras	1999	77 095	11.3	68.8	4.8	29.8	41.3	56.0
	2000	87 523	12.0	70.0	4.6	27.2	42.3	56.1
Hungary [2]	1998	10 087 434	21.7	50.8[4]	6.0	23.6	50.6	52.7
Hongrie [2]	1999	11 393 499	21.5	52.4[4]	4.6	23.9	53.0	55.5
	2000	13 075 210	21.1	52.4[4]	6.2	24.3	61.6	65.6
Iceland [2]	1998	579 286	22.1	57.4[4]	0.2	25.0	35.2	39.7
Islande [2]	1999	623 419	23.0	58.7[4]	0.0	22.9	34.2	38.7
	2000	673 660	23.5	59.2[4]	0.4	23.8	34.4	41.4

21
Expenditure on gross domestic product in current prices
Percentage distribution *[cont.]*
Dépenses imputées au produit intérieur brut aux prix courants
Répartition en pourcentage *[suite]*

Country or area Pays ou zone	Year Année	GDP in current prices (Million nat. cur.) PIB aux prix courants (Mil. monnaie nat.)	% of GDP − en % du PIB					
			Govt. final consumption expenditure Consom. finale des admin. publiques	Household final consumption expenditure Consom. finale des ménages	Changes in inventories Variation des stocks	Gross fixed capital formation Formation brute de capital fixe	Exports of goods and services Exportations de biens et services	Imports of goods and services Importations de biens et services
India [9]	1998	17 409 350[3]	12.3	65.1	−0.1	21.5	11.2	12.9
Inde [9]	1999	19 296 410[3]	12.9	65.4	1.7	21.6	11.8	13.8
	2000	20 879 880[3]	13.2	64.2	1.0	21.9	13.9	14.7
Indonesia	1998	955 754 000	5.7	67.8[4]	−8.7	25.4	53.0	43.2
Indonésie	1999	1 109 980 000	6.5	73.3[4]	−9.5	21.7	35.2	27.2
	2000	1 290 684 000	2.4	71.9[4]	−6.5	24.3	38.5	30.7
Iran (Islamic Republic of) [2] [15]	1998	317 084 200[3]	15.9	56.9[4]	0.6	30.4	14.2	15.9
Iran (Rép. islamique d') [2] [15]	1999	426 367 300	15.3	52.8[4]	−2.4	28.4	20.9	15.1
	2000	582 050 300	14.4	45.3[4]	−3.0	27.1	32.5	16.3
Iraq	1998	4 570 100	...	86.9	...	3.8[5]	...	...
Iraq	1999	6 809 790	...	67.4	...	3.9[5]	...	...
	2000	7 398 604	...	66.0	...	7.3[5]	...	...
Ireland [2]	1998	77 110[3]	14.5	49.7[4]	1.5[7]	22.1	86.6	75.2
Irlande [2]	1999	89 029[3]	14.0	48.2[4]	0.0[7]	23.5	88.7	74.8
	2000	103 470[3]	13.4	47.7[4]	0.3[7]	23.6	94.9	80.7
Israel [2]	1998	405 021	27.7	54.6[4]	0.0	21.2	30.2	33.7
Israël [2]	1999	443 048	27.6	54.3[4]	1.2	20.9	34.1	38.1
	2000	480 780	26.9	54.0[4]	1.1	19.1	38.3	39.4
Italy [2]	1999	1 108 497	18.0	60.2[4]	0.6[7]	19.1	25.5	23.5
Italie [2]	2000	1 164 767	18.2	60.4[4]	0.5[7]	19.8	28.4	27.4
	2001	1 216 583	18.5	60.2[4]	−0.1[7]	19.8	28.3	26.7
Jamaica [2]	1996	221 763	14.4	66.5	0.2	31.6	47.8	60.4
Jamaïque [2]	1997	242 762	16.4	65.7	0.2	31.5	42.6	56.5
	1998	257 392	17.8	64.8	0.2	28.2	44.3	55.3
Japan [2]	1998	515 834 800	15.7	55.6[4]	0.0	26.9	10.7	8.8
Japon [2]	1999	511 837 100	16.2	56.4[4]	−0.3	26.2	10.0	8.5
	2000	513 534 000	16.7	55.9[4]	−0.3	26.3	10.8	9.3
Jordan	1996	4 983	24.2	70.7[4]	1.0	29.0	52.1	77.1
Jordanie	1997	5 193	25.3	71.3[4]	−0.1	25.5	48.8	70.8
	1998	5 646	24.2	73.4[4]	0.6	21.0	44.6	63.9
Kazakhstan [2]	1998	1 733 264	10.8	73.3	0.1	14.2	30.3	34.9
Kazakhstan [2]	1999	2 016 456	10.6	72.4	1.6	13.0	42.5	40.1
	2000	2 599 902	14.8	62.3	0.8	17.0	58.8	49.3
Kenya	1999	37 107	17.0	72.6	1.0	15.2	25.5	31.3
Kenya	2000	39 799	17.5	76.6	0.8	14.6	26.6	36.1
	2001	44 764	16.8	77.7	0.6	13.9	26.2	35.1
Korea, Republic of [2]	1998	444 366 540[3]	11.0	54.6[4]	−8.6[7]	29.8	49.7	36.3
Corée, Rép. de [2]	1999	482 744 175[3]	10.4	56.2[4]	−1.1[7]	27.8	42.3	35.5
	2000	517 096 590[3]	10.2	57.3[4]	0.0[7]	28.7	45.0	42.2
Kuwait	1998	7 742	31.1	55.7	...	20.6	44.8	52.2
Koweït	1999	9 075	27.1	49.9	...	16.4	46.4	39.9
	2000	11 590	22.1	40.7	...	11.1	57.2	31.2
Kyrgyzstan [2]	1998	34 181	17.9	88.2[4]	2.6[7]	12.9	36.5	58.0
Kirghizistan [2]	1999	48 744	19.1	77.6[4]	2.3[7]	15.7	42.2	57.0
	2000	65 358	20.0	65.7[4]	2.0[7]	18.0	41.8	47.6
Latvia [2]	1999	3 897	20.5	62.8	1.9	25.1	43.8	54.1
Lettonie [2]	2000	4 336	19.8	62.1	0.2	26.6	45.8	54.4
	2001	4 741	20.0	62.5	3.2	25.7	45.7	57.2
Lebanon	1994	14 992 000	10.6	110.8	0.0	36.4	8.4	66.3
Liban	1995	17 779 000	9.9	107.7	0.0	36.3	11.0	64.9
Lesotho [2]	1997	4 720	16.9	113.5[4]	−1.0	55.0	27.6	112.0
Lesotho [2]	1998	4 921	20.8	112.6[4]	−1.9	49.0	26.8	107.4
	1999	5 637	21.1	105.4[4]	−1.0	47.0	24.1	96.6
Liberia	1987	1 090[3]	13.2	65.5	0.6	11.1	40.2	32.7
Libéria	1988	1 158[3]	11.8	63.3	0.3	10.0	39.0	27.8
	1989	1 194[3]	11.9	55.0	0.3	8.1	43.7	23.1
Libyan Arab Jamah.	1983	8 805	32.7	39.2	−1.1	25.1	42.1	38.0
Jamah. arabe libyenne	1984	8 013	33.6	38.6	0.5	25.3	41.4	39.4
	1985	8 277	31.7	37.6	0.4	19.7	37.4	26.7

21
Expenditure on gross domestic product in current prices
Percentage distribution [cont.]
Dépenses imputées au produit intérieur brut aux prix courants
Répartition en pourcentage [suite]

Country or area Pays ou zone	Year Année	GDP in current prices (Million nat. cur.) PIB aux prix courants (Mil. monnaie nat.)	% of GDP − en % du PIB					
			Govt. final consumption expenditure Consom. finale des admin. publiques	Household final consumption expenditure Consom. finale des ménages	Changes in inventories Variation des stocks	Gross fixed capital formation Formation brute de capital fixe	Exports of goods and services Exportations de biens et services	Imports of goods and services Importations de biens et services
Lithuania [2] Lithuanie [2]	1999	42 655	22.2	65.5[4]	0.6[7]	22.1	39.7	50.1
	2000	45 148	21.4	64.5[4]	2.0[7]	18.5	45.3	51.7
	2001	47 968	20.1	63.8[4]	2.1[7]	19.4	50.4	55.8
Luxembourg [2] Luxembourg [2]	1998	16 975	16.8	43.2[4]	0.7[7]	21.3	126.7	108.7
	1999	18 449	17.1	41.2[4]	0.4[7]	23.8	137.4	119.9
	2000	20 564	16.3	39.2[4]	0.5[7]	21.3	154.2	131.4
Madagascar Madagascar	1990	4 601 600	8.0	86.0	...	17.0	15.9	26.9
	1991	4 906 400	8.6	92.2	...	8.2	17.3	26.2
	1992	5 584 500	8.2	90.0	...	11.6	15.6	25.3
Malawi Malawi	1994	10 319	28.3	74.4[16]	...	12.0	31.8	40.7
	1995	20 923	21.9	30.4[16]	...	11.9	32.2	38.2
	1996	33 918	17.5	56.1[16]	...	11.2	15.5	27.1
Malaysia Malaisie	1998	283 243	9.8	41.6[4]	−0.2	26.8	115.7	93.7
	1999	300 340	11.1	41.5[4]	0.1	22.1	121.7	96.6
	2000	340 706	10.6	42.6[4]	1.2	25.6	125.4	105.4
Maldives Maldives	1982	454	14.3	80.8	0.4	22.7	−18.3[1]	...
	1983	466	16.3	82.6	2.6	35.6	−37.1[1]	...
	1984	537	17.7	77.5	1.5	39.5	−36.1[1]	...
Mali Mali	1990	683 300	15.2	79.0	2.2	20.0	17.3	33.7
	1991	691 400	15.3	85.1	−2.4	20.0	17.5	35.5
	1992	737 400	14.2	82.2	2.7	17.6	17.8	34.6
Malta Malte	1997	1 288	20.5	62.4	0.2[3]	25.3	85.1	93.5
	1998	1 362	19.7	62.1	−0.8[3]	24.5	87.7	93.2
	1999	1 447	18.7	63.1	0.8[3]	22.8	91.3	96.7
Martinique Martinique	1990	19 320	29.7	83.6	1.9	26.7	8.4	50.3
	1991	20 787	28.8	84.0	1.4	25.6	7.4	47.1
	1992	22 093	28.7	84.3	−0.9	23.6	6.8	42.5
Mauritania Mauritanie	1986	59 715	14.3	85.4	1.5	22.7	55.4	79.4
	1987	67 216	13.6	82.6	1.7	20.8	48.3	67.0
	1988	72 635	14.2	79.6	1.4	17.0	49.1	61.3
Mauritius [2] Maurice [2]	1999	107 370	13.2	64.0	−1.3	27.6	64.4	67.9
	2000	118 478	13.1	62.4	1.4	23.7	62.3	62.9
	2001	131 465	12.8	62.0	1.6	23.0	62.7	62.0
Mexico [2] Méxique [2]	1998	3 846 350	10.4	67.4[4]	3.4[17]	20.9	30.7	32.8
	1999	4 583 762	10.9	67.1[4]	2.3[17]	21.2	30.9	32.4
	2000	5 426 786	11.0	67.6[4]	2.3[17]	20.9	31.4	33.3
Mongolia Mongolie	1996	659 698	71.2[12]	...	...	22.4[2]	...	...
	1997	846 344	70.0[12]	...	...	25.3[2]	...	...
	1998	833 727	81.0[12]	...	...	27.3[2]	...	...
Montserrat Montserrat	1984	94	20.6	96.4	2.7	23.7	13.6	56.9
	1985	100	20.3	96.3	1.5	24.7	11.7	54.4
	1986	114	18.7	89.5	2.8	33.0	10.1	53.9
Morocco Maroc	1997	318 342	17.8	65.3	0.0	20.7	23.1	26.9
	1998	342 558	18.1	64.0	0.1	22.4	22.7	27.3
	1999	343 131	19.3	61.1	−0.2	24.3	24.4	29.0
Mozambique Mozambique	1992	2 764 000	21.6	93.5	...	43.5[2]	26.7	85.3
	1997	40 126 200[2]	8.4	89.2	...	18.9[2]	12.8	29.2
	1998	43 557 100[2]	9.4	88.2	...	23.3[2]	11.6	32.5
Myanmar [9] Myanmar [9]	1996	791 980	88.5[12]	...	−2.7	14.9	0.7	1.5
	1997	1 109 554	88.1[12]	...	−0.9	13.5	0.6	1.3
	1998	1 559 996	89.4[12]	...	−0.7	11.8	0.5	1.0
Namibia [2] Namibie [2]	1999	20 681[3]	30.3	59.2[4]	0.3	23.0	46.2	56.9
	2000	23 995[3]	28.4	59.1[4]	0.7	18.6	45.1	50.5
	2001	27 231[3]	27.8	60.6[4]	1.5	22.2	44.3	54.3
Nepal [18] Népal [18]	1996	248 913	9.2	76.9	4.8	22.5	22.3	35.8
	1997	280 513	8.9	77.1	3.7	21.7	26.3	37.7
	1998	296 547	9.3	81.2	−0.5	21.2	23.1	34.3
Netherlands [2] Pays−Bas [2]	1998	354 194	22.7	49.7[4]	0.7[7]	21.5	61.0	55.5
	1999	373 664	23.0	50.2[4]	0.1[7]	22.5	60.6	56.3
	2000	401 089	22.7	49.8[4]	−0.1[7]	22.7	67.2	62.4

21
Expenditure on gross domestic product in current prices
Percentage distribution *[cont.]*
Dépenses imputées au produit intérieur brut aux prix courants
Répartition en pourcentage *[suite]*

Country or area Pays ou zone	Year Année	GDP in current prices (Million nat. cur.) PIB aux prix courants (Mil. monnaie nat.)	% of GDP – en % du PIB					
			Govt. final consumption expenditure Consom. finale des admin. publiques	Household final consumption expenditure Consom. finale des ménages	Changes in inventories Variation des stocks	Gross fixed capital formation Formation brute de capital fixe	Exports of goods and services Exportations de biens et services	Imports of goods and services Importations de biens et services
Netherlands Antilles	1992	3548	25.3	58.3[4]	2.3	22.1	81.5	89.6
Antilles néerlandaises	1993	3766	27.7	57.6[4]	0.4	20.9	76.1	82.7
	1994	4218	26.2	64.2[4]	0.7	18.5	72.8	82.4
New Caledonia	1990	250 427[3]	32.6	57.3	−1.1	24.4	22.0	35.4
Nouvelle−Calédonie	1991	272 235[3]	32.8	53.8	1.3	23.9	20.1	32.2
	1992	281 427[3]	33.7	56.7	0.1	23.7	16.8	31.4
New Zealand [2][9]	1998	101 169[3]	18.8	60.8[4]	−0.1	19.7	30.0	29.8
Nouvelle−Zélande [2][9]	1999	105 852[3]	19.1	60.2[4]	1.2	19.7	31.3	32.5
	2000	111 776[3]	18.2	59.1[4]	1.0	19.0	36.7	35.1
Nicaragua	1998	21 881	16.7	93.2	0.4	33.4	36.8	80.5
Nicaragua	1999	26 130	18.9	95.2	0.2	43.1	34.5	91.9
	2000	30 740	18.7	92.3	−0.2	35.4	36.0	82.2
Niger	1988	678 200	15.5	65.9	7.9	11.9	20.7	21.9
Niger	1989	692 600	18.0	73.0	−0.1	12.3	18.6	21.8
	1990	682 300	17.2	74.1	1.1	11.7	16.8	20.9
Nigeria	1992	549 809	3.7	73.5	0.1	10.7	35.8	23.8
Nigéria	1993	701 473	3.9	76.6	0.1	11.5	32.6	24.8
	1994	914 334	3.5	82.1	0.0	9.3	23.8	18.6
Norway [2]	1998	1 114 827	21.4	49.6[4]	2.7	26.0	36.9	36.0
Norvège [2]	1999	1 197 457	21.3	48.1[4]	...	22.6	39.0	32.8
	2000	1 423 864	19.0	42.7[4]	...	19.8	46.6	30.4
Oman [2]	1998	5 416	25.9	57.6	0.0	24.0	41.2	48.6
Oman [2]	1999	6 041	23.8	50.2	0.1	14.9	47.8	36.7
	2000	7 623	20.7	39.5	0.0	12.0	58.5	30.7
Pakistan [6]	1998	2 938 379	10.4	75.7	1.6	13.9	15.4	17.0
Pakistan [6]	1999	3 182 822	11.0	75.0	1.6	14.0	16.2	17.8
	2000	3 472 149	10.5	76.8	1.6	13.1	17.4	19.4
Panama	1998	9 345	16.1	56.5	4.0	28.1	89.9	94.6
Panama	1999	9 637	15.6	55.3	2.9	30.2	76.7	80.6
	2000	10 019	16.0	56.6	2.4	26.3	79.3	80.6
Papua New Guinea [2]	1997	7 064	19.3	58.3	5.8	15.3	46.9	45.5
Papouasie−Nouvelle−	1998	7 863	17.9	59.7	3.9	13.8	50.1	45.5
Guinée [2]	1999	8 781	16.9	69.7	4.3	12.1	47.3	50.4
Paraguay	1993	11 991 719	6.7	81.3	0.9	22.0	36.9	47.9
Paraguay	1994	14 960 131	6.8	88.4	0.9	22.5	34.2	52.8
	1995	17 699 000	7.2	85.3	0.9	23.1	35.0	51.2
Peru [2]	1998	166 513	10.6	71.2	0.1	23.5	13.3	18.6
Pérou [2]	1999	174 719	10.9	69.9	−0.2	21.7	14.8	17.1
	2000	186 757	11.2	70.6	0.0	20.1	16.0	17.9
Philippines	1998	2 665 060[3]	13.3	74.3	−0.8	21.1	52.2	58.8
Philippines	1999	2 976 904[3]	13.1	72.6	−0.3	19.1	51.5	51.3
	2000	3 302 589[3]	12.8	70.7	−0.2	18.1	56.3	50.2
Poland [2]	1998	553 560	15.4	63.6[4]	1.0	25.1	28.2	33.4
Pologne [2]	1999	615 115	15.5	64.4[4]	0.9	25.5	26.1	32.5
	2000	684 926	15.5	65.3[4]	1.2	24.9	29.4	36.3
Portugal [2]	1998	101 323	18.9	62.2[4]	0.9[7]	26.8	30.8	39.6
Portugal [2]	1999	108 217	19.6	62.4[4]	1.0[7]	27.4	29.7	40.0
	2000	115 262	20.1	61.8[4]	0.8[7]	28.6	31.8	43.1
Puerto Rico [6]	1998	57 841	13.0	58.8	0.9	19.8	69.7	62.1
Porto Rico [6]	1999	61 045	11.8	58.9	0.5	19.4	72.5	63.2
	2000	67 897	11.4	55.4	0.7	17.2	78.3	63.1
Qatar [2]	1998	37 330	31.6	25.3	1.1	30.9	51.1	40.0
Qatar [2]	1999	45 111	25.7	21.1	0.5	18.3	60.0	25.7
	2000	59 893	20.0	16.1	0.4	16.9	71.9	25.2
Republic of Moldova [2]	1999	12 322	15.3	74.7[4]	4.4	18.4	52.3	65.2
Rép. de Moldova [2]	2000	16 020	14.7	88.4[4]	8.5	15.4	49.6	76.6
	2001	19 019	14.0	90.3[4]	6.5	13.5	49.6	74.0
Réunion	1992	33 787	28.4	76.1	2.1	28.6	3.4	38.6
Réunion	1993	33 711	28.6	76.4	−0.4	25.7	3.1	36.2
	1994	35 266	28.9	78.0	0.1	28.1	2.9	38.0

21
Expenditure on gross domestic product in current prices
Percentage distribution *[cont.]*
Dépenses imputées au produit intérieur brut aux prix courants
Répartition en pourcentage *[suite]*

% of GDP – en % du PIB

Country or area Pays ou zone	Year Année	GDP in current prices (Million nat. cur.) PIB aux prix courants (Mil. monnaie nat.)	Govt. final consumption expenditure Consom. finale des admin. publiques	Household final consumption expenditure Consom. finale des ménages	Changes in inventories Variation des stocks	Gross fixed capital formation Formation brute de capital fixe	Exports of goods and services Exportations de biens et services	Imports of goods and services Importations de biens et services
Romania [2] Roumanie [2]	1998	371 193 800	14.2	76.0[4]	−0.4[7]	18.3	23.5	31.5
	1999	539 356 900	12.7	74.4[4]	−0.8[7]	18.0	29.0	33.4
	2000	796 533 700	12.5	73.9[4]	1.0[7]	18.5	34.1	39.9
Russian Federation [2] Féderation de Russie [2]	1999	4 766 800[3]	14.7	54.1[4]	0.2[7]	14.5	43.8	26.5
	2000	7 302 200[3]	14.8	46.8[4]	2.6[7]	16.0	44.3	24.1
	2001	9 040 800[3]	14.3	50.9[4]	4.4[7]	17.7	36.9	24.0
Rwanda Rwanda	1990	192 900	17.2	82.9	−0.9	12.4	7.7	19.2
	1991	212 900	21.6	82.2	−1.5	11.9	9.8	23.9
	1992	217 300	25.1	76.8	0.0	14.9	7.4	24.2
Saint Kitts−Nevis Saint−Kitts−et−Nevis	1997	742	19.3	52.0	...	44.1[5]	53.6	68.8
	1998	775	19.1	54.3	...	43.0[5]	53.5	69.9
	1999	812	21.6	64.7	...	37.3[5]	46.2	69.8
Saint Lucia Sainte−Lucie	1996	1 543	16.9	64.4	...	24.7	61.8	67.9
	1997	1 562	18.2	65.5	...	26.8	62.0	72.4
	1998	1 695	18.5	65.5	...	24.7	60.7	69.4
Saint Vincent−Grenadines St.−Vincent−et−Grenadines	1998	858	18.3	78.8	...	31.7	49.5	78.3
	1999	890	18.8	69.8	...	32.5	52.9	73.8
	2000	924	19.3	62.9	...	25.8	51.4	59.3
Sao Tome and Principe Sao Tomé−et−Principe	1986	2 478[3]	30.3	76.1	0.9	13.6	...	50.8
	1987	3 003[3]	24.8	63.1	1.1	15.4	...	43.1
	1988	4 221[3]	21.2	71.8		15.7	...	66.8
Saudi Arabia [6] Arabie saoudite [6]	1997	548 620	27.6	37.6	1.0	18.7	45.8	30.7
	1998	480 773	32.6	41.3	1.1	20.2	35.5	30.7
	1999	521 988	29.9	38.8	1.0	18.3	39.8	27.9
Senegal Sénégal	1998	2 746 000	11.8	75.5	2.1	17.7	29.9	37.0
	1999	2 925 000	12.7	74.3	1.1	19.6	30.4	38.0
	2000	3 114 000	14.0	72.9	5.6	17.3	29.7	39.6
Serbia and Montenegro [2] Serbie−et−Monténégro [2]	1996	79 396	22.1	72.6	4.9	11.9	15.8	27.4
	1997	112 355	25.0	65.5[4]	6.4[7]	11.7	17.8	26.3
	1998	154 584	27.0	69.0[4]	1.8[7]	11.2	22.5	31.5
Seychelles Seychelles	1997	2 830	25.9	53.1	3.9	28.1	−10.9[1]	...
	1998	3 201	26.5	54.5	0.6	34.0	−15.5[1]	...
	1999	3 379	31.1	51.8	−0.3	30.3	−12.9[1]	...
Sierra Leone [6] Sierra Leone [6]	1988	43 947	7.5	86.7	0.8	12.7	14.5	22.3
	1989	82 837	6.6	84.7	0.5	13.5	19.7	25.1
	1990	150 175	10.4	77.9	1.8	10.1	25.4	25.7
Singapore Singapour	1998	137 464[3]	10.1	39.4	−4.6	37.2	19.9[1]	...
	1999	142 111[3]	9.8	40.4	−0.7	33.1	19.3[1]	...
	2000	159 042[3]	10.5	40.0	1.8	29.5	18.5[1]	...
Slovakia [2] Slovaquie [2]	1998	750 761	21.5	53.3[4]	−1.9	38.0	61.2	72.2
	1999	815 330	19.5	54.0[4]	1.1	30.8	61.5	66.9
	2000	887 198	19.0	53.4[4]	0.1	30.0	73.5	76.0
Slovenia [2] Slovénie [2]	1999	3 648 401	20.2	55.8	1.0[7]	27.4	52.5	56.9
	2000	4 035 518	20.8	54.9	1.1[7]	26.7	59.1	62.7
	2001	4 566 191	21.3	53.6	0.5[7]	24.9	60.1	60.5
Solomon Islands Iles Salomon	1986	253	33.3	63.1	1.0	25.2	52.6	75.2
	1987	293	36.3	63.1	2.7	20.4	55.9	78.4
	1988	367	31.4	68.6	2.7	30.0	52.4	85.0
Somalia Somalie	1985	87 290	10.6	90.5	2.9	8.9	4.2	17.0
	1986	118 781	9.7	89.1	1.0	16.8	5.8	22.4
	1987	169 608	11.1	88.8	4.8	16.8	5.9	27.2
South Africa [2] Afrique du Sud [2]	1998	739 504[3]	19.0	63.1	−0.4	17.0	25.7	24.6
	1999	802 840[3]	18.4	63.0	0.5	15.5	25.6	22.9
	2000	887 795[3]	18.0	62.9	1.1	14.9	28.6	25.7
Spain [2] Espagne [2]	1998	527 957	17.5	59.3[4]	0.4	22.8	27.2	27.2
	1999	565 483	17.4	59.4[4]	0.5	24.0	27.5	28.8
	2000	608 787	17.4	59.2[4]	0.3	25.3	30.0	32.2
Sri Lanka Sri Lanka	1998	1 011 349[3]	14.2	66.1	0.1	25.6	36.5	42.5
	1999	1 100 825[3]	13.9	68.1	0.2	25.6	35.7	43.6
	2000	1 245 041[3]	14.2	70.6	0.2	25.5	39.5	50.1

21
Expenditure on gross domestic product in current prices
Percentage distribution *[cont.]*
Dépenses imputées au produit intérieur brut aux prix courants
Répartition en pourcentage *[suite]*

			% of GDP — en % du PIB					
Country or area Pays ou zone	Year Année	GDP in current prices (Million nat. cur.) PIB aux prix courants (Mil. monnaie nat.)	Govt. final consumption expenditure Consom. finale des admin. publiques	Household final consumption expenditure Consom. finale des ménages	Changes in inventories Variation des stocks	Gross fixed capital formation Formation brute de capital fixe	Exports of goods and services Exportations de biens et services	Imports of goods and services Importations de biens et services
Sudan [6]	1994	5 522 838	4.6	84.1	6.8	9.4	4.6	9.5
Soudan [6]	1996	10 330 678	7.5	81.9	9.6	12.3	8.0	19.2
	1997	16 769 372	5.4	85.6	5.7	12.2	10.2	19.2
Suriname	1996	303 970	14.7	58.9	6.2	29.1	65.5	74.4
Suriname	1997	340 220	17.7	60.2	5.9	24.0	57.4	65.1
	1998	407 130	18.7	71.5	...	23.2[5]	42.3	55.7
Swaziland [2 10]	1998	7 449	24.2	72.5	...	22.4	79.4	98.5
Swaziland [2 10]	1999	8 410	22.2	73.9	...	18.8	72.7	87.6
	2000	9 673	19.9	75.5	...	19.8	63.5	78.8
Sweden [2]	1999	2 004 651	26.7	50.1[4]	0.2	17.0	43.5	37.6
Suède [2]	2000	2 098 451	26.2	50.5[4]	0.7	17.3	47.2	41.8
	2001	2 167 196	26.7	49.8[4]	0.1	17.5	46.5	40.6
Switzerland	1998	379 989	14.0	61.2	0.9	20.0	40.3	36.3
Suisse	1999	388 569	13.7	61.3	−0.5	20.3	42.2	37.0
	2000	404 392	13.4	60.7	0.1	21.1	46.4	41.6
Syrian Arab Rep.	1999	819 092	10.6	70.3	...	18.8	32.3	32.0
Rép. arabe syrienne	2000	903 944	12.4	63.4	...	17.3	36.1	29.2
	2001	947 808	14.6	60.9	...	18.3	37.7	31.4
Tajikistan [2]	1997	518 400[3]	10.6	60.0[4]	2.0	17.7	81.8	85.4
Tadjikistan [2]	1998	1 025 200[3]	7.8	68.9[4]	2.0	13.4	49.7	57.5
	1999	1 344 900[3]	8.6	70.0[4]	1.9	17.2	67.9	66.4
Thailand	1997	4 740 249[3]	10.1	54.7	0.0	33.4	47.8	46.4
Thaïlande	1998	4 628 431[3]	11.1	54.4	−1.9	22.2	58.7	42.8
	1999	4 615 388[3]	11.3	56.4	−0.1	20.1	58.5	45.8
TFYR of Macedonia [2]	1997	186 019	19.7	72.8[4]	3.6	17.3	37.3	50.8
L'ex–République yougo–	1998	194 979	20.3	72.4[4]	4.8	17.4	41.2	56.1
slave de Macédoine [2]	1999	209 010	20.6	69.7[4]	3.1	16.6	42.2	52.2
Togo	1984	304 800	14.0	66.0	−1.5	21.2	51.9	51.6
Togo	1985	332 500	14.2	66.0	5.2	22.9	48.3	56.7
	1986	363 600	14.4	69.0	5.3	23.8	35.6	48.2
Tonga [9]	1981	54	14.2	122.8	2.2	23.9	26.3	67.3
Tonga [9]	1982	64	16.8	121.0	1.4	23.1	25.7	63.9
	1983	73	14.2	125.9	1.0	28.1	19.7	70.0
Trinidad and Tobago [2]	1998	39 796	14.5	63.6	0.6	26.4	46.4	51.5
Trinité–et–Tobago [2]	1999	43 254	14.0	59.4	0.4	20.5	49.6	43.9
	2000	50 872	12.1	56.3	0.0	...	59.8	45.8
Tunisia [2]	1997	20 898	15.8	60.2	1.8	24.7	43.8	46.2
Tunisie [2]	1998	22 581	15.7	60.7	2.0	24.9	43.0	46.4
	1999	24 672	15.6	60.4	0.8	25.4	42.6	44.8
Turkey	1998	52 224 945 000[3]	12.7	69.2	−0.4	24.6	24.3	27.9
Turquie	1999	77 415 272 000[3]	15.2	72.2	1.5	21.9	23.2	26.9
	2000	124 982 454 000[3]	14.0	71.2	1.9	22.2	23.8	31.2
Turkmenistan [2]	1995	652 044	8.4	60.6	10.4	23.1	142.5	145.0
Turkménistan [2]	1996	7 751 754[3]	7.1	49.2	8.7	41.3	105.8	107.0
	1997	11 108 783[3]	13.3	68.4	7.7	40.9	51.3	82.4
Uganda	1997	7 230 521[3]	9.6	92.3	−0.1	16.9	11.5	25.5
Ouganda	1998	8 298 977[3]	9.2	90.6	0.0	17.3	10.4	28.2
	1999	9 132 410[3]	9.2	91.0	0.0	20.1	10.3	28.5
Ukraine [2]	1999	130 442	19.8	57.2[4]	−1.8[7]	19.3	54.3	48.8
Ukraine [2]	2000	170 070	19.2	56.6[4]	0.1[7]	19.7	62.4	58.0
	2001	201 927	20.5	57.5[4]	0.2[7]	20.2	56.1	54.4
United Arab Emirates	1990	124 008	16.3	38.6	1.0	19.4	65.4	40.8
Emirats arabes unis	1991	124 500	16.9	41.4	1.1	20.7	67.6	47.7
	1992	128 400	17.8	45.5	1.2	23.2	69.1	56.8
United Kingdom [2]	1998	859 805	18.0	64.9[4]	0.6[7]	17.6	26.6	27.7
Royaume–Uni [2]	1999	901 269	18.5	65.5[4]	0.6[7]	17.2	26.3	28.0
	2000	944 724	18.6	65.4[4]	0.2[7]	17.5	28.1	29.8
United Rep. of Tanzania	1992	1 130 596	7.1	90.7	2.8	29.9	15.1	45.7
Rép.–Unie de Tanzanie	1993	1 404 369	9.1	86.8	3.2	29.0	20.5	48.6
	1994	1 822 570	7.7	89.6	3.2	27.5	26.4	54.3

21
Expenditure on gross domestic product in current prices
Percentage distribution [cont.]
Dépenses imputées au produit intérieur brut aux prix courants
Répartition en pourcentage [suite]

Country or area Pays ou zone	Year Année	GDP in current prices (Million nat. cur.) PIB aux prix courants (Mil. monnaie nat.)	% of GDP – en % du PIB					
			Govt. final consumption expenditure Consom. finale des admin. publiques	Household final consumption expenditure Consom. finale des ménages	Changes in inventories Variation des stocks	Gross fixed capital formation Formation brute de capital fixe	Exports of goods and services Exportations de biens et services	Imports of goods and services Importations de biens et services
United States [2] Etats–Unis [2]	1998	8 720 200	14.3	67.2[4]	0.8	19.4	11.1	12.8
	1999	9 206 900	14.3	67.9[4]	0.6	19.9	10.8	13.5
	2000	9 810 200	14.4	68.6[4]	0.5	20.2	11.2	15.0
Uruguay Uruguay	1998	234 267	12.5	72.3[4]	0.7	15.2	19.9	20.6
	1999	237 142	13.0	73.1[4]	0.6	14.5	18.0	19.3
	2000	242 637	13.0	74.5[4]	0.7	13.2	19.3	20.7
Uzbekistan [2] Ouzbékistan [2]	1998	1 416 200	20.8	63.0[4]	−15.6	30.4	23.7	22.0
	1999	2 128 700	20.6	62.1[4]	−10.0	27.1	0.1	...
	2000	3 194 500	19.7	63.7[4]	−9.1	25.0	0.7	...
Vanuatu Vanuatu	1993	23 779[3]	28.4	49.2	2.3	25.5	45.3	53.8
	1994	24 961[3]	27.7	49.2	2.3	26.5	47.3	57.2
	1995	27 255[3]	25.4	46.9	2.1	29.8	44.2	53.6
Venezuela Venezuela	1998	52 482 466	7.5	71.8[4]	2.8	19.0	19.9	21.1
	1999	62 577 039	7.5	69.1[4]	2.4	15.7	21.6	16.4
	2000	82 450 674	7.2	63.4[4]	3.0	14.2	28.4	16.3
Viet Nam [2] Viet Nam [2]	1998	361 017 000[3]	7.6	70.9	2.0	27.0	−7.3[1]	...
	1999	399 942 000[3]	6.8	68.6	1.9	25.7	−2.9[1]	...
	2000	444 139 000[3]	6.4	66.6	2.0	27.4	−2.3[1]	...
Yemen [2] Yémen [2]	1998	849 321	14.7	67.8	1.0	31.5	27.6	42.6
	1999	1 132 619	13.8	68.0	1.2	23.4	36.3	42.7
	2000	1 379 812	14.1	57.8	0.9	18.2	50.5	41.5
Yugoslavia, SFR Yougoslavie, SFR	1988	15 833[3]	14.2	50.1	19.9	17.2	29.5	30.4
	1989	235 395[3]	14.4	47.4	28.0	14.5	25.3	29.2
	1990	1 147 787[3]	17.6	66.1	7.3	14.7	23.7	29.4
Zambia Zambie	1989	58 706	73.3	13.5	...	19.9	25.2	31.8
	1990	123 487	54.7	14.1	...	30.7	34.3	33.8
	1991	234 504	60.4	14.3	...	24.6	26.4	25.7
Zimbabwe Zimbabwe	1996	84 759	17.1	64.0[4]	0.5	18.2	36.5	36.3
	1997	102 074	16.7	72.2[4]	0.1	18.0	37.6	44.6
	1998	135 722	15.6	69.0[4]	−0.4	17.6	45.9	47.8

Source:
United Nations Statistics Division, New York, national accounts database.

Source:
Organisation des Nations Unies, Division de statistique,
New York, la base de données sur les comptes nationaux.

1 Net exports.
2 Data are classified according to 1993 SNA.
3 Including statistical discrepancy.
4 Including "Non–profit institutions serving households" (NPISHs) final consumption expenditure.
5 Gross capital formation.
6 Data refer to fiscal years beginning 1 July.

7 Including acquisitions less disposals of valuables.
8 Data in Belarussian roubles.
9 Data refer to fiscal years beginning 1 April.

10 Data refer to fiscal years ending 30 June.
11 Including government consumption expenditure on collective goods.

12 Including household final consumption expenditure.

13 Data refer to fiscal years ending 7 July.

14 Data refer to fiscal years ending 30 September.

15 Data refer to fiscal years beginning 21 March.
16 Including changes in inventories.
17 Excluding acquisitions less disposals of valuables.
18 Data refer to fiscal years ending 15 July.

1 Exportations nettes.
2 Les données sont classifiées selon le SCN 1993.
3 Y compris divergence statistique.
4 Y compris la consommation finale des institutions sans but lucratif au service des ménages.
5 Formation brute de capital.
6 Les données se réfèrent aux exercises budgétaires commençant le 1er juillet.
7 Y compris les acquisitions moins cessions d'objets de valeur.
8 Les données sont exprimées en roubles Belarussian.
9 Les données se réfèrent aux exercises budgétaires commençant le 1er avril.
10 Les données se réfèrent aux exercises budgétaires finissant le 30 juin.
11 Y compris la consommation des administrations publiques sur des biens collectifs.
12 Y compris la consommation finale des ménages.
13 Les données se réfèrent aux exercises budgétaires commençant le 7 juillet.
14 Les données se réfèrent aux exercises budgétaires finissant le 30 septembre.
15 Les données se réfèrent aux exercises budgétaires commençant le 21 mars.
16 Y compris les variations des stocks.
17 Non compris les acquisitions moins cessions d'objets de valeur.
18 Les données se réfèrent aux exercises budgétaires finissant le 15 juillet.

22
Value added by industries in current prices
Percentage distribution
Valeur ajoutée par branche d'activité aux prix courants
Répartition en pourcentage

% of Value added — % de la valeur ajoutée

Country or area Pays ou zone	Year Année	Value added, gross (Mil. nat.cur.) Valeur ajoutée, brute (Mil. mon.nat.)	Agriculture, hunting, forestry and fishing Agriculture, chasse, sylviculture et pêche	Mining and quarrying Activités extractives	Manufac- turing Activités de fabri- cation	Electricity, gas and water supply Electricité, gaz et eau	Con- struc- tion Con- struc- tion	Wholesale, retail trade, restaurants and hotels Commerce, restaurants, hôtels	Transport, storage & commu- nication Transports, entrepôts, communi- cations	Other activities Autres activités
Albania [1] Albanie [1]	1997	341 716	56.0	12.4[2 3]	...	...	11.2	17.6[4]	2.7	...
	1998	460 631	54.4	11.9[2 3]	...	...	12.6	18.0[4]	3.0	...
	1999	506 205	52.6	11.9[2 3]	...	...	13.5	18.8[4]	3.3	...
Algeria Algérie	1998	2 655 621	11.5	25.6	8.1	1.4	10.0	15.8	7.8	19.9
	1999	3 067 846	11.0	30.4	7.4	1.3	8.8	14.8	7.8	18.5
	2000	3 915 728	8.3	42.7	6.0	1.1	7.5	12.2	7.0	15.2
Angola Angola	1988	236 682	16.0	27.1	8.3	0.2	4.1	11.7[5]	3.5	29.1
	1989	276 075	19.3	29.7	6.2	0.2	3.3	11.4[5]	3.0	27.1
	1990	305 831	18.0	32.9	5.0	0.1	2.9	10.7[5]	3.2	27.0
Anguilla Anguilla	1999	259[6]	2.7	0.9	1.2	3.8	15.2	34.4	13.1	28.9
	2000	265[6]	2.5	0.9	1.2	2.9	13.6	32.4	13.8	32.5
	2001	273[6]	2.6	0.7	1.1	3.3	11.0	33.7	13.9	34.1
Antigua and Barbuda Antigua-et-Barbuda	1986	567[6]	4.3	1.7	3.8	3.5	8.9	23.6	15.6	38.5
	1987	649[6]	4.5	2.2	3.5	3.5	11.3	24.1	15.6	35.3
	1988	776[6]	4.1	2.2	3.1	4.0	12.7	23.7	14.3	35.9
Argentina [1] Argentine [1]	1998	272 917[6]	5.8	1.6	17.5	2.1	6.0	18.4	8.9	39.8
	1999	260 646[6]	4.8	1.8	16.4	2.3	5.9	17.5	9.0	42.3
	2000	260 898[6]	5.1	2.7	15.9	2.5	5.0	16.8	9.3	42.8
Armenia Arménie	1998	884 500	33.4	...	22.3[3 7]	...	8.7	9.4	7.4	18.8
	1999	921 400	28.9	...	23.5[3 7]	...	8.9	9.7	8.1	20.9
	2000	951 800	25.1	...	24.9[3 7]	...	11.1	10.0	7.8	21.0
Aruba [1] Aruba [1]	1996	2 379	0.5[7]	...	2.5	5.8[9]	7.1	24.6	8.3	51.2
	1997	2 667	0.4[7]	...	2.5	6.5[9]	7.8	23.8	8.4	50.7
	1998	2 845	0.4[7]	...	2.7	6.8[9]	7.7	24.3	8.2	49.9
Australia [1 8] Australie [1 8]	1998	542 580	3.3	4.5	13.2	2.6	6.0	14.0	8.9	47.4
	1999	577 845	3.5	4.9	12.8	2.7	6.2	13.8	8.6	47.6
	2000	611 896	3.5	5.2	12.8	2.7	5.5	13.3	8.5	48.5
Austria [1] Autriche [1]	1998	178 963	2.4	0.3	20.2	2.6	8.1	16.6	7.3	42.5
	1999	183 536	2.1	0.4	20.4	2.6	8.2	16.7	7.1	42.4
	2000	192 932	...	0.4	21.0	2.4	7.8	16.9	6.8	42.5
Azerbaijan [1] Azerbaïdjan [1]	1997	14 675 500	21.5	...	28.4[3 7]	...	12.6	6.2	11.3	20.0
	1998	16 591 100	18.6	...	23.5[3 7]	...	13.4	6.1	12.4	25.9
	1999	15 328 900	23.3	...	25.2[3 7]	...	10.1	5.5	15.5	20.5
Bahamas [1] Bahamas [1]	1993	2 404	3.3[10]	0.7	3.7	4.0[11]	3.6	27.0	10.9	46.8
	1994	2 608	3.8[10]	0.7	3.4	4.6[11]	3.1	26.0	11.9	46.4
	1995	2 656	3.8[10]	1.0	3.0	4.4[11]	2.7	26.5	11.1	46.6
Bahrain Bahreïn	1998	2 575	0.8	12.3	11.5	1.7	3.7	11.2	7.5	51.3
	1999	2 745	0.8	16.5	11.2	1.6	3.8	9.6	7.1	49.3
	2000	3 336	0.7	25.2	10.3	1.3	3.2	9.0	6.3	44.0
Bangladesh [1 8] Bangladesh [1 8]	1997	1 925 917	25.4	1.0	16.2	1.4	7.2	13.5	8.7	26.5
	1998	2 119 211	26.2	1.0	15.5	1.3	7.4	13.5	8.5	26.7
	1999	2 287 605	25.5	1.0	15.2	1.3	7.7	13.4	8.6	27.2
Barbados Barbade	1998	3 913[6]	3.9	0.6	6.2	3.3	5.7	30.3	10.2	39.8
	1999	4 145[6]	4.9	0.7	6.3	3.2	5.8	29.1	10.4	39.7
	2000	4 309[6]	4.4	0.7	6.2	3.2	5.8	29.5	10.3	39.9
Belarus [1] Bélarus [1]	1999	2 687 694 200[12]	14.3	...	33.6[3 7]	...	6.5	10.8	12.9	21.9
	2000	7 970 800	13.9	...	32.7[3 7]	...	7.4	10.9	12.7	22.5
	2001	14 911 000	10.7	...	33.6[3 7]	...	6.0	10.9	12.9	25.8
Belgium [1] Belgique [1]	1998	210 963	1.5	0.2	19.4	2.9	4.7	13.2	6.9	51.2
	1999	218 222	1.3	0.2	19.0	2.7	5.0	13.4	6.9	51.6
	2000	229 730	1.4	0.2	18.9	2.6	5.0	13.4	6.8	51.8
Belize [1] Belize [1]	1998	1 051	19.1	0.6	13.2	3.4	5.7	18.9	10.4	37.9
	1999	1 154	19.7	0.6	13.0	3.4	6.5	20.8	11.0	36.1
	2000	1 311	17.2	0.7	13.1	3.3	7.1	21.6	9.9	29.8
Benin Bénin	1987	430 800	36.3	1.2	7.8	0.9	3.5	17.0	8.5	24.7
	1988	451 080	37.2	0.9	8.9	1.0	3.3	18.7	8.1	21.9
	1989	465 735	38.0	0.9	9.2	0.9	3.3	17.6	7.8	22.2

22
Value added by industries in current prices
Percentage distribution *[cont.]*
Valeur ajoutée par branche d'activité aux prix courants
Répartition en pourcentage *[suite]*

			% of Value added — % de la valeur ajoutée							
Country or area Pays ou zone	Year Année	Value added, gross (Mil. nat.cur.) Valeur ajoutée, brute (Mil. mon.nat.)	Agriculture, hunting, forestry and fishing Agriculture, chasse, sylviculture et pêche	Mining and quarrying Activités extractives	Manufac- turing Activités de fabri- cation	Electricity, gas and water supply Electricité, gaz et eau	Con- struc- tion Con- struc- tion	Wholesale, retail trade, restaurants and hotels Commerce, restaurants, hôtels	Transport, storage & commu- nication Transports, entrepôts, communi- cations	Other activities Autres activités
Bermuda [1] [13]	1998	3 021[14]	0.8	0.2	2.5	2.4	4.2	18.8	7.4	64.6
Bermudes [1] [13]	1999	3 270[14]	0.8	0.2	2.5	2.3	5.9	17.3	7.2	63.9
	2000	3 387[14]	0.7	0.2	2.5	2.3	6.1	16.9	7.2	64.0
Bhutan	1998	16 537[6]	36.6	1.6	9.8	11.7	10.2	7.0	8.3	14.8
Bhoutan	1999	18 957[6]	35.0	1.7	9.3	12.2	11.1	6.8	8.6	15.2
	2000	21 654[6]	35.9	1.6	8.0	11.6	12.5	6.8	8.6	15.0
Bolivia [1]	1998	42 012	13.6	5.1	15.4	3.1	4.2	11.6	14.1	32.8
Bolivie [1]	1999	44 714	14.9	6.5	15.1	2.9	3.4	11.6	12.6	33.0
	2000	46 916	14.8	9.2	14.0	2.8	2.8	11.6	12.5	32.2
Botswana [1] [15]	1998	19 320	3.6	39.7	5.2	1.9	6.0	10.4	3.5	29.7
Botswana [1] [15]	1999	20 477	3.2	32.7	5.5	2.2	6.6	11.4	4.0	34.3
	2000	23 815	2.8	35.2	5.2	2.4	6.0	11.5	3.9	33.0
Brazil [1]	1998	862 794	7.8	0.6	19.7	3.0	9.6	6.7[5] [16]	5.3	47.2
Brésil [1]	1999	901 474	7.8	1.5	20.3	3.2	9.0	6.8[5] [16]	5.7	45.7
	2000	1 006 931	7.4	2.4	21.5	3.4	8.8	7.0[5] [16]	6.0	43.6
British Virgin Islands	1987	108	4.0	0.2	3.2	3.8	6.0	29.8	11.4	41.6
Iles Vierges brit.	1988	121	3.6	0.2	3.1	4.0	6.1	28.3	11.9	42.8
	1989	141	3.4	0.2	3.0	3.7	6.7	27.9	15.0	40.1
Brunei Darussalam	1996	7 886	2.5	34.7[2]	...	1.0	5.8	11.9	4.8	39.3
Brunéi Darussalam	1997	8 268	2.6	33.6[2]	...	1.0	6.2	12.1	4.9	39.6
	1998	8 331	2.8	31.6[2]	...	1.1	6.5	12.6	5.1	40.4
Bulgaria [1]	1998	19 203 204	21.1	1.5	19.1	4.3	3.7	9.7	8.2	32.3
Bulgarie[1]	1999	19 890 889	17.3	1.7	16.6	4.8	3.7	9.7	8.7	37.5
	2000	22 532 628	14.5	1.7	17.4	5.0	3.6	11.7	10.5	35.5
Burkina Faso	1991	780 492	33.8	0.9	14.2	0.9	5.7	1.7	4.1	1.6
Burkina Faso	1992	782 551	32.7	0.9	19.5	1.1	5.7	1.6	4.2	1.6
	1993	808 487	33.9	0.8	14.7	1.3	5.6	1.7	4.4	1.5
Burundi	1988	149 067	48.9	1.0[3]	16.5	...	2.9	12.9	2.6	15.2
Burundi	1989	175 627	47.0	1.2[3]	18.5	...	3.3	10.8	3.3	16.0
	1990	192 050	52.4	0.8[3]	16.8	...	3.4	4.9	3.1	18.5
Cambodia	1998	10 088 610	43.8	0.2	13.3	0.5	4.1	16.4	5.8	16.0
Cambodge	1999	11 150 270	42.2	0.2	13.3	0.4	5.3	16.7	6.4	15.6
	2000	11 444 080	37.1	0.2	17.4	0.4	5.7	16.6	6.8	15.9
Cameroon [1] [8]	1996	4 467 110	22.0	5.5	21.3	0.9	3.2	21.0	5.2	20.9
Cameroun [1] [8]	1997	5 013 530	23.6	5.6	21.3	0.8	2.1	19.9	5.8	20.8
	1998	5 362 130	23.6	5.6	21.3	0.8	2.1	19.9	5.8	20.8
Canada [1]	1996	774 342	3.0	4.4	17.9	3.6	5.0	13.3	7.2	45.6
Canada [1]	1997	816 905	2.5	4.2	18.0	3.4	5.3	13.6	7.4	45.7
	1998	844 981	2.6	3.2	18.4	3.2	5.3	13.9	7.3	46.1
Cape Verde	1993	27 264	14.7	1.0	7.5	1.4	11.6	17.8	18.9	27.0
Cap-Vert	1994	31 175	13.8	0.9	7.5	1.4	11.1	18.9	20.2	26.2
	1995	35 256	14.6	1.1	7.3	1.9	10.1	18.6	18.0	28.5
Cayman Islands	1989	473	0.4	0.6	1.9	3.2	11.0	24.5	11.0	47.6
Iles Caïmanes	1990	580	0.3	0.3	1.6	3.1	9.7	24.5	10.9	49.8
	1991	605	0.3	0.3	1.5	3.1	9.1	22.8	10.7	52.1
Central African Rep.	1983	243 350	40.8	2.5	7.8	0.5	2.1	21.2[5]	4.2	20.8
Rép. centrafricaine	1984	268 725	40.7	2.8	8.1	0.9	2.7	21.7[5]	4.3	18.8
	1985	308 549	42.4	2.5	7.5	0.8	2.6	22.0[5]	4.2	17.9
Chad	1992	297 361[6]	34.7	0.3	18.1	0.7	1.2	34.3[17]	...	10.7[18]
Tchad	1993	250 850[6]	32.1	0.2	18.7	0.9	1.1	33.8[17]	...	13.1[18]
	1994	347 578[6]	29.4	0.3	17.9	0.7	1.6	40.1[17]	...	10.0[18]
Chile	1996	26 361 928[14]	7.2	7.5	20.4	3.2	7.6	13.6	7.6	33.0
Chili	1997	29 476 765[14]	7.1	6.9	20.3	3.1	8.2	13.7	7.9	32.7
	1998	31 767 117[14]	7.2	4.5	19.2	2.9	8.5	14.8	8.3	34.6
China	1995	5 847 810	20.5	42.3[2] [3]	...	...	6.5	8.4	5.2	17.0
Chine	1996	6 788 460	20.4	42.8[2] [3]	...	...	6.7	8.2	5.1	16.8
	1997	7 477 240	18.7	42.5[2] [3]	...	...	6.7	8.4	6.1	17.7

22

Value added by industries in current prices
Percentage distribution [cont.]
Valeur ajoutée par branche d'activité aux prix courants
Répartition en pourcentage [suite]

% of Value added – % de la valeur ajoutée

Country or area Pays ou zone	Year Année	Value added, gross (Mil. nat.cur.) Valeur ajoutée, brute (Mil. mon.nat.)	Agriculture, hunting, forestry and fishing Agriculture, chasse, sylviculture et pêche	Mining and quarrying Activités extractives	Manufac- turing Activités de fabri- cation	Electricity, gas and water supply Electricité, gaz et eau	Con- struc- tion Con- struc- tion	Wholesale, retail trade, restaurants and hotels Commerce, restaurants, hôtels	Transport, storage & commu- nication Transports, entrepôts, communi- cations	Other activities Autres activités
China, Hong Kong SAR	1998	1 258 510[6]	0.1[10]	0.0	5.6	2.7	5.6	22.9[16]	8.6	54.5
Chine, Hong Kong RAS	1999	1 233 943[6]	0.1[10]	0.0	5.3	2.8	5.4	22.9[16]	8.8	54.7
	2000	1 280 617[6]	0.1[10]	0.0	5.3	2.8	4.9	24.3[16]	9.3	53.2
Colombia [1]	1998	138 713 130	13.3	3.2	14.0	3.7	5.8	11.5	7.7	40.7
Colombie [1]	1999	145 573 338	13.2	5.6	13.1	3.8	4.3	11.1	8.3	40.6
	2000	164 170 747	13.2	7.9	13.3	4.3	3.8	11.5	8.9	38.4
Comoros	1989	64 731	40.0	...	3.9	0.8	3.4	25.1	3.9	22.8
Comores	1990	67 992	40.4	...	4.1	0.9	3.1	25.1	4.1	22.3
	1991	71 113	40.8	...	4.2	0.9	2.7	25.1	4.2	22.1
Congo	1987	678 106	12.2	22.9	8.8	1.6	3.2	15.1	10.5	25.8
Congo	1988	643 830	14.2	17.1	8.8	2.0	2.7	16.7	11.3	27.2
	1989	757 088	13.3	28.6	7.2	1.9	1.8	14.7	9.3	23.3
Cook Islands	1984	44	14.9	0.2	4.8	1.0	2.1	25.4	10.3	41.3
Iles Cook	1985	53	14.1	0.1	4.5	0.1	2.6	25.6	10.6	42.3
	1986	64	12.5	0.1	5.0	1.1	3.7	22.6	12.0	43.1
Costa Rica [1]	1998	3 416 676	12.5	0.1	22.4	2.4	4.0	19.7	8.1	30.7
Costa Rica [1]	1999	4 265 974	10.2	0.1	28.1	2.2	3.6	18.1	7.4	30.3
	2000	4 632 634	9.2	0.2	23.8	2.4	3.9	18.7	8.1	33.7
Côte d'Ivoire	1994	4 551 000	25.6	0.2	17.6	1.7	1.8	...	6.0	18.7
Côte d'Ivoire	1995	5 110 000	26.6	0.3	18.1	1.7	2.2	...	5.4	18.0
	1996	5 684 000	27.2	0.4	19.0	1.7	2.6	...	5.0	17.1
Croatia [1]	1999	122 948	9.2	0.5	21.5	3.1	6.5	14.5	8.5	36.2
Croatie [1]	2000	136 480	9.1	25.8[2 3]	...	...	5.6	15.1	9.2	35.2
	2001	147 208	8.9	25.8[2 3]	...	...	5.6	16.3	10.3	33.1
Cuba	1998	23 515[14]	6.3	1.5	37.9	2.0	5.5	21.4	4.5	20.9
Cuba	1999	25 094[14]	6.5	1.5	39.3	1.9	5.5	20.1	4.5	20.6
	2000	27 240[14]	6.8	1.8	37.7	2.0	5.7	21.2	4.7	20.3
Cyprus	1997	4 162	4.3	0.3	11.8	2.1	8.4	22.1	8.6	42.5
Chypre	1998	4 497	4.4	0.3	11.3	2.1	8.0	22.4	8.9	42.6
	1999	4 820	4.2	0.3	10.8	2.0	7.7	22.3	8.7	49.6
Czech Republic [1]	1998	1 716 882	4.7	1.7	27.0	4.0	7.1	15.6	8.4	31.5
République tchèque [1]	1999	1 745 046	3.9	1.5	26.3	4.0	7.4	15.9	7.8	33.1
	2000	1 807 966	3.9	1.5	27.8	3.6	7.1	16.3	7.4	...
Denmark [1]	1998	1 013 188	2.8	1.1	16.7	2.4	5.0	14.5	7.5	49.9
Danemark [1]	1999	1 066 468	2.6	1.5	16.4	2.3	4.8	14.8	8.1	49.5
	2000	1 150 415	2.5	3.1	16.3	2.2	4.9	14.2	8.6	48.3
Djibouti	1996	76 435[6]	3.5[19]	0.2	2.8	6.8[11]	5.7	15.9	21.7	43.4
Djibouti	1997	75 964[6]	3.6[19]	0.2	2.8	6.6[11]	6.0	16.1	23.1	41.6
	1998	78 263[6]	3.6[19]	0.2	2.7	5.3[11]	6.4	16.4	26.0	39.4
Dominica	1989	367[6]	24.4	0.8	6.7	2.7	6.8	11.9	14.7	32.1
Dominique	1990	402[6]	24.1	0.8	6.6	2.8	7.0	12.1	14.9	31.8
	1991	427[6]	23.8	0.9	6.4	3.0	6.8	12.3	15.2	31.6
Dominican Republic [1]	1994	165 808	10.8	1.1	20.2	1.4	7.7	16.4	9.8	32.6
Rép. dominicaine [1]	1995	193 436	10.1	1.3	19.6	1.7	7.7	17.3	9.0	33.3
	1996	228 022	8.9	1.0	19.3	1.8	7.3	20.4	8.8	32.5
Ecuador	1998	103 676 217[14]	12.5	5.8[20]	22.7	0.3	5.1	20.9	9.9	22.8
Equateur	1999	156 065 932[14]	12.6	11.8[20]	22.0	0.3	4.7	19.0	9.7	20.0
	2000	320 099 401[14]	10.6	20.9[20]	18.0	0.3	3.6	18.1	9.7	18.9
Egypt [8]	1989	81 341[6]	19.5	4.8[21]	18.0	1.3[22]	5.5	21.9	9.2	19.8
Egypte [8]	1990	103 344[6]	17.2	10.6[21]	16.9	1.4[22]	5.1	21.0	10.5	17.3
	1991	125 485[6]	16.5	10.6[21]	17.1	1.6[22]	4.8	21.2	11.3	16.8
El Salvador	1998	102 135[14]	12.4	0.4	22.0	2.0	4.6	19.9[5]	8.3	30.4
El Salvador	1999	106 413[14]	10.7	0.4	23.2	2.0	4.5	19.6[5]	8.5	31.1
	2000	112 841[14]	9.9	0.4	24.1	2.2	4.5	19.2[5]	8.6	31.0
Equatorial Guinea	1989	40 948	56.1	...	1.3	3.1	3.7	8.8	2.0	25.0
Guinée équatoriale	1990	42 765	53.6	...	1.3	3.4	3.8	7.6	2.2	28.0
	1991	43 932	53.1	...	1.4	3.1	3.0	7.6	1.9	30.0

22
Value added by industries in current prices
Percentage distribution *[cont.]*
Valeur ajoutée par branche d'activité aux prix courants
Répartition en pourcentage *[suite]*

% of Value added − % de la valeur ajoutée

Country or area Pays ou zone	Year Année	Value added, gross (Mil. nat.cur.) Valeur ajoutée, brute (Mil. mon.nat.)	Agriculture, hunting, forestry and fishing Agriculture, chasse, sylviculture et pêche	Mining and quarrying Activités extractives	Manufac− turing Activités de fabri− cation	Electricity, gas and water supply Electricité, gaz et eau	Con− struc− tion Con− struc− tion	Wholesale, retail trade, restaurants and hotels Commerce, restaurants, hôtels	Transport, storage & commu− nication Transports, entrepôts, communi− cations	Other activities Autres activités
Estonia [1] Estonie [1]	1999	69 011	6.7	1.1	16.5	3.6	6.0	15.8	15.2	35.2
	2000	76 290	6.3	1.1	17.9	3.3	5.8	15.8	15.4	34.3
	2001	85 175	6.3	1.1	17.9	3.2	5.8	15.9	16.2	33.7
Ethiopia incl. Eritrea [23] Ethiopie y comp. Eryth. [23]	1990	11 436[6]	41.1	0.2	11.1	1.5	3.6	9.6	7.2	25.7
	1991	12 295[6]	41.0	0.3	10.3	1.5	3.2	9.4	7.1	27.3
	1992	12 544[6]	50.3	0.3	9.1	1.3	2.8	10.2	5.4	20.6
Fiji Fidji	1987	1 399[6]	21.9	2.2	11.2	3.1	3.6	14.9	9.5	33.5
	1988	1 518[6]	18.4	4.1	9.0	3.4	4.0	18.6	10.7	31.8
	1989	1 759[6]	18.5	3.2	9.9	3.1	3.8	21.5	9.6	30.3
Finland [1] Finlande [1]	1998	102 547	3.8	0.3	25.1	2.3	5.0	12.0	10.0	41.6
	1999	106 476	3.7	0.3	24.5	2.1	5.4	11.8	10.2	41.9
	2000	117 020	3.6	0.2	25.7	1.7	5.7	11.2	10.3	41.6
French Guiana Guyane française	1990	6 454	10.1	7.6	...	0.7	12.8	13.5	7.7	47.5
	1991	7 385	7.4	7.6	...	0.5	12.1	13.1	12.3	47.0
	1992	8 052	7.2	9.0	...	0.6	10.8	11.9	11.4	49.1
French Polynesia Polynésie française	1991	305 211	4.1	...	7.5	1.8	5.7	...	...	29.3
	1992	314 265	3.8	...	7.5	2.1	5.9	...	...	29.5
	1993	329 266	3.9	...	6.7	2.1	5.7	...	...	29.0
Gabon Gabon	1987	986 000	10.9	28.4	7.1[24]	2.7	7.2	9.2	8.1	26.5
	1988	965 700	11.2	22.6	7.3[24]	3.0	5.2	14.4	9.1	27.3
	1989	1 128 400	10.4	32.3	5.7[24]	2.5	5.5	12.4	8.2	23.1
Gambia [8] Gambie [8]	1991	2 962	22.3	0.0	5.5	0.9	4.4	39.1	10.9	17.0
	1992	3 100	18.4	0.0	5.7	1.0	4.7	41.7	11.2	17.4
	1993	3 296	20.2	0.0	5.1	1.0	4.5	38.3	12.5	18.4
Georgia [1] Géorgie [1]	1999	5 392	26.0	...	18.4[3 7]	...	3.9	14.7	12.5	24.6
	2000	5 657	21.2	...	18.4[3 7]	...	4.0	16.0	15.2	25.3
	2001	6 142	20.3	...	18.2[3 7]	...	4.2	16.8	15.1	25.5
Germany [1] Allemagne [1]	1998	1 810 240	1.2	0.3	22.5	2.3	5.6	11.8	5.7	50.5
	1999	1 838 320	1.2	0.3	22.3	2.1	5.5	11.7	5.8	51.2
	2000	1 886 030	1.2	0.3	23.2	1.8	5.1	11.7	5.9	50.9
Ghana Ghana	1994	4 686 000	42.0	6.3	10.1	3.0	8.3	6.4	4.8	18.2
	1995	7 040 200	42.7	5.3	10.3	2.9	8.3	6.5	4.3	18.8
	1996	10 067 000	43.9	5.3	9.7	3.0	8.5	6.5	4.2	17.9
Greece [1] Grèce [1]	1998	96 750	8.2	0.6	11.8	2.1	7.1	21.3	6.7	42.2
	1999	102 554	7.8	0.6	11.0	2.0	7.4	20.9	7.4	42.8
	2000	110 520	7.3	0.6	11.1	1.8	6.9	21.6	8.5	42.3
Grenada Grenade	1989	393	18.7	0.4	5.3	2.9	10.3	18.8	13.9	34.4
	1990	440	16.2	0.4	5.1	3.0	10.1	18.7	13.7	32.8
	1991	463	14.9	0.4	5.3	3.1	10.4	19.5	14.3	32.1
Guadeloupe Guadeloupe	1990	15 036	6.7	5.4[2]	...	1.0	7.4	18.3	5.9	55.2
	1991	16 278	7.3	6.1[2]	...	1.4	7.0	16.5	6.0	55.5
	1992	17 968	6.7	6.9[2]	...	1.7	6.5	16.2	7.9	54.1
Guinea−Bissau Guinée−Bissau	1989	358 875	44.6	7.9[2 3]	...	...	9.7	25.7	3.6	8.5
	1990	510 094	44.6	8.2[2 3]	...	...	10.0	25.7	3.7	7.8
	1991	854 985	44.7	8.5[2 3]	...	...	8.4	25.8	3.9	8.7
Guyana Guyana	1999	105 095[6]	41.2[20]	15.4	3.5[3]	...	4.5	4.1[5]	6.8	24.5
	2000	108 087[6]	36.1[20]	15.9	3.2[3]	...	4.9	4.4[5]	7.8	27.7
	2001	112 360[6]	34.7[20]	16.0	3.2[3]	...	5.0	4.4[5]	8.9	27.8
Honduras Honduras	1998	60 068[6]	19.1	1.8	18.6	5.1	5.1	12.3	5.0	33.0
	1999	65 881[6]	15.9	2.0	19.6	4.9	5.9	12.7	5.2	33.8
	2000	75 924[6]	15.0	2.0	19.8	4.8	5.7	12.8	5.2	34.7
Hungary [1] Hongrie [1]	1998	8 873 463	5.5	0.3	24.1	3.9	4.6	13.4	9.9	38.4
	1999	9 973 026	4.8	0.3	23.5	3.9	4.7	12.8	10.2	39.8
	2000	11 414 378	4.1	0.3	25.2	3.8	4.6	12.5	9.6	39.9
Iceland [1] Islande [1]	1995	382 752	11.7	0.1	16.4	3.9	7.1	14.1	8.8	31.9[25]
	1996	411 859	11.4	0.1	16.4	3.7	6.6	14.3	8.5	32.5[25]
	1997	449 589	9.6	0.1	17.0	3.8	7.1	13.3	7.8	34.2[25]

22
Value added by industries in current prices
Percentage distribution [cont.]
Valeur ajoutée par branche d'activité aux prix courants
Répartition en pourcentage [suite]

			% of Value added − % de la valeur ajoutée							
Country or area Pays ou zone	Year Année	Value added, gross (Mil. nat.cur.) Valeur ajoutée, brute (Mil. mon.nat.)	Agriculture, hunting, forestry and fishing Agriculture, chasse, sylviculture et pêche	Mining and quarrying Activités extractives	Manufac− turing Activités de fabri− cation	Electricity, gas and water supply Electricité, gaz et eau	Con− struc− tion Con− struc− tion	Wholesale, retail trade, restaurants and hotels Commerce, restaurants, hôtels	Transport, storage & commu− nication Transports, entrepôts, communi− cations	Other activities Autres activités
India [13] Inde [13]	1998	15 980 770[6]	27.7	2.2	15.8	2.7	5.8	13.8	7.0	24.9
	1999	17 556 380[6]	26.2	2.3	15.2	2.5	6.0	13.8	7.1	26.9
	2000	18 958 430[6]	24.9	2.4	15.8	2.6	6.1	13.8	7.3	27.1
Indonesia Indonésie	1996	532 567 000[14]	16.7	8.7	25.6	1.3	7.9	16.4[5]	6.6	17.0
	1997	627 695 000[14]	16.1	8.9	26.8	1.2	7.5	15.9[5]	6.1	17.6
	1998	1 002 334 000[14]	18.1	13.7	24.5	1.1	5.6	16.7[5]	5.2	15.2
Iran (Islamic Rep. of) [1][26] Iran (Rép. islamique d') [1][26]	1998	320 751 900	16.4	9.5	13.7	1.1	3.8	17.2	7.8	30.5
	1999	430 103 800	14.0	15.5	13.5	1.0	3.9	15.8	6.9	29.4
	2000	585 644 700	12.8	22.7	12.7	0.8	3.4	14.3	6.2	27.0
Iraq Iraq	1998	4653524	36.6	0.3	3.0	...	0.8	21.4[27]	26.7	12.5
	1999	6 301 285	34.6	0.5	3.9	...	0.7	21.0[27]	28.5	12.3
	2000	7 377 758	31.3	0.5	4.7	...	1.2	19.3[27]	28.8	15.8
Ireland [1] Irlande [1]	1997	59 583	5.6	0.9	30.1	1.7	5.7	13.6	5.6	36.8
	1998	69 152	4.7	0.6	30.7	1.5	6.1	13.2	5.7	37.6
	1999	78 089	3.8	0.7	27.7	1.6	6.0	12.9	5.8	41.6
Israel [1] Israël [1]	1998	360 400	2.1	17.7	...	1.9	6.1	9.7	8.5	54.9
	1999	390 905	1.8	18.1	...	1.9	5.4	10.1	8.3	55.5
	2000	425 391	1.8	17.6	...	1.9	4.8	10.1	8.0	57.1
Italy [1] Italie [1]	1999	1 025 827	3.0	0.4	20.7	2.2	4.8	16.7	7.3	44.8
	2000	1 080 291	2.8	0.5	20.6	2.1	4.8	16.7	7.2	45.3
	2001	1 135 037	2.7	0.5	20.2	2.2	4.9	16.9	7.1	45.5
Jamaica [1] Jamaïque [1]	1997	240 562[14]	7.3	5.1	14.9	3.0	10.6	21.0	9.5	28.5
	1998	254 167[14]	7.3	4.4	14.0	3.2	10.3	21.0	10.2	29.5
	1999	277 101[14]	6.6	4.1	13.9	3.6	10.4	20.2	10.4	30.8
Japan [1] Japon [1]	1998	537 475 600	1.5	0.1	21.1	2.7	7.4	14.4	6.4	46.3
	1999	532 957 800	1.4	0.1	20.8	2.7	7.2	13.7	6.2	47.8
	2000	533 952 700	1.3	0.1	20.8	2.7	7.0	13.4	6.2	48.5
Jordan Jordanie	1996	4 292[6]	3.7	3.6	13.3	2.4	5.9	11.5	15.0	44.6
	1997	4 588[6]	3.2	3.7	13.5	2.6	4.9	12.7	14.7	44.7
	1998	4 867[6]	3.0	3.5	14.9	2.5	4.0	12.5	14.7	44.8
Kazakhstan [1] Kazakhstan [1]	1995	976 600	12.8	...	33.7[3][7]	...	6.7	17.9	11.1	17.8
	1996	1 356 000	12.7	...	32.3[3][7]	...	4.6	18.0	11.8	20.6
	1997	1 603 300	11.9	...	32.8[3][7]	...	4.4	16.3	12.2	22.4
Kenya Kenya	1999	34 062[6]	21.9	0.1	11.6	1.1	4.0	20.3	6.7	30.2
	2000	35 846[6]	18.9	0.2	12.4	1.1	4.1	22.7	7.0	29.3
	2001	40 066[6]	18.3	0.2	12.1	1.1	4.1	24.3	6.6	28.8
Korea, Republic of [1] Corée, Rép. de [1]	1998	448 988 063[14]	4.9	0.4	30.5	2.4	10.0	10.2	7.0	34.6
	1999	485 659 596[14]	5.0	0.3	30.6	2.7	8.7	11.2	6.8	34.7
	2000	517 227 986[14]	4.6	0.3	31.5	2.8	8.2	12.0	6.5	34.3
Kuwait Koweït	1998	8 041[14]	0.4	29.5	11.4	−0.3	3.0	8.2	5.7	39.0
	1999	9 429[14]	0.4	35.6	11.7	−0.5	2.4	7.1	5.4	35.3
	2000	11 977[14]	0.3	46.6	10.2	−0.7	1.9	5.6	4.5	29.3
Kyrgyzstan [1] Kirghizistan [1]	1999	45 201	37.6	0.2	23.7[3]	...	3.3	13.9	5.2	16.2
	2000	61 018	36.7	0.2	25.4[3]	...	4.1	12.9	4.1	16.7
	2001	68 815	37.9	0.2	23.3[3]	...	4.4	12.8	2.5	18.9
Latvia [1] Lettonie [1]	1999	3 411	4.5	0.1	15.3	4.4	7.1	18.9	15.3	34.3
	2000	3 823	4.6	0.1	14.7	3.9	6.7	19.2	15.5	35.3
	2001	4 204	4.5	0.1	14.9	3.8	6.2	20.1	15.4	35.1
Lebanon Liban	1982	12 600	8.5	...	13.0	5.4	3.4	28.3	3.7	37.5
	1994	14 992 000	12.1	...	17.7[3]	...	9.5	28.8	2.8	29.5
	1995	17 779 000	12.6	...	17.5[3]	...	9.4	30.4	2.9	28.4
Lesotho [1] Lesotho [1]	1997	4 293[6]	16.0	0.1	15.9	7.3	18.2	10.6	3.8	28.1
	1998	4 521[6]	17.4	0.1	17.2	5.0	15.8	10.3	3.6	30.7
	1999	5 182[6]	16.9	0.1	16.4	5.9	17.9	9.4	3.3	30.5
Liberia Libéria	1987	1 009[6]	37.8	10.4	7.2	1.9	3.2	6.0	7.5	26.0
	1988	1 080[6]	38.2	10.7	7.4	1.7	2.7	5.9	7.3	26.1
	1989	1 119[6]	36.7	10.9	7.3	1.7	2.4	5.7	7.1	28.3

22
Value added by industries in current prices
Percentage distribution [cont.]
Valeur ajoutée par branche d'activité aux prix courants
Répartition en pourcentage [suite]

% of Value added − % de la valeur ajoutée

Country or area Pays ou zone	Year Année	Value added, gross (Mil. nat.cur.) Valeur ajoutée, brute (Mil. mon.nat.)	Agriculture, hunting, forestry and fishing Agriculture, chasse, sylviculture et pêche	Mining and quarrying Activités extractives	Manufac- turing Activités de fabri- cation	Electricity, gas and water supply Electricité, gaz et eau	Con- struc- tion Con- struc- tion	Wholesale, retail trade, restaurants and hotels Commerce, restaurants, hôtels	Transport, storage & commu- nication Transports, entrepôts, communi- cations	Other activities Autres activités
Libyan Arab Jamah.	1983	8 482[6]	3.0	48.8[28]	3.2	0.9	10.4	6.1	4.6	23.0
Jamah. arabe libyenne	1984	7 681[6]	3.4	40.9[28]	3.9	1.2	11.1	7.9	5.3	26.4
	1985	8 050[6]	3.5	41.6[28]	4.5	1.3	11.4	7.0	5.0	25.8
Lithuania [1]	1999	38 054	8.4	0.7	17.6	4.5	7.9	16.9	11.4	32.4
Lithuanie [1]	2000	40 788	7.7	0.9	20.9	4.0	6.1	17.1	12.2	31.0
	2001	41 901	7.2	1.2	23.7	4.4	6.3	17.3	12.7	27.2
Luxembourg [1]	1998	16 911	0.7	0.1	12.5	1.2	6.2	12.8	10.1	56.4
Luxembourg [1]	1999	18 114	0.8	0.1	11.8	1.2	6.1	12.4	9.6	57.9
	2000	19 542	0.7	0.1	11.8	1.1	6.3	12.6	10.2	57.2
Madagascar	1983	1 187 400	44.2	15.6[2 3]	...	...	...	30.4	...	9.7
Madagascar	1984	1 323 100	43.9	16.2[2 3]	...	...	...	30.3	...	9.7
	1985	1 500 600	43.5	16.9[2 3]	...	...	...	30.1	...	9.5
Malawi	1987	2 505[29]	28.1	...	17.7	1.1	2.4	17.0	3.9	23.9
Malawi	1988	3 200[29]	29.5	...	17.4	1.2	1.8	17.2	3.7	22.2
	1989	3 961[29]	31.2	...	16.5	1.8	2.2	15.2	4.3	23.1
Malaysia	1998	300 687	12.5	6.3	27.1	3.1	4.8	14.4	6.5	25.3
Malaisie	1999	315 934	10.3	6.6	30.0	3.1	4.4	13.9	6.5	25.2
	2000	357 187	8.2	9.7	32.7	2.9	3.9	13.0	6.2	23.3
Mali	1990	655 600	47.8	1.6	8.1[30]	3.8[31]	...	18.8	4.9	15.1
Mali	1991	662 500	46.1	1.7	6.9[30]	4.3[31]	...	20.2	5.0	15.9
	1992	707 000	47.2	1.5	7.0[30]	4.4[31]	...	19.3	5.0	15.6
Malta	1995	989[6]	2.8	3.5[31]	24.4	6.2	...	13.3[5]	6.7	43.1
Malte	1996	1 053[6]	2.9	3.4[31]	23.6	5.6	...	12.6[5]	6.5	45.4
	1997	1 111[6]	3.0	3.4[31]	22.7	6.7	...	12.2[5]	6.2	46.1
Marshall Islands	1995	105	14.9	0.3	2.6	2.0	10.2	17.0	6.2	46.8
Iles Marshall	1996	95	14.3	0.3	1.6	2.7	7.0	18.7	7.3	48.2
	1997	90	14.3	0.4	1.7	3.1	7.0	17.9	7.9	47.7
Martinique	1990	18 835	5.7	7.9[2]	...	2.5	4.9	18.9	6.2	53.9
Martinique	1991	20 377	5.7	7.8[2]	...	2.4	5.3	18.9	6.3	53.6
	1992	21 869	5.1	8.1[2]	...	2.2	5.2	18.4	6.5	54.5
Mauritania	1987	60 302[6]	32.3	8.3	12.1	...	6.3	13.0	5.1	22.8
Mauritanie	1988	65 069[6]	32.4	7.7	13.0	...	6.3	13.2	5.1	22.3
	1989	75 486[6]	34.2	10.4	10.3	...	6.4	...	4.9	14.5
Mauritius [1]	1999	97 922	5.7	0.1	22.9	1.4	5.7	18.3	11.9	33.9
Maurice [1]	2000	109 223	6.3	0.1	22.6	1.6	5.7	17.2	12.2	34.3
	2001	122 200	6.1	0.1	22.3	1.8	5.4	16.9	12.6	34.8
Mexico [1]	1997	2 915 601	5.5	1.5	21.1	1.2	4.4	21.0	10.4	34.9
Mexique [1]	1998	3 553 149	5.2	1.4	21.1	1.2	4.6	19.7	10.7	36.0
	1999	4 253 513	4.6	1.4	20.8	1.3	4.9	19.7	11.0	36.3
Mongolia	1996	625 005	45.2	10.8	5.2	2.4	2.8	11.8	7.7	14.1
Mongolie	1997	792 989	37.6	15.0	5.7	3.2	2.3	15.9	8.1	12.1
	1998	775 578	39.5	8.8	5.0	4.3	2.6	15.3	10.4	14.2
Montserrat	1985	90[6]	4.8	1.3	5.7	3.7	7.9	18.0	11.5	47.2
Montserrat	1986	103[6]	4.3	1.4	5.6	3.7	11.3	18.7	11.6	43.4
	1987	118[6]	4.1	1.3	5.7	3.2	11.5	22.1	11.1	41.0
Morocco	1997	292 940	16.8	2.4	19.2	9.2[11 20]	5.0	26.2	6.3	14.8
Maroc	1998	315 766	18.4	2.3	18.5	8.9[11 20]	4.9	25.7	6.3	15.0
	1999	316 631	16.0	2.3	18.8	9.1[11 20]	5.1	26.4	6.6	15.6
Mozambique [1]	1997	40 126 200	8.2[10]	0.0	...	...	0.4	...	...	...
Mozambique [1]	1998	43 557 100	7.6[10]	0.3	...	...	0.6	...	...	...
Myanmar [13]	1996	791 980	60.1	0.6	7.1	0.3[22]	2.4	22.6[5]	3.5	3.4
Myanmar [13]	1997	1 109 554	59.4	0.6	7.1	0.1[22]	2.4	23.2[5]	3.9	3.1
	1998	1 559 996	59.1	0.5	7.2	0.1[22]	2.4	23.9[5]	4.0	2.7
Namibia [1]	1999	18 228	11.4	10.7	11.4	3.0	2.6	12.1	6.7	43.6
Namibie [1]	2000	21 343	11.0	12.2	11.1	2.8	2.2	14.5	6.4	41.1
	2001	24 401	10.0	14.3	10.8	2.7	3.2	14.3	5.9	40.3

22
Value added by industries in current prices
Percentage distribution *[cont.]*
Valeur ajoutée par branche d'activité aux prix courants
Répartition en pourcentage *[suite]*

Country or area Pays ou zone	Year Année	Value added, gross (Mil. nat.cur.) Valeur ajoutée, brute (Mil. mon.nat.)	Agriculture, hunting, forestry and fishing Agriculture, chasse, sylviculture et pêche	Mining and quarrying Activités extractives	Manufac- turing Activités de fabri- cation	Electricity, gas and water supply Electricité, gaz et eau	Con- struc- tion Con- struc- tion	Wholesale, retail trade, restaurants and hotels Commerce, restaurants, hôtels	Transport, storage & commu- nication Transports, entrepôts, communi- cations	Other activities Autres activités
Nepal [32]	1997	269 570[6]	40.4	0.6	9.2[33]	1.7	10.9	11.3	7.2	18.9
Népal [32]	1998	285 702[6]	39.4	0.5	9.3[33]	1.6	10.2	11.8	7.8	19.5
	1999	323 009[6]	40.1	0.5	9.1[33]	1.5	9.9	12.0	7.5	19.4
Netherlands [1]	1997	307 406	3.1	2.9	17.1	1.7	5.4	14.8	7.4	47.7
Pays–Bas [1]	1998	325 762	3.0	2.4	17.0	1.7	5.4	14.9	7.5	48.1
	1999	343 349	2.7	1.9	16.6	1.7	5.7	14.9	7.4	49.1
Netherlands Antilles	1992	3 755	0.7[7]	...	6.9	4.2	6.1	25.3	11.6	45.3
Antilles néerlandaises	1993	3 994	0.8[7]	...	6.1	3.4	6.0	24.4	12.3	46.9
	1994	4 476	0.8[7]	...	6.3	2.8	5.7	24.1	13.8	46.4
New Caledonia	1994	306 748	1.9	7.4	6.6	1.5	6.0	23.0[5]	6.3	47.4
Nouvelle–Calédonie	1995	329 296	1.8	8.7	6.0	1.5	5.7	22.2[5]	6.3	47.7
	1996	335 482	1.7	8.5	5.7	1.6	5.0	22.8[5]	6.7	47.8
New Zealand [1 13]	1994	83 587	7.3	1.3	18.6	2.9	4.0	16.1	8.2	41.7
Nouvelle–Zélande [1 13]	1995	88 763	7.2	1.2	18.0	2.7	4.2	16.0	8.5	42.3
	1996	92 555	7.3	1.4	17.4	2.7	4.4	15.1	8.1	43.6
Nicaragua	1998	21 881	32.4	1.0	15.6	1.2	4.4	23.5	3.5	18.5
Nicaragua	1999	26 130	31.6	1.0	14.8	1.1	6.0	23.0	3.4	19.1
	2000	30 740	32.8	0.7	14.3	1.1	6.2	22.5	3.3	18.9
Niger	1985	627 027	37.9	8.3	7.4	2.3	3.6	16.3	4.4	19.9
Niger	1986	622 426	37.3	7.6	7.9	2.6	4.6	14.6	4.2	21.1
	1987	632 248	34.6	7.8	9.0	2.8	5.3	14.1	4.3	22.2
Nigeria	1992	549 809	26.5	46.6	5.7	0.3	1.1	11.5[34]	1.7	6.7
Nigéria	1993	701 473	33.1	35.9	6.2	0.2	1.1	14.6[34]	2.2	6.8
	1994	914 334	38.2	25.0	7.1	0.2	1.1	17.5[34]	3.5	7.3
Norway [1]	1995	831 067	2.8	13.4	13.4	2.9	4.0	12.7	10.6	40.2
Norvège [1]	1996	907 645	2.4	17.2	12.3	2.7	4.0	12.2	10.2	39.0
	1997	977 083	2.2	17.7	12.4	2.7	4.3	12.0	10.3	38.5
Oman [1]	1998	5 532[14]	2.8	30.5	4.5	1.2	3.7	16.1	8.1	33.0
Oman [1]	1999	6 155[14]	2.6	38.7	4.3	1.2	2.3	13.4	7.1	30.5
	2000	7 790[14]	1.9	48.0	5.3	0.9	1.9	11.0	5.8	25.3
Pakistan [8]	1998	2 735 943[6]	27.0	0.5	15.5	4.5	3.2	15.0[5]	10.1	24.1
Pakistan [8]	1999	2 951 680[6]	26.3	0.6	15.1	3.8	3.3	15.0[5]	10.7	25.2
	2000	3 191 813[6]	25.0	0.6	15.7	3.6	3.1	15.5[5]	11.1	25.4
Panama	1998	9 391[14]	7.0	0.4	8.0	3.4	4.6	19.4	14.8	42.4
Panama	1999	9 733[14]	6.9	0.5	7.5	3.6	4.9	17.7	15.8	43.1
	2000	10 194[14]	6.7	0.4	7.0	3.9	4.8	17.3	17.0	42.9
Papua New Guinea [1]	1997	7 064[29]	31.3	18.5	9.2	1.1	5.3	9.5[5]	5.0	17.2
Papouasie–Nouv.– Guinée [1]	1998	7 863[29]	30.9	20.8	9.2	1.1	4.7	9.0[5]	4.9	16.7
	1999	8 781[29]	28.7	23.8	9.1	1.1	4.1	9.5[5]	4.9	15.8
Paraguay	1993	11 991 719	24.5	0.4	16.5	3.4	5.9	30.4[5]	3.9	15.0
Paraguay	1994	14 960 131	23.7	0.4	15.7	3.9	6.0	30.5[5]	3.9	15.9
	1995	17 699 000	24.8	0.3	15.7	4.3	6.0	29.5[5]	3.7	15.8
Peru [1]	1998	150 719	9.0	4.4	15.7	2.3	7.3	20.3	8.5	32.3
Pérou [1]	1999	159 025	8.8	5.4	15.8	2.5	6.5	19.6	8.7	32.8
	2000	170 563	8.5	5.8	16.3	2.3	6.0	19.6	9.1	32.2
Philippines	1998	2 665 060	16.9	0.8	21.9	2.9	5.9	15.4	5.2	30.9
Philippines	1999	2 976 904	17.1	0.6	21.6	2.9	5.5	16.0	5.4	30.8
	2000	3 302 589	15.9	0.6	22.6	3.0	5.0	16.2	6.0	30.7
Poland [1]	1998	485 177	4.8	2.9	21.5	3.2	8.7	21.8	6.4	30.8
Pologne [1]	1999	535 829	4.0	2.6	21.1	3.4	8.8	21.9	6.8	31.5
	2000	601 427	3.8	2.8	20.6	3.3	8.3	22.1	6.8	32.3
Portugal [1]	1997	80 887	4.4	0.5	20.4	2.9	7.6	18.5	6.7	38.9
Portugal [1]	1998	87 520	4.1	0.4	20.0	2.9	7.8	18.6	7.0	39.1
	1999	92 891	4.1	0.4	19.3	2.9	7.9	18.6	7.1	39.8
Puerto Rico [8]	1998	57 312	0.6	0.1	40.7	2.3	2.8[35]	15.3	4.8	33.5
Porto Rico [8]	1999	60 340	0.9	0.1	38.7	2.5	3.0[35]	15.0	4.6	35.2
	2000	67 062	0.7	0.1	40.4	2.3	2.9[35]	13.9	4.7	35.0

22
Value added by industries in current prices
Percentage distribution *[cont.]*
Valeur ajoutée par branche d'activité aux prix courants
Répartition en pourcentage *[suite]*

Country or area Pays ou zone	Year Année	Value added, gross (Mil. nat.cur.) Valeur ajoutée, brute (Mil. mon.nat.)	% of Value added – % de la valeur ajoutée							
			Agriculture, hunting, forestry and fishing Agriculture, chasse, sylviculture et pêche	Mining and quarrying Activités extractives	Manufacturing Activités de fabrication	Electricity, gas and water supply Electricité, gaz et eau	Construction Construction	Wholesale, retail trade, restaurants and hotels Commerce, restaurants, hôtels	Transport, storage & communication Transports, entrepôts, communications	Other activities Autres activités
Qatar [1] Qatar [1]	1998	38 356	0.7	33.9	7.7	1.6	7.1	8.2	4.9	36.0
	1999	46 170	0.6	44.7	6.2	1.6	5.2	7.2	4.1	30.3
	2000	60 948	0.4	57.3	5.7	1.1	3.3	5.3	3.3	23.5
Republic of Moldova [1] Rép. de Moldova [1]	1999	11 692	26.2	0.2	13.8	3.9	3.5	17.0	8.7	26.7
	2000	14 402	28.3	0.2	15.8	2.1	3.0	14.7	10.6	25.3
	2001	17 033	25.4	0.2	17.7	2.3	3.4	15.4	10.8	24.9
Réunion Réunion	1990	27 417	4.0	9.1[2]	...	4.7	5.9	20.5	4.0	51.7
	1991	30 371	3.7	9.1[2]	...	4.1	7.1	19.9	4.6	51.5
	1992	32 832	3.5	9.0[2]	...	4.1	6.8	20.0	4.5	50.1
Romania [1] Roumanie [1]	1998	340 128 600	15.8	2.3	25.1	2.9	5.5	14.6	10.1	23.7
	1999	488 059 000	14.8	...	29.9[3][7]	...	5.4	14.5	11.3	24.1
	2000	719 834 000	12.6	...	30.5[3][7]	...	5.3	...	...	...
Russian Federation [1] Fédération de Russie [1]	1999	4 282 900	7.7	...	31.6[3][7]	...	6.1	23.1	9.7	21.8
	2000	6 527 300	6.7	...	32.7[3][7]	...	7.2	23.4	9.1	20.9
	2001	7 979 200	7.0	...	30.0[3][7]	...	8.3	22.7	10.2	21.8
Rwanda Rwanda	1987	166 760	39.2	0.2	15.0	0.6	7.2	14.2	7.1	16.5
	1988	171 700	39.3	0.2	14.5	0.7	7.1	13.2	7.4	17.6
	1989	184 380	41.1	0.4	13.5	0.5	7.0	13.2	7.0	17.3
Saint Kitts–Nevis Saint–Kitts–et–Nevis	1997	671[6]	5.2	0.3	9.7	1.8	10.4	22.5	7.0	43.2
	1998	697[6]	3.9	0.3	9.2	1.8	11.5	23.0	6.8	43.6
	1999	731[6]	3.4	0.3	9.7	1.8	12.2	22.3	7.0	43.4
Saint Lucia Sainte–Lucie	1996	1 409	8.2	0.4	6.2	3.6	7.1	24.7	17.4	32.4
	1997	1 454	7.0	0.4	5.8	3.7	7.0	25.4	17.7	32.9
	1998	1 544	7.5	0.4	5.3	4.1	7.2	25.6	17.3	32.6
Saint Vincent–Grenadines St.–Vincent–et–Gren.	1998	764[6]	10.2	0.3	6.5	5.4	13.4	17.4	19.6	27.2
	1999	792[6]	10.0	0.3	5.9	5.6	12.2	18.3	19.7	28.0
	2000	813[6]	10.1	0.2	4.9	5.8	11.1	18.3	19.3	30.3
Sao Tome and Principe Sao Tomé–et–Principe	1986	2 259	29.2	...	2.3	0.3	3.4	19.4	5.3	40.1
	1987	2 797	31.5	...	1.3	1.4	3.8	17.1	5.6	39.2
	1988	3 800	32.1	...	1.7	1.0	4.2	18.8	4.1	38.1
Saudi Arabia [8] Arabie saoudite [8]	1997	545 481	6.1	37.3	9.3	0.2	8.5	6.8	6.0	25.8
	1998	477 210	7.1	27.6	10.0	0.2	9.9	7.8	7.0	30.4
	1999	519 419	6.6	31.8	9.6	0.2	9.3	7.2	6.6	8.8
Senegal Sénégal	1998	2 746 000	17.9	1.0	12.3	2.3	4.0	27.5	11.1	23.1
	1999	2 925 000	18.6	1.1	12.1	2.2	4.4	27.0	11.3	22.6
	2000	3 114 000	19.4	1.1	12.0	2.2	4.3	25.7	11.9	22.4
Serbia and Montenegro [1] Serbie–et–Monténégro [1]	1997	103 160	19.3	5.5	22.8	4.7	5.3	8.4	8.6	25.4
	1998	141 182	18.1	5.1	24.3	4.3	5.3	9.7	9.7	23.6
Seychelles Seychelles	1998	3 013	2.8	...	16.0[7][30]	2.7	8.8	9.6	32.0	28.2
	1999	3 244	2.5	...	15.8[7][30]	2.5	9.6	8.6	34.1	27.0
	2000	3 319	2.5	...	15.0[7][30]	2.6	10.3	8.9	33.8	26.8
Sierra Leone [8] Sierra Leone [8]	1988	42 364	39.3	6.3	7.7	0.3	2.6	20.9	10.5	12.3
	1989	81 921	37.3	7.0	7.1	0.2	1.9	25.0	10.8	10.6
	1990	148 652	35.3	9.5	8.7	0.1	1.3	20.3	8.9	15.9
Singapore Singapour	1998	145 835	...	...	22.5[7][36]	1.9	8.8	16.3	10.8	39.7
	1999	151 236	...	...	23.7[7][36]	1.6	7.4	17.1	11.0	39.2
	2000	168 108	...	...	25.2[7][36]	1.6	5.8	18.5	10.7	38.2
Slovakia [1] Slovaquie [1]	1997	632 861	5.0	1.0	24.4	3.7	7.5	15.6	10.5	32.4
	1998	680 357	5.1	0.9	23.6	3.6	7.4	16.4	10.8	32.4
	1999	736 202	4.5	1.0	24.2	4.1	5.8	0.0	11.1	18.4
Slovenia [1] Slovénie [1]	1999	3 179 760	3.6	1.2	27.0	3.1	6.2	14.5	8.1	36.3
	2000	3 562 382[6]	3.2	1.0	27.2	3.2	6.0	14.5	7.9	36.9
	2001	4 043 150	3.1	0.9	26.8	3.3	5.8	14.6	7.7	37.7
Solomon Islands Iles Salomon	1984	199	53.5	−0.2	3.6	0.9	3.8	10.6	5.2	22.6
	1985	213	50.4	−0.7	3.8	1.0	4.2	10.4	5.1	25.8
	1986	224	48.3	−1.2	4.5	1.2	5.1	8.4	5.8	27.9

22
Value added by industries in current prices
Percentage distribution *[cont.]*
Valeur ajoutée par branche d'activité aux prix courants
Répartition en pourcentage *[suite]*

Country or area Pays ou zone	Year Année	Value added, gross (Mil. nat.cur.) Valeur ajoutée, brute (Mil. mon.nat.)	Agriculture, hunting, forestry and fishing Agriculture, chasse, sylviculture et pêche	Mining and quarrying Activités extractives	Manufac- turing Activités de fabri- cation	Electricity, gas and water supply Electricité, gaz et eau	Con- struc- tion Con- struc- tion	Wholesale, retail trade, restaurants and hotels Commerce, restaurants, hôtels	Transport, storage & commu- nication Transports, entrepôts, communi- cations	Other activities Autres activités
Somalia	1985	84 050[6]	66.1	0.3	4.9	0.1	2.2	10.1	6.7	9.5
Somalie	1986	112 584[6]	62.5	0.4	5.5	0.2	2.7	10.3	7.3	11.1
	1987	163 175[6]	64.9	0.3	5.1	−0.5	2.9	10.7	6.8	9.8
South Africa [1]	1998	674 454	3.6	6.4	19.1	3.3	3.2	13.3	9.4	41.6
Afrique du Sud [1]	1999	730 584	3.4	6.6	18.6	3.0	3.1	13.1	9.7	42.6
	2000	808 017	3.2	7.3	18.5	2.8	3.0	13.1	9.9	42.3
Spain [1]	1996	444 763	4.8	0.5	18.6	2.9	7.2	18.6	7.9	39.4
Espagne [1]	1997	471 233	4.4	0.5	18.9	2.8	7.2	18.7	8.1	39.3
	1998	499 873	4.1	0.4	18.9	2.7	7.4	18.4	8.3	39.4
Sri Lanka	1998	985 609	17.8	0.9	18.8	2.1	6.9	23.8	10.7	19.1
Sri Lanka	1999	1 076 965	17.5	1.1	18.7	2.1	7.0	23.4	10.8	19.4
	2000	1 221 356	16.3	1.2	19.0	2.0	6.9	24.5	10.7	19.3
Sudan [8]	1994	4 440 648	40.5	6.5[2]	...	0.7	3.8	46.6[17]	...	1.9[18]
Soudan [8]	1996	9 015 824	37.1	9.6[2]	...	0.9	5.0	44.4[17]	...	3.0[18]
	1997	15 865 432	40.5	9.1[2]	...	0.8	6.9	39.8[17]	...	2.8[18]
Suriname	1998	315 526[6]	10.1	6.4	12.0	6.4	4.8	14.6	6.2	39.6
Suriname	1999	536 873[6]	9.2	11.7	12.5	6.1	4.8	14.3	6.4	35.0
	2000	824 075[6]	8.8	11.7	12.5	5.2	10.1	11.6	7.0	33.1
Swaziland [1] [15]	1998	5 752	16.5	0.9	35.6	1.9	4.8	8.8	4.6	24.3
Swaziland [1] [15]	1999	6 235	16.6	1.0	34.8	1.8	5.3	8.9	4.6	24.4
	2000	6 902	16.3	0.6	34.7	1.5	6.5	9.0	4.5	24.0
Sweden [1]	1995	1 576 849	2.5	0.4	22.1	2.9	4.4	11.8	7.9	47.9
Suède [1]	1996	1 615 329	2.1	0.3	21.3	2.9	4.3	11.7	8.1	49.2
Switzerland	1985	234 650	3.5	0.0	25.1	2.1	7.4	17.8	6.2	37.9
Suisse	1990	324 289	3.0	...	23.7	1.9	8.1	18.7	5.7	39.0
	1991	343 983	2.9	...	22.6	1.9	7.8	16.6	5.8	42.4
Syrian Arab Rep.	1999	819 092	24.3	19.9	5.6	1.1	3.4	18.7	12.7	14.3
Rép. arabe syrienne	2000	903 944	24.7	27.5	1.5	1.1	3.2	14.9	12.6	14.4
	2001	947 808	25.9	20.3	5.6	1.0	3.2	15.6	12.7	15.7
Tajikistan [1]	1997	472 200	35.1	...	25.9[3] [7]	...	3.0	22.7	3.2	10.1
Tadjikistan [1]	1998	950 700	27.1	...	23.2[3] [7]	...	4.2	24.2	4.5	16.9
	1999	1 209 300	18.7	...	21.6[3] [7]	...	3.4	16.0	2.1	38.2
Thailand	1997	4 200 698	12.6	1.7	26.8	2.7	5.9	14.1	8.7	27.5
Thaïlande	1998	4 152 782	14.1	1.7	27.6	3.0	3.7	14.5	8.6	26.7
	1999	4 145 154	12.4	1.8	29.2	3.0	3.5	14.5	9.0	26.5
TFYR of Macedonia [1]	1998	169 094	11.8	...	27.0[7]	2.9	6.4	14.3	7.2	30.4
L'ex–R.y. Macédoine [1]	1999	171 948	11.0	...	25.8[7]	2.8	7.2	15.0	8.2	30.0
	2000	191 066	9.4	...	26.1[7]	2.8	6.7	18.2	8.6	28.2
Trinidad and Tobago [1]	1998	37 682	1.5	9.1	17.5	2.3	12.4	18.4	10.4	31.4
Trinité–et–Tobago [1]	1999	41 140	1.6	10.4	23.0	2.2	11.7	18.5	10.1	30.8
	2000	49 654	1.3	11.7	19.8	1.9	10.5	18.3	9.2	27.2
Tunisia [1]	1997	18 850[6]	14.6	4.1	20.5	2.2[11]	4.9	16.1[5]	8.6	29.0
Tunisie [1]	1998	20 232[6]	14.0	3.7	20.6	2.3[11]	5.1	16.7[5]	8.6	29.1
	1999	22 093[6]	14.5	4.2	20.1	2.1[11]	5.1	16.8[5]	8.6	28.6
Turkey	1995	7 748 669 630	15.7	1.3	22.6	2.5	5.5	20.5	12.7	19.3
Turquie	1996	15 022 756 540	16.6	1.2	20.8	2.7	5.7	20.1	12.9	19.9
	1997	29 235 581 840	15.0	1.2	21.3	2.5	5.9	20.7	13.8	20.9
Turkmenistan [1]	1998	13 629 143	25.9	...	31.2[3] [7]	...	13.4	3.7	8.0	17.8
Turkménistan [1]	1999	20 056 000	24.8	...	31.4[3] [7]	...	12.2	4.1	6.7	20.8
	2000	22 895 000	25.8	...	37.8[3] [7]	...	9.8	4.4	4.6	17.7
Uganda	1997	6 565 455[6]	42.4	0.6	8.7	1.4	7.5	13.9	4.5	20.9
Ouganda	1998	7 568 986[6]	43.5	0.6	8.8	1.3	7.6	13.7	4.5	20.0
	1999	8 356 013[6]	42.5	0.6	9.2	1.3	8.2	13.7	5.0	19.6
Ukraine [1]	1998	88 000	14.1	...	31.4[3] [7]	...	5.6	8.6	14.3	25.9
Ukraine [1]	1999	109 600	14.1	...	34.4[3] [7]	...	4.9	8.5	14.1	24.2
	2000	146 000	16.8	...	32.7[3] [7]	...	4.2	10.4	13.6	22.3

22
Value added by industries in current prices
Percentage distribution [cont.]
Valeur ajoutée par branche d'activité aux prix courants
Répartition en pourcentage [suite]

% of Value added − % de la valeur ajoutée

Country or area Pays ou zone	Year Année	Value added, gross (Mil. nat.cur.) Valeur ajoutée, brute (Mil. mon.nat.)	Agriculture, hunting, forestry and fishing Agriculture, chasse, sylviculture et pêche	Mining and quarrying Activités extractives	Manufac- turing Activités de fabri- cation	Electricity, gas and water supply Electricité, gaz et eau	Con- struc- tion Con- struc- tion	Wholesale, retail trade, restaurants and hotels Commerce, restaurants, hôtels	Transport, storage & commu- nication Transports, entrepôts, communi- cations	Other activities Autres activités
United Arab Emirates	1988	90 137[6]	1.8	33.2	9.1	2.3	9.8	11.3	5.6	26.8
Emirats arabes unis	1989	104 730[6]	1.8	37.3	8.3	2.1	9.1	10.2	5.4	25.7
	1990	127 737[6]	1.6	45.4	7.2	1.8	7.8	8.8	4.6	22.7
United Kingdom [1]	1998	789 312	1.2	1.9	19.2	2.0	4.9	14.7	7.9	47.4
Royaume−Uni [1]	1999	825 844	1.1	2.2	17.9	2.2	5.0	14.2	8.4	48.1
	2000	868 287	1.0	3.2	17.0	2.1	5.0	13.9	8.1	48.4
United Rep. of Tanzania	1992	1 060 631[6]	54.4	1.8	7.8[30]	1.9	4.5	15.4	5.1	9.1
Rép.−Unie de Tanzanie	1993	1 343 237[6]	54.4	1.4	7.8[30]	2.1	4.9	14.6	6.3	8.5
	1994	1 740 521[6]	54.5	1.5	7.3[30]	2.2	5.0	14.6	6.2	8.8
United States [1]	1997	7 613 500	1.7	1.6	18.1	2.7	4.4	19.3	7.1	53.1
Etats−Unis [1]	1998	8 109 000	1.6	1.3	17.7	2.5	4.7	19.6	7.2	53.4
	1999	8 634 800	1.5	1.3	17.4	2.5	4.8	19.6	7.3	53.4
Uruguay	1998	239 783[14]	6.8	0.3	18.0	3.9	5.7	13.8	7.9	43.6
Uruguay	1999	246 753[14]	5.4	0.3	16.0	3.8	6.1	13.5	8.5	46.3
	2000	255 121[14]	5.7	0.3	16.1	4.0	5.6	12.7	8.7	46.9
Uzbekistan [1]	1998	1 212 700	31.3	...	17.4[3 7]	...	8.8	9.9	7.9	24.7
Ouzbékistan [1]	1999	1 842 900	33.5	...	16.5[3 7]	...	7.8	10.4	8.0	23.7
	2000	2 788 100	34.9	...	15.8[3 7]	...	7.0	10.9	9.3	22.2
Vanuatu	1996	28 227	24.9	...	5.0	1.7	5.6	32.0	7.3	23.5
Vanuatu	1997	29 477	25.2	...	4.9	1.7	5.5	32.4	7.3	23.1
	1998	29 545	23.1	...	4.9	1.8	4.6	34.3	7.4	23.9
Venezuela	1998	50 571 369	4.9	10.7[37]	14.8[20]	1.7[11]	6.8	17.4	9.7	34.1
Venezuela	1999	60 336 461	4.8	13.8[37]	13.6[20]	1.5[11]	5.6	16.2	9.5	34.9
	2000	79 740 289	4.1	20.0[37]	13.3[20]	1.4[11]	4.8	14.7	8.7	33.1
Viet Nam [1]	1998	361 017 000	25.8	6.7	17.1	2.9	5.8	18.9	3.9	18.9
Viet Nam [1]	1999	399 942 000	25.4	8.4	17.7	2.9	5.4	18.2	3.9	18.0
	2000	444 140 000	24.3	9.5	18.7	2.9	5.5	17.7	4.0	17.4
Yemen [1]	1998	847 533	19.4	16.4	10.2	0.9	5.3	11.2	14.4	22.2
Yémen [1]	1999	1 132 153	16.1	29.2	8.2	0.7	4.7	9.0	11.6	20.8
	2000	1 380 603	15.3	33.8	7.5	0.7	4.2	8.6	10.3	19.4
Yugoslavia, SFR	1988	14 645	11.2	2.7	40.3	2.2	6.2	7.6	11.1	18.6
Yougoslavie, SFR	1989	224 684	11.3	2.4	41.4	1.7	6.4	6.6	10.5	19.7
	1990	966 420	12.9	2.5	31.2	1.7	7.9	8.5	12.3	23.1
Zambia	1989	55 850[6]	11.4	18.0	23.3	0.6	5.4	16.0	5.6	19.7
Zambie	1990	114 675[6]	12.4	22.0	22.2	0.6	5.5	11.5	6.0	19.9
	1991	220 351[6]	12.8	15.3	28.0	0.9	5.0	10.9	7.2	20.0
Zimbabwe	1996	76 274[6]	21.9	1.7	17.4	3.2[11]	2.2	19.8	5.5	28.3
Zimbabwe	1997	90 246[6]	18.9	1.5	17.0	3.2[11]	2.8	19.0	5.7	31.8
	1998	118 145[6]	19.3	2.1	16.4	2.6[11]	3.1	19.2	5.7	31.7

Source:
United Nations Statistics Division, New York,
national accounts database.

1 Data classified according to 1993 SNA.
2 Including "manufacturing".
3 Including "electricity, gas and water".
4 Including "other activities".
5 Restaurants and hotels are included in "other activities".
6 Value added at factor cost.
7 Including mining and quarrying.

Source:
Organisation des Nations Unies, Division de statistique,
New York, la base de données sur les comptes nationaux.

1 Les données sont classifiées selon le SCN 1993.
2 Y compris les industries manufacturières.
3 Y compris l'électricité, le gaz et l'eau.
4 Y compris "autres activités".
5 Restaurants et hôtels sont incluses dans "autres activités".
6 Valeur ajoutée au coût des facteurs.
7 Y compris industries extractives.

22
Value added by kind of economic activity in current prices
Percentage distribution *[cont.]*
Valeur ajoutée par genre d'activité économique aux prix courants
Répartition en pourcentage *[suite]*

8	Data refer to fiscal years beginning 1 July.	8	Les données se réfèrent aux exercices budgétaires commençant le 1er juillet.
9	Oil refining is incuded in "Electricity, gas and water".	9	Le raffinage du pétrole est compris dans "électricité, gaz et eau".
10	Excluding hunting and forestry.	10	Non compris le chasse et le sylviculture.
11	Excluding gas.	11	Non compris le gaz.
12	Data in Belarussian roubles.	12	Les données sont exprimées en roubles bélarussiens.
13	Data refer to fiscal years beginning 1 April.	13	Les données se réfèrent aux exercices budgétaires commençant le 1er avril.
14	Value added at producer's prices.	14	Valeur ajoutée aux prix à la production.
15	Data refer to fiscal years ending 30 June.	15	Les données se réfèrent aux exercices budgétaires finissant le 30 juin.
16	Excluding repair of motor vehicles, motorcycles and personal and household goods.	16	Non compris les réparations de véhicules à moteur, de motorcycles et d'articles personnels et ménagers.
17	Including "Transport, storage and communication" .	17	Y compris transports, entrepôts et communications.
18	"Other activities," refer only to public administration and defence; compulsory social security; all other services and activities are included in "wholesale and retail trade".	18	Les "autres activités" ne comprennent que l'administration publique et la défense, et la sécurité sociale obligatoire. Tous les autres services et activités sont compris dans le commerce de gros et de détail.
19	Excluding hunting.	19	Non compris le chasse.
20	Including petroleum refining.	20	Y compris le raffinage du pétrole.
21	Refers to oil and oil products.	21	Concerne le pétrole et les produits pétroliers.
22	Electricity only. Gas and water are included in "other activities".	22	Seulement électricité. Le gaz et l'eau sont incluses dans les "autres activités".
23	Data refer to fiscal years ending 7 July.	23	Les données se réfèrent aux exercices budgétaires finissant le 7 juillet.
24	Including repair services.	24	Y compris les services de réparation.
25	Excluding education.	25	Non compris le éducation.
26	Data refer to fiscal years beginning 21 March.	26	Les données se réfèrent aux exercices budgétaires commençant le 21 mars.
27	Distribution of petroleum products and gas is included in wholesale and retail trade.	27	La distribution des produits pétroliers et du gaz est comprise dans le commerce de gros et de détail.
28	Including gas and oil production.	28	Y compris la production de gaz et de pétrole.
29	Gross domestic product.	29	Produit intérieur brut.
30	Including handicrafts.	30	Y compris l'artisanat.
31	Including construction.	31	Y compris construction.
32	Data refer to fiscal years ending 15 July.	32	Les données se réfèrent aux exercices budgétaires finissant le 15 juillet.
33	Including cottage industries.	33	Y compris artisanat.
34	Including import duties.	34	Droits d'importation compris.
35	Contract construction only.	35	Construction sous contrat seulement.
36	Including agriculture.	36	Y compris l'agriculture.
37	Including crude petroleum and natural gas production.	37	Y compris la production de pétrole brut et de gas naturel.

23
Relationships among the principal national accounting aggregates
As a percentage of GDP
Relations entre les principaux agrégats de comptabilité nationale
En pourcentage du PIB

As a percentage of GDP − En pourcentage du PIB

Country or area Pays ou zone	Year Année	GDP in current prices (Mil. nat.cur.) PIB aux prix courants (Mil. mon.nat.)	Plus: Compensation of employees and property income from and to the rest of the world, net Plus: Rémunération des salariés et revenus de la propriété – du et au reste du monde, net	Equals: Gross national income Égale: Revenu national brut	Plus: Net current transfers from/to the rest of the world Plus: Transfers courants du/au reste du monde, net	Equals: Gross national disposable income Égale: Revenu national disponible brut	Less: Final consumption expenditure Moins: Dépense de consommation finale	Equals: Gross savings Égale: Épargne brute	Less: Consumption of fixed capital Moins: Consommation de capital fixe
Algeria Algérie	1998	2 810 124	−4.101	95.9	3.3	99.3	73.3	26.0	7.8
	1999	3 215 126	−4.601	95.4	3.0	98.5	68.8	29.7	8.2
	2000	4 078 676	−4.301	95.7	1.9	97.6	55.7	41.9	8.8
Angola Angola	1988	239 640	−11.1	88.9	−1.9	87.0	78.4	8.6	...
	1989	278 866	−10.5	89.5	−1.6	87.9	77.1	10.8	...
	1990	308 062	−12.4	87.6	−4.2	83.4	73.2	10.2	...
Anguilla Anguilla	1999	283	−3.1	96.9	−0.3	96.6	101.3	−4.6	...
	2000	292	−2.7	97.3	1.4	98.6	106.8	−8.2	...
	2001	298	−0.7	99.0	−0.7	98.3	93.3	5.4	...
Argentina [2] Argentine [2]	1998	298 948	−2.5	97.5	0.1	97.7	81.5	16.1	...
	1999	283 523	−2.6	97.4	0.1	97.5	83.9	13.6	...
	2000	284 204	−2.6	97.4	0.1	97.5	83.1	14.4	...
Armenia [2] Arménie [2]	1997	804 300	0.1[1]	100.1	9.3	109.5	114.7	−5.3	14.4
	1998	955 400	−0.7[1]	99.3	7.5	106.8	111.1	−4.3	13.7
	1999	987 400	−0.9[1]	99.1	9.2	108.3	108.3	0.0	14.1
Australia [2][3] Australie [2][3]	1998	591 592	−3.1	96.9	−0.1	96.8	78.3	18.5	15.4
	1999	629 212	−3.1	96.9	0.0	97.0	78.3	18.6	15.5
	2000	670 029	−2.9	97.1	0.0	97.1	78.8	18.3	15.6
Austria [2] Autriche [2]	1998	189 937	−0.8	99.2	−0.6	98.6	76.7	21.9	14.3
	1999	196 658	−1.7	98.3	−0.5	97.8	76.8	21.0	14.3
	2000	204 843	−1.4	98.6	−0.4	98.2	76.4	21.8	14.4
Azerbaijan [2] Azerbaïdjan [2]	1997	15 791 400	0.1	100.1	1.2	101.3	87.1	14.3	14.1
	1998	17 203 100	0.8	100.8	1.7	102.5	95.2	7.4	16.7
	1999	18 875 400	1.0	101.0	1.9	102.9	91.4	11.5	15.6
Bahamas [2] Bahamas [2]	1993	2 854	−2.6	97.4	0.5	97.9	83.9	14.0	6.0
	1994	3 053	−2.9	97.1	0.5	97.6	84.0	13.6	5.9
	1995	3 069	−3.2	96.8	0.2	97.0	83.4	13.6	4.9
Bahrain Bahreïn	1998	2 325	−2.6[1]	97.4	−10.7	86.7	77.9	...	14.7
	1999	2 489	−4.1[1]	95.9	−12.4	83.5	76.2	...	14.2
	2000	2 997	−2.8[1]	97.2	−12.4	84.8	64.7	...	12.1
Bangladesh [2][3] Bangladesh [2][3]	1997	2 001 766	3.2	103.2	1.1	104.4	82.6	21.8	8.0
	1998	2 196 972	3.4	103.4	1.2	104.6	82.3	22.3	8.0
	1999	2 370 856	3.7	103.7	1.5	105.2	82.1	23.1	7.9
Belarus [2] Bélarus [2]	1998	702 161 100[4]	0.0	100.0	0.6	100.6	77.7	22.9	...
	1999	3 026 063 700[4]	0.1	100.1	1.0	101.1	78.1	23.0	...
	2000	9 133 800	0.1	100.1	1.3	101.4	76.4	25.0	...
Belgium [2] Belgique [2]	1998	225 873	2.0	102.0	−1.1	100.9	75.4	25.5	14.5
	1999	235 538	2.0	102.0	−1.0	101.0	75.0	26.0	14.6
	2000	248 338	2.4	102.4	−1.0	101.5	75.2	26.2	16.2
Belize [2] Belize [2]	1997	1 231	...	96.1	...	100.2	83.5	...	4.9
	1998	1 258	...	94.9	...	100.2	84.8	...	4.7
	1999	1 377	...	95.1	...	...	82.3	...	5.9
Benin Bénin	1987	469 554	...	98.2	8.7	106.9	96.5	10.4	...
	1988	482 434	...	97.9	9.3	107.2	95.3	11.9	...
	1989	479 200	...	99.2	11.1	110.2	94.4	12.6	...
Bermuda [2][5] Bermudes [2][5]	1998	3 053	4.2	104.2	...	...	71.4	...	...
	1999	3 272	4.6	104.6	...	...	72.0	...	...
	2000	3 397	4.9	104.9	...	...	72.0	...	...

23
Relationships among the principal national accounting aggregates
As a percentage of GDP *[cont.]*
Relations entre les princtipaux agrégats de comptabilité nationale
En pourcentage du PIB *[suite]*

			As a percentage of GDP – En pourcentage du PIB						
Country or area Pays ou zone	Year Année	GDP in current prices (Mil. nat.cur.) PIB aux prix courants (Mil. mon.nat.)	Plus: Compen- sation of employees and property income from and to the rest of the world, net Plus : Rémunéra- tion des salariés et revenus de la propriété – du et au reste du monde, net	Equals: Gross national income Égale : Revenu national brut	Plus: Net current transfers from/to the rest of the world Plus : Transferts courants du/au reste du monde, net	Equals: Gross national disposable income Égale : Revenu national disponible brut	Less: Final con- sumption expen- diture Moins : Dépense de con- somma- tion de finale	Equals: Gross savings Égale : Épargne brute	Less: Con- sumption of fixed capital Moins : Consom- mation de capital fixe
Bhutan Bhoutan	1998 1999 2000	16 337 19 123 21 698	−14.2 −16.1 −15.9	94.1 83.9 84.1	4.2 4.5 5.8	99.0 88.4 89.8	77.3 75.0 72.6	36.6	8.1 8.2 8.1
Bolivia Bolivie	1990 1991 1992	15 443 19 132 22 014[2]	−4.6 −4.0 −3.5	95.4 96.0 96.5	2.9 2.6 2.8	98.3 98.6 99.3	88.6 89.9 92.3	9.7 8.7 7.0	... ...
Botswana [2][6] Botswana [2][6]	1998 1999 2000	20 163 21 524 25 363	−0.1 −1.6 −5.2	99.9 98.4 94.8	−0.4 −0.1 −0.1	99.5 98.2 94.6	57.5 62.8 60.5	42.0 35.4 34.1	12.0 12.3 12.1
Brazil [2] Brésil [2]	1998 1999 2000	914 188 963 869 1 086 700	−2.3 −3.5 −3.2	97.7 96.5 96.8	0.2 0.3 0.3	97.9 96.8 97.1	81.1 81.3 79.9	16.8 15.5 17.2	... ...
British Virgin Islands Iles Vierges britanniques	1987 1988 1989	117 131 156	9.3 8.8 8.5	109.3 108.8 108.5	1.7 1.6 1.5	110.9 110.4 109.9	91.0 88.9 85.6	19.9 21.5 24.3	11.6 10.8 14.9
Bulgaria [2] Bulgarie [2]	1995 1996 1997	880 322 1 748 701 17 055 205	−3.3 −4.0 −3.5	96.7 96.0 96.5	0.1 1.0 2.3	96.8 97.0 98.9	85.9 88.5 83.1	... ...	8.7 8.2 6.8
Burkina Faso Burkina Faso	1991 1992 1993	811 676 812 590 832 349	0.3 0.2 −0.1	100.3 100.2 99.9	1.5 1.9 1.9	... ...	90.9 90.6 91.6	... ...	... ...
Burundi Burundi	1990 1991 1992	196 656 211 898 226 384	... ...	98.0 99.0 98.7	... ...	... ...	102.5 100.9 98.5	... ...	4.2 ... ...
Cameroon [2][3] Cameroun [2][3]	1994 1995 1996	3 754 530 4 465 080 4 793 080	... ...	94.6 95.2 95.7	0.0 0.5 0.3	94.7 95.8 95.9	84.4 80.3 79.8	10.2 15.5 16.1	... ...
Canada [2] Canada [2]	1998 1999 2000	901 239 960 206 1 040 426	−3.2 −3.0 −2.3	96.8 97.0 97.7	0.1 0.1 0.1	96.8 97.1 97.8	77.4 76.1 74.1	19.5 21.0 23.7	13.6 13.3 12.9
Cape Verde Cap–Vert	1993 1994 1995	29 078 33 497 37 705	... ...	166.4 161.3 163.5	... ...	... ...	106.8 104.5 109.1	... ...	... ...
Cayman Islands Iles Caïmanes	1989 1990 1991	474 590 616	−10.8 −10.3 −9.4	89.2 89.7 90.6	... ...	92.0 92.2 93.0	79.3 76.8 77.6	12.7 15.4 15.4	8.0 7.1 7.6
Chile Chili	1998 1999 2000	33 630 367 34 422 796 37 774 743	−2.7[7] −2.7[7] −3.4[7]	97.3 97.3 96.6	0.6 0.7 0.8	97.9 97.9 97.4	76.7 76.1 75.5	21.2 21.8 21.9	9.6 ... ...
China [2] Chine [2]	1997 1998 1999	7 446 260 7 834 520 8 191 090	... ... −1.8	98.2 98.2 98.2	... ...	... ...	... ...	... ...	... ...
China, Hong Kong SAR Chine, Hong Kong RAS	1998 1999 2000	1 259 306 1 227 658 1 267 175	2.3 2.8 1.7	102.3 102.8 101.7	−1.0 −1.0 −1.0	101.3 101.9 100.7	69.9 69.6 67.7	31.4 32.2 33.0	... ...
Colombia [2] Colombie [2]	1997 1998 1999	121 707 501 140 953 206 149 042 204	−2.2 −2.4 −1.7	97.8 97.6 98.3	3.0 3.2 1.7	101.2 100.8 100.0	85.0 86.2 87.5	16.2 14.6 12.5	... ...

23

Relationships among the principal national accounting aggregates
As a percentage of GDP *[cont.]*
Relations entre les printicpaux agrégats de comptabilité nationale
En pourcentage du PIB *[suite]*

As a percentage of GDP – En pourcentage du PIB

Country or area Pays ou zone	Year Année	GDP in current prices (Mil. nat.cur.) PIB aux prix courants (Mil. mon.nat.)	Plus: Compensation of employees and property income from and to the rest of the world, net Plus: Rémunération des salariés et revenus de la propriété – du et au reste du monde, net	Equals: Gross national income Égale: Revenu national brut	Plus: Net current transfers from/to the rest of the world Plus: Transfers courants du/au reste du monde, net	Equals: Gross national disposable income Égale: Revenu national disponible brut	Less: Final consumption expenditure Moins: Dépense de consommation de finale	Equals: Gross savings Égale: Épargne brute	Less: Consumption of fixed capital Moins: Consommation de capital fixe
Comoros	1989	63 397	...	100.7	...	...	...	...	...
Comores	1990	66 370	...	99.8	12.3	112.1	105.5	6.7	...
	1991	69 248	...	99.6	...	...	...	...	...
Congo	1986	640 407	−6.5	93.5	−1.3	92.2	84.4	7.8	24.4
Congo	1987	690 523	−11.1	88.9	−1.6	87.3	77.2	10.2	23.8
	1988	658 964	−13.7	86.3	−1.8	84.5	81.2	3.3	22.0
Costa Rica [2]	1998	3 625 330	−3.3	96.7	0.8	97.5	82.2	15.3	5.6
Costa Rica [2]	1999	4 512 763	−11.5	88.5	0.6	89.1	77.2	12.0	5.9
	2000	4 915 089	−7.8	92.2	0.6	92.7	81.1	11.6	6.0
Côte d'Ivoire	1994	4 616 000	−8.0	91.9	2.4	...	78.5	...	...
Côte d'Ivoire	1995	5 543 000	−7.8	92.4	−1.2	...	81.0	...	...
	1996	6 177 000	−8.6	91.4	−2.7	...	81.1	...	...
Cuba	1998	23 901	−1.9[7]	98.1	3.4	101.5	95.2	6.3	...
Cuba	1999	25 504	−2.0[7]	98.0	3.1	101.1	94.4	6.7	...
	2000	27 635	−2.5[7]	97.5	3.0	100.5	92.1	8.5	...
Cyprus	1997	4 371	0.9	100.9	...	101.7	84.8	...	10.6
Chypre	1998	4 695	0.6	100.6	...	101.2	86.8	...	10.6
	1999	5 009	0.4	100.4	...	100.7	83.6	...	10.5
Czech Republic [2]	1998	1 837 060	−1.7	98.3	0.7	99.0	71.3	26.4	19.9
République tchèque [2]	1999	1 887 325	−2.3	97.7	0.9	98.6	73.6	25.0	20.6
	2000	1 959 479	...	98.5	...	...	74.0	...	...
Dem. Rep. of the Congo	1983	59 134	...	95.7	...	...	76.9	...	2.9
Rép. dém. du Congo	1984	99 723	...	88.5	...	...	49.5	...	2.5
	1985	147 263	...	97.2	...	...	59.4	...	2.9
Denmark [2]	1999	1 213 595	−0.8	99.2	−2.3	96.9	75.1	21.8	16.4
Danemark [2]	2000	1 296 137	−1.7	98.3	−2.5	95.7	72.4	23.3	16.6
	2001	1 352 069	−1.8	98.2	−2.2	95.9	72.3	23.7	16.1
Djibouti	1996	88 233	1.0[1]	100.0	9.4	109.4	97.3	12.1	...
Djibouti	1997	87 289	1.2[1]	99.9	8.3	108.2	94.2	14.0	...
	1998	88 461	1.2[1]	99.9	8.3	108.3	96.4	11.8	...
Dominica	1989	423	...	101.0	...	...	92.0	...	...
Dominique	1990	452	...	101.1	...	...	84.4	...	...
	1991	479	...	101.0	...	...	91.4	...	...
Dominican Republic [2]	1994	179 130	−2.2	97.8	6.7	104.5	81.4	23.1	3.6
Rép. dominicaine [2]	1995	209 646	−2.3	97.7	6.2	103.9	82.9	21.0	4.0
	1996	243 973	−5.4	94.6	6.1	100.7	82.2	18.5	3.8
Ecuador	1998	107 421 048	−8.2	91.8	3.9	95.7	82.0	13.7	...
Equateur	1999	161 350 379	−12.7	87.3	8.1	95.3	75.8	19.5	...
	2000	340 021 704	−12.8	87.2	9.9	97.2	71.6	25.6	...
Egypt [3]	1980	17 149	4.3	104.3	1.5	...	81.6	...	...
Egypte [3]	1981	20 222	1.3	101.3	1.3	...	81.7	...	...
El Salvador	1998	105 074	−1.4	98.6	12.7	111.4	94.7	16.6	...
El Salvador	1999	109 115	−2.3	97.7	12.5	110.1	95.8	14.3	...
	2000	115 610	−1.9	98.1	13.8	111.9	98.2	13.8	...
Estonia [2]	1996	52 446	0.0	100.0	2.3	102.4	84.8	17.6	10.8
Estonie [2]	1997	64 324	−3.1	96.9	2.5	99.4	81.2	18.2	11.5
	1998	73 325	−1.6	98.4	2.8	101.3	81.3	19.9	13.7

23
Relationships among the principal national accounting aggregates
As a percentage of GDP [cont.]
Relations entre les printicpaux agrégats de comptabilité nationale
En pourcentage du PIB [suite]

As a percentage of GDP – En pourcentage du PIB

Country or area Pays ou zone	Year Année	GDP in current prices (Mil. nat.cur.) PIB aux prix courants (Mil. mon.nat.)	Plus: Compensation of employees and property income from and to the rest of the world, net Plus: Rémunération des salariés et revenus de la propriété – du et au reste du monde, net	Equals: Gross national income Égale: Revenu national brut	Plus: Net current transfers from/to the rest of the world Plus: Transfers courants du/au reste du monde, net	Equals: Gross national disposable income Égale: Revenu national disponible brut	Less: Final consumption expenditure Moins: Dépense de consommation de finale	Equals: Gross savings Égale: Épargne brute	Less: Consumption of fixed capital Moins: Consommation de capital fixe
Ethiopia [8]	1997	41 465	−0.5[7]	99.5	7.0	106.5	...	7.0	...
Ethiopie [8]	1998	44 896	−0.4[7]	99.6	8.3	107.9	...	8.3	...
	1999	48 949	−0.4[7]	99.6	7.6	107.2	...	7.6	...
Fiji	1991	2 042	−1.4	105.1	−1.6	103.6	92.1	11.5	8.2
Fidji	1992	2 302	−1.7	101.5	−0.9	100.7	88.1	12.5	7.9
	1993	2 522	−0.6	100.2	−0.5	99.7	87.4	12.3	7.3
Finland [2]	1999	120 485	−1.6	98.4	−0.8	97.6	72.4	25.1	16.2
Finlande [2]	2000	131 229	−1.5	98.5	−0.6	97.9	70.1	27.8	16.0
	2001	135 057	−1.7	98.3	−0.7	97.6	71.2	26.4	16.4
France [2]	1998	1 305 851	0.5	100.5	−0.7	99.7	78.3	21.4	14.0
France [2]	1999	1 350 159	0.7	100.7	−0.7	99.9	78.1	21.8	14.0
	2000	1 404 775	0.8	100.8	−0.8	100.0	78.0	22.0	14.1
French Guiana	1990	6 526	−1.9[1]	98.1	36.3	134.4	99.4	35.0	...
Guyane française	1991	7 404	−5.8[1]	94.2	35.9	130.1	94.5	35.6	...
	1992	7 976	−6.9[1]	93.1	36.4	129.6	93.1	36.4	...
Gabon	1987	1 020 600	−6.2[1]	93.8	−4.2	89.7	72.4	17.3	19.2
Gabon	1988	1 013 600	−7.4[1]	92.6	−7.6	85.0	69.9	15.1	12.0
	1989	1 168 066	−8.6[1]	91.4	−6.1	85.3	66.8	18.5	14.5
Gambia [3]	1991	2 920	...	98.3	...	115.7	96.7	19.0	11.7
Gambie [3]	1992	3 078	...	98.7	...	114.1	94.4	19.7	12.3
	1993	3 243	...	98.5	...	114.4	93.3	21.1	12.9
Georgia [2]	1995	3 694	−2.1	97.9	4.0	101.9	91.2	10.7	11.2
Georgie [2]	1996	5 300	1.7	101.7	2.0	103.7	93.2	10.5	11.6
	1997	6 431	2.6	102.6	3.9	106.5	100.0	6.5	11.7
Germany [2]	1999	1 974 300	−0.6	99.4	−1.0	98.4	77.4	21.0	14.8
Allemagne [2]	2000	2 025 500	−0.4	99.6	−1.0	98.7	77.4	21.3	14.9
	2001	2 063 000	−0.4	99.6	−1.0	98.6	78.1	20.5	15.1
Ghana	1994	5 205 200	...	98.0	...	...	...	...	7.9
Ghana	1995	7 752 600	...	98.0	...	...	...	...	6.6
	1996	11 339 200	...	98.1	...	...	...	...	7.1
Greece [2]	1998	105 773	2.7	102.7	2.1	104.8	87.0	17.8	9.0
Grèce [2]	1999	112 660	2.0	102.0	2.6	104.6	85.9	18.7	9.1
	2000	121 516	1.6	101.6	1.9	103.5	85.3	18.2	9.3
Grenada	1984	275	...	98.9	...	...	99.1	...	...
Grenade	1985	311	...	98.9	...	...	99.0	...	...
	1986	350	...	99.2	...	...	97.7	...	...
Guadeloupe	1990	15 201	−2.5	97.5	37.3	134.8	123.6	11.2	...
Guadeloupe	1991	16 415	−3.4	96.6	35.4	132.0	118.3	13.7	...
	1992	17 972	−3.0	97.0	36.6	133.6	113.4	20.2	...
Guatemala	1996	95 479	−1.5[1]	98.5	3.4	101.9	92.1	10.2	...
Guatemala	1997	107 943	−1.3[1]	98.7	3.4	102.1	91.8	10.8	...
	1998	121 548	−0.8[1]	99.2	3.8	103.0	92.8	10.6	...
Guinea−Bissau	1986	46 973	−1.7	98.3	2.9	101.3	102.8	−1.5	...
Guinée−Bissau	1987	92 375	−0.5	99.5	4.1	103.6	100.8	2.8	...
Guyana	1999	123 665	...	90.1	...	...	68.0	...	...
Guyana	2000	130 013	...	93.8	...	...	...	...	...
	2001	133 544	...	92.8	...	...	...	...	...

23
Relationships among the principal national accounting aggregates
As a percentage of GDP [cont.]
Relations entre les princtipaux agrégats de comptabilité nationale
En pourcentage du PIB [suite]

As a percentage of GDP – En pourcentage du PIB

Country or area Pays ou zone	Year Année	GDP in current prices (Mil. nat.cur.) PIB aux prix courants (Mil. mon.nat.)	Plus: Compen- sation of employees and property income from and to the rest of the world, net Plus : Rémunération des salariés et revenus de la propriété – du et au reste du monde, net	Equals: Gross national income Égale : Revenu national brut	Plus: Net current transfers from/to the rest of the world Plus : Transfers courants du/au reste du monde, net	Equals: Gross national disposable income Égale : Revenu national disponible brut	Less: Final con- sumption expen- diture Moins : Dépense de con- somma- tion de finale	Equals: Gross savings Égale : Épargne brute	Less: Con- sumption of fixed capital Moins : Consom- mation de capital fixe
Haiti [9]	1995	35 207	...	98.7	22.8	121.5	108.1	13.4	2.2
Haïti [9]	1996	43 234	...	99.6	17.1	116.7	104.9	11.8	2.3
	1997	51 789	...	99.6	14.1	113.7	103.7	10.0	2.0
Honduras	1998	70 438	...	95.9	9.3	105.2	77.1	28.1	5.8
Honduras	1999	77 095	...	96.9	13.6	110.5	80.1	30.4	6.0
	2000	87 523	...	97.0	12.5	109.6	82.0	27.6	6.0
Hungary [2]	1997	8 540 669	-8.4	91.6	...	...	72.3	...	...
Hongrie [2]	1998	10 087 434	-8.7	91.3	...	...	72.4	...	...
	1999	11 393 499	-7.8	92.2	...	...	74.0	...	...
Iceland [2]	1998	579 286	-2.2	97.8	-0.2	97.6	79.4	18.2	13.0
Islande [2]	1999	623 419	-2.2	97.8	-0.1	97.7	81.7	16.0	13.1
	2000	673 660	-2.9	97.1	-0.1	97.0	82.7	14.3	12.9
India [5]	1998	17 409 350	-0.9	99.1	2.5	101.6	77.4	21.7	9.7
Inde [5]	1999	19 296 410	-0.8	99.2	2.8	102.0	78.2	23.2	9.5
	2000	20 879 880	-0.8	99.2	2.8	102.0	77.4	23.4	9.5
Indonesia	1998	955 754 000	...	94.4	...	...	73.5	...	5.0
Indonésie	1999	1 109 980 000	...	92.9	...	...	79.8	...	5.0
	2000	1 290 684 000	...	93.1	...	...	74.3	...	5.0
Iran (Islamic Rep. of) [2] [10]	1998	317 084 200	0.5	100.5	...	100.5	72.8	27.7	25.4
Iran (Rép. islamique d') [2] [10]	1999	426 367 300	0.0	100.0	...	100.0	68.1	31.9	22.1
	2000	582 050 300	-0.5	99.5	...	99.5	59.7	39.8	20.0
Iraq	1989	21 026	...	96.7	...	95.9	81.9	14.0	8.7
Iraq	1990	23 297	...	96.7	...	96.5	76.8	19.6	8.8
	1991	19 940	...	96.7	...	97.4	83.5	13.9	9.6
Ireland [2]	1998	77 110	-10.8	89.2	0.3	89.5	64.2	25.3	9.5
Irlande [2]	1999	89 029	-13.8	86.2	0.2	86.5	62.2	24.3	9.6
	2000	103 470	-15.0	85.0	0.2	85.2	61.1	24.1	9.8
Israel [2]	1998	405 021	-3.5	96.5	5.8	102.3	82.3	20.0	13.8
Israël [2]	1999	443 048	-4.8	95.2	5.9	101.2	81.9	19.3	14.0
	2000	480 780	-5.6	94.4	5.6	99.9	80.9	19.1	13.3
Italy [2]	1999	1 108 497	-0.7	99.3	-0.4	98.9	78.2	20.8	13.0
Italie [2]	2000	1 164 767	-0.8	99.2	-0.3	98.9	78.7	20.2	13.1
	2001	1 216 583	-0.6	99.4	-0.4	99.0	78.7	20.4	13.1
Jamaica	1985	11 674	-12.6	83.4	7.1	90.5	81.5	9.0	9.3
Jamaïque	1986	13 898	-11.2	85.2	5.7	90.9	75.7	15.2	8.3
	1987	16 640	-11.4	84.8	3.7	88.4	73.5	14.9	7.9
Japan [2]	1998	515 834 800	1.3	101.3	-0.2	101.2	71.3	29.1	18.6
Japon [2]	1999	511 837 100	1.2	101.2	-0.2	101.0	72.6	27.6	18.7
	2000	513 534 000	1.3	101.3	-0.2	101.1	72.6	27.7	19.1
Jordan	1996	4 983	-2.3	97.7	24.0	121.8	94.9	26.9	10.4
Jordanie	1997	5 193	-0.9	99.1	23.3	122.4	96.6	25.9	10.8
	1998	5 646	-0.1	99.9	19.7	119.6	97.7	22.0	10.8
Kazakhstan [2]	1998	1 733 264	-1.3	98.7	0.4	99.0	84.1	15.0	13.8
Kazakhstan [2]	1999	2 016 456	-3.1	96.9	0.9	97.8	84.0	13.8	14.2
	2000	2 599 902	-6.5	93.5	1.1	94.6	77.1	17.5	16.2
Kenya	1999	37 107	...	98.4	6.4	...	89.6	...	...
Kenya	2000	39 799	...	98.7	8.8	...	94.1	...	...
	2001	44 764	...	98.7	7.5	...	94.4	...	...

23
Relationships among the principal national accounting aggregates
As a percentage of GDP *[cont.]*
Relations entre les princtcpaux agrégats de comptabilité nationale
En pourcentage du PIB *[suite]*

As a percentage of GDP – En pourcentage du PIB

Country or area Pays ou zone	Year Année	GDP in current prices (Mil. nat.cur.) PIB aux prix courants (Mil. mon.nat.)	Plus: Compensation of employees and property income from and to the rest of the world, net Plus : Rémunération des salariés et revenus de la propriété – du et au reste du monde, net	Equals: Gross national income Égale : Revenu national brut	Plus: Net current transfers from/to the rest of the world Plus : Transfers courants du/au reste du monde, net	Equals: Gross national disposable income Égale : Revenu national disponible brut	Less: Final consumption expenditure Moins : Dépense de consommation de finale	Equals: Gross savings Égale : Épargne brute	Less: Consumption of fixed capital Moins : Consommation de capital fixe
Korea, Republic of [2]	1998	444 366 540	−1.7	98.3	1.1	99.3	65.6	33.7	13.1
Corée, Rép. de [2]	1999	482 744 175	−1.3	98.7	0.5	99.2	66.5	32.6	12.6
	2000	517 096 590	−0.5	99.5	0.1	99.6	67.5	32.1	11.6
Kuwait	1998	7 742	23.1	123.1	−7.0	116.1	86.8	29.3	9.1
Koweït	1999	9 075	17.1	117.1	−6.7	110.4	77.1	33.3	7.2
	2000	11 590	18.3	118.3	−5.0	113.3	62.8	50.5	5.9
Krygyzstan [2]	1998	34 181	−5.1	94.9	3.1	97.9	106.1	−8.2	...
Kirghizistan [2]	1999	48 744	−6.0	94.0	4.0	98.0	96.8	1.2	...
	2000	65 358	−5.9	94.1	6.0	100.1	85.7	14.4	...
Latvia [2]	1994	2 043	−0.2	99.8	3.6	103.4	78.8	24.6	12.5
Lettonie [2]	1995	2 349	0.5	100.5	1.5	102.0	84.8	17.2	12.2
	1996	2 829	0.8	100.8	1.8	102.6	89.3	13.4	10.7
Lesotho [2]	1997	4 720	38.4[1]	138.4	24.0	162.4	130.5	31.9	...
Lesotho [2]	1998	4 921	32.3[1]	132.3	19.5	151.8	133.4	18.4	...
	1999	5 637	27.1[1]	127.1	20.0	147.2	126.5	20.7	...
Liberia	1987	1 090	...	83.2	...	...	...	...	8.6
Libéria	1988	1 158	...	84.2	...	...	...	...	8.3
	1989	1 194	...	84.9	...	...	...	...	8.5
Libyan Arab Jamah.	1983	8 805	...	91.0	−0.2	90.9	72.0	18.9	5.0
Jamah. arabe libyenne	1984	8 013	...	92.7	−0.3	92.4	72.2	20.2	5.7
	1985	8 277	...	96.7	−0.2	96.5	69.2	27.3	5.8
Lithuania [2]	1995	24 103	−0.2	99.8	1.8	101.6	87.1	14.5	8.7
Lituanie [2]	1996	31 569	−1.2	98.8	1.8	100.7	85.3	15.3	9.7
	1997	38 340	−2.1	97.6	2.4	100.0	84.0	13.5	10.0
Luxembourg [2]	1998	16 975	0.9	100.9	...	...	60.0	...	13.8
Luxembourg [2]	1999	18 449	−2.3	97.7	...	...	58.3	...	13.7
	2000	20 564	−9.4	90.6	...	...	55.5	...	13.4
Madagascar									
Madagascar	1980	689 800	...	99.9	...	...	...	...	...
Malawi	1994	10 319	...	104.7	...	...	...	...	11.8
Malawi	1995	20 923	...	93.7	...	...	...	...	7.6
	1996	33 918	...	69.5	...	...	...	...	5.4
Malaysia	1998	283 243	−5.4[1]	94.6	−3.4	91.2	51.3	39.9	...
Malaisie	1999	300 340	−7.0[1]	93.0	−2.2	90.9	52.7	38.2	...
	2000	340 706	−8.4[1]	91.6	−2.2	89.4	53.3	36.2	...
Mali	1990	683 300	−1.2[1]	98.8	11.5	110.3	94.3	16.1	3.9
Mali	1991	691 400	−1.3[1]	98.7	13.0	111.9	100.4	11.5	4.0
	1992	737 400	−1.2[1]	98.8	11.4	110.2	96.4	13.8	3.5
Malta	1997	1 288	0.3[1]	100.3	...	...	...	...	...
Malte	1998	1 362	−2.0[1]	98.0	...	...	...	...	...
	1999	1 447	0.0[1]	100.0	...	...	...	...	...
Martinique	1990	19 320	−4.2	95.8	33.7	...	113.3	...	...
Martinique	1991	20 787	−4.4	95.6	30.7	...	112.8	...	...
	1992	22 093	−3.9	96.1	33.4	...	113.1	...	...
Mauritania	1987	67 216	−5.1	94.9	8.1	103.0	96.2	6.7	...
Mauritanie	1988	72 635	−5.6	94.4	7.9	102.3	93.7	8.5	...
	1989	83 520	−3.6	96.4	9.0	105.4	...	...	...

23

Relationships among the principal national accounting aggregates
As a percentage of GDP *[cont.]*
Relations entre les princticpaux agrégats de comptabilité nationale
En pourcentage du PIB *[suite]*

As a percentage of GDP − En pourcentage du PIB

Country or area Pays ou zone	Year Année	GDP in current prices (Mil. nat.cur.) PIB aux prix courants (Mil. mon.nat.)	Plus: Compen− sation of employees and property income from and to the rest of the world, net Plus : Rémunération des salariés et revenus de la propriété − du et au reste du monde, net	Equals: Gross national income Égale : Revenu national brut	Plus: Net current transfers from/to the rest of the world Plus : Transfers courants du/au reste du monde, net	Equals: Gross national disposable income Égale : Revenu national disponible brut	Less: Final con− sumption expen− diture Moins : Dépense de con− somma− tion de finale	Equals: Gross savings Égale : Épargne brute	Less: Con− sumption of fixed capital Moins : Consom− mation de capital fixe
Mauritius [2]	1999	107 370	−0.4	99.6	3.4	102.9	77.2	25.7	...
Maurice [2]	2000	118 478	−0.7	99.3	1.4	100.7	75.5	25.2	...
	2001	131 465	−0.3	99.7	1.7	101.2	74.7	26.7	...
Mexico [2]	1997	3 174 275	−3.1	96.9	1.3	98.2	74.2	24.0	10.2
Mexique [2]	1998	3 846 350	−3.1	96.9	1.4	98.3	77.8	20.5	10.3
	1999	4 583 762	−2.7	97.3	1.3	98.6	78.1	20.6	10.1
Mongolia	1996	659 698	...	98.8	...	...	...	...	6.0
Mongolie	1997	846 344	...	95.0	...	...	...	...	8.4
	1998	833 727	...	99.3	...	...	...	...	10.5
Morocco	1995	281 702	−4.0	96.1	7.0	103.1	85.8	17.3	...
Maroc	1996	319 630	...	...	7.0	103.9	83.9	20.0	...
	1997	319 290	...	...	6.6	103.5	83.2	20.4	...
Mozambique	1984	109 000	...	100.0	...	106.4	...	3.7	
Mozambique	1985	147 000	...	100.0	...	102.7	...	2.7	
	1986	167 000	...	100.6	...	101.2	...	...	
Myanmar [5]	1996	791 980	0.0[1]	100.0	...	100.0	88.5	11.4	2.3
Myanmar [5]	1997	1 109 554	0.0[1]	100.0	...	100.0	88.1	11.9	1.9
	1998	1 559 996	0.0[1]	100.0	...	100.0	89.4	10.6	1.7
Namibia [2]	1999	20 681	−0.4	99.5	12.3	111.8	89.5	22.3	13.8
Namibie [2]	2000	23 995	1.0	101.0	12.5	113.5	87.6	25.9	12.9
	2001	27 231	1.1	101.0	11.0	112.0	88.4	23.6	13.1
Nepal [11]	1996	248 913	1.4[1]	101.4	0.4	101.8	86.2	15.6	1.8
Népal [11]	1997	280 513	1.7[1]	101.7	0.4	102.0	86.0	16.0	2.0
	1998	296 547	2.0[1]	102.0	0.4	102.4	90.5	11.9	2.4
Netherlands [2]	1998	354 194	−1.6	98.4	−0.8	97.6	72.4	25.2	15.0
Pays−Bas [2]	1999	373 664	0.4	100.4	−0.6	99.8	73.1	26.7	15.3
	2000	401 089	0.9	100.9	−0.7	100.2	72.6	27.6	15.4
Netherlands Antilles	1992	3 548	3.4	103.4	...	107.9	83.6	24.3	11.4
Antilles néerlandaises	1993	3 766	1.6	101.6	...	105.8	85.4	20.4	12.6
	1994	4 218	3.8	103.8	...	106.6	90.4	16.2	13.1
New Zealand [2] [5]	1997	99 631	−6.4	93.6	0.5	94.1	78.4	15.7	13.5
Nouvelle−Zélande [2] [5]	1998	101 169	−4.9	95.1	0.4	95.4	79.6	15.8	14.0
	1999	105 852	−6.2	93.8	0.5	94.2	79.3	14.9	13.8
Nicaragua	1998	21 881	−4.2	95.8	9.7	105.5	109.9	−4.4	...
Nicaragua	1999	26 130	−3.1	96.9	13.6	110.5	114.1	−3.6	...
	2000	30 740	−2.9	97.1	13.2	110.3	111.0	−0.6	...
Niger	1982	663 022	−3.1	96.9	1.5	98.4	85.1	13.3	8.7
Niger	1983	687 142	−3.1	96.9	1.1	98.0	88.8	9.2	9.3
	1984	638 406	...	96.2	1.6	97.8	88.2	9.6	10.4
Nigeria	1992	549 809	−11.7	88.3	2.3	90.6	77.2	13.4	3.0
Nigéria	1993	701 473	−10.5	89.5	2.5	92.0	80.6	11.5	2.5
	1994	914 334	−7.2	92.8	1.2	94.0	85.5	8.5	2.0
Norway [2]	1998	1 114 826	−0.7	99.3	−1.0	98.2	71.0	27.3	16.2
Norvège [2]	1999	1 197 457	−1.1	98.9	−0.9	98.0	69.4	28.6	16.3
	2000	1 423 865	−0.9	99.1	−0.9	98.1	61.7	36.4	14.9
Oman [2]	1998	5 416	−3.7	96.3	...	86.7	83.5	3.2	12.0
Oman [2]	1999	6 041	−2.9	95.1	...	87.7	74.0	13.6	11.2
	2000	7 623	−2.0	...	...	...	60.2	...	9.1

23
Relationships among the principal national accounting aggregates
As a percentage of GDP [cont.]
Relations entre les printicpaux agrégats de comptabilité nationale
En pourcentage du PIB [suite]

As a percentage of GDP¹ – En pourcentage du PIB

Country or area Pays ou zone	Year Année	GDP in current prices (Mil. nat.cur.) PIB aux prix courants (Mil. mon.nat.)	Plus: Compen- sation of employees and property income from and to the rest of the world, net Plus : Rémunération des salariés et revenus de la propriété – du et au reste du monde, net	Equals: Gross national income Égale : Revenu national brut	Plus: Net current transfers from/to the rest of the world Plus : Transferts courants du/au reste du monde, net	Equals: Gross national disposable income Égale : Revenu national disponible brut	Less: Final con- sumption expen- diture Moins : Dépense de con- somma- tion de finale	Equals: Gross savings Égale : Épargne brute	Less: Con- sumption of fixed capital Moins : Consom- mation de capital fixe
Pakistan [3]	1998	2 938 379	...	99.1	...	...	86.0	...	6.4
Pakistan [3]	1999	3 182 822	...	98.6	...	...	86.0	...	6.6
	2000	3 472 149	...	98.2	...	...	87.3	...	6.6
Panama	1998	9 345	−6.5	93.5	1.7	95.2	72.7	23.1	7.1
Panama	1999	9 637	−8.2	91.8	1.8	93.6	70.9	22.7	7.5
	2000	10 019	−7.0	93.0	1.8	94.8	72.6	22.1	7.5
Papua New Guinea [2]	1997	7 064	−4.4	88.0	1.5	89.6	77.6	12.0	...
Papouasie–Nouv.–	1998	7 863	−4.4	88.8	0.7	89.5	77.6	11.9	...
Guinée [2]	1999	8 781	−4.1	89.9	0.9	90.8	86.7	4.1	...
Paraguay	1993	11 991 719	...	100.4	...	100.4	88.0	12.4	7.8
Paraguay	1994	14 960 131	...	100.5	...	100.5	95.2	5.3	7.8
	1995	17 699 000	...	100.9	...	100.9	92.5	8.4	7.8
Peru	1989	115	−0.9	99.1	0.9	100.0	79.1	20.0	7.0
Pérou	1990	6 790	−2.4	97.0	0.6	97.6	84.4	13.3	6.3
	1991	32 936	−2.1	96.9	...	98.1	81.7	16.4	4.3
Philippines	1998	2 665 060	5.1	105.1	5.0	110.2	87.6	22.6	8.9
Philippines	1999	2 976 904	5.3	105.3	2.0	107.4	85.7	21.7	8.5
	2000	3 302 589	5.7	105.7	0.1	105.8	83.5	22.3	8.3
Poland [2]	1998	553 560	−0.7	99.3	1.8	101.1	79.0	22.0	...
Pologne [2]	1999	615 115	−0.7	99.3	1.5	100.8	80.0	20.9	...
	2000	684 926	−0.9	99.1	...	...	80.8	...	...
Portugal [2]	1998	101 323	−1.6	98.4	3.2	101.6	81.1	20.5	15.5
Portugal [2]	1999	108 217	−1.5	98.5	3.0	101.5	82.0	19.4	15.5
	2000	115 262	−2.1	97.9	3.0	100.9	81.9	19.0	15.6
Puerto Rico [3]	1998	57 841	−34.3	65.7	15.2	80.9	71.8	6.0	7.5
Porto Rico [3]	1999	61 045	−32.6	67.4	13.5	81.6	70.8	5.2	7.6
	2000	67 897	−35.5	64.5	13.2	77.6	66.9	3.3	7.1
Republic of Moldova [2]	1999	12 322	2.9	102.9	6.5	109.4	90.0	19.4	...
République de Moldova [2]	2000	16 020	5.0	105.0	11.2	116.2	103.0	13.1	...
	2001	19 019	4.2	...	...	...	...	...	...
Réunion	1990	28 374	−2.5¹	97.5	44.3	141.7	108.1	33.6	...
Réunion	1991	31 339	0.1¹	100.7	42.7	143.4	103.5	39.9	...
	1992	33 787	−1.5¹	98.4	43.6	142.1	104.5	37.6	...
Romania [2]	1994	49 773 200	...	100.0	2.2	102.2	77.3	24.9	...
Roumanie [2]	1995	72 135 500	...	100.0	1.2	101.2	81.3	19.9	...
	1996	108 390 900	...	100.0	...	101.2	83.0	18.3	...
Russian Federation [2]	1998	2 741 050	−4.2	95.8	−0.1	95.7	76.6	19.0	...
Fédération de Russie [2]	1999	4 766 835	−4.0	96.0	0.3	96.3	68.8	27.5	...
	2000	7 302 233	−2.6	97.4	0.0	97.4	61.6	35.8	...
Rwanda	1987	171 430	−1.6	98.4	2.5	100.9	93.5	7.4	6.5
Rwanda	1988	177 920	−2.0	98.0	2.9	100.9	93.6	7.3	6.9
	1989	190 220	−1.2	98.8	2.4	101.3	95.4	5.9	7.6
Saint Kitts–Nevis	1996	663	...	108.8	6.8	115.6	81.2	34.4	...
Saint–Kitts–et–Nevis	1997	742	...	107.6	5.8	113.3	71.3	42.0	...
	1998	775	...	106.2	10.6	116.8	73.4	43.4	...
Saint Lucia	1996	1 543	...	92.6	3.6	96.2	81.4	14.8	...
Sainte–Lucie	1997	1 562	...	92.3	3.6	95.9	83.7	12.3	...
	1998	1 695	...	92.8	3.4	96.2	84.0	12.2	...

23
Relationships among the principal national accounting aggregates
As a percentage of GDP *[cont.]*
Relations entre les printicpaux agrégats de comptabilité nationale
En pourcentage du PIB *[suite]*

As a percentage of GDP — En pourcentage du PIB

Country or area Pays ou zone	Year Année	GDP in current prices (Mil. nat.cur.) PIB aux prix courants (Mil. mon.nat.)	Plus: Compen- sation of employees and property income from and to the rest of the world, net Plus : Rémunération des salariés et revenus de la propriété – du et au reste du monde, net	Equals: Gross national income Égale : Revenu national brut	Plus: Net current transfers from/to the rest of the world Plus : Transfers courants du/au reste du monde, net	Equals: Gross national disposable income Égale : Revenu national disponible brut	Less: Final con- sumption expen- diture Moins : Dépense de con- somma- tion de finale	Equals: Gross savings Égale : Épargne brute	Less: Con- sumption of fixed capital Moins : Consom- mation de capital fixe
Saint Vincent–Grenadines	1998	858	−4.5	95.3	3.3	98.6	87.9	10.7	...
St.–Vincent–et–Gren.	1999	890	−6.6	95.6	4.4	100.0	85.8	14.2	...
	2000	924	−5.8	94.2	5.5	99.7	82.1	17.5	...
Saudi Arabia [3]	1996	529 250	−2.8	97.2	−13.2	84.0	65.5	18.5	10.0
Arabie saoudite [3]	1997	548 620	−2.6	97.4	−12.3	85.1	65.2	19.9	10.0
	1998	480 773	−1.6	98.4	−13.4	84.9	73.9	11.1	10.0
Senegal	1996	2 380 000	...	108.1	...	...	91.0	...	...
Sénégal	1997	2 554 300	...	104.1	...	...	88.8	...	...
	1998	2 746 000	...	104.5	...	...	87.3	...	...
Seychelles	1997	2 830	...	98.4	...	...	79.0	...	...
Seychelles	1998	3 201	...	97.2	...	...	80.9	...	...
	1999	3 379	...	95.9	...	...	82.9	...	...
Sierra Leone [3]	1988	43 947	...	100.9	0.6	101.5	94.3	7.3	5.8
Sierra Leone [3]	1989	82 837	...	100.8	0.5	101.3	91.3	10.0	5.9
	1990	150 175	...	95.0	0.7	95.7	88.4	7.3	5.6
Singapore	1998	137 464	6.2	106.2	−1.3	104.9	49.5	57.3	13.9
Singapour	1999	142 111	8.0	108.0	−1.4	106.6	50.3	58.4	14.3
	2000	159 042	6.6	106.6	−1.5	105.2	50.4	54.9	13.2
Slovakia [2]	1996	606 094	−0.2	99.7	1.03	100.8	74.4	26.4	17.3
Slovaquie [2]	1997	686 087	−0.6	99.4	0.9	100.3	73.2	27.1	18.9
	1998	750 761	−0.7	99.3	1.7	101.0	74.8	26.2	19.8
Slovenia [2] Slovénie [2]	1993	1 435 095	−0.4	...	...	...	...	...	...
Solomon Islands	1984	222	...	94.2	...	100.8	78.2	22.6	5.9
Iles Salomon	1985	237	...	95.0	...	101.0	91.6	9.4	6.7
	1986	253	...	92.6	...	115.7	94.8	20.9	7.6
Somalia	1985	87 290	...	97.8	10.1	107.9	101.1	6.8	...
Somalie	1986	118 781	...	96.3	14.2	110.5	98.8	11.7	...
	1987	169 608	...	96.8	21.3	118.0	99.9	18.2	...
South Africa [2]	1998	739 504	−2.3[1]	97.7	−0.6	97.0	82.1	14.9	13.1
Afrique du Sud [2]	1999	802 840	−2.4[1]	97.6	−0.7	96.9	81.4	15.5	13.4
	2000	887 795	−2.5[1]	97.5	−0.7	96.5	80.9	15.6	13.4
Spain [2]	1998	527 957	−0.9	99.1	0.2	99.3	76.7	22.6	12.9
Espagne [2]	1999	565 483	−1.2	98.8	0.3	99.0	76.8	22.2	13.1
	2000	608 787	−1.1	98.9	0.0	98.9	76.6	22.3	13.6
Sri Lanka	1998	1 011 349	−1.1[1]	98.9	5.4	104.3	80.3	24.0	5.1
Sri Lanka	1999	1 100 825	−1.6[1]	98.4	5.7	104.1	82.0	22.1	5.1
	2000	1 245 041	−1.8[1]	98.2	5.9	104.1	84.8	19.3	5.1
Sudan [3]	1991	421 819	...	85.5	...	104.0	86.0	18.0	7.0
Soudan [3]	1992	948 448	...	99.7	...	102.2	88.2	14.0	6.4
	1993	1 881 289	...	99.8	...	100.6	88.3	12.3	7.1
Suriname	1998	358 114	−0.1	99.9	−0.2	99.7	105.3	−5.6	10.8
Suriname	1999	603 483	0.0	100.0	−0.2	99.7	...	...	...
	2000	873 865	1.3	101.3	−0.3	101.0	...	...	...
Swaziland [2][6]	1998	7 449	...	104.1	9.9	114.0	96.7	3.3	...
Swaziland [2][6]	1999	8 410	...	106.3	9.1	115.4	96.1	3.9	...
	2000	9 673	...	105.5	6.9	112.4	95.5	4.5	...

23

Relationships among the principal national accounting aggregates
As a percentage of GDP *[cont.]*
Relations entre les printicpaux agrégats de comptabilité nationale
En pourcentage du PIB *[suite]*

As a percentage of GDP – En pourcentage du PIB

Country or area Pays ou zone	Year Année	GDP in current prices (Mil. nat.cur.) PIB aux prix courants (Mil. mon.nat.)	Plus: Compen- sation of employees and property income from and to the rest of the world, net Plus : Rémunération des salariés et revenus de la propriété – du et au reste du monde, net	Equals: Gross national income Égale : Revenu national brut	Plus: Net current transfers from/to the rest of the world Plus : Transfers courants du/au reste du monde, net	Equals: Gross national disposable income Égale : Revenu national disponible brut	Less: Final con- sumption expen- diture Moins : Dépense de con- somma- tion de finale	Equals: Gross savings Égale : Épargne brute	Less: Con- sumption of fixed capital Moins : Consom- mation de capital fixe
Sweden [2]	1999	2 004 651	−1.0	99.0	−0.9	98.0	76.9	21.2	13.9
Suède [2]	2000	2 098 451	−0.8	99.2	−0.9	98.3	76.7	21.6	14.4
	2001	2 167 196	−1.6	98.4	−1.0	97.4	76.5	20.9	15.2
Switzerland	1998	379 989	7.3	107.3	−1.4	105.9	75.2	30.7	15.8
Suisse	1999	388 568	8.0	108.0	−1.4	106.7	75.0	31.6	16.0
	2000	404 392	10.2	110.2	...	...	74.0	...	...
Thailand	1997	4 740 249	−2.6	97.4	0.4	97.8	64.8	33.0	13.3
Thaïlande	1998	4 628 431	−3.5	96.5	0.4	97.0	65.5	31.5	14.6
	1999	4 615 388	−2.7	97.3	0.3	97.6	67.7	29.9	15.2
TYFR of Macedonia [2]	1991	935	...	99.4	−0.4	99.0	85.5	13.5	12.0
L'ex−R.y. Macédoine [2]	1992	12 005	...	96.9	−0.4	96.6	83.8	12.8	27.1
	1993	58 145	...	97.7	0.7	98.4	88.9	9.5	22.2
Togo [6] Togo [6]	1980	238 872	−1.8	98.2	6.3	104.4	80.3	24.1	7.5
Tonga [6]	1981	54	6.3	106.3	23.7	130.0	136.9	15.1	4.6
Tonga [6]	1982	64	6.9	106.9	35.8	142.7	137.9	29.0	4.5
	1983	73	4.4	104.4	27.1	130.5	140.0	10.2	4.0
Trinidad and Tobago [2]	1998	39 796	−6.3	93.7	0.4	94.0	78.1	15.9	11.1
Trinité−et−Tobago [2]	1999	43 254	−5.8	94.2	0.5	94.7	73.4	21.2	12.0
	2000	50 872	−7.8	92.2	0.5	92.7	68.5	24.2	11.9
Tunisia [2]	1997	20 898	−4.8	95.2	4.1	99.3	76.0	23.3	9.5
Tunisie [2]	1998	22 581	−4.2	95.8	4.1	100.0	76.5	23.5	9.6
	1999	24 672	−4.1	95.9	4.2	100.1	76.0	24.1	9.6
Turkey	1998	52 224 945 000	2.5	102.5	0.0	102.5	81.9	20.6	6.3
Turquie	1999	77 415 272 000	1.1	101.1	0.0	101.1	87.4	13.7	6.9
	2000	124 982 454 000	0.8	100.8	0.0	100.8	85.2	15.6	6.9
Ukraine [2]	1998	102 593	−2.0	98.0	2.6	100.6	81.5	19.1	18.8
Ukraine [2]	1999	130 442	−2.7	97.3	2.2	99.5	77.0	22.5	17.8
	2000	170 070	−3.0	97.0	2.9	99.9	75.8	24.1	17.8
United Arab Emirates	1988	87 106	0.3	100.3	−1.2	99.1	65.8	33.3	16.5
Emirats arabes unis	1989	100 976	0.4	100.4	−0.7	99.7	61.7	38.0	15.0
	1990	124 008	−1.0	99.0	−8.9	90.1	54.9	35.1	13.0
United Kingdom [2]	1998	859 805	1.1	101.1	−0.5	100.6	82.9	17.7	11.2
Royaume−Uni [2]	1999	901 269	0.1	100.1	−0.4	99.7	83.9	15.8	11.2
	2000	944 724	0.6	100.6	−0.7	99.9	84.0	15.9	11.2
United Rep. of Tanzania	1992	1 130 596	...	93.8	25.0	118.8	97.8	20.9	3.2
Rép.−Unie de Tanzanie	1993	1 404 369	...	95.7	20.8	116.5	95.9	20.6	2.6
	1994	1 822 570	...	96.2	20.9	117.1	97.3	19.8	2.7
United States [2]	1998	8 720 200	0.0	100.3	−0.5	99.8	81.5	18.3	11.6
Etats−Unis [2]	1999	9 206 900	−0.1	100.7	−0.5	100.2	82.2	18.0	11.8
	2000	9 810 200	−0.1	101.2	−0.6	100.6	83.0	17.7	12.0
Uruguay	1998	234 267	−1.4[1]	98.6	0.3	98.9	84.9	14.1	...
Uruguay	1999	237 142	−1.4[1]	98.6	0.4	99.0	86.1	12.9	...
	2000	242 637	−1.7[1]	98.3	0.3	98.6	87.5	11.1	...
Vanuatu	1996	28 227	...	91.1	...	...	...	...	...
Vanuatu	1997	29 477	...	91.7	...	...	...	...	...
	1998	29 545	...	93.5	...	...	...	...	...

23
Relationships among the principal national accounting aggregates
As a percentage of GDP *[cont.]*
Relations entre les printicpaux agrégats de comptabilité nationale
En pourcentage du PIB *[suite]*

As a percentage of GDP − En pourcentage du PIB

Country or area Pays ou zone	Year Année	GDP in current prices (Mil. nat.cur.) PIB aux prix courants (Mil. mon.nat.)	Plus: Compen− sation of employees and property income from and to the rest of the world, net Plus : Rémunération des salariés et revenus de la propriété − du et au reste du monde, net	Equals: Gross national income Égale : Revenu national brut	Plus: Net current transfers from/to the rest of the world Plus : Transfers courants du/au reste du monde, net	Equals: Gross national disposable income Égale : Revenu national disponible brut	Less: Final con− sumption expen− diture Moins : Dépense de con− somma− tion de finale	Equals: Gross savings Égale : Épargne brute	Less: Con− sumption of fixed capital Moins : Consom− mation de capital fixe
Venezuela	1998	52 482 466	−2.0	98.0	−0.1	97.9	79.3	18.5	7.8
Venezuela	1999	62 577 039	−1.5	98.5	0.1	98.6	76.6	22.0	7.6
	2000	82 450 674	−1.0	99.0	−0.2	98.8	70.7	28.2	7.2
Yemen [2]	1998	849 321	−5.6	94.4	19.1	113.5	82.5	31.0	9.3
Yémen [2]	1999	1 132 619	−9.3	90.7	17.2	107.9	81.8	24.7	8.6
	2000	1 379 812	−13.4	86.6	17.6	104.1	71.8	37.3	8.2
Yugoslavia, SFR	1988	15 833	...	105.0	...	...	64.3	...	12.2
Yougoslavie, SFR	1989	235 395	...	106.9	...	...	61.9	...	12.1
	1990	1 147 787	...	108.7	...	...	83.7	...	11.2
Zimbabwe	1996	84 759	−3.5	96.5	2.8	99.3	81.1	18.2	...
Zimbabwe	1997	102 074	−4.9	95.1	2.9	98.0	88.9	9.1	...
	1998	135 722	−6.7	93.3	4.0	97.2	84.6	12.6	...

Source:
United Nations Statistics Division, New York, the
national accounts database.

Source:
Organisation des Nations Unies, Division de statistique,
New York, la base de données sur les comptes nationaux.

1   Property income − from and to the rest of the world, net.
2   Data classified according to SNA 93.
3   Data refer to fiscal years beginning 1 July.

4   Data in Russian rubles.
5   Data refer to fiscal years beginning 1 April.

6   Data refer to fiscal years ending 30 June.

7   Compensation of employees − from and to the rest of the world, net.
8   Data refer to fiscal years ending 7 July.

9   Data refer to fiscal years ending 30 September.

10   Data refer to fiscal years beginning 21 March.

11   Data refer to fiscal years ending 15 July.

12   Thousands.

1   Revenus de la propriété − du et au reste du monde, net.
2   Les données sont classifiées selon le SCN 1993.
3   Les données se réfèrent aux exercices budgétaires
    commençant le 1er juillet.
4   Les données sont exprimées en roubles russiens.
5   Les données se réfèrent aux exercices budgétaires
    commençant le 1er avril.
6   Les données se réfèrent aux exercices budgétaires
    finissant le 30 juin.
7   Rémunération des salariés − du et au reste du monde, net.
8   Les données se réfèrent aux exercices budgétaires
    finissant le 7 juillet.
9   Les données se réfèrent aux exercices budgétaires
    finissant le 30 septembre.
10   Les données se réfèrent aux exercices budgétaires
    commençant le 21 mars.
11   Les données se réfèrent aux exercices budgétaires
    finissant le 15 juillet.
12   Milliers.

24
Government final consumption expenditure by function in current prices
Percentage distribution
Dépenses de consommation finale des administrations publiques, par fonction, aux prix courants
Répartition en pourcentage

Country or area Pays ou zone	Year Année	General govt. final consumption expenditure (M. nat'l. curr.) Dépenses de consommation finale des administrations publiques (M. monn. nat.)	General public services Services généraux des administrations publiques (%)	Defence Défense (%)	Public order and safety Ordre et sécurité publics (%)	Environment protection Protection de l'environnement (%)	Health Santé (%)	Education Enseignement (%)	Social protection Protection sociale (%)	Other functions Autres fonctions (%)
Anguilla	1998	54	40.7	...	9.3	...	18.5	16.7	1.9	14.8
Anguilla	1999	64	42.2	...	9.4	...	15.6	17.2	1.6	15.6
	2000	58	41.4	...	10.3	...	15.5	19.0	3.4	10.3
Argentina	1996	43 617	10.8	4.5	3.2	0.2	8.4	5.9[1]	43.2	8.1
Argentine	1997	45 156	9.4	4.4	3.1	0.2	7.1	6.0[1]	42.0	8.0
	1998	46 463	9.5	4.2	3.0	0.2	6.6	6.0[1]	41.0	7.9
Australia [2]	1994	79 341	15.1	11.6	7.3	...	17.6	20.7	5.6	21.9
Australie [2]	1995	83 437	15.0	10.9	7.6	...	18.2	20.3	5.8	22.2
	1996	86 419	15.4	10.1	7.8	...	18.5	21.0	5.8	21.5
Austria [3]	1998	37 248	14.9	4.8	7.4	0.8	27.6	27.2	4.0	13.4
Autriche [3]	1999	38 671	14.9	4.8	7.4	0.8	27.1	27.3	4.6	13.2
	2000	39 739	14.7	4.7	7.3	0.7	27.5	27.5	4.4	13.1
Bahamas [3]	1993	408	17.4	4.2	14.5	...	18.6	24.0	4.2	17.4
Bahamas [3]	1994	511	20.2	3.7	13.3	...	18.0	23.1	3.5	18.8
	1995	484	18.4	3.9	14.5	...	18.0	22.1	3.9	19.4
Bangladesh [2,3]	1998	88 546	15.3	24.3	13.0	...	10.3	17.1	1.0	19.0
Bangladesh [2,3]	1999	92 450	12.9	24.0	13.4	...	12.3	16.6	1.4	19.2
	2000	105 351	12.9	22.0	12.9	...	12.0	16.5	1.4	22.3
Belgium [3]	1998	47 711	12.0	6.4	6.6	1.1	28.0	29.1	6.0	10.9
Belgique [3]	1999	50 002	12.8	6.0	6.7	0.9	28.3	28.3	6.0	11.1
	2000	52 529	12.6	5.8	6.7	1.0	28.8	27.8	6.2	11.1
Belize	1990	279	12.7	3.4	7.9	...	6.8	15.3	3.3	50.7
Belize	1991	321	16.6	3.4	7.0	...	6.6	16.8	4.0	45.7
Bolivia [3]	1991	2 310	74.7	...	...	...	...	7.7	1.9	15.6
Bolivie [3]	1992	2 833	76.2	...	...	...	...	8.1	1.9	13.7
	1993	3 270	75.9	...	...	...	...	9.0	2.4	12.7
Botswana [3,4]	1998	5 453	46.6[5]	...	...	...	6.1	25.0	3.6	18.6
Botswana [3,4]	1999	6 579	45.4[5]	...	...	...	6.2	25.0	2.9	20.6
	2000	7 525	44.0[5]	...	...	...	6.5	26.4	3.4	19.7
Brazil [3]	1998	174 847	71.1	...	...	...	11.5	16.5	...	...
Brésil [3]	1999	185 858	72.0	...	...	...	11.5	16.5	...	...
	2000	209 334	73.1	...	...	...	11.3	15.7	...	...
Cayman Islands	1990	94	26.6[17]	...	14.9	...	16.0	14.9	4.3	23.4
Iles Caïmanes	1991	103	27.2[17]	...	14.6	...	14.6	14.6	5.8	23.3
Colombia	1992	3 965 104	29.5	10.8	...	...	7.7	24.8	8.9	18.2
Colombie	1993	5 108 076	28.5	10.2	...	...	11.0	24.0	8.2	18.0
	1994	7 652 736	36.2	9.8	...	...	14.3	21.0	8.6	10.1
Costa Rica [3]	1998	469 886	35.6	...	...	...	32.6	31.7	...	...
Costa Rica [3]	1999	565 207	34.9	...	...	...	33.1	31.9	...	...
	2000	652 509	34.4	...	...	...	32.8	32.8	...	...
Croatia [3]	1996	30 973	6.2	25.1	12.0	...	0.5	11.6	14.2	30.4
Croatie [3]	1997	34 395	6.3	20.3	12.1	...	0.5	11.8	18.8	30.1
	1998	41 390	8.2	17.8	10.3	...	2.0	11.3	19.4	31.1
Cyprus	1992	591	10.3	32.3	8.7	...	9.5	16.3	11.6	11.2
Chypre	1993	553	13.0	16.3	10.2	...	11.7	19.7	15.0	14.1
	1994	608	11.8	16.2	9.4	...	11.6	20.4	16.1	14.5
Denmark [3]	1998	300 452	7.3	6.3	3.3	...	19.4	22.9	26.2	14.6
Danemark [3]	1999	313 888	7.5	6.2	3.3	...	19.6	22.7	26.4	14.4
	2000	325 784	7.7	6.0	3.3	...	19.7	22.3	27.0	14.0
Dominican Republic [3]	1994	8 265	66.3	...	2.7	...	12.8	18.1	...	...
République dominicaine [3]	1995	9 115	61.2	...	2.7	...	12.6	23.4	...	...
	1996	10 843	61.1	...	2.3	...	12.5	24.1	...	...

24

Government final consumption expenditure by function in current prices
Dépenses de consommation finale des administrations publiques, par fonction, aux prix courants
Percentage distribution [cont.]
Répartition en pourcentage [suite]

Country or area Pays ou zone	Year Année	General govt. final consumption expenditure (M. nat'l. curr.) Dépenses de consommation finale des administrations publiques (M. monn. nat.)	General public services Services généraux des adminis- trations publiques (%)	Defence Défense (%)	Public order and safety Ordre et sécurité publics (%)	Environ- ment protection Protection de l'envir- onnement (%)	Health Santé (%)	Education Enseigne- ment (%)	Social protection Protection sociale (%)	Other functions Autres fonctions (%)
Ecuador	1990	777 131	13.0	14.5	7.0	...	4.8	27.5	6.1	27.0
Equateur	1991	1 009 000	13.0	15.0	7.1	...	4.6	27.8	6.2	26.4
	1992	1 498 000	12.8	15.9	7.3	...	3.9	26.8	7.8	25.4
Estonia [3]	1994	6 790	12.9	4.3	12.5	...	16.5	29.2	4.3	20.3
Estonie [3]	1995	10 350	11.2	4.5	11.2	...	17.7	27.8	3.9	23.8
	1996	12 632	11.0	4.6	11.7	...	17.3	27.8	4.1	23.4
Fiji	1993	467	28.1	9.9	...	...	11.6	24.8	0.2	25.5
Fidji	1994	441	25.6	10.2	...	...	13.2	25.4	0.2	25.2
	1995	451	26.8	10.0	...	...	12.9	24.8	0.2	25.3
Finland [3]	1998	25 132	8.7	7.5	5.3	1.0	23.5	23.6	15.9	14.5
Finlande [3]	1999	26 124	9.8	6.8	5.3	1.0	23.5	23.5	15.8	14.4
	2000	27 068	10.0	6.5	5.3	1.0	24.0	23.3	16.2	13.7
France	1991	1 238 998	12.2	15.7	4.6	...	17.4	26.2	7.4	16.5
France	1992	1 320 450	12.1	15.9	4.6	...	17.3	26.2	7.4	16.5
	1993	1 402 898	12.1	15.8	4.7	...	17.3	26.0	7.5	16.6
Gambia [2]	1990	819[6]	22.0	...	...	...	6.4	12.9[7]	0.1	58.7
Gambie [2]	1991	804[6]	22.2	...	...	...	5.7	12.6[7]	0.1	59.5
Georgia [3]	1993	1 213[8]	...	1.9	8.2	...	0.6	5.7	0.5	83.2
Géorgie [3]	1994	119 012[8]	...	5.4	10.1	...	3.2	4.8	9.0	67.5
	1995	295	...	12.9	45.8	...	6.1	10.2	12.5	12.5
Germany [3]	1998	369 536	11.9	6.8	8.5	0.4	32.0	19.0	15.7	5.8
Allemagne [3]	1999	378 402	11.8	6.8	8.4	0.4	32.0	18.8	16.0	5.9
	2000	384 481	11.9	6.4	8.4	0.4	32.3	18.6	16.1	5.9
Greece	1990	2 220 840	41.4	25.3	...	...	11.9	15.7	1.5	4.3
Grèce	1991	2 548 186	42.6	24.7	...	...	11.7	15.6	1.3	4.1
Honduras	1995	3 495	27.8	9.5	...	...	20.5	39.1	...	3.1
Honduras	1996	4 556	26.0	8.2	...	...	27.6	36.7	...	1.6
	1997	5 377	31.0	7.3	...	...	24.9	35.2	...	1.5
Hungary	1992	780 638	15.0	6.3	7.5	...	16.3	22.2	9.4	23.3
Hongrie	1993	1 013 524	15.1	12.8	7.3	...	14.4	20.4	8.7	21.3
	1994	1 145 444	17.1	6.2	8.0	...	15.7	21.4	9.3	22.3
Iceland [3]	1996	98 630	7.9	...	5.7	...	32.1	21.2	8.2	17.8
Islande [3]	1997	105 445	7.9	...	5.7	...	31.8	21.6	8.2	18.0
	1998	120 166	7.9	...	5.9	...	32.3	22.3	8.7	16.7
India [9]	1997	1 335 550[6]	23.1	31.2[10]	...	...	6.3	16.1	3.5	19.8
Inde [9]	1998	1 679 310[6]	23.3	29.4[10]	...	...	6.3	16.1	3.5	21.4
	1999	1 968 680[6]	23.3	28.5[10]	...	...	6.5	16.7	3.5	21.5
Iran, Islamic Rep. of [3][11]	1998	50 460 600	3.7	19.7	4.2	...	5.1	18.9	10.6	37.7
Iran, Rép. islamique d' [3][11]	1999	65 412 400	3.9	20.1	4.4	...	5.3	19.6	10.9	35.8
	2000	83 794 900	3.8	22.4	4.3	...	5.1	19.1	10.6	34.5
Ireland [3]	1998	11 207	10.5	5.2	9.9	...	34.7	17.5	3.3	19.0
Irlande [3]	1999	12 464	11.5	4.7	9.1	...	36.9	17.2	3.1	17.5
	2000	13 880	11.5	4.7	9.1	...	36.9	17.2	3.1	17.5
Israel [3]	1997	102 754	7.3	31.5	5.3	3.0	16.6	24.4	4.0	7.8
Israël [3]	1998	112 189	7.8	31.5	5.5	3.1	16.5	24.1	4.1	7.4
	1999	122 274	7.9	31.5	5.5	3.0	16.3	24.0	4.1	7.6
Italy [3]	1998	192 517	12.3	5.6	11.2	0.9	29.7	25.6	3.7	11.0
Italie [3]	1999	200 488	12.1	6.2	10.9	1.2	30.0	25.3	3.7	10.6
	2000	209 500	12.0	6.2	10.8	1.4	30.6	24.4	4.0	10.6
Japan [3][9]	1997	79 618 500	9.4	5.3	7.2	6.0	31.6	22.4	4.7	13.3
Japon [3][9]	1998	81 220 900	9.6	5.2	7.2	6.1	31.2	22.1	4.9	13.7
	1999	83 288 400	9.8	5.0	7.0	6.3	31.6	21.5	4.9	13.8
Jordan	1993	939	53.6[5]	...	...	...	10.2	21.9	1.0	13.4
Jordanie	1994	986	59.3[5]	...	...	...	8.2	20.4	1.0	11.1
	1995	1 111	60.0[5]	...	...	...	8.3	21.3	0.9	9.5

24

Government final consumption expenditure by function in current prices
Dépenses de consommation finale des administrations publiques, par fonction, aux prix courants
Percentage distribution *[cont.]*
Répartition en pourcentage *[suite]*

Country or area Pays ou zone	Year Année	General govt. final consumption expenditure (M. nat'l. curr.) Dépenses de consommation finale des administrations publiques (M. monn. nat.)	General public services Services généraux des adminis– trations publiques (%)	Defence Défense (%)	Public order and safety Ordre et securité publics (%)	Environ– ment protection Protection de l'envir– onnement (%)	Health Santé (%)	Education Enseigne– ment (%)	Social protection Protection sociale (%)	Other functions Autres fonctions (%)
Kazakhstan [3]	1998	186 870	13.5	9.4	17.1	...	11.9	34.0	2.6	11.5
Kazakhstan [3]	1999	232 713	14.3	7.7	12.5	...	17.4	30.6	5.6	11.8
	2000	384 819	11.6	5.5	12.2	...	13.5	20.1	18.1	19.0
Kenya	1998	5 678	29.4	10.8	...	...	10.2	33.9	...	...
Kenya	1999	6 297	29.8	10.4	...	...	10.0	35.2	...	...
	2000	6 958	27.7	9.6	...	...	9.4	36.8	...	...
Korea, Republic of [3]	1996	42 477 400	19.0	28.5	11.8	...	1.7	25.0	4.2	9.9
Corée, Rép. de [3]	1997	45 659 700	19.1	28.3	11.9	...	1.7	24.9	4.3	9.8
	1998	48 782 109	19.0	27.5	11.7	...	1.7	24.8	4.9	10.5
Kyrgyzstan [3]	1998	6 103	28.0	8.2	2.5	...	16.5	23.9	4.3	16.7
Kirghizistan [3]	1999	9 320	32.0	12.3	2.4	...	13.8	20.0	4.1	15.4
	2000	13 099	38.7	11.8	3.2	...	13.0	17.4	4.6	11.4
Lesotho [3]	1997	800	23.4	...	21.8	...	13.0	6.9	...	18.9
Lesotho [3]	1998	1 023	24.4	...	22.6	...	13.5	6.4	...	18.5
	1999	1 188	26.1	...	21.1	...	13.6	6.1	...	18.5
Luxembourg [3]	1998	2 853	15.3	3.3	4.2	4.0	24.8	24.9	5.2	18.3
Luxembourg [3]	1999	3 157	15.3	1.5	5.6	3.9	23.7	24.5	7.8	17.8
	2000	3 342	14.9	1.4	5.5	3.9	25.0	24.5	6.1	18.5
Malaysia	1997	30 341	13.0	19.4	8.7	...	10.7	31.5	5.3[7][12]	11.4
Malaisie	1998	28 454	15.4	16.2	8.4	...	12.4	31.0	6.4[7][12]	10.1
	1999	33 467	14.7	19.1	7.8	...	11.9	28.8	5.9[7][12]	11.8
Malta	1994	210	17.6	12.4	...	...	24.3	27.6	2.4	15.2
Malte	1995	235	19.6	11.9	...	...	23.4	28.1	2.6	14.5
	1996	260	18.8	12.3	...	...	23.1	27.7	2.3	15.8
Mauritius [3]	1998	12 648	26.0	1.6	14.8	...	16.0	19.4	2.4	19.8
Maurice [3]	1999	14 192	25.8	1.6	14.7	...	16.1	19.0	2.5	20.4
	2000	15 509	26.9	1.6	14.1	...	16.5	18.8	2.4	19.7
Mozambique [3]	1997	9 113	...	9.2[10]	...	...	...	...	3.9	33.7
Mozambique [3]	1998	10 042	...	10.1[10]	...	...	...	...	4.1	37.5
Netherlands [3]	1998	80 442	7.6	6.6	5.6	1.4	17.4	18.5	21.1	21.9
Pays–Bas [3]	1999	85 759	7.4	7.2	5.5	1.3	17.1	18.4	21.3	21.8
	2000	91 189	8.3	6.8	5.7	1.3	17.4	18.3	21.4	20.6
New Zealand [9]	1992	12 658	22.5	8.0	9.7	...	20.1	26.3	7.7	5.8
Nouvelle–Zélande [9]	1993	12 692	22.3	8.2	10.2	...	19.9	26.3	7.4	5.6
	1994	12 682	22.9	7.3	10.3	...	20.1	26.1	7.5	5.9
Norway	1990	139 115	7.9	15.9	4.2	...	22.4	25.7	10.0	13.9
Norvège	1991	147 478	8.1	15.1	4.3	...	22.6	25.7	10.5	13.7
Oman [3]	1998	1 402	10.7	31.9[13]	11.9	...	9.8	19.6	1.2	15.0
Oman [3]	1999	1 440	10.5	30.6[13]	11.4	...	9.9	20.8	1.2	15.7
	2000	1 580	10.5	29.3[13]	11.6	...	10.1	21.4	1.2	8.2
Pakistan [2]	1998	304 769	48.4	...	6.1	...	4.7	17.4	6.0	17.3
Pakistan [2]	1999	351 302	55.1	...	7.0	...	3.9	18.6	0.5	14.9
	2000	366 083	45.9	...	5.8	...	3.8	19.6	4.0	21.0
Panama	1998	1 508	14.7	...	14.1	...	12.1	27.9	20.8	10.5
Panama	1999	1 500	14.5	...	13.7	...	11.5	28.0	21.2	10.1
	2000	1 605	21.6	...	13.6	...	9.8	25.9	21.6	7.6
Portugal [3]	1997	17 704	7.1	7.7	8.8	1.9	26.4	30.7	4.0	13.5
Portugal [3]	1998	19 124	7.9	7.2	8.5	2.0	26.8	30.6	4.0	12.9
	1999	21 205	7.7	7.1	8.5	2.1	27.1	30.6	4.1	12.9
Romania [3]	1993	2 473 200	36.5[5]	...	...	...	22.3	22.6	2.1	16.4
Roumanie [3]	1994	6 851 800	39.0[5]	...	...	...	28.6	19.4	2.2	13.0
	1995	9 877 000	37.3[5]	...	...	...	19.0	21.4	2.3	20.0
Russian Federation [3]	1998	512 586	0.6	...	2.8	52.8	19.9	20.1	...	3.7
Fédération de Russie [3]	1999	702 832	0.6	...	1.6	56.0	20.6	18.0	...	3.1
	2000	1 082 786	1.0	...	1.4	58.7	18.9	16.9	...	3.2

24

Government final consumption expenditure by function in current prices
Dépenses de consommation finale des administrations publiques, par fonction, aux prix courants
Percentage distribution [cont.]
Répartition en pourcentage [suite]

Country or area Pays ou zone	Year Année	General govt. final consumption expenditure (M. nat'l. curr.) Dépenses de consommation finale des administrations publiques (M. monn. nat.)	General public services Services généraux des administrations publiques (%)	Defence Défense (%)	Public order and safety Ordre et sécurité publics (%)	Environment protection Protection de l'environnement (%)	Health Santé (%)	Education Enseignement (%)	Social protection Protection sociale (%)	Other functions Autres fonctions (%)
Saint Vincent−Grenadines	1998	157	10.2	...	10.2	...	19.7	26.8	7.6	25.5
St.−Vincent−et−Grenad.	1999	167	8.4	...	12.0	...	19.8	27.5	7.2	25.1
	2000	178	12.4	...	11.8	...	19.7	26.4	8.4	21.3
Saudi Arabia [2]	1996	140 275	19.8	36.4	...	...	6.6	20.1	0.4	16.7
Arabie saoudite [2]	1997	151 652	19.6	36.8	...	...	6.7	19.9	0.5	16.4
	1998	156 652	20.5	35.9	...	...	6.9	19.8	0.5	16.4
Senegal	1994	258 400	8.8	14.6	8.1	...	5.8	31.4	...	5.4
Sénégal	1995	278 500	8.8	14.6	7.3	...	5.7	30.2	...	5.0
	1996	289 100	9.0	15.4	8.0	...	5.6	30.1	...	5.2
Seychelles	1990	544	9.5	10.2	5.1	...	12.8	29.2	3.5	29.8
Seychelles	1991	558	10.3	11.0	5.7	...	13.7	26.4	5.2	27.7
Sierra Leone [2]										
Sierra Leone [2]	1990	32 337[6]	11.9	5.6	...	...	2.1	6.2	0.6	73.5
Slovenia [3]	1991	65 845	35.5	7.6	...	...	25.6	21.0	7.3	3.0
Slovénie [3]	1992	213 669	34.1	7.6	...	...	28.6	19.8	7.0	2.9
	1993	297 449	40.5	...	...	...	28.8	24.3	2.0	4.4
Spain	1993	10 700 500	8.4	9.6	11.8	...	24.7	22.2	5.3	18.1
Espagne	1994	10 963 200	8.0	8.7	11.9	...	25.8	22.3	4.9	18.3
	1995	11 647 100	8.3	9.0	12.5	...	24.1	22.9	4.8	18.4
Sri Lanka	1998	143 298	18.9	31.6	...	...	8.0	14.4	16.4	10.7
Sri Lanka	1999	152 958	17.4	31.9	...	...	9.1	14.3	15.3	11.9
	2000	176 856	16.6	34.9	...	...	9.9	13.2	14.3	11.1
Sweden [3]	1997	484 001	7.9	8.2	5.0	0.2	22.5	23.3	21.8	11.1
Suède [3]	1998	509 385	7.1	8.0	4.9	0.2	22.6	23.5	22.5	11.2
	1999	536 139	6.6	8.1	4.8	0.2	22.8	24.0	22.0	11.5
Thailand	1997	479 047	20.6	31.1[14]	...	...	11.1	32.1	0.6	4.5
Thaïlande	1998	512 905	20.4	28.0[14]	...	...	11.6	34.9	0.5	4.5
	1999	523 429	24.3	26.0[14]	...	...	10.8	34.0	0.5	4.3
TFYR of Macedonia [3]	1991	199	37.6	...	...	...	21.8	27.1	6.7	6.9
L'ex−R.y. Macédoine [3]	1992	2 302	38.3	...	...	...	28.9	23.4	4.7	4.7
	1993	12 472	42.6	...	...	...	24.3	23.5	5.5	4.2
Trinidad and Tobago [3]	1998	5 782	26.7	...	17.5	...	10.0	19.5	0.5	26.0
Trinité−et−Tobago [3]	1999	6 058	28.6	...	17.5	...	10.6	18.7	0.6	24.0
	2000	6 171	23.7	...	18.9	...	11.5	18.7	0.7	26.5
United Kingdom	1993	137 800	5.4	17.2	9.5	...	25.8	20.2	8.5	13.4
Royaume−Uni	1994	144 117	5.6	16.1	9.5	...	26.4	20.6	8.4	13.1
	1995	149 256	5.9	15.0	9.3	...	27.0	21.2	9.1	12.6
United Rep. of Tanzania [2]	1992	225 639[6]	17.5	8.5	8.5	...	5.9	7.7	0.7	51.2
Rép.−Unie de Tanzanie [2]	1993	336 855[6]	21.5	6.8	6.8	...	5.7	7.5	0.2	51.6
	1994	408 440[6]	21.1	4.9	7.5	...	7.2	7.6	0.2	51.6
Vanuatu	1991	4 693	20.5	8.4	...	...	10.3	19.8	...	41.0[15]
Vanuatu	1992	5 112	22.6	8.7	...	...	10.1	21.2	...	37.4[15]
	1993	5 194	27.1	9.2	...	...	9.7	20.0	...	34.0[15]
Zimbabwe	1990	7 425[6]	28.1	13.1	4.9	...	6.5	19.9	3.1	24.3
Zimbabwe	1991	7 788[6]	16.7	14.3	6.1	...	7.4	26.7	4.1	27.5

Source:
United Nations Statistics Division, New York, the
national accounts database.

1 Including expenditure on culture.
2 Data refer to fiscal years beginning 1 July.

Source:
Organisation des Nations Unies, Division de statistique,
New York, la base de données sur les comptes nationaux.

1 Y compris dépenses de culture.
2 Les données se réfèrent aux exercices budgétaires commençant
le 1er juillet.

24

Government final consumption expenditure by function in current prices
Dépenses de consommation finale des administrations publiques, par fonction, aux prix courants
Percentage distribution *[cont.]*
Répartition en pourcentage *[suite]*

3	Data are classified according to the 1993 SNA.
4	Data refer to fiscal years ending 30 June.
5	Including defence and public order and safety.
6	Central government estimates only (India: including state government).
7	Including recreational, cultural and religious affairs.
8	Data in Georgian coupons.
9	Data refer to fiscal years beginning 1 April.
10	Including public order and safety.
11	Data refer to fiscal years beginning 21 March.
12	Including housing and community amenities.
13	Data refer to defense affairs and services.
14	Including justice and police.
15	Including "Social protection".
16	Total government current expenditure only.

3	Les données sont classifiées selon le SCN 1993.
4	Les données se réfèrent aux exercices budgétaires finissant le 30 juin.
5	Y compris défense et ordre et securité publics.
6	Administration centrale seulement (India : y compris administration publiques).
7	Y compris loisirs, affaires culturelles et religieuses.
8	Les données sont exprimées en coupons géorgiens.
9	Les données se réfèrent aux exercices budgétaires commençant le 1er avril.
10	Y compris ordre et securité publics.
11	Les données se réfèrent aux exercices budgétaires commençant le 21 mars.
12	Y compris logement et équipements collectifs.
13	Les données se réfèrent aux affaires et services de la défense.
14	Y compris justice et police.
15	Y compris "protection sociale".
16	Dépenses publiques courants seulement.

25
Household consumption expenditure by purpose in current prices
Percentage distribution
Dépenses de consommation des ménages par fonction aux prix courants
Répartition en pourcentage

Country or area / Pays ou zone	Year / Année	Household final consumption expenditure (M. nat.curr.) / Dépense de consommation finale des ménages (M.monn.nat.)	Food, beverages, tobacco and narcotics / Alimentation, boissons, tabac et stupéfiants (%)	Clothing and footwear / Articles d'habillement et chaussures (%)	Housing, water, electricity, gas and other fuels / Logement, eau, gaz, électricité et autres combustibles (%)	Furnishings, household equipment, routine maintenance of the house / Meubles, articles de ménage et entretien courant de l'habitation (%)	Health / Santé (%)	Transport and communication / Transports et communication (%)	Recreation, culture, education, restaurants, hotels / Loisirs, culture, enseignement, restaurants et hôtels (%)	Other functions / Autres fonctions (%)
Azerbaijan [2] / Azerbaïdjan [2]	1998	13 510 800	78.6	5.8	1.3	1.7	1.8	6.2	4.0	0.6
	1999	14 019 900	78.6	5.8	1.3	1.7	1.8	6.2	4.0	0.6
	2000	14 864 500	78.6	5.8	1.3	1.7	1.8	6.2	4.0	0.6
Australia [1][2] / Australie [1][2]	1998	354 951	14.7	4.1	20.8	5.4	4.1	14.5	22.1	14.3
	1999	374 712	14.6	4.1	20.9	5.6	4.2	14.3	22.3	14.0
	2000	402 685	14.7	3.8	20.8	5.3	4.6	14.7	22.2	13.8
Austria [2] / Autriche [2]	1998	104 971	16.5	7.2	19.9	8.8	3.3	15.6	24.2	4.5
	1999	108 651	16.0	7.0	20.0	8.7	3.3	16.2	24.6	4.1
	2000	113 113	15.9	6.9	20.1	8.5	3.4	16.2	25.0	4.1
Belarus [2] / Bélarus [2]	1998	389 246 900[4]	61.0	8.8	8.1	4.0	1.4	7.6	6.0	3.0
	1999	1 714 505 600[4]	63.8	10.1	5.0	3.9	1.4	7.1	5.7	3.0
	2000	5 011 900	65.5	8.5	5.6	3.2	1.6	7.5	5.1	3.1
Belgium [2] / Belgique [2]	1998	119 723	17.3	5.6	23.0	5.7	3.7	16.2	14.9	13.6
	1999	123 493	16.5	5.4	22.9	5.5	3.7	17.0	15.2	13.8
	2000	131 145	16.5	5.3	22.3	5.4	3.7	17.6	15.1	14.1
Bolivia [2] / Bolivie [2]	1994	21 444	34.7	6.7	...	...	...	...	9.2	...
	1995	24 440	34.4	6.5	...	...	...	...	9.5	...
	1996	28 200	35.7	6.5	...	...	...	...	9.8	...
Botswana [2][3] / Botswana [2][3]	1998	5 852	41.7	5.9	12.3	3.9	2.2	8.9	7.5	...
	1999	6 619	43.3	5.4	12.2	4.1	2.3	7.9	7.9	...
	2000	7 469	42.7	5.3	13.6	3.7	2.5	7.1	8.4	...
Canada [2] / Canada [2]	1998	510 392	14.1	5.5	24.3	6.4	4.2	17.1	19.2	9.2
	1999	536 218	13.9	5.5	23.9	6.5	4.2	17.7	19.3	9.1
	2000	566 853	13.7	5.4	23.5	6.5	4.2	18.1	19.5	9.2
China, Hong Kong SAR / Chine, Hong Kong RAS	1998	707 532	14.0	18.3[5]	21.5	10.0	5.2	9.5	8.6	12.9
	1999	676 229	14.4	16.3[5]	21.8	10.2	5.6	9.7	8.2	13.8
	2000	679 624	14.2	15.8[5]	20.9	11.3	5.6	10.3	8.8	13.1
Colombia [2] / Colombie [2]	1997	79 037 154	33.3	5.5	17.5	5.7	3.6	12.8	15.5	6.0
	1998	92 337 668	33.4	5.6	17.5	5.5	3.8	12.7	15.7	5.8
	1999	95 736 626	32.8	5.3	16.6	5.6	4.2	13.6	16.0	5.9
Cyprus / Chypre	1994	2 068	36.3	11.1	10.3	15.1	5.4	...	33.1	9.1
	1995	2 552	31.4	10.4	9.0	13.2	4.9	...	27.6	7.9
	1996	2 704	30.8	10.1	9.2	13.0	5.7	...	27.0	8.3
Czech Republic [2] / République tchéque [2]	1997	887 974	33.2	6.2	17.4	5.8	1.2	10.1	15.0	11.2
	1998	947 451	32.8	5.9	20.9	5.2	1.2	9.6	15.0	9.4
	1999	1 005 895	31.8	5.7	19.9	5.7	1.1	12.8	14.2	8.9
Denmark [2] / Danemark [2]	1998	572 152	17.7	5.1	27.2	5.8	2.5	15.5	16.7	9.6
	1999	587 646	17.4	5.0	27.5	5.8	2.5	15.2	16.7	9.8
	2000	602 638	17.5	4.9	27.9	5.8	2.6	14.5	16.8	9.9
Dominican Republic [2] / Rép. dominicaine [2]	1994	137 616	33.3	4.1	20.6	6.4	5.2	14.2	10.2	5.9
	1995	164 689	34.1	4.0	20.3	6.2	5.2	13.5	11.1	5.6
	1996	189 675	32.0	3.4	20.1	6.5	5.0	14.1	14.1	4.8
Ecuador / Equateur	1991	8 432 000	38.9	9.9	5.3	7.4	4.2	...	4.2	17.5
	1992	13 147 000	38.7	9.5	5.1	7.2	4.5	...	4.4	18.3
	1993	19 374 000	37.8	9.2	5.2	6.6	4.6	...	4.4	18.6
Fiji / Fidji	1990	1 277	31.6	8.2	13.1	7.8	2.0	...	...	9.0
	1991	1 405	31.2	7.9	13.2	7.9	2.0	...	...	10.7
Finland [2] / Finlande [2]	1998	55 745	19.0	4.7	25.6	4.6	3.4	16.3	18.9	7.3
	1999	58 476	18.7	4.6	25.6	4.6	3.6	17.0	18.8	7.1
	2000	62 014	18.2	4.5	25.6	4.6	3.7	17.0	18.7	7.7

25
Household consumption expenditure by purpose in current prices
Dépenses de consommation des ménages par fonction aux prix courants
Percentage distribution [cont.]
Répartition en pourcentage [suite]

Country or area Pays ou zone	Year Année	Household final consump- tion expenditure (M. nat.curr.) Dépense de consomma- tion finale des ménages (M.monn.nat.)	Food, beverages, tobacco and narcotics Alimen- tation, boissons, tabac et stupéfiants (%)	Clothing and footwear Articles d'habille- ment et chaussures (%)	Housing, water, electricity, gas and other fuels Logement, eau, gaz, électricité et autres combustibles (%)	Furnishings, household equipment, routine maintenance of the house Muebles, articles de ménage et entretien courant de l'habitation (%)	Health Santé (%)	Transport and commu- nication Transports et commu- nication (%)	Recreation, culture, education, restau- rants, hotels Loisirs, culture, enseigne- ment, restau- rants et hôtels (%)	Other functions Autres fonctions (%)
France [2] France [2]	1998 1999 2000	708 107 730 725 760 297	18.4 18.1 18.0	5.3 5.2 5.1	24.4 24.4 24.3	6.4 6.5 6.4	3.6 3.6 3.7	16.7 17.3 17.7	17.0 17.1 17.3	8.1 7.8 7.6
Germany [2] Allemagne [2]	1998 1999 2000	1 076 620 1 112 160 1 144 020	15.6 15.3 15.2	6.5 6.4 6.3	23.7 23.6 23.9	7.2 7.0 7.0	4.0 3.9 3.9	16.5 16.9 16.4	14.8 15.0 15.0	11.7 12.0 12.3
Greece [2] Grèce [2]	1998 1999 2000	75 558 79 376 84 462	23.0 22.7 22.8	11.6 11.7 11.7	18.6 18.3 18.2	6.8 6.8 6.9	5.9 6.0 5.4	11.2 11.4 11.7	24.1 23.6 23.9	-1.1 -0.4 -0.6
Hungary Hungary	1990 1991	1 052 078 1 303 792	43.8 40.9	7.8 7.4	10.6 12.0	8.4 8.7	1.4 1.5	... ...	8.0 7.7	... ...
Iceland [2] Islande [2]	1998 1999 2000	320 495 352 715 384 400	23.6 22.7 21.8	7.0 6.8 6.4	16.1 16.1 17.0	7.3 7.3 6.8	2.7 2.7 2.8	14.6 15.3 15.1	19.1 19.4 19.9	9.6 9.8 10.2
India [6] Inde [6]	1998 1999 2000	11 394 110[7] 12 653 490[7] 13 409 620[7]	52.6 50.2 46.7	4.6 4.9 4.9	9.9 10.1 11.3	2.9 2.8 3.0	5.7 6.6 7.3	12.6 12.6 13.3	4.6 4.9 5.0	7.1 8.0 8.3
Iran, Islamic Republic of [2 8] Iran, Rép. islamique d' [2 8]	1998 1999 2000	179 402 400 223 325 300 261 809 400	35.9 35.1 34.9	9.9 9.1 9.1	29.5 29.2 29.4	6.5 6.5 6.5	4.4 5.2 5.2	7.4 8.4 8.5	3.2 3.0 3.0	3.2 3.5 3.4
Ireland [2] Irlande [2]	1998 1999 2000	36 598[7] 41 078[7] 47 311[7]	19.3 18.4 17.4	7.3 7.0 7.1	18.4 18.7 19.4	7.3 7.5 7.2	2.7 2.6 2.5	14.2 14.2 14.9	23.3 22.9 22.2	7.6 8.6 9.3
Israel [2] Israël [2]	1998 1999 2000	216 325 235 176 253 573	22.3 22.2 21.8	3.9 3.7 3.9	27.2 27.0 26.1	8.5 8.6 9.0	5.1 4.9 4.8	11.9 12.8 13.5	13.0 13.9 14.1	8.1 6.9 6.8
Italy [2] Italie [2]	1999 2000 2001	661 737 698 745 726 704	17.5 17.2 17.2	9.7 9.5 9.7	19.8 19.8 20.0	9.7 9.5 9.4	3.3 3.2 3.0	15.7 15.9 15.4	17.7 18.4 18.6	6.7 6.5 6.8
Japan [2] Japon [2]	1998 1999 2000	280 826 500 282 398 100 281 309 300	18.6 18.1 17.2	6.8 6.2 6.0	24.3 24.6 25.1	4.8 4.7 4.6	3.3 3.4 3.5	12.3 12.1 12.6	19.2 19.1 19.2	10.8 11.8 11.9
Korea, Republic of [2] Corée, République de [2]	1998 1999 2000	237 996 661 266 031 046 290 681 584	18.9 18.8 17.6	4.1 3.9 4.1	18.9 17.2 17.5	4.6 4.6 4.6	7.5 7.5 7.2	16.1 16.5 16.8	19.3 19.6 19.7	10.7 11.9 12.4
Malta Malte	1994 1995 1996	608[7] 700[7] 765[7]	37.5 36.0 34.5	8.7 8.3 8.6	7.2 6.6 6.3	11.2 10.9 10.7	4.3 3.9 3.9	... ...	30.6 27.7 26.7	6.6 6.7 6.7
Mexico [2] Mexique [2]	1997 1998 1999	2 021 232[7] 2 573 467[7] 3 054 141[7]	28.5 27.5 27.9	4.3 4.1 3.8	14.3 14.3 13.9	8.9 8.8 8.2	4.4 4.1 4.3	17.6 18.7 19.2	14.1 14.1 14.3	10.5 10.6 10.1
Namibia [2] Namibie [2]	1998 1999 2000	10 475 11 566 13 439	43.8 45.9 39.9	5.6 5.3 4.5	15.9 16.0 15.4	... ...	... ...	... ...	... ...	35.7 32.8 40.1
Netherlands [2] Pays-Bas [2]	1997 1998 1999	163 183 174 079 185 403	15.6 15.1 14.5	6.2 6.2 6.1	21.3 20.7 20.5	7.1 7.2 7.3	3.9 3.8 3.9	14.4 14.8 15.3	17.2 17.3 17.2	14.3 14.5 14.8
New Zealand [2 6] Nouvelle-Zélande [2 6]	1998 1999 2000	60 463 62 681 64 992	17.2 17.3 16.8	4.6 4.8 4.8	21.4 20.9 20.4	11.0 11.1 11.1	3.0 3.1 3.2	14.8 15.2 15.4	19.2 19.6 20.4	8.7 8.0 7.7
Norway [2] Norvège [2]	1995 1996 1997	435 247 465 695 495 077	21.0 20.5 20.4	6.2 6.1 6.1	22.8 22.5 21.9	6.5 6.2 6.3	2.6 2.7 2.7	15.8 16.6 16.8	17.2 17.2 17.4	7.9 8.1 8.3

25
Household consumption expenditure by purpose in current prices
Dépenses de consommation des ménages par fonction aux prix courants
Percentage distribution [cont.]
Répartition en pourcentage [suite]

Country or area Pays ou zone	Year Année	Household final consump- tion expenditure (M. nat.curr.) Dépense de consomma- tion finale des ménages (M.monn.nat.)	Food, beverages, tobacco and narcotics Alimen- tation, boissons, tabac et stupéfiants (%)	Clothing and footwear Articles d'habille- ment et chaussures (%)	Housing, water, electricity, gas and other fuels Logement, eau, gaz, électricité et autres combustibles (%)	Furnishings, household equipment, routine maintenance of the house Muebles, articles de ménage et entretien courant de l'habitation (%)	Health Santé (%)	Transport and commu- nication Transports et commu- nication (%)	Recreation, culture, education, restau- rants, hotels Loisirs, culture, enseigne- ment, restau- rants et hôtels (%)	Other functions Autres fonctions (%)
Philippines	1998	1 980 088	54.2	2.9	4.2	14.4	...	4.5	...	19.9
Philippines	1999	2 161 645	53.4	2.9	4.3	14.4	...	4.5	...	20.6
	2000	2 335 290	51.7	2.8	4.6	14.2	...	5.2	...	21.4
Poland [2]	1997	296 649	34.4	5.6	20.8	5.2	3.8	12.8	10.9	6.5
Pologne [2]	1998	346 936	31.8	5.2	21.9	5.0	4.0	13.4	11.2	7.5
	1999	390 474	29.4	5.0	23.4	5.0	4.2	14.3	10.9	7.8
Portugal [2]	1998	61 484	24.1	8.3	11.1	7.7	4.9	20.6	18.7	4.6
Portugal [2]	1999	65 826	23.8	8.2	11.0	7.8	4.9	20.9	18.6	4.8
	2000	69 396	23.6	8.3	11.2	7.8	5.0	20.8	18.8	4.4
Puerto Rico [1]	1998	32 630	19.5	7.9	15.2	7.4	14.2	16.4	11.4	10.9
Porto Rico [1]	1999	34 502	18.4	8.0	16.2	6.6	14.6	16.4	11.7	11.3
	2000	36 047	19.6	7.2	17.3	6.6	14.4	15.7	11.7	11.1
Republic of Moldova [2]	1993	728	49.4	6.5	6.0	5.7	8.6	4.2	17.7	1.9
République de Moldova [2]	1996	5 243	42.9	6.6	5.0	2.9	9.9	9.3	16.2	7.2
Saudi Arabia [1]	1996	206 336	34.6	7.8	14.7	9.2	0.9	17.9	2.1	12.8
Arabie saoudite [1]	1997	206 185	34.7	7.7	14.7	9.1	0.9	17.8	2.1	13.1
	1998	198 574	37.3	8.2	15.7	9.7	1.0	18.9	2.2	7.0
Singapore	1995	50 020	15.6	5.9	13.7	8.3	4.9	21.1	23.9	6.5
Singapour	1996	53 920	15.4	5.5	13.7	8.4	5.0	19.4	23.0	9.6
	1997	58 067	14.7	5.2	13.6	8.3	4.9	18.1	21.9	13.2
Slovakia [2]	1996	315 800	38.5	9.2	18.0	4.9	1.0	10.4	14.0	4.0
Slovaquie [2]	1997	353 700	38.7	9.1	17.7	5.0	1.0	9.8	13.8	4.9
	1998	395 400	37.0	8.4	17.0	5.4	0.9	10.8	14.3	6.2
South Africa [2]	1998	466 552	31.3	5.6	12.1	8.9	7.0	14.3	9.3	11.5
Afrique du Sud [2]	1999	505 698	30.6	5.1	12.2	8.9	7.3	14.4	9.4	12.0
	2000	558 425	30.0	5.0	12.0	8.8	7.4	15.6	9.4	11.9
Spain [2]	1997	289 675	21.0	7.0	15.8	6.4	3.5	15.4	30.7	−0.2
Espagne [2]	1998	309 279	20.3	6.9	15.8	6.5	3.6	15.8	31.1	−0.4
	1999	331 825	20.1	6.9	15.6	6.5	3.7	16.6	30.9	−0.7
Sri Lanka	1997	596 917	55.1	7.9	3.9	5.5	1.6	14.9	3.9	7.3
Sri Lanka	1998	668 901	54.6	8.0	3.6	5.0	1.8	15.0	4.3	7.7
	1999	749 533	54.3	8.1	3.4	5.1	1.8	15.3	4.1	8.0
Sweden [2]	1997	895 968	17.3	5.2	32.8	4.5	2.3	15.1	15.3	7.5
Suède [2]	1998	929 240	16.9	5.2	32.0	4.6	2.4	15.3	15.8	7.8
	1999	977 354	16.6	5.4	30.3	4.8	2.4	16.0	16.1	8.0
Switzerland	1994	204 965	24.7	5.2	24.0	5.2	12.5	...	...	1.4
Suisse	1995	209 548	24.6	4.8	24.4	5.0	12.7	...	...	1.4
	1996	213 441	...	4.6	24.7	4.8	13.0	...	...	1.5
Thailand	1997	2 592 314	32.0	13.9	8.7	10.4	6.7	14.2	15.7	−1.6
Thaïlande	1998	2 516 512	35.1	12.8	9.6	10.1	6.9	13.2	15.7	−3.4
	1999	2 600 896	33.4	12.9	9.5	10.0	7.1	13.9	15.8	−2.7
United Kingdom [2]	1998	536 525	14.5	6.0	17.9	5.8	1.5	17.0	25.1	12.2
Royaume−Umi [2]	1999	567 555	14.3	5.9	17.7	5.8	1.5	16.9	25.2	12.6
	2000	595 236	13.9	5.8	17.7	5.9	1.5	16.7	25.1	13.4
United States [2]	1998	5 856 000	9.4	5.4	17.3	5.2	16.7	12.7	17.8	15.5
Etats−Unis [2]	1999	6 250 200	9.4	5.4	17.1	5.2	16.6	13.0	17.8	15.6
	2000	6 728 400	9.3	5.3	16.8	5.2	16.4	13.4	17.8	15.9
Venezuela	1998	36 718 686	36.2	2.8	11.0	2.7	3.3	11.1	17.3	15.5
Venezuela	1999	42 041 902	35.0	2.4	11.9	2.5	3.9	9.2	19.0	16.0
	2000	50 918 722	32.9	2.4	12.0	2.6	4.0	10.1	18.7	17.3

25
Household consumption expenditure by purpose in current prices
Dépenses de consommation des ménages par fonction aux prix courants
Percentage distribution *[cont.]*
Répartition en pourcentage *[suite]*

Source:
United Nations Statistics Division, New York, the
national accounts database.

1   Data refer to fiscal year beginning 1 July.

2   Data classified according to the 1993 SNA.
3   Data refer to fiscal years ending 30 June.
4   Data in Belarussian rubles.
5   Including personal effects.
6   Data refer to fiscal years beginning 1 April.

7   Including "Non−profit institutions serving households" (NPISHs).
8   Data refer to fiscal years beginning 21 March.

Source:
Organisation des Nations Unies, Division de statistique,
New York, la base de données sur les comptes nationaux.

1   Les données se réfèrent aux exercises budgétaires commençant
le 1er juillet.
2   Les données sont classifiées selon le SCN 1993.
3   Les données se réfèrent aux exercises budgétaires finissant le 30 juin.
4   Les données sont exprimées en roubles bélarussiens.
5   Y compris les effets personnels.
6   Les données se réfèrent aux exercises budgétaires commençant
le 1er avril.
7   Y compris les institutions sans but lucratif au service des ménages.
8   Les données se réfèrent aux exercises budgétaires commençant
le 21 mars.

26
# Index numbers of industrial production
# Indices de la production industrielle
1995=100

Country or area and industry [ISIC Rev.3] Pays ou zone et industrie [CITI Rév.3]	1994	1995	1996	1997	1998	1999	2000	2001
Africa · Afrique								
Algeria Algérie								
Total industry [CDE]								
Total, industrie [CDE]	101.0	100.0	92.6	89.6	95.7	96.0	97.3	97.0
Total mining [C]								
Total, industries extractives [C]	101.6	100.0	95.7	84.1	87.3	93.0	92.5	92.2
Total manufacturing [D]								
Total, industries manufacturières [D]	104.3	100.0	88.7	82.3	89.7	88.3	86.8	86.0
Food, beverages, tobacco								
Aliments, boissons, tabac	108.3	100.0	95.5	93.4	107.1	105.5	96.1	84.0
Textiles,wearing apparel, leather, footwear								
Textiles, habillement, cuir et chaussures	113.2	100.0	70.8	63.7	69.5	51.0	45.7	41.3
Chemicals, petroleum, rubber and plastic prod.								
Prod. chimiques, pétroliers, caoutch. et plast.	98.6	100.0	94.1	100.9	99.7	103.8	104.8	108.8
Basic metals								
Métaux de base	88.2	100.0	66.5	53.9	62.9	75.1	72.2	77.9
Metal products								
Produits métalliques	89.9	100.0	76.5	60.7	64.7	72.0	74.5	85.5
Electricity [E]								
Électricité [E]	100.5	100.0	104.5	108.5	118.0	126.4	129.4	135.9
Cameroon [1] Cameroun [1]								
Total industry [DE]								
Total, industrie [DE]	93.2	100.0	118.9	117.1	121.1	...	...	...
Total manufacturing [D]								
Total, industries manufacturières [D]	91.1	100.0	120.2	117.5	121.1	...	...	...
Electricity, gas and water [E]								
Électricité, gaz et eau [E]	99.6	100.0	108.5	113.7	121.0	...	...	...
Central African Republic République centrafricaine								
Total industry [CDE]								
Total, industrie [CDE]	111.2	100.0	100.9	...	...	...	...	...
Total mining [C]								
Total, industries extractives [C]	109.4	100.0	93.8	...	...	...	...	...
Total manufacturing [D]								
Total, industries manufacturières [D]	70.5	100.0	81.7	...	...	...	...	...
Electricity, gas and water [E]								
Électricité, gaz et eau [E]	84.4	100.0	96.5	...	...	...	...	...
Côte d'Ivoire Côte d'Ivoire								
Total industry [CDE]								
Total, industrie [CDE]	90.7	100.0	112.1	125.0	138.8	143.2	132.0	126.5
Total mining [C]								
Total, industries extractives [C]	9.2	100.0	238.5	220.0	165.5	169.5	146.5	99.1
Total manufacturing [D]								
Total, industries manufacturières [D]	97.4	100.0	106.6	119.2	139.5	139.6	126.9	121.5
Food, beverages, tobacco								
Aliments, boissons, tabac	102.6	100.0	108.3	116.8	127.1	139.5	133.0	130.2
Textiles and wearing apparel								
Textiles et habillement	76.0	100.0	100.8	117.6	164.0	157.6	106.4	92.8
Chemicals, petroleum, rubber and plastic prod.								
Prod. chimiques, pétroliers, caoutch. et plast.	102.4	100.0	107.6	124.6	137.8	129.0	121.9	120.9
Metal products								
Produits métalliques	102.0	100.0	107.8	108.1	112.4	106.1	89.5	76.3
Electricity and water [E]								
Électricité et eau [E]	83.2	100.0	110.3	132.8	134.7	157.0	156.5	159.7
Egypt [2] Egypte [2]								
Total industry [CDE]								
Total, industrie [CDE]	99.1	100.0	111.0	124.5	127.2	134.6	...	...
Total mining [C]								
Total, industries extractives [C]	101.8	100.0	98.2	113.8	99.3	143.8	...	...
Total manufacturing [D]								
Total, industries manufacturières [D]	100.1	100.0	120.4	134.0	144.7	133.8	...	...
Food, beverages, tobacco								
Aliments, boissons, tabac	95.4	100.0	112.8	118.0	147.1	153.1	...	...

26
Index numbers of industrial production [*cont.*]
Indices de la production industrielle [*suite*]
1995=100

Country or area and industry [ISIC Rev.3] Pays ou zone et industrie [CITI Rév.3]	1994	1995	1996	1997	1998	1999	2000	2001
Textiles and wearing apparel								
Textiles et habillement	95.4	100.0	87.7	117.5	113.8	111.8	...	...
Chemicals, petroleum, rubber and plastic prod.								
Prod. chimiques, pétroliers, caoutch. et plast.	106.7	100.0	135.5	129.5	97.8	121.2	...	...
Basic metals								
Métaux de base	94.3	100.0	120.7	110.0	139.0	156.3	...	...
Metal products								
Produits métalliques	98.5	100.0	136.0	182.7	236.8	173.3	...	...
Electricity, gas and water [E]								
Electricité, gaz et eau [E]	**98.0**	**100.0**	**105.6**	**110.6**	**117.3**	**127.1**	...	...
Ethiopia [2] **Ethiopie** [2]								
Total industry [CDE]								
Total, industrie [CDE]	92.4	100.0	104.8	111.3	119.3	129.4	...	...
Total mining [C]								
Total, industries extractives [C]	91.8	100.0	113.1	127.8	143.7	161.0	...	...
Total manufacturing [D]								
Total, industries manufacturières [D]	91.8	100.0	107.6	113.9	122.5	129.6	...	...
Electricity and water [E]								
Electricité et eau [E]	**95.9**	**100.0**	**104.7**	**109.3**	**110.6**	**121.5**	...	...
Gabon Gabon								
Total industry [CDE]								
Total, industrie [CDE]	82.5	100.0	101.5	98.1	...	...	...	...
Total mining [C]								
Total, industries extractives [C]	78.4	100.0	99.6	94.7	...	...	...	...
Total manufacturing [D]								
Total, industries manufacturières [D]	94.5	100.0	105.1	104.7	...	...	...	...
Food, beverages, tobacco								
Aliments, boissons, tabac	94.2	100.0	104.1	105.2	110.0	106.4	117.6	134.3
Textiles								
Textiles	90.9	100.0	79.3	72.5	...	...	...	...
Chemicals and chemical products								
Produits chimiques	83.1	100.0	117.1	126.3	131.8	141.0	110.7	119.6
Electricity and water [E]								
Electricité et eau [E]	**95.1**	**100.0**	**105.3**	**107.0**	**121.8**	**121.7**	**118.5**	**130.3**
Ghana Ghana								
Total industry [CDE] [3]								
Total, industrie [CDE] [3]	92.1	100.0	104.4	96.6	103.3	109.3	110.9	...
Total mining [C]								
Total, industries extractives [C]	86.4	100.0	100.3	109.3	140.8	158.8	153.8	...
Total manufacturing [D]								
Total, industries manufacturières [D]	92.1	100.0	104.6	91.9	94.3	98.4	101.7	...
Food, beverages, tobacco								
Aliments, boissons, tabac	99.0	100.0	103.5	106.9	107.6	101.4	102.0	...
Textiles,wearing apparel, leather, footwear								
Textiles, habillement, cuir et chaussures	87.6	100.0	102.4	101.3	102.0	102.2	102.6	...
Chemicals, petroleum, rubber and plastic prod.								
Prod. chimiques, pétroliers, caoutch. et plast.	92.9	100.0	104.3	110.7	90.3	97.5	106.0	...
Basic metals								
Métaux de base	74.6	100.0	104.7	124.5	114.1	133.1	133.2	...
Metal products								
Produits métalliques	107.5	100.0	116.6	125.3	121.8	119.7	119.8	...
Electricity [E]								
Electricité [E]	**99.1**	**100.0**	**108.0**	**112.2**	**115.9**	**119.6**	**117.8**	...
Kenya Kenya								
Total industry [CD] [3]								
Total, industrie [CD] [3]	96.4	100.0	104.5	111.2	120.9	108.5	106.7	108.2
Total mining [C]								
Total, industries extractives [C]	95.3	100.0	103.4	111.6	110.6	122.3	110.6	138.2
Total manufacturing [D]								
Total, industries manufacturières [D]	96.5	100.0	104.5	111.2	121.2	108.2	106.6	107.5
Food, beverages, tobacco								
Aliments, boissons, tabac	88.3	100.0	97.7	97.7	99.6	97.2	95.5	95.3
Textiles,wearing apparel, leather, footwear								
Textiles, habillement, cuir et chaussures	135.1	100.0	96.1	90.0	89.4	87.7	89.9	91.8

26
Index numbers of industrial production [*cont.*]
Indices de la production industrielle [*suite*]
1995=100

Country or area and industry [ISIC Rev.3] Pays ou zone et industrie [CITI Rév.3]	1994	1995	1996	1997	1998	1999	2000	2001
Chemicals, petroleum, rubber and plastic prod.								
Prod. chimiques, pétroliers, caoutch. et plast.	95.1	100.0	104.3	115.3	121.5	125.8	133.2	144.2
Metal products								
Produits métalliques	97.6	100.0	118.9	114.0	100.1	95.1	74.1	85.0
Madagascar Madagascar								
Total industry [CDE]								
Total, industrie [CDE]	95.3	100.0	100.2	120.5	124.2	129.0	147.5	...
Total mining [C]								
Total, industries extractives [C]	87.7	100.0	119.7	106.8	124.8	75.2	109.2	...
Total manufacturing [D]								
Total, industries manufacturières [D]	94.9	100.0	99.0	122.1	124.5	131.0	148.3	...
Food, beverages, tobacco								
Aliments, boissons, tabac	90.6	100.0	103.0	97.6	107.6	131.8	139.1	...
Textiles,wearing apparel, leather, footwear								
Textiles, habillement, cuir et chaussures	154.5	100.0	92.8	91.5	106.1	119.7	152.1	...
Chemicals, petroleum products								
Produits chimiques et pétroliers	90.8	100.0	95.0	157.8	146.7	145.9	163.8	...
Basic metals								
Métaux de base	117.6	100.0	142.6	151.1	162.3	167.8	121.3	...
Metal products								
Produits métalliques	98.9	100.0	107.9	100.3	107.4	111.1	99.9	...
Electricity [E]								
Electricité [E]	100.1	100.0	102.7	112.3	121.1	129.7	152.4	...
Malawi Malawi								
Total industry [DE]								
Total, industrie [DE]	98.7	100.0	103.5	102.7	99.4	90.4	91.2	81.8
Total manufacturing [D]								
Total, industries manufacturières [D]	98.4	100.0	103.5	100.2	94.4	81.2	80.2	68.1
Food, beverages, tobacco								
Aliments, boissons, tabac	105.2	100.0	101.9	103.1	65.1	50.0	48.5	43.4
Textiles,wearing apparel, leather, footwear								
Textiles, habillement, cuir et chaussures	126.9	100.0	90.3	146.2	181.8	222.5	137.3	111.9
Electricity and water [E]								
Electricité et eau [E]	100.2	100.0	103.5	112.8	120.3	118.7	128.1	131.6
Mali Mali								
Total industry [DE]								
Total, industrie [DE]	82.5	100.0	106.2	121.5	140.2	133.4	...	...
Food, beverages, tobacco								
Aliments, boissons, tabac	100.4	100.0	104.3	110.1	104.3	98.7	...	...
Wearing apparel								
Habillement	89.5	100.0	108.3	138.4	141.4	121.8	...	...
Chemicals and chemical products								
Produits chimiques	91.6	100.0	112.6	106.5	101.2	91.3	...	...
Mauritius Maurice								
Total industry [CDE]								
Total, industrie [CDE]	...	100.0	106.5	111.6	90.7	87.6	93.1	...
Total mining [C]								
Total, industries extractives [C]	...	100.0	106.0	110.2	84.5	84.5	84.5	...
Total manufacturing [D]								
Total, industries manufacturières [D]	...	100.0	106.4	112.9	91.5	87.8	93.3	...
Food, beverages, tobacco								
Aliments, boissons, tabac	...	100.0	106.5	114.7	127.1	110.0	121.0	...
Textiles,wearing apparel, leather, footwear								
Textiles, habillement, cuir et chaussures	...	100.0	108.7	114.9	90.4	89.8	89.8	...
Chemicals, petroleum, rubber and plastic prod.								
Prod. chimiques, pétroliers, caoutch. et plast.	...	100.0	98.6	103.9	91.6	89.8	91.3	...
Basic metals								
Métaux de base	...	100.0	104.4	107.4	84.1	80.3	80.3	...
Metal products								
Produits métalliques	...	100.0	101.0	108.4	77.5	73.9	73.7	...
Electricity [E]								
Electricité [E]	...	100.0	107.5	116.4	85.3	83.9	95.2	...

26
Index numbers of industrial production [*cont.*]
Indices de la production industrielle [*suite*]
1995=100

Country or area and industry [ISIC Rev.3] Pays ou zone et industrie [CITI Rév.3]	1994	1995	1996	1997	1998	1999	2000	2001
Morocco Maroc								
Total industry [CDE] [3]								
Total, industrie [CDE] [3]	96.6	100.0	103.3	108.3	110.6	11.6	114.6	119.7
Total mining [C] [4]								
Total, industries extractives [C] [4]	101.2	100.0	102.5	111.6	109.8	107.5	103.8	106.3
Total manufacturing [D] [5]								
Total, industries manufacturières [D] [5]	96.8	100.0	103.2	107.5	110.2	112.7	116.6	120.4
Food, beverages, tobacco								
Aliments, boissons, tabac	99.3	100.0	102.8	101.8	112.4	114.6	120.6	130.0
Textiles,wearing apparel, leather, footwear								
Textiles, habillement, cuir et chaussures	96.8	100.0	103.2	108.9	110.7	109.2	110.5	109.1
Chemicals, petroleum, rubber and plastic prod.								
Prod. chimiques, pétroliers, caoutch. et plast.	98.0	100.0	101.3	108.6	109.5	116.5	118.1	123.3
Basic metals								
Métaux de base	88.3	100.0	98.1	110.5	109.3	122.0	122.2	130.8
Metal products								
Produits métalliques	98.7	100.0	98.9	102.5	103.0	109.6	114.9	120.1
Electricity [E]								
Electricité [E]	91.0	100.0	104.4	111.2	112.6	109.7	111.1	126.6
Nigeria Nigéria								
Total industry [CDE]								
Total, industrie [CDE]	100.4	100.0	102.8	109.2	104.0	...	...	...
Total mining [C]								
Total, industries extractives [C]	97.3	100.0	103.7	113.7	107.8	...	...	...
Total manufacturing [D]								
Total, industries manufacturières [D]	105.8	100.0	101.2	101.6	97.7	...	...	...
Electricity [E]								
Electricité [E]	101.7	100.0	97.6	95.7	92.2	...	...	...
Senegal Sénégal								
Total industry [CDE]								
Total, industrie [CDE]	86.1	100.0	96.5	98.2	102.1	104.1	103.7	...
Total mining [C]								
Total, industries extractives [C]	98.8	100.0	99.3	111.5	107.0	123.9	126.0	...
Total manufacturing [D] [3]								
Total, industries manufacturières [D] [3]	82.7	100.0	95.4	94.2	100.1	98.5	97.1	...
Food, beverages, tobacco								
Aliments, boissons, tabac	91.6	100.0	85.5	80.6	89.3	90.9	88.3	...
Textiles								
Textiles	114.0	100.0	108.3	107.5	104.5	84.1	86.4	...
Chemicals, petroleum, rubber and plastic prod.								
Prod. chimiques, pétroliers, caoutch. et plast.	76.6	100.0	93.2	107.1	106.6	97.4	91.6	...
Metal products								
Produits métalliques	78.7	100.0	92.6	92.8	94.4	94.4	91.9	...
Electricity and water [E]								
Electricité et eau [E]	92.0	100.0	103.1	109.6	113.6	116.8	121.6	...
South Africa Afrique du Sud								
Total industry [CDE] [3]								
Total, industrie [CDE] [3]	96.0	100.0	101.4	104.4	101.7	101.3	104.5	106.1
Total mining [C]								
Total, industries extractives [C]	100.8	100.0	98.3	100.3	99.3	97.3	96.3	94.2
Total manufacturing [D]								
Total, industries manufacturières [D]	94.0	100.0	101.5	104.3	101.1	101.4	105.9	109.2
Food and beverages								
Aliments et boissons	95.9	100.0	101.2	102.2	100.9	99.7	97.0	101.8
Textiles,wearing apparel, leather, footwear								
Textiles, habillement, cuir et chaussures	91.2	100.0	93.1	96.3	89.1	88.5	86.4	83.6
Chemicals, petroleum, rubber and plastic prod.								
Prod. chimiques, pétroliers, caoutch. et plast.	94.4	100.0	100.8	103.7	103.3	106.7	108.6	112.0
Basic metals								
Métaux de base	86.5	100.0	110.3	114.7	111.8	114.4	130.9	131.2
Metal products								
Produits métalliques	88.8	100.0	103.8	106.8	101.8	100.5	109.4	117.0
Electricity [E]								
Electricité [E]	97.4	100.0	107.2	112.6	110.1	108.8	112.8	112.5

26

Index numbers of industrial production [*cont.*]

Indices de la production industrielle [*suite*]

1995=100

Country or area and industry [ISIC Rev.3] Pays ou zone et industrie [CITI Rév.3]	1994	1995	1996	1997	1998	1999	2000	2001
Swaziland Swaziland								
Total industry [CDE] [3]								
Total, industrie [CDE] [3]	92.1	100.0	100.1	112.0	114.1	109.7	110.1	...
Total mining [C]								
Total, industries extractives [C]	103.2	100.0	96.5	78.4	99.6	85.6	65.9	...
Total manufacturing [D]								
Total, industries manufacturières [D]	91.3	100.0	99.3	112.6	114.0	109.0	110.6	...
Electricity, gas and water [E]								
Electricité, gaz et eau [E]	98.8	100.0	112.7	115.1	120.4	126.4	117.9	...
Tunisia Tunisie								
Total industry [CDE]								
Total, industrie [CDE]	97.0	100.0	102.7	107.2	114.6	120.7	128.3	136.0
Total mining [C]								
Total, industries extractives [C]	98.9	100.0	105.4	102.6	109.8	112.9	109.6	106.1
Total manufacturing [D]								
Total, industries manufacturières [D]	96.5	100.0	101.9	108.2	115.9	122.5	133.2	144.1
Food, beverages, tobacco								
Aliments, boissons, tabac	100.0	100.0	102.3	113.4	117.9	132.7	143.4	144.1
Textiles,wearing apparel, leather, footwear								
Textiles, habillement, cuir et chaussures	92.7	100.0	100.9	106.0	114.6	117.8	133.0	147.7
Chemicals, petroleum, rubber and plastic prod.								
Prod. chimiques, pétroliers, caoutch. et plast.	92.3	100.0	101.3	105.7	108.1	108.3	112.1	113.0
Basic metals								
Métaux de base	100.2	100.0	100.7	105.0	100.3	119.6	124.5	118.5
Metal products								
Produits métalliques	100.1	100.0	105.1	111.7	129.9	141.3	153.7	169.9
Electricity and water [E]								
Electricité et eau [E]	94.9	100.0	102.1	108.4	114.5	124.7	131.7	140.3
Uganda Ouganda								
Total manufacturing [D]								
Total, industries manufacturières [D]	78.6	100.0	119.1	137.9	153.5	165.1	164.4	178.1
Food, beverages, tobacco								
Aliments, boissons, tabac	80.5	100.0	122.4	125.9	138.8	148.5	149.0	147.6
Textiles,wearing apparel, leather, footwear								
Textiles, habillement, cuir et chaussures	86.9	100.0	85.5	160.1	152.8	159.7	123.9	89.4
Chemicals, rubber and plastic prod.								
Prod. chimiques, caoutchouc et plastiques	72.4	100.0	101.0	146.9	174.8	192.1	199.1	227.0
Basic metals								
Métaux de base	79.5	100.0	98.0	255.6	280.6	319.2	286.8	307.1
Metal products								
Produits métalliques	95.5	100.0	128.0	106.4	81.6	73.1	65.6	58.3
United Rep. of Tanzania Rép.–Unie de Tanzanie								
Total manufacturing [D]								
Total, industries manufacturières [D]	96.3	100.0	101.0	106.7	115.4	119.2	...	...
Food, beverages, tobacco								
Aliments, boissons, tabac	89.9	100.0	117.9	133.7	139.8	130.5	...	...
Textiles, leather and footwear								
Textiles, cuir et chaussures	106.0	100.0	97.8	91.2	104.6	106.0	...	...
Chemicals, rubber and plastic prod.								
Prod. chimiques, caoutchouc et plastiques	129.1	100.0	104.1	82.8	80.0	86.6	...	...
Basic metals								
Métaux de base	231.2	100.0	31.3	29.2	81.3	16.7	...	...
Metal products								
Produits métalliques	133.8	100.0	117.5	119.9	122.3	132.1	...	...
Zambia Zambie								
Total industry [CDE] [3]								
Total, industrie [CDE] [3]	107.3	100.0	103.5	105.9	108.6	93.4	95.8	...
Total mining [C]								
Total, industries extractives [C]	111.7	100.0	114.3	114.5	129.5	92.8	96.1	...
Total manufacturing [D]								
Total, industries manufacturières [D]	102.6	100.0	91.6	94.8	82.0	87.5	95.4	...
Food, beverages, tobacco								
Aliments, boissons, tabac	100.4	100.0	72.0	54.7	52.2	57.1	57.6	...

26
Index numbers of industrial production [*cont.*]
Indices de la production industrielle [*suite*]
1995=100

Country or area and industry [ISIC Rev.3] Pays ou zone et industrie [CITI Rév.3]	1994	1995	1996	1997	1998	1999	2000	2001
Textiles and wearing apparel Textiles et habillement	113.0	100.1	128.2	218.3	165.1	179.5	187.3	...
Chemicals, petroleum, rubber and plastic prod. Prod. chimiques, pétroliers, caoutch. et plast.	111.1	100.0	138.9	115.4	112.7	96.3	169.4	...
Basic metals Métaux de base	105.6	100.0	80.0	68.1	74.4	76.4	78.1	...
Metal products Produits métalliques	95.4	100.1	68.0	65.3	70.2	58.3	65.0	...
Electricity and water [E] Electricité et eau [E]	**98.4**	**100.0**	**86.4**	**100.1**	**92.0**	**93.0**	**94.5**	...
Zimbabwe Zimbabwe								
Total industry [CDE] [3] Total, industrie [CDE] [3]	**104.1**	**100.0**	**108.9**	**106.8**	**109.9**	**103.2**	**96.6**	**87.8**
Total mining [C] Total, industries extractives [C]	**96.0**	**100.0**	**99.0**	**90.9**	**108.6**	**103.4**	**95.0**	**81.7**
Total manufacturing [D] Total, industries manufacturières [D]	**106.7**	**100.0**	**113.0**	**112.9**	**112.0**	**103.7**	**97.4**	**88.6**
Food, beverages, tobacco Aliments, boissons, tabac	98.7	100.0	102.0	105.7	111.8	101.6	108.8	90.2
Textiles,wearing apparel, leather, footwear Textiles, habillement, cuir et chaussures	145.0	100.0	123.6	125.4	137.7	148.3	132.2	130.0
Chemicals, petroleum, rubber and plastic prod. Prod. chimiques, pétroliers, caoutch. et plast.	105.3	100.0	106.2	126.8	120.0	107.0	75.5	75.4
Basic metals and metal products Métaux de base et produtis métalliques	84.3	100.0	107.0	96.2	81.1	78.7	76.7	68.4
Electricity [E] Electricité [E]	**104.2**	**100.0**	**96.3**	**94.1**	**87.3**	**94.6**	**93.2**	**104.9**
America, North · Amérique du Nord								
Barbados Barbade								
Total industry [CDE] Total, industrie [CDE]	**93.1**	**100.0**	**100.2**	**104.3**	**112.1**	**112.9**	**111.1**	**104.3**
Total mining [C] Total, industries extractives [C]	**99.5**	**100.0**	**89.5**	**92.9**	**141.4**	**164.8**	**140.4**	**121.9**
Total manufacturing [D] Total, industries manufacturières [D]	**92.5**	**100.0**	**100.1**	**104.3**	**109.1**	**107.2**	**106.5**	**98.3**
Food, beverages, tobacco Aliments, boissons, tabac	95.5	100.0	100.5	106.2	114.5	112.7	109.8	106.7
Wearing apparel Habillement	109.1	100.0	90.9	94.4	69.2	65.0	69.9	44.1
Chemicals, petroleum products Produits chimiques et pétroliers	72.9	100.0	101.1	118.6	105.3	104.7	83.8	78.7
Metal products Produits métalliques	92.1	100.0	106.5	103.3	87.5	80.8	78.9	54.9
Electricity and gas [E] Electricité et gaz [E]	**93.6**	**100.0**	**103.8**	**107.8**	**117.3**	**123.6**	**123.5**	**128.0**
Belize Belize								
Total industry [DE] Total, industrie [DE]	**96.4**	**100.0**	**100.6**	**106.0**	**105.0**	**105.0**	**120.0**	**120.2**
Total manufacturing [D] Total, industries manufacturières [D]	**96.4**	**100.0**	**100.2**	**105.2**	**101.8**	**107.2**	**125.4**	**125.2**
Food, beverages, tobacco Aliments, boissons, tabac	95.1	100.0	99.0	105.2	102.4	107.0	124.8	125.3
Wearing apparel Habillement	167.2	100.0	100.7	100.9	108.6	108.4	89.1	76.3
Chemicals and chemical products Produits chimiques	103.1	100.0	93.0	80.9	80.1	94.8	87.5	89.2
Metal products Produits métalliques	127.7	100.0	80.6	66.1	54.6	46.3	40.2	31.0
Electricity and water [E] Electricité et eau [E]	**96.6**	**100.0**	**102.7**	**111.0**	**122.3**	**93.1**	**91.4**	**93.3**
Canada Canada								
Total industry [CDE] Total, industrie [CDE]	**95.7**	**100.0**	**101.2**	**106.2**	**109.9**	**115.4**	**121.9**	**118.0**

26
Index numbers of industrial production [*cont.*]
Indices de la production industrielle [*suite*]
1995=100

Country or area and industry [ISIC Rev.3] Pays ou zone et industrie [CITI Rév.3]	1994	1995	1996	1997	1998	1999	2000	2001
Total mining [C]								
Total, industries extractives [C]	**96.5**	**100.0**	**101.1**	**104.1**	**105.7**	**104.0**	**111.8**	**113.7**
Total manufacturing [D]								
Total, industries manufacturières [D]	**95.3**	**100.0**	**101.1**	**107.7**	**113.0**	**120.9**	**127.4**	**121.7**
Food, beverages, tobacco								
Aliments, boissons, tabac	99.1	100.0	99.1	100.0	105.2	105.2	108.3	113.2
Textiles,wearing apparel, leather, footwear								
Textiles, habillement, cuir et chaussures	95.8	100.0	97.0	102.8	106.2	100.3	98.2	90.2
Chemicals, petroleum, rubber and plastic prod.								
Prod. chimiques, pétroliers, caoutch. et plast.	95.7	100.0	102.9	99.8	101.8	106.4	108.6	110.1
Basic metals								
Métaux de base	97.3	100.0	101.6	107.2	116.3	121.3	123.1	121.0
Metal products								
Produits métalliques	90.8	100.0	100.5	109.3	116.5	132.5	147.9	132.6
Electricity, gas and water [E]								
Electricité, gaz et eau [E]	**96.4**	**100.0**	**102.0**	**101.4**	**99.6**	**102.1**	**106.8**	**104.7**
Costa Rica Costa Rica								
Total industry [DE] [3]								
Total, industrie [DE] [3]	**96.2**	**100.0**	**100.8**	**108.2**	**120.1**	**146.3**	**142.0**	**134.3**
Total manufacturing [D]								
Total, industries manufacturières [D]	**96.0**	**100.0**	**100.5**	**108.2**	**120.5**	**150.3**	**143.8**	**133.4**
Food, beverages, tobacco								
Aliments, boissons, tabac	92.2	100.0	101.9	109.3	115.9	118.7	117.0	113.6
Textiles,wearing apparel, leather, footwear								
Textiles, habillement, cuir et chaussures	102.9	100.0	91.2	87.5	91.5	83.1	74.1	67.2
Chemicals, petroleum, rubber and plastic prod.								
Prod. chimiques, pétroliers, caoutch. et plast.	101.3	100.0	97.2	101.7	96.1	95.3	97.5	109.5
Metal products								
Produits métalliques	99.2	100.0	100.1	109.7	113.8	112.1	106.2	104.6
Electricity and water [E]								
Electricité et eau [E]	**97.0**	**100.0**	**102.6**	**108.2**	**117.7**	**125.0**	**132.5**	**139.3**
Cuba Cuba								
Total industry [CDE]								
Total, industrie [CDE]	**96.4**	**100.0**	**113.8**	**117.0**	**111.4**	**118.7**	**128.2**	**...**
Total mining [C]								
Total, industries extractives [C]	**89.4**	**100.0**	**106.4**	**108.1**	**121.8**	**163.7**	**201.9**	**...**
Total manufacturing [D]								
Total, industries manufacturières [D]	**89.9**	**100.0**	**109.3**	**114.2**	**113.4**	**116.7**	**126.8**	**...**
Food, beverages, tobacco								
Aliments, boissons, tabac	103.4	100.0	105.7	111.3	116.8	127.1	124.2	...
Textiles,wearing apparel, leather, footwear								
Textiles, habillement, cuir et chaussures	100.9	100.0	110.5	118.2	122.5	132.8	126.0	
Chemicals, petroleum, rubber and plastic prod.								
Prod. chimiques, pétroliers, caoutch. et plast.	82.2	100.0	108.9	114.0	94.6	94.4	122.7	...
Basic metals								
Métaux de base	65.7	100.0	122.7	141.4	149.9	147.8	158.0	...
Metal products								
Produits métalliques	93.6	100.0	166.2	165.4	110.1	136.8	121.9	...
Electricity and water [E]								
Electricité et eau [E]	**96.0**	**100.0**	**106.2**	**113.4**	**113.4**	**116.3**	**120.5**	**...**
Dominican Republic Rép. dominicaine								
Total industry [CDE]								
Total, industrie [CDE]	**98.3**	**100.0**	**103.6**	**111.1**	**115.5**	**121.9**	**131.6**	**130.9**
Total mining [C]								
Total, industries extractives [C]	**91.4**	**100.0**	**102.4**	**105.6**	**88.8**	**87.4**	**99.0**	**84.0**
Total manufacturing [D]								
Total, industries manufacturières [D]	**98.7**	**100.0**	**103.1**	**110.8**	**117.1**	**124.2**	**133.6**	**131.9**
Electricity [E]								
Electricité [E]	**104.2**	**100.0**	**120.2**	**131.7**	**139.0**	**162.4**	**170.3**	**189.2**
El Salvador El Salvador								
Total industry [CDE]								
Total, industrie [CDE]	**93.6**	**100.0**	**102.1**	**110.2**	**117.5**	**121.7**	**126.4**	**131.8**
Total mining [C]								
Total, industries extractives [C]	**93.8**	**100.0**	**101.1**	**107.5**	**113.2**	**113.7**	**108.4**	**121.3**

26
Index numbers of industrial production [*cont.*]
Indices de la production industrielle [*suite*]
1995＝100

Country or area and industry [ISIC Rev.3] Pays ou zone et industrie [CITI Rév.3]	1994	1995	1996	1997	1998	1999	2000	2001
Total manufacturing [D]								
Total, industries manufacturières [D]	**93.6**	**100.0**	**101.7**	**109.9**	**117.2**	**121.5**	**126.5**	**131.8**
Food, beverages, tobacco								
Aliments, boissons, tabac	96.1	100.0	101.6	106.2	111.4	114.3	118.0	120.8
Textiles,wearing apparel, leather, footwear								
Textiles, habillement, cuir et chaussures	96.2	100.0	99.1	102.2	108.4	111.7	113.6	107.6
Chemicals, petroleum, rubber and plastic prod.								
Prod. chimiques, pétroliers, caoutch. et plast.	104.3	100.0	101.1	106.9	114.4	124.2	121.6	128.6
Basic metals and metal products								
Métaux de base et produtis métalliques	92.4	100.0	107.3	117.4	129.9	132.3	135.3	145.1
Electricity [E]								
Electricité [E]	**94.3**	**100.0**	**139.1**	**142.0**	**156.8**	**160.2**	**146.0**	**150.4**
Guatemala Guatemala								
Total industry [CDE]								
Total, industrie [CDE]	**95.8**	**100.0**	**103.1**	...	...	...	...	...
Total mining [C]								
Total, industries extractives [C]	**87.8**	**100.0**	**123.9**	...	...	...	...	...
Total manufacturing [D]								
Total, industries manufacturières [D]	**96.9**	**100.0**	**101.9**	...	...	...	...	...
Food, beverages, tobacco								
Aliments, boissons, tabac	96.5	100.0	102.2	...	...	...	...	...
Textiles,wearing apparel, leather, footwear								
Textiles, habillement, cuir et chaussures	97.7	100.0	101.4	...	...	...	...	...
Chemicals, rubber and plastic products								
Prod. chimiques, caoutchouc et plastiques	96.6	100.0	101.9	...	...	...	...	...
Basic metals and metal products								
Métaux de base et produtis métalliques	97.0	100.0	101.8	...	...	...	...	...
Electricity and water [E]								
Electricité et eau [E]	**92.1**	**100.0**	**106.0**	...	...	...	...	...
Haiti [6] Haïti [6]								
Total industry [DE] [3]								
Total, industrie [DE] [3]	**76.5**	**100.0**	**101.5**	**108.1**	**112.2**	**115.2**	**120.8**	**114.8**
Total manufacturing [D]								
Total, industries manufacturières [D]	**83.3**	**100.0**	**99.2**	**102.0**	**107.4**	**110.9**	**118.2**	**120.9**
Food, beverages, tobacco								
Aliments, boissons, tabac	104.6	100.0	103.5	112.9	105.9	152.4	182.2	185.5
Chemicals and chemical products								
Produits chimiques	79.1	100.0	96.1	94.2	101.7	101.9	104.7	108.3
Electricity and water [E]								
Electricité et eau [E]	**50.1**	**100.0**	**110.4**	**131.6**	**130.7**	**132.0**	**130.8**	**91.0**
Honduras Honduras								
Total industry [CDE]								
Total, industrie [CDE]	**93.0**	**100.0**	**106.3**	**113.0**	**117.1**	**120.3**	**127.5**	**131.6**
Total mining [C]								
Total, industries extractives [C]	**86.5**	**100.0**	**107.3**	**112.5**	**116.7**	**122.9**	**125.0**	**120.8**
Total manufacturing [D]								
Total, industries manufacturières [D]	**94.8**	**100.0**	**104.6**	**111.0**	**114.8**	**117.8**	**124.3**	**130.8**
Food, beverages, tobacco								
Aliments, boissons, tabac	79.9	100.0	121.2	149.0	162.9	180.0	195.9	211.5
Textiles,wearing apparel, leather, footwear								
Textiles, habillement, cuir et chaussures	71.9	100.0	133.5	166.0	193.6	221.4	246.3	271.7
Chemicals, petroleum, rubber and plastic prod.								
Prod. chimiques, pétroliers, caoutch. et plast.	65.3	100.0	106.3	124.1	140.1	157.0	172.3	192.1
Basic metals								
Métaux de base	73.7	100.0	115.5	136.6	143.7	155.9	174.8	194.0
Metal products								
Produits métalliques	82.8	100.0	116.8	134.0	153.4	174.4	193.1	209.6
Electricity, gas and water [E]								
Electricité, gaz et eau [E]	**87.2**	**100.0**	**115.4**	**124.2**	**130.2**	**132.9**	**147.0**	**143.6**
Mexico Mexique								
Total industry [CDE] [7]								
Total, industrie [CDE] [7]	**108.5**	**100.0**	**110.1**	**120.3**	**127.8**	**133.3**	**141.5**	**136.4**
Total mining [C]								
Total, industries extractives [C]	**103.2**	**100.0**	**108.1**	**112.9**	**116.0**	**113.6**	**117.9**	**117.2**

26

Index numbers of industrial production [*cont.*]

Indices de la production industrielle [*suite*]

1995=100

Country or area and industry [ISIC Rev.3] Pays ou zone et industrie [CITI Rév.3]	1994	1995	1996	1997	1998	1999	2000	2001
Total manufacturing [D]								
Total, industries manufacturières [D]	**105.3**	**100.0**	**110.8**	**121.8**	**130.8**	**136.3**	**145.7**	**140.0**
Food, beverages, tobacco								
Aliments, boissons, tabac	100.0	100.0	103.2	106.6	113.6	118.3	123.0	125.2
Textiles and wearing apparel								
Textiles et habillement	109.6	100.0	113.5	122.6	124.5	125.5	129.3	115.1
Chemicals, petroleum, rubber and plastic prod.								
Prod. chimiques, pétroliers, caoutch. et plast.	101.2	100.0	106.3	113.4	120.1	122.7	126.5	120.9
Basic metals								
Métaux de base	96.7	100.0	119.1	132.5	137.7	138.3	142.5	134.5
Metal products								
Produits métalliques	115.8	100.0	123.5	148.9	166.2	175.8	199.3	189.4
Electricity, gas and water [E]								
Electricité, gaz et eau [E]	**97.9**	**100.0**	**104.6**	**110.1**	**112.1**	**120.9**	**122.1**	**124.2**
Panama Panama								
Total industry [CDE] [3]								
Total, industrie [CDE] [3]	**98.3**	**100.0**	**102.6**	**110.2**	**115.6**	**112.2**	**110.3**	**106.6**
Total mining [C]								
Total, industries extractives [C]	**104.4**	**100.0**	**79.9**	**160.5**	**202.2**	**230.5**	**228.6**	**137.1**
Total manufacturing [D]								
Total, industries manufacturières [D]	**99.5**	**100.0**	**99.9**	**105.6**	**109.9**	**105.3**	**99.9**	**93.2**
Food, beverages, tobacco								
Aliments, boissons, tabac	100.3	100.0	102.3	110.7	119.7	111.8	108.4	107.1
Textiles,wearing apparel, leather, footwear								
Textiles, habillement, cuir et chaussures	101.0	100.0	90.4	85.2	80.4	68.9	62.6	56.0
Chemicals, petroleum, rubber and plastic prod.								
Prod. chimiques, pétroliers, caoutch. et plast.	93.8	100.0	117.7	121.5	126.5	125.8	116.9	117.6
Basic metals								
Métaux de base	84.0	100.0	112.1	148.9	124.3	177.1	135.6	55.1
Metal products								
Produits métalliques	89.6	100.0	104.7	111.0	116.3	112.3	120.3	111.0
Electricity and water [E]								
Electricité et eau [E]	**95.4**	**100.0**	**109.2**	**120.3**	**127.6**	**126.3**	**132.7**	**137.8**
Trinidad and Tobago Trinité−et−Tobago								
Total industry [DE]								
Total, industrie [DE]	**93.0**	**100.0**	**105.7**	**112.4**	**125.0**	**139.0**	**146.4**	**157.6**
Total manufacturing [D] [3]								
Total, industries manufacturières [D] [3]	**92.8**	**100.0**	**106.0**	**113.0**	**125.4**	**140.1**	**148.7**	**162.2**
Food, beverages, tobacco								
Aliments, boissons, tabac	99.3	100.0	106.4	122.3	174.0	183.4	234.2	266.7
Textiles, leather and footwear								
Textiles, cuir et chaussures	105.5	100.0	101.3	135.6	180.8	364.1	458.0	434.1
Chemicals and petroleum products								
Produits chimiques et pétroliers	95.7	100.0	116.5	134.5	175.6	236.6	270.6	264.1
Metal products								
Produits métalliques	94.7	100.0	121.8	110.6	154.3	154.4	155.4	172.2
Electricity [E]								
Electricité [E]	**95.3**	**100.0**	**102.6**	**106.3**	**120.1**	**127.1**	**121.5**	**106.4**
United States Etats−Unis								
Total industry [CDE]								
Total, industrie [CDE]	**95.4**	**100.0**	**104.6**	**111.8**	**117.6**	**121.9**	**127.4**	**122.5**
Total mining [C]								
Total, industries extractives [C]	**100.3**	**100.0**	**101.5**	**103.2**	**100.9**	**96.3**	**98.7**	**99.3**
Total manufacturing [D]								
Total, industries manufacturières [D]	**95.0**	**100.0**	**104.9**	**113.2**	**119.9**	**125.0**	**130.9**	**125.1**
Food, beverages, tobacco								
Aliments, boissons, tabac	97.7	100.0	99.9	101.4	104.1	104.3	105.9	105.1
Textiles,wearing apparel, leather, footwear								
Textiles, habillement, cuir et chaussures	100.6	100.0	98.6	100.0	96.9	95.8	91.6	82.1
Chemicals, petroleum, rubber and plastic prod.								
Prod. chimiques, pétroliers, caoutch. et plast.	97.8	100.0	102.7	109.0	111.6	113.3	115.7	113.7
Basic metals								
Métaux de base	97.9	100.0	103.0	107.9	109.9	111.3	113.5	100.6

26
Index numbers of industrial production [*cont.*]
Indices de la production industrielle [*suite*]
1995=100

Country or area and industry [ISIC Rev.3] Pays ou zone et industrie [CITI Rév.3]	1994	1995	1996	1997	1998	1999	2000	2001
Metal products Produits métalliques	89.8	100.0	111.2	128.7	147.7	167.6	195.3	185.2
Electricity and gas [E] Électricité et gaz [E]	**96.6**	**100.0**	**103.3**	**103.3**	**104.8**	**107.5**	**110.6**	**109.8**
America, South · Amérique du Sud								
Argentina Argentine								
Total manufacturing [D] Total, industries manufacturières [D]	**107.5**	**100.0**	**106.4**	**116.3**	**118.7**	**108.8**	**107.4**	**97.8**
Food, beverages, tobacco Aliments, boissons, tabac	98.7	100.0	100.4	105.1	113.7	114.7	112.0	104.5
Textiles,wearing apparel, leather, footwear Textiles, habillement, cuir et chaussures	110.1	100.0	111.8	111.0	101.3	87.0	83.0	69.4
Chemicals, petroleum, rubber and plastic prod. Prod. chimiques, pétroliers, caoutch. et plast.	107.0	100.0	107.1	116.4	120.0	115.5	115.8	112.3
Basic metals Métaux de base	94.7	100.0	111.6	124.2	126.4	108.5	121.3	115.0
Metal products Produits métalliques	116.5	100.0	108.5	124.5	128.6	100.7	98.8	82.3
Bolivia Bolivie								
Total industry [CDE] [3] Total, industrie [CDE] [3]	**89.8**	**100.0**	**101.4**	**104.8**	**109.8**	**104.9**	**104.6**	**102.4**
Total mining [C] Total, industries extractives [C]	**84.6**	**100.0**	**98.5**	**100.6**	**106.7**	**95.1**	**93.6**	**90.5**
Total manufacturing [D] Total, industries manufacturières [D]	**95.6**	**100.0**	**104.1**	**108.4**	**112.0**	**114.1**	**114.8**	**113.5**
Food, beverages, tobacco Aliments, boissons, tabac	94.7	100.0	105.8	106.3	111.5	115.0	120.0	119.8
Textiles,wearing apparel, leather, footwear Textiles, habillement, cuir et chaussures	93.2	100.0	99.5	105.1	103.5	93.1	94.5	81.2
Chemicals, petroleum, rubber and plastic prod. Prod. chimiques, pétroliers, caoutch. et plast.	97.4	100.0	111.6	121.5	123.5	125.1	113.5	110.6
Basic metals Métaux de base	130.7	100.0	93.4	108.4	84.7	87.1	90.5	79.1
Metal products Produits métalliques	103.0	100.0	92.0	92.9	95.0	88.2	75.6	70.4
Electricity, gas and water [E] Électricité, gaz et eau [E]	**91.3**	**100.0**	**109.3**	**118.5**	**126.2**	**131.6**	**135.7**	**136.5**
Brazil Brésil								
Total industry [CD] Total, industrie [CD]	**98.2**	**100.0**	**101.8**	**105.7**	**103.5**	**102.9**	**109.7**	**111.3**
Total mining [C] Total, industries extractives [C]	**96.8**	**100.0**	**109.8**	**117.7**	**132.4**	**144.4**	**161.6**	**167.2**
Total manufacturing [D] Total, industries manufacturières [D]	**98.3**	**100.0**	**101.1**	**104.7**	**101.4**	**99.7**	**105.8**	**107.0**
Food, beverages, tobacco Aliments, boissons, tabac	92.7	100.0	104.7	107.1	106.0	108.3	106.4	110.8
Textiles,wearing apparel, leather, footwear Textiles, habillement, cuir et chaussures	106.9	100.0	95.9	89.6	84.5	83.9	89.2	83.7
Chemicals, petroleum, rubber and plastic prod. Prod. chimiques, pétroliers, caoutch. et plast.	99.6	100.0	105.3	110.3	113.3	113.8	115.9	114.3
Basic metals and metal products Métaux de base et produtis métalliques	98.2	100.0	98.2	103.8	95.9	90.6	102.8	106.9
Chile Chili								
Total industry [CDE] [3] Total, industrie [CDE] [3]	**93.1**	**100.0**	**108.3**	**115.6**	**118.8**	**124.8**	**130.1**	**132.2**
Total mining [C] Total, industries extractives [C]	**89.9**	**100.0**	**122.3**	**134.8**	**142.5**	**164.6**	**173.7**	**176.4**
Total manufacturing [D] Total, industries manufacturières [D]	**94.2**	**100.0**	**102.7**	**108.0**	**109.0**	**108.7**	**112.3**	**113.6**
Food, beverages, tobacco Aliments, boissons, tabac	95.3	100.0	101.5	102.6	100.2	101.6	104.5	108.3
Textiles,wearing apparel, leather, footwear Textiles, habillement, cuir et chaussures	102.8	100.0	97.8	90.2	77.6	68.7	67.2	59.3

26

Index numbers of industrial production [*cont.*]

Indices de la production industrielle [*suite*]

1995=100

Country or area and industry [ISIC Rev.3] Pays ou zone et industrie [CITI Rév.3]	1994	1995	1996	1997	1998	1999	2000	2001
Chemicals, petroleum, rubber and plastic prod. Prod. chimiques, pétroliers, caoutch. et plast.	91.7	100.0	106.9	116.5	123.2	128.3	140.6	148.1
Basic metals Métaux de base	93.8	100.0	102.8	111.3	119.9	123.5	92.3	96.5
Metal products Produits métalliques	95.5	100.0	101.4	114.0	106.8	97.6	105.6	104.7
Electricity [E] **Electricité [E]**	**94.1**	**100.0**	**112.7**	**121.2**	**129.9**	**139.6**	**147.4**	**153.7**
Colombia Colombie								
Total manufacturing [D] **Total, industries manufacturières [D]**	**97.9**	**100.0**	**97.3**	**99.7**	**98.2**	**85.0**	**93.2**	**94.4**
Food, beverages, tobacco Aliments, boissons, tabac	96.4	100.0	101.1	101.5	102.2	93.2	92.7	94.3
Textiles,wearing apparel, leather, footwear Textiles, habillement, cuir et chaussures	103.2	100.0	96.2	101.3	119.0	102.7	120.6	117.0
Chemicals, petroleum, rubber and plastic prod. Prod. chimiques, pétroliers, caoutch. et plast.	98.3	100.0	98.1	98.3	94.6	86.0	93.1	89.7
Basic metals Métaux de base	97.9	100.0	94.6	107.0	97.9	93.3	123.7	118.0
Metal products Produits métalliques	98.0	100.0	92.8	100.0	91.4	66.6	75.1	83.7
Ecuador Equateur								
Total manufacturing [D] **Total, industries manufacturières [D]**	**95.2**	**100.0**	**102.3**	**104.4**	**105.2**	**100.0**	**114.9**	**127.6**
Food, beverages, tobacco Aliments, boissons, tabac	96.9	100.0	102.0	103.3	105.9	104.5	107.7	119.6
Textiles, leather and footwear Textiles, cuir et chaussures	98.1	100.0	101.9	104.0	101.3	95.8	114.7	118.0
Chemicals, petroleum, rubber and plastic prod. Prod. chimiques, pétroliers, caoutch. et plast.	98.2	100.0	102.3	104.7	106.8	97.0	107.4	112.5
Basic metals Métaux de base	101.0	100.0	101.4	102.4	102.7	95.5	127.1	129.6
Metal products Produits métalliques	94.8	100.0	99.4	100.8	101.6	67.1	97.0	151.8
Paraguay Paraguay								
Total manufacturing [D] **Total, industries manufacturières [D]**	**97.2**	**100.0**	**97.8**	**97.6**	**98.6**	**98.6**	**99.6**	**101.0**
Food, beverages, tobacco Aliments, boissons, tabac	96.5	100.0	101.2	105.0	106.6	110.0	112.5	114.2
Textiles, wearing apparel, leather and footwear Textiles, habillement, cuir et chaussures	91.1	100.0	97.7	81.2	88.3	84.9	92.3	99.1
Chemicals, petroleum, rubber and plastic prod. Prod. chimiques, pétroliers, caoutch. et plast.	123.9	100.0	85.6	76.9	72.0	68.6	64.2	67.3
Basic metals Métaux de base	96.1	100.0	96.0	90.7	86.3	82.5	83.2	79.9
Metal products Produits métalliques	99.7	100.0	99.6	99.1	99.1	99.1	99.1	99.1
Peru Pérou								
Total industry [CDE] **Total, industrie [CDE]**	**92.1**	**100.0**	**102.5**	**109.4**	**108.8**	**109.9**	**113.3**	**113.5**
Total mining [C] **Total, industries extractives [C]**	**96.0**	**100.0**	**105.1**	**114.6**	**118.9**	**134.3**	**137.5**	**152.9**
Total manufacturing [D] **Total, industries manufacturières [D]**	**94.8**	**100.0**	**101.5**	**106.9**	**103.4**	**102.9**	**109.8**	**108.6**
Food, beverages, tobacco Aliments, boissons, tabac	100.6	100.0	100.3	103.8	99.0	112.4	122.0	118.1
Textiles,wearing apparel, leather, footwear Textiles, habillement, cuir et chaussures	90.5	100.0	102.6	107.2	99.9	97.2	110.1	105.6
Chemicals, petroleum, rubber and plastic prod. Prod. chimiques, pétroliers, caoutch. et plast.	96.6	100.0	106.3	118.3	114.1	114.3	118.6	122.9
Basic metals Métaux de base	94.9	100.0	108.6	115.6	121.4	121.9	128.1	132.7
Metal products Produits métalliques	79.4	100.0	90.9	98.3	91.7	75.6	83.4	82.1

26
Index numbers of industrial production [*cont.*]
Indices de la production industrielle [*suite*]
1995=100

Country or area and industry [ISIC Rev.3] Pays ou zone et industrie [CITI Rév.3]	1994	1995	1996	1997	1998	1999	2000	2001
Electricity [E] **Électricité [E]**	**99.8**	**100.0**	**105.9**	**119.4**	**129.2**	**132.5**	**138.6**	**144.0**
Suriname Suriname								
Total industry [CDE] **Total, industrie [CDE]**	**91.4**	**100.0**	**103.8**	**107.6**	**106.7**	**99.0**	...	...
Total mining [C] **Total, industries extractives [C]**	**98.1**	**100.0**	**103.9**	**168.9**	**194.2**	...	...	...
Total manufacturing [D] **Total, industries manufacturières [D]**	**75.7**	**100.0**	**101.8**	**104.5**	**86.5**	**79.3**	...	...
Food, beverages, tobacco Aliments, boissons, tabac	105.5	100.0	120.3	118.4	125.8	142.2	...	...
Electricity, gas and water [E] **Électricité, gaz et eau [E]**	**71.3**	**100.0**	**121.3**	**140.4**	**159.6**	**86.2**	**62.8**	...
Uruguay Uruguay								
Total manufacturing [D] **Total, industries manufacturières [D]**	**96.9**	**100.0**	**104.1**	**110.0**	**116.1**	**106.1**	**108.2**	**102.3**
Food, beverages, tobacco Aliments, boissons, tabac	99.9	100.0	106.3	115.7	118.6	120.1	114.3	107.6
Textiles,wearing apparel, leather, footwear Textiles, habillement, cuir et chaussures	121.7	100.0	100.6	108.5	89.0	64.0	64.5	52.6
Chemicals, petroleum, rubber and plastic prod. Prod. chimiques, pétroliers, caoutch. et plast.	59.1	100.0	106.4	100.4	114.8	103.1	112.6	102.8
Basic metals Métaux de base	105.5	100.0	98.1	107.0	111.5	105.2	101.0	99.7
Metal products Produits métalliques	166.8	100.0	70.5	83.8	115.8	92.5	111.9	87.0
Venezuela Venezuela								
Total industry [CDE] **Total, industrie [CDE]**	**100.0**	**95.8**	**100.1**	**95.2**	**87.3**	**90.5**	...	...
Total mining [C] **Total, industries extractives [C]**	**100.0**	**104.0**	**110.0**	**106.0**	**94.0**	**102.0**	...	...
Total manufacturing [D] **Total, industries manufacturières [D]**	**100.0**	**94.8**	**98.9**	**99.3**	**86.8**	**91.0**	...	...
Electricity, gas and water [E] **Électricité, gaz et eau [E]**	**100.0**	**101.0**	**106.1**	**110.5**	**109.9**	**114.6**	...	...
Asia · Asie								
Armenia Arménie								
Total industry [CDE] **Total, industrie [CDE]**	...	**100.0**	**101.4**	**102.4**	**100.2**	**105.5**	**112.3**	**116.6**
Total mining [C] **Total, industries extractives [C]**	...	**100.0**	**116.1**	**110.2**	**143.1**	**166.3**	**207.4**	**248.3**
Total manufacturing [D] **Total, industries manufacturières [D]**	...	**100.0**	**99.0**	**101.9**	**97.1**	**107.3**	**114.7**	**123.3**
Food, beverages, tobacco Aliments, boissons, tabac	...	100.0	101.5	113.5	101.4	112.1	117.0	124.4
Textiles,wearing apparel, leather, footwear Textiles, habillement, cuir et chaussures	...	100.0	104.9	133.0	117.5	75.1	73.0	84.2
Chemicals, petroleum, rubber and plastic prod. Prod. chimiques, pétroliers, caoutch. et plast.	...	100.0	107.5	78.1	93.0	101.5	115.3	97.9
Basic metals Métaux de base	...	100.0	76.9	44.5	184.7	151.3	318.0	457.3
Metal products Produits métalliques	...	100.0	93.9	81.0	68.2	74.4	88.1	117.5
Electricity [E] **Électricité [E]**	...	**100.0**	**108.3**	**105.2**	**105.7**	**100.0**	**102.6**	**95.1**
Azerbaijan Azerbaïdjan								
Total industry [CDE] **Total, industrie [CDE]**	**127.2**	**100.0**	**93.3**	**93.6**	**95.6**	**99.1**	**105.9**	**111.3**
Total mining [C] **Total, industries extractives [C]**	**135.9**	**100.0**	**97.9**	**97.3**	**121.2**	**145.3**	**146.9**	**155.5**
Total manufacturing [D] **Total, industries manufacturières [D]**	**128.5**	**100.0**	**90.0**	**90.7**	**80.1**	**72.8**	**84.0**	**86.3**
Electricity [E] **Électricité [E]**	**106.6**	**100.0**	**105.8**	**98.6**	**103.6**	**104.7**	**108.6**	**109.3**

26
Index numbers of industrial production [*cont.*]
Indices de la production industrielle [*suite*]
1995=100

Country or area and industry [ISIC Rev.3] Pays ou zone et industrie [CITI Rév.3]	1994	1995	1996	1997	1998	1999	2000	2001
Bangladesh [2] Bangladesh [2]								
Total industry [CDE]								
Total, industrie [CDE]	**93.7**	**100.0**	**106.2**	**110.3**	**112.5**	**121.4**	**131.5**	**140.9**
Total mining [C]								
Total, industries extractives [C]	**90.5**	**100.0**	**107.3**	**106.4**	**113.5**	**114.6**	**134.5**	**150.8**
Total manufacturing [D]								
Total, industries manufacturières [D]	**94.2**	**100.0**	**106.2**	**109.8**	**120.0**	**123.8**	**132.8**	**139.9**
Food, beverages, tobacco								
Aliments, boissons, tabac	93.2	100.0	96.1	94.4	99.4	98.0	105.2	108.3
Textiles,wearing apparel, leather, footwear								
Textiles, habillement, cuir et chaussures	99.7	100.0	106.6	111.8	122.8	127.7	132.3	141.9
Chemicals, petroleum, rubber and plastic prod.								
Prod. chimiques, pétroliers, caoutch. et plast.	101.6	100.0	106.8	99.1	104.4	98.2	103.5	112.7
Basic metals								
Métaux de base	60.0	100.0	87.0	94.3	105.1	89.3	93.0	103.0
Metal products								
Produits métalliques	95.7	100.0	93.6	108.5	151.9	116.6	117.5	117.3
Electricity [E]								
Electricité [E]	**90.2**	**100.0**	**105.8**	**109.3**	**118.8**	**127.3**	**135.8**	**149.8**
China, Hong Kong SAR Chine, Hong Kong RAS								
Total industry [DE] [3]								
Total, industrie [DE] [3]	**98.6**	**100.0**	**97.0**	**96.6**	**90.2**	**84.7**	**85.1**	**82.4**
Total manufacturing [D]								
Total, industries manufacturières [D]	**99.0**	**100.0**	**96.3**	**95.6**	**87.2**	**81.7**	**81.2**	**77.7**
Food, beverages, tobacco								
Aliments, boissons, tabac	100.4	100.0	99.1	98.6	89.7	88.2	85.5	84.0
Textiles and wearing apparel								
Textiles and habillement	101.1	100.0	94.8	93.9	86.2	84.1	86.9	86.7
Chemicals and other non−metallic mineral prod.								
Prod. chimiques et minéraux non−métalliques	105.4	100.0	100.2	101.4	88.1	74.9	64.1	59.2
Basic metals and metal products								
Métaux de base et produtis métalliques	93.6	100.0	94.1	91.3	84.0	80.0	79.2	72.5
Electricity and gas [E]								
Electricité et gaz [E]	**95.5**	**100.0**	**102.3**	**104.6**	**111.9**	**106.8**	**113.4**	**116.9**
Cyprus Chypre								
Total industry [CDE]								
Total, industrie [CDE]	**98.5**	**100.0**	**96.8**	**96.7**	**99.4**	**100.9**	**105.4**	**105.1**
Total mining [C]								
Total, industries extractives [C]	**108.5**	**100.0**	**97.6**	**101.4**	**121.1**	**130.2**	**135.3**	**131.6**
Total manufacturing [D]								
Total, industries manufacturières [D]	**99.5**	**100.0**	**94.9**	**94.3**	**95.4**	**96.3**	**100.1**	**98.1**
Food, beverages, tobacco								
Aliments, boissons, tabac	99.7	100.0	95.1	93.9	94.5	98.1	102.0	100.8
Textiles,wearing apparel, leather, footwear								
Textiles, habillement, cuir et chaussures	104.5	100.0	83.9	80.2	81.7	76.0	70.1	67.2
Chemicals, petroleum, rubber and plastic prod.								
Prod. chimiques, pétroliers, caoutch. et plast.	96.7	100.0	98.1	102.9	101.7	101.8	102.6	105.7
Metal products								
Produits métalliques	96.5	100.0	98.6	100.0	103.2	109.2	117.4	120.3
Electricity, gas and water [E]								
Electricité, gaz et eau [E]	**93.0**	**100.0**	**105.6**	**107.8**	**116.0**	**123.5**	**131.7**	**141.6**
India [8] Inde [8]								
Total industry [CDE]								
Total, industrie [CDE]	**88.5**	**100.0**	**106.1**	**113.1**	**117.8**	**125.6**	**131.9**	**135.4**
Total mining [C]								
Total, industries extractives [C]	**91.2**	**100.0**	**98.0**	**104.9**	**104.1**	**105.1**	**108.1**	**109.5**
Total manufacturing [D]								
Total, industries manufacturières [D]	**87.6**	**100.0**	**107.3**	**114.5**	**119.5**	**128.0**	**134.9**	**138.7**
Food, beverages, tobacco								
Aliments, boissons, tabac	94.1	100.0	105.5	110.9	113.3	118.9	125.8	124.6
Textiles,wearing apparel, leather, footwear								
Textiles, habillement, cuir et chaussures	84.8	100.0	109.5	112.9	109.7	117.0	123.9	124.0
Chemicals, petroleum, rubber and plastic prod.								
Prod. chimiques, pétroliers, caoutch. et plast.	90.6	100.0	104.1	116.4	125.2	134.8	146.4	154.3

26
Index numbers of industrial production [*cont.*]
Indices de la production industrielle [*suite*]
1995=100

Country or area and industry [ISIC Rev.3] Pays ou zone et industrie [CITI Rév.3]	1994	1995	1996	1997	1998	1999	2000	2001
Basic metals								
Métaux de base	86.4	100.0	106.7	109.5	106.8	112.1	114.2	119.0
Metal products								
Produits métalliques	88.6	100.0	108.4	113.2	125.2	137.7	145.2	145.1
Electricity [E]								
Electricité [E]	**92.5**	**100.0**	**104.0**	**110.8**	**118.0**	**126.6**	**131.7**	**135.7**
Indonesia Indonésie								
Total industry [CDE] [3]								
Total, industrie [CDE] [3]	**95.1**	**100.0**	**101.6**	**105.2**	**97.6**	**95.1**	**108.2**	**112.6**
Total mining [C]								
Total, industries extractives [C]	**98.6**	**100.0**	**101.8**	**103.3**	**103.8**	**96.9**	**117.7**	**125.9**
Total manufacturing [D]								
Total, industries manufacturières [D]	**91.4**	**100.0**	**100.6**	**106.0**	**86.7**	**88.3**	**91.5**	**91.5**
Food, beverages, tobacco								
Aliments, boissons, tabac	86.9	100.0	103.9	100.8	93.5	87.3	85.4	...
Textiles,wearing apparel, leather, footwear								
Textiles, habillement, cuir et chaussures	96.1	100.0	98.4	100.0	99.1	107.1	100.7	...
Chemicals, petroleum, rubber and plastic prod.								
Prod. chimiques, pétroliers, caoutch. et plast.	92.8	100.0	107.0	113.8	104.3	109.6	106.7	...
Basic metals								
Métaux de base	82.6	100.0	99.2	104.1	81.1	89.3	109.3	...
Metal products								
Produits métalliques	88.0	100.0	98.2	106.2	50.6	59.4	95.2	...
Electricity [E]								
Electricité [E]	**86.4**	**100.0**	**114.4**	**130.1**	**147.6**	**167.5**	**185.2**	**187.2**
Iran (Islamic Rep. of) Iran (Rép. islamique d')								
Total manufacturing [D]								
Total, industries manufacturières [D]	**93.7**	**100.0**	**105.8**	**108.6**	**130.3**	**135.8**	**141.2**	**146.6**
Food and beverages								
Aliments et boissons	89.2	100.0	109.2	119.2	123.5	131.7	139.3	133.8
Textiles, wearing apparel, leather, footwear								
Textiles, habillement, cuir et chaussures	100.8	100.0	107.0	109.5	104.9	102.0	97.7	98.9
Chemical, rubber and plastic products								
Prod. chimiques, caoutchouc et plastiques	92.0	100.0	110.7	117.7	115.2	124.4	129.6	137.6
Metal products								
Produits métalliques	92.4	100.0	110.7	146.4	154.2	173.3	187.1	212.2
Israel Israël								
Total industry [CD]								
Total, industrie [CD]	**92.3**	**100.0**	**105.4**	**107.2**	**110.2**	**111.8**	**123.1**	**116.3**
Total mining [C]								
Total, industries extractives [C]	**90.7**	**100.0**	**107.8**	**104.9**	**109.2**	**108.2**	**105.6**	**107.8**
Total manufacturing [D]								
Total, industries manufacturières [D]	**92.3**	**100.0**	**105.4**	**107.3**	**110.3**	**112.0**	**123.6**	**116.6**
Food, beverages, tobacco								
Aliments, boissons, tabac	91.8	100.0	100.1	103.1	103.9	105.3	105.5	104.3
Textiles								
Textiles	93.4	100.0	94.6	94.6	97.7	102.3	96.6	88.3
Chemicals, petroleum, rubber and plastic prod.								
Prod. chimiques, pétroliers, caoutch. et plast.	92.7	100.0	108.2	108.8	119.1	118.1	122.1	124.2
Basic metals								
Métaux de base	83.6	100.0	105.9	107.4	101.1	100.6	102.5	95.2
Metal products								
Produits métalliques	91.0	100.0	104.9	107.5	106.6	104.4	114.4	108.7
Japan Japon								
Total industry [CDE]								
Total, industrie [CDE]	**96.9**	**100.0**	**102.4**	**106.0**	**99.0**	**99.9**	**105.5**	**97.7**
Total mining [C]								
Total, industries extractives [C]	**103.7**	**100.0**	**101.4**	**92.8**	**86.4**	**86.1**	**85.8**	**85.6**
Total manufacturing [D]								
Total, industries manufacturières [D]	**96.8**	**100.0**	**102.3**	**106.0**	**98.5**	**99.3**	**105.2**	**96.9**
Food, beverages, tobacco								
Aliments, boissons, tabac	100.7	100.0	100.9	100.4	97.8	99.1	100.1	98.1
Textiles,wearing apparel, leather, footwear								
Textiles, habillement, cuir et chaussures	107.5	100.0	96.4	92.6	82.4	77.0	70.7	64.1

26

Index numbers of industrial production [*cont.*]

Indices de la production industrielle [*suite*]

1995=100

Country or area and industry [ISIC Rev.3] Pays ou zone et industrie [CITI Rév.3]	1994	1995	1996	1997	1998	1999	2000	2001
Chemicals, petroleum, rubber and plastic prod.								
Prod. chimiques, pétroliers, caoutch. et plast.	96.0	100.0	101.0	104.0	100.5	103.0	103.5	102.6
Basic metals								
Métaux de base	96.6	100.0	99.1	103.7	92.0	91.7	100.2	97.8
Metal products								
Produits métalliques	95.4	100.0	105.2	110.3	102.7	103.5	111.2	102.2
Electricity and gas [E]								
Electricité et gaz [E]	**97.8**	**100.0**	**103.2**	**105.6**	**106.8**	**108.2**	**111.5**	**111.2**
Jordan Jordanie								
Total industry [CDE]								
Total, industrie [CDE]	**88.9**	**100.0**	**94.8**	**99.6**	**102.1**	**102.5**	**106.5**	**117.2**
Total mining [C]								
Total, industries extractives [C]	**86.1**	**100.0**	**101.4**	**104.0**	**99.4**	**106.6**	**108.0**	**111.4**
Total manufacturing [D]								
Total, industries manufacturières [D]	**92.9**	**100.0**	**95.2**	**100.9**	**104.1**	**102.0**	**107.3**	**120.7**
Food, beverages, tobacco								
Aliments, boissons, tabac	88.2	100.0	92.1	83.4	107.7	119.0	140.5	166.4
Textiles,wearing apparel, leather, footwear								
Textiles, habillement, cuir et chaussures	108.4	100.0	108.7	100.6	100.5	82.9	74.9	55.8
Chemicals, petroleum, rubber and plastic prod.								
Prod. chimiques, pétroliers, caoutch. et plast.	82.9	100.0	90.8	109.2	103.0	94.7	97.1	107.8
Basic metals								
Métaux de base	105.3	100.0	108.7	78.1	64.4	75.3	70.7	88.1
Electricity and gas [E]								
Electricité et gaz [E]	**88.3**	**100.0**	**107.2**	**112.1**	**123.9**	**130.1**	**131.2**	**134.6**
Korea, Republic of Corée, Rép. de								
Total industry [CDE]								
Total, industrie [CDE]	**89.3**	**100.0**	**108.4**	**113.6**	**106.2**	**131.9**	**154.0**	**156.7**
Total mining [C]								
Total, industries extractives [C]	**107.0**	**100.0**	**98.0**	**93.9**	**72.8**	**78.6**	**77.4**	**75.1**
Total manufacturing [D]								
Total, industries manufacturières [D]	**89.3**	**100.0**	**108.3**	**113.2**	**105.7**	**132.2**	**154.7**	**157.0**
Food, beverages, tobacco								
Aliments, boissons, tabac	99.9	100.0	105.0	104.0	95.2	103.0	106.0	110.8
Textiles,wearing apparel, leather, footwear								
Textiles, habillement, cuir et chaussures	104.2	100.0	93.5	82.8	69.6	74.0	75.0	66.8
Chemicals, petroleum, rubber and plastic prod.								
Prod. chimiques, pétroliers, caoutch. et plast.	92.9	100.0	111.7	125.3	115.1	128.0	134.6	135.1
Basic metals								
Métaux de base	91.1	100.0	106.1	112.2	98.6	112.6	122.2	123.3
Metal products								
Produits métalliques	83.3	100.0	112.8	120.7	118.8	163.5	205.0	211.6
Electricity and gas [E]								
Electricité et gaz [E]	**88.1**	**100.0**	**112.3**	**123.3**	**119.1**	**133.8**	**149.9**	**160.3**
Malaysia Malaisie								
Total industry [CDE]								
Total, industrie [CDE]	**88.4**	**100.0**	**111.0**	**122.8**	**114.0**	**124.3**	**148.0**	**142.1**
Total mining [C]								
Total, industries extractives [C]	**91.8**	**100.0**	**105.9**	**108.4**	**109.6**	**106.1**	**105.9**	**108.7**
Total manufacturing [D]								
Total, industries manufacturières [D]	**87.6**	**100.0**	**112.3**	**126.2**	**113.3**	**127.7**	**159.6**	**149.3**
Food, beverages, tobacco								
Aliments, boissons, tabac	94.4	100.0	108.8	117.8	113.1	127.1	150.9	158.8
Textiles,wearing apparel, leather, footwear								
Textiles, habillement, cuir et chaussures	96.4	100.0	99.9	103.9	97.8	101.4	112.0	103.9
Chemicals, petroleum, rubber and plastic prod.								
Prod. chimiques, pétroliers, caoutch. et plast.	89.2	100.0	115.8	136.6	134.8	152.7	174.4	168.4
Basic metals								
Métaux de base	88.7	100.0	117.2	132.5	93.7	134.6	141.7	140.9
Metal products								
Produits métalliques	83.2	100.0	110.8	125.4	111.1	128.2	176.9	153.8
Electricity [E]								
Electricité [E]	**87.6**	**100.0**	**112.8**	**128.8**	**133.2**	**138.3**	**146.8**	**159.6**

26
Index numbers of industrial production [*cont.*]
Indices de la production industrielle [*suite*]
1995=100

Country or area and industry [ISIC Rév.3] Pays ou zone et industrie [CITI Rév.3]	1994	1995	1996	1997	1998	1999	2000	2001
Mongolia Mongolie								
Total industry [CDE]								
Total, industrie [CDE]	**89.4**	**100.0**	**97.5**	**101.9**	**186.2**	**106.7**	**108.9**	**121.9**
Total mining [C]								
Total, industries extractives [C]	**82.6**	**100.0**	**107.3**	**125.5**	**116.5**	**121.0**	**128.1**	**141.1**
Total manufacturing [D]								
Total, industries manufacturières [D]	**89.5**	**100.0**	**89.5**	**82.1**	**73.3**	**71.1**	**65.9**	**81.1**
Food and beverages								
Aliments et boissons	83.8	100.0	75.5	70.8	69.6	60.7	59.5	70.4
Textiles,wearing apparel, leather, footwear								
Textiles, habillement, cuir et chaussures	77.8	100.0	92.1	80.8	80.6	88.4	83.0	121.6
Chemicals and chemical products								
Produits chimiques	97.4	100.0	97.4	96.1	103.0	108.0	108.4	117.3
Basic metals								
Métaux de base	48.6	100.0	92.9	167.3	143.1	145.1	133.3	158.9
Electricity and gas [E]								
Electricité et gaz [E]	**94.9**	**100.0**	**96.2**	**93.7**	**98.1**	**101.1**	**103.6**	**108.4**
Pakistan [1] Pakistan [1]								
Total industry [CDE] [3]								
Total, industrie [CDE] [3]	**96.7**	**100.0**	**97.9**	**104.7**	**107.4**	**108.0**	**115.2**	**122.9**
Total mining [C]								
Total, industries extractives [C]	**96.3**	**100.0**	**102.1**	**96.1**	**101.0**	**104.1**	**113.1**	**112.7**
Total manufacturing [D]								
Total, industries manufacturières [D]	**96.9**	**100.0**	**97.9**	**105.3**	**109.1**	**109.1**	**118.4**	**124.6**
Electricity and gas [E]								
Electricité et gaz [E]	**95.5**	**100.0**	**96.7**	**105.1**	**100.5**	**103.9**	**98.2**	**117.5**
Singapore Singapour								
Total manufacturing [D]								
Total, industries manufacturières [D]	**90.7**	**100.0**	**103.4**	**108.2**	**107.7**	**122.6**	**141.4**	**125.1**
Food, beverages, tobacco								
Aliments, boissons, tabac	99.2	100.0	101.8	98.9	87.8	92.0	93.5	97.5
Textiles,wearing apparel, leather, footwear								
Textiles, habillement, cuir et chaussures	123.0	100.0	81.1	79.1	84.4	88.1	101.0	86.3
Chemicals, petroleum, rubber and plastic prod.								
Prod. chimiques, pétroliers, caoutch. et plast.	98.6	100.0	104.2	119.7	136.0	159.9	168.7	174.4
Basic metals								
Métaux de base	109.7	100.0	100.1	105.2	87.3	92.7	98.4	99.4
Metal products								
Produits métalliques	94.4	100.0	98.8	102.3	100.0	114.5	138.2	115.7
Sri Lanka Sri Lanka								
Total manufacturing [D]								
Total, industries manufacturières [D]	**95.0**	**100.0**	**93.5**	**91.0**	**85.9**	**92.0**	...	...
Food, beverages, tobacco								
Aliments, boissons, tabac	95.3	100.0	89.3	89.4	83.0	93.3	...	...
Textiles,wearing apparel, leather, footwear								
Textiles, habillement, cuir et chaussures	107.9	100.0	98.1	106.4	106.3	116.4	...	...
Chemicals, petroleum, rubber and plastic prod.								
Prod. chimiques, pétroliers, caoutch. et plast.	87.6	100.0	120.0	95.1	93.3	100.2	...	...
Basic metals								
Métaux de base	100.3	100.0	95.8	90.7	71.0	66.4	...	...
Metal products								
Produits métalliques	92.3	100.0	95.6	120.1	115.7	116.2	...	...
Syrian Arab Republic Rép. arabe syrienne								
Total industry [CDE]								
Total, industrie [CDE]	**97.0**	**100.0**	**101.0**	**107.0**	**109.0**	**109.0**	**109.0**	...
Total mining [C]								
Total, industries extractives [C]	**96.0**	**100.0**	**100.0**	**101.0**	**102.0**	**101.0**	**97.0**	...
Total manufacturing [D]								
Total, industries manufacturières [D]	**97.0**	**100.0**	**101.0**	**109.0**	**110.0**	**110.0**	**109.0**	...
Food, beverages, tobacco								
Aliments, boissons, tabac	91.1	100.0	101.3	108.0	102.1	108.3	107.6	...
Textiles,wearing apparel, leather, footwear								
Textiles, habillement, cuir et chaussures	103.7	100.0	98.7	106.9	108.3	113.7	126.3	...

26
Index numbers of industrial production [*cont.*]
Indices de la production industrielle [*suite*]
1995=100

Country or area and industry [ISIC Rev.3] Pays ou zone et industrie [CITI Rév.3]	1994	1995	1996	1997	1998	1999	2000	2001
Chemicals, petroleum, rubber and plastic prod. Prod. chimiques, pétroliers, caoutch. et plast.	99.8	100.0	95.4	109.6	109.3	95.1	95.1	...
Basic metals Métaux de base	102.0	100.0	146.0	163.0	159.0	147.0	138.0	...
Metal products Produits métalliques	86.2	100.0	96.3	88.9	85.4	93.2	60.6	...
Electricity and water [E] **Électricité et eau [E]**	**91.4**	**100.0**	**108.0**	**115.0**	**129.6**	**143.6**	**155.9**	...
Tajikistan Tadjikistan								
Total industry [CDE] Total, industrie [CDE]	116.3	100.0	76.7	74.4	81.4	86.0	88.4	93.0
Total mining [C] Total, industries extractives [C]	101.6	100.0	96.9	118.8	131.3	131.3	132.8	134.4
Total manufacturing [D] Total, industries manufacturières [D]	119.5	100.0	73.2	65.9	68.3	78.0	82.9	87.8
Electricity, gas and water [E] Électricité, gaz et eau [E]	101.1	100.0	97.9	109.5	112.6	126.3	131.6	136.8
Thailand Thaïlande								
Total manufacturing [D] Total, industries manufacturières [D]	92.0	100.0	108.3	107.8	96.5	108.6	111.9	113.5
Turkey Turquie								
Total industry [CDE] Total, industrie [CDE]	92.1	100.0	105.9	117.2	118.3	112.3	118.4	107.9
Total mining [C] Total, industries extractives [C]	99.5	100.0	103.3	109.4	120.2	110.0	105.1	96.8
Total manufacturing [D] Total, industries manufacturières [D]	92.2	100.0	106.5	118.8	118.4	111.6	118.1	106.4
Food, beverages, tobacco Aliments, boissons, tabac	97.5	100.0	109.4	118.1	120.4	119.2	124.3	123.1
Textiles,wearing apparel, leather, footwear Textiles, habillement, cuir et chaussures	85.9	100.0	108.3	115.1	111.6	105.0	114.2	108.2
Chemicals, petroleum, rubber and plastic prod. Prod. chimiques, pétroliers, caoutch. et plast.	84.6	100.0	105.0	118.5	120.4	118.3	123.1	116.4
Basic metals Métaux de base	94.0	100.0	107.7	118.1	118.7	116.5	120.9	113.0
Metal products Produits métalliques	80.9	100.0	115.1	140.4	138.5	127.6	148.2	115.0
Electricity, gas and water [E] **Électricité, gaz et eau [E]**	**90.8**	**100.0**	**110.5**	**119.6**	**128.7**	**135.0**	**144.9**	**142.6**
Europe · Europe								
Albania Albanie								
Total industry [CDE] Total, industrie [CDE]	115.6	100.0	82.8	53.6	82.5	59.7	121.3	91.3
Total mining [C] Total, industries extractives [C]	107.7	100.0	87.7	54.5	56.2	41.4	36.4	32.1
Total manufacturing [D] Total, industries manufacturières [D]	119.6	100.0	81.1	74.8	68.5	77.7	116.0	77.6
Electricity, gas and water [E] **Électricité, gaz et eau [E]**	**88.5**	**100.0**	**131.1**	**116.0**	**114.6**	**121.5**	**104.5**	**81.5**
Austria Autriche								
Total industry [CDE] Total, industrie [CDE]	83.3	100.0	101.0	107.4	116.2	123.2	134.1	134.2
Total mining [C] Total, industries extractives [C]	84.1	100.0	100.2	96.7	103.9	107.4	112.3	110.5
Total manufacturing [D] Total, industries manufacturières [D]	81.5	100.0	100.7	108.0	117.8	124.9	137.3	137.5
Food, beverages, tobacco Aliments, boissons, tabac	96.5	100.0	100.0	108.4	113.2	117.1	121.2	121.1
Textiles,wearing apparel, leather, footwear Textiles, habillement, cuir et chaussures	107.0	100.0	94.3	95.3	97.5	90.8	88.9	87.5
Chemicals, petroleum, rubber and plastic prod. Prod. chimiques, pétroliers, caoutch. et plast.	87.1	100.0	101.0	103.7	112.1	116.8	126.6	132.4
Basic metals Métaux de base	85.5	100.0	96.3	111.2	114.6	113.9	126.5	129.1

26
Index numbers of industrial production [*cont.*]
Indices de la production industrielle [*suite*]
1995=100

Country or area and industry [ISIC Rev.3] Pays ou zone et industrie [CITI Rév.3]	1994	1995	1996	1997	1998	1999	2000	2001
Metal products								
Produits métalliques	74.3	100.0	102.6	111.5	128.4	142.3	162.2	162.2
Electricity, gas and water [E]								
Electricité, gaz et eau [E]	104.5	100.0	102.9	104.8	106.6	112.9	114.6	114.6
Belarus Belarus								
Total industry [CDE]								
Total, industrie [CDE]	...	100.0	103.5	123.0	138.3	152.5	164.4	173.3
Total mining [C]								
Total, industries extractives [C]	...	100.0	99.0	111.7	118.6	123.9	117.5	131.6
Total manufacturing [D]								
Total, industries manufacturières [D]	...	100.0	104.3	125.6	143.9	159.8	174.3	184.4
Electricity, gas and water [E]								
Electricité, gaz et eau [E]	...	100.0	98.4	103.9	96.2	101.4	98.6	97.4
Belgium Belgique								
Total industry [CDE]								
Total, industrie [CDE]	94.1	100.0	100.8	105.4	108.9	110.1	115.5	115.8
Total mining [C]								
Total, industries extractives [C]	71.2	100.0	106.7	113.4	116.6	125.2	138.1	142.0
Total manufacturing [D]								
Total, industries manufacturières [D]	94.0	100.0	100.5	105.4	108.4	109.7	116.2	116.9
Food, beverages, tobacco								
Aliments, boissons, tabac	93.1	100.0	100.4	105.0	107.3	103.0	107.3	111.3
Textiles,wearing apparel, leather, footwear								
Textiles, habillement, cuir et chaussures	106.7	100.0	91.3	93.9	91.0	85.2	87.0	83.2
Chemicals, petroleum, rubber and plastic prod.								
Prod. chimiques, pétroliers, caoutch. et plast.	92.0	100.0	103.3	113.7	115.1	122.5	134.9	131.8
Basic metals								
Métaux de base	96.7	100.0	97.8	98.2	101.2	101.5	106.9	94.8
Metal products								
Produits métalliques	92.8	100.0	101.2	105.3	111.8	112.3	119.2	122.1
Electricity, gas and water [E]								
Electricité, gaz et eau [E]	96.8	100.0	103.6	105.6	112.7	112.8	109.8	106.4
Bulgaria Bulgarie								
Total industry [CDE]								
Total, industrie [CDE]	...	100.0	105.1	85.8	78.5	70.9	78.2	76.3
Total mining [C]								
Total, industries extractives [C]	...	100.0	115.5	93.3	90.9	78.1	80.7	74.4
Total manufacturing [D]								
Total, industries manufacturières [D]	...	100.0	104.8	84.2	74.8	68.1	74.7	72.1
Food, beverages, tobacco								
Aliments, boissons, tabac	...	100.0	102.0	75.5	78.2	70.8	73.3	71.9
Textiles,wearing apparel, leather, footwear								
Textiles, habillement, cuir et chaussures	...	100.0	114.0	91.8	87.9	74.5	85.5	94.1
Chemicals, petroleum, rubber and plastic prod.								
Prod. chimiques, pétroliers, caoutch. et plast.	...	100.0	113.4	84.4	61.9	51.6	49.7	44.3
Basic metals								
Métaux de base	...	100.0	102.8	100.7	82.7	66.4	80.9	67.9
Metal products								
Produits métalliques	...	100.0	96.6	87.2	84.0	70.6	72.3	67.4
Electricity, gas and water [E]								
Electricité, gaz et eau [E]	...	100.0	101.6	98.6	109.2	94.8	112.3	120.7
Croatia Croatie								
Total industry [CDE]								
Total, industrie [CDE]	99.5	100.0	103.0	110.0	114.2	112.5	114.4	121.3
Total mining [C]								
Total, industries extractives [C]	97.6	100.0	97.0	96.6	94.2	96.0	97.8	99.7
Total manufacturing [D]								
Total, industries manufacturières [D]	100.3	100.0	101.2	105.2	108.6	105.4	108.5	115.4
Food, beverages, tobacco								
Aliments, boissons, tabac	97.8	100.0	102.9	95.8	99.1	94.1	94.3	100.5
Textiles,wearing apparel, leather, footwear								
Textiles, habillement, cuir et chaussures	112.3	100.0	87.8	89.1	88.3	79.4	78.4	82.1
Chemicals, petroleum, rubber and plastic prod.								
Prod. chimiques, pétroliers, caoutch. et plast.	79.3	100.0	96.6	91.6	88.8	91.5	96.7	92.4

26
Index numbers of industrial production [*cont.*]
Indices de la production industrielle [*suite*]
1995=100

Country or area and industry [ISIC Rev.3] Pays ou zone et industrie [CITI Rév.3]	1994	1995	1996	1997	1998	1999	2000	2001
Basic metals								
Métaux de base	121.5	100.0	91.0	114.1	133.3	115.6	120.6	125.7
Metal products								
Produits métalliques	102.5	100.0	101.0	111.4	118.4	120.4	121.1	137.0
Electricity, gas and water [E]								
Electricité, gaz et eau [E]	**95.3**	**100.0**	**125.3**	**155.7**	**169.3**	**181.0**	**172.4**	**180.7**
Czech Republic Rép. tchèque								
Total industry [CDE]								
Total, industrie [CDE]	**92.0**	**100.0**	**102.0**	**106.5**	**108.2**	**104.8**	**110.4**	...
Total mining [C]								
Total, industries extractives [C]	**101.4**	**100.0**	**101.4**	**98.5**	**92.8**	**81.6**	**87.9**	...
Total manufacturing [D]								
Total, industries manufacturières [D]	**92.3**	**100.0**	**101.6**	**108.1**	**110.9**	**107.9**	**113.4**	...
Food, beverages, tobacco								
Aliments, boissons, tabac	...	100.0	103.8	108.0	107.8	107.3	104.1	...
Textiles,wearing apparel, leather, footwear								
Textiles, habillement, cuir et chaussures	...	100.0	94.0	95.4	92.0	81.1	93.3	...
Chemicals, petroleum, rubber and plastic prod.								
Prod. chimiques, pétroliers, caoutch. et plast.	...	100.0	104.6	108.0	107.1	105.0	108.0	...
Basic metals								
Métaux de base	...	100.0	88.8	92.6	86.2	69.0	59.1	...
Metal products								
Produits métalliques	...	100.0	110.4	125.2	139.9	134.6	165.9	...
Electricity, gas and water [E]								
Electricité, gaz et eau [E]	**95.9**	**100.0**	**103.7**	**100.9**	**99.4**	**95.9**	**101.8**	...
Denmark Danemark								
Total industry [CD]								
Total, industrie [CD]	**95.7**	**100.0**	**101.7**	**107.0**	**109.3**	**111.4**	**118.3**	**120.1**
Total mining [C]								
Total, industries extractives [C]	**100.0**	**100.0**	**103.4**	**88.4**	**94.3**	**94.0**	**94.5**	**96.4**
Total manufacturing [D]								
Total, industries manufacturières [D]	**95.7**	**100.0**	**101.7**	**107.2**	**109.4**	**111.5**	**118.5**	**120.3**
Food, beverages, tobacco								
Aliments, boissons, tabac	103.4	100.0	98.0	103.5	102.3	102.0	104.8	103.6
Textiles,wearing apparel, leather, footwear								
Textiles, habillement, cuir et chaussures	101.5	100.0	103.6	101.3	106.1	100.7	104.9	94.9
Chemicals, petroleum, rubber and plastic prod.								
Prod. chimiques, pétroliers, caoutch. et plast.	94.0	100.0	103.2	112.0	117.5	132.0	146.9	156.3
Basic metals								
Métaux de base	97.9	100.0	94.3	104.3	102.4	100.8	119.5	109.8
Metal products								
Produits métalliques	92.9	100.0	102.7	107.9	111.5	110.0	118.9	123.3
Estonia Estonie								
Total industry [CDE]								
Total, industrie [CDE]	**98.1**	**100.0**	**102.9**	**117.9**	**122.8**	**118.6**	**135.9**	**146.5**
Total mining [C]								
Total, industries extractives [C]	**104.6**	**100.0**	**105.7**	**105.3**	**100.8**	**86.9**	**91.3**	**98.0**
Total manufacturing [D]								
Total, industries manufacturières [D]	**97.2**	**100.0**	**102.2**	**121.1**	**127.9**	**124.7**	**145.4**	**157.7**
Food, beverages, tobacco								
Aliments, boissons, tabac	103.4	100.0	92.9	108.7	103.4	83.1	89.0	94.9
Textiles,wearing apparel, leather, footwear								
Textiles, habillement, cuir et chaussures	89.2	100.0	115.0	127.5	134.0	135.6	160.7	180.0
Chemicals, petroleum, rubber and plastic prod.								
Prod. chimiques, pétroliers, caoutch. et plast.	92.4	100.0	105.8	126.1	123.7	115.7	133.8	146.4
Metal products								
Produits métalliques	89.3	100.0	102.9	122.0	141.2	149.4	188.3	196.2
Electricity [E]								
Electricité [E]	**102.0**	**100.0**	**106.3**	**103.0**	**99.3**	**93.8**	**94.3**	**95.4**
Finland Finlande								
Total industry [CDE]								
Total, industrie [CDE]	**94.2**	**100.0**	**103.3**	**112.0**	**122.2**	**129.4**	**144.1**	**142.5**
Total mining [C]								
Total, industries extractives [C]	**101.5**	**100.0**	**100.6**	**127.1**	**92.8**	**128.2**	**95.7**	**108.4**

26
Index numbers of industrial production [*cont.*]
Indices de la production industrielle [*suite*]
1995=100

Country or area and industry [ISIC Rev.3] Pays ou zone et industrie [CITI Rév.3]	1994	1995	1996	1997	1998	1999	2000	2001
Total manufacturing [D]								
Total, industries manufacturières [D]	**93.4**	**100.0**	**102.8**	**111.9**	**123.5**	**131.0**	**147.5**	**145.1**
Food, beverages, tobacco								
Aliments, boissons, tabac	96.4	100.0	103.2	106.3	106.8	110.7	111.0	112.4
Textiles,wearing apparel, leather, footwear								
Textiles, habillement, cuir et chaussures	110.3	100.0	100.8	101.5	100.5	100.4	98.1	95.1
Chemicals, petroleum, rubber and plastic prod.								
Prod. chimiques, pétroliers, caoutch. et plast.	98.2	100.0	103.0	108.3	114.5	117.3	125.2	122.5
Basic metals								
Métaux de base	94.2	100.0	105.6	111.9	118.2	122.3	129.9	130.5
Metal products								
Produits métalliques	83.6	100.0	106.6	118.0	140.0	154.0	191.5	194.3
Electricity, gas and water [E]								
Electricité, gaz et eau [E]	**101.6**	**100.0**	**109.0**	**108.9**	**110.2**	**109.9**	**110.9**	**117.0**
France France								
Total industry [CDE]								
Total, industrie [CDE]	**97.6**	**100.0**	**100.9**	**104.7**	**110.2**	**112.4**	**116.4**	**117.3**
Total mining [C]								
Total, industries extractives [C]	**100.4**	**100.0**	**91.7**	**89.5**	**88.8**	**89.8**	**91.3**	**89.1**
Total manufacturing [D]								
Total, industries manufacturières [D]	**97.8**	**100.0**	**100.6**	**105.4**	**111.6**	**113.8**	**117.9**	**118.6**
Food, beverages, tobacco								
Aliments, boissons, tabac	98.5	100.0	102.0	104.8	105.9	107.7	107.3	108.3
Textiles,wearing apparel, leather, footwear								
Textiles, habillement, cuir et chaussures	105.3	100.0	88.2	86.0	83.4	75.3	69.0	63.6
Chemicals, petroleum, rubber and plastic prod.								
Prod. chimiques, pétroliers, caoutch. et plast.	97.6	100.0	102.0	106.9	112.4	114.4	120.2	122.4
Basic metals								
Métaux de base	99.5	100.0	97.4	105.1	108.1	105.9	112.8	109.3
Metal products								
Produits métalliques	96.6	100.0	102.3	108.9	118.8	123.0	128.9	130.6
Electricity and gas [E]								
Electricité et gaz [E]	**95.9**	**100.0**	**103.7**	**101.8**	**102.8**	**105.2**	**108.6**	**111.3**
Germany Allemagne								
Total industry [CDE]								
Total, industrie [CDE]	**97.9**	**100.0**	**100.6**	**104.1**	**108.5**	**110.2**	**117.6**	**117.6**
Total mining [C]								
Total, industries extractives [C]	**104.0**	**100.0**	**94.3**	**91.1**	**84.8**	**83.7**	**79.2**	**73.4**
Total manufacturing [D]								
Total, industries manufacturières [D]	**97.8**	**100.0**	**100.4**	**104.4**	**109.5**	**111.3**	**119.6**	**119.9**
Food, beverages, tobacco								
Aliments, boissons, tabac	99.5	100.0	101.3	102.4	101.9	104.7	111.6	105.5
Textiles,wearing apparel, leather, footwear								
Textiles, habillement, cuir et chaussures	104.6	100.0	93.0	90.6	89.0	82.1	81.1	77.6
Chemicals, petroleum, rubber and plastic prod.								
Prod. chimiques, pétroliers, caoutch. et plast.	97.1	100.0	103.1	108.6	110.4	114.1	118.1	116.2
Basic metals								
Métaux de base	98.6	100.0	94.7	103.8	104.7	101.2	108.7	108.7
Metal products								
Produits métalliques	98.7	100.0	100.9	106.1	114.7	116.7	129.7	132.8
Electricity and gas [E]								
Electricité et gaz [E]	**98.0**	**100.0**	**105.5**	**104.7**	**104.9**	**105.5**	**106.2**	**104.5**
Greece Grèce								
Total industry [CDE]								
Total, industrie [CDE]	**97.7**	**100.0**	**100.9**	**102.8**	**112.0**	**114.2**	**122.5**	**123.8**
Total mining [C]								
Total, industries extractives [C]	**97.5**	**100.0**	**103.6**	**103.9**	**102.6**	**96.4**	**109.3**	**107.7**
Total manufacturing [D]								
Total, industries manufacturières [D]	**98.0**	**100.0**	**99.6**	**101.9**	**110.2**	**109.2**	**114.8**	**117.0**
Food, beverages, tobacco								
Aliments, boissons, tabac	96.1	100.0	97.9	102.4	111.8	111.6	113.5	116.0
Textiles,wearing apparel, leather, footwear								
Textiles, habillement, cuir et chaussures	104.8	100.0	94.3	92.7	91.4	85.9	86.6	83.2

26
Index numbers of industrial production [*cont.*]
Indices de la production industrielle [*suite*]
1995=100

Country or area and industry [ISIC Rev.3] Pays ou zone et industrie [CITI Rév.3]	1994	1995	1996	1997	1998	1999	2000	2001
Chemicals, petroleum, rubber and plastic prod.								
Prod. chimiques, pétroliers, caoutch. et plast.	97.5	100.0	108.1	110.7	124.8	121.6	130.9	137.4
Basic metals								
Métaux de base	91.5	100.0	97.8	106.2	98.3	109.7	125.5	127.4
Metal products								
Produits métalliques	98.1	100.0	97.8	97.5	108.0	110.4	119.1	122.5
Electricity and gas [E]								
Electricité et gaz [E]	**96.4**	**100.0**	**103.8**	**104.5**	**120.0**	**135.1**	**151.0**	**149.9**
Hungary Hongrie								
Total industry [CDE]								
Total, industrie [CDE]	**95.6**	**100,0**	**103.4**	**114.8**	**129.0**	**142.4**	**168.4**	**174.3**
Total mining [C]								
Total, industries extractives [C]	**115.4**	**100.0**	**102.5**	**93.9**	**74.7**	**75.3**	**68.2**	**79.4**
Total manufacturing [D]								
Total, industries manufacturières [D]	**95.1**	**100.0**	**103.4**	**118.5**	**137.7**	**154.7**	**186.8**	**194.7**
Food, beverages, tobacco								
Aliments, boissons, tabac	98.2	100.0	99.6	92.4	93.1	95.6	101.8	101.1
Textiles,wearing apparel, leather, footwear								
Textiles, habillement, cuir et chaussures	105.4	100.0	97.3	98.9	112.4	122.4	134.0	137.2
Chemicals, petroleum, rubber and plastic prod.								
Prod. chimiques, pétroliers, caoutch. et plast.	100.6	100.0	97.3	101.7	105.9	97.0	103.8	106.0
Basic metals								
Métaux de base	88.1	100.0	109.4	122.4	118.8	113.3	132.3	127.8
Metal products								
Produits métalliques	89.0	100.0	111.2	158.7	216.4	301.4	404.3	411.9
Electricity and gas [E]								
Electricité et gaz [E]	**98.1**	**100.0**	**105.0**	**106.0**	**105.9**	**104.4**	**102.6**	**102.1**
Ireland Irlande								
Total industry [CDE]								
Total, industrie [CDE]	**83.0**	**100.0**	**107.6**	**127.0**	**152.1**	**174.6**	**201.5**	**222.2**
Total mining [C]								
Total, industries extractives [C]	**67.8**	**100.0**	**98.4**	**84.2**	**77.6**	**92.3**	**113.6**	**108.3**
Total manufacturing [D]								
Total, industries manufacturières [D]	**82.5**	**100.0**	**108.0**	**129.5**	**157.0**	**180.6**	**209.1**	**231.3**
Food, beverages, tobacco								
Aliments, boissons, tabac	90.3	100.0	101.6	103.8	109.1	114.4	120.5	126.1
Textiles,wearing apparel, leather, footwear								
Textiles, habillement, cuir et chaussures	120.2	100.0	100.5	100.3	102.1	90.0	73.6	75.6
Chemicals, rubber and plastic prod.								
Prod. chimiques, caoutch. et plast.	78.8	100.0	115.9	157.3	218.9	273.1	310.3	376.2
Basic metals								
Métaux de base	83.1	100.0	98.5	95.0	93.6	92.0	94.2	85.6
Metal products								
Produits métalliques	76.9	100.0	108.8	126.0	143.9	161.6	213.5	220.7
Electricity, gas and water [E]								
Electricité, gaz et eau [E]	**98.4**	**100.0**	**105.7**	**110.2**	**113.3**	**122.9**	**129.3**	**137.8**
Italy Italie								
Total industry [CDE]								
Total, industrie [CDE]	**94.9**	**100.0**	**99.1**	**102.4**	**104.3**	**104.4**	**107.7**	**107.0**
Total mining [C]								
Total, industries extractives [C]	**93.0**	**100.0**	**102.4**	**108.5**	**107.9**	**107.8**	**98.4**	**91.1**
Total manufacturing [D]								
Total, industries manufacturières [D]	**94.7**	**100.0**	**98.9**	**102.2**	**103.9**	**103.6**	**106.7**	**105.9**
Food, beverages, tobacco								
Aliments, boissons, tabac	99.5	100.0	99.7	102.2	104.4	107.6	109.9	110.6
Textiles,wearing apparel, leather, footwear								
Textiles, habillement, cuir et chaussures	96.8	100.0	98.8	102.1	99.9	95.2	95.6	98.6
Chemicals, petroleum, rubber and plastic prod.								
Prod. chimiques, pétroliers, caoutch. et plast.	98.0	100.0	99.6	105.2	106.8	106.3	108.4	106.2
Basic metals								
Métaux de base	96.3	100.0	99.9	102.0	101.8	94.1	100.8	94.2
Metal products								
Produits métalliques	90.4	100.0	99.4	102.2	104.0	102.5	106.5	104.4

26
Index numbers of industrial production [*cont.*]
Indices de la production industrielle [*suite*]
1995=100

Country or area and industry [ISIC Rev.3] Pays ou zone et industrie [CITI Rév.3]	1994	1995	1996	1997	1998	1999	2000	2001
Electricity and gas [E]								
Électricité et gaz [E]	**96.1**	**100.0**	**100.6**	**103.4**	**107.3**	**111.4**	**118.3**	**120.3**
Latvia Lettonie								
Total industry [CDE]								
Total, industrie [CDE]	**103.8**	**100.0**	**105.5**	**120.1**	**123.8**	**101.7**	**104.9**	**112.1**
Total mining [C]								
Total, industries extractives [C]	**120.2**	**100.0**	**102.4**	**110.4**	**117.2**	**123.9**	**134.9**	**141.4**
Total manufacturing [D]								
Total, industries manufacturières [D]	**104.7**	**100.0**	**107.3**	**125.6**	**130.2**	**103.6**	**108.4**	**116.5**
Food, beverages, tobacco								
Aliments, boissons, tabac	102.6	100.0	111.6	127.7	124.0	102.0	100.6	107.0
Textiles,wearing apparel, leather, footwear								
Textiles, habillement, cuir et chaussures	112.5	100.0	126.5	138.9	140.8	121.3	133.1	137.9
Chemicals, rubber and plastic prod.								
Prod. chimiques, caoutch. et plast.	98.0	100.0	98.1	115.6	105.5	56.5	48.7	54.7
Basic metals								
Métaux de base	121.4	100.0	99.7	139.7	237.6	325.9	325.8	379.9
Metal products								
Produits métalliques	109.6	100.0	92.8	103.2	91.7	72.9	91.3	94.5
Electricity, gas and water [E]								
Électricité, gaz et eau [E]	**100.2**	**100.0**	**98.1**	**97.4**	**98.5**	**92.5**	**89.8**	**94.6**
Lithuania Lituanie								
Total industry [CDE]								
Total, industrie [CDE]	**...**	**100.0**	**104.1**	**108.9**	**117.8**	**104.6**	**110.1**	**128.7**
Total mining [C]								
Total, industries extractives [C]	**...**	**100.0**	**122.0**	**136.3**	**185.7**	**177.1**	**198.1**	**271.4**
Total manufacturing [D]								
Total, industries manufacturières [D]	**...**	**100.0**	**100.9**	**106.6**	**115.4**	**102.8**	**111.9**	**130.4**
Food, beverages, tobacco								
Aliments, boissons, tabac	...	100.0	100.0	102.9	107.1	99.8	102.2	101.4
Textiles,wearing apparel, leather, footwear								
Textiles, habillement, cuir et chaussures	...	100.0	108.3	111.6	109.9	111.1	115.0	124.4
Chemicals, rubber and plastic prod.								
Prod. chimiques, caoutch. et plast.	...	100.0	111.9	120.7	137.5	138.5	165.0	158.4
Basic metals								
Métaux de base	...	100.0	75.4	69.2	79.3	134.6	160.3	165.6
Metal products								
Produits métalliques	...	100.0	100.1	103.2	114.4	115.7	138.9	158.2
Electricity, gas and water [E]								
Électricité, gaz et eau [E]	**...**	**100.0**	**106.7**	**96.8**	**99.9**	**80.7**	**68.7**	**79.7**
Luxembourg Luxembourg								
Total industry [CDE]								
Total, industrie [CDE]	**98.9**	**100.0**	**100.1**	**105.3**	**114.5**	**116.3**	**122.1**	**126.1**
Total mining [C]								
Total, industries extractives [C]	**109.2**	**100.0**	**89.9**	**89.4**	**100.2**	**107.8**	**108.8**	**111.0**
Total manufacturing [D]								
Total, industries manufacturières [D]	**99.1**	**100.0**	**100.3**	**106.1**	**115.7**	**117.7**	**123.6**	**127.8**
Food and beverages								
Aliments et boissons	101.4	100.0	99.5	99.6	101.2	105.6	106.6	115.1
Textiles,wearing apparel, leather, footwear								
Textiles, habillement, cuir et chaussures	102.9	100.0	81.4	93.2	98.8	91.6	98.4	100.5
Chemicals, rubber and plastic products								
Prod. chimiques, caoutchouc et plastiques	96.3	100.0	104.5	109.9	129.6	119.5	128.3	139.0
Basic metals								
Métaux de base	108.7	100.0	93.7	102.9	90.1	114.2	120.6	118.4
Metal products								
Produits métalliques	91.2	100.0	106.4	106.9	121.6	122.0	122.5	125.9
Electricity and gas [E]								
Électricité et gaz [E]	**94.5**	**100.0**	**99.2**	**98.2**	**102.0**	**99.8**	**106.9**	**107.2**
Malta Malte								
Total industry [CDE]								
Total, industrie [CDE]	**90.1**	**100.0**	**95.3**	**...**	**...**	**...**	**...**	**...**
Total mining [C]								
Total, industries extractives [C]	**79.0**	**100.0**	**111.1**	**...**	**...**	**...**	**...**	**...**

26
Index numbers of industrial production [*cont.*]
Indices de la production industrielle [*suite*]
1995=100

Country or area and industry [ISIC Rev.3] Pays ou zone et industrie [CITI Rév.3]	1994	1995	1996	1997	1998	1999	2000	2001
Total manufacturing [D]								
Total, industries manufacturières [D]	**92.5**	**100.0**	**93.8**	...	...	...	...	...
Food, beverages, tobacco								
Aliments, boissons, tabac	96.5	100.0	104.5	...	...	...	...	...
Textiles,wearing apparel, leather, footwear								
Textiles, habillement, cuir et chaussures	108.1	100.0	107.7	...	...	...	...	...
Chemicals, petroleum, rubber and plastic prod.								
Prod. chimiques, pétroliers, caoutch. et plast.	85.1	100.0	101.8	...	...	...	...	...
Metal products								
Produits métalliques	86.1	100.0	90.6	...	...	...	...	...
Electricity and water [E]								
Electricité et eau [E]	**95.8**	**100.0**	**103.7**	...	...	...	...	...
Netherlands Pays–Bas								
Total industry [CDE]								
Total, industrie [CDE]	**97.1**	**100.0**	**102.4**	**102.6**	**104.9**	**106.9**	**110.9**	**110.1**
Total mining [C]								
Total, industries extractives [C]	**99.2**	**100.0**	**113.4**	**104.1**	**103.2**	**94.8**	**92.8**	**98.8**
Total manufacturing [D]								
Total, industries manufacturières [D]	**96.7**	**100.0**	**100.5**	**103.1**	**106.1**	**109.2**	**114.3**	**111.9**
Food, beverages, tobacco								
Aliments, boissons, tabac	96.6	100.0	101.7	102.1	102.2	104.8	106.9	105.9
Textiles,wearing apparel, leather, footwear								
Textiles, habillement, cuir et chaussures	105.4	100.0	99.1	99.3	103.1	101.1	104.1	101.9
Chemicals, petroleum, rubber and plastic prod.								
Prod. chimiques, pétroliers, caoutch. et plast.	94.9	100.0	97.6	99.2	100.1	106.7	113.5	112.3
Basic metals								
Métaux de base	98.9	100.0	97.5	105.5	107.6	108.3	111.3	109.2
Metal products								
Produits métalliques	95.8	100.0	102.1	105.8	110.1	112.3	120.8	117.6
Electricity, gas and water [E]								
Electricité, gaz et eau [E]	**97.7**	**100.0**	**104.8**	**97.4**	**97.8**	**103.8**	**105.5**	**107.8**
Norway Norvège								
Total industry [CDE]								
Total, industrie [CDE]	**94.4**	**100.0**	**105.4**	**109.0**	**108.3**	**108.1**	**111.2**	**110.9**
Total mining [C] [9]								
Total, industries extractives [C] [9]	**97.1**	**100.0**	**99.5**	**103.3**	**99.4**	**98.3**	**101.7**	**107.1**
Total manufacturing [D]								
Total, industries manufacturières [D]	**97.0**	**100.0**	**102.8**	**106.2**	**109.4**	**107.0**	**104.1**	**103.1**
Food, beverages, tobacco								
Aliments, boissons, tabac	98.4	100.0	101.9	102.9	102.1	98.8	97.1	96.3
Textiles,wearing apparel, leather, footwear								
Textiles, habillement, cuir et chaussures	103.6	100.0	101.3	99.9	95.1	83.1	76.4	72.5
Chemicals, petroleum, rubber and plastic prod.								
Prod. chimiques, pétroliers, caoutch. et plast.	99.0	100.0	101.9	103.3	105.7	105.9	104.3	104.2
Basic metals								
Métaux de base	101.2	100.0	102.8	106.6	112.0	115.5	116.7	111.7
Metal products								
Produits métalliques	96.6	100.0	103.9	108.1	117.3	115.2	109.6	109.9
Electricity and gas [E]								
Electricité et gaz [E]	**92.0**	**100.0**	**85.1**	**90.8**	**95.1**	**99.8**	**116.0**	**99.0**
Poland Pologne								
Total industry [CDE]								
Total, industrie [CDE]	**91.2**	**100.0**	**109.4**	**121.7**	**127.4**	**133.5**	**143.5**	**144.1**
Total mining [C]								
Total, industries extractives [C]	**100.6**	**100.0**	**101.3**	**99.7**	**86.6**	**83.2**	**82.1**	**77.9**
Total manufacturing [D]								
Total, industries manufacturières [D]	**89.6**	**100.0**	**111.5**	**126.6**	**134.9**	**142.4**	**153.7**	**153.5**
Food, beverages, tobacco								
Aliments, boissons, tabac	92.3	100.0	111.9	118.3	127.0	129.0	130.1	133.9
Textiles,wearing apparel, leather, footwear								
Textiles, habillement, cuir et chaussures	92.2	100.0	108.5	118.1	120.0	115.9	114.5	110.3
Chemicals, petroleum, rubber and plastic prod.								
Prod. chimiques, pétroliers, caoutch. et plast.	87.5	100.0	108.3	121.3	124.9	132.8	147.1	153.2

26
Index numbers of industrial production [cont.]
Indices de la production industrielle [suite]
1995=100

Country or area and industry [ISIC Rev.3] Pays ou zone et industrie [CITI Rév.3]	1994	1995	1996	1997	1998	1999	2000	2001
Basic metals								
Métaux de base	86.7	100.0	100.3	112.9	107.2	97.2	106.5	89.8
Metal products								
Produits métalliques	84.7	100.0	116.6	136.6	152.3	163.8	180.1	181.1
Electricity, gas and water [E]								
Electricité, gaz et eau [E]	**99.1**	**100.0**	**100.4**	**102.8**	**104.7**	**107.1**	**116.9**	**126.3**
Portugal Portugal								
Total industry [CDE]								
Total, industrie [CDE]	**95.5**	**100.0**	**107.0**	**109.6**	**114.0**	**117.6**	**118.1**	**121.0**
Total mining [C]								
Total, industries extractives [C]	**102.1**	**100.0**	**103.3**	**103.3**	**105.2**	**102.2**	**103.8**	**113.5**
Total manufacturing [D]								
Total, industries manufacturières [D]	**96.5**	**100.0**	**105.3**	**110.0**	**112.8**	**114.4**	**114.8**	**116.3**
Food, beverages, tobacco								
Aliments, boissons, tabac	97.3	100.0	102.5	105.4	109.3	113.5	116.8	112.2
Textiles,wearing apparel, leather, footwear								
Textiles, habillement, cuir et chaussures	98.0	100.0	96.4	95.1	91.4	86.2	80.4	80.4
Chemicals, petroleum, rubber and plastic prod.								
Prod. chimiques, pétroliers, caoutch. et plast.	98.3	100.0	101.8	107.7	110.3	115.0	114.2	114.2
Basic metals								
Métaux de base	94.3	100.0	96.6	109.9	112.5	126.3	124.1	117.2
Metal products								
Produits métalliques	93.1	100.0	112.6	121.9	130.7	134.8	136.2	145.5
Electricity and gas [E]								
Electricité et gaz [E]	**91.1**	**100.0**	**117.9**	**113.1**	**124.3**	**144.3**	**145.6**	**157.3**
Romania Roumanie								
Total industry [CDE]								
Total, industrie [CDE]	**91.4**	**100.0**	**105.7**	**98.7**	**81.9**	**77.7**	**83.2**	**90.3**
Total mining [C]								
Total, industries extractives [C]	**100.6**	**100.0**	**100.7**	**95.0**	**81.6**	**76.1**	**79.8**	**84.0**
Total manufacturing [D]								
Total, industries manufacturières [D]	**89.3**	**100.0**	**107.2**	**100.8**	**82.5**	**78.5**	**85.1**	**93.6**
Food, beverages, tobacco								
Aliments, boissons, tabac	96.9	100.0	101.3	86.2	85.0	85.9	97.2	114.2
Textiles,wearing apparel, leather, footwear								
Textiles, habillement, cuir et chaussures	89.9	100.0	109.4	111.1	71.8	73.8	82.5	90.7
Chemicals, petroleum, rubber and plastic prod.								
Prod. chimiques, pétroliers, caoutch. et plast.	93.4	100.0	91.0	75.3	64.7	59.1	66.9	73.3
Basic metals								
Métaux de base	84.8	100.0	91.7	93.0	92.4	63.9	79.9	93.3
Metal products								
Produits métalliques	83.6	100.0	117.8	119.5	97.0	92.2	84.2	88.5
Electricity, gas and water [E]								
Electricité, gaz et eau [E]	**96.8**	**100.0**	**100.6**	**88.8**	**77.8**	**72.9**	**72.7**	**72.0**
Russian Federation Fédération de Russie								
Total industry [CDE]								
Total, industrie [CDE]	**102.6**	**100.0**	**95.5**	**97.4**	**92.3**	**102.5**	**114.7**	**...**
Total mining [C]								
Total, industries extractives [C]	**102.2**	**100.0**	**98.4**	**97.5**	**105.9**	**111.4**	**121.4**	**...**
Total manufacturing [D]								
Total, industries manufacturières [D]	**104.1**	**100.0**	**85.5**	**78.8**	**73.0**	**84.0**	**96.1**	**...**
Food, beverages, tobacco								
Aliments, boissons, tabac	...	100.0	89.6	87.1	87.5	95.5	105.4	
Textiles,wearing apparel, leather, footwear								
Textiles, habillement, cuir et chaussures	...	100.0	77.7	69.2	55.5	67.3	76.8	...
Chemicals, petroleum, rubber and plastic prod.								
Prod. chimiques, pétroliers, caoutch. et plast.	...	100.0	93.5	92.0	86.6	101.6	114.7	...
Basic metals								
Métaux de base	...	100.0	98.4	100.1	95.0	107.3	121.9	
Metal products								
Produits métalliques	...	100.0	77.4	65.8	54.9	64.1	79.6	...
Electricity and gas [E]								
Electricité et gaz [E]	**103.4**	**100.0**	**96.8**	**95.1**	**93.5**	**92.8**	**95.6**	**...**

26
Index numbers of industrial production [*cont.*]
Indices de la production industrielle [*suite*]
1995=100

Country or area and industry [ISIC Rev.3] Pays ou zone et industrie [CITI Rév.3]	1994	1995	1996	1997	1998	1999	2000	2001
Serbia and Montenegro Serbie–et–Monténégro								
Total industry [CDE]								
Total, industrie [CDE]	**95.7**	**100.0**	**107.3**	**117.2**	**121.2**	**91.7**	**102.1**	**102.2**
Total mining [C]								
Total, industries extractives [C]	**95.1**	**100.0**	**99.2**	**106.0**	**105.4**	**86.0**	**93.8**	**81.9**
Total manufacturing [D]								
Total, industries manufacturières [D]	**97.4**	**100.0**	**111.1**	**127.8**	**133.4**	**94.7**	**108.4**	**109.3**
Food, beverages, tobacco								
Aliments, boissons, tabac	94.4	100.0	102.0	98.2	113.5	109.5	110.5	107.5
Textiles,wearing apparel, leather, footwear								
Textiles, habillement, cuir et chaussures	118.5	100.0	106.2	112.3	127.2	90.3	106.4	108.0
Chemicals, petroleum, rubber and plastic prod.								
Prod. chimiques, pétroliers, caoutch. et plast.	90.8	100.0	136.0	194.1	226.0	124.6	·141.3	164.2
Basic metals								
Métaux de base	83.6	100.0	143.3	177.4	192.6	105.2	142.2	138.3
Metal products								
Produits métalliques	98.3	100.0	101.8	120.3	134.4	94.7	114.8	101.5
Electricity, gas and water [E]								
Electricité, gaz et eau [E]	**95.1**	**100.0**	**102.5**	**108.4**	**109.3**	**103.1**	**104.6**	**105.3**
Slovakia Slovaquie								
Total industry [CDE]								
Total, industrie [CDE]	**92.4**	**100.0**	**102.5**	**103.8**	**108.6**	**105.8**	**115.0**	**122.8**
Total mining [C]								
Total, industries extractives [C]	**100.5**	**100.0**	**105.6**	**118.0**	**104.9**	**103.8**	**101.4**	**88.4**
Total manufacturing [D]								
Total, industries manufacturières [D]	**90.7**	**100.0**	**102.3**	**104.0**	**110.4**	**105.7**	**116.2**	**127.6**
Electricity, gas and water [E]								
Electricité, gaz et eau [E]	**101.7**	**100.0**	**104.8**	**101.5**	**95.6**	**98.5**	**104.7**	**103.2**
Slovenia Slovénie								
Total industry [CDE]								
Total, industrie [CDE]	**98.1**	**100.0**	**101.0**	**102.0**	**105.8**	**105.3**	**111.9**	**115.1**
Total mining [C]								
Total, industries extractives [C]	**99.2**	**100.0**	**100.5**	**102.3**	**102.0**	**97.8**	**95.5**	**87.7**
Total manufacturing [D]								
Total, industries manufacturières [D]	**97.4**	**100.0**	**101.2**	**101.4**	**105.4**	**105.4**	**112.9**	**116.0**
Food, beverages, tobacco								
Aliments, boissons, tabac	100.3	100.0	105.1	101.5	100.2	100.4	99.0	98.2
Textiles,wearing apparel, leather, footwear								
Textiles, habillement, cuir et chaussures	102.6	100.0	94.8	96.8	95.8	94.6	94.6	94.0
Chemicals, petroleum, rubber and plastic prod.								
Prod. chimiques, pétroliers, caoutch. et plast.	97.4	100.0	101.4	74.7	77.7	74.1	70.6	70.5
Basic metals								
Métaux de base	94.7	100.0	92.7	80.6	82.1	76.9	72.3	69.8
Metal products								
Produits métalliques	96.0	100.0	101.1	90.9	101.3	102.5	105.3	113.0
Electricity [E]								
Electricité [E]	**100.3**	**100.0**	**100.7**	**109.0**	**112.7**	**107.5**	**109.1**	**118.1**
Spain Espagne								
Total industry [CDE]								
Total, industrie [CDE]	**95.5**	**100.0**	**99.3**	**106.1**	**111.9**	**114.8**	**119.3**	**118.0**
Total mining [C]								
Total, industries extractives [C]	**95.2**	**100.0**	**94.4**	**92.0**	**92.1**	**90.2**	**91.2**	**88.3**
Total manufacturing [D]								
Total, industries manufacturières [D]	**95.1**	**100.0**	**99.3**	**106.6**	**113.2**	**115.8**	**119.7**	**117.3**
Food, beverages, tobacco								
Aliments, boissons, tabac	101.5	100.0	96.9	104.6	109.1	109.3	108.3	109.5
Textiles,wearing apparel, leather, footwear								
Textiles, habillement, cuir et chaussures	102.6	100.0	95.4	99.5	101.5	99.4	97.6	94.3
Chemicals, petroleum, rubber and plastic prod.								
Prod. chimiques, pétroliers, caoutch. et plast.	96.6	100.0	100.3	107.0	112.6	118.7	119.7	119.7
Basic metals								
Métaux de base	94.1	100.0	97.2	103.8	108.5	109.5	124.7	120.2
Metal products								
Produits métalliques	88.5	100.0	102.4	111.5	121.0	122.7	128.8	123.8

26

Index numbers of industrial production [*cont.*]
Indices de la production industrielle [*suite*]
1995=100

Country or area and industry [ISIC Rev.3] Pays ou zone et industrie [CITI Rév.3]	1994	1995	1996	1997	1998	1999	2000	2001
Electricity and gas [E] **Electricité et gaz [E]**	**98.6**	**100.0**	**100.6**	**107.0**	**108.4**	**115.1**	**124.9**	**130.3**
Sweden Suède								
Total industry [CDE] **Total, industrie [CDE]**	**91.6**	**100.0**	**100.9**	**107.0**	**111.5**	**114.5**	**123.5**	**121.5**
Total mining [C] **Total, industries extractives [C]**	**93.9**	**100.0**	**98.3**	**94.4**	**94.2**	**91.7**	**93.4**	**90.4**
Total manufacturing [D] **Total, industries manufacturières [D]**	**91.1**	**100.0**	**101.0**	**107.8**	**112.4**	**116.0**	**125.8**	**123.8**
Food, beverages, tobacco Aliments, boissons, tabac	96.9	100.0	104.5	103.1	103.8	103.9	103.0	105.8
Textiles,wearing apparel, leather, footwear Textiles, habillement, cuir et chaussures	97.5	100.0	97.6	97.7	94.6	86.6	87.8	86.9
Chemicals, petroleum, rubber and plastic prod. Prod. chimiques, pétroliers, caoutch. et plast.	101.4	100.0	103.9	109.6	112.2	116.0	125.6	129.8
Basic metals Métaux de base	94.2	100.0	101.5	105.6	105.4	105.0	110.4	119.1
Metal products Produits métalliques	81.5	100.0	101.6	111.7	119.7	126.0	142.1	136.8
Electricity and gas [E] **Electricité et gaz [E]**	**95.5**	**100.0**	**100.6**	**101.9**	**106.2**	**105.2**	**106.1**	**104.5**
Switzerland Suisse								
Total industry [CDE] **Total, industrie [CDE]**	**98.0**	**100.0**	**100.0**	**104.6**	**108.4**	**112.2**	**121.6**	**121.3**
Total mining [C] **Total, industries extractives [C]**	**...**	**100.0**	**98.3**	**100.5**	**87.9**	**93.4**	**94.2**	**96.2**
Total manufacturing [D] **Total, industries manufacturières [D]**	**97.0**	**100.0**	**100.3**	**104.9**	**109.1**	**112.7**	**123.2**	**122.4**
Food, beverages, tobacco Aliments, boissons, tabac	102.6	100.0	101.2	92.2	88.2	86.8	88.5	86.0
Textiles and wearing apparel Textiles et habillement	97.6	100.0	99.0	99.0	93.1	87.5	87.6	79.3
Chemicals and chemical products Produits chimiques	91.0	100.0	110.2	125.7	135.8	152.0	163.0	172.0
Basic metals and metal products Métaux de base et produtis métalliques	97.7	100.0	99.1	106.3	108.6	108.8	123.8	125.5
Electricity, gas and water [E] **Electricité, gaz et eau [E]**	**104.0**	**100.0**	**97.5**	**101.5**	**102.4**	**108.1**	**107.5**	**112.1**
TFYR of Macedonia L'ex−R.y. Macédonie								
Total industry [CDE] **Total, industrie [CDE]**	**111.9**	**100.0**	**103.2**	**104.7**	**109.5**	**106.7**	**110.4**	**99.2**
Ukraine Ukraine								
Total industry [CDE] **Total, industrie [CDE]**	**113.7**	**100.0**	**94.9**	**93.1**	**91.6**	**95.9**	**108.2**	**122.4**
Total mining [C] **Total, industries extractives [C]**	**112.9**	**100.0**	**94.8**	**97.9**	**95.3**	**98.3**	**104.0**	**107.4**
Total manufacturing [D] **Total, industries manufacturières [D]**	**115.9**	**100.0**	**94.9**	**94.5**	**93.7**	**97.1**	**112.6**	**132.0**
Electricity, gas and water [E] **Electricité, gaz et eau [E]**	**106.3**	**100.0**	**93.2**	**90.8**	**90.6**	**88.3**	**86.7**	**89.3**
United Kingdom Royaume−Uni								
Total industry [CDE] **Total, industrie [CDE]**	**98.3**	**100.0**	**101.3**	**102.4**	**103.3**	**104.1**	**105.9**	**103.6**
Total mining [C] **Total, industries extractives [C]**	**96.7**	**100.0**	**103.2**	**102.1**	**104.2**	**108.1**	**106.8**	**101.5**
Total manufacturing [D] **Total, industries manufacturières [D]**	**98.5**	**100.0**	**100.6**	**102.0**	**102.8**	**103.1**	**105.2**	**102.6**
Food, beverages, tobacco Aliments, boissons, tabac	102.2	100.0	101.4	103.6	101.8	101.2	99.9	101.2
Textiles,wearing apparel, leather, footwear Textiles, habillement, cuir et chaussures	103.3	100.0	98.3	96.8	89.1	82.5	78.4	68.7
Chemicals, petroleum, rubber and plastic prod. Prod. chimiques, pétroliers, caoutch. et plast.	95.3	100.0	99.1	100.4	101.6	102.4	105.3	106.0

26
Index numbers of industrial production [*cont.*]
Indices de la production industrielle [*suite*]
1995=100

Country or area and industry [ISIC Rev.3] Pays ou zone et industrie [CITI Rév.3]	1994	1995	1996	1997	1998	1999	2000	2001
Basic metals								
Métaux de base	96.6	100.0	101.1	102.3	99.1	94.2	89.8	85.3
Metal products								
Produits métalliques	97.2	100.0	102.5	104.6	108.0	110.2	115.9	111.0
Electricity, gas and water [E]								
Electricité, gaz et eau [E]	**97.7**	**100.0**	**105.2**	**105.7**	**107.5**	**109.4**	**111.4**	**114.1**
Oceania · Océanie								
Australia [2] Australie [2]								
Total industry [CDE]								
Total, industrie [CDE]	**96.9**	**100.0**	**103.3**	**104.9**	**108.3**	**111.7**	**116.6**	**118.8**
Total mining [C] [10]								
Total, industries extractives [C] [10]	**93.8**	**100.0**	**107.8**	**109.2**	**112.6**	**114.0**	**123.8**	**133.7**
Total manufacturing [D]								
Total, industries manufacturières [D]	**97.9**	**100.0**	**102.2**	**104.3**	**107.7**	**112.0**	**115.1**	**114.5**
Food, beverages, tobacco								
Aliments, boissons, tabac	99.0	100.0	103.7	105.1	113.6	120.8	128.4	136.7
Textiles,wearing apparel, leather, footwear								
Textiles, habillement, cuir et chaussures	102.4	100.0	94.8	94.1	95.8	97.0	91.0	85.4
Chemicals, petroleum, rubber and plastic prod.								
Prod. chimiques, pétroliers, caoutch. et plast.	97.1	100.0	105.7	108.0	110.8	117.7	117.2	122.9
Basic metals and metal products								
Métaux de base et produtis métalliques	97.5	100.0	103.4	106.2	109.0	112.0	116.4	114.8
Electricity, gas and water [E]								
Electricité, gaz et eau [E]	**97.4**	**100.0**	**101.4**	**101.1**	**104.7**	**106.1**	**109.2**	**112.6**
Fiji Fidji								
Total industry [CDE]								
Total, industrie [CDE]	**97.3**	**100.0**	**86.8**	**90.9**	**92.5**	**98.7**	**91.8**	...
Total mining [C]								
Total, industries extractives [C]	**101.2**	**100.0**	**127.4**	**133.7**	**106.6**	**126.8**	**108.6**	...
Total manufacturing [D]								
Total, industries manufacturières [D]	**97.8**	**100.0**	**73.8**	**78.5**	**81.1**	**84.3**	**76.5**	...
Food, beverages, tobacco								
Aliments, boissons, tabac	103.8	100.0	99.0	86.1	89.1	96.7	88.6	...
Textiles and wearing apparel								
Textiles et habillement	73.8	100.0	132.0	169.3	220.9	240.6	227.3	...
Chemicals and chemical products								
Produits chimiques	105.9	100.0	93.2	113.5	124.7	109.2	95.0	...
Electricity and water [E]								
Electricité et eau [E]	**95.8**	**100.0**	**108.3**	**111.7**	**115.7**	**127.8**	**124.5**	...
New Zealand [11] Nouvelle−Zélande [11]								
Total industry [CDE]								
Total, industrie [CDE]	**95.1**	**100.0**	**102.3**	**104.0**	**103.6**	**100.8**	**104.3**	**106.7**
Total mining [C] [12]								
Total, industries extractives [C] [12]	**101.6**	**100.0**	**102.0**	**112.6**	**113.9**	**112.7**	**116.3**	**119.0**
Total manufacturing [D]								
Total, industries manufacturières [D]	**93.8**	**100.0**	**101.9**	**103.5**	**102.9**	**99.0**	**103.3**	**105.4**
Food, beverages, tobacco								
Aliments, boissons, tabac	95.9	100.0	104.2	104.3	108.6	104.3	106.3	110.0
Textiles,wearing apparel, leather, footwear								
Textiles, habillement, cuir et chaussures	97.2	100.0	95.6	103.2	95.3	92.9	96.3	96.7
Chemicals, petroleum, rubber and plastic prod.								
Prod. chimiques, pétroliers, caoutch. et plast.	92.0	100.0	99.7	102.0	95.8	95.2	98.5	108.7
Basic metals and metal products								
Métaux de base et produtis métalliques	92.1	100.0	103.1	105.3	104.7	100.7	107.5	109.6
Electricity, gas and water [E]								
Electricité, gaz et eau [E]	**96.5**	**100.0**	**105.2**	**97.3**	**97.3**	**100.8**	**97.3**	**102.4**

26
Index numbers of industrial production [*cont.*]
Indices de la production industrielle [*suite*]
1995=100

Source:
United Nations Statistics Division, New York, "Industrial Commodity Statistics Yearbook 2000" and the industrial statistics database.

1   Figures relate to 12 months beginning 1 July of the year stated.
2   Figures relate to 12 months ending 30 June of the year stated.
3   Calculated by the Statistics Division of the United Nations from component national indices.
4   Excluding coal mining and crude petroleum.
5   Excluding petroleum refineries.
6   Figures relate to 12 months ending 30 September of the year stated.
7   Including construction.
8   Figures relate to 12 months beginning 1 April of the year stated.
9   Excluding gas and oil extraction.
10   Excluding services to mining.
11   Figures relate to 12 months ending 31 March of the year stated.
12   Including forestry and fishing.

Source:
Organisation des Nations Unies, New York, "Annuaire de statistiques industrielles par produit 2000" et la base de données pour les statistiques industrielles.

1   Les chiffres se rapportent à 12 mois commençant le 1er juillet de l'année indiquée.
2   Les chiffres se rapportent à 12 mois finissant le 30 juin de l'année indiquée.
3   Calculé par la Division de Statistiques de l'Organisation des Nations Unies à partir d'indices nationaux plus détaillés.
4   Non compris l'extraction du charbon et de pétrole brut.
5   Non compris les raffineries de pétrole.
6   Les chiffres se rapportent à 12 mois finissant le 30 septembre de l'année indiquée.
7   Y compris la construction.
8   Les chiffres se rapportent à 12 mois commençant le 1er avril de l'année indiquée.
9   Non compris l'extraction de gaz et de pétrole brut.
10   Non compris les services relatifs aux mines.
11   Les chiffres se rapportent à 12 mois finissant le 31 mars de l'année indiquée.
12   Y compris l'exploitation forestière et la pêche.

Technical notes, tables 20-26

Detailed internationally comparable data on national accounts are compiled and published annually by the Statistics Division, Department of Economic and Social Affairs of the United Nations Secretariat. Data for national accounts aggregates for countries or areas are based on the concepts and definitions contained in *A System of National Accounts* (1968 SNA) [58] and in *System of National Accounts 1993* (1993 SNA) [59]. A summary of the conceptual framework, classifications and definitions of transactions is found in the annual United Nations publication, *National Accounts Statistics: Main Aggregates and Detailed Tables* [27].

The national accounts data shown in this publication offer, in the form of analytical tables, a summary of selected principal national accounts aggregates based on official detailed national accounts data of some 180 countries and areas. Every effort has been made to present the estimates of the various countries or areas in a form designed to facilitate international comparability. The data for the majority of countries or areas has been compiled according to the 1968 SNA. Data for those countries or areas which have started to follow the concepts and definitions of the 1993 SNA is indicated with a footnote. To the extent possible, any other differences in concept, scope, coverage and classification are footnoted as well. Detailed footnotes identifying these differences are also available in the annual national accounts publication mentioned above. Such differences should be taken into account in order to avoid misleading comparisons among countries or areas.

Table 20 shows gross domestic product (GDP) and GDP per capita in US dollars in current prices, and GDP in constant 1990 prices and the corresponding rates of growth. The table is designed to facilitate international comparisons of levels of income generated in production. In order to present comparable coverage for as many countries as possible, the official GDP national currency data are supplemented by estimates prepared by the Statistics Division, based on a variety of data derived from national and international sources. The conversion rates used to translate national currency data into US dollars are the period averages of market exchange rates (MERs) for members of the International Monetary Fund (IMF). These rates, which are published in the *International Financial Statistics* [15], are communicated to the IMF by national central banks and consist of three types: (a) market rates, determined largely by market forces; (b) official rates, determined by government authorities; and (c) principal rates for countries maintaining multiple exchange rate arrangements. Market rates always take priority and official rates are used only when a free market rate is not available.

Notes techniques, tableaux 20 à 26

La Division de statistique du Département des affaires économiques et sociales du Secrétariat de l'Organisation des Nations Unies établit et publie chaque année des données détaillées, comparables au plan international, sur les comptes nationaux. Les données relatives aux agrégats des différents pays et territoires sont établies en fonction des concepts et des définitions du *Système de comptabilité nationale* (SCN de 1968) [58] et du *Système de comptabilité nationale* (SCN de 1993) [59]. On trouvera un résumé de l'appareil conceptuel, des classifications et des définitions des opérations dans *National Accounts Statistics: Main Aggregates and Detailed Tables* [27], publication annuelle des Nations Unies.

Les chiffres de comptabilité nationale présentés ici récapitulent sous forme de tableaux analytiques un choix d'agrégats essentiels de comptabilité nationale, issus des comptes nationaux détaillés de quelque 180 pays et territoires. On n'a rien négligé pour présenter les chiffres des différents pays et territoires sous une forme facilitant les comparaisons internationales. Pour la plupart des pays, les chiffres ont été établis selon le SCN de 1968. Les données des pays et territoires qui ont commencé à appliquer les concepts et les définitions du SCN de 1993 sont signalées par une note. Dans toute la mesure possible, on signale également au moyen de notes les cas où les concepts, la portée, la couverture et la classification ne seraient pas les mêmes. Il y a en outre des notes détaillées explicitant ces différences dans la publication annuelle mentionnée plus haut. Il y a lieu de tenir compte de ces différences pour éviter de tenter des comparaisons qui donneraient matière à confusion.

Le *tableau 20* fait apparaître le produit intérieur brut (PIB) total et par habitant, exprimé en dollars des États-Unis aux prix courants et à prix constants (base 1990), ainsi que les taux de croissance correspondants. Le tableau est conçu pour faciliter les comparaisons internationales du revenu issu de la production. Afin que la couverture soit comparable pour le plus grand nombre possible de pays, la Division de statistique s'appuie non seulement sur les chiffres officiels du PIB exprimé dans la monnaie nationale, mais aussi sur diverses données provenant de sources nationales et internationales. Les taux de conversion utilisés pour exprimer les données nationales en dollars des États-Unis sont, pour les membres du Fonds monétaire international (FMI), les moyennes pour la période considérée des taux de change du marché. Ces derniers, publiés dans *Statistiques financières internationales* [15], sont communiqués au FMI par les banques centrales des pays et reposent sur trois types de taux : a) taux du marché, déterminés dans une large mesure par les facteurs du marché; b) taux officiels, déterminés par les pouvoirs publics; c) taux principaux, pour les pays pratiquant diffé-

For non-members of the IMF, averages of the United Nations operational rates, used for accounting purposes in United Nations transactions with member countries, are applied. These are based on official, commercial and/or tourist rates of exchange.

It should be noted that there are practical constraints in the use of MERs for conversion purposes. Their use may result in excessive fluctuations or distortions in the dollar income levels of a number of countries particularly in those with multiple exchange rates, those coping with inordinate levels of inflation or countries experiencing misalignments caused by market fluctuations. Caution is therefore urged when making intercountry comparisons of incomes as expressed in US dollars.

The GDP constant price series, based primarily on data officially provided by countries or areas and partly on estimates made by the Statistics Division, are transformed into index numbers and rebased to 1990=100. The resulting data are then converted into US dollars at the rate prevailing in the base year 1990. The growth rates are based on the estimates of GDP at constant 1990 prices. The growth rate of the year in question is obtained by dividing the GDP of that year by the GDP of the preceding year.

Table 21 features the percentage distribution of GDP in current prices by expenditure breakdown. It shows the portions of GDP spent on consumption by the government and the household (including the non-profit institutions serving households) sector, the portions spent on gross fixed capital formation, on changes in inventories, and on exports of goods and services, deducting imports of goods and services. The percentages are derived from official data reported to the United Nations by the countries and published in the annual national accounts publication.

Table 22 shows the percentage distribution of value added originating from the various industry components of the *International Standard Industrial Classification of All Economic Activities, Revision 3* (ISIC Rev. 3) [50]. This table reflects the economic structure of production in the different countries or areas. The percentages are based on official value added estimates at current prices broken down by the kind of economic activity: agriculture, hunting, forestry and fishing (categories A+B); mining and quarrying (C); manufacturing (D); electricity, gas and water supply (E); construction (F); wholesale and retail trade, repair of motor vehicles, motorcycles and personal and household goods, restaurants and hotels (G+H); transport, storage and communication (I) and other activities comprised of financial intermediation (J), real estate, renting and business activities (K), public administration and defence, compulsory social security (L), education (M), health and social

rents arrangements en matière de taux de change. On donne toujours la priorité aux taux du marché, n'utilisant les taux officiels que lorsqu'on n'a pas de taux du marché libre.

Pour les pays qui ne sont pas membres du FMI, on utilise les moyennes des taux de change opérationnels de l'ONU (qui servent à des fins comptables pour les opérations de l'ONU avec les pays qui en sont membres). Ces taux reposent sur les taux de change officiels, les taux du commerce et/ou les taux touristiques.

Il est à noter que l'utilisation des taux de change du marché pour la conversion des données se heurte à des obstacles pratiques. On risque, ce faisant, d'aboutir à des fluctuations excessives ou à des distorsions du revenu en dollars de certains pays, surtout dans le cas des pays qui pratiquent plusieurs taux de change et de ceux qui connaissent des taux d'inflation exceptionnels ou des décalages provenant des fluctuations du marché. Les comparaisons de revenu entre pays sont donc sujettes à caution lorsqu'on se fonde sur le revenu exprimé en dollars des États-Unis.

La série de statistiques du PIB à prix constants est fondée principalement sur des données officiellement communiquées par les pays, et en partie sur des estimations de la Division de statistique; les données permettent de calculer des indices, la base 100 correspondant à 1990. Les chiffres ainsi obtenus sont alors convertis en dollars des États-Unis au taux de change de l'année de base (1990). Les taux de croissance sont calculés à partir des estimations du PIB aux prix constants de 1990. Le taux de croissance de l'année considérée est obtenu en divisant le PIB de l'année par celui de l'année précédente.

Le *tableau 21* montre la répartition (en pourcentage) du PIB aux prix courants par catégorie de dépense. Il indique la part du PIB consacrée aux dépenses de consommation des administrations publiques et du secteur des ménages (y compris les institutions sans but lucratif au service des ménages), celle qui est consacrée à la formation brute de capital fixe, celle qui correspond aux variations de stocks et celle qui correspond aux exportations de biens et services, déduction faite des importations de biens et services. Ces pourcentages sont calculés à partir des chiffres officiels communiqués à l'ONU par les pays, publiés dans l'ouvrage annuel.

Le *tableau 22* montre la répartition (en pourcentage) de la valeur ajoutée par branche d'activité, selon le classement retenu dans la *Classification internationale type, par industrie, de toutes les branches d'activité économique, Révision 3* (CITI Rev. 3) [50]. Il rend donc compte de la structure économique de la production dans chaque pays. Les pourcentages sont établis à partir des chiffres officiels de valeur ajoutée, aux prix courants, ventilés selon les différentes catégories d'activité économique : agriculture, chasse, sylviculture et pêche (catégories

work (N), other community, social and personal service activities (O) and private households with employed persons (P).

Table 23 presents the relationships among the principal national accounting aggregates, namely: gross domestic product (GDP), gross national income (GNI), gross national disposable income (GNDI) and gross saving. GNI is the term used in the 1993 SNA instead of the term Gross National Product (GNP) which was used in the 1968 SNA. The ratio of each aggregate to GDP is derived cumulatively by adding net primary income (or net factor income) from the rest of the world, (GNI); adding net current transfers from the rest of the world, (GNDI) and deducting final consumption to arrive at gross saving. Net national income, net national disposable income and net saving can be derived by deducting consumption of fixed capital from the corresponding gross values mentioned above.

Table 24 presents the distribution of government final consumption expenditure by function in current prices. The breakdown by function includes: general public services; defence; public order and safety; environment protection; health; education; social protection; and other functions which include housing, community amenities, recreational, cultural and religious affairs. The government expenditure is equal to the service produced by general government for its own use. These services are not sold; they are valued in the GDP at their cost to the government.

Table 25 shows the distribution of total household consumption expenditure by purpose in current prices. Household consumption expenditure measures the expenditure of all resident non-government units which includes all households and private non-profit institutions serving households. The percentage shares include: food, beverages, tobacco and narcotics; clothing and footwear; housing, water, electricity, gas and other fuels; furnishings, household equipment, routine maintenance of the house; health; transport and communication; recreation, culture, education, restaurants, hotels; and other functions which include miscellaneous goods and services, purchases abroad by resident households deducting the expenditure of non-resident in the domestic market and the expenditure of private non-profit institutions serving households.

Table 26:The national indices in this table are shown for the categories "Mining and Quarrying", "Manufacturing" and "Electricity, gas and water". These categories are classified according to Tabulation Categories C, D and E of the ISIC Revision 3 [50]. Major deviations from ISIC in the scope of the indices for the above categories are indicated by footnotes to the table.

The category "Total industry" covers Mining, Manufacturing and Electricity, gas and water. The indices for "Total industry", however, are the combination

A + B); activités extractives (C); activités de fabrication (D); production et distribution d'électricité, de gaz et d'eau (E); construction (F); commerce de gros et de détail, réparation de véhicules automobiles, de motocycles et de biens personnels et domestiques, hôtels et restaurants (G + H); transports, entreposage et communications (I) et intermédiation financière (J); immobilier, locations et activités de services aux entreprises (K); administration publique et défense, sécurité sociale obligatoire (L); éducation (M); santé et action sociale (N); autres activités de services collectifs, sociaux et personnels (O); et ménages privés employant du personnel domestique (P).

Le *tableau 23* montre les rapports entre les principaux agrégats de la comptabilité nationale, à savoir le produit intérieur brut (PIB), le revenu national brut (RNB), le revenu national brut disponible et l'épargne brute. Le revenu national brut est l'agrégat qui remplace dans le SCN de 1993 le produit national brut, utilisé dans le SCN de 1968. Chacun d'entre eux est obtenu par rapport au PIB, en ajoutant les revenus primaires nets (ou revenus nets de facteurs) engendrés dans le reste du monde, pour obtenir le revenu national brut; en ajoutant les transferts courants nets reçus de non-résidents, pour obtenir le revenu national disponible; en soustrayant la consommation finale pour obtenir l'épargne brute. Le revenu national net, le revenu national disponible net et l'épargne nette s'obtiennent en déduisant de la valeur brute correspondante la consommation de capital fixe.

Le *tableau 24* donne la répartition des dépenses de consommation finale des administrations publiques, par fonction, aux prix courants. La répartition par fonction est la suivante: services généraux des administrations publiques; protection de l'environnement; santé; éducation; protection sociale; défense; ordre et sécurité publics; et autres fonctions incluant le logement, les aménagements collectifs, les équipements de loisir et les activités culturelles et religieuses. Les dépenses des administrations sont considérées comme égales aux services produits par l'administration pour son propre usage. Ces services ne sont pas vendus et ils sont évalués, dans le PIB, à leur coût pour l'administration.

Le *tableau 25* donne la répartition des dépenses de consommation finale des ménages par fonction aux prix courants. Les dépenses de consommation des ménages mesurent donc les dépenses de toutes les entités résidentes autres que les administrations, y compris tous les ménages et les entités privées à but non lucratif fournissant des services aux ménages. La répartition en pourcentage distingue les rubriques suivantes: alimentation, boissons, tabac et stupéfiants; articles d'habillement et chaussures; logement, eau, gaz, électricité et autres combustibles; meubles, articles de ménage et entretien courant de l'habitation; santé; transports et communication; loisirs, culture; enseignement, restaurants et hôtels; et autres fonctions, y compris les biens et services divers, achats à

of the components shown and share all deviations from ISIC as footnoted for the component series.

For the purpose of presentation, the national indices have been rebased to 1995=100, where necessary.

l'étranger effectués par les ménages résidents, moins les dépenses des non-résidents sur le marché intérieur, et dépenses des institutions privées à but non lucratif fournissant des services aux ménages.

Tableau 26: Les définitions des catégories "Industries extractives", "Industries manufacturières" et "Electricité, gaz et eau", pour lesquelles des indices nationaux sont donnés dans ce tableau correspondent aux catégories C, D et E des tableaux de la CITI Révision 3 [50]. Toutes différences importantes par rapport à la CITI dans la portée des indices de ces catégories sont indiquées dans les notes du tableau.

La catégorie "Total, industrie" couvre Industries extractives, Industries manufacturières et Electricité, gaz et eau. Toutefois, les indices de cette catégorie "Total, industrie" ne portent que sur la combinaison des indices partiels indiqués, et partagent toutes les différences par rapport à la CITI notées dans le cas des indices partiels.

Pour les besoins de la présentation, les indices nationaux ont été dans certains cas recalculés en prenant 1995=100 comme base de référence.

27

Rates of discount of central banks
Per cent per annum, end of period

Taux d'escompte des banques centrales
Pour cent par année, fin de la période

Country or area Pays ou zone	1992	1993	1994	1995	1996	1997	1998	1999	2000	2001
Albania Albanie	40.00	34.00	25.00	20.50	24.00	32.00	23.44	18.00	10.82	...
Algeria Algérie	11.50	11.50	21.00	#14.00	13.00	11.00	9.50	8.50	6.00	6.00
Angola Angola	...	...	...	160.00	2.00	48.00	58.00	120.00	150.00	150.00
Armenia Arménie	30.00	210.00	210.00	77.80	26.00	65.10	...	...	...	...
Aruba Aruba	9.50	9.50	9.50	9.50	9.50	9.50	9.50	6.50	6.50	6.50
Australia Australie	6.96	5.83	5.75	5.75	...	...	...	...	...	...
Austria Autriche	8.00	5.25	4.50	3.00	2.50	2.50	2.50	...	...	...
Azerbaijan Azerbaïdjan	12.00	100.00	200.00	80.00	20.00	12.00	14.00	10.00	10.00	10.00
Bahamas Bahamas	7.50	7.00	6.50	6.50	6.50	6.50	6.50	5.75	5.75	5.75
Bangladesh Bangladesh	8.50	6.00	5.50	6.00	7.00	8.00	8.00	7.00	7.00	6.00
Barbados Barbade	12.00	8.00	9.50	12.50	12.50	9.00	9.00	10.00	10.00	7.50
Belarus Bélarus	30.00	210.00	480.00	66.00	8.30	8.90	9.60	23.40	#80.00	48.00
Belgium Belgique	7.75	5.25	4.50	3.00	2.50	2.75	2.75	...	...	...
Belize Belize	12.00	12.00	12.00	12.00	12.00	12.00	12.00	12.00	12.00	12.00
Benin Bénin	12.50	10.50	10.00	7.50	6.50	6.00	6.25	5.75	6.50	6.50
Bolivia Bolivie	...	...	...	...	16.50	13.25	14.10	12.50	10.00	8.50
Botswana Botswana	14.25	14.25	13.50	13.00	13.00	12.50	12.50	13.25	14.25	14.25
Brazil Brésil	...	...	...	...	25.34	45.09	39.41	21.37	#18.52	21.43
Bulgaria Bulgarie	41.00	52.00	#72.00	34.00	180.00	6.65	5.08	4.46	4.63	4.65
Burkina Faso Burkina Faso	12.50	10.50	10.00	7.50	6.50	6.00	6.25	5.75	6.50	6.50
Burundi Burundi	11.00	10.00	10.00	10.00	10.00	12.00	12.00	12.00	14.00	14.00
Cameroon Cameroun	12.00	11.50	# 7.75	8.60	7.75	7.50	7.00	7.30	7.00	6.50
Canada Canada	7.36	4.11	7.43	5.79	3.25	4.50	5.25	5.00	6.00	2.50
Central African Rep. Rép. centrafricaine	12.00	11.50	# 7.75	8.60	7.75	7.50	7.00	7.60	7.00	6.50
Chad Tchad	12.00	11.50	# 7.75	8.60	7.75	7.50	7.00	7.60	7.00	6.50
Chile Chili	...	7.96	13.89	7.96	11.75	7.96	9.12	7.44	8.73	6.50

27
Rates of discount of central banks
Per cent per annum, end of period *[cont.]*

Taux d'escompte des banques centrales
Pour cent par année, fin de la période *[suite]*

Country or area Pays ou zone	1992	1993	1994	1995	1996	1997	1998	1999	2000	2001
China Chine	7.20	10.08	10.08	10.44	9.00	8.55	4.59	3.24	3.24	3.24
China, Hong Kong SAR Chine, Hong Kong RAS	4.00	4.00	5.75	6.25	6.00	7.00	6.25	7.00	8.00	3.25
Colombia Colombie	34.42	33.49	44.90	40.42	35.05	31.32	42.28	23.05	18.28	16.40
Congo Congo	12.00	11.50	# 7.75	8.60	7.75	7.50	7.00	7.60	7.00	6.50
Costa Rica Costa Rica	29.00	35.00	37.75	38.50	35.00	31.00	37.00	34.00	31.50	28.75
Côte d'Ivoire Côte d'Ivoire	12.50	10.50	10.00	7.50	6.50	6.00	6.25	5.75	6.50	6.50
Croatia Croatie	1 889.39	34.49	8.50	8.50	6.50	5.90	5.90	7.90	5.90	5.90
Cyprus Chypre	6.50	6.50	6.50	6.50	7.50	7.00	7.00	7.00	7.00	5.50
Czech Republic République tchèque	...	8.00	8.50	11.30	12.40	14.75	9.50	5.25	5.25	4.50
Dem. Rep. of the Congo Rép. dém. du Congo	55.00	95.00	145.00	125.00	238.00	13.00	22.00	120.00	120.00	...
Denmark Danemark	9.50	6.25	5.00	4.25	3.25	3.50	3.50	3.00	4.75	3.25
Ecuador Equateur	49.00	33.57	44.88	59.41	46.38	37.46	61.84	64.40	#13.16	16.44
Egypt Egypte	18.40	16.50	14.00	13.50	13.00	12.25	12.00	12.00	12.00	11.00
Equatorial Guinea Guinée équatoriale	12.00	11.50	# 7.75	8.60	7.75	7.50	7.00	7.60	7.00	6.50
Ethiopia Ethiopie	5.25	12.00	12.00	12.00	...	...	...	...	...	...
Fiji Fidji	6.00	6.00	6.00	6.00	6.00	1.88	2.50	2.50	8.00	1.75
Finland Finlande	9.50	5.50	5.25	4.88	4.00	4.00	3.50	...	...	...
Gabon Gabon	12.00	11.50	# 7.75	8.60	7.75	7.50	7.00	7.60	7.00	6.50
Gambia Gambie	17.50	13.50	13.50	14.00	14.00	14.00	12.00	10.50	10.00	13.00
Germany Allemagne	8.25	5.75	4.50	3.00	2.50	2.50	2.50	...	...	...
Ghana Ghana	30.00	35.00	33.00	45.00	45.00	45.00	37.00	27.00	27.00	27.00
Greece Grèce	19.00	21.50	20.50	18.00	16.50	14.50	...	#11.81	8.10	...
Guinea Guinée	19.00	17.00	17.00	18.00	18.00	15.00	...	...	11.50	16.25
Guinea-Bissau Guinée-Bissau	45.50	41.00	26.00	39.00	54.00	6.00	6.25	5.75	6.50	6.50
Guyana Guyana	24.30	17.00	20.25	17.25	12.00	11.00	11.25	13.25	11.75	8.75
Hungary Hongrie	21.00	22.00	25.00	28.00	23.00	20.50	17.00	14.50	11.00	9.75

27

Rates of discount of central banks
Per cent per annum, end of period *[cont.]*

Taux d'escompte des banques centrales
Pour cent par année, fin de la période *[suite]*

Country or area Pays ou zone	1992	1993	1994	1995	1996	1997	1998	1999	2000	2001
Iceland Islande	16.63	...	4.70	5.93	5.70	6.55	# 8.50	10.00	12.40	12.00
India Inde	12.00	12.00	12.00	12.00	12.00	9.00	9.00	8.00	8.00	6.50
Indonesia Indonésie	13.50	8.82	12.44	13.99	12.80	20.00	38.44	12.51	14.53	17.62
Ireland Irlande	...	7.00	6.25	6.50	6.25	6.75	4.06	...	...	...
Israel Israël	10.39	9.78	17.01	14.19	15.30	13.72	13.47	11.20	8.21	5.67
Italy Italie	12.00	8.00	7.50	9.00	7.50	5.50	3.00	...	...	...
Japan Japon	3.25	1.75	1.75	0.50	0.50	0.50	0.50	0.50	0.50	0.10
Jordan Jordanie	8.50	8.50	8.50	8.50	8.50	7.75	9.00	8.00	6.50	5.00
Kazakhstan Kazakhstan	...	170.00	230.00	#52.50	35.00	18.50	25.00	18.00	14.00	9.00
Kenya Kenya	20.46	45.50	21.50	24.50	26.88	32.27	17.07	26.46	...	...
Korea, Republic of Corée, République de	7.00	5.00	5.00	5.00	5.00	5.00	3.00	3.00	3.00	2.50
Kuwait Koweït	7.50	5.75	7.00	7.25	7.25	7.50	7.00	6.75	7.25	4.25
Lao People's Dem. Rep. Rép. dém. pop. lao	23.67	25.00	30.00	32.08	35.00	...	35.00	34.89	35.17	35.00
Latvia Lettonie	...	27.00	25.00	24.00	9.50	4.00	4.00	4.00	3.50	3.50
Lebanon Liban	16.00	20.22	16.49	19.01	25.00	30.00	30.00	25.00	20.00	20.00
Lesotho Lesotho	15.00	13.50	13.50	15.50	17.00	15.60	19.50	19.00	15.00	13.00
Libyan Arab Jamah. Jamah. arabe libyenne	5.00	5.00	...	...	...	...	3.00	5.00	5.00	5.00
Malawi Malawi	20.00	25.00	40.00	50.00	27.00	23.00	43.00	47.00	50.23	46.80
Malaysia Malaisie	7.10	5.24	4.51	6.47	7.28	...	...	...	...	...
Mali Mali	12.50	10.50	10.00	7.50	6.50	6.00	6.25	5.75	6.50	6.50
Malta Malte	5.50	5.50	5.50	5.50	5.50	5.50	5.50	4.75	4.75	4.25
Mauritius Maurice	8.30	8.30	13.80	11.40	11.82	10.46	17.19	...	...	...
Mongolia Mongolie	...	628.80	180.00	150.00	109.00	45.50	23.30	11.40	8.65	8.60
Morocco Maroc	...	...	7.17	...	...	...	6.04	5.42	5.00	4.71
Mozambique Mozambique	...	...	69.70	57.75	32.00	12.95	9.95	9.95	9.95	9.95
Myanmar Myanmar	11.00	11.00	11.00	12.50	15.00	15.00	15.00	12.00	10.00	10.00

27
Rates of discount of central banks
Per cent per annum, end of period *[cont.]*
Taux d'escompte des banques centrales
Pour cent par année, fin de la période *[suite]*

Country or area Pays ou zone	1992	1993	1994	1995	1996	1997	1998	1999	2000	2001
Namibia Namibie	16.50	14.50	15.50	17.50	17.75	16.00	18.75	11.50	11.25	9.25
Nepal Népal	13.00	11.00	11.00	11.00	11.00	9.00	9.00	9.00	7.50	6.50
Netherlands Pays-Bas	7.75	5.00	...	...	...	...	...	...	...	...
Netherlands Antilles Antilles néerlandaises	6.00	5.00	5.00	6.00	6.00	6.00	6.00	6.00	6.00	6.00
New Zealand Nouvelle-Zélande	9.15	5.70	9.75	9.80	8.80	9.70	5.60	5.00	6.50	4.75
Niger Niger	12.50	10.50	10.00	7.50	6.50	6.00	6.25	5.75	6.50	6.50
Nigeria Nigéria	17.50	26.00	13.50	13.50	13.50	13.50	13.50	18.00	14.00	20.50
Norway Norvège	11.00	7.00	6.75	6.75	6.00	5.50	10.00	7.50	9.00	8.50
Pakistan Pakistan	10.00	10.00	#15.00	17.00	20.00	18.00	16.50	13.00	13.00	10.00
Papua New Guinea Papouasie-Nvl-Guinée	7.12	# 6.30	6.55	18.00	10.30	10.20	18.15	12.80	4.41	11.25
Paraguay Paraguay	24.00	27.17	19.15	20.50	15.00	20.00	20.00	20.00	20.00	20.00
Peru Pérou	48.50	28.63	16.08	18.44	18.16	15.94	18.72	17.80	14.00	14.00
Philippines Philippines	14.30	9.40	8.30	10.83	11.70	14.64	12.40	7.89	13.81	8.30
Poland Pologne	32.00	29.00	28.00	25.00	22.00	24.50	18.25	19.00	21.50	14.00
Portugal Portugal	21.96	11.00	8.88	8.50	6.70	5.31	3.00	...	...	...
Russian Federation Fédération de Russie	...	...	...	160.00	48.00	28.00	60.00	55.00	25.00	25.00
Rwanda Rwanda	11.00	11.00	11.00	16.00	16.00	10.75	11.38	11.19	11.69	13.00
Sao Tome and Principe Sao Tomé-et-Principe	45.00	30.00	32.00	50.00	35.00	55.00	29.50	17.00	17.00	15.50
Senegal Sénégal	12.50	10.50	10.00	7.50	6.50	6.00	6.25	5.75	6.50	6.50
Seychelles Seychelles	1.00	1.00	1.00	1.00	1.00	1.00	1.00	1.00	1.00	1.00
Slovakia Slovaquie	...	12.00	12.00	9.75	8.80	8.80	8.80	8.80	8.80	...
Slovenia Slovénie	...	...	...	14.62	11.42	13.78	8.55	8.35	11.85	...
South Africa Afrique du Sud	14.00	12.00	13.00	15.00	17.00	16.00	#19.32	12.00	12.00	9.50
Spain Espagne	13.25	9.00	7.38	9.00	6.25	4.75	3.00	...	...	...
Sri Lanka Sri Lanka	17.00	17.00	17.00	17.00	17.00	17.00	17.00	16.00	25.00	...
Swaziland Swaziland	12.00	11.00	12.00	15.00	16.75	15.75	18.00	12.00	11.00	9.50

27

Rates of discount of central banks
Per cent per annum, end of period *[cont.]*

Taux d'escompte des banques centrales
Pour cent par année, fin de la période *[suite]*

Country or area Pays ou zone	1992	1993	1994	1995	1996	1997	1998	1999	2000	2001
Sweden Suède	10.00	5.00	7.00	7.00	3.50	2.50	2.00	1.50	2.00	2.00
Switzerland Suisse	6.00	4.00	3.50	1.50	1.00	1.00	1.00	0.50	# 3.20	1.59
Syrian Arab Republic Rép. arabe syrienne	5.00	5.00	5.00	5.00	5.00	5.00	5.00	5.00	5.00	5.00
Thailand Thaïlande	11.00	9.00	9.50	10.50	10.50	12.50	12.50	4.00	4.00	3.75
TFYR of Macedonia L'ex-R.y. Macédoine	...	295.00	33.00	15.00	9.20	8.90	8.90	8.90	7.90	10.70
Togo Togo	12.50	10.50	10.00	7.50	6.50	6.00	6.25	5.75	6.50	6.50
Trinidad and Tobago Trinité-et-Tobago	13.00	13.00	13.00	13.00	13.00	13.00	13.00	13.00	13.00	13.00
Tunisia Tunisie	11.38	8.88	8.88	8.88	7.88	...	...	...	...	...
Turkey Turquie	48.00	48.00	55.00	50.00	50.00	67.00	67.00	60.00	60.00	60.00
Uganda Ouganda	41.00	24.00	15.00	13.30	15.85	14.08	9.10	15.75	18.86	8.88
Ukraine Ukraine	34.33	190.00	228.92	125.83	60.25	24.83	61.08	49.17	30.25	19.46
United Rep. of Tanzania Rép.-Unie de Tanzanie	14.50	14.50	67.50	47.90	19.00	16.20	17.60	20.20	10.70	8.70
United States Etats-Unis	3.00	3.00	4.75	5.25	5.00	5.00	4.50	5.00	6.00	1.25
Uruguay Uruguay	162.40	164.30	182.30	178.70	160.30	95.50	73.70	66.39	57.26	71.66
Vanuatu Vanuatu	...	...	...	...	...	...	7.00	7.00	7.00	6.50
Venezuela Venezuela	52.20	71.25	48.00	49.00	45.00	45.00	60.00	38.00	38.00	37.00
Viet Nam Viet Nam	...	...	...	...	18.90	10.80	12.00	6.00	6.00	4.80
Yemen Yémen	...	...	...	27.40	28.51	15.00	19.95	18.53	15.89	15.16
Zambia Zambie	47.00	72.50	20.50	40.20	47.00	17.70	...	32.93	25.67	40.10
Zimbabwe Zimbabwe	29.50	28.50	29.50	29.50	27.00	31.50	#39.50	74.41	57.84	57.20

Source:
International Monetary Fund (IMF), Washington, D.C., "International Financial Statistics," January 2003 and the IMF database.

Source:
Fonds monétaire international (FMI), Washington, D.C.,"Statistiques Financières Internationales," janvier 2003 et la base de données du FMI.

28

Short-term interest rates
Treasury bill and money market rates: per cent per annum

Taux d'intérêt à court terme
Taux des bons du Trésor et du marché monétaire : pour cent par année

Country or area Pays ou zone	1992	1993	1994	1995	1996	1997	1998	1999	2000	2001
Albania Albanie										
Treasury bill										
Bons du trésor	...	...	...	13.84	17.81	32.59	27.49	17.54	10.80	...
Algeria Algérie										
Treasury bill										
Bons du trésor	9.50	9.50	16.50	...	...	...	# 9.96	10.05	7.95	5.69
Money market										
Marché monétaire	...	...	19.80	# 21.05	18.47	11.80	10.40	10.43	6.77	3.35
Antigua and Barbuda Antigua-et-Barbuda										
Treasury bill										
Bons du trésor	7.00	7.00	7.00	7.00	7.00	7.00	7.00	7.00	7.00	7.00
Argentina Argentine										
Money market										
Marché monétaire	15.11	6.31	7.66	9.46	6.23	6.63	6.81	6.99	8.15	24.90
Armenia Arménie										
Treasury bill										
Bons du trésor	...	...	...	37.81	# 43.95	57.54	46.99	55.10	24.40	19.92
Money market										
Marché monétaire	...	...	...	...	48.56	36.41	27.84	23.65	18.63	19.40
Australia Australie										
Treasury bill										
Bons du trésor	6.27	5.00	5.69	# 7.64	7.02	5.29	4.84	4.76	5.98	4.80
Money market										
Marché monétaire	6.44	5.11	5.18	# 7.50	7.20	5.50	4.99	# 4.78	5.90	5.06
Austria Autriche										
Money market										
Marché monétaire	9.35	7.22	5.03	4.36	3.19	3.27	3.36	2.97[1]	4.39[1]	4.26[1]
Azerbaijan Azerbaïdjan										
Treasury bill										
Bons du trésor	...	...	...	...	...	12.23	14.10	18.31	16.73	16.51
Bahamas Bahamas										
Treasury bill										
Bons du trésor	5.32	3.96	1.88	3.01	4.45	4.35	3.84	1.97	1.03	1.94
Bahrain Bahreïn										
Treasury bill										
Bons du trésor	3.78	3.33	4.81	6.07	5.49	5.68	5.53	5.46	6.56	3.78
Money market										
Marché monétaire	3.99	3.53	5.18	6.24	5.69	...	5.69	5.58	6.89	3.85
Barbados Barbade										
Treasury bill										
Bons du trésor	10.88	5.44	7.26	8.01	6.85	3.61	5.61	5.83	5.29	3.14
Belgium Belgique										
Treasury bill										
Bons du trésor	9.36	8.52	5.57	4.67	3.19	3.38	3.51	2.72	4.02	4.16
Money market										
Marché monétaire	9.38	8.21	5.72	4.80	3.24	3.46	3.58	2.97[1]	4.39[1]	4.26[1]
Belize Belize										
Treasury bill										
Bons du trésor	5.38	4.59	4.27	4.10	3.78	3.51	3.83	5.91	5.91	5.91
Benin Bénin										
Money market										
Marché monétaire	11.44	...	...	...	...	...	4.81	4.95	4.95	4.95
Bolivia Bolivie										
Treasury bill										
Bons du trésor	...	...	17.89	24.51	19.93	13.65	12.33	14.07	10.99	11.48
Money market										
Marché monétaire	...	...	...	22.42	20.27	13.97	12.57	13.49	7.40	6.99
Brazil Brésil										
Treasury bill										
Bons du trésor	...	...	...	49.93	25.73	24.79	28.57	26.39	18.51	20.06

28

Short-term interest rates
Treasury bill and money market rates: per cent per annum *[cont.]*

Taux d'intérêt à court terme
Taux des bons du Trésor et du marché monétaire : pour cent par année *[suite]*

Country or area Pays ou zone	1992	1993	1994	1995	1996	1997	1998	1999	2000	2001
Money market Marché monétaire	1 574.28	3 284.44	4 820.64	53.37	27.45	25.00	29.50	26.26	17.59	17.47
Bulgaria Bulgarie										
Treasury bill Bons du trésor	48.11	45.45	57.72	48.27	114.31	78.35	6.02	5.43	4.21	4.57
Money market Marché monétaire	52.39	48.07	66.43	53.09	119.88	66.43	2.48	2.93	3.02	3.74
Burkina Faso Burkina Faso										
Money market Marché monétaire	11.44	...	...	...	...	...	4.81	4.95	4.95	4.95
Canada Canada										
Treasury bill Bons du trésor	6.59	4.84	5.54	6.89	4.21	3.26	4.73	4.72	5.49	3.77
Money market Marché monétaire	6.64	4.63	5.05	6.92	4.33	3.26	4.87	4.74	5.52	4.11
Chile Chili										
Money market Marché monétaire	...	...	...	...	...	...	...	...	10.09	6.81
China, Hong Kong SAR Chine, Hong Kong RAS										
Treasury bill Bons du trésor	3.83	3.17	5.66	5.55	4.45	7.50	5.04	4.94	5.69	1.69
Money market Marché monétaire	3.81	4.00	5.44	6.00	5.13	4.50	5.50	5.75	7.13	2.69
China, Macao SAR Chine, Macao RAS										
Money market Marché monétaire	4.41	3.79	5.91	6.01	5.60	7.54	5.41	6.11	6.20	1.93
Colombia Colombie										
Money market Marché monétaire	...	...	...	22.40	28.37	23.83	35.00	18.81	10.87	10.43
Côte d'Ivoire Côte d'Ivoire										
Money market Marché monétaire	11.44	...	...	...	...	...	4.81	4.95	4.95	4.95
Croatia Croatie										
Money market Marché monétaire	951.20	1 370.50	26.93	21.13	19.26	10.18	14.48	13.72	8.85	3.90
Cyprus Chypre										
Treasury bill Bons du trésor	6.00	6.00	6.00	6.00	6.05	5.38	5.59	5.59	6.01	...
Money market Marché monétaire	...	...	...	...	6.85	4.82	4.80	5.15	5.96	4.93
Czech Republic République tchèque										
Treasury bill Bons du trésor	...	6.62	6.98	8.99	11.91	11.21	10.51	5.71	5.37	5.06
Money market Marché monétaire	...	8.00	12.65	10.93	12.67	17.50	10.08	5.58	5.42	4.69
Denmark Danemark										
Money market Marché monétaire	11.35	# 11.49	6.30	6.19	3.98	3.71	4.27	3.37	4.98	...
Dominica Dominique										
Treasury bill Bons du trésor	6.48	6.40	6.40	6.40	6.40	6.40	6.40	6.40	6.40	6.40
Dominican Republic Rép. dominicaine										
Money market Marché monétaire	...	...	...	...	14.70	13.01	16.68	15.30	18.28	13.47
Egypt Egypte										
Treasury bill Bons du trésor	...	...	...	...	...	8.80	8.80	9.00	9.10	7.20
El Salvador El Salvador										
Money market Marché monétaire	...	...	...	...	10.43	9.43	10.68	6.93	5.28	

28

Short-term interest rates
Treasury bill and money market rates: per cent per annum *[cont.]*

Taux d'intérêt à court terme
Taux des bons du Trésor et du marché monétaire : pour cent par année *[suite]*

Country or area Pays ou zone	1992	1993	1994	1995	1996	1997	1998	1999	2000	2001
Estonia Estonie										
Money market										
Marché monétaire	...	...	5.67	4.94	3.53	6.45	11.66	5.39	4.57	4.92
Ethiopia Ethiopie										
Treasury bill										
Bons du trésor	5.25	12.00	12.00	12.00	7.22	3.97	3.48	3.65	2.74	3.06
Fiji Fidji										
Treasury bill										
Bons du trésor	3.65	2.91	2.69	3.15	2.98	2.60	2.00	2.00	3.63	1.51
Money market										
Marché monétaire	3.06	2.91	4.10	3.95	2.43	1.91	1.27	1.27	2.58	0.79
Finland Finlande										
Money market										
Marché monétaire	13.25	7.77	5.35	5.75	3.63	3.23	3.57	2.96	4.39	4.26
France France										
Treasury bill										
Bons du trésor	10.49	8.41	5.79	6.58	3.84	3.35	3.45	2.72	4.23	4.26
Money market										
Marché monétaire	10.35	8.75	5.69	6.35	3.73	3.24	3.39	2.97[1]	4.39[1]	4.26[1]
Georgia Géorgie										
Money market										
Marché monétaire	...	...	...	...	43.39	26.58	43.26	34.61	18.17	17.50
Germany Allemagne										
Treasury bill										
Bons du trésor	8.32	6.22	5.05	4.40	3.30	3.32	3.42	2.88	4.32	3.66
Money market										
Marché monétaire	9.42	7.49	5.35	4.50	3.27	3.18	3.41	2.73	4.11	4.37
Ghana Ghana										
Treasury bill										
Bons du trésor	19.38	30.95	27.72	35.38	41.64	42.77	34.33	26.37	36.28	40.96
Greece Grèce										
Treasury bill										
Bons du trésor	22.50	20.25	17.50	14.20	11.20	11.38	10.30	8.30	# 6.22	4.08
Money market										
Marché monétaire	...	...	24.60	16.40	13.80	12.80	13.99	2.97[1]	4.39[1]	4.26[1]
Grenada Grenade										
Treasury bill										
Bons du trésor	6.50	6.50	6.50	6.50	6.50	6.50	6.50	6.50	6.50	6.50
Guatemala Guatemala										
Money market										
Marché monétaire	...	...	...	...	...	7.77	6.62	9.23	9.33	10.58
Guinea-Bissau Guinée-Bissau										
Money market										
Marché monétaire	11.45	...	...	...	...	...	4.81	4.95	4.95	4.95
Guyana Guyana										
Treasury bill										
Bons du trésor	25.75	16.83	17.66	17.51	11.35	8.91	8.33	11.31	9.88	7.78
Haiti Haïti										
Treasury bill										
Bons du trésor	...	...	...	...	...	14.13	16.21	7.71	12.33	13.53
Hungary Hongrie										
Treasury bill										
Bons du trésor	22.65	17.22	26.93	32.04	23.96	20.13	17.83	14.68	11.03	10.79
Iceland Islande										
Treasury bill										
Bons du trésor	11.30	8.35	4.95	7.22	6.97	7.04	7.40	8.61	11.12	11.03
Money market										
Marché monétaire	12.38	8.61	4.96	6.58	6.96	7.38	8.12	9.24	11.61	14.51

28

Short-term interest rates
Treasury bill and money market rates: per cent per annum *[cont.]*

Taux d'intérêt à court terme
Taux des bons du Trésor et du marché monétaire : pour cent par année *[suite]*

Country or area Pays ou zone	1992	1993	1994	1995	1996	1997	1998	1999	2000	2001
India Inde										
Money market										
Marché monétaire	15.23	8.64	7.14	15.57	11.04	5.29	...	...	...	...
Indonesia Indonésie										
Money market										
Marché monétaire	11.99	8.66	9.74	13.64	13.96	27.82	62.79	23.58	10.32	15.03
Ireland Irlande										
Treasury bill										
Bons du trésor	...	# 9.06	5.87	6.19	5.36	6.03	5.37	...	...	...
Money market										
Marché monétaire	15.12	10.49	# 5.75	5.45	5.74	6.43	3.23	3.14	4.84	3.31
Israel Israël										
Treasury bill										
Bons du trésor	11.79	10.54	11.77	14.37	15.34	13.39	11.33	11.41	8.81	6.50
Italy Italie										
Treasury bill										
Bons du trésor	14.32	10.58	9.17	10.85	8.46	6.33	4.59	3.01	4.53	4.05
Money market										
Marché monétaire	14.02	10.20	8.51	10.46	8.82	6.88	4.99	2.95	4.39	4.26
Jamaica Jamaïque										
Treasury bill										
Bons du trésor	34.36	28.85	42.98	27.65	37.95	21.14	25.65	20.75	18.24	16.71
Japan Japon										
Money market										
Marché monétaire	4.58	# 3.06	2.20	1.21	0.47	0.48	0.37	0.06	0.11	0.06
Kazakhstan Kazakhstan										
Treasury bill										
Bons du trésor	...	...	214.34	48.98	28.91	15.15	23.59	15.63	6.59	5.28
Kenya Kenya										
Treasury bill										
Bons du trésor	16.53	49.80	23.32	18.29	22.25	22.87	22.83	13.87	12.05	12.60
Korea, Republic of Corée, République de										
Money market										
Marché monétaire	14.32	12.12	12.45	12.57	12.44	13.24	14.98	5.01	5.16	4.69
Kuwait Koweït										
Treasury bill										
Bons du trésor	...	...	6.32	7.35	6.93	6.98	...	...	...	...
Money market										
Marché monétaire	...	7.43	6.31	7.43	6.98	7.05	7.24	6.32	6.82	4.62
Kyrgyzstan Kirghizistan										
Treasury bill										
Bons du trésor	...	...	143.13	34.90	40.10	35.83	43.67	47.19	32.26	19.08
Money market										
Marché monétaire	...	...	...	...	...	...	43.98	43.71	24.26	11.92
Lao People's Dem. Rep. Rép. dém. pop. lao										
Treasury bill										
Bons du trésor	...	...	...	20.46	...	...	23.66	30.00	29.94	22.70
Latvia Lettonie										
Treasury bill										
Bons du trésor	...	...	...	28.24	16.27	4.73	5.27	6.23	3.83	5.14
Money market										
Marché monétaire	...	...	37.18	22.39	13.08	3.76	4.42	4.72	2.97	5.23
Lebanon Liban										
Treasury bill										
Bons du trésor	22.40	18.27	15.09	19.40	15.19	13.42	12.70	11.57	11.18	11.18
Lesotho Lesotho										
Treasury bill										
Bons du trésor	14.20	# 10.01	9.44	12.40	13.89	14.83	15.47	12.45	9.06	9.49

28

Short-term interest rates
Treasury bill and money market rates: per cent per annum *[cont.]*
Taux d'intérêt à court terme
Taux des bons du Trésor et du marché monétaire : pour cent par année *[suite]*

Country or area Pays ou zone	1992	1993	1994	1995	1996	1997	1998	1999	2000	2001
Libyan Arab Jamah. Jamah. arabe libyenne										
Money market										
Marché monétaire	4.00	4.00	...	...	...	...	4.00	4.00	4.00	4.00
Lithuania Lituanie										
Treasury bill										
Bons du trésor	...	...	...	26.82	20.95	8.64	10.69	11.14	...	...
Money market										
Marché monétaire	...	...	69.48	26.73	20.26	9.55	6.12	6.26	3.60	3.37
Luxembourg Luxembourg										
Money market										
Marché monétaire	8.93	8.09	5.16	4.26	3.29	3.36	3.48	2.97[1]	4.39[1]	4.26[1]
Madagascar Madagascar										
Treasury bill										
Bons du trésor	...	...	...	...	...	...	...	...	...	10.28
Money market										
Marché monétaire	15.00	...	...	29.00	10.00	...	11.24	...	16.00	...
Malawi Malawi										
Treasury bill										
Bons du trésor	15.62	23.54	27.68	46.30	30.83	18.31	32.98	42.85	39.52	42.41
Malaysia Malaisie										
Treasury bill										
Bons du trésor	7.66	6.48	3.68	5.50	6.41	6.41	6.86	3.53	2.86	2.79
Money market										
Marché monétaire	8.01	6.53	4.65	5.78	# 6.98	7.61	8.46	3.38	2.66	2.79
Maldives Maldives										
Money market										
Marché monétaire	7.00	5.00	5.00	6.80	6.80	6.80	6.80	6.80	6.80	6.80
Mali Mali										
Money market										
Marché monétaire	11.44	...	...	...	...	...	4.81	4.95	4.95	4.95
Malta Malte										
Treasury bill										
Bons du trésor	4.58	4.60	4.29	4.65	4.99	5.08	5.41	5.15	4.89	4.93
Mauritius Maurice										
Money market										
Marché monétaire	9.05	7.73	10.23	10.35	9.96	9.43	8.99	10.01	7.66	7.25
Mexico Mexique										
Treasury bill										
Bons du trésor	15.62	14.99	14.10	48.44	31.39	19.80	24.76	21.41	15.24	11.31
Money market										
Marché monétaire	18.87	17.39	16.47	# 60.92	33.61	21.91	26.89	24.10	16.96	12.89
Morocco Maroc										
Money market										
Marché monétaire	...	...	12.29	10.06	8.42	7.89	6.30	5.64	5.41	4.44
Mozambique Mozambique										
Treasury bill										
Bons du trésor	...	...	...	...	...	...	...	...	16.97	24.77
Money market										
Marché monétaire	...	...	...	...	...	...	...	9.92	16.12	33.64
Namibia Namibie										
Treasury bill										
Bons du trésor	13.88	12.16	11.35	13.91	15.25	15.69	17.24	13.28	10.26	9.29
Nepal Népal										
Treasury bill										
Bons du trésor	9.00	4.50	6.50	9.90	11.51	2.52	3.70	4.30	5.30	5.00
Netherlands Pays-Bas										
Money market										
Marché monétaire	9.27	7.10	5.14	4.22	2.89	3.07	3.21	2.97[1]	4.39[1]	4.26[1]

28

Short-term interest rates
Treasury bill and money market rates: per cent per annum *[cont.]*

Taux d'intérêt à court terme
Taux des bons du Trésor et du marché monétaire : pour cent par année *[suite]*

Country or area Pays ou zone	1992	1993	1994	1995	1996	1997	1998	1999	2000	2001
Netherlands Antilles Antilles néerlandaises										
Treasury bill										
Bons du trésor	...	4.83	4.48	5.46	5.66	5.77	5.82	6.15	6.15	6.15
New Zealand Nouvelle-Zélande										
Treasury bill										
Bons du trésor	6.72	6.21	6.69	8.82	9.09	7.53	7.10	4.58	6.39	5.56
Money market										
Marché monétaire	6.63	6.25	6.13	8.91	9.38	7.38	6.86	4.33	6.12	5.76
Niger Niger										
Money market										
Marché monétaire	11.44	...	...	...	...	...	4.81	4.95	4.95	4.95
Nigeria Nigéria										
Treasury bill										
Bons du trésor	17.89	24.50	12.87	12.50	12.25	12.00	12.26	17.82	15.50	17.50
Norway Norvège										
Money market										
Marché monétaire	13.71	7.64	5.70	5.54	4.97	3.77	6.03	6.87	6.72	7.38
Pakistan Pakistan										
Treasury bill										
Bons du trésor	12.47	13.03	11.26	12.49	13.61	# 15.74	...	...	8.38	10.71
Money market										
Marché monétaire	7.51	11.00	8.36	11.52	11.40	12.10	10.76	9.04	8.57	8.49
Papua New Guinea Papouasie-Nvl-Guinée										
Treasury bill										
Bons du trésor	8.88	6.25	6.85	17.40	14.44	9.94	21.18	22.70	17.00	12.36
Paraguay Paraguay										
Money market										
Marché monétaire	21.59	22.55	18.64	20.18	16.35	12.48	20.74	17.26	10.70	13.45
Philippines Philippines										
Treasury bill										
Bons du trésor	16.02	12.45	12.71	11.76	12.34	12.89	15.00	10.00	9.91	9.73
Poland Pologne										
Treasury bill										
Bons du trésor	44.03	33.16	28.81	25.62	20.32	21.58	19.09	13.14	16.62	...
Money market										
Marché monétaire	29.49	24.51	23.32	25.82	20.63	22.43	20.59	13.58	18.16	16.23
Portugal Portugal										
Treasury bill										
Bons du trésor	12.88	...	...	7.75	5.75	4.43	...	...	...	...
Money market										
Marché monétaire	17.48	13.25	10.62	8.91	7.38	5.78	4.34	2.71	4.39[1]	4.26[1]
Republic of Moldova République de Moldova										
Treasury bill										
Bons du trésor	...	...	...	52.90	39.01	23.63	30.54	28.49	22.20	14.24
Money market										
Marché monétaire	...	...	...	...	...	28.10	30.91	32.60	20.77	11.04
Romania Roumanie										
Treasury bill										
Bons du trésor	...	...	...	51.09	85.72	63.99	74.21	51.86	42.18
Russian Federation Fédération de Russie										
Treasury bill										
Bons du trésor	...	...	...	168.04	86.07	23.43	...	...	12.12	12.45
Money market										
Marché monétaire	...	...	...	190.43	47.65	20.97	50.56	14.79	7.14	10.10
Saint Kitts and Nevis[2] Saint-Kitts-et-Nevis[2]										
Treasury bill										
Bons du trésor	6.50	6.50	6.50	6.50	6.50	6.50	6.50	6.50	6.50	6.17
Saint Lucia Sainte-Lucie										
Treasury bill										
Bons du trésor	7.00	7.00	7.00	7.00	7.00	7.00	7.00	7.00	7.00	7.00

28

Short-term interest rates
Treasury bill and money market rates: per cent per annum *[cont.]*

Taux d'intérêt à court terme
Taux des bons du Trésor et du marché monétaire : pour cent par année *[suite]*

Country or area Pays ou zone	1992	1993	1994	1995	1996	1997	1998	1999	2000	2001
St. Vincent-Grenadines St. Vincent-Grenadines										
Treasury bill										
Bons du trésor	6.50	6.50	6.50	6.50	6.50	6.50	6.50	6.50	6.50	6.50
Senegal Sénégal										
Money market										
Marché monétaire	11.44	...	...	...	...	...	4.81	4.95	4.95	4.95
Seychelles Seychelles										
Treasury bill										
Bons du trésor	13.00	12.91	12.36	12.15	11.47	10.50	7.96	4.50	4.50	4.50
Sierra Leone Sierra Leone										
Treasury bill										
Bons du trésor	78.63	28.64	12.19	14.73	29.25	12.71	22.10	32.42	26.22	13.74
Singapore Singapour										
Treasury bill										
Bons du trésor	1.73	0.92	1.94	1.05	1.38	2.32	2.12	1.12	2.18	1.69
Money market										
Marché monétaire	2.74	2.50	3.68	2.56	2.93	4.35	5.00	2.04	2.57	1.99
Slovakia Slovaquie										
Money market										
Marché monétaire	...	...	...	...	...	...	...	...	8.08	7.76
Slovenia Slovénie										
Treasury bill										
Bons du trésor	...	...	...	...	...	...	...	8.63	10.94	10.88
Money market										
Marché monétaire	67.58	39.15	29.08	12.18	13.98	9.71	7.45	6.87	6.95	6.90
Solomon Islands Iles Salomon										
Treasury bill										
Bons du trésor	13.50	12.15	11.25	12.50	12.75	12.88	6.00	6.00	...	...
South Africa Afrique du Sud										
Treasury bill										
Bons du trésor	13.77	11.31	10.93	13.53	15.04	15.26	16.53	12.85	10.11	9.68
Money market										
Marché monétaire	14.11	10.83	10.24	13.07	15.54	15.59	17.11	13.06	9.54	8.84
Spain Espagne										
Treasury bill										
Bons du trésor	12.44	10.53	8.11	9.79	7.23	5.02	3.79	3.01	4.61	3.92
Money market										
Marché monétaire	13.01	12.33	7.81	8.98	7.65	5.49	4.34	2.72	4.11	4.36
Sri Lanka Sri Lanka										
Treasury bill										
Bons du trésor	16.19	16.52	12.68	16.81	# 17.40	...	12.59	12.51	14.02	17.57
Money market										
Marché monétaire	21.63	25.65	18.54	41.87	24.33	18.42	15.74	16.69	17.30	21.24
Swaziland Swaziland										
Treasury bill										
Bons du trésor	12.34	8.25	8.35	10.87	13.68	14.37	13.09	11.19	8.30	7.16
Money market										
Marché monétaire	10.25	9.73	7.01	8.52	9.77	10.35	10.63	8.86	5.54	5.06
Sweden Suède										
Treasury bill										
Bons du trésor	12.85	8.35	7.40	8.75	5.79	4.11	4.19	3.12	3.95	...
Money market										
Marché monétaire	18.42	9.08	7.36	8.54	6.28	4.21	4.24	3.14	3.81	4.08
Switzerland Suisse										
Treasury bill										
Bons du trésor	7.76	4.75	3.97	2.78	1.72	1.45	1.32	1.17	2.93	2.68
Money market										
Marché monétaire	7.47	4.94	3.85	2.89	1.78	1.35	1.22	0.93	# 3.50	1.65

28

Short-term interest rates
Treasury bill and money market rates: per cent per annum [cont.]

Taux d'intérêt à court terme
Taux des bons du Trésor et du marché monétaire : pour cent par année [suite]

Country or area Pays ou zone	1992	1993	1994	1995	1996	1997	1998	1999	2000	2001
Thailand Thaïlande										
Money market										
Marché monétaire	6.93	6.54	7.25	10.96	9.23	14.59	13.02	1.77	1.95	2.00
Togo Togo										
Money market										
Marché monétaire	11.44	...	...	...	...	...	4.81	4.95	4.95	4.95
Trinidad and Tobago Trinité-et-Tobago										
Treasury bill										
Bons du trésor	9.26	9.45	10.00	8.41	10.44	9.83	11.93	10.40	10.56	8.55
Tunisia Tunisie										
Money market										
Marché monétaire	11.73	10.48	8.81	8.81	8.64	6.88	6.89	5.99	5.88	6.04
Turkey Turquie										
Treasury bill										
Bons du trésor	72.17	...	...	...	...	...	...	...	33.32	64.61
Money market										
Marché monétaire	65.35	62.83	136.47	72.30	76.24	70.32	74.60	73.53	56.72	91.95
Uganda Ouganda										
Treasury bill										
Bons du trésor	...	# 21.30	12.52	8.75	11.71	10.59	7.77	7.43	13.19	11.00
Ukraine Ukraine										
Money market										
Marché monétaire	...	...	...	...	...	22.05	40.41	44.98	18.34	16.57
United Kingdom Royaume-Uni										
Treasury bill										
Bons du trésor	8.94	5.21	5.15	6.33	5.78	6.48	6.82	5.04	5.80	4.77
Money market										
Marché monétaire	9.37	5.91	4.88	6.08	5.96	6.61	7.21	5.20	5.77	5.08
United Rep. of Tanzania Rép.-Unie de Tanzanie										
Treasury bill										
Bons du trésor	...	34.00	35.09	40.33	15.30	9.59	11.83	10.05	9.78	4.14
United States Etats-Unis										
Treasury bill										
Bons du trésor	3.46	3.02	4.27	5.51	5.02	5.07	4.82	4.66	5.84	3.45
Money market[3]										
Marché monétaire[3]	3.52	3.02	4.20	5.84	5.30	5.46	5.35	4.97	6.24	3.89
Uruguay Uruguay										
Treasury bill										
Bons du trésor	...	...	44.60	39.40	29.20	23.18	...	...	...	...
Money market										
Marché monétaire	...	...	39.82	36.81	28.47	23.43	20.48	13.96	14.82	22.10
Vanuatu Vanuatu										
Money market										
Marché monétaire	5.92	6.00	6.00	6.00	6.00	6.00	8.65	6.99	5.58	5.50
Venezuela Venezuela										
Money market										
Marché monétaire	...	...	...	...	16.70	12.47	18.58	7.48	8.14	13.33
Viet Nam Viet Nam										
Treasury bill										
Bons du trésor	...	26.40	...	...	...	...	...	...	5.42	5.49
Yemen Yémen										
Treasury bill										
Bons du trésor	...	...	...	...	25.20	15.97	12.53	20.57	14.16	13.27
Zambia Zambie										
Treasury bill										
Bons du trésor	...	124.03	74.21	39.81	52.78	29.48	24.94	36.19	31.37	44.28
Zimbabwe Zimbabwe										
Treasury bill										
Bons du trésor	26.16	33.04	29.22	27.98	24.53	22.07	32.78	50.48	64.78	17.60

28

Short-term interest rates
Treasury bill and money market rates: per cent per annum *[cont.]*

Taux d'intérêt à court terme
Taux des bons du Trésor et du marché monétaire : pour cent par année *[suite]*

Country or area Pays ou zone	1992	1993	1994	1995	1996	1997	1998	1999	2000	2001
Money market Marché monétaire	34.77	34.18	30.90	29.64	26.18	25.15	37.22	53.13	64.98	21.52

Source:
International Monetary Fund (IMF), Washington, D.C., "International Financial Statistics," January 2003 and the IMF database.

Source:
Fonds monétaire international (FMI), Washington, D.C.,"Statistiques Financières Internationales," janvier 2003 et la base de données du FMI.

1 Euro area interbank rate (3 month).
2 Including Anguilla.
3 Federal funds rate.

1 Taux interbancaire (3 mois) du zone euro.
2 Y compris Anguilla.
3 Taux des fonds du système fédérale.

Technical notes, tables 27 and 28

Detailed information and current figures relating to tables 27 and 28 are contained in *International Financial Statistics*, published by the International Monetary Fund [15] (see also <www.imf.org>) and in the United Nations *Monthly Bulletin of Statistics* [26].

Table 27: The discount rates shown represent the rates at which the central bank lends or discounts eligible paper for deposit money banks, typically shown on an end-of-period basis.

Table 28: The rates shown represent short-term treasury bill rates and money market rates. The treasury bill rate is the rate at which short-term securities are issued or traded in the market. The money market rate is the rate on short-term lending between financial institutions.

Notes techniques, tableaux 27 et 28

Les informations détaillées et les chiffres courants concernant les tableaux 27 et 28 figurent dans les *Statistiques financières internationales* publiées par le Fonds monétaire international [15] (voir aussi <www.imf.org>) et dans le *Bulletin mensuel de statistique* des Nations Unies [26].

Tableau 27: Les taux d'escomptes indiqués représentent les taux que la banque centrale applique à ses prêts ou auquel elle réescompte les effets escomptables des banques créatrices de monnaie (généralement, taux de fin de période).

Tableau 28: Les taux indiqués représentent le taux des bons du Trésor et le taux du marché monétaire à court terme. Le taux des bons du Trésor est le taux auquel les effets à court terme sont émis ou négociés sur le marché. Le taux du marché monétaire est le taux prêteur à court terme entre institutions financières.

29
Employment by industry
Total employment and persons employed by branch of economic activity (thousands)
Emploi par industrie
Emploi total et personnes employées par branches d'activité économique (milliers)

A. ISIC Rev. 2[+] - CITI Rév. 2[+]

Country or area / Pays ou zone	Year / Année	Total employment / Emploi total		Major division 1 / Branche 1		Major division 2 / Branche 2		Major division 3 / Branche 3		Major division 4 / Branche 4	
		M	F	M	F	M	F	M	F	M	F
Bangladesh [1]	1989	29 386.0	20 761.0	17 735.0	14 836.0	82.0	6.0	2 491.0	4 484.0	14.0	3.
Bangladesh [1]	1990	30 443.0	19 716.0	16 560.0	16 743.0	15.0	...	4 240.0	1 685.0	39.0	1.
	1996[2]	33 765.0	20 832.0	18 382.0	16 148.0	22.0	1.0	2 586.0	1 499.0	90.0	13.
Barbados [3][4]	1994	54.1	46.6	3.5	2.4	...	...	5.2	4.8	0.9	0.
Barbade [3][4]	1995	57.7	52.1	3.2	1.9	...	...	5.4	6.3	0.8	0.
	1999	65.5	56.9	3.4	1.8	...	...	5.4	4.9	1.4	0.
Belarus [7]	1992	4 891.4	...	1 089.7	...	24.5	...	1 329.1	...	34.7	.
Belarus [7]	1993	4 827.7	...	1 048.8	...	29.6	...	1 311.8	...	38.1	.
	1994	4 700.9	...	995.7	...	27.2	...	1 245.6	...	38.7	.
Belize [8]	1993	43.4	18.7	14.7	0.9	0.3	0.0	5.0	2.2	1.0	0.
Belize [8]	1994	43.0	19.0	13.3	0.8	0.3	0.0	5.0	1.7	1.0	0.
	1995	43.7	18.8	...	...	...	...	...	...	...	
Brazil [1][9][10]	1997	41 978.0	27 354.0	11 254.0	5 516.0	658.0[11]	116.0[11]	6 101.0	2 406.0	...	
Brésil [1][9][10]	1998	42 312.0	27 650.0	10 996.0	5 342.0	712.0[11]	150.0[11]	5 910.0	2 320.0		
	1999	42 813.0	28 864.0	11 470.0	5 902.0	657.0[11]	126.0[11]	5 849.0	2 430.0		
Chile [3][4][16]	1998	3 624.8	1 807.6	702.1	82.3	76.6	5.3	591.3	227.3	34.0	3.
Chili [3][4][16]	1999	3 603.6	1 800.9	696.7	83.3	70.4	2.9	568.2	207.3	23.7	4.8
	2000	3 600.5	1 781.0	695.3	81.6	68.4	1.9	552.2	201.9	23.3	5.
China [7][9][17][18]	1998	699 570.0	...	332 320.0	...	7 210.0	...	83 190.0	...	2 830.0	
Chine [7][9][17][18]	1999	705 860.0	...	334 930.0	...	6 670.0	...	81 090.0	...	2 850.0	
	2000	711 500.0	...	333 550.0	...	5 970.0	...	80 430.0	...	2 840.0	
China, Hong Kong SAR [3][44]	1998	1 869.1	1 281.0	6.5	2.9	0.2	...	243.3	142.3	15.6	2.
Chine, Hong Kong RAS [3][44]	1999	1 821.5	1 311.5	6.5	2.7	0.3	...	223.8	135.6	15.2	1.9
	2000	1 849.1	1 365.3	6.2	3.1	0.3	...	213.5	124.6	14.7	1.8
China, Macao SAR [3][20]	1995	101.9	78.5	0.3	0.1	0.0	...	14.4	24.8	1.2	0.
Chine, Macao RAS [3][20]	1996	109.7	87.8	0.3	0.1	...	...	14.0	26.6	1.1	0.2
	1997	110.9	89.7	0.2	0.1	...	...	14.0	27.4	1.3	0.2
Colombia [9][21][22][23]	1998	3 194.6	2 460.3	43.3	14.8	11.0	3.4	624.7	474.4	23.4	9.4
Colombie [9][21][22][23]	1999	3 121.8	2 518.8	50.6	13.2	12.8	2.5	573.1	466.6	26.4	7.0
	2000	3 237.3	2 672.4	51.7	13.5	10.9	1.5	684.8	509.5	29.2	8.1
Ecuador [1][9][24]	1996	1 794.5	1 094.4	170.2	20.9	15.2	1.6	283.0	141.1	8.1	3.2
Equateur [1][9][24]	1997	1 909.6	1 152.6	187.2	22.2	10.7	0.5	307.5	167.8	8.4	4.8
	1998	1 920.8	1 230.4	202.4	28.2	10.4	0.2	303.7	159.3	12.9	2.6
Honduras [1][3][9]	1997	1 374.5	714.0	722.0	50.7	2.9	0.1	170.6	191.1	5.6	1.0
Honduras [1][3][9]	1998	1 400.8	734.2	680.9	57.6	4.4	0.1	177.1	191.3	5.8	1.2
	1999	1 472.1	826.9	732.5	73.6	2.3	1.5	180.2	196.6	6.6	1.6
Indonesia [4][9]	1997	53 971.0	33 079.0	21 960.0	13 889.0	710.0	186.0	6 189.0	5 026.0	214.0	19.0
Indonésie [4][9]	1998	53 800.5	33 773.1	23 871.3	15 543.5	573.9	100.7	5 482.4	4 451.2	131.1	16.8
	1999	54 908.0	33 908.3	23 764.0	14 613.8	621.0	104.6	6 481.0	5 034.7	178.0	10.1
Jamaica [3][20]	1996	553.3	406.5	171.6	45.8	5.5	0.8	57.4	43.0	5.4	1.5
Jamaïque [3][20]	1997	556.9	399.4	162.5	40.2	4.6	0.8	52.4	35.0	4.0	1.8
	1998	553.7	400.6	160.5	39.6	4.5	0.7	55.7	29.1	4.0	1.7
Japan [4][25]	1998	38 580.0	26 560.0	1 860.0	1 580.0	50.0	10.0	8 920.0	4 900.0	330.0	40.0
Japon [4][25]	1999	38 310.0	26 320.0	1 850.0	1 510.0	50.0	10.0	8 730.0	4 710.0	320.0	50.0
	2000	38 180.0	26 300.0	1 910.0	1 450.0	50.0	10.0	8 600.0	4 610.0	300.0	50.0
Malaysia [3][28]	1998	5 718.9	2 880.7	1 185.0	431.5	25.3	3.1	1 146.9	761.0	44.2	5.9
Malaisie [3][28]	1999	5 851.2	2 986.6	1 222.3	401.4	33.9	3.9	1 187.9	802.9	43.5	6.6
	2000	6 096.2	3 235.5	1 257.3	454.4	23.8	3.5	1 248.1	877.7	43.0	5.1
Morocco [4][24]	1997	3 222.0	1 001.8	172.6	44.1	35.3	1.1	589.2	453.9	35.1	3.0
Maroc [4][24]	1998	3 238.3	930.0	160.7	44.9	42.3	1.4	599.5	389.8	36.5	2.9
	1999	3 226.3	948.2	181.1	57.3	39.1	1.7	584.5	366.2	33.0	2.4
Myanmar [3][7]	1994	16 817.0	...	11 551.0	...	87.0	...	1 250.0	...	17.0	...
Myanmar [3][7]	1997	17 964.0	...	11 381.0	...	132.0	...	1 573.0	...	21.0	...
	1998	18 359.0	...	11 507.0	...	121.0	...	1 666.0	...	48.0	...
Nicaragua [7]	1998	1 441.8	...	609.2	...	9.7	...	122.0	...	5.8	...
Nicaragua [7]	1999	1 544.2	...	655.3	...	11.7	...	125.3	...	5.8	...
	2000	1 637.1	...	711.8	...	11.9	...	127.6	...	5.9	...

Major division 5 Branche 5		Major division 6 Branche 6		Major division 7 Branche 7		Major division 8 Branche 8		Major division 9 Branche 9	
M	F	M	F	M	F	M	F	M	F
610.0	51.0	3 909.0	220.0	1 268.0	9.0	229.0	8.0	1 606.0	188.0
485.0	41.0	4 262.0	123.0	1 600.0	11.0	284.0	12.0	1 647.0	262.0
936.0	80.0	5 573.0	488.0	2 263.0	45.0	197.0	16.0	3 343.0	1 748.0
7.4[5]	0.3[5]	6.9[6]	8.4[6]	3.1	1.1	2.2	4.1	10.8	19.8
8.5[5]	0.3[5]	8.1[6]	8.5[6]	3.7	1.3	2.3	5.3	20.3	21.8
13.2	0.8	12.5	17.0	3.3	1.2	13.6	16.7	12.7	13.7
418.8	...	340.8	...	350.9	...	31.0	...	1 069.6	...
369.1	...	405.3	...	328.9	...	33.6	...	1 075.6	...
328.9	...	422.3	...	318.0	...	40.9	...	1 099.7	...
3.8	0.1	1.1	2.0	2.9	0.5	0.3	0.6	1.6	1.1
3.5	0.1	1.3	1.9	3.2	0.5	0.5	0.7	1.4	1.4
...	...	...	...	...	...	...	...	...	...
4 486.0	98.0	5 614.0[12]	3 609.0[12]	2 507.0[13]	252.0[13]	818.0[14]	460.0[14]	10 538.0[15]	14 898.0[15]
4 787.0	193.0	5 639.0[12]	3 778.0[12]	2 501.0[13]	285.0[13]	842.0[14]	467.0[14]	10 925.0[15]	15 115.0[15]
4 558.0	185.0	5 731.0[12]	3 887.0[12]	2 542.0[13]	274.0[13]	844.0[14]	400.0[14]	11 162.0[15]	15 560.0[15]
434.6	13.9	545.1	460.4	373.6	59.1	252.4	153.3	615.2	802.5
376.8	11.8	558.6	468.6	354.9	48.4	247.4	143.0	706.9	830.9
397.2	8.9	550.4	445.1	371.0	59.2	270.0	155.8	672.7	821.5
33 270.0	...	46 450.0	...	20 090.0	...	4 080.0[19]	...	19 650.0	...
34 120.0	...	47 510.0	...	20 220.0	...	4 240.0[19]	...	20 250.0	...
35 520.0	...	46 860.0	...	20 290.0	...	4 270.0[19]	...	20 250.0	...
290.6	18.9	514.4	447.3	285.7	67.3	242.7	168.9	270.2	431.1
270.0	19.2	493.5	447.8	275.1	67.6	261.5	176.1	270.0	460.6
283.9	19.4	500.0	485.2	285.9	72.8	267.6	181.1	276.9	477.3
15.1	2.1	24.9	21.3	8.3	2.1	6.1	5.0	31.5	22.7
13.1	1.7	29.1	25.3	9.5	2.8	7.9	5.2	34.5	25.8
12.8	1.6	27.9	25.3	9.7	3.7	8.3	5.4	36.5	25.9
326.2	26.2	763.7	668.1	355.4	56.3	312.3	206.8	730.5	997.6
244.1	25.4	784.4	698.7	386.3	55.7	305.2	194.6	728.9	1 050.2
253.9	11.7	814.4	720.4	342.9	59.2	276.8	204.7	770.7	1 140.3
164.1	7.3	447.4	426.5	156.3	11.1	90.8	42.3	458.7	440.3
178.7	6.4	458.9	412.0	164.2	11.4	96.5	42.0	495.9	487.3
181.0	4.9	489.9	462.6	181.3	17.7	113.0	50.8	425.3	502.6
86.7	1.6	157.3	236.5	43.0	3.8	26.8	14.6	159.6	214.5
108.8	1.8	183.5	256.4	48.9	5.7	36.5	15.9	154.8	204.3
114.3	3.5	182.3	306.8	51.8	4.2	31.2	18.7	170.8	220.3
4 050.0	150.0	8 404.0	8 817.0	4 023.0	115.0	447.0	209.0	7 972.0	4 666.0
3 385.9	135.8	8 245.0	8 570.2	4 023.6	130.2	412.0	205.8	7 775.3	4 618.9
3 295.0	120.0	8 456.0	9 073.4	4 083.0	123.5	445.0	188.9	7 585.0	4 639.3
78.8	2.4	72.3	126.8	39.8	8.6	27.4	27.1	94.9	150.2
77.6	1.9	80.4	125.8	43.6	10.7	35.8	30.7	95.2	151.3
75.8	2.6	77.2	127.2	46.6	11.3	27.5	30.4	101.0	157.6
5 550.0	1 070.0	7 290.0[26]	7 540.0[26]	3 290.0	760.0	3 310.0	2 630.0	7 770.0[27]	7 890.0[27]
5 550.0	1 020.0	7 250.0[26]	7 590.0[26]	3 310.0	750.0	3 350.0	2 630.0	7 650.0[27]	7 890.0[27]
5 550.0	980.0	7 170.0[26]	7 570.0[26]	3 370.0	780.0	3 460.0	2 700.0	7 630.0[27]	8 000.0[27]
700.4	45.5	982.6	633.3	364.7	57.0	247.4	178.4	1 022.6	764.9
677.6	45.2	1 006.2	654.5	361.8	58.5	274.2	192.0	1 043.8	821.6
750.0	48.9	1 073.8	716.2	368.7	54.0	271.9	190.1	1 049.7	885.5
371.6	5.4	810.4	75.7	186.8	10.3	65.9	29.9	932.8[29]	371.3[29]
338.7	4.9	860.2	88.2	191.9	7.9	60.6	25.4	923.2[29]	357.6[29]
362.4	4.5	825.7	89.2	204.8	12.0	69.3	30.8	918.7[29]	380.2[29]
292.0	...	1 450.0	...	420.0	...	486.0	...	1 264.0	...
378.0	...	1 746.0	...	470.0	...	577.0	...	1 686.0	...
400.0	...	1 781.0	...	495.0	...	597.0	...	1 744.0	...
63.2	...	245.5	...	46.8	...	17.4	...	251.0	...
88.1	...	259.2	...	49.7	...	20.1	...	261.5	...
97.3	...	268.3	...	51.2	...	21.8	...	278.8	...

29

Employment by industry *[cont]*
Total employment and persons employed by branch of economic activity (thousands)

Emploi par industrie *[suite]*
Emploi total et personnes employées, par branches d'activité économique (milliers)

A. ISIC Rev. 2[+] – CITI Rév. 2[+]

Country or area Pays ou zone	Year Année	Total employment Emploi total		Major division 1 Branche 1		Major division 2 Branche 2		Major division 3 Branche 3		Major division 4 Branche 4	
		M	F	M	F	M	F	M	F	M	F
Pakistan [1 3 30]	1996	28 275.0	3 913.0	12 426.0	2 635.0	39.0	...	2 969.0	371.0	263.0	1
Pakistan [1 3 30]	1997	29 581.0	4 599.0	12 040.0	3 051.0	35.0	...	3 336.0	457.0	332.0	2
	1998	30 927.0	5 007.0	13 501.0	3 479.0	63.0	6.0	3 139.0	440.0	244.0	7
Paraguay [1 3 24]	1994	616.0	433.6	36.9	3.5	1.8	...	126.7	53.1	10.1	1
Paraguay [1 3 24]	1995	644.8	505.6	...	...	...	...	...	...	...	
	1996	684.8	505.6	48.1	14.1	0.1	...	121.3	49.2	6.3	2
Philippines [4 9 31]	1998	17 654.0	10 608.0	8 375.0	2 898.0	98.0	6.0	1 480.0	1 207.0	119.0	21
Philippines [4 9 31]	1999	17 131.0	10 631.0	7 773.0	2 730.0	81.0	7.0	1 454.0	1 342.0	115.0	25
	2000	17 258.0	10 516.0	7 823.0	2 578.0	101.0	5.0	1 453.0	1 339.0	97.0	19
Puerto Rico [3 32]	1998	667.0	470.0	27.0	1.0	1.0	...	98.0	62.0	12.0	2
Porto Rico [3 32]	1999	669.0	480.0	23.0	1.0	1.0	...	94.0	62.0	11.0	3
	2000	677.0	497.0	21.0	1.0	1.0	...	96.0	67.0	11.0	2
Sri Lanka [1 16 34]	1995	3 661.0	1 655.0	1 298.5	686.9	49.3	7.2	415.7	448.4	23.9	0
Sri Lanka [1 16 34]	1996	3 797.4	1 789.5	1 244.2	718.5	58.4	10.3	429.9	408.2	20.8	3
	1998	3 855.3	2 090.8	1 451.6	1 020.7	68.3	9.8	479.5	435.1	30.2	5
Suriname [20]	1997	55.2	27.6	3.5	0.8	3.5	0.1	5.2	1.0	1.2	0
Suriname [20]	1998	59.8	28.5	4.0	0.9	3.3	0.1	5.2	1.9	1.6	0
	1999[35]	47.8	25.1	4.0		1.7		2.9		1.0	
Thailand [3 35 36]	1998	17 666.8	14 471.1	9 231.2	7 240.5	33.1	8.1	2 135.4[37]	2 054.0[37]	149.8[39]	27
Thaïlande [3 35 36]	1999	17 721.2	14 365.9	8 826.0	6 737.3	40.6	11.2	2 224.8[37]	2 169.6[37]	124.6[39]	33
	2000	18 164.9	14 836.1	9 049.2	7 046.3	31.6	7.3	2 454.7[37]	2 330.1[37]	134.0[39]	38
Trinidad and Tobago [4]	1997	294.5	165.3	37.2	6.5	15.5	2.1	33.2	13.6	4.8	1
Trinité–et–Tobago [4]	1998	305.5	173.8	33.1	5.9	16.0	2.5	37.2	14.3	5.1	1
	1999	310.1	179.3	34.6	5.1	13.2	2.4	37.3	15.7	5.3	0
Turkey [3 19 21]	1997	15 364.0	5 450.0	4 657.0	3 562.0	174.0	3.0	2 919.0	684.0	101.0	11
Turquie [3 19 21]	1998	15 587.0	6 371.0	5 074.0	4 460.0	167.0	4.0	2 667.0	632.0	96.0	10
	1999	15 167.0	6 882.0	5 127.0	4 970.0	131.0	2.0	2 479.0	638.0	71.0	7
Ukraine [7]	1998	19 415.0	...	5 060.0	...	687.0	...	3 540.0	...	...	
Ukraine [7]	1999	18 790.0	...	4 961.0	...	639.0	...	3 319.0	...	...	
	2000	18 063.0	...	4 977.0	...	618.0	...	2 914.0	...	...	
United States [3 32 41]	1998	70 693.0	60 771.0	2 657.0	852.0	535.0	85.0	14 138.0	6 595.0	1 162.0	334
Etats–Unis [3 32 41]	1999	71 446.0	62 042.0	2 539.0	877.0	495.0	69.0	13 647.0	6 423.0	1 145.0	324
	2000	72 293.0	62 915.0	2 552.0	905.0	450.0	71.0	13 458.0	6 482.0	1 146.0	301
Uruguay [20 24 43]	1998	635.3	468.4	36.4	6.9	1.4	0.2	116.1	61.8	8.5	2
Uruguay [24 43]	1999	623.7	458.4	36.2	5.7	1.4	...	112.2	58.5	7.2	3
	2000	613.4	454.2	37.2	5.2	1.6	0.1	103.9	54.3	10.0	3
Uzbekistan	1993	...	...	...	...	...	...	560.2	519.2	...	
Ouzbékistan	1994	...	...	...	...	...	...	537.8	506.3	...	
	1995	...	...	...	...	...	...	498.3	469.3	...	
Venezuela [3 4]	1996	5 249.6	2 569.6	1 013.1	43.3	69.1	8.6	715.0	290.4	50.2	13
Venezuela [3 4]	1997	5 451.8	2 835.0	852.8	41.3	80.1	10.4	789.9	332.6	55.3	10
	1998	5 631.0	3 079.7	...	...	...	...	...	...	...	
Viet Nam [7]	1995	...	...	...	...	...	...	3 227.2	...	...	
Viet Nam [7]	1996	...	...	...	...	...	...	3 288.8	...	...	
	1997	...	...	...	...	...	...	3 292.5	...	...	

[+] Major divisions of ISIC Rev. 2:

1. Agriculture, hunting, forestry and fishing.
2. Mining and quarrying.
3. Manufacturing.
4. Electricity, gas and water.
5. Construction.
6. Wholesale and retail trade and restaurants and hotels.
7. Transport, storage and communication.
8. Financing, insurance, real estate and business services.
9. Community, social and personal services.

[+] Branches de la CITI Rév. 2:

1. Agriculture, chasse, sylviculture et pêche.
2. Industries extractives.
3. Industries manufacturières.
4. Electricité, gaz et eau.
5. Bâtiment et travaux publics.
6. Commerce de gros et de détail; restaurants et hôtels.
7. Transports, entrepôts et communications.
8. Banques, assurances, affaires immobilières et services fournis aux entreprise
9. Services fournis à la collectivité, services sociaux et services personnels.

Major division 5 Branche 5		Major division 6 Branche 6		Major division 7 Branche 7		Major division 8 Branche 8		Major division 9 Branche 9	
M	F	M	F	M	F	M	F	M	F
2 273.0	46.0	4 557.0	111.0	1 597.0	35.0	240.0	8.0	3 891.0	704.0
2 284.0	23.0	4 868.0	128.0	1 934.0	16.0	333.0	3.0	4 407.0	917.0
2 221.0	30.0	4 895.0	89.0	1 940.0	30.0	299.0	13.0	4 609.0	913.0
89.2	...	151.1	159.0	48.7	6.2	30.5	16.8	121.0	193.4
...	...	...	...	...	...	...	...	...	...
82.5	...	198.9	199.7	56.5	5.2	41.0	15.9	130.0	219.5
1 480.0	31.0	1 511.0[12]	2 817.0[12]	1 780.0	105.0	408.0	287.0	2 398.0[33]	3 234.0[33]
1 457.0	19.0	1 610.0[12]	2 856.0[12]	1 852.0	116.0	404.0	309.0	2 377.0[33]	3 226.0[33]
1 404.0	27.0	1 593.0[12]	2 994.0[12]	1 916.0	108.0	380.0	298.0	2 489.0[33]	3 147.0[33]
70.0	3.0	134.0[26]	96.0[26]	33.0	13.0	18.0	23.0	272.0[27]	271.0[27]
80.0	4.0	138.0[26]	93.0[26]	34.0	10.0	17.0	25.0	271.0[27]	281.0[27]
79.0	4.0	145.0[26]	101.0[26]	31.0	10.0	16.0	25.0	275.0[27]	286.0[27]
281.7	18.7	469.4	87.7	230.0	14.7	57.2	34.3	573.0	320.5
309.2	11.7	552.6	152.5	234.2	25.3	78.8	39.2	691.1	392.0
295.2	14.0	469.5	124.2	251.5	16.5	85.5	31.6	607.7	398.9
7.0	0.3	9.4	6.9	4.9	0.6	2.2	2.1	15.0	15.3
9.2	0.7	10.0	6.4	5.0	0.8	2.2	1.5	16.4	15.6
4.8	0.1	9.9	7.4	4.2	1.6	2.7	1.9	13.9	13.4
1 082.4	197.1	2 076.5[38]	2 387.0[38]	798.7	124.0	...	...	2 156.8[33 40]	2 427.4[33 40]
1 064.4	220.9	2 229.0[38]	2 506.9[38]	873.3	115.8	...	...	2 331.0[33 40]	2 561.4[33 40]
1 089.5	190.5	2 258.8[38]	2 542.7[38]	836.6	114.6	...	...	2 304.6[33 40]	2 560.2[33 40]
47.0	3.8	37.5	43.5	25.6	6.2	20.7	18.1	72.9	70.2
53.9	4.9	38.4	44.9	29.3	6.2	19.0	20.0	73.2	73.9
56.6	4.2	39.5	49.3	29.5	6.2	18.6	19.0	75.2	76.3
1 296.0	27.0	2 617.0	298.0	882.0	44.0	373.0	143.0	2 345.0	679.0
1 306.0	30.0	2 601.0	300.0	917.0	36.0	358.0	157.0	2 400.0	742.0
1 170.0	22.0	2 636.0	308.0	830.0	32.0	374.0	146.0	2 350.0	757.0
1 097.0	...	1 514.0	...	1 400.0	...	213.0	...	...	...
974.0	...	1 604.0	...	1 329.0	...	197.0	...	...	...
895.0	...	1 406.0	...	1 228.0	...	196.0	...	...	...
7 721.0	798.0	14 367.0[26]	12 836.0[26]	5 436.0	2 375.0	7 431.0	8 021.0	17 246.0[42]	28 875.0[42]
8 101.0	886.0	14 448.0[26]	13 124.0[26]	5 670.0	2 416.0	7 871.0	8 182.0	17 530.0[42]	29 740.0[42]
8 520.0	913.0	14 705.0[26]	13 127.0[26]	5 800.0	2 494.0	8 039.0	8 477.0	17 625.0[42]	30 144.0[42]
81.0	1.7	127.7	95.9	57.0	9.9	39.5	30.9	167.6	258.7
88.7	2.2	120.6	93.7	54.1	12.3	40.1	31.7	163.2	251.3
86.8	1.8	121.0	93.1	52.3	9.2	38.4	33.6	161.9	253.7
...	...	...	...	...	...	...	...	...	...
...	...	...	...	...	...	...	...	...	...
580.9	19.2	1 027.7	765.5	485.0	36.8	299.1	182.9	1 001.8	1 204.1
668.0	26.4	1 130.7	854.9	487.8	46.6	281.0	185.3	1 092.3	1 319.4
...	...	...	...	...	...	...	...	...	...
995.6	...	...	...	781.0	...	...	...	...	...
975.1	...	...	...	855.6	...	...	...	...	...
976.5	...	...	...	856.0	...	...	...	...	...

29
Employment by industry [*cont.*]
Emploi par industrie [*suite*]

B. ISIC Rev. 3[+] - CITI Rév. 3[+]

Country or area Pays ou zone	Sex	Year Année	Total employment Emploi total	ISIC Rev. 3 Tabulation categories [+] CITI Rév. 3 Catégories de classement [+]					
				Categ. A Catég. A	Categ. B Catég. B	Categ. C Catég. C	Categ. D Catég. D	Categ. E Catég. E	Categ. F Catég. F
Algeria [47]	MF	1996	4 957.0	...				...	...
Algérie [47]	MF	1997	5 708.0	884.0[45]		584.0[46]		...	588
	MF	2000	5 725.9	898.0[45]		720.9[46]		...	669
Argentina [135]	M	1998	5 057.0	50.1	5.9	18.0	966.8	47.6	685
Argentine [135]	F	1998	3 221.6	7.0	0.0	1.0	312.8	8.6	12
	M	1999	4 971.4	49.4	4.8	13.0	872.2	44.8	673
	F	1999	3 313.8	7.5	...	2.2	327.1	6.5	16
	M	2000	4 942.0	42.0	5.6	14.9	846.8	40.7	634
	F	2000	3 319.8	7.7	0.0	0.6	308.6	7.7	19
Australia [3 75]	M	1998	4 838.6	279.8	10.6	69.4	812.5	54.0	537
Australie [3 75]	F	1998	3 714.6	127.6	2.7	7.3	285.8	11.1	84
	M	1999	4 945.3	287.0	12.0	63.7	787.6	53.1	580
	F	1999	3 802.2	131.2	2.3	6.1	287.5	11.3	82
	M	2000	5 062.6	289.7	14.3	60.9	832.6	53.7	613
	F	2000	3 947.4	131.6	3.3	7.5	308.6	11.2	87
Austria [4]	M	1998	2 125.7	124.5	0.2	9.8	560.3	31.8	293
Autriche [4]	F	1998	1 597.5	117.2	0.1	1.8	196.7	4.1	24
	M	1999	2 139.7	119.8	0.2	9.9	564.4	27.4	310
	F	1999	1 622.7	110.5	0.1	1.3	198.9	3.8	26
	M	2000	2 145.6	118.1	0.1	8.7	566.3	25.3	313
	F	2000	1 631.0	99.6	0.2	0.9	197.6	4.7	25
Azerbaijan	M	1999	1 936.6	725.6	0.5	29.7	81.2	29.3	135
Azerbaïdjan	F	1999	1 766.2	840.7	...	9.9	99.4	9.5	19
	M	2000	1 937.5	725.4	0.5	29.7	81.3	29.2	135
	F	2000	1 767.0	841.1	...	9.9	99.4	9.6	19
Bahamas [9 48]	M	1996	70.4	5.7[45]	...	1.3[49]	2.8	...	11
Bahamas [9 48]	F	1996	59.4	0.7[45]	...	0.4[49]	2.6	...	0
	M	1997	71.3	4.3[45]	...	1.4[49]	2.7	...	11
	F	1997	63.9	0.9[45]	...	0.5[49]	2.7	...	0
	M	1998	74.6	4.4[45]	...	1.2[49]	2.9	...	14
	F	1998	69.8	0.6[45]	...	0.3[49]	2.5	...	1
Belgium [4 43]	M	1998[9]	2 270.4	61.4	...	8.8	570.4	33.1	236
Belgique [4 43]	F	1998[9]	1 587.1	24.9	...	1.4	178.6	4.4	18
	M	1999	2 321.4	54.9	...	8.1	578.6	29.0	252
	F	1999	1 685.5	24.6	...	2.1	172.4	4.5	20
	M	2000	2 367.6	53.2	...	7.0	588.9	30.0	243
	F	2000	1 724.5	19.2	...	0.7	183.7	4.6	17
Bolivia [1 3 24]	M	1997	1 065.6	74.0	0.1	43.9	214.8	9.7	153
Bolivie [1 3 24]	F	1997	812.0	32.9	...	4.9	124.0	1.3	4
	M	1999	1 130.2	55.6	1.0	16.3	224.9	4.8	174
	F	1999	886.8	20.9	...	0.0	145.6	0.8	1
	M	2000	1 171.1	71.7	...	30.1	203.9	14.5	210
	F	2000	924.9	31.0	...	5.3	116.2	1.4	8
Bulgaria [7 48]	MF	1997	3 157.4	800.4	...	60.5	752.4	58.5	139
Bulgarie [7 48]	MF	1998	3 152.5	825.2	...	55.5	723.2	57.8	129
	MF	1999	3 072.0	818.2	...	47.9	663.0	57.9	123
Canada [4 52]	M	1998	7 802.6	359.0	29.2	151.6	1 556.7	90.8	674
Canada [4 52]	F	1998	6 523.8	141.1	4.8	30.0	589.9	26.6	82
	M	1999[53]	7 865.8	349.0	28.9	132.8	1 589.2	87.8	691
	F	1999[53]	6 665.3	139.2	4.4	23.5	628.1	28.0	77
	M	2000	8 049.3	334.8	28.5	135.0	1 644.5	90.2	723
	F	2000	6 860.4	122.6	6.4	28.3	635.7	26.1	84
China, Macao SAR [3 20]	M	1998	109.8	0.2	...	...	13.4	1.1	19
Chine, Macao RAS [3 20]	F	1998	91.2	0.1	...	...	28.0	0.3	1
	M	1999	106.4	0.1	...	...	13.6	1.0	15
	F	1999	96.1	...	...	...	30.9	0.2	1
	M	2000	103.8	0.3	...	...	12.0	0.7	14
	F	2000	96.2	0.2	...	...	27.3	0.1	1

Categ. G / Catég. G	Categ. H / Catég. H	Categ. I / Catég. I	Categ. J / Catég. J	Categ. K / Catég. K	Categ. L / Catég. L	Categ. M / Catég. M	Categ. N / Catég. N	Categ. O / Catég. O	Categ. P / Catég. P	Categ. Q / Catég. Q
	...	...	...	...	...	...	...	...	...	...
838.0[43]		...	...	...	1 317.0	1 496.0[47]	...	...	...	...
669.8[43]	...	...	...	...	1 773.2	932.6[47]		...	...	...
								...	...	...
1 070.2	133.4	562.4	115.0	358.7	412.5	131.0	161.3	281.0	37.4	...
597.3	96.3	72.4	86.9	213.1	241.8	472.6	335.4	166.7	584.7	1.7
1 067.2	127.5	578.3	117.5	387.8	400.9	117.7	155.6	302.0	42.2	0.1
573.0	108.7	89.9	83.1	247.1	241.9	489.5	331.5	180.9	596.3	1.9
1 074.7	142.2	589.4	128.8	381.8	389.2	138.0	153.9	294.7	40.7	1.2
608.6	112.7	85.0	78.3	218.7	244.3	487.8	320.6	190.1	614.5	1.3
975.2	183.4	401.2	140.1	541.1	254.0	194.1	184.8	198.6	1.7	0.6
799.5	224.4	143.6	182.6	411.4	174.3	399.0	625.5	224.8	9.0	0.7
1 001.3	188.5	415.1	142.2	552.8	266.7	202.0	184.3	206.7	1.4	0.5
839.6	230.0	155.0	172.3	430.2	184.0	411.5	631.6	218.7	8.1	0.3
949.3	205.4	436.7	148.1	596.9	269.9	197.9	184.0	208.0	1.6	0.5
830.1	251.8	155.4	187.4	470.7	186.9	414.5	665.3	229.5	5.0	0.9
265.7	82.5	190.9	71.8	113.2	161.7	69.8	72.4	73.2	0.4	4.0
315.9	133.5	51.0	67.1	119.7	90.8	148.0	226.3	85.2	13.6	1.8
269.5	76.4	197.1	71.8	114.2	157.4	71.1	74.6	72.6	0.4	2.7
323.3	135.8	57.2	70.0	126.3	90.3	149.2	226.7	89.0	11.9	2.1
270.7	76.2	185.2	71.4	132.1	160.3	70.8	75.0	69.5	0.2	2.3
323.0	137.8	60.5	67.1	137.2	92.7	154.8	224.9	89.9	11.6	2.7
296.2	6.4	127.4	8.3	58.2	163.5	125.4	73.2	76.2	0.2	...
280.2	3.4	41.0	6.9	40.5	96.7	174.2	95.0	49.3	0.1	...
296.7	6.4	127.5	8.3	58.2	163.5	125.4	73.4	76.3	0.2	...
280.3	3.4	41.1	6.9	40.5	96.7	174.2	95.0	49.3	0.1	...
8.0	8.7	7.7	4.9[50]	...	...	...	...	...	19.2[51]	...
10.4	11.7	3.7	6.2[50]	...	...	...	...	...	23.0[51]	...
8.0	9.2	7.9	5.0[50]	...	...	...	...	...	20.7[51]	...
9.6	12.2	4.0	7.4[50]	...	...	...	...	...	25.9[51]	...
8.7	9.3	7.5	5.9[50]	...	...	...	...	...	20.3[51]	...
11.4	12.8	4.3	8.1[50]	...	...	...	...	...	28.4[51]	...
299.3	69.2	215.1	260.6	...	507.3	...	...	...	9.0	...
264.6	64.4	53.6	187.6	...	772.8	...	...	...	16.7	...
310.1	67.5	231.4	259.5	...	514.7	...	...	...	15.2	...
279.2	68.6	64.7	205.9	...	817.1	...	...	...	26.0	...
297.2	64.6	250.0	297.6	...	522.0	...	...	...	13.6	...
275.2	68.2	67.6	214.9	...	849.3	...	...	...	23.6	...
179.7	21.8	141.4	12.2	36.5	58.9	46.5	22.3	37.4	11.0	1.6
271.4	88.9	10.2	7.3	20.7	14.8	74.1	35.6	28.3	91.4	0.4
206.0	34.6	164.0	9.1	43.7	59.9	63.3	20.1	41.8	3.1	1.2
336.5	92.2	9.0	8.5	28.0	18.8	66.3	43.1	34.9	80.0	...
209.0	29.9	131.0	13.5	71.4	54.6	56.6	21.1	47.2	5.2	1.0
327.1	94.5	13.4	6.4	24.5	18.1	76.2	27.7	51.6	121.6	1.8
310.4	72.1	228.2	40.0	98.7	78.9	242.6	177.6	98.1	...	...
337.2	70.5	236.7	37.6	102.9	80.7	233.1	167.1	95.9	...	...
337.7	68.2	232.9	35.8	95.2	91.7	232.0	165.1	102.7		...
1 359.7	383.6	737.6	207.7	903.4	435.5	349.3	281.2	267.5	14.7	...
1 092.8	532.9	343.5	387.9	730.1	352.7	593.4	1 184.0	353.3	77.0	1.5
1 391.5	374.0	775.3	213.4	912.7	415.0	354.6	271.1	272.7	5.7	...
1 122.1	550.7	328.6	405.5	739.9	357.3	628.0	1 173.3	365.5	92.7	1.5
1 412.1	390.5	795.0	220.1	955.9	404.5	343.2	288.7	277.3	4.5	0.3
1 165.5	570.1	350.0	394.6	788.0	354.6	631.6	1 237.7	387.4	75.0	1.9
19.2	12.0	10.3	2.2	6.2	11.0	2.1	1.3	11.0	0.4	...
14.3	11.1	3.4	3.4	2.1	5.4	4.6	2.8	9.0	4.5	...
17.1	11.0	11.2	2.7	6.6	12.0	2.9	1.6	11.3	0.2	...
14.2	10.7	3.8	3.4	3.1	4.8	6.3	3.6	8.4	5.4	...
17.1	10.2	11.1	3.3	7.1	11.9	2.5	1.7	11.0	0.4	...
13.8	11.4	3.9	3.8	3.7	4.8	5.8	3.7	11.1	5.1	...

29
Employment by industry [*cont.*]
Emploi par industrie [*suite*]

B. ISIC Rev. 3⁺ − CITI Rév. 3⁺

Country or area Pays ou zone	Sex Sex	Year Année	Total employment Emploi total	ISIC Rev. 3 Tabulation categories [+] CITI Rév. 3 Catégories de classement [+] Categ. A Catég. A	Categ. B Catég. B	Categ. C Catég. C	Categ. D Catég. D	Categ. E Catég. E	Categ. F Catég. F
Costa Rica [3 9 21] Costa Rica [3 9 21]	M	1998	887.5	233.1	5.6	1.6	132.4	11.1	80.2
	F	1998	412.5	22.7	0.1	...	71.1	2.0	1.0
	M	1999	879.6	230.5	6.2	1.9	133.4	11.8	81.6
	F	1999	420.5	19.7	0.1	0.2	70.6	1.4	1.0
	M	2000	902.5	239.7	7.0	2.4	125.6	9.3	87.5
	F	2000	416.1	22.4	0.2	0.2	64.7	1.6	2.2
Croatia [4] Croatie [4]	M	1998	832.2	264.0	2.4	7.3	184.3	22.8	87.9
	F	1998	711.6	123.1	...	...	139.1	5.8	11.0
	M	1999	802.2	125.2	3.6	7.6	188.5	20.8	87.5
	F	1999	689.5	118.3	0.3	1.2	136.5	5.4	9.6
	M	2000	848.7	113.2	4.5	6.7	188.9	23.7	88.5
	F	2000	704.3	107.0	0.5	0.5	122.0	6.0	11.4
Cyprus [4 16 54] Chypre [4 16 54]	M	1999	172.9	7.3	1.0	0.3	23.6	1.8	25.7
	F	1999	106.3	4.4	...	0.1	13.1	0.5	1.4
	M	2000	176.1	9.4	0.4	0.7	23.3	2.2	26.1
	F	2000	112.5	5.4	...	...	12.7	0.5	1.7
Czech Republic [4 16] Rép. tchèque [4 16]	M	1998	2 751.0	171.0	0.0	73.0	806.0	74.0	415.0
	F	1998	2 101.0	85.0	0.0	10.0	538.0	20.0	35.0
	M	1999	2 691.0	165.0	0.0	66.0	787.0	64.0	413.0
	F	1999	2 074.0	78.0	0.0	9.0	515.0	17.0	32.0
	M	2000	2 687.0	161.0	0.0	56.0	787.0	60.0	402.0
	F	2000	2 064.0	76.0	0.0	12.0	502.0	21.0	40.0
Denmark [55] Danemark [55]	M	1996	1 440.7	74.4	5.4	2.8	351.0	13.4	155.5
	F	1996	1 186.5	23.7	0.0	0.7	159.6	3.3	14.7
	M	1997	1 464.7	73.3	5.3	2.4	353.6	13.3	159.4
	F	1997	1 217.3	20.3	...	0.6	159.1	3.3	16.7
	M	1998	1 460.1	72.0	4.7	2.4	356.1	16.9	159.3
	F	1998	1 232.3	19.9	0.0	0.8	160.0	3.6	18.3
Dominican Republic Rép. dominicaine	M	1997	1 891.4	502.5	0.0	7.5	332.7	13.7	150.4
	F	1997	760.6	16.5	0.0	0.9	150.7	6.6	3.1
Egypt [3 28 35] Egypte [3 28 35]	M	1997	12 813.0	3 642.3	87.0	41.2	1 925.4	177.1	1 134.3
	F	1997	3 017.0	1 218.0	3.9	0.8	208.1	15.6	18.6
	M	1998	13 187.0	3 665.1	98.8	57.6	1 814.5	187.1	1 269.8
	F	1998	2 996.0	1 058.0	0.8	11.4	227.7	16.3	17.3
	M	1999	13 611.0	3 688.1	117.1	46.4	1 897.8	188.3	1 299.8
	F	1999	3 139.2	996.3	5.5	1.0	309.8	18.7	20.3
El Salvador [1] El Salvador [1]	M	1998	1 345.8	485.3	16.9	1.7	199.7	7.7	117.9
	F	1998	881.7	54.1	1.8	0.2	215.9	1.0	3.3
	M	1999	1 349.1	444.3	15.4	1.8	207.0	8.1	126.4
	F	1999	925.6	42.2	1.4	...	219.6	0.4	4.5
Estonia [56] Estonie [56]	M	1998	330.7	33.1	4.5	7.0	76.2	13.2	42.0
	F	1998	309.5	19.8	...	...	63.3	5.0	5.0
	M	1999[16]	316.0	30.1	3.1	7.3	70.9	11.8	37.9
	F	1999[16]	298.0	17.7	...	...	59.3	5.7	3.9
	M	2000	313.8	28.2	3.0	6.3	77.0	11.4	38.5
	F	2000	294.8	13.8	...	...	60.8	4.3	4.0
Finland [56] Finlande [56]	M	1998	1 199.0	95.0	2.0	5.0	314.0	18.0	129.0
	F	1998	1 048.0	47.0	...	1.0	133.0	4.0	10.6
	M	1999	1 227.0	97.0	2.0	4.0	321.0	18.0	138.0
	F	1999	1 090.0	46.0	...	1.0	140.0	4.0	11.6
	M	2000	1 248.0	97.0	2.0	3.0	329.0	17.0	139.0
	F	2000	1 108.0	43.0	...	1.0	138.0	5.0	10.0
Georgia [4] Georgie [4]	M	1998	898.5	414.9	1.9	4.5	85.3	18.1	23.3
	F	1998	832.4	422.5	0.2	1.5	38.0	5.6	1.9
	M	1999	884.2	444.7	1.1	5.0	76.0	17.1	23.5
	F	1999	847.4	458.6	0.1	1.1	35.5	4.0	1.5
	M	2000	934.8	442.3	0.8	5.5	77.8	25.7	29.2
	F	2000	814.0	468.1	...	0.8	26.1	3.4	2.8

Categ. G Catég. G	Categ. H Catég. H	Categ. I Catég. I	Categ. J Catég. J	Categ. K Catég. K	Categ. L Catég. L	Categ. M Catég. M	Categ. N Catég. N	Categ. O Catég. O	Categ. P Catég. P	Categ. Q Catég. Q
129.4	26.3	65.4	19.0	3.5	...	21.5	27.4	114.8	6.9	1.9
63.9	32.2	7.9	10.5	1.1	...	50.3	32.0	42.9	71.1	1.0
126.1	30.4	66.9	12.9	3.8	...	21.2	24.7	115.1	6.9	1.4
77.7	34.4	7.7	7.5	1.6	...	44.2	31.1	43.7	76.6	0.8
128.8	29.6	69.9	15.2	3.0	...	23.3	23.6	121.9	8.3	1.3
75.5	33.0	8.9	8.7	2.4	...	51.4	28.2	40.7	73.1	0.2
89.0	38.7	86.9	7.9	34.0	67.4	21.1	20.0	28.9	...	...
117.1	43.7	23.6	24.9	26.4	41.0	54.2	72.6	23.0	3.8	...
90.2	34.3	79.1	9.6	29.9	62.3	18.7	19.3	25.9	0.3	...
107.0	39.7	22.0	25.0	26.7	43.1	62.1	69.6	19.0	3.1	...
107.3	40.1	80.6	11.5	33.3	74.4	24.1	21.2	28.4	2.3	...
112.5	39.6	27.5	25.7	34.9	49.3	63.9	70.1	29.8	1.5	...
30.3	13.2	13.6	6.7	7.0	15.1	5.1	4.0	7.2	0.1	1.7
19.9	13.8	5.3	7.1	8.6	6.3	9.8	6.8	4.9	3.6	0.7
31.3	13.9	11.2	7.2	7.5	17.0	4.6	3.2	7.1	0.1	1.6
19.9	13.0	5.1	8.4	8.7	7.7	11.2	7.2	5.4	5.0	0.7
300.0	69.0	266.0	37.0	139.0	191.0	65.0	51.0	91.0	...	1.0
355.0	96.0	113.0	65.0	110.0	138.0	216.0	214.0	102.0	1.0	1.0
299.0	67.0	252.0	322.0	145.0	202.0	67.0	53.0	79.0	...	1.0
338.0	92.0	118.0	67.0	118.0	134.0	229.0	235.0	90.0	2.0	2.0
286.0	66.0	257.0	38.0	147.0	207.0	72.0	62.0	85.0	...	1.0
329.0	89.0	115.0	65.0	119.0	134.0	228.0	232.0	99.0	2.0	1.0
212.6	26.7	132.0	39.2	115.4	86.7	88.9	75.7	56.9	0.6	0.6
146.6	42.5	52.5	44.1	73.7	80.8	104.3	368.3	62.6	6.6	0.5
214.7	29.6	134.5	36.1	128.6	88.3	86.0	74.1	61.7	0.6	0.4
151.0	44.4	50.9	43.7	80.5	80.0	113.4	383.2	63.3	4.1	0.3
211.6	28.1	131.9	37.9	138.1	89.5	80.1	70.5	56.7	0.8	0.4
156.1	43.2	50.0	41.3	89.5	78.8	113.7	388.3	61.8	4.6	0.5
356.1	59.5	190.0	17.3	...	99.5	...	...	152.2	...	...
176.1	55.8	12.9	16.8	...	25.9	...	...	295.3	...	...
1 550.6	203.9	881.4	138.1	182.4	1 221.8	1 040.2	228.9	280.1	30.2	...
195.2	13.2	41.8	41.9	24.6	343.5	674.9	181.5	24.3	9.3	...
1 676.1	244.7	909.9	139.7	240.9	1 279.8	1 028.0	250.4	292.0	31.5	...
273.8	32.3	44.2	34.6	25.3	348.8	637.2	235.4	24.3	8.8	...
1 741.8	257.2	1 019.6	143.6	239.0	1 292.2	1 061.7	255.2	333.5	28.8	...
278.4	42.4	40.6	41.6	34.0	339.5	702.8	275.9	23.0	9.2	...
228.4[33]	...	84.8	49.7	...	74.1	26.0	46.7	5.5	...	...
327.5[33]	...	5.2	32.9	...	30.6	40.0	77.4	90.6	...	...
229.9[33]	...	92.5	52.2	...	82.4	26.4	51.8	10.5	...	...
348.7[33]	...	7.8	32.3	...	30.8	48.2	88.3	100.7	...	...
40.1	2.4	41.8	2.7	21.6	19.0	11.9	4.8	10.3	...	...
50.5	11.9	16.5	5.9	17.3	17.6	44.6	30.3	19.9	...	...
37.2	2.9	45.2	3.5	22.0	18.4	10.0	4.4	11.3	...	...
49.7	10.9	17.6	5.6	17.1	18.5	42.6	28.2	19.8	...	...
37.0	4.7	441.7	3.7	21.7	17.7	7.9	3.5	11.6	...	...
47.5	16.4	18.8	4.5	20.1	18.7	38.8	26.2	19.3	...	...
141.0	22.0	122.0	15.0	117.0	81.0	50.0	37.0	47.0	...	...
128.0	49.0	47.0	31.0	87.0	56.0	104.0	277.0	68.0	3.0	...
143.0	24.0	121.0	14.0	125.0	79.0	53.0	38.0	47.0	...	...
135.0	52.0	48.0	32.0	97.0	59.0	102.0	283.0	74.0	4.0	...
144.0	22.0	125.0	15.0	138.0	74.0	54.0	37.0	48.0	...	...
134.0	54.0	46.0	34.0	100.0	60.0	110.0	289.0	75.0	4.0	...
93.0	7.9	60.0	6.3	21.4	79.2	31.5	18.3	23.1	8.4	1.2
66.0	8.0	15.7	6.8	21.6	35.3	112.9	64.5	24.7	6.6	0.6
87.6	9.0	52.8	4.8	22.3	73.1	25.8	15.0	21.2	3.7	1.3
66.2	6.4	15.7	6.1	18.0	33.3	112.7	63.0	21.4	3.2	0.6
91.1	7.6	59.9	3.3	29.2	83.5	21.6	26.5	27.2	2.0	1.5
83.7	7.4	12.0	5.7	8.5	22.3	92.6	58.7	18.1	1.2	0.4

29
Employment by industry [cont.]
Emploi par industrie [suite]

B. ISIC Rev. 3+ — CITI Rév. 3+

Country or area Pays ou zone	Sex	Year Année	Total employment Emploi total	ISIC Rev. 3 Tabulation categories + CITI Rév. 3 Catégories de classement +					
				Categ. A Catég. A	Categ. B Catég. B	Categ. C Catég. C	Categ. D Catég. D	Categ. E Catég. E	Categ. F Catég. F
Germany [49] Allemagne [49]	M	1998	20 509.0	639.0	6.0	167.0	6 068.0	241.0	2 769.(
	F	1998	15 351.0	377.0	...	15.0	2 393.0	64.0	414.(
	M	1999	20 659.0	653.0	5.0	148.0	6 115.0	249.0	2 746.(
	F	1999	15 743.0	367.0	...	13.0	2 417.0	62.0	400.(
	M	2000	20 680.0	635.0	4.0	139.0	6 128.0	235.0	2 729.(
	F	2000	15 924.0	347.0	2.0	13.0	2 414.0	55.0	389.(
Greece [4][16][43] Grèce [4][16][43]	M	1998	2 504.2	396.8	10.1	17.4	406.7	29.4	280.:
	F	1998	1 463.0	296.7	0.6	0.9	171.2	5.9	1.:
	M	1999	2 466.5	374.5	10.8	17.5	394.9	33.8	268.(
	F	1999	1 473.3	282.9	0.9	1.2	173.9	7.1	4.:
	M	2000	2 457.3	374.1	9.7	15.5	387.1	29.9	271.
	F	2000	1 489.0	285.4	1.4	1.0	169.9	8.2	5.:
Hungary [56] Hongrie [56]	M	1998	2 041.7	211.6	...	21.4	535.5	72.6	210.(
	F	1998	1 656.0	67.2	...	4.3	376.6	23.9	19.:
	M	1999	2 103.1	204.5	...	19.4	551.7	65.4	232.(
	F	1999	1 708.4	65.9	...	5.0	377.2	24.4	20.(
	M	2000	2 122.4	190.3	...	15.4	542.6	60.5	247.(
	F	2000	1 726.7	61.4	...	3.8	388.7	19.6	20.8
Iceland [3][35][66] Islande [3][35][66]	M	1998	79.1	3.9	5.6	0.1	15.3	1.2	10..
	F	1998	68.9	2.7	0.6	...	9.4	0.3	0.(
	M	1999	82.2	4.2	6.3	0.3	15.6	1.0	10.:
	F	1999	71.2	2.4	0.9	...	7.7	0.1	0.:
	M	2000	83.6	4.5	5.3	0.2	16.6	1.0	10.:
	F	2000	72.8	2.4	0.8	...	7.3	0.3	0.
Ireland [4][35] Irlande [4][35]	M	1997	840.3	123.2	2.2	6.0	183.9	10.5	104.
	F	1997	539.7	16.0	...	0.4	86.0	1.7	6.(
	M	1998	899.9	116.1	3.4	4.7	193.8	9.9	129.:
	F	1998	594.6	16.1	0.4	0.4	90.4	2.0	6.(
	M	1999	947.3	117.7	2.7	5.3	200.4	10.0	135.
	F	1999	643.9	15.1	0.4	0.4	91.0	1.8	6.
Israel [3][4][57] Israël [3][4][57]	M	1998[53]	1 155.2	37.7[45]	...	279.5[58]	...	16.4	121.
	F	1998[53]	917.2	9.8[45]	...	106.7[58]	...	3.6	9.
	M	1999	1 176.2	38.8[45]	...	281.1[58]	...	15.9	111.
	F	1999	960.5	10.8[45]	...	108.7[58]	...	3.3	8.
	M	2000	1 211.7	39.2[45]	...	286.3[58]	...	16.0	107.
	F	2000	1 009.5	8.7[45]	...	110.3[58]	...	3.3	8.
Italy [5][59][60] Italie [5][59][60]	M	1998	13 273.0	767.0	43.0	65.0	3 421.0	169.0	1 452.
	F	1998	7 345.0	389.0	2.0	9.0	1 500.0	22.0	92.
	M	1999	13 330.0	737.0	42.0	61.0	3 442.0	156.0	1 481.(
	F	1999	7 533.0	352.0	3.0	10.0	1 487.0	20.0	94.
	M	2000	13 461.0	723.0	46.0	55.0	3 417.0	146.0	1 516.(
	F	2000	7 764.0	348.0	3.0	9.0	1 501.0	21.0	102.
Kazakhstan [7] Kazakhstan [7]	MF	1996	6 361.0	...	...	...	...	...	.
	MF	1997	6 308.0	...	...	...	...	...	
	MF	1998	6 127.0	1 353.9	5.9	123.7	627.0	125.5	222.
Korea, Republic of [34] Corée, République de [34]	M	1998	11 910.0	1 241.0	58.0	21.0	2 553.0	52.0	1 435.(
	F	1998	8 084.0	1 158.0	24.0	...	1 345.0	9.0	143.
	M	1999	11 978.0	1 189.0	59.0	19.0	2 563.0	52.0	1 354.(
	F	1999	8 303.0	1 075.0	26.0	1.0	1 443.0	9.0	122.
	M	2000	12 353.0	1 140.0	59.0	18.0	2 713.0	52.0	1 449.(
	F	2000	8 707.0	1 063.0	26.0	...	1 530.0	11.0	132.
Kyrgyzstan Kirghizistan	M	1997	907.9	435.1	...	6.9	82.4	14.3	46.
	F	1997	781.4	380.5	...	2.0	61.3	4.7	10.
	M	1998	918.7	450.4	...	6.3	78.7	15.3	41.
	F	1998	786.2	385.0	...	1.9	64.6	5.0	9.
	M	1999	971.6	501.9	0.5	7.7	74.1	16.6	38.
	F	1999	792.7	421.9	0.1	1.8	52.9	5.5	6.
Latvia [49][61] Lettonie [49][61]	M	1998	533.5	108.5	3.7	1.1	105.3	17.8	49.
	F	1998	473.7	75.6	1.2	0.2	77.1	6.6	6.
	M	1999	515.0	83.5	3.2	1.1	102.6	16.6	58.
	F	1999	474.5	63.5	0.8	0.1	72.9	6.4	5.
	M	2000	492.0	74.7	1.3	1.7	98.4	17.0	51.
	F	2000	474.8	53.7	0.8	0.3	72.9	6.3	6.

Categ. G Catég. G	Categ. H Catég. H	Categ. I Catég. I	Categ. J Catég. J	Categ. K Catég. K	Categ. L Catég. L	Categ. M Catég. M	Categ. N Catég. N	Categ. O Catég. O	Categ. P Catég. P	Categ. Q Catég. Q
2 435.0	482.0	1 382.0	638.0	1 348.0	1 872.0	697.0	914.0	820.0	9.0	22.0
2 719.0	648.0	538.0	635.0	1 233.0	1 302.0	1 230.0	2 620.0	1 006.0	141.0	14.0
2 442.0	492.0	1 396.0	639.0	1 422.0	1 859.0	697.0	927.0	839.0	8.0	22.0
2 766.0	696.0	557.0	652.0	1 316.0	1 319.0	1 251.0	2 738.0	1 040.0	133.0	15.0
2 393.0	507.0	1 426.0	648.0	1 530.0	1 804.0	669.0	939.0	868.0	7.0	19.0
2 797.0	712.0	582.0	685.0	1 393.0	1 299.0	1 259.0	2 757.0	1 076.0	130.0	14.0
413.1	145.9	212.2	50.9	109.3	185.5	92.8	65.4	84.6	2.5	1.3
254.7	103.4	32.5	45.4	85.0	93.1	148.2	119.8	50.9	52.2	0.7
416.1	147.6	208.1	48.4	112.0	182.9	98.4	67.5	81.6	2.9	0.7
257.7	105.2	40.1	45.3	87.0	94.6	145.7	118.8	59.5	48.6	0.2
422.1	143.7	208.4	56.2	108.5	196.1	94.7	63.9	72.6	3.1	0.2
255.8	109.0	43.0	51.5	87.1	97.0	147.4	119.8	55.8	51.5	...
220.2	57.2	216.0	26.6	91.4	160.7	73.5	57.0	84.4	0.7	1.8
252.0	64.4	85.9	55.2	71.6	133.6	232.0	180.8	87.4	0.8	1.2
241.6	63.9	222.8	26.6	102.2	160.8	71.9	56.5	81.9	0.6	0.7
275.9	69.3	85.5	54.3	81.7	141.1	235.0	182.7	87.9	1.4	0.7
262.8	63.3	225.8	28.2	111.0	164.9	70.5	59.7	78.7	0.5	1.2
278.1	70.0	86.0	55.5	93.6	134.1	247.3	182.0	84.1	1.4	0.3
11.2	2.0	6.6	1.8	5.7	4.1	3.1	3.0	4.4	...	0.7
9.4	2.5	4.1	2.8	3.8	2.9	6.5	17.7	5.4	...	0.1
11.3	2.3	7.2	2.5	6.7	4.2	2.8	3.1	4.1	...	0.5
9.9	3.6	4.4	3.2	4.4	3.4	6.3	18.3	5.8	...	0.1
11.5	3.1	6.2	2.6	7.9	3.8	2.7	2.7	4.5	...	0.6
10.4	3.4	4.3	4.0	5.1	3.2	7.1	17.9	5.9	...	0.2
108.8	32.7	51.4	22.7	48.7	45.0	33.4	27.1	36.3	1.4	0.6
84.5	43.7	13.6	27.6	35.6	27.2	59.8	92.6	37.2	5.2	0.6
115.3	39.4	59.9	22.8	58.8	45.0	33.9	25.8	33.9	0.6	0.1
92.3	53.7	20.2	32.5	51.5	27.4	66.2	86.9	34.4	8.3	0.1
118.2	41.8	72.0	26.3	72.9	45.1	32.6	24.9	35.9	0.9	0.3
105.1	60.8	23.9	34.8	61.8	29.3	67.9	95.1	38.1	7.6	0.3
164.7	45.6	92.7	31.6	119.7	67.0	62.8	52.4	51.6	2.5	1.2
107.7	35.0	29.7	41.2	97.0	45.4	199.4	150.4	47.1	29.9	1.0
169.3	51.1	100.3	31.9	127.4	65.6	64.2	52.2	50.2	5.0	1.1
112.3	39.0	35.3	41.8	97.3	50.6	203.6	159.7	49.0	35.1	0.7
175.5	57.3	102.8	30.5	147.2	66.9	61.3	51.1	52.5	4.1	0.6
120.1	44.4	42.1	42.7	111.5	53.0	211.1	162.5	53.9	30.6	0.7
2 077.0	378.0	884.0	439.0	729.0	1 345.0	422.0	557.0	471.0	43.0	12.0
1 189.0	298.0	213.0	235.0	488.0	594.0	1 004.0	724.0	407.0	172.0	6.0
2 066.0	400.0	910.0	434.0	774.0	1 343.0	416.0	547.0	469.0	43.0	11.0
1 242.0	339.0	223.0	236.0	562.0	600.0	1 029.0	742.0	428.0	158.0	6.0
2 110.0	434.0	954.0	419.0	854.0	1 327.0	421.0	518.0	467.0	46.0	11.0
1 267.0	380.0	236.0	243.0	624.0	615.0	1 046.0	770.0	438.0	150.0	9.0
...	...	...	...	...	...	...	...	...	...	...
...	...	...	...	...	...	...	...	...	...	...
1 404.6	67.9	560.2	37.9	183.5	178.7	521.7	325.9	186.8	0.1	...
2 151.0	563.0	1 045.0	357.0	771.0	571.0	488.0	113.0	467.0	5.0	18.0
1 667.0	1 190.0	124.0	404.0	323.0	174.0	656.0	247.0	421.0	197.0	1.0
2 172.0	586.0	1 080.0	351.0	855.0	610.0	463.0	120.0	483.0	4.0	17.0
1 732.0	1 234.0	122.0	372.0	347.0	260.0	659.0	261.0	442.0	197.0	...
2 040.0	608.0	1 121.0	337.0	942.0	538.0	466.0	123.0	725.0	4.0	18.0
1 786.0	1 317.0	144.0	392.0	414.0	215.0	697.0	289.0	520.0	191.0	1.0
86.2	6.0	65.4	3.1	21.7	44.6	46.6	23.0	26.5	...	...
88.5	6.1	13.9	4.1	19.6	15.8	92.8	65.6	15.6	...	...
82.9	6.9	61.9	4.4	23.5	47.2	47.7	23.2	28.9	...	...
97.3	7.0	13.4	3.7	15.4	15.8	91.6	61.3	15.0	...	...
102.5	5.7	52.6	3.3	17.4	50.0	46.4	22.3	28.4	3.5	...
81.2	5.8	13.2	3.8	11.3	15.7	94.3	62.9	14.6	1.3	...
65.2	3.8	57.4	4.6	20.0	41.3	20.5	11.8	21.4	1.0	...
86.6	13.0	24.6	8.0	16.7	29.5	62.1	41.6	24.1	0.9	0.1
72.2	5.4	56.8	3.5	23.5	43.6	19.9	8.4	20.3	1.0	...
78.8	16.2	28.0	7.3	21.5	34.8	70.2	43.5	23.1	2.3	...
64.7	5.7	58.6	5.2	24.2	38.9	18.0	7.8	22.6	1.3	...
89.8	17.3	23.3	8.5	21.8	32.4	71.8	42.0	25.7	2.0	...

29
Employment by industry [cont.]
Emploi par industrie [suite]

B. ISIC Rev. 3[+] — CITI Rév. 3[+]

Country or area / Pays ou zone	Sex	Year / Année	Total employment Emploi total	Categ. A / Catég. A	Categ. B / Catég. B	Categ. C / Catég. C	Categ. D / Catég. D	Categ. E / Catég. E	Categ. F / Catég. F
Lithuania[3] Lituanie[3]	M	1998[20]	823.3	199.5[45]	...	155.1[58]	...	28.1	92.6
	F	1998[20]	774.3	136.6[45]	...	146.2[58]	...	9.9	9.5
	M	1999[20]	812.0	194.7[45]	...	145.1[58]	...	29.3	90.6
	F	1999[20]	786.3	128.1[45]	...	145.3[58]	...	10.6	8.6
	M	2000[4]	759.8	178.2[45]	...	141.9[58]	...	25.2	80.8
	F	2000[4]	758.1	119.6[45]	...	133.4[58]	...	10.9	7.4
Luxembourg[7 62] Luxembourg[7 62]	MF	1996	219.8	4.9[45]	...	0.3	32.7	1.5	24.5
	MF	1997	227.1	5.1[45]	...	0.3	32.4	1.5	24.7
	MF	1998	237.0	5.0[45]	...	0.3	32.5	1.5	25.4
Maldives Maldives	M	1995	48.9	0.9	12.3	0.4	4.5	0.7	2.8
	F	1995	18.1	1.4	0.2	0.0	7.6	0.1	0.0
	M	2000	57.9	1.1	9.2	0.4	4.3	1.0	3.6
	F	2000	28.9	1.4	0.1	0.0	6.8	0.1	0.1
Mauritius[3 21] Maurice[3 21]	M	1995	299.3	45.9[45]	...	1.9	68.1	4.1	41.4
	F	1995	137.0	17.3[45]	...	0.1	57.4	0.3	0.5
Mexico[16 21] Mexique[16 21]	M	1998	25 663.1	6 508.6	171.4	140.8	4 473.5	155.1	2 058.6
	F	1998	12 954.4	1 133.3	4.0	11.9	2 510.5	27.6	66.9
	M	1999	26 049.7	6 855.8	153.3	122.5	4 675.5	168.7	2 116.4
	F	1999	13 019.4	1 192.8	6.7	10.8	2 669.3	24.5	41.6
	M	2000	25 672.6	5 949.2	150.2	137.6	4 715.5	157.2	2 461.7
	F	2000	13 311.2	925.6	8.8	18.0	2 831.2	31.3	66.0
Netherlands[28] Pays–Bas[28]	M	1998	4 289.0	167.0	...	10.0	856.0	40.0	413.0
	F	1998	3 109.0	70.0	...	...	247.0	7.0	38.0
	M	1999	4 361.0	158.0	3.0	8.0	855.0	31.0	437.0
	F	1999	3 241.0	69.0	...	2.0	256.0	6.0	34.0
	M	2000	4 420.0	167.0	4.0	10.0	866.0	27.0	424.0
	F	2000	3 311.0	76.0	...	2.0	255.0	8.0	41.0
Netherlands Antilles[4 9 65] Antilles néerlandaises[4 9 65]	M	1997	30.5	0.5[45]	...	0.0	4.3	0.8	4.3
	F	1997	25.8	0.1[45]	...	0.0	1.0	0.1	0.3
	M	1998	29.5	0.5[45]	...	0.0	4.0	0.8	3.9
	F	1998	24.7	0.0[45]	...	0.0	0.9	0.1	0.3
	M	2000	27.3	0.5[45]	...	0.1	3.6	0.8	3.4
	F	2000	24.9	0.0[45]	...	0.0	1.0	0.1	0.3
New Zealand[34] Nouvelle–Zealande[34]	M	1998	947.5	98.8	3.5	3.6	202.1	8.1	97.7
	F	1998	777.5	44.1	0.5	0.6	87.6	2.0	13.3
	M	1999	956.6	108.5	3.8	3.1	195.3	7.1	98.1
	F	1999	793.7	52.6	0.6	0.4	83.1	1.8	11.4
	M	2000	972.7	104.4	3.7	3.4	197.0	6.3	107.2
	F	2000	806.3	46.9	0.6	0.5	84.4	2.3	11.2
Norway[62 66] Norvège[62 66]	M	1998	1 211.0	60.0	17.0	28.0	239.0	16.0	134.0
	F	1998	1 036.0	26.0	2.0	6.0	82.0	3.0	11.0
	M	1999	1 209.0	60.0	16.0	26.0	222.0	15.0	134.0
	F	1999	1 050.0	25.0	2.0	6.0	77.0	3.0	12.0
	M	2000	1 212.0	55.0	14.0	28.0	214.0	16.0	135.0
	F	2000	1 057.0	22.0	2.0	6.0	76.0	4.0	12.0
Panama[49] Panama[49]	M	1997	603.1	153.2	9.3	1.8	65.9	6.9	57.6
	F	1997	306.0	6.7	0.3	0.2	30.3	2.2	2.0
	M	1998	624.3	151.7	8.8	0.7	63.1	6.6	65.3
	F	1998	312.2	5.4	0.4	0.1	29.1	2.5	1.5
	M	1999	638.0	151.4	10.0	0.9	64.2	5.8	70.4
	F	1999	323.4	5.7	0.4	0.0	29.8	1.1	2.5
Peru[16 20 24] Pérou[16 20 24]	M	1998	3 918.5	247.6	25.5	59.2	608.2	21.6	381.1
	F	1998	3 010.8	94.4	0.4	3.4	317.4	3.1	6.0
	M	1999	3 980.4	250.9	63.1	28.3	555.7	35.1	370.0
	F	1999	3 230.8	104.1	2.2	3.0	341.9	6.3	8.2
	M	2000	4 067.6	339.3	24.4	48.7	631.1	24.4	287.4
	F	2000	3 060.7	117.0	1.4	3.8	332.4	3.7	12.1
Poland[4 67] Pologne[4 67]	M	1998	8 470.0	1 631.0	11.0	339.0	1 970.0	210.0	977.0
	F	1998	6 884.0	1 304.0	1.0	41.0	1 235.0	55.0	94.0
	M	1999[35]	8 132.0	1 496.0	9.0	277.0	1 900.0	195.0	918.0
	F	1999[35]	6 624.0	1 161.0	1.0	38.0	1 149.0	51.0	94.0
	M	2000	8 004.0	1 521.0	10.0	250.0	1 847.0	210.0	936.0
	F	2000	6 522.0	1 195.0	1.0	43.0	1 054.0	53.0	89.0

Categ. G Catég. G	Categ. H Catég. H	Categ. I Catég. I	Categ. J Catég. J	Categ. K Catég. K	Categ. L Catég. L	Categ. M Catég. M	Categ. N Catég. N	Categ. O Catég. O	Categ. P Catég. P	Categ. Q Catég. Q
110.9	6.2	69.1	7.2	23.2	48.3	35.8	19.1	27.5	0.7	...
114.5	19.6	34.9	12.4	21.8	28.9	114.8	87.0	36.8	1.5	...
113.7	6.8	69.6	5.9	24.3	51.5	36.0	17.4	26.5	0.6	...
109.8	23.5	30.8	10.6	21.7	34.0	126.8	95.3	37.4	3.4	0.6
113.7	8.3	67.7	6.9	25.3	46.3	38.1	14.9	25.0	0.2	...
118.2	21.7	30.3	8.8	22.0	35.0	131.4	87.3	30.8	1.3	...
34.7	10.4	16.3	22.4	23.0	11.7	10.1	13.5	9.0	4.9	...
35.5	10.9	17.2	22.9	25.8	11.5	10.9	14.1	9.2	5.3	...
37.2	11.0	19.0	24.0	29.3	11.4	11.1	14.4	9.4	5.6	...
4.5	6.9	5.8	1.4[50]	...	7.2	...	...	...	...	...
0.8	0.3	0.7	0.7[50]	...	5.7	...	...	...	...	...
4.8	9.2	7.2	1.1[50]	...	9.7	...	...	...	...	...
1.0	0.5	0.6	0.6[50]	...	8.4	...	...	...	...	...
41.9	11.2	24.9	8.6[50]	...	21.2	18.0[63]	...	12.1[64]	...	...
15.4	3.3	2.7	4.6[50]	...	5.4	16.1[63]	...	13.9[64]	...	...
3 643.5	815.2	1 539.5	175.8	766.1	1 134.1	785.2	341.6	2 628.1	187.6	120.0
3 160.7	1 009.6	153.6	140.0	390.1	472.9	1 108.0	668.8	482.1	1 583.8	24.4
3 502.0	827.2	1 548.2	178.7	732.8	1 186.7	731.4	365.1	2 573.0	179.0	124.5
3 080.4	980.2	190.3	124.0	423.9	541.6	991.5	659.6	521.5	1 528.4	26.5
5 239.9	842.7	1 571.2	150.8	773.7	1 171.8	768.2	362.8	890.5	206.2	123.3
3 284.6	1 001.7	159.4	142.2	404.2	567.6	1 109.3	699.8	432.1	1 564.7	36.5
686.0	120.0	333.0	148.0	498.0	348.0	219.0	221.0	147.0	...	...
534.0	147.0	109.0	116.0	334.0	117.0	246.0	807.0	171.0	20.0	...
672.0	128.0	339.0	156.0	532.0	353.0	218.0	227.0	146.0	1.0	2.0
566.0	153.0	125.0	132.0	359.0	165.0	263.0	821.0	164.0	16.0	...
705.0	138.0	349.0	156.0	568.0	320.0	202.0	230.0	159.0	1.0	2.0
586.0	151.0	123.0	120.0	377.0	168.0	256.0	841.0	197.0	4.0	...
5.3	1.6	2.9	1.4	2.4	3.6	0.9	0.9	1.3	0.1	0.1
5.4	2.4	1.3	2.3	1.4	2.2	1.9	3.4	2.0	2.0	0.1
5.1	1.7	2.7	1.4	2.5	3.4	1.0	0.9	1.4	0.1	0.1
5.1	2.1	1.4	2.3	1.5	2.0	1.9	3.4	1.9	1.7	0.1
4.7	1.7	2.5	1.3	2.4	3.0	1.0	0.8	1.3	0.1	0.1
5.2	1.9	1.5	2.2	1.6	1.9	1.9	3.5	2.0	1.7	0.1
146.8	34.9	72.2	22.4	92.9	46.2	37.8	24.6	51.9	1.0	0.3
134.7	53.6	31.0	31.1	75.4	50.8	89.2	108.9	44.6	7.4	0.4
155.6	33.2	75.1	23.1	93.5	48.2	34.3	25.8	48.9	0.8	0.4
129.2	53.4	35.4	30.7	81.3	50.3	91.1	115.2	47.6	7.2	0.2
159.2	35.7	77.4	23.6	93.3	46.0	34.8	25.2	50.2	0.0	0.5
136.4	57.2	33.5	31.8	80.8	45.3	94.9	117.2	51.5	7.7	0.4
181.0	25.0	119.0	25.0	109.0	89.0	64.0	65.0	37.0	...	...
160.0	45.0	51.0	26.0	70.0	63.0	109.0	324.0	51.0	6.0	...
187.0	23.0	120.0	26.0	121.0	89.0	61.0	66.0	39.0	...	...
151.0	49.0	50.0	28.0	79.0	63.0	118.0	330.0	51.0	5.0	...
189.0	26.0	117.0	24.0	126.0	90.0	65.0	68.0	41.0	...	...
157.0	47.0	51.0	25.0	80.0	67.0	119.0	335.0	48.0	4.0	...
105.2	16.6	51.9	8.9	19.8	40.8	16.0	10.5	28.5	5.8	4.3
62.9	17.5	10.2	13.9	8.8	28.4	32.1	18.3	24.3	46.4	1.5
113.3	16.5	55.2	10.0	24.4	40.8	17.0	11.7	31.8	5.9	1.2
64.6	17.4	8.1	14.1	9.7	27.1	35.0	19.7	29.2	47.1	1.2
113.7	18.1	62.2	10.0	25.8	41.1	17.4	11.7	27.8	5.7	1.6
69.0	21.4	10.8	13.9	13.6	27.0	32.8	19.1	29.8	45.4	0.8
925.3	139.2	522.1	39.6	262.9	233.4	231.9	72.9	128.9	19.2	...
1 116.0	373.5	58.0	35.9	97.3	74.1	289.1	100.2	156.0	286.1	...
956.6	111.0	568.9	42.6	270.4	258.2	225.3	63.4	169.8	11.3	...
1 120.4	359.6	49.3	33.7	137.1	90.7	326.2	101.7	203.2	342.4	...
952.5	109.7	591.0	42.0	283.7	255.3	213.2	50.1	196.4	11.3	...
1 108.0	322.2	48.0	24.6	129.7	91.4	266.5	112.6	171.8	315.5	...
1 003.0	72.0	710.0	110.0	275.0	440.0	239.0	188.0	294.0	...	1.0
1 114.0	147.0	247.0	244.0	189.0	340.0	732.0	868.0	263.0	8.0	...
997.0	72.0	663.0	132.0	290.0	436.0	276.0	193.0	277.0	...	...
1 098.0	150.0	232.0	255.0	216.0	336.0	753.0	835.0	250.0	5.0	...
969.0	75.0	669.0	120.0	303.0	416.0	258.0	166.0	254.0	1.0	...
1 074.0	165.0	225.0	260.0	228.0	348.0	755.0	773.0	253.0	7.0	...

29

Employment by industry [cont.]
Emploi par industrie [suite]

B. ISIC Rev. 3[+] — CITI Rév. 3[+]

Country or area Pays ou zone	Sex	Year Année	Total employment Emploi total	ISIC Rev. 3 Tabulation categories [+] CITI Rév. 3 Catégories de classement [+]					
				Categ. A Catég. A	Categ. B Catég. B	Categ. C Catég. C	Categ. D Catég. D	Categ. E Catég. E	Categ. F Catég. F
Portugal [4]	M	1998	2 641.4	299.9	20.5	14.0	635.5	27.9	497
Portugal [4]	F	1998	2 110.5	317.4	1.6	1.9	494.6	4.0	19
	M	1999	2 663.1	281.2	19.0	12.3	610.5	30.8	521
	F	1999	2 173.8	312.7	0.4	0.8	496.0	3.2	19
	M	2000	2 707.3	284.2	18.1	15.0	594.2	25.4	570
	F	2000	2 213.8	312.9	...	...	487.0	...	22
Republic of Moldova [4]	M	1999	739.1	...	...	...	...	...	
République de Moldova [4]	F	1999	755.3	...	...	...	...	...	
	M	2000	747.4	387.3	1.3	1.6	70.0	22.8	37
	F	2000	767.2	381.7	0.1	0.2	65.8	5.7	6
Romania [4]	M	1998	5 885.1	2 166.3	6.6	171.1	1 284.9	183.2	379
Roumanie [4]	F	1998	4 959.8	2 168.3	0.9	30.8	1 028.8	51.8	54
	M	1999	5 799.1	2 249.8	6.5	158.8	1 198.5	178.5	348
	F	1999	4 976.6	2 241.8	1.1	27.6	966.3	45.1	49
	M	2000	5 772.2	2 325.7	7.0	141.8	1 118.5	151.4	352
	F	2000	4 991.6	2 273.1	0.9	21.4	935.3	44.4	50
Russian Federation [9][68]	M	1997	31 554.0	4 874.0	180.0	878.0	6 511.0	1 082.0	2 928
Fédération de Russie [9][68]	F	1997	28 467.0	2 214.0	28.0	250.0	5 065.0	425.0	873
	M	1998	30 486.0	4 540.0	135.0	802.0	6 146.0	1 173.0	2 634
	F	1998	27 374.0	1 962.0	19.0	247.0	4 743.0	459.0	785
	M	1999	31 524.0	4 659.0	133.0	925.0	6 513.0	1 126.0	2 627
	F	1999	28 884.0	2 328.0	25.0	285.0	5 002.0	451.0	818
San Marino [20][69]	M	1997	10.6	0.1	...	...	3.9	...	1
Saint–Marin [20][69]	F	1997	6.7	0.1	...	...	1.6	...	0
	M	1998	11.0	0.1	...	...	4.1	...	1
	F	1998	6.9	0.1	...	...	1.7	...	0
	M	1999	11.3	0.1	...	...	4.2	...	1
	F	1999	7.3	0.1	...	...	1.7	...	0
Singapore [4][9]	M	1998	1 089.6	3.5	...	1.3	245.2	6.7	111
Singapour [4][9]	F	1998	780.1	0.9	...	0.2	159.2	1.6	19
	M	1999	1 087.2	4.5	...	1.0	236.2	7.3	110
	F	1999	798.6	1.0	...	0.4	159.4	1.5	20
	M	2000[73]	1 270.8	4.3	...	0.5	279.3	5.8	257
	F	2000[73]	824.0	0.8	...	0.1	155.6	1.3	16
Slovakia [3][4][70]	M	1998	1 210.4	125.8[45]	...	30.6	337.1	45.5	186
Slovaquie [3][4][70]	F	1998	988.2	55.6[45]	...	5.0	236.6	7.7	17
	M	1999	1 163.7	111.8[45]	...	25.9	325.8	43.6	171
	F	1999	968.4	45.4[45]	...	3.9	221.7	9.3	18
	M	2000	1 137.3	101.3[45]	...	21.7	320.3	41.2	153
	F	2000	964.4	38.4[45]	...	3.1	220.1	8.8	13
Slovenia [4][16]	M	1997	482.0	57.0	...	6.0	171.0	12.0	49
Slovénie [4][16]	F	1997	416.0	52.0	...	...	119.0	2.0	6
	M	1998	487.0	57.0	...	8.0	171.0	7.0	45
	F	1998	420.0	51.0	...	...	118.0	1.0	6
	M	1999	482.0	51.0	...	6.0	169.0	6.0	41
	F	1999	410.0	45.0	...	...	109.0	1.0	4
Spain [32][61]	M	1998	8 517.4	741.7	49.6	54.4	1 984.3	77.0	1 259
Espagne [32][61]	F	1998	4 687.4	263.7	5.6	5.3	578.9	8.0	47
	M	1999	8 790.9	701.9	49.5	56.3	2 018.2	74.9	1 403
	F	1999	5 026.6	256.5	6.8	6.8	616.3	11.4	60
	M	2000	9 086.7	670.0	52.6	56.1	2 038.8	79.3	1 515
	F	2000	5 387.1	257.2	9.2	4.5	686.7	13.6	76
Sweden [71]	M	1998	2 079.0	74.0	2.0	8.0	560.0	25.0	202
Suède [71]	F	1998	1 901.0	26.0	...	1.0	202.0	7.0	19
	M	1999	2 121.0	76.0	2.0	8.0	558.0	23.0	206
	F	1999	1 946.0	26.0	...	1.0	198.0	8.0	19
	M	2000	2 167.0	73.0	3.0	8.0	557.0	21.0	208
	F	2000	1 992.0	23.0	...	1.0	200.0	8.0	18
Switzerland [3][4][16][76]	M	1998	2 146.3	119.0[45]	...	507.0[74]	...	...	226
Suisse [3][4][16][76]	F	1998	1 686.7	63.0[45]	...	186.0[74]	...	...	32
	M	1999	2 157.3	126.0[45]	...	501.0[74]	...	...	226
	F	1999	1 704.7	65.0[45]	...	177.0[74]	...	...	37
	M	2000	2 172.0	115.0[45]	...	515.0[74]	...	...	234
	F	2000	1 707.0	66.0[45]	...	178.0[74]	...	...	33

Categ. G Catég. G	Categ. H Catég. H	Categ. I Catég. I	Categ. J Catég. J	Categ. K Catég. K	Categ. L Catég. L	Categ. M Catég. M	Categ. N Catég. N	Categ. O Catég. O	Categ. P Catég. P	Categ. Q Catég. Q
388.4	103.3	140.2	55.8	91.0	196.1	67.1	38.8	62.2	1.7	1.6
266.2	141.7	37.4	31.4	84.7	104.4	208.3	161.7	91.5	143.2	1.0
407.1	102.5	130.2	53.8	100.5	202.1	69.4	45.8	71.6	1.7	2.5
286.3	146.3	37.6	30.6	102.7	105.0	208.4	186.1	94.1	142.9	1.1
404.8	98.9	143.2	54.7	103.8	206.6	63.2	49.9	71.4	...	...
318.3	154.7	37.2	33.4	101.7	112.7	208.0	193.1	80.4	144.9	...
...	...	...	...	...	...	...	...	...	...	...
...	...	...	...	...	...	...	...	...	...	...
65.3	4.2	48.0	3.4	10.7	42.8	21.7	14.2	13.1	3.3	...
82.0	13.8	15.8	4.6	8.8	21.7	79.8	60.0	15.1	5.3	...
421.4	49.8	399.6	26.8	85.6	392.5	125.8	80.4	112.0	...	...
504.5	92.3	129.7	54.9	68.4	112.1	302.3	255.0	105.6	...	...
412.8	42.2	369.3	25.0	74.7	411.5	129.1	72.2	122.1	...	...
513.4	81.7	130.4	62.0	66.4	121.1	294.1	268.3	108.2	...	...
407.2	47.1	388.9	27.9	74.5	422.0	117.7	65.6	124.4	...	...
521.2	75.8	122.4	64.6	57.8	141.1	297.3	280.1	105.2	...	...
2 961.0	124.0	3 805.0	260.0	939.0	2 714.0	1 104.0	760.0	2 434.0	...	...
4 178.0	561.0	1 711.0	626.0	921.0	1 515.0	4 583.0	3 416.0	2 100.0	...	...
2 914.0	130.0	3 743.0	243.0	988.0	2 723.0	1 145.0	767.0	2 404.0	...	...
4 113.0	559.0	1 590.0	569.0	889.0	1 534.0	4 476.0	3 368.0	2 064.0	...	...
2 933.0	177.0	3 772.0	264.0	938.0	3 082.0	1 186.0	778.0	2 411.0	...	...
4 275.0	661.0	1 715.0	540.0	852.0	1 507.0	4 697.0	3 555.0	2 173.0	...	...
1.1	0.3	0.3	0.3	0.5	1.5	0.2	0.3	0.3	0.0	...
1.1	0.3	0.1	0.2	0.4	0.7	0.7	0.7	0.4	0.1	0.0
1.1	0.3	0.3	0.3	0.5	1.5	0.2	0.3	0.3	0.0	...
1.1	0.3	0.1	0.2	0.4	0.8	0.8	0.7	0.4	0.1	0.0
1.2	0.3	0.3	0.3	0.6	1.5	0.2	0.3	0.4	0.0	...
1.3	0.3	0.1	0.2	0.5	0.8	0.8	0.7	0.5	0.1	0.0
166.1	61.0	157.2	45.4	104.3	93.4	41.7[63]	...	50.5[51]	...	1.6
115.1	57.9	49.2	63.1	80.0	25.1	95.9[63]	...	111.4[51]	...	1.1
165.8	61.6	152.8	43.9	110.6	94.8	44.5[63]	...	52.5[51]	...	1.2
113.1	59.7	50.9	60.7	86.2	27.0	97.5[63]	...	119.9[51]	...	1.0
171.2	58.9	147.5	41.9	136.2	82.3	39.5[63]	...	44.8[51]	...	1.1
115.6	55.6	49.0	54.4	90.0	23.6	87.9[63]	...	172.5[51]	...	0.9
110.8	21.2	118.7	9.6	45.1	80.2	32.0	29.9	37.2	0.1	0.1
151.5	41.4	50.9	27.5	32.2	73.7	133.3	116.4	35.7	2.7	0.2
103.1	23.9	116.5	10.6	48.6	80.5	35.0	28.7	38.0	0.1	0.1
157.3	41.0	49.5	26.1	31.5	69.9	131.8	126.3	34.9	1.9	0.1
106.6	25.3	115.8	11.7	55.1	76.9	35.0	26.3	45.5	0.2	0.1
153.0	39.9	51.4	25.4	35.7	81.5	126.6	121.5	41.1	3.7	0.3
51.0	14.0	41.0	6.0	20.0	17.0	11.0	8.0	17.0	...	...
56.0	25.0	10.0	14.0	20.0	19.0	41.0	34.0	16.0	1.0	...
55.0	15.0	39.0	5.0	26.0	19.0	14.0	9.0	15.0	...	...
56.0	23.0	12.0	13.0	21.0	22.0	46.0	33.0	15.0	1.0	...
53.0	14.0	42.0	5.0	25.0	25.0	14.0	9.0	17.0	...	...
56.0	19.0	11.0	15.0	24.0	24.0	46.0	36.0	19.0	...	...
1 252.5	437.1	640.2	228.6	454.7	532.7	293.3	205.8	256.5	48.8	0.5
927.0	360.6	131.4	104.6	403.8	293.4	493.5	508.4	240.0	313.4	2.4
1 261.8	453.4	654.3	241.8	495.4	553.9	297.4	226.7	255.6	45.6	0.7
1 004.0	395.4	151.6	121.2	435.6	333.7	504.5	516.7	260.5	344.4	0.8
1 298.0	477.3	692.5	243.1	531.2	572.4	309.1	227.8	277.0	45.2	1.3
1 054.4	427.6	170.6	140.1	505.4	355.2	497.0	561.5	282.3	344.8	0.4
288.0	44.0	192.0	36.0	250.0	105.0[72]	94.0	103.0	93.0[51]	...	...
215.0	67.0	79.0	48.0	161.0	103.0[72]	199.0	667.0	106.0[51]	...	...
289.0	49.0	197.0	37.0	271.0	104.0[72]	104.0	103.0	92.0[51]	...	...
223.0	65.0	78.0	48.0	175.0	104.0[72]	212.0	673.0	114.0[51]	...	...
290.0	51.0	200.0	38.0	287.0	111.0[72]	107.0	100.0	93.0[51]	...	...
230.0	66.0	79.0	48.0	194.0	112.0[72]	222.0	670.0	118.0[51]	...	...
307.0	38.0	158.0	119.0	245.0	120.0[72]	91.0	117.0	96.0[51]	...	...
312.0	79.0	65.0	84.0	148.0	94.0[72]	148.0	294.0	176.0[51]	...	...
315.0	39.0	156.0	116.0	247.0	120.0[72]	99.0	115.0	92.0[51]	...	...
295.0	73.0	82.0	80.0	151.0	94.0[72]	152.0	313.0	183.0[51]	...	...
312.0	44.0	149.0	115.0	239.0	122.0[72]	105.0	114.0	103.0[51]	...	...
279.0	74.0	75.0	81.0	151.0	97.0[72]	164.0	331.0	174.0[51]	...	...

29
Employment by industry [cont.]
Emploi par industrie [suite]

B. ISIC Rev. 3⁺ — CITI Rév. 3⁺

Country or area Pays ou zone	Sex Sex	Year Année	Total employment Emploi total	ISIC Rev. 3 Tabulation categories⁺ CITI Rév. 3 Catégories de classement⁺					
				Categ. A Catég. A	Categ. B Catég. B	Categ. C Catég. C	Categ. D Catég. D	Categ. E Catég. E	Categ. F Catég. F
Tajikistan Tadjikistan	M	1995	1 038.0	1 095.0⁷	...	...	183.0⁷	24.0⁷	81
	F	1995	815.0	...	...	...	...	...	
	M	1996	927.0	1 026.0⁷	...	...	181.0⁷	21.0⁷	68
	F	1996	804.0	...	...	...	...	...	
	M	1997	...	527.6⁷	...	...	136.5⁷	18.0⁷	44
United Arab Emirates Emirats arabes unis	M	1995[73]	1 159.7	96.7	8.1	29.4	125.2	13.0	252
	F	1995[73]	152.1	0.1	0.0	0.9	18.4	0.1	1.
	M	2000	1 553.0	129.5	10.8	39.4	167.7	17.4	337
	F	2000	226.0	0.1	0.0	1.3	27.3	0.1	2
United Kingdom[32][35] Rouyame—Uni[32][35]	M	1997	14 792.3	355.3	13.6	92.1	3 646.5	139.5	1 708
	F	1997	12 022.0	124.0	1.6	12.7	1 360.3	40.2	166
	M	1998	14 998.6	337.5	16.4	86.4	3 673.1	138.7	1 730
	F	1998	12 117.0	108.5	2.6	13.8	1 337.5	41.9	176
	M	1999	15 138.5	317.2	14.4	87.6	3 586.9	134.9	1 754
	F	1999	12 303.9	91.4	1.6	13.6	1 299.3	52.7	174

Source:
International Labour Office (ILO), Geneva, "Yearbook of Labour Statistics 2000" and the ILO labour statistics database.

Source:
Bureau international du travail (BIT), Genève, "Annuaire des statistiques du travail 2000" et la base de données du BIT.

+ Countries using the latest version of the International Standard Industrial Classification of all Economic Activities, Revision 3 (ISIC Revision 3), are presented in Part B. Countries using the former classification, ISIC Revision 2, are presented in Part A.

+ On trouvera dans la partie B les chiffres relatifs aux pays qui appliquent la version la plus récente de la Classification internationale type, par industrie, de toutes les branches d'activité économique, Révision 3 (CITI Rév. 3). Les pays qui utilisent encore la classification dans sa version précédente (Révision 2) figurent à la partie A.

+ Tabulation categories of ISIC Rev. 3:
A. Agriculture, hunting and forestry.
B. Fishing.
C. Mining and quarrying.
D. Manufacturing.
E. Electricity, gas and water supply.
F. Construction.
G. Wholesale and retail trade; repair of motor vehicles, motorcycles and personal and household goods.
H. Hotels and restaurants.
I. Transport, storage and communications.
J. Financial intermediation.
K. Real estate, renting and business activities.
L. Public administration and defence; compulsory social security.
M. Education.
N. Health and social work.
O. Other community, social and personal service activities.
P. Private households with employed persons.
Q. Extra—territorial organizations and bodies.

+ Catégories de classement de la CITI Rév. 3:
A. Agriculture, chasse et sylviculture.
B. Pêche.
C. Activités extractives.
D. Activités de fabrication.
E. Production et distribution d'électricité, de gaz et d'eau.
F. Construction.
G. Commerce de gros et de détail; réparation de véhicules automobiles, de motocycles et de biens personneles et domestiques.
H. Hôtels et restaurants.
I. Transports, entreposage et communications.
J. Intermédiation financière.
K. Immobilier, locations et activités de services aux entreprises.
L. Administration publique et défense; sécurité sociale obligatoire.
M. Education.
N. Santé et action sociale.
O. Autres activités de services collectifs, sociaux et personnels.
P. Ménages privés employant du personnel domestique.
Q. Organisations et organismes extraterritoriaux.

1 Persons aged 10 years and over.
2 Year ending in June of the year indicated.
3 Civilian labour force employed.
4 Persons aged 15 years and over.
5 Including quarrying.
6 Wholesale and retail trade.
7 Both sexes.
8 Persons aged 15 to 69 years.
9 One month of each year.
10 Excluding rural population of Rondônia, Acre, Amazonas, Roraima, Pará and Amapa.
11 Including electricity, gas, water and sanitary services.
12 Excluding restaurants and hotels.
13 Excluding storage.
14 Including international and other extra—territorial bodies and activities not adequately defined.

1 Personnes âgées de 10 ans et plus.
2 Année se terminant en juin de l'année indiquée.
3 Main—d'oeuvre civile occupée.
4 Personnes âgées de 15 ans et plus.
5 Y compris les carrières.
6 Commerce de gros et de détail.
7 Les deux sexes.
8 Personnes âgées de 15 à 69 ans.
9 Un mois de chaque année.
10 Non compris la population rurale de Rondônia, Acre, Amazonas, Roraima, Pará et Amapá.
11 Y compris l'électricité, le gaz, l'eau et les services sanitaires.
12 Non compris les restaurants et hôtels.
13 Non compris les entrepôts.
14 Y compris les organisations internationales et autres organismes extra—territoriaux et les activitiés mal designées.

Categ. G / Catég. G	Categ. H / Catég. H	Categ. I / Catég. I	Categ. J / Catég. J	Categ. K / Catég. K	Categ. L / Catég. L	Categ. M / Catég. M	Categ. N / Catég. N	Categ. O / Catég. O	Categ. P / Catég. P	Categ. Q / Catég. Q
87.0[7]	...	58.0[7]	...	...	...	168.0[7]	88.0[7]	...	...	...
69.0[7]	...	58.0[7]	...	...	...	161.0[7]	84.0[7]	...	...	...
...	...	...	...	...	...	...	...	...	...	...
40.2[7]	...	50.9[7]	...	...	...	160.0[7]	82.3[7]	...	...	...
173.1	42.2	89.6	13.8	30.6	168.3	24.2	12.7	38.1	40.7	1.0
10.0	3.6	4.2	3.0	3.0	6.7	25.0	10.9	1.8	62.5	0.2
231.9	56.5	119.9	18.4	40.9	225.4	32.4	17.0	51.1	54.5	1.3
14.8	5.4	6.3	4.4	4.4	10.0	37.2	16.2	2.7	92.8	0.4
2 122.7	502.2	1 305.8	563.4	1 535.5	876.9	606.8	545.6	655.8	42.7	16.8
2 043.5	736.6	413.4	623.8	1 110.0	717.5	1 390.3	2 397.3	730.0	116.4	8.9
2 127.7	491.3	1 331.6	590.7	1 611.2	878.8	596.4	582.7	702.9	32.4	16.9
2 003.0	752.6	437.8	607.5	1 180.1	696.3	1 455.9	2 399.2	757.9	112.5	4.4
2 152.2	459.4	1 359.5	558.1	1 751.1	902.1	664.2	601.6	694.4	35.9	12.1
2 110.3	705.6	453.2	613.7	1 242.2	734.5	1 518.0	2 413.1	745.7	102.5	6.2

15 Including restaurants, hotels and storage; excluding sanitary services and international bodies.
16 One quarter of each year.
17 Excluding armed forces and reemployed retired persons.
18 Whole national economy.
19 Excluding business services.
20 Persons aged 14 years and over.
21 Persons aged 12 years and over.
22 7 main cities of the country.
23 Estimates based on the 1993 Census results.
24 Urban areas.
25 Including self-defence forces.
26 Excluding hotels.
27 Including hotels.
28 Persons aged 15 to 64 years.
29 Including repairs.
30 July of preceding year to June of current year.
31 Including members of the armed forces living in private households.
32 Persons aged 16 years and over.
33 Including restaurants and hotels.
34 Excluding Northern and Eastern provinces.
35 Average of less than 12 months.
36 Persons aged 13 years and over.
37 Including repair and installation services.
38 Including financing, insurance and real estate; excl. restaurants and hotels.
39 Including sanitary services.
40 Excluding repair and installation services and sanitary services.

41 Estimates based on 1990 census benchmarks.
42 Including hotels, excluding sanitary services.
43 Including professional army; excluding compulsory military service.
44 Including unpaid family workers who worked for one hour or more.
45 Including tabulation category B - Fishing
46 Including tabulation categories D - manufacturing and E - electricity, gas and water supply.
47 Including major divisions 1 and 4.
48 Excluding armed forces.
49 Including electricity, gas and water.
50 Including tabulation category K - real estate, renting and business activities.
51 Including private households with employed persons.
52 Excluding full-time members of the armed forces.

15 Y compris les restaurants, hôtels et entrepôts; non compris les services sanitaires et les organismes internationaux.
16 Un trimestre de chaque année.
17 Non compris les forces armées et les retraités réemployés.
18 Ensemble de l'économie nationale.
19 Non compris les services aux entreprises.
20 Personnes âgées de 14 ans et plus.
21 Personnes âgées de 12 ans et plus.
22 7 villes principales du pays.
23 Estimations basées sur les résultats du Recensement de 1993.
24 Régions urbaines.
25 Y compris les forces d'autodéfense.
26 Non compris les hôtels.
27 Y compris les hôtels.
28 Personnes âgées de 15 à 64 ans.
29 Y compris les réparations.
30 Juillet de l'année précédente à juin de l'année en cours.
31 Y compris les membres des forces armées vivant en ménages privés.
32 Personnes âgées de 16 ans et plus.
33 Y compris les restaurants et hôtels.
34 Non compris les provinces du Nord et de l'Est.
35 Moyenne de moins de douze mois.
36 Personnes âgées de 13 ans et plus.
37 Y compris les services de réparation et d'installation.
38 Y compris les banques, les assurances et affaires immobilières; non compris les restaurants et hôtels.
39 Y compris les services sanitaires.
40 Non compris les services de réparation et d'installation, et les services sanitaires.

41 Estimations basées sur les données de calage du recensement de 1990.
42 Y compris les hôtels; non compris les services sanitaires.
43 Y compris les militaires de carrière; non compris les militaires du contingent.
44 Y compris les travailleurs familiaux non rémunérés ayant travaillé une heure ou plus.
45 Y compris la catégorie de classement B - pêche.
46 Y compris la catégories de classement D - activités de fabrication et E - production et distribution d'électricité, de gaz et d'eau.
47 Y compris les branches 1 et 4.
48 Non compris les forces armées.
49 Y compris l'électricité, le gaz et l'eau.
50 Y compris la catégorie de classement K - immobilier, locations et activitiés de services aux entreprises.
51 Y compris les ménages privés employant du personnel domestique.
52 Non compris les membres à temps complet des forces armées.

29
Employment by industry [*cont.*]
Emploi par industrie [*suite*]

53 Beginning this year, methodology revised; data not strictly comparable.	53 A partir de cette année, méthodologie révisée; les données ne sont pas strictement comparables.
54 Government−controlled areas.	54 Région sous contrôle gouvernemental.
55 Persons aged 15 to 66 years.	55 Personnes âgées de 15 à 66 ans.
56 Persons aged 15 to 74 years.	56 Personnes âgées de 15 à 74 ans.
57 Including workers from the Judea, Samaria and Gaza areas.	57 Y compris les travailleurs des régions de Judée, Samarie et Gaza.
58 Including manufacturing.	58 Y compris les activités de fabrication.
59 Including permanent members of institutional households.	59 Y compris les membres permanents des ménages collectifs.
60 Including conscripts.	60 Y compris les conscrits.
61 Excluding compulsory military service.	61 Non compris les militaires du contingent.
62 Including armed forces.	62 Y compris les forces armées.
63 Including tabulation category N − health and social work.	63 Y compris la catégorie de classement N − santé et action socials.
64 Including tabulation categories P and Q.	64 Y compris les catégories de classement P et Q.
65 Curaçao.	65 Curaçao.
66 Persons aged 16 to 74 years.	66 Personnes âgées de 16 à 74 ans.
67 Excluding regular military living in barracks and conscripts.	67 Non compris les militaires de carrière vivant dans des casernes et les conscrits.
68 Persons aged 15 to 72 years.	68 Personnes âgées de 15 à 72 ans.
69 31st Dec. of each year.	69 31 déc. de chaque année.
70 Excluding persons on child−care leave.	70 Non compris les personnes en congé parental.
71 Persons aged 16 to 64 years.	71 Personnes âgées de 16 à 64 ans.
72 Including tabulation category Q − extra−territorial organizations and bodies	72 Y compris la catégorie de classement Q − organisation et organismes extraterritoriaux.
73 Population census.	73 Recensement de population.
74 Including tabulation categories C, D and E.	74 Y compris les catégories de classement C, D et E.
75 Estimates based on 1996 census of population benchmarks.	75 Estimations basées sur les données de calage du recensement de population de 1996.
76 Excluding seasonal/border workers.	76 Non compris les travailleurs saisonniers et frontaliers.

30
Unemployment
Number (thousands) and percentage unemployed
Chômage
Nombre (milliers) et pourcentage des chômeurs

Country or area [§] Pays ou zone [§]	1991	1992	1993	1994	1995	1996	1997	1998	1999	2000
Albania Albanie										
MF [IV]	139.8	...	...	...	...	...	...	...	...	...
% MF [IV]	9.1	...	...	...	...	...	...	...	...	...
Algeria Algérie										
MF [IV][1]	1 261.0	1 482.0	1 519.0	1 660.0	2 105.0	...	2 049.0	...	...	2 427.7
M [IV][1]	1 155.0	1 348.0	...	...	1 626.0	...	1 769.0	...	...	2 132.7
F [IV][1]	106.0	134.0	...	...	478.0	...	280.0	...	...	295.0
% MF [IV][1]	20.6	23.0	23.2	24.4	27.9	...	26.4	...	...	29.8
% M [IV][1]	21.7	24.2	...	...	26.0	...	26.9	...	...	33.9
% F [IV][1]	17.0	20.3	...	...	38.4	...	24.0	...	...	29.7
Angola Angola										
MF [III][2]	...	...	...	...	...	19.0	...	...	...	...
M [III][2]	...	...	...	...	...	15.5	...	...	...	...
F [III][2]	...	...	...	...	...	3.5	...	...	...	...
Argentina Argentine										
MF [I][4]	257.3[3 5]	305.2[5 6]	493.9[5 6]	595.1[5 6]	963.6[5 6]	1 531.4[6 7]	1 375.1[6 7]	1 218.7[6 7]	1 359.6[6 7]	1 460.9[6 7]
M [I][4]	158.4[3 5]	186.2[5 6]	253.9[5 6]	325.0[5 6]	508.1[5 6]	866.1[6 7]	731.4[6 7]	680.0[6 7]	764.9[6 7]	809.9[6 7]
F [I][4]	98.8[3 5]	119.0[5 6]	240.1[5 6]	270.1[5 6]	455.6[5 6]	665.3[6 7]	643.7[6 7]	538.7[6 7]	594.7[6 7]	651.0[6 7]
% MF [I][4]	5.8[3 5]	6.7[5 6]	10.1[5 6]	12.1[5 6]	18.8[5 6]	17.2[6 7]	14.9[6 7]	12.8[6 7]	14.1[6 7]	15.0[6 7]
% M [I][4]	5.6[3 5]	6.4[5 6]	8.5[5 6]	10.7[5 6]	16.5[5 6]	15.8[6 7]	13.0[6 7]	11.9[6 7]	13.3[6 7]	14.1[6 7]
% F [I][4]	6.1[3 5]	7.0[5 6]	12.7[5 6]	14.4[5 6]	22.3[5 6]	19.4[6 7]	17.9[6 7]	14.3[6 7]	15.2[6 7]	16.4[6 7]
Armenia Arménie										
MF [I][1 8]	...	...	...	...	...	...	423.7	...	...	...
M [I][1 8]	...	...	...	...	...	...	247.0	...	...	...
F [I][1 8]	...	...	...	...	...	...	176.7	...	...	...
% MF [I][1 8]	...	...	...	...	...	...	36.4	...	...	...
% M [I][1 8]	...	...	...	...	...	...	38.0	...	...	...
% F [I][1 8]	...	...	...	...	...	...	34.4	...	...	...
Australia Australie										
MF [I][1]	814.5[9]	925.1[9]	939.2[9]	855.5[9]	764.5[10]	779.4[10]	786.5[10]	746.5[10]	685.4[10]	641.0[10]
M [I][1]	489.5[9]	566.2[9]	574.0[9]	505.6[9]	453.4[10]	456.0[10]	457.9[10]	434.5[10]	393.4[10]	363.3[10]
F [I][1]	325.0[9]	358.9[9]	365.1[9]	349.9[9]	311.1[10]	323.4[10]	328.7[10]	312.0[10]	292.0[10]	277.7[10]
% MF [I][1]	9.6[9]	10.8[9]	10.9[9]	9.7[9]	8.5[10]	8.5[10]	8.6[10]	8.0[10]	7.2[10]	6.6[10]
% M [I][1]	9.9[9]	11.4[9]	11.5[9]	10.0[9]	8.8[10]	8.8[10]	8.7[10]	8.2[10]	7.3[10]	6.7[10]
% F [I][1]	9.2[9]	10.0[9]	10.1[9]	9.4[9]	8.1[10]	8.3[10]	8.3[10]	7.7[10]	7.1[10]	6.6[10]
Austria Autriche										
MF [I][1]	125.4	132.4	158.8	138.4	143.7	160.4	164.8	165.0	146.7	138.8
M [I][1]	70.9	74.4	88.1	72.6	71.4	86.5	87.3	88.4	81.7	73.8
F [I][1]	54.5	58.0	70.7	65.7	72.2	73.9	77.5	76.6	65.0	65.0
MF [III][1]	185.0	193.1	222.3	214.9	215.7	230.5	233.3	237.8	221.7	194.3
M [III][1]	99.0	107.2	126.7	120.6	120.0	128.0	128.6	129.4	121.5	107.5
F [III][1]	86.0	85.9	95.6	94.4	95.7	102.5	104.8	108.4	100.2	86.2
% MF [I][1]	3.5	3.7	4.3	3.6	3.7	4.1	4.2	4.2	3.8	3.6
% M [I][1]	3.3	3.5	4.1	3.3	3.2	3.9	3.9	4.0	3.7	3.3
% F [I][1]	3.7	3.8	4.5	4.0	4.3	4.5	4.6	4.6	3.9	3.8
% MF [III][1]	5.8	5.9	6.8	6.5	6.6	7.0	7.1	7.2	6.7	5.8
% M [III][1]	5.3	5.7	6.7	6.4	6.4	6.9	6.9	6.9	6.5	5.8
% F [III][1]	6.5	6.2	6.9	6.7	6.8	7.3	7.4	7.5	6.9	5.9
Azerbaijan Azerbaïdjan										
MF [III][11]	4.0	6.4	19.5	23.6	28.3	31.9	38.3	42.3	45.2	43.7
M [III][11]	1.5	2.8	7.7	9.2	11.4	13.1	16.2	18.2	19.6	19.3
F [III][11]	2.5	3.6	11.8	14.4	16.9	18.8	22.1	24.1	25.6	24.5
% MF [III][11]	0.1	0.2	0.5	0.7	0.8	0.9	1.0	1.1	1.2	1.2
% M [III][11]	0.1	0.1	0.4	0.5	0.6	0.7	0.8	0.9	1.0	1.0
% F [III][11]	0.2	0.2	0.7	0.9	1.0	1.1	1.2	1.4	1.4	1.4
Bahamas Bahamas										
MF [I][1 3]	16.0	20.0	18.0	18.4	15.6	16.9	14.7	12.1	...	...
M [I][1 3]	8.4	9.8	9.2	9.2	7.5	6.6	6.5	4.7	...	...
F [I][1 3]	7.7	10.2	8.7	9.3	8.1	10.3	8.2	7.4	...	...
% MF [I][1 3]	12.3	14.8	13.1	13.3	10.9	11.5	9.8	7.7	...	...
% M [I][1 3]	12.2	13.8	12.8	12.6	10.1	8.6	8.3	5.9	...	...
% F [I][1 3]	12.4	16.0	13.4	14.0	11.8	14.7	11.3	9.6	...	...

30
Unemployment
Number (thousands) and percentage unemployed [*cont.*]
Chômage
Nombre (milliers) et pourcentage des chômeurs [*suite*]

Country or area § Pays ou zone §	1991	1992	1993	1994	1995	1996	1997	1998	1999	2000
Bahrain Bahreïn										
MF [III] [12]	3.3	3.0	3.6	4.2	5.1	...	6.1	4.1	3.8	6.2
M [III] [12]	2.4	2.2	2.9	2.7	3.4	...	4.1	2.7	2.6	4.2
F [III] [12]	0.9	0.9	0.7	1.4	1.7	...	2.0	1.4	1.1	2.0
Bangladesh Bangladesh										
MF [I] [4 13]	...	...	...	...	...	1 417.0	...	...	...	...
M [I] [4 13]	...	...	...	...	...	933.0	...	...	...	...
F [I] [4 13]	...	...	...	...	...	484.0	...	...	...	...
% MF [I] [4 13]	...	...	...	...	...	2.5	...	...	...	...
% M [I] [4 13]	...	...	...	...	...	2.7	...	...	...	...
% F [I] [4 13]	...	...	...	...	...	2.3	...	...	...	...
Barbados Barbade										
MF [I] [1]	20.9	28.7	30.9	28.2	26.9	21.1	19.6	16.7	14.3	...
M [I] [1]	8.6	13.2	14.0	12.1	11.4	8.6	7.9	5.9	5.5	...
F [I] [1]	12.3	15.5	16.9	16.1	15.5	12.6	11.7	10.8	8.7	...
% MF [I] [1]	17.1	23.0	24.5	21.9	19.7	15.8	14.5	12.3	10.5	...
% M [I] [1]	13.3	20.4	21.5	18.3	16.5	12.4	11.3	8.4	7.7	...
% F [I] [1]	21.4	25.7	27.7	25.6	22.9	18.9	17.8	16.4	13.3	...
Belarus Bélarus										
MF [III] [3]	2.3	24.0	66.3	101.2	131.0	182.5	126.2	105.9	95.4	95.8
M [III] [3]	0.5	4.4	22.3	36.7	46.7	66.1	42.1	35.3	34.2	37.6
F [III] [3]	1.8	19.6	44.0	64.5	84.3	116.4	84.1	70.6	61.2	58.2
% MF [III] [3]	0.1	0.5	1.4	2.1	2.9	4.0	2.8	2.3	2.1	2.1
% M [III] [3]	0.0	0.2	0.9	1.6	2.2	3.0	1.9	1.6	1.6	1.7
% F [III] [3]	0.1	0.8	1.8	2.6	3.5	5.0	3.6	3.0	2.6	2.4
Belgium Belgique										
MF [I] [2 3]	282.4	316.1	335.2	405.4	390.1	404.0	375.1	384.0	375.2	309.4
M [I] [2 3]	110.9	137.1	149.1	188.5	178.9	181.7	173.2	179.3	179.4	144.7
F [I] [2 3]	171.5	179.0	186.1	216.9	211.2	222.3	201.9	204.7	195.8	163.8
MF [III] [14]	429.5	472.9	549.7	588.7	596.9	588.2	570.0	541.0	507.5	474.4
M [III] [14]	178.0	199.1	237.5	257.0	259.6	255.5	249.6	237.4	224.7	208.7
F [III] [14]	251.5	273.8	312.2	331.6	337.3	332.7	320.5	303.6	282.9	265.8
% MF [I] [2 3]	7.0	7.7	8.2	9.8	9.3	9.6	8.9	9.1	8.6	7.0
% M [I] [2 3]	4.6	5.7	6.2	7.7	7.3	7.4	7.1	7.3	7.2	5.8
% F [I] [2 3]	10.7	10.7	11.1	12.7	12.2	12.8	11.4	11.4	10.4	8.7
% MF [III] [14]	10.2	11.2	12.9	13.8	13.9	13.7	13.1	12.4	11.6	10.9
% M [III] [14]	7.3	8.1	9.7	10.6	10.7	10.5	10.2	9.7	9.2	8.6
% F [III] [14]	14.3	15.3	17.1	18.0	18.1	17.7	16.8	15.9	14.7	13.8
Belize Belize										
MF [I] [15]	...	...	6.7	7.7	...	...	...	...	...	...
M [I] [15]	...	...	3.5	4.3	...	...	...	...	...	...
F [I] [15]	...	...	3.2	3.5	...	...	...	...	...	...
% MF [I] [15]	...	...	9.8	11.1	...	...	...	...	...	...
% M [I] [15]	...	...	7.5	9.0	...	...	...	...	...	...
% F [I] [15]	...	...	14.5	15.1	...	...	...	...	...	...
Bermuda Bermudes										
MF [III]	0.2	...	...	...	...	...	...	...	...	...
MF [IV] [1]	1 261.0	1 482.0	1 519.0	1 660.0	2 105.0	...	2 311.0	...	...	...
Bolivia Bolivie										
MF [I] [4]	62.1[16]	59.3[16]	69.6[16]	38.8[16]	47.5[16]	73.6[8]	71.2[8]	...	156.7[8]	167.5[8]
M [I] [4]	34.6[16]	34.5[16]	43.2[16]	23.5[16]	24.3[16]	37.6[8]	40.8[8]	...	74.4[8]	77.0[8]
F [I] [4]	27.4[16]	24.8[16]	26.3[16]	15.3[16]	23.1[16]	36.0[8]	30.4[8]	...	82.3[8]	90.5[8]
% MF [I] [4]	5.9[16]	5.5[16]	6.0[16]	3.1[16]	3.6[16]	3.8[8]	3.7[8]	...	7.2[8]	7.4[8]
% M [I] [4]	5.7[16]	5.5[16]	6.5[16]	3.4[16]	3.3[16]	3.6[8]	3.7[8]	...	6.2[8]	6.2[8]
% F [I] [4]	6.2[16]	5.6[16]	5.3[16]	2.9[16]	4.0[16]	4.1[8]	3.6[8]	...	8.5[8]	8.9[8]
Brazil Brésil										
MF [I] [3 4 17]	...	4 573.3[18]	4 395.6	...	4 509.8	5 076.2	5 881.8	6 922.6	7 639.1	...
M [I] [3 4 17]	...	2 355.1[18]	2 305.9	...	2 327.9	2 498.3	2 854.9	3 301.1	3 667.9	...
F [I] [3 4 17]	...	2 218.2[18]	2 089.7	...	2 181.9	2 577.9	3 026.9	3 621.5	3 971.2	...
% MF [I] [3 4 17]	...	6.5[18]	6.2	...	6.1	7.0	7.8	9.0	9.6	...
% M [I] [3 4 17]	...	5.6[18]	5.4	...	5.3	5.7	6.4	7.2	7.9	...
% F [I] [3 4 17]	...	8.0[18]	7.4	...	7.3	8.8	10.0	11.6	12.1	...

30
Unemployment
Number (thousands) and percentage unemployed [*cont.*]
Chômage
Nombre (milliers) et pourcentage des chômeurs [*suite*]

Country or area [§] Pays ou zone [§]	1991	1992	1993	1994	1995	1996	1997	1998	1999	2000
Bulgaria Bulgarie										
MF [I] [1]	...	...	814.7	731.1	589.7	505.2	512.8	497.4	534.0	536.7
M [I] [1]	...	...	421.3	392.0	305.9	268.6	271.9	269.2	288.0	288.0
F [I] [1]	...	...	393.4	339.1	283.8	236.6	240.9	228.2	245.9	278.6
MF [III] [3]	419.1	576.9	626.1	488.4	423.8	478.8	523.5	465.2	610.6	682.8
M [III] [3 19]	190.7	274.5	298.4	223.0	188.0	215.4	236.5	211.1	284.5	323.4
F [III] [3 20]	228.4	302.4	327.7	265.4	235.8	263.4	287.1	254.1	326.1	359.4
% MF [I] [1]	...	...	21.4	20.2	16.5	14.2	14.4	14.1	15.7	16.4
% M [I] [1]	...	...	20.9	20.2	16.2	14.2	14.3	14.3	15.8	16.5
% F [I] [1]	...	...	22.0	20.3	16.8	14.1	14.4	...	...	...
% MF [III] [3]	11.1	15.3	16.4	12.8	11.1	12.5	13.7	12.2	16.0	17.9
Burkina Faso Burkina Faso										
MF [III] [21]	34.8	29.8	29.6	26.6	13.9	13.5	9.2	9.4	7.5	6.6
M [III] [21]	30.4	25.9	24.9	24.0	11.8	11.0	7.6	7.8	6.2	5.4
F [III] [21]	4.4	3.9	4.6	2.7	2.1	2.5	1.6	1.6	1.4	1.2
Burundi Burundi										
MF [III] [22]	13.8	7.3	...	...	...	...	...	...	...	...
M [III] [22]	9.6	...	...	...	...	...	...	...	...	...
F [III] [22]	4.2	...	...	...	...	...	...	...	...	...
Canada Canada										
MF [I] [1 23 24]	1 491.7	1 640.2	1 648.8	1 540.7	1 422.1	1 469.2	1 413.5	1 305.1	1 190.1[18]	1 089.6
M [I] [1 23 24]	866.1	966.2	952.0	884.5	801.1	822.5	779.1	727.4	668.2[18]	600.0
F [I] [1 23 24]	625.6	674.0	696.8	656.2	621.0	646.7	634.3	577.7	521.9[18]	489.6
% MF [I] [1 23 24]	10.4	11.3	11.2	10.4	9.5	9.7	9.2	8.3	7.6[18]	6.8
% M [I] [1 23 24]	10.9	12.1	11.8	10.8	9.8	9.9	9.2	8.5	7.8[18]	6.9
% F [I] [1 23 24]	9.7	10.4	10.6	9.9	9.2	9.4	9.2	8.1	7.3[18]	6.7
Cape Verde Cap—Vert										
MF [III]	0.3	0.2	0.6	0.6	0.6	...	...	...	...	...
Central African Republic République centrafricaine										
MF [III] [25]	7.7	5.8	5.6	9.9	7.6	...	...	...	...	...
M [III] [25]	7.2	5.2	5.2	9.2	6.7	...	...	...	...	...
F [III] [25]	0.5	0.5	0.4	0.6	0.9	...	...	...	...	...
Chad Tchad										
MF [III]	4.4	...	16.3	...	...	...	...	...	...	...
M [III]	2.8	...	13.3	...	...	...	...	...	...	...
F [III]	0.1	...	2.9	...	...	...	...	...	...	...
Chile Chili										
MF [I] [1 26]	253.6	217.1	233.6	311.3	248.1	302.0[27]	303.6	419.2	529.1	489.4
M [I] [1 26]	168.6	132.1	147.6	193.9	158.4	180.9[27]	180.8	271.1	322.9	312.5
F [I] [1 26]	85.0	85.1	86.0	117.4	89.8	121.1[27]	122.8	148.1	206.2	176.9
% MF [I] [1 26]	5.3	4.4	4.5	5.9	4.7	5.4[27]	5.3	7.2	8.9	8.3
% M [I] [1 26]	5.1	4.1	4.2	5.4	4.4	4.8[27]	4.7	7.0	8.2	8.0
% F [I] [1 26]	5.8	5.6	5.1	6.8	5.3	6.7[27]	6.6	7.6	10.3	9.0
China Chine										
MF [IV] [3 28]	3 522.0	3 603.0	4 201.0	4 764.0	5 196.0	5 528.0	5 768.0	5 710.0	5 750.0	5 950.0
M [IV] [3 28 29]	1 207.0	1 298.0	1 394.0	1 258.0	...	2 637.0	2 737.0	2 705.0	...	...
F [IV] [3 28 29]	1 677.0	1 700.0	1 925.0	1 752.0	...	2 891.0	3 031.0	3 005.0	...	...
% MF [IV] [3 28]	2.3	2.3	2.6	2.8	2.9	3.0	3.0	3.1	3.1	3.1
% M [IV] [3 28 29]	0.8	...	0.9	0.8	...	...	...	...	...	...
% F [IV] [3 28 29]	1.1	...	1.2	1.1	...	...	...	...	...	...
China, Hong Kong SAR Chine, Hong Kong RAS										
MF [I] [1]	50.4[30]	54.7[30]	56.3[30]	56.2[30]	95.6[30]	88.8[30]	72.6[30]	155.4[30]	209.4[30]	168.3
M [I] [1]	33.8[30]	35.3[30]	35.8[30]	37.7[30]	62.3[30]	59.8[30]	46.3[30]	102.3[30]	142.1[30]	110.7
F [I] [1]	16.6[30]	19.4[30]	20.6[30]	18.6[30]	33.3[30]	29.0[30]	26.4[30]	53.1[30]	67.3[30]	57.6
% MF [I] [1]	1.8[30]	2.0[30]	2.0[30]	1.9[30]	3.2[30]	2.8[30]	2.2[30]	4.7[30]	6.3[30]	5.0
% M [I] [1]	1.9[30]	2.0[30]	2.0[30]	2.1[30]	3.4[30]	3.1[30]	2.3[30]	5.2[30]	7.2[30]	5.6
% F [I] [1]	1.6[30]	1.9[30]	1.9[30]	1.7[30]	2.9[30]	2.3[30]	2.0[30]	4.0[30]	4.9[30]	4.0
China, Macao SAR Chine, Macao RAS										
MF [I] [2]	5.33	3.8	3.7	4.4	6.7	8.7	6.5	9.6	13.8	14.5
M [I] [2]	2.63	2.1	2.2	2.4	4.3	5.4	4.2	6.6	9.4	9.9
F [I] [2]	2.73	1.8	1.5	2.0	2.4	3.3	2.3	3.1	4.4	4.7

30
Unemployment
Number (thousands) and percentage unemployed [*cont.*]
Chômage
Nombre (milliers) et pourcentage des chômeurs [*suite*]

Country or area [§] Pays ou zone [§]	1991	1992	1993	1994	1995	1996	1997	1998	1999	2000
% MF [I] [2]	3.03	2.2	2.1	2.5	3.6	4.3	3.2	4.6	6.4	6.8
% M [I] [2]	2.53	2.1	2.2	2.4	4.1	4.7	2.7	5.7	8.1	8.7
% F [I] [2]	3.73	2.4	2.0	2.6	3.0	3.7	2.5	3.3	4.4	4.6
Colombia　Colombie										
MF [I] [3 31 32 33]	522.0	505.3	447.0	442.3	521.9	735.2	782.1	998.3	1 415.4	1 526.0
M [I] [3 31 32 33]	225.9	204.0	174.0	163.3	230.2	336.3	353.5	457.2	649.8	660.2
F [I] [3 31 32 33]	296.1	301.3	273.1	279.0	291.7	398.9	428.6	541.1	765.6	865.8
% MF [I] [3 31 32 33]	9.8	9.2	7.8	7.6	8.7	12.0	12.1	15.0	20.1	20.5
% M [I] [3 31 32 33]	7.4	6.5	5.3	4.9	6.8	9.6	9.8	12.5	17.2	16.9
% F [I] [3 31 32 33]	13.1	12.6	11.0	11.2	11.3	15.1	15.1	18.0	23.3	24.5
Costa Rica　Costa Rica										
MF [I] [3 31]	59.1	44.0	46.9	49.4	63.5	75.9	74.3	76.5	83.3	71.9
M [I] [3 31]	35.5	26.4	28.9	28.7	39.1	45.3	43.5	40.6	45.6	41.2
F [I] [3 31]	23.5	17.6	18.0	20.7	24.4	30.6	30.8	36.0	37.7	30.8
% MF [I] [3 31]	5.5	4.1	4.1	4.2	5.2	6.2	5.7	5.6	6.0	5.2
% M [I] [3 31]	4.8	3.5	3.6	3.5	4.6	5.3	4.9	4.4	4.9	4.4
% F [I] [3 31]	7.4	5.4	5.3	5.8	6.5	8.3	7.5	8.0	8.2	6.9
Côte d'Ivoire　Côte d'Ivoire										
MF [III] [11 34]	136.9	114.9	...	...	...	...	...	...	...	...
M [III] [11 34]	...	88.2	...	...	...	...	...	...	...	...
F [III] [11 34]	...	26.7	...	...	...	...	...	...	...	...
Croatia　Croatie										
MF [I] [1]	...	...	...	...	...	170.2[3]	175.2[3]	198.5	234.0	297.2
M [I] [1]	...	...	...	...	...	88.3[3]	90.7[3]	100.9	117.4	149.8
F [I] [1]	...	...	...	...	...	82.0[3]	84.5[3]	97.5	116.6	147.4
MF [III]	254.0	267.0	251.0	243.0	241.0	261.0	278.0	288.0	322.0	358.0
M [III]	121.0	126.0	113.0	113.0	117.0	131.0	141.0	139.0	153.0	169.0
F [III]	133.0	141.0	138.0	130.0	124.0	130.0	137.0	149.0	169.0	189.0
% MF [I] [1]	...	...	...	...	...	10.0[3]	9.9[3]	11.4	13.5	16.1
% M [I] [1]	...	...	...	...	...	9.5[3]	9.5[3]	11.9	12.8	15.0
% F [I] [1]	...	...	...	...	...	10.5[3]	10.4[3]	12.1	14.5	17.3
% MF [III]	14.9	15.3	14.8	14.5	14.5	16.4	17.5	17.2	19.1	21.1
% M [III]	...	...	...	...	...	...	...	15.6	17.2	19.0
% F [III]	...	...	...	...	...	...	...	19.0	21.2	23.4
Cyprus　Chypre										
MF [I] [26 35 36]	...	...	...	...	...	...	...	...	16.9	14.5
M [I] [26 35 36]	...	...	...	...	...	...	...	...	7.7	5.5
F [I] [26 35 36]	...	...	...	...	...	...	...	...	9.1	8.9
% MF [III] [2 36]	8.3	5.2	7.6	8.0	7.9	9.4	10.4	10.4	11.4	10.9
% M [III] [2 36]	3.8	2.4	3.2	3.7	3.6	4.3	5.0	5.4	5.6	...
% F [III] [2 36]	4.5	2.8	4.4	4.3	4.3	5.1	5.4	5.0	5.8	...
% MF [I] [26 35 36]	...	...	...	...	...	...	...	...	5.7	4.9
% M [I] [26 35 36]	...	...	...	...	...	...	...	...	4.3	3.2
% F [I] [26 35 36]	...	...	...	...	...	...	...	...	7.9	7.4
% MF [III] [2 36]	3.0	1.8	2.7	2.7	2.6	3.1	3.4	3.3	3.6	...
% M [III] [2 36]	2.2	1.8	1.8	2.0	1.9	2.3	2.7	2.8	2.9	...
% F [III] [2 36]	4.4	2.6	4.1	3.9	3.7	4.3	4.5	4.2	4.8	...
Czech Republic　République tchèque										
MF [I] [1 26]	...	...	214.6[37]	222.4[37]	192.8[37]	210.3[37]	280.7[37]	379.6	470.4	430.4
M [I] [1 26]	...	...	93.5[37]	106.1[37]	90.2[37]	97.5[37]	122.7[37]	165.4	222.3	196.5
F [I] [1 26]	...	...	121.1[37]	116.3[37]	102.7[37]	112.8[37]	158.0[37]	214.3	248.1	233.9
MF [III] [3]	222.0	135.0	185.0	166.0	153.0	186.0	269.0	387.0	488.0	457.0
M [III] [3]	95.0	57.0	81.0	70.0	65.0	81.0	117.0	182.0	240.0	227.0
F [III] [3]	127.0	78.0	104.0	96.0	88.0	105.0	152.0	205.0	248.0	230.0
% MF [I] [1 26]	...	...	4.2[37]	4.3[37]	3.7[37]	4.1[37]	5.4[37]	7.3	9.0	8.3
% M [I] [1 26]	...	...	3.3[37]	3.7[37]	3.1[37]	3.4[37]	4.2[37]	5.7	7.6	6.8
% F [I] [1 26]	...	...	5.3[37]	5.1[37]	4.5[37]	4.9[37]	6.9[37]	9.3	10.7	10.2
% MF [III] [3]	4.1	2.6	3.5	3.2	2.9	3.5	5.2	7.5	9.4	8.8
% M [III] [3]	3.5	2.2	3.0	2.5	2.3	2.8	4.1	6.3	8.2	7.8
% F [III] [3]	4.8	3.0	4.1	4.0	3.6	4.3	6.7	9.0	10.8	10.0

30
Unemployment
Number (thousands) and percentage unemployed [*cont.*]
Chômage
Nombre (milliers) et pourcentage des chômeurs [*suite*]

Country or area [§] Pays ou zone [§]	1991	1992	1993	1994	1995	1996	1997	1998	1999	2000
Denmark Danemark										
MF [I] [26]	264.8[38]	261.8[38]	308.8[38]	222.0[39]	195.5[39]	194.5[39]	174.2[39]	155.3[39]	...	...
M [I] [26]	129.3[38]	127.9[38]	159.2[38]	107.0[39]	85.6[39]	87.6[39]	74.8[39]	68.5[39]	...	...
F [I] [26]	135.5[38]	134.0[38]	149.6[38]	115.0[39]	109.9[39]	107.0[39]	99.5[39]	86.9[39]	...	...
MF [III] [40]	296.1	318.3	348.8	343.4	288.4	245.6	220.2	182.7	158.2	150.5
M [III] [40]	137.2	148.8	168.6	163.9	134.1	115.8	99.4	81.0	72.8	68.5
F [III] [40]	158.9	169.5	180.2	179.6	154.3	129.8	120.8	101.8	85.4	82.0
% MF [I] [26] [39]	...	...	...	8.0	7.0	6.9	6.1	5.5	...	...
% M [I] [26] [39]	...	...	...	7.1	5.6	5.7	4.9	4.5	...	...
% F [I] [26] [39]	...	...	...	9.0	8.6	8.3	7.6	6.6	...	...
% MF [III] [40]	10.6	11.3	12.4	12.2	10.3	8.8	7.9	6.6	5.7	5.4
% M [III] [40]	9.2	10.0	11.3	11.0	9.0	7.8	6.7	5.5	4.9	4.6
% F [III] [40]	12.1	12.9	13.7	13.6	12.0	10.1	9.4	7.8	6.5	6.3
Dominican Republic République dominicaine										
MF [IV]	547.5[2]	611.8[2]	599.3[2]	456.6[2]	452.1[2]	505.7[4]	503.7[2]	...	...	...
M [IV]	229.7[2]	223.5[2]	217.9[2]	185.1[2]	187.3[2]	218.6[4]	199.0[2]	...	...	...
F [IV]	317.8[2]	388.3[2]	381.4[2]	271.6[2]	264.8[2]	287.2[4]	304.7[2]	...	...	...
% MF [IV]	19.7[2]	20.3[2]	19.9[2]	16.0[2]	15.8[2]	16.6[4]	15.9[2]	...	...	...
% M [IV]	12.5[2]	11.7[2]	11.4[2]	10.0[2]	10.2[2]	10.6[4]	9.5[2]	...	...	...
% F [IV]	33.1[2]	34.9[2]	34.8[2]	26.0[2]	26.2[2]	28.4[4]	28.6[2]	...	...	...
Ecuador Equateur [3 4 8]										
MF [I] [3 4 8]	158.0	263.2	240.8	207.2	212.7	334.6	311.6	409.3	...	...
M [I] [3 4 8]	69.0	105.3	108.6	101.8	104.2	156.1	143.4	174.5	...	...
F [I] [3 4 8]	89.1	157.9	132.3	105.4	108.4	178.5	168.3	233.8	...	...
% MF [I] [3 4 8]	5.8	8.9	8.3	7.1	6.9	10.4	9.2	11.5	...	...
% M [I] [3 4 8]	4.1	6.0	6.2	5.8	5.5	8.0	7.0	8.4	...	...
% F [I] [3 4 8]	8.5	13.2	11.5	9.3	8.8	14.0	12.7	16.0	...	...
Egypt Egypte										
MF [I]	1 463.4[3 41]	1 415.7[6 41]	1 800.6[6 41]	1 877.4[6 41]	1 916.9[6 41]	...	1 446.4[6 41]	1 447.5[6 35]	1 480.5[6 35]	...
M [I]	692.1[3 41]	768.1[6 41]	955.8[6 41]	963.3[6 41]	997.2[6 41]	...	701.5[6 41]	703.3[6 35]	726.2[6 35]	...
F [I]	771.3[3 41]	647.6[6 41]	844.8[6 41]	914.1[6 41]	919.7[6 41]	...	744.9[6 41]	744.5[6 35]	754.3[6 35]	...
% MF [I]	9.6[3 41]	9.0[6 41]	10.9[6 41]	11.0[6 41]	11.3[6 41]	...	8.4[6 41]	8.2[6 35]	8.1[6 35]	...
% M [I]	5.9[3 41]	6.4[6 41]	7.5[6 41]	7.4[6 41]	7.6[6 41]	...	5.2[6 41]	5.1[6 35]	5.1[6 35]	...
% F [I]	21.3[3 41]	17.0[6 41]	22.3[6 41]	22.8[6 41]	24.1[6 41]	...	19.8[6 41]	19.9[6 35]	19.4[6 35]	...
El Salvador El Salvador [4]										
MF [I] [4]	72.5[8]	81.0[8]	109.0	162.3	163.4	171.0	180.0	175.7	170.2	...
M [I] [4]	43.9[8]	47.5[8]	148.0	110.7	116.8	117.5	136.0	119.9	125.2	...
F [I] [4]	28.6[8]	33.5[8]	51.0	51.6	46.6	53.4	44.0	55.8	45.0	...
% MF [I] [4]	7.5[8]	7.9[8]	9.9	7.7	7.7	7.7	8.0	7.3	7.0	...
% M [I] [4]	8.3[8]	8.4[8]	11.8	8.4	8.7	8.4	9.5	8.2	8.5	...
% F [I] [4]	6.6[8]	7.2[8]	6.8	6.4	5.9	6.5	5.3	6.0	4.6	...
Estonia Estonie										
MF [I]	12.0[15]	29.1[15]	49.6[15]	56.7[15]	70.9[15]	71.9[15]	69.4[38]	70.2[38]	86.2[38]	96.5[38]
M [I]	6.1[15]	16.3[15]	26.0[15]	28.9[15]	40.6[15]	40.4[15]	37.9[38]	40.0[38]	49.6[38]	53.6[38]
F [I]	6.0[15]	12.8[15]	23.7[15]	27.8[15]	30.3[15]	31.6[15]	31.5[38]	30.2[38]	36.7[38]	42.8[38]
MF [III] [42]	0.9	14.9	16.3	15.3	15.6	17.3	...	18.8	44.0	46.3
M [III] [42]	0.3	7.5	7.5	6.4	5.1	5.2	...	...	...	...
F [III] [42]	0.6	7.4	8.8	8.9	10.5	12.1	...	...	...	...
% MF [I]	1.5[15]	3.7[15]	6.5[15]	7.6[15]	9.7[15]	10.0[15]	9.7[38]	9.9[38]	12.3[38]	13.7[38]
% M [I]	1.4[15]	3.9[15]	6.5[15]	7.3[15]	10.6[15]	10.7[15]	10.1[38]	10.8[38]	13.6[38]	14.6[38]
% F [I]	1.5[15]	3.4[15]	6.6[15]	7.9[15]	8.8[15]	9.2[15]	9.2[38]	8.9[38]	11.0[38]	12.7[38]
% MF [III] [42]	0.1	1.7	1.9	2.2	...	...	...	2.2	5.1	5.3
% M [III] [42]	0.1	1.6	1.7	...	...	...	...	...	...	...
% F [III] [42]	0.2	1.8	2.1	...	...	...	...	...	...	...
Ethiopia Ethiopie										
MF [III] [13]	44.3	70.9	62.9	64.7	37.5	44.9	34.6	29.5	25.7	...
M [III] [13]	24.9	52.0	40.4	37.5	14.0	16.6	19.1	16.6	14.3	...
F [III] [13]	19.4	18.8	22.6	27.2	23.5	28.3	15.4	12.9	11.4	...
Fiji Fidji										
MF [IV] [1]	15.0	14.2	15.8	16.1	15.4	...	...	...	...	...
% MF [IV] [1]	5.9	5.4	5.9	5.7	5.4	...	...	...	...	...

30
Unemployment
Number (thousands) and percentage unemployed [*cont.*]
Chômage
Nombre (milliers) et pourcentage des chômeurs [*suite*]

Country or area [§] Pays ou zone [§]	1991	1992	1993	1994	1995	1996	1997	1998	1999	2000
Finland Finlande										
MF [I] [38 43]	169.0	292.0	405.0	408.0	382.0	363.0	314.0	285.0	261.0	253.0
M [I] [38 43]	106.0	178.0	235.0	235.0	204.0	186.0	160.0	143.0	130.0	122.0
F [I] [38 43]	62.0	114.0	170.0	174.0	178.0	176.0	154.0	142.0	131.0	131.0
MF [III] [1 43 44]	181.0	319.0	436.0	467.0	451.0	434.0	398.0	362.0	337.0	321.0
M [III] [1 43 44]	108.0	186.0	245.0	257.0	244.0	231.0	207.0	183.0	169.0	162.0
F [III] [1 43 44]	73.0	133.0	191.0	210.0	207.0	203.0	191.0	179.0	168.0	159.0
% MF [I] [38 43]	6.6	11.6	16.2	16.4	15.2	14.4	12.5	11.3	10.1	9.7
% M [I] [38 43]	7.8	13.3	17.7	17.8	15.3	14.0	12.1	10.7	9.6	8.9
% F [I] [38 43]	5.1	9.6	14.4	14.9	15.1	14.8	13.0	11.9	10.7	10.6
France France										
MF [I] [1 3]	2 213.7	2 476.1	2 756.7	3 075.3	2 899.2	3 059.3	3 104.9	3 006.6	3 014.3	2 590.2
M [I] [1 3]	966.6	1 087.9	1 288.5	1 480.1	1 339.3	1 438.0	1 495.7	1 411.0	1 424.6	1 185.0
F [I] [1 3]	1 247.0	1 388.3	1 468.3	1 595.2	1 559.9	1 621.3	1 609.2	1 595.6	1 589.7	1 405.1
MF [III] [42 45]	2 709.1	2 911.2	3 172.0	3 329.2	2 976.2[46]	3 063.0	3 102.4	2 976.8	2 772.1	2 338.2
M [III] [42 45]	1 266.4	1 404.6	1 603.9	1 664.5	1 457.7[46]	1 519.8	1 545.7	1 464.1	1 357.5	1 129.5
F [III] [42 45]	1 442.7	1 506.6	1 568.1	1 664.7	1 518.5[46]	1 543.2	1 556.7	1 512.6	1 414.2	1 208.7
MF [IV] [1]	2 328.5	2 560.2	2 891.5	3 053.9	2 887.1	3 088.7	3 144.6	3 003.5	2 870.5	2 517.6
M [IV] [1]	1 022.5	1 150.8	1 377.8	1 456.3	1 343.4	1 470.6	1 514.3	1 417.4	1 345.5	1 142.7
F [IV] [1]	1 306.0	1 409.4	1 513.6	1 597.6	1 543.7	1 618.1	1 630.3	1 586.1	1 525.1	1 374.9
% MF [I] [1 3]	9.0	10.0	11.1	12.3	11.6	12.1	12.3	11.8	11.7	10.0
% M [I] [1 3]	7.0	7.9	9.4	10.7	9.7	10.3	10.8	10.2	10.2	8.4
% F [I] [1 3]	11.6	12.7	13.3	14.3	13.8	14.2	14.1	13.8	13.6	11.9
% MF [IV] [1]	9.3	10.2	11.5	12.1	11.4	12.1	12.3	11.7	11.0	9.6
% M [IV] [1]	7.3	8.2	9.9	10.4	9.6	10.4	10.7	10.0	9.4	8.0
% F [IV] [1]	12.0	12.8	13.6	14.2	13.7	14.2	14.2	13.7	13.0	11.6
French Guiana Guyane française										
MF [III] [42 47]	4.7	6.9	8.1	...	...	...	...	...	...	...
M [III] [42 47]	2.5	4.0	4.7	...	...	...	...	...	...	...
F [III] [42 47]	2.2	3.0	3.4	...	...	...	...	...	...	...
% MF [III] [42 47]	9.7	...	...	...	...	...	...	...	...	...
% M [III] [42 47]	8.2	...	...	...	...	...	...	...	...	...
% F [III] [42 47]	11.6	...	...	...	...	...	...	...	...	...
French Polynesia Polynésie française										
MF [III] [2]	0.6	...	...	...	...	...	...	3.8	...	...
Georgia Géorgie										
MF [I] [1]	...	...	...	...	...	...	...	291.0	277.5	212.2
M [I] [1]	...	...	...	...	...	...	...	159.7	160.1	116.7
F [I] [1]	...	...	...	...	...	...	...	131.3	117.4	95.5
% MF [I] [1]	...	...	...	...	...	...	...	14.5	13.8	10.8
% M [I] [1]	...	...	...	...	...	...	...	15.4	15.3	11.1
% F [I] [1]	...	...	...	...	...	...	...	13.9	12.2	10.5
Germany Allemagne										
MF [I] [1 3]	2 642.0	3 186.0	3 799.0	4 160.0	4 035.0	3 473.0	3 890.0	3 849.0	3 503.0	3 127.0
M [I] [1 3]	1 251.0	1 422.0	1 792.0	2 051.0	1 991.0	1 858.0	2 083.0	2 074.0	1 905.0	1 691.0
F [I] [1 3]	1 392.0	1 764.0	2 007.0	2 110.0	2 044.0	1 614.0	1 806.0	1 775.0	1 598.0	1 436.0
MF [III] [3 35]	...	2 894.2	3 447.1	3 493.3	3 521.0	3 848.4	4 308.1	3 965.4	3 943.0	3 685.0
M [III] [3 35]	...	1 344.6	1 672.3	1 721.2	1 764.9	1 996.1	2 220.5	2 046.8	2 013.0	1 899.0
F [III] [3 35]	...	1 549.6	1 774.8	1 772.1	1 756.1	1 852.3	2 087.6	1 918.6	1 930.0	1 786.0
% MF [I] [1 3]	6.6	7.9	9.5	10.3	10.1	8.8	9.8	9.7	8.8	7.9
% M [I] [1 3]	5.4	6.2	7.8	8.9	8.7	8.2	9.2	9.2	8.4	7.6
% F [I] [1 3]	8.2	10.3	11.7	12.3	11.9	9.6	10.6	10.4	9.2	8.3
% MF [III] [3 35]	...	8.2	9.9	10.0	10.2	11.2	12.5	11.4	11.2	10.0
% M [III] [3 35]	...	...	...	...	9.2	10.4	11.6	10.7	10.5	9.6
% F [III] [3 35]	...	...	...	...	11.4	12.1	13.5	12.2	12.0	10.4
Ghana Ghana										
MF [III] [48]	30.7	30.6	39.4	37.0	40.5	...	...	...	...	...
M [III] [48]	27.5	27.5	36.2	34.5	...	...	...	...	...	...
F [III] [48]	3.3	3.1	3.2	2.4	...	...	...	...	...	...

30
Unemployment
Number (thousands) and percentage unemployed [*cont.*]
Chômage
Nombre (milliers) et pourcentage des chômeurs [*suite*]

Country or area § Pays ou zone §	1991	1992	1993	1994	1995	1996	1997	1998	1999	2000
Gibraltar Gibraltar										
MF [III] [49]	0.9	1.8	2.1	2.4	2.1	1.9	1.7	0.5	...	...
M [III] [49]	0.7	1.3	1.4	1.5	1.3	1.2	1.1	0.3	...	...
F [III] [49]	0.2	0.5	0.8	0.9	0.8	0.7	0.6	0.2	...	...
Greece Grèce										
MF [I] [26]	301.1[2]	349.8[2]	398.2[2]	403.8[2]	424.7[2]	446.4[2]	440.4[2]	478.5[1]	523.4[1]	491.1[1]
M [I] [26]	120.8[2]	137.9[2]	164.5[2]	170.4[2]	176.1[2]	167.1[2]	173.0[2]	188.8[1]	201.8[1]	193.4[1]
F [I] [26]	180.3[2]	211.9[2]	233.7[2]	233.4[2]	248.6[2]	279.3[2]	267.3[2]	289.8[1]	321.6[1]	297.7[1]
MF [III] [1]	173.2	184.7	175.9	179.8	...	...	...	...	...	...
M [III] [1]	83.9	89.7	87.9	87.3	...	...	...	...	...	...
F [III] [1]	89.3	95.0	87.9	92.4	...	...	...	...	...	...
% MF [I] [26]	7.7[2]	8.7[2]	9.7[2]	9.6[2]	10.0[2]	10.3[2]	10.3[2]	10.8[1]	11.7[1]	11.1[1]
% M [I] [26]	4.8[2]	5.4[2]	6.4[2]	6.5[2]	6.7[2]	6.3[2]	6.6[2]	7.0[1]	7.6[1]	7.3[1]
% F [I] [26]	12.9[2]	14.2[2]	15.2[2]	14.9[2]	15.4[2]	16.6[2]	15.9[2]	16.5[1]	17.9[1]	16.7[1]
% MF [III] [1]	7.3	7.6	7.1	7.2	...	...	...	...	...	...
Greenland Groenland										
MF [III]	1.7	1.9	1.8	1.8	2.0	2.0	1.9	...	...	...
Guadeloupe Guadeloupe										
MF [III] [42]	34.3[3]	...	38.8	42.9	...	...	...	...	...	...
Guam Guam										
MF [I] [42]	1.7	1.8	2.6	...	...	...	...	...	...	...
% MF [I] [42]	3.5	3.9	5.5	...	...	...	...	...	...	...
Guatemala Guatemala										
MF [III] [4 50]	1.7	1.6	1.0	1.3	1.4	...	...	...	...	...
M [III] [4 50]	1.0	1.1	0.7	0.9	0.9	...	...	...	...	...
F [III] [4 50]	0.7	0.5	0.3	0.4	0.5	...	...	...	...	...
Honduras Honduras										
MF [I] [3 4]	72.1	53.9	...	...	59.1	89.4	69.4	87.7	89.3	...
M [I] [3 4]	46.0	37.8	...	...	40.3	58.9	45.4	55.5	56.7	...
F [I] [3 4]	26.1	16.1	...	...	18.8	30.4	23.9	32.2	32.6	...
% MF [I] [3 4]	4.6	3.1	...	...	3.2	4.3	3.2	3.9	3.7	...
% M [I] [3 4]	4.2	3.2	...	...	3.1	4.2	3.2	3.8	3.7	...
% F [I] [3 4]	5.6	3.0	...	...	3.4	4.4	3.2	4.2	3.8	...
Hungary Hongrie										
MF [I] [38]	...	444.2	518.9	451.2	416.5	400.1	348.8	313.0	284.7	262.5
M [I] [38]	...	265.9	316.0	274.8	261.5	243.7	214.1	189.2	170.7	159.5
F [I] [38]	...	178.3	202.9	176.4	155.0	156.4	134.7	123.8	114.0	103.0
MF [III] [3]	406.1[51]	663.0[51]	632.1[51]	519.6[51]	495.9	477.5	464.0	404.1	404.5	372.4
M [III] [3]	239.0[51]	390.0[51]	376.1[51]	302.6[51]	285.3	275.4	...	...	...	...
F [III] [3]	167.1[51]	273.0[51]	256.0[51]	217.0[51]	210.6	202.1	...	...	...	...
% MF [I] [38]	...	9.8	11.9	10.7	10.2	9.9	8.7	7.8	7.0	6.4
% M [I] [38]	...	10.7	13.2	11.8	10.7	10.7	9.5	8.5	7.5	7.0
% F [I] [38]	...	8.7	10.4	9.4	8.7	8.8	7.8	7.0	6.3	5.6
% MF [III] [3]	8.5[51]	12.3[51]	12.1[51]	10.4[51]	12.0	10.7	10.4	9.6	9.6	...
% M [III] [3 51]	9.2	14.0	14.2	11.7	...	...	...	...	...	...
% F [III] [3 51]	7.6	10.5	10.1	8.9	...	...	...	...	...	...
Iceland Islande										
MF [I] [6 52]	3.6	6.2	7.6	7.7	7.2	5.5	5.7	4.2	3.1	3.7
M [I] [6 52]	1.7	2.9	3.8	4.0	3.8	2.7	2.6	1.8	1.2	1.5
F [I] [6 52]	1.9	3.2	3.8	3.8	3.4	2.8	3.1	2.3	1.9	2.2
MF [III] [42]	1.9	3.9	5.6	6.2	6.5	5.8	5.2	3.8	2.6	1.9
M [III] [42]	1.0	1.9	2.7	2.9	3.1	2.5	2.0	1.4	1.0	0.7
F [III] [42]	0.9	1.9	2.9	3.4	3.5	3.3	3.2	2.4	1.6	1.1
% MF [I] [6 52]	2.5	4.3	5.3	5.3	4.9	3.7	3.9	2.7	2.0	2.3
% M [I] [6 52]	2.3	3.8	5.0	5.1	4.8	3.4	3.3	2.3	1.5	1.8
% F [I] [6 52]	2.9	4.9	5.6	5.5	4.9	4.1	4.5	3.3	2.6	2.9
% MF [III] [42]	1.5	3.0	4.3	4.8	5.0	4.3	3.9	2.8	1.9	1.3
% M [III] [42]	1.3	2.6	3.6	3.9	4.1	3.2	2.6	1.8	...	...
% F [III] [42]	1.7	3.6	5.4	6.1	6.2	5.8	5.6	5.5	...	...

30
Unemployment
Number (thousands) and percentage unemployed [*cont.*]
Chômage
Nombre (milliers) et pourcentage des chômeurs [*suite*]

Country or area § Pays ou zone §	1991	1992	1993	1994	1995	1996	1997	1998	1999	2000
India Inde										
MF [III] [2 3]	36 300.0	36 758.4	36 275.5	36 691.5	36 742.3	37 430.0	39 140.0	40 090.0	40 371.0	...
M [III] [2 3]	28 992.0	29 105.0	28 410.0	28 647.0	28 722.0	29 050.0	30 107.0	30 563.0	30 438.0	...
F [III] [2 3]	7 308.0	7 653.0	7 865.0	8 045.0	8 020.0	8 380.0	9 033.0	9 526.0	9 933.0	...
Indonesia Indonésie										
MF [I] [3]	2 032.4[4]	2 198.8[4]	...	...	...	3 624.8[4]	4 197.3[1]	5 062.5[1]	6 030.3[1]	5 872.0[1]
M [I] [3 4]	1 147.3	1 292.1	...	...	...	1 851.8	...	2 862.2[1]	...	...
F [I] [3 4]	885.1	906.7	...	...	...	1 773.0	...	2 200.3[1]	...	...
MF [III] [1]	782.9	814.9	754.1	1 198.3	953.2	1 041.8	1 542.2	1 191.7	...	...
% MF [I] [3]	...	...	...	...	...	4.0[4]	4.7[1]	5.5[1]	...	...
% M [I] [3 4]	...	...	...	...	...	3.3	...	...	...	...
% F [I] [3 4]	...	...	...	...	...	5.1	...	...	...	...
Ireland Irlande										
MF [I] [1 6]	198.5	206.6	220.1	211.0	177.4	179.0	159.0	126.6	96.9	...
M [I] [1 6]	124.9	132.3	138.6	131.9	110.4	109.8	97.1	78.8	59.4	...
F [I] [1 6]	73.6	74.4	81.4	79.1	67.1	69.1	62.0	47.8	37.5	...
MF [III] [42]	254.0	283.1	294.3	282.4	276.9	279.2	254.4	227.1	192.2	...
M [III] [42]	170.5	187.2	193.8	184.4	178.5	175.6	155.8	135.7	112.7	...
F [III] [42]	83.5	96.0	100.5	98.0	99.3	103.6	98.5	91.4	79.5	...
% MF [I] [1 6]	14.7	15.1	15.7	14.7	12.2	11.9	10.3	7.8	5.7	...
% M [I] [1 6]	14.2	15.0	15.6	14.7	12.1	11.9	10.4	8.1	5.9	...
% F [I] [1 6]	15.5	15.2	15.8	14.8	12.2	11.9	10.3	7.4	5.5	...
% MF [III] [42]	19.0	...	16.7	15.1	14.1	11.8	10.1	7.6	5.8	...
Isle of Man Ile de Man										
MF [III]	1.0	1.4	1.7	1.6	1.5	1.2	0.7	0.4	0.3	0.2
M [III]	0.7	1.0	1.2	1.2	1.1	0.9	0.5	0.3	0.2	0.2
F [III]	0.3	0.4	0.4	0.4	0.4	0.3	0.2	0.1	0.1	0.1
% MF [III]	3.0[53]	4.3	4.9	4.7	4.4	3.4	...	...	0.8	0.6
% M [III]	3.9[53]	5.4	...	...	...	4.4	...	...	1.0	0.8
% F [III]	1.9[53]	2.7	...	...	...	2.1	...	...	0.5	0.4
Israel Israël										
MF [I] [1 54]	187.4[55]	207.5[55]	194.9[55]	158.3[55]	145.0	144.1	169.8	193.4[18]	208.5	213.8
M [I] [1 54]	89.9[55]	99.7[55]	96.2[55]	71.7[55]	66.6	70.8	84.6	100.4[18]	108.8	111.7
F [I] [1 54]	97.5[55]	107.8[55]	98.7[55]	86.6[55]	78.4	73.3	85.2	93.0[18]	99.7	102.1
% MF [I] [1 54]	10.6[55]	11.2[55]	10.0[55]	7.8[55]	6.9	6.7	7.7	8.5[18]	8.9	8.8
% M [I] [1 54]	8.6[55]	9.2[55]	8.5[55]	6.2[55]	5.6	5.8	6.8	8.0[18]	8.5	8.4
% F [I] [1 54]	13.4[55]	13.9[55]	12.1[55]	10.0[55]	8.6	7.8	8.8	9.2[18]	9.4	9.2
Italy Italie										
MF [I]	2 653.0[2]	2 799.0[2]	2 299.0[1 18]	2 508.0[1]	2 638.0[1]	2 653.0[1]	2 688.0[1]	2 745.0[1]	2 669.0[1]	2 495.0[1]
M [I]	1 142.0[2]	1 226.0[2]	1 094.0[1 18]	1 234.0[1]	1 280.0[1]	1 286.0[1]	1 294.0[1]	1 313.0[1]	1 266.0[1]	1 179.0[1]
F [I]	1 511.0[2]	1 572.0[2]	1 205.0[1 18]	1 274.0[1]	1 358.0[1]	1 367.0[1]	1 394.0[1]	1 431.0[1]	1 404.0[1]	1 316.0[1]
% MF [I]	10.9[2]	11.4[2]	9.8[1 18]	10.7[1]	11.3[1]	11.4[1]	11.5[1]	11.7[1]	11.4[1]	10.5[1]
% M [I]	7.5[2]	7.9[2]	7.6[1 18]	8.6[1]	8.9[1]	8.9[1]	9.0[1]	9.1[1]	8.8[1]	8.1[1]
% F [I]	16.8[2]	17.2[2]	13.5[1 18]	14.3[1]	15.2[1]	15.3[1]	15.6[1]	16.0[1]	15.7[1]	14.5[1]
Jamaica Jamaïque										
MF [I] [2]	168.7	169.2	176.7	167.4	186.7	183.0	186.9	175.0	...	...
M [I] [2]	54.2	54.1	62.1	54.9	66.9	61.3	64.8	61.4	...	...
F [I] [2]	114.5	115.2	114.6	112.5	119.8	121.7	122.1	113.5	...	...
% MF [I] [2]	15.7	15.4	16.3	15.4	16.2	16.0	...	...	...	...
% M [I] [2]	9.4	9.4	10.9	9.6	10.8	9.9	...	...	...	...
% F [I] [2]	22.8	22.2	22.4	21.8	22.5	23.0	...	...	...	...
Japan Japon										
MF [I] [1]	1 360.0	1 420.0	1 660.0	1 920.0	2 100.0	2 250.0	2 300.0	2 790.0	3 170.0	3 200.0
M [I] [1]	780.0	820.0	950.0	1 120.0	1 230.0	1 340.0	1 350.0	1 680.0	1 940.0	1 960.0
F [I] [1]	590.0	600.0	710.0	800.0	870.0	910.0	950.0	1 110.0	1 230.0	1 230.0
% MF [I] [1]	2.1	2.2	2.5	2.9	3.2	3.4	3.4	4.1	4.7	4.7
% M [I] [1]	2.0	2.1	2.4	2.8	3.1	3.4	3.4	4.2	4.8	4.9
% F [I] [1]	2.2	2.2	2.6	3.0	3.2	3.3	3.4	4.0	4.5	4.5
Kazakhstan Kazakhstan										
MF [III] [11]	6.0	34.0	40.5	70.1	139.6	282.4	257.5	251.9	251.4	...
M [III] [11]	2.0	9.0	12.1	24.7	55.7	104.0	86.0	95.5	102.0	...
F [III] [11]	4.0	25.0	28.4	45.4	83.9	178.4	171.5	156.4	149.4	...

30
Unemployment
Number (thousands) and percentage unemployed [*cont.*]
Chômage
Nombre (milliers) et pourcentage des chômeurs [*suite*]

Country or area [§] Pays ou zone [§]	1991	1992	1993	1994	1995	1996	1997	1998	1999	2000
MF [IV]	6.0	70.5	78.1	170.0	203.2	391.7	382.8	382.0	264.0	...
M [IV]	1.0	21.0	...	103.8	88.5	156.6	139.5	161.9	117.0	...
F [IV]	5.0	19.0	...	66.2	114.7	235.1	243.3	220.1	147.0	...
% MF [III] [11]	0.1	0.4	0.6	1.1	2.1	4.2	3.8	3.7	3.9	...
% M [III] [11]	...	...	...	0.7	1.6	2.9	2.4	2.6	...	...
% F [III] [11]	...	...	...	1.4	2.7	5.6	5.5	5.0	...	...
% MF [IV]	...	...	...	7.5	11.0	13.0	13.0	13.7		
Korea, Republic of Corée, République de										
MF [I] [1 56]	438.0	466.0	551.0	490.0	420.0	426.0	556.0	1 461.0	1 353.0	889.0
M [I] [1 56]	289.0	306.0	376.0	335.0	280.0	291.0	352.0	983.0	911.0	597.0
F [I] [1 56]	149.0	161.0	175.0	155.0	140.0	135.0	204.0	478.0	442.0	293.0
% MF [I] [1 56]	2.3	2.4	2.8	2.4	2.0	2.0	2.6	6.8	6.3	4.1
% M [I] [1 56]	2.5	2.6	3.2	2.7	2.3	2.3	2.8	7.6	7.1	4.6
% F [I] [1 56]	1.9	2.1	2.2	1.9	1.7	1.6	2.3	5.6	5.1	3.3
Kuwait Koweït										
MF [III] [11]	...	...	...	...	...	...	8.6	8.9	...	...
M [III] [11]	...	...	...	...	...	...	7.2	7.3	...	...
F [III] [11]	...	...	...	...	...	...	1.4	1.6	...	...
Kyrgyzstan Kirghizistan										
MF [III]	...	1.8	2.9	12.6	50.4	77.2	54.6	55.9	54.7	...
M [III]	...	0.5	0.9	4.9	20.5	32.5	22.7	22.6	24.2	...
F [III]	...	1.3	2.0	7.7	29.9	44.7	31.9	33.3	30.6	...
Latvia Lettonie										
MF [I] [3]	...	...	...	...	227.0[15]	216.7[1]	171.2[1]	160.6[1]	167.3[1]	165.1[1]
M [I] [3]	...	...	...	...	126.5[15]	117.9[1]	88.0[1]	82.9[1]	94.4[1]	91.2[1]
F [I] [3]	...	...	...	...	100.5[15]	98.8[1]	83.2[1]	77.7[1]	72.9[1]	73.9[1]
MF [III] [11]	...	31.3	76.7	83.9	83.2	90.8	84.9	111.4	109.5	93.3
M [III] [11]	...	12.9	35.9	40.4	39.7	41.1	34.5	46.2	46.7	39.5
F [III] [11]	...	18.4	40.8	43.6	43.5	49.7	50.4	65.2	62.8	53.8
% MF [I] [3]	...	...	...	...	18.9[15]	18.3[1]	14.4[1]	13.8[1]	14.5[1]	14.6[1]
% M [I] [3]	...	...	...	...	19.7[15]	18.9[1]	14.3[1]	13.5[1]	15.5[1]	15.6[1]
% F [I] [3]	...	...	...	...	18.0[15]	17.7[1]	14.6[1]	14.1[1]	13.3[1]	13.5[1]
% MF [III] [11]	...	2.3	5.8	6.5	6.6	7.2	7.0	9.2	9.1	7.8
% M [III] [11]	...	1.8	5.2	6.1	6.1	6.4	5.6	7.5	7.6	6.5
% F [III] [11]	...	2.8	6.4	6.9	7.0	8.1	8.5	11.0	10.7	9.2
Lebanon Liban										
MF [IV]	...	...	...	...	...	...	116.1	...	...	...
Lithuania Lituanie										
MF [I]	...	...	...	347.2[2]	347.1[2]	317.4[2]	257.2[2]	244.9[2]	263.3[2]	275.7[1]
M [I]	...	...	...	...	...	155.4[2]	137.1[2]	137.2[2]	150.3[2]	159.0[1]
F [I]	...	...	...	...	...	162.0[2]	120.1[2]	107.7[2]	113.0[2]	116.7[1]
MF [III] [11]	4.8	66.5	65.5	78.0	127.7	109.4	120.2	122.8	177.4	225.9
M [III] [11]	...	38.1	33.5	36.7	57.4	49.8	58.3	61.7	94.6	123.1
F [III] [11]	...	28.4	32.0	41.3	70.3	59.6	61.9	61.1	82.8	102.8
% MF [I]	...	...	...	17.4[2]	17.1[2]	16.4[2]	14.1[2]	13.3[2]	14.1[2]	15.4[1]
% M [I]	...	...	...	...	...	...	14.2[2]	14.3[2]	15.6[2]	17.3[1]
% F [I]	...	...	...	...	...	...	13.9[2]	12.2[2]	12.6[2]	13.3[1]
% MF [III] [11]	0.3	3.5	3.5	4.5	7.3	6.2	6.7	6.5	10.0	12.6
% M [III] [11]	...	4.3	3.7	4.4	6.6	5.7	6.6	6.5	10.6	13.5
% F [III] [11]	...	2.8	3.3	4.5	8.1	6.7	6.9	7.0	9.3	11.6
Luxembourg Luxembourg										
MF [III] [57]	2.3	2.7	3.5	4.6	5.1	5.7	6.4[58]	5.5	5.4	5.0
M [III] [57]	1.4	1.6	2.0	2.8	2.9	3.2	3.6[58]	2.9	2.8	2.6
F [III] [57]	0.9	1.2	1.5	1.9	2.2	2.5	2.8[58]	2.6	2.5	2.3
% MF [III] [57]	1.4	1.6	2.1	2.7	3.0	3.3	3.3[58]	3.1	2.9	2.7
Madagascar Madagascar										
MF [III] [3 59]	9.3	6.2	5.3	3.6	3.3	...	...	...	...	...
Malaysia Malaisie										
MF [I] [35]	...	271.2	316.8	...	248.1	216.8	214.9	284.0	313.7	294.4
MF [III] [1]	48.6	45.2	35.6	26.8	24.0	23.3	23.1	33.4	31.8	...
% MF [I] [35]	...	3.7	3.0	...	2.8	2.5	2.5	3.2	3.4	3.1

30
Unemployment
Number (thousands) and percentage unemployed [*cont.*]
Chômage
Nombre (milliers) et pourcentage des chômeurs [*suite*]

Country or area [§] Pays ou zone [§]	1991	1992	1993	1994	1995	1996	1997	1998	1999	2000
Malta Malte										
MF [III] [3 60]	4.9	5.5	6.2	5.6	5.2	6.2	7.1	7.4	7.7	...
M [III] [3 60]	4.0	4.5	5.3	4.8	4.4	5.2	6.0	6.4	6.6	...
F [III] [3 60]	0.9	1.1	0.9	0.8	0.8	1.1	1.1	1.0	1.1	...
% MF [III] [3 60]	3.6	4.0	4.5	4.1	3.7	4.4	5.0	5.1	5.3	...
% M [III] [3 60]	4.0	4.4	5.2	4.8	4.3	5.0	5.8	6.1	6.3	...
% F [III] [3 60]	2.6	3.0	2.5	2.2	2.3	2.9	2.8	2.5	2.6	...
Mauritius Maurice										
MF [I] [31]	...	...	...	...	47.6	...	...	...	...	...
M [I] [31]	...	...	...	...	25.5	...	...	...	...	...
F [I] [31]	...	...	...	...	22.1	...	...	...	...	...
MF [III] [1 61]	10.6	7.9	6.7	6.6	8.5	10.4	10.7	10.7	12.1	18.0
M [III] [1 61]	5.2	3.4	2.6	2.5	3.4	4.5	4.6	4.6	5.3	8.6
F [III] [1 61]	5.4	4.6	4.1	4.2	5.0	5.9	6.0	6.1	6.8	9.5
% MF [I] [31]	...	...	...	...	9.8	...	...	...	...	...
% M [I] [31]	...	...	...	...	7.8	...	...	...	...	...
% F [I] [31]	...	...	...	...	13.9	...	...	...	...	...
Mexico Mexique										
MF [I] [26 31]	694.9	...	819.1	...	1 677.4	1 354.7	984.9	889.6	682.3	650.0
M [I] [26 31]	373.1	...	495.4	...	1 100.2	860.7	544.7	513.0	387.2	400.9
F [I] [26 31]	321.8	...	323.7	...	577.2	494.0	440.2	376.6	295.1	249.1
% MF [I] [26 31]	2.2	...	2.4	...	4.7	3.7	2.6	2.3	1.7	1.6
% M [I] [26 31]	1.7	...	2.1	...	4.6	3.5	2.1	2.0	1.5	1.5
% F [I] [26 31]	3.4	...	3.1	...	5.0	4.1	3.4	2.8	2.2	1.8
Mongolia Mongolie										
MF [III] [11]	...	...	...	...	...	...	...	48.3	...	...
M [III] [11]	...	...	...	...	...	...	...	22.7	...	...
F [III] [11]	...	...	...	...	...	...	...	25.6	...	...
% MF [III] [11]	...	...	...	...	...	...	...	5.7	...	...
% M [III] [11]	...	...	...	...	...	...	...	5.2	...	...
% F [III] [11]	...	...	...	...	...	...	...	6.3	...	...
Morocco Maroc										
MF [I] [1 8]	695.5	649.9	680.8	...	1 111.7	871.2	844.7	969.2	1 161.8	...
M [I] [1 8]	459.3	400.7	469.1	...	631.5	568.1	574.8	676.1	808.2	...
F [I] [1 8]	236.2	249.2	211.7	...	480.2	303.1	269.9	293.0	353.6	...
% MF [I] [1 8]	17.3	16.0	15.9	...	22.9	18.1	16.9	19.1	22.0	...
% M [I] [1 8]	15.3	13.0	14.2	...	18.7	16.1	15.3	17.5	20.3	...
% F [I] [1 8]	23.3	25.3	21.7	...	32.2	23.6	21.8	24.4	27.6	...
Myanmar Myanmar										
MF [III] [62]	559.0	502.6	518.2	541.5	...	...	535.3	451.5	425.3	
Netherlands Pays–Bas										
MF [I] [35 63]	490.0	386.0	437.0	493.0	523.0	489.0	422.0	337.0	277.0	262.0
M [I] [35 63]	226.0	181.0	217.0	254.0	255.0	228.0	196.0	155.0	124.0	118.0
F [I] [35 63]	264.0	205.0	220.0	239.0	268.0	262.0	227.0	181.0	153.0	144.0
MF [III] [35 63]	319.0	336.0	415.0	486.0	464.0	440.0	375.0	286.0	221.5	187.0
M [III] [35 63]	187.0	195.0	241.0	283.0	260.0	240.0	199.0	156.0	...	...
F [III] [35 63]	132.0	141.0	174.0	203.0	204.0	201.0	176.0	132.0	...	...
% MF [I] [35 63]	7.0	5.5	6.2	6.8	7.1	6.6	5.5	4.4	3.5	3.3
% M [I] [35 63]	5.3	4.3	5.2	6.0	5.9	5.3	4.5	3.5	2.8	2.6
% F [I] [35 63]	9.5	7.3	7.6	8.1	8.8	8.4	7.0	5.5	4.5	4.2
% MF [III] [35]	5.4	5.3	6.5	7.5	7.0	6.6	5.5	4.1	3.2	2.6
% M [III] [35]	4.9	4.9	6.0	7.0	6.4	5.9	4.8	...	...	...
% F [III] [35]	6.3	6.1	7.3	8.3	8.1	7.8	6.5	...	...	...
Netherlands Antilles Antilles néerlandaises										
MF [I] [1 65]	8.6	8.2	8.2	8.0	8.2	9.3	10.1	10.5	...	8.5
M [I] [1 65]	3.8	3.5	3.8	3.7	3.3	3.7	4.3	4.7	...	3.7
F [I] [1 65]	4.7	4.8	4.4	4.3	4.9	5.6	5.8	5.8	...	4.8
% MF [I] [1 65]	14.6	13.9	13.6	12.8	13.1	14.0	15.3	16.6	...	14.0
% M [I] [1 65]	11.7	10.5	11.4	11.0	9.9	10.5	12.4	13.7	...	12.0
% F [I] [1 65]	18.1	17.9	16.2	15.0	17.0	10.1	10.4	19.2	...	16.2
New Caledonia Nouvelle–Calédonie										
MF [III] [42]	6.3	6.6	6.8	7.4	7.4	7.7	7.9	8.3	8.8	9.4

30
Unemployment
Number (thousands) and percentage unemployed [*cont.*]
Chômage
Nombre (milliers) et pourcentage des chômeurs [*suite*]

Country or area [§] Pays ou zone [§]	1991	1992	1993	1994	1995	1996	1997	1998	1999	2000
New Zealand Nouvelle–Zélande										
MF [I] [1]	167.6	169.8	158.8	140.4	111.5	112.3	123.3	139.1	127.8	113.4
M [I] [1]	99.8	101.1	94.0	81.7	61.8	61.9	67.9	77.4	72.4	63.4
F [I] [1]	67.7	68.7	64.8	58.6	49.7	50.4	55.5	61.8	55.4	50.0
MF [III] [48 6]	196.0	216.9	212.7	186.5	157.7	154.0	168.9	193.9[3]	213.8[3]	...
M [III] [48 66]	135.9	149.8	143.2	124.1	103.1	100.0	107.3	121.8[3]	126.3[3]	...
F [III] [48 66]	60.1	67.1	69.4	62.4	54.6	54.0	61.6	68.0[3]	87.5[3]	...
% MF [I] [1]	10.3	10.3	9.5	8.1	6.3	6.1	6.6	7.5	6.8	6.0
% M [I] [1]	10.9	10.9	10.0	8.5	6.2	6.1	6.6	7.6	7.0	6.1
% F [I] [1]	9.5	9.6	8.9	7.7	6.3	6.1	6.7	7.4	6.5	5.8
Nicaragua Nicaragua										
MF [IV] [4]	194.2	...	...	...	244.7	225.1	208.4	215.5	185.1	178.0
M [IV] [4]	104.8	...	...	...	162.3	149.2	138.2	142.9	122.8	118.0
F [IV] [4]	89.4	...	...	...	82.4	75.9	70.2	72.6	62.3	60.0
% MF [IV] [4]	14.0	...	...	...	16.9	14.9	13.3	13.3	10.9	9.8
% M [IV] [4]	11.3	...	...	...	15.9	14.0	12.6	8.8	...	...
% F [IV] [4]	19.4	...	...	...	19.3	17.1	14.8	14.5	...	...
Nigeria Nigéria										
MF [III] [1]	60.2	64.0	68.6	...	...	...	...	...	...	...
Norway Norvège										
MF [I] [52]	116.0	126.0	127.0	116.0	107.0	108.0	92.0	74.0	75.0	81.0
M [I] [52]	68.0	76.0	77.0	70.0	61.0	58.0	49.0	40.0	42.0	46.0
F [I] [52]	48.0	50.0	50.0	46.0	46.0	50.0	44.0	35.0	33.0	35.0
MF [III] [42]	100.7	114.4	118.1	110.3	102.2	90.9	73.5	56.0	59.6[18]	62.6
M [III] [42]	62.8	71.0	73.3	65.7	57.7	50.4	39.9	29.8	33.5[18]	36.3
F [III] [42]	37.9	43.3	44.8	44.5	44.5	40.6	33.6	26.2	26.0[18]	26.4
% MF [I] [52]	5.5	5.9	6.0	5.4	4.9	4.8	4.0	3.2	3.2	3.4
% M [I] [52]	5.9	6.5	6.6	6.0	5.2	4.8	3.9	3.2	3.4	3.6
% F [I] [52]	5.0	5.1	5.2	4.7	4.6	4.9	4.2	3.3	3.0	3.2
% MF [III] [42]	4.7	5.4	5.5	5.2	4.7	4.2	3.3	2.4	2.6[18]	2.7
% M [III] [42]	5.3	6.1	6.3	5.6	4.9	4.1	...	...	...	...
% F [III] [42]	3.9	4.5	4.7	4.5	4.5	3.9	...	...	...	...
Pakistan Pakistan										
MF [I] [4 67]	1 922.0	1 845.0	1 516.0	1 591.0	1 783.0	1 827.0	2 227.0	2 240.0	...	...
M [I] [4 67]	1 190.0	1 134.0	1 024.0	1 083.0	1 179.0	1 208.0	1 302.0	1 363.0	...	...
F [I] [4 67]	732.0	711.0	492.0	508.0	604.0	619.0	925.0	877.0	...	...
MF [III] [68]	221.7	204.3	...	...	...	...	...	...	...	...
% MF [I] [4 67]	6.3	5.9	4.7	4.8	5.4	5.4	6.1	5.9	...	...
% M [I] [4 67]	4.5	4.3	3.8	3.9	4.1	4.1	4.2	4.2	...	...
% F [I] [4 67]	16.8	14.2	10.3	10.0	13.7	13.7	16.8	15.0	...	...
Panama Panama										
MF [I] [1 3]	138.4	134.4	124.7	135.5	141.2	144.9	140.3	147.1	128.0	...
M [I] [1 3]	72.8	65.6	60.2	67.7	70.7	74.8	72.5	69.5	62.1	...
F [I] [1 3]	65.6	68.7	64.5	67.7	70.5	70.1	67.8	77.6	65.9	...
% MF [I] [1 3]	16.2	14.7	13.3	14.0	14.0	14.3	13.4	13.6	11.8	...
% M [I] [1 3]	12.6	10.8	9.7	10.7	10.8	11.3	10.7	10.0	8.9	...
% F [I] [1 3]	22.6	22.3	20.2	20.4	20.1	20.0	18.1	19.9	16.9	...
Paraguay Paraguay										
MF [I]	26.6[31 69]	29.1[31 69]	30.5[4 69]	48.1[4 8]	...	105.7[4 8]	...	...	...	...
M [I]	16.6[31 69]	20.1[31 69]	19.1[4 69]	31.7[4 8]	...	58.1[4 8]	...	...	...	...
F [I]	10.0[31 69]	8.9[31 69]	11.4[4 69]	16.5[4 8]	...	47.5[4 8]	...	...	...	...
% MF [I]	5.1[31 69]	5.3[31 69]	5.1[4 69]	4.4[4 8]	...	8.2[4 8]	...	...	...	...
% M [I]	5.4[31 69]	6.4[31 69]	5.5[4 69]	4.9[4 8]	...	7.8[4 8]	...	...	...	...
% F [I]	4.7[31 69]	3.8[31 69]	4.5[4 69]	3.7[4 8]	...	8.6[4 8]	...	...	...	...
Peru Pérou										
MF [I] [2 8 26]	...	...	...	...	...	461.6	565.0	582.5	624.9	566.5
M [I] [2 8 26]	...	...	...	...	...	247.4	279.9	274.4	322.8	318.8
F [I] [2 8 26]	...	...	...	...	...	214.2	285.1	308.1	392.2	247.7
% MF [I] [2 8 26]	...	...	...	...	...	7.0	7.7	7.8	8.0	7.4
% M [I] [2 8 26]	...	...	...	...	...	6.4	6.8	6.5	7.5	7.3
% F [I] [2 8 26]	...	...	...	...	...	7.9	8.9	9.3	8.6	7.5

30
Unemployment
Number (thousands) and percentage unemployed [*cont.*]
    Chômage
    Nombre (milliers) et pourcentage des chômeurs [*suite*]

Country or area § Pays ou zone §	1991	1992	1993	1994	1995	1996	1997	1998	1999	2000
Philippines Philippines										
MF [I] [1 3]	2 267.0	2 263.0	2 379.0	2 317.0	2 342.0	2 195.0	2 377.0	3 016.0	2 931.0	3 133.0
M [I] [1 3]	1 290.0	1 303.0	1 384.0	1 362.0	1 354.0	1 293.0	1 411.0	1 857.0	1 835.0	1 978.0
F [I] [1 3]	977.0	959.0	995.0	955.0	988.0	902.0	966.0	1 159.0	1 096.0	1 156.0
% MF [I] [1 3]	9.0	8.6	8.9	8.4	8.4	7.4	7.9	9.6	9.6	10.1
% M [I] [1 3]	8.1	7.9	8.2	7.9	7.7	7.0	7.5	9.5	9.7	10.3
% F [I] [1 3]	10.5	9.8	10.0	9.4	9.4	8.2	8.5	9.8	9.3	9.9
Poland Pologne										
MF [I] [1]	...	2 394.0	2 427.0	2 474.0	2 277.0	2 108.0	1 923.0	1 808.0	2 391.0[6]	2 785.0
M [I] [1]	...	1 172.0	1 183.0	1 207.0	1 119.0	1 015.0	889.0	843.0	1 147.0[6]	1 344.0
F [I] [1]	...	1 221.0	1 244.0	1 266.0	1 157.0	1 093.0	1 035.0	965.0	1 244.0[6]	1 440.0
MF [III] [1 11]	2 155.6	2 509.3	2 889.6	2 838.0	2 628.8	2 359.5	1 826.4	1 831.4	2 349.8	2 702.6
M [III] [1 11]	1 021.5	1 170.5	1 382.3	1 343.0	1 180.2	983.9	723.2	760.1	1 042.5	1 211.0
F [III] [1 11]	1 134.1	1 338.8	1 507.3	1 495.0	1 448.6	1 375.6	1 103.2	1 071.3	1 307.3	1 491.6
% MF [I] [1]	...	...	14.0	14.4	13.3	12.3	11.2	10.5	13.9[6]	16.1
% M [I] [1]	...	...	12.6	13.1	12.1	11.0	9.6	9.1	12.4[6]	14.4
% F [I] [1]	...	...	15.6	16.0	14.7	13.9	13.2	12.3	15.8[6]	18.1
% MF [III] [1 11]	11.8	13.6	16.4	16.0	15.2	13.2	10.5	10.4	13.0	15.0
% M [III] [1 11]	10.6	11.9	15.0	14.7	...	...	...	...	...	...
% F [III] [1 11]	13.5	15.5	17.9	17.3	...	...	...	...	...	...
Portugal Portugal										
MF [I]	207.5[4]	194.1[2]	257.5[2]	323.8[2]	338.4[2]	343.9[2]	324.1[2]	247.9[1]	221.6[1]	204.6[1]
M [I]	77.6[4]	90.7[2]	120.0[2]	155.8[2]	165.8[2]	167.0[2]	158.5[2]	107.6[1]	105.9[1]	87.9[1]
F [I]	129.9[4]	103.4[2]	137.5[2]	168.1[2]	172.1[2]	177.0[2]	165.6[2]	140.4[1]	115.7[1]	116.7[1]
% MF [I]	4.1[4]	4.1[2]	5.4[2]	6.7[2]	7.1[2]	7.2[2]	6.7[2]	5.0[1]	4.4[1]	4.0[1]
% M [I]	2.8[4]	3.4[2]	4.5[2]	5.9[2]	6.3[2]	6.4[2]	6.0[2]	3.9[1]	3.8[1]	3.2[1]
% F [I]	5.8[4]	4.9[2]	6.5[2]	7.8[2]	8.1[2]	8.2[2]	7.5[2]	6.2[1]	5.1[1]	5.0[1]
Puerto Rico Porto Rico										
MF [I] [42 44]	186.0	197.0	206.0	175.0	170.0	172.0	176.0	175.0	153.0	132.0
M [I] [42 44]	131.0	139.0	144.0	121.0	117.0	114.0	112.0	112.0	102.0	91.0
F [I] [42 44]	55.0	58.0	62.0	54.0	53.0	58.0	64.0	63.0	51.0	42.0
% MF [I] [42 44]	16.0	16.6	17.0	14.6	13.7	13.4	13.5	13.3	11.8	10.1
% M [I] [42 44]	17.9	19.0	19.5	16.5	15.6	14.9	14.4	14.4	13.2	11.8
% F [I] [42 44]	12.6	12.8	13.2	11.5	10.8	11.2	12.1	11.8	9.6	7.7
Republic of Moldova Réublique de Moldova										
MF [I] [1]	...	...	...	...	...	...	...	...	187.2	140.1
M [I] [1]	...	...	...	...	...	...	...	...	113.6	80.6
F [I] [1]	...	...	...	...	...	...	...	...	73.6	59.5
MF [III] [3]	0.1	15.0	14.1	20.6	24.5	23.4	28.0	32.0	34.9	28.9
M [III] [3]	...	5.9	5.5	7.7	8.4	7.5	10.3	13.0	13.3	11.9
F [III] [3]	0.1	9.1	8.9	12.9	16.1	15.9	17.7	19.0	21.6	17.0
% MF [I] [1]	...	...	...	...	...	...	...	...	11.1	8.5
% M [I] [1]	...	...	...	...	...	...	...	...	13.3	9.7
% F [I] [1]	...	...	...	...	...	...	...	...	8.9	7.2
% MF [III] [3]	...	0.7	0.7	1.1	1.0	1.5	1.5	1.9	2.1	2.1
Réunion Réunion										
MF [III] [42]	59.3	80.1	80.2	...	...	...	...	...	...	...
M [III] [3 42]	30.4	41.9	43.1	...	...	...	...	...	...	...
F [III] [3 42]	28.8	38.2	37.1	...	...	...	...	...	...	...
% MF [III] [42]	25.4	34.3	34.4	...	...	...	...	...	...	...
Romania Roumanie										
MF [I]	...	...	...	971.0[2 3]	967.9[2 3]	790.9[1]	706.5[1]	732.4[1]	789.9[1]	821.2[1]
M [I]	...	...	...	488.2[2 3]	487.6[2 3]	399.1[1]	364.2[1]	410.3[1]	462.5[1]	481.6[1]
F [I]	...	...	...	482.8[2 3]	480.3[2 3]	391.7[1]	342.2[1]	322.1[1]	327.4[1]	339.6[1]
MF [III] [3]	337.4	929.0	1 164.7	1 223.9	998.4	657.6	881.4	1 025.1	1 130.3	1 007.1
M [III] [3]	129.0	366.0	479.2	530.6	446.9	302.2	452.8	539.9	600.2	535.5
F [III] [3]	208.4	563.0	685.5	693.3	551.5	355.4	428.6	485.2	530.1	471.6
% MF [I]	...	...	...	8.2[2 3]	8.0[2 3]	6.7[1]	6.0[1]	6.3[1]	6.8[1]	7.1[1]
% M [I]	...	...	...	7.7[2 3]	7.5[2 3]	6.3[1]	5.7[1]	6.5[1]	7.4[1]	7.7[1]
% F [I]	...	...	...	8.7[2 3]	8.6[2 3]	7.3[1]	6.4[1]	6.1[1]	6.2[1]	6.4[1]

30
Unemployment
Number (thousands) and percentage unemployed [*cont.*]
Chômage
Nombre (milliers) et pourcentage des chômeurs [*suite*]

Country or area [§] Pays ou zone [§]	1991	1992	1993	1994	1995	1996	1997	1998	1999	2000
% MF [III] [3]	3.0	8.2	10.4	10.9	9.5	6.6	10.4	10.3	11.8	10.5
% M [III] [3]	2.2	6.2	8.1	9.0	7.9	5.7	10.4	10.2	12.1	10.8
% F [III] [3]	4.0	10.3	12.9	12.9	11.4	7.5	10.4	10.5	11.6	10.3
Russian Federation Fédération de Russie										
MF [I] [3 70]	...	3 877.0	4 305.0	5 702.0	6 712.0	6 732.0	8 058.0	8 876.0	9 323.0	...
M [I] [3 70]	...	2 026.0	2 280.0	3 074.0	3 616.0	3 662.0	4 371.0	4 787.0	4 966.0	...
F [I] [3 70]	...	1 851.0	2 025.0	2 628.0	3 096.0	3 070.0	3 687.0	4 090.0	4 357.0	...
MF [III] [3]	61.9	577.7	836.0	1 637.0	2 327.0	2 506.0	1 990.0	1 929.0	1 263.0	...
M [III] [3]	18.8	160.7	268.0	586.0	872.0	930.0	721.0	682.0	383.0	...
F [III] [3]	43.1	417.0	567.0	1 051.0	1 455.0	1 576.0	1 278.0	1 247.0	880.0	...
% MF [I] [3 70]	...	5.2	5.9	8.1	9.5	9.7	11.8	13.3	13.4	...
% M [I] [3 70]	...	5.2	5.9	8.3	9.7	10.0	12.2	13.6	13.6	...
% F [I] [3 70]	...	5.2	5.8	7.9	9.2	9.3	11.5	13.0	13.1	...
% MF [III] [3]	0.1	0.8	5.7	7.5	8.9	9.9	11.3	13.3	...	...
Saint Helena Sainte-Hélène										
MF [III]	0.2	0.2	0.2	0.3	0.3	0.4	0.4	0.5	...	...
M [III]	0.1	0.1	0.1	0.2	0.2	0.2	0.3	0.3	...	...
F [III]	0.1	0.1	0.1	0.1	0.1	0.1	0.1	0.1	...	...
Saint Pierre and Miquelon Sainte-Pierre-et-Miquelon										
MF [III] [19]	...	...	0.4	...	...	...	...	...	...	...
San Marino Saint-Marin										
MF [IV] [11]	0.5[2]	0.5[2]	0.6[2]	0.6[2]	0.5[2]	0.6[1]	0.5[1]	0.6[1]	0.4[1]	...
M [IV] [11]	0.1[2]	0.1[2]	0.2[2]	0.1[2]	0.1[2]	0.1[1]	0.1[1]	0.1[1]	0.1[1]	...
F [IV] [11]	0.3[2]	0.4[2]	0.4[2]	0.4[2]	0.4[2]	0.5[1]	0.4[1]	0.4[1]	0.3[1]	...
% MF [IV] [11]	4.3[2]	4.2[2]	5.1[2]	3.9[2]	3.9[2]	5.1[1]	4.4[1]	4.1[1]	3.0[1]	...
% M [IV] [11]	2.3[2]	2.0[2]	2.6[2]	1.6[2]	1.5[2]	2.0[1]	1.9[1]	1.8[1]	1.6[1]	...
% F [IV] [11]	6.9[2]	7.1[2]	8.1[2]	7.4[2]	7.0[2]	8.8[1]	7.3[1]	6.9[1]	4.6[1]	...
Senegal Sénégal										
MF [III] [34 71]	14.4	12.0	10.2	...	...	...	...	...	...	...
M [III] [34 71]	13.1	10.0	9.0	...	...	...	...	...	...	...
F [III] [34 71]	1.3	2.0	1.2	...	...	...	...	...	...	...
Singapore Singapour										
MF [I] [1 3]	30.0	43.4	43.7	43.8	47.2	53.8	45.5	62.1	90.1	97.5
M [I] [1 3]	18.7	26.4	25.2	24.9	28.4	31.0	26.8	35.5	51.4	53.5
F [I] [1 3]	11.3	17.0	18.5	18.9	18.8	22.8	18.7	26.6	38.7	44.0
MF [III] [2]	1.2	1.0	1.0	1.0	1.1	1.5	2.6	4.4	5.9	4.2
M [III] [2]	0.8	0.7	0.7	0.7	0.7	0.8	1.2	2.3	3.2	2.3
F [III] [2]	0.4	0.3	0.3	0.4	0.4	0.7	1.4	2.1	2.7	1.8
% MF [I] [1 3]	1.9	2.7	2.7	2.6	2.7	3.0	2.4	3.2	4.6	4.4
% M [I] [1 3]	2.0	2.7	2.6	2.5	2.7	2.9	2.4	3.2	4.5	4.0
% F [I] [1 3]	1.8	2.6	2.8	2.8	2.8	3.1	2.4	3.3	4.6	5.1
Slovakia Slovaquie										
MF [I] [1 72]	...	...	...	333.5	323.7	284.2	297.5	317.1	416.8	485.2
M [I] [1 72]	...	...	...	179.9	171.4	140.7	151.8	167.5	226.6	265.5
F [I] [1 72]	...	...	...	153.5	152.4	143.5	145.6	149.6	190.3	219.7
MF [III]	169.0	285.5	323.2	366.2	349.8	324.3	336.7	379.5	485.2	519.1
M [III]	83.4	141.1	167.2	189.5	174.8	155.1	162.9	193.0	265.8	294.6
F [III]	85.6	144.4	156.0	176.6	175.0	169.2	173.8	186.5	219.4	224.5
% MF [I] [1 72]	...	...	...	13.7	13.1	11.3	11.8	12.5	16.2	18.6
% M [I] [1 72]	...	...	...	13.3	12.6	10.2	10.9	11.9	16.0	18.6
% F [I] [1 72]	...	...	...	14.1	13.8	12.7	12.8	13.2	16.4	18.6
% MF [III]	6.6	11.4	12.9	14.4	13.8	12.6	12.9	13.7	17.3	18.3
% M [III]	6.4	11.1	12.7	13.9	12.8	11.3	11.7	13.3	17.9	19.7
% F [III]	6.9	11.7	13.0	15.0	14.8	14.1	14.3	14.1	16.6	16.9
Slovenia Slovénie										
MF [I] [1 3]	...	...	85.0	85.0	70.0	69.0	69.0	75.0	71.0	...
M [I] [1 3]	...	...	49.0	48.0	39.0	38.0	36.0	40.0	37.0	...
F [I] [1 3]	...	...	36.0	37.0	31.0	31.0	32.0	35.0	34.0	...
MF [III] [1]	75.1	102.6	129.1	127.1	...	...	125.2	126.1	119.0	106.6
M [III] [1]	41.5	57.5	72.5	70.0	...	...	64.1	63.2	58.8	52.5
F [III] [1]	33.6	45.1	56.6	57.0	...	...	61.1	62.9	60.2	54.1
% MF [I] [1 3]	...	...	9.1	9.0	7.4	7.3	7.1	7.7	7.4	...

30
Unemployment
Number (thousands) and percentage unemployed [*cont.*]
Chômage
Nombre (milliers) et pourcentage des chômeurs [*suite*]

Country or area § Pays ou zone §	1991	1992	1993	1994	1995	1996	1997	1998	1999	2000
% M [I] [1 3]	...	...	9.9	9.5	7.7	7.5	7.0	7.6	7.2	...
% F [I] [1 3]	...	...	8.3	8.4	7.0	7.0	7.3	7.7	7.6	
% MF [III] [1]	8.2	11.5	14.4	14.4	...	...	...	...	...	...
% M [III] [1]	8.5	12.1	15.3	15.1	...	...	...	...	...	...
% F [III] [1]	7.9	10.8	13.5	13.7	...	...	...	...	...	...
South Africa Afrique du Sud										
MF [III] [1 73 74]	247.8	287.8	313.3	271.3	273.0	295.7	309.6	...	...	...
M [III] [1 73 74]	176.6	201.1	221.3	184.8	186.7	197.4	207.8	...	...	...
F [III] [1 73 74]	71.2	86.7	92.6	86.6	86.2	98.3	101.8	...	...	...
% MF [III]	...	...	...	4.4	4.5	5.1	5.4	...	...	...
Spain Espagne										
MF [I] [42]	2 463.7	2 788.5	3 481.3	3 738.1	3 583.5	3 540.0	3 356.5	3 060.3	2 605.5	2 370.4
M [I] [42]	1 191.9	1 384.5	1 836.7	1 911.9	1 753.9	1 724.0	1 581.6	1 364.3	1 102.0	980.7
F [I] [42]	1 271.8	1 404.1	1 644.6	1 826.2	1 829.7	1 816.1	1 774.9	1 696.1	1 503.5	1 389.7
MF [III] [57]	2 289.0	2 259.9	2 537.9	2 647.0	2 449.0	2 275.4	2 118.7	1 889.5	1 651.6	1 557.5
M [III] [57]	910.7	954.2	1 193.0	1 283.5	1 156.0	1 064.9	968.4	818.2	682.2	615.9
F [III] [57]	1 378.3	1 305.7	1 344.9	1 363.5	1 292.9	1 210.4	1 150.3	1 071.3	964.4	941.6
% MF [I] [42]	16.4	18.4	22.7	24.2	22.9	22.2	20.8	18.8	15.9	14.1
% M [I] [42]	12.3	14.3	19.0	18.8	18.2	17.6	16.1	13.8	11.1	9.7
% F [I] [42]	23.8	25.6	29.2	31.4	30.6	29.6	28.3	26.6	23.0	20.5
% MF [III] [57]	15.2	14.9	16.6	17.1	20.3	...	...	...	...	...
% M [III] [57]	9.4	9.9	12.3	13.3	12.0	...	...	...	...	...
% F [III] [57]	25.8	23.8	23.9	23.4	21.6	...	...	...	...	...
Sri Lanka Sri Lanka										
MF [I] [5 25 75]	843.3	817.6	874.1	813.3	759.1	710.3	...	701.0	612.7	546.0
M [I] [5 25 75]	380.0	408.7	349.3	390.5	352.9	328.2	...	296.2	330.7	...
F [I] [5 25 75]	463.3	409.0	524.8	422.8	406.2	382.0	...	404.8	282.0	...
% MF [I] [5 25 75]	14.1	14.1	14.7	13.6	12.5	11.3	10.7	10.6	9.1	8.0
% M [I] [5 25 75]	10.0	10.6	9.1	9.9	8.8	8.0	8.0	7.1	7.4	6.4
% F [I] [5 25 75]	21.2	21.0	25.2	20.8	19.7	17.6	16.2	16.2	12.6	11.1
Sudan Soudan										
MF [III] [76]	19.9	5.3	...	...	...	...	...	...	...	...
M [III] [76]	10.2	3.7	...	...	...	...	...	...	...	...
F [III] [76]	9.7	1.6	...	...	...	...	...	...	...	...
Suriname Suriname										
MF [I] [2]	...	18.5	14.4	11.3	7.6	10.7	9.7	10.5	11.8[6]	...
M [I] [2]	...	9.1	7.3	6.6	4.1	4.9	4.4	4.6	5.4[6]	...
F [I] [2]	...	9.4	7.1	4.7	3.4	5.8	5.3	5.8	6.5[6]	...
MF [III] [77]	3.7	1.4	1.0	0.6	0.9	0.9	...	...	...	...
M [III] [77]	1.1	0.5	0.4	0.1	0.3	0.3	...	...	...	...
F [III] [77]	2.6	0.9	0.6	0.4	0.6	0.6	...	...	...	...
% MF [I] [2]	...	17.2	14.7	12.7	8.4	11.0	10.5	10.6	14.0[6]	...
% M [I] [2]	...	13.7	12.0	11.4	7.0	7.9	7.4	7.2	10.0[6]	...
% F [I] [2]	...	23.1	19.2	15.0	10.9	16.4	16.0	17.0	20.0[6]	...
Sweden Suède										
MF [I] [57]	134.0	233.0	356.0[18]	340.0	333.0	347.0	342.0	276.0	241.0	203.0
M [I] [57]	78.0	144.0	218.0[18]	202.0	190.0	192.0	188.0	154.0	133.0	114.0
F [I] [57]	56.0	89.0	137.0[18]	138.0	142.0	155.0	154.0	122.0	107.0	89.0
MF [III] [57]	114.6	309.8	447.4	438.4	436.2	407.6	367.0	285.6	276.7	231.2
M [III] [57]	66.4	186.1	262.6	250.7	238.2	220.2	199.5	156.3	151.7	126.9
F [III] [57]	48.1	123.7	184.8	187.7	198.0	187.3	167.4	129.3	125.0	104.3
% MF [I] [57]	3.0	5.2	8.2[18]	8.0	7.7	8.0	8.0	6.5	5.6	4.7
% M [I] [57]	3.3	6.3	9.7[18]	9.1	8.5	8.5	8.4	6.9	5.9	5.0
% F [I] [57]	2.6	4.2	6.6[18]	6.7	6.9	7.5	7.5	6.0	5.2	4.3
% MF [III] [57]	2.1	5.7	8.2	8.0	7.9	7.4	6.6	5.1	5.0	4.1
% M [III] [57]	2.4	6.7	9.5	9.0	8.5	7.8	7.1	5.5	5.4	4.5
% F [III] [57]	1.8	4.6	6.9	7.0	7.3	6.9	6.1	4.7	4.6	3.8
Switzerland Suisse										
MF [I] [1 26]	68.2	108.7	144.6	150.1	129.0	144.6	162.1	141.8	121.6	105.9
M [I] [1 26]	26.7	49.7	68.0	76.3	63.6	74.7	94.7	70.0	59.2	51.0
F [I] [1 26]	41.4	59.0	76.7	73.8	65.4	69.9	67.4	71.8	62.4	55.0
MF [III] [1]	39.2	92.3	163.1	171.0	153.3	168.6	188.3	139.7	98.6	72.0

30
Unemployment
Number (thousands) and percentage unemployed [*cont.*]
Chômage
Nombre (milliers) et pourcentage des chômeurs [*suite*]

Country or area [§] Pays ou zone [§]	1991	1992	1993	1994	1995	1996	1997	1998	1999	2000
M [III] [1]	22.7	54.7	96.6	98.0	85.5	96.8	108.7	77.1	52.6	37.8
F [III] [1]	16.5	37.6	66.6	73.1	67.8	71.8	79.6	62.6	46.0	34.2
% MF [I] [1 26]	1.8	2.8	3.7	3.9	3.3	3.7	4.1	3.6	3.1	2.7
% M [I] [1 26]	1.2	2.3	3.1	3.5	2.9	3.4	4.3	3.2	2.7	2.3
% F [I] [1 26]	2.5	3.5	4.6	4.4	3.9	4.1	3.9	4.1	3.5	3.1
% MF [III] [1]	1.1	2.5	4.5	4.7	4.2	4.7	5.2	3.9	2.7	2.0
% M [III] [1]	1.1	2.5	4.4	4.4	3.9	4.4	4.9	3.5	2.4	1.7
% F [III] [1]	1.2	2.7	4.7	5.2	4.8	5.1	5.7	4.4	3.3	2.4
Tajikistan Tadjikistan										
MF [III]	...	6.8	21.6	32.1	37.5	45.7	51.1	...	...	...
M [III]	...	4.2	12.4	17.1	20.2	22.8	24.1	...	...	...
F [III]	...	2.6	9.2	15.0	17.3	22.9	27.0	...	...	...
% MF [III]	...	0.4	1.2	1.7	2.0	2.6	2.7	...	...	...
% M [III]	...	0.4	1.2	1.6	1.9	2.4	2.4	...	...	...
% F [III]	...	0.4	1.1	1.8	2.1	2.8	2.9	...	...	...
Thailand Thaïlande										
MF [I] [6 78]	869.3	456.3	494.4	422.8	375.0	353.9	292.5	1 137.9	985.7	812.6
M [I] [6 78]	350.1	224.1	217.3	196.2	167.1	186.5	154.4	625.2	546.4	454.5
F [I] [6 78]	519.1	232.2	277.0	226.5	207.9	167.4	138.1	512.7	439.3	358.0
% MF [I] [6 78]	2.7	1.4	1.5	1.3	1.1	1.1	0.9	3.4	3.0	2.4
% M [I] [6 78]	2.0	1.3	1.2	1.1	0.9	1.0	0.8	3.4	3.0	2.4
% F [I] [6 78]	3.5	1.5	1.8	1.5	1.4	1.1	0.9	3.4	3.0	2.3
TFYR of Macedonia L'ex−R.y. Macédoine										
MF [III]	164.8	172.1	174.8	185.9	216.2	238.0	253.0	...	...	...
M [III]	82.0	87.0	89.0	96.0	101.0	110.0	138.0	...	...	...
F [III]	83.0	85.0	86.0	90.0	115.0	128.0	115.0	...	...	...
% MF [III]	24.5	26.3	27.7	30.0	35.6	38.8	...	...	...	...
% M [III]	20.1	22.1	23.6	25.8	31.9	35.0	...	...	...	...
% F [III]	31.3	32.5	33.7	36.4	41.7	44.5	...	...	...	...
Trinidad and Tobago Trinité−et−Tobago										
MF [I] [1 79 80]	91.2	99.2	99.9	93.9	89.4	86.1	81.2	79.4	74.0	...
M [I] [1 79 80]	49.6	54.3	56.3	51.5	49.5	43.1	41.3	39.0	37.9	...
F [I] [1 79 80]	41.5	44.9	43.7	42.4	39.9	43.0	39.9	40.4	36.1	...
% MF [I] [1 79 80]	18.5	19.6	19.8	18.4	17.2	16.2	15.0	14.2	13.1	...
% M [I] [1 79 80]	15.7	17.0	17.6	16.1	15.1	13.2	12.3	11.3	10.9	...
% F [I] [1 79 80]	23.4	23.9	23.4	22.3	20.6	21.0	19.4	18.9	16.8	...
Tunisia Tunisie										
MF [I] [62]	...	...	...	...	...	...	474.7	...	509.9	510.8
MF [III] [62]	133.1	136.9	142.2	160.2	189.7	180.9	...	...	...	...
M [III] [62]	89.4	89.0	94.8	132.7	160.4	115.9	...	...	...	...
F [III] [62]	43.7	47.9	47.4	27.5	29.3	64.9	...	...	...	...
% MF [I] [62]	...	...	...	...	...	...	15.7	...	15.8	15.6
Turkey Turquie										
MF [I] [3 31 81]	1 787.0	1 745.0	1 722.0	1 740.0	1 522.0	1 332.0	1 545.0	1 547.0	1 730.0	...
M [I] [3 31 81]	1 300.0	1 237.0	1 225.0	1 218.0	1 052.0	956.0	994.0	1 041.0	1 259.0	...
F [I] [3 31 81]	486.0	508.0	497.0	522.0	470.0	376.0	550.0	416.0	471.0	...
MF [III] [2]	859.0[82]	840.1[82]	682.6[82]	469.3[3]	401.3[3]	416.8[3]	463.0[3]	465.2[3]	...	...
M [III] [2]	706.8[82]	695.5[82]	571.7[82]	382.2[3]	324.7[3]	341.8[3]	382.1[3]	386.0[3]	...	...
F [III] [2]	152.2[82]	144.6[82]	111.0[82]	87.1[3]	76.6[3]	75.0[3]	81.2[3]	79.2[3]	...	...
% MF [I] [3 31 81]	8.4	8.0	8.0	7.9	6.6	5.8	6.9	6.2	7.3	...
% M [I] [3 31 81]	8.9	8.2	8.2	7.7	6.6	5.9	6.1	6.3	7.7	...
% F [I] [3 31 81]	7.3	7.6	7.5	8.2	6.8	5.5	9.2	6.1	6.4	...
Ukraine Ukraine										
MF [I] [3 83]	...	...	...	...	1 437.0	1 997.5	2 330.1	2 937.1	2 698.8	2 707.6
M [I] [3 83]	...	...	...	...	805.7	1 057.2	1 216.9	1 515.1	1 435.5	1 392.2
F [I] [3 83]	...	...	...	...	631.3	940.3	1 113.2	1 422.0	1 263.3	1 315.4
MF [III] [11 84]	...	...	83.9	82.2	126.9	351.1	637.1	1 003.2	1 174.5	1 155.2
M [III] [11 84]	...	...	21.2	22.5	34.7	115.3	220.6	382.8	444.9	424.8
F [III] [11 84]	...	...	62.7	59.7	92.2	235.8	416.5	620.4	729.6	730.4
% MF [I] [3 83]	...	...	...	...	5.6	7.6	8.9	11.3	11.9	11.7
% M [I] [3 83]	...	...	...	...	6.3	8.0	9.5	11.9	12.2	11.7
% F [I] [3 83]	...	...	...	...	4.9	7.3	8.4	10.8	11.5	11.7

30
Unemployment
Number (thousands) and percentage unemployed [*cont.*]
Chômage
Nombre (milliers) et pourcentage des chômeurs [*suite*]

Country or area [§] Pays ou zone [§]	1991	1992	1993	1994	1995	1996	1997	1998	1999	2000
%MF [III] [11 84]	...	...	0.4	0.4	0.6	1.6	3.1	4.8	5.8	5.8
%M [III] [11 84]	...	...	0.2	0.2	0.3	1.1	2.2	3.7	4.4	4.3
%F [III] [11 84]	...	...	0.6	0.6	0.9	2.3	4.0	5.9	7.1	7.2
United Arab Emirates										
MF [IV]	...	...	...	...	24.1[85]	...	...	...	...	41.0
M [IV]	...	...	...	...	20.4[85]	...	...	...	...	34.7
F [IV]	...	...	...	...	3.7[85]	...	...	...	...	6.3
% MF [IV]	...	...	...	...	1.8[85]	...	...	...	...	2.3
% M [IV]	...	...	...	...	1.7[85]	...	...	...	...	2.2
% F [IV]	...	...	...	...	2.4[85]	...	...	...	...	2.6
United Kingdom Royaume–Uni										
MF [I] [6 42]	2 413.6	2 769.2	2 935.5	2 737.6	2 460.4	2 340.1	2 037.3	1 776.4	1 751.7	1 619.1
M [I] [6 42]	1 513.9	1 865.2	1 986.4	1 826.1	1 611.8	1 549.0	1 305.8	1 097.8	1 095.2	991.5
F [I] [6 42]	899.7	903.9	949.2	911.6	848.6	791.0	731.5	678.6	656.5	627.6
MF [II] [44 86 87]	2 291.9	2 778.6	2 919.2	2 636.5	2 325.7	2 122.2	1 602.4	1 362.4	1 263.1	1 102.3
M [II] [44 86 87]	1 737.1	2 126.0	2 236.0	2 014.4	1 770.0	1 610.3	1 225.5	1 037.7	963.5	839.6
F [II] [44 86 87]	554.9	652.6	683.1	622.6	555.6	511.9	377.3	324.7	299.5	262.6
% MF [I] [6 42]	8.4	9.7	10.3	9.6	8.6	8.2	7.1	6.1	6.0	5.5
% M [I] [6 42]	9.2	11.5	12.4	11.4	10.1	9.6	8.1	6.8	6.7	6.1
% F [I] [6 42]	7.2	7.3	7.6	7.3	6.8	6.3	5.7	5.3	5.1	4.8
% MF [II] [44 86 87]	8.1	9.9	10.4	9.4	8.3	7.6	5.7	4.7	4.3	3.8
% M [II] [44 86 87]	10.7	13.3	14.0	12.6	11.3	10.3	7.7	6.5	6.0	5.2
% F [II] [44 86 87]	4.6	5.4	5.6	5.1	4.5	4.2	2.9	2.5	2.3	2.0
United States Etats–Unis										
MF [I] [42 88]	8 628.0	9 613.0	8 940.0	7 996.0[18]	7 404.0	7 236.0	6 739.0	6 210.0	5 880.0	5 655.0
M [I] [42 88]	4 946.0	5 523.0	5 055.0	4 367.0[18]	3 983.0	3 880.0	3 577.0	3 266.0	3 066.0	2 954.0
F [I] [42 88]	3 683.0	4 090.0	3 885.0	3 629.0[18]	3 421.0	3 356.0	3 162.0	2 944.0	2 814.0	2 701.0
% MF [I] [42 88]	6.8	7.5	6.9	6.1[18]	5.6	5.4	4.9	4.5	4.2	4.0
% M [I] [42 88]	7.2	7.9	7.2	6.2[18]	5.6	5.4	4.9	4.4	4.1	3.9
% F [I] [42 88]	6.4	7.0	6.6	6.0[18]	5.6	5.4	5.0	4.6	4.3	4.1
United States Virgin Is. Iles Vierges américaines										
MF [III] [89]	1.4	1.7	1.9	2.8	2.7	2.4	2.7	...	...	...
% MF [III] [89]	2.8	3.5	3.5	5.6	5.7	5.2	5.9	...	...	...
Uruguay Uruguay										
MF [I] [2 8]	111.0	112.8	105.0	120.1	137.5	...	...	123.8	137.7	167.7
M [I] [2 8]	52.6	49.6	46.9	53.2	61.5	...	...	53.7	59.4	74.7
F [I] [2 8]	58.4	63.2	58.1	66.9	76.0	...	...	70.1	78.3	93.0
% MF [I] [2 8]	9.0	9.0	8.3	9.2	10.2	...	...	10.1	11.3	13.6
% M [I] [2 8]	7.2	6.9	6.5	7.1	8.0	...	...	7.8	8.7	10.9
% F [I] [2 8]	11.6	11.9	10.9	12.1	13.2	...	...	13.0	14.6	17.0
Uzbekistan Ouzbékistan										
MF [III]	...	20.2	29.0	29.4	31.0	...	...	...	...	...
M [III]	...	7.9	11.3	12.1	12.1	...	...	...	...	...
F [III]	...	12.3	17.7	17.3	18.9	...	...	...	...	...
% MF [III]	...	0.2	0.4	0.4	0.4	...	...	...	...	...
% M [III]	...	0.2	0.2	0.3	0.3	...	...	...	...	...
% F [III]	...	0.3	0.5	0.5	0.5	...	...	...	...	...
Venezuela Venezuela										
MF [I] [1]	701.7	582.4	503.5	687.4	874.7	1 042.9	1 060.7	1 092.6	1 525.5	...
M [I] [1]	481.7	418.7	371.2	442.4	1 016.8	1 210.0	592.4	616.4	...	...
F [I] [1]	220.0	163.7	132.3	245.0	366.3	437.9	468.3	476.2	...	...
% MF [I] [1]	9.5	7.7	6.7	8.7	10.3	11.8	11.4	11.2	14.9	...
% M [I] [1]	9.6	8.1	7.1	8.2	9.1	10.4	9.8	9.9	...	...
% F [I] [1]	9.4	6.8	5.6	9.7	12.9	14.5	14.2	13.4	...	...

30
Unemployment
Number (thousands) and percentage unemployed [*cont.*]
Chômage
Nombre (milliers) et pourcentage des chômeurs [*suite*]

Source:
International Labour Office (ILO), Geneva, "Yearbook of Labour Statistics 2001" and the ILO labour statistics database.

§   I = Labour force sample surveys.
    II = Social insurance statistics.
    III = Employment office statistics.
    IV = Official estimates.

1 Persons aged 15 years and over.
2 Persons aged 14 years and over.
3 One month of each year.
4 Persons aged 10 years and over.
5 Gran Buenos Aires.
6 Average of less than 12 months.
7 28 urban agglomerations.
8 Urban areas.
9 Estimates based on the 1991 Census of Population and Housing.
10 Estimates based on 1996 census of population benchmarks.

11 31st December of each year.
12 Private sector.
13 Year ending in June of the year indicated.
14 Beginning April 1985, excluding some elderly unemployed no longer applicants for work.
15 Persons aged 15 to 69 years.
16 Main towns.
17 Excluding rural population of Rondônia, Acre, Amazonas, Roraima, Pará and Amapá.
18 Beginning this year, methodology revised; data not strictly comparable.
19 Persons aged 16 to 60 years.
20 Persons aged 16 to 55 years.
21 Four employment offices.
22 Bujumbura.
23 Excluding full-time members of the armed forces.
24 Excluding residents of the Territories and indigenous persons living on reserves.
25 Bangui.
26 One quarter of each year.
27 Beginning this year, sample design revised.
28 Unemployed in urban areas.
29 Young people aged 16 to 25 years.
30 Excluding unpaid family workers who worked for one hour or more.
31 Persons aged 12 years and over.
32 7 main cities of the country.
33 Estimates based on the 1993 Census results.
34 Persons aged 14 to 55 years.
35 Persons aged 15 to 64 years.
36 The data relate to the government-controlled areas.

37 Excluding persons on child care leave actively seeking a job.
38 Persons aged 15 to 74 years.
39 Persons aged 15 to 66 years.

Source:
Bureau international du Travail (BIT), Genève, "Annuaire des statistiques du travail 2001" et la base de données du BIT.

§   I = Enquêtes par sondage sur la main-d'oeuvre.
    II = Statistiques d'assurances sociales.
    III = Statistiques des bureaux de placement.
    IV = Evaluations officielles.

1 Personnes âgées de 15 ans et plus.
2 Personnes âgées de 14 ans et plus.
3 Un mois de chaque année.
4 Personnes âgées de 10 ans et plus.
5 Gran Buenos Aires.
6 Moyenne de moins de douze mois.
7 28 agglomérations urbaines.
8 Régions urbaines.
9 Estimations basées sur le recensement de la population et de l'habitat de 1991.
10 Estimations basées sur les données de calage du recensement de population de 1996.

11 31 décembre de chaque année.
12 Secteur privé.
13 Année se terminant en juin de l'année indiquée.
14 A partir d'avril 1985, non compris certains chômeurs âgés devenus non demandeurs d'emploi.
15 Personnes âgées de 15 à 69 ans.
16 Villes principales.
17 Non compris la population rurale de Rondônia, Acre, Amazonas, Roraima, Pará et Amapá.
18 A partir de cette année, méthodologie révisée; les données ne sont pas strictement comparables.
19 Personnes âgées de 16 à 60 ans.
20 Personnes âgées de 16 à 55 ans.
21 Quatre bureaux de placement.
22 Bujumbura.
23 Non compris les membres à temps complet des forces armées.
24 Non compris les habitants des Territoires " et les populations indigènes vivant dans les réserves."
25 Bangui.
26 Un trimestre de chaque année.
27 A partir de cette année, plan d'échantillonnage révisé.
28 Chômeurs dans les régions urbaines.
29 Jeunes gens de 16 à 25 ans.
30 Non compris les travailleurs familiaux non rémunérés ayant travaillé une heure ou plus.
31 Personnes âgées de 12 ans et plus.
32 7 villes principales du pays.
33 Estimations basées sur les résultats du Recensement de 1993.
34 Personnes âgées de 14 à 55 ans.
35 Personnes âgées de 15 à 64 ans.
36 Les données se réfèrent aux régions sous contrôle gouvernemental.

37 Non compris les personnes en congé parental cherchant activement un travail.
38 Personnes âgées de 15 à 74 ans.
39 Personnes âgées de 15 à 66 ans.

30
Unemployment
Number (thousands) and percentage unemployed [*cont.*]
Chômage
Nombre (milliers) et pourcentage des chômeurs [*suite*]

40 Persons aged 16 to 66 years.	40 Personnes âgées de 16 à 66 ans.
41 Persons aged 12 to 64.	41 Personnes âgées de 12 à 64 ans.
42 Persons aged 16 years and over.	42 Personnes âgées de 16 ans et plus.
43 Excluding elderly unemployment pensioners no longer seeking work.	43 Non compris les chômeurs indemnisés âgés ne recherchant plus de travail.
44 Excluding persons temporarily laid off.	44 Non compris les personnes temporairement mises à pied.
45 Beginning October 1982: series revised on the basis of new administrative procedures adopted in 1986.	45 A partir d'octobre 1982: série révisée sur la base de nouvelles procédures administratives adoptées en 1986.
46 Excluding registered applicants for work who worked more than 78 hours during the month.	46 Non compris les demandeurs d'emploi inscrits ayant travaillé plus de 78 heures dans le mois.
47 Cayenne and Kourou.	47 Cayenne et Kourou.
48 Persons aged 15 to 60 years.	48 Personnes âgées de 15 à 60 ans.
49 Persons aged 15 to 65 years.	49 Personnes âgées de 15 à 65 ans.
50 Guatemala city.	50 Ville de Guatemala.
51 Including unemployed temporarily unable to undertake work (child−care allowance, military service, etc.).	51 Y compris chômeurs qui temporairement ne peuvent travailler (allocation congé parental, service militaire, etc.).
52 Persons aged 16 to 74 years.	52 Personnes âgées de 16 à 74 ans.
53 Rates calculated on basis of 1991 Census.	53 Taux calculés sur la base du Recensement de 1991.
54 Including the residents of East Jerusalem.	54 Y compris les résidents de Jérusalem−Est.
55 Including workers from the Judea, Samaria and Gaza areas.	55 Y compris les travailleurs des régions de Judée, Samarie et Gaza.
56 Beginning 1992, series revised on basis of 1995 Population Census.	56 A partir de 1992, série révisée sur la base du Recensement de la population de 1995.
57 Persons aged 16 to 64 years.	57 Personnes âgées de 16 à 64 ans.
58 Beginning this year, series revised.	58 A partir de cette année, série révisée.
59 6 provincial capitals.	59 6 chefs−lieux de province.
60 Persons aged 16 to 61 years.	60 Personnes âgées de 16 à 61 ans.
61 Excluding Rodrigues.	61 Non compris Rodriguez.
62 Persons aged 18 years and over.	62 Personnes âgées de 18 ans et plus.
63 Beginning 1993, persons working or seeking work for less than 12 hours per week are no longer included.	63 A partir de 1993, ne sont plus comprises les personnes qui travaillent, ou qui cherchent moins de 12 heures de travail par semaine.
64 Persons seeking work for 20 hours or more a week.	64 Personnes à la recherche d'un travail de 20 heures ou plus par semaine.
65 Curaçao.	65 Curaçao.
66 Including students seeking vacation work.	66 Y compris les étudiants qui cherchent un emploi pendant les vacances.
67 July of preceding year to June of current year.	67 Juillet de l'année précédente à juin de l'année en cours.
68 Persons aged 18 to 60 years.	68 Personnes âgées de 18 à 60 ans.
69 Asunción metropolitan area.	69 Région métropolitaine d'Asunción.
70 Persons aged 15 to 72 years.	70 Personnes âgées de 15 à 72 ans.
71 Dakar.	71 Dakar.
72 Excluding persons on child−care leave.	72 Non compris les personnes en congé parental.
73 Excluding Transkei, Bophuthatswana, Venda, Ciskei, Kwazulu, KaNgwane, Qwa Qwa, Gazankulu, Lebowa and KwaNdebele.	73 Non compris Transkei, Bophuthatswana, Venda, Ciskei, Kwazulu, KaNgwane, Qwa Qwa, Gazankulu, Lebowa et KwaNdebele.
74 Whites, Coloureds and Asians; eligibility rules for registration not specified.	74 Blancs, personnes de couleur et asiatiques; conditions d'éligibilité pour l'enregistrement non spécifiées.
75 Excluding Northern and Eastern provinces.	75 Non compris les provinces du Nord et de l'Est.
76 Khartoum province.	76 Province de Khartoum.
77 Beginning 1987, change in registration system; unemployed must re−register every 3 months.	77 A partir de 1987, modification du système d'enregistrement; les chômeurs doivent se réinscrire tous les 3 mois.
78 Persons aged 13 years and over.	78 Personnes âgées de 13 ans et plus.
79 New series according to 1980 population census.	79 Nouvelle série selon le recensement de population de 1980.
80 Excluding unemployed not previously employed.	80 Non compris les chômeurs n'ayant jamais travaillé.
81 Beginning 1988, figures revised on the basis of the 1990 census results.	81 A partir de 1988, données révisées sur la base des résultats du Recensement de 1990.
82 Annual averages.	82 Moyennes annuelles.

30
Unemployment
Number (thousands) and percentage unemployed [*cont.*]
Chômage
Nombre (milliers) et pourcentage des chômeurs [*suite*]

83   Persons aged 15 to 70 years.

84   Men aged 16 to 59 years; women aged 16 to 54 years.

85   Population census.

86   Claimants at unemployment benefits offices.

87   Beginning April 1983: excluding some categories of men aged 60 and over; February 1986:

88   Estimates based on 1990 census benchmarks.

89   Persons aged 16 to 65 years.

83   Personnes âgées de 15 à 70 ans.

84   Hommes âgés de 16 à 59 ans; femmes âgées de 16 à 54 ans.

85   Recensement de population.

86   Demandeurs auprès des bureaux de prestations de chômage.

87   A partir d'avril 1983: non compris certaines catégories d'hommes âgés de 60 ans et plus; de février 1986:

88   Estimations basées sur les données de calage du recensement de 1990.

89   Personnes âgées de 16 à 65 ans.

Technical notes, tables 29 and 30

Detailed data on labour force and related topics are published in the ILO *Yearbook of Labour Statistics* [13] and on the ILO Web site <http://laborsta.ilo.org>. The series shown in the *Statistical Yearbook* give an overall picture of the availability and disposition of labour resources and, in conjunction with other macro-economic indicators, can be useful for an overall assessment of economic performance. The ILO *Yearbook of Labour Statistics* provides a comprehensive description of the methodology underlying the labour series. Brief definitions of the major categories of labour statistics are given below.

"Employment" is defined to include persons above a specified age who, during a specified period of time, were in one of the following categories:

(a)   "Paid employment", comprising persons who perform some work for pay or profit during the reference period or persons with a job but not at work due to temporary absence, such as vacation, strike, education leave;

(b)   "Self-employment", comprising employers, own-account workers, members of producers cooperatives, persons engaged in production of goods and services for own consumption and unpaid family workers;

(c)   Members of the armed forces, students, homemakers and others mainly engaged in non-economic activities during the reference period who, at the same time, were in paid employment or self-employment are considered as employed on the same basis as other categories.

"Unemployment" is defined to include persons above a certain age and who, during a specified period of time were:

(a)   "Without work", i.e. were not in paid employment or self-employment;

(b)   "Currently available for work", i.e. were available for paid employment or self-employment during the reference period; and

(c)   "Seeking work", i.e. had taken specific steps in a specified period to find paid employment or self-employment.

Persons not considered to be unemployed include:

(a)   Persons intending to establish their own business or farm, but who had not yet arranged to do so and who were not seeking work for pay or profit;

(b)   Former unpaid family workers not at work and not seeking work for pay or profit.

For various reasons, national definitions of employment and unemployment often differ from the recommended international standard definitions and thereby limit international comparability. Intercountry

Notes techniques, tableaux 29 et 30

Des données détaillées sur la main-d'oeuvre et des sujets connexes sont publiées dans l'*Annuaire des Statistiques du Travail* du BIT [13] et sur le site Web du BIT <http://laborsta.ilo.org>. Les séries indiquées dans l'*Annuaire des Statistiques* donnent un tableau d'ensemble des disponibilités de main-d'œuvre et de l'emploi de ces ressources et, combinées à d'autres indicateurs économiques, elles peuvent être utiles pour une évaluation générale de la performance économique. L'*Annuaire des statistiques du Travail* du BIT donne une description complète de la méthodologie employée pour établir les séries sur la main-d'œuvre. On trouvera ci-dessous quelques brèves définitions des grandes catégories de statistiques du travail.

Le terme "Emploi" désigne les personnes dépassant un âge déterminé qui, au cours d'une période donnée, se trouvaient dans l'une des catégories suivantes:

(a)   La catégorie "emploi rémunéré", composée des personnes faisant un certain travail en échange d'une rémunération ou d'un profit pendant la période de référence, ou les personnes ayant un emploi, mais qui ne travaillaient pas en raison d'une absence temporaire (vacances, grève, congé d'études);

(b)   La catégorie "emploi indépendant" regroupe les employeurs, les travailleurs indépendants, les membres de coopératives de producteurs et les personnes s'adonnant à la production de biens et de services pour leur propre consommation et la main-d'œuvre familiale non rémunérée;

(c)   Les membres des forces armées, les étudiants, les aides familiales et autres personnes qui s'adonnaient essentiellement à des activités non économiques pendant la période de référence et qui, en même temps, avaient un emploi rémunéré ou indépendant, sont considérés comme employés au même titre que les personnes des autres catégories.

Par "chômeurs", on entend les personnes dépassant un âge déterminé et qui, pendant une période donnée, étaient:

(a)   "sans emploi", c'est-à-dire sans emploi rémunéré ou indépendant;

(b)   "disponibles", c'est-à-dire qui pouvaient être engagées pour un emploi rémunéré ou pouvaient s'adonner à un emploi indépendant au cours de la période de référence; et

(c)   "à la recherche d'un emploi", c'est-à-dire qui avaient pris des mesures précises à un certain moment pour trouver un emploi rémunéré ou un emploi indépendant.

Ne sont pas considérés comme chômeurs:

(a)   Les personnes qui, pendant la période de ré-

comparisons are also complicated by a variety of types of data collection systems used to obtain information on employed and unemployed persons.

Table 29 presents absolute figures on the distribution of employed persons by economic activity. In part A the figures are according to Revision 2 (ISIC 2) of the *International Standard Industrial Classification* [50], and in part B according to ISIC 3. In part A, the column for total employment includes economic activities not adequately defined and that are not accounted for in the other categories. Data are arranged as far as possible according to the major divisions of economic activity of the *International Standard Industrial Classification of All Economic Activities* [50].

Table 30: Figures are presented in absolute numbers and in percentages. Data are normally annual averages of monthly, quarterly or semi-annual data.

The series generally represent the total number of persons wholly unemployed or temporarily laid off. Percentage figures, where given, are calculated by comparing the number of unemployed to the total members of that group of the labour force on which the unemployment data are based.

férence, avaient l'intention de créer leur propre entreprise ou exploitation agricole, mais n'avaient pas encore pris les dispositions nécessaires à cet effet et qui n'étaient pas à la recherche d'un emploi en vue d'une rémunération ou d'un profit;

(b)   Les anciens travailleurs familiaux non rémunérés qui n'avaient pas d'emploi et n'étaient pas à la recherche d'un emploi en vue d'une rémunération ou d'un profit.

Pour diverses raisons, les définitions nationales de l'emploi et du chômage diffèrent souvent des définitions internationales types recommandées, limitant ainsi les possibilités de comparaison entre pays. Ces comparaisons se trouvent en outre compliquées par la diversité des systèmes de collecte de données utilisés pour recueillir des informations sur les personnes employées et les chômeurs.

Le *tableau 29* présente les effectifs de personnes employées par activité économique. Dans la partie A, les chiffres sont classés en fonction de la Révision 2 de la *Classification internationale type, par Industrie, de toutes les branches d'activité économique* [50] et dans la partie B en fonction de la Révision 3. Dans la partie A, l'emploi total inclut les personnes employées à des activités économiques mal définies et qui ne sont pas classées ailleurs. Les données sont ventilées autant que possible selon les branches d'activité économique de la *Classification internationale type, par industrie, de toutes les activités économiques* [50].

Tableau 30: Les chiffres sont présentés en valeur absolue et en pourcentage. Les données sont normalement des moyennes annuelles des données mensuelles, trimestrielles ou semestrielles.

Les séries représentent généralement le nombre total des chômeurs complets ou des personnes temporairement mises à pied. Les données en pourcentage, lorsqu'elles figurent au tableau, sont calculées par comparaison du nombre de chômeurs au nombre total des personnes du groupe de main-d'œuvre sur lequel sont basées les données relatives au chômage.

31
Wages in manufacturing
Salaires dans les industries manufacturières
By hour, day, week or month
Par heure, jour, semaine ou mois

Country or area and unit Pays ou zone et unité	1991	1992	1993	1994	1995	1996	1997	1998	1999	2000
Albania: lek Albanie : lek										
MF - month mois[1 2]	665.0	...	...	...	...	...	...	...	...	...
Algeria: Algerian dinar Algérie : dinar algérien										
MF - month mois[3]	...	6 430.0	8 012.0	8 937.0	10 462.0	12 323.0	...	...	...	...
Anguilla: EC dollar Anguilla : dollar des Carraïbes orientales										
MF - month mois	1 235.3	...	...	...	1 358.9	...	...	...	...	1 494.7[3]
Argentina: Argentine peso Argentine : peso argentin										
MF - hour heure[3 4 5]	24 941.2[6]	3.2	3.6	3.8	3.9	4.0	4.1	4.1	4.2	4.2
Armenia: dram Arménie : dram										
MF - month mois[3]	348.0[7]	1 574.0[7]	13 208.0[7]	2 470.0	7 680.0	12 464.0	17 656.0	21 278.0	...	...
Australia: Australian dollar Australie : dollar australien										
MF - hour heure[8 9]	13.3	13.7	14.0	14.7[10]	15.6	16.4[3]	...	17.4[3]	...	...
M - hour heure[8 9]	13.8	14.2	14.6	15.2[10]	16.1	16.9[3]	...	18.0[3]	...	...
F - hour heure[8 9]	11.7	12.0	12.4	13.0[10]	13.7	14.3[3]	...	15.2[3]	...	...
Austria: Austrian schilling Autriche : schilling autrichien										
MF - month mois[3]	...	...	...	...	26 020.0	27 239.0	27 776.0	28 455.0	...	...
M - month mois[3]	...	...	...	...	28 815.0	30 084.0	30 667.0	31 471.0	...	...
F - month mois[3]	...	...	...	...	19 903.0	20 667.0	21 051.0	21 480.0	...	...
MF - month mois[1]	26 583.0	28 183.0	29 572.0	30 790.0	32 173.0	...	...	...	...	...
Azerbaijan: manat Azerbaïdjan : manat										
MF - month mois	400.2[11]	3 282.6[11]	3 109.2	21 009.0	95 556.7	146 174.7	200 030.1[3]	202 082.6[3]	244 087.1[3]	299 523.8[3]
Bahrain: Bahrain dinar Bahreïn : dinar de Bahreïn										
MF - month mois[12 13]	277.0	271.0	254.0	250.0	...	...	...	257.0	227.0	231.0
M - month mois[12 13]	286.0	288.0	277.0	275.0	...	...	...	276.0	250.0	255.0
F - month mois[12 13]	155.0	120.0	103.0	100.0	...	...	...	125.0	109.0	107.0
Bangladesh: taka Bangladesh : taka										
MF - day jour[14 15 16]	56.1	59.9	...	...	...	...	...	...	...	...
M - day jour[14 15 16]	60.9	62.1	...	...	...	...	...	...	...	...
F - day jour[14 15 16]	30.1	31.3	...	...	...	...	...	...	...	...
MF - day jour[15 17 18]	21.8	23.0	...	...	...	...	...	...	...	...
M - day jour[15 17 18]	22.8	24.0	...	...	...	...	...	...	...	...
F - day jour[15 17 18]	15.9	17.2	...	...	...	...	...	...	...	...
Barbados: Barbados dollar Barbade : dollar de la Barbade										
MF - week semaine[5]	255.7	...	...	...	...	...	...	...	...	...
Belarus: Belarussian rouble Bélarus : rouble bélarussien										
MF - month mois	596.0	5 852.0	68 866.0	115 536.0	...	...	...	...	...	...
Belgium: Belgian franc Belgique : franc belge										
MF - hour heure[5 8]	363.1	379.6	395.9	411.8	388.2[3]	398.2[3]	406.8[3]	417.6[3]	...	...
M - hour heure[5 8]	385.7	403.8	420.7	438.0	405.5[3]	416.2[3]	425.2[3]	436.1[3]	...	...
F - hour heure[5 8]	287.7	300.2	313.4	325.3	320.9[3]	331.0[3]	335.8[3]	345.5[3]	...	...
MF - month mois[8 19]	91 950.0	95 615.0	98 702.0	101 426.0	104 773.0[3]	106 983.0[3]	109 980.0[3]	112 682.0[3]	...	...

31
Wages in manufacturing
By hour, day, week or month [cont.]
Salaires dans les industries manufacturières
Par heure, jour, semaine ou mois [suite]

Country or area and unit Pays ou zone et unité	1991	1992	1993	1994	1995	1996	1997	1998	1999	2000
M - month mois[8 19]	101 007.0	104 757.0	107 877.0	110 656.0	113 618.0[3]	116 279.0[3]	119 233.0[3]	122 031.0[3]	...	...
F - month mois[8 19]	64 116.0	67 524.0	70 506.0	73 061.0	80 118.0[3]	82 096.0[3]	85 194.0[3]	87 869.0[3]	...	...
Bolivia: boliviano Bolivie : boliviano										
MF - month mois[20]	620.9[8 21]	689.6[8 21]	761.3[8 21]	891.5[8 21]	959.0[8 21]	1 094.0[8 21]	873.0[3 22]	972.0[3 22]	1 055.0[3 22]	1 120.0[3 22]
Botswana: pula Botswana : pula										
MF - month mois[8 23]	403.0	511.0	606.0	537.0	582.0	617.0	633.0	632.0[3]	...	...
M - month mois[3 8 23]	...	...	...	...	...	...	...	821.0	...	...
F - month mois[3 8 23]	...	...	...	...	...	...	...	447.0	...	...
Brazil: real Brésil : real										
MF - month mois[8]	136 699.0[24]	1 562.0[24 25]	33 978.0[24 25]	479.1[3]	629.0[3]	696.6[3]	734.4[3]	715.0[3]	727.6[3]	...
M - month mois[8]	156 457.0[24]	2 779.0[24 25]	38 861.0[24 25]	547.1[3]	711.0[3]	784.0[3]	824.4[3]	799.5[3]	814.6[3]	...
F - month mois[8]	84 818.0[24]	963.0[24 25]	20 895.0[24 25]	297.0[3]	403.0[3]	455.8[3]	483.6[3]	486.2[3]	503.2[3]	...
British Virgin Islands: US dollar Iles Vierges britanniques : dollar des Etats-Unis										
MF - hour heure[3]	6.1	6.0	6.3	6.1	...	...	...	...	...	...
M - hour heure[3]	...	...	...	7.2	...	...	...	...	...	...
F - hour heure[3]	...	...	...	4.4	...	...	...	...	...	...
Bulgaria: lev Bulgarie : lev										
MF - month mois[26]	916.9	2 244.2[27]	3 481.2[27]	5 356.0[27]	8 448.0[27]	15 276.0[3 28]	148 460.0[3 28]	194 612.0[3 28]	203.0[3 29]	228.0[3 29]
M - month mois[3 28]	...	...	...	...	...	17 794.0	172 043.0	224 492.0	232.0[29]	...
F - month mois[3 28]	...	...	...	...	...	12 658.0	123 423.0	163 045.0	172.0[29]	...
Canada: Canadian dollar Canada : dollar canadien										
MF - hour heure[3 5 30 31]	14.9	15.4	15.7	16.0	16.2	16.7	16.9	17.2	17.2	...
MF - week semaine[3 31]	624.7	652.9	669.4	685.8	694.6	716.6	736.7	755.9	755.9	...
Chile: Chilean peso Chili : peso chilien										
MF - month mois[8 32]	173 012.0	211 780.0	116 457.0[3 33]	141 844.0	159 085.0	176 480.0	189 753.0	200 773.0	203 540.0	208 257.0
China: yuan Chine : yuan										
MF - month mois[3 34]	190.8	219.6	279.0	356.9	430.8	470.2	494.4	588.7	649.5	729.0
China, Hong Kong SAR: Hong Kong dollar Chine, Hong Kong RAS : dollar de Hong Kong										
MF - month mois[19 20]	6 382.8	7 163.5	7 897.5	8 780.4	9 508.3	10 323.8	11 331.2	11 711.6	11 853.0	...
M - month mois[19 20]	7 020.7	7 878.2	8 677.8	9 499.6	10 421.4	11 260.0	12 165.2	12 555.7	12 893.2	...
F - month mois[19 20]	5 718.4	6 445.4	7 180.2	8 098.4	8 684.2	9 390.4	10 467.0	10 915.9	10 846.7	...
MF - day jour[5 15]	200.7	218.6	241.7	266.6	278.0	296.9	322.6	335.3	334.7	...
M - day jour[5 15]	249.9	274.8	313.8	333.5	357.7	386.3	423.8	430.6	422.6	...
F - day jour[5 15]	173.6	189.6	206.8	226.3	233.5	245.3	258.8	262.9	268.9	...
China, Macao SAR: Macao pataca Chine, Macao RAS : pataca de Macao										
MF - month mois[35 36]	2 232.0[8]	2 509.0	2 926.0	3 111.0	3 210.0	3 124.0	3 323.0	3 138.0[3]	2 911.0[3]	...
M - month mois[35 36]	...	3 321.0	3 865.0	4 015.0	4 388.0	4 541.0	5 016.0	4 789.0[3]	4 701.0[3]	...
F - month mois[35 36]	...	2 222.0	2 447.0	2 624.0	2 682.0	2 677.0	2 842.0	2 694.0[3]	2 501.0[3]	...

31
Wages in manufacturing
By hour, day, week or month [cont.]
Salaires dans les industries manufacturières
Par heure, jour, semaine ou mois [suite]

Country or area and unit Pays ou zone et unité	1991	1992	1993	1994	1995	1996	1997	1998	1999	2000
Colombia: Colombian peso Colombie : peso colombien										
MF - month mois[8 37 38]	94 946.0	177 028.0	145 767.0	209 630.0	225 995.0	275 905.0	322 695.0	441 965.0	455 252.0	...
MF - month mois[8 35 37 38]	95 496.0	117 853.0	163 389.0	225 272.0	248 615.0	274 231.0	329 437.0	446 445.0	427 313.0	...
Cook Islands: Cook Islands dollar Iles Cook : dollar des Iles Cook										
MF - week semaine[8]	...	...	187.0	...	...	...	...	...	...	...
M - week semaine[8]	...	...	194.0	...	...	...	...	...	...	...
F - week semaine[8]	...	...	177.0	...	...	...	...	...	...	...
Costa Rica: Costa Rican colón Costa Rica : colón costa-ricien										
MF - month mois[8]	27 229.0	32 949.0	38 631.0	44 720.0	54 365.0	63 894.0	75 672.0	85 899.0[3]	97 774.5[3]	108 777.0[3]
M - month mois[8]	30 152.0	36 427.0	42 225.0	49 059.0	60 273.0	69 627.0	78 917.0	91 493.0[3]	106 594.0[3]	115 642.0[3]
F - month mois[8]	21 733.0	26 282.0	30 556.0	35 335.0	42 739.0	50 028.0	67 531.0	73 122.0[3]	77 969.3[3]	93 773.0[3]
Croatia: kuna Croatie : kuna										
MF - month mois	7 447.0[39]	34 024.0[39]	518.0	1 186.0	1 672.0	3 034.0[3]	3 358.0[3]	3 681.0[3]	3 869.0[3]	4 100.0[3]
Cuba: Cuban peso Cuba : peso cubain										
MF - month mois[2]	180.0	179.0	180.0	192.0	211.0	210.0	212.0	214.0	225.0	234.0
Cyprus: Cyprus pound Chypre : livre chypriote										
MF - month mois[8 19 32 40]	542.0	558.0	640.0	672.0	710.0	758.0	762.0	769.2[3]	806.0[3]	...
M - month mois[8 19 32 40]	626.0	678.0	738.0	770.0	822.0	864.0	871.0	897.1[3]	932.4[3]	...
F - month mois[8 19 32 40]	349.0	384.0	419.0	455.0	476.0	504.0	530.0	520.5[3]	560.7[3]	...
MF - week semaine[5 8 32 40]	80.3	89.0	101.0	104.1	113.4	130.1	117.5	...	...	...
M - week semaine[5 8 32 40]	105.6	116.4	134.2	132.3	143.4	170.8	145.0	166.5[3]	...	...
F - week semaine[5 8 32 40]	63.0	69.9	75.8	81.2	86.1	90.1	92.4	96.4[3]	...	...
Czech Republic: Czech koruna République tchèque : couronne tchèque										
MF - month mois[3]	...	...	5 652.0[41]	6 631.0[41]	7 854.0[42]	9 259.0[42]	10 411.0[43]	11 513.0[43]	12 271.0[43]	13 177.0[43]
Denmark: Danish krone Danemark : couronne danoise										
MF - hour heure[3]	...	...	...	...	152.8	163.5	167.3	174.6	182.3	...
M - hour heure[3]	...	...	...	...	160.2	172.9	176.5	183.3	192.2	...
F - hour heure[3]	...	...	...	...	135.5	143.1	147.4	154.8	160.3	...
MF - hour heure[5 40 44]	104.6	108.3	...	...	...	...	...	...	...	...
M - hour heure[5 40 44]	108.5	112.2	...	...	...	...	...	...	...	...
F - hour heure[5 40 44]	92.1	95.4	...	...	...	...	...	...	...	...
Dominican Republic: Dominican peso Rép. dominicaine : peso dominicain										
MF - hour heure[35 45]	10.4	12.2	11.3	17.4	16.6	18.0	21.6	...	...	...
MF - month mois[20]	1 456.0	1 456.0	1 456.0	1 675.0	2 010.0	...	...	...	...	...
Ecuador: sucre Equateur : sucre										
MF - hour heure[5]	669.4	1 088.6	1 676.1	2 113.1	2 469.3[3]	3 226.7[3]	4 380.4[3]	...	...	...
MF - month mois[3 25]	...	...	...	...	1 302.7	1 726.4	2 179.7	...	...	...
Egypt: Egyptian pound Egypte : livre égyptienne										
MF - week semaine[5 8 12]	55.0	62.0	70.0	77.0	84.0	93.0[3]	103.0[3]	107.0[3]	...	...

31
Wages in manufacturing
By hour, day, week or month [cont.]
Salaires dans les industries manufacturières
Par heure, jour, semaine ou mois [suite]

Country or area and unit Pays ou zone et unité	1991	1992	1993	1994	1995	1996	1997	1998	1999	2000
M - week semaine[5 8 12]	57.0	64.0	72.0	80.0	87.0	97.0[3]	107.0[3]	112.0[3]	...	...
F - week semaine[5 8 12]	41.0	48.0	54.0	57.0	64.0	87.0[3]	80.0[3]	77.0[3]	...	...
El Salvador: El Salvadoran colón El Salvador : colón salvadorien										
MF - hour heure[5]	4.1	4.6	5.4	6.2	6.9	7.5	...	10.3	10.7	10.1
M - hour heure[5]	4.5	4.8	5.6	6.4	7.0	7.7	...	12.0	12.1	11.4
F - hour heure[5]	3.7	4.5	5.2	6.0	6.8	7.3	...	9.0	9.2	9.0
MF - month mois[3 20]	...	...	...	...	...	...	...	1 993.4	1 746.6	...
M - month mois[3 20]	...	...	...	...	...	...	...	2 348.5	2 157.8	...
F - month mois[3 20]	...	...	...	...	...	...	...	1 646.0	1 337.1	...
Eritrea: Nakfa Erythrée : Nakfa										
MF - month mois[3 20]	...	...	...	...	...	478.5	...	...	...	...
M - month mois[3 20]	...	...	...	...	...	522.0	...	...	...	...
F - month mois[3 20]	...	...	...	...	...	346.5	...	...	...	...
Estonia: Estonian kroon Estonie : couronne estonienne										
MF - month mois	850.7[46]	536.0[3]	1 036.0[3]	1 784.0[3]	2 421.0[3]	2 991.0[3]	3 578.0[3]	4 081.0[3]	4 117.0[3]	4 772.0[3]
Fiji: Fiji dollar Fidji : dollar des Fidji										
MF - day jour[5 8 15]	...	...	13.9	...	...	16.3	15.1	14.5	...	...
Finland: Finnish markka Finlande : markka finlandais										
MF - hour heure[5 47]	50.7	52.3	53.5	55.8	60.1	...	...	...	...	...
M - hour heure[5 47]	53.9	55.4	56.8	59.2	63.4	...	...	...	...	...
F - hour heure[5 47]	42.1	43.4	44.4	46.6	50.3	...	...	...	...	...
MF - month mois[3 48]	...	...	...	...	11 004.0	11 434.0	11 677.0	12 054.0	12 510.0	...
M - month mois[3 48]	...	...	...	...	11 810.0	12 240.0	12 523.0	12 880.0	13 305.0	...
F - month mois[3 48]	...	...	...	...	9 232.0	9 674.0	9 842.0	10 237.0	10 683.0	...
France: French franc France : franc français										
MF - hour heure[5 8]	47.5	49.4	50.6	51.8	52.8	54.2	55.4	...	...	...
M - hour heure[5 8]	50.5	52.4	53.7	54.9	55.8	57.2	58.5	...	...	...
F - hour heure[5 8]	39.7	41.2	42.5	43.3	44.3	45.4	46.3	...	...	...
MF - month mois[3]	...	...	...	...	...	...	13 600.0	13 860.0	14 110.0	...
M - month mois[3]	...	...	...	...	...	...	14 520.0	14 770.0	...	...
F - month mois[3]	...	...	...	...	...	...	11 210.0	11 490.0	...	...
Gambia: dalasi Gambie : dalasi										
MF - month mois[3 49 50]	...	...	1 008.6	1 045.5	...	...	...	969.7	...	...
MF - day jour	...	...	...	...	...	...	...	...	...	...
Georgia: lari Géorgie : lari										
MF - month mois[3]	...	...	...	...	...	...	51.2	68.9	87.4	103.4[51]
M - month mois[3]	...	...	...	...	...	...	...	...	101.1	120.7[51]
F - month mois[3]	...	...	...	...	...	...	...	...	63.3	71.7[51]

31
Wages in manufacturing
By hour, day, week or month [*cont.*]
Salaires dans les industries manufacturières
Par heure, jour, semaine ou mois [*suite*]

Country or area and unit Pays ou zone et unité	1991	1992	1993	1994	1995	1996	1997	1998	1999	2000
Germany: deutsche mark Allemagne : deutsche mark										
MF - hour heure[35]	...	...	...	...	...	25.7	26.2	26.8	27.5	28.8
M - hour heure[35]	...	...	...	...	...	27.0	27.4	28.0	28.8	30.1
F - hour heure[35]	...	...	...	...	...	20.0	20.3	20.8	21.4	22.4
F. R. Germany: deutsche mark R. f. Allemagne : deutsche mark										
MF - hour heure[5]	21.3[52]	22.5[52]	23.8[52]	24.6[52]	25.5[3]	26.4[3]	26.8[3]	27.4[3]	...	19.6[3]
M - hour heure[5]	22.6[52]	23.8[52]	25.0[52]	25.8[52]	26.8[3]	27.7[3]	28.0[3]	28.6[3]	...	20.8[3]
F - hour heure[5]	16.5[52]	17.5[52]	18.5[52]	19.0[52]	19.7[3]	20.5[3]	20.8[3]	21.3[3]	...	15.9[3]
German D. R.(former): deutsche mark R. d. allemande (anc.) : deutsche mark										
MF - hour heure[5]	9.4	11.9	13.9	15.5	17.0[3]	18.0[3]	18.6[3]	19.2[3]	...	27.8[3]
M - hour heure[5]	9.7	12.3	14.4	16.2	17.8[3]	18.8[3]	19.5[3]	20.1[3]	...	29.1[3]
F - hour heure[5]	8.4	10.5	11.9	13.0	14.1[3]	15.0[3]	15.4[3]	15.9[3]	...	21.4[3]
Ghana: cedi Ghana : cedi										
MF - month mois[8]	34 226.0	...	...	...	...	...	...	...	...	...
Gibraltar: Gibraltar pound Gibraltar : livre de Gibraltar										
MF - week semaine[5 8 53]	214.1	239.4	252.2	233.3	279.3	307.3	...	...	...	...
M - week semaine[5 8 53]	254.4	254.5	272.7	246.0	295.3	345.0	...	...	...	...
F - week semaine[5 8 53]	148.8	161.7	166.0	171.5	193.8	192.5	...	...	...	...
Greece: drachma Grèce : drachme										
MF - hour heure[5 12]	772.1	878.2	970.8	1 097.9	1 243.3	1 349.9	1 470.5	1 539.8	...	...
M - hour heure[5 12]	854.7	967.5	1 063.6	1 200.1	1 353.3	1 459.8	1 585.9	1 653.0	...	...
F - hour heure[5 12]	673.2	765.3	851.4	963.4	1 088.6	1 183.4	1 287.8	1 355.8	...	...
MF - month mois[12 19]	200 303.0	229 596.0	259 853.0	293 627.0	332 568.0	363 857.0	399 599.0	423 142.0	...	...
M - month mois[12 19]	216 176.0	247 723.0	280 219.0	319 082.0	358 318.0	391 700.0	430 889.0	456 488.0	...	...
F - month mois[12 19]	148 938.0	171 921.0	195 542.0	218 400.0	244 904.0	278 996.0	303 900.0	323 153.0	...	...
Guam: US dollar Guam : dollar des Etats-Unis										
MF - hour heure[5 8 13]	9.1	9.3	10.1	10.4	10.6	...	...	...	...	...
Guatemala: quetzal Guatemala : quetzal										
MF - month mois	577.9	686.2	775.2	868.1	1 138.0	1 368.9	1 430.0	1 541.0	1 602.3	1 655.3
Guinea: Guinean franc Guinée : franc guinéen										
MF - month mois[20]	85 000.0	110 000.0	110 000.0	130 000.0	130 000.0	153 000.0	...	...	...	...
Hungary: forint Hongrie : forint										
MF - month mois[3 48]	...	21 107.0[43]	26 317.0[43]	32 500.0[43]	39 554.0[43]	48 195.0[43]	58 915.0[43]	68 872.0[43]	76 099.0[54]	88 136.0[54]
M - month mois[3 48]	...	24 319.0[43]	30 422.0[43]	37 429.0[43]	45 466.0[43]	55 437.0[43]	68 396.0[43]	79 892.0[43]	86 866.0[54]	...
F - month mois[3 48]	...	17 014.0[43]	21 109.0[43]	26 175.0[43]	31 853.0[43]	38 897.0[43]	46 897.0[43]	54 985.0[43]	61 898.0[54]	...
MF - month mois[5 43]	13 992.0[55]	17 636.0	21 751.0	...	...	...	...	...	...	...
Iceland: Icelandic króna Islande : couronne islandaise										
MF - month mois[3 56]	...	...	...	...	...	...	...	...	119 800.0	129 800.0
India: Indian rupee Inde : roupie indienne										
MF - month mois[5]	1 019.3	932.6	977.4	960.5	1 211.0	1 188.8	1 137.3	...	...	...

31
Wages in manufacturing
By hour, day, week or month [cont.]
Salaires dans les industries manufacturières
Par heure, jour, semaine ou mois [suite]

Country or area and unit Pays ou zone et unité	1991	1992	1993	1994	1995	1996	1997	1998	1999	2000
Indonesia: Indonesian rupiah Indonésie : roupie indonésien										
MF - week semaine[5 8 25 57 58]	...	...	...	...	...	...	...	64.2	75.3	...
Ireland: Irish pound Irlande : livre irlandaise										
MF - hour heure[5 8 59]	5.6	5.9	6.2	6.3	6.5	6.6	6.9	7.2	...	...
M - hour heure[5 8 40]	6.3	6.6	7.0	7.0	7.1	7.3	7.5	7.9	...	...
F - hour heure[5 8 40]	4.4	4.7	5.0	5.1	5.3	5.4	5.6	5.9	...	...
Isle of Man: pound sterling Ile de Man : livre sterling										
MF - hour heure[3 8]	...	...	...	...	6.9	6.6	7.1	7.8	9.1	8.9
M - hour heure[3 8]	...	...	...	...	6.9	7.0	7.6	8.9	9.4	9.3
F - hour heure[3 8]	...	...	...	...	6.7	5.0	5.7	5.7	7.5	7.3
MF - week semaine[8]	...	207.0	225.0	238.1	285.2[3]	272.4[3]	292.7[3]	313.3[3]	377.1[3]	394.8[3]
M - week semaine[8]	...	...	276.0	251.8	288.6[3]	294.6[3]	320.5[3]	366.0[3]	408.9[3]	411.2[3]
F - week semaine[8]	...	...	148.0	199.4	266.2[3]	196.1[3]	215.8[3]	209.6[3]	241.1[3]	332.3[3]
Israel: new sheqel Israël : nouveau sheqel										
MF - month mois[60]	3 080.0	3 514.0	3 917.0	4 427.0[3]	5 061.0[3]	5 757.0[3]	6 676.0[3]	7 418.0[3]	8 227.0[3]	8 665.0[3]
Italy: Italian lira Italie : lire italienne										
MF - month mois[35]	109.5[61]	115.7[61]	120.5[61]	124.3[61]	128.7[61]	101.8[62]	105.7[62]	108.6[62]	110.9[62]	113.1[62]
MF - month mois[3 19]	110.2[61]	116.8[61]	121.9[61]	126.1[61]	131.3[61]	102.2[62]	106.4[62]	109.6[62]	112.1[62]	114.4[62]
Jamaica: Jamaican dollar Jamaïque : dollar jamaïcain										
MF - week semaine	701.0	895.0	...	...	...	...	...	...	...	...
Japan: yen Japon : yen										
MF - month mois[8 63 64]	...	...	...	276 700.0	278 800.0	283 700.0	287 200.0	289 600.0	291 100.0	293 100.0
M - month mois[8 63 64]	...	...	...	317 000.0	318 200.0	322 500.0	325 600.0	327 900.0	327 700.0	328 100.0
F - month mois[8 63 64]	...	...	...	175 500.0	177 900.0	181 800.0	184 500.0	187 300.0	189 000.0	190 700.0
MF - month mois[65]	368 011.0	372 594.0	371 356.0	...	...	...	...	...	...	...
M - month mois[65]	450 336.0	454 482.0	...	...	...	...	...	...	...	...
F - month mois[65]	193 112.0	198 058.0	...	...	...	...	...	...	...	...
Jordan: Jordan dinar Jordanie : dinar jordanien										
MF - day jour[8 49]	4.6	4.8	4.9	5.2	5.3	5.6	5.7	5.9	...	...
M - day jour[8 49]	4.9	5.0	5.1	5.4	5.5	5.8	6.0	6.2	...	...
F - day jour[8 49]	3.0	2.9	3.1	3.3	3.4	3.6	3.6	3.7	...	...
Kazakhstan: tenge Kazakhstan : tenge										
MF - month mois	489.0[66]	5 675.0[66]	144.0	2 263.0	6 520.0	9 288.0	11 092.0	11 357.0[3]	13 434.0[3]	...
M - month mois[3]	...	...	...	...	...	...	...	12 246.0	...	...
F - month mois[3]	...	...	...	...	...	...	...	9 641.0	...	...
Kenya: Kenya shilling Kenya : shilling du Kenya										
MF - month mois[8 67]	3 324.2	...	...	4 920.5	6 228.7	4 998.6	5 510.8	...	...	...
M - month mois[8 67]	3 430.1	...	...	4 878.6	6 867.7	...	5 294.3	...	...	...
F - month mois[8 67]	2 515.8	...	...	5 168.5	3 314.4	...	6 509.5	...	...	...

31
Wages in manufacturing
By hour, day, week or month [cont.]
Salaires dans les industries manufacturières
Par heure, jour, semaine ou mois [suite]

Country or area and unit Pays ou zone et unité	1991	1992	1993	1994	1995	1996	1997	1998	1999	2000
Korea, Republic of: Korean won Corée, République de : won coréen										
MF - month mois[25 32]	690.3	798.5	885.4[3]	1 022.5[3]	1 123.9[3]	1 261.2[3]	1 326.2[3]	1 284.5[3]	1 475.5[3]	1 601.5[3]
M - month mois[25 32]	842.8	963.8	1 055.5[3]	1 206.7[3]	1 314.7[3]	1 463.4[3]	1 527.2[3]	1 467.3[3]	1 686.3[3]	1 826.4[3]
F - month mois[25 32]	428.1	497.3	551.4[3]	638.9[3]	711.1[3]	795.6[3]	852.0[3]	820.1[3]	933.1[3]	1 055.8[3]
Kyrgyzstan: Kyrgyz som Kirghizistan : som kirghize										
MF - month mois[3]	2.1	15.1	118.1	280.4	377.1	652.1	844.7	988.8	1 280.8	...
Latvia: lats Lettonie : lats										
MF - month mois[3]	3.2[2]	22.5	46.2	60.5[44]	86.5[44]	95.2[44]	114.7[44]	128.3[44]	129.0[44]	135.1[44]
M - month mois[3]	...	24.0	...	66.2[44]	94.6[44]	101.4[44]	121.5[44]	136.1[44]	137.5[44]	146.0[44]
F - month mois[3]	...	20.1	...	54.8[44]	77.8[44]	88.3[44]	107.9[44]	119.2[44]	118.5[44]	122.9[44]
Lithuania: litas Lituanie : litas										
MF - hour heure[3 8 48 68]	...	...	...	...	...	...	4.9	5.9	6.2	6.2
M - hour heure[3 8 48 68]	...	...	...	...	...	...	5.4	6.6	6.9	6.9
F - hour heure[3 8 48 68]	...	...	...	...	...	...	4.4	5.1	5.4	5.5
MF - month mois[3 8 48]	...	...	...	...	...	...	824.0	973.0	1 010.0	...
M - month mois[3 8 48]	...	...	...	...	...	...	909.0	1 089.0	1 135.0	...
F - month mois[3 8 48]	...	...	...	...	...	...	733.0	847.0	875.0	...
Luxembourg: Luxembourg franc Luxembourg : franc luxembourgeois										
MF - hour heure[5 8]	400.0	425.0	446.0	468.0	478.0	484.0	465.0[3]	470.0[3]	493.0[3]	506.0[3]
M - hour heure[5 8]	420.0	446.0	466.0	486.0	495.0	504.0	485.0[3]	490.0[3]	514.0[3]	527.0[3]
F - hour heure[5 8]	265.0	278.0	300.0	314.0	316.0	320.0	335.0[3]	337.0[3]	351.0[3]	377.0[3]
MF - month mois[8 19]	124 885.0	133 958.0	136 802.0	138 170.0	139 190.0	140 155.0	145 433.0[3]	144 697.0[3]	148 436.0[3]	150 348.0[3]
M - month mois[8 19]	135 258.0	144 648.0	146 876.0	148 197.0	147 878.0	148 131.0	156 574.0[3]	155 036.0[3]	159 116.0[3]	161 161.0[3]
F - month mois[8 19]	77 096.0	83 632.0	88 607.0	89 493.0	93 576.0	95 441.0	97 209.0[3]	98 614.0[3]	102 264.0[3]	105 723.0[3]
Malawi: Malawi kwacha Malawi : kwacha malawien										
MF - month mois	154.8	167.8	173.8	184.7	195.8	...	...	...	...	...
Malaysia: ringgit Malaisie : ringgit										
MF - month mois	719.0	794.0	848.0	928.0	1 002.0	1 115.0	1 210.0	...	...	...
M - month mois	952.0	1 037.0	1 082.0	1 161.0	1 242.0	1 343.0	1 449.0	...	...	...
F - month mois	495.0	558.0	612.0	677.0	719.0	842.0	912.0	...	...	...
Mauritius: Mauritian rupee Maurice : roupie mauricienne										
MF - month mois[8 19]	3 684.0	4 016.0	4 411.0	5 162.0	5 659.0	5 972.0	6 282.0	6 912.0	7 034.0	7 638.0
MF - day jour[8 69]	84.0	93.0	109.0	122.0	132.0	138.0	148.7	161.4	166.0	174.3
Mexico: Mexican peso Mexique : peso mexicain										
MF - hour heure[3 5]	5.2	6.4	6.5	7.2	8.3	10.2	12.4	14.8	17.8	...
MF - month mois[5]	1 023.9[25 70]	1 255.7[25 70]	1 400.1	1 415.0	1 605.0	1 963.0	...	...	...	...
MF - month mois[3]	947.8	...	1 014.9	...	1 220.6	1 404.2	1 651.8	2 077.2	2 377.7	2 909.6
M - month mois[3]	1 124.1	...	1 122.3	...	1 338.3	1 526.3	1 816.7	2 286.0	2 632.9	3 253.4
F - month mois[3]	558.9	...	750.1	...	919.9	1 104.1	1 281.7	1 622.4	1 835.9	2 240.4

31
Wages in manufacturing
By hour, day, week or month [*cont.*]
Salaires dans les industries manufacturières
Par heure, jour, semaine ou mois [*suite*]

Country or area and unit Pays ou zone et unité	1991	1992	1993	1994	1995	1996	1997	1998	1999	2000
Myanmar: kyat Myanmar : kyat										
M - month mois[51 71]	631.9	880.5	985.3	...	...	...	1 043.3	1 054.3	1 066.0	...
F - month mois[51 71]	670.9	866.8	940.2	...	...	...	998.9	1 010.6	1 190.9	
Netherlands: Netherlands guilder Pays-Bas : florin néerlandais										
MF - hour heure	22.3[8 59]	22.7[8 59]	23.4[8 59]	27.9[3 872]	28.9[3 872]	30.2[3 72]	31.1[3 72]	32.0[3 872]	33.3[3 872]	...
M - hour heure	23.5[8 40]	23.9[8 40]	24.5[8 40]	29.1[3 872]	30.1[3 872]	31.4[3 72]	32.3[3 72]	33.4[3 872]	34.7[3 872]	...
F - hour heure	17.8[8 40]	18.3[8 40]	19.0[8 40]	22.2[3 872]	22.6[3 872]	24.0[3 72]	24.8[3 72]	25.7[3 872]	26.9[3 872]	...
MF - month mois[3 48 72]	...	...	...	4 052.0[8]	4 184.0[8]	4 369.0	4 472.0	4 614.0[8]	4 797.0[8]	...
M - month mois[3 48 72]	...	...	...	4 186.0[8]	4 318.0[8]	4 497.0	4 601.0	4 750.0[8]	4 932.0[8]	...
F - month mois[3 48 72]	...	...	...	3 194.0[8]	3 270.0[8]	3 474.0	3 567.0	3 684.0[8]	3 870.0[8]	...
Netherlands Antilles: Netherlands Antillean guilder Antilles néerlandaises : florin des Antilles néerlandaises										
MF - month mois[3 73]	2 319.0	2 416.0	2 441.0	2 445.0	2 364.0	2 475.0	2 591.0	2 462.0	...	2 565.0
New Zealand: New Zealand dollar Nouvelle-Zélande : dollar néo-zélandais										
MF - hour heure[8]	13.8	14.2	14.3	14.4[3 74]	14.8[3 74]	15.4[3 74]	15.9[3 74]	16.3[3 74]	16.9[3 74]	17.0[3 75]
M - hour heure[8]	14.8	15.1	15.2	15.3[3 74]	15.7[3 74]	16.3[3 74]	16.8[3 74]	17.2[3 74]	17.7[3 74]	17.9[3 75]
F - hour heure[8]	11.0	11.5	11.6	11.9[3 74]	12.2[3 74]	12.7[3 74]	13.2[3 74]	13.7[3 74]	14.3[3 74]	14.5[3 75]
Nicaragua: córdoba Nicaragua : córdoba										
MF - hour heure	4.7	8.0	8.8	9.4	10.0	11.0	11.2	12.0	12.0	...
MF - month mois	1 140.6	1 951.2	2 150.0	2 282.4	2 443.6	2 672.0	2 724.0	2 846.0	3 014.3	...
Norway: Norwegian krone Norvège : couronne norvégienne										
MF - hour heure[5 40 67]	97.3	100.4	103.2	106.1	109.8	114.4	118.9	125.5	...	...
M - hour heure[5 40 67]	99.5	102.7	105.4	108.5	112.3	117.0	121.6	128.3	...	...
F - hour heure[5 40 67]	86.7	89.2	91.8	94.6	97.8	102.2	106.1	112.4	...	...
MF - month mois[3 8 48 72]	...	...	...	...	...	...	20 005.0	21 417.0	22 441.0	23 388.0
M - month mois[3 8 48 72]	...	...	...	...	...	...	...	...	23 039.0	23 964.0
F - month mois[3 8 48 72]	...	...	...	...	...	...	...	...	20 017.0	21 091.0
Pakistan: Pakistan rupee Pakistan : roupie pakistanaise										
MF - month mois	...	...	1 502.0	1 956.0	2 970.0	2 878.0	3 211.5	3 706.0	2 865.8	...
Panama: balboa Panama : balboa										
MF - month mois[3 8 36]	...	...	...	...	...	...	...	247.0	250.9	...
M - month mois[3 8 36]	...	...	...	...	...	...	...	249.8	259.0	...
F - month mois[3 8 36]	...	...	...	...	...	...	...	238.5	241.3	...
MF - month mois	537.0[49]	524.0[49]	590.0[49]	587.0[49]	...	597.0[3 76]	...	...	...	...
Paraguay: guaraní Paraguay : guaraní										
MF - month mois	273 537.0	298 682.0	380 096.0	480 081.0	610 414.0	686 436.0	761 675.0	898 598.0	741 416.0	...
M - month mois	292 787.0	342 552.0	407 117.0	507 072.0	645 759.0	721 289.0	800 340.0	947 853.0	923 124.0	...
F - month mois	196 738.0	177 754.0	298 952.0	389 558.0	485 113.0	563 271.0	628 963.0	729 160.0	404 458.0	...
Peru: new sol Pérou : nouveau sol										
MF - month mois[19 20]	322.7[8]	565.0[8]	860.6[8]	1 451.1[8]	...	1 624.6[3 77]	1 875.2[3 77]	2 067.0[3 77]	2 155.6[3 77]	2 315.7[3 77]

31
Wages in manufacturing
By hour, day, week or month [*cont.*]
Salaires dans les industries manufacturières
Par heure, jour, semaine ou mois [*suite*]

Country or area and unit / Pays ou zone et unité	1991	1992	1993	1994	1995	1996	1997	1998	1999	2000
MF - day jour[5 15]	6.0[8]	10.1[8]	14.8[8]	21.9[8]	24.0[3 8 78]	22.6[3 77]	24.5[3 77]	24.9[3 77]	25.6[3 77]	27.2[3 77]
Philippines: Philippine peso Philippines : peso philippin										
MF - month mois	4 831.0[12 79]	5 386.0[12 79]	5 584.0[12 79]	6 272.0[12 79]	6 654.0[12 79]	6 815.0[3 79]	7 281.0[3 79]	6 400.0[3 80]	6 900.0[3 80]	...
M - month mois[79]	...	...	6 223.0[12]	7 063.0[12]	7 529.0[12]	7 605.0[3]	8 065.0[3]	...	...	...
F - month mois[79]	...	...	4 741.0[12]	5 277.0[12]	5 592.0[12]	5 814.0[3]	631.0[3]	...	...	...
Poland: new zloty Pologne : nouveau zloty										
MF - month mois[67]	1 620.1[25 81]	2 679.4[25 81]	361.9[3]	494.9[3]	656.7[3]	832.8[3]	1 014.9[3]	1 164.4[3]	1 598.9[3]	...
Portugal: Portuguese escudo Portugal : escudo portugais										
MF - hour heure[5]	370.0	419.0	436.4	...	470.0	498.0	539.0	703.0[3]	718.0[3]	...
M - hour heure[5]	419.0	480.0	485.7	...	551.0	586.0	626.0	832.0[3]	856.0[3]	...
F - hour heure[5]	295.0	326.0	390.1	...	378.0	402.0	434.0	545.0[3]	554.0[3]	...
MF - month mois	...	...	...	...	100 700.0	107 800.0	116 100.0	120 803.0[3]	122 327.0[3]	...
M - month mois	...	...	...	...	118 900.0	127 200.0	136 900.0	140 720.0[3]	146 138.0[3]	...
F - month mois	...	...	...	...	78 100.0	83 900.0	88 900.0	94 837.0[3]	94 057.0[3]	...
Puerto Rico: US dollar Porto Rico : dollar des Etats-Unis										
MF - hour heure[5]	6.3	6.6	7.0	7.2	7.4	7.7	8.0	8.4	8.9	9.4
Republic of Moldova: Moldovan leu République de Moldova : leu moldove										
MF - month mois	475.2[82]	3 676.2[82]	37.8	143.2	209.5	282.2[3 43]	352.0[3 43]	399.0[3 43]	492.6[3 43]	677.7[3 43]
Romania: Romanian leu Roumanie : leu roumain										
MF - month mois[3]	...	23 582.0	71 779.0	169 435.0	268 436.0	424 587.0	826 902.0	1 198 560.0	1 712 748.0	...
MF - month mois[5]	6 842.0[26]	17 959.0	54 245.0	126 260.0	...	...	...	...	...	...
Russian Federation: ruble Fédération de Russie : ruble										
MF - month mois	584.0	6 466.0	57 633.0	198 593.0	464 792.0[3]	748 189.0[3]	919.0[3 83]	1 026.0[3 83]	...	...
San Marino: Italian lira Saint-Marin : lire italienne										
MF - day jour	102 579.0	111 611.0	113 772.0	120 131.0	127 347.0	135 278.0	142 712.0	149 357.0	157 158.0	...
Serbia and Montenegro: Yugoslav dinar Serbie-et-Monténégro : dinar yougoslave										
MF - month mois[3 84 85 86]	...	...	...	...	...	...	647.0	897.0	1 126.0[87]	...
Seychelles: Seychelles rupee Seychelles : roupie seychelloises										
MF - month mois[88]	2 259.0[89]	2 349.0	2 454.0	2 422.0	2 513.0	2 646.0	2 727.0	2 853.0	2 962.0	...
Singapore: Singapore dollar Singapour : dollar singapourien										
MF - month mois	1 551.8	1 686.2	1 817.8	1 995.3	2 157.3	2 319.5	2 486.7	2 716.0[3 90]	2 803.0[3]	3 036.0[3]
M - month mois	1 970.1	2 127.4	2 266.2	2 473.8	2 644.0	2 815.2	2 999.7	3 311.0[3 90]	3 384.0[3]	3 653.0[3]
F - month mois	1 096.8	1 190.7	1 294.5	1 415.4	1 541.2	1 674.4	1 811.0	1 916.0[3 90]	2 007.0[3]	2 181.0[3]
Slovakia: Slovak koruna Slovaquie : couronne slovaque										
MF - month mois[3]	3 757.0[91]	4 370.0[91]	5 234.0[91]	6 193.0[91]	7 194.0[91]	8 230.0[91]	9 197.0[92]	10 001.0[92]	10 758.0	11 722.0
Slovenia: tolar Slovénie : tolar										
MF - month mois[3]	14 737.0	43 305.0	62 491.0	79 347.0	92 877.0	106 144.0	118 960.0	132 080.0	144 110.0	161 269.0
Solomon Islands: Solomon Islands dollar Iles Salomon : dollar des Iles Salomon										
MF - month mois[18]	403.0	...	572.0	579.0	632.0	987.0	...	...	...	...

31
Wages in manufacturing
By hour, day, week or month [*cont.*]
Salaires dans les industries manufacturières
Par heure, jour, semaine ou mois [*suite*]

Country or area and unit Pays ou zone et unité	1991	1992	1993	1994	1995	1996	1997	1998	1999	2000
South Africa: rand Afrique du Sud : rand										
MF - month mois[93]	1 890.0	2 195.0	2 446.0	...	...	...	...	...	...	...
Spain: peseta Espagne : peseta										
MF - hour heure	994.0	1 080.0	1 159.0	1 221.0	1 263.0	1 311.0[3]	1 372.0[3]	1 429.0[3]	1 463.0[3]	1 499.0[3]
Sri Lanka: Sri Lanka rupee Sri Lanka : roupie sri-lankaise										
MF - hour heure[5][51]	11.2	11.8	13.7	15.1	16.5	17.9	18.2	20.3	22.0	...
M - hour heure[5][51]	11.7	12.3	14.1	15.6	17.1	17.9	18.4	20.8	22.3	...
F - hour heure[5][51]	9.4	10.4	12.7	13.8	16.2	17.6	16.3	16.4	18.1	...
MF - day jour[5][51]	100.5	104.8	116.8	134.6	145.4	151.2	166.3	174.2	199.2	...
M - day jour[5][51]	106.1	107.7	120.3	139.0	151.7	151.6	167.8	175.6	203.9	...
F - day jour[5][51]	79.2	96.7	105.7	120.0	136.2	138.7	142.5	145.7	165.8	...
Sudan: Sudanese pound Soudan : livre soudanaise										
MF - month mois[5]	...	1 210.3	...	...	...	...	...	...	...	...
Swaziland: lilangeni Swaziland : lilangeni										
M - month mois[8][13][14]	1 415.0	1 486.0	1 146.0	1 861.0	2 134.0	2 388.0	2 948.0	...	...	...
F - month mois[8][13][14]	845.0	835.0	1 869.0	1 252.0	1 507.0	1 530.0	1 850.0	...	...	...
M - month mois[8][13][17]	318.0	372.0	409.0	424.0	558.0	681.0	863.0	...	...	...
F - month mois[8][13][17]	286.0	305.0	382.0	346.0	483.0	572.0	542.0	...	...	...
Sweden: Swedish krona Suède : couronne suédoise										
MF - hour heure[5][40]	91.7[94]	98.3[94]	98.5[94][95]	102.4[94][95]	107.0[94][95]	115.0[94][95]	101.2[95][96]	105.1[95][97]	106.9[95][97]	111.3[95][97]
M - hour heure[5][40]	93.8[94]	100.7[94]	100.7[94][95]	104.5[94][95]	109.1[94][95]	117.4[94][95]	103.3[95][96]	107.0[95][97]	108.7[95][97]	113.3[95][97]
F - hour heure[5][40]	83.7[94]	90.1[94]	90.1[94][95]	94.2[94][95]	98.2[94][95]	105.7[94][95]	93.3[95][96]	97.6[95][97]	99.6[95][97]	103.4[95][97]
Switzerland: Swiss franc Suisse : franc suisse										
M - hour heure[5][8][40]	25.0	26.2	26.8	...	...	...	...	...	...	...
F - hour heure[5][8][40]	17.0	17.8	18.4	...	...	...	...	...	...	...
MF - month mois[3][98]	...	...	...	5 462.0	...	5 565.0	...	5 717.0	...	...
M - month mois[3][98]	...	...	...	5 881.0	...	5 970.0	...	6 128.0	...	...
F - month mois[3][98]	...	...	...	4 151.0	...	4 280.0	...	4 413.0	...	...
Tajikistan: somoni Tadjikistan : somoni										
MF - month mois[27]	405.4[99]	2 522.9[99]	26 905.1[99]	65 162.0[99]	1 559.0	8 080.0	14 977.0	...	...	...
Thailand: baht Thaïlande : baht										
MF - month mois[8][20][100]	3 688.0	3 986.0	4 138.0	4 229.0[101]	4 994.0[101]	5 502.0[101]	5 935.0[101]	6 389.0[101]	5 907.0[101]	...
M - month mois[8][20][100]	4 728.0	5 159.0	5 145.0	5 205.0[101]	6 234.0[101]	...	...	...	...	...
F - month mois[8][20][100]	3 016.0	3 329.0	3 558.0	3 715.0[101]	4 250.0[101]	...	...	...	...	...
Tonga: pa'anga Tonga : pa'anga										
MF - week semaine[8]	51.4	51.3	58.3	62.6	...	...	...	...	...	...
Trinidad and Tobago: Trinidad and Tobago dollar Trinité-et-Tobago : dollar de la Trinité-et-Tobago										
MF - week semaine[3]	731.3	732.3	755.0	739.9	790.6	810.1	865.4	908.7	938.8	...

31
Wages in manufacturing
By hour, day, week or month [cont.]
Salaires dans les industries manufacturières
Par heure, jour, semaine ou mois [suite]

Country or area and unit Pays ou zone et unité	1991	1992	1993	1994	1995	1996	1997	1998	1999	2000
Turkey: Turkish lira Turquie : livre turque										
MF - hour heure[3 12 25 51 102]	...	...	...	...	...	173.6	333.3	...	...	...
MF - month mois[3 12 25 51 103]	...	...	...	...	...	38 992.0	77 250.0	...	...	...
MF - day jour[8]	61 620.4	88 144.3	135 236.0	191 118.5	...	757 277.0	1 640 856.4	...	...	...
M - day jour[8]	62 140.3	91 204.1	138 746.1	191 858.8	...	758 475.1	1 661 886.1	...	...	...
F - day jour[8]	56 660.2	84 558.2	122 720.8	189 297.3	...	747 788.8	1 611 526.4	...	...	...
Ukraine: hryvnia Ukraine : hryvnia										
MF - month mois	532.2[104]	7 494.8[104]	173.3[105]	1 499.9[105]	7 716.7[105]	131.7	148.9	157.4	188.0	289.0
United Kingdom: pound sterling Royaume-Uni : livre sterling										
MF - hour heure[3 8 72 106 107]	6.7	7.1	7.5	7.6	7.9	8.2	8.5	9.1	9.5	9.7
M - hour heure[3 8 72 106 107]	7.2	7.7	8.0	8.1	8.4	8.8	9.1	9.7	10.1	10.3
F - hour heure[3 8 72 106 107]	4.9	5.3	5.6	5.7	6.0	6.2	6.6	7.0	7.5	7.7
United States: US dollar Etats-Unis : dollar des Etats-Unis										
MF - hour heure[5 108]	11.2	11.5	11.7	12.1	12.4	12.8	13.2	13.5	13.9	14.4
United States Virgin Is.: US dollar Iles Vierges américaines : dollar des Etats-Unis										
MF - hour heure[5]	12.5	13.7	15.0	15.2	15.8	17.0	18.1	...	...	...
Uruguay: Uruguayan peso Uruguay : peso uruguayen										
MF - month mois[13]	7 371.5[109]	12 564.4[109]	20 197.5[109]	28 849.4[109]	38 710.5[109]	113.3[110]	135.2[110]	151.2[110]	159.7[110]	165.2[110]
Zimbabwe: Zimbabwe dollar Zimbabwe : dollar zimbabwéen										
MF - month mois	844.1	1 008.2	1 200.3	1 391.9	1 702.5	2 056.7	2 619.8	3 276.8	4 700.4	...

Source:
International Labour Office (ILO), Geneva, "Yearbook of Labour Statistics, 2001" and the ILO database.

1 Including mining and quarrying.
2 State sector.
3 Data classified according to ISIC, Rev.3.
4 Hourly wage rates.
5 Wages earners.
6 Australes; 1 peso = 10,000 australes.
7 Roubles; 1 dram = 200 roubles.
8 One month of each year.
9 Full-time adult non-managerial employees.

10 New industrial classification.
11 Roubles; 1 manat is equivalent to 10 roubles.
12 Establishments with 10 or more persons employed.
13 Private sector.
14 Skilled wage earners.
15 Daily wage rates.
16 Managerial, administrative, technical, and production workers.
17 Unskilled wage earners.
18 Clerical, sales and service workers.

19 Salaried employees.

Source:
Bureau international du Travail (BIT), Genève, "Annuaire des statistiques du travail, 2001" et la base de données du BIT.

1 Y compris les industries extractives.
2 Secteur d'Etat.
3 Données classifiées selon la CITI, Rev.3.
4 Taux de salaire horaires.
5 Ouvriers.
6 Australes; 1 peso = 10,000 australes.
7 Roubles; 1 dram = 200 roubles.
8 Un mois de chaque année.
9 Salariés adultes à plein temps, non compris les cadres dirigeants.
10 Nouvelle classification industrielle.
11 Roubles; 1 manat équivaut à 10 roubles.
12 Etablissements occupant 10 personnes et plus.
13 Secteur privé.
14 Ouvriers qualifiés.
15 Taux de salaire journaliers.
16 Directeurs, cadres administratifs supérieurs, personnel technique et travailleurs à la production.
17 Ouvriers non qualifiés.
18 Personnel administratif, personnel commercial et spécialisé dans les services.
19 Employés.

31
Wages in manufacturing
By hour, day, week or month [cont.]
Salaires dans les industries manufacturières
Par heure, jour, semaine ou mois [suite]

20 Monthly wage rates.
21 Private sector establishments with 5 or more employees. La Paz and El Alto.
22 Main cities, except Pando.
23 Citizens only.
24 Cruzeiros; 1 real = approximately 2750 x 1000 cruzeiros.
25 Figures in thousands.
26 State and cooperative sector.
27 Including major divisions 2 and 4.
28 Employees under labour contract.
29 Employees under labour contract. New denomination: 1 new lev = 1000 old leva.
30 Employees paid by the hour.
31 Including overtime payments.
32 Including family allowances and the value of payments in kind.
33 Beginning April: sample design and methodology revised.

34 State-owned units, urban collective-owned units and other ownership units.
35 Total employment.
36 Median.
37 7 main cities.
38 Estimates based on the results of the 1993 Census.
39 Dinars; 1 kuna = 1,000 dinars.
40 Adults.
41 Enterprises with 25 or more employees.
42 Enterprises with 100 or more employees.
43 Enterprises with 20 or more employees.
44 One quarter of each year.
45 Estimations based on National Accounts.
46 Roubles; 1 kroon = 10 roubles.
47 Including mining, quarrying and electricity.
48 Full-time employees.
49 Establishments with 5 or more persons employed.
50 Survey results influenced by a low response rate.

51 Average of less than 12 months.
52 Including family allowances paid directly by the employers.

53 Excluding part-time workers and juveniles.
54 Enterprises with 5 or more employees.
55 All legal economic units.

56 Adult employees; excluding overtime payments and payments in kind.
57 Production workers.
58 Weekly wage rates.
59 Including juveniles.
60 Including payments subject to income tax.
61 Index of hourly wage rates (1990=100).
62 Index of hourly wage rates (Dec.1995=100).
63 Regular scheduled cash earnings.
64 Private sector; establishments with 10 or more regular employees.
65 Including family allowances and mid- and end-of-year bonuses.
66 Roubles; 1 tenge = 500 roubles.
67 Including the value of payments in kind.
68 Excluding individual unincorporated enterprises.

69 Wage-earners on daily rates of pay.

70 Pesos; 1 new peso = 1,000 pesos.

20 Taux de salaire mensuels.
21 Etablissements du secteur privé occupant 5 salariés ou plus. La Paz et El Alto.
22 Villes prinipales, sauf Pando.
23 Nationaux seulement.
24 Cruzeiros; 1 real = environ 2750 x 1000 cruzeiros.
25 Données en milliers.
26 Secteur d'Etat et coopératif.
27 Y compris les branches 2 et 4.
28 Salariés sous contrat de travail.
29 Salariés sous contrat de travail. Nouvelle dénomination: 1 nouveau lev = 1000 anciens leva.
30 Salariés rémunérés à l'heure.
31 Y compris la rémunération des heures supplémentaires.
32 Y compris les allocations familiales et la valeur des paiements en nature.
33 A partir d'avril: plan d'échantillonnage et méthodologie révisés.

34 Unités d'Etat, unités collectives urbaines et autres.
35 Emploi total.
36 Médiane.
37 7 villes principales.
38 Estimations basées sur les résultats du Recensement de 1993.
39 Dinars; 1 kuna = 1?000 dinars.
40 Adultes.
41 Entreprises occupant 25 salariés et plus.
42 Entreprises occupant 100 salariés et plus.
43 Entreprises occupant 20 salariés et plus.
44 Un trimestre de chaque année.
45 Estimations basées sur la Comptabilité nationale.
46 Roubles; 1 couronne = 10 roubles.
47 Y compris les industries extractives et l'électricité.
48 Salariés à plein temps.
49 Etablissements occupant 5 personnes et plus.
50 Résultats de l'enquête influencés par un taux de réponse faible.

51 Moyenne de moins de douze mois.
52 Y compris les allocations familiales payées directement par l'employeur.

53 Non compris les travailleurs à temps partiel et les jeunes.
54 Entreprises occupant 5 salariés et plus.
55 Ensemble des unités économiques dotées d'un statut juridique.
56 Salariés adultes; n.c. la rémunération des heures supplémentaires et la valeur des paiements en nature.
57 Travailleurs à la production.
58 Taux de salaire hebdomadaires.
59 Y compris les jeunes gens.
60 Y compris les versements soumis à l'impôt sur le revenu.
61 Indice des taux de salaires horaires (1990=100).
62 Indice des taux de salaires horaires (déc.1995=100).
63 Gains en espèce tarifés réguliers.
64 Secteur privé; établissements occupant 10 salariés stables ou plus.
65 Y compris les allocations familiales et les primes de milieu et de fin d'année.
66 Roubles; 1 tenge = 500 roubles.
67 Y compris la valeur des paiements en nature.
68 Non compris les entreprises individuelles non constituées en société.

69 Ouvriers rémunérés sur la base de taux de salaire journaliers.

70 Pesos; 1 nouveau peso = 1,000 peos.

31
Wages in manufacturing
By hour, day, week or month [*cont.*]
Salaires dans les industries manufacturières
Par heure, jour, semaine ou mois [*suite*]

71 Regular employees.
72 Excluding overtime payments.
73 Curaçao.
74 Establishments with the equivalent of more than 2 full-time paid employees.
75 Full-time employees. Establishments with the equivalent of more than 0.5 full-time paid employees.
76 Incorporated entreprises.
77 Urban areas. Annual averages.
78 Lima.
79 Computed on the basis of annual wages.
80 Establishments with 20 or more persons employed.
81 Zlotyche; 1 new zloty = 10,000 zlotyche.
82 Roubles; 1 leu = approximately 417 roubles.
83 New denomination: 1 new rouble = 1000 old roubles.

84 Data refer to the Fed.Rep of Yugoslavia composed of two republics (Serbia and Montenegro).
85 Net earnings.
86 Excluding private sector.
87 Excluding Kosovo and Metohia.
88 Earnings are exempted from income tax.
89 Including electricity and water.
90 Beginning this year, methodology revised.
91 Excluding enterprises with less than 25 employees.
92 Excluding enterprises with less than 20 employees.
93 Including employers' non-statutory contributions to certain funds.
94 Including holidays and sick-leave payments and the value of payments in kind. One quarter of each year.

95 Data classified according to ISIC, Rev.3. Private sector.
96 Excluding holidays, sick-leave and overtime payments. One quarter of each year.

97 Average of less than 12 months. Excluding holidays, sick-leave and overtime payments.

98 Standardised monthly earnings (40 hours x 4 1/3 weeks).
99 Roubles; 1 Tajik rouble = 100 roubles.
100 Average wage rates for normal/usual hours of work.

101 Excluding public enterprises.
102 Excluding overtime payments and irregular bonuses and allowances.
103 Including overtime payments and irregular bonuses and allowances.
104 Roubles; 1 rouble = 25 karbovanets.
105 Figures in thousands. Karbovanets: 1 hrivna = 100,000 karbovanets.
106 Full-time employees on adult rates of pay.

107 Excluding Northern Ireland.
108 Private sector; production workers.
109 Index of average monthly earnings (October-December 1984=100).
110 Index of average monthly earnings (December 1995=100).

71 Salariés stables.
72 Non compris la rémunération des heures supplémentaires.
73 Curaçao.
74 Etablissements occupant plus de l'équivalent de 2 salariés à plein temps.
75 Salariés à plein temps. Etablissements occupant plus de l'équivalent de 0.5 salarié à plein temps.
76 Entreprises constituées en sociétés.
77 Régions urbaines. Moyennes annuelles.
78 Lima.
79 Calculés sur la base de salaires annuels.
80 Etablissements occupant 20 personnes et plus.
81 Zlotyche; 1 nouveau zloty = 10?000 zlotyche.
82 Roubles; 1 leu = environ 417 roubles.
83 Nouvelle dénomination: 1 nouveau rouble = 1000 anciens roubles.

84 Données se rapportant à la Rép.féd. De Yougoslavie, qui est composée de deux républiques (Serbie et Monténégro).
85 Gains nets.
86 Non compris le secteur privé.
87 Non compris Kosovo et Metohia.
88 Les gains sont exempts de l'impôt sur le revenu.
89 Y compris l'électricité et l'eau.
90 A partir de cette année, méthodologie révisée.
91 Non compris les entreprises occupant moins de 25 salariés.
92 Non compris les entreprises occupant moins de 20 salariés.
93 Y compris les cotisations des employeurs à certains fonds privés.
94 Y compris les versements pour les vacances et congés de maladie et la valeur des paiements en nature. Un trimestre de chaque année.

95 Données classifiées selon la CITI, Rev.3. Secteur privé.
96 Non compris les versements pour les vacances, congés maladie ainsi que la rémunération des heures supplémentaires. Un trimestre de chaque année.

97 Moyenne de moins de douze mois. Non compris les versements pour les vacances, congés maladie ainsi que la rémunération des heures supplémentaires.

98 Gains mensuels standardisés (40 heures x 4 1/3 semaines).
99 Roubles; 1 rouble Tajik = 100 roubles.
100 Taux de salaire moyens pour la durée normale/usuelle du travail.

101 Non compris les entreprises publiques.
102 Non compris la rémunération des heures supplémentaires et les prestations versées irrégulièrement.
103 Y compris la rémunération des heures suppl émentaires et les prestations versées irrégulièrement.
104 Roubles; 1 rouble = 25 karbovanets.
105 Données en milliers. Karbovanets; 1 hrivna = 100 000 karbovanets.
106 Salariés à plein temps rémunérés sur la base de taux de salaire pour adultes.

107 Non compris l'Irlande du Nord.
108 Secteur privé; travailleurs à la production.
109 Indices des gains mensuels moyens (octobre-decembre 1984=100).
110 Indices des gains mensuels moyens (decembre 1995=100).

32

Producers' prices or wholesale prices
Index numbers: 1990 = 100

Prix à la production ou prix de gros
Indices : 1990 = 100

Country or area	1995	1996	1997	1998	1999	2000	2001	Pays ou zone
Argentina								**Argentine**
Domestic supply [1,2]	241	248	249	241	232	241	234	Offre intérieure [1,2]
Domestic production	243	252	253	245	236	246	241	Production intérieure
Agricultural products [2]	245	283	254	237	189	184	180	Produits agricoles [2]
Industrial products [2,3]	247	248	252	249	241	244	233	Produits industriels [2,3]
Imported goods [3]	211	204	196	187	177	177	172	Produits importés [3]
Australia [4,5]								**Australie [4,5]**
Industrial products [2,3,6]	110	111	112	109	114	118	122	Produits industriels [2,3,6]
Raw materials	106	102	105	102	111	121	117	Matières premières
Austria								**Autriche**
Domestic supply [2,7]	102	102	102	102	101	105	106	Offre intérieure [2,7]
Agricultural products	86	76	74	77	75	77	80	Produits agricoles
Consumers' goods [2]	107	106	106	107	106	110	113	Biens de consommation [2]
Capital goods [2]	100	101	101	100	98	96	96	Biens d'équipement [2]
Bangladesh [5]								**Bangladesh [5]**
Domestic supply [2,7]	121	127	128	135	144	141	141	Offre intérieure [2,7]
Agricultural products [2,8]	119	126	126	133	146	142	141	Produits agricoles [2,8]
Industrial products [2,3,8]	125	131	132	137	128	138	140	Produits industriels [2,3,8]
Raw materials	117	120	123	...	134	131	132	Matières premières
Belgium								**Belgique**
Domestic supply	102	102	104	103	...	...	...	Offre intérieure
Domestic production [9]	...	...	...	...	...	100	...	Production intérieure [9]
Agricultural products [2]	106	107	111	109	107	111	116	Produits agricoles [2]
Industrial products	101	102	104	103	102	111	113	Produits industriels
Intermediate products	97	98	99	97	97	111	112	Produits intermédiaires
Consumers' goods	107	108	111	110	109	112	116	Biens de consommation
Capital goods	108	109	109	109	108	108	110	Biens d'équipement
Bolivia								**Bolivie**
Agricultural products	167	185	...	...	...	...	...	Produits agricoles
Industrial products	...	174	179	187	190	200	202	Produits industriels
Imported goods	179	194	...	...	...	...	...	Produits importés
Raw materials	169	197	204	204	192	181	176	Matières premières
Consumers' goods	157	170	175	185	190	204	208	Biens de consommation
Capital goods	139	150	157	159	161	164	146	Biens d'équipement
Brazil [10]								**Brésil [10]**
Domestic supply [11]	159	169	181	189	220	261	293	Offre intérieure [11]
Agricultural products [11]	163	172	200	215	252	306	358	Produits agricoles [11]
Industrial products [11]	155	165	172	175	203	237	262	Produits industriels [11]
Raw materials [11]	150	162	179	179	212	251	284	Matières premières [11]
Consumers' goods [11]	169	177	192	212	243	288	314	Biens de consommation [11]
Capital goods	155	172	176	178	198	220	239	Biens d'équipement
Bulgaria [12]								**Bulgarie [12]**
Domestic supply	100	233	2 500	2 914	3 010	3 521	3 674	Offre intérieure
Canada [13]								**Canada [13]**
Raw materials	118	122	120	103	111	136	134	Matières premières
Chile								**Chili**
Domestic supply	171	181	184	188	198	220	237	Offre intérieure
Domestic production	178	190	195	197	205	229	243	Production intérieure
Agricultural products	180	193	197	204	200	216	214	Produits agricoles
Industrial products [7]	179	190	193	198	210	235	252	Produits industriels [7]
Imported goods	140	147	145	152	165	182	207	Produits importés
China, Hong Kong SAR								**Chine, Hong Kong RAS**
Industrial products	111	111	111	109	107	107	106	Produits industriels
Colombia [14]								**Colombie [14]**
Domestic supply [2]	58	67	84	95	100 [15]	119	128	Offre intérieure [2]
Domestic production	62	71	84	95	100 [15]	118	127	Production intérieure
Agricultural products	63	73	88	97	100 [15]	114	123	Produits agricoles
Industrial products	62	71	83	95	100 [15]	120	...	Produits industriels
Imported goods	69	73	85	96	100 [15]	125	131	Produits importés
Raw materials	62	71	83	93	100 [15]	...	...	Matières premières
Intermediate products	65	73	86	96	100 [15]	120	127	Produits intermédiaires

32

Producers' prices or wholesale prices
Index numbers: 1990 = 100 *[cont.]*

Prix à la production ou prix de gros
Indices : 1990 = 100 *[suite]*

Country or area	1995	1996	1997	1998	1999	2000	2001	Pays ou zone
Croatia [16]								**Croatie** [16]
Industrial products	93	94	96	# 86	88	97	100	Produits industriels
Consumers' goods	95	99	101	# 99	99	100	100	Biens de consommation
Capital goods	97	99	97	# 93	96	102	100	Biens d'équipement
Cyprus								**Chypre**
Industrial products	117	122	122	124	126	135	...	Produits industriels
Czech Republic								**République tchèque**
Agricultural products	129	140	144	147	130	142	153	Produits agricoles
Denmark								**Danemark**
Domestic supply [2,11]	103	104	106	105	106	112	115	Offre intérieure [2,11]
Domestic production [2,11]	103	105	107	106	107	113	116	Production intérieure [2,11]
Imported goods [11]	103	103	105	104	104	111	112	Produits importés [11]
Consumers' goods	103	104	106	106	106	109	112	Biens de consommation
Ecuador								**Equateur**
Agricultural products	12	...	...	...	...	110	128	Produits agricoles
Egypt [5]								**Egypte** [5]
Domestic supply [7]	163	176	183	186	188	185	181	Offre intérieure [7]
Raw materials	113	133	140	133	132	129	126	Matières premières
Intermediate products	151	162	165	169	163	162	159	Produits intermédiaires
Capital goods	153	158	163	165	159	158	157	Biens d'équipement
El Salvador								**El Salvador**
Domestic supply [17]	138	145	147	138	136	140	...	Offre intérieure [17]
Domestic production	133	147	148	142	147	148	...	Production intérieure
Imported goods	125	130	126	119	119	123	...	Produits importés
Finland								**Finlande**
Domestic supply	107	106	108	106	106	115	115	Offre intérieure
Domestic production	104	102	104	105	104	111	113	Production intérieure
Imported goods	119	120	121	115	115	130	126	Produits importés
Raw materials	108	105	107	100	98	109	107	Matières premières
Consumers' goods [18]	107	108	109	112	113	114	116	Biens de consommation [18]
Capital goods	105	105	108	109	109	113	114	Biens d'équipement
France								**France**
Agricultural products	89	89	90	90	86	88	91	Produits agricoles
Germany [19]								**Allemagne** [19]
Domestic supply	104	104	105	103	102	106	110	Offre intérieure
Domestic production	103	100	101	100	...	...	...	Production intérieure
Agricultural products	92	91	93	88	84	89	92	Produits agricoles
Imported goods	97	96	97	97	97	108	109	Produits importés
Greece [20]								**Grèce** [20]
Domestic supply [21]	166	176	182	189	193	208	215	Offre intérieure [21]
Domestic production [21]	166	179	186	192	199	215	224	Production intérieure [21]
Agricultural products [22]	164	171	178	192	198	204	228	Produits agricoles [22]
Industrial products [21]	166	180	187	193	200	217	223	Produits industriels [21]
Imported goods [21]	166	170	174	183	184	196	201	Produits importés [21]
Guatemala								**Guatemala**
Domestic supply	166	202	222	228	236	260	274	Offre intérieure
Domestic production	178	205	221	231	238	263	281	Production intérieure
Agricultural products	180	200	213	235	246	272	294	Produits agricoles
Industrial products	176	209	226	229	233	258	273	Produits industriels
Imported goods	147	197	223	222	234	256	264	Produits importés
India [23]								**Inde** [23]
Domestic supply	165	174	184	197	203	210	220	Offre intérieure
Agricultural products	173	189	201	225	237	249	240	Produits agricoles
Industrial products [3]	162	169	176	184	188	188	192	Produits industriels [3]
Raw materials [24]	170	181	189	210	219	223	224	Matières premières [24]
Indonesia								**Indonésie**
Domestic supply [21]	135	145	158	319	355	404	462	Offre intérieure [21]
Domestic production	157	168	179	296	326	406	469	Production intérieure
Agricultural products	186	209	233	393	533	604	746	Produits agricoles
Industrial products [3]	146	151	156	258	325	344	383	Produits industriels [3]
Imported goods [21]	120	127	136	313	325	349	393	Produits importés [21]

32

Producers' prices or wholesale prices
Index numbers: 1990 = 100 *[cont.]*

Prix à la production ou prix de gros
Indices : 1990 = 100 *[suite]*

Country or area	1995	1996	1997	1998	1999	2000	2001	Pays ou zone
Raw materials	125	141	161	357	352	452	496	Matières premières
Intermediate products	135	141	148	317	342	376	430	Produits intermédiaires
Consumers' goods	141	151	164	299	395	440	522	Biens de consommation
Capital goods	128	132	139	248	291	296	320	Biens d'équipement
Iran (Islamic Rep. of) [2,8]								**Iran (Rép. islamique d')** [2,8]
Domestic supply	483	582	644	740	860	1 013	1 111	Offre intérieure
Domestic production	423	573	619	749	868	1 015	...	Production intérieure
Agricultural products	409	505	541	690	822	943	1 021	Produits agricoles
Industrial products	415	493	486	536	663	882	820	Produits industriels
Imported goods	477	668	731	798	910	1 067	1 587	Produits importés
Raw materials	410	572	598	608	691	832	934	Matières premières
Ireland								**Irlande**
Domestic supply [2,25]	110	111	110	112	112	119	119	Offre intérieure [2,25]
Agricultural products [2,25]	108	103	96	96	91	98	103	Produits agricoles [2,25]
Industrial products [2,3,25]	111	112	111	112	113	120	...	Produits industriels [2,3,25]
Capital goods [8]	113	115	117	120	123	128	...	Biens d'équipement [8]
Israel [21]								**Israël** [21]
Industrial products	166	180	192	201	214	218	219	Produits industriels
Italy								**Italie**
Domestic supply [2,21]	130	132	134	135	134	142	145	Offre intérieure [2,21]
Agricultural products [2,8]	122	127	124	...	...	...	...	Produits agricoles [2,8]
Industrial products [2,21]	130	133	136	...	...	...	...	Produits industriels [2,21]
Intermediate products	123	124	126	125	123	135	138	Produits intermédiaires
Consumers' goods	129	133	134	136	137	139	143	Biens de consommation
Capital goods	130	133	137	139	141	142	144	Biens d'équipement
Japan								**Japon**
Domestic supply [2]	94	93	95	93	91	91	91	Offre intérieure [2]
Domestic production	96	95	94	94	92	93	92	Production intérieure
Agricultural products [8]	90	90	90	85	88	86	86	Produits agricoles [8]
Industrial products [8]	96	95	95	94	92	93	92	Produits industriels [8]
Imported goods	104	103	102	92	93	102	98	Produits importés
Raw materials	80	88	93	83	78	89	92	Matières premières
Intermediate products	93	92	94	92	90	91	91	Produits intermédiaires
Consumers' goods	97	96	97	96	95	94	94	Biens de consommation
Capital goods	95	93	93	93	90	88	87	Biens d'équipement
Jordan [2]								**Jordanie** [2]
Domestic supply	117	119	121	122	116	112	115	Offre intérieure
Korea, Republic of								**Corée, République de**
Domestic supply	117	121	125	141	107	140	143	Offre intérieure
Agricultural products [8,26]	134	134	136	142	157	151	154	Produits agricoles [8,26]
Industrial products	115	117	121	139	134	137	139	Produits industriels
Raw materials	118	126	140	169	157	192	199	Matières premières
Intermediate products	116	117	123	153	139	145	150	Produits intermédiaires
Consumers' goods	121	126	131	144	147	147	150	Biens de consommation
Capital goods	112	112	114	139	132	128	131	Biens d'équipement
Kuwait								**Koweït**
Domestic supply	110	115	114	112	111	111	...	Offre intérieure
Agricultural products	113	111	112	115	109	...	...	Produits agricoles
Raw materials	103	110	115	114	115	...	...	Matières premières
Intermediate products	111	119	123	121	114	...	...	Produits intermédiaires
Consumers' goods	117	126	128	128	126	...	...	Biens de consommation
Capital goods	95	98	89	84	86	...	...	Biens d'équipement
Latvia [27]								**Lettonie** [27]
Domestic supply	284	323	336	343	329	331	...	Offre intérieure
Lithuania								**Lituanie**
Domestic supply	36 504	42 796	44 611	41 636	42 912	51 238	50 358	Offre intérieure
Luxembourg								**Luxembourg**
Industrial products	98	94	95	97	93	97	98	Produits industriels
Imported goods	111	106	109	112	110	116	119	Produits importés
Intermediate products	92	86	88	90	84	90	88	Produits intermédiaires
Consumers' goods [18]	103	104	104	104	104	105	115	Biens de consommation [18]

32

Producers' prices or wholesale prices
Index numbers: 1990 = 100 *[cont.]*

Prix à la production ou prix de gros
Indices : 1990 = 100 *[suite]*

Country or area	1995	1996	1997	1998	1999	2000	2001	Pays ou zone
Capital goods	108	111	112	114	113	117	120	Biens d'équipement
Malaysia								**Malaisie**
Domestic supply	113	115	118	131	127	131	...	Offre intérieure
Domestic production	115	118	121	135	130	134	...	Production intérieure
Imported goods	104	104	107	117	116	118	...	Produits importés
Mexico								**Mexique**
Domestic supply [7,28]	214	278	327	379	438	474	500	Offre intérieure [7,28]
Agricultural products	206	287	333	349	434	514	496	Produits agricoles
Raw materials	211	287	325	358	400	447	...	Matières premières
Consumers' goods [8,28]	222	288	349	404	455	503	536	Biens de consommation [8,28]
Capital goods [7,8,28]	207	266	312	363	418	457	479	Biens d'équipement [7,8,28]
Morocco								**Maroc**
Domestic supply	125	130	128	132	134	...	...	Offre intérieure
Agricultural products	132	140	134	138	136	141	141	Produits agricoles
Industrial products	120	124	126	129	130	135	132	Produits industriels
Netherlands								**Pays-Bas**
Industrial products	100	101	104	102	102	110	113	Produits industriels
Imported goods	100	104	109	102	106	132	128	Produits importés
Raw materials	100	101	104	99	99	111	122	Matières premières
Intermediate products	100	101	104	100	100	111	114	Produits intermédiaires
Consumers' goods	100	102	104	103	104	111	114	Biens de consommation
Capital goods	100	101	103	105	106	107	108	Biens d'équipement
New Zealand [29]								**Nouvelle-Zélande** [29]
Agricultural products [2]	101	99	100	99	99	110	137	Produits agricoles [2]
Industrial products [2,30]	102	101	100	101	102	109	114	Produits industriels [2,30]
Intermediate products [31]	99	100	100	101	102	108	116	Produits intermédiaires [31]
Norway								**Norvège**
Domestic supply	107	108	110	110	112	117	122	Offre intérieure
Imported goods	99	98	97	98	96	101	108	Produits importés
Raw materials	98	97	101	100	101	109	108	Matières premières
Intermediate products	109	110	111	113	113	116	...	Produits intermédiaires
Consumers' goods	109	111	113	114	116	119	...	Biens de consommation
Capital goods	111	112	113	114	115	116	119	Biens d'équipement
Pakistan [5]								**Pakistan** [5]
Domestic supply [2,7]	168	199	237	227	229	238	250	Offre intérieure [2,7]
Agricultural products	184	206	221	236	237	241	249	Produits agricoles
Industrial products	165	185	189	195	201	204	211	Produits industriels
Raw materials	179	216	233	256	245	236	247	Matières premières
Panama								**Panama**
Domestic supply	111	113	111	106	109	119	...	Offre intérieure
Peru								**Pérou**
Domestic supply	1 228	1 344	1 443	1 548	1 624	1 694	1 708	Offre intérieure
Domestic production	1 226	1 341	...	1 545	1 606	1 673	1 698	Production intérieure
Agricultural products [32]	1 468	1 592	1 763	2 061	1 891	1 793	1 863	Produits agricoles [32]
Industrial products [3,8]	1 155	1 264	1 355	1 437	1 525	1 616	1 642	Produits industriels [3,8]
Imported goods	1 116	1 230	1 295	1 376	1 513	1 608	1 623	Produits importés
Philippines [33]								**Philippines** [33]
Domestic supply	131	143	...	162	172	175	179	Offre intérieure
Portugal								**Portugal**
Domestic supply	117	121	124	119	121	140	141	Offre intérieure
Intermediate products	114	114	115	115	114	120	121	Produits intermédiaires
Romania								**Roumanie**
Industrial products	7 391	11 236	28 390	37 810	53 757	81 488	118 223	Produits industriels
Serbia and Montenegro								**Serbie-et-Monténégro**
Domestic supply [34]	28	64	75	100	135	...	...	Offre intérieure [34]
Agricultural products [14]	20	44	52	69	100	258	439	Produits agricoles [14]
Industrial products [14]	24	47	55	69	100	207	382	Produits industriels [14]
Consumers' goods [14]	25	46	56	70	100	185	373	Biens de consommation [14]
Capital goods [14]	23	42	47	62	100	225	321	Biens d'équipement [14]
Singapore								**Singapour**
Domestic supply [7]	87	85	81	79	80	88	87	Offre intérieure [7]

32

Producers' prices or wholesale prices
Index numbers: 1990 = 100 *[cont.]*

Prix à la production ou prix de gros
Indices : 1990 = 100 *[suite]*

Country or area	1995	1996	1997	1998	1999	2000	2001	Pays ou zone
Domestic production [2,3,35]	81	77	70	67	67	72	70	Production intérieure [2,3,35]
Imported goods [35]	91	87	84	83	85	92	92	Produits importés [35]
Slovenia								**Slovénie**
Agricultural products	972	1 077	1 149	1 198	1 206	...	...	Produits agricoles
Industrial products	1 149	1 226	1 300	1 379	1 408	1 515	1 652	Produits industriels
Consumers' goods [9]	72	77	84	90	94	100	110	Biens de consommation [9]
Capital goods [9]	82	88	89	92	96	100	104	Biens d'équipement [9]
South Africa								**Afrique du Sud**
Domestic supply [36]	152	164	175	181	190	209	226	Offre intérieure [36]
Domestic production [36]	157	168	181	188	197	212	229	Production intérieure [36]
Agricultural products	166	174	188	191	194	202	228	Produits agricoles
Industrial products [3]	153	166	180	188	195	210	226	Produits industriels [3]
Imported goods	134	141	148	153	164	189	208	Produits importés
Spain								**Espagne**
Domestic supply [21]	118	120	121	120	121	128	130	Offre intérieure [21]
Consumers' goods	121	126	127	127	129	131	135	Biens de consommation
Capital goods	113	116	117	118	119	121	123	Biens d'équipement
Sri Lanka								**Sri Lanka**
Domestic supply	146	172	188	199	198	212	...	Offre intérieure
Domestic production	151	168	179	188	194	212	...	Production intérieure
Imported goods	134	151	161	161	161	189	...	Produits importés
Consumers' goods	138	173	189	203	203	201	...	Biens de consommation
Capital goods	172	182	192	210	227	219	...	Biens d'équipement
Sweden [21,37]								**Suède** [21,37]
Domestic supply [2]	120	118	119	119	120	127	131	Offre intérieure [2]
Domestic production [2]	116	116	117	117	117	121	124	Production intérieure [2]
Imported goods	124	120	122	121	124	134	140	Produits importés
Switzerland								**Suisse**
Domestic supply [2,7]	100	98	98	97	95	98	98	Offre intérieure [2,7]
Domestic production [2,7]	102	99	99	98	98	98	99	Production intérieure [2,7]
Agricultural products [2]	91	85	84	81	79	83	92	Produits agricoles [2]
Industrial products	103	101	100	99	98	98	96	Produits industriels
Imported goods [7]	96	92	94	92	90	96	95	Produits importés [7]
Raw materials	93	88	89	84	81	88	78	Matières premières
Consumers' goods	104	103	103	103	104	104	106	Biens de consommation
Thailand								**Thaïlande**
Domestic supply [2,11]	119	125	130	147	138	157	145	Offre intérieure [2,11]
Agricultural products	133	145	148	171	147	145	152	Produits agricoles
Industrial products [3]	117	120	125	139	136	141	144	Produits industriels [3]
Raw materials	134	138	144	173	138	139	149	Matières premières
Intermediate products	118	123	128	150	144	142	144	Produits intermédiaires
Consumers' goods	123	130	137	160	148	151	159	Biens de consommation
TFYR of Macedonia [34]								**L'ex-R.y. Macédoine** [34]
Domestic supply	93	92	96	100	100	109	...	Offre intérieure
Consumers' goods	90	92	97	100	101	103	...	Biens de consommation
Capital goods	90	92	96	100	102	103	...	Biens d'équipement
Trinidad and Tobago								**Trinité-et-Tobago**
Industrial products	116	119	122	124	126	127	...	Produits industriels
Tunisia								**Tunisie**
Agricultural products	135	140	147	153	156	160	163	Produits agricoles
Industrial products	129	134	138	142	144	146	149	Produits industriels
Turkey								**Turquie**
Domestic supply [2,21,38]	1 638	2 881	5 238	9 000	13 776	20 861	33 718	Offre intérieure [2,21,38]
Agricultural products	1 638	3 054	5 707	10 659	15 117	20 860	29 678	Produits agricoles
Industrial products	1 611	2 746	4 959	8 265	12 991	20 282	33 807	Produits industriels
United Kingdom								**Royaume-Uni**
Agricultural products	116	114	99	90	86	84	...	Produits agricoles
Industrial products [3]	120	123	123	123	122	130	124	Produits industriels [3]
Raw materials	103	102	94	85	87	97	96	Matières premières
United States								**Etats-Unis**
Domestic supply [2]	107	110	110	107	108	114	115	Offre intérieure [2]

32

Producers' prices or wholesale prices
Index numbers: 1990 = 100 *[cont.]*

Prix à la production ou prix de gros
Indices : 1990 = 100 *[suite]*

Country or area	1995	1996	1997	1998	1999	2000	2001	Pays ou zone
Agricultural products [2]	96	109	101	93	88	89	93	Produits agricoles [2]
Industrial products [2,39]	109	110	111	108	109	116	117	Produits industriels [2,39]
Raw materials	94	104	102	89	90	110	110	Matières premières
Intermediate products	109	110	110	107	108	113	113	Produits intermédiaires
Consumers' goods	106	110	110	109	111	202	120	Biens de consommation
Capital goods	111	113	113	112	112	113	114	Biens d'équipement
Uruguay [40]								**Uruguay [40]**
Domestic supply [2,7]	703	887	1 032	1 128	1 118	1 194	...	Offre intérieure [2,7]
Domestic production	735	919	1 069	1 168	1 158	1 237	1 319	Production intérieure
Agricultural products	748	918	1 067	1 170	1 062	1 146	1 256	Produits agricoles
Industrial products [7]	742	934	1 086	1 184	1 208	1 285	1 356	Produits industriels [7]
Venezuela [7]								**Venezuela [7]**
Domestic supply	573	1 164	1 511	1 846	2 145	2 427	2 801	Offre intérieure
Domestic production	597	1 191	1 580	1 966	2 313	2 703	3 109	Production intérieure
Agricultural products	500	793	1 089	1 635	2 265	3 682	5 186	Produits agricoles
Industrial products	579	1 194	1 545	1 863	2 136	2 438	2 722	Produits industriels
Imported goods	514	1 098	1 339	1 548	1 727	1 894	2 043	Produits importés
Zambia								**Zambie**
Domestic supply	2 603	...	...	...	...	...	...	Offre intérieure
Domestic production	2 081	...	...	...	...	...	...	Production intérieure
Agricultural products	2 900	...	...	...	...	...	...	Produits agricoles
Industrial products	2 751	...	...	...	...	...	...	Produits industriels
Consumers' goods	5 475	...	...	...	...	...	...	Biens de consommation
Capital goods	1 718	...	...	...	...	...	...	Biens d'équipement
Zimbabwe								**Zimbabwe**
Domestic supply	380	445	503	662	1 048	...	...	Offre intérieure
Domestic production	381	446	503	661	1 048	...	...	Production intérieure

Source:
United Nations Statistics Division, New York, price statistics database.

Source:
Organisation des Nations Unies, Division de statistique, New York, la base de données pour les statistiques des prix.

1 Domestic agricultural products only.
2 Including exported products.
3 Manufacturing industry only.
4 Including service industries.
5 Annual average refers to average of 12 months ending June.
6 Prices relate only to products for sale or transfer to other sectors or for use as capital equipment.
7 Excluding mining and quarrying.
8 Including imported products.
9 Base: 2000=100.
10 Base: 1994=100.
11 Agricultural products and products of the manufacturing industry.
12 Base: 1995=100.
13 Valued at purchasers' values.
14 Base: 1999=100.
15 Beginning 1999, annual average refers to average of 12 months ending May.
16 Base: 2001=100.
17 San Salvador.
18 Durable goods only (Finland: beginning 1994; Luxembourg: beginning 1995).
19 Base: 1991=100.
20 Finished products only.
21 Excluding electricity, gas and water.
22 Including mining and quarrying.
23 Annual average refers to average of 12 months ending March.

1 Produits agricoles intériéurs seulement.
2 Y compris les produits exportés.
3 Industries manufacturières seulement.
4 Y compris industries de service.
5 La moyenne annuelle est la moyenne de douze mois finissant juin.
6 Uniquement les prix des produits destinés à être vendus ou transférés à d'autres secteurs ou à être utilisés comme biens d'équipment.
7 Non compris les industries extractives.
8 Y compris les produits importés.
9 Base: 2000=100.
10 Base: 1994=100.
11 Produits agricoles et produits des industries manufacturières.
12 Base: 1995=100.
13 A la valeur d'acquisition.
14 Base: 1999=100.
15 A partir de 1999, la moyenne annuelle est la moyenne de 12 mois finissant mai.
16 Base: 2001=100.
17 San Salvador.
18 Biens durables seulement (Finlande: à partir de 1995; Luxembourg: à partir de 1994).
19 Base: 1991=100.
20 Produits finis uniquement.
21 Non compris l'électricité, le gaz et l'eau.
22 Y compris les industries extractives.
23 La moyenne annuelle est la moyenne de 12 mois finissant mars.

32

Producers' prices or wholesale prices
Index numbers: 1990 = 100 *[cont.]*

Prix à la production ou prix de gros
Indices : 1990 = 100 *[suite]*

24 Primary articles include food, non-food articles and minerals.

25 Excluding Value Added Tax.
26 Including marine foods.
27 Base: 1992=100.
28 Mexico City.
29 Base: 1997=100.
30 Including all outputs of manufacturing.
31 Including all industrial inputs.
32 Excluding fishing.
33 Metro Manila.
34 Base: 1998=100.
35 Not a sub-division of the domestic supply index.
36 Excluding gold mining.
37 Excluding agriculture.
38 Excluding industrial finished goods.
39 Excluding foods and feeds production.
40 Montevideo.

24 Les articles primaires comprennent des articles des produits alimentaires, non- alimentaires et des minéraux.

25 Non compris taxe sur la valeur ajoutée.
26 Y compris l'alimentation marine.
27 Base: 1992=100.
28 Mexico.
29 Base: 1997=100.
30 Y compris toute la production du secteur manufacturière.
31 Tous les intrants industriels.
32 Non compris la pêche.
33 L'agglomération de Manille.
34 Base: 1998=100.
35 N'est pas un élément de l'indice de l'offre intérieure.
36 Non compris l'extraction de l'or.
37 Non compris l'agriculture.
38 Non compris les produits finis industriels.
39 Non compris les produits alimentaires et d'affouragement.
40 Montevideo.

33
Consumer price index numbers
Indices des prix à la consommation

All items and food; 1990 = 100

Ensemble des prix et alimentation; 1990 = 100

Country or area Pays ou zone	1991	1992	1993	1994	1995	1996	1997	1998	1999	2000
Afghanistan[12] **Afghanistan**[12]	144	...	...	...	...	...	...	...	...	...
Albania[3] **Albanie**[3]	31	100	185	227[4]	246	276	367	444	446	447
Food[36] Aliments[36]	45[5]	100	187	214[4]	229	263	358	433	432	...
Algeria **Algérie**	125	164	200	263	338	407	431	458	468	465
Food Aliments	121	152	189	266	343	417	437	467	472	462
American Samoa[2] **Samoa américaines**[2]	104	109	109	111	113	118	...	...	...	...
Food Aliments	104	108	107	108	109	112	...	...	...	...
Angola[1] **Angola**[1]	100[7]	399[7]	5 904[7]	61 982[7]	2 771[8]	117 653[8]	375 531[8]	778 445[8]	2 710 680[8]	11 521 164[8]
Food[1] Aliments[1]	100[7]	409[7]	6 856[7]	70 425[7]	2 533[8]	100 167[8]	201 844[8]	...	...	...
Anguilla **Anguilla**	105	108	111	116	117	121	122	125	126	136
Food Aliments	104	107	111	113	116	119	120	119	122	123
Antigua and Barbuda **Antigua-et-Barbuda**	106	...	100[9]	106[9]	108[9 10]	112[9]	112[9]	116[9]	117[9]	...
Food Aliments	106	...	100[9]	112[9]	115[9 10]	119[9]	118[9]	119[9]	123[9]	...
Argentina[1 11] **Argentine**[1 11]	272	339	375	391	404	405	407	411	406	402
Food[1 11] Aliments[1 11]	261	340	375	380	391	389	387	393	379	369
Armenia[8] **Arménie**[8]	...	...	0	100	276	328	373	406	408	405
Food[8] Aliments[8]	...	...	0	100	291	334	362	384	362	341
Aruba **Aruba**	106	110	115	123	127[4]	131	135	137	140	146
Food Aliments	105	109	113	120	125[4]	130	134	136	...	...
Australia **Australie**	103	104	106	108	113	116	116	117	119	124
Food Aliments	103	105	107	109	113	116	119	122	126	129
Austria **Autriche**	103	107	111	115	117	119[4]	121	122	123	126
Food Aliments	104	108	111	113	113	114[4]	116	118	118	119
Azerbaijan[9] **Azerbaïdjan**[9]	1	8	100	1 764	9 025	10 817	11 218	11 131	10 182	10 366
Food[69] Aliments[69]	1	7	100	1 793	9 369	11 016	10 964	10 817	9 630	9 853
Bahamas **Bahamas**	107	113	116	118	121[4]	122	123	125	126	...
Food Aliments	109	111	112	111	113[4]	116	118	121	121	...

33
Consumer price index numbers
All items and food; 1990 = 100 [*cont.*]
Indices des prix à la consommation
Ensemble des prix et alimentation; 1990 = 100 [*suite*]

Country or area Pays ou zone	1991	1992	1993	1994	1995	1996	1997	1998	1999	2000
Bahrain **Bahreïn**	**101**	**101**	**103**	**104**	**107**	**107**	**100**[12]	**100**[12]	**98**[12]	...
Food Aliments	102	102	102	101	107	108	100[12]	101[12]	100[12]	...
Bangladesh[8 13] **Bangladesh**[8 13]	...	...	...	**100**	**110**	**113**	**119**	**129**	**137**	**140**
Food[8 13] Aliments[8 13]	...	...	...	100	111	113	118	130	141	143
Barbados **Barbade**	**106**	**113**	**114**	**114**	**117**[4]	**120**	**129**	**127**	**129**	**132**
Food Aliments	105	105	105	105	110[4]	115	130	124	128	131
Belarus[3] **Bélarus**[3]	**9**	**100**	**1 290**	**29 946**	**242 349**	**370 043**	**606 280**	**1 049 047**	**4 130 518**	**11 092 521**
Food[3] Aliments[3]	9	100	1 515	37 477	285 492	427 011	725 423	1 275 657	5 264 124	12 872 715
Belgium **Belgique**	**103**[4]	**106**	**109**	**111**	**113**	**115**[4]	**117**	**118**	**119**	**123**
Food Aliments	102[4]	102	101	103	104	105[4]	107	109	109	110
Belize **Belize**	**106**	**108**	**110**	**113**	**116**	**123**	**125**	**123**	**122**	...
Food[6] Aliments[6]	106	102	111	112	115	123	125	124	121	...
Benin[1 3] **Bénin**[1 3]	...	**100**	**101**[10]	**140**	**160**	**166**	**172**[4]	**182**	**182**	...
Food[1] Aliments[1]	100	100[3]	100[3 10]	135[3]	161[3]	183[3 4]	189[3]	203[3]	202[3]	...
Bermuda **Bermudes**	**104**	**107**	**110**	**112**	**115**	**118**	**121**	**123**	**126**	**129**
Food Aliments	103	103	105	106	110	113	116	119	121	124
Bhutan **Bhoutan**	**112**	**130**	**145**	**155**	**170**	**185**	**197**	**217**	**232**	...
Food[6] Aliments[6]	113	134	145	150	165	180	187	208	220	...
Bolivia[14] **Bolivie**[14]	**120**	**136**	**148**	**159**	**176**	**197**	**207**	**223**	**227**	**238**
Food[14] Aliments[14]	120	138	147	160	180	205	212	224	220	225
Botswana **Botswana**	**112**	**130**[4]	**148**	**164**	**181**	**200**[4]	**217**	**231**	**248**	**271**
Food Aliments	112	133[4]	151	165	183	207[4]	228	242	259	271
Brazil **Brésil**	**533**	**5 605**	**113 626**	**100**[8]	**166**[8]	**192**[8]	**205**[8]	**212**[8]	**222**[8]	**238**[8]
Food Aliments	489	5 367	109 994	100[8]	158[8]	168[8]	169[8]	174[8]	180[8]	189[8]
British Virgin Islands **Iles Vierges britanniques**	**106**	**110**	**113**	**117**	**123**	**129**	...	...	...	...
Food Aliments	107	109	109	115	120	124	...	...	...	...

33
Consumer price index numbers
All items and food; 1990 = 100 [cont.]
Indices des prix à la consommation
Ensemble des prix et alimentation; 1990 = 100 [suite]

Country or area Pays ou zone	1991	1992	1993	1994	1995	1996	1997	1998	1999	2000
Brunei Darussalam **Brunéi Darussalam**	**102**	**103**	**107**	**110**	**117**	**119**	**121**	**120**	...	...
Food Aliments	103	103	106	107	110	113	118	118	...	...
Bulgaria **Bulgarie**	**439**	**787**	**1 228**	**2 296**	**3 722**	**222**[15]	**2 567**[15]	**3 046**[15]	**3 125**[15]	**3 447**[15]
Food Aliments	475	830	1 296	2 484	3 968	223[15]	2 666[15]	2 962[15]	2 724[15]	3 003[15]
Burkina Faso[1] **Burkina Faso**[1]	**103**	**100**	**101**	**126**	**136**	**144**	**148**	**156**[4]	**154**	...
Food[1] Aliments[1]	110	101	96	113	126	145	149	166[4]	156	...
Burundi[1] **Burundi**[1]	**109**[4]	**111**[4]	**122**	**140**	**166**	...	...	...	...	...
Food[1] Aliments[1]	107[4]	105[4]	121	143	171	...	...	...	...	...
Cambodia[1 15] **Cambodge**[1 15]	...	...	...	...	**100**	**107**	**116**	**133**	**138**	**137**
Food[1 15] Aliments[1 15]	...	...	...	...	100	108	115[6]	131[6]	141[6]	136[6]
Cameroon[8] **Cameroun**[8]	...	...	...	**100**	**109**	**113**	**119**	**123**	**125**	...
Food[8] Aliments[8]	...	...	...	100	108	112	120	123	125	...
Canada **Canada**	**106**	**107**[4]	**109**	**109**	**112**	**114**	**115**	**116**	**118**	**122**
Food Aliments	105	104[4]	106	107	109	111	112	114	116	117
Cape Verde **Cap-Vert**	**106**	**112**	**119**	**122**	**133**	**141**	**153**	**160**	**166**	...
Food Aliments	109	119	123	126	140	148	162	170	176	...
Cayman Islands **Iles Caïmanes**	**108**	**111**	**114**	**118**	**120**	**123**	**126**	**130**	...	...
Food Aliments	102	103	106	108	110	114	119	121	...	...
Central African Rep.[1 2] **Rép. centrafricaine**[1 2]	**97**	**96**	**94**	**117**	**139**	**144**	**146**	**145**	**142**	**146**
Food[1] Aliments[1]	96	95	91	113	139	147	148	144	140	145
Chad[1] **Tchad**[1]	**104**	**101**	**92**	**131**	**143**	**161**	**170**	**193**	**162**	**168**
Food[1] Aliments[1]	109	104	90	136	143	164	178	184	161	173
Chile[1] **Chili**[1]	**122**	**141**	**158**	**177**	**191**	**205**	**218**	**229**[4]	**236**	**246**
Food[1] Aliments[1]	126	148	165	181	196	207	222	231[4]	231	234
China **Chine**	**105**	**113**	**132**	**166**	**193**	**210**	**215**	**214**	**211**	**211**
Food Aliments	102	113	132	174	214	230	230	223	213	208
China, Hong Kong SAR **Chine, Hong Kong RAS**	**111**	**122**	**133**	**144**	**157**	**167**	**177**	**182**	**175**	**168**[4]

33
Consumer price index numbers
All items and food; 1990 = 100 [*cont.*]
Indices des prix à la consommation
Ensemble des prix et alimentation; 1990 = 100 [*suite*]

Country or area Pays ou zone	1991	1992	1993	1994	1995	1996	1997	1998	1999	2000
Food Aliments	111	122	131	140	149	155	161	164	161	158[4]
China, Macao SAR **Chine, Macao RAS**	**110**[2]	**118**[2]	**126**[2]	**134**[2 4]	**145**[2]	**152**[2]	**158**[2 4]	**158**[2]	**97**[16 17]	**95**[16 17]
Food Aliments	109	118	126	135[4]	146	152	158[4]	159	152	149
Colombia[18] **Colombie**[18]	**130**	**167**	**203**	**250**	**302**	**364**	**432**	**520**[4]	**578**	**634**
Food[18] Aliments[18]	130	168	194	234	280	326	379	465[4]	491	535
Congo[1] **Congo**[1]	**98**	**94**	**99**	**141**	**154**	**170**	**202**	**194**	**202**	**200**
Food[1] Aliments[1]	96	88	94	139	149	159	199	198	207	197
Cook Islands[1] **Iles Cook**[1]	**106**	**110**	**118**	**121**	**122**	**121**	**120**	**121**	**...**	**...**
Food[1 19] Aliments[1 19]	102	106	113	115	115	114	114	116	...	...
Costa Rica[20] **Costa Rica**[20]	**129**	**157**	**172**	**195**	**241**	**283**	**320**	**358**	**394**	**437**
Food[20] Aliments[20]	126	156	173	197	100[15 21]	119[15 21]	136[15 21]	156[15 21]	171[15 21]	188[15 21]
Côte d'Ivoire[1 7 18] **Côte d'Ivoire**[1 7 18]	**100**	**104**	**107**	**135**[4]	**...**	**...**	**...**	**...**	**...**	**...**
Food[1 7 18] Aliments[1 7 18]	100	103	107	131[4]	...	...	...	...	...	...
Croatia **Croatie**	**224**	**1 646**	**26 104**	**54 088**	**56 251**	**58 670**	**61 074**	**65 032**	**67 259**	**70 519**[22]
Food Aliments	223	1 832	26 707	53 696	54 112	55 844	58 305	62 270	62 294	62 507[22]
Cyprus **Chypre**	**105**	**112**	**117**	**123**[4]	**126**	**130**	**134**	**137**	**140**	**145**
Food Aliments	107	115	117	126[4]	128	132	139	145	101	106
Czech Republic **République tchèque**	**157**	**174**	**210**	**231**[4]	**252**	**275**	**298**	**330**	**337**	**350**
Food[23] Aliments[23]	144	158	184	201[4]	222	240	252	267	261	266
Denmark **Danemark**	**102**	**105**	**106**	**108**	**110**	**113**	**115**	**117**	**120**	**124**[4]
Food Aliments	101	102	102	105	108	110	114	116	117	120[4]
Dominica **Dominique**	**106**	**111**	**113**	**113**[22]	**115**	**116**	**119**	**121**	**122**	**...**
Food Aliments	105	114	117	112[22]	114	116	120	120	121	...
Dominican Republic[24] **Rép. dominicaine**[24]	**147**	**153**	**161**	**175**	**197**	**207**	**224**	**235**[4]	**251**	**270**
Food Aliments	149	149	154	164	188	197	212	225[4]	238	239
Ecuador **Equateur**	**149**	**230**	**333**	**424**	**522**[22]	**649**	**847**	**1 153**	**1 749**	**3 444**
Food[6] Aliments[6]	149	229	325	405	489[22]	598	814	1 146	1 574	3 468

33
Consumer price index numbers
All items and food; 1990 = 100 [cont.]
Indices des prix à la consommation
Ensemble des prix et alimentation; 1990 = 100 [suite]

Country or area Pays ou zone	1991	1992	1993	1994	1995	1996	1997	1998	1999	2000
Egypt										
Egypte Food[6]	**120**	**136**	**153**	**165**	**179**	**192**	**200**	**207**	**218**[4]	**224**
Aliments[6]	117	127	136	149	164	176	184	191	203[4]	209
El Salvador[14]										
El Salvador[14] Food[6,14]	**114**	**127**	**151**	**167**	**183**	**201**	**210**	**216**	**217**	**222**
Aliments[6,14]	118	133	167	193	206	232	244	248	246	247
Estonia										
Estonie Food	**100**[7]	**1 176**[7]	**2 232**[7]	**3 296**[7]	**4 252**[7]	**5 232**[7]	**5 817**[7]	**108**[12]	**112**[12]	**116**[12]
Aliments	100[7]	1 037[7]	1 804[7]	2 451[7]	2 838[7]	3 355[7]	3 540[7]	105[12]	101[12]	103[12]
Ethiopia[1]										
Ethiopie[1] Food[1]	**136**[2]	**150**[2]	**155**[2]	**167**[2]	**184**[2]	**178**[2,10]	**100**[12,25]	**101**[12,25]	**105**[12,25]	**107**[12,25]
Aliments[1]	141	158	160	177	199	189[10]	100[12,26]	102[12,26]	111[12,26]	110[12,26]
Faeroe Islands										
Iles Féroé Food	**104**	**106**	**111**	**114**	**118**	**121**	...	...	**137**	...
Aliments	105	110	116	123	133	138	...	...	...	...
Falkland Is. (Malvinas)[1]										
Iles Falkland (Malvinas)[1] Food[1]	**105**	**112**	**113**	**113**	**117**	**123**	**125**	**128**	...	...
Aliments[1]	104	110	116	119	124	128	124	...	...	...
Fiji										
Fidji Food[27]	**107**	**112**	**118**	**118**[4]	**121**	**125**	**129**	**136**	**139**	**141**
Aliments[27]	102	101	108	109[4]	109	112	117	126	128	124
Finland										
Finlande Food[28]	**104**	**107**	**110**	**111**	**112**[4]	**113**	**114**	**116**	**117**	**121**
Aliments[28]	103	103	102	102	95[4]	93	94	96	96	97
France										
France Food	**103**	**106**	**108**	**110**	**112**	**114**	**115**	**116**	**117**[4]	**119**
Aliments	103	104	104	105	106	107	109	111	111[4]	114
French Guiana										
Guyane française Food	...	**105**	**107**	**109**	**111**	**112**	**113**	**114**	**114**[4]	**115**
Aliments	...	102	104	105	107	108	109	111	110[4]	111
French Polynesia										
Polynésie française Food	**101**	**102**	**104**	**106**	**107**	**108**	**109**	**111**	**112**	**113**
Aliments	99	100	102	105	107	108	111	112	112	113
Gabon[17]										
Gabon[17] Food[17]	**100**[22]	**90**	**91**	**121**	**133**	**138**	**144**	**147**	**146**	...
Aliments[17]	100[22]	83	85	111	120	121	129	133	132	...
Gambia[1]										
Gambie[1] Food[1]	**119**	**119**	**127**	**129**	**138**	**139**	**143**	**144**	**142**	...
Aliments[1]	108	118	128	126	137	139	141	146	151	...
Georgia[15]										
Géorgie[15]	...	...	...	**38**	**100**	**139**	**149**	**155**	**184**	**192**

33
Consumer price index numbers
All items and food; 1990 = 100 [cont.]
Indices des prix à la consommation
Ensemble des prix et alimentation; 1990 = 100 [suite]

Country or area Pays ou zone	1991	1992	1993	1994	1995	1996	1997	1998	1999	2000
Food[6][15] Aliments[6][15]	...	...	...	42	100	133	139	145	171	174
Germany[7] Allemagne[7]	100	105	110	113	115[22]	116	118	120	120	123
Food[7] Aliments[7]	100[29]	103[29]	105[29]	107[29]	105[22][28]	106[28]	107[28]	109[28]	107[28]	107[28]
Ghana Ghana	118	130	163	203	323	474	606	720[4]	810	1 014
Food Aliments	109	120	150	189	307	417	504	610[4]	663	741
Gibraltar Gibraltar	108	115	121	121	124	126	128	130	131[4]	132
Food Aliments	107	112	114	113	114	117	120	122	124[4]	125
Greece Grèce	120	138	158	176[4]	191	207	218	229	235	242
Food Aliments	119	136	153	164[22]	178	190	198	207	212	216
Greenland Groenland	104	106	107	108	109	111	112	113	114[4]	115
Food[6] Aliments[6]	105	106	107	107	113	118	120	122	101[16]	104[16]
Grenada Grenade	103	107	109	112	115	118	120	...	...	...
Food[6] Aliments[6]	102	102	107	112	118	123	123	...	...	...
Guadeloupe Guadeloupe	103	106	108[4][30]	110	112	114	115	117[4]	118	118
Food Aliments	102	103	106[4][30]	108	111	113	114	117[4]	117	115
Guam Guam	110	121	132	154	162	...	100[12]	100[12]	99[12]	...
Food Aliments	118	136	160	208	226	...	100[12]	101[12]	101[12]	...
Guatemala[1] Guatemala[1]	135	149	169	190	206	229	250	266	280	297
Food[1] Aliments[1]	132	142	162	189	205	229	244	256	261	273
Guinea[1] Guinée[1]	119	140	149	156	164	169	...	...	...	...
Food[1] Aliments[1]	116	131	148	154	167	169	...	...	...	...
Guyana[1][7] Guyana[1][7]	100	126	138	155[4]	174	186	193	202	217	230
Food[1][7][14] Aliments[1][7][14]	100	125	133	149[4]	174	187	189	196	213	221
Haïti[11] Haïti[11]	115	131	166	243	228	...	100[22]	111	120	137
Food[11] Aliments[11]	115	126	160	226	216	...	100[22]	110	112	123
Honduras Honduras	134	146	161	196	254	315	378	430	480	509[4]
Food Aliments	144	153	172	219	281	350	420	469	506	531[4]
Hungary Hongrie	135	166[4]	203	242	310	383	453	518	570	625

33
Consumer price index numbers
All items and food; 1990 = 100 [*cont.*]
Indices des prix à la consommation
Ensemble des prix et alimentation; 1990 = 100 [*suite*]

Country or area Pays ou zone	1991	1992	1993	1994	1995	1996	1997	1998	1999	2000
Food Aliments	122	146[4]	188	232	304	357	419	480	494	539
Iceland **Islande**	**107**	**111**	**115**	**117**	**119**	**122**	**124**	**126**	**130**	**137**
Food[19] Aliments[19]	103	104	106	104	107	110	114	117	121	126
India[1 31] **Inde**[1 31]	**112**	**127**	**139**	**153**	**168**	**177**	**195**	**229**	**246**	**264**
Food[1 31] Aliments[1 31]	116	129	144	160	179	187	201	236	230	240
Indonesia **Indonésie**	**109**	**118**	**129**	**140**	**153**	**165**	**176**	**278**[4]	**335**[32]	**348**
Food Aliments	108	116	124	138	156	171	186	358[4]	448[32]	426
Iran (Islamic Rep. of) **Iran (Rép. islamique d')**	**118**	**148**	**180**	**236**	**353**	**455**	**534**	**637**	**771**	...
Food[6] Aliments[6]	119	159	193	255	405	506	557	688	856	...
Ireland **Irlande**	**103**	**106**	**108**	**111**	**113**	**115**	**117**[4]	**120**	**122**	**128**
Food Aliments	101	103	103	107	110	112	114[4]	119	123	128
Isle of Man **Ile de Man**	**107**	**112**	**115**	**118**	**121**	**124**	**127**	**131**	**133**	**137**[4]
Food Aliments	108	113	118	121	126	133	135	143	148	153[4]
Israel **Israël**	**119**	**133**	**148**[4]	**166**	**183**	**203**	**222**	**234**[4]	**246**	**249**
Food Aliments	114	128	135[4]	150	161	177	193	204[4]	218	223
Italy **Italie**	**106**	**112**	**117**	**121**	**128**[4]	**133**	**135**	**138**	**140**	**144**
Food Aliments	107[33]	112[33 34]	114[33 35]	118[33 35]	126[4 33 35]	131[33 35]	131[33 35]	132[33 35]	133[29]	135[29]
Jamaica **Jamaïque**	**151**	**268**	**327**	**442**	**530**	**669**	**734**	**797**	**845**	**914**
Food Aliments	155	275	333	461	554	688	742	794	812	869
Japan **Japon**	**103**	**105**	**106**	**107**	**107**[4]	**107**	**109**	**110**	**109**	**109**
Food Aliments	105	105	107	107	106[4]	106	108	109	109	107
Jordan **Jordanie**	**108**	**112**[4]	**116**	**120**	**123**	**131**	**135**[4]	**139**	**140**	**141**
Kazakhstan[3] **Kazakhstan**[3]	**3**[5]	**100**	**703**	**13 899**	**38 389**	**53 476**	**62 776**	**67 246**	**72 834**	**82 394**
Food[3] Aliments[3]	5[5]	100	691	13 465	35 521	47 882	50 946	53 208	57 162	...
Kenya[1 18] **Kenya**[1 18]	**119**	**154**	**225**	**291**	**297**	**319**	**357**	**378**	**388**	**410**
Food[1 18] Aliments[1 18]	124	167	242	317	310	335	388	402	408	422
Kiribati[1] **Kiribati**[1]	**106**	**110**	**117**	**123**	**127**	**127**	**127**[10]	...	...	...

33
Consumer price index numbers
All items and food; 1990 = 100 [*cont.*]
Indices des prix à la consommation
Ensemble des prix et alimentation; 1990 = 100 [*suite*]

Country or area Pays ou zone	1991	1992	1993	1994	1995	1996	1997	1998	1999	2000
Food[1] Aliments[1]	104	107	113	117	123	121	120[10]	...	...	...
Korea, Republic of **Corée, République de**	**109**	**116**	**122**	**129**	**135**[4]	**142**	**148**	**159**	**160**	**164**
Food Aliments	112	119	124	135	140[4]	145	151	164	169	170
Kuwait[36] **Koweït**[36]	**120**[10]	**119**	**120**	**123**	**126**	**130**	**131**	**131**	**135**	**138**
Food[36] Aliments[36]	124[10]	121	115	117	120	127	127	128	134	135
Kyrgyzstan[3] **Kirghizistan**[3]	...	**100**	**1 186**	**3 329**	**4 776**[4]	**6 303**	**7 780**	**8 593**	**11 678**	**13 862**
Food[3] Aliments[3]	...	100	1 066	2 785	3 898[4]	5 504	6 874	7 593	10 605	12 465
Latvia[7] **Lettonie**[7]	**100**	**1 051**	**2 199**[4]	**2 989**	**3 735**[4]	**4 393**	**4 766**	**4 986**	**5 102**	**5 240**
Lebanon Liban Food[1] Aliments[1]	143	258	301	324	350	379	377	...	...	...
Lesotho **Lesotho**	**118**	**138**	**157**	**168**	**185**	**202**	...	...	...	...
Food[6] Aliments[6]	118	146	161	171	193	214	...	...	...	...
Lithuania[7] **Lituanie**[7]	**100**	**1 121**	**5 718**	**9 845**	**13 749**	**17 135**	**18 656**	**19 602**	**19 751**	**19 937**
Food[7] Aliments[7]	100	1 187	6 187	9 874	13 846	17 687	18 760	18 732	17 997	17 563
Luxembourg[17] **Luxembourg**[17]	**103**	**106**	**110**	**113**	**115**	**116**	**118**	**119**	**120**	**124**
Food[28] Aliments[28]	103	104	104	105	108	109	110[4]	113	114	116
Madagascar[1 2 37] **Madagascar**[1 2 37]	**109**	**124**	**137**	**190**	**283**	**339**	**355**	**377**	**414**	**463**
Food[1 37] Aliments[1 37]	109	127	138	193	291	346	360	382	428	489
Malawi **Malawi**	**108**	**133**	**164**	**221**	**404**	**556**	**607**	**788**	**1 141**	**1 478**
Food Aliments	108	139	176	243	469	681	737	941	1 346	1 612
Malaysia **Malaisie**	**104**	**109**	**113**	**117**[4]	**121**	**126**	**129**	**136**	**140**	**142**
Food Aliments	105	112	114	120[4]	126	133	139	151	158	161
Maldives[1] **Maldives**[1]	**115**	**134**	**161**	**166**	**176**	**187**	**201**	**198**	**204**	**202**
Food[1 6] Aliments[1 6]	113	129	152	158	177	193	231	220	229	...
Mali **Mali**	**101**	**95**	**95**	**117**	...	**142**	...	...	...	...
Food Aliments	103	93	93	116	...	147	...	...	...	...
Malta **Malte**	**103**[4]	**104**	**109**	**113**	**118**[4]	**120**	**124**	**127**	**129**	**132**

33
Consumer price index numbers
All items and food; 1990 = 100 [*cont.*]
Indices des prix à la consommation
Ensemble des prix et alimentation; 1990 = 100 [*suite*]

Country or area Pays ou zone	1991	1992	1993	1994	1995	1996	1997	1998	1999	2000
Food[27] Aliments[27]	102[4]	102	107	111	115[4]	119	120	123	124	126
Marshall Islands[13] **Iles Marshall**[13]	...	**100**	**105**	**111**	**119**	...	...	...	...	...
Martinique **Martinique**	**103**	**107**	**111**[4]	**113**	**116**	**117**	**119**	**120**[4]	**120**	**122**
Food[6] Aliments[6]	103	106	109[4]	111	113	114	115	118[4]	118	118
Mauritania **Mauritanie**	**106**	**116**	**127**	**132**	**141**	**148**	**154**	**167**	**173**	**179**
Food Aliments	103	110	121	125	135	145	151	165	171	177
Mauritius **Maurice**	**107**	**112**[4]	**124**	**133**	**141**	**150**	**160**[4]	**171**	**183**	**190**
Food Aliments	104	100[3]	114[3]	124[3]	132[3]	139[3]	146[3 4]	158[3]	168[3]	170[3]
Mexico **Mexique**	**123**	**142**	**156**	**166**[4]	**225**	**302**	**364**	**422**	**492**	**539**
Food[6] Aliments[6]	120	134	142	150[4]	209	296	352	409	474	503
Morocco **Maroc**	**108**	**114**	**120**	**126**	**134**	**138**	**139**	**143**	**144**	**147**
Food[6] Aliments[6]	109	116	123	132	143	144	142	146	145	147
Myanmar[1] **Myanmar**[1]	**132**	**161**	**213**	**264**	**330**	**384**	**498**	**755**	**893**	...
Food[1] Aliments[1]	137	168	234	281	354	421	548	835	997	...
Namibia[1] **Namibie**[1]	**112**	**132**	**143**	**158**	**174**	**188**	**205**	**218**	**236**	**258**
Food[1] Aliments[1]	106	127	135	153	170	182	196	201	212	227
Nepal **Népal**	**116**	**135**	**145**	**158**	**170**	**185**[22]	**198**	**221**	**236**	...
Food Aliments	118	139	147	159	171	189[22]	199	229	247	...
Netherlands **Pays-Bas**	**103**	**106**	**109**	**112**	**114**[4]	**117**	**119**	**122**	**124**	**127**
Food[6] Aliments[6]	103	106	107	109	109	100[15 35]	102[15 35]	104[15 35]	105[15 35]	106[15 35]
Netherlands Antilles[1] **Antilles néerlandaises**[1]	**104**	**105**	**108**	**110**	**113**	**117**[4]	**120**	**122**	**122**	**129**
Food[1] Aliments[1]	107	110	114	116	122	129[4]	132	133	136	145
New Caledonia[1] **Nouvelle-Calédonie**[1]	**104**	**107**	**110**[4]	**113**	**114**	**116**	**118**	**119**	**120**	**122**
Food[1] Aliments[1]	103	106	110[4]	114	115	118	123	124	125	126
New Zealand **Nouvelle-Zélande**	**103**	**104**	**105**	**107**	**111**	**113**	**115**	**116**	**116**	**119**
Food Aliments	101	101	102	102	103	104	107	110	111	113
Nicaragua **Nicaragua**	**2 842**	**3 767**	**4 534**	**4 886**[4]	**5 421**	**6 050**	**6 608**	**7 470**	**8 308**	**9 267**

33
Consumer price index numbers
All items and food; 1990 = 100 [*cont.*]
Indices des prix à la consommation
Ensemble des prix et alimentation; 1990 = 100 [*suite*]

Country or area Pays ou zone	1991	1992	1993	1994	1995	1996	1997	1998	1999	2000
Food Aliments	2 851	3 503	3 904	4 208[4]	4 711	5 248	5 724	6 541	6 898	7 243
Niger[12] Niger[12]	92[4]	90	90	122	136	143	147	154[4]	151	155
Food[1] Aliments[1]	88[4]	86	87	125	136	153	161	173[4]	164	169
Nigeria[38] Nigéria[38]	113	163	257	403	688	901	975	1 076	...	...
Food[38] Aliments[38]	112	164	259	380	654	851	924	985	...	...
Niue Nioué	105	110	112	114	115	...	...	...	...	...
Food Aliments	104	107	110	111	113	...	...	...	...	...
Norfolk Island[7] Ile Norfolk[7]	100	102	106	110	113	117	...	...	...	...
Food[7] Aliments[7]	100	101	103	106	112	117	...	...	...	...
Northern Mariana Islands[1] Iles Mariannes du Nord[1]	107	117	122	125	128	131	133	133	...	...
Food[1] Aliments[1]	108	112	116	118	119	121	121	120	...	...
Norway Norvège	103	106	108	110	112	114	117	119[4]	122	126
Food Aliments	102	103	102	103	105	107	110	116[4]	120	122
Oman[1] Oman[1]	105	106	107	106	105[22]	105	105	104	105	104
Food[16] Aliments[16]	103	102	101	100	102[22]	104	105	104	104	103
Pakistan Pakistan	112	122[4]	135	151	170	188	209	222	231	241
Food Aliments	111	123[4]	135	155	177	193	217	229	238	246
Panama[1] Panama[1]	101	103	104	105	106	107	109	109	111	112
Food[1] Aliments[1]	102	106	106	108	108	109	110	110	111	111
Papua New Guinea Papouasie-Nvl-Guinée	107	112	117	120	141	158	164	186	214	...
Food Aliments	108	111	114	116	137	156	166	188	220	...
Paraguay[1] Paraguay[1]	124	143	169	204	231	254	272	303	324	...
Food[1] Aliments[1]	120	138	161	195	224	237	247	275	284	...
Peru[1 11] Pérou[1 11]	510	884	1 314	1 626[4]	1 806	2 015	2 187	2 346	2 427	2 518
Food[1 11] Aliments[1 11]	448	770	1 150	1 352[22]	1 479	1 659	1 776	1 923	1 918	1 933
Philippines Philippines	119	129	139	149[22]	161	176	186	204	217	227
Food[6] Aliments[6]	115	123	131	141[22]	154	170	175	191	201	205

33
Consumer price index numbers
All items and food; 1990 = 100 [cont.]
Indices des prix à la consommation
Ensemble des prix et alimentation; 1990 = 100 [suite]

Country or area Pays ou zone	1991	1992	1993	1994	1995	1996	1997	1998	1999	2000
Poland **Pologne**	**170**	**244**	**330**	**436**	**557**	**668**	**767**	**100**[16]	**107**[16]	**118**[16]
Food[33] Aliments[33]	151	207	274	363	462	550	620	100[16]	102[16]	112[16]
Portugal[2] **Portugal**[2]	**111**	**121**[4]	**129**	**136**	**142**	**146**	**149**[4]	**153**	**157**	**161**
Food[29] Aliments[29]	110	118[4]	121	127	132	135	136[4]	140	143	147
Puerto Rico **Porto Rico**	**103**	**106**	**109**	**113**	**118**	**124**	**131**	**138**	**146**	**155**
Food Aliments	105	114	118	128	142	156	174	195	215	235
Qatar **Qatar**	**104**	**108**	**107**	**108**	**111**	**119**	**122**	**126**	**129**	**...**
Food[6] Aliments[6]	106	106	98	93	104	108	108	112	112	...
Republic of Moldova[3] **République de Moldova**[3]	**7**	**100**	**1 714**	**10 059**	**13 064**	**16 135**	**18 034**	**19 422**	**27 046**	**35 512**
Food[3] Aliments[3]	7	100	1 418	7 844	10 168	12 148	13 004	13 525	17 954	24 487
Réunion **Réunion**	**104**	**107**	**111**	**114**	**116**	**118**	**119**	**121**[4]	**122**	**124**
Food Aliments	105	107	111	112	113	115	117	120[4]	119	119
Romania **Roumanie**	**275**	**310**[7]	**1 105**[7]	**2 617**[7]	**3 461**[7]	**4 805**[7]	**12 241**[7]	**19 474**[7]	**28 394**[7]	**41 361**[7]
Food Aliments	299	337[7]	1 174[7]	2 774[7]	3 657[7]	4 987[7]	12 536[7]	18 607[7]	23 789[7]	34 188[7]
Russian Federation[7] **Fédération de Russie**[7]	**100**	**1 630**	**15 869**	**64 688**	**192 521**	**284 429**[4]	**326 484**	**416 814**[4]	**773 814**	**934 450**
Food[7] Aliments[7]	100	1 690	16 760	67 339	210 975	287 151[4]	323 749	412 044[4]	810 254	952 104
Rwanda[1] **Rwanda**[1]	**120**	**131**	**147**	**...**	**...**	**...**	**...**	**...**	**...**	**...**
Food[1] Aliments[1]	114	122	...	...	...	...	...	...	...	...
Saint Helena **Sainte-Hélène**	**104**	**109**[4]	**118**	**123**	**128**	**134**	**137**	**139**	**142**	**...**
Food Aliments	102	106[4]	112	116	121	126	126	124	126	...
Saint Kitts and Nevis[1] **Saint-Kitts-et-Nevis**[1]	**104**	**107**	**109**	**111**	**114**	**116**	**127**	**131**	**135**	**138**
Food[1] Aliments[1]	106	111	113	117	119	123	134	141	141	145
Saint Lucia **Sainte-Lucie**	**106**	**113**	**113**	**116**	**123**	**124**	**124**	**128**	**132**	**137**
Food Aliments	109	114	114	119	128	128	124	130	133	135
Saint Pierre and Miquelon **Saint-Pierre-et-Miquelon**	**105**	**...**	**...**	**...**	**...**	**...**	**100**[12]	**101**[12]	**102**[12]	**...**
Food Aliments	104	...	...	...	...	...	100[12]	102[12]	104[12]	...
St. Vincent-Grenadines[1] **St. Vincent-Grenadines**[1]	**106**	**110**	**115**	**115**	**118**	**123**	**124**	**126**	**128**	**128**

33
Consumer price index numbers
All items and food; 1990 = 100 [*cont.*]
Indices des prix à la consommation
Ensemble des prix et alimentation; 1990 = 100 [*suite*]

Country or area Pays ou zone	1991	1992	1993	1994	1995	1996	1997	1998	1999	2000
Food[1] Aliments[1]	109	113	116	116	120	128	127	124	125	123
Samoa[2] **Samoa[2]**	**99**	**107**	**109**	**129**	**130**	**139**	**155**	**137**	...	...
Food Aliments	92	102	102	127	128	144	160	123	...	...
San Marino **Saint-Marin**	**107**	**115**	**121**	**125**[4]	**132**	**137**[4]	**140**	**143**	**148**	...
Food Aliments	105	111	118	123[4]	128	132[4]	136	139	142	...
Saudi Arabia[39] **Arabie saoudite[39]**	**105**	**104**	**105**	**106**	**111**	**112**	**112**	**111**	**110**	**109**
Food[6,39] Aliments[6,39]	108	112	113	111	112	114	116	117	114	113
Senegal[1] **Sénégal[1]**	**98**	**98**	**98**	**129**	**139**	**143**	**146**	**147**[4]	**148**	**149**
Food[1] Aliments[1]	97	96	94	131	143	145	146	152[4]	152	150
Serbia and Montenegro **Serbie-et-Monténégro**	**222**	**20 021**	...	**24**[12]	**43**[12]	**82**[12]	**100**[12]	**130**[12]	**188**[12]	**350**[12]
Food Aliments	200	19 217	...	27[12]	46[12]	84[12]	100[12]	133[12]	193[12]	396[12]
Seychelles **Seychelles**	**102**	**105**	**107**	**109**	**108**	**107**	**108**	**111**	**118**	**125**
Food Aliments	102	104	107	100	99	96	98	101	100	101
Sierra Leone[1] **Sierra Leone[1]**	**183**	**258**	...	...	...	...	...	...	...	...
Food[1] Aliments[1]	186	264	...	...	...	...	...	...	...	...
Singapore **Singapour**	**103**	**106**	**108**[22]	**112**	**113**	**115**	**117**[22]	**117**	**117**	**119**
Food Aliments	101	103	104[22]	107	110	112	114[22]	115	116	116
Slovakia **Slovaquie**	**161**	**177**	**218**	**248**	**272**	**288**	**305**	**326**	**360**	**403**
Food[28] Aliments[28]	152	163	197	231	260	270	286	303	311	327
Slovenia[14] **Slovénie[14]**	**215**	**662**	**880**	**1 065**	**1 208**	**1 327**	**1 438**	**1 552**	**1 647**	**1 793**
Food[14,19] Aliments[14,19]	212	649	816	1 005	1 162	1 271	1 378	1 495	1 555	1 640
Solomon Islands[1] **Iles Salomon[1,33]**	**114**	**126**	**134**[4]	**152**	**167**	**186**	**202**	**226**	**245**	...
Food[1,33] Aliments[1,33]	117	130	136[4]	152	163	185	205	232	258	...
South Africa **Afrique du Sud**	**115**	**131**	**144**	**157**	**171**	**183**	**199**	**213**	**224**	**236**
Food Aliments	120	150	160	182	198	210	230	244	256	276
Spain **Espagne**	**106**	**112**[22]	**117**	**123**	**129**	**133**	**136**	**138**	**142**	**146**
Food[6] Aliments[6]	104	107[22]	102	107	112	116	115	117	118	121

33
Consumer price index numbers
All items and food; 1990 = 100 [cont.]
Indices des prix à la consommation
Ensemble des prix et alimentation; 1990 = 100 [suite]

Country or area Pays ou zone	1991	1992	1993	1994	1995	1996	1997	1998	1999	2000
Sri Lanka[1] **Sri Lanka**[1]	**112**	**125**	**140**	**151**	**163**	**189**	**207**	**227**	**237**	**252**
Food[1] Aliments[1]	112	125	139	152	162	193	214	238	247	258
Sudan[18] **Soudan**[18]	**222**	**473**	**953**	**2 068**	**3 482**	**8 192**	...	...	...	...
Food[6][18] Aliments[6][18]	236	457	...	...	...	...	...	...	...	...
Suriname[1] **Suriname**[1]	**126**	**181**	**441**	**2 065**	**6 934**	**6 879**	**7 371**	**8 773**	**17 446**	**27 797**
Food[1] Aliments[1]	119	184	485	2 364	7 842	7 267	7 209	8 244	15 708	...
Swaziland[18] **Swaziland**[18]	**102**	**122**	**137**	**157**	**180**	**204**	**212**[4]	**228**	**246**	...
Food[18] Aliments[18]	114	128	144	172	206	233	265[4]	281	...	...
Sweden **Suède**	**109**	**112**	**117**	**120**	**123**	**123**	**124**	**124**	**125**	**126**
Food Aliments	105	99	100	102	103	96	96	97	99	99
Switzerland **Suisse**	**106**	**110**	**114**	**115**	**117**	**118**	**118**	**118**	**119**	**121**[4]
Food Aliments	104	104	104	105	105	105	106	106	106	108[4]
Syrian Arab Republic **Rép. arabe syrienne**	**109**	**121**	**137**	**154**	**170**	**185**	**189**	**188**	**184**	**183**
Food Aliments	106	113	126	145	155	169	173	169	162	159
Tajikistan **Tadjikistan**	**184**	**1 951**	**43 622**	**148 095**	**804 305**	**2 977 539**	**5 112 434**	**73106505**	**92114196**	**114221600**
Food Aliments	189	2 477	75 096	189 918	1 066 009	4 065 760	7 172 001	...	...	...
Thailand **Thaïlande**	**106**	**110**	**114**	**120**[4]	**126**	**134**	**141**	**153**	**153**	**156**
Food Aliments	107	112	114	122[4]	132	144	154	168	167	165
TFYR of Macedonia **L'ex-R.y. Macédoine**	**211**	**3 397**	**15 692**	**35 826**	**41 444**	**42 401**	**43 499**	**43 468**	**43 154**	**45 657**
Food Aliments	205	3 462	15 434	34 419	37 382	37 336	38 910	38 833	38 216	38 063
Togo[1] **Togo**[1][27]	**100**	**102**	**102**	**143**[4]	**165**	**173**	**187**	**184**	...	...
Food Aliments[1][27]	96	99	98	129	100[15]	106[15]	121[15]	117[15]	...	...
Tonga[2] **Tonga**[2]	**109**	**118**	**119**	**120**[4]	**122**	**126**	**129**	**133**	**138**	...
Food Aliments	106	119	115	114	117	126	130	138	145	...
Trinidad and Tobago **Trinité-et-Tobago**	**104**	**111**	**122**	**133**[4]	**140**	**145**	**150**	**159**	**164**	...
Food Aliments	106	115	137	161[4]	188	208	228	262	285	...
Tunisia **Tunisie**	**108**	**115**	**119**	**125**	**132**	**137**	**142**	**147**	**151**	**155**

33
Consumer price index numbers
All items and food; 1990 = 100 [cont.]
Indices des prix à la consommation
Ensemble des prix et alimentation; 1990 = 100 [suite]

Country or area Pays ou zone	1991	1992	1993	1994	1995	1996	1997	1998	1999	2000
Food Aliments	109	114	117	122	132	137	143	147	150	157
Turkey Turquie	166	282	469	967	1 872	339[8]	630[8]	1 163[8]	1 917[8]	2 970[8]
Food[6] Aliments[6]	167	286	468	983	1 938	331[8]	637[8]	1 162[8]	1 727[8]	...
Tuvalu[1,14] Tuvalu[1,14]	106	100	102	104	109	110	112	112	...	...
Food[1] Aliments[1]	106	97	99	103	109	110	110	110	...	...
Uganda[14] Ouganda[14]	128	198	208	229	244	261	282	282	300	...
Food[14] Aliments[14]	124	205	197	228	238	254	300	291	311	...
Ukraine[3] Ukraine[3]	...	100	4 835	47 923	228 471	411 775	477 190	527 663	647 356	829 931
Food[3,6] Aliments[3,6]	...	100	5 514	49 582	226 059	357 921	399 575	446 690	570 891	767 855
United Kingdom Royaume-Uni	106	110	112	114	118	121	125	129	131	135
Food Aliments	105	107	109	110	115	118	119	120	120	120
United Rep. of Tanzania[40] Rép.-Unie de Tanzanie[40]	129	157	197	254	336	406	471	532	574	608
Food[40] Aliments[40]	132	160	196	260	347	417	490	562	612	653
United States Etats-Unis	104	107	111	113	117	120	123	125	127	132
Food Aliments	103	104	106	109	112	116	119	121	124	127
Uruguay[1] Uruguay[1]	202	340	524	759	1 079	1 385	1 661[4]	1 839	1 943	2 036
Food[1] Aliments[1]	185	297	449	632	894	1 105	1 308[4]	1 444	1 498	1 582
Vanuatu[14] Vanuatu[14]	106	111	115	117	120	121	124	129	...	...
Food[14] Aliments[14]	103	104	108	109	113	112	113	117	...	...
Venezuela Venezuela	133	175	239	381	609	1 224	1 819	2 448	2 986	...
Food[6] Aliments[6]	134	175	231	366	585	1 096	1 585	2 182	2 516	...
Viet Nam Viet Nam	182	250	271	287	347	367	379	408	426	419
Zambia[18] Zambie[18]	193	573	1 655	2 521	3 381	4 590[22]	5 662	7 045	...	...
Food[6,18] Aliments[6,18]	191	608	1 781	2 665	3 568	5 203[22]	6 279	7 803	...	...
Zimbabwe Zimbabwe	123	175	224	273	335	407	484	637	1 010	1 574
Food[27] Aliments[27]	113	193	267	337	429	545	641	893	1 500	2 234

33
Consumer price index numbers
All items and food; 1990 = 100 [*cont.*]

Indices des prix à la consommation
Ensemble des prix et alimentation; 1990 = 100 [*suite*]

Source:
International Labour Office (ILO), Geneva, "Yearbook of
Labour Statistics 2001" and the ILO labour statistics
database.

1 Data refer to the index of the capital city.
2 Excluding Rent.
3 Index base: 1992 = 100.
4 Series linked to former series.
5 One month of each year.
6 Including tobacco.
7 Index base: 1991 = 100.
8 Index base: 1994 = 100.
9 Index base 1993 = 100.
10 Average of less than twelve months.
11 Metropolitan area.
12 Index base 1997 = 100.
13 Government officials.
14 Urban areas.
15 Index base: 1995 = 100.
16 Index base 1998 = 100.
17 Including rent.
18 Low income group.
19 Excluding beverages.
20 Central area.
21 Including alcoholic beverages and tobacco.
22 Series replacing former series.
23 Including tobacco, beverages and public catering.
24 Including direct taxes.
25 Beginning September 1996: including "rent".
26 Beginning September 1996: excluding beverages.
27 Excluding beverages and tobacco.
28 Excluding alcoholic beverages and tobacco.
29 Excluding alcoholic beverages.
30 All households.
31 Industrial workers.
32 Since November 1999: exclude Dili.
33 Including alcoholic beverages.
34 Beginning February 1992: excluding tobacco.
35 Excluding tobacco.
36 Index base: 1989 = 100.
37 Madagascans.
38 Rural and urban areas.
39 All cities.
40 Tanganyika.

Source:
Bureau international du Travail (BIT), Genève, "Annuaire des
statistiques du travail 2001" et la base de données du BIT.

1 Les données se referènt à l'indice de la capitale.
2 Non compris le groupe loyer.
3 Indices base: 1992 = 100.
4 Série enchaînée à la précédente.
5 Un mois de chaque année.
6 Y compris le tabac.
7 Indices base: 1991 = 100.
8 Indices base: 1994 = 100.
9 Indices base 1993 = 100.
10 Moyenne de moins de douze mois.
11 Région métropolitaine.
12 Indices base 1997 = 100.
13 Fonctionnaires.
14 Régions urbaines.
15 Indices base: 1995 = 100.
16 Indices base 1998 = 100.
17 Y compris le groupe loyer.
18 Familles à revenu modique.
19 Non compris les boissons.
20 Région centrale.
21 Y compris les boissons alcoolisées et le tabac.
22 Série remplaçant la précédente.
23 Y compris le tabac, les boissons et la restauration.
24 Y compris les impôts directs.
25 A partir de septembre 1996: y compris le groupe loyer.
26 A partir de septembre 1996: non compris les boissons.
27 Non compris les boissons et le tabac.
28 Non compris les boissons alcoolisées et le tabac.
29 Non compris les boissons alcooliques.
30 Ensemble des ménages.
31 Travailleurs de l'industrie.
32 A partir de novembre 1999, non compris Dili.
33 Y compris les boissons alcoolisées.
34 A partir de février 1992: non compris le tabac.
35 Non compris le tabac.
36 Indices base: 1989 = 100.
37 Malgaches.
38 Régions rurales et urbaines.
39 Ensemble des villes.
40 Tanganyika.

Technical notes, tables 31-33

Table 31: The series generally relate to the average earnings per worker in manufacturing industries, according to the *International Standard Industrial Classification of All Economic Activities* (ISIC) Revision 2 or Revision 3 [50]. The data are published in the ILO *Yearbook of Labour Statistics* [13] and on the ILO Web site <http://laborsta.ilo.org> and cover all employees (i.e. wage earners and salaried employees) of both sexes, irrespective of age. Data which refer exclusively to wage earners (i.e. manual or production workers), or to salaried employees (i.e. non-manual workers) are footnoted. Earnings generally include bonuses, cost of living allowances, taxes, social insurance contributions payable by the employed person and, in some cases, payments in kind, and normally exclude social insurance contributions payable by the employers, family allowances and other social security benefits. The time of year to which the figures refer is not the same for all countries. In some cases, the series may show wage rates instead of earnings; this is indicated in footnotes.

Table 32: Producer prices are prices at which producers sell their output on the domestic market or for export. Wholesale prices, in the strict sense, are prices at which wholesalers sell their goods on the domestic market or for export. In practice, many national wholesale price indexes are a mixture of producer and wholesale prices for domestic goods representing prices for purchases in large quantities from either source. In addition, these indexes may cover the prices of goods imported in quantity for the domestic market either by producers or by retail or wholesale distributors.

Producer or wholesale price indexes normally cover the prices of the characteristic products of agriculture, forestry and fishing, mining and quarrying, manufacturing, and electricity, gas and water supply. Prices are normally measured in terms of transaction prices, including non-deductible indirect taxes less subsidies, in the case of domestically-produced goods and import duties and other non-deductible indirect taxes less subsidies in the case of imported goods.

The Laspeyres index number formula is generally used and, for the purpose of the presentation, the national index numbers have been recalculated, where necessary, on the reference base 1990=100.

The price index numbers for each country are arranged according to the following scheme:

(a)   Components of supply
       Domestic supply
       Domestic production for domestic market
       Agricultural products

Notes techniques, tableaux 31 à 33

Tableau 31: Les séries se rapportent généralement aux gains moyens des salariés des industries manufacturières (activités de fabrication), suivant la *Classification internationale type, par industrie, de toutes les branches d'activité économique* (CITI, Rev. 2 ou Rev.3) [50]. Les données sont publiées dans *l'Annuaire des statistiques du travail* du BIT [13] et sur le site Web du BIT <http://laborsta.ilo.org> et portent sur l'ensemble des salariés (qu'ils perçoivent un salaire ou un traitement au mois) des deux sexes, indépendamment de leur âge. Lorsque les données portent exclusivement sur les salariés horaires (ouvriers, travailleurs manuels) ou sur les employés percevant un traitement (travailleurs autres que manuels, cadres), le fait est signalé par une note. Les gains comprennent en général les primes, les indemnités pour coût de la vie, les impôts, les cotisations de sécurité sociale à la charge de l'employé, et dans certains cas des paiements en nature, mais ne comprennent pas en règle générale la part patronale des cotisations d'assurance sociale, les allocations familiales et les autres prestations de sécurité sociale. La période de l'année visée par les données n'est pas la même pour tous les pays. Dans certains cas, les séries visent les taux horaires et non pas les gains, ce qui est alors signalé en note.

Tableau 32: Les prix à la production sont les prix auxquels les producteurs vendent leur production sur le marché intérieur ou à l'exportation. Les prix de gros, au sens strict du terme, sont les prix auxquels les grossistes vendent sur le marché intérieur ou à l'exportation. En pratique, les indices nationaux des prix de gros combinent souvent les prix à la production et les prix de gros de biens nationaux représentant les prix d'achat par grandes quantités au producteur ou au grossiste. En outre, ces indices peuvent s'appliquer aux prix de biens importés en quantités pour être vendus sur le marché intérieur par les producteurs, les détaillants ou les grossistes.

Les indices de prix de gros ou de prix à la production comprennent aussi en général les prix des produits provenant de l'agriculture, de la sylviculture et de la pêche, des industries extractives (mines et carrières), de l'industrie manufacturière ainsi que les prix de l'électricité, de gaz et de l'eau. Les prix sont normalement ceux auxquels s'effectue la transaction, y compris les impôts indirects non déductibles, mais non compris les subventions dans le cas des biens produits dans le pays et y compris les taxes à l'importation et autres impôts indirects non déductibles, mais non compris les subventions dans le cas des biens importés.

On utilise généralement la formule de Laspeyres

Industrial products
Imported goods
(b)   Stage of processing
Raw materials
Intermediate products
(c)   End-use
Consumers' goods
Capital goods

A description of the general methods used in compiling the related national indexes is given in the United Nations *1977 Supplement to the Statistical Yearbook and the Monthly Bulletin of Statistics* [57].

Table 33: Unless otherwise stated, the consumer price index covers all the main classes of expenditure on all items and on food. Monthly data for many of these series and descriptions of them may be found in the United Nations *Monthly Bulletin of Statistics* [26] and the United Nations *1977 Supplement to the Statistical Yearbook and the Monthly Bulletin of Statistics* [57].

et, pour la présentation, on a recalculé les indices nationaux, le cas échéant, en prenant comme base de référence 1990=100.

Les indices des prix pour chaque pays sont présentés suivant la classification ci-après:
(a)   Eléments de l'offre
Offre intérieure
Production nationale pour le marché intérieur
Produits agricoles
Produits industriels
Produits importés
(b)   Stade de la transformation
Matières premières
Produits intermédiaires
(c)   Utilisation finale
Biens de consommation
Biens d'équipement

Les méthodes générales utilisées pour calculer les indices nationaux correspondants sont exposées dans: *1977 Supplément à l'Annuaire statistique et au Bulletin mensuel de statistique* des Nations Unies [57].

Tableau 33: Sauf indication contraire, les indices des prix à la consommation donnés englobent tous les groupes principaux de dépenses pour l'ensemble des prix et alimentation. Les données mensuelles pour plusieurs de ces séries et définitions figurent dans le *Bulletin mensuel de statistique* [26] et dans le *1977 Supplément à l'Annuaire statistique et au Bulletin mensuel de statistique* des Nations Unies [57].

34

Agricultural production
Index numbers: 1989-91 = 100

Production agricole
Indices: 1989-91 = 100

Country or area Pays ou zone	Agriculture Agriculture					Food Produits alimentaires				
	1997	1998	1999	2000	2001	1997	1998	1999	2000	2001
Africa · Afrique										
Algeria Algérie	112.2	127.8	132.2	126.2	137.4	113.0	129.1	133.6	127.1	138.6
Angola Angola	127.4	146.0	139.1	146.1	146.5	128.9	148.2	141.6	148.4	148.9
Benin Bénin	168.4	165.3	160.9	173.1	170.2	153.8	151.4	153.5	159.9	159.4
Botswana Botswana	94.5	90.3	93.6	96.3	96.3	94.6	90.4	93.7	96.4	96.4
Burkina Faso Burkina Faso	127.3	144.0	147.5	129.7	139.7	116.8	137.2	143.4	126.2	136.6
Burundi Burundi	94.5	89.6	91.7	86.0	94.9	97.1	91.7	92.1	87.4	95.9
Cameroon Cameroun	119.4	127.0	132.2	128.5	131.4	122.4	126.9	132.9	127.8	131.7
Cape Verde Cap-Vert	109.4	127.5	153.1	132.8	135.8	109.7	127.9	153.5	133.2	136.2
Central African Rep. Rép. centrafricaine	125.8	128.1	130.5	136.9	137.6	125.8	130.2	132.9	142.4	142.9
Chad Tchad	139.6	152.4	140.9	130.1	132.1	135.9	159.5	143.9	135.3	134.8
Comoros Comores	113.9	123.1	130.0	118.8	120.2	115.5	123.8	131.8	120.6	121.6
Congo Congo	118.6	116.6	125.4	127.7	129.2	119.5	117.7	126.3	128.6	130.1
Côte d'Ivoire Côte d'Ivoire	128.1	124.5	129.8	144.3	130.8	131.6	133.0	136.4	143.4	134.1
Dem. Rep. of the Congo Rép. dém. du Congo	88.1	89.2	86.2	83.8	81.8	88.6	90.3	87.5	85.1	83.3
Djibouti Djibouti	87.7	88.4	89.6	90.1	90.2	87.7	88.4	89.6	90.1	90.2
Egypt Egypte	140.2	138.4	148.2	152.7	152.8	141.8	142.0	152.3	157.6	157.7
Equatorial Guinea Guinée équatoriale	96.3	95.8	101.1	100.0	99.3	111.1	110.9	117.0	115.5	114.6
Eritrea Erythrée	103.4	148.9	134.7	118.1	126.1	103.5	150.0	135.4	118.5	126.6
Ethiopia Ethiopie	136.3	125.9	133.6	142.3	138.9	138.6	127.5	136.3	145.3	141.7
Gabon Gabon	113.0	116.4	117.4	119.6	119.8	110.2	113.3	114.3	116.6	116.7
Gambia Gambie	88.9	85.8	124.9	138.7	150.6	89.6	86.8	126.4	140.4	152.5
Ghana Ghana	145.1	158.6	165.8	171.0	175.1	144.2	157.3	164.9	170.0	174.0
Guinea Guinée	135.4	144.7	148.4	160.0	160.0	137.8	146.1	148.6	158.7	158.7
Guinea-Bissau Guinée-Bissau	125.2	128.1	135.1	139.9	144.4	125.6	128.5	135.3	140.1	144.6

34

Agricultural production
Index numbers: 1989-91=100 *[cont.]*

Production agricole
Indices: 1989-91 = 100 *[suite]*

Country or area Pays ou zone	Agriculture Agriculture					Food Produits alimentaires				
	1997	1998	1999	2000	2001	1997	1998	1999	2000	2001
Kenya Kenya	105.8	110.8	109.7	108.8	106.8	106.1	109.2	109.4	107.7	106.1
Lesotho Lesotho	115.7	95.4	93.3	124.6	125.1	114.9	96.5	94.2	128.0	128.5
Libyan Arab Jamah. Jamah. arabe libyenne	132.1	157.0	145.8	158.6	160.9	133.3	160.1	147.5	160.9	163.4
Madagascar Madagascar	109.4	108.9	112.4	105.5	105.5	111.7	110.8	114.4	107.4	107.4
Malawi Malawi	121.9	134.6	136.1	145.3	146.8	114.7	141.7	157.2	161.8	163.4
Mali Mali	117.2	125.6	129.4	109.3	135.7	105.2	114.6	121.9	111.9	124.6
Mauritania Mauritanie	105.2	106.5	106.1	110.5	111.6	105.2	106.5	106.1	110.5	111.6
Mauritius Maurice	110.7	105.9	83.0	100.7	106.8	116.2	111.3	86.7	105.9	112.4
Morocco Maroc	96.6	112.0	105.9	99.9	105.4	96.5	112.3	106.2	99.8	105.5
Mozambique Mozambique	131.0	140.9	143.1	122.4	125.3	130.1	139.2	141.4	120.5	123.5
Namibia Namibie	85.8	95.1	123.1	116.6	115.3	85.2	94.7	122.9	116.3	114.9
Niger Niger	101.0	151.9	137.4	127.4	147.1	100.5	151.7	135.7	125.9	146.4
Nigeria Nigéria	142.8	149.2	153.3	156.8	156.8	143.2	149.6	153.8	157.4	157.4
Réunion Réunion	121.0	115.9	124.1	124.7	125.3	121.7	116.6	124.8	125.4	126.0
Rwanda Rwanda	78.2	84.1	89.2	109.0	108.5	78.6	84.7	90.0	111.2	110.3
Sao Tome and Principe Sao Tomé-et-Principe	139.4	147.8	159.1	166.3	166.3	139.2	147.6	158.8	166.4	166.4
Senegal Sénégal	101.3	98.2	134.6	133.6	136.2	101.1	100.0	137.0	135.6	137.3
Seychelles Seychelles	142.1	128.0	133.8	136.2	136.2	142.7	128.3	134.9	137.5	137.5
Sierra Leone Sierra Leone	103.0	95.0	82.8	78.2	78.2	101.9	94.7	85.3	80.1	80.2
South Africa Afrique du Sud	103.5	98.1	104.5	107.9	101.8	106.4	100.6	107.1	111.3	104.8
Sudan Soudan	153.7	156.9	154.2	157.2	164.7	156.6	160.6	157.8	159.6	167.6
Swaziland Swaziland	86.1	86.4	90.2	84.5	84.6	88.0	90.1	93.1	86.9	86.9
Togo Togo	134.2	131.4	134.2	133.8	135.4	130.4	121.6	135.3	131.5	132.0
Tunisia Tunisie	97.0	122.9	134.3	132.1	126.0	97.7	124.4	136.2	133.7	127.4
Uganda Ouganda	110.0	121.3	132.4	132.4	139.5	105.9	118.0	127.3	131.3	136.9

34

Agricultural production
Index numbers: 1989-91=100 *[cont.]*
Production agricole
Indices: 1989-91 = 100 *[suite]*

Country or area Pays ou zone	Agriculture Agriculture					Food Produits alimentaires				
	1997	1998	1999	2000	2001	1997	1998	1999	2000	2001
United Rep. of Tanzania Rép.-Unie de Tanzanie	99.7	104.2	105.1	101.1	106.0	97.3	104.7	105.8	101.4	104.3
Zambia Zambie	100.1	95.0	106.5	106.1	109.0	98.7	93.4	105.0	105.0	108.1
Zimbabwe Zimbabwe	114.3	110.0	110.3	126.8	116.2	105.8	93.5	103.0	116.6	110.3
America, North · Amérique du Nord										
Antigua and Barbuda Antigua-et-Barbuda	98.6	98.6	98.6	98.6	98.6	98.9	98.9	98.9	98.9	98.9
Bahamas Bahamas	137.9	148.0	146.7	137.9	139.8	137.9	148.0	146.7	137.9	139.8
Barbados Barbade	96.7	97.2	99.1	100.1	100.1	96.7	97.2	99.1	100.1	100.1
Belize Belize	159.3	149.5	161.2	173.6	175.9	159.3	149.5	161.2	173.6	175.9
Bermuda Bermudes	78.4	78.4	78.4	78.4	78.4	78.4	78.4	78.4	78.4	78.4
British Virgin Islands Iles Vierges britanniques	104.0	104.0	104.0	104.0	104.0	104.0	104.0	104.0	104.0	104.0
Canada Canada	116.1	124.2	131.5	129.4	118.1	116.0	123.9	131.5	130.1	118.5
Cayman Islands Iles Caïmanes	84.9	84.9	84.9	84.9	84.9	84.9	84.9	84.9	84.9	84.9
Costa Rica Costa Rica	126.7	138.8	141.0	142.4	144.0	132.5	144.0	147.5	147.3	149.1
Cuba Cuba	63.0	59.3	62.6	64.5	62.2	62.2	58.3	61.8	63.5	61.3
Dominica Dominique	92.1	84.3	85.8	86.0	86.0	91.3	83.5	85.0	85.2	85.2
Dominican Republic Rép. dominicaine	102.9	104.2	99.8	106.1	113.2	103.4	102.4	103.4	109.1	117.7
El Salvador El Salvador	107.7	104.1	116.4	109.0	105.9	114.3	110.8	118.7	118.1	114.3
Greenland Groenland	105.9	105.8	105.8	105.9	105.9	106.3	106.1	106.1	106.3	106.3
Grenada Grenade	99.0	85.1	92.6	93.8	94.4	99.0	85.1	92.6	93.8	94.3
Guadeloupe Guadeloupe	111.3	95.8	114.3	114.3	114.3	111.3	95.8	114.3	114.3	114.3
Guatemala Guatemala	123.0	126.0	128.5	133.3	133.0	128.1	132.4	131.3	135.2	137.6
Haiti Haïti	94.1	93.3	95.0	101.7	97.7	95.7	94.9	96.5	103.4	99.5
Honduras Honduras	125.6	125.1	113.9	121.8	122.9	122.4	120.5	109.6	113.6	113.2
Jamaica Jamaïque	117.4	117.7	120.8	116.2	118.3	117.7	118.3	121.3	116.4	118.6
Martinique Martinique	122.8	114.2	122.1	123.4	123.0	122.8	114.1	122.1	123.3	123.0

34

Agricultural production
Index numbers: 1989-91=100 *[cont.]*

Production agricole
Indices: 1989-91 = 100 *[suite]*

Country or area Pays ou zone	Agriculture Agriculture					Food Produits alimentaires				
	1997	1998	1999	2000	2001	1997	1998	1999	2000	2001
Mexico Mexique	121.7	122.0	128.0	130.1	135.3	122.6	123.0	130.0	132.7	138.0
Montserrat Montserrat	110.2	110.2	110.2	110.2	110.2	110.2	110.2	110.2	110.2	110.2
Netherlands Antilles Antilles néerlandaises	163.4	170.7	161.4	163.8	163.8	163.4	170.7	161.4	163.8	163.8
Nicaragua Nicaragua	118.5	124.2	130.4	140.3	147.2	122.7	130.2	131.9	145.6	154.8
Panama Panama	100.6	103.0	101.8	113.4	103.9	100.8	103.2	101.9	114.3	103.8
Puerto Rico Porto Rico	81.7	83.2	83.9	84.4	84.4	81.5	82.6	83.5	84.0	84.0
Saint Kitts and Nevis Saint-Kitts-et-Nevis	134.3	112.5	96.5	93.9	93.9	134.6	112.8	96.7	94.2	94.2
Saint Lucia Sainte-Lucie	81.0	67.3	70.6	71.7	74.4	81.0	67.3	70.6	71.7	74.4
St. Vincent-Grenadines St. Vincent-Grenadines	71.3	76.1	73.5	77.2	77.2	70.7	75.6	72.9	76.6	76.7
Trinidad and Tobago Trinité-et-Tobago	110.6	99.2	112.0	113.9	113.9	111.2	100.4	113.5	115.2	115.3
United States Etats-Unis	118.7	119.2	120.9	123.1	121.7	118.6	120.4	121.6	123.9	121.8
United States Virgin Is. Iles Vierges américaines	103.4	103.4	103.4	103.4	103.4	103.4	103.4	103.4	103.4	103.4
America, South · Amérique du Sud										
Argentina Argentine	123.0	131.3	137.8	135.5	140.4	125.8	134.6	142.3	140.6	145.8
Bolivia Bolivie	134.1	135.6	136.8	148.1	145.7	133.5	136.7	137.9	149.5	146.9
Brazil Brésil	126.7	128.9	139.4	142.6	148.4	130.3	131.6	142.3	144.8	150.6
Chile Chili	131.8	133.6	131.3	135.2	143.6	133.0	134.8	132.2	136.3	145.0
Colombia Colombie	110.0	110.1	109.6	113.6	113.3	116.9	115.0	117.8	120.8	121.6
Ecuador Equateur	147.4	125.4	145.3	151.6	157.7	154.0	132.2	149.6	156.4	162.3
Falkland Is. (Malvinas) Iles Falkland (Malvinas)	91.9	90.2	89.6	90.2	88.8	87.0	85.9	83.9	85.9	80.6
French Guiana Guyane française	130.1	129.4	121.1	121.2	121.2	130.1	129.4	121.1	121.2	121.2
Guyana Guyana	203.8	179.5	199.6	196.2	192.8	204.4	180.1	200.3	196.9	193.5
Paraguay Paraguay	108.8	113.0	117.4	117.9	127.9	124.8	127.9	134.0	134.1	144.4
Peru Pérou	140.8	142.4	161.6	169.9	170.5	144.8	146.6	165.8	174.2	175.5
Suriname Suriname	90.2	77.4	77.7	75.2	77.0	90.2	77.4	77.8	75.2	77.1

34

Agricultural production
Index numbers: 1989-91=100 *[cont.]*

Production agricole
Indices: 1989-91 = 100 *[suite]*

Country or area Pays ou zone	Agriculture Agriculture					Food Produits alimentaires				
	1997	1998	1999	2000	2001	1997	1998	1999	2000	2001
Uruguay Uruguay	129.8	129.6	130.2	123.1	123.2	136.7	137.8	141.4	134.1	134.3
Venezuela Venezuela	117.7	113.6	118.3	123.8	120.6	119.3	115.3	120.5	126.1	123.1
Asia · Asie										
Armenia Arménie	71.5	78.0	77.8	73.5	71.1	72.1	78.7	78.0	72.8	71.0
Azerbaijan Azerbaïdjan	54.0	58.2	62.9	67.7	74.6	59.7	64.6	71.4	76.7	86.0
Bahrain Bahreïn	89.8	108.6	125.7	137.5	138.9	89.8	108.6	125.7	137.5	138.9
Bangladesh Bangladesh	111.6	114.4	127.0	134.7	139.2	111.3	115.2	129.0	136.7	141.2
Bhutan Bhoutan	119.7	119.7	117.5	117.5	117.5	119.8	119.8	117.5	117.5	117.5
Brunei Darussalam Brunéi Darussalam	175.8	193.7	182.0	229.4	203.6	176.7	194.8	182.9	230.9	204.8
Cambodia Cambodge	132.3	134.4	149.6	150.7	155.9	132.4	134.5	150.7	151.7	157.4
China Chine	154.7	160.5	166.1	169.7	173.0	158.1	166.2	172.8	176.0	178.9
Cyprus Chypre	103.6	110.4	116.4	116.4	129.0	103.3	110.3	116.4	116.4	129.0
Georgia Géorgie	80.4	72.4	77.4	62.8	69.2	92.6	80.4	84.6	72.2	79.2
India Inde	121.6	123.3	129.6	130.2	127.8	122.3	123.6	130.1	130.7	128.8
Indonesia Indonésie	117.9	117.4	117.7	120.3	116.9	118.3	117.3	117.5	120.3	117.0
Iran (Islamic Rep. of) Iran (Rép. islamique d')	134.6	154.4	144.7	143.2	130.9	134.6	155.1	144.2	142.8	130.1
Iraq Iraq	90.3	93.1	82.6	68.9	67.6	91.4	94.2	83.2	69.0	67.6
Israel Israël	111.5	116.4	112.9	112.1	111.6	110.5	116.0	115.1	115.2	114.6
Japan Japon	95.1	91.0	92.3	92.1	91.5	95.6	91.6	92.8	92.7	92.1
Jordan Jordanie	136.3	146.4	113.6	144.6	135.8	136.9	147.9	115.8	147.6	138.9
Kazakhstan Kazakhstan	60.8	49.3	68.0	64.9	72.7	62.2	50.2	70.3	66.7	73.9
Korea, Republic of Corée, République de	125.3	124.2	129.4	130.6	128.6	126.7	125.5	130.5	131.7	129.9
Kuwait Koweït	144.0	163.4	179.4	211.8	227.3	145.2	165.1	181.1	213.7	229.4
Kyrgyzstan Kirghizistan	98.0	101.9	107.1	113.2	110.3	109.1	112.8	118.2	124.8	121.2
Lao People's Dem. Rep. Rép. dém. pop. lao	124.5	128.6	149.7	161.1	166.6	126.2	130.4	156.2	164.1	170.3

34

Agricultural production
Index numbers: 1989-91=100 *[cont.]*
Production agricole
Indices: 1989-91 = 100 *[suite]*

Country or area Pays ou zone	Agriculture Agriculture					Food Produits alimentaires				
	1997	1998	1999	2000	2001	1997	1998	1999	2000	2001
Lebanon Liban	137.3	144.9	140.7	147.3	151.1	135.1	142.4	138.2	144.6	148.4
Malaysia Malaisie	121.2	119.2	124.6	127.3	131.7	131.2	130.1	138.7	142.6	148.3
Maldives Maldives	115.5	120.2	130.4	131.2	129.9	115.5	120.2	130.4	131.2	129.9
Mongolia Mongolie	88.2	90.9	104.5	102.5	103.4	88.2	90.7	104.8	102.3	103.1
Myanmar Myanmar	136.4	138.7	154.5	164.5	170.3	136.0	138.1	155.0	164.9	170.8
Nepal Népal	118.2	118.1	121.3	128.4	132.1	118.5	118.4	121.6	128.8	132.5
Occupied Palestinian Terr. Terr. palestinien occupé	102.0	102.0	102.0	102.0	102.0	102.0	102.0	102.0	102.0	102.0
Oman Oman	132.6	149.5	165.1	160.7	157.9	133.4	150.5	166.4	161.9	159.1
Pakistan Pakistan	129.3	134.9	138.6	140.2	136.9	137.3	144.6	144.6	147.4	143.5
Philippines Philippines	123.0	114.0	124.1	128.9	133.7	124.6	115.4	126.2	131.1	136.1
Qatar Qatar	173.2	137.8	170.3	173.1	177.8	173.2	137.8	170.3	173.1	177.8
Saudi Arabia Arabie saoudite	89.7	89.2	84.5	84.1	84.1	89.0	88.4	83.6	83.2	83.2
Singapore Singapour	37.5	41.4	39.5	39.5	39.5	37.5	41.4	39.5	39.5	39.5
Sri Lanka Sri Lanka	111.2	115.4	119.8	123.3	122.5	108.9	114.8	120.4	123.0	123.3
Syrian Arab Republic Rép. arabe syrienne	137.4	165.0	136.5	156.1	155.1	132.0	165.8	134.2	153.7	153.1
Tajikistan Tadjikistan	50.3	47.2	46.0	46.2	49.2	53.3	47.1	49.4	50.6	54.6
Thailand Thaïlande	118.9	114.0	116.6	121.3	122.5	117.1	112.0	114.9	119.7	120.2
Turkey Turquie	108.5	116.2	110.6	114.6	109.8	107.7	115.9	110.4	114.6	109.6
Turkmenistan Turkménistan	76.9	85.2	100.3	94.0	117.3	102.9	125.9	138.1	126.8	137.4
United Arab Emirates Emirats arabes unis	252.3	263.2	262.5	255.5	289.2	253.8	264.9	264.0	257.1	291.0
Uzbekistan Ouzbékistan	93.0	97.3	94.2	98.4	106.1	106.6	110.8	111.2	119.1	123.6
Viet Nam Viet Nam	143.3	150.3	157.8	165.2	164.9	138.6	145.8	151.6	155.2	154.8
Yemen Yémen	122.2	133.2	131.5	138.4	138.4	120.5	131.4	129.6	136.4	136.4
Europe **Europe**										
Austria Autriche	104.3	106.4	110.6	107.9	104.3	104.3	106.5	110.6	107.9	104.3

34

Agricultural production
Index numbers: 1989-91=100 *[cont.]*

Production agricole
Indices: 1989-91 = 100 *[suite]*

Country or area Pays ou zone	Agriculture Agriculture					Food Produits alimentaires				
	1997	1998	1999	2000	2001	1997	1998	1999	2000	2001
Belarus Bélarus	62.3	65.6	59.0	58.3	60.6	62.7	65.8	59.4	58.3	60.8
Belgium-Luxembourg Belgique-Luxembourg	113.8	113.7	113.8	114.7	112.5	113.8	113.7	113.8	114.6	112.4
Bulgaria Bulgarie	68.7	67.3	68.5	61.7	62.8	69.4	68.9	70.3	63.3	64.5
Croatia Croatie	59.4	71.3	67.8	67.1	67.8	58.9	70.8	67.5	66.8	67.5
Czech Republic République tchèque	77.5	79.6	78.6	73.6	79.0	77.8	79.8	78.6	73.6	79.0
Denmark Danemark	104.0	106.0	104.2	103.7	104.6	104.0	106.0	104.2	103.7	104.6
Estonia Estonie	44.3	41.1	43.5	43.3	43.3	44.4	41.1	43.5	43.3	43.3
Faeroe Islands Iles Féroé	105.8	105.7	96.7	96.7	96.7	105.8	105.7	96.7	96.7	96.7
Finland Finlande	95.2	84.8	88.5	90.5	90.4	95.2	84.8	88.5	90.5	90.4
France France	106.6	107.6	108.1	105.4	102.4	106.6	107.7	108.1	105.4	102.4
Germany Allemagne	92.6	93.8	98.3	98.0	98.7	92.5	93.7	98.1	97.9	98.6
Greece Grèce	104.8	101.8	106.1	110.2	106.3	101.7	98.0	102.6	105.8	101.7
Hungary Hongrie	78.3	78.1	72.3	72.1	84.1	78.5	78.2	72.3	72.3	84.2
Iceland Islande	94.1	96.6	101.3	107.7	108.2	95.2	97.7	103.0	108.0	109.8
Ireland Irlande	103.1	108.3	115.3	110.3	112.9	103.6	108.9	116.0	110.9	113.6
Italy Italie	100.3	101.4	106.8	103.2	102.6	100.9	102.0	107.5	103.8	103.3
Latvia Lettonie	52.2	46.0	41.4	42.2	42.2	52.4	46.1	41.3	42.2	42.2
Liechtenstein Liechtenstein	91.1	91.1	91.1	91.1	91.1	91.1	91.1	91.1	91.1	91.1
Lithuania Lituanie	71.5	66.2	60.7	62.9	55.5	71.7	66.4	60.9	63.0	55.5
Malta Malte	137.4	136.9	128.2	123.4	117.8	137.5	137.1	128.3	123.6	117.9
Netherlands Pays-Bas	95.8	97.8	103.5	104.0	100.7	96.0	98.0	103.7	104.2	100.8
Norway Norvège	96.2	95.6	93.0	93.4	89.6	96.1	95.5	92.9	93.3	89.4
Poland Pologne	84.9	90.8	86.2	84.4	85.8	85.4	91.2	86.5	84.8	86.4
Portugal Portugal	96.5	94.2	106.6	101.7	100.2	96.5	94.0	106.7	101.7	100.2
Republic of Moldova République de Moldova	63.3	45.6	42.0	49.0	46.3	64.3	45.8	42.1	49.5	46.0

34
Agricultural production
Index numbers: 1989-91=100 *[cont.]*

Production agricole
Indices: 1989-91 = 100 *[suite]*

Country or area Pays ou zone	Agriculture Agriculture					Food Produits alimentaires				
	1997	1998	1999	2000	2001	1997	1998	1999	2000	2001
Romania Roumanie	102.9	88.5	99.3	87.3	98.9	104.0	89.4	100.5	88.2	100.1
Russian Federation Fédération de Russie	67.8	58.7	60.6	62.5	65.4	68.5	59.4	61.4	63.3	66.3
Serbia and Montenegro Serbie-et-Monténégro	99.6	94.4	83.2	80.3	82.3	99.7	94.5	83.1	80.4	82.4
Slovakia Slovaquie	82.8	79.1	70.8	62.8	72.1	83.3	79.7	71.3	63.1	72.5
Slovenia Slovénie	99.7	102.0	98.1	114.9	113.8	99.7	102.0	98.1	114.9	113.7
Spain Espagne	114.3	111.7	111.8	118.2	115.7	114.0	111.2	111.1	117.9	115.3
Sweden Suède	101.2	100.6	96.3	98.0	97.2	101.1	100.6	96.0	98.0	97.2
Switzerland Suisse	93.1	99.1	93.0	95.9	93.2	93.2	99.1	93.1	96.0	93.2
TFYR of Macedonia L'ex-R.y. Macédoine	94.3	97.5	100.9	98.7	89.3	93.7	95.2	98.8	97.7	87.4
Ukraine Ukraine	55.3	47.2	45.5	49.0	53.0	55.7	47.5	45.8	49.3	53.4
United Kingdom Royaume-Uni	99.2	100.2	99.9	97.6	89.1	99.2	100.1	99.5	97.7	89.4
Oceania · Océanie										
American Samoa Samoa américaines	96.2	96.2	96.2	96.2	96.2	96.2	96.2	96.2	96.2	96.2
Australia Australie	118.3	123.5	131.5	130.1	131.3	129.6	136.9	147.4	144.6	145.2
Cocos (Keeling) Islands Iles des Cocos (Keeling)	127.1	127.1	127.1	127.1	127.1	127.1	127.1	127.1	127.1	127.1
Cook Islands Iles Cook	89.4	103.0	96.9	96.9	96.9	89.0	102.7	96.8	96.8	96.8
Fiji Fidji	97.2	81.5	100.2	98.0	98.8	97.4	81.7	100.5	98.2	99.1
French Polynesia Polynésie française	94.1	79.0	92.6	92.6	92.6	94.1	78.9	92.5	92.5	92.5
Guam Guam	129.0	129.0	129.0	129.0	129.1	129.0	129.0	129.0	129.0	129.1
Kiribati Kiribati	127.2	133.1	134.6	127.9	134.2	127.2	133.1	134.6	127.9	134.2
Marshall Islands Iles Marshall	120.0	85.4	67.3	54.5	54.5	120.0	85.4	67.3	54.5	54.5
Nauru Nauru	105.6	105.6	105.6	105.6	105.6	105.6	105.6	105.6	105.6	105.6
New Caledonia Nouvelle-Calédonie	125.9	129.4	129.8	126.2	127.1	127.6	131.1	131.6	127.9	128.8
New Zealand Nouvelle-Zélande	120.2	120.7	114.3	120.9	123.8	127.2	128.4	121.6	129.2	133.1
Niue Nioué	106.8	106.8	106.8	106.8	106.8	106.8	106.8	106.8	106.8	106.8

34

Agricultural production
Index numbers: 1989-91=100 *[cont.]*

Production agricole
Indices: 1989-91 = 100 *[suite]*

Country or area Pays ou zone	Agriculture Agriculture					Food Produits alimentaires				
	1997	1998	1999	2000	2001	1997	1998	1999	2000	2001
Papua New Guinea Papouasie-Nvl-Guinée	113.4	116.3	123.2	125.4	125.6	114.5	114.2	121.2	123.5	123.6
Samoa Samoa	94.0	94.7	92.3	99.1	99.1	93.7	94.3	91.8	98.9	99.0
Solomon Islands Iles Salomon	131.1	134.6	138.2	146.6	147.0	131.1	134.8	138.3	146.7	147.1
Tokelau Tokélaou	108.5	108.5	108.5	108.5	108.5	108.5	108.5	108.5	108.5	108.5
Tonga Tonga	96.0	91.5	98.3	97.5	97.6	96.0	91.6	98.4	97.6	97.6
Tuvalu Tuvalu	105.5	107.0	110.3	110.6	100.4	105.5	107.0	110.3	110.6	100.4
Vanuatu Vanuatu	122.7	126.9	107.9	110.8	111.1	122.7	126.9	107.8	110.8	111.0
Wallis and Futuna Islands Iles Wallis et Futuna	101.5	101.5	101.5	101.5	101.5	101.5	101.5	101.5	101.5	101.5

Source:
Food and Agriculture Organization of the United Nations (FAO), Rome, "FAO Production Yearbook 2001" and the FAOSTAT database.

Source:
Organisation des Nations Unies pour l'alimentation et l'agriculture (FAO), Rome, "Annuaire FAO de la production 2001" et la base de données FAOSTAT.

35
Cereals
Céréales
Production: thousand metric tons
Production : milliers de tonnes

Region, country or area Région, pays ou zone	1992	1993	1994	1995	1996	1997	1998	1999	2000	2001
World *Monde*	1 973 109	1 902 742	1 956 419	1 896 376	2 070 972	2 094 448	2 082 765	2 084 468	2 063 521	2 086 123
Africa **Afrique**	88 984	99 608	110 352	97 278	124 913	110 170	115 673	112 873	114 068	116 503
Algeria Algérie	3 330	1 454	965	2 140	4 902	870	3 026	2 021	935	2 502
Angola Angola	402	322	285	296	525	457	621	550	575 [1]	585 [1]
Benin Bénin	609	625	645	734	714	906	867	890	878	878 [1]
Botswana Botswana	20	43	52	42	111	31	12	20	22	22 [1]
Burkina Faso Burkina Faso	2 479	2 527	2 232	2 308	2 482	2 014	2 657	2 700	2 286	2 796
Burundi Burundi	306	300	* 225	* 269	* 273	* 305	261	265	245	272
Cameroon Cameroun	1 019	986	961	1 180	1 296	1 268	1 418	1 196	1 411	1 441 [1]
Cape Verde Cap-Vert	10	12	8 [1]	8	10	5	3	36	21	21 [1]
Central African Rep. Rép. centrafricaine	94	94	101	113	126	138	148	173	184	195
Chad Tchad	977	680	1 073	907	878	986	1 342	1 230	1 156	1 156 [1]
Comoros Comores	20	21	21	21	21	21	21	21	21	21
Congo Congo	6	7	7	9	* 10	10	11	7	8	8
Côte d'Ivoire Côte d'Ivoire	1 262	1 286	1 331	1 409	1 800	1 961	1 878	1 858	1 970	1 808 [1]
Dem. Rep. of the Congo Rép. dém. du Congo	1 553	1 655	1 708	1 475	1 557	1 584	1 675	1 643	1 616	1 590
Egypt Egypte	14 611	14 961	15 012	16 097	16 542	18 071	17 964	19 401	20 106	19 464
Eritrea Erythrée	...	87	259	* 123	* 83	* 95	450	315	169	197 [1]
Ethiopia incl. Eritrea Ethiopie comp. Erythrée	5 035	...	...	...	...	...	...	...	...	...
Ethiopia Ethiopie	...	5 295	5 245	6 740	9 379	9 473	7 197	8 013	9 691	8 732 [1]
Gabon Gabon	26	27	29	24	24	25	26	26	27	27 [1]
Gambia Gambie	96	97	95	98	103	100	106	151	176	190
Ghana Ghana	1 254	1 645	1 594	1 797	1 770	1 669	1 788	1 686	1 711	1 711 [1]
Guinea Guinée	683	711	718	825	879	927	985	952	1 103	1 103 [1]
Guinea-Bissau Guinée-Bissau	169	181	190	201	174	142	137	139	166	166 [1]

35

Cereals
Production: thousand metric tons [*cont.*]
Céréales
Production : milliers de tonnes [*suite*]

Region, country or area Région, pays ou zone	1992	1993	1994	1995	1996	1997	1998	1999	2000	2001
Kenya Kenya	2 849	2 530	3 663	3 275	2 714	2 711	2 962	2 778	2 663	3 167
Lesotho Lesotho	94	153	223	81	256	206	171	174	394	398[1]
Liberia Libéria	110[1]	* 65	* 50	* 56	* 94	168	209	196	183	183[1]
Libyan Arab Jamah. Jamah. arabe libyenne	218[1]	180[1]	165[1]	146	160	206	213[1]	213[1]	213	218[1]
Madagascar Madagascar	2 591	2 724	2 517	2 642	2 685	2 742	2 610	2 829	2 460	2 460[1]
Malawi Malawi	689	2 137	1 109	1 778	1 943	1 349	1 904	2 635	2 658	2 658[1]
Mali Mali	1 809	2 228	2 457	2 173	2 201	2 124	2 529	2 894	2 310	2 866
Mauritania Mauritanie	107	169	207	222	234	154	189	146	185	201[1]
Mauritius Maurice	2	2	1	0	0	0	0	0	1	1[1]
Morocco Maroc	2 950	2 818	9 639	1 783	10 104	4 098	6 632	3 860	2 009	4 607
Mozambique Mozambique	242	765	791	1 127	1 379	1 531	1 688	1 822	1 473	1 674
Namibia Namibie	31	75	116	62	89	173	55	72	139	107
Niger Niger	2 255	2 024	2 430	2 096	2 232	1 725	2 982	2 864	2 127	3 161
Nigeria Nigéria	19 597	20 091	20 373	22 513	21 665	21 853	22 040	22 405	22 891	22 891[1]
Réunion Réunion	16	14	17	17	16	17[1]	17[1]	17[1]	17[1]	17[1]
Rwanda Rwanda	240	234	133	142	183	223	194	179	240	297
Sao Tome and Principe Sao Tomé-et-Principe	4	4	4	* 3	3[1]	1	* 1	1	2	2[1]
Senegal Sénégal	856	1 086	943	1 059	976	781	717	1 131	1 026	1 026[1]
Sierra Leone Sierra Leone	534	542	466	408	444	467	373	280	222	222[1]
Somalia Somalie	209	165	405	285	290	284[1]	232	208	313	313[1]
South Africa Afrique du Sud	5 044	12 792	15 967	7 491	13 648	13 230	10 191	10 035	13 732	9 603
Sudan Soudan	5 438	3 102	5 146	3 305	5 202	4 261	5 530	3 108	3 332	3 365
Swaziland Swaziland	58	75	101	79	152	110	126	114	86	86[1]
Togo Togo	495	633	561	550	687	748	620	759	736	740[1]
Tunisia Tunisie	2 213	1 931	675	637	2 885	1 072	1 684	1 836	1 088	1 820

35
Cereals
Production: thousand metric tons [*cont.*]
Céréales
Production : milliers de tonnes [*suite*]

Region, country or area Région, pays ou zone	1992	1993	1994	1995	1996	1997	1998	1999	2000	2001
Uganda Ouganda	1 743	1 880	1 936	2 030	1 588	1 625	2 085	2 178	2 112	2 309
United Rep. of Tanzania Rép.-Unie de Tanzanie	3 533	3 917	3 550	4 629	4 719	3 390	4 495	3 801	3 429	4 131
Zambia Zambie	612	1 758	1 170	882	1 573	1 137	798	1 057	1 037	1 069[1]
Zimbabwe Zimbabwe	481	2 498	2 780	987	3 127	2 723	1 829	1 987	2 513	2 027
America, North **Amérique du Nord**	**435 375**	**341 071**	**434 470**	**359 141**	**429 143**	**419 410**	**434 680**	**422 366**	**427 752**	**405 011**
Bahamas Bahamas	1[1]	0[1]	0	0	0	0	0	0	0	0[1]
Barbados[1] Barbade[1]	2	2	2	2	2	2	2	2	2	2
Belize Belize	32	37	30	38	50	54	47	53	39	48[1]
Canada Canada	49 636	51 420	46 773	49 336	58 459	49 526	50 901	53 951	51 315	44 251
Costa Rica Costa Rica	272	208	229	223	329	271	314	317	318	323
Cuba Cuba	418	227	301	305	474	546	392	555	511	556[1]
Dominican Republic Rép. dominicaine	629	498	417	548	535	564	530	605	610	763
El Salvador El Salvador	992	909	727	899	867	773	783	857	779	751
Guatemala Guatemala	1 514	1 446	1 296	1 164	1 140	954	1 164	1 134	1 161	1 199
Haiti Haïti	452	420[1]	425[1]	410[1]	412	490[1]	403	450[1]	431	363
Honduras Honduras	687	691	674	770	784	757	590	562	607	599
Jamaica Jamaïque	4	4	4	4	4	3	2	2	2	2[1]
Mexico Mexique	26 889	25 200	26 810	26 883	29 311	28 062	29 123	27 419	28 059	29 737
Nicaragua Nicaragua	498	588	521	622	674	608	618	559	717	770
Panama Panama	337	329	348	310	323	239	338	322	401	317
Puerto Rico Porto Rico	0	0	1	1[1]	1[1]	1	1	1[1]	1[1]	1[1]
St. Vincent-Grenadines St. Vincent-Grenadines	2	2	2	2	1	1	2	2	2	2
Trinidad and Tobago Trinité-et-Tobago	26	21	23	15	23	12	12	12[1]	12[1]	12[1]
United States Etats-Unis	352 983	259 067	355 887	277 610	335 754	336 546	349 455	335 563	342 785	325 315
America, South **Amérique du Sud**	**85 406**	**84 577**	**88 048**	**91 812**	**93 297**	**99 104**	**96 103**	**100 791**	**104 421**	**115 076**

35
Cereals
Production: thousand metric tons [*cont.*]
Céréales
Production : milliers de tonnes [*suite*]

Region, country or area Région, pays ou zone	1992	1993	1994	1995	1996	1997	1998	1999	2000	2001
Argentina Argentine	25 598	25 175	25 371	24 307	30 700	35 907	37 808	35 036	38 785	38 372
Bolivia Bolivie	941	1 114	960	1 092	1 139	920	1 146	1 128	1 245	1 279
Brazil Brésil	44 058	43 073	45 849	49 642	44 962	44 876	40 743	47 431	45 897	56 329
Chile Chili	2 901	2 643	2 619	2 766	2 578	3 077	3 098	2 168	2 590	3 116
Colombia Colombie	3 674	3 522	3 631	3 435	3 177	3 207	2 893	3 396	3 740	3 731
Ecuador Equateur	1 631	1 902	2 061	1 900	1 947	1 815	1 485	1 847	2 025	2 084
French Guiana Guyane française	24	28	25	25	31	31	25	20	20[1]	20[1]
Guyana Guyana	288	349	396	507	547	576	535	603	544	544[1]
Paraguay Paraguay	985	950	815	1 522	1 210	1 450	1 156	1 199	1 012	1 249
Peru Pérou	1 522	2 013	2 408	2 135	2 338	2 583	2 830	3 398	3 557	3 854
Suriname Suriname	261	217	218	242	220	213	189	180	164	165[1]
Uruguay Uruguay	1 558	1 491	1 515	1 811	2 222	2 057	2 046	2 218	1 894	2 053
Venezuela Venezuela	1 966	2 100	2 181	2 428	2 225	2 391	2 149	2 167	2 948	2 281
Asia Asie	930 603	936 942	923 425	944 052	997 072	992 839	1 016 453	1 036 368	995 610	984 539
Afghanistan Afghanistan	2 420	2 900	3 102	3 052	3 252	3 683	3 876	3 257	2 095	2 046
Armenia Arménie	307	312	233	257	323	254	323	297	231	374
Azerbaijan Azerbaïdjan	1 325	1 137	1 024	880	1 010	1 119	940	1 088	1 503	1 994
Bangladesh Bangladesh	28 654	28 297	26 513	27 702	29 622	29 674	31 576	36 480	39 349	41 177
Bhutan Bhoutan	106	118[1]	133[1]	151[1]	165[1]	174	174	159	159[1]	159[1]
Brunei Darussalam Brunéi Darussalam	1	1	* 1	* 1	* 0	* 0	* 0	0[1]	1[1]	1[1]
Cambodia Cambodge	2 281	2 429	2 268	3 373	3 523	3 457	3 558	4 136	4 183	4 273
China Chine	404 269	407 931	396 460	418 665	453 665	445 931	458 396	455 192	407 335	404 126
Cyprus Chypre	182	205	162	145	141	48	66	127	48	125
Georgia Géorgie	496	403	471	501	630	892	589	771	348	545
India Inde	201 468	208 627	211 941	210 013	218 750	223 232	227 133	236 836	235 494	230 611

35
Cereals
Production: thousand metric tons [*cont.*]
Céréales
Production : milliers de tonnes [*suite*]

Region, country or area Région, pays ou zone	1992	1993	1994	1995	1996	1997	1998	1999	2000	2001
Indonesia Indonésie	56 235	54 641	53 510	57 990	60 409	58 148	59 406	60 070	61 575	59 186
Iran (Islamic Rep. of) Iran (Rép. islamique d')	15 811	16 287	16 691	17 032	16 083	15 823	18 985	14 186	12 874	11 909
Iraq Iraq	2 959	3 239	2 829	2 538	2 999	2 211	2 427	1 845	1 170[1]	1 207[1]
Israel Israël	343	297	184	309	264	187	235	122	197	272
Japan Japon	14 286	10 737	15 787	14 122	13 668	13 320	11 934	12 283	12 796	12 270
Jordan Jordanie	157	114	111	125	97	96	76	27	57	65
Kazakhstan Kazakhstan	29 649	21 533	16 375	9 476	11 210	12 359	6 380	14 248	11 547	16 353
Korea, Dem. P. R. Corée, R. p. dém. de	8 681	9 137	7 215	3 787	2 596	2 866	4 422	3 845	2 951	3 854
Korea, Republic of Corée, République de	7 846	7 042	7 305	6 877	7 617	7 676	7 132	7 458	7 428	7 791
Kuwait Koweït	2[1]	2[1]	2	2	3	2	3	3	3	4
Kyrgyzstan Kirghizistan	1 603	1 597	1 065	1 045	1 407	1 615	1 608	1 617	1 550	* 1 804
Lao People's Dem. Rep. Rép. dém. pop. lao	1 561	1 298	1 633	1 466	1 490	1 738	1 784	2 199	2 319	2 319[1]
Lebanon Liban	88	81	79	100	94	90	94	93[1]	96[1]	96[1]
Malaysia Malaisie	2 049	2 142	2 179	2 170	2 273	2 168	1 994	2 094	* 2 260	* 2 282
Mongolia Mongolie	496	474	328	261	219	240	194	168	140	160
Myanmar Myanmar	15 342	17 263	18 727	18 483	18 238	17 195	17 641	20 773	21 963	21 230
Nepal Népal	4 902	5 773	5 375	6 078	6 367	6 416	6 331	6 465	6 985	7 172
Occupied Palestinian Terr.[2] Terr. palestinien occupé[2]	1	1	1	1	1	1	1	1	1	1
Oman Oman	5[1]	5[1]	6[1]	6[1]	6[1]	6[1]	5	5	5[1]	5[1]
Pakistan Pakistan	22 123	23 870	22 338	25 036	25 395	25 260	27 985	27 755	30 471	27 821
Philippines Philippines	14 132	14 232	14 669	14 702	15 629	15 600	12 377	16 371	16 901	17 480
Qatar Qatar	4	5	4	4	5	6	6	6	6	6
Saudi Arabia Arabie saoudite	4 703	5 043	4 860	2 669	1 932	2 339	2 202	2 452	2 214	2 214
Sri Lanka Sri Lanka	2 374	2 609	2 722	2 850	2 099	2 269	2 731	2 905	2 895	2 904
Syrian Arab Republic Rép. arabe syrienne	4 360	5 386	5 392	6 093	5 989	4 321	5 270	3 300	3 510	5 158

35

Cereals
Production: thousand metric tons [*cont.*]
   Céréales
   Production : milliers de tonnes [*suite*]

Region, country or area Région, pays ou zone	1992	1993	1994	1995	1996	1997	1998	1999	2000	2001
Tajikistan Tadjikistan	276	258	250	249	548	559	500	475	359	316
Thailand Thaïlande	23 864	22 013	25 339	26 399	27 124	27 605	27 801	28 638	30 191	30 111
Turkey Turquie	29 157	31 749	27 014	28 134	29 344	29 747	33 175	28 877	32 039	25 571
Turkmenistan Turkménistan	732	1 009	1 120	1 102	545	759	1 278	1 567	1 208	1 299
United Arab Emirates Emirats arabes unis	3	1	1	1	1	1[1]	0	0	0[1]	0[1]
Uzbekistan Ouzbékistan	2 178	2 165	2 502	3 223	3 558	3 768	4 132	4 304	3 916	3 502
Viet Nam Viet Nam	22 338	23 719	24 672	26 141	27 933	29 175	30 758	33 147	34 535	34 043
Yemen Yémen	811	834	802	810	660	646	833	694	672	672[1]
Europe **Europe**	**406 878**	**413 000**	**383 816**	**375 980**	**390 743**	**440 808**	**386 434**	**376 093**	**385 360**	**427 588**
Albania Albanie	430	686	666	662	519	616	621	512	581	581
Austria Autriche	4 323	4 206	4 436	4 455	4 493	5 009	4 776	4 806	4 490	4 538
Belarus Bélarus	7 061	7 315	5 938	5 314	5 478	5 920	4 495	3 412	* 4 548	* 4 823
Belgium-Luxembourg Belgique-Luxembourg	2 165	2 311	2 174	2 144	2 571	2 393	2 601	2 449	2 576	2 430
Bosnia and Herzegovina Bosnie-Herzégovine	1 080[1]	962[1]	847[1]	* 671	* 841	* 1 242	* 1 327	* 1 369	* 935	* 1 031
Bulgaria Bulgarie	6 560	5 666	6 409	6 514	3 380	6 152	5 345	5 132	4 677	5 238
Croatia Croatie	2 356	2 733	2 596	2 760	2 762	3 179	3 210	2 883	2 766	3 018
Czech Republic République tchèque	...	6 486	6 790	6 611	6 654	6 995	6 676	6 935	6 455	7 432
Denmark Danemark	6 954	8 203	7 800	9 043	9 218	9 529	9 344	8 782	9 421	9 358
Estonia Estonie	592	811	510	513	629	651	576	402	697	570
Finland Finlande	2 603	3 340	3 400	3 333	3 697	3 807	2 773	2 879	4 100	3 670
France France	60 639	55 626	53 407	53 545	62 599	63 432	68 664	64 342	65 762	60 477
Germany Allemagne	34 758	35 549	36 336	39 863	42 136	45 486	44 575	44 461	45 435	50 056
Greece Grèce	5 035	4 856	5 272	4 903	4 683	4 705	4 359	4 620	4 793	3 876
Hungary Hongrie	10 007	8 543	11 749	11 297	11 344	14 139	13 038	11 422	10 056	14 881
Ireland Irlande	2 017	1 627	1 610	1 796	2 142	1 944	1 865	2 011	1 963	2 156

35
Cereals
Production: thousand metric tons [*cont.*]
Céréales
Production : milliers de tonnes [*suite*]

Region, country or area Région, pays ou zone	1992	1993	1994	1995	1996	1997	1998	1999	2000	2001
Italy Italie	19 891	19 772	19 187	19 693	20 900	19 898	20 711	21 068	20 616	20 067
Latvia Lettonie	1 146	1 234	899	692	961	1 036	964	784	924	938
Lithuania Lituanie	2 198	2 673	2 098	1 907	2 615	2 945	2 717	2 049	2 658	* 2 293
Malta Malte	7	7	7	7	7	11	11	11	12	12
Netherlands Pays-Bas	1 350	1 466	1 355	1 505	1 659	1 373	1 497	1 387	1 714	1 732
Norway Norvège	1 010	1 402	1 271	1 227	1 345	1 288	1 412	1 215	1 349	1 307
Poland Pologne	19 962	23 417	21 763	25 905	25 298	25 399	27 159	25 750	22 341	27 231
Portugal Portugal	1 338	1 449	1 645	1 446	1 673	1 559	1 622	1 678	1 619	1 347
Republic of Moldova République de Moldova	1 978	3 219	1 628	2 611	1 976	3 487	2 385	2 138	2 021	2 086
Romania Roumanie	12 288	15 493	18 184	19 883	14 200	22 107	15 453	17 034	10 478	16 550
Russian Federation Fédération de Russie	103 794	96 225	78 650	61 902	67 589	86 801	46 969	53 845	64 342	83 623
Serbia and Montenegro Serbie-et-Monténégro	7 019	7 411	8 409	9 245	7 294	10 355	8 667	8 615	5 391	9 144
Slovakia Slovaquie	...	3 157	3 700	3 489	3 322	3 740	3 485	2 829	2 201	3 478
Slovenia Slovénie	429	457	571	453	487	544	557	469	499	499[1]
Spain Espagne	14 479	17 479	15 231	11 574	22 366	19 324	22 557	18 002	24 633	18 187
Sweden Suède	3 760	5 242	4 472	4 791	5 954	5 986	5 618	4 931	5 770	5 548
Switzerland Suisse	1 213	1 292	1 249	1 281	1 348	1 223	1 263	1 055	1 206	1 106
TFYR of Macedonia L'ex-R.y. Macédoine	624	479	648	725	546	610	660	740	567	487
Ukraine Ukraine	35 550	42 725	32 960	32 360	23 486	34 396	25 689	23 952	23 780	38 837
United Kingdom Royaume-Uni	22 063	19 482	19 948	21 859	24 571	23 527	22 795	22 126	23 985	18 983
Oceania **Océanie**	**25 863**	**27 542**	**16 308**	**28 113**	**35 804**	**32 118**	**33 422**	**35 977**	**36 311**	**37 406**
Australia Australie	25 097	26 709	15 437	27 331	34 870	31 107	32 533	35 067	35 423	36 487
Fiji Fidji	23	23	20	20	19	19	6	19	15	17
New Caledonia Nouvelle-Calédonie	1	1	1	1	2	2	2	2	2[1]	2[1]
New Zealand Nouvelle-Zélande	736	803	843	752	904	980	869	873	854	883

35

Cereals
Production: thousand metric tons [*cont.*]
Céréales
Production : milliers de tonnes [*suite*]

Region, country or area Région, pays ou zone	1992	1993	1994	1995	1996	1997	1998	1999	2000	2001
Papua New Guinea Papouasie-Nvl-Guinée	5	6	7	8	9	10	10	11	11	11[1]
Solomon Islands Iles Salomon	0[1]	0[1]	0[1]	0[1]	0[1]	0[1]	* 1	* 5	5[1]	5[1]
Vanuatu Vanuatu	1[1]	1[1]	1[1]	1[1]	1[1]	1	1	1[1]	1[1]	1[1]

Source:
Food and Agriculture Organization of the United
Nations (FAO), Rome, "FAO Production Yearbook 2001" and the
FAOSTAT database.

1 FAO estimate.
2 Data refer to the Gaza Strip.

Source:
Organisation des Nations Unies pour l'alimentation et
l'agriculture (FAO), Rome, "Annuaire FAO de la production
2001" et la base de données FAOSTAT.

1 Estimation de la FAO.
2 Les données se rapportent à la Zone de Gaza.

36
Oil crops, in oil equivalent
Production : thousand metric tons
Cultures d'huile, en équivalent d'huile
Production : milliers de tonnes

Region, country or area Région, pays ou zone	1992	1993	1994	1995	1996	1997	1998	1999	2000	2001
World **Monde**	**78 827**	**79 918**	**88 311**	**91 839**	**93 415**	**98 020**	**102 623**	**109 111**	**109 904**	**111 194**
Africa **Afrique**	**5 452**	**5 745**	**5 838**	**6 110**	**7 098**	**6 620**	**6 769**	**7 586**	**6 946**	**6 919**
Algeria Algérie	97	84	76	67	108	109	67	119	87	105[1]
Angola Angola	68	70	73	72	74	73	75	72	74[1]	74[1]
Benin Bénin	63	74	70	92	100	96	97	101	94	91
Botswana Botswana	1[1]	1	1[1]	1	2	2[1]	3[1]	3[1]	3	3[1]
Burkina Faso Burkina Faso	85	97	97	94	109	98	118	136	96	98
Burundi Burundi	8	8	6	7	6	6	6	6	5	5
Cameroon Cameroun	206	212	224	221	277	225	228	244	223	228[1]
Cape Verde Cap-Vert	1	1	1	1	1	1	1	1	1	1
Central African Rep. Rép. centrafricaine	52	53	57	61	64	67	68	67	67	67
Chad Tchad	91	78	87	113	122	146	174	143	126	128[1]
Comoros Comores	7	7	7	9	10	10	10	10	10	10[1]
Congo Congo	26	26	27	27	27	25	25	27	27	27
Côte d'Ivoire Côte d'Ivoire	396	394	395	392	416	374	400	398	410	338
Dem. Rep. of the Congo Rép. dém. du Congo	401	417	407	372	356	335	327	333	328	324
Egypt Egypte	171	215	183	206	224	211	189	223	215	211
Equatorial Guinea Guinée équatoriale	7[1]	7[1]	7[1]	7[1]	7[1]	6[1]	6[1]	6	6[1]	6[1]
Eritrea Erythrée	...	7	8	11	7	6	8	7	7	7[1]
Ethiopia incl. Eritrea Ethiopie comp. Erythrée	144	...	...	...	...	...	...	...	...	...
Ethiopia Ethiopie	...	72	75[1]	80	117	82	83	86	104	105
Gabon Gabon	12	13	13	13	12	13	12	13	13	13[1]
Gambia Gambie	20	27	28	26	17	27	25	40	45	49[1]
Ghana Ghana	189	198	219	216	202	210	249	239	245	247[1]
Guinea Guinée	105	114	114	118	126	130	131	137	144	144[1]

36

Oil crops, in oil equivalent
Production: thousand metric tons *[cont.]*

Cultures d'huile, en equivalent d'huile
Production : milliers de tonnes *[suite]*

Region, country or area Région, pays ou zone	1992	1993	1994	1995	1996	1997	1998	1999	2000	2001
Guinea-Bissau Guinée-Bissau	18	18	19	19	19	20	20	21	20	20
Kenya Kenya	27	30	33	32	32	35	35	41	40	40 [1]
Liberia Libéria	41	41	42	41	53	50	50	50	50	50 [1]
Libyan Arab Jamah. Jamah. arabe libyenne	26	31	35	41	45	46	47	47	47	47
Madagascar Madagascar	26	30	27	28	30	31	30	30	30	30 [1]
Malawi Malawi	11	25	15	21	29	28	38	46	42	43 [1]
Mali Mali	96	95	120	108	106	109	110	112	98	121
Mauritania Mauritanie	1	1	1	2	2	2	2	2 [1]	2 [1]	2 [1]
Mauritius Maurice	1	1	1	1	0	1	0	0	0	0 [1]
Morocco Maroc	157	122	141	104	229	158	183	177	110	117
Mozambique Mozambique	104	106	102	112	118	124	132	132	92	90
Namibia Namibie	0	1	0	0	0	0	0	1	1	1
Niger Niger	18	9	22	33	61	28	36	35	41	49
Nigeria Nigéria	1 613	1 695	1 767	1 889	2 036	2 162	2 202	2 357	2 172	2 172
Rwanda Rwanda	8	5	4	5	4	3	3	3	7	5
Sao Tome and Principe Sao Tomé-et-Principe	5	5	5	4	5	5	5	5	7	7 [1]
Senegal Sénégal	184	199	214	250	207	179	184	316	330	332
Sierra Leone Sierra Leone	70	69	79	71	74	78	64	55	51	51 [1]
Somalia Somalie	8	12	12	13	13	13	11 [1]	12 [1]	13 [1]	13 [1]
South Africa Afrique du Sud	137	209	227	278	417	273	323	597	323	343
Sudan Soudan	280	251	352	420	476	488	394	478	441	469 [1]
Swaziland Swaziland	2	3	2	2	4	5	6	5	4	4 [1]
Togo Togo	37	37	42	41	47	44	43	41	38	43 [1]
Tunisia Tunisie	153	236	83	72	347	116	215	255	254	172
Uganda Ouganda	95	103	99	101	99	100	106	116	122	131
United Rep. of Tanzania Rép.-Unie de Tanzanie	137	129	122	139	141	134	122	125	128	139

36
Oil crops, in oil equivalent
Production: thousand metric tons *[cont.]*

Cultures d'huile, en equivalent d'huile
Production : milliers de tonnes *[suite]*

Region, country or area Région, pays ou zone	1992	1993	1994	1995	1996	1997	1998	1999	2000	2001
Zambia Zambie	11	32	22	28	32	29	28	30	31	31[1]
Zimbabwe Zimbabwe	38	77	77	49	89	106	76	86	122	* 116
America, North **Amérique du Nord**	**15 463**	**14 637**	**19 478**	**17 152**	**17 547**	**19 773**	**20 894**	**20 844**	**20 407**	**20 445**
Canada Canada	1 926	2 745	3 653	3 360	2 718	3 350	3 907	4 362	3 559	2 609
Costa Rica Costa Rica	86	96	101	106	110	115	122	122	148	144
Cuba Cuba	7	8	8	8	8	8	8	8	8	8
Dominica Dominique	2	2	2[1]	2[1]	2[1]	2[1]	1[1]	1[1]	1[1]	1[1]
Dominican Republic Rép. dominicaine	42	44	50	49	50	48	50	52	72	73
El Salvador El Salvador	17	17	13	15	15	15	15	16	15	15
Grenada [1] Grenade [1]	1	1	1	1	1	1	1	1	1	1
Guatemala Guatemala	49	46	53	59	73	82	79	83	77	83
Haiti Haïti	13	13[1]	13[1]	13[1]	13	14[1]	12	13[1]	12	12
Honduras Honduras	95	92	92	91	94	92	108	105	107	109
Jamaica Jamaïque	16	16	16	16	16	16	16	16	16	16[1]
Mexico Mexique	323	313	335	331	347	365	383	361	295	331
Nicaragua Nicaragua	18	20	35	28	32	31	27	35	34	38
Panama Panama	3	3[1]	2	2	2	2[1]	2[1]	2[1]	2	2[1]
Puerto Rico Porto Rico	1	1	1	1	1	1	0	0[1]	0[1]	0[1]
Saint Lucia [1] Sainte-Lucie [1]	3	3	2	2	2	3	2	2	2	2
St. Vincent-Grenadines St. Vincent-Grenadines	3	3	3	3	3	3	3	3	3	3
Trinidad and Tobago [1] Trinité-et-Tobago [1]	7	7	4	3	3	3	3	3	3	3
United States Etats-Unis	12 851	11 207	15 093	13 062	14 057	15 622	16 153	15 658	16 050	16 995
America, South **Amérique du Sud**	**9 079**	**9 192**	**10 355**	**11 498**	**11 155**	**11 568**	**14 132**	**14 924**	**15 119**	**16 231**
Argentina Argentine	3 865	3 438	4 009	4 854	4 921	4 483	6 083	6 779	6 397	6 382
Bolivia Bolivie	78	103	146	183	180	231	249	224	277	222

36

Oil crops, in oil equivalent
Production: thousand metric tons *[cont.]*

Cultures d'huile, en equivalent d'huile
Production : milliers de tonnes *[suite]*

Region, country or area Région, pays ou zone	1992	1993	1994	1995	1996	1997	1998	1999	2000	2001
Brazil Brésil	3 995	4 463	4 918	5 057	4 573	5 270	6 198	6 228	6 678	7 654
Chile Chili	36	16	14	15	16	16	23	32	24	28
Colombia Colombie	375	394	435	469	492	522	497	582	607	648
Ecuador Equateur	215	221	255	221	226	275	299	208	298	340
Guyana Guyana	6	7	8	10	14	17	8	10	11	10
Paraguay Paraguay	369	404	413	490	520	542	599	626	622	722
Peru Pérou	41	48	54	64	69	61	53	61	70	69
Suriname Suriname	4	4	3	3	2	1	1	1	1	1 [1]
Uruguay Uruguay	31	27	30	54	51	51	37	71	17	31
Venezuela Venezuela	63	66	71	78	91	99	84	102	117	124
Asia **Asie**	**37 468**	**39 618**	**41 809**	**44 178**	**45 651**	**46 800**	**46 936**	**49 548**	**52 983**	**53 703**
Afghanistan Afghanistan	31	29	30	29	28	28	28	28	27	27 [1]
Azerbaijan Azerbaïdjan	31	26	27	24	23	12	11	10	9	9
Bangladesh Bangladesh	159	163	157	161	159	162	165	162	161	166
Bhutan [1] Bhoutan [1]	1	1	1	1	1	1	1	1	1	1
Cambodia Cambodge	19	19	16	15	20	25	20	23	22	24
China Chine	9 885	10 908	11 882	12 508	12 157	12 458	12 886	13 585	15 221	15 531
Cyprus Chypre	5	3	3	3	3	2	3	4	5	5
Georgia Géorgie	3	1	3	3	2	13	10	17	2	17 [1]
India Inde	8 396	8 094	8 528	8 707	9 313	8 975	8 773	7 872	8 163	7 316
Indonesia Indonésie	6 035	6 268	6 902	7 472	7 928	8 366	8 986	9 381	10 071	10 337
Iran (Islamic Rep. of) Iran (Rép. islamique d')	80	80	117	92	106	102	106	105	109	109
Iraq Iraq	36	44	37	39	41	40	41	39	38	39 [1]
Israel Israël	39	31	27	36	39	34	33	23	32	28
Japan Japon	50	30	36	38	45	36	36	42	51	52

36

Oil crops, in oil equivalent
Production: thousand metric tons *[cont.]*

Cultures d'huile, en equivalent d'huile
Production : milliers de tonnes *[suite]*

Region, country or area Région, pays ou zone	1992	1993	1994	1995	1996	1997	1998	1999	2000	2001
Jordan Jordanie	18	7	21	14	20	13	30	8	30	22
Kazakhstan Kazakhstan	109	81	86	82	57	56	66	89	88	101
Korea, Dem. P. R. Corée, R. p. dém. de	75	72	76	73	76	68	65	65	67	67[1]
Korea, Republic of Corée, République de	62	52	53	57	53	54	50	43	45	46
Kyrgyzstan Kirghizistan	5	5	5	7	8	7	8	10	10	10[1]
Lao People's Dem. Rep. Rép. dém. pop. lao	7	7	7	9	9	9	10	8	8	8[1]
Lebanon Liban	26	14[1]	20	15[1]	24	23	25	23[1]	26[1]	26[1]
Malaysia Malaisie	7 397	8 615	8 398	9 080	9 692	10 431	9 567	12 072	12 423	13 340
Maldives Maldives	2	* 2	* 2	* 2	2[1]	2[1]	2[1]	* 2	* 2	2[1]
Myanmar Myanmar	264	311	299	376	433	416	392	408	461	594
Nepal Népal	38	39	44	48	47	49	45	48	49	53
Occupied Palestinian Terr. [2] Terr. palestinien occupé [2]	1	1	1	1	1	1	1	1	1	1
Pakistan Pakistan	657	593	628	763	717	725	700	836	817	806
Philippines Philippines	1 298	1 551	1 535	1 660	1 626	1 851	1 731	1 646	1 763	1 795
Saudi Arabia Arabie saoudite	2	2	2	2	2	2	2	2	2[1]	2[1]
Sri Lanka Sri Lanka	230	221	264	277	255	264	254	284	310	310[1]
Syrian Arab Republic Rép. arabe syrienne	211	169	192	176	243	213	296	208	323	235
Tajikistan Tadjikistan	46	50	51	39	29	33	33	28	28	38
Thailand Thaïlande	674	678	722	779	805	838	863	886	964	951
Turkey Turquie	755	646	815	749	959	721	975	784	956	825
Turkmenistan Turkménistan	132	115	133	125	42	61	68	125	99	173
Uzbekistan Ouzbékistan	400	413	390	391	336	366	320	368	301	329
Viet Nam Viet Nam	244	265	266	291	315	307	295	276	260	267
Yemen Yémen	6	6	6	7	8	9	10	10	11	11[1]
Europe **Europe**	**10 585**	**9 903**	**10 041**	**12 009**	**10 941**	**12 097**	**12 323**	**14 357**	**12 835**	**12 224**

36

Oil crops, in oil equivalent
Production: thousand metric tons *[cont.]*

Cultures d'huile, en equivalent d'huile
Production : milliers de tonnes *[suite]*

Region, country or area Région, pays ou zone	1992	1993	1994	1995	1996	1997	1998	1999	2000	2001
Albania Albanie	6	6	7	9	7	8	12	11	12	12 [1]
Austria Autriche	98	113	142	134	71	76	90	112	79	86
Belarus Bélarus	23	17	16	22	20	20	30	34	43 [1]	36 [1]
Belgium-Luxembourg Belgique-Luxembourg	9	10	12	14	13	* 12	* 13	15	* 16	16
Bosnia and Herzegovina Bosnie-Herzégovine	3 [1]	3 [1]	2 [1]	2	2	* 2	* 2	* 2	* 1	* 1
Bulgaria Bulgarie	254	183	252	323	222	186	221	255	179	133
Croatia Croatie	38	39	33	38	26	28	52	71	49	59
Czech Republic République tchèque	...	161	195	280	221	237	298	412	362	418
Denmark Danemark	155	159	141	119	96	112	137	158	112	134
Estonia Estonie	1 [1]	1 [1]	1	3	4	4	7	11	15	15 [1]
Finland Finlande	50	48	41	49	34	35	27	34	33	33 [1]
France France	1 598	1 317	1 590	1 946	1 986	2 221	2 195	2 530	2 135	1 849
Germany Allemagne	1 090	1 185	1 241	1 245	821	1 169	1 394	1 784	1 453	1 673
Greece Grèce	497	457	547	616	571	571	581	621	654	618
Hungary Hongrie	346	300	304	368	420	289	342	474	277	382
Ireland Irlande	7	3	6	5	4	5	6	2	3	3 [1]
Italy Italie	860	911	976	1 139	888	1 240	1 018	1 226	1 021	1 022
Latvia Lettonie	1	2	1	1	1	1	1	4	5	7
Lithuania Lituanie	4	2	6	10	10	15	28	45	32	31
Netherlands Pays-Bas	7	6	6	5	3	4	3	4	3	3
Norway Norvège	3	6	5	* 5	*5	* 5	5	4	4	4
Poland Pologne	292	230	295	532	177	231	425	438	372	416
Portugal Portugal	61	85	73	87	84	78	84	86	76	78
Republic of Moldova République de Moldova	82	81	62	96	130	83	83	120	115	117
Romania Roumanie	350	315	335	407	473	382	492	612	338	332
Russian Federation Fédération de Russie	1 476	1 313	1 209	1 865	1 273	1 283	1 370	1 840	1 723	1 217

36

Oil crops, in oil equivalent
Production: thousand metric tons *[cont.]*

Cultures d'huile, en equivalent d'huile
Production : milliers de tonnes *[suite]*

Region, country or area Région, pays ou zone	1992	1993	1994	1995	1996	1997	1998	1999	2000	2001
Serbia and Montenegro Serbie-et-Monténégro	165	174	138	146	196	138	146	167	127	231
Slovakia Slovaquie	...	52	62	94	100	105	91	146	102	152
Slovenia Slovénie	2	2	2	1	1	0	0	0	0	0 [1]
Spain Espagne	1 278	1 170	1 050	645	1 544	1 890	1 486	1 066	1 484	1 643
Sweden Suède	108	137	81	76	54	50	49	73	49	41
Switzerland Suisse	18	20	14	18	18	21	21	18	20	19
TFYR of Macedonia L'ex-R.y. Macédoine	17	8	8	10	10	7	6	6	4	4 [1]
Ukraine Ukraine	953	891	666	1 203	888	971	966	1 214	1 484	986
United Kingdom Royaume-Uni	517	496	520	498	566	617	645	766	455	454
Oceania **Océanie**	**781**	**823**	**790**	**892**	**1 023**	**1 162**	**1 569**	**1 851**	**1 615**	**1 673**
American Samoa [1] Samoa américaines [1]	1	1	1	1	1	1	1	1	1	1
Australia Australie	249	260	248	361	396	554	936	1 187	948	1 006 [1]
Cocos (Keeling) Islands Iles des Cocos (Keeling)	1 [1]	1 [1]	1 [1]	1 [1]	*1	* 1	* 1	* 1	* 1	1 [1]
Cook Islands Iles Cook	0	1	0	1 [1]	1 [1]	1	1	1 [1]	1 [1]	1 [1]
Fiji Fidji	32	26	25	25 [1]	28 [1]	28	27	28 [1]	28 [1]	28 [1]
French Polynesia [1] Polynésie française [1]	11	11	11	12	12	11	8	10	10	10
Guam Guam	5 [1]	5 [1]	5 [1]	5 [1]	*7	* 7	* 7	* 7	* 7	7 [1]
Kiribati Kiribati	* 11	* 11	* 11	* 11	*13	* 13	* 14	* 14	* 12	12 [1]
Marshall Islands [1] Iles Marshall [1]	4	3	3	5	5	4	3	2	2	2
New Caledonia [1] Nouvelle-Calédonie [1]	2	2	2	2	2	2	2	2	2	2
New Zealand Nouvelle-Zélande	1	1	2	2	2	2	2	2	2	2
Papua New Guinea Papouasie-Nvl-Guinée	332	363	344	337	426	394	420	464	465	465 [1]
Samoa Samoa	13 [1]	17 [1]	17 [1]	17 [1]	17 [1]	17 [1]	17 [1]	15	18	18 [1]
Solomon Islands Iles Salomon	61	62	61	69	69	71	72	72	77	77
Tonga Tonga	4 [1]	6 [1]	6 [1]	5	5 [1]	6 [1]	7 [1]	8	8	8 [1]

36

Oil crops, in oil equivalent
Production: thousand metric tons *[cont.]*

Cultures d'huile, en equivalent d'huile
Production : milliers de tonnes *[suite]*

Region, country or area Région, pays ou zone	1992	1993	1994	1995	1996	1997	1998	1999	2000	2001
Vanuatu Vanuatu	34	34	34	36	38	48	51	37	33	33[1]

Source:
United Nations Statistics Division, New York, "Industrial Commodity Statistics Yearbook 2000" and the industrial statistics database.

1 FAO estimate.
2 Data refer to the Gaza Strip.

Source:
Organisation des Nations Unies, Division de statistique, New York, "Annuaire de statistiques industrielles par produit 2000" et la base de données pour les statistiques industrielles.

1 Estimation de la FAO.
2 Les données se rapportent à la Bande de Gaza.

37
Livestock
Stocks: thousand head
Cheptel
Effectifs : milliers de têtes

Region, country or area	1994	1995	1996	1997	1998	1999	2000	2001	Région, pays ou zone
World									**Monde**
Cattle and buffaloes	1475055	1489993	1495586	1488152	1492092	1494316	1510876	1517516	Bovins et buffles
Sheep and goats	1756533	1750364	1763545	1733179	1752071	1766097	1783297	1794430	Ovins et caprins
Pigs	882 055	900 208	861 445	835 309	875 724	904 142	908 166	922 929	Porcins
Horses	59 930	60 515	60 100	58 628	58 310	58 345	58 128	58 244	Chevaux
Asses	43 741	44 151	43 327	42 338	41 925	42 822	42 771	42 822	Anes
Mules	14 900	14 948	14 123	13 515	13 500	13 538	13 543	13 463	Mulets
Africa									**Afrique**
Cattle and buffaloes	199 714	204 304	213 362	219 262	225 270	229 004	233 820	233 477	Bovins et buffles
Sheep and goats	414 777	418 264	427 775	442 460	450 152	457 704	467 025	468 773	Ovins et caprins
Pigs	17 421	17 782	17 792	18 316	18 656	18 606	18 517	18 467	Porcins
Horses	4 734	4 757	4 763	4 774	4 771	4 812	4 848	4 879	Chevaux
Asses	14 805	14 970	14 892	15 081	15 081	15 161	15 245	15 338	15 374	Anes
Mules	1 367	1 379	1 358	1 345	1 331	1 335	1 327	1 329	Mulets
Algeria									**Algérie**
Cattle and buffaloes	1 269	1 267	1 228	1 255	1 317	1 650	1 650	1 700[1]	Bovins et buffles
Sheep and goats	20 386	20 081	20 460	20 509	21 206	21 600	22 900	22 800[1]	Ovins et caprins
Pigs [1]	6	6	6	6	6	6	6	6	Porcins [1]
Horses	67	62	60	52	46	46	47[1]	48[1]	Chevaux
Asses	226	224	210	199	183	180[1]	180[1]	180[1]	Anes
Mules	81	80	76	69	50	50[1]	50[1]	50[1]	Mulets
Angola									**Angola**
Cattle and buffaloes	3 000[1]	3 000	3 309	* 3 556	* 3 898	* 3 900	* 4 042	4 042[1]	Bovins et buffles
Sheep and goats	1 690[1]	* 1 700	1 850[1]	* 2 000	* 2 166	* 2 336	* 2 500	2 500[1]	Ovins et caprins
Pigs	790[1]	800	810[1]	820[1]	810[1]	800[1]	800[1]	800[1]	Porcins
Horses [1]	1	1	1	1	1	1	1	1	Chevaux [1]
Asses [1]	5	5	5	5	5	5	5	5	Anes [1]
Benin									**Bénin**
Cattle and buffaloes	1 223	1 294	1 350	1 399	1 345	1 438	1 500	1 500[1]	Bovins et buffles
Sheep and goats	2 150[1]	1 575[1]	1 614	1 688[1]	1 721	1 828	1 828[1]	1 828[1]	Ovins et caprins
Pigs	555	566	584	580[1]	470	470[1]	470[1]	470[1]	Porcins
Horses [1]	6	6	6	6	6	6	6	6	Chevaux [1]
Asses [1]	1	1	1	1	1	1	1	1	Anes [1]
Botswana									**Botswana**
Cattle and buffaloes	2 200[1]	2 530	2 249	2 270[1]	2 250[1]	2 300[1]	2 350[1]	2 400[1]	Bovins et buffles
Sheep and goats	2 088	2 961	2 554	2 580[1]	2 400[1]	2 470[1]	2 550[1]	2 620[1]	Ovins et caprins
Pigs	4[1]	1	3	5[1]	2[1]	5[1]	6[1]	7[1]	Porcins
Horses	31	35	30[1]	33[1]	32[1]	33[1]	33[1]	33[1]	Chevaux
Asses	231	303	336	330[1]	320[1]	325[1]	330[1]	330[1]	Anes
Mules [1]	3	3	3	3	3	3	3	3	Mulets [1]
Burkina Faso									**Burkina Faso**
Cattle and buffaloes	4 261	4 346	4 433	4 522	4 612	4 704	4 798	4 798[1]	Bovins et buffles
Sheep and goats	12 923	13 310	13 709	14 121	14 544	14 980	15 430	15 430[1]	Ovins et caprins
Pigs	552	563	575	587	598	610	622	622[1]	Porcins
Horses	* 23	23	23	24	24	24	26	26[1]	Chevaux
Asses	445	454	463	472	482	491	501	501[1]	Anes
Burundi									**Burundi**
Cattle and buffaloes	400[1]	350[1]	330[1]	* 311	346	329	320[1]	315[1]	Bovins et buffles
Sheep and goats [1]	1 270	1 150	1 000	850	859	920	820	830	Ovins et caprins [1]
Pigs	85[1]	80[1]	75[1]	70[1]	73	61	70[1]	70[1]	Porcins
Cameroon									**Cameroun**
Cattle and buffaloes	4 700[1]	4 650[1]	4 623	4 737	4 846	5 500	5 882	5 900[1]	Bovins et buffles
Sheep and goats	6 950[1]	7 020[1]	7 100[1]	7 200[1]	7 300[1]	7 450[1]	8 163	8 200[1]	Ovins et caprins
Pigs	1 000[1]	1 000[1]	1 000[1]	1 000	1 200	1 000	1 346	1 350[1]	Porcins
Horses [1]	15	16	16	16	16	17	17	17	Chevaux [1]
Asses [1]	36	36	37	37	37	37	38	38	Anes [1]
Cape Verde									**Cap-Vert**
Cattle and buffaloes	18	19	21	21[1]	22[1]	22	22	22[1]	Bovins et buffles
Sheep and goats	143[1]	122	118	119[1]	125[1]	121	118	118[1]	Ovins et caprins
Pigs [1]	133	239	100	143	185	200	186	200	Porcins [1]
Asses	13[1]	13	14[1]	14[1]	14[1]	14[1]	14[1]	14[1]	Anes

37

Livestock

Stocks: thousand head [*cont.*]

Cheptel

Effectifs : milliers de têtes [*suite*]

Region, country or area	1994	1995	1996	1997	1998	1999	2000	2001	Région, pays ou zone
Mules [1]	2	2	2	2	2	2	2	2	Mulets [1]
Central African Rep.									**Rép. centrafricaine**
Cattle and buffaloes	2 735	2 797	2 861	2 926	2 992	2 951	3 129	3 100 [1]	Bovins et buffles
Sheep and goats	2 037	2 152	2 274	2 404	2 540	2 683	2 836	2 820 [1]	Ovins et caprins
Pigs	524	547	571	596	622	649	678	680 [1]	Porcins
Chad									**Tchad**
Cattle and buffaloes	4 653	4 746	4 860	5 451	5 582	5 715	5 852	5 900 [1]	Bovins et buffles
Sheep and goats	5 330	5 490	6 235	7 189	7 371	7 404	7 642	7 650 [1]	Ovins et caprins
Pigs	17	18	* 18	* 19	* 20	* 21	* 22	22 [1]	Porcins
Horses	214	224	* 224	190	194	198	202	205 [1]	Chevaux
Asses	253	258	* 275	346	347	350	357	360 [1]	Anes
Comoros									**Comores**
Cattle and buffaloes	* 45	* 46	* 47	* 48	* 50	50	51 [1]	52 [1]	Bovins et buffles
Sheep and goats	* 134	* 135	* 137	* 138	* 160	190	191 [1]	193 [1]	Ovins et caprins
Asses [1]	5	5	5	5	5	5	5	5	Anes [1]
Congo									**Congo**
Cattle and buffaloes	69 [1]	70 [1]	72 [1]	75	72	83	87	90	Bovins et buffles
Sheep and goats	409 [1]	409 [1]	409 [1]	401	394 [1]	395 [1]	376	376 [1]	Ovins et caprins
Pigs	47 [1]	46 [1]	46 [1]	45	44 [1]	45 [1]	46 [1]	46 [1]	Porcins
Côte d'Ivoire									**Côte d'Ivoire**
Cattle and buffaloes	1 231	1 258	1 286	1 316	1 346	1 377	1 409	1 409 [1]	Bovins et buffles
Sheep and goats	2 229	2 284	2 341	2 399	2 460	2 527	2 585	2 585 [1]	Ovins et caprins
Pigs	403	414	264	271	278	327	336	336 [1]	Porcins
Dem. Rep. of the Congo									**Rép. dém. du Congo**
Cattle and buffaloes	1 127	1 113	1 060	853	822	853	822	793	Bovins et buffles
Sheep and goats	5 372	5 329	5 286	5 134	5 600	5 136	5 056	4 978	Ovins et caprins
Pigs	1 152	1 084	1 117	1 100	1 049	1 100	1 049	1 000	Porcins
Djibouti									**Djibouti**
Cattle and buffaloes	* 213	* 247	* 266	267 [1]	268 [1]	269 [1]	269 [1]	269 [1]	Bovins et buffles
Sheep and goats	* 971	* 965	* 972	973 [1]	974 [1]	977 [1]	978 [1]	978 [1]	Ovins et caprins
Asses	8 [1]	* 8	* 8	8 [1]	9 [1]	9 [1]	9 [1]	9 [1]	Anes
Egypt									**Egypte**
Cattle and buffaloes	* 5 909	6 014	* 6 014	6 213	6 366	6 747	6 909	7 066	Bovins et buffles
Sheep and goats	* 7 003	7 352	* 7 352	7 447	7 613	7 699	7 894 [1]	8 073 [1]	Ovins et caprins
Pigs	27	27 [1]	27 [1]	28 [1]	29 [1]	29 [1]	30 [1]	30 [1]	Porcins
Horses	* 39	* 42	* 41	43 [1]	45 [1]	46 [1]	46 [1]	46 [1]	Chevaux
Asses [1]	3 100	3 112	2 980	2 990	2 995	3 000	3 050	3 050	Anes [1]
Mules [1]	1	1	1	1	1	1	1	1	Mulets [1]
Equatorial Guinea [1]									**Guinée équatoriale** [1]
Cattle and buffaloes	5	5	5	5	5	5	5	5	Bovins et buffles
Sheep and goats	44	45	45	45	46	46	46	47	Ovins et caprins
Pigs	5	6	6	6	6	6	6	6	Porcins
Eritrea									**Erythrée**
Cattle and buffaloes	* 1 290	* 1 312	* 1 600	* 1 928	* 2 026	2 100 [1]	2 150 [1]	2 200 [1]	Bovins et buffles
Sheep and goats [1]	2 970	3 030	3 090	3 150	3 210	3 270	3 270	3 270	Ovins et caprins [1]
Ethiopia									**Ethiopie**
Cattle and buffaloes	29 450 [1]	29 825	31 207	32 612	35 372	35 095	35 480 [1]	34 500 [1]	Bovins et buffles
Sheep and goats [1]	38 400	38 500	38 600	38 700	38 800	38 950	39 500	39 500	Ovins et caprins [1]
Pigs [1]	20	21	22	23	24	25	25	25	Porcins [1]
Horses [1]	2 750	2 750	2 750	2 750	2 750	2 750	2 750	2 750	Chevaux [1]
Asses [1]	5 200	5 200	5 200	5 200	5 200	5 200	5 200	5 200	Anes [1]
Mules [1]	630	630	630	630	630	630	630	630	Mulets [1]
Gabon									**Gabon**
Cattle and buffaloes	38 [1]	* 38	36	33	34 [1]	35 [1]	36 [1]	36 [1]	Bovins et buffles
Sheep and goats [1]	260	265	270	275	280	285	289	289	Ovins et caprins [1]
Pigs [1]	207	208	209	210	211	212	213	213	Porcins [1]
Gambia									**Gambie**
Cattle and buffaloes	348	351	353	356	359	361	364	365 [1]	Bovins et buffles
Sheep and goats	318	305	293	282	271	261	251	251 [1]	Ovins et caprins
Pigs	14	14	14	14	14 [1]	14 [1]	14 [1]	14 [1]	Porcins
Horses	18	18 [1]	13	16	17 [1]	17 [1]	17 [1]	17 [1]	Chevaux

37

Livestock
Stocks: thousand head [*cont.*]
Cheptel
Effectifs : milliers de têtes [*suite*]

Region, country or area	1994	1995	1996	1997	1998	1999	2000	2001	Région, pays ou zone
Asses	33	34[1]	25	33	34[1]	35[1]	35[1]	35[1]	Anes
Ghana									**Ghana**
Cattle and buffaloes	1 187	1 217	1 248	1 260	1 273	1 288	1 302	1 302[1]	Bovins et buffles
Sheep and goats	4 410	4 214	4 759	5 101	5 256	5 589	5 820	5 820[1]	Ovins et caprins
Pigs	419	351	318	353	352	332	324	324[1]	Porcins
Horses	2	2[1]	3	3[1]	3[1]	3[1]	3[1]	3[1]	Chevaux
Asses	12	12[1]	13	14[1]	14[1]	14[1]	15[1]	15[1]	Anes
Guinea									**Guinée**
Cattle and buffaloes	1 874	2 202	2 246	2 291	2 337	2 368	2 679	2 679[1]	Bovins et buffles
Sheep and goats	1 074	1 341	1 389	1 438	1 489	1 635	1 904	1 904[1]	Ovins et caprins
Pigs	40	46	54	62	72	84	98	98[1]	Porcins
Horses[1]	2	3	3	3	3	3	3	3	Chevaux[1]
Asses	2[1]	* 2	2[1]	2[1]	2[1]	2[1]	2[1]	2[1]	Anes
Guinea-Bissau									**Guinée-Bissau**
Cattle and buffaloes	442	453	464	475	487	500	512	515[1]	Bovins et buffles
Sheep and goats[1]	540	550	565	580	595	610	605	610	Ovins et caprins[1]
Pigs[1]	320	325	330	335	340	345	345	350	Porcins[1]
Horses[1]	2	2	2	2	2	2	2	2	Chevaux[1]
Asses[1]	5	5	5	5	5	5	5	5	Anes[1]
Kenya									**Kenya**
Cattle and buffaloes	13 250[1]	* 13 567	* 13 838	13 414	* 13 002	* 13 392	* 13 794	12 500[1]	Bovins et buffles
Sheep and goats	18 666	18 317	18 330[1]	18 400	18 600[1]	17 700[1]	16 600[1]	15 500[1]	Ovins et caprins
Pigs	201	231	285	313	291	301	315	315[1]	Porcins
Horses[1]	2	2	2	2	2	2	2	2	Chevaux[1]
Lesotho									**Lesotho**
Cattle and buffaloes	578	580	539	601	496	510[1]	520[1]	510[1]	Bovins et buffles
Sheep and goats	2 152	1 880	1 683	1 749	1 243	1 280[1]	1 330[1]	1 300[1]	Ovins et caprins
Pigs	46	66	64	58	60[1]	63[1]	65[1]	60[1]	Porcins
Horses	113	100	98	100[1]	95[1]	98[1]	100[1]	100[1]	Chevaux
Asses	140	146	153	155[1]	150[1]	152[1]	154[1]	154[1]	Anes
Mules[1]	1	1	1	1	1	1	1	1	Mulets[1]
Liberia[1]									**Libéria[1]**
Cattle and buffaloes	36	36	36	36	36	36	36	36	Bovins et buffles
Sheep and goats	430	430	430	430	430	430	430	430	Ovins et caprins
Pigs	120	120	120	120	120	120	130	130	Porcins
Libyan Arab Jamah.									**Jamah. arabe libyenne**
Cattle and buffaloes	* 140	* 145	* 145	142[1]	180[1]	190[1]	210[1]	220[1]	Bovins et buffles
Sheep and goats[1]	6 260	* 6 400	* 7 200	8 420	8 800	6 800	7 000	7 050	Ovins et caprins[1]
Horses	* 30	* 35	* 40	43[1]	44[1]	45[1]	46[1]	46[1]	Chevaux
Asses	* 20	* 21	* 25	27[1]	28[1]	29[1]	30[1]	30[1]	Anes
Madagascar									**Madagascar**
Cattle and buffaloes	10 298	10 309	10 320	10 331	10 342	10 353	10 364	10 300[1]	Bovins et buffles
Sheep and goats	* 2 173	* 2 220	2 085	2 110[1]	2 130[1]	2 150[1]	2 170[1]	2 140[1]	Ovins et caprins
Pigs	1 558	1 592	1 629	1 662	1 650[1]	1 500[1]	900[1]	850[1]	Porcins
Malawi									**Malawi**
Cattle and buffaloes	680[1]	690[1]	700	750[1]	740[1]	712	750[1]	750[1]	Bovins et buffles
Sheep and goats	1 100[1]	1 200[1]	1 358	1 370[1]	1 355[1]	1 530	1 555[1]	1 560[1]	Ovins et caprins
Pigs	245[1]	247	220	230[1]	220[1]	230[1]	240[1]	250[1]	Porcins
Asses	2[1]	2	2[1]	2[1]	2[1]	2[1]	2[1]	2[1]	Anes
Mali									**Mali**
Cattle and buffaloes	5 380	5 541	5 708	5 882	6 240	6 428	6 620	6 819	Bovins et buffles
Sheep and goats	12 553	13 179	13 838	* 14 500[1]	14 500	* 15 986	16 049[1]	16 300[1]	Ovins et caprins
Pigs	62	63	64	65	65	65	66	66[1]	Porcins
Horses	101	112	123	136	150	165	165[1]	165[1]	Chevaux
Asses	612	625	638	652	666	680	680[1]	680[1]	Anes
Mauritania									**Mauritanie**
Cattle and buffaloes	1 100	1 111	1 122	1 353	1 394	1 433	1 476	1 500[1]	Bovins et buffles
Sheep and goats	* 8 800	* 8 814	10 332	10 500[1]	* 11 390	* 11 960	* 12 558	12 700[1]	Ovins et caprins
Horses	* 19	* 19	* 19	20[1]	20[1]	20[1]	20[1]	20[1]	Chevaux
Asses[1]	155	155	155	156	156	157	157	158	Anes[1]

37

Livestock
Stocks: thousand head [*cont.*]
    Cheptel
        Effectifs : milliers de têtes [*suite*]

Region, country or area	1994	1995	1996	1997	1998	1999	2000	2001	Région, pays ou zone
Mauritius									**Maurice**
Cattle and buffaloes [1]	24	23	23	21	22	25	27	28	Bovins et buffles [1]
Sheep and goats [1]	97	98	97	98	99	100	101	102	Ovins et caprins [1]
Pigs	17 [1]	18 [1]	19 [1]	* 20	* 20	* 20	* 20	21 [1]	Porcins
Morocco									**Maroc**
Cattle and buffaloes	2 343	2 371	2 408	2 547	2 569	2 560	2 675	2 663	Bovins et buffles
Sheep and goats	17 282	17 403	19 131	20 077	19 743	21 691	22 420	22 500 [1]	Ovins et caprins
Pigs	10 [1]	10 [1]	10 [1]	10	8	8 [1]	8 [1]	8 [1]	Porcins
Horses	165	162	156	145	147	149	154	155 [1]	Chevaux
Asses	916	954	919	949	980	1 001	985	985 [1]	Anes
Mules	527	540	523	516	524	527	518	520 [1]	Mulets
Mozambique [1]									**Mozambique** [1]
Cattle and buffaloes	1 240	1 250	1 270	1 290	1 300	1 310	1 320	1 320	Bovins et buffles
Sheep and goats	497	501	504	508	511	514	517	517	Ovins et caprins
Pigs	168	170	172	174	176	178	180	180	Porcins
Asses	18	19	20	21	22	23	23	23	Anes
Namibia									**Namibie**
Cattle and buffaloes	2 036	2 031	1 990	2 055	2 192	2 279	2 505	2 100 [1]	Bovins et buffles
Sheep and goats	4 259	4 026	3 985	4 250	3 797	3 864	4 296	3 900 [1]	Ovins et caprins
Pigs	18	20	19	17	15	19	23	18 [1]	Porcins
Horses	59	58	57	57	53	66	62 [1]	63 [1]	Chevaux
Asses [1]	72	71	70	71	69	70	68	69	Anes [1]
Mules [1]	7	7	7	7	7	7	7	7	Mulets [1]
Niger									**Niger**
Cattle and buffaloes	1 968	2 008	2 048	2 089	2 131	2 174	2 217	2 260 [1]	Bovins et buffles
Sheep and goats	9 244	9 504	9 718	* 10 176	* 10 447	10 826	11 116	11 400 [1]	Ovins et caprins
Pigs [1]	39	39	39	39	39	39	39	39	Porcins [1]
Horses	* 90	* 93	* 96	* 99	* 102	103 [1]	104 [1]	105 [1]	Chevaux
Asses	476	481	506	516	562	570 [1]	570 [1]	580 [1]	Anes
Nigeria									**Nigéria**
Cattle and buffaloes	14 881	15 405	18 680	19 610	19 700 [1]	19 830	19 830 [1]	19 830 [1]	Bovins et buffles
Sheep and goats [1]	38 500	38 500	38 500	42 660	43 700	44 800	44 800	44 800	Ovins et caprins [1]
Pigs	3 989	4 149	4 315	4 487	4 667 [1]	4 855 [1]	4 855 [1]	4 855 [1]	Porcins
Horses [1]	204	204	204	204	204	204	204	204	Chevaux [1]
Asses [1]	1 000	1 000	1 000	1 000	1 000	1 000	1 000	1 000	Anes [1]
Réunion									**Réunion**
Cattle and buffaloes	26	26	26	* 27	27 [1]	27	28	28 [1]	Bovins et buffles
Sheep and goats	33	32	32	* 40	40 [1]	39	39	40 [1]	Ovins et caprins
Pigs	82	86	86	* 89	82 [1]	77	76	77 [1]	Porcins
Rwanda									**Rwanda**
Cattle and buffaloes	454	465	500 [1]	570 [1]	657	749	732	800 [1]	Bovins et buffles
Sheep and goats	* 1 655	* 770	* 869	* 921	* 977	912	1 005	960 [1]	Ovins et caprins
Pigs	* 150	* 120	* 134	* 142	* 149	160	177	180 [1]	Porcins
Sao Tome and Principe [1]									**Sao Tomé-et-Principe** [1]
Cattle and buffaloes	4	4	4	4	4	4	4	4	Bovins et buffles
Sheep and goats	7	7	7	7	7	7	7	7	Ovins et caprins
Pigs	2	2	2	2	2	2	2	2	Porcins
Senegal									**Sénégal**
Cattle and buffaloes	2 760	2 800	2 870	2 898	2 912	2 927	3 073	* 3 227	Bovins et buffles
Sheep and goats	7 034	7 183	7 485	7 811	8 047	8 330	8 421	* 8 813	Ovins et caprins
Pigs	161	163	171	191	213	240	269	* 280	Porcins
Horses	434	434	436	465	445	446	471	* 492	Chevaux
Asses	366	366	367	393	375	377	399	410 [1]	Anes
Seychelles [1]									**Seychelles** [1]
Cattle and buffaloes	2	2	1	1	1	1	1	2	Bovins et buffles
Sheep and goats	5	5	5	5	5	5	5	5	Ovins et caprins
Pigs	18	18	18	18	18	18	18	18	Porcins
Sierra Leone									**Sierra Leone**
Cattle and buffaloes [1]	370	380	390	400	410	420	420	420	Bovins et buffles [1]
Sheep and goats [1]	488	510	525	540	553	565	565	565	Ovins et caprins [1]
Pigs	50 [1]	50 [1]	50 [1]	50 [1]	50 [1]	52	52 [1]	52 [1]	Porcins

37

Livestock

Stocks: thousand head [*cont.*]

Cheptel

Effectifs : milliers de têtes [*suite*]

Region, country or area	1994	1995	1996	1997	1998	1999	2000	2001	Région, pays ou zone
Somalia									**Somalie**
Cattle and buffaloes	5 000	5 200[1]	5 400[1]	5 600[1]	5 300[1]	5 000[1]	5 100[1]	5 200[1]	Bovins et buffles
Sheep and goats	25 000	26 000[1]	26 600[1]	27 000[1]	26 000[1]	25 000[1]	25 400[1]	25 700[1]	Ovins et caprins
Pigs [1]	4	4	4	5	4	4	4	4	Porcins [1]
Horses [1]	1	1	1	1	1	1	1	1	Chevaux [1]
Asses [1]	19	20	20	21	19	19	20	20	Anes [1]
Mules [1]	19	19	20	20	18	18	19	19	Mulets [1]
South Africa									**Afrique du Sud**
Cattle and buffaloes	12 584	13 015	13 389	13 667	13 772	13 580	13 461	* 13 740	Bovins et buffles
Sheep and goats	35 536	35 241	35 608	35 830	35 903	35 137	35 257	35 350[1]	Ovins et caprins
Pigs	1 511	1 628	1 603	1 617	1 641	1 531	1 556	1 540[1]	Porcins
Horses [1]	240	245	250	255	260	258	255	258	Chevaux [1]
Asses [1]	210	210	210	210	210	210	210	210	Anes [1]
Mules [1]	14	14	14	14	14	14	14	14	Mulets [1]
Sudan									**Soudan**
Cattle and buffaloes	29 000[1]	30 077	31 669	33 103	34 584	35 825	37 093	38 325	Bovins et buffles
Sheep and goats	70 464	72 395[1]	72 418	75 872	78 861	82 148	84 643	86 000[1]	Ovins et caprins
Horses [1]	23	24	24	25	25	26	26	26	Chevaux [1]
Asses [1]	675	678	680	700	720	730	740	750	Anes [1]
Mules [1]	1	1	1	1	1	1	1	1	Mulets [1]
Swaziland									**Swaziland**
Cattle and buffaloes	626	642	656	658	660	602	608	615[1]	Bovins et buffles
Sheep and goats	455[1]	459	465	465[1]	462[1]	458[1]	449	477[1]	Ovins et caprins
Pigs	30[1]	30	31	32[1]	30[1]	31[1]	30	34[1]	Porcins
Horses	1	1[1]	1[1]	1[1]	1[1]	1[1]	1[1]	1[1]	Chevaux
Asses	15	15[1]	15[1]	15[1]	15[1]	15[1]	15[1]	15[1]	Anes
Togo									**Togo**
Cattle and buffaloes	227	202	217	206	223	275	277	277[1]	Bovins et buffles
Sheep and goats	1 656	1 315	1 932	1 598	1 850	2 197	2 425[1]	2 425[1]	Ovins et caprins
Pigs	421	331	288	360	320	284	289	289[1]	Porcins
Horses [1]	2	2	2	2	2	2	2	2	Chevaux [1]
Asses [1]	3	3	3	3	3	3	3	3	Anes [1]
Tunisia									**Tunisie**
Cattle and buffaloes	662	654	680[1]	701	770[1]	780[1]	790[1]	795[1]	Bovins et buffles
Sheep and goats	7 488	7 426	7 650[1]	7 554	7 900[1]	7 950[1]	8 000[1]	8 050[1]	Ovins et caprins
Pigs [1]	6	6	6	6	6	6	6	6	Porcins [1]
Horses [1]	56	56	56	56	56	56	56	56	Chevaux [1]
Asses [1]	230	230	230	230	230	230	230	230	Anes [1]
Mules [1]	81	81	81	81	81	81	81	81	Mulets [1]
Uganda									**Ouganda**
Cattle and buffaloes	5 106	5 233	5 301	5 460	5 651	5 820	5 966	5 900[1]	Bovins et buffles
Sheep and goats	6 280	6 469	6 635	6 805	7 013	7 224	7 250[1]	7 300[1]	Ovins et caprins
Pigs	1 304	1 343	1 383	1 425	1 475	1 520	1 550[1]	1 550[1]	Porcins
Asses [1]	17	17	18	18	18	18	18	18	Anes [1]
United Rep. of Tanzania									**Rép.-Unie de Tanzanie**
Cattle and buffaloes	* 13 752	* 13 888	* 14 025	* 14 163	* 14 302	14 350[1]	14 380[1]	14 400[1]	Bovins et buffles
Sheep and goats	* 13 637	13 670[1]	13 750[1]	13 850[1]	13 950[1]	14 050[1]	14 150[1]	14 250[1]	Ovins et caprins
Pigs	* 335	340[1]	330[1]	335[1]	340[1]	345[1]	350[1]	355[1]	Porcins
Asses [1]	178	178	176	177	178	179	180	180	Anes [1]
Zambia									**Zambie**
Cattle and buffaloes	3 200[1]	3 000[1]	2 800[1]	* 2 100	* 2 176	* 2 273	* 2 373	2 400[1]	Bovins et buffles
Sheep and goats	700[1]	724[1]	747[1]	* 780	* 989	* 1 189	* 1 389	1 420[1]	Ovins et caprins
Pigs	310[1]	300[1]	320[1]	* 316	* 320	* 324	* 330	340[1]	Porcins
Asses [1]	2	2	2	2	2	2	2	2	Anes [1]
Zimbabwe									**Zimbabwe**
Cattle and buffaloes	4 300[1]	4 500	5 436	5 400[1]	5 450	5 500[1]	5 550[1]	5 550[1]	Bovins et buffles
Sheep and goats	3 030[1]	3 102	3 236	3 210[1]	3 270	3 295[1]	3 320[1]	3 335[1]	Ovins et caprins
Pigs	* 246	277	266	260[1]	270	272[1]	275[1]	278[1]	Porcins
Horses [1]	24	25	25	25	25	26	26	26	Chevaux [1]

37

Livestock

Stocks: thousand head [*cont.*]

Cheptel

Effectifs : milliers de têtes [*suite*]

Region, country or area	1994	1995	1996	1997	1998	1999	2000	2001	Région, pays ou zone
Asses [1]	104	105	105	104	105	106	107	107	Anes [1]
Mules [1]	1	1	1	1	1	1	1	1	Mulets [1]
America, North									**Amérique du Nord**
Cattle and buffaloes	163 999	165 365	166 183	165 460	163 478	160 992	160 767	160 681	**Bovins et buffles**
Sheep and goats	32 794	31 809	30 962	29 932	29 014	28 442	28 433	29 015	Ovins et caprins
Pigs	91 208	93 760	92 402	90 735	95 749	97 872	95 526	97 445	Porcins
Horses	13 997	14 055	14 116	14 119	14 078	14 010	14 084	14 138	Chevaux
Asses	3 699	3 730	3 750	3 750	3 750	3 751	3 757	3 768	Anes
Mules	3 706	3 736	3 755	3 753	3 749	3 763	3 764	3 764	Mulets
Antigua and Barbuda [1]									**Antigua-et-Barbuda** [1]
Cattle and buffaloes	16	16	16	16	16	16	16	16	Bovins et buffles
Sheep and goats	25	24	24	24	24	24	24	24	Ovins et caprins
Pigs	2	2	2	2	2	2	2	2	Porcins
Horses	1	0	0	0	0	0	0	0	Chevaux
Asses	2	1	1	1	1	1	1	1	Anes
Bahamas									**Bahamas**
Cattle and buffaloes	1	1	1	1 [1]	1 [1]	1	1	1	Bovins et buffles
Sheep and goats	20	21	22	22 [1]	22 [1]	20	20	20	Ovins et caprins
Pigs	5	* 5	5	5 [1]	5 [1]	6	5	5	Porcins
Barbados [1]									**Barbade** [1]
Cattle and buffaloes	28	28	28	24	23	23	23	23	Bovins et buffles
Sheep and goats	46	46	46	46	46	46	46	46	Ovins et caprins
Pigs	30	30	30	31	33	33	33	33	Porcins
Horses	1	1	1	1	1	1	1	1	Chevaux
Asses	2	2	2	2	2	2	2	2	Anes
Mules	2	2	2	2	2	2	2	2	Mulets
Belize									**Belize**
Cattle and buffaloes	59 [1]	60	62 [1]	61 [1]	59 [1]	53 [1]	44 [1]	45 [1]	Bovins et buffles
Sheep and goats [1]	4	4	4	4	4	4	4	5	Ovins et caprins [1]
Pigs	24 [1]	22	23 [1]	23 [1]	23 [1]	24 [1]	24 [1]	24 [1]	Porcins
Horses [1]	5	5	5	5	5	5	5	5	Chevaux [1]
Mules [1]	4	4	4	4	4	4	4	4	Mulets [1]
Bermuda									**Bermudes**
Cattle and buffaloes [1]	1	1	1	1	1	1	1	1	Bovins et buffles [1]
Sheep and goats	1	0 [1]	0	0 [1]	0 [1]	0 [1]	0 [1]	0 [1]	Ovins et caprins
Pigs	1 [1]	1 [1]	1	1 [1]	1 [1]	1 [1]	1 [1]	1 [1]	Porcins
Horses	1	1 [1]	1 [1]	1 [1]	1 [1]	1 [1]	1 [1]	1 [1]	Chevaux
British Virgin Islands [1]									**Iles Vierges britanniques** [1]
Cattle and buffaloes	2	2	2	2	2	2	2	2	Bovins et buffles
Sheep and goats	16	16	16	16	16	16	16	16	Ovins et caprins
Pigs	2	2	2	2	2	2	2	2	Porcins
Canada									**Canada**
Cattle and buffaloes	12 012	12 709	13 402	13 409	13 215	12 902	12 815	12 996	Bovins et buffles
Sheep and goats [1]	667	645	672	656	642	679	725	871	Ovins et caprins [1]
Pigs	10 534	11 291	11 588	11 480	11 985	12 409	12 254	12 600	Porcins
Horses [1]	350	380	376	400	380	380	385	385	Chevaux [1]
Mules [1]	4	4	4	4	4	4	4	4	Mulets [1]
Cayman Islands [1]									**Iles Caïmanes** [1]
Cattle and buffaloes	1	1	1	1	1	1	1	1	Bovins et buffles
Costa Rica									**Costa Rica**
Cattle and buffaloes	* 1 894	* 1 645	* 1 585	* 1 529	* 1 527	* 1 617	1 715	1 720 [1]	Bovins et buffles
Sheep and goats [1]	4	4	4	4	4	4	4	4	Ovins et caprins [1]
Pigs	350	300	300	315 [1]	360 [1]	390 [1]	440 [1]	430 [1]	Porcins
Horses [1]	114	115	115	115	115	115	115	115	Chevaux [1]
Asses [1]	7	8	8	8	8	8	8	8	Anes [1]
Mules [1]	5	5	5	5	5	5	5	5	Mulets [1]
Cuba									**Cuba**
Cattle and buffaloes	4 617	4 632	4 601	4 606	4 644	4 406	4 110	4 400 [1]	Bovins et buffles
Sheep and goats [1]	410	415	429	449	472	518	559	550	Ovins et caprins [1]
Pigs [1]	2 300	2 300	2 400	2 400	2 400	2 500	2 600	2 700	Porcins [1]
Horses	597	583	568	525	434	430	415	400 [1]	Chevaux

37

Livestock
Stocks: thousand head [*cont.*]
Cheptel
Effectifs : milliers de têtes [*suite*]

Region, country or area	1994	1995	1996	1997	1998	1999	2000	2001	Région, pays ou zone
Asses	6	6	6	6	6	6	7	7[1]	Anes
Mules	33	32	30	28	24	24	23	23[1]	Mulets
Dominica[1]									**Dominique**[1]
Cattle and buffaloes	13	13	13	13	13	13	13	13	Bovins et buffles
Sheep and goats	17	17	17	17	17	17	17	17	Ovins et caprins
Pigs	5	5	5	5	5	5	5	5	Porcins
Dominican Republic									**Rép. dominicaine**
Cattle and buffaloes	* 2 366	2 302	2 435	2 481	2 528	1 954	2 018	2 107	Bovins et buffles
Sheep and goats	700[1]	705[1]	705[1]	705	435[1]	269	284	293	Ovins et caprins
Pigs	900[1]	950[1]	950[1]	960	960	540	539	566	Porcins
Horses[1]	329	329	329	329	330	330	330	330	Chevaux[1]
Asses[1]	145	145	145	145	145	145	145	145	Anes[1]
Mules[1]	135	135	135	135	135	138	138	138	Mulets[1]
El Salvador									**El Salvador**
Cattle and buffaloes	1 262	1 125	1 287	1 162	1 038	1 141	1 212	1 216	Bovins et buffles
Sheep and goats[1]	20	21	21	21	21	21	20	20	Ovins et caprins[1]
Pigs	223	190	194	182	175	248	186	150	Porcins
Horses[1]	96	96	96	96	96	96	96	96	Chevaux[1]
Asses[1]	3	3	3	3	3	3	3	3	Anes[1]
Mules[1]	24	24	24	24	24	24	24	24	Mulets[1]
Greenland[1]									**Groenland**[1]
Sheep and goats	22	22	22	22	22	22	22	22	Ovins et caprins
Grenada									**Grenade**
Cattle and buffaloes	4[1]	4	4[1]	4[1]	4[1]	4[1]	4[1]	4[1]	Bovins et buffles
Sheep and goats	21[1]	20	20[1]	20[1]	20[1]	20[1]	20[1]	20[1]	Ovins et caprins
Pigs	5[1]	5	5[1]	5[1]	5[1]	5[1]	5[1]	5[1]	Porcins
Asses[1]	1	1	1	1	1	1	1	1	Anes[1]
Guadeloupe									**Guadeloupe**
Cattle and buffaloes	60	61	80	85	85	85[1]	85[1]	85[1]	Bovins et buffles
Sheep and goats	43	43	43	33	31	31[1]	31[1]	31[1]	Ovins et caprins
Pigs	49	37	31	26	20	19[1]	19[1]	19[1]	Porcins
Horses[1]	1	1	1	1	1	1	1	1	Chevaux[1]
Guatemala									**Guatemala**
Cattle and buffaloes	2 300	2 293	2 291	* 2 337	* 2 330	2 500[1]	2 500[1]	2 500[1]	Bovins et buffles
Sheep and goats	604	628	660	661[1]	662[1]	662[1]	662[1]	664[1]	Ovins et caprins
Pigs	796	1 000[1]	1 258	1 296	1 336	1 376	1 424	1 450[1]	Porcins
Horses[1]	116	117	118	118	118	119	120	120	Chevaux[1]
Asses[1]	9	9	10	10	10	10	10	10	Anes[1]
Mules[1]	38	38	38	38	38	39	39	39	Mulets[1]
Haiti									**Haïti**
Cattle and buffaloes	* 1 234	1 250	1 246	1 270	1 300	1 300[1]	1 430	1 440[1]	Bovins et buffles
Sheep and goats	1 245[1]	* 1 242	* 1 380	* 1 605	* 1 756	1 757[1]	2 094	2 094[1]	Ovins et caprins
Pigs	* 360	390	485	600	800	800[1]	1 000	1 001[1]	Porcins
Horses[1]	470	480	490	490	490	490	500	501	Chevaux[1]
Asses[1]	210	210	210	210	210	210	215	215	Anes[1]
Mules[1]	80	80	80	80	80	80	82	82	Mulets[1]
Honduras									**Honduras**
Cattle and buffaloes	* 2 286	2 111	2 127	2 061	* 1 945	1 715	1 780	1 715[1]	Bovins et buffles
Sheep and goats[1]	41	41	41	43	43	44	45	46	Ovins et caprins[1]
Pigs	400[1]	415[1]	445[1]	455[1]	455[1]	473	470	480[1]	Porcins
Horses[1]	173	174	175	176	177	178	179	180	Chevaux[1]
Asses[1]	23	23	23	23	23	23	23	23	Anes[1]
Mules[1]	69	69	69	69	69	70	70	70	Mulets[1]
Jamaica[1]									**Jamaïque**[1]
Cattle and buffaloes	440	450	420	400	400	400	400	400	Bovins et buffles
Sheep and goats	441	441	441	442	442	441	441	441	Ovins et caprins
Pigs	200	200	180	180	180	180	180	180	Porcins
Horses	4	4	4	4	4	4	4	4	Chevaux
Asses	23	23	23	23	23	23	23	23	Anes
Mules	10	10	10	10	10	10	10	10	Mulets
Martinique									**Martinique**
Cattle and buffaloes	30	30[1]	28	26	25	25[1]	25[1]	25[1]	Bovins et buffles

37

Livestock
Stocks: thousand head [*cont.*]
Cheptel
Effectifs : milliers de têtes [*suite*]

Region, country or area	1994	1995	1996	1997	1998	1999	2000	2001	Région, pays ou zone
Sheep and goats [1]	70	64	64	55	53	51	51	51	Ovins et caprins [1]
Pigs [1]	36	33	33	32	34	35	35	35	Porcins [1]
Horses [1]	2	2	2	2	2	2	2	2	Chevaux [1]
Mexico									**Mexique**
Cattle and buffaloes	* 30 702	* 30 191	29 301	30 772	31 060	30 193	30 492	30 600[1]	Bovins et buffles
Sheep and goats	* 16 355[1]	16 328	15 750	* 15 195	14 844	15 017	14 750	15 250[1]	Ovins et caprins
Pigs	16 200	15 923	15 405	15 735	14 972	15 748	16 088	17 750[1]	Porcins
Horses [1]	6 190	6 200	6 250	6 250	6 250	6 250	6 250	6 255	Chevaux [1]
Asses [1]	3 200	3 230	3 250	3 250	3 250	3 250	3 250	3 260	Anes [1]
Mules [1]	3 220	3 250	3 270	3 270	3 270	3 280	3 280	3 280	Mulets [1]
Montserrat [1]									**Montserrat** [1]
Cattle and buffaloes	10	10	10	10	10	10	10	10	Bovins et buffles
Sheep and goats	12	12	12	12	12	12	12	12	Ovins et caprins
Pigs	1	1	1	1	1	1	1	1	Porcins
Netherlands Antilles [1]									**Antilles néerlandaises** [1]
Cattle and buffaloes	1	1	1	1	1	1	1	1	Bovins et buffles
Sheep and goats	20	19	20	19	20	20	20	20	Ovins et caprins
Pigs	2	2	2	2	2	2	2	2	Porcins
Asses	3	3	3	3	3	3	3	3	Anes
Nicaragua									**Nicaragua**
Cattle and buffaloes	1 730	1 750	1 807	* 1 712	* 1 668	* 1 693	2 050[1]	* 2 280	Bovins et buffles
Sheep and goats [1]	10	10	11	10	10	10	11	11	Ovins et caprins [1]
Pigs [1]	330	392	366	385	400	400	400	400	Porcins [1]
Horses [1]	247	246	245	245	245	245	246	248	Chevaux [1]
Asses [1]	8	8	8	9	9	9	9	9	Anes [1]
Mules [1]	46	46	46	46	46	46	46	46	Mulets [1]
Panama									**Panama**
Cattle and buffaloes	1 454	1 456	1 442	1 362	1 382	1 360	1 360	1 342	Bovins et buffles
Sheep and goats	* 5	5[1]	5[1]	5[1]	5[1]	5[1]	5	5	Ovins et caprins
Pigs	257	261	244	240	252	278	280	278	Porcins
Horses	* 164	165[1]	165[1]	165[1]	165[1]	166[1]	166[1]	166[1]	Chevaux
Mules	* 4	4[1]	4[1]	4[1]	4[1]	4[1]	4[1]	4[1]	Mulets
Puerto Rico									**Porto Rico**
Cattle and buffaloes	429	368	371	388	387	390[1]	390[1]	390[1]	Bovins et buffles
Sheep and goats	34[1]	33[1]	24[1]	29[1]	26	25[1]	25[1]	25[1]	Ovins et caprins
Pigs	196	205	182	175	115	118[1]	118[1]	118[1]	Porcins
Horses [1]	24	24	24	24	25	25	26	26	Chevaux [1]
Asses [1]	2	2	2	2	2	2	2	2	Anes [1]
Mules [1]	3	3	3	3	3	3	3	3	Mulets [1]
Saint Kitts and Nevis									**Saint-Kitts-et-Nevis**
Cattle and buffaloes	4[1]	4[1]	4[1]	4	4[1]	4[1]	4[1]	4[1]	Bovins et buffles
Sheep and goats	24[1]	24	26	24[1]	21[1]	22[1]	22[1]	22[1]	Ovins et caprins
Pigs	2	2	3	3[1]	3[1]	3	3[1]	3[1]	Porcins
Saint Lucia									**Sainte-Lucie**
Cattle and buffaloes [1]	12	12	12	12	12	12	12	12	Bovins et buffles [1]
Sheep and goats	24[1]	23[1]	22	22[1]	22[1]	22[1]	22[1]	22[1]	Ovins et caprins
Pigs	14[1]	14[1]	15	15[1]	15[1]	15[1]	15[1]	15[1]	Porcins
Horses [1]	1	1	1	1	1	1	1	1	Chevaux [1]
Asses [1]	1	1	1	1	1	1	1	1	Anes [1]
Mules [1]	1	1	1	1	1	1	1	1	Mulets [1]
St. Vincent-Grenadines [1]									**St. Vincent-Grenadines** [1]
Cattle and buffaloes	6	6	6	6	6	6	6	6	Bovins et buffles
Sheep and goats	18	19	19	19	19	19	19	19	Ovins et caprins
Pigs	9	9	9	9	9	9	10	10	Porcins
Asses	1	1	1	1	1	1	1	1	Anes
Trinidad and Tobago									**Trinité-et-Tobago**
Cattle and buffaloes	41	41	41[1]	40[1]	39[1]	40[1]	40[1]	40[1]	Bovins et buffles
Sheep and goats	71	71	71[1]	71[1]	71[1]	71[1]	71[1]	71[1]	Ovins et caprins
Pigs	31	32	34	43[1]	40[1]	41[1]	41[1]	41[1]	Porcins
Horses [1]	1	1	1	1	1	1	1	1	Chevaux [1]
Asses [1]	2	2	2	2	2	2	2	2	Anes [1]
Mules [1]	2	2	2	2	2	2	2	2	Mulets [1]

37

Livestock
Stocks: thousand head [*cont.*]
Cheptel
Effectifs : milliers de têtes [*suite*]

Region, country or area	1994	1995	1996	1997	1998	1999	2000	2001	Région, pays ou zone
United States									**États-Unis**
Cattle and buffaloes	100 976	102 785	103 548	101 656	99 744	99 115	98 198	97 277	Bovins et buffles
Sheep and goats	11 796	10 839	10 365	9 674	9 225	8 565	8 382[1]	8 315[1]	Ovins et caprins
Pigs	57 940	59 738	58 201	56 124	61 158	62 206	59 342	59 138	Porcins
Horses	5 110[1]	5 130[1]	5 150[1]	* 5 170	* 5 237	5 170	5 240	5 300[1]	Chevaux
Asses[1]	52	52	52	52	52	52	52	52	Anes[1]
Mules[1]	28	28	28	28	28	28	28	28	Mulets[1]
United States Virgin Is.[1]									**Îles Vierges américaines[1]**
Cattle and buffaloes	8	8	8	8	8	8	8	8	Bovins et buffles
Sheep and goats	7	7	7	7	7	7	7	7	Ovins et caprins
Pigs	3	3	3	3	3	3	3	3	Porcins
America, South									**Amérique du Sud**
Cattle and buffaloes	290 988	295 733	291 881	294 240	294 400	296 305	302 383	309 719	**Bovins et buffles**
Sheep and goats	109 966	108 564	99 921	98 483	97 339	97 460	97 813	97 460	**Ovins et caprins**
Pigs	56 337	57 603	50 862	52 108	53 479	56 423	57 867	55 399	Porcins
Horses	15 308	15 587	15 004	15 093	15 128	15 464	15 541	15 651	Chevaux
Asses	4 030	4 062	3 951	3 969	3 954	3 984	4 009	4 039	Anes
Mules	3 342	3 311	2 611	2 621	2 620	2 684	2 712	2 775	Mulets
Argentina									**Argentine**
Cattle and buffaloes	53 157	52 649	50 861	50 059	48 049	49 057	48 674	* 50 167	Bovins et buffles
Sheep and goats	20 901	18 792	17 683	16 626	16 900[1]	17 106	17 052	17 000[1]	Ovins et caprins
Pigs	3 300	3 100	3 100	3 200	3 500[1]	4 200[1]	4 200[1]	4 200[1]	Porcins
Horses[1]	3 300	3 300	3 300	3 300	3 300	3 600	3 600	3 600	Chevaux[1]
Asses[1]	90	90	90	90	90	95	95	95	Anes[1]
Mules[1]	175	175	175	175	175	180	180	180	Mulets[1]
Bolivia									**Bolivie**
Cattle and buffaloes	5 912	6 000	6 118	6 238	6 387	6 556	6 725	6 725[1]	Bovins et buffles
Sheep and goats	9 165	9 380	9 539[1]	9 728	9 905	10 075	10 252[1]	10 252[1]	Ovins et caprins
Pigs	2 331	2 405	2 482	2 569	2 637	2 715	2 793	2 800[1]	Porcins
Horses[1]	322	322	322	322	322	322	322	322	Chevaux[1]
Asses[1]	631	631	631	631	631	631	631	631	Anes[1]
Mules[1]	81	81	81	81	81	81	81	81	Mulets[1]
Brazil									**Brésil**
Cattle and buffaloes	159 815	162 870	159 335	162 394	164 172	165 689	170 978	172 936	Bovins et buffles
Sheep and goats	29 315	29 608	22 162	22 502	22 433	23 023	24 132	23 700[1]	Ovins et caprins
Pigs	35 142	36 062	29 202	29 637	30 007	30 839	31 562	29 424	Porcins
Horses	6 356	6 394	5 705	5 832	5 867	5 831	5 832	5 850[1]	Chevaux
Asses	1 313	1 344	1 232	1 249	1 233	1 236	1 242	1 250[1]	Anes
Mules	1 987	1 990	1 286	1 295	1 292	1 336	1 348	1 400[1]	Mulets
Chile									**Chili**
Cattle and buffaloes	3 692	3 814	3 858	4 142	4 160	4 134	4 068	4 150[1]	Bovins et buffles
Sheep and goats	5 249[1]	5 225[1]	5 116[1]	4 573	4 494[1]	4 856[1]	4 889[1]	4 950[1]	Ovins et caprins
Pigs	1 407	1 490	1 486	1 655	1 962	2 221	2 465	2 500[1]	Porcins
Horses[1]	500	550	580	600	600	610	620	650	Chevaux[1]
Asses[1]	28	28	28	28	28	28	29	29	Anes[1]
Mules[1]	10	10	10	10	10	10	10	11	Mulets[1]
Colombia									**Colombie**
Cattle and buffaloes	* 25 634	25 551	* 26 088	25 673	25 764	24 363	25 206	* 28 332	Bovins et buffles
Sheep and goats	3 500[1]	* 3 505	* 3 503	3 332	3 045	3 311	3 473	3 500[1]	Ovins et caprins
Pigs	2 600[1]	2 500	2 431	2 480	2 452	2 765	2 712	2 750[1]	Porcins
Horses	2 300[1]	2 450	2 450[1]	2 450[1]	2 450[1]	2 500[1]	2 550[1]	2 600[1]	Chevaux
Asses[1]	710	710	710	710	710	715	718	720	Anes[1]
Mules	622[1]	586	590[1]	590[1]	590[1]	595[1]	595[1]	595[1]	Mulets
Ecuador									**Equateur**
Cattle and buffaloes	4 937	4 995	5 105	5 150	5 076	5 106	5 104	5 574	Bovins et buffles
Sheep and goats	2 059	1 987	2 018	2 112	2 361	2 472	2 198	2 249	Ovins et caprins
Pigs	2 546	2 618	2 621	2 708	2 708	2 786	2 783	2 392	Porcins
Horses[1]	515	520	520	520	520	521	523	525	Chevaux[1]
Asses[1]	264	265	266	267	268	269	270	270	Anes[1]
Mules[1]	153	154	155	156	157	157	158	158	Mulets[1]
Falkland Is. (Malvinas)									**Îles Falkland (Malvinas)**
Cattle and buffaloes	5	5	4	5	4	4[1]	4[1]	4[1]	Bovins et buffles

37

Livestock
Stocks: thousand head [*cont.*]
Cheptel
Effectifs : milliers de têtes [*suite*]

Region, country or area	1994	1995	1996	1997	1998	1999	2000	2001	Région, pays ou zone
Sheep and goats	727	717	686	707	708	700[1]	710[1]	690[1]	Ovins et caprins
Horses	1	1	1	1	1	1[1]	1[1]	1[1]	Chevaux
French Guiana									**Guyane française**
Cattle and buffaloes	8	8	9	10	9	9[1]	9[1]	9[1]	Bovins et buffles
Sheep and goats	4	4	4[1]	3[1]	3[1]	3[1]	3[1]	3[1]	Ovins et caprins
Pigs	9	9	10	10	10	10[1]	11[1]	11[1]	Porcins
Guyana [1]									**Guyana** [1]
Cattle and buffaloes	260	250	240	230	220	220	220	220	Bovins et buffles
Sheep and goats	209	209	209	209	209	209	209	209	Ovins et caprins
Pigs	25	20	20	20	20	20	20	20	Porcins
Horses	2	2	2	2	2	2	2	2	Chevaux
Asses	1	1	1	1	1	1	1	1	Anes
Paraguay									**Paraguay**
Cattle and buffaloes	9 100[1]	9 788	9 765	9 794	* 9 833	9 647	9 737	9 737[1]	Bovins et buffles
Sheep and goats	508	509[1]	511[1]	510	* 525	520	525	525[1]	Ovins et caprins
Pigs [1]	2 500	2 525	2 268	2 300	2 300	2 500	2 700	2 700	Porcins [1]
Horses	370	411[1]	478[1]	400[1]	400[1]	400[1]	400[1]	400[1]	Chevaux
Asses [1]	32	32	32	32	32	32	32	32	Anes [1]
Mules [1]	14	14	14	14	14	14	14	14	Mulets [1]
Peru									**Pérou**
Cattle and buffaloes	4 062	4 513	4 646	4 560	4 657	4 903	4 927	4 930	Bovins et buffles
Sheep and goats	13 950	14 614	14 736	15 156	15 585	16 365	16 709	16 500	Ovins et caprins
Pigs	2 442	2 401	2 533	2 481	2 531	2 788	2 819	2 800	Porcins
Horses [1]	665	665	665	665	665	675	690	700	Chevaux [1]
Asses [1]	520	520	520	520	520	535	550	570	Anes [1]
Mules [1]	224	224	224	224	224	235	250	260	Mulets [1]
Suriname									**Suriname**
Cattle and buffaloes	100[1]	103	99	98	112	121	130	136[1]	Bovins et buffles
Sheep and goats	16[1]	13	16	17	15	16	14	15[1]	Ovins et caprins
Pigs	37	20	17[1]	21	20	20	22	23[1]	Porcins
Uruguay									**Uruguay**
Cattle and buffaloes	10 511	10 450	10 651	10 553	10 297	10 504	* 10 800	10 800[1]	Bovins et buffles
Sheep and goats [1]	21 245	20 220	19 762	18 295	16 510	14 424	13 047	13 047	Ovins et caprins [1]
Pigs	280	270[1]	270	270[1]	330[1]	360[1]	380[1]	380[1]	Porcins
Horses [1]	480	470	480	500	500	500	500	500	Chevaux [1]
Asses [1]	1	1	1	1	1	1	1	1	Anes [1]
Mules [1]	4	4	4	4	4	4	4	4	Mulets [1]
Venezuela									**Venezuela**
Cattle and buffaloes	13 796	14 737	15 103	15 337	15 661	15 992	15 800[1]	16 000[1]	Bovins et buffles
Sheep and goats	3 119[1]	3 781	3 978	4 714	4 647	4 381	4 600[1]	4 820[1]	Ovins et caprins
Pigs	3 716	4 182	4 422	4 756	5 000[1]	5 200[1]	5 400[1]	5 400[1]	Porcins
Horses [1]	495	500	500	500	500	500	500	500	Chevaux [1]
Asses [1]	440	440	440	440	440	440	440	440	Anes [1]
Mules [1]	72	72	72	72	72	72	72	72	Mulets [1]
Asia									**Asie**
Cattle and buffaloes	597 092	610 336	615 452	607 688	616 403	620 938	629 843	631 812	**Bovins et buffles**
Sheep and goats	802 691	821 995	849 467	812 386	833 199	847 902	856 899	871 782	**Ovins et caprins**
Pigs	489 861	511 342	486 989	464 925	501 372	521 332	531 044	552 372	**Porcins**
Horses	17 722	17 855	18 019	16 538	16 573	16 592	16 302	16 190	**Chevaux**
Asses	20 228	20 445	19 806	18 615	18 216	19 014	18 853	18 843	**Anes**
Mules	6 171	6 221	6 113	5 512	5 528	5 488	5 475	5 332	**Mulets**
Afghanistan									**Afghanistan**
Cattle and buffaloes	1 900[1]	2 095	* 2 641	* 2 895	3 008	2 600[1]	2 200[1]	* 2 000	Bovins et buffles
Sheep and goats	17 750[1]	17 957	* 18 574	* 20 641	22 851	20 000[1]	17 500[1]	* 16 000	Ovins et caprins
Horses	100[1]	100[1]	100[1]	100[1]	100[1]	104	104[1]	104[1]	Chevaux
Asses	600[1]	* 704	* 753	* 805	* 860	920	920[1]	920[1]	Anes
Mules [1]	23	23	24	26	28	30	30	30	Mulets [1]
Armenia									**Arménie**
Cattle and buffaloes	502[1]	504[1]	508[1]	510[1]	466[1]	469	479	485	Bovins et buffles
Sheep and goats	* 736	* 636	604	* 579	* 546	520	508	507	Ovins et caprins
Pigs	81	82	80	54	57	86	71	69	Porcins

37

Livestock

Stocks: thousand head [cont.]

Cheptel

Effectifs : milliers de têtes [suite]

Region, country or area	1994	1995	1996	1997	1998	1999	2000	2001	Région, pays ou zone
Horses	11	12	12	13	13	12	12	11	Chevaux
Asses [1]	3	3	3	3	3	3	2	3	Anes [1]
Azerbaijan									**Azerbaïdjan**
Cattle and buffaloes	1 911 [1]	1 928 [1]	1 980	2 083	2 136	2 210	2 252	2 301 [1]	Bovins et buffles
Sheep and goats	* 4 539	* 4 558	4 644	4 922	5 512	6 229	6 528	* 5 976	Ovins et caprins
Pigs	48	33	30	23	21	26	20	19	Porcins
Horses	35	38	43	49	53	56	61	64	Chevaux
Asses	20	22	25	28	31	33	36	38	Anes
Bahrain									**Bahreïn**
Cattle and buffaloes	12 [1]	11	12	12	13	13 [1]	11	11 [1]	Bovins et buffles
Sheep and goats	35 [1]	33	34	35	33	33 [1]	34 [1]	34 [1]	Ovins et caprins
Bangladesh									**Bangladesh**
Cattle and buffaloes	* 24 643	* 24 859	24 401	* 24 816	24 220	24 480 [1]	24 730 [1]	24 730 [1]	Bovins et buffles
Sheep and goats	* 29 080 [1]	* 31 400 [1]	34 436	35 636	34 610	34 921 [1]	35 232 [1]	35 232 [1]	Ovins et caprins
Bhutan									**Bhoutan**
Cattle and buffaloes	439 [1]	439 [1]	439 [1]	439 [1]	439 [1]	439 [1]	439	439	Bovins et buffles
Sheep and goats [1]	101	101	101	101	101	101	101	101	Ovins et caprins [1]
Pigs [1]	75	75	75	75	75	75	75	75	Porcins [1]
Horses [1]	30	30	30	30	30	30	30	30	Chevaux [1]
Asses [1]	18	18	18	18	18	18	18	18	Anes [1]
Mules [1]	10	10	10	10	10	10	10	10	Mulets [1]
Brunei Darussalam									**Brunéi Darussalam**
Cattle and buffaloes	6	6	6	8	8	10 [1]	12 [1]	14 [1]	Bovins et buffles
Sheep and goats	4	4	3	3	4	4 [1]	4 [1]	4 [1]	Ovins et caprins
Pigs [1]	5	4	5	5	5	6	6	6	Porcins [1]
Cambodia									**Cambodge**
Cattle and buffaloes	3 431	3 543	3 544	3 514	3 374	3 480	3 686	3 495	Bovins et buffles
Pigs	2 024	2 039	2 151	2 438	2 339	2 189	1 934	2 118	Porcins
Horses [1]	21	21	22	22	23	25	26	26	Chevaux [1]
China									**Chine**
Cattle and buffaloes	113 473	123 484	123 055	*112 570	121 964	124 552	127 181	*128 456	Bovins et buffles
Sheep and goats	217 670	240 840	277 542	237 593	256 073	269 309	279 496	290 522	Ovins et caprins
Pigs	402 943	424 787	*398 617	373 644	408 425	429 212	437 551	454 420	Porcins
Horses	9 961	10 040	10 074	8 717	8 914	8 983	8 916	8 768	Chevaux
Asses	10 891	10 923	10 745	9 444	9 528	9 558	9 348	9 227	Anes
Mules	5 498	5 552	5 389	4 780	4 806	4 739	4 673	4 530	Mulets
Cyprus									**Chypre**
Cattle and buffaloes	61	64	68	70	62	56	54	54	Bovins et buffles
Sheep and goats	473	465	470	492	535	562	579	625	Ovins et caprins
Pigs	369	356	374	400	415	431	419	419 [1]	Porcins
Horses [1]	1	1	1	1	1	1	1	1	Chevaux [1]
Asses [1]	5	5	5	5	5	5	5	5	Anes [1]
Mules [1]	2	2	2	2	2	2	2	2	Mulets [1]
Georgia									**Géorgie**
Cattle and buffaloes	* 949	* 964	* 994	1 034 [1]	1 055 [1]	1 084 [1]	1 157 [1]	1 212 [1]	Bovins et buffles
Sheep and goats	958	793	725	652	584	587	633	* 623	Ovins et caprins
Pigs	365	367	353	333	330	366	411	443	Porcins
Horses	20	21	24	26	28	30	30 [1]	30 [1]	Chevaux
Asses [1]	2	3	3	3	3	3	2	3	Anes [1]
India									**Inde**
Cattle and buffaloes	293 220	295 868	298 552	301 273	*303 030	*306 967	*312 572	*313 774	Bovins et buffles
Sheep and goats	170 358	172 550	174 773	177 032	*178 462	*180 130	*180 900	181 700 [1]	Ovins et caprins
Pigs	13 783	14 306	14 848	15 411	* 16 005	16 500 [1]	17 000 [1]	17 500 [1]	Porcins
Horses [1]	800	800	800	800	800	800	800	800	Chevaux [1]
Asses [1]	1 000	1 000	1 000	1 000	1 000	1 000	1 000	1 000	Anes [1]
Mules [1]	200	200	200	200	200	200	200	200	Mulets [1]
Indonesia									**Indonésie**
Cattle and buffaloes	14 472	14 670	14 987	15 003	14 463	13 779	14 047	13 479	Bovins et buffles
Sheep and goats	19 511	20 336	21 565	21 860	20 704	19 927	20 012	19 883 [1]	Ovins et caprins
Pigs	8 858	7 720	7 597	8 233	7 798	7 042	5 357	5 897	Porcins
Horses	611	609	579	582	566	484	517	517 [1]	Chevaux

37

Livestock
Stocks: thousand head [*cont.*]
Cheptel
Effectifs : milliers de têtes [*suite*]

Region, country or area	1994	1995	1996	1997	1998	1999	2000	2001	Région, pays ou zone
Iran (Islamic Rep. of)									**Iran (Rép. islamique d')**
Cattle and buffaloes	8 640	8 794	8 948	9 103	9 259	8 521	7 960[1]	7 460[1]	Bovins et buffles
Sheep and goats	76 042	76 646	77 256	78 117	79 002	79 657	79 000[1]	78 200[1]	Ovins et caprins
Horses [1]	150	150	150	150	130	120	150	150	Chevaux [1]
Asses	* 1 400	* 1 400	* 1 400	* 1 490	* 1 400	* 1 554	1 600[1]	1 600[1]	Anes
Mules	* 137	* 137	* 137	* 147	* 137	* 173	175[1]	175[1]	Mulets
Iraq									**Iraq**
Cattle and buffaloes	* 1 441[1]	* 1 260[1]	1 100[1]	* 1 363	1 384[1]	1 389[1]	1 415[1]	1 415[1]	Bovins et buffles
Sheep and goats	9 825[1]	8 850[1]	6 405[1]	* 8 050	8 200[1]	8 300[1]	8 380[1]	8 380[1]	Ovins et caprins
Horses	51[1]	* 47	46[1]	47[1]	48[1]	46[1]	47[1]	47[1]	Chevaux
Asses	380[1]	* 396	368[1]	380[1]	385[1]	375[1]	380[1]	380[1]	Anes
Mules [1]	12	12	12	12	13	11	11	11	Mulets [1]
Israel									**Israël**
Cattle and buffaloes	387	391	391	380	388	395	395	390	Bovins et buffles
Sheep and goats	435	421	420	435	424	425	455	457	Ovins et caprins
Pigs [1]	120	143	145	165	163	150	150	150	Porcins [1]
Horses [1]	4	4	4	4	4	4	4	4	Chevaux [1]
Asses [1]	5	5	5	5	5	5	5	5	Anes [1]
Mules [1]	2	2	2	2	2	2	2	2	Mulets [1]
Japan									**Japon**
Cattle and buffaloes	4 989	4 916	4 828	4 750	4 708	4 658	4 588	4 530	Bovins et buffles
Sheep and goats	56	50	47	45	42[1]	43[1]	42[1]	42[1]	Ovins et caprins
Pigs	10 621	10 250	9 900	9 823	9 904	9 879	9 806	9 785	Porcins
Horses	28	29[1]	26[1]	27	26[1]	25[1]	25[1]	25[1]	Chevaux
Jordan									**Jordanie**
Cattle and buffaloes	62	58	62	62	* 61	* 65	* 65	66[1]	Bovins et buffles
Sheep and goats	2 979	3 227	2 951	2 717	2 213	2 575	2 536	2 490	Ovins et caprins
Horses [1]	4	4	4	4	4	4	4	4	Chevaux [1]
Asses [1]	19	18	18	18	18	18	18	18	Anes [1]
Mules [1]	3	3	3	3	3	3	3	3	Mulets [1]
Kazakhstan									**Kazakhstan**
Cattle and buffaloes [1]	9 358	8 083	6 870	5 435	4 316	3 967	4 007	4 116	Bovins et buffles [1]
Sheep and goats	34 209	25 132	19 585	13 679	10 384	9 527	9 657	9 981	Ovins et caprins
Pigs	2 445	1 983	1 623	1 036	879	892	984	1 076	Porcins
Horses	1 777	1 636	1 557	1 310	1 083	986	970	976	Chevaux
Asses [1]	40	40	40	35	29	29	30	30	Anes [1]
Korea, Dem. P. R.									**Corée, R. p. dém. de**
Cattle and buffaloes	911	886	615	545	565	577	579	570	Bovins et buffles
Sheep and goats	1 401	972[1]	960	1 237	1 673	2 085	2 461	2 755	Ovins et caprins
Pigs	3 572	2 674	2 674	1 859	2 475	2 970	3 120	3 137	Porcins
Horses [1]	47	45	40	40	44	45	46	46	Chevaux [1]
Korea, Republic of									**Corée, République de**
Cattle and buffaloes	2 945	3 147	3 395	3 280	2 922	2 486	2 134	1 954	Bovins et buffles
Sheep and goats	605	682	676	605	540	463	446	431[1]	Ovins et caprins
Pigs	5 955	6 461	6 517	7 096	7 544	7 864	8 214	8 720	Porcins
Horses	6	6	7	8	8	8	8[1]	8[1]	Chevaux
Kuwait									**Koweït**
Cattle and buffaloes	15	20	19	21	18	20	20[1]	21[1]	Bovins et buffles
Sheep and goats	258	376	491	564	551	635	654	760	Ovins et caprins
Horses [1]	1	1	1	1	1	1	1	1	Chevaux [1]
Kyrgyzstan									**Kirghizistan**
Cattle and buffaloes	1 062	920	869	848	885	911	932	985	Bovins et buffles
Sheep and goats	7 322	5 076	4 275	3 716	* 3 405	* 3 536	* 3 498	* 4 396	Ovins et caprins
Pigs	169	118	114	88	93	105	105	117	Porcins
Horses	322	299	308	314	320[1]	325[1]	328[1]	346[1]	Chevaux
Asses [1]	10	10	10	9	8	8	8	7	Anes [1]
Lao People's Dem. Rep.									**Rép. dém. pop. lao**
Cattle and buffaloes	2 249	2 337	2 398	2 451	2 219	2 085	2 153	2 108[1]	Bovins et buffles
Sheep and goats	142	153	159	172	186	200	217	240[1]	Ovins et caprins
Pigs	1 673	1 724	1 772	1 813	1 432	1 036	1 326	1 500[1]	Porcins
Horses [1]	29	29	26	26	27	28	29	29	Chevaux [1]

37

Livestock
Stocks: thousand head [*cont.*]
Cheptel
Effectifs : milliers de têtes [*suite*]

Region, country or area	1994	1995	1996	1997	1998	1999	2000	2001	Région, pays ou zone
Lebanon									**Liban**
Cattle and buffaloes	77	* 60	70	69	80	76	75[1]	74[1]	Bovins et buffles
Sheep and goats	662	* 688[1]	795	819	800	814	825[1]	825[1]	Ovins et caprins
Pigs	53	54[1]	58	59[1]	60	62[1]	64[1]	64[1]	Porcins
Horses	* 7	* 5	5	5[1]	6[1]	6[1]	6[1]	6[1]	Chevaux
Asses [1]	23	24	24	25	25	25	25	25	Anes [1]
Mules	7[1]	6[1]	5	6[1]	6[1]	6[1]	6[1]	6[1]	Mulets
Malaysia									**Malaisie**
Cattle and buffaloes	893	881	850	842	875	879	879[1]	879[1]	Bovins et buffles
Sheep and goats	554	504	442	409	402	406	406[1]	406[1]	Ovins et caprins
Pigs	3 203	3 150	3 103	3 171	2 934	1 829	1 829[1]	1 829[1]	Porcins
Horses [1]	5	4	4	4	5	5	5	5	Chevaux [1]
Mongolia									**Mongolie**
Cattle and buffaloes	2 731	3 005	3 317	3 476	3 613	3 825	3 098	2 477	Bovins et buffles
Sheep and goats	19 886	21 028	22 239	22 695	24 431	26 225	24 146	27 471	Ovins et caprins
Pigs	29	23	24	19	21	22	15	16[1]	Porcins
Horses	2 190	2 409	2 648	2 771	2 893	3 059	2 800[1]	2 750[1]	Chevaux
Myanmar									**Myanmar**
Cattle and buffaloes	11 821	12 060	12 386	12 600	12 829	13 131	13 405	13 718	Bovins et buffles
Sheep and goats	1 417	1 492	1 558	1 632	1 688	1 732	1 782	1 842	Ovins et caprins
Pigs	2 728	2 944	3 229	3 358	3 501	3 715	3 914	4 139	Porcins
Horses [1]	120	120	120	120	120	120	120	120	Chevaux [1]
Mules [1]	8	8	8	8	8	8	8	8	Mulets [1]
Nepal									**Népal**
Cattle and buffaloes	9 722	10 116	10 311	10 387	10 438	10 501	10 549	10 607	Bovins et buffles
Sheep and goats	6 439	6 568	6 642	6 792	6 950	7 060	7 177	7 329[1]	Ovins et caprins
Pigs	612	636	670	724	766	825	878	913	Porcins
Occ. Palestinian Terr. [1,2]									**Terr. palestinien occ. [1,2]**
Cattle and buffaloes	3	3	3	3	3	3	3	3	Bovins et buffles
Sheep and goats	40	40	40	40	40	40	40	40	Ovins et caprins
Oman									**Oman**
Cattle and buffaloes	* 223	* 234	* 245	256[1]	271	285	290[1]	290[1]	Bovins et buffles
Sheep and goats	* 1 123	* 1 153	* 1 183	1 220[1]	1 252	1 286	1 310[1]	1 315[1]	Ovins et caprins
Asses [1]	26	26	27	27	28	28	29	29	Anes [1]
Pakistan									**Pakistan**
Cattle and buffaloes	37 033	37 559	40 697	41 640	42 614	43 600	44 700	45 700	Bovins et buffles
Sheep and goats	70 315	72 829	64 713	66 318	67 983	69 700	71 500	73 300	Ovins et caprins
Horses	350	346	334	331	327	300	300	300	Chevaux
Asses	3 901	4 000	3 600	3 600	3 200	3 800	3 800	3 900	Anes
Mules	77	78	132	142	151	150	200	200	Mulets
Philippines									**Philippines**
Cattle and buffaloes	4 496	4 728	4 970	5 234	5 408	5 432	5 505	5 561	Bovins et buffles
Sheep and goats [1]	6 025	6 213	6 260	6 530	6 810	6 830	6 960	6 980	Ovins et caprins [1]
Pigs	8 227	8 941	9 026	9 752	10 210	10 397	10 711	11 063	Porcins
Horses [1]	220	220	220	230	230	230	230	230	Chevaux [1]
Qatar									**Qatar**
Cattle and buffaloes	13	14	14	14	14	15	15	15[1]	Bovins et buffles
Sheep and goats	340	360	372	376	381	389	393	394[1]	Ovins et caprins
Horses	1	1	1	4	4[1]	4[1]	4[1]	4[1]	Chevaux
Saudi Arabia									**Arabie saoudite**
Cattle and buffaloes	243	253	259	277	294	297	297[1]	297[1]	Bovins et buffles
Sheep and goats	11 840	11 961	12 193	11 886	* 11 771	* 11 881	11 881[1]	11 881[1]	Ovins et caprins
Horses	3	3	3	3[1]	3[1]	3[1]	3[1]	3[1]	Chevaux
Asses	107	102	101	101[1]	100[1]	100[1]	100[1]	100[1]	Anes
Singapore [1]									**Singapour [1]**
Sheep and goats	1	0	0	0	0	0	0	0	Ovins et caprins
Pigs	180	190	190	190	190	190	190	190	Porcins
Sri Lanka									**Sri Lanka**
Cattle and buffaloes	2 494	2 468	2 405	2 305	2 320	2 344	2 251	2 250[1]	Bovins et buffles
Sheep and goats	608	610	547	531	531	527	506	* 511	Ovins et caprins
Pigs	94	87	85	80	76	74	71	68[1]	Porcins

37

Livestock
Stocks: thousand head [*cont.*]
Cheptel
Effectifs : milliers de têtes [*suite*]

Region, country or area	1994	1995	1996	1997	1998	1999	2000	2001	Région, pays ou zone
Horses [1]	2	2	2	2	2	2	2	2	Chevaux [1]
Syrian Arab Republic									**Rép. arabe syrienne**
Cattle and buffaloes	722	776	812	858	933	981	987	839	Bovins et buffles
Sheep and goats	12 292	13 138	14 201	14 930	16 526	15 044	14 555	13 341	Ovins et caprins
Pigs	1	1 [1]	1 [1]	1 [1]	1 [1]	1 [1]	1 [1]	1 [1]	Porcins
Horses	27	27	28	27	28 [1]	29 [1]	30 [1]	30 [1]	Chevaux
Asses	201	200	191	190	195 [1]	196 [1]	198 [1]	198 [1]	Anes
Mules	18	17	18	18	19 [1]	19 [1]	20 [1]	20 [1]	Mulets
Tajikistan									**Tadjikistan**
Cattle and buffaloes	1 250	1 199	1 147	1 082	1 050	1 037	1 042	1 053 [1]	Bovins et buffles
Sheep and goats *	2 906	2 700	2 494	2 293	2 222	2 195	2 183	1 938 [1]	Ovins et caprins *
Pigs	46	32	6	2	1	1	1	1 [1]	Porcins
Horses [1]	50	48	47	45	45	46	46	45	Chevaux [1]
Asses [1]	35	34	33	32	33	32	30	32	Anes [1]
Thailand									**Thaïlande**
Cattle and buffaloes	11 862	11 004	10 611	9 643	8 614	7 589	8 000 [1]	8 200 [1]	Bovins et buffles
Sheep and goats	232	208	140	167	* 171 [1]	* 172	173 [1]	175 [1]	Ovins et caprins
Pigs	5 435	5 369	6 129	6 894	7 082	6 370	6 500 [1]	8 300 [1]	Porcins
Horses	14	17	12	15	15 [1]	16 [1]	16 [1]	16 [1]	Chevaux
Turkey									**Turquie**
Cattle and buffaloes	12 226	12 206	12 044	12 121	11 379	11 207	* 11 075	* 10 970	Bovins et buffles
Sheep and goats	47 674	45 210	42 902	42 023	38 614	37 492	37 492 [1]	37 492 [1]	Ovins et caprins
Pigs	9	8	5	5	5	5	5 [1]	5 [1]	Porcins
Horses	450	437	415	391	345	330	330 [1]	330 [1]	Chevaux
Asses	841	809	731	689	640	603	603 [1]	603 [1]	Anes
Mules	172	169	169	154	142	133	133 [1]	133 [1]	Mulets
Turkmenistan									**Turkménistan**
Cattle and buffaloes	1 104	1 181	1 199	* 959	950 [1]	880 [1]	850 [1]	860 [1]	Bovins et buffles
Sheep and goats	* 6 314	* 6 503	* 6 574	* 5 775	5 870 [1]	6 025 [1]	5 968 [1]	6 375 [1]	Ovins et caprins
Pigs	159	128	82	65 [1]	55 [1]	48 [1]	46 [1]	45 [1]	Porcins
Horses [1]	20	18	17	17	16	16	16	17	Chevaux [1]
Asses [1]	25	25	26	26	25	25	24	25	Anes [1]
United Arab Emirates									**Emirats arabes unis**
Cattle and buffaloes	65	69	74	* 79	98	106	110 [1]	110 [1]	Bovins et buffles
Sheep and goats	1 194	1 277	1 367	* 1 398 [1]	1 565	1 674	1 667 [1]	1 667 [1]	Ovins et caprins
Uzbekistan									**Ouzbékistan**
Cattle and buffaloes	5 431	5 484	5 204	5 100	5 200	5 225	5 268	5 344	Bovins et buffles
Sheep and goats	* 10 400	10 049	* 9 322	* 8 200	* 8 600	* 8 724	* 8 886	* 8 930	Ovins et caprins
Pigs	391	350	208	100	70	80	80	89	Porcins
Horses	120 [1]	145	146	* 146	150 [1]	155 [1]	155 [1]	150 [1]	Chevaux
Asses [1]	162	165	168	169	165	165	160	165	Anes [1]
Viet Nam									**Viet Nam**
Cattle and buffaloes	6 444	6 602	6 754	6 848	6 939	7 019	7 025	7 150	Bovins et buffles
Sheep and goats	428	551	513	515	514	471	544	600 [1]	Ovins et caprins
Pigs	15 588	16 306	16 922	17 636	18 132	18 886	20 194	20 200	Porcins
Horses	131	127	126	120	123	150	127	190 [1]	Chevaux
Yemen									**Yémen**
Cattle and buffaloes	1 151	1 174	1 181	1 201	1 263	1 282	1 339	1 339 [1]	Bovins et buffles
Sheep and goats	6 941	7 080	7 480	8 148	8 616	8 871	9 056	9 056 [1]	Ovins et caprins
Horses [1]	3	3	3	3	3	3	3	3	Chevaux [1]
Asses	* 500	500 [1]	500 [1]	500 [1]	500 [1]	500 [1]	500 [1]	500 [1]	Anes
Europe									**Europe**
Cattle and buffaloes	187 860	178 493	172 552	164 815	156 056	150 790	146 599	144 105	**Bovins et buffles**
Sheep and goats	213 461	199 271	186 177	182 114	178 170	172 761	168 504	162 716	**Ovins et caprins**
Pigs	222 023	214 576	208 329	204 099	201 135	204 667	200 160	194 153	**Porcins**
Horses	7 758	7 860	7 807	7 712	7 379	7 092	6 978	7 010	**Chevaux**
Asses	970	935	919	914	835	819	805	789	**Anes**
Mules	314	303	288	286	272	269	265	263	**Mulets**
Albania									**Albanie**
Cattle and buffaloes	820	840	806	771	705	720	720 [1]	720 [1]	Bovins et buffles
Sheep and goats	4 177	4 130	3 232	3 006	2 923	3 061	3 061 [1]	3 061 [1]	Ovins et caprins

37
Livestock
Stocks: thousand head [*cont.*]
Cheptel
Effectifs : milliers de têtes [*suite*]

Region, country or area	1994	1995	1996	1997	1998	1999	2000	2001	Région, pays ou zone
Pigs	98	100	98	97	83	81	81[1]	81[1]	Porcins
Horses	62	71	74	70	65	65[1]	65[1]	65[1]	Chevaux
Asses[1]	113	113	113	113	113	113	113	113	Anes[1]
Mules[1]	25	25	25	25	25	25	25	25	Mulets[1]
Austria									**Autriche**
Cattle and buffaloes	2 334	2 329	2 326	2 272	2 198	* 2 172	2 172	2 155	Bovins et buffles
Sheep and goats	381	392	419	435	442	415	424	428	Ovins et caprins
Pigs	3 820	3 729	3 706	3 664	3 680	3 810	3 431	3 427	Porcins
Horses	65	67	72	73	74	75	82	85[1]	Chevaux
Belarus									**Bélarus**
Cattle and buffaloes	5 851	5 403	5 054	4 855	4 801	4 686	4 326	4 221	Bovins et buffles
Sheep and goats	301	284	262	213	186	162	150	* 191	Ovins et caprins
Pigs	4 181	4 005	3 895	3 715	3 686	3 698	3 566	3 431	Porcins
Horses	215	220	229	232	233	229	221	221[1]	Chevaux
Asses[1]	8	8	8	8	9	9	8	9	Anes[1]
Belgium-Luxembourg									**Belgique-Luxembourg**
Cattle and buffaloes	3 289	3 369	3 363	3 280	3 184	3 395	3 288	3 245	Bovins et buffles
Sheep and goats	176	170	170	174	* 166	* 171	* 166	169[1]	Ovins et caprins
Pigs	6 948	7 053	7 225	7 194	7 436	7 632	7 404	7 349	Porcins
Horses	66	66	66	67	67[1]	67[1]	67[1]	67[1]	Chevaux
Bosnia and Herzegovina									**Bosnie-Herzégovine**
Cattle and buffaloes[1]	571	520	391	413	* 427	* 443	* 463	441	Bovins et buffles[1]
Sheep and goats	600[1]	520[1]	473[1]	378[1]	* 581	* 633	* 662	640[1]	Ovins et caprins
Pigs	300[1]	290[1]	180[1]	162[1]	* 373	350[1]	355[1]	330[1]	Porcins
Horses	17[1]	18[1]	18	19	19	20[1]	* 18	18[1]	Chevaux
Bulgaria									**Bulgarie**
Cattle and buffaloes	768	652	645	593	622	681	691	649[1]	Bovins et buffles
Sheep and goats	4 440	4 193	4 216	3 868	3 814	3 822	3 595	3 256	Ovins et caprins
Pigs	2 071	1 986	2 140	1 500	1 480	1 721	1 512	1 144	Porcins
Horses	113	133	151	170	126	133	141	140	Chevaux
Asses	297	276	281	287	225	221	208	196	Anes
Mules	23	16	17	17	17	16[1]	16[1]	16[1]	Mulets
Croatia									**Croatie**
Cattle and buffaloes	519	493	462	451	443	439	427	438	Bovins et buffles
Sheep and goats	552	560	532	552	511	566	608[1]	619[1]	Ovins et caprins
Pigs	1 347	1 175	1 196	1 175	1 166	1 362	1 233	1 234	Porcins
Horses	22	21	21	19	16	13	11	11[1]	Chevaux
Asses	7	4[1]	4[1]	4[1]	4[1]	4[1]	4[1]	4[1]	Anes
Czech Republic									**République tchèque**
Cattle and buffaloes	2 161	2 030	1 989	1 866	1 701	1 657	1 574	1 582	Bovins et buffles
Sheep and goats	241	210	176	159	128	120	116	119	Ovins et caprins
Pigs	4 071	3 867	4 016	4 080	4 013	4 001	3 688	3 594	Porcins
Horses	18	19	19	19	20	23	24	24[1]	Chevaux
Denmark									**Danemark**
Cattle and buffaloes	2 105	2 091	2 093	2 004	1 977	1 887	1 868	* 1 891	Bovins et buffles
Sheep and goats	145	145	170	142	156	143	145	145[1]	Ovins et caprins
Pigs	10 923	11 084	10 842	11 383	12 095	11 626	11 922	* 12 125	Porcins
Horses	18	18	20	39	38	40	40[1]	40[1]	Chevaux
Estonia									**Estonie**
Cattle and buffaloes	463	420	370	343	326	308	267	253	Bovins et buffles
Sheep and goats	83	62	50	39	36	29	28	29	Ovins et caprins
Pigs	424	460	449	298	306	326	286	300	Porcins
Horses	5	5	5	4	4	4	4	4	Chevaux
Faeroe Islands[1]									**Iles Féroé**[1]
Cattle and buffaloes	2	2	2	2	2	2	2	2	Bovins et buffles
Sheep and goats	68	68	68	68	68	68	68	68	Ovins et caprins
Finland									**Finlande**
Cattle and buffaloes	1 230	1 185	1 179	1 150	1 101	1 087	1 068	1 085[1]	Bovins et buffles
Sheep and goats	84	85	120	157	135	115	108[1]	108[1]	Ovins et caprins
Pigs	1 300	1 295	1 395	1 467	1 401	1 351	1 296	1 300[1]	Porcins
Horses	49	50	52	55	56	56	58	57[1]	Chevaux

37

Livestock
Stocks: thousand head [*cont.*]
Cheptel
Effectifs : milliers de têtes [*suite*]

Region, country or area	1994	1995	1996	1997	1998	1999	2000	2001	Région, pays ou zone
France									**France**
Cattle and buffaloes	20 099	20 524	20 661	20 664	20 023	20 265	20 527	20 500[1]	Bovins et buffles
Sheep and goats	12 560	11 389	11 744	11 665	11 516	11 439	11 195	11 200[1]	Ovins et caprins
Pigs	14 291	14 593	14 530	14 976	14 501	14 682	14 635	14 635[1]	Porcins
Horses	332	338	338	340	347	348	349	349[1]	Chevaux
Asses[1]	18	18	18	17	17	16	16	16	Anes[1]
Mules	13	13	14	14	14	14	15	15[1]	Mulets
Germany									**Allemagne**
Cattle and buffaloes	15 897	15 962	15 890	15 760	15 227	14 942	14 658	14 568	Bovins et buffles
Sheep and goats	2 461	2 435	2 495	2 429	2 417	2 405	2 285	2 280	Ovins et caprins
Pigs	26 075	24 698	23 737	24 283	24 795	26 294	26 001	25 767	Porcins
Horses	599	652	652	670	600	524	476	* 520	Chevaux
Greece									**Grèce**
Cattle and buffaloes	580	579	582	581	581	584[1]	591[1]	* 586[1]	Bovins et buffles
Sheep and goats	14 084	14 181	14 394	14 466	14 484	14 450	* 14 334	14 300[1]	Ovins et caprins
Pigs	1 014	1 009	994	987	998	933	906	* 905	Porcins
Horses	38	36	35	33	32	31	33[1]	33[1]	Chevaux
Asses	103	95	89	83	78	73	72[1]	72[1]	Anes
Mules	47	44	41	39	37	35	35[1]	35[1]	Mulets
Hungary									**Hongrie**
Cattle and buffaloes	999	910	928	909	871	873	857	805	Bovins et buffles
Sheep and goats	1 288	999	1 065	980	987	1 058	1 123	1 279[1]	Ovins et caprins
Pigs	5 002	4 356	5 032	5 289	4 931	5 479	5 335	4 834	Porcins
Horses	72	78	71	79	72	70	65[1]	70	Chevaux
Asses[1]	4	4	4	4	4	4	4	4	Anes[1]
Iceland									**Islande**
Cattle and buffaloes	72	73	75	75	76	75	72	72[1]	Bovins et buffles
Sheep and goats	499	459	464	478	490	491	466	465[1]	Ovins et caprins
Pigs[1]	41	42	43	43	43	44	44	44	Porcins[1]
Horses	79	78	81	80	78	77	74	78[1]	Chevaux
Ireland									**Irlande**
Cattle and buffaloes	6 308	6 410	6 532	6 757	6 992	7 093	6 708	6 459	Bovins et buffles
Sheep and goats	5 991	5 775	5 583	5 391	5 634	5 624	5 393	5 130	Ovins et caprins
Pigs	1 487	1 498	1 542	1 665	1 717	1 801	1 763	1 732	Porcins
Horses	48[1]	40[1]	45[1]	52[1]	50[1]	76	70	70[1]	Chevaux
Asses[1]	10	10	10	10	10	10	10	10	Anes[1]
Mules[1]	1	1	1	1	1	1	1	1	Mulets[1]
Italy									**Italie**
Cattle and buffaloes	7 560	7 272	7 414	7 313	7 328	7 315	7 363	7 401	Bovins et buffles
Sheep and goats	11 839	12 129	12 041	12 363	12 241	12 225	12 414	12 464	Ovins et caprins
Pigs	8 348	8 023	8 061	8 171	8 281	8 323	8 415	8 329	Porcins
Horses	323	324	315	305[1]	290[1]	288[1]	280[1]	285[1]	Chevaux
Asses	33	* 30	26	25[1]	23[1]	23[1]	23[1]	23[1]	Anes
Mules	17	16	12	12[1]	11[1]	10[1]	10[1]	10[1]	Mulets
Latvia									**Lettonie**
Cattle and buffaloes	678	551	537	509	477	434	378	367	Bovins et buffles
Sheep and goats	120	94	81	49	38	37	35	39	Ovins et caprins
Pigs	482	501	553	460	430	421	405	394	Porcins
Horses	26	27	27	26	23	19	19	20	Chevaux
Liechtenstein[1]									**Liechtenstein[1]**
Cattle and buffaloes	6	6	6	6	6	6	6	6	Bovins et buffles
Sheep and goats	3	3	3	3	3	3	3	3	Ovins et caprins
Pigs	3	3	3	3	3	3	3	3	Porcins
Lithuania									**Lituanie**
Cattle and buffaloes	1 384	1 152	1 065	1 054	1 016	923	898	748	Bovins et buffles
Sheep and goats	55	52	47	45	43	40	39	35	Ovins et caprins
Pigs	1 196	1 260	1 270	1 128	1 200	1 159	936	856	Porcins
Horses	81	78	78	81	78	74	75	68	Chevaux
Malta									**Malte**
Cattle and buffaloes	20	19	21	21[1]	19[1]	20[1]	19	19	Bovins et buffles
Sheep and goats	25[1]	25	25	25[1]	25[1]	25[1]	25[1]	25[1]	Ovins et caprins
Pigs	111[1]	103	69	70[1]	70[1]	70[1]	80	80	Porcins

37

Livestock

Stocks: thousand head [*cont.*]

Cheptel

Effectifs : milliers de têtes [*suite*]

Region, country or area	1994	1995	1996	1997	1998	1999	2000	2001	Région, pays ou zone
Horses [1]	1	1	1	1	1	1	1	1	Chevaux [1]
Asses [1]	1	1	1	1	1	1	1	1	Anes [1]
Netherlands									**Pays-Bas**
Cattle and buffaloes	4 716	4 654	4 557	4 411	4 283	4 206	4 097	4 050 [1]	Bovins et buffles
Sheep and goats	1 830	1 750	1 729	1 584	1 526	1 554	1 487	1 580 [1]	Ovins et caprins
Pigs	14 565	14 397	* 13 958	* 14 253	13 446	13 567	13 139	12 822	Porcins
Horses	97	100	107	112	114	116	116 [1]	116 [1]	Chevaux
Norway									**Norvège**
Cattle and buffaloes	980	998	1 006	1 018	1 036	1 047	1 019	980	Bovins et buffles
Sheep and goats	2 524	2 586	2 620	2 511	2 481	2 348	2 385	2 451	Ovins et caprins
Pigs	748	768	768 [1]	692	689	439	412	391	Porcins
Horses	22	22	23	24	26	26 [1]	26 [1]	26 [1]	Chevaux
Poland									**Pologne**
Cattle and buffaloes	7 696	7 306	7 136	7 307	7 029	6 455	6 093	5 723	Bovins et buffles
Sheep and goats	870	713	552	491	453	392	372	337	Ovins et caprins
Pigs	19 467	20 418	17 964	18 135	19 168	18 538	18 224	16 992	Porcins
Horses	622	636	569	558	561	551	550	550 [1]	Chevaux
Portugal									**Portugal**
Cattle and buffaloes	* 1 323	* 1 329	* 1 324	* 1 311	* 1 285	* 1 267	* 1 245	1 250 [1]	Bovins et buffles
Sheep and goats	6 827	6 719 [1]	6 599 [1]	7 081 [1]	6 585 [1]	6 600 [1]	6 660 [1]	6 660 [1]	Ovins et caprins
Pigs	2 666	2 430	2 375	2 394	2 385	2 350	* 2 330	2 350 [1]	Porcins
Horses [1]	25	23	25	22	24	19	17	17	Chevaux [1]
Asses [1]	160	160	150	150	140	135	135	130	Anes [1]
Mules [1]	70	70	60	60	50	50	45	45	Mulets [1]
Republic of Moldova									**République de Moldova**
Cattle and buffaloes	916	832	726	646	551	452	416	402	Bovins et buffles
Sheep and goats	1 445	1 507	1 423	1 372	1 128	* 1 105	* 1 069	* 959	Ovins et caprins
Pigs	1 165	1 061	1 015	950	798	807	705	543	Porcins
Horses	55	59	61	63	66	68 [1]	68 [1]	68 [1]	Chevaux
Asses	2	2 [1]	2 [1]	2 [1]	2 [1]	2 [1]	2 [1]	2 [1]	Anes
Romania									**Roumanie**
Cattle and buffaloes	3 957	3 481	3 496	3 435	3 235	3 143	3 051	2 965	Bovins et buffles
Sheep and goats	12 275	11 642	11 086	10 317	9 547	8 994	8 679	* 8 374	Ovins et caprins
Pigs	9 262	7 758	7 960	8 235	7 097	7 194	5 848	5 076	Porcins
Horses	751	784	806	816	822	839	858	858 [1]	Chevaux
Asses [1]	33	32	31	30	31	31	31	31	Anes [1]
Russian Federation									**Fédération de Russie**
Cattle and buffaloes	48 932	43 320	39 720	35 124	31 536	28 496	27 516 [1]	27 316 [1]	Bovins et buffles
Sheep and goats	43 713	34 540	28 027	22 772	18 774	15 556	* 15 720	* 15 700	Ovins et caprins
Pigs	28 557	24 859	22 631	19 115	17 348	17 248	18 300	15 700	Porcins
Horses	2 500	2 431	2 363	2 197	2 013	1 800	1 750 [1]	1 750 [1]	Chevaux
Asses	26	26 [1]	27 [1]	26 [1]	25 [1]	25 [1]	25 [1]	25 [1]	Anes
Serbia and Montenegro									**Serbie-et-Monténégro**
Cattle and buffaloes	1 832	1 968	1 944	1 915	1 910	1 852	1 481	1 860 [1]	Bovins et buffles
Sheep and goats	2 914	3 004	2 966	2 859	2 714	2 521	2 158	2 158 [1]	Ovins et caprins
Pigs	3 693	4 192	4 446	4 216	4 150	4 372	4 087	4 372 [1]	Porcins
Horses	82	96	93	90	86	76	76 [1]	76 [1]	Chevaux
Slovakia									**Slovaquie**
Cattle and buffaloes	993	916	929	892	803	705	665	646	Bovins et buffles
Sheep and goats	436	422	453	445	444	377	391	399	Ovins et caprins
Pigs	2 179	2 037	2 076	1 985	1 810	1 593	1 562	1 488	Porcins
Horses	11	10	10	10	10	10 [1]	10 [1]	10 [1]	Chevaux
Slovenia									**Slovénie**
Cattle and buffaloes	478	477	496	486	446	453	471	494	Bovins et buffles
Sheep and goats	39	50	52	74	88	89	87	118	Ovins et caprins
Pigs	592	571	592	552	578	592	558	604	Porcins
Horses	9	8	8	8	10	12	14	14 [1]	Chevaux
Spain									**Espagne**
Cattle and buffaloes	5 018	5 248	5 512	5 925	5 884	5 951	6 291	6 164	Bovins et buffles
Sheep and goats	26 819	26 215	23 928	26 917	27 864	26 969	26 592	27 230	Ovins et caprins
Pigs	18 234	19 288	18 731	18 517	19 397	21 668	21 526	23 348	Porcins
Horses	248	248	248	248	248	248	248 [1]	248 [1]	Chevaux

37

Livestock
Stocks: thousand head [*cont.*]
Cheptel
Effectifs : milliers de têtes [*suite*]

Region, country or area	1994	1995	1996	1997	1998	1999	2000	2001	Région, pays ou zone
Asses	140	140	140	140	140	140	140[1]	140[1]	Anes
Mules	117	117	117	117	117	117	117	115[1]	Mulets
Sweden									**Suède**
Cattle and buffaloes	1 827	1 777	1 790	1 781	1 739	1 713	1 684	1 652	Bovins et buffles
Sheep and goats	484	462	469	442	421	437	432	452	Ovins et caprins
Pigs	2 328	2 313	2 349	2 351	2 286	2 115	1 918	1 891	Porcins
Horses	86	83	85[1]	87	87[1]	87[1]	87[1]	87[1]	Chevaux
Switzerland									**Suisse**
Cattle and buffaloes	1 755	1 756	1 772	1 673	1 641	1 609	1 588	1 611	Bovins et buffles
Sheep and goats	496	489	495	478	482	485	483	528	Ovins et caprins
Pigs	1 660	1 611	1 580	1 395	1 487	1 452	1 498	1 556	Porcins
Horses	51[1]	46[1]	43	46	46[1]	46[1]	45[1]	45[1]	Chevaux
Asses[1]	2	2	2	2	2	2	2	2	Anes[1]
TFYR of Macedonia									**L'ex-R.y. Macédoine**
Cattle and buffaloes	281	282	284	296	298	291	* 281[1]	* 266[1]	Bovins et buffles
Sheep and goats	2 459	2 466	2 320	1 814	1 805	1 550	* 1 400	1 251	Ovins et caprins
Pigs	185	172	175	192	184	197	* 200	204	Porcins
Horses	62	62	66	66	60	60	60[1]	60[1]	Chevaux
Ukraine									**Ukraine**
Cattle and buffaloes	21 607	19 624	17 557	15 313	12 759	11 722	10 627	9 914	Bovins et buffles
Sheep and goats	6 863	5 575	4 099	3 047	2 362	2 026	1 885	* 1 770	Ovins et caprins
Pigs	15 298	13 946	13 144	11 236	9 479	10 083	10 073	9 078	Porcins
Horses	716	737	756	754	737	721	698	675[1]	Chevaux
Asses[1]	15	15	14	13	13	12	12	12	Anes[1]
United Kingdom									**Royaume-Uni**
Cattle and buffaloes	11 834	11 733	11 913	11 633	11 519	11 423	11 133	10 600	Bovins et buffles
Sheep and goats	43 295	42 771	41 530	42 823	44 471	44 656	42 261	36 697	Ovins et caprins
Pigs	7 892	7 627	7 590	8 072	8 146	7 284	6 482	5 845	Porcins
Horses[1]	174	175	176	177	178	180	182	184	Chevaux[1]
Oceania									**Océanie**
Cattle and buffaloes	**35 403**	**35 762**	**36 155**	**36 687**	**36 485**	**36 288**	**37 464**	**37 722**	**Bovins et buffles**
Sheep and goats	**182 845**	**170 461**	**169 243**	**167 805**	**164 198**	**161 828**	**164 624**	**164 685**	**Ovins et caprins**
Pigs	**5 205**	**5 146**	**5 071**	**5 127**	**5 333**	**5 242**	**5 052**	**5 094**	**Porcins**
Horses	**412**	**402**	**392**	**392**	**382**	**376**	**376**	**376**	**Chevaux**
Asses	**9**	**9**	**9**	**9**	**9**	**9**	**9**	**9**	**Anes**
American Samoa[1]									**Samoa américaines**[1]
Pigs	11	11	11	11	11	11	11	11	Porcins
Australia									**Australie**
Cattle and buffaloes	25 758	25 731	26 377	26 780	26 852	26 578	27 588	27 588[1]	Bovins et buffles
Sheep and goats	132 801	121 092[1]	121 346[1]	120 458[1]	117 711	115 656[1]	118 752[1]	120 200[1]	Ovins et caprins
Pigs	2 775	2 653	2 526	2 555	2 768	2 626	2 433	2 433[1]	Porcins
Horses[1]	250	240	230	230	220	220	220	220	Chevaux[1]
Asses[1]	2	2	2	2	2	2	2	2	Anes[1]
Cook Islands									**Iles Cook**
Sheep and goats	8	7	3	3[1]	3[1]	3[1]	3[1]	3[1]	Ovins et caprins
Pigs	28	32	40	40[1]	40[1]	40[1]	40[1]	40[1]	Porcins
Fiji									**Fidji**
Cattle and buffaloes	334	354	350[1]	350[1]	345	330[1]	335[1]	340[1]	Bovins et buffles
Sheep and goats	211	218	214	237	242[1]	244[1]	248[1]	253[1]	Ovins et caprins
Pigs	115	121	120[1]	115[1]	112	146	135	137	Porcins
Horses[1]	44	44	44	44	44	44	44	44	Chevaux[1]
French Polynesia									**Polynésie française**
Cattle and buffaloes	7	8[1]	6[1]	8[1]	9[1]	10[1]	10[1]	10[1]	Bovins et buffles
Sheep and goats	16	16[1]	16[1]	16[1]	16[1]	17[1]	17[1]	17[1]	Ovins et caprins
Pigs	40	39[1]	37[1]	35[1]	35[1]	37[1]	37[1]	37[1]	Porcins
Horses[1]	2	2	2	2	2	2	2	2	Chevaux[1]
Guam[1]									**Guam**[1]
Sheep and goats	1	1	1	1	1	1	1	1	Ovins et caprins
Pigs	4	4	4	4	4	5	5	5	Porcins
Kiribati									**Kiribati**
Pigs	9[1]	9[1]	10[1]	10[1]	10[1]	10	12[1]	13[1]	Porcins

37

Livestock

Stocks: thousand head [*cont.*]

Cheptel

Effectifs : milliers de têtes [*suite*]

Region, country or area	1994	1995	1996	1997	1998	1999	2000	2001	Région, pays ou zone
Micronesia (Fed. States)[1]									**Micronésie (Etats féd. de)**[1]
Cattle and buffaloes	...	14	14	14	14	14	14	14	Bovins et buffles
Sheep and goats	...	4	4	4	4	4	4	4	Ovins et caprins
Pigs	...	32	32	32	32	32	32	32	Porcins
Nauru[1]									**Nauru**[1]
Pigs	3	3	3	3	3	3	3	3	Porcins
New Caledonia									**Nouvelle-Calédonie**
Cattle and buffaloes	113	110[1]	120[1]	120[1]	122[1]	124[1]	122[1]	123[1]	Bovins et buffles
Sheep and goats[1]	16	16	3	3	2	2	2	2	Ovins et caprins[1]
Pigs[1]	38	37	38	38	40	38	40	40	Porcins[1]
Horses[1]	12	12	12	12	12	12	12	12	Chevaux[1]
New Zealand									**Nouvelle-Zélande**
Cattle and buffaloes	8 887	9 272	9 017	9 145	8 873	8 960	9 120	9 370	Bovins et buffles
Sheep and goats	49 750	49 072	47 622	47 049	46 184	45 866	45 562	44 170	Ovins et caprins
Pigs	423	431	424	407	351	369	369	354	Porcins
Horses[1]	85	85	85	85	85	80	80	80	Chevaux[1]
Niue[1]									**Nioué**[1]
Pigs	2	2	2	2	2	2	2	2	Porcins
Papua New Guinea									**Papouasie-Nvl-Guinée**
Cattle and buffaloes	93[1]	90[1]	88[1]	87	86[1]	87[1]	87[1]	88[1]	Bovins et buffles
Sheep and goats	7[1]	7[1]	6[1]	* 8	8[1]	8[1]	8[1]	8[1]	Ovins et caprins
Pigs	1 300[1]	1 400[1]	1 450[1]	1 500	1 550[1]	1 550[1]	1 550[1]	1 600[1]	Porcins
Horses[1]	2	2	2	2	2	2	2	2	Chevaux[1]
Samoa									**Samoa**
Cattle and buffaloes	26[1]	26[1]	26[1]	26[1]	27[1]	28	* 28	28[1]	Bovins et buffles
Pigs	179[1]	170[1]	170[1]	170[1]	170[1]	167	170[1]	170[1]	Porcins
Horses	3[1]	3[1]	2[1]	2[1]	2[1]	2	2[1]	2[1]	Chevaux
Asses[1]	7	7	7	7	7	7	7	7	Anes[1]
Solomon Islands[1]									**Iles Salomon**[1]
Cattle and buffaloes	10	10	10	10	10	10	11	13	Bovins et buffles
Pigs	55	55	56	57	57	58	64	67	Porcins
Tokelau[1]									**Tokélaou**[1]
Pigs	1	1	1	1	1	1	1	1	Porcins
Tonga									**Tonga**
Cattle and buffaloes	10[1]	9	10[1]	10[1]	10[1]	10	11[1]	11[1]	Bovins et buffles
Sheep and goats	14[1]	14	13[1]	12[1]	12[1]	* 12	13[1]	13[1]	Ovins et caprins
Pigs	94[1]	81	81[1]	81[1]	81[1]	81[1]	81[1]	81[1]	Porcins
Horses[1]	11	11	11	11	11	11	11	11	Chevaux[1]
Tuvalu									**Tuvalu**
Pigs[1]	13	13	13	13	13	13	13	13	Porcins[1]
Vanuatu									**Vanuatu**
Cattle and buffaloes	* 151	* 151	151[1]	151[1]	151[1]	151[1]	151[1]	151[1]	Bovins et buffles
Sheep and goats	12	12	12[1]	12[1]	12[1]	12[1]	12[1]	12[1]	Ovins et caprins
Pigs	60	60	61[1]	61[1]	62[1]	62[1]	62[1]	62[1]	Porcins
Horses[1]	3	3	3	3	3	3	3	3	Chevaux[1]
Wallis and Futuna Is.[1]									**Iles Wallis et Futuna**[1]
Sheep and goats	7	7	7	7	7	7	7	7	Ovins et caprins
Pigs	25	25	25	25	25	25	25	25	Porcins

Source:
Food and Agriculture Organization of the United Nations (FAO), Rome, "FAO Production Yearbook 2001" and the FAOSTAT database.

1 FAO estimate.
2 Data refer to the Gaza Strip.

Source:
Organisation des Nations Unies pour l'alimentation et l'agriculture (FAO), Rome, "Annuaire FAO de la production 2001" et la base de données FAOSTAT.

1 Estimation de la FAO.
2 Les données se rapportent à la Bande de Gaza.

38

Roundwood
Production (solid volume of roundwood without bark): million cubic metres

Bois rond
Production (volume solide de bois rond sans écorce) : millions de mètres cubes

Region, country or area Région, pays ou zone	1992	1993	1994	1995	1996	1997	1998	1999	2000	2001
World **Monde**	**3 201.4**	**3 188.6**	**3 194.1**	**3 244.1**	**3 237.5**	**3 307.7**	**3 224.0**	**3 333.6**	**3 377.3**	**3 327.6**
Africa **Afrique**	**522.4**	**538.1**	**551.1**	**568.3**	**576.2**	**582.5**	**584.9**	**588.4**	**595.4**	**602.6**
Algeria Algérie	6.3	6.6	6.7	6.8	7.0	7.2	7.3	7.4	7.2	7.4
Angola Angola	3.4	3.7	3.7	3.8	3.9	4.0	4.1	4.2	4.3	4.4
Benin Bénin	6.0 [1]	6.0 [1]	6.1 [1]	6.1	6.2	6.2	6.2	6.2	6.2 [1]	6.3 [1]
Botswana [1] Botswana [1]	0.7	0.7	0.7	0.7	0.7	0.7	0.7	0.7	0.7	0.7
Burkina Faso Burkina Faso	10.0 [1]	10.3 [1]	10.6	10.8	11.0	11.1	11.3	7.8	8.0	11.8 [1]
Burundi Burundi	6.1	6.3	6.6	6.8	7.1	7.4 [1]	7.7	5.6	5.8	8.3 [1]
Cameroon Cameroun	11.0	11.3	11.9	12.3	12.6	12.2	11.1	10.9	11.0	11.0
Central African Rep. Rép. centrafricaine	3.7	3.7	3.6	3.6	3.2	3.4	3.5	2.9	3.0	3.1
Chad Tchad	5.4	5.6	5.8 [1]	5.9 [1]	6.0 [1]	6.2 [1]	6.3 [1]	6.5 [1]	6.6 [1]	6.8 [1]
Congo Congo	2.3	2.3	2.4	2.5	2.2	2.7	2.7	2.4	2.4	2.4
Côte d'Ivoire Côte d'Ivoire	10.9	11.2	11.9	11.9	11.7	11.6	11.8	11.7	11.9	12.1
Dem. Rep. of the Congo Rép. dém. du Congo	52.9	57.0	60.1	62.1	63.7	64.9	66.0	67.3 [1]	68.6 [1]	69.7 [1]
Egypt Egypte	14.7 [1]	15.1 [1]	15.4 [1]	15.5 [1]	15.8	16.0 [1]	16.1	16.3	16.4	16.6 [1]
Equatorial Guinea Guinée équatoriale	0.6	0.6	0.7	0.8	0.8 [1]	0.8 [1]	0.8 [1]	0.8 [1]	0.8 [1]	0.8 [1]
Eritrea Erythrée	...	1.7	1.8	1.9	1.9	2.0	2.1	2.2	2.2 [1]	2.3 [1]
Ethiopia incl. Eritrea Ethiopie comp. Erythrée	79.1	...	...	...	...	...	...	...	...	...
Ethiopia Ethiopie	...	78.5	80.8	82.5	83.7	85.5	86.5	88.2	89.9	91.3
Gabon Gabon	2.0	2.3	2.6	2.8	2.9	3.3	3.3 [1]	2.8	3.1	3.1 [1]
Gambia Gambie	0.6 [1]	0.6	0.6	0.6	0.6	0.6	0.6	0.6	0.7 [1]	0.7 [1]
Ghana Ghana	16.3	19.9	22.5	22.0	21.9	22.0	21.9	21.9	21.8	22.0
Guinea Guinée	8.2	8.3	8.6	12.6 [1]	12.7 [1]	8.7	8.7	12.2 [1]	12.1 [1]	12.1 [1]
Guinea-Bissau [1] Guinée-Bissau [1]	0.6	0.6	0.6	0.6	0.6	0.6	0.6	0.6	0.6	0.6
Kenya Kenya	19.6	20.1	20.4	20.8	21.0	21.3	21.3	21.5	21.6	21.8

38
Roundwood
Production (solid volume of roundwood without bark): million cubic metres *[cont.]*
Bois rond
Production (volume solide de bois rond sans écorce) : millions de mètres cubes *[suite]*

Region, country or area Région, pays ou zone	1992	1993	1994	1995	1996	1997	1998	1999	2000	2001
Lesotho Lesotho	1.4	1.4	1.4	1.5	1.5	1.6	1.6	2.0 [1]	2.0 [1]	2.0 [1]
Liberia Libéria	4.2	3.8	3.4 [1]	3.0 [1]	3.1	3.5	4.1	4.5 [1]	5.1 [1]	5.3 [1]
Libyan Arab Jamah. [1] Jamah. arabe libyenne [1]	0.6	0.6	0.6	0.6	0.6	0.7	0.7	0.7	0.7	0.7
Madagascar Madagascar	8.9	9.1	9.4	9.8	10.1	9.2	9.2	9.5	9.7	10.0
Malawi Malawi	5.7	5.5	5.6 [1]	5.4 [1]	5.3 [1]	5.3 [1]	5.4 [1]	5.4 [1]	5.5 [1]	5.5 [1]
Mali Mali	4.5 [1]	4.6 [1]	4.8 [1]	4.8	4.9	5.0 [1]	5.0 [1]	5.1 [1]	5.1 [1]	5.2 [1]
Mauritania [1] Mauritanie [1]	1.2	1.2	1.3	1.3	1.3	1.3	1.4	1.4	1.4	1.5
Morocco Maroc	7.6	7.3	1.6	1.5	1.5	0.8	1.7	1.1	1.1	1.0
Mozambique Mozambique	16.4	16.8 [1]	17.3	17.9	17.9 [1]	18.0 [1]	18.0 [1]	18.0 [1]	18.0 [1]	18.0 [1]
Niger Niger	6.5 [1]	6.8 [1]	7.0 [1]	7.2 [1]	7.4 [1]	7.6 [1]	7.8 [1]	8.0 [1]	8.2 [1]	3.3
Nigeria Nigéria	61.1	62.3	63.8	65.0	66.2	67.7	67.8	68.3 [1]	68.8 [1]	69.1 [1]
Rwanda Rwanda	3.1	3.1	2.6	5.4	5.8	7.4	7.5	7.8	7.8 [1]	7.8 [1]
Senegal Sénégal	5.5	5.6 [1]	5.6 [1]	5.6 [1]	5.7 [1]	5.8 [1]	5.8 [1]	5.9 [1]	5.9 [1]	5.9 [1]
Sierra Leone Sierra Leone	4.7	4.6	4.5 [1]	4.7 [1]	4.7 [1]	5.1 [1]	5.2 [1]	5.3 [1]	5.5 [1]	5.5 [1]
Somalia [1] Somalie [1]	7.1	7.2	7.4	7.6	8.0	8.3	8.6	9.0	9.3	9.6
South Africa Afrique du Sud	27.9	28.2	30.5	32.0	32.4	33.2	30.6	30.6	30.6	30.6
Sudan Soudan	18.0	18.0	18.1	18.3 [1]	18.4 [1]	18.4 [1]	18.6 [1]	18.7 [1]	18.9 [1]	19.0 [1]
Swaziland Swaziland	1.5	1.5	1.5	1.5	1.5	1.5	0.9	0.9	0.9	0.9
Togo Togo	5.1	5.3	5.4	5.5	5.5	5.6	5.7	5.7	5.8	5.8
Tunisia Tunisie	2.1	2.2	2.2	2.2	2.2	2.3	2.3	2.3	2.3	2.3
Uganda Ouganda	32.7	33.4	34.4 [1]	34.9	35.4	36.0	36.4	36.9	37.3 [1]	37.8 [1]
United Rep. of Tanzania Rép.-Unie de Tanzanie	21.7	22.0	22.3	22.6	22.8	22.9	23.0	23.1	23.1	23.3
Zambia Zambie	7.6	7.9	8.3	8.2 [1]	8.1 [1]	8.0 [1]	8.0 [1]	8.1 [1]	8.1 [1]	8.1 [1]
Zimbabwe Zimbabwe	7.0	7.0	8.1	8.4	8.6	8.9	9.0	9.3	9.1	9.1
America, North Amérique du Nord	**749.3**	**751.4**	**769.6**	**777.4**	**770.8**	**769.6**	**764.5**	**783.6**	**771.9**	**751.1**

38

Roundwood

Production (solid volume of roundwood without bark): million cubic metres *[cont.]*

Bois rond

Production (volume solide de bois rond sans écorce) : millions de mètres cubes *[suite]*

Region, country or area Région, pays ou zone	1992	1993	1994	1995	1996	1997	1998	1999	2000	2001
Bahamas Bahamas	0.1	0.1	0.1	0.1	0.1	0.1	0.0	0.0	0.0	0.0
Belize [1] Belize [1]	0.2	0.2	0.2	0.2	0.2	0.2	0.2	0.2	0.2	0.2
Canada Canada	169.9	176.2	183.2	188.4	189.8	191.2	177.0	193.2	178.1	176.7
Costa Rica Costa Rica	4.6	4.6	5.1	5.2	5.2	5.2	5.2	5.2	5.2	5.2
Cuba Cuba	3.4	3.5	3.6 [1]	3.6 [1]	3.5 [1]	3.5 [1]	3.5 [1]	1.6	1.8	1.7
Dominican Republic Rép. dominicaine	0.6	0.6	0.6 [1]	0.6 [1]	0.6 [1]	0.6 [1]	0.6 [1]	0.6 [1]	0.6 [1]	0.6 [1]
El Salvador El Salvador	3.8 [1]	3.9 [1]	3.9 [1]	4.7	4.3	5.2	5.1	5.2	5.2	5.2
Guatemala Guatemala	12.2	13.0	13.4	13.6	13.5	13.8	14.1 [1]	14.7	15.0	15.3
Haiti [1] Haïti [1]	2.0	2.0	2.1	2.1	2.2	2.2	2.2	2.2	2.2	2.2
Honduras Honduras	9.1	9.1	9.3	9.1	9.3	9.4	9.5	9.6	9.5	9.6
Jamaica Jamaïque	0.7	0.6	0.7	0.6	0.8	0.8	0.8	0.9	0.9 [1]	0.9 [1]
Mexico Mexique	42.0	41.3	41.6	42.5	43.3	44.3	45.0	45.4	45.7	45.2
Nicaragua Nicaragua	5.8	5.8	5.8	5.8	5.9	5.8	5.9 [1]	5.9 [1]	6.0 [1]	5.9
Panama Panama	1.5	1.5	1.5	1.5	1.4	1.4	1.3	1.3	1.3	1.3
Trinidad and Tobago Trinité-et-Tobago	0.1	0.1	0.1	0.2	0.1	0.1	0.1	0.1	0.1	0.1
United States Etats-Unis	493.4	488.8	498.4	499.3	490.6	485.9	494.0	497.6	500.2	481.1
America, South **Amérique du Sud**	**286.5**	**289.6**	**300.4**	**306.5**	**304.8**	**303.8**	**305.5**	**331.3**	**339.3**	**340.3**
Argentina Argentine	10.4	9.8	10.1	10.6	11.4	6.9	5.7	10.6	10.0	10.0
Bolivia Bolivie	2.6	2.7	2.9	2.9	2.9	3.0	2.9	2.6	2.6	2.7
Brazil Brésil	202.5	205.7	208.9	211.1	212.3	213.5	213.7	231.6	235.4	236.4
Chile Chili	28.4	29.9	31.1	34.6	29.8	30.0	31.7	34.0	36.6	37.8
Colombia Colombie	9.7	9.6	9.5	9.5	9.5	9.6	10.1	10.6	13.1	12.5
Ecuador Equateur	6.4	4.7	9.4	10.0	10.6	11.5	10.9	10.7	10.8	10.9
French Guiana Guyane française	0.2 [1]	0.1	0.1	0.1 [1]	0.1 [1]	0.1 [1]	0.1 [1]	0.1 [1]	0.1 [1]	0.1 [1]
Guyana Guyana	1.1	1.2	1.3	1.4	1.4	1.5	1.3	1.3	1.2	1.2

38

Roundwood
Production (solid volume of roundwood without bark): million cubic metres *[cont.]*

Bois rond
Production (volume solide de bois rond sans écorce) : millions de mètres cubes *[suite]*

Region, country or area Région, pays ou zone	1992	1993	1994	1995	1996	1997	1998	1999	2000	2001
Paraguay Paraguay	8.6	8.8	9.0	9.3	9.3	9.4	9.5	9.6	9.6 [1]	9.7 [1]
Peru Pérou	7.8	8.2	9.0	8.0	7.9	8.4	9.2	9.2	9.3	8.4
Suriname Suriname	0.1	0.1	0.1	0.1	0.3	0.2	0.2	0.1	0.2	0.2
Uruguay Uruguay	4.2	4.4	4.5	4.6	4.7	5.0	5.5	5.6	5.7	5.8
Venezuela Venezuela	4.3	4.4	4.4	4.3	4.6	4.7	4.6	5.3	4.7	4.6
Asia **Asie**	**1 057.0**	**1 058.4**	**1 053.2**	**1 052.1**	**1 066.5**	**1 071.7**	**1 044.4**	**1 037.0**	**1 020.0**	**1 011.5**
Afghanistan [1] Afghanistan [1]	2.3	2.4	2.5	2.6	2.7	2.8	2.9	3.0	3.0	3.1
Armenia Arménie	...	...	...	...	...	0.1	...	...	0.1	0.0
Bangladesh Bangladesh	28.6	28.6	28.6	28.5	28.5	28.5	28.5	28.5	28.5	28.4
Bhutan Bhoutan	4.0	3.9	3.9 [1]	3.9 [1]	4.0 [1]	4.0 [1]	4.1 [1]	4.3	4.4	4.4 [1]
Brunei Darussalam Brunéi Darussalam	0.2	0.2	0.2 [1]	0.2 [1]	0.2 [1]	0.2 [1]	0.2 [1]	0.2 [1]	0.2 [1]	0.2 [1]
Cambodia Cambodge	11.8	11.8	12.1	12.0	11.9 [1]	11.8 [1]	11.6 [1]	11.2	10.3	10.0
China Chine	289.0	298.8	303.5	305.7	312.8	311.2	298.5	291.4	287.5	284.9
Cyprus Chypre	0.0	0.1	0.0	0.0	0.0	0.0	0.0	0.0	0.0	0.0
India Inde	308.5	311.3	312.8	313.4	296.8	296.5	296.3	296.7	296.2	296.2
Indonesia Indonésie	158.8	154.8	148.2	143.6	143.1	139.1	135.6	130.2	122.5	119.2
Iran (Islamic Rep. of) Iran (Rép. islamique d')	1.4	1.6	1.6	1.5	1.4	1.5	1.3	1.1	1.1	1.3
Iraq Iraq	0.1 [1]	0.1 [1]	0.1 [1]	0.1 [1]	0.1 [1]	0.2	0.2	0.1 [1]	0.1 [1]	0.1 [1]
Israel Israël	0.1	0.1	0.1	0.1	0.1	0.1	0.1	0.1	0.1	0.0
Japan Japon	27.3	25.7	24.6	23.1	23.2	22.3	19.6	19.0	18.1	16.2
Jordan [1] Jordanie [1]	0.1	0.2	0.2	0.2	0.2	0.1	0.2	0.2	0.2	0.2
Kazakhstan Kazakhstan	0.5	0.3	0.3	0.3	0.3	0.3	0.0 [1]	0.0 [1]	0.0 [1]	0.0 [1]
Korea, Dem. P. R. Corée, R. p. dém. de	5.2	5.4	5.5	5.6	6.1 [1]	6.5 [1]	6.9 [1]	6.9 [1]	7.0 [1]	7.1 [1]
Korea, Republic of Corée, République de	3.7	3.7	3.7	3.8	3.6	3.5	3.9	4.1	4.0	4.0
Lao People's Dem. Rep. Rép. dém. pop. lao	6.0	6.3	6.4	6.7	6.5	6.5	6.4 [1]	6.7 [1]	6.4	6.5

38

Roundwood
Production (solid volume of roundwood without bark): million cubic metres [cont.]

Bois rond
Production (volume solide de bois rond sans écorce) : millions de mètres cubes [suite]

Region, country or area Région, pays ou zone	1992	1993	1994	1995	1996	1997	1998	1999	2000	2001
Lebanon Liban	0.1	0.1	0.1 [1]	0.1 [1]	0.1 [1]	0.1 [1]	0.1 [1]	0.0	0.0	0.1 [1]
Malaysia Malaisie	48.9	41.8	40.1	39.3	35.1	36.0	26.4	26.6	18.4	16.3
Mongolia [1] Mongolie [1]	0.9	0.9	0.8	0.6	0.6	0.6	0.6	0.6	0.6	0.6
Myanmar Myanmar	21.7	21.2	20.7	21.1	21.5	34.8	34.3	37.6	38.1	39.4
Nepal Népal	13.0 [1]	13.1 [1]	13.0 [1]	13.1 [1]	13.1 [1]	13.2 [1]	13.9	13.9	14.0	14.0
Pakistan Pakistan	24.2	24.2	24.3	24.2	29.0	30.9	31.8	33.1	33.6	33.2
Philippines Philippines	18.2	17.7	17.5	17.2	40.3	41.0	42.0	43.0	44.0	44.4
Sri Lanka Sri Lanka	9.7	9.9	10.2	10.4	10.4	6.8	6.6	6.6	6.6	6.5
Syrian Arab Republic Rép. arabe syrienne	0.1	0.1	0.1 [1]	0.1 [1]	0.1 [1]	0.1 [1]	0.1 [1]	0.1 [1]	0.1 [1]	0.1 [1]
Thailand Thaïlande	24.2	24.0	23.7	23.5	23.4	23.4	23.4	23.4	26.8	27.5
Turkey Turquie	17.0	18.9	16.8	19.3	19.4	18.1	17.7	17.6	16.8	16.2
Viet Nam Viet Nam	31.2	31.2	31.2	31.6	31.6	31.3	31.0	30.2	30.9	30.8 [1]
Yemen [1] Yémen [1]	0.2	0.2	0.2	0.2	0.3	0.3	0.3	0.3	0.3	0.3
Europe **Europe**	**541.6**	**503.2**	**469.5**	**488.1**	**468.0**	**527.6**	**472.4**	**538.7**	**590.8**	**560.6**
Albania Albanie	2.6	0.6	0.4	0.4	0.4	0.4	* 0.0	0.2	0.4	0.5
Austria Autriche	12.8	12.9	15.0	14.4	15.6	15.3	14.0	14.1	13.3	13.5
Belarus Bélarus	11.4	10.0	10.0	10.0	15.7	17.6	5.9	6.6	6.1	6.3
Belgium Belgique	...	...	...	...	...	...	...	4.8	4.5 [1]	4.2
Belgium-Luxembourg Belgique-Luxembourg	4.2	4.2	4.3	4.1	4.0	4.0	4.8	...	...	...
Bosnia and Herzegovina Bosnie-Herzégovine	0.0	0.0	0.0	0.0	0.0	4.0	* 4.1	* 4.1	4.3	3.8
Bulgaria Bulgarie	3.5	3.5	2.7	2.8	3.2	3.0	3.2	4.4	4.8	4.0
Croatia Croatie	2.0	2.5	2.8	2.6	2.5	3.1	3.4	3.5	3.7	3.5
Czech Republic République tchèque	...	10.4	12.0	12.4	12.6	13.5	14.0	14.2	14.4	14.4
Denmark Danemark	2.2	2.3	2.3	2.3	2.3	2.1	1.6	1.6	3.0	1.4
Estonia Estonie	2.1	2.4	3.6	3.7	3.9	5.4	6.1	6.7	8.9	10.2

38
Roundwood
Production (solid volume of roundwood without bark): million cubic metres *[cont.]*

Bois rond
Production (volume solide de bois rond sans écorce) : millions de mètres cubes *[suite]*

Region, country or area Région, pays ou zone	1992	1993	1994	1995	1996	1997	1998	1999	2000	2001
Finland Finlande	38.5	42.2	48.7	50.2	46.6	51.3	53.7	53.6	54.3	52.2
France France	42.4	39.4	42.2	43.4	40.4	41.1	35.5	43.0	45.8	38.8
Germany Allemagne	33.0	33.2	39.8	39.3	37.0	38.2	39.1	37.6	53.7	39.5
Greece Grèce	2.3	2.2	2.1	2.0	2.0	1.7	1.7	2.2	2.2	2.2
Hungary Hongrie	5.0	4.5	4.5	4.3	3.7	4.2	4.2	5.8	5.9	5.8
Ireland Irlande	2.0	1.8	2.0	2.2	2.3	2.2	2.3	2.6	2.7	2.5
Italy Italie	8.4	8.8	9.5	9.7	9.1	9.1	9.6	11.1	9.3	7.4
Latvia Lettonie	2.5	4.9	5.7	6.9	8.1	8.7	10.0	14.0	14.3	12.8
Lithuania Lituanie	3.2	4.5	4.0	6.0	5.5	5.1	4.9	4.9	5.5	5.7
Luxembourg Luxembourg	...	...	...	...	...	...	...	0.3	0.3 [1]	0.3 [1]
Netherlands Pays-Bas	1.3	1.1	1.0	1.1	1.0	1.1	1.0	1.0	1.0	0.9
Norway Norvège	10.1	9.7	8.7	9.0	8.4	8.3	8.2	8.4	8.2	8.4
Poland Pologne	18.8	18.6	18.8	20.4	20.3	21.7	23.1	24.3	26.0	25.3
Portugal Portugal	10.3	10.2	9.8	9.4	9.0	9.0	8.5	9.0	10.8	11.3
Republic of Moldova République de Moldova	...	...	...	...	0.4	0.4	0.4	0.0	0.1	0.1
Romania Roumanie	12.4	8.8	11.9	12.2	12.3	13.5	11.6	12.7	13.1	12.4
Russian Federation Fédération de Russie	227.9	174.6	111.8	116.2	96.8	134.7	95.0	143.6	158.1	162.3
Serbia and Montenegro Serbie-et-Monténégro	2.8	2.6	2.8	3.1	3.1	2.8	2.7	2.5	3.4	2.5
Slovakia Slovaquie	...	5.2	5.3	5.3	5.5	4.9	5.5	5.3	5.2	5.2
Slovenia Slovénie	1.7	1.1	1.9	1.9	2.0	2.2	2.1	2.1	2.3	2.3
Spain Espagne	13.9	13.8	15.3	16.1	15.6	15.6	14.9	14.8	14.3	15.1
Sweden Suède	53.5	54.0	56.3	63.6	56.3	60.2	60.6	58.7	63.3	62.8
Switzerland Suisse	4.6	4.4	4.7	4.7	4.1	4.5	4.3	4.7	9.2	5.0
TFYR of Macedonia L'ex-R.y. Macédoine	...	0.9	0.8	0.8	0.8	0.8	0.7	0.8	1.1	0.7
Ukraine Ukraine	...	...	...	...	10.4	10.1	8.5	7.9	9.9	9.9 [1]

38

Roundwood
Production (solid volume of roundwood without bark): million cubic metres *[cont.]*

Bois rond
Production (volume solide de bois rond sans écorce) : millions de mètres cubes *[suite]*

Region, country or area Région, pays ou zone	1992	1993	1994	1995	1996	1997	1998	1999	2000	2001
United Kingdom Royaume-Uni	6.3	7.8	8.6	7.6	7.1	7.5	7.3	7.5	7.5	7.6
Oceania **Océanie**	**44.7**	**48.0**	**50.3**	**51.7**	**51.2**	**52.7**	**52.3**	**54.5**	**59.9**	**61.5**
Australia Australie	20.7	21.9	23.3	24.3	24.4	25.2	26.8	26.6	30.4	30.9
Fiji Fidji	0.3	0.5	0.6	0.6	0.6	0.5	0.5	0.5	0.5	0.5
New Zealand Nouvelle-Zélande	15.1	16.0	16.3	16.9	16.4	17.1	15.3	17.7	19.3	20.5
Papua New Guinea Papouasie-Nvl-Guinée	8.0	8.8	9.3	8.8	8.8	8.8	8.6	8.6	8.6	8.6
Samoa [1] Samoa [1]	0.1	0.1	0.1	0.1	0.1	0.1	0.1	0.1	0.1	0.1
Solomon Islands Iles Salomon	0.5	0.5	0.8	0.9	0.9 [1]	0.9 [1]	0.9 [1]	0.9 [1]	0.9 [1]	0.7
Vanuatu Vanuatu	0.1 [1]	0.1 [1]	0.1 [1]	0.1 [1]	0.1 [1]	0.1 [1]	0.1	0.1	0.1	0.1

Source:
Food and Agriculture Organization of the United Nations (FAO), Rome, "FAO Yearbook of Forest Products 2001" and the FAOSTAT database.

Source:
Organisation des Nations Unies pour l'alimentation et l'agriculture (FAO), Rome, "Annuaire FAO des produits forestiers 2001" et la base de données FAOSTAT.

1 FAO estimate.

1 Estimation de la FAO.

39
Fish production
Production halieutique
Capture and aquaculture: metric tons
Capture et aquaculture : tonnes

Country or area Pays ou zone	Capture production Captures					Aquaculture production Production de l'aquaculture				
	1996	1997	1998	1999	2000	1996	1997	1998	1999	2000
Afghanistan[1] Afghanistan[1]	1 300	1 250	1 200	1 200	1 000	...	...	...	...	...
Albania Albanie	2 125	1 013	2 683	2 745	3 320	323	97	124	310	307
Algeria Algérie	81 989	91 580	92 346	102 396	100 000	322	322	283	250	275
American Samoa Samoa américaines	210	420	594	504	866	...	...	...	...	...
Angola Angola	137 815	146 304	163 149	175 799	238 351	...	...	...	...	...
Anguilla Anguilla	200	250	250	250	250	...	...	...	...	...
Antigua and Barbuda Antigua-et-Barbuda	1 209	1 437	1 415	1 361	1 481	...	...	...	...	...
Argentina Argentine	1 256 270	1 361 254	1 138 689	1 037 804	917 725	1 322	1 314	1 040	1 218	1 784
Armenia Arménie	580	580	698	1 111	1 105	650	670	437	901	902
Aruba Aruba	150	205	182	175	163	...	...	...	...	...
Australia Australie	203 963	198 010	204 710	240 044	211 391	25 323	26 637	28 106	33 729	39 909
Austria Autriche	450	465	451	432	859	2 952	3 021	2 912	3 070	2 847
Azerbaijan Azerbaïdjan	6 627	5 119	4 678	20 861	18 797	419	364	211	148	120
Bahamas Bahamas	9 866	10 439	10 124	10 473	10 500	1	1	1	1	2
Bahrain Bahreïn	12 940	10 050	9 849	10 620	11 718	3	4[1]	4[1]	5	12
Bangladesh Bangladesh	814 787	829 426	839 141	959 215	1 004 264	379 088	432 135	514 842	620 114	657 121
Barbados Barbade	3 512	2 809	3 644	3 250	3 100	...	...	...	...	...
Belarus Bélarus	821	499	457	514	553	6 038	4 322	4 727	5 289	6 716
Belgium Belgique	30 823	30 500	30 835	29 876	29 800	946	846	846	1 597	1 641
Belize Belize	977	10 070	15 553	36 761	61 059	1 004	1 397	1 642	3 163	2 648
Benin Bénin	42 175	43 784	42 139	40 436	32 324	...	...	...	...	...
Bermuda Bermudes	465	461	465	452	286	...	...	...	...	...
Bhutan[1] Bhoutan[1]	300	300	300	300	300	30	30	30	30	30
Bolivia Bolivie	5 988	6 038	6 055	6 052	6 106	380	387	385	398	405

39
Fish production
Capture and aquaculture: metric tons [*cont.*]
Production halieutique
Capture et aquaculture : tonnes [*suite*]

Country or area Pays ou zone	Capture production Captures					Aquaculture production Production de l'aquaculture				
	1996	1997	1998	1999	2000	1996	1997	1998	1999	2000
Bosnia and Herzegovina Bosnie-Herzégovine	2 500	2 500	2 500	2 500	2 500	...	...	...	...	...
Botswana Botswana	81	160	191	157	166	...	...	...	...	...
Brazil Brésil	715 482	744 585	706 789	703 941	693 710	77 690	87 674	103 915	140 657	153 558
British Virgin Islands Iles Vierges britanniques	506	105	116	115	43	...	...	...	...	...
Brunei Darussalam Brunéi Darussalam	7 405	4 521	5 049	3 186	2 487	119	156	172	122	107
Bulgaria Bulgarie	8 854	11 237	18 946	10 556	6 998	4 727	5 437	4 252	7 780	3 654
Burkina Faso Burkina Faso	8 000	8 000	8 335	7 600	8 500	30	45	40	25	5
Burundi Burundi	3 041	20 296	13 426	9 199	10 000[1]	50[1]	50[1]	55[1]	55[1]	55[1]
Cambodia Cambodge	94 710	102 800	107 900	269 100	284 368	9 600	11 800	14 100	15 000	14 430
Cameroon Cameroun	98 400	102 000	106 800	110 000	112 109	58	67	67	67[1]	50
Canada Canada	904 726	971 021	1 013 810	1 027 258	993 605	72 376	81 676	91 046	113 016	123 297
Cape Verde Cap-Vert	9 155	9 627	9 461	10 371	10 821	...	...	...	...	...
Cayman Islands Iles Caïmanes	110	125	125	125	125	...	...	...	...	...
Central African Rep. Rép. centrafricaine	14 000[1]	14 250[1]	14 500[1]	15 000[1]	15 000[1]	150[1]	80	80	117	120
Chad Tchad	100 000	85 000	84 000	84 000[1]	84 000[1]	...	...	...	...	...
Channel Islands Iles Anglo-Normandes	4 346	4 238	4 117	3 601	3 589	191	130	196	249	390
Chile Chili	6 690 942	5 810 764	3 265 383	5 050 528	4 300 160	217 903	272 346	293 044	274 216	391 587
China Chine	14 182 107	15 722 344	17 229 927	17 240 032	16 987 325	17 714 570	19 315 623	20 795 367	22 789 887	24 580 671
China, Hong Kong SAR Chine, Hong Kong RAS	183 856	186 000	180 000	127 780	157 012	8 418	8 310	6 439	6 052	4 989
China, Macao SAR Chine, Macao RAS	1 418	1 500	1 500	1 500	1 500	...	...	...	...	...
Colombia Colombie	130 829	147 918	132 908	117 995	129 644	29 990	43 710	45 933	52 947	61 786
Comoros Comores	12 700	12 500	12 500	12 000	13 200	...	...	...	...	...
Congo Congo	45 473	38 082	44 455	43 696	49 980	106	99	140[1]	190	200
Cook Islands Iles Cook	900	800	700	600	500	0	0	0	0	0

39
Fish production
Capture and aquaculture: metric tons [*cont.*]
Production halieutique
Capture et aquaculture : tonnes [*suite*]

Country or area Pays ou zone	Capture production Captures					Aquaculture production Production de l'aquaculture				
	1996	1997	1998	1999	2000	1996	1997	1998	1999	2000
Costa Rica Costa Rica	23 377	24 066	20 577	24 152	27 950	6 986	7 000	7 937	9 324	9 708
Côte d'Ivoire Côte d'Ivoire	72 711	67 167	72 528	78 272	80 322	1 128	450	862	1 000	1 197
Croatia Croatie	18 233	17 035	22 318	19 280	21 388	2 889	3 510	5 958	6 228	6 674
Cuba Cuba	85 603	84 911	67 076	67 381	56 146	36 337	44 050	46 712	55 163	52 700
Cyprus Chypre	5 246	16 019	18 865	5 273	2 308	787	969	1 178	1 422	1 878
Czech Republic République tchèque	3 524	3 321	3 952	4 190	4 654	18 200	17 560	17 231	18 775	19 475
Dem. Rep. of the Congo Rép. dém. du Congo	163 010	162 211	178 041	208 448	208 448	600[1]	550[1]	500[1]	414	414
Denmark Danemark	1 681 517	1 826 852	1 557 335	1 405 005	1 534 089	41 924	39 697	42 368	42 670	43 609
Djibouti Djibouti	350	350	350	350	350	...	...	...	...	...
Dominica Dominique	1 030	1 079	1 212	1 200	1 150	4[1]	5[1]	5[1]	5[1]	7
Dominican Republic Rép. dominicaine	12 894	14 535	10 171	8 402	11 029	789	677	810	748	2 125
Ecuador Equateur	702 974	548 988	310 022	497 872	592 547	108 720	135 297	146 590	127 375	62 111
Egypt Egypte	320 230	342 759	362 741	380 504	384 314	75 837	73 454	139 389	226 276	340 093
El Salvador El Salvador	14 434	11 897	10 977	9 914	9 590	358	384	399	279	261
Equatorial Guinea Guinée équatoriale	5 040	6 090	6 005	7 001[1]	3 634	...	...	...	...	...
Eritrea Erythrée	3 252	1 038	1 629	6 891	12 612	...	...	...	...	...
Estonia Estonie	108 446	123 613	118 714	111 793	113 146	272	260	260	200	225
Ethiopia Ethiopie	8 770	10 370	14 000	15 858	15 681	38[1]	24[1]	14[1]	0	0
Faeroe Islands Iles Féroé	305 160	329 825	376 353	358 666	365 802	17 584	22 538	20 558	39 507	29 297
Falkland Is. (Malvinas) Iles Falkland (Malvinas)	31 540	17 113	43 616	39 164	62 928	...	...	...	...	...
Fiji Fidji	25 029	27 755	28 158	36 713	37 600	235	345	298	1 758	1 779
Finland Finlande	179 077	180 185	171 681	160 560	162 906	17 659	16 426	16 024	15 449	15 400
France France	559 046	568 833	544 330	588 523	596 926	285 464	287 181	267 795	264 830	267 747
French Guiana Guyane française	7 377	6 602	6 709	6 271	5 237	...	7	18	31	31

39
Fish production
Capture and aquaculture: metric tons [*cont.*]
Production halieutique
Capture et aquaculture : tonnes [*suite*]

Country or area Pays ou zone	Capture production Captures					Aquaculture production Production de l'aquaculture				
	1996	1997	1998	1999	2000	1996	1997	1998	1999	2000
French Polynesia Polynésie française	9 910	11 670	12 473	12 336	13 899	67	56	53	48	53
Gabon Gabon	46 113	43 584	53 609	51 143	47 470	62	57	158	558	558
Gambia Gambie	31 601	32 254	29 002	29 000	29 016	4	4	4	4	0
Georgia Géorgie	2 453	2 583	3 001	1 680	2 450	101	61	96	83	86
Germany Allemagne	236 411	259 352	266 622	238 925	205 689	75 237	59 433	67 020	73 567	59 891
Ghana Ghana	477 173	447 088	442 641	492 776	452 070	550	400	420	430	511
Greece Grèce	149 435	157 088	108 580	118 771	99 280	39 852	48 838	59 926	79 474	79 879
Greenland Groenland	116 018	120 596	128 590	160 253	165 000	...	...	...	...	...
Grenada Grenade	1 574	1 548	1 852	1 802	1 696	0	0	0	1	4
Guadeloupe Guadeloupe	9 570	10 480	9 084	9 114	10 100	30	20	14	20	20
Guam Guam	121	158	253	223	275	220	220	220	230	232
Guatemala Guatemala	7 653	6 896	10 847	11 028	40 078	3 421	4 407	3 124	4 850	3 963
Guinea Guinée	63 360	62 441	69 764	87 314	91 513	4	0	0	0	0
Guinea-Bissau Guinée-Bissau	7 000	7 250	6 000	5 000	5 000	...	...	...	...	...
Guyana Guyana	48 583	53 998	52 840	53 844	48 818	250	270	300	606	606
Haiti Haïti	5 245	5 301	5 259	5 000[1]	5 000[1]	...	...	...	...	...
Honduras Honduras	11 478	13 787	8 338	9 007	15 320	10 065	9 274	8 147	8 180	8 542
Hungary Hongrie	7 606	7 406	7 265	7 514	7 101	8 080	9 334	10 222	11 947	12 886
Iceland Islande	2 060 168	2 205 944	1 681 951	1 736 267	1 982 522	3 687	3 663	3 868	3 897	3 623
India Inde	3 447 954	3 523 448	3 373 492	3 472 150	3 594 396	1 783 491	1 862 288	1 902 167	2 120 316	2 095 072
Indonesia Indonésie	3 557 826	3 791 025	3 964 897	3 986 919	4 140 045	733 098	662 547	629 797	749 269	788 500
Iran (Islamic Rep. of) Iran (Rép. islamique d')	351 725	342 287	367 212	387 200	411 500	29 977	30 279	33 237	31 800	40 550
Iraq Iraq	30 737	31 302	22 574	24 606	20 766	2 500	3 400	7 500	2 183	1 745
Ireland Irlande	333 030	292 673	324 274	280 957	273 231	34 925	36 854	42 375	43 856	51 247

39
Fish production
Capture and aquaculture: metric tons [*cont.*]
Production halieutique
Capture et aquaculture : tonnes [*suite*]

Country or area Pays ou zone	Capture production Captures					Aquaculture production Production de l'aquaculture				
	1996	1997	1998	1999	2000	1996	1997	1998	1999	2000
Isle of Man Ile de Man	3 537	4 289	2 214	2 608	2 600	...	...	...	...	...
Israel Israël	5 229	5 204	6 300	5 884	5 818	17 553	18 264	18 556	18 777	20 098
Italy Italie	365 899	343 693	317 789	294 155	299 949	184 373	190 719	205 625	207 368	213 525
Jamaica Jamaïque	12 504	8 198	6 560	8 508	5 676	3 500[1]	3 450[1]	3 410	4 150	4 512
Japan Japon	5 933 661	5 926 113	5 263 384	5 201 805	4 989 354	829 354	806 534	766 812	759 262	762 824
Jordan Jordanie	440	450	470	510	550	181	200	293	515	569
Kazakhstan Kazakhstan	44 273	31 826	23 089	21 004	25 774	1 682	1 921	1 106	1 193	1 153
Kenya Kenya	180 988	161 054	172 592	205 287	215 106	579	199	153	300	512
Kiribati Kiribati	31 829	28 661	33 484	50 886	40 000	9	7	4	13	9
Korea, Dem. P. R. Corée, R. p. dém. de	253 125	236 462	220 000	210 000	200 850	80 896	70 174	68 500[1]	68 500[1]	66 700[1]
Korea, Republic of Corée, République de	2 413 713	2 204 047	2 026 934	2 119 678	1 823 175	358 046	392 367	327 462	303 106	323 218
Kuwait Koweït	8 255	7 826	7 799	6 271	6 300	90	204	220	264	376
Kyrgyzstan Kirghizistan	160	120	80	48	52	161[1]	127[1]	97[1]	71	58
Lao People's Dem. Rep.[1] Rép. dém. pop. lao	23 000	18 857	19 642	30 041	29 250	16 000	21 143	21 216	30 362	42 066
Latvia Lettonie	142 644	105 682	102 331	125 389	136 403	380	345	425	468	325
Lebanon Liban	4 135	3 655	3 520	3 560	3 666	350	300	400	300	400
Lesotho Lesotho	28[1]	30[1]	30[1]	30[1]	32[1]	14[1]	14[1]	8	4	8
Liberia Libéria	7 408	8 580	10 830	15 472	11 726	0	0	0	0	22
Libyan Arab Jamah. Jamah. arabe libyenne	32 976	31 877	32 911	32 850	33 387	100[1]	100[1]	100[1]	100[1]	100[1]
Lithuania Lituanie	88 514	44 002	66 578	33 594	78 987	1 537	1 516	1 516	1 650	1 996
Madagascar Madagascar	114 475	116 391	126 395	129 630	132 093	5 075	8 582	4 503	5 811	7 280
Malawi Malawi	63 569	56 340	41 111	45 392	45 000[1]	240	231	229	590	530
Malaysia Malaisie	1 130 372	1 172 922	1 153 719	1 251 768	1 289 245	109 063	107 984	133 635	155 127	151 773
Maldives Maldives	120 508	116 257	128 968	133 547	132 427	...	...	...	...	...

39
Fish production
Capture and aquaculture: metric tons [*cont.*]
Production halieutique
Capture et aquaculture : tonnes [*suite*]

Country or area Pays ou zone	Capture production Captures					Aquaculture production Production de l'aquaculture				
	1996	1997	1998	1999	2000	1996	1997	1998	1999	2000
Mali Mali	111 910	99 550	98 000	98 536	109 870	60	60	60	80	30
Malta Malte	9 027	875	980	1 033	1 039	1 552	1 800	1 950	2 002	1 746
Marshall Islands Iles Marshall	2 772	370	400	400	7 960	...	...	...	...	...
Martinique Martinique	3 500	5 500	5 500	6 000	6 314	58	66	55	60	51
Mauritania Mauritanie	45 482	37 267	37 916	37 811	38 096	...	...	...	...	...
Mauritius Maurice	11 869	14 025	12 093	12 312	9 299	165	118	83	85	87
Mayotte Mayotte	1 300[1]	1 600[1]	1 700[1]	2 000[1]	5 000[1]	1	2[1]	2[1]	2[1]	3[1]
Mexico Mexique	1 464 084	1 489 020	1 174 742	1 202 178	1 314 219	31 339	39 500	40 989	48 414	53 802
Micronesia (Fed. States of) Micron (Etats fédérés de)	9 724	10 332	15 523	12 205	27 974	...	...	...	...	...
Monaco[1] Monaco[1]	3	3	3	3	3	...	...	...	...	...
Mongolia Mongolie	221	180	311	524	425	...	...	...	...	...
Montserrat Montserrat	38	45	46	50	50	...	...	...	...	...
Morocco Maroc	642 886	791 906	710 436	745 431	896 620	2 057	2 184	2 104	2 720	1 847
Mozambique Mozambique	34 915	39 703	36 677	33 989	39 065	4	0	0	0	0
Myanmar Myanmar	601 788	780 295	830 117	919 410	1 069 726	71 508	82 740	81 968	91 114	98 912
Namibia Namibie	266 912	282 151	337 482	299 151	282 965	50[1]	45[1]	45[1]	45[1]	50[1]
Nauru[1] Nauru[1]	400	350	300	250	250	...	...	...	...	...
Nepal Népal	11 230	11 230	12 000	12 752	16 700	10 649	11 977	12 866	13 028	15 023
Netherlands Pays-Bas	410 798	451 799	536 626	514 611	495 804	99 871	98 210	120 094	108 785	75 339
Netherlands Antilles Antilles néerlandaises	1 000	950	950	950	19 974	4[1]	5[1]	5[1]	5[1]	5[1]
New Caledonia Nouvelle-Calédonie	2 998	2 438	3 105	3 152	3 250	1 005	1 152	1 596	1 936	1 754
New Zealand Nouvelle-Zélande	421 104	596 017	636 219	594 084	561 324	74 800	76 850	93 807	91 650	85 640
Nicaragua Nicaragua	15 442	16 176	19 892	20 569	28 008	2 299	3 452	4 788	4 198	5 429
Niger Niger	4 156	6 328	7 013	11 000	16 250	11	13	12	14	15

39
Fish production
Capture and aquaculture: metric tons [*cont.*]
Production halieutique
Capture et aquaculture : tonnes [*suite*]

Country or area Pays ou zone	Capture production Captures					Aquaculture production Production de l'aquaculture				
	1996	1997	1998	1999	2000	1996	1997	1998	1999	2000
Nigeria Nigéria	337 993	387 923	463 024	455 628	441 377	19 491	24 297	20 458	21 737	25 718
Niue Nioué	120	120	120	120	120	...	...	...	...	...
Northern Mariana Islands Iles Mariannes du Nord	225	250	235	193	189	...	...	...	...	...
Norway Norvège	2 648 457	2 863 059	2 861 223	2 620 073	2 703 415	321 516	367 617	410 748	475 830	487 920
Occupied Palestinian Terr.[2] Terr. palestinien occupé[2]	2 493	3 791	3 625	3 600	3 600	...	...	...	...	...
Oman Oman	112 477	112 338	102 536	108 808	118 855	4 968	4 698	4 081	6 454	4 851
Pakistan Pakistan	537 432	589 731	596 980	654 530	614 829	13 557	15 464	17 369	23 076	12 485
Palau Palaos	1 990	1 751	1 777	1 800	2 000	2	2	1	1	2
Panama Panama	153 564	166 159	202 687	120 577	223 502	5 079	7 217	10 161	3 236	2 394
Papua New Guinea Papouasie-Nvl-Guinée	38 865	45 276	71 252	59 725	50 537	23[1]	20[1]	17[1]	17[1]	19[1]
Paraguay Paraguay	22 000[1]	28 000[1]	25 000[1]	25 000[1]	25 000[1]	350	350	95	95[1]	103[1]
Peru Pérou	9 515 048	7 869 871	4 338 437	8 428 601	10 658 620	6 912	7 381	7 732	8 275	6 801
Philippines Philippines	1 783 601	1 805 806	1 833 458	1 872 827	1 892 832	349 442	330 441	312 077	328 375	387 680
Pitcairn Pitcairn	8	8	8	8	8	...	...	...	...	...
Poland Pologne	341 299	353 661	238 262	235 111	218 354	27 700	28 680	29 791	33 711	35 795
Portugal Portugal	260 422	221 923	224 228	208 429	187 153	5 364	7 185	7 536	6 268	7 538
Puerto Rico Porto Rico	2 701	3 187	3 006	3 020	4 154	58	13	164	138	154
Qatar Qatar	4 739	5 032	5 279	4 207	7 142	1	2	0	0	0
Republic of Moldova République de Moldova	603	569	491	129	151	1 067	1 202	1 129	1 007	1 168
Réunion Réunion	3 607	4 288	5 169	5 155	5 091	4	134	124	138	142
Romania Roumanie	18 259	8 446	9 061	7 843	7 372	13 900	11 168	9 614	8 998	9 727
Russian Federation Fédération de Russie	4 676 666	4 661 853	4 454 759	4 141 158	3 973 535	52 899	53 171	63 195	68 615	74 124
Rwanda Rwanda	2 952	4 428	6 641	6 433	6 726	100[1]	118[1]	128	300	270
Saint Helena Sainte-Hélène	744	862	1 007	572	658	...	...	...	...	...

39
Fish production
Capture and aquaculture: metric tons [*cont.*]
Production halieutique
Capture et aquaculture : tonnes [*suite*]

Country or area Pays ou zone	Capture production Captures					Aquaculture production Production de l'aquaculture				
	1996	1997	1998	1999	2000	1996	1997	1998	1999	2000
Saint Kitts and Nevis Saint-Kitts-et-Nevis	352	216	407	348	257	4[1]	4[1]	4[1]	5[1]	5[1]
Saint Lucia Sainte-Lucie	1 274	1 311	1 314	1 718	1 759	2	3	2	1	1
Saint Pierre and Miquelon Saint-Pierre-et-Miquelon	747	3 571	6 108	5 892	6 485	...	...	...	...	...
St. Vincent-Grenadines St. Vincent-Grenadines	921	6 092	33 891	15 573	7 294	...	...	...	...	...
Samoa Samoa	2 727	7 041	7 547	10 204	13 004	0	1	0	0	0
Sao Tome and Principe Sao Tomé-et-Principe	3 980	3 338	3 477	3 756	3 500	...	...	...	...	...
Saudi Arabia Arabie saoudite	47 698	49 314	51 206	46 618	49 650	3 835	4 690	5 101	5 052	6 004
Senegal Sénégal	411 759	457 366	403 872	412 125	402 047	78	74	23	155	155
Serbia and Montenegro Serbie-et-Monténégro	4 030	3 873	2 610	1 251	1 096	2 896	3 493	6 560	3 435	2 843
Seychelles Seychelles	4 707	14 043	23 885	34 050	40 183	278	584	649	227	425
Sierra Leone Sierra Leone	67 304	72 628	63 065	59 407	74 730	30[1]	30[1]	30[1]	30[1]	30[1]
Singapore Singapour	9 943	9 250	7 733	6 489	5 371	3 567	4 088	3 706	4 029	5 112
Slovakia Slovaquie	1 456	1 434	1 414	1 391	2 255	954	1 254	648	872	887
Slovenia Slovénie	2 343	2 345	2 210	2 009	1 859	869	917	909	1 206	1 181
Solomon Islands Iles Salomon	50 490	63 005	60 332	57 428	23 443	13	13	13	13	15
Somalia[1] Somalie[1]	26 050	24 150	22 250	20 250	20 200	...	...	...	...	...
South Africa Afrique du Sud	440 428	514 826	559 390	588 644	643 812	2 981	4 186	5 072	4 143	3 951
Spain Espagne	1 168 943	1 199 141	1 262 954	1 190 071	976 910	231 633	239 136	315 477	321 145	312 171
Sri Lanka Sri Lanka	228 945	235 099	269 443	294 819	300 316	6 102	6 440	10 020	8 305	12 360
Sudan Soudan	45 000	47 000	49 500	49 500	50 000[1]	1 000[1]	1 000	1 000	1 000	1 000
Suriname Suriname	13 000	14 000	16 195	16 200	16 200[1]	1	1	106	200	345
Swaziland Swaziland	60[1]	65[1]	70[1]	70[1]	70[1]	93	66	81	61	69
Sweden Suède	370 881	357 406	410 886	351 254	338 534	8 267	6 709	5 504	6 035	4 834
Switzerland Suisse	1 841	1 859	1 809	1 840	1 659	1 161	1 150	1 150	1 135	1 100

39
Fish production
Capture and aquaculture: metric tons [*cont.*]
Production halieutique
Capture et aquaculture : tonnes [*suite*]

Country or area Pays ou zone	Capture production Captures					Aquaculture production Production de l'aquaculture				
	1996	1997	1998	1999	2000	1996	1997	1998	1999	2000
Syrian Arab Republic Rép. arabe syrienne	5 773	6 131	7 097	7 938	6 572	6 355	5 596	7 233	6 079	6 797
Tajikistan Tadjikistan	80	70	60	48	59	93	71	81	74	86
Thailand Thaïlande	3 004 681	2 889 665	2 927 544	2 928 806	2 923 579	556 155	539 855	594 593	691 790	706 999
TFYR of Macedonia L'ex-R.y. Macédoine	78	130	131	135	208	911	879	1 257	1 669	1 626
Timor-Leste Timor-Leste	...	...	...	406	356	...	...	...	...	...
Togo Togo	15 098	14 290	16 655	22 924	22 277	21	20	25	150	102
Tokelau Tokélaou	200	200	200	200	200	...	...	...	...	...
Tonga Tonga	2 915	2 739	3 903	3 663	3 531	...	...	...	...	...
Trinidad and Tobago Trinité-et-Tobago	9 205	11 088	9 027	8 728	9 661	17	18	20	21	22
Tunisia Tunisie	83 734	87 012	88 075	92 075	95 550	1 351	1 875	1 842	1 095	1 553
Turkey Turquie	527 826	459 153	487 200	574 031	503 345	33 201	45 450	56 700	63 000	79 031
Turkmenistan Turkménistan	9 014	8 169	7 010	9 058	12 228	307	605	559	549	547
Turks and Caicos Islands Iles Turques et Caïques	1 297	1 250	1 318	1 300	1 300	3	4	4	4	5
Tuvalu Tuvalu	400	400	400	400	400	...	...	...	...	...
Uganda Ouganda	195 088	218 026	220 628	226 097	355 831	210	360	200	200	201
Ukraine Ukraine	417 119	373 005	462 308	407 853	392 724	32 709	30 000	28 332	33 816	30 969
United Arab Emirates Emirats arabes unis	107 000	114 358	114 739	117 607	105 456	0	0	0	0	0
United Kingdom Royaume-Uni	865 145	886 252	920 354	837 767	746 291	109 901	129 715	137 421	154 800	152 485
United Rep. of Tanzania Rép.-Unie de Tanzanie	323 921	356 960	348 000	310 509	332 779	200[1]	200[1]	200[1]	200[1]	210
United States Etats-Unis	5 001 483	4 983 440	4 708 980	4 749 646	4 745 321	393 331	438 331	445 123	478 679	428 262
United States Virgin Is. Iles Vierges américaines	400	350	300	263	300	0	0	0	0	0
Uruguay Uruguay	123 330	136 954	140 707	103 012	116 588	21	19	19	31	85
Uzbekistan Ouzbékistan	1 494	3 075	2 799	2 871	3 387	5 006	7 490	6 966	5 665	5 142
Vanuatu Vanuatu	49 752	66 191	77 319	96 961	73 490	...	...	...	...	...

39
Fish production
Capture and aquaculture: metric tons [*cont.*]
Production halieutique
Capture et aquaculture : tonnes [*suite*]

Country or area Pays ou zone	Capture production Captures					Aquaculture production Production de l'aquaculture				
	1996	1997	1998	1999	2000	1996	1997	1998	1999	2000
Venezuela Venezuela	496 196	469 805	505 680	412 777	391 255	7 330	8 914	9 670	10 860	12 670
Viet Nam Viet Nam	1 223 644	1 276 325	1 293 954	1 386 300	1 441 590	414 038	404 593	413 031	467 267	510 555
Wallis and Futuna Islands Iles Wallis et Futuna	180	176	300	300	300	...	...	...	...	...
Yemen Yémen	104 955	115 600	127 620	124 385	114 751	...	...	...	...	...
Zambia Zambie	66 332	65 923	69 938	67 327	66 671	4 770	4 718	4 159	4 180	4 240
Zimbabwe Zimbabwe	16 387	18 156	16 371	12 410	13 114	170	170	170	185	185

Source:
Food and Agriculture Organization of the United
Nations (FAO), Rome, FAOSTAT Fisheries database.

†† For statistical purposes, the data for
China do not include those for Hong Kong Special
Administrative Region (Hong Kong SAR) and Macao Special
Administrative Region (Macao SAR).

1 FAO estimate.
2 Data refer to the Gaza Strip.

Source:
Organisation des Nations Unies pour l'alimentation et
l'agriculture (FAO), Rome, les données des pêches de
FAOSTAT.

†† Les données statistiques relatives à
la Chine ne comprennent pas celles qui concernent la région
administrative spéciale de Hong Kong (la RAS de Hong Kong)
et la région administrative spéciale de Macao (la RAS de
Macao).

1 Estimation de la FAO.
2 Les données se rapportent à la Zone de Gaza.

40
Fertilizers
Nitrogenous, phosphate and potash: thousand metric tons
Engrais
Azotés, phosphatés et potassiques : milliers de tonnes

Country or area Pays ou zone	Production Production					Consumption Consommation				
	1996/97	1997/98	1998/99	1999/00	2000/01	1996/97	1997/98	1998/99	1999/00	2000/01
World Monde										
Nitrogenous fertilizers										
Engrais azotés	90 418.5	87 540.0	88 303.0	87 751.7	84 615.8	82 590.2	81 317.0	82 767.2	84 950.9	81 624.5
Phosphate fertilizers										
Engrais phosphatés	33 607.7	32 927.4	33 086.5	32 514.9	31 704.4	31 103.7	33 320.5	33 347.4	33 464.6	32 654.9
Potash fertilizers										
Engrais potassiques	22 962.8	26 014.4	25 006.6	25 011.0	25 541.2	20 885.4	22 586.4	22 044.8	22 121.4	22 155.7
Africa Afrique										
Nitrogenous fertilizers										
Engrais azotés	2 605.5	2 451.2	2 680.4	2 890.0	2 686.0	2 313.7	2 257.0	2 339.9	2 443.5	2 444.1
Phosphate fertilizers										
Engrais phosphatés	2 458.5	2 264.2	2 430.6	2 522.0	2 524.3	971.7	944.0	942.0	999.4	954.8
Potash fertilizers										
Engrais potassiques	...	...	...	...	...	468.1	473.3	501.1	484.0	481.5
Algeria Algérie										
Nitrogenous fertilizers										
Engrais azotés	8.3	28.4	40.7	54.4	77.7	14.0	36.0	44.0	47.0	44.3
Phosphate fertilizers *										
Engrais phosphatés *	...	...	23.4	8.7	8.3	11.0	35.0	30.8	25.0	25.0
Potash fertilizers *										
Engrais potassiques *	...	...	...	...	...	13.0	26.0	33.2	21.0	23.0
Angola Angola										
Nitrogenous fertilizers *										
Engrais azotés *	...	...	...	...	...	2.0	2.0	2.3	2.3	1.4
Phosphate fertilizers *										
Engrais phosphatés *	...	...	...	...	...	2.0	...	...	...	...
Potash fertilizers *										
Engrais potassiques *	...	...	...	...	...	2.0	...	1.1	1.1	...
Benin Bénin										
Nitrogenous fertilizers										
Engrais azotés	...	...	...	...	...	14.5	18.8	* 15.3	* 34.6	* 14.3
Phosphate fertilizers										
Engrais phosphatés	...	...	...	...	...	10.3	12.6	* 14.6	* 10.4	* 11.4
Potash fertilizers										
Engrais potassiques	...	...	...	...	...	* 5.9	* 7.6	* 7.8	* 11.7	9.5
Botswana Botswana										
Nitrogenous fertilizers										
Engrais azotés	...	...	...	...	...	3.2	* 3.5	3.7	* 4.1	* 4.1
Phosphate fertilizers										
Engrais phosphatés	...	...	...	...	...	0.1	* 0.2	* 0.3	* 0.3	* 0.3
Potash fertilizers										
Engrais potassiques	...	...	...	...	...	0.0	* 0.1	* 0.2	* 0.2	* 0.2
Burkina Faso Burkina Faso										
Nitrogenous fertilizers										
Engrais azotés	...	...	...	...	...	11.5	24.4	* 16.4	* 16.9	* 9.9
Phosphate fertilizers										
Engrais phosphatés	* 0.3	* 0.3	* 0.3	0.9	0.4	6.3	9.9	* 17.8	18.5	15.1
Potash fertilizers										
Engrais potassiques	...	...	...	...	...	6.3	8.3	* 16.0	* 8.0	9.0
Burundi Burundi										
Nitrogenous fertilizers *										
Engrais azotés *	...	...	...	...	...	1.0	1.0	1.4	1.8	1.5
Phosphate fertilizers										
Engrais phosphatés	...	...	...	...	...	* 1.8	...	1.2	* 1.4	* 1.0
Potash fertilizers										
Engrais potassiques	...	...	...	...	...	0.0	0.0	1.0	0.8	* 1.0
Cameroon Cameroun										
Nitrogenous fertilizers										
Engrais azotés	...	...	...	...	...	* 18.0	* 18.9	16.5	* 24.7	23.0
Phosphate fertilizers										
Engrais phosphatés	...	...	...	...	...	* 5.0	7.0	7.6	* 10.0	6.9
Potash fertilizers										
Engrais potassiques	...	...	...	...	...	* 11.0	13.3	15.4	* 13.5	18.0

40

Fertilizers

Nitrogenous, phosphate and potash: thousand metric tons [*cont.*]

Engrais

Azotés, phosphatés et potassiques : milliers de tonnes [*suite*]

Country or area	Production Production					Consumption Consommation				
Pays ou zone	1996/97	1997/98	1998/99	1999/00	2000/01	1996/97	1997/98	1998/99	1999/00	2000/01
Cape Verde Cap−Vert										
Nitrogenous fertilizers										
Engrais azotés	...	...	...	...	...	0.0	0.0	0.1	0.2	0.1
Central African Rep. Rép. centrafricaine										
Nitrogenous fertilizers *										
Engrais azotés *	...	...	...	...	...	0.1	0.1	0.2	0.2	0.2
Phosphate fertilizers *										
Engrais phosphatés *	...	...	...	...	...	0.1	0.1	0.2	0.2	0.2
Potash fertilizers *										
Engrais potassiques *	...	...	...	...	...	0.1	0.1	0.2	0.2	0.2
Chad Tchad										
Nitrogenous fertilizers *										
Engrais azotés *	...	...	...	...	...	7.5	3.5	10.7	11.0	11.0
Phosphate fertilizers										
Engrais phosphatés	...	...	...	...	...	* 2.4	* 2.4	1.7	* 2.0	* 2.0
Potash fertilizers										
Engrais potassiques	...	...	...	...	...	* 2.0	* 2.0	4.4	* 4.5	* 4.5
Comoros Comores										
Nitrogenous fertilizers *										
Engrais azotés *	...	...	...	...	...	0.1	0.1	0.1	0.1	0.1
Phosphate fertilizers *										
Engrais phosphatés *	...	...	...	...	...	0.1	0.1	0.1	0.1	0.1
Potash fertilizers *										
Engrais potassiques *	...	...	...	...	...	0.1	0.1	0.1	0.1	0.1
Congo Congo										
Nitrogenous fertilizers *										
Engrais azotés *	...	...	...	...	...	2.0	2.0	2.0	2.0	2.0
Phosphate fertilizers *										
Engrais phosphatés *	...	...	...	...	...	1.0	1.0	1.0	1.0	1.0
Potash fertilizers *										
Engrais potassiques *	...	...	...	...	...	1.0	1.0	2.0	2.0	2.0
Côte d'Ivoire Côte d'Ivoire										
Nitrogenous fertilizers *										
Engrais azotés *	...	...	...	...	...	41.5	60.0	50.0	41.2	45.6
Phosphate fertilizers *										
Engrais phosphatés *	...	...	...	...	...	15.0	25.0	25.0	14.4	11.1
Potash fertilizers *										
Engrais potassiques *	...	...	...	...	...	14.0	25.0	15.0	15.0	16.2
Dem. Rep. of the Congo Rép. dém. du Congo										
Nitrogenous fertilizers										
Engrais azotés	...	...	...	...	...	* 2.0	...	1.7	0.3	* 0.3
Phosphate fertilizers										
Engrais phosphatés	...	...	...	...	...	* 2.0	...	0.3	0.3	* 0.3
Potash fertilizers										
Engrais potassiques	...	...	...	...	...	* 2.0	...	1.0	0.2	0.2
Egypt Egypte										
Nitrogenous fertilizers										
Engrais azotés	1 019.4	* 943.8	* 1 111.0	* 1 268.5	1 287.5	* 1 002.6	* 915.0	* 1 014.0	* 1 003.0	1 073.4
Phosphate fertilizers										
Engrais phosphatés	* 201.6	* 195.3	* 174.0	* 203.0	170.8	* 121.9	* 134.5	* 128.6	* 149.0	151.3
Potash fertilizers										
Engrais potassiques	...	...	...	...	...	* 33.0	29.2	28.5	45.0	* 45.0
Eritrea Erythrée										
Nitrogenous fertilizers										
Engrais azotés	...	...	...	...	...	3.8	* 5.0	* 5.0	5.4	* 5.4
Phosphate fertilizers										
Engrais phosphatés	...	...	...	...	...	* 1.2	* 1.0	* 1.5	5.5	* 5.5
Ethiopia Ethiopie										
Nitrogenous fertilizers										
Engrais azotés	...	...	...	...	...	81.0	54.1	* 75.1	79.8	76.5
Phosphate fertilizers										
Engrais phosphatés	...	...	...	...	...	* 96.5	77.6	89.0	88.1	81.0

40

Fertilizers

Nitrogenous, phosphate and potash: thousand metric tons [*cont.*]

Engrais

Azotés, phosphatés et potassiques : milliers de tonnes [*suite*]

Country or area	Production Production					Consumption Consommation				
Pays ou zone	1996/97	1997/98	1998/99	1999/00	2000/01	1996/97	1997/98	1998/99	1999/00	2000/01
Gabon Gabon										
Nitrogenous fertilizers *										
Engrais azotés *	...	...	...	...	...	0.1	0.1	0.1	0.1	0.1
Phosphate fertilizers *										
Engrais phosphatés *	...	...	...	...	...	0.1	0.1	0.2	0.1	0.1
Potash fertilizers										
Engrais potassiques	...	...	...	...	...	0.0	0.0	* 0.1	* 0.1	* 0.1
Gambia Gambie										
Nitrogenous fertilizers										
Engrais azotés	...	...	...	...	...	0.2	* 0.3	* 2.3	* 1.0	* 0.6
Phosphate fertilizers *										
Engrais phosphatés *	...	...	...	...	...	0.4	0.5	0.1	0.1	0.1
Potash fertilizers *										
Engrais potassiques *	...	...	...	...	...	0.2	0.3	0.1	0.1	0.1
Ghana Ghana										
Nitrogenous fertilizers										
Engrais azotés	...	...	...	...	...	* 7.2	8.7	7.3	8.0	7.0
Phosphate fertilizers										
Engrais phosphatés	...	...	...	...	...	* 3.5	6.0	3.7	4.2	2.7
Potash fertilizers										
Engrais potassiques	...	...	...	...	...	* 6.7	6.7	4.3	3.2	2.1
Guinea Guinée										
Nitrogenous fertilizers										
Engrais azotés	...	...	...	...	...	2.4	0.7	1.1	* 1.0	* 1.0
Phosphate fertilizers										
Engrais phosphatés	...	...	...	...	...	1.0	0.6	1.4	* 1.4	* 1.4
Potash fertilizers										
Engrais potassiques	...	...	...	...	...	0.8	0.5	0.7	* 0.8	* 0.8
Guinea−Bissau Guinée−Bissau										
Nitrogenous fertilizers *										
Engrais azotés *	...	...	...	...	...	0.1	0.1	0.2	0.2	1.0
Phosphate fertilizers *										
Engrais phosphatés *	...	...	...	...	...	0.1	0.1	0.2	0.2	0.7
Potash fertilizers *										
Engrais potassiques *	...	...	...	...	...	0.1	0.1	0.2	0.2	0.7
Kenya Kenya										
Nitrogenous fertilizers *										
Engrais azotés *	...	...	...	...	...	63.0	51.0	53.0	54.2	56.8
Phosphate fertilizers *										
Engrais phosphatés *	...	...	...	...	...	75.8	69.4	57.1	84.9	73.5
Potash fertilizers *										
Engrais potassiques *	...	...	...	...	...	22.0	14.0	17.0	11.0	11.0
Lesotho Lesotho										
Nitrogenous fertilizers										
Engrais azotés	...	...	...	...	...	2.1	1.6	* 1.8	1.9	* 2.0
Phosphate fertilizers										
Engrais phosphatés	...	...	...	...	...	* 2.0	* 2.0	* 2.1	1.9	* 2.0
Potash fertilizers										
Engrais potassiques	...	...	...	...	...	* 2.0	* 2.0	* 2.1	1.3	1.5
Libyan Arab Jamah. Jamah. arabe libyenne										
Nitrogenous fertilizers										
Engrais azotés	* 398.8	* 383.4	408.2	386.9	* 407.1	* 16.6	* 17.5	* 20.0	* 43.6	* 31.7
Phosphate fertilizers *										
Engrais phosphatés *	...	...	...	...	...	40.4	40.9	27.0	34.7	18.0
Potash fertilizers *										
Engrais potassiques *	...	...	...	...	...	5.4	3.3	3.5	8.2	7.3
Madagascar Madagascar										
Nitrogenous fertilizers										
Engrais azotés	...	...	...	...	...	8.9	3.6	3.6	4.3	3.8
Phosphate fertilizers										
Engrais phosphatés	...	...	...	...	...	4.6	3.0	2.7	2.3	3.0
Potash fertilizers										
Engrais potassiques	...	...	...	...	...	3.1	2.9	2.4	1.3	2.4

40

Fertilizers
Nitrogenous, phosphate and potash: thousand metric tons [*cont.*]
Engrais
Azotés, phosphatés et potassiques : milliers de tonnes [*suite*]

Country or area Pays ou zone	Production Production					Consumption Consommation				
	1996/97	1997/98	1998/99	1999/00	2000/01	1996/97	1997/98	1998/99	1999/00	2000/01
Malawi Malawi										
Nitrogenous fertilizers *										
Engrais azotés *	...	...	...	...	...	37.9	41.2	34.8	30.0	22.8
Phosphate fertilizers										
Engrais phosphatés	...	...	...	...	...	14.3	12.6	11.9	16.6	6.5
Potash fertilizers *										
Engrais potassiques *	...	...	...	...	...	6.0	3.0	3.5	3.5	3.5
Mali Mali										
Nitrogenous fertilizers *										
Engrais azotés *	...	...	...	...	...	12.0	25.6	17.4	18.1	20.8
Phosphate fertilizers										
Engrais phosphatés	...	...	...	...	...	* 8.7	* 12.0	* 15.8	16.1	* 15.6
Potash fertilizers										
Engrais potassiques	...	...	...	...	...	* 6.6	* 10.2	* 12.7	15.6	* 15.6
Mauritania Mauritanie										
Nitrogenous fertilizers										
Engrais azotés	...	...	...	...	...	* 5.0	1.5	* 1.8	* 2.4	...
Phosphate fertilizers										
Engrais phosphatés	...	...	...	...	...	...	* 0.2	...	...	...
Mauritius Maurice										
Nitrogenous fertilizers										
Engrais azotés	16.2	14.3	* 14.4	* 14.4	* 12.4	13.1	11.8	* 12.4	* 14.0	* 14.0
Phosphate fertilizers *										
Engrais phosphatés *	...	...	...	...	...	8.0	7.0	6.0	5.7	6.0
Potash fertilizers										
Engrais potassiques	...	...	...	...	...	16.7	14.7	* 14.7	* 15.1	* 16.0
Morocco Maroc										
Nitrogenous fertilizers										
Engrais azotés	* 257.7	* 261.9	* 271.0	* 272.2	* 297.4	* 124.5	174.1	* 176.0	* 201.9	207.6
Phosphate fertilizers										
Engrais phosphatés	* 990.0	923.9	* 958.6	* 961.6	* 1 124.9	* 109.0	* 98.0	* 98.0	99.3	103.3
Potash fertilizers *										
Engrais potassiques *	...	...	...	...	...	56.5	55.2	51.0	57.5	51.0
Mozambique Mozambique										
Nitrogenous fertilizers										
Engrais azotés	0.0	0.0	0.0	0.0	0.0	* 7.0	* 1.5	* 3.8	* 8.0	* 9.7
Phosphate fertilizers										
Engrais phosphatés	0.0	0.0	0.0	0.0	0.0	* 0.3	* 2.6	* 1.6	...	* 3.4
Potash fertilizers										
Engrais potassiques	...	...	...	...	...	* 0.8	* 2.4	* 2.6	...	* 1.2
Namibia Namibie										
Nitrogenous fertilizers *										
Engrais azotés *	...	...	...	...	...	...	...	0.1	0.1	0.1
Phosphate fertilizers *										
Engrais phosphatés *	...	...	...	...	...	...	...	...	0.2	0.2
Niger Niger										
Nitrogenous fertilizers										
Engrais azotés	...	...	...	...	...	* 5.5	* 0.5	* 0.5	1.7	2.5
Phosphate fertilizers										
Engrais phosphatés	...	...	...	...	...	* 2.0	...	...	1.4	1.2
Potash fertilizers										
Engrais potassiques	...	...	...	...	...	* 1.5	* 0.2	...	1.1	0.8
Nigeria Nigéria										
Nitrogenous fertilizers										
Engrais azotés	* 114.3	* 41.2	* 71.0	* 85.0	...	105.0	* 77.3	* 100.0	* 122.0	* 105.6
Phosphate fertilizers										
Engrais phosphatés	* 9.5	* 5.0	* 10.5	...	...	* 32.5	* 21.4	* 39.2	* 34.7	* 44.0
Potash fertilizers *										
Engrais potassiques *	...	...	...	...	...	36.0	39.0	24.8	26.0	37.1
Réunion Réunion										
Nitrogenous fertilizers *										
Engrais azotés *	...	...	...	...	...	3.5	2.0	2.1	2.1	2.0
Phosphate fertilizers *										
Engrais phosphatés *	...	...	...	...	...	1.6	2.0	1.5	1.5	1.5

40
Fertilizers
Nitrogenous, phosphate and potash: thousand metric tons [*cont.*]
Engrais
Azotés, phosphatés et potassiques : milliers de tonnes [*suite*]

Country or area	Production Production					Consumption Consommation				
Pays ou zone	1996/97	1997/98	1998/99	1999/00	2000/01	1996/97	1997/98	1998/99	1999/00	2000/01
Potash fertilizers *										
Engrais potassiques *	...	...	...	...	...	4.0	3.0	2.0	2.0	1.3
Rwanda Rwanda										
Nitrogenous fertilizers *										
Engrais azotés *	...	...	...	...	...	0.1	0.1	0.1	0.1	0.1
Phosphate fertilizers *										
Engrais phosphatés *	...	...	...	...	...	0.1	0.2	0.1	0.1	0.1
Potash fertilizers *										
Engrais potassiques *	...	...	...	...	...	0.1	0.1	0.1	0.1	0.1
Senegal Sénégal										
Nitrogenous fertilizers *										
Engrais azotés *	24.8	30.4	38.8	24.5	19.4	8.0	7.1	8.8	14.4	16.9
Phosphate fertilizers *										
Engrais phosphatés *	35.4	55.0	67.5	45.0	32.4	9.6	10.8	11.0	15.4	17.4
Potash fertilizers *										
Engrais potassiques *	...	...	...	...	...	4.0	5.0	7.0	11.0	11.0
Sierra Leone Sierra Leone										
Nitrogenous fertilizers										
Engrais azotés	...	...	...	...	...	* 1.0	* 1.0	* 0.1	0.0	0.1
Phosphate fertilizers										
Engrais phosphatés	...	...	...	...	...	* 1.0	* 1.0	* 0.1	0.0	0.1
Potash fertilizers										
Engrais potassiques	...	...	...	...	...	* 1.0	* 1.0	* 0.1	0.0	0.1
Somalia Somalie										
Nitrogenous fertilizers *										
Engrais azotés *	...	...	...	...	...	0.5	0.5	0.5	0.5	0.5
South Africa Afrique du Sud										
Nitrogenous fertilizers										
Engrais azotés	* 452.0	* 465.0	* 423.0	* 443.0	244.4	405.0	405.0	406.0	* 413.0	* 411.0
Phosphate fertilizers										
Engrais phosphatés	* 397.7	* 378.4	378.8	391.2	* 267.9	255.9	225.0	218.0	* 227.3	* 218.0
Potash fertilizers										
Engrais potassiques	...	...	...	...	...	143.0	131.0	* 158.8	* 136.4	* 129.0
Sudan Soudan										
Nitrogenous fertilizers *										
Engrais azotés *	...	...	...	...	...	76.8	69.0	26.2	25.9	29.7
Phosphate fertilizers										
Engrais phosphatés	...	...	...	...	...	* 18.6	* 8.4	* 11.5	* 12.1	7.3
Potash fertilizers										
Engrais potassiques	...	...	...	...	...	...	...	...	0.6	0.6
Swaziland Swaziland										
Nitrogenous fertilizers										
Engrais azotés	...	...	...	...	...	1.5	* 1.6	* 2.0	* 1.7	* 2.0
Phosphate fertilizers										
Engrais phosphatés	...	...	...	...	...	1.7	* 1.8	* 1.9	* 1.9	* 1.9
Potash fertilizers *										
Engrais potassiques *	...	...	...	...	...	1.0	1.8	1.9	1.9	1.9
Togo Togo										
Nitrogenous fertilizers										
Engrais azotés	...	...	...	...	...	8.1	* 6.0	* 6.6	* 8.5	9.0
Phosphate fertilizers										
Engrais phosphatés	...	...	...	...	...	4.7	* 5.4	* 5.3	* 4.2	5.4
Potash fertilizers										
Engrais potassiques	...	...	...	...	...	4.8	* 5.4	* 5.3	* 4.2	5.4
Tunisia Tunisie										
Nitrogenous fertilizers										
Engrais azotés	223.9	* 190.4	* 225.9	* 253.4	* 267.9	* 52.0	* 51.5	63.3	* 65.0	* 62.1
Phosphate fertilizers										
Engrais phosphatés	* 788.0	* 673.3	782.0	873.6	* 889.6	* 41.0	40.0	44.5	* 43.0	* 45.0
Potash fertilizers										
Engrais potassiques	...	...	...	...	...	* 4.0	* 5.0	* 6.0	* 4.2	4.2
Uganda Ouganda										
Nitrogenous fertilizers										
Engrais azotés	...	...	...	...	...	* 0.2	* 0.2	1.8	2.1	* 2.2

40

Fertilizers
Nitrogenous, phosphate and potash: thousand metric tons [cont.]
Engrais
Azotés, phosphatés et potassiques : milliers de tonnes [suite]

Country or area	Production					Consumption Consommation				
Pays ou zone	1996/97	1997/98	1998/99	1999/00	2000/01	1996/97	1997/98	1998/99	1999/00	2000/01
Phosphate fertilizers										
Engrais phosphatés	...	...	...	...	...	* 0.2	* 0.2	0.9	1.3	* 1.5
Potash fertilizers										
Engrais potassiques	...	...	...	...	...	* 0.2	* 0.2	0.8	1.1	* 1.1
United Rep. of Tanzania Rép. – Unie de Tanzanie										
Nitrogenous fertilizers										
Engrais azotés	...	...	...	...	...	20.2	24.9	19.3	12.5	14.1
Phosphate fertilizers										
Engrais phosphatés	...	...	...	...	...	7.0	* 8.3	* 4.9	6.2	6.0
Potash fertilizers										
Engrais potassiques	...	...	...	...	...	4.0	6.7	5.6	2.2	2.3
Zambia Zambie										
Nitrogenous fertilizers										
Engrais azotés	* 4.1	* 4.0	* 2.3	1.7	* 0.9	* 27.5	* 32.6	* 13.2	10.6	6.9
Phosphate fertilizers										
Engrais phosphatés	...	...	...	...	...	* 13.9	* 14.1	* 13.5	* 13.4	13.4
Potash fertilizers *										
Engrais potassiques *	...	...	...	...	...	10.0	10.0	10.0	10.0	10.0
Zimbabwe Zimbabwe										
Nitrogenous fertilizers *										
Engrais azotés *	86.0	88.4	74.1	86.0	71.4	94.0	94.0	95.0	100.0	87.4
Phosphate fertilizers *										
Engrais phosphatés *	36.0	33.0	35.5	38.0	30.0	37.0	44.0	42.0	43.0	43.4
Potash fertilizers										
Engrais potassiques	...	...	...	...	...	* 37.0	* 37.0	* 38.0	42.0	* 34.5
America, North Amérique du Nord										
Nitrogenous fertilizers										
Engrais azotés	20 966.5	19 111.8	18 749.2	16 408.2	13 039.2	14 636.5	14 668.8	14 844.3	14 720.5	13 748.9
Phosphate fertilizers										
Engrais phosphatés	11 717.0	9 840.5	9 838.1	9 240.3	7 931.9	5 391.7	5 399.1	5 133.1	5 071.2	4 943.6
Potash fertilizers										
Engrais potassiques	8 985.4	10 970.4	9 508.6	9 096.0	9 984.0	5 622.1	5 644.3	5 327.0	5 278.2	5 175.5
Bahamas Bahamas										
Nitrogenous fertilizers *										
Engrais azotés *	...	...	...	...	...	0.2	0.1	0.1	0.1	0.1
Phosphate fertilizers *										
Engrais phosphatés *	...	...	...	...	...	0.1	0.1	0.1	0.1	0.1
Potash fertilizers										
Engrais potassiques	...	...	...	...	...	* 0.1	0.1	* 0.1	* 0.1	* 0.1
Barbados Barbade										
Nitrogenous fertilizers *										
Engrais azotés *	...	...	...	...	...	2.0	2.0	1.8	1.8	1.8
Phosphate fertilizers										
Engrais phosphatés	...	...	...	...	...	* 0.2	* 0.2	0.2	* 0.2	* 0.2
Potash fertilizers *										
Engrais potassiques *	...	...	...	...	...	1.0	1.0	1.0	1.0	1.0
Belize Belize										
Nitrogenous fertilizers										
Engrais azotés	...	...	...	...	...	* 1.0	* 1.3	1.9	* 2.3	2.8
Phosphate fertilizers										
Engrais phosphatés	...	...	...	...	...	* 1.3	2.5	* 2.7	* 2.8	* 1.9
Potash fertilizers *										
Engrais potassiques *	...	...	...	...	...	1.0	1.0	1.0	1.0	1.4
Bermuda Bermudes										
Nitrogenous fertilizers *										
Engrais azotés *	...	...	...	...	...	0.1	0.1	0.1	0.1	0.1
Canada Canada										
Nitrogenous fertilizers										
Engrais azotés	* 3 864.2	* 3 654.3	* 3 737.1	4 165.9	3 590.0	1 670.6	* 1 652.7	* 1 625.8	1 682.1	1 554.4
Phosphate fertilizers										
Engrais phosphatés	* 383.0	* 372.6	* 357.8	249.1	239.7	* 703.5	* 717.0	* 666.6	667.9	613.5
Potash fertilizers										
Engrais potassiques	* 8 151.4	* 9 535.1	* 8 605.9	* 8 230.5	* 9 173.9	* 322.2	* 356.3	* 356.6	339.3	309.4

40

Fertilizers

Nitrogenous, phosphate and potash: thousand metric tons [*cont.*]

Engrais

Azotés, phosphatés et potassiques : milliers de tonnes [*suite*]

Country or area	Production Production					Consumption Consommation				
Pays ou zone	1996/97	1997/98	1998/99	1999/00	2000/01	1996/97	1997/98	1998/99	1999/00	2000/01
Costa Rica Costa Rica										
Nitrogenous fertilizers *										
Engrais azotés *	56.0	41.0	32.0	35.0	19.9	89.0	100.0	104.0	82.2	86.6
Phosphate fertilizers *										
Engrais phosphatés *	...	...	...	...	...	28.2	31.0	33.0	32.0	34.4
Potash fertilizers										
Engrais potassiques	...	...	...	...	...	* 32.0	* 60.0	* 61.0	* 72.0	73.4
Cuba Cuba										
Nitrogenous fertilizers										
Engrais azotés	* 60.0	* 62.0	* 50.0	* 50.0	50.0	* 100.0	* 133.0	* 107.0	* 72.3	* 78.0
Phosphate fertilizers *										
Engrais phosphatés *	...	...	...	5.0	5.0	32.0	35.0	14.8	23.4	29.3
Potash fertilizers *										
Engrais potassiques *	...	...	...	...	...	103.0	71.4	47.5	59.8	28.1
Dominica Dominique										
Nitrogenous fertilizers										
Engrais azotés	...	...	...	...	...	0.9	* 1.0	* 1.0	* 1.0	* 1.0
Phosphate fertilizers										
Engrais phosphatés	...	...	...	...	...	0.9	* 1.0	* 1.0	* 1.0	* 1.0
Potash fertilizers										
Engrais potassiques	...	...	...	...	...	0.9	* 1.0	* 1.0	* 1.0	* 1.0
Dominican Republic Rép. dominicaine										
Nitrogenous fertilizers *										
Engrais azotés *	...	...	...	...	...	50.0	55.4	51.3	52.9	48.5
Phosphate fertilizers *										
Engrais phosphatés *	...	...	...	...	...	17.9	22.0	20.3	18.3	15.4
Potash fertilizers *										
Engrais potassiques *	...	...	...	...	...	24.0	31.5	26.2	22.5	22.7
El Salvador El Salvador										
Nitrogenous fertilizers										
Engrais azotés	...	...	...	...	...	* 60.0	* 72.1	* 58.4	56.7	51.3
Phosphate fertilizers *										
Engrais phosphatés *	...	...	...	...	...	22.0	13.1	16.0	16.7	16.1
Potash fertilizers *										
Engrais potassiques *	...	...	...	...	...	9.8	9.2	9.8	10.5	16.0
Guadeloupe Guadeloupe										
Nitrogenous fertilizers *										
Engrais azotés *	...	...	...	...	...	1.5	1.5	6.1	6.8	7.0
Phosphate fertilizers										
Engrais phosphatés	...	...	...	...	...	* 1.0	* 1.0	4.8	* 7.0	* 6.5
Potash fertilizers *										
Engrais potassiques *	...	...	...	...	...	1.0	1.0	6.7	5.8	5.8
Guatemala Guatemala										
Nitrogenous fertilizers										
Engrais azotés	...	...	...	...	...	* 110.0	118.6	* 101.0	* 123.0	* 124.0
Phosphate fertilizers *										
Engrais phosphatés *	...	...	...	...	...	37.0	76.0	81.0	36.2	46.1
Potash fertilizers										
Engrais potassiques	...	...	...	...	...	* 36.0	* 42.0	* 27.3	* 36.3	41.5
Haiti Haïti										
Nitrogenous fertilizers										
Engrais azotés	...	...	...	...	...	* 4.0	8.5	6.3	5.0	8.9
Phosphate fertilizers										
Engrais phosphatés	...	...	...	...	...	* 2.0	2.0	2.2	1.7	2.7
Potash fertilizers										
Engrais potassiques	...	...	...	...	...	* 1.0	2.0	2.5	2.0	2.9
Honduras Honduras										
Nitrogenous fertilizers *										
Engrais azotés *	...	...	...	...	...	49.8	82.9	93.9	109.5	135.9
Phosphate fertilizers										
Engrais phosphatés	...	...	...	...	...	* 19.2	* 24.2	* 23.0	* 30.3	21.6
Potash fertilizers										
Engrais potassiques	...	...	...	...	...	* 13.6	* 36.6	* 23.0	* 24.0	23.0

40

Fertilizers
Nitrogenous, phosphate and potash: thousand metric tons [*cont.*]
Engrais
Azotés, phosphatés et potassiques : milliers de tonnes [*suite*]

Country or area	Production Production					Consumption Consommation				
Pays ou zone	1996/97	1997/98	1998/99	1999/00	2000/01	1996/97	1997/98	1998/99	1999/00	2000/01
Jamaica　　Jamaïque										
Nitrogenous fertilizers										
Engrais azotés	...	...	...	...	...	* 8.1	9.0	8.9	9.2	9.9
Phosphate fertilizers										
Engrais phosphatés	...	...	...	...	...	* 5.3	6.0	5.2	5.0	* 5.2
Potash fertilizers										
Engrais potassiques	...	...	...	...	...	* 10.4	8.4	9.3	8.8	* 7.3
Martinique　　Martinique										
Nitrogenous fertilizers *										
Engrais azotés *	...	...	...	...	...	5.3	3.9	6.4	3.0	2.3
Phosphate fertilizers *										
Engrais phosphatés *	...	...	...	...	...	0.6	1.0	4.4	0.6	1.1
Potash fertilizers *										
Engrais potassiques *	...	...	...	...	...	9.8	4.7	10.3	7.6	7.7
Mexico　　Mexique										
Nitrogenous fertilizers										
Engrais azotés	* 1 487.4	* 1 290.9	* 1 190.2	* 650.8	* 700.0	1 207.4	* 1 197.0	* 1 336.0	* 1 300.0	* 1 342.0
Phosphate fertilizers										
Engrais phosphatés	* 434.0	* 462.8	* 479.4	* 515.9	434.9	* 309.0	* 257.0	* 295.0	* 306.0	315.0
Potash fertilizers										
Engrais potassiques	...	...	...	...	...	* 120.0	* 190.1	* 173.3	* 170.0	175.0
Nicaragua　　Nicaragua										
Nitrogenous fertilizers										
Engrais azotés	...	...	...	...	...	25.9	20.0	* 21.9	* 20.2	* 14.9
Phosphate fertilizers										
Engrais phosphatés	...	...	...	...	...	* 10.6	* 8.9	* 9.0	9.4	9.4
Potash fertilizers										
Engrais potassiques	...	...	...	...	...	4.2	6.8	* 7.7	* 6.3	5.0
Panama　　Panama										
Nitrogenous fertilizers										
Engrais azotés	...	...	...	...	...	* 27.4	21.4	21.3	* 17.7	18.4
Phosphate fertilizers										
Engrais phosphatés	...	...	...	...	...	* 12.5	9.5	9.2	* 9.0	9.0
Potash fertilizers										
Engrais potassiques	...	...	...	...	...	* 4.4	5.5	9.4	* 7.3	6.2
Saint Kitts and Nevis　　Saint−Kitts−et−Nevis										
Nitrogenous fertilizers										
Engrais azotés	...	...	...	...	...	0.6	* 0.8	* 0.8	* 0.8	* 0.8
Phosphate fertilizers										
Engrais phosphatés	...	...	...	...	...	0.4	* 0.5	* 0.5	* 0.5	* 0.5
Potash fertilizers										
Engrais potassiques	...	...	...	...	...	0.3	* 0.4	* 0.4	* 0.4	* 0.4
Saint Lucia　　Sainte−Lucie										
Nitrogenous fertilizers										
Engrais azotés	...	...	...	...	...	9.0	9.6	* 2.2	* 2.0	2.0
Phosphate fertilizers *										
Engrais phosphatés *	...	...	...	...	...	2.0	2.0	...	2.5	2.5
Potash fertilizers *										
Engrais potassiques *	...	...	...	...	...	2.0	2.0	...	0.8	0.8
St. Vincent−Grenadines　　St. Vincent−Grenadines										
Nitrogenous fertilizers *										
Engrais azotés *	...	...	...	...	...	1.0	1.0	1.3	1.3	1.3
Phosphate fertilizers										
Engrais phosphatés	...	...	...	...	...	* 1.0	* 1.0	* 1.3	* 1.3	1.3
Potash fertilizers										
Engrais potassiques	...	...	...	...	...	* 1.0	* 1.0	* 1.3	* 1.3	1.3
Trinidad and Tobago　　Trinité−et−Tobago										
Nitrogenous fertilizers										
Engrais azotés	* 272.9	* 277.5	* 240.7	* 276.0	275.3	* 6.0	* 6.0	* 5.0	* 4.9	5.3
Phosphate fertilizers										
Engrais phosphatés	...	...	...	...	...	* 1.0	* 1.0	* 0.4	* 0.3	0.3
Potash fertilizers										
Engrais potassiques	...	...	...	...	...	3.4	* 3.6	* 1.4	* 0.9	0.3

40
Fertilizers
Nitrogenous, phosphate and potash: thousand metric tons [*cont.*]
Engrais
Azotés, phosphatés et potassiques : milliers de tonnes [*suite*]

Country or area Pays ou zone	Production Production					Consumption Consommation				
	1996/97	1997/98	1998/99	1999/00	2000/01	1996/97	1997/98	1998/99	1999/00	2000/01
United States Etats–Unis										
Nitrogenous fertilizers										
Engrais azotés	15 226.0	13 786.1	13 499.2	11 230.5	8 403.9	11 205.6	11 169.7	11 281.5	11 165.3	10 251.3
Phosphate fertilizers										
Engrais phosphatés	10 900.0	9 005.2	9 000.9	8 470.3	7 252.3	4 183.7	4 186.8	3 942.1	3 898.6	3 810.2
Potash fertilizers										
Engrais potassiques	834.0	1 435.3	902.7	865.5	810.1	4 921.0	4 808.7	4 550.3	4 499.5	4 445.3
United States Virgin Is. Iles Vierges américaines										
Nitrogenous fertilizers										
Engrais azotés	...	...	...	...	...	* 1.0	* 1.0	* 0.3	* 0.3	0.3
Phosphate fertilizers										
Engrais phosphatés	...	...	...	...	...	* 0.3	* 0.3	* 0.3	* 0.3	0.3
America, South Amérique du Sud										
Nitrogenous fertilizers										
Engrais azotés	1 565.8	1 575.9	1 421.1	1 483.0	1 340.4	2 675.2	2 896.9	2 913.2	3 082.5	3 534.1
Phosphate fertilizers										
Engrais phosphatés	1 400.3	1 418.7	1 463.4	1 447.1	1 572.8	2 503.9	2 839.9	2 871.2	2 805.9	3 392.8
Potash fertilizers										
Engrais potassiques	419.5	516.4	636.5	709.8	761.2	2 430.0	2 805.1	2 715.1	2 702.6	3 357.1
Argentina Argentine										
Nitrogenous fertilizers										
Engrais azotés	* 80.7	* 97.1	* 98.6	* 79.8	* 91.3	* 510.3	* 476.4	* 422.7	457.3	* 481.3
Phosphate fertilizers *										
Engrais phosphatés *	...	...	...	...	...	306.9	302.6	320.7	340.2	314.5
Potash fertilizers										
Engrais potassiques	...	...	...	...	...	* 38.0	* 30.6	32.1	* 26.0	* 28.2
Bolivia Bolivie										
Nitrogenous fertilizers										
Engrais azotés	...	...	...	...	...	4.0	4.9	1.3	0.9	3.2
Phosphate fertilizers										
Engrais phosphatés	...	...	...	...	...	4.3	7.1	2.9	0.7	3.6
Potash fertilizers										
Engrais potassiques	...	...	...	...	...	0.8	0.6	0.8	0.4	0.7
Brazil Brésil										
Nitrogenous fertilizers										
Engrais azotés	779.0	808.4	728.0	847.6	772.2	1 250.9	1 438.1	1 545.5	1 660.8	1 999.3
Phosphate fertilizers										
Engrais phosphatés	1 305.1	1 354.1	1 369.0	1 357.8	1 496.1	1 704.8	2 004.4	2 022.4	1 953.7	2 544.3
Potash fertilizers										
Engrais potassiques	240.7	281.4	326.5	347.8	353.2	2 064.3	2 397.4	2 283.2	2 255.3	2 889.9
Chile Chili										
Nitrogenous fertilizers *										
Engrais azotés *	111.0	115.0	97.0	95.0	112.5	225.0	220.0	215.5	236.0	237.0
Phosphate fertilizers *										
Engrais phosphatés *	4.0	...	...	...	...	145.0	160.0	173.0	164.7	174.0
Potash fertilizers *										
Engrais potassiques *	178.8	235.0	310.0	362.0	408.0	53.0	55.0	81.6	74.5	78.0
Colombia Colombie										
Nitrogenous fertilizers *										
Engrais azotés *	109.0	92.3	93.0	75.5	72.0	236.0	265.2	296.8	299.8	334.3
Phosphate fertilizers *										
Engrais phosphatés *	10.0	9.2	9.3	9.3	7.8	113.0	123.1	127.0	116.7	131.8
Potash fertilizers *										
Engrais potassiques *	...	...	...	...	...	136.0	168.4	172.1	169.4	192.0
Ecuador Equateur										
Nitrogenous fertilizers *										
Engrais azotés *	...	...	...	...	...	65.0	90.6	88.1	69.8	71.6
Phosphate fertilizers										
Engrais phosphatés	...	...	...	...	...	23.0	* 32.1	* 29.5	* 37.1	* 35.4
Potash fertilizers *										
Engrais potassiques *	...	...	...	...	...	30.0	39.9	44.1	68.6	57.4
French Guiana Guyane française										
Nitrogenous fertilizers *										
Engrais azotés *	...	...	...	...	...	1.0	1.0	0.4	0.4	0.4

40

Fertilizers
Nitrogenous, phosphate and potash: thousand metric tons [*cont.*]
Engrais
Azotés, phosphatés et potassiques : milliers de tonnes [*suite*]

Country or area	Production Production					Consumption Consommation				
Pays ou zone	1996/97	1997/98	1998/99	1999/00	2000/01	1996/97	1997/98	1998/99	1999/00	2000/01
Phosphate fertilizers *										
Engrais phosphatés *	...	...	...	...	...	0.3	0.3	0.4	0.4	0.4
Potash fertilizers *										
Engrais potassiques *	...	...	...	...	...	0.1	0.1	0.4	0.4	0.4
Guyana Guyana										
Nitrogenous fertilizers										
Engrais azotés	...	...	...	...	...	* 10.9	14.0	* 13.8	* 15.5	10.7
Phosphate fertilizers										
Engrais phosphatés	...	...	...	...	...	* 1.4	* 0.7	* 0.9	* 2.8	1.2
Potash fertilizers *										
Engrais potassiques *	...	...	...	...	...	1.0	1.0	0.2	0.6	0.6
Paraguay Paraguay										
Nitrogenous fertilizers *										
Engrais azotés *	...	...	...	...	...	14.0	15.0	20.5	18.5	18.3
Phosphate fertilizers *										
Engrais phosphatés *	...	...	...	...	...	5.0	22.0	29.4	25.9	25.9
Potash fertilizers *										
Engrais potassiques *	...	...	...	...	...	14.0	22.0	22.0	21.0	21.0
Peru Pérou										
Nitrogenous fertilizers										
Engrais azotés	* 12.6	* 11.5	* 3.0	* 1.5	...	* 133.1	* 149.7	121.8	171.0	190.1
Phosphate fertilizers										
Engrais phosphatés	* 2.4	* 2.5	* 3.0	3.5	3.3	* 33.6	* 45.8	* 47.4	43.7	30.7
Potash fertilizers										
Engrais potassiques	...	...	...	...	...	* 18.6	* 26.7	* 24.8	33.2	22.8
Suriname Suriname										
Nitrogenous fertilizers *										
Engrais azotés *	...	...	...	...	...	7.0	6.8	5.7	4.8	5.3
Phosphate fertilizers										
Engrais phosphatés	...	...	...	...	...	* 0.1	* 0.1	0.8	0.0	0.0
Potash fertilizers *										
Engrais potassiques *	...	...	...	...	...	0.2	0.2	1.1	0.5	0.5
Uruguay Uruguay										
Nitrogenous fertilizers										
Engrais azotés	...	...	...	...	...	* 47.0	* 47.0	52.5	* 41.6	37.5
Phosphate fertilizers										
Engrais phosphatés	* 9.3	* 9.3	* 9.3	* 10.0	* 15.0	* 102.5	* 80.4	* 65.5	68.0	78.0
Potash fertilizers										
Engrais potassiques	...	...	...	...	...	* 4.0	* 1.8	* 11.0	11.0	* 11.6
Venezuela Venezuela										
Nitrogenous fertilizers *										
Engrais azotés *	473.5	451.6	401.5	383.6	292.4	171.0	168.3	128.6	106.0	145.0
Phosphate fertilizers *										
Engrais phosphatés *	69.5	43.6	72.8	66.5	50.5	64.0	61.3	51.4	52.0	53.0
Potash fertilizers *										
Engrais potassiques *	...	...	...	...	...	70.0	61.4	41.7	41.7	54.0
Asia Asie										
Nitrogenous fertilizers										
Engrais azotés	42 871.8	43 563.5	45 799.0	46 976.9	46 814.7	47 703.8	46 433.7	47 612.5	49 453.9	47 286.6
Phosphate fertilizers										
Engrais phosphatés	11 888.6	12 800.1	13 294.0	13 220.9	13 566.1	15 745.0	17 825.7	18 268.0	18 663.4	17 686.3
Potash fertilizers										
Engrais potassiques	2 801.6	2 532.0	2 812.9	3 019.1	3 199.4	6 225.0	7 421.7	7 571.8	8 038.9	7 881.9
Afghanistan Afghanistan										
Nitrogenous fertilizers *										
Engrais azotés *	5.0	5.0	5.0	5.0	5.0	5.0	5.0	6.0	5.0	5.0
Phosphate fertilizers *										
Engrais phosphatés *	...	...	...	...	...	...	...	1.0	...	...
Armenia Arménie										
Nitrogenous fertilizers										
Engrais azotés	...	...	...	...	...	* 8.0	* 8.0	9.6	6.2	7.0
Azerbaijan Azerbaïdjan										
Nitrogenous fertilizers *										
Engrais azotés *	...	...	...	...	...	16.6	20.0	13.0	13.8	2.1

40
Fertilizers
Nitrogenous, phosphate and potash: thousand metric tons [*cont.*]
Engrais
Azotés, phosphatés et potassiques : milliers de tonnes [*suite*]

Country or area	Production Production					Consumption Consommation				
Pays ou zone	1996/97	1997/98	1998/99	1999/00	2000/01	1996/97	1997/98	1998/99	1999/00	2000/01
Phosphate fertilizers *										
Engrais phosphatés *	...	...	...	...	...	...	2.7	2.8	...	...
Potash fertilizers										
Engrais potassiques	* 3.0	* 5.0	...	...	...	...	1.0	...	...	...
Bahrain Bahreïn										
Nitrogenous fertilizers										
Engrais azotés	...	...	214.3	223.4	247.0	* 0.2	* 0.2	0.7	0.1	0.1
Phosphate fertilizers										
Engrais phosphatés	...	...	0.3	...	...	* 0.2	* 0.2	* 0.3	0.1	0.1
Potash fertilizers										
Engrais potassiques	...	...	...	...	...	* 0.2	* 0.2	0.1	0.1	0.1
Bangladesh Bangladesh										
Nitrogenous fertilizers										
Engrais azotés	* 965.7	868.2	* 1 010.1	* 1 049.2	* 1 143.0	* 996.1	876.6	* 882.5	1 014.0	994.0
Phosphate fertilizers										
Engrais phosphatés	49.4	38.9	* 41.1	50.0	50.0	117.5	116.8	* 161.4	207.0	231.0
Potash fertilizers										
Engrais potassiques	...	...	...	...	...	* 117.0	115.8	* 126.6	144.0	101.0
Bhutan Bhoutan										
Nitrogenous fertilizers										
Engrais azotés	...	...	...	...	...	* 0.1	* 0.1	0.0	0.0	0.0
Cambodia Cambodge										
Nitrogenous fertilizers										
Engrais azotés	...	...	...	...	...	* 4.3	* 18.9	3.2	...	...
Phosphate fertilizers *										
Engrais phosphatés *	...	...	...	...	...	2.7	3.0	4.4	...	...
Potash fertilizers *										
Engrais potassiques *	...	...	...	...	...	0.8	...	...	...	...
China Chine										
Nitrogenous fertilizers *										
Engrais azotés *	21 042.8	20 232.1	21 530.0	22 833.1	22 181.7	25 275.0	22 949.7	22 887.0	24 142.0	22 688.0
Phosphate fertilizers										
Engrais phosphatés	* 5 822.0	* 6 419.0	* 6 713.0	6 430.0	* 6 700.0	* 8 118.0	* 9 277.0	* 9 457.0	* 8 907.0	* 8 491.0
Potash fertilizers										
Engrais potassiques	* 218.0	* 170.0	* 213.0	* 218.0	* 275.0	2 591.0	3 420.0	* 3 486.0	* 3 390.0	* 3 466.0
Cyprus Chypre										
Nitrogenous fertilizers										
Engrais azotés	...	...	...	...	...	13.8	10.8	10.8	10.9	7.8
Phosphate fertilizers										
Engrais phosphatés	...	...	...	...	...	9.5	7.8	7.5	7.4	4.9
Potash fertilizers										
Engrais potassiques	...	...	...	...	...	2.2	1.8	2.0	1.9	1.7
Georgia Géorgie										
Nitrogenous fertilizers *										
Engrais azotés *	53.7	76.3	55.3	93.9	99.4	27.2	31.5	30.0	40.0	40.0
Phosphate fertilizers *										
Engrais phosphatés *	...	...	...	...	...	5.0	5.0	4.0	...	...
India Inde										
Nitrogenous fertilizers										
Engrais azotés	8 592.3	10 083.1	10 477.3	10 872.8	10 942.8	10 315.9	10 901.9	11 353.8	11 586.3	10 910.5
Phosphate fertilizers										
Engrais phosphatés	2 595.6	3 079.5	3 194.1	3 447.7	3 734.1	2 979.0	3 913.6	* 4 112.2	4 796.3	4 251.1
Potash fertilizers										
Engrais potassiques	...	...	...	...	...	1 043.1	1 372.5	1 331.5	1 674.2	1 564.8
Indonesia Indonésie										
Nitrogenous fertilizers										
Engrais azotés	* 2 986.4	* 2 992.6	* 2 899.1	2 667.4	2 852.2	* 2 084.0	* 1 706.6	* 2 120.9	* 1 985.0	1 955.0
Phosphate fertilizers										
Engrais phosphatés	* 355.0	* 282.9	* 237.6	299.8	193.0	* 331.9	* 280.0	* 361.8	* 324.0	252.3
Potash fertilizers *										
Engrais potassiques *	...	...	...	...	...	300.0	241.0	245.0	275.0	267.8
Iran (Islamic Rep. of) Iran (Rép. islamique d')										
Nitrogenous fertilizers										
Engrais azotés	* 688.8	* 727.8	* 863.7	* 714.5	* 742.6	685.2	* 830.0	* 878.0	* 859.0	* 819.6

40
Fertilizers
Nitrogenous, phosphate and potash: thousand metric tons [*cont.*]
Engrais
Azotés, phosphatés et potassiques : milliers de tonnes [*suite*]

Country or area Pays ou zone	Production Production					Consumption Consommation				
	1996/97	1997/98	1998/99	1999/00	2000/01	1996/97	1997/98	1998/99	1999/00	2000/01
Phosphate fertilizers										
Engrais phosphatés	* 136.1	* 93.3	* 113.6	103.6	* 130.5	* 374.1	340.0	* 330.0	* 364.0	* 393.3
Potash fertilizers										
Engrais potassiques	...	...	...	...	...	* 20.0	37.1	60.0	* 121.4	* 106.8
Iraq Iraq										
Nitrogenous fertilizers *										
Engrais azotés *	235.0	235.0	235.0	238.0	238.0	240.5	242.7	251.2	254.7	250.6
Phosphate fertilizers *										
Engrais phosphatés *	90.0	90.0	90.0	90.0	90.0	103.9	111.6	132.1	132.7	117.2
Potash fertilizers										
Engrais potassiques	...	...	...	...	...	* 10.0	* 2.5	0.0	0.7	* 3.5
Israel Israël										
Nitrogenous fertilizers *										
Engrais azotés *	76.0	88.0	87.0	82.0	82.0	65.0	61.0	61.0	60.0	55.0
Phosphate fertilizers										
Engrais phosphatés	* 222.0	* 244.0	* 250.0	* 285.0	* 306.0	* 19.0	* 23.0	23.0	* 23.0	* 22.0
Potash fertilizers										
Engrais potassiques	* 1 500.0	* 1 488.0	* 1 668.0	* 1 701.6	* 1 747.8	* 35.0	* 36.0	37.0	* 30.0	* 30.0
Japan Japon										
Nitrogenous fertilizers										
Engrais azotés	883.4	829.7	799.4	803.0	768.0	511.7	495.2	476.0	480.2	487.0
Phosphate fertilizers										
Engrais phosphatés	278.0	263.0	248.9	234.1	215.0	610.1	592.5	561.3	570.4	584.0
Potash fertilizers										
Engrais potassiques	* 21.4	* 19.6	* 15.7	* 17.5	* 15.0	* 441.2	* 422.0	381.3	388.8	383.0
Jordan Jordanie										
Nitrogenous fertilizers										
Engrais azotés	120.8	127.9	* 149.6	* 137.3	121.1	* 5.0	10.9	14.8	12.3	9.3
Phosphate fertilizers										
Engrais phosphatés	308.7	279.4	338.9	* 316.4	253.2	11.2	9.1	4.6	* 4.0	3.8
Potash fertilizers										
Engrais potassiques	* 1 059.2	849.4	916.2	1 081.1	1 161.6	* 3.0	* 4.0	* 4.0	* 5.0	6.8
Kazakhstan Kazakhstan										
Nitrogenous fertilizers *										
Engrais azotés *	78.7	17.0	5.1	7.7	5.4	67.1	15.1	12.6	23.0	30.0
Phosphate fertilizers										
Engrais phosphatés	* 125.0	* 74.0	* 10.0	* 27.5	* 3.5	* 57.9	* 35.0	* 0.2	2.9	4.9
Potash fertilizers										
Engrais potassiques	...	...	...	...	...	* 6.0	* 6.0	* 0.2	* 2.1	2.1
Korea, Dem. P. R. Corée, R. p. dém. de										
Nitrogenous fertilizers *										
Engrais azotés *	72.0	72.0	72.0	72.0	72.0	72.4	149.3	128.3	152.0	228.0
Phosphate fertilizers *										
Engrais phosphatés *	20.0	20.0	10.0	32.0	32.0	20.0	21.0	26.0	61.0	76.0
Potash fertilizers *										
Engrais potassiques *	...	...	...	...	...	0.6	0.8	2.9	59.0	47.0
Korea, Republic of Corée, République de										
Nitrogenous fertilizers										
Engrais azotés	663.0	* 659.0	* 584.0	542.5	471.5	455.9	* 507.0	* 451.0	428.3	421.3
Phosphate fertilizers										
Engrais phosphatés	* 409.0	* 438.0	* 421.0	421.5	421.9	* 209.0	* 223.0	* 188.0	179.8	161.7
Potash fertilizers										
Engrais potassiques	...	...	...	...	...	* 244.0	* 262.0	* 228.0	200.6	198.7
Kuwait Koweït										
Nitrogenous fertilizers										
Engrais azotés	* 356.3	* 348.5	361.3	330.7	287.6	* 2.0	* 1.2	* 1.0	* 1.1	0.6
Kyrgyzstan Kirghizistan										
Nitrogenous fertilizers										
Engrais azotés	...	...	...	...	...	* 25.0	* 25.0	* 27.7	26.6	27.5
Phosphate fertilizers										
Engrais phosphatés	...	...	...	...	...	* 1.0	* 1.0	1.1	1.2	1.4
Potash fertilizers										
Engrais potassiques	...	...	...	...	...	* 5.0	* 5.0	* 0.3	0.0	0.1

40
Fertilizers
Nitrogenous, phosphate and potash: thousand metric tons [*cont.*]
Engrais
Azotés, phosphatés et potassiques : milliers de tonnes [*suite*]

Country or area Pays ou zone	Production Production					Consumption Consommation				
	1996/97	1997/98	1998/99	1999/00	2000/01	1996/97	1997/98	1998/99	1999/00	2000/01
Lao People's Dem. Rep. **Rép. dém. pop. lao**										
Nitrogenous fertilizers										
Engrais azotés	...	...	...	...	...	* 2.0	* 5.0	2.9	4.5	* 4.2
Phosphate fertilizers										
Engrais phosphatés	...	...	...	...	...	* 1.3	* 2.6	1.5	3.4	* 2.5
Potash fertilizers *										
Engrais potassiques *	...	...	...	...	...	0.5	0.2	0.3	2.0	2.0
Lebanon Liban										
Nitrogenous fertilizers										
Engrais azotés	...	...	...	...	...	* 22.0	21.9	* 23.4	* 22.0	24.2
Phosphate fertilizers *										
Engrais phosphatés *	95.0	115.0	134.0	85.0	130.0	30.0	32.0	32.0	32.0	32.5
Potash fertilizers										
Engrais potassiques	...	...	...	...	...	* 4.0	* 8.3	* 8.3	* 9.7	9.6
Malaysia Malaisie										
Nitrogenous fertilizers *										
Engrais azotés *	290.0	231.7	316.6	399.2	566.0	255.0	344.0	417.0	453.7	525.0
Phosphate fertilizers *										
Engrais phosphatés *	...	...	...	...	...	230.0	238.0	233.0	264.0	253.2
Potash fertilizers *										
Engrais potassiques *	...	...	...	...	...	646.0	670.0	756.0	730.6	650.0
Mongolia Mongolie										
Nitrogenous fertilizers										
Engrais azotés	...	...	...	...	...	* 2.0	5.0	* 4.2	* 2.8	* 3.4
Phosphate fertilizers										
Engrais phosphatés	...	...	...	...	...	0.0	1.0	...	...	...
Myanmar Myanmar										
Nitrogenous fertilizers										
Engrais azotés	73.6	56.1	51.6	* 65.5	71.3	130.9	135.5	* 135.0	* 125.0	* 165.0
Phosphate fertilizers										
Engrais phosphatés	...	...	...	...	...	* 33.0	35.2	34.5	* 28.1	34.5
Potash fertilizers										
Engrais potassiques	...	...	...	...	...	* 10.0	* 7.2	* 2.3	* 9.0	10.3
Nepal Népal										
Nitrogenous fertilizers *										
Engrais azotés *	...	...	...	...	...	75.0	77.4	87.4	57.2	53.6
Phosphate fertilizers *										
Engrais phosphatés *	...	...	...	...	...	25.0	28.5	32.3	25.8	19.3
Potash fertilizers *										
Engrais potassiques *	...	...	...	...	...	3.0	1.6	1.8	2.0	3.1
Oman Oman										
Nitrogenous fertilizers										
Engrais azotés	...	...	...	...	...	4.9	3.5	6.7	5.7	* 3.7
Phosphate fertilizers										
Engrais phosphatés	...	...	...	...	...	* 0.9	1.0	0.7	0.8	* 0.8
Potash fertilizers										
Engrais potassiques	...	...	...	...	...	* 0.9	1.0	0.7	* 0.8	* 0.8
Pakistan Pakistan										
Nitrogenous fertilizers										
Engrais azotés	1 681.5	1 660.5	1 795.2	2 039.3	2 053.7	1 985.1	2 087.6	2 091.9	2 218.1	2 265.7
Phosphate fertilizers										
Engrais phosphatés	80.6	67.5	90.8	223.4	244.0	419.5	551.3	465.0	596.8	677.7
Potash fertilizers										
Engrais potassiques	...	...	...	...	...	8.4	20.4	* 21.2	18.1	22.9
Philippines Philippines										
Nitrogenous fertilizers										
Engrais azotés	255.7	213.0	164.6	166.1	141.5	* 482.5	* 548.1	408.9	481.4	488.2
Phosphate fertilizers										
Engrais phosphatés	* 273.4	217.1	192.7	134.1	81.9	* 145.8	* 148.7	118.5	142.6	124.1
Potash fertilizers										
Engrais potassiques	...	...	...	...	...	* 108.5	112.3	* 100.4	121.1	122.2
Qatar Qatar										
Nitrogenous fertilizers										
Engrais azotés	400.3	* 672.3	* 767.0	757.2	* 748.1	1.2	1.2	* 1.0	* 0.8	* 0.5

40
Fertilizers
Nitrogenous, phosphate and potash: thousand metric tons [cont.]
Engrais
Azotés, phosphatés et potassiques : milliers de tonnes [suite]

Country or area	Production Production					Consumption Consommation				
Pays ou zone	1996/97	1997/98	1998/99	1999/00	2000/01	1996/97	1997/98	1998/99	1999/00	2000/01
Saudi Arabia Arabie saoudite										
Nitrogenous fertilizers										
Engrais azotés	* 1 063.7	* 981.1	* 1 079.8	1 071.7	1 271.2	* 171.0	* 181.0	* 200.0	* 210.0	242.0
Phosphate fertilizers										
Engrais phosphatés	* 129.7	* 119.8	* 136.9	156.3	144.2	* 138.0	* 131.0	* 121.0	128.0	133.0
Potash fertilizers										
Engrais potassiques	0.0	0.0	0.0	* 0.9	...	* 8.0	* 9.0	* 9.0	* 20.0	* 21.0
Singapore Singapour										
Nitrogenous fertilizers										
Engrais azotés	...	...	...	...	...	2.8	1.9	2.5	2.3	1.6
Phosphate fertilizers										
Engrais phosphatés	...	...	...	...	...	0.2	0.1	* 0.9	0.7	* 0.7
Potash fertilizers										
Engrais potassiques	...	...	...	...	...	* 0.2	* 0.1	* 0.7	0.7	* 0.7
Sri Lanka Sri Lanka										
Nitrogenous fertilizers										
Engrais azotés	...	...	...	...	...	117.6	122.5	142.2	163.8	157.1
Phosphate fertilizers										
Engrais phosphatés	9.5	8.3	10.2	8.5	9.8	35.0	30.1	29.1	33.7	29.9
Potash fertilizers										
Engrais potassiques	...	...	...	...	...	58.6	56.1	61.6	61.6	59.2
Syrian Arab Republic Rép. arabe syrienne										
Nitrogenous fertilizers										
Engrais azotés	* 71.3	* 68.7	* 113.2	103.9	* 82.0	227.4	236.8	218.4	250.5	236.2
Phosphate fertilizers										
Engrais phosphatés	91.7	* 84.2	* 96.5	66.1	* 112.7	124.0	124.6	105.1	111.9	* 121.5
Potash fertilizers										
Engrais potassiques	...	...	...	...	...	5.8	7.0	7.4	8.5	8.1
Tajikistan Tadjikistan										
Nitrogenous fertilizers										
Engrais azotés	* 4.1	* 4.0	* 4.0	* 4.0	* 4.0	* 32.1	41.2	28.3	* 10.7	* 9.0
Phosphate fertilizers *										
Engrais phosphatés *	...	...	...	...	...	25.0	6.5	8.5	...	...
Potash fertilizers *										
Engrais potassiques *	...	...	...	...	...	5.0	5.0	0.1	...	...
Thailand Thaïlande										
Nitrogenous fertilizers										
Engrais azotés	...	* 56.0	* 79.0	* 70.4	* 83.0	810.8	* 784.0	* 905.0	1 057.4	* 896.4
Phosphate fertilizers										
Engrais phosphatés	...	43.0	85.0	* 70.0	* 90.0	* 436.0	* 423.0	* 455.0	* 415.0	* 400.9
Potash fertilizers *										
Engrais potassiques *	...	...	...	...	...	273.0	274.0	277.0	278.0	253.1
Turkey Turquie										
Nitrogenous fertilizers										
Engrais azotés	* 923.5	* 921.6	* 922.4	572.4	515.5	1 147.8	* 1 167.0	* 1 392.0	1 485.4	1 378.6
Phosphate fertilizers										
Engrais phosphatés	* 424.9	* 501.8	* 491.1	385.0	311.0	578.0	* 592.4	* 700.2	637.9	628.8
Potash fertilizers										
Engrais potassiques	...	...	...	...	...	* 73.5	* 66.3	* 88.5	80.7	82.0
Turkmenistan Turkménistan										
Nitrogenous fertilizers *										
Engrais azotés *	110.0	110.0	57.0	60.0	60.0	110.0	159.0	57.0	72.2	86.5
Phosphate fertilizers										
Engrais phosphatés	...	* 5.0	* 5.0	* 5.0	* 5.0	* 20.0	* 5.0	* 5.0	* 5.0	* 5.0
Potash fertilizers *										
Engrais potassiques *	...	...	...	...	...	12.0	14.0	14.0	14.0	14.0
United Arab Emirates Emirats arabes unis										
Nitrogenous fertilizers										
Engrais azotés	* 258.4	* 299.6	* 258.9	271.9	* 243.4	* 24.5	* 24.2	* 24.7	* 25.1	* 23.8
Phosphate fertilizers										
Engrais phosphatés	...	...	...	...	...	* 3.3	* 3.7	* 5.0	* 5.0	5.0
Potash fertilizers *										
Engrais potassiques *	...	...	...	...	...	4.4	4.4	5.7	6.1	6.3

40

Fertilizers
Nitrogenous, phosphate and potash: thousand metric tons [*cont.*]
Engrais
Azotés, phosphatés et potassiques : milliers de tonnes [*suite*]

Country or area	Production Production					Consumption Consommation				
Pays ou zone	1996/97	1997/98	1998/99	1999/00	2000/01	1996/97	1997/98	1998/99	1999/00	2000/01
Uzbekistan Ouzbékistan										
Nitrogenous fertilizers										
Engrais azotés	* 825.3	* 809.3	* 731.8	* 699.8	* 680.8	* 220.0	* 678.0	* 643.0	622.0	* 607.0
Phosphate fertilizers										
Engrais phosphatés	* 194.3	* 122.1	* 141.4	* 170.9	* 116.2	* 150.0	* 122.1	* 141.4	137.0	* 116.2
Potash fertilizers										
Engrais potassiques	...	...	...	...	...	* 75.0	* 75.0	* 40.0	15.8	4.0
Viet Nam Viet Nam										
Nitrogenous fertilizers *										
Engrais azotés *	94.5	117.4	109.8	23.0	35.0	995.3	922.9	1 186.1	1 068.0	1 158.0
Phosphate fertilizers *										
Engrais phosphatés *	178.8	194.2	241.9	179.0	192.0	380.2	386.8	399.8	515.0	506.0
Potash fertilizers *										
Engrais potassiques *	...	...	...	...	...	109.0	162.0	271.0	367.0	433.0
Yemen Yémen										
Nitrogenous fertilizers										
Engrais azotés	...	...	...	...	...	* 8.1	* 19.3	* 15.9	14.8	* 18.5
Phosphate fertilizers *										
Engrais phosphatés *	...	...	...	...	...	...	...	0.8	...	...
Potash fertilizers *										
Engrais potassiques	...	...	...	...	...	...	...	* 0.9	0.3	* 0.3
Europe Europe										
Nitrogenous fertilizers										
Engrais azotés	**22 060.2**	**20 505.7**	**19 261.7**	**19 569.6**	**20 294.2**	**14 277.6**	**14 063.3**	**13 912.0**	**13 960.4**	**13 355.5**
Phosphate fertilizers										
Engrais phosphatés	**5 569.9**	**5 950.5**	**5 443.4**	**5 341.0**	**5 320.5**	**5 112.8**	**4 834.1**	**4 711.7**	**4 483.3**	**4 115.3**
Potash fertilizers										
Engrais potassiques	**10 756.4**	**11 995.6**	**12 048.7**	**12 186.1**	**11 596.6**	**5 791.7**	**5 850.1**	**5 556.6**	**5 268.0**	**4 911.3**
Albania Albanie										
Nitrogenous fertilizers *										
Engrais azotés *	...	...	...	...	...	5.5	4.2	18.0	5.8	5.8
Phosphate fertilizers *										
Engrais phosphatés *	3.0	3.0	2.0	2.0	2.0	1.0	1.0	6.9	5.0	3.4
Potash fertilizers										
Engrais potassiques	...	...	...	...	...	0.0	0.0	0.1	0.1	* 0.1
Austria Autriche										
Nitrogenous fertilizers										
Engrais azotés	* 240.0	* 227.0	* 254.0	* 227.0	* 187.0	* 133.0	* 128.0	* 128.0	122.0	* 117.0
Phosphate fertilizers *										
Engrais phosphatés *	72.0	64.0	62.0	58.0	54.0	60.0	57.0	57.0	48.0	47.0
Potash fertilizers										
Engrais potassiques	...	...	...	...	...	72.0	* 63.0	62.0	* 60.0	* 59.0
Belarus Bélarus										
Nitrogenous fertilizers *										
Engrais azotés *	449.6	378.9	442.5	534.4	588.0	260.0	280.0	280.0	286.0	280.0
Phosphate fertilizers										
Engrais phosphatés	* 91.5	* 128.2	* 127.0	* 120.0	87.0	* 95.0	* 100.0	* 100.0	* 105.0	* 75.0
Potash fertilizers *										
Engrais potassiques *	2 716.0	3 247.0	3 451.0	3 613.0	3 372.0	422.0	475.0	545.0	475.0	450.0
Belgium−Luxembourg Belgique−Luxembourg										
Nitrogenous fertilizers *										
Engrais azotés *	660.0	808.0	748.0	916.0	900.0	172.0	171.0	171.0	171.0	159.0
Phosphate fertilizers *										
Engrais phosphatés *	108.0	104.0	78.0	166.0	166.0	46.0	44.0	47.0	45.0	44.0
Potash fertilizers *										
Engrais potassiques *	...	...	...	...	...	96.0	92.0	91.0	88.0	84.0
Bosnia and Herzegovina Bosnie−Herzégovine										
Nitrogenous fertilizers *										
Engrais azotés *	...	...	...	...	...	3.0	3.0	23.0	28.0	27.8
Phosphate fertilizers *										
Engrais phosphatés *	...	...	...	...	...	3.0	3.0	12.0	7.0	7.0
Potash fertilizers *										
Engrais potassiques *	...	...	...	...	...	3.0	3.0	12.0	7.0	7.0

40
Fertilizers
Nitrogenous, phosphate and potash: thousand metric tons [*cont.*]
Engrais
Azotés, phosphatés et potassiques : milliers de tonnes [*suite*]

Country or area	Production Production					Consumption Consommation				
Pays ou zone	1996/97	1997/98	1998/99	1999/00	2000/01	1996/97	1997/98	1998/99	1999/00	2000/01
Bulgaria Bulgarie										
Nitrogenous fertilizers										
Engrais azotés	835.2	* 694.9	* 362.9	270.9	322.7	* 152.0	* 157.8	* 135.0	110.6	137.7
Phosphate fertilizers										
Engrais phosphatés	* 80.0	109.8	* 83.1	52.0	* 94.2	13.0	11.0	* 9.0	6.0	7.1
Potash fertilizers *										
Engrais potassiques *	...	...	...	...	...	27.0	31.0	25.0	0.8	0.8
Croatia Croatie										
Nitrogenous fertilizers										
Engrais azotés	* 305.9	324.1	248.0	309.8	327.5	* 101.6	* 152.0	95.0	99.8	115.7
Phosphate fertilizers										
Engrais phosphatés	86.8	* 90.0	* 96.0	* 118.0	100.7	48.2	* 56.0	* 38.0	43.8	48.5
Potash fertilizers										
Engrais potassiques	...	...	...	...	...	52.5	67.9	43.4	51.0	57.4
Czech Republic République tchèque										
Nitrogenous fertilizers										
Engrais azotés	* 305.0	264.4	284.4	269.3	306.2	* 262.3	* 225.8	218.8	209.5	235.8
Phosphate fertilizers										
Engrais phosphatés	* 24.8	24.6	25.6	18.3	22.1	* 50.4	46.9	51.2	35.4	43.3
Potash fertilizers										
Engrais potassiques	...	...	...	...	...	* 34.0	41.4	29.9	24.0	20.7
Denmark Danemark										
Nitrogenous fertilizers										
Engrais azotés	* 150.0	* 160.0	* 146.0	* 164.0	* 133.0	* 288.0	* 283.0	* 263.0	252.0	* 244.0
Phosphate fertilizers										
Engrais phosphatés	* 46.0	* 47.0	* 47.0	* 38.0	* 27.0	* 53.0	* 50.0	47.0	* 41.0	* 37.0
Potash fertilizers *										
Engrais potassiques *	...	...	...	...	...	108.0	104.0	102.0	86.6	85.0
Estonia Estonie										
Nitrogenous fertilizers										
Engrais azotés	* 52.3	* 41.8	* 29.3	* 40.4	37.9	* 16.6	20.5	24.9	19.6	16.0
Phosphate fertilizers										
Engrais phosphatés	...	...	...	...	...	2.6	4.3	4.4	* 5.3	* 6.5
Potash fertilizers										
Engrais potassiques	...	...	...	...	...	* 3.0	* 3.0	3.1	3.7	* 6.5
Finland Finlande										
Nitrogenous fertilizers										
Engrais azotés	* 231.0	* 238.0	* 227.0	* 227.0	249.0	174.0	177.0	* 175.0	* 176.0	* 175.0
Phosphate fertilizers										
Engrais phosphatés	105.0	* 95.0	96.0	* 96.0	* 101.0	57.0	56.0	* 53.0	* 52.0	* 53.0
Potash fertilizers *										
Engrais potassiques *	...	...	...	...	...	82.0	81.0	81.0	82.0	80.0
France France										
Nitrogenous fertilizers										
Engrais azotés	* 1 616.0	* 1 484.0	* 1 436.0	* 1 319.4	* 983.0	2 523.9	* 2 513.1	* 2 488.1	* 2 571.4	* 2 316.0
Phosphate fertilizers *										
Engrais phosphatés *	558.0	527.6	489.7	437.2	318.0	1 051.9	1 038.8	1 011.2	965.6	795.0
Potash fertilizers										
Engrais potassiques	* 751.0	* 665.3	* 417.1	* 311.3	* 321.0	1 488.2	* 1 436.9	* 1 337.7	* 1 216.4	* 1 034.0
Germany Allemagne										
Nitrogenous fertilizers										
Engrais azotés	* 1 269.0	* 1 125.0	* 1 175.0	* 1 265.0	* 1 101.5	1 758.0	1 788.4	1 903.0	2 014.0	1 847.6
Phosphate fertilizers										
Engrais phosphatés	* 203.0	194.0	* 184.0	* 94.9	* 69.3	415.1	409.5	406.7	421.0	351.3
Potash fertilizers										
Engrais potassiques	* 3 334.0	* 3 423.1	* 3 582.0	* 3 291.0	* 3 145.0	645.8	658.9	628.7	619.0	544.0
Greece Grèce										
Nitrogenous fertilizers *										
Engrais azotés *	316.0	240.0	231.0	225.0	224.0	340.0	307.0	292.0	291.0	285.0
Phosphate fertilizers *										
Engrais phosphatés *	162.0	125.0	115.0	114.0	108.0	145.0	132.0	120.0	119.0	113.0
Potash fertilizers *										
Engrais potassiques *	...	...	...	...	...	75.0	65.0	60.0	59.0	59.5

40

Fertilizers
Nitrogenous, phosphate and potash: thousand metric tons [*cont.*]
Engrais
Azotés, phosphatés et potassiques : milliers de tonnes [*suite*]

Country or area	Production Production					Consumption Consommation				
Pays ou zone	1996/97	1997/98	1998/99	1999/00	2000/01	1996/97	1997/98	1998/99	1999/00	2000/01
Hungary Hongrie										
Nitrogenous fertilizers										
Engrais azotés	260.9	251.4	* 213.5	* 314.3	* 330.4	318.5	* 285.8	* 282.0	* 320.6	344.2
Phosphate fertilizers										
Engrais phosphatés	28.5	* 26.5	* 20.0	* 4.9	25.3	* 74.7	* 73.5	* 37.6	* 48.6	57.6
Potash fertilizers										
Engrais potassiques	...	...	...	...	...	* 61.7	67.8	* 51.0	* 63.4	69.7
Iceland Islande										
Nitrogenous fertilizers										
Engrais azotés	12.3	* 12.0	* 11.5	* 12.0	* 12.0	11.6	* 11.8	* 12.5	* 13.5	* 13.0
Phosphate fertilizers *										
Engrais phosphatés *	...	...	...	...	...	3.5	4.1	4.2	4.2	4.0
Potash fertilizers *										
Engrais potassiques *	...	...	...	...	...	3.8	3.4	2.0	4.2	4.0
Ireland Irlande										
Nitrogenous fertilizers *										
Engrais azotés *	288.0	326.0	311.0	170.0	170.9	394.0	397.0	444.0	407.6	394.0
Phosphate fertilizers *										
Engrais phosphatés *	...	...	...	...	...	128.0	113.0	116.0	115.0	98.0
Potash fertilizers										
Engrais potassiques	...	...	...	...	...	160.0	150.0	152.0	148.0	134.0
Italy Italie										
Nitrogenous fertilizers *										
Engrais azotés *	535.0	537.0	463.0	430.0	427.0	876.0	855.0	845.0	868.0	828.0
Phosphate fertilizers *										
Engrais phosphatés *	198.0	170.0	153.0	64.0	116.0	575.0	501.0	508.0	514.0	504.0
Potash fertilizers *										
Engrais potassiques *	...	...	...	...	...	414.0	402.0	395.0	402.0	394.0
Latvia Lettonie										
Nitrogenous fertilizers										
Engrais azotés	...	...	...	...	...	* 14.0	* 19.0	* 31.5	* 33.6	28.5
Phosphate fertilizers										
Engrais phosphatés	...	...	...	...	...	* 6.0	* 8.1	* 10.7	* 10.6	10.4
Potash fertilizers										
Engrais potassiques	...	...	...	...	...	* 5.0	* 8.0	* 7.0	10.3	11.6
Lithuania Lituanie										
Nitrogenous fertilizers										
Engrais azotés	* 300.2	* 322.9	* 447.3	* 454.7	531.0	* 79.0	* 81.1	* 83.4	* 94.0	* 100.0
Phosphate fertilizers										
Engrais phosphatés	* 146.1	* 192.8	* 230.5	299.6	296.6	* 10.0	* 18.2	* 18.4	20.0	20.0
Potash fertilizers *										
Engrais potassiques *	...	...	...	...	...	30.0	38.0	38.0	35.0	40.0
Malta Malte										
Nitrogenous fertilizers										
Engrais azotés	...	...	...	...	...	* 1.0	* 1.0	1.2	0.5	* 0.5
Phosphate fertilizers										
Engrais phosphatés	...	...	...	...	...	0.0	0.0	0.2	0.1	* 0.2
Potash fertilizers										
Engrais potassiques	...	...	...	...	...	0.0	0.0	0.2	0.1	* 0.2
Netherlands Pays–Bas										
Nitrogenous fertilizers *										
Engrais azotés *	1 513.0	1 586.0	1 548.0	1 081.0	1 109.0	390.0	375.0	350.0	345.0	300.0
Phosphate fertilizers										
Engrais phosphatés	* 271.0	* 402.0	* 343.0	* 105.0	* 53.0	* 65.0	60.0	* 62.0	* 59.0	* 55.0
Potash fertilizers *										
Engrais potassiques *	...	...	...	...	...	72.0	73.0	73.0	73.0	70.0
Norway Norvège										
Nitrogenous fertilizers *										
Engrais azotés *	* 595.0	* 570.0	* 470.0	* 511.0	* 618.2	* 112.0	* 112.0	* 106.0	* 106.0	103.0
Phosphate fertilizers *										
Engrais phosphatés	265.0	236.0	194.0	229.0	247.0	32.0	30.0	31.0	30.0	30.0
Potash fertilizers *										
Engrais potassiques *	...	...	...	...	...	65.0	63.0	64.0	63.0	63.0

40
Fertilizers
Nitrogenous, phosphate and potash: thousand metric tons [*cont.*]
Engrais
Azotés, phosphatés et potassiques : milliers de tonnes [*suite*]

Country or area	Production Production					Consumption Consommation				
Pays ou zone	1996/97	1997/98	1998/99	1999/00	2000/01	1996/97	1997/98	1998/99	1999/00	2000/01
Poland Pologne										
Nitrogenous fertilizers										
Engrais azotés	1 548.0	* 1 557.4	* 1 575.6	* 1 359.5	1 492.7	* 910.0	* 1 009.7	862.0	861.3	878.4
Phosphate fertilizers										
Engrais phosphatés	* 442.0	* 473.6	* 480.2	* 473.0	* 430.2	310.0	* 289.6	308.4	296.3	* 270.0
Potash fertilizers										
Engrais potassiques	...	...	...	...	...	376.1	* 400.9	386.7	368.7	370.0
Portugal Portugal										
Nitrogenous fertilizers *										
Engrais azotés *	135.0	143.0	134.0	123.0	117.0	132.0	121.0	131.0	121.0	113.0
Phosphate fertilizers *										
Engrais phosphatés *	57.0	56.0	62.0	56.0	58.0	76.0	67.0	71.0	68.0	66.0
Potash fertilizers *										
Engrais potassiques *	...	...	...	...	...	50.0	48.0	50.0	50.0	49.0
Republic of Moldova République de Moldova										
Nitrogenous fertilizers *										
Engrais azotés *	...	...	...	...	...	60.0	9.5	6.8	3.1	5.0
Phosphate fertilizers *										
Engrais phosphatés *	...	...	...	...	...	40.0	0.5	0.1	0.1	0.1
Potash fertilizers										
Engrais potassiques	...	...	...	...	...	* 16.0	* 0.2	* 0.1	0.0	0.0
Romania Roumanie										
Nitrogenous fertilizers										
Engrais azotés	* 1 250.0	663.7	* 314.1	517.7	869.0	* 266.0	* 220.0	* 268.0	* 182.0	* 300.0
Phosphate fertilizers										
Engrais phosphatés	202.0	* 135.8	* 96.2	* 111.2	99.2	* 141.0	* 85.0	* 80.0	* 46.0	* 56.0
Potash fertilizers *										
Engrais potassiques *	...	...	...	...	...	15.0	10.0	12.0	8.6	9.0
Russian Federation Fédération de Russie										
Nitrogenous fertilizers										
Engrais azotés	* 4 900.0	* 4 094.7	* 4 135.0	* 4 966.1	* 5 464.0	* 984.0	* 950.0	* 831.0	* 959.0	960.0
Phosphate fertilizers										
Engrais phosphatés	* 1 575.0	* 1 853.0	* 1 688.0	* 2 017.4	* 2 319.8	* 376.0	* 320.0	* 280.0	* 220.0	280.0
Potash fertilizers										
Engrais potassiques	* 2 618.0	* 3 403.0	* 3 461.0	* 4 050.0	* 3 716.0	* 220.0	* 280.0	* 153.0	* 182.0	180.0
Serbia and Montenegro Serbie—et—Monténégro										
Nitrogenous fertilizers *										
Engrais azotés *	95.0	171.0	185.1	72.0	85.0	160.5	185.0	154.0	138.1	153.0
Phosphate fertilizers *										
Engrais phosphatés *	14.0	16.0	24.0	12.0	12.0	19.0	35.0	24.0	26.0	17.0
Potash fertilizers *										
Engrais potassiques *	...	...	...	...	...	35.0	24.0	25.0	29.0	29.0
Slovakia Slovaquie										
Nitrogenous fertilizers										
Engrais azotés	* 210.8	* 283.8	* 245.9	* 204.0	* 262.3	77.6	* 72.5	82.8	65.3	72.7
Phosphate fertilizers										
Engrais phosphatés	* 36.7	* 16.0	* 15.0	* 15.0	* 15.0	20.9	* 17.8	* 20.5	13.1	15.7
Potash fertilizers										
Engrais potassiques	...	...	...	...	...	* 20.2	* 17.1	* 17.1	10.6	12.9
Slovenia Slovénie										
Nitrogenous fertilizers										
Engrais azotés	...	...	...	...	...	24.2	34.1	34.8	34.4	34.8
Phosphate fertilizers										
Engrais phosphatés	...	...	...	...	...	* 17.5	17.5	18.8	19.8	18.4
Potash fertilizers										
Engrais potassiques	...	...	...	...	...	* 21.6	22.3	23.0	24.5	22.1
Spain Espagne										
Nitrogenous fertilizers										
Engrais azotés	881.7	918.5	* 878.0	* 745.6	* 677.2	1 153.1	1 041.9	* 1 199.0	1 180.7	1 113.7
Phosphate fertilizers										
Engrais phosphatés	* 333.0	* 349.0	* 407.0	* 357.6	* 326.4	* 581.0	* 589.0	* 655.0	* 643.0	568.1
Potash fertilizers										
Engrais potassiques	680.1	640.0	* 496.0	* 452.0	* 454.3	* 458.0	* 477.0	* 513.0	* 495.0	467.6

40
Fertilizers
Nitrogenous, phosphate and potash: thousand metric tons [*cont.*]
Engrais
Azotés, phosphatés et potassiques : milliers de tonnes [*suite*]

Country or area	Production Production					Consumption Consommation				
Pays ou zone	1996/97	1997/98	1998/99	1999/00	2000/01	1996/97	1997/98	1998/99	1999/00	2000/01
Sweden Suède										
Nitrogenous fertilizers										
Engrais azotés	* 107.0	* 103.0	* 94.0	* 103.0	* 97.0	207.8	207.0	* 196.0	* 197.0	* 192.0
Phosphate fertilizers										
Engrais phosphatés	* 16.0	* 15.0	* 18.0	* 9.0	* 22.0	49.9	49.0	47.0	* 43.0	* 38.0
Potash fertilizers										
Engrais potassiques	...	...	...	...	...	52.8	* 54.0	* 51.0	50.0	50.1
Switzerland Suisse										
Nitrogenous fertilizers *										
Engrais azotés *	13.0	19.0	18.0	11.0	15.0	62.0	60.0	59.0	53.0	55.0
Phosphate fertilizers *										
Engrais phosphatés *	...	...	...	...	...	26.0	25.0	25.0	18.0	17.0
Potash fertilizers *										
Engrais potassiques *	...	...	...	...	...	37.0	36.0	36.0	31.0	30.0
TFYR of Macedonia L'ex−R.y. Macédoine										
Nitrogenous fertilizers *										
Engrais azotés *	6.0	6.5	6.5	7.0	8.0	30.4	28.1	25.2	25.0	24.2
Phosphate fertilizers										
Engrais phosphatés	* 8.0	* 7.0	* 7.0	7.5	* 8.5	* 7.0	* 9.2	* 9.5	10.5	* 12.5
Potash fertilizers										
Engrais potassiques	...	...	...	...	...	* 6.0	* 9.4	* 4.5	8.0	* 9.0
Ukraine Ukraine										
Nitrogenous fertilizers *										
Engrais azotés *	2 083.3	2 001.7	1 687.1	1 959.5	2 250.2	373.0	413.0	406.0	327.0	350.0
Phosphate fertilizers										
Engrais phosphatés	* 326.5	* 299.6	* 231.1	* 211.4	* 83.1	* 97.0	* 104.0	76.0	* 62.0	* 62.0
Potash fertilizers										
Engrais potassiques	* 39.3	* 52.2	* 33.6	* 11.8	* 19.3	* 55.0	* 45.0	32.0	* 28.0	* 28.0
United Kingdom Royaume−Uni										
Nitrogenous fertilizers *										
Engrais azotés *	896.0	952.0	940.0	760.0	398.5	1 451.0	1 363.0	1 286.0	1 268.0	1 030.0
Phosphate fertilizers *										
Engrais phosphatés *	111.0	190.0	69.0	54.0	59.0	416.0	408.0	345.0	317.0	284.0
Potash fertilizers *										
Engrais potassiques *	618.0	565.0	608.0	457.0	569.0	509.0	499.0	450.0	411.0	380.0
Oceania Océanie										
Nitrogenous fertilizers										
Engrais azotés	**348.7**	**331.8**	**391.5**	**424.0**	**441.3**	**983.3**	**997.3**	**1 145.3**	**1 290.2**	**1 255.3**
Phosphate fertilizers										
Engrais phosphatés	**573.4**	**653.4**	**617.0**	**743.6**	**788.9**	**1 378.7**	**1 477.6**	**1 421.4**	**1 441.5**	**1 562.0**
Potash fertilizers										
Engrais potassiques	...	...	...	...	...	348.5	391.8	373.2	349.7	348.3
Australia Australie										
Nitrogenous fertilizers *										
Engrais azotés *	278.7	250.8	299.0	316.0	347.0	824.6	839.4	979.0	1 099.4	1 002.2
Phosphate fertilizers										
Engrais phosphatés	* 333.4	* 383.4	* 357.0	* 428.6	473.9	* 985.3	* 1 090.1	* 1 039.0	* 1 034.9	* 1 096.6
Potash fertilizers *										
Engrais potassiques *	...	...	...	...	...	206.0	254.6	231.9	206.9	202.6
Fiji Fidji										
Nitrogenous fertilizers *										
Engrais azotés *	...	...	...	...	...	10.0	10.2	8.9	6.4	2.5
Phosphate fertilizers *										
Engrais phosphatés *	...	...	...	...	...	4.0	4.0	3.2	2.0	2.0
Potash fertilizers *										
Engrais potassiques *	...	...	...	...	...	5.0	5.0	6.3	6.0	3.0
French Polynesia Polynésie française										
Nitrogenous fertilizers										
Engrais azotés	...	...	...	...	...	* 0.4	* 0.4	* 0.4	0.5	* 0.5
Phosphate fertilizers										
Engrais phosphatés	...	...	...	...	...	* 0.4	* 0.4	* 0.4	0.3	* 0.3
Potash fertilizers										
Engrais potassiques	...	...	...	...	...	* 0.2	* 0.2	* 0.2	0.4	* 0.4

40

Fertilizers
Nitrogenous, phosphate and potash: thousand metric tons [*cont.*]
    Engrais
    Azotés, phosphatés et potassiques : milliers de tonnes [*suite*]

Country or area	Production Production					Consumption Consommation				
Pays ou zone	1996/97	1997/98	1998/99	1999/00	2000/01	1996/97	1997/98	1998/99	1999/00	2000/01
New Caledonia Nouvelle – Calédonie										
Nitrogenous fertilizers *										
Engrais azotés *	...	...	...	...	...	0.3	0.3	0.3	0.3	0.3
Phosphate fertilizers *										
Engrais phosphatés *	...	...	...	...	...	1.0	1.0	0.3	0.3	0.3
Potash fertilizers *										
Engrais potassiques *	...	...	...	...	...	0.3	0.3	0.3	0.3	0.3
New Zealand Nouvelle – Zélande										
Nitrogenous fertilizers *										
Engrais azotés *	70.0	81.0	92.5	108.0	94.3	140.0	138.9	153.5	180.0	242.0
Phosphate fertilizers *										
Engrais phosphatés *	240.0	270.0	260.0	315.0	315.0	385.0	379.1	376.0	400.0	458.0
Potash fertilizers *										
Engrais potassiques *	...	...	...	...	...	135.0	129.7	132.0	133.0	138.0
Papua New Guinea Papouasie – Nvl – Guinée										
Nitrogenous fertilizers *										
Engrais azotés *	...	...	...	...	...	8.0	8.1	3.2	2.7	4.7
Phosphate fertilizers *										
Engrais phosphatés *	...	...	...	...	...	3.0	3.0	2.5	3.8	4.0
Potash fertilizers *										
Engrais potassiques *	...	...	...	...	...	2.0	2.0	2.5	2.8	3.0
Samoa Samoa										
Nitrogenous fertilizers										
Engrais azotés	...	...	...	...	...	0.0	0.0	0.0	0.9	3.1
Phosphate fertilizers										
Engrais phosphatés	...	...	...	...	...	0.0	0.0	0.0	0.2	0.8
Potash fertilizers										
Engrais potassiques	...	...	...	...	...	0.0	0.0	0.0	0.2	1.0

Source:
Food and Agriculture Organization of the United
Nations (FAO), Rome, FAOSTAT Agriculture Database
and the Fertilizer Yearbook 2001.

Source:
Organisation des Nations Unies pour l'alimentation et
l'agriculture (FAO), Rome, les données de l'agriculture de
FAOSTAT et l'Annuaire des Engrais 2001.

1   FAO estimate.

1   Estimation de FAO.

Technical notes, tables 34-40

The series shown on agriculture and fishing have been furnished by the Food and Agriculture Organization of the United Nations (FAO). They refer mainly to:

    (a)   Long-term trends in the growth of agricultural output and the food supply;

    (b)   Output of principal agricultural commodities.

Agricultural production is defined to include all crops and livestock products except those used for seed and fodder and other intermediate uses in agriculture; for example deductions are made for eggs used for hatching. Intermediate input of seeds and fodder and similar items refer to both domestically produced and imported commodities. For further details, reference may be made to FAO Yearbooks [4, 6, 7, 8, 9, 10]. FAO data are also available through the Internet (http://www.fao.org).

Table 34: "Agriculture" relates to the production of all crops and livestock products. The "Food Index" includes those commodities which are considered edible and contain nutrients.

The index numbers of agricultural output and food production are calculated by the Laspeyres formula with the base year period 1989-1991. The latter is provided in order to diminish the impact of annual fluctuations in agricultural output during base years on the indices for the period. Production quantities of each commodity are weighted by 1989-1991 average national producer prices and summed for each year. The index numbers are based on production data for a calendar year. These may differ in some instances from those actually produced and published by the individual countries themselves due to variations in concepts, coverage, weights and methods of calculation. Efforts have been made to estimate these methodological differences to achieve a better international comparability of data. The series include a large amount of estimates made by FAO in cases where no official or semi-official figures are available from the countries.

Detailed data on agricultural production are published by FAO in its *Production Yearbook* [6].

Table 35: The data on the production of cereals relate to crops harvested for dry grain only. Cereals harvested for hay, green feed or used for grazing are excluded.

Table 36: Oil crops, or oil-bearing crops, are those crops yielding seeds, nuts or fruits which are used mainly for the extraction of culinary or industrial oils, excluding essential oils. In this table, data for oil crops represent the total production of oil seeds, oil nuts and oil fruits harvested in the year indicated and expressed in terms of oil equivalent and cake/meal equivalent. That is

Notes techniques, tableaux 34 à 40

Les séries présentées sur l'agriculture et la pêche ont été fournies par l'Organisation des Nations Unies pour l'alimentation et l'agriculture (FAO) et portent principalement sur:

    (a)   Les tendances à long terme de la croissance de la production agricole et des approvisionnements alimentaires;

    (b)   La production des principales denrées agricoles.

La production agricole se définit comme comprenant l'ensemble des produits agricoles et des produits de l'élevage à l'exception de ceux utilisés comme semences et comme aliments pour les animaux, et pour les autres utilisations intermédiaires en agriculture; par exemple, on déduit les œufs utilisés pour la reproduction. L'apport intermédiaire de semences et d'aliments pour les animaux et d'autres éléments similaires se rapportent à la fois à des produits locaux et importés. Pour tous détails complémentaires, on se reportera aux annuaires de la FAO [4, 6, 7, 8, 9, 10]. Des statistiques peuvent également être consultées sur le site Web de la FAO (http://www.fao.org).

Tableau 34: L'"Agriculture" se rapporte à la production de tous les produits de l'agriculture et de l'élevage. L'"Indice des produits alimentaires" comprend les produits considérés comme comestibles et qui contiennent des éléments nutritifs.

Les indices de la production agricole et de la production alimentaire sont calculés selon la formule de Laspeyres avec les années 1989-1991 pour période de base. Le choix d'une période de plusieurs années permet de diminuer l'incidence des fluctuations annuelles de la production agricole pendant les années de base sur les indices pour cette période. Les quantités produites de chaque denrée sont pondérées par les prix nationaux moyens à la production de 1989-1991, et additionnées pour chaque année. Les indices sont fondés sur les données de production d'une année civile. Ils peuvent différer dans certains cas des indices effectivement établis et publiés par les pays eux-mêmes par suite de différences dans les concepts, la couverture, les pondérations et les méthodes de calcul. On s'est efforcé d'estimer ces différences méthodologiques afin de rendre les données plus facilement comparables à l'échelle internationale. Les séries comprennent une grande quantité d'estimations faites par la FAO dans les cas où les pays n'avaient pas fourni de chiffres officiels ou semi-officiels.

Des chiffres détaillés de production sont publiés dans l'*Annuaire FAO de la production* [6].

Tableau 35: Les données sur la production de céréales se rapportent uniquement aux céréales récoltées

to say, these figures do not relate to the actual production of vegetable oils and cake/meal, but to the potential production if the total amounts produced from all oil crops were processed into oil and cake/meal in producing countries in the same year in which they were harvested. Naturally, the total production of oil crops is never processed into oil in its entirety, since depending on the crop, important quantities are also used for seed, feed and food. However, although oil and cake/meal extraction rates vary from country to country, in this table the same extraction rate for each crop has been applied for all countries. Moreover. it should be borne in mind that the crops harvested during the latter months of the year are generally processed into oil during the following year.

In spite of these deficiencies in coverage, extraction rates and time reference, the data reported here are useful as they provide a valid indication of year-to-year changes in the size of total oil-crop production. The actual production of vegetable oils in the world is about 80 percent of the production reported here. In addition, about two million tonnes of vegetable oils are produced every year from crops which are not included among those defined above. The most important of these oils are maize-germ oil and rice-bran oil. The actual world production of cake/meal derived from oil crops is also about 80 percent of the production reported in the table.

Table 37: The data refer to livestock numbers grouped into twelve-month periods ending 30 September of the year stated and cover all domestic animals irrespective of their age and place or purpose of their breeding.

Table 38: The data on roundwood refer to wood in the rough, wood in its natural state as felled or otherwise harvested, with or without bark, round, split, roughly squared or in other form (i.e. roots, stumps, burls, etc.). It may also be impregnated (e.g. telegraph poles) or roughly shaped or pointed. It comprises all wood obtained from removals, i.e. the quantities removed from forests and from trees outside the forest, including wood recovered from natural, felling and logging losses during the period — calendar year or forest year.

Table 39: The data cover (i) capture production from marine and inland fisheries and (ii) aquaculture, and are expressed in terms of live weight. They include fish, crustaceans and molluscs but exclude sponges and corals, seaweed, crocodiles, and aquatic mammals (such as whales and dolphins).

The flag of the vessel is considered as the paramount indication of the nationality of the catch. Marine fisheries data include landings by domestic craft in foreign ports and exclude landings by foreign craft in domestic ports.

pour le grain sec; celles cultivées pour le foin, le fourrage vert ou le pâturage en sont exclues.

Tableau 36: On désigne sous le nom de cultures oléagineuses l'ensemble des cultures produisant des graines, des noix ou des fruits, essentiellement destinées à l'extraction d'huiles alimentaires ou industrielles, à l'exclusion des huiles essentielles. Dans ce tableau, les chiffres se rapportent à la production totale de graines, noix et fruits oléagineux récoltés au cours de l'année de référence et sont exprimés en équivalent d'huile et en équivalent de tourteau/farine. En d'autres termes, ces chiffres ne se rapportent pas à la production effective mais à la production potentielle d'huiles végétales et de tourteau/farine dans l'hypothèse où les volumes totaux de produits provenant de toutes les cultures d'oléagineux seraient transformés en huile et en tourteau/farine dans les pays producteurs l'année même où ils ont été récoltés. Bien entendu, la production totale d'oléagineux n'est jamais transformée intégralement en huile, car des quantités importantes qui varient suivant les cultures sont également utilisées pour les semailles, l'alimentation animale et l'alimentation humaine. Toutefois, bien que les taux d'extraction d'huile et de tourteau/farine varient selon les pays, on a appliqué dans ce tableau le même taux à tous les pays pour chaque oléagineux. En outre, il ne faut pas oublier que les produits récoltés au cours des derniers mois de l'année sont généralement transformés en huile dans le courant de l'année suivante.

En dépit de ces imperfections qui concernent le champ d'application, les taux d'extraction et les périodes de référence, les chiffres présentés ici sont utiles, car ils donnent une indication valable des variations de volume que la production totale d'oléagineux enregistre d'une année à l'autre. La production mondiale effective d'huiles végétales atteint 80 pour cent environ de la production indiquée ici. En outre, environ 2 millions de tonnes d'huiles végétales sont produites chaque année à partir de cultures non comprises dans les catégories définies ci-dessus. Les principales sont l'huile de germes de maïs et l'huile de son de riz. La production mondiale effective tourteau/farine d'oléagineux représente environ 80 pour cent de production indiquée dans le tableau.

Tableau 37: Les statistiques sur les effectifs du cheptel sont groupées en périodes de 12 mois se terminant le 30 septembre de l'année indiquée et s'entendent de tous les animaux domestiques, quel que soit leur âge, leur emplacement ou le but de leur élevage.

Tableau 38: Les données sur le bois rond se réfèrent au bois brut, bois à l'état naturel, tel qu'il a été abattu ou récolté autrement, avec ou sans écorce, fendu, grossièrement équarri ou sous une autre forme (par exemple, racines, souches, loupes, etc.). Il peut être éga-

To separate capture fisheries from aquaculture production, at least two criteria must apply i.e., the human intervention in one or more of the phases of the growth cycle, and individual, corporate or state ownership of the organism reared and harvested.

Data on aquaculture production are published in the *FAO Yearbook of Fishery Statistics, Aquaculture Production* [7]; capture production statistics are published in the *Yearbook of Fishery Statistics, Capture Production* [8].

Table 40: The data generally refer to the fertilizer year 1 July-30 June.

Nitrogenous fertilizers: data refer to the nitrogen content of commercial inorganic fertilizers.

Phosphate fertilizers: data refer to commercial phosphoric acid (P_2O_5) and cover the P_2O_5 of superphosphates, ammonium phosphate and basic slag.

Potash fertilizers: data refer to K_2O content of commercial potash, muriate, nitrate and sulphate of potash, manure salts, kainit and nitrate of soda potash.

Data on fertilizer production, consumption and trade are available in FAO's *Fertilizer Yearbook* [4].

lement imprégné (par exemple, dans le cas des poteaux télégraphiques) et dégrossi ou taillé en pointe. Cette catégorie comprend tous les bois provenant des quantités enlevées en forêt ou provenant des arbres poussant hors forêt, y compris le volume récupéré sur les déchets naturels et les déchets d'abattage et de transport pendant la période envisagée (année civile ou forestière).

Tableau 39: Les données ont trait (i) à la pêche maritime et intérieure et (ii) à l'aquaculture, et sont exprimées en poids vif. Elles comprennent poissons, crustacés et mollusques, mais excluent éponges, coraux, algues, crocodiles et les mammifères aquatiques (baleines, dauphins, etc.).

Le pavillon du navire est considéré comme la principale indication de la nationalité de la prise.

Les données de pêche maritime comprennent les quantités débarquées par des bateaux nationaux dans des ports étrangers et excluent les quantités débarquées par des bateaux étrangers dans des ports nationaux.

Pour séparer la production d'aquaculture de la pêche de capture, au moins deux critères doivent se vérifier, c'est-à-dire l'intervention humaine dans une ou plusieurs des phases du cycle de croissance, et l'appartenance de l'organisme élevé et récolté à une personne physique, à une personne morale ou à l'état.

Les données sur la production de l'aquaculture sont publiées dans l'*Annuaire statistique des pêches, production de l'aquaculture* [7] ; celles sur les captures sont publiées dans l'*Annuaire statistique des pêches, captures* [8].

Tableau 40: Les données sur les engrais se rapportent en général à une période d'un an comptée du 1er juillet au 30 juin.

Engrais azotés: les données se rapportent à la teneur en azote des engrais commerciaux inorganiques.

Engrais phosphatés: les données se rapportent à l'acide phosphorique (P_2O_5) et englobent la teneur en (P_2O_5) des superphosphates, du phosphate d'ammonium et des scories de déphosphoration.

Engrais potassiques: les données se rapportent à la teneur en K_2O des produits potassiques commerciaux, muriate, nitrate et sulfate de potasse, sels d'engrais, kainite et nitrate de soude potassique.

On trouvera des chiffres relatifs à la production, à la consommation et aux échanges d'engrais dans l'*Annuaire FAO des engrais* [4].

41
Sugar
Production and consumption: thousand metric tons; consumption per capita: kilograms
Sucre
Production et consommation : milliers de tonnes ; consommation per habitant : kilogrammes

Country or area	1995	1996	1997	1998	1999	2000	2001	Pays ou zone
World								**Monde**
Production	**117 883**	**125 014**	**125 037**	**125 893**	**135 005**	**130 037**	**130 616**	**Production**
Consumption	**116 416**	**119 878**	**122 980**	**122 607**	**126 183**	**127 307**	**130 939**	**Consommation**
Consumption per cap. kg.)	**20**	**21**	**21**	**20**	**21**	**21**	**21**	**Consom. par hab. (kg.)**
Afghanistan								**Afghanistan**
Consumption *	50	45	50	55	60	60	60	Consommation *
Consumption per cap. (kg.)	3	2	3	3	3	3	3	Consom. par hab.(kg.)
Albania								**Albanie**
Production	* 10	9	* 3	* 3	* 3	* 3	* 3	Production
Consumption *	80	80	65	65	65	68	68	Consommation *
Consumption per cap. (kg.)	24	24	20	20	20	22	22	Consom. par hab.(kg.)
Algeria								**Algérie**
Consumption *	775	750	650	800	900	935	965	Consommation *
Consumption per cap. (kg.)	28	26	22	27	29	31	32	Consom. par hab.(kg.)
Angola								**Angola**
Production *	30	25	28	32	32	30	30	Production *
Consumption *	100	110	110	85	120	130	155	Consommation *
Consumption per cap. (kg.)	9	10	9	7	10	10	11	Consom. par hab.(kg.)
Argentina								**Argentine**
Production	1 612	1 393	1 649	1 749	* 1 882	* 1 580	* 1 630	Production
Consumption	1 350	1 347	* 1 350	* 1 350	* 1 450	* 1 485	* 1 520	Consommation
Consumption per cap. (kg.)	39	39	38	38	40	41	41	Consom. par hab.(kg.)
Armenia								**Arménie**
Consumption *	50	60	60	65	70	72	73	Consommation *
Consumption per cap. (kg.)	13	16	16	17	19	19	19	Consom. par hab.(kg.)
Australia								**Australie**
Production	5 119	5 618	5 883	5 085	5 514	4 417	4 768	Production
Consumption	926	976	1 003	1 003	* 1 005	1 048	1 068	Consommation
Consumption per cap. (kg.)	51	53	54	54	53	55	55	Consom. par hab.(kg.)
Austria *[1]								**Autriche *[1]**
Production	481	535	529	533	545	447	478	Production
Azerbaijan								**Azerbaïdjan**
Consumption	* 170	* 170	123	157	* 160	* 160	* 160	Consommation
Consumption per cap. (kg.)	22	22	16	20	20	20	20	Consom. par hab.(kg.)
Bahamas								**Bahamas**
Consumption	11	12	10	10	10	11	8	Consommation
Consumption per cap. (kg.)	41	44	36	36	35	35	28	Consom. par hab.(kg.)
Bangladesh								**Bangladesh**
Production	* 278	* 194	* 138	* 159	* 162	* 110	109	Production
Consumption *	285	290	300	270	300	325	335	Consommation *
Consumption per cap. (kg.)	2	2	2	2	3	3	3	Consom. par hab.(kg.)
Barbados								**Barbade**
Production	* 55	59	62	46	53	58	* 50	Production
Consumption	* 14	16	16	15	* 15	* 16	* 15	Consommation
Consumption per cap. (kg.)	54	60	62	55	56	57	56	Consom. par hab.(kg.)
Belarus								**Bélarus**
Production	139	144	179	180	151	186	196	Production
Consumption	355	358	380	405[2]	* 357	380	422	Consommation
Consumption per cap. (kg.)	34	35	37	39	35	38	42	Consom. par hab.(kg.)
Belgium-Luxembourg[1]								**Belgique-Luxembourg[1]**
Production	999	1 036	1 106	863	1 187	* 1 024	* 874	Production
Belize								**Belize**
Production	115	113	131	123	124	128	114	Production
Consumption	13	15	16	15	15	15	12[3]	Consommation
Consumption per cap. (kg.)	60	69	68	64	61	58	45	Consom. par hab.(kg.)
Benin								**Bénin**
Production *	5	5	4	4	4	5	5	Production *
Consumption	* 45	* 45	* 40	* 40	* 45	* 46	22	Consommation
Consumption per cap. (kg.)	8	8	7	7	8	8	3	Consom. par hab.(kg.)
Bermuda								**Bermudes**
Consumption	2	2	1	2	1	2	2	Consommation

41

Sugar
Production and consumption: thousand metric tons; consumption per capita: kilograms *[cont.]*
Sucre
Production et consommation : milliers de tonnes ; consommation par habitant : kilogrammes *[suite]*

Country or area	1995	1996	1997	1998	1999	2000	2001	Pays ou zone
Consumption per cap. (kg.)	25	25	17	25	17	25	25	Consom. par hab.(kg.)
Bolivia								**Bolivie**
Production	* 230	* 270	* 277	282	293	311	* 288	Production
Consumption	* 215	* 225	* 235	287	290	* 293	* 295	Consommation
Consumption per cap. (kg.)	29	30	30	36	36	35	35	Consom. par hab.(kg.)
Bosnia and Herzegovina								**Bosnie-Herzégovine**
Production *	10	15	0	0	0	0	0	Production *
Consumption *	30	30	30	75	80	90	110	Consommation *
Consumption per cap. (kg.)	7	7	9	21	21	23	27	Consom. par hab.(kg.)
Botswana								**Botswana**
Consumption	40	40	30	45	45	46	46	Consommation
Consumption per cap. (kg.)	27	27	20	29	28	28	27	Consom. par hab.(kg.)
Brazil								**Brésil**
Production	13 835	14 718	16 371	19 168	20 646	16 464	20 336	Production
Consumption *	8 230	8 490	8 900	9 150	9 500	9 725	9 800	Consommation *
Consumption per cap. (kg.)	53	54	56	57	57	58	58	Consom. par hab.(kg.)
Brunei Darussalam								**Brunéi Darussalam**
Consumption	8	6	4	7	5	6	10	Consommation
Consumption per cap. (kg.)	25	19	11	20	15	18	29	Consom. par hab.(kg.)
Bulgaria								**Bulgarie**
Production *	15	7	6	5	2	2	3	Production *
Consumption *	260	260	260	260	225	230	235	Consommation *
Consumption per cap. (kg.)	31	30	31	32	27	29	30	Consom. par hab.(kg.)
Burkina Faso								**Burkina Faso**
Production	* 32	* 33	* 34	* 30	30	* 30	* 35	Production
Consumption *	35	35	42	50	45	46	50	Consommation *
Consumption per cap. (kg.)	3	3	4	5	4	4	4	Consom. par hab.(kg.)
Burundi								**Burundi**
Production	10	8	8	24	23	24	20	Production
Consumption	25	20	12	22	23	24	23	Consommation
Consumption per cap. (kg.)	4	3	2	4	4	4	4	Consom. par hab.(kg.)
Cambodia								**Cambodge**
Consumption *	22	40	55	65	75	85	90	Consommation *
Consumption per cap. (kg.)	2	4	5	5	6	7	7	Consom. par hab.(kg.)
Cameroon								**Cameroun**
Production	* 59	* 52	* 44	* 46	* 52	41	94	Production
Consumption	* 85	* 85	* 80	* 95	* 95	* 95	112	Consommation
Consumption per cap. (kg.)	6	6	6	7	7	6	8	Consom. par hab.(kg.)
Canada								**Canada**
Production *	167	158	115	104	118	123	95	Production *
Consumption *	1 200	1 225	1 225	1 200	1 200	1 235	1 240	Consommation *
Consumption per cap. (kg.)	41	41	41	40	39	40	40	Consom. par hab.(kg.)
Cape Verde								**Cap-Vert**
Consumption *	15	17	18	12	12	13	20	Consommation *
Consumption per cap. (kg.)	39	40	42	33	31	31	46	Consom. par hab.(kg.)
Central African Rep.								**Rép. centrafricaine**
Consumption *	3	5	5	5	4	4	4	Consommation *
Consumption per cap. (kg.)	1	1	2	1	1	1	1	Consom. par hab.(kg.)
Chad								**Tchad**
Production *	30	30	34	31	32	32	32	Production *
Consumption *	47	50	46	55	55	57	57	Consommation *
Consumption per cap. (kg.)	8	7	6	7	7	7	7	Consom. par hab.(kg.)
Chile								**Chili**
Production	596	459	390	511	487	457	430	Production
Consumption	650	* 700	* 720	728	729	683	685	Consommation
Consumption per cap. (kg.)	46	49	49	49	49	45	44	Consom. par hab.(kg.)
China								**Chine**
Production	6 148	* 7 091	7 415	8 904	8 527	7 616	7 160	Production
Consumption *	8 200	8 250	8 250	8 300	8 300	8 500	8 900	Consommation *
Consumption per cap. (kg.)	7	7	6	7	7	7	7	Consom. par hab.(kg.)

41

Sugar
Production and consumption: thousand metric tons; consumption per capita: kilograms *[cont.]*

Sucre
Production et consommation : milliers de tonnes ; consommation par habitant : kilogrammes *[suite]*

Country or area	1995	1996	1997	1998	1999	2000	2001	Pays ou zone
China, Hong Kong SAR								**Chine, Hong Kong RAS**
Consumption *	160	180	180	180	180	181	185	Consommation *
Consumption per cap. (kg.)	26	28	28	28	27	27	28	Consom. par hab.(kg.)
China, Macao SAR								**Chine, Macao RAS**
Consumption	5	6	7	7	7	7	7	Consommation
Consumption per cap. (kg.)	12	13	17	17	16	17	16	Consom. par hab.(kg.)
Colombia								**Colombie**
Production	2 069	2 149	2 136	2 126	2 241	2 391	2 260	Production
Consumption [4]	1 128	1 206	1 192	1 240	1 281	1 343	1 309	Consommation [4]
Consumption per cap. (kg.)	29	31	30	30	31	32	30	Consom. par hab.(kg.)
Comoros								**Comores**
Consumption	3	3	2	5	5	6	8	Consommation
Consumption per cap. (kg.)	5	4	3	8	7	8	11	Consom. par hab.(kg.)
Congo								**Congo**
Production	38	42	* 45	* 45	* 35	* 40	* 45	Production
Consumption *	28	28	30	30	30	40	45	Consommation *
Consumption per cap. (kg.)	11	11	11	11	10	13	15	Consom. par hab.(kg.)
Costa Rica								**Costa Rica**
Production	* 355	* 332	* 319	* 381	* 378	338	358	Production
Consumption	* 195	* 225	* 220	* 210	* 210	208	* 210	Consommation
Consumption per cap. (kg.)	62	70	67	62	61	59	58	Consom. par hab.(kg.)
Côte d'Ivoire								**Côte d'Ivoire**
Production	* 160	* 134	* 132	126	152	189	* 155	Production
Consumption	* 160	* 170	* 170	137	* 170	* 180	* 190	Consommation
Consumption per cap. (kg.)	11	12	11	9	11	11	11	Consom. par hab.(kg.)
Croatia								**Croatie**
Production	191	212	154	151	114	57	130	Production
Consumption *	180	190	190	195	180	180	180	Consommation *
Consumption per cap. (kg.)	39	42	42	43	40	41	41	Consom. par hab.(kg.)
Cuba								**Cuba**
Production	3 259	4 529	4 318	3 291	3 875	4 057	3 548	Production
Consumption	581	* 670	733	713	711	705	698	Consommation
Consumption per cap. (kg.)	53	61	66	64	64	63	62	Consom. par hab.(kg.)
Cyprus								**Chypre**
Consumption *	35	30	30	30	30	31	31	Consommation *
Consumption per cap. (kg.)	49	41	41	40	40	41	42	Consom. par hab.(kg.)
Czech Republic								**République tchèque**
Production	550	654	648	535	420	434	484	Production
Consumption	* 435	412	* 425	438	* 450	440	* 450	Consommation
Consumption per cap. (kg.)	42	40	41	43	44	43	44	Consom. par hab.(kg.)
Dem. Rep. of the Congo								**Rép. dém. du Congo**
Production	* 80	* 50	* 86	* 51	* 65	* 75	60	Production
Consumption *	110	110	90	80	75	75	75	Consommation *
Consumption per cap. (kg.)	3	2	2	2	2	2	1	Consom. par hab.(kg.)
Denmark [1]								**Danemark [1]**
Production	448	536	603	585	589	595	* 514	Production
Djibouti								**Djibouti**
Consumption	12	11	10	10	12	13	13	Consommation
Consumption per cap. (kg.)	21	19	17	16	19	20	20	Consom. par hab.(kg.)
Dominican Republic								**Rép. dominicaine**
Production	508	* 670	687	409	421	438	491	Production
Consumption	300	* 350	274	337	* 350	298	352	Consommation
Consumption per cap. (kg.)	39	45	34	42	42	35	41	Consom. par hab.(kg.)
Ecuador								**Equateur**
Production	358	419	190	* 354	* 420	* 500	* 495	Production
Consumption	355	* 375	396	* 410	* 425	* 440	* 465	Consommation
Consumption per cap. (kg.)	31	32	33	34	34	35	36	Consom. par hab.(kg.)
Egypt								**Egypte**
Production *	1 125	1 222	1 228	1 152	1 269	1 450	1 585	Production *
Consumption *	1 775	1 850	2 000	2 075	2 150	2 250	2 325	Consommation *
Consumption per cap. (kg.)	30	31	33	34	34	35	36	Consom. par hab.(kg.)

41

Sugar
Production and consumption: thousand metric tons; consumption per capita: kilograms *[cont.]*

Sucre
Production et consommation : milliers de tonnes ; consommation par habitant : kilogrammes *[suite]*

Country or area	1995	1996	1997	1998	1999	2000	2001	Pays ou zone
El Salvador								**El Salvador**
Production	* 300	* 352	414	487	585	562	527	Production
Consumption	* 190	* 210	232	237	234	236	244	Consommation
Consumption per cap. (kg.)	34	36	39	39	38	38	39	Consom. par hab.(kg.)
Eritrea								**Erythrée**
Consumption	...	...	10	10	8	8	8	Consommation
Estonia								**Estonie**
Consumption	* 40	37	* 50	* 55	* 65	* 70	* 73	Consommation
Consumption per cap. (kg.)	27	25	34	38	46	51	51	Consom. par hab.(kg.)
Ethiopia								**Ethiopie**
Production	128	180	126	219	235	251	* 305	Production
Consumption	96	206	145	185	199	246	* 250	Consommation
Consumption per cap. (kg.)	2	4	3	3	3	4	4	Consom. par hab.(kg.)
Fiji								**Fidji**
Production	458	474	369	278	377	353	327	Production
Consumption [5]	48	48	51	44	38	41	45	Consommation [5]
Consumption per cap. (kg.)	63	62	64	55	47	51	56	Consom. par hab.(kg.)
Finland [1]								**Finlande** [1]
Production	164	135	175	133	180	* 166	* 158	Production
France [1]								**France** [1]
Production	4 564	4 543	5 134	4 637	4 914	* 4 685	* 4 195	Production
Gabon								**Gabon**
Production *	16	15	16	17	16	17	18	Production *
Consumption *	17	16	16	17	18	19	19	Consommation *
Consumption per cap. (kg.)	16	14	14	15	15	15	15	Consom. par hab.(kg.)
Gambia								**Gambie**
Consumption *	45	30	40	45	50	58	60	Consommation *
Consumption per cap. (kg.)	41	26	34	37	36	41	43	Consom. par hab.(kg.)
Georgia								**Géorgie**
Production	0	0	0	0	0	0	0	Production
Consumption *	70	90	95	100	105	108	110	Consommation *
Consumption per cap. (kg.)	13	17	18	19	21	21	22	Consom. par hab.(kg.)
Germany [1]								**Allemagne** [1]
Production	3 826	4 203	4 045	4 037	4 401	4 361	3 736	Production
Ghana								**Ghana**
Consumption *	120	120	130	140	145	150	155	Consommation *
Consumption per cap. (kg.)	7	7	7	8	8	8	8	Consom. par hab.(kg.)
Gibraltar								**Gibraltar**
Consumption	4	4	4	3	3	3	2	Consommation
Consumption per cap. (kg.)	133	133	133	100	83	83	73	Consom. par hab.(kg.)
Greece * [1]								**Grèce** * [1]
Production	312	288	396	220	252	373	341	Production
Guadeloupe [1]								**Guadeloupe** [1]
Production	33	49	57	38	65	65 [6]	65 [6]	Production
Guatemala								**Guatemala**
Production	1 362	1 318	1 390	1 682	1 687	1 675	1 661	Production
Consumption	417	372	392	408	460	468	496	Consommation
Consumption per cap. (kg.)	42	36	37	38	42	41	42	Consom. par hab.(kg.)
Guinea								**Guinée**
Production *	20	21	22	22	25	25	25	Production *
Consumption *	75	75	80	80	85	90	95	Consommation *
Consumption per cap. (kg.)	10	10	10	10	11	11	12	Consom. par hab.(kg.)
Guinea-Bissau								**Guinée-Bissau**
Consumption	4	4	7	4	5	7	7	Consommation
Consumption per cap. (kg.)	3	4	6	4	4	6	6	Consom. par hab.(kg.)
Guyana								**Guyana**
Production	258	287	283	263	336	273	284	Production
Consumption	24	24	25	25	25	24	24	Consommation
Consumption per cap. (kg.)	31	31	32	32	32	31	35	Consom. par hab.(kg.)
Haiti								**Haïti**
Production *	5	8	9	5	5	5	5	Production *

41

Sugar
Production and consumption: thousand metric tons; consumption per capita: kilograms *[cont.]*
  Sucre
  Production et consommation : milliers de tonnes ; consommation par habitant : kilogrammes *[suite]*

Country or area	1995	1996	1997	1998	1999	2000	2001	Pays ou zone
Consumption *	120	115	120	130	160	165	170	Consommation *
Consumption per cap. (kg.)	17	16	16	17	21	21	21	Consom. par hab.(kg.)
Honduras								**Honduras**
Production	* 215	* 240	* 251	* 277	190	320	316	Production
Consumption	* 225	* 235	* 235	* 230	235	236	237	Consommation
Consumption per cap. (kg.)	40	41	39	37	37	37	37	Consom. par hab.(kg.)
Hungary								**Hongrie**
Production	515	554	460	461	446	309	434	Production
Consumption	430	462	448	386	399	367	317	Consommation
Consumption per cap. (kg.)	42	45	44	38	40	37	32	Consom. par hab.(kg.)
Iceland								**Islande**
Consumption *	16	15	13	13	12	13	12	Consommation *
Consumption per cap. (kg.)	57	50	43	46	43	46	41	Consom. par hab.(kg.)
India								**Inde**
Production	15 337	16 892	14 440	14 281	17 406	20 247	19 906	Production
Consumption	* 13 900	15 254	14 971	15 272	15 750	16 546	17 274	Consommation
Consumption per cap. (kg.)	15	16	16	16	17	17	17	Consom. par hab.(kg.)
Indonesia								**Indonésie**
Production	2 103	2 100	2 189	1 493	* 1 490	* 1 685	* 1 850	Production
Consumption	3 341	3 074	* 3 350	2 736	* 3 000	* 3 375	* 3 400	Consommation
Consumption per cap. (kg.)	17	16	17	14	15	16	16	Consom. par hab.(kg.)
Iran (Islamic Rep. of)								**Iran (Rép. islamique d')**
Production	905	692	848	863	* 940	* 920	* 900	Production
Consumption *	1 675	1 750	1 800	1 800	1 900	1 960	1 965	Consommation *
Consumption per cap. (kg.)	28	29	30	29	30	31	30	Consom. par hab.(kg.)
Iraq								**Iraq**
Consumption *	285	250	350	350	400	405	415	Consommation *
Consumption per cap. (kg.)	14	12	17	16	18	18	18	Consom. par hab.(kg.)
Ireland *[1]								**Irlande *[1]**
Production	242	247	223	238	235	238	223	Production
Israel								**Israël**
Production	0	0	0	0	0	0	0	Production
Consumption *	330	340	350	360	370	380	400	Consommation *
Consumption per cap. (kg.)	60	60	60	60	61	62	66	Consom. par hab.(kg.)
Italy [1]								**Italie [1]**
Production	1 621	1 561	1 891	* 1 735	* 1 705	* 1 552	* 1 430	Production
Jamaica								**Jamaïque**
Production	214	236	233	183	212	210	205	Production
Consumption	92	115	113	120	98	129	136	Consommation
Consumption per cap. (kg.)	37	46	44	47	38	49	52	Consom. par hab.(kg.)
Japan								**Japon**
Production	870	882	783	870	913	842	823	Production
Consumption	2 600	2 579	2 471	2 427	2 541	2 413	2 339	Consommation
Consumption per cap. (kg.)	21	21	20	19	20	19	18	Consom. par hab.(kg.)
Jordan								**Jordanie**
Consumption	174	170	* 170	* 150	* 180	* 185	* 190	Consommation
Consumption per cap. (kg.)	41	39	37	32	38	38	38	Consom. par hab.(kg.)
Kazakhstan								**Kazakhstan**
Production	45	* 50	* 45	* 40	* 25	* 30	* 25	Production
Consumption *	390	360	325	300	310	375	390	Consommation *
Consumption per cap. (kg.)	24	22	21	20	21	25	26	Consom. par hab.(kg.)
Kenya								**Kenya**
Production	418	423	436	488	512	437	377	Production
Consumption	* 510	* 500	* 525	* 650	662	663	* 625	Consommation
Consumption per cap. (kg.)	17	16	19	20	22	22	21	Consom. par hab.(kg.)
Korea, Dem. P. R.								**Corée, R. p. dém. de**
Consumption	* 55	* 55	* 48	30	* 60	* 65	* 70	Consommation
Consumption per cap. (kg.)	3	3	2	1	3	3	3	Consom. par hab.(kg.)
Korea, Republic of								**Corée, République [7]**
Consumption [7]	1 041	1 107	1 113	986	966	1 012	1 086	Consommation [7]
Consumption per cap. (kg.)	23	25	24	21	21	21	23	Consom. par hab.(kg.)

41

Sugar
Production and consumption: thousand metric tons; consumption per capita: kilograms *[cont.]*

Sucre
Production et consommation : milliers de tonnes ; consommation par habitant : kilogrammes *[suite]*

Country or area	1995	1996	1997	1998	1999	2000	2001	Pays ou zone
Kuwait								**Koweït**
Consumption *	60	65	65	70	70	73	75	Consommation *
Consumption per cap. (kg.)	33	34	33	35	33	33	33	Consom. par hab.(kg.)
Kyrgyzstan								**Kirghizistan**
Production	* 35	* 35	26	36	45	57	29	Production
Consumption *	125	125	110	110	100	110	110	Consommation *
Consumption per cap. (kg.)	27	27	23	23	21	22	22	Consom. par hab.(kg.)
Lao People's Dem. Rep.								**Rép. dém. pop. lao**
Consumption *	15	15	15	16	20	21	25	Consommation *
Consumption per cap. (kg.)	3	3	3	3	4	4	5	Consom. par hab.(kg.)
Latvia								**Lettonie**
Production	* 35	* 40	* 49	71	* 70	68	56	Production
Consumption	* 100	* 90	* 90	* 85	82	78	78	Consommation
Consumption per cap. (kg.)	40	36	37	35	34	32	33	Consom. par hab.(kg.)
Lebanon								**Liban**
Production	29	30	32	37	40	34	30	Production
Consumption	* 125	* 125	* 125	* 125	* 130	122	* 135	Consommation
Consumption per cap. (kg.)	42	40	39	37	38	35	38	Consom. par hab.(kg.)
Liberia								**Libéria**
Production	0	0	0	0	0	0	...	Production
Consumption	8	7	6	10	8	10	9	Consommation
Consumption per cap. (kg.)	3	3	2	4	3	3	3	Consom. par hab.(kg.)
Libyan Arab Jamah.								**Jamah. arabe libyenne**
Consumption *	150	180	220	220	220	225	225	Consommation *
Consumption per cap. (kg.)	32	37	44	44	43	43	42	Consom. par hab.(kg.)
Lithuania								**Lituanie**
Production	105	* 75	117	137	121	137	118	Production
Consumption	104	* 125	98	119	* 110	95	111	Consommation
Consumption per cap. (kg.)	28	28	27	32	30	26	32	Consom. par hab.(kg.)
Madagascar								**Madagascar**
Production	94	* 95	* 96	95	* 85	* 70	* 50	Production
Consumption	78	* 90	* 93	* 93	* 95	* 98	* 98	Consommation
Consumption per cap. (kg.)	6	6	6	6	6	6	6	Consom. par hab.(kg.)
Malawi								**Malawi**
Production	241	234	210	210	187	209	* 205	Production
Consumption	164	173	178	158	137	127	* 140	Consommation
Consumption per cap. (kg.)	17	17	17	15	12	11	12	Consom. par hab.(kg.)
Malaysia								**Malaisie**
Production *	110	107	108	100	107	108	105	Production *
Consumption *	950	1 025	1 050	1 060	1 070	1 080	1 085	Consommation *
Consumption per cap. (kg.)	47	49	49	48	47	46	45	Consom. par hab.(kg.)
Maldives								**Maldives**
Consumption	8	8	7	8	5	6	5	Consommation
Consumption per cap. (kg.)	32	31	26	30	18	22	17	Consom. par hab.(kg.)
Mali								**Mali**
Production *	25	26	26	33	31	32	32	Production *
Consumption *	90	65	60	80	75	85	80	Consommation *
Consumption per cap. (kg.)	9	6	6	7	7	7	7	Consom. par hab.(kg.)
Malta								**Malte**
Consumption *	19	20	20	20	22	23	23	Consommation *
Consumption per cap. (kg.)	51	54	53	53	56	58	59	Consom. par hab.(kg.)
Martinique [1]								**Martinique** [1]
Production	8	8	7	7	6	6 [6]	6 [6]	Production
Mauritania								**Mauritanie**
Consumption *	80	85	90	120	125	130	135	Consommation *
Consumption per cap. (kg.)	35	37	37	48	48	49	49	Consom. par hab.(kg.)
Mauritius								**Maurice**
Production	572	624	658	667	396	604	685	Production
Consumption	39	40	42	43	42	42	44	Consommation
Consumption per cap. (kg.)	36	36	37	37	36	35	36	Consom. par hab.(kg.)

41

Sugar

Production and consumption: thousand metric tons; consumption per capita: kilograms *[cont.]*

Sucre

Production et consommation : milliers de tonnes ; consommation par habitant : kilogrammes *[suite]*

Country or area	1995	1996	1997	1998	1999	2000	2001	Pays ou zone
Mexico								**Mexique**
Production	4 588	4 784	5 048	5 287	5 030	4 816	5 614	Production
Consumption	4 423	4 229	4 231	4 293	* 4 400	4 619	4 857	Consommation
Consumption per cap. (kg.)	48	45	45	44	45	46	48	Consom. par hab.(kg.)
Mongolia								**Mongolie**
Consumption	45	40	40	19	10	20	20	Consommation
Consumption per cap. (kg.)	20	18	17	8	4	8	8	Consom. par hab.(kg.)
Morocco								**Maroc**
Production	455	434	442	499	522	556	530	Production
Consumption	894	967	996	1 002	1 018	1 034	1 050	Consommation
Consumption per cap. (kg.)	34	36	37	36	36	36	36	Consom. par hab.(kg.)
Mozambique								**Mozambique**
Production	* 30	* 30	* 42	39	46	* 45	* 60	Production
Consumption *	60	55	50	60	70	75	80	Consommation *
Consumption per cap. (kg.)	4	3	3	4	4	4	4	Consom. par hab.(kg.)
Myanmar								**Myanmar**
Production	42	46	55	51	43	75	* 125	Production
Consumption	* 50	* 55	* 50	31	69	* 85	* 90	Consommation
Consumption per cap. (kg.)	1	1	1	1	2	2	2	Consom. par hab.(kg.)
Namibia *								**Namibie ***
Consumption	16	25	35	40	45	46	46	Consommation
Nepal								**Népal**
Production *	60	80	90	120	150	110	65	Production *
Consumption *	75	80	95	105	110	115	120	Consommation *
Consumption per cap. (kg.)	4	4	5	5	5	5	5	Consom. par hab.(kg.)
Netherlands *[1]								**Pays-Bas *[1]**
Production	1 074	1 125	1 109	897	1 217	1 153	1 031	Production
Netherlands Antilles								**Antilles néerlandaises**
Consumption *	9	8	12	15	20	21	22	Consommation *
Consumption per cap. (kg.)	45	38	57	71	95	96	96	Consom. par hab.(kg.)
New Zealand								**Nouvelle-Zélande**
Consumption	* 185	* 200	* 220	158	198	212	* 215	Consommation
Consumption per cap. (kg.)	52	56	59	42	52	56	56	Consom. par hab.(kg.)
Nicaragua								**Nicaragua**
Production	* 220	* 314	* 354	330	351	398	* 390	Production
Consumption	* 160	* 180	* 180	217	179	157	* 160	Consommation
Consumption per cap. (kg.)	35	40	39	45	36	31	31	Consom. par hab.(kg.)
Niger								**Niger**
Production	* 10	15	15	* 5	* 10	* 10	* 10	Production
Consumption *	30	35	40	45	50	55	55	Consommation *
Consumption per cap. (kg.)	3	4	4	5	5	5	...	Consom. par hab.(kg.)
Nigeria								**Nigéria**
Production	* 37	* 27	* 15	* 15	* 17	36	7	Production
Consumption	* 500	* 600	* 650	* 700	* 700	* 760	975	Consommation
Consumption per cap. (kg.)	5	6	6	7	6	7	...	Consom. par hab.(kg.)
Norway								**Norvège**
Consumption	177	* 180	* 185	* 185	* 185	* 186	* 186	Consommation
Consumption per cap. (kg.)	41	41	42	42	42	41	41	Consom. par hab.(kg.)
Pakistan								**Pakistan**
Production	3 116	2 662	2 635	3 503	3 709	2 053	2 720	Production
Consumption	2 971	3 033	* 3 023	* 3 085	* 3 196	* 3 330	* 3 440	Consommation
Consumption per cap. (kg.)	23	23	22	24	24	24	24	Consom. par hab.(kg.)
Panama								**Panama**
Production	127	142	166	181	177	161	146	Production
Consumption	66	69	73	* 75	* 85	* 95	* 105	Consommation
Consumption per cap. (kg.)	25	26	27	27	30	33	36	Consom. par hab.(kg.)
Papua New Guinea								**Papouasie-Nvl-Guinée**
Production	* 35	* 35	39	41	47	41	45	Production
Consumption	* 27	* 30	37	36	38	35	35	Consommation
Consumption per cap. (kg.)	7	7	9	8	8	7	7	Consom. par hab.(kg.)

41

Sugar
Production and consumption: thousand metric tons; consumption per capita: kilograms *[cont.]*

Sucre
Production et consommation : milliers de tonnes ; consommation par habitant : kilogrammes *[suite]*

Country or area	1995	1996	1997	1998	1999	2000	2001	Pays ou zone
Paraguay								**Paraguay**
Production *	90	116	108	114	112	90	95	Production *
Consumption *	103	105	105	105	108	108	110	Consommation *
Consumption per cap. (kg.)	21	21	21	20	20	20	20	Consom. par hab.(kg.)
Peru								**Pérou**
Production	633	612	693	570	* 655	* 725	* 755	Production
Consumption	730	745	826	* 850	* 900	* 950	* 975	Consommation
Consumption per cap. (kg.)	31	31	34	34	36	37	37	Consom. par hab.(kg.)
Philippines								**Philippines**
Production	1 562	1 895	1 954	1 549	1 913	1 826	1 895	Production
Consumption	1 765	1 956	1 959	1 958	1 854	2 052	1 974	Consommation
Consumption per cap. (kg.)	26	28	28	27	25	28	26	Consom. par hab.(kg.)
Poland								**Pologne**
Production	1 734	2 380	2 112	2 242	1 968	2 104	1 626	Production
Consumption	* 1 700	* 1 700	* 1 750	1 708	* 1 720	* 1 730	* 1 740	Consommation
Consumption per cap. (kg.)	44	44	45	44	45	45	45	Consom. par hab.(kg.)
Portugal *[1]								**Portugal *[1]**
Production	6	3	71	66	76	60	60	Production
Republic of Moldova								**République de Moldova**
Production	215	231	203	186	108	102	130	Production
Consumption *	175	175	160	150	125	105	105	Consommation *
Consumption per cap. (kg.)	40	40	37	41	34	29	29	Consom. par hab.(kg.)
Réunion [1]								**Réunion [1]**
Production	195	205	207	* 195	* 234	* 219	* 231	Production
Romania								**Roumanie**
Production	202	226	204	189	86	54	71	Production
Consumption *	480	500	510	520	530	550	565	Consommation *
Consumption per cap. (kg.)	21	22	23	23	24	25	25	Consom. par hab.(kg.)
Russian Federation								**Fédération de Russie**
Production	2 241	1 851	1 337	1 370	1 651	1 705	1 757	Production
Consumption	5 108	5 235	5 308	* 5 450	5 565	5 707	5 848	Consommation
Consumption per cap. (kg.)	35	35	36	37	38	39	40	Consom. par hab.(kg.)
Rwanda								**Rwanda**
Production	1	0	0	0	0	0	0	Production
Consumption *	4	4	4	3	3	3	10	Consommation *
Consumption per cap. (kg.)	1	1	1	0	0	0	...	Consom. par hab.(kg.)
Saint Kitts and Nevis								**Saint-Kitts-et-Nevis**
Production	* 25	20	30	24	* 20	* 20	* 20	Production
Consumption *	2	2	2	2	2	3	3	Consommation *
Consumption per cap. (kg.)	50	50	50	50	50	63	63	Consom. par hab.(kg.)
Samoa								**Samoa**
Production	2	2	2	2	2	2	2	Production
Consumption	4	3	3	3	2	2	2	Consommation
Consumption per cap. (kg.)	14	10	10	10	8	8	8	Consom. par hab.(kg.)
Saudi Arabia								**Arabie saoudite**
Consumption *	550	550	550	550	520	560	600	Consommation *
Consumption per cap. (kg.)	31	30	30	29	26	27	28	Consom. par hab.(kg.)
Senegal								**Sénégal**
Production	* 81	* 85	* 91	90	* 95	* 90	* 95	Production
Consumption *	165	175	180	170	170	165	170	Consommation *
Consumption per cap. (kg.)	19	20	20	18	18	18	...	Consom. par hab.(kg.)
Serbia and Montenegro								**Serbie-et-Monténégro**
Production	* 156	* 285	239	213	248	* 170	209	Production
Consumption	* 300	* 300	299	* 300	* 300	* 275	* 300	Consommation
Consumption per cap. (kg.)	28	28	28	28	28	26	28	Consom. par hab.(kg.)
Sierra Leone								**Sierra Leone**
Production *	4	5	6	6	7	7	7	Production *
Consumption *	18	19	14	15	15	20	20	Consommation *
Consumption per cap. (kg.)	4	4	3	3	3	4	...	Consom. par hab.(kg.)
Singapore								**Singapour**
Consumption *	250	280	290	270	280	285	300	Consommation *

41

Sugar
Production and consumption: thousand metric tons; consumption per capita: kilograms *[cont.]*

Sucre
Production et consommation : milliers de tonnes ; consommation par habitant : kilogrammes *[suite]*

Country or area	1995	1996	1997	1998	1999	2000	2001	Pays ou zone
Consumption per cap. (kg.)	71	76	77	69	71	69	69	Consom. par hab.(kg.)
Slovakia								**Slovaquie**
Production	* 145	* 140	237	170	213	140	173	Production
Consumption *	175	200	220	220	225	230	235	Consommation *
Consumption per cap. (kg.)	33	37	41	41	42	43	43	Consom. par hab.(kg.)
Slovenia								**Slovénie**
Production	65	71	67	51	* 60	44	* 50	Production
Consumption *	110	110	110	110	105	110	108	Consommation *
Consumption per cap. (kg.)	55	52	52	53	53	53	54	Consom. par hab.(kg.)
Somalia								**Somalie**
Production *	20	20	19	19	20	15	20	Production *
Consumption *	110	110	135	150	170	180	185	Consommation *
Consumption per cap. (kg.)	13	13	15	16	18	18	...	Consom. par hab.(kg.)
South Africa								**Afrique du Sud**
Production	1 732	2 471	2 419	2 985	2 547	2 691	2 311	Production
Consumption	1 381	1 330	1 743	1 508	1 385	1 453	1 341	Consommation
Consumption per cap. (kg.)	35	33	42	36	32	33	30	Consom. par hab.(kg.)
Spain[1]								**Espagne**[1]
Production	1 111	1 228	1 142	1 327	1 071	* 1 208	* 1 068	Production
Sri Lanka								**Sri Lanka**
Production	70	73	63	20	* 19	* 15	* 20	Production
Consumption *	500	525	535	550	550	560	565	Consommation *
Consumption per cap. (kg.)	28	29	29	30	29	29	29	Consom. par hab.(kg.)
Sudan								**Soudan**
Production	486	543	538	610	635	680	719	Production
Consumption	* 460	* 480	* 480	391	396	430	523	Consommation
Consumption per cap. (kg.)	17	17	16	13	13	14	16	Consom. par hab.(kg.)
Suriname								**Suriname**
Production *	10	7	10	5	7	10	10	Production *
Consumption *	17	17	17	18	18	19	19	Consommation *
Consumption per cap. (kg.)	42	42	41	44	42	45	46	Consom. par hab.(kg.)
Swaziland								**Swaziland**
Production	419	458	457	537	571	553	567	Production
Consumption *	104	108	99	101	103	105	107	Consommation *
Consumption per cap. (kg.)	114	115	114	113	113	113	107	Consom. par hab.(kg.)
Sweden[1]								**Suède**[1]
Production	357	398	396	400	448	448	402	Production
Switzerland								**Suisse**
Production	* 140	* 194	* 200	191	177	* 231	* 187	Production
Consumption	* 315	* 310	* 315	206	328	* 338	* 360	Consommation
Consumption per cap. (kg.)	45	44	44	29	46	47	50	Consom. par hab.(kg.)
Syrian Arab Republic								**Rép. arabe syrienne**
Production	172	197	191	107	* 102	* 100	* 115	Production
Consumption *	650	675	695	715	720	730	745	Consommation *
Consumption per cap. (kg.)	46	46	46	46	45	45	45	Consom. par hab.(kg.)
Tajikistan								**Tadjikistan**
Consumption *	95	80	70	65	60	60	60	Consommation *
Consumption per cap. (kg.)	16	14	12	11	10	9	10	Consom. par hab.(kg.)
Thailand								**Thaïlande**
Production	5 447	6 154	6 243	4 143	5 456	6 157	5 370	Production
Consumption	1 645	1 706	1 829	1 834	1 776	1 816	1 955	Consommation
Consumption per cap. (kg.)	28	28	30	30	29	29	31	Consom. par hab.(kg.)
TFYR of Macedonia								**L'ex-R.y. Macédoine**
Production	7	18	* 15	40	43	32	20	Production
Consumption *	45	50	50	60	80	85	80	Consommation *
Consumption per cap. (kg.)	23	25	25	30	40	39	40	Consom. par hab.(kg.)
Togo								**Togo**
Production *	5	5	3	3	3	3	5	Production *
Consumption *	32	35	45	45	50	50	50	Consommation *
Consumption per cap. (kg.)	8	8	11	10	11	11	11	Consom. par hab.(kg.)

41

Sugar
Production and consumption: thousand metric tons; consumption per capita: kilograms *[cont.]*
Sucre
Production et consommation : milliers de tonnes ; consommation par habitant : kilogrammes *[suite]*

Country or area	1995	1996	1997	1998	1999	2000	2001	Pays ou zone
Trinidad and Tobago								**Trinité-et-Tobago**
Production	117	117	120	79	92	115	89	Production
Consumption	84	73	87	72	70	78	79	Consommation
Consumption per cap. (kg.)	66	57	67	56	55	60	61	Consom. par hab.(kg.)
Tunisia								**Tunisie**
Production	29	29	28	15	9	2	0	Production
Consumption	257	272	283	287	292	294	309	Consommation
Consumption per cap. (kg.)	29	30	31	31	31	31	30	Consom. par hab.(kg.)
Turkey								**Turquie**
Production	1 405	2 002	2 187	2 784	2 491	2 273	2 360	Production
Consumption	* 1 800	* 1 900	2 107	2 074	1 836	* 1 925	1 973	Consommation
Consumption per cap. (kg.)	30	31	34	33	29	29	28	Consom. par hab.(kg.)
Turkmenistan								**Turkménistan**
Consumption *	80	75	70	70	70	70	70	Consommation *
Consumption per cap. (kg.)	20	18	16	16	15	15	15	Consom. par hab.(kg.)
Uganda								**Ouganda**
Production *	76	109	145	111	137	130	140	Production *
Consumption *	100	100	150	150	150	155	160	Consommation *
Consumption per cap. (kg.)	5	5	7	7	7	7	7	Consom. par hab.(kg.)
Ukraine								**Ukraine**
Production	3 801	* 2 935	* 2 170	2 041	1 640	1 686	1 802	Production
Consumption	* 2 200	* 2 100	* 1 800	1 739	* 1 800	* 1 875	* 2 005	Consommation
Consumption per cap. (kg.)	43	41	35	34	36	38	41	Consom. par hab.(kg.)
United Kingdom [1]								**Royaume-Uni** [1]
Production	* 1 326	1 605	1 592	1 439	1 540	1 325	1 200	Production
United Rep. of Tanzania								**Rép.-Unie de Tanzanie**
Production	* 110	* 100	84	* 110	114	* 130	* 115	Production
Consumption *	120	160	175	200	200	208	210	Consommation *
Consumption per cap. (kg.)	4	6	6	6	6	6	6	Consom. par hab.(kg.)
United States								**Etats-Unis**
Production	7 238	6 593	6 731	7 159	* 8 243	8 080	7 774	Production
Consumption	8 580	8 701	8 800	9 049	8 993	8 992	9 139 [8]	Consommation
Consumption per cap. (kg.)	33	33	33	34	33	32	32	Consom. par hab.(kg.)
Uruguay								**Uruguay**
Production *	20	15	19	14	9	8	7	Production *
Consumption	* 105	* 105	* 110	* 115	101	* 102	* 105	Consommation
Consumption per cap. (kg.)	33	33	34	35	31	30	31	Consom. par hab.(kg.)
Uzbekistan								**Ouzbékistan**
Production	...	...	...	11	* 20	11	* 7	Production
Consumption *	360	350	350	350	355	359	360	Consommation *
Consumption per cap. (kg.)	16	15	15	15	15	15	14	Consom. par hab.(kg.)
Venezuela								**Venezuela**
Production *	523	559	594	590	535	645	585	Production *
Consumption *	800	820	840	855	870	893	910	Consommation *
Consumption per cap. (kg.)	37	37	37	37	37	37	37	Consom. par hab.(kg.)
Viet Nam								**Viet Nam**
Production	* 525	* 550	* 559	657	* 878	1 155	* 850	Production
Consumption *	625	640	675	700	750	810	825	Consommation *
Consumption per cap. (kg.)	8	9	9	9	10	10	11	Consom. par hab.(kg.)
Yemen								**Yémen**
Consumption *	285	350	375	375	390	410	420	Consommation *
Consumption per cap. (kg.)	19	22	23	22	22	22	22	Consom. par hab.(kg.)
Zambia								**Zambie**
Production	151	166	174	173	* 210	* 190	199	Production
Consumption	152	154	74	* 85	* 115	* 145	102	Consommation
Consumption per cap. (kg.)	17	16	8	8	11	14	11	Consom. par hab.(kg.)
Zimbabwe								**Zimbabwe**
Production	512	337	574	571	583	571	548	Production
Consumption	292	287	335	305	376	374	305	Consommation
Consumption per cap. (kg.)	25	24	27	24	29	30	24	Consom. par hab.(kg.)

41

Sugar
Production and consumption: thousand metric tons; consumption per capita: kilograms *[cont.]*

Sucre
Production et consommation : milliers de tonnes ; consommation par habitant : kilogrammes *[suite]*

Source:
International Sugar Organization (ISO), London, "Sugar Yearbook 2001" and the ISO database.

1   Source: Food and Agriculture Organization of the United Nations (FAO), (Rome).
2   Including non-human consumption: 1998 - 15,652 tons.

3   Including store losses of 1,159 tons and accidental losses of 129 tons.

4   Including non-human consumption: 1983 - 6,710 tons; 1984 - 19,797 tons; 1985-79,908 tons; 1986- 98,608 tons; 1987- 147,262 tons; 1988- 122,058 tons; 1989- 52,230 tons; 1991- 13,541 tons; 1994- 12,178 tons; 1995- 10,211 tons; 1996- 14,648 tons; 2000- 31,836 tons.

5   Including 11,572 tons sold to other Pacific Island nations in 1994; 12,520 tons in 1995; 14,154 tons in 1996; 13,109 tons in 1997; 5,305 tons in 1998; and 6,444 tons in 2001.

6   FAO estimate.
7   Including consumption of mono-sodium glutamate, lysine and other products: 1987- 44,600 tons; 1988- 92,200 tons; 1989- 94,500 tons; 1990- 89,400 tons; 1991- 77,300 tons; 1992- 75,800 tons; 1993- 89,800 tons; 1994- 170,384 tons; 1995- 200,863 tons; 1996- 257,763 tons; 1997- 257,310 tons; 1998- 258,247 tons; 2000- 159,027 tons.

8   Including 19,780 tons used for livestock feed.

Source:
Organisation internationale du sucre (OIS), Londres, "Annuaire du sucre 2001" et la base de données de l'OIS.

1   Source: Organisation des Nations Unies pour l'alimentation et l'agriculture (FAO), (Rome).
2   Dont la consommation non humaine: 1998 - 15 652 tonnes.

3   Y compris des pertes de 1 159 tonnes au cours de stockage et des pertes accidentelles de 129 tonnes.

4   Dont consommation non humaine : 1983 - 6 710 tonnes; 1984 - 19 797 tonnes; 1985-79 908 tonnes; 1986- 98 608 tonnes; 1987- 147 262 tonnes; 1988- 122 058 tonnes; 1989- 52 230 tonnes; 1991- 13 541 tonnes; 1994- 12 178 tonnes; 1995- 10 211 tonnes; 1996- 14 648 tonnes; 2000- 31 836 tonnes.

5   Y compris 11 572 tonnes vendues à autres îles pacifiques en 1994; 12 520 tonnes en 1995; 14 154 tonnes en 1996; 13 109 tonnes en 1997; 5,305 tonnes in 1998; et 6,444 tonnes en 2001.

6   Estimation de la FAO.
7   Y compris la consommation des produits du glutamate monosodium, lysine et autres: 1987- 44 600 tonnes ; 1988- 92 200 tonnes; 1989- 94 500 tonnes; 1990- 89 400 tonnes; 1991- 77 300 tonnes ; 1992- 75 800 tonnes; 1993- 89 800 tonnes; 1994- 170 384 tonnes; 1995- 200 863 tonnes; 1996-257 763 tonnes; 1997- 257 310 tonnes; 1998- 258 247 tonnes; 2000- 159 027 tonnes; 2001-210,498 tonnes.

8   Y compris 19 780 tonnes utilisées pour les aliments du bétail.

42

Meat

Production: thousand metric tons

Viande

Production: milliers de tonnes

Country or area	1994	1995	1996	1997	1998	1999	2000	2001	Pays ou zone
World									**Monde**
Total	143 867	146 041	146 161	151 028	156 413	160 087	160 633	162 259	Totale
Beef, veal and buffalo	55 946	56 930	57 435	58 262	58 107	59 282	59 612	59 779	Bœuf, veau et buffle
Pork	77 581	78 558	78 440	82 173	87 623	89 698	89 584	91 188	Porc
Mutton, lamb and goat	10 340	10 553	10 286	10 593	10 683	11 107	11 437	11 291	Mouton, agneau et caprin
Africa									**Afrique**
Total	5 797	5 938	6 065	6 304	6 535	6 718	6 875	7 003	Totale
Beef, veal and buffalo	3 551	3 582	3 682	3 840	3 973	4 113	4 248	4 370	Bœuf, veau et buffle
Pork	541	602	578	593	610	620	604	605	Porc
Mutton, lamb and goat	1 704	1 755	1 805	1 871	1 953	1 984	2 023	2 027	Mouton, agneau et caprin
Algeria									**Algérie**
Total	279	279	289	281	282	293	309	310	Totale
Beef, veal and buffalo	101	101	99	102	103	117	133	133[1]	Bœuf, veau et buffle
Mutton, lamb and goat	178	178	190	179	179	175	176	177[1]	Mouton, agneau et caprin
Angola									**Angola**
Total	96	97	107	115	123	124	125	125	Totale
Beef, veal and buffalo [1]	65	65	71	77	85	85	85	85	Bœuf, veau et buffle [1]
Pork [1]	25	26	28	29	29	29	29	29	Porc [1]
Mutton, lamb and goat	6	6	8	9	9	10	11	11	Mouton, agneau et caprin
Benin									**Bénin**
Total	30	32	33	34	33	33	33	33	Totale
Beef, veal and buffalo	17	18	19	20	20	21	21[1]	21[1]	Bœuf, veau et buffle
Pork	6	7	8	8	6	6	6	6	Porc
Mutton, lamb and goat	6	7	6	6	7	6	6[1]	6[1]	Mouton, agneau et caprin
Botswana									**Botswana**
Total	45	55	52	47	45	45	46	46	Totale
Beef, veal and buffalo	38	46	44	38	37	37	38	38[1]	Bœuf, veau et buffle
Pork	0	0	1	0	1	1	1	1	Porc
Mutton, lamb and goat	6	9	8	8	7	7	8	8	Mouton, agneau et caprin
Burkina Faso									**Burkina Faso**
Total	77	78	88	91	94	96	96	96	Totale
Beef, veal and buffalo	40	40	47	50	51	52	52[1]	52[1]	Bœuf, veau et buffle
Pork	6	6	7	8	8	8	8[1]	8[1]	Porc
Mutton, lamb and goat	31	32	33	34	35	36	36[1]	36[1]	Mouton, agneau et caprin
Burundi									**Burundi**
Total	23	22	22	18	19	18	17	17	Totale
Beef, veal and buffalo	12	12	13	10	11	9	9	9	Bœuf, veau et buffle
Pork	5	5	5	4	4	4	5	5	Porc
Mutton, lamb and goat	6	5	5	4	3	4	4	4	Mouton, agneau et caprin
Cameroon									**Cameroun**
Total	114	113	113	116	120	133	141	143	Totale
Beef, veal and buffalo	75[1]	73[1]	73[1]	76[1]	77[1]	* 91	* 93	* 95	Bœuf, veau et buffle
Pork	12	12	12	12	14	12	16	16	Porc
Mutton, lamb and goat	27	28	28	28	29	29	32	32	Mouton, agneau et caprin
Cape Verde									**Cap-Vert**
Total	6	9	4	6	8	8	7	8	Totale
Beef, veal and buffalo	0[1]	0[1]	1	1[1]	1	0	0	0[1]	Bœuf, veau et buffle
Pork	5	8	3	5[1]	6	7[1]	7	7[1]	Porc
Mutton, lamb and goat	1[1]	0[1]	0[1]	0[1]	1[1]	1	0	0	Mouton, agneau et caprin
Central African Rep.									**Rép. centrafricaine**
Total	61	66	81	70	72	72	83	83	Totale
Beef, veal and buffalo	45[1]	48	* 61	* 50	* 51	* 51	* 60	* 60	Bœuf, veau et buffle
Pork	9[1]	10[1]	11	12	12[1]	12[1]	* 12	12[1]	Porc
Mutton, lamb and goat	7[1]	8[1]	8	8	9[1]	9[1]	* 11	11[1]	Mouton, agneau et caprin
Chad									**Tchad**
Total	79	90	98	104	111	109	106	101	Totale
Beef, veal and buffalo	57	68	74	73	80	78	74	74	Bœuf, veau et buffle
Mutton, lamb and goat	21	22	24	30	31	31	32	27	Mouton, agneau et caprin
Comoros									**Comores**
Total	1	1	1	1	1	2	2	2	Totale
Beef, veal and buffalo	1	1	1	1	1	1	1	1	Bœuf, veau et buffle

42

Meat
Production: thousand metric tons *[cont.]*
Viande
Production: milliers de tonnes *[suite]*

Country or area	1994	1995	1996	1997	1998	1999	2000	2001	Pays ou zone
Mutton, lamb and goat	0	0	0	0	1	1	1	1	Mouton, agneau et caprin
Congo									**Congo**
Total	5	5	5	5	5	5	5	5	Totale
Beef, veal and buffalo	2	2	2	2	2	2	2	2	Bœuf, veau et buffle
Pork	2	2	2	2	2	2	2	2	Porc
Mutton, lamb and goat	1	1	1	1	1	1	1	1	Mouton, agneau et caprin
Côte d'Ivoire									**Côte d'Ivoire**
Total	60	64	61	72	75	70	72	63	Totale
Beef, veal and buffalo	34	36	40[1]	50	52	47	48	40	Bœuf, veau et buffle
Pork	16	19	11	11	11	13	* 13	13	Porc
Mutton, lamb and goat	9	9	10[1]	* 11	* 12	* 11	* 10	10	Mouton, agneau et caprin
Dem. Rep. of the Congo									**Rép. dém. du Congo**
Total	82	83	79	82	82	77	76	76	Totale
Beef, veal and buffalo	16	16	15	16	14	14	14	13	Bœuf, veau et buffle
Pork [1]	43	44	42	43	43	41	41	41	Porc [1]
Mutton, lamb and goat	23	23	23	24	24	22	22	22	Mouton, agneau et caprin
Djibouti									**Djibouti**
Total	8	8	8	8	8	8	8	8	Totale
Beef, veal and buffalo	3	3	3	4	4	4	4	4	Bœuf, veau et buffle
Mutton, lamb and goat	4	4	4	4	4	4	4	4	Mouton, agneau et caprin
Egypt									**Egypte**
Total	472	488	546	600	616	625	661	697	Totale
Beef, veal and buffalo	382[1]	394	453	504[1]	518	510	541[1]	576[1]	Bœuf, veau et buffle
Pork [1]	3	3	3	3	3	3	3	3	Porc [1]
Mutton, lamb and goat	87[1]	91[1]	91[1]	93	95	113	117[1]	118[1]	Mouton, agneau et caprin
Eritrea									**Erythrée**
Total	20	20	22	25	27	28	28	28	Totale
Beef, veal and buffalo [1]	10	10	12	14	16	16	16	17	Bœuf, veau et buffle [1]
Mutton, lamb and goat [1]	10	10	10	10	11	12	12	12	Mouton, agneau et caprin [1]
Ethiopia									**Ethiopie**
Total	374	379	412	415	420	436	446	446	Totale
Beef, veal and buffalo	230[1]	235[1]	267	270	274	290	298[1]	298[1]	Bœuf, veau et buffle
Pork [1]	1	1	1	1	1	1	1	1	Porc [1]
Mutton, lamb and goat [1]	143	143	144	144	144	145	147	147	Mouton, agneau et caprin [1]
Gabon									**Gabon**
Total	5	5	5	5	5	5	5	5	Totale
Beef, veal and buffalo	1	1	1	1	1	1	1	1	Bœuf, veau et buffle
Pork	3	3	3	3	3	3	3	3	Porc
Mutton, lamb and goat	1	1	1	1	1	1	1	1	Mouton, agneau et caprin
Gambia									**Gambie**
Total	5	5	5	5	5	5	5	5	Totale
Beef, veal and buffalo	3	3	3	3	3	3	3	3	Bœuf, veau et buffle
Mutton, lamb and goat	1	1	1	1	1	1	1	1	Mouton, agneau et caprin
Ghana									**Ghana**
Total	43	43	43	44	45	45	55	55	Totale
Beef, veal and buffalo	20	21	21	21	21	21	24	24	Bœuf, veau et buffle
Pork	11	11	10	11	11	10	11	11	Porc
Mutton, lamb and goat	11	11	12	13	13	14	20	20	Mouton, agneau et caprin
Guinea									**Guinée**
Total	17	20	21	22	27	29	33	33	Totale
Beef, veal and buffalo	12	15	15	15	20	21	23	23	Bœuf, veau et buffle
Pork	1	1	2	2	2	2	3	3	Porc
Mutton, lamb and goat	3	4	5	5	5	6	6	6	Mouton, agneau et caprin
Guinea-Bissau									**Guinée-Bissau**
Total	15	15	16	16	16	17	17	17	Totale
Beef, veal and buffalo	4	4	4	4	4	4	5	5	Bœuf, veau et buffle
Pork	10	10	10	10	10	11	11	11	Porc
Mutton, lamb and goat	1	1	1	2	2	2	2	2	Mouton, agneau et caprin
Kenya									**Kenya**
Total	308	305	320	330	340	349	355	358	Totale
Beef, veal and buffalo	242	239	252	261	270	279	287	290[1]	Bœuf, veau et buffle

42

Meat
Production: thousand metric tons *[cont.]*

Viande
Production: milliers de tonnes *[suite]*

Country or area	1994	1995	1996	1997	1998	1999	2000	2001	Pays ou zone
Pork	7	8	10	11	10	10	12	12	Porc
Mutton, lamb and goat	59	58	58	58	61	59	56	56	Mouton, agneau et caprin
Lesotho									**Lesotho**
Total	22	23	21	24	20	19	19	19	Totale
Beef, veal and buffalo	13	14	12	15	12	11	11	11	Bœuf, veau et buffle
Pork	2	3	3	3	3	3	3	3	Porc
Mutton, lamb and goat	7	6	6	6	5	5	5	5	Mouton, agneau et caprin
Liberia									**Libéria**
Total	6	6	6	6	6	6	7	7	Totale
Beef, veal and buffalo	1	1	1	1	1	1	1	1	Bœuf, veau et buffle
Pork	4	4	4	4	4	4	4	4	Porc
Mutton, lamb and goat	1	1	1	1	1	1	1	1	Mouton, agneau et caprin
Libyan Arab Jamah.									**Jamah. arabe libyenne**
Total	53	58	59	82	130	74	80	88	Totale
Beef, veal and buffalo	* 22	22[1]	15[1]	39[1]	43[1]	15[1]	* 20	* 27	Bœuf, veau et buffle
Mutton, lamb and goat	31[1]	36[1]	45[1]	43[1]	* 87	59[1]	60[1]	62[1]	Mouton, agneau et caprin
Madagascar									**Madagascar**
Total	217	224	226	229	230	231	202	202	Totale
Beef, veal and buffalo	145	146	147	147	148	148	148	148	Bœuf, veau et buffle
Pork	62	68	70	72	72	74	44	44	Porc
Mutton, lamb and goat	10	10	9	10	10	10	10	10	Mouton, agneau et caprin
Malawi									**Malawi**
Total	30	31	32	35	33	34	34	34	Totale
Beef, veal and buffalo	14	14	16	18	17	17	17	17[1]	Bœuf, veau et buffle
Pork	12	12	11	12	11	12	12	12	Porc
Mutton, lamb and goat	4	4	5	5	5	5	5	5	Mouton, agneau et caprin
Mali									**Mali**
Total	130	135	138	146	152	152	157	160	Totale
Beef, veal and buffalo	83	85	86	88	91	89	91	91	Bœuf, veau et buffle
Pork	2	2	2	2	2	2	2	2	Porc
Mutton, lamb and goat	45	48	50	55	58	61	64	67	Mouton, agneau et caprin
Mauritania									**Mauritanie**
Total	30	31	35	35	37	39	40	41	Totale
Beef, veal and buffalo	9	10	10	10	* 10	* 10	* 10	* 11	Bœuf, veau et buffle
Mutton, lamb and goat	21	21	25	25	27	29	30	30	Mouton, agneau et caprin
Mauritius									**Maurice**
Total	4	4	4	3	4	4	4	4	Totale
Beef, veal and buffalo	3	2	2	2	3	3	3	3[1]	Bœuf, veau et buffle
Pork	1	1	1	1	1	1	1	1[1]	Porc
Morocco									**Maroc**
Total	250	255	216	268	256	278	288	298	Totale
Beef, veal and buffalo	125	122	103	125	120	130	140	150	Bœuf, veau et buffle
Pork	1[1]	1[1]	1[1]	1	1	1	* 1	1[1]	Porc
Mutton, lamb and goat	125	132	112	142	135	147	147	147	Mouton, agneau et caprin
Mozambique									**Mozambique**
Total	51	52	52	53	53	54	54	54	Totale
Beef, veal and buffalo	36	37	37	38	38	38	38	38	Bœuf, veau et buffle
Pork	12	12	12	13	13	13	13	13	Porc
Mutton, lamb and goat	3	3	3	3	3	3	3	3	Mouton, agneau et caprin
Namibia									**Namibie**
Total	69	62	60	46	50	91	74	68	Totale
Beef, veal and buffalo	49	48	46	30	38	78	61	55	Bœuf, veau et buffle
Pork[1]	2	2	2	1	1	1	1	1	Porc[1]
Mutton, lamb and goat	17	13	13	15	11	12	12	12	Mouton, agneau et caprin
Niger									**Niger**
Total	69	71	74	76	78	80	81	84	Totale
Beef, veal and buffalo	34[1]	35[1]	36[1]	38[1]	39[1]	40[1]	* 41	* 42	Bœuf, veau et buffle
Pork	1	1	1	1	1	1	1	1	Porc
Mutton, lamb and goat	34	35	36	37	38	39	39	40	Mouton, agneau et caprin
Nigeria									**Nigéria**
Total	478	514	545	584	602	622	622	622	Totale

42

Meat
Production: thousand metric tons *[cont.]*

Viande
Production: milliers de tonnes *[suite]*

Country or area	1994	1995	1996	1997	1998	1999	2000	2001	Pays ou zone
Beef, veal and buffalo	264	267	280	294	297	298	298[1]	298[1]	Bœuf, veau et buffle
Pork	34	67	47	56	65	78	78	78	Porc
Mutton, lamb and goat	180	180	218	234	240	246	246	246	Mouton, agneau et caprin
Réunion									**Réunion**
Total	12	12	12	14	13	14	14	14	Totale
Beef, veal and buffalo	1	1	1	1	* 1	* 2	2	2[1]	Bœuf, veau et buffle
Pork	10	10	10	12	* 11	* 12	12	12[1]	Porc
Rwanda									**Rwanda**
Total	18	16	17	19	22	24	27	29	Totale
Beef, veal and buffalo	10	10	11	14	16	18	20	22	Bœuf, veau et buffle
Pork	3	2	2	2	2	2	2	2	Porc
Mutton, lamb and goat	5	3	4	4	5	5	5	5	Mouton, agneau et caprin
Senegal									**Sénégal**
Total	75	77	79	81	83	85	88	93	Totale
Beef, veal and buffalo	45	46	47	47	47	48	50	53	Bœuf, veau et buffle
Pork	4	4	4	5	5	6	7	7	Porc
Mutton, lamb and goat	26	27	28	29	30	31	32	33	Mouton, agneau et caprin
Seychelles									**Seychelles**
Total	1	1	1	1	1	1	1	1	Totale
Pork	1	1	1	1	1	1	1	1	Porc
Sierra Leone									**Sierra Leone**
Total	9	10	10	10	10	10	10	10	Totale
Beef, veal and buffalo	6	6	6	6	6	7	7	7	Bœuf, veau et buffle
Pork	2	2	2	2	2	2	2	2	Porc
Mutton, lamb and goat	1	1	1	1	2	2	2	2	Mouton, agneau et caprin
Somalia									**Somalie**
Total	99	107	114	122	135	131	135	135	Totale
Beef, veal and buffalo	44	50	54	61	62	58	59	59	Bœuf, veau et buffle
Mutton, lamb and goat	55	57	60	61	73	73	75	75	Mouton, agneau et caprin
South Africa									**Afrique du Sud**
Total	828	794	744	732	770	818	838	838	Totale
Beef, veal and buffalo	554	521	481	484	518	553	568	568[1]	Bœuf, veau et buffle
Pork	119	127	128	120	124	117	116	116[1]	Porc
Mutton, lamb and goat [1]	155	146	135	128	128	148	154	154	Mouton, agneau et caprin [1]
Sudan									**Soudan**
Total	417	462	469	505	529	532	557	629	Totale
Beef, veal and buffalo	212	225	226	250[1]	265[1]	276[1]	296[1]	367[1]	Bœuf, veau et buffle
Mutton, lamb and goat	205	237	242	255[1]	264[1]	256[1]	261[1]	262[1]	Mouton, agneau et caprin
Swaziland									**Swaziland**
Total	18	18	18	18	19	19	23	23	Totale
Beef, veal and buffalo	14[1]	14	13	* 14	14[1]	14[1]	18	18[1]	Bœuf, veau et buffle
Pork	1	1	1	2	2	2	2	2	Porc
Mutton, lamb and goat	3	3	3	3	3	4	4	4	Mouton, agneau et caprin
Togo									**Togo**
Total	15	12	13	13	14	15	16	16	Totale
Beef, veal and buffalo	4	4	4	4	4	5	5	5	Bœuf, veau et buffle
Pork	6	5	4	6	5	4	4	4	Porc
Mutton, lamb and goat	4	3	5	4	5	5	6	6	Mouton, agneau et caprin
Tunisia									**Tunisie**
Total	101	105	108	106	112	120	123	123	Totale
Beef, veal and buffalo	49	50	52	50	53	58	60	60[1]	Bœuf, veau et buffle
Mutton, lamb and goat	52	54	56	55	58	63	63	63[1]	Mouton, agneau et caprin
Uganda									**Ouganda**
Total	174	179	183	186	193	200	203	204	Totale
Beef, veal and buffalo	84[1]	86[1]	88[1]	89	93[1]	96[1]	97[1]	97[1]	Bœuf, veau et buffle
Pork [1]	65	67	69	71	72	75	78	78	Porc [1]
Mutton, lamb and goat [1]	25	26	26	27	28	29	29	29	Mouton, agneau et caprin [1]
United Rep. of Tanzania									**Rép.-Unie de Tanzanie**
Total	250	251	254	257	264	269	271	271	Totale
Beef, veal and buffalo [1]	205	206	209	211	218	223	224	224	Bœuf, veau et buffle [1]
Pork	9	10	9	9	10	10	10	10	Porc

42

Meat
Production: thousand metric tons *[cont.]*

Viande
Production: milliers de tonnes *[suite]*

Country or area	1994	1995	1996	1997	1998	1999	2000	2001	Pays ou zone
Mutton, lamb and goat	35	36	36	36	36	37	37	37	Mouton, agneau et caprin
Zambia									**Zambie**
Total	56	50	53	41	42	44	48	48	Totale
Beef, veal and buffalo	43	38	40	28	27	29	32	32[1]	Bœuf, veau et buffle
Pork	10	10	10	10	10	11	11	11	Porc
Mutton, lamb and goat	3	3	3	3	4	4	5	5	Mouton, agneau et caprin
Zimbabwe									**Zimbabwe**
Total	88	98	92	98	99	121	127	127	Totale
Beef, veal and buffalo	67	73	67	74	74	95	101	101[1]	Bœuf, veau et buffle
Pork	10	13	13	12	13	13	13	13	Porc
Mutton, lamb and goat	11	11	12	12	12	13	13	13	Mouton, agneau et caprin
America, North									**Amérique du Nord**
Total	24 648	25 274	25 062	25 232	26 413	27 187	27 316	27 407	Totale
Beef, veal and buffalo	14 027	14 489	14 675	14 712	14 923	15 342	15 519	15 233	Bœuf, veau et buffle
Pork	10 386	10 561	10 173	10 309	11 280	11 637	11 589	11 967	Porc
Mutton, lamb and goat	235	224	214	211	209	208	208	207	Mouton, agneau et caprin
Antigua and Barbuda									**Antigua-et-Barbuda**
Total	1	1	1	1	1	1	1	1	Totale
Beef, veal and buffalo [1]	1	1	1	1	1	1	1	1	Bœuf, veau et buffle [1]
Barbados									**Barbade**
Total	5	5	5	5	5	5	5	5	Totale
Beef, veal and buffalo	1	1	1	1	1	1[1]	1[1]	1[1]	Bœuf, veau et buffle
Pork	4	4	4	4	4	4	4	4	Porc
Belize									**Belize**
Total	3	3	3	3	3	3	2	2	Totale
Beef, veal and buffalo	1	1	1	2	1[1]	1[1]	1[1]	1[1]	Bœuf, veau et buffle
Pork	1	1	1	1	1	1	1	1	Porc
Canada									**Canada**
Total	2 139	2 214	2 255	2 356	2 585	2 842	2 895	3 061	Totale
Beef, veal and buffalo	899	928	1 017	1 089	1 183	1 265	1 246	1 250	Bœuf, veau et buffle
Pork	1 229	1 276	1 228	1 257	1 392	1 566	1 638	1 800	Porc
Mutton, lamb and goat	11	10	11	10	10	11	11	11[1]	Mouton, agneau et caprin
Costa Rica									**Costa Rica**
Total	115	116	117	107	107	113	113	113	Totale
Beef, veal and buffalo	91	92	96	86	82	84	82	* 83	Bœuf, veau et buffle
Pork	23	24	20	21	25	29	31	30[1]	Porc
Cuba									**Cuba**
Total	130	137	144	147	169	178	178	191	Totale
Beef, veal and buffalo	60	64	68	68	69	73	73	77[1]	Bœuf, veau et buffle
Pork	69	72	74	78	98	103	103	112[1]	Porc
Mutton, lamb and goat	1	1	2	2	2	2	2	2	Mouton, agneau et caprin
Dominica									**Dominique**
Total	1	1	1	1	1	1	1	1	Totale
Beef, veal and buffalo	0	0	1	1	1	1	1	1	Bœuf, veau et buffle
Dominican Republic									**Rép. dominicaine**
Total	140	144	146	146	146	124	131	135	Totale
Beef, veal and buffalo	81	80	80	79	80	66	69	71	Bœuf, veau et buffle
Pork	57[1]	62[1]	63[1]	64	64	58	61	63	Porc
Mutton, lamb and goat	3	3	3	3	2	1	1	1	Mouton, agneau et caprin
El Salvador									**El Salvador**
Total	35	36	34	42	41	43	41	41	Totale
Beef, veal and buffalo	27	29	27	35	34	34	35	35[1]	Bœuf, veau et buffle
Pork	8	6	6	7	6	9	7	5	Porc
Guadeloupe									**Guadeloupe**
Total	5	5	4	5	5	5	5	5	Totale
Beef, veal and buffalo	3	3	3	3	3	3	3[1]	3[1]	Bœuf, veau et buffle
Pork	1	1	1	1[1]	1[1]	1[1]	1[1]	1[1]	Porc
Guatemala									**Guatemala**
Total	70	73	74	74	75	89	90	90	Totale
Beef, veal and buffalo	52	54	54	54	54	62	62[1]	62[1]	Bœuf, veau et buffle
Pork	15	16	16	17	18	24	25[1]	25[1]	Porc

42

Meat
Production: thousand metric tons *[cont.]*
Viande
Production: milliers de tonnes *[suite]*

Country or area	1994	1995	1996	1997	1998	1999	2000	2001	Pays ou zone
Mutton, lamb and goat	3	3	3	3	3	3	3	3	Mouton, agneau et caprin
Haiti									**Haïti**
Total	53	51	57	59	64	64	76	77	Totale
Beef, veal and buffalo	* 28	24	28	28	31	31[1]	40	41[1]	Bœuf, veau et buffle
Pork	21[1]	23	24	25	27	27[1]	28	29[1]	Porc
Mutton, lamb and goat	4[1]	4[1]	* 5	* 5	* 6	6[1]	7	7[1]	Mouton, agneau et caprin
Honduras									**Honduras**
Total	81	73	77	73	66	64	65	65	Totale
Beef, veal and buffalo	73	64	68	63	57	55	55	55	Bœuf, veau et buffle
Pork	8	8	9	9	9	9	10	10	Porc
Jamaica									**Jamaïque**
Total	25	25	24	23	23	23	22	22	Totale
Beef, veal and buffalo	16	17	16	15	14	15	14	14[1]	Bœuf, veau et buffle
Pork	7	7	7	7	7	7	7	6[1]	Porc
Mutton, lamb and goat [1]	2	2	2	2	2	2	2	2	Mouton, agneau et caprin [1]
Martinique									**Martinique**
Total	4	4	4	4	4	4	4	4	Totale
Beef, veal and buffalo	2	2	3	2	2	2	2[1]	2[1]	Bœuf, veau et buffle
Pork	2	2	2	1	2	2	2[1]	2[1]	Porc
Mexico									**Mexique**
Total	2 307	2 401	2 306	2 345	2 409	2 462	2 511	2 647	Totale
Beef, veal and buffalo	1 365	1 412	1 330	1 340	1 380	1 400	1 409	1 428	Bœuf, veau et buffle
Pork	873	922	910	939	961	994	1 030	1 144	Porc
Mutton, lamb and goat	69	68	65	65	69	68	72	75	Mouton, agneau et caprin
Montserrat									**Montserrat**
Total	1	1	1	1	1	1	1	1	Totale
Beef, veal and buffalo	1	1	1	1	1	1	1	1	Bœuf, veau et buffle
Nicaragua									**Nicaragua**
Total	56	54	55	57	52	54	58	60	Totale
Beef, veal and buffalo	51	49	50	52	46	48	52	54	Bœuf, veau et buffle
Pork	5	5	5	5	6	6	6	6	Porc
Panama									**Panama**
Total	76	78	84	79	82	81	78	76	Totale
Beef, veal and buffalo	60	61	66	60	64	60	57	57	Bœuf, veau et buffle
Pork	16	17	19	19[1]	19	21[1]	21[1]	19	Porc
Puerto Rico									**Porto Rico**
Total	34	32	29	29	28	29	30	30	Totale
Beef, veal and buffalo	18	16	14	16	14[1]	15[1]	15[1]	15[1]	Bœuf, veau et buffle
Pork	15	15	15	13	14[1]	14[1]	15[1]	15[1]	Porc
Saint Lucia									**Sainte-Lucie**
Total	1	1	1	1	1	1	1	1	Totale
Beef, veal and buffalo	1	1	1	1	1	1	1[1]	1	Bœuf, veau et buffle
Pork	1	1	1	1	1	1	1	1	Porc
St. Vincent-Grenadines									**St. Vincent-Grenadines**
Total	1	1	1	1	1	1	1	1	Totale
Pork	1	1	1	1	1	1	1	1	Porc
Trinidad and Tobago									**Trinité-et-Tobago**
Total	3	3	3	4	3	3	3	3	Totale
Beef, veal and buffalo	1	1	1	1	1	1	1[1]	1[1]	Bœuf, veau et buffle
Pork	2	2	2	2	2	2	2[1]	2[1]	Porc
United States									**Etats-Unis**
Total	19 361	19 812	19 635	19 667	20 540	20 994	21 002	20 773	Totale
Beef, veal and buffalo	11 194	11 585	11 749	11 714	11 803	12 123	12 298	11 980	Bœuf, veau et buffle
Pork	8 027	8 097	7 764	7 835	8 623	8 758	8 597	8 690	Porc
Mutton, lamb and goat	140	130	122	118	114	113	107	103	Mouton, agneau et caprin
United States Virgin Is.									**Iles Vierges américaines**
Total	1	1	1	1	1	1	1	1	Totale
Beef, veal and buffalo [1]	1	1	1	1	1	1	1	1	Bœuf, veau et buffle [1]
America, South									**Amérique du Sud**
Total	12 808	13 442	14 187	14 015	13 795	14 733	15 069	15 274	Totale
Beef, veal and buffalo	10 114	10 639	11 264	11 180	10 815	11 620	11 721	11 813	Bœuf, veau et buffle

42

Meat
Production: thousand metric tons *[cont.]*

Viande
Production: milliers de tonnes *[suite]*

Country or area	1994	1995	1996	1997	1998	1999	2000	2001	Pays ou zone
Pork	2 322	2 445	2 596	2 506	2 670	2 790	3 015	3 130	Porc
Mutton, lamb and goat	372	358	327	329	310	323	333	331	Mouton, agneau et caprin
Argentina									**Argentine**
Total	3 106	2 988	2 945	2 938	2 710	2 988	2 956	2 913	Totale
Beef, veal and buffalo	2 783	2 688	2 694	2 712	2 469	2 720	2 683	* 2 640	Bœuf, veau et buffle
Pork	230	211	180	161	184	215	214	214[1]	Porc
Mutton, lamb and goat	92	88	71	* 65	* 57	* 54	59[1]	59[1]	Mouton, agneau et caprin
Bolivia									**Bolivie**
Total	214	221	229	236	248	250	258	258	Totale
Beef, veal and buffalo	136	140	143	147	155	155	160	160[1]	Bœuf, veau et buffle
Pork	60	62	66	69	72	74	76	76	Porc
Mutton, lamb and goat	19	20	20	20	21	21	21	22	Mouton, agneau et caprin
Brazil									**Brésil**
Total	6 556	7 265	7 884	7 541	7 549	8 207	8 538	8 746	Totale
Beef, veal and buffalo	5 136	5 710	6 187	5 922	5 794	6 413	6 540	6 671	Bœuf, veau et buffle
Pork	1 300	1 430	1 600	1 518	1 652	1 684	1 888	1 968	Porc
Mutton, lamb and goat	* 120	125[1]	97[1]	101[1]	102[1]	110[1]	110[1]	107[1]	Mouton, agneau et caprin
Chile									**Chili**
Total	417	445	458	486	508	488	504	537	Totale
Beef, veal and buffalo	240	258	259	262	256	226	226	218	Bœuf, veau et buffle
Pork	161	172	185	209	235	244	261	303	Porc
Mutton, lamb and goat	17	15	13	15	17	18	16	16	Mouton, agneau et caprin
Colombia									**Colombie**
Total	793	849	875	884	851	835	839	843	Totale
Beef, veal and buffalo	646	702	730	763	766	716	745	746[1]	Bœuf, veau et buffle
Pork	133	133[1]	129[1]	103	75	107	78	81[1]	Porc
Mutton, lamb and goat	13[1]	14[1]	16[1]	18	9	12	* 16	16[1]	Mouton, agneau et caprin
Ecuador									**Equateur**
Total	216	245	264	270	265	282	290	285	Totale
Beef, veal and buffalo	127	149	153	156	158	164	174	179	Bœuf, veau et buffle
Pork	82	89	103	107	100	110	108	98[1]	Porc
Mutton, lamb and goat	6	7	7	8	7	7	8	8	Mouton, agneau et caprin
Falkland Is. (Malvinas)									**Iles Falkland (Malvinas)**
Total	1	1	1	1	1	1	1	1	Totale
Mutton, lamb and goat	1	1	1	1	1	1	1	1	Mouton, agneau et caprin
French Guiana									**Guyane française**
Total	1	1	2	2	2	2	2	2	Totale
Pork	1	1	1	1	1	1	1[1]	1[1]	Porc
Guyana									**Guyana**
Total	6	5	4	3	3	3	3	3	Totale
Beef, veal and buffalo	5	4	3	2	2	2	2	2[1]	Bœuf, veau et buffle
Pork	1	1	1[1]	1[1]	1[1]	1[1]	1[1]	1[1]	Porc
Mutton, lamb and goat	1	1	1	1	1	1	1	1	Mouton, agneau et caprin
Paraguay									**Paraguay**
Total	356	359	345	347	353	369	390	390	Totale
Beef, veal and buffalo	* 225	* 226	226[1]	226	* 231	* 246	239	239[1]	Bœuf, veau et buffle
Pork	128	130	116	117	119	120	148	148	Porc
Mutton, lamb and goat	3	3	3	3	3	3	3	3	Mouton, agneau et caprin
Peru									**Pérou**
Total	205	213	220	233	243	263	269	270	Totale
Beef, veal and buffalo	102	107	110	118	124	134	136	138	Bœuf, veau et buffle
Pork	78	80	83	87	91	93	95	94	Porc
Mutton, lamb and goat	26	26	27	28	29	37	38	38	Mouton, agneau et caprin
Suriname									**Suriname**
Total	3	3	2	3	3	3	3	3	Totale
Beef, veal and buffalo	2	2	2	2	2	2	2	2[1]	Bœuf, veau et buffle
Pork	2[1]	1	1	1	1	1	1	1[1]	Porc
Uruguay									**Uruguay**
Total	450	412	491	536	531	536	530	530	Totale
Beef, veal and buffalo	361	338	407	454	450	458	453	453[1]	Bœuf, veau et buffle
Pork	23	22	21	22	26	27	26	26[1]	Porc

42

Meat
Production: thousand metric tons *[cont.]*

Viande
Production: milliers de tonnes *[suite]*

Country or area	1994	1995	1996	1997	1998	1999	2000	2001	Pays ou zone
Mutton, lamb and goat	66	52	* 64	* 60	* 55	* 51	* 51	51[1]	Mouton, agneau et caprin
Venezuela									**Venezuela**
Total	483	435	469	535	528	505	485	491	Totale
Beef, veal and buffalo	351	316	350	415	406	384	360[1]	* 365	Bœuf, veau et buffle
Pork	125	112	113	111	113	114	117[1]	118[1]	Porc
Mutton, lamb and goat	8	7	7	9	9	8	8[1]	8[1]	Mouton, agneau et caprin
Asia									**Asie**
Total	**55 199**	**56 951**	**56 551**	**62 377**	**65 894**	**67 576**	**68 415**	**70 050**	**Totale**
Beef, veal and buffalo	**11 028**	**11 810**	**11 771**	**12 871**	**13 270**	**13 552**	**13 854**	**14 011**	**Bœuf, veau et buffle**
Pork	**39 145**	**39 843**	**39 643**	**44 019**	**46 865**	**48 105**	**48 418**	**49 938**	**Porc**
Mutton, lamb and goat	**5 027**	**5 298**	**5 137**	**5 486**	**5 759**	**5 920**	**6 143**	**6 101**	**Mouton, agneau et caprin**
Afghanistan									**Afghanistan**
Total	248	267	283	312	338	297	255	226	Totale
Beef, veal and buffalo [1]	113	130	143	156	171	149	126	108	Bœuf, veau et buffle [1]
Mutton, lamb and goat [1]	134	137	141	156	167	147	129	118	Mouton, agneau et caprin [1]
Armenia									**Arménie**
Total	42	42	44	45	47	45	45	45	Totale
Beef, veal and buffalo	29	30	33	35	35	32	33	32	Bœuf, veau et buffle
Pork	6	5	6	5	7	8	6	6	Porc
Mutton, lamb and goat	7	7	6	5	5	5	6	7	Mouton, agneau et caprin
Azerbaijan									**Azerbaïdjan**
Total	68	66	71	76	83	88	92	96	Totale
Beef, veal and buffalo	44	41	44	48	50	52	54	* 56	Bœuf, veau et buffle
Pork	2	2	2	2	1	2	2	* 2	Porc
Mutton, lamb and goat	22	23	26	26	32	35	36	* 38	Mouton, agneau et caprin
Bahrain									**Bahreïn**
Total	10	9	9	9	8	8	8	8	Totale
Beef, veal and buffalo	1[1]	1[1]	1[1]	1[1]	1[1]	1	1[1]	1[1]	Bœuf, veau et buffle
Mutton, lamb and goat	9[1]	9[1]	9[1]	9[1]	7[1]	7	7[1]	7[1]	Mouton, agneau et caprin
Bangladesh									**Bangladesh**
Total	250	258	273	294	293	303	307	307	Totale
Beef, veal and buffalo	150[1]	151[1]	156	169[1]	165	174[1]	176[1]	176[1]	Bœuf, veau et buffle
Mutton, lamb and goat	100[1]	107[1]	118	126[1]	129	130[1]	132[1]	132[1]	Mouton, agneau et caprin
Bhutan									**Bhoutan**
Total	7	7	7	7	7	7	7	7	Totale
Beef, veal and buffalo	6	6	6	6	6	6	6	6	Bœuf, veau et buffle
Pork	1	1	1	1	1	1	1	1	Porc
Brunei Darussalam									**Brunéi Darussalam**
Total	2	1	2	2	2	5	5	17	Totale
Beef, veal and buffalo	2	1	2	2	2	5	5	16	Bœuf, veau et buffle
Cambodia									**Cambodge**
Total	129	134	139	151	155	158	175	179	Totale
Beef, veal and buffalo	48	52	53	54	55	55	70	71	Bœuf, veau et buffle
Pork	81	82	86	97	100	103	105	108	Porc
China									**Chine**
Total	36 902	38 748	38 414	43 718	47 073	48 644	49 467	51 009	Totale
Beef, veal and buffalo *	2 806	3 598	3 585	4 431	4 824	5 078	5 352	5 534	Bœuf, veau et buffle *
Pork	* 32 613	* 33 401	33 015	37 155	39 899	41 048	41 371	* 42 787	Porc
Mutton, lamb and goat	* 1 483	* 1 749	* 1 815	* 2 132	* 2 350	* 2 517	* 2 744	2 689[1]	Mouton, agneau et caprin
Cyprus									**Chypre**
Total	54	56	58	60	61	64	67	65	Totale
Beef, veal and buffalo	4	5	5	5	4	4	4	5	Bœuf, veau et buffle
Pork	43	43	46	46	47	49	52	50	Porc
Mutton, lamb and goat	7	8	8	8	10	11	11	11	Mouton, agneau et caprin
Georgia									**Géorgie**
Total	98	105	109	109	93	89	94	106	Totale
Beef, veal and buffalo	44	53	54	56	43	41	48	55[1]	Bœuf, veau et buffle
Pork	47	44	46	47	42	41	37	44[1]	Porc
Mutton, lamb and goat	7	8	9	7	8	7	9	7[1]	Mouton, agneau et caprin
India									**Inde**
Total	3 814	3 875	3 937	3 995	4 011	4 086	4 137	4 184	Totale

42

Meat
Production: thousand metric tons *[cont.]*
Viande
Production: milliers de tonnes *[suite]*

Country or area	1994	1995	1996	1997	1998	1999	2000	2001	Pays ou zone
Beef, veal and buffalo	2 682	2 716	2 751	2 782	2 781	2 832	2 863	2 890	Bœuf, veau et buffle
Pork	477	495	514	533	543	560	578	595	Porc
Mutton, lamb and goat	655	663	672	680	688	694	696	699	Mouton, agneau et caprin
Indonesia									**Indonésie**
Total	1 144	1 026	1 094	1 141	1 092	984	890	887	Totale
Beef, veal and buffalo	385	359	396	401	389	357	397	392[1]	Bœuf, veau et buffle
Pork	660	572	600	633	622	550	413	413	Porc
Mutton, lamb and goat	100	94	99	107	82	77	81	83[1]	Mouton, agneau et caprin
Iran (Islamic Rep. of)									**Iran (Rép. islamique d')**
Total	628	642	668	715	744	703	650	625	Totale
Beef, veal and buffalo	* 256	* 265	287	309	326	306	262[1]	243[1]	Bœuf, veau et buffle
Mutton, lamb and goat	* 372	* 377	380	406	418	397	388[1]	382[1]	Mouton, agneau et caprin
Iraq									**Iraq**
Total	84	73	59	73	75	76	76	76	Totale
Beef, veal and buffalo [1]	51	43	37	46	47	47	48	48	Bœuf, veau et buffle [1]
Mutton, lamb and goat [1]	33	31	22	27	28	28	29	28	Mouton, agneau et caprin [1]
Israel									**Israël**
Total	57	58	61	65	62	61	68	71	Totale
Beef, veal and buffalo	41	41	44	46	44	46	52	54	Bœuf, veau et buffle
Pork	9	11	11	12	12	9	10	11	Porc
Mutton, lamb and goat *	7	7	7	6	6	6	6	6	Mouton, agneau et caprin *
Japan									**Japon**
Total	1 993	1 923	1 821	1 814	1 816	1 818	1 800	1 770	Totale
Beef, veal and buffalo	602	601	555	530	529	540	531	* 520	Bœuf, veau et buffle
Pork	1 390	1 322	1 266	1 283	1 286	1 277	1 269	* 1 250	Porc
Jordan									**Jordanie**
Total	16	16	16	15	22	21	15	15	Totale
Beef, veal and buffalo	4	4[1]	3	4	3	4	3	3	Bœuf, veau et buffle
Mutton, lamb and goat	12	12	13	12	19	17	11	11	Mouton, agneau et caprin
Kazakhstan									**Kazakhstan**
Total	1 052	867	740	627	546	540	531	524	Totale
Beef, veal and buffalo	642	548	463	398	348	344	306	306[1]	Bœuf, veau et buffle
Pork	158	113	110	82	79	98	133	126[1]	Porc
Mutton, lamb and goat	* 252	* 206	* 167	* 147	119	* 99	* 91	92[1]	Mouton, agneau et caprin
Korea, Dem. P. R.									**Corée, R. p. dém. de**
Total	173	150	131	108	139	164	172	178	Totale
Beef, veal and buffalo	32	31	22	19	20	20	20	21	Bœuf, veau et buffle
Pork	135	115	105	84	112	134	140	145	Porc
Mutton, lamb and goat	6	4	4	6	8	11	12	12	Mouton, agneau et caprin
Korea, Republic of									**Corée, République de**
Total	1 003	1 023	1 138	1 237	1 318	1 342	1 225	1 156	Totale
Beef, veal and buffalo	214	221	248	338	376	342	306	226	Bœuf, veau et buffle
Pork	786	799	887	896	939	996	916	928	Porc
Mutton, lamb and goat	3	3	3	4	3	3	3	3	Mouton, agneau et caprin
Kuwait									**Koweït**
Total	50	40	41	41	41	40	38	38	Totale
Beef, veal and buffalo	1[1]	* 2	2[1]	2[1]	2[1]	2[1]	2[1]	2[1]	Bœuf, veau et buffle
Mutton, lamb and goat	* 49	* 38	* 39	39[1]	38[1]	39[1]	36[1]	36[1]	Mouton, agneau et caprin
Kyrgyzstan									**Kirghizistan**
Total	177	167	169	165	168	170	170	161	Totale
Beef, veal and buffalo	82	85	86	95	95	95	98	93[1]	Bœuf, veau et buffle
Pork	18	28	29	26	30	29	29	25[1]	Porc
Mutton, lamb and goat	* 76	* 54	* 54	45	43	47	43	43[1]	Mouton, agneau et caprin
Lao People's Dem. Rep.									**Rép. dém. pop. lao**
Total	48	58	58	61	63	70	67	79	Totale
Beef, veal and buffalo	22[1]	28	28	30	31	38	33	43	Bœuf, veau et buffle
Pork	26	29	30	31	31	32	33	* 35	Porc
Mutton, lamb and goat	0	0	0	0	0	0	0	1	Mouton, agneau et caprin
Lebanon									**Liban**
Total	38	33	32	43	47	50	49	49	Totale
Beef, veal and buffalo	15	12	10	20	22	25	24	24	Bœuf, veau et buffle

42

Meat
Production: thousand metric tons *[cont.]*

Viande
Production: milliers de tonnes *[suite]*

Country or area	1994	1995	1996	1997	1998	1999	2000	2001	Pays ou zone
Pork	6	7	8	8	8	9	9	9	Porc
Mutton, lamb and goat	17	14	14	14	16	16	16	16	Mouton, agneau et caprin
Malaysia									**Malaisie**
Total	305	305	301	305	285	274	274	274	Totale
Beef, veal and buffalo	19	21	22	23	22	24	24	24	Bœuf, veau et buffle
Pork	285	283	278	282	262	250[1]	250[1]	250[1]	Porc
Mutton, lamb and goat	1	1	1	1	1	1	1	1	Mouton, agneau et caprin
Mongolia									**Mongolie**
Total	177	182	212	191	199	234	234	236	Totale
Beef, veal and buffalo	64	69	90	87	86	105	113	115	Bœuf, veau et buffle
Pork	1	1	0	0	1	0	1	1	Porc
Mutton, lamb and goat	112	112	121	104	112	129	120	121	Mouton, agneau et caprin
Myanmar									**Myanmar**
Total	182	190	196	216	220	237	244	250	Totale
Beef, veal and buffalo	111	113	116	119	121	121	122	125	Bœuf, veau et buffle
Pork	63	69	72	89	91	107	113	116	Porc
Mutton, lamb and goat	7	8	8	8	9	9	9	9	Mouton, agneau et caprin
Nepal									**Népal**
Total	188	195	199	211	217	220	224	225	Totale
Beef, veal and buffalo	144	150	152	161	165	167	170	169	Bœuf, veau et buffle
Pork	11	11	12	12	13	14	15	15	Porc
Mutton, lamb and goat	34	34	35	37	39	39	40	41	Mouton, agneau et caprin
Occup. Palestinian Terr. [2]									**Terr. palestinien occupé** [2]
Total	3	3	3	3	3	3	3	3	Totale
Beef, veal and buffalo	1	1	1	1	1	1	1	1	Bœuf, veau et buffle
Mutton, lamb and goat	1	1	1	1	1	1	1	1	Mouton, agneau et caprin
Oman									**Oman**
Total	19	18	19	20	20	20	21	19	Totale
Beef, veal and buffalo	3	3	4	4	4	5	5	3	Bœuf, veau et buffle
Mutton, lamb and goat	16	15	15	15	16	16	16	16	Mouton, agneau et caprin
Pakistan									**Pakistan**
Total	1 444	1 530	1 275	1 307	1 342	1 375	1 410	1 445	Totale
Beef, veal and buffalo	807	847	* 811	* 830	* 853	* 875	* 897	* 918	Bœuf, veau et buffle
Mutton, lamb and goat	637	683	* 464	* 477	* 489	* 500	* 513	* 527	Mouton, agneau et caprin
Philippines									**Philippines**
Total	930	983	1 051	1 121	1 175	1 265	1 304	1 353	Totale
Beef, veal and buffalo	* 136	147	161	189	212	259	262	255	Bœuf, veau et buffle
Pork	765	805	860	901	933	973	1 008	1 064	Porc
Mutton, lamb and goat	* 30	* 31	* 30	* 31	* 31	33	34	34	Mouton, agneau et caprin
Qatar									**Qatar**
Total	13	14	8	8	8	8	9	9	Totale
Beef, veal and buffalo	0	0	0	0	0	0	0	1	Bœuf, veau et buffle
Mutton, lamb and goat	13	14	8	8	8	8	8	8	Mouton, agneau et caprin
Saudi Arabia									**Arabie saoudite**
Total	119	114	106	101	104	110	110	110	Totale
Beef, veal and buffalo	* 30	* 26	* 18	* 16	19	19	19[1]	19[1]	Bœuf, veau et buffle
Mutton, lamb and goat	89[1]	88[1]	88[1]	* 85	* 85	* 91	91[1]	91[1]	Mouton, agneau et caprin
Singapore									**Singapour**
Total	88	87	84	84	84	50	50	50	Totale
Beef, veal and buffalo	0	0	0	0	0	0	0[1]	0[1]	Bœuf, veau et buffle
Pork	87	86	84	84	84	50	50[1]	50[1]	Porc
Mutton, lamb and goat	1	0	0	0	0	0	0	0	Mouton, agneau et caprin
Sri Lanka									**Sri Lanka**
Total	36	37	33	34	33	31	32	32	Totale
Beef, veal and buffalo	31	32	29	30	29	28	29	29[1]	Bœuf, veau et buffle
Pork	2	2	2	2	2	2	2	2[1]	Porc
Mutton, lamb and goat	3	3	2	2	2	2	2	2[1]	Mouton, agneau et caprin
Syrian Arab Republic									**Rép. arabe syrienne**
Total	156	170	190	196	204	229	236	242	Totale
Beef, veal and buffalo	31	34	40	42	43	47	47	42	Bœuf, veau et buffle
Mutton, lamb and goat	126	137	150	154	160	182	189	200[1]	Mouton, agneau et caprin

42

Meat
Production: thousand metric tons *[cont.]*

Viande
Production: milliers de tonnes *[suite]*

Country or area	1994	1995	1996	1997	1998	1999	2000	2001	Pays ou zone
Tajikistan									**Tadjikistan**
Total	58	51	45	29	28	28	28	33	Totale
Beef, veal and buffalo	36	* 31	34	26	15	* 15	* 12	* 17	Bœuf, veau et buffle
Pork	1	* 1	0	* 0	* 0	* 0	* 0	* 0	Porc
Mutton, lamb and goat	21	* 19	11	3	13	* 13	* 16	* 15	Mouton, agneau et caprin
Thailand									**Thaïlande**
Total	839	827	841	849	750	671	675	710	Totale
Beef, veal and buffalo	348	337	329	300	275	244	224	234	Bœuf, veau et buffle
Pork	489	489	511	549	475	426	450	475	Porc
Mutton, lamb and goat	1	1	1	1	1	1	1	1	Mouton, agneau et caprin
Turkey									**Turquie**
Total	697	671	672	763	738	738	744	750	Totale
Beef, veal and buffalo	325	299	305	385	364	* 370	* 376	* 382	Bœuf, veau et buffle
Pork	0	0	1	0	0	0[1]	0[1]	0[1]	Porc
Mutton, lamb and goat	* 372	* 372	* 366	* 378	* 374	* 368	368[1]	368[1]	Mouton, agneau et caprin
Turkmenistan									**Turkménistan**
Total	100	104	107	107	123	127	127	128	Totale
Beef, veal and buffalo	51	51	52	55	61	63	65[1]	67[1]	Bœuf, veau et buffle
Pork	4	3	1	1	1	1	1[1]	1[1]	Porc
Mutton, lamb and goat	* 45	* 50	* 53	* 51	* 61	* 63	62[1]	60[1]	Mouton, agneau et caprin
United Arab Emirates									**Emirats arabes unis**
Total	44	46	48	50	45	46	47	47	Totale
Beef, veal and buffalo	7	9	10	13	14	15	15	15	Bœuf, veau et buffle
Mutton, lamb and goat	36	38	39	37	30	31	31	31	Mouton, agneau et caprin
Uzbekistan									**Ouzbékistan**
Total	483	491	447	457	497	465	516	524	Totale
Beef, veal and buffalo	390	392	362	387	400	* 372	* 413	420[1]	Bœuf, veau et buffle
Pork	20	16	9	4	15	* 20	* 17	16[1]	Porc
Mutton, lamb and goat	73	83	76	* 66	82	* 73	* 87	88[1]	Mouton, agneau et caprin
Viet Nam									**Viet Nam**
Total	1 137	1 191	1 232	1 334	1 400	1 499	1 598	1 614	Totale
Beef, veal and buffalo	176	180	175[1]	175[1]	167	176	185	194[1]	Bœuf, veau et buffle
Pork	958	1 007	1 052	1 154	1 228	1 318	1 409	1 416	Porc
Mutton, lamb and goat	3	4	5	5	5	5	5	5	Mouton, agneau et caprin
Yemen									**Yémen**
Total	78	79	81	86	90	93	98	98	Totale
Beef, veal and buffalo	40	41	42	43	45	47	52	52[1]	Bœuf, veau et buffle
Mutton, lamb and goat [1]	38	38	39	43	45	46	47	47	Mouton, agneau et caprin [1]
Europe									**Europe**
Total	**41 400**	**40 358**	**40 361**	**39 058**	**39 815**	**39 651**	**38 674**	**38 136**	**Totale**
Beef, veal and buffalo	**14 843**	**13 959**	**13 644**	**13 182**	**12 516**	**12 061**	**11 687**	**11 698**	**Bœuf, veau et buffle**
Pork	**24 740**	**24 649**	**25 010**	**24 301**	**25 721**	**26 074**	**25 487**	**25 049**	**Porc**
Mutton, lamb and goat	**1 818**	**1 751**	**1 708**	**1 575**	**1 579**	**1 517**	**1 500**	**1 390**	**Mouton, agneau et caprin**
Albania									**Albanie**
Total	60	63	56	55	55	58	62	65	Totale
Beef, veal and buffalo *	28	31	33	33	32	34	36	38	Bœuf, veau et buffle *
Pork	* 14	* 14	* 6	* 7	* 7	* 6	* 7	8[1]	Porc
Mutton, lamb and goat	* 19	* 18	* 17	* 16	* 17	* 18	* 20	20[1]	Mouton, agneau et caprin
Austria									**Autriche**
Total	757	723	766	769	796	832	774	733	Totale
Beef, veal and buffalo	212	196	221	206	197	203	203	215	Bœuf, veau et buffle
Pork	* 539	* 521	* 538	* 556	* 592	* 622	* 563	510[1]	Porc
Mutton, lamb and goat	6	7	7	7	7	7	8	8[1]	Mouton, agneau et caprin
Belarus									**Bélarus**
Total	641	582	554	556	594	570	519	562	Totale
Beef, veal and buffalo	384	316	277	256	271	262	* 269	295[1]	Bœuf, veau et buffle
Pork	252	263	273	298	320	* 305	* 247	265[1]	Porc
Mutton, lamb and goat	5	4	4	* 3	3	* 3	* 3	2[1]	Mouton, agneau et caprin
Belgium-Luxembourg									**Belgique-Luxembourg**
Total	1 380	1 405	1 436	1 377	1 393	1 290	1 332	1 271	Totale
Beef, veal and buffalo	355	357	362	340	303	281	274	296	Bœuf, veau et buffle

42

Meat
Production: thousand metric tons *[cont.]*
    Viande
    Production: milliers de tonnes *[suite]*

Country or area	1994	1995	1996	1997	1998	1999	2000	2001	Pays ou zone
Pork	1 019	1 043	1 070	1 033	1 085	1 005	1 053	* 970	Porc
Mutton, lamb and goat	5	5	5	4	4	5	4	* 5	Mouton, agneau et caprin
Bosnia and Herzegovina									**Bosnie-Herzégovine**
Total	40	35	27	24	27	27	20	18	Totale
Beef, veal and buffalo	23[1]	16	* 13	10	12	12[1]	* 13	* 13	Bœuf, veau et buffle
Pork [1]	15	17	11	11	12	12	5	2	Porc [1]
Mutton, lamb and goat	2[1]	3[1]	3	3[1]	3[1]	3[1]	3	3[1]	Mouton, agneau et caprin
Bulgaria									**Bulgarie**
Total	343	366	388	334	357	389	363	355	Totale
Beef, veal and buffalo	* 89	* 65	* 80	* 57	* 56	* 64	68[1]	64[1]	Bœuf, veau et buffle
Pork	207	256	252	227	248	267	* 243	242[1]	Porc
Mutton, lamb and goat	* 47	* 45	* 56	* 50	* 53	* 58	52[1]	48[1]	Mouton, agneau et caprin
Croatia									**Croatie**
Total	91	83	80	83	88	94	92	91	Totale
Beef, veal and buffalo	28	26	22	26	26	28	30	* 19	Bœuf, veau et buffle
Pork *	60	56	56	55	60	64	60	70	Porc *
Mutton, lamb and goat	* 2	* 2	* 2	* 2	* 2	* 2	2[1]	2[1]	Mouton, agneau et caprin
Czech Republic									**République tchèque**
Total	645	676	669	623	613	576	527	523	Totale
Beef, veal and buffalo	170	170	164	156	134	121	107	103	Bœuf, veau et buffle
Pork	471	502	502	464	476	452	417	417	Porc
Mutton, lamb and goat	* 4	* 4	* 4	* 4	3	3	3	3[1]	Mouton, agneau et caprin
Denmark									**Danemark**
Total	1 712	1 677	1 673	1 697	1 793	1 800	1 780	1 864	Totale
Beef, veal and buffalo	189	182	178	175	162	157	154	158[1]	Bœuf, veau et buffle
Pork	1 521	1 494	1 494	1 521	1 629	1 642	1 625	* 1 705	Porc
Mutton, lamb and goat	2	2	2	2	2	1	1	1[1]	Mouton, agneau et caprin
Estonia									**Estonie**
Total	63	62	54	49	52	53	46	51	Totale
Beef, veal and buffalo	31	26	22	19	19	22	15	19[1]	Bœuf, veau et buffle
Pork	30	35	32	30	32	31	30	32[1]	Porc
Mutton, lamb and goat	1	1	1	0	0	0	0	0[1]	Mouton, agneau et caprin
Faeroe Islands									**Iles Féroé**
Total	1	1	1	1	1	1	1	1	Totale
Mutton, lamb and goat	1	1	1	1	1	1	1	1	Mouton, agneau et caprin
Finland									**Finlande**
Total	280	265	270	281	279	273	264	261	Totale
Beef, veal and buffalo	108	96	97	100	94	90	90	90[1]	Bœuf, veau et buffle
Pork	171	168	172	180	185	182	173	170[1]	Porc
Mutton, lamb and goat	1	2	1	1	1	1	1	1[1]	Mouton, agneau et caprin
France									**France**
Total	3 890	3 975	4 053	4 089	4 104	4 100	3 966	3 968	Totale
Beef, veal and buffalo	1 627	1 683	1 737	1 720	1 632	1 609	1 514	* 1 571	Bœuf, veau et buffle
Pork	2 116	2 144	2 161	2 219	2 328	2 353	2 312	* 2 255	Porc
Mutton, lamb and goat	147	148	155	150	144	138	140	143[1]	Mouton, agneau et caprin
Germany									**Allemagne**
Total	5 064	5 052	5 160	5 056	5 246	5 521	5 329	5 475	Totale
Beef, veal and buffalo	1 420	1 408	1 482	1 448	1 367	1 374	1 303	1 360	Bœuf, veau et buffle
Pork	3 604	3 602	3 635	3 564	3 834	4 103	3 981	4 071	Porc
Mutton, lamb and goat	40	42	43	44	44	44	45	44	Mouton, agneau et caprin
Greece									**Grèce**
Total	349	353	352	349	348	331	334	334	Totale
Beef, veal and buffalo	71	72	71	72	69	67	66	* 66	Bœuf, veau et buffle
Pork	137	137	136	133	134	138	143	* 142	Porc
Mutton, lamb and goat	142	143	145	143	145	* 127	* 125	* 126	Mouton, agneau et caprin
Hungary									**Hongrie**
Total	682	638	723	638	619	680	694	648	Totale
Beef, veal and buffalo	72	* 58	* 50	55	47	51	51[1]	40[1]	Bœuf, veau et buffle
Pork	608	* 578	* 671	581	570	626	* 640	605[1]	Porc
Mutton, lamb and goat	1	* 2	* 2	2	3	4	3[1]	3[1]	Mouton, agneau et caprin

42

Meat
Production: thousand metric tons *[cont.]*

Viande
Production: milliers de tonnes *[suite]*

Country or area	1994	1995	1996	1997	1998	1999	2000	2001	Pays ou zone
Iceland									**Islande**
Total	16	15	15	15	16	17	18	19	Totale
Beef, veal and buffalo	4	3	3	3	3	4	4	4[1]	Bœuf, veau et buffle
Pork	3	3	4	4	4	5	5	5[1]	Porc
Mutton, lamb and goat	9	9	8	8	8	9	10	10[1]	Mouton, agneau et caprin
Ireland									**Irlande**
Total	753	779	836	866	921	984	886	896	Totale
Beef, veal and buffalo	445	477	535	568	594	644	577	579	Bœuf, veau et buffle
Pork	215	212	211	220	242	250	226	238	Porc
Mutton, lamb and goat	93	89	90	79	86	90	83	78	Mouton, agneau et caprin
Italy									**Italie**
Total	2 619	2 603	2 670	2 633	2 598	2 711	2 703	2 708	Totale
Beef, veal and buffalo	1 171	1 181	1 182	1 161	1 113	1 166	1 156	1 134[1]	Bœuf, veau et buffle
Pork	1 369	1 346	1 410	1 396	1 412	1 472	1 478	1 510	Porc
Mutton, lamb and goat	79	76	78	76	73	73	69	64	Mouton, agneau et caprin
Latvia									**Lettonie**
Total	124	112	67	63	63	57	54	46	Totale
Beef, veal and buffalo	68	48	27	26	26	23	22	17	Bœuf, veau et buffle
Pork	54	63	40	37	36	35	32	29	Porc
Mutton, lamb and goat	2	1	1	0	0	0	0	0	Mouton, agneau et caprin
Lithuania									**Lituanie**
Total	199	182	173	178	178	170	161	155	Totale
Beef, veal and buffalo	116	87	83	90	81	77	75	64	Bœuf, veau et buffle
Pork	82	93	89	87	96	91	85	90	Porc
Mutton, lamb and goat	2	2	1	1	1	1	1	1	Mouton, agneau et caprin
Malta									**Malte**
Total	11	10	10	12	12	12	11	11	Totale
Beef, veal and buffalo	2	2	2	2	2	2	2	2	Bœuf, veau et buffle
Pork	9	9	9	10	10	10	9	10	Porc
Netherlands									**Pays-Bas**
Total	2 294	2 218	2 222	1 956	2 277	2 237	2 112	2 069	Totale
Beef, veal and buffalo	603	* 580	580	565	535	508	471	475[1]	Bœuf, veau et buffle
Pork	1 673	1 622	1 624	1 376	1 725	1 711	1 623	* 1 575	Porc
Mutton, lamb and goat	17	16	18	15	17	18	* 19	19[1]	Mouton, agneau et caprin
Norway									**Norvège**
Total	206	208	217	221	221	228	218	213	Totale
Beef, veal and buffalo	88	85	86	89	91	96	91	84	Bœuf, veau et buffle
Pork	91	96	103	105	106	109	103	105	Porc
Mutton, lamb and goat	27	27	27	26	24	23	24	24	Mouton, agneau et caprin
Poland									**Pologne**
Total	2 111	2 354	2 483	2 323	2 457	2 429	2 273	1 971	Totale
Beef, veal and buffalo	421	386	415	429	430	385	349	300[1]	Bœuf, veau et buffle
Pork	1 681	1 962	2 064	1 891	2 026	2 043	1 923	1 670[1]	Porc
Mutton, lamb and goat	8	6	5	3	1	2	1	1[1]	Mouton, agneau et caprin
Portugal									**Portugal**
Total	438	435	450	442	454	468	456	463	Totale
Beef, veal and buffalo	95	104	99	109	96	97	100	* 99	Bœuf, veau et buffle
Pork	316	305	325	306	332	346	329	* 340	Porc
Mutton, lamb and goat	27	27	26	27	26	25	27	* 24	Mouton, agneau et caprin
Republic of Moldova									**République de Moldova**
Total	127	110	106	104	86	88	72	63	Totale
Beef, veal and buffalo	62	47	39	35	24	24	* 21	21[1]	Bœuf, veau et buffle
Pork	61	60	64	66	58	61	* 48	39[1]	Porc
Mutton, lamb and goat	4	3	3	3	4	4	* 3	3[1]	Mouton, agneau et caprin
Romania									**Roumanie**
Total	1 114	950	880	916	862	817	845	869	Totale
Beef, veal and buffalo	* 258	202	177	185	183	153	162	175[1]	Bœuf, veau et buffle
Pork	* 775	673	631	667	620	610	626[1]	635[1]	Porc
Mutton, lamb and goat	* 81	75	71	64	* 60	54	57[1]	59[1]	Mouton, agneau et caprin
Russian Federation									**Fédération de Russie**
Total	5 659	4 859	4 565	4 140	3 931	3 497	3 623	3 660	Totale

42

Meat
Production: thousand metric tons *[cont.]*

Viande
Production: milliers de tonnes *[suite]*

Country or area	1994	1995	1996	1997	1998	1999	2000	2001	Pays ou zone
Beef, veal and buffalo	3 240	2 733	2 630	2 394	2 247	1 868	1 897	* 1 916	Bœuf, veau et buffle
Pork	2 103	1 865	1 705	1 546	1 505	1 485	1 603	* 1 620	Porc
Mutton, lamb and goat	316	261	230	200	178	143	* 123	* 124	Mouton, agneau et caprin
Serbia and Montenegro									**Serbie-et-Monténégro**
Total	794	899	986	883	782	767	782	717	Totale
Beef, veal and buffalo	197	227	* 242	* 209	127	104	* 104	* 104	Bœuf, veau et buffle
Pork	571	644	* 713	* 644	* 625	* 640	655[1]	590[1]	Porc
Mutton, lamb and goat	26	29	31	31	30	23	23[1]	23[1]	Mouton, agneau et caprin
Slovakia									**Slovaquie**
Total	314	304	314	322	288	227	208	197	Totale
Beef, veal and buffalo	67	59	61	66	59	50	43	38	Bœuf, veau et buffle
Pork	244	243	251	255	227	176	164	157	Porc
Mutton, lamb and goat	2	2	2	2	2	2	2	2	Mouton, agneau et caprin
Slovenia									**Slovénie**
Total	123	112	117	114	106	111	102	103	Totale
Beef, veal and buffalo	52	51	54	54	45	43	42	42[1]	Bœuf, veau et buffle
Pork	71	61	63	59	61	67	59	60[1]	Porc
Mutton, lamb and goat	* 0	0[1]	0[1]	1	1	1	1	1[1]	Mouton, agneau et caprin
Spain									**Espagne**
Total	2 849	2 925	3 159	3 238	3 645	3 809	3 795	3 875	Totale
Beef, veal and buffalo	484	508	565	592	651	678	632	* 616	Bœuf, veau et buffle
Pork	2 124	2 175	2 356	2 401	2 744	2 893	2 912	* 3 000	Porc
Mutton, lamb and goat	241	242	238	245	250	239	251	* 259	Mouton, agneau et caprin
Sweden									**Suède**
Total	454	456	460	482	477	474	431	424	Totale
Beef, veal and buffalo	142	143	138	149	143	145	150	143	Bœuf, veau et buffle
Pork	308	309	319	329	330	325	277	276	Porc
Mutton, lamb and goat	4	3	4	4	3	4	4	5	Mouton, agneau et caprin
Switzerland									**Suisse**
Total	394	404	385	373	385	379	359	383	Totale
Beef, veal and buffalo	142	147	159	152	147	146	128	140	Bœuf, veau et buffle
Pork	246	251	220	214	232	226	225	237	Porc
Mutton, lamb and goat	6	6	6	6	6	7	6	6	Mouton, agneau et caprin
TFYR of Macedonia									**L'ex-R.y. Macédoine**
Total	30	26	26	23	22	22	22	24	Totale
Beef, veal and buffalo	8	7	7	8	7	7[1]	* 7	* 9	Bœuf, veau et buffle
Pork	10	9	9	9	9	9[1]	9[1]	9[1]	Porc
Mutton, lamb and goat	13	10	10	7	6	6[1]	6[1]	6[1]	Mouton, agneau et caprin
Ukraine									**Ukraine**
Total	2 387	2 032	1 869	1 664	1 482	1 467	1 452	1 359	Totale
Beef, veal and buffalo	1 427	1 186	1 048	930	793	791	754	* 735	Bœuf, veau et buffle
Pork	916	807	789	710	668	656	676	* 609	Porc
Mutton, lamb and goat	44	40	32	24	21	19	* 22	* 15	Mouton, agneau et caprin
United Kingdom									**Royaume-Uni**
Total	2 387	2 409	2 094	2 111	2 190	2 086	1 990	1 692	Totale
Beef, veal and buffalo	943	996	708	696	697	678	708	652	Bœuf, veau et buffle
Pork	1 053	1 012	1 004	1 094	1 142	1 047	923	782	Porc
Mutton, lamb and goat	391	401	382	321	351	361	359	258	Mouton, agneau et caprin
Oceania									**Océanie**
Total	4 015	4 078	3 935	4 043	3 961	4 221	4 283	4 390	Totale
Beef, veal and buffalo	2 383	2 452	2 398	2 478	2 611	2 593	2 583	2 654	Bœuf, veau et buffle
Pork	448	459	441	445	477	472	470	499	Porc
Mutton, lamb and goat	1 184	1 167	1 096	1 121	873	1 156	1 230	1 236	Mouton, agneau et caprin
Australia									**Australie**
Total	2 827	2 786	2 662	2 721	2 647	3 009	3 039	3 100	Totale
Beef, veal and buffalo	1 825	1 803	1 745	1 810	1 955	2 011	1 988	* 2 040	Bœuf, veau et buffle
Pork	344	351	334	336	366	362	362	* 389	Porc
Mutton, lamb and goat	658	631	583	575	325	637	689	* 671	Mouton, agneau et caprin
Cook Islands									**Iles Cook**
Total	0	0	1	1	1	1	1	1	Totale
Pork	0	0	1	1	1	1	1	1	Porc

42

Meat
Production: thousand metric tons *[cont.]*

Viande
Production: milliers de tonnes *[suite]*

Country or area	1994	1995	1996	1997	1998	1999	2000	2001	Pays ou zone
Fiji									**Fidji**
Total	13	13	13	14	14	14	14	14	Totale
Beef, veal and buffalo	9	9	9	9	9	9	9	9	Bœuf, veau et buffle
Pork	4	3	3	4	3	4	4	4	Porc
Mutton, lamb and goat	1	1	1	1	1	1[1]	1[1]	1[1]	Mouton, agneau et caprin
French Polynesia									**Polynésie française**
Total	2	2	1	1	1	1	1	1	Totale
Pork	1	1	1	1	1	1[1]	1[1]	1[1]	Porc
Kiribati									**Kiribati**
Total	1	1	1	1	1	1	1	1	Totale
Pork	1	1	1	1	1	1	1	1	Porc
Micronesia (Fed. States)									**Micronésie (Etats féd. de)**
Total	...	1	1	1	1	1	1	1	Totale
Pork	...	1	1	1	1	1	1	1	Porc
New Caledonia									**Nouvelle-Calédonie**
Total	5	5	6	5	6	6	5	5	Totale
Beef, veal and buffalo	4	4	4	4	4	4	4	4[1]	Bœuf, veau et buffle
Pork	1	1	1	1	1	1	1	1[1]	Porc
New Zealand									**Nouvelle-Zélande**
Total	1 111	1 215	1 194	1 240	1 231	1 127	1 158	1 200	Totale
Beef, veal and buffalo	537	629	633	646	634	561	572	590	Bœuf, veau et buffle
Pork	49	51	50	49	50	48	46	46	Porc
Mutton, lamb and goat	525	535	511	544	547	519	540	564	Mouton, agneau et caprin
Papua New Guinea									**Papouasie-Nvl-Guinée**
Total	38	41	42	44	46	46	46	48	Totale
Beef, veal and buffalo	2	2	2	2	2	3	3	3	Bœuf, veau et buffle
Pork	36	39	40	42	44	44	44	45	Porc
Samoa									**Samoa**
Total	5	4	4	4	4	4	5	5	Totale
Beef, veal and buffalo [1]	1	1	1	1	1	1	1	1	Bœuf, veau et buffle [1]
Pork [1]	4	3	3	3	3	3	4	4	Porc [1]
Solomon Islands									**Iles Salomon**
Total	2	2	2	3	2	2	3	3	Totale
Beef, veal and buffalo	0	0	0	1	0	0	1	1	Bœuf, veau et buffle
Pork	2	2	2	2	2	2	2	2	Porc
Tonga									**Tonga**
Total	2	2	2	2	2	2	2	2	Totale
Pork [1]	1	1	1	1	1	1	1	1	Porc [1]
Vanuatu									**Vanuatu**
Total	7	6	6	7	6	7	9	9	Totale
Beef, veal and buffalo	4	4	4	4	4	4	6	6[1]	Bœuf, veau et buffle
Pork	3	3	3	3	3	3	3	3[1]	Porc

Source:
Food and Agriculture Organization of the United Nations (FAO), Rome, "FAO Production Yearbook 2001" and the FAOSTAT Database.

Source:
Organisation de Nations Unies pour l'alimentation at l'agriculture (FAO), Rome, "Annuaire FAO de la production 2001" et la base de données FAOSTAT.

[1] FAO estimate.
[2] Data refer to the Gaza Strip.

[1] FAO estimation.
[2] Les données se rapportent à la Zone de Gaza.

43

Beer
Production: thousand hectolitres

Bière
Production: milliers d'hectolitres

Country or area Pays ou zone	1991	1992	1993	1994	1995	1996	1997	1998	1999	2000
Albania Albanie	76	18	5	72	89	9	151	92	82	82
Algeria Algérie	301	337	421	398	402	377	379	382	383	453
Angola Angola	484	345	...	...	...	...	...	...	...	...
Argentina Argentine	7 979	9 518	10 305	11 272	10 913	11 615	12 687	12 395	12 133	12 090
Armenia Arménie	419	149	70	70	53	29	50	133	84	79
Australia [1] Australie [1]	18 970	18 040	17 760	17 840	17 700	17 424	17 349	17 570	17 378	17 679
Austria Autriche	9 971	10 176	11 465	10 070	9 767	9 445	9 303	8 837	8 884	8 725
Azerbaijan Azerbaïdjan	5 159	1 855	148	114	22	13	16	12	69	71
Barbados Barbade	66	58	67	73	74	76	75	87	76	69
Belarus Bélarus	3 389	2 736	2 146	1 489	1 518	2 013	2 413	2 604	2 728	2 371
Belgium Belgique	13 799	14 259	...	15 055	15 110	14 648	14 758	14 763	15 166	...
Belize Belize	36	38	68	56	49	41	37	42	66	92
Bolivia Bolivie	1 278	1 333	1 121	1 262	*1 429	...	...	...	...	...
Botswana Botswana	1 211	1 289	1 374	1 305	1 366	1 351	1 005	1 019	1 591	1 976
Brazil Brésil	54 545	43 509	45 336	52 556	67 284	63 559	66 582	66 453	62 491	66 954
Bulgaria Bulgarie	4 880	4 695	4 247	4 792	4 331	4 402	3 031	3 796	4 045	4 048
Burkina Faso Burkina Faso	394	71	258	...	...	...	...	...	...	...
Burundi Burundi	981	1 007	1 044	...	...	...	...	...	...	...
Cameroon Cameroun	4 324	3 834	4 373	2 073	2 933	...	...	...	...	...
Central African Rep. Rép. centrafricaine	270	285	124	450	269	...	...	...	...	...
Chad Tchad	144	129	117	110	95	...	...	...	...	...
Chile Chili	2 791	3 349	3 623	3 303	3 551	3 459	3 640	3 666	3 343	3 221
China [2] Chine [2]	68 590	83 536	97 565	115 752	128 406	137 664	154 610	162 693	...	...
Colombia Colombie	...	14 574	...	15 739	20 525	...	18 290	16 461	14 213	...
Congo Congo	686	708	759	...	...	...	...	...	...	...

43

Beer
Production: thousand hectolitres *[cont.]*
Bière
Production: milliers d'hectolitres *[suite]*

Country or area Pays ou zone	1991	1992	1993	1994	1995	1996	1997	1998	1999	2000
Croatia Croatie	2 248	2 720	2 481	3 122	3 166	3 292	3 607	3 759	3 663	3 847
Cyprus Chypre	331	370	341	359	352	331	333	365	405	409
Czech Republic République tchèque	17 902	18 982	17 366	17 876	17 687	18 057	18 558	18 290	17 945	17 796
Denmark [3] Danemark [3]	...	9 775	9 435	9 410	9 903	9 591	9 181	8 044	8 205	7 455
Dominica Dominique	...	...	...	...	3	14	11	11	8	11
Dominican Republic Rép. dominicaine	1 459	1 956	1 992	2 190	2 082	447	2 593	2 993	3 484	...
Ecuador Equateur	...	1 826	1 525	1 131	3 201	2 163	238	633	555	...
Egypt Egypte	440	420	350	360	360	380	...	...	...	...
Estonia Estonie	675	426	419	477	492	459	543	744	957	950
Ethiopia [4] Ethiopie [4]	435	428	522	634	724	876	843	831	921	1 111
Fiji Fidji	183	173	167	160	150	170	170	170	...	...
Finland Finlande	4 418	4 685	4 579	4 524	4 702	4 980	4 840	4 341	4 733	4 559
France France	18 654	18 512	18 291	17 688	18 311	17 140	17 010	16 551	...	...
French Polynesia Polynésie française	124	129	...	...	...	...	...	...	...	...
Gabon Gabon	814	785	905	801	816	...	...	...	...	...
Georgia Géorgie	...	235	120	63	65	48	79	97	126	234
Germany Allemagne	112 071	114 089	111 075	113 428	111 875	108 938	108 729	106 993	...	...
Greece Grèce	3 772	4 025	4 088	4 376	4 024	3 766	3 950	3 886	4 129	4 223
Grenada Grenade	25	26	18	24	...	...	...	...	...	...
Guatemala Guatemala	974	1 172	1 327	805	1 471	1 655	1 303	1 363	1 443	1 406
Guyana Guyana	124	143	145	97	...	...	...	...	...	...
Hungary Hongrie	9 570	9 162	7 877	8 082	7 697	7 270	6 973	7 163	6 996	5 984
Iceland Islande	30	32	41	54	52	63	64	71	77	81
India [5] Inde [5]	2 136	2 233	3 053	2 778	3 700	4 255	4 331	4 332	3 632	3 025
Indonesia Indonésie	1 043	1 145	871	779	1 136	...	531	502	401	...

43

Beer
Production: thousand hectolitres *[cont.]*

Bière
Production: milliers d'hectolitres *[suite]*

Country or area Pays ou zone	1991	1992	1993	1994	1995	1996	1997	1998	1999	2000
Ireland Irlande	...	...	...	...	8 132	10 765	12 095	12 580	...	...
Israel Israël	532	511	587	508	...	...	...	...	...	...
Italy Italie	11 049	10 489	9 873	10 258	10 616	9 559	10 379	11 073	11 123	11 173
Jamaica Jamaïque	715	828	786	760	662	690	674	670	656	...
Japan [6] Japon [6]	69 157	70 106	69 642	71 007	67 971	69 082	66 370	61 759	58 901	54 638
Kazakhstan Kazakhstan	31 330	23 011	1 692	129	812	636	693	850	824	1 357
Kenya Kenya	3 140	3 686	3 589	3 250	3 474	2 759	...	...	...	...
Korea, Republic of Corée, République de	15 928	15 673	15 252	17 176	17 554	17 210	16 907	14 080	14 866	16 544
Kyrgyzstan Kirghizistan	45	31	19	12	12	14	14	13	12	12
Lao People's Dem. Rep. Rép. dém. pop. lao	...	...	...	102	151	...	...	...	...	...
Latvia Lettonie	1 295	859	546	638	653	645	715	721	953	945
Lithuania Lituanie	1 412	1 426	1 164	1 353	1 093	1 139	1 413	1 559	1 848	2 080
Luxembourg Luxembourg	572	569	558	531	518	484	481	469	450	438
Madagascar Madagascar	236	226	228	219	246	347	234	297	...	...
Malawi Malawi	763	774	763	811	289	277	292	206	684	...
Malaysia Malaisie	1 413	...	...	...	...	...	...	...	...	...
Mali Mali	38	41	40	43	52	60	...	...	...	...
Mauritius Maurice	291	295	292	283	309	312	340	376	358	* 375
Mexico Mexique	41 092	42 262	43 630	45 060	44 205	48 111	51 315	54 569	57 905	59 851
Mozambique Mozambique	227	211	204	118	244	374	631	75	95	989
Myanmar [7] Myanmar [7]	30	19	24	13	...	...	...	...	...	...
Nepal [8] Népal [8]	...	123	144	149	168	183	215	139	188	217
Netherlands [3,9] Pays-Bas [3,9]	19 863	20 419	19 720	21 200	22 380	22 670	23 780	23 040	23 799	24 956
New Zealand [3] Nouvelle-Zélande [3]	3 627	3 637	3 519	3 568	3 488	3 435	3 214	3 206	3 148	2 980
Nigeria Nigéria	8 108	11 438	16 860	1 561	1 461	...	...	...	...	...

43

Beer
Production: thousand hectolitres *[cont.]*

Bière
Production: milliers d'hectolitres *[suite]*

Country or area Pays ou zone	1991	1992	1993	1994	1995	1996	1997	1998	1999	2000
Norway Norvège	...	2 273	...	...	2 255	...	2 396	1 833	2 651	...
Panama Panama	1 219	1 163	1 204	1 291	1 274	1 229	1 335	1 448	1 461	1 399
Paraguay Paraguay	1 150	1 140	1 710	...	...	...	...	...	...	...
Peru Pérou	6 774	6 764	7 060	6 957	7 817	7 435	7 431	6 557	6 168	5 706
Poland Pologne	13 633	14 139	12 585	14 099	15 205	16 667	19 281	21 017	23 360	...
Portugal Portugal	6 309	6 923	6 662	6 902	7 220	6 958	6 766	7 072	6 945	7 044
Puerto Rico Porto Rico	773	654	477	438	397	360	317	263	259	...
Republic of Moldova République de Moldova	660	410	297 [10]	233 [10]	276 [10]	226 [10]	238 [10]	278 [10]	202 [10]	248 [10]
Romania Roumanie	9 803	10 014	9 929	9 047	8 768	8 118	7 651	9 989	11 133	12 664
Russian Federation Fédération de Russie	33 300	27 900	24 700	21 800	21 400	20 800	26 100	33 600	44 500	51 600
Saint Kitts and Nevis Saint-Kitts-et-Nevis	17	16	17	17	17	20	19	...	...	...
Serbia and Montenegro Serbie-et-Monténégro	5 460	4 413	3 019	5 043	5 611	5 987	6 106	6 630	6 786	6 735
Seychelles Seychelles	59	70	65	58	58	63	71	72	68	70
Slovakia Slovaquie	4 082	3 686	3 967	4 974	4 369	4 666	5 577	4 478	4 473	4 491
Slovenia Slovénie	2 203	1 783	1 978	2 075	2 087	2 223	2 138	2 000	2 022	2 571
South Africa Afrique du Sud	17 710	18 290	...	...	...	...	...	...	...	...
Spain Espagne	26 482	24 279	21 353	25 587	25 396	24 520	24 786	22 428	26 007	26 388
Suriname Suriname	122	71	107	69	65	72	...	...	...	...
Sweden Suède	4 663	4 969	5 087	5 379	5 471	5 318	5 078	4 763	4 718	4 663
Switzerland [3] Suisse [3]	4 137	4 020	3 804	3 828	3 672	...	...	...	...	...
Syrian Arab Republic Rép. arabe syrienne	99	102	104	102	102	102	97	97	121	91
Tajikistan Tadjikistan	364	135	82	67	47	6	6	9	7	4
Thailand Thaïlande	2 840	3 252	4 153	5 230	6 473	7 591	8 742	9 770	10 422	11 650
TFYR of Macedonia L'ex-R.y. Macédoine	928	861	952	725	620	622	600	578	652	661
Trinidad and Tobago Trinité-et-Tobago	487	395	424	482	428	419	407	517	522	625

43

Beer
Production: thousand hectolitres *[cont.]*
Bière
Production: milliers d'hectolitres *[suite]*

Country or area Pays ou zone	1991	1992	1993	1994	1995	1996	1997	1998	1999	2000
Tunisia Tunisie	407	494	601	689	659	662	780	813	912	1 066
Turkey Turquie	4 188	4 843	5 524	6 019	6 946	7 381	7 656	7 130	7 188	7 649
Turkmenistan Turkménistan	465	372	287	218	113	17	44	29	37	52
Uganda Ouganda	195	187	239	308	512	642	896	1 105	1 178	...
Ukraine Ukraine	13 093	10 997	9 086	9 087	7 102	6 025	6 125	6 842	8 407	10 765
United Kingdom Royaume-Uni	...	...	...	66 161	59 337	61 262	64 816	60 915	62 510	58 913
United Rep. of Tanzania Rép.-Unie de Tanzanie	498	493	570	568	893	125	148	...	...	...
United States [11] Etats-Unis [11]	...	237 029	237 345	237 987	...	233 485	...	...	...	...
Uruguay Uruguay	...	...	817	...	998	913	939	860	741	706
Uzbekistan Ouzbékistan	1 759	1 434	1 363	1 291	724	677	619	...	...	...
Viet Nam Viet Nam	1 312	1 685	...	...	4 650	5 330	5 810	6 700	* 6 480	7 791
Yemen Yémen	100	40	...	...	...	...	...	...	...	...

Source:
United Nations Statistics Division, New York, "Industrial Commodity Statistics Yearbook 2000" and the industrial statistics database.

Source:
Organisation des Nations Unies, Division de statistique, New York, "Annuaire de statistiques industrielles par produit 2000" et la base de données pour les statistiques industrielles.

1 Twelve months ending 30 June of the year stated.
2 Original data in metric tons.
3 Sales.
4 Twelve months ending 7 July of the year stated.
5 Production by large and medium scale establishments only.
6 Twelve months beginning 1 April of the year stated.

7 Government production only.
8 Twelve months beginning 16 July of the year stated.

9 Production by establishments employing 20 or more persons.
10 Excluding the Transnistria region.
11 Twelve months ending 30 September of the year stated.

1 Période de douze mois finissant le 30 juin de l'année indiquée.
2 Données d'origine exprimées en tonnes.
3 Ventes.
4 Période de douze mois finissant le 7 juillet de l'année indiquée.
5 Production des grandes et moyennes entreprises seulement.
6 Période de douze mois commençant le 1er avril de l'année indiquée.
7 Production de l'Etat seulement.
8 Période de douze mois commençant le 16 juillet de l'année indiquée.
9 Production des établissements occupant 20 personnes ou plus.
10 Non compris la région de Transnistria.
11 Période de douze mois finissant le 30 septembre de l'année indiquée.

44
Cigarettes
Production: millions

Cigarettes
Production: millions

Country or area Pays ou zone	1991	1992	1993	1994	1995	1996	1997	1998	1999	2000
Albania [1] Albanie [1]	1 703	1 393	1 395	929	685	4 830	414	764	63	62
Algeria [1] Algérie [1]	17 848	16 426	16 260	16 345	...	...	...	...	...	...
Angola [2] Angola [2]	2 400	2 400	...	...	...	...	...	...	...	...
Argentina Argentine	1 727	1 845	1 929	1 975	1 963	1 971	1 940	1 967	1 996	1 843
Armenia Arménie	6 614	3 927	1 878	2 014	1 043	152	815	2 489	3 132	2 096
Australia [3] Australie [3]	34 977	* 34 000	...	...	...	...	...	...	...	...
Austria Autriche	16 406	15 836	16 247	16 429	16 297	...	...	...	...	...
Azerbaijan Azerbaïdjan	7 256	4 855	5 277	3 179	1 926	766	827	241	416	2 362
Bangladesh [4] Bangladesh [4]	13 604	12 535	11 516	12 655	17 379	16 222	18 601	19 889	19 558	19 732
Barbados Barbade	124 [1]	115 [1]	133 [1]	150 [1]	65	...	...	...	...	...
Belarus Bélarus	15 009	8 847	8 670	7 378	6 228	6 267	6 787	7 296	9 259	10 356
Belgium Belgique	27 303 [5]	29 576 [5]	27 173 [5]	21 366	18 826	17 471	18 061	17 519	14 712	...
Belize Belize	104	104	105	101	95	79	88	94	91	84
Bolivia Bolivie	102	116	119	1 490	*170	...	...	...	...	...
Brazil [2] Brésil [2]	175 396	169 000	...	...	...	...	...	...	...	...
Bulgaria Bulgarie	79 749	48 558	32 098	53 664	74 603	57 238	43 315	33 181	25 715	26 681
Burkina Faso Burkina Faso	983	979	943	...	...	...	...	...	...	...
Burundi Burundi	450	453	517	...	...	...	...	...	...	...
Cambodia [2] Cambodge [2]	4 200	4 200	...	...	...	...	...	...	...	...
Cameroon [2] Cameroun [2]	5 000	5 000	...	...	...	...	...	...	...	...
Canada Canada	46 815 [2]	45 500 [2]	...	...	50 775	49 362	47 263	24 022	46 908	45 252
Central African Rep. Rép. centrafricaine	26	21	12	21	30	...	...	...	...	...
Chad Tchad	476	415	499	508	569	...	...	...	...	...
Chile Chili	10 259	11 167	10 793	10 801	10 891	11 569	12 522	12 904	13 271	13 796
China Chine	1613245	1642340	1655630	...	...	...	...	...	...	...

44

Cigarettes
Production: millions *[cont.]*

Cigarettes
Production: millions *[suite]*

Country or area Pays ou zone	1991	1992	1993	1994	1995	1996	1997	1998	1999	2000
China, Hong Kong SAR [5,6] Chine, Hong Kong RAS [5,6]	32 721	36 513	25 759	24 747	22 767	21 386	20 929	13 470	...	...
China, Macao SAR [1,7,8] Chine, Macao RAS [1,7,8]	500	500	500	450	450	450	...	...	...	...
Colombia Colombie	13 585 [2]	14 877	...	11 566	10 491	...	11 662	12 472	15 182	...
Congo [1] Congo [1]	581	431	...	...	...	...	...	...	...	...
Costa Rica Costa Rica	2 000 [2]	2 000 [2]	16 [1,8]	16 [1,8]	16 [1,8]	16 [1,8]	...	...	...	...
Côte d'Ivoire [2] Côte d'Ivoire [2]	4 500	4 500	...	...	...	...	...	...	...	...
Croatia Croatie	11 655	12 833	11 585	12 672	12 110	11 548	11 416	11 987	12 785	13 692
Cyprus Chypre	5 497	6 177	3 530	2 493	2 528	2 728	3 662	4 362	4 783	4 980
Dem. Rep. of the Congo [2] Rép. dém. du Congo [2]	5 200	5 200	...	...	...	...	...	...	...	...
Denmark [9] Danemark [9]	11 407	11 439	10 980	11 448	11 902	11 804	12 262	12 392	11 749	11 413
Dominican Republic Rép. dominicaine	4 170	4 432	4 356	4 696	4 092	4 192	3 972	4 098	4 005	...
Ecuador Equateur	* 4 600	3 000	3 079	2 515	1 734	1 745	1 678	1 997	2 178	...
Egypt Egypte	40 154	42 516	38 844	39 145	42 469	46 000	50 000	52 000	51 000	53 000
El Salvador El Salvador	1 620 [2]	1 620 [2]	...	...	1 701	1 756	...	...	...	...
Estonia Estonie	3 577	1 780	2 630	2 287	1 864	954	...	...	...	...
Ethiopia [10] Ethiopie [10]	2 416	1 879	1 932	1 468	1 583	1 862	2 024	2 029	1 829	1 931
Fiji Fidji	514	484	506	483	437	439	450	410	446	396
Finland Finlande	8 180	8 106	7 237	7 232	6 542	5 910	...	...	4 877	3 981
France France	50 311	* 53 312	47 912	48 188	46 361	46 931	44 646	43 304	...	...
Gabon Gabon	358	399	334	288	297	...	...	...	...	...
Georgia Géorgie	...	4 953	3 593	3 256	1 840	1 183	917	601	1 327	296
Germany Allemagne	...	...	204 730	222 791	...	...	...	...	...	...
Ghana Ghana	* 2 100	* 2 100	...	...	...	...	...	...	...	...
Greece Grèce	27 700	* 29 250	30 427	32 843	39 291	38 268	36 909	21 427	34 322	34 381
Grenada Grenade	20	20	19	15	...	...	...	...	...	...

44

Cigarettes
Production: millions *[cont.]*

Cigarettes
Production: millions *[suite]*

Country or area Pays ou zone	1991	1992	1993	1994	1995	1996	1997	1998	1999	2000
Guatemala Guatemala	870	2 001 [2]	2 010	1 390	2 616	1 725	2 198	4 184	4 376	4 262
Guyana Guyana	307	318	302	314	...	...	...	...	...	...
Haiti Haïti	985	970	1 110	722	...	...	...	...	...	...
Honduras [2] Honduras [2]	2 300	2 200	...	...	...	...	...	...	...	...
Hungary Hongrie	26 124	26 835	28 728	29 518	25 709	27 594	26 057	26 849	22 985	21 608
India [11] Inde [11]	65 130	61 413	71 842	71 038	69 589	73 841	83 162	79 313	82 504	75 085
Indonesia Indonésie	...	34 382	34 757	36 421	38 768	...	220 157	271 177	254 276	
Iran (Islamic Rep. of) Iran (Rép. islamique d')	* 11 565 [12]	10 171 [12]	7 835 [12]	7 939 [12]	9 787 [13]	11 860 [13]	10 304 [13]	14 335 [13]	20 143 [13]	13 811 [13]
Iraq [2] Iraq [2]	13 000	5 794	...	...	...	...	...	...	...	...
Ireland Irlande	6 377	* 7 850	7 300 [1,8]	7 000 [1,8]	7 500 [1,8]	7 500 [1,8]	4 605	6 452	6 176	6 461
Israel [1] Israël [1]	5 590	5 742	5 525	5 638	4 933	4 793	...	...	...	...
Italy Italie	57 634 [1]	53 799 [1]	54 943 [1]	55 175 [1]	50 247 [1]	51 489 [1]	51 894 [1]	50 785	45 159	43 694 [1]
Jamaica Jamaïque	1 219	1 299	1 224	1 273	1 216	1 219	1 175	1 160	1 078	991
Japan [14] Japon [14]	275 000	279 000	...	...	...	...	...	...	...	...
Jordan Jordanie	3 719	3 091	3 465	4 191	3 675	4 738	...	...	...	...
Kazakhstan Kazakhstan	9 536	8 997	10 664	9 393	12 080	19 121	24 109	21 747	18 773	19 293
Kenya Kenya	6 473	7 193	7 267	7 319	7 932	8 436	...	...	...	
Korea, Republic of Corée, République de	94 336	96 648	96 887	90 774	87 959	94 709	96 725	101 011	95 995	98 231
Kyrgyzstan Kirghizistan	4 015	3 120	3 428	1 943	1 332	975	716	862	2 103	3 169
Lao People's Dem. Rep. Rép. dém. pop. lao	1 200 [2]	1 200 [2]	...	936	1 062	...	...	...	...	...
Latvia Lettonie	4 765	3 435	2 589	2 093	2 101	1 876	1 775	2 018	1 916	...
Lebanon Liban	4 000 [2]	4 000 [2]	...	...	535 [1,1][5]	539 [1]	793 [1]	672 [1]	945 [1]	1 009 [1]
Liberia [2] Libéria [2]	22	22	...	...	...	...	...	...	...	...
Libyan Arab Jamah. [2] Jamah. arabe libyenne [2]	3 500	3 500	...	...	...	...	...	...	...	...
Lithuania Lituanie	6 438	5 269	3 435	3 860	4 876	4 538	5 755	7 427	8 217	7 207

44

Cigarettes
Production: millions *[cont.]*

Cigarettes
Production: millions *[suite]*

Country or area Pays ou zone	1991	1992	1993	1994	1995	1996	1997	1998	1999	2000
Madagascar [1] Madagascar [1]	1 950	2 223	2 304	2 003	2 354	2 957	2 826	3 303	...	...
Malawi Malawi	951	1 000	1 020	1 127	1 160	975	731	501	...	...
Malaysia [1] Malaisie [1]	17 498	16 574	15 568	15 762	15 918	16 896	20 236	18 410	15 504	27 271
Mali Mali	23	24	23	20	22	21	...	...	...	...
Malta [2] Malte [2]	1 475	1 475	...	...	...	...	...	...	...	...
Mauritius Maurice	1 034	1 060	1 269	1 300	1 215	1 193	1 144	1 034	979	976
Mexico Mexique	54 680	55 988	53 435	53 402	56 821	59 907	57 618	60 407	59 492	56 383
Morocco Maroc	602	515	...	...	...	...	...	...	...	...
Mozambique Mozambique	217	124	377	343	106	250	250	950	1 084	1 417
Myanmar [16] Myanmar [16]	682	396	426	440	752	1 727	1 991	2 040	2 270	2 559
Nepal [17] Népal [17]	...	6 963	7 846	6 894	7 430	8 067	7 944	8 127	7 315	6 587
Netherlands [9,18] Pays-Bas [9,18]	74 767	78 479	71 254	88 069	97 727	...	...	...	...	...
New Zealand Nouvelle-Zélande	4 014	3 466	3 381	3 396 [9]	3 338 [9]	3 660 [9]	3 449 [9]	3 263 [9]	3 010 [9]	3 277
Nicaragua [2] Nicaragua [2]	2 400	2 400 [19]	...	...	...	...	...	...	...	...
Nigeria Nigéria	9 405	8 608	9 384	338	256	...	...	...	...	...
Norway [2] Norvège [2]	1 730	1 825	...	...	...	...	...	...	...	...
Pakistan [4] Pakistan [4]	29 887	29 673	29 947	35 895	32 747	45 506	46 101	48 215	51 579	46 976
Panama Panama	771	806	903	1 204	1 136	663	752	320	...	...
Paraguay Paraguay	827	777	...	...	...	...	...	...	...	...
Peru Pérou	2 696	2 501	2 511	2 752	3 041	3 358	3 028	3 115	3 580	3 605
Philippines [1,8] Philippines [1,8]	7 071	6 771	7 135	7 300	7 440	7 440	...	...	...	...
Poland Pologne	90 407	86 571	90 713	98 394	100 627	95 293	95 798	96 741	95 056	83 800
Portugal Portugal	17 361	15 619	15 335	13 610	13 215	12 780	13 234	15 781	17 742	21 377
Republic of Moldova République de Moldova	9 164	8 582	8 790 [20]	8 001 [20]	7 108 [20]	9 657 [20]	9 539 [20]	7 512 [20]	8 731 [20]	9 262 [20]
Romania [3] Roumanie [3]	17 722	17 781	15 222	14 532	14 747	16 536	25 943	...	...	...

44

Cigarettes
Production: millions *[cont.]*

Cigarettes
Production: millions *[suite]*

Country or area Pays ou zone	1991	1992	1993	1994	1995	1996	1997	1998	1999	2000
Russian Federation Fédération de Russie	112 326	107 763	100 162	91 601	99 545	112 319	140 077	195 806	266 031	333 953
Senegal [2] Sénégal [2]	3 350	3 350	...	...	...	...	...	...	...	...
Serbia and Montenegro Serbie-et-Monténégro	17 605	15 654	16 053	12 972	12 686	13 176	10 988	14 597	13 126	14 451
Seychelles Seychelles	69	62	65	49	56	62	70	61	60	40
Sierra Leone [2] Sierra Leone [2]	1 200	1 200	...	...	...	...	...	...	...	...
Singapore [2] Singapour [2]	10 500	11 760	...	...	...	...	...	...	...	...
Slovakia Slovaquie	8 721	...	...	...	...	...	...	...	...	...
Slovenia Slovénie	4 798	5 278	4 851	4 722	4 543	4 909	5 767	7 555	8 032	7 855
South Africa Afrique du Sud	40 163	35 563	34 499	...	...	...	...	...	...	...
Spain Espagne	81 843	76 696	80 103	81 886	78 676	77 675	77 315	81 940	74 873	74 799
Sri Lanka Sri Lanka	5 789	5 359	5 649	5 656	5 822	6 160	5 712	5 797	5 333	4 889
Sudan [2] Soudan [2]	750	750	...	...	...	...	...	...	...	...
Suriname Suriname	337	419	454	443	472	483	...	...	...	...
Sweden Suède	9 594	9 841	7 420	8 032	7 193	7 251	6 237	5 692	6 060	5 958
Switzerland Suisse	32 943	33 740	34 713	39 906	41 976	42 955	37 638	34 453	32 139	34 299
Syrian Arab Republic [1] Rép. arabe syrienne [1]	7 974	8 093	7 185	7 773	9 699	8 528	10 137	10 398	10 991	11 097
Tajikistan Tadjikistan	4 467	2 607	1 901	1 644	964	604	153	191	209	667
Thailand Thaïlande	39 697	40 691	42 043	45 359	43 020	48 173	43 387	34 585	31 146	30 732
Trinidad and Tobago Trinité-et-Tobago	881 [1]	656 [1]	638	593	920	1 102	1 386	1 680	1 945	2 050
Tunisia Tunisie	7 790	7 797	6 965	7 128	7 421	7 159	7 735	9 813	11 066	12 231
Turkey [1] Turquie [1]	71 106	67 549	74 845	85 093	80 700	73 787	74 984	81 616	75 135	76 613
Uganda Ouganda	1 688	1 575	1 412	1 459	1 576	1 702	1 864	1 866	1 688	...
Ukraine Ukraine	66 645	60 990	40 571	47 083	48 033	44 900	54 488	59 275	54 052	58 679
United Kingdom Royaume-Uni	127 000	*126 538	146 138	165 479	155 103	166 496	167 670	152 998	143 794	139 125
United Rep. of Tanzania Rép.-Unie de Tanzanie	3 870	3 789	3 893	3 383	3 699	3 733	4 710	...	...	...

44

Cigarettes
Production: millions *[cont.]*

Cigarettes
Production: millions *[suite]*

Country or area Pays ou zone	1991	1992	1993	1994	1995	1996	1997	1998	1999	2000
United States Etats-Unis	694 500	718 500	661 000	725 500	746 500	754 500	719 600	679 700	611 929	...
Uruguay Uruguay	3 900 [2]	3 900 [2]	3 736	...	3 561	6 018	6 872	10 187	11 161	10 894
Uzbekistan Ouzbékistan	4 897	4 150	4 151	3 379	2 742	5 172	8 521	...	...	...
Venezuela [2] Venezuela [2]	24 236	24 400	...	...	...	...	...	...	...	...
Viet Nam Viet Nam	25 960	* 24 600	...	...	...	...	...	...	...	...
Yemen Yémen	6 790 [1,8]	6 294 [1,8]	8 844 [1,8]	5 423 [1,8]	6 540	6 740	6 800	...	...	...
Zambia [2] Zambie [2]	1 500	1 500	...	...	...	...	...	...	...	...
Zimbabwe [2] Zimbabwe [2]	3 240	3 025	...	...	...	...	...	...	...	...

Source:
United Nations Statistics Division, New York, "Industrial Commodity Statistics Yearbook 2000" and the industrial statistics database.

1 Original data in units of weight. Computed on the basis of one million cigarettes per ton.
2 Source: U.S. Department of Agriculture, (Washington, D.C.).
3 Including cigars.
4 Twelve months ending 30 June of the year stated.
5 Including cigarillos.
6 Beginning 1999, data are confidential.
7 Beginning 1997, data are confidential.
8 Source: Food and Agriculture Organization of the United Nations (FAO), (Rome).
9 Sales.
10 Twelve months ending 7 July of the year stated.
11 Production by large and medium scale establishments only.
12 Production by establishments employing 50 or more persons.
13 Production by establishments employing 10 or more persons.
14 Twelve months beginning 1 April of the year stated.

15 Break in series; data prior to the sign not comparable to following years.
16 Government production only.
17 Twelve months beginning 16 July of the year stated.

18 Production by establishments employing 20 or more persons.
19 Beginning August 1999, national production discontinued.
20 Excluding the Transnistria region.

Source:
Organisation des Nations Unies, Division de statistique, New York, "Annuaire de statistiques industrielles par produit 2000" et la base de données pour les statistiques industrielles.

1 Données d'origine exprimées en poids. Calcul sur la base d'un million cigarettes par tonne.
2 Source: "U.S. Department of Agriculture" (Washington, D.C.).
3 Y compris les cigares.
4 Période de douze mois finissant le 30 juin de l'année indiquée.
5 Y compris les cigarillos.
6 A partir de 1999, les données sont confidentielles.
7 A partir 1997, les données sont confidentielles.
8 Source: Organisation des Nations Unies pour l'alimentation et l'agriculture (FAO), (Rome).
9 Ventes.
10 Période de douze mois finissant le 7 juillet de l'année indiquée.
11 Production des grandes et moyennes entreprises seulement.
12 Production des établissements occupant 50 personnes ou plus.
13 Production des établissements occupant 10 personnes ou plus.
14 Période de douze mois commençant le 1er avril de l'année indiquée.
15 Marque une interruption dans la série et la non-comparabilité des données précédant le symbole.
16 Production de l'Etat seulement.
17 Période de douze mois commençant le 16 juillet de l'année indiquée.
18 Production des établissements occupant 20 personnes ou plus.
19 A partir d'août 1999, la production nationale a été discontinuée.
20 Non compris la région de Transnistria.

45
Fabrics
Woven cotton, wool, cellulosic and non-cellulosic fibres: million square metres
Tissus
Tissus de coton, laines, fibres cellulosiques et non cellulosiques : millions de mètres carrés

Country or area Pays ou zone	1991	1992	1993	1994	1995	1996	1997	1998	1999	2000
Algeria[1] Algérie[1]										
Wool										
Laines	16	13	...		...		...	...		...
Armenia Arménie										
Cotton										
Coton	10	5	2	0	0	1	0	0	0	0
Wool										
Laines	4	3	1	0	0	0	0	0	0	0
Australia[2] Australie[2]										
Cotton										
Coton	36[3]	40	41	50	52	64	61	62	56	47
Wool										
Laines	8	8	8	8	8	7	6	7	6	5
Cellulosic and non-cellulosic fibres										
Fibres cellulosiques et non cellulosiques	185	186	185	...	...		...	...	...	...
Austria Autriche										
Cotton										
Coton	100	86	83	83	101	96	95	101	74	58
Wool										
Laines	8	8	5	3	2	12	13	17	13	15
Cellulosic and non-cellulosic fibres										
Fibres cellulosiques et non cellulosiques	66	73	47	41	60	...	...	...	...	...
Azerbaijan Azerbaïdjan										
Cotton										
Coton	95	77	98	78	58	24	17	7	1	1
Wool										
Laines	9	7	5	2	1	0	0	0	0	0
Bangladesh[2] Bangladesh[2]										
Cotton										
Coton	63	63	63	63	63	63	63	63	63	63
Belarus Bélarus										
Cotton										
Coton	144	119	92	25	34	45	48	72	50	65
Wool										
Laines	49	39	40	20	8	8	9	10	10	9
Cellulosic and non-cellulosic fibres[5]										
Fibres cellulosiques et non cellulosiques[5]	175	147	135	80	35	39	67	77	71	62
Belgium Belgique										
Cotton										
Coton	379	337	331	255	256[8]	294[8]	298[8]	311[8]	301[8]	...
Wool[6]										
Laines[6]	6	4	4	...	...	...	...	...	...	...
Cellulosic and non-cellulosic fibres										
Fibres cellulosiques et non cellulosiques	3 883[7]	4 259[7]	4 776[7]	643[8]	878[8]	900[8]	972[8]	1 017[8]	1 014[8]	...
Bolivia[1] Bolívie[1]										
Cotton										
Coton	1	1	0	0	*0	...	...	...	...	...
Cellulosic and non-cellulosic fibres[5]										
Fibres cellulosiques et non cellulosiques[5]	1	1	2	2	*2	...	...	...	...	...
Brazil[1] Brésil[1]										
Cotton										
Coton	1 679[9,10]	1 616[9,10]	1 568[9,10]	1 566[9]	1 354	1 318	1 278	1 209	1 270	1 339
Bulgaria Bulgarie										
Cotton										
Coton	138[11]	102[11]	83[11]	86[11]	93[11]	85[11]	98[11]	96[1]	62[1]	59[1]
Wool[11]										
Laines[11]	26	22	23	21	20	18	17	10[1]	8[1]	8[1]
Cameroon[1] Cameroun[1]										
Cotton										
Coton	18	21	18	35	24	...	...	...	...	...

45

Fabrics
Woven cotton, wool, cellulosic and non-cellulosic fibres: million square metres *[cont.]*

Tissus
Tissus de coton, laines, fibres cellulosiques et non cellulosiques : millions de mètres carrés *[suite]*

Country or area Pays ou zone	1991	1992	1993	1994	1995	1996	1997	1998	1999	2000
Chad Tchad										
Cotton										
Coton	60	81	...	...	...	...	...	...	...	...
Chile[1] Chili[1]										
Cotton										
Coton	24	23	32	28	29	34	31	27	21	25
China[1] Chine[1]										
Cotton										
Coton	21 719	22 783	24 263	25 243	31 091	24 987	29 730	28 800	29 875	33 102
Wool										
Laines	514	558	388	413	1 079	758	640	442	451	459
China, Hong Kong SAR Chine, Hong Kong RAS										
Cotton[12]										
Coton[12]	753	807	755	692	658	540	506	...		...
Cellulosic and non-cellulosic fibres[12,13]										
Fibres cellulosiques et non cellulosiques[12,13]	1	2	3	3	1	...	21	...		...
China, Macao SAR Chine, Macao RAS										
Cotton										
Coton	...	...	15	10	8	9	9	10	11	7
Colombia Colombie										
Cotton[1]										
Coton[1]	...	249	238	210	90	...	88	76	54	...
Wool[1]										
Laines[1]	...	1	1	1	1	...	1	1	1	...
Cellulosic and non-cellulosic fibres										
Fibres cellulosiques et non cellulosiques	...	3[8]	24[8]	20[8]	22[8]	...	98[1]	91[1]	16[1]	...
Congo[1] Congo[1]										
Cotton										
Coton	7	6	2	...	...	...	...	...	...	...
Croatia Croatie										
Cotton										
Coton	30	29	29	23	22	19	34	39	34	34
Wool										
Laines	5	6	7	7	7	5	3	2	2	2
Cellulosic and non-cellulosic fibres										
Fibres cellulosiques et non cellulosiques	12	12	14	11	9	8	11	11	9	9
Czech Republic République tchèque										
Cotton										
Coton	381	293	337	340	358	330	346	331	265	313
Wool										
Laines	49	46	43	34	32	30	28	28	17	14
Cellulosic and non-cellulosic fibres										
Fibres cellulosiques et non cellulosiques	32	35	29	...	...	...	...	...	...	346
Denmark[14] Danemark[14]										
Cotton										
Coton	...	...	...	...	...	5	19	6	2	1
Wool										
Laines	1[15]	1[15]	1	1	1	1	1	0	0	1
Ecuador[1] Equateur[1]										
Wool										
Laines	...	3	2	2	3	2	0	2	2	...
Cellulosic and non-cellulosic fibres										
Fibres cellulosiques et non cellulosiques	...	23	39	36	36	21	0	21	20	...
Egypt Egypte										
Cotton										
Coton	609	613	329	494	414	1 561	1 474	1 559	1 524	1 559
Wool										
Laines	23	23	9	14	14	8	8	8	7	6

45

Fabrics
Woven cotton, wool, cellulosic and non-cellulosic fibres: million square metres *[cont.]*

Tissus
Tissus de coton, laines, fibres cellulosiques et non cellulosiques : millions de mètres carrés *[suite]*

Country or area Pays ou zone	1991	1992	1993	1994	1995	1996	1997	1998	1999	2000
Estonia Estonie										
Cotton Coton	168	111	55	74	90	120	130	127	95	124
Wool Laines	7	4	1	0	0	0	0	0	0	0
Ethiopia Ethiopie										
Cotton[16] Coton[16]	32	30	36	61	50	48	35	38	43	38
Cellulosic and non-cellulosic fibres[4,16] Fibres cellulosiques et non cellulosiques[4,16]	3	2	4	4	5	5	4	5	4	3
Finland[11] Finlande[11]										
Cotton Coton	24	20	20	19	8	9	...	...	...	...
Cellulosic and non-cellulosic fibres * Fibres cellulosiques et non cellulosiques *	17	14	14	11	8	8	...	...	...	...
France France										
Cotton[8] Coton[8]	760	753	761	691	682	672	689	658	702	...
Wool Laines	14	13	9	37	...	...	...	...	...	...
Cellulosic and non-cellulosic fibres Fibres cellulosiques et non cellulosiques	2 763	3 517	2 891	2 885	...	...	...	...	...	...
Georgia Géorgie										
Cotton Coton	...	13	7	2	1	1	0	0	0	0
Wool Laines	...	0	2	1	0	0	0	0	0	0
Germany Allemagne										
Cotton Coton	929	763	687	635	444	466	489	506	...	...
Wool Laines	121	119	97	...	87	87	87	79	...	...
Cellulosic and non-cellulosic fibres Fibres cellulosiques et non cellulosiques	1 477	1 359	1 154	1 116	1 329	1 175	1 225	1 269	...	...
Greece Grèce										
Cotton Coton	...	...	119[9]	94[9]	72[9]	...	...	29	...	...
Wool Laines	3[8,11]	2[8,11]	3	2	2	2	3	3	...	...
Cellulosic and non-cellulosic fibres[17,18] Fibres cellulosiques et non cellulosiques[17,18]	...	...	19	29	15	...	...	...	...	...
Hungary[11] Hongrie[11]										
Cotton Coton	133	86	78	76	66	...	79	44	48	47
Wool Laines	7	4	3	1	1	...	0	...	...	...
Cellulosic and non-cellulosic fibres Fibres cellulosiques et non cellulosiques	35	22	20	19	19	...	...	* 97	231	255
India Inde										
Cotton Coton	16 478	17 582	19 648	...	...	...	...	...	...	...
Indonesia Indonésie										
Wool Laines	...	1[8]	1[1]	...	...	...	...	...	...	...
Italy[8] Italie[8]										
Cotton Coton	1 682	1 487	1 422	1 521	1 585	1 555	1 609	1 657	1 570	...
Wool Laines	428	445	426	443	433	431	445	396	...	...

45

Fabrics
Woven cotton, wool, cellulosic and non-cellulosic fibres: million square metres *[cont.]*

Tissus
Tissus de coton, laines, fibres cellulosiques et non cellulosiques : millions de mètres carrés *[suite]*

Country or area Pays ou zone	1991	1992	1993	1994	1995	1996	1997	1998	1999	2000
Japan Japon										
Cotton										
Coton	1 603	1 465	1 205	1 180	1 029	916	917	842	774	664
Wool[15]										
Laines[15]	345	326	287	286	249	247	247	213	199	98
Cellulosic and non-cellulosic fibres[15]										
Fibres cellulosiques et non cellulosiques[15]	3 263	3 175	2 758	2 578	2 458	2 438	2 496	2 133	1 933	1 846
Kazakhstan Kazakhstan										
Cotton										
Coton	134	135	136	85	21	21	14	10	9	5
Wool										
Laines	31	23	20	10	3	2	2	1	0	0
Kenya Kenya										
Cotton										
Coton	27	31	28	27	22	28	...	...	...	...
Wool										
Laines	...	...	0	9	1	1	...	...	...	...
Korea, Republic of Corée, République de										
Cotton[11]										
Coton[11]	608	483	480	447	379	...	...	...	...	...
Wool										
Laines	20[11]	20[11]	19[11]	20	18	17	14	7	6	6
Cellulosic and non-cellulosic fibres[4]										
Fibres cellulosiques et non cellulosiques[4]	3 479	3 094	2 459	2 540	2 594	...	...	...	...	...
Kyrgyzstan Kirghizistan										
Cotton										
Coton	119	119	65	49	21	25	20	13	12	6
Wool										
Laines	13	11	9	4	2	3	3	2	1	1
Latvia Lettonie										
Cotton										
Coton	45	22	0	0	2	6	9	12	12	13
Wool										
Laines	11	8	2	0[11]	0[11]	0[11]	0[11]	0[11]	...	...
Lithuania Lituanie										
Cotton										
Coton	106	89	48	42	35	35	62	64	57	55
Wool										
Laines	22	17	12	9	10	13	12	14	11	15
Cellulosic and non-cellulosic fibres										
Fibres cellulosiques et non cellulosiques	35	26	18	...	8	6	43	47	40	19
Madagascar[1] Madagascar[1]										
Cotton										
Coton	57	50	42	44	34	27	32	23	...	...
Mexico[8] Mexique[8]										
Cotton										
Coton	368	313	454	320	304	282	271	300	285	311
Wool										
Laines	8	11	12	9	12	16	20	19	19	18
Cellulosic and non-cellulosic fibres										
Fibres cellulosiques et non cellulosiques	452	453	558	527	489	624	638	623	626	622
Mongolia[1] Mongolie[1]										
Wool										
Laines	1	1	0	0	0	0	0	0	0	0
Myanmar[1,19] Myanmar[1,19]										
Cotton										
Coton	27	22	16	13	16	12	11	13	21	26
Nepal[1,4] Népal[1,4]										
Cellulosic and non-cellulosic fibres										
Fibres cellulosiques et non cellulosiques	...	16	18	23	20	25	25	26	24	33

45

Fabrics
Woven cotton, wool, cellulosic and non-cellulosic fibres: million square metres *[cont.]*
Tissus
Tissus de coton, laines, fibres cellulosiques et non cellulosiques : millions de mètres carrés *[suite]*

Country or area Pays ou zone	1991	1992	1993	1994	1995	1996	1997	1998	1999	2000
Netherlands Pays-Bas										
Cotton[8]										
Coton[8]	81	70	...	...	...	...	...	...	...	...
Wool[11]										
Laines[11]	4	4	...	...	...	...	...	...	...	...
Cellulosic and non-cellulosic fibres[8,20]										
Fibres cellulosiques et non cellulosiques[8,20]	203	189	...	...	...	...	...	...	...	...
Nigeria Nigéria										
Cotton										
Coton	395	420	393	124	113	...	...	...	...	...
Norway[8] Norvège[8]										
Cotton										
Coton	11	10	7	8	6	7	...	...	* 8	6[21]
Wool										
Laines	1	2	1	2	2	2	2	2	...	...
Pakistan[22] Pakistan[22]										
Cotton										
Coton	293[15]	308[15]	325[15]	315	322	327	333	340	385	437
Paraguay[1] Paraguay[1]										
Cotton										
Coton	23	23	24	...	...	...	...	...	...	...
Poland[11] Pologne[11]										
Cotton[23]										
Coton[23]	332	290	284	321	263	295	303	275	234	...
Wool[24]										
Laines[24]	67	50	48	51	50	50	49	45	35	...
Cellulosic and non-cellulosic fibres										
Fibres cellulosiques et non cellulosiques	88	98	85	106	103	95	95	87	58	...
Portugal Portugal										
Cotton										
Coton	511[8]	355[8]	388	421	418	401	412	444	410	385
Wool										
Laines	29[8]	12	10	9	8	6	6	8	9	12
Cellulosic and non-cellulosic fibres										
Fibres cellulosiques et non cellulosiques	429[8]	142	133	129	127	131	138	151	134	146
Republic of Moldova République de Moldova										
Cotton										
Coton	165	150	1[26]	0[26]	0[26]	0[26]	0[26]	0[26]	0[26]	0[26]
Wool										
Laines	0	0	0[26]	0[26]	0[26]	0[26]	0[26]	0[26]	0[26]	0[26]
Cellulosic and non-cellulosic fibres[5,25]										
Fibres cellulosiques et non cellulosiques[5,25]	44	22	...	...	...	...	...	...	...	...
Romania[11] Roumanie[11]										
Cotton										
Coton	437	289	271	294	275	212	173	170	143	145
Wool										
Laines	100	69	68	65	68	50	34	22	18	13
Russian Federation Fédération de Russie										
Cotton										
Coton	5 949	3 799	2 822	1 631	1 401	1 120	1 374	1 241	1 455	2 026
Wool										
Laines	492	351	270	114	107	67	63	52	61	67
Cellulosic and non-cellulosic fibres[1]										
Fibres cellulosiques et non cellulosiques[1]	673	536	391	167	114	65	56	50	77	...
Serbia and Montenegro Serbie-et-Monténégro										
Cotton[10,27]										
Coton[10,27]	45	39	27	24	19	22	18	23	21	20
Wool[27,28]										
Laines[27,28]	24	21	13	13	11	11	10	9	7	6
Cellulosic and non-cellulosic fibres[5]										
Fibres cellulosiques et non cellulosiques[5]	4	4	4	2	2	1	1	1	0	0

45

Fabrics
Woven cotton, wool, cellulosic and non-cellulosic fibres: million square metres *[cont.]*

Tissus
Tissus de coton, laines, fibres cellulosiques et non cellulosiques : millions de mètres carrés *[suite]*

Country or area Pays ou zone	1991	1992	1993	1994	1995	1996	1997	1998	1999	2000
Slovakia Slovaquie										
Cotton										
Coton	...	...	78	76	90	57	61[1]	125[8]	32[8]	49[8]
Wool										
Laines	12[11]	11[11]	10[11]	10[11]	10[1]	11[1]	11[1]	10[8]	7[8]	9[8]
Cellulosic and non-cellulosic fibres								8,		
Fibres cellulosiques et non cellulosiques	26	18[1]	...	13	...	...	...	79[29]	68[8]	73[8]
Slovenia Slovénie										
Cotton										
Coton	102[23]	78[23]	81	81	71	53	...	...	...	...
Wool										
Laines	15	15	13	10	7	3	...	...	1	2
Cellulosic and non-cellulosic fibres										
Fibres cellulosiques et non cellulosiques	7	6	5	10	24	42	...	...	34	51
South Africa Afrique du Sud										
Cotton										
Coton	170	138	166	195	228	246	269	223	224	219
Wool[30]										
Laines[30]	15	11	10	11	10	9	9	8	7	7
Spain Espagne										
Cotton										
Coton	773[8,31]	748[8,31]	523	622	689	...	...	...	...	...
Wool[8]										
Laines[8]	31[31]	28[31]	17	14	15	...	...	...	...	...
Cellulosic and non-cellulosic fibres[4,8]										
Fibres cellulosiques et non cellulosiques[4,8]	533[31]	466[31]	626	785	1 003	...	...	...	...	...
Sweden[8] Suède[8]										
Cellulosic and non-cellulosic fibres										
Fibres cellulosiques et non cellulosiques	29	21	18	23	24	38	28	28	21	18
Switzerland Suisse										
Cotton[1]										
Coton[1]	81	77	74	82	70	...	...	...	...	...
Wool[30]										
Laines[30]	10	8	7	7	5	...	...	...	...	...
Syrian Arab Republic[8] Rép. arabe syrienne[8]										
Cotton										
Coton	221	205	222	213	184	186	198	199	186	...
Wool										
Laines	0	1	2	2	4	5	8	14	19	...
Tajikistan Tadjikistan										
Cotton										
Coton	102	58	57	34	28	17	8	13	11	11
Wool										
Laines	2	3	3	1	0	0	0	0	0	0
TFYR of Macedonia L'ex-R.y. Macédoine										
Cotton										
Coton	25	21	19	23	15	16	8	12	6	6
Wool										
Laines	10	9	7	5	6	4	4	4	3	2
Cellulosic and non-cellulosic fibres[5]										
Fibres cellulosiques et non cellulosiques[5]	5	3	2	1	1	1	1	1	0	0
Turkey[1] Turquie[1]										
Cotton										
Coton	626	648	532	432	414	395	580	479	471	567
Wool										
Laines	36	35	38	38	50	59	78	77	78	91
Cellulosic and non-cellulosic fibres[5]										
Fibres cellulosiques et non cellulosiques[5]	110	151	178	254	225	246	224	240	215	228
Turkmenistan Turkménistan										
Cotton										
Coton	28	29	29	20	17	18	14	15	21	34

45

Fabrics
Woven cotton, wool, cellulosic and non-cellulosic fibres: million square metres *[cont.]*

Tissus
Tissus de coton, laines, fibres cellulosiques et non cellulosiques : millions de mètres carrés *[suite]*

Country or area Pays ou zone	1991	1992	1993	1994	1995	1996	1997	1998	1999	2000
Wool										
Laines	3	3	3	3	3	3	3	3	...	...
Uganda[11] Ouganda[11]										
Cotton										
Coton	9[27]	10[27]	7[27]	4	...	...	...	...	...	...
Ukraine Ukraine										
Cotton										
Coton	561	509	262	145	87	54	28	57	27	37
Wool										
Laines	79	76	60	26	19	12	14	8	6	8
Cellulosic and non-cellulosic fibres[1]										
Fibres cellulosiques et non cellulosiques[1]	194	152	132	42	15	6	5	5	3	5
United Kingdom Royaume-Uni										
Cotton[1]										
Coton[1]	184	170	130	103	96	99	93	88	...	...
Wool *										
Laines *	39	37	33	38	...	...	...	...	...	...
Cellulosic and non-cellulosic fibres										
Fibres cellulosiques et non cellulosiques	...	...	26	19	...	...	...	...	...	...
United Rep. of Tanzania Rép.-Unie de Tanzanie										
Cotton										
Coton	38	49	40	24	10	13	27	...	...	...
United States Etats-Unis										
Cotton										
Coton	3 682	3 846	3 682	3 740	3 753	4 010	4 246	3 974	3 721	...
Wool										
Laines	142	147	154	149	136	127	138	111	65	57
Uzbekistan Ouzbékistan										
Cotton										
Coton	392	474	482	433	456	445	425	...	...	...
Wool										
Laines	1	1	1	1	1	1	0	...	...	...
Viet Nam[1] Viet Nam[1]										
Cotton										
Coton	335	325	...	...	...	...	...	...	...	...

Source:
United Nations Statistics Division, New York, "Industrial Commodity Statistics Yearbook 2000" and the industrial statistics database.

Source:
Organisation des Nations Unies, Division de statistique, New York, "Annuaire de statistiques industrielles par produit 2000" et la base de données pour les statistiques industrielles.

1 Original data in metres.
2 Twelve months ending 30 June of the year stated.
3 Including pile and chemille fabrics of non-cellulosic fibres.

4 Non-cellulosic fabrics only.

5 Cellulosic fabrics only.

6 Including woollen blankets and carpets.
7 Including blankets and carpets of cellulosic and non-cellulosic fibres.
8 Original data in metric tons.
9 Including cotton fabrics after undergoing finishing processes.
10 Including mixed cotton fabrics.
11 After undergoing finishing processes.
12 1998 data are confidential.
13 1996 data are confidential.
14 Sales.
15 Including finished fabrics and blanketing made of synthetic

1 Données d'origine exprimées en mètres.
2 Période de douze mois finissant le 30 juin de l'année indiquée.
3 Y compris les tissus bouclés et tissus chenille de fibres non-cellulosiques.
4 Les tissus en fibres non cellulosiques seulement.

5 Les tissus en fibres cellulosiques seulement.

6 Y compris les couvertures et tapis en laine.
7 Y compris les couvertures et les tapis en fibres cellulosiques.
8 Données d'origine exprimées en tonnes.
9 Y compris les tissus de cotton, après opérations de finition.
10 Y compris les tissus de cotton mélangé.
11 Après opérations de finition.
12 Pour 1998, les données sont confidentielles.
13 Pour 1996, les données sont confidentielles.
14 Ventes.
15 Y compris les tissus finis et les couvertures en fibres

45

Fabrics
Woven cotton, wool, cellulosic and non-cellulosic fibres: million square metres *[cont.]*

Tissus
Tissus de coton, laines, fibres cellulosiques et non cellulosiques : millions de mètres carrés *[suite]*

fibers.	synthétiques.
16 Twelve months ending 7 July of the year stated.	16 Période de douze mois finissant le 7 juillet de l'année indiquée.
17 Including fabrics after undergoing finishing processes.	17 Y compris les tissus, après opérations de finition.
18 Including mixed fabrics.	18 Y compris les tissus mélangés.
19 Production by government-owned enterprises only.	19 Production des établissements d'Etat seulement.
20 Including linen and jute fabrics.	20 Y compris les tissus de lin y de jute.
21 Incomplete coverage.	21 Couverture incomplète.
22 Factory production only.	22 Production des fabriques seulement.
23 Including fabrics of cotton substitutes.	23 Y compris les tissus de succédanés de coton.
24 Including fabrics of wool substitutes.	24 Y compris les tissus de succédanés de laine.
25 Including silk fabrics.	25 Y compris les tissus de soie.
26 Excluding the Transnistria region.	26 Non compris la région de Transnistria.
27 Including cellulosic fabrics.	27 Y compris les tissus en fibres cellulosiques.
28 Including mixed wool fabrics.	28 Y compris les tissus de laine mélangée.
29 Break in series; data prior to the sign not comparable to following years.	29 Marque une interruption dans la série et la non-comparabilité des données précédant le symbole.
30 Pure woollen fabrics only.	30 Tissus de laine pure seulement.
31 Including household production.	31 Y compris la production ménagère.

46

Leather footwear
Production: thousand pairs

Chaussures de cuir
Production : milliers de paires

Country or area Pays ou zone	1991	1992	1993	1994	1995	1996	1997	1998	1999	2000
Albania Albanie	1 881	1 214	1 818	266	267	...	...	...	...	...
Algeria Algérie	11 824	9 040	7 171	6 467	3 986	2 320	2 542	1 249	1 529	1 278
Angola Angola	95	48	...	...	...	...	...	...		...
Armenia Arménie	11 340	5 661	3 517	1 612	656	305	87	65	31	53
Australia [1,2] Australie [1,2]	1 935	383	283	315	278	...	...	...		
Austria Autriche	16 760	14 842	13 229	12 767	12 743	10 120	10 615	10 919	...	...
Azerbaijan Azerbaïdjan	10 491	5 221	4 329	3 057	799	495	313	315	54	122
Belarus Bélarus	45 343	37 207	33 412	26 358	13 004	11 381	15 587	16 223	16 538	15 388
Belgium Belgique	3 454	3 190	2 267	...	...	...	...	...	...	...
Bolivia Bolivie	862	1 152	1 308	1 381	*1 222	...	...	...	...	...
Brazil Brésil	152 925	156 540	190 026	146 540	124 272	163 042	159 861	142 734	145 393	146 938
Bulgaria Bulgarie	17 048	13 421	10 785	10 244	11 980	8 915	6 838	6 401	4 591	4 790
Burkina Faso Burkina Faso	1 271	1 200 [3]	...	...	...	...	...	...	...	...
Cameroon [3] Cameroun [3]	1 800	1 900	...	...	...	...	...	...	...	...
Canada [3] Canada [3]	16 000	16 000	...	...	...	...	...	...	...	...
Cape Verde Cap-Vert	...	...	...	...	192	...	...	...	...	...
Central African Rep. [3] Rép. centrafricaine [3]	200	200	...	...	...	...	...	...	...	...
Chile Chili	9 231	9 311	9 270	8 317	7 410	7 134	7 008	6 777	6 237	5 735
China Chine	1 328 950	1 613 647	...	...	...	...	...	...	...	...
China, Hong Kong SAR Chine, Hong Kong RAS	140 000 [3]	8 433	...	...	...	1 499	752 [4]	178 [4]	120 [4]	437 [4]
Colombia Colombie	30 000 [3]	20 651	19 471	20 933	18 277	...	18 736 [5]	16 635 [5]	12 541 [5]	...
Congo [3] Congo [3]	300	300	...	...	...	...	...	...	...	...
Côte d'Ivoire [3] Côte d'Ivoire [3]	1 800	1 800	...	...	...	...	...	...	...	...
Croatia Croatie	11 717	11 240	13 449	12 459	9 521	9 271	9 598	9 350	8 367	8 402
Cuba [3] Cuba [3]	13 000	13 400	...	...	...	...	...	...	...	...

46

Leather footwear
Production: thousand pairs *[cont.]*

Chaussures de cuir
Production : milliers de paires *[suite]*

Country or area Pays ou zone	1991	1992	1993	1994	1995	1996	1997	1998	1999	2000
Cyprus Chypre	10 591	6 199	3 835	3 820 [6]	3 444 [6]	2 507 [6]	2 192 [6]	2 100 [6]	1 208 [6]	1 416 [6]
Czechoslovakia-former Tchécoslovaquie (anc.)	72 134	...	...	...	...	...	...	...	...	...
Czech Republic République tchèque	41 400	36 948	32 293	23 323	22 115	21 572	13 455	10 099	7 146	6 109
Dem. Rep. of the Congo [3] Rép. dém. du Congo [3]	900	900	...	...	...	...	...	...	...	...
Denmark Danemark	4 400 [3]	4 600 [3]	...	...	...	8 387 [7]	10 118 [7]	10 390 [7]	10 114 [7]	10 025 [7]
Dominican Republic [3] Rép. dominicaine [3]	2 000	2 200	...	...	...	...	...	...	...	...
Ecuador Equateur	1 600 [3]	1 936	1 691	1 672	1 744	1 507	2	1	1	...
Egypt Egypte	48 311	48 390	48 385	48 394	48 444	48 300	48 131	48 171	...	49 077
El Salvador [3] El Salvador [3]	3 700	3 800	...	...	...	...	...	...	...	...
Estonia Estonie	6 301	3 208	1 035	827	682	711	793	803	840	886
Ethiopia [8] Ethiopie [8]	3 374	2 419	3 083	2 871	3 751	3 773	6 925	6 252	7 477 [9]	5 022
Finland Finlande	3 683	3 606	3 291	3 421	3 186	3 220	2 928	3 499	2 650	2 612
France [9] France [9]	169 221	160 320	151 124	154 898	151 704	139 442	135 447	125 524	114 540	...
Georgia Géorgie	...	2 614	1 046	224	50	48	101	95	101	90
Germany Allemagne	84 435	63 672	55 485	47 193	45 491	40 675	36 948	38 441	...	...
Greece Grèce	10 712	9 264	8 166	6 922	7 032	6 769	6 202	5 716	...	...
Haiti [3] Haïti [3]	500	600	...	...	...	...	...	...	...	...
Hungary Hongrie	20 757	14 752	12 783	12 499	12 178	...	...	...	14 386	15 045
Iceland Islande	46	18	...	...	...	9	8	...	...	...
India [10] Inde [10]	201 449	207 181	188 746	158 263	181 462	157 095	137 837	180 490	134 524	141 941
Indonesia [11] Indonésie [11]	87 571	...	# 250 053 [12]	272 529	249 509	...	238 335	258 780	332 478	...
Iran (Islamic Rep. of) Iran (Rép. islamique d')	20 944 [13]	25 129 [13]	21 756 [13]	17 598 [13]	29 807 [14]	28 310 [14]	27 267 [14]	22 362 [14]	...	...
Iraq Iraq	5 000 [3]	4 087	...	...	...	...	...	...	...	...
Ireland [3] Irlande [3]	3 000	3 200	...	...	...	...	...	...	...	...
Italy [3] Italie [3]	310 200	295 000	...	...	...	...	...	...	...	...

46

Leather footwear
Production: thousand pairs *[cont.]*

Chaussures de cuir
Production : milliers de paires *[suite]*

Country or area Pays ou zone	1991	1992	1993	1994	1995	1996	1997	1998	1999	2000
Jamaica [3] Jamaïque [3]	700	800	...	...	...	...	...	...	...	...
Japan [14,15] Japon [14,15]	53 351	52 455	47 703	51 503	49 525	48 819	47 573	42 573	37 546	35 961
Kenya Kenya	1 190	1 480	1 571	1 774	2 018	2 089		...	...	...
Korea, Republic of Corée, République de	28 923	27 617	19 085	16 806	15 309	...	...	...	...	...
Kyrgyzstan Kirghizistan	9 646	5 757	3 528	1 512	755	605	332	135	85	137
Lao People's Dem. Rep. Rép. dém. pop. lao	...	...	...	240	150	...	...	...	...	...
Latvia Lettonie	7 778	5 764	2 687	1 633	1 032	939	753	753	451	371
Lithuania Lituanie	11 154	7 702	3 657	1 565	1 961	2 004	1 663	1 654	1 783	744
Madagascar Madagascar	837 [11]	702 [11]	306 [11]	180	136	158	126	115	...	...
Mali Mali	127	104	86	106	99	98	...	...	...	...
Mexico Mexique	36 911	33 141	62 315	56 948	44 006	50 340	52 586	47 072	43 916	42 434
Mongolia Mongolie	3 994	2 245	1 031	407	325	146	41	33	7	6
Mozambique Mozambique	242	148	153	87	29	...	12	10	7	7
Nepal Népal	700 [3]	800 [16]	823 [16]	700 [16]	685 [16]	649 [16]	550 [16]	550 [16]	* 605 [16]	650 [16]
Netherlands [7,9,17] Pays-Bas [7,9,17]	5 255	5 289	6 315	5 455	5 492	...	...	...	...	...
New Zealand [1,18] Nouvelle-Zélande [1,18]	4 022	3 765	3 525	3 590	3 119	2 676	2 222	1 484	1 650	...
Nicaragua [3] Nicaragua [3]	1 200	1 300	...	...	...	...	...	...	...	...
Nigeria Nigéria	7 093	4 538	4 554	1 182	1 255	...	...	...	...	...
Norway [3] Norvège [3]	900	1 000	...	...	...	...	...	...	...	...
Panama Panama	1 600 [3]	1 377	1 483	1 294	1 287	1 058	1 104	753	799	...
Paraguay [3] Paraguay [3]	5 500	5 600	...	...	...	...	...	...	...	...
Peru [3] Pérou [3]	19 000	20 000	...	...	...	...	...	...	...	...
Philippines [3] Philippines [3]	12 000	15 000	...	...	...	...	...	...	...	...
Poland Pologne	66 857	55 181	47 905	53 236	59 783	66 620	68 513	54 491	48 538	...
Portugal Portugal	39 658	60 463	75 422	71 648	68 070	69 439	71 949	68 176	76 149	75 953

46

Leather footwear
Production: thousand pairs *[cont.]*

Chaussures de cuir
Production : milliers de paires *[suite]*

Country or area Pays ou zone	1991	1992	1993	1994	1995	1996	1997	1998	1999	2000
Republic of Moldova République de Moldova	20 751	14 504	4 897 [19]	2 267 [19]	1 506 [19]	1 429 [19]	1 032 [19]	739 [19]	705 [19]	1 003 [19]
Romania Roumanie	63 196	41 237	41 893	45 666	48 239	44 838	34 365	30 341	30 491	36 863
Russian Federation Fédération de Russie	356 147	231 005	153 343	80 776	54 254	36 764	33 030	23 816	29 864	32 939
Senegal Sénégal	153	644	508	...	...	...	...	...	...	...
Serbia and Montenegro Serbie-et-Monténégro	18 149	16 169	10 590	8 824	5 982	6 461	6 848	6 976	3 892	4 248
Singapore [3] Singapour [3]	3 000	3 100	...	...	...	...	...	...	...	...
Slovakia Slovaquie	26 744	22 875	18 332	13 577	46 438	13 188	10 300	9 772	7 643	8 503
Slovenia Slovénie	9 124	9 492	8 923	8 683	6 951	5 739	5 976	5 641	4 779	3 404
South Africa [9] Afrique du Sud [9]	49 318	42 251	44 492	41 078	39 071 [20]	38 858 [20]	35 486 [20]	29 581 [20]	24 257 [20]	20 195 [20]
Spain Espagne	115 190	106 959	74 883	104 788	140 141	155 218	165 417	177 464		...
Sri Lanka Sri Lanka	276	272	274	...	...	...	...	...	...	...
Sudan [3] Soudan [3]	3 000	3 000	...	...	...	...	...	...	...	...
Sweden Suède	2 500 [3]	3 000 [3]	1 013	676	372	1 104	1 202	430	956	944
Switzerland Suisse	3 385	3 065	3 291	3 232	2 490	...	...	...	...	...
Tajikistan Tadjikistan	8 567	5 476	4 044	929	612	394	107	123	72	110
TFYR of Macedonia L'ex-R.y. Macédoine	4 238	3 786	2 031	1 760	1 121	* 1 230	* 1 509	* 1 722	* 2 172	* 2 059
Togo [3] Togo [3]	100	100	...	...	...	...	...	...	...	...
Tunisia Tunisie	11 590	13 220	12 870	14 100	16 580	18 380	20 300	...	...	...
Turkmenistan Turkménistan	4 246	3 231	3 358	1 938	1 910	1 546	1 108	561	416	478
Ukraine Ukraine	183 888	147 703	105 814	40 309	20 757	13 175	10 580	11 389	11 875	17 451
United Kingdom Royaume-Uni	41 000 [3]	43 000 [3]	70 837	69 637	61 141	62 157	55 418	44 862	37 148	28 313
United Rep. of Tanzania Rép.-Unie de Tanzanie	328	168	55	89	339	121	152	...	...	...
United States Etats-Unis	168 992	164 904	171 733	156 712	146 979	127 315	127 876	115 808	85 332	76 045
Uzbekistan Ouzbékistan	45 443	40 491	40 466	28 202	5 654	5 591	5 547	...	...	...
Viet Nam Viet Nam	6 188	5 672	...	...	46 440	61 785	79 289	77 037	* 81 780	32 391

46

Leather footwear
Production: thousand pairs *[cont.]*

Chaussures de cuir
Production : milliers de paires *[suite]*

Source:

United Nations Statistics Division, New York, "Industrial Commodity Statistics Yearbook 2000" and the industrial statistics database.

1 Twelve months ending 30 June of the year stated.
2 Excluding sporting footwear.
3 Source: Food and Agriculture Organization of the United Nations (FAO), (Rome).
4 Excluding other footwear for confidentiality purposes.

5 Including rubber and plastic footwear.

6 Including other footwear, house footwear, sandals and other light footwear. Also including rubber footwear.

7 Sales.
8 Twelve months ending 7 July of the year stated.
9 Including rubber footwear.
10 Production by large and medium scale establishments only.
11 Including plastic footwear.
12 Break in series; data prior to the sign not comparable to following years.
13 Production by establishments employing 50 or more persons.
14 Production by establishments employing 10 or more persons.
15 Shipments.
16 Twelve months beginning 16 July of the year stated.

17 Production by establishments employing 20 or more persons.
18 Including non-leather footwear.
19 Excluding the Transnistria region.
20 Excluding children's footwear.

Source:

Organisation des Nations Unies, Division de statistique, New York, "Annuaire de statistiques industrielles par produit 2000" et la base de données pour les statistiques industrielles.

1 Période de douze mois finissant le 30 juin de l'année indiquée.
2 Y compris les chaussures sportif.
3 Source: Organisation des Nations Unies pour l'alimentation et l'agriculture (FAO), (Rome).
4 A l'exclusion d'autres chaussures, pour raisons de confidentialité
5 Y compris les chaussures en caoutchouc et en matière plastique.
6 Y compris les autres chaussures, chaussures de maison, sandales et autres chaussures légères. Y compris également les chaussures en caoutchouc.
7 Ventes.
8 Période de douze mois finissant le 7 juillet de l'année indiquée.
9 Y compris les chaussures en caoutchouc.
10 Production des grandes et moyennes entreprises seulement.
11 Y compris les chaussures en matière plastique.
12 Marque une interruption dans la série et la non-comparabilité des données précédant le symbole.
13 Production des établissements occupant 50 personnes ou plus.
14 Production des établissements occupant 10 personnes ou plus.
15 Expéditions.
16 Période de douze mois commençant le 16 juillet de l'année indiquée.
17 Production des établissements occupant 20 personnes ou plus.
18 Y compris les chaussures en matières autres que le cuir.
19 Non compris la région de Transnistria.
20 Non compris les chaussures pour enfants.

47
Sawnwood
Production (sawn): thousand cubic metres

Sciages
Production (sciés): milliers de mètres cubes

Region, country or area Région, pays ou zone	1992	1993	1994	1995	1996	1997	1998	1999	2000	2001
World **Monde**	**437 623**	**431 143**	**433 911**	**425 238**	**424 190**	**430 934**	**374 406**	**383 159**	**388 430**	**377 570**
Africa **Afrique**	**8 102**	**7 850**	**8 490**	**8 243**	**7 867**	**7 505**	**7 423**	**7 415**	**8 096**	**8 414**
Algeria [1] Algérie [1]	13	13	13	13	13	13	13	13	13	13
Angola [1] Angola [1]	5	5	5	5	5	5	5	5	5	5
Benin Bénin	24	24 [1]	24 [1]	15	11	12	13	13	13 [1]	13 [1]
Burkina Faso Burkina Faso	2 [1]	2 [1]	1	1	1	2	1	1	1 [1]	1 [1]
Burundi Burundi	3	20	21	43	33	33 [1]	33 [1]	80 [1]	83 [1]	83 [1]
Cameroon Cameroun	577 [1]	579 [1]	647 [1]	676 [1]	685 [1]	560	588	600	900	1 150
Central African Rep. Rép. centrafricaine	68	60 [1]	73	70	61	72	91	79	102	150
Chad Tchad	2	2	2 [1]	2	2	2 [1]	2 [1]	2 [1]	2 [1]	2 [1]
Congo Congo	52	52 [1]	57	62	59	64	73	74	93	95
Côte d'Ivoire Côte d'Ivoire	623	587	708	706	596	613	623	611	603	630
Dem. Rep. of the Congo Rép. dém. du Congo	105 [1]	105 [1]	75	65	85	90	80	70	70	70
Egypt Egypte	0	0	0	0	0	0	3	4	4	4 [1]
Equatorial Guinea Guinée équatoriale	8	7	4	4	4 [1]	4 [1]	4 [1]	4 [1]	4 [1]	4 [1]
Ethiopia incl. Eritrea [1] Ethiopie comp. Erythrée [1]	12	...	...	...	...	...	...	...	...	...
Ethiopia Ethiopie	...	33	45	40	33	60	60 [1]	60 [1]	60 [1]	60 [1]
Gabon Gabon	* 155	* 153	* 173	100 [1]	50 [1]	30 [1]	60	98	88	142
Gambia [1] Gambie [1]	1	1	1	1	1	1	1	1	1	1
Ghana Ghana	420	504	801	612	604	575	590	454	475	480
Guinea Guinée	63	65	72	85	85 [1]	25	26	26 [1]	26 [1]	26 [1]
Guinea-Bissau [1] Guinée-Bissau [1]	16	16	16	16	16	16	16	16	16	16
Kenya [1] Kenya [1]	185	185	185	185	185	185	185	185	185	185
Liberia Libéria	* 125	* 90	90 [1]	90 [1]	90 [1]	90 [1]	6	4	10	20
Libyan Arab Jamah. [1] Jamah. arabe libyenne [1]	31	31	31	31	31	31	31	31	31	31

47

Sawnwood
Production (sawn): thousand cubic metres *[cont.]*

Sciages
Production (sciés): milliers de mètres cubes *[suite]*

Region, country or area Région, pays ou zone	1992	1993	1994	1995	1996	1997	1998	1999	2000	2001
Madagascar Madagascar	238 [1]	144	74	84 [1]	84 [1]	84 [1]	84 [1]	102	485	400
Malawi Malawi	43 [1]	45	45 [1]	45 [1]	45 [1]	45 [1]	45 [1]	45 [1]	45 [1]	45 [1]
Mali [1] Mali [1]	13	13	13	13	13	13	13	13	13	13
Mauritius Maurice	4	5	4	2	3	3 [1]	5	5	3	3
Morocco [1] Maroc [1]	83	83	83	83	83	83	83	83	83	83
Mozambique Mozambique	16 [1]	30 [1]	30	42	42 [1]	33	28	28 [1]	28 [1]	28 [1]
Niger [1] Niger [1]	1	4	4	4	4	4	4	4	4	4
Nigeria Nigéria	2 715	2 711	2 533	2 356	2 178	2 000	2 000 [1]	2 000 [1]	2 000 [1]	2 000 [1]
Réunion [1] Réunion [1]	2	2	2	2	2	2	2	2	2	2
Rwanda Rwanda	36	36	26	54	59	74	76	79	79 [1]	79 [1]
Sao Tome and Principe [1] Sao Tomé-et-Principe [1]	5	5	5	5	5	5	5	5	5	5
Senegal [1] Sénégal [1]	23	23	23	23	23	23	23	23	23	23
Sierra Leone Sierra Leone	9 [1]	5	5 [1]	5 [1]	5 [1]	5 [1]	5 [1]	5 [1]	5 [1]	5 [1]
Somalia [1] Somalie [1]	14	14	14	14	14	14	14	14	14	14
South Africa Afrique du Sud	1 818	1 383	1 499	1 574	1 574 [1]	1 574 [1]	1 498	1 498 [1]	1 498 [1]	1 498 [1]
Sudan Soudan	3	3	45	45	45 [1]	45 [1]	51 [1]	51 [1]	51 [1]	51 [1]
Swaziland Swaziland	75	75	80 [1]	90 [1]	100 [1]	102	102 [1]	102 [1]	102 [1]	102 [1]
Togo Togo	3	3 [1]	8	14	15	17	18	21	19	15
Tunisia Tunisie	6	19	20	20 [1]	20 [1]	20 [1]	20 [1]	20 [1]	20 [1]	20 [1]
Uganda Ouganda	96	107	140 [1]	200	215	229	245	264	264 [1]	264 [1]
United Rep. of Tanzania [1] Rép.-Unie de Tanzanie [1]	48	39	24	24	24	24	24	24	24	24
Zambia Zambie	112	318	367	320 [1]	245 [1]	157 [1]	157 [1]	157 [1]	157 [1]	157 [1]
Zimbabwe Zimbabwe	250 [1]	250 [1]	401	401	418	465	416	438	386	397
America, North **Amérique du Nord**	**168 640**	**169 803**	**175 837**	**169 948**	**177 007**	**181 173**	**141 383**	**148 105**	**146 710**	**140 382**
Bahamas [1] Bahamas [1]	1	1	1	1	1	1	1	1	1	1

47

Sawnwood
Production (sawn): thousand cubic metres *[cont.]*

Sciages
Production (sciés): milliers de mètres cubes *[suite]*

Region, country or area Région, pays ou zone	1992	1993	1994	1995	1996	1997	1998	1999	2000	2001
Belize [1] Belize [1]	14	14	20	35	35	35	35	35	35	35
Canada Canada	56 318	59 774	61 650	60 436	62 828	64 764	47 185	50 412	50 465	47 696
Costa Rica Costa Rica	772	798	746 [1]	780 [1]	780 [1]	780 [1]	780 [1]	780 [1]	812	812 [1]
Cuba Cuba	130 [1]	130 [1]	130 [1]	130 [1]	130 [1]	130 [1]	130 [1]	146 [1]	179	190
El Salvador El Salvador	70 [1]	70 [1]	70 [1]	70 [1]	70 [1]	58	58 [1]	58 [1]	58 [1]	58 [1]
Guadeloupe [1] Guadeloupe [1]	1	1	1	1	1	1	1	1	1	1
Guatemala Guatemala	90 [1]	398	417	355	355 [1]	355 [1]	308	235	220	220
Haiti [1] Haïti [1]	14	14	14	14	14	14	14	14	14	14
Honduras Honduras	411	364	361	231	322	379	369	419	444	417
Jamaica Jamaïque	27	24	63	63	64	65	66	66 [1]	66 [1]	66 [1]
Martinique Martinique	1	1 [1]	1 [1]	1 [1]	1 [1]	1 [1]	1 [1]	1 [1]	1 [1]	1 [1]
Mexico Mexique	2 696 [1]	2 560	2 693	2 329	2 543	2 961	3 260	3 110 [1]	3 110 [1]	3 387
Nicaragua Nicaragua	61	65	27	74	160	148	148 [1]	148 [1]	148 [1]	65
Panama Panama	37	37	37	37	19	17	8	46	48	42
Trinidad and Tobago Trinité-et-Tobago	59	35	58	64	29	38	27	18	32	41
United States Etats-Unis	107 937	105 516	109 547	105 326	109 654	111 425	88 991	92 615	91 076	87 335
America, South **Amérique du Sud**	**26 705**	**25 474**	**27 190**	**28 390**	**29 990**	**29 926**	**29 799**	**28 307**	**33 659**	**33 721**
Argentina Argentine	1 472	998	1 080	1 329	1 711	1 170	1 377	1 408	821	821 [1]
Bolivia Bolivie	230	268	185	162	181	180	515	259	239	308
Brazil Brésil	18 628 [1]	18 628 [1]	18 691	19 091	19 091 [1]	19 091 [1]	18 591	17 280	23 100	23 100 [1]
Chile Chili	3 020	3 113	3 364	3 802	4 140	4 661	4 551	5 254	5 698	5 872
Colombia Colombie	758	694	644	644	1 134	1 085	910	730	587	539
Ecuador Equateur	908	196	1 600	1 696	1 886	2 075	2 079	1 455	1 455 [1]	1 455 [1]
French Guiana Guyane française	19 [1]	18	15	15 [1]	15 [1]	15 [1]	15 [1]	15 [1]	15 [1]	15 [1]
Guyana Guyana	50 [1]	50 [1]	77	101	97	57	50	50	50	30

47

Sawnwood
Production (sawn): thousand cubic metres *[cont.]*

Sciages
Production (sciés): milliers de mètres cubes *[suite]*

Region, country or area Région, pays ou zone	1992	1993	1994	1995	1996	1997	1998	1999	2000	2001
Paraguay Paraguay	357	357 [1]	357 [1]	400 [1]	500 [1]	550 [1]	550 [1]	550 [1]	550 [1]	550 [1]
Peru Pérou	500	592	649	630	693	482	590	835	646	494
Suriname Suriname	43	33	29	29 [1]	40	41	41 [1]	28	54	57
Uruguay Uruguay	269	269 [1]	269 [1]	269 [1]	269 [1]	269 [1]	269 [1]	269 [1]	269 [1]	269 [1]
Venezuela Venezuela	451	258	230	222	233	250	261	174	175	211
Asia **Asie**	**97 204**	**101 601**	**98 045**	**96 652**	**92 089**	**90 246**	**71 051**	**70 986**	**62 368**	**60 425**
Afghanistan [1] Afghanistan [1]	400	400	400	400	400	400	400	400	400	400
Armenia Arménie	0	0	0	0	0	0	0	0	4	4
Azerbaijan Azerbaïdjan	0	0	0	0	0	0	0	0	1	0
Bangladesh [1] Bangladesh [1]	79	79	79	70	70	70	70	70	70	70
Bhutan Bhoutan	21	18	18 [1]	18 [1]	18 [1]	18 [1]	18 [1]	22 [1]	31 [1]	31 [1]
Brunei Darussalam Brunéi Darussalam	90	90	90 [1]	90 [1]	90 [1]	90 [1]	90 [1]	90 [1]	90 [1]	90 [1]
Cambodia Cambodge	132 [1]	155 [1]	195	140	100	71	40	26	20	5
China Chine	19 756 [1]	25 709 [1]	25 603 [1]	25 603 [1]	27 410 [1]	20 982	18 716 [1]	16 700 [1]	7 345 [1]	8 549 [1]
Cyprus Chypre	14	17	15	15	16	14	11	12	9	9
India Inde	17 460 [1]	17 460 [1]	17 460 [1]	17 460 [1]	10 624 [1]	18 520 [1]	8 400	8 400	7 900	7 900
Indonesia Indonésie	8 438	8 338	6 838	6 638	7 338	7 238	7 125	6 625	6 500	6 400
Iran (Islamic Rep. of) Iran (Rép. islamique d')	187	170	178	159	144	141	129	96	106	106 [1]
Iraq Iraq	8 [1]	8 [1]	8 [1]	8 [1]	8 [1]	8 [1]	12	12 [1]	12 [1]	12 [1]
Japan Japon	27 277 [1]	26 260 [1]	25 906 [1]	24 493 [1]	23 844 [1]	21 709	18 625	17 952	17 094	15 485
Kazakhstan Kazakhstan	0	0	0	0	0	0	* 182	* 337	* 460	460 [1]
Korea, Dem. P. R. [1] Corée, R. p. dém. de [1]	280	280	280	280	280	280	280	280	280	280
Korea, Republic of Corée, République de	3 513	3 249	3 862	3 440	4 291	4 759	2 240	4 300	4 544	4 420
Kyrgyzstan Kirghizistan	0	0	0	0	0	2	* 23	* 23	* 6	* 6
Lao People's Dem. Rep. Rép. dém. pop. lao	170 [1]	262	331	465	320	560	250 [1]	350 [1]	208	227

47

Sawnwood
Production (sawn): thousand cubic metres *[cont.]*

Sciages
Production (sciés): milliers de mètres cubes *[suite]*

Region, country or area Région, pays ou zone	1992	1993	1994	1995	1996	1997	1998	1999	2000	2001
Lebanon Liban	9	9	9 [1]	9 [1]	9 [1]	9 [1]	9 [1]	9 [1]	9 [1]	9 [1]
Malaysia Malaisie	9 369	9 395	8 858	8 382 [1]	8 382 [1]	7 326	5 091	5 237	5 590	4 700
Mongolia Mongolie	124	84	50	61	170 [1]	200 [1]	300 [1]	300 [1]	300 [1]	300 [1]
Myanmar Myanmar	302	339	347 [1]	347 [1]	351	372	299	298	545	671
Nepal Népal	620 [1]	620 [1]	620 [1]	620 [1]	620 [1]	620 [1]	630	630	630	630
Pakistan Pakistan	1 450	1 503	1 127	1 266	1 280	1 024	1 051	1 075	1 087	1 180
Philippines Philippines	651	440	407	286	313	351	222	288	151	199
Singapore [1] Singapour [1]	25	25	25	25	25	25	25	25	25	25
Sri Lanka Sri Lanka	5	5 [1]	5 [1]	6	5	5 [1]	5 [1]	5 [1]	29	29 [1]
Syrian Arab Republic [1] Rép. arabe syrienne [1]	9	9	9	9	9	9	9	9	9	9
Thailand Thaïlande	1 076	715	568	426	307	426	103	178	220	233
Turkey Turquie	4 891	5 241	4 037	4 331	4 268	3 833	3 990	4 300	5 743	5 036
Viet Nam Viet Nam	849	721	721 [1]	1 606	1 398	1 184	2 705	2 937	2 950	2 950
Europe **Europe**	**131 066**	**120 148**	**117 683**	**115 000**	**110 310**	**115 072**	**117 460**	**120 681**	**129 357**	**126 933**
Albania Albanie	382 [1]	4	5	5 [1]	5 [1]	5	28	35	90	90 [1]
Austria Autriche	7 020	6 786	7 572	7 804	8 200	8 450	8 737	9 628	10 390	10 227
Belarus Bélarus	1 693	1 545	1 545 [1]	1 545 [1]	1 545 [1]	1 545 [1]	* 2 131	2 175	1 808	1 721
Belgium Belgique	...	...	...	...	...	...	...	1 056	* 1 150	* 1 300
Belgium-Luxembourg Belgique-Luxembourg	1 184	1 184 [1]	1 209	1 150	1 100	1 150	1 267	...	...	...
Bosnia and Herzegovina Bosnie-Herzégovine	20	20	20	20	20	320	* 330	* 330	* 320	* 310
Bulgaria Bulgarie	324	253	253 [1]	253 [1]	253 [1]	253 [1]	253 [1]	325	312	312 [1]
Croatia Croatie	651	699	601	578	598	644	676	685	642	634
Czech Republic République tchèque	...	3 025	3 155	3 490	3 405	3 393	3 427	3 584	4 106	3 889
Denmark Danemark	620	583	583 [1]	583 [1]	583 [1]	583 [1]	238	344	364	281
Estonia Estonie	300	300 [1]	341	350	400	729 [1]	850	1 200	1 436	1 670

47

Sawnwood
Production (sawn): thousand cubic metres *[cont.]*

Sciages
Production (sciés): milliers de mètres cubes *[suite]*

Region, country or area Région, pays ou zone	1992	1993	1994	1995	1996	1997	1998	1999	2000	2001
Finland Finlande	7 330	8 570	10 290	9 940	9 780	11 430	12 300	12 768	13 420	12 770
France France	10 488	9 132	9 649	9 848	9 600	9 607	10 220	10 236	10 536	10 700
Germany Allemagne	13 496	11 522	13 567	14 105	14 267	14 730	14 972	16 096	16 340	16 189
Greece Grèce	337	337 [1]	337 [1]	337 [1]	337 [1]	130	137	140	137	137 [1]
Hungary Hongrie	667	480	417	230	285	317	298	308	291	219
Ireland Irlande	575	637	709	678	687	642	675	811	888	925
Italy Italie	1 823	1 700	1 808	1 850	1 650	1 751	1 600	1 630	1 630	1 600
Latvia Lettonie	740	446	950	1 300	1 614	2 700	3 200	3 640	3 900	3 840
Lithuania Lituanie	105 [1]	699	760	940	1 450	1 250	1 150	1 150	1 300	1 250
Luxembourg Luxembourg	...	...	...	...	...	...	...	133	133 [1]	133 [1]
Netherlands Pays-Bas	405	389	383	426	359	401	349	362	390	268
Norway Norvège	2 362	2 315	2 415	2 210	2 420	2 520	2 525	2 336	2 280	2 253
Poland Pologne	4 082	4 260	5 300	3 842	3 747	4 214	4 320	4 137	4 262	3 550
Portugal Portugal	1 550	1 494	1 670	1 731	1 731 [1]	1 731 [1]	1 490	1 430	1 427	1 410
Republic of Moldova République de Moldova	0	0	31	25	29	30	30	6	5	5 [1]
Romania Roumanie	2 460	2 460 [1]	1 727	1 777	1 693	1 861	2 200	2 818	3 396	3 059
Russian Federation Fédération de Russie	53 370	40 890	30 720	26 500	21 913	20 600	19 580	19 100	20 000	20 000
Serbia and Montenegro Serbie-et-Monténégro	461	315	280	304	378	391	438	364	504	391
Slovakia Slovaquie	...	550	700	646	629	767	1 265	1 265 [1]	1 265 [1]	1 265 [1]
Slovenia Slovénie	403	513	513	511	496	510	664	455	439	460
Spain Espagne	2 468	2 717	2 755	3 262	3 080	3 080	3 178	3 178 [1]	3 760	4 185
Sweden Suède	12 128	12 738	13 816	14 944	14 370	15 669	15 124	14 858	16 176	15 810
Switzerland Suisse	1 525	1 410	1 320	1 479	1 355	1 280	1 400 [1]	1 525	1 625	1 400
TFYR of Macedonia L'ex-R.y. Macédoine	...	63	57	42	40	34	27	37	36	23
Ukraine Ukraine	...	...	...	...	...	...	...	...	* 2 117	2 117 [1]

47

Sawnwood
Production (sawn): thousand cubic metres *[cont.]*

Sciages
Production (sciés): milliers de mètres cubes *[suite]*

Region, country or area Région, pays ou zone	1992	1993	1994	1995	1996	1997	1998	1999	2000	2001
United Kingdom Royaume-Uni	2 097	2 112	2 225	2 295	2 291	2 356	2 382	2 537	2 482	2 540
Oceania **Océanie**	**5 907**	**6 268**	**6 667**	**7 006**	**6 927**	**7 013**	**7 291**	**7 664**	**8 239**	**7 695**
Australia Australie	3 041	3 187	3 431	3 691	3 530	3 481	3 711	3 673	3 983	3 525
Fiji Fidji	91 [1]	111	112	102	102 [1]	133	131	64	72	79
New Caledonia Nouvelle-Calédonie	2	2	3	3 [1]	3 [1]	3 [1]	3 [1]	3 [1]	3 [1]	3 [1]
New Zealand Nouvelle-Zélande	2 544	2 805	2 861	2 950	3 032	3 136	3 178	3 653	3 910	3 807
Papua New Guinea Papouasie-Nvl-Guinée	183	118	218	218	218 [1]	218 [1]	218 [1]	218 [1]	218 [1]	218 [1]
Samoa Samoa	21	21	21 [1]	21 [1]	21 [1]	21 [1]	21 [1]	21 [1]	21 [1]	21 [1]
Solomon Islands Iles Salomon	16 [1]	16 [1]	12	12 [1]	12 [1]	12 [1]	12 [1]	12 [1]	12 [1]	12 [1]
Tonga Tonga	1 [1]	1 [1]	1 [1]	1 [1]	1 [1]	1 [1]	1 [1]	2	2 [1]	2 [1]	2 [1]
Vanuatu Vanuatu	7	7	7 [1]	7 [1]	7 [1]	7 [1]	15	18	18	28

Source:
Food and Agriculture Organization of the United Nations (FAO), Rome, "FAO Yearbook of Forest Products 2001" and the FAOSTAT database.

Source:
Organisation des Nations Unies pour l'alimentation et l'agriculture (FAO), Rome, "Annuaire FAO des produits forestiers 2001" et la base de données FAOSTAT.

1 FAO estimate.

1 Estimation de la FAO.

48
Paper and paperboard
Production: thousand metric tons
Papiers et cartons
Production: milliers de tonnes

Region, country or area Région, pays ou zone	1992	1993	1994	1995	1996	1997	1998	1999	2000	2001
World **Monde**	**245 404**	**252 250**	**268 515**	**282 286**	**284 297**	**301 413**	**301 736**	**315 678**	**324 046**	**320 256**
Africa **Afrique**	**2 605**	**2 519**	**2 437**	**2 624**	**2 634**	**2 885**	**2 980**	**2 897**	**3 012**	**3 278**
Algeria Algérie	91 [1]	93	87	* 78	*56	* 65	* 55	26	41 [1]	41 [1]
Cameroon Cameroun	5 [1]	5 [1]	5 [1]	5 [1]	5 [1]	0	0	0 [1]	0 [1]	0 [1]
Dem. Rep. of the Congo Rép. dém. du Congo	3	3 [1]	3 [1]	3 [1]	3 [1]	3 [1]	3 [1]	3 [1]	3 [1]	3 [1]
Egypt Egypte	201	* 220	* 219	* 221	221 [1]	* 282	343	343 [1]	440 [1]	460 [1]
Ethiopia incl. Eritrea Ethiopie comp. Erythrée	3	...	...	...	...	...	...	...	...	
Ethiopia Ethiopie	...	7	7	6	8	10	6	10	12	12 [1]
Kenya Kenya	176	176 [1]	* 108	* 113	129	129 [1]	129 [1]	129 [1]	129 [1]	129 [1]
Libyan Arab Jamah. [1] Jamah. arabe libyenne [1]	6	6	6	6	6	6	6	6	6	6
Madagascar Madagascar	5	6	5	4	3	4	5	2	4 [1]	4 [1]
Morocco Maroc	102	99	103	106	106	107	110	109	109	129
Mozambique Mozambique	2 [1]	1 [1]	1 [1]	1 [1]	1 [1]	0	0	0 [1]	0 [1]	0 [1]
Nigeria Nigéria	21	5	3	6	21	19	19	19	19	19
South Africa Afrique du Sud	* 1 800	* 1 710	* 1 684	1 871	1 871 [1]	2 047	2 105	2 041	2 041 [1]	2 267
Sudan [1] Soudan [1]	3	3	3	3	3	3	3	3	3	3
Tunisia Tunisie	71	* 80	* 92	* 90	90 [1]	97	88	* 94	94 [1]	94 [1]
Uganda [1] Ouganda [1]	3	3	3	3	3	3	3	3	3	3
United Rep. of Tanzania [1] Rép.-Unie de Tanzanie [1]	25	25	25	25	25	25	25	25	25	25
Zambia Zambie	2	4	2	2 [1]	2 [1]	4 [1]	4 [1]	4 [1]	4 [1]	4 [1]
Zimbabwe Zimbabwe	86	73	81	81	81	81	76	80	80 [1]	80 [1]
America, North **Amérique du Nord**	**94 724**	**97 399**	**101 968**	**107 536**	**105 823**	**111 272**	**109 388**	**113 229**	**111 720**	**105 802**
Canada Canada	16 585	17 557	18 348	18 713	18 414	18 969	18 875	20 280	20 921	19 828
Costa Rica Costa Rica	19 [1]	19 [1]	* 20	20 [1]	20 [1]	20 [1]	20 [1]	20 [1]	20 [1]	20 [1]
Cuba Cuba	* 60	* 57	57 [1]	57 [1]	57 [1]	57 [1]	57 [1]	57 [1]	57 [1]	57 [1]

48

Paper and paperboard
Production: thousand metric tons *[cont.]*

Papiers et cartons
Production: milliers de tonnes *[suite]*

Region, country or area Région, pays ou zone	1992	1993	1994	1995	1996	1997	1998	1999	2000	2001
Dominican Republic Rép. dominicaine	10	7	7	7	21	21 [1]	130	130 [1]	130 [1]	130 [1]
El Salvador El Salvador	17	17	17	17	56	56 [1]	56 [1]	56 [1]	56 [1]	56 [1]
Guatemala Guatemala	14	14	25	31	31 [1]	31 [1]	31 [1]	31 [1]	31 [1]	31 [1]
Honduras Honduras	...	...	...	90	103	88	95	95 [1]	95 [1]	95 [1]
Jamaica Jamaïque	5	3	3 [1]	0	0 [1]	0 [1]	0 [1]	0 [1]	0 [1]	0 [1]
Mexico Mexique	* 2 825	2 447	2 518	* 3 047	3 047 [1]	3 491	3 673	3 784	3 865	4 056
Panama Panama	28	28	28 [1]	28 [1]	28 [1]	28 [1]	0	0	0 [1]	0 [1]
United States Etats-Unis	75 161	77 250	80 945	85 526	84 046	88 511	86 451	88 776	86 545	81 529
America, South Amérique du Sud	**8 082**	**8 208**	**8 812**	**9 204**	**9 247**	**9 970**	**9 606**	**9 655**	**10 607**	**12 015**
Argentina Argentine	976	850	* 961	1 025	991	1 133	978	1 012	1 270	1 374
Bolivia Bolivie	0	0	0 [1]	2	2	2 [1]	2 [1]	0 [1]	0 [1]	0 [1]
Brazil Brésil	4 913	5 352	5 730	5 856	5 885	6 475	6 524	6 255	6 473	7 354
Chile Chili	508	526	553	573	680	614	642	815	1 240	1 668
Colombia Colombie	629	595	672	690	693	704	712	733	771 [1]	771 [1]
Ecuador Equateur	160	103	78	83	86	91	91 [1]	91 [1]	91 [1]	91 [1]
Paraguay Paraguay	13	13	13 [1]	13 [1]	13 [1]	13 [1]	13 [1]	13 [1]	13 [1]	13 [1]
Peru Pérou	141	79	94	140	140 [1]	140 [1]	63	63 [1]	63 [1]	63 [1]
Uruguay Uruguay	83	83 [1]	83 [1]	86	86 [1]	* 90	* 88	* 92	92 [1]	92 [1]
Venezuela Venezuela	659	607	628	736	671	708	493	581	594 [1]	589 [1]
Asia Asie	**63 168**	**65 822**	**71 791**	**77 457**	**81 636**	**85 208**	**85 584**	**91 731**	**94 739**	**97 248**
Armenia Arménie	0	0	0	0	0	0	0	0	20 [1]	21 [1]
Azerbaijan Azerbaïdjan	0	0	0	0	0	0	0	0	28 [1]	140 [1]
Bangladesh Bangladesh	97 [1]	* 150	* 160	120 [1]	90 [1]	70	46	46 [1]	46 [1]	46 [1]
China Chine	20 049	22 077	25 627	28 517	30 913	31 763	* 32 303	34 137	35 439	37 929
India Inde	2 528	2 626	* 2 859	* 3 025	3 025 [1]	2 922	3 320	3 845	3 673	3 973

48

Paper and paperboard
Production: thousand metric tons *[cont.]*

Papiers et cartons
Production: milliers de tonnes *[suite]*

Region, country or area Région, pays ou zone	1992	1993	1994	1995	1996	1997	1998	1999	2000	2001
Indonesia Indonésie	* 2 263	2 600 [1]	* 3 054	* 3 425	*4 121	* 4 822	* 5 487	6 978	6 977	6 995
Iran (Islamic Rep. of) Iran (Rép. islamique d')	190	260	205	205	205	205	20	25	46	46 [1]
Iraq Iraq	13 [1]	13 [1]	* 18	18 [1]	18 [1]	18 [1]	20	20 [1]	20 [1]	20 [1]
Israel Israël	215	213	229	275	275 [1]	275 [1]	242	275 [1]	275 [1]	275
Japan Japon	28 324	27 764	28 527	29 664	30 014	31 014	29 886	30 631	31 828	30 717
Jordan Jordanie	15	29	31	31	31	32	32	32	19 [1]	27 [1]
Kazakhstan Kazakhstan	0	0	0	0	0	0	0	0	19 [1]	22 [1]
Korea, Dem. P. R. [1] Corée, R. p. dém. de [1]	80	80	80	80	80	80	80	80	80	80
Korea, Republic of Corée, République de	5 504	5 804	6 435	* 6 878	7 681	8 334	7 750	8 875	9 308	9 332
Kyrgyzstan Kirghizistan	0	0	0	0	0	0	0	0	2 [1]	2 [1]
Lebanon [1] Liban [1]	42	42	42	42	42	42	42	42	42	42
Malaysia Malaisie	636	663	574	665	674	711	761	859	791	851
Myanmar Myanmar	11	15	15	15	15	39	41	37	39	42
Nepal [1] Népal [1]	13	13	13	13	13	13	13	13	13	13
Pakistan Pakistan	229	362	403	420	447	500	527	574	592	1 165
Philippines Philippines	570	* 518	* 518	* 613	613 [1]	613 [1]	987	1 010	1 107	1 056
Singapore Singapour	85 [1]	* 96	* 97	* 87	87 [1]	87 [1]	87 [1]	87 [1]	87 [1]	87 [1]
Sri Lanka Sri Lanka	26	29	31	28	25	25 [1]	25 [1]	25 [1]	24 [1]	24 [1]
Syrian Arab Republic [1] Rép. arabe syrienne [1]	1	1	1	1	1	1	1	1	1	1
Thailand Thaïlande	1 150	1 306	1 664	1 970	2 036	2 271	2 367	2 434	2 312	2 445
Turkey Turquie	1 013	1 032	1 102	1 240	1 105	1 246	1 357	1 349	1 567	1 512
Viet Nam Viet Nam	115	129	* 106	* 125	125 [1]	125 [1]	190	356	384	384 [1]
Europe **Europe**	**74 097**	**75 427**	**80 446**	**82 310**	**81 773**	**88 771**	**90 794**	**94 785**	**100 254**	**98 421**
Albania Albanie	44 [1]	44 [1]	44 [1]	44 [1]	44 [1]	44 [1]	44 [1]	1	3	3 [1]
Austria Autriche	3 252	3 301	3 603	3 599	3 653	3 816	4 009	4 142	4 386	4 250

48

Paper and paperboard
Production: thousand metric tons *[cont.]*

Papiers et cartons
Production: milliers de tonnes *[suite]*

Region, country or area Région, pays ou zone	1992	1993	1994	1995	1996	1997	1998	1999	2000	2001
Belarus Bélarus	267	175	131	131	131	131	195	208	236	241
Belgium Belgique	...	...	...	...	...	...	...	1 727	1 727	1 662
Belgium-Luxembourg Belgique-Luxembourg	1 147	1 147 [1]	1 088	1 088 [1]	1 432	1 432 [1]	1 831	...	...	...
Bulgaria Bulgarie	153	139	148	150	150	150	153	126	136	136 [1]
Croatia Croatie	100	114	248	325	304	393	403	417	406 [1]	407
Czech Republic République tchèque	...	643	700	738	714	772	768	770	804	865
Denmark Danemark	317	339	345	345 [1]	345 [1]	391	393	397	263 [1]	253 [1]
Estonia Estonie	42	42	42	42	53	35	43	48	54 [1]	54 [1]
Finland Finlande	9 153	9 990	10 909	10 942	10 442	12 149	12 703	12 947	13 509	12 503
France France	7 691	7 975	8 701	8 619	8 556	9 143	9 161	9 603	10 006	9 630
Germany Allemagne	13 214	13 034	14 457	14 827	14 733	15 930	16 311	16 742	18 182	17 879
Greece Grèce	387 [1]	750	750 [1]	750 [1]	750 [1]	478	622	545	350	350 [1]
Hungary Hongrie	348	292	328	321	363	820	434	456	506	495 [1]
Ireland Irlande	0	0	0	0	0 [1]	0 [1]	42	42	43	43 [1]
Italy Italie	6 040	6 019	6 705	6 810	6 954	8 032	8 254	8 568	9 129	8 924
Latvia Lettonie	45	10	4	6	8	16	18	19	16 [1]	24 [1]
Lithuania Lituanie	50	31	23	29	31	25	37	37	53	68 [1]
Netherlands Pays-Bas	2 835	2 855	3 011	2 967	2 987	3 159	3 180	3 256	3 332	3 174
Norway Norvège	1 683	1 958	2 148	2 261	2 096	2 129	2 260	2 241	2 300	2 220
Poland Pologne	1 147	1 183	1 326	1 477	1 528	1 660	1 718	1 839	1 934	1 950 [1]
Portugal Portugal	959	878	949	977	1 026	1 080	1 136	1 163	1 290 [1]	1 419 [1]
Romania Roumanie	359 [1]	359 [1]	288	364	332	324	301	289	340	395
Russian Federation Fédération de Russie	5 765	4 459	3 412	4 073	3 224	3 339	3 595	4 535	5 310	5 596
Serbia and Montenegro Serbie-et-Monténégro	402	222	238	245	249	300	326	230	180	241
Slovakia Slovaquie	...	303	299	327	467	526	597	803	925	954

48

Paper and paperboard
Production: thousand metric tons *[cont.]*

Papiers et cartons
Production: milliers de tonnes *[suite]*

Region, country or area Région, pays ou zone	1992	1993	1994	1995	1996	1997	1998	1999	2000	2001
Slovenia Slovénie	413	401	460	449	456	430	491	417	411	411 [1]
Spain Espagne	3 449	3 348	3 503	3 684	3 768	3 968	3 545	4 435	4 765	5 131
Sweden Suède	8 378	8 781	9 284	9 159	9 018	9 756	9 879	10 071	10 786	10 535
Switzerland Suisse	1 305	1 332	1 450	1 435	1 461	1 583	1 592	1 748	1 616	1 754
TFYR of Macedonia L'ex-R.y. Macédoine	...	22	24	34	21	21	15	14	17	14 [1]
Ukraine Ukraine	...	...	...	...	288	261	261 [1]	373	373	373 [1]
United Kingdom Royaume-Uni	5 152	5 282	5 829	6 093	6 189	6 479	6 477	6 576	6 868	6 467
Oceania **Océanie**	**2 728**	**2 875**	**3 061**	**3 155**	**3 185**	**3 308**	**3 385**	**3 381**	**3 713**	**3 491**
Australia Australie	1 990	2 039	2 197	2 252	2 320	2 418	2 541	2 564	2 836	2 652
New Zealand Nouvelle-Zélande	738	836	864	903	865	890	844	817	877	839

Source:
Food and Agriculture Organization of the United Nations (FAO),
Rome, "FAO Yearbook of Forest Products 2001" and the FAOSTAT
database.

Source:
Organisation des Nations Unies pour l'alimentation et l'agriculture
(FAO), Rome, "Annuaire FAO des produits forestiers 2001" et la base
de données FAOSTAT.

1 FAO estimate.

1 Estimation de la FAO.

49
Cement
Production: thousand metric tons
Ciment
Production: milliers de tonnes

Country or area Pays ou zone	1991	1992	1993	1994	1995	1996	1997	1998	1999	2000
Afghanistan Afghanistan	109 [1]	* 115 [2]	* 115 [2]	* 115 [2]	*115 [2]	* 116 [2]	* 116 [2]	* 116 [2]	* 116 [2]	* 120 [2]
Albania Albanie	311	197	198	240	240	204	100	84	107	180
Algeria Algérie	6 323	7 093	6 951	6 093	6 783	7 470	7 146	7 836	7 685	8 406
Angola Angola	314	370	* 250 [2]	* 240 [2]	*200 [2]	* 270 [2]	301 [2]	* 350 [2]	* 350 [2]	* 350 [2]
Argentina Argentine	4 399	5 051	5 647	6 306	5 477	5 117	6 769	7 092	7 187	6 119
Armenia Arménie	1 507	368	198	122	228	281	293	314	287	219
Australia Australie	5 725	5 897	6 628	7 017	6 606	6 397 [3]	6 701	7 235 [3]	7 705 [3]	7 937 [3]
Austria Autriche	5 017	5 029	4 941	4 828	3 806	3 900 [4]	...	...	...	...
Azerbaijan Azerbaïdjan	923	827	643	467	196	223	303	201	171	251
Bahrain Bahreïn	...	...	...	...	...	192 [2]	172	230	156 [2]	89 [2]
Bangladesh [3] Bangladesh [3]	275	272	207	324	316	426	610	543	1 514	1 868
Barbados Barbade	144	71	64	76	76	108	176	257	257	268
Belarus Bélarus	2 402	2 263	1 908	1 488	1 235	1 467	1 876	2 035	1 998	1 847
Belgium Belgique	7 184	8 073	7 569	7 542	7 501	6 996	6 996	6 852	9 252	8 000 [2]
Benin Bénin	320 [2]	370 [2]	506 [2]	465 [2]	579 [2]	* 360 [2]	* 450 [2]	* 520 [2]	* 520 [2]	759
Bhutan [2] Bhoutan [2]	116	116	108	* 120	*140	* 160	* 160	* 150	* 150	* 150
Bolivia Bolivie	587	650	718	776	877	897	1 048	1 167	1 201	1 072
Brazil Brésil	27 491	23 902	24 845	25 229	28 256	34 559	37 995	39 942	40 248	39 559
Bulgaria Bulgarie	2 374	2 132	2 007	1 910	2 070	2 137	1 654	1 742	2 060	2 209
Cameroon Cameroun	521 [2]	620 [2]	* 620 [2]	* 479 [2]	522	305 [2]	350 [2]	400 [2]	* 500 [2]	500 [2]
Canada Canada	9 372	8 592	9 394	10 584	10 440	11 587	11 736	12 064	12 624	12 612
Chile Chili	2 251	2 660	3 024	3 001	3 304	3 627	3 718	3 890	2 508	2 686
China Chine	244656	308217	367878	421180	475606	491189	511738	536000	573000	597000
China, Hong Kong SAR Chine, Hong Kong RAS	1 677	1 644	1 712	1 927	1 913	2 027	1 925	1 539	1 387	1 284
Colombia Colombie	6 389	9 163	18 205	9 273	9 908	...	10 878	8 673	6 677	7 131

49

Cement
Production: thousand metric tons *[cont.]*

Ciment
Production: milliers de tonnes *[suite]*

Country or area Pays ou zone	1991	1992	1993	1994	1995	1996	1997	1998	1999	2000
Congo Congo	102	124	95	87	98	43	20	0	0	0
Costa Rica [2] Costa Rica [2]	* 700	* 700	860	940	865	830	940	1 200	1 260	1 150
Côte d'Ivoire [*2] Côte d'Ivoire [*2]	500	510	500	1 100	1 000	1 000	1 100	650	650	650
Croatia Croatie	1 742	1 771	1 683	2 055	1 708	1 842	2 184	3 873	2 712	2 769
Cuba Cuba	1 851 [5]	1 134 [5]	1 049 [5]	1 085 [5]	1 456 [5]	1 438	1 701	1 713	1 785	1 633
Cyprus Chypre	1 134	1 132	1 089	1 053	1 024	1 021	910	1 207	1 157	1 398
Czech Republic République tchèque	5 610	6 145	5 393	5 252	4 831	5 016	4 874	4 599	4 241	4 093
Dem. Rep. of the Congo [2] Rép. dém. du Congo [2]	* 250	174	149	166	235	241	125	* 100	* 100	...
Denmark [6] Danemark [6]	2 019	2 072	2 270	2 427	2 584	2 629	2 683	2 667	2 534	2 639
Dominican Republic Rép. dominicaine	1 235	1 365	1 271	1 276	1 450	1 642	1 822	1 872	2 295	2 000 [2]
Ecuador Equateur	1 774	2 072	2 155	2 452	2 549	2 601	2 900 [2]	2 539	2 262	2 800 [2]
Egypt Egypte	16 427	15 454	12 576	13 544	14 237	15 569	15 569	15 480	11 933	3 725
El Salvador El Salvador	694 [5]	760 [5]	659 [5]	915 [5]	914 [5]	948 [2]	1 020 [2]	1 076 [2]	1 031 [2]	1 064 [2]
Estonia Estonie	905	483	354	403	418	388	422	321	358	329
Ethiopia [7] Ethiopie [7]	270	237	377	464	609	672	775	783	767	816
Fiji Fidji	79	85	80	94	91	84	96	89	99	87
Finland Finlande	1 343	1 133	835	864	907	975	* 960 [2]	* 1 104	* 1 164	1 422
France France	25 089	21 584	19 222	20 020	19 724	18 337	18 309	19 434	20 302	20 000 [2]
Gabon Gabon	126	116 [2]	132 [2]	126 [2]	154 [2]	185	200	198	162	166
Georgia Géorgie	...	426	278	89	59	85	94	199	341	348
Germany Allemagne	...	37 331	36 649	40 217	38 858	37 006	37 210	38 464	*38 100	38 000 [2]
Ghana Ghana	750 [2]	1 020 [2]	1 200 [2]	1 350 [2]	*1 300 [2]	* 1 500 [2]	1 446	1 573	1 851	1 673
Greece Grèce	13 151	12 761	12 492	12 633	10 914	13 391	13 660	14 207	13 624	14 147
Guadeloupe Guadeloupe	339	292	276	283	*230	* 230 [2]	* 230 [2]	* 230 [2]	* 230 [2]	* 230 [2]
Guatemala Guatemala	450	658 [5]	1 018 [5]	1 163 [5]	1 257	1 173	1 480	1 496	2 120	2 039

49

Cement
Production: thousand metric tons *[cont.]*

Ciment
Production: milliers de tonnes *[suite]*

Country or area Pays ou zone	1991	1992	1993	1994	1995	1996	1997	1998	1999	2000
Haiti Haïti	211	216 [5]	228 [5]	228 [5]	...	...	...	...	...	...
Honduras Honduras	402	760 [5]	933 [5]	1 000 [5]	995 [5]	952 [2]	* 980 [2]	1 020 [2]	1 200 [2]	1 280 [2]
Hungary Hongrie	2 529	2 236	2 533	2 793	2 875	2 747	2 811	2 999	2 980	3 326
Iceland Islande	106	100	86	81	82	90	110	118	131	144
India Inde	52 013	53 936	57 326	63 461	67 722	73 261	82 873	87 646	100230	99 227
Indonesia Indonésie	13 480	14 048	19 610	24 564	23 136	* 24 648	20 702	*22 344	22 806	22 789 [2]
Iran (Islamic Rep. of) Iran (Rép. islamique d')	13 996 [8]	15 094 [8]	16 321 [8]	16 250 [8]	16 904 [8]	17 703 [8]	18 349 [8]	20 049 [8]	22 219	23 277
Iraq Iraq	* 5 000	2 453	* 2 000 [2]	* 2 000 [2]	2 108 [2]	* 1 600 [2]	* 1 700 [2]	* 2 000 [2]	* 2 000 [2]	* 2 000 [2]
Ireland [2] Irlande [2]	* 1 600	* 1 600	1 450	1 623	1 730	1 933	2 100	* 2 000	* 2 000	* 2 000
Israel Israël	3 340	3 960	4 536	4 800	6 204	6 723	5 916	6 476 [2]	6 354 [2]	6 600 [2]
Italy Italie	40 301	41 034	33 771	32 698	33 716	33 327	33 718	35 512	36 827	38 302
Jamaica Jamaïque	390	480	441	445	518	559	588	558	504 [5]	521 [5]
Japan Japon	89 564	88 252	88 046	91 624	90 474	94 492	91 938	81 328	80 120	81 097
Jordan Jordanie	1 675	2 651	3 437	3 392	3 415	3 512	3 250	2 650	2 688	2 640
Kazakhstan Kazakhstan	7 575	6 436	3 963	2 033	1 772	1 115	657	622	838	1 175
Kenya Kenya	1 423	1 507	1 417	1 470	1 670	1 575	1 440	1 200 [2]	1 204 [2]	1 071 [2]
Korea, Dem. P. R. [2] Corée, R. p. dém. de [2]	*16 000	*17 000	*17 000	*17 000	*17 000	* 17 000	*17 000	*17 000	*16 000	15 000
Korea, Republic of Corée, République de	39 167	44 444	47 313	52 088	56 101	58 434	60 317	46 791	48 579	51 424
Kuwait Koweït	300 [2]	534	956	1 232	*1 363	1 113 [9]	2 000 [2]	2 310	2 000 [2]	2 000 [2]
Kyrgyzstan Kirghizistan	1 320	1 096	692	426	310	546	658	709	386	453
Lao People's Dem. Rep. Rép. dém. pop. lao	...	...	...	7	59	78 [2]	84 [2]	80 [2]	80 [2]	80 [2]
Latvia Lettonie	720	340	114	244	204	325	246	366	301	...
Lebanon Liban	* 900 [2]	2 163	2 591	2 948	3 470	3 430	3 126	3 316	2 714	2 808
Liberia [2] Libéria [2]	* 2	* 8	* 8	* 3	*5	* 15	* 7	* 10	* 15	15
Libyan Arab Jamah. Jamah. arabe libyenne	4	4	4	4	3	3	3	3	3	3 [2]

49

Cement
Production: thousand metric tons *[cont.]*
Ciment
Production: milliers de tonnes *[suite]*

Country or area Pays ou zone	1991	1992	1993	1994	1995	1996	1997	1998	1999	2000
Lithuania Lituanie	3 126	1 485	727	736	649	656	714	788	666	573
Luxembourg Luxembourg	688	695	719	711	714	667	683	699	742	749
Madagascar Madagascar	32	30	36	8	38	44	36	44	46 [2]	48 [2]
Malawi Malawi	112	108	117	122	124	88	70	83	104	198 [2]
Malaysia Malaisie	7 451	8 366	8 797	9 928	10 713	12 349	12 668	10 397	10 104	11 445
Mali Mali	11	16	14	14	13	21	10 [2]	10 [2]	10 [2]	10 [2]
Martinique Martinique	291	262	234	231	*225	* 220 [2]	* 220 [2]	* 220 [2]	* 220 [2]	* 220 [2]
Mauritania [2] Mauritanie [2]	105	122	111	374	120	* 100	* 80	* 50	* 50	* 50
Mexico Mexique	25 208	27 114	28 725	31 594	25 295	26 174	29 685	30 915	31 958	33 429
Mongolia Mongolie	227	133	82	86	109	106	* 112 [2]	109	104	92
Morocco Maroc	5 777	6 223	6 175	6 284	6 399	6 585	7 236	7 155	7 194	7 497
Mozambique Mozambique	63	73	60	62	146	179	217	264	266	348
Myanmar [10] Myanmar [10]	443	472	400	477	525	513	524	371	343	400
Nepal [11] Népal [11]	136 [2]	237	248	315	327	309	227	139	191	206
Netherlands Pays-Bas	3 571 [6,12]	3 296 [6,12]	3 142 [6,12]	3 180 [2]	3 180 [2]	3 140 [2]	3 230 [2]	3 200 [2]	3 200 [2]	3 200 [2]
New Caledonia Nouvelle-Calédonie	* 68	90	100	97	98	89	84	0 [2]	0 [2]	100 [2]
New Zealand Nouvelle-Zélande	581	599	684	* 900 [2]	*950 [2]	974 [2]	976 [2]	950 [2]	960 [2]	950 [2]
Nicaragua [2] Nicaragua [2]	239	277	255	309	324	360	377	480	570	650
Niger Niger	20	29	31	26	31	29 [2]	* 30 [2]	* 30 [2]	* 30 [2]	* 30 [2]
Nigeria Nigéria	3 418	3 367	3 247	1 275	1 573	2 545 [2]	2 520 [2]	2 700 [2]	2 500 [2]	2 500 [2]
Norway Norvège	1 293	1 242	1 368	1 464	1 613	1 690	1 724 [2]	1 676 [2]	1 700 [2]	1 720 [2]
Oman Oman	1 100 [9]	1 103 [13]	1 130 [13]	1 191 [13]	1 280 [13]	1 206 [13]	1 233 [13]	1 217 [13]	1 990 [13]	* 1 815 [13]
Pakistan [3] Pakistan [3]	7 762	8 321	8 558	8 100	7 913	9 567	9 536	9 364	9 635	9 314
Panama Panama	300 [2]	473	620 [5]	678 [5]	658 [5]	651	752	814	976	849 [5]
Paraguay Paraguay	343	476	476	529	624	627	603	586	556	516

49

Cement
Production: thousand metric tons *[cont.]*
   Ciment
   Production: milliers de tonnes *[suite]*

Country or area Pays ou zone	1991	1992	1993	1994	1995	1996	1997	1998	1999	2000
Peru Pérou	2 137	2 080	2 327	3 177	3 645	3 678	4 092	4 069	3 327	3 265
Philippines Philippines	6 804	6 540	7 932	9 576	10 566	12 429 [2]	14 681 [2]	12 888 [2]	12 557	11 959
Poland Pologne	12 012	11 908	12 200	13 834	13 914	13 959	15 003	14 970	15 555	15 046
Portugal Portugal	7 342	7 728	7 662	7 756	8 030	8 444	9 395	9 784	10 079	10 343
Puerto Rico Porto Rico	1 296	1 266	1 303	1 356	1 398	1 508	1 586	1 646	1 757	...
Qatar Qatar	367	354	400	470	475	486	584	857	959	1 029
Republic of Moldova République de Moldova	1 809	705	110 [14]	39 [14]	49 [14]	40 [14]	122 [14]	74 [14]	50 [14]	222 [14]
Réunion Réunion	350	344	325	321	313	229	200	342	263	258
Romania Roumanie	6 692	6 271	6 158	5 998	6 842	6 956	6 553	7 300	6 252	8 411
Russian Federation Fédération de Russie	77 463	61 699	49 903	37 220	36 466	27 791	26 688	26 018	28 529	32 389
Rwanda Rwanda	60	60	60	10	36	42	61	60	66	70 [2]
Saudi Arabia Arabie saoudite	12 106 [9]	15 301 [9]	16 584	17 013	15 772	16 391	15 448	15 776	16 381	15 000 [2]
Senegal Sénégal	503	602	591	697	694	810	854	847	1 030	1 000 [2]
Serbia and Montenegro Serbie-et-Monténégro	2 411	2 036	1 088	1 612	1 696	2 212	2 011	2 253	1 575	2 117
Singapore Singapour	2 199	* 1 900 [2]	* 2 980 [2]	* 3 100 [2]	*3 200 [2]	* 3 300 [2]	* 3 300 [2]	* 3 300 [2]	* 3 250 [2]	* 3 250 [2]
Slovakia Slovaquie	2 680	3 374	2 656	2 879	2 981	4 234	5 856	3 066	3 084	3 045
Slovenia Slovénie	1 801	1 568	1 291	1 667	1 807	1 064	1 113	1 149	1 222	1 252
South Africa Afrique du Sud	6 147	5 850	6 135	7 068	7 437	7 664	7 891	7 676	8 211	8 715
Spain Espagne	27 576	24 612	21 658	25 884	27 220	26 339	27 860	27 943 [2]	30 800 [2]	30 000 [2]
Sri Lanka Sri Lanka	620	553	466	* 925 [2]	956	670	966	2 151	2 354	2 432
Sudan [2] Soudan [2]	* 170	* 250	* 250	* 160	391	* 380	291	* 206	* 267	* 300
Suriname Suriname	24	11	17	18	*60 [2]	* 60 [2]	* 65 [2]	* 65 [2]	* 65 [2]	65 [2]
Sweden Suède	4 493	2 289	2 152	2 138	2 550	2 503	2 272	2 372	2 293	2 613
Switzerland Suisse	4 716	4 260	* 4 000 [2]	* 4 370 [2]	4 024 [2]	3 638 [2]	3 568 [2]	* 3 600 [2]	* 3 600 [2]	3 600 [2]
Syrian Arab Republic Rép. arabe syrienne	3 078	3 515	3 906	4 344	4 804	4 817	4 838	5 016	5 134	4 631

49

Cement
Production: thousand metric tons *[cont.]*

Ciment
Production: milliers de tonnes *[suite]*

Country or area Pays ou zone	1991	1992	1993	1994	1995	1996	1997	1998	1999	2000
Tajikistan Tadjikistan	1 013	447	262	178	78	49	36	18	33	55
Thailand Thaïlande	19 164	21 711	26 300	29 929	34 051	38 749	37 136	22 722	25 354	25 499
TFYR of Macedonia L'ex-R.y. Macédoine	606	516	499	486	523	490	610	461	563	801
Togo [2] Togo [2]	388	350	* 350	* 286	350	413	421	565	* 560	* 560
Trinidad and Tobago Trinité-et-Tobago	486	482	527	583	559	617	677	700	740	743
Tunisia Tunisie	4 195	4 184	4 508	4 605	4 998	4 566	4 378	4 588	4 864	5 647
Turkey Turquie	26 029	28 455	31 134	29 356	33 153	35 214	36 035	38 175	34 258	35 825
Turkmenistan Turkménistan	904	1 050	1 118	690	437	438	601	750	780	420
Uganda Ouganda	27	38	52	45	84	195	290	321	347	320 [2]
Ukraine Ukraine	21 745	20 121	15 012	11 435	7 627	5 021	5 101	5 591	5 828	5 311
United Arab Emirates Emirats arabes unis	3 710 [9]	4 328 [9]	4 734 [9]	4 968 [9]	5 071 [9]	* 6 000 [2]	* 5 250 [2]	* 6 000 [2]	* 6 000 [2]	* 6 000 [2]
United Kingdom Royaume-Uni	12 297	11 006	11 039	12 307	11 805	12 214	12 638 [2]	12 409 [2]	12 697 [2]	12 800 [2]
United Rep. of Tanzania Rép.-Unie de Tanzanie	1 022	677	749	686	739	726	621	178 [2]	833 [2]	833 [2]
United States Etats-Unis	67 193	69 585	73 807	77 948	76 906	79 266	82 582	83 931	85 952	87 846
Uruguay Uruguay	458	552	610	701	593	631	818	940	839	688
Uzbekistan Ouzbékistan	6 191	5 934	5 277	4 780	3 419	3 277	3 286	3 400 [2]	3 300 [2]	3 400 [2]
Venezuela Venezuela	6 336	6 585	6 876	4 562	*6 900	7 556 [2]	8 145 [2]	8 202 [2]	8 500 [2]	8 600 [2]
Viet Nam Viet Nam	3 127	3 926	* 4 200 [2]	* 4 700 [2]	5 828	6 585	8 019	9 738	*10 381	13 298
Yemen Yémen	718	820	1 000	898	1 100	1 028	1 038	1 195	1 454	1 406
Zambia Zambie	376	347 [2]	* 350 [2]	280 [2]	312 [2]	348 [2]	384 [2]	351 [2]	300 [2]	380 [2]
Zimbabwe Zimbabwe	949	829	816	624	948	996	954	1 000 [2]	1 000 [2]	1 000 [2]

Source:
United Nations Statistics Division, New York, "Industrial Commodity Statistics Yearbook 2000" and the industrial statistics database.

Source:
Organisation des Nations Unies, Division de statistique, New York, "Annuaire de statistiques industrielles par produit 2000" et la base de données pour les statistiques industrielles.

1 Twelve months beginning 21 March of the year stated.

2 Source: U.S. Geological Survey (Washington, D. C).

3 Twelve months ending 30 June of the year stated.

1 Période de douze mois commençant le 21 mars de l'année indiquée.

2 Source : U.S. Geological Survey (Washington, D. C.).

3 Période de douze mois finissant le 30 juin de l'année indiquée.

49

Cement
Production: thousand metric tons *[cont.]*

Ciment
Production: milliers de tonnes *[suite]*

4 Beginning 1997, data are confidential.	4 A partir 1997, les données sont confidentielles.
5 Source: United Nations Economic Commission for Latin America and the Caribbean (ECLAC), (Santiago).	5 Source: Commission économique des Nations Unies pour l'Amérique Latine et des Caraïbes (CEPAL), (Santiago).
6 Sales.	6 Ventes.
7 Twelve months ending 7 July of the year stated.	7 Période de douze mois finissant le 7 juillet de l'année indiquée.
8 Production by establishments employing 50 or more persons.	8 Production des établissements occupant 50 personnes ou plus.
9 Source: Arab Gulf Cooperation Council (GCC).	9 Source: "Arab Gulf Cooperation Council", (GCC).
10 Government production only.	10 Production de l'Etat seulement.
11 Twelve months beginning 16 July of the year stated.	11 Période de douze mois commençant le 16 juillet de l'année indiquée.
12 Production by establishments employing 20 or more persons.	12 Production des établissements occupant 20 personnes ou plus.
13 Source: Bulletin of Industrial Statistics for the Arab Countries.	13 Source: 'Bulletin of Industrial Statistics for the Arab Countries'.
14 Excluding the Transnistria region.	14 Non compris la région de Transnistria.

50
Sulphuric acid
Production: thousand metric tons
Acide sulfurique
Production: milliers de tonnes

Country or area Pays ou zone	1991	1992	1993	1994	1995	1996	1997	1998	1999	2000
Albania Albanie	21	11	6	4	...	0	0	0	0	0
Algeria Algérie	46	52	55	40	45	42	55	45	48	36
Argentina Argentine	243	219	206	204	226	220	...	...	...	...
Australia [1] Australie [1]	986	816	868	833	...	...	...	...	...	...
Azerbaijan Azerbaïdjan	552	269	141	56	24	31	53	24	26	52
Bangladesh [1] Bangladesh [1]	7	4	7	6	5	9	4	4	4	5
Belarus Bélarus	998	616	399	291	437	549	698	640	614	584
Belgium Belgique	1 936 [2]	1 906 [2]	1 593 [2]	717 [3]	673 [3]	678 [3]	668 [3]	596 [3]	709 [3]	...
Bolivia Bolivie	1	0	1	3	*1	...	...	...	...	...
Brazil Brésil	3 634	3 257	3 724	4 112	4 043	4 308	4 638	4 624	4 882	...
Bulgaria Bulgarie	356	404	409	428	454	525	556	499	456	641
Canada Canada	3 676	3 776	3 713	4 059	3 844	4 278	* 4 100	4 333	4 194	3 804
Chile Chili	804	887	920	1 174	1 427	1 518	1 864	1 983	2 436	2 363
China Chine	13 329	14 087	13 365	15 365	18 110	18 836	20 369	21 710	23 560	24 270
Colombia Colombie	...	91	77	103	86	...	95	93	92	...
Croatia Croatie	187	278	178	206	233	223	202	164	193	200
Cyprus Chypre	0	...	...	...	...	...	...	...	...	...
Czech Republic République tchèque	588	522	383	337	340	345	333	327	318	274
Denmark Danemark	37 [4,5]	38 [4,5]	...	5 [4]	25 [4]	19 [4]	2 [4]	...	0 [6]	...
Egypt Egypte	101	111	122	112	133	299	84	82	83	75
Estonia Estonie	460	46	...	0	...	...	...	...	...	...
Finland Finlande	1 015	1 087	1 179	1 084	1 159	1 288	2 182	2 496	2 857	1 211
France France	3 627	2 871	2 357	2 227	2 382 [6]	2 263 [6]	2 250 [6]	2 214 [6]	2 177 [6]	...
Germany Allemagne	3 064	...	...	2 781 [6]	1 387	1 225	1 370	1 601	...	...
Greece Grèce	841	617	550	623	753	1 544	1 655	814	911	966

50

Sulphuric acid
Production: thousand metric tons *[cont.]*

Acide sulfurique
Production: milliers de tonnes *[suite]*

Country or area Pays ou zone	1991	1992	1993	1994	1995	1996	1997	1998	1999	2000
Hungary [7] Hongrie [7]	141	99	77	80	114	94	89	62	53	80
India Inde	3 904	4 183	3 730	3 745	4 402	4 988	4 830	5 366	5 686	5 540
Indonesia Indonésie	52	52	42	35	35	...	224	314	981	...
Italy Italie	1 853	1 733	1 430	1 975	2 161	2 214	2 214	2 013	1 017	1 048
Japan Japon	7 057	7 100	6 937	6 594	6 888	6 851	6 828	6 739	6 943	7 059
Kazakhstan Kazakhstan	2 815	2 349	1 179	681	695	653	635	605	685	635
Lithuania Lituanie	368	141	129	212	344	425	504	619	800	807
Mexico Mexique	362	195	178	375	...	...	...	...	...	...
Netherlands Pays-Bas	...	...	...	...	500 [6]	418 [6]	356 [6]	429 [6]	465 [4,8]	...
Norway Norvège	...	615	...	...	...	...	...	...	...	...
Pakistan [1] Pakistan [1]	93	98	100	102	80	69	31	28	27	58
Peru Pérou	207	143	229	215	216	429	411	541	592	594
Poland Pologne	1 088	1 244	1 145	1 452	1 861	1 761	1 741	1 707	1 505	...
Portugal Portugal	51	...	...	2 [6]	3 [6]	10 [6]	11 [6]	15 [6]	16 [6]	...
Romania Roumanie	745	572	527	491	477	422	329	229	234	181
Russian Federation Fédération de Russie	11 597	9 704	8 243	6 334	6 946	5 764	6 247	5 840	7 148	8 258
Serbia and Montenegro Serbie-et-Monténégro	582	302	80	24	87	231	177	211	30	98
Slovakia Slovaquie	94	...	...	...	...	62 [6]	73	68	16	15
Slovenia Slovénie	86	121	114	123	116	103	109	128	126	133
Spain Espagne	1 628	1 724	1 199	1 375	2 847	2 265	2 817	3 896 [6]	3 334 [6]	...
Sweden Suède	928	...	...	487	507	572 [6]	566	383	415	356
Syrian Arab Republic Rép. arabe syrienne	8	10	10	...	...	...	...	...	...	...
Thailand [9] Thaïlande [9]	82	...	...	...	...	...	...	...	...	...
TFYR of Macedonia L'ex-R.y. Macédoine	102	95	89	72	82	99	105	101	88	109
Tunisia Tunisie	3 421	3 644	3 547	4 161	4 239	4 423	4 256	4 657	4 858	...

50

Sulphuric acid
Production: thousand metric tons *[cont.]*

Acide sulfurique
Production: milliers de tonnes *[suite]*

Country or area Pays ou zone	1991	1992	1993	1994	1995	1996	1997	1998	1999	2000
Turkey Turquie	532	642	757	730	765	798 [6]	947	913	828	678
Turkmenistan Turkménistan	788	353	206	70	76	120	31	47	104	93
Ukraine Ukraine	4 186	3 000	1 843	1 646	1 593	1 577	1 438	1 354	1 393	1 036
United Kingdom Royaume-Uni	1 852	1 568	1 268	1 266	1 293	643 [6]	698	716	908	581
United States [10] Etats-Unis [10]	12 842	12 340	11 900	11 300	11 500	10 900	10 700	10 600	10 400	9 620
Uzbekistan Ouzbékistan	2 393	1 476	1 361	805	1 016	984	870	...	...	...
Venezuela Venezuela	277	253	...	...	...	...	...	...	...	...
Viet Nam Viet Nam	9	7	...	...	10	18	15	23	* 24	35

Source:
United Nations Statistics Division, New York, "Industrial Commodity Statistics Yearbook 2000" and the industrial statistics database.

Source:
Organisation des Nations Unies, Division de statistique, New York, "Annuaire de statistiques industrielles par produit 2000" et la base de données pour les statistiques industrielles.

1 Twelve months ending 30 June of the year stated.
2 Production by establishments employing 5 or more persons.
3 Incomplete coverage.
4 Sales.
5 Excluding quantities consumed by superphosphate industry.

6 Source: United Nations Economic Commission for Europe (ECE), (Geneva).
7 Including regenerated sulphuric acid.
8 Production by establishments employing 20 or more persons.
9 Strength of acid not known.
10 Sold or used by producers.

1 Période de douze mois finissant le 30 juin de l'année indiquée.
2 Production des établissements occupant 5 personnes ou plus.
3 Couverture incomplète.
4 Ventes.
5 Non compris les quantités utilisées par l'industrie des superphosphates.
6 Source: Commission économique des Nations Unies pour l'Europe (CEE), (Genève).
7 Y compris l'acide sulfurique régénéré.
8 Production des établissements occupant 20 personnes ou plus.
9 Titre de l'acide inconnu.
10 Vendu ou utilisé par les producteurs.

51

Pig iron and crude steel
Production: thousand metric tons

Fonte et acier brut
Production : milliers de tonnes

Country or area Pays ou zone	1991	1992	1993	1994	1995	1996	1997	1998	1999	2000
Albania Albanie										
Pig-iron [*1,2] Fonte [*1,2]	50	10	10	10	10	10	10	10	10	10
Crude steel Acier brut	16	0	15	19	22	22	22	22	16	65
Algeria Algérie										
Pig-iron Fonte	893	944	925	919	962	850	526	757	807	767
Crude steel Acier brut	797	768	798	772	780	590	361	581	675	689
Angola [*1,3] Angola [*1,3]										
Crude steel Acier brut	10	10	9	9	9	9	9	9	9	9
Argentina Argentine										
Pig-iron Fonte	1 366	971	980	1 392	1 524	1 966[1]	2 080[1]	* 2 122[1]	* 1 985[1]	* 2 188[1]
Crude steel Acier brut	2 972	2 680	2 870	3 274	3 575	4 069	4 157	4 210	3 797	4 472
Australia Australie										
Pig-iron[4] Fonte[4]	5 600	6 394	7 209	7 449	7 449	7 554	7 545	7 928	7 513	6 489
Crude steel Acier brut	7 141[4]	5 205	7 628[4]	7 807[4]	8 052[4]	7 944[4]	8 088[4]	8 356[4]	7 678[4]	6 742[4]
Austria Autriche										
Pig-iron Fonte	3 439	3 074[5]	3 070[5]	3 320[5]	3 878[5]	3 416[1]	3 965[1]	4 022[1]	3 913[1,2]	4 318[1,2]
Crude steel Acier brut	4 186	3 953	4 149[5]	4 398[5]	* 4 990	* 4 442	* 5 181	* 5 283	1 406[3]	1 417[3]
Azerbaijan Azerbaïdjan										
Crude steel Acier brut	1 127	809	461	77	39	3	25	8	0	0[6]
Bangladesh[3] Bangladesh[3]										
Crude steel Acier brut	58[1,4]	36[1,4]	32[1,4]	34[1,4]	36[1,4]	27[4]	23[4]	35[1]	36[1]	* 35[1]
Belarus Bélarus										
Crude steel Acier brut	1 123	1 105[5]	946[5]	880	744	886	1 220	1 411	1 449	1 623
Belgium Belgique										
Pig-iron[2] Fonte[2]	9 353	8 524	8 179	8 976	9 204	8 628	8 076	8 616	8 436	8 472[1]
Crude steel Acier brut	11 419	10 386	10 237	11 268	11 544	10 752	10 716	11 400	10 908	...
Bosnia and Herzegovina Bosnie-Herzégovine										
Pig-iron [*1,2] Fonte [*1,2]	...	150	100	100	100	100	100	100	100	100
Crude steel[3,5] Acier brut[3,5]	...	...	...	...	...	52	72	75	60	...
Brazil Brésil										
Pig-iron Fonte	22 695	23 057	23 900	25 092	25 021	23 978	25 013	25 111	24 549	27 723
Crude steel Acier brut	22 617	23 934	25 207	25 747	25 093	25 237	26 153	25 760	24 996	27 865
Bulgaria Bulgarie										
Pig-iron Fonte	961	849	1 014	1 470	1 607	1 504	1 643	1 389[1]	1 130[1]	1 220[1]
Crude steel Acier brut	1 615	1 551	1 941	2 491	2 724	2 457	2 628	2 216[1]	1 846[1]	* 1 900[1]
Canada Canada										
Pig-iron Fonte	8 268	8 621	8 628	8 112	8 460	8 638[1]	8 679[1]	8 937[1]	8 783[1]	8 780[1]

51

Pig iron and crude steel
Production: thousand metric tons *[cont.]*

Fonte et acier brut
Production : milliers de tonnes *[suite]*

Country or area Pays ou zone	1991	1992	1993	1994	1995	1996	1997	1998	1999	2000
Crude steel Acier brut	13 079	14 027	14 369[1]	13 897[1]	14 415[1]	14 735[1]	15 554[1]	15 930[1]	16 300[1]	16 500[1]
Chile Chili										
Pig-iron[2] Fonte[2]	700	873[1]	917[1]	886[1]	855[1]	* 996[1]	* 941[1]	* 993[1]	* 1 033[1]	* 1 026[1]
Crude steel[3] Acier brut[3]	804	1 008	1 020	996	948	1 178[1]	1 167[1]	1 171[1]	1 291[1]	1 352[1]
China Chine										
Pig-iron Fonte	67 000	75 890	87 389[2]	97 410[2]	105 293[2]	107 225[2]	115 114[2]	118 629[2]	125 392[2]	131 015[2]
Crude steel Acier brut	73 881	84 252	89 556	92 617	95 360	100 056	108 942	115 590	124 260[3]	128 500[3]
China, Hong Kong SAR *[1,6] Chine, Hong Kong RAS *[1,6]										
Crude steel Acier brut	350	350	350	350	350	350	350	350	450	500
Colombia Colombie										
Pig-iron Fonte	300	308[1]	238[1]	245[1]	282[1]	286[1]	324[1]	* 256[1]	* 264[1]	* 285[1]
Crude steel Acier brut	700	657	715	702	714[1]	695[1]	734[1]	636[1]	* 534[1]	* 660[1]
Croatia Croatie										
Pig-iron Fonte	69	* 40[1]	* 40[1]	* 40[1]	* 0[1]	* 0[1]	* 0[1]	...	...	...
Crude steel Acier brut	214[3]	102[3]	74[3,5]	63[3]	46	47	70	101	76	69
Cuba[3] Cuba[3]										
Crude steel Acier brut	270	134[1]	91[1]	131[1]	207[1]	229	335	283	303	327
Czech Republic République tchèque										
Pig-iron Fonte	5 090	5 010	4 656	5 274	5 545	4 898	5 276	5 165	4 137	4 603
Crude steel Acier brut	...	7 349	6 732	7 075	7 003	6 519	6 593	6 059	5 453	# 2 613[3]
Denmark[3,7] Danemark[3,7]										
Crude steel Acier brut	...	...	...	2	6	4	3	3	10	...
Dominican Republic[1] Rép. dominicaine[1]										
Crude steel Acier brut	39	33	0	0	0	42	82	36	43	* 36
Ecuador[3] Equateur[3]										
Crude steel Acier brut	20	20[1]	27[1]	32[1]	35[1]	* 20[1]	44[1]	46[1]	53[1]	* 65[1]
Egypt[1] Egypte[1]										
Pig-iron Fonte	1 250	1 062	1 326	1 148	1 062	1 050	1 000	1 334	700	700
Crude steel Acier brut	2 541	2 524	2 772	2 622	2 642	2 618	2 717	* 2 870	* 2 619	* 2 820
El Salvador[1] El Salvador[1]										
Crude steel Acier brut	* 19	* 28	* 37	* 40	28	41	45	43	34	41
Finland Finlande										
Pig-iron[2] Fonte[2]	2 332	2 452	2 595	2 597	2 242	2 457	2 784	2 916	2 954[1]	2 983[1]
Crude steel Acier brut	2 890	3 077	3 257	3 420	3 176	3 301	3 734	3 952[5]	3 956[5]	...
France France										
Pig-iron Fonte	13 416	13 057	12 396	13 008	12 860	12 108	13 424	13 602	13 852	13 621[1,2]
Crude steel Acier brut	18 708	18 190	17 313	18 242	18 100	17 633	19 767	20 126	20 200	...

51

Pig iron and crude steel
Production: thousand metric tons *[cont.]*

Fonte et acier brut
Production : milliers de tonnes *[suite]*

Country or area Pays ou zone	1991	1992	1993	1994	1995	1996	1997	1998	1999	2000
Georgia Géorgie										
Pig-iron Fonte	501[2,5]	242[2]	12	1	4	4	4	1	1[8]	...
Crude steel Acier brut	...	532[3]	224	122	175	165	205	112	14	...
Germany Allemagne										
Pig-iron[5] Fonte[5]	30 608	28 202	26 705	29 632	29 599	27 340	30 462	29 705	27 934	...
Crude steel Acier brut	41 997	39 962	37 705	40 963	42 051[5]	39 792[5]	10 591	10 218	42 062[5]	...
Greece Grèce										
Pig-iron[1] Fonte[1]	160	...	...	...	...	...	...	...	...	...
Crude steel Acier brut	980	924	980	852	936	852	1 020	1 104	960	...
Hungary Hongrie										
Pig-iron Fonte	1 314	1 179	1 407	1 595[5]	1 515[5]	1 496[1]	1 141[1]	1 258[1]	1 309[1]	1 340[1,2]
Crude steel Acier brut	1 860	1 560	1 752	1 932	1 860	1 878[5]	1 690[5]	1 940	1 920	1 970[3]
India Inde										
Pig-iron[1] Fonte[1]	14 176	15 126	17 913	20 593	21 499	23 168	23 325	23 170	23 340	24 426
Crude steel Acier brut	17 577	18 723	13 351	13 356	13 378	13 439	13 416	23 899[1]	24 704[1]	* 27 322[1]
Indonesia[1] Indonésie[1]										
Crude steel Acier brut	3 250	3 171	1 948	3 220	3 500	4 100	3 800	* 2 700	* 2 890	* 3 010
Iran (Islamic Rep. of)[1] Iran (Rép. islamique d')[1]										
Pig-iron Fonte	1 952[2]	2 053[2]	1 961[2]	1 883[2]	1 532[2]	1 867[2]	2 053	* 2 087	* 2 147	* 2 202
Crude steel Acier brut	2 200	2 940	3 672	4 498	4 696	5 415	6 322	5 608	6 070	6 600
Iraq *[1,3] Iraq *[1,3]										
Crude steel Acier brut	20	100	300	300	300	300	200	200	200	200
Ireland Irlande										
Crude steel Acier brut	293	257	326	288	312	336	336	355	337	...
Israel *[1] Israël *[1]										
Crude steel Acier brut	90	109	120	180	200	246	268	244	280	285
Italy Italie										
Pig-iron Fonte	10 561	10 432	11 188	11 161	11 677	10 321	11 477	10 791	10 829	11 195
Crude steel Acier brut	25 270	24 924	25 967	26 212	27 907	24 391	25 870	25 782	24 780	26 760
Japan Japon										
Pig-iron Fonte	79 985	73 144	73 738	73 776	74 905	74 597	78 520	74 981	74 520	81 071
Crude steel Acier brut	109 648	98 132	99 632	98 295	101 640	98 801	104 545	93 548	94 192	105 869
Kazakhstan Kazakhstan										
Pig-iron[8] Fonte[8]	4 953	4 666	3 552	2 435	2 530	2 536	3 089	2 594	3 438	4 010
Crude steel Acier brut	6 377	6 063	4 557	2 968	3 026	3 216	3 880	3 116	4 105[3]	4 799[6]
Korea, Dem. P. R. *[1] Corée, R. p. dém. de *[1]										
Pig-iron Fonte	...	...	...	...	500	500	500	250	250	250

51

Pig iron and crude steel
Production: thousand metric tons *[cont.]*

Fonte et acier brut
Production : milliers de tonnes *[suite]*

Country or area Pays ou zone	1991	1992	1993	1994	1995	1996	1997	1998	1999	2000
Crude steel										
Acier brut	8 000	8 100	8 100	8 100	1 500	1 500	1 000	1 000	1 000	1 000
Korea, Republic of Corée, République de										
Pig-iron										
Fonte	18 883	19 581	22 193	21 169	22 344	23 010	22 712	23 093	23 328	24 828
Crude steel										
Acier brut	26 126	28 177	33 141	33 887	37 639	39 643[3]	43 405[3]	40 299[3]	41 502[3]	43 392[3]
Latvia Lettonie										
Crude steel										
Acier brut	374	246	300	332	280	293	465	471	484[5]	...
Libyan Arab Jamah.[1] Jamah. arabe libyenne[1]										
Crude steel										
Acier brut	718	789	920	874	909	* 863	897	874	925	1 055
Lithuania[6] Lituanie[6]										
Crude steel										
Acier brut	4	3	2	1	1	0	1	1	1	0
Luxembourg Luxembourg										
Pig-iron[2]										
Fonte[2]	2 463	2 255	2 412	1 927	1 028	829	438	0	0	0
Crude steel[3]										
Acier brut[3]	3 379	3 068	3 293	3 073	2 613	2 501	2 580	2 477	2 600	2 571
Malaysia[1] Malaisie[1]										
Crude steel										
Acier brut	1 130	1 559	1 808	2 046	2 450	3 216	2 962	1 921	2 200	2 430
Mexico Mexique										
Pig-iron										
Fonte	2 313	2 220	2 515	3 359	3 660	4 404	4 464	4 532	4 808[1]	4 856[1]
Crude steel										
Acier brut	7 462	7 848	8 188	8 690	9 948	9 852	10 560	10 812[3]	...	...
Morocco[1] Maroc[1]										
Pig-iron[2]										
Fonte[2]	15	15	15	* 15	* 15	* 15	* 15	* 15	* 15	* 15
Crude steel										
Acier brut	* 7	* 7	* 7	* 7	* 7	* 5	5	* 5	* 5	* 5
Myanmar[1] Myanmar[1]										
Pig-iron[2]										
Fonte[2]	1	1	1	1	1	1	0	2	2	* 2
Crude steel										
Acier brut	25	10	11	17	20	40	0	* 24	* 24	* 24
Netherlands Pays-Bas										
Pig-iron[2]										
Fonte[2]	4 697	4 849	5 405	5 443[7,9]	5 530[7,9]	5 544[7,9]	5 805[7,9]	5 562[7,9]	5 320[1]	4 969[1]
Crude steel										
Acier brut	5 171	5 439	6 000	6 172	6 409	6 326	6 641	6 377[3]	6 075[3]	...
New Zealand[1] Nouvelle-Zélande[1]										
Pig-iron[2]										
Fonte[2]	594	625	653	563	631	619	534	609	620	* 600
Crude steel[3]										
Acier brut[3]	806	759	853	766	842	680	680	* 756	* 744	* 765
Nigeria[3] Nigéria[3]										
Crude steel										
Acier brut	200	* 200[1]	* 150[1]	* 58[1]	* 36[1]	* 0[1]	* 0[1]	* 2[1]	* 0[1]	* 0[1]
Norway Norvège										
Pig-iron[1,2]										
Fonte[1,2]	61	70	73	* 70	* 70	* 70	* 70	* 70	* 60	* 60
Crude steel[5]										
Acier brut[5]	438	446	505	456	503	511	564	639	595	...
Pakistan[1] Pakistan[1]										
Pig-iron *[2]										
Fonte *[2]	1 100	1 100	1 200	1 045	1 100	1 500	1 400	1 500	1 500	1 500

51

Pig iron and crude steel
Production: thousand metric tons *[cont.]*

Fonte et acier brut
Production : milliers de tonnes *[suite]*

Country or area Pays ou zone	1991	1992	1993	1994	1995	1996	1997	1998	1999	2000
Crude steel Acier brut	* 1 000	* 1 000	* 1 100	344	409	416	479	494	* 500	* 500
Paraguay[1] Paraguay[1]										
Pig-iron[2] Fonte[2]	68	92	81	90	103	104	79	66	61	82
Crude steel Acier brut	61	86	77	87	95	96	66	56	56	* 77
Peru Pérou										
Pig-iron[1] Fonte[1]	207	147	147	* 150	* 247	* 273	* 264	* 283	* 237	* 327
Crude steel Acier brut	404	343	417	506[1]	* 512[1]	* 678[1]	* 607[1]	* 631[1]	* 559[1]	* 749[1]
Philippines[1] Philippines[1]										
Crude steel Acier brut	605	497	623	473	* 923	* 920	* 950	* 880	* 530	* 530
Poland Pologne										
Pig-iron Fonte	6 297	6 315	6 105	6 866	7 373	6 540	7 295	6 129	5 233	...
Crude steel Acier brut	10 440	9 864	9 936	11 112	11 892	10 668[5]	11 592	9 916[5]	8 759[5]	...
Portugal Portugal										
Pig-iron Fonte	252	408	396	420	408[2]	420[2]	431[1,2]	365[1,2]	* 389[1,2]	* 382[1,2]
Crude steel Acier brut	576	768	780	744	828	840[5]	879[5]	907[5]	1 013[5]	...
Qatar[1] Qatar[1]										
Crude steel Acier brut	561	588	620	572	614	626	616	646	629	* 729
Republic of Moldova[6] République de Moldova[6]										
Crude steel Acier brut	623	653	# 1[10]	1[10]	0[10]	0[10]	0[10]	0[10]	0[10]	0[10]
Romania Roumanie										
Pig-iron Fonte	4 525	3 110	3 190	3 496	4 203	4 025	4 557	4 541	2 969	3 066
Crude steel Acier brut	7 509	5 614	5 629	5 943	6 697	6 216	6 790	6 405	4 431	4 742
Russian Federation Fédération de Russie										
Pig-iron Fonte	48 628	45 990	40 744	36 480	39 676	37 079	37 277	34 582	40 695	44 492
Crude steel Acier brut	77 100	67 028	58 346	48 812	51 590	49 253	48 502	43 673	51 517	59 150
Saudi Arabia[1,3] Arabie saoudite[1,3]										
Crude steel Acier brut	1 785	1 825	2 318	2 411	2 451	2 683	2 539	2 356	* 2 610	* 2 973
Serbia and Montenegro Serbie-et-Monténégro										
Pig-iron[2] Fonte[2]	526	512	62	17	109	565	907	792	128	560
Crude steel Acier brut	164	96	51	44	28	45	46	45	29	26
Singapore *[1] Singapour *[1]										
Crude steel Acier brut	490	500	500	500	500	500	500	500	500	500
Slovakia Slovaquie										
Pig-iron[2] Fonte[2]	3 163	2 952[5]	3 205	3 330	3 207	2 928	3 072[5]	2 756[5]	2 897[5]	3 166
Crude steel[3] Acier brut[3]	4 107	4 498	3 922	3 974	3 958	253	255	36	16	17
Slovenia Slovénie										
Crude steel Acier brut	289	401	357	424	408	94	99	98	79	95

51

Pig iron and crude steel
Production: thousand metric tons *[cont.]*

Fonte et acier brut
Production : milliers de tonnes *[suite]*

Country or area Pays ou zone	1991	1992	1993	1994	1995	1996	1997	1998	1999	2000
South Africa Afrique du Sud										
Pig-iron[1]										
Fonte[1]	6 968	7 352	6 940	6 982	7 137	6 876	6 192	* 5 650	* 4 587	* 4 573
Crude steel										
Acier brut	9 358	8 970[1]	8 726[1]	8 525[1]	8 741[1]	7 999[1]	8 311[1]	7 506[1]	6 830[1]	7 019[1]
Spain Espagne										
Pig-iron										
Fonte	5 397[5]	4 764[5]	5 394[5]	5 447[5]	5 106[5]	4 128[1]	3 926[1]	4 278[1]	4 146[1,2]	4 059[1,2]
Crude steel										
Acier brut	12 846	12 600	12 960	13 440	13 932	12 166[5]	13 677[5]	14 819[5]	14 875[5]	...
Sri Lanka *[1] Sri Lanka *[1]										
Crude steel										
Acier brut	30	30	30	30	30	30	30	30	30	30
Sweden Suède										
Pig-iron										
Fonte	2 851	2 883	2 844	3 036	3 020	1 223	1 317	1 272	1 281	1 411
Crude steel										
Acier brut	4 248	4 356	4 596	4 956	4 920	4 908	5 148	5 172	5 066[5]	...
Switzerland Suisse										
Pig-iron										
Fonte	105	102	82	88	97	100[1]	* 100[1]	* 100[1]	* 100[1]	100[1]
Crude steel[3]										
Acier brut[3]	955[5]	1 238[5]	1 254[5]	1 100[5]	850[5]	750[5]	1 047[1]	1 018[1]	1 037[1]	* 1 140[1]
Syrian Arab Republic *[1] Rép. arabe syrienne *[1]										
Crude steel										
Acier brut	63	70	70	70	70	70	70	70	70	70
Thailand[3] Thaïlande[3]										
Crude steel										
Acier brut	711[1]	779[1]	972[1]	1 391[1]	2 134[1]	2 143[1]	2 101	1 619	1 474	1 648
TFYR of Macedonia L'ex-R.y. Macédoine										
Pig-iron[2]										
Fonte[2]	...	13	20	20	* 20[1]	* 20[1]	* 0[1]	* 0[1]	* 0[1]	* 0[1]
Crude steel[3]										
Acier brut[3]	209	162	133	67	31	21	27	45	47	...
Trinidad and Tobago[1] Trinité-et-Tobago[1]										
Crude steel										
Acier brut	440	553	496	631	738	695	736	777	* 729	* 741
Tunisia Tunisie										
Pig-iron[8]										
Fonte[8]	162	147	154	145	152	145	152	123	180	195
Crude steel[6]										
Acier brut[6]	193	182	182	183	201	186	195	171	231	237
Turkey Turquie										
Pig-iron										
Fonte	332	286	296	326	246[8]	363[8]	337[8]	171[8]	192[8]	250[8]
Crude steel										
Acier brut	12 323	15 387	15 198	15 861	14 438	17 189	17 795	17 002	16 821	17 051
Uganda[1] Ouganda[1]										
Crude steel										
Acier brut	20	30	20	10	12	12	15	15	15	7
Ukraine Ukraine										
Pig-iron										
Fonte	36 435	36 948	28 160	20 837	18 314	18 110	21 060	21 239	23 315	26 052
Crude steel										
Acier brut	46 767	43 285	33 709	24 635	22 761	22 718	25 972	24 789	27 713	32 264
United Arab Emirates[3,11] Emirats arabes unis[3,11]										
Crude steel										
Acier brut	30	40	40	...	...	...	...	...	...	...

51

Pig iron and crude steel
Production: thousand metric tons *[cont.]*

Fonte et acier brut
Production : milliers de tonnes *[suite]*

Country or area Pays ou zone	1991	1992	1993	1994	1995	1996	1997	1998	1999	2000
United Kingdom Royaume-Uni										
Pig-iron Fonte	11 884	11 542	11 534	11 943	12 236	12 830	13 056	12 746	12 139[2]	10 989[1,2]
Crude steel Acier brut	16 475	16 212	16 625	17 286	17 604	17 992	18 499	17 315	16 284	...
United States Etats-Unis										
Pig-iron Fonte	44 123	47 377	48 200	49 400	50 900	49 400	49 600	48 200	46 300	47 900
Crude steel Acier brut	79 738	84 322	88 800	91 200	95 200	95 500	98 500	98 600	97 400	102 000
Uruguay[1,3] Uruguay[1,3]										
Crude steel Acier brut	41	55	36	36	40	34	39	52	45	38
Uzbekistan[1] Ouzbékistan[1]										
Crude steel Acier brut	...	630	573	364	352	444	365	344	* 343	* 420
Venezuela Venezuela										
Crude steel Acier brut	2 933	2 446	2 568	3 524[1]	3 568[1]	3 956[1]	3 987[1]	3 553[1]	3 261[1]	* 3 835[1]
Viet Nam[3] Viet Nam[3]										
Crude steel Acier brut	149	196	* 270[1]	* 301[1]	* 271[1]	* 311[1]	* 330	* 306[1]	* 308[1]	109
Zimbabwe[1] Zimbabwe[1]										
Pig-iron * Fonte *	535	507	211	100	209	210	216	217	228	240
Crude steel[3] Acier brut[3]	581	547	221	187	210	212	214	212	255	269

Source:
United Nations Statistics Division, New York, "Industrial Commodity Statistics Yearbook 2000" and the industrial statistics database.

Source:
Organisation des Nations Unies, Division de statistique, New York, "Annuaire de statistiques industrielles par produit 2000" et la base de données pour les statistiques industrielles.

1 Source: U.S. Geological Survey (Washington, D. C).
2 Pig-iron for steel making only.
3 Ingots only.
4 Twelve months ending 30 June of the year stated.
5 Source: Annual Bulletin of Steel Statistics for Europe, America and Asia, United Nations Economic Commission of Europe (Geneva).
6 Crude steel for casting only.
7 Sales.
8 Foundry pig-iron only.
9 Production by establishments employing 20 or more persons.
10 Excluding the Transnistria region.
11 Source: Statistical Yearbook of the OIC countries.

1 Source : U.S. Geological Survey (Washington, D. C.).
2 La fonte d'affinage seulement.
3 L'acier brut (lingots) seulement.
4 Période de douze mois finissant le 30 juin de l'année indiquée.
5 Source: Bulletin annuel de statistiques de l'acier pour l'Europe, l'Amérique et l'Asie, Commission économique des Nations Unies pour l'Europe (Genève).
6 L'acier brut pour moulages seulement.
7 Ventes.
8 La fonte de moulage seulement.
9 Production des établissements occupant 20 personnes ou plus.
10 Non compris la région de Transnistria.
11 Source: Annuaire statistique des pays de OCI.

52
Aluminum
Production: thousand metric tons
Aluminium
Production : milliers de tonnes

Country or area Pays ou zone	1991	1992	1993	1994	1995	1996	1997	1998	1999	2000
Argentina Argentine										
Primary										
Neuf	166	153	171	173	183	185	187	187	206	261
Secondary[1]										
Récupéré[1]	18	19	14	14	10	16	13	17	14	23
Australia[2] Australie[2]										
Primary										
Neuf	1 235	1 194	1 306	1 384	1 285	1 331	1 395	1 589	1 686	1 742
Secondary										
Récupéré	30	40[1]	35[1]	55[1]	...	...	...	...	...	...
Austria Autriche										
Primary										
Neuf	89	33	0[1]	0[1]	0[1]	0[1]	0[1]	0[1]	0[1]	0[1]
Secondary										
Récupéré	117[3]	45[1]	43[1]	53[1]	94[1]	98[1]	119[1]	128[1]	143[1]	158[1]
Azerbaijan[4] Azerbaïdjan[4]										
Primary										
Neuf	...	* 25	* 20	* 5	4	1	5	* 0	0	0
Bahrain Bahreïn										
Primary										
Neuf	214	293	448	451	449	456	490[4]	501[4]	502	512
Belgium[1] Belgique[1]										
Secondary										
Récupéré	3	0	0	0	0	0	0	0	0	0
Bosnia and Herzegovina *[4] Bosnie-Herzégovine *[4]										
Primary										
Neuf	...	30	15	10	10	10	15	28	70	90
Brazil[1] Brésil[1]										
Primary										
Neuf	1 139	1 193	1 172	1 185	1 188	1 197	1 189	1 208	1 250	1 271
Secondary										
Récupéré	66	67	77	91	117	146	163	180	186	229
Cameroon Cameroun										
Primary										
Neuf	86[1]	83[1]	87[1]	81[1]	71	82[1]	* 91[1]	82[1]	92[4]	* 95[4]
Canada Canada										
Primary										
Neuf	1 822	1 972[1]	2 309[1]	2 255[1]	2 172[1]	2 283[1]	2 327[1]	2 374[1]	2 390[1]	2 374[1]
Secondary[1]										
Récupéré[1]	68	86	90	97	97	101	106	111	112	112
China Chine										
Primary										
Neuf	900	1 096	1 255	1 498	1 870	1 896	2 180	2 362	2 809	2 989
Colombia Colombie										
Total										
Totale	...	0	1	...	0	...	...	...	...	...
Croatia Croatie										
Primary										
Neuf	54	29	26	26	31	33	35[4]	16	14	14
Czechoslovakia-former Tchécoslovaquie (anc.)										
Primary										
Neuf	49	...	...	...	...	...	...	...	...	...
Secondary										
Récupéré	17	...	...	...	...	...	...	...	...	...
Denmark Danemark										
Secondary										
Récupéré	12[1]	16[5]	21[5]	22[5]	28[5]	27[5]	35[5]	34[5]	34[5]	32[5]
Egypt[6] Egypte[6]										
Primary										
Neuf	141	139	139	149	136	150	119	187[1]	193[4]	193[4]

52

Aluminum
Production: thousand metric tons *[cont.]*

Aluminium
Production : milliers de tonnes *[suite]*

Country or area Pays ou zone	1991	1992	1993	1994	1995	1996	1997	1998	1999	2000
Finland * Finlande *										
Secondary										
Récupéré	4	5	4	4	5	5	...	...	...	...
France France										
Primary										
Neuf	255	414	425	481	364	380	399	424	455	...
Secondary[7]										
Récupéré[7]	217	222	203	227	...	...	...	...	...	...
Germany Allemagne										
Primary										
Neuf	690	603	552	503	576	577	572	612[4]	634	644[4]
Secondary										
Récupéré	50	52	58	56	...	...	...	...	...	...
Ghana Ghana										
Primary										
Neuf	175	180[1]	175[1]	141[1]	135[1]	137[1]	152[1]	56[1]	114[1]	156[1]
Greece Grèce										
Primary										
Neuf	175	174	148	142	132	141	132	146	161	...
Hungary Hongrie										
Primary										
Neuf	63	27	29	31	35	94	98	92	89	...
Iceland Islande										
Primary										
Neuf	89	89	94	99	100	102	123	160	161	167
India Inde										
Primary										
Neuf	504	499	478	479	518	516	539	542[4]	* 550[4]	* 560[4]
Indonesia Indonésie										
Primary										
Neuf	173	213	202	222[1]	228[1]	223[1]	219[1]	133[1]	112[1]	191[1]
Iran (Islamic Rep. of)[1] Iran (Rép. islamique d')[1]										
Primary										
Neuf	70	79	92	116	115	78	91	111	138	140
Secondary										
Récupéré	39	39	15	26	26	26	26	26	26	10
Italy Italie										
Primary										
Neuf	218	161	156	175	178	184	188	187	187	190
Secondary										
Récupéré	348	353	346	376	412	377	443	503	502	568
Japan Japon										
Primary										
Neuf	52	38	39	41	46	46	53	51	...	...
Secondary[7]										
Récupéré[7]	1 096	1 074	1 006	1 175	1 181	1 191	1 277	1 155	1 158	1 214
Korea, Republic of Corée, République de										
Primary										
Neuf	14	...	...	...	...	...	...	...	...	...
Mexico Mexique										
Primary										
Neuf	43	17	25	29	33	69	71	68	70	63
Secondary[4]										
Récupéré[4]	80	62	74	46	59	98	112	118	126	...
Netherlands Pays-Bas										
Primary										
Neuf	254	227	228	230	216	227[4]	232[4]	264[4]	286[4]	300[4]
Secondary										
Récupéré	114	150	139	175	192	150[4]	150[4]	102[4]	105[4]	105[4]

52

Aluminum
Production: thousand metric tons *[cont.]*
Aluminium
Production : milliers de tonnes *[suite]*

Country or area Pays ou zone	1991	1992	1993	1994	1995	1996	1997	1998	1999	2000
New Zealand[1] Nouvelle-Zélande[1]										
Primary										
Neuf	259	243	277	269	273	285	310	318	327	328
Secondary										
Récupéré	5	7	7	8	8	8	8	8	...	...
Norway Norvège										
Primary										
Neuf	858	838	887	857	847	863	919[1]	996[1]	1 020[1]	1 026[1]
Secondary[1]										
Récupéré[1]	31	40	56	49	72	60	59	62	178	255
Poland Pologne										
Primary										
Neuf	46	44	47	50	56	52	54	54	51	...
Portugal Portugal										
Secondary										
Récupéré	8	12	12	12	14[1]	16[1]	16[1]	18[1]	18[1]	18[1]
Romania Roumanie										
Primary										
Neuf	158[7,8]	112[7,8]	112[7,8]	120[7,8]	141[7,8]	141[7,8]	162[7,8]	174[7,8]	174[7,8]	179
Secondary[7]										
Récupéré[7]	9	8	4	3	3	4	2	1[8]	0[8]	2[8]
Russian Federation[4] Fédération de Russie[4]										
Primary										
Neuf	...	2 700	2 820	2 670	2 724	2 874	2 906	3 005	3 146	3 245
Serbia and Montenegro Serbie-et-Monténégro										
Primary										
Neuf	76	67	26	4	17	37	66	61	73	88
Secondary										
Récupéré	0	0	0	0	0	0	1	0	...	...
Slovakia Slovaquie										
Primary										
Neuf	49	...	18	4	25	311	110[1]	115	109[1]	110[1]
Secondary										
Récupéré	17	...	1	...	...	...	...	6	...	...
Slovenia Slovénie										
Primary										
Neuf	90	85	83	77	58	27	9	10	9	9
South Africa[4] Afrique du Sud[4]										
Primary										
Neuf	169	173	175	172	229	570	673	677	679	* 671
Spain[1] Espagne[1]										
Primary										
Neuf	355	359	356	338	362	362	360	360	364	366
Secondary										
Récupéré	96	97	100	104	107	154	173	210	224	240
Suriname Suriname										
Primary										
Neuf	31	32	30	27	28	29	32[4]	29[4]	10[4]	0[4]
Sweden[1] Suède[1]										
Primary										
Neuf	97	77	82	84	95	98	98	96	99	100
Secondary										
Récupéré	17	19	19	22	23	25	25	27	28	30
Switzerland Suisse										
Primary										
Neuf	66	52	36	24	21	27[1]	27[1]	32[1]	34[1]	36[1]
Secondary[1]										
Récupéré[1]	36	11	4	6	5	6	8	15	6	6

52

Aluminum
Production: thousand metric tons *[cont.]*

Aluminium
Production : milliers de tonnes *[suite]*

Country or area Pays ou zone	1991	1992	1993	1994	1995	1996	1997	1998	1999	2000
Tajikistan Tadjikistan										
Primary										
Neuf	...	* 400[4]	252	237	237	198	189	196	229	...
TFYR of Macedonia L'ex-R.y. Macédoine										
Total										
Totale	6	6	6	7	5	5	5	7	6	4
Turkey Turquie										
Primary										
Neuf	56	61	59	60	62	62	62	62	62	62
Ukraine *[4] Ukraine *[4]										
Primary										
Neuf	...	100	100	100	98	90	101	107	112	104
United Kingdom Royaume-Uni										
Primary										
Neuf	294[7]	244[7]	239[7]	231[7]	238[7]	240[7]	248[4]	258[4]	272[4]	305[4]
Secondary										
Récupéré	195	197	236	224	230	261	258[4]	236[4]	275[4]	285[4]
United States Etats-Unis										
Primary										
Neuf	4 121	4 042	3 695	3 299	3 375	3 577	3 603	3 713	3 779	3 668
Secondary										
Récupéré	2 290[7]	2 760[7]	2 940[7]	3 090[7]	3 190[7]	3 310[7]	3 550[7]	3 440[7]	3 690	3 450
Venezuela Venezuela										
Primary										
Neuf	610	508	568	585[1]	627[1]	635[1]	641[1]	584[1]	567[1]	569[1]
Secondary[1]										
Récupéré[1]	10	35	35	32	28	21	27	33	27	24

Source:
United Nations Statistics Division, New York, "Industrial Commodity Statistics Yearbook 2000" and the industrial statistics database.

1 Source: World Metal Statistics, (London).
2 Twelve months ending 30 June of the year stated.
3 Secondary aluminium produced from old scrap only.

4 Source: U.S. Geological Survey (Washington, D. C).
5 Sales.
6 Including aluminium plates, shapes and bars.
7 Including alloys.
8 Including pure content of virgin alloys.

Source:
Organisation des Nations Unies, Division de statistique, New York, "Annuaire de statistiques industrielles par produit 2000" et la base de données pour les statistiques industrielles.

1 Source: "World Metal Statistics," (Londres).
2 Période de douze mois finissant le 30 juin de l'année indiquée.
3 Aluminum de deuxième fusion obtenu à partir de vieux déchets seulement.
4 Source : U.S. Geological Survey (Washington, D. C.).
5 Ventes.
6 Aluminum de deuxième fusion produit de débris de metal.
7 Y compris les alliages.
8 Y compris la teneur pure des alliages de première fusion.

53
Radio and television receivers
Production: thousands
Récepteurs de radio et de télévision
Production : milliers

Country or area Pays ou zone	Radio receivers Récepteurs radio					Television receivers Récepteurs télévision				
	1996	1997	1998	1999	2000	1996	1997	1998	1999	2000
Albania Albanie	0	0	0	0	0	0	0	0	0	0
Algeria Algérie	...	...	...	...	...	250	172	251	173	194
Argentina Argentine	...	...	...	...	...	1 096	1 630	1 592	1 335	1 556
Armenia Arménie	0	0	0	0		...	...	...	...	...
Azerbaijan Azerbaïdjan	0	0	0	0	...	1	1	3	0	0
Bangladesh Bangladesh	11	20	10	13	6	61	93	152	107	127
Belarus Bélarus	138	170	114	195	101	314	454	468	516	532
Brazil Brésil	2 941	4 211	2 753	2 039	1 629	8 644	7 976	5 711	4 328	6 078
Bulgaria Bulgarie	0	...	0	0	0	11	6	3	2	...
China Chine	...	...	...	...	...	35 418	36 372	42 809	49 113	45 012
Colombia Colombie	...	...	...	...	...	...	58	50	19	...
Croatia Croatie	0	...	...	...	...	0	...	...	...	...
Czech Republic République tchèque	...	...	...	...	...	74	180	567	707	1 141
Egypt Egypte	...	...	...	...	...	336	114	43	30	27
Finland Finlande	...	...	...	...	...	191	...	...	...	92
France France	...	3 853	4 586	2 961	...	...	...	...	...	...
Georgia Géorgie	...	...	...	...	...	2	2	1	1	2
Germany Allemagne	3 342	3 632	3 884	...	...	1 965	...	1 269	...	...
Hungary Hongrie	310	528	2 328	2 412	2 320	...	...	...	...	...
India Inde	47	33	2	0	0	1 949	2 370	2 461	2 561	2 399
Indonesia [1] Indonésie [1]	...	4 177	# 80 [2]	4 937	...	...	...	...	...	...
Iran (Islamic Rep. of) Iran (Rép. islamique d')	56 [3]	76 [3]	127 [3]	114	139	453 [3]	751 [3]	769 [3]	...	...
Italy Italie	...	...	...	...	...	2 677	1 920	1 659	1 627	1 350
Japan Japon	2 638	2 434	2 623	2 678	2 384	7 568	7 559	6 567	4 386	3 382
Kazakhstan Kazakhstan	3	3	3	0	0	74	61	103	112	338

53

Radio and television receivers
Production: thousands *[cont.]*

Récepteurs de radio et de télévision
Production : milliers *[suite]*

Country or area Pays ou zone	Radio receivers Récepteurs radio					Television receivers Récepteurs télévision				
	1996	1997	1998	1999	2000	1996	1997	1998	1999	2000
Korea, Republic of Corée, République de	...	...	...	...	...	21 469	16 428	12 763	15 556	16 952
Kyrgyzstan Kirghizistan	...	...	...	...	...	0	0	4	1	3
Latvia Lettonie	10	10	2	2	...	...	...	...	...	...
Lithuania Lituanie	...	...	...	...	...	57	52	84	187	207
Malaysia Malaisie	29 431	33 491	30 265	32 957	36 348	8 901	7 774	8 035	7 611	10 551
Mexico Mexique	...	...	...	...	...	205	...	...	...	0
Pakistan Pakistan	...	...	...	...	...	278	186	107	128	122
Poland Pologne	206	143	154	132	...	1 615	3 020	4 436	5 121	6 287
Portugal Portugal	4 372	4 552	5 076	5 939	6 848	...	...	...	...	...
Republic of Moldova [4] République de Moldova [4]	67	94	51	10	18	31	19	10	3	2
Romania Roumanie	76 [1]	28 [1]	10 [1]	0 [1]	0	275	89	134	56	32
Russian Federation Fédération de Russie	477	342	235	332	390	313	327	329	281	1 116
Serbia and Montenegro Serbie-et-Monténégro	1	0	0	0	0	24	25	30	13	6
Slovakia Slovaquie	...	...	...	...	...	...	...	304	311	431
Slovenia Slovénie	0	0	0	0	0	179	0	231	244	349
South Africa Afrique du Sud	...	...	...	...	...	...	...	273	273	290
Spain Espagne	82	313	508	357	57	...	...	...	...	...
Syrian Arab Republic Rép. arabe syrienne	...	...	...	...	...	124	128	151	150	169
Trinidad and Tobago Trinité-et-Tobago	0	...	...	...	...	1	...	...	...	...
Tunisia Tunisie	...	...	...	...	...	90	108	90	104	99
Turkey Turquie	...	...	...	...	...	2 510	4 657	5 795	6 941	8 789
Ukraine Ukraine	47	25	10	27	36	118	50	93	81	62
United Kingdom Royaume-Uni	1 531	2 062	...	...	545	...	...	...	...	...
United Rep. of Tanzania Rép.-Unie de Tanzanie	54	56	...	...	...	...	...	...	...	...
United States [5] Etats-Unis [5]	...	...	...	...	...	11 440	11 476	10 715	10 914	9 581

53

Radio and television receivers
Production: thousands *[cont.]*

Récepteurs de radio et de télévision
Production : milliers *[suite]*

Country or area Pays ou zone	Radio receivers Récepteurs radio					Television receivers Récepteurs télévision				
	1996	1997	1998	1999	2000	1996	1997	1998	1999	2000
Uzbekistan Ouzbékistan	...	...	...	...	...	140	269	...	...	...

Source:
United Nations Statistics Division, New York, "Industrial Commodity Statistics Yearbook 2000" and the industrial statistics database.

1 Including radios with tape recording units and clocks.

2 Break in series; data prior to the sign not comparable to following years.

3 Production by establishments employing 10 or more persons.

4 Excluding the Transnistria region.

5 Shipments.

Source:
Organisation des Nations Unies, Division de statistique, New York, "Annuaire de statistiques industrielles par produit 2000" et la base de données pour les statistiques industrielles.

1 Y compris les récepteurs de radio avec appareil enregistreur à bande magnétique incorporés.

2 Marque une interruption dans la série et la non-comparabilité des données précédant le symbole.

3 Production des établissements occupant 10 personnes ou plus.

4 Non compris la région de Transnistria.

5 Expéditions.

54

Passengers cars
Production: thousands

Voitures de tourisme
Production: milliers

Country or area Pays ou zone	1991	1992	1993	1994	1995	1996	1997	1998	1999	2000
Argentina [1] Argentine [1]	114	221	287	338	227	269	366	353	225	239
Australia Australie	278	270	285	310	294	305	304	313	323	330
Austria Autriche	14	...	...	...	...	...	...	...	...	...
Brazil [2] Brésil [2]	293	338	392	367	271	245	253	242	221	257
Canada Canada	890	901	838	...	...	...	...	...	...	...
China * Chine *	40	...	...	...	...	...	...	...	...	...
Colombia [3] Colombie [3]	...	...	63	65	66	63	69	50	25	38
Ecuador Equateur	...	...	...	...	...	...	...	27	...	...
Egypt Egypte	9	7	4	7	8	14	13	13	12	11
Finland Finlande	39 [1]	13 [1]	7 [1]	...	...	0 [1]	...	...	34	38
France France	3 190	3 326	2 837	3 176	...	...	...	...	...	...
Germany Allemagne	4 647	4 895	3 875	4 222	...	4 713 [1]	...	...	...	...
Hungary Hongrie	...	...	...	...	...	...	...	90	125	...
India Inde	164 [4]	162 [4]	210 [4]	262 [4]	331 [4]	400 [4]	384 [4]	393 [4]	577 [4]	506
Indonesia Indonésie	26	28	20	85	19	...	11	56	39	...
Italy [4] Italie [4]	1 632	1 475	1 116	1 340	1 422	1 244	1 563	1 379	1 384	1 423
Japan Japon	9 753	9 379	8 494	7 801	7 611	7 864	8 491	8 056	8 100	8 363
Korea, Republic of [1] Corée, République de [1]	1 119	1 259	1 528	1 755	1 999	2 256	2 313	1 577	2 158	2 198
Mexico Mexique	730 [1]	799 [1]	861	887	705	802	858	947	988	1 294
Netherlands [1,5,6] Pays-Bas [1,5,6]	84	95	80	92	98	...	...	...	...	...
Poland Pologne	167	219	334	338	366	441	520	592	647	532
Romania Roumanie	84	74	93	56	70	97	109	104	89	64
Russian Federation Fédération de Russie	1 030	963	956	798	835	868	986	840	954	969
Serbia and Montenegro Serbie-et-Monténégro	76	22	8	8	8	9	10	12	8	12
Slovakia Slovaquie	4	...	5	8	22	32	42	125	127	181

54

Passengers cars
Production: thousands *[cont.]*

Voitures de tourisme
Production: milliers *[suite]*

Country or area Pays ou zone	1991	1992	1993	1994	1995	1996	1997	1998	1999	2000
Slovenia Slovénie	79	84	58	74	88	89	...	...	119	123
Spain Espagne	1 787	1 817	1 774 [1,5]	2 146 [1,5]	2 254 [1,5]	2 334 [1,5]	2 278 [1,5]	2 468 [1,5]	2 473 [1,5]	2 619 [1,5]
Sweden Suède	178	205	173	193	...	207	219	214	235	278
Ukraine Ukraine	156	135	140	94	59	7	2	26	10	17
United Kingdom Royaume-Uni	1 340	1 291	1 504	1 654	1 735	1 707	1 818	1 709	...	...
United States [7] Etats-Unis [7]	5 441	5 684	5 956	* 6 614	...	...	...	...	...	...

Source:
United Nations Statistics Division, New York, "Industrial Commodity Statistics Yearbook 2000" and the industrial statistics database.

Source:
Organisation des Nations Unies, Division de statistique, New York, "Annuaire de statistiques industrielles par produit 2000" et la base de données pour les statistiques industrielles.

1 Including assembly.
2 Excluding station wagons.
3 Source: United Nations Economic Commission for Latin America and the Caribbean (ECLAC), (Santiago).
4 Excluding production for armed forces.
5 Sales.
6 Production by establishments employing 20 or more persons.
7 Factory sales.

1 Y compris le montage.
2 Non compris les stations-wagons.
3 Source: Commission économique des Nations Unies pour l'Amérique Latine et des Caraïbes (CEPAL), (Santiago).
4 Non compris la production destinée aux forces armées.
5 Ventes.
6 Production des établissements occupant 20 personnes ou plus.
7 Ventes des fabriques.

55

Refrigerators for household use
Production: thousands

Réfrigérateurs à usage domestique
Production: milliers

Country or area Pays ou zone	1991	1992	1993	1994	1995	1996	1997	1998	1999	2000
Algeria Algérie	388	317	183	119	131	137	175	215	181	117
Angola Angola	2	2	...	...	...	...	...	...	...	...
Antigua and Barbuda [1] Antigua-et-Barbuda [1]	...	...	3	3	...	...	...	...	...	...
Argentina Argentine	439	554	688	494	49	45	401	424	354	325
Australia Australie	389	363	421	444	423	403	398	441	427	...
Azerbaijan Azerbaïdjan	313	223	228	97	25	7	0	3	1	1
Belarus Bélarus	743	740	738	742	746	754	795	802	802	812
Brazil Brésil	2 445	1 704	2 098	2 721	3 242	3 776	3 592	3 034	2 796	2 921
Bulgaria Bulgarie	65	106	81	69	49	36	21	56	45	18
Chile Chili	86	136	192	221	272	213	268	229	242	271
China Chine	4 699	4 858	5 967	7 681	9 185	9 797	10 444	10 600	12 100	12 790
Colombia Colombie	...	306	396	465	465	...	...	...	...	...
Denmark [2] Danemark [2]	269	294	261	808	1 502	1 276	1 523	1 589	1 560	1 475
Ecuador Equateur	...	66	72	111	156	17	133	88	38	...
Egypt Egypte	260	232	204	236	236	250	2	5	3	...
Finland Finlande	150	144	128	134	104	68	102	107	...	...
France France	556	566	487	554	...	...	...	...	...	...
Germany Allemagne	4 226	4 298	3 838	3 794	...	2 747	...	...	...	...
Greece Grèce	85	80	...	...	...	...	...	...	...	...
Guyana Guyana	8	6	5	5	...	...	...	...	...	...
Hungary Hongrie	443	483	520	603	714	736	835	708	849	995
India Inde	1 133	997	1 382	1 668	1 913	1 705	1 600	1 902	2 012	2 009
Indonesia Indonésie	194	...	172	469	291	...	573	417	240	...
Iran (Islamic Rep. of) Iran (Rép. islamique d')	829 [3]	896 [3]	789 [3]	629 [3]	575 [4]	756 [4]	702 [4]	1 104 [4]	...	...
Iraq Iraq	...	35	...	...	...	...	...	...	...	...

55

Refrigerators for household use
Production: thousands *[cont.]*

Réfrigérateurs à usage domestique
Production: milliers *[suite]*

Country or area Pays ou zone	1991	1992	1993	1994	1995	1996	1997	1998	1999	2000
Italy Italie	4 484	4 285	4 753	5 033	5 908	5 402	5 562	6 280	6 582	6 987
Japan Japon	5 212	4 425	4 351	4 952	5 013	5 163	5 369	4 851	4 543	4 224
Kazakhstan Kazakhstan	...	...	13	...	...	...	...	...	...	...
Korea, Republic of Corée, République de	3 228	3 296	3 585	3 943	3 975	4 292	4 257	3 790	4 235	5 224
Kyrgyzstan Kirghizistan	0	1	0	3	1	0	0	...	...	...
Lithuania Lituanie	254	137	207	183	187	138	172	154	153	154
Malaysia Malaisie	266	288	250	266	295	257	249	206	194	215
Mexico Mexique	487	541	1 065	1 356	1 256	1 447	1 942	1 986	2 083	2 049
Myanmar [5] Myanmar [5]	0	...	...	...	...	...	...	...	...	...
Nigeria Nigéria	77	52	53	20	19	...	...	...	...	...
Peru Pérou	70	54	57	86	161	81	101	118	42	51
Poland Pologne	553	500	588	605	585	584	705	714	726	693
Portugal Portugal	529	251	224	244	...	173	211	257	300	302
Republic of Moldova République de Moldova	118	55	58 [6]	53 [6]	24 [6]	1 [6]	2 [6]	0 [6]	...	...
Romania [7] Roumanie [7]	389	402	435	383	435	446	429	366	323	341
Russian Federation Fédération de Russie	3 566	2 972	3 049	2 283	1 531	966	1 108	956	1 041	1 151
Serbia and Montenegro Serbie-et-Monténégro	109	85	39	41	50	51	81	48	5	20
Slovakia Slovaquie	515	552	482	371	330	393	258	228	206	177
Slovenia Slovénie	720	661	665	797	863	592	692	756	780	841
South Africa [8] Afrique du Sud [8]	356	318	318	321	365	411	388	399	440	508
Spain Espagne	1 410	1 322	1 240	1 461	1 269	1 260	1 960	2 415	2 107	2 153
Sweden Suède	562	562	549	582	610	478	523	545	604	620
Syrian Arab Republic Rép. arabe syrienne	85	129	150	148	156	155	138	137	120	...
Tajikistan Tadjikistan	145	61	18	3	0	1	2	1	2	2
Thailand [9] Thaïlande [9]	789	...	...	...	...	2 246	2 384	1 631	...	...

55

Refrigerators for household use
Production: thousands *[cont.]*

Réfrigérateurs à usage domestique
Production: milliers *[suite]*

Country or area Pays ou zone	1991	1992	1993	1994	1995	1996	1997	1998	1999	2000
TFYR of Macedonia L'ex-R.y. Macédoine	136	139	98	95	51	20	12	* 4	0	0
Trinidad and Tobago Trinité-et-Tobago	13	10	3	3	1	0	...	...	...	...
Tunisia Tunisie	82	123	141	129	...	...	...	...	...	...
Turkey Turquie	1 019	1 040	1 254	1 258	1 680	1 612	1 945	1 993	2 079	2 401
Ukraine Ukraine	883	838	757	653	562	431	382	390	409	451
United Kingdom Royaume-Uni	...	...	1 033	1 094	1 256	1 225	1 251	1 095	912	
United States [10,11] Etats-Unis [10,11]	7 599	9 676	10 306	11 276	11 005	11 132	12 092	11 279	11 716	12 532
Uzbekistan Ouzbékistan	212	85	82	20	19	13	13	...		...

Source:
United Nations Statistics Division, New York, "Industrial Commodity Statistics Yearbook 2000" and the industrial statistics database.

1 Twelve months beginning 21 March of the year stated.
2 Sales.
3 Production by establishments employing 50 or more persons.
4 Production by establishments employing 10 or more persons.
5 Government production only.
6 Excluding the Transnistria region.
7 Including freezers.
8 Including deep freezers and deep freeze-refrigerator combinations.
9 Beginning 1999, series discontinued.
10 Electric domestic refrigerators only.
11 Shipments.

Source:
Organisation des Nations Unies, Division de statistique, New York, "Annuaire de statistiques industrielles par produit 2000" et la base de données pour les statistiques industrielles.

1 Période de douze mois commençant le 21 mars de l'année indiquée.
2 Ventes.
3 Production des établissements occupant 50 personnes ou plus.
4 Production des établissements occupant 10 personnes ou plus.
5 Production de l'Etat seulement.
6 Non compris la région de Transnistria.
7 Y compris les congélateurs.
8 Y compris congélateurs-conservateurs et congélateurs combinés avec un réfrigérateur.
9 A partir de 1999, les séries ont été discontinuées.
10 Réfrigérateurs électriques de ménage seulement.
11 Expéditions.

56
Washing machines for household use
Production: thousands
Machines à laver à usage domestique
Production: en milliers

Country or area Pays ou zone	1991	1992	1993	1994	1995	1996	1997	1998	1999	2000
Argentina Argentine	436	756	801	702	458	524	603	...	...	...
Armenia Arménie	74	9	0	0	1	0	...	...	...	...
Australia Australie	295	295	328	314	310	266	268	321	354	...
Belarus Bélarus	57	62	71	77	37	61	88	91	92	88
Belgium [1,2] Belgique [1,2]	99	138	49	...	...	...	...	...	...	...
Brazil Brésil	948	849	1 167	1 461	1 681	2 160	2 095	1 851	1 940	2 302
Bulgaria Bulgarie	74	69	42	41	26	24	5	...	...	...
Chile Chili	203	301	386	447	434	310	...	...	...	...
China Chine	6 872	7 079	8 959	10 941	9 484	10 747	12 545	12 073	13 422	14 430
Colombia Colombie	...	41	41	50	45	...	...	...	...	...
Croatia Croatie	1	1	0	0	0	0	0	...	...	...
Ecuador Equateur	...	...	...	...	11	12	...	...	...	...
Egypt Egypte	202	198	200	209	198	200	201	201	252	...
France [1] France [1]	1 645	1 713	1 943	2 244	2 200	1 868	1 933	1 941	2 229	...
Germany Allemagne	...	...	...	...	2 703	2 816	3 035	3 370	...	...
Greece Grèce	...	...	31	20	15	10	...	5 741	...	...
Hungary Hongrie	220	219	...	...	...	...	...	...	...	...
Indonesia Indonésie	19	27	32	44	13	...	86	33	48	...
Iran (Islamic Rep. of) Iran (Rép. islamique d')	43 [4]	63 [4]	59 [4]	79 [4]	98 [5]	159 [5]	194 [5]	190 [5]	182	189
Italy Italie	5 044	5 140	5 693	6 251	6 996	7 135	7 967	8 119	7 367	8 186
Japan Japon	5 587	5 225	5 163	5 042	4 876	5 006	4 818	4 468	4 287	4 179
Kazakhstan Kazakhstan	391	370	255	88	46	23	11	3	2	5
Korea, Republic of Corée, République de	2 157	1 896	2 199	2 443	2 827	2 878	2 967	2 643	2 822	3 271
Kyrgyzstan Kirghizistan	209	94	77	17	4	3	2	0	...	...
Latvia Lettonie	427	18	18	10	8	3	3	2	2	...
Mexico Mexique	611	646	1 085	1 185	882	1 091	1 448	1 512	1 593	1 720

56

Washing machines for household use
Production: thousands [cont.]

Machines à laver à usage domestique
Production: en milliers [suite]

Country or area Pays ou zone	1991	1992	1993	1994	1995	1996	1997	1998	1999	2000
Peru Pérou	6	5	3	5	6	3	1	0	0	0
Poland Pologne	336	363	402	449	419	445	412	416	448	457
Portugal Portugal	7	...	...	...	...	...	...	...	...	...
Republic of Moldova République de Moldova	194	102	123 [6]	81 [6]	49 [6]	54 [6]	46 [6]	43 [6]	18 [6]	25 [6]
Romania Roumanie	188	159	161	109	125	138	82	36	28	25
Russian Federation Fédération de Russie	5 541	4 289	3 901	2 122	1 294	762	800	862	999	954
Serbia and Montenegro Serbie-et-Monténégro	94	68	39	63	36	33	33	30	12	9
Slovakia Slovaquie	144	122	100	...	...	...	...	...	...	...
Slovenia Slovénie	318	188	189	200	220	291	405	474	447	488
South Africa Afrique du Sud	87	44	52	55	57	55	44	44	45	35
Spain Espagne	1 522	1 540	1 334	1 632	1 655	1 945	2 270	2 281	...	...
Sweden Suède	103	91	94	113	106	103	120	119	122	117
Syrian Arab Republic Rép. arabe syrienne	29	41	47	50	78	80	72	68	65	...
Thailand [7] Thaïlande [7]	...	...	...	...	...	541	794	800	...	...
Turkey Turquie	837	802	980	780	873	1 015	1 485	1 408	1 249	1 346
Ukraine Ukraine	830	805	643	422	213	149	147	138	127	125
United Kingdom Royaume-Uni	...	...	...	...	...	...	1 148	1 111	...	...
United States Etats-Unis	6 404 [1]	6 566 [1]	6 739 [1]	7 081 [1]	6 605 [1]	6 873 [1]	6 942 [1]	7 504 [1]	7 991 [1]	8 043
Uzbekistan Ouzbékistan	13	9	10	9	14	4	4	...	...	...

Source:
United Nations Statistics Division, New York, "Industrial Commodity Statistics Yearbook 2000" and the industrial statistics database.

1 Shipments.
2 Production by establishments employing 5 or more persons.
3 Sales.
4 Production by establishments employing 50 or more persons.
5 Production by establishments employing 10 or more persons.
6 Excluding the Transnistria region.
7 Beginning 1999, series discontinued.

Source:
Organisation des Nations Unies, Division de statistique, New York, "Annuaire de statistiques industrielles par produit 2000" et la base de données pour les statistiques industrielles.

1 Expéditions.
2 Production des établissements occupant 5 personnes ou plus.
3 Ventes.
4 Production des établissements occupant 50 personnes ou plus.
5 Production des établissements occupant 10 personnes ou plus.
6 Non compris la région de Transnistria.
7 A partir de 1999, les séries ont été discontinuées.

57

Machine tools
Production: number

Machines-outils
Production : nombre

Country or area Pays ou zone	1991	1992	1993	1994	1995	1996	1997	1998	1999	2000
Algeria Algérie										
Drilling and boring machines										
Perceuses	210	122	30	...	...	...	...	...	...	...
Lathes										
Tours	273	310	194	118	196	189	110	14	177	38
Milling machines										
Fraiseuses	150	103	81	124	119	124	75	80	72	69
Armenia Arménie										
Lathes										
Tours	2 633	1 079	486	395	190	141	81	71	33	40
Milling machines										
Fraiseuses	759	410	0	63	73	47	188	82	27	18
Metal-working presses										
Presses pour de travail de métaux	206	45	100	29	43	34	31	18	11	11
Austria[1] Autriche[1]										
Lathes										
Tours	1 647	1 421	915	709	1 482	1 452	801	1 914	...	...
Milling machines										
Fraiseuses	526	844	223	209	625	362	284	279		
Azerbaijan Azerbaïdjan										
Drilling and boring machines										
Perceuses	643	428	86	102	112	49	24	29	1	...
Bangladesh[2] Bangladesh[2]										
Lathes										
Tours	13	3	1	1	...	...	...	...	...	...
Belarus Bélarus										
Lathes										
Tours	...	162	332	57	70	93	117	131	96	122
Milling machines										
Fraiseuses	150	56	13	0	1	3	5	3	2	16
Brazil Brésil										
Metal-working presses										
Presses pour de travail de métaux	1 853	1 194	1 763	1 836	1 858	1 657	1 678	1 531	1 102	1 386
Bulgaria Bulgarie										
Drilling and boring machines										
Perceuses	1 959	996	759	850	864	953	906	* 1 025	* 940	* 1 429
Lathes										
Tours	4 744	3 587	2 197	1 979	2 496	2 513	2 315	1 761	1 611	1 563
Milling machines										
Fraiseuses	961	432	324	200	227	295	412	104	139	218
Colombia Colombie										
Lathes										
Tours	...	97	103	155	112	...	...	...	...	...
Metal-working presses										
Presses pour de travail de métaux	...	16 992	13 366	22 661	26 344	...	...	...	...	...
Croatia Croatie										
Drilling and boring machines										
Perceuses	458	346	255	...	4 369	3 212	1 134	31	28	16
Lathes										
Tours	584	463	358	...	52	68	98	144	186	122
Milling machines										
Fraiseuses	212	168	192	...	77	90	165	224	196	162
Czech Republic République tchèque										
Drilling and boring machines										
Perceuses	1 131	...	...	...	...	1 235	1 263	1 352	986	982
Lathes										
Tours	1 405	1 017	709	685	735	943	932	994	989	1 032
Milling machines										
Fraiseuses	1 706	1 358	...	...	...	1 109	1 039	1 117	821	860
Metal-working presses										
Presses pour de travail de métaux	82	106	47	60	114	231	239	...	...	...

57

Machine tools
Production: number *[cont.]*

Machines-outils
Production : nombre *[suite]*

Country or area Pays ou zone	1991	1992	1993	1994	1995	1996	1997	1998	1999	2000
Denmark[3] Danemark[3]										
Drilling and boring machines										
Perceuses	394	223	197	...	...	...	...	...	...	...
Lathes										
Tours	384	279	374	...	...	...	...	...	...	...
Milling machines										
Fraiseuses	201	200	0	0	0	...	...	...	...	...
Finland Finlande										
Drilling and boring machines										
Perceuses	42	54	78	88	106	109	...	67	13	89
Lathes										
Tours	1	1	1	2	3	2	...	...	...	...
Metal-working presses										
Presses pour de travail de métaux	98	17	6	180	1 764	2 159	2 101	2 285	2 315	2 735
France France										
Drilling and boring machines[4]										
Perceuses[4]	1 460	1 212	...	...	...	...	...	...	...	...
Lathes[5]										
Tours[5]	988	942	11	546	...	...	...	...	...	...
Milling machines[5]										
Fraiseuses[5]	496	401	7	394	...	...	...	...	...	...
Metal-working presses[5]										
Presses pour de travail de métaux[5]	1 235	1 385	970	605	...	...	...	...	...	...
Georgia Géorgie										
Lathes										
Tours	...	1 001	348	109	57	18	28	21	2	
Germany Allemagne										
Drilling and boring machines										
Perceuses	...	15 085	21 222	15 955	13 049	11 730	...	11 396	...	...
Lathes										
Tours	...	7 689	4 755	5 322	8 232	6 375	5 542	6 070	...	...
Milling machines										
Fraiseuses	...	...	6 680	6 327	...	5 213	5 335	5 348	...	...
Metal-working presses										
Presses pour de travail de métaux	17 726	55 997	18 939	23 284	16 399	...	21 531	...	...	...
Greece Grèce										
Milling machines										
Fraiseuses	1 452	...	...	...	...	...	...	4	...	...
Metal-working presses										
Presses pour de travail de métaux	320	355	...	...	...	...	...	...	...	...
Hungary Hongrie										
Drilling and boring machines										
Perceuses	1 257	75	78	15	4	...	...	...	...	167
Lathes										
Tours	304	63	135	33	7	...	...	...	...	100
Milling machines										
Fraiseuses	297	256	50	3	...	...	...	...	...	...
India Inde										
Lathes										
Tours	...	...	...	6 747 000	6 279 000	4 685 000	4 881 000	6 902 000	12 436 000	21 579 000
Indonesia Indonésie										
Drilling and boring machines										
Perceuses	437	1 000	52	...	12 155	...	...	5 153	14	...
Lathes										
Tours	45	42	46	96	166	...	23	4	4	...
Milling machines										
Fraiseuses	...	...	50	...	...	...	...	...	...	...
Metal-working presses										
Presses pour de travail de métaux	...	...	54	...	...	...	...	...	...	...

57

Machine tools
Production: number *[cont.]*

Machines-outils
Production : nombre *[suite]*

Country or area Pays ou zone	1991	1992	1993	1994	1995	1996	1997	1998	1999	2000
Japan Japon										
Drilling and boring machines										
Perceuses	33 929	22 973	14 496	11 936	14 678	16 414	17 097	12 531	9 377	12 784
Lathes										
Tours	26 216	16 155	12 343	14 961	20 339	21 443	23 357	22 652	16 924	22 027
Milling machines										
Fraiseuses	7 584	3 913	2 007	1 791	1 832	2 198	2 368	2 019	1 022	1 260
Metal-working presses										
Presses pour de travail de métaux	19 173	12 458	9 516	9 531	10 512	10 068	11 575	8 546	7 285	8 884
Korea, Republic of Corée, République de										
Drilling and boring machines[6]										
Perceuses[6]	8 150	7 336	7 416	11 107	10 861	8 025	8 741	1 491	2 805	...
Lathes										
Tours	11 324	6 643	6 931	10 265	12 526	11 094	8 357	4 809	6 542	8 424
Milling machines										
Fraiseuses	3 994	2 509	2 824	4 667	5 293	3 952	2 900	825	2 242	3 664
Latvia Lettonie										
Lathes										
Tours	...	...	28	87	36	26	20	29	...	...
Milling machines										
Fraiseuses	...	...	12	44	44	9	26	78	...	...
Metal-working presses										
Presses pour de travail de métaux	3	...	...	...	...	...	...	...	...	...
Lithuania Lituanie										
Drilling and boring machines										
Perceuses	...	...	...	...	749	437	333	192	171	105
Lathes										
Tours	95	110	93	27	64	4	1	6	6	6
Milling machines										
Fraiseuses	1 303	1 035	450	341	255	213	161	130	58	55
Mexico Mexique										
Drilling and boring machines										
Perceuses	2 187	855	487	...	...	...	...	...	...	...
Poland Pologne										
Drilling and boring machines										
Perceuses	2 995	1 858	1 348	998	771	840	1 253	917	624	...
Lathes										
Tours	2 184	1 105	910	900	1 012	1 037	900	963	732	...
Milling machines										
Fraiseuses	834	500	248	260	274	281	354	257	222	...
Metal-working presses										
Presses pour de travail de métaux	44	13	11	8	2	2	15			
Portugal Portugal										
Drilling and boring machines										
Perceuses	...	75	52	...	...	...	...	...	...	...
Lathes										
Tours	87	...	...	...	...	...	...	...	...	...
Metal-working presses										
Presses pour de travail de métaux	102	742	670	649	...	...	...	...	...	...
Romania Roumanie										
Lathes										
Tours	2 883	1 583	489	312	471	587	681	573	330	307
Milling machines										
Fraiseuses	1 355	764	436	162	341	458	403	321	333	242
Russian Federation Fédération de Russie										
Drilling and boring machines										
Perceuses	16 020	12 835	10 607	5 291	5 021	3 088	2 522	1 877	1 898	1 669
Lathes										
Tours	9 850	7 079	6 506	3 807	3 269	2 095	2 135	1 798	1 681	2 067
Milling machines										
Fraiseuses	4 233	4 144	3 424	1 560	897	622	591	641	724	1 163

57

Machine tools
Production: number *[cont.]*

Machines-outils
Production : nombre *[suite]*

Country or area Pays ou zone	1991	1992	1993	1994	1995	1996	1997	1998	1999	2000
Serbia and Montenegro Serbie-et-Monténégro										
Drilling and boring machines										
Perceuses	924	607	276	206	328	100	106	133	111	97
Lathes										
Tours	514	338	67	135	206	110	256	213	231	181
Milling machines										
Fraiseuses	15	...	...	...	...	...	...	...	3	...
Metal-working presses										
Presses pour de travail de métaux	979	1 046	167	54	114	53	47	66	29	28
Slovakia Slovaquie										
Drilling and boring machines										
Perceuses	10	...	0	...	...	...	...	...	...	...
Lathes										
Tours	4 417	...	1 637	1 566	1 549	3 121	3 084	1 660	1 786	1 769
Metal-working presses										
Presses pour de travail de métaux	829	261	184	301	282	199	73	276	195	147
Slovenia Slovénie										
Drilling and boring machines										
Perceuses	114	60	0	...	...	...	4	0	...	...
Milling machines										
Fraiseuses	13	12	15	26	27	...	...	...	...	...
Metal-working presses										
Presses pour de travail de métaux	119	92	145	153	215	719	...	...	...	91
Spain Espagne										
Drilling and boring machines										
Perceuses	2 567	2 060	886	1 738	2 313	2 185	2 689	3 317	4 732	4 976
Lathes										
Tours	1 265	925	1 237	1 713	2 475	2 887	3 080	3 509	3 559	3 492
Milling machines										
Fraiseuses	4 169	4 553	788	1 458	1 600	1 852	1 605	2 986	3 075	3 964
Metal-working presses										
Presses pour de travail de métaux	2 152	1 687	2 436	723	5 452	...	...	...	...	...
Sweden Suède										
Drilling and boring machines										
Perceuses	...	...	...	...	...	...	3 158	3 661	3 003	2 232
Lathes										
Tours	...	...	...	...	...	259	40	22	25	17
Milling machines										
Fraiseuses	...	48	22	27	25	...	...	...	...	...
Turkey Turquie										
Drilling and boring machines										
Perceuses	57	239	41	185	12	57	22	21	7	85
Lathes										
Tours	23	2	10	59	12	16	0	0	0	0
Milling machines										
Fraiseuses	86	39	85	107	84	169	75	1	0	0
Ukraine Ukraine										
Drilling and boring machines										
Perceuses	7 970	11 113	12 996	3 745	1 337	563	750	418	306	225
Lathes										
Tours	3 300	2 420	1 619	867	808	338	352	234	213	260
Milling machines										
Fraiseuses	1 208	1 040	752	195	90	48	161	168	45	77
Metal-working presses										
Presses pour de travail de métaux	666	268	277	117	146	35	42	38	29	34
United Kingdom Royaume-Uni										
Drilling and boring machines										
Perceuses	...	...	901	1 061	...	...	...	...	...	...
Lathes										
Tours	...	...	2 429	2 941	3 568	3 845	3 102	3 478	2 047	...

57

Machine tools
Production: number *[cont.]*

Machines-outils
Production : nombre *[suite]*

Country or area Pays ou zone	1991	1992	1993	1994	1995	1996	1997	1998	1999	2000
Milling machines Fraiseuses	...	...	824	856	493	268	529	...	...	132
Metal-working presses Presses pour de travail de métaux	...	...	667	615	...	...	827	...	...	...
United States[5] Etats-Unis[5]										
Drilling and boring machines Perceuses	7 603	7 542	7 182	...	10 465	7 927	6 234	5 812	5 096	4 277
Lathes Tours	2 658	2 409	3 042	3 662	4 643	4 190	5 058	5 089	3 807	3 278
Milling machines Fraiseuses	2 772	2 581	3 386	4 087	4 747	4 102	4 240	3 416	2 749	3 545
Metal-working presses Presses pour de travail de métaux	5 912	5 822	6 236	10 947	5 045	11 023	12 084	12 559	12 301	11 079

Source:
United Nations Statistics Division, New York, "Industrial Commodity Statistics Yearbook 2000" and the industrial statistics database.

Source:
Organisation des Nations Unies, Division de statistique, New York, "Annuaire de statistiques industrielles par produit 2000" et la base de données pour les statistiques industrielles.

1 Beginning 1999, data are confidential.
2 Twelve months ending 30 June of the year stated.
3 Sales.
4 Limited coverage.
5 Shipments.
6 Drilling machines only.

1 A partir de 1999, les données sont confidentielles.
2 Période de douze mois finissant le 30 juin de l'année indiquée.
3 Ventes.
4 Couverture limitée.
5 Expéditions.
6 Perceuses seulement.

58

Lorries (trucks)
Production or assembly from imported parts: number

Camions
Production ou montage avec des pièces importées : nombre

Country or area Pays ou zone	1991	1992	1993	1994	1995	1996	1997	1998	1999	2000
Algeria Algérie										
Assembled										
Assemblés	3 164	2 434	2 304	1 230	2 570	2 136	1 293	1 798	1 583	1 719
Argentina[1] Argentine[1]										
Produced										
Fabriqués	22 388	36 999	50 805	64 022	...	...	...	...	...	...
Armenia Arménie										
Produced										
Fabriqués	6 823	3 171	1 247	446	232	114	27	51	2	...
Australia[2,3] Australie[2,3]										
Produced										
Fabriqués	17 666	14 550	15 459	...	...	...	...	...	...	...
Austria Autriche										
Produced										
Fabriqués	5 168	4 089	3 565	3 098	2 903[4]	...	...	...	...	...
Azerbaijan Azerbaïdjan										
Produced										
Fabriqués	3 246	402	93	8	2	1	0	0	0	0
Bangladesh Bangladesh										
Assembled										
Assemblés	713	549	236	430	830	797	887	788	793	629
Belarus Bélarus										
Produced										
Fabriqués	38 178	32 951	30 771	21 264	12 902	10 671	13 002	12 799	13 370	14 656
Belgium[5,6] Belgique[5,6]										
Assembled										
Assemblés	88 937	70 532	56 244	...	...	...	...	...	...	...
Brazil[7] Brésil[7]										
Produced										
Fabriqués	49 295	32 025	47 876	64 137	70 495	48 712	63 744	63 773	55 277	...
Bulgaria Bulgarie										
Produced										
Fabriqués	2 778[1]	945[1]	406[1]	321	259	66	43	...	...	...
Canada[8] Canada[8]										
Produced										
Fabriqués	789 600	901 000	838 000	...	...	...	...	...	...	...
Chile[9] Chili[9]										
Assembled										
Assemblés	9 400	14 352	16 584	15 960	...	...	...	...	...	...
China Chine										
Produced										
Fabriqués	382 500	476 700	597 897	662 600	595 997	625 100	573 600	...	...	...
Colombia Colombie										
Assembled										
Assemblés	8 900[9]	10 116[9]	13 992[9]	15 660[9]	...	...	736	903	219	...
Croatia Croatie										
Produced										
Fabriqués	...	4	7	...	5	8	10	96	10	0
Czech Republic République tchèque										
Produced										
Fabriqués	20 419	14 030	33 873	30 103	22 052	27 036	39 537	39 098	23 113	23 641
Egypt Egypte										
Produced										
Fabriqués	1 127	1 529	1 208	1 379	1 241	738	328	467	444	180
Finland[1] Finlande[1]										
Produced										
Fabriqués	545	578	435	546	540	492	493	687	721	655
France France										
Produced										
Fabriqués	461 640	494 124	373 200	453 344	...	...	...	...	...	...

58

Lorries (trucks)
Production or assembly from imported parts: number *[cont.]*

Camions
Production ou montage avec des pièces importées : nombre *[suite]*

Country or area Pays ou zone	1991	1992	1993	1994	1995	1996	1997	1998	1999	2000
Georgia Géorgie										
Produced										
Fabriqués	...	650	384	137	209	95	82	39	38	...
Germany Allemagne										
Produced										
Fabriqués	356 059	325 901	240 014	259 575	...	240 604[1]	272 916[1]	292 581[1]	...	...
Greece Grèce										
Assembled										
Assemblés	1 534	1 920	62	...	57	128	...	219	...	...
Hungary[9] Hongrie[9]										
Produced										
Fabriqués	480	360	...	...	...	...	...	...	...	...
India[8,9] Inde[8,9]										
Produced										
Fabriqués	146 400	141 600	148 800	163 200	...	...	...	...	...	...
Indonesia Indonésie										
Produced										
Fabriqués	26	174	...	2 890	4 755	...	575	#465464[10]	...	...
Iran (Islamic Rep. of) Iran (Rép. islamique d')										
Assembled										
Assemblés	32 672[11]	34 842[11]	21 234[11]	15 785[11]	8 836[12]	19 777[12]	16 761[12]	38 141[12]	...	...
Israel Israël										
Assembled										
Assemblés	864	852	836	1 260	1 217	1 199	...	...	...	...
Italy Italie										
Produced										
Fabriqués	229 860	194 616	155 476	191 288	234 354	188 852	256 062	278 322	288 038	283 266
Japan Japon										
Produced										
Fabriqués	3433790	3053477	2674941	2689340	2519319	2417370	2410124	1930965	1742111	1719584
Kenya Kenya										
Assembled										
Assemblés	1 296	315	310	428	1 103	1 430	...	...	...	...
Korea, Republic of[1] Corée, République de[1]										
Produced										
Fabriqués	245 232	293 260	310 639	332 263	331 328	340 179	297 565	182 218	264 212	265 448
Kyrgyzstan Kirghizistan										
Produced										
Fabriqués	23 621	14 818	5 026	206	8	1	12	...	...	...
Latvia Lettonie										
Assembled										
Assemblés	...	...	...	...	...	...	...	...	5	...
Malaysia[13] Malaisie[13]										
Assembled										
Assemblés	78 926	34 711	34 711	42 618	55 961	78 571	94 977	19 693	44 951	55 721
Mexico Mexique										
Produced										
Fabriqués	238 804[1]	269 591[1]	222 807	217 359	210 072	396 377	468 931	445 125	451 880	542 809
Morocco[9] Maroc[9]										
Assembled										
Assemblés	12 775	11 976	9 734	...	...	...	...	...	...	...
Myanmar[14] Myanmar[14]										
Assembled										
Assemblés	117	85	172	846	500	550	255	31	102	135
Netherlands[15,16] Pays-Bas[15,16]										
Produced										
Fabriqués	10 316	10 034	9 538	13 938	15 818	...	...	...	...	...
New Zealand *[13] Nouvelle-Zélande *[13]										
Assembled										
Assemblés	13 500	10 210	...	...	...	...	...	...	...	...

58

Lorries (trucks)
Production or assembly from imported parts: number *[cont.]*

Camions
Production ou montage avec des pièces importées : nombre *[suite]*

Country or area Pays ou zone	1991	1992	1993	1994	1995	1996	1997	1998	1999	2000
Nigeria Nigéria										
Assembled										
Assemblés	4 378	2 683	1 097	696	715	...	...	...	...	...
Pakistan[3] Pakistan[3]										
Assembled										
Assemblés	13 911	13 270	13 700	6 522	5 857	9 864	12 733	11 736	9 210	8 164
Peru[9] Pérou[9]										
Assembled										
Assemblés	2 000	600	768	...	...	...	...	...	...	...
Poland[17] Pologne[17]										
Produced										
Fabriqués	20 100	17 657	18 811	21 356	30 662	44 159	57 254	56 080	62 719	58 267
Romania Roumanie										
Produced										
Fabriqués	7 592	4 456	4 433	3 044	3 098	3 142	1 956	1 263	900	762
Russian Federation Fédération de Russie										
Produced										
Fabriqués	615 868	582 963	466 925	185 018	142 483	134 130	145 850	141 484	176 207	184 489
Serbia and Montenegro Serbie-et-Monténégro										
Produced										
Fabriqués	8 601	4 169	287	685	708	824	1 278	1 139	407	710
Slovakia Slovaquie										
Assembled										
Assemblés	...	...	...	...	...	1 421	709	312	72	37
Produced										
Fabriqués	...	...	744	369	663	1 421	709	312	72	37
Slovenia Slovénie										
Assembled										
Assemblés	611	...	1	...	...	...	...	...	...	...
Produced										
Fabriqués	1 513	377	424	397	277	195	...	...	16	16
South Africa Afrique du Sud										
Assembled										
Assemblés	97 178	93 599	96 772	118 221	147 792	132 383	132 338	117 092	113 310	130 589
Spain Espagne										
Produced										
Fabriqués	244 164	256 070	17 923[1,15]	32 217[1,15]	50 255[1,15]	73 319[1,15]	280 708[1,15]	343 699[1,15]	366 702[1,15]	404 249[1,15]
Sweden Suède										
Produced										
Fabriqués	75 000[8]	...	...	...	...	...	51 378	30 582	30 399	32 546
Thailand[9] Thaïlande[9]										
Assembled										
Assemblés	206 172	223 680	323 508	324 780	...	...	...	...	...	...
Trinidad and Tobago[9] Trinité-et-Tobago[9]										
Assembled										
Assemblés	1 711	1 698	1 083	621	0	0	...	...	...	...
Tunisia Tunisie										
Assembled										
Assemblés	1 065	768	922	1 084	616	954	1 003	1 016	770	1 130
Turkey Turquie										
Assembled										
Assemblés	29 967	37 195	49 827	21 591	35 930	50 471	73 946	67 985	44 457	77 514
Ukraine Ukraine										
Produced										
Fabriqués	25 096	33 386	23 052	11 741	6 492	4 164	3 386	4 768	7 769	11 185
United Kingdom Royaume-Uni										
Produced										
Fabriqués	207 304	239 936	320 456	372 633	247 022	188 215	189 464	185 152	...	...

58

Lorries (trucks)
Production or assembly from imported parts: number *[cont.]*

Camions
Production ou montage avec des pièces importées : nombre *[suite]*

Country or area Pays ou zone	1991	1992	1993	1994	1995	1996	1997	1998	1999	2000
United Rep. of Tanzania[18] **Rép.-Unie de Tanzanie**[18]										
Assembled										
Assemblés	479	171	40	115	0	0	0	...	...	...
United States Etats-Unis										
Produced										
Fabriqués	3372000	4118578	...	...	...	...	...	...	...	...
Venezuela Venezuela										
Assembled										
Assemblés	24 000	30 000	...	...	...	...	...	...	...	...

Source:
United Nations Statistics Division, New York, "Industrial Commodity Statistics Yearbook 2000" and the industrial statistics database.

Source:
Organisation des Nations Unies, Division de statistique, New York, "Annuaire de statistiques industrielles par produit 2000" et la base de données pour les statistiques industrielles.

1 Including assembly.
2 Finished and partly finished.
3 Twelve months ending 30 June of the year stated.
4 Beginning 1995, data are confidential.
5 Production by establishments employing 5 or more persons.
6 Shipments.
7 Trucks only.
8 Excluding production for armed forces.
9 Including motor coaches and buses.
10 Break in series; data prior to the sign not comparable to following years.
11 Production by establishments employing 50 or more persons.
12 Production by establishments employing 10 or more persons.
13 Including vans and buses.
14 Government production only.
15 Sales.
16 Production by establishments employing 20 or more persons.
17 Including special-purpose vehicles.
18 Including buses.

1 Y compris le montage.
2 Finis et semi-finis.
3 Période de douze mois finissant le 30 juin de l'année indiquée.
4 A partir de 1995, les données sont confidentielles.
5 Production des établissements occupant 5 personnes ou plus.
6 Expéditions.
7 Camions seulement.
8 Non compris la production destinée aux forces armées.
9 Y compris les autocars et autobus.
10 Marque une interruption dans la série et la non-comparabilité des données précédant le symbole.
11 Production des établissements occupant 50 personnes ou plus.
12 Production des établissements occupant 10 personnes ou plus.
13 Y compris les autobus et les camionnettes.
14 Production de l'Etat seulement.
15 Ventes.
16 Production des établissements occupant 20 personnes ou plus.
17 Y compris véhicules à usages spéciaux.
18 Y compris les autobus.

Technical notes, tables 41-58

Industrial activity includes mining and quarrying, manufacturing and the production of electricity, gas and water. These activities correspond to the major divisions 2, 3 and 4 respectively of the *International Standard Industrial Classification of All Economic Activities* [50].

Many of the tables are based primarily on data compiled for the United Nations *Industrial Commodity Statistics Yearbook* [24]. Data taken from alternate sources are footnoted.

The methods used by countries for the computation of industrial output are, as a rule, consistent with those described in the United Nations *International Recommendations for Industrial Statistics* [49] and provide a satisfactory basis for comparative analysis. In some cases, however, the definitions and procedures underlying computations of output differ from approved guidelines. The differences, where known, are indicated in the footnotes to each table.

A.   Food, beverages and tobacco

Table 41: The statistics on sugar were obtained from the database and the *Sugar Yearbook* [16] of the International Sugar Organization. The data shown cover the production and consumption of centrifugal sugar from both beet and cane, and refer to calendar years.

The consumption data relate to the apparent consumption of centrifugal sugar in the country concerned, including sugar used for the manufacture of sugar-containing products whether exported or not and sugar used for purposes other than human consumption as food. Unless otherwise specified, the statistics are expressed in terms of raw value (i.e. sugar polarizing at 96 degrees). The world and regional totals also include data for countries not shown separately whose sugar consumption was less than 10,000 metric tons.

Table 42: The data refer to meat from animals slaughtered within the national boundaries irrespective of the origin of the animals. Production figures of beef, veal, buffalo meat, pork (including bacon and ham), mutton, lamb and goat meat are in terms of carcass weight, excluding edible offals, tallow and lard. All data refer to total meat production, i.e from both commercial and farm slaughter.

Table 43: The data refer to beer made from malt, including ale, stout, porter.

Table 44 presents data on cigarettes only.

B.   Textiles and leather products

Table 45: The data on cotton fabrics refer to woven fabrics of cotton at the loom stage before undergoing finishing processes such as bleaching, dyeing,

Notes techniques, tableaux 41 à 58

L'activité industrielle comprend les industries extractives (mines et carrières), les industries manufacturières et la production d'électricité, de gaz et d'eau. Ces activités correspondent aux grandes divisions 2, 3 et 4, respectivement, de la *Classification internationale type par industrie de toutes les branches d'activité économique* [50].

Un grand nombre de ces tableaux sont établis principalement sur la base de données compilées pour l'*Annuaire de statistiques industrielles par produit* des Nations Unies [24]. Les données tirées des autres sources sont signalées par une note.

En règle générale, les méthodes employées par les pays pour le calcul de leur production industrielle sont conformes à celles dans *Recommandations internationales concernant les statistiques industrielles* des Nations Unies [49] et offrent une base satisfaisante pour une analyse comparative. Toutefois, dans certains cas, les définitions des méthodes sur lesquelles reposent les calculs de la production diffèrent des directives approuvées. Lorsqu'elles sont connues, les différences sont indiquées par une note.

A.   Alimentation, boissons et tabac

Tableau 41: Les données sur le sucre proviennent de la base de données et de l'*Annuaire du sucre* [16] de l'Organisation internationale du sucre. Les données présentées portent sur la production et la consommation de sucre centrifugé à partir de la betterave et de la canne à sucre, et se rapportent à des années civiles.

Les données de la consommation se rapportent à la consommation apparente de sucre centrifugé dans le pays en question, y compris le sucre utilisé pour la fabrication de produits à base de sucre, exportés ou non, et le sucre utilisé à d'autres fins que pour la consommation alimentaire humaine. Sauf indication contraire, les statistiques sont exprimés en valeur brute (sucre polarisant à 96°). Les totaux mondiaux et régionaux comprennent également les données relatives aux pays où la consommation de sucre est inférieure à 10.000 tonnes.

Le *tableau 42* indique la production de viande provenant des animaux abattus à l'intérieur des frontières nationales, quelle que soit leur origine. Les chiffres de production de viande de bœuf, de veau, de la viande de buffle, de porc (y compris le bacon et le jambon), de mouton et d'agneau (y compris la viande de chèvre) se rapportent à la production en poids de carcasses et ne comprennent pas le saindoux, le suif et les abats comestibles. Toutes les données se rapportent à la production totale de viande, c'est-à-dire à la fois aux animaux abattus à des fins commerciales et des animaux sacrifiés à la ferme.

printing, mercerizing, lazing, etc.; those on wool refer to woollen and worsted fabrics before undergoing finishing processes. Fabrics of fine hair are excluded.

The data on woven fabrics of cellulosic and non-cellulosic fibres include fabrics of continuous and discontinuous rayon and acetate fibres, and non-cellulosic fibres other than textile glass fibres. Pile and chenille fabrics at the loom stage are also included.

Table 46: The data refer to the total production of leather footwear for children, men and women and all other footwear such as footwear with outer soles of wood or cork, sports footwear and orthopedic leather footwear. House slippers and sandals of various types are included, but rubber footwear is excluded.

C.   *Wood and wood products; paper and paper products*

Table 47: The data refer to the aggregate of sawnwood and sleepers, coniferous or non-coniferous. The data cover wood planed, unplaned, grooved, tongued and the like, sawn lengthwise or produced by a profile-chipping process, and planed wood which may also be finger-jointed, tongued or grooved, chamfered, rabbeted, V-jointed, beaded and so on. Wood flooring is excluded. Sleepers may be sawn or hewn.

Table 48 presents statistics on the production of all paper and paper board. The data cover newsprint, printing and writing paper, construction paper and paperboard, household and sanitary paper, special thin paper, wrapping and packaging paper and paperboard.

D.   *Chemicals and related products*

Table 49: Statistics on all hydraulic cements used for construction (portland, metallurgic, aluminous, natural, and so on) are shown.

Table 50: The data refer to H_2SO_4 in terms of pure monohydrate sulphuric acid, including the sulphuric acid equivalent of oleum or fuming sulphuric acid.

E.   *Basic metal industries*

Table 51 includes foundry and steel making pig-iron. Figures on crude steel include both ingots and steel for castings. In selected cases, data are obtained from the United States Bureau of Mines (Washington, D.C.), the Latin American Iron and Steel Institute (Santiago) and the United Nations Economic Commission for Europe. Detailed references to sources of data are given in the United Nations *Industrial Commodity Statistics Yearbook* [24].

Table 52: The data refer to aluminium obtained by electrolytic reduction of alumina (primary) and re-melting metal waste or scrap (secondary).

Tableau 43: Les données se rapportent à la bière produite à partir du malte, y compris ale, stout et porter (bière anglaise, blonde et brune).

Le *Tableau 44* se rapporte seulement aux cigarettes.

B.   *Textiles et articles en cuir*

Tableau 45: Les données sur les tissus de coton et de laine se rapportent aux tissus de coton, avant les opérations de finition, c'est-à-dire avant d'être blanchis teints, imprimés, mercerisés, glacés, etc., et aux tissus de laine cardée ou peignée, avant les opérations de finition. A l'exclusion des tissus de poils fins.

Les données sur les tissus de fibres cellulosiques et non-cellulosiques comprennent les tissus sortant du métier à tisser de fibres de rayonne et d'acétate et tissus composés de fibres non cellulosiques, autres que les fibres de verre, continues ou discontinues. Cette rubrique comprend les velours, peluches, tissus boucles et tissus chenille.

Tableau 46: Les données se rapportent à la production totale de chaussures de cuir pour enfants, hommes et dames et toutes les autres chaussures telles que chaussures à semelles en bois ou en liège, chaussures pour sports et orthopédiques en cuir. Chaussures en caoutchouc ne sont pas compris.

C.   *Bois et produits dérivés; papier et produits dérivés*

Tableau 47: Les données sont un agrégat des sciages de bois de conifères et de non-conifères et des traverses de chemins de fer. Elles comprennent les bois rabotés, non rabotés, rainés, languetés, etc. sciés en long ou obtenus à l'aide d'un procédé de profilage par enlèvement de copeaux et les bois rabotés qui peuvent être également à joints digitiformes languetés ou rainés, chanfreinés, à feuillures, à joints en V, à rebords, etc. Cette rubrique ne comprend pas les éléments de parquet en bois. Les traverses de chemin de fer comprennent les traverses sciées ou équaries à la hache.

Le *tableau 48* présente les statistiques sur la production de tout papier et carton. Les données comprennent le papier journal, les papiers d'impression et d'écriture, les papiers et cartons de construction, les papiers de ménage et les papiers hygiéniques, les papiers minces spéciaux, les papiers d'empaquetage et d'emballage et carton.

D.   *Produits chimiques et apparentés*

Tableau 49: Les données sur tous les ciments hydrauliques utilisés dans la construction (portland métallurgique, alumineux, naturel, etc.) sont présentées.

Tableau 50: Les données se rapportent au H_2SO_4 sur la base de l'acide sulfurique monohydraté, y compris l'équivalent en acide sulfurique de l'oléum ou acide sulfurique fumant.

*F.   Fabricated metal products, machinery and
equipment*

Table 53 presents data on the total production of
all kinds of radio and television receivers.

Table 54: Passenger cars include three-and four-
wheeled road motor vehicles other than motorcycle
combinations, intended for the transport of passengers
and seating not more than nine persons (including the
driver), which are manufactured wholly or mainly from
domestically-produced parts and passenger cars shipped
in "knocked-down" form for assembly abroad.

Table 55: The data refer to refrigerators of the
compression type or of the absorption type, of the sizes
commonly used in private households. Insulated cabi-
nets to contain an active refrigerating element (block
ice) but no machine are excluded.

Table 56: These washing machines usually include
electrically-driven paddles or rotating cylinders (for
keeping the cleaning solution circulating through the
fabrics) or alternative devices. Washing machines with
attached wringers or centrifugal spin driers, and centrifugal spin driers designed as independent units, are
included.

Table 57: The data on machine tools presented in
this table include drilling and boring machines, lathes,
milling machines, and metal-working presses. Drilling
and boring machines refer to metal-working machines
fitted with a baseplate, stand or other device for mount-
ing on the floor, or on a bench, wall or another machine.
Lathes refer to metal-working lathes of all kinds,
whether or not automatic, including slide lathes, vertical
lathes, capstan and turret lathes, production (or copying)
lathes. Milling machines refer to metal-working machines designed to work a plane or profile surface by
means of rotating tools, known as milling cutters. Metal-
working presses are mechanical, hydraulic and pneu-
matic presses used for forging, stamping, cutting out,
etc. Forge hammers are excluded. Detailed product definitions are given in the United Nations *Industrial
Commodity Statistics Yearbook* [24].

Table 58 presents data on lorries, distinguishing
between lorries assembled from imported parts and
those manufactured wholly or mainly from domestically-produced parts. Both include road motor vehicles
designed for the conveyance of goods, including vehicles specially equipped for the transport of certain
goods, and articulated vehicles (that is, units made up of
a road motor vehicle and a semi-trailer). Ambulances,
prison vans and special purpose lorries and vans, such as
fire-engines are excluded.

E.   Industries métallurgiques de base

Tableau 51: Les données se rapportent à la production de fonte et d'acier. Les données sur l'acier brut comprennent les lingots et l'acier pour moulage. Dans certains
cas, les données proviennent du United States Bureau of
Mines (Washington, D.C.), de l'Institut latino-américain
du fer et de l'acier (Santiago) et de la Commission économique pour l'Europe. Pour plus de détails sur les sources de données, se reporter à *l'Annuaire des statistiques
industrielles par produit* des Nations Unies [24].

Tableau 52: Les données se rapportent à la production d'aluminium obtenue par réduction électrolytique de
l'alumine (production primaire) et par refusion de déchets
métalliques (production secondaire).

*F.   Fabrications métallurgiques, machines et
équipements*

Tableau 53: Les données sur la production totale de
postes récepteurs de radiodiffusion et de télévision de
toutes sortes sont présentées.

Tableau 54: Les voitures de tourisme comprennent
les véhicules automobiles routiers à trois ou quatre roues,
autres que les motocycles, destinés au transport de passagers, dont le nombre de places assises (y compris celle du
conducteur) n'est pas supérieur à neuf et qui sont cons-
truits entièrement ou principalement avec des pièces fabriqués dans le pays, et les voitures destinées au transport
de passagers exportées en pièces détachées pour être mon-
tées à l'étranger.

Tableau 55: Les données se rapportent aux appareils
frigorifiques du type à compression ou à absorption de la
taille des appareils communément utilisés dans les ménages. Cette rubrique ne comprend pas les glacières conçues
pour contenir un élément frigorifique actif (glace en bloc)
mais non un équipement frigorifique.

Tableau 56: Ces machines à laver comprennent généralement des pales ou des cylindres rotatifs (destinés à
assurer le brassage continu du liquide et du linge) ou des
dispositifs à mouvements alternés, mus électriquement.
Cette rubrique comprend les machines à laver avec essoreuses à rouleau ou essoreuses centrifuges et les essoreuses centrifuges conçues comme des appareils indépendants.

Tableau 57: Les données sur les machines-outils
présentés dans ce tableau comprennent les perceuses,
tours, fraiseuses, et presses pour le travail des métaux.
Perceuses se rapportent aux machines-outils pour le travail des métaux, munies d'un socle, d'un pied ou d'un
autre dispositif permettant de les fixer au sol, à un établi,
à une paroi ou à une autre machine. Tours se rapportent
aux tours à métaux, de tous types, automatiques ou non, y
compris les tours parallèles, les tours verticaux, les tours
à revolver, les tours à reproduire. Fraiseuses se rapportent

aux machines-outils pour le travail des métaux conçues pour usiner une surface plane ou un profil au moyen d'outils tournants appelés fraises. Presses pour le travail des métaux se rapportent aux presses à commande mécanique, hydraulique et pneumatique servant à forger, à estamper, à matricer etc. Cette rubrique ne comprend pas les outils agissant par chocs. Pour plus de détails sur les description des produits se reporter à l'*Annuaire des statistiques industrielles par produit* [24] des Nations Unies.

Tableau 58 présente les données sur les camions et fait la distinction entre les camions assemblés à partir de pièces importées et les camions qui sont montés entièrement ou principalement avec des pièces importées. Les deux comprennent les véhicules automobiles routiers conçus pour le transport des marchandises, y compris les véhicules spécialement équipés pour le transport de certaines marchandises, et les véhicules articulés (c'est-à-dire les ensembles composés d'un véhicule automobile routier et d'une semi-remorque). Cette rubrique ne comprend pas les ambulances, les voitures cellulaires et les camions à usages spéciaux, tels que les voitures-pompes à incendie.

59

Railways: traffic
Passenger and net ton-kilometres: millions
Chemins de fer : trafic
Voyageurs et tonnes-kilomètres nettes : millions

Country or area Pays ou zone	1992	1993	1994	1995	1996	1997	1998	1999	2000	2001
Albania Albanie										
Passenger-kilometres										
Voyageurs-kilomètres	191	223	215	197	168	95	116	121	183	138
Net ton-kilometres										
Tonnes-kilomètres nettes	60	54	53	53	42	23	25	26	28	19
Algeria Algérie										
Passenger-kilometres										
Voyageurs-kilomètres	2 904	3 009	2 234	1 574	1 826	1 360	1 163	1 069	1 142	...
Net ton-kilometres										
Tonnes-kilomètres nettes	2 523	2 296	2 261	1 946	2 194	2 892	2 174	2 033	1 980	...
Argentina Argentine										
Passenger-kilometres[1]										
Voyageurs-kilomètres[1]	6 749	4 171	4 905	7 017	8 524	9 324	9 652	9 102	8 939	7 934
Net ton-kilometres										
Tonnes-kilomètres nettes	4 388	4 477	6 613	7 613	8 505	9 835	9 852	9 101	8 696	8 989
Armenia Arménie										
Passenger-kilometres										
Voyageurs-kilomètres	446	435	353	166	84	84	52	46	47	47
Net ton-kilometres										
Tonnes-kilomètres nettes	1 260	451	378	403	351	381	419	323	354	344
Australia[2] Australie[2]										
Net ton-kilometres										
Tonnes-kilomètres nettes	89 276	92 123	97 779	99 727	104 311	114 500	125 200	127 400	134 200	139 700
Austria Autriche										
Passenger-kilometres										
Voyageurs-kilomètres	9 501	9 342	9 629	9 625	9 689	8 140	7 971	7 997	8 206	...
Net ton-kilometres										
Tonnes-kilomètres nettes	12 207	11 798	13 050	13 715	13 909	14 791	15 348	15 556	17 110	17 387
Azerbaijan Azerbaïdjan										
Passenger-kilometres										
Voyageurs-kilomètres	1 629	1 330	1 081	791	558	491	533	422	493	...
Net ton-kilometres										
Tonnes-kilomètres nettes	13 781	7 300	3 312	2 384	2 778	3 515	4 702	5 052	5 770	...
Bangladesh[3] Bangladesh[3]										
Passenger-kilometres										
Voyageurs-kilomètres	5 348	5 112	4 570	4 037	3 333	3 754	3 855	...	...	...
Net ton-kilometres										
Tonnes-kilomètres nettes	718	641	641	760	689	782	804	...	...	...
Belarus Bélarus										
Passenger-kilometres[4]										
Voyageurs-kilomètres[4]	18 017	19 500	16 063	12 505	11 657	12 909	13 268	16 874	17 722	15 264
Net ton-kilometres										
Tonnes-kilomètres nettes	56 441	42 919	27 963	25 510	26 018	30 636	30 370	30 529	31 425	29 727
Belgium Belgique										
Passenger-kilometres										
Voyageurs-kilomètres	6 798	6 694	6 638	6 757	6 788	6 984	7 097	7 354	7 755	...
Net ton-kilometres										
Tonnes-kilomètres nettes	8 346	7 581	8 081	7 287	7 244	7 465	7 600	7 392	7 674	...
Benin Bénin										
Passenger-kilometres										
Voyageurs-kilomètres	62	75	107	116	117	121	111	108	100	...
Net ton-kilometres										
Tonnes-kilomètres nettes	238	225	253	207	178	218	219	204	89	...
Bolivia Bolivie										
Passenger-kilometres										
Voyageurs-kilomètres	334	279	277	240	197	225	270	271	259	267
Net ton-kilometres										
Tonnes-kilomètres nettes	714	695	782	758	780	839	908	832	856	750
Botswana Botswana										
Passenger-kilometres										
Voyageurs-kilomètres	75	95	119	110	81	82	71	75	...	...

59

Railways: traffic
Passenger and net ton-kilometres: millions *[cont.]*

Chemins de fer : trafic
Voyageurs et tonnes-kilomètres nettes : millions *[suite]*

Country or area Pays ou zone	1992	1993	1994	1995	1996	1997	1998	1999	2000	2001
Net ton-kilometres Tonnes-kilomètres nettes	...	585	569	687	668	1 049	1 278	1 037	...	...
Brazil Brésil										
Passenger-kilometres Voyageurs-kilomètres[5]	15 668	14 040	15 758	9 936	9 048	7 876	7 224	6 528	5 852	...
Net ton-kilometres Tonnes-kilomètres nettes[6]	116 599	124 677	133 735	136 460	128 976	138 724	142 446	140 957	154 870	...
Bulgaria Bulgarie										
Passenger-kilometres Voyageurs-kilomètres	5 393	5 837	5 059	4 693	5 065	5 886	4 740	3 819	3 472	2 990
Net ton-kilometres Tonnes-kilomètres nettes[7]	7 758	7 702	7 774	8 595	7 549	7 444	6 152	5 297	5 538	4 904
Cambodia Cambodge										
Passenger-kilometres Voyageurs-kilomètres	69	97	39	38	22	51	44	50	15	...
Net ton-kilometres Tonnes-kilomètres nettes	22	28	16	6	4	37	76	76	91	...
Cameroon Cameroun										
Passenger-kilometres Voyageurs-kilomètres	445	352	317	301	306	283	292	311	...	...
Net ton-kilometres Tonnes-kilomètres nettes	613	653	812	607	869	850	888	916	...	...
Canada Canada										
Passenger-kilometres Voyageurs-kilomètres	1 439	1 413	1 440	1 473	1 519	1 515	1 458	1 593	...	...
Net ton-kilometres Tonnes-kilomètres nettes	252 454[7]	257 805[7]	288 864[7]	280 474	282 489	306 943	299 508	298 836	...	...
Chile Chili										
Passenger-kilometres Voyageurs-kilomètres	1 010	938	816	691	644	552	519	637	736	...
Net ton-kilometres Tonnes-kilomètres nettes	2 738	2 496	2 371	2 262	2 366	2 330	2 650	2 896	3 141	...
China[8] Chine[8]										
Passenger-kilometres Voyageurs-kilomètres	315 224	348 330	363 605	354 570	332 537	358 486	377 342	413 593	453 300	476 700
Net ton-kilometres Tonnes-kilomètres nettes	1157555	1195464	1245750	1287025	1297046	1325330	1251707	1283840	1390200	1457500
China, Hong Kong SAR[9] Chine, Hong Kong RAS[9]										
Passenger-kilometres Voyageurs-kilomètres	3 121	3 269	3 497	3 662	3 914	4 172	4 252	4 321	4 533	...
Net ton-kilometres Tonnes-kilomètres nettes	61	51	47	41	30	24	15	15	15	...
Colombia Colombie										
Passenger-kilometres Voyageurs-kilomètres	16	...	...	...	...	...	...	...	...	...
Net ton-kilometres Tonnes-kilomètres nettes[7]	243	459	666	753	747	736	658	373	...	...
Congo Congo										
Passenger-kilometres Voyageurs-kilomètres	421	312	227	302	360	235	242	9	...	...
Net ton-kilometres Tonnes-kilomètres nettes	350	257	122	267	289	139	135	21	...	...
Croatia Croatie										
Passenger-kilometres Voyageurs-kilomètres[10]	981	1 094	1 182	1 139	1 205	1 158	1 092	1 137	1 252	1 241
Net ton-kilometres Tonnes-kilomètres nettes	1 770	1 592	1 563	1 974	1 717	1 876	2 001	1 849	1 928	2 249
Cuba Cuba										
Passenger-kilometres Voyageurs-kilomètres	2 594	2 512	2 353	2 188	2 156	1 962	1 750	1 499	1 737	1 740

59

Railways: traffic
Passenger and net ton-kilometres: millions *[cont.]*

Chemins de fer : trafic
Voyageurs et tonnes-kilomètres nettes : millions *[suite]*

Country or area Pays ou zone	1992	1993	1994	1995	1996	1997	1998	1999	2000	2001
Net ton-kilometres										
Tonnes-kilomètres nettes	1 059	764	653	745	871	859	822	806	808	828
Czech Republic République tchèque										
Passenger-kilometres										
Voyageurs-kilomètres	11 753	8 548	8 481	8 023	8 111	7 710	7 001	6 929	7 266	7 262
Net ton-kilometres[11]										
Tonnes-kilomètres nettes[11]	31 116	25 579	24 393	25 395	24 174	22 173	19 529	17 625	18 183	17 365
Denmark Danemark										
Passenger-kilometres										
Voyageurs-kilomètres	4 798	4 737	4 847	4 783	4 718	4 990	5 369	...	...	...
Net ton-kilometres[12]										
Tonnes-kilomètres nettes[12]	1 870	1 751	2 008	1 985	1 757	1 983	2 058	...	...	...
Ecuador Equateur										
Passenger-kilometres										
Voyageurs-kilomètres	53	39	27	47	51	47	44	5	5	...
Net ton-kilometres										
Tonnes-kilomètres nettes	3	3	9	3	1	0	14	0	0	...
Egypt[2] Egypte[2]										
Passenger-kilometres										
Voyageurs-kilomètres	46 517	49 025	51 098	52 839	55 888	60 617	64 077	68 423	...	...
Net ton-kilometres										
Tonnes-kilomètres nettes	3 213	3 142	3 621	4 073	4 117	3 969	4 012	3 464	...	...
El Salvador El Salvador										
Passenger-kilometres										
Voyageurs-kilomètres	6	6	6	5	7	7	6	8	...	...
Net ton-kilometres										
Tonnes-kilomètres nettes	38	35	30	13	17	17	24	19	...	...
Estonia Estonie										
Passenger-kilometres										
Voyageurs-kilomètres	950	722	537	421	309	261	236	238	263	683
Net ton-kilometres										
Tonnes-kilomètres nettes	3 646	4 152	3 612	3 846	4 198	5 141	6 079	7 295	8 102	8 557
Ethiopia[13,14] Ethiopie[13,14]										
Passenger-kilometres										
Voyageurs-kilomètres	152	230	280	293	218	206	151	...	...	...
Net ton-kilometres										
Tonnes-kilomètres nettes	118	112	102	93	104	106	90	...	...	...
Finland Finlande										
Passenger-kilometres										
Voyageurs-kilomètres	3 057	3 007	3 037	3 184	3 254	3 376	3 377	3 415	3 405	...
Net ton-kilometres[15]										
Tonnes-kilomètres nettes[15]	7 848	9 259	9 949	9 293	8 806	9 856	9 885	9 753	10 107	...
France France										
Passenger-kilometres										
Voyageurs-kilomètres	62 230	58 610	58 930	55 560	59 770	61 830	64 460	66 590	69 870	...
Net ton-kilometres[16]										
Tonnes-kilomètres nettes[16]	50 380	45 830	49 720	49 170	50 500	54 820	55 090	54 350	55 470	...
Georgia Géorgie										
Passenger-kilometres										
Voyageurs-kilomètres	1 210	917	1 165	371	380	294	397	349	450	...
Net ton-kilometres										
Tonnes-kilomètres nettes	3 512	1 554	955	1 246	1 141	2 006	2 574	3 139	3 910	...
Germany Allemagne										
Passenger-kilometres										
Voyageurs-kilomètres	57 240	58 003	61 962	74 970	75 975	73 917	72 389	73 587	75 111	75 403
Net ton-kilometres										
Tonnes-kilomètres nettes	70 204	64 902	70 980	68 788	67 740	72 703	73 560	71 356	76 032	74 260
Ghana Ghana										
Passenger-kilometres										
Voyageurs-kilomètres	135	118	196	213	209	...	...	...	...	...

59

Railways: traffic
Passenger and net ton-kilometres: millions *[cont.]*

Chemins de fer : trafic
Voyageurs et tonnes-kilomètres nettes : millions *[suite]*

Country or area Pays ou zone	1992	1993	1994	1995	1996	1997	1998	1999	2000	2001
Net ton-kilometres										
Tonnes-kilomètres nettes	109	137	149	157	160	...	...	...	...	...
Greece Grèce										
Passenger-kilometres										
Voyageurs-kilomètres	2 004	1 726	1 399	1 569	1 752	1 783	1 552	1 453	1 629	...
Net ton-kilometres[17]										
Tonnes-kilomètres nettes[17]	563	523	325	306	350	330	322	347	427	...
Guatemala Guatemala										
Passenger-kilometres										
Voyageurs-kilomètres	9 151	3 427	991	...	...	...	...	...	...	...
Net ton-kilometres										
Tonnes-kilomètres nettes	66 472	29 186	25 295	14 242	836	...	...	...	...	...
Hungary Hongrie										
Passenger-kilometres										
Voyageurs-kilomètres	9 184	8 432	8 508	8 441	8 582	8 669	8 884	9 514	9 693	10 005
Net ton-kilometres										
Tonnes-kilomètres nettes	10 015	7 708	7 707	8 422	7 634	8 149	8 150	7 734	8 095	7 731
India[18] Inde[18]										
Passenger-kilometres										
Voyageurs-kilomètres	300 103	296 245	319 365	341 999	357 013	379 897	403 884	430 666	457 022	...
Net ton-kilometres										
Tonnes-kilomètres nettes	252 388	252 411	249 564	270 489	277 567	284 249	281 513	305 201	312 371	...
Indonesia Indonésie										
Passenger-kilometres										
Voyageurs-kilomètres	10 458	12 337	13 728	15 500	15 223	15 518	16 970	17 820	19 228	18 270
Net ton-kilometres										
Tonnes-kilomètres nettes	3 779	3 955	3 854	4 172	4 700	5 030	4 963	5 035	4 997	4 859
Iran (Islamic Rep. of) Iran (Rép. islamique d')										
Passenger-kilometres										
Voyageurs-kilomètres	5 298	6 422	6 479	7 294	7 044	6 103	5 637	6 451	7 128	...
Net ton-kilometres										
Tonnes-kilomètres nettes	8 002	9 124	10 700	11 865	13 638	14 400	12 638	14 082	14 179	...
Iraq Iraq										
Passenger-kilometres										
Voyageurs-kilomètres	926	1 566	2 334	2 198	...	...	...	...	...	...
Net ton-kilometres[19]										
Tonnes-kilomètres nettes[19]	1 100	1 587	1 901	1 120	...	...	...	...	...	...
Ireland Irlande										
Passenger-kilometres										
Voyageurs-kilomètres	1 226	1 274	1 260	1 291	1 295	1 388	1 490	...	...	...
Net ton-kilometres										
Tonnes-kilomètres nettes	633	575	569	602	570	522	469	523	...	...
Israel Israël										
Passenger-kilometres										
Voyageurs-kilomètres	198	214	231	269	294	346	383	529	781	961
Net ton-kilometres										
Tonnes-kilomètres nettes	1 098	1 072	1 089	1 176	1 152	992	1 049	1 128	1 173	1 098
Italy Italie										
Passenger-kilometres										
Voyageurs-kilomètres	48 361	47 101	48 900	49 700	50 300	49 500	47 285	49 424	# 47 133	46 675
Net ton-kilometres[19]										
Tonnes-kilomètres nettes[19]	21 830	20 226	22 564	24 050	23 314	25 285	24 704	23 781	# 24 995	24 352
Japan Japon										
Passenger-kilometres										
Voyageurs-kilomètres	403 245	401 864	402 513	393 907	400 712	301 510	391 073	384 943	384 906	...
Net ton-kilometres										
Tonnes-kilomètres nettes	26 899	25 619	25 946	23 695	24 991	18 661	23 136	22 676	22 131	...
Jordan Jordanie										
Passenger-kilometres										
Voyageurs-kilomètres	2	2	2	1	1	2	2	2	2	4

59

Railways: traffic
Passenger and net ton-kilometres: millions *[cont.]*

Chemins de fer : trafic
Voyageurs et tonnes-kilomètres nettes : millions *[suite]*

Country or area Pays ou zone	1992	1993	1994	1995	1996	1997	1998	1999	2000	2001
Net ton-kilometres										
Tonnes-kilomètres nettes	797	711	676	698	735	625	596	585	671	371
Kazakhstan Kazakhstan										
Passenger-kilometres										
Voyageurs-kilomètres	19 671	20 507	17 362	13 159	14 188	12 802	10 668	8 859	10 215	10 384
Net ton-kilometres										
Tonnes-kilomètres nettes	286 109	192 258	146 778	124 502	112 688	106 425	103 045	91 700	124 983	135 653
Kenya Kenya										
Passenger-kilometres										
Voyageurs-kilomètres	566	395	408	363	385	393	432	306	302	166
Net ton-kilometres										
Tonnes-kilomètres nettes	1 784	1 479	1 282	1 371	1 338	1 068	1 111	1 492	1 557	1 603
Korea, Republic of Corée, République de										
Passenger-kilometres										
Voyageurs-kilomètres	32 118	31 048	28 859	29 292	29 580	30 073	32 976	28 606	27 017	...
Net ton-kilometres										
Tonnes-kilomètres nettes	14 256	14 658	14 070	13 838	12 947	12 710	10 372	10 072	10 803	...
Kyrgyzstan Kirghizistan										
Passenger-kilometres										
Voyageurs-kilomètres	235	296	172	87	92	93	59	31	44	50
Net ton-kilometres										
Tonnes-kilomètres nettes	1 589	923	629	403	481	472	466	354	338	332
Latvia Lettonie										
Passenger-kilometres										
Voyageurs-kilomètres	3 656	2 359	1 794	1 256	1 149	1 154	1 059	984	715	706
Net ton-kilometres[12]										
Tonnes-kilomètres nettes[12]	10 115	9 852	9 520	9 757	12 412	13 970	12 995	12 210	13 310	14 179
Lithuania Lituanie										
Passenger-kilometres										
Voyageurs-kilomètres	2 740	2 700	1 574	1 130	954	842	800	745	611	533
Net ton-kilometres[20]										
Tonnes-kilomètres nettes[20]	11 337	11 030	7 996	7 220	8 103	8 622	8 265	7 849	8 918	7 741
Luxembourg Luxembourg										
Passenger-kilometres										
Voyageurs-kilomètres	255	262	289	286	284	295	300	310	332	346
Net ton-kilometres										
Tonnes-kilomètres nettes	672	647	686	566	574	613	624	660	683	634
Madagascar Madagascar										
Passenger-kilometres										
Voyageurs-kilomètres	...	...	...	...	...	81	35	28	19	...
Net ton-kilometres[7,21]										
Tonnes-kilomètres nettes[7,21]	...	...	...	...	...	81	71	44	26	...
Malawi[18] Malawi[18]										
Passenger-kilometres										
Voyageurs-kilomètres	72	46	20	22	26	17	21	19	...	...
Net ton-kilometres										
Tonnes-kilomètres nettes	52	43	58	74	57	46	55	62	...	...
Malaysia[22] Malaisie[22]										
Passenger-kilometres										
Voyageurs-kilomètres	1 618	1 543	1 348	1 270	1 370	1 492	1 397	1 313	1 220	1 181
Net ton-kilometres										
Tonnes-kilomètres nettes	1 081	1 157	1 463	1 416	1 397	1 336	992	908	917	1 094
Mali Mali										
Net ton-kilometres										
Tonnes-kilomètres nettes	208	191	220	254	405	...	...	...	...	...
Mexico Mexique										
Passenger-kilometres										
Voyageurs-kilomètres	4 794	3 219	1 855	1 899	1 799	1 508	460	254	82	78
Net ton-kilometres										
Tonnes-kilomètres nettes	34 197	35 672	37 315	37 613	41 723	42 442	46 873	47 273	48 333	48 816

59

Railways: traffic
Passenger and net ton-kilometres: millions *[cont.]*

Chemins de fer : trafic
Voyageurs et tonnes-kilomètres nettes : millions *[suite]*

Country or area Pays ou zone	1992	1993	1994	1995	1996	1997	1998	1999	2000	2001
Mongolia Mongolie										
Passenger-kilometres										
Voyageurs-kilomètres	630	583	790	680	733	951	981	1 010	1 067	...
Net ton-kilometres										
Tonnes-kilomètres nettes	2 756	2 531	2 132	2 280	2 529	2 254	2 815	3 492	4 283	...
Morocco Maroc										
Passenger-kilometres										
Voyageurs-kilomètres	2 233	1 904	1 881	1 564	1 776	1 856	1 875	1 880	1 956	...
Net ton-kilometres										
Tonnes-kilomètres nettes	5 001	4 415	4 679	4 621	4 757	4 835	4 827	4 795	4 650	4 699
Myanmar Myanmar										
Passenger-kilometres										
Voyageurs-kilomètres	4 606	4 706	4 390	4 178	4 294	3 784	3 948	4 112	4 451	...
Net ton-kilometres[7]										
Tonnes-kilomètres nettes[7]	601	663	726	659	748	674	988	1 043	1 222	...
Netherlands Pays-Bas										
Passenger-kilometres										
Voyageurs-kilomètres	14 980	14 788	14 439	13 977	14 131	14 485	14 879	...	...	...
Net ton-kilometres										
Tonnes-kilomètres nettes	2 764	2 681	2 830	3 097	3 123	3 406	3 778	...	...	...
New Zealand[2] Nouvelle-Zélande[2]										
Net ton-kilometres										
Tonnes-kilomètres nettes	2 475	2 468	2 835	3 202	3 260	3 505	3 547	3 636	4 040	
Nigeria Nigéria										
Passenger-kilometres										
Voyageurs-kilomètres	451	55	220	161	170	179	...	...	...	...
Net ton-kilometres										
Tonnes-kilomètres nettes	203	162	141	108	114	120	...	...	...	...
Norway Norvège										
Passenger-kilometres										
Voyageurs-kilomètres	2 201	2 341	2 398	2 381	2 120	2 425	2 495	2 689	2 634	2 470
Net ton-kilometres										
Tonnes-kilomètres nettes	2 294	2 873	2 678	2 715	2 641	2 401	2 144	2 454	2 399	2 448
Pakistan[3] Pakistan[3]										
Passenger-kilometres										
Voyageurs-kilomètres	16 759	16 274	18 044	18 905	19 114	18 771	18 979	18 761	19 292	20 004
Net ton-kilometres										
Tonnes-kilomètres nettes	5 860	5 940	5 660	5 078	4 538	4 444	3 939	3 612	3 799	4 681
Panama[23] Panama[23]										
Passenger-kilometres										
Voyageurs-kilomètres	4 731[25]	2 315[25]	2 619[26,27]	1 069[27]	122[27]	9[27]	...	...	...	...
Net ton-kilometres[24]										
Tonnes-kilomètres nettes[24]	2 475	1 669	1 199	1 728	710	306	...	...	...	...
Paraguay Paraguay										
Passenger-kilometres										
Voyageurs-kilomètres	1	1	...	...	...	...	...	...	...	...
Net ton-kilometres										
Tonnes-kilomètres nettes	3	3	...	...	...	...	...	...	...	...
Peru[7] Pérou[7]										
Passenger-kilometres										
Voyageurs-kilomètres	226	165	240	231	222	210	180	144	...	...
Net ton-kilometres										
Tonnes-kilomètres nettes	837	850	864	843	878	833	892	891	...	...
Philippines Philippines										
Passenger-kilometres										
Voyageurs-kilomètres	121	102	106	163	69	175	181	171	123	110
Net ton-kilometres										
Tonnes-kilomètres nettes	1	5	3	4	0[28]	0	0	...	49	67
Poland Pologne										
Passenger-kilometres										
Voyageurs-kilomètres	32 571	30 865	27 610	26 635	26 569	25 806	25 664	26 198	24 093	22 469

59

Railways: traffic
Passenger and net ton-kilometres: millions *[cont.]*

Chemins de fer : trafic
Voyageurs et tonnes-kilomètres nettes : millions *[suite]*

Country or area Pays ou zone	1992	1993	1994	1995	1996	1997	1998	1999	2000	2001
Net ton-kilometres Tonnes-kilomètres nettes	57 763	64 359	65 788	69 116	68 332	68 651	61 760	55 471	54 448	47 913
Portugal Portugal										
Passenger-kilometres Voyageurs-kilomètres	5 494	5 397	5 149	4 840	4 503[29]	4 563[29]	4 602[29]	4 380	3 834	...
Net ton-kilometres Tonnes-kilomètres nettes	1 767	1 786	1 826	2 342	2 178	2 632	2 340	2 562	2 569	...
Republic of Moldova République de Moldova										
Passenger-kilometres[4] Voyageurs-kilomètres[4]	1 718	1 661	1 204	1 019	882	789	656	343	315	325
Net ton-kilometres Tonnes-kilomètres nettes	7 861	4 965	3 533	3 134	2 897	2 937	2 575	1 191	1 513	1 980
Romania Roumanie										
Passenger-kilometres[30] Voyageurs-kilomètres[30]	24 269	19 402	18 313	18 879	18 356	15 795	13 422	12 304	11 632	10 966
Net ton-kilometres Tonnes-kilomètres nettes	24 387	22 046	21 746	17 907	24 254	22 111	16 619	14 679	16 354	16 102
Russian Federation Fédération de Russie										
Passenger-kilometres Voyageurs-kilomètres	253 200	272 200	227 100	192 200	181 200	170 300	152 900	141 000	167 100	157 900
Net ton-kilometres Tonnes-kilomètres nettes	1967000	1608000	1195000	1214000	1131000	1100000	1020000	1205000	1373000	1434000
Saudi Arabia Arabie saoudite										
Passenger-kilometres Voyageurs-kilomètres	135	136	153	159	170	192	222	224	...	...
Net ton-kilometres Tonnes-kilomètres nettes	915	868	927	728	691	726	856	938	...	...
Serbia and Montenegro Serbie-et-Monténégro										
Passenger-kilometres Voyageurs-kilomètres	2 800	3 379	2 525	2 611	1 830	1 744	1 622	860	1 436	...
Net ton-kilometres[7] Tonnes-kilomètres nettes[7]	4 409	1 699	1 387	1 855	2 062	2 432	2 793	1 267	1 969	...
Slovakia Slovaquie										
Passenger-kilometres Voyageurs-kilomètres	5 453	4 569	4 548	4 202	3 769	3 057	3 092	2 968	2 870	2 805
Net ton-kilometres Tonnes-kilomètres nettes	16 697	14 201	12 236	13 674	12 017	12 373	11 753	9 859	11 234	10 929
Slovenia Slovénie										
Passenger-kilometres Voyageurs-kilomètres	547	566	590	595	613	616	645	623	705	715
Net ton-kilometres Tonnes-kilomètres nettes	2 573	2 262	2 448	3 076	2 550	2 852	2 859	2 784	2 857	2 837
South Africa[31,32] Afrique du Sud[31,32]										
Passenger-kilometres Voyageurs-kilomètres	1 038	895	686	1 007	1 198	1 393	1 775	1 794	3 930	...
Net ton-kilometres Tonnes-kilomètres nettes	88 817	91 472	92 538	98 798	99 818	99 773	103 866	102 777	106 786	...
Spain Espagne										
Passenger-kilometres Voyageurs-kilomètres	17 579	16 490	16 142	16 582	16 637	17 883	18 875	19 659	18 547	19 190
Net ton-kilometres[7] Tonnes-kilomètres nettes[7]	9 550	8 132	9 048	10 419	10 219	11 488	11 801	12 029	11 620	11 748
Sri Lanka[33] Sri Lanka[33]										
Passenger-kilometres Voyageurs-kilomètres	2 613	2 822	3 202	3 321	3 103	3 146	3 206	3 393	3 691	...
Net ton-kilometres Tonnes-kilomètres nettes	177	159	154	136	107	98	108	106	90	...
Sudan Soudan										
Passenger-kilometres Voyageurs-kilomètres	177	1 183	...	...	...	...	...	...	...	...

59

Railways: traffic
Passenger and net ton-kilometres: millions *[cont.]*

Chemins de fer : trafic
Voyageurs et tonnes-kilomètres nettes : millions *[suite]*

Country or area Pays ou zone	1992	1993	1994	1995	1996	1997	1998	1999	2000	2001
Net ton-kilometres										
Tonnes-kilomètres nettes	2 120	2 240	...	...	...	...	...	...	...	...
Swaziland Swaziland										
Net ton-kilometres										
Tonnes-kilomètres nettes	...	...	675	743	684	670	653	677	875	...
Sweden Suède										
Passenger-kilometres										
Voyageurs-kilomètres	5 587	6 001	6 063	6 364	6 216[34]	6 770[34]	6 997[34]	7 434[34]	...	...
Net ton-kilometres										
Tonnes-kilomètres nettes	19 204	18 581	19 062	19 390	18 835[34]	19 114[34]	19 019[34]	18 905[34]	19 668[34]	19 129[34]
Switzerland Suisse										
Passenger-kilometres										
Voyageurs-kilomètres	13 209	13 384	13 836	13 408	13 326	14 104	...	...	...	...
Net ton-kilometres										
Tonnes-kilomètres nettes	8 212	7 821	8 586	8 626	7 847	8 629	...	...	...	...
Syrian Arab Republic Rép. arabe syrienne										
Passenger-kilometres										
Voyageurs-kilomètres	1 254	855	769	498	454	294	182	187	197	...
Net ton-kilometres										
Tonnes-kilomètres nettes	1 699	1 097	1 190	1 285	1 864	1 472	1 430	1 577	1 568	...
Tajikistan[35] Tadjikistan[35]										
Passenger-kilometres										
Voyageurs-kilomètres	103	117	366	134	95	129	121	61	73	...
Net ton-kilometres										
Tonnes-kilomètres nettes	641	329	2 169	2 115	1 719	1 384	1 458	1 282	1 326	...
Thailand[33] Thaïlande[33]										
Passenger-kilometres										
Voyageurs-kilomètres	13 669	13 702	13 814	12 975	12 205	11 804	10 947	9 894	10 040	...
Net ton-kilometres										
Tonnes-kilomètres nettes	3 075	3 059	3 072	3 242	3 286	3 410	2 874	2 929	3 347	...
TFYR of Macedonia L'ex-R.y. Macédoine										
Passenger-kilometres										
Voyageurs-kilomètres	109	66	67	65	120	141	150	150	176	133
Net ton-kilometres										
Tonnes-kilomètres nettes	577	493	151	169	271	279	408	380	527	462
Tunisia Tunisie										
Passenger-kilometres[17]										
Voyageurs-kilomètres[17]	1 078	1 057	1 038	996	988	1 094	1 133	1 196	1 258	1 285
Net ton-kilometres[7,36]										
Tonnes-kilomètres nettes[7,36]	2 015	2 012	2 225	2 317	2 329	2 338	2 349	2 365	2 274	2 285
Turkey Turquie										
Passenger-kilometres										
Voyageurs-kilomètres	6 259	7 147	6 335	5 797	5 229	5 840	6 161	6 146	5 833	5 568
Net ton-kilometres										
Tonnes-kilomètres nettes	8 383	8 517	8 339	8 632	9 018	9 717	8 466	8 446	9 895	7 562
Uganda Ouganda										
Passenger-kilometres										
Voyageurs-kilomètres	63	60	35	30	25	5	0[37]	0[37]	0[37]	0[37]
Net ton-kilometres										
Tonnes-kilomètres nettes	119	130	208	245	184	148	148	200	210	220
Ukraine Ukraine										
Passenger-kilometres										
Voyageurs-kilomètres	76 196	75 896	70 882	63 759	59 080	54 540	49 938	47 600	51 767	52 661
Net ton-kilometres										
Tonnes-kilomètres nettes	307 761	246 356	200 422	195 762	160 384	160 433	158 693	156 336	172 840	177 465
United Kingdom[18,38] Royaume-Uni[18,38]										
Passenger-kilometres										
Voyageurs-kilomètres	31 718	30 363	28 650	30 039	32 135	34 660	36 270	38 349	...	...
Net ton-kilometres										
Tonnes-kilomètres nettes	15 550	13 765	12 979	13 136	15 144	16 949	17 369	18 409	...	...

59

Railways: traffic
Passenger and net ton-kilometres: millions *[cont.]*

Chemins de fer : trafic
Voyageurs et tonnes-kilomètres nettes : millions *[suite]*

Country or area Pays ou zone	1992	1993	1994	1995	1996	1997	1998	1999	2000	2001
United States Etats-Unis										
Passenger-kilometres[39] Voyageurs-kilomètres[39]	9 803	9 976	9 529	8 924	8 127	8 317	8 573	8 515	8 974	8 969
Net ton-kilometres[40] Tonnes-kilomètres nettes[40]	1557492	1619588	1753020	1906300	1984654	1974337	2015138	2098066	2145632	2188827
Uruguay Uruguay										
Passenger-kilometres Voyageurs-kilomètres	0[41]	221	467	...	...	17	14	10	9	...
Net ton-kilometres Tonnes-kilomètres nettes	215	178	188	184	182	204	244	272	239	...
Uzbekistan Ouzbékistan										
Passenger-kilometres Voyageurs-kilomètres	6	5	5	3	2	2	2	2	2	2
Net ton-kilometres Tonnes-kilomètres nettes	41	36	19	17	20	17	16	14	15	16
Venezuela Venezuela										
Passenger-kilometres Voyageurs-kilomètres	47	44	31	12	...	...	...	...	...	...
Net ton-kilometres Tonnes-kilomètres nettes	36	26	47	53	...	...	...	...	...	...
Viet Nam Viet Nam										
Passenger-kilometres Voyageurs-kilomètres	1 752	1 921	1 796	2 133	2 261	2 476	2 542	2 722	3 200	3 426
Net ton-kilometres Tonnes-kilomètres nettes	1 077	978	1 370	1 751	1 684	1 533	1 369	1 446	1 955	2 044
Yemen Yémen										
Passenger-kilometres Voyageurs-kilomètres	...	...	1 714	2 051	2 260	2 492				
Zambia Zambie										
Passenger-kilometres Voyageurs-kilomètres	547	690	702	778	749	755	586	...	...	...
Net ton-kilometres Tonnes-kilomètres nettes	...	123	151	90	666	758	702	...	...	...
Zimbabwe[2,42] Zimbabwe[2,42]										
Net ton-kilometres Tonnes-kilomètres nettes	5 887	4 581	4 489	7 180	4 990	5 115	9 122	4 375	3 326	...

Source:
United Nations Statistics Division, New York, transport statistics database.

1 Including urban transport only.
2 Data refer to fiscal years ending 30 June.

3 Data refer to fiscal years beginning 1 July.

4 Including passengers carried without revenues.
5 Including urban railways traffic.
6 Including service traffic, animals, baggage and parcels.

7 Including service traffic.
8 May include service traffic.
9 Kowloon - Canton Railway only.
10 Beginning 1993, railway transport of passengers includes urban transport of passengers organized by ZET City Rail and HZ State Rail.
11 Including only state-owned railways.
12 Including passengers' baggage and parcel post (Latvia: also mail).
13 Including traffic of the Djibouti portion of the Djibouti-Addis

Source:
Organisation des Nations Unies, Division de statistique, New York, la base de données pour les statistiques des transports.

1 Les chemins de fer urbains seulement.
2 Les données se réfèrent aux exercices budgétaires finissant le 30 juin.
3 Les données se réfèrent aux exercices budgétaires commençant le 1er juillet.
4 Y compris passagers transportés gratuitement.
5 Y compris le trafic de chemins-de-fer urbains.
6 Y compris le trafic de service, les animaux, les baggages et les colis.
7 Y compris le trafic de service.
8 Le trafic de service peut être compris.
9 Chemin de fer de Kowloon-Canton seulement.
10 A compter de l'annee 1993 y compris le transport urbain de passagers organisés par ZET City Rail et HZ State Rail.
11 Y compris chemins-de-fer de l'état seulement.
12 Y compris les bagages des voyageurs et les colis postaux (Lettonie : courrier aussi).
13 Y compris le trafic de la ligne Djibouti-Addis Abeba en Djibouti.

59

Railways: traffic
Passenger and net ton-kilometres: millions *[cont.]*
Chemins de fer : trafic
Voyageurs et tonnes-kilomètres nettes : millions *[suite]*

Ababa line.

14 Data refer to fiscal years beginning 7 July.	14 Les données se réfèrent aux exercices budgétaires commençant le 7 juillet.
15 Beginning 1995, wagon loads traffic only.	15 A compter de 1995, y compris trafic de charge de waggon seulement.
16 Including passengers' baggage.	16 Y compris les bagages des voyageurs.
17 Including military traffic (Greece: also government traffic).	17 Y compris le trafic militaire (Grèce: et de l'Etat aussi).
18 Data refer to fiscal years beginning 1 April.	18 Les données se réfèrent aux exercices budgétaires commençant le 1er avril.
19 Excluding livestock.	19 Non compris le bétail.
20 Prior to 1994, data refer to operated ton-kilometres which is the weight in tons of freight carried multiplied by the distance in kilometres actually run; beginning 1994, data refer to net ton-kilometres which is the weight in tons of freight carried multi	20 Avant de 1994, les données se réfèrent aux tonnes-kilomètres transportées, c'est-à-dire le produit du poids et de la distance effectivement parcourue. A partir de l'année 1994, l'unité utilisée est la tonne-kilomètre nette, c'est-à-dire le produit du poid
21 Including baggage and service traffic.	21 Y compris bagages et les transports pour les besoins du service.
22 Data refer to Peninsular Malaysia only.	22 Les données se rapportent à Malasie péninsulaire seulement.
23 Beginning August 1997, railways operations closed.	23 A cessé de fonctionner en août 1997.
24 Panama Railway only.	24 Chemin de fer de Panama seulement.
25 National Railway of Chiriqui only.	25 Chemin de fer national de Chiriqui seulement.
26 Beginning April, Panama Railway resumed operations.	26 A compter d'avril, le Chemin de fer de Panama a recommencé des opérations.
27 Panama Railway and National Railway of Chiriqui.	27 Chemin de fer de Panama et chemin de fer national de Chiriqui.
28 Freight train operations suspended from November 1995 to August 1996 due to typhoon damages.	28 Les opérations de train de marchandises interrompues pendant la période de novembre 1995 à août 1996 à cause des dommages de typhon.
29 Excluding river traffic of the railway company.	29 Non compris le trafic fluvial de la compagnie des chemins de fer.
30 Including military and government personnel.	30 Y compris les militaires et les fonctionnaires.
31 Beginning 1988, excluding Namibia.	31 A partir de 1988, non compris la Namibie.
32 Data refer to fiscal years ending 31 March.	32 Les données se réfèrent aux exercices budgétaires finissant le 31 mars.
33 Data refer to fiscal years ending 30 September.	33 Les données se réfèrent aux exercices budgétaires finissant le 30 septembre.
34 Including Swedish State Railways and MTAB.	34 Y compris chemins-de-fer de l'état y MTAB.
35 Beginning 1992, decline due to border changes affecting the Dushanbe branch of the Csredniya Niyatskaya (Central Asia) Railway Co.	35 A compter de 1992, réduction imputable à des changements de frontière affectant la ligne de Douchanbé de la Compagnie Csredniya Niyatskaya (Asie centrale).
36 Ordinary goods only.	36 Petite vitesse seulement.
37 Beginning late 1997, passenger services suspended.	37 A compter de l'année de 1997, transport passager interrompu.
38 Excluding Northern Ireland.	38 Non compris l'Irlande du Nord.
39 Beginning 1986, excluding commuter railroads.	39 A partir de 1986, non compris les chemins de fer de banlieue.
40 Class I railways only.	40 Réseaux de catégorie 1 seulement.
41 Passenger transport suspended from 1988 to 1992.	41 Transport passager interrompu pendant la période 1988 à 1992.
42 Including traffic in Botswana.	42 Y compris le trafic en Botswana.

60
Motor vehicles in use
Passenger cars and commercial vehicles: thousands
Véhicules automobiles en circulation
Voitures de tourisme et véhicules utilitaires : milliers

Country or area Pays ou zone	1992	1993	1994	1995	1996	1997	1998	1999	2000	2001
Afghanistan Afghanistan										
Passenger cars										
Voitures de tourisme	31.0	1.6	1.6	1.6	4.1	4.6	4.9	5.4	6.2	...
Commercial vehicles										
Véhicules utilitaires	25.0	0.6	0.6	0.6	4.5	5.3	5.4	6.2	7.0	...
Albania Albanie										
Passenger cars										
Voitures de tourisme	...	56.7	67.9	58.6	67.2	76.8	90.7	99.0	114.5	133.5
Commercial vehicles										
Véhicules utilitaires	...	39.3	51.1	29.1	30.6	33.2	37.1	40.9	43.0	73.0
Algeria Algérie										
Passenger cars										
Voitures de tourisme	1 528.3	1 547.8	1 555.8	1 562.1	1 588.0	1 615.1	1 634.4	1 676.8	1 721.8	...
Commercial vehicles										
Véhicules utilitaires	917.2	926.0	930.8	933.1	958.1	952.7	963.9	986.7	1 010.5	...
American Samoa Samoa américaines										
Passenger cars										
Voitures de tourisme	5.0	4.6	4.6	4.7	5.4	5.3	5.7	6.2	...	...
Commercial vehicles										
Véhicules utilitaires	0.3	0.5	0.4	0.4	0.5	0.5	0.7	0.7	...	...
Angola[1] Angola[1]										
Passenger cars										
Voitures de tourisme	122.0	...	...	...	...	...	103.4	107.1	...	...
Commercial vehicles										
Véhicules utilitaires	42.2	...	...	...	...	...	107.6	110.5	...	...
Antigua and Barbuda Antigua-et-Barbuda										
Passenger cars										
Voitures de tourisme	13.5	14.8	15.0	15.1	21.6[2]	23.7[2]	24.0[2]	...	...	...
Commercial vehicles										
Véhicules utilitaires	3.5	4.6	4.8	4.8	...	...	...	...	...	...
Argentina Argentine										
Passenger cars										
Voitures de tourisme	4 809.0	4 856.0	4 427.0	4 665.0	4 783.9	4 904.3	5 047.8	5 056.7	5 386.7	...
Commercial vehicles										
Véhicules utilitaires	1 648.0	1 664.0	1 342.0	1 233.0	4 254.0	1 172.0	1 094.0	1 029.0	1 004.0	...
Australia[3] Australie[3]										
Passenger cars										
Voitures de tourisme	7 913.2	8 050.0	8 209.0	8 660.6	9 021.5	9 239.5	9 526.7	9 686.2	...	9 835.9
Commercial vehicles										
Véhicules utilitaires	2 041.3	2 043.0	2 151.0	1 990.3	2 075.6	2 111.7	2 177.5	2 214.9	...	2 236.4
Austria[4] Autriche[4]										
Passenger cars										
Voitures de tourisme	3 244.9	3 367.6	3 479.6	3 593.6	3 690.7	3 782.5	3 887.2	4 009.6	4 097.1	4 182.0
Commercial vehicles[5]										
Véhicules utilitaires[5]	674.6	685.7	698.2	710.1	721.1	736.2	752.1	767.8	779.7	787.9
Azerbaijan Azerbaïdjan										
Passenger cars										
Voitures de tourisme	258.3	263.3	276.4	278.3	273.7	271.3	281.3	311.6	332.1	343.0
Commercial vehicles										
Véhicules utilitaires	141.3	132.3	127.5	125.5	122.9	115.6	117.6	122.8	133.4	127.6
Bahamas Bahamas										
Passenger cars										
Voitures de tourisme	44.7[1]	46.1[1]	54.4	67.1	86.6[6]	89.7[6]	67.4[1]	...	...	...
Commercial vehicles										
Véhicules utilitaires	11.5[1]	11.9[1]	9.3	13.7	16.9[6]	17.6[6]	16.8[1]	...	...	...
Bahrain Bahreïn										
Passenger cars										
Voitures de tourisme	113.8	122.9	130.7	135.4	140.0	147.9	160.2	169.6	...	...
Commercial vehicles										
Véhicules utilitaires	26.5	28.2	29.4	30.5	31.5	32.8	34.5	35.7	...	...

60

Motor vehicles in use
Passenger cars and commercial vehicles: thousands *[cont.]*

Véhicules automobiles en circulation
Voitures de tourisme et véhicules utilitaires : milliers *[suite]*

Country or area Pays ou zone	1992	1993	1994	1995	1996	1997	1998	1999	2000	2001
Bangladesh Bangladesh										
Passenger cars										
Voitures de tourisme	45.6	46.6	48.1	51.1	55.8	61.2	65.0	...	...	...
Commercial vehicles										
Véhicules utilitaires	87.5	92.4	99.4	111.7	126.8	138.1	145.9	...	...	...
Barbados Barbade										
Passenger cars[7]										
Voitures de tourisme[7]	41.3	46.4	43.5	47.2	49.8	53.6	57.5	62.1	...	...
Commercial vehicles[8]										
Véhicules utilitaires[8]	5.6	5.8	5.8	7.1	6.9	7.9	8.6	9.4	...	...
Belarus Bélarus										
Passenger cars										
Voitures de tourisme	722.8	773.6	875.6	939.6	1 035.8	1 132.8	1 279.2	1 351.1	1 421.9	1 467.6
Belgium Belgique										
Passenger cars										
Voitures de tourisme	3 991.6	4 079.5	4 208.1	4 270.3	4 336.1	4 412.1	4 488.5	4 580.0	4 675.1	4 736.6
Commercial vehicles										
Véhicules utilitaires	420.0	427.7	444.4	457.1	471.8	491.3	510.1	539.0	563.2	587.3
Belize[6,9] Belize[6,9]										
Passenger cars										
Voitures de tourisme	...	...	...	16.1	17.0	19.1	19.3	21.0	21.5	...
Commercial vehicles										
Véhicules utilitaires	...	...	...	3.0	3.1	3.6	3.7	3.9	3.9	...
Benin[1] Bénin[1]										
Passenger cars										
Voitures de tourisme	22.0	7.1	7.3	7.3	7.3	7.3	7.3	...	...	...
Commercial vehicles										
Véhicules utilitaires	12.2	5.3	5.5	5.7	5.8	6.0	6.2	...	...	...
Bermuda Bermudes										
Passenger cars										
Voitures de tourisme	19.7	20.1	20.7	21.1	21.2	21.6	22.0	22.6	...	...
Commercial vehicles										
Véhicules utilitaires	3.9	4.0	4.2	4.4	4.1	4.2	5.0	4.2	...	...
Bolivia Bolivie										
Passenger cars										
Voitures de tourisme	146.6	164.7	183.7	201.9	220.3	234.1	274.1	295.1	310.5	316.3
Commercial vehicles										
Véhicules utilitaires	87.7	95.3	103.4	112.2	119.8	124.8	138.0	147.2	153.2	155.5
Botswana Botswana										
Passenger cars										
Voitures de tourisme	23.4	26.3	27.1	30.5	26.7	28.2	37.0	44.5	...	...
Commercial vehicles										
Véhicules utilitaires	49.2	55.0	60.9	63.7	48.1	52.3	58.7	67.9	...	...
Brazil[1] Brésil[1]										
Passenger cars										
Voitures de tourisme	7 855.5	8 098.4	9 524.0	10 320.5	12 666.0	9 385.8	10 828.8	11 630.7	...	...
Commercial vehicles										
Véhicules utilitaires	1 170.8	1 839.0	2 378.7	2 520.4	2 896.0	2 087.5	2 429.5	2 630.1	...	...
British Virgin Islands[2] Iles Vierges britanniques[2]										
Passenger cars										
Voitures de tourisme	6.9	6.7	7.0	...	...	...	...	...	...	...
Brunei Darussalam Brunéi Darussalam										
Passenger cars										
Voitures de tourisme	122.0	130.0	135.9	141.7	150.1	163.1	170.2	176.0	...	...
Commercial vehicles										
Véhicules utilitaires	13.7	14.5	15.4	16.3	17.3	18.3	19.1	19.4	...	...
Bulgaria Bulgarie										
Passenger cars										
Voitures de tourisme	1 411.3	1 505.5	1 587.9	1 647.6	1 707.0	1 730.5	1 809.4	1 908.4	1 992.8	2 085.7

60

Motor vehicles in use
Passenger cars and commercial vehicles: thousands *[cont.]*

Véhicules automobiles en circulation
Voitures de tourisme et véhicules utilitaires : milliers *[suite]*

Country or area Pays ou zone	1992	1993	1994	1995	1996	1997	1998	1999	2000	2001
Commercial vehicles Véhicules utilitaires	224.5	243.2	255.4	264.2	270.7	273.2	283.8	293.5	301.7	312.5
Burkina Faso Burkina Faso										
Passenger cars Voitures de tourisme	27.4	29.9	32.0	35.5[1]	35.5[1]	35.5[1]	25.3[1]	26.3[1]	...	...
Commercial vehicles Véhicules utilitaires	22.2	23.4	24.0	19.5[1]	19.5[1]	19.5[1]	14.9[1]	19.6[1]		...
Burundi Burundi										
Passenger cars Voitures de tourisme	17.5	18.5	17.5	8.2[1]	8.2[1]	8.2[1]	6.6[1]	6.9[1]	...	...
Commercial vehicles Véhicules utilitaires	11.8	12.3	10.2	11.8[1]	11.8[1]	11.8[1]	9.3[1]	9.3[1]	...	...
Cambodia Cambodge										
Passenger cars Voitures de tourisme	10.8	6.8	7.4	8.0	6.3	8.4	8.0	8.5	8.3	...
Commercial vehicles Véhicules utilitaires	0.9	0.7	1.7	2.1	1.4	1.8	1.6	1.5	3.1	
Cameroon Cameroun										
Passenger cars Voitures de tourisme	98.1	92.8	88.3	94.7	100.9	102.2	105.8	110.7	115.9	...
Commercial vehicles Véhicules utilitaires	42.9	39.0	37.6	39.6	40.6	41.6	43.2	45.3	47.4	...
Canada[4] Canada[4]										
Passenger cars Voitures de tourisme	12 781.1	12 926.8	13 122.5	13 182.9	13 251.1	13 486.9	13 887.3	16 538.0	16 860.5	...
Commercial vehicles Véhicules utilitaires	3 349.5	3 346.1	3 401.8	3 420.3	3 476.2	3 526.9	3 625.8	649.1[10]	668.0[10]	...
Cape Verde Cap-Vert										
Passenger cars Voitures de tourisme	5.5	6.5	7.7	8.0	9.3	10.3	11.4	13.5	...	...
Commercial vehicles Véhicules utilitaires	1.2	1.3	2.0	2.0	2.2	2.5	2.8	3.1	...	...
Cayman Islands Iles Caïmanes										
Passenger cars Voitures de tourisme	11.3	11.6	12.3	13.5	14.9	16.0	15.8	17.9	19.8	...
Commercial vehicles Véhicules utilitaires	2.6	2.7	2.8	9.1	3.4	3.7	3.6	4.1	4.4	...
Central African Rep. Rép. centrafricaine										
Passenger cars Voitures de tourisme	8.0	10.4	11.9	8.9	...	...	4.5[1]	4.9[1]	...	...
Commercial vehicles Véhicules utilitaires	1.7	2.4	2.8	3.5	...	...	5.4[1]	5.8[1]	...	...
Chad[11] Tchad[11]										
Passenger cars Voitures de tourisme	9.0	9.5	9.5	8.7	...	...	...	...	...	...
Commercial vehicles Véhicules utilitaires	7.0	7.2	7.2	12.4	...					
Chile Chili										
Passenger cars Voitures de tourisme	826.8	896.5	914.3	1 026.0	1 121.2	1 175.8	1 236.9	1 323.8	1 320.5	...
Commercial vehicles[12] Véhicules utilitaires[12]	198.8[13]	211.0[13]	492.7[14]	540.0[14]	585.7[14]	635.2[14]	672.2[14]	708.5[14]	701.3	...
China Chine										
Passenger cars Voitures de tourisme	2 261.6	2 859.8	3 497.4	4 179.0	4 880.2	5 805.6	6 548.3	...	...	...
Commercial vehicles Véhicules utilitaires	4 414.5	5 010.0	5 603.3	5 854.3	5 750.3	6 012.3	6 278.9	...	...	...
China, Hong Kong SAR Chine, Hong Kong RAS										
Passenger cars Voitures de tourisme	254.6	277.5	297.3	303.3	311.2	332.8	336.2	339.6	350.4	...

60

Motor vehicles in use
Passenger cars and commercial vehicles: thousands *[cont.]*
Véhicules automobiles en circulation
Voitures de tourisme et véhicules utilitaires : milliers *[suite]*

Country or area Pays ou zone	1992	1993	1994	1995	1996	1997	1998	1999	2000	2001
Commercial vehicles										
Véhicules utilitaires	134.4	135.6	137.0	134.2	133.7	135.9	133.4	132.3	133.2	...
China, Macao SAR[12] Chine, Macao RAS[12]										
Passenger cars										
Voitures de tourisme	29.9	32.6	34.0	34.5	38.9	42.9	46.3	47.8	48.9	49.9
Commercial vehicles										
Véhicules utilitaires	6.5	6.6	6.3	6.2	6.3	6.6	6.6	7.4	7.1	6.6
Colombia[1] Colombie[1]										
Passenger cars										
Voitures de tourisme	715.0	761.7	688.1	718.9	800.0	584.1	714.3	762.0	...	...
Commercial vehicles										
Véhicules utilitaires	665.0	672.6	385.1	405.6	530.0	339.1	495.7	542.0	...	...
Congo[1] Congo[1]										
Passenger cars										
Voitures de tourisme	26.0	29.0	29.0	29.0	29.0	29.0	24.9	26.2	...	...
Commercial vehicles										
Véhicules utilitaires	20.1	16.6	16.6	16.6	16.6	16.6	19.2	20.4	...	...
Costa Rica Costa Rica										
Passenger cars										
Voitures de tourisme	204.2[4]	220.1[4]	238.5[4]	254.8[4]	272.9[4]	294.1	316.8	326.5	342.0	...
Commercial vehicles										
Véhicules utilitaires	110.3[4]	114.9[4]	127.1[4]	141.4[4]	151.1[4]	153.1	164.8	169.8	177.9	
Côte d'Ivoire[1] Côte d'Ivoire[1]										
Passenger cars										
Voitures de tourisme	155.3	109.9	109.9	111.9	74.2	76.2	98.4	109.6	...	...
Commercial vehicles										
Véhicules utilitaires	90.3	46.1	47.1	50.3	35.3	35.3	45.4	54.1	...	...
Croatia Croatie										
Passenger cars										
Voitures de tourisme	669.8	646.2	698.4	710.9	835.7	932.3	1 000.0	1 063.5	1 124.8	1 195.5
Commercial vehicles										
Véhicules utilitaires	53.6	55.0	68.5	77.4	99.5	114.5	120.6	123.4	127.2	134.3
Cuba Cuba										
Commercial vehicles										
Véhicules utilitaires	...	...	10.0	10.0	9.9	10.3	10.5	11.0	10.1	...
Cyprus Chypre										
Passenger cars										
Voitures de tourisme	198.2	203.6	210.4	219.7	226.8	235.0	249.2	257.0	267.6	280.1
Commercial vehicles										
Véhicules utilitaires	89.9	93.5	98.0	104.9	108.0	109.7	113.6	115.8	119.6	123.2
Czech Republic[15] République tchèque[15]										
Passenger cars										
Voitures de tourisme	2 522.4	2 693.9	2 967.3[17]	3 113.5[17]	3 192.5[17]	3 391.5[17]	3 493.0[17]	3 439.7[17]	3 438.9[17]	3 529.8
Commercial vehicles[16]										
Véhicules utilitaires[16]	523.3	515.2	469.5[18]	490.0[18]	381.1[18]	305.1[18]	320.6[18]	329.9[18]	339.3[18]	364.1
Dem. Rep. of the Congo[1] Rép. dém. du Congo[1]										
Passenger cars										
Voitures de tourisme	...	...	...	...	...	...	172.6	172.6	...	...
Commercial vehicles										
Véhicules utilitaires	...	...	...	...	...	...	28.2	34.6	...	...
Denmark[4,19] Danemark[4,19]										
Passenger cars										
Voitures de tourisme	1 604.6	1 618.3	1 611.2	1 679.0	1 738.9	1 783.1	1 817.1	1 853.8[1]	...	...
Commercial vehicles										
Véhicules utilitaires	376.6	326.4	335.6	347.6	353.6	359.8	371.5	375.6[1]	...	...
Djibouti[11] Djibouti[11]										
Passenger cars										
Voitures de tourisme	13.0	13.5	13.5	...	...	...	...	...	...	...
Commercial vehicles										
Véhicules utilitaires	3.0	3.0	3.0	...	...	...	...	...	...	...

60

Motor vehicles in use
Passenger cars and commercial vehicles: thousands *[cont.]*

Véhicules automobiles en circulation
Voitures de tourisme et véhicules utilitaires : milliers *[suite]*

Country or area Pays ou zone	1992	1993	1994	1995	1996	1997	1998	1999	2000	2001
Dominica Dominique										
Passenger cars										
Voitures de tourisme	4.8	5.8	7.0	7.4	7.9	8.3	8.7	...	...	...
Commercial vehicles[20]										
Véhicules utilitaires[20]	2.8	2.7	2.8	2.9	3.3	3.3	3.4	...	...	...
Dominican Republic Rép. dominicaine										
Passenger cars										
Voitures de tourisme	138.1	174.4	...	183.8	271.0	331.0	384.7	445.9	455.6	561.3
Commercial vehicles										
Véhicules utilitaires	97.5[21]	118.5[21]	...	117.5	164.8	202.3	236.7	247.2	283.0	284.7
Ecuador Equateur										
Passenger cars										
Voitures de tourisme	194.5	202.4	219.8	253.5	268.2	276.5	301.4	322.3	...	...
Commercial vehicles										
Véhicules utilitaires	232.7	231.4	243.4	244.0	248.4	256.3	257.6	272.0	...	...
Egypt Egypte										
Passenger cars										
Voitures de tourisme	1 117.0	1 143.0	1 225.0	1 313.0	1 372.0	1 439.0	1 525.0	1 616.0	1 700.0	...
Commercial vehicles										
Véhicules utilitaires	408.0	423.0	445.0	466.0	484.0	508.0	539.0	577.0	600.0	...
El Salvador El Salvador										
Passenger cars										
Voitures de tourisme	80.5	88.4	86.9	113.8	121.8	129.8	136.6	142.2	148.0	...
Commercial vehicles										
Véhicules utilitaires	140.2	165.9	195.5	209.9	218.6	227.3	235.4	243.0	250.8	...
Estonia Estonie										
Passenger cars										
Voitures de tourisme	283.5	317.4	337.8	383.4	406.6	427.7	451.0	458.7	463.9	407.3
Commercial vehicles										
Véhicules utilitaires	83.0	82.8	60.0	72.6	78.0	83.1	86.9	87.2	88.2	80.5
Ethiopia[22] Ethiopie[22]										
Passenger cars										
Voitures de tourisme	40.0	47.0	52.7	60.0	62.4	66.2	68.9	71.0	...	...
Commercial vehicles										
Véhicules utilitaires	18.8	16.0	17.0	23.3	29.0	30.3	34.0	34.6	...	...
Fiji Fidji										
Passenger cars[23]										
Voitures de tourisme[23]	44.0	45.3	47.7	49.7	51.7	50.4	51.7	...	...	...
Commercial vehicles[24]										
Véhicules utilitaires[24]	43.8	44.8	46.4	47.5	48.5	48.0	48.6	...	...	...
Finland Finlande										
Passenger cars										
Voitures de tourisme	1 936.3	1 872.9	1 872.6	1 900.9	1 942.8	1 948.1	2 021.1	2 082.6	2 134.7	...
Commercial vehicles[25]										
Véhicules utilitaires[25]	271.2	261.4	257.5	260.1	266.9	275.4	289.7	303.2	314.2	...
France France										
Passenger cars										
Voitures de tourisme	24 020.0	24 385.0	24 900.0	25 100.0	25 500.0	26 090.0	26 810.0	27 480.0	28 060.0	...
Commercial vehicles[26]										
Véhicules utilitaires[26]	5 209.0	5 238.0	5 314.0	5 374.0	5 437.0	5 561.0	5 680.0	5 790.0	5 933.0	...
French Guiana[1] Guyane française[1]										
Passenger cars										
Voitures de tourisme	27.7	29.1	24.4	26.5	28.2	28.2	32.9	32.9	...	...
Commercial vehicles										
Véhicules utilitaires	10.4	10.6	7.6	8.1	8.9	9.4	11.9	11.9	...	...
Gabon[11] Gabon[11]										
Passenger cars										
Voitures de tourisme	23.0	24.0	24.0	23.0	...	...	...	...	...	...
Commercial vehicles										
Véhicules utilitaires	17.0	17.5	18.0	10.0	...	...	...	...	...	...

60

Motor vehicles in use
Passenger cars and commercial vehicles: thousands *[cont.]*

Véhicules automobiles en circulation
Voitures de tourisme et véhicules utilitaires : milliers *[suite]*

Country or area Pays ou zone	1992	1993	1994	1995	1996	1997	1998	1999	2000	2001
Gambia Gambie										
Passenger cars										
Voitures de tourisme	7.4	6.1	6.2	6.4	...	...	...	...	...	...
Commercial vehicles										
Véhicules utilitaires	2.8	3.4	3.5	3.5	...	...	...	...	...	
Georgia Géorgie										
Passenger cars										
Voitures de tourisme	479.0	485.9	452.3	360.6	323.6	265.6	260.4	247.9	244.9	...
Commercial vehicles										
Véhicules utilitaires	138.6	147.7	101.2	104.3	90.7	79.6	71.0	68.9	66.8	...
Germany[27] Allemagne[27]										
Passenger cars										
Voitures de tourisme	36 042.4	38 772.5	39 765.4	40 404.3	40 987.5	41 372.0	41 673.8	42 323.7	42 839.9	43 772.2
Commercial vehicles										
Véhicules utilitaires	...	...	2 619.3	2 754.9	2 851.4	2 931.3	3 023.9	3 166.4	...	3 378.7
Ghana[1] Ghana[1]										
Passenger cars										
Voitures de tourisme	90.0	30.4	30.7	30.8	31.2	31.9	63.5	90.4	...	...
Commercial vehicles										
Véhicules utilitaires	44.2	31.5	33.1	35.7	38.4	38.4	109.0	119.9	...	
Gibraltar Gibraltar										
Passenger cars										
Voitures de tourisme	24.0	18.0	18.5	18.4	19.0[1]	20.5[1]	21.8[1]	22.4[1]	...	...
Commercial vehicles										
Véhicules utilitaires	2.9	1.1	1.2	1.0	12.2[1]	12.3[1]	1.1[1]	1.8[1]	...	...
Greece Grèce										
Passenger cars										
Voitures de tourisme	1 829.1	1 958.5	2 074.1	2 204.8	2 339.4	2 500.1	2 675.7	2 928.9	3 195.1	3 423.7
Commercial vehicles										
Véhicules utilitaires	820.5	848.9	872.6	908.4	939.9	977.5	1 013.7	1 050.8	1 084.5	1 112.9
Greenland[4] Groenland[4]										
Passenger cars										
Voitures de tourisme	2.0	2.1	1.9	1.9	2.6	1.8	2.0	2.4	1.9	2.5
Commercial vehicles										
Véhicules utilitaires	1.5	1.4	1.6	1.4	1.2	1.5	1.4	1.5	0.9	1.8
Grenada Grenade										
Passenger cars[28]										
Voitures de tourisme[28]	...	...	...	9.0	9.7	10.7	12.0	13.3	14.6	15.8
Commercial vehicles										
Véhicules utilitaires	...	...	...	2.2	2.4	2.7	3.1	3.6	3.9	4.2
Guadeloupe[1] Guadeloupe[1]										
Passenger cars										
Voitures de tourisme	94.7	101.6	90.5	97.0	106.5	107.6	117.7	117.7	...	...
Commercial vehicles										
Véhicules utilitaires	36.0	37.5	26.6	28.9	32.5	34.1	31.4	31.4		
Guam Guam										
Passenger cars										
Voitures de tourisme	76.7	74.7	65.1	79.8	79.1	67.8	69.0	66.4	64.5	...
Commercial vehicles										
Véhicules utilitaires	30.2	30.6	27.5	34.7	33.8	28.9	28.9	27.4	26.6	...
Guatemala Guatemala										
Passenger cars										
Voitures de tourisme	...	...	...	...	...	...	646.5	...	...	...
Commercial vehicles										
Véhicules utilitaires	...	...	...	...	...	...	21.2	...	...	...
Guinea[11] Guinée[11]										
Passenger cars										
Voitures de tourisme	23.1	24.0	24.0	23.2	...	...	...	...	...	
Commercial vehicles										
Véhicules utilitaires	13.0	13.5	14.0	13.0	...	...	...	...		

60

Motor vehicles in use
Passenger cars and commercial vehicles: thousands *[cont.]*

Véhicules automobiles en circulation
Voitures de tourisme et véhicules utilitaires : milliers *[suite]*

Country or area Pays ou zone	1992	1993	1994	1995	1996	1997	1998	1999	2000	2001
Guinea-Bissau[11] Guinée-Bissau[11]										
Passenger cars										
Voitures de tourisme	3.5	...	...	...	...	...	...	...	...	...
Commercial vehicles										
Véhicules utilitaires	2.5	...	...	...	...	...	...	...	...	...
Guyana[1] Guyana[1]										
Passenger cars										
Voitures de tourisme	24.0	9.5	9.5	9.5	9.5	9.5	9.5	...	...	...
Commercial vehicles										
Véhicules utilitaires	9.0	2.6	2.7	2.9	3.0	3.1	3.2	...	...	...
Haiti Haïti										
Passenger cars										
Voitures de tourisme	32.0	32.0	30.0	49.0	59.0	...	...	93.0	...	...
Commercial vehicles										
Véhicules utilitaires	21.0	21.0	30.0	29.0	35.0	...	...	61.6	...	...
Honduras Honduras										
Passenger cars										
Voitures de tourisme	68.5	...	15.1[1]	16.1[1]	16.3[1]	16.5[1]	17.2[1]	...	...	...
Commercial vehicles										
Véhicules utilitaires	102.0	...	45.3[1]	48.0[1]	48.6[1]	49.1[1]	53.9[1]	...	...	...
Hungary Hongrie										
Passenger cars										
Voitures de tourisme	2 058.3	2 091.6	2 176.9	2 245.4	2 264.2	2 297.1	2 218.0	2 255.5	2 364.7	2 482.8
Commercial vehicles										
Véhicules utilitaires	288.9	296.2	318.5	345.0	351.3	360.9	355.4	363.0	384.3	398.3
Iceland Islande										
Passenger cars										
Voitures de tourisme	120.1	116.2	116.2	119.2	124.9	132.5	140.4	151.4	158.9	...
Commercial vehicles[29]										
Véhicules utilitaires[29]	16.0	15.6	15.6	16.0	16.6	17.5	18.1	19.4	21.1	...
India Inde										
Passenger cars										
Voitures de tourisme	3 205.0	3 361.0	3 569.0	3 841.0	4 204.0	4 662.0	5 056.0	...	...	...
Commercial vehicles[30]										
Véhicules utilitaires[30]	4 641.0	4 961.0	5 192.0	5 623.0	6 327.0	6 876.0	7 541.0	...	...	...
Indonesia Indonésie										
Passenger cars										
Voitures de tourisme	1 590.8	1 700.5	1 890.3	2 107.3	2 409.1	2 639.5	2 772.5	2 897.8	3 038.9	3 244.7
Commercial vehicles										
Véhicules utilitaires	1 666.0	1 729.0	1 903.6	2 024.7	2 030.2	2 160.0	2 220.5	2 273.2	2 373.4	2 482.4
Iran (Islamic Rep. of)[1,31] Iran (Rép. islamique d')[1,31]										
Passenger cars										
Voitures de tourisme	1 557.0	779.8	819.6	819.6	454.2	572.9	684.5	847.9	935.9	...
Commercial vehicles										
Véhicules utilitaires	584.1	589.2	589.2	589.2	346.4	346.4	355.1	378.8	384.9	...
Iraq Iraq										
Passenger cars										
Voitures de tourisme	670.2	672.4	678.5	680.1	...	...	...	...	...	...
Commercial vehicles										
Véhicules utilitaires	299.5	309.3	317.2	319.9	...	...	...	...	...	...
Ireland[32] Irlande[32]										
Passenger cars[33,34]										
Voitures de tourisme[33,34]	865.4	898.3	947.2	999.7	1 067.8	1 145.9	1 209.2	1 283.4	...	...
Commercial vehicles[20]										
Véhicules utilitaires[20]	152.0	142.9	143.9	150.5	155.9	168.2	181.0	193.1	...	...
Israel Israël										
Passenger cars										
Voitures de tourisme	932.4	992.9	1 064.9	1 131.0	1 195.1	1 252.0	1 298.0	1 341.3	1 422.0	1 474.0
Commercial vehicles										
Véhicules utilitaires	200.0	217.0	250.0	263.0	279.0	292.0	297.9	308.8	328.0	350.2

60

Motor vehicles in use
Passenger cars and commercial vehicles: thousands *[cont.]*

Véhicules automobiles en circulation
Voitures de tourisme et véhicules utilitaires : milliers *[suite]*

Country or area Pays ou zone	1992	1993	1994	1995	1996	1997	1998	1999	2000	2001
Italy Italie										
Passenger cars										
Voitures de tourisme	29 429.6	29 652.0	29 665.3	30 149.6	30 467.1	30 741.9	31 370.8	31 953.2	32 583.8	...
Commercial vehicles										
Véhicules utilitaires	2 763.0	2 663.0	2 745.5	2 863.5	3 177.7	3 253.7	3 336.4	3 409.5	3 377.6	...
Jamaica Jamaïque										
Passenger cars										
Voitures de tourisme	73.0	81.1	86.8	104.0	120.7	156.8	140.4[1]	140.4[1]	...	...
Commercial vehicles										
Véhicules utilitaires	30.5	36.2	41.3	49.1	52.8	56.1	54.7[1]	56.6[1]	...	...
Japan[35] Japon[35]										
Passenger cars[36]										
Voitures de tourisme[36]	38 964.0	40 772.0	42 679.0	44 680.0	46 869.0	48 611.0	49 896.0	51 165.0	52 738.0	53 541.2
Commercial vehicles										
Véhicules utilitaires	21 383.0	21 132.0	20 916.0	20 676.0	20 334.0	19 859.0	19 821.0	18 869.0	18 463.6	18 103.6
Jordan[4] Jordanie[4]										
Passenger cars										
Voitures de tourisme	181.5	175.3	164.0	188.0	212.2	202.1	200.0	213.0	255.8	322.4
Commercial vehicles										
Véhicules utilitaires	51.5	63.8	75.3	76.7	80.6	85.1	106.9	109.0	104.5	138.6
Kazakhstan Kazakhstan										
Passenger cars										
Voitures de tourisme	916.1	955.9	991.7	1 034.1	997.5	973.3	971.2	987.7	1 000.3	...
Commercial vehicles										
Véhicules utilitaires	456.9	456.4	428.1	390.9	360.4	315.3	277.1	257.4	256.6	...
Kenya Kenya										
Passenger cars										
Voitures de tourisme	165.1	171.5	171.6	172.8	202.7	211.9	225.1	238.9	244.8	255.4
Commercial vehicles										
Véhicules utilitaires	158.1	162.2	162.3	163.3	187.7	196.1	239.4	249.8	256.2	263.7
Korea, Republic of[37] Corée, République de[37]										
Passenger cars										
Voitures de tourisme	3 461.1	4 271.3	5 148.7	6 006.3	6 893.6	7 586.5	7 580.9	7 837.2	...	...
Commercial vehicles										
Véhicules utilitaires	1 745.1	1 976.6	2 226.7	2 429.2	2 625.6	2 791.2	2 854.0	3 291.3	...	...
Kuwait Koweït										
Passenger cars										
Voitures de tourisme	579.8	600.0	629.7	662.9	701.2	540.0	585.0	624.0	...	...
Commercial vehicles										
Véhicules utilitaires	151.1	147.0	148.7	153.5	160.0	115.0	124.0	130.0	...	...
Kyrgyzstan Kirghizistan										
Passenger cars										
Voitures de tourisme	215.0	188.3	140.0	197.5	172.4	176.1	187.7	187.3	189.8	191.6
Latvia Lettonie										
Passenger cars										
Voitures de tourisme	350.0	367.5	251.6	331.8	379.9	431.8	482.7	525.6	556.8	586.2
Commercial vehicles										
Véhicules utilitaires	83.3	72.1	73.5	85.1	90.2	95.4	96.5	101.8	108.6	111.0
Lebanon Liban										
Passenger cars										
Voitures de tourisme	...	943.1	1 141.7	1 197.5	1 250.5	1 299.4[38]	1 335.7[38]	...	...	...
Commercial vehicles										
Véhicules utilitaires	...	77.3	82.9	84.7	87.4	92.1[38]	95.4[38]	...	...	...
Liberia[1] Libéria[1]										
Passenger cars										
Voitures de tourisme	...	17.4	17.4	17.4	17.4	17.4	17.4	15.3	16.0	...
Commercial vehicles										
Véhicules utilitaires	...	10.7	10.7	10.7	10.7	10.7	10.7	11.9	12.5	...
Libyan Arab Jamah. Jamah. arabe libyenne										
Passenger cars										
Voitures de tourisme	448.0[11]	448.0[11]	448.0[11]	448.0[11]	829.0	859.0	...	...	...	...

60

Motor vehicles in use
Passenger cars and commercial vehicles: thousands *[cont.]*
Véhicules automobiles en circulation
Voitures de tourisme et véhicules utilitaires : milliers *[suite]*

Country or area Pays ou zone	1992	1993	1994	1995	1996	1997	1998	1999	2000	2001
Commercial vehicles Véhicules utilitaires	322.0[11]	322.0[11]	322.0[11]	322.0[11]	357.5	362.4	...	...	...	...
Lithuania Lituanie										
Passenger cars Voitures de tourisme	565.3	597.7	652.8	718.5	785.1	882.1	980.9	1 089.3	1 172.4	1 133.5
Commercial vehicles Véhicules utilitaires	112.5	115.1	118.2	125.9	104.8	108.6	114.6	112.2	113.7	115.6
Luxembourg Luxembourg										
Passenger cars Voitures de tourisme	200.7	208.8	217.8	229.0	231.7	236.8	244.1	253.4	272.1	280.7
Commercial vehicles Véhicules utilitaires	21.1	22.4	25.0	26.1	25.5	26.2	27.3	28.8	48.6	48.7
Madagascar Madagascar										
Passenger cars Voitures de tourisme	10.9[1]	11.1[1]	11.1[1]	11.1[1]	11.1[1]	11.3[1]	64.0	...	...	...
Commercial vehicles Véhicules utilitaires	12.6[1]	13.3[1]	13.3[1]	13.3[1]	13.9[1]	15.5[1]	9.1	...	...	...
Malawi[4] Malawi[4]										
Passenger cars Voitures de tourisme	5.3	1.8	2.3	1.5	1.6	...	6.3[1]	12.6[1]	...	...
Commercial vehicles Véhicules utilitaires	2.7	1.4	1.8	2.2	1.9	...	19.6[1]	22.7[1]	...	...
Malaysia Malaisie										
Passenger cars Voitures de tourisme	131.0	132.8	186.6	256.4	325.7	379.5	163.8	300.4	350.4	400.4
Commercial vehicles[25] Véhicules utilitaires[25]	43.7	33.5	49.9	74.9	102.7	96.5	19.0	28.6	36.8	40.1
Maldives Maldives										
Passenger cars Voitures de tourisme	0.1	0.1	0.2	0.1	0.2	0.2	0.2	0.2	0.3	0.1
Commercial vehicles Véhicules utilitaires	0.1	0.2	0.2	0.1	0.1	0.2	0.2	0.2	0.4	0.1
Mali Mali										
Passenger cars Voitures de tourisme	21.0	6.3	6.3	6.3	6.3[1]	6.3[1]	15.8[1]	17.6[1]	...	...
Commercial vehicles Véhicules utilitaires	8.4	6.6	6.8	7.2	7.6[1]	7.6[1]	21.5[1]	28.1[1]	...	...
Malta Malte										
Passenger cars Voitures de tourisme	125.0	152.6	170.6	199.3	166.2	183.8	191.8	201.8	210.9	219.0
Commercial vehicles Véhicules utilitaires	35.4	50.9	55.7	40.8	39.4	47.4	49.5	51.2	51.4	52.6
Martinique[1] Martinique[1]										
Passenger cars Voitures de tourisme	102.6	80.8	86.7	95.0	...	...	...	...	...	...
Commercial vehicles Véhicules utilitaires	31.9	19.3	20.0	21.5	...	...	...	...	...	...
Mauritania[1] Mauritanie[1]										
Passenger cars Voitures de tourisme	8.0	5.0	5.1	5.1	5.2	5.3	8.6	9.9	...	...
Commercial vehicles Véhicules utilitaires	5.5	5.0	5.3	5.6	6.0	6.3	16.7	17.3	...	...
Mauritius Maurice										
Passenger cars Voitures de tourisme	52.4	55.8	59.6	63.6	68.1	73.4	78.5	83.0	87.5	92.7
Commercial vehicles Véhicules utilitaires	20.6	22.1	23.3	24.4	25.3	26.6	29.1	31.7	34.2	36.5
Mexico[4] Mexique[4]										
Passenger cars Voitures de tourisme	7 750.0	8 112.0	7 772.0	8 074.0	8 437.0	9 023.0	9 761.0	10 282.0	10 832.0	11 004.0

60
Motor vehicles in use
Passenger cars and commercial vehicles: thousands *[cont.]*

Véhicules automobiles en circulation
Voitures de tourisme et véhicules utilitaires : milliers *[suite]*

Country or area Pays ou zone	1992	1993	1994	1995	1996	1997	1998	1999	2000	2001
Commercial vehicles										
Véhicules utilitaires	3 601.0	3 695.0	3 759.0	3 751.0	3 773.0	4 034.0	4 282.0	4 569.0	4 822.0	4 887.0
Morocco[12] Maroc[12]										
Passenger cars										
Voitures de tourisme	778.9	849.3	944.0	992.0	1 018.1	1 060.3	1 108.7	1 161.9	1 211.1	...
Commercial vehicles										
Véhicules utilitaires	307.4	316.7	332.1	343.2	351.6	365.7	382.0	400.3	415.7	...
Mozambique[1] Mozambique[1]										
Passenger cars										
Voitures de tourisme	84.0	84.0	27.2	27.2	27.2	27.2	52.2	78.6	...	...
Commercial vehicles										
Véhicules utilitaires	26.2	26.8	14.3	14.4	14.5	14.5	26.5	46.9	...	...
Myanmar[4] Myanmar[4]										
Passenger cars										
Voitures de tourisme	100.2	115.9	125.4	145.4	171.3	177.9	177.6	171.1	173.9	175.4
Commercial vehicles										
Véhicules utilitaires	59.7	66.6	58.2	63.1	68.3	74.8	75.9	83.4	90.4	98.9
Nepal Népal										
Passenger cars										
Voitures de tourisme	26.2	28.4	31.5	34.5	39.8	42.8	46.9	49.4	...	...
Commercial vehicles										
Véhicules utilitaires	9.3	103.7	99.5	113.8	131.8	147.9	164.2	185.8	...	...
Netherlands[4,39] Pays-Bas[4,39]										
Passenger cars										
Voitures de tourisme	5 247.0	5 341.0	5 456.0	5 581.0	5 664.0	5 810.0	5 931.0	6 120.0	...	...
Commercial vehicles										
Véhicules utilitaires	590.0	631.0	652.0	654.0	666.0	695.0	738.0	806.0	...	...
New Caledonia Nouvelle-Calédonie										
Passenger cars										
Voitures de tourisme	56.7[1]	58.5[1]	50.4[1]	52.8[1]	55.1[1]	57.9[1]	76.4[2]	80.3[2]	83.5[2]	85.5[2]
Commercial vehicles[1]										
Véhicules utilitaires[1]	21.2	22.6	17.2	18.4	20.8	23.0	...	...	...	...
New Zealand[40] Nouvelle-Zélande[40]										
Passenger cars										
Voitures de tourisme	1 554.9	1 575.6	1 615.9	1 665.0	1 655.8	1 697.2	1 768.2	1 855.8	1 905.6	1 936.8
Commercial vehicles										
Véhicules utilitaires	330.9	344.9	396.2	411.9	403.0	407.8	422.6	433.6	438.1	436.3
Nicaragua Nicaragua										
Passenger cars										
Voitures de tourisme	67.2	68.4	72.4	44.9	50.7	57.6	62.9	67.9	73.0	82.2
Commercial vehicles										
Véhicules utilitaires	69.5	66.3	69.5	56.7	63.8	72.8	81.7	91.1	98.1	107.7
Niger Niger										
Passenger cars										
Voitures de tourisme	16.0[1]	16.0[11]	16.0[11]	16.0[11]	...	...	12.1[1]	26.0[1]	...	...
Commercial vehicles										
Véhicules utilitaires	18.0[1]	18.0[11]	18.0[11]	18.0[11]	...	...	30.6[1]	35.6[1]	...	...
Nigeria[41] Nigéria[41]										
Passenger cars										
Voitures de tourisme	37.4	63.6	45.4	46.1	40.7	52.3	...	...	...	...
Commercial vehicles										
Véhicules utilitaires	4.6	1.4	6.8	8.6	10.5	13.5	...	...	...	...
Norway[4] Norvège[4]										
Passenger cars										
Voitures de tourisme	1 619.4	1 633.0	1 653.7	1 684.7	1 661.2	1 758.0	1 786.0	1 813.6	1 851.9	1 872.9
Commercial vehicles[42]										
Véhicules utilitaires[42]	341.6	352.5	366.3	382.0	392.1	412.2	427.0	440.0	451.0	463.7
Oman Oman										
Passenger cars[43]										
Voitures de tourisme[43]	171.3	184.3	194.5	204.0	220.4	245.1	279.1	310.4	344.0	359.2

60

Motor vehicles in use
Passenger cars and commercial vehicles: thousands *[cont.]*
Véhicules automobiles en circulation
Voitures de tourisme et véhicules utilitaires : milliers *[suite]*

Country or area Pays ou zone	1992	1993	1994	1995	1996	1997	1998	1999	2000	2001
Commercial vehicles[44] Véhicules utilitaires[44]	84.4	86.6	88.2	89.3	92.0	101.2	110.7	117.6	124.6	132.9
Pakistan[3,4] Pakistan[3,4]										
Passenger cars Voitures de tourisme	659.0	670.0	690.9	772.6	816.1	863.0	930.1	1 004.3	1 066.1	1 130.6
Commercial vehicles Véhicules utilitaires	262.9	269.6	285.8	305.8	333.6	351.7	379.0	406.4	434.5	463.0
Panama Panama										
Passenger cars Voitures de tourisme	149.9	161.2	169.8	178.3	188.3	198.7	212.6	222.4	223.1	...
Commercial vehicles Véhicules utilitaires	50.4	55.0	56.5	60.4	60.5	64.2	68.4	71.9	74.4	...
Papua New Guinea Papouasie-Nvl-Guinée										
Passenger cars Voitures de tourisme	11.5[11]	13.0[11]	11.5[11]	20.0[11]	21.7[1]	21.7[1]	21.7[1]	...	...	...
Commercial vehicles Véhicules utilitaires	29.8[11]	32.0[11]	30.8[11]	35.0[11]	81.1[1]	85.5[1]	89.7[1]			
Paraguay Paraguay										
Passenger cars Voitures de tourisme	221.1	250.7	...	...	...	...	...	...	...	...
Commercial vehicles Véhicules utilitaires	34.9	37.7	...	...	...	...	...	...	...	...
Peru Pérou										
Passenger cars Voitures de tourisme	402.4	418.6	444.2	505.8	557.0	595.8	645.9	684.6	731.3	...
Commercial vehicles Véhicules utilitaires	270.6	288.8	316.6	356.8	379.5	389.9	409.8	429.7	459.6	...
Philippines[45] Philippines[45]										
Passenger cars Voitures de tourisme	1 227.8	1 365.4	1 485.4	1 624.9	1 803.7	1 934.7	1 993.2	2 084.7	2 156.1	2 218.6
Commercial vehicles Véhicules utilitaires	172.5	189.9	207.4	221.0	249.7	274.8	263.1	276.6	282.3	285.3
Poland Pologne										
Passenger cars Voitures de tourisme	6 504.7	6 770.6	7 153.1	7 517.3	8 054.4	8 533.5	8 890.8	9 282.8	9 991.3	10 503.1
Commercial vehicles[46] Véhicules utilitaires[46]	1 299.5	1 321.9	1 394.3	1 440.1	1 517.6	1 569.9	1 644.4	1 762.9	1 962.7	2 062.9
Portugal[47] Portugal[47]										
Passenger cars[48] Voitures de tourisme[48]	3 049.8	3 295.1	3 532.0	3 751.0	4 002.6[49]	4 272.5[49]	4 587.3[49]	4 931.7[49]	5 260.3	...
Commercial vehicles Véhicules utilitaires	964.0	1 050.1	1 158.6	1 218.8	1 292.2[49]	1 383.9[49]	1 492.4[49]	1 600.1[49]	1 727.9	...
Puerto Rico[3] Porto Rico[3]										
Passenger cars Voitures de tourisme	1 347.0	1 393.3	1 484.7	1 597.0	1 726.4	1 840.6	1 962.4	2 038.9	2 035.3	2 064.1
Commercial vehicles Véhicules utilitaires	201.5	239.6	257.7	270.6	290.2	288.9	298.9	306.6	...	...
Qatar Qatar										
Passenger cars Voitures de tourisme	123.6	132.1	137.6	143.4	151.9	164.7	178.0	188.0	199.6	...
Commercial vehicles Véhicules utilitaires	57.5	61.5	65.8	69.5	73.8	79.1	85.0	88.9	92.9	
Republic of Moldova[50] République de Moldova[50]										
Passenger cars Voitures de tourisme	166.3	166.4	169.4	165.9	173.6	206.0	222.8	232.3	238.4	256.5
Commercial vehicles[51] Véhicules utilitaires[51]	10.1	8.9	7.8	12.9	11.5	10.4	9.2	8.1	6.9	6.3
Réunion Réunion										
Passenger cars Voitures de tourisme	119.3	127.8	133.1	142.1	150.6	159.3	167.9	180.6	247.8[2]	...

60

Motor vehicles in use
Passenger cars and commercial vehicles: thousands *[cont.]*

Véhicules automobiles en circulation
Voitures de tourisme et véhicules utilitaires : milliers *[suite]*

Country or area Pays ou zone	1992	1993	1994	1995	1996	1997	1998	1999	2000	2001
Commercial vehicles										
Véhicules utilitaires	36.6	39.2	40.9	43.6	46.2	49.0	51.6	54.0	...	...
Romania Roumanie										
Passenger cars										
Voitures de tourisme	1 593.0	1 793.0	2 020.0	2 197.0	2 392.0	2 605.0	2 822.0	2 980.0	3 129.0	3 226.0
Commercial vehicles										
Véhicules utilitaires	311.0	336.0	362.0	385.0	409.0	428.0	456.0	489.0	497.0	504.0
Russian Federation Fédération de Russie										
Passenger cars[52]										
Voitures de tourisme[52]	10 531.3	11 518.3	12 863.5	14 195.3	15 815.0	17 631.6	18 819.6	19 717.8	20 353.0	21 231.8
Commercial vehicles										
Véhicules utilitaires	2 847.9	2 924.0	3 006.0	3 078.1	3 041.1	3 103.1	3 108.2	3 196.2	3 232.4	3 329.4
Rwanda Rwanda										
Passenger cars										
Voitures de tourisme	7.9[11]	...	...	1.2	3.2	5.8	7.7	9.2	10.7	...
Commercial vehicles										
Véhicules utilitaires	2.0[11]	...	...	1.7	4.6	9.0	11.3	13.6	16.3	...
Saint Kitts and Nevis Saint-Kitts-et-Nevis										
Passenger cars										
Voitures de tourisme	4.1	4.5	4.8	5.2	5.5	6.3	6.3	7.7	...	...
Commercial vehicles										
Véhicules utilitaires	2.3	2.4	2.4	2.3	2.5	2.4	2.9	3.9	...	...
Saint Lucia Sainte-Lucie										
Passenger cars										
Voitures de tourisme	9.3	10.1	11.4	12.5	13.5	...	...	...	...	...
Commercial vehicles										
Véhicules utilitaires	9.3	10.5	9.5	...	10.8					
St. Vincent-Grenadines St. Vincent-Grenadines										
Passenger cars										
Voitures de tourisme	5.0	5.4	5.7	5.3	6.1	7.4	8.0	8.7	9.1	9.9
Commercial vehicles										
Véhicules utilitaires	2.0	3.1	3.2	3.7	3.2	3.8	4.1	3.9	4.0	4.0
Saudi Arabia[2,53] Arabie saoudite[2,53]										
Passenger cars										
Voitures de tourisme	5 328.5	5 588.0	5 861.6	6 111.1	6 333.9	6 580.0	7 046.0	...	...	...
Senegal[11] Sénégal[11]										
Passenger cars										
Voitures de tourisme	100.0	102.0	105.0	106.0	...	...	...	...	...	...
Commercial vehicles										
Véhicules utilitaires	45.0	46.0	45.0	48.0	...	...	...	...	...	...
Seychelles Seychelles										
Passenger cars										
Voitures de tourisme	4.9	6.1	5.6	5.5	6.2	6.7	6.5	6.4	...	...
Commercial vehicles										
Véhicules utilitaires	1.5	1.8	1.8	1.9	2.0	2.1	2.2	2.2	...	...
Sierra Leone[1] Sierra Leone[1]										
Passenger cars										
Voitures de tourisme	36.0	32.4	32.4	32.4	32.4	32.4	18.5	19.2	...	...
Commercial vehicles										
Véhicules utilitaires	12.0	11.9	11.9	11.9	11.9	11.9	14.8	14.8	...	...
Singapore Singapour										
Passenger cars										
Voitures de tourisme	302.8	321.9	340.6	363.9	384.5	396.4	395.2	403.2	413.5	426.4
Commercial vehicles										
Véhicules utilitaires	131.5	135.2	136.8	140.0	142.7	144.8	142.6	141.3	137.2	139.9
Slovakia Slovaquie										
Passenger cars										
Voitures de tourisme	953.2	994.9	994.0	1 015.8	1 058.4	1 135.9	1 196.1	1 236.4	1 274.2	1 292.8
Commercial vehicles										
Véhicules utilitaires	134.7	130.6	131.2	131.5	127.2	135.0	144.4	149.4	153.2	161.5

60

Motor vehicles in use
Passenger cars and commercial vehicles: thousands *[cont.]*

Véhicules automobiles en circulation
Voitures de tourisme et véhicules utilitaires : milliers *[suite]*

Country or area Pays ou zone	1992	1993	1994	1995	1996	1997	1998	1999	2000	2001
Slovenia Slovénie										
Passenger cars										
Voitures de tourisme	615.7	641.7	667.2	709.6	740.9	778.3	813.4	848.3	868.3	884.2
Commercial vehicles										
Véhicules utilitaires	34.0	34.7	36.6	40.2	42.6	44.9	52.0	54.3	56.8	58.6
Somalia[11] Somalie[11]										
Passenger cars										
Voitures de tourisme	10.5	10.7	11.8	12.0	...	...	...	...	...	...
Commercial vehicles										
Véhicules utilitaires	11.5	12.0	12.2	12.0	...	...	...	...	...	...
South Africa Afrique du Sud										
Passenger cars										
Voitures de tourisme	3 739.2[33]	3 488.6[1]	3 814.9[1]	3 830.8[1]	3 846.8[1]	3 664.0[1]	3 540.6[1]	3 966.3[55]	...	...
Commercial vehicles										
Véhicules utilitaires	1 551.4[54]	1 784.9[1]	1 596.8[1]	1 625.5[1]	1 653.5[1]	1 868.0[1]	1 736.0[1]	2 248.1[56]	...	...
Spain Espagne										
Passenger cars										
Voitures de tourisme	13 102.3	13 440.7	13 733.8	14 212.3	14 753.8	15 297.4	16 050.1	16 847.4	17 449.2	18 150.8
Commercial vehicles										
Véhicules utilitaires	2 773.4	2 859.6	2 952.8	3 071.6	3 200.3	3 360.1	3 561.5	3 788.7	3 977.9	4 161.1
Sri Lanka[4] Sri Lanka[4]										
Passenger cars										
Voitures de tourisme	189.5	197.3	210.1	228.9	246.5	261.6	284.3	309.5	335.0	...
Commercial vehicles										
Véhicules utilitaires	159.9	166.3	175.3	184.3	191.5	199.2	211.2	227.1	236.9	...
Sudan Soudan										
Passenger cars										
Voitures de tourisme	116.0[11]	30.8[11]	30.8[11]	30.8[11]	...	...	38.0[1]	40.6[1]	...	...
Commercial vehicles										
Véhicules utilitaires	57.0[11]	35.9[11]	35.9[11]	35.9[11]	...	...	50.4[1]	53.9[1]	...	...
Suriname Suriname										
Passenger cars										
Voitures de tourisme	42.6	46.6	42.2	49.3	46.4	50.2	55.4	59.9	61.4	...
Commercial vehicles										
Véhicules utilitaires	16.0	18.2	17.9	17.3	19.5	20.5	21.1	22.5	23.5	...
Swaziland[6] Swaziland[6]										
Passenger cars										
Voitures de tourisme	74.8	79.0	82.2	86.7	91.7	97.8	102.2	108.7	...	...
Commercial vehicles										
Véhicules utilitaires	35.5	37.2	36.6	40.0	42.1	44.8	46.6	49.5	...	...
Sweden Suède										
Passenger cars										
Voitures de tourisme	3 588.4	3 566.0	3 594.2	3 630.8	3 654.9	3 702.8	3 790.7	3 890.2	3 998.6	4 018.5
Commercial vehicles										
Véhicules utilitaires	319.2	316.0	317.8	322.3	326.5	336.6	352.9	369.2	388.6	409.9
Switzerland[32] Suisse[32]										
Passenger cars										
Voitures de tourisme	3 091.2	3 109.5	3 165.0	3 229.2	3 268.1	3 323.4	3 383.2	3 467.3	3 545.2	...
Commercial vehicles										
Véhicules utilitaires	291.3	288.8	292.4	299.3	300.7	302.7	306.4	313.6	318.8	...
Syrian Arab Republic Rép. arabe syrienne										
Passenger cars										
Voitures de tourisme	128.0	149.8	159.1	166.5	173.6	175.9	179.0	180.7	181.7	...
Commercial vehicles										
Véhicules utilitaires	136.7	162.3	188.4	224.0	251.4	269.1	282.6	313.5	345.6	...
Tajikistan Tadjikistan										
Passenger cars										
Voitures de tourisme	...	...	175.0	166.4	151.5	154.1	146.6	141.7	117.1	...
Commercial vehicles										
Véhicules utilitaires	...	...	10.9	9.8	9.6	10.2	13.3	16.4	16.8	...

60

Motor vehicles in use
Passenger cars and commercial vehicles: thousands *[cont.]*

Véhicules automobiles en circulation
Voitures de tourisme et véhicules utilitaires : milliers *[suite]*

Country or area Pays ou zone	1992	1993	1994	1995	1996	1997	1998	1999	2000	2001
Thailand Thaïlande										
Passenger cars[57]										
Voitures de tourisme[57]	1 396.6	1 598.2	1 798.8	1 913.2	2 098.6	2 350.4	2 529.2	2 650.5	2 665.4	...
Commercial vehicles[58]										
Véhicules utilitaires[58]	1 763.5	2 091.1	2 384.1	2 735.6	3 149.3	3 534.9	3 746.7	4 065.3	4 220.1	...
TFYR of Macedonia L'ex-R.y. Macédoine										
Passenger cars										
Voitures de tourisme	280.0	290.0	263.0	286.0	284.0	289.0	289.0	290.0	300.0	...
Commercial vehicles										
Véhicules utilitaires	22.1	23.0	19.9	22.1	21.8	22.2	22.6	22.5	23.3	...
Togo[1] Togo[1]										
Passenger cars										
Voitures de tourisme	25.0	18.2	74.6	74.7	74.7	74.7	27.2	36.0	...	...
Commercial vehicles										
Véhicules utilitaires	16.1	11.6	34.6	34.6	34.6	34.6	11.0	17.6	...	...
Tonga Tonga										
Passenger cars										
Voitures de tourisme	3.3	4.7	5.3	7.7	8.6	9.0	9.7	10.8	...	...
Commercial vehicles										
Véhicules utilitaires	3.7	5.0	5.9	8.1	9.7	8.9	9.4	10.4	...	...
Trinidad and Tobago Trinité-et-Tobago										
Passenger cars										
Voitures de tourisme	166.7	159.0	162.1	166.8	180.2	194.3	213.4	229.4	...	...
Commercial vehicles										
Véhicules utilitaires	40.8	39.2	40.2	42.2	44.9	47.7	51.1	53.9	...	...
Tunisia Tunisie										
Passenger cars										
Voitures de tourisme	277.6	299.1	327.0	356.3	379.2	415.2	445.6	482.2	516.5	552.9
Commercial vehicles[59]										
Véhicules utilitaires[59]	151.6	165.3	177.7	189.3	201.5	217.1	233.0	250.3	265.7	281.5
Turkey Turquie										
Passenger cars[60]										
Voitures de tourisme[60]	2 181.4	2 619.9	2 861.6	3 058.5	3 274.1	3 570.1	3 838.3	4 072.3	4 422.2	4 534.8
Commercial vehicles[29]										
Véhicules utilitaires[29]	841.0	929.6	968.5	1 010.2	1 083.9	1 215.7	1 353.6	1 443.2	1 583.7	1 629.9
Uganda Ouganda										
Passenger cars										
Voitures de tourisme	19.0	20.5	24.2	28.9	35.6	42.0	46.9	48.3	49.0	53.1
Commercial vehicles										
Véhicules utilitaires	26.9	29.4	35.0	44.1	52.4	59.1	66.7	72.6	74.3	79.9
Ukraine Ukraine										
Passenger cars										
Voitures de tourisme	3 884.8	4 206.5	4 384.1	4 603.1	4 872.3	5 024.0	5 127.3	5 210.8	5 250.1	5 312.6
United Arab Emirates Emirats arabes unis										
Passenger cars										
Voitures de tourisme	257.8	297.1	332.5	321.6	346.3	...	...	...	...	...
Commercial vehicles										
Véhicules utilitaires	65.8	78.8	87.2	84.2	89.3					
United Kingdom[61] Royaume-Uni[61]										
Passenger cars										
Voitures de tourisme	20 973.0	21 291.0	21 740.0	21 949.9	22 819.0	23 450.0	23 881.0	24 594.0	...	...
Commercial vehicles										
Véhicules utilitaires	3 008.0	2 990.0	2 994.0	2 987.3	3 035.0	3 104.0	3 167.0	3 333.0		
United Rep. of Tanzania[1] Rép.-Unie de Tanzanie[1]										
Passenger cars										
Voitures de tourisme	44.0	13.6	13.6	13.8	13.8	13.8	31.2	33.9	...	...
Commercial vehicles										
Véhicules utilitaires	57.2	33.7	35.4	37.5	42.5	42.5	87.3	98.8	...	...
United States Etats-Unis										
Passenger cars[62]										
Voitures de tourisme[62]	187 737.4	187 291.5	191 071.6	193 963.4	198 662.0	199 973.0	203 168.7	207 788.4	212 706.4	221 821.1

60

Motor vehicles in use
Passenger cars and commercial vehicles: thousands *[cont.]*

Véhicules automobiles en circulation
Voitures de tourisme et véhicules utilitaires : milliers *[suite]*

Country or area Pays ou zone	1992	1993	1994	1995	1996	1997	1998	1999	2000	2001
Commercial vehicles Véhicules utilitaires	7 780.8	7 959.6	7 258.3	7 404.9	7 707.4	7 780.8	8 447.8	8 520.2	8 768.8	8 607.2
Uruguay Uruguay										
Passenger cars Voitures de tourisme	418.0	425.6	444.8	464.5	485.1	516.9	578.3	662.3	652.3	...
Commercial vehicles Véhicules utilitaires	45.0	44.3	46.2	45.8	48.4	50.3	53.9	57.8	56.1	...
Vanuatu[1] Vanuatu[1]										
Passenger cars Voitures de tourisme	4.0	2.7	7.1	7.4	2.7	2.7	2.5	2.6	...	...
Commercial vehicles Véhicules utilitaires	2.2	2.7	1.7	1.8	3.2	3.5	3.8	4.1	...	...
Venezuela Venezuela										
Passenger cars Voitures de tourisme	1 753.0	1 805.0	1 813.0	1 823.0	1 393.5[1]	1 313.9[1]	1 402.9[1]	1 420.0[1]	...	...
Commercial vehicles Véhicules utilitaires	559.0	576.0	578.0	581.0	664.6[1]	352.1[1]	786.2[1]	846.0[1]	...	...
Viet Nam Viet Nam										
Commercial vehicles Véhicules utilitaires	38.7	41.5	33.8	39.1	41.5	41.5	49.4	57.8	69.9	...
Yemen Yémen										
Passenger cars Voitures de tourisme	140.6	176.1	196.5	224.1	259.4	327.1	380.6	...	...	...
Commercial vehicles Véhicules utilitaires	223.0	251.8	266.4	291.7	345.3	413.1	422.1	...	...	...
Zambia Zambie										
Passenger cars Voitures de tourisme	3.0	3.0	3.9	5.7	3.7	...	...	...	...	...
Commercial vehicles Véhicules utilitaires	4.0	2.7	4.2	7.3	3.9	...	...	...	...	...
Zimbabwe Zimbabwe										
Passenger cars Voitures de tourisme	310.0	328.3	349.1	384.0	422.4	464.7	521.0	534.6	544.5	...
Commercial vehicles Véhicules utilitaires	30.4	32.5	34.5	37.9	42.2	46.4	54.3	58.5	67.7	

Source:
United Nations Statistics Division, New York, transport statistics
database.

Source:
Organisation des Nations Unies, Division de statistique, New York, la
base de données pour les statistiques des transports.

1 Source: World Automotive Market Report, Auto and Truck
   International (Illinois).
2 Including commercial vehicles.
3 Data refer to fiscal years beginning 1 July.

4 Including vehicles operated by police or other governmental
   security organizations.
5 Including farm tractors.
6 Excluding government vehicles.
7 Including buses and coaches.
8 Including pick-ups.
9 Number of licensed vehicles.
10 Including only vehicles (trucks) weighing 4,500 kilograms to
    14,999 kilograms and vehicles (tractor-trailers and Class A
    trucks) weighing 15,000 kilograms or more.

11 Source: AAMA Motor Vehicle Facts and Figures, American
    Automobile Manufacturers Association (Michigan).
12 Including special-purpose vehicles.
13 Excluding pick-ups.

1 Source : "World Automotive Market Report, Auto and Truck
   International" (Illinois).
2 Y compris véhicules utilitaires.
3 Les données se réfèrent aux exercices budgétaires
   commençant le 1er juillet.
4 Y compris véhicules de la police ou d'autres services
   gouvernementales d'ordre public.
5 Y compris tracteurs agricoles.
6 Non compris les véhicules des administrations publiques.
7 Y compris autobus et autocars.
8 Y compris fourgonnettes.
9 Nombre de véhicules automobiles licensés.
10 Y compris seulement véhicules (camions) pesant de 4,500
    kilogrammes à 14,999 kilogrammes et véhicules (semi-
    remorques et camions de Classe A) pesant 15,000
    kilogrammes ou plus.
11 Source: AAMA Motor Vehicle Facts and Figures, American
    Automobile Manufacturers Association (Michigan).
12 Y compris véhicules à usages spéciaux.
13 Non compris fourgonnettes.

60

Motor vehicles in use
Passenger cars and commercial vehicles: thousands *[cont.]*
Véhicules automobiles en circulation
Voitures de tourisme et véhicules utilitaires : milliers *[suite]*

14 Including minibuses.	14 Y compris minibuses.
15 Beginning 1996, methodological change in calculation.	15 Changement de méthode de calcul introduit en 1996.
16 Including special-purpose commercial vehicles and farm tractors.	16 Y compris véhicules utilitaires à usages spéciaux et tracteurs agricoles.
17 Including vans.	17 Y compris fourgons.
18 Excluding vans.	18 Non compris fourgons.
19 Excluding Faeroe Islands.	19 Non compris les Iles Féroés.
20 Including large public service excavators and trench diggers.	20 Y compris les grosses excavatrices et machines d'excavation de tranchées de travaux publics.
21 Including dump trucks and motor scooters.	21 Y compris camions-bennes et scooters.
22 Data refer to fiscal years ending 7 July.	22 Les données se réfèrent aux exercices budgétaires finissant le 7 juillet.
23 Including private and government cars, rental and hired cars.	23 Y compris les voitures particulières et celles des administrations publiques, les voitures de location et de louage.
24 Including pick-ups, ambulances, light and heavy fire engines and all other vehicles such as trailers, cranes, loaders, forklifts, etc.	24 Y compris les fourgonnettes, les ambulances, les voitures de pompiers légères pompiers légères et lourdes, et tous autres véhicules tels que remoques, grues, chargeuses, chariots élévateurs à fourches, etc.
25 Excluding tractors.	25 Non compris tracteurs.
26 Including only trailers and semi-trailer combinations less than 10 years old.	26 Y compris les légères remorques et semi-remorques de moins de 10 ans seulement.
27 Beginning 2001, data refer to fiscal years ending 1 January. For all previous years data refer to fiscal years ending 1 July.	27 A compter de l'année 2001, les données se réfèrent aux exercices budgétaires finissant le 1er janvier. Pour toutes les années antérieures, les données se réfèrent aux exercices budgétaires finissant le 1er juillet.
28 Including "other, not specified", registered motor vehicles.	28 Y compris "autres, non-spécifiés", véhicules automobiles enregistrés.
29 Excluding tractors and semi-trailer combinations.	29 Non compris ensembles tracteur-remorque et semi-remorque.
30 Including goods vehicles, tractors, trailers, three-wheeled passengers and goods vehicles and other miscellaneous vehicles which are not separately classified.	30 Y compris véhicules de transport de marchandises, camions-remorques, remorques, véhicules à trois roues (passagers et marchandises) et autres véhicules divers qui ne font pas l'objet d'une catégories separée.
31 Data refer to fiscal years ending 20 March.	31 Les données se réfèrent aux exercices budgétaires finissant le 20 mars.
32 Data refer to fiscal years ending 30 September.	32 Les données se réfèrent aux exercices budgétaires finissant le 30 septembre.
33 Including mini-buses equipped for transport of nine to fifteen passengers.	33 Y compris mini-buses ayant une capacité de neuf à quinze passagers.
34 Including school buses.	34 Y compris l'autobus de l'école.
35 Excluding small vehicles.	35 Non compris véhicules petites.
36 Including cars with a seating capacity of up to 10 persons.	36 Y compris véhicules comptant jusqu'à 10 places.
37 Numbered of registered motor vehicles.	37 Nombre de véhicules automobiles enregistrès.
38 Source: United Nations Economic and Social Commission for Western Asia (ESCWA).	38 Source : Commission économique et sociale pour l'Asie occidentale (CESAO).
39 Excluding diplomatic corps vehicles.	39 Non compris véhicules des diplomates.
40 Data refer to fiscal years ending 31 March.	40 Les données se réfèrent aux exercices budgétaires finissant le 31 mars.
41 Newly registered.	41 Enregistrés récemment.
42 Including hearses (Norway: registered before 1981).	42 Y compris corbillards (Norvège : enregistrés avant de 1981).
43 Excluding taxis.	43 Non compris taxis.
44 Trucks only.	44 Camions seulement.
45 Data prior to 1987 do not include diplomatic vehicles and tax-exempt vehicles.	45 Avant 1987, les données n'incluyaient pas les véhicules diplomatiques et les véhicules exempts d'impôts.
46 Excluding buses and tractors, but including special lorries.	46 Non compris autobus et tracteurs, mais y compris camions spéciaux.
47 Excluding Madeira and Azores.	47 Non compris Madère et Azores.
48 Including light miscellaneous vehicles.	48 Y compris les véhicules légers divers.
49 Including vehicles no longer in circulation.	49 Non compris véhicules retirés de la circulation.
50 Excluding the Transnistria region.	50 Non compris la région de Transnistria.
51 For the period 1980 - 1994, including motor vehicles for general use owned by Ministry of Transport. For the period 1995 - 2000, including motor vehicles owned by enterprises with main activity as road transport enterprises.	51 Pour la période 1980 - 1994, y compris les véhicules à moteur d'usage général appartenant au Ministère des transports. Pour la période 1995-2000, y compris les véhicules pour les entreprises de transport.
52 Beginning 1996, data provided by State Inspection for security	52 A partir de 1996, données fournies par l'Inspecteurat d'Etat

60

Motor vehicles in use
Passenger cars and commercial vehicles: thousands *[cont.]*
Véhicules automobiles en circulation
Voitures de tourisme et véhicules utilitaires : milliers *[suite]*

of road traffic of the Russian Federation Ministry of Internal Affairs.

53 Including motorcycles.

54 Including hearses, ambulances, fire-engines and jeeps specifically registered as commercial vehicles.

55 Including all minibuses and passenger vehicles which transport fewer than 12 persons.

56 Including vehicles which transport 12 persons or more and all light and heavy load vehicles, whether self-propelled or semi-trailer.

57 Including micro-buses and passenger pick-ups.

58 Including pick-ups, taxis, cars for hire, small rural buses.

59 Beginning 1987, including trailers.

60 Including vehicles seating not more than eight persons, including the driver.

61 Figures prior to 1992 were derived from vehicle taxation class; beginning 1992, figures derived from vehicle body type.

62 Including motorcycles (prior to 1993 only), mini-vans, sport-utility vehicles and pick-up trucks.

pour la sécurité routière du Ministère de l'Intérieur de la Fédération de Russie.

53 Y compris motocyclettes.

54 Y compris corbillards, ambulances, voitures de pompiers et jeeps spécifiquement immatriculés comme véhicules utilitaires.

55 Y compris tous les minibus et véhicules qui transportant moins de 12 passagers.

56 Y compris véhicules transportant 12 personnes ou plus et tous véhicules poids légèrs ou poids lourds, auto-propulsés ou semi-remorque.

57 Y compris les microbus et les camionnettes de transport de passagers.

58 Y compris les camionnettes, les taxis, les voitures de louage, les petits autobus ruraux.

59 A compter de l'année 1987, y compris remorques.

60 Y compris véhicules dont le nombre de places assises (y compris celle du conducteur) n'est pas supérieur à huit.

61 Les chiffres antérieurs à 1992 ont été calculés selon les catégories fiscales de véhicules; à partir de 1992, ils ont été calculés selan les types de carrosserie.

62 Y compris motocyclettes (antérieur à 1993 seulement), fourgonettes, véhicules de la classe quatre-x-quatre et camionettes légères.

61
Merchant shipping: fleets
All ships, oil tankers, and ore and bulk carrier fleets: thousand gross registered tons

Transports maritimes : flotte marchande
Tous les navires, pétroliers, et minéraliers et transporteurs de vracs : milliers de tonneaux de jauge brute

Country or area	1994	1995	1996	1997	1998	1999	2000	2001	Pays ou zone
World									**Monde**
All ships	**475 859**	**490 662**	**507 873**	**522 197**	**531 893**	**543 610**	**558 054**	**574 551**	**Tous les navires**
Oil tankers	**144 595**	**143 521**	**146 366**	**147 108**	**151 036**	**154 092**	**155 429**	**156 068**	**Pétroliers**
Ore and bulk carriers	**144 914**	**151 694**	**157 382**	**162 169**	**158 565**	**158 957**	**161 186**	**168 000**	**Minéral. et transp. de vracs**
Albania									**Albanie**
All ships	59	63	43	30	29	21	24	25	Tous les navires
Algeria									**Algérie**
All ships	936	980	983	983	1 005	1 005	961	964	Tous les navires
Oil tankers	35	35	34	34	33	33	19	19	Pétroliers
Ore and bulk carriers	172	172	172	172	172	172	173	173	Minéral. et transp. de vracs
Angola									**Angola**
All ships	90	90	82	68	74	66	66	63	Tous les navires
Oil tankers	2	2	2	3	3	3	3	3	Pétroliers
Anguilla									**Anguilla**
All ships	3	2	2	2	1	1	1	1	Tous les navires
Antigua and Barbuda									**Antigua-et-Barbuda**
All ships	1 507	1 842	2 176	2 214	2 788	3 622	4 224	4 688	Tous les navires
Oil tankers	2	4	4	4	7	5	5	5	Pétroliers
Ore and bulk carriers	93	102	174	174	294	196	194	251	Minéral. et transp. de vracs
Argentina									**Argentine**
All ships	716	595	586	579	499	477	464	422	Tous les navires
Oil tankers	124	107	114	105	102	100	83	49	Pétroliers
Ore and bulk carriers	62	62	34	34	34	34	34	34	Minéral. et transp. de vracs
Australia									**Australie**
All ships	3 012	2 853	2 718	2 607	2 188	2 084	1 912	1 888	Tous les navires
Oil tankers	779	579	467	380	226	226	226	226	Pétroliers
Ore and bulk carriers	1 049	1 011	1 039	1 036	893	801	624	624	Minéral. et transp. de vracs
Austria									**Autriche**
All ships	134	92	95	83	68	71	90	35	Tous les navires
Ore and bulk carriers	49	...	...	...	...	...	...	...	Minéral. et transp. de vracs
Azerbaijan									**Azerbaïdjan**
All ships	621	655	636	633	651	654	647	641	Tous les navires
Oil tankers	180	188	181	180	176	176	176	175	Pétroliers
Bahamas									**Bahamas**
All ships	22 915	23 603	24 409	25 523	27 716	29 483	31 445	33 386	Tous les navires
Oil tankers	10 393	10 326	10 863	10 810	11 982	13 158	13 504	14 469	Pétroliers
Ore and bulk carriers	4 269	4 501	4 425	4 728	4 990	4 943	4 833	5 339	Minéral. et transp. de vracs
Bahrain									**Bahreïn**
All ships	167	166	164	194	284	292	256	338	Tous les navires
Oil tankers	55	54	54	55	54	54	1	81	Pétroliers
Ore and bulk carriers	8	8	8	33	33	33	43	43	Minéral. et transp. de vracs
Bangladesh									**Bangladesh**
All ships	380	379	436	419	414	378	370	388	Tous les navires
Oil tankers	51	51	59	59	59	61	62	63	Pétroliers
Ore and bulk carriers	...	7	7	7	6	6	6	6	Minéral. et transp. de vracs
Barbados									**Barbade**
All ships	76	292	497	888	688	725	733	687	Tous les navires
Oil tankers	44	44	22	350	350	350	350	350	Pétroliers
Ore and bulk carriers	...	74	226	268	174	174	174	174	Minéral. et transp. de vracs
Belgium									**Belgique**
All ships	233	240	278	169	127	132	144	151	Tous les navires
Oil tankers	3	2	2	2	4	4	4	4	Pétroliers
Ore and bulk carriers	...	...	56	...	...	...	...	...	Minéral. et transp. de vracs
Belize									**Belize**
All ships	280	517	1 016	1 761	2 382	2 368	2 251	1 828	Tous les navires
Oil tankers	59	22	67	338	360	321	348	311	Pétroliers
Ore and bulk carriers	5	20	160	195	190	210	178	145	Minéral. et transp. de vracs
Benin									**Bénin**
All ships	1	1	1	1	1	1	1	1	Tous les navires
Bermuda									**Bermudes**
All ships	2 904	3 048	3 462	4 610	4 811	6 187	5 752	5 313	Tous les navires

61

Merchant shipping: fleets
All ships, oil tankers, and ore and bulk carrier fleets: thousand gross registered tons *[cont.]*

Transports maritimes : flotte marchande
Tous les navires, pétroliers, et minéraliers et transporteurs de vracs : milliers de tonneaux de jauge brute *[suite]*

Country or area	1994	1995	1996	1997	1998	1999	2000	2001	Pays ou zone
Oil tankers	1 569	1 586	1 586	2 069	2 144	2 652	2 152	1 661	Pétroliers
Ore and bulk carriers	165	248	301	1 018	1 089	1 910	1 911	1 885	Minéral. et transp. de vracs
Bolivia									**Bolivie**
All ships	...	...	...	2	16	179	178	174	Tous les navires
Oil tankers	...	...	...	...	...	18	25	65	Pétroliers
Ore and bulk carriers	...	...	...	...	7	49	28	25	Minéral. et transp. de vracs
Brazil									**Brésil**
All ships	5 283	5 077	4 530	4 372	4 171	3 933	3 809	3 687	Tous les navires
Oil tankers	2 112	2 090	1 803	1 854	1 825	1 770	1 642	1 564	Pétroliers
Ore and bulk carriers	2 214	2 077	1 890	1 706	1 501	1 453	1 437	1 418	Minéral. et transp. de vracs
British Virgin Islands									**Iles Vierges britanniques**
All ships	5	5	5	5	4	4	74	3	Tous les navires
Brunei Darussalam									**Brunéi Darussalam**
All ships	366	366	369	369	362	362	362	363	Tous les navires
Bulgaria									**Bulgarie**
All ships	1 295	1 166	1 150	1 128	1 091	1 036	990	955	Tous les navires
Oil tankers	256	216	194	163	145	145	143	114	Pétroliers
Ore and bulk carriers	578	502	532	542	532	518	518	517	Minéral. et transp. de vracs
Cambodia									**Cambodge**
All ships	6	60	206	439	616	999	1 447	1 997	Tous les navires
Oil tankers	...	...	...	...	...	7	31	111	Pétroliers
Ore and bulk carriers	...	...	95	146	169	305	405	511	Minéral. et transp. de vracs
Cameroon									**Cameroun**
All ships	36	37	37	11	13	14	14	14	Tous les navires
Canada									**Canada**
All ships	2 490	2 401	2 406	2 527	2 501	2 496	2 658	2 727	Tous les navires
Oil tankers	153	118	110	254	255	250	329	338	Pétroliers
Ore and bulk carriers	1 371	1 335	1 347	1 352	1 352	1 338	1 307	1 321	Minéral. et transp. de vracs
Cape Verde									**Cap-Vert**
All ships	22	16	15	21	20	21	21	17	Tous les navires
Oil tankers	0	0	0	1	1	1	1	1	Pétroliers
Cayman Islands									**Iles Caïmanes**
All ships	383	368	827	844	1 282	1 165	1 796	2 054	Tous les navires
Oil tankers	6	6	87	114	318	123	304	519	Pétroliers
Ore and bulk carriers	136	104	282	282	455	526	634	602	Minéral. et transp. de vracs
Channel Islands									**Iles Anglo-Normandes**
All ships	3	2	3	3	2	2	2	1	Tous les navires
Chile									**Chili**
All ships	721	761	691	722	753	820	842	880	Tous les navires
Oil tankers	41	71	93	93	100	100	100	100	Pétroliers
Ore and bulk carriers	306	294	191	213	188	203	217	224	Minéral. et transp. de vracs
China									**Chine**
All ships	15 827	16 943	16 993	16 339	16 503	16 315	16 499	16 646	Tous les navires
Oil tankers	2 278	2 295	2 190	2 014	2 029	2 084	2 250	2 352	Pétroliers
Ore and bulk carriers	5 960	6 677	6 781	6 464	6 832	6 648	6 618	6 634	Minéral. et transp. de vracs
China, Hong Kong SAR									**Chine, Hong Kong RAS**
All ships	7 703	8 795	7 863	5 771	6 171	7 973	10 242	13 710	Tous les navires
Oil tankers	697	669	396	22	340	515	734	1 537	Pétroliers
Ore and bulk carriers	5 570	6 405	5 749	4 211	4 208	5 233	6 947	8 740	Minéral. et transp. de vracs
China, Macao SAR									**Chine, Macao RAS**
All ships	2	2	2	2	2	4	4	4	Tous les navires
Colombia									**Colombie**
All ships	142	144	122	118	112	97	81	66	Tous les navires
Oil tankers	6	6	6	6	6	6	6	6	Pétroliers
Comoros									**Comores**
All ships	2	2	2	2	1	1	20	54	Tous les navires
Oil tankers	...	...	...	...	...	...	...	37	Pétroliers
Congo									**Congo**
All ships	9	12	6	7	4	4	3	3	Tous les navires
Cook Islands									**Iles Cook**
All ships	5	4	5	6	7	7	6	5	Tous les navires

61

Merchant shipping: fleets

All ships, oil tankers, and ore and bulk carrier fleets: thousand gross registered tons *[cont.]*

Transports maritimes : flotte marchande

Tous les navires, pétroliers, et minéraliers et transporteurs de vracs : milliers de tonneaux de jauge brute *[suite]*

Country or area	1994	1995	1996	1997	1998	1999	2000	2001	Pays ou zone
Costa Rica									**Costa Rica**
All ships	8	7	6	6	6	6	6	3	Tous les navires
Côte d'Ivoire									**Côte d'Ivoire**
All ships	62	40	13	11	10	10	9	9	Tous les navires
Oil tankers	1	1	1	1	1	1	1	1	Pétroliers
Croatia									**Croatie**
All ships	247	333	580	871	896	869	734	775	Tous les navires
Oil tankers	19	6	8	13	11	11	9	9	Pétroliers
Ore and bulk carriers	19	19	186	469	517	504	438	527	Minéral. et transp. de vracs
Cuba									**Cuba**
All ships	444	410	291	203	158	130	120	101	Tous les navires
Oil tankers	71	64	27	8	8	3	3	3	Pétroliers
Ore and bulk carriers	1	1	1	2	2	2	2	5	Minéral. et transp. de vracs
Cyprus									**Chypre**
All ships	23 293	24 653	23 799	23 653	23 302	23 641	23 206	22 762	Tous les navires
Oil tankers	4 634	4 341	3 733	3 779	3 848	3 987	4 165	3 803	Pétroliers
Ore and bulk carriers	12 317	13 084	12 653	11 819	11 090	11 511	11 437	11 776	Minéral. et transp. de vracs
Czech Republic									**République tchèque**
All ships	173	140	78	16	...	...	...	...	Tous les navires
Ore and bulk carriers	112	98	78	16	...	...	...	...	Minéral. et transp. de vracs
Dem. Rep. of the Congo									**Rép. dém. du Congo**
All ships	15	15	15	15	13	13	13	13	Tous les navires
Denmark									**Danemark**
All ships	5 698	5 747	5 885	5 754	5 687	5 809	6 823	6 913	Tous les navires
Oil tankers	788	1 053	1 024	741	379	494	1 171	1 230	Pétroliers
Ore and bulk carriers	569	493	521	522	522	464	356	204	Minéral. et transp. de vracs
Djibouti									**Djibouti**
All ships	4	4	4	4	4	4	4	2	Tous les navires
Dominica									**Dominique**
All ships	2	2	2	3	3	2	2	2	Tous les navires
Dominican Republic									**Rép. dominicaine**
All ships	12	12	12	11	9	10	10	9	Tous les navires
Oil tankers	1	1	1	1	...	...	...	...	Pétroliers
Ecuador									**Equateur**
All ships	270	168	178	145	171	309	301	306	Tous les navires
Oil tankers	77	77	81	80	93	223	219	219	Pétroliers
Ore and bulk carriers	22	...	...	...	...	...	...	...	Minéral. et transp. de vracs
Egypt									**Egypte**
All ships	1 262	1 269	1 230	1 288	1 368	1 368	1 346	1 350	Tous les navires
Oil tankers	245	222	222	223	210	209	208	207	Pétroliers
Ore and bulk carriers	420	510	487	575	613	601	546	586	Minéral. et transp. de vracs
El Salvador									**El Salvador**
All ships	1	1	1	1	1	2	2	1	Tous les navires
Equatorial Guinea									**Guinée équatoriale**
All ships	3	3	21	35	59	44	46	37	Tous les navires
Oil tankers	...	...	...	...	5	...	...	...	Pétroliers
Eritrea									**Erythrée**
All ships	0	12	1	7	7	16	16	21	Tous les navires
Oil tankers	...	...	...	...	2	2	2	2	Pétroliers
Estonia									**Estonie**
All ships	695	598	545	602	522	453	379	347	Tous les navires
Oil tankers	10	10	6	6	7	8	6	9	Pétroliers
Ore and bulk carriers	160	160	160	160	96	65	33	33	Minéral. et transp. de vracs
Ethiopia									**Ethiopie**
All ships	83	80	86	86	83	96	92	82	Tous les navires
Oil tankers	4	4	4	...	2	2	2	2	Pétroliers
Faeroe Islands									**Iles Féroé**
All ships	100	104	109	105	103	104	103	195	Tous les navires
Oil tankers	1	1	3	2	2	2	2	80	Pétroliers
Falkland Is. (Malvinas)									**Iles Falkland (Malvinas)**
All ships	16	20	30	38	39	45	53	55	Tous les navires

61

Merchant shipping: fleets
All ships, oil tankers, and ore and bulk carrier fleets: thousand gross registered tons *[cont.]*

Transports maritimes : flotte marchande
Tous les navires, pétroliers, et minéraliers et transporteurs de vracs : milliers de tonneaux de jauge brute *[suite]*

Country or area	1994	1995	1996	1997	1998	1999	2000	2001	Pays ou zone
Fiji									**Fidji**
All ships	31	32	36	36	29	29	29	29	Tous les navires
Oil tankers	3	3	3	3	3	3	3	3	Pétroliers
Finland									**Finlande**
All ships	1 404	1 519	1 511	1 559	1 629	1 658	1 620	1 595	Tous les navires
Oil tankers	303	303	303	303	303	303	304	304	Pétroliers
Ore and bulk carriers	71	80	80	80	90	90	90	105	Minéral. et transp. de vracs
France [1]									**France** [1]
All ships	4 242	4 086	4 291	4 570	4 738	4 766	4 681	4 495	Tous les navires
Oil tankers	1 957	1 943	1 797	2 049	2 248	2 198	2 108	1 900	Pétroliers
Ore and bulk carriers	462	291	448	355	354	539	538	355	Minéral. et transp. de vracs
Gabon									**Gabon**
All ships	28	32	33	35	27	16	13	13	Tous les navires
Oil tankers	1	1	1	1	1	1	1	1	Pétroliers
Ore and bulk carriers	11	24	24	24	12	...	...	...	Minéral. et transp. de vracs
Gambia									**Gambie**
All ships	3	1	1	2	2	2	2	2	Tous les navires
Georgia									**Géorgie**
All ships	439	282	206	128	118	132	119	277	Tous les navires
Oil tankers	220	136	115	73	73	76	8	21	Pétroliers
Ore and bulk carriers	170	104	48	0	0	0	0	5	Minéral. et transp. de vracs
Germany									**Allemagne**
All ships	5 696	5 626	5 842	6 950	8 084	6 514	6 552	6 300	Tous les navires
Oil tankers	83	14	11	17	9	8	29	51	Pétroliers
Ore and bulk carriers	285	238	48	2	2	2	2	2	Minéral. et transp. de vracs
Ghana									**Ghana**
All ships	106	114	135	130	115	118	119	123	Tous les navires
Oil tankers	1	1	1	2	6	6	6	7	Pétroliers
Gibraltar									**Gibraltar**
All ships	331	307	306	297	314	451	604	816	Tous les navires
Oil tankers	271	272	272	263	233	288	342	342	Pétroliers
Ore and bulk carriers	28	...	...	...	...	16	16	85	Minéral. et transp. de vracs
Greece									**Grèce**
All ships	30 162	29 435	27 507	25 288	25 225	24 833	26 402	28 678	Tous les navires
Oil tankers	13 386	12 836	13 066	11 894	12 587	13 158	13 681	14 889	Pétroliers
Ore and bulk carriers	12 988	12 795	10 705	9 472	8 771	7 709	8 077	9 026	Minéral. et transp. de vracs
Grenada									**Grenade**
All ships	1	5	1	1	1	1	1	1	Tous les navires
Guatemala									**Guatemala**
All ships	1	1	1	1	1	5	5	5	Tous les navires
Guinea									**Guinée**
All ships	8	7	7	9	11	11	11	11	Tous les navires
Guinea-Bissau									**Guinée-Bissau**
All ships	5	5	6	6	6	6	7	6	Tous les navires
Guyana									**Guyana**
All ships	15	15	16	17	16	14	16	15	Tous les navires
Haiti									**Haïti**
All ships	1	0	1	2	1	1	1	1	Tous les navires
Honduras									**Honduras**
All ships	1 206	1 206	1 198	1 053	1 083	1 220	1 111	967	Tous les navires
Oil tankers	85	97	103	107	108	131	143	184	Pétroliers
Ore and bulk carriers	118	138	115	114	77	133	101	74	Minéral. et transp. de vracs
Hungary									**Hongrie**
All ships	45	45	50	27	15	12	...	...	Tous les navires
Iceland									**Islande**
All ships	175	209	218	215	198	192	187	193	Tous les navires
Oil tankers	2	2	2	2	2	2	2	1	Pétroliers
Ore and bulk carriers	0	0	0	0	0	0	0	0	Minéral. et transp. de vracs
India									**Inde**
All ships	6 485	7 127	7 127	6 934	6 777	6 915	6 662	6 688	Tous les navires
Oil tankers	2 337	2 553	2 622	2 515	2 530	2 698	2 526	2 522	Pétroliers

61

Merchant shipping: fleets
All ships, oil tankers, and ore and bulk carrier fleets: thousand gross registered tons *[cont.]*

Transports maritimes : flotte marchande
Tous les navires, pétroliers, et minéraliers et transporteurs de vracs : milliers de tonneaux de jauge brute *[suite]*

Country or area	1994	1995	1996	1997	1998	1999	2000	2001	Pays ou zone
Ore and bulk carriers	2 740	3 183	3 081	3 013	2 832	2 748	2 663	2 706	Minéral. et transp. de vracs
Indonesia									**Indonésie**
All ships	2 678	2 771	2 973	3 195	3 252	3 241	3 384	3 613	Tous les navires
Oil tankers	646	738	849	844	841	830	805	831	Pétroliers
Ore and bulk carriers	170	205	222	335	358	380	335	344	Minéral. et transp. de vracs
Iran (Islamic Rep. of)									**Iran (Rép. islamique d')**
All ships	3 803	2 902	3 567	3 553	3 347	3 546	4 234	3 944	Tous les navires
Oil tankers	2 135	1 234	1 860	1 844	1 592	1 754	2 101	1 846	Pétroliers
Ore and bulk carriers	1 048	1 015	1 015	1 015	990	957	1 148	1 142	Minéral. et transp. de vracs
Iraq									**Iraq**
All ships	885	858	857	572	511	511	511	241	Tous les navires
Oil tankers	719	698	698	422	361	361	361	102	Pétroliers
Ireland									**Irlande**
All ships	190	213	219	235	184	219	248	300	Tous les navires
Oil tankers	9	9	3	3	0	0	0	...	Pétroliers
Ore and bulk carriers	3	...	...	...	...	8	26	26	Minéral. et transp. de vracs
Isle of Man									**Ile de Man**
All ships	2 093	2 300	3 140	4 759	4 203	4 729	5 431	6 057	Tous les navires
Oil tankers	1 059	872	1 023	2 401	1 893	2 409	2 877	3 154	Pétroliers
Ore and bulk carriers	223	414	756	831	783	732	795	911	Minéral. et transp. de vracs
Israel									**Israël**
All ships	646	599	679	794	752	728	612	611	Tous les navires
Oil tankers	1	1	1	1	1	1	1	1	Pétroliers
Ore and bulk carriers	23	12	12	12	...	...	...	...	Minéral. et transp. de vracs
Italy									**Italie**
All ships	6 818	6 699	6 594	6 194	6 819	8 048	9 049	9 655	Tous les navires
Oil tankers	2 181	1 956	1 781	1 608	1 547	1 660	1 639	1 426	Pétroliers
Ore and bulk carriers	1 549	1 535	1 553	1 303	1 525	1 851	2 049	1 829	Minéral. et transp. de vracs
Jamaica									**Jamaïque**
All ships	7	9	9	10	4	4	4	23	Tous les navires
Oil tankers	2	2	2	2	2	2	2	2	Pétroliers
Japan									**Japon**
All ships	22 102	19 913	19 201	18 516	17 780	17 063	15 257	14 565	Tous les navires
Oil tankers	6 421	6 033	5 819	5 510	5 434	5 006	3 742	3 341	Pétroliers
Ore and bulk carriers	6 615	5 445	4 956	4 558	3 869	3 556	3 243	3 093	Minéral. et transp. de vracs
Jordan									**Jordanie**
All ships	61	21	41	43	42	42	42	42	Tous les navires
Oil tankers	50	...	...	...	...	...	...	...	Pétroliers
Ore and bulk carriers	10	21	40	40	21	21	11	...	Minéral. et transp. de vracs
Kazakhstan									**Kazakhstan**
All ships	9	12	9	10	9	9	11	13	Tous les navires
Kenya									**Kenya**
All ships	16	18	20	21	21	21	21	19	Tous les navires
Oil tankers	4	4	5	5	5	5	5	5	Pétroliers
Kiribati									**Kiribati**
All ships	5	6	6	6	4	4	4	4	Tous les navires
Oil tankers	...	2	2	2	...	...	...	...	Pétroliers
Korea, Dem. P. R.									**Corée, R. p. dém. de**
All ships	696	715	693	667	631	658	653	698	Tous les navires
Oil tankers	115	116	4	5	6	6	6	12	Pétroliers
Ore and bulk carriers	128	107	107	96	50	53	63	63	Minéral. et transp. de vracs
Korea, Republic of									**Corée, République de**
All ships	7 004	6 972	7 558	7 430	5 694	5 735	6 200	6 395	Tous les navires
Oil tankers	524	399	380	385	328	404	607	843	Pétroliers
Ore and bulk carriers	3 659	3 706	3 650	3 542	2 809	2 708	2 915	2 874	Minéral. et transp. de vracs
Kuwait									**Koweït**
All ships	2 017	2 057	2 028	1 984	2 459	2 456	2 415	2 292	Tous les navires
Oil tankers	1 343	1 343	1 343	1 313	1 662	1 644	1 628	1 628	Pétroliers
Ore and bulk carriers	...	...	...	...	17	17	17	17	Minéral. et transp. de vracs
Lao People's Dem. Rep.									**Rép. dém. pop. lao**
All ships	3	3	3	3	2	2	2	2	Tous les navires

61

Merchant shipping: fleets
All ships, oil tankers, and ore and bulk carrier fleets: thousand gross registered tons *[cont.]*

Transports maritimes : flotte marchande
Tous les navires, pétroliers, et minéraliers et transporteurs de vracs : milliers de tonneaux de jauge brute *[suite]*

Country or area	1994	1995	1996	1997	1998	1999	2000	2001	Pays ou zone
Latvia									**Lettonie**
All ships	1 034	798	723	319	118	118	98	68	Tous les navires
Oil tankers	483	323	279	137	9	9	7	4	Pétroliers
Lebanon									**Liban**
All ships	258	285	275	297	263	322	363	302	Tous les navires
Oil tankers	2	1	2	2	1	1	1	1	Pétroliers
Ore and bulk carriers	46	81	73	124	108	152	191	126	Minéral. et transp. de vracs
Liberia									**Libéria**
All ships	57 648	59 801	59 989	60 058	60 492	54 107	51 451	51 784	Tous les navires
Oil tankers	28 275	29 002	28 044	26 699	26 361	21 298	19 759	18 733	Pétroliers
Ore and bulk carriers	15 970	16 373	16 744	17 711	16 739	14 426	10 533	11 747	Minéral. et transp. de vracs
Libyan Arab Jamah.									**Jamah. arabe libyenne**
All ships	739	733	681	686	567	439	434	251	Tous les navires
Oil tankers	579	572	505	511	395	267	267	81	Pétroliers
Lithuania									**Lituanie**
All ships	661	610	572	510	481	424	434	393	Tous les navires
Oil tankers	13	8	5	5	4	4	4	5	Pétroliers
Ore and bulk carriers	111	111	110	110	110	110	100	80	Minéral. et transp. de vracs
Luxembourg									**Luxembourg**
All ships	1 143	881	878	820	932	1 343	1 079	1 469	Tous les navires
Oil tankers	3	3	165	165	244	543	311	630	Pétroliers
Ore and bulk carriers	555	365	86	86	86	93	6	14	Minéral. et transp. de vracs
Madagascar									**Madagascar**
All ships	36	38	39	40	42	43	44	43	Tous les navires
Oil tankers	9	11	11	11	11	11	11	11	Pétroliers
Malaysia									**Malaisie**
All ships	2 728	3 283	4 175	4 842	5 209	5 245	5 328	5 207	Tous les navires
Oil tankers	382	412	589	689	854	918	868	871	Pétroliers
Ore and bulk carriers	798	982	1 272	1 305	1 448	1 513	1 568	1 447	Minéral. et transp. de vracs
Maldives									**Maldives**
All ships	68	85	96	98	101	90	78	67	Tous les navires
Oil tankers	6	6	6	6	6	4	3	4	Pétroliers
Ore and bulk carriers	11	11	11	...	...	...	...	...	Minéral. et transp. de vracs
Malta									**Malte**
All ships	15 455	17 678	19 479	22 984	24 075	28 205	28 170	27 053	Tous les navires
Oil tankers	5 699	6 793	7 370	9 043	9 848	12 151	11 595	10 546	Pétroliers
Ore and bulk carriers	6 196	6 857	7 478	8 623	8 616	9 984	10 533	10 661	Minéral. et transp. de vracs
Marshall Islands									**Iles Marshall**
All ships	2 149	3 099	4 897	6 314	6 442	6 762	9 745	11 719	Tous les navires
Oil tankers	1 560	1 502	2 721	3 388	3 561	4 313	5 462	5 955	Pétroliers
Ore and bulk carriers	539	701	1 095	1 666	1 602	1 255	2 067	2 747	Minéral. et transp. de vracs
Mauritania									**Mauritanie**
All ships	42	39	43	43	48	49	49	47	Tous les navires
Mauritius									**Maurice**
All ships	206	238	244	275	206	150	91	97	Tous les navires
Oil tankers	...	53	53	53	...	...	...	...	Pétroliers
Ore and bulk carriers	120	2	2	4	4	4	4	4	Minéral. et transp. de vracs
Mexico									**Mexique**
All ships	1 179	1 129	1 128	1 145	1 085	918	883	908	Tous les navires
Oil tankers	425	425	425	435	409	464	460	454	Pétroliers
Micronesia (Fed. States)									**Micronésie (Etats féd. de)**
All ships	9	8	9	9	10	10	10	9	Tous les navires
Morocco									**Maroc**
All ships	362	383	403	417	444	448	467	461	Tous les navires
Oil tankers	14	14	12	12	12	12	12	9	Pétroliers
Mozambique									**Mozambique**
All ships	36	38	45	39	35	36	37	38	Tous les navires
Myanmar									**Myanmar**
All ships	683	523	687	568	492	540	446	380	Tous les navires
Oil tankers	3	3	45	3	3	3	3	3	Pétroliers
Ore and bulk carriers	358	215	310	298	283	301	231	162	Minéral. et transp. de vracs

61

Merchant shipping: fleets
All ships, oil tankers, and ore and bulk carrier fleets: thousand gross registered tons *[cont.]*

Transports maritimes : flotte marchande
Tous les navires, pétroliers, et minéraliers et transporteurs de vracs : milliers de tonneaux de jauge brute *[suite]*

Country or area	1994	1995	1996	1997	1998	1999	2000	2001	Pays ou zone
Namibia									**Namibie**
All ships	44	52	59	55	55	55	63	66	Tous les navires
Netherlands									**Pays-Bas**
All ships	3 349	3 409	3 995	3 880	4 263	4 814	5 168	5 605	Tous les navires
Oil tankers	403	405	412	18	16	25	29	37	Pétroliers
Ore and bulk carriers	99	99	68	68	77	77	10	9	Minéral. et transp. de vracs
Netherlands Antilles									**Antilles néerlandaises**
All ships	1 047	1 197	1 168	1 067	971	1 110	1 235	1 250	Tous les navires
Oil tankers	32	139	215	158	135	135	135	0	Pétroliers
Ore and bulk carriers	146	71	108	108	...	...	2	72	Minéral. et transp. de vracs
New Zealand									**Nouvelle-Zélande**
All ships	246	307	386	367	336	265	180	175	Tous les navires
Oil tankers	54	76	61	61	73	73	20	50	Pétroliers
Ore and bulk carriers	25	25	25	12	12	12	12	12	Minéral. et transp. de vracs
Nicaragua									**Nicaragua**
All ships	4	4	4	4	4	4	4	4	Tous les navires
Nigeria									**Nigéria**
All ships	473	479	447	452	452	432	438	404	Tous les navires
Oil tankers	245	251	252	250	252	265	265	287	Pétroliers
Ore and bulk carriers	1	...	...	...	...	...	...	...	Minéral. et transp. de vracs
Norway									**Norvège**
All ships	22 388	21 551	21 806	22 839	23 136	23 446	22 604	22 591	Tous les navires
Oil tankers	8 962	8 779	8 895	9 244	8 993	9 195	7 949	7 575	Pétroliers
Ore and bulk carriers	4 865	4 010	3 858	3 908	4 041	3 913	3 863	4 048	Minéral. et transp. de vracs
Oman									**Oman**
All ships	15	16	16	15	15	17	19	20	Tous les navires
Oil tankers	0	0	0	0	0	0	0	0	Pétroliers
Pakistan									**Pakistan**
All ships	375	398	444	435	401	308	260	247	Tous les navires
Oil tankers	50	49	49	50	50	50	50	50	Pétroliers
Ore and bulk carriers	88	115	159	158	125	30	...	...	Minéral. et transp. de vracs
Panama									**Panama**
All ships	64 710	71 922	82 131	91 128	98 222	105 248	114 382	122 352	Tous les navires
Oil tankers	18 649	19 513	20 910	21 272	22 680	23 856	27 588	28 528	Pétroliers
Ore and bulk carriers	22 169	26 726	33 019	38 617	40 319	42 726	45 734	49 947	Minéral. et transp. de vracs
Papua New Guinea									**Papouasie-Nvl-Guinée**
All ships	47	49	57	60	61	65	73	77	Tous les navires
Oil tankers	3	3	7	4	3	3	2	2	Pétroliers
Paraguay									**Paraguay**
All ships	33	39	44	44	45	43	45	47	Tous les navires
Oil tankers	2	2	4	4	4	4	4	4	Pétroliers
Peru									**Pérou**
All ships	321	341	346	337	270	285	257	240	Tous les navires
Oil tankers	68	80	76	76	31	31	19	14	Pétroliers
Ore and bulk carriers	31	31	15	...	...	15	...	...	Minéral. et transp. de vracs
Philippines									**Philippines**
All ships	9 413	8 744	9 034	8 849	8 508	7 650	7 002	6 030	Tous les navires
Oil tankers	419	147	158	163	162	159	154	142	Pétroliers
Ore and bulk carriers	6 496	6 138	6 334	5 951	5 597	4 822	4 366	3 751	Minéral. et transp. de vracs
Poland									**Pologne**
All ships	2 610	2 358	2 293	1 878	1 424	1 319	1 119	618	Tous les navires
Oil tankers	88	7	6	5	5	5	6	5	Pétroliers
Ore and bulk carriers	1 511	1 455	1 455	1 360	1 082	993	851	391	Minéral. et transp. de vracs
Portugal									**Portugal**
All ships	882	897	676	952	1 130	1 165	1 191	1 199	Tous les navires
Oil tankers	552	490	217	349	416	416	354	424	Pétroliers
Ore and bulk carriers	85	127	128	128	188	160	261	214	Minéral. et transp. de vracs
Qatar									**Qatar**
All ships	557	482	562	648	744	749	715	691	Tous les navires
Oil tankers	177	105	183	263	263	263	214	214	Pétroliers
Ore and bulk carriers	141	142	142	142	142	142	142	142	Minéral. et transp. de vracs

61

Merchant shipping: fleets
All ships, oil tankers, and ore and bulk carrier fleets: thousand gross registered tons *[cont.]*

Transports maritimes : flotte marchande
Tous les navires, pétroliers, et minéraliers et transporteurs de vracs : milliers de tonneaux de jauge brute *[suite]*

Country or area	1994	1995	1996	1997	1998	1999	2000	2001	Pays ou zone
Romania									**Roumanie**
All ships	2 689	2 536	2 568	2 345	2 088	1 221	767	638	Tous les navires
Oil tankers	438	429	429	249	204	68	67	64	Pétroliers
Ore and bulk carriers	980	850	865	865	788	320	138	143	Minéral. et transp. de vracs
Russian Federation									**Fédération de Russie**
All ships	16 504	15 202	13 755	12 282	11 090	10 649	10 486	10 248	Tous les navires
Oil tankers	2 378	2 294	1 917	1 646	1 608	1 429	1 402	1 430	Pétroliers
Ore and bulk carriers	1 757	1 768	1 767	1 568	1 031	889	864	783	Minéral. et transp. de vracs
Saint Helena									**Sainte-Hélène**
All ships	...	...	0	1	1	1	1	1	Tous les navires
Saint Kitts and Nevis									**Saint-Kitts-et-Nevis**
All ships	0	0	0	0	0	0	0	0	Tous les navires
Saint Lucia									**Sainte-Lucie**
All ships	2	1	1	...	...	...	...	...	Tous les navires
St. Vincent-Grenadines									**St. Vincent-Grenadines**
All ships	5 420	6 165	7 134	8 374	7 875	7 105	7 026	7 073	Tous les navires
Oil tankers	941	1 101	1 228	1 061	913	569	450	459	Pétroliers
Ore and bulk carriers	1 939	2 328	2 627	3 202	2 858	2 656	2 672	3 019	Minéral. et transp. de vracs
Samoa									**Samoa**
All ships	6	6	...	1	3	3	2	10	Tous les navires
Sao Tome and Principe									**Sao Tomé-et-Principe**
All ships	3	3	3	3	10	42	173	190	Tous les navires
Oil tankers	...	...	...	...	...	1	7	11	Pétroliers
Ore and bulk carriers	...	...	...	...	...	...	10	62	Minéral. et transp. de vracs
Saudi Arabia									**Arabie saoudite**
All ships	1 064	1 187	1 208	1 164	1 278	1 208	1 260	1 133	Tous les navires
Oil tankers	210	238	258	203	220	218	219	224	Pétroliers
Ore and bulk carriers	12	12	12	12	12	...	...	...	Minéral. et transp. de vracs
Senegal									**Sénégal**
All ships	50	48	50	51	51	48	50	48	Tous les navires
Serbia and Montenegro									**Serbie-et-Monténégro**
All ships	2	2	2	2	5	4	4	3	Tous les navires
Seychelles									**Seychelles**
All ships	4	5	4	5	18	24	22	34	Tous les navires
Sierra Leone									**Sierra Leone**
All ships	24	23	19	19	19	17	17	13	Tous les navires
Oil tankers	1	1	1	1	1	3	...	...	Pétroliers
Singapore									**Singapour**
All ships	11 895	13 611	16 448	18 875	20 370	21 780	21 491	21 023	Tous les navires
Oil tankers	4 959	5 102	6 614	7 787	8 781	9 619	9 118	8 647	Pétroliers
Ore and bulk carriers	3 209	3 766	4 344	4 358	4 585	4 695	4 753	4 800	Minéral. et transp. de vracs
Slovakia									**Slovaquie**
All ships	6	19	19	15	15	15	15	15	Tous les navires
Slovenia									**Slovénie**
All ships	9	2	2	2	2	2	2	2	Tous les navires
Solomon Islands									**Iles Salomon**
All ships	8	8	10	10	10	10	9	8	Tous les navires
Somalia									**Somalie**
All ships	17	16	14	11	11	6	7	6	Tous les navires
Oil tankers	...	...	...	...	...	1	1	1	Pétroliers
South Africa									**Afrique du Sud**
All ships	331	340	371	383	384	379	380	382	Tous les navires
Oil tankers	1	1	4	3	3	3	3	3	Pétroliers
Spain									**Espagne**
All ships	1 560	1 619	1 675	1 688	1 838	1 903	2 030	2 148	Tous les navires
Oil tankers	430	437	515	510	585	583	600	598	Pétroliers
Ore and bulk carriers	59	68	23	39	42	42	42	42	Minéral. et transp. de vracs
Sri Lanka									**Sri Lanka**
All ships	294	227	242	217	189	195	150	154	Tous les navires
Oil tankers	74	3	5	5	5	5	2	6	Pétroliers
Ore and bulk carriers	93	93	93	95	77	77	77	77	Minéral. et transp. de vracs

61

Merchant shipping: fleets
All ships, oil tankers, and ore and bulk carrier fleets: thousand gross registered tons *[cont.]*

Transports maritimes : flotte marchande
Tous les navires, pétroliers, et minéraliers et transporteurs de vracs : milliers de tonneaux de jauge brute *[suite]*

Country or area	1994	1995	1996	1997	1998	1999	2000	2001	Pays ou zone
Sudan									**Soudan**
All ships	57	48	42	42	43	43	43	43	Tous les navires
Oil tankers	1	1	1	1	1	1	1	1	Pétroliers
Suriname									**Suriname**
All ships	8	8	8	8	6	6	5	5	Tous les navires
Oil tankers	2	2	2	2	2	2	2	2	Pétroliers
Sweden									**Suède**
All ships	2 797	2 955	3 002	2 754	2 552	2 947	2 887	2 958	Tous les navires
Oil tankers	370	385	392	307	105	102	103	101	Pétroliers
Ore and bulk carriers	45	52	44	38	32	32	29	29	Minéral. et transp. de vracs
Switzerland									**Suisse**
All ships	336	381	400	434	383	439	429	502	Tous les navires
Ore and bulk carriers	307	351	370	389	349	393	393	463	Minéral. et transp. de vracs
Syrian Arab Republic									**Rép. arabe syrienne**
All ships	279	352	420	415	428	440	465	498	Tous les navires
Oil tankers	...	...	...	...	...	...	1	1	Pétroliers
Ore and bulk carriers	48	48	45	14	22	30	26	54	Minéral. et transp. de vracs
Thailand									**Thaïlande**
All ships	1 374	1 743	2 042	2 158	1 999	1 956	1 945	1 771	Tous les navires
Oil tankers	190	196	385	411	364	361	364	231	Pétroliers
Ore and bulk carriers	224	387	480	567	491	476	443	392	Minéral. et transp. de vracs
Togo									**Togo**
All ships	1	1	1	2	2	43	5	8	Tous les navires
Tonga									**Tonga**
All ships	10	12	11	12	22	25	25	338	Tous les navires
Oil tankers	...	...	...	...	...	...	...	31	Pétroliers
Ore and bulk carriers	...	...	...	...	...	...	...	49	Minéral. et transp. de vracs
Trinidad and Tobago									**Trinité-et-Tobago**
All ships	27	28	19	19	19	22	22	27	Tous les navires
Oil tankers	...	...	...	...	...	1	1	1	Pétroliers
Tunisia									**Tunisie**
All ships	141	160	158	180	193	200	208	203	Tous les navires
Oil tankers	6	9	7	7	22	20	20	20	Pétroliers
Ore and bulk carriers	37	38	38	38	27	17	17	17	Minéral. et transp. de vracs
Turkey									**Turquie**
All ships	5 453	6 268	6 426	6 567	6 251	6 325	5 833	5 897	Tous les navires
Oil tankers	954	821	709	514	503	584	625	772	Pétroliers
Ore and bulk carriers	3 253	4 007	4 168	4 444	4 023	3 939	3 303	3 178	Minéral. et transp. de vracs
Turkmenistan									**Turkménistan**
All ships	23	32	40	39	38	44	42	46	Tous les navires
Oil tankers	1	3	3	3	2	2	2	6	Pétroliers
Ore and bulk carriers	...	...	...	...	...	5	3	3	Minéral. et transp. de vracs
Turks and Caicos Islands									**Iles Turques et Caïques**
All ships	3	2	2	2	1	1	1	1	Tous les navires
Oil tankers	1	...	...	...	...	...	...	...	Pétroliers
Tuvalu									**Tuvalu**
All ships	51	64	57	55	49	43	59	36	Tous les navires
Ukraine									**Ukraine**
All ships	5 279	4 613	3 825	2 690	2 033	1 775	1 546	1 408	Tous les navires
Oil tankers	84	81	79	89	62	56	56	45	Pétroliers
Ore and bulk carriers	1 196	729	452	254	207	161	100	100	Minéral. et transp. de vracs
United Arab Emirates									**Emirats arabes unis**
All ships	1 016	961	890	924	933	786	979	746	Tous les navires
Oil tankers	502	519	410	426	369	248	240	233	Pétroliers
Ore and bulk carriers	47	35	37	20	20	20	0	0	Minéral. et transp. de vracs
United Kingdom									**Royaume-Uni**
All ships	4 430	4 413	3 872	3 486	4 085	4 331	5 532	6 029	Tous les navires
Oil tankers	1 185	1 115	876	476	625	544	538	562	Pétroliers
Ore and bulk carriers	74	74	67	64	48	33	52	78	Minéral. et transp. de vracs
United Rep. of Tanzania									**Rép.-Unie de Tanzanie**
All ships	43	46	45	46	36	36	38	38	Tous les navires

61

Merchant shipping: fleets
All ships, oil tankers, and ore and bulk carrier fleets: thousand gross registered tons *[cont.]*

Transports maritimes : flotte marchande
Tous les navires, pétroliers, et minéraliers et transporteurs de vracs : milliers de tonneaux de jauge brute *[suite]*

Country or area	1994	1995	1996	1997	1998	1999	2000	2001	Pays ou zone
Oil tankers	4	5	5	5	4	4	4	4	Pétroliers
United States									**Etats-Unis**
All ships	13 655	12 761	12 025	11 789	11 852	12 026	11 111	10 907	Tous les navires
Oil tankers	4 500	3 987	3 630	3 372	3 436	3 491	3 176	2 965	Pétroliers
Ore and bulk carriers	1 546	1 513	1 301	1 275	1 268	1 268	1 271	1 339	Minéral. et transp. de vracs
Uruguay									**Uruguay**
All ships	125	124	100	121	107	62	67	73	Tous les navires
Oil tankers	46	46	48	48	48	6	6	6	Pétroliers
Vanuatu									**Vanuatu**
All ships	1 998	1 874	1 711	1 578	1 602	1 444	1 379	1 496	Tous les navires
Oil tankers	15	38	40	14	11	11	11	4	Pétroliers
Ore and bulk carriers	1 008	841	706	620	708	518	506	529	Minéral. et transp. de vracs
Venezuela									**Venezuela**
All ships	920	787	697	705	665	657	667	872	Tous les navires
Oil tankers	420	361	275	275	222	222	212	374	Pétroliers
Ore and bulk carriers	147	111	111	111	126	116	126	121	Minéral. et transp. de vracs
Viet Nam									**Viet Nam**
All ships	773	700	808	766	784	865	1 002	1 074	Tous les navires
Oil tankers	94	19	20	22	63	105	136	158	Pétroliers
Ore and bulk carriers	21	21	63	94	94	94	122	122	Minéral. et transp. de vracs
Wallis and Futuna Islands									**Iles Wallis et Futuna**
All ships	105	108	92	111	111	159	135	183	Tous les navires
Oil tankers	75	75	75	75	75	75	50	50	Pétroliers
Yemen									**Yémen**
All ships	25	27	25	26	25	25	28	74	Tous les navires
Oil tankers	2	2	2	2	2	2	5	51	Pétroliers

Source:
Lloyd's Register of Shipping, London, "World Fleet Statistics 2001"
and previous issues.

Source:
"Lloyd's Register of Shipping", Londres, "World Fleet Statistics 2001"
et éditions précédentes.

1 Including the French Antarctic Territory.

1 Y compris le territoire antarctique français.

62

International maritime transport
Vessels entered and cleared: thousand net registered tons

Transports maritimes internationaux
Navires entrés et sortis : milliers de tonneaux de jauge nette

Country or area Pays ou zone	1992	1993	1994	1995	1996	1997	1998	1999	2000	2001
Albania Albanie										
Vessels entered										
Navires entrés	...	288	576	1 002	1 218	1 053	1 419	1 115	2 212	2 558
Vessels cleared										
Navires sortis	...	121	198	309	213	123	61	29	72	69
Algeria Algérie										
Vessels entered										
Navires entrés	85 577	84 744	86 500	88 502	93 913	103 201	106 256	113 681	117 918	...
Vessels cleared										
Navires sortis	85 730	84 659	86 767	88 865	93 676	103 187	106 036	113 627	117 937	...
American Samoa[1] Samoa américaines[1]										
Vessels entered										
Navires entrés	618	440	581	526	452	725	589	884	...	
Vessels cleared										
Navires sortis	618	440	581	526	452	725	589	884	...	
Antigua and Barbuda Antigua-et-Barbuda										
Vessels entered										
Navires entrés	...	...	...	...	57 386	94 907	...	...	...	
Vessels cleared										
Navires sortis	...	...	...	...	544 328	667 126	...	...	...	
Argentina[2] Argentine[2]										
Vessels entered										
Navires entrés	11 379[3]	20 092[4]	12 345[3]	...	...	...	...	...	...	...
Australia[1,5] Australie[1,5]										
Vessels entered										
Navires entrés	...	...	...	2 299	2 268	2 231	...	1 864	1 730	...
Azerbaijan Azerbaïdjan										
Vessels entered										
Navires entrés	115	142	127	925	1 022	2 007	3 967	4 015	5 118	...
Vessels cleared										
Navires sortis	1 849	1 568	2 289	1 751	1 702	1 737	1 483	624	703	...
Bahrain Bahreïn										
Vessels entered										
Navires entrés	1	1	1	1	2	2	...	...	...	
Bangladesh[6] Bangladesh[6]										
Vessels entered										
Navires entrés	5 375	4 835	4 832	6 013	5 928	5 488	5 794	6 509	...	...
Vessels cleared										
Navires sortis	2 943	3 103	2 556	3 094	3 136	2 866	2 556	2 949	...	...
Barbados Barbade										
Vessels entered										
Navires entrés	13 342	12 195	13 703	12 780	14 002	15 146	16 893	14 470	15 875	...
Belgium Belgique										
Vessels entered										
Navires entrés	236 323	229 915	239 678	253 427	297 664	337 862	367 684	386 211	415 640	436 927
Vessels cleared										
Navires sortis	189 286	190 795	201 448	210 144	297 610	333 694	360 987	375 519	404 159	422 703
Benin Bénin										
Vessels entered										
Navires entrés	937	1 134	1 163	1 192	1 321	1 296	1 289	1 095	1 184	...
Brazil Brésil										
Vessels entered										
Navires entrés	65 794	74 314	78 757	79 732	82 593	86 720	92 822	78 775	84 355	...
Vessels cleared										
Navires sortis	164 152	173 624	185 291	197 955	192 889	209 331	216 273	217 811	230 157	...
Cambodia Cambodge										
Vessels entered[7]										
Navires entrés[7]	468	463	608	647	726	715	781	1 056	1 313	...
Vessels cleared										
Navires sortis	124	193	182	214	145	293	319	191	179	...

62

International maritime transport
Vessels entered and cleared: thousand net registered tons *[cont.]*

Transports maritimes internationaux
Navires entrés et sortis : milliers de tonneaux de jauge nette *[suite]*

Country or area Pays ou zone	1992	1993	1994	1995	1996	1997	1998	1999	2000	2001
Cameroon[2,8] Cameroun[2,8]										
Vessels entered										
Navires entrés	5 344	5 279	964	1 543	1 157	1 159	1 154	1 234	1 215	1 243
Canada[9] Canada[9]										
Vessels entered										
Navires entrés	58 724	56 769	60 417	62 415	66 166	74 422	81 539	82 976	...	...
Vessels cleared										
Navires sortis	109 263	108 587	116 279	114 040	117 452	124 999	120 349	122 282	...	...
Cape Verde Cap-Vert										
Vessels entered										
Navires entrés	...	...	3 409	3 628	3 601	3 590	4 296	...	...	
China, Hong Kong SAR Chine, Hong Kong RAS										
Vessels entered										
Navires entrés	160 193	184 166	201 919	216 437	229 444	250 303	261 694	267 255	300 606	...
Vessels cleared										
Navires sortis	160 436	184 023	201 607	217 539	229 474	250 399	261 552	267 419	300 522	...
China, Macao SAR[2] Chine, Macao RAS[2]										
Vessels cleared										
Navires sortis	...	...	...	...	...	...	...		10 736[5]	1 975
Colombia Colombie										
Vessels entered[2]										
Navires entrés[2]	21 967	24 874	28 138	32 191	35 787	40 863	50 712	68 649	52 442	...
Vessels cleared										
Navires sortis	22 056	24 967	27 919	31 813	34 585	39 562	48 530	65 790	50 787	...
Congo Congo										
Vessels entered										
Navires entrés	6 318	6 176	5 665	6 449	7 645	...	...	...	...	...
Costa Rica Costa Rica										
Vessels entered										
Navires entrés	3 326	3 684	4 004	4 202	4 135	3 555	4 024	2 168	2 019	1 923
Vessels cleared										
Navires sortis	2 510	2 760	2 983	3 070	2 992	2 941	3 405	2 168	2 019	1 923
Croatia Croatie										
Vessels entered										
Navires entrés	4 419	4 686	5 028	6 023	13 587[5]	16 131[5]	16 410[5]	14 685[5]	13 925	22 425
Vessels cleared										
Navires sortis	2 156	3 251	4 161	4 297	10 393[5]	11 502[5]	11 912[5]	11 374[5]	12 686	20 560
Cyprus Chypre										
Vessels entered										
Navires entrés	14 791	14 918	15 350	15 700	19 033	16 478	15 955	18 001	20 571	20 310
Dominica Dominique										
Vessels entered										
Navires entrés	...	...	2 214	2 252	2 289	2 145	2 218	...	...	...
Dominican Republic Rép. dominicaine										
Vessels entered										
Navires entrés	7 489	7 563	8 421	8 751	9 238	10 113	10 719	13 603	14 245	13 892
Vessels cleared										
Navires sortis	796	788	770	1 162	1 341	1 822	1 673	1 609	2 170	2 507
Ecuador Equateur										
Vessels entered										
Navires entrés	2 563	2 719	3 006	3 665	3 283	3 263	3 158	2 019	4 711	...
Vessels cleared										
Navires sortis	15 208	15 459	16 958	18 010	17 450	18 277	16 937	18 051	16 779	...
Egypt Egypte										
Vessels entered										
Navires entrés	39 606	41 253	44 726	48 008	47 824	48 866	40 834	36 333	...	...
Vessels cleared										
Navires sortis	33 059	34 307	37 377	41 257	43 386	40 924	33 711	32 186	...	...

62

International maritime transport
Vessels entered and cleared: thousand net registered tons *[cont.]*

Transports maritimes internationaux
Navires entrés et sortis : milliers de tonneaux de jauge nette *[suite]*

Country or area Pays ou zone	1992	1993	1994	1995	1996	1997	1998	1999	2000	2001
El Salvador El Salvador										
Vessels entered										
Navires entrés	3 008	3 012	3 393	3 185	3 345	5 633	7 969	3 374	...	...
Vessels cleared										
Navires sortis	834	938	861	625	822	550	490	566	...	...
Estonia Estonie										
Vessels entered										
Navires entrés	...	3 419	2 376[5]	...	...	...	...	...	...	...
Vessels cleared										
Navires sortis	...	3 087	3 813[5]	...	...	...	...	...	...	...
Fiji Fidji										
Vessels entered										
Navires entrés	3 381	2 876	2 843	4 065	4 070	...	...	...	...	...
Finland[2] Finlande[2]										
Vessels entered										
Navires entrés	119 238	117 003	111 934	127 711	131 338	144 923	148 690	153 149	155 635	...
Vessels cleared										
Navires sortis	119 040	121 946	117 143	132 879	135 650	148 366	150 969	154 700	152 143	...
France[10,11] France[10,11]										
Vessels entered										
Navires entrés	1 825 276	1 861 742	1 941 433	1 921 826	2 202 359	2 235 210	2 164 285	2 119 434	2 087 368	...
Gambia[1] Gambie[1]										
Vessels entered										
Navires entrés	1 117	1 153	...	...	...	...	...	...	...	...
Germany Allemagne										
Vessels entered										
Navires entrés	225 984	221 741	223 363	221 226	251 500	260 553	263 470	271 978	959 448[12]	953 366[12]
Vessels cleared										
Navires sortis	199 441	196 456	201 316	197 339	229 959	235 110	237 071	249 225	938 028[12]	953 287[12]
Gibraltar Gibraltar										
Vessels entered										
Navires entrés	321	307	276	256	...	...	...	...	...	...
Greece Grèce										
Vessels entered										
Navires entrés	37 789	32 429	33 048	38 573	38 549	38 704	43 786	44 662	45 072	45 973
Vessels cleared										
Navires sortis	20 401	18 467	21 087	21 940	21 356	19 359	21 865	22 302	22 526	23 970
Guatemala Guatemala										
Vessels entered										
Navires entrés	2 747	3 367	4 008	3 976	3 680	4 505	...	...	...	...
Vessels cleared										
Navires sortis	2 025	2 266	2 280	2 854	3 275	3 815	...	...	...	...
Haiti[13] Haïti[13]										
Vessels entered										
Navires entrés	583	897	529	1 285	1 680	1 304	...	...	...	...
India[14,15] Inde[14,15]										
Vessels entered										
Navires entrés	30 125	27 825	39 619	47 857	48 358	47 055	48 512	60 850	55 466	...
Vessels cleared										
Navires sortis	34 660	36 325	42 885	48 497	44 494	45 819	39 031	41 187	38 043	...
Indonesia Indonésie										
Vessels entered										
Navires entrés	128 571	140 861	155 869	163 597	259 096	286 314	246 838	252 893	303 587	320 657
Vessels cleared										
Navires sortis	38 178	41 993	48 857	48 753	75 055	97 885	82 711	73 938	79 813	83 115
Iran (Islamic Rep. of) Iran (Rép. islamique d')										
Vessels entered										
Navires entrés	12 772	11 218	13 795	14 686	17 155	27 756	46 937	62 828	64 114	67 267

62

International maritime transport
Vessels entered and cleared: thousand net registered tons *[cont.]*

Transports maritimes internationaux
Navires entrés et sortis : milliers de tonneaux de jauge nette *[suite]*

Country or area Pays ou zone	1992	1993	1994	1995	1996	1997	1998	1999	2000	2001
Ireland Irlande										
Vessels entered[2]										
Navires entrés[2]	33 857	36 408	37 896	45 968	54 602	165 925[5]	176 228[5]	190 818[5]	...	...
Vessels cleared										
Navires sortis	12 109	13 199	15 113	15 890	16 787	16 463	16 669	17 645		
Italy Italie										
Vessels entered										
Navires entrés	175 940	168 545	180 175	181 733	190 910	226 977	250 830	277 384	211 242	...
Vessels cleared										
Navires sortis	79 600	84 044	91 288	96 505	160 757	132 532	152 655	167 550	137 864	...
Jamaica Jamaïque										
Vessels entered										
Navires entrés	...	...	9 892	10 531	12 339	12 815	...	...	...	...
Vessels cleared										
Navires sortis	4 859	5 576	5 599	5 730	6 043	6 457	6 553	...	...	...
Japan[2] Japon[2]										
Vessels entered										
Navires entrés	398 240	397 582	410 164	412 163	422 256	438 111	425 193	446 482	461 903	459 840
Jordan Jordanie										
Vessels entered										
Navires entrés	2 041	2 143	1 910	2 382	2 735	2 997	2 608	2 551	2 505	2 673
Vessels cleared										
Navires sortis	392	347	576	...	...	...	...	...	...	...
Kenya[2,8] Kenya[2,8]										
Vessels entered										
Navires entrés	7 112	7 102	7 108	7 973	8 694	8 442	8 561	8 188	9 126	10 600
Korea, Republic of Corée, République de										
Vessels entered										
Navires entrés	348 767	383 311	430 872	487 851	537 163	578 373	586 629	691 166	755 225	...
Vessels cleared										
Navires sortis	350 906	381 545	429 538	485 357	542 600	584 164	595 072	695 598	737 999	...
Kuwait Koweït										
Vessels entered										
Navires entrés	6 230	6 248	9 775	10 723	9 676	9 171	9 357	...	...	...
Vessels cleared										
Navires sortis	619	944	1 184	1 222	1 223	1 285	1 178	...	...	...
Libyan Arab Jamah. Jamah. arabe libyenne										
Vessels entered										
Navires entrés	5 850	6 492	5 277	5 142	5 638	5 980	6 245	5 304	...	...
Vessels cleared										
Navires sortis	456	556	572	751	624	647	739	815	...	...
Lithuania[2,5] Lituanie[2,5]										
Vessels entered										
Navires entrés	...	...	...	25 642	32 187	34 259	35 680	32 438	37 138	34 310
Vessels cleared										
Navires sortis	...	...	...	25 477	31 383	34 161	35 658	32 419	37 044	33 932
Madagascar[2] Madagascar[2]										
Vessels entered										
Navires entrés	...	...	...	...	...	4 169	3 920	2 629	4 842	...
Malaysia[16] Malaisie[16]										
Vessels entered										
Navires entrés	108 170	109 300	110 330	...	...	...	...	...	...	...
Vessels cleared										
Navires sortis	109 070	109 000	110 650	...	...	...	...	...	...	...
Malta Malte										
Vessels entered										
Navires entrés	7 049	6 802	7 657	9 404	9 830	11 597	13 738	16 725	17 299	18 279
Vessels cleared										
Navires sortis	3 160	3 534	2 471	2 887	3 779	4 976	2 493	5 084	7 528	7 795

62

International maritime transport
Vessels entered and cleared: thousand net registered tons *[cont.]*

Transports maritimes internationaux
Navires entrés et sortis : milliers de tonneaux de jauge nette *[suite]*

Country or area Pays ou zone	1992	1993	1994	1995	1996	1997	1998	1999	2000	2001
Mauritius Maurice										
Vessels entered[2]										
Navires entrés[2]	5 277	5 271	5 500	5 356	4 999	5 485	5 925	6 725	6 387	7 026
Vessels cleared										
Navires sortis	5 447	5 219	5 550	5 313	5 140	5 263	5 924	6 129	6 087	6 482
Mexico Mexique										
Vessels entered										
Navires entrés	21 520	20 241	21 919	19 697	27 533	33 317	43 185	44 614	45 276	52 728
Vessels cleared										
Navires sortis	97 464	101 688	100 757	103 355	117 598	125 571	125 682	119 284	125 864	126 752
Morocco[17] Maroc[17]										
Vessels entered										
Navires entrés	21 578	22 436	22 633	24 034	26 271	27 088	27 478	29 918	30 170	30 664
Myanmar Myanmar										
Vessels entered										
Navires entrés	879	1 278	1 587	2 388	2 286	2 230	2 955	2 729	4 545	...
Vessels cleared										
Navires sortis	1 205	1 408	1 612	1 624	1 108	794	1 235	1 656	2 252	...
Netherlands[5] Pays-Bas[5]										
Vessels entered										
Navires entrés	383 164	375 906	403 355	431 997	441 281	456 522	472 977	...	...	...
Vessels cleared										
Navires sortis	239 572	237 817	258 152	280 667	291 089	290 813	301 559	...	...	...
New Zealand[5] Nouvelle-Zélande[5]										
Vessels entered										
Navires entrés	27 983	37 603	39 700	48 827	...	...	...	...	...	...
Vessels cleared										
Navires sortis	27 508	35 128	37 421	42 985	...	...	...	...	...	...
Nigeria Nigéria										
Vessels entered										
Navires entrés	2 352	2 776	1 908	1 846[18]	2 043	2 464	...	...	...	...
Vessels cleared										
Navires sortis	2 275	2 830	1 879	1 852[18]	2 104	2 510	...	...	...	...
Norway[19] Norvège[19]										
Vessels entered										
Navires entrés	...	82 369	112 247	139 252	147 192	148 060	148 764	155 805	...	...
Oman Oman										
Vessels entered										
Navires entrés	1 819	2 190	2 119	2 099	2 110	2 226	2 102	2 087	2 142	2 457
Vessels cleared										
Navires sortis	2 745	1 146	1 192	1 309	5 529	6 781	7 147	7 008	...	...
Pakistan[6] Pakistan[6]										
Vessels entered										
Navires entrés	19 401	18 785	20 195	21 268	22 632	26 915	26 502	26 702	27 005	26 453
Vessels cleared										
Navires sortis	7 382	7 284	8 287	7 411	7 728	5 748	6 983	7 296	7 500	9 173
Panama Panama										
Vessels entered										
Navires entrés	1 959	2 178	2 404	2 766	3 263	4 431	9 879	12 008	13 301	...
Vessels cleared										
Navires sortis	1 513	1 560	1 643	1 972	2 367	2 927	6 453	7 298	7 369	...
Peru Pérou										
Vessels entered										
Navires entrés	7 012	6 066	7 145	7 454	7 516	6 701	7 675	6 948	6 901	...
Vessels cleared										
Navires sortis	8 852	9 186	4 930	4 640	4 731	6 082	4 688	5 696	6 499	...
Philippines Philippines										
Vessels entered										
Navires entrés	29 876	32 388	38 222	40 876	...	...	...	...	...	...

62

International maritime transport
Vessels entered and cleared: thousand net registered tons *[cont.]*

Transports maritimes internationaux
Navires entrés et sortis : milliers de tonneaux de jauge nette *[suite]*

Country or area Pays ou zone	1992	1993	1994	1995	1996	1997	1998	1999	2000	2001
Vessels cleared										
Navires sortis	19 411	22 431	25 582	27 829	...	...	...	...	...	...
Poland Pologne										
Vessels entered										
Navires entrés	15 573	15 544	14 816	18 316	20 997	24 280	25 549	24 161	26 176	26 568
Vessels cleared										
Navires sortis	20 031	23 222	25 552	25 269	25 566	28 877	30 065	30 062	32 225	31 730
Portugal Portugal										
Vessels entered										
Navires entrés	36 415	32 654	34 544	36 095	...	...	...	...	...	...
Réunion[17] Réunion[17]										
Vessels entered										
Navires entrés	2 375	2 421	2 349	2 715	2 595	2 755	3 065	3 059	3 266	...
Russian Federation[2] Fédération de Russie[2]										
Vessels entered										
Navires entrés	...	...	...	...	...	...	67 110	82 544	76 376	83 581
Vessels cleared										
Navires sortis	...	...	...	...	...	...	68 830	82 939	76 369	81 830
Saint Helena Sainte-Hélène										
Vessels entered										
Navires entrés	244	319	254	55	...	...	...	...	...	...
Saint Lucia Sainte-Lucie										
Vessels entered										
Navires entrés	1 331	...	...	4 755	5 317	6 803	...	...	...	...
St. Vincent-Grenadines St. Vincent-Grenadines										
Vessels entered										
Navires entrés	1 233	1 336	1 037	932	1 204	1 253	1 274	1 478	1 674	1 790
Vessels cleared										
Navires sortis	1 233	1 336	1 037	932	1 204	1 253	1 274	1 478	1 674	1 790
Samoa Samoa										
Vessels entered										
Navires entrés	425	530	563	579	544	662	685	827	...	...
Senegal Sénégal										
Vessels entered										
Navires entrés	9 447	9 625	...	...	...	...	...	...	...	...
Vessels cleared										
Navires sortis	9 477	9 769	...	...	...	...	...	...	...	...
Serbia and Montenegro Serbie-et-Monténégro										
Vessels entered										
Navires entrés	626	...	...	805	1 960	1 828	1 589	1 810	...	...
Vessels cleared										
Navires sortis	511	...	...	769	1 155	1 360	1 091	1 083	...	...
Seychelles Seychelles										
Vessels entered										
Navires entrés	778	871	764	879	872	1 059	1 099	1 139	...	...
Singapore[20] Singapour[20]										
Vessels entered										
Navires entrés	81 334	92 655	101 107	104 014	117 723	130 333	140 922	141 523	145 383	...
Vessels cleared										
Navires sortis	81 245	92 477	101 017	104 123	117 662	130 237	140 838	141 745	145 415	...
Slovakia[21] Slovaquie[21]										
Vessels entered										
Navires entrés	...	387	379	374	401	367	381	336	...	...
Slovenia Slovénie										
Vessels entered										
Navires entrés	3 774	3 963	4 049	4 280	5 067	5 960	6 686	7 762	6 605	6 444
Vessels cleared										
Navires sortis	2 128	2 362	2 095	2 388	2 251	3 254	3 652	4 394	3 969	3 986

62

International maritime transport
Vessels entered and cleared: thousand net registered tons *[cont.]*

Transports maritimes internationaux
Navires entrés et sortis : milliers de tonneaux de jauge nette *[suite]*

Country or area Pays ou zone	1992	1993	1994	1995	1996	1997	1998	1999	2000	2001
South Africa[5] Afrique du Sud[5]										
Vessels entered										
Navires entrés	13 309	13 437	13 037	13 285	14 075	14 383	13 559	12 695	12 041	12 763
Vessels cleared										
Navires sortis	439 645	441 053	472 025	515 278	586 492	629 033	631 059	606 231	577 520	634 997
Spain Espagne										
Vessels entered										
Navires entrés	134 847	130 171	137 951	154 134	149 874	152 951	170 817	184 362	194 911	198 696
Vessels cleared										
Navires sortis	43 255	46 942	47 813	48 176	51 657	54 243	56 449	56 817	59 247	59 297
Sri Lanka Sri Lanka										
Vessels entered										
Navires entrés	22 087	24 955	25 120	25 368	29 882	33 188	36 011	37 399	37 418	34 690
Suriname Suriname										
Vessels entered										
Navires entrés	1 335	1 265	1 301	1 167	1 270	1 307	1 411	1 344	1 120	...
Vessels cleared										
Navires sortis	1 723	1 595	1 714	1 926	2 018	2 135	2 206	2 391	2 186	...
Sweden Suède										
Vessels entered										
Navires entrés	64 654[5]	62 159[5]	74 334[5]	82 386[5]	88 828[5]	95 655[5]	101 977[5]	158 718[22]	935 481[23]	925 202[23]
Vessels cleared										
Navires sortis	58 075[5]	55 058[5]	63 026[5]	73 139[5]	79 888[5]	82 877[5]	84 722[5]	143 200[22]	917 926[23]	910 735[23]
Syrian Arab Republic[2] Rép. arabe syrienne[2]										
Vessels entered[8]										
Navires entrés[8]	2 836	3 525	3 433	2 884	2 901	2 640	2 622	2 928	2 798	...
Vessels cleared										
Navires sortis	2 992	3 459	3 537	2 701	2 792	2 573	2 562	2 845	2 696	...
Thailand Thaïlande										
Vessels entered										
Navires entrés	47 639	39 647	46 527	58 759	53 033	54 489	35 764	41 106	...	...
Vessels cleared										
Navires sortis	23 584	22 205	24 692	28 689	22 231	23 757	24 920	31 125	...	...
Tunisia[5] Tunisie[5]										
Vessels entered										
Navires entrés	26 842	28 746	32 498	36 205	38 513	42 749	43 546	52 441	56 632	58 610
Vessels cleared										
Navires sortis	26 883	28 753	32 462	36 232	38 541	42 561	43 513	52 464	56 551	58 595
Turkey Turquie										
Vessels entered										
Navires entrés	46 990	56 687	52 925	57 170	59 861	78 474	142 303[5]	136 456[5]	152 191[5]	...
Vessels cleared										
Navires sortis	45 961	55 329	51 303	56 221	58 766	77 952	89 712[5]	88 761[5]	92 406[5]	...
Ukraine Ukraine										
Vessels entered										
Navires entrés	16 640	5 072	3 381	4 270	3 287	3 108	4 843	5 085	6 840	7 404
Vessels cleared										
Navires sortis	45 374	29 120	25 189	21 916	21 550	28 765	36 027	44 030	42 704	49 310
United States[9,24] Etats-Unis[9,24]										
Vessels entered										
Navires entrés	321 169	340 507	363 896	352 411	371 107	410 157	431 565	440 341	464 358	451 929
Vessels cleared										
Navires sortis	293 452	277 520	281 709	303 707	305 250	318 435	327 092	302 344	332 445	310 973
Uruguay Uruguay										
Vessels entered										
Navires entrés	3 862	4 036	5 297	5 414	5 505	5 844	5 262	4 386	5 257	...
Vessels cleared										
Navires sortis	13 141	16 059	20 266	24 608	24 975	26 844	24 499	21 596	19 587	...
Venezuela Venezuela										
Vessels entered										
Navires entrés	19 758	22 087	21 657	21 009	...	...	...	...	...	...

62

International maritime transport
Vessels entered and cleared: thousand net registered tons *[cont.]*

Transports maritimes internationaux
Navires entrés et sortis : milliers de tonneaux de jauge nette *[suite]*

Country or area Pays ou zone	1992	1993	1994	1995	1996	1997	1998	1999	2000	2001
Vessels cleared Navires sortis	15 194	17 211	12 045	8 461	...	...	...	...	...	...
Yemen Yémen										
Vessels entered Navires entrés	11 439	12 459	9 323	10 353	10 477	10 268	11 210	...	...	...
Vessels cleared Navires sortis	11 207	12 243	10 386	10 524	4 562	5 958	9 851	...	...	...

Source:
United Nations Statistics Division, New York, transport statistics database.

Source:
Organisation des Nations Unies, Division de statistique, New York, la base de données pour les statistiques des transports.

1 Data refer to fiscal years ending 30 June.

2 Including vessels in ballast.
3 Buenos Aires only.
4 Comprising Buenos Aires, Rosario, Lib. Gral. San Martin, Quequén and La Plata.
5 Gross registered tons.
6 Data refer to fiscal years beginning 1 July.

7 Sihanoukville Port and Phnom Penh Port.
8 All entrances counted.
9 Including Great Lakes international traffic (Canada: also St. Lawrence).
10 Taxable volume in thousands of cubic metres.
11 Including national maritime transport.
12 Beginning 2000, gross registered tons.
13 Port-au-Prince.
14 Data refer to fiscal years beginning 1 April.

15 Excluding minor and intermediate ports.
16 Data for Sarawak include vessels in ballast and all entrances counted.
17 Including vessels cleared.
18 Data cover only the first three quarters of the year.

19 Gross tonnage for a sample of Norwegian ports.
20 Vessels exceeding 75 gross registered tons.
21 Inland waterway system.
22 Break in series. Beginning 1999, data are based on a survey of all ports in Sweden.

23 Beginning 2000, including all passenger vessels and ferries.

24 Excluding traffic with United States Virgin Islands.

1 Les données se réfèrent aux exercices budgétaires finissant le 30 juin.
2 Y compris navires sur lest.
3 Buenos Aires seulement.
4 Buenos Aires, Rosario, Lib. Gral, San Martín, Quequén et La Plata.
5 Tonneaux de jauge brute.
6 Les données se réfèrent aux exercices budgétaires commençant le 1er juillet.
7 Port de Sihanoukville et Port de Phnom Penh.
8 Toutes entrées comprises.
9 Y compris trafic international des Grands Lacs (Canada: et du St. Laurent).
10 Volume taxable en milliers de mètres cubes.
11 Y compris transports martimes nationaux.
12 De compter à l'année 2000, tonneaux de jauge brute.
13 Port-au-Prince.
14 Les données se réfèrent aux exercices budgétaires commençant le 1er avril.
15 Non compris les ports petits et moyens.
16 Les données pour Sarawak comprennent navires sur lest et toutes entrées comprises.
17 Y compris navires sortis.
18 Les données se réfèrent aux premières trois trimestres de l'année.
19 Tonnage brute pour un échantillon de ports norvègiens.
20 Navires dépassant 75 tonneaux de jauge brute.
21 Transport fluvial.
22 Discontinuité dans la série. A compter de 1999, les données sont basées sur une enquête menée auprès de tous les ports de Suède.
23 De compter à l'année 2000, y compris tous les navires à passagers et les transbordeurs.
24 Non compris le trafic avec les Iles Vierges américaines.

63

Civil Aviation
Passengers on scheduled services (thousands); Kilometers (millions)

Aviation civile
Passagers sur les services réguliers (milliers) ; Kilomètres (millions)

Country or area and traffic	Total Totale 1997	1998	1999	2000	International Internationaux 1997	1998	1999	2000	Région, pays ou zone et trafic
World									**Monde**
Kilometers flown	21 635	22 430	23 672	25 155	9 963	10 589	11 231	12 043	Kilomètres parcourus
Passengers carried	1 456 147	1 470 730	1 558 628	1 655 164	437 688	457 151	491 126	538 200	Passagers transportés
Passenger-km	2 571 962	2 627 056	2 793 003	3 014 211	1 467 863	1 511 533	1 619 369	1 778 860	Passagers-km
Total ton-km	344 013	348 480	369 881	400 740	227 282	231 389	247 284	271 482	Total tonnes-km
Africa[1]									**Afrique**[1]
Kilometers flown	522	532	574	595	388	408	445	456	Kilomètres parcourus
Passengers carried	29 696	29 076	31 195	32 057	15 517	16 062	17 617	18 420	Passagers transportés
Passenger-km	56 258	55 736	62 223	66 637	46 988	47 448	53 226	57 204	Passagers-km
Total ton-km	6 657	6 830	7 598	8 278	5 778	6 031	6 719	7 331	Total tonnes-km
Algeria									**Algérie**
Kilometers flown	34	31	32	34	17	16	21	19	Kilomètres parcourus
Passengers carried	3 518	3 382	2 937	2 997	1 525	1 436	1 663	1 863	Passagers transportés
Passenger-km	3 130	3 012	2 991	3 051	1 874	1 785	2 226	2 389	Passagers-km
Total ton-km	299	292	286	287	183	177	214	225	Total tonnes-km
Angola									**Angola**
Kilometers flown	8	8	7	6	5	5	4	5	Kilomètres parcourus
Passengers carried	555	553	531	235	125	125	120	142	Passagers transportés
Passenger-km	620	622	597	619	368	369	355	565	Passagers-km
Total ton-km	97	95	92	116	73	71	68	111	Total tonnes-km
Benin[2]									**Bénin**[2]
Kilometers flown	3	3	3	3	3	3	3	3	Kilomètres parcourus
Passengers carried	86	91	84	77	86	91	84	77	Passagers transportés
Passenger-km	242	258	235	216	242	258	235	216	Passagers-km
Total ton-km	38	38	36	32	38	38	36	32	Total tonnes-km
Botswana									**Botswana**
Kilometers flown	2	3	3	3	2	2	2	2	Kilomètres parcourus
Passengers carried	116	124	144	164	88	92	108	121	Passagers transportés
Passenger-km	55	57	67	74	41	42	50	53	Passagers-km
Total ton-km	5	5	6	7	4	4	5	5	Total tonnes-km
Burkina Faso[2]									**Burkina Faso**[2]
Kilometers flown	3	3	4	4	3	3	4	4	Kilomètres parcourus
Passengers carried	97	102	147	144	94	99	132	128	Passagers transportés
Passenger-km	248	264	269	253	247	263	264	247	Passagers-km
Total ton-km	39	39	39	35	39	39	39	35	Total tonnes-km
Burundi									**Burundi**
Kilometers flown	1	1	...	...	1	1	...	...	Kilomètres parcourus
Passengers carried	12	12	...	...	12	12	...	...	Passagers transportés
Passenger-km	8	8	...	...	8	8	...	...	Passagers-km
Total ton-km	1	1	...	...	1	1	...	...	Total tonnes-km
Cameroon									**Cameroun**
Kilometers flown	6	6	6	6	5	5	5	5	Kilomètres parcourus
Passengers carried	279	290	293	312	175	189	204	221	Passagers transportés
Passenger-km	547	568	597	646	490	492	533	580	Passagers-km
Total ton-km	84	108	106	115	78	100	99	108	Total tonnes-km
Cape Verde									**Cap-Vert**
Kilometers flown	5	5	5	6	3	3	4	4	Kilomètres parcourus
Passengers carried	237	236	252	264	87	87	114	120	Passagers transportés
Passenger-km	268	269	334	356	218	219	287	307	Passagers-km
Total ton-km	25	26	32	34	20	21	27	29	Total tonnes-km
Central African Rep.[2]									**Rép. centrafricaine**[2]
Kilometers flown	3	3	3	3	3	3	3	3	Kilomètres parcourus
Passengers carried	86	91	84	77	86	91	84	77	Passagers transportés
Passenger-km	242	258	235	216	242	258	235	216	Passagers-km
Total ton-km	38	38	36	32	38	38	36	32	Total tonnes-km
Chad[2]									**Tchad**[2]
Kilometers flown	3	3	3	3	3	3	3	3	Kilomètres parcourus
Passengers carried	93	98	84	77	86	91	84	77	Passagers transportés
Passenger-km	247	263	235	216	242	258	235	216	Passagers-km

63
Civil Aviation
Passengers on scheduled services (thousands); Kilometers (millions)
Aviation civile
Passagers sur les services réguliers (milliers) ; Kilomètres (millions)

Country or area and traffic	Total Totale				International Internationaux				Région, pays ou zone et trafic
	1997	1998	1999	2000	1997	1998	1999	2000	
Total ton-km	39	38	36	32	38	38	36	32	Total tonnes-km
Congo [2]									**Congo [2]**
Kilometers flown	5	5	4	4	3	3	3	3	Kilomètres parcourus
Passengers carried	237	241	132	128	88	93	87	81	Passagers transportés
Passenger-km	305	321	263	245	245	261	240	222	Passagers-km
Total ton-km	44	44	39	34	39	38	36	32	Total tonnes-km
Côte d'Ivoire [2]									**Côte d'Ivoire [2]**
Kilometers flown	4	4	6	3	4	4	6	3	Kilomètres parcourus
Passengers carried	158	162	260	108	148	153	233	103	Passagers transportés
Passenger-km	302	318	381	242	297	313	366	240	Passagers-km
Total ton-km	44	44	50	34	43	43	48	34	Total tonnes-km
Egypt									**Egypte**
Kilometers flown	65	63	68	64	59	58	62	58	Kilomètres parcourus
Passengers carried	4 416	4 022	4 620	4 522	2 931	2 793	3 065	2 860	Passagers transportés
Passenger-km	9 018	8 036	9 074	8 828	8 310	7 470	8 355	8 065	Passagers-km
Total ton-km	1 029	989	1 097	1 085	965	938	1 032	1 015	Total tonnes-km
Equatorial Guinea									**Guinée équatoriale**
Kilometers flown	0	0	...	...	0	0	...	...	Kilomètres parcourus
Passengers carried	21	21	...	...	8	7	...	...	Passagers transportés
Passenger-km	4	4	...	...	1	1	...	...	Passagers-km
Total ton-km	0	0	...	...	0	0	...	...	Total tonnes-km
Ethiopia									**Ethiopie**
Kilometers flown	28	27	29	29	24	22	25	26	Kilomètres parcourus
Passengers carried	772	790	861	945	496	460	617	683	Passagers transportés
Passenger-km	1 966	1 881	2 458	2 753	1 834	1 743	2 358	2 641	Passagers-km
Total ton-km	317	318	371	383	305	304	362	373	Total tonnes-km
Gabon									**Gabon**
Kilometers flown	8	8	8	8	6	6	6	7	Kilomètres parcourus
Passengers carried	469	467	423	447	195	194	226	244	Passagers transportés
Passenger-km	826	829	782	847	745	748	712	774	Passagers-km
Total ton-km	112	111	124	135	105	103	117	128	Total tonnes-km
Ghana									**Ghana**
Kilometers flown	6	6	9	9	6	6	9	9	Kilomètres parcourus
Passengers carried	211	210	304	314	211	210	304	314	Passagers transportés
Passenger-km	702	705	1 097	1 204	702	705	1 097	1 204	Passagers-km
Total ton-km	99	97	151	162	99	97	151	162	Total tonnes-km
Guinea									**Guinée**
Kilometers flown	1	1	1	...	1	1	1	...	Kilomètres parcourus
Passengers carried	36	36	59	...	31	31	59	...	Passagers transportés
Passenger-km	55	55	94	...	50	50	94	...	Passagers-km
Total ton-km	6	6	10	...	5	5	10	...	Total tonnes-km
Guinea-Bissau									**Guinée-Bissau**
Kilometers flown	0	0	...	...	0	0	...	...	Kilomètres parcourus
Passengers carried	21	20	...	...	8	8	...	...	Passagers transportés
Passenger-km	10	10	...	...	6	6	...	...	Passagers-km
Total ton-km	1	1	...	...	1	1	...	...	Total tonnes-km
Kenya									**Kenya**
Kilometers flown	19	21	24	34	15	17	19	27	Kilomètres parcourus
Passengers carried	836	1 138	1 358	1 555	470	658	808	973	Passagers transportés
Passenger-km	1 824	2 091	2 513	3 271	1 689	1 883	2 286	3 040	Passagers-km
Total ton-km	216	243	292	377	203	223	271	355	Total tonnes-km
Lesotho									**Lesotho**
Kilometers flown	0	1	0	...	0	1	0	...	Kilomètres parcourus
Passengers carried	10	28	1	...	7	23	1	...	Passagers transportés
Passenger-km	3	9	0	...	3	8	0	...	Passagers-km
Total ton-km	0	1	0	...	0	1	0	...	Total tonnes-km
Libyan Arab Jamah.									**Jamah. arabe libyenne**
Kilometers flown	4	4	4	4	...	...	...	...	Kilomètres parcourus
Passengers carried	571	571	571	601	...	...	...	...	Passagers transportés
Passenger-km	377	377	377	409	...	...	...	...	Passagers-km

63

Civil Aviation

Passengers on scheduled services (thousands); Kilometers (millions)

Aviation civile

Passagers sur les services réguliers (milliers) ; Kilomètres (millions)

Country or area and traffic	Total Totale 1997	1998	1999	2000	International Internationaux 1997	1998	1999	2000	Région, pays ou zone et trafic
Total ton-km	30	27	27	33	...	...	...	...	Total tonnes-km
Madagascar									**Madagascar**
Kilometers flown	9	9	12	14	4	7	7	9	Kilomètres parcourus
Passengers carried	575	318	635	667	131	145	168	183	Passagers transportés
Passenger-km	758	718	1 037	1 146	570	646	841	907	Passagers-km
Total ton-km	98	94	126	137	79	86	107	114	Total tonnes-km
Malawi									**Malawi**
Kilometers flown	3	3	2	3	2	2	1	2	Kilomètres parcourus
Passengers carried	158	158	112	116	79	79	63	64	Passagers transportés
Passenger-km	336	337	224	210	299	300	150	136	Passagers-km
Total ton-km	33	33	21	22	31	31	14	15	Total tonnes-km
Mali [2]									**Mali** [2]
Kilometers flown	3	3	3	3	3	3	3	3	Kilomètres parcourus
Passengers carried	86	91	84	77	86	91	84	77	Passagers transportés
Passenger-km	242	258	235	216	242	258	235	216	Passagers-km
Total ton-km	38	38	36	32	38	38	36	32	Total tonnes-km
Mauritania [2]									**Mauritanie** [2]
Kilometers flown	4	4	4	4	3	3	3	3	Kilomètres parcourus
Passengers carried	245	250	187	185	110	115	103	98	Passagers transportés
Passenger-km	324	340	290	275	267	283	255	238	Passagers-km
Total ton-km	46	46	41	37	41	40	38	34	Total tonnes-km
Mauritius									**Maurice**
Kilometers flown	26	24	29	29	25	23	28	27	Kilomètres parcourus
Passengers carried	804	810	831	949	743	743	756	865	Passagers transportés
Passenger-km	3 917	3 826	4 073	4 888	3 881	3 788	4 027	4 837	Passagers-km
Total ton-km	538	526	539	647	535	523	535	643	Total tonnes-km
Morocco									**Maroc**
Kilometers flown	49	56	63	64	45	51	59	60	Kilomètres parcourus
Passengers carried	2 638	3 012	3 392	3 671	2 023	2 265	2 587	2 800	Passagers transportés
Passenger-km	5 321	5 868	6 614	7 185	5 124	5 625	6 355	6 904	Passagers-km
Total ton-km	417	573	667	722	401	549	641	693	Total tonnes-km
Mozambique									**Mozambique**
Kilometers flown	4	4	5	6	1	2	2	3	Kilomètres parcourus
Passengers carried	188	201	235	260	65	73	87	93	Passagers transportés
Passenger-km	291	295	326	376	170	163	171	207	Passagers-km
Total ton-km	32	33	36	41	19	19	20	24	Total tonnes-km
Namibia									**Namibie**
Kilometers flown	8	9	7	8	7	7	5	6	Kilomètres parcourus
Passengers carried	214	229	201	247	183	200	165	212	Passagers transportés
Passenger-km	906	630	548	740	882	614	528	720	Passagers-km
Total ton-km	118	59	49	151	116	57	47	149	Total tonnes-km
Niger [2]									**Niger** [2]
Kilometers flown	3	3	3	3	3	3	3	3	Kilomètres parcourus
Passengers carried	86	91	84	77	86	91	84	77	Passagers transportés
Passenger-km	242	258	235	216	242	258	235	216	Passagers-km
Total ton-km	38	38	36	32	38	38	36	32	Total tonnes-km
Nigeria									**Nigéria**
Kilometers flown	5	5	7	7	2	2	4	2	Kilomètres parcourus
Passengers carried	318	313	668	507	44	49	162	48	Passagers transportés
Passenger-km	221	245	560	565	100	122	370	63	Passagers-km
Total ton-km	27	32	82	57	14	18	61	8	Total tonnes-km
Sao Tome and Principe									**Sao Tomé-et-Principe**
Kilometers flown	0	0	0	0	0	0	0	0	Kilomètres parcourus
Passengers carried	25	24	34	35	15	15	20	21	Passagers transportés
Passenger-km	9	9	13	14	5	5	6	7	Passagers-km
Total ton-km	1	1	1	1	0	0	1	1	Total tonnes-km
Senegal [2]									**Sénégal** [2]
Kilometers flown	4	3	3	3	3	3	3	3	Kilomètres parcourus
Passengers carried	166	121	103	98	135	91	84	77	Passagers transportés
Passenger-km	265	267	241	222	256	258	235	216	Passagers-km

63

Civil Aviation

Passengers on scheduled services (thousands); Kilometers (millions)

Aviation civile

Passagers sur les services réguliers (milliers) ; Kilomètres (millions)

Country or area and traffic	Total Totale 1997	1998	1999	2000	International Internationaux 1997	1998	1999	2000	Région, pays ou zone et trafic
Total ton-km	40	39	37	32	40	38	36	32	Total tonnes-km
Seychelles									**Seychelles**
Kilometers flown	8	9	9	9	7	8	8	8	Kilomètres parcourus
Passengers carried	384	369	347	394	133	113	110	127	Passagers transportés
Passenger-km	847	755	735	807	836	743	725	795	Passagers-km
Total ton-km	106	84	85	94	105	83	84	93	Total tonnes-km
Sierra Leone									**Sierra Leone**
Kilometers flown	...	...	0	1	...	...	0	1	Kilomètres parcourus
Passengers carried	...	...	19	19	...	...	19	19	Passagers transportés
Passenger-km	...	...	30	93	...	...	30	93	Passagers-km
Total ton-km	...	...	3	18	...	...	3	18	Total tonnes-km
South Africa									**Afrique du Sud**
Kilometers flown	131	128	144	151	69	75	84	87	Kilomètres parcourus
Passengers carried	7 274	6 480	7 374	8 001	1 808	1 913	2 189	2 483	Passagers transportés
Passenger-km	16 825	16 997	19 021	21 015	11 928	12 869	14 247	15 857	Passagers-km
Total ton-km	1 918	2 046	2 381	2 579	1 449	1 636	1 904	2 041	Total tonnes-km
Sudan									**Soudan**
Kilometers flown	7	6	7	6	5	4	4	5	Kilomètres parcourus
Passengers carried	333	499	390	414	211	311	245	265	Passagers transportés
Passenger-km	471	148	693	748	384	126	588	639	Passagers-km
Total ton-km	66	19	94	101	50	16	80	87	Total tonnes-km
Swaziland									**Swaziland**
Kilometers flown	1	1	1	2	1	1	1	2	Kilomètres parcourus
Passengers carried	41	41	12	90	41	41	12	90	Passagers transportés
Passenger-km	43	43	13	68	43	43	13	68	Passagers-km
Total ton-km	4	4	1	6	4	4	1	6	Total tonnes-km
Togo [2]									**Togo** [2]
Kilometers flown	3	3	3	3	3	3	3	3	Kilomètres parcourus
Passengers carried	86	91	84	77	86	91	84	77	Passagers transportés
Passenger-km	242	258	235	216	242	258	235	216	Passagers-km
Total ton-km	38	38	36	32	38	38	36	32	Total tonnes-km
Tunisia									**Tunisie**
Kilometers flown	24	27	27	27	24	27	27	27	Kilomètres parcourus
Passengers carried	1 779	1 888	1 923	1 908	1 779	1 888	1 923	1 908	Passagers transportés
Passenger-km	2 479	2 683	2 762	2 690	2 479	2 683	2 762	2 690	Passagers-km
Total ton-km	249	266	282	284	249	266	282	284	Total tonnes-km
Uganda									**Ouganda**
Kilometers flown	2	2	5	2	2	2	2	2	Kilomètres parcourus
Passengers carried	100	100	179	39	100	100	36	39	Passagers transportés
Passenger-km	110	110	356	215	110	110	198	215	Passagers-km
Total ton-km	11	11	54	40	11	11	37	40	Total tonnes-km
United Rep. of Tanzania									**Rép.-Unie de Tanzanie**
Kilometers flown	4	5	3	4	3	3	2	3	Kilomètres parcourus
Passengers carried	218	220	190	193	93	89	75	90	Passagers transportés
Passenger-km	231	236	176	198	165	171	115	146	Passagers-km
Total ton-km	26	25	18	21	18	18	12	15	Total tonnes-km
Zambia									**Zambie**
Kilometers flown	1	1	1	2	1	1	1	1	Kilomètres parcourus
Passengers carried	50	49	42	90	42	42	36	45	Passagers transportés
Passenger-km	45	44	34	51	43	42	32	38	Passagers-km
Total ton-km	5	4	3	5	4	4	3	4	Total tonnes-km
Zimbabwe									**Zimbabwe**
Kilometers flown	16	19	13	17	13	16	10	14	Kilomètres parcourus
Passengers carried	771	706	567	605	302	310	248	288	Passagers transportés
Passenger-km	914	955	918	771	724	791	788	653	Passagers-km
Total ton-km	224	234	114	228	208	221	102	217	Total tonnes-km
America, North [1]									**Amérique du Nord** [1]
Kilometers flown	9 912	10 224	10 908	11 553	2 240	2 473	2 601	2 754	**Kilomètres parcourus**
Passengers carried	639 612	640 789	688 567	721 303	82 704	85 779	91 296	98 240	**Passagers transportés**

63

Civil Aviation

Passengers on scheduled services (thousands); Kilometers (millions)

Aviation civile

Passagers sur les services réguliers (milliers) ; Kilomètres (millions)

Country or area and traffic	Total Totale				International Internationaux				Région, pays ou zone et trafic
	1997	1998	1999	2000	1997	1998	1999	2000	
Passenger-km	1 058 636	1 086 197	1 154 217	1 226 291	328 718	339 436	361 495	387 991	Passagers-km
Total ton-km	127 555	130 124	137 802	147 429	47 720	49 173	52 481	57 021	Total tonnes-km
Antigua and Barbuda									**Antigua-et-Barbuda**
Kilometers flown	12	12	11	10	12	12	11	10	Kilomètres parcourus
Passengers carried	1 250	1 245	1 371	1 426	1 250	1 245	1 371	1 426	Passagers transportés
Passenger-km	250	251	276	298	250	251	276	298	Passagers-km
Total ton-km	23	23	26	28	23	23	26	28	Total tonnes-km
Bahamas									**Bahamas**
Kilometers flown	2	2	7	7	1	1	3	3	Kilomètres parcourus
Passengers carried	704	701	1 719	1 861	296	294	944	1 016	Passagers transportés
Passenger-km	140	140	366	415	76	76	244	280	Passagers-km
Total ton-km	13	13	42	47	7	7	28	32	Total tonnes-km
Canada									**Canada**
Kilometers flown	519	547	570	598	293	317	337	370	Kilomètres parcourus
Passengers carried	23 981	24 653	24 039	25 281	10 945	11 382	11 875	12 775	Passagers transportés
Passenger-km	61 862	63 801	65 323	69 985	40 928	42 071	43 728	47 408	Passagers-km
Total ton-km	7 667	7 751	7 929	8 293	5 382	5 402	5 599	5 882	Total tonnes-km
Costa Rica									**Costa Rica**
Kilometers flown	24	28	27	20	23	25	24	18	Kilomètres parcourus
Passengers carried	992	1 070	1 055	878	899	933	923	742	Passagers transportés
Passenger-km	1 915	2 004	2 145	2 358	1 903	1 983	2 112	2 334	Passagers-km
Total ton-km	248	289	245	252	247	287	242	250	Total tonnes-km
Cuba									**Cuba**
Kilometers flown	26	34	26	20	20	28	22	16	Kilomètres parcourus
Passengers carried	1 117	1 138	1 259	1 007	592	647	684	598	Passagers transportés
Passenger-km	3 543	4 791	3 712	2 964	3 228	4 470	3 463	2 769	Passagers-km
Total ton-km	388	524	421	335	362	497	392	312	Total tonnes-km
Dominican Republic									**Rép. dominicaine**
Kilometers flown	1	1	0	...	1	1	0	...	Kilomètres parcourus
Passengers carried	34	34	10	...	34	34	10	...	Passagers transportés
Passenger-km	16	16	5	...	16	16	5	...	Passagers-km
Total ton-km	1	1	0	...	1	1	0	...	Total tonnes-km
El Salvador									**El Salvador**
Kilometers flown	17	22	28	34	17	22	26	30	Kilomètres parcourus
Passengers carried	1 006	1 585	1 624	2 476	1 006	1 525	1 467	1 960	Passagers transportés
Passenger-km	1 898	2 292	5 091	3 020	1 898	2 284	5 025	2 829	Passagers-km
Total ton-km	190	253	502	302	190	252	496	284	Total tonnes-km
Guatemala									**Guatemala**
Kilometers flown	5	7	5	...	4	7	5	...	Kilomètres parcourus
Passengers carried	508	794	506	...	432	760	472	...	Passagers transportés
Passenger-km	368	480	342	...	337	469	331	...	Passagers-km
Total ton-km	77	50	33	...	75	49	32	...	Total tonnes-km
Jamaica									**Jamaïque**
Kilometers flown	22	23	35	32	22	23	35	32	Kilomètres parcourus
Passengers carried	1 400	1 454	1 670	1 922	1 400	1 454	1 670	1 922	Passagers transportés
Passenger-km	2 677	2 961	3 495	4 087	2 677	2 961	3 495	4 087	Passagers-km
Total ton-km	264	293	377	400	264	293	377	400	Total tonnes-km
Mexico									**Mexique**
Kilometers flown	308	360	368	359	141	176	179	160	Kilomètres parcourus
Passengers carried	17 752	18 685	19 263	20 894	4 773	4 728	5 049	6 137	Passagers transportés
Passenger-km	24 065	25 976	27 847	30 299	11 228	11 703	12 939	15 059	Passagers-km
Total ton-km	2 333	2 566	2 742	3 061	1 142	1 241	1 377	1 635	Total tonnes-km
Nicaragua									**Nicaragua**
Kilometers flown	1	1	1	1	1	1	1	1	Kilomètres parcourus
Passengers carried	51	52	59	61	51	52	59	61	Passagers transportés
Passenger-km	85	93	67	72	85	93	67	72	Passagers-km
Total ton-km	17	10	7	7	17	10	7	7	Total tonnes-km
Panama									**Panama**
Kilometers flown	18	21	24	34	18	21	24	34	Kilomètres parcourus
Passengers carried	772	856	933	1 117	772	856	933	1 117	Passagers transportés

63

Civil Aviation

Passengers on scheduled services (thousands); Kilometers (millions)

Aviation civile

Passagers sur les services réguliers (milliers) ; Kilomètres (millions)

	Total Totale				International Internationaux				
Country or area and traffic	1997	1998	1999	2000	1997	1998	1999	2000	Région, pays ou zone et trafic
Passenger-km	1 094	1 373	1 697	2 604	1 094	1 373	1 697	2 604	Passagers-km
Total ton-km	152	174	215	312	152	174	215	312	Total tonnes-km
Trinidad and Tobago									**Trinité-et-Tobago**
Kilometers flown	18	21	25	28	18	21	24	28	Kilomètres parcourus
Passengers carried	807	880	1 112	1 254	807	880	1 046	1 126	Passagers transportés
Passenger-km	2 392	2 567	2 720	2 765	2 392	2 567	2 715	2 754	Passagers-km
Total ton-km	239	315	309	300	239	315	309	299	Total tonnes-km
United States									**Etats-Unis**
Kilometers flown	8 928	9 134	9 759	10 386	1 659	1 809	1 888	2 030	Kilomètres parcourus
Passengers carried	587 992	586 402	632 440	661 461	58 580	60 126	63 644	68 037	Passagers transportés
Passenger-km	957 379	978 498	1 039 643	1 105 728	261 741	268 253	284 008	305 895	Passagers-km
Total ton-km	115 856	117 773	124 817	133 937	39 541	40 540	43 254	47 431	Total tonnes-km
America, South									**Amérique du Sud**
Kilometers flown	**1 023**	**1 099**	**1 088**	**1 049**	**466**	**445**	**426**	**412**	**Kilomètres parcourus**
Passengers carried	**58 522**	**63 745**	**62 391**	**64 647**	**13 332**	**13 731**	**13 523**	**12 992**	**Passagers transportés**
Passenger-km	**86 036**	**91 204**	**86 711**	**91 229**	**53 012**	**53 043**	**49 626**	**51 849**	**Passagers-km**
Total ton-km	**12 035**	**12 559**	**11 599**	**12 245**	**8 277**	**8 568**	**7 735**	**8 174**	**Total tonnes-km**
Argentina									**Argentine**
Kilometers flown	155	157	170	160	74	54	53	58	Kilomètres parcourus
Passengers carried	8 603	8 623	9 192	8 904	2 120	2 108	1 980	2 305	Passagers transportés
Passenger-km	14 348	14 379	14 024	15 535	8 602	8 447	7 621	9 287	Passagers-km
Total ton-km	1 566	1 597	1 559	1 751	1 055	1 055	970	1 171	Total tonnes-km
Bolivia									**Bolivie**
Kilometers flown	28	28	21	20	17	19	15	15	Kilomètres parcourus
Passengers carried	2 251	2 115	1 873	1 757	705	773	659	657	Passagers transportés
Passenger-km	2 143	2 179	1 851	1 809	1 548	1 629	1 398	1 403	Passagers-km
Total ton-km	274	273	186	181	215	218	147	143	Total tonnes-km
Brazil									**Brésil**
Kilometers flown	468	535	530	519	172	173	156	151	Kilomètres parcourus
Passengers carried	24 196	29 137	28 273	31 819	4 582	4 648	3 980	3 903	Passagers transportés
Passenger-km	42 242	46 978	42 224	45 812	25 492	25 479	21 504	22 812	Passagers-km
Total ton-km	5 716	5 980	5 333	5 712	3 697	3 627	3 088	3 246	Total tonnes-km
Chile									**Chili**
Kilometers flown	109	117	107	108	59	63	65	67	Kilomètres parcourus
Passengers carried	4 693	5 095	5 188	5 175	1 613	1 768	2 056	2 059	Passagers transportés
Passenger-km	8 769	9 679	10 650	10 859	5 691	6 300	7 438	7 678	Passagers-km
Total ton-km	1 865	2 124	2 107	2 296	1 543	1 768	1 766	1 955	Total tonnes-km
Colombia									**Colombie**
Kilometers flown	117	125	120	120	50	57	60	65	Kilomètres parcourus
Passengers carried	9 099	9 051	8 665	8 570	1 136	1 320	1 553	1 773	Passagers transportés
Passenger-km	6 934	7 350	7 848	8 662	3 400	3 835	4 659	5 366	Passagers-km
Total ton-km	1 392	1 436	1 348	1 384	855	1 061	985	1 046	Total tonnes-km
Ecuador									**Equateur**
Kilometers flown	23	23	16	12	18	18	11	6	Kilomètres parcourus
Passengers carried	1 791	2 048	1 387	1 319	503	674	351	163	Passagers transportés
Passenger-km	2 035	2 282	1 388	1 042	1 455	1 788	976	544	Passagers-km
Total ton-km	235	286	157	108	180	239	118	62	Total tonnes-km
Guyana									**Guyana**
Kilometers flown	3	3	2	2	2	2	2	2	Kilomètres parcourus
Passengers carried	126	126	70	73	59	59	70	73	Passagers transportés
Passenger-km	248	249	277	299	230	231	277	299	Passagers-km
Total ton-km	26	26	28	30	23	24	28	30	Total tonnes-km
Paraguay									**Paraguay**
Kilometers flown	4	5	5	5	4	5	4	4	Kilomètres parcourus
Passengers carried	196	222	232	266	196	222	217	249	Passagers transportés
Passenger-km	215	247	244	270	215	247	239	266	Passagers-km
Total ton-km	19	22	22	24	19	22	21	24	Total tonnes-km
Peru									**Pérou**
Kilometers flown	40	41	27	24	17	18	6	8	Kilomètres parcourus

63

Civil Aviation

Passengers on scheduled services (thousands); Kilometers (millions)

Aviation civile

Passagers sur les services réguliers (milliers) ; Kilomètres (millions)

Country or area and traffic	Total Totale				International Internationaux				Région, pays ou zone et trafic
	1997	1998	1999	2000	1997	1998	1999	2000	
Passengers carried	2 725	2 774	1 900	1 595	510	508	150	145	Passagers transportés
Passenger-km	2 964	3 014	1 590	1 555	1 521	1 526	450	548	Passagers-km
Total ton-km	276	286	149	196	140	144	42	95	Total tonnes-km
Suriname									**Suriname**
Kilometers flown	7	7	6	6	7	7	6	5	Kilomètres parcourus
Passengers carried	279	278	194	233	275	274	190	227	Passagers transportés
Passenger-km	1 068	1 072	726	1 151	1 067	1 071	725	1 149	Passagers-km
Total ton-km	127	127	91	130	127	127	91	129	Total tonnes-km
Uruguay									**Uruguay**
Kilometers flown	6	7	8	8	6	7	8	8	Kilomètres parcourus
Passengers carried	544	557	728	642	544	557	728	642	Passagers transportés
Passenger-km	627	642	839	747	627	642	839	747	Passagers-km
Total ton-km	57	70	94	82	57	70	94	82	Total tonnes-km
Venezuela									**Venezuela**
Kilometers flown	63	52	75	66	40	22	39	23	Kilomètres parcourus
Passengers carried	4 020	3 720	4 690	4 295	1 090	820	1 590	795	Passagers transportés
Passenger-km	4 444	3 133	5 050	3 487	3 164	1 848	3 500	1 750	Passagers-km
Total ton-km	483	332	526	350	364	213	383	190	Total tonnes-km
Asia [1]									**Asie** [1]
Kilometers flown	**4 102**	**4 189**	**4 321**	**4 627**	**2 540**	**2 593**	**2 729**	**2 959**	Kilomètres parcourus
Passengers carried	**345 483**	**336 963**	**351 455**	**379 120**	**117 496**	**116 720**	**127 479**	**143 253**	Passagers transportés
Passenger-km	**636 050**	**621 807**	**665 643**	**737 948**	**445 638**	**439 870**	**480 286**	**544 206**	Passagers-km
Total ton-km	**93 944**	**91 631**	**100 049**	**109 528**	**76 098**	**74 427**	**82 323**	**90 964**	Total tonnes-km
Afghanistan									**Afghanistan**
Kilometers flown	6	3	3	3	6	2	2	2	Kilomètres parcourus
Passengers carried	90	53	140	150	51	27	36	40	Passagers transportés
Passenger-km	158	88	129	143	136	72	90	101	Passagers-km
Total ton-km	50	24	19	21	48	22	15	17	Total tonnes-km
Armenia									**Arménie**
Kilometers flown	8	9	8	7	8	9	8	7	Kilomètres parcourus
Passengers carried	368	365	343	298	368	365	343	298	Passagers transportés
Passenger-km	767	765	639	572	767	765	639	572	Passagers-km
Total ton-km	80	80	70	61	80	80	70	61	Total tonnes-km
Azerbaijan									**Azerbaïdjan**
Kilometers flown	17	9	10	10	13	7	8	7	Kilomètres parcourus
Passengers carried	982	669	572	546	517	311	188	146	Passagers transportés
Passenger-km	1 283	843	614	503	1 021	632	390	272	Passagers-km
Total ton-km	159	169	113	93	119	145	90	70	Total tonnes-km
Bahrain [3]									**Bahreïn** [3]
Kilometers flown	19	19	21	28	19	19	21	28	Kilomètres parcourus
Passengers carried	1 165	1 207	1 307	1 382	1 165	1 207	1 307	1 382	Passagers transportés
Passenger-km	2 501	2 653	2 836	3 185	2 501	2 653	2 836	3 185	Passagers-km
Total ton-km	333	357	387	510	333	357	387	510	Total tonnes-km
Bangladesh									**Bangladesh**
Kilometers flown	20	20	21	25	19	19	20	23	Kilomètres parcourus
Passengers carried	1 315	1 162	1 215	1 331	846	855	892	969	Passagers transportés
Passenger-km	3 233	3 422	3 515	3 988	3 141	3 358	3 448	3 910	Passagers-km
Total ton-km	494	524	545	632	486	519	538	626	Total tonnes-km
Bhutan									**Bhoutan**
Kilometers flown	1	1	1	1	1	1	1	1	Kilomètres parcourus
Passengers carried	36	36	31	34	36	36	31	34	Passagers transportés
Passenger-km	49	49	41	47	49	49	41	47	Passagers-km
Total ton-km	4	4	4	4	4	4	4	4	Total tonnes-km
Brunei Darussalam									**Brunéi Darussalam**
Kilometers flown	28	35	25	25	28	35	25	25	Kilomètres parcourus
Passengers carried	1 088	877	808	864	1 088	877	808	864	Passagers transportés
Passenger-km	2 906	2 972	2 563	3 001	2 906	2 972	2 563	3 001	Passagers-km
Total ton-km	378	386	380	410	378	386	380	410	Total tonnes-km

63

Civil Aviation

Passengers on scheduled services (thousands); Kilometers (millions)

Aviation civile

Passagers sur les services réguliers (milliers) ; Kilomètres (millions)

Country or area and traffic	Total Totale				International Internationaux				Région, pays ou zone et trafic
	1997	1998	1999	2000	1997	1998	1999	2000	
China									**Chine**
Kilometers flown	639	730	784	854	107	127	138	153	Kilomètres parcourus
Passengers carried	52 277	53 481	55 853	61 892	4 790	5 086	6 005	6 417	Passagers transportés
Passenger-km	72 964	75 823	80 575	90 960	15 781	17 181	19 877	22 232	Passagers-km
Total ton-km	8 259	8 893	10 115	11 603	2 709	3 047	3 845	4 465	Total tonnes-km
China, Hong Kong SAR [4]									**Chine, Hong Kong RAS [4]**
Kilometers flown	112	228	228	251	112	228	228	251	Kilomètres parcourus
Passengers carried	5 957	12 203	12 593	14 378	5 957	12 203	12 593	14 378	Passagers transportés
Passenger-km	20 283	42 964	43 907	50 248	20 283	42 964	43 907	50 248	Passagers-km
Total ton-km	4 278	8 274	8 759	9 933	4 278	8 274	8 759	9 933	Total tonnes-km
China, Macao SAR									**Chine, Macao RAS**
Kilometers flown	...	...	...	14	...	...	...	14	Kilomètres parcourus
Passengers carried	...	...	...	1 532	...	...	...	1 532	Passagers transportés
Passenger-km	...	...	...	1 730	...	...	...	1 730	Passagers-km
Total ton-km	...	...	...	195	...	...	...	195	Total tonnes-km
Cyprus									**Chypre**
Kilometers flown	20	20	20	21	20	20	20	21	Kilomètres parcourus
Passengers carried	1 278	1 346	1 337	1 396	1 278	1 346	1 337	1 396	Passagers transportés
Passenger-km	2 657	2 711	2 687	2 785	2 657	2 711	2 687	2 785	Passagers-km
Total ton-km	278	284	285	297	278	284	285	297	Total tonnes-km
Georgia									**Géorgie**
Kilometers flown	3	7	5	4	3	5	5	4	Kilomètres parcourus
Passengers carried	110	205	159	118	110	175	159	118	Passagers transportés
Passenger-km	206	409	307	230	206	340	307	230	Passagers-km
Total ton-km	20	45	30	23	20	34	30	23	Total tonnes-km
India									**Inde**
Kilometers flown	194	200	190	202	66	68	66	65	Kilomètres parcourus
Passengers carried	16 536	16 547	16 005	17 303	3 447	3 478	3 640	3 748	Passagers transportés
Passenger-km	24 620	24 722	24 215	25 905	12 700	12 947	13 100	13 798	Passagers-km
Total ton-km	2 737	2 776	2 734	2 903	1 573	1 607	1 624	1 693	Total tonnes-km
Indonesia									**Indonésie**
Kilometers flown	199	155	122	138	88	56	47	48	Kilomètres parcourus
Passengers carried	12 937	9 603	8 047	9 916	3 120	2 017	1 927	2 192	Passagers transportés
Passenger-km	23 718	15 974	14 544	16 764	15 670	9 770	9 329	10 706	Passagers-km
Total ton-km	2 797	1 826	1 560	1 865	2 007	1 173	1 022	1 252	Total tonnes-km
Iran (Islamic Rep. of)									**Iran (Rép. islamique d')**
Kilometers flown	70	68	63	66	21	22	23	25	Kilomètres parcourus
Passengers carried	9 804	9 303	8 277	8 722	1 309	1 404	1 388	1 775	Passagers transportés
Passenger-km	8 963	8 539	7 852	8 202	2 642	2 632	2 704	3 220	Passagers-km
Total ton-km	901	856	799	801	324	322	339	350	Total tonnes-km
Israel									**Israël**
Kilometers flown	75	79	86	92	69	72	80	82	Kilomètres parcourus
Passengers carried	3 754	3 699	4 033	4 443	2 714	2 741	2 984	3 102	Passagers transportés
Passenger-km	11 776	12 418	13 515	14 507	11 493	12 152	13 225	14 127	Passagers-km
Total ton-km	2 195	2 241	2 259	2 200	2 175	2 217	2 233	2 166	Total tonnes-km
Japan									**Japon**
Kilometers flown	777	828	841	878	399	426	440	471	Kilomètres parcourus
Passengers carried	94 998	101 701	105 960	109 123	16 235	16 388	18 057	20 571	Passagers transportés
Passenger-km	151 048	154 402	162 798	174 149	84 098	85 608	91 463	102 683	Passagers-km
Total ton-km	20 627	20 896	22 348	23 868	14 755	14 905	16 144	17 572	Total tonnes-km
Jordan									**Jordanie**
Kilometers flown	40	35	36	37	40	35	36	37	Kilomètres parcourus
Passengers carried	1 353	1 187	1 252	1 282	1 353	1 187	1 252	1 282	Passagers transportés
Passenger-km	4 900	4 065	4 195	4 207	4 900	4 065	4 195	4 207	Passagers-km
Total ton-km	721	596	579	591	721	596	579	591	Total tonnes-km
Kazakhstan									**Kazakhstan**
Kilometers flown	20	35	33	15	7	25	25	10	Kilomètres parcourus
Passengers carried	568	726	667	461	158	318	318	234	Passagers transportés
Passenger-km	1 330	1 533	1 477	1 208	640	1 149	1 149	916	Passagers-km
Total ton-km	137	162	156	133	72	123	123	104	Total tonnes-km

63

Civil Aviation

Passengers on scheduled services (thousands); Kilometers (millions)

Aviation civile

Passagers sur les services réguliers (milliers) ; Kilomètres (millions)

Country or area and traffic	Total Totale 1997	1998	1999	2000	International Internationaux 1997	1998	1999	2000	Région, pays ou zone et trafic
Korea, Dem. P. R.									**Corée, R. p. dém. de**
Kilometers flown	5	3	2	1	3	3	2	1	Kilomètres parcourus
Passengers carried	280	64	59	83	64	64	59	83	Passagers transportés
Passenger-km	286	192	178	37	192	192	178	37	Passagers-km
Total ton-km	30	19	18	5	19	19	18	5	Total tonnes-km
Korea, Republic of									**Corée, République de**
Kilometers flown	365	319	336	367	306	266	285	309	Kilomètres parcourus
Passengers carried	35 506	27 109	31 319	34 331	10 262	8 973	10 646	12 137	Passagers transportés
Passenger-km	59 372	47 711	56 116	62 837	50 485	40 982	48 806	54 926	Passagers-km
Total ton-km	13 210	11 605	13 424	13 302	12 346	10 929	12 692	12 526	Total tonnes-km
Kuwait									**Koweït**
Kilometers flown	43	45	36	37	43	45	36	37	Kilomètres parcourus
Passengers carried	2 114	2 190	2 130	2 113	2 114	2 190	2 130	2 113	Passagers transportés
Passenger-km	5 997	6 207	6 158	6 134	5 997	6 207	6 158	6 134	Passagers-km
Total ton-km	912	932	829	805	912	932	829	805	Total tonnes-km
Kyrgyzstan									**Kirghizistan**
Kilometers flown	8	9	9	6	2	6	6	5	Kilomètres parcourus
Passengers carried	423	427	312	241	52	143	136	114	Passagers transportés
Passenger-km	531	519	532	423	189	407	463	373	Passagers-km
Total ton-km	52	60	56	44	19	50	50	39	Total tonnes-km
Lao People's Dem. Rep.									**Rép. dém. pop. lao**
Kilometers flown	1	1	2	2	1	1	1	1	Kilomètres parcourus
Passengers carried	125	124	197	211	31	31	54	61	Passagers transportés
Passenger-km	48	48	78	85	20	20	34	38	Passagers-km
Total ton-km	5	5	8	9	2	2	4	4	Total tonnes-km
Lebanon									**Liban**
Kilometers flown	21	20	20	20	21	20	20	20	Kilomètres parcourus
Passengers carried	857	716	719	806	857	716	719	806	Passagers transportés
Passenger-km	2 116	1 504	1 288	1 484	2 116	1 504	1 288	1 484	Passagers-km
Total ton-km	319	247	222	223	319	247	222	223	Total tonnes-km
Malaysia									**Malaisie**
Kilometers flown	183	189	207	220	128	140	158	171	Kilomètres parcourus
Passengers carried	15 592	13 654	14 985	16 561	6 274	6 105	6 770	7 390	Passagers transportés
Passenger-km	28 698	29 372	33 708	37 939	24 004	25 392	29 253	32 905	Passagers-km
Total ton-km	3 777	3 777	4 431	5 346	3 332	3 407	4 014	4 875	Total tonnes-km
Maldives									**Maldives**
Kilometers flown	3	4	5	6	2	3	4	4	Kilomètres parcourus
Passengers carried	189	247	344	315	170	192	273	222	Passagers transportés
Passenger-km	292	355	501	425	283	331	470	385	Passagers-km
Total ton-km	33	42	62	54	32	40	59	50	Total tonnes-km
Mongolia									**Mongolie**
Kilometers flown	4	8	6	6	2	4	3	3	Kilomètres parcourus
Passengers carried	240	255	225	254	121	95	98	118	Passagers transportés
Passenger-km	195	469	436	520	147	331	325	401	Passagers-km
Total ton-km	18	50	46	51	14	35	35	41	Total tonnes-km
Myanmar									**Myanmar**
Kilometers flown	9	8	9	...	6	5	5	...	Kilomètres parcourus
Passengers carried	575	522	537	...	192	148	145	...	Passagers transportés
Passenger-km	385	345	355	...	206	156	152	...	Passagers-km
Total ton-km	46	40	40	...	33	25	24	...	Total tonnes-km
Nepal									**Népal**
Kilometers flown	11	11	9	10	7	7	8	9	Kilomètres parcourus
Passengers carried	755	754	583	643	385	385	452	506	Passagers transportés
Passenger-km	908	908	1 023	1 155	855	855	1 004	1 135	Passagers-km
Total ton-km	99	99	108	121	94	94	106	119	Total tonnes-km
Oman [3]									**Oman** [3]
Kilometers flown	26	27	30	32	24	26	29	31	Kilomètres parcourus
Passengers carried	1 678	1 768	1 933	2 118	1 507	1 590	1 768	1 942	Passagers transportés
Passenger-km	3 197	3 405	3 435	4 148	3 055	3 257	3 295	4 002	Passagers-km
Total ton-km	384	415	437	549	374	404	427	533	Total tonnes-km

63

Civil Aviation

Passengers on scheduled services (thousands); Kilometers (millions)

Aviation civile

Passagers sur les services réguliers (milliers) ; Kilomètres (millions)

Country or area and traffic	Total Totale				International Internationaux				Région, pays ou zone et trafic
	1997	1998	1999	2000	1997	1998	1999	2000	
Pakistan									**Pakistan**
Kilometers flown	78	75	73	76	56	53	52	57	Kilomètres parcourus
Passengers carried	5 883	5 414	4 972	5 294	2 632	2 568	2 443	2 785	Passagers transportés
Passenger-km	11 658	10 972	10 466	12 054	9 413	8 922	8 550	10 103	Passagers-km
Total ton-km	1 479	1 408	1 293	1 452	1 243	1 186	1 085	1 243	Total tonnes-km
Philippines									**Philippines**
Kilometers flown	96	40	53	67	73	28	37	50	Kilomètres parcourus
Passengers carried	7 475	3 944	5 004	5 756	2 902	1 306	1 922	2 343	Passagers transportés
Passenger-km	16 392	7 503	10 292	13 063	13 966	5 918	8 405	10 958	Passagers-km
Total ton-km	2 086	925	1 303	1 661	1 847	785	1 112	1 438	Total tonnes-km
Qatar [3]									**Qatar** [3]
Kilometers flown	19	19	21	48	19	19	21	48	Kilomètres parcourus
Passengers carried	1 165	1 207	1 307	2 673	1 165	1 207	1 307	2 673	Passagers transportés
Passenger-km	2 501	2 653	2 836	6 042	2 501	2 653	2 836	6 042	Passagers-km
Total ton-km	333	357	387	823	333	357	387	823	Total tonnes-km
Saudi Arabia									**Arabie saoudite**
Kilometers flown	117	120	128	133	68	71	76	79	Kilomètres parcourus
Passengers carried	11 738	11 816	12 328	12 566	3 895	3 895	4 074	4 246	Passagers transportés
Passenger-km	18 949	18 820	19 618	20 229	13 061	12 875	13 357	13 807	Passagers-km
Total ton-km	2 650	2 645	2 783	2 836	2 038	2 030	2 138	2 173	Total tonnes-km
Singapore									**Singapour**
Kilometers flown	270	293	326	346	270	293	326	346	Kilomètres parcourus
Passengers carried	12 981	13 316	15 283	16 704	12 981	13 316	15 283	16 704	Passagers transportés
Passenger-km	55 459	58 174	65 471	71 786	55 459	58 174	65 471	71 786	Passagers-km
Total ton-km	10 128	10 381	11 824	12 986	10 128	10 381	11 824	12 986	Total tonnes-km
Sri Lanka									**Sri Lanka**
Kilometers flown	22	23	28	47	22	23	28	47	Kilomètres parcourus
Passengers carried	1 232	1 213	1 422	1 756	1 232	1 213	1 422	1 756	Passagers transportés
Passenger-km	4 249	4 136	5 156	6 840	4 249	4 136	5 156	6 840	Passagers-km
Total ton-km	569	553	669	1 125	569	553	669	1 125	Total tonnes-km
Syrian Arab Republic									**Rép. arabe syrienne**
Kilometers flown	12	13	12	15	11	13	12	14	Kilomètres parcourus
Passengers carried	694	665	668	750	615	643	581	640	Passagers transportés
Passenger-km	1 235	1 410	1 287	1 422	1 205	1 398	1 259	1 381	Passagers-km
Total ton-km	127	140	134	149	124	139	131	145	Total tonnes-km
Tajikistan									**Tadjikistan**
Kilometers flown	7	5	4	4	2	3	3	4	Kilomètres parcourus
Passengers carried	594	217	156	168	44	105	79	99	Passagers transportés
Passenger-km	1 825	322	229	286	222	275	197	257	Passagers-km
Total ton-km	166	32	23	29	19	28	20	26	Total tonnes-km
Thailand									**Thaïlande**
Kilometers flown	153	158	163	172	131	136	142	147	Kilomètres parcourus
Passengers carried	14 236	15 015	15 950	17 392	8 445	9 147	10 100	11 054	Passagers transportés
Passenger-km	30 827	34 340	38 345	42 236	27 633	31 049	35 057	38 676	Passagers-km
Total ton-km	4 460	4 682	5 184	5 571	4 139	4 355	4 854	5 215	Total tonnes-km
Turkey									**Turquie**
Kilometers flown	113	123	134	142	84	90	98	106	Kilomètres parcourus
Passengers carried	9 380	10 132	10 097	11 513	3 812	3 988	4 065	5 075	Passagers transportés
Passenger-km	12 379	13 037	13 350	16 492	9 372	9 792	10 002	12 938	Passagers-km
Total ton-km	1 363	1 371	1 514	1 865	1 107	1 092	1 223	1 555	Total tonnes-km
Turkmenistan									**Turkménistan**
Kilometers flown	15	11	9	20	...	6	9	10	Kilomètres parcourus
Passengers carried	523	890	220	1 284	...	250	220	315	Passagers transportés
Passenger-km	1 093	832	640	1 466	...	511	640	1 007	Passagers-km
Total ton-km	101	79	74	144	...	49	74	102	Total tonnes-km
United Arab Emirates [3]									**Emirats arabes unis** [3]
Kilometers flown	85	94	106	123	85	94	106	123	Kilomètres parcourus
Passengers carried	4 720	5 264	5 848	6 893	4 720	5 264	5 848	6 893	Passagers transportés
Passenger-km	13 519	15 633	18 154	22 691	13 519	15 633	18 154	22 691	Passagers-km
Total ton-km	2 107	2 403	2 950	3 649	2 107	2 403	2 950	3 649	Total tonnes-km

63

Civil Aviation

Passengers on scheduled services (thousands); Kilometers (millions)

Aviation civile

Passagers sur les services réguliers (milliers) ; Kilomètres (millions)

Country or area and traffic	Total Totale				International Internationaux				Région, pays ou zone et trafic
	1997	1998	1999	2000	1997	1998	1999	2000	
Uzbekistan									**Ouzbékistan**
Kilometers flown	23	33	37	39	2	23	27	30	Kilomètres parcourus
Passengers carried	1 566	1 401	1 658	1 745	36	673	878	950	Passagers transportés
Passenger-km	3 460	2 609	3 328	3 732	145	2 258	2 952	3 332	Passagers-km
Total ton-km	321	284	370	417	20	252	335	380	Total tonnes-km
Viet Nam									**Viet Nam**
Kilometers flown	35	33	31	34	22	20	18	21	Kilomètres parcourus
Passengers carried	2 527	2 373	2 600	2 878	925	899	994	1 165	Passagers transportés
Passenger-km	3 785	3 644	3 831	4 499	2 511	2 371	2 523	3 099	Passagers-km
Total ton-km	448	426	445	524	306	285	303	375	Total tonnes-km
Yemen									**Yémen**
Kilometers flown	13	12	15	16	12	11	13	15	Kilomètres parcourus
Passengers carried	707	765	731	842	408	462	480	585	Passagers transportés
Passenger-km	1 076	1 104	1 031	1 588	987	1 017	960	1 498	Passagers-km
Total ton-km	115	120	114	179	106	111	107	170	Total tonnes-km
Europe [1]									**Europe [1]**
Kilometers flown	**5 299**	**5 629**	**6 045**	**6 482**	**3 969**	**4 310**	**4 679**	**5 033**	**Kilomètres parcourus**
Passengers carried	**337 120**	**356 166**	**381 397**	**409 735**	**195 590**	**212 517**	**229 568**	**251 520**	**Passagers transportés**
Passenger-km	**627 072**	**669 007**	**720 219**	**777 230**	**518 162**	**560 344**	**603 478**	**656 321**	**Passagers-km**
Total ton-km	**90 617**	**94 522**	**99 950**	**109 339**	**79 625**	**83 633**	**88 458**	**97 401**	**Total tonnes-km**
Albania									**Albanie**
Kilometers flown	1	0	0	3	1	0	0	3	Kilomètres parcourus
Passengers carried	55	21	20	137	55	21	20	137	Passagers transportés
Passenger-km	35	7	7	101	35	7	7	101	Passagers-km
Total ton-km	3	1	1	9	3	1	1	9	Total tonnes-km
Austria									**Autriche**
Kilometers flown	118	126	131	139	113	121	127	135	Kilomètres parcourus
Passengers carried	5 154	5 880	6 057	6 642	4 829	5 510	5 694	6 261	Passagers transportés
Passenger-km	10 066	11 923	13 380	14 232	9 959	11 814	13 271	14 121	Passagers-km
Total ton-km	1 201	1 411	1 694	1 885	1 191	1 400	1 683	1 874	Total tonnes-km
Belarus									**Bélarus**
Kilometers flown	9	9	8	7	9	9	8	7	Kilomètres parcourus
Passengers carried	231	226	212	211	231	226	212	211	Passagers transportés
Passenger-km	399	397	338	317	399	397	338	317	Passagers-km
Total ton-km	39	40	33	31	39	40	33	31	Total tonnes-km
Belgium									**Belgique**
Kilometers flown	159	197	219	216	159	197	219	216	Kilomètres parcourus
Passengers carried	6 872	8 748	9 965	10 738	6 872	8 748	9 965	10 738	Passagers transportés
Passenger-km	11 277	15 338	17 692	19 379	11 277	15 338	17 692	19 379	Passagers-km
Total ton-km	1 706	1 853	2 128	2 921	1 706	1 853	2 128	2 921	Total tonnes-km
Bosnia and Herzegovina									**Bosnie-Herzégovine**
Kilometers flown	...	1	1	2	...	1	1	2	Kilomètres parcourus
Passengers carried	...	50	60	69	...	50	60	69	Passagers transportés
Passenger-km	...	40	42	48	...	40	42	48	Passagers-km
Total ton-km	...	5	5	6	...	5	5	6	Total tonnes-km
Bulgaria									**Bulgarie**
Kilometers flown	20	22	20	14	19	21	18	12	Kilomètres parcourus
Passengers carried	722	828	735	535	655	750	650	466	Passagers transportés
Passenger-km	1 796	2 026	1 512	834	1 766	1 992	1 478	804	Passagers-km
Total ton-km	194	214	149	70	192	211	146	68	Total tonnes-km
Croatia									**Croatie**
Kilometers flown	9	10	10	10	8	8	8	9	Kilomètres parcourus
Passengers carried	767	828	833	929	417	465	503	583	Passagers transportés
Passenger-km	469	544	560	644	367	436	460	538	Passagers-km
Total ton-km	45	52	53	61	35	42	44	51	Total tonnes-km
Czech Republic									**République tchèque**
Kilometers flown	30	32	36	39	29	32	36	39	Kilomètres parcourus
Passengers carried	1 448	1 606	1 853	2 229	1 437	1 606	1 853	2 204	Passagers transportés
Passenger-km	2 442	2 637	2 870	3 313	2 439	2 637	2 870	3 306	Passagers-km

63

Civil Aviation

Passengers on scheduled services (thousands); Kilometers (millions)

Aviation civile

Passagers sur les services réguliers (milliers) ; Kilomètres (millions)

Country or area and traffic	Total Totale				International Internationaux				Région, pays ou zone et trafic
	1997	1998	1999	2000	1997	1998	1999	2000	
Total ton-km	244	264	286	333	244	264	286	332	Total tonnes-km
Denmark [5]									**Danemark [5]**
Kilometers flown	80	81	82	85	66	69	72	76	Kilomètres parcourus
Passengers carried	6 236	5 947	5 971	5 923	3 832	3 976	4 249	4 305	Passagers transportés
Passenger-km	5 669	5 658	5 883	6 128	4 891	4 990	5 300	5 543	Passagers-km
Total ton-km	729	725	769	810	651	657	708	747	Total tonnes-km
Estonia									**Estonie**
Kilometers flown	5	6	7	6	5	6	7	6	Kilomètres parcourus
Passengers carried	231	297	302	278	231	294	300	275	Passagers transportés
Passenger-km	147	177	228	235	147	177	228	235	Passagers-km
Total ton-km	14	17	22	23	14	17	22	23	Total tonnes-km
Finland									**Finlande**
Kilometers flown	92	95	81	92	72	73	60	70	Kilomètres parcourus
Passengers carried	6 002	6 771	6 050	6 427	3 577	3 986	3 391	3 622	Passagers transportés
Passenger-km	9 575	10 714	7 802	7 556	8 475	9 467	6 592	6 270	Passagers-km
Total ton-km	1 170	1 250	967	984	1 073	1 140	861	871	Total tonnes-km
France [6]									**France [6]**
Kilometers flown	669	726	819	961	432	486	564	643	Kilomètres parcourus
Passengers carried	42 344	43 826	48 693	52 581	17 329	18 494	21 437	24 103	Passagers transportés
Passenger-km	84 037	90 225	101 449	113 438	54 823	59 584	67 462	75 250	Passagers-km
Total ton-km	13 750	14 033	14 279	15 639	10 622	10 784	10 909	11 871	Total tonnes-km
Germany									**Allemagne**
Kilometers flown	704	736	788	850	593	625	680	736	Kilomètres parcourus
Passengers carried	45 805	49 417	54 247	58 679	29 202	31 281	34 963	38 568	Passagers transportés
Passenger-km	86 189	90 393	104 602	114 124	79 338	82 922	96 402	105 552	Passagers-km
Total ton-km	14 822	15 301	16 950	18 495	14 093	14 522	16 108	17 619	Total tonnes-km
Greece									**Grèce**
Kilometers flown	68	68	75	90	52	53	54	70	Kilomètres parcourus
Passengers carried	7 061	6 403	6 267	7 937	2 872	2 621	2 630	3 384	Passagers transportés
Passenger-km	9 261	8 561	8 306	9 841	8 026	7 455	7 234	8 504	Passagers-km
Total ton-km	1 013	936	899	1 067	891	829	796	939	Total tonnes-km
Hungary									**Hongrie**
Kilometers flown	32	35	39	42	32	35	39	42	Kilomètres parcourus
Passengers carried	1 635	1 749	1 944	2 198	1 635	1 749	1 944	2 198	Passagers transportés
Passenger-km	2 346	2 510	2 861	3 573	2 346	2 510	2 861	3 573	Passagers-km
Total ton-km	249	267	301	377	249	267	301	377	Total tonnes-km
Iceland									**Islande**
Kilometers flown	28	33	35	34	25	31	35	34	Kilomètres parcourus
Passengers carried	1 334	1 593	1 350	1 432	1 056	1 298	1 350	1 432	Passagers transportés
Passenger-km	3 216	3 774	4 096	3 937	3 147	3 712	4 096	3 937	Passagers-km
Total ton-km	351	426	458	491	344	420	458	491	Total tonnes-km
Ireland									**Irlande**
Kilometers flown	70	78	90	106	68	77	88	104	Kilomètres parcourus
Passengers carried	8 964	10 401	11 949	13 983	8 522	9 917	11 398	13 431	Passagers transportés
Passenger-km	7 260	8 510	11 026	13 664	7 201	8 442	10 953	13 584	Passagers-km
Total ton-km	767	889	1 121	1 396	762	883	1 115	1 389	Total tonnes-km
Italy									**Italie**
Kilometers flown	338	344	368	392	242	239	254	274	Kilomètres parcourus
Passengers carried	28 184	28 037	28 049	30 418	11 507	11 113	11 092	12 246	Passagers transportés
Passenger-km	38 240	38 122	39 519	44 389	29 289	28 889	29 951	34 271	Passagers-km
Total ton-km	5 247	5 261	5 526	6 136	4 327	4 338	4 586	5 147	Total tonnes-km
Latvia									**Lettonie**
Kilometers flown	6	6	5	7	6	6	5	7	Kilomètres parcourus
Passengers carried	229	222	199	278	229	222	199	278	Passagers transportés
Passenger-km	217	174	132	236	217	174	132	236	Passagers-km
Total ton-km	20	16	12	22	20	16	12	22	Total tonnes-km
Lithuania									**Lituanie**
Kilometers flown	9	10	11	10	9	10	11	10	Kilomètres parcourus
Passengers carried	237	259	250	284	236	259	249	284	Passagers transportés
Passenger-km	301	307	272	322	301	307	272	322	Passagers-km

63

Civil Aviation

Passengers on scheduled services (thousands); Kilometers (millions)

Aviation civile

Passagers sur les services réguliers (milliers) ; Kilomètres (millions)

Country or area and traffic	Total Totale				International Internationaux				Région, pays ou zone et trafic
	1997	1998	1999	2000	1997	1998	1999	2000	
Total ton-km	30	31	27	31	30	31	27	31	Total tonnes-km
Luxembourg									**Luxembourg**
Kilometers flown	36	43	57	61	36	43	57	61	Kilomètres parcourus
Passengers carried	560	701	843	871	560	701	843	871	Passagers transportés
Passenger-km	281	454	738	557	281	454	738	557	Passagers-km
Total ton-km	2 286	2 287	2 573	3 573	2 286	2 287	2 573	3 573	Total tonnes-km
Malta									**Malte**
Kilometers flown	20	20	24	26	20	20	24	26	Kilomètres parcourus
Passengers carried	1 054	1 143	1 421	1 365	1 054	1 143	1 421	1 365	Passagers transportés
Passenger-km	1 681	1 888	2 320	2 384	1 681	1 888	2 320	2 384	Passagers-km
Total ton-km	157	177	214	229	157	177	214	229	Total tonnes-km
Monaco									**Monaco**
Kilometers flown	0	0	1	1	0	0	1	1	Kilomètres parcourus
Passengers carried	44	44	75	83	44	44	75	83	Passagers transportés
Passenger-km	1	1	2	2	1	1	2	2	Passagers-km
Total ton-km	0	0	0	0	0	0	0	0	Total tonnes-km
Netherlands [7]									**Pays-Bas** [7]
Kilometers flown	364	390	422	445	363	390	421	444	Kilomètres parcourus
Passengers carried	17 161	17 950	18 540	19 556	17 084	17 879	18 409	19 393	Passagers transportés
Passenger-km	66 132	68 597	70 117	73 030	66 124	68 590	70 099	73 008	Passagers-km
Total ton-km	10 590	10 864	11 204	11 811	10 589	10 864	11 202	11 809	Total tonnes-km
Norway [5]									**Norvège** [5]
Kilometers flown	130	134	151	149	60	62	70	71	Kilomètres parcourus
Passengers carried	13 759	14 279	15 020	15 182	3 871	4 068	4 367	4 646	Passagers transportés
Passenger-km	9 158	9 480	9 874	10 367	5 041	5 171	5 432	5 870	Passagers-km
Total ton-km	1 061	1 082	1 154	1 218	663	673	722	777	Total tonnes-km
Poland									**Pologne**
Kilometers flown	45	46	49	55	42	42	45	51	Kilomètres parcourus
Passengers carried	1 998	2 061	2 141	2 341	1 690	1 724	1 791	1 928	Passagers transportés
Passenger-km	4 204	4 255	4 632	4 757	4 111	4 155	4 528	4 635	Passagers-km
Total ton-km	478	483	498	547	470	475	489	537	Total tonnes-km
Portugal [8]									**Portugal** [8]
Kilometers flown	95	98	102	105	76	78	83	87	Kilomètres parcourus
Passengers carried	5 296	5 832	6 054	6 721	3 170	3 462	3 604	4 019	Passagers transportés
Passenger-km	9 342	10 107	10 070	11 217	7 889	8 475	8 595	9 594	Passagers-km
Total ton-km	1 094	1 157	1 128	1 252	936	981	976	1 088	Total tonnes-km
Republic of Moldova									**République de Moldova**
Kilometers flown	2	4	2	4	2	4	2	4	Kilomètres parcourus
Passengers carried	46	118	43	118	46	118	43	118	Passagers transportés
Passenger-km	61	146	97	125	61	146	97	125	Passagers-km
Total ton-km	6	14	9	13	6	14	9	13	Total tonnes-km
Romania									**Roumanie**
Kilometers flown	26	22	24	30	23	20	22	29	Kilomètres parcourus
Passengers carried	995	921	980	1 218	775	758	844	1 105	Passagers transportés
Passenger-km	1 702	1 712	1 757	2 098	1 617	1 647	1 704	2 053	Passagers-km
Total ton-km	167	167	171	202	159	161	166	198	Total tonnes-km
Russian Federation									**Fédération de Russie**
Kilometers flown	609	581	550	534	198	212	196	189	Kilomètres parcourus
Passengers carried	20 419	18 685	18 600	17 688	5 915	5 960	5 190	5 480	Passagers transportés
Passenger-km	49 278	46 158	45 863	42 950	18 135	18 811	16 862	17 584	Passagers-km
Total ton-km	5 269	4 931	5 036	4 948	2 145	2 179	2 088	2 285	Total tonnes-km
Slovakia									**Slovaquie**
Kilometers flown	2	3	3	2	2	3	2	2	Kilomètres parcourus
Passengers carried	81	107	111	57	59	82	75	44	Passagers transportés
Passenger-km	103	128	117	108	95	119	105	103	Passagers-km
Total ton-km	10	11	10	10	9	10	9	10	Total tonnes-km
Slovenia									**Slovénie**
Kilometers flown	7	8	9	10	7	8	9	10	Kilomètres parcourus
Passengers carried	404	460	555	628	404	460	555	628	Passagers transportés
Passenger-km	375	411	515	563	375	411	515	563	Passagers-km

63

Civil Aviation

Passengers on scheduled services (thousands); Kilometers (millions)

Aviation civile

Passagers sur les services réguliers (milliers) ; Kilomètres (millions)

Country or area and traffic	Total Totale				International Internationaux				Région, pays ou zone et trafic
	1997	1998	1999	2000	1997	1998	1999	2000	
Total ton-km	37	41	50	55	37	41	50	55	Total tonnes-km
Spain									**Espagne**
Kilometers flown	305	331	365	418	159	179	200	235	Kilomètres parcourus
Passengers carried	30 316	31 594	33 559	39 712	8 227	8 971	9 581	11 911	Passagers transportés
Passenger-km	37 240	40 042	44 172	52 427	23 595	26 027	29 035	35 003	Passagers-km
Total ton-km	4 093	4 378	4 828	5 635	2 780	3 038	3 360	3 966	Total tonnes-km
Sweden[5]									**Suède**[5]
Kilometers flown	132	143	150	167	83	89	94	92	Kilomètres parcourus
Passengers carried	11 327	11 878	12 933	13 354	5 264	5 571	5 785	5 901	Passagers transportés
Passenger-km	9 749	10 249	10 607	11 192	6 972	7 198	7 312	7 765	Passagers-km
Total ton-km	1 191	1 234	1 309	1 387	939	959	1 001	1 064	Total tonnes-km
Switzerland									**Suisse**
Kilometers flown	230	263	295	317	225	258	289	311	Kilomètres parcourus
Passengers carried	12 482	14 299	16 209	17 268	11 204	12 868	14 735	15 800	Passagers transportés
Passenger-km	26 314	29 415	33 309	36 625	26 072	29 147	33 030	36 339	Passagers-km
Total ton-km	4 462	4 897	5 195	5 616	4 438	4 870	5 167	5 588	Total tonnes-km
TFYR of Macedonia									**L'ex-R.y. Macédoine**
Kilometers flown	5	5	7	10	5	5	7	10	Kilomètres parcourus
Passengers carried	250	295	488	599	250	295	488	599	Passagers transportés
Passenger-km	285	328	599	740	285	328	599	740	Passagers-km
Total ton-km	27	31	57	70	27	31	57	70	Total tonnes-km
Ukraine									**Ukraine**
Kilometers flown	36	37	31	32	29	30	24	25	Kilomètres parcourus
Passengers carried	1 190	1 064	891	951	887	807	661	704	Passagers transportés
Passenger-km	1 853	1 720	1 312	1 387	1 658	1 556	1 165	1 240	Passagers-km
Total ton-km	186	188	138	145	168	173	125	132	Total tonnes-km
United Kingdom[9,10]									**Royaume-Uni**[9,10]
Kilometers flown	809	885	977	1 013	698	768	845	893	Kilomètres parcourus
Passengers carried	56 227	61 625	67 928	70 115	40 360	45 017	48 941	52 131	Passagers transportés
Passenger-km	136 371	151 880	161 541	170 388	129 725	144 933	153 697	162 865	Passagers-km
Total ton-km	17 912	19 589	20 692	21 839	17 331	18 984	20 021	21 191	Total tonnes-km
Oceania[1]									**Océanie**[1]
Kilometers flown	777	757	735	850	360	360	351	429	Kilomètres parcourus
Passengers carried	45 714	43 990	43 622	48 303	13 048	12 343	11 643	13 776	Passagers transportés
Passenger-km	107 911	103 104	103 991	114 876	75 345	71 392	71 257	81 288	Passagers-km
Total ton-km	13 205	12 813	12 883	13 921	9 783	9 558	9 568	10 590	Total tonnes-km
Australia									**Australie**
Kilometers flown	500	479	474	558	196	193	194	248	Kilomètres parcourus
Passengers carried	30 954	30 180	30 007	32 578	6 783	6 894	6 579	7 508	Passagers transportés
Passenger-km	75 873	73 647	75 575	81 689	47 771	46 525	47 436	53 007	Passagers-km
Total ton-km	9 137	8 929	9 107	9 806	6 243	6 116	6 236	6 936	Total tonnes-km
Fiji									**Fidji**
Kilometers flown	20	20	20	23	13	13	13	16	Kilomètres parcourus
Passengers carried	517	516	525	586	334	334	361	399	Passagers transportés
Passenger-km	2 000	2 000	2 159	2 385	1 956	1 956	2 120	2 355	Passagers-km
Total ton-km	200	200	218	309	196	196	214	307	Total tonnes-km
Kiribati									**Kiribati**
Kilometers flown	1	1	...	...	0	0	...	...	Kilomètres parcourus
Passengers carried	28	28	...	...	3	3	...	...	Passagers transportés
Passenger-km	11	11	...	...	7	7	...	...	Passagers-km
Total ton-km	2	2	...	...	1	1	...	...	Total tonnes-km
Marshall Islands									**Iles Marshall**
Kilometers flown	2	1	1	1	1	1	0	0	Kilomètres parcourus
Passengers carried	33	32	19	16	11	9	5	1	Passagers transportés
Passenger-km	26	20	12	22	17	12	7	2	Passagers-km
Total ton-km	2	2	1	2	2	1	1	0	Total tonnes-km
Nauru									**Nauru**
Kilometers flown	2	2	3	3	2	2	3	3	Kilomètres parcourus
Passengers carried	137	137	143	161	137	137	143	161	Passagers transportés

63

Civil Aviation

Passengers on scheduled services (thousands); Kilometers (millions)

Aviation civile

Passagers sur les services réguliers (milliers) ; Kilomètres (millions)

Country or area and traffic	Total Totale 1997	1998	1999	2000	International Internationaux 1997	1998	1999	2000	Région, pays ou zone et trafic
Passenger-km	243	243	254	287	243	243	254	287	Passagers-km
Total ton-km	24	24	25	28	24	24	25	28	Total tonnes-km
New Zealand									**Nouvelle-Zélande**
Kilometers flown	173	174	172	198	93	98	100	121	Kilomètres parcourus
Passengers carried	9 435	8 655	8 892	10 781	3 324	2 773	2 829	3 673	Passagers transportés
Passenger-km	20 983	19 014	19 322	23 374	18 273	16 352	16 679	20 338	Passagers-km
Total ton-km	2 816	2 700	2 746	3 006	2 492	2 479	2 529	2 762	Total tonnes-km
Papua New Guinea									**Papouasie-Nvl-Guinée**
Kilometers flown	15	15	12	17	5	5	3	7	Kilomètres parcourus
Passengers carried	1 114	1 110	1 102	1 100	159	159	110	271	Passagers transportés
Passenger-km	735	736	641	1 036	361	361	250	628	Passagers-km
Total ton-km	86	87	80	118	49	49	39	77	Total tonnes-km
Samoa									**Samoa**
Kilometers flown	3	4	3	2	3	3	3	1	Kilomètres parcourus
Passengers carried	75	149	92	164	75	77	77	88	Passagers transportés
Passenger-km	247	250	244	290	247	242	242	281	Passagers-km
Total ton-km	30	24	23	28	30	23	23	28	Total tonnes-km
Solomon Islands									**Iles Salomon**
Kilometers flown	3	3	4	3	1	1	1	1	Kilomètres parcourus
Passengers carried	94	94	98	75	28	28	23	18	Passagers transportés
Passenger-km	74	74	80	50	58	58	47	37	Passagers-km
Total ton-km	9	9	9	6	7	7	6	4	Total tonnes-km
Tonga									**Tonga**
Kilometers flown	1	1	1	1	...	...	...	...	Kilomètres parcourus
Passengers carried	49	49	91	52	...	...	...	...	Passagers transportés
Passenger-km	10	10	19	11	...	...	...	...	Passagers-km
Total ton-km	1	1	2	1	...	...	...	...	Total tonnes-km
Vanuatu									**Vanuatu**
Kilometers flown	2	3	3	3	2	3	3	3	Kilomètres parcourus
Passengers carried	75	89	86	102	75	89	86	102	Passagers transportés
Passenger-km	156	179	178	221	156	179	178	221	Passagers-km
Total ton-km	15	19	18	22	15	19	18	22	Total tonnes-km

Source:
International Civil Aviation Organization (ICAO), Montreal, "Digest of Statistics – Traffic 1996 – 2000" and the ICAO database.

Source:
Organisation de l'aviation civile international (OACI), Montréal, " Recueil de statistiques – trafic, 1996 – 2000" et la base de données de l'OCAI.

1   The statistics of France, the Netherlands, Portugal, United Kingdom and United States have been distributed between two or more regions - France (Europe, Africa, North America and Oceania), Netherlands (Europe and North America), Portugal (1997 only; Europe and Asia), United Kingdom (Europe, Asia and North America) and United States (North America and Oceania).
2   Includes apportionment (1/10) of the traffic of Air Afrique, a multinational airline with headquarters in Cote d'Ivoire and operated by 10 African states unitl 1991. From 1992 includes apportionment (1/11) of the traffic of Air Afrique and operated by 11 African states.

3   Includes apportionment (1/4) of the traffic of Gulf Air, a multinational airline with headquarters in Bahrain and operated by four Gulf States.
4   Data refer to the last six months of 1997.
5   Includes the apportionment of international operations performed by Scandinavian Airlines System (SAS) Denmark (2/7), Norway (2/7), Sweden (3/7).
6   Includes data for airlines based in the territories and dependancies of France.

1   Les statistiques de la France, des Pays-Bas, du Portugal, du Royaume-Uni et des Etats-Unis concernent deux régions ou plus; France (Europe, Afrique, Amérique du Nord et Océanie), Pays-Bas (Europe et Amérique du Nord), Portugal (1997 seulement; Europe et Asie), Royaume-Uni (Europe, Asie et Amérqiue du Nord) et Etats-Unis (Amérique du Nord et Océanie).
2   Ces chiffres comprennent une partie du trafic (1/10) assurée par Air Afrique, compagnie aérienne multinationale dont le siège est situé en Côte d'Ivoire et est exploitée conjointement par 10 Etats Africains jusqu'à 1991. A partir de 1992 ces chiffres comprennent une partie du trafic (1/11) assurée par Air Afrique et exploitée conjointement par11 Etats Africains.
3   Ces chiffres comprennent une partie du trafic (1/4) assurée par Gulf Air, compagnie aérienne multinationale dont le siège est situé en Bahreïn et est exploitée conjointement par 4 Etats Gulf.
4   Pour 1997, les données se rapportent au second semestre de 1997.
5   Y compris une partie des vols internationaux effectués parle SAS; Danemark (2/7), Norvège (2/7) et Suède (3/7).
6   Y compris les données relatives aux compagnies aériennes ayant des bases d'opérations dans les territoires et dépendances de France.

63

Civil Aviation

Passengers on scheduled services (thousands); Kilometers (millions)

Aviation civile

Passagers sur les services réguliers (milliers) ; Kilomètres (millions)

7 Includes data for airlines based in the territories and dependancies of Netherlands.	7 Y compris les données relatives aux compagnies aériennes ayant des bases d'opérations dans les territoires et dépendances des Pays-Bas.
8 Prior to 2000, data include those for Macao (SAR) of China.	8 Avant 2000, y compris Macao.
9 Beginning the second half of 1997, data exclude those for Hong Kong Special Administrative Region (SAR) of China.	9 A partir du second semestre de 1997, les données ne comprennent pas celles relatives à la RAS de Hong Kong de la Chine.
10 Includes data for airlines based in the territories and dependancies of United Kingdom.	10 Y compris les données relatives aux compagnies aériennes ayant des bases d'opération dans les territoires et dépendances du Royaume-Uni.

Technical notes, tables 59-63

Table 59: Data refer to domestic and international traffic on all railway lines within each country shown, except railways entirely within an urban unit, and plantation, industrial mining, funicular and cable railways. The figures relating to passenger-kilometres include all passengers except military, government and railway personnel when carried without revenue. Those relating to ton-kilometres are freight net ton-kilometres and include both fast and ordinary goods services but exclude service traffic, mail, baggage and non-revenue governmental stores.

Table 60: For years in which a census or registration took place, the census or registration figure is shown; for other years, unless otherwise indicated, the officially estimated number of vehicles in use is shown. The time of year to which the figures refer is variable. Special purpose vehicles such as two- or three-wheeled cycles and motorcycles, trams, trolley-buses, ambulances, hearses, military vehicles operated by police or other governmental security organizations are excluded. Passenger cars includes vehicles seating not more than nine persons (including the driver), such as taxis, jeeps and station wagons. Commercial vehicles include: vans, lorries (trucks), buses, tractor and semi-trailer combinations but excludes trailers and farm tractors.

Table 61: Data refer to merchant fleets registered in each country as at 31 December, except for data prior to 1992 which refer to 30 June of the year stated. They are given in gross registered tons (100 cubic feet or 2.83 cubic metres) and represent the total volume of all the permanently enclosed spaces of the vessels to which the figures refer. Vessels without mechanical means of propulsion are excluded, but sailing vessels with auxiliary power are included.

Part A of the table refers to the total of merchant fleets registered. Part B shows data for oil tanker fleets and part C data for ore/oil and bulk carrier fleets. The data are published by Lloyd's Register of Shipping in *World Fleet Statistics* [19]. (See also <www.lrfairplay.com>).

Table 62: The figures for vessels entered and cleared, unless otherwise stated, represent the sum of the net registered tonnage of sea-going foreign and domestic merchant vessels (power and sailing) entered with cargo from or cleared with cargo to a foreign port and refer to only one entrance or clearance for each foreign voyage. Where possible, the data exclude vessels "in ballast", i.e. entering without unloading or clearing without loading goods.

Table 63: Data for total services cover both domestic and international scheduled services operated

Notes techniques, tableaux 59 à 63

Tableau 59: Les données se rapportent au trafic intérieur et international de toutes les lignes de chemins de fer du pays indiqué, à l'exception des lignes situées entièrement à l'intérieur d'une agglomération urbaine ou desservant une plantation ou un complexe industriel minier, des funiculaires et des téléfériques. Les chiffres relatifs aux voyageurs-kilomètres se rapportent à tous les voyageurs sauf les militaires, les fonctionnaires et le personnel des chemins de fer, qui sont transportés gratuitement. Les chiffres relatifs aux tonnes-kilomètres se rapportent aux tonnes-kilomètres nettes de fret et comprennent les services rapides et ordinaires de transport de marchandises, à l'exception des transports pour les besoins du service, du courrier, des bagages et des marchandises transportées gratuitement pour les besoins de l'Etat.

Tableau 60: Pour les années où a eu lieu un recensement ou un enregistrement des véhicules, le chiffre indiqué est le résultat de cette opération; pour les autres années, sauf indication contraire, le chiffre indiqué correspond à l'estimation officielle du nombre de véhicules en circulation. L'époque de l'année à laquelle se rapportent les chiffres varie. Les véhicules à usage spécial, tels que les cycles à deux ou trois roues et motocyclettes, les tramways, les trolley-bus, les ambulances, les corbillards, les véhicules militaires utilisés par la police ou par d'autres services publics de sécurité ne sont pas compris dans ces chiffres. Les voitures de tourisme comprennent les véhicules automobiles dont le nombre de places assises (y compris celle du conducteur) n'est pas supérieur à neuf, tels que les taxis, jeeps et breaks. Les véhicules utilitaires comprennent les fourgons, camions, autobus et autocars, les ensembles tracteurs-remorques et semi-remorques, mais ne comprennent pas les remorques et les tracteurs agricoles.

Tableau 61: Les données se rapportent à la flotte marchande enregistrée dans chaque pays au 31 décembre de l'année indiquée à l'exception des données qui se rapportent aux années avant 1992, qui se réfèrent à la flotte marchande au 30 juin. Elles sont exprimées en tonneaux de jauge brute (100 pieds cubes ou 2,83 mètres cubes) et représentent le volume total de tous les espaces clos en permanence dans les navires auxquels elle s'appliquent. Elles excluent les navires sans moteur, mais pas les voiliers avec moteurs auxiliaires.

Les données de la Partie A du tableau se rapportent au total de la flotte marchande enregistrée. Celles de la Partie B se rapportent à la flotte des pétroliers, et celles de la Partie C à la flotte des minéraliers et des transporteurs de vrac et d'huile. Les données sont publiées par Lloyd's Register of Shipping dans *World Fleet*

airlines registered in each country. Scheduled services include supplementary services occasioned by overflow traffic on regularly scheduled trips and preparatory flights for newly scheduled services. Freight means all goods, except mail and excess baggage, carried for remuneration. The data are published by the International Civil Aviation Organization in *Civil Aviation Statistics of the World* [11] and in the *Digest of Statistics—Traffic* [12]. (See also <www.icao.org>).

Statistics [19]. (Voir aussi <www.lrfairplay.com>).

Tableau 62: Sauf indication contraire, les données relatives aux navires entrés et sortis représentent la jauge nette totale des navires marchands de haute mer (à moteur ou à voile) nationaux ou étrangers, qui entrent ou sortent chargés, en provenance ou à destination d'un port étranger. On ne compte qu'une seule entrée et une seule sortie pour chaque voyage international. Dans la mesure du possible, le tableau exclut les navires sur lest (c'est-à-dire les navires entrant sans décharger ou sortant sans avoir chargé).

Tableau 63: Les données relatives au total des services se rapportent aux services réguliers, intérieurs ou internationaux des compagnies de transport aérien enregistrées dans chaque pays. Les services réguliers comprennent aussi les vols supplémentaires nécessités par un surcroît d'activité des services réguliers et les vols préparatoires en vue de nouveaux services réguliers. Par fret, on entend toutes les marchandises transportées contre paiement, mais non le courrier et les excédents de bagage. Les données sont publiées par l'Organisation de l'aviation civile internationale dans les *Statistiques de l'Aviation civile dans le monde* [11] et dans le *Recueil de statistiques—trafic* [12]. (Voir aussi <www.icao.org>).

64
Production, trade and consumption of commercial energy
Thousand metric tons of oil equivalent and kilograms per capita
Production, commerce et consommation d'énergie commerciale
Milliers de tonnes d'équivalent pétrole et kilogrammes par habitant

Region, country or area	Year	Primary energy production – Production d'énergie primaire					Changes in stocks	Imports	Exports
		Total Totale	Solids Solides	Liquids Liquides	Gas Gaz	Electricity Electricité	Variations des stocks	Imports Importations	Exports Exportations
World	**1996**	**8 850 528**	**2 361 410**	**3 442 999**	**2 152 096**	**894 023**	**1 803**	**3 210 555**	**3 149 577**
	1997	**8 966 415**	**2 379 338**	**3 542 876**	**2 152 762**	**891 439**	**25 326**	**3 340 746**	**3 298 078**
	1998	**9 001 683**	**2 307 393**	**3 593 221**	**2 192 847**	**908 221**	**53 041**	**3 381 342**	**3 393 649**
	1999	**8 861 452**	**2 183 749**	**3 516 092**	**2 227 619**	**933 992**	**- 83 437**	**3 412 729**	**3 387 099**
Africa	**1996**	**617 031**	**149 546**	**367 270**	**91 367**	**8 849**	**6 153**	**60 526**	**374 700**
	1997	**651 345**	**159 164**	**381 696**	**101 125**	**9 360**	**8 541**	**67 107**	**403 764**
	1998	**651 160**	**160 945**	**376 437**	**103 778**	**9 999**	**16 623**	**69 293**	**396 969**
	1999	**650 538**	**161 018**	**366 177**	**113 352**	**9 992**	**4 661**	**74 007**	**407 605**
Algeria	1996	126 709	*15	64 093	62 589	*11	195	689	88 658
	1997	137 134	*16	66 487	70 624	6	*-327	733	97 728
	1998	144 359	*16	68 911	75 423	*9	- 28	772	102 142
	1999	146 632	*17	66 544	80 062	*9	343	*709	109 679
Angola	1996	35 400	...	34 812	*509	80	831	225	31 428
	1997	35 777	...	35 184	*518	75	448	237	33 382
	1998	37 036	...	36 418	*527	91	153	91	34 997
	1999	38 652	...	38 066	*509	*77	184	105	35 124
Benin	1996	112	...	112	...	...	...	*333	119
	1997	90	...	90	...	...	...	*332	97
	1998	62	...	62	...	...	...	*348	69
	1999	44	...	44	...	...	...	368	53
Burkina Faso	1996	10	...	...	...	10	...	*326	...
	1997	*10	...	...	...	*10	...	*328	...
	1998	*10	...	...	...	*10	...	*334	...
	1999	*10	...	...	...	*10	...	*334	...
Burundi	1996	*14	*4	...	...	*10	1	*76	...
	1997	*15	*4	...	...	*10	...	*77	...
	1998	*15	*4	...	...	*10	...	*78	...
	1999	*15	*4	...	...	*11	...	*82	...
Cameroon	1996	5 468	*1	5 220	...	247	- 325	*978	5 037
	1997	5 782	*1	5 516	...	266	- 95	*1274	5 381
	1998	6 180	*1	5 911	...	268	...	*1176	5 508
	1999	7 144	*1	6 857	...	287	*-12	*206	5 539
Cape Verde	1996	...	...	...	...	...	...	*41	...
	1997	...	...	...	...	...	...	*41	...
	1998	...	...	...	...	...	...	*41	...
	1999	...	...	...	...	...	...	*46	...
Central African Rep.	1996	*7	...	...	...	*7	*1	*95	...
	1997	*7	...	...	...	*7	*1	*98	...
	1998	*7	...	...	...	*7	*1	*99	...
	1999	*7	...	...	...	*7	*1	*105	...
Chad	1996	...	...	...	...	...	3	*57	...
	1997	...	...	...	...	...	...	*58	...
	1998	...	...	...	...	...	...	*58	...
	1999	...	...	...	...	...	...	*62	...
Comoros	1996	*0	...	...	...	*0	...	*23	...
	1997	*0	...	...	...	*0	...	*23	...
	1998	*0	...	...	...	*0	...	*24	...
	1999	*0	...	...	...	*0	...	*27	...
Congo	1996	10 509	...	10 380	*99	30	*9	*58	9 823
	1997	11 771	...	11 610	*123	39	*5	*60	11 055
	1998	12 884	...	12 723	*123	39	*5	62	12 163
	1999	13 421	...	13 258	133	30	150	67	12 517
Côte d'Ivoire	1996	1 802	...	1 264	416	122	...	3 954	1 349
	1997	2 116	...	1 273	682	161	...	*3537	1 419
	1998	2 858	...	1 900	841	117	...	*3798	2 344
	1999	3 038	...	1 485	1 409	144	...	4 214	2 503
Dem. Rep. of the Congo	1996	*1680	*66	*1149	...	*464	...	*699	*1029
	1997	*1683	*66	*1152	...	*465	...	*699	*1034
	1998	*1689	*67	*1156	...	*465	...	*709	*1036
	1999	1 625	*67	1 069	...	489	...	*726	1 102
Djibouti	1996	...	...	...	...	...	...	*545	...
	1997	...	...	...	...	...	...	*550	...
	1998	...	...	...	...	...	...	*550	...
	1999	...	...	...	...	...	...	*560	...

Bunkers – Soutes			Consumption – Consommation							
Air Avion	Sea Maritime	Unallocated Nondistribué	Per capita Par habitant	Total Totale	Solids Solides	Liquids Liquides	Gas Gaz	Electricity Electricité	Année	Région, pays ou zone
73 488	125 577	366 340	1 405	8 344 298	2 407 786	2 894 092	2 148 397	894 023	1996	**Monde**
77 569	128 318	405 499	1 393	8 372 371	2 394 305	2 923 989	2 162 637	891 439	1997	
79 580	133 250	377 855	1 370	8 345 651	2 329 935	2 942 904	2 164 591	908 221	1998	
83 457	137 864	367 733	1 358	8 381 464	2 237 332	2 972 947	2 237 193	933 992	1999	
2 333	8 318	17 968	349	268 085	113 189	92 433	53 614	8 849	1996	**Afrique**
2 236	7 525	25 354	343	271 032	116 072	90 415	55 185	9 360	1997	
1 962	7 249	20 211	344	277 439	114 288	98 363	54 790	9 999	1998	
2 282	8 038	14 561	347	287 399	117 871	102 834	56 703	9 992	1999	
*268	334	*4946	1 155	32 997	238	8 180	24 568	*11	1996	Algérie
*279	266	*5269	1 193	34 652	402	9 250	24 993	6	1997	
*279	239	*5127	1 267	37 372	456	10 361	26 547	*9	1998	
*279	238	– 170	1 234	36 973	*459	11 765	24 740	*9	1999	
334	7	1 514	129	1 510	...	921	*509	80	1996	Angola
341	2	313	127	1 527	...	934	*518	75	1997	
220	...	264	120	1 493	...	875	*527	91	1998	
301	...	1 618	120	1 529	...	944	*509	*77	1999	
*22	...	...	*54	*304	...	*304		...	1996	Bénin
*22	...	0	*54	*303	...	*303	...	...	1997	
*23	...	...	*55	*318	...	*318	...	...	1998	
*23	...	...	56	336	...	336	...	...	1999	
...	...	...	*32	*336	...	*326	...	10	1996	Burkina Faso
...	...	...	*31	*338	...	*328	...	*10	1997	
...	...	...	*32	*344	...	*334	...	*10	1998	
...	...	...	*31	*344	...	*334	...	*10	1999	
*6	...	...	*14	*83	*4	*69	...	*10	1996	Burundi
*6	...	...	*14	*85	*4	*71	...	*10	1997	
*6	...	...	*14	*87	*4	*72	...	*10	1998	
*6	...	...	*14	*91	*4	*76	...	*11	1999	
*21	...	105	*118	*1608	*1	*1361	...	247	1996	Cameroun
*21	3	66	*118	*1681	*1	*1414	...	266	1997	
*21	5	132	*117	*1690	*1	*1421	...	268	1998	
*22	8	129	*114	*1664	*1	*1377	...	287	1999	
...	...	...	*104	*41	...	*41	...	...	1996	Cap–Vert
...	...	...	*101	*41	...	*41	...	...	1997	
...	...	...	*99	*41	...	*41	...	...	1998	
...	...	...	*108	*46	...	*46	...	...	1999	
*14	...	...	*25	*86	...	*79	...	*7	1996	Rép. centrafricaine
*14	...	...	*28	*89	...	*82	...	*7	1997	
*14	...	...	*25	*90	...	*83	...	*7	1998	
*14	...	...	*27	*97	...	*89	...	*7	1999	
*20	...	...	*5	*34	...	*34	...	...	1996	Tchad
*20	...	...	*5	*38	...	*38	...	...	1997	
*20	...	...	*5	*38	...	*38	...	...	1998	
*21	...	...	*5	*41	...	*41	...	...	1999	
...	...	...	*36	*23	...	*23	...	*0	1996	Comores
...	...	...	*35	*23	...	*23	...	*0	1997	
...	...	...	*36	*24	...	*24	...	*0	1998	
...	...	...	*39	*27	...	*27	...	*0	1999	
...	*10	30	*259	*695	...	*566	*99	30	1996	Congo
...	*10	26	*266	*735	...	*573	*123	39	1997	
...	*10	20	*263	*748	...	*587	*123	39	1998	
...	*10	62	*256	*749	...	*586	133	30	1999	
*131	79	1 261	199	2 936	...	2 398	416	122	1996	Côte d'Ivoire
*132	82	*797	214	3 222	...	2 379	682	161	1997	
*139	82	*641	224	3 449	...	2 491	841	117	1998	
*145	83	504	256	4 015	...	2 463	1 409	144	1999	
*114	*2	*66	*25	*1168	*226	*478	...	*464	1996	Rép. Dém. du Congo
*116	*2	*64	*25	*1166	*228	*474	...	*465	1997	
*117	*2	*22	*25	*1221	*228	*528	...	*465	1998	
*117	*2	*–110	*25	*1241	*233	*519	...	489	1999	
*68	*356	...	*217	*121	...	*121	...	...	1996	Djibouti
*69	*360	...	*210	*121	...	*121	...	...	1997	
*69	*360	...	*203	*121	...	*121	...	...	1998	
*70	*363	...	*206	*127	...	*127	...	...	1999	

64
Production, trade and consumption of commercial energy
Thousand metric tons of oil equivalent and kilograms per capita [*cont.*]
Production, commerce et consommation d'énergie commerciale
Milliers de tonnes d'équivalent pétrole et kilogrammes par habitant [*suite*]

Region, country or area	Year	Primary energy production – Production d'énergie primaire					Changes in stocks	Imports	Exports
		Total Totale	Solids Solides	Liquids Liquides	Gas Gaz	Electricity Electricité	Variations des stocks	Imports Importations	Exports Exportations
Egypt	1996	59 917	...	45 461	13 462	994	7 661	2 202	13 834
	1997	59 439	...	44 515	13 893	1 031	6 381	2 343	13 440
	1998	55 774	...	43 200	11 523	1 051	8 203	2 932	9 602
	1999	59 094	...	42 179	15 601	1 315	6 956	9 668	14 074
Equatorial Guinea	1996	858	...	858	...	*0	*2	*44	853
	1997	3 256	...	3 256	...	*0	*3	*48	3 041
	1998	4 172	...	4 172	...	*0	*2	*49	4 134
	1999	4 826	...	4 826	...	*0	*2	*53	4 665
Eritrea	1996	...	...	...	...	...	...	95	...
	1997							141	
	1998	...		...		...	...	*171	...
	1999	...		...				184	...
Ethiopia	1996	135	...	...	...	135	*11	*1363	*79
	1997	140		...		140	*12	*1579	*127
	1998	142		...		142	*20	*1660	*119
	1999	144		...		144	*−23	*1804	*40
Gabon	1996	19 179	...	18 295	821	63	*−88	193	17 675
	1997	19 462	...	18 616	782	64	− 113	269	18 057
	1998	18 974	...	18 213	698	63	− 117	*261	17 649
	1999	17 357	...	16 537	761	60	*11	*262	15 796
Gambia	1996	...	...	...	...	...	...	*74	*2
	1997							*74	*2
	1998	...		...		...		*80	*2
	1999	...		...		...	...	*88	*2
Ghana	1996	570	...	...	...	570	...	*1859	*122
	1997	590	...	...	...	590	...	*1941	*138
	1998	520	...	...	...	520	...	*2140	*155
	1999	468	...	9	...	459	...	1 821	174
Guinea	1996	*16	...	...	...	*16	...	*376	...
	1997	*16	...	...	...	*16	...	*378	...
	1998	*17	...	...	...	*17	...	*383	...
	1999	*17	...	...	...	*17	...	*392	...
Guinea−Bissau	1996	...	...	...	...	...	...	*82	...
	1997							*83	...
	1998	...		...		...		*85	...
	1999	...		...		...	...	*93	...
Kenya	1996	629	...	...	...	629	...	*3119	429
	1997	596	...	...	...	596	...	2 850	669
	1998	623	...	...	...	623	...	3 648	651
	1999	580	...	...	...	580	...	3 550	635
Liberia	1996	*15	...	...	...	*15	...	*126	*1
	1997	*16	...	...	...	*16	...	*132	*1
	1998	*16	...	...	...	*16	...	*142	*1
	1999	*17	...	...	...	*17	...	*147	*1
Libyan Arab Jamah.	1996	75 102	...	69 115	5 987	...	...	*7	59 555
	1997	77 202	...	71 075	6 127	...	...	*7	58 931
	1998	75 121	...	69 190	5 931	...	...	*7	60 924
	1999	70 283	...	65 433	4 850	...	− 4 058	*7	58 123
Madagascar	1996	38	...	...	...	38	*1	*488	*20
	1997	42	...	...	...	42	...	*579	*21
	1998	44	...	...	...	44	...	*597	*21
	1999	44	...	...	...	44	...	673	*31
Malawi	1996	*74	...	...	...	*74	...	*233	...
	1997	*74	...	...	...	*74	...	*234	...
	1998	*74	...	...	...	*74	...	*238	...
	1999	*74	...	...	...	*74	...	*243	...
Mali	1996	18	...	...	...	18	...	*176	...
	1997	20	...	...	...	20	...	*176	...
	1998	*20	...	...	...	*20	...	*179	...
	1999	*20	...	...	...	*20	...	*183	...
Mauritania	1996	*2	...	...	...	*2	...	*1063	...
	1997	*2	...	...	...	*2	...	*1064	...
	1998	*2	...	...	...	*2	...	*1068	...
	1999	*3	...	...	...	*3	...	*1106	...

Bunkers – Soutes			Consumption – Consommation							
Air Avion	Sea Maritime	Unallocated Nondistribué	Per capita Par habitant	Total Totale	Solids Solides	Liquids Liquides	Gas Gaz	Electricity Electricité	Année	Région, pays ou zone
*361	3 055	2 422	592	34 785	903	19 426	13 462	994	1996	Egypte
*310	3 011	2 425	603	36 215	756	20 535	13 893	1 031	1997	
*337	2 228	2 155	590	36 181	743	22 864	11 523	1 051	1998	
516	2 708	4 840	633	39 669	609	22 144	15 601	1 315	1999	
...	...	3	*108	*44	...	*44	...	*0	1996	Guinée équatoriale
...	...	212	*115	*48	...	*48	...	*0	1997	
...	...	36	*114	*49	...	*49	...	*0	1998	
...	...	159	*120	*53	...	*53	...	*0	1999	
...	...	...	29	95	...	95	...	...	1996	Erythree
...	...	...	42	141	...	141	...	...	1997	
...	...	...	*50	*171	...	*171	...	...	1998	
...	...	...	52	184	...	184	...	...	1999	
*55	*14	− 18	*26	*1357	...	*1222	...	135	1996	Ethiopie
*55	*14	*42	*27	*1469	...	*1329	...	140	1997	
*57	*14	*103	*26	*1489	...	*1347	...	142	1998	
*57	*15	*0	*32	*1860	...	*1716	...	144	1999	
39	318	113	1 173	1 314	...	430	821	63	1996	Gabon
34	290	*42	1 269	1 422	...	576	782	64	1997	
*39	*285	31	1 174	1 348	...	587	698	63	1998	
*47	*289	52	1 211	1 425	...	604	761	60	1999	
...	...	...	*63	*72	...	*72	...	...	1996	Gambie
...	...	...	*61	*72	...	*72	...	...	1997	
...	...	...	*64	*78	...	*78	...	...	1998	
...	...	...	*62	*85	...	*85	...	...	1999	
*29	*25	*49	124	2 204	*2	*1632	...	570	1996	Ghana
*29	*25	*56	*126	*2283	*2	*1690	...	590	1997	
*30	*26	*50	*130	*2399	*2	*1877	...	520	1998	
*30	*28	66	105	1 990	*2	1 529	...	459	1999	
*14	...	...	*50	*379	...	*363	...	*16	1996	Guinée
*14	...	...	*49	*381	...	*365	...	*16	1997	
*15	...	...	*49	*386	...	*369	...	*17	1998	
*15	...	...	*49	*394	...	*377	...	*17	1999	
*6	...	...	*69	*76	...	*76	...	...	1996	Guinée – Bissau
*6	...	...	*69	*77	...	*77	...	...	1997	
*6	...	...	*68	*78	...	*78	...	...	1998	
*6	...	...	*74	*87	...	*87	...	...	1999	
...	37	*158	98	3 124	93	2 402	...	629	1996	Kenya
...	57	159	77	2 561	93	1 872	...	596	1997	
...	72	300	111	3 248	66	2 559	...	623	1998	
...	110	454	98	2 931	69	2 282	...	580	1999	
*4	*12	...	*44	*125	...	*109	...	*15	1996	Libéria
*4	*12	...	*45	*130	...	*114	...	*16	1997	
*2	*12	...	*57	*143	...	*127	...	*16	1998	
*3	*12	...	*54	*147	...	*131	...	*17	1999	
*134	89	*1310	2 889	14 021	*4	9 120	4 897	...	1996	Jamah. arabe libyenne
*52	89	4 912	2 668	13 225	*4	8 093	5 128	...	1997	
*52	89	*859	2 608	13 205	*4	8 096	5 105	...	1998	
*52	89	*3695	2 394	12 389	*4	8 407	3 978	...	1999	
*2	*15	*10	*34	*478	*9	*431	...	38	1996	Madagascar
*2	*15	*8	*39	*575	*10	*523	...	42	1997	
*2	*15	*51	*37	*552	*10	*498	...	44	1998	
2	*15	82	*38	*587	8	*535	...	44	1999	
*18	...	...	*29	*289	*12	*204	...	*74	1996	Malawi
*18	...	...	*28	*291	*12	*205	...	*74	1997	
*19	...	...	*27	*293	*12	*207	...	*74	1998	
*19	...	...	*27	*298	*12	*212	...	*74	1999	
*18	...	...	*17	*177	...	*159	...	18	1996	Mali
*18	...	...	*16	*178	...	*159	...	20	1997	
*18	...	...	*17	*182	...	*162	...	*20	1998	
*18	...	...	*17	*186	...	*166	...	*20	1999	
*12	*10	*90	*405	*953	*4	*946	...	*2	1996	Mauritanie
*12	*10	*85	*396	*959	*4	*952	...	*2	1997	
*12	*10	*85	*385	*963	*4	*956	...	*2	1998	
*12	*10	*102	*381	*985	*4	*978	...	*3	1999	

64

Production, trade and consumption of commercial energy
Thousand metric tons of oil equivalent and kilograms per capita [*cont.*]
Production, commerce et consommation d'énergie commerciale
Milliers de tonnes d'équivalent pétrole et kilogrammes par habitant [*suite*]

Region, country or area	Year	Total Totale	Solids Solides	Liquids Liquides	Gas Gaz	Electricity Electricité	Changes in stocks Variations des stocks	Imports Importations	Exports Exportations
Mauritius	1996	9	...	...	...	9	*−39	778	...
	1997	8	...	...	...	8	22	867	...
	1998	9	...	...	...	9	36	972	...
	1999	3	...	...	...	3	*−27	1 019	...
Morocco	1996	543	354	5	17	167	*−236	8 613	...
	1997	484	263	12	32	177	178	8 850	...
	1998	386	188	12	35	151	*−163	9 224	...
	1999	213	90	11	41	70	*−324	10 404	...
Mozambique	1996	52	*14	...	...	38	...	*359	...
	1997	96	*13	...	...	83	...	*372	...
	1998	600	*13	...	...	587	...	380	...
	1999	604	*14	...	...	590	...	*382	...
Niger	1996	*121	*121	...	...	...	...	*231	...
	1997	*122	*122	...	...	...	...	*231	...
	1998	*122	*122	...	...	...	...	*231	...
	1999	*122	*122	...	...	...	...	*242	...
Nigeria	1996	110 061	98	104 543	4 956	463	...	70	94 524
	1997	116 921	98	111 169	5 182	471	...	70	100 678
	1998	109 106	41	103 034	5 559	471	...	1 894	95 223
	1999	101 867	42	94 801	6 549	476	...	640	86 983
Réunion	1996	54	...	...	...	54	1	637	...
	1997	47	...	...	...	47	...	673	...
	1998	48	...	...	...	48	...	717	...
	1999	48	...	...	...	48	...	743	...
Rwanda	1996	*14	...	...	*0	*14	...	*171	...
	1997	*14	...	...	*0	*14	...	*175	...
	1998	*14	...	...	*0	*14	...	*177	...
	1999	*14	...	...	*0	*14	...	*186	...
Saint Helena	1996	...	...	...	...	...	...	*5	...
	1997	...	...	...	...	...	...	*5	...
	1998	...	...	...	...	...	...	*6	...
	1999	...	...	...	...	...	...	7	...
Sao Tome and Principe	1996	*1	...	...	...	*1	...	*26	...
	1997	*1	...	...	...	*1	...	*26	...
	1998	*1	...	...	...	*1	...	*27	...
	1999	*1	...	...	...	*1	...	*30	...
Senegal	1996	...	...	...	...	...	...	*1343	*56
	1997	...	...	...	...	...	...	*1363	*60
	1998	...	...	...	...	...	...	*1384	*63
	1999	...	...	...	...	...	...	1 418	*67
Seychelles	1996	...	...	...	...	...	...	*175	...
	1997	...	...	...	...	...	...	*181	...
	1998	...	...	...	...	...	...	*181	...
	1999	...	...	...	...	...	...	*188	...
Sierra Leone	1996	...	...	...	...	...	...	*290	*3
	1997	...	...	...	...	...	...	*295	*3
	1998	...	...	...	...	...	...	*297	*3
	1999	...	...	...	...	...	...	*306	*3
Southern African Customs Union	1996	157 817	145 053	7 652	1 716	3 396	*−1986	18 397	45 288
	1997	167 607	154 699	7 652	1 532	3 723	1 712	24 627	54 227
	1998	169 225	156 836	7 186	1 290	3 913	8 553	23 139	46 826
	1999	170 033	157 065	7 627	1 688	3 654	1 173	21 686	52 838
Sudan	1996	184	...	102	...	*82	88	1 030	*41
	1997	339	...	255	...	*84	*−88	958	*43
	1998	421	...	330	...	*90	...	*594	*43
	1999	3 548	...	3 453	...	95	...	472	2 912
Togo	1996	*1	...	...	...	*1	...	*255	*6
	1997	*0	...	...	...	*0	...	*260	*6
	1998	*0	...	...	...	*0	...	*286	*6
	1999	0	...	...	...	0	...	372	*6
Tunisia	1996	5 008	...	4 208	795	6	115	5 193	4 579
	1997	5 468	...	3 835	1 630	4	238	4 672	4 034
	1998	5 854	...	4 019	1 829	6	194	4 900	3 082
	1999	5 735	...	3 978	1 751	*6	286	4 808	4 574

Bunkers – Soutes			Consumption – Consommation							
Air Avion	Sea Maritime	Unallocated Nondistribué	Per capita Par habitant	Total Totale	Solids Solides	Liquids Liquides	Gas Gaz	Electricity Electricité	Année	Région, pays ou zone
46	129	...	574	651	29	613	...	9	1996	Maurice
56	132	...	578	664	32	625	...	8	1997	
55	164	...	627	727	50	668	...	9	1998	
80	170	...	680	798	95	700	...	3	1999	
*77	...	1 210	302	8 104	2 298	5 622	17	167	1996	Maroc
*77	...	806	303	8 273	2 170	5 894	32	177	1997	
*88	...	926	315	8 759	2 586	5 987	35	151	1998	
*88	...	1 167	343	9 686	2 498	7 077	41	70	1999	
2	3	...	*25	*406	*25	*342	...	38	1996	Mozambique
2	2	...	*28	*463	*24	*357	...	83	1997	
2	1	...	58	976	*24	365	...	587	1998	
*2	*1	...	57	984	*26	*367	...	590	1999	
*22	...	...	*35	*331	*121	*210	...	...	1996	Niger
*22	...	...	*34	*332	*122	*210	...	...	1997	
*22	...	...	*33	*332	*122	*210	...	...	1998	
*23	...	...	*33	*341	*122	*219	...	...	1999	
*5	*343	740	142	14 519	102	8 997	4 956	463	1996	Nigéria
*5	*343	750	145	15 214	102	9 458	5 182	471	1997	
*5	*343	441	139	14 988	46	8 912	5 559	471	1998	
*5	*343	509	132	14 667	45	8 295	5 851	476	1999	
...	*10	...	1 006	679	...	626	...	54	1996	Réunion
...	*11	...	1 031	708	...	662	...	47	1997	
...	14	...	1 074	751	...	703	...	48	1998	
...	15	...	1 093	776	...	728	...	48	1999	
*9	...	...	*34	*175	...	*161	*0	*14	1996	Rwanda
*9	...	...	*31	*180	...	*165	*0	*14	1997	
*9	...	...	*28	*182	...	*167	*0	*14	1998	
*9	...	...	*27	*191	...	*177	*0	*14	1999	
...	...	...	*1039	*5	...	*5	...	...	1996	Saint–Hélène
...	...	...	*1039	*5	...	*5	...	...	1997	
...	...	...	*1242	*6	...	*6	...	...	1998	
...	...	...	1 452	7	...	7	...	...	1999	
...	...	...	*205	*26	...	*26	...	*1	1996	Sao Tomé–et–Principe
...	...	...	*202	*26	...	*26	...	*1	1997	
...	...	...	*206	*27	...	*27	...	*1	1998	
...	...	...	*226	*30	...	*30	...	*1	1999	
*109	*144	*52	*114	*981	...	*981	...	...	1996	Sénégal
*110	*148	*45	*114	*1000	...	*1000	...	...	1997	
*110	*148	*33	*114	*1029	...	*1029	...	...	1998	
*111	*153	− 29	*120	*1115	...	*1115	...	...	1999	
*34	78	...	*832	*63	...	*63	...	...	1996	Seychelles
*35	*80	...	*848	*65	...	*65	...	...	1997	
*35	*80	...	*826	*65	...	*65	...	...	1998	
*36	*80	...	*893	*71	...	*71	...	...	1999	
*19	*83	*53	*32	*132	...	*132	...	...	1996	Sierra Leone
*19	*85	*52	*33	*136	...	*136	...	...	1997	
*19	*85	*53	*33	*137	...	*137	...	...	1998	
*19	*86	*53	*34	*145	...	*145	...	...	1999	
...	3 132	4 045	2 715	125 735	105 190	15 433	1 716	3 396	1996	Union douanière
...	2 443	9 128	2 641	124 724	108 359	11 110	1 532	3 723	1997	d'Afrique australe
...	2 858	7 893	2 616	126 235	106 205	14 827	1 290	3 913	1998	
...	3 166	1 655	2 690	132 888	110 148	17 398	1 688	3 654	1999	
*38	*8	− 165	*42	*1204	...	*1122	...	*82	1996	Soudan
*38	*8	84	*42	*1212	...	*1128	...	*84	1997	
*38	*8	− 325	*42	*1250	...	*1160	...	*90	1998	
*39	*8	− 246	43	1 306	*1	1 211	...	95	1999	
12	...	...	*60	*237	...	*237	...	*1	1996	Togo
12	...	...	*59	*242	...	*241	...	*0	1997	
19	...	...	*62	*261	...	*261	...	*0	1998	
*19	...	...	79	348	...	348	...	0	1999	
*196	...	*−67	592	5 378	63	3 155	2 154	6	1996	Tunisie
*217	...	*−43	618	5 696	68	3 304	2 320	4	1997	
4	74	1 395	643	6 005	55	3 400	2 543	6	1998	
...	10	*−57	606	5 730	*55	3 676	1 992	*6	1999	

64
Production, trade and consumption of commercial energy
Thousand metric tons of oil equivalent and kilograms per capita [*cont.*]
Production, commerce et consommation d'énergie commerciale
Milliers de tonnes d'équivalent pétrole et kilogrammes par habitant [*suite*]

| Region, country or area | Year | Primary energy production – Production d'énergie primaire | | | | | Changes in stocks | Imports | Exports |
		Total Totale	Solids Solides	Liquids Liquides	Gas Gaz	Electricity Electricité	Variations des stocks	Importations	Exportations
Uganda	1996	100	...	...	...	100	...	315	*3
	1997	108	...	...	...	108	...	336	*3
	1998	109	...	...	...	109	...	397	*3
	1999	109	...	...	...	109	...	412	*4
United Rep. of Tanzania	1996	*133	*4	...	...	*129	...	*751	*29
	1997	*140	*4	...	...	*137	...	*760	*32
	1998	*173	*4	...	...	*170	...	*765	*32
	1999	*189	*4	...	...	*185	...	*785	*33
Western Sahara	1996	...	...	...	...	...	...	*74	...
	1997	...	...	...	...	...	...	*77	...
	1998	...	...	...	...	...	...	*79	...
	1999	...	...	...	...	...	...	*84	...
Zambia	1996	859	*192	...	...	667	...	*584	*44
	1997	850	*165	...	...	685	...	*589	*44
	1998	795	121	...	...	674	...	406	43
	1999	798	109	...	...	690	...	472	4
Zimbabwe	1996	3 810	3 623	...	...	186	*−92	1 631	113
	1997	3 900	3 713	...	...	*187	163	1 777	110
	1998	3 699	3 533	...	...	166	*−237	1 459	128
	1999	3 738	3 484	...	...	254	...	*1468	*122
America, North	**1996**	**2 267 968**	**589 982**	**675 741**	**700 065**	**302 180**	**− 6 899**	**682 904**	**363 936**
	1997	**2 293 700**	**605 486**	**694 805**	**708 769**	**284 639**	**− 7 450**	**733 467**	**379 340**
	1998	**2 296 079**	**613 242**	**682 352**	**711 100**	**289 386**	**17 923**	**772 011**	**389 330**
	1999	**2 267 554**	**600 079**	**647 428**	**710 436**	**309 612**	**− 28 404**	**791 327**	**376 794**
Antigua and Barbuda	1996	...	...	...	...	...	...	*158	*7
	1997	...	...	...	...	...	...	*164	*7
	1998	...	...	...	...	...	...	*164	*7
	1999	...	...	...	...	...	...	*170	*7
Aruba	1996	...	...	...	...	...	...	*602	...
	1997	...	...	...	...	...	...	*615	...
	1998	...	...	...	...	...	...	*619	...
	1999	...	...	...	...	...	...	*626	...
Bahamas	1996	...	...	...	...	...	− 18	*2876	*2096
	1997	...	...	...	...	...	− 5	*2888	*2096
	1998	...	...	...	...	...	*2	*2912	*2096
	1999	...	...	...	...	...	*2	*2913	*2096
Barbados	1996	77	...	50	27	...	7	508	158
	1997	67	...	45	22	...	5	590	199
	1998	115	...	80	35	...	6	827	188
	1999	141	...	97	44	...	*−10	847	186
Belize	1996	5	...	...	...	5	...	115	...
	1997	6	...	...	...	6	...	145	...
	1998	6	...	...	...	6	...	148	...
	1999	7	...	...	...	7	...	226	...
Bermuda	1996	...	...	...	...	...	...	*171	...
	1997	...	...	...	...	...	...	*171	...
	1998	...	...	...	...	...	...	*171	...
	1999	...	...	...	...	...	...	*171	...
British Virgin Islands	1996	...	...	...	...	...	...	*20	...
	1997	...	...	...	...	...	...	*20	...
	1998	...	...	...	...	...	...	*20	...
	1999	...	...	...	...	...	...	*20	...
Canada	1996	365 684	39 721	113 262	157 875	54 825	7	47 172	163 841
	1997	376 583	41 103	123 362	160 390	51 727	1 782	54 361	170 819
	1998	364 931	38 947	114 465	164 250	47 269	2 000	56 975	180 861
	1999	359 917	37 336	111 831	161 907	48 843	*−3511	58 569	181 815
Cayman Islands	1996	...	...	...	...	...	...	*111	...
	1997	...	...	...	...	...	...	*111	...
	1998	...	...	...	...	...	...	*113	...
	1999	...	...	...	...	...	...	*112	...
Costa Rica	1996	779	...	...	...	779	− 50	1 584	162
	1997	886	...	...	...	886	− 88	1 625	166
	1998	924	...	...	...	924	*−17	1 659	154
	1999	1 155	...	...	...	1 155	39	1 943	55

Air Avion	Sea Maritime	Unallocated Nondistribué	Per capita Par habitant	Total Totale	Solids Solides	Liquids Liquides	Gas Gaz	Electricity Electricité	Année	Région, pays ou zone
...	...	...	21	412	...	312	...	100	1996	Ouganda
...	...	...	22	440	...	333	...	108	1997	
...	...	...	24	503	...	394	...	109	1998	
...	...	...	24	517	...	408	...	109	1999	
*31	*23	− 2	*28	*803	*4	*670	...	*129	1996	République − Unie de
*31	*24	− 2	*27	*815	*4	*675	...	*137	1997	Tanzanie
*31	*24	− 3	*26	*855	*4	*681	...	*170	1998	
*34	*25	*−11	*26	*892	*4	704	...	*185	1999	
*4	...	...	*316	*70	...	*70	...	...	1996	Sahara occidental
*4	...	...	*319	*73	...	*73	...	...	1997	
*4	...	...	*317	*75	...	*75	...	...	1998	
*5	...	...	*324	*79	...	*79	...	...	1999	
*36	...	*42	*140	*1321	*189	*465	...	667	1996	Zambie
*26	...	*57	134	1 312	*162	*465	...	685	1997	
25	...	*−77	120	1 210	120	416	...	674	1998	
37	...	37	115	1 192	104	398	...	690	1999	
...	...	...	455	5 419	3 673	1 560	...	186	1996	Zimbabwe
...	...	...	440	5 404	3 513	1 703	...	*187	1997	
...	...	...	415	5 267	3 548	1 554	...	166	1998	
...	...	...	389	5 084	3 368	*1462	...	254	1999	
19 473	31 303	60 858	5 435	2 482 202	534 261	945 876	699 885	302 180	1996	**Amérique du Nord**
20 993	27 618	78 138	5 468	2 528 528	566 845	968 495	708 549	284 639	1997	
21 557	27 794	71 776	5 426	2 539 711	575 254	982 558	692 514	289 386	1998	
22 983	31 010	53 171	5 491	2 603 328	574 772	997 289	721 654	309 612	1999	
*43	...	...	*1561	*108	...	*108	...	...	1996	Antigua − et − Barbuda
*44	...	...	*1763	*113	...	*113	...	...	1997	
*44	...	...	*1763	*113	...	*113	...	...	1998	
*45	...	...	*1799	*117	...	*117	...	...	1999	
...	...	*315	*3333	*287	...	*287	...	...	1996	Aruba
...	...	*321	*3264	*294	...	*294	...	...	1997	
...	...	*322	*3228	*297	...	*297	...	...	1998	
...	...	*325	*3203	*301	...	*301	...	...	1999	
*41	*184	...	*2016	*572	*1	*571	...	...	1996	Bahamas
*36	*184	...	*2002	*577	*1	*575	...	...	1997	
*36	*184	...	*2026	*593	1	*593	...	...	1998	
*36	*184	...	*1994	*594	*1	*593	...	...	1999	
136	...	*−44	1 236	328	...	300	27	...	1996	Barbade
179	...	*−54	1 243	329	...	308	22	...	1997	
162	...	*234	1 319	351	...	*316	35	...	1998	
166	...	*262	1 438	384	...	340	44	...	1999	
7	4	...	490	109	...	103	...	5	1996	Belize
5	9	...	596	137	...	131	...	6	1997	
*5	*8	...	590	140	...	135	...	6	1998	
8	*7	...	978	217	...	211	...	7	1999	
*17	...	...	*2579	*155	...	*155	...	...	1996	Bermudes
*17	...	...	*2579	*155	...	*155	...	...	1997	
*17	...	...	*2495	*155	...	*155	...	...	1998	
*17	...	...	*2456	*155	...	*155	...	...	1999	
...	...	...	*932	*20	...	*20	...	...	1996	Iles Vierges britanniques
...	...	...	*890	*20	...	*20	...	...	1997	
...	...	...	*890	*20	...	*20	...	...	1998	
...	...	...	*851	*20	...	*20	...	...	1999	
996	636	3 700	8 212	243 676	24 167	78 769	85 915	54 825	1996	Canada
970	546	4 403	8 418	252 424	26 011	88 430	86 255	51 727	1997	
932	1 163	− 7 305	8 075	244 255	26 903	88 124	81 959	47 269	1998	
1 010	1 108	− 6 795	8 030	244 858	25 885	90 966	79 164	48 843	1999	
*17	...	...	*2778	*94	...	*94	...	...	1996	Iles Caïmanes
*17	...	...	*2778	*94	...	*94	...	...	1997	
*17	...	...	*2681	*97	...	*97	...	...	1998	
*18	...	...	*2553	*94	...	*94	...	...	1999	
...	...	*51	648	2 201	...	1 422	...	779	1996	Costa Rica
...	...	*46	689	2 387	...	1 501	...	886	1997	
...	...	*−114	726	2 560	...	1 636	...	924	1998	
...	...	*−1	837	3 004	...	1 849	...	1 155	1999	

64

Production, trade and consumption of commercial energy

Thousand metric tons of oil equivalent and kilograms per capita [*cont.*]

Production, commerce et consommation d'énergie commerciale

Milliers de tonnes d'équivalent pétrole et kilogrammes par habitant [*suite*]

Region, country or area	Year	Primary energy production – Production d'énergie primaire					Changes in stocks Variations des stocks	Imports Importations	Exports Exportations
		Total Totale	Solids Solides	Liquids Liquides	Gas Gaz	Electricity Electricité			
Cuba	1996	1 503	...	1 477	18	8	59	6 526	74
	1997	1 509	...	1 463	35	11	41	7 057	...
	1998	1 804	...	1 680	116	8	103	6 546	...
	1999	2 576	...	2 138	429	9	*−22	5 994	...
Dominica	1996	3	...	...	...	3	...	25	...
	1997	3	...	...	...	3	...	27	...
	1998	3	...	...	...	3	...	28	...
	1999	3	...	...	...	3	...	27	...
Dominican Republic	1996	*174		...	...	*174	*−10	5 633	...
	1997	*189		...	...	*189	− 130	5 560	...
	1998	*208		...	...	*208	...	7 247	...
	1999	119	...	...	...	119	...	7 419	...
El Salvador	1996	533	...	...	...	533	8	1 549	114
	1997	*550	...	...	...	*550	8	1 902	220
	1998	547	...	...	...	547	3	2 039	219
	1999	666	...	...	...	666	*−23	1 983	230
Greenland	1996	...	...	...	...	...	...	*178	*7
	1997	...	...	...	...	...	...	*180	*7
	1998	...	...	...	...	...	...	*182	*7
	1999	...	...	...	...	...	...	*186	*7
Grenada	1996	...	...	...	...	...	1	62	...
	1997	...	...	...	...	...	1	68	...
	1998	...	...	...	...	...	1	71	...
	1999	...	...	...	...	...	...	74	...
Guadeloupe	1996	...	...	...	...	...	...	*544	...
	1997	...	...	...	...	...	...	*552	...
	1998	...	...	...	...	...	...	*556	...
	1999	...	...	...	...	...	...	*581	...
Guatemala	1996	938	...	730	10	198	4	1 921	642
	1997	1 167	...	976	10	181	27	2 276	893
	1998	1 462	...	1 273	10	179	59	2 839	1 104
	1999	1 403	...	1 164	*10	229	*−5	2 680	960
Haiti	1996	*22	...	...	...	*22	...	368	...
	1997	*22	...	...	...	*22	...	478	...
	1998	*24	...	...	...	*24	...	436	...
	1999	23	...	...	...	23	...	487	...
Honduras	1996	186	...	...	...	186	28	1 213	25
	1997	119	...	...	...	119	1	1 234	21
	1998	165	...	...	...	165	*−30	1 442	12
	1999	183	...	...	...	183	*−17	1 472	16
Jamaica	1996	11	...	...	...	11	*−113	3 200	57
	1997	12	...	...	...	12	*−122	3 390	58
	1998	12	...	...	...	12	*−129	3 682	32
	1999	10	...	...	...	10	*−134	3 250	69
Martinique	1996	...	...	...	...	...	...	*857	*197
	1997	...	...	...	...	...	...	*865	*201
	1998	...	...	...	...	...	...	*870	*202
	1999	...	...	...	...	...	...	*880	*208
Mexico	1996	209 157	3 157	165 847	30 462	9 690	423	9 167	83 985
	1997	219 516	3 222	175 160	31 424	9 710	334	15 053	94 492
	1998	225 194	3 501	178 356	33 927	9 410	*−474	17 041	95 893
	1999	218 142	3 515	171 908	32 563	10 155	*−170	16 999	38 470
Montserrat	1996	...	...	...	...	...	...	*14	...
	1997	...	...	...	...	...	...	*16	...
	1998	...	...	...	...	...	...	*16	...
	1999	...	...	...	...	...	...	*18	...
Netherland Antilles	1996	...	...	...	...	...	...	*15650	*9479
	1997	...	...	...	...	...	...	*15673	*9599
	1998	...	...	...	...	...	...	*16037	*9621
	1999	...	...	...	...	...	...	*16557	*10066
Nicaragua	1996	*547	...	...	...	*547	54	957	...
	1997	*547	...	...	...	*547	2	965	...
	1998	*600	...	...	...	*600	33	1 132	...
	1999	459	...	...	...	459	*−64	1 112	11

| Bunkers – Soutes | | | Consumption – Consommation | | | | | | | |
Air Avion	Sea Maritime	Unallocated Nondistribué	Per capita Par habitant	Total Totale	Solids Solides	Liquids Liquides	Gas Gaz	Electricity Electricité	Année	Région, pays ou zone
266	...	1 225	582	6 405	8	6 371	18	8	1996	Cuba
304	...	1 132	641	7 089	8	7 035	35	11	1997	
277	...	1 386	592	6 585	10	6 451	116	8	1998	
259	...	1 853	581	6 480	10	6 032	429	9	1999	
...	...	...	371	28	...	25	...	3	1996	Dominique
...	...	...	392	30	...	27	...	3	1997	
1	...	...	392	30	...	27	...	3	1998	
...	...	...	419	30	...	27	...	3	1999	
...	...	152	723	5 664	90	5 401	...	*174	1996	Rép. dominicaine
...	...	*16	736	5 863	97	5 577	...	*189	1997	
...	...	911	807	6 544	57	6 279	...	*208	1998	
...	...	489	847	7 048	55	6 875	...	119	1999	
...	...	43	331	1 915	...	1 383	...	533	1996	El Salvador
...	...	52	368	2 172	...	1 622	...	*550	1997	
...	...	38	386	2 325	...	1 778	...	547	1998	
...	...	33	392	2 410	...	1 743	...	666	1999	
...	...	...	*3054	*171	...	*171	...	...	1996	Groenland
...	...	...	*3091	*173	...	*173	...	...	1997	
...	...	...	*3127	*175	...	*175	...	...	1998	
...	...	...	*3201	*179	...	*179	...	...	1999	
*2	...	...	595	59	...	59	...	...	1996	Grenade
*2	...	...	701	65	...	65	...	...	1997	
*2	...	...	734	68	...	68	...	...	1998	
*2	...	...	707	71	...	71	...	...	1999	
*79	...	...	*1127	*465	...	*465	...	...	1996	Guadeloupe
*80	...	...	*1136	*473	...	*473	...	...	1997	
*80	...	...	*1135	*477	...	*477	...	...	1998	
*81	...	...	*1181	*501	...	*501	...	...	1999	
...	...	*−42	220	2 255	...	2 047	10	198	1996	Guatemala
...	...	70	233	2 453	...	2 262	10	181	1997	
...	...	129	279	3 008	...	2 819	10	179	1998	
...	...	140	270	2 989	...	2 749	*10	229	1999	
*8	...	...	52	381	...	360	...	*22	1996	Haïti
*15	...	...	65	484	...	462	...	*22	1997	
*15	...	...	58	444	...	421	...	*24	1998	
*14	...	...	63	495	...	472	...	23	1999	
...	...	...	232	1 345	...	1 160	...	186	1996	Honduras
...	...	...	222	1 331	...	1 212	...	119	1997	
...	...	...	263	1 626	...	1 460	...	165	1998	
...	...	...	259	1 656	...	1 473	...	183	1999	
*36	...	2	1 278	3 228	45	3 172	...	11	1996	Jamaïque
*36	...	50	1 324	3 379	47	3 321	...	12	1997	
*36	...	471	1 277	3 284	50	3 222	...	12	1998	
*39	...	− 84	1 301	3 370	50	3 309	...	10	1999	
...	*39	*44	*1542	*577	...	*577	...	...	1996	Martinique
...	*39	*48	*1527	*576	...	*576	...	...	1997	
...	*39	*50	*1525	*578	...	*578	...	...	1998	
...	*40	*46	*1538	*586	...	*586	...	...	1999	
2 134	575	9 297	1 315	121 911	4 657	76 671	30 893	9 690	1996	Mexique
2 267	796	10 464	1 339	126 215	4 859	79 581	32 065	9 710	1997	
2 503	785	9 835	1 395	133 694	4 958	84 342	34 984	9 410	1998	
2 604	835	13 035	1 328	130 368	4 719	82 859	32 635	10 155	1999	
...	*1	...	*1487	*13	...	*13	...	...	1996	Montserrat
...	*1	...	*1931	*15	...	*15	...	...	1997	
...	*1	...	*2575	*15	...	*15	...	...	1998	
...	*1	...	*3307	*17	...	*17	...	...	1999	
*63	*1714	*3564	*4048	*830	...	*830	...	...	1996	Antilles néerlandaises
*65	*1720	*3442	*4073	*847	...	*847	...	...	1997	
*68	*1726	*3650	*4677	*973	...	*973	...	...	1998	
*70	*1759	*4064	2 916	598	...	598	...	...	1999	
...	...	11	316	1 438	...	892	...	*547	1996	Nicaragua
...	...	5	322	1 505	...	958	...	*547	1997	
...	...	14	351	1 685	...	1 085	...	*600	1998	
...	...	− 5	330	1 629	...	1 169	...	459	1999	

64
Production, trade and consumption of commercial energy
Thousand metric tons of oil equivalent and kilograms per capita [*cont.*]
Production, commerce et consommation d'énergie commerciale
Milliers de tonnes d'équivalent pétrole et kilogrammes par habitant [*suite*]

Region, country or area	Year	Primary energy production – Production d'énergie primaire					Changes in stocks Variations des stocks	Imports Importations	Exports Exportations
		Total Totale	Solids Solides	Liquids Liquides	Gas Gaz	Electricity Electricité			
Panama	1996	258	...	...	...	258	4	2 846	1 343
	1997	250	...	...	...	250	86	2 874	356
	1998	184	...	...	...	184	45	3 257	469
	1999	269	...	...	...	269	*−64	3 137	621
Puerto Rico	1996	12	...	...	...	12	− 74	5 657	*466
	1997	8	...	...	...	8	− 79	5 613	*437
	1998	10	...	...	...	10	− 28	5 471	*437
	1999	*10	...	...	...	*10	− 100	5 340	*394
Saint Kitts and Nevis	1996	...	...	...	...	...	...	*34	...
	1997	...	...	...	...	...	...	*34	...
	1998	...	...	...	...	...	...	*34	...
	1999	...	...	...	...	...	...	*34	...
Saint Lucia	1996	...	...	...	...	...	...	108	...
	1997	...	...	...	...	...	...	101	...
	1998	...	...	...	...	...	...	98	...
	1999	...	...	...	...	...	...	108	...
Saint Pierre and Miquelon	1996	...	...	...	...	...	...	28	...
	1997	...	...	...	...	...	...	19	...
	1998	...	...	...	...	...	...	*22	...
	1999	...	...	...	...	...	...	*22	...
Saint Vincent and the Grenadines	1996	*2	...	...	...	*2	...	*44	...
	1997	2	...	...	...	2	...	44	...
	1998	2	...	...	...	2	...	55	...
	1999	*2	...	...	...	*2	...	*55	...
Trinidad and Tobago	1996	13 829	...	6 717	7 112	...	87	2 303	7 144
	1997	13 789	...	6 218	7 572	...	33	2 065	6 605
	1998	14 294	...	6 391	7 903	...	100	3 760	8 511
	1999	16 171	...	6 509	9 662	...	*−173	4 082	9 553
United States	1996	1 674 249	547 104	387 656	504 560	234 928	*−7432	553 117	80 195
	1997	1 678 477	561 161	387 581	509 317	220 418	*−9520	588 984	79 188
	1998	1 685 593	570 794	380 107	504 860	229 834	16 060	617 712	75 517
	1999	1 666 300	559 228	353 780	505 820	247 471	*−24269	634 971	67 989
U.S. Virgin Islands	1996	...	...	...	...	...	*115	*17587	*13944
	1997	...	...	...	...	...	*175	*17744	*13976
	1998	...	...	...	...	...	*189	*17830	*14000
	1999	...	...	...	...	...	*118	*18261	*14040
America, South	**1996**	**448 399**	**24 847**	**317 384**	**63 189**	**42 979**	**6 372**	**77 635**	**221 870**
	1997	**480 301**	**28 191**	**335 730**	**70 867**	**45 513**	**− 658**	**81 574**	**249 271**
	1998	**489 647**	**30 399**	**339 838**	**73 064**	**46 346**	**1 128**	**84 571**	**249 775**
	1999	**487 787**	**29 163**	**337 637**	**74 179**	**46 808**	**− 4 114**	**78 349**	**241 456**
Argentina	1996	70 510	183	41 741	24 661	3 924	*−71	4 575	19 447
	1997	78 050	148	44 388	29 034	4 480	241	4 059	21 464
	1998	78 032	171	43 812	29 835	4 215	365	4 978	22 410
	1999	78 983	198	42 697	32 403	3 684	*−319	3 377	21 306
Bolivia	1996	5 537	...	1 824	3 587	126	− 21	139	*2082
	1997	5 143	...	1 805	3 205	133	*−270	249	2 075
	1998	5 291	...	2 085	3 067	139	16	303	1 677
	1999	*5593	...	1 784	*3662	147	*−25	359	2 052
Brazil	1996	71 203	2 135	40 418	5 160	23 490	974	48 752	1 720
	1997	76 783	2 509	43 726	5 729	24 819	211	48 910	1 827
	1998	85 120	2 451	50 747	6 012	25 910	522	47 662	3 965
	1999	91 062	2 489	56 389	5 958	26 226	*−102	43 617	3 163
Chile	1996	4 685	703	877	1 653	1 452	511	13 047	85
	1997	4 910	731	754	1 797	1 629	*−109	15 044	185
	1998	4 438	658	789	1 620	1 371	92	16 601	143
	1999	4 055	340	704	1 843	1 168	*−584	17 914	186
Colombia	1996	59 893	19 237	32 629	4 972	3 056	172	1 105	36 226
	1997	63 934	21 185	33 970	6 051	2 729	145	1 389	39 253
	1998	68 318	21 886	37 457	6 327	2 647	170	1 305	43 624
	1999	73 058	21 240	42 100	*6263	3 454	*−801	428	49 934
Ecuador	1996	20 727	...	19 431	618	679	...	734	12 882
	1997	21 517	...	20 313	*581	624	...	906	15 414
	1998	21 124	...	19 798	704	622	...	1 495	14 303
	1999	21 011	...	19 689	702	620	...	1 221	14 239

Energy   Energie

Air Avion	Sea Maritime	Unallocated Nondistribué	Per capita Par habitant	Total Totale	Solids Solides	Liquids Liquides	Gas Gaz	Electricity Electricité	Année	Région, pays ou zone
...	...	28	647	1 729	70	1 344	*57	258	1996	Panama
...	...	864	669	1 818	40	1 472	*57	250	1997	
...	...	55	1 039	2 871	39	2 591	*57	184	1998	
...	...	214	938	2 635	49	2 260	*57	269	1999	
...	*172	− 186	1 417	5 291	*119	5 160	...	12	1996	Porto Rico
...	*175	127	*1304	*4961	*121	*4832	...	8	1997	
...	*175	53	*1264	*4845	*122	*4712	...	10	1998	
...	*160	− 67	1 276	4 963	*112	4 841	...	*10	1999	
...	...	...	*847	*34	...	*34	...	...	1996	Saint−Kitts−et−Nevis
...	...	...	*869	*34	...	*34	...	...	1997	
...	...	...	*869	*34	...	*34	...	...	1998	
...	...	...	*807	*34	...	*34	...	...	1999	
...	...	...	736	108	...	108	...	...	1996	Saint−Lucie
...	...	...	673	101	...	101	...	...	1997	
...	...	...	645	98	...	98	...	...	1998	
...	...	...	741	108	...	108	...	...	1999	
...	4	...	3 350	23	...	23	...	...	1996	Saint−Pierre−et−
...	4	...	2 185	15	...	15	...	...	1997	Miquelon
...	4	...	*2625	*18	...	*18	...	...	1998	
...	4	...	*2625	*18	...	*18	...	...	1999	
...	...	...	*417	*46	...	*44	...	*2	1996	Saint−Vincent−et−les−
...	...	...	414	46	...	44	...	2	1997	Grenadines
...	...	...	510	57	...	55	...	2	1998	
...	...	...	*505	*57	...	*55	...	*2	1999	
*58	*161	132	6 764	8 549	...	1 437	7 112	...	1996	Trinité−et−Tobago
*58	*152	28	7 043	8 979	...	1 408	7 572	...	1997	
*63	185	234	7 011	8 960	...	1 058	7 903	...	1998	
30	186	237	8 084	10 421	...	*759	9 662	...	1999	
5 570	27 620	41 854	7 796	2 069 558	504 929	753 849	575 853	234 928	1996	Etats−Unis
6 898	23 798	56 353	7 838	2 100 745	535 484	762 310	582 533	220 418	1997	
7 299	23 325	61 007	7 799	2 110 097	542 936	769 877	567 450	229 834	1998	
8 583	26 523	38 193	7 973	2 174 252	543 713	783 415	599 653	247 471	1999	
...	*193	*709	*22638	*2626	*175	*2451	...	...	1996	Iles Vierges américaines
...	*195	*770	*22463	*2628	*176	*2452	...	...	1997	
...	*198	*806	*22355	*2638	*178	*2460	...	...	1998	
...	*203	*1230	*22255	*2671	*178	*2492	...	...	1999	
876	3 430	24 112	837	269 374	20 734	142 918	62 743	42 979	1996	**Amérique du Sud**
960	3 702	22 496	876	286 104	21 908	148 587	70 097	45 513	1997	
1 131	3 394	25 136	886	293 654	21 822	152 864	72 622	46 346	1998	
894	4 547	30 839	865	292 515	21 214	152 428	72 065	46 808	1999	
...	579	4 480	1 438	50 650	818	19 428	26 480	3 924	1996	Argentine
...	704	5 658	1 515	54 042	733	19 025	29 804	4 480	1997	
...	550	5 740	1 493	53 945	750	19 513	29 466	4 215	1998	
...	736	5 823	1 499	54 812	569	20 893	29 666	3 684	1999	
...	...	268	441	3 347	...	1 504	1 718	126	1996	Bolivie
...	...	423	407	3 164	...	1 665	1 367	133	1997	
...	...	591	417	3 311	...	1 767	1 406	139	1998	
...	...	373	*437	*3552	...	1 795	*1610	147	1999	
779	1 347	9 103	672	106 031	12 364	65 017	5 160	23 490	1996	Brésil
858	1 713	9 105	701	111 979	12 571	68 861	5 729	24 819	1997	
963	1 703	9 755	716	115 875	12 315	71 637	6 012	25 910	1998	
*748	2 642	12 076	702	116 152	12 824	70 774	6 328	26 226	1999	
...	...	519	1 152	16 617	3 807	10 100	1 258	1 452	1996	Chili
5	...	556	1 321	19 317	4 913	10 680	2 095	1 629	1997	
27	...	712	1 354	20 064	4 671	10 816	3 207	1 371	1998	
1	56	1 146	1 409	21 163	4 892	10 955	4 148	1 168	1999	
...	191	2 314	562	22 095	3 301	10 767	4 972	3 056	1996	Colombie
...	207	2 823	571	22 894	3 242	10 872	6 051	2 729	1997	
...	203	3 215	549	22 411	2 668	10 769	6 327	2 647	1998	
...	174	2 065	532	22 113	2 505	9 890	*6263	3 454	1999	
*31	*223	1 118	616	7 208	...	5 911	618	679	1996	Equateur
*26	*151	*−222	591	7 054	...	5 849	*581	624	1997	
*57	*148	398	634	7 714	...	6 387	704	622	1998	
*41	*146	872	559	6 934	...	5 612	702	620	1999	

64
Production, trade and consumption of commercial energy
Thousand metric tons of oil equivalent and kilograms per capita [*cont.*]
Production, commerce et consommation d'énergie commerciale
Milliers de tonnes d'équivalent pétrole et kilogrammes par habitant [*suite*]

| Region, country or area | Year | Primary energy production – Production d'énergie primaire | | | | | Changes in stocks Variations des stocks | Imports Importations | Exports Exportations |
		Total Totale	Solids Solides	Liquids Liquides	Gas Gaz	Electricity Electricité			
Falkland Is. (Malvinas)	1996	3	3	...	...	...	...	10	
	1997	*3	*3	...	...	...	...	*11	
	1998	3	3	...	...	...	...	9	
	1999	*3	*3	...	...	...	...	*9	
French Guiana	1996	...	...	...	...	...	...	304	
	1997	...	...	...	...	...	...	*304	
	1998	...	...	...	...	...	...	*309	
	1999	...	...	...	...	...	...	*313	
Guyana	1996	*0	...	...	...	*0	...	516	
	1997	*0	...	...	...	*0	...	542	
	1998	*0	...	...	...	*0	...	559	
	1999	*0	...	...	...	*0	...	569	
Paraguay	1996	3 850	...	...	...	3 850	*−116	1 105	
	1997	4 369	...	...	...	4 369	...	1 273	
	1998	4 371	...	...	...	4 371	3	1 299	
	1999	4 464	...	...	...	4 464	*−69	1 337	
Peru	1996	7 729	40	6 027	497	1 165	454	4 618	2 7
	1997	7 527	15	5 992	383	1 136	13	5 803	3 2
	1998	7 424	14	5 691	530	1 188	197	6 297	3 8
	1999	7 961	11	5 981	719	1 251	*−1161	4 954	2 6
Suriname	1996	356	...	245	...	110	...	483	
	1997	357	...	246	...	111	1	488	
	1998	360	...	248	...	111	1	493	
	1999	361	...	248	...	113	...	496	
Uruguay	1996	496	...	...	...	496	*−50	2 168	
	1997	558	...	...	...	558	*−16	2 128	
	1998	787	...	...	...	787	*−23	2 115	
	1999	473	...	...	...	473	42	2 604	
Venezuela	1996	203 410	2 546	174 193	22 041	4 631	4 519	*79	146 6
	1997	217 148	3 600	184 536	24 087	4 925	*−874	467	165 7
	1998	214 380	5 216	179 210	24 969	4 984	*−215	1 145	159 7
	1999	200 764	4 883	168 045	22 628	5 208	*−1095	*1152	147 8
Asia	**1996**	**3 060 808**	**1 038 492**	**1 414 934**	**433 009**	**174 373**	**2 112**	**1 063 575**	**1 172 2**
	1997	**3 110 219**	**1 030 917**	**1 459 165**	**438 949**	**181 188**	**23 024**	**1 129 103**	**1 224 7**
	1998	**3 142 978**	**970 254**	**1 525 887**	**455 843**	**190 994**	**13 891**	**1 095 175**	**1 293 2**
	1999	**3 024 197**	**862 590**	**1 490 994**	**480 472**	**190 142**	**− 41 729**	**1 122 268**	**1 289 7**
Afghanistan	1996	*183	2	...	*149	*31	*10	*277	
	1997	*166	*1	...	*137	*28	*10	*259	
	1998	*156	*1	...	*128	*27	*10	*247	
	1999	*146	*1	...	*118	*27	*10	*229	
Armenia	1996	742	...	...	...	742	...	1 135	
	1997	537	...	...	...	537	...	1 455	
	1998	547	...	...	...	547	...	1 514	
	1999	646	...	...	...	646	...	1 321	
Azerbaijan	1996	14 939	...	9 125	5 681	132	*−3	103	2 29
	1997	14 568	...	9 047	5 374	147	300	330	2 33
	1998	16 636	...	11 449	5 019	168	2 304	308	2 14
	1999	19 558	...	13 833	5 595	130	4 252	244	2 30
Bahrain	1996	8 910	...	2 375	6 536	...	*−374	11 060	10 88
	1997	9 402	...	2 361	7 041	...	*−166	10 584	10 28
	1998	9 714	...	2 293	7 421	...	*−484	10 540	10 27
	1999	9 970	...	2 280	7 690	...	*−257	11 259	10 81
Bangladesh	1996	6 687	...	66	6 557	64	*−274	2 724	
	1997	6 551	...	45	6 444	62	*−25	3 276	
	1998	7 103	...	*37	6 992	74	251	3 040	
	1999	7 738	...	*37	7 630	72	*−7	3 045	
Bhutan	1996	214	45	...	...	170	...	*43	2
	1997	196	38	...	...	158	...	75	2
	1998	190	*35	...	...	155	...	*79	*2
	1999	*190	*35	...	...	*155	...	*80	*2
Brunei Darussalam	1996	18 640	...	8 679	9 962	...	89	59	16 62
	1997	*18524	...	8 563	*9961	...	*25	80	*1646
	1998	*18116	...	*8472	*9644	...	− 50	14	*1600
	1999	*18313	...	9 358	*8954	...	*89	4	16 52

Air Avion	Sea Maritime	Unallocated Nondistribué	Per capita Par habitant	Total Totale	Solids Solides	Liquids Liquides	Gas Gaz	Electricity Electricité	Année	Région, pays ou zone
...	...	...	6 825	14	3	10	...	...	1996	Iles Falkland (Malvinas)
...	...	...	*7332	*15	*3	*11	...	...	1997	
...	...	...	5 958	12	3	9	...	...	1998	
...	...	...	*5959	*12	*3	*9	...	...	1999	
*17	...	...	2 012	288	...	288	...	...	1996	Guyane française
*17	...	...	1 944	288	...	288	...	...	1997	
*17	...	...	*1901	*293	...	*293	...	...	1998	
*18	...	...	*1861	*296	...	*296	...	...	1999	
12	*2	...	673	502	...	502	...	*0	1996	Guyana
13	*2	...	703	527	...	527	...	*0	1997	
12	*2	...	723	545	...	545	...	*0	1998	
12	...	...	723	557	...	557	...	*0	1999	
*2	...	*−1	1 023	5 070	...	1 220	...	3 850	1996	Paraguay
...	...	2	1 109	5 640	...	1 271	...	4 369	1997	
...	...	*−1	1 086	5 668	...	1 297	...	4 371	1998	
...	...	2	1 096	5 868	...	1 404	...	4 464	1999	
...	...	*−76	387	9 264	347	7 255	497	1 165	1996	Pérou
...	...	661	385	9 385	333	7 532	383	1 136	1997	
...	...	− 285	403	9 983	412	7 853	530	1 188	1998	
...	...	799	420	10 598	307	8 321	719	1 251	1999	
...	...	189	1 458	602	...	492	...	110	1996	Suriname
...	...	189	1 450	608	...	497	...	111	1997	
...	...	191	1 443	613	...	502	...	111	1998	
...	...	191	1 437	618	...	505	...	113	1999	
35	409	37	680	2 205	1	1 708	...	496	1996	Uruguay
41	318	69	692	2 261	1	1 702	...	558	1997	
56	281	81	762	2 508	1	1 719	...	787	1998	
73	293	141	762	2 524	1	2 051	...	473	1999	
...	680	6 161	2 039	45 481	*92	18 718	22 041	4 631	1996	Venezuela
...	606	3 231	2 148	48 930	*111	19 808	24 087	4 925	1997	
...	507	*4739	2 182	50 713	1 002	19 757	24 969	4 984	1998	
...	500	*7351	1 996	47 316	*114	19 366	22 628	5 208	1999	
7 759	40 364	205 520	767	2 686 355	1 158 628	916 465	436 889	174 373	1996	Asie
8 618	43 533	221 995	763	2 707 430	1 138 848	931 149	456 245	181 188	1997	
7 959	47 462	205 452	739	2 660 155	1 085 687	917 374	466 100	190 994	1998	
6 811	48 387	204 138	721	2 629 092	1 002 780	939 192	496 978	190 142	1999	
*5	...	...	*22	*444	2	*261	*149	*31	1996	Afghanistan
*5	...	...	*20	*410	*1	*244	*137	*28	1997	
*5	...	...	*19	*388	*1	*232	*128	*27	1998	
*5	...	...	*17	*360	*1	*214	*118	*27	1999	
...	...	...	497	1 877	4	141	991	742	1996	Arménie
...	...	...	526	1 992	4	150	1 302	537	1997	
...	...	...	543	2 061	4	155	1 356	547	1998	
...	...	...	517	1 966	2	213	1 105	646	1999	
230	...	1 341	1 454	11 175	4	5 336	5 703	132	1996	Azerbaïdjan
199	...	1 413	1 372	10 648	4	5 123	5 374	147	1997	
184	...	1 629	1 363	10 686	1	5 559	4 958	168	1998	
159	...	2 195	1 368	10 827	...	5 019	5 678	130	1999	
...	...	2 112	12 268	7 349	...	813	6 536	...	1996	Bahreïn
...	...	2 138	12 465	7 728	...	687	7 041	...	1997	
...	...	2 135	12 953	8 329	...	908	7 421	...	1998	
...	...	2 083	12 889	8 584	...	894	7 690	...	1999	
...	14	775	73	8 897	179	2 097	6 557	64	1996	Bangladesh
...	9	622	74	9 222	323	2 393	6 444	62	1997	
...	*7	221	73	9 664	86	2 511	6 992	74	1998	
...	...	500	76	10 290	46	2 542	7 630	72	1999	
...	...	...	127	237	24	*43	...	170	1996	Bhoutan
...	...	...	130	249	50	*41	...	158	1997	
...	...	...	125	247	*48	*44	...	155	1998	
...	...	...	*121	*246	*46	*45	...	*155	1999	
...	...	*−338	7 610	2 321	...	949	1 372	...	1996	Brunéi Darussalam
...	...	− 288	*7798	*2402	...	977	*1424	...	1997	
...	...	*−272	*7582	*2388	...	906	*1482	...	1998	
...	...	− 166	*5641	*1867	...	*1058	*809	...	1999	

64

Production, trade and consumption of commercial energy
Thousand metric tons of oil equivalent and kilograms per capita [cont.]
Production, commerce et consommation d'énergie commerciale
Milliers de tonnes d'équivalent pétrole et kilogrammes par habitant [suite]

Region, country or area	Year	Primary energy production – Production d'énergie primaire					Changes in stocks Variations des stocks	Imports Importations	Exports Exportations
		Total Totale	Solids Solides	Liquids Liquides	Gas Gaz	Electricity Electricité			
Cambodia	1996	*7	...	...	...	*7	...	*166	
	1997	*7	...	...	...	*7	...	*170	
	1998	*7	...	...	...	*7	...	*170	
	1999	*7	...	...	...	*7	...	*174	
China	1996	898 324	697 802	157 491	23 134	19 897	*−5483	46 244	45 68
	1997	891 083	685 724	160 902	23 840	20 618	9 860	65 694	49 33
	1998	833 878	624 375	161 161	26 774	21 568	*−8221	56 667	45 36
	1999	732 548	521 978	160 160	28 981	21 430	*−15873	63 827	39 98
China, Hong Kong SAR	1996	...	...	...	...	...	− 5	22 352	8 77
	1997	...	...	...	...	...	177	24 468	10 27
	1998	...	...	...	...	...	75	25 472	8 54
	1999	...	...	...	...	...	281	23 007	3 49
China, Macao SAR	1996	...	...	...	...	...	2	465	
	1997	...	...	...	...	...	*−11	486	
	1998	...	...	...	...	...	10	522	
	1999	...	...	...	...	...	4	502	
Cyprus	1996	...	...	...	...	...	56	1 993	
	1997	...	...	...	...	...	*−8	1 999	
	1998	...	...	...	...	...	*−12	2 122	
	1999	...	...	...	...	...	68	2 297	
Georgia	1996	661	13	128	3	517	43	1 612	11
	1997	657	3	134	...	520	63	1 801	13
	1998	675	8	119	...	548	25	1 954	8
	1999	670	9	107	...	554	61	1 997	6
India	1996	240 369	170 750	36 841	24 404	8 374	*−1026	59 640	58
	1997	241 379	177 148	37 600	17 489	9 142	471	62 536	88
	1998	249 163	178 145	36 860	23 811	10 347	985	68 670	1 22
	1999	245 501	177 209	36 841	20 921	10 530	*−7918	67 089	1 21
Indonesia	1996	212 376	35 232	102 983	71 291	2 870	− 1 009	17 479	101 98
	1997	216 369	38 226	103 912	71 294	2 937	− 2 647	21 087	109 55
	1998	211 091	42 225	95 211	70 198	3 457	6 671	18 271	115 02
	1999	206 357	49 492	90 587	62 735	3 543	− 17 224	18 764	124 74
Iran (Islamic Rep. of)	1996	225 296	848	186 138	37 676	634	2 048	3 555	129 28
	1997	230 778	717	183 246	46 221	594	10 400	3 260	117 84
	1998	233 028	818	184 977	46 629	603	11 547	3 335	117 89
	1999	236 134	936	181 841	52 930	427	*2949	3 436	124 98
Iraq	1996	31 652	...	28 581	3 022	49	...	...	5 64
	1997	59 990	...	57 096	2 844	50	*−3199	...	36 64
	1998	107 480	...	104 679	2 751	50	3 439	...	76 80
	1999	127 863	...	124 848	2 966	50	...	...	102 25
Israel	1996	224	206	4	12	2	*−805	16 972	1 78
	1997	251	231	5	12	2	239	19 753	2 36
	1998	243	225	5	11	2	830	21 506	2 78
	1999	247	232	4	9	1	*−715	20 152	2 44
Japan	1996	96 374	3 764	697	2 186	89 727	3 336	401 832	8 50
	1997	100 589	2 486	700	2 234	95 168	3 595	405 375	9 37
	1998	103 674	2 132	655	2 256	98 630	*−4606	387 818	7 49
	1999	98 936	2 272	602	2 235	93 828	*−3166	395 139	6 13
Jordan	1996	207	...	2	203	2	72	4 450	
	1997	227	...	2	224	1	*−66	4 383	
	1998	231	...	2	228	1	175	4 719	
	1999	229	...	2	226	1	64	4 615	
Kazakhstan	1996	63 407	33 761	23 137	5 878	630	...	6 705	27 21
	1997	65 883	32 009	26 005	7 311	559	...	6 369	29 10
	1998	64 684	30 804	26 191	7 161	528	...	6 397	31 90
	1999	65 656	25 743	30 425	8 962	527	*−799	5 164	35 51
Korea, Dem. People's Republic of	1996	*61925	*59990	...	...	*1935	...	*5441	*27
	1997	57 714	55 911	...	...	1 803	...	5 071	25
	1998	54 828	53 115	...	...	1 713	...	4 818	24
	1999	*50352	*48636	...	...	*1716	...	*4850	*24
Korea, Republic of	1996	21 969	2 227	...	...	19 741	1 985	158 552	17 70
	1997	22 615	2 031	...	...	20 584	2 332	179 828	26 36
	1998	25 895	1 962	...	...	23 933	1 245	167 413	33 86
	1999	29 310	1 888	...	...	27 421	1 543	179 997	33 95

Bunkers – Soutes		Unallocated	Consumption – Consommation							
Air Avion	Sea Maritime	Nondistribué	Per capita Par habitant	Total Totale	Solids Solides	Liquids Liquides	Gas Gaz	Electricity Electricité	Année	Région, pays ou zone
...	...	...	*16	*173	...	*166	...	*7	1996	Cambodge
...	...	...	*15	*177	...	*170	...	*7	1997	
...	...	...	*16	*177	...	*170	...	*7	1998	
...	...	...	*14	*182	...	*174	...	*7	1999	
...	983	37 794	703	865 593	683 339	139 223	23 134	19 897	1996	Chine
...	940	45 535	685	851 108	657 744	148 906	23 840	20 618	1997	
...	2 267	45 292	643	805 843	605 525	151 976	26 774	21 568	1998	
...	*2379	44 503	574	725 381	509 873	165 098	28 981	21 430	1999	
2 859	2 389	...	1 285	8 334	3 623	3 183	1 528	...	1996	Chine, Hong Kong
2 991	2 159	...	1 351	8 870	3 055	3 427	2 387	...	1997	RAS
2 708	2 891	...	1 693	11 252	3 800	5 213	2 240	...	1998	
2 268	3 625	...	1 984	13 335	3 420	7 446	2 470	...	1999	
...	...	...	1 116	463	...	463	...	...	1996	Chine, Macao RAS
...	...	...	1 186	497	...	497	...	...	1997	
...	...	...	1 202	512	...	512	...	...	1998	
...	...	...	1 149	499	...	499	...	...	1999	
257	90	20	2 127	1 570	12	1 558	...	...	1996	Chypre
253	98	25	2 191	1 628	13	1 615	...	...	1997	
266	98	26	2 329	1 745	18	1 726	...	...	1998	
272	154	22	2 365	1 781	21	1 760	...	...	1999	
...	...	4	389	2 107	42	844	705	517	1996	Géorgie
...	...	8	424	2 251	8	872	851	520	1997	
...	...	18	473	2 503	11	1 179	765	548	1998	
...	...	14	469	2 532	16	1 194	767	554	1999	
671	...	20 826	297	278 955	177 344	68 832	24 404	8 374	1996	Inde
676	...	19 255	296	282 632	185 157	70 845	17 489	9 142	1997	
681	...	21 493	302	293 450	186 392	72 899	23 811	10 347	1998	
*681	...	20 349	302	298 261	197 082	69 727	20 921	10 530	1999	
*619	341	31 115	488	96 807	13 183	39 958	40 796	2 870	1996	Indonésie
*645	313	33 723	476	95 868	9 070	44 055	39 806	2 937	1997	
722	339	27 808	386	78 793	8 782	42 541	24 013	3 457	1998	
*464	317	28 372	426	88 451	11 272	45 733	27 903	3 543	1999	
*5	552	9 094	1 336	87 869	1 071	*48488	37 676	634	1996	Iran (Rép. islamique d')
*5	433	7 837	1 600	97 521	955	*49379	46 593	594	1997	
*5	694	8 268	*1584	*97954	1 077	*47893	48 381	603	1998	
*5	811	9 756	1 611	101 064	1 195	*44521	54 921	427	1999	
...	...	2 428	1 143	23 575	...	20 505	3 022	49	1996	Iraq
...	...	2 733	1 131	23 961	...	21 067	2 844	50	1997	
...	...	2 821	1 122	24 413	...	21 612	2 751	50	1998	
...	...	1 721	1 070	23 892	...	20 876	2 966	50	1999	
*4	93	887	2 678	15 237	5 673	9 551	12	2	1996	Israël
*4	180	1 254	2 739	15 967	6 279	9 673	12	2	1997	
*4	153	1 391	2 778	16 586	6 724	9 848	11	2	1998	
4	148	952	2 868	17 568	6 664	10 894	9	1	1999	
5 909	4 335	17 202	3 649	458 915	90 031	216 814	62 343	89 727	1996	Japon
6 287	5 186	20 886	3 654	460 633	92 583	209 223	63 659	95 168	1997	
6 344	5 648	14 781	3 653	461 829	90 746	206 206	66 246	98 630	1998	
6 166	5 352	15 438	3 665	464 150	94 352	206 894	69 075	93 828	1999	
303	1	89	950	4 189	...	3 985	203	2	1996	Jordanie
280	2	62	954	4 333	...	4 108	224	1	1997	
226	1	80	958	4 467	...	4 238	228	1	1998	
226	4	73	935	4 476	...	4 249	226	1	1999	
343	...	82	2 668	42 472	25 359	7 764	8 719	630	1996	Kazakhstan
317	...	4 569	2 429	38 266	21 758	8 123	7 826	559	1997	
326	...	1 952	2 448	36 903	21 244	7 298	7 833	528	1998	
236	...	1 999	2 269	33 868	20 127	5 569	7 644	527	1999	
...	...	– 697	*3139	*67785	*61483	*4367	...	*1935	1996	Corée, Rép. populaire
...	...	*–649	2 900	63 175	57 302	4 069	...	1 803	1997	démocratique de
...	...	*–617	2 734	60 016	54 437	3 866	...	1 713	1998	
...	...	– 621	*2513	*55573	*49966	*3891	...	*1716	1999	
756	5 386	13 787	3 094	140 906	32 920	76 293	11 952	19 741	1996	Corée, République de
760	5 983	19 665	3 204	147 336	34 760	77 424	14 567	20 584	1997	
516	6 230	20 113	2 829	131 340	35 959	57 810	13 637	23 933	1998	
476	6 732	21 459	3 098	145 144	37 601	63 495	16 627	27 421	1999	

64
Production, trade and consumption of commercial energy
Thousand metric tons of oil equivalent and kilograms per capita [*cont.*]
Production, commerce et consommation d'énergie commerciale
Milliers de tonnes d'équivalent pétrole et kilogrammes par habitant [*suite*]

Region, country or area	Year	Primary energy production – Production d'énergie primaire					Changes in stocks Variations des stocks	Imports Importations	Exports Exportations
		Total Totale	Solids Solides	Liquids Liquides	Gas Gaz	Electricity Electricité			
Kuwait [1]	1996	114 275	...	105 600	8 675	...	...	1	88 1
	1997	114 224	...	105 579	8 645	...	− 141	1	88 4
	1998	116 472	...	107 620	8 851	...	...	1	88 2
	1999	106 843	...	98 742	8 101	...	...	1	78 5
Kyrgystan	1996	1 311	133	100	24	1 054	62	1 894	
	1997	1 233	170	85	37	940	*−133	1 540	
	1998	1 087	137	78	17	855	...	1 830	
	1999	1 274	129	77	23	1 044	*−41	1 287	
Lao People's Dem. Rep.	1996	*104	*1	...	...	*104	...	*111	
	1997	*102	*1	...	...	*101	...	*116	
	1998	*102	*1	...	...	*102	...	*123	
	1999	*102	*1	...	...	*102	...	*123	
Lebanon	1996	69	...	...	...	69	...	4 146	
	1997	63	...	...	...	63	...	4 731	
	1998	68	...	...	...	68	...	4 931	
	1999	28	...	...	...	28	...	5 191	
Malaysia	1996	68 732	58	35 341	32 891	442	*573	11 544	36 8
	1997	72 558	70	34 811	37 213	*464	*700	13 047	38 5
	1998	72 621	246	36 170	35 788	418	565	13 547	41 2
	1999	72 810	193	33 219	38 752	647	*−960	12 755	39 7
Maldives	1996	...	...	...	...	...	...	155	
	1997	...	...	...	...	...	...	177	
	1998	...	...	...	...	...	...	179	
	1999	...	...	...	...	...	...	227	
Mongolia	1996	*1828	*1828	...	...	...	...	404	*
	1997	1 687	1 687	...	...	...	...	448	
	1998	1 632	1 632	...	...	...	...	435	
	1999	1 562	1 562	...	...	...	...	463	
Myanmar	1996	2 045	28	408	1 470	140	*−244	687	
	1997	2 168	28	402	1 588	150	17	942	
	1998	3 092	29	390	2 591	82	15	1 229	1 0
	1999	4 924	58	443	4 338	85	46	1 577	2 89
Nepal	1996	103	4	...	...	99	*−7	721	
	1997	106	6	...	...	100	*−4	826	
	1998	101	11	...	...	90	...	898	
	1999	119	13	...	...	106	...	972	
Oman	1996	48 312	...	44 091	4 221	...	41	65	41 49
	1997	50 010	...	45 004	5 006	...	182	315	43 02
	1998	50 281	...	44 659	*5622	...	*−66	108	42 76
	1999	49 356	...	44 990	4 366	...	*−761	254	43 42
Pakistan	1996	21 198	1 720	2 959	14 396	2 122	...	15 121	28
	1997	21 637	1 680	2 980	15 093	1 884	...	14 799	4
	1998	21 552	1 494	2 889	15 174	1 995	...	15 759	22
	1999	22 623	1 637	2 833	16 149	2 005	...	16 002	43
Philippines	1996	*6661	524	47	...	*6090	1 395	21 236	62
	1997	*6970	511	42	...	*6417	44	22 714	58
	1998	*7077	473	41	...	*6563	*−1	21 923	17
	1999	*7356	557	47	...	*6752	379	21 554	52
Qatar	1996	34 073	...	21 296	12 776	...	*−1783	...	20 96
	1997	45 104	...	28 878	16 227	...	731	...	27 67
	1998	50 060	...	31 800	18 260	...	*−1769	...	34 72
	1999	59 636	...	31 826	27 810	...	*−1952	...	38 35
Saudi Arabia [1]	1996	500 968	...	459 459	41 509	...	− 22	...	368 05
	1997	498 299	...	455 550	42 749	...	*49	...	375 64
	1998	510 138	...	466 568	43 570	...	*136	...	387 53
	1999	471 682	...	428 597	43 085	...	− 413	21	353 28
Singapore	1996	...	...	...	...	...	...	83 839	44 72
	1997	...	...	...	...	...	452	85 583	41 39
	1998	...	...	...	...	...	*1	83 951	42 03
	1999	...	...	...	...	...	*1	82 928	40 36
Sri Lanka	1996	280	...	...	...	280	*−14	2 902	7
	1997	296	...	...	...	296	28	3 023	7
	1998	337	...	...	...	337	15	3 061	2
	1999	359	...	...	...	359	33	3 252	2

| Bunkers – Soutes | | Unallocated | Consumption – Consommation | | | | | | | |
Air Avion	Sea Maritime	Nondistribué	Per capita Par habitant	Total Totale	Solids Solides	Liquids Liquides	Gas Gaz	Electricity Electricité	Année	Région, pays ou zone
*103	554	*5378	10 631	20 134	...	11 459	8 675	...	1996	Koweït [1]
*181	662	*4587	10 356	20 505	...	11 860	8 645	...	1997	
*196	621	*3945	11 575	23 462	...	14 611	8 851	...	1998	
*206	644	*5511	10 407	21 928	...	13 827	8 101	...	1999	
...	...	17	662	3 063	458	569	982	1 054	1996	Kirghizistan
...	...	4	601	2 817	474	595	808	940	1997	
...	...	7	610	2 901	477	620	949	855	1998	
...	...	5	536	2 589	483	503	559	1 044	1999	
...	...	...	*45	*215	*1	*111	...	*104	1996	Rép. démocratique populaire lao
...	...	...	*44	*218	*1	*116	...	*101	1997	
...	...	...	*45	*226	*1	*123	...	*102	1998	
...	...	...	*44	*226	*1	*123	...	*102	1999	
*175	...	...	1 243	4 039	157	3 813	...	69	1996	Liban
*181	...	...	1 391	4 614	160	4 390	...	63	1997	
*186	...	...	1 424	4 813	86	4 659	...	68	1998	
120	...	...	1 483	5 100	*82	4 990	...	28	1999	
...	162	3 286	1 863	39 444	2 041	19 348	17 612	442	1996	Malaisie
...	156	3 319	1 977	42 832	1 928	20 752	19 688	*464	1997	
...	445	3 619	1 817	40 297	1 852	20 191	17 837	418	1998	
...	390	816	2 005	45 532	1 526	20 257	23 102	647	1999	
...	...	...	422	106	...	106	...	...	1996	Maldives
...	...	...	471	122	...	122	...	...	1997	
...	...	...	415	111	...	111	...	...	1998	
...	...	...	557	155	...	155	...	...	1999	
...	...	...	*924	*2157	*1770	387	...	...	1996	Mongolie
...	...	...	872	2 066	1 687	378	...	...	1997	
...	...	...	859	2 066	1 658	408	...	...	1998	
...	...	...	859	2 025	1 622	403	...	...	1999	
12	5	67	64	2 893	32	1 251	1 470	140	1996	Myanmar
17	4	132	63	2 941	33	1 169	1 588	150	1997	
*13	2	142	66	3 088	33	1 443	1 531	82	1998	
13	1	172	72	3 379	55	1 791	1 447	85	1999	
...	...	...	40	827	196	532	...	99	1996	Népal
...	...	...	44	936	214	622	...	100	1997	
...	...	...	46	999	237	672	...	90	1998	
...	...	...	49	1 091	293	691	...	106	1999	
131	*454	*−302	2 964	6 563	...	2 342	4 221	...	1996	Oman
36	*396	*−440	3 162	7 130	...	2 125	5 006	...	1997	
25	150	*−50	*3333	*7623	...	2 001	*5622	...	1998	
...	54	*−522	3 190	7 416	...	3 050	4 366	...	1999	
129	12	907	279	34 981	2 469	15 995	14 396	2 122	1996	Pakistan
135	18	716	273	35 095	2 262	15 856	15 093	1 884	1997	
138	15	713	275	36 217	2 159	16 890	15 174	1 995	1998	
121	15	782	277	37 273	2 267	16 852	16 149	2 005	1999	
527	162	1 469	330	23 719	2 113	15 516	...	*6090	1996	Philippines
628	128	2 957	345	25 337	2 592	16 328	...	*6417	1997	
448	218	1 927	349	26 238	2 616	17 058	...	*6563	1998	
513	241	1 548	344	25 699	3 131	15 816	...	*6752	1999	
180	...	*158	27 817	14 548	...	1 772	12 776	...	1996	Qatar
203	...	*825	29 348	15 672	...	2 022	13 650	...	1997	
185	...	*857	29 531	16 065	...	2 121	13 944	...	1998	
174	...	957	39 828	22 104	...	1 592	20 512	...	1999	
2 535	*6486	*34611	4 743	89 300	...	47 791	41 509	...	1996	Arabie saoudite [1]
2 526	*6385	*25025	4 552	88 674	...	45 925	42 749	...	1997	
*2453	*6334	*21933	4 546	91 744	...	48 174	43 570	...	1998	
2 320	*5471	*21379	4 290	89 660	...	46 574	43 085	...	1999	
1 104	15 247	11 549	3 056	11 214	*0	11 214	...	...	1996	Singapour
1 118	17 040	13 932	3 069	11 645	...	11 645	...	...	1997	
1 191	17 750	10 932	3 070	12 042	...	12 042	...	...	1998	
1 233	17 601	8 429	3 873	15 301	...	15 301	...	...	1999	
101	379	127	137	2 511	1	2 230	...	280	1996	Sri Lanka
104	273	103	147	2 732	2	2 434	...	296	1997	
90	257	138	153	2 878	1	2 540	...	337	1998	
101	231	137	162	3 088	1	2 728	...	359	1999	

64

Production, trade and consumption of commercial energy
Thousand metric tons of oil equivalent and kilograms per capita [*cont.*]
Production, commerce et consommation d'énergie commerciale
Milliers de tonnes d'équivalent pétrole et kilogrammes par habitant [*suite*]

Region, country or area	Year	Primary energy production – Production d'énergie primaire					Changes in stocks Variations des stocks	Imports Importations	Exports Exportation
		Total Totale	Solids Solides	Liquids Liquides	Gas Gaz	Electricity Electricité			
Syrian Arab Republic	1996	32 228	...	29 571	*2438	*219	− 684	566	18
	1997	32 607	...	29 037	*3346	*224	− 1 103	800	19
	1998	34 021	...	29 009	*4780	*232	− 1 075	780	18
	1999	34 521	...	29 149	*5138	*234	− 1 789	716	18
Tajikistan	1996	1 345	5	20	45	1 275	...	*2211	
	1997	1 244	5	25	35	1 179	...	*1881	
	1998	1 268	5	19	27	1 217	...	1 903	
	1999	1 383	5	19	32	1 327	...	1 893	
Thailand	1996	25 044	9 449	4 223	10 740	633	1 199	41 558	4
	1997	29 369	10 291	5 060	13 398	621	229	41 241	5
	1998	28 479	8 870	5 266	13 896	447	*−79	36 289	4
	1999	29 062	8 035	5 721	15 000	306	*−688	38 829	5
Turkey	1996	19 602	12 356	3 504	189	3 554	565	42 922	1
	1997	20 288	13 107	3 452	232	3 497	*−427	44 386	
	1998	21 939	14 490	3 226	517	3 706	*−132	45 550	1
	1999	20 999	14 358	2 944	643	3 054	*−31	46 267	1
Turkmenistan	1996	35 729	...	4 029	31 700	0	...	248	22
	1997	20 759	...	5 154	15 604	0	...	558	8
	1998	18 771	...	6 826	11 945	0	...	1 344	8
	1999	27 840	...	7 167	20 672	0	...	688	14
United Arab Emirates	1996	145 311	...	113 789	31 521		...	453	102	110
	1997	149 775	...	115 913	33 862		...	198	102	112
	1998	154 109	...	119 538	34 571		...	− 48	*102	116
	1999	144 031	...	109 732	*34299		...	286	*102	106
Uzbekistan	1996	51 688	779	7 729	42 619	561	135	3 863	8
	1997	53 499	806	8 020	44 176	497	*−481	2 541	9
	1998	59 090	801	8 179	49 615	495	...	35	4
	1999	60 033	814	8 399	50 331	489	19	8	6
Viet Nam	1996	17 463	6 876	8 714	307	1 566	497	5 884	11
	1997	20 991	7 972	10 920	553	1 546	1 049	6 138	13
	1998	22 906	8 170	12 412	819	1 504	1 698	7 076	14
	1999	24 739	6 740	15 232	1 023	1 744	*385	7 493	17
Yemen	1996	17 747	...	17 747	...	...	− 500	*200	14
	1997	18 582	...	18 582	...	...	− 691	*153	14
	1998	19 032	...	19 032	...	...	− 691	*127	15
	1999	20 887	...	20 887	...	...	− 691	*127	*157
Europe	1996	2 247 356	422 745	633 566	831 033	360 012	− 5 152	1 294 093	901 0
	1997	2 212 156	410 478	637 151	799 408	365 119	− 119	1 296 746	918 5
	1998	2 189 040	376 712	631 708	814 901	365 719	3 108	1 327 679	930 2
	1999	2 201 227	372 938	642 919	813 743	371 626	− 9 685	1 307 533	933 5
Albania	1996	1 028	26	488	21	492	...	109	
	1997	834	19	366	17	432	...	116	
	1998	821	14	368	15	423	...	184	
	1999	797	10	323	13	451	...	154	
Austria	1996	5 679	288	992	1 339	3 060	98	20 628	9
	1997	5 781	295	999	1 281	3 207	*−461	20 725	1 2
	1998	6 201	297	1 167	1 408	3 330	*−209	21 605	1 4
	1999	6 491	297	1 040	1 564	3 590	*−670	20 982	1 4
Belarus	1996	2 742	649	1 862	230	1	*−1425	24 740	3 4
	1997	2 684	631	1 824	227	2	453	26 251	2 9
	1998	2 531	464	1 832	233	2	*−120	25 552	3 7
	1999	2 784	705	1 842	236	2	131	26 219	4 9
Belgium	1996	11 754	337	...	2	11 414	248	68 308	20 0
	1997	12 741	257	...	0	12 484	65	68 555	20 0
	1998	12 367	188	...	*0	12 179	746	72 023	22 8
	1999	13 142	219	...	0	12 923	*−617	70 058	21 3
Bosnia & Herzegovina	1996	653	527	...	...	126		807	
	1997	672	543	...	...	130		832	
	1998	693	559	...	...	134		857	
	1999	714	576	...	...	138		882	
Bulgaria	1996	9 728	4 689	32	37	4 970	481	15 032	1 6
	1997	9 416	4 472	28	31	4 886	*−17	12 611	1 5
	1998	9 725	4 970	33	26	4 697	64	11 747	1 2
	1999	8 647	4 199	40	24	4 384	*−352	10 736	1 6

Air Avion	Sea Maritime	Unallocated Nondistribué	Per capita Par habitant	Total Totale	Solids Solides	Liquids Liquides	Gas Gaz	Electricity Electricité	Année	Région, pays ou zone
*98	...	*773	933	13 636	3	10 976	*2438	*219	1996	Rép. arabe syrienne
*93	...	*1012	944	14 260	3	10 688	*3346	*224	1997	
*93	...	*920	1 051	16 396	...	11 384	*4780	*232	1998	
*95	...	*1391	1 052	16 948	3	11 573	*5138	*234	1999	
...	...	20	597	3 536	50	*1167	1 044	1 275	1996	Tadjikistan
...	...	25	526	3 100	53	*1167	700	1 179	1997	
...	...	14	517	3 152	52	1 167	716	1 217	1998	
...	...	13	522	3 257	51	1 167	712	1 327	1999	
...	...	3 135	967	57 994	11 725	34 896	10 740	633	1996	Thaïlande
...	...	3 945	1 003	60 773	12 018	34 736	13 398	621	1997	
...	...	4 334	908	55 555	10 082	31 111	13 915	447	1998	
...	...	5 162	938	57 766	10 323	32 110	15 027	306	1999	
328	126	3 229	927	57 055	19 012	26 721	7 768	3 554	1996	Turquie
448	160	3 731	957	59 782	21 120	25 892	9 274	3 497	1997	
498	161	4 400	961	60 893	22 539	24 702	9 946	3 706	1998	
495	284	3 584	949	61 043	20 844	25 396	11 750	3 054	1999	
...	...	464	2 773	12 671	70	2 525	10 075	0	1996	Turkménistan
...	...	71	2 842	12 581	...	2 298	10 283	0	1997	
...	...	102	2 441	11 861	...	2 126	9 735	0	1998	
...	...	106	3 080	14 279	...	2 367	11 912	0	1999	
*310	214	*1882	13 197	32 240	...	7 004	25 236	...	1996	Emirats arabes unis
*464	207	*1735	13 345	34 430	...	7 385	27 045	...	1997	
*392	*91	*2069	12 982	35 362	...	7 058	28 304	...	1998	
*392	*91	*2056	*11974	*35180	...	7 231	*27950	...	1999	
...	...	1 584	1 952	45 152	932	5 923	37 736	561	1996	Ouzbékistan
...	...	1 661	1 922	45 277	767	6 157	37 856	497	1997	
...	...	1 377	2 205	53 040	800	6 226	45 519	495	1998	
...	...	1 739	2 177	52 160	794	6 071	44 806	489	1999	
...	...	...	154	11 583	3 891	5 818	307	1 566	1996	Viet Nam
...	...	...	170	12 742	4 322	6 321	553	1 546	1997	
...	...	− 49	180	13 707	4 313	7 070	819	1 504	1998	
...	...	− 171	192	14 839	4 409	7 664	1 023	1 744	1999	
*63	100	*524	224	3 560	...	3 560	...	...	1996	Yémen
*63	100	*121	268	4 422	...	4 422	...	...	1997	
*63	100	*92	260	4 435	...	4 435	...	...	1998	
*63	*100	1 691	*234	*4130	...	*4130	...	...	1999	
29 963	40 685	58 027	2 939	2 516 876	532 629	752 562	871 673	360 012	1996	**Europe**
31 578	44 515	55 666	2 873	2 458 743	500 406	744 690	848 529	365 119	1997	
33 573	46 065	52 962	2 865	2 450 773	479 909	750 893	854 251	365 719	1998	
36 998	44 523	62 039	2 854	2 441 368	466 543	738 992	864 206	371 626	1999	
...	...	94	286	1 043	26	504	21	492	1996	Albanie
...	...	67	237	884	19	415	17	432	1997	
...	...	87	242	918	14	466	15	423	1998	
...	...	62	284	889	10	416	13	451	1999	
256	...	327	3 060	24 662	3 426	10 706	7 470	3 060	1996	Autriche
265	...	429	3 101	25 033	3 638	10 989	7 200	3 207	1997	
279	...	897	3 143	25 432	3 643	11 053	7 407	3 330	1998	
505	127	364	3 175	25 697	3 455	11 137	7 515	3 590	1999	
...	...	1 834	2 304	23 614	1 308	8 827	13 478	1	1996	Bélarus
...	...	1 364	2 367	24 191	1 076	7 793	15 320	2	1997	
...	...	1 092	2 295	23 390	998	7 364	15 026	2	1998	
...	...	1 152	2 269	22 773	785	6 454	15 532	2	1999	
998	4 591	2 726	5 078	51 475	8 785	18 138	13 137	11 414	1996	Belgique
1 281	5 197	3 218	5 059	51 505	8 604	17 892	12 524	12 484	1997	
1 512	5 563	1 158	5 150	52 602	8 667	17 888	13 869	12 179	1998	
1 482	4 494	3 675	5 163	52 800	7 575	17 471	14 832	12 923	1999	
...	...	...	350	1 460	527	558	249	126	1996	Bosnie−Herzégovine
...	...	...	402	1 504	543	575	257	130	1997	
...	...	...	424	1 550	559	592	265	134	1998	
...	...	...	415	1 596	576	610	273	138	1999	
...	238	1 098	2 549	21 319	6 795	4 354	5 199	4 970	1996	Bulgarie
25	9	898	2 356	19 586	7 082	3 505	4 113	4 886	1997	
21	71	929	2 313	19 096	7 187	3 733	3 479	4 697	1998	
51	8	743	2 105	17 281	6 295	3 615	2 987	4 384	1999	

64
Production, trade and consumption of commercial energy
Thousand metric tons of oil equivalent and kilograms per capita [*cont.*]
Production, commerce et consommation d'énergie commerciale
Milliers de tonnes d'équivalent pétrole et kilogrammes par habitant [*suite*]

Region, country or area	Year	Primary energy production – Production d'énergie primaire					Changes in stocks Variations des stocks	Imports Importations	Exports Exportations
		Total Totale	Solids Solides	Liquids Liquides	Gas Gaz	Electricity Electricité			
Croatia	1996	4 201	45	1 913	1 622	622	145	5 340	1 596
	1997	4 026	34	1 977	1 560	456	*−19	5 219	1 351
	1998	3 920	36	1 989	1 426	470	*−61	5 539	1 465
	1999	3 647	10	1 661	1 408	567	*−21	6 162	1 651
Czech Republic	1996	31 444	27 529	152	202	3 561	636	19 350	7 734
	1997	30 372	26 587	163	182	3 440	572	18 783	7 048
	1998	28 779	24 809	179	188	3 602	222	18 899	6 983
	1999	25 846	21 792	183	195	3 677	*−973	17 761	6 392
Denmark	1996	18 847	38	10 131	8 566	112	*−1058	17 372	11 648
	1997	19 729	14	11 371	8 170	174	1 424	17 446	14 323
	1998	18 312	...	11 443	6 617	252	*−445	14 775	14 352
	1999	21 609	...	14 479	6 859	270	*−1019	13 561	17 944
Estonia	1996	3 257	3 257	...	...	0	*−84	2 706	393
	1997	3 161	3 161	...	...	0	*−111	3 072	790
	1998	2 846	2 845	...	...	0	*−55	2 892	596
	1999	2 540	2 540	...	...	0	*−180	2 779	700
Faeroe Islands	1996	*7	...	...	...	*7	...	*210	...
	1997	*7	...	...	...	*7	...	*211	...
	1998	*7	...	...	...	*7	...	*213	...
	1999	*7	...	...	...	*7	...	*215	...
Finland	1996	8 320	2 216	...	...	6 104	*−1000	21 224	4 699
	1997	9 134	2 627	...	...	6 508	503	21 437	3 839
	1998	7 424	424	...	...	7 000	*−1257	20 942	4 457
	1999	9 661	2 043	519	...	7 100	*−1285	20 270	4 783
France [2]	1996	121 151	5 360	3 307	2 676	109 809	*−1830	149 811	16 464
	1997	119 160	4 501	3 202	2 365	109 092	705	147 664	17 689
	1998	115 767	3 790	2 861	2 102	107 014	*−1206	159 212	19 128
	1999	118 079	3 559	3 004	1 919	109 598	1 156	154 545	17 160
Germany	1996	137 969	73 504	2 877	17 348	44 240	*−3495	226 346	17 844
	1997	136 628	70 140	2 807	17 159	46 522	1 512	225 369	18 101
	1998	128 245	64 016	2 937	16 863	44 429	*−705	229 207	18 130
	1999	127 640	62 058	2 749	18 050	44 783	*−2155	221 594	20 574
Gibraltar	1996	...	...	...	...	...	...	*1719	...
	1997	...	...	...	...	...	...	2 156	...
	1998	...	...	...	...	...	...	*2167	...
	1999	...	...	...	...	...	...	*2191	...
Greece	1996	8 727	7 783	501	50	392	335	23 031	3 680
	1997	8 582	7 709	458	49	367	275	22 660	2 703
	1998	8 691	7 976	317	44	355	941	24 170	2 227
	1999	8 622	8 129	38	3	453	*−610	23 588	2 840
Hungary	1996	13 705	3 123	2 863	4 000	3 719	757	16 024	1 688
	1997	13 326	3 214	2 712	3 735	3 664	596	15 635	1 603
	1998	12 551	3 021	2 579	3 297	3 654	761	16 413	1 201
	1999	11 544	3 000	2 274	2 576	3 695	*−8	16 084	1 629
Iceland	1996	712	...	...	...	712	*−28	798	...
	1997	771	...	...	...	771	*−12	794	...
	1998	1 048	...	...	...	1 048	4	831	...
	1999	1 113	...	...	...	1 113	32	853	...
Ireland	1996	3 791	1 261	...	2 410	119	154	9 516	939
	1997	2 978	740	...	2 119	119	*−57	10 890	1 255
	1998	2 530	813	...	1 564	152	7	11 997	1 144
	1999	2 670	1 252	...	1 275	143	308	12 970	1 014
Italy [3]	1996	31 008	69	5 459	18 194	7 287	1 490	150 420	17 625
	1997	30 896	24	5 956	17 544	7 372	*−996	152 838	19 852
	1998	30 715	44	5 629	17 309	7 732	*−379	160 227	21 289
	1999	29 519	27	5 005	16 213	8 275	*−972	161 647	18 415
Latvia	1996	249	89	...	...	160	243	3 560	111
	1997	343	89	...	...	254	*−105	2 873	63
	1998	385	14	...	...	371	58	3 029	125
	1999	325	87	...	...	237	*−171	2 433	190
Lithuania	1996	3 887	18	155	...	3 714	81	8 172	2 475
	1997	3 437	20	212	...	3 204	25	8 899	3 405
	1998	3 906	14	277	...	3 615	*−155	9 669	4 333
	1999	2 899	19	232	...	2 648	*−183	7 183	2 633

Bunkers – Soutes			Consumption – Consommation							
Air Avion	Sea Maritime	Unallocated Nondistribué	Per capita Par habitant	Total Totale	Solids Solides	Liquids Liquides	Gas Gaz	Electricity Electricité	Année	Région, pays ou zone
56	37	1 084	1 474	6 624	150	3 442	2 410	622	1996	Croatie
59	24	989	1 496	6 841	296	3 591	2 498	456	1997	
63	26	931	1 563	7 035	277	3 887	2 401	470	1998	
37	22	759	1 616	7 361	243	4 116	2 435	567	1999	
133	...	1 673	3 938	40 618	22 366	6 307	8 384	3 561	1996	République tchèque
125	...	1 290	3 894	40 120	22 002	6 151	8 526	3 440	1997	
118	...	1 299	3 794	39 056	20 413	6 496	8 545	3 602	1998	
115	...	1 333	3 573	36 741	18 131	6 340	8 594	3 677	1999	
709	1 518	*−133	4 473	23 536	8 879	8 171	6 372	112	1996	Danemark
697	1 507	*−235	3 683	19 459	6 584	7 974	4 727	174	1997	
712	1 400	*−29	3 225	17 097	5 500	7 552	3 794	252	1998	
763	1 316	*−435	3 121	16 601	4 539	7 730	4 062	270	1999	
17	93	...	3 774	5 544	3 532	1 298	714	0	1996	Estonie
21	102	...	3 725	5 432	3 520	1 217	694	0	1997	
13	108	...	3 500	5 076	3 217	1 200	659	0	1998	
18	185	...	3 188	4 596	2 942	1 014	640	0	1999	
...	...	...	*4917	*216	...	*210	...	*7	1996	Iles Féroé
...	...	...	*4940	*217	...	*211	...	*7	1997	
...	...	...	*4879	*220	...	*213	...	*7	1998	
...	...	...	*4822	*222	...	*215	...	*7	1999	
314	380	*−2410	5 378	27 561	7 487	10 671	3 299	6 104	1996	Finlande
326	413	*−1330	5 218	26 820	6 966	10 115	3 232	6 508	1997	
334	528	*−1229	4 955	25 533	4 765	10 059	3 709	7 000	1998	
356	566	*−990	5 131	26 501	5 467	10 223	3 711	7 100	1999	
4 138	2 749	9 010	4 117	240 430	16 928	74 713	38 981	109 809	1996	France [2]
4 247	2 993	8 851	3 962	232 339	14 758	72 727	35 762	109 092	1997	
4 528	2 894	8 483	4 095	241 151	17 693	76 367	40 077	107 014	1998	
5 160	2 926	7 898	4 030	238 325	15 686	74 642	38 400	109 598	1999	
5 871	2 040	5 338	4 112	336 716	90 632	118 937	82 907	44 240	1996	Allemagne
6 064	2 166	6 353	3 995	327 801	86 301	116 501	78 478	46 522	1997	
6 241	2 051	8 427	3 941	323 309	83 847	114 731	80 302	44 429	1998	
6 699	2 089	8 809	3 817	313 219	79 414	109 501	79 521	44 783	1999	
*4	*1654	...	*2249	*61	...	*61	...	...	1996	Gibraltar
2	2 124	...	*1087	*29	...	*29	...	...	1997	
*3	*2128	...	*1306	*35	...	*35	...	...	1998	
*3	*2129	...	*2156	*58	...	*58	...	...	1999	
818	3 165	*−1025	2 366	24 784	8 523	15 815	54	392	1996	Grèce
792	3 174	*−1030	2 412	25 328	8 556	16 217	189	367	1997	
831	3 542	*−1058	2 508	26 378	8 769	16 449	805	355	1998	
933	3 147	*−1460	2 597	27 360	8 647	16 906	1 354	453	1999	
194	...	1 677	2 493	25 413	4 191	6 133	11 370	3 719	1996	Hongrie
185	...	1 708	2 449	24 870	4 062	6 349	10 795	3 664	1997	
193	...	1 895	2 463	24 914	4 007	6 384	10 870	3 654	1998	
207	...	1 394	2 424	24 405	3 822	6 217	10 671	3 695	1999	
85	38	...	5 260	1 415	64	639	...	712	1996	Islande
93	47	...	5 305	1 438	56	611	...	771	1997	
110	57	...	6 232	1 708	66	594	...	1 048	1998	
119	52	...	6 366	1 763	57	593	...	1 113	1999	
345	160	13	3 226	11 696	3 105	5 524	2 948	119	1996	Irlande
414	152	64	3 289	12 040	3 111	5 728	3 082	119	1997	
427	159	*−32	3 460	12 821	3 095	6 457	3 116	152	1998	
505	173	43	3 631	13 597	2 738	7 336	3 380	143	1999	
2 631	2 297	*−1287	2 764	158 673	11 290	88 878	51 218	7 287	1996	Italie [3]
2 723	2 391	*−3335	2 834	163 098	11 229	91 701	52 796	7 372	1997	
2 889	2 634	599	2 845	163 910	11 225	88 109	56 844	7 732	1998	
3 289	2 425	605	2 903	167 404	11 807	85 241	62 082	8 275	1999	
...	...	...	1 387	3 455	221	2 101	973	160	1996	Latvie
...	...	...	1 320	3 258	168	1 653	1 184	254	1997	
...	...	...	1 319	3 231	133	1 578	1 148	371	1998	
...	...	...	1 126	2 738	96	1 304	1 100	237	1999	
33	...	*−452	2 674	9 921	255	3 541	2 411	3 714	1996	Lettonie
32	62	*−429	2 494	9 241	198	3 613	2 226	3 204	1997	
29	31	*−292	2 601	9 629	168	3 897	1 950	3 615	1998	
27	74	*−87	2 059	7 619	139	2 802	2 030	2 648	1999	

64
Production, trade and consumption of commercial energy
Thousand metric tons of oil equivalent and kilograms per capita [*cont.*]
Production, commerce et consommation d'énergie commerciale
Milliers de tonnes d'équivalent pétrole et kilogrammes par habitant [*suite*]

Region, country or area	Year	Primary energy production – Production d'énergie primaire					Changes in stocks	Imports	Exports
		Total Totale	Solids Solides	Liquids Liquides	Gas Gaz	Electricity Electricité	Variations des stocks	Imports Importations	Exports Exportations
Luxembourg	1996	75	...	...	...	75	16	3 018	5
	1997	81	...	...	...	81	*−8	2 915	5
	1998	90	...	...	...	90	36	2 964	17
	1999	69	...	...	...	69	*−47	3 046	19
Malta	1996	...	...	...	...	...	...	*966	...
	1997	...	...	...	...	...	...	*991	...
	1998	...	...	...	...	...	...	*1083	...
	1999	...	...	...	...	...	...	*1165	...
Netherlands	1996	80 099	...	3 175	75 794	1 130	190	99 301	87 180
	1997	70 930	...	3 000	67 253	677	1 103	104 781	83 772
	1998	67 747	...	2 738	63 950	1 060	*−442	107 578	85 212
	1999	63 746	...	2 611	60 071	1 064	1 681	107 309	82 579
Norway [4]	1996	209 774	154	153 908	46 734	8 977	1 632	4 847	184 261
	1997	211 677	259	153 690	48 045	9 683	*−43	5 350	189 928
	1998	205 697	220	147 294	48 066	10 117	151	5 528	183 661
	1999	209 886	328	149 773	49 184	10 601	*−15	5 313	185 286
Poland	1996	95 860	91 714	317	3 491	337	437	27 118	19 083
	1997	95 647	91 467	289	3 562	329	4 033	29 260	20 403
	1998	83 191	78 845	360	3 612	374	*−582	29 851	19 820
	1999	79 558	75 303	434	3 449	371	*−649	28 768	17 369
Portugal	1996	1 330	...	...	...	1 330	*−226	17 926	2 055
	1997	1 186	...	...	...	1 186	308	19 046	1 983
	1998	1 187	...	...	...	1 187	*−154	20 438	1 729
	1999	744	...	...	...	744	469	22 725	1 153
Republic of Moldova	1996	31	...	...	...	31	*−156	4 574	...
	1997	33	...	...	...	33	106	4 725	...
	1998	7	...	...	...	7	*−112	4 015	...
	1999	7	...	...	...	7	*−118	2 715	...
Romania	1996	29 897	7 531	6 876	13 773	1 717	*−61	18 550	3 685
	1997	27 836	6 229	6 776	11 916	2 915	1 094	17 490	2 797
	1998	25 588	4 844	6 579	11 157	3 009	*−450	14 800	3 157
	1999	24 732	4 199	6 404	11 200	2 930	*−690	9 923	2 081
Russian Federation	1996	971 681	101 021	299 797	529 109	41 754	343	21 369	368 411
	1997	950 054	96 397	304 172	507 593	41 892	*−12855	22 548	376 968
	1998	959 728	91 081	301 707	525 712	41 228	2 492	21 846	382 805
	1999	973 124	98 095	303 542	525 776	45 711	*−2506	16 344	382 187
Serbia and Montenegro	1996	10 818	8 193	1 031	605	989	...	3 615	...
	1997	11 228	8 668	980	620	961	...	4 501	...
	1998	12 454	9 398	1 234	713	1 109	...	4 168	140
	1999	9 932	7 093	1 031	658	1 150	...	3 157	...
Slovakia	1996	4 793	1 121	71	272	3 329	207	15 304	1 968
	1997	4 653	1 146	64	250	3 193	31	15 012	2 188
	1998	4 808	1 157	60	224	3 367	*−224	15 101	2 407
	1999	5 182	1 097	66	184	3 834	*−577	15 400	2 896
Slovenia	1996	2 557	1 037	1	12	1 507	31	3 741	7
	1997	2 540	952	1	11	1 576	30	3 987	7
	1998	2 544	923	1	8	1 613	*−51	3 789	112
	1999	2 422	868	1	5	1 547	121	4 123	235
Spain	1996	29 101	9 384	801	635	18 282	*−605	79 031	5 028
	1997	27 974	9 318	670	383	17 603	*−1458	84 613	4 772
	1998	28 584	8 743	873	375	18 594	1 984	93 090	6 323
	1999	27 097	8 267	652	392	17 785	1 429	99 044	4 487
Sweden	1996	24 101	297	*4	...	23 801	*−332	29 347	9 116
	1997	24 478	266	...	...	24 212	428	29 147	9 749
	1998	25 967	331	...	...	25 636	702	29 131	8 674
	1999	25 548	255	...	...	25 294	*−1089	27 950	9 349
Switzerland [5]	1996	9 220	...	...	...	9 220	*−16	15 509	664
	1997	9 733	...	...	...	9 733	102	15 740	522
	1998	9 820	...	...	...	9 820	19	16 178	473
	1999	10 356	...	...	...	10 356	*−597	15 300	558
TFYR of Macedonia	1996	2 002	1 929	...	...	73	*−6	1 293	37
	1997	1 886	1 809	...	...	77	...	1 079	5
	1998	2 301	2 208	...	...	93	90	1 222	34
	1999	2 111	1 991	...	...	119	*−104	1 055	81

Bunkers – Soutes			Consumption – Consommation							
Air Avion	Sea Maritime	Unallocated Nondistribué	Per capita Par habitant	Total Totale	Solids Solides	Liquids Liquides	Gas Gaz	Electricity Electricité	Année	Région, pays ou zone
206	...	...	6 888	2 865	485	1 625	679	75	1996	Luxembourg
252	...	...	6 525	2 747	312	1 658	696	81	1997	
284	...	...	6 380	2 718	205	1 719	703	90	1998	
333	...	...	6 503	2 809	210	1 802	729	69	1999	
*52	*30	...	*2371	*885	*185	*699	...	...	1996	Malte
*52	*30	...	*2417	*909	*185	*724	...	...	1997	
54	*33	...	*2642	*996	*191	*805	...	...	1998	
*54	*34	...	*2841	*1077	*192	*884	...	...	1999	
2 705	11 646	*−9115	5 588	86 794	9 239	34 981	41 444	1 130	1996	Pays–Bas
2 930	12 354	*−6290	5 243	81 842	8 898	33 097	39 170	677	1997	
3 191	12 446	*−7429	5 243	82 347	8 879	33 660	38 748	1 060	1998	
3 314	12 867	*−7103	4 915	77 717	7 289	31 015	38 350	1 064	1999	
57	775	*−22	6 373	27 919	1 026	8 738	9 178	8 977	1996	Norvège [4]
131	964	*−757	6 085	26 803	1 033	9 287	6 800	9 683	1997	
129	901	*−572	6 083	26 955	1 048	8 916	6 874	10 117	1998	
570	861	*−256	6 444	28 754	1 059	11 694	5 399	10 601	1999	
382	224	1 395	2 627	101 456	74 520	16 097	10 502	337	1996	Pologne
262	153	1 193	2 558	98 862	71 303	16 822	10 408	329	1997	
258	268	1 150	2 383	92 128	64 383	17 123	10 248	374	1998	
257	549	644	2 332	90 155	61 591	18 255	9 939	371	1999	
469	507	829	1 574	15 622	3 398	10 894	...	1 330	1996	Portugal
482	504	772	1 627	16 183	3 497	11 403	96	1 186	1997	
485	388	1 452	1 778	17 723	3 139	12 622	775	1 187	1998	
536	598	1 299	1 944	19 415	3 820	12 694	2 157	744	1999	
...	...	...	1 100	4 761	523	952	3 255	31	1996	Rép. de Moldova
...	...	...	1 273	4 652	263	878	3 478	33	1997	
...	...	...	1 132	4 133	259	721	3 145	7	1998	
...	...	...	779	2 840	119	459	2 255	7	1999	
10	...	2 778	1 859	42 034	9 892	10 994	19 431	1 717	1996	Roumanie
124	...	2 261	1 732	39 050	9 144	11 042	15 949	2 915	1997	
105	...	1 792	1 590	35 785	7 411	10 432	14 933	3 009	1998	
131	...	1 959	1 388	31 175	6 156	8 349	13 740	2 930	1999	
...	...	23 763	4 065	600 533	106 590	108 981	343 209	41 754	1996	Fédération de Russie
...	...	22 897	3 981	585 592	96 333	105 788	341 579	41 892	1997	
...	...	17 058	3 953	579 219	90 641	106 413	340 936	41 228	1998	
...	...	21 119	4 034	588 669	92 821	105 225	344 912	45 711	1999	
57	...	813	1 282	13 563	8 237	1 840	2 497	989	1996	Serbie–et–Monténégro
98	...	704	1 408	14 928	8 706	2 782	2 480	961	1997	
68	...	1 032	1 449	15 383	9 425	2 519	2 330	1 109	1998	
186	...	679	1 150	12 224	7 175	2 285	1 614	1 150	1999	
...	...	1 294	3 094	16 628	4 987	2 137	6 176	3 329	1996	Slovaquie
...	...	1 290	3 001	16 156	4 659	2 039	6 266	3 193	1997	
...	...	1 153	3 074	16 574	4 463	2 377	6 367	3 367	1998	
...	...	1 145	3 173	17 117	4 749	2 089	6 444	3 834	1999	
18	...	61	3 105	6 182	1 208	2 657	810	1 507	1996	Slovénie
19	...	66	3 224	6 406	1 281	2 665	884	1 576	1997	
19	...	54	3 126	6 200	1 287	2 389	911	1 613	1998	
21	...	46	3 083	6 122	1 226	2 400	949	1 547	1999	
2 150	4 727	7 968	2 263	88 865	18 370	42 443	9 770	18 282	1996	Espagne
2 322	5 830	7 465	2 382	93 656	17 994	45 285	12 775	17 603	1997	
2 450	6 138	6 515	2 496	98 265	17 264	49 238	13 168	18 594	1998	
2 535	5 990	6 734	2 663	104 965	20 539	51 619	15 022	17 785	1999	
431	1 131	1 340	4 724	41 762	3 059	14 093	809	23 801	1996	Suède
446	1 341	1 064	4 589	40 598	2 511	13 076	799	24 212	1997	
451	1 601	1 546	4 759	42 124	2 534	13 163	792	25 636	1998	
481	1 543	1 508	4 707	41 707	2 520	13 100	794	25 294	1999	
1 287	14	46	3 158	22 734	146	10 725	2 642	9 220	1996	Suisse [5]
1 343	13	*−82	3 252	23 575	111	11 180	2 551	9 733	1997	
1 440	11	*−17	3 320	24 072	92	11 535	2 626	9 820	1998	
1 466	12	*−13	3 342	24 229	97	11 056	2 720	10 356	1999	
18	...	*−23	1 655	3 269	2 011	1 186	...	73	1996	L'ex–Rép. yougoslave
21	...	12	1 466	2 927	1 879	970	...	77	1997	de Macédoine
17	...	23	1 673	3 359	2 385	861	20	93	1998	
*37	...	*0	1 563	3 152	2 160	837	37	119	1999	

64
Production, trade and consumption of commercial energy
Thousand metric tons of oil equivalent and kilograms per capita [cont.]
Production, commerce et consommation d'énergie commerciale
Milliers de tonnes d'équivalent pétrole et kilogrammes par habitant [suite]

Region, country or area	Year	Primary energy production – Production d'énergie primaire					Changes in stocks	Imports	Exports
		Total Totale	Solids Solides	Liquids Liquides	Gas Gaz	Electricity Electricité	Variations des stocks	Imports Importations	Exports Exportations
Ukraine	1996	81 810	39 012	4 102	17 167	21 529	...	91 583	4 71
	1997	82 255	39 613	4 138	16 909	21 595	...	78 235	4 10
	1998	81 381	39 715	3 904	16 756	21 006	...	70 841	3 56
	1999	82 895	42 582	3 804	16 682	19 827	*−18	76 068	4 02
United Kingdom	1996	275 349	30 545	132 750	86 746	25 308	*−2356	71 780	101 87
	1997	275 285	29 278	131 295	88 427	26 284	2 657	72 289	103 57
	1998	280 482	24 956	135 346	93 236	26 944	1 438	73 905	107 44
	1999	285 523	22 339	141 212	95 806	26 166	611	75 259	115 87
Oceania	**1996**	**208 965**	**135 798**	**34 105**	**33 432**	**5 630**	**− 783**	**31 822**	**115 74**
	1997	**218 694**	**145 102**	**34 328**	**33 644**	**5 621**	**1 988**	**32 749**	**122 46**
	1998	**232 779**	**155 842**	**36 999**	**34 161**	**5 777**	**368**	**32 613**	**134 10**
	1999	**230 148**	**157 961**	**30 937**	**35 438**	**5 812**	**− 4 166**	**39 244**	**137 96**
American Samoa	1996	...	...	...	...	...	...	*186	...
	1997	...	...	...	...	...	...	*186	...
	1998	...	...	...	...	...	...	*186	...
	1999	...	...	...	...	...	...	*182	...
Australia	1996	191 686	133 798	27 977	28 525	1 385	*−558	22 481	109 36
	1997	200 690	143 212	27 579	28 415	1 483	2 115	23 263	115 909
	1998	215 784	153 998	30 846	29 552	1 389	428	22 676	127 77
	1999	212 430	155 880	24 984	30 099	1 466	*−4576	29 020	131 638
Cook Islands	1996	...	...	...	...	...	...	*15	
	1997	...	...	...	...	...	...	*15	
	1998	...	...	...	...	...	...	*15	
	1999	...	...	...	...	...	...	*19	...
Fiji	1996	*37	...	...	...	*37	...	*416	*12
	1997	*37	...	...	...	*37	...	*409	*11
	1998	*37	...	...	...	*37	...	*377	*10
	1999	*37	...	...	...	*37	...	*364	*9
French Polynesia	1996	12	...	...	...	12	...	*230	..
	1997	12	...	...	...	12	...	*230	..
	1998	13	...	...	...	13	...	*230	
	1999	8	...	...	...	8	...	*217	
Guam	1996	...	...	...	...	...	...	*1465	
	1997	...	...	...	...	...	...	*1465	
	1998	...	...	...	...	...	...	*1476	
	1999	...	...	...	...	...	...	*1463	
Kiribati	1996	...	...	...	...	...	...	*7	
	1997	...	...	...	...	...	...	*7	
	1998	...	...	...	...	...	...	*7	
	1999	...	...	...	...	...	...	*8	
Nauru	1996	...	...	...	...	...	...	*50	
	1997	...	...	...	...	...	...	*50	
	1998	...	...	...	...	...	...	*50	
	1999	...	...	...	...	...	...	*50	..
New Caledonia	1996	34	...	...	...	34	...	*567	*12
	1997	31	...	...	...	31	...	*567	*12
	1998	34	...	...	...	34	...	*568	*12
	1999	40	...	...	...	40	...	*559	*12
New Zealand	1996	13 028	2 000	2 124	4 829	4 075	*−224	4 990	2 287
	1997	13 817	1 889	2 785	5 151	3 992	*−127	5 132	2 502
	1998	12 851	1 845	2 249	4 531	4 226	*−61	5 630	2 339
	1999	13 540	2 081	2 019	5 261	4 179	409	5 951	2 338
Niue	1996	...	...	...	...	...	...	*1	...
	1997	...	...	...	...	...	...	*1	...
	1998	...	...	...	...	...	...	*1	...
	1999	...	...	...	...	...	...	*1	...
Palau	1996	*3	...	...	...	*3	...	*98	...
	1997	*3	...	...	...	*3	...	*96	...
	1998	*3	...	...	...	*3	...	*97	...
	1999	*3	...	...	...	*3	...	*96	...
Papua New Guinea	1996	*4164	...	*4004	*78	82	...	*724	*3964
	1997	*4103	...	*3964	*78	61	...	*736	*3919
	1998	*4056	...	*3904	*78	74	...	*709	*3869
	1999	*4090	...	*3934	*78	78	...	*716	*3880

Bunkers – Soutes			Consumption – Consommation							
Air Avion	Sea Maritime	Unallocated Nondistribué	Per capita Par habitant	Total Totale	Solids Solides	Liquids Liquides	Gas Gaz	Electricity Electricité	Année	Région, pays ou zone
771	...	1 104	3 249	166 804	45 263	17 188	82 823	21 529	1996	Ukraine
658	...	1 041	3 033	154 687	43 551	15 790	73 751	21 595	1997	
684	...	1 050	2 936	146 920	43 711	16 058	66 145	21 006	1998	
679	...	1 052	3 058	153 227	46 578	15 860	70 962	19 827	1999	
4 751	2 670	6 228	3 979	233 964	45 000	76 805	86 852	25 308	1996	Royaume – Uni
5 091	2 963	5 158	3 866	228 134	39 977	74 646	87 228	26 284	1997	
5 637	3 086	4 997	3 913	231 783	38 351	75 241	91 247	26 944	1998	
6 133	2 337	9 363	3 806	226 466	35 819	75 431	89 050	26 166	1999	
3 084	**1 477**	**− 145**	**4 220**	**121 406**	**48 347**	**43 837**	**23 593**	**5 630**	**1996**	**Oceanie**
3 183	**1 426**	**1 850**	**4 172**	**120 534**	**50 227**	**40 654**	**24 033**	**5 621**	**1997**	
3 398	**1 286**	**2 317**	**4 192**	**123 919**	**52 975**	**40 851**	**24 315**	**5 777**	**1998**	
3 489	**1 359**	**2 986**	**4 269**	**127 763**	**54 151**	**42 212**	**25 587**	**5 812**	**1999**	
...	*91	...	*1605	*95	...	*95	...	...	1996	Samoa américaines
...	*91	...	*1552	*95	...	*95	...	...	1997	
...	*91	...	*1503	*95	...	*95	...	...	1998	
...	*86	...	*1473	*96	...	*96	...	...	1999	
2 029	871	*−17	5 597	102 480	46 846	35 562	18 687	1 385	1996	Australie
2 102	805	1 970	5 455	101 052	48 643	32 122	18 804	1 483	1997	
2 325	708	2 308	5 601	104 912	51 571	32 245	19 706	1 389	1998	
2 336	810	2 921	5 720	108 320	52 857	33 749	20 249	1 466	1999	
*8	...	...	*359	*7	...	*7	...	...	1996	Iles Cook
*8	...	...	*399	*7	...	*7	...	...	1997	
*8	...	...	*422	*7	...	*7	...	...	1998	
*9	...	...	*578	*9	...	*9	...	...	1999	
*26	*29	...	*358	*277	*15	*225	...	*37	1996	Fidji
*26	*29	...	*344	*271	*15	*219	...	*37	1997	
*21	*27	...	*329	*262	*14	*211	...	*37	1998	
*19	*27	...	*323	*260	*13	*210	...	*37	1999	
*5	*38	...	*907	*199	...	*187	...	12	1996	Polynésie française
*5	*38	...	*895	*199	...	*187	...	12	1997	
*5	*38	...	*894	*200	...	*187	...	13	1998	
*4	*32	...	*826	*188	...	*181	...	8	1999	
*11	*90	...	*8910	*1363	...	*1363	...	...	1996	Guam
*11	*90	...	*8739	*1363	...	*1363	...	...	1997	
*11	*90	...	*9225	*1374	...	*1374	...	...	1998	
*11	*90	...	*8955	*1361	...	*1361	...	...	1999	
...	...	...	*92	*7	...	*7	...	...	1996	Kiribati
...	...	...	*89	*7	...	*7	...	...	1997	
...	...	...	*88	*7	...	*7	...	...	1998	
...	...	...	*100	*8	...	*8	...	...	1999	
*5	...	...	*4093	*45	...	*45	...	...	1996	Nauru
*5	...	...	*4093	*45	...	*45	...	...	1997	
*5	...	...	*3752	*45	...	*45	...	...	1998	
*6	...	...	*3666	*44	...	*44	...	...	1999	
*17	*9	...	*2856	*563	*118	*411	...	34	1996	Nouvelle – Calédonie
*17	*9	...	*2785	*560	*118	*411	...	31	1997	
18	*9	...	*2757	*562	*116	*413	...	34	1998	
*18	*10	...	*2716	*559	*112	*407	...	40	1999	
540	332	*−132	4 097	15 217	1 367	4 946	4 828	4 075	1996	Nouvelle – Zélande
563	347	*−127	4 199	15 791	1 450	5 197	5 151	3 992	1997	
561	306	8	4 042	15 327	1 274	5 296	4 531	4 226	1998	
641	285	45	4 139	15 772	1 169	5 164	5 260	4 179	1999	
...	...	...	*507	*1	...	*1	...	...	1996	Nioué
...	...	...	*507	*1	...	*1	...	...	1997	
...	...	...	*507	*1	...	*1	...	...	1998	
...	...	...	*507	*1	...	*1	...	...	1999	
*15	...	...	*4703	*85	...	*82	...	*3	1996	Palaos
*15	...	...	*4590	*83	...	*80	...	*3	1997	
*15	...	...	*4402	*84	...	*81	...	*3	1998	
*14	...	...	*4404	*84	...	*81	...	*3	1999	
*21	*3	*4	*204	*896	*1	*736	*78	82	1996	Papouasie – Nouvelle – Guinée
*23	*3	*7	*211	*886	*1	*747	*78	61	1997	
*21	*3	*1	*189	*871	*1	*719	*78	74	1998	
*21	*3	*20	*188	*882	*1	*726	*78	78	1999	

64

Production, trade and consumption of commercial energy

Thousand metric tons of oil equivalent and kilograms per capita [cont.]

Production, commerce et consommation d'énergie commerciale

Milliers de tonnes d'équivalent pétrole et kilogrammes par habitant [suite]

Region, country or area	Year	Primary energy production – Production d'énergie primaire					Changes in stocks Variations des stocks	Imports Importations	Exports Exportations
		Total Totale	Solids Solides	Liquids Liquides	Gas Gaz	Electricity Electricité			
Samoa	1996	*2	...	...	...	*2	...	*44	...
	1997	*2	...	...	...	*2	...	*44	...
	1998	*2	...	...	...	*2	...	*44	...
	1999	*2	...	...	...	*2	...	*46	...
Solomon Islands	1996	...	...	...	...	...	...	*55	...
	1997	...	...	...	...	...	...	*55	...
	1998	...	...	...	...	...	...	*55	...
	1999	...	...	...	...	...	...	*57	...
Tonga	1996	...	...	...	...	...	...	*42	...
	1997	...	...	...	...	...	...	43	...
	1998	...	...	...	...	...	...	42	...
	1999	...	...	...	...	...	...	*43	...
Vanuatu	1996	...	...	...	...	...	...	28	...
	1997	...	...	...	...	...	...	29	...
	1998	...	...	...	...	...	...	27	...
	1999	...	...	...	...	...	...	*27	...
Wake Island	1996	...	...	...	...	...	...	*421	...
	1997	...	...	...	...	...	...	*421	...
	1998	...	...	...	...	...	...	*421	...
	1999	...	...	...	...	...	...	*424	...

Source:

United Nations Statistics Division, New York, "Energy Statistics Yearbook 1999" and the energy statistics database.

1   Including part of the Neutral Zone.
2   Including Monaco.
3   Including San Marino.
4   Including Svalbard and Jan Mayen Islands.
5   Including Liechtenstein.

Source:

Organisation des Nations Unies, Division de statistique, New York, "Annuaire des statistique de l'énergie 1999" et la base de données pour les statistiques énergétiques.

1   Y compris une partie de la Zone Neutrale.
2   Y compris Monaco.
3   Y compris Saint–Marin.
4   Y compris îles Svalbard et Jan Mayen.
5   Y compris Liechtenstein.

Bunkers – Soutes			Consumption – Consommation							
Air Avion	Sea Maritime	Unallocated Nondistribué	Per capita Par habitant	Total Totale	Solids Solides	Liquids Liquides	Gas Gaz	Electricity Electricité	Année	Région, pays ou zone
...	...	...	*294	*46	...	*44	...	*2	1996	Samoa
...	...	...	*294	*46	...	*44	...	*2	1997	
...	...	...	*277	*46	...	*44	...	*2	1998	
...	...	...	*287	*49	...	*46	...	*2	1999	
*2	...	...	*136	*53	...	*53	...	...	1996	Iles Salomon
*2	...	...	*132	*53	...	*53	...	...	1997	
*2	...	...	*127	*53	...	*53	...	...	1998	
*2	...	...	*128	*55	...	*55	...	...	1999	
*3	...	...	*396	*39	...	*39	...	...	1996	Tonga
3	...	...	411	40	...	40	...	...	1997	
3	...	...	400	39	...	39	...	...	1998	
*3	...	...	*406	*40	...	*40	...	...	1999	
...	...	...	156	28	...	28	...	...	1996	Vanuatu
...	...	...	157	29	...	29	...	...	1997	
...	...	...	142	27	...	27	...	...	1998	
...	...	...	*138	*27	...	*27	...	...	1999	
*402	*13	...	*6125	*6	...	*6	...	...	1996	Ile de Wake
*402	*13	...	*6125	*6	...	*6	...	...	1997	
*402	*13	...	*6125	*6	...	*6	...	...	1998	
*404	*14	...	*6125	*6	...	*6	...	...	1999	

65

Production of selected energy commodities
Thousand metric tons of oil equivalent

Production des principaux biens de l'énergie
Milliers de tonnes d'équivalent pétrole

Region, country or area Région, pays ou zone	Year Anneé	Hard coal, lignite and peat Houille, lignite et tourbe	Briquettes and cokes Agglom-érés et cokes	Crude petroleum and NGL Pétrole Brut et GNL	Light petroleum products Produits pétroliers légers	Heavy petroleum products Produits pétroliers lourds	Other petroleum products Autres produits pétroliers	LPG and refinery gas GLP et gas de raffinerie	Natural gas Gaz naturel	Electricity Electricité
World	**1996**	**2 361 410**	246 394	3 442 999	1 311 153	1 587 576	245 254	182 051	2 152 096	1 646 454
Monde	1997	2 379 338	246 181	3 542 876	1 352 527	1 625 827	255 763	187 989	2 152 762	1 669 585
	1998	2 307 393	234 255	3 593 221	1 372 850	1 625 254	258 131	193 028	2 192 847	1 710 266
	1999	2 183 749	224 533	3 516 092	1 380 458	1 616 351	273 446	195 248	2 227 619	1 771 045
Africa	**1996**	149 546	3 294	367 270	43 748	68 620	3 301	2 524	91 367	35 679
Afrique	1997	159 164	3 338	381 696	44 342	71 514	3 232	2 575	101 125	37 481
	1998	160 945	2 957	376 437	42 133	67 099	3 364	2 488	103 778	38 415
	1999	161 018	2 497	366 177	43 415	73 041	3 444	2 686	113 352	38 919
Algeria	1996	* 15	..	64 093	7 553	11 173	324	507	62 589	* 1 776
Algérie	1997	* 16	..	66 487	7 920	12 127	281	519	70 624	1 848
	1998	* 16	..	68 911	7 530	11 306	275	507	75 423	* 2 031
	1999	* 17	..	66 544	8 147	12 181	297	631	80 062	2 120
Angola	1996	..	..	34 812	607	1 160	1	36	* 509	88
Angola	1997	..	..	35 184	622	1 186	5	38	* 518	99
	1998	..	..	36 418	575	1 119	5	32	* 527	113
	1999	..	..	38 066	692	1 231	6	33	* 509	* 115
Benin	1996	..	..	112	..	..	..	..	..	4
Bénin	1997	..	..	90	..	..	..	..	..	4
	1998	..	..	62	..	..	..	..	..	5
	1999	..	..	44	..	..	..	..	..	5
Burkina Faso *	1996	..	..	..	..	..	..	..	..	23
Burkina Faso *	1997	..	..	..	..	..	..	..	..	24
	1998	..	..	..	..	..	..	..	..	24
	1999	..	..	..	..	..	..	..	..	24
Burundi *	1996	4	..	..	..	..	..	..	..	10
Burundi *	1997	4	..	..	..	..	..	..	..	10
	1998	4	..	..	..	..	..	..	..	11
	1999	4	..	..	..	..	..	..	..	11
Cameroon	1996	* 1	..	5 220	* 606	* 676	* 43	* 24	..	255
Cameroun	1997	* 1	..	5 516	* 611	* 761	* 47	* 27	..	274
	1998	* 1	..	5 911	* 613	* 785	* 48	* 30	..	276
	1999	* 1	..	6 857	* 627	* 709	* 45	36	..	295
Cape Verde *	1996	..	..	..	..	..	..	..	..	4
Cap-Vert *	1997	..	..	..	..	..	..	..	..	4
	1998	..	..	..	..	..	..	..	..	4
	1999	..	..	..	..	..	..	..	..	4
Central African Rep. *	1996	..	..	..	..	..	..	..	..	9
Rép. centrafricaine *	1997	..	..	..	..	..	..	..	..	9
	1998	..	..	..	..	..	..	..	..	9
	1999	..	..	..	..	..	..	..	..	9
Chad *	1996	..	..	..	..	..	..	..	..	8
Tchad *	1997	..	..	..	..	..	..	..	..	8
	1998	..	..	..	..	..	..	..	..	8
	1999	..	..	..	..	..	..	..	..	8
Comoros *	1996	..	..	..	..	..	..	..	..	1
Comores *	1997	..	..	..	..	..	..	..	..	1
	1998	..	..	..	..	..	..	..	..	1
	1999	..	..	..	..	..	..	..	..	1
Congo	1996	..	..	10 380	* 186	* 351	* 11	* 4	* 99	31
Congo	1997	..	..	11 610	* 187	* 356	* 12	* 4	* 123	39
	1998	..	..	12 723	* 189	* 367	* 12	* 4	* 123	39
	1999	..	..	13 258	* 191	* 359	* 13	* 5	133	30
Côte d'Ivoire	1996	..	..	1 264	1 514	1 418	* 101	100	416	207
Côte d'Ivoire	1997	..	..	1 273	1 525	1 376	* 104	99	682	253
	1998	..	..	1 900	1 725	2 175	* 104	111	841	225
	1999	..	..	1 485	1 781	2 238	* 107	113	1 409	251

65

Production of selected energy commodities
Thousand metric tons of oil equivalent *[cont.]*

Production des principaux biens de l'énergie
Milliers de tonnes d'équivalent pétrole *[suite]*

Region, country or area Région, pays ou zone	Year Anneé	Hard coal, lignite and peat Houille, lignite et tourbe	Briquettes and cokes Agglomérés et cokes	Crude petroleum and NGL Pétrole Brut et GNL	Light petroleum products Produits pétroliers légers	Heavy petroleum products Produits pétroliers lourds	Other petroleum products Autres produits pétroliers	LPG and refinery gas GLP et gas de raffinerie	Natural gas Gaz naturel	Electricity Electricité
Dem. Rep. of the Congo	1996 *	66	..	1 149	77	26	12	..	..	466
Rép. dém. du Congo	1997 *	66	..	1 152	84	27	13	..	..	466
	1998 *	67	..	1 156	129	27	13	..	..	467
	1999	* 67	..	1 069	158	* 30	* 15	..	..	490
Djibouti *	1996	..	..	..	..	..	..	..	..	16
Djibouti *	1997	..	..	..	..	..	..	..	..	16
	1998	..	..	..	..	..	..	..	..	16
	1999	..	..	..	..	..	..	..	..	16
Egypt	1996	..	* 1 175	45 461	7 276	18 367	1 240	482	13 462	4 786
Egypte	1997	..	1 189	44 515	7 471	18 770	1 287	499	13 893	5 070
	1998	..	1 227	43 200	7 557	19 168	1 496	473	11 523	5 461
	1999	..	1 070	42 179	7 390	18 442	1 564	529	15 601	5 938
Equatorial Guinea	1996	..	..	858	..	..	..	..	..	* 2
Guinée équatoriale	1997	..	..	3 256	..	..	..	..	..	* 2
	1998	..	..	4 172	..	..	..	..	..	* 2
	1999	..	..	4 826	..	..	..	..	..	* 2
Eritrea	1996	..	..	..	..	..	..	..	..	14
Erythrée	1997	..	..	..	..	..	..	..	..	16
	1998	..	..	..	..	..	..	..	..	17
	1999	..	..	..	..	..	..	..	..	18
Ethiopia	1996	..	..	..	* 24	* 558	* 2	* 3	..	139
Ethiopie	1997	..	..	..	* 19	* 607	* 2	* 3	..	144
	1998	..	..	..	* 19	* 474	* 2	* 3	..	146
	1999	..	..	..	* 20	* 613	* 2	* 3	..	148
Gabon	1996	..	..	18 295	184	473	33	* 40	821	110
Gabon	1997	..	..	18 616	186	516	28	* 41	782	114
	1998	..	..	18 213	* 202	* 512	* 31	44	698	117
	1999	..	..	16 537	222	* 506	32	47	761	115
Gambia	1996 *	..	..	..	..	..	..	..	..	7
Gambie	1997 *	..	..	..	..	..	..	..	..	7
	1998 *	..	..	..	..	..	..	..	..	7
	1999	..	..	..	..	..	..	..	..	8
Ghana	1996	..	..	...	367	* 557	* 59	* 38	..	570
Ghana	1997	..	..	...	368	* 557	* 59	* 31	..	592
	1998	..	..	...	* 381	* 561	* 60	* 35	..	528
	1999	..	..	9	253	624	* 60	47	..	468
Guinea *	1996	..	..	..	..	..	..	..	..	47
Guinée *	1997	..	..	..	..	..	..	..	..	47
	1998	..	..	..	..	..	..	..	..	48
	1999	..	..	..	..	..	..	..	..	48
Guinea-Bissau	1996	..	..	..	..	..	..	..	..	4
Guinée-Bissau	1997	..	..	..	..	..	..	..	..	5
	1998 *	..	..	..	..	..	..	..	..	5
	1999 *	..	..	..	..	..	..	..	..	5
Kenya	1996	..	..	..	* 712	937	* 103	* 35	..	664
Kenya	1997	..	..	..	739	912	108	26	..	656
	1998	..	..	..	892	937	117	32	..	686
	1999	..	..	..	* 718	940	111	29	..	682
Liberia *	1996	..	..	..	..	..	..	..	..	42
Libéria *	1997	..	..	..	..	..	..	..	..	43
	1998	..	..	..	..	..	..	..	..	43
	1999	..	..	..	..	..	..	..	..	45
Libyan Arab Jamah.	1996	..	..	69 115	4 991	9 063	103	259	5 987	1 574
Jamah. arabe libyenne	1997	..	..	71 075	4 938	9 127	106	286	6 127	1 632
	1998	..	..	69 190	4 938	9 127	106	286	5 931	1 677
	1999	..	..	65 433	4 976	9 248	100	259	4 850	1 724

65

Production of selected energy commodities
Thousand metric tons of oil equivalent [cont.]
Production des principaux biens de l'énergie
Milliers de tonnes d'équivalent pétrole [suite]

Region, country or area Région, pays ou zone	Year Anneé	Hard coal, lignite and peat Houille, lignite et tourbe	Briquettes and cokes Agglom-érés et cokes	Crude petroleum and NGL Pétrole Brut et GNL	Light petroleum products Produits pétroliers légers	Heavy petroleum products Produits pétroliers lourds	Other petroleum products Autres produits pétroliers	LPG and refinery gas GLP et gas de raffinerie	Natural gas Gaz naturel	Electricity Electricité
Madagascar	1996	..	..	..	131	* 122	* 10	* 5	..	59
Madagascar	1997	..	..	..	188	* 124	* 10	* 5	..	63
	1998	..	..	..	131	* 126	* 10	* 7	..	68
	1999	..	..	..	* 172	* 130	* 10	* 7	..	68
Malawi *	1996	..	..	..	..	..	..	..	..	75
Malawi *	1997	..	..	..	..	..	..	..	..	75
	1998	..	..	..	..	..	..	..	..	75
	1999	..	..	..	..	..	..	..	..	76
Mali	1996	..	..	..	..	..	..	..	..	29
Mali	1997	..	..	..	..	..	..	..	..	34
	1998 *	..	..	..	..	..	..	..	..	34
	1999 *	..	..	..	..	..	..	..	..	35
Mauritania *	1996	..	..	..	310	505	98	41	..	13
Mauritanie *	1997	..	..	..	313	507	99	41	..	13
	1998	..	..	..	313	510	99	41	..	13
	1999	..	..	..	317	514	101	44	..	13
Mauritius	1996	..	..	..	..	..	..	..	..	100
Maurice	1997	..	..	..	..	..	..	..	..	109
	1998	..	..	..	..	..	..	..	..	119
	1999	..	..	..	..	..	..	..	..	124
Morocco	1996	354	..	5	981	3 893	254	264	17	1 067
Maroc	1997	263	..	12	1 062	4 126	260	260	32	1 136
	1998	188	..	12	1 140	4 170	260	274	35	1 156
	1999	90	..	11	1 332	5 063	266	290	41	1 132
Mozambique	1996 *	14	..	..	..	..	..	..	..	83
Mozambique	1997	* 13	..	..	..	..	..	..	..	128
	1998	* 13	..	..	..	..	..	..	..	632
	1999	* 14	..	..	..	..	..	..	..	633
Niger *	1996	121	..	..	..	..	..	..	..	20
Niger *	1997	122	..	..	..	..	..	..	..	20
	1998	122	..	..	..	..	..	..	..	20
	1999	122	..	..	..	..	..	..	..	20
Nigeria	1996	98	..	104 543	5 656	6 879	..	220	4 956	1 289
Nigéria	1997	98	..	111 169	5 636	6 856	..	219	5 182	1 319
	1998	41	..	103 034	3 326	4 046	..	129	5 559	1 352
	1999	42	..	94 801	3 839	4 670	..	149	6 549	1 388
Réunion	1996	..	..	..	..	..	..	..	..	119
Réunion	1997	..	..	..	..	..	..	..	..	127
	1998	..	..	..	..	..	..	..	..	135
	1999	..	..	..	..	..	..	..	..	135
Rwanda *	1996	..	..	..	..	..	..	..	0	14
Rwanda *	1997	..	..	..	..	..	..	..	0	14
	1998	..	..	..	..	..	..	..	0	14
	1999	..	..	..	..	..	..	..	0	15
Saint Helena	1996	..	..	..	..	..	..	..	..	1
Sainte-Hélène	1997	..	..	..	..	..	..	..	..	1
	1998	..	..	..	..	..	..	..	..	1
	1999	..	..	..	..	..	..	..	..	1
Sao Tome and Principe *	1996	..	..	..	..	..	..	..	..	1
Sao Tomé-et-Principe *	1997	..	..	..	..	..	..	..	..	1
	1998	..	..	..	..	..	..	..	..	1
	1999	..	..	..	..	..	..	..	..	1
Senegal	1996	..	..	..	* 293	* 525	* 12	* 3	..	87
Sénégal	1997	..	..	..	* 298	* 527	* 12	* 5	..	101
	1998	..	..	..	* 305	* 533	* 12	* 7	..	107
	1999	..	..	..	* 325	* 548	* 13	9	..	118

65

Production of selected energy commodities
Thousand metric tons of oil equivalent *[cont.]*

Production des principaux biens de l'énergie
Milliers de tonnes d'équivalent pétrole *[suite]*

Region, country or area Région, pays ou zone	Year Anneé	Hard coal, lignite and peat Houille, lignite et tourbe	Briquettes and cokes Agglom- érés et cokes	Crude petroleum and NGL Pétrole Brut et GNL	Light petroleum products Produits pétroliers légers	Heavy petroleum products Produits pétroliers lourds	Other petroleum products Autres produits pétroliers	LPG and refinery gas GLP et gas de raffinerie	Natural gas Gaz naturel	Electricity Electricité
Seychelles	1996	..	..	..	..	..	..	..	..	11
Seychelles	1997	..	..	..	..	..	..	..	..	13
	1998	..	..	..	..	..	..	..	..	14
	1999	..	..	..	..	..	..	..	..	14
Sierra Leone *	1996	..	..	..	64	122	27	..	..	21
Sierra Leone *	1997	..	..	..	64	125	27	..	..	21
	1998	..	..	..	65	125	27	..	..	21
	1999	..	..	..	66	128	31	..	..	21
Somalia *	1996	..	..	..	..	..	..	..	..	24
Somalie *	1997	..	..	..	..	..	..	..	..	24
	1998	..	..	..	..	..	..	..	..	24
	1999	..	..	..	..	..	..	..	..	24
South Africa [1]	1996	145 053	1 789	7 652	11 023	9 236	736	279	1 716	* 19 389
Afrique du Sud [1]	1997	154 699	1 789	7 652	10 715	10 343	640	311	1 532	* 20 394
	1998	156 836	1 349	7 186	10 953	8 489	557	309	1 290	* 20 165
	1999	157 065	1 123	7 627	11 072	12 534	532	316	1 688	19 825
Sudan	1996		..	102	* 257	* 650	* 107	10	..	* 133
Soudan	1997		..	255	* 259	* 652	* 107	9	..	* 135
	1998		..	330	* 265	* 668	* 107	* 8	..	* 150
	1999		..	3 453	* 212	* 658	* 109	* 5	..	181
Togo	1996	..	..	..	..	..	..	..	..	8
Togo	1997	..	..	..	..	..	..	..	..	8
	1998 *	..	..	..	..	..	..	..	..	8
	1999 *	..	..	..	..	..	..	..	..	8
Tunisia	1996	..	..	4 208	546	1 217	..	154	795	674
Tunisie	1997	..	..	3 835	756	1 220	..	133	1 630	721
	1998	..	..	4 019	507	1 198	..	138	1 829	770
	1999	..	..	3 978	622	1 138	..	122	1 751	866
Uganda	1996	..	..	..	..	..	..	..	..	101
Ouganda	1997	..	..	..	..	..	..	..	..	108
	1998	..	..	..	..	..	..	..	..	109
	1999	..	..	..	..	..	..	..	..	110
United Rep. of Tanzania	1996 *	4	..	..	191	395	3	7	..	155
Rép.-Unie de Tanzanie	1997 *	4	..	..	194	397	4	7	..	166
	1998 *	4	..	..	196	399	4	7	..	203
	1999	* 4	..	..	201	* 413	* 5	* 8	..	* 219
Western Sahara *	1996	..	..	..	..	..	..	..	..	7
Sahara occidental *	1997	..	..	..	..	..	..	..	..	7
	1998	..	..	..	..	..	..	..	..	7
	1999	..	..	..	..	..	..	..	..	8
Zambia	1996	* 192	* 20	..	* 199	* 316	* 20	* 13	..	670
Zambie	1997	* 165	* 20	..	* 190	* 317	* 18	11	..	689
	1998	121	* 20	..	183	276	15	11	..	677
	1999	109	* 21	..	80	127	21	4	..	694
Zimbabwe	1996	3 623	311		..	..	..	..	..	672
Zimbabwe	1997	3 713	340		..	..	..	..	..	* 673
	1998	3 533	360	..	..	..	..	..	..	574
	1999	3 484	* 284	..	..	..	..	..	..	* 610
America, North	**1996**	**589 982**	**17 387**	**675 741**	**514 859**	**309 585**	**101 864**	**63 869**	**700 065**	**548 787**
Amérique du Nord	**1997**	**605 486**	**16 794**	**694 805**	**523 285**	**314 709**	**105 171**	**65 295**	**708 769**	**541 837**
	1998	**613 242**	**15 453**	**682 352**	**531 176**	**320 246**	**108 738**	**65 156**	**711 100**	**560 041**
	1999	**600 079**	**15 563**	**647 428**	**534 358**	**315 042**	**120 628**	**65 021**	**710 436**	**588 631**
Antigua and Barbuda *	1996	..	..	..	..	..	..	..	..	8
Antigua-et-Barbuda *	1997	..	..	..	..	..	..	..	..	9
	1998	..	..	..	..	..	..	..	..	9
	1999	..	..	..	..	..	..	..	..	9

65

Production of selected energy commodities
Thousand metric tons of oil equivalent *[cont.]*
Production des principaux biens de l'énergie
Milliers de tonnes d'équivalent pétrole *[suite]*

Region, country or area / Région, pays ou zone	Year / Anneé	Hard coal, lignite and peat / Houille, lignite et tourbe	Briquettes and cokes / Agglom-érés et cokes	Crude petroleum and NGL / Pétrole Brut et GNL	Light petroleum products / Produits pétroliers légers	Heavy petroleum products / Produits pétroliers lourds	Other petroleum products / Autres produits pétroliers	LPG and refinery gas / GLP et gas de raffinerie	Natural gas / Gaz naturel	Electricity / Electricité
Aruba / Aruba	1996	..	..	..	..	..	..	..	..	55
	1997	..	..	..	..	..	..	..	..	58
	1998	..	..	..	..	..	..	..	..	63
	1999	..	..	..	..	..	..	..	..	63
Bahamas / Bahamas	1996	..	..	..	..	..	..	..	..	115
	1997	..	..	..	..	..	..	..	..	122
	1998	..	..	..	..	..	..	..	..	132
	1999 *	..	..	..	..	..	..	..	..	143
Barbados / Barbade	1996	..	..	50	61	195	5	1	27	56
	1997	..	..	45	74	204	5	1	22	58
	1998	..	..	80	...	...	* 5	2	35	64
	1999	..	..	97	...	...	* 5	4	44	69
Belize / Belize	1996	..	..	..	..	..	..	..	..	13
	1997	..	..	..	..	..	..	..	..	14
	1998	..	..	..	..	..	..	..	..	16
	1999	..	..	..	..	..	..	..	..	11
Bermuda / Bermudes	1996	..	..	..	..	..	..	..	..	45
	1997 *	..	..	..	..	..	..	..	..	46
	1998 *	..	..	..	..	..	..	..	..	46
	1999	..	..	..	..	..	..	..	..	47
British Virgin Islands * / Iles Vierges britanniques *	1996	..	..	..	..	..	..	..	..	4
	1997	..	..	..	..	..	..	..	..	4
	1998	..	..	..	..	..	..	..	..	4
	1999	..	..	..	..	..	..	..	..	4
Canada / Canada	1996	39 721	2 196	113 262	40 705	31 944	10 216	5 282	157 875	65 511
	1997	41 103	2 205	123 362	40 409	34 685	11 739	6 117	160 390	63 776
	1998	38 947	2 055	114 465	40 417	32 939	12 561	6 370	164 250	60 871
	1999	37 336	2 163	111 831	42 319	33 430	11 944	6 293	161 907	62 527
Cayman Islands / Iles Caïmanes	1996 *	..	..	..	..	..	..	..	..	26
	1997 *	..	..	..	..	..	..	..	..	26
	1998 *	..	..	..	..	..	..	..	..	26
	1999	..	..	..	..	..	..	..	..	28
Costa Rica / Costa Rica	1996	..	..	..	128	485	23	2	..	814
	1997	..	..	..	135	501	26	2	..	895
	1998	..	..	..	6	165	12	...	..	956
	1999	..	..	..	2	..	* 12	...	..	1 168
Cuba / Cuba	1996	..	..	1 477	694	1 069	136	* 147	18	1 138
	1997	..	..	1 463	569	691	157	* 154	35	1 217
	1998	..	..	1 680	415	618	165	* 135	116	1 217
	1999	..	..	2 138	449	471	161	* 139	429	1 247
Dominica / Dominique	1996	..	..	..	..	..	..	..	..	5
	1997	..	..	..	..	..	..	..	..	6
	1998	..	..	..	..	..	..	..	..	6
	1999	..	..	..	..	..	..	..	..	6
Dominican Republic / Rép. dominicaine	1996	..	..	..	642	1 489	..	42	..	* 569
	1997	..	..	..	664	1 567	..	39	..	* 622
	1998	..	..	..	494	1 081	..	45	..	* 662
	1999	..	..	..	666	1 064	..	75	..	799
El Salvador / El Salvador	1996	..	..	..	280	415	28	15	..	630
	1997	..	..	..	211	501	35	15	..	* 648
	1998	..	..	..	204	641	31	17	..	704
	1999	..	..	..	205	716	* 31	20	..	787
Greenland * / Groenland *	1996	..	..	..	..	..	..	..	..	22
	1997	..	..	..	..	..	..	..	..	22
	1998	..	..	..	..	..	..	..	..	22
	1999	..	..	..	..	..	..	..	..	22

65

Production of selected energy commodities
Thousand metric tons of oil equivalent *[cont.]*

Production des principaux biens de l'énergie
Milliers de tonnes d'équivalent pétrole *[suite]*

Region, country or area Région, pays ou zone	Year Anneé	Hard coal, lignite and peat Houille, lignite et tourbe	Briquettes and cokes Agglom- érés et cokes	Crude petroleum and NGL Pétrole Brut et GNL	Light petroleum products Produits pétroliers légers	Heavy petroleum products Produits pétroliers lourds	Other petroleum products Autres produits pétroliers	LPG and refinery gas GLP et gas de raffinerie	Natural gas Gaz naturel	Electricity Electricité
Grenada	1996	..	..	..	..	..	..	..	..	8
Grenade	1997	..	..	..	..	..	..	..	..	9
	1998	..	..	..	..	..	..	..	..	10
	1999	..	..	..	..	..	..	..	..	10
Guadeloupe	1996	..	..	..	..	..	..	..	..	97
Guadeloupe	1997	..	..	..	..	..	..	..	..	104
	1998	..	..	..	..	..	..	..	..	104
	1999	..	..	..	..	..	..	..	..	105
Guatemala	1996	..	..	730	176	526	..	8	10	318
Guatemala	1997	..	..	976	187	564	..	5	10	355
	1998	..	..	1 273	168	591	..	5	10	386
	1999	..	..	1 164	197	620	..	13	* 10	450
Haiti	1996 *	..	..	..	..	..	..	..	..	54
Haïti	1997 *	..	..	..	..	..	..	..	..	54
	1998 *	..	..	..	..	..	..	..	..	59
	1999	..	..	..	..	..	..	..	..	55
Honduras	1996	..	..	..	...	...	..	...	..	257
Honduras	1997 *	..	..	..	...	...	..	...	..	269
	1998	..	..	..	...	...	..	...	..	305
	1999	..	..	..	...	...	..	...	..	295
Jamaica	1996	..	..	..	273	770	* 17	* 24	..	519
Jamaïque	1997	..	..	..	301	791	* 14	* 25	..	538
	1998	..	..	..	190	519	* 14	* 26	..	557
	1999	..	..	..	* 134	372	* 20	* 18	..	568
Martinique	1996	..	..	..	* 296	* 433	..	* 23	..	88
Martinique	1997	..	..	..	* 296	* 435	..	* 23	..	93
	1998 *	..	..	..	298	435	..	23	..	93
	1999 *	..	..	..	301	440	..	24	..	93
Mexico	1996	3 157	1 456	165 847	22 163	37 771	3 892	3 216	30 462	19 771
Mexique	1997	3 222	1 426	175 160	20 435	38 246	3 404	2 766	31 424	20 721
	1998	3 501	1 469	178 356	21 727	40 177	3 744	2 445	33 927	21 797
	1999	3 515	1 486	171 908	20 749	38 404	3 680	2 438	32 563	25 714
Montserrat *	1996	..	..	..	..	..	..	..	..	1
Montserrat *	1997	..	..	..	..	..	..	..	..	2
	1998	..	..	..	..	..	..	..	..	2
	1999	..	..	..	..	..	..	..	..	1
Netherlands Antilles	1996	..	..	..	* 2 829	* 7 219	* 2 394	* 79	..	91
Antilles néerlandaises	1997	..	..	..	* 2 847	* 7 309	* 2 499	* 98	..	91
	1998	..	..	..	* 2 766	* 7 523	* 2 661	* 100	..	96
	1999	..	..	..	* 2 680	7 612	* 2 949	106	..	96
Nicaragua	1996	..	..	..	144	424	* 24	32	..	* 629
Nicaragua	1997	..	..	..	137	575	* 24	* 30	..	* 628
	1998	..	..	..	145	662	* 24	* 27	..	* 694
	1999	..	..	..	135	650	* 24	* 31	..	566
Panama	1996	..	..	..	277	1 700	* 10	* 61	..	334
Panama	1997	..	..	..	314	1 125	* 10	* 57	..	360
	1998	..	..	..	361	1 916	* 10	* 70	..	373
	1999	..	..	..	323	1 902	* 10	* 72	..	424
Puerto Rico	1996	..	..	..	* 2 111	1 371	* 1 627	* 122	..	1 645
Porto Rico	1997	..	..	..	* 2 021	* 1 248	* 1 635	* 125	..	1 720
	1998	..	..	..	* 2 014	* 1 248	* 1 635	* 125	..	1 751
	1999	..	..	..	* 1 691	976	1 560	* 120	..	* 1 752
Saint Kitts and Nevis	1996	..	..	..	..	..	..	..	..	7
Saint-Kitts-et-Nevis	1997	..	..	..	..	..	..	..	..	8
	1998	..	..	..	..	..	..	..	..	8
	1999	..	..	..	..	..	..	..	..	8

65

Production of selected energy commodities
Thousand metric tons of oil equivalent *[cont.]*

Production des principaux biens de l'énergie
Milliers de tonnes d'équivalent pétrole *[suite]*

Region, country or area Région, pays ou zone	Year Anneé	Hard coal, lignite and peat Houille, lignite et tourbe	Briquettes and cokes Agglomérés et cokes	Crude petroleum and NGL Pétrole Brut et GNL	Light petroleum products Produits pétroliers légers	Heavy petroleum products Produits pétroliers lourds	Other petroleum products Autres produits pétroliers	LPG and refinery gas GLP et gas de raffinerie	Natural gas Gaz naturel	Electricity Electricité
Saint Lucia	1996	..	..	..	..	..	..	..	..	17
Sainte-Lucie	1997	..	..	..	..	..	..	..	..	18
	1998	..	..	..	..	..	..	..	..	20
	1999	..	..	..	..	..	..	..	..	22
Saint Pierre and Miquelon	1996	..	..	..	..	..	..	..	..	4
Saint-Pierre-et-Miquelon	1997	..	..	..	..	..	..	..	..	4
	1998	..	..	..	..	..	..	..	..	4
	1999 *	..	..	..	..	..	..	..	..	4
St. Vincent-Grenadines	1996	..	..	..	..	..	..	..	..	7
St. Vincent-Grenadines	1997	..	..	..	..	..	..	..	..	7
	1998	..	..	..	..	..	..	..	..	7
	1999 *	..	..	..	..	..	..	..	..	7
Trinidad and Tobago	1996	..	..	6 717	1 434	3 612	* 43	491	7 112	391
Trinité-et-Tobago	1997	..	..	6 218	1 284	3 620	* 42	466	7 572	416
	1998	..	..	6 391	2 075	4 532	* 42	509	7 903	446
	1999	..	..	6 509	2 031	4 966	* 42	643	9 662	451
Turks and Caicos Islands *	1996	..	..	..	..	..	..	..	..	0
Iles Turques et Caïques *	1997	..	..	..	..	..	..	..	..	0
	1998	..	..	..	..	..	..	..	..	0
	1999	..	..	..	..	..	..	..	..	0
United States	1996	547 104	13 735	387 656	438 520	213 455	78 934	54 064	504 560	455 444
Etats-Unis	1997	561 161	13 163	387 581	449 259	215 933	81 045	55 116	509 317	448 824
	1998	570 794	11 929	380 107	455 742	220 478	83 292	54 999	504 860	468 439
	1999	559 228	11 913	353 780	458 284	216 690	95 644	54 767	505 820	490 984
United States Virgin Is. *	1996	..	..	..	4 125	6 706	4 515	261	..	92
Iles Vierges américaines *	1997	..	..	..	4 141	6 714	4 536	256	..	93
	1998	..	..	..	4 154	6 722	4 541	258	..	93
	1999	..	..	..	4 191	6 730	4 546	259	..	93
America, South	**1996**	**24 847**	**7 209**	**317 384**	**63 380**	**97 365**	**10 049**	**11 953**	**63 189**	**53 168**
Amérique du Sud	**1997**	**28 191**	**7 020**	**335 730**	**67 343**	**102 999**	**11 615**	**12 307**	**70 867**	**56 155**
	1998	**30 399**	**7 007**	**339 838**	**71 604**	**104 075**	**11 629**	**13 834**	**73 064**	**58 183**
	1999	**29 163**	**6 855**	**337 637**	**73 183**	**104 346**	**12 060**	**14 006**	**74 179**	**59 956**
Argentina	1996	183	467	41 741	8 438	11 536	1 802	1 507	24 661	7 317
Argentine	1997	148	478	44 388	8 305	13 082	1 869	1 466	29 034	7 650
	1998	171	673	43 812	7 909	13 544	2 226	1 584	29 835	7 688
	1999	198	692	42 697	9 608	13 603	2 090	1 635	32 403	8 191
Bolivia	1996	..	..	1 824	577	404	22	66	3 587	277
Bolivie	1997	..	..	1 805	627	401	19	56	3 205	297
	1998	..	..	2 085	651	420	* 19	56	3 067	317
	1999	..	..	1 784	626	395	* 20	57	* 3 662	335
Brazil	1996	2 135	6 096	40 418	20 595	36 929	3 919	6 526	5 160	25 472
Brésil	1997	2 509	5 949	43 726	22 567	39 481	4 576	6 795	5 729	27 041
	1998	2 451	5 770	50 747	24 687	42 905	4 727	6 914	6 012	28 228
	1999	2 489	5 534	56 389	25 029	43 799	4 967	7 302	5 958	29 274
Chile	1996	703	319	877	2 850	4 505	130	629	1 653	2 797
Chili	1997	731	301	754	3 165	4 629	133	616	1 797	2 863
	1998	658	328	789	3 277	5 028	126	762	1 620	3 053
	1999	340	415	704	3 371	4 900	761	785	1 843	3 301
Colombia	1996	19 237	328	32 629	5 884	6 254	* 1	* 1 116	4 972	3 858
Colombie	1997	21 185	293	33 970	5 532	6 355	* 1	1 095	6 051	3 989
	1998	21 886	236	37 457	5 504	5 949	* 1	1 093	6 327	3 953
	1999	21 240	213	42 100	6 274	5 981	* 1	1 125	* 6 263	3 797
Ecuador	1996	..	..	19 431	1 906	4 927	89	275	618	793
Equateur	1997	..	..	20 313	1 743	5 635	* 95	224	* 581	822
	1998	..	..	19 798	1 785	5 079	* 85	113	704	937
	1999	..	..	19 689	1 722	4 751	* 90	83	702	886

65

Production of selected energy commodities
Thousand metric tons of oil equivalent *[cont.]*

Production des principaux biens de l'énergie
Milliers de tonnes d'équivalent pétrole *[suite]*

Region, country or area Région, pays ou zone	Year Anneé	Hard coal, lignite and peat Houille, lignite et tourbe	Briquettes and cokes Agglomérés et cokes	Crude petroleum and NGL Pétrole Brut et GNL	Light petroleum products Produits pétroliers légers	Heavy petroleum products Produits pétroliers lourds	Other petroleum products Autres produits pétroliers	LPG and refinery gas GLP et gas de raffinerie	Natural gas Gaz naturel	Electricity Electricité
Falkland Is. (Malvinas)	1996	3	..	..	..	..	..	..	..	1
Iles Falkland (Malvinas)	1997 *	3	..	..	..	..	..	..	..	1
	1998	3	..	..	..	..	..	..	..	1
	1999 *	3	..	..	..	..	..	..	..	1
French Guiana *	1996	..	..	..	..	..	..	..	..	39
Guyane française *	1997	..	..	..	..	..	..	..	..	39
	1998	..	..	..	..	..	..	..	..	39
	1999	..	..	..	..	..	..	..	..	39
Guyana	1996	..	..	..	..	..	..	..	..	60
Guyana	1997	..	..	..	..	..	..	..	..	68
	1998	..	..	..	..	..	..	..	..	73
	1999	..	..	..	..	..	..	..	..	77
Paraguay	1996	..	..	..	38	125	..	..	..	3 854
Paraguay	1997	..	..	..	32	104	..	..	..	4 374
	1998	..	..	..	30	103	..	..	..	4 375
	1999	..	..	..	20	98	..	..	..	4 469
Peru	1996	40	..	6 027	2 439	4 428	* 254	263	497	1 486
Pérou	1997	15	..	5 992	2 353	4 435	427	327	383	1 544
	1998	14	..	5 691	2 902	5 394	* 279	356	530	1 598
	1999	11	..	5 981	2 924	4 588	404	313	719	1 638
Suriname	1996	..	..	245	..	..	..	..	..	139
Suriname	1997	..	..	246	..	..	..	..	..	140
	1998	..	..	248	..	..	..	..	..	139
	1999	..	..	248	..	..	..	..	..	141
Uruguay	1996	..	..	..	349	1 199	61	70	..	573
Uruguay	1997	..	..	..	360	907	80	81	..	615
	1998	..	..	..	461	1 161	106	121	..	823
	1999	..	..	..	467	913	108	108	..	619
Venezuela	1996	2 546	..	174 193	20 303	27 058	3 772	1 500	22 041	6 501
Venezuela	1997	3 600	..	184 536	22 659	27 970	4 416	1 647	24 087	6 714
	1998	5 216	..	179 210	24 398	24 492	4 060	2 836	24 969	6 958
	1999	4 883	..	168 045	23 142	25 318	3 619	2 598	22 628	7 187
Asia	**1996**	**1 038 492**	**139 697**	**1 414 934**	**361 609**	**584 101**	**53 307**	**46 754**	**433 009**	**430 248**
Asie	**1997**	**1 030 917**	**140 985**	**1 459 165**	**383 558**	**604 092**	**57 805**	**49 842**	**438 949**	**450 178**
	1998	**970 254**	**135 879**	**1 525 887**	**391 512**	**594 318**	**57 767**	**50 730**	**455 843**	**466 020**
	1999	**862 590**	**127 612**	**1 490 994**	**403 820**	**609 405**	**57 819**	**53 163**	**480 472**	**484 770**
Afghanistan	1996	2	..	..	..	..	..	..	* 149	* 49
Afghanistan	1997 *	1	..	..	..	..	..	..	137	43
	1998 *	1	..	..	..	..	..	..	128	42
	1999 *	1	..	..	..	..	..	..	118	42
Armenia	1996	..	..	..	..	..	..	..	..	941
Arménie	1997	..	..	..	..	..	..	..	..	798
	1998	..	..	..	..	..	..	..	..	811
	1999	..	..	..	..	..	..	..	..	855
Azerbaijan	1996	..	..	9 125	1 474	6 068	360	243	5 681	1 470
Azerbaïdjan	1997	..	..	9 047	1 571	5 793	212	229	5 374	1 444
	1998	..	..	11 449	1 388	6 080	134	292	5 019	1 548
	1999	..	..	13 833	1 083	6 005	117	278	5 595	1 563
Bahrain	1996	..	..	2 375	4 991	7 715	288	36	6 536	431
Bahreïn	1997	..	..	2 361	4 782	7 374	367	33	7 041	433
	1998	..	..	2 293	4 700	7 387	315	28	7 421	496
	1999	..	..	2 280	4 975	7 930	269	32	7 690	512
Bangladesh	1996	..	..	66	418	251	...	14	6 557	1 067
Bangladesh	1997	..	..	45	467	279	...	17	6 444	1 103
	1998	..	..	* 37	295	214	...	15	6 992	1 192
	1999	..	..	* 37	319	213	11	11	7 630	1 327

65

Production of selected energy commodities
Thousand metric tons of oil equivalent [cont.]

Production des principaux biens de l'énergie
Milliers de tonnes d'équivalent pétrole [suite]

Region, country or area Région, pays ou zone	Year Anneé	Hard coal, lignite and peat Houille, lignite et tourbe	Briquettes and cokes Agglom- érés et cokes	Crude petroleum and NGL Pétrole Brut et GNL	Light petroleum products Produits pétroliers légers	Heavy petroleum products Produits pétroliers lourds	Other petroleum products Autres produits pétroliers	LPG and refinery gas GLP et gas de raffinerie	Natural gas Gaz naturel	Electricity Electricité
Bhutan	1996	45	..	..	..	..	..	..	..	170
Bhoutan	1997	38	..	..	..	..	..	..	..	158
	1998	* 35	..	..	..	..	..	..	..	155
	1999 *	35					..	..	..	155
Brunei Darussalam	1996	..	..	8 679	369	192	..	10	9 962	* 144
Brunéi Darussalam	1997	..	..	8 563	381	204	..	2	* 9 961	* 147
	1998	..	..	* 8 472	377	209	..	1	* 9 644	* 148
	1999	..	..	9 358	381	216	..		* 8 954	* 209
Cambodia *	1996	..	..	..	..	..	..	..	..	17
Cambodge *	1997	..	..	..	..	..	..	..	..	18
	1998	..	..	..	..	..	..	..	..	18
	1999	..	..	..	..	..	..	..	..	19
China	1996	697 802	91 205	157 491	58 108	69 672	9 782	11 093	23 134	95 495
Chine	1997	685 724	91 517	160 902	65 067	72 888	11 744	12 607	23 840	100 088
	1998	624 375	87 585	161 161	65 923	70 527	12 286	13 581	26 774	102 761
	1999	521 978	81 980	160 160	67 864	82 070	11 231	15 066	28 981	109 196
China, Hong Kong SAR	1996	..	..	..	..	..	..	..	..	2 446
Chine, Hong Kong RAS	1997	..	..	..	..	..	..	..	..	2 489
	1998	..	..	..	..	..	..	..	..	2 702
	1999	..	..	..	..	..	..	..	..	2 537
China, Macao SAR	1996	..	..	..	..	..	..	..	..	118
Chine, Macao RAS	1997	..	..	..	..	..	..	..	..	121
	1998	..	..	..	..	..	..	..	..	132
	1999	..	..	..	..	..	..	..	..	132
Cyprus	1996	..	..	..	120	575	30	45	..	223
Chypre	1997	..	..	..	174	789	37	56	..	233
	1998	..	..	..	177	826	37	55	..	254
	1999	..	..	..	187	908	37	65	..	270
Georgia	1996	13	..	128	...	11	1	..	3	621
Géorgie	1997	3	..	134	5	17	1	..	0	617
	1998	8	..	119	5	33	...	..		694
	1999	9	..	107	7	48	...	..	...	692
India	1996	170 750	7 476	36 841	19 711	31 965	5 693	1 704	24 404	39 159
Inde	1997	177 148	7 841	37 600	20 244	34 332	5 491	1 807	17 489	41 825
	1998	178 145	7 484	36 860	20 330	36 213	5 717	1 823	23 811	44 822
	1999	177 209	7 215	36 841	21 572	43 827	6 976	2 225	20 921	48 119
Indonesia	1996	35 232	..	102 983	17 640	24 658	1 635	3 160	71 291	8 429
Indonésie	1997	38 226	..	103 912	16 756	23 529	1 761	3 026	71 294	9 120
	1998	42 225	..	95 211	16 632	25 080	1 526	2 444	70 198	9 749
	1999	49 492	..	90 587	18 046	25 511	1 622	2 463	62 735	10 363
Iran (Islamic Rep. of)	1996	848	80	186 138	15 292	* 34 066	3 455	1 586	37 676	7 813
Iran (Rép. islamique d')	1997	717	35	183 246	15 655	* 35 069	3 513	1 681	46 221	8 406
	1998	818	* 35	184 977	18 175	* 36 427	3 535	1 739	46 629	8 893
	1999	936	* 32	181 841	18 789	* 38 291	2 784	1 802	52 930	10 115
Iraq	1996	..	..	28 581	5 148	14 135	761	1 065	3 022	* 2 498
Iraq	1997	..	..	57 096	5 221	14 334	771	1 080	2 844	* 2 542
	1998	..	..	104 679	5 392	14 804	796	* 1 116	2 751	* 2 610
	1999	..	..	124 848	5 201	14 280	768	1 077	2 966	* 2 622
Israel	1996	206	..	4	3 974	5 804	362	481	12	2 797
Israël	1997	231	..	5	4 271	5 768	355	536	12	3 016
	1998	225	..	5	4 551	6 140	370	542	11	3 265
	1999	232	..	4	4 037	5 907	344	509	9	3 370
Japan	1996	3 764	26 083	697	83 116	104 958	11 596	14 154	2 186	142 532
Japon	1997	2 486	26 021	700	87 026	106 460	11 686	14 821	2 234	148 022
	1998	2 132	24 946	655	88 558	102 471	11 338	14 406	2 256	150 902
	1999	2 272	23 002	602	88 399	98 913	11 223	14 431	2 235	149 766

65

Production of selected energy commodities
Thousand metric tons of oil equivalent *[cont.]*

Production des principaux biens de l'énergie
Milliers de tonnes d'équivalent pétrole *[suite]*

Region, country or area Région, pays ou zone	Year Anneé	Hard coal, lignite and peat Houille, lignite et tourbe	Briquettes and cokes Agglomérés et cokes	Crude petroleum and NGL Pétrole Brut et GNL	Light petroleum products Produits pétroliers légers	Heavy petroleum products Produits pétroliers lourds	Other petroleum products Autres produits pétroliers	LPG and refinery gas GLP et gas de raffinerie	Natural gas Gaz naturel	Electricity Electricité
Jordan	1996	..	..	2	1 075	1 877	163	209	203	521
Jordanie	1997		..	2	1 069	2 125	149	222	224	539
	1998	..	..	2	1 013	2 184	162	212	228	580
	1999	..	..	2	1 021	2 193	156	202	226	609
Kazakhstan	1996	33 761	..	23 137	3 011	6 462	239	336	5 878	5 045
Kazakhstan	1997	32 009	..	26 005	2 418	5 854	660	269	7 311	4 472
	1998	30 804	..	26 191	2 339	5 557	893	141	7 161	4 226
	1999	25 743	..	30 425	1 666	3 971	679	96	8 962	* 4 085
Korea, Dem. P. R.	1996 *	59 990	2 174	..	1 204	1 645	..	..	..	3 010
Corée, R. p. dém. de	1997	55 911	2 025	..	1 121	1 533	..	..	..	2 805
	1998	53 115	1 924	..	1 066	1 457	..	..	..	2 665
	1999 *	48 636	1 952	..	1 064	1 473	..	..	..	2 705
Korea, Republic of	1996	2 227	8 286	..	33 258	62 557	2 950	1 498	..	32 506
Corée, République de	1997	2 031	8 496	..	43 596	72 727	3 403	1 948	..	34 874
	1998	1 962	8 565	..	44 785	64 092	2 845	2 569	..	36 386
	1999	1 888	8 560	..	48 266	66 713	3 040	2 823	..	40 983
Kuwait [2]	1996	..	..	105 600	16 662	21 080	1 721	334	8 675	2 236
Koweït [2]	1997	..	..	105 579	18 534	24 824	1 691	333	8 645	2 344
	1998	..	..	107 620	19 047	23 608	1 576	341	8 851	2 624
	1999	..	..	98 742	20 589	24 653	1 854	420	8 101	2 761
Kyrgyzstan	1996	133	..	100	3	9	..	..	24	1 183
Kirghizistan	1997	170	..	85	173	66	..	..	37	1 087
	1998	137	..	78	56	77	..	..	17	999
	1999	129	..	77	76	102	..	..	23	1 132
Lao People's Dem. Rep. *	1996	1	..	..	..	..	..	..	..	107
Rép. dém. pop. lao *	1997	1	..	..	..	..	..	..	..	105
	1998	1	..	..	..	..	..	..	..	105
	1999	1	..	..	..	..	..	..	..	105
Lebanon	1996	..	..	..	..	..	..	..	..	644
Liban	1997	..	..	..	..	..	..	..	..	716
	1998	..	..	..	..	..	..	..	..	775
	1999	..	..	..	..	..	..	..	..	777
Malaysia	1996	58	..	35 341	5 048	* 9 047	* 350	538	32 891	4 558
Malaisie	1997	70	..	34 811	5 222	* 9 841	* 365	544	37 213	* 5 046
	1998	246	..	36 170	6 137	9 151	* 148	641	35 788	5 219
	1999	193	..	33 219	7 027	9 308	261	847	38 752	5 606
Maldives	1996	..	..	..	..	..	..	..	..	5
Maldives	1997	..	..	..	..	..	..	..	..	6
	1998	..	..	..	..	..	..	..	..	7
	1999	..	..	..	..	..	..	..	..	8
Mongolia	1996	* 1 828	..	..	..	..	..	..	..	225
Mongolie	1997	1 687	..	..	..	..	..	..	..	234
	1998	1 632	..	..	..	..	..	..	..	238
	1999	1 562	..	..	..	..	..	..	..	252
Myanmar	1996	28	..	408	236	447	50	4	1 470	366
Myanmar	1997	28	..	402	324	574	54	7	1 588	391
	1998	29	..	390	331	557	47	7	2 591	356
	1999	58	..	443	340	512	50	9	4 338	392
Nepal	1996	4	..	..	..	..	..	..	..	104
Népal	1997	6	..	..	..	..	..	..	..	108
	1998	11	..	..	..	..	..	..	..	103
	1999	13	..	..	..	..	..	..	..	120
Oman	1996	..	..	44 091	1 070	2 835	...	38	4 221	772
Oman	1997	..	..	45 004	992	2 648	...	39	5 006	831
	1998	..	..	44 659	1 052	2 712	...	39	* 5 622	918
	1999	..	..	44 990	978	3 035	...	41	4 366	966

65

Production of selected energy commodities
Thousand metric tons of oil equivalent *[cont.]*
Production des principaux biens de l'énergie
Milliers de tonnes d'équivalent pétrole *[suite]*

Region, country or area / Région, pays ou zone	Year / Anneé	Hard coal, lignite and peat / Houille, lignite et tourbe	Briquettes and cokes / Agglomérés et cokes	Crude petroleum and NGL / Pétrole Brut et GNL	Light petroleum products / Produits pétroliers légers	Heavy petroleum products / Produits pétroliers lourds	Other petroleum products / Autres produits pétroliers	LPG and refinery gas / GLP et gas de raffinerie	Natural gas / Gaz naturel	Electricity / Electricité
Pakistan / Pakistan	1996	1 720	...	2 959	2 320	3 618	470	39	14 396	4 982
	1997	1 680	...	2 980	2 149	3 398	436	45	15 093	5 145
	1998	1 494	...	2 889	2 278	3 622	401	60	15 174	5 407
	1999	1 637	...	2 833	2 303	3 650	420	74	16 149	5 674
Philippines / Philippines	1996	524	..	47	4 388	11 729	96	450	..	* 8 110
	1997	511	..	42	4 492	11 146	109	494	..	* 8 649
	1998	473	..	41	4 155	10 750	114	465	..	* 8 917
	1999	557	..	47	4 355	10 581	287	533	..	* 9 048
Qatar / Qatar	1996	..	..	21 296	1 131	1 694	..	97	12 776	569
	1997	..	..	28 878	999	1 547	..	75	16 227	594
	1998	..	..	31 800	1 106	1 652	..	85	18 260	703
	1999	..	..	31 826	1 057	1 677	..	71	27 810	702
Saudi Arabia [2] / Arabie saoudite [2]	1996	..	..	459 459	26 304	52 991	* 2 212	3 200	41 509	8 888
	1997	..	..	455 550	25 096	49 492	* 2 234	3 136	42 749	9 227
	1998	..	..	466 568	25 817	49 964	* 2 257	3 196	43 570	9 691
	1999	..	..	428 597	25 692	47 099	* 2 280	2 999	43 085	10 459
Singapore / Singapour	1996	..	..	..	20 825	27 392	2 210	952	..	2 017
	1997	..	..	..	17 633	26 911	2 822	1 050	..	2 252
	1998	..	..	..	17 832	26 909	2 895	1 093	..	2 432
	1999	..	..	..	15 833	23 411	3 138	1 058	..	2 539
Sri Lanka / Sri Lanka	1996	..	..	..	593	1 382	68	68	..	389
	1997	..	..	..	508	1 235	67	55	..	442
	1998	..	..	..	595	1 441	94	70	..	489
	1999	..	..	..	506	1 255	76	55	..	532
Syrian Arab Republic / Rép. arabe syrienne	1996	..	..	29 571	2 233	9 402	530	199	* 2 438	* 1 486
	1997	..	..	29 037	2 304	9 568	554	203	* 3 346	* 1 570
	1998	..	..	29 009	2 236	9 691	611	208	* 4 780	* 1 706
	1999	..	..	29 149	2 082	9 631	660	210	* 5 138	* 1 855
Tajikistan / Tadjikistan	1996	5	...	20	19	..	..	..	45	1 290
	1997	5	3	25	24	..	..	..	35	1 204
	1998	5	1	19	13	..	..	..	27	1 240
	1999	5	1	19	13	..	..	..	32	1 359
Thailand / Thaïlande	1996	9 449	..	4 223	8 807	19 859	355	1 017	10 740	7 865
	1997	10 291		5 060	9 900	23 035	615	1 147	13 398	8 389
	1998	8 870		5 266	9 246	21 447	697	1 059	13 896	8 150
	1999	8 035		5 721	9 839	21 104	847	1 253	15 000	8 184
Turkey / Turquie	1996	12 356	2 249	3 504	6 820	16 678	1 723	1 448	189	8 223
	1997	13 107	2 253	3 452	7 389	16 089	1 968	1 491	232	8 948
	1998	14 490	2 140	3 226	7 568	16 228	2 488	1 521	517	9 614
	1999	14 358	1 962	2 944	6 630	16 130	1 925	1 381	643	10 075
Turkmenistan / Turkménistan	1996	..	..	4 029	711	2 561	..	193	31 700	* 869
	1997	..	..	5 154	804	3 128	..	250	15 604	817
	1998	..	..	6 826	1 158	4 505	..	360	11 945	810
	1999	..	..	7 167	1 184	4 608	..	368	20 672	762
United Arab Emirates / Emirats arabes unis	1996	..	..	113 789	5 279	5 507	* 60	281	31 521	2 285
	1997	..	..	115 913	6 155	5 453	* 65	296	33 862	2 448
	1998	..	..	119 538	5 703	5 135	* 65	296	34 571	2 700
	1999	..	..	109 732	5 841	5 595	* 65	314	* 34 299	* 2 743
Uzbekistan / Ouzbékistan	1996	779	..	7 729	1 648	4 050	723	213	42 619	3 906
	1997	806	..	8 020	1 773	4 027	829	232	44 176	3 961
	1998	801	..	8 179	2 083	4 220	823	230	49 615	3 947
	1999	814	..	8 399	2 155	3 988	802	248	50 331	3 896
Viet Nam / Viet Nam	1996	6 876	..	8 714	...	...	...	..	307	1 937
	1997	7 972	..	10 920	...	...	...	..	553	* 2 135
	1998	8 170	..	12 412	...	...	...	..	819	* 2 359
	1999	6 740	..	15 232	...	...	...	..	1 023	* 2 529

65

Production of selected energy commodities
Thousand metric tons of oil equivalent *[cont.]*
Production des principaux biens de l'énergie
Milliers de tonnes d'équivalent pétrole *[suite]*

Region, country or area / Région, pays ou zone	Year / Anneé	Hard coal, lignite and peat / Houille, lignite et tourbe	Briquettes and cokes / Agglomérés et cokes	Crude petroleum and NGL / Pétrole Brut et GNL	Light petroleum products / Produits pétroliers légers	Heavy petroleum products / Produits pétroliers lourds	Other petroleum products / Autres produits pétroliers	LPG and refinery gas / GLP et gas de raffinerie	Natural gas / Gaz naturel	Electricity / Electricité
Yemen	1996	..	..	17 747	1 882	2 329	60	21	..	201
Yémen	1997	..	..	18 582	2 123	2 937	59	22	..	220
	1998	..	..	19 032	2 123	2 966	59	22	..	216
	1999	..	..	20 887	* 1 928	* 2 994	* 59	18	..	255
Europe	**1996**	**422 745**	**75 768**	**633 566**	**306 208**	**513 010**	**73 374**	**54 542**	**831 033**	**558 050**
Europe	**1997**	**410 478**	**75 140**	**637 151**	**312 372**	**517 086**	**74 673**	**55 495**	**799 408**	**562 794**
	1998	**376 712**	**70 017**	**631 708**	**314 483**	**523 894**	**73 087**	**58 491**	**814 901**	**565 098**
	1999	**372 938**	**69 245**	**642 919**	**303 656**	**499 559**	**76 396**	**57 970**	**813 743**	**575 574**
Albania	1996	26	..	488	150	209	20	40	21	510
Albanie	1997	19	..	366	127	148	17	30	17	446
	1998	14	..	368	103	154	16	30	15	436
	1999	10	..	323	100	136	17	30	13	464
Austria	1996	288	1 061	992	2 912	5 066	1 519	381	1 339	4 716
Autriche	1997	295	1 109	999	3 053	5 501	1 577	400	1 281	4 889
	1998	297	1 137	1 167	2 824	5 285	809	381	1 408	4 940
	1999	297	1 136	1 040	2 772	5 068	1 408	362	1 564	5 686
Belarus	1996	649	..	1 862	1 930	7 986	680	717	230	2 041
Bélarus	1997	631	..	1 824	2 140	7 645	755	650	227	2 241
	1998	464	..	1 832	2 106	7 582	768	687	233	2 020
	1999	705	..	1 842	1 875	7 715	602	708	236	2 280
Belgium	1996	337	2 500	..	9 504	19 590	5 516	1 197	2	14 159
Belgique	1997	257	2 390	..	9 875	20 091	6 110	1 224	0	15 081
	1998	188	2 114	..	10 788	20 603	5 951	1 352	* 0	15 241
	1999	219	2 201	..	10 436	18 758	6 039	1 206	0	15 842
Bosnia and Herzegovina	1996	527	..	..	..	..	..	..	..	206
Bosnie-Herzégovine	1997	543	..	..	..	..	..	..	..	212
	1998	559	..	..	..	..	..	..	..	218
	1999	576	..	..	..	..	..	..	..	225
Bulgaria	1996	4 689	1 248	32	2 203	4 106	312	238	37	6 838
Bulgarie	1997	4 472	1 241	28	1 978	3 534	215	214	31	6 745
	1998	4 970	1 087	33	1 810	3 301	357	211	26	6 544
	1999	4 199	1 063	40	1 826	3 343	422	300	24	6 057
Croatia	1996	45	..	1 913	1 475	2 869	291	399	1 622	907
Croatie	1997	34	..	1 977	1 441	2 985	346	374	1 560	833
	1998	36	..	1 989	1 493	2 927	341	451	1 426	937
	1999	10	..	1 661	1 483	3 275	300	490	1 408	1 053
Czech Republic	1996	27 529	3 414	152	1 970	4 239	1 524	245	202	* 7 775
République tchèque	1997	26 587	2 955	163	1 856	4 001	1 386	306	182	* 7 742
	1998	24 809	2 692	179	1 715	4 017	1 233	254	188	7 906
	1999	21 792	2 246	183	1 588	3 322	1 209	246	195	7 901
Denmark	1996	38	..	10 131	3 319	6 933	..	587	8 566	4 712
Danemark	1997	14	..	11 371	2 973	5 507	..	531	8 170	4 138
	1998	...	..	11 443	2 688	4 839	..	442	6 617	3 969
	1999		..	14 479	2 923	4 907	..	474	6 859	3 835
Estonia	1996	3 257	26	..	..	..	..	..	..	783
Estonie	1997	3 161	25	..	..	..	..	..	..	793
	1998	2 845	16	..	..	..	..	..	..	733
	1999	2 540	10	..	..	..	..	..	..	711
Faeroe Islands *	1996	..	..	..	..	..	..	..	..	15
Iles Féroé *	1997	..	..	..	..	..	..	..	..	16
	1998	..	..	..	..	..	..	..	..	16
	1999	..	..	..	..	..	..	..	..	16
Finland	1996	2 216	573	..	5 669	5 942	274	988	..	9 374
Finlande	1997	2 627	554	..	5 049	5 535	335	864	..	9 865
	1998	424	575	..	5 571	6 627	377	945	..	10 103
	1999	2 043	567	..	5 800	6 320	346	796	..	10 214

65

Production of selected energy commodities
Thousand metric tons of oil equivalent *[cont.]*

Production des principaux biens de l'énergie
Milliers de tonnes d'équivalent pétrole *[suite]*

Region, country or area Région, pays ou zone	Year Anneé	Hard coal, lignite and peat Houille, lignite et tourbe	Briquettes and cokes Agglom-érés et cokes	Crude petroleum and NGL Pétrole Brut et GNL	Light petroleum products Produits pétroliers légers	Heavy petroleum products Produits pétroliers lourds	Other petroleum products Autres produits pétroliers	LPG and refinery gas GLP et gas de raffinerie	Natural gas Gaz naturel	Electricity Electricité
France [3] France [3]	1996	5 360	4 022	3 307	30 189	44 258	9 710	5 440	2 676	113 554
	1997	4 501	3 897	3 202	32 798	46 591	10 394	5 489	2 365	113 439
	1998	3 790	3 911	2 861	33 212	48 568	10 143	5 727	2 102	111 183
	1999	3 559	3 832	3 004	30 294	43 813	10 420	4 920	1 919	114 573
Germany Allemagne	1996	73 504	11 653	2 877	40 784	61 404	8 819	7 102	17 348	75 836
	1997	70 140	10 943	2 807	39 659	58 310	8 831	6 759	17 159	77 485
	1998	64 016	9 904	2 937	41 556	62 007	9 361	6 884	16 863	76 571
	1999	62 058	8 514	2 749	42 798	58 566	9 484	6 856	18 050	76 559
Gibraltar Gibraltar	1996	..	..	..	..	..	..	..	..	9
	1997	..	..	..	..	..	..	..	..	10
	1998	..	..	..	..	..	..	..	..	10
	1999	..	..	..	..	..	..	..	..	8
Greece Grèce	1996	7 783	32	501	6 749	12 189	693	1 082	50	3 680
	1997	7 709	36	458	6 846	12 306	697	1 114	49	3 767
	1998	7 976	28	317	6 896	12 524	761	1 200	44	4 003
	1999	8 129	27	38	6 267	11 208	727	1 015	3	4 287
Hungary Hongrie	1996	3 123	823	2 863	2 647	3 806	671	280	4 000	5 499
	1997	3 214	763	2 712	2 820	3 971	775	283	3 735	5 488
	1998	3 021	756	2 579	2 887	3 867	918	282	3 297	5 639
	1999	3 000	713	2 274	2 682	4 082	600	462	2 576	5 662
Iceland Islande	1996	..	..	..	..	..	..	..	..	713
	1997	..	..	..	..	..	..	..	..	771
	1998	..	..	..	..	..	..	..	..	1 048
	1999	..	..	..	..	..	..	..	..	1 114
Ireland Irlande	1996	1 261	146		619	1 566	...	86	2 410	1 685
	1997	740	134	..	805	2 028	19	101	2 119	1 751
	1998	813	139	..	837	2 228	31	115	1 564	1 887
	1999	1 252	168	..	801	1 976	* 25	98	1 275	2 039
Italy [4] Italie [4]	1996	69	3 473	5 459	30 328	50 326	5 035	5 345	18 194	24 524
	1997	24	3 653	5 956	32 444	54 324	5 654	5 595	17 544	25 227
	1998	44	3 634	5 629	33 269	57 118	5 894	5 340	17 309	26 321
	1999	27	3 493	5 005	29 726	54 279	6 317	5 493	16 213	27 025
Latvia Lettonie	1996	89	..	..	..	..	..	..	..	269
	1997	89	..	..	..	..	..	..	..	387
	1998	14	..	..	..	..	..	..	..	499
	1999	87	..	..	..	..	..	..	..	353
Lithuania Lituanie	1996	18	..	155	1 628	2 195	44	396	..	3 884
	1997	20	..	212	1 979	3 018	68	454	..	3 382
	1998	14	..	277	2 603	3 587	120	473	..	3 888
	1999	19	..	232	1 751	2 357	98	341	..	2 890
Luxembourg Luxembourg	1996	..	..	..	..	..	..	..	..	101
	1997	..	..	..	..	..	..	..	..	100
	1998	..	..	..	..	..	..	..	..	109
	1999	..	..	..	..	..	..	..	..	95
Malta Malte	1996	..	..	..	..	..	..	..	..	143
	1997	..	..	..	..	..	..	..	..	145
	1998	..	..	..	..	..	..	..	..	148
	1999	..	..	..	..	..	..	..	..	158
Netherlands Pays-Bas	1996	..	1 988	3 175	33 927	36 035	5 161	7 885	75 794	8 045
	1997	..	1 977	3 000	33 595	34 645	5 532	7 764	67 253	7 872
	1998	..	1 931	2 738	32 960	35 888	5 780	7 512	63 950	8 485
	1999	..	1 584	2 611	31 249	33 052	6 151	7 848	60 071	8 517
Norway [5] Norvège [5]	1996	154	..	153 908	5 211	8 397	131	1 056	46 734	9 040
	1997	259	..	153 690	5 344	8 928	166	1 106	48 045	9 745
	1998	220	..	147 294	5 068	8 778	168	1 104	48 066	10 172
	1999	328	..	149 773	5 200	9 242	165	1 059	49 184	10 662

65

Production of selected energy commodities
Thousand metric tons of oil equivalent *[cont.]*

Production des principaux biens de l'énergie
Milliers de tonnes d'équivalent pétrole *[suite]*

Region, country or area / Région, pays ou zone	Year / Anneé	Hard coal, lignite and peat Houille, lignite et tourbe	Briquettes and cokes Agglom- érés et cokes	Crude petroleum and NGL Pétrole Brut et GNL	Light petroleum products Produits pétroliers légers	Heavy petroleum products Produits pétroliers lourds	Other petroleum products Autres produits pétroliers	LPG and refinery gas GLP et gas de raffinerie	Natural gas Gaz naturel	Electricity Electricité
Poland	1996	91 714	6 927	317	4 375	9 179	793	505	3 491	12 313
Pologne	1997	91 467	7 153	289	4 551	9 502	1 081	610	3 562	12 280
	1998	78 845	6 613	360	4 672	10 339	1 078	758	3 612	12 280
	1999	75 303	5 676	434	5 438	10 691	1 296	853	3 449	12 223
Portugal	1996	..	222	..	4 596	6 827	777	413	..	3 015
Portugal	1997	..	228	..	5 039	7 025	791	494	..	2 996
	1998	..	236	..	5 028	7 590	1 263	446	..	3 404
	1999	..	243	..	4 916	7 456	1 065	371	..	3 793
Republic of Moldova	1996	..	..	..	..	..	..	..	..	526
République de Moldova	1997	..	..	..	..	..	..	..	..	454
	1998 *	..	..	..	..	..	..	..	..	394
	1999 *	..	..	..	..	..	..	..	..	328
Romania	1996	7 531	1 986	6 876	4 048	6 644	1 661	1 087	13 773	5 519
Roumanie	1997	6 229	2 089	6 776	3 998	6 073	1 267	1 147	11 916	5 860
	1998	4 844	1 973	6 579	3 997	6 019	1 981	1 212	11 157	5 529
	1999	4 199	1 081	6 404	3 382	4 993	1 285	960	11 200	5 271
Russian Federation	1996	101 021	16 289	299 797	37 391	110 331	15 580	9 421	529 109	91 959
Fédération de Russie	1997	96 397	16 323	304 172	37 560	109 530	14 424	10 162	507 593	90 745
	1998	91 081	13 940	301 707	35 583	103 042	10 259	12 925	525 712	89 590
	1999	98 095	16 809	303 542	36 227	102 549	13 453	13 528	525 776	94 125
Serbia and Montenegro	1996	8 193	..	1 031	795	954	321	29	605	* 3 276
Serbie-et-Monténégro	1997	8 668	..	980	1 179	1 746	293	51	620	* 3 467
	1998	9 398	..	1 234	1 272	1 331	312	96	713	* 3 251
	1999	7 093	..	1 031	684	724	261	39	658	* 2 870
Slovakia	1996	1 121	1 102	71	1 654	2 884	675	133	272	4 145
Slovaquie	1997	1 146	1 116	64	1 671	2 944	746	133	250	4 024
	1998	1 157	977	60	1 914	3 133	630	126	224	4 184
	1999	1 097	1 042	66	1 870	3 077	702	103	184	4 681
Slovenia	1996	1 037	..	1	220	312	3	..	12	1 896
Slovénie	1997	952	..	1	175	375	3	..	11	2 011
	1998	923	..	1	73	174	...	..	8	2 062
	1999	868	..	1	123	165	...	...	5	1 962
Spain	1996	9 384	1 745	801	16 206	29 972	5 066	3 147	635	25 002
Espagne	1997	9 318	1 914	670	16 654	32 310	5 089	3 363	383	26 212
	1998	8 743	1 903	873	18 320	35 191	6 399	3 282	375	27 342
	1999	8 267	1 686	652	17 824	34 672	6 093	3 287	392	28 579
Sweden	1996	297	770	* 4	6 358	13 004	1 103	283	..	25 063
Suède	1997	266	777	...	6 485	13 906	1 113	295	..	25 115
	1998	331	769	...	6 357	13 528	1 188	320	..	26 509
	1999	255	767	...	6 539	13 186	1 545	292	..	26 216
Switzerland [6]	1996	..	..	..	1 590	3 214	134	420	..	9 413
Suisse [6]	1997	..	..	..	1 682	2 872	126	424	..	9 924
	1998	..	..	..	1 723	2 845	144	471	..	10 028
	1999	..	..	..	1 839	2 828	133	441	..	10 570
TFYR of Macedonia	1996	1 929	..	..	61	611	..	8	..	555
L'ex-R.y. Macédoine	1997	1 809	..	..	37	348	..	3	..	574
	1998	2 208	..	..	161	566	..	10	..	606
	1999	1 991	..	..	139	451	..	8	..	590
Ukraine	1996	39 012	11 232	4 102	2 943	8 945	1 068	357	17 167	29 577
Ukraine	1997	39 613	11 326	4 138	3 594	8 123	996	341	16 909	29 209
	1998	39 715	11 370	3 904	3 773	8 529	1 045	358	16 756	28 030
	1999	42 582	12 192	3 804	3 743	8 460	932	354	16 682	27 420
United Kingdom	1996	30 545	4 533	132 750	44 760	43 016	5 792	5 276	86 746	46 775
Royaume-Uni	1997	29 278	4 536	131 295	44 964	43 264	5 865	5 213	88 427	47 353
	1998	24 956	4 312	135 346	43 226	41 708	5 759	5 101	93 236	48 862
	1999	22 339	4 196	141 212	41 362	38 887	5 302	5 034	95 806	48 718

65

Production of selected energy commodities
Thousand metric tons of oil equivalent [cont.]

Production des principaux biens de l'énergie
Milliers de tonnes d'équivalent pétrole [suite]

Region, country or area Région, pays ou zone	Year Anneé	Hard coal, lignite and peat Houille, lignite et tourbe	Briquettes and cokes Agglomérés et cokes	Crude petroleum and NGL Pétrole Brut et GNL	Light petroleum products Produits pétroliers légers	Heavy petroleum products Produits pétroliers lourds	Other petroleum products Autres produits pétroliers	LPG and refinery gas GLP et gas de raffinerie	Natural gas Gaz naturel	Electricity Electricité
Oceania	**1996**	**135 798**	**3 040**	**34 105**	**21 349**	**14 895**	**3 359**	**2 410**	**33 432**	**20 521**
Océanie	**1997**	**145 102**	**2 903**	**34 328**	**21 626**	**15 426**	**3 267**	**2 475**	**33 644**	**21 141**
	1998	**155 842**	**2 941**	**36 999**	**21 941**	**15 621**	**3 546**	**2 328**	**34 161**	**22 509**
	1999	**157 961**	**2 761**	**30 937**	**22 026**	**14 959**	**3 099**	**2 402**	**35 438**	**23 196**
American Samoa *	1996	..	..	..	..	..	..	..	..	11
Samoa américaines *	1997	..	..	..	..	..	..	..	..	11
	1998	..	..	..	..	..	..	..	..	11
	1999	..	..	..	..	..	..	..	..	11
Australia	1996	133 798	3 040	27 977	18 990	12 946	3 105	2 219	28 525	15 280
Australie	1997	143 212	2 903	27 579	19 123	13 271	3 044	2 225	28 415	15 754
	1998	153 998	2 941	30 846	19 414	13 453	3 314	2 086	29 552	16 854
	1999	155 880	2 761	24 984	19 702	12 684	2 838	2 193	30 099	17 491
Cook Islands	1996	..	..	..	..	..	..	..	..	2
Iles Cook	1997	..	..	..	..	..	..	..	..	2
	1998	..	..	..	..	..	..	..	..	2
	1999	..	..	..	..	..	..	..	..	2
Fiji *	1996	..	..	..	..	..	..	..	..	47
Fidji *	1997	..	..	..	..	..	..	..	..	47
	1998	..	..	..	..	..	..	..	..	46
	1999	..	..	..	..	..	..	..	..	47
French Polynesia	1996	..	..	..	..	..	..	..	..	31
Polynésie française	1997	..	..	..	..	..	..	..	..	31
	1998	..	..	..	..	..	..	..	..	30
	1999	..	..	..	..	..	..	..	..	31
Guam *	1996	..	..	..	..	..	..	..	..	71
Guam *	1997	..	..	..	..	..	..	..	..	71
	1998	..	..	..	..	..	..	..	..	71
	1999	..	..	..	..	..	..	..	..	71
Kiribati *	1996	..	..	..	..	..	..	..	..	1
Kiribati *	1997	..	..	..	..	..	..	..	..	1
	1998	..	..	..	..	..	..	..	..	1
	1999	..	..	..	..	..	..	..	..	1
Nauru *	1996	..	..	..	..	..	..	..	..	3
Nauru *	1997	..	..	..	..	..	..	..	..	3
	1998	..	..	..	..	..	..	..	..	3
	1999	..	..	..	..	..	..	..	..	3
New Caledonia	1996	..	..	..	..	..	..	..	..	128
Nouvelle-Calédonie	1997	..	..	..	..	..	..	..	..	131
	1998	..	..	..	..	..	..	..	..	136
	1999	..	..	..	..	..	..	..	..	139
New Zealand	1996	2 000	..	2 124	2 338	1 919	254	191	4 829	4 800
Nouvelle-Zélande	1997	1 889	..	2 785	2 482	2 122	223	250	5 151	4 929
	1998	1 845	..	2 249	2 509	2 137	232	243	4 531	5 161
	1999	2 081	..	2 019	2 305	2 244	261	210	5 261	5 213
Niue *	1996	..	..	..	..	..	..	..	..	0
Nioué *	1997	..	..	..	..	..	..	..	..	0
	1998	..	..	..	..	..	..	..	..	0
	1999	..	..	..	..	..	..	..	..	0
Palau *	1996	..	..	..	..	..	..	..	..	18
Palaos *	1997	..	..	..	..	..	..	..	..	18
	1998	..	..	..	..	..	..	..	..	18
	1999	..	..	..	..	..	..	..	..	18
Papua New Guinea	1996	..	..	* 4 004	* 21	* 30	..	..	* 78	116
Papouasie-Nvl-Guinée	1997	..	..	* 3 964	* 21	* 32	..	..	* 78	131
	1998	..	..	* 3 904	* 19	* 30	..	..	* 78	160
	1999	..	..	* 3 934	* 19	* 31	..	..	* 78	153

65

Production of selected energy commodities
Thousand metric tons of oil equivalent *[cont.]*
Production des principaux biens de l'énergie
Milliers de tonnes d'équivalent pétrole *[suite]*

Region, country or area Région, pays ou zone	Year Anneé	Hard coal, lignite and peat Houille, lignite et tourbe	Briquettes and cokes Agglom-érés et cokes	Crude petroleum and NGL Pétrole Brut et GNL	Light petroleum products Produits pétroliers légers	Heavy petroleum products Produits pétroliers lourds	Other petroleum products Autres produits pétroliers	LPG and refinery gas GLP et gas de raffinerie	Natural gas Gaz naturel	Electricity Electricité
Samoa *	1996	..	..	..	..	..	..	..	..	6
Samoa *	1997	..	..	..	..	..	..	..	..	6
	1998	..	..	..	..	..	..	..	..	6
	1999	..	..	..	..	..	..	..	..	6
Solomon Islands *	1996	..	..	..	..	..	..	..	..	3
Iles Salomon *	1997	..	..	..	..	..	..	..	..	3
	1998	..	..	..	..	..	..	..	..	3
	1999	..	..	..	..	..	..	..	..	3
Tonga	1996	..	..	..	..	..	..	..	..	3
Tonga	1997 *	..	..	..	..	..	..	..	..	3
	1998	..	..	..	..	..	..	..	..	3
	1999 *	..	..	..	..	..	..	..	..	3
Vanuatu *	1996	..	..	..	..	..	..	..	..	3
Vanuatu *	1997	..	..	..	..	..	..	..	..	3
	1998	..	..	..	..	..	..	..	..	3
	1999	..	..	..	..	..	..	..	..	3

Source:
United Nations Statistics Division, New York, "Energy Statistics Yearbook 1999" and the energy statistics database.

Source:
Organisation des Nations Unies, Division de statistique, New York, "Annuaire des statistiques de l'énergie 1999" et la base de données pour les statistiques énergétiques.

1 Refers to the Southern African Customs Union.
2 Including part of the Neutral Zone.
3 Including Monaco.
4 Including San Marino.
5 Including Svalbard and Jan Mayen Islands.
6 Including Liechtenstein.

1 Se rèfèrent à l'Union douanière d'afrique australe.
2 Y compris une partie de la Zone Neutrale.
3 Y compris Monaco.
4 Y compris Saint-Marin.
5 Y compris îles Svalbard et Jan Mayen.
6 Y compris Liechtenstein.

Technical notes, tables 64 and 65

Tables 64 and 65: Data are presented in metric tons of oil equivalent (TOE), to which the individual energy commodities are converted in the interests of international uniformity and comparability.

To convert from original units to TOE, the data in original units (metric tons, terajoules, kilowatt hours, cubic metres) are multiplied by conversion factors. For a list of the relevant conversion factors and a detailed description of methods, see the United Nations *Energy Statistics Yearbook* and related methodological publications [23, 45, 46].

Table 64: Included in the production of commercial primary energy for *solids* are hard coal, lignite, peat and oil shale; *liquids* are comprised of crude petroleum and natural gas liquids; *gas* comprises natural gas; and *electricity* is comprised of primary electricity generation from hydro, nuclear, geothermal, wind, tide, wave and solar sources.

In general, data on stocks refer to changes in stocks of producers, importers and/or industrial consumers at the beginning and end of each year.

International trade of energy commodities is based on the "general trade" system, that is, all goods entering and leaving the national boundary of a country are recorded as imports and exports.

Sea/air bunkers refer to the amounts of fuels delivered to ocean-going ships or aircraft of all flags engaged in international traffic. Consumption by ships engaged in transport in inland and coastal waters, or by aircraft engaged in domestic flights, is not included.

Data on consumption refer to "apparent consumption" and are derived from the formula "production + imports - exports - bunkers +/- stock changes". Accordingly, the series on apparent consumption may in some cases represent only an indication of the magnitude of actual gross inland availability.

Included in the consumption of commercial energy for *solids* are consumption of primary forms of solid fuels, net imports and changes in stocks of secondary fuels; *liquids* are comprised of consumption of energy petroleum products including feedstocks, natural gasolene, condensate, refinery gas and input of crude petroleum to thermal power plants; *gases* include the consumption of natural gas, net imports and changes in stocks of gasworks and coke-oven gas; and *electricity* is comprised of production of primary electricity and net imports of electricity.

Table 65: The definitions of the energy commodities are as follows:

— Hard coal: Coal that has a high degree of coalification with a gross calorific value above 23,865 KJ/kg (5,700 kcal/kg) on an ash-free but moist basis, and a mean random reflectance of vitrinite of at least 0.6. Slurries, middlings and

Notes techniques, tableaux 64 et 65

Tableaux 64 et 65: Les données relatives aux divers produits énergétiques ont été converties en tonnes d'équivalent pétrole (TEP), dans un souci d'uniformité et pour permettre les comparaisons entre la production de différents pays.

Pour passer des unités de mesure d'origine à l'unité commune, les données en unités d'origine (tonnes, terajoules, kilowatt-heures, mètres cubes) sont multipliées pour les facteurs de conversion. Pour une liste des facteurs de conversion appropriée et pour des descriptions détaillées des méthodes appliquées, se reporter à *l'Annuaire des statistiques de l'énergie* des Nations Unies et aux publications méthodologiques connexes [23, 45, 46].

Tableau 64: Sont compris dans la production d'énergie primaire commerciale: pour *les solides*, la houille, le lignite, la tourbe et le schiste bitumineux; pour *les liquides*, le pétrole brut et les liquides de gaz naturel; pour *les gaz*, le gaz naturel; pour *l'électricité*, l'électricité primaire de source hydraulique, nucléaire, géothermique, éolienne, marémotrice, des vagues et solaire.

En général, les variations des stocks se rapportent aux différences entre les stocks des producteurs, des importateurs ou des consommateurs industriels au début et à la fin de chaque année.

Le commerce international des produits énergétiques est fondé sur le système du "commerce général", c'est-à-dire que tous les biens entrant sur le territoire national d'un pays ou en sortant sont respectivement enregistrés comme importations et exportations.

Les soutages maritimes/aériens se rapportent aux quantités de combustibles livrées aux navires de mer et aéronefs assurant des liaisons commerciales internationales, quel que soit leur pavillon. La consommation des navires effectuant des opérations de transport sur les voies navigables intérieures ou dans les eaux côtières n'est pas incluse, non plus que celle des aéronefs effectuant des vols intérieurs.

Les données sur la consommation se rapportent à la "consommation apparente" et sont obtenues par la formule "production + importations - exportations - soutage +/- variations des stocks". En conséquence, les séries relatives à la consommation apparente peuvent occasionnellement ne donner qu'une indication de l'ordre de grandeur des disponibilités intérieures brutes réelles.

Sont compris dans la consommation d'énergie commerciale: pour *les solides*, la consommation de combustibles solides primaires, les importations nettes et les variations de stocks de combustibles solides secondaires; pour *les liquides*, la consommation de produits pétroliers énergétiques y compris les charges d'alimentation des usines de traitement, l'essence naturelle, le condensat et le gaz de raffinerie ainsi que le pétrole brut consommé dans les centrales thermiques pour la production d'électricité; pour *les gaz*, la consommation de gaz naturel, les importations nettes et

other low-grade coal products, which cannot be classified according to the type of coal from which they are obtained, are included under hard coal.

— Lignite: Non-agglomerating coal with a low degree of coalification which retained the anatomical structure of the vegetable matter from which it was formed. Its gross calorific value is less than 17,435 KJ/kg (4,165 kcal/kg), and it contains greater than 31 per cent volatile matter on a dry mineral matter free basis.

— Peat: A solid fuel formed from the partial decomposition of dead vegetation under conditions of high humidity and limited air access (initial stage of coalification). Only peat used as fuel is included.

— Patent fuel (hard coal briquettes): A composition fuel manufactured from coal fines by shaping with the addition of a binding agent (pitch).

— Lignite briquettes: A composition fuel manufactured from lignite. The lignite is crushed, dried and molded under high pressure into an even-shaped briquette without the addition of binders.

— Peat briquettes: A composition fuel manufactured from peat. Raw peat, after crushing and drying, is molded under high pressure into an even-shaped briquette without the addition of binders.

— Coke: The solid residue obtained from coal or lignite by heating it to a high temperature in the absence or near absence of air. It is high in carbon and low in moisture and volatile matter. Several categories are distinguished: coke-oven coke; gas coke; and brown coal coke.

— Crude oil: A mineral oil consisting of a mixture of hydrocarbons of natural origin, yellow to black in color, of variable density and viscosity. Data in this category also includes lease or field condensate (separator liquids) which is recovered from gaseous hydrocarbons in lease separation facilities, as well as synthetic crude oil, mineral oils extracted from bituminous minerals such as shales and bituminous sand, and oils from coal liquefaction.

— Natural gas liquids (NGL): Liquid or liquefied hydrocarbons produced in the manufacture, purification and stabilization of natural gas. NGLs include, but are not limited to, ethane, propane, butane, pentane, natural gasolene, and plant condensate.

— Light petroleum products: Light products are defined in the table as liquid products obtained by distillation of crude petroleum at temperatures between 30°C and 350°C, and/or which have a specific gravity between 0.625 and 0.830. They comprise: aviation gasolene; motor gasolene; natural gasolene; jet fuel; kerosene; naphtha; and white spirit/industrial spirit.

— Heavy petroleum products: are defined in the table as products obtained by the distillation of crude petroleum at temperatures above 350°C, and which have a specific gravity higher than 0.83. Products which are

les variations de stocks de gaz d'usines à gaz et de gaz de cokerie; pour *l'électricité*, la production d'électricité primaire et les importations nettes d'électricité.

Tableau 65: Les définitions des produits énergétiques sont données ci-après :

— Houille: Charbon à haut degré de houillification et de pouvoir calorifique brut supérieur à 23 865 kJ/kg (5 700 kcal/kg), valeur mesurée pour un combustible exempt de cendres, mais humide et ayant un indice moyen de réflectance de la vitrinite au moins égal à 0,6. Les schlamms, les mixtes et autres produits du charbon de faible qualité qui ne peuvent être classés en fonction du type de charbon dont ils sont dérivés, sont inclus dans cette rubrique.

— Lignite: Le charbon non agglutinant d'un faible degré de houillification qui a gardé la structure anatomique des végétaux dont il est issu. Son pouvoir calorifique supérieur est inférieur à 17 435 kJ/kg (4 165 kcal/kg) et il contient plus de 31% de matières volatiles sur produit sec exempt de matières minérales.

— Tourbe: Combustible solide issu de la décomposition partielle de végétaux morts dans des conditions de forte humidité et de faible circulation d'air (phase initiale de la houillification). N'est prise en considération ici que la tourbe utilisée comme combustible.

— Agglomérés (briquettes de houille): Combustibles composites fabriqués par moulage au moyen de fines de charbon avec l'addition d'un liant (brai).

— Briquettes de lignite: Combustibles composites fabriqués au moyen de lignite. Le lignite est broyé, séché et moulé sous pression élevée pour donner une briquette de forme régulière sans l'addition d'un élément liant.

— Briquettes de tourbe: Combustibles composites fabriqués au moyen de tourbe. La tourbe brute, après broyage et séchage, est moulée sous pression élevée pour donner une briquette de forme régulière sans l'addition d'un élément liant.

— Coke: Résidu solide obtenu lors de la distillation de houille ou de lignite en l'absence totale ou presque total d'air. Il a un haut contenu de carbone, et a peu d'humidité et matières volatiles. On distingue plusieurs catégories de coke: coke de four; coke de gaz; et coke de lignite.

— Pétrole brut: Huile minérale constituée d'un mélange d'hydrocarbures d'origine naturelle, de couleur variant du jaune au noir, d'une densité et d'une viscosité variable. Figurent également dans cette rubrique les condensats directement récupérés sur les sites d'exploitation des hydrocarbures gazeux (dans les installations prévues pour la séparation des phases liquide et gazeuse), le pétrole brut synthétique, les huiles minérales brutes extraites des roches bitumineuses telles que schistes, sables asphaltiques et les huiles issues de la liquéfaction du charbon.

— Liquides de gaz naturel (LGN): Hydrocarbures liquides ou liquéfiés produits lors de la fabrication, de la purification et de la stabilisation du gaz naturel. Les liquides de gaz naturel comprennent l'éthane, le propane, le butane, le pentane, l'essence naturelle et les conden-

not used for energy purposes, such as insulating oils, lubricants, paraffin wax, bitumen and petroleum coke, are excluded. Heavy products comprise residual fuel oil and gas-diesel oil (distillate fuel oil).

— Liquefied petroleum gas (LPG): Hydrocarbons which are gaseous under conditions of normal temperature and pressure but are liquefied by compression or cooling to facilitate storage, handling and transportation. It comprises propane, butane, or a combination of the two. Also included is ethane from petroleum refineries or natural gas producers' separation and stabilization plants.

— Refinery gas: Non-condensable gas obtained during distillation of crude oil or treatment of oil products (e.g. cracking) in refineries. It consists mainly of hydrogen, methane, ethane and olefins.

— Natural gas: Gases consisting mainly of methane occurring naturally in underground deposits. It includes both non-associated gas (originating from fields producing only hydrocarbons in gaseous form) and associated gas (originating from fields producing both liquid and gaseous hydrocarbons), as well as methane recovered from coal mines and sewage gas. Production of natural gas refers to dry marketable production, measured after purification and extraction of natural gas liquids and sulphur. Extraction losses and the amounts that have been reinjected, flared, and vented are excluded from the data on production.

— Electricity production refers to gross production, which includes the consumption by station auxiliaries and any losses in the transformers that are considered integral parts of the station. Included also is total electric energy produced by pumping installations without deduction of electric energy absorbed by pumping.

le butane, le pentane, l'essence naturelle et les condensats d'usine, sans que la liste soit limitative.

— Produits pétroliers légers: Les produits légers sont définis ici comme des produits liquides obtenus par distillation du pétrole brut à des températures comprises entre 30°C et 350°C et/ou ayant une densité comprise entre 0,625 et 0,830. Ces produits sont les suivants: l'essence aviation; l'essence auto; l'essence naturelle; les carburéacteurs du type essence et du type kérosène; le pétrole lampant; les naphtas; et le white spirit/essences spéciales.

— Produits pétroliers lourds sont définis ici comme des produits obtenus par distillation du pétrole brut à des températures supérieures à 350°C et ayant une densité supérieure à 0,83. En sont exclus les produits qui ne sont pas utilisés à des fins énergétiques, tels que les huiles isolantes, les lubrifiants, les paraffines, le bitume et le coke de pétrole. Les produits lourds comprennent le mazout résiduel et le gazole/carburant diesel (mazout distillé).

— Gaz de pétrole liquéfiés (GPL): Hydrocarbures qui sont à l'état gazeux dans des conditions de température et de pression normales mais sont liquéfiés par compression ou refroidissement pour en faciliter l'entreposage, la manipulation et le transport. Dans cette rubrique figurent le propane et le butane ou un mélange de ces deux hydrocarbures. Est également inclus l'éthane produit dans les raffineries ou dans les installations de séparation et de stabilisation des producteurs de gaz naturel.

— Gaz de raffinerie: Comprend les gaz non condensables obtenus dans les raffineries lors de la distillation du pétrole brut ou du traitement des produits pétroliers (par craquage par exemple). Il s'agit principalement d'hydrogène, de méthane, d'éthane et d'oléfines.

— Gaz naturel: Est constitué de gaz, méthane essentiellement, extraits de gisements naturels souterrains. Il peut s'agir aussi bien de gaz non associé (provenant de gisements qui produisent uniquement des hydrocarbures gazeux) que de gaz associé (provenant de gisements qui produisent à la fois des hydrocarbures liquides et gazeux) ou de méthane récupéré dans les mines de charbon et le gaz de gadoues. La production de gaz naturel se rapporte à la production de gaz commercialisable sec, mesurée après purification et extraction des condensats de gaz naturel et du soufre. Les quantités réinjectées, brûlées à la torchère ou éventées et les pertes d'extraction sont exclus des données sur la production.

— Production d'électricité se rapporte à la production brute, qui comprend la consommation des équipements auxiliaires des centrales et les pertes au niveau des transformateurs considérés comme faisant partie intégrante de ces centrales, ainsi que la quantité totale d'énergie électrique produits par les installations de pompage sans déductions de l'énergie électrique absorbée par ces dernières.

66
Land   Terres

Country or area Pays ou zone	2000 Land area Superficie des terres	2000 Arable land Terres arables	Permanent crops Cultures permanentes	2000 Forest cover Superficie forestière	Net change − Variation nette 1990 − 2000 Arable land Terres arables	Net change − Variation nette 1990 − 2000 Permanent crops Cultures permanentes	1990−2000 Forest cover Superficie forestière	1997 Protected areas Aires protégées	Protected areas Aires protégées %[1]
	Area in thousand hectares − Superficie en milliers de hectares								
Africa · Afrique									
Algeria Algérie	238 174	7 675[2]	520[2]	2145	594	− 34	27	5890.8	2.5
Angola Angola	124 670	3 000[2]	300[2]	69756	100	− 200	−124	8181.2	6.6
Benin Bénin	11 062	1 950[2]	265[2]	2650	335	160	−70	1262.5	11.2
Botswana Botswana	56 673	370[2]	3[2]	12427	− 48	0	−118	10498.7	18.3
Burkina Faso Burkina Faso	27 360	3 800[2]	50[2]	7089	280	− 5	−15	2855.2	10.4
Burundi Burundi	2 568	900[2]	360[2]	94	− 30	0	−15	146.2	5.3
Cameroon Cameroun	46 540	5 960[2]	1 200[2]	23858	20	− 30	−222	2097.7	4.4
Cape Verde Cap−Vert	403	39[2]	2[2]	85	− 2	0	5	0.0	0.0
Central African Republic République centrafricaine	62 298	1 930[2]	90[2]	22907	10	4	−30	5445.6	8.7
Chad Tchad	125 920	3 520[2]	30[2]	12692	247	3	−82	11494.0	9.0
Comoros Comores	223	78[2]	50[2]	8	0	15	...	0.0	0.0
Congo Congo	34 150	175[2]	45[2]	22060	21	3	−17	1699.8	5.0
Côte d'Ivoire Côte d'Ivoire	31 800	2 950[2]	4 400[2]	7117	520	900	−265	1985.5	6.2
Dem. Republic of the Congo République dém. du Congo	226 705	6 700[2]	1 180[2]	135207	30	− 10	−532	14637.4	6.2
Djibouti Djibouti	2 318	...	...	6	...	...	...	10.0	0.4
Egypt Egypte	99 545	2 825[2]	466[2]	72	541	102	2	793.8	0.8
Equatorial Guinea Guinée équatoriale	2 805	130[2]	100[2]	1752	0	0	−11	0.0	0.0
Eritrea Erythrée	10 100	498[2]	3[2]	1585	...	...	−5	500.6	4.3
Ethiopia Ethiopie	100 000	10 000[2]	728[2]	4593	...	...	−40	18699.8	16.9
Gabon Gabon	25 767	325[2]	170[2]	21826	30	8	−10	723.0	2.7
Gambia Gambie	1 000	230[2]	5[2]	481	48	0	4	22.5	2.1
Ghana Ghana	22 754	3 609[2]	2 200[2]	6335	909	700	−120	1268.4	5.3
Guinea Guinée	24 572	885[2]	600[2]	6929	157	100	−35	163.5	0.7
Guinea−Bissau Guinée−Bissau	2 812	300[2]	50[2]	2187	0	10	−22	0.0	0.0
Kenya Kenya	56 914	4 000[2]	520[2]	17096	0	20	−93	4538.3	7.8
Lesotho Lesotho	3 035	325[2]	...	14	8	...	...	6.8	0.2
Liberia Libéria	9 632	380[2]	215[2]	3481	− 20	0	−76	129.2	1.2
Libyan Arab Jamahiriya Jamah. arabe libyenne	175 954	1 815[2]	335[2]	358	10	− 15	5	173.0	0.1

66
Land [*cont.*]
Terres [*suite*]

		2000		2000	Net change − Variation nette			1997	
					1990 − 2000		1990−2000		
Country or area Pays ou zone	Land area Superficie des terres	Arable land Terres arables	Permanent crops Cultures permanentes	Forest cover Superficie forestière	Arable land Terres arables	Permanent crops Cultures permanentes	Forest cover Superficie forestière	Protected areas Aires protégées	Protected areas Aires protégées
	Area in thousand hectares − Superficie en milliers de hectares								%[1]
Madagascar Madagascar	58 154	2 900[2]	600[2]	11727	180	− 5	−117	1231.9	2.1
Malawi Malawi	9 408	2 100[2]	140[2]	2562	285	25	−71	1058.5	11.3
Mali Mali	122 019	4 630[2]	44[2]	13186	2 577	4	−99	4531.9	3.7
Mauritania Mauritanie	102 522	488[2]	12[2]	317	88	6	−10	1746.0	1.7
Mauritius Maurice	203	100[2]	6[2]	16	0	0	...	15.7	8.4
Mayotte Mayotte	...	...	...	...	...	...	...	4.5	12.0
Morocco Maroc	44 630	8 767	967	3025	60	231	−1	317.4	0.7
Mozambique Mozambique	78 409	3 900[2]	235[2]	30601	450	5	−64	6979.0	8.9
Namibia Namibie	82 329	816[2]	4[2]	8040	156	2	−73	11215.8	13.6
Niger Niger	126 670	4 490[2]	10[2]	1328	895	0	−62	9694.1	8.2
Nigeria Nigéria	91 077	28 200[2]	2 650[2]	13517	−1 339	115	−398	3021.4	3.3
Reunion Réunion	250	34	4	71	− 13	− 1	−1	13.0	5.2
Rwanda Rwanda	2 467	900[2]	250[2]	307	20	− 55	−15	396.4	15.1
Saint Helena Sainte−Hélène	31	4[2]	...	2	2	...	...	7.6	18.5
Sao Tome and Principe Sao Tomé−et−Principe	96	4[2]	43[2]	27	2	4	...	...	...
Senegal Sénégal	19 253	2 362[2]	38[2]	6205	37	13	−45	2242.1	11.4
Seychelles Seychelles	45	1[2]	6[2]	30	0	1	...	44.9	99.8
Sierra Leone Sierra Leone	7 162	490[2]	60[2]	1055	4	6	−36	153.3	2.1
Somalia Somalie	62 734	1 043[2]	24[2]	7515	21	4	−77	524.5	0.8
South Africa Afrique du Sud	122 104	14 753	959	8917	1 313	99	−8	6645.1	5.6
Sudan Soudan	237 600	16 233	200[2]	61627	3 233	− 35	−959	12249.0	4.9
Swaziland Swaziland	1 720	178	12[2]	522	− 2	0	6	60.0	3.5
Togo Togo	5 439	2 510[2]	120[2]	510	410	30	−21	429.1	7.6
Tunisia Tunisie	15 536	2 909[2]	2 105[2]	510	0	163	1	44.5	0.3
Uganda Ouganda	19 710	5 060[2]	1 900[2]	4190	60	190	−91	4915.3	20.8
United Republic of Tanzania Rép.−Unie de Tanzanie	88 359	4 000[2]	950[2]	38811	500	50	−91	26261.8	27.9
Western Sahara Sahara occidental	26 600	2[2]	...	...	0	...	...	...	...
Zambia Zambie	74 339	5 260[2]	19[2]	31246	11	0	−851	22649.1	30.1
Zimbabwe Zimbabwe	38 685	3 220[2]	130[2]	19040	330	10	−320	4996.8	12.8

66
Land [*cont.*]
Terres [*suite*]

Country or area Pays ou zone	2000 Land area Superficie des terres	2000 Arable land Terres arables	Permanent crops Cultures permanentes	2000 Forest cover Superficie forestière	1990−2000 Arable land Terres arables	1990−2000 Permanent crops Cultures permanentes	1990−2000 Forest cover Superficie forestière	1997 Protected areas Aires protégées	Protected areas Aires protégées %[1]
America, North · Amérique du Nord									
Antigua and Barbuda Antigua−et−Barbuda	44	8[2]	...	9	0	...	...	6.6	14.9
Aruba Aruba	19	2[2]	...	...	0	...	...	0.0	0.0
Bahamas Bahamas	1 001	7	4	842	− 1	2	...	145.7	10.5
Barbados Barbade	43	16[2]	1[2]	2	0	0	...	0.2	0.5
Belize Belize	2 280	64[2]	25[2]	1348	14	7	−36	913.0	39.8
Bermuda Bermudes	5	...	...	...	...	...	...	12.5	231.5
British Virgin Islands Iles Vierges britanniques	15	3[2]	1[2]	3	0	0	...	2.0	13.1
Canada Canada	922 097	45 560[2]	140[2]	244571	− 260	10	...	95310.3	9.6
Cayman Islands Iles Caïmanes	26	...	...	13	...	...	...	8.8	34.0
Costa Rica Costa Rica	5 106	225[2]	280[2]	1968	− 35	30	−16	1204.4	23.7
Cuba Cuba	10 982	3 630[2]	835[2]	2348	380	25	28	1908.9	16.7
Dominica Dominique	75	3[2]	12[2]	46	− 2	1	...	17.0	22.6
Dominican Republic Rép. dominicaine	4 838	1 096[2]	500[2]	1376	46	50	...	8404.3	173.5
El Salvador El Salvador	2 072	560[2]	250[2]	121	10	− 10	−7	5.2	0.2
Greenland Groenland	34 170[5]	...	...	...	...	...	...	98250.0	45.2
Grenada Grenade	34	1	10	5	− 1	0	...	0.6	1.7
Guadeloupe Guadeloupe	169	19	6	82	− 2	− 2	2	21.0	11.8
Guatemala Guatemala	10 843	1 360[2]	545[2]	2850	60	60	−54	2166.6	19.9
Haiti Haïti	2 756	560[2]	350[2]	88	5	0	−7	9.7	0.3
Honduras Honduras	11 189	1 068	359	5383	− 394	1	−59	1130.9	10.1
Jamaica Jamaïque	1 083	174[2]	100[2]	325	55	0	−5	98.2	8.6
Martinique Martinique	106	11	10	47	1	0	...	71.2	66.0
Mexico Mexique	190 869	24 800[2]	2 500[2]	55205	800	600	−631	15975.9	8.1
Montserrat Montserrat	10	2[2]	...	3	0	...	...	1.0	9.6
Netherland Antilles Antilles néerlandaises	80	8[2]	...	1	0	...	...	7.7	9.6
Nicaragua Nicaragua	12 140	2 457[2]	289[2]	3278	494	38	−117	1637.5	11.1
Panama Panama	7 443	500[2]	155	2876	1	0	−52	1547.3	19.7
Puerto Rico Porto Rico	887	35[2]	46[2]	229	− 30	− 4	−1	29.5	3.3
Saint Kitts and Nevis Saint−Kitts−et−Nevis	36	7[2]	1[2]	4	− 1	− 1	...	2.6	10.0
Saint Lucia Sainte−Lucie	61	3[2]	14[2]	9	− 2	1	−1	9.7	15.7

66
Land [cont.]
Terres [suite]

Country or area Pays ou zone	2000 Land area Superficie des terres	2000 Arable land Terres arables	Permanent crops Cultures permanentes	2000 Forest cover Superficie forestière	Net change – Variation nette 1990 – 2000 Arable land Terres arables	1990 – 2000 Permanent crops Cultures permanentes	1990–2000 Forest cover Superficie forestière	1997 Protected areas Aires protégées	Protected areas Aires protégées %[1]
	Area in thousand hectares – Superficie en milliers de hectares								
Saint Pierre and Miquelon Saint–Pierre–et–Miquelon	23	3[2]	...	...	0	...	...	0.0	0.0
Saint Vincent – Grenadines Saint–Vincent–Grenadines	39	4[2]	7[2]	6	0	0	...	8.2	21.1
Trinidad and Tobago Trinité–et–Tobago	513	75[2]	47[2]	259	1	1	−2	21.0	4.1
Turks and Caicos Islands Iles Turques et Caïques	43	1[2]	...	...	0	...	...	71.6	166.5
United States Etats–Unis	915 896	176 950[2]	2 050[2]	225993	−8 792	16	388	198844.4	21.2
United States Virgin Islands Iles Vierges américaines	34	4[2]	1[2]	14	0	0	...	5.7	16.2
America, South · Amérique du Sud									
Argentina Argentine	273 669	25 000[2]	2 200[2]	34648	0	0	−285	9126.1	3.3
Bolivia Bolivie	108 438	1 944	262	53068	44	41	−161	17818.5	16.2
Brazil Brésil	845 651	53 200[2]	12 000[2]	543905	7 600	1 000	−2309	52671.7	6.2
Chile Chili	74 880	1 979[2]	318[2]	15536	− 823	71	−20	14137.2	18.8
Colombia Colombie	103 870	2 818	1 727	49601	− 487	32	−190	9365.2	8.2
Ecuador Equateur	27 684	1 574[2]	1 427[2]	10557	− 30	106	−137	15551.7	33.7
Falkland Islands (Malvinas) Iles Falkland (Malvinas)	1 217	...	...	...	...	...	...	11.1	0.9
French Guiana Guyane française	8 815	9	4	7926	− 1	2	...	100.1	1.1
Guyana Guyana	19 685	480[2]	16[2]	16879	0	1	−49	58.5	0.3
Paraguay Paraguay	39 730	2 290[2]	88	23372	180	− 1	−123	1401.1	3.4
Peru Pérou	128 000	3 700[2]	510[2]	65215	200	90	−269	6760.4	5.3
Suriname Suriname	15 600	57[2]	10[2]	14113	0	− 1	...	804.2	4.9
Uruguay Uruguay	17 502	1 300[2]	40	1292	40	− 5	50	47.5	0.3
Venezuela Venezuela	88 205	2 440[2]	960[2]	49506	− 260	50	−218	56040.4	61.4
Asia · Asie									
Afghanistan Afghanistan	65 209	7 910[2]	144[2]	1351	0	0	...	218.6	0.3
Armenia Arménie	2 820	495[2]	65[2]	351	...	...	4	213.4	7.2
Azerbaijan Azerbaïdjan	8 660	1 644[2]	263[2]	1094	...	...	13	477.6	5.5
Bahrain Bahreïn	71	2[2]	4	...	0	2	...	0.8	1.2
Bangladesh Bangladesh	13 017	8 139[2]	345[2]	1334	− 998	45	17	98.0	0.7
Bhutan Bhoutan	4 700	140[2]	20[2]	3016	27	1	...	997.8	21.4
Brunei Darussalam Brunéi Darussalam	527	3[2]	4[2]	442	0	0	−1	121.2	21.0
Cambodia Cambodge	17 652	3 700[2]	107[2]	9335	5	7	−56	3267.1	18.1
China [3] Chine [3]	932 742	124 136[2]	11 421[2]	163480	458	3 702	1806	68240.7	7.1
China, Hong Kong SAR Chine, Hong Kong RAS	...	...	...	...	...	...	...	46.1	43.4

66
Land [*cont.*]
Terres [*suite*]

| | 2000 | | | 2000 | Net change − Variation nette | | | 1997 | |
| | | | | | 1990 − 2000 | | 1990−2000 | | |
Country or area Pays ou zone	Land area Superficie des terres	Arable land Terres arables	Permanent crops Cultures permanentes	Forest cover Superficie forestière	Arable land Terres arables	Permanent crops Cultures permanentes	Forest cover Superficie forestière	Protected areas Aires protégées	Protected areas Aires protégées % [1]
	Area in thousand hectares − Superficie en milliers de hectares								
Cyprus Chypre	924	101	42	172	− 5	− 9	5	78.1	8.4
Georgia Gerogie	6 949	793	269	2 988	...	...	...	195.3	2.8
India Inde	297 319	161 800[2]	7 900[2]	64113	−1 338	1 600	38	14312.0	4.5
Indonesia Indonésie	181 157	20 500[2]	13 046[2]	104986	247	1 326	−1312	34511.8	18.0
Iran (Islamic Rep. of) Iran (Rép. islamique d')	163 620	14 324[2]	2 002	7299	− 866	692		8303.1	5.0
Iraq Iraq	43 737	5 200[2]	340[2]	799	− 100	50	...	0.5	0.0
Israel Israël	2 062	333[2]	85[2]	132	− 10	− 3	5	325.6	15.7
Japan Japon	36 450	4 474	356	24081	− 294	− 119	3	2559.0	6.9
Jordan Jordanie	8 893	244[2]	157	86	− 46	67	...	298.0	3.1
Kazakhstan Kazakhstan	269 970	21 535	136	12 148	...	...	239	7 337.3	2.7
Korea, Dem.People's Rep. Corée, R. p. dém. de	12 041	1 700[2]	300[2]	8210	0	0	...	315.8	2.6
Korea, Republic of Corée, République de	9 873	1 719	200	6248	− 234	44	−5	...	6.9
Kuwait Koweït	1 782	8[2]	2[2]	5	4	1	...	27.2	1.1
Kyrgyzstan Kirghizistan	19 180	1 368[2]	67[2]	1 003	.....	...	23	693.9	3.5
Lao People's Dem. Rep. Rép. dém. pop. lao	23 080	877	81	12561	78	20	−53	2756.3	11.6
Lebanon Liban	1 023	190[2]	142[2]	36	7	20	...	4.8	0.5
Malaysia Malaisie	32 855	1 820[2]	5 785[2]	19292	120	537	−237	1527.4	4.6
Maldives Maldives	30	1[2]	2[2]	1	0	0	...	0.0	0.0
Mongolia Mongolie	156 650	1 175[2]	1[2]	10645	− 195	0	−60	16129.1	10.3
Myanmar Myanmar	65 755	9 900[2]	595[2]	34419	333	93	−517	173.5	0.3
Nepal Népal	14 300	2 898[2]	70[2]	3900	612	6	−78	1270.5	9.0
Occ. Palestinian Territory [4] Terr. palestinien occupé [4]	38	11[2]	8	...	2	− 2	...	...	...
Oman Oman	30 950	19[2]	61[2]	1	3	16	...	3428.0	12.6
Pakistan Pakistan	77 088	21 302	658	2361	818	202	−39	3744.7	4.7
Philippines Philippines	29 817	5 550[2]	4 500[2]	5789	70	100	−89	1454.0	4.8
Qatar Qatar	1 100	18[2]	3	1	8	2	...	1.6	0.1
Saudi Arabia Arabie saoudite	214 969	3 594[2]	191[2]	1504	204	100	...	82562.0	34.4
Singapore Singapour	61	1[2]	0	2	0	0	0	2.9	4.7
Sri Lanka Sri Lanka	6 463	890[2]	1 020[2]	1940	15	− 5	−35	869.4	13.3
Syrian Arab Republic Rep. arabe syrienne	18 378	4 542	810	461	− 343	69	...	0.0	0.0
Tajikistan Tadjikistan	14 060	730[2]	130[2]	400	...	...	2	587.0	4.1

66
Land [*cont.*]
Terres [*suite*]

Country or area Pays ou zone	2000 Land area Superficie des terres	2000 Arable land Terres arables	Permanent crops Cultures permanentes	2000 Forest cover Superficie forestière	Net change − Variation nette 1990 − 2000 Arable land Terres arables	1990 − 2000 Permanent crops Cultures permanentes	1990−2000 Forest cover Superficie forestière	1997 Protected areas Aires protégées	Protected areas Aires protégées %[1]
			Area in thousand hectares −		Superficie en milliers de hectares				
Thailand Thaïlande	51 089	14 700[2]	3 300[2]	14762	−2 794	191	−112	7077.1	13.8
Timor−Leste Timor−Leste	1 487	70[2]	10[2]	507	0	0	−3	...	...
Turkey Turquie	76 963	24 138	2 534	10225	− 509	− 496	22	1289.8	1.7
Turkmenistan Turkménistan	46 993	1 630[2]	65[2]	3 755	...	...	...	1 977.3	4.1
United Arab Emirates Emirats arabes unis	8 360	60	187	321	25	167	8	0.0	0.0
Uzbekistan Ouzbékistan	41 424	4 475[2]	375[2]	1 969	...	...	5	818.4	1.8
Viet Nam Viet Nam	32 549	5 750[2]	1 600[2]	9819	411	555	52	995.1	3.0
Yemen Yémen	52 797	1 545[2]	124	449	22	21	−9	0.0	0.0
Europe · Europe									
Albania Albanie	2 740	578	121	991	− 1	− 4	−8	102.5	3.6
Andorra Andorre	45	1[2]	...	...	0	...	...	0.0	0.0
Austria Autriche	8 273	1 399[2]	71[2]	3886	− 27	− 8	8	2451.2	29.2
Belarus Bélarus	20 748	6 133	124	9 402	...	...	256	875.4	4.2
Belgium−Luxembourg Belgique−Luxembourg	3 282	815	22	728	49	7	−1	85.9	2.8
Bosnia and Herzegovina Bosnie−Herzégovine	5 100	500[2]	150[2]	2 273	...	...	...	26.7	0.5
Bulgaria Bulgarie	11 055	4 424	212	3690	568	− 88	20	499.8	4.5
Croatia Craotie	5 592	1 458	128	1 783	...	...	2	396.4	7.0
Czech Republic République tchèque	7 728	3 082	236	2632	...	...	1	1277.6	16.2
Denmark Danemark	4 243	2 281	8	455	− 280	− 2	1	1379.6	32.0
Estonia Estonie	4 227	1 120	14	2 060	...	...	13	536.4	11.9
Faeroe Islands Iles Féroé	140	3[2]	...	...	0	...	...	...	...
Finland Finlande	30 459	2 187	4	21935	− 85	1	8	2840.7	8.4
France France	55 010	18 440	1 142	15341	441	− 49	62	5572.3	10.2
Germany Allemagne	35 668	11 804	216	10740	− 167	− 227	...	9619.3	27.0
Gibraltar Gibraltar	1	...	...	...	...	...	...	0.0	0.0
Greece Grèce	12 890	2 741	1 113	3599	− 158	45	30	340.8	2.6
Hungary Hongrie	9 234	4 602	201	1840	− 452	− 33	7	649.0	7.0
Iceland Islande	10 025	7	...	31	0	...	1	980.5	9.5
Ireland Irlande	6 889	1 050[2]	3[2]	659	9	0	17	65.3	0.9
Italy Italie	29 411	7 984[2]	2 841[2]	10003	−1 028	− 119	30	2203.7	7.3
Latvia Lettonie	6 205	1 845	29	2 923	...	...	13	821.7	12.9

66

Land [*cont.*]

Terres [*suite*]

		2000		2000	Net change — Variation nette			1997	
					1990 — 2000		1990—2000		
Country or area Pays ou zone	Land area Superficie des terres	Arable land Terres arables	Permanent crops Cultures permanentes	Forest cover Superficie forestière	Arable land Terres arables	Permanent crops Cultures permanentes	Forest cover Superficie forestière	Protected areas Aires protégées	Protected areas Aires protégées
	Area in thousand hectares — Superficie en milliers de hectares								%[1]
Liechtenstein Liechtenstein	16	4[2]	...	7	0	...	...	6.1	38.1
Lithuania Lituanie	6 480	2933	59	1 994	...	...	5	645.4	9.9
Malta Malte	32	8[2]	1[2]	...	− 4	0	...	0.4	1.2
Netherlands Pays−Bas	3 388	909[2]	35[2]	375	30	5	1	482.0	11.7
Norway Norvège	30 683	883	...	8868	19	...	31	2086.5	6.4
Poland Pologne	30 442	13 993	337	9047	− 395	− 8	18	2929.1	9.4
Portugal Portugal	9 150	1 990[2]	715[2]	3666	− 354	− 66	57	603.6	6.5
Republic of Moldova République de Moldova	3 291	1 820[2]	370[2]	325	...	...	1	50.6	1.5
Romania Roumanie	23 034	9 365	500	6448	− 85	− 91	15	1089.4	4.6
Russian Federation Fédération de Russie	1 688 850	124 975[2]	1 845[2]	851 392	...	...	135	51 668.8	3.0
San Marino Saint−Marin	6	1[2]	...	...	0	...	...	...	...
Serbia and Montenegro Serbie−et−Monténégro	10 200	3 406	330	2 887	...	...	− 1	338.9	3.3
Slovakia Slovaquie	4 808	1 450	126	2177	...	...	18	1060.5	21.6
Slovenia Slovénie	2 012	173	31	1107	...	...	2	120.2	5.9
Spain Espagne	49 944	13 317*	4 900[2]	14370	−2 018	63	86	4241.8	8.4
Svalbard and Jan Mayen Islands Svalbard et Ile Jan−Mayen	...	...	...	...	...	...	...	7 289.0	116.8
Sweden Suède	41 162	2 706	...	27134	− 139	...	1	3654.7	8.3
Switzerland Suisse	3 955	413	24	1199	22	3	4	744.7	18.0
TFYR of Macedonia L'ex−R.y Macédoine	2 543	555	44	906	...	...	...	181.3	7.1
Ukraine Ukraine	57 935	32 564	932	9584	...	...	31	898.5	1.5
United Kingdom Royaume−Uni	24 088	5 876	52	2794	− 744	− 14	17	5000.1	20.4
Oceania · Océanie									
American Samoa Samoa américaines	20	2[2]	3[2]	12	0	1	...	4.3	21.8
Australia Australie	768 230	50 304[2][6]	296[2]	154539	2 404	115	−282	104568.6	13.6
Cook Islands Iles Cook	23	4[2]	3[2]	...	2	− 1	...	0.2	0.9
Fiji Fidji	1 827	200[2]	85[2]	815	40	5	−2	20.0	1.1
French Polynesia Polynésie française	366	3[2]	20[2]	105	1	− 1	...	19.8	5.0
Guam Guam	55	6[2]	6[2]	21	0	0	...	8.6	19.1
Kiribati Kiribati	73	...	37[2]	28	...	0	...	26.7	39.0
Marshall Islands Iles Marshall	18	3[2]	...	...	3	...	...	...	...
Micronesia (Federated States of) Micronésie (Etats fédérés de)	70	4[2]	32[2]	15	4	32	−1	...	...

66
Land [*cont.*]
Terres [*suite*]

Country or area Pays ou zone	2000 Land area Superficie des terres	2000 Arable land Terres arables	2000 Permanent crops Cultures permanentes	2000 Forest cover Superficie forestière	Net change – Variation nette 1990 – 2000 Arable land Terres arables	Net change – Variation nette 1990 – 2000 Permanent crops Cultures permanentes	Net change – Variation nette 1990–2000 Forest cover Superficie forestière	1997 Protected areas Aires protégées	Protected areas Aires protégées %[1]
	Area in thousand hectares – Superficie en milliers de hectares								
New Caledonia Nouvelle–Calédonie	1 828	7[2]	6[2]	372	0	0	...	115.4	6.0
New Zealand Nouvelle–Zélande	26 799	1 555[2]	1 725[2]	7946	– 956	371	39	6333.8	23.9
Niue Nioué	26	5[2]	2[2]	6	0	0	...	5.4	20.8
Northern Mariana Islands Iles Mariannes du Nord	46	6[2]	2[2]	14	6	2	...	1.7	3.6
Palau Palaos	46	10[2]	...	35	10	...	...	4.0	8.1
Papua New Guinea Papouasie–Nvl–Guinée	45 286	205[2]	650[2]	30601	13	70	–113	1034.1	2.2
Samoa Samoa	283	55[2]	67[2]	105	0	0	–3	11.5	4.0
Solomon Islands Iles Salomon	2 799	42[2]	18[2]	2536	2	1	–4	8.2	0.3
Tonga Tonga	72	17[2]	31[2]	4	0	0	...	3.6	5.2
Tuvalu Tuvalu	3	...	...	...	...	...	...	3.3	132.0
Vanuatu Vanuatu	1 219	30[2]	90[2]	447	0	0	1	3.4	0.2
Wallis and Futuna Islands Iles Wallis et Futuna	20	1[2]	4[2]	...	0	0	...	...	...

Sources:
Food and Agriculture Organization of the United Nations (FAO), Rome, "FAO Production Yearbook 2001", the FAOSTAT database and the "Global Forest Resources Assessment 2000;" and the United Nations Environment Programme (UNEP), World Conservation Monitoring Centre, "United Nations List of Protected Areas".

1   Calculated by the World Conservation Monitoring Centre based on total area which includes land area and inland waters. Percentages are inflated due to the inclusion of marine protected areas.
2   FAO estimate.
3   Data generally include those for Taiwan Province of China, except for data on protected areas.
4   Data refer to the Gaza Strip.
5   Area free from ice.
6   Includes about 27 million hectares of cultivated grassland.

Sources:
Organisation des Nations Unies pour l'alimentation et l'agriculture (FAO), Rome "Annuaire FAO de la production 2001" et la base de données de FAOSTAT et "Global Forest Resources Assessment 2000;" et le Programme des Nations Unies pour l'environnement (PNUE), Centre mondial de surveillance pour la conservation, "United Nations List of Protected Areas".

1   Les pourcentages sont calculés par le Centre mondial de surveillance pour la conservation par rapport à la superficie totale des pays, qui comprend la superficie des terres et celle des eaux intérieures. Les pourcentages sont majorés, du fait qu'on tient compte des zones marines protégées.
2   Estimation de la FAO.
3   Les données comprennent en général les chiffres pour la province de Taiwan, les données sur les aires protégées exceptées.
4   Les données se rapportent à la Zone de Gaza.
5   Superficie non couverte de glace.
6   Y compris 27 millions d'hectares d'herbages cultivés.

67
CO$_2$ emission estimates
From fossil fuel combustion, cement production and gas flared (thousand metric tons of carbon dioxide)
Estimation des émissions de CO$_2$
Dues à la combustion de combustibles fossiles, à la production de ciment et au gaz brûlés à la torche

Country or area Pays ou zone	1990	1993	1994	1995	1996	1997	1998	1999	2000	Change: 1990 - latest year Variation : 1990 à l'année la plus récente (%)
Afghanistan Afghanistan	2 614	1 342	1 291	1 239	1 177	1 096	1 038	964	...	-63
Albania Albanie	7 274	2 339	1 925	2 086	2 002	1 569	1 756	1 514	...	-79
Algeria Algérie	80 490	82 561	86 180	94 520	96 420	99 529	106 531	90 869	...	13
Angola Angola	4 649	5 877	4 198	11 303	9 932	6 255	6 046	10 277	...	121
Antigua and Barbuda Antigua-et-Barbuda	301	304	312	323	323	337	337	348	...	16
Argentina Argentine	109 798	122 688	131 462	129 145	128 928	135 564	133 687	137 885	...	26
Armenia Arménie	...	2 783	2 852	3 512	2 621	3 296	3 424	3 080	...	...
Aruba Aruba	1 840	1 767	1 782	1 800	1 833	1 873	1 884	1 906	...	4
Australia [1] Australie [1]	277 867	285 480	291 431	301 101	310 586	318 222	334 904	339 385	347 006	25
Austria [1] Autriche [1]	62 297	60 717	61 995	64 015	65 386	67 012	65 464	66 025	66 102	6
Azerbaijan Azerbaïdjan	...	44 762	41 675	33 429	31 306	30 731	32 043	33 649	...	...
Bahamas Bahamas	1 950	1 716	1 719	1 730	1 730	1 741	1 793	1 796	...	-8
Bahrain Bahreïn	11 717	14 881	15 013	15 849	16 550	17 199	18 724	19 024	...	62
Bangladesh Bangladesh	15 369	17 122	18 412	21 891	23 127	24 025	23 376	25 462	...	66
Barbados Barbade	1 078	1 115	748	825	876	891	1 862	2 035	...	89
Belarus Bélarus	...	78 444	69 945	63 269	64 248	62 517	59 496	57 667	...	...
Belgium [1] Belgique [1]	117 966	120 887	124 072	127 647	130 367	125 579	128 607	125 639	127 040	8
Belize Belize	312	378	374	378	308	389	400	620	...	99
Benin Bénin	719	1 078	1 104	1 140	1 082	1 126	1 203	1 258	...	75
Bermuda Bermudes	590	462	458	455	462	462	462	462	...	-22
Bhutan Bhoutan	128	187	216	253	301	392	389	385	...	200
Bolivia Bolivie	5 503	7 967	8 810	10 137	10 379	11 145	12 289	11 248	...	104
Bosnia and Herzegovina Bosnie-Herzégovine	...	3 743	4 205	4 260	4 348	4 506	4 689	4 825	...	...

67

CO₂ emission estimates
From fossil fuel combustion, cement production and gas flared (thousand metric tons of carbon dioxide) *[cont.]*
Estimation des émissions de CO₂
Dues à la combustion de combustibles fossiles, à la production de ciment et au gaz brûlés à la torche *[suite]*

Country or area Pays ou zone	1990	1993	1994	1995	1996	1997	1998	1999	2000	Change: 1990 - latest year Variation : 1990 à l'année la plus récente (%)
Botswana Botswana	2 170	3 483	3 479	3 512	3 113	3 377	3 780	3 879	...	79
Brazil Brésil	202 738	225 007	234 825	249 769	276 632	288 382	298 725	300 844	...	48
British Virgin Islands Iles Vierges britanniques	48	51	51	51	59	59	59	59	...	23
Brunei Darussalam Brunéi Darussalam	5 822	5 283	5 100	5 210	5 147	5 496	5 400	4 671	...	-20
Bulgaria [1] Bulgarie [1]	103 856	61 859	59 178	62 332	66 825	58 742	52 277	48 440	...	-53
Burkina Faso Burkina Faso	994	920	950	972	983	994	1 012	1 016	...	2
Burundi Burundi	194	205	213	216	224	227	231	242	...	25
Cambodia Cambodge	451	477	539	550	601	612	664	675	...	50
Cameroon Cameroun	3 685	4 004	4 147	4 136	4 484	4 539	4 784	4 697	...	27
Canada [1] Canada [1]	471 563	473 976	488 138	500 627	513 343	524 505	534 224	550 073	571 427	21
Cape Verde Cap-Vert	84	106	117	117	121	121	121	139	...	65
Cayman Islands Iles Caïmanes	249	286	286	286	282	282	290	282	...	13
Central African Rep. Rép. centrafricaine	198	224	235	235	235	246	249	268	...	35
Chad Tchad	143	92	95	95	103	114	114	121	...	-15
Chile Chili	35 354	35 706	41 202	44 230	50 455	58 111	60 237	62 554	...	77
China Chine	2400350	2788067	2959913	3199640	3344814	3295326	3118886	2826783	...	18
China, Hong Kong SAR Chine, Hong Kong RAS	26 199	34 888	29 851	29 888	27 460	27 772	35 504	41 216	...	57
China, Macao SAR Chine, Macao RAS	1 027	1 181	1 272	1 232	1 408	1 511	1 558	1 518	...	48
Colombia Colombie	55 977	63 115	66 275	68 303	67 852	71 800	71 643	63 680	...	14
Comoros Comores	66	66	66	66	66	66	70	81	...	22
Congo Congo	2 005	2 207	2 530	2 134	2 189	2 229	2 244	2 405	...	20
Cook Islands Iles Cook	22	22	22	22	22	22	22	29	...	33
Costa Rica Costa Rica	2 918	3 945	5 235	4 861	4 733	5 012	5 100	6 123	...	110

67

CO$_2$ emission estimates
From fossil fuel combustion, cement production and gas flared (thousand metric tons of carbon dioxide) *[cont.]*

Estimation des émissions de CO$_2$
Dues à la combustion de combustibles fossiles, à la production de ciment et au gaz brûles à la torche *[suite]*

Country or area Pays ou zone	1990	1993	1994	1995	1996	1997	1998	1999	2000	Change: 1990 - latest year Variation : 1990 à l'année la plus récente (%)
Côte d'Ivoire Côte d'Ivoire	10 783	10 797	10 981	9 382	12 330	11 435	11 453	12 124	...	12
Croatia Croatie	...	17 012	16 942	17 759	18 504	19 600	20 209	20 802	...	...
Cuba Cuba	32 069	29 008	31 867	23 387	23 406	25 349	24 546	25 393	...	-21
Cyprus Chypre	4 649	5 107	5 261	5 133	5 276	5 415	5 921	6 024	...	30
Czech Republic [1] République tchèque [1]	163 990	134 851	127 745	128 817	132 780	137 357	128 268	121 093	127 902	-22
Dem. Rep. of the Congo Rép. dém. du Congo	3 974	3 168	2 596	2 552	2 577	2 508	2 548	2 145	...	-46
Denmark [1] Danemark [1]	52 635	59 884	63 855	61 001	74 514	65 161	60 006	57 245	52 852	0
Djibouti Djibouti	352	378	367	370	367	367	367	385	...	9
Dominica Dominique	59	62	70	81	73	81	81	81	...	38
Dominican Republic Rép. dominicaine	9 569	11 937	12 671	16 249	17 847	18 137	22 742	23 288	...	143
Ecuador Equateur	16 579	25 151	14 456	23 255	24 729	20 498	24 351	23 281	...	40
Egypt Egypte	75 481	92 273	84 790	95 085	103 488	107 602	108 933	123 664	...	64
El Salvador El Salvador	2 618	3 894	4 425	5 122	4 704	5 470	5 928	5 774	...	121
Equatorial Guinea Guinée équatoriale	117	125	128	132	143	796	257	649	...	453
Estonia [1] Estonie [1]	38 107	20 553	21 378	19 315	20 264	20 225	18 318	16 771	16 849	-56
Ethiopia Ethiopie	2 966	5 096	3 201	2 445	3 985	4 521	4 770	5 507	...	86
Faeroe Islands Iles Féroé	616	576	513	620	631	634	642	649	...	5
Falkland Is. (Malvinas) Iles Falkland (Malvinas)	37	37	37	40	44	48	37	37	...	0
Fiji Fidji	814	711	722	755	774	759	730	726	...	-11
Finland [1] Finlande [1]	62 466	59 172	65 468	62 684	68 130	66 842	64 601	64 073	62 305	0
France [1,2] France [1,2]	394 067	388 491	384 050	390 492	404 177	398 310	419 453	407 004	401 923	2
Gabon Gabon	5 452	3 252	2 973	3 050	3 325	3 498	3 296	3 556	...	-35
Gambia Gambie	191	209	209	216	216	216	235	253	...	33

67

CO$_2$ emission estimates
From fossil fuel combustion, cement production and gas flared (thousand metric tons of carbon dioxide) *[cont.]*
Estimation des émissions de CO$_2$
Dues à la combustion de combustibles fossiles, à la production de ciment et au gaz brûles à la torche *[suite]*

Country or area Pays ou zone	1990	1993	1994	1995	1996	1997	1998	1999	2000	Change: 1990 - latest year Variation : 1990 à l'année la plus récente (%)
Georgia Géorgie	...	9 848	6 024	2 288	4 169	4 429	5 276	5 378	...	...
Germany [1] Allemagne [1]	1014501	918 268	904 111	903 665	923 085	892 649	885 963	859 246	857 908	-15
Ghana Ghana	3 699	4 462	4 946	5 224	5 661	5 961	6 467	5 580	...	51
Gibraltar Gibraltar	62	293	356	301	180	84	103	176	...	182
Greece [1] Grèce [1]	84 336	85 847	87 479	87 644	90 163	94 668	99 419	98 626	103 727	17
Greenland Groenland	554	499	502	502	517	521	528	539	...	-3
Grenada Grenade	121	143	165	172	176	194	202	213	...	76
Guatemala Guatemala	5 089	5 657	6 867	7 208	6 607	7 688	9 804	9 679	...	90
Guinea Guinée	1 012	1 063	1 188	1 206	1 228	1 236	1 247	1 265	...	25
Guinea-Bissau Guinée-Bissau	209	227	227	231	231	235	235	260	...	25
Guyana Guyana	1 133	1 049	1 327	1 474	1 518	1 595	1 650	1 686	...	49
Haiti Haïti	994	664	301	942	1 078	1 393	1 261	1 415	...	42
Honduras Honduras	2 592	2 849	3 336	3 879	3 974	4 139	4 905	5 030	...	94
Hungary [1] Hongrie [1]	83 676	60 826	59 196	59 758	60 475	58 893	57 601	60 117	59 445	-29
Iceland [1] Islande [1]	2 065	2 228	2 193	2 228	2 313	2 388	2 411	2 494	2 444	18
India Inde	675 681	807 850	860 762	908 097	1003395	1026093	1060541	1077659	...	59
Indonesia Indonésie	165 804	197 536	201 121	209 730	274 714	277 633	220 787	235 771	...	42
Iran (Islamic Rep. of) Iran (Rép. islamique d')	216 857	227 632	292 049	272 265	275 374	290 428	285 915	301 621	...	39
Iraq Iraq	49 293	64 116	72 761	74 000	73 604	76 688	79 041	74 286	...	51
Ireland [1] Irlande [1]	31 599	32 458	33 893	34 529	35 729	38 102	40 062	41 932	43 925	39
Israel Israël	34 973	46 232	48 252	54 448	53 883	56 978	59 529	61 165	...	75
Italy [1] Italie [1]	439 478	425 929	419 673	445 009	439 066	442 116	454 352	457 202	463 381	5
Jamaica Jamaïque	7 963	8 418	8 630	9 547	10 101	10 731	11 710	10 222	...	28

67

CO₂ emission estimates
From fossil fuel combustion, cement production and gas flared (thousand metric tons of carbon dioxide) *[cont.]*

Estimation des émissions de CO₂
Dues à la combustion de combustibles fossiles, à la production de ciment et au gaz brûlés à la torche *[suite]*

Country or area Pays ou zone	1990	1993	1994	1995	1996	1997	1998	1999	2000	Change: 1990 - latest year Variation : 1990 à l'année la plus récente (%)
Japan [1] Japon [1]	1119319	1136428	1194757	1207994	1219442	1219422	1191671	1232770	1237107	11
Jordan Jordanie	10 189	12 099	13 631	13 573	14 181	14 416	14 544	14 581	...	43
Kazakhstan Kazakhstan	...	214 195	196 938	165 709	137 823	135 447	122 358	112 907	...	...
Kenya Kenya	5 826	6 240	6 526	6 878	8 722	6 973	9 180	8 843	...	52
Kiribati Kiribati	22	22	22	22	22	22	22	26	...	17
Korea, Dem. P. R. Corée, R. p. dém. de	244 787	262 088	259 591	257 146	254 484	237 755	226 290	208 780	...	-15
Korea, Republic of Corée, République de	241 329	317 540	343 047	373 832	408 182	424 071	363 563	393 755	...	63
Kuwait [3] Koweït [3]	42 232	27 479	33 195	44 193	45 051	42 173	49 649	47 999	...	14
Kyrgyzstan Kirghizistan	...	8 355	6 086	4 627	5 796	5 620	6 020	4 719	...	...
Lao People's Dem. Rep. Rép. dém. pop. lao	231	275	301	315	370	389	407	407	...	76
Latvia [1] Lettonie [1]	23 527	12 861	11 911	10 145	9 550	8 619	8 287	7 545	6 847	-71
Lebanon Liban	9 100	11 655	12 740	13 620	13 796	15 182	16 011	16 924	...	86
Lesotho [1] Lesotho [1]	...	...	636	...	...	...	...	...	...	...
Liberia Libéria	466	315	312	323	337	348	385	400	...	-14
Libyan Arab Jamah. Jamah. arabe libyenne	37 796	39 772	39 244	44 281	40 806	48 736	36 468	42 796	...	13
Liechtenstein [1] Liechtenstein [1]	195	...	...	...	...	...	...	196	...	1
Lithuania [1] Lituanie [1]	39 535	...	...	15 200	16 200	16 200	16 694	...	...	-58
Luxembourg [1] Luxembourg [1]	12 750	...	11 998	9 545	...	...	...	5 432	5 399	-58
Madagascar Madagascar	946	1 030	1 276	1 331	1 364	1 639	1 697	1 899	...	101
Malawi Malawi	601	682	700	711	697	744	730	770	...	28
Malaysia Malaisie	55 313	90 465	92 706	119 066	122 322	130 619	123 931	123 730	...	124
Maldives Maldives	154	216	220	275	319	367	334	466	...	202
Mali Mali	422	455	462	473	480	477	488	499	...	18

67

CO₂ emission estimates
From fossil fuel combustion, cement production and gas flared (thousand metric tons of carbon dioxide) *[cont.]*
Estimation des émissions de CO₂
Dues à la combustion de combustibles fossiles, à la production de ciment et au gaz brûles à la torche *[suite]*

Country or area Pays ou zone	1990	1993	1994	1995	1996	1997	1998	1999	2000	Change: 1990 - latest year Variation : 1990 à l'année la plus récente (%)
Malta Malte	2 064	2 486	2 621	2 687	2 838	2 911	3 179	3 424	...	66
Mauritania Mauritanie	2 636	2 907	3 065	2 944	2 940	2 933	2 929	3 039	...	15
Mauritius Maurice	1 463	1 774	1 624	1 829	1 950	1 998	2 200	2 471	...	69
Mexico Mexique	343 824	340 311	357 305	339 230	339 292	359 585	377 117	378 730	...	10
Micronesia (Fed. States) [1] Micronésie (Etats féd. de) [1]	...	...	236	...	141	...	...	...	...	...
Monaco [1] Monaco [1]	98	121	123	120	126	125	121	129	...	32
Mongolia Mongolie	9 987	9 283	7 941	7 919	8 040	7 710	7 703	7 553	...	-24
Montserrat Montserrat	33	37	37	44	40	48	48	48	...	44
Morocco Maroc	23 501	28 216	29 646	30 349	31 185	30 540	32 476	35 860	...	53
Mozambique Mozambique	997	1 067	1 063	1 206	1 214	1 272	1 316	1 335	...	34
Myanmar Myanmar	4 150	5 393	6 299	6 984	7 267	7 487	8 146	9 206	...	122
Namibia Namibie	7	18	29	33	48	73	92	128	...	1 650
Nauru Nauru	132	136	136	139	139	139	139	136	...	3
Nepal Népal	631	1 467	1 697	2 038	2 486	2 783	3 047	3 322	...	427
Netherlands [1] Pays-Bas [1]	159 630	167 935	168 764	172 659	179 706	168 973	175 057	172 061	173 527	9
Netherlands Antilles Antilles néerlandaises	895	7 215	6 970	6 849	6 486	5 844	6 368	5 609	...	527
New Zealand [1] Nouvelle-Zélande [1]	25 267	27 136	27 199	27 206	28 223	30 210	28 684	30 331	30 852	22
Nicaragua Nicaragua	2 603	2 299	2 537	2 790	2 867	3 054	3 516	3 758	...	44
Niger Niger	1 049	1 096	1 089	1 100	1 104	1 107	1 107	1 137	...	8
Nigeria Nigéria	45 367	60 050	46 650	32 381	41 880	43 764	41 484	40 413	...	-11
Niue Nioué	4	4	4	4	4	4	4	4	...	0
Norway [1] Norvège [1]	35 163	35 822	37 659	37 756	40 940	41 193	41 314	41 743	41 273	17
Oman Oman	11 545	13 309	15 351	17 235	16 256	17 884	20 425	19 901	...	72

67

CO$_2$ emission estimates
From fossil fuel combustion, cement production and gas flared (thousand metric tons of carbon dioxide) *[cont.]*
Estimation des émissions de CO$_2$
Dues à la combustion de combustibles fossiles, à la production de ciment et au gaz brûles à la torche *[suite]*

Country or area Pays ou zone	1990	1993	1994	1995	1996	1997	1998	1999	2000	Change: 1990 - latest year Variation : 1990 à l'année la plus récente (%)
Pakistan Pakistan	68 068	77 776	84 544	84 533	93 391	93 267	96 328	98 931	...	45
Palau Palaos	235	231	231	238	246	238	242	242	...	3
Panama Panama	3 131	4 121	4 781	3 274	4 836	7 703	8 663	8 256	...	164
Papua New Guinea Papouasie-Nvl-Guinée	2 431	2 530	2 504	2 409	2 409	2 453	2 346	2 427	...	0
Paraguay Paraguay	2 262	2 948	3 498	4 011	3 960	4 154	4 191	4 532	...	100
Peru Pérou	21 671	24 274	23 904	24 579	25 246	27 644	26 386	30 412	...	40
Philippines Philippines	44 333	51 566	56 439	63 317	66 268	77 366	75 841	73 260	...	65
Poland [1] Pologne [1]	476 625	363 133	371 588	348 172	372 530	361 626	337 448	329 697	314 812	-34
Portugal [1] Portugal [1]	44 109	48 620	48 713	52 688	50 986	53 102	56 894	64 062	63 150	45
Qatar Qatar	11 857	31 050	30 595	31 193	32 362	36 901	37 909	51 731	...	336
Republic of Moldova République de Moldova	...	15 659	12 143	11 233	11 582	10 860	9 664	6 500	...	...
Romania [1] Roumanie [1]	194 826	127 086	125 597	...	...	...	...	...	...	-36
Russian Federation [1] Fédération de Russie [1]	2372300	1855302	1660000	1590420	1495920	...	...	...	...	-37
Rwanda Rwanda	528	502	484	491	510	528	535	565	...	7
Saint Helena Sainte-Hélène	7	7	7	11	15	15	18	22	...	200
Saint Kitts and Nevis Saint-Kitts-et-Nevis	66	84	88	95	103	103	103	103	...	56
Saint Lucia Sainte-Lucie	161	172	260	308	323	301	293	323	...	100
St. Vincent-Grenadines St. Vincent-Grenadines	81	103	121	128	132	132	161	161	...	100
Samoa Samoa	125	128	121	132	132	132	132	139	...	12
Sao Tome and Principe Sao Tomé-et-Principe	66	73	73	77	77	77	81	88	...	33
Saudi Arabia [3] Arabie saoudite [3]	123 499	200 047	264 240	256 266	279 675	246 524	240 739	235 555	...	91
Senegal Sénégal	2 900	3 109	3 208	3 307	3 501	3 553	3 677	3 743	...	29
Serbia and Montenegro Serbie-et-Monténégro	...	38 984	37 964	39 772	45 242	49 095	51 717	39 534	...	...

67

CO$_2$ emission estimates
From fossil fuel combustion, cement production and gas flared (thousand metric tons of carbon dioxide) *[cont.]*
Estimation des émissions de CO$_2$
Dues à la combustion de combustibles fossiles, à la production de ciment et au gaz brûlés à la torche *[suite]*

Country or area Pays ou zone	1990	1993	1994	1995	1996	1997	1998	1999	2000	Change: 1990 - latest year Variation : 1990 à l'année la plus récente (%)
Seychelles Seychelles	114	161	176	187	191	198	198	216	...	90
Sierra Leone Sierra Leone	334	436	502	506	543	499	528	543	...	63
Singapore Singapour	45 095	50 569	61 007	43 456	50 697	60 992	51 482	54 294	...	20
Slovakia [1] Slovaquie [1]	59 746	46 232	43 365	44 898	45 156	45 556	44 811	43 600	41 472	-31
Slovenia [1] Slovénie [1]	13 935	...	...	...	...	...	...	...	...	0
Solomon Islands Iles Salomon	161	158	154	161	161	161	161	165	...	2
Somalia Somalie	18	11	11	11	...	...	...	...	...	-40
South Africa Afrique du Sud	285 658	296 972	312 701	325 624	325 778	334 772	337 829	334 790	...	17
Spain [1] Espagne [1]	227 233	229 942	242 657	254 411	242 215	261 369	270 130	295 233	306 632	35
Sri Lanka Sri Lanka	3 857	5 034	5 518	5 914	7 094	7 677	7 926	8 652	...	124
Sudan Soudan	2 882	1 199	2 218	2 647	2 698	3 435	2 229	2 636	...	-9
Suriname Suriname	1 811	2 126	2 137	2 156	2 101	2 119	2 141	2 152	...	19
Swaziland Swaziland	425	132	484	455	341	400	400	385	...	-9
Sweden [1] Suède [1]	56 065	54 879	59 233	58 574	62 062	57 056	58 142	56 458	55 855	0
Switzerland [1] Suisse [1]	44 420	43 570	42 946	43 825	44 227	43 561	44 833	44 843	43 853	-1
Syrian Arab Republic Rép. arabe syrienne	35 867	45 891	43 977	45 788	45 554	46 796	50 991	53 392	...	49
Tajikistan Tadjikistan	...	13 613	5 096	5 184	5 796	5 092	5 114	5 103	...	...
Thailand Thaïlande	95 800	142 523	158 240	181 419	202 522	209 774	189 664	199 783	...	109
TFYR of Macedonia L'ex-R.y. Macédoine	...	10 207	10 343	10 691	11 703	10 632	12 363	11 384	...	...
Togo Togo	752	803	774	876	917	931	1 063	1 327	...	77
Tonga Tonga	77	103	106	114	117	121	117	121	...	57
Trinidad and Tobago Trinité-et-Tobago	16 935	16 799	19 296	20 828	22 430	22 196	22 742	25 103	...	48
Tunisia Tunisie	13 268	16 484	15 937	15 721	16 381	16 645	22 375	17 492	...	32

67

CO$_2$ emission estimates
From fossil fuel combustion, cement production and gas flared (thousand metric tons of carbon dioxide) *[cont.]*

Estimation des émissions de CO$_2$
Dues à la combustion de combustibles fossiles, à la production de ciment et au gaz brûles à la torche *[suite]*

Country or area Pays ou zone	1990	1993	1994	1995	1996	1997	1998	1999	2000	Change: 1990 - latest year Variation : 1990 à l'année la plus récente (%)
Turkey Turquie	143 909	159 864	155 744	171 010	188 286	198 133	202 162	198 617	...	38
Turkmenistan Turkménistan	...	27 658	33 469	33 858	30 415	28 718	27 211	32 436	...	...
Tuvalu [1] Tuvalu [1]	...	...	5	...	...	...	...	...	...	...
Uganda Ouganda	814	818	744	953	1 052	1 126	1 316	1 371	...	68
Ukraine [1] Ukraine [1]	703 792	504 222	406 838	380 928	346 768	322 907	314 445	...	...	-55
United Arab Emirates Emirats arabes unis	55 178	58 437	76 435	76 277	79 808	85 241	88 255	88 031	...	60
United Kingdom [1] Royaume-Uni [1]	583 705	558 945	555 933	547 374	566 961	542 718	545 116	536 490	542 743	-7
United Rep. of Tanzania Rép.-Unie de Tanzanie	2 273	2 277	2 170	2 335	2 409	2 368	2 460	2 530	...	11
United States [1,2] Etats-Unis [1,2]	4998516	5157298	5260956	5305896	5483671	5567981	5575083	5665472	5840039	17
Uruguay Uruguay	3 912	4 407	4 018	4 524	5 411	5 477	5 496	6 552	...	67
Uzbekistan [1] Ouzbékistan [1]	114 559	...	102 157	...	...	...	...	...	...	-11
Vanuatu Vanuatu	66	62	62	66	84	84	81	81	...	22
Venezuela Venezuela	117 798	118 769	151 953	124 316	117 640	121 955	127 367	125 904	...	7
Viet Nam Viet Nam	21 440	24 296	26 273	31 083	36 172	40 512	44 021	46 598	...	117
Western Sahara Sahara occidental	198	202	202	209	213	220	227	238	...	20
Yemen Yémen	...	8 594	10 643	11 288	12 722	14 229	14 167	18 269	...	...
Yugoslavia, SFR Yougoslavie, Rfs	130 534	...	...	...	...	...	...	...	...	...
Zambia Zambie	2 445	2 497	2 420	2 412	2 387	2 357	1 628	1 807	...	-26
Zimbabwe Zimbabwe	16 656	17 334	18 544	19 505	19 083	18 951	18 650	17 635	...	6

Source:
Carbon Dioxide Information Analysis Center (CDIAC) of the Oak Ridge National Laboratory, Oak Ridge, Tennessee, U.S.A., database on national CO$_2$ emission estimates from fossil fuel burning, cement production and gas flaring: 1751- 1999 and the Secretariat of the United Nations Framework Convention on Climate Change (UNFCCC), Bonn, Secretariat of the UNFCCC database.

Source:
"Carbon Dioxide Information Analysis Center (CDIAC) of the Oak Ridge National Laboratory, Oak Ridge, Tennessee, U.S.A., database on national CO$_2$ emission estimates from fossil fuel burning, cement production and gas flaring: 1751- 1999" et le Secrétariat de la convention-cadre concernant les changements climatiques (CCCC) des Nations Unies, Bonn, la base de données du Secrétariat de la CCCC.

67

CO$_2$ emission estimates
From fossil fuel combustion, cement production and gas flared (thousand metric tons of carbon dioxide) *[cont.]*
Estimation des émissions de CO$_2$
Dues à la combustion de combustibles fossiles, à la production de ciment et au gaz brûles à la torche *[suite]*

The majority of the data have been taken from the CDIAC database; all other data have been taken from the UNFCCC database and are footnoted accordingly.

1 Source: Secretariat of the UNFCCC.
2 Including territories.
3 Including part of the Neutral Zone.

La majorité des données proviennent de la base de données du CDIAC ; les autres, qui proviennent de la base de données du Secrétariat de la CCCC, sont signalées par une note.

1 Source : Secrétariat de la CCC des Nations Unies.
2 Y compris les territoires.
3 Y compris une partie de la Zone Neutrale.

68

Ozone-depleting chlorofluorocarbons (CFCs)
Consumption: ozone-depleting potential (ODP) metric tons
Chlorofluorocarbones (CFC) qui appauvrissent la couche d'ozone
Consommation : tonnes de potentiel de destruction de l'ozone (PDO)

Region, country or area Région, pays ou zone	1989	1991	1993	1994	1995	1996	1997	1998	1999	2000
Algeria Algérie	3 570	...	2 146	2 226	2 292	2 292	1 774	1 549	1 502	1 475
Antigua and Barbuda Antigua-et-Barbuda	428	428	426	12	12	10	10	26	-2	5
Argentina Argentine	3 463	2 797	1 806	4 569	6 366	4 202	3 524	3 546	4 316	2 397
Armenia Arménie	...	...	...	...	...	...	...	...	9	25
Australia Australie	14 293	6 812	3 409	3 895	2 585	234	184	195	274	6
Azerbaijan Azerbaïdjan	481	...	...	...	...	456	201	152	100	88
Bahamas Bahamas	57	...	66	68	70	72	53	55	54	66
Bahrain Bahreïn	92	85	111	118	122	137	147	150	129	113
Bangladesh Bangladesh	205	93	227	181	281	628	832	830	801	805
Barbados Barbade	27	25	30	35	25	22	17	22	17	8
Belarus Bélarus	1 680	1 185	914	900	579	524	372	256	194	0
Belize Belize	20	...	...	...	16	11	20	25	25	9
Benin Bénin	79	37	37	37	62	58	60	54	57	55
Bolivia Bolivie	23	14	...	76	82	87	58	74	72	...
Bosnia and Herzegovina Bosnie-Herzégovine	219	145	...	...	...	...	...	45	151	176
Botswana Botswana	6	...	15	8	8	5	7	3	3	2
Brazil Brésil	9 110	8 504	9 818	10 778	10 896	10 872	9 810	9 543	11 612	9 275
Brunei Darussalam Brunéi Darussalam	64	...	81	63	65	80	90	63	37	47
Bulgaria Bulgarie	2 612	1 556	690	684	322	4	0	0	0	0
Burkina Faso Burkina Faso	26	29	31	34	34	38	38	37	31	25
Burundi Burundi	40	46	...	...	56	59	62	64	60	54
Cameroon Cameroun	79	67	157	157	231	280	260	312	362	...
Canada Canada	18 843	8 819	4 521	4 853	4 816	129	136	42	-5	10
Central African Rep. Rép. centrafricaine	26	43	31	31	27	6	0	7	1	4
Chad Tchad	24	28	31	32	33	35	36	38	37	37

68

Ozone-depleting chlorofluorocarbons (CFCs) *[cont]*
Consumption: ozone-depleting potential (ODP) metric tons *[cont]*
Chlorofluorocarbones (CFC) qui appauvrissent la couche d'ozone *[suite]*
Consommation : tonnes de potentiel de destruction de l'ozone (PDO) *[suite]*

Region, country or area Région, pays ou zone	1989	1991	1993	1994	1995	1996	1997	1998	1999	2000
Chile Chili	906	675	892	853	933	878	674	738	658	576
China Chine	34 783	50 263	66 283	70 779	75 291	47 089	51 076	55 414	42 983	...
Colombia Colombie	1 520	1 686	...	2 115	2 156	2 302	2 166	1 224	986	1 149
Comoros Comores	1	1	...	...	2	2	3	4	2	3
Congo Congo	8	53	...	27	14	13	9	7	9	11
Costa Rica Costa Rica	342	267	222	184	159	497	95	-204	152	106
Côte d'Ivoire Côte d'Ivoire	188	258	204	342	354	384	144	268	166	...
Croatia Croatie	515	337	253	314	194	184	280	86	142	171
Cuba Cuba	974	328	122	150	546	664	665	531	571	534
Cyprus Chypre	309	249	429	196	165	141	143	81	115	165
Czech Republic République tchèque	5 498	...	1 039	403	369	50	12	8	11	5
Dem. Rep. of the Congo Rép. dém. du Congo	...	...	...	...	793	735	469	...	371	387
Dominica Dominique	...	...	1	1	1	2	2	2	1	...
Dominican Republic Rép. dominicaine	256	...	330	433	634	559	427	311	752	399
Ecuador Equateur	458	691	261	78	315	269	320	272	153	230
Egypt Egypte	2 373	1 960	1 746	1 870	1 640	1 732	1 632	1 540	1 374	1 267
El Salvador El Salvador	384	423	398	256	330	312	278	195	110	99
Estonia Estonie	190	...	...	...	765	-442	45	70	56	16
Ethiopia Ethiopie	33	...	...	...	33	34	35	38	39	39
Fiji Fidji	40	42	7	0	60	27	14	13	9	0
Gabon Gabon	13	10	13	12	7	11	12	12	8	14
Gambia Gambie	7	11	21	23	23	21	28	11	7	6
Georgia Géorgie	766	...	...	53	13	23	31	26	22	22
Ghana Ghana	98	97	24	39	44	14	49	50	47	47
Grenada Grenade	4	...	4	4	7	5	7	4	...	...

68

Ozone-depleting chlorofluorocarbons (CFCs) *[cont]*

Consumption: ozone-depleting potential (ODP) metric tons *[cont]*

Chlorofluorocarbones (CFC) qui appauvrissent la couche d'ozone *[suite]*
Consommation : tonnes de potentiel de destruction de l'ozone (PDO) *[suite]*

Region, country or area Région, pays ou zone	1989	1991	1993	1994	1995	1996	1997	1998	1999	2000
Guatemala Guatemala	421	357	357	269	231	236	207	189	191	188
Guinea Guinée	27	29	30	32	37	44	46	42	40	38
Guyana Guyana	30	17	59	42	91	41	28	29	40	24
Honduras Honduras	...	...	...	115	118	523	354	157	335	172
Hungary Hongrie	4 848	2 290	1 381	844	566	0	4	1	1	1
Iceland Islande	140	93	62	31	0	0	0	0	0	0
India Inde	4 358	...	5 277	6 387	6 402	6 937	6 703	5 265	4 143	5 614
Indonesia Indonésie	1 457	...	4 363	6 910	8 351	9 012	7 635	6 183	5 866	5 411
Iran (Islamic Rep. of) Iran (Rép. islamique d')	2 235	4 750	4 495	4 328	4 140	3 692	5 883	5 571	4 399	4 157
Israel Israël	4 560	...	3 524	897	1 095	7	0	0	0	0
Jamaica Jamaïque	400	350	66	49	82	91	107	199	210	60
Japan Japon	146 609	88 436	47 452	19 713	23 064	-614	-113	-208	23	-24
Jordan Jordanie	594	545	580	520	535	627	857	647	398	354
Kazakhstan Kazakhstan	1 395	1 206	2 218	...	...	826	669	1 025	...	...
Kenya Kenya	230	105	47	273	301	167	251	245	241	203
Kiribati Kiribati	...	...	1	1	1	1	1	0	...	...
Korea, Dem. P. R. Corée, R. p. dém. de	950	...	...	...	825	267	233	112	106	77
Korea, Republic of Corée, République de	24 126	...	8 728	10 070	10 039	8 220	9 220	5 299	7 403	...
Kuwait Koweït	1 757	...	546	600	485	472	485	399	450	420
Kyrgyzstan Kirghizistan	...	118	93	85	82	67	9	57	...	54
Lao People's Dem. Rep. Rép. dém. pop. lao	...	...	...	...	...	...	...	43	44	45
Latvia Lettonie	4 736	...	...	...	665	307	23	25	22	35
Lebanon Liban	432	...	908	726	820	735	621	475	463	528
Lesotho Lesotho	6	...	...	5	6	6	4	3	3	2
Libyan Arab Jamah. Jamah. arabe libyenne	...	...	...	...	773	730	647	660	894	985

68

Ozone-depleting chlorofluorocarbons (CFCs) *[cont]*
Consumption: ozone-depleting potential (ODP) metric tons *[cont]*

Chlorofluorocarbones (CFC) qui appauvrissent la couche d'ozone *[suite]*
Consommation : tonnes de potentiel de destruction de l'ozone (PDO) *[suite]*

Region, country or area Région, pays ou zone	1989	1991	1993	1994	1995	1996	1997	1998	1999	2000
Liechtenstein Liechtenstein	13	19	6	4	1	0	0	0	0	...
Lithuania Lituanie	5 528	3 814	...	596	361	289	100	104	85	37
Madagascar Madagascar	...	...	...	...	19	21	104	24	26	14
Malawi Malawi	...	23	88	30	62	56	56	57	51	...
Malaysia Malaisie	3 442	3 829	3 624	4 730	3 427	3 038	3 348	2 334	2 010	1 980
Maldives Maldives	2	6	6	7	6	0	8	1	1	...
Mali Mali	...	...	...	...	104	109	111	113	37	29
Malta Malte	366	85	62	61	63	70	60	107	97	68
Marshall Islands Iles Marshall	1	1	1	...	...	...	1	1	1	...
Mauritania Mauritanie	17	...	...	17	23	8	16	15	13	...
Mauritius Maurice	76	...	64	42	24	36	27	39	19	19
Mexico Mexique	9 223	10 291	9 198	9 652	4 859	4 859	4 157	3 483	2 838	3 060
Monaco Monaco	0	...	9	5	0	0	0	0	0	...
Mongolia Mongolie	7	...	...	...	7	12	13	20	21	14
Morocco Maroc	559	691	630	757	707	814	886	924	871	564
Mozambique Mozambique	18	...	...	18	20	22	13	3	14	...
Myanmar Myanmar	...	...	...	2	49	59	55	52	31	26
Namibia Namibie	21	...	34	35	27	19	19	14	21	22
Nepal Népal	25	20	20	20	25	27	29	33	25	...
New Zealand Nouvelle-Zélande	1 185	752	805	338	189	2	0	0	0	-3
Nicaragua Nicaragua	87	90	100	106	110	83	56	37	53	...
Niger Niger	15	17	18	17	19	18	59	61	58	40
Nigeria Nigéria	568	1 020	1 996	1 795	1 536	4 548	4 866	4 762	4 286	4 095
Norway Norvège	908	414	222	173	3	3	3	-16	-60	...
Oman Oman	...	...	244	309	230	265	250	261	260	282

68

Ozone-depleting chlorofluorocarbons (CFCs) *[cont]*
Consumption: ozone-depleting potential (ODP) metric tons *[cont]*
Chlorofluorocarbones (CFC) qui appauvrissent la couche d'ozone *[suite]*
Consommation : tonnes de potentiel de destruction de l'ozone (PDO) *[suite]*

Region, country or area Région, pays ou zone	1989	1991	1993	1994	1995	1996	1997	1998	1999	2000
Pakistan Pakistan	927	674	1 781	1 823	2 104	1 671	1 264	1 196	1 422	...
Panama Panama	226	377	359	254	440	355	358	346	301	250
Papua New Guinea Papouasie-Nvl-Guinée	...	28	39	53	10	63	36	45	...	48
Paraguay Paraguay	176	...	191	221	211	127	102	113	345	153
Peru Pérou	540	541	279	249	367	243	259	327	296	347
Philippines Philippines	3 273	2 023	3 779	3 959	3 382	3 039	2 747	2 130	2 088	2 905
Poland Pologne	4 986	2 562	2 589	1 678	1 756	549	308	314	187	176
Qatar Qatar	85	...	...	...	91	102	111	121	89	86
Republic of Moldova République de Moldova	...	...	...	...	85	51	83	40	11	32
Romania Roumanie	...	...	1 649	960	544	763	720	582	338	361
Russian Federation Fédération de Russie	100 102	38 949	30 130	23 413	20 990	12 345	10 986	11 821	14 824	23 821
Saint Kitts and Nevis Saint-Kitts-et-Nevis	6	...	5	5	4	3	4	2	3	...
Saint Lucia Sainte-Lucie	8	...	11	8	8	8	8	6	3	...
St. Vincent-Grenadines St. Vincent-Grenadines	2	...	...	...	2	1	2	2	...	...
Samoa Samoa	4	4	4	4	4	5	5	3	5	...
Saudi Arabia Arabie saoudite	3 688	...	645	2 082	1 828	1 668	1 899	1 922	1 710	1 594
Senegal Sénégal	94	100	156	118	151	178	138	128	121	117
Serbia and Montenegro Serbie-et-Monténégro	1 749	1 199	999	868	820	896	832	519	549	...
Seychelles Seychelles	1	4	10	4	4	2	2	2	1	1
Singapore Singapour	679	639	1 482	792	774	37	-179	24	24	110
Slovakia Slovaquie	1 979	...	986	229	381	0	1	1	1	2
Slovenia Slovénie	2 391	222	594	564	354	1	0	0	0	0
Solomon Islands Iles Salomon	0	2	5	0	2	2	2	1	6	...
South Africa Afrique du Sud	10 656	4 795	4 127	2 417	1 680	0	98	155	117	81
Sri Lanka Sri Lanka	...	185	294	347	520	498	183	250	216	220

68

Ozone-depleting chlorofluorocarbons (CFCs) *[cont]*
Consumption: ozone-depleting potential (ODP) metric tons *[cont]*
Chlorofluorocarbones (CFC) qui appauvrissent la couche d'ozone *[suite]*
Consommation : tonnes de potentiel de destruction de l'ozone (PDO) *[suite]*

Region, country or area Région, pays ou zone	1989	1991	1993	1994	1995	1996	1997	1998	1999	2000
Sudan Soudan	501	601	320	338	635	430	306	295	295	292
Swaziland Swaziland	10	...	83	83	35	22	16	2	2	0
Switzerland Suisse	4 023	2 186	1 206	741	275	-43	-41	-28	-5	-6
Syrian Arab Republic Rép. arabe syrienne	1 195	1 326	1 406	2 380	2 370	2 260	2 044	1 246	1 281	1 175
Tajikistan Tadjikistan	189	91	...	...	32	35	48	56	51	28
Thailand Thaïlande	4 595	7 904	8 053	6 865	8 248	5 550	4 448	3 783	3 611	3 568
TFYR of Macedonia L'ex-R.y. Macédoine	1 174	...	...	206	558	514	487	63	192	49
Togo Togo	39	43	46	48	50	34	35	37	42	37
Tonga Tonga	...	...	...	...	2	1	1	...	...	...
Trinidad and Tobago Trinité-et-Tobago	143	116	97	109	111	114	135	156	82	101
Tunisia Tunisie	725	1 055	581	508	758	882	970	791	566	555
Turkey Turquie	3 131	3 223	4 451	2 661	3 789	3 759	3 870	3 985	1 791	820
Turkmenistan Turkménistan	171	97	61	57	56	30	26	25	19	...
Tuvalu Tuvalu	0	...	0	0	0	0	0	0	0	...
Uganda Ouganda	14	15	16	9	12	13	14	11	12	...
Ukraine Ukraine	4 518	4 518	1 703	2 421	746	1 401	1 405	1 101	951	839
United Arab Emirates Emirats arabes unis	414	522	478	425	514	511	563	737	529	476
United Rep. of Tanzania Rép.-Unie de Tanzanie	88	...	185	263	280	294	188	132	89	...
United States Etats-Unis	317 543	174 262	111 459	72 534	35 530	1 015	-967	1 180	2 123	2 145
Uruguay Uruguay	531	416	223	312	232	172	193	194	111	107
Uzbekistan Ouzbékistan	2 454	...	585	250	294	260	53	120	53	...
Venezuela Venezuela	3 451	3 786	3 624	3 093	3 220	3 041	3 704	3 214	1 922	2 706
Viet Nam Viet Nam	303	303	...	380	480	520	500	392	294	220
Yemen Yémen	...	...	...	...	306	329	412	453	1 041	1 045
Zambia Zambie	22	22	25	38	23	30	29	27	24	23

68

Ozone-depleting chlorofluorocarbons (CFCs) *[cont]*

Consumption: ozone-depleting potential (ODP) metric tons *[cont]*

Chlorofluorocarbones (CFC) qui appauvrissent la couche d'ozone *[suite]*
Consommation : tonnes de potentiel de destruction de l'ozone (PDO) *[suite]*

Region, country or area Région, pays ou zone	1989	1991	1993	1994	1995	1996	1997	1998	1999	2000
Zimbabwe Zimbabwe	476	...	218	476	462	457	435	390	229	145

Source:
United Nations Environment Programme (UNEP) Ozone Secretariat, Nairobi, "Production and Consumption of Ozone Depleting Substances, 1986 – 1998".

Source:
Programme des Nations Unies pour l'environnement (PNUE), Nairobi, "Production et consommation des substances qui appauvrissent la couche d'ozone, 1986 – 1998".

Technical notes, tables 66-68

Table 66: The data on land and forest cover are compiled by the Food and Agriculture Organization of the United Nations (FAO). The protected areas data are taken from the United Nations Environment Programme (UNEP) World Conservation Monitoring Centre.

FAO's definitions of the land categories and forest cover are as follows:

Land area: Total area excluding area under inland water bodies. The definition of inland water bodies generally includes major rivers and lakes.

Arable land: Land under temporary crops (double-cropped areas are counted only once); temporary meadows for mowing or pasture; land under market and kitchen gardens; and land temporarily fallow (less than five years). Abandoned land resulting from shifting cultivation is not included in this category. Data for "arable land" are not meant to indicate the amount of land that is potentially cultivable.

Permanent crops: Land cultivated with crops that occupy the land for long periods and need not be replanted after each harvest, such as cocoa, coffee and rubber. This category includes land under flowering shrubs, fruit trees, nut trees and vines, but excludes land under trees grown for wood or timber.

Forest: In the *Global Forest Resources Assessment 2000* [10] the following definition is used for forest. Forest includes natural forests and forest plantations and is used to refer to land with a tree crown cover (or equivalent stocking level) of more than 10 per cent and area of more than 0.5 ha. The trees should be able to reach a minimum height of 5 m at maturity *in situ*. Forest may consist either of closed forest formations where trees of various storeys and undergrowth cover a high proportion of the ground; or open forest formations with a continuous vegetation cover in which the tree crown cover exceeds 10 per cent. Young natural stands and all plantations established for forestry purposes that have yet to reach a crown density of 10 per cent or tree height of 5 m are included under forest, as are areas normally forming part of the forest area that are temporarily unstocked as a result of human intervention or natural causes but that are expected to revert to forest.

The *United Nations List of Protected Areas* [33] is the definitive list of the world's national parks and reserves. It is compiled by the UNEP World Conservation Monitoring Centre working in close collaboration with the World Conservation Union (IUCN) World Commission on Protected Areas. Information is provided by national protected areas authorities and the secretariats of international conventions and programmes.

Notes techniques, tableaux 66 à 68

Tableau 66: Les données relatives aux terres et à la superficie forestière sont compilées par l'Organisation des Nations Unies pour l'alimentation et l'agriculture (FAO). Les données relatives aux aires protégées viennent du Centre mondial de surveillance pour la conservation du Programme des Nations Unies pour l'environnement (PNUE).

Les définitions de la FAO en ce qui concerne les terres et la superficie forestière sont les suivantes:

Superficie totale des terres: Superficie totale, à l'exception des eaux intérieures. Les eaux intérieures désignent généralement les principaux fleuves et lacs.

Terres arables: Terres affectées aux cultures temporaires (les terres sur lesquelles est pratiquée la double culture ne sont comptabilisées qu'une fois), prairies temporaires à faucher ou à pâturer, jardins maraîchers ou potagers et terres en jachère temporaire (moins de cinq ans). Cette définition ne comprend pas les terres abandonnées du fait de la culture itinérante. Les données relatives aux terres arables ne peuvent être utilisées pour calculer la superficie des terres aptes à l'agriculture.

Cultures permanentes: Superficie des terres avec des cultures qui occupent la terre pour de longues périodes et qui ne nécessitent pas d'être replantées après chaque récolte, comme le cacao, le café et le caoutchouc. Cette catégorie comprend les terres plantées d'arbustes à fleurs, d'arbres fruitiers, d'arbres à noix et de vignes, mais ne comprend pas les terres plantées d'arbres destinés à la coupe.

Superficie forestière: Dans *l'Évaluation des ressources forestières mondiales 2000* [10], la FAO a défini les forêts comme suit : les forêts, qui comprennent les forêts naturelles et les plantations forestières, sont des terres où le couvert arboré (ou la densité de peuplement équivalente) est supérieur à 10 % et représente une superficie de plus de 0,5 ha. Les arbres doivent être susceptibles d'atteindre sur place, à leur maturité, une hauteur de 5 m minimum. Il peut s'agir de forêts denses, où les arbres de différente hauteur et le sous-bois couvrent une proportion importante du sol, ou de forêts claires, avec un couvert végétal continu, où le couvert arboré est supérieur à 10 %. Les jeunes peuplements naturels et toutes les plantations d'exploitation forestière n'ayant pas encore atteint une densité de couvert arboré de 10 % ou une hauteur de 5 m sont inclus dans les forêts, de même que les aires formant naturellement partie de la superficie forestière mais temporairement déboisées du fait d'une intervention de l'homme ou de causes naturelles, mais devant redevenir boisées.

Countries vary considerably in their mechanisms for creating and maintaining systems of protected areas. In order to facilitate international comparisons for protected areas, IUCN has adopted a definition of a protected area which is, an area of land and/or sea especially dedicated to the protection and maintenance of biological diversity, and of natural and associated cultural resources, and managed through legal or other effective means.

IUCN has defined a series of six protected area management categories, based on primary management objectives. These categories are as follows:

Category Ia: Strict Nature Reserve;
Category Ib: Wilderness Area;
Category II: National Park;
Category III: Natural Monument;
Category IV: Habitat/Species Management Area;
Category V: Protected Landscape/Seascape;
Category VI: Managed Resource Protected Area.

Table 67: The sources of the data presented on the emissions of carbon dioxide (CO_2) are the Carbon Dioxide Information Analysis Center (CDIAC) of the Oak Ridge National Laboratory in the USA and the Secretariat of the United Nations Framework Convention on Climate Change (UNFCCC). The majority of the data have been taken from the CDIAC database. The data taken from the UNFCCC database are footnoted accordingly.

The CDIAC estimates of CO_2 emissions are derived primarily from United Nations energy statistics on the consumption of liquid and solid fuels and gas consumption and flaring, and from cement production estimates from the Bureau of Mines of the U.S. Department of Interior. The emissions presented in the table are in units of 1,000 metric tons of carbon dioxide (CO_2); to convert CO_2 into carbon, multiply the data by 0.272756. Full details of the procedures for calculating emissions are given in *Global, Regional, and National Annual C0₂ Emissions Estimates from Fossil Fuel Burning, Hydraulic Cement Production, and Gas Flaring* [3] and in the CDIAC Web site (see <http://cdiac.esd.ornl.gov>. Relative to other industrial sources for which CO_2 emissions are estimated, statistics on gas flaring activities are sparse and sporadic. In countries where gas flaring activities account for a considerable proportion of the total CO_2 emissions, the sporadic nature of gas flaring statistics may produce spurious or misleading trends in national CO_2 emissions over the period covered by the table.

The UNFCCC data in the table are indicated by a footnote, and cover (a) the countries that joined the convention (except for Belarus which joined in May 2000) and (b) countries which voluntarily reported time-series

La *Liste des Nations Unies des zones protégées* [33] est la liste la plus fiable des parcs et réserves naturels du monde. Elle est établie par le Centre mondial de surveillance pour la conservation du PNUE, en collaboration étroite avec la Commission mondiale des aires protégées de l'Union mondiale pour la nature (UICN). Les renseignements sont communiqués par les services nationaux responsables des aires protégées et les secrétariats des conventions et programmes internationaux.

Les mécanismes nationaux de création et d'entretien des systèmes de zones protégées sont très différents d'un pays à l'autre. Pour faciliter les comparaisons internationales, l'UICN a adopté une définition des aires protégées, zone terrestre ou marine (ou les deux) spécialement consacrée à la protection et à la sauvegarde de la diversité biologique et des ressources naturelles, ainsi que des ressources culturelles qui y sont associées, dont la gestion est assurée par des moyens juridiques ou autres moyens efficaces.

L'UICN a défini une série de six catégories de gestion des aires protégées, en fonction des objectifs principaux:

Catégorie Ia:: Réserve naturelle intégrale;
Catégorie Ib: Zone vierge;
Catégorie II: Parc national;
Catégorie III: Monument naturel;
Catégorie IV: Aire de gestion des habitats/des espèces;
Catégorie V: Paysage terrestre/marin protégé;
Catégorie VI: Aire protégée de ressources naturelles.

Tableau 67: Les données sur les émissions de dioxyde de carbone (CO_2) proviennent du Carbon Dioxide Information Analysis Center (CDIAC) du Oak Ridge National Laboratory (États-Unis) et du Secrétariat de la convention-cadre concernant les changements climatiques (CCCC) des Nations Unies. La majorité des données proviennent de la base de données du CDIAC. Les données qui proviennent du Secrétariat de la CCCC sont signalées par une note.

Les estimations du Carbon Dioxide Information Analysis Center sont obtenues essentiellement à partir des statistiques de l'énergie des Nations Unies relatives à la consommation de combustibles liquides et solides, à la production et à la consommation de gaz de torche, et des chiffres de production de ciment du Bureau of Mines du Department of Interior des États-Unis. Les émissions sont indiquées en milliers de tonnes de dioxyde de carbone (à multiplier par 0,272756 pour avoir les chiffres de carbone). On peut voir dans le détail les méthodes utilisées pour calculer les émissions dans *Global, Regional, and National Annual C0₂ Emissions Estimates from Fossil Fuel Burning, Hydraulic Cement Production, and Gas Flaring* [3] et sur le site Web du Carbon Dioxide

data on their emissions to the UNFCCC. The CO_2 data from national reports to the Secretariat of the UNFCCC are based on the methodology of the Intergovernmental Panel for Climate Change (IPCC) 1996 Guidebook.

Table 68: Chlorofluorocarbons (CFCs) are synthetic compounds formerly used as refrigerants and aerosol propellants and known to be harmful to the ozone layer of the atmosphere. In the Montreal Protocol on Substances that Deplete the Ozone Layer, CFCs to be measured are found in vehicle air conditioning units, domestic and commercial refrigeration and air conditioning/heat pump equipment, aerosol products, portable fire extinguishers, insulation boards, panels and pipe covers, and pre-polymers.

The Parties to the Montreal Protocol on Substances that Deplete the Ozone Layer report data on CFCs to the Ozone Secretariat of the United Nations Environment Programme. The data on CFCs are shown in ozone depleting potential (ODP) tons that are calculated by multiplying the quantities in metric tons reported by the Parties, by the ODP of that substance, and added together.

Consumption is defined as production plus imports, minus exports of controlled substances. Feedstocks are exempt and are therefore subtracted from the imports and/or production. Similarly, the destroyed amounts are also subtracted. Negative numbers can occur when destruction and/or exports exceed production plus imports, implying that the destruction and/or exports are from stockpiles.

Information Analysis Center (voir <http://cdiac.esd.ornl.gov>. Par rapport à d'autres sources industrielles pour lesquelles on calcule les émissions de CO_2, les statistiques sur la production de gaz de torche sont rares et sporadiques. Dans les pays où cette production représente une proportion considérable de l'ensemble des émissions de dioxyde de carbone, on peut voir apparaître de ce fait des chiffres parasites ou trompeurs pour ce qui est des tendances des émissions nationales de dioxyde de carbone durant la période visée par le tableau.

Les données provenant du secrétariat de la Convention-cadre, qui sont signalées par une note, couvrent (a) les pays qui ont adhéré à la Convention (sauf pour le Bélarus, qui y a adhéré en mai 2000), et (b) les pays qui ont bénévolement communiqué des séries chronologiques sur leurs émissions au secrétariat. Les données sur le CO_2 tirées des rapports de pays au secrétariat de la Convention-cadre ont été obtenues par les méthodes recommandées dans le Manuel de 1996 du Groupe intergouvernemental d'experts pour l'étude du changement climatique.

Tableau 68: Les chlorofluorocarbones (CFC) sont des substances de synthèse utilisées comme réfrigérants et propulseurs d'aérosols, dont on sait qu'elles appauvrissent la couche d'ozone. Aux termes du Protocole de Montréal relatif à des substances qui appauvrissent la couche d'ozone, la production de certains CFC doit être mesurée : ils sont utilisés dans les climatiseurs de véhicules, le matériel domestique et commercial de réfrigération et de climatisation (pompes à chaleur), les produits sous forme d'aérosols, les extincteurs d'incendie portables, les planches, panneaux et gaines isolants, et les prépolymères.

Les Parties au Protocole de Montréal communiquent leurs données concernant les CFC au secrétariat de l'ozone du Programme des Nations Unies pour l'environnement. Les données sur les CFC, indiquées en tonnes de potentiel d'appauvrissement de la couche d'ozone (PAO), sont calculées en multipliant le nombre de tonnes signalé par les Parties par le potentiel d'appauvrissement (coefficient) de la substance considérée, et en faisant la somme de ces PAO.

La consommation est définie comme production de substances contrôlées, plus les importations, moins les exportations. Les produits intermédiaires de l'industrie sont exemptés, et on les soustrait donc des importations et/ou de la production. De même, on soustrait aussi les quantités détruites. On peut obtenir des quantités négatives, lorsque les quantités détruites et/ou exportées sont supérieures à la somme production + importations, ce qui signifie que les quantités détruites ou exportées ont été prélevées sur les stocks accumulés.

69
Researchers, technicians and other supporting staff engaged in research and development
Full−time equivalent (FTE)
Chercheurs, techniciens et autre personnel de soutien employés à des travaux de recherche et de développement
Equivalent plein temps (EPT)

Country or area Pays ou zone	Year Année	Total	Researchers Chercheurs		Technicians Techniciens		Other supporting staff Autre personnel de soutien	
			Total M & W Total H & F	Women Femmes	Total M & W Total H & F	Women Femmes	Total M & W Total H & F	Women Femmes
Africa • Afrique								
Benin [1]								
Bénin [1]	1989	2 687	794	100	242	64	1 651	339
Burkino Faso	1996	738	162	32	158	13	418	...
Burkina Faso	1997	780	176	34	165	16	439	...
Burundi [23]	1984	515	114	10	90	...	311	...
Burundi [23]	1989	814	170	17	168	...	476	...
Cameroon	1998	198	43	...	55	...	100	...
Cameroun	1999	196	43	...	53	...	100	...
Central African Rep.	1990	...	162	16	92	5	...	...
Rép. centrafricaine	1996	19 500	...	...	...	2 555	...	...
Congo	1999	227	110	15	114	22	2	...
Congo	2000[4]	217	101	13	111	22	3	...
Egypt	1990	89 154	24 599	8 055	17 150	1 200	47 405	25 471
Egypte	1991	102 296	26 415		19 607		56 274	
Libyan Arab Jamahiriya								
Jamah. arabe libyenne	1980	3 600	1 100	...	1 500	...	1 000	...
Madagascar	1999	1 114	227	...	862	...	25	...
Madagascar	2000	985	240	...	730	...	15	...
Mauritius	1989	1 021	193	33	172	46	656	97
Maurice	1992	1 162	389	...	170	...	603	...
Nigeria	1986	12 845	1 499	...	6 005	...	5 341	...
Nigéria	1987	12 880	1 338	...	6 042	...	5 500	...
Rwanda	1984	164	69	...	60	...	35	...
Rwanda	1995	315	181	18	40	31	94	33
Saint Helena [6]	1999	40	4	1	38	13	...	...
Saint Hélène [6]	2000	33	2	...	8	4	23	...
Senegal [5]	1996	78	19	5	29	7	30	...
Sénégal [5]	1997	66	16	...	23	...	27	...
South Africa	1991	22 223	12 102	...	5 006	...	5 115	...
Afrique du Sud	1993	60 464	37 192	...	11 343	...	11 929	...
Togo	1989	1 200	277	...	183	...	740	...
Togo	1994	1 473	387	...	249	...	837	...
Tunisia	1999	5 363	3 149[7]	...	292	...	1 922	...
Tunisie	2000	5 708	...	...	303	...	1 943	...
Uganda	1999	1 102	503	189	309	25	290	...
Ouganda	2000	1 187	549	206	330	27	308	...
America, North • Amérique du Nord								
Canada	1997	146 190	93 440	...	33 660	...	19 090	...
Canada	1998[8]	139 570	90 200	...	31 380	...	17 990	...
Costa Rica	1988[39]	1 528	1 528	...	...	...	...	...
Costa Rica	1996	1 866	...	...	...	...	...	...
Cuba [10]	1999	62 512	5 468	...	23 595	...	33 449	...
Cuba [10]	2000	64 074	5 378	...	24 190	...	34 506	...
El Salvador	1999	...	199	...	...	...	...	...
El Salvador	2000	...	293	...	...	...	...	...
Guatemala [11]								
Guatemala [11]	1988	2 575	858	...	925	...	792	...
Jamaica [12]	1985	121	21	...	31	...	69	...
Jamaïque [12]	1986	104	18	10	15	3	71	...
Mexico	1998	40 520	22 190	...	18 330	...	...	...
Mexique	1999	39 736	21 879	...	17 857	...	...	...
Nicaragua	1987[3]	2 005	725	...	302	...	978	...
Nicaragua	1997	620	340	...	153	...	127	...
Panama	1998	1 614	461	...	733	...	420	...
Panama	1999	1 750	350	...	687	...	713	...
Trinidad and Tobago								
Trinité−et−Tobago	1997	515	185	80	330	129	515	...

69
Researchers, technicians and other supporting staff engaged in research and development
Full—time equivalent (FTE) *[cont.]*
Chercheurs, techniciens et autre personnel de soutien employés à des travaux de recherche
et de développement
Equivalent plein temps (EPT) *[suite]*

Country or area Pays ou zone	Year Année	Total	Researchers Chercheurs		Technicians Techniciens		Other supporting staff Autre personnel de soutien	
			Total M & W Total H & F	Women Femmes	Total M & W Total H & F	Women Femmes	Total M & W Total H & F	Women Femmes
United States	1996	...	1 040 900	...	...	...	...	...
Etats—Unis	1997	...	1 114 100	...	...	...	...	...
America, South • Amérique du Sud								
Argentina	1999	36 939	26 004	11 825	5 707	...	5 228	...
Argentine	2000	37 515	26 420	...	5 836	...	5 259	...
Bolivia	1999	830	600	...	200	...	30	...
Bolivie	2000	820	600	...	170	...	50	...
Brazil	1995	...	26 754[13]	...	9 327	...	...	...
Brésil	2000[10]	78 565	55 103	21 252[32]	21 914	...	1 548	...
Chile *	1999	14 957	5 549	...	...	...	...	...
Chili *	2000	15 415	5 629	...	...	...	...	...
Colombia	1999	5 925	4 065	1 860	...	...	...	...
Colombie	2000	6 262	4 240	2 022	...	...	...	...
Ecuador	1997	2 735	932	...	885	...	918	...
Ecuador	1998	2 907	1 014	...	874	...	1 019	...
Paraguay [3]								
Paraguay [3]	1981	...	807	...	...	...	1 545	...
Peru	1996	5 785	5 522	...	220	...	...	...
Pérou	1997	5 610	5 576	...	34	...	...	...
Uruguay	1987[3]	...	2 093	720	...	...	...	...
Uruguay	1999	949	724	...	68	...	157	...
Venezuela	1999	...	4 435	...	...	...	...	...
Venezuela	2000	...	4 688[15]	1 969	...	...	...	...
Asia • Asie								
Armenia	1999	6 523	4 856	...	903	...	764	...
Arménie	2000	...	4 971	...	846	...	529	...
Azerbaijan	1996	25 556	21 234	8 889	1 428	...	2 894	...
Azerbaïdjan	1997	25 322	21 387	...	1 226	...	2 742	...
Bangladesh	1994	15 010	5 418	568	2 055	404	7 537	...
Bangladesh	1995	16 629	6 097	851	3 825	728	6 707	...
China [16][26]	1999	821 700	531 100	...	...	...	...	...
Chine [16][26]	2000	922 131	695 062	...	...	...	...	...
China, Hong Kong SAR	1995[17]	1 627	574	...	613	...	440	...
Chine, Hong Kong RAS	1998	5 809					...	
China, Macao SAR [19]	1999	18	12	2	6	...	...	...
Chine, Macao RAS [19]	2000	28	18	2	10	2	...	...
Cyprus	1998	564	237	69	168	60	159	...
Chypre	1999	681	278	81	198	71	205	...
Georgia [21]	1998	17 009	13 692	...	...	...	3 317	...
Géorgie [21]	1999	15 138	12 786	...	...	...	2 353	...
India	1992[22]	315 448	117 586	7 737	98 202	7 096	99 660	...
Inde	1996	357 172	149 326	11 078	108 817	9 121	99 029	...
Indonesia [3]	1984	36 185	24 895	...	4 125	...	7 165	...
Indonésie [3]	1985	...	21 160	...	3 888	...	...	...
Iran, Islamic Rep. of	1985	5 048[23]	3 194	...	1 854	...	...	...
Iran, Rép. islamique d'	1994	50 326	34 256	...	10 104	...	5 966	...
Israel [10]	1996	12 267	7 620	...	3 558	...	789	...
Israël [10]	1997	13 110	9 161	...	3 023	...	926	...
Japan	1999	919 132	658 910	...	84 527	...	175 695	...
Japon	2000	896 847	647 572	...	...	...	...	...
Jordan								
Jordanie	1998	23 946	9 090	1 629	3 345	737	11 511	...
Kazakhstan	1996	20 620	14 600	...	5 140	...	880	...
Kazakhstan	1997	18 980	11 720	...	4 800	...	2 500	...
Korea, Republic of [24]	1999	137 874	100 210	...	26 160	...	11 504	...
Corée, République de [24]	2000	138 077	108 370	...	...	...	...	...
Kuwait	1999	750	397	115	96	38	257	...
Koweït	2000	746	406	120	102	46	256	...
Kyrgzstan	1996	4 126	2 629	...	256	...	1 241	...
Kirghizistan	1997	4 161	2 685	1 249	226	...	1 250	...
Malaysia	1996	4 437	1 894	509	655	146	1 889	...
Malaisie	1998	6 656	3 415	935	966	201	2 274	...
Mongolia	1999	2 141	1 114	557	219	96	808	...
Mongolie	2000	2 531	1 344	746	294	150	893	...

69
Researchers, technicians and other supporting staff engaged in research and development
Full−time equivalent (FTE) *[cont.]*
Chercheurs, techniciens et autre personnel de soutien employés à des travaux de recherche
et de développement
Equivalent plein temps (EPT) *[suite]*

Country or area Pays ou zone	Year Année	Total	Researchers Chercheurs Total M & W Total H & F	Women Femmes	Technicians Techniciens Total M & W Total H & F	Women Femmes	Other supporting staff Autre personnel de soutien Total M & W Total H & F	Women Femmes
Oman [18]	1999	9	8	...	1	...	...	...
Oman [18]	2000	10	9	...	1	...	...	...
Pakistan	1990[25]	29 040	6 626	464	9 314	...	13 100	...
Pakistan	1997	36 706	9 977	859	1 749	27	24 980	...
Philippines								
Philippines	1992	14 578	9 960	5 260	1 399	374	3 219	1 338
Qatar [3 25]								
Qatar [3 25]	1986	290	229	58	61	2	...	...
Singapore	1999	15 098	12 598	...	...	...	...	...
Singapour	2000	19 365	16 633	...	...	...	...	...
Sri Lanka	1985	3 483[23]	2 790	667	693	188	...	...
Sri Lanka	1996	4 281	3 448	1 103	833	...	...	...
Syrian Arab Republic								
Rép. arabe syrienne	1997	804	440	...	364	...	...	...
Tajikistan [3]	1992	...	3 974	1 144	...	...	...	...
Tadjikistan [3]	1993		3 722	...	...	...	...	...
Thailand	1996	10 209	6 038	5 846	2 303	2 129	1 868	...
Thaïlande	1997	14 022	4 409	5 455	4 446	7 318	5 167	...
Turkey [26]	1998	22 892	18 925	...	...	...	...	...
Turquie [26]	1999	24 267	20 065	...	...	...	...	...
Uzbekistan [15]								...
Ouzbékistan [15]	1992	...	37 625	17 005	6 687	...	...	...
Viet Nam [27]								
Viet Nam [27]	1995	...	20 000	...	...	...	...	...
Europe · Europe								
Austria	1993	24 458	12 821	2 008	6 397	1 945	5 240	2 119
Autriche	1998[26]	31 308	18 715	...	7 919	...	4 674	...
Belarus	1996	38 030	23 324	...	2 758	...	8 816	...
Bélarus	1997	33 200	19 598	...	2 830	...	10 772	...
Belgium	1998	46 428	28 149	...	11 142	...	7 136	...
Belgique	1999	49 477	30 219	...	11 843	...	7 415	...
Bulgaria	1998	19 116	11 972	5 321	4 862	3 295	2 282	...
Bulgarie	1999	16 087	10 580	4 656	3 829	2 578	1 678	...
Croatia	1998	7 642	4 736	2 007	1 493	906	1 413	...
Croatie	1999	8 827	5 523	2 426	1 615	954	1 689	...
Czech Republic	1999	24 106	13 535	...	...	...	...	...
République tchèque	2000	24 198	13 852	...	...	...	...	...
Denmark	1997	34 187	17 511	...	13 344	...	3 330	...
Danemark	1999	35 650	18 438	...	13 758	...	3 454	...
Estonia	1998[24]	4 713	3 045	1 239	782	547	886	...
Estonie	1999	4 545[28]	3 001[28]	1 251[24]	749[24]	538[24]	795[24]	...
Finland	1999	50 604	25 398	...	...	...	...	...
Finlande	2000	52 604	26 162	...	...	...	...	...
France	1998	309 161	155 727	...	...	...	...	...
France	1999	314 452	160 424	...	...	...	...	...
Germany	1999	480 415	255 260	...	110 364	...	114 415	...
Allemagne	2000[8]	488 097	259 214	...	...	...	...	...
Greece	1997	20 173	10 972	...	4 265	...	4 935	...
Grèce	1999	26 495	14 828	...	5 867	...	5 800	...
Hungary [29]	1999	21 329	12 579	...	5 037	...	3 713	...
Hongrie [29]	2000	23 534	14 406	...	5 166	...	3 962	...
Iceland	1998[8]	2 273	1 414	...	...	...	...	...
Islande	1999	2 390	1 578	...	...	...	...	...
Ireland [8]	1998	11 613	7 720	...	...	...	...	...
Irlande [8]	1999	12 289	8 217	...	...	...	...	...
Italy	1998	145 969	65 354	...	...	...	...	...
Italie	1999	142 506	64 886	...	...	...	...	...
Latvia	1998	4 437	2 557	1 201	777	422	1 103	...
Lettonie	1999	4 301	2 626	1 277	726	419	949	...
Lithuania								...
Lituanie	1996	12 569	7 532	...	2 344	1 546	2 693	...
Malta [17]								
Malte [17]	1988	46	34	...	5	..	7	...

69
Researchers, technicians and other supporting staff engaged in research and development
Full−time equivalent (FTE) *[cont.]*
Chercheurs, techniciens et autre personnel de soutien employés à des travaux de recherche
et de développement
Equivalent plein temps (EPT) *[suite]*

Country or area Pays ou zone	Year Année	Total	Researchers Chercheurs Total M & W Total H & F	Women Femmes	Technicians Techniciens Total M & W Total H & F	Women Femmes	Other supporting staff Autre personnel de soutien Total M & W Total H & F	Women Femmes
Monaco [30]								
Monaco [30]	1998	48	22	...	15	...	11	...
Netherlands	1998	85 486	39 081	...	...	...	...	...
Pays−Bas	1999	87 006	40 623	...	...	...	...	...
Norway	1997	24 877	17 490	...	...	...	...	...
Norvège	1999	25 400	18 295	...	...	...	...	...
Poland	1999	82 368	56 433	...	...	...	...	...
Pologne	2000	78 925	55 174	...	...	...	...	...
Portugal	1997	18 035	13 642	...	4 393			
Portugal	1999	20 806	15 752	...	5 054			
Republic of Moldova	1999	8 957	...					
Moldova, Rep. de	2000	8 173	...					
Romania	1999	44 091	23 473	...	...	...	...	...
Roumanie	2000	33 892	20 476					
Russian Federation	1999	989 291	497 030	186 264	80 498	...	411 763	...
Fédération de Russie	2000	1 007 257	506 420					
Serbia and Montenegro	1995	25 392	11 611	4 150	5 436	2 950	8 345	4 713
Serbie−et−Monténégro	1996	22 195		...	4 274		6 438	
Slovakia [29]	1999	14 849	9 204	...	...	...	...	...
Slovaquie [29]	2000	15 221	9 955	...	...	...	...	...
Slovenia [29]	1999	8 495	4 427	...	...	...	...	...
Slovénie [29]	2000	9 568	4 336	...	...	...	...	...
Spain	1999	102 237	61 568	...	40 670[8]	...	...	...
Espagne	2000[8]	103 259	76 670	...	...	...	...	...
Sweden	1997	65 495	36 878	...	...	...	...	...
Suède	1999	66 674	39 921	...	...	...	...	...
Switzerland	1996	50 265	21 635	...	...	...	...	...
Suisse	2000	52 225	25 755					
TFYR Macedonia								
L'ex−R.y. Macédoine	1995	5 043	2 620	1 081	1 070	794	1 353	898
Ukraine	1999	170 599	102 196	...	27 851	...	40 552	...
Ukraine	2000	170 079	104 970	...	29 465	...	35 664	...
United Kingdom	1997	...	145 946	...	...	...	...	...
Royaume−Uni	1998	...	157 662	...	...	...	...	...
Oceania · Océanie								
Australia	1996	90 744	61 073	...	...	...	29 671[31]	...
Australie	1998	91 490	62 790	...	...	...	28 700[31]	...
Fiji [5]								
Fidji [5]	1986	156	36	4	90	10	30	...
Guam	1989[15]	52[17]	21	4	11	4	20	2
Guam	1991	55[17]	23	5	11	5	21	1
New Caledonia [14]								
Nouvelle−Calédonie [14]	1985	334	77	7	71	11	186	37
New Zealand	1995[20]	10 547	6 104	...	2 838	...	1 606	...
Nouvelle−Zélande	1997	12 908	8 264	...	...	...	...	...

Source:
United Nations Educational, Scientific and Cultural Organization (UNESCO) Institute for Statistics, Montreal, the UNESCO statistics database.

1   Not including data for the productive sector (non−integrated R & D).
2   Not including data for the productive sector.
3   Data refer to full−time plus part−time personnel.

4   Data relate to persons employed in government institutions only.
5   Data relate to one research institute only.
6   Includes only private research into class teacher attrition, and these sectors: tourism, electricity, gas and water supply, agriculture.

7   Secondary or higher education teachers who reserve 35%

Source:
L'Institut de statistique de l'Organisation des Nations Unies pour l'éducation, la science et la culture (UNESCO), Montréal, la base de données de l'UNESCO.

1   Non compris les données relatives au secteur de la production (activités de R − D non intégrées).
2   Non compris les données relatives au secteur de la production.
3   Les données se réfèrent au personnel à plein temps et à temps partiel.
4   Données concernant exclusivement le personnel des institutions gouvernementales.
5   Les données ne concernent qu'un institut de recherche.
6   Données provenant exclusivement d?études privées portant sur la réduction naturelle des effectifs du corps enseignant et sur les secteurs suivants : tourisme, électricité, alimentation en gaz et en eau, agriculture.

7   Sont comptabilisés comme chercheurs, les enseignants de

69
Researchers, technicians and other supporting staff engaged in research and development
Full−time equivalent (FTE) *[cont.]*
Chercheurs, techniciens et autre personnel de soutien employés à des travaux de recherche
et de développement
Equivalent plein temps (EPT) *[suite]*

of their time for research and development activities.	l'enseignement supérieur qui réservent 35% de leur activités pour les r&d.
8 National estimate or projection adjusted, if necessary, by OECD.	8 Estimation nationale ou projection corrigée, le cas échéant, par l'OCDE.
9 Data refer to researchers only.	9 Les données se réfèrent aux chercheurs seulement.
10 Employed persons engaged in r&d (not full time equivalent).	10 Personnel affecté à la recherche−développement (ne correspond pas à un équivalent plein temps).
11 Data relate to the productive sector (integrated R&D) and the higher education sector only.	11 Les données se réfèrent au secteur de la production (activités de R−D intégrées) et au secteur de l'enseignement supérieur seulement.
12 Data relate to the Scientific Research Council only.	12 Les données se réfèrent au 'Scientific Research Council' seulement.
13 Data refer to researchers listed in the directory of research group in Brazil by the Conselho Nacional de Desenvolvimento Cientifico e Tecnologica (CNPq).	13 Les données se réfèrent aux chercheurs figurant dans le répertoire du groupe de chercheurs brésiliens élaboré par le Conselho Nacional de Desenvolvimento Cientifico e Tecnológico (CNPq).
14 Data refer only to 6 out of 11 research institutes.	14 Les données concernent 6 des 11 instituts de recherche.
15 Number of researchers who applied to the research program (expressed in number of persons).	15 Nombre de chercheurs ayant demandé à suivre le programme de recherche (en nombre de personnes).
16 The sum of the breakdown does not add to the total.	16 La somme de toutes les valeurs diffère du total.
17 Data refer to the higher education sector only.	17 Les données se réfèrent au secteur de l'enseignement supérieur seulement.
18 Data refer only to the animal production center (ministry of agriculture and fisheries).	18 Les données concernent uniquement le centre de la production animale (Ministère de l?agriculture et de la pêche).
19 Includes only three faculties' r&d projects from the University of Macao: faculty of science and technology (fst), faculty of business administration (gfba), faculty of social science and humanity (fsh).	19 Ne comprend que les projets de recherche−développement de trois facultés de l'Université de Macao, à savoir la faculté de sciences et technologies, la faculté de hautes études commerciales et la la faculté de sciences sociales et humanités.
20 Data are from OECD.	20 Les données sont de l'OCDE.
21 Includes part−time.	21 Y compris le personnel à temps partiel.
22 Not including data for the higher education sector.	22 Non compris les données pour le secteur de l'enseignement supérieur.
23 Not including data for other supporting staff.	23 Non compris les données pour le personnel de soutien.
24 Excluding R&D in the social sciences and humanities.	24 À l'exclusion de la recherche−développement en sciences sociales et humanités.
25 Not including social sciences and humanities in the higher education sector.	25 Non inclus les sciences sociales et humanités dans le secteur de la production et le secteur de service général.
26 Under−estimated or based on under−estimated data.	26 Sous−estimation ou chiffre établi sur la base de données sous−estimées
27 Not including general service sector.	27 Non compris le secteur de service général.
28 Excluding the business enterprise sector.	28 Non compris le secteur des entreprises.
29 Defence excluded (all or mostly).	29 À l'exclusion de la défense (en totalité ou en grande partie).
30 Personnel in public or parapublic sector only.	30 Personnel du secteur public or parapublic seulement.
31 Includes other classes.	31 Comprend d'autres catégories.
32 The number of female researchers is not available for the business enterprise sector.	32 Le nombre de femmes chercheurs n'est pas disponible pour le secteur des entreprises industrielles.

70
Gross domestic expenditure on R & D by source of funds
National currency
Dépenses intérieures brutes de recherche et développement par source de fonds
Monnaie nationale

Country or area (Monetary unit) Pays ou zone (Unité monétaire)	Years Années	Gross domestic exp on R&D Dép int. brutes de R–D (thousands)	Source of funds (%) / Source de fonds (%)					
			Business enterprises Enterprises	Gov't Etat	Higher education Enseigne-ment supérieur	Private non–profit Inst. privées sans but lucratif	Funds from abroad Fonds de l'étranger	Not dis-tributed Non répartis
Africa · Afrique								
Burkino Faso (CFA franc)	1996	2 095 055	...	...	...	...	...	...
Burkina Faso (franc CFA)	1997	2 586 461	...	...	...	...	...	...
Burundi (franc)[1 2]								
Burundi (franc)[1 2]	1989	536 187	...	39.4	...	...	60.6	
Central African Rep. (CFA franc)								
Rép. centrafricaine (franc CFA)	1996	130 899[3]	...	100.0		...	...	
Congo (CFA franc)								
Congo (franc CFA)	1984	25 530	25.5	68.8	...		5.7	
Egypt (Eg. pound)	1999	573 700	...	...	...	...	...	
Egypte (livre)	2000	654 600	...	...	...	...	...	
Madagascar (franc)	1999	22 425 000	...	...	...	...	...	
Madagascar (franc)	2000	31 428 000	...	...	...	...	...	
Mauritius (rupee)	1989[5]	54 300	2.4	35.0	62.6	...	...	
Maurice (roupie)	1997	246 000	...	94.7	...	...	5.3	
Nigeria (naira)[7]								
Nigéria (naira)[7]	1987	86 270	...	100.0	...		...	
Rwanda (franc)								
Rwanda (franc)	1984	260 750	...	72.5	...	...	17.8	9.7
Saint Helena (pound)	1999	40 390	...	...	...	...	...	
Saint–Hélène (livre)	2000	151 774	...	42.6	...	...	...	57.4
Senegal (CFA franc)	1996	410 160						
Sénégal (franc CFA)	1997	314 000	...	...	...	...	...	
Seychelles (rupee)[7]	1983	12 854	...	48.8	...	...	51.2	
Seychelles (roupie)[7]	1991	4 593	...	100.0	...	...	...	
South Africa (rand)	1991	2 786 086	46.8	32.4	20.8	...	...	...
Afrique du sud (rand)	1993	2 594 107	54.4	42.7	1.8	...	1.0[27]	...
Togo (CFA franc)[8]								
Togo (CFA franc)[8]	1995	52 737 405	...	...	...	...	100.0	
Tunisia (dinar)	1999	108 249	...	...	...	...	...	
Tunisie (dinar)	2000	120 402	7.0	45.1	44.9	...	3.0	
Uganda (shilling)	1996	34 866 530	2.2	6.6	0.6	0.3	90.3	...
Ouganda (shilling)	1999	65 740 280	2.2	6.6	0.6	0.3	90.3	...
America, North · Amérique du Nord								
Canada (dollar)	1999	17 243 000	57.0	12.1	29.9	1.0	...	...
Canada (dollar)	2000	* 19 129 000	56.8	11.3	31.0	1.0	...	...
Costa Rica (colón)	1997	6 395 014	...	...	...	...	...	...
Costa Rica (colón)	1998	7 252 307	...	...	...	...	...	...
Cuba (peso)	1999	130 000	...	...	...	...	...	...
Cuba (peso)	2000	136 000	...	...	...	...	...	...
El Salvador (colón)[10]	1989[7]	290 881	...	100.0	...	...	...	...
El Salvador (colón)[10]	1992	1 083 559	...	47.4	...	...	52.6	...
Guatemala (quetzal)								
Guatemala (quetzal)	1988	31 859[11]	0.5	36.7	45.7	...	17.0[27]	...
Jamaica (dollar)								
Jamaïque (dollar)	1986	4 016[12]	...	100.0	...	...	...	...
Mexico (peso)	1998	14 524 570	23.2	38.3	36.9	1.6	...	...
Mexique (peso)	1999	19 746 068	27.2	32.5	38.6	1.7	...	...
Nicaragua (córdoba)	1987	* 988 970[5]	...	* 80.8	...	...	* 19.2	...
Nicaragua (córdoba)	1997	27 000	...	...	...	...	...	...
Panama (balboa)	1998	31 164	...	...	...	...	...	...
Panama (balboa)	1999	33 000	...	...	...	...	...	...
Trinidad and Tobago (dollar)	1996	45 600	...	...	...	...	...	...
Trinité-et-Tobago (dollar)	1997	49 200	...	...	...	...	...	...
United States (dollar)	1999	244 143 000	74.7	7.7	13.9	3.6	...	...
Etats–Unis (dollar)	2000	264 622 000	75.3	7.5	13.6	3.6	...	...
America, South · Amérique du Sud								
Argentina (peso)	1999	1 285 400	...	...	...	...	...	...
Argentine (peso)	2000	1 271 200	...	...	...	...	...	...
Bolivia (peso)	1999	143 000	...	...	...	...	...	...
Bolivie (peso)	2000	149 000	...	...	...	...	...	...

70
Gross domestic expenditure on R & D by source of funds
National currency [*cont.*]

Dépenses intérieures brutes de recherche et développement par source de fonds
Monnaie nationale [*suite*]

Country or area (Monetary unit) Pays ou zone (Unité monétaire)	Years Années	Gross domestic exp on R&D Dép int. brutes de R−D (thousands)	Source of funds (%) / Source de fonds (%)					
			Business enterprises Enterprises	Gov't Etat	Higher education Enseigne- ment supérieur	Private non−profit Inst. privées sans but lucratif	Funds from abroad Fonds de l'étranger	Not dis− tributed Non répartis
Brazil (reais)	1996	6 035 023	...	...	...	...	...	...
Brésil (reais)	1999	8 395 900	...	...	...	...	...	...
Chile (peso)	1999	188 605 370	...	...	...	...	...	...
Chili (peso)	2000	203 491 020	18.0	71.2	...	5.8	4.9	
Colombia (peso)	1999	348 146 567	...	...	...	...	...	...
Colombie (peso)	2000	426 820 731	...	...	...	...	...	...
Ecuador (US dollar)	1997	70 488 000	...	...	...	...	...	...
Equateur (dollar E.U.)	1998	99 274 000	...	...	...	...	...	...
Peru (sol)	1998	89 210	...	...	...	...	...	...
Pérou (sol)	1999	146 290	...	...	...	...	...	...
Uruguay (peso)	1998	510 049	...	...	...	...	...	...
Uruguay (peso)	1999	609 655	...	...	...	...	...	...
Venezuela (bolívar)	1999	206 299 200	...	...	...	...	...	...
Venezuela (bolívar)	2000	275 279 510	...	...	...	...	...	...
Asia • Asie								
China, Hong Kong SAR (dollar)	1995	2 742 000[21]	2.8	91.0	5.7	...	0.5	...
Chine, Hong Kong RAS (dollar)	1998	5 603 000	...	...	...	...	...	...
Cyprus (pound)	1992	6 037	13.1	76.4	8.8	...	1.7[27]	...
Chypre (livre)	1999	12 417	17.4	68.5	1.8	4.6	7.7	
Georgia (lari)	1998	16 200[7]	...	...	...	...	...	...
Georgie (lari)	1999	18 600[7]	...	...	...	...	...	...
India (rupee)	1990	41 864 300	12.6	87.4	...	...	...	...
Inde (roupie)	1994	75 063 500	24.0	75.0	1.0	...	...	...
Indonesia (rupiah)	1986[7 22]	241 750 000	...	100.0	...	...	...	...
Indonésie (rupiah)	1994	244 843 000[23]	76.4	15.8	0.5	...	7.2	...
Iran, Islamic Rep. of (rial)	1985[7]	22 010 713	...	100.0	...	...	...	...
Iran, Rép. Islamique d' (rial)	1994	620 849 320	...	86.8	13.2	...	...	...
Israel (sheqel)	1998	12 563 400	...	...	...	...	...	...
Israël (sheqel)	1999	15 096 700	...	...	...	...	...	...
Japan (yen)	1998	15 169 203 000	71.2	9.2	14.8	4.7	...	...
Japon (yen)	1999	15 032 660 000	70.7	9.9	14.8	4.6	...	...
Kazakhstan (tenge)								
Kazakhstan (tenge)	1997	4 905 637	1.1	44.1	...	6.2	0.7	48.0
Korea, Republic of (won) [25]	1998	11 336 617 000	70.3	17.5	11.2	1.1	...	...
Corée, République de (won) [25]	1999	11 921 752 000	71.4	14.5	12.0	2.1	...	...
Kuwait (dinar)								
Koweït (dinar)	1984	71 163[20]	64.3	34.3	1.4	...	...	...
Kyrgyzstan (som)	1995	46 309	29.4	67.3	1.8	...	1.5[27]	...
Kirghizistan (som)	1997	59 466	24.8	63.3	3.5	...	8.5[27]	...
Malaysia (ringgit)	1996	549 196	8.3	13.5	...	...	1.6	76.6
Malaisie (ringgit)	1998	1 127 010	...	...	...	...	...	...
Pakistan (rupee)	1984	3 834 287[7 26]	...	100.0	...	...	...	...
Pakistan (roupie)	1987	5 582 081[7 26]	...	100.0	...	...	...	...
Philippines (peso)	1984	614 080	23.6	60.8	2.4	...	13.0	0.1
Philippines (peso)	1992	* 2 940 549	* 1.9	* 3.2	* 70.2	...	* 24.7[27]	...
Qatar (riyal)								
Qatar (riyal)	1986	6 650	...	100.0	...	...	...	...
Singapore (dollar)	1987	374 700[16 25]	59.6	38.8	1.6	...	...	...
Singapour (dollar)	1995	1 366 570[25]	62.5	31.4	2.4	...	3.7[27]	...
Sri Lanka (rupee)	1984	256 799	...	83.7	...	...	16.3	...
Sri Lanka (roupie)	1996	1 410 000	...	...	...	...	...	...
Syrian Arab Republic (pound)								
Rép. arabe syrienne (pound)	1997	1 368 000	...	...	100.	...	...	...
Thailand (baht)	1996	5 528 134	18.4	61.1	6.8	8.7	5.0	...
Thaïlande (baht)	1997	4 811 233	...	...	...	...	...	...
Turkey (lira)	1998	260 422 137 000	31.6	7.3	...	...	...	...
Turquie (livre)	1999	489 162 882 000	38.0	6.7	...	...	...	...
Viet Nam (dong) [7]	1984	516 000	...	100.0	...	...	...	...
Viet Nam (dong) [7]	1985	498 000	...	100.0	...	...	...	...
Europe • Europe								
Austria (schilling) [13]	1999	3 599 800	...	...	...	...	...	...
Autriche (schilling) [13]	2000	* 3 687 500	...	...	...	...	...	...

70

Gross domestic expenditure on R & D by source of funds
National currency [*cont.*]

Dépenses intérieures brutes de recherche et développement par source de fonds
Monnaie nationale [*suite*]

Country or area (Monetary unit) Pays ou zone (Unité monétaire)	Years Années	Gross domestic exp on R&D Dép int. brutes de R−D (thousands)	Source of funds (%) / Source de fonds (%)					
			Business enterprises Enterprises	Gov't Etat	Higher education Enseigne- ment supérieur	Private non−profit Inst. privées sans but lucratif	Funds from abroad Fonds de l'étranger	Not dis− tributed Non répartis
Belarus (rouble)	1995	1 325 959 800	59.5	40.1	0.4	...	...	...
Bélarus (rouble)	1997	2 098 170 700	27.9	67.2	0.1	...	4.8	...
Belgium (euro)	1998	4 276 800	71.0	3.4	24.3	1.3	...	...
Belgique (euro)	1999	4 618 100	71.6	3.3	23.9	1.2	...	...
Bulgaria (lev)	1996	9 148 000	60.5	35.1	3.8	0.4	0.1	...
Bulgarie (lev)	1999[18]	134 449	22.8	69.7	3.2	0.2	4.1	...
Croatia (kuna)	1997[17]	484 897	...	...	...	...	...	...
Croatie (kuna)	1999	1 397 761	53.3	42.6			0.8	3.3
Czech Republic (koruna)	1999	23 646 700	62.9	24.3	12.3	0.5	...	...
Rép. tchèque (couronne)	2000	26 487 200	60.0	25.3	14.2	0.5	...	...
Denmark (krone)	1998[13]	23 793 100	64.7	14.3	20.1	0.9	...	...
Danemark (couronne)	1999	25 317 700	63.4	15.2	20.3	1.2	...	...
Estonia (kroon)	1998	451 000	...	...	...	...	...	...
Estonie (couronne)	1999	573 000	24.3	64.6	0.7	1.6	8.9	...
Finland (euro)	1999[13]	* 3 878 800	68.2	11.4	19.7	...	...	...
Finlande (euro)	2000	4 354 400	71.1	11.1		...	...	...
France (euro)	1999	29 528 400	63.2	18.1	17.2	1.5	...	...
France (euro)	2000	30 152 700	64.0	17.8	16.7	1.5	...	...
Germany (euro)	1999	48 190 700	69.8	13.8	16.5	...	...	...
Allemagne (euro)	2000[13]	49 822 400	70.5	13.4	16.1	...	...	...
Greece (euro)	1997	492 231	25.6	23.4	50.6	0.4	...	...
Grèce (euro)	1999	* 760 413	28.5	21.7	49.5	0.3	...	...
Hungary (forint) [9]	1999	78 187 900	40.2	32.3	...	...	...	...
Hongrie (forint) [9]	2000	105 387 600	44.3	26.1	24.0	...	...	...
Iceland (króna) [13]	1998	11 772 451	36.6	37.3	24.9	1.2	...	...
Islande (couronne) [13]	1999	14 521 644	46.7	30.2	20.9	2.2	...	...
Ireland (euro)	1996	808 932	72.4	7.9	18.9	0.8	...	...
Irlande (euro)	1997	929 160	73.1	7.0	19.2	0.7	...	...
Italy (euro)	1998	* 10 552 387	52.4	21.8	25.7	...	...	...
Italie (euro)	1999	* 11 425 791	52.8	22.0	25.2	...	...	...
Latvia (lat)	1997	13 893	14.1	59.0	...	...	26.9	...
Lettonie (lat)	1999	15 512	15.7	55.6	...	7.1	21.6	...
Malta (lira)								
Malte (lira)	1988	10[21]	...	100.0	...	...	...	...
Monaco (euro) [6]								
Monaco (euro) [6]	1998	132 671	85.8	14.2			...	...
Netherlands (euro)	1998	6 868 871	54.2	17.7	27.1	1.0	...	...
Pays−Bas (euro)	1999	7 563 609	56.4	16.5	26.2	0.9	...	...
Norway (krone)	1997	18 187 200	56.9	16.4	...	...	...	...
Norvège (couronne)	1999	20 318 700	56.0	15.4	...	...	...	...
Poland (zloty)	1999	4 590 500	41.3	30.8	27.8	0.1	...	...
Pologne (zloty)	2000	4 796 100	36.1	32.2	31.5	0.1	...	...
Portugal (euro)	1998	115 654 600	22.5	24.2	40.0	13.3	...	...
Portugal (euro)	2000	163 342 100	22.7	27.9	38.6	10.8	...	...
Republic of Moldova (leu)	1999	78 900	...	...	...	...	...	...
Moldova, Rép de (leu)	2000	99 400	...	...	...	...	...	...
Romania (leu) [19]	1991	17 369 000	54.3[5]	22.9[5]	8.1[5]	...	0.7[5]	14.0
Roumanie (leu) [19]	1995	514 420 000	23.1	63.4	10.4	...	3.2	...
Russian Federation (rouble)	1998	25 082 066	...	...	...	...	...	...
Fédération de Russie (rouble)	1999	48 050 525	31.6	51.1	0.4	...	16.9	...
Slovakia (koruna)	1999	5 552 000	62.6	27.5	9.9	...	...	...
Slovaquie (couronne)	2000	6 086 000	65.8	24.7	9.5	...	...	...
Slovenia (tolar)	1996	36 816 000	49.1	43.4	4.5	0.4	2.7	...
Slovénie (tolar)	1998	48 015 000	52.5	39.9	0.8	...	6.7	...
Spain (peseta)	1999	4 995 358	52.0	16.9	30.1	1.0	...	...
Espagne (peseta)	2000[13]	5 459 828	53.0	16.5	29.5	1.0	...	...
Sweden (krona) [4]	1997	66 920 700	74.9	3.5	21.4	0.1	...	...
Suède (couronne) [4]	1999	75 813 500	75.1	3.4	21.4	0.1	...	...
Switzerland (franc)	1992	9 090 000	67.4	28.4	2.3	...	1.9[27]	...
Suisse (franc)	1996	9 990 000	70.7	2.5	24.3	2.5	...	...
TFYR of Macedonia (dinar)								
L'ex−R.y. Macédoine (dinar)	1995	876 244[5]	48.4	41.9	7.5		2.2[27]	...
Ukraine (hyrvnais)	1997	1 113 188	40.3	41.9	...	...	24.6	...
Ukraine (hyrvnais)	2000	1 636 362	31.4	39.3	0.1	...	29.2	...

70

Gross domestic expenditure on R & D by source of funds
National currency [*cont.*]

Dépenses intérieures brutes de recherche et développement par source de fonds
Monnaie nationale [*suite*]

Country or area (Monetary unit) Pays ou zone (Unité monétaire)	Years Années	Gross domestic exp on R&D Dép int. brutes de R−D (thousands)	Source of funds (%) / Source de fonds (%)					
			Business enterprises Enterprises	Gov't Etat	Higher education Enseigne-ment supérieur	Private non−profit Inst. privées sans but lucratif	Funds from abroad Fonds de l'étranger	Not dis-tributed Non répartis
United Kingdom (pound)	1998	15 454 600	65.6	13.4	19.7	1.3	...	...
Royaume−Uni (livre)	1999	16 664 000	67.8	10.7	20.0	1.4	...	...
Oceania · Océanie								
Australia (dollar)	1996	8 795 100	48.2	23.6	26.2	2.0	...	...
Australie (dollar)	1998	8 925 800	45.6	23.2	29.2	2.1	...	...
Fiji (dollar) [24]								
Fidji (dollar) [24]	1986	3 800	...	73.7	...	...	26.3	...
Guam (US dollar) [5]	1989	* 1 926	...	* 88.6	* 11.4	...	...	...
Guam (dollar E.U.) [5]	1991	2 215	...	87.7	12.3	...	...	...
New Zealand (dollar)	1993	825 200	33.9	54.7	8.9	...	2.4	...
Nouvelle−Zélande (dollar)	1997	1 107 355	28.2	35.3	...	...	...	...

Source:
United Nations Educational, Scientific and Cultural Organization (UNESCO), Institute for Statistics, Montreal, the UNESCO statistics database.

1   Not including data for the productive sector.
2   Not including labour costs at the Ministry of Public Health.
3   Figures in millions.
4   Under−estimated or based on under−estimated data.

5   Data refer to current expenditure only.
6   Partial estimates.
7   Data refer to government funds only.
8   Data refer to funds from abroad only.
9   Defence excluded (all or mostly).
10   Data refer to R&D activites performed in public enterprises.

11   Not including data for the productive sector (non−integrated R&D) and the general service sector.
12   Data relate to the Scientific Research Council only.
13   National estimate or projection adjusted, if necessary, by OECD.
14   Receipts from R&D.
15   Not including data for law, humanities and education.

16   Not including funds from abroad.
17   Part of the total revenue data which could be defined as "revenue for R&D purposes"; detailed specification of sources are not available.

18   Denomination change in 1999.
19   Due to methodological changes in 1991 data are not comparable with previous years.
20   Data refer to scientific and technological activities (STA).

21   Data refer to the higher education sector only.

22   Data refer to the general service sector only.
23   Data refer to the productive sector only.
24   Data relate to one research institute only.
25   Not including data for social sciences and humanities.
26   Data refer to R&D activities which are concentrated mainly in government−financed research establishments. Social sciences and the humanities in the higher education and general service sectors are not included.
27   Including funds from private non−profit institutions.

Source:
L'Institut de statistique de l'Organisation des Nations Unies pour l'éducation, la science et la culture (UNESCO), Montréal, la base de données de l'UNESCO.

1   Non compris les données du secteur de la production.
2   Non compris les coûts salariaux du Ministère de la Santé Publique.
3   Chiffres en millions.
4   Sous−estimation ou chiffre établi sur la base de données sous−estimées.
5   Les données se réfèrent aux dépenses courantes seulement.
6   Estimations partielles.
7   Les données se réfèrent aux fonds publics seulement.
8   Les données se réfèrent aux fonds étrangers seulement.
9   Non compris la défense.
10   Les données se réfèrent aux activités de R−D dans les entreprises publiques.
11   Non compris les données du secteur de la production (activités de R−D non intégrées) et du secteur de service général.
12   Les données se réfèrent au 'Scientific Research Council' seulement.
13   Estimations ou projections adjustées pour OCED s'il le faut.
14   Recettes de la recherche et développement.
15   Non compris les données pour droit, sciences humaines et sciences de l'éducation.
16   Non compris les fonds étrangers.
17   Partie des données du révenu total que peut être définie comme révenu pour la recherche et développement. Une spécification détaillée des sources n'est pas disponible.
18   Changement de dénomination en 1999.
19   Suite à des changements de méthodologie en 1991, les données ne sont pas comparables avec celles des années précédentes.
20   Les données se réfèrent aux activités scientifiques et technologiques (AST).
21   Les données se réfèrent au secteur de l'enseignement supérieur seulement.
22   Les données se réfèrent au secteur de service général seulement.
23   Les données se réfèrent au secteur de la production seulement.
24   Les données ne concernent qu'un institut de recherche.
25   Non compris les données pour les sciences sociales et humaines.
26   Les données se réfèrent aux activités de R−D concentrées pour la plupart dans les établissements de recherche financés par le gouvernement. Les sciences sociales et humaines dans le secteur de service général ne sont pas inclus.
27   Y compris fonds des institutions privées sans but lucratif.

71
Patents
Applications, grants, patents in force: number
Brevets
Demandes, délivrances, brevets en vigueur: nombre

Country or area Pays ou zone	Applications for patents Demandes de brevets			Grants of patents Brevets délivrés			Patents in force Brevets en vigueur		
	1998	1999	2000	1998	1999	2000	1998	1999	2000
Albania Albanie	35 159	89 519	111 610	...	52	203	...	...	...
Algeria Algérie	306	282	33 650	...	...	...	...	1 501	1 484
Antigua and Barbuda Antigua-et-Barbuda	...	3	32 394	...	...	...	...	...	...
Argentina Argentine	6 320	6 457	6 634	1 689	1 241	1 587	...	...	...
Armenia Arménie	33 899	40 272	58 277	85	205	168	261	279	285
Australia Australie	57 706	63 355	80 721	14 784	13 528	13 916	83 429	88 361	93 211
Austria Autriche	147 040	162 121	201 030	14 963	14 347	11 266	13 621	12 845	12 132
Azerbaijan Azerbaïdjan	33 507	40 042	58 076	19	...	...	...	...	...
Bangladesh Bangladesh	216	...	...	140	...	...	...	...	...
Barbados Barbade	35 001	41 272	58 943	...	3	...	...	9	...
Belarus Bélarus	35 269	41 792	59 430	687	550	537	...	...	...
Belgium Belgique	112 652	120 981	141 766	16 093	15 802	12 122	88 752	85 370	...
Belize Belize	...	...	21 308	...	...	...	...	...	...
Bosnia and Herzegovina Bosnie-Herzégovine	34 441	41 224	59 188	...	5	1	...	79	79
Botswana Botswana	92	54	15	21	26	43	...	...	...
Brazil Brésil	41 621	52 295	64 686	...	3 219	...	...	22 375	...
Bulgaria Bulgarie	36 575	42 952	60 480	534	533	481	1 754	2 136	1 460
Canada Canada	65 682	69 777	85 926	9 572	13 778	12 125	235 916	209 333	196 519
Chile Chili	...	2 812	3 120	...	418	601	...	...	...
China Chine	82 289	89 042	122 306	4 735	7 637	13 356	...	49 402	34 848
China, Hong Kong SAR Chine, Hong Kong RAS	14 667	6 040	8 295	2 453	2 502	2 737	...	...	...
China, Macao SAR Chine, Macao RAS	...	...	...	4	9	1	...	...	...
Colombia Colombie	1 736	1 683	1 799	476	590	595	417	...	...
Costa Rica Costa Rica	...	9 105	52 437	...	...	...	...	...	...
Croatia Croatie	12 906	40 279	58 936	244	275	379	...	...	...

71

Patents
Applications, grants, patents in force: number *[cont.]*

Brevets
Demandes, délivrances, brevets en vigueur: nombre *[suite]*

Country or area Pays ou zone	Applications for patents Demandes de brevets			Grants of patents Brevets délivrés			Patents in force Brevets en vigueur		
	1998	1999	2000	1998	1999	2000	1998	1999	2000
Cuba Cuba	33 997	41 039	58 418	...	70	...	...	1 427	...
Cyprus Chypre	77 374	118 767	139 700	...	3	23	...	...	...
Czech Republic République tchèque	39 196	45 309	62 645	1 451	1 482	1 611	7 001	7 249	7 789
Denmark Danemark	146 357	161 564	200 652	11 018	10 754	8 484	...	...	...
Dominica Dominique	...	8 500	52 176	...	...	...	...	...	...
Ecuador Equateur	...	490	11	...	142	...	...	...	...
Egypt Egypte	1 633	1 682	1 615	118	410	453	...	...	...
Estonia Estonie	35 501	41 756	60 237	82	103	84	212	320	390
Ethiopia Ethiopie	...	12	7	...	1	1	...	1	4
European Patent Office [1] Office européen de brevets [1]	113 408	121 816	143 074	36 718	35 358	27 523	...	...	...
Finland Finlande	146 884	159 033	198 293	2 329	1 618	2 557	20 274	...	...
France France	130 015	138 455	160 178	46 213	44 287	36 404	326 447	345 808	371 428
Gambia Gambie	60 272	79 703	115 420	18	26	51	...	...	...
Georgia Géorgie	35 728	41 960	59 368	536	398	451	961	728	1 163
Germany Allemagne	202 771	220 761	262 550	51 685	49 548	41 585	354 879	371 816	377 001
Ghana Ghana	66 173	80 028	115 543	13	17	64	...	...	...
Greece Grèce	111 339	119 774	140 540	7 857	7 598	6 059	...	...	...
Grenada Grenade	3 330	34 698	57 014	...	...	...	...	...	...
Guatemala Guatemala	207	231	226	17	36	23	...	...	...
Guinea-Bissau Guinée-Bissau	15 568	1	...	...	...	...	...	...	...
Haiti Haïti	...	6	...	...	7	...	...	...	...
Honduras Honduras	151	156	139	58	77	63	...	198	375
Hungary Hongrie	38 707	44 974	62 438	1 257	1 881	1 605	10 896	11 438	11 441
Iceland Islande	35 182	41 570	59 656	35	27	16	275	248	237
India Inde	282	41 496	60 942	...	2 160	...	...	8 639	...

71

Patents
Applications, grants, patents in force: number *[cont.]*
Brevets
Demandes, délivrances, brevets en vigueur: nombre *[suite]*

Country or area Pays ou zone	Applications for patents Demandes de brevets			Grants of patents Brevets délivrés			Patents in force Brevets en vigueur		
	1998	1999	2000	1998	1999	2000	1998	1999	2000
Indonesia Indonésie	32 910	42 503	60 363	...	...	...	...	...	...
Iran (Islamic Rep. of) Iran (Rép. islamique d')	496	543	616	241	322	448	...	...	...
Ireland Irlande	112 344	120 795	140 519	7 088	7 288	5 916	...	23 209	...
Israel Israël	42 271	49 414	67 858	2 021	2 024	2 033	12 017	12 040	...
Italy Italie	123 606	128 260	151 188	38 988	32 476	24 937	...	...	...
Jamaica Jamaïque	...	...	101	...	17	20	...	...	...
Japan Japon	437 375	442 245	486 204	141 448	150 059	125 880	935 858	1 005 304	1 040 607
Kazakhstan Kazakhstan	35 338	41 828	59 587	1 192	1 553	1 417	5 830	6 658	3 717
Kenya Kenya	67 830	80 544	115 936	101	94	117	...	...	...
Kiribati Kiribati	...	2	...	...	2	...	...	17	...
Korea, Dem. P. R. Corée, R. p. dém. de	33 918	40 391	57 805	...	...	...	...	...	...
Korea, Republic of Corée, République de	46 517	133 127	172 184	...	62 635	34 956	...	...	215 882
Kyrgyzstan Kirghizistan	33 905	40 191	58 196	105	93	104	579	501	446
Latvia Lettonie	35 963	90 276	112 228	297	353	644	2 160	1 883	1 903
Lebanon Liban	...	115 822	104	...	80	...	...	...	...
Lesotho Lesotho	67 491	80 315	115 822	36	43	80	...	...	...
Liberia Libéria	34 862	41 120	58 896	...	...	...	...	...	...
Lithuania Lituanie	35 838	90 417	112 240	165	440	798	1 219	1 137	1 047
Luxembourg Luxembourg	144 401	159 601	198 631	8 023	7 490	5 901	30 681	30 503	29 575
Madagascar Madagascar	34 941	41 246	59 029	...	35	...	...	81	187
Malawi Malawi	67 756	80 431	115 894	76	84	110	631	...	817
Malta Malte	34	83	116	28	35	89	110	237	332
Mauritius Maurice	15	...	...	3	...	...	96	...	...
Mexico Mexique	44 721	50 000	66 916	3 219	3 899	5 527	36 817	38 965	20 414
Monaco Monaco	111 088	119 539	140 333	4 061	4 137	3 502	241	6 287	6 519

71

Patents
Applications, grants, patents in force: number *[cont.]*
Brevets
Demandes, délivrances, brevets en vigueur: nombre *[suite]*

Country or area Pays ou zone	Applications for patents Demandes de brevets			Grants of patents Brevets délivrés			Patents in force Brevets en vigueur		
	1998	1999	2000	1998	1999	2000	1998	1999	2000
Mongolia Mongolie	35 154	41 240	58 983	172	161	...	...	...	...
Morocco Maroc	...	3 649	52 011	...	...	...	6 331	...	...
Mozambique Mozambique	...	...	56 555	...	...	...	...	...	...
Netherlands Pays-Bas	115 076	123 513	144 341	22 411	21 403	17 052	117 453	120 748	120 181
New Zealand Nouvelle-Zélande	39 734	47 640	67 938	4 058	2 463	4 587	...	...	...
Nicaragua Nicaragua	154	145	143	18	12	136	...	205	343
Norway Norvège	44 258	50 662	68 055	2 560	2 362	2 412	...	...	...
OAPI [2] OAPI [2]	34 995	41 098	58 146	265	380	364	1 229	1 494	1 684
Pakistan Pakistan	...	...	1 195	...	...	381	...	...	...
Panama Panama	...	...	160	...	...	15	...	...	414
Peru Pérou	...	992	1 078	...	271	308	...	1 007	1 183
Philippines Philippines	3 443	3 361	3 636	565	648	566	...	...	...
Poland Pologne	41 352	47 480	64 873	2 416	2 236	2 463	13 589	13 614	13 851
Portugal Portugal	145 142	159 666	198 700	8 947	8 493	6 354	...	22 219	22 573
Republic of Moldova République de Moldova	34 111	40 455	58 418	220	231	234	774	1 006	1 216
Romania Roumanie	37 826	91 304	113 379	1 818	1 083	1 320	20 100	18 425	15 574
Russian Federation Fédération de Russie	58 532	67 876	89 429	23 368	19 508	17 592	173 081	191 129	144 325
Rwanda Rwanda	...	4	...	...	4	...	...	47	...
Saint Lucia Sainte-Lucie	34 087	40 901	58 724	...	...	...	...	...	...
St. Vincent-Grenadines St. Vincent-Grenadines	...	...	2	...	...	2	...	...	...
Saudi Arabia Arabie saoudite	1 331	1 216	873	3	16	8	8	22	28
Serbia and Montenegro Serbie-et-Monténégro	34 541	42 084	59 669	342	175	8	2 059	2 238	2 242
Sierra Leone Sierra Leone	33 154	72 449	116 129	...	1	...	...	...	...
Singapore Singapour	44 948	51 495	70 191	2 291	4 410	5 090	...	...	...
Slovakia Slovaquie	36 852	43 079	60 511	845	773	894	2 436	...	...

71

Patents
Applications, grants, patents in force: number *[cont.]*
Brevets
Demandes, délivrances, brevets en vigueur: nombre *[suite]*

Country or area Pays ou zone	Applications for patents Demandes de brevets			Grants of patents Brevets délivrés			Patents in force Brevets en vigueur		
	1998	1999	2000	1998	1999	2000	1998	1999	2000
Slovenia Slovénie	36 297	90 972	112 864	466	871	1 276	2 905	3 218	3 407
South Africa Afrique du Sud	8	26 470	58 166	...	...	...	...	...	...
Spain Espagne	147 889	163 090	202 439	20 128	20 066	15 809	...	178 782	142 188
Sri Lanka Sri Lanka	34 974	41 263	58 929	...	...	...	...	...	...
Sudan Soudan	67 719	80 426	115 860	64	59	97	...	...	...
Swaziland Swaziland	34 535	40 673	58 033	63	57	85	...	...	...
Sweden Suède	149 493	165 051	204 173	18 482	17 649	13 812	97 435	97 980	97 345
Switzerland Suisse	147 579	162 403	201 571	16 253	15 434	12 258	87 527	87 033	87 008
Syrian Arab Republic Rép. arabe syrienne	...	...	296	...	...	50	...	...	...
Tajikistan Tadjikistan	33 779	40 141	58 133	57	42	43	177	222	281
Thailand Thaïlande	5 071	...	5 665	723	...	541	...	...	352
TFYR of Macedonia L'ex-R.y. Macédoine	35 133	89 425	111 683	80	55	86	360	378	434
Trinidad and Tobago Trinité-et-Tobago	34 969	41 238	58 974	...	...	...	...	...	...
Turkey Turquie	37 386	43 833	77 274	796	1 122	1 157	12 786	21 183	22 040
Turkmenistan Turkménistan	33 705	40 114	58 061	154	95	...	...	...	...
Uganda Ouganda	67 610	80 421	115 875	66	74	112	...	...	...
Ukraine Ukraine	41 950	48 273	65 917	4 336	1 294	5 772	19 587	16 270	15 005
United Arab Emirates Emirats arabes unis	8	24 218	56 158	...	...	...	...	...	...
United Kingdom Royaume-Uni	176 187	192 875	233 223	43 181	40 683	33 756	...	...	312 802
United Rep. of Tanzania Rép.-Unie de Tanzanie	...	14 467	108 930	10	8	...	...	...	...
United States Etats-Unis	262 787	294 706	331 773	147 520	153 487	157 496	1 173 145	1 242 853	1 295 176
Uruguay Uruguay	496	552	616	73	113	140	386	356	396
Uzbekistan Ouzbékistan	35 110	42 365	59 859	...	512	476	...	727	2 586
Venezuela Venezuela	...	...	2 348	...	...	756	...	...	...
Viet Nam Viet Nam	35 748	42 212	59 776	...	490	727	...	...	...

71

Patents
Applications, grants, patents in force: number *[cont.]*
Brevets
Demandes, délivrances, brevets en vigueur: nombre *[suite]*

Country or area Pays ou zone	Applications for patents Demandes de brevets			Grants of patents Brevets délivrés			Patents in force Brevets en vigueur		
	1998	1999	2000	1998	1999	2000	1998	1999	2000
Zambia Zambie	93	92	10	20	67	46	...	1 346	...
Zimbabwe Zimbabwe	66 272	80 168	115 750	30	34	86	...	...	...

Source:
World Intellectual Property Organization (WIPO), Geneva, "Industrial Property Statistics 2000, Publication A" and previous issues.

1 In 1992, the European Patent Office (EPO) was constituted by the following member countries: Austria, Belgium, Denmark, France, Germany, Greece, Ireland, Italy, Liechtenstein, Luxembourg, Monaco, Netherlands, Portugal, Spain, Sweden, Switzerland, United Kingdom.
2 Members of the African Intellectual Property Organization (OAPI), which includes Benin, Burkina Faso, Cameroon, Central African Republic, Chad, Congo, Côte d'Ivoire, Gabon, Guinea, Mali, Mauritania, Niger, Senegal, Togo.

Source :
Organisation mondiale de la propriété intellectuelle (OMPI), Genève, « Statistiques de propriété industrielle 2000, Publication A » et éditions précédentes.

1 En 1992, l'Office européen de brevets (OEB) comprenait les pays membres suivants: Allemagne, Autriche, Belgique, Danemark, Espagne, France, Grèce, Irlande, Italie, Liechtenstein, Luxembourg, Monaco, Pays-Bas, Portugal, Royaume-Uni, Suède, Suisse.
2 Les membres de l'Organisation africaine de la propriété intellectuelle (OAPI): Bénin, Burkina Faso, Cameroun, Congo, Côte d'Ivoire, Gabon, Guinée, Mali, Mauritanie, Niger, République centrafricaine, Sénégal, Tchad, Togo.

Technical notes, tables 69-71

Table 69: The data presented on personnel engaged in research and experimental development (R&D) are compiled by the UNESCO Institute for Statistics. The definitions and classifications applied by UNESCO in the table are based on those set out in the *Recommendation concerning the International Standardization of Statistics on Science and Technology* (for data covering the years prior to 1998) and in the *Frascati Manual* (for data referring to 1998 and on).

The three categories of personnel shown are defined as follows:

Researchers are professionals engaged in the conception or creation of new knowledge, products, processes, methods and systems, and in the planning and management of R&D projects. Post-graduate students engaged in R&D are considered as researchers. The data shown for researchers for the years prior to 1998 refer to "R&D scientists and engineers".

Technicians (and equivalent staff) comprise persons whose main tasks require technical knowledge and experience in one or more fields of engineering, physical and life sciences, or social sciences and humanities.

Other supporting staff includes skilled and unskilled craftsmen, secretarial and clerical staff participating in or directly associated with R&D projects.

More information can be found on the UNESCO Institute for Statistics Web site <www.uis.unesco.org>.

Table 70: The data presented on gross domestic expenditure on research and development are compiled by the UNESCO Institute for Statistics.

Gross domestic expenditure on R&D (GERD) is total intramural expenditure on R&D performed on the national territory during a given period. It includes R&D performed within a country and funded from abroad but excludes payments made abroad for R&D.

The sources of funds for GERD are classified according to the following five categories:

Business enterprise funds include funds allocated to R&D by all firms, organizations and institutions whose primary activity is the market production of goods and services (other than the higher education sector) for sale to the general public at an economically significant price, and those private non-profit institutes mainly serving these firms, organizations and institutions.

Government funds refer to funds allocated to R&D by the central (federal), state or local government authorities. Public enterprises funds are included in the business enterprise funds sector. These authorities also include private non-profit institutes controlled and

Notes techniques, tableaux 69 à 71

Le *tableau 69:* Les données présentées sur le personnel employé à des travaux de recherche scientifique et le développement expérimental (R-D) sont compilées par l'Institut de statistique de l'UNESCO. Les définitions et classifications appliquées par l'UNESCO sont basées sur la *Recommandation concernant la normalisation internationale des statistiques relatives à la science et à la technologie* (pour les chiffres des années antérieures à 1998) et sur le *Manuel de Frascati* (à compter de 1998).

Les trois catégories du personnel présentées sont définies comme suivant:

Les chercheurs sont des spécialistes travaillant à la conception ou à la création de connaissances, de produits, de procédés, de méthodes et de systèmes, et dans la planification et la gestion de projets de R-D. Les étudiants diplômés ayant des activités de R-D sont également considérés comme des chercheurs. Les données relatives aux chercheurs pour les années antérieures à 1998 se rapportent aux « scientifiques et ingénieurs employés à des travaux de R-D ».

Techniciens (et personnel assimilé) comprend des personnes dont les tâches principales requièrent des connaissances et une expérience technique dans un ou plusieurs domaines de l'ingénierie, des sciences physiques et de la vie ou des sciences sociales et humaines.

Autre personnel de soutien comprend les travailleurs, qualifiés ou non, et le personnel de secrétariat et de bureau qui participent à l'exécution des projets de R-D ou qui sont directement associés à l'exécution de tels projets.

Pour tout renseignement complémentaire, voir le site Web de l'Institut de statistique de l'UNESCO <www.uis.unesco.org>.

Tableau 70: Les données présentées sur les dépenses intérieures brutes de recherche et développement sont compilées par l'Institut de statistique de l'UNESCO.

Dépense intérieure brute de R-D (DIRD) est la dépense totale intra-muros afférente aux travaux de R-D exécutés sur le territoire national pendant une période donnée. Elle comprend la R-D exécutée sur le territoire national et financée par l'étranger mais ne tient pas compte des paiements effectués à l'étranger pour des travaux de R-D.

Les sources de financement pour la DIRD sont classées selon les cinq catégories suivantes:

Fonds des entreprises inclut les fonds alloués à la R-D par toutes les firmes, organismes et institutions dont l'activité première est la production marchande de biens ou de services (autres que dans le secteur

mainly financed by government.

Higher education funds include funds allocated to R&D by institutions of higher education comprising all universities, colleges of technology, other institutes of post-secondary education, and all research institutes, experimental stations and clinics operating under the direct control of or administered by or associated with higher educational establishments.

Private non-profit funds are funds allocated to R&D by non-market, private non-profit institutions serving the general public, as well as by private individuals and households.

Funds from abroad refer to funds allocated to R&D by institutions and individuals located outside the political frontiers of a country except for vehicles, ships, aircraft and space satellites operated by domestic organizations and testing grounds acquired by such organizations, and by all international organizations (except business enterprises) including their facilities and operations within the frontiers of a country.

The absolute figures for R&D expenditure should not be compared country by country. Such comparisons would require the conversion of national currencies into a common currency by means of special R&D exchange rates. Official exchange rates do not always reflect the real costs of R&D activities and comparisons are based on such rates can result in misleading conclusions, although they can be used to indicate a gross order of magnitude.

More information can be found on the UNESCO Institute for Statistics Web site <www.uis.unesco.org>.

Table 71: Data on patents include patent applications filed directly with the office concerned and grants made on the basis of such applications; inventors' certificates; patents of importation, including patents of introduction, revalidation patents and "patentes precaucionales"; petty patents; patents applied and granted under the Patent Cooperation Treaty (PCT), the European Patent Convention, the Havana Agreement, the Harare Protocol of the African Regional Industrial Property Organization (ARIPO) and the African Intellectual Property Organization (OAPI). The data are compiled and published by the World Intellectual Property Organization (see [37] and <www.wipo.int>).

d'enseignement supérieur) en vue de leur vente au public, à un prix qui correspond à la réalité économique, et les institutions privées sans but lucratif principalement au service de ces entreprises, organismes et institutions.

Fonds de l'Etat sont les fonds fournis à la R-D par le gouvernement central (fédéral), d'état ou par les autorités locales. Les fonds des entreprises publiques sont comprises dans ceux du secteur des entreprises. Les fonds de l'Etat incluent également les institutions privées sans but lucratif contrôlées et principalement financées par l'Etat.

Fonds de l'enseignement supérieur inclut les fonds fournis à la R-D par les établissements d'enseignement supérieur tels que toutes les universités, grandes écoles, instituts de technologie et autres établissements post-secondaires, ainsi que tous les instituts de recherche, les stations d'essais et les cliniques qui travaillent sous le contrôle direct des établissements d'enseignement supérieur ou qui sont administrés par ces derniers ou leur sont associés.

Fonds d'institutions privées à but non lucratif sont les fonds destinés à la R-D par les institutions privées sans but lucratif non marchandes au service du public, ainsi que par les simples particuliers ou les ménages.

Fonds étrangers concernent les fonds destinés à la R-D par les institutions et les individus se trouvant en dehors des frontières politiques d'un pays, à l'exception des véhicules, navires, avions et satellites utilisés par des institutions nationales, ainsi que des terrains d'essai acquis par ces institutions, et par toutes les organisations internationales (à l'exception des entreprises), y compris leurs installations et leurs activités à l'intérieur des frontières d'un pays.

Il faut éviter de comparer les chiffres absolus concernant les dépenses de R-D d'un pays à l'autre. On ne pourrait procéder à des comparaisons détaillées qu'en convertissant en une même monnaie les sommes libellées en monnaie nationale au moyen de taux de change spécialement applicables aux activités de R-D. Les taux de change officiels ne reflètent pas toujours le coût réel des activités de R-D, et les comparaisons établies sur la base de ces taux peuvent conduire à des conclusions trompeuses; toutefois, elles peuvent être utilisées pour donner une idée de l'ordre de grandeur.

Pour tout renseignement complémentaire, voir le site Web de l'Institut de statistique de l'UNESCO <www.uis.unesco.org>.

Tableau 71: Les données relatives aux brevets comprennent les demandes de brevet déposées directement auprès de l'office intéressé et brevets délivrés sur la base de telles demandes; les brevets d'invention; les brevets d'importation; y compris les brevets d'introduction, les brevets de revalidation et les brevets

"precaucionales"; les petits brevets, les brevets demandés et délivrés en vertu du traité de coopération sur les brevets, de la Convention européenne relative aux brevets, de l'Accord de la Havane, du Protocole d'Hararé de l'Organisation régionale africaine de la propriété industrielle (ARIPO) et de l'Organisation africaine de la propriété intellectuelle (OAPI). Les données sont compilées et publiées par l'Organisation mondiale de la propriété intellectuelle (voir [37] et <www.wipo.int>).

Part Four
International Economic Relations

Chapter XVI
International merchandise trade
(tables 72-74)
Chapter XVII
International tourism (tables 75-77)
Chapter XVIII
Balance of payments (table 78)
Chapter XIX
International finance (tables 79 and 80)
Chapter XX
Development assistance (tables 81-83)

Part Four of the *Yearbook* presents statistics on international economic relations in areas of international merchandise trade, international tourism, balance of payments and assistance to developing countries. The series cover all countries or areas of the world for which data are available.

Quatrième partie
Relations économiques internationales

Chapitre XVI
Commerce international des marchandises
(tableaux 72 à 74)
Chapitre XVII
Tourisme international (tableaux 75 à 77)
Chapitre XVIII
Balance des paiements (tableau 78)
Chapitre XIX
Finances internationales (tableaux 79 et 80)
Chapitre XX
Aide au développement (tableaux 81 à 83)

La quatrième partie de l'*Annuaire* présente des statistiques sur les relations économiques internationales dans les domaines du commerce international des marchandises, du tourisme international, de la balance des paiements et de l'assistance aux pays en développement. Les séries couvrent tous les pays ou les zones du monde pour lesquels des données sont disponibles.

72
Total imports and exports
Imports c.i.f., exports f.o.b. and balance, value in million US dollars
Importations et exportations totales
Importations c.a.f., exportations f.o.b., et balance, valeur en millions de dollars E.−U.

Country or area	Sys.[1]	1995	1996	1997	1998	1999	2000	2001	Pays ou zone
World									*Monde*
Imports		*4939813*	*5184473*	*5354673*	*5295049*	*5511403*	*6203546*	*5981409*	*Importations*
Exports		*4910018*	*5114661*	*5302472*	*5238965*	*5421505*	*6048039*	*5814640*	*Exportations*
Balance		*−29795*	*−69812*	*−52201*	*−56085*	*−89898*	*−155507*	*−166770*	*Balance*
Developed economies [23]									Économies développées [23]
Imports		3419133	3542314	3625426	3711817	3894242	4287194	4099857	Importations
Exports		3452404	3545581	3631076	3652682	3702776	3947264	3817707	Exportations
Balance		33272	3267	5649	−59135	−191466	−339930	−282150	Balance
Developing economies [3]									Écon. en dévelop. [3]
Imports		1347439	1445950	1517947	1369240	1425553	1694678	1637180	Importations
Exports		1275544	1370541	1465891	1385815	1519980	1850271	1732587	Exportations
Balance		−71895	−75409	−52056	16575	94427	155593	95406	Balance
Other [4]									Autres [4]
Imports		173241	196209	211300	213992	191608	221674	244372	Importations
Exports		182069	198540	205506	200468	198748	250504	264346	Exportations
Balance		8828	2330	−5794	−13524	7140	28830	19974	Balance

Americas · Amériques

Country or area	Sys.	1995	1996	1997	1998	1999	2000	2001	Pays ou zone
Developed economies [3]									Économies développées [3]
Imports		886786	939950	1037793	1085185	1208522	1414250	1321315	Importations
Exports		728927	773940	845918	836244	874811	973908	911039	Exportations
Balance		−157859	−166010	−191875	−248941	−333711	−440342	−410277	Balance
Canada [5]									Canada [5]
Imports	G	163954	170694	195980	201061	214791	238812	221757	Importations
Exports	G	192204	201636	214428	214335	238422	276645	259857	Exportations
Balance	G	28250	30942	18448	13274	23631	37833	38100	Balance
United States [6]									États−Unis [6]
Imports	G	770852	822025	899019	944353	1059440	1259300	1179180	Importations
Exports	G	584743	625073	688696	682138	702098	781125	730803	Exportations
Balance	G	−186109	−196952	−210323	−262215	−357342	−478175	−448377	Balance
Developing economies [3]									Écon. en dévelop. [3]
Imports		248520	278422	322130	336963	324773	376280	368590	Importations
Exports		225103	253309	279057	276799	295260	353931	338594	Exportations
Balance		−23417	−25112	−43073	−60164	−29513	−22349	−29997	Balance
LAIA+									ALAI +
Imports		209170	233989	279925	291375	277565	325971	317873	Importations
Exports		205834	232225	257375	254265	271975	328598	314554	Exportations
Balance		−3336	−1764	−22550	−37109	−5591	2627	−3319	Balance
Argentina									Argentine
Imports	S	20122	23762	30450	31404	25508	25243	20311	Importations
Exports	S	20967	23811	26370	26441	23333	26409	26655	Exportations
Balance	S	846	49	−4080	−4963	−2175	1166	6344	Balance
Bolivia									Bolivie
Imports	G	1424	1635	1851	1983	1755	1830	1724	Importations
Exports	G	1101	1137	1167	1104	1051	1230	1285	Exportations
Balance	G	−323	−498	−684	−879	−704	−600	−440	Balance
Brazil									Brésil
Imports	G	53783	56947	64996	60631	51675	58532	...	Importations
Exports	G	46506	47747	52994	51140	48011	55086	58223	Exportations
Balance	G	−7277	−9200	−12001	−9491	−3664	−3446	...	Balance
Chile									Chili
Imports	S	15900	19123	20825	19880	15988	18507	17814	Importations
Exports	S	16024	15657	17902	16353	17194	19246	18505	Exportations
Balance	S	124	−3466	−2923	−3527	1206	739	691	Balance
Colombia									Colombie
Imports	G	13853	13684	15378	14635	10659	11539	12834	Importations
Exports	G	10056	10587	11522	10852	11576	13040	12257	Exportations
Balance	G	−3797	−3097	−3855	−3782	918	1502	−577	Balance
Ecuador									Équateur
Imports	G	4153	3935	4955	5576	3017	3721	5363	Importations
Exports	G	4307	4900	5264	4203	4451	4927	4678	Exportations
Balance	G	155	965	310	−1373	1434	1205	−685	Balance

72
Total imports and exports
Imports c.i.f., exports f.o.b. and balance, value in million US dollars
Importations et exportations totales
Importations c.a.f., exportations f.o.b., et balance, valeur en millions de dollars E.–U.

Country or area	Sys.[1]	1995	1996	1997	1998	1999	2000	2001	Pays ou zone
Mexico [57]									**Mexique** [57]
Imports	G	72453	89469	109808	125373	141975	174500	168276	Importations
Exports	G	79542	96000	110431	117460	136391	166367	158547	Exportations
Balance	G	7089	6531	623	−7913	−5584	−8133	−9729	Balance
Paraguay									**Paraguay**
Imports	S	2782	2850	3099	2471	1725	...	...	Importations
Exports	S	919	1044	1089	1014	741	...	...	Exportations
Balance	S	−1863	−1807	−2011	−1457	−984	...	...	Balance
Peru									**Pérou**
Imports	S	9224	9473	10264	9867	8075	8797	...	Importations
Exports	S	5575	5897	6841	5757	6113	7028	7100	Exportations
Balance	S	−3649	−3575	−3423	−4110	−1962	−1769	...	Balance
Uruguay									**Uruguay**
Imports	G	2867	3323	3727	3811	3357	3466	3061	Importations
Exports	G	2106	2397	2726	2771	2237	2295	2060	Exportations
Balance	G	−761	−926	−1001	−1040	−1120	−1171	−1000	Balance
Venezuela									**Venezuela**
Imports	G	12619	9794	14577	15750	13835	16142	18263	Importations
Exports	G	18740	23053	21073	17175	20880	31737	24345	Exportations
Balance	G	6121	13260	6496	1425	7045	15596	6082	Balance
CACM+									**MCAC+**
Imports		**12817**	**13110**	**15355**	**18029**	**18380**	**19571**	**20731**	**Importations**
Exports		**8284**	**8568**	**10005**	**11455**	**11861**	**11893**	**10613**	**Exportations**
Balance		**−4534**	**−4543**	**−5349**	**−6574**	**−6519**	**−7678**	**−10118**	**Balance**
Costa Rica									**Costa Rica**
Imports	S	4036	4300	4924	6230	6320	6372	6564	Importations
Exports	S	3453	3730	4268	5511	6577	5865	5010	Exportations
Balance	S	−583	−569	−656	−719	257	−508	−1555	Balance
El Salvador									**El Salvador**
Imports	S	2853	2671	2981	3121	3140	3795	3866	Importations
Exports	S	998	1024	1371	1256	1177	1332	1214	Exportations
Balance	S	−1855	−1647	−1609	−1865	−1963	−2462	−2652	Balance
Guatemala									**Guatemala**
Imports	S	3293	3146	3852	4651	4382	4791	5607	Importations
Exports	S	2156	2031	2344	2582	2398	2696	2466	Exportations
Balance	S	−1137	−1115	−1508	−2070	−1984	−2095	−3141	Balance
Honduras									**Honduras**
Imports	S	1643	1840	2149	2535	2676	2855	2918	Importations
Exports	S	1220	1316	1446	1533	1164	1370	1318	Exportations
Balance	S	−423	−524	−703	−1002	−1512	−1485	−1600	Balance
Nicaragua									**Nicaragua**
Imports	G	993	1154	1450	1492	1862	1759	1776	Importations
Exports	G	457	466	577	573	545	631	606	Exportations
Balance	G	−536	−688	−873	−918	−1317	−1128	−1171	Balance
Other America									**Autres pays d'Amérique**
Imports		**26532**	**31322**	**26850**	**27559**	**28828**	**30738**	**29986**	**Importations**
Exports		**10985**	**12517**	**11676**	**11078**	**11424**	**13440**	**13427**	**Exportations**
Balance		**−15547**	**−18806**	**−15173**	**−16481**	**−17403**	**−17298**	**−16560**	**Balance**
Antigua and Barbuda									**Antigua–et–Barbuda**
Imports	G	346	365	370	385	414	...	...	Importations
Exports	G	53	38	38	36	38	...	...	Exportations
Balance	G	−293	−328	−333	−349	−376	...	...	Balance
Aruba									**Aruba**
Imports	S	567	578	614	815	782	...	...	Importations
Exports	S	15	12	24	29	29	...	...	Exportations
Balance	S	−552	−566	−590	−786	−753	...	...	Balance
Bahamas [16]									**Bahamas** [16]
Imports	G	1243	1366	1666	1873	1772	1764	1797	Importations
Exports	G	176	180	181	300	532	805	614	Exportations
Balance	G	−1067	−1186	−1484	−1573	−1240	−959	−1183	Balance
Barbados									**Barbade**
Imports	G	771	834	996	1010	1108	1156	1087	Importations
Exports	G	239	281	283	252	264	272	259	Exportations
Balance	G	−532	−553	−713	−758	−844	−884	−827	Balance

72
Total imports and exports
Imports c.i.f., exports f.o.b. and balance, value in million US dollars
Importations et exportations totales
Importations c.a.f., exportations f.o.b., et balance, valeur en millions de dollars E.-U.

Country or area	Sys. [1]	1995	1996	1997	1998	1999	2000	2001	Pays ou zone
Belize									**Belize**
Imports	G	257	255	286	295	370	452	434	Importations
Exports	G	162	168	176	172	186	185	174	Exportations
Balance	G	−96	−88	−110	−123	−184	−268	−260	Balance
Bermuda									**Bermudes**
Imports	G	550	569	619	629	712	720	721	Importations
Exports	G	56	68	57	45	...	...	...	Exportations
Balance	G	−494	−501	−562	−584	...	...	...	Balance
Cayman Islands									**Iles Caïmanes**
Imports	G	399	378	...	...	...	...	...	Importations
Exports	G	4	3	...	...	...	...	...	Exportations
Balance	G	−395	−375	...	...	...	...	...	Balance
Cuba									**Cuba**
Imports	S	2805	3205	...	...	...	...	...	Importations
Exports	S	1625	2015	...	...	...	...	...	Exportations
Balance	S	−1180	−1190	...	...	...	...	...	Balance
Dominica									**Dominique**
Imports	S	117	130	125	136	141	147	130	Importations
Exports	S	45	51	53	63	54	53	46	Exportations
Balance	S	−72	−79	−72	−73	−87	−94	−84	Balance
Dominican Republic [58]									**Rép. dominicaine** [58]
Imports	G	3164	3581	4192	4897	5207	6416	5937	Importations
Exports	G	872	945	1017	880	805	966	805	Exportations
Balance	G	−2292	−2635	−3175	−4016	−4402	−5450	−5132	Balance
French Guiana [13]									**Guyane française** [13]
Imports	S	752	...	...	...	...	...	...	Importations
Exports	S	131	...	...	...	...	...	...	Exportations
Balance	S	−622	...	...	...	...	...	...	Balance
Greenland									**Groenland**
Imports	G	435	469	397	409	...	...	...	Importations
Exports	G	373	369	293	254	...	...	...	Exportations
Balance	G	−63	−100	−104	−155	...	...	...	Balance
Grenada									**Grenade**
Imports	S	124	152	173	200	...	...	...	Importations
Exports	S	22	20	23	27	...	...	...	Exportations
Balance	S	−102	−132	−151	−173	...	...	...	Balance
Guadeloupe [13]									**Guadeloupe** [13]
Imports	S	1890	...	...	...	...	...	...	Importations
Exports	S	159	...	...	...	...	...	...	Exportations
Balance	S	−1731	...	...	...	...	...	...	Balance
Guyana									**Guyana**
Imports	S	528	598	629	...	...	...	584	Importations
Exports	S	455	517	643	485	523	498	478	Exportations
Balance	S	−73	−81	14	...	...	...	−106	Balance
Haiti									**Haiti**
Imports	G	654	666	648	800	1035	1041	1017	Importations
Exports	G	112	90	212	320	338	313	275	Exportations
Balance	G	−542	−576	−436	−480	−697	−728	−742	Balance
Jamaica									**Jamaique**
Imports	G	2808	5217	3128	3033	2899	3326	3361	Importations
Exports	G	1420	2579	1382	1312	1241	1304	1220	Exportations
Balance	G	−1388	−2638	−1746	−1721	−1658	−2022	−2140	Balance
Martinique [13]									**Martinique** [13]
Imports	S	1963	...	...	...	...	...	...	Importations
Exports	S	224	...	...	...	...	...	...	Exportations
Balance	S	−1739	...	...	...	...	...	...	Balance
Netherlands Antilles [9]									**Antilles néerlandaises** [9]
Imports	S	1841	2519	2083	...	...	...	...	Importations
Exports	S	1522	1269	1488	...	...	...	...	Exportations
Balance	S	−319	−1249	−594	...	...	...	...	Balance
Panama [10]									**Panama** [10]
Imports	S	2511	2780	3002	3398	3516	3379	2964	Importations
Exports	S	625	723	723	784	822	859	911	Exportations
Balance	S	−1886	−2057	−2279	−2614	−2694	−2519	−2053	Balance

72
Total imports and exports
Imports c.i.f., exports f.o.b. and balance, value in million US dollars
Importations et exportations totales
Importations c.a.f., exportations f.o.b., et balance, valeur en millions de dollars E.–U.

Country or area	Sys.[1]	1995	1996	1997	1998	1999	2000	2001	Pays ou zone
Saint Kitts and Nevis									**Saint–Kitts–et–Nevis**
Imports	S	133	149	148	148	...	...	...	Importations
Exports	S	19	22	36	...	...	...	...	Exportations
Balance	S	−114	−127	−112	...	...	...	...	Balance
Saint Lucia									**Sainte–Lucie**
Imports	S	306	304	332	335	...	...	...	Importations
Exports	S	124	82	66	...	...	...	...	Exportations
Balance	S	−182	−222	−266	...	...	...	...	Balance
Saint Vincent–Grenadines									**St.Vincent–Grenadines**
Imports	S	136	132	182	193	201	163	186	Importations
Exports	S	43	46	46	50	49	47	41	Exportations
Balance	S	−93	−85	−136	−143	−152	−116	−144	Balance
Suriname									**Suriname**
Imports	G	583	501	657	551	...	...	...	Importations
Exports	G	478	433	700	435	...	...	...	Exportations
Balance	G	−105	−68	43	−116	...	...	...	Balance
Trinidad and Tobago									**Trinité–et–Tobago**
Imports	S	1714	2144	2990	2999	2740	3308	...	Importations
Exports	S	2456	2500	2542	2258	2803	4654	...	Exportations
Balance	S	742	356	−448	−741	63	1346	...	Balance

Europe · Europe

Country or area	Sys.[1]	1995	1996	1997	1998	1999	2000	2001	Pays ou zone
Developed economies [3]									**Economies développées [3]**
Imports		2075553	2126485	2122016	2228376	2252935	2361253	2311652	**Importations**
Exports		2179826	2249802	2249162	2327200	2307768	2374280	2388776	**Exportations**
Balance		104273	123316	127146	98823	54833	13027	77124	**Balance**
EU+									**UE+**
Imports		1959683	2010317	2009359	2111690	2136716	2245182	2195731	**Importations**
Exports		2055694	2120170	2124285	2207818	2182428	2237255	2248341	**Exportations**
Balance		96011	109854	114925	96129	45713	−7927	52611	**Balance**
Austria									**Autriche**
Imports	S	66400	67336	64786	68187	69557	68986	70461	Importations
Exports	S	57655	57822	58599	62747	64126	64167	66671	Exportations
Balance	S	−8745	−9514	−6187	−5441	−5431	−4819	−3789	Balance
Belgium [11]									**Belgique [11]**
Imports	S	159716	163615	157283	162212	164620	177001	178715	Importations
Exports	S	175884	175367	171906	177666	178965	187885	190352	Exportations
Balance	S	16169	11752	14623	15454	14345	10884	11637	Balance
Denmark									**Danemark**
Imports	S	45082	44434	44044	45427	44067	43713	43430	Importations
Exports	S	49769	50099	47720	47481	48698	49480	50409	Exportations
Balance	S	4687	5665	3676	2054	4632	5767	6980	Balance
Finland									**Finlande**
Imports	G	28114	29265	29786	32301	31617	33900	32114	Importations
Exports	G	39574	38435	39318	42963	41841	45482	42802	Exportations
Balance	G	11460	9171	9533	10662	10224	11582	10688	Balance
France [13]									**France [13]**
Imports	S	281497	281776	272721	288412	294916	310321	298884	Importations
Exports	S	284914	287643	290972	305664	302472	299650	295671	Exportations
Balance	S	3417	5867	18252	17252	7556	−10672	−3213	Balance
Germany [12]									**Allemagne [12]**
Imports	S	464366	458808	445683	471448	473551	495480	486053	Importations
Exports	S	523909	524226	512503	543431	542884	550260	571460	Exportations
Balance	S	59544	65418	66820	71983	69334	54780	85407	Balance
Greece									**Grèce**
Imports	S	22929	29672	27899	29388	28720	29221	29928	Importations
Exports	S	10961	11948	11128	10732	10475	10747	9483	Exportations
Balance	S	−11968	−17724	−16771	−18656	−18244	−18474	−20444	Balance
Ireland									**Irlande**
Imports	G	41987	45577	49814	56684	47195	51444	51304	Importations
Exports	G	56677	61798	67951	81576	71221	77097	83015	Exportations
Balance	G	14689	16221	18137	24893	24026	25653	31711	Balance

72
Total imports and exports
Imports c.i.f., exports f.o.b. and balance, value in million US dollars
Importations et exportations totales
Importations c.a.f., exportations f.o.b., et balance, valeur en millions de dollars E.−U.

Country or area	Sys. [1]	1995	1996	1997	1998	1999	2000	2001	Pays ou zone
Italy									**Italie**
Imports	S	206059	208097	210297	218459	220327	238071	233024	Importations
Exports	S	234020	252045	240438	245716	235180	239934	241772	Exportations
Balance	S	27960	43948	30141	27257	14852	1863	8748	Balance
Luxembourg [29]									**Luxembourg** [29]
Imports	S	...	...	9380	7409	10787	10615	10681	Importations
Exports	S	...	...	7000	7912	7849	7825	7922	Exportations
Balance	S	...	...	−2380	503	−2937	−2790	−2759	Balance
Netherlands									**Pays−Bas**
Imports	S	176874	180642	178133	187754	190285	197535	194925	Importations
Exports	S	196276	197420	194909	201382	200267	208899	216117	Exportations
Balance	S	19402	16778	16776	13628	9981	11364	21193	Balance
Portugal									**Portugal**
Imports	S	33315	35179	35066	38539	39826	38257	37902	Importations
Exports	S	23212	24606	23974	24816	25228	23315	23901	Exportations
Balance	S	−10103	−10572	−11092	−13723	−14599	−14943	−14001	Balance
Spain									**Espagne**
Imports	S	113316	121792	122721	133164	144438	152901	153634	Importations
Exports	S	91041	102003	104368	109240	109966	113348	115175	Exportations
Balance	S	−22275	−19788	−18353	−23923	−34473	−39553	−38459	Balance
Sweden									**Suède**
Imports	G	64752	66931	65697	68633	68588	72643	62640	Importations
Exports	G	79813	84904	82956	85003	84796	86919	75153	Exportations
Balance	G	15061	17973	17258	16370	16208	14276	12513	Balance
United Kingdom									**Royaume−Uni**
Imports	G	265322	287472	306592	314036	317963	334371	320956	Importations
Exports	G	242036	262130	281083	271851	268203	281525	267357	Exportations
Balance	G	−23286	−25342	−25509	−42185	−49760	−52846	−53599	Balance
EFTA+									**AELE+**
Imports		**111734**	**112118**	**108781**	**112570**	**111990**	**111327**	**111518**	**Importations**
Exports		**121862**	**127489**	**122905**	**117139**	**123020**	**134287**	**138112**	**Exportations**
Balance		**10128**	**15371**	**14124**	**4569**	**11030**	**22960**	**26593**	**Balance**
Iceland									**Islande**
Imports	G	1756	2031	1992	2489	2503	2591	2253	Importations
Exports	G	1804	1638	1852	2050	2005	1891	2021	Exportations
Balance	G	48	−393	−140	−438	−498	−700	−232	Balance
Norway									**Norvège**
Imports	G	32972	35616	35713	36196	34047	32655	32180	Importations
Exports	G	41997	49646	48547	39649	44892	57519	57964	Exportations
Balance	G	9024	14030	12834	3453	10845	24865	25784	Balance
Switzerland									**Suisse**
Imports	S	77006	74471	71075	73885	75440	76082	77086	Importations
Exports	S	78061	76205	72506	75439	76124	74876	78126	Exportations
Balance	S	1055	1735	1431	1554	684	−1206	1041	Balance
Other developed Europe [3]									**Autres pays dév. d'Eur.** [3]
Imports		**4136**	**4051**	**3876**	**4117**	**4230**	**4743**	**4404**	**Importations**
Exports		**2270**	**2143**	**1973**	**2243**	**2320**	**2738**	**2323**	**Exportations**
Balance		**−1866**	**−1908**	**−1903**	**−1874**	**−1910**	**−2006**	**−2080**	**Balance**
Faeroe Islands									**Iles Féroé**
Imports	G	316	365	...	...	...	...	...	Importations
Exports	G	362	437	...	...	...	...	...	Exportations
Balance	G	46	71	...	...	...	...	...	Balance
Malta									**Malte**
Imports	G	2942	2796	2552	2666	2841	3399	2726	Importations
Exports	G	1913	1731	1630	1833	1980	2447	1958	Exportations
Balance	G	−1029	−1064	−922	−834	−861	−952	−768	Balance
Developing economies [3]									**Econ. en dévelop.** [3]
Imports		**21487**	**23029**	**27989**	**28130**	**26374**	**26278**	**28744**	**Importations**
Exports		**15770**	**15892**	**16598**	**17964**	**16746**	**17408**	**17482**	**Exportations**
Balance		**−5717**	**−7137**	**−11391**	**−10166**	**−9629**	**−8870**	**−11262**	**Balance**
Croatia									**Croatie**
Imports	G	7510	7788	9104	8383	7799	7887	9044	Importations
Exports	G	4633	4512	4171	4541	4303	4432	4659	Exportations
Balance	G	−2877	−3276	−4933	−3842	−3496	−3455	−4384	Balance
Serbia and Montenegro [28]									**Serbie−et−Monténégro** [28]
Imports	S	2666	4102	4799	4622	...	...	...	Importations
Exports	S	1531	1842	2368	2604	...	...	...	Exportations
Balance	S	−1135	−2260	−2431	−2018	...	...	...	Balance

72
Total imports and exports
Imports c.i.f., exports f.o.b. and balance, value in million US dollars
Importations et exportations totales
Importations c.a.f., exportations f.o.b., et balance, valeur en millions de dollars E.−U.

Country or area	Sys. [1]	1995	1996	1997	1998	1999	2000	2001	Pays ou zone
Slovenia									**Slovénie**
Imports	S	9492	9423	9357	10110	9952	10107	10144	Importations
Exports	S	8316	8312	8372	9048	8604	8733	9251	Exportations
Balance	S	−1175	−1111	−985	−1062	−1348	−1374	−892	Balance
TFYR of Macedonia									**L'ex−Ry de Macédonie**
Imports	S	1719	1627	1779	1915	1796	2085	1688	Importations
Exports	S	1204	1148	1237	1311	1192	1319	1155	Exportations
Balance	S	−515	−479	−542	−604	−604	−766	−533	Balance
Eastern Europe									**Europe de l'est**
Imports		**96065**	**113395**	**118464**	**132624**	**130461**	**147177**	**160227**	**Importations**
Exports		**79242**	**85649**	**89592**	**100201**	**101311**	**116084**	**129539**	**Exportations**
Balance		**−16823**	**−27746**	**−28872**	**−32422**	**−29150**	**−31094**	**−30687**	**Balance**
Albania									**Albanie**
Imports	G	1161	841	649	829	1140	1091	1331	Importations
Exports	G	367	208	139	205	264	261	305	Exportations
Balance	G	−794	−633	−510	−624	−876	−829	−1026	Balance
Bulgaria									**Bulgarie**
Imports	S	5651	6861	5223	4954	5454	6505	7263	Importations
Exports	S	5353	6602	5322	4197	3964	4809	5115	Exportations
Balance	S	−298	−259	99	−757	−1490	−1696	−2148	Balance
Czech Rep. [5]									**République tchèque [5]**
Imports	S	25306	27724	27189	28814	28087	32180	36473	Importations
Exports	S	21686	21917	22751	26417	26245	29057	33399	Exportations
Balance	S	−3620	−5807	−4438	−2396	−1842	−3123	−3075	Balance
Hungary [17][27]									**Hongrie [17][27]**
Imports	S	15379	18058	21116	25679	27923	31955	33725	Importations
Exports	S	12439	15631	18989	22992	24950	28016	30530	Exportations
Balance	S	−2940	−2426	−2126	−2687	−2973	−3939	−3195	Balance
Poland									**Pologne**
Imports	S	29064	37045	42237	46803	45778	48970	50378	Importations
Exports	S	22890	24389	25708	27370	27323	31684	36159	Exportations
Balance	S	−6173	−12656	−16529	−19433	−18455	−17285	−14219	Balance
Romania									**Roumanie**
Imports	S	10278	11435	11280	11821	10392	13055	15561	Importations
Exports	S	7910	8085	8431	8300	8505	10367	11391	Exportations
Balance	S	−2368	−3351	−2849	−3521	−1887	−2688	−4170	Balance
Slovakia									**Slovaquie**
Imports	S	9226	11431	10770	13725	11688	13423	15496	Importations
Exports	S	8596	8818	8251	10721	10062	11889	12641	Exportations
Balance	S	−630	−2613	−2519	−3004	−1625	−1534	−2855	Balance
Former USSR−Europe									**anc. URSS−Europe**
Imports		77176	82814	92836	81369	61146	74497	84145	Importations
Exports		102827	112890	115914	100266	97437	134421	134807	Exportations
Balance		25651	30076	23078	18898	36290	59924	50662	Balance
Belarus									**Belarus**
Imports	G	5563	6939	8689	8549	6674	8646	8141	Importations
Exports	G	4707	5652	7301	7070	5909	7326	7485	Exportations
Balance	G	−856	−1287	−1388	−1479	−765	−1320	−656	Balance
Estonia [15]									**Estonie [15]**
Imports	G	2545	3245	4429	4611	4094	4242	7493	Importations
Exports	G	1838	2087	2924	3130	2937	3132	6105	Exportations
Balance	G	−707	−1157	−1506	−1482	−1157	−1109	−1388	Balance
Latvia									**Lettonie**
Imports	S	1818	2320	2721	3191	2945	3187	3504	Importations
Exports	S	1305	1443	1672	1811	1723	1867	2001	Exportations
Balance	S	−513	−876	−1049	−1380	−1222	−1320	−1504	Balance
Lithuania									**Lituanie**
Imports	G	3649	4559	5644	5794	4835	5457	6353	Importations
Exports	G	2705	3355	3860	3711	3004	3810	4583	Exportations
Balance	G	−944	−1204	−1784	−2083	−1831	−1647	−1770	Balance
Republic of Moldova									**Rép. de Moldova**
Imports	G	841	1079	1200	1018	...	...	...	Importations
Exports	G	739	805	890	644	...	...	...	Exportations
Balance	G	−102	−275	−310	−374	...	...	...	Balance

72
Total imports and exports
Imports c.i.f., exports f.o.b. and balance, value in million US dollars
Importations et exportations totales
Importations c.a.f., exportations f.o.b., et balance, valeur en millions de dollars E.–U.

Country or area	Sys.[1]	1995	1996	1997	1998	1999	2000	2001	Pays ou zone
Russian Federation									**Fédération de Russie**
Imports	G	46709	46034	53039	43530	30185	33884	41879	Importations
Exports	G	78217	85107	85036	71265	71817	103070	99955	Exportations
Balance	G	31508	39073	31997	27735	41632	69186	58076	Balance
Ukraine									**Ukraine**
Imports	G	16052	18639	17114	14676	11846	...	...	Importations
Exports	G	13317	14441	14232	12637	11582	...	...	Exportations
Balance	G	−2735	−4198	−2882	−2039	−265	...	...	Balance

Africa · Afrique

Country or area	Sys.[1]	1995	1996	1997	1998	1999	2000	2001	Pays ou zone
South Africa [18][19]									**Afrique du Sud [18][19]**
Imports		29608	29105	31939	28277	25890	28980	27494	Importations
Exports		26917	28145	29964	25396	25901	29267	28464	Exportations
Balance		−2690	−960	−1975	−2881	11	287	970	Balance
Developing economies [3]									**Econ. en dévelop. [3]**
Imports		87238	89159	90254	101984	99662	99346	105307	**Importations**
Exports		77617	86359	86065	81144	90653	104137	99490	**Exportations**
Balance		−9622	−2801	−4189	−20840	−9009	4791	−5817	**Balance**
North Africa									**Afrique du Nord**
Imports		45943	45701	46310	50954	48785	48773	50291	**Importations**
Exports		35725	38835	39670	36559	39573	44451	43414	**Exportations**
Balance		−10218	−6866	−6640	−14394	−9212	−4323	−6877	**Balance**
Algeria									**Algérie**
Imports	S	10250	8690	...	...	...	...	...	Importations
Exports	S	10250	12621	...	...	...	...	...	Exportations
Balance	S	0	3931	...	...	...	...	...	Balance
Egypt [20]									**Egypte [20]**
Imports	S	11760	13038	13211	16166	16022	14010	12756	Importations
Exports	S	3450	3539	3921	3130	3559	4691	4126	Exportations
Balance	S	−8310	−9499	−9290	−13036	−12463	−9319	−8630	Balance
Libyan Arab Jamah.									**Jamah. arabe libyenne**
Imports	G	5033	5295	5605	5600	3862	3751	4458	Importations
Exports	G	9364	9895	9057	6032	7374	10247	9038	Exportations
Balance	G	4331	4601	3452	433	3512	6496	4580	Balance
Morocco									**Maroc**
Imports	S	10024	9704	9526	10290	9925	11534	11038	Importations
Exports	S	6882	6881	7033	7153	7367	6956	7144	Exportations
Balance	S	−3142	−2823	−2493	−3137	−2558	−4577	−3894	Balance
Sudan									**Soudan**
Imports	G	1219	1504	1580	1925	1415	1553	1586	Importations
Exports	G	556	620	594	596	780	1807	1699	Exportations
Balance	G	−663	−884	−986	−1329	−635	254	113	Balance
Tunisia									**Tunisie**
Imports	G	7903	7700	7914	8338	8474	8567	9579	Importations
Exports	G	5475	5517	5559	5738	5872	5850	6609	Exportations
Balance	G	−2428	−2184	−2355	−2600	−2603	−2717	−2970	Balance
Other Africa									**Autres pays d'Afrique**
Imports		41295	43458	43944	51030	50876	50573	55016	**Importations**
Exports		41891	47524	46395	44585	51079	59687	56077	**Exportations**
Balance		597	4065	2451	−6445	203	9113	1060	**Balance**
EMCCA+									**CEMAC+**
Imports		3345	4498	4192	4002	3749	3760	4627	**Importations**
Exports		6047	6855	7443	5816	6608	8265	8158	**Exportations**
Balance		2703	2357	3251	1814	2859	4505	3531	**Balance**
Cameroon									**Cameroun**
Imports	S	1201	1226	1359	1503	1314	...	...	Importations
Exports	S	1654	1768	1860	1675	1595	...	...	Exportations
Balance	S	453	542	501	172	281	...	...	Balance
Central African Rep.									**Rép. centrafricaine**
Imports	S	174	141	141	146	131	116	109	Importations
Exports	S	171	147	163	151	147	161	147	Exportations
Balance	S	−3	5	22	5	15	45	39	Balance
Chad									**Tchad**
Imports	S	365	332	335	356	317	318	621	Importations
Exports	S	243	238	238	262	202	184	166	Exportations
Balance	S	−122	−94	−97	−94	−115	−135	−456	Balance

72
Total imports and exports
Imports c.i.f., exports f.o.b. and balance, value in million US dollars
Importations et exportations totales
Importations c.a.f., exportations f.o.b., et balance, valeur en millions de dollars E.−U.

Country or area	Sys.[1]	1995	1996	1997	1998	1999	2000	2001	Pays ou zone
Congo									**Congo**
Imports	S	670	1550	925	577	718	464	...	Importations
Exports	S	1176	1343	1666	1373	1555	2477	...	Exportations
Balance	S	506	−207	741	797	837	2013	...	Balance
Equatorial Guinea									**Guinée équatoriale**
Imports	G	50	292	330	317	425	451	...	Importations
Exports	G	86	175	495	438	708	1097	...	Exportations
Balance	G	36	−117	165	122	284	646	...	Balance
Gabon									**Gabon**
Imports	S	884	956	1103	1103	844	996	...	Importations
Exports	S	2718	3183	3021	1916	2401	2465	...	Exportations
Balance	S	1834	2227	1918	813	1557	1470	...	Balance
ECOWAS+									**CEDEAO+**
Imports		**18966**	**17743**	**20353**	**20769**	**21355**	**20038**	**23458**	**Importations**
Exports		**21753**	**26367**	**25114**	**20512**	**24740**	**30510**	**26871**	**Exportations**
Balance		**2787**	**8624**	**4761**	**−257**	**3385**	**10472**	**3412**	**Balance**
Benin									**Benin**
Imports	S	746	654	681	736	749	613	652	Importations
Exports	S	417	653	417	407	416	384	343	Exportations
Balance	S	−329	−1	−264	−328	−333	−229	−308	Balance
Burkina Faso									**Burkina Faso**
Imports	G	455	647	588	732	579	550	656	Importations
Exports	G	276	234	232	319	255	213	175	Exportations
Balance	G	−180	−413	−355	−412	−324	−337	−481	Balance
Cape Verde									**Cap−Vert**
Imports	G	252	...	235	231	262	237	248	Importations
Exports	G	9	...	14	10	11	11	10	Exportations
Balance	G	−243	...	−221	−220	−251	−227	−238	Balance
Côte d'Ivoire									**Côte d'Ivoire**
Imports	S	2929	2900	2782	3002	3262	2532	2548	Importations
Exports	S	3812	4444	4460	4610	4675	3905	3659	Exportations
Balance	S	883	1543	1679	1608	1413	1372	1112	Balance
Gambia									**Gambie**
Imports	G	182	258	174	245	192	...	...	Importations
Exports	G	16	21	15	27	7	...	...	Exportations
Balance	G	−166	−237	−159	−218	−185	...	...	Balance
Ghana									**Ghana**
Imports	G	1896	2101	2310	2561	3505	2973	...	Importations
Exports	G	1754	1670	1636	1792	...	...	...	Exportations
Balance	G	−142	−431	−674	−769	...	...	...	Balance
Guinea−Bissau									**Guinée−Bissau**
Imports	G	134	85	89	69	69	71	86	Importations
Exports	G	45	28	49	26	51	62	62	Exportations
Balance	G	−89	−57	−40	−43	−18	−9	−24	Balance
Mali									**Mali**
Imports	S	774	772	738	761	824	830	1011	Importations
Exports	S	443	433	561	561	566	547	723	Exportations
Balance	S	−331	−340	−177	−199	−258	−283	−288	Balance
Niger									**Niger**
Imports	S	373	448	374	470	395	395	320	Importations
Exports	S	289	325	272	334	288	285	270	Exportations
Balance	S	−85	−123	−102	−136	−107	−111	−50	Balance
Nigeria									**Nigeria**
Imports	G	8222	6438	9501	9211	8588	8721	11586	Importations
Exports	G	12342	16154	15207	9855	13856	20975	17261	Exportations
Balance	G	4121	9715	5706	644	5268	12254	5675	Balance
Senegal									**Sénégal**
Imports	G	1411	1435	1333	1455	1561	1519	1544	Importations
Exports	G	993	987	904	968	1025	920	1000	Exportations
Balance	G	−419	−448	−429	−487	−535	−599	−544	Balance
Sierra Leone									**Sierra Leone**
Imports	S	134	211	92	95	80	149	182	Importations
Exports	S	42	47	17	7	6	13	29	Exportations
Balance	S	−91	−164	−75	−88	−74	−136	−153	Balance

72

Total imports and exports
Imports c.i.f., exports f.o.b. and balance, value in million US dollars
Importations et exportations totales
Importations c.a.f., exportations f.o.b., et balance, valeur en millions de dollars E.–U.

Country or area	Sys.[1]	1995	1996	1997	1998	1999	2000	2001	Pays ou zone
Togo									**Togo**
Imports	S	594	664	645	589	593	541	590	Importations
Exports	S	378	441	424	969	389	361	389	Exportations
Balance	S	−215	−224	−221	381	−204	−180	−201	Balance
Rest of Africa									**Afrique NDA**
Imports		18984	21217	19399	26259	25773	26775	26931	Importations
Exports		14091	14302	13838	18256	19732	20911	21048	Exportations
Balance		−4893	−6915	−5561	−8003	−6041	−5864	−5883	Balance
Angola									**Angola**
Imports	S	427	...	...	...	...	...	...	Importations
Exports	S	3642	...	...	...	...	...	...	Exportations
Balance	S	3215	...	...	...	...	...	...	Balance
Botswana									**Botswana**
Imports	G	...	...	...	2942	2909	2816	...	Importations
Exports	G	...	...	...	2783	3610	3752	...	Exportations
Balance	G	...	...	...	−159	701	937	...	Balance
Burundi									**Burundi**
Imports	S	234	127	121	158	118	148	139	Importations
Exports	S	106	40	87	65	54	50	39	Exportations
Balance	S	−129	−87	−35	−93	−64	−98	−101	Balance
Comoros									**Comores**
Imports	S	63	...	...	...	...	...	...	Importations
Exports	S	11	...	...	...	...	...	...	Exportations
Balance	S	−51	...	...	...	...	...	...	Balance
Dem. Rep. of the Congo									**Rép. dém. du Congo**
Imports	S	397	424	...	...	...	...	...	Importations
Exports	S	438	592	...	...	...	...	...	Exportations
Balance	S	41	167	...	...	...	...	...	Balance
Djibouti									**Djibouti**
Imports	G	177	179	148	158	153	...	...	Importations
Exports	G	14	14	11	12	12	...	...	Exportations
Balance	G	−163	−165	−137	−146	−140	...	...	Balance
Eritrea									**Érythrée**
Imports	G	...	450	425	356	329	...	...	Importations
Exports	G	...	76	52	26	17	...	...	Exportations
Balance	G	...	−374	−373	−330	−312	...	...	Balance
Ethiopia									**Éthiopie**
Imports	G	1142	1401	...	...	1317	...	...	Importations
Exports	G	422	417	587	560	...	...	...	Exportations
Balance	G	−720	−984	...	...	...	...	...	Balance
Kenya									**Kenya**
Imports	G	3006	2949	3296	3195	2833	3105	3189	Importations
Exports	G	1890	2068	2054	2007	1747	1734	1943	Exportations
Balance	G	−1116	−881	−1243	−1188	−1086	−1372	−1246	Balance
Lesotho									**Lesotho**
Imports	G	...	...	...	863	781	728	681	Importations
Exports	G	...	...	...	194	172	221	280	Exportations
Balance	G	...	...	...	−670	−609	−507	−401	Balance
Madagascar									**Madagascar**
Imports	S	543	507	467	514	377	...	...	Importations
Exports	S	370	299	222	243	221	...	...	Exportations
Balance	S	−174	−208	−245	−271	−156	...	...	Balance
Malawi									**Malawi**
Imports	G	475	623	791	515	673	532	530	Importations
Exports	G	405	481	537	430	453	379	463	Exportations
Balance	G	−69	−143	−255	−85	−221	−152	−67	Balance
Mauritius									**Maurice**
Imports	G	1976	2289	2181	2073	2248	2088	1990	Importations
Exports	G	1538	1802	1592	1645	1554	1498	1615	Exportations
Balance	G	−438	−487	−588	−428	−694	−591	−374	Balance
Mozambique									**Mozambique**
Imports	S	704	759	739	790	1139	1158	...	Importations
Exports	S	168	217	222	230	263	364	...	Exportations
Balance	S	−536	−542	−517	−560	−876	−794	...	Balance

72
Total imports and exports
Imports c.i.f., exports f.o.b. and balance, value in million US dollars
Importations et exportations totales
Importations c.a.f., exportations f.o.b., et balance, valeur en millions de dollars E.–U.

Country or area	Sys. [1]	1995	1996	1997	1998	1999	2000	2001	Pays ou zone
Namibia									**Namibie**
Imports	S	...	...	...	1662	...	...	...	Importations
Exports	S	...	...	...	1214	1244	...	...	Exportations
Balance	S	...	...	...	−448	...	...	...	Balance
Réunion [13]									**Réunion** [13]
Imports	G	2625	...	...	...	...	...	...	Importations
Exports	G	207	...	...	...	...	...	...	Exportations
Balance	G	−2418	...	...	...	...	...	...	Balance
Rwanda									**Rwanda**
Imports	G	241	256	297	285	253	213	250	Importations
Exports	G	52	60	87	60	61	53	85	Exportations
Balance	G	−189	−196	−210	−225	−192	−160	−165	Balance
Sao Tome and Principe									**Sao Tomé−et−Principe**
Imports	S	29	22	16	...	...	...	...	Importations
Exports	S	5	5	5	...	...	...	...	Exportations
Balance	S	−24	−18	−11	...	...	...	...	Balance
Seychelles									**Seychelles**
Imports	G	233	379	340	384	434	342	523	Importations
Exports	G	53	139	113	122	145	194	216	Exportations
Balance	G	−180	−239	−227	−261	−289	−149	−307	Balance
Uganda									**Ouganda**
Imports	G	1056	1190	1317	1414	1342	1512	1594	Importations
Exports	G	461	587	555	501	517	469	457	Exportations
Balance	G	−595	−603	−762	−913	−825	−1043	−1137	Balance
United Rep. of Tanzania									**Rép.−Unie de Tanzanie**
Imports	G	1679	1386	1336	1453	1550	1523	1712	Importations
Exports	G	685	783	752	589	543	663	776	Exportations
Balance	G	−994	−603	−584	−864	−1007	−860	−936	Balance
Zambia									**Zambie**
Imports	S	702	836	819	...	...	...	...	Importations
Exports	S	1046	1049	914	...	...	...	...	Exportations
Balance	S	344	213	96	...	...	...	...	Balance
Zimbabwe									**Zimbabwe**
Imports	G	2661	2817		...	...	...	...	Importations
Exports	G	2114	2419		...	...	...	...	Exportations
Balance	G	−548	−399		...	...	...	...	Balance

Asia · Asie

Country or area	Sys. [1]	1995	1996	1997	1998	1999	2000	2001	Pays ou zone
Developed economies [3]									**Economies développées** [3]
Imports		355048	369841	356580	296211	326856	401048	366221	**Importations**
Exports		453076	422252	432218	399238	429180	496439	416378	**Exportations**
Balance		98028	52411	75638	103027	102324	95391	50157	**Balance**
Israel [21] [22]									**Israël** [21] [22]
Imports	S	28287	29951	29084	27470	31090	35750	33319	Importations
Exports	S	19046	20610	22503	22993	25794	31404	29048	Exportations
Balance	S	−9241	−9341	−6582	−4477	−5296	−4345	−4271	Balance
Japan									**Japon**
Imports	G	335990	349174	338830	280632	310039	379491	349189	Importations
Exports	G	443259	410926	421050	388135	417659	479227	403616	Exportations
Balance	G	107269	61752	82220	107503	107620	99736	54427	Balance
Developing economies [3] [23]									**Econ. en dévelop.** [3] [23]
Imports		983350	1047961	1070047	894835	967120	1185193	1126205	**Importations**
Exports		951254	1009329	1078881	1005200	1112315	1369377	1272052	**Exportations**
Balance		−32096	−38632	8834	110365	145195	184185	145847	**Balance**
Asia Middle East									**Moyen−Orient d'Asie**
Imports		136403	153339	163444	157805	153564	179687	170173	**Importations**
Exports		152666	175698	187914	159212	202139	268495	251096	**Exportations**
Balance		16263	22359	24471	1406	48575	88809	80922	**Balance**
Bahrain									**Bahreïn**
Imports	G	3716	4273	4026	3566	3698	4634	4263	Importations
Exports	G	4113	4702	4384	3270	4140	5703	5545	Exportations
Balance	G	397	429	358	−296	443	1070	1282	Balance
Cyprus									**Chypre**
Imports	G	3694	3983	3655	3687	3618	3846	3938	Importations
Exports	G	1231	1391	1250	1062	997	954	976	Exportations
Balance	G	−2463	−2591	−2405	−2625	−2621	−2893	−2962	Balance

72
Total imports and exports
Imports c.i.f., exports f.o.b. and balance, value in million US dollars
Importations et exportations totales
Importations c.a.f., exportations f.o.b., et balance, valeur en millions de dollars E.–U.

Country or area	Sys.[1]	1995	1996	1997	1998	1999	2000	2001	Pays ou zone
Iran (Islamic Rep. of) [25]									**Iran (Rép. islamique d')**[25]
Imports	S	13882	16274	14196	14323	12683	14296	17938	Importations
Exports	S	18360	22391	18381	13118	21030	28345	23716	Exportations
Balance	S	4478	6117	4185	−1205	8347	14049	5778	Balance
Jordan									**Jordanie**
Imports	G	3696	4293	4102	3828	3717	4597	4844	Importations
Exports	G	1769	1817	1836	1802	1832	1899	2293	Exportations
Balance	G	−1928	−2476	−2266	−2026	−1885	−2698	−2551	Balance
Kuwait									**Koweït**
Imports	S	7792	8373	8246	8617	7617	7157	5716	Importations
Exports	S	12785	14889	14225	9554	12164	19436	15869	Exportations
Balance	S	4992	6515	5979	936	4547	12280	10153	Balance
Lebanon									**Liban**
Imports	G	5480	7540	7467	7070	6207	6228	...	Importations
Exports	G	656	736	643	662	677	714	...	Exportations
Balance	G	−4825	−6804	−6824	−6408	−5530	−5514	...	Balance
Oman									**Oman**
Imports	G	4248	4578	5026	5682	4674	5040	5811	Importations
Exports	G	6068	7346	7630	5508	...	...	...	Exportations
Balance	G	1821	2768	2604	−173	...	...	...	Balance
Qatar									**Qatar**
Imports	S	3398	2868	3322	3409	2499	...	...	Importations
Exports	S	3481	3752	3791	4880	7059	...	...	Exportations
Balance	S	83	884	470	1471	4560	...	...	Balance
Saudi Arabia									**Arabe saoudite**
Imports	S	28091	27744	28732	30013	28010	30237	31223	Importations
Exports	S	50040	60729	60732	38822	50760	77583	...	Exportations
Balance	S	21949	32985	32000	8809	22750	47345	...	Balance
Syrian Arab Republic									**Rep. arabe syrienne**
Imports	S	4709	5380	4028	3895	3832	4055	4757	Importations
Exports	S	3563	3999	3916	2890	3464	4674	5254	Exportations
Balance	S	−1146	−1381	−111	−1005	−368	620	497	Balance
Turkey									**Turquie**
Imports	S	35709	43627	48559	45921	40692	53499	41124	Importations
Exports	S	21637	23224	26261	26974	26588	26572	31169	Exportations
Balance	S	−14072	−20403	−22298	−18947	−14104	−26927	−9954	Balance
United Arab Emirates									**Emirats arabes unis**
Imports	G	20984	22638	29952	24728	33231	38139	...	Importations
Exports	G	27753	28085	39613	42666	43307	...	...	Exportations
Balance	G	6769	5447	9661	17938	10076	...	...	Balance
Yemen [24]									**Yémen** [24]
Imports	S	1817	2442	2017	2172	2006	2326	2309	Importations
Exports	S	1917	3206	2509	1501	2438	4078	3214	Exportations
Balance	S	101	763	491	−671	432	1751	905	Balance
Non Petrol. Export [26]									**Pétrole non Compris** [26]
Imports		...	...	...	...	...	...	...	Importations
Exports		96706	111242	62312	60768	73025	102397	100182	Exportations
Balance		...	...	...	...	...	...	...	Balance
Other Asia									**Autres Pays d'Asie**
Imports		836436	880807	892875	724049	802180	992378	941465	**Importations**
Exports		786134	818873	875444	832764	896560	1083691	1004662	**Exportations**
Balance		−50302	−61934	−17431	108715	94380	91313	63197	**Balance**
ASEAN+									**ANASE+**
Imports		354158	375044	370102	280212	299125	364456	334739	**Importations**
Exports		320457	340148	350769	327659	357417	424545	378605	**Exportations**
Balance		−33701	−34897	−19333	47446	58292	60089	43866	**Balance**
Brunei Darussalam									**Brunéi Darussalam**
Imports	S	2078	2494	2203	1552	...	...	...	Importations
Exports	S	2389	2481	2467	2058	...	...	...	Exportations
Balance	S	311	−13	264	506	...	...	...	Balance
Cambodia									**Cambodge**
Imports	S	...	...	1116	1129	1243	1424	1456	Importations
Exports	S	...	...	626	933	1040	1123	1296	Exportations
Balance	S	...	...	−491	−195	−203	−302	−160	Balance

72

Total imports and exports
Imports c.i.f., exports f.o.b. and balance, value in million US dollars
Importations et exportations totales
Importations c.a.f., exportations f.o.b., et balance, valeur en millions de dollars E.−U.

Country or area	Sys.[1]	1995	1996	1997	1998	1999	2000	2001	Pays ou zone
Indonesia									**Indonésie**
Imports	S	40630	42929	41694	27337	24004	33515	31010	Importations
Exports	S	45417	49814	53443	48847	48665	62124	52115	Exportations
Balance	S	4787	6885	11749	21511	24661	28609	21105	Balance
Lao People's Dem.Rep.									**Rép. dém. populaire lao**
Imports	S	589	690	706	553	525	535	528	Importations
Exports	S	311	323	359	370	311	330	331	Exportations
Balance	S	−278	−367	−347	−183	−214	−205	−197	Balance
Malaysia									**Malaisie**
Imports	G	77545	78408	79030	58277	65385	81963	73867	Importations
Exports	G	73779	78318	78741	73256	84617	98230	88006	Exportations
Balance	G	−3766	−90	−289	14978	19231	16266	14139	Balance
Myanmar									**Myanmar**
Imports	G	1335	1355	2037	2667	2301	2371	2848	Importations
Exports	G	851	744	866	1066	1125	1621	2359	Exportations
Balance	G	−484	−611	−1171	−1601	−1176	−750	−489	Balance
Philippines									**Philippines**
Imports	G	28328	34127	38604	31542	32569	33808	31359	Importations
Exports	G	17492	20408	24895	29449	36577	39794	32664	Exportations
Balance	G	−10836	−13719	−13709	−2093	4008	5986	1306	Balance
Singapore									**Singapour**
Imports	G	124502	131340	132443	104728	111062	134546	116004	Importations
Exports	G	118263	125016	124990	109905	114682	137806	121755	Exportations
Balance	G	−6239	−6324	−7453	5177	3620	3259	5752	Balance
Thailand									**Thaïlande**
Imports	S	70787	72336	62880	42971	50343	61924	62058	Importations
Exports	S	56440	55721	57402	54458	58440	69057	65114	Exportations
Balance	S	−14347	−16616	−5479	11487	8098	7133	3055	Balance
Viet Nam									**Viet Nam**
Imports	G	8155	11144	11592	11500	11742	15638	15999	Importations
Exports	G	5449	7256	9185	9361	11540	14449	15100	Exportations
Balance	G	−2707	−3888	−2407	−2139	−202	−1189	−899	Balance
Rest of Asia									**Asie NDA**
Imports		482279	505762	522774	443837	503055	627922	606726	**Importations**
Exports		465677	478725	524675	505106	539143	659146	626057	**Exportations**
Balance		−16601	−27037	1902	61269	36088	31224	19331	**Balance**
Afghanistan									**Afghanistan**
Imports	G	50	...	...	...	...	...	...	Importations
Exports	G	26	...	...	...	...	...	...	Exportations
Balance	G	−24	...	...	...	...	...	...	Balance
Bangladesh									**Bangladesh**
Imports	G	6501	6621	6896	6978	7685	8358	8349	Importations
Exports	G	3173	3297	3778	3831	3919	4787	4826	Exportations
Balance	G	−3328	−3324	−3117	−3147	−3766	−3572	−3523	Balance
Bhutan									**Bhoutan**
Imports	G	113	128	137	135	182	...	...	Importations
Exports	G	103	100	118	108	116	...	...	Exportations
Balance	G	−9	−27	−19	−26	−66	...	...	Balance
China									**Chine**
Imports	S	129113	138944	142189	140305	165788	206132	243521	Importations
Exports	S	148797	151197	182877	183589	195150	249297	266620	Exportations
Balance	S	19684	12253	40688	43284	29362	43165	23099	Balance
China, Hong Kong SAR									**Chine, Hong Kong RAS**
Imports	G	192751	198550	208614	184518	179520	212805	201076	Importations
Exports	G	173750	180750	188059	174002	173885	201860	189894	Exportations
Balance	G	−19001	−17800	−20555	−10516	−5635	−10945	−11182	Balance
China, Macao SAR									**Chine, Macao RAS**
Imports	G	2042	2000	2082	1955	2040	2255	2386	Importations
Exports	G	1997	1996	2148	2141	2200	2539	2300	Exportations
Balance	G	−44	−4	66	186	160	284	−87	Balance
India									**Inde**
Imports	G	34710	37944	41430	42999	46971	51563	50390	Importations
Exports	G	30628	33107	35006	33463	35666	42378	43338	Exportations
Balance	G	−4082	−4837	−6425	−9536	−11305	−9185	−7052	Balance

72
Total imports and exports
Imports c.i.f., exports f.o.b. and balance, value in million US dollars
Importations et exportations totales
Importations c.a.f., exportations f.o.b., et balance, valeur en millions de dollars E.-U.

Country or area	Sys. [1]	1995	1996	1997	1998	1999	2000	2001	Pays ou zone
Korea, Republic of									**Corée, République**
Imports	G	135119	150339	144616	93282	119752	160481	141098	Importations
Exports	G	125058	129715	136164	132313	143686	172268	150439	Exportations
Balance	G	−10061	−20624	−8452	39031	23934	11787	9341	Balance
Maldives									**Maldives**
Imports	G	268	302	349	354	402	389	393	Importations
Exports	G	50	59	73	74	64	76	76	Exportations
Balance	G	−218	−243	−276	−280	−338	−313	−317	Balance
Mongolia									**Mongolie**
Imports	G	415	451	468	503	426	...	...	Importations
Exports	G	473	424	452	345	233	...	...	Exportations
Balance	G	58	−27	−17	−158	−193	...	...	Balance
Nepal									**Népal**
Imports	G	1333	1398	1693	1245	1418	1573	1475	Importations
Exports	G	346	385	406	474	600	804	738	Exportations
Balance	G	−988	−1013	−1287	−772	−818	−768	−737	Balance
Pakistan									**Pakistan**
Imports	G	11517	12191	11652	9331	10163	11293	10192	Importations
Exports	G	8031	9367	8760	8515	8387	9028	9238	Exportations
Balance	G	−3486	−2824	−2893	−816	−1776	−2265	−953	Balance
Sri Lanka									**Sri Lanka**
Imports	G	5307	5442	5864	5877	5961	7210	5924	Importations
Exports	G	3798	4095	4639	4787	4594	5416	4817	Exportations
Balance	G	−1509	−1347	−1225	−1091	−1367	−1794	−1107	Balance
Former USSR − Asia									**anc. URSS − Asie**
Imports		**10511**	**13815**	**13728**	**12981**	**11376**	**13128**	**14567**	**Importations**
Exports		**12454**	**14758**	**15523**	**13224**	**13616**	**17191**	**16294**	**Exportations**
Balance		**1943**	**943**	**1795**	**244**	**2240**	**4062**	**1727**	**Balance**
Armenia									**Arménie**
Imports		674	856	892	902	800	882	874	Importations
Exports		271	290	233	221	232	294	343	Exportations
Balance		−403	−566	−660	−682	−568	−588	−532	Balance
Azerbaijan									**Azerbaidjan**
Imports		668	961	794	1077	1036	...	...	Importations
Exports		637	631	781	606	929	...	...	Exportations
Balance		−30	−329	−13	−471	−107	...	...	Balance
Georgia									**Géorgie**
Imports		412	687	944	878	...	...	...	Importations
Exports		158	199	240	192	...	...	...	Exportations
Balance		−255	−489	−704	−686	...	...	...	Balance
Kazakhstan									**Kazakhstan**
Imports		3807	4241	4301	4350	3687	5051	6363	Importations
Exports		5250	5911	6497	5436	5598	9126	8647	Exportations
Balance		1444	1670	2196	1086	1912	4075	2284	Balance
Kyrgyzstan									**Kirghizistan**
Imports		522	838	709	842	600	554	468	Importations
Exports		409	505	604	514	454	504	460	Exportations
Balance		−113	−332	−105	−328	−146	−50	−8	Balance
Tajikistan									**Tadjikistan**
Imports		810	763	750	771	664	...	...	Importations
Exports		749	651	746	602	689	...	...	Exportations
Balance		−61	−112	−5	−170	25	...	...	Balance
Turkmenistan									**Turkménistan**
Imports		777	...	...	...	...	...	...	Importations
Exports		1939	...	...	...	...	...	...	Exportations
Balance		1162	...	...	...	...	...	...	Balance
Uzbekistan									**Ouzbékistan**
Imports		2900	4721	4523	3289	...	...	...	Importations
Exports		3100	4590	4388	3528	...	...	...	Exportations
Balance		200	−131	−136	240	...	...	...	Balance

72
Total imports and exports
Imports c.i.f., exports f.o.b. and balance, value in million US dollars
Importations et exportations totales
Importations c.a.f., exportations f.o.b., et balance, valeur en millions de dollars E.−U.

Country or area	Sys.[1]	1995	1996	1997	1998	1999	2000	2001	Pays ou zone
Oceania · Océanie									
Developed economies[3]									**Economies développées**[3]
Imports		72138	76932	77098	73768	80039	81663	73175	Importations
Exports		63658	71441	73814	64605	65116	73370	73051	Exportations
Balance		−8480	−5490	−3285	−9163	−14923	−8293	−124	Balance
Australia									**Australie**
Imports	G	61283	65428	65892	64630	69158	71537	63890	Importations
Exports	G	53115	60300	62910	55893	56080	63878	63389	Exportations
Balance	G	−8167	−5128	−2982	−8737	−13078	−7659	−501	Balance
New Zealand									**Nouvelle−Zélande**
Imports	G	13958	14724	14519	12496	14299	13906	13347	Importations
Exports	G	13645	14362	14216	12069	12454	13272	13724	Exportations
Balance	G	−312	−362	−303	−427	−1844	−634	377	Balance
Developing economies[3]									**Econ. en dévelop.**[3]
Imports		6844	7380	7528	7328	7625	7581	8334	Importations
Exports		5800	5652	5290	4708	5008	5417	4969	Exportations
Balance		−1044	−1727	−2238	−2620	−2617	−2164	−3365	Balance
Cook Islands									**Iles Cook**
Imports	G	49	43	48	38	37	50	47	Importations
Exports	G	5	3	3	3	3	9	7	Exportations
Balance	G	−44	−40	−45	−35	−34	−41	−40	Balance
Fiji									**Fidji**
Imports	G	892	987	965	721	...	830	...	Importations
Exports	G	619	749	619	510	...	585	...	Exportations
Balance	G	−273	−239	−346	−211	...	−246	...	Balance
French Polynesia									**Polynésie française**
Imports	S	1019	1016	936	...	...	...	...	Importations
Exports	S	196	251	222	...	...	...	...	Exportations
Balance	S	−823	−765	−714	...	...	...	...	Balance
Kiribati[5]									**Kiribati**[5]
Imports	G	35	38	39	33	...	...	...	Importations
Exports	G	7	5	6	6	...	...	...	Exportations
Balance	G	−28	−33	−33	−27	...	...	...	Balance
Micronesia									**Micronésie**
Imports	S	100	84	...	...	...	...	...	Importations
Exports	S	43	14	...	...	...	...	...	Exportations
Balance	S	−56	−70	...	...	...	...	...	Balance
New Caledonia									**Nouvelle−Calédonie**
Imports	S	967	1001	928	938	1009	925	977	Importations
Exports	S	570	554	542	382	468	606	465	Exportations
Balance	S	−397	−447	−386	−555	−541	−319	−512	Balance
Papua New Guinea									**Papouaise−Nvl−Guinée**
Imports	G	1452	1741	1709	1240	1236	1151	1073	Importations
Exports	G	2654	2531	2160	1772	1927	2096	1813	Exportations
Balance	G	1202	789	451	532	691	945	740	Balance
Samoa									**Samoa**
Imports	S	95	100	97	97	115	106	130	Importations
Exports	S	9	10	15	15	20	14	16	Exportations
Balance	S	−86	−90	−82	−82	−95	−92	−115	Balance
Solomon Islands									**Iles Salomon**
Imports	S	154	151	183	150	...	...	...	Importations
Exports	S	168	162	174	126	...	...	...	Exportations
Balance	S	14	11	−10	−24	...	...	...	Balance
Tonga									**Tonga**
Imports	G	77	75	73	69	73	70	...	Importations
Exports	G	15	13	10	8	12	9	...	Exportations
Balance	G	−63	−61	−63	−61	−60	−61	...	Balance
Vanuatu									**Vanuatu**
Imports	G	95	97	94	88	96	89	...	Importations
Exports	G	28	30	35	34	26	26	...	Exportations
Balance	G	−67	−67	−59	−54	−70	−63	...	Balance
ANCOM+									**ANCOM+**
Imports		41263	38515	47021	47806	37338	42025	47262	Importations
Exports		39769	45570	45864	39087	44068	57959	49662	Exportations
Balance		−1494	7055	−1157	−8719	6730	15933	2400	Balance

72
Total imports and exports
Imports c.i.f., exports f.o.b. and balance, value in million US dollars
Importations et exportations totales
Importations c.a.f., exportations f.o.b., et balance, valeur en millions de dollars E.−U.

Country or area	Sys. [1]	1995	1996	1997	1998	1999	2000	2001	Pays ou zone
APEC+									**CEAP+**
Imports		2200316	2331190	2453260	2277375	2501549	2999632	2818936	Importations
Exports		2143210	2215301	2368559	2266288	2414602	2824902	2591961	Exportations
Balance		−57107	−115889	−84701	−11087	−86947	−174730	−226975	Balance
CARICOM+									**CARICOM+**
Imports		9423	12500	12060	12270	12169	13132	13074	Importations
Exports		5457	6640	6058	5421	6237	8205	7893	Exportations
Balance		−3966	−5859	−6002	−6849	−5932	−4927	−5181	Balance
CIS+									**CEI+**
Imports		79675	86507	93769	80753	60649	74740	81362	Importations
Exports		109433	120763	122981	104840	103388	142803	138412	Exportations
Balance		29758	34256	29212	24087	42739	68062	57050	Balance
COMESA+									**COMESA+**
Imports		26552	30620	31605	37205	36002	35267	34729	Importations
Exports		16446	16649	16913	17408	18852	21772	21996	Exportations
Balance		−10106	−13971	−14692	−19797	−17150	−13495	−12733	Balance
LDC+									**PMA+**
Imports		29623	33300	34585	37231	38053	39867	41701	Importations
Exports		20529	21719	21862	22349	24951	29871	30700	Exportations
Balance		−9094	−11581	−12723	−14883	−13102	−9996	−11001	Balance
MERCOSUR+									**MERCOSUR+**
Imports		79554	86882	102272	98316	82265	90938	84522	Importations
Exports		70499	74998	83179	81366	74322	85027	87840	Exportations
Balance		−9055	−11884	−19093	−16950	−7943	−5911	3318	Balance
NAFTA+									**ALENA+**
Imports		959239	1029419	1147601	1210558	1350497	1588750	1489591	Importations
Exports		808469	869940	956349	953704	1011202	1140275	1069586	Exportations
Balance		−150770	−159479	−191252	−256854	−339295	−448475	−420006	Balance
OECD+									**OCDE+**
Imports		3679358	3856899	3964983	4031732	4249139	4732948	4521423	Importations
Exports		3696019	3814377	3925354	3966480	4044218	4349927	4210968	Exportations
Balance		16661	−42522	−39630	−65252	−204921	−383021	−310455	Balance
OPEC+									**OPEP+**
Imports		151323	151512	165649	149638	145670	167805	173656	Importations
Exports		209060	241957	253013	212491	256529	345219	303210	Exportations
Balance		57737	90444	87364	62853	110859	177414	129554	Balance
EU−15 [30]									**U.E.−15** [30]
Imports		...	...	...	...	829780	950433	914064	Importations
Exports		...	...	...	...	808092	866124	872808	Exportations
Balance		...	...	...	...	−21688	−84309	−41257	Balance

Source:
United Nations Statistics Division, New York, trade
statistics database.

+ For member states of this grouping, see Annex I − Other groupings.
  The totals have been re−calculated for all periods shown according
  to the current composition.

1 Systems of trade: Two systems of recording trade, the General trade
  system (G) and the Special trade system (S), are in common use. They
  differ mainly in the way warehoused and re−exported goods are recorded.
  See the Technical notes for an explanation of the trade systems.

2 United States, Canada, Developed Economies of Europe, Israel, Japan,
  Australia, New Zealand and South Africa.

3 This classification is intended for statistical convenience and
  does not necessarily express a judgement about the stage
  reached by a particular country in the development process.
4 Comprises Eastern Europe and the European countries of the former USSR.

5 Imports FOB.
6 Including the trade of the U.S. Virgin Islands and Puerto Rico, but
  excluding shipments of merchandise between the United States
  and its other possessions (Guam, American Samoa, etc). Data

Source:
Organisation des Nations Unies, Division de statistique, New York, la
base de données pour les statistiques de commerce extérieur.

+ Pour les Etats membres de ce groupements, voir annexe I − Autres
  groupements. Les totaux ont été récalculés pour toutes les périodes
  données suivant la composition présente.

1 Systèmes de commerce: Deux systèmes d'enregistrement du
  commerce sont couramment utilisés, le Commerce général (G) et le
  Commerce spécial (S). Ils ne diffèrent que par la façon dont sont
  enregistrées les marchandises entreposées et les marchandises
  réexportées. Voir les Notes techniques pour une explication des
  Systèmes de commerce.

2 Etats−Unis, Canada, pays aux économies développés d'Europe, Israë
  Japon, Australie, Nouvelle Zélande et l'Afrique du Sud.

3 Cette classification est utilisée pour plus de commodité dans la
  présentation des statistiques et n'implique pas nécessairement un
  jugement quant au stage de développement auquel est parvenu un
  pays donné.
4 Compris de l'Europe l'Est et les pays européennes de l'ancienne
  URSS.

5 Importations FOB.
6 Y compris le commerce des isles Vierges américaines et de Porto
  Rico mais non compris les échanges de merchandises entre les
  Etats−Unis et leurs autres possessions (Guam, Samoa américaines,

72
Total imports and exports
Imports c.i.f. and exports f.o.b., value in million US dollars
Importations et exportations totales
Importations c.a.f. et exportations f.o.b., valeur en millions de dollars E.−U.

include imports and exports of non−monetary gold.

7 Trade data include maquiladoras and exclude goods from customs−bonded warehouses. Total exports include revaluation and exports of silver.

8 Export and import values exclude trade in the processing zone.

9 Prior to 1986, includes Aruba.

10 Exports include re−exports and petroleum products.

11 Economic Union of Belgium and Luxembourg. Intertrade between the two countries is excluded. Beginning January 1997, data refer to Belgium only and include trade between Belgium and Luxembourg.

12 Prior to January 1991, excludes trade conducted in accordance with the supplementary protocol to the treaty on the basis of relations between the Federal Republic of Germany and the former German Democratic Republic.

13 Beginning 1997, trade data for France include the import and export values of French Guiana, Guadeloupe, Martinique, and Reunion.

14 Data prior to January 1991 pertaining to the territorial boundaries of the Federal Republic of Germany prior to 3 October 1990.

15 Beginning January 1994, foreign trade statistics exclude re−exports.

16 Beginning 1990, trade statistics exclude certain oil and chemical products.

17 Prior to 1996 data exclude customs free zones, repairs on goods, and operational leasing.

18 Exports include gold.

19 Beginning in January 1998, foreign trade data refer to South Africa only, excluding intra−trade of the Southern African Common Customs Area. Prior to January 1998, trade data refer to the Southern African Common Customs Area, which includes Botswana, Lesotho, Namibia, South Africa and Swaziland.

20 Imports exclude petroleum imported without stated value. Exports cover domestic exports.

21 Imports and exports net of returned goods. The figures also exclude Judea and Samaria and the Gaza area.

22 Imports exclude military imports.

23 Data include Armenia, Azerbaijan, Georgia, Kazakhstan, Kyrgyzstan, Tajikistan, Turkmenistan, and Uzbekistan.

24 Comprises trade of the former Democratic Yemen and the former Yemen Arab Republic including any inter−trade between them.

25 Data include oil and gas. Data on the value and volume of oil exports and on the value of total exports are rough estimates based on information published in various petroleum industry journals.

26 Data refer to total exports less petroleum exports of Asia Middle East countries where petroleum, in this case, is the sum of SITC groups 333, 334 and 335.

27 Beginning 1989, data exclude re−exports.

28 Prior to January 1992, data refer to the Socialist Federal Republic of Yugoslavia.

29 Prior to 1997, included under Belgium. See also footnote for Belgium.

30 Excluding intra−EU trade.

etc). Les données comprennent les importations et exportations d'or non monétaire.

7 Les statistiques du commerce extérieur comprennent maquiladoras et et ne comprennent maquiladoras et ne comprennent pas les marchandises provenant des entrepôts en douane. Les exportations comprennent la réevaluation et les données sur les exportations d'argent.

8 Les valeurs à l'exportation et à l'importation excluent le commerce de la zone de transformation.

9 Avant 1986, comprend Aruba.

10 Exportations comprennent re−exportations et produits pétroliers.

11 L'Union économique belgo−luxembourgeoise. Non compris le commerce entre ces pays. A partir de janvier 1997, les données se rapportent à Belgique seulement et recouvrent les échanges entre la Belgique et le Luxembourg.

12 Avant janvier 1991, non compris le commerce effectué en accord avec le protocole additionnel au traité définissant la base des relations entre la République Fédérale d'Allemagne et l'ancienne République Démocratique Allemagne.

13 A compter de 1997, les valeurs de commerce pour la France comprennent les valeurs des importations et des exportations de la Guyane franç, la Guadeloupe, la Martinique, et la Réunion.

14 Les données relatives à la période précédantjanvier 1991 correspondentaux limites territoriales de la République fédérales d'Allemagne autérieur au 3 octobre 1990.

15 A partir de janvier 1994, les statistiques du commerce exterieur non compris les réexportations.

16 A compter de 1990, les statistiques commerciales font exclusion de certains produits pétroliers et chimiques.

17 Avant de 1996 les données excluent des zones franches, des réparations sur des marchandises, et le crédit−bail opérationnel.

18 Les exportations comprennent l'or.

19 A compter de janvier 1998, les données sur le commerce extérieur ne se rapportent qu'à l'Afrique du Sud. et ne tiennent pas compte des échanges commerciaux entre les pays de l'Union douanière de l'Afrique, du Sud, qui incluait l'Afrique du Sud le Botswana, le Lesotho, la Namibie, et le Swaziland.

20 Non compris le petrole brute dont la valeur des importations n'sont pas stipulée. Les exportations sont les exportations d'intérieur.

21 Importations et exportations nets, ne comprennant pas les marchandises retournées. Sont egalement exclues les données de la Judée et de Samaria et ainsi que la zone de Gaza.

22 Non compris les importations des economats militaires.

23 Données compris Arménie, Azerbaïdjan, Georgie, Kazakhstan, Kirghizistan, Ouzbékistan, Tadjikistan et Turkménistan.

24 Y compris le commerce de l'ancienne République populaire démocratique de Yémen, le commerce de l'ancienne République arabe de Yémen et le commerce entre eux.

25 Les données comprennent le pétrole et le gaz. Les données relatives à la valeur et au volume des exportations de pétrole et à la valeur des exportations totales sont des estimations approximatives établies syr la base des données des journaux de l'industrie pétrolier.

26 Les données se rapportent aux exportations totales moins les exportations pétrolières de moyen−orient d'Asie. Dans ce cas, le pétrole est la somme des groupes CTCI 333, 334 et 335.

27 A compter de 1989, les données non compris les réexportations.

28 Avant 1992, les données se rapportent à la République fédérative socialiste de Yougoslavie.

29 Avant 1997, inclus sous la Belgique. Voir également l'apostille pour la Belgique.

30 Non compris le commerce l'intra−UE.

73
Total imports and exports : index numbers
Importations et exportations : indices

1990 = 100

Country or area	1993	1994	1995	1996	1997	1998	1999	2000	2001	Pays ou zone
Argentina										**Argentine**
Imports: Quantum	399	459	503	603	782	856	733	794	605	Imp.: quantum
Imports: Unit value	98	100	98	104	95	90	98	107	...	Imp.: valeur unitaire
Exports: Quantum	136	179	152	162	181	208	202	221	222	Exp.: quantum
Exports: Unit value	111	115	111	129	114	104	106	123	...	Exp.: valeur unitaire
Terms of trade	113	115	113	124	120	115	108	114	...	Termes de l'échange
Purchasing power	154	206	173	202	216	239	217	252	...	Pouvoir d'achat
Australia										**Australie**
Imports: Quantum	115	133	148	161	180	195	215	233	223	Imp.: quantum
Imports: Unit value [1]	99	105	109	109	103	95	95	94	88	Imp.: valeur unitaire [1]
Exports: Quantum	128	139	141	157	179	178	187	205	211	Exp.: quantum
Exports: Unit value [1]	82	86	94	95	91	81	77	80	79	Exp.: valeur unitaire [1]
Terms of trade	83	82	85	87	88	85	81	86	89	Termes de l'échange
Purchasing power	106	114	120	136	158	152	151	176	188	Pouvoir d'achat
Austria										**Autriche**
Imports: Quantum	106	140	125	129	164	188	206	223	...	Imp.: quantum
Imports: Unit value	93	94	108	98	80	74	69	60	58	Imp.: valeur unitaire
Exports: Quantum	108	152	140	147	192	220	269	268	...	Exp.: quantum
Exports: Unit value	88	84	97	89	72	67	56	54	51	Exp.: valeur unitaire
Terms of trade	95	90	90	91	90	91	81	89	88	Termes de l'échange
Purchasing power	102	138	126	134	173	200	218	240	...	Pouvoir d'achat
Belgium										**Belgique**
Imports: Quantum	106	115	121	126	131	141	141	155	161	Imp.: quantum
Imports: Unit value	88	91	106	105	96	93	90	88	87	Imp.: valeur unitaire
Exports: Quantum	111	123	131	134	144	151	156	171	175	Exp.: quantum
Exports: Unit value	92	94	110	107	98	96	92	87	86	Exp.: valeur unitaire
Terms of trade	104	103	103	102	102	104	102	99	99	Termes de l'échange
Purchasing power	116	127	135	137	146	156	159	170	174	Pouvoir d'achat
Bolivia										**Bolivie**
Exports: Quantum	93	95	91	93	98	93	85	97	103	Exp.: quantum
Exports: Unit value	64	66	73	72	55	49	48	61	58	Exp.: valeur unitaire
Brazil										**Brésil**
Imports: Quantum	136	142	176	190	161	162	150	163	164	Imp.: quantum
Imports: Unit value	91	113	136	133	180	167	152	158	158	Imp.: valeur unitaire
Exports: Quantum	109	116	120	119	125	138	137	146	163	Exp.: quantum
Exports: Unit value	113	119	124	128	136	119	112	120	114	Exp.: valeur unitaire
Terms of trade	125	106	91	96	75	71	74	76	72	Termes de l'échange
Purchasing power	136	123	109	115	94	98	101	111	118	Pouvoir d'achat
Canada										**Canada**
Imports: Quantum	120	133	143	151	179	190	207	226	226	Imp.: quantum
Imports: Unit value	98	98	102	102	101	98	97	100	96	Imp.: valeur unitaire
Exports: Quantum	123	138	152	161	175	189	210	229	229	Exp.: quantum
Exports: Unit value	93	94	102	103	101	94	94	102	98	Exp.: valeur unitaire
Terms of trade	95	96	100	101	100	96	97	103	103	Termes de l'échange
Purchasing power	118	133	152	163	174	182	204	234	235	Pouvoir d'achat
China, Hong Kong SAR										**Chine, Hong Kong RAS**
Imports: Quantum	164	187	213	222	238	221	221	261	256	Imp.: quantum
Imports: Unit value	102	105	110	109	106	101	99	99	96	Imp.: valeur unitaire
Exports: Quantum	160	176	197	207	219	210	218	255	246	Exp.: quantum
Exports: Unit value	104	105	109	108	107	103	100	99	97	Exp.: valeur unitaire
Terms of trade	102	100	99	100	100	102	101	100	101	Termes de l'échange
Purchasing power	162	177	195	206	220	213	220	255	248	Pouvoir d'achat
Colombia										**Colombie**
Imports: Unit value	84	94	100	101	99	91	85	82	...	Imp.: valeur unitaire
Exports: Unit value	77	104	112	104	116	103	96	100	88	Exp.: valeur unitaire
Terms of trade	92	111	112	104	117	113	113	122	...	Termes de l'échange
Denmark										**Danemark**
Imports: Quantum	114	118	126	128	139	145	148	156	...	Imp.: quantum
Imports: Unit value	89	93	107	104	94	93	88	82	...	Imp.: valeur unitaire
Exports: Quantum	113	122	116	119	127	128	135	144	...	Exp.: quantum
Exports: Unit value	91	94	107	105	94	92	89	83	...	Exp.: valeur unitaire
Terms of trade	103	102	100	101	100	99	100	102	...	Termes de l'échange
Purchasing power	116	124	116	120	126	127	136	146	...	Pouvoir d'achat

73
Total imports and exports : index numbers
Importations et exportations : indices

1990 = 100

Country or area	1993	1994	1995	1996	1997	1998	1999	2000	2001	Pays ou zone
Dominica										**Dominique**
Exports: Quantum	95	107	68	...	...	...	...	...	...	Exp.: quantum
Exports: Unit value	89	97	100	...	...	...	...	...	...	Exp.: valeur unitaire
Dominican Republic										**Rép. dominicaine**
Exports: Quantum	95	92	96	101	104	99	...	...	...	Exp.: quantum
Exports: Unit value	75	90	101	102	106	83	...	...	...	Exp.: valeur unitaire
Ecuador										**Equateur**
Imports: Quantum	...	103	138	133	182	228	132	137	171	Imp.: quantum
Exports: Quantum	124	138	154	157	157	149	143	154	156	Exp.: quantum
Exports: Unit value	74	83	84	96	94	70	85	110	95	Exp.: valeur unitaire
Ethiopia										**Ethiopie**
Exports: Quantum	125	94	80	...	...	...	...	...	...	Exp.: quantum
Exports: Unit value	65	94	118	...	...	...	...	...	...	Exp.: valeur unitaire
Finland										**Finlande**
Imports: Quantum	79	95	102	110	119	129	129	135	132	Imp.: quantum
Imports: Unit value	85	91	108	104	95	92	92	90	89	Imp.: valeur unitaire
Exports: Quantum	117	133	143	151	169	178	185	200	199	Exp.: quantum
Exports: Unit value	75	83	106	100	90	90	87	85	82	Exp.: valeur unitaire
Terms of trade	89	92	98	96	95	97	95	94	92	Termes de l'échange
Purchasing power	104	122	141	146	161	173	176	189	183	Pouvoir d'achat
France										**France**
Imports: Quantum	107	117	123	126	135	146	152	168	...	Imp.: quantum
Imports: Unit value	87	92	104	103	92	90	86	79	...	Imp.: valeur unitaire
Exports: Quantum	111	120	129	134	147	157	166	185	...	Exp.: quantum
Exports: Unit value	90	99	111	109	98	96	91	80	...	Exp.: valeur unitaire
Terms of trade	104	107	107	105	106	106	106	101	...	Termes de l'échange
Purchasing power	115	127	137	141	155	166	175	187	...	Pouvoir d'achat
Germany										**Allemagne**
Imports: Quantum	104	114	115	122	133	146	153	172	173	Imp.: quantum
Imports: Unit value	91	94	110	102	91	88	82	79	77	Imp.: valeur unitaire
Exports: Quantum	98	112	116	125	140	152	159	182	188	Exp.: quantum
Exports: Unit value	92	93	107	100	87	85	80	72	72	Exp.: valeur unitaire
Terms of trade	101	98	98	98	96	97	98	91	93	Termes de l'échange
Purchasing power	99	110	114	123	134	148	155	166	174	Pouvoir d'achat
Greece										**Grèce**
Imports: Quantum	143	150	163	178	180	219	231	...	...	Imp.: quantum
Imports: Unit value	77	72	77	69	65	66	64	58	64	Imp.: valeur unitaire
Exports: Quantum	143	149	164	175	194	221	235	...	...	Exp.: quantum
Exports: Unit value	76	79	84	69	58	61	72	68	75	Exp.: valeur unitaire
Terms of trade	98	110	109	100	90	93	112	118	117	Termes de l'échange
Purchasing power	140	164	179	175	174	205	263	...	...	Pouvoir d'achat
Guatemala										**Guatemala**
Imports: Quantum	133	148	...	...	...	...	...	...	...	Imp.: quantum
Imports: Unit value	119	109	...	...	...	...	...	...	...	Imp.: valeur unitaire
Exports: Quantum	136	147	...	...	...	...	...	...	...	Exp.: quantum
Exports: Unit value	85	88	98	89	...	...	...	...	...	Exp.: valeur unitaire
Terms of trade	72	81	...	...	...	...	...	...	...	Termes de l'échange
Purchasing power	97	119	...	...	...	...	...	...	...	Pouvoir d'achat
Honduras										**Honduras**
Exports: Quantum	90	79	83	99	86	86	...	...	...	Exp.: quantum
Exports: Unit value	78	89	123	115	119	116	...	...	...	Exp.: valeur unitaire
Hungary										**Hongrie**
Imports: Quantum	119	136	131	138	174	217	248	299	313	Imp.: quantum
Imports: Unit value	120	121	134	133	123	120	114	108	109	Imp.: valeur unitaire
Exports: Quantum	84	97	106	110	143	175	203	247	267	Exp.: quantum
Exports: Unit value	109	113	126	123	115	114	106	98	99	Exp.: valeur unitaire
Terms of trade	91	93	94	93	93	95	93	90	90	Termes de l'échange
Purchasing power	76	91	99	102	134	167	189	224	241	Pouvoir d'achat
Iceland										**Islande**
Imports: Quantum	84	90	96	111	118	147	154	160	145	Imp.: quantum
Imports: Unit value	97	99	111	111	104	103	99	98	96	Imp.: valeur unitaire
Exports: Quantum	96	108	105	115	117	113	122	122	131	Exp.: quantum
Exports: Unit value	92	94	108	104	100	107	104	98	97	Exp.: valeur unitaire
Terms of trade	95	96	97	93	96	105	104	100	101	Termes de l'échange
Purchasing power	91	103	102	107	113	119	127	122	133	Pouvoir d'achat

73
Total imports and exports : index numbers
Importations et exportations : indices

1990 = 100

Country or area	1993	1994	1995	1996	1997	1998	1999	2000	2001	Pays ou zone
India										**Inde**
Imports: Quantum	138	168	261	186	199	292	309	346	...	Imp.: quantum
Imports: Unit value	68	68	59	83	102	59	58	62	...	Imp.: valeur unitaire
Exports: Quantum	140	154	189	236	205	206	213	287	...	Exp.: quantum
Exports: Unit value	89	94	90	78	91	85	93	84	...	Exp.: valeur unitaire
Terms of trade	132	137	152	93	89	143	161	134	...	Termes de l'échange
Purchasing power	185	211	286	220	182	294	343	384	...	Pouvoir d'achat
Indonesia										**Indonésie**
Exports: Quantum	148	163	171	179	230	214	...	...	253	Exp.: quantum
Exports: Unit value	77	97	111	117	111	87	...	...	97	Exp.: valeur unitaire
Ireland										**Irlande**
Imports: Quantum	113	128	146	161	185	218	236	275	274	Imp.: quantum
Imports: Unit value	93	98	109	107	102	99	96	90	90	Imp.: valeur unitaire
Exports: Quantum	133	153	184	202	232	289	336	401	422	Exp.: quantum
Exports: Unit value	92	94	102	102	97	94	94	85	84	Exp.: valeur unitaire
Terms of trade	99	96	94	94	95	95	97	94	93	Termes de l'échange
Purchasing power	132	147	173	191	221	275	328	379	391	Pouvoir d'achat
Israel										**Israël**
Imports: Quantum	146	166	182	194	197	197	226	257	238	Imp.: quantum
Imports: Unit value	92	94	102	101	96	91	88	91	90	Imp.: valeur unitaire
Exports: Quantum	121	140	150	161	177	188	204	256	245	Exp.: quantum
Exports: Unit value	102	100	105	105	104	101	102	102	98	Exp.: valeur unitaire
Terms of trade	111	107	103	104	108	111	115	112	110	Termes de l'échange
Purchasing power	134	150	155	167	191	208	235	286	269	Pouvoir d'achat
Italy										**Italie**
Imports: Quantum	114	108	119	113	124	135	145	158	157	Imp.: quantum
Imports: Unit value	84	85	73	78	71	68	64	63	63	Imp.: valeur unitaire
Exports: Quantum	112	125	141	138	145	149	149	167	166	Exp.: quantum
Exports: Unit value	115	116	96	106	96	95	91	83	84	Exp.: valeur unitaire
Terms of trade	137	136	131	136	135	140	141	130	133	Termes de l'échange
Purchasing power	153	169	184	188	195	209	211	218	222	Pouvoir d'achat
Japan										**Japon**
Imports: Quantum	107	121	136	141	145	137	150	166	164	Imp.: quantum
Imports: Unit value	97	97	105	105	100	87	88	97	90	Imp.: valeur unitaire
Exports: Quantum	102	103	107	107	117	116	118	129	116	Exp.: quantum
Exports: Unit value	124	134	145	133	125	116	123	129	121	Exp.: valeur unitaire
Terms of trade	129	138	138	127	125	134	140	133	134	Termes de l'échange
Purchasing power	131	143	147	136	147	155	166	172	155	Pouvoir d'achat
Jordan										**Jordanie**
Imports: Quantum	224	219	152	164	160	151	149	178	186	Imp.: quantum
Imports: Unit value	86	83	94	101	99	98	96	98	100	Imp.: valeur unitaire
Exports: Quantum	143	153	137	134	143	147	151	163	200	Exp.: quantum
Exports: Unit value	92	96	111	117	113	107	104	100	101	Exp.: valeur unitaire
Terms of trade	107	115	118	115	114	109	109	101	101	Termes de l'échange
Purchasing power	153	176	162	154	163	160	164	165	202	Pouvoir d'achat
Kenya										**Kenya**
Imports: Quantum	97	121	141	140	149	150	136	157	...	Imp.: quantum
Imports: Unit value	84	78	96	95	100	98	92	94	...	Imp.: valeur unitaire
Exports: Quantum	133	153	183	...	...	...	...	...	...	Exp.: quantum
Exports: Unit value	105	111	129	123	141	138	112	110	...	Exp.: valeur unitaire
Terms of trade	126	143	134	130	142	141	122	118	...	Termes de l'échange
Purchasing power	167	219	246	...	...	...	...	...	...	Pouvoir d'achat
Korea, Republic of										**Corée, République de**
Imports: Quantum	236	287	187	216	220	165	212	253	247	Imp.: quantum
Imports: Unit value	95	95	104	99	99	82	81	93	84	Imp.: valeur unitaire
Exports: Quantum	230	264	181	213	244	291	326	393	396	Exp.: quantum
Exports: Unit value	113	117	106	92	79	62	61	61	53	Exp.: valeur unitaire
Terms of trade	120	123	102	93	80	76	75	66	63	Termes de l'échange
Purchasing power	276	324	185	197	195	222	243	257	248	Pouvoir d'achat
Malaysia										**Malaisie**
Exports: Quantum	86	84	84	...	...	...	...	...	...	Exp.: quantum
Mauritius										**Maurice**
Imports: Unit value	99	105	115	119	103	96	98	97	94	Imp.: valeur unitaire
Exports: Unit value	104	107	117	126	110	111	105	99	91	Exp.: valeur unitaire
Terms of trade	104	102	102	106	107	115	108	102	97	Termes de l'échange

73
Total imports and exports : index numbers
Importations et exportations : indices

1990 = 100

Country or area	1993	1994	1995	1996	1997	1998	1999	2000	2001	Pays ou zone
Mexico										**Mexique**
Imports: Unit value	102	...	...	...	...	...	...	...	...	Imp.: valeur unitaire
Exports: Unit value	89	...	...	...	...	...	...	...	...	Exp.: valeur unitaire
Terms of trade	87	...	...	...	...	...	...	...	...	Termes de l'échange
Morocco										**Maroc**
Imports: Quantum	120	96	...	...	...	...	...	...	...	Imp.: quantum
Imports: Unit value	89	102	...	...	...	...	...	...	...	Imp.: valeur unitaire
Exports: Quantum	105	115	...	...	...	...	...	...	...	Exp.: quantum
Exports: Unit value	85	84	124	...	...	...	...	...	...	Exp.: valeur unitaire
Terms of trade	95	82	...	...	...	...	...	...	...	Termes de l'échange
Purchasing power	100	95	...	...	...	...	...	...	...	Pouvoir d'achat
Myanmar										**Myanmar**
Exports: Quantum	149	145	151	104	110	...	...	...	...	Exp.: quantum
Exports: Unit value	82	91	150	138	132	...	...	...	...	Exp.: valeur unitaire
Netherlands										**Pays–Bas**
Imports: Quantum	110	121	136	143	152	166	179	187	188	Imp.: quantum
Imports: Unit value	90	92	104	100	92	88	84	81	81	Imp.: valeur unitaire
Exports: Quantum	116	129	140	146	159	171	179	195	195	Exp.: quantum
Exports: Unit value	90	92	106	101	93	89	83	82	82	Exp.: valeur unitaire
Terms of trade	100	100	102	101	102	101	98	100	101	Termes de l'échange
Purchasing power	116	129	143	148	162	173	176	195	197	Pouvoir d'achat
New Zealand										**Nouvelle–Zélande**
Imports: Quantum	104	122	129	134	139	142	161	157	160	Imp.: quantum
Imports: Unit value	97	104	113	115	110	92	93	93	87	Imp.: valeur unitaire
Exports: Quantum	118	130	134	140	147	146	149	157	165	Exp.: quantum
Exports: Unit value	96	102	110	111	104	89	89	89	90	Exp.: valeur unitaire
Terms of trade	99	98	97	97	95	96	96	96	103	Termes de l'échange
Purchasing power	117	127	130	135	140	141	142	152	170	Pouvoir d'achat
Norway										**Norvège**
Imports: Quantum [2]	107	122	134	147	160	181	182	194	196	Imp.: quantum [2]
Imports: Unit value [2]	85	86	97	94	84	78	73	67	65	Imp.: valeur unitaire [2]
Exports: Quantum [2]	121	136	145	163	172	172	176	185	194	Exp.: quantum [2]
Exports: Unit value [2]	77	75	86	91	84	70	77	98	92	Exp.: valeur unitaire [2]
Terms of trade	91	87	89	97	100	89	105	147	140	Termes de l'échange
Purchasing power	110	119	128	158	172	154	186	273	271	Pouvoir d'achat
Pakistan										**Pakistan**
Imports: Quantum	124	120	129	127	130	130	140	138	155	Imp.: quantum
Imports: Unit value	91	98	107	103	47	41	44	50	45	Imp.: valeur unitaire
Exports: Quantum	112	139	110	130	123	119	134	150	153	Exp.: quantum
Exports: Unit value	90	96	117	114	114	117	108	102	93	Exp.: valeur unitaire
Terms of trade	98	99	110	111	245	282	244	205	206	Termes de l'échange
Purchasing power	110	137	121	144	300	336	326	307	315	Pouvoir d'achat
Panama										**Panama**
Exports: Quantum	126	...	...	...	...	113	84	79	...	Exp.: quantum
Papua New Guinea										**Papouasie–Nvl–Guinée**
Exports: Unit value	110	124	137	132	135	105	95	...	...	Exp.: valeur unitaire
Peru										**Pérou**
Exports: Quantum	121	132	133	141	153	132	148	168	191	Exp.: quantum
Exports: Unit value	75	86	106	112	109	84	90	120	100	Exp.: valeur unitaire
Phillipines										**Phillipines**
Imports: Quantum	58	70	41	48	52	41	46	49	48	Imp.: quantum
Imports: Unit value [1]	97	101	101	104	94	70	68	58	48	Imp.: valeur unitaire [1]
Exports: Quantum	78	93	60	67	79	85	93	107	95	Exp.: quantum
Exports: Unit value [1]	...	...	...	...	...	69	79	65	54	Exp.: valeur unitaire [1]
Terms of trade	...	...	...	...	...	98	116	112	112	Termes de l'échange
Purchasing power	...	...	...	...	...	84	108	120	107	Pouvoir d'achat
Poland										**Pologne**
Imports: Quantum	186	211	254	325	397	473	492	526	562	Imp.: quantum
Imports: Unit value [1]	92	94	100	105	98	97	90	85	88	Imp.: valeur unitaire [1]
Exports: Quantum	94	111	130	142	162	173	183	226	257	Exp.: quantum
Exports: Unit value [1]	99	102	116	113	105	107	100	92	95	Exp.: valeur unitaire [1]
Terms of trade	107	109	117	108	107	109	110	108	107	Termes de l'échange
Purchasing power	101	121	152	154	174	189	202	245	276	Pouvoir d'achat

73
Total imports and exports : index numbers
Importations et exportations : indices

1990 = 100

Country or area	1993	1994	1995	1996	1997	1998	1999	2000	2001	Pays ou zone
Rwanda										**Rwanda**
Exports: Quantum	73	30	51	49	121	129	...	...	...	Exp.: quantum
Exports: Unit value	74	61	127	123	139	67	...	...	...	Exp.: valeur unitaire
Serbia and Montenegro										**Serbie−et−Monténégro**
Imports: Unit Value	121	...	...	...	...	...	...	...	...	Imp.: valeur unitaire
Seychelles										**Seychelles**
Imports: Quantum	147	124	135	227	200	...	...	...	...	Imp.: quantum
Imports: Unit value	87	89	92	89	91	85	...	...	...	Imp.: valeur unitaire
Exports: Quantum	106	172	139	256	421	...	...	...	...	Exp.: quantum
Exports: Unit value	104	95	125	116	117	152	117	...	...	Exp.: valeur unitaire
Terms of trade	119	106	135	130	128	179	...	...	...	Termes de l'échange
Purchasing power	126	183	187	333	538	...	...	...	...	Pouvoir d'achat
Singapore										**Singapour**
Imports: Quantum	137	157	177	188	203	184	194	220	196	Imp.: quantum
Imports: Unit value [1]	103	108	116	115	107	94	94	100	97	Imp.: valeur unitaire [1]
Exports: Quantum	145	187	216	229	245	248	261	302	288	Exp.: quantum
Exports: Unit value [1]	97	98	104	103	97	84	83	86	80	Exp.: valeur unitaire [1]
Terms of trade	94	91	90	90	90	90	89	86	83	Termes de l'échange
Purchasing power	137	171	194	207	221	223	232	260	238	Pouvoir d'achat
South Africa										**Afrique du Sud**
Imports: Quantum	108	125	136	155	...	...	...	...	...	Imp.: quantum
Imports: Unit value	99	100	112	100	...	...	...	...	...	Imp.: valeur unitaire
Exports: Quantum	109	115	119	169	...	...	...	...	...	Exp.: quantum
Exports: Unit value	96	100	114	106	...	...	...	...	...	Exp.: valeur unitaire
Terms of trade	98	99	102	106	...	...	...	...	...	Termes de l'échange
Purchasing power	106	114	122	179	...	...	...	...	...	Pouvoir d'achat
Spain										**Espagne**
Imports: Quantum	118	131	...	...	...	...	...	...	...	Imp.: quantum
Imports: Unit value [1]	81	81	91	90	81	77	74	72	70	Imp.: valeur unitaire [1]
Exports: Quantum	135	160	...	...	...	...	...	...	...	Exp.: quantum
Exports: Unit value [1]	84	83	95	94	84	83	78	72	72	Exp.: valeur unitaire [1]
Terms of trade	104	102	104	105	105	107	106	100	103	Termes de l'échange
Purchasing power	140	164	...	...	...	...	...	...	...	Pouvoir d'achat
Sri Lanka										**Sri Lanka**
Imports: Quantum	136	153	178	179	201	218	218	244	221	Imp.: quantum
Imports: Unit value	95	98	109	112	109	...	...	...	...	Imp.: valeur unitaire
Exports: Quantum	108	118	145	151	167	165	173	205	188	Exp.: quantum
Exports: Unit value	95	98	132	136	140	146	133	133	129	Exp.: valeur unitaire
Terms of trade	100	100	120	122	128	...	...	...	...	Termes de l'échange
Purchasing power	108	117	175	184	214	...	...	...	...	Pouvoir d'achat
Sweden										**Suède**
Imports: Quantum	97	108	109	102	110	110	103	112	94	Imp.: quantum
Imports: Unit value [1]	85	90	103	106	95	90	89	86	80	Imp.: valeur unitaire [1]
Exports: Quantum	107	114	112	106	111	100	106	111	96	Exp.: quantum
Exports: Unit value [1]	82	85	97	98	87	83	79	74	67	Exp.: valeur unitaire [1]
Terms of trade	97	94	94	93	92	92	89	86	83	Termes de l'échange
Purchasing power	104	108	105	98	102	92	94	95	80	Pouvoir d'achat
Switzerland										**Suisse**
Imports: Quantum	93	102	109	110	117	126	137	146	146	Imp.: quantum
Imports: Unit value	94	97	109	104	94	90	85	80	82	Imp.: valeur unitaire
Exports: Quantum	104	109	114	115	124	130	135	144	147	Exp.: quantum
Exports: Unit value	97	104	117	113	100	99	97	89	91	Exp.: valeur unitaire
Terms of trade	103	107	107	108	107	110	114	111	111	Termes de l'échange
Purchasing power	107	117	122	125	132	143	153	160	164	Pouvoir d'achat
Syrian Arab Republic										**Rép. arabe syrienne**
Imports: Quantum	225	276	248	250	218	...	...	...	...	Imp.: quantum
Imports: Unit value	93	105	118	125	107	...	...	...	...	Imp.: valeur unitaire
Exports: Quantum	158	171	167	164	183	...	...	...	...	Exp.: quantum
Exports: Unit value	67	72	90	95	75	...	...	...	...	Exp.: valeur unitaire
Terms of trade	72	69	76	76	70	...	...	...	...	Termes de l'échange
Purchasing power	114	117	127	125	128	...	...	...	...	Pouvoir d'achat

73
Total imports and exports : index numbers
Importations et exportations : indices

1990 = 100

Country or area	1993	1994	1995	1996	1997	1998	1999	2000	2001	Pays ou zone
Thailand										**Thaïlande**
Imports: Quantum	130	151	170	154	137	100	124	150	134	Imp.: quantum
Imports: Unit value	107	111	125	139	136	122	119	125	136	Imp.: valeur unitaire
Exports: Quantum	149	177	243	219	235	254	284	346	327	Exp.: quantum
Exports: Unit value	107	111	121	132	126	110	106	104	102	Exp.: valeur unitaire
Terms of trade	100	100	97	95	93	90	89	83	75	Termes de l'échange
Purchasing power	149	177	235	207	218	229	253	287	246	Pouvoir d'achat
Tunisia										**Tunisie**
Imports: Quantum	116	120	...	...	...	...	...	...	...	Imp.: quantum
Imports: Unit value	82	...	...	...	...	...	...	...	...	Imp.: valeur unitaire
Exports: Quantum	121	137	...	...	...	...	...	...	...	Exp.: quantum
Exports: Unit value	84	87	...	...	...	...	...	...	...	Exp.: valeur unitaire
Terms of trade	102	...	...	...	...	...	...	...	...	Termes de l'échange
Purchasing power	123	...	...	...	...	...	...	...	...	Pouvoir d'achat
Turkey										**Turquie**
Imports: Quantum	134	99	128	166	205	200	198	262	197	Imp.: quantum
Imports: Unit value	89	95	111	105	96	92	87	91	90	Imp.: valeur unitaire
Exports: Quantum	117	134	143	157	178	195	201	224	274	Exp.: quantum
Exports: Unit value	98	95	107	102	97	93	87	83	81	Exp.: valeur unitaire
Terms of trade	110	99	96	97	102	102	100	92	90	Termes de l'échange
Purchasing power	128	133	137	153	181	199	202	206	246	Pouvoir d'achat
United Kingdom										**Royaume−Uni**
Imports: Quantum	101	108	112	123	135	148	159	178	183	Imp.: quantum
Imports: Unit value [1]	94	99	112	111	109	103	99	97	92	Imp.: valeur unitaire [1]
Exports: Quantum	103	116	125	136	146	148	155	173	174	Exp.: quantum
Exports: Unit value [1]	97	101	111	111	110	105	102	99	94	Exp.: valeur unitaire [1]
Terms of trade	103	102	99	100	101	102	102	102	102	Termes de l'échange
Purchasing power	106	118	124	135	147	151	159	176	178	Pouvoir d'achat
United States										**Etats−Unis**
Imports: Quantum	117	131	140	148	166	186	206	230	224	Imp.: quantum
Imports: Unit value [1]	100	102	106	107	105	98	99	106	102	Imp.: valeur unitaire [1]
Exports: Quantum [3]	116	126	137	145	162	166	173	190	179	Exp.: quantum [3]
Exports: Unit value [1,3]	101	104	109	109	108	104	103	105	104	Exp.: valeur unitaire [1,3]
Terms of trade	101	102	102	102	103	106	104	99	102	Termes de l'échange
Purchasing power	118	128	140	148	167	176	179	188	182	Pouvoir d'achat
Uruguay										**Uruguay**
Exports: Unit value	93	95	105	102	...	...	...	...	...	Exp.: valeur unitaire
Venezuela										**Venezuela**
Imports: Unit value [1]	98	108	139	122	129	134	135	131	133	Imp.: valeur unitaire [1]
Exports: Unit value	66	64	...	...	...	...	...	...	...	Exp.: valeur unitaire
Terms of trade	67	59	...	...	...	...	...	...	...	Termes de l'échange

Source:
United Nations Statistics Division, New York, trade statistics
database.

Source:
Organisation des Nations Unies, Division de statistique, New York, la base de
données pour les statistiques du commerce extérieur.

1 Price index numbers. For Philippines beginning 1998, for the
  United States beginning 1989, for the United Kingdom
  starting 1999.
2 Excluding ships.
3 Excludes military exports.

1 Indices des prix. Pour Philippines, à partir de 1998; pour les Etats−Unis
  à partir de 1989; pour le Royaume−Uni, à partir de 1999.

2 Non compris les navires.
3 Non compris les exportations militaires.

74

Manufactured goods exports
Unit value and quantum indices: 1990 = 100; value: thousand million US dollars

Exportations des produits manufacturés
Indices de valeur unitaire et de volume: 1990 = 100; valeur: milliards de dollars des E.-U.

Country or area Pays ou zone	1992	1993	1994	1995	1996	1997	1998	1999	2000	2001
Total Total										
Unit value indices, US $[1]										
Ind. de valeur unitaire, $ des E.-U.[1]	103	98	100	110	106	99	95	91	88	...
Unit value indices, SDR										
Ind. de valeur unitaire, DTS	99	96	95	99	99	97	95	90	91	...
Quantum indices[1]										
Indices de volume[1]	111	115	130	141	152	171	172	180	206	...
Value, thousand million US $[1]										
Valeur, millards de $ des E.-U.[1]	2 747.30	2 729.60	3 141.80	3 744.20	3 872.70	4 068.50	3 935.30	3 931.70	4 355.20	...
Developed economies Economies développées										
Unit value indices, US $										
Ind. de valeur unitaire, $ des E.-U.	103	97	99	110	106	99	95	91	87	84
Unit value indices, SDR										
Ind. de valeur unitaire, DTS	100	95	94	98	99	97	95	91	89	90
Quantum indices										
Indices de volume	106	108	121	129	137	153	161	170	189	195
Value, thousand million US $										
Valeur, millards de $ des E.-U.	2 148.10	2 064.30	2 346.20	2 774.60	2 847.20	2 959.80	2 993.30	3 031.70	3 211.60	3 213.20
America Amérique										
Unit value indices, US $										
Ind. de valeur unitaire, $ des E.-U.	100	99	99	102	102	103	102	101	102	101
Quantum indices										
Indices de volume	114	121	137	152	162	179	183	193	207	214
Value, thousand million US $										
Valeur, millards de $ des E.-U.	413.80	435.09	490.11	557.03	593.68	667.70	675.62	703.74	763.59	781.36
Canada Canada										
Unit value indices, US $										
Ind. de valeur unitaire, $ des E.-U.	91	88	84	87	88	89	85	83	84	81
Unit value indices, national currency										
Ind. de val. unitaire, monnaie nat.	94	98	99	102	103	105	108	106	106	108
Quantum indices										
Indices de volume	119	135	164	187	193	204	223	253	254	263
Value, thousand million US $										
Valeur, millards de $ des E.-U.	84.61	93.80	109.17	128.22	134.01	142.90	148.67	165.60	167.30	168.78
United States Etats-Unis										
Unit value indices, US $[2]										
Ind. de valeur unitaire, $ des E.-U.[2]	103	103	104	107	106	108	108	108	109	108
Unit value indices, national currency[2]										
Ind. de val. unitaire, monnaie nat.[2]	103	103	104	107	106	108	108	108	109	108
Quantum indices										
Indices de volume	113	117	130	142	153	172	172	176	194	200
Value, thousand million US $										
Valeur, millards de $ des E.-U.	329.19	341.29	380.94	428.81	459.67	524.79	526.96	538.14	596.29	612.57
Europe Europe										
Unit value indices, US $										
Ind. de valeur unitaire, $ des E.-U.	102	91	93	107	103	93	89	84	77	76
Quantum indices										
Indices de volume	104	106	119	126	135	153	165	172	194	204
Value, thousand million US $										
Valeur, millards de $ des E.-U.	1 372.70	1 244.10	1 432.40	1 741.30	1 803.10	1 830.80	1 894.10	1 866.90	1 922.40	1 982.40
EU+ UE+										
Unit value indices, US $										
Ind. de valeur unitaire, $ des E.-U.	102	91	93	106	103	92	88	84	76	75
Quantum indices										
Indices de volume	105	106	120	128	137	156	168	174	197	208
Value, thousand million US $										
Valeur, millards de $ des E.-U.	1 294.70	1 170.60	1 352.80	1 646.90	1 709.30	1 739.00	1 798.60	1 767.80	1 824.90	1 886.40
Austria Autriche										
Unit value indices, US $[3]										
Ind. de valeur unitaire, $ des E.-U.[3]	99	91	90	104	94	77	68	...	...	...

74

Manufactured goods exports
Unit value and quantum indices: 1990 = 100; value: thousand million US dollars *[cont.]*

Exportations des produits manufacturés
Indices de valeur unitaire et de volume: 1990 = 100; valeur: milliards de dollars des E.-U. *[suite]*

Country or area Pays ou zone	1992	1993	1994	1995	1996	1997	1998	1999	2000	2001
Unit value indices, national currency[3] Ind. de val. unitaire, monnaie nat.[3]	96	93	91	92	88	83	74	...	...	...
Quantum indices Indices de volume	108	107	119	130	147	181	201	...	...	...
Value, thousand million US $ Valeur, millards de $ des E.-U.	40.66	36.70	40.88	51.38	52.28	53.05	51.65	50.44	49.82	...
Belgium-Luxembourg Belgique-Luxembourg										
Unit value indices, US $ Ind. de valeur unitaire, $ des E.-U.	99	87	91	105	103	94	93	88	83	82
Unit value indices, national currency Ind. de val. unitaire, monnaie nat.	...	90	91	93	95	100	101	100	109	111
Quantum indices Indices de volume	104	116	128	133	137	147	163	170	192	200
Value, thousand million US $ Valeur, millards de $ des E.-U.	97.60	95.90	110.73	133.05	133.30	131.23	143.26	142.52	151.41	156.72
Denmark Danemark										
Unit value indices, US $ Ind. de valeur unitaire, $ des E.-U.	102	92	97	112	108	98	97	94	...	...
Unit value indices, national currency Ind. de val. unitaire, monnaie nat.	100	97	100	102	102	105	105	106	...	...
Quantum indices Indices de volume	114	111	118	125	128	145	152	170	...	...
Value, thousand million US $ Valeur, millards de $ des E.-U.	24.66	21.65	24.30	29.43	29.22	30.17	31.22	33.76	31.83	33.45
Finland Finlande										
Unit value indices, US $ Ind. de valeur unitaire, $ des E.-U.	90	74	83	105	99	89	88	85	82	...
Unit value indices, national currency Ind. de val. unitaire, monnaie nat.	106	112	112	120	119	121	123	124	138	...
Quantum indices Indices de volume	97	117	132	144	153	172	188	188	211	...
Value, thousand million US $ Valeur, millards de $ des E.-U.	20.05	20.05	25.11	34.68	34.77	35.12	38.00	36.70	39.71	38.85
France France										
Unit value indices, US $ Ind. de valeur unitaire, $ des E.-U.	100	94	98	111	107	96	96	90	80	78
Unit value indices, national currency Ind. de val. unitaire, monnaie nat.	97	98	100	101	101	103	104	102	104	105
Quantum indices Indices de volume	112	104	116	122	129	143	154	163	189	225
Value, thousand million US $ Valeur, millards de $ des E.-U.	184.58	162.83	187.22	222.89	229.44	225.78	244.30	242.53	249.20	290.20
Germany Allemagne										
Unit value indices, US $ Ind. de valeur unitaire, $ des E.-U.	103	93	94	108	101	87	89	80	72	72
Unit value indices, national currency Ind. de val. unitaire, monnaie nat.	100	95	94	96	94	94	97	92	95	97
Quantum indices Indices de volume	104	100	112	116	126	145	148	158	184	...
Value, thousand million US $ Valeur, millards de $ des E.-U.	387.53	334.59	380.38	455.79	459.69	455.26	477.85	461.09	481.03	...
Greece Grèce										
Unit value indices, US $ Ind. de valeur unitaire, $ des E.-U.	94	81	82	88	84	72	66	...	...	...
Unit value indices, national currency Ind. de val. unitaire, monnaie nat.	114	112	127	128	128	123	123	...	...	...
Quantum indices Indices de volume	127	134	133	153	169	195	216	...	...	...
Value, thousand million US $ Valeur, millards de $ des E.-U.	5.31	4.83	4.88	5.99	6.29	6.21	6.34	5.58	6.06	5.99

74

Manufactured goods exports
Unit value and quantum indices: 1990 = 100; value: thousand million US dollars *[cont.]*

Exportations des produits manufacturés
Indices de valeur unitaire et de volume: 1990 = 100; valeur: milliards de dollars des E.-U. *[suite]*

Country or area Pays ou zone	1992	1993	1994	1995	1996	1997	1998	1999	2000	2001
Ireland Irlande										
Unit value indices, US $[4]										
Ind. de valeur unitaire, $ des E.-U.[4]	97	96	89	98	97	81	75	...	...	...
Quantum indices										
Indices de volume	122	124	166	193	232	320	434	...	...	...
Value, thousand million US $										
Valeur, millards de $ des E.-U.	19.56	19.58	24.29	31.21	36.99	42.82	53.58	59.55	65.59	75.13
Italy Italie										
Unit value indices, US $[4]										
Ind. de valeur unitaire, $ des E.-U.[4]	105	89	86	96	98	90	70	67	59	59
Unit value indices, national currency										
Ind. de val. unitaire, monnaie nat.	...	...	...	...	...	...	102	101	103	107
Quantum indices										
Indices de volume	100	112	132	144	153	159	208	206	238	253
Value, thousand million US $										
Valeur, millards de $ des E.-U.	158.35	150.13	170.55	208.98	226.89	215.04	219.73	206.69	212.62	223.24
Netherlands Pays-Bas										
Unit value indices, US $										
Ind. de valeur unitaire, $ des E.-U.	102	92	92	109	102	91	89	85	77	...
Unit value indices, national currency										
Ind. de val. unitaire, monnaie nat.	98	94	92	96	95	97	97	97	102	
Quantum indices										
Indices de volume	105	107	121	130	139	184	170	180	205	...
Value, thousand million US $										
Valeur, millards de $ des E.-U.	85.31	79.18	89.86	113.91	114.03	133.46	121.70	122.17	127.52	120.92
Portugal Portugal										
Unit value indices, US $[4]										
Ind. de valeur unitaire, $ des E.-U.[4]	106	98	94	111	105	96	96	...	...	...
Quantum indices										
Indices de volume	110	100	120	132	143	154	166	...	...	...
Value, thousand million US $										
Valeur, millards de $ des E.-U.	15.38	12.88	14.86	19.45	19.85	19.48	21.10	21.33	20.96	...
Spain Espagne										
Unit value indices, US $[4]										
Ind. de valeur unitaire, $ des E.-U.[4]	109	85	86	99	99	88	86	...	...	...
Quantum indices										
Indices de volume	109	132	157	169	191	220	231	...	...	...
Value, thousand million US $										
Valeur, millards de $ des E.-U.	50.61	47.54	57.74	71.35	80.45	82.32	84.75	88.72	89.43	91.38
Sweden Suède										
Unit value indices, US $										
Ind. de valeur unitaire, $ des E.-U.	102	82	85	105	106	94	90	85	80	...
Unit value indices, national currency										
Ind. de val. unitaire, monnaie nat.	100	108	111	126	120	121	120	119	124	...
Quantum indices										
Indices de volume	97	108	128	131	131	156	157	171	171	...
Value, thousand million US $										
Valeur, millards de $ des E.-U.	48.49	43.13	53.35	67.44	67.70	71.39	68.70	71.11	67.16	58.69
United Kingdom Royaume-Uni										
Unit value indices, US $										
Ind. de valeur unitaire, $ des E.-U.	102	98	103	114	113	113	112	106	98	...
Unit value indices, national currency										
Ind. de val. unitaire, monnaie nat.	104	117	120	129	129	123	121	117	116	...
Quantum indices										
Indices de volume	101	95	108	116	128	139	139	140	156	...
Value, thousand million US $										
Valeur, millards de $ des E.-U.	156.62	141.64	168.65	201.32	218.42	237.73	236.39	225.63	232.53	210.23
EFTA+ AELE+										
Unit value indices, US $										
Ind. de valeur unitaire, $ des E.-U.	101	87	96	116	114	101	99	97	90	95

74

Manufactured goods exports
Unit value and quantum indices: 1990 = 100; value: thousand million US dollars *[cont.]*

Exportations des produits manufacturés
Indices de valeur unitaire et de volume: 1990 = 100; valeur: milliards de dollars des E.-U. *[suite]*

Country or area Pays ou zone	1992	1993	1994	1995	1996	1997	1998	1999	2000	2001
Quantum indices Indices de volume	101	111	108	106	108	119	125	134	141	131
Value, thousand million US $ Valeur, millards de $ des E.-U.	76.60	72.26	78.21	92.70	92.26	90.34	93.84	97.39	95.38	94.31
Iceland Islande										
Unit value indices, US $[4] Ind. de valeur unitaire, $ des E.-U.[4]	86	76	80	114	106	101	89	...	...	...
Quantum indices Indices de volume	94	102	131	120	130	149	168	...	...	...
Value, thousand million US $ Valeur, millards de $ des E.-U.	0.23	0.23	0.31	0.40	0.40	0.44	0.44	0.56	0.61	0.67
Norway Norvège										
Unit value indices, US $ Ind. de valeur unitaire, $ des E.-U.	92	80	82	102	96	88	85	80	75	73
Unit value indices, national currency Ind. de val. unitaire, monnaie nat.	92	92	93	104	99	100	103	100	107	106
Quantum indices Indices de volume	106	105	96	100	106	136	147	149	155	142
Value, thousand million US $ Valeur, millards de $ des E.-U.	13.84	12.05	11.20	14.46	14.39	17.01	17.67	16.84	16.60	14.82
Switzerland Suisse										
Unit value indices, US $ Ind. de valeur unitaire, $ des E.-U.	103	88	99	120	118	105	104	101	93	...
Quantum indices Indices de volume	100	112	111	107	108	114	120	130	138	...
Value, thousand million US $ Valeur, millards de $ des E.-U.	62.53	59.98	66.70	77.84	77.47	72.88	75.73	79.99	78.18	78.82
Other developed economies Autres economies développées										
Unit value indices, US $ Ind. de valeur unitaire, $ des E.-U.	113	120	129	138	128	121	115	113	116	107
Quantum indices Indices de volume	104	104	107	112	115	124	120	133	148	137
Value, thousand million US $ Valeur, millards de $ des E.-U.	361.60	385.08	423.70	476.20	450.37	461.27	423.65	461.04	525.60	449.46
Australia Australie										
Unit value indices, US $ Ind. de valeur unitaire, $ des E.-U.	86	81	88	96	94	89	78	78	80	72
Unit value indices, national currency Ind. de val. unitaire, monnaie nat.	91	94	94	102	94	94	97	94	108	112
Quantum indices Indices de volume	138	161	180	196	254	277	267	291	320	323
Value, thousand million US $ Valeur, millards de $ des E.-U.	9.83	10.85	13.07	15.63	19.75	20.43	17.29	18.73	21.21	19.32
Israel Israël										
Unit value indices, US $ Ind. de valeur unitaire, $ des E.-U.	101	102	101	105	105	102	105	114	137	...
Quantum indices Indices de volume	111	126	146	155	170	194	197	203	207	...
Value, thousand million US $ Valeur, millards de $ des E.-U.	11.74	13.48	15.50	17.09	18.79	20.84	21.67	24.22	29.71	...
Japan Japon										
Unit value indices, US $ Ind. de valeur unitaire, $ des E.-U.	115	124	134	144	133	126	121	119	121	...
Unit value indices, national currency Ind. de val. unitaire, monnaie nat.	101	95	95	93	101	106	109	94	91	...
Quantum indices Indices de volume	103	101	103	107	107	115	110	121	135	...
Value, thousand million US $ Valeur, millards de $ des E.-U.	328.52	348.56	381.06	425.75	393.58	402.10	369.56	397.48	454.78	378.01

74

Manufactured goods exports
Unit value and quantum indices: 1990 = 100; value: thousand million US dollars *[cont.]*

Exportations des produits manufacturés
Indices de valeur unitaire et de volume: 1990 = 100; valeur: milliards de dollars des E.-U. *[suite]*

Country or area Pays ou zone	1992	1993	1994	1995	1996	1997	1998	1999	2000	2001
New Zealand Nouvelle-Zélande										
Unit value indices, US $										
Ind. de valeur unitaire, $ des E.-U.	89	89	98	112	109	102	84	80	83	...
Unit value indices, national currency										
Ind. de val. unitaire, monnaie nat.	99	98	99	101	94	92	93	90	109	...
Quantum indices										
Indices de volume	120	132	152	155	162	178	203	221	222	...
Value, thousand million US $										
Valeur, millards de $ des E.-U.	2.73	2.98	3.78	4.38	4.46	4.60	4.32	4.50	4.69	4.95
South Africa Afrique du Sud										
Unit value indices, US $										
Ind. de valeur unitaire, $ des E.-U.	101	100	101	123	107	...	...	...	...	...
Unit value indices, national currency										
Ind. de val. unitaire, monnaie nat.	111	127	139	173	178	...	...	...	...	...
Quantum indices										
Indices de volume	107	113	126	134	159	...	...	...	...	...
Value, thousand million US $										
Valeur, millards de $ des E.-U.	8.78	9.22	10.28	13.36	13.79	13.31	10.81	16.12	15.21	17.49
Developing economies Economies en voie de développement										
Unit value indices, US $										
Ind. de valeur unitaire, $ des E.-U.	101	102	104	111	105	99	96	89	92	...
Unit value indices, SDR										
Ind. de valeur unitaire, DTS	97	99	99	99	98	97	96	88	95	...
Quantum indices										
Indices de volume	133	146	171	196	218	250	221	226	278	...
Value, thousand million US $										
Valeur, millards de $ des E.-U.	599.24	665.29	795.55	969.59	1 025.50	1 108.70	942.00	900.00	1 143.60	
China, Hong Kong SAR Chine, Hong Kong RAS										
Unit value indices, US $										
Ind. de valeur unitaire, $ des E.-U.	104	104	105	108	108	104	101	99	97	93
Unit value indices, national currency										
Ind. de val. unitaire, monnaie nat.	103	103	105	107	107	103	100	98	97	93
Quantum indices										
Indices de volume	100	95	93	95	87	90	84	78	84	74
Value, thousand million US $										
Valeur, millards de $ des E.-U.	28.42	27.12	27.11	28.22	25.83	25.69	23.26	21.16	22.43	18.94
India Inde										
Unit value indices, US $										
Ind. de valeur unitaire, $ des E.-U.	92	89	88	86	69	84	79	90	74	...
Unit value indices, national currency										
Ind. de val. unitaire, monnaie nat.	136	154	158	160	141	174	187	221	190	
Quantum indices										
Indices de volume	132	147	181	215	278	246	253	259	375	...
Value, thousand million US $										
Valeur, millards de $ des E.-U.	15.35	16.42	20.15	23.34	24.32	25.97	25.28	29.27	35.01	...
Korea, Republic of Corée, République de										
Unit value indices, US $										
Ind. de valeur unitaire, $ des E.-U.	96	95	98	103	94	86	77	72	77	...
Unit value indices, national currency[5]										
Ind. de val. unitaire, monnaie nat.[5]	106	108	111	112	107	114	150	122	120	...
Quantum indices										
Indices de volume	122	132	151	184	202	228	249	295	335	...
Value, thousand million US $										
Valeur, millards de $ des E.-U.	71.38	76.79	89.86	115.54	115.97	119.96	116.33	130.55	156.87	137.26
Pakistan Pakistan										
Unit value indices, US $										
Ind. de valeur unitaire, $ des E.-U.	101	98	107	125	123	129	127	118	110	...
Unit value indices, national currency										
Ind. de val. unitaire, monnaie nat.	117	127	151	182	203	245	265	270	269	...
Quantum indices										
Indices de volume	130	136	137	124	146	132	128	145	161	...

74

Manufactured goods exports
Unit value and quantum indices: 1990 = 100; value: thousand million US dollars *[cont.]*

Exportations des produits manufacturés
Indices de valeur unitaire et de volume: 1990 = 100; valeur: milliards de dollars des E.-U. *[suite]*

Country or area Pays ou zone	1992	1993	1994	1995	1996	1997	1998	1999	2000	2001
Value, thousand million US $ Valeur, millards de $ des E.-U.	5.72	5.79	6.38	6.74	7.76	7.40	7.08	7.41	7.73	7.79
Singapore Singapour										
Unit value indices, US $ Ind. de valeur unitaire, $ des E.-U.	103	99	108	112	109	102	92	90	88	...
Quantum indices Indices de volume	125	155	195	236	255	274	267	292	354	...
Value, thousand million US $ Valeur, millards de $ des E.-U.	49.33	58.74	80.54	100.99	105.95	106.55	94.15	99.68	119.26	103.68
Turkey Turquie										
Unit value indices, US $[6] Ind. de valeur unitaire, $ des E.-U.[6]	100	95	90	106	97	89	84	80	85	...
Quantum indices Indices de volume	119	130	164	170	197	250	279	294	297	...
Value, thousand million US $ Valeur, millards de $ des E.-U.	10.64	11.17	13.30	16.32	17.32	20.02	21.04	21.19	22.70	25.98

Source:
United Nations Statistics Division, New York, trade statistics database.

Source:
Organisation des Nations Unies, Division de statistique, New York, la base de données pour les statistiques du commerce extérieur.

+ For Member States of this grouping, see Annex I – Other groupings.

1 Excludes trade of the countries of Eastern Europe and the former USSR.
2 Derived from price indices; national unit value index is discontinued.
3 Series linked at 1988 by a factor calculated by the United Nations Statistics Division.
4 Indices are calculated by the United Nations Statistics Division.
5 Average price indexes of manufacturing industry products.
6 Industrial product.

+ Pour les Etats membres de ce groupement, voir annexe I – Autres groupements.

1 Non compris le commerce des pays de l'Europe de l'Est et l'ex-URSS.
2 Calculés à partir des indices des prix; l'indice de la valeur unitaire nationale est discontinué.
3 Les seriessont enchainées à 1988 par un facteur calculé par la Division de Statistique des Nations Unies.
4 Les indices sont calculés par la Division de statistique des Nations Unies.
5 Les indices moyens de prix des produits de l'industrie manufacturière.
6 Produit industriel.

Technical notes, tables 72-74

Tables 72-74: Current data (annual, monthly and/or quarterly) for most of the series are published regularly by the Statistics Division in the United Nations *Monthly Bulletin of Statistics* [26]. More detailed descriptions of the tables and notes on methodology appear in the United Nations *1977 Supplement to the Statistical Yearbook and Monthly Bulletin of Statistics* [57], *International Trade Statistics: Concepts and Definitions* [51] and the *International Trade Statistics Yearbook* [25]. More detailed data including series for individual countries showing the value in national currencies for imports and exports and notes on these series can be found in the *International Trade Statistics Yearbook* [25] and in the *Monthly Bulletin of Statistics* [26].

Data are obtained from national published sources; from data supplied by the governments for publication in United Nations publications and from publications of other United Nations agencies.

Territory

The statistics reported by a country refer to the customs area of the country. In most cases, this coincides with the geographical area of the country.

Systems of trade

Two systems of recording trade are in common use, differing mainly in the way warehoused and re-exported goods are recorded:

(a)   Special trade (S): special imports are the combined total of imports for direct domestic consumption (including transformation and repair) and withdrawals from bonded warehouses or free zones for domestic consumption. Special exports comprise exports of national merchandise, namely, goods wholly or partly produced or manufactured in the country, together with exports of nationalized goods. (Nationalized goods are goods which, having been included in special imports, are then exported without transformation);

(b)   General trade (G): general imports are the combined total of imports for direct domestic consumption and imports into bonded warehouses or free zones. General exports are the combined total of national exports and re-exports. Re-exports, in the general trade system, consist of the outward movement of nationalized goods plus goods which, after importation, move outward from bonded warehouses or free zones without having been transformed.

Valuation

Goods are, in general, valued according to the transaction value. In the case of imports, the transaction value is the value at which the goods were purchased by

Notes techniques, tableaux 72 à 74

Tableaux 72-74: La Division de statistique des Nations Unies publie régulièrement dans le *Bulletin mensuel de statistique* [26] des données courantes (annuelles, mensuelles et/ou trimestrielles) pour la plupart des séries de ces tableaux. Des descriptions plus détaillées des tableaux et des notes méthodologiques figurent dans *1977 Supplément à l'Annuaire statistique et au Bulletin mensuel de statistique* des Nations Unies [57], dans la publication *Statistiques du commerce international, Concepts et définitions* [51] et dans l'*Annuaire statistique du Commerce international* [25]. Des données plus détaillées, comprenant des séries indiquant la valeur en monnaie nationale des importations et des exportations des divers pays et les notes accompagnant ces séries figurent dans l'*Annuaire statistique du Commerce international* [25] et dans le *Bulletin mensuel de statistique* [26].

Les données proviennent de publications nationales et des informations fournies par les gouvernements pour les publications des Nations Unies ainsi que de publications d'autres institutions des Nations Unies.

Territoire

Les statistiques fournies par pays se rapportent au territoire douanier de ce pays. Le plus souvent, ce territoire coïncide avec l'étendue géographique du pays.

Systèmes de commerce

Deux systèmes d'enregistrement du commerce sont couramment utilisés, qui ne diffèrent que par la façon dont sont enregistrées les marchandises entreposées et les marchandises réexportées:

(a)   Commerce spécial (S): les importations spéciales représentent le total combiné des importations destinées directement à la consommation intérieure (transformations et réparations comprises) et les marchandises retirées des entrepôts douaniers ou des zones franches pour la consommation intérieure. Les exportations spéciales comprennent les exportations de marchandises nationales, c'est-à-dire des biens produits ou fabriqués en totalité ou en partie dans le pays, ainsi que les exportations de biens nationalisés. (Les biens nationalisés sont des biens qui, ayant été inclus dans les importations spéciales, sont ensuite réexportés tels quels.)

(b)   Commerce général (G): les importations générales sont le total combiné des importations destinées directement à la consommation intérieure et des importations placées en entrepôt douanier ou destinées aux zones franches. Les exportations générales sont le total combiné des exportations de biens nationaux et des réexportations. Ces dernières, dans le système du com-

the importer plus the cost of transportation and insurance to the frontier of the importing country (c.i.f. valuation). In the case of exports, the transaction value is the value at which the goods were sold by the exporter, including the cost of transportation and insurance to bring the goods onto the transporting vehicle at the frontier of the exporting country (f.o.b. valuation).

Currency conversion

Conversion of values from national currencies into United States dollars is done by means of external trade conversion factors which are generally weighted averages of exchange rates, the weight being the corresponding monthly or quarterly value of imports or exports.

Coverage

The statistics relate to merchandise trade. Merchandise trade is defined to include, as far as possible, all goods which add to or subtract from the material resources of a country as a result of their movement into or out of the country. Thus, ordinary commercial transactions, government trade (including foreign aid, war reparations and trade in military goods), postal trade and all kinds of silver (except silver coins after their issue), are included in the statistics. Since their movement affects monetary rather than material resources, monetary gold, together with currency and titles of ownership after their issue into circulation, are excluded.

Commodity classification

The commodity classification of trade is in accordance with the United Nations *Standard International Trade Classification* (SITC) [56].

World and regional totals

The regional, economic and world totals have been adjusted: (a) to include estimates for countries or areas for which full data are not available; (b) to include insurance and freight for imports valued f.o.b.; (c) to include countries or areas not listed separately; (d) to approximate special trade; (e) to approximate calendar years; and (f) where possible, to eliminate incomparabilities owing to geographical changes, by adjusting the figures for periods before the change to be comparable to those for periods after the change.

Quantum and unit value index numbers

These index numbers show the changes in the volume of imports or exports (quantum index) and the average price of imports or exports (unit value index).

Description of tables

Table 72: World imports and exports are the sum of imports and exports of Developed economies, Developing economies and other. The regional totals for imports and exports are the sum of imports and exports of Developed economies, Developing economies and other. The regional totals for im-

merce général, comprennent les exportations de biens nationalisés et de biens qui, après avoir été importés, sortent des entrepôts de douane ou des zones franches sans avoir été transformés.

Evaluation

En général, les marchandises sont évaluées à la valeur de la transaction. Dans le cas des importations, cette valeur est celle à laquelle les marchandises ont été achetées par l'importateur plus le coût de leur transport et de leur assurance jusqu'à la frontière du pays importateur (valeur c.a.f.). Dans le cas des exportations, la valeur de la transaction est celle à laquelle les marchandises ont été vendues par l'exportateur, y compris le coût de transport et d'assurance des marchandises jusqu'à leur chargement sur le véhicule de transport à la frontière du pays exportateur (valeur f.à.b.).

Conversion des monnaies

Le conversion en dollars des Etats-Unis de valeurs exprimées en monnaie nationale se fait par application de coefficients de conversion du commerce extérieur, qui sont généralement les moyennes pondérées des taux de change, le poids étant la valeur mensuelle ou trimestrielle correspondante des importations ou des exportations.

Couverture

Les statistiques se rapportent au commerce des marchandises. Le commerce des marchandises se définit comme comprenant, dans toute la mesure du possible, toutes les marchandises qui ajoutent ou retranchent aux ressources matérielles d'un pays par suite de leur importation ou de leur exportation par ce pays. Ainsi, les transactions commerciales ordinaires, le commerce pour le compte de l'Etat (y compris l'aide extérieure, les réparations pour dommages de guerre et le commerce des fournitures militaires), le commerce par voie postale et les transactions de toutes sortes sur l'argent (à l'exception des transactions sur les pièces d'argent après leur émission) sont inclus dans ces statistiques. La monnaie or ainsi que la monnaie et les titres de propriété après leur mise en circulation sont exclus, car leurs mouvements influent sur les ressources monétaires plutôt que sur les ressources matérielles.

Classification par marchandise

La classification par marchandise du commerce extérieur est celle adoptée dans la *Classification type pour le commerce international* des Nations Unies (CTCI) [56].

Totaux mondiaux et régionaux

Les totaux économiques, régionaux et mondiaux ont été ajustés de manière: (a) à inclure les estimations

ports and exports and have been adjusted to exclude the re-exports of countries or areas comprising each region. Estimates for certain countries or areas not shown separately as well as for those shown separately but for which no data are yet available are included in the regional and world totals. Export and import values in terms of U.S. dollars are derived by the United Nations Statistics Division from data published in national publications, from data in the replies to the *Monthly Bulletin of Statistics* questionnaires and from data published by the International Monetary Fund (IMF) in the publication *International Financial Statistics* [15].

Table 73: These index numbers show the changes in the volume (quantum index) and the average price (unit value index) of total imports and exports. The terms of trade figures are calculated by dividing export unit value indices by the corresponding import unit value indices. The product of the net terms of trade and the quantum index of exports is called the index of the purchasing power of exports. The footnotes to countries appearing in table 72 also apply to the index numbers in this table.

Table 74: Manufactured goods are defined here to comprise sections 5 through 8 of the Standard International Trade Classification (SITC). These sections are: chemicals and related products, manufactured goods classified chiefly by material, machinery and transport equipment and miscellaneous manufactured articles. The economic and geographic groupings in this table are in accordance with those of table 72, although table 72 includes more detailed geographical sub-groups which make up the groupings "other developed market economies" and "developing market economies" of this table.

The unit value indices are obtained from national sources, except those of a few countries which the United Nations Statistics Division compiles using their quantity and value figures. For countries that do not compile indices for manufactured goods exports conforming to the above definition, sub-indices are aggregated to approximate an index of SITC sections 5-8. Unit value indices obtained from national indices are rebased, where necessary, so that 1990=100. Indices in national currency are converted into US dollars using conversion factors obtained by dividing the weighted average exchange rate of a given currency in the current period by the weighted average exchange rate in the base period. All aggregate unit value indices are current period weighted.

The indices in Special Drawing Rights (SDRs) are calculated by multiplying the equivalent aggregate indices in United States dollars by conversion factors obtained by dividing the SDR/US $ exchange rate in the

ont été ajustés de manière: (a) à inclure les estimations pour les pays ou régions pour lesquels on ne disposait pas de données complètes; (b) à inclure l'assurance et le fret dans la valeur f.o.b. des importations; (c) à inclure les pays ou régions non indiqués séparément; (d) à donner une approximation du commerce spécial; (e) à les ramener à des années civiles; et (f) à éliminer, dans la mesure du possible, les données non comparables par suite de changements géographiques, en ajustant les chiffres correspondant aux périodes avant le changement de manière à les rendre comparables à ceux des périodes après le changement.

Indices de quantum et de valeur unitaire

Ces indices indiquent les variations du volume des importations ou des exportations (indice de quantum) et du prix moyen des importations ou des exportations (indice de valeur unitaire).

Description des tableaux

Tableau 72: Les importations et les exportations totales pour le monde se composent des importations et exportations des Economies développées, des Economies en développement et des autres. Les totaux régionaux pour importations et exportations ont été ajustés pour exclure les re-exportations des pays ou zones qui comprennent la région. Les totaux régionaux et mondiaux comprennent des estimations pour certains pays ou zones ne figurant pas séparément mais pour lesquels les données ne sont pas encore disponibles. Les valeurs en dollars des E.U. des exportations et des importations ont été obtenues par la Division de statistique des Nations Unies à partir des réponses aux questionnaires du *Bulletin Mensuel de Statistique*, des données publiées par le Fonds Monétaire International dans la publication *Statistiques financières internationales* [15].

Tableau 73: Ces indices indiquent les variations du volume (indice de quantum) et du prix moyen (indice de valeur unitaire) des importations et des exportations totales. Les chiffres relatifs aux termes de l'échange se calculent en divisant les indices de valeur unitaire des exportations par les indices correspondants de valeur unitaire des importations. Le produit de la valeur nette des termes de l'échange et de l'indice du quantum des exportations est appelé indice du pouvoir d'achat des exportations. Les notes figurant au bas du tableau 72 concernant certains pays s'appliquent également aux indices du présent tableau.

Tableau 74: Les produits manufacturés se définissent comme correspondant aux sections 5 à 8 de la Classification type pour le commerce international (CTCI). Ces sections sont: produits chimiques et produits connexes, biens manufacturés classés principalement par

current period by the rate in the base period.

The quantum indices are derived from the value data and the unit value indices. All aggregate quantum indices are base period weighted.

matière première, machines et équipements de transport et articles divers manufacturés. Les groupements économiques et géographiques de ce tableau sont conformes à ceux du tableau 72; toutefois, le tableau 72 comprend des subdivisions géographiques plus détaillées qui composent les groupements "autres pays développés à économie de marché" et "pays en développement à économie de marché" du présent tableau.

Les indices de valeur unitaire sont obtenus de sources nationales, à l'exception de ceux de certains pays que la Division de statistique des Nations Unies compile en utilisant les chiffres de ces pays relatifs aux quantités et aux valeurs. Pour les pays qui n'établissent pas d'indices conformes à la définition ci-dessus pour leurs exportations de produits manufacturés, on fait la synthèse de sous-indices de manière à établir un indice proche de celui des sections 5 à 8 de la CTCI. Le cas échéant, les indices de valeur unitaire obtenus à partir des indices nationaux sont ajustés sur la base 1990=100. On convertit les indices en monnaie nationale en indices en dollars des Etats-Unis en utilisant des facteurs de conversion obtenus en divisant la moyenne pondérée des taux de change d'une monnaie donnée pendant la période courante par la moyenne pondérée des taux de change de la période de base. Tous les indices globaux de valeur unitaire sont pondérés pour la période courante.

On calcule les indices en droits de tirages spécial (DTS) en multipliant les indices globaux équivalents en dollars des Etats-Unis par les facteurs de conversion obtenus en divisant le taux de change DTS/dollars E.U. de la période courante par le taux correspondant de la période de base.

On détermine les indices de quantum à partir des données de valeur et des indices de valeur unitaire. Tous les indices globaux de quantum sont pondérés par rapport à la période de base.

75

Tourist/visitor arrivals by region of origin
Arrivées de touristes/visiteurs par région de provenance

Country or area of destination and region of origin +	1996	1997	1998	1999	2000	Pays ou zone de destination et région de provenance +
Albania						**Albanie**
Total [1]	56 276	19 154	27 709	38 963	...	Totale [1]
Africa	195	...	...	...	...	Afrique
Americas	4 752	1 177	1 545	2 150	...	Amériques
Europe	29 052	11 849	13 854	18 520	...	Europe
Asia, East and South East/Oceania	1 582	185	310	417	...	Asie. Est et Sud-Est et Océanie
Southern Asia	234	...	...	...	...	Asie du Sud
Western Asia	3 594	105	2 370	3 056	...	Asie occidentale
Region not specified	16 867	5 838	9 630	14 820	...	Région non spécifiée
Algeria						**Algérie**
Total [2,3]	604 968	634 761	678 436	748 536	865 984	Totale [2,3]
Africa	35 029	34 027	37 373	51 303	55 508	Afrique
Americas	1 770	1 838	2 297	2 563	3 207	Amériques
Europe	45 570	48 440	56 509	72 573	98 563	Europe
Asia, East and South East/Oceania	1 107	1 342	2 609	4 414	5 080	Asie. Est et Sud-Est et Océanie
Western Asia	10 015	9 194	8 414	10 008	13 180	Asie occidentale
Region not specified	511 477	539 920	571 234	607 675	690 446	Région non spécifiée
American Samoa						**Samoa américaines**
Total [4,5]	21 295	15 809	...	27 201	...	Totale [4,5]
Africa	19	10	...	10	...	Afrique
Americas	9 108	8 646	...	17 111	...	Amériques
Europe	2 965	1 396	...	774	...	Europe
Asia, East and South East/Oceania	8 618	5 631	...	8 948	...	Asie. Est et Sud-Est et Océanie
Southern Asia	531	61	...	92	...	Asie du Sud
Western Asia	29	20	...	66	...	Asie occidentale
Region not specified	25	45	...	200	...	Région non spécifiée
Angola						**Angola**
Total [5]	20 978	45 139	52 011	45 477	50 765	Totale [5]
Africa	4 524	13 863	7 332	7 887	8 343	Afrique
Americas	2 133	3 154	7 509	6 074	7 666	Amériques
Europe	13 079	27 422	34 444	29 113	30 868	Europe
Asia, East and South East/Oceania	1 152	674	2 125	2 009	3 028	Asie. Est et Sud-Est et Océanie
Southern Asia	90	26	359	328	661	Asie du Sud
Western Asia	...	...	242	66	199	Asie occidentale
Anguilla						**Anguilla**
Total [5,6]	37 498	43 181	43 874	46 782	43 789	Totale [5,6]
Americas	33 748	36 642	34 658	33 449	33 127	Amériques
Europe	2 926	5 455	7 986	11 720	9 422	Europe
Region not specified	824	1 084	1 230	1 613	1 240	Région non spécifiée
Antigua and Barbuda						**Antigua-et-Barbuda**
Total [5,6,7]	220 475	232 141	226 121	...	...	Totale [5,6,7]
Americas	128 266	138 028	133 607	...	...	Amériques
Europe	87 935	89 884	88 082	...	...	Europe
Region not specified	4 274	4 229	4 432	...	...	Région non spécifiée
Argentina						**Argentine**
Total [5,6,8]	2 613 909	2 764 226	3 012 472	2 898 241	2 949 139	Totale [5,6,8]
Americas	2 252 082	2 378 327	2 595 379	2 490 667	2 519 898	Amériques
Europe	298 858	319 787	344 323	336 676	353 983	Europe
Region not specified	62 969	66 112	72 770	70 898	75 258	Région non spécifiée
Armenia						**Arménie**
Total [9]	13 388	23 430	31 837	40 745	45 222	Totale [9]
Africa	44	10	32	43	48	Afrique
Americas	1 011	3 282	5 028	6 156	8 117	Amériques
Europe	11 245	16 109	23 099	26 880	25 487	Europe
Asia, East and South East/Oceania	232	602	906	923	787	Asie. Est et Sud-Est et Océanie
Southern Asia	638	2 203	1 300	4 845	8 704	Asie du Sud
Western Asia	218	1 224	1 472	1 898	2 079	Asie occidentale
Aruba						**Aruba**
Total [5]	640 836	649 893	647 437	683 320	721 224	Totale [5]
Americas	582 140	587 776	595 186	629 597	670 271	Amériques
Europe	55 333	57 335	49 042	49 370	47 063	Europe
Asia, East and South East/Oceania	284	346	320	273	215	Asie. Est et Sud-Est et Océanie

75

Tourist/visitor arrivals by region of origin *[cont.]*

Arrivées de touristes/visiteurs par région de provenance *[suite]*

Country or area of destination and region of origin +	1996	1997	1998	1999	2000	Pays ou zone de destination et région de provenance +
Region not specified	3 079	4 436	2 889	4 080	3 675	Région non spécifiée
Australia						**Australie**
Total [2,6,10]	4 164 800	4 317 867	4 167 204	4 459 181	4 946 200	Totale [2,6,10]
Africa	53 400	56 220	70 849	71 480	...	Afrique
Americas	401 300	420 040	473 551	533 953	482 200	Amériques
Europe	810 500	885 103	963 571	1 083 978	1 201 900	Europe
Asia, East and South East/Oceania	2 842 900	2 892 508	2 583 820	2 683 321	2 566 300	Asie. Est et Sud-Est et Océanie
Southern Asia	33 100	37 765	42 741	50 160	...	Asie du Sud
Western Asia	20 100	21 120	28 003	34 449	...	Asie occidentale
Region not specified	3 500	5 111	4 669	1 840	695 800	Région non spécifiée
Austria						**Autriche**
Total [9,11]	17 089 973	16 647 281	17 352 477	17 466 714	17 982 204	Totale [9,11]
Africa	21 783	23 080	32 818	32 575	35 511	Afrique
Americas	707 509	718 578	827 764	767 196	933 841	Amériques
Europe	15 569 746	15 063 175	15 680 020	15 843 176	16 084 063	Europe
Asia, East and South East/Oceania	514 877	530 304	499 515	534 948	623 939	Asie. Est et Sud-Est et Océanie
Southern Asia	27 742	24 174	21 533	30 685	35 357	Asie du Sud
Western Asia	20 582	25 703	25 583	25 030	28 858	Asie occidentale
Region not specified	227 734	262 267	265 244	233 104	240 635	Région non spécifiée
Azerbaijan						**Azerbaïdjan**
Total [5]	...	305 830	483 163	602 047	681 000	Totale [5]
Americas	...	4 895	3 350	1 815	...	Amériques
Europe	...	182 506	331 377	446 415	367 443	Europe
Southern Asia	...	106 183	140 459	122 231	242 354	Asie du Sud
Western Asia	...	405	208	94	...	Asie occidentale
Region not specified	...	11 841	7 769	31 492	71 203	Région non spécifiée
Bahamas						**Bahamas**
Total [5]	1 633 105	1 617 595	1 527 707	1 576 888	1 596 159	Totale [5]
Americas	1 445 460	1 413 485	1 333 112	1 381 208	1 396 800	Amériques
Europe	127 600	130 365	117 954	125 484	128 163	Europe
Asia, East and South East/Oceania	25 680	...	...	...	...	Asie. Est et Sud-Est et Océanie
Region not specified	34 365	73 745	76 641	70 196	71 196	Région non spécifiée
Bahrain						**Bahreïn**
Total [2,6]	1 987 604	2 600 320	2 897 562	3 280 452	3 868 738	Totale [2,6]
Africa	11 713	18 389	21 910	26 396	32 442	Afrique
Americas	76 746	86 358	96 881	101 859	120 801	Amériques
Europe	147 574	173 258	179 472	191 040	215 951	Europe
Asia, East and South East/Oceania	84 318	82 767	96 886	100 646	107 445	Asie. Est et Sud-Est et Océanie
Southern Asia	193 465	221 615	260 817	299 168	331 893	Asie du Sud
Western Asia	1 473 748	2 017 933	2 241 596	2 561 343	3 060 206	Asie occidentale
Region not specified	40	...	...	...	...	Région non spécifiée
Bangladesh						**Bangladesh**
Total [5,6]	165 887	182 420	171 961	172 781	199 211	Totale [5,6]
Africa	1 381	1 150	1 609	1 511	1 787	Afrique
Americas	13 984	15 435	15 653	12 444	15 110	Amériques
Europe	51 034	47 934	36 920	39 599	46 036	Europe
Asia, East and South East/Oceania	29 875	33 609	35 757	34 865	38 429	Asie. Est et Sud-Est et Océanie
Southern Asia	66 307	81 728	77 692	78 878	93 709	Asie du Sud
Western Asia	3 282	2 548	4 291	5 333	3 893	Asie occidentale
Region not specified	24	16	39	151	247	Région non spécifiée
Barbados						**Barbade**
Total [5]	447 083	472 290	512 397	514 614	544 695	Totale [5]
Africa	...	...	...	563	646	Afrique
Americas	238 721	245 004	254 982	264 129	277 985	Amériques
Europe	200 960	220 618	251 735	245 143	263 165	Europe
Asia, East and South East/Oceania	1 615	1 490	1 515	4 242	2 296	Asie. Est et Sud-Est et Océanie
Southern Asia	...	...	...	363	439	Asie du Sud
Western Asia	...	...	...	174	164	Asie occidentale
Region not specified	5 787	5 178	4 165	...	...	Région non spécifiée
Belarus						**Bélarus**
Total [5]	234 226	254 023	355 342	...	...	Totale [5]
Africa	171	235	703	...	...	Afrique

75

Tourist/visitor arrivals by region of origin *[cont.]*

Arrivées de touristes/visiteurs par région de provenance *[suite]*

Country or area of destination and region of origin +	1996	1997	1998	1999	2000	Pays ou zone de destination et région de provenance +
Americas	7 808	9 214	9 607	...	...	Amériques
Europe	222 177	241 549	339 587	...	...	Europe
Asia, East and South East/Oceania	2 883	2 311	4 388	...	...	Asie. Est et Sud-Est et Océanie
Southern Asia	502	508	676	...	...	Asie du Sud
Western Asia	685	206	381	...	...	Asie occidentale
Belgium						**Belgique**
Total [9]	5 829 257	6 037 031	6 179 254	6 369 030	6 457 325	Totale [9]
Africa	63 451	63 003	61 028	57 058	64 094	Afrique
Americas	388 850	410 712	420 335	434 012	448 770	Amériques
Europe	5 046 096	5 197 330	5 363 775	5 522 422	5 549 692	Europe
Asia, East and South East/Oceania	266 218	286 455	266 801	287 214	297 402	Asie. Est et Sud-Est et Océanie
Southern Asia	30 305	27 946	17 149	19 211	23 448	Asie du Sud
Western Asia	16 036	18 083	19 275	17 898	20 363	Asie occidentale
Region not specified	18 301	33 502	30 891	31 215	53 556	Région non spécifiée
Belize						**Belize**
Total [2,12]	367 602	328 143	299 725	339 581	373 995	Totale [2,12]
Americas	322 529	275 704	248 188	288 212	320 283	Amériques
Europe	38 808	47 489	45 130	44 364	47 993	Europe
Asia, East and South East/Oceania	4 975	3 780	3 972	3 917	2 654	Asie. Est et Sud-Est et Océanie
Region not specified	1 290	1 170	2 435	3 088	3 065	Région non spécifiée
Bermuda						**Bermudes**
Total [5,13]	390 395	380 058	368 756	354 026	328 305	Totale [5,13]
Americas	351 229	338 725	323 609	311 015	284 331	Amériques
Europe	30 273	31 646	37 096	35 597	35 312	Europe
Asia, East and South East/Oceania	1 260	1 010	978	851	1 114	Asie. Est et Sud-Est et Océanie
Region not specified	7 633	8 677	7 073	6 563	7 548	Région non spécifiée
Bhutan						**Bhoutan**
Total [5]	5 150	5 362	6 203	7 158	7 559	Totale [5]
Africa	...	5	8	12	7	Afrique
Americas	1 072	1 046	1 622	2 346	3 024	Amériques
Europe	2 365	2 576	3 145	3 140	3 029	Europe
Asia, East and South East/Oceania	1 597	1 679	1 403	1 576	1 425	Asie. Est et Sud-Est et Océanie
Southern Asia	15	33	24	23	50	Asie du Sud
Region not specified	101	23	1	61	24	Région non spécifiée
Bolivia						**Bolivie**
Total [1,14]	376 855	397 517	420 491	409 142	381 077	Totale [1,14]
Africa	683	641	1 016	943	1 117	Afrique
Americas	226 084	257 203	269 344	242 075	219 636	Amériques
Europe	135 084	124 895	135 759	146 138	142 170	Europe
Asia, East and South East/Oceania	15 004	14 778	14 372	19 986	18 154	Asie. Est et Sud-Est et Océanie
Bonaire						**Bonaire**
Total [5]	65 080	62 776	61 737	61 495	51 269	Totale [5]
Americas	41 650	40 495	39 976	40 883	33 067	Amériques
Europe	23 188	22 090	21 605	20 393	17 950	Europe
Asia, East and South East/Oceania	74	38	25	19	16	Asie. Est et Sud-Est et Océanie
Region not specified	168	153	131	200	236	Région non spécifiée
Botswana						**Botswana**
Total [5]	512 118	606 781	749 535	843 314	...	Totale [5]
Africa	439 333	516 328	629 033	720 310	...	Afrique
Americas	7 644	8 614	10 714	12 070	...	Amériques
Europe	31 235	38 311	38 755	44 024	...	Europe
Asia, East and South East/Oceania	7 949	9 281	9 127	9 841	...	Asie. Est et Sud-Est et Océanie
Southern Asia	721	1 174	1 063	1 384	...	Asie du Sud
Region not specified	25 236	33 073	60 843	55 665	...	Région non spécifiée
Brazil						**Brésil**
Total [5]	2 665 508	2 849 750	4 818 084 [15]	5 107 169	5 313 463	Totale [5]
Africa	23 187	23 747	40 959	41 294	34 503	Afrique
Americas	1 830 419	1 998 967	3 449 456	3 643 223	3 803 069	Amériques
Europe	681 340	713 059	1 160 673	1 246 155	1 320 325	Europe
Asia, East and South East/Oceania	109 638	95 228	121 692	130 070	121 791	Asie. Est et Sud-Est et Océanie
Western Asia	7 344	7 674	13 661	15 254	11 174	Asie occidentale
Region not specified	13 580	11 075	31 643	31 173	22 601	Région non spécifiée

75

Tourist/visitor arrivals by region of origin *[cont.]*

Arrivées de touristes/visiteurs par région de provenance *[suite]*

Country or area of destination and region of origin +	1996	1997	1998	1999	2000	Pays ou zone de destination et région de provenance +
British Virgin Islands						**Iles Vierges britanniques**
Total [5]	243 683	244 318	279 097	285 858	...	Totale [5]
Americas	213 311	214 316	223 729	238 435	...	Amériques
Europe	23 043	22 137	31 457	32 614	...	Europe
Region not specified	7 329	7 865	23 911	14 809	...	Région non spécifiée
Brunei Darussalam						**Brunéi Darussalam**
Total [2]	...	...	964 080	966 684	984 093	Totale [2]
Americas	...	...	10 184	8 751	9 469	Amériques
Europe	...	...	48 152	44 865	41 728	Europe
Asia, East and South East/Oceania	...	...	892 624	896 925	912 667	Asie. Est et Sud-Est et Océanie
Southern Asia	...	...	13 100	12 501	16 168	Asie du Sud
Western Asia	...	...	...	886	781	Asie occidentale
Region not specified	...	...	20	2 756	3 280	Région non spécifiée
Bulgaria						**Bulgarie**
Total [2]	6 810 688	7 543 185	5 239 691 [16]	5 056 240 [16]	4 922 118 [16]	Totale [2]
Africa	3 254	6 838	6 675	4 418	3 523	Afrique
Americas	18 672	21 515	39 788	39 241	42 435	Amériques
Europe	6 406 574	7 247 812	4 821 516	4 911 853	4 780 489	Europe
Asia, East and South East/Oceania	13 812	19 054	20 715	21 275	23 674	Asie. Est et Sud-Est et Océanie
Southern Asia	10 086	15 963	14 778	14 570	15 917	Asie du Sud
Western Asia	18 201	21 438	19 840	17 964	17 403	Asie occidentale
Region not specified	340 089	210 565	316 379	46 919	38 677	Région non spécifiée
Burkina Faso						**Burkina Faso**
Total [1]	131 113	138 364	160 284	...	...	Totale [1]
Africa	54 460	57 459	62 673	...	...	Afrique
Americas	7 780	8 209	10 062	...	...	Amériques
Europe	54 942	57 997	77 785	...	...	Europe
Asia, East and South East/Oceania	2 039	2 153	3 199	...	...	Asie. Est et Sud-Est et Océanie
Western Asia	642	677	1 016	...	...	Asie occidentale
Region not specified	11 250	11 869	5 549	...	...	Région non spécifiée
Burundi						**Burundi**
Total [3,5]	27 391	10 553	15 404	...	...	Totale [3,5]
Africa	13 004	5 011	7 394	...	...	Afrique
Americas	1 660	639	1 092	...	...	Amériques
Europe	10 514	4 051	5 700	...	...	Europe
Asia, East and South East/Oceania	2 213	852	1 218	...	...	Asie. Est et Sud-Est et Océanie
Cambodia						**Cambodge**
Total [5,17]	260 489	218 843	186 333	262 907	351 661	Totale [5,17]
Africa	...	...	...	4 592	...	Afrique
Americas	27 812	24 561	21 773	36 324	42 156	Amériques
Europe	53 761	43 331	46 165	60 031	65 657	Europe
Asia, East and South East/Oceania	174 406	147 470	105 422	135 502	152 383	Asie. Est et Sud-Est et Océanie
Southern Asia	3 609	2 735	1 999	2 445	2 967	Asie du Sud
Western Asia	...	...	...	24 013	...	Asie occidentale
Region not specified	901	746	10 974	...	88 498	Région non spécifiée
Cameroon						**Cameroun**
Total [1]	101 106	132 839	...	...	...	Totale [1]
Africa	26 912	47 689	...	...	...	Afrique
Americas	7 728	14 080	...	...	...	Amériques
Europe	62 228	66 034	...	...	...	Europe
Asia, East and South East/Oceania	1 874	2 736	...	...	...	Asie. Est et Sud-Est et Océanie
Western Asia	1 328	1 308	...	...	...	Asie occidentale
Region not specified	1 036	992	...	...	...	Région non spécifiée
Canada						**Canada**
Total [5]	17 329 000	17 669 000	18 870 000	19 411 000	19 650 300	Totale [5]
Africa	55 500	58 700	59 200	66 300	73 300	Afrique
Americas	13 240 500	13 741 900	15 256 000	15 564 300	15 627 500	Amériques
Europe	2 371 200	2 329 900	2 273 800	2 381 800	2 497 200	Europe
Asia, East and South East/Oceania	1 509 400	1 392 600	1 145 400	1 251 000	1 342 000	Asie. Est et Sud-Est et Océanie
Southern Asia	73 400	77 700	55 700	62 500	74 000	Asie du Sud
Western Asia	35 400	34 900	38 000	40 700	36 300	Asie occidentale
Region not specified	43 600	33 300	41 900	44 400	...	Région non spécifiée

75

Tourist/visitor arrivals by region of origin *[cont.]*

Arrivées de touristes/visiteurs par région de provenance *[suite]*

Country or area of destination and region of origin +	1996	1997	1998	1999	2000	Pays ou zone de destination et région de provenance +
Cape Verde						**Cap-Vert**
Total[5,13]	37 000	45 000	52 000	67 042	83 259	Totale[5,13]
Americas	...	...	...	...	3 039	Amériques
Europe	31 108	37 834	44 408	...	70 600	Europe
Region not specified	5 892	7 166	7 592	67 042	9 620	Région non spécifiée
Cayman Islands						**Îles Caïmanes**
Total[5,13]	373 245	381 188	404 205	394 534	354 087	Totale[5,13]
Africa	374	374	514	661	...	Afrique
Americas	335 548	344 391	365 319	355 605	297 174	Amériques
Europe	33 440	32 746	34 690	34 501	22 590	Europe
Asia, East and South East/Oceania	2 462	2 861	2 800	2 870	...	Asie. Est et Sud-Est et Océanie
Region not specified	1 421	816	882	897	34 323	Région non spécifiée
Central African Rep.						**Rép. centrafricaine**
Total[5]	...	...	7 478	...	...	Totale[5]
Africa	...	...	3 439	...	...	Afrique
Americas	...	...	455	...	...	Amériques
Europe	...	...	3 054	...	...	Europe
Asia, East and South East/Oceania	...	...	313	...	...	Asie. Est et Sud-Est et Océanie
Western Asia	...	...	89	...	...	Asie occidentale
Region not specified	...	...	128	...	...	Région non spécifiée
Chad						**Tchad**
Total[1]	19 962	26 980	41 244	46 603	43 034	Totale[1]
Africa	2 400	3 700	12 160	13 649	12 542	Afrique
Americas	1 023	615	3 963	4 546	8 216	Amériques
Europe	5 246	4 764	21 206	24 134	21 306	Europe
Asia, East and South East/Oceania	98	180	216	420	436	Asie. Est et Sud-Est et Océanie
Western Asia	124	116	139	591	534	Asie occidentale
Region not specified	11 071	17 605	3 560	3 263	...	Région non spécifiée
Chile						**Chili**
Total[5]	1 449 528	1 643 640	1 759 279	1 622 252	1 742 407	Totale[5]
Africa	...	1 794	2 092	2 470	2 392	Afrique
Americas	1 242 865	1 402 868	1 492 699	1 356 414	1 456 648	Amériques
Europe	167 986	203 373	226 653	223 731	240 144	Europe
Asia, East and South East/Oceania	27 745	32 023	34 281	35 511	36 996	Asie. Est et Sud-Est et Océanie
Southern Asia	...	1 818	2 442	2 232	2 746	Asie du Sud
Western Asia	...	519	455	646	912	Asie occidentale
Region not specified	10 932	1 245	657	1 248	2 569	Région non spécifiée
China						**Chine**
Total[5,18]	6 744 150	7 427 934	7 107 529	8 432 050	10 160 432	Totale[5,18]
Africa[18]	38 479	38 027	39 167	42 851	54 015	Afrique[18]
Americas	809 185	867 166	947 927	1 025 996	1 217 091	Amériques
Europe	1 770 216	2 039 424	1 896 160	2 148 520	2 537 222	Europe
Asia, East and South East/Oceania	3 972 408	4 312 645	4 057 595	5 022 581	6 103 863	Asie. Est et Sud-Est et Océanie
Southern Asia	119 692	130 716	132 853	160 990	210 347	Asie du Sud
Western Asia	17 769	21 644	20 993	26 051	34 658	Asie occidentale
Region not specified	16 401	18 312	12 834	5 061	3 236	Région non spécifiée
China, Hong Kong SAR						**Chine, Hong Kong RAS**
Total[2,19]	12 973 764	11 273 377	10 159 646	11 328 272	13 059 477	Totale[2,19]
Africa	64 831	73 559	63 939	65 027	73 093	Afrique
Americas	1 083 247	1 125 138	1 104 888	1 155 313	1 295 908	Amériques
Europe	1 373 747	1 195 345	1 042 231	1 059 155	1 117 435	Europe
Asia, East and South East/Oceania	10 256 102	8 695 439	7 761 524	8 852 807	10 335 534	Asie. Est et Sud-Est et Océanie
Southern Asia	179 845	167 690	167 766	171 615	205 899	Asie du Sud
Western Asia	15 992	16 206	19 298	24 355	31 608	Asie occidentale
China, Macao SAR						**Chine, Macao RAS**
Total[2,20]	8 151 055	7 000 370	6 948 535	7 443 924	9 162 212	Totale[2,20]
Africa	6 595	5 579	4 786	4 111	4 333	Afrique
Americas	149 327	121 286	110 619	105 715	117 989	Amériques
Europe	293 355	239 364	262 783	163 427	148 361	Europe
Asia, East and South East/Oceania	7 493 180	6 434 682	6 498 013	7 154 937	8 871 880	Asie. Est et Sud-Est et Océanie
Southern Asia	18 489	16 221	12 532	14 010	17 008	Asie du Sud
Western Asia	562	586	719	682	771	Asie occidentale

75

Tourist/visitor arrivals by region of origin *[cont.]*

Arrivées de touristes/visiteurs par région de provenance *[suite]*

Country or area of destination and region of origin +	1996	1997	1998	1999	2000	Pays ou zone de destination et région de provenance +
Region not specified	189 547	182 652	59 083	1 042	1 870	Région non spécifiée
Colombia						**Colombie**
Total [5,21]	756 606	639 250	674 425	546 035	557 280	Totale [5,21]
Americas	499 884	512 979	561 292	475 322	485 613	Amériques
Europe	61 372	69 797	69 664	70 617	69 920	Europe
Region not specified	195 350	56 474	43 469	96	1 747	Région non spécifiée
Comoros						**Comores**
Total [5,13]	23 775	26 219	27 474	24 479	23 893	Totale [5,13]
Africa	11 355	14 202	11 155	14 420	15 812	Afrique
Americas	130	337	783	144	230	Amériques
Europe	10 623	11 143	12 799	9 083	7 240	Europe
Asia, East and South East/Oceania	215	537	460	210	153	Asie. Est et Sud-Est et Océanie
Region not specified	1 452	...	2 277	622	458	Région non spécifiée
Congo						**Congo**
Total [1]	39 114	26 738	20 315	13 964	18 798	Totale [1]
Africa	14 337	10 351	7 425	5 540	9 301	Afrique
Americas	2 792	1 812	1 110	627	785	Amériques
Europe	20 926	13 891	11 063	7 293	8 294	Europe
Region not specified	1 059	684	717	504	418	Région non spécifiée
Cook Islands						**Iles Cook**
Total [5,7]	48 354	49 866	48 629	55 599	72 994	Totale [5,7]
Americas	8 845	9 491	8 987	11 083	12 726	Amériques
Europe	18 024	19 896	19 290	18 382	23 683	Europe
Asia, East and South East/Oceania	21 268	20 293	20 239	25 974	36 359	Asie. Est et Sud-Est et Océanie
Region not specified	217	186	113	160	226	Région non spécifiée
Costa Rica						**Costa Rica**
Total [5]	781 127	811 490	942 853	1 031 585	1 088 075	Totale [5]
Africa	714	689	748	897	789	Afrique
Americas	629 879	661 574	791 219	863 324	907 381	Amériques
Europe	132 435	130 713	131 657	145 586	156 562	Europe
Asia, East and South East/Oceania	14 638	14 484	14 447	15 885	15 993	Asie. Est et Sud-Est et Océanie
Region not specified	3 461	4 030	4 782	5 893	7 350	Région non spécifiée
Côte d'Ivoire						**Côte d'Ivoire**
Total [5,22]	236 913	274 094	301 039	...	...	Totale [5,22]
Africa	113 324	137 886	158 808	...	...	Afrique
Americas	19 478	20 703	23 328	...	...	Amériques
Europe	96 620	107 304	109 176	...	...	Europe
Asia, East and South East/Oceania	5 440	5 649	6 172	...	...	Asie. Est et Sud-Est et Océanie
Southern Asia	720	...	1 000	...	...	Asie du Sud
Western Asia	1 331	2 552	2 555	...	...	Asie occidentale
Croatia						**Croatie**
Total [9,23]	2 914 434	4 177 764	4 499 138	3 805 343	5 831 180	Totale [9,23]
Americas	65 229	60 353	52 764	46 672	66 869	Amériques
Europe	2 814 575	4 072 325	4 411 729	3 730 199	5 719 995	Europe
Asia, East and South East/Oceania	7 987	10 938	16 072	15 013	23 305	Asie. Est et Sud-Est et Océanie
Region not specified	26 643	34 148	18 573	13 459	21 011	Région non spécifiée
Cuba						**Cuba**
Total [2]	1 004 336	1 170 083	1 415 832	1 602 781	1 773 986	Totale [2]
Africa	3 036	5 178	5 919	6 269	7 262	Afrique
Americas	418 378	496 913	594 354	696 521	783 425	Amériques
Europe	562 575	648 265	793 246	874 444	949 328	Europe
Asia, East and South East/Oceania	15 287	13 775	16 368	20 060	27 103	Asie. Est et Sud-Est et Océanie
Southern Asia	3 141	4 083	4 278	3 366	4 442	Asie du Sud
Western Asia	1 045	1 554	1 319	1 782	2 168	Asie occidentale
Region not specified	874	315	348	339	258	Région non spécifiée
Curaçao						**Curaçao**
Total [3,5,13]	214 325	205 045	198 570	198 271	191 246	Totale [3,5,13]
Americas	127 386	125 078	125 419	120 121	32 020	Amériques
Europe	83 664	76 926	69 462	68 001	61 105	Europe
Region not specified	3 275	3 041	3 689	10 149	98 121	Région non spécifiée

75

Tourist/visitor arrivals by region of origin *[cont.]*

Arrivées de touristes/visiteurs par région de provenance *[suite]*

Country or area of destination and region of origin +	1996	1997	1998	1999	2000	Pays ou zone de destination et région de provenance +
Cyprus						**Chypre**
Total [5]	1 950 000	2 088 000	2 222 706	2 434 285	2 686 205	Totale [5]
Africa	...	...	5 769	8 509	10 247	Afrique
Americas	...	...	26 030	30 747	38 737	Amériques
Europe	1 772 500	1 978 509	2 111 879	2 312 058	2 553 842	Europe
Asia, East and South East/Oceania	...	...	9 921	11 358	14 031	Asie. Est et Sud-Est et Océanie
Southern Asia	...	...	11 304	13 053	15 820	Asie du Sud
Western Asia	105 000	52 825	51 133	55 674	51 388	Asie occidentale
Region not specified	72 500	56 666	6 670	2 886	2 140	Région non spécifiée
Czech Republic						**République tchèque**
Total [9]	4 558 322	4 975 658	5 482 080	5 609 700	* 4 666 305	Totale [9]
Africa	15 321	15 538	22 089	26 317	14 122	Afrique
Americas	234 065	257 313	317 618	313 151	284 537	Amériques
Europe	4 149 631	4 507 425	4 925 570	5 037 345	4 167 620	Europe
Asia, East and South East/Oceania	159 305	195 382	216 803	232 887	200 026	Asie. Est et Sud-Est et Océanie
Dem. Rep. of the Congo						**Rép. dém. du Congo**
Total [5,24]	37 000	30 000	53 139	79 922	102 770	Totale [5,24]
Africa	...	...	22 223	73 428	96 594	Afrique
Americas	...	...	1 231	799	495	Amériques
Europe	...	...	7 975	4 295	5 681	Europe
Asia, East and South East/Oceania	...	...	1 333	1 400	...	Asie. Est et Sud-Est et Océanie
Region not specified	37 000	30 000	20 377	...	...	Région non spécifiée
Denmark						**Danemark**
Total [9,25]	2 124 572	2 157 665	2 072 800	2 023 056	2 087 681	Totale [9,25]
Americas	93 551	95 437	100 781	101 039	112 706	Amériques
Europe	1 823 769	1 850 525	1 792 981	1 748 024	1 795 286	Europe
Asia, East and South East/Oceania	55 673	51 230	55 921	60 947	62 474	Asie. Est et Sud-Est et Océanie
Region not specified	151 579	160 473	123 117	113 046	117 215	Région non spécifiée
Dominica						**Dominique**
Total [5]	63 259	65 446	65 501	73 500	...	Totale [5]
Americas	50 542	52 295	52 776	60 400	...	Amériques
Europe	11 898	12 215	11 710	12 600	...	Europe
Asia, East and South East/Oceania	277	806	339	...	...	Asie. Est et Sud-Est et Océanie
Region not specified	542	130	676	500	...	Région non spécifiée
Dominican Republic						**Rép. dominicaine**
Total [3,5,26]	1 948 464	2 184 688	2 334 493	2 651 249	2 972 552	Totale [3,5,26]
Americas	701 555	732 535	804 941	924 553	1 131 479	Amériques
Europe	863 492	1 013 863	1 063 766	1 206 007	1 301 563	Europe
Asia, East and South East/Oceania	2 790	2 553	2 455	1 841	3 132	Asie. Est et Sud-Est et Océanie
Region not specified	380 627	435 737	463 331	518 848	536 378	Région non spécifiée
Ecuador						**Equateur**
Total [2,6]	493 727	529 492	510 626	517 670	615 493	Totale [2,6]
Africa	1 023	1 033	980	1 054	1 253	Afrique
Americas	373 652	406 379	387 560	395 808	470 603	Amériques
Europe	105 452	108 473	107 845	107 124	127 367	Europe
Asia, East and South East/Oceania	13 561	13 595	14 195	13 681	16 266	Asie. Est et Sud-Est et Océanie
Region not specified	39	12	46	3	4	Région non spécifiée
Egypt						**Egypte**
Total [2]	3 895 942	3 961 416	3 453 866	4 796 520	5 506 179	Totale [2]
Africa	115 808	120 145	130 671	150 552	147 425	Afrique
Americas	259 057	256 668	217 403	276 769	340 770	Amériques
Europe	2 342 709	2 394 414	1 956 833	3 224 097	3 805 389	Europe
Asia, East and South East/Oceania	251 789	230 769	130 835	211 107	280 831	Asie. Est et Sud-Est et Océanie
Southern Asia	36 539	29 549	30 193	34 682	39 304	Asie du Sud
Western Asia	828 727	893 351	985 947	897 108	889 886	Asie occidentale
Region not specified	61 313	36 520	1 984	2 205	2 574	Région non spécifiée
El Salvador						**El Salvador**
Total [5,6]	282 835	387 052	541 863	658 191	794 678	Totale [5,6]
Africa	150	...	...	...	...	Afrique
Americas	244 818	343 209	498 160	596 044	719 615	Amériques
Europe	32 613	27 401	27 107	26 469	27 012	Europe
Asia, East and South East/Oceania	5 224	3 719	3 965	3 406	3 075	Asie. Est et Sud-Est et Océanie

75

Tourist/visitor arrivals by region of origin *[cont.]*

Arrivées de touristes/visiteurs par région de provenance *[suite]*

Country or area of destination and region of origin +	1996	1997	1998	1999	2000	Pays ou zone de destination et région de provenance +
Western Asia	30	...	...	...	...	Asie occidentale
Region not specified	...	12 723	12 631	32 272	44 976	Région non spécifiée
Eritrea						**Erythrée**
Total [2,3]	416 596	409 544	187 647	56 699	70 355	Totale [2,3]
Africa	254 996	279 666	119 357	3 729	4 023	Afrique
Americas	2 564	2 960	2 088	783	2 093	Amériques
Europe	11 611	11 948	7 757	3 605	6 276	Europe
Asia, East and South East/Oceania	1 521	1 614	1 406	2 126	2 960	Asie. Est et Sud-Est et Océanie
Southern Asia	167	475	408	345	562	Asie du Sud
Western Asia	1 302	1 403	1 543	1 501	1 512	Asie occidentale
Region not specified	144 435	111 478	55 088	44 610	52 929	Région non spécifiée
Estonia						**Estonie**
Total [2]	2 443 871	2 618 484	2 908 819	3 180 530	3 310 300	Totale [2]
Americas	55 568	44 519	78 590	65 448	99 652	Amériques
Europe	2 364 836	2 547 620	2 783 501	3 090 765	3 186 491	Europe
Asia, East and South East/Oceania	16 196	24 338	28 156	14 142	13 521	Asie. Est et Sud-Est et Océanie
Region not specified	7 271	2 007	18 572	10 175	10 636	Région non spécifiée
Ethiopia						**Ethiopie**
Total [5,27,28]	108 885	114 732	90 847	91 859	135 954	Totale [5,27,28]
Africa	27 658	29 255	25 368	28 496	48 796	Afrique
Americas	14 917	15 957	15 126	16 162	14 279	Amériques
Europe	39 198	40 905	29 536	25 704	34 941	Europe
Asia, East and South East/Oceania	4 246	4 705	4 297	4 462	6 951	Asie. Est et Sud-Est et Océanie
Southern Asia	2 069	2 066	1 642	1 755	3 480	Asie du Sud
Western Asia	12 739	13 538	14 814	15 221	8 605	Asie occidentale
Region not specified	8 058	8 306	64	59	18 902	Région non spécifiée
Fiji						**Fidji**
Total [5,6]	339 560	359 441	371 342	409 955	294 070	Totale [5,6]
Americas	50 138	57 735	61 227	75 683	63 066	Amériques
Europe	60 782	67 825	68 675	67 394	51 721	Europe
Asia, East and South East/Oceania	227 211	232 157	239 600	263 734	177 697	Asie. Est et Sud-Est et Océanie
Region not specified	1 429	1 724	1 840	3 144	1 586	Région non spécifiée
Finland						**Finlande**
Total [9]	* 1 724 000	1 831 500	1 866 842	1 830 560	1 970 817	Totale [9]
Africa	3 796	4 032	3 583	3 495	4 051	Afrique
Americas	108 015	114 740	113 959	113 986	123 479	Amériques
Europe	1 422 712	1 511 328	1 539 863	1 502 238	1 589 433	Europe
Asia, East and South East/Oceania	116 669	123 961	110 937	119 036	133 492	Asie. Est et Sud-Est et Océanie
Southern Asia	4 408	4 682	4 756	3 995	5 610	Asie du Sud
Western Asia	1 571	1 669	1 729	1 358	2 023	Asie occidentale
Region not specified	66 829	71 088	92 015	86 452	112 729	Région non spécifiée
France						**France**
Total [5,29]	62 406 000	67 310 000	70 040 300	73 042 300	75 595 376	Totale [5,29]
Africa	996 000	1 086 000	1 117 800	986 700	1 051 425	Afrique
Americas	4 191 000	4 433 000	4 703 700	4 609 400	5 053 201	Amériques
Europe	54 788 000	59 180 000	61 556 000	64 784 600	66 604 944	Europe
Asia, East and South East/Oceania	1 986 000	2 133 000	2 229 000	2 235 700	2 423 611	Asie. Est et Sud-Est et Océanie
Western Asia	262 000	288 000	246 100	234 100	258 600	Asie occidentale
Region not specified	183 000	190 000	187 700	191 800	203 595	Région non spécifiée
French Polynesia						**Polynésie française**
Total [5,6,13]	163 774	180 440	188 933	210 800	252 000 [30]	Totale [5,6,13]
Africa	171	207	161	212	...	Afrique
Americas	54 970	53 811	62 225	80 148	...	Amériques
Europe	73 827	83 697	87 454	91 785	...	Europe
Asia, East and South East/Oceania	34 138	42 020	38 381	37 780	...	Asie. Est et Sud-Est et Océanie
Southern Asia	14	32	33	44	...	Asie du Sud
Western Asia	199	186	213	283	...	Asie occidentale
Region not specified	455	487	466	548	...	Région non spécifiée
Gabon						**Gabon**
Total * [5,31]	144 509	167 197	195 323	177 834	155 432	Totale * [5,31]
Africa	28 338	33 341	47 819	37 995	37 712	Afrique
Americas	20 911	24 094	26 562	6 000	2 000	Amériques

75

Tourist/visitor arrivals by region of origin *[cont.]*

Arrivées de touristes/visiteurs par région de provenance *[suite]*

Country or area of destination and region of origin +	1996	1997	1998	1999	2000	Pays ou zone de destination et région de provenance +
Europe	81 819	93 699	103 294	103 839	112 000	Europe
Asia, East and South East/Oceania	1 115	1 285	1 416	5 000	1 000	Asie. Est et Sud-Est et Océanie
Western Asia	2 788	3 212	3 541	5 000	2 000	Asie occidentale
Region not specified	9 538	11 566	12 691	20 000	720	Région non spécifiée
Gambia						**Gambie**
Total [5,32]	76 814	84 751	91 106	96 126	...	Totale [5,32]
Africa	319	549	986	928	...	Afrique
Americas	528	575	779	890	...	Amériques
Europe	71 935	80 694	85 994	90 087	...	Europe
Region not specified	4 032	2 933	3 347	4 221	...	Région non spécifiée
Georgia						**Géorgie**
Total [5]	116 980	313 290	317 063	383 817	387 258	Totale [5]
Africa	57	139	140	340	326	Afrique
Americas	2 918	4 248	5 278	8 919	10 958	Amériques
Europe	106 564	304 547	303 572	362 548	357 798	Europe
Asia, East and South East/Oceania	326	1 091	1 513	4 784	7 327	Asie. Est et Sud-Est et Océanie
Southern Asia	2 071	2 522	4 832	4 872	6 058	Asie du Sud
Western Asia	249	685	774	1 877	2 167	Asie occidentale
Region not specified	4 795	58	954	477	2 624	Région non spécifiée
Germany						**Allemagne**
Total [9,33]	15 204 707	15 836 797	16 511 486	17 115 685	18 983 264	Totale [9,33]
Africa	124 108	133 811	136 740	141 843	159 991	Afrique
Americas	1 942 264	2 127 253	2 351 112	2 399 923	2 865 485	Amériques
Europe	11 112 158	11 490 712	11 979 093	12 497 088	13 515 662	Europe
Asia, East and South East/Oceania	1 573 285	1 589 968	1 514 879	1 567 293	1 799 132	Asie. Est et Sud-Est et Océanie
Western Asia	75 854	83 888	96 820	93 341	106 459	Asie occidentale
Region not specified	377 038	411 165	432 842	416 197	536 535	Région non spécifiée
Ghana						**Ghana**
Total [5]	304 860	325 433	347 949	372 651	...	Totale [5]
Africa	103 726	110 725	118 384	126 788	...	Afrique
Americas	25 603	27 331	29 222	31 297	...	Amériques
Europe	75 572	80 672	86 255	92 378	...	Europe
Asia, East and South East/Oceania	14 663	15 652	16 736	17 924	...	Asie. Est et Sud-Est et Océanie
Western Asia	2 312	2 468	2 639	2 827	...	Asie occidentale
Region not specified	82 984	88 585	94 713	101 437	...	Région non spécifiée
Greece						**Grèce**
Total [5,34]	9 233 295	10 070 325	10 916 046	12 164 088	...	Totale [5,34]
Africa	23 706	23 072	21 134	23 995	...	Afrique
Americas	298 144	314 057	291 507	305 261	...	Amériques
Europe	8 541 456	9 404 889	10 333 580	11 555 502	...	Europe
Asia, East and South East/Oceania	314 038	280 749	224 193	225 275	...	Asie. Est et Sud-Est et Océanie
Southern Asia	5 319	3 730	3 848	3 809	...	Asie du Sud
Western Asia	50 632	43 828	41 784	50 246	...	Asie occidentale
Grenada						**Grenade**
Total [5]	108 230	110 749	115 794	125 289	128 864	Totale [5]
Africa	144	238	337	481	612	Afrique
Americas	49 753	51 727	54 578	64 000	62 214	Amériques
Europe	37 587	37 796	38 081	40 549	46 325	Europe
Asia, East and South East/Oceania	1 039	977	1 279	1 802	1 394	Asie. Est et Sud-Est et Océanie
Western Asia	49	75	104	118	122	Asie occidentale
Region not specified	19 658	19 936	21 415	18 339	18 197	Région non spécifiée
Guadeloupe						**Guadeloupe**
Total [1,35]	146 878	147 010	133 030	146 201	623 134	Totale [1,35]
Americas	11 040	16 740	7 097	8 435	125 871	Amériques
Europe	134 799	129 436	125 231	137 030	495 385	Europe
Region not specified	1 039	834	702	736	1 878	Région non spécifiée
Guam						**Guam**
Total [5,7]	1 362 600	1 381 513	1 137 026	1 161 803	1 288 002	Totale [5,7]
Americas	35 836	44 087	42 415	41 798	42 284	Amériques
Europe	1 278	1 786	1 890	1 628	1 618	Europe
Asia, East and South East/Oceania	1 307 561	1 323 597	1 079 175	1 105 064	1 231 413	Asie. Est et Sud-Est et Océanie
Region not specified	17 925	12 043	13 546	13 313	12 687	Région non spécifiée

75

Tourist/visitor arrivals by region of origin *[cont.]*

Arrivées de touristes/visiteurs par région de provenance *[suite]*

Country or area of destination and region of origin +	1996	1997	1998	1999	2000	Pays ou zone de destination et région de provenance +
Guatemala						**Guatemala**
Total[5]	520 085	576 361	636 278	822 695	...	Totale[5]
Americas	409 374	457 156	504 757	692 626	...	Amériques
Europe	96 830	104 475	115 406	113 698	...	Europe
Asia, East and South East/Oceania	12 029	13 746	14 739	15 084	...	Asie. Est et Sud-Est et Océanie
Southern Asia	267	...	...	...	...	Asie du Sud
Western Asia	318	261	296	345	...	Asie occidentale
Region not specified	1 267	723	1 080	942	...	Région non spécifiée
Guinea						**Guinée**
Total[5,36]	...	17 000	23 000	27 345	32 598	Totale[5,36]
Africa	...	2 886	4 400	9 098	12 308	Afrique
Americas	...	2 300	2 434	3 638	3 636	Amériques
Europe	...	8 966	11 562	11 173	14 315	Europe
Asia, East and South East/Oceania	...	353	489	2 408	1 160	Asie. Est et Sud-Est et Océanie
Southern Asia	...	...	...	229	373	Asie du Sud
Western Asia	...	2 495	4 115	409	290	Asie occidentale
Region not specified	...	...	...	390	516	Région non spécifiée
Guyana						**Guyana**
Total[5]	92 232	75 794	68 403	...	...	Totale[5]
Africa	137	128	63	...	...	Afrique
Americas	84 533	69 419	62 930	...	...	Amériques
Europe	6 348	5 425	4 927	...	...	Europe
Asia, East and South East/Oceania	839	543	265	...	...	Asie. Est et Sud-Est et Océanie
Southern Asia	358	268	207	...	...	Asie du Sud
Western Asia	17	11	11	...	...	Asie occidentale
Haiti						**Haïti**
Total[5]	150 147	148 735	146 837	143 362	140 492	Totale[5]
Americas	133 475	132 706	131 385	129 854	128 048	Amériques
Europe	14 625	14 112	13 607	11 783	10 960	Europe
Region not specified	2 047	1 917	1 845	1 725	1 484	Région non spécifiée
Honduras						**Honduras**
Total[2]	263 317	306 646	321 149	370 847	470 727	Totale[2]
Africa	237	231	168	222	204	Afrique
Americas	224 926	265 600	280 437	330 821	420 112	Amériques
Europe	31 666	32 954	32 892	33 670	43 022	Europe
Asia, East and South East/Oceania	6 462	7 823	7 618	5 767	6 914	Asie. Est et Sud-Est et Océanie
Southern Asia	...	...	...	156	168	Asie du Sud
Western Asia	...	...	...	150	132	Asie occidentale
Region not specified	26	38	34	61	175	Région non spécifiée
Hungary						**Hongrie**
Total[37]	20 674 199[5]	17 248 257[5]	33 624 091[2]	28 802 636[2]	31 141 271[2]	Totale[37]
Africa	29 757	26 219	11 762	13 680	15 630	Afrique
Americas	329 686	372 537	451 965	405 275	448 433	Amériques
Europe	20 054 714	16 575 893	32 967 543	28 147 860	30 407 612	Europe
Asia, East and South East/Oceania	260 042	273 608	124 281	166 156	197 898	Asie. Est et Sud-Est et Océanie
Southern Asia	...	...	14 593	17 831	21 546	Asie du Sud
Western Asia	...	...	30 743	23 901	22 667	Asie occidentale
Region not specified	...	...	23 204	27 933	27 485	Région non spécifiée
Iceland						**Islande**
Total[5]	200 835	201 666	232 219	262 604	302 913	Totale[5]
Africa	294	407	487	706	945	Afrique
Americas	33 759	35 757	44 414	48 568	58 679	Amériques
Europe	160 370	158 767	179 783	204 837	232 697	Europe
Asia, East and South East/Oceania	6 129	6 187	7 001	7 701	9 754	Asie. Est et Sud-Est et Océanie
Southern Asia	185	205	421	615	551	Asie du Sud
Western Asia	77	314	82	133	243	Asie occidentale
Region not specified	21	29	31	44	44	Région non spécifiée
India						**Inde**
Total[5,6]	2 287 860	2 374 094	2 358 629	2 481 928	2 641 157	Totale[5,6]
Africa	85 663	98 910	106 045	129 520	138 441	Afrique
Americas	322 240	339 875	348 621	372 857	448 341	Amériques
Europe	897 010	898 929	924 753	895 300	895 784	Europe

75

Tourist/visitor arrivals by region of origin *[cont.]*

Arrivées de touristes/visiteurs par région de provenance *[suite]*

Country or area of destination and region of origin +	1996	1997	1998	1999	2000	Pays ou zone de destination et région de provenance +
Asia, East and South East/Oceania	335 165	358 472	343 102	368 703	389 282	Asie. Est et Sud-Est et Océanie
Southern Asia	543 967	583 706	558 772	624 945	663 581	Asie du Sud
Western Asia	96 857	93 555	77 153	90 359	105 728	Asie occidentale
Region not specified	6 958	647	183	244	...	Région non spécifiée
Indonesia						**Indonésie**
Total [5]	5 034 472	5 185 243	4 606 416	4 727 520	5 064 217	Totale [5]
Africa	29 051	24 253	52 312	37 551	37 573	Afrique
Americas	244 497	208 726	201 488	186 727	232 117	Amériques
Europe	754 412	820 340	641 374	688 234	799 769	Europe
Asia, East and South East/Oceania	3 936 282	4 061 865	3 608 283	3 747 388	3 909 094	Asie. Est et Sud-Est et Océanie
Southern Asia	46 370	39 580	58 707	35 484	50 260	Asie du Sud
Western Asia	23 860	30 479	44 252	32 136	35 404	Asie occidentale
Iran (Islamic Rep. of)						**Iran (Rép. islamique d')**
Total [5]	567 334	739 711	1 007 597	1 320 690	...	Totale [5]
Africa	1 966	2 596	2 914	3 410	...	Afrique
Americas	3 350	2 640	2 986	1 825	...	Amériques
Europe	260 958	449 115	631 020	735 202	...	Europe
Asia, East and South East/Oceania	17 063	10 847	17 800	20 805	...	Asie. Est et Sud-Est et Océanie
Southern Asia	208 752	194 409	255 776	298 954	...	Asie du Sud
Western Asia	75 200	80 104	97 101	113 494	...	Asie occidentale
Region not specified	45	...	...	147 000	...	Région non spécifiée
Iraq						**Iraq**
Total [2]	51 330	14 906	44 885	30 328	78 457	Totale [2]
Africa	777	264	250	207	256	Afrique
Americas	761	143	88	145	183	Amériques
Europe	3 052	1 287	1 088	685	1 461	Europe
Asia, East and South East/Oceania	1 541	229	65	42	134	Asie. Est et Sud-Est et Océanie
Southern Asia	9 087	9 704	40 018	28 139	76 367	Asie du Sud
Western Asia	34 812	3 279	3 376	1 110	56	Asie occidentale
Region not specified	1 300	...	...	...	...	Région non spécifiée
Ireland						**Irlande**
Total [5]	5 289 000	5 587 000	6 064 000	6 403 000	6 749 000	Totale [5]
Americas	738 000	787 000	871 000	961 000	1 070 000	Amériques
Europe	4 374 000	4 598 000	4 984 000	5 211 000	5 428 000	Europe
Asia, East and South East/Oceania	157 000	180 000	184 000	205 000	223 000	Asie. Est et Sud-Est et Océanie
Region not specified	20 000	22 000	25 000	26 000	28 000	Région non spécifiée
Israel						**Israël**
Total [5,6]	2 100 051	2 010 242	1 941 620	2 312 411	2 416 756	Totale [5,6]
Africa	42 172	42 837	37 085	36 173	45 381	Afrique
Americas	558 964	548 385	571 409	645 040	683 917	Amériques
Europe	1 246 091	1 178 934	1 117 249	1 340 682	1 442 158	Europe
Asia, East and South East/Oceania	111 002	107 478	66 303	98 734	111 238	Asie. Est et Sud-Est et Océanie
Southern Asia	12 834	14 480	12 715	17 152	19 052	Asie du Sud
Western Asia	106 039	94 094	100 507	111 684	107 882	Asie occidentale
Region not specified	22 949	24 034	36 352	62 946	7 128	Région non spécifiée
Italy						**Italie**
Total [2,38]	57 249 184	57 998 188	58 499 261	59 521 444	62 702 228	Totale [2,38]
Africa	168 162	241 635	181 150	155 103	212 873	Afrique
Americas	2 034 016	2 645 989	2 474 646	2 004 432	2 292 254	Amériques
Europe	52 905 181	52 920 478	54 049 369	55 840 818	58 643 827	Europe
Asia, East and South East/Oceania	1 973 565	2 018 245	1 626 810	1 346 538	1 362 568	Asie. Est et Sud-Est et Océanie
Southern Asia	71 851	72 052	73 450	74 396	93 151	Asie du Sud
Western Asia	96 176	99 789	93 751	100 157	97 555	Asie occidentale
Region not specified	233	...	85	...	...	Région non spécifiée
Jamaica						**Jamaïque**
Total [3,5,13]	1 162 449	1 192 194	1 225 287	1 248 397	1 322 690	Totale [3,5,13]
Africa	1 063	1 023	1 026	1 361	1 388	Afrique
Americas	925 859	959 027	995 137	1 024 015	1 108 727	Amériques
Europe	209 050	211 551	213 893	209 576	200 269	Europe
Asia, East and South East/Oceania	25 266	19 621	14 144	12 248	11 194	Asie. Est et Sud-Est et Océanie
Southern Asia	484	700	595	751	670	Asie du Sud
Western Asia	...	63	423	367	361	Asie occidentale

75

Tourist/visitor arrivals by region of origin *[cont.]*

Arrivées de touristes/visiteurs par région de provenance *[suite]*

Country or area of destination and region of origin +	1996	1997	1998	1999	2000	Pays ou zone de destination et région de provenance +
Region not specified	727	209	69	79	81	Région non spécifiée
Japan						**Japon**
Total [5,6]	3 837 113	4 218 208	4 106 057	4 437 863	4 757 146	Totale [5,6]
Africa	10 914	11 928	12 556	12 939	14 512	Afrique
Americas	749 000	780 711	828 240	852 751	899 277	Amériques
Europe	484 394	545 783	577 278	580 135	624 850	Europe
Asia, East and South East/Oceania	2 540 221	2 817 089	2 622 286	2 925 323	3 148 918	Asie. Est et Sud-Est et Océanie
Southern Asia	47 123	55 525	57 662	60 114	63 725	Asie du Sud
Western Asia	2 659	2 841	3 095	3 317	3 154	Asie occidentale
Region not specified	2 802	4 331	4 940	3 284	2 710	Région non spécifiée
Jordan						**Jordanie**
Total [5]	1 102 752	1 127 028	1 256 428	1 357 822	1 426 879	Totale [5]
Africa	2 313	2 338	2 750	2 811	32 758	Afrique
Americas	107 960	107 676	108 612	123 525	126 411	Amériques
Europe	373 016	365 036	338 706	418 285	463 311	Europe
Asia, East and South East/Oceania	46 806	47 877	33 933	47 379	55 787	Asie. Est et Sud-Est et Océanie
Southern Asia	...	...	...	4 224	4 203	Asie du Sud
Western Asia	572 657	604 101	772 427	761 598	744 409	Asie occidentale
Kazakhstan						**Kazakhstan**
Total [2]	202 000	284 000	257 000	394 000	1 682 604	Totale [2]
Africa	...	...	...	...	441	Afrique
Americas	...	...	...	...	18 017	Amériques
Europe	...	...	...	...	1 583 711	Europe
Asia, East and South East/Oceania	...	...	...	...	68 835	Asie. Est et Sud-Est et Océanie
Southern Asia	...	...	...	...	9 177	Asie du Sud
Western Asia	...	...	...	...	2 423	Asie occidentale
Kenya						**Kenya**
Total [2,6,39]	1 003 000	1 000 600	894 300	969 419	1 036 628	Totale [2,6,39]
Africa	216 353	272 674	251 243	264 145	282 458	Afrique
Americas	59 982	85 161	79 864	82 496	88 216	Amériques
Europe	485 580	573 672	504 204	556 577	595 162	Europe
Asia, East and South East/Oceania	35 766	44 313	38 145	42 927	45 903	Asie. Est et Sud-Est et Océanie
Southern Asia	12 100	24 026	20 844	23 274	24 889	Asie du Sud
Region not specified	193 219	754	...	...	...	Région non spécifiée
Kiribati						**Kiribati**
Total [2,13,40]	4 205	5 054	5 679	4 865	4 035	Totale [2,13,40]
Americas	791	1 039	1 460	1 452	1 202	Amériques
Europe	282	289	144	254	152	Europe
Asia, East and South East/Oceania	2 616	2 819	3 200	2 756	2 229	Asie. Est et Sud-Est et Océanie
Region not specified	516	907	875	403	452	Région non spécifiée
Korea, Republic of						**Corée, République de**
Total [2,41]	3 683 779	3 908 140	4 250 176	4 659 785	5 321 792	Totale [2,41]
Africa	8 639	10 681	11 368	13 986	14 085	Afrique
Americas	464 509	493 942	471 317	463 937	534 519	Amériques
Europe	444 691	436 078	401 309	408 481	479 238	Europe
Asia, East and South East/Oceania	2 381 766	2 582 236	2 977 078	3 380 795	3 916 518	Asie. Est et Sud-Est et Océanie
Southern Asia	74 352	71 251	65 727	81 044	95 677	Asie du Sud
Western Asia	7 456	6 907	9 382	10 515	4 232	Asie occidentale
Region not specified	302 366	307 045	313 995	301 027	277 523	Région non spécifiée
Kuwait						**Koweït**
Total [2]	1 555 285	1 637 805	1 762 641	1 883 633	1 944 233	Totale [2]
Africa	10 797	13 885	18 648	17 679	17 093	Afrique
Americas	26 311	31 807	33 428	39 191	39 389	Amériques
Europe	58 383	66 155	65 998	73 638	71 409	Europe
Asia, East and South East/Oceania	56 670	54 516	65 908	81 737	95 263	Asie. Est et Sud-Est et Océanie
Southern Asia	459 051	471 276	513 475	537 496	518 160	Asie du Sud
Western Asia	930 385	983 464	1 045 852	1 117 588	1 191 168	Asie occidentale
Region not specified	13 688	16 702	19 332	16 304	11 751	Région non spécifiée
Kyrgyzstan						**Kirghizistan**
Total [5]	41 650	87 386	59 363	68 863	...	Totale [5]
Americas	...	...	1 386	3 224	...	Amériques
Europe	28 625	72 202	46 287	50 352	...	Europe

75

Tourist/visitor arrivals by region of origin *[cont.]*

Arrivées de touristes/visiteurs par région de provenance *[suite]*

Country or area of destination and region of origin +	1996	1997	1998	1999	2000	Pays ou zone de destination et région de provenance +
Asia, East and South East/Oceania	...	...	6 791	8 786	...	Asie. Est et Sud-Est et Océanie
Southern Asia	...	...	2 656	2 930	...	Asie du Sud
Western Asia	...	...	90	160	...	Asie occidentale
Region not specified	13 025	15 184	2 153	3 411	...	Région non spécifiée
Lao People's Dem. Rep.						**Rép. dém. pop. lao**
Total [2]	403 000	463 200	500 200	614 278	737 208	Totale [2]
Americas	14 102	18 213	25 326	31 780	42 111	Amériques
Europe	30 582	39 096	52 749	70 755	89 703	Europe
Asia, East and South East/Oceania	337 437	397 253	410 888	503 324	599 908	Asie. Est et Sud-Est et Océanie
Southern Asia	20 255	6 528	10 308	7 379	4 346	Asie du Sud
Region not specified	624	2 110	929	1 040	1 140	Région non spécifiée
Latvia						**Lettonie**
Total [9]	188 269	219 939	238 835	240 799	268 083	Totale [9]
Africa	...	68	144	77	136	Afrique
Americas	9 812	9 312	10 762	10 991	11 574	Amériques
Europe	165 829	199 147	214 066	217 050	240 686	Europe
Asia, East and South East/Oceania	2 707	4 010	4 097	5 928	6 816	Asie. Est et Sud-Est et Océanie
Southern Asia	84	214	286	793	285	Asie du Sud
Western Asia	46	79	106	157	257	Asie occidentale
Region not specified	9 791	7 109	9 374	5 803	8 329	Région non spécifiée
Lebanon						**Liban**
Total [5,42]	424 000	557 568	630 781	673 261	741 648	Totale [5,42]
Africa	13 527	19 380	23 497	27 887	24 183	Afrique
Americas	46 917	59 404	68 321	84 516	89 962	Amériques
Europe	142 100	173 887	195 950	223 945	228 960	Europe
Asia, East and South East/Oceania	33 604	40 683	40 962	46 986	55 638	Asie. Est et Sud-Est et Océanie
Southern Asia	20 213	26 598	35 273	36 004	51 313	Asie du Sud
Western Asia	138 891	207 866	235 992	253 423	288 083	Asie occidentale
Region not specified	28 748	29 750	30 786	500	3 509	Région non spécifiée
Lesotho						**Lesotho**
Total [2]	311 802	323 868	289 819	...	...	Totale [2]
Africa	304 368	313 323	285 734	...	...	Afrique
Americas	1 242	2 861	794	...	...	Amériques
Europe	4 708	5 682	2 311	...	...	Europe
Asia, East and South East/Oceania	1 484	2 002	980	...	...	Asie. Est et Sud-Est et Océanie
Libyan Arab Jamah.						**Jamah. arabe libyenne**
Total [2]	1 276 000	913 251	850 292	965 307	962 559	Totale [2]
Africa	829 000	571 868	461 533	531 123	533 223	Afrique
Americas	3 030	861	456	463	647	Amériques
Europe	54 733	28 140	22 649	33 409	34 296	Europe
Asia, East and South East/Oceania	18 500	3 177	3 088	2 841	1 669	Asie. Est et Sud-Est et Océanie
Southern Asia	8 000	2 100	1 271	867	977	Asie du Sud
Western Asia	361 938	307 105	361 295	396 604	391 747	Asie occidentale
Region not specified	799	...	...	...	...	Région non spécifiée
Liechtenstein						**Liechtenstein**
Total [1]	56 168	57 077	59 228	59 502	61 550	Totale [1]
Africa	209	155	173	176	224	Afrique
Americas	4 504	5 252	4 879	4 861	4 728	Amériques
Europe	49 031	49 237	52 319	52 554	54 759	Europe
Asia, East and South East/Oceania	1 733	2 433	1 857	1 911	1 839	Asie. Est et Sud-Est et Océanie
Region not specified	691	...	...	...	...	Région non spécifiée
Lithuania						**Lituanie**
Total [9,43]	255 301	288 028	306 228	293 120	299 976	Totale [9,43]
Africa	170	234	208	166	220	Afrique
Americas	11 344	12 407	14 918	15 194	15 120	Amériques
Europe	237 682	267 822	284 489	270 082	275 503	Europe
Asia, East and South East/Oceania	6 105	7 565	6 613	7 678	9 133	Asie. Est et Sud-Est et Océanie
Luxembourg						**Luxembourg**
Total [9]	724 279	778 304	789 176	836 921	807 002	Totale [9]
Americas	30 463	35 911	40 172	40 576	39 145	Amériques
Europe	671 770	718 864	721 519	768 875	740 117	Europe
Region not specified	22 046	23 529	27 485	27 470	27 740	Région non spécifiée

75

Tourist/visitor arrivals by region of origin *[cont.]*

Arrivées de touristes/visiteurs par région de provenance *[suite]*

Country or area of destination and region of origin +	1996	1997	1998	1999	2000	Pays ou zone de destination et région de provenance +
Madagascar						**Madagascar**
Total [5]	82 681	100 762	121 207	138 253	160 071	Totale [5]
Africa	9 303	5 844	15 515	20 461	24 534	Afrique
Americas	5 606	2 015	2 424	6 913	6 402	Amériques
Europe	63 462	64 488	82 421	95 395	110 449	Europe
Asia, East and South East/Oceania	4 205	1 008	1 454	2 489	2 055	Asie. Est et Sud-Est et Océanie
Region not specified	105	27 407	19 393	12 995	16 631	Région non spécifiée
Malawi						**Malawi**
Total [5,37]	193 628	207 259	219 570	* 254 352	* 228 106	Totale [5,37]
Africa	142 840	152 876	161 955	187 610	179 000	Afrique
Americas	9 681	10 362	10 979	12 718	10 000	Amériques
Europe	30 980	33 161	35 131	40 696	26 106	Europe
Asia, East and South East/Oceania	7 745	8 290	8 783	10 174	10 000	Asie. Est et Sud-Est et Océanie
Southern Asia	2 188	2 342	2 481	2 874	3 000	Asie du Sud
Western Asia	194	228	241	280	...	Asie occidentale
Malaysia						**Malaisie**
Total [5,44]	7 138 452	6 210 921	5 550 748	7 931 149	10 221 582	Totale [5,44]
Africa	30 039	23 502	25 519	29 863	74 314	Afrique
Americas	145 991	137 164	121 569	122 079	307 692	Amériques
Europe	407 537	386 790	367 660	308 713	590 304	Europe
Asia, East and South East/Oceania	6 335 909	5 449 937	4 696 660	6 826 835	8 716 429	Asie. Est et Sud-Est et Océanie
Southern Asia	62 985	53 644	56 117	68 992	180 016	Asie du Sud
Western Asia	31 371	16 460	19 571	19 128	44 665	Asie occidentale
Region not specified	124 620	143 424	263 652	555 539	308 162	Région non spécifiée
Maldives						**Maldives**
Total [5,13]	338 733	365 563	395 725	429 666	467 154	Totale [5,13]
Africa	7 584	7 962	7 168	1 846	2 311	Afrique
Americas	4 125	6 101	6 119	6 082	7 108	Amériques
Europe	252 781	273 066	304 905	340 469	362 196	Europe
Asia, East and South East/Oceania	52 634	60 644	56 983	60 598	73 411	Asie. Est et Sud-Est et Océanie
Southern Asia	19 782	16 443	19 284	19 393	20 648	Asie du Sud
Western Asia	1 819	1 347	1 266	1 278	1 480	Asie occidentale
Region not specified	8	...	...	...	...	Région non spécifiée
Mali						**Mali**
Total [1]	53 893	65 649	83 000	82 159	86 469	Totale [1]
Africa	11 541	14 321	18 000	15 852	18 962	Afrique
Americas	5 814	6 841	8 000	8 671	9 306	Amériques
Europe	31 137	38 278	49 000	49 733	48 304	Europe
Asia, East and South East/Oceania	1 467	1 621	2 000	782	1 020	Asie. Est et Sud-Est et Océanie
Western Asia	171	321	400	1 369	2 206	Asie occidentale
Region not specified	3 763	4 267	5 600	5 752	6 671	Région non spécifiée
Malta						**Malte**
Total [5]	1 053 788 [37]	1 111 161 [37]	1 182 240 [37]	1 214 230 [37]	1 215 713 [45]	Totale [5]
Africa	4 383	5 730	6 342	7 387	9 691	Afrique
Americas	17 662	21 197	25 258	25 951	26 932	Amériques
Europe	952 940	1 023 222	1 087 709	1 107 725	1 103 937	Europe
Asia, East and South East/Oceania	11 952	13 930	15 706	17 620	21 162	Asie. Est et Sud-Est et Océanie
Southern Asia	1 336	1 250	1 987	2 054	1 944	Asie du Sud
Western Asia	53 328	42 117	41 067	48 480	46 384	Asie occidentale
Region not specified	12 187	3 715	4 171	5 013	5 663	Région non spécifiée
Marshall Islands						**Iles Marshall**
Total [5,13]	6 229	6 354	6 374	4 622	5 246	Totale [5,13]
Americas	2 055	2 471	2 388	2 064	2 022	Amériques
Europe	367	354	229	220	129	Europe
Asia, East and South East/Oceania	3 664	3 411	3 497	2 234	2 673	Asie. Est et Sud-Est et Océanie
Region not specified	143	118	260	104	422	Région non spécifiée
Martinique						**Martinique**
Total [5]	476 880	513 229	548 767	564 304	526 291	Totale [5]
Americas	66 226	77 759	77 270	85 291	80 168	Amériques
Europe	406 423	431 096	467 263	474 475	443 046	Europe
Region not specified	4 231	4 374	4 234	4 538	3 077	Région non spécifiée

75

Tourist/visitor arrivals by region of origin *[cont.]*

Arrivées de touristes/visiteurs par région de provenance *[suite]*

Country or area of destination and region of origin +	1996	1997	1998	1999	2000	Pays ou zone de destination et région de provenance +
Mauritius						**Maurice**
Total [5]	486 867	536 125	558 195	578 085	656 453	Totale [5]
Africa	163 435	164 082	163 024	156 228	163 763	Afrique
Americas	4 265	5 509	5 842	5 820	7 643	Amériques
Europe	281 817	326 522	352 688	379 051	440 279	Europe
Asia, East and South East/Oceania	23 887	25 283	22 677	21 531	24 083	Asie. Est et Sud-Est et Océanie
Southern Asia	13 075	13 998	13 395	14 694	19 598	Asie du Sud
Western Asia	...	682	509	527	591	Asie occidentale
Region not specified	388	49	60	234	496	Région non spécifiée
Mexico						**Mexique**
Total [3,5]	21 404 674	19 350 900	19 392 005	19 042 726	20 641 358	Totale [3,5]
Americas	21 019 950	18 940 859	18 550 480	18 182 563	19 949 917	Amériques
Europe	340 593	346 530	476 654	562 790	400 566	Europe
Region not specified	44 131	63 511	364 871	297 373	290 875	Région non spécifiée
Micronesia (Fed. States)						**Micronésie (Etats féd. de)**
Total [5,46]	...	28 245	27 222	27 853	32 530	Totale [5,46]
Americas	...	8 008	7 499	8 113	8 789	Amériques
Europe	...	295	361	452	358	Europe
Asia, East and South East/Oceania	...	16 797	15 645	15 205	18 140	Asie. Est et Sud-Est et Océanie
Region not specified	...	3 145	3 717	4 083	5 243	Région non spécifiée
Monaco						**Monaco**
Total [1]	226 421	258 604	278 474	278 448	300 185	Totale [1]
Africa	466	576	555	2 326	2 459	Afrique
Americas	31 309	45 817	42 929	41 660	43 622	Amériques
Europe	159 163	172 201	194 000	202 394	210 506	Europe
Asia, East and South East/Oceania	12 051	14 202	12 061	11 689	19 311	Asie. Est et Sud-Est et Océanie
Western Asia	3 516	3 660	4 816	3 717	4 173	Asie occidentale
Region not specified	19 916	22 148	24 113	16 662	20 114	Région non spécifiée
Mongolia						**Mongolie**
Total [5]	70 853	82 084	197 424	158 734	158 205	Totale [5]
Africa	...	81	72	115	183	Afrique
Americas	3 834	5 129	5 442	6 059	7 217	Amériques
Europe	21 800	25 956	79 818	72 430	69 354	Europe
Asia, East and South East/Oceania	44 733	50 328	111 493	79 421	80 720	Asie. Est et Sud-Est et Océanie
Southern Asia	464	526	490	584	625	Asie du Sud
Western Asia	22	64	109	115	106	Asie occidentale
Region not specified	...	...	...	10	...	Région non spécifiée
Montserrat						**Montserrat**
Total [3,5,13]	8 703	5 132	7 467	9 900	...	Totale [3,5,13]
Americas	6 771	3 770	5 560	6 900	...	Amériques
Europe	1 631	1 085	1 496	2 300	...	Europe
Region not specified	301	277	411	700	...	Région non spécifiée
Morocco						**Maroc**
Total [3,5]	2 693 338	3 071 668	3 242 105	3 816 641	4 113 037	Totale [3,5]
Africa	75 658	78 327	80 687	87 888	88 689	Afrique
Americas	119 534	129 530	141 676	178 642	178 625	Amériques
Europe	1 337 213	1 507 819	1 655 935	1 875 824	2 055 919	Europe
Asia, East and South East/Oceania	32 480	36 041	38 992	45 397	49 486	Asie. Est et Sud-Est et Océanie
Southern Asia	3 350	3 490	4 013	5 256	5 116	Asie du Sud
Western Asia	62 910	66 022	76 795	78 271	78 514	Asie occidentale
Region not specified	1 062 193	1 250 439	1 244 007	1 545 363	1 656 688	Région non spécifiée
Myanmar						**Myanmar**
Total [5,47]	172 000	189 000	201 000	198 210	206 243	Totale [5,47]
Africa	...	...	...	316	304	Afrique
Americas	13 654	14 747	13 304	12 748	14 197	Amériques
Europe	50 818	54 859	51 659	51 627	54 905	Europe
Asia, East and South East/Oceania	98 377	113 927	119 721	126 136	129 040	Asie. Est et Sud-Est et Océanie
Southern Asia	1 805	1 948	10 816	5 967	6 534	Asie du Sud
Western Asia	...	...	...	1 416	1 263	Asie occidentale
Region not specified	7 346	3 519	5 500	...	...	Région non spécifiée
Namibia						**Namibie**
Total [5]	461 310	502 012	559 674	...	...	Totale [5]

75

Tourist/visitor arrivals by region of origin *[cont.]*

Arrivées de touristes/visiteurs par région de provenance *[suite]*

Country or area of destination and region of origin +	1996	1997	1998	1999	2000	Pays ou zone de destination et région de provenance +
Africa	351 398	383 515	429 532	...	...	Afrique
Americas	8 452	9 181	10 074	...	...	Amériques
Europe	93 946	101 162	111 113	...	...	Europe
Region not specified	7 514	8 154	8 955	...	...	Région non spécifiée
Nepal						**Népal**
Total [5]	393 613	421 857	463 684	491 504	463 646	Totale [5]
Africa	1 982	1 734	1 803	1 891	2 038	Afrique
Americas	33 269	38 797	47 348	51 422	52 964	Amériques
Europe	139 366	146 889	160 539	173 976	169 367	Europe
Asia, East and South East/Oceania	78 522	84 765	87 514	95 565	111 667	Asie. Est et Sud-Est et Océanie
Southern Asia	140 444	149 662	166 475	168 649	127 602	Asie du Sud
Region not specified	30	10	5	1	8	Région non spécifiée
Netherlands						**Pays-Bas**
Total [9]	6 580 300	7 841 000	9 312 000	9 874 000	10 003 000	Totale [9]
Africa	55 000	72 000	80 000	107 000	108 000	Afrique
Americas	664 200	900 000	1 144 000	1 162 000	1 216 000	Amériques
Europe	5 340 000	6 149 000	7 371 000	7 905 000	7 956 000	Europe
Asia, East and South East/Oceania	521 100	720 000	717 000	700 000	723 000	Asie. Est et Sud-Est et Océanie
New Caledonia						**Nouvelle-Calédonie**
Total [3,5]	91 121	105 137	103 835	99 735	109 587	Totale [3,5]
Africa	472	480	511	597	583	Afrique
Americas	1 355	1 311	1 529	1 738	2 523	Amériques
Europe	29 823	32 608	31 421	32 111	33 651	Europe
Asia, East and South East/Oceania	59 080	70 475	70 005	64 749	72 129	Asie. Est et Sud-Est et Océanie
Region not specified	391	263	369	540	701	Région non spécifiée
New Zealand						**Nouvelle-Zélande**
Total [2,48]	1 528 720	1 497 183	1 484 512	1 607 241	1 786 765	Totale [2,48]
Africa	13 686	15 529	17 499	17 135	19 241	Afrique
Americas	187 490	185 257	205 738	228 654	245 000	Amériques
Europe	270 179	280 766	294 904	317 810	371 684	Europe
Asia, East and South East/Oceania	982 665	941 659	887 317	958 485	1 068 933	Asie. Est et Sud-Est et Océanie
Southern Asia	5 838	6 255	6 751	8 307	10 494	Asie du Sud
Western Asia	3 894	3 535	3 691	4 558	4 726	Asie occidentale
Region not specified	64 968	64 182	68 612	72 292	66 687	Région non spécifiée
Nicaragua						**Nicaragua**
Total [5]	302 694	358 439	405 702	468 159	485 909	Totale [5]
Africa	106	121	155	192	563	Afrique
Americas	266 880	322 241	365 011	424 072	437 062	Amériques
Europe	29 761	30 315	33 639	35 521	38 357	Europe
Asia, East and South East/Oceania	5 474	5 318	6 170	7 763	9 189	Asie. Est et Sud-Est et Océanie
Southern Asia	410	359	647	461	531	Asie du Sud
Western Asia	63	85	80	97	128	Asie occidentale
Region not specified	...	...	...	53	79	Région non spécifiée
Niger						**Niger**
Total [5,49]	37 561	44 018	41 961	42 826	50 263	Totale [5,49]
Africa	7 388	7 500	8 000	26 618	28 181	Afrique
Americas	1 923	2 030	3 000	1 383	2 500	Amériques
Europe	7 104	8 000	7 902	9 380	14 083	Europe
Asia, East and South East/Oceania	508	500	1 000	706	...	Asie. Est et Sud-Est et Océanie
Western Asia	...	500	...	...	...	Asie occidentale
Region not specified	20 638	25 488	22 059	4 739	5 499	Région non spécifiée
Nigeria						**Nigéria**
Total [2]	1 230 155	1 292 247	1 356 958	1 424 840	1 491 767	Totale [2]
Africa	866 709	909 867	955 362	1 003 133	1 050 993	Afrique
Americas	48 018	50 421	52 944	55 593	58 242	Amériques
Europe	189 927	200 178	210 301	220 817	230 316	Europe
Asia, East and South East/Oceania	75 855	79 650	83 606	87 815	91 997	Asie. Est et Sud-Est et Océanie
Southern Asia	28 016	29 418	30 892	32 435	33 978	Asie du Sud
Western Asia	20 635	21 668	22 756	23 895	25 034	Asie occidentale
Region not specified	995	1 045	1 097	1 152	1 207	Région non spécifiée
Niue						**Nioué**
Total [5,13,50]	1 522	1 820	1 736	2 252	2 010	Totale [5,13,50]

75

Tourist/visitor arrivals by region of origin *[cont.]*

Arrivées de touristes/visiteurs par région de provenance *[suite]*

Country or area of destination and region of origin +	1996	1997	1998	1999	2000	Pays ou zone de destination et région de provenance +
Africa	...	...	...	15	4	Afrique
Americas	55	98	86	247	163	Amériques
Europe	74	81	78	226	111	Europe
Asia, East and South East/Oceania	1 360	1 623	1 552	1 617	1 416	Asie. Est et Sud-Est et Océanie
Western Asia	...	...	...	1	10	Asie occidentale
Region not specified	33	18	20	146	306	Région non spécifiée
Northern Mariana Islands						**Iles Mariannes du Nord**
Total [2]	736 117	694 888	490 165	501 788	528 600	Totale [2]
Africa	22	39	34	15	36	Afrique
Americas	84 856	76 217	61 491	49 892	52 331	Amériques
Europe	2 000	2 860	2 852	2 374	2 166	Europe
Asia, East and South East/Oceania	648 188	614 558	425 178	449 339	473 875	Asie. Est et Sud-Est et Océanie
Southern Asia	306	187	141	66	93	Asie du Sud
Western Asia	32	63	100	74	49	Asie occidentale
Region not specified	713	964	369	28	50	Région non spécifiée
Norway						**Norvège**
Total [9]	...	...	4 538 221	4 481 400	4 348 039	Totale [9]
Africa	...	...	9 316	7 763	7 964	Afrique
Americas	...	...	277 624	302 965	296 410	Amériques
Europe	...	...	3 960 482	3 846 408	3 697 345	Europe
Asia, East and South East/Oceania	...	...	187 482	209 961	243 073	Asie. Est et Sud-Est et Océanie
Region not specified	...	...	103 317	114 303	103 247	Région non spécifiée
Occupied Palestinian Terr.						**Terr. palestinien occupé**
Total [2]	...	685 000	767 000	907 000	1 055 000	Totale [2]
Africa	...	21 000	15 000	18 000	21 000	Afrique
Americas	...	143 000	176 000	181 000	211 000	Amériques
Europe	...	418 000	499 000	608 000	717 000	Europe
Asia, East and South East/Oceania	...	41 000	33 000	38 000	43 000	Asie. Est et Sud-Est et Océanie
Southern Asia	...	14 000	13 000	17 000	21 000	Asie du Sud
Western Asia	...	48 000	31 000	45 000	42 000	Asie occidentale
Oman						**Oman**
Total [1]	349 000	375 753	423 953	502 788	571 110	Totale [1]
Africa	22 000	21 747	26 752	37 345	20 033	Afrique
Americas	25 000	12 355	49 617	58 626	34 089	Amériques
Europe	110 000	159 675	176 123	172 022	227 143	Europe
Asia, East and South East/Oceania	65 000	69 837	54 977	84 692	98 295	Asie. Est et Sud-Est et Océanie
Southern Asia	...	31 200	39 466	53 887	65 555	Asie du Sud
Western Asia	58 000	80 939	77 018	96 216	125 995	Asie occidentale
Region not specified	69 000	...	...	...	...	Région non spécifiée
Pakistan						**Pakistan**
Total [5]	368 662	374 800	428 781	432 217	556 805	Totale [5]
Africa	9 776	8 261	8 330	9 694	16 499	Afrique
Americas	54 070	54 169	61 073	60 676	89 783	Amériques
Europe	152 998	153 788	183 855	189 979	257 504	Europe
Asia, East and South East/Oceania	43 987	41 935	48 798	44 484	49 654	Asie. Est et Sud-Est et Océanie
Southern Asia	87 502	97 000	107 302	107 214	108 960	Asie du Sud
Western Asia	20 274	19 587	19 375	19 792	33 107	Asie occidentale
Region not specified	55	60	48	378	1 298	Région non spécifiée
Palau						**Palaos**
Total [5,51]	69 330	73 719	64 194	55 493	57 732	Totale [5,51]
Africa	...	...	6	16	...	Afrique
Americas	9 955	10 481	6 347	5 818	6 704	Amériques
Europe	2 870	1 767	1 257	1 779	974	Europe
Asia, East and South East/Oceania	55 897	59 909	54 926	46 886	48 630	Asie. Est et Sud-Est et Océanie
Southern Asia	...	...	141	105	...	Asie du Sud
Western Asia	...	...	10	19	...	Asie occidentale
Region not specified	608	1 562	1 507	870	1 424	Région non spécifiée
Panama						**Panama**
Total [2,52]	376 672	418 846	422 228	445 957	467 228	Totale [2,52]
Africa	215	276	216	228	324	Afrique
Americas	331 908	370 752	377 594	398 852	419 348	Amériques
Europe	29 985	32 415	30 934	33 729	35 350	Europe

75

Tourist/visitor arrivals by region of origin *[cont.]*

Arrivées de touristes/visiteurs par région de provenance *[suite]*

Country or area of destination and region of origin +	1996	1997	1998	1999	2000	Pays ou zone de destination et région de provenance +
Asia, East and South East/Oceania	14 504	15 338	13 426	13 098	12 151	Asie. Est et Sud-Est et Océanie
Western Asia	60	65	58	50	55	Asie occidentale
Papua New Guinea						**Papouasie-Nvl-Guinée**
Total [5]	61 385	66 143	67 465	67 357	58 448	Totale [5]
Africa	...	...	310	320	...	Afrique
Americas	6 192	6 878	7 013	6 542	7 191	Amériques
Europe	5 770	5 984	6 646	7 282	5 198	Europe
Asia, East and South East/Oceania	44 391	53 019	53 316	53 055	45 847	Asie. Est et Sud-Est et Océanie
Western Asia	...	...	162	142	...	Asie occidentale
Region not specified	5 032	262	18	16	212	Région non spécifiée
Paraguay						**Paraguay**
Total [5,6,10]	425 561	395 058	349 592	269 021	323 041	Totale [5,6,10]
Africa	...	1 541	723	289	388	Afrique
Americas	349 283	316 244	282 668	213 662	264 603	Amériques
Europe	40 226	41 995	33 280	32 200	36 536	Europe
Asia, East and South East/Oceania	7 929	11 219	3 852	4 260	4 522	Asie. Est et Sud-Est et Océanie
Region not specified	28 123	24 059	29 069	18 610	16 992	Région non spécifiée
Peru						**Pérou**
Total [5]	584 388	649 287	723 668	...	...	Totale [5]
Africa	1 088	1 435	1 541	...	...	Afrique
Americas	372 079	436 479	483 106	...	...	Amériques
Europe	166 648	172 204	199 495	...	...	Europe
Asia, East and South East/Oceania	42 643	36 940	36 054	...	...	Asie. Est et Sud-Est et Océanie
Southern Asia	1 626	1 888	2 566	...	...	Asie du Sud
Western Asia	248	271	349	...	...	Asie occidentale
Region not specified	56	70	557	...	...	Région non spécifiée
Philippines						**Philippines**
Total [3,5]	2 049 367	2 222 523	2 149 357	2 170 514	1 992 169	Totale [3,5]
Africa	1 802	1 888	2 054	1 824	1 192	Afrique
Americas	434 828	496 213	540 596	534 480	510 862	Amériques
Europe	272 987	294 679	310 762	293 722	252 195	Europe
Asia, East and South East/Oceania	1 133 893	1 232 487	1 050 917	1 076 862	1 021 967	Asie. Est et Sud-Est et Océanie
Southern Asia	25 861	27 384	30 954	25 920	24 092	Asie du Sud
Western Asia	18 406	15 104	16 123	15 868	14 711	Asie occidentale
Region not specified	161 590	154 768	197 951	221 838	167 150	Région non spécifiée
Poland						**Pologne**
Total [2]	87 438 583	87 817 369	88 592 355	89 117 875	84 514 858	Totale [2]
Africa	5 543	5 558	7 988	8 387	9 496	Afrique
Americas	251 164	276 272	307 205	297 944	329 591	Amériques
Europe	87 022 729	87 369 361	88 145 239	88 677 996	84 043 059	Europe
Asia, East and South East/Oceania	67 373	74 777	71 173	77 679	87 690	Asie. Est et Sud-Est et Océanie
Southern Asia	11 546	10 558	9 234	9 198	8 990	Asie du Sud
Western Asia	8 147	8 121	7 123	6 430	6 763	Asie occidentale
Region not specified	72 081	72 722	44 393	40 241	29 269	Région non spécifiée
Portugal						**Portugal**
Total [5,6,53]	9 730 200	10 172 423	11 294 973	11 631 996	12 096 680	Totale [5,6,53]
Americas	337 004	373 915	408 580	417 122	479 501	Amériques
Europe	9 150 847	9 550 552	10 588 648	10 869 577	11 191 804	Europe
Asia, East and South East/Oceania	37 502	37 769	44 209	40 570	46 135	Asie. Est et Sud-Est et Océanie
Region not specified	204 847	210 187	253 536	304 727	379 240	Région non spécifiée
Puerto Rico						**Porto Rico**
Total [5,54]	3 065 056	3 241 774	3 396 115	3 024 088	3 341 400	Totale [5,54]
Americas	2 237 540	2 474 433	2 569 596	2 284 058	2 500 800	Amériques
Region not specified	827 516	767 341	826 519	740 030	840 600	Région non spécifiée
Republic of Moldova						**République de Moldova**
Total [2,55]	28 900	21 169	19 896	14 088	18 964	Totale [2,55]
Africa	23	13	42	10	20	Afrique
Americas	773	1 050	894	910	1 109	Amériques
Europe	27 642	19 692	18 634	12 832	17 230	Europe
Asia, East and South East/Oceania	220	277	187	224	398	Asie. Est et Sud-Est et Océanie
Southern Asia	52	48	75	23	48	Asie du Sud
Western Asia	190	89	64	89	159	Asie occidentale

75

Tourist/visitor arrivals by region of origin *[cont.]*

Arrivées de touristes/visiteurs par région de provenance *[suite]*

Country or area of destination and region of origin +	1996	1997	1998	1999	2000	Pays ou zone de destination et région de provenance +
Réunion						**Réunion**
Total[5]	346 898	370 255	391 000	394 000	430 000	Totale[5]
Africa	40 073	40 626	43 000	53 000	...	Afrique
Americas	794	1 269	1 000	1 000	...	Amériques
Europe	303 772	325 045	345 000	338 000	359 689	Europe
Asia, East and South East/Oceania	1 402	1 351	1 000	1 000	...	Asie. Est et Sud-Est et Océanie
Southern Asia	77	285	1 000	1 000	...	Asie du Sud
Region not specified	780	1 679	...	...	70 311	Région non spécifiée
Romania						**Roumanie**
Total	3 027 596[5]	2 957 161[5]	2 965 707[5]	5 223 896[2]	5 263 715[2]	Totale
Africa	4 466	4 224	3 751	4 667	5 131	Afrique
Americas	66 866	70 933	79 351	84 184	94 642	Amériques
Europe	2 895 069	2 825 926	2 831 628	5 048 614	5 074 204	Europe
Asia, East and South East/Oceania	27 435	27 549	27 642	36 020	37 260	Asie. Est et Sud-Est et Océanie
Southern Asia	6 305	5 516	5 332	16 174	16 909	Asie du Sud
Western Asia	20 501	21 458	16 926	32 140	33 647	Asie occidentale
Region not specified	6 954	1 555	1 077	2 097	1 922	Région non spécifiée
Russian Federation						**Fédération de Russie**
Total[2,56]	16 208 339	17 462 627	15 805 242	18 493 012	21 169 100	Totale[2,56]
Africa	25 378	33 593	31 321	28 616	...	Afrique
Americas	245 747	293 230	291 751	255 017	198 800	Amériques
Europe	15 196 814	16 034 061	14 286 682	16 780 247	18 964 000	Europe
Asia, East and South East/Oceania	652 297	757 046	754 049	747 677	752 600	Asie. Est et Sud-Est et Océanie
Southern Asia	34 726	51 155	51 851	43 137	...	Asie du Sud
Western Asia	45 004	39 429	64 264	28 290	...	Asie occidentale
Region not specified	8 373	254 113	325 324	610 028	1 253 700	Région non spécifiée
Saba						**Saba**
Total[5,57]	9 785	10 556	10 565	9 252	...	Totale[5,57]
Americas	7 540	8 295	8 172	6 922	...	Amériques
Europe	990	994	1 110	850	...	Europe
Region not specified	1 255	1 267	1 283	1 480	...	Région non spécifiée
Saint Eustatius						**Saint-Eustache**
Total[2,13]	19 912	19 128	19 072	19 065	...	Totale[2,13]
Americas	15 331	14 396	14 076	13 835	...	Amériques
Europe	3 816	4 125	4 309	4 293	...	Europe
Region not specified	765	607	687	937	...	Région non spécifiée
Saint Kitts and Nevis						**Saint-Kitts-et-Nevis**
Total[5,7]	84 176	88 297	93 190	84 002	...	Totale[5,7]
Americas	71 365	74 662	77 056	67 684	...	Amériques
Europe	11 944	13 068	15 166	15 759	...	Europe
Asia, East and South East/Oceania	151	62	91	114	...	Asie. Est et Sud-Est et Océanie
Region not specified	716	505	877	445	...	Région non spécifiée
Saint Lucia						**Sainte-Lucie**
Total[5,6]	235 659	248 406	252 237	263 793	269 850	Totale[5,6]
Americas	148 353	149 334	161 000	162 010	168 150	Amériques
Europe	84 376	96 398	88 642	98 555	98 869	Europe
Asia, East and South East/Oceania	...	207	179	237	503	Asie. Est et Sud-Est et Océanie
Region not specified	2 930	2 467	2 416	2 991	2 328	Région non spécifiée
Saint Maarten						**Saint-Martin**
Total[5,58]	350 641	418 340	458 486	444 812	...	Totale[5,58]
Americas	214 955	271 923	289 670	281 213	...	Amériques
Europe	100 936	110 030	132 881	125 828	...	Europe
Region not specified	34 750	36 387	35 935	37 771	...	Région non spécifiée
St. Vincent-Grenadines						**St. Vincent-Grenadines**
Total[5]	57 882	65 143	67 228	68 293	72 895	Totale[5]
Americas	39 186	45 722	46 186	46 980	...	Amériques
Europe	18 045	18 625	20 301	20 264	...	Europe
Region not specified	651	796	741	1 049	...	Région non spécifiée
Samoa						**Samoa**
Total[5]	73 155	67 960	77 926	85 124	87 688	Totale[5]
Americas	8 434	6 956	8 037	8 252	9 422	Amériques
Europe	4 799	4 494	4 917	5 460	6 396	Europe

75

Tourist/visitor arrivals by region of origin *[cont.]*

Arrivées de touristes/visiteurs par région de provenance *[suite]*

Country or area of destination and region of origin +	1996	1997	1998	1999	2000	Pays ou zone de destination et région de provenance +
Asia, East and South East/Oceania	58 252	55 370	64 695	70 603	71 314	Asie. Est et Sud-Est et Océanie
Region not specified	1 670	1 140	277	809	556	Région non spécifiée
San Marino [2,59]						**Saint-Marin** [2,59]
Total	3 345 381	3 307 983	3 264 385	3 148 477	3 071 005	Totale
Sao Tome and Principe						**Sao Tomé-et-Principe**
Total [5]	6 436	4 924	...	...	...	Totale [5]
Africa	1 742	1 109	...	...	...	Afrique
Americas	320	236	...	...	...	Amériques
Europe	4 101	3 395	...	...	...	Europe
Asia, East and South East/Oceania	219	146	...	...	...	Asie. Est et Sud-Est et Océanie
Southern Asia	17	17	...	...	...	Asie du Sud
Western Asia	37	21	...	...	...	Asie occidentale
Senegal						**Sénégal**
Total [1]	282 169	313 642	352 389	369 116	389 433	Totale [1]
Africa	67 267	70 224	84 244	81 101	96 834	Afrique
Americas	12 803	11 597	11 632	10 057	13 192	Amériques
Europe	194 705	224 971	247 533	269 692	274 035	Europe
Asia, East and South East/Oceania	3 542	3 583	2 588	2 680	2 669	Asie. Est et Sud-Est et Océanie
Western Asia	1 572	1 335	1 611	955	988	Asie occidentale
Region not specified	2 280	1 932	4 781	4 631	1 715	Région non spécifiée
Serbia and Montenegro						**Serbie-et-Monténégro**
Total [9]	301 428	298 415	282 639	151 650	238 957	Totale [9]
Americas	5 864	6 288	9 952	2 595	3 631	Amériques
Europe	285 005	280 363	258 992	140 806	222 074	Europe
Asia, East and South East/Oceania	2 073	1 942	2 156	1 525	2 360	Asie. Est et Sud-Est et Océanie
Region not specified	8 486	9 822	11 539	6 724	10 892	Région non spécifiée
Seychelles						**Seychelles**
Total [5]	130 955	130 070	128 258	124 865	130 046	Totale [5]
Africa	13 330	13 966	12 675	14 188	13 746	Afrique
Americas	6 657	6 726	6 787	4 144	6 239	Amériques
Europe	103 495	102 510	102 736	101 320	104 545	Europe
Asia, East and South East/Oceania	4 408	3 523	2 916	2 543	2 716	Asie. Est et Sud-Est et Océanie
Southern Asia	1 828	1 875	1 782	1 251	1 288	Asie du Sud
Western Asia	1 237	1 470	1 362	1 419	1 512	Asie occidentale
Sierra Leone						**Sierra Leone**
Total [5,13]	21 877	...	...	...	...	Totale [5,13]
Africa	7 313	...	...	...	...	Afrique
Americas	3 932	...	...	...	...	Amériques
Europe	4 481	...	...	...	...	Europe
Region not specified	6 151	...	...	...	...	Région non spécifiée
Singapore						**Singapour**
Total [2,60]	7 292 366	7 197 871	6 242 152	6 958 201	7 691 399	Totale [2,60]
Africa	75 036	64 978	72 197	83 808	92 003	Afrique
Americas	459 471	460 435	425 424	444 252	482 984	Amériques
Europe	1 011 044	996 814	990 805	1 058 433	1 138 518	Europe
Asia, East and South East/Oceania	5 329 485	5 216 166	4 287 819	4 849 620	5 347 318	Asie. Est et Sud-Est et Océanie
Southern Asia	367 208	396 147	394 617	444 088	516 293	Asie du Sud
Western Asia	49 860	48 106	59 976	66 045	70 628	Asie occidentale
Region not specified	262	15 225	11 314	11 955	43 655	Région non spécifiée
Slovakia						**Slovaquie**
Total [9]	951 355	814 138	896 100	975 105	1 045 614 [61]	Totale [9]
Africa	2 481	2 305	3 039	2 664	2 670	Afrique
Americas	28 189	25 982	30 206	30 683	35 821	Amériques
Europe	897 505	762 025	839 445	917 862	980 250	Europe
Asia, East and South East/Oceania	23 180	21 143	22 901	23 204	25 417	Asie. Est et Sud-Est et Océanie
Southern Asia	...	...	...	425	1 117	Asie du Sud
Western Asia	...	...	...	180	238	Asie occidentale
Region not specified	...	2 683	509	87	101	Région non spécifiée
Slovenia						**Slovénie**
Total [9]	831 895	974 350	976 514	884 048	1 089 549	Totale [9]
Americas	16 926	17 193	20 510	22 290	30 221	Amériques
Europe	800 426	942 022	940 365	844 728	1 037 797	Europe

75

Tourist/visitor arrivals by region of origin *[cont.]*

Arrivées de touristes/visiteurs par région de provenance *[suite]*

Country or area of destination and region of origin +	1996	1997	1998	1999	2000	Pays ou zone de destination et région de provenance +
Asia, East and South East/Oceania	4 786	5 820	7 775	8 286	11 725	Asie. Est et Sud-Est et Océanie
Region not specified	9 757	9 315	7 864	8 744	9 806	Région non spécifiée
Solomon Islands						**Iles Salomon**
Total [5]	11 217	15 894	13 229	21 318	...	Totale [5]
Americas	988	1 145	789	1 824	...	Amériques
Europe	1 517	1 356	1 073	2 193	...	Europe
Asia, East and South East/Oceania	8 664	13 318	11 278	16 247	...	Asie. Est et Sud-Est et Océanie
Region not specified	48	75	89	1 054	...	Région non spécifiée
South Africa						**Afrique du Sud**
Total [2,6,62]	5 186 221	5 170 096	5 898 236	6 026 086	6 000 538	Totale [2,6,62]
Africa	3 790 167	3 676 810	4 304 878	4 362 677	4 309 893	Afrique
Americas	178 347	207 891	254 840	245 297	257 697	Amériques
Europe	817 071	924 497	1 015 942	1 048 633	1 070 284	Europe
Asia, East and South East/Oceania	180 213	190 022	199 248	187 576	189 717	Asie. Est et Sud-Est et Océanie
Southern Asia	27 008	29 918	33 666	38 656	38 839	Asie du Sud
Western Asia	8 058	7 095	10 614	10 582	10 210	Asie occidentale
Region not specified	185 357	133 863	79 048	132 665	123 898	Région non spécifiée
Spain						**Espagne**
Total [63]	36 221 008	39 552 719	43 396 083	46 775 869	47 897 915	Totale [63]
Americas	...	1 904 078	2 165 477	2 238 148	2 518 590	Amériques
Europe	...	39 743 065	40 261 677	43 587 460	44 499 469	Europe
Asia, East and South East/Oceania	...	299 337	387 815	359 113	300 828	Asie. Est et Sud-Est et Océanie
Region not specified	36 221 008	606 239	581 114	591 148	579 028	Région non spécifiée
Sri Lanka						**Sri Lanka**
Total [5,6]	302 265	366 165	381 063	436 440	400 414	Totale [5,6]
Africa	2 376	1 533	1 035	1 236	894	Afrique
Americas	12 798	16 455	17 937	18 849	17 766	Amériques
Europe	171 888	218 481	246 198	282 000	267 664	Europe
Asia, East and South East/Oceania	51 402	58 632	54 474	66 528	58 197	Asie. Est et Sud-Est et Océanie
Southern Asia	59 919	66 645	57 387	63 006	51 552	Asie du Sud
Western Asia	3 882	4 419	4 032	4 821	4 341	Asie occidentale
Suriname						**Suriname**
Total [5,64]	53 228	61 361	54 585	...	...	Totale [5,64]
Africa	74	70	62	...	...	Afrique
Americas	10 419	9 553	5 501	...	...	Amériques
Europe	39 149	49 929	46 061	...	...	Europe
Asia, East and South East/Oceania	3 390	1 744	1 714	...	...	Asie. Est et Sud-Est et Océanie
Southern Asia	159	59	45	...	...	Asie du Sud
Region not specified	37	6	1 202	...	...	Région non spécifiée
Swaziland						**Swaziland**
Total [1,65]	314 921	269 113	284 116	289 383	280 870	Totale [1,65]
Africa	264 037	131 440	201 288	198 921	177 216	Afrique
Americas	6 464	17 616	5 121	9 733	10 823	Amériques
Europe	38 122	104 338	76 288	72 916	84 514	Europe
Asia, East and South East/Oceania	4 094	13 550	1 298	6 313	7 053	Asie. Est et Sud-Est et Océanie
Region not specified	2 204	2 169	121	1 500	1 264	Région non spécifiée
Switzerland						**Suisse**
Total [1]	6 729 797	7 039 225	7 185 379	7 153 967	7 821 158	Totale [1]
Africa	79 804	81 015	82 431	73 139	77 345	Afrique
Americas	946 349	990 354	1 074 217	1 019 743	1 198 553	Amériques
Europe	4 556 622	4 846 684	5 050 341	5 029 798	5 343 044	Europe
Asia, East and South East/Oceania	1 057 519	1 026 559	879 624	923 645	1 079 068	Asie. Est et Sud-Est et Océanie
Southern Asia	37 276	42 190	55 102	64 543	71 912	Asie du Sud
Western Asia	52 227	52 423	43 664	43 099	51 236	Asie occidentale
Syrian Arab Republic						**Rép. arabe syrienne**
Total [2,6]	2 435 381	2 331 628	2 463 724	2 681 534	3 014 758	Totale [2,6]
Africa	71 636	76 116	70 906	64 920	66 131	Afrique
Americas	21 375	26 265	27 766	30 591	38 209	Amériques
Europe	332 005	342 767	342 615	369 479	397 871	Europe
Asia, East and South East/Oceania	13 027	18 215	16 319	22 287	26 115	Asie. Est et Sud-Est et Océanie
Southern Asia	199 324	139 693	170 143	220 741	242 529	Asie du Sud
Western Asia	1 745 916	1 696 803	1 799 683	1 928 846	2 196 287	Asie occidentale

75

Tourist/visitor arrivals by region of origin *[cont.]*

Arrivées de touristes/visiteurs par région de provenance *[suite]*

Country or area of destination and region of origin +	1996	1997	1998	1999	2000	Pays ou zone de destination et région de provenance +
Region not specified	52 098	31 769	36 292	44 670	47 616	Région non spécifiée
Thailand						**Thaïlande**
Total [3,5]	7 244 400	7 293 957	7 842 760	8 651 260	9 578 826	Totale [3,5]
Africa	47 449	50 963	72 097	73 233	80 389	Afrique
Americas	384 012	388 190	448 761	514 595	584 967	Amériques
Europe	1 651 788	1 635 581	1 946 154	2 055 430	2 242 466	Europe
Asia, East and South East/Oceania	4 765 104	4 840 429	4 931 506	5 546 527	6 134 335	Asie. Est et Sud-Est et Océanie
Southern Asia	275 966	235 623	258 815	280 422	339 413	Asie du Sud
Western Asia	67 826	70 559	107 597	110 125	127 053	Asie occidentale
Region not specified	52 255	72 612	77 830	70 928	70 203	Région non spécifiée
TFYR of Macedonia						**L'ex-R.y. Macédoine**
Total [9]	136 137	121 337	156 670	180 788	224 016	Totale [9]
Americas	6 083	5 424	8 788	15 526	17 023	Amériques
Europe	126 679	112 752	143 830	158 754	198 298	Europe
Asia, East and South East/Oceania	1 672	1 644	2 280	2 440	2 803	Asie. Est et Sud-Est et Océanie
Region not specified	1 703	1 517	1 772	4 068	5 892	Région non spécifiée
Togo						**Togo**
Total [1]	58 049	92 081	69 461	69 818	59 541	Totale [1]
Africa	30 650	52 275	39 026	41 268	29 546	Afrique
Americas	2 846	4 263	4 853	3 339	2 050	Amériques
Europe	22 683	30 488	21 857	21 336	25 376	Europe
Asia, East and South East/Oceania	731	1 739	1 091	1 453	1 271	Asie. Est et Sud-Est et Océanie
Western Asia	1 057	3 163	2 588	2 344	1 203	Asie occidentale
Region not specified	82	153	46	78	95	Région non spécifiée
Tonga						**Tonga**
Total [5,13]	26 642	26 162	27 132	30 949	34 694	Totale [5,13]
Americas	5 681	5 166	6 093	6 153	7 980	Amériques
Europe	4 485	4 225	4 031	4 855	5 977	Europe
Asia, East and South East/Oceania	16 389	16 712	16 921	19 790	20 659	Asie. Est et Sud-Est et Océanie
Southern Asia	72	51	72	84	...	Asie du Sud
Region not specified	15	8	15	67	78	Région non spécifiée
Trinidad and Tobago						**Trinité-et-Tobago**
Total [5,13]	265 900	324 293	334 037	358 220	398 559	Totale [5,13]
Africa	483	613	736	904	996	Afrique
Americas	208 398	249 552	254 963	277 819	309 122	Amériques
Europe	52 790	69 887	73 970	74 260	82 661	Europe
Asia, East and South East/Oceania	2 088	1 758	2 098	3 141	3 507	Asie. Est et Sud-Est et Océanie
Southern Asia	1 017	937	876	1 093	1 196	Asie du Sud
Western Asia	141	233	110	267	279	Asie occidentale
Region not specified	983	1 313	1 284	736	798	Région non spécifiée
Tunisia						**Tunisie**
Total [5,6]	3 884 593	4 263 107	4 717 705	4 831 658	5 057 193	Totale [5,6]
Africa	719 410	671 432	750 322	671 501	665 812	Afrique
Americas	26 945	26 689	27 831	27 050	31 275	Amériques
Europe	2 522 893	2 845 952	3 011 383	3 460 857	3 615 793	Europe
Asia, East and South East/Oceania	4 706	5 506	8 354	9 314	8 343	Asie. Est et Sud-Est et Océanie
Western Asia	571 010	675 264	879 931	634 898	712 932	Asie occidentale
Region not specified	39 629	38 264	39 884	28 038	23 038	Région non spécifiée
Turkey						**Turquie**
Total [5]	7 966 004	9 039 671	8 959 712	6 892 636	9 585 695	Totale [5]
Africa	90 714	95 596	95 504	82 332	106 289	Afrique
Americas	220 032	267 575	317 451	282 616	360 920	Amériques
Europe	6 854 575	7 874 694	7 786 373	5 786 258	8 234 233	Europe
Asia, East and South East/Oceania	169 973	204 510	194 838	166 139	229 285	Asie. Est et Sud-Est et Océanie
Southern Asia	398 671	348 318	320 779	366 621	397 348	Asie du Sud
Western Asia	218 971	233 183	231 436	199 750	246 736	Asie occidentale
Region not specified	13 068	15 795	13 331	8 920	10 884	Région non spécifiée
Turkmenistan						**Turkménistan**
Total [2]	281 988	332 425	...	...	...	Totale [2]
Africa	248	109	...	...	...	Afrique
Americas	3 684	2 647	...	...	...	Amériques
Europe	162 804	150 705	...	...	...	Europe

75

Tourist/visitor arrivals by region of origin *[cont.]*

Arrivées de touristes/visiteurs par région de provenance *[suite]*

Country or area of destination and region of origin +	1996	1997	1998	1999	2000	Pays ou zone de destination et région de provenance +
Asia, East and South East/Oceania	2 668	2 189	...	...	...	Asie. Est et Sud-Est et Océanie
Southern Asia	108 502	175 542	...	...	...	Asie du Sud
Western Asia	4 082	1 233	...	...	...	Asie occidentale
Turks and Caicos Islands						**Iles Turques et Caïques**
Total [5]	87 794	93 011	110 855	120 898	152 211	Totale [5]
Americas	73 446	78 736	90 321	98 316	134 286	Amériques
Europe	11 431	9 121	11 887	11 498	11 503	Europe
Region not specified	2 917	5 154	8 647	11 084	6 422	Région non spécifiée
Tuvalu						**Tuvalu**
Total [5]	1 039	1 029	1 077	...	...	Totale [5]
Americas	89	76	118	...	...	Amériques
Europe	88	127	123	...	...	Europe
Asia, East and South East/Oceania	849	822	804	...	...	Asie. Est et Sud-Est et Océanie
Region not specified	13	4	32	...	...	Région non spécifiée
Uganda						**Ouganda**
Total [5]	173 623	171 438	192 012	186 937	191 276	Totale [5]
Africa	102 755	99 609	115 847	116 207	131 687	Afrique
Americas	12 535	13 857	14 550	12 898	11 947	Amériques
Europe	43 198	43 656	45 720	43 133	36 050	Europe
Asia, East and South East/Oceania	6 268	6 107	6 738	6 123	4 868	Asie. Est et Sud-Est et Océanie
Southern Asia	7 349	6 926	7 950	7 048	5 569	Asie du Sud
Western Asia	524	616	836	773	553	Asie occidentale
Region not specified	994	667	371	755	602	Région non spécifiée
Ukraine						**Ukraine**
Total [5]	3 853 944	7 658 235	6 207 640	4 232 357	4 405 746	Totale [5]
Africa	729	10 551	3 843	6 927	15 278	Afrique
Americas	26 116	79 638	63 941	70 159	70 500	Amériques
Europe	3 611 514	7 465 648	6 091 006	4 098 337	4 258 339	Europe
Asia, East and South East/Oceania	4 009	28 129	22 473	23 979	26 586	Asie. Est et Sud-Est et Océanie
Southern Asia	2 507	36 381	12 675	10 774	11 263	Asie du Sud
Western Asia	205 273	28 585	8 940	14 195	18 345	Asie occidentale
Region not specified	3 796	9 303	4 762	7 986	5 435	Région non spécifiée
United Arab Emirates						**Emirats arabes unis**
Total [1,66,67]	2 572 382	2 475 868	2 990 539	3 392 614	3 906 545	Totale [1,66,67]
Africa	99 551	118 629	145 851	153 899	173 601	Afrique
Americas	84 332	80 290	110 618	130 280	139 474	Amériques
Europe	964 084	787 395	947 183	1 016 869	1 076 813	Europe
Asia, East and South East/Oceania	216 067	199 633	235 811	247 673	263 609	Asie. Est et Sud-Est et Océanie
Southern Asia	328 813	372 242	425 982	500 985	568 453	Asie du Sud
Western Asia	646 588	641 607	797 285	923 248	1 088 753	Asie occidentale
Region not specified	232 947	276 072	327 809	419 660	595 842	Région non spécifiée
United Kingdom						**Royaume-Uni**
Total [2,37]	25 163 000	25 515 000	25 744 000	25 396 000	25 211 000	Totale [2,37]
Africa	510 000	525 000	570 000	588 000	618 000	Afrique
Americas	4 017 000	4 509 000	5 053 000	5 000 000	5 287 000	Amériques
Europe	17 856 000	17 644 000	17 581 000	17 046 000	16 307 000	Europe
Asia, East and South East/Oceania	2 166 000	2 155 000	1 872 000	2 062 000	2 256 000	Asie. Est et Sud-Est et Océanie
Southern Asia	238 000	269 000	264 000	291 000	314 000	Asie du Sud
Western Asia	376 000	413 000	404 000	409 000	429 000	Asie occidentale
United Rep. of Tanzania						**Rép.-Unie de Tanzanie**
Total [2]	326 188	360 500	482 331	627 417	501 669	Totale [2]
Africa	136 502	150 861	201 845	262 559	209 934	Afrique
Americas	32 184	35 570	47 594	61 908	49 501	Amériques
Europe	96 861	107 051	143 229	186 311	148 970	Europe
Asia, East and South East/Oceania	24 902	27 520	36 824	47 898	38 299	Asie. Est et Sud-Est et Océanie
Southern Asia	16 012	17 696	23 677	30 797	24 626	Asie du Sud
Western Asia	19 727	21 802	29 162	37 944	30 339	Asie occidentale
United States						**Etats-Unis**
Total [5]	46 489 166	47 766 476	46 395 587	48 491 187	50 890 701	Totale [5]
Africa	204 322	233 972	258 228	273 762	295 090	Afrique
Americas	27 948 403	28 155 272	27 512 761	28 746 665	30 010 382	Amériques
Europe	10 028 117	10 734 881	11 040 602	11 634 166	12 052 331	Europe

75

Tourist/visitor arrivals by region of origin *[cont.]*

Arrivées de touristes/visiteurs par région de provenance *[suite]*

Country or area of destination and region of origin +	1996	1997	1998	1999	2000	Pays ou zone de destination et région de provenance +
Asia, East and South East/Oceania	7 928 682	8 201 299	7 081 823	7 301 839	7 921 004	Asie. Est et Sud-Est et Océanie
Southern Asia	201 723	235 416	282 112	300 673	362 634	Asie du Sud
Western Asia	177 919	205 636	220 061	234 082	249 260	Asie occidentale
United States Virgin Is.						**Iles Vierges américaines**
Total [1]	229 237	386 740	480 064	484 156	496 349	Totale [1]
Africa	254	248	539	322	140	Afrique
Americas	213 318	360 897	453 047	451 618	435 544	Amériques
Europe	11 868	14 875	14 570	19 435	10 285	Europe
Asia, East and South East/Oceania	395	1 063	764	783	653	Asie. Est et Sud-Est et Océanie
Region not specified	3 402	9 657	11 144	11 998	49 727	Région non spécifiée
Uruguay						**Uruguay**
Total [2,3]	2 258 616	2 462 532	2 323 993	2 273 164	2 235 887	Totale [2,3]
Americas	1 749 878	1 888 852	1 809 579	1 759 517	1 758 399	Amériques
Europe	60 101	83 626	96 190	86 167	85 039	Europe
Asia, East and South East/Oceania	...	...	...	...	6 515	Asie. Est et Sud-Est et Océanie
Western Asia	...	...	...	...	201	Asie occidentale
Region not specified	448 637	490 054	418 224	427 480	385 733	Région non spécifiée
Vanuatu						**Vanuatu**
Total [5]	46 123	49 605	52 085	50 746	57 591	Totale [5]
Americas	1 223	1 248	1 297	1 343	1 547	Amériques
Europe	2 644	2 788	2 337	3 063	3 401	Europe
Asia, East and South East/Oceania	42 199	44 623	47 547	45 525	51 803	Asie. Est et Sud-Est et Océanie
Region not specified	57	946	904	815	840	Région non spécifiée
Venezuela						**Venezuela**
Total [5]	758 503	813 862	685 429	586 900	469 047	Totale [5]
Africa	866	929	3 364	860	380	Afrique
Americas	423 517	454 427	366 315	296 212	172 071	Amériques
Europe	322 606	346 182	301 795	277 014	288 037	Europe
Asia, East and South East/Oceania	6 597	7 065	9 179	5 069	3 286	Asie. Est et Sud-Est et Océanie
Southern Asia	900	966	462	686	256	Asie du Sud
Western Asia	1 619	1 716	1 051	519	462	Asie occidentale
Region not specified	2 398	2 577	3 263	6 540	4 555	Région non spécifiée
Viet Nam						**Viet Nam**
Total [2,3]	1 607 155	1 715 637	1 520 128	1 781 754	2 140 000	Totale [2,3]
Africa	...	626	...	4 599	1 707	Afrique
Americas	146 488	176 159	176 578	243 549	241 708	Amériques
Europe	128 487	218 502	123 002	241 537	271 183	Europe
Asia, East and South East/Oceania	705 895	1 033 527	679 577	1 059 357	1 398 885	Asie. Est et Sud-Est et Océanie
Southern Asia	...	6 151	...	6 428	6 639	Asie du Sud
Region not specified	626 285	280 672	540 971	226 284	219 878	Région non spécifiée
Yemen						**Yémen**
Total [1]	74 476	80 451	87 627	58 370	72 836	Totale [1]
Africa	1 610	2 156	2 696	4 312	5 658	Afrique
Americas	3 293	4 676	5 585	6 732	8 161	Amériques
Europe	48 597	50 560	54 163	22 201	24 825	Europe
Asia, East and South East/Oceania	5 475	8 447	7 437	4 862	8 788	Asie. Est et Sud-Est et Océanie
Western Asia	15 501	14 612	17 746	20 263	25 404	Asie occidentale
Zambia						**Zambie**
Total [5]	270 747	340 897	362 025	404 247	457 419	Totale [5]
Africa	192 923	203 777	260 162	301 942	294 479	Afrique
Americas	12 438	27 819	14 893	15 121	27 469	Amériques
Europe	44 023	71 427	67 055	67 253	105 409	Europe
Asia, East and South East/Oceania	16 364	34 419	17 494	17 451	27 709	Asie. Est et Sud-Est et Océanie
Southern Asia	4 560	3 455	2 421	2 480	2 353	Asie du Sud
Western Asia	353	...	...	...	...	Asie occidentale
Region not specified	86	...	...	...	...	Région non spécifiée
Zimbabwe						**Zimbabwe**
Total [5,68]	1 577 005	1 281 205	1 986 474	2 100 520	1 868 412	Totale [5,68]
Africa	1 241 827	935 089	1 485 774	1 508 326	1 403 774	Afrique
Americas	48 450	62 224	119 521	114 865	116 128	Amériques
Europe	229 988	227 606	301 884	377 377	268 980	Europe
Asia, East and South East/Oceania	56 740	56 286	79 295	99 952	79 530	Asie. Est et Sud-Est et Océanie

75

Tourist/visitor arrivals by region of origin *[cont.]*
Arrivées de touristes/visiteurs par région de provenance *[suite]*

Source:
World Tourism Organization (WTO), Madrid, WTO statistics database
and the "Yearbook of Tourism Statistics", 2002 edition.

Source:
Organisation mondiale du tourisme (OMT), Madrid, la base de
données de l'OMT, et "l'Annuaire des statistiques du tourisme", 2002
édition.

+   For a listing of the Member States of the regions of origin, see
Annex I, with the following exceptions:
   Africa includes the countries and territories listed under Africa in
Annex I but excludes Egypt, Guinea-Bissau, Liberia, Libyan Arab
Jamahiriya, Mozambique and Western Sahara.
   Americas is as shown In Annex I, but excludes Falkland Islands
(Malvinas), French Guyana, Greenland and Saint Pierre and
Miquelon.
   Europe is as shown in Annex I, but excludes Andorra, Channel
Islands, Faeroe Islands, Holy See, Isle of Man and Svalbard and Jan
Mayen Islands. The Europe group also includes Armenia, Azerbaijan,
Cyprus, Israel, Kyrgyzstan, Turkey and Turkmenistan.
   Asia, East and South East/Oceania includes the countries and
territories listed under Eastern Asia and South-eastern Asia in Annex I
(except for Timor-Leste), and under Oceania except for Christmas
Island, Cocos Island, Norfolk Island, Nauru, Wake Island, Johnston
Island, Midway Islands, Pitcairn, Tokelau and Wallis and Futuna
Islands. The Asia, East and South East/Oceania group also includes
Taiwan Province of China.
   Southern Asia is as shown in Annex I under South-central Asia, but
excludes Kazakhstan, Kyrgyzstan, Tajikistan, Turkmenistan and
Uzbekistan.
   Western Asia is as shown in Annex I but excludes Armenia,
Azerbaijan, Cyprus, Georgia, Israel, Occupied Palestinian Territory,
and Turkey. The Western Asia group also includes Egypt and the
Libyan Arab Jamahiriya.

+   On se reportera à l'Annexe I pour les États Membres classés dans
les différentes régions de provenance, avec les exceptions ci-après ;
   Afrique – Comprend les États et territoires énumérés à l'Annexe I,
sauf l'Égypte, la Guinée-Bissau, le Libéria, la Jamahiriya arabe
libyenne, le Mozambique et le Sahara occidental.
   Amériques – Comprend les États et territoires énumérés à
l'Annexe I, sauf les îles Falkland (Malvinas), le Groënland, la Guyane
française et Saint-Pierre-et-Miquelon.
   Europe – Comprend les États et territoires énumérés à l'Annexe I,
sauf l'Andorre, les îles Anglo-normandes, les îles Féroé, l'île de Man,
le Saint-Siège et les îles Svalbard et Jan Mayen. Le Groupe
comprend en revanche l'Arménie, l'Azerbaïdjan, Chypre, Israël,
l'Kirghizistan, la Turquie et le Turkménistan.
   L'Asie de l'Est et du Sud-Est/Océanie – Comprend les États et
territoires énumérés à l'Annexe I dans les Groupes Asie de l'Est et
Asie de Sud-Est sauf le Timor-Leste, et les États et territoires
énumérés dans le Groupe Océanie sauf les îles Christmas, les îles
Cocos, l'île Johnston, les îles Midway, Nauru, l'îles Norfolk, Pitcairn,
Tokélou, l'île Wake et Wallis-et-Futuna. Le Groupe Asie de l'Est et du
Sud-Est/Océanie comprend en revanche la Province chinoise de
Taiwan.
   Asie du Sud – Comprend les États et territoires énumérés à
l'Annexe I, sauf le Kazakhstan, le Kirghizistan, l'Ouzbékistan, le
Tadjikistan et le Turkménistan.
   Asie occidentale – Comprend les États et territoires énumérés à
l'Annexe I, sauf l'Arménie, l'Azerbaïdjan, Chypre, la Géorgie, Israël, le
territoire Palestinien Occupé et la Turquie. Le Groupe comprend en
revanche l'Égypte et la Jamahiriya arabe libyenne.

1 Arrivals of non-resident tourists at hotels and similar
   establishments.
2 Arrivals of non-resident tourists at national borders (including
   tourists and same-day visitors).
3 Including nationals of the country residing abroad.
4 Including arrivals from Western Samoa. Beginning 1990,
   excluding arrivals from Western Samoa.

5 Arrivals of non-resident tourists at national borders (excluding
   same-day visitors).
6 Excluding nationals of the country residing abroad.
7 Air and sea arrivals.
8 Arrivals correspond to a new series and source of data from
   1990 to 1999.
9 Arrivals of non-resident tourists in all types of tourism
   accommodation establishments.
10 Excluding crew members.
11 Including private accommodation.
12 Including transit passengers, border permits and returning
    residents.
13 Air arrivals.
14 International tourist arrivals in hotels of regional capitals.

15 Change in methodology.
16 Excluding children without own passports. (Bulgaria: 1998-
    2000).
17 Air arrivals at Pochentong and Siem Reap Airports. Region Not
    Specified 1998 and 2000: Including arrivals at Siem Reap
    Airport by direct-flights; 1998: 10,423; 2000: 87,012.

1 Arrivées de touristes non résidents dans les hôtels et
   établissements assimilés.
2 Arrivées de visiteurs non résidents aux frontières nationales (y
   compris touristes et visiteurs de la journée).
3 Y compris les nationaux du pays résidant à l'étranger.
4 Y compris des arrivées en provenance de Samoa occidentale.
   A partir de 1990, à l'exclusion des arrivées en provenance de
   Samoa occidentale.
5 Arrivées de touristes non résidents aux frontières nationales(à
   l'exclusion de visiteurs de la journée).
6 A l'exclusion des nationaux du pays résidant à l'étranger.
7 Arrivées par voie aérienne et maritime.
8 Les arrivées constituent une nouvelle série et source de
   données de 1990 à 1999.
9 Arrivées de touristes non résidents dans tous les types
   d'établissements d'hébergement touristique.
10 A l'exclusion des membres des équipages.
11 Y compris hébergement privé.
12 Y compris passagers en transit, passages à la frontière et
    résidents de retour de voyage.
13 Arrivées par voie aérienne.
14 Arrivées de touristes internationaux dans les hôtels des
    capitales de département.
15 Changement de méthode.
16 A l'exclusion d'enfants sans passeports personnels (Bulgarie :
    1998-2000).
17 Arrivées par voie aérienne aux aéroports de Pochentong et de
    Siem Reap. Région non spécifiée 1998 et 2000: Y compris les
    arrivées à l'aéroport de Siem Reap en vols directs; 1998:

75

Tourist/visitor arrivals by region of origin *[cont.]*

Arrivées de touristes/visiteurs par région de provenance *[suite]*

10.423; 2000: 87.012.

18 Excluding ethnic Chinese arriving from "China, Hong Kong SAR", Macao SAR and Taiwan: 1987: 25,174,446; 1988: 29,852,598; 1989: 28,040,424; 1990: 25,714,506; 1991: 30,639,658; 1992: 34,108,578; 1993: 36,871,088; 1994: 38,502,396; 1995: 40,499,795;1996: 44,383,182; 1997: 50,159,917; 1998: 56,370,654; 1999: 64,363,298; 2000: 73,283,449. Also including stateless persons and employees of the United Nations Organizations.

19 From 1996 and onwards, figures adjusted to include non-Macanese arrivals via Macao.

20 Including arrivals by sea, land and by air (helicopter). 1995, Nov.: Arrivals by air began (Macao SAR International Airport). Including stateless and Chinese people whodo not have permanent residency in Hong Kong SAR, China: 1992: 93,965; 1993: 92,679; 1994: 147,304; 1995: 167,361; 1996: 189,364; 1997: 182,344.

21 Beginning 1996, change in national source.

22 Prior to 1997. air arrivals at the International FHB Airport at Port Bouet. Arrivals at land frontiers, Bouake Airport and Air Ivoire Airport at Abidjan are not taken into consideration. 1997-1998: Air arrivals at the International FHB Airport at Port Bouet and arrivals at land frontiers.

23 Including arrivals in ports of nautical tourism.

24 1991: January-June; 1992: Incomplete; 1993: July-December; 1994: January-June; 1995: estimate.

25 Beginning 1996, including camp sites with more than 74 units only.

26 Departures by air.

27 Prior to 1996, international tourist arrivals at Addis Ababa Airport.

28 Including nationals of the country residing abroad. 1996-1999: Arrivals at Bole airport only. 1998-1999: Arrivals compiled by country of residence. 2000: Arrivals through all ports of entry.

29 Since 1989 survey at frontiers and car study realized by SOFRES. 1992 and 1993: Estimates based on the frontier survey. 1994 and 1996: Frontier survey. 1997: Update of the frontier survey 1996. 1995, 1998 - 2000: Estimates.

30 2000: Estimated by the "Institut de la Statistique (ISPF)".

31 Arrivals at Libreville Airport.

32 Charter tourists only.

33 The data relate to the territory of the Federal Republic of Germany prior to 3 October 1990. As of 1990, tourists from the former German Democratic Republic will be regarded as domestic tourists.

34 Data based on surveys.

35 Arrivals at 21 traditional hotel establishments. 2000: Arrivals at 83 traditional hotel establishments.

36 Air arrivals at Conakry airport.

37 Departures.

38 Prior to 1996: travellers. From 1996 New methodology, excluding seasonal and border workers.

39 Excluding nationals of the country residing abroad. All data are estimates, projected using 1989 market shares. Source: Economic survey various years.

18 A l'exclusion des arrivées de personnes d'ethnie chinoise en provenance de "Chine, Hong Kong RAS", Macao et Taiwan: 1987: 25.174.446; 1988: 29.852.598; 1989: 28,040,424;1990: 25,714,506; 1991: 30,639,658; 1992: 34.108.578; 1993: 36,871,088; 1994: 38,502,396; 1994: 38,502,396; 1995: 40,499,795; 1996: 44,383,182;1997: 50,159,917; 1998: 56,370,654; 1999: 64,363,298; 2000: 73,283,449. Y compris également les apatrides et les employés des organisations des Nations Unis.

19 A partir de 1996, les chiffres ont été ajustés pour inclure les arrivées de non-macanais arrivant via Macao.

20 Y compris les arrivées par mer, terre et air (hélicoptère). 1995, Nov.: Début de l'inclusion des arrivées par air (Aéroport international de Macao SAR). Y compris les aptrides et les chinois qui ne résident pas de manière permanente à Hong Kong SAR, Chine: 1992: 93 .965; 1993: 92.679; 1994: 147.304; 1995: 167.361; 1996: 189.364; 1997: 182.344.

21 A partir de 1996, changement de la source national des données.

22 Avant 1997, arrivées par voie aérienne à l'aéroport international FHB de Port-Bouet. Les arrivées aux frontières terrestres, à l'aéroport de Bouaké, ainsi qu'à l'aéroport Air Ivoire d'Abidjan ne sont pas prises en compte. 1997-1998 : Arrivées par voie aérienne à l'aéroport international FHB de Port-Bouet et arrivées aux frontières terrestres.

23 Y compris les arrivées dans des ports à tourisme nautique.

24 1991: Janvier-juin; 1992: Incomplet; 1993: Juillet-décembre; 1994: Janvier-juin; 1995: estimation.

25 A partir de 1996, y compris terrains de camping de plus de 74 unités seulement.

26 Départs par voie aérienne.

27 Avant 1996, arrivées par voie aérienne (Aéroport Addis-Abeba).

28 Y compris les nationaux du pays résidant à l'étranger. 1996-1999: Arrivées à l'aéroport de Bole seulement. 1998-1999: Arrivées compilées par pays de residence. 2000: Arrivées à travers tous les ports d'entrée.

29 A partir de 1989 enquête aux frontières et étude autocar réalisée par la SOFRES. 1992 et 1993: Estimation sur la base des enquêtes aux frontières. 1994 et 1996: Enquêtes aux frontières. 1997 : Actualisation de l'enquête aux frontière 1996. 1995, 1998 à 2000 : Estimation.

30 2000 : Estimation de la fréquentation touristique réalisée par l'Institut de la Statistique (ISPF)".

31 Arrivées à l'aéroport de Libreville.

32 Arrivées en vols à la demande seulement.

33 Les données se réfèrent au territoire de la République fédérale d'Allemagne avant le 3 octobre 1990. A partir de 1990, les touristes en provenance de l'ancienne République Démocratique Allemande seront considérés comme des touristes nationaux.

34 Données obtenues au moyen d'enquêtes.

35 Arrivées dans 21 établissements hôteliers. 2000: Arrivées dans 83 établissements hôteliers.

36 Arrivées par voie aérienne à l'aéroport de Conakry.

37 Départs.

38 Avant 1996: voyageurs. A partir de 1996 Nouvelle méthodologie, à l'exclusion des travailleurs saisoniers et frontaliers.

39 A l'exclusion des nationaux du pays résidant à l'étranger. Toutes les données représentent des estimations, dont la projection a été faite sur la base des taux de marché de l'année 1989. Source: Enquête économique de diverses années.

75

Tourist/visitor arrivals by region of origin *[cont.]*

Arrivées de touristes/visiteurs par région de provenance *[suite]*

40 Prior to 1996, arrivals at Tarawa and Christmas Islands.	40 Avant 1996, arrivées aux Iles Tarawa et Christmas.
41 Including nationals residing abroad and from June 1988, also crew members.	41 Y compris les nationaux résidant à l'étranger, à partir de juin 1988, également membres des équipages.
42 Excluding Syrian nationals, Palestinians and students.	42 A l'exclusion des ressortissants syriens, palestiniens et sous-études.
43 Excluding sanatoria and rest houses.	43 A l'exclusion des sanatoria et des maisons de repos.
44 Foreign tourist departures; includes Singapore residents crossing the frontier by road through Johore Causeway.	44 Départs de touristes étrangers; y compris les résidents de Singapour traversant la frontière par voie terrestre à travers le Johore Causeway.
45 Tourist arrivals.	45 Arrivées de touristes.
46 Arrivals in the States of Kosrae, Chuuk, Pohnpei and Yap.	46 Arrivées dans les États de Kosrae, Chuuk, Pohnpei et Yap.
47 Arrivals at Yangon by air.	47 Arrivées à Yangon par voie aérienne.
48 Data regarding to short term movements are compiled from a random sample of passenger declarations. Including nationals of the country residing abroad. Source: Statistivs New Zealand, External Migration.	48 Les données relatives aux mouvements de courte durée sont obtenues à partir d'un échantillon aléatoire de déclarations des passagers. Y compris les nationaux du pays résidant à l'étranger. Source : Statistiques de la Nouvelle Zélande, Immigration.
49 Air arrivals (Niamey Airport).	49 Arrivées par voie aérienne (Aéroport de Niamey).
50 Including Niuans residing usually in New Zealand.	50 Y compris les nationaux de Niue résidant habituellement en Nouvelle-Zélande.
51 Air arrivals (Palau International Airport). 1996-1997: arrivals by nationality. 1998-2000: arrivals by country of residence.	51 Arrivées par voie aérienne (Aéroport international de Palau). 1996-1997 : arrivées par nationalité. 1998-2000 : arrivées par pays de résidence.
52 Total number of visitors broken down by permanent residence who arrived in Panama at Tocumen International Airport and Paso Canoa border post.	52 Nombre total de visiteurs arrivées au Panama par l'aéroport international de Tocúmen et le poste frontière de Paso Canoa, classes selon leur résidence permanente.
53 Including arrivals from abroad to insular possessions of Madeira and the Azores.	53 Y compris les arrivées en provenance de l'étranger aux possessions insulaires de Madère et des Açores.
54 Arrivals by air. Fiscal year July to June. Figures for fiscal year 2000 have been rounded up to the nearest hundred.	54 Arrivées par voie aérienne. Année fiscale de juillet à juin. Les chiffres pour l'année fiscale 2000 ont été arrondis au centième près.
55 Persons who enjoyed the services of the economic agents which carry out the tourist's activity in the republic (except left-bank Dniester river regions and municipality of Bender).	55 Personnes qui ont bénéficié des services des agents économiques chargés de l'activité touristique dans le pays (à l'exception des régions de la rive gauche du Dniester et la municipalité de Bender).
56 Data for 1992 correspond to all CIS countries. 1994: Excluding arrivals by road from Belarus, Kazakhstan and Uzbekistan.	56 Les données de 1992 couvrent l'ensemble des pays CEI. 1994: Exception faite des arrivées per le route en provenance de Bélarus, Kazakhstan et Ouzbékistan.
57 Prior to 1994, air arrivals. Beginning 1994, air and sea arrivals.	57 Avant 1996, arrivées par voie aérienne. A partir de 1994, arrivées par voie aérienne et maritime.
58 Arrivals at Princess Juliana International airport. Including visitors to St. Maarten (the French side of the island).	58 Arrivées à l'aéroport international "Princess Juliana". Y compris les visiteurs à Saint-Martin (partie française de l'île).
59 Including Italian visitors.	59 Y compris les visiteurs italiens.
60 Including Malaysian citizens arriving by land.	60 Y compris les arrivées de malaysiens par voie terrestre.
61 2000: Excluding arrivals in private accommodation = 7,086.	61 2000: A l'exclusion des arrivées dans l'hébergement privé = 7.086.
62 Beginning January 1992, contract and border traffic concession workers are excluded.	62 A partir de janvier 1992, les données excluent les travailleurs contractuels et ceux de la zone frontière.
63 The 1995-2000 series have been technically adjusted and refer to arrivals of non-resident tourists at national borders (excluding same-day visitors). They now exclude passengers residing in Spain who enter the country by international air transport. This statistical improvement has resulted in the revision of the data published until now with a decrease in the number of arrivals.	63 La série 1995-2000 a été modifiée. Cette série exclue maintenant les passagers résidents en Espagne qui rentrent dans le pays par vols internationaux. Cette amélioration statistique a donné lieu à une révision qui montre une diminution dans le chiffre des arrivées (par rapport aux chiffres publiés jusqu'à présent).
64 Arrivals at Zanderij Airport.	64 Arrivées à l'aéroport de Zanderij.
65 Arrivals in hotels only.	65 Arrivées dans les hôtels uniquement.
66 Including domestic tourism and nationals of the country residing abroad.	66 Y compris le tourisme interne et les nationaux résidant à l'étranger.
67 Data refer to Dubai only.	67 Les données se réfèrent au Dubai seulement.
68 Excluding transit passengers.	68 A l'exclusion des passagers en transit.

76
Tourist/visitor arrivals and tourism expenditure
Arrivées de touristes/visiteurs et dépenses touristiques

Region, country or area Région, pays ou zone	Number of tourist/visitor arrivals (thousands) Nombre d'arrivées de touristes/visiteurs (milliers)					Tourism expenditure (million US dollars) Dépenses touristiques (millions de dollars E. –U.)				
	1996	1997	1998	1999	2000	1996	1997	1998	1999	2000
World [1] Monde [1]	586 167	610 088	628 923	652 298	696 837	437 721	441 707	444 506	456 294	474 385
Africa · Afrique										
Algeria Algérie	605	635	678	749	866	45	28	74	80	102
Angola Angola	21	45	52	45	51	9	9	8	13	18
Benin Bénin	143	148	152	...	...	29	31	33	...	...
Botswana Botswana	512	607	750	843	995	93	136	175	234	313
Burkina Faso Burkina Faso	131	138	160	117	126	31	39	42	...	...
Burundi Burundi	27	11	15	26	30	1	1	1	1	1
Cameroon Cameroun	101	133	135	...	...	38	39	40	...	...
Cape Verde Cap-Vert	37 [2]	45 [2]	52 [2]	67 [2]	83 [2]	11	15	20	23	...
Central African Rep. Rép. centrafricaine	21 [2]	17 [2]	7 [2]	10 [2]	...	5	5	6	...	...
Chad Tchad	20	27	41	47	54	10	9	10	...	...
Comoros Comores	24 [2]	26 [2]	27 [2]	24 [2]	24 [2]	23	26	16	19	15
Congo Congo	39	27	20	14	19	10	10	9	12	11
Côte d'Ivoire Côte d'Ivoire	237	274	301	...	...	93	90	98	100	57
Dem. Rep. of the Congo Rép. dém. du Congo	37	30	53	80	103	5	2	2	...	...
Djibouti Djibouti	20	20	21	...	...	4	4	4	...	...
Egypt Egypte	3 528	3 656	3 213	4 490	5 116	3 204	3 727	2 565	3 903	4 345
Equatorial Guinea Guinée équatoriale	...	...	...	...	...	2	2	2	...	...
Eritrea Erythrée	417	410	188	57	70	69	90	34	28	36
Ethiopia Ethiopie	109 [2]	115 [2]	91 [2]	92 [2]	136 [3]	28	36	16	16	68 [4]
Gabon Gabon	145 [2]	167 [2]	195 [2]	177 [2]	155 [2]	7	7	8	11	7
Gambia Gambie	77 [2]	85 [2]	91 [2]	96 [2]	...	31	32	49	...	...
Ghana Ghana	305	325	348	373	399	249	266	284	304	386
Guinea Guinée	12	17	23	27	33	6	5	1	7	12

76

Tourist/visitor arrivals and tourism expenditure
[cont.]

Arrivées de touristes/visiteurs et dépenses touristiques
[suite]

Region, country or area Région, pays ou zone	Number of tourist/visitor arrivals (thousands) Nombre d'arrivées de touristes/visiteurs (milliers)					Tourism expenditure (million US dollars) Dépenses touristiques (millions de dollars E. –U.)				
	1996	1997	1998	1999	2000	1996	1997	1998	1999	2000
Kenya Kenya	925	907	857	862	899	448	385	290	304	257
Lesotho Lesotho	134	144	150	186	...	32	32	24	23	24
Libyan Arab Jamah. Jamah. arabe libyenne	88	50	32	178	174	6	6	18	28	...
Madagascar Madagascar	83²	101²	121²	138²	160²	65	74	91	100	119
Malawi Malawi	194	207	220	254	228	5	11	15	20	27
Mali Mali	98²	75²	83²	82²	86²	29	26	89	77	71
Mauritania Mauritanie	...	...	...	24	30	19	21	20	28	...
Mauritius Maurice	487	536	558	578	656	452	485	503	545	542
Morocco Maroc	2 693	3 072	3 242	3 817	4 113	1 674	1 449	1 712	1 880	2 040
Namibia Namibie	461	502	614	...	...	293	333	288	...	...
Niger Niger	38²	44²	42²	43²	50²	17	18	18	24	...
Nigeria Nigéria	822	611	739	776	813	85	118	142	171	200
Réunion Réunion	350	374	400	394	430	258	249	265	270	276
Rwanda Rwanda	* 1	* 1	* 2	...	...	4	17	19	17	24
Sao Tome and Principe Sao Tomé-et-Principe	6	5	5	...	...	2	2	2	...	...
Senegal Sénégal	282²	314²	352²	369²	389²	149	153	178	166	140
Seychelles Seychelles	131	130	128	125	130	107	122	111	112	115
Sierra Leone Sierra Leone	22	23	6	6	10	10	...	8	8	12
Somalia Somalie	* 10	* 10	* 10	...	...	...	...	...	...	...
South Africa Afrique du Sud	5 186	5 170	5 898	6 026	6 001	2 575	2 769	2 717	2 637	2 707
Sudan Soudan	28²	30²	38²	39²	38²	25	17	21	22	30
Swaziland Swaziland	315	269	284	289	281	38	40	47	50	34
Togo Togo	58	92	69	70	60	11⁵	12⁵	13⁵	9⁵	5⁵
Tunisia Tunisie	3 885	4 263	4 718	4 832	5 057	1 411	1 361	1 557	1 560	1 496
Uganda Ouganda	174	171	192	187	191	117	135	144	149	...

76

Tourist/visitor arrivals and tourism expenditure
[cont.]

Arrivées de touristes/visiteurs et dépenses touristiques
[suite]

Region, country or area Région, pays ou zone	Number of tourist/visitor arrivals (thousands) Nombre d'arrivées de touristes/visiteurs (milliers)					Tourism expenditure (million US dollars) Dépenses touristiques (millions de dollars E. –U.)				
	1996	1997	1998	1999	2000	1996	1997	1998	1999	2000
United Rep. of Tanzania Rép.-Unie de Tanzanie	315	347	450	564	459	322	392	570	733	739
Zambia Zambie	264	341	362	404	457	60	75	75	85	91
Zimbabwe Zimbabwe	1 577	1 281	1 986	2 101	1 868	232	205	158	202	125
America, North · Amérique du Nord										
Anguilla Anguilla	37	43	44	47	44	48	57	58	56	55
Antigua and Barbuda Antigua-et-Barbuda	228	240	234	240	237	258	269	256	290	290
Aruba Aruba	641	650	647	683	721	613	668	732	778	638
Bahamas Bahamas	1 633	1 618	1 528	1 577	1 596	1 398	1 416	1 354	1 583	1 814
Barbados Barbade	447	472	512	515	544	644	657	703	677	711
Belize Belize	133	146	177	181	196	89	88	108	112	121
Bermuda Bermudes	390[2]	380[2]	369[2]	354[2]	328[2]	472	478	487	479	431
British Virgin Islands Iles Vierges britanniques	244	244	279	286	281	228	220	255	300	315
Canada Canada	17 329	17 669	18 870	19 411	19 663	8 616	8 828	9 396	10 171	10 704
Cayman Islands Iles Caïmanes	373[2]	381[2]	404[2]	395[2]	354[2]	368	436	450	439	...
Costa Rica Costa Rica	781	811	943	1 032	1 088	689	719	884	1 036	1 229
Cuba Cuba	999[2]	1 153[2]	1 390[2]	1 561[2]	1 741[2]	1 185	1 326	1 571	1 714	1 756
Dominica Dominique	63	65	66	74	69	37	40	38	49	47
Dominican Republic Rép. dominicaine	1 926[2]	2 211[2]	2 309[2]	2 649[2]	2 972[2]	1 766	2 099	2 153	2 483	2 860
El Salvador El Salvador	283	387	542	658	795	44	75	125	211	254
Grenada Grenade	108	111	116	125	129	55	55	59	63	67
Guadeloupe Guadeloupe	625	660	693	711	807	496	372	466	375	418
Guatemala Guatemala	520	576	636	823	826	284	325	394	570	518
Haiti Haïti	150[2]	149[2]	147[2]	143[2]	140[2]	58	57	56	55	54
Honduras Honduras	263	307	321	371	471	115	146	168	195	262
Jamaica Jamaïque	1 162[2]	1 192[2]	1 225[2]	1 248[2]	1 323[2]	1 092	1 131	1 197	1 279	1 333

76

Tourist/visitor arrivals and tourism expenditure
[cont.]

Arrivées de touristes/visiteurs et dépenses touristiques
[suite]

Region, country or area Région, pays ou zone	Number of tourist/visitor arrivals (thousands) Nombre d'arrivées de touristes/visiteurs (milliers)					Tourism expenditure (million US dollars) Dépenses touristiques (millions de dollars E. –U.)				
	1996	1997	1998	1999	2000	1996	1997	1998	1999	2000
Martinique Martinique	477	513	549	564	526	382	400	415	404	302
Mexico Mexique	21 405	19 351	19 392	19 043	20 641	6 934[6]	7 593[6]	7 493[6]	7 223[6]	8 295[6]
Montserrat Montserrat	9	5	7	10	10	10	5	8	11	9
Netherlands Antilles Antilles néerlandaises	648	706	739	722	692	550	624	734	773	812
Nicaragua Nicaragua	303	358	406	468	486	54	74	90	107	111
Panama Panama	362	421	431	457	484	425	457	494	538	576
Puerto Rico Porto Rico	3 065[2]	3 242[2]	3 396[2]	3 024[2]	3 341[2]	1 898	2 046	2 233	2 139	2 388
Saint Kitts and Nevis Saint-Kitts-et-Nevis	84	88	93	84	73	67	67	76	70	58
Saint Lucia Sainte-Lucie	236	248	252	264	270	269	284	291	311	277
St. Vincent-Grenadines St. Vincent-Grenadines	58	65	67	68	73	64	70	71	74	79
Trinidad and Tobago Trinité-et-Tobago	266[2]	324[2]	334[2]	358[2]	399[2]	110	193	201	210	...
Turks and Caicos Islands Iles Turques et Caïques	88	93	111	121	152	99	113	157	238	285
United States Etats-Unis	46 489	47 752	46 404	48 497	50 945	69 809	73 426	71 286	74 731	82 042
United States Virgin Is. Iles Vierges américaines	373	411	422	484	607	781	894	940	955	1 157
America, South · Amérique du Sud										
Argentina Argentine	2 614	2 764	3 012	2 898	2 909	2 542	2 693	2 936	2 813	2 817
Bolivia Bolivie	313	355	387	342	306	155	181	200	174	160
Brazil Brésil	2 666	2 850	4 818[7]	5 107	5 313	2 469[8]	2 595[8]	3 678[7,8]	3 994[8]	4 228[8]
Chile Chili	1 450	1 644	1 759	1 622	1 742	905	1 020	1 062	898	827
Colombia Colombie	757[7]	639	674	546	557	1 120	1 044	929	928	1 028
Ecuador Equateur	494	529	511	518	615	281	290	291	343	402
French Guiana Guyane française	...	...	68	70	...	...	...	51	50	...
Guyana Guyana	92	76	68	75	105	70	60	54	59	...
Paraguay Paraguay	426	395	350	269	323	140	128	111	81	101
Peru Pérou	663	747	820	944	1 027	670	817	845	890	911

76

Tourist/visitor arrivals and tourism expenditure
[cont.]

Arrivées de touristes/visiteurs et dépenses touristiques
[suite]

Region, country or area Région, pays ou zone	Number of tourist/visitor arrivals (thousands) Nombre d'arrivées de touristes/visiteurs (milliers)					Tourism expenditure (million US dollars) Dépenses touristiques (millions de dollars E. –U.)				
	1996	1997	1998	1999	2000	1996	1997	1998	1999	2000
Suriname Suriname	53[2]	61[2]	55[2]	63[2]	58[2]	14	9	2	9	16
Uruguay Uruguay	2 152	2 316	2 163	2 073	1 968	717	759	695	653	652
Venezuela Venezuela	759	814	685	587	469	944	1 086	961	673	563
Asia · Asie										
Afghanistan Afghanistan	* 4	* 4	* 4	...	...	1	1	1	...	...
Armenia Arménie	13	23	32	41	45	5	7	10	27	45
Azerbaijan Azerbaïdjan	210	306	483	602	681	46	162	125	81	63
Bahrain Bahreïn	1 201	1 611	1 640	2 019	2 420	263	311	366	408	469
Bangladesh Bangladesh	166	182	172	173	199	32	59	51	50	50
Bhutan Bhoutan	5	5	6	7	8	6	6	8	9	10
Brunei Darussalam Brunéi Darussalam	837	643	964	967	984	38	39	37	...	...
Cambodia Cambodge	260	219	286	368	466	118	103	166	190	228
China Chine	* 22 765	* 23 770	* 25 073	* 27 047	*31 229	10 200	12 074	12 602	14 099	16 224
China, Hong Kong SAR Chine, Hong Kong RAS	12 974	11 273	10 160	11 328	13 059	11 994[9]	9 979[9]	7 496[9]	7 210[9]	7 886[9]
China, Macao SAR Chine, Macao RAS	* 4 690	* 3 836	* 4 517	* 5 050	*5 197	3 085[10]	2 947[10]	2 638[10]	2 466[10]	2 999[10]
Cyprus Chypre	1 950	2 088	2 223	2 434	2 686	1 669	1 639	1 696	1 878	1 894
Georgia Géorgie	117	313	317	384	387	170	416	423	400	413
India Inde	2 288	2 374	2 359	2 482	2 649	2 832	2 889	2 948	3 009	3 168
Indonesia Indonésie	5 034	5 185	4 606	4 728	5 064	6 307	5 321	4 331	4 710	5 749
Iran (Islamic Rep. of) Iran (Rép. islamique d')	573	764	1 008	1 321	1 342	244	327	477	662	850
Iraq Iraq	51	15	45	30	78	13	13	13	...	...
Israel Israël	2 100	2 010	1 942	2 312	2 417	2 955	2 836	2 657	2 974	3 819
Japan Japon	3 837	4 218	4 106	4 438	4 757	4 078	4 326	3 742	3 428	3 373
Jordan Jordanie	1 103	1 127	1 256	1 358	1 427	743	774	773	795	722
Kazakhstan Kazakhstan	...	...	...	...	1 471	199	289	407	363	356

76

Tourist/visitor arrivals and tourism expenditure
[cont.]

Arrivées de touristes/visiteurs et dépenses touristiques
[suite]

Region, country or area Région, pays ou zone	Number of tourist/visitor arrivals (thousands) Nombre d'arrivées de touristes/visiteurs (milliers)					Tourism expenditure (million US dollars) Dépenses touristiques (millions de dollars E. –U.)				
	1996	1997	1998	1999	2000	1996	1997	1998	1999	2000
Korea, Dem. P. R. [*] Corée, R. p. dém. de [*]	127	128	130	...	...	...	...	...	...	...
Korea, Republic of Corée, République de	3 684	3 908	4 250	4 660	5 322	5 430[11]	5 116[11]	6 865[11]	6 802[11]	6 811[11]
Kuwait Koweït	72	76	77	...	79	184	188	207	92	98
Kyrgyzstan Kirghizistan	42	87	59	69	...	4	7	8	14	15
Lao People's Dem. Rep. Rép. dém. pop. lao	93	193	200	259	191	44	73	80	97	114
Lebanon Liban	424	558	631	673	742	715	1 000	1 221	673[12]	742[12]
Malaysia Malaisie	7 138	6 211	5 551	7 931	10 222	4 447	2 702	2 456	3 540	4 936
Maldives Maldives	339[2]	366[2]	396[2]	430[2]	467[2]	266	286	303	314	321
Mongolia Mongolie	71	82	197	159	158	10	13	35	36	...
Myanmar Myanmar	172[2]	189[2]	201[2]	198[2]	208[2]	33	34	35	35	42
Nepal Népal	394	422	464	492	464	117	116	153	168	167
Occupied Palestinian Terr. Terr. palestinien occupé	...	...	201	271	330	104	96	114	132	155
Oman Oman	349	376	424	503	571	105[13]	111[13]	114[13]	106[13]	120[13]
Pakistan Pakistan	369	375	429	432	557	146	117	98	76	84
Philippines Philippines	2 049	2 223	2 149	2 171	1 992	2 701	2 831	2 413	2 531	2 134
Qatar Qatar	327	435	451	...	...	...	...	...	...	...
Saudi Arabia Arabie saoudite	...	...	...	...	6 295	...	...	...	...	...
Singapore Singapour	6 608	6 531	5 631	6 258	6 917	8 012	6 073	5 402	5 859	6 018
Sri Lanka Sri Lanka	302	366	381	436	400	173	217	231	275	253
Syrian Arab Republic Rép. arabe syrienne	830	891	1 267[7]	1 386	1 416	1 165	1 013	1 017	1 031	1 082
Tajikistan Tadjikistan	...	...	...	2	4	...	...	...	...	...
Thailand Thaïlande	7 244	7 294	7 843	8 651	9 579	8 664	7 048	5 934	6 695	7 112
Turkey Turquie	7 966	9 040	8 960	6 893	9 586	5 962	8 088	7 809	5 203	7 636
Turkmenistan Turkménistan	217	257	300	...	...	66	74	192	...	...
United Arab Emirates [14] Emirats arabes unis [14]	2 572	2 476	2 991	3 393	3 907	743	814	859	893	1 012

76

Tourist/visitor arrivals and tourism expenditure
[cont.]

Arrivées de touristes/visiteurs et dépenses touristiques
[suite]

Region, country or area Région, pays ou zone	Number of tourist/visitor arrivals (thousands) Nombre d'arrivées de touristes/visiteurs (milliers)					Tourism expenditure (million US dollars) Dépenses touristiques (millions de dollars E. –U.)				
	1996	1997	1998	1999	2000	1996	1997	1998	1999	2000
Uzbekistan Ouzbékistan	174	253	272	...	...	15	19	21	...	...
Viet Nam Viet Nam	975[7]	1 114	978	1 211	1 383	87	88	86	...	...
Yemen Yémen	74	80	88	58	73	56	70	84	61	76
Europe · Europe										
Albania Albanie	64	23	22	26	32	77	27	54	211	389
Andorra Andorre	...	...	...	2 347	2 949	...	...	...	...	...
Austria Autriche	17 090	16 647	17 352	17 467	17 982	13 930[15]	12 248[15]	12 628[15]	12 533[15]	10 031
Belarus Bélarus	234	254	355	...	...	55	25	22	12	19
Belgium Belgique	5 829	6 037	6 179	6 369	6 457	...	...	...	...	...
Belgium-Luxembourg Belgique-Luxembourg	...	...	...	...	...	4 893	5 267	5 443	7 331	7 422
Bosnia and Herzegovina Bosnie-Herzégovine	99	100	90	89	110	16	15	21	21	17
Bulgaria Bulgarie	2 795	2 980	2 667	2 472	2 785	450	496	966[16]	932[16]	1 074[16]
Croatia Croatie	2 914	4 178	4 499	3 805	5 831	2 014	2 523	2 733	2 493	2 758
Czech Republic République tchèque	4 558	4 976	5 482	5 610	4 666	4 075	3 647	3 719	3 035	2 869
Denmark Danemark	2 125	2 158	2 073	2 023	2 088	3 425	3 185	3 211	3 460	4 025
Estonia Estonie	665	730	825	950	1 240	470	465	534	560	506
Finland Finlande	1 724	1 832	2 644	2 454	2 714	1 637[17]	1 644[17]	1 631[17]	1 517[17]	1 397[17]
France France	62 406	67 310	70 040	73 042	75 595	28 357	28 009	29 931	31 507[18]	30 686[18]
Germany Allemagne	15 205	15 837	16 511	17 116	18 983	17 706[19]	16 696[19]	16 766[19]	16 730[19]	17 879[19]
Greece Grèce	9 233	10 070	10 916	12 164	13 096	3 723	5 151	6 188[20]	8 783[20]	9 219[20]
Hungary Hongrie	19 917	18 658	16 812	14 402	15 571	3 222	3 440	3 514	3 394	3 429
Iceland Islande	201	202	232	263	303	176	173	207	221	227
Ireland Irlande	5 289	5 587	6 064	6 403	6 749	3 022	3 189	3 267	3 392	3 387
Italy Italie	32 943	34 692	34 933	36 516	41 181	30 017	29 714	29 866	28 359	27 500
Latvia Lettonie	565	635	576	544	509	215	192	182	118	131

76

Tourist/visitor arrivals and tourism expenditure
[cont.]

Arrivées de touristes/visiteurs et dépenses touristiques
[suite]

Region, country or area Région, pays ou zone	Number of tourist/visitor arrivals (thousands) Nombre d'arrivées de touristes/visiteurs (milliers)					Tourism expenditure (million US dollars) Dépenses touristiques (millions de dollars E. –U.)				
	1996	1997	1998	1999	2000	1996	1997	1998	1999	2000
Liechtenstein Liechtenstein	56	57	59	60	62	...	...	...	...	...
Lithuania Lituanie	832	1 012	1 416	1 422	1 083	316	360	460	550	391
Luxembourg Luxembourg	724	778	789	863	835	...	...	...	...	...
Malta Malte	1 054	1 111	1 182	1 214	1 216	635	648	656	679	614
Monaco Monaco	226	259	278	278	300	...	...	...	...	...
Netherlands Pays-Bas	6 580	7 841	9 312	9 874	10 003	6 548	6 319	6 792	6 998	7 206
Norway Norvège	2 746	2 702	4 538	4 481	4 348	2 402	2 183	2 172	2 115	1 937
Poland Pologne	19 410	19 520	18 780	17 950	17 400	8 444[21]	8 679[21]	7 946[21]	6 100[21]	6 100[21]
Portugal Portugal	9 730	10 172	11 295	11 632	12 097	4 265	4 619	5 302	5 261	5 257
Republic of Moldova République de Moldova	29	21	19	14	18	33	50	40	38	46
Romania Roumanie	3 028	2 957	2 966	3 209	3 274	529	526	260	254	359
Russian Federation Fédération de Russie	16 208	17 463	15 805	18 496	21 169	6 868	7 164	6 508	7 510	...
San Marino Saint-Marin	* 530	* 532	* 532	...	...	...	...	...	...	...
Serbia and Montenegro Serbie-et-Monténégro	301	298	283	152	239	43	41	35	17	26
Slovakia Slovaquie	951	814	896	975	1 053	* 673	* 546	* 489	* 461	* 432
Slovenia Slovénie	832	974	977	884	1 090	1 240[22]	1 187[22]	1 088[22]	954[22]	961[22]
Spain Espagne	36 221	39 553	43 396	46 776	47 898	26 690	26 651	29 839	32 497	31 454
Sweden Suède	2 376	2 388	2 573	2 595	2 746	3 657	3 730	4 189	3 894	4 034
Switzerland Suisse	* 10 600	* 10 600	* 10 900	* 10 700	*11 000	8 826	7 915	7 973	7 769	7 500
TFYR of Macedonia L'ex-R.y. Macédoine	136	121	157	181	224	21	14	15	37	37
Ukraine Ukraine	3 854	7 558	6 208	4 232	4 406	3 416	3 865	3 317	2 124	2 207
United Kingdom Royaume-Uni	25 163	25 515	25 745	25 394	25 209	19 173	20 039	20 978	20 223	19 544
Oceania · Océanie										
American Samoa Samoa américaines	21	16	...	27	...	9	10	10	...	...
Australia Australie	4 165	4 318	4 167	4 459	4 946	9 113	9 057	7 335	7 525	8 006

76

Tourist/visitor arrivals and tourism expenditure
[cont.]

Arrivées de touristes/visiteurs et dépenses touristiques
[suite]

Region, country or area Région, pays ou zone	Number of tourist/visitor arrivals (thousands) Nombre d'arrivées de touristes/visiteurs (milliers)					Tourism expenditure (million US dollars) Dépenses touristiques (millions de dollars E.–U.)				
	1996	1997	1998	1999	2000	1996	1997	1998	1999	2000
Cook Islands Iles Cook	48	50	49	56	73	50	35	34	39	36
Fiji Fidji	340	359	371	410	294	299	297	244	284	195
French Polynesia Polynésie française	164	180	189	211	252	322	345	354	394	...
Guam Guam	1 373	1 382	1 137	1 162	1 287	1 415	2 818	2 361	1 908	...
Kiribati Kiribati	3[2]	5[2]	2[2]	1[2]	1[2]	2	2	3	2	2
Marshall Islands Iles Marshall	6[2]	6[2]	6[2]	5[2]	5[2]	3	3	3	4	4
Micronesia (Fed. States) Micronésie (Etats féd. de)	...	28	27	28	33	...	...	...	...	...
New Caledonia Nouvelle-Calédonie	91	105	104	100	110	114	117	110	112	110
New Zealand Nouvelle-Zélande	1 529	1 497	1 485	1 607	1 789	1 546	1 406	1 441	1 737	2 062
Niue Nioué	2[2]	2[2]	2[2]	2[2]	2[2]	1	2	1	...	...
Northern Mariana Islands Iles Mariannes du Nord	728[2]	685[2]	481[2]	493[2]	517[2]	670	672	647	...	...
Palau [2] Palaos [2]	69	74	64	55	58	...	...	...	...	...
Papua New Guinea Papouasie-Nvl-Guinée	61	66	67	67	58	68	71	75	76	92
Samoa Samoa	73	68	78	85	88	41	37	38	42	40
Solomon Islands Iles Salomon	11	16	13	21	...	14	7	7	6	...
Tonga Tonga	27[2]	26[2]	27[2]	31[2]	35[2]	13	16	8	9	7
Tuvalu Tuvalu	1	1	1	1	1	...	...	...	...	...
Vanuatu Vanuatu	46	50	52	51	58	50	46	52	56	58

Source:
World Tourism Organization (WTO), Madrid, "Yearbook of Tourism Statistics - 2002 Edition" and the WTO Statistics Database.

Source:
Organisation mondiale du tourisme (OMT), Madrid, "Annuaire des statistiques du tourisme - 2002 édition" et la base de données de l'OMT.

1 The World totals are global estimates prepared by WTO. The estimated part relates only to those countries that were unable to provide the information contained in WTO Database as of June 2002.
2 Air arrivals.
3 Arrivals through all ports of entry.
4 Incorporates all revenues obtained from the sector based on estimation.
5 Hotel receipts.
6 Including receipts from cruise passengers and frontier visitors.

1 Les chiffres mondials sont des estimations globales de l'OMT. La partie estimative ne concerne que les pays qui n'ont pas été en mesure de comuniquer les données intégrées à la base de l'OMT au 1er juin 2002.
2 Arrivées par voie aérienne.
3 Arrivées à travers tous les ports d'entrée.
4 Comporte une estimation de toutes les recettes du secteur.
5 Recettes des hôtels.
6 Y compris les recettes provenant des passagers de navires de

76

Tourist/visitor arrivals and tourism expenditure
[cont.]

Arrivées de touristes/visiteurs et dépenses touristiques
[suite]

7 Change in methodology.
8 Data based on the sample survey conducted by EMBRATUR.

9 Including receipts from servicemen, air crew members and transit passengers.
10 Including gambling receipts.
11 Excluding expenses of students studying overseas.

12 Due to the lack of data on international tourism receipts concerning statistics on inbound tourism, the Department of "Internet and Statistics Service of the Ministry of Tourism" considers that a tourist spends an average of US$ 1,000.

13 Hotel sales.
14 Data refer to Dubai only.
15 Including international transport.
16 New methodology of the Bulgarian Central Bank and Ministry of Economy.
17 Data collected by travel surveys.
18 New series since 1999 excluding frontier workers paid in foreign currency.
19 Including border merchandise transactions and purchases of inward-bound and outward-bound commuters.
20 Including registrations through new methodology.

21 Based on surveys and estimations by the Institute of Tourism.

22 Data refer to the item "travel" of the Balance of Payments.

croisière et des visiteurs frontaliers.
7 Changement de méthode.
8 Données basées sur une enquête sur échantillon réalisée par EMBRATUR.

9 Y compris les recettes provenant des militaires, des équipages d'avions et des passagers en transit.
10 Y compris les recettes tirées des jeux de hasard.
11 Non compris les dépenses des étudiants poursuivant leurs études à l'étranger.

12 Du fait d'un manque de données sur les recettes du tourisme international concernant les statistiques sur le tourisme récepteur, le Département "Internet et Service Statistique du Ministère du Tourisme" considère qu'un touriste dépense en moyenne 1.000$E.U.

13 Chiffre d'affaires des hôtels.
14 Les données se réfèrent au Dubai seulement.
15 Y compris les transports internationaux.
16 Nouvelle méthodologie élaborée par la Banque Centrale de la Bulgarie et le Ministère de l'Economie.
17 Données collectées au moyen d'enquêtes sur les voyages.
18 A partir de 1999, non compris les travailleurs frontaliers rémunérés en devises.
19 Y compris les transactions frontalières en marchandises, et les achats des migrants quotidiens entrant et sortant.
20 Y compris les mouvements enregistrés selon la nouvelle méthode.

21 Chiffres basés sur des enquêtes et des estimations de l'Institut du tourisme.

22 Données relatives à la rubrique "Voyages" de la balance des paiements.

77

Tourism expenditure in other countries
Million US dollars

Dépenses touristiques dans d'autres pays
Millions de dollars E.-U.

Region, country or area Région, pays ou zone	1991	1992	1993	1994	1995	1996	1997	1998	1999	2000
World **Monde**	**249 585**	**286 436**	**280 418**	**313 271**	**362 822**	**383 382**	**378 998**	...	...	...
Africa **Afrique**	**5 594**	**5 529**	**6 013**	**6 452**	**7 377**	**7 845**	**8 536**	...	...	...
Algeria Algérie	140	163	163	24	186	188	144	269	250	193
Angola Angola	65	75	66	88	75	73	98	75	127	...
Benin Bénin	10	12	12	6	5	6	7	7	...	...
Botswana Botswana	67	75	79	76	145	78	92	126	143	...
Burkina Faso Burkina Faso	22	21	21	23	30	32	32	...	...	...
Burundi Burundi	18	21	20	18	25	12	12	11	8	14
Cameroon Cameroun	414	228	225	58	105	107	107	...	...	...
Cape Verde Cap-Vert	3	8	9	12	16	18	17	24		
Central African Rep. Rép. centrafricaine	43	51	50	43	37	39	39	...	...	...
Chad Tchad	63	80	86	26	23	24	24	...		
Comoros Comores	7	7	6	6	7	8	8	3	...	
Congo Congo	106	95	70	34	52	77	64	57	60	58
Côte d'Ivoire Côte d'Ivoire	163	168	169	157	190	221	200	213	222	226
Dem. Rep. of the Congo Rép. dém. du Congo	16	16	16	12	10	7	7	...	...	...
Djibouti Djibouti	...	3	5	3	4	5	5	...	...	...
Egypt Egypte	225	918	1 048	1 067	1 278	1 317	1 347	1 148	1 078	1 073
Equatorial Guinea Guinée équatoriale	9	9	9	8	7	8	8	...	...	...
Ethiopia Ethiopie	7	10	11	15	25	25	40	50	51	74
Gabon Gabon	112	143	154	143	173	176	178	180	183	174
Gambia Gambie	15	13	14	14	14	15	16	...	...	...
Ghana Ghana	14	17	20	20	21	22	23	85	91	100
Guinea Guinée	27	17	28	24	21	27	23	27	31	35
Kenya Kenya	24	29	48	114	145	167	194	190	115	132
Lesotho Lesotho	11	11	6	7	13	12	14	13	14	9

77

Tourism expenditure in other countries
Million US dollars *[cont.]*

Dépenses touristiques dans d'autres pays
Millions de dollars E.-U. *[suite]*

Region, country or area Région, pays ou zone	1991	1992	1993	1994	1995	1996	1997	1998	1999	2000
Libyan Arab Jamah. Jamah. arabe libyenne	877	154	206	210	212	215	154	143	150	...
Madagascar Madagascar	32	37	34	47	59	72	80	119	111	114
Malawi Malawi	27	24	11	15	16	17	17	...	...	...
Mali Mali	60	71	58	42	49	46	42	52	44	41
Mauritania Mauritanie	26	31	20	18	23	36	48	42	55	...
Mauritius Maurice	110	142	128	143	159	179	173	185	187	182
Morocco Maroc	190	242	245	303	304	300	316	424	440	430
Namibia Namibie	69	72	71	77	90	89	99	88	...	...
Niger Niger	40	30	29	21	21	23	24	25	26	28
Nigeria Nigéria	839	348	298	858	906	1 304	1 816	1 567	620	730
Rwanda Rwanda	17	17	18	18	10	12	13	17	18	20
Sao Tome and Principe Sao Tomé-et-Principe	2	2	2	1	1	1	1	...	...	...
Senegal Sénégal	105	112	50	48	72	53	53	54	54	...
Seychelles Seychelles	24	28	35	31	39	30	30	26	21	20
Sierra Leone Sierra Leone	4	3	4	4	2	2	...	4	4	6
South Africa Afrique du Sud	1 148	1 554	1 868	1 861	1 849	1 754	1 961	1 908	2 028	2 004
Sudan Soudan	12	33	15	47	43	28	33	29	35	55
Swaziland Swaziland	41	40	43	38	43	42	38	40	40	36
Togo Togo	29	30	20	18	18	3	5	3	3	...
Tunisia Tunisie	128	167	203	216	251	251	235	235	239	263
Uganda Ouganda	16	18	40	78	80	135	113	95	141	...
United Rep. of Tanzania Rép.-Unie de Tanzanie	60	73	180	206	360	412	407	493	368	337
Zambia Zambie	87	56	56	58	57	59	59	...	...	...
Zimbabwe Zimbabwe	70	55	44	96	106	118	120	131	110	...
America, North **Amérique du Nord**	**55 253**	**58 771**	**59 834**	**61 866**	**61 379**	**65 927**	**70 956**	...	...	...
Anguilla Anguilla	3	4	5	6	6	6	6	...	...	...

77

Tourism expenditure in other countries
Million US dollars *[cont.]*

Dépenses touristiques dans d'autres pays
Millions de dollars E.-U. *[suite]*

Region, country or area Région, pays ou zone	1991	1992	1993	1994	1995	1996	1997	1998	1999	2000
Antigua and Barbuda Antigua-et-Barbuda	20	23	23	24	23	26	26	...	...	...
Aruba Aruba	47	51	58	65	73	96	131	111	122	...
Bahamas Bahamas	200	187	171	193	213	235	250	256	309	293
Barbados Barbade	44	42	53	59	71	74	79	82	87	...
Belize Belize	8	14	20	19	25	26	34	24	24	24
Bermuda Bermudes	126	134	140	143	145	148	148	...	...	...
British Virgin Islands Iles Vierges britanniques	26	30	33	36	40	42	42	...	...	...
Canada Canada	12 002	11 796	11 133	10 014	10 267	11 253	11 464	10 765	11 345	12 140
Costa Rica Costa Rica	149	223	267	300	321	335	358	408	446	482
Dominica Dominique	5	6	5	6	6	7	7	8	...	...
Dominican Republic Rép. dominicaine	154	164	128	145	173	198	221	254	264	309
El Salvador El Salvador	57	58	61	70	72	73	153	179	169	171
Grenada Grenade	5	4	4	4	5	5	5	5	...	...
Guatemala Guatemala	67	103	117	151	141	135	119	157	183	182
Haiti Haïti	35	11	10	14	35	37	35	37	...	...
Honduras Honduras	37	38	55	57	57	60	62	81	94	99
Jamaica Jamaïque	71	87	82	81	148	157	181	198	227	209
Mexico [1] Mexique [1]	5 812	6 107	5 562	5 338	3 171	3 387	3 891	4 209	4 541	5 499
Montserrat Montserrat	2	1	3	3	2	3	3	...	...	...
Netherlands Antilles [2] Antilles néerlandaises [2]	95	105	125	147	209	236	243	109	179	218
Nicaragua Nicaragua	28	30	31	30	40	60	65	70	78	79
Panama Panama	109	120	123	123	128	136	164	176	184	187
Puerto Rico Porto Rico	689	736	776	797	833	821	869	874	815	931
Saint Kitts and Nevis Saint-Kitts-et-Nevis	5	5	5	6	5	6	6	6	...	...
Saint Lucia Sainte-Lucie	18	21	20	23	25	29	29	...	...	...
St. Vincent-Grenadines St. Vincent-Grenadines	4	4	5	6	7	8	7	8	...	...

77

Tourism expenditure in other countries
Million US dollars *[cont.]*

Dépenses touristiques dans d'autres pays
Millions de dollars E.-U. *[suite]*

Region, country or area Région, pays ou zone	1991	1992	1993	1994	1995	1996	1997	1998	1999	2000
Trinidad and Tobago Trinité-et-Tobago	113	115	106	90	69	76	72	67	...	...
Turks and Caicos Islands Iles Turques et Caïques	...	...	...	134	153	174	235	194	244	154
United States Etats-Unis	35 322	38 552	40 713	43 782	44 916	48 078	52 051	56 509	58 865	65 537
America, South **Amérique du Sud**	**6 317**	**7 392**	**9 230**	**10 632**	**11 155**	**14 565**	**15 094**	...	...	...
Argentina Argentine	2 145	2 613	3 117	3 306	3 190	3 497	3 874	3 993	4 107	4 338
Bolivia Bolivie	129	135	137	140	112	140	142	150	130	101
Brazil Brésil	1 224	1 332	1 892	2 931	3 412	5 825	5 446	5 731	3 085	3 893
Chile Chili	409	536	560	535	774	806	945	906	806	752
Colombia Colombie	509	641	694	841	878	1 116	1 209	1 120	1 078	1 057
Ecuador Equateur	177	178	190	203	235	219	227	241	271	299
Guyana Guyana	...	14	18	23	21	22	22	...	...	...
Paraguay [3] Paraguay [3]	118	135	138	177	133	139	139	143	109	97
Peru Pérou	263	255	269	266	296	350	434	453	444	530
Suriname Suriname	16	21	3	3	3	8	11	11	13	23
Uruguay Uruguay	100	104	129	234	236	192	264	265	280	281
Venezuela Venezuela	1 227	1 428	2 083	1 973	1 865	2 251	2 381	2 451	1 646	1 824
Asia **Asie**	**46 929**	**55 403**	**57 745**	**64 487**	**75 912**	**82 292**	**78 540**	...	...	...
Afghanistan Afghanistan	1	1	1	1	1	1	1	...	...	...
Armenia Arménie	...	...	...	1	3	22	41	45	34	37
Azerbaijan Azerbaïdjan	...	...	...	...	146	100	186	170	139	132
Bahrain Bahreïn	98	141	130	146	122	109	122	142	159	169
Bangladesh Bangladesh	83	111	153	210	229	200	170	198	212	301
Cambodia Cambodge	...	...	4	8	8	15	13	7	18	19
China Chine	511	2 512	2 797	3 036	3 688	4 474	8 130	9 205	10 864	13 114
Cyprus Chypre	113	132	133	176	241	263	278	276	289	285

77

Tourism expenditure in other countries
Million US dollars *[cont.]*

Dépenses touristiques dans d'autres pays
Millions de dollars E.-U. *[suite]*

Region, country or area Région, pays ou zone	1991	1992	1993	1994	1995	1996	1997	1998	1999	2000
Georgia Géorgie	...	...	...	...	...	...	156	226	130	110
India Inde	434	470	474	769	996	913	1 341	1 712	2 010	2 567
Indonesia Indonésie	969	1 166	1 539	1 900	2 172	2 399	2 411	2 102	2 353	3 197
Iran (Islamic Rep. of) Iran (Rép. islamique d')	734	1 109	862	149	241	529	677	788	918	1 350
Israel Israël	1 551	1 674	2 052	2 135	2 120	2 278	2 283	2 376	2 566	2 804
Japan Japon	23 983	26 837	26 860	30 715	36 792	37 040	33 041	28 815	32 808	31 886
Jordan [4] Jordanie [4]	281	350	344	394	420	381	398	353	355	387
Kazakhstan Kazakhstan	...	...	...	...	283	319	445	498	394	408
Korea, Republic of [5] Corée, République de [5]	3 784	3 794	3 259	4 088	5 903	6 963	6 262	2 640	3 975	6 174
Kuwait Koweït	2 012	1 797	1 819	2 146	2 248	2 492	2 377	2 517	2 270	2 451
Kyrgyzstan Kirghizistan	...	...	...	2	7	6	4	3	11	16
Lao People's Dem. Rep. Rép. dém. pop. lao	6	10	11	18	30	22	21	23	12	17
Malaysia Malaisie	1 584	1 770	1 838	1 994	2 314	2 569	2 590	1 785	1 973	...
Maldives Maldives	19	22	29	28	31	38	39	42	45	46
Mongolia Mongolie	2	4	3	3	20	19	14	45	41	...
Myanmar Myanmar	24	16	10	12	18	28	33	27	21	25
Nepal Népal	38	52	93	112	136	125	103	78	71	73
Oman Oman	47	47	47	47	47	255	252	289	323	341
Pakistan Pakistan	555	680	633	397	449	900	364	352	180	252
Philippines Philippines	61	102	130	196	422	1 266	1 935	1 950	1 308	1 005
Singapore Singapour	2 080	2 489	3 412	3 368	4 631	5 797	4 605	4 707	4 666	4 970
Sri Lanka Sri Lanka	97	111	121	170	186	176	180	202	219	244
Syrian Arab Republic Rép. arabe syrienne	256	260	300	512	498	513	545	580	630	640
Thailand Thaïlande	1 266	1 590	2 092	2 906	3 373	4 171	1 888	1 448	1 843	2 065
Turkey Turquie	592	776	934	886	912	1 265	1 716	1 754	1 471	1 711
Turkmenistan Turkménistan	...	...	...	...	...	73	125	...	...	...

77

Tourism expenditure in other countries
Million US dollars *[cont.]*

Dépenses touristiques dans d'autres pays
Millions de dollars E.-U. *[suite]*

Region, country or area Région, pays ou zone	1991	1992	1993	1994	1995	1996	1997	1998	1999	2000
Yemen Yémen	70	101	80	78	76	78	124	130	136	...
Europe **Europe**	**130 147**	**153 954**	**143 005**	**164 511**	**201 439**	**206 212**	**199 584**	...	...	...
Albania Albanie	3	1	7	6	7	12	5	5	12	272
Austria Autriche	7 362	7 891	7 776	8 788	11 663[6]	11 782[6]	10 712[6]	10 324[6]	9 803[6]	9 291[6]
Belarus Bélarus	...	...	56	74	87	119	114	124	116	133
Belgium-Luxembourg Belgique-Luxembourg	5 543	6 714	6 338	7 773	9 003	8 562	8 281	8 794	10 426	10 151
Bulgaria Bulgarie	128	313	257	244	195	199	222	519[7]	526[7]	538[7]
Croatia Croatie	231	158	375	396	422	510	530	600	751	568
Czech Republic République tchèque	274	467	527	1 585	1 633	2 953	2 380	1 869	1 474	1 257
Denmark [8] Danemark [8]	3 377	3 779	3 214	3 583	4 280	4 142	4 137	4 462	4 884	5 139
Estonia Estonie	...	19	25	48	90	98	118	133	217	204
Finland [9] Finlande [9]	2 677	2 386	1 617	1 608	2 272	2 287	2 082	2 063	2 021	1 836
France [10] France [10]	12 321	13 914	12 836	13 773	16 328	17 746	16 576	17 791	18 631	17 718
Germany [11] Allemagne [11]	35 819	41 174	40 878	45 198	54 007	52 938	47 920	48 911	48 495	47 785
Greece [12] Grèce [12]	1 015	1 186	1 003	1 125	1 323	1 210	1 327	1 756	3 989	4 558
Hungary Hongrie	443	640	739	925	1 071	957	925	1 115	1 193	1 094
Iceland Islande	299	294	270	247	282	308	324	396	434	467
Ireland [13] Irlande [13]	1 128	1 361	1 220	1 615	2 034	2 198	2 210	2 374	2 620	2 957
Italy Italie	12 288	19 583	15 903	13 941	14 827	15 805	16 631	17 653	16 913	15 693
Latvia Lettonie	...	13	29	31	24	373	326	305	268	248
Lithuania Lituanie	...	...	12	50	106	266	277	292	341	253
Malta Malte	133	138	154	177	214	219	191	193	201	201
Netherlands Pays-Bas	8 149	9 634	8 920	9 371	11 661	11 528	11 285	11 996	12 045	12 198
Norway Norvège	3 413	3 870	3 364	3 712	4 247	4 536	4 306	4 551	4 609	4 335
Poland [4] Pologne [4]	143	132	181	316	5 500	6 240	5 750	4 430	3 600	3 600
Portugal Portugal	1 024	1 165	1 893	1 698	2 141	2 283	2 161	2 319	2 260	2 230

77
Tourism expenditure in other countries
Million US dollars *[cont.]*

Dépenses touristiques dans d'autres pays
Millions de dollars E.-U. *[suite]*

Region, country or area Région, pays ou zone	1991	1992	1993	1994	1995	1996	1997	1998	1999	2000
Republic of Moldova République de Moldova	...	...	...	...	56	52	65	59	58	78
Romania Roumanie	143	260	195	449	697	666	783	451	395	420
Russian Federation Fédération de Russie	...	...	...	7 092	11 599	10 270	9 363	8 279	7 434	...
Slovakia Slovaquie *	119	155	262	284	330	483	439	475	339	295
Slovenia [14] Slovénie [14]	...	282	305	369	573	602	518	558	539	521
Spain Espagne	4 544	5 542	4 735	4 129	4 461	4 919	4 467	5 001	5 523	5 572
Sweden Suède	6 286	7 059	4 483	4 864	5 624	6 448	6 898	7 723	7 557	8 015
Switzerland Suisse	5 735	6 099	5 954	6 370	7 346	7 570	6 960	6 798	6 718	6 238
TFYR of Macedonia L'ex-R.y. Macédoine	...	...	...	22	27	26	27	30	32	34
Ukraine Ukraine	...	...	...	2 650	3 041	2 596	2 564	2 021	1 774	2 017
United Kingdom Royaume-Uni	17 550	19 725	19 477	21 998	24 268	25 309	27 710	32 267	35 631	36 267
Oceania **Océanie**	**5 345**	**5 387**	**4 591**	**5 323**	**5 560**	**6 541**	**7 288**	...	...	...
Australia Australie	4 247	4 301	3 451	3 969	4 587	5 445	6 150	5 388	5 792	5 740
Fiji Fidji	36	34	47	62	64	70	69	52	66	...
Kiribati Kiribati	2	3	3	3	3	4	4	2	2	...
New Zealand Nouvelle-Zélande	987	977	1 002	1 194	824	923	965	1 143	1 195	1 420
Papua New Guinea Papouasie-Nvl-Guinée	57	57	69	71	58	72	78	52	53	...
Samoa Samoa	2	2	2	4	3	4	5	4	4	...
Solomon Islands Iles Salomon	12	11	12	13	13	15	9	6	7	...
Tonga Tonga	1	1	1	3	3	3	3	...	...	...
Vanuatu Vanuatu	1	1	4	4	5	5	5	8	9	9

Source:
World Tourism Organisation (WTO), Madrid, "Yearbook of Tourism Statistics – 2000 edition", and the WTO Statistics Database.

Source:
Organisation mondiale du tourisme (OMT), Madrid, "Annuaire des statistiques du tourisme – 2002 édition", et la base de données de l'OMT.

1 Including expenditure from frontier visitors.
2 Prior to 1995, data refer to Curaçao only; between 1995 and 1997, to Curaçao and Saint-Maarten; beginning 1998, to Bonaire and Saint Maarten.
3 Beginning 1995, change in methodology. The data reported

1 Y compris les dépenses des visiteurs frontaliers.
2 Avant 1995, les données ne se rapportent qu'à Curaçao; de 1995 à 1997, les données se rapportent à Curaçao et Saint-Maarten; à partir de 1998, à Bonaire et Saint-Maarten.
3 Avant 1995, changement de méthode. Les données

77

Tourism expenditure in other countries
Million US dollars *[cont.]*

Dépenses touristiques dans d'autres pays
Millions de dollars E.-U. *[suite]*

relate only to expenditure by tourists; expenditure by same-day visitors are not included.

4   Based on surveys and estimations by the Institute of Tourism.

5   Excluding expenses of students studying overseas.

6   Including international transport.
7   Change in methodology.
8   Including international fare expenditure.
9   Data collected by travel surveys.
10 New series since 1999 excluding frontier workers paid in foreign currency.
11 Including border merchandise transactions and purchases of inward-bound and outward-bound commuters.
12 Including registrations through new methodology.

13 Excluding fare paid to national carriers.
14 Data refer to the item "travel" of the Balance of Payments.

communiquées ne se rapportent qu'aux dépenses des touristes, à l'exclusion de celles des visiteurs ne restant pas au-delà d'une journée.

4   Chiffres basés sur des enquêtes et des estimations de l'Institut du tourisme.
5   Non compris les dépenses des étudiants poursuivant leurs études à l'étranger.
6   Y compris les transports internationaux.
7   Changement de méthode.
8   Y compris les dépenses de billets internationaux.
9   Données collectées au moyen d'enquêtes sur les voyages.
10 A partir de 1999, non compris les travailleurs frontaliers rémunérés en devises.
11 Y compris les transactions frontalières en marchandises, et les achats des migrants quotidiens entrant et sortant.
12 Y compris les mouvements enregistrés selon la nouvelle méthode.
13 Non compris les billets achetés à des transporteurs nationaux.
14 Données relatives à la rubrique "Voyages" de la balance des paiements.

Technical notes, tables 75-77

The data on international tourism have been supplied by the World Tourism Organization (WTO), which publishes detailed tourism information in the *Yearbook of Tourism Statistics* [38]. Additional information on data collection methods and definitions can be found in the *Methodological Supplement to World Travel and Tourism Statistics* [63] also published by the WTO. (See also [54] and [55]).

For statistical purposes, the term "international visitor" describes "any person who travels to a country other than that in which he/she has his/her usual residence but outside his/her usual environment for a period not exceeding 12 months and whose main purpose of visit is other than the exercise of an activity remunerated from within the country visited".

International visitors include:

(a) *Tourists* (overnight visitors): "visitors who stay at least one night in a collective or private accommodation in the country visited"; and

(b) *Same-day visitors*: "visitors who do not spend the night in a collective or private accommodation in the country visited".

The figures do not include immigrants, residents in a frontier zone, persons domiciled in one country or area and working in an adjoining country or area, members of the armed forces and diplomats and consular representatives when they travel from their country of origin to the country in which they are stationed and vice-versa.

The figures also exclude persons in transit who do not formally enter the country through passport control, such as air transit passengers who remain for a short period in a designated area of the air terminal or ship passengers who are not permitted to disembark. This category includes passengers transferred directly between airports or other terminals. Other passengers in transit through a country are classified as visitors.

Tables 75 and 76: Data on arrivals of international (or non-resident) visitors may be obtained from different sources. In some cases data are obtained from border statistics derived from administrative records (police, immigration, traffic and other type of controls applied at national borders), and eventually, completed by means of border statistical surveys. In other cases, data are obtained from different types of tourism accommodation establishments (hotels and similar establishments and/or all types of tourism accommodation establishments).

Unless otherwise stated, table 75 shows the number of tourist/visitor arrivals at frontiers classified by their region of origin. Totals correspond to the total number of arrivals from the regions indicated in the ta-

Notes techniques, tableaux 75 à 77

Les données sur le tourisme international ont été fournies par l'Organisation mondiale du tourisme (l'OMT) qui publie des renseignements détaillés sur le tourisme dans l'*Annuaire des statistiques du tourisme* [38]. On trouvera plus de renseignements sur les méthodes de collecte et sur les définitions dans « *Methodological Supplement to World Travel and Tourism Statistics* » [63] publié par l'OMT. (Voir aussi [54] et [55]).

A des fins statistiques, l'expression "*visiteur international*" désigne "toute personne qui se rend dans un pays autre que celui où elle a son lieu de résidence habituelle, mais différent de son environnement habituel, pour une période de 12 mois au maximum, dans un but principal autre que celui d'y exercer une profession rémunérée".

Entrent dans cette catégorie:

(a) Les *touristes* (visiteurs passant la nuit), c'est à dire "les visiteurs qui passent une nuit au moins en logement collectif ou privé dans le pays visité";

(b) Les *visiteurs ne restant que la journée*, c'est à dire "les visiteurs qui ne passent pas la nuit en logement collectif ou privé dans le pays visité".

Ces chiffres ne comprennent pas les immigrants, les résidents frontaliers, les personnes domiciliées dans une zone ou un pays donné et travaillant dans une zone ou pays limitrophe, les membres des forces armées et les membres des corps diplomatique et consulaire lorsqu'ils se rendent de leur pays d'origine au pays où ils sont en poste, et vice versa.

Ne sont pas non plus inclus les voyageurs en transit, qui ne pénètrent pas officiellement dans le pays en faisant contrôler leurs passeports, tels que les passagers d'un vol en escale, qui demeurent pendant un court laps de temps dans une aire distincte de l'aérogare, ou les passagers d'un navire qui ne sont pas autorisés à débarquer. Cette catégorie comprend également les passagers transportés directement d'une aérogare à l'autre ou à un autre terminal. Les autres passagers en transit dans un pays sont classés parmi les visiteurs.

Tableaux 75 et 76: Les données relatives aux arrivées des visiteurs internationaux (ou non résidents) peuvent être obtenues de différentes sources. Dans certains cas, elles proviennent des statistiques des frontières tirées des registres administratifs (contrôles de police, de l'immigration, de la circulation et autres effectués aux frontières nationales) et, éventuellement, complétées à l'aide d'enquêtes statistiques aux frontières. Dans d'autres cas, elles proviennent de différents types d'établissements d'hébergement touristique (hôtels et établissements assimilés et/ou tous types

ble. However, these totals may not correspond to the number of tourist arrivals shown in table 76. The latter excludes same-day visitors whereas they may be included in table 75. More detailed information can be found in the *Yearbook of Tourism Statistics* [38].

When a person visits the same country several times a year, an equal number of arrivals is recorded. Likewise, if a person visits several countries during the course of a single trip, his/her arrival in each country is recorded separately. Consequently, *arrivals* cannot be assumed to be equal to the number of persons traveling.

Tourism expenditure (in the country of reference) corresponds to the "expenditure of non-resident visitors (tourists and same-day visitors)" within the economic territory of the country of reference. International transport is excluded. The data are obtained by the WTO from the item "Travel receipts" of the Balance of Payments of each country shown in the *Balance of Payments Statistics Yearbook* published by the International Monetary Fund [14].

Table 77: The data on tourism expenditure in other countries are obtained from the item "Travel expenditure" of the Balance of Payments of each country and corresponds to the "expenditure of resident visitors (tourists and same-day visitors)" outside the economic territory of the country of reference.

For more information, see the *Yearbook of Tourism Statistics* published by the World Tourism Organization.[38] and the *Balance of Payments Statistics Yearbook* published by the International Monetary Fund [14].

d'établissements d'hébergement touristique).

Sauf indication contraire, le tableau 75 indique le nombre d'arrivées de touristes/visiteurs par région de provenance. Les totaux correspondent au nombre total d'arrivées de touristes des régions indiquées sur le tableau. Les chiffres totaux peuvent néanmoins, ne pas coïncider avec le nombre des arrivées de touristes indiqué dans le tableau 76, qui ne comprend pas les visiteurs ne restant que la journée, lesquels peuvent au contraire être inclus dans les chiffres du tableau 75. Pour plus de renseignements, consulter l'*Annuaire des statistiques du tourisme* [38].

Lorsqu'une personne visite le même pays plusieurs fois dans l'année, il est enregistré un nombre égal d'arrivées. En outre, si une personne visite plusieurs pays au cours d'un seul et même voyage, son arrivée dans chaque pays est enregistrée séparément. Par conséquent, on ne peut pas partir du postulat que les *arrivées* sont égales au nombre de personnes qui voyagent.

Dépenses touristiques (dans le pays de référence) correspondent aux «dépenses des visiteurs (touristes et visiteurs de la journée) non résidents» dans le territoire économique du pays dont il s'agit. Les données excluent les dépenses du transport international. Ils sont tirées par l'OMT du poste «recettes au titre des voyages» de la balance des paiements de chaque pays presentée dans le *"Balance of Payments Statistics Yearbook"* publié par le Fonds monétaire international [14].

Tableau 77: Les dépenses touristiques dans d'autres pays sont tirées du poste «dépenses au titre des voyages» de la balance des paiements de chaque pays et correspondent aux «dépenses des visiteurs (touristes et visiteurs de la journée) résidents» en dehors du territoire économique du pays de référence.

On trouvera plus de renseignements dans l'*Annuaire des statistiques du tourisme* publié par l'Organisation mondiale du tourisme [38] et dans *"Balance of Payments Statistics Yearbook"* publié par le Fonds monétaire international [14].

78
Summary of balance of payments
Millions of US dollars
Résumé des balances des paiements
Millions de dollars des E.-U.

Country or area	1995	1996	1997	1998	1999	2000	2001	Pays ou zone
Albania								**Albanie**
Goods: Exports fob	204.9	243.7	158.6	208.0	275.0	255.7	304.5	Biens : exportations, fab
Goods: Imports fob	-679.7	-922.0	-693.6	-811.7	-938.0	-1 070.0	-1 331.6	Biens : importations, fab
Serv. & Income: Credit	170.8	212.9	125.2	172.6	354.9	563.7	693.8	Serv. & revenu : crédit
Serv. & Income: Debit	-184.9	-201.3	-127.0	-138.0	-173.3	-438.6	-457.6	Serv & revenu : débit
Current Trans.,nie: Credit	521.2	595.9	299.8	560.8	508.9	629.0	647.5	Transf. cour.,nia : crédit
Current Transfers: Debit	-43.8	-36.5	-35.2	-56.9	-182.9	-96.1	-76.9	Transf. courants : débit
Capital Acct.,nie: Credit	389.4	4.8	2.0	31.0	22.6	78.0	117.7	Compte de cap.,nia : crédit
Capital Account: Debit	0.0	0.0	0.0	0.0	0.0	0.0	0.0	Compte de capital : débit
Financial Account, nie	-411.0	61.5	151.4	15.4	33.7	188.4	110.0	Compte d'op. fin., nia
Net Errors and Omissions	53.7	96.9	158.4	71.1	206.2	9.8	139.3	Erreurs et omissions nettes
Reserves & Related Items	-20.6	-55.9	-39.5	-52.4	-107.1	-119.9	-146.7	Rés. et postes appareutés
Angola								**Angola**
Goods: Exports fob	3 722.7	5 095.0	5 006.8	3 542.9	5 156.5	7 920.7	...	Biens : exportations, fab
Goods: Imports fob	-1 467.7	-2 040.5	-2 597.0	-2 079.4	-3 109.1	-3 039.5	...	Biens : importations, fab
Serv. & Income: Credit	129.0	311.0	250.7	156.3	177.1	301.7	...	Serv. & revenu : crédit
Serv. & Income: Debit	-2 834.6	-3 940.0	-3 638.5	-3 638.5	-3 990.7	-4 414.6	...	Serv & revenu : débit
Current Trans.,nie: Credit	312.2	3 949.4	176.4	238.2	154.5	123.5	...	Transf. cour.,nia : crédit
Current Transfers: Debit	-156.7	-108.6	-81.8	-86.7	-98.7	-95.9	...	Transf. courants : débit
Capital Acct.,nie: Credit	0.0	0.0	11.2	8.4	6.8	18.3	...	Compte de cap.,nia : crédit
Capital Account: Debit	0.0	0.0	0.0	0.0	0.0	0.0	...	Compte de capital : débit
Financial Account, nie	-924.8	-654.5	489.5	368.4	1 739.6	-494.1	...	Compte d'op. fin., nia
Net Errors and Omissions	-19.4	149.2	-182.1	378.4	-78.8	-50.5	...	Erreurs et omissions nettes
Reserves & Related Items	1 239.3	-2 761.0	564.8	1 112.0	42.9	-269.5	...	Rés. et postes appareutés
Anguilla								**Anguilla**
Goods: Exports fob	1.2	1.8	1.6	3.2	2.9	4.4	4.0	Biens : exportations, fab
Goods: Imports fob	-47.0	-52.9	-54.3	-63.0	-80.9	-83.3	-68.5	Biens : importations, fab
Serv. & Income: Credit	57.6	59.5	69.3	81.0	72.5	69.2	72.5	Serv. & revenu : crédit
Serv. & Income: Debit	-37.4	-36.1	-36.0	-43.5	-45.2	-47.5	-43.4	Serv & revenu : débit
Current Trans.,nie: Credit	21.5	12.6	7.2	8.8	6.8	8.9	7.8	Transf. cour.,nia : crédit
Current Transfers: Debit	-5.4	-5.2	-6.5	-6.4	-7.2	-7.3	-7.6	Transf. courants : débit
Capital Acct.,nie: Credit	6.7	6.5	3.9	3.4	4.0	6.2	8.3	Compte de cap.,nia : crédit
Capital Account: Debit	-1.3	-1.3	-1.4	-1.3	-1.3	-1.3	-1.3	Compte de capital : débit
Financial Account, nie	-1.0	35.7	19.2	10.8	58.4	40.9	18.8	Compte d'op. fin., nia
Net Errors and Omissions	5.0	-19.3	-1.1	8.9	-8.2	10.3	13.3	Erreurs et omissions nettes
Reserves & Related Items	0.0	-1.4	-1.9	-1.8	-1.8	-0.4	-3.9	Rés. et postes appareutés
Antigua and Barbuda								**Antigua-et-Barbuda**
Goods: Exports fob	53.1	38.9	38.8	37.4	36.8	42.3	38.6	Biens : exportations, fab
Goods: Imports fob	-291.0	-309.9	-313.9	-320.8	-352.7	-342.4	-321.2	Biens : importations, fab
Serv. & Income: Credit	353.7	369.4	408.2	441.2	450.9	431.9	421.3	Serv. & revenu : crédit
Serv. & Income: Debit	-180.0	-189.4	-190.3	-202.7	-217.5	-202.7	-192.2	Serv & revenu : débit
Current Trans.,nie: Credit	78.0	35.2	19.9	12.4	23.6	17.9	15.4	Transf. cour.,nia : crédit
Current Transfers: Debit	-14.4	-3.6	-10.1	-14.3	-3.9	-8.9	-9.4	Transf. courants : débit
Capital Acct.,nie: Credit	7.0	4.4	9.2	13.5	10.3	17.8	18.4	Compte de cap.,nia : crédit
Capital Account: Debit	0.0	0.0	0.0	0.0	0.0	0.0	0.0	Compte de capital : débit
Financial Account, nie	-10.7	55.0	50.5	49.1	55.2	65.0	23.6	Compte d'op. fin., nia
Net Errors and Omissions	17.8	-11.2	-9.4	-6.9	7.7	-27.1	21.6	Erreurs et omissions nettes
Reserves & Related Items	-13.6	11.3	-3.0	-8.7	-10.4	6.2	-16.2	Rés. et postes appareutés
Argentina								**Argentine**
Goods: Exports fob	21 161.7	24 042.7	26 430.8	26 433.7	23 308.6	26 409.5	26 610.0	Biens : exportations, fab
Goods: Imports fob	-18 804.3	-22 283.2	-28 553.5	-29 530.9	-24 103.2	-23 851.5	-19 159.3	Biens : importations, fab
Serv. & Income: Credit	8 204.7	8 781.4	9 985.9	10 830.7	10 715.8	12 224.6	9 969.4	Serv. & revenu : crédit
Serv. & Income: Debit	-16 290.9	-17 811.7	-20 568.8	-22 671.4	-22 219.6	-23 903.3	-22 157.8	Serv & revenu : débit
Current Trans.,nie: Credit	822.5	703.0	759.8	719.2	703.7	601.1	571.9	Transf. cour.,nia : crédit
Current Transfers: Debit	-269.1	-256.7	-296.7	-313.6	-306.8	-359.8	-388.6	Transf. courants : débit
Capital Acct.,nie: Credit	25.4	71.5	111.8	91.5	97.6	101.6	108.7	Compte de cap.,nia : crédit
Capital Account: Debit	-11.2	-20.7	-17.4	-18.6	-11.5	-14.9	-8.2	Compte de capital : débit
Financial Account, nie	4 989.8	11 712.9	16 754.9	18 996.2	14 925.8	8 770.4	-13 589.8	Compte d'op. fin., nia
Net Errors and Omissions	-2 140.0	-1 681.5	-1 276.3	-446.5	-1 097.8	-1 154.1	-3 361.3	Erreurs et omissions nettes
Reserves & Related Items	2 311.4	-3 257.7	-3 330.6	-4 090.3	-2 012.7	1 176.4	21 405.0	Rés. et postes appareutés
Armenia								**Arménie**
Goods: Exports fob	270.9	290.4	233.6	228.9	247.3	309.9	353.1	Biens : exportations, fab

78

Summary of balance of payments
Millions of US dollars *[cont.]*

Résumé des balances des paiements
Millions de dollars des E.-U. *[suite]*

Country or area	1995	1996	1997	1998	1999	2000	2001	Pays ou zone
Goods: Imports fob	-673.9	-759.6	-793.1	-806.3	-721.4	-773.4	-773.3	Biens : importations, fab
Serv. & Income: Credit	83.2	155.8	235.6	234.3	229.4	240.7	289.6	Serv. & revenu : crédit
Serv. & Income: Debit	-66.9	-161.8	-199.8	-252.2	-236.5	-243.6	-243.9	Serv & revenu : débit
Current Trans.,nie: Credit	170.0	199.0	252.4	203.0	200.6	208.5	200.8	Transf. cour.,nia : crédit
Current Transfers: Debit	-1.7	-14.4	-35.2	-25.6	-26.5	-20.5	-26.8	Transf. courants : débit
Capital Acct.,nie: Credit	8.1	13.4	10.9	9.7	16.9	29.5	32.6	Compte de cap.,nia : crédit
Capital Account: Debit	0.0	0.0	0.0	0.0	-4.3	-1.2	-2.5	Compte de capital : débit
Financial Account, nie	227.5	216.8	334.8	390.4	286.2	249.9	176.9	Compte d'op. fin., nia
Net Errors and Omissions	12.4	15.1	10.8	18.4	13.1	17.0	12.1	Erreurs et omissions nettes
Reserves & Related Items	-29.5	45.5	-50.0	-0.6	-4.8	-16.9	-18.6	Rés. et postes appareutés
Aruba								**Aruba**
Goods: Exports fob	1 347.2	1 735.7	1 728.7	1 164.8	1 413.5	2 582.1	...	Biens : exportations, fab
Goods: Imports fob	-1 772.5	-2 043.4	-2 115.9	-1 518.2	-2 005.2	-2 610.4	...	Biens : importations, fab
Serv. & Income: Credit	661.5	789.1	836.5	932.6	1 027.0	1 078.7	...	Serv. & revenu : crédit
Serv. & Income: Debit	-270.1	-546.9	-634.0	-593.2	-781.9	-732.2	...	Serv & revenu : débit
Current Trans.,nie: Credit	71.5	18.4	18.4	29.3	59.3	46.2	...	Transf. cour.,nia : crédit
Current Transfers: Debit	-37.9	-22.0	-29.5	-34.1	-45.9	-82.2	...	Transf. courants : débit
Capital Acct.,nie: Credit	3.1	28.7	21.6	10.2	0.9	10.5	...	Compte de cap.,nia : crédit
Capital Account: Debit	-3.6	-0.7	-0.6	-5.0	-0.9	-0.6	...	Compte de capital : débit
Financial Account, nie	41.6	10.7	158.9	64.2	336.4	-314.6	...	Compte d'op. fin., nia
Net Errors and Omissions	2.0	4.3	-2.5	0.6	-0.7	6.5	...	Erreurs et omissions nettes
Reserves & Related Items	-42.7	26.1	18.4	-51.3	-2.5	15.9	...	Rés. et postes appareutés
Australia								**Australie**
Goods: Exports fob	53 219.6	60 396.9	64 892.7	55 883.6	56 096.0	64 040.8	63 673.1	Biens : exportations, fab
Goods: Imports fob	-57 442.8	-61 031.7	-63 043.6	-61 215.2	-65 826.0	-68 751.8	-61 761.2	Biens : importations, fab
Serv. & Income: Credit	21 413.4	24 558.0	25 650.3	22 713.8	24 262.6	26 975.6	24 170.0	Serv. & revenu : crédit
Serv. & Income: Debit	-36 403.6	-39 826.3	-39 844.2	-35 114.2	-37 515.5	-37 608.4	-34 978.8	Serv & revenu : débit
Current Trans.,nie: Credit	2 364.2	2 698.9	2 765.1	2 650.6	3 002.7	2 621.8	2 242.4	Transf. cour.,nia : crédit
Current Transfers: Debit	-2 473.6	-2 606.2	-2 804.7	-2 932.7	-3 031.7	-2 669.1	-2 221.4	Transf. courants : débit
Capital Acct.,nie: Credit	1 250.0	1 674.1	1 606.1	1 315.3	1 534.7	1 405.9	1 319.8	Compte de cap.,nia : crédit
Capital Account: Debit	-691.7	-709.8	-703.3	-645.6	-715.5	-790.9	-728.9	Compte de capital : débit
Financial Account, nie	18 631.8	16 069.5	16 820.4	15 116.5	27 968.6	14 313.4	8 002.7	Compte d'op. fin., nia
Net Errors and Omissions	528.7	1 248.0	-2 465.6	187.8	929.4	-902.0	1 378.1	Erreurs et omissions nettes
Reserves & Related Items	-395.9	-2 471.5	-2 873.3	2 040.0	-6 705.5	1 364.7	-1 095.7	Rés. et postes appareutés
Austria								**Autriche**
Goods: Exports fob	57 695.2	57 937.3	58 662.3	63 299.1	64 421.7	64 684.0	66 899.0	Biens : exportations, fab
Goods: Imports fob	-64 351.6	-65 251.9	-62 936.3	-66 983.3	-68 050.8	-67 420.7	-68 226.9	Biens : importations, fab
Serv. & Income: Credit	41 111.6	43 828.9	39 998.0	39 715.8	43 978.5	43 333.2	45 193.1	Serv. & revenu : crédit
Serv. & Income: Debit	-38 201.1	-39 621.5	-39 251.5	-39 356.2	-44 973.7	-44 108.5	-46 827.3	Serv & revenu : débit
Current Trans.,nie: Credit	2 972.3	3 144.8	2 911.6	2 940.4	2 924.8	2 914.2	3 263.6	Transf. cour.,nia : crédit
Current Transfers: Debit	-4 674.3	-4 928.0	-4 605.2	-4 874.0	-4 956.1	-4 266.6	-4 404.4	Transf. courants : débit
Capital Acct.,nie: Credit	540.0	591.3	590.0	483.3	554.6	530.2	484.8	Compte de cap.,nia : crédit
Capital Account: Debit	-601.7	-513.0	-563.7	-830.6	-820.0	-962.1	-998.6	Compte de capital : débit
Financial Account, nie	7 365.0	5 324.9	1 665.9	9 534.8	4 788.7	3 407.2	1 809.4	Compte d'op. fin., nia
Net Errors and Omissions	-464.0	562.1	475.5	-447.2	-39.7	1 143.2	919.1	Erreurs et omissions nettes
Reserves & Related Items	-1 391.3	-1 075.0	3 053.3	-3 481.9	2 171.9	745.8	1 888.1	Rés. et postes appareutés
Azerbaijan								**Azerbaïdjan**
Goods: Exports fob	612.3	643.7	808.3	677.8	1 025.2	1 858.3	2 078.9	Biens : exportations, fab
Goods: Imports fob	-985.4	-1 337.6	-1 375.2	-1 723.9	-1 433.4	-1 539.0	-1 465.1	Biens : importations, fab
Serv. & Income: Credit	182.3	164.3	364.6	370.0	267.8	315.7	331.3	Serv. & revenu : crédit
Serv. & Income: Debit	-320.6	-468.1	-758.2	-752.3	-541.1	-875.9	-1 073.5	Serv & revenu : débit
Current Trans.,nie: Credit	129.3	107.2	95.7	145.0	134.5	135.0	176.5	Transf. cour.,nia : crédit
Current Transfers: Debit	-18.5	-40.7	-50.9	-80.9	-52.8	-62.0	-99.9	Transf. courants : débit
Capital Acct.,nie: Credit	0.0	0.0	0.0	0.0	0.0	0.0	0.0	Compte de cap.,nia : crédit
Capital Account: Debit	-1.6	0.0	-10.2	-0.7	0.0	0.0	0.0	Compte de capital : débit
Financial Account, nie	400.3	822.5	1 092.1	1 326.0	690.2	493.4	126.0	Compte d'op. fin., nia
Net Errors and Omissions	59.7	23.6	-27.0	-20.1	42.4	0.0	-0.9	Erreurs et omissions nettes
Reserves & Related Items	-57.8	85.0	-139.2	59.2	-132.9	-325.6	-73.4	Rés. et postes appareutés
Bahamas								**Bahamas**
Goods: Exports fob	225.4	273.3	295.0	362.9	379.9	805.3	614.1	Biens : exportations, fab
Goods: Imports fob	-1 156.7	-1 287.4	-1 410.7	-1 737.1	-1 808.1	-2 176.4	-1 764.7	Biens : importations, fab
Serv. & Income: Credit	1 617.4	1 662.8	1 698.6	1 680.9	2 040.8	2 248.6	1 983.7	Serv. & revenu : crédit

78
Summary of balance of payments
Millions of US dollars *[cont.]*
Résumé des balances des paiements
Millions de dollars des E.-U. *[suite]*

Country or area	1995	1996	1997	1998	1999	2000	2001	Pays ou zone
Serv. & Income: Debit	-849.9	-949.2	-1 094.3	-1 336.3	-1 321.0	-1 392.2	-1 222.9	Serv & revenu : débit
Current Trans.,nie: Credit	25.1	45.9	50.0	45.0	49.0	53.8	52.7	Transf. cour.,nia : crédit
Current Transfers: Debit	-7.2	-8.7	-10.7	-10.8	-12.5	-10.5	-10.9	Transf. courants : débit
Capital Acct.,nie: Credit	0.0	0.0	0.0	0.0	0.0	0.0	0.0	Compte de cap.,nia : crédit
Capital Account: Debit	-12.5	-24.4	-12.9	-11.7	-14.5	-16.4	-20.3	Compte de capital : débit
Financial Account, nie	104.6	181.1	412.0	817.7	611.4	429.3	279.8	Compte d'op. fin., nia
Net Errors and Omissions	50.9	99.0	129.5	308.6	140.2	-2.6	58.6	Erreurs et omissions nettes
Reserves & Related Items	2.9	7.6	-56.5	-119.2	-65.2	61.0	29.9	Rés. et postes appareutés
Bahrain								**Bahreïn**
Goods: Exports fob	4 114.4	4 702.1	4 383.0	3 270.2	4 362.8	6 195.0	5 544.7	Biens : exportations, fab
Goods: Imports fob	-3 488.3	-4 037.0	-3 778.2	-3 298.7	-3 468.4	-4 393.6	-4 008.2	Biens : importations, fab
Serv. & Income: Credit	4 770.2	4 481.4	4 908.0	5 488.6	5 977.4	7 261.4	4 744.7	Serv. & revenu : crédit
Serv. & Income: Debit	-4 780.1	-4 452.9	-5 141.8	-5 577.9	-6 089.1	-7 289.9	-4 859.8	Serv & revenu : débit
Current Trans.,nie: Credit	120.7	126.3	232.7	65.2	36.7	22.3	22.9	Transf. cour.,nia : crédit
Current Transfers: Debit	-499.7	-559.3	-634.8	-725.0	-856.1	-1 012.8	-1 287.0	Transf. courants : débit
Capital Acct.,nie: Credit	156.9	50.0	125.0	100.0	100.0	50.0	100.0	Compte de cap.,nia : crédit
Capital Account: Debit	0.0	0.0	0.0	0.0	0.0	0.0	0.0	Compte de capital : débit
Financial Account, nie	-1 726.6	-510.4	15.4	22.3	230.1	-29.8	-417.0	Compte d'op. fin., nia
Net Errors and Omissions	1 501.4	193.3	-6.5	638.7	-268.1	-602.6	283.3	Erreurs et omissions nettes
Reserves & Related Items	-168.9	6.4	-102.8	16.6	-25.3	-200.1	-123.5	Rés. et postes appareutés
Bangladesh								**Bangladesh**
Goods: Exports fob	3 733.3	4 009.3	4 839.9	5 141.5	5 458.3	6 399.2	6 084.7	Biens : exportations, fab
Goods: Imports fob	-6 057.4	-6 284.6	-6 550.7	-6 715.7	-7 535.5	-8 052.9	-8 133.4	Biens : importations, fab
Serv. & Income: Credit	968.3	734.2	773.9	815.4	872.0	893.4	826.2	Serv. & revenu : crédit
Serv. & Income: Debit	-1 733.0	-1 359.1	-1 481.7	-1 443.2	-1 655.2	-1 965.0	-1 835.5	Serv & revenu : débit
Current Trans.,nie: Credit	2 266.8	1 912.8	2 136.5	2 172.9	2 501.4	2 426.5	2 572.8	Transf. cour.,nia : crédit
Current Transfers: Debit	-1.8	-4.0	-4.3	-5.9	-5.3	-7.0	-4.9	Transf. courants : débit
Capital Acct.,nie: Credit	0.0	371.2	366.8	238.7	364.1	248.7	235.4	Compte de cap.,nia : crédit
Capital Account: Debit	0.0	0.0	0.0	0.0	0.0	0.0	0.0	Compte de capital : débit
Financial Account, nie	178.8	92.4	-140.2	-116.0	-446.9	-256.0	261.5	Compte d'op. fin., nia
Net Errors and Omissions	133.3	113.5	-75.5	201.0	258.0	282.4	-150.7	Erreurs et omissions nettes
Reserves & Related Items	511.7	414.3	135.1	-288.5	189.2	30.7	143.9	Rés. et postes appareutés
Barbados								**Barbade**
Goods: Exports fob	245.4	286.7	289.0	270.1	275.3	286.4	...	Biens : exportations, fab
Goods: Imports fob	-691.2	-743.0	-887.7	-920.7	-989.4	-1 030.3	...	Biens : importations, fab
Serv. & Income: Credit	915.0	981.0	1 019.7	1 087.1	1 096.1	1 160.4	...	Serv. & revenu : crédit
Serv. & Income: Debit	-459.3	-493.4	-517.6	-551.7	-596.4	-639.8	...	Serv & revenu : débit
Current Trans.,nie: Credit	56.2	64.8	71.7	78.4	94.0	108.9	...	Transf. cour.,nia : crédit
Current Transfers: Debit	-23.6	-26.6	-25.1	-26.2	-27.7	-31.0	...	Transf. courants : débit
Capital Acct.,nie: Credit	0.0	0.4	0.0	0.7	0.7	0.0	...	Compte de cap.,nia : crédit
Capital Account: Debit	0.0	0.0	0.0	0.0	0.0	-1.8	...	Compte de capital : débit
Financial Account, nie	-26.4	-22.2	20.0	55.5	118.4	302.9	...	Compte d'op. fin., nia
Net Errors and Omissions	26.0	38.5	47.4	0.7	65.5	22.1	...	Erreurs et omissions nettes
Reserves & Related Items	-42.1	-86.4	-17.4	6.1	-36.3	-177.6	...	Rés. et postes appareutés
Belarus								**Bélarus**
Goods: Exports fob	4 803.0	5 790.1	6 918.7	6 172.3	5 646.4	6 640.5	7 256.2	Biens : exportations, fab
Goods: Imports fob	-5 468.7	-6 938.6	-8 325.7	-7 673.4	-6 216.4	-7 524.6	-8 063.1	Biens : importations, fab
Serv. & Income: Credit	468.0	982.1	950.0	951.9	774.1	1 041.3	1 040.1	Serv. & revenu : crédit
Serv. & Income: Debit	-336.6	-440.8	-480.6	-562.9	-501.6	-635.0	-672.5	Serv & revenu : débit
Current Trans.,nie: Credit	107.2	135.5	106.1	120.9	137.0	177.1	202.6	Transf. cour.,nia : crédit
Current Transfers: Debit	-31.2	-44.2	-27.7	-25.3	-33.2	-22.4	-48.5	Transf. courants : débit
Capital Acct.,nie: Credit	7.3	257.2	248.0	261.3	131.1	125.6	132.3	Compte de cap.,nia : crédit
Capital Account: Debit	0.0	-156.1	-114.8	-91.2	-70.7	-56.2	-76.0	Compte de capital : débit
Financial Account, nie	204.0	378.7	738.1	354.8	399.5	140.1	250.0	Compte d'op. fin., nia
Net Errors and Omissions	168.6	-178.1	53.0	172.3	-246.3	238.9	-102.5	Erreurs et omissions nettes
Reserves & Related Items	78.4	214.2	-65.1	319.3	-19.9	-125.3	81.4	Rés. et postes appareutés
Belgium-Luxembourg [1]								**Belgique-Luxembourg [1]**
Goods: Exports fob	155 219.0	154 695.0	149 497.0	153 558.0	161 263.0	164 677.0	163 498.0	Biens : exportations, fab
Goods: Imports fob	-145664.0	-146004.0	-141794.0	-146577.0	-154237.0	-162086.0	-159790.0	Biens : importations, fab
Serv. & Income: Credit	110 263.7	97 585.7	93 739.2	103 332.2	117 183.2	125 461.8	129 219.4	Serv. & revenu : crédit
Serv. & Income: Debit	-101123.8	-87 907.4	-83 546.1	-93 725.8	-105292.2	-112493.2	-119314.9	Serv & revenu : débit
Current Trans.,nie: Credit	7 821.8	7 473.8	7 142.1	7 005.7	7 040.6	7 013.9	7 315.7	Transf. cour.,nia : crédit

78

Summary of balance of payments
Millions of US dollars [cont.]

Résumé des balances des paiements
Millions de dollars des E.-U. [suite]

Country or area	1995	1996	1997	1998	1999	2000	2001	Pays ou zone
Current Transfers: Debit	-12 284.7	-12 080.6	-11 124.3	-11 425.5	-11 871.8	-11 192.8	-11 535.3	Transf. courants : débit
Capital Acct.,nie: Credit	734.4	673.5	782.5	323.1	419.8	222.5	479.7	Compte de cap.,nia : crédit
Capital Account: Debit	-356.4	-494.3	-379.2	-436.3	-497.5	-435.8	-454.1	Compte de capital : débit
Financial Account, nie	-12 912.4	-12 257.2	-12 090.7	-16 042.8	-13 465.9	-9 235.7	-7 979.4	Compte d'op. fin., nia
Net Errors and Omissions	-1 455.5	-1 090.9	-1 171.0	1 893.0	-2 410.3	-2 891.0	3.5	Erreurs et omissions nettes
Reserves & Related Items	-242.6	-592.6	-1 056.0	2 095.0	1 867.4	959.0	-1 442.1	Rés. et postes appareutés
Belize								**Belize**
Goods: Exports fob	164.6	171.3	193.4	186.2	213.2	212.3	...	Biens : exportations, fab
Goods: Imports fob	-230.6	-229.5	-282.9	-290.9	-337.5	-403.7	...	Biens : importations, fab
Serv. & Income: Credit	135.6	144.2	145.3	147.7	164.3	177.2	...	Serv. & revenu : crédit
Serv. & Income: Debit	-120.0	-123.7	-122.5	-138.3	-154.7	-178.6	...	Serv & revenu : débit
Current Trans.,nie: Credit	38.3	34.2	38.2	38.4	40.6	56.6	...	Transf. cour.,nia : crédit
Current Transfers: Debit	-5.2	-3.1	-3.4	-2.8	-3.5	-3.2	...	Transf. courants : débit
Capital Acct.,nie: Credit	0.0	0.0	0.0	0.0	0.5	0.9	...	Compte de cap.,nia : crédit
Capital Account: Debit	0.0	-2.2	-3.4	-1.9	-2.4	-0.5	...	Compte de capital : débit
Financial Account, nie	-1.0	11.0	27.6	23.5	91.5	88.4	...	Compte d'op. fin., nia
Net Errors and Omissions	22.4	18.4	9.1	24.5	0.9	7.3	...	Erreurs et omissions nettes
Reserves & Related Items	-4.1	-20.6	-1.4	13.7	-12.9	43.3	...	Rés. et postes appareutés
Benin								**Bénin**
Goods: Exports fob	419.9	527.7	424.0	414.3	421.5	392.4	...	Biens : exportations, fab
Goods: Imports fob	-622.5	-559.7	-576.9	-572.6	-635.2	-516.1	...	Biens : importations, fab
Serv. & Income: Credit	218.4	155.8	140.4	170.1	204.5	164.1	...	Serv. & revenu : crédit
Serv. & Income: Debit	-297.4	-239.4	-216.7	-232.7	-254.4	-232.0	...	Serv & revenu : débit
Current Trans.,nie: Credit	105.4	92.4	77.8	102.0	87.1	91.3	...	Transf. cour.,nia : crédit
Current Transfers: Debit	-30.5	-34.2	-18.5	-32.7	-14.9	-10.7	...	Transf. courants : débit
Capital Acct.,nie: Credit	85.6	6.4	84.5	66.6	69.9	73.4	...	Compte de cap.,nia : crédit
Capital Account: Debit	0.0	0.0	0.0	0.0	0.0	-0.1	...	Compte de capital : débit
Financial Account, nie	-132.9	-104.2	-21.3	-8.9	25.4	10.8	...	Compte d'op. fin., nia
Net Errors and Omissions	-1.0	6.3	6.7	7.1	7.3	6.7	...	Erreurs et omissions nettes
Reserves & Related Items	254.9	149.0	100.0	86.7	88.7	20.3	...	Rés. et postes appareutés
Bolivia								**Bolivie**
Goods: Exports fob	1 041.4	1 132.0	1 166.6	1 104.0	1 051.2	1 246.0	1 284.9	Biens : exportations, fab
Goods: Imports fob	-1 223.7	-1 368.0	-1 643.6	-1 759.5	-1 539.0	-1 610.1	-1 493.9	Biens : importations, fab
Serv. & Income: Credit	220.7	209.5	345.4	378.6	416.7	363.8	357.0	Serv. & revenu : crédit
Serv. & Income: Debit	-585.1	-600.2	-713.4	-729.8	-803.0	-833.4	-833.5	Serv & revenu : débit
Current Trans.,nie: Credit	248.0	226.2	300.3	352.3	414.7	419.9	428.4	Transf. cour.,nia : crédit
Current Transfers: Debit	-3.8	-3.8	-8.8	-11.7	-28.6	-33.2	-35.4	Transf. courants : débit
Capital Acct.,nie: Credit	2.0	2.8	25.3	9.9	0.0	0.0	3.2	Compte de cap.,nia : crédit
Capital Account: Debit	0.0	0.0	0.0	0.0	0.0	0.0	0.0	Compte de capital : débit
Financial Account, nie	505.2	701.0	889.8	1 181.9	868.6	428.2	330.8	Compte d'op. fin., nia
Net Errors and Omissions	-112.3	-31.6	-260.6	-401.0	-353.6	-20.7	-78.8	Erreurs et omissions nettes
Reserves & Related Items	-92.4	-268.0	-101.0	-124.7	-27.0	39.5	37.3	Rés. et postes appareutés
Bosnia and Herzegovina								**Bosnie-Herzégovine**
Goods: Exports fob	...	...	...	652.0	816.2	1 151.5	1 166.4	Biens : exportations, fab
Goods: Imports fob	...	...	...	-3 807.0	-4 149.3	-3 811.4	-3 917.9	Biens : importations, fab
Serv. & Income: Credit	...	...	...	786.0	739.6	653.0	689.5	Serv. & revenu : crédit
Serv. & Income: Debit	...	...	...	-282.8	-311.2	-292.5	-293.4	Serv & revenu : débit
Current Trans.,nie: Credit	...	...	...	1 404.9	1 361.5	1 020.9	994.3	Transf. cour.,nia : crédit
Current Transfers: Debit	...	...	...	-2.4	-2.5	-2.8	-3.4	Transf. courants : débit
Capital Acct.,nie: Credit	...	...	...	435.2	531.5	406.0	386.7	Compte de cap.,nia : crédit
Capital Account: Debit	...	...	...	0.0	0.0	0.0	0.0	Compte de capital : débit
Financial Account, nie	...	...	...	110.5	486.7	732.8	1 508.6	Compte d'op. fin., nia
Net Errors and Omissions	...	...	...	175.0	194.1	111.1	124.7	Erreurs et omissions nettes
Reserves & Related Items	...	...	...	528.7	333.3	31.4	-655.4	Rés. et postes appareutés
Botswana								**Botswana**
Goods: Exports fob	2 160.2	2 217.5	2 819.8	2 060.6	2 671.0	...	...	Biens : exportations, fab
Goods: Imports fob	-1 605.4	-1 467.7	-1 924.5	-1 983.1	-1 996.5	...	...	Biens : importations, fab
Serv. & Income: Credit	743.6	664.7	832.3	878.0	802.4	...	...	Serv. & revenu : crédit
Serv. & Income: Debit	-959.8	-1 098.4	-1 207.5	-1 025.5	-1 211.9	...	...	Serv & revenu : débit
Current Trans.,nie: Credit	330.7	355.4	456.8	460.9	474.4	...	...	Transf. cour.,nia : crédit
Current Transfers: Debit	-369.5	-176.6	-255.5	-220.8	-222.6	...	...	Transf. courants : débit
Capital Acct.,nie: Credit	15.4	18.0	29.4	44.2	33.5	...	...	Compte de cap.,nia : crédit

78

Summary of balance of payments
Millions of US dollars *[cont.]*

Résumé des balances des paiements
Millions de dollars des E.-U. *[suite]*

Country or area	1995	1996	1997	1998	1999	2000	2001	Pays ou zone
Capital Account: Debit	-0.9	-11.9	-12.5	-12.4	-12.9	...	...	Compte de capital : débit
Financial Account, nie	-33.9	42.4	5.6	-202.4	-175.2	...	...	Compte d'op. fin., nia
Net Errors and Omissions	-73.6	-32.9	-108.9	44.6	8.7	...	...	Erreurs et omissions nettes
Reserves & Related Items	-206.6	-510.7	-635.1	-44.2	-371.0	...	...	Rés. et postes appareutés
Brazil								**Brésil**
Goods: Exports fob	46 506.0	47 851.0	53 189.0	51 136.0	48 011.0	55 087.0	58 224.0	Biens : exportations, fab
Goods: Imports fob	-49 663.0	-53 304.0	-59 841.0	-57 739.0	-49 272.0	-55 783.0	-55 579.0	Biens : importations, fab
Serv. & Income: Credit	9 592.0	10 005.0	11 333.0	12 545.0	11 125.0	13 002.0	12 602.4	Serv. & revenu : crédit
Serv. & Income: Debit	-28 192.0	-30 241.0	-36 986.0	-41 207.0	-36 952.0	-38 460.0	-40 097.4	Serv & revenu : débit
Current Trans.,nie: Credit	3 861.0	2 699.0	2 130.0	1 795.0	1 969.0	1 828.0	1 934.0	Transf. cour.,nia : crédit
Current Transfers: Debit	-240.0	-258.0	-316.0	-359.0	-281.0	-306.0	-295.0	Transf. courants : débit
Capital Acct.,nie: Credit	363.0	507.0	519.0	488.0	361.0	300.0	329.0	Compte de cap.,nia : crédit
Capital Account: Debit	-11.0	-13.0	-37.0	-113.0	-22.0	-28.0	-365.0	Compte de capital : débit
Financial Account, nie	29 306.0	33 428.0	24 918.0	20 063.0	8 056.0	29 369.0	20 078.7	Compte d'op. fin., nia
Net Errors and Omissions	1 446.7	-1 991.6	-3 160.2	-2 910.7	239.6	2 971.0	-249.8	Erreurs et omissions nettes
Reserves & Related Items	-12 968.7	-8 682.4	8 251.2	16 301.7	16 765.4	-7 980.0	3 418.2	Rés. et postes appareutés
Bulgaria								**Bulgarie**
Goods: Exports fob	5 345.0	4 890.2	4 939.6	4 193.5	4 006.4	4 824.6	5 106.8	Biens : exportations, fab
Goods: Imports fob	-5 224.0	-4 702.6	-4 559.3	-4 574.2	-5 087.4	-6 000.1	-6 682.4	Biens : importations, fab
Serv. & Income: Credit	1 581.1	1 547.0	1 548.2	2 094.5	2 051.8	2 498.2	2 770.8	Serv. & revenu : crédit
Serv. & Income: Debit	-1 859.8	-1 823.1	-1 738.4	-2 005.4	-1 955.3	-2 313.6	-2 530.4	Serv & revenu : débit
Current Trans.,nie: Credit	256.8	231.8	275.5	261.4	328.7	354.1	588.5	Transf. cour.,nia : crédit
Current Transfers: Debit	-124.9	-127.6	-38.7	-31.6	-28.9	-64.4	-100.1	Transf. courants : débit
Capital Acct.,nie: Credit	0.0	65.9	0.0	0.0	0.0	25.0	0.0	Compte de cap.,nia : crédit
Capital Account: Debit	0.0	0.0	0.0	0.0	-2.4	0.0	0.0	Compte de capital : débit
Financial Account, nie	326.6	-715.0	462.0	266.7	777.4	881.5	1 002.1	Compte d'op. fin., nia
Net Errors and Omissions	143.8	-105.3	256.4	-299.2	6.1	-68.3	288.5	Erreurs et omissions nettes
Reserves & Related Items	-444.6	738.7	-1 145.4	94.3	-96.4	-137.0	-443.8	Rés. et postes appareutés
Burundi								**Burundi**
Goods: Exports fob	112.9	40.4	87.5	64.0	55.0	49.1	...	Biens : exportations, fab
Goods: Imports fob	-175.6	-100.0	-96.1	-123.5	-97.3	-107.9	...	Biens : importations, fab
Serv. & Income: Credit	26.8	16.9	13.0	11.2	8.2	8.5	...	Serv. & revenu : crédit
Serv. & Income: Debit	-106.3	-58.7	-62.2	-61.4	-43.9	-57.9	...	Serv & revenu : débit
Current Trans.,nie: Credit	154.7	62.5	61.3	59.3	52.9	61.1	...	Transf. cour.,nia : crédit
Current Transfers: Debit	-2.1	-1.1	-4.5	-3.3	-1.8	-1.8	...	Transf. courants : débit
Capital Acct.,nie: Credit	0.0	0.0	0.0	0.0	0.0	0.0	...	Compte de cap.,nia : crédit
Capital Account: Debit	-0.8	-0.3	-0.1	0.0	0.0	0.0	...	Compte de capital : débit
Financial Account, nie	21.1	14.1	13.7	28.8	17.0	58.9	...	Compte d'op. fin., nia
Net Errors and Omissions	5.9	-9.2	-2.4	5.4	8.7	-6.2	...	Erreurs et omissions nettes
Reserves & Related Items	-36.7	35.3	-10.2	19.5	1.2	-3.9	...	Rés. et postes appareutés
Cambodia								**Cambodge**
Goods: Exports fob	855.2	643.6	736.0	903.4	886.4	1 264.0	1 377.5	Biens : exportations, fab
Goods: Imports fob	-1 186.8	-1 071.8	-1 064.0	-1 149.1	-1 239.0	-1 628.2	-1 725.0	Biens : importations, fab
Serv. & Income: Credit	123.7	175.4	176.4	127.6	219.3	276.2	277.9	Serv. & revenu : crédit
Serv. & Income: Debit	-254.8	-313.1	-246.5	-214.6	-256.0	-322.7	-307.7	Serv & revenu : débit
Current Trans.,nie: Credit	277.9	383.4	188.5	224.0	235.9	305.3	273.1	Transf. cour.,nia : crédit
Current Transfers: Debit	-0.9	-2.4	-0.3	-0.6	-1.6	-0.4	-0.4	Transf. courants : débit
Capital Acct.,nie: Credit	78.0	75.8	65.2	42.0	44.0	38.1	63.3	Compte de cap.,nia : crédit
Capital Account: Debit	0.0	0.0	0.0	0.0	0.0	0.0	0.0	Compte de capital : débit
Financial Account, nie	122.4	259.1	219.8	154.1	126.2	99.3	74.8	Compte d'op. fin., nia
Net Errors and Omissions	11.5	-78.0	-41.2	-56.1	34.8	54.3	39.0	Erreurs et omissions nettes
Reserves & Related Items	-26.2	-72.0	-33.9	-30.7	-50.0	-85.9	-72.5	Rés. et postes appareutés
Cameroon								**Cameroun**
Goods: Exports fob	1 735.9	...	...	...	...	...	...	Biens : exportations, fab
Goods: Imports fob	-1 109.0	...	...	...	...	...	...	Biens : importations, fab
Serv. & Income: Credit	316.7	...	...	...	...	...	...	Serv. & revenu : crédit
Serv. & Income: Debit	-923.3	...	...	...	...	...	...	Serv & revenu : débit
Current Trans.,nie: Credit	100.7	...	...	...	...	...	...	Transf. cour.,nia : crédit
Current Transfers: Debit	-31.2	...	...	...	...	...	...	Transf. courants : débit
Capital Acct.,nie: Credit	21.1	...	...	...	...	...	...	Compte de cap.,nia : crédit
Capital Account: Debit	-0.7	...	...	...	...	...	...	Compte de capital : débit
Financial Account, nie	43.3	...	...	...	...	...	...	Compte d'op. fin., nia

78

Summary of balance of payments
Millions of US dollars *[cont.]*

Résumé des balances des paiements
Millions de dollars des E.-U. *[suite]*

Country or area	1995	1996	1997	1998	1999	2000	2001	Pays ou zone
Net Errors and Omissions	-138.1	...	...	...	...	...	...	Erreurs et omissions nettes
Reserves & Related Items	-15.4	...	...	...	...	...	...	Rés. et postes appareutés
Canada								**Canada**
Goods: Exports fob	193 373.0	205 443.0	219 063.0	220 539.0	247 240.0	286 476.0	267 915.0	Biens : exportations, fab
Goods: Imports fob	-167517.0	-174352.0	-200498.0	-204617.0	-220159.0	-244714.0	-226490.0	Biens : importations, fab
Serv. & Income: Credit	45 015.6	48 446.4	55 594.1	55 665.9	57 880.1	65 306.7	59 209.2	Serv. & revenu : crédit
Serv. & Income: Debit	-75 082.1	-76 660.9	-82 890.6	-79 971.6	-84 275.9	-89 462.7	-82 410.6	Serv & revenu : débit
Current Trans.,nie: Credit	2 878.2	3 593.5	3 634.0	3 406.8	3 796.0	4 109.0	4 535.2	Transf. cour.,nia : crédit
Current Transfers: Debit	-2 995.0	-3 091.8	-3 135.5	-2 862.9	-3 113.7	-3 119.9	-3 280.2	Transf. courants : débit
Capital Acct.,nie: Credit	5 415.9	6 262.1	5 862.3	3 793.7	3 857.8	4 044.0	4 162.9	Compte de cap.,nia : crédit
Capital Account: Debit	-466.2	-428.7	-433.0	-457.5	-457.6	-492.1	-490.2	Compte de capital : débit
Financial Account, nie	-1 277.4	-9 276.8	3 393.6	4 944.4	-6 470.5	-14 295.0	-15 007.6	Compte d'op. fin., nia
Net Errors and Omissions	3 366.2	5 562.8	-2 983.0	4 555.1	7 636.6	-4 132.5	-5 971.6	Erreurs et omissions nettes
Reserves & Related Items	-2 710.8	-5 497.7	2 393.1	-4 996.3	-5 933.1	-3 720.0	-2 172.2	Rés. et postes appareutés
Cape Verde								**Cap-Vert**
Goods: Exports fob	16.6	23.9	43.2	32.7	26.2	...	...	Biens : exportations, fab
Goods: Imports fob	-233.6	-207.5	-215.1	-218.8	-240.9	...	...	Biens : importations, fab
Serv. & Income: Credit	70.9	80.5	96.2	89.0	107.8	...	...	Serv. & revenu : crédit
Serv. & Income: Debit	-67.1	-77.4	-80.4	-98.7	-127.2	...	...	Serv & revenu : débit
Current Trans.,nie: Credit	156.0	148.4	129.9	142.5	168.4	...	...	Transf. cour.,nia : crédit
Current Transfers: Debit	-4.4	-2.9	-3.6	-5.1	-9.1	...	...	Transf. courants : débit
Capital Acct.,nie: Credit	20.9	12.8	6.3	19.0	4.5	...	...	Compte de cap.,nia : crédit
Capital Account: Debit	0.0	0.0	0.0	0.0	0.0	...	...	Compte de capital : débit
Financial Account, nie	44.5	46.0	44.1	37.0	128.9	...	...	Compte d'op. fin., nia
Net Errors and Omissions	-35.6	-1.3	-20.4	13.3	-8.8	...	...	Erreurs et omissions nettes
Reserves & Related Items	31.9	-22.5	-0.2	-10.8	-49.8	...	...	Rés. et postes appareutés
Chile								**Chili**
Goods: Exports fob	16 025.0	16 653.0	17 900.0	16 355.0	17 192.0	19 246.0	18 508.0	Biens : exportations, fab
Goods: Imports fob	-14 644.0	-17 699.0	-19 297.0	-18 364.0	-14 737.0	-17 093.0	-16 413.0	Biens : importations, fab
Serv. & Income: Credit	4 201.4	4 539.0	5 025.0	5 187.0	4 738.0	5 306.0	5 077.0	Serv. & revenu : crédit
Serv. & Income: Debit	-7 239.0	-7 144.0	-7 820.0	-7 647.0	-7 924.0	-8 990.0	-8 838.0	Serv & revenu : débit
Current Trans.,nie: Credit	482.0	664.0	836.0	810.0	769.0	821.0	795.0	Transf. cour.,nia : crédit
Current Transfers: Debit	-175.0	-158.0	-312.0	-349.0	-339.0	-368.0	-372.0	Transf. courants : débit
Capital Acct.,nie: Credit	0.0	0.0	0.0	0.0	0.0	0.0	0.0	Compte de cap.,nia : crédit
Capital Account: Debit	0.0	0.0	0.0	0.0	0.0	0.0	0.0	Compte de capital : débit
Financial Account, nie	2 356.6	4 185.2	6 741.0	1 968.0	236.0	829.0	1 758.0	Compte d'op. fin., nia
Net Errors and Omissions	131.5	77.6	245.4	-123.3	-588.2	566.5	-1 114.5	Erreurs et omissions nettes
Reserves & Related Items	-1 138.5	-1 117.8	-3 318.5	2 163.3	653.2	-317.5	599.5	Rés. et postes appareutés
China								**Chine**
Goods: Exports fob	128 110.0	151 077.0	182 670.0	183 529.0	194 716.0	249 131.0	266 075.0	Biens : exportations, fab
Goods: Imports fob	-110060.0	-131542.0	-136448.0	-136915.0	-158734.0	-214657.0	-232058.0	Biens : importations, fab
Serv. & Income: Credit	24 321.6	27 919.0	30 279.0	29 479.0	34 578.0	42 980.4	42 722.0	Serv. & revenu : crédit
Serv. & Income: Debit	-42 187.9	-42 340.0	-44 682.0	-48 900.0	-54 389.0	-63 246.9	-67 830.0	Serv & revenu : débit
Current Trans.,nie: Credit	1 826.7	2 368.0	5 477.0	4 661.0	5 368.0	6 860.8	9 125.0	Transf. cour.,nia : crédit
Current Transfers: Debit	-392.1	-239.0	-333.0	-382.0	-424.0	-549.5	-633.0	Transf. courants : débit
Capital Acct.,nie: Credit	0.0	0.0	0.0	0.0	0.0	0.0	0.0	Compte de cap.,nia : crédit
Capital Account: Debit	0.0	0.0	-21.0	-47.0	-26.0	-35.3	-54.0	Compte de capital : débit
Financial Account, nie	38 673.8	39 966.0	21 037.0	-6 275.0	5 204.0	1 957.9	34 832.0	Compte d'op. fin., nia
Net Errors and Omissions	-17 823.2	-15 504.0	-22 121.8	-18 901.8	-17 640.5	-11 747.9	-4 732.5	Erreurs et omissions nettes
Reserves & Related Items	-22 469.0	-31 705.0	-35 857.2	-6 248.2	-8 652.5	-10 693.1	-47 446.5	Rés. et postes appareutés
China, Hong Kong SAR								**Chine, Hong Kong RAS**
Goods: Exports fob	...	...	...	175 833.0	174 719.0	202 698.0	190 926.0	Biens : exportations, fab
Goods: Imports fob	...	...	...	-183666.0	-177878.0	-210891.0	-199257.0	Biens : importations, fab
Serv. & Income: Credit	...	...	...	81 963.3	83 013.6	94 253.0	89 438.5	Serv. & revenu : crédit
Serv. & Income: Debit	...	...	...	-68 107.8	-66 273.4	-75 282.9	-67 690.9	Serv & revenu : débit
Current Trans.,nie: Credit	...	...	...	668.7	569.5	538.2	813.5	Transf. cour.,nia : crédit
Current Transfers: Debit	...	...	...	-2 265.0	-2 109.3	-2 208.3	-2 494.5	Transf. courants : débit
Capital Acct.,nie: Credit	...	...	...	377.4	103.3	56.5	35.8	Compte de cap.,nia : crédit
Capital Account: Debit	...	...	...	-2 759.0	-1 883.3	-1 602.2	-1 197.5	Compte de capital : débit
Financial Account, nie	...	...	...	-8 475.8	1 060.9	4 165.4	-5 145.7	Compte d'op. fin., nia
Net Errors and Omissions	...	...	...	-358.1	-1 294.6	-1 682.5	-744.1	Erreurs et omissions nettes
Reserves & Related Items	...	...	...	6 789.1	-10 027.7	-10 043.7	-4 684.0	Rés. et postes appareutés

78

Summary of balance of payments
Millions of US dollars *[cont.]*
Résumé des balances des paiements
Millions de dollars des E.-U. *[suite]*

Country or area	1995	1996	1997	1998	1999	2000	2001	Pays ou zone
Colombia								**Colombie**
Goods: Exports fob	10 594.0	10 966.2	12 065.0	11 480.0	12 037.3	13 620.4	12 775.4	Biens : exportations, fab
Goods: Imports fob	-13 139.0	-13 057.7	-14 702.6	-13 929.9	-10 261.9	-11 089.6	-12 267.1	Biens : importations, fab
Serv. & Income: Credit	2 377.0	2 898.7	3 036.9	2 833.4	2 673.7	2 861.9	2 896.2	Serv. & revenu : crédit
Serv. & Income: Debit	-5 157.0	-6 158.4	-6 897.5	-6 054.2	-5 530.9	-6 698.4	-7 286.9	Serv & revenu : débit
Current Trans.,nie: Credit	963.0	814.0	830.9	607.5	1 683.0	1 900.0	2 395.4	Transf. cour.,nia : crédit
Current Transfers: Debit	-234.0	-217.3	-217.3	-161.9	-248.3	-238.1	-301.5	Transf. courants : débit
Capital Acct.,nie: Credit	0.0	0.0	0.0	0.0	0.0	0.0	0.0	Compte de cap.,nia : crédit
Capital Account: Debit	0.0	0.0	0.0	0.0	0.0	0.0	0.0	Compte de capital : débit
Financial Account, nie	4 476.0	6 850.9	6 731.0	3 717.9	-592.7	489.5	2 477.1	Compte d'op. fin., nia
Net Errors and Omissions	115.1	-367.0	-568.4	109.4	-72.2	16.7	537.1	Erreurs et omissions nettes
Reserves & Related Items	4.9	-1 729.4	-278.0	1 397.8	312.0	-862.4	-1 225.7	Rés. et postes appareutés
Comoros								**Comores**
Goods: Exports fob	11.3	...	...	...	...	...	...	Biens : exportations, fab
Goods: Imports fob	-53.5	...	...	...	...	...	...	Biens : importations, fab
Serv. & Income: Credit	37.9	...	...	...	...	...	...	Serv. & revenu : crédit
Serv. & Income: Debit	-52.2	...	...	...	...	...	...	Serv & revenu : débit
Current Trans.,nie: Credit	41.1	...	...	...	...	...	...	Transf. cour.,nia : crédit
Current Transfers: Debit	-3.5	...	...	...	...	...	...	Transf. courants : débit
Capital Acct.,nie: Credit	0.0	...	...	...	...	...	...	Compte de cap.,nia : crédit
Capital Account: Debit	0.0	...	...	...	...	...	...	Compte de capital : débit
Financial Account, nie	10.9	...	...	...	...	...	...	Compte d'op. fin., nia
Net Errors and Omissions	-1.8	...	...	...	...	...	...	Erreurs et omissions nettes
Reserves & Related Items	9.9	...	...	...	...	...	...	Rés. et postes appareutés
Congo								**Congo**
Goods: Exports fob	1 167.0	1 554.5	1 744.1	...	...	...	...	Biens : exportations, fab
Goods: Imports fob	-650.7	-1 361.0	-802.9	...	...	...	...	Biens : importations, fab
Serv. & Income: Credit	79.3	102.8	60.8	...	...	...	...	Serv. & revenu : crédit
Serv. & Income: Debit	-1 237.9	-1 391.3	-1 234.1	...	...	...	...	Serv & revenu : débit
Current Trans.,nie: Credit	30.9	29.9	24.7	...	...	...	...	Transf. cour.,nia : crédit
Current Transfers: Debit	-38.3	-44.0	-44.5	...	...	...	...	Transf. courants : débit
Capital Acct.,nie: Credit	0.0	0.0	0.0	...	...	...	...	Compte de cap.,nia : crédit
Capital Account: Debit	0.0	0.0	0.0	...	...	...	...	Compte de capital : débit
Financial Account, nie	-80.3	657.2	-173.7	...	...	...	...	Compte d'op. fin., nia
Net Errors and Omissions	120.7	102.1	-122.1	...	...	...	...	Erreurs et omissions nettes
Reserves & Related Items	609.3	349.7	547.7	...	...	...	...	Rés. et postes appareutés
Costa Rica								**Costa Rica**
Goods: Exports fob	3 481.8	3 774.1	4 220.6	5 538.3	6 576.8	5 813.7	4 907.8	Biens : exportations, fab
Goods: Imports fob	-3 804.4	-4 023.3	-4 718.2	-5 937.4	-5 996.3	-6 024.8	-6 117.9	Biens : importations, fab
Serv. & Income: Credit	1 115.5	1 196.0	1 314.0	1 526.1	1 858.8	2 143.0	2 611.6	Serv. & revenu : crédit
Serv. & Income: Debit	-1 284.9	-1 360.0	-1 422.8	-1 761.0	-3 221.8	-2 781.7	-2 250.7	Serv & revenu : débit
Current Trans.,nie: Credit	165.2	192.7	191.2	190.5	190.8	192.0	248.9	Transf. cour.,nia : crédit
Current Transfers: Debit	-31.3	-43.2	-65.7	-77.3	-88.4	-100.0	-101.2	Transf. courants : débit
Capital Acct.,nie: Credit	0.0	28.2	0.0	0.0	0.0	8.8	12.4	Compte de cap.,nia : crédit
Capital Account: Debit	0.0	0.0	0.0	0.0	0.0	0.0	0.0	Compte de capital : débit
Financial Account, nie	517.3	47.5	129.7	199.0	568.0	-84.1	383.1	Compte d'op. fin., nia
Net Errors and Omissions	57.1	118.7	157.8	-182.6	213.4	218.2	19.2	Erreurs et omissions nettes
Reserves & Related Items	-216.2	69.3	193.3	504.3	-101.3	614.9	286.8	Rés. et postes appareutés
Côte d'Ivoire								**Côte d'Ivoire**
Goods: Exports fob	3 805.9	4 446.1	4 451.2	4 606.5	4 661.4	3 888.1	3 947.4	Biens : exportations, fab
Goods: Imports fob	-2 430.3	-2 622.4	-2 658.4	-2 886.5	-2 766.0	-2 401.8	-2 407.8	Biens : importations, fab
Serv. & Income: Credit	720.4	736.4	740.8	783.5	748.6	623.8	629.3	Serv. & revenu : crédit
Serv. & Income: Debit	-2 351.8	-2 379.8	-2 307.4	-2 400.0	-2 378.4	-2 021.6	-1 951.9	Serv & revenu : débit
Current Trans.,nie: Credit	277.7	204.1	137.7	148.1	136.8	79.4	85.0	Transf. cour.,nia : crédit
Current Transfers: Debit	-514.3	-546.6	-518.3	-541.7	-522.7	-409.4	-359.7	Transf. courants : débit
Capital Acct.,nie: Credit	291.3	49.8	50.5	35.9	17.4	9.8	11.5	Compte de cap.,nia : crédit
Capital Account: Debit	0.0	-2.7	-9.9	-10.3	-3.6	-1.4	-1.5	Compte de capital : débit
Financial Account, nie	-88.6	-717.8	-323.0	-417.0	-577.2	-362.5	-23.5	Compte d'op. fin., nia
Net Errors and Omissions	35.6	-15.4	-39.6	32.0	-24.0	-10.2	-23.0	Erreurs et omissions nettes
Reserves & Related Items	254.2	848.4	476.6	649.6	707.8	605.9	94.2	Rés. et postes appareutés
Croatia								**Croatie**
Goods: Exports fob	4 517.3	4 677.5	4 021.1	4 580.6	4 394.7	4 567.1	4 758.7	Biens : exportations, fab

78

Summary of balance of payments
Millions of US dollars [cont.]

Résumé des balances des paiements
Millions de dollars des E.-U. [suite]

Country or area	1995	1996	1997	1998	1999	2000	2001	Pays ou zone
Goods: Imports fob	-7 744.8	-8 165.5	-9 404.1	-8 652.1	-7 693.4	-7 770.7	-8 737.2	Biens : importations, fab
Serv. & Income: Credit	2 442.2	3 463.1	4 348.3	4 343.9	3 955.6	4 412.3	5 269.4	Serv. & revenu : crédit
Serv. & Income: Debit	-1 608.8	-2 046.7	-2 660.0	-2 446.2	-2 701.8	-2 545.4	-2 873.9	Serv & revenu : débit
Current Trans.,nie: Credit	971.2	1 173.3	963.8	919.1	967.3	1 101.0	1 174.6	Transf. cour.,nia : crédit
Current Transfers: Debit	-168.9	-150.8	-94.5	-213.3	-334.9	-218.0	-208.9	Transf. courants : débit
Capital Acct.,nie: Credit	0.0	18.0	23.5	24.1	28.3	24.5	137.6	Compte de cap.,nia : crédit
Capital Account: Debit	0.0	-1.8	-2.2	-5.0	-3.3	-3.6	-4.6	Compte de capital : débit
Financial Account, nie	1 135.3	2 996.3	3 020.8	1 610.3	2 758.1	1 793.1	2 371.4	Compte d'op. fin., nia
Net Errors and Omissions	496.9	-946.1	173.7	-0.9	-960.6	-749.5	-544.9	Erreurs et omissions nettes
Reserves & Related Items	-40.4	-1 017.3	-390.4	-160.5	-410.0	-610.8	-1 342.2	Rés. et postes appareutés
Cyprus								**Chypre**
Goods: Exports fob	1 228.7	1 392.4	1 245.8	1 064.6	1 000.3	951.0	976.5	Biens : exportations, fab
Goods: Imports fob	-3 314.2	-3 575.7	-3 317.2	-3 490.4	-3 309.5	-3 556.5	-3 526.9	Biens : importations, fab
Serv. & Income: Credit	3 362.4	3 231.5	3 209.8	3 371.4	3 608.4	3 714.9	3 916.8	Serv. & revenu : crédit
Serv. & Income: Debit	-1 469.7	-1 547.0	-1 502.4	-1 577.9	-1 603.8	-1 690.9	-1 782.7	Serv & revenu : débit
Current Trans.,nie: Credit	46.4	43.1	40.9	49.6	113.6	153.3	49.3	Transf. cour.,nia : crédit
Current Transfers: Debit	-17.7	-9.9	-15.0	-20.3	-26.3	-27.5	-27.7	Transf. courants : débit
Capital Acct.,nie: Credit	0.0	0.0	0.0	0.0	0.0	0.0	0.0	Compte de cap.,nia : crédit
Capital Account: Debit	0.0	0.0	0.0	0.0	0.0	0.0	0.0	Compte de capital : débit
Financial Account, nie	-140.8	419.0	383.7	657.9	1 006.4	263.5	845.7	Compte d'op. fin., nia
Net Errors and Omissions	-58.2	-13.3	-92.5	-137.6	-150.0	184.0	161.4	Erreurs et omissions nettes
Reserves & Related Items	363.1	59.8	47.0	82.5	-639.0	8.2	-612.3	Rés. et postes appareutés
Czech Republic								**République tchèque**
Goods: Exports fob	21 476.8	21 950.3	22 318.6	25 885.5	26 259.0	29 019.3	33 403.6	Biens : exportations, fab
Goods: Imports fob	-25 162.2	-27 656.2	-27 257.1	-28 532.5	-28 161.4	-32 114.5	-36 481.7	Biens : importations, fab
Serv. & Income: Credit	7 922.5	9 350.6	8 536.6	9 377.9	8 907.9	8 791.6	9 261.6	Serv. & revenu : crédit
Serv. & Income: Debit	-6 182.5	-8 156.2	-7 585.4	-8 556.1	-9 059.0	-8 759.0	-9 277.8	Serv & revenu : débit
Current Trans.,nie: Credit	664.1	616.6	866.0	1 066.5	1 309.7	948.0	958.9	Transf. cour.,nia : crédit
Current Transfers: Debit	-92.1	-232.6	-500.6	-549.7	-722.0	-575.1	-488.9	Transf. courants : débit
Capital Acct.,nie: Credit	11.7	1.0	16.7	13.8	18.4	5.8	2.4	Compte de cap.,nia : crédit
Capital Account: Debit	-4.9	-0.5	-5.5	-11.6	-20.5	-10.9	-11.3	Compte de capital : débit
Financial Account, nie	8 224.6	4 202.5	1 122.2	2 908.3	3 079.9	3 834.9	4 057.9	Compte d'op. fin., nia
Net Errors and Omissions	595.5	-900.7	730.0	288.3	27.2	-296.6	362.4	Erreurs et omissions nettes
Reserves & Related Items	-7 453.4	825.2	1 758.4	-1 890.4	-1 639.3	-843.6	-1 787.1	Rés. et postes appareutés
Denmark								**Danemark**
Goods: Exports fob	50 348.2	50 734.7	48 102.9	47 907.8	49 932.0	50 754.4	50 942.6	Biens : exportations, fab
Goods: Imports fob	-43 820.5	-43 202.5	-42 734.2	-44 021.5	-43 533.0	-44 000.5	-43 983.0	Biens : importations, fab
Serv. & Income: Credit	43 739.6	54 128.5	32 817.7	25 612.8	29 189.9	36 222.4	37 910.6	Serv. & revenu : crédit
Serv. & Income: Debit	-47 021.5	-57 005.8	-35 929.8	-30 026.4	-29 942.6	-37 477.3	-38 101.6	Serv & revenu : débit
Current Trans.,nie: Credit	2 579.6	2 398.3	3 632.9	3 442.8	4 156.2	3 303.4	3 629.2	Transf. cour.,nia : crédit
Current Transfers: Debit	-3 970.4	-3 963.4	-4 968.0	-4 923.7	-6 887.6	-6 295.7	-6 255.9	Transf. courants : débit
Capital Acct.,nie: Credit	0.0	0.0	127.8	81.3	1 330.8	320.1	253.1	Compte de cap.,nia : crédit
Capital Account: Debit	0.0	0.0	0.0	-31.3	-247.7	-334.0	-278.0	Compte de capital : débit
Financial Account, nie	-431.6	1 882.0	8 495.6	-1 489.1	6 247.2	-3 688.6	-3 837.5	Compte d'op. fin., nia
Net Errors and Omissions	1 074.7	-1 408.3	-3 012.5	-792.3	-807.8	-4 453.5	2 990.2	Erreurs et omissions nettes
Reserves & Related Items	-2 497.9	-3 563.3	-6 532.1	4 239.4	-9 437.3	5 649.3	-3 269.7	Rés. et postes appareutés
Djibouti								**Djibouti**
Goods: Exports fob	33.5	...	...	...	...	...	...	Biens : exportations, fab
Goods: Imports fob	-205.0	...	...	...	...	...	...	Biens : importations, fab
Serv. & Income: Credit	177.3	...	...	...	...	...	...	Serv. & revenu : crédit
Serv. & Income: Debit	-95.9	...	...	...	...	...	...	Serv & revenu : débit
Current Trans.,nie: Credit	85.4	...	...	...	...	...	...	Transf. cour.,nia : crédit
Current Transfers: Debit	-18.4	...	...	...	...	...	...	Transf. courants : débit
Capital Acct.,nie: Credit	0.0	...	...	...	...	...	...	Compte de cap.,nia : crédit
Capital Account: Debit	0.0	...	...	...	...	...	...	Compte de capital : débit
Financial Account, nie	-2.1	...	...	...	...	...	...	Compte d'op. fin., nia
Net Errors and Omissions	0.7	...	...	...	...	...	...	Erreurs et omissions nettes
Reserves & Related Items	24.5	...	...	...	...	...	...	Rés. et postes appareutés
Dominica								**Dominique**
Goods: Exports fob	50.3	52.9	53.8	63.2	56.0	54.7	44.4	Biens : exportations, fab
Goods: Imports fob	-103.2	-117.2	-118.7	-116.4	-121.6	-130.4	-115.3	Biens : importations, fab
Serv. & Income: Credit	64.7	71.8	87.0	93.1	105.4	94.4	79.4	Serv. & revenu : crédit

78

Summary of balance of payments
Millions of US dollars *[cont.]*

Résumé des balances des paiements
Millions de dollars des E.-U. *[suite]*

Country or area	1995	1996	1997	1998	1999	2000	2001	Pays ou zone
Serv. & Income: Debit	-60.3	-68.8	-74.7	-75.7	-89.3	-90.4	-74.8	Serv & revenu : débit
Current Trans.,nie: Credit	16.3	17.8	17.4	19.9	20.5	25.1	24.8	Transf. cour.,nia : crédit
Current Transfers: Debit	-8.4	-7.7	-7.1	-7.2	-6.9	-7.0	-7.3	Transf. courants : débit
Capital Acct.,nie: Credit	24.7	25.4	22.6	14.9	12.1	9.7	18.1	Compte de cap.,nia : crédit
Capital Account: Debit	-0.1	-0.1	-0.1	-0.1	-0.3	-1.5	-0.1	Compte de capital : débit
Financial Account, nie	42.1	6.1	25.8	-1.7	37.3	46.4	27.5	Compte d'op. fin., nia
Net Errors and Omissions	-17.6	22.0	-5.5	13.5	-2.1	-0.6	7.9	Erreurs et omissions nettes
Reserves & Related Items	-8.3	-2.2	-0.6	-3.5	-11.0	-0.5	-4.5	Rés. et postes appareutés
Dominican Republic								**Rép. dominicaine**
Goods: Exports fob	3 779.5	4 052.8	4 613.7	4 980.5	5 136.7	5 736.7	5 332.9	Biens : exportations, fab
Goods: Imports fob	-5 170.4	-5 727.0	-6 608.7	-7 597.3	-8 041.1	-9 478.5	-8 784.2	Biens : importations, fab
Serv. & Income: Credit	2 079.4	2 270.3	2 587.0	2 669.7	3 068.6	3 527.3	3 270.0	Serv. & revenu : crédit
Serv. & Income: Debit	-1 863.5	-1 976.5	-2 107.1	-2 377.8	-2 441.2	-2 714.3	-2 685.1	Serv. & revenu : débit
Current Trans.,nie: Credit	1 007.7	1 187.6	1 373.1	2 016.9	1 997.1	2 095.6	2 232.0	Transf. cour.,nia : crédit
Current Transfers: Debit	-15.5	-19.9	-21.0	-30.4	-149.3	-193.3	-204.5	Transf. courants : débit
Capital Acct.,nie: Credit	0.0	0.0	0.0	0.0	0.0	0.0	0.0	Compte de cap.,nia : crédit
Capital Account: Debit	0.0	0.0	0.0	0.0	0.0	0.0	0.0	Compte de capital : débit
Financial Account, nie	253.6	64.1	447.6	688.1	1 061.0	1 596.6	1 722.9	Compte d'op. fin., nia
Net Errors and Omissions	75.3	108.8	-193.7	-338.6	-480.4	-618.5	-371.1	Erreurs et omissions nettes
Reserves & Related Items	-146.1	39.8	-90.9	-11.1	-151.4	48.4	-512.9	Rés. et postes appareutés
Ecuador								**Equateur**
Goods: Exports fob	4 468.3	4 929.4	5 360.5	4 326.2	4 615.5	5 137.2	4 862.3	Biens : exportations, fab
Goods: Imports fob	-4 534.6	-4 008.1	-4 869.1	-5 457.9	-3 027.9	-3 742.6	-5 324.7	Biens : importations, fab
Serv. & Income: Credit	826.2	763.3	814.5	797.7	804.7	919.8	959.0	Serv. & revenu : crédit
Serv. & Income: Debit	-2 201.9	-2 231.2	-2 383.6	-2 531.4	-2 563.7	-2 745.2	-2 840.8	Serv. & revenu : débit
Current Trans.,nie: Credit	506.1	615.9	738.2	933.0	1 188.2	1 436.8	1 550.1	Transf. cour.,nia : crédit
Current Transfers: Debit	-64.2	-124.2	-117.3	-166.1	-98.7	-85.0	-5.6	Transf. courants : débit
Capital Acct.,nie: Credit	21.3	18.1	17.0	22.7	11.3	8.1	16.7	Compte de cap.,nia : crédit
Capital Account: Debit	-4.0	-3.7	-6.0	-8.6	-9.2	-9.5	-84.1	Compte de capital : débit
Financial Account, nie	-43.2	103.4	-14.1	1 447.6	-1 343.5	-6 602.3	1 007.2	Compte d'op. fin., nia
Net Errors and Omissions	-433.0	-189.1	-61.6	-147.3	-521.0	-14.5	-399.5	Erreurs et omissions nettes
Reserves & Related Items	1 459.0	126.2	521.4	784.1	944.3	5 697.3	259.3	Rés. et postes appareutés
Egypt								**Egypte**
Goods: Exports fob	4 670.0	4 779.0	5 525.3	4 403.0	5 236.5	7 061.0	7 024.9	Biens : exportations, fab
Goods: Imports fob	-12 267.0	-13 169.0	-14 156.8	-14 617.0	-15 164.8	-15 382.0	-13 959.6	Biens : importations, fab
Serv. & Income: Credit	10 168.0	11 172.0	11 501.4	10 171.0	11 281.5	11 674.0	10 510.7	Serv. & revenu : crédit
Serv. & Income: Debit	-6 856.0	-6 640.0	-7 955.0	-7 567.0	-7 496.4	-8 496.0	-7 921.6	Serv. & revenu : débit
Current Trans.,nie: Credit	4 284.0	3 888.0	4 737.7	5 166.0	4 563.8	4 224.0	4 055.6	Transf. cour.,nia : crédit
Current Transfers: Debit	-253.0	-222.0	-363.1	-122.0	-55.4	-52.0	-98.4	Transf. courants : débit
Capital Acct.,nie: Credit	0.0	0.0	0.0	0.0	0.0	0.0	0.0	Compte de cap.,nia : crédit
Capital Account: Debit	0.0	0.0	0.0	0.0	0.0	0.0	0.0	Compte de capital : débit
Financial Account, nie	-1 845.0	-1 459.0	1 957.8	1 901.0	-1 421.4	-1 646.0	189.8	Compte d'op. fin., nia
Net Errors and Omissions	272.0	-73.6	-1 882.3	-721.9	-1 557.6	586.8	-1 146.1	Erreurs et omissions nettes
Reserves & Related Items	1 827.0	1 724.6	635.1	1 386.9	4 613.8	2 030.2	1 344.7	Rés. et postes appareutés
El Salvador								**El Salvador**
Goods: Exports fob	1 651.1	1 787.4	2 437.1	2 459.5	2 534.3	2 963.2	2 901.0	Biens : exportations, fab
Goods: Imports fob	-3 113.5	-3 029.7	-3 580.3	-3 765.2	-3 890.4	-4 702.9	-4 813.9	Biens : importations, fab
Serv. & Income: Credit	442.6	458.5	550.9	699.8	753.4	839.7	1 244.7	Serv. & revenu : crédit
Serv. & Income: Debit	-630.5	-639.1	-866.4	-1 011.7	-1 218.0	-1 327.7	-1 512.5	Serv. & revenu : débit
Current Trans.,nie: Credit	1 393.2	1 258.6	1 363.6	1 534.1	1 590.5	1 830.3	2 022.4	Transf. cour.,nia : crédit
Current Transfers: Debit	-4.6	-4.8	-2.7	-7.3	-9.0	-33.2	-18.6	Transf. courants : débit
Capital Acct.,nie: Credit	0.0	0.0	11.6	28.9	78.8	109.4	197.8	Compte de cap.,nia : crédit
Capital Account: Debit	0.0	0.0	0.0	-0.3	-0.2	-0.4	-0.1	Compte de capital : débit
Financial Account, nie	438.3	358.1	653.2	1 034.3	574.3	287.4	145.7	Compte d'op. fin., nia
Net Errors and Omissions	-28.4	-24.2	-204.4	-668.9	-205.9	-11.3	-344.2	Erreurs et omissions nettes
Reserves & Related Items	-148.3	-164.8	-362.7	-303.3	-207.8	45.5	177.7	Rés. et postes appareutés
Equatorial Guinea								**Guinée équatoriale**
Goods: Exports fob	89.9	175.3	...	...	...	...	...	Biens : exportations, fab
Goods: Imports fob	-120.6	-292.0	...	...	...	...	...	Biens : importations, fab
Serv. & Income: Credit	4.3	5.0	...	...	...	...	...	Serv. & revenu : crédit
Serv. & Income: Debit	-100.6	-229.8	...	...	...	...	...	Serv & revenu : débit
Current Trans.,nie: Credit	6.8	4.0	...	...	...	...	...	Transf. cour.,nia : crédit

78

Summary of balance of payments
Millions of US dollars *[cont.]*

Résumé des balances des paiements
Millions de dollars des E.-U. *[suite]*

Country or area	1995	1996	1997	1998	1999	2000	2001	Pays ou zone
Current Transfers: Debit	-3.3	-6.6	...	...	...	...	...	Transf. courants : débit
Capital Acct.,nie: Credit	0.0	0.0	...	...	...	...	...	Compte de cap.,nia : crédit
Capital Account: Debit	0.0	0.0	...	...	...	...	...	Compte de capital : débit
Financial Account, nie	101.6	313.8	...	...	...	...	...	Compte d'op. fin., nia
Net Errors and Omissions	10.3	24.8	...	...	...	...	...	Erreurs et omissions nettes
Reserves & Related Items	11.5	5.5	...	...	...	...	...	Rés. et postes appareutés
Estonia								**Estonie**
Goods: Exports fob	1 696.3	1 812.4	2 289.6	2 690.1	2 453.1	3 311.4	3 338.1	Biens : exportations, fab
Goods: Imports fob	-2 362.3	-2 831.5	-3 413.7	-3 805.4	-3 330.6	-4 079.5	-4 125.0	Biens : importations, fab
Serv. & Income: Credit	940.4	1 220.5	1 433.1	1 613.2	1 623.5	1 616.5	1 813.5	Serv. & revenu : crédit
Serv. & Income: Debit	-558.5	-700.2	-987.4	-1 124.7	-1 153.1	-1 258.1	-1 516.7	Serv & revenu : débit
Current Trans.,nie: Credit	134.5	116.8	135.3	172.9	153.7	144.7	180.4	Transf. cour.,nia : crédit
Current Transfers: Debit	-8.2	-16.3	-18.6	-24.6	-41.3	-29.1	-29.3	Transf. courants : débit
Capital Acct.,nie: Credit	1.4	0.2	0.7	2.1	1.4	16.8	5.5	Compte de cap.,nia : crédit
Capital Account: Debit	-2.2	-0.8	-0.9	-0.3	-0.2	-0.2	-0.4	Compte de capital : débit
Financial Account, nie	233.4	540.9	802.8	508.1	418.2	406.7	306.4	Compte d'op. fin., nia
Net Errors and Omissions	8.7	-35.6	-25.1	5.9	-5.5	-1.6	-12.8	Erreurs et omissions nettes
Reserves & Related Items	-83.5	-106.3	-215.9	-37.3	-119.3	-127.6	40.3	Rés. et postes appareutés
Ethiopia								**Ethiopie**
Goods: Exports fob	423.0	417.5	588.3	560.3	467.4	486.0	433.3	Biens : exportations, fab
Goods: Imports fob	-1 092.8	-1 002.8	-1 001.6	-1 359.8	-1 387.2	-1 131.4	-1 626.1	Biens : importations, fab
Serv. & Income: Credit	412.9	418.4	415.0	412.5	490.3	522.4	539.2	Serv. & revenu : crédit
Serv. & Income: Debit	-440.0	-424.9	-459.8	-519.8	-516.8	-542.7	-573.8	Serv & revenu : débit
Current Trans.,nie: Credit	737.3	679.0	425.5	589.8	500.7	697.9	774.6	Transf. cour.,nia : crédit
Current Transfers: Debit	-1.1	-7.5	-7.6	-15.7	-19.7	-17.6	-24.0	Transf. courants : débit
Capital Acct.,nie: Credit	2.6	0.9	0.0	1.4	1.8	0.0	0.0	Compte de cap.,nia : crédit
Capital Account: Debit	0.0	0.0	0.0	0.0	0.0	0.0	0.0	Compte de capital : débit
Financial Account, nie	-24.9	-499.6	241.2	-21.3	-180.1	22.8	-139.6	Compte d'op. fin., nia
Net Errors and Omissions	-122.4	-45.8	-629.5	-7.9	407.2	-233.0	51.6	Erreurs et omissions nettes
Reserves & Related Items	105.2	464.8	428.6	360.4	236.3	195.6	564.9	Rés. et postes appareutés
Euro Area								**Zone euro**
Goods: Exports fob	...	...	...	878 680.0	870 873.0	911 008.0	924 619.0	Biens : exportations, fab
Goods: Imports fob	...	...	...	-756380.0	-790369.0	-882167.0	-857031.0	Biens : importations, fab
Serv. & Income: Credit	...	...	...	482 260.0	483 768.0	510 488.0	539 869.0	Serv. & revenu : crédit
Serv. & Income: Debit	...	...	...	-515660.0	-534987.0	-546033.0	-574717.0	Serv & revenu : débit
Current Trans.,nie: Credit	...	...	...	70 140.0	69 671.7	63 096.4	68 151.7	Transf. cour.,nia : crédit
Current Transfers: Debit	...	...	...	-123150.0	-119078.0	-111747.0	-113211.0	Transf. courants : débit
Capital Acct.,nie: Credit	...	...	...	19 840.0	20 309.7	16 804.4	15 199.1	Compte de cap.,nia : crédit
Capital Account: Debit	...	...	...	-5 930.0	-6 725.8	-7 761.2	-7 211.1	Compte de capital : débit
Financial Account, nie	...	...	...	-87 320.0	1 381.0	51 832.5	-51 211.1	Compte d'op. fin., nia
Net Errors and Omissions	...	...	...	27 920.0	-6 420.0	-21 673.5	38 652.2	Erreurs et omissions nettes
Reserves & Related Items	...	...	...	9 640.0	11 576.6	16 152.4	16 890.2	Rés. et postes appareutés
Fiji								**Fidji**
Goods: Exports fob	519.6	672.2	535.6	428.9	537.7	...	...	Biens : exportations, fab
Goods: Imports fob	-761.4	-839.9	-818.9	-614.6	-653.3	...	...	Biens : importations, fab
Serv. & Income: Credit	619.5	676.2	729.7	557.8	572.4	...	...	Serv. & revenu : crédit
Serv. & Income: Debit	-493.3	-504.5	-504.8	-462.6	-472.6	...	...	Serv & revenu : débit
Current Trans.,nie: Credit	36.0	44.1	54.6	45.3	42.7	...	...	Transf. cour.,nia : crédit
Current Transfers: Debit	-33.1	-34.6	-30.3	-14.7	-14.2	...	...	Transf. courants : débit
Capital Acct.,nie: Credit	120.1	114.5	88.9	100.6	59.3	...	...	Compte de cap.,nia : crédit
Capital Account: Debit	-33.1	-43.8	-40.5	-40.0	-45.3	...	...	Compte de capital : débit
Financial Account, nie	88.3	3.6	-15.1	28.7	-104.0	...	...	Compte d'op. fin., nia
Net Errors and Omissions	30.4	-9.7	-24.3	-24.6	32.5	...	...	Erreurs et omissions nettes
Reserves & Related Items	-93.0	-78.1	25.1	-4.9	44.9	...	...	Rés. et postes appareutés
Finland								**Finlande**
Goods: Exports fob	40 558.0	40 725.0	41 148.2	43 393.4	41 983.0	45 703.2	42 979.6	Biens : exportations, fab
Goods: Imports fob	-28 120.7	-29 410.6	-29 604.4	-30 902.9	-29 815.1	-32 018.9	-30 322.6	Biens : importations, fab
Serv. & Income: Credit	10 293.5	9 996.7	10 776.1	10 934.6	12 185.7	13 442.2	14 335.2	Serv. & revenu : crédit
Serv. & Income: Debit	-16 902.4	-15 319.5	-14 834.7	-15 087.1	-15 664.1	-17 428.7	-17 677.5	Serv & revenu : débit
Current Trans.,nie: Credit	1 536.4	1 253.0	1 209.8	1 522.7	1 607.8	1 714.9	1 549.5	Transf. cour.,nia : crédit
Current Transfers: Debit	-2 133.3	-2 242.0	-2 062.2	-2 521.1	-2 640.7	-2 334.0	-2 233.3	Transf. courants : débit
Capital Acct.,nie: Credit	113.7	129.9	247.5	90.7	149.3	99.7	75.2	Compte de cap.,nia : crédit

78

Summary of balance of payments
Millions of US dollars *[cont.]*

Résumé des balances des paiements
Millions de dollars des E.-U. *[suite]*

Country or area	1995	1996	1997	1998	1999	2000	2001	Pays ou zone
Capital Account: Debit	-48.0	-74.3	0.0	0.0	-36.3	-7.4	-9.8	Compte de capital : débit
Financial Account, nie	-4 284.3	-7 718.4	-2 975.8	-1 722.3	-5 995.7	-8 210.9	-10 733.2	Compte d'op. fin., nia
Net Errors and Omissions	-1 384.5	-375.5	-1 600.3	-5 412.2	-1 761.1	-608.8	2 447.1	Erreurs et omissions nettes
Reserves & Related Items	371.7	3 035.7	-2 304.2	-295.8	-12.8	-351.3	-410.1	Rés. et postes appareutés
France								**France**
Goods: Exports fob	278 627.0	281 846.0	286 071.0	303 025.0	300 052.0	295 533.0	291 410.0	Biens : exportations, fab
Goods: Imports fob	-267629.0	-266911.0	-259172.0	-278084.0	-282064.0	-294402.0	-288557.0	Biens : importations, fab
Serv. & Income: Credit	129 272.1	131 078.2	137 920.6	151 623.9	147 348.3	153 098.3	159 960.5	Serv. & revenu : crédit
Serv. & Income: Debit	-120263.1	-117529.5	-114202.0	-125732.4	-117473.6	-120275.8	-126666.3	Serv & revenu : débit
Current Trans.,nie: Credit	22 005.7	22 759.8	19 614.0	19 653.9	18 880.0	17 346.3	17 161.9	Transf. cour.,nia : crédit
Current Transfers: Debit	-31 172.6	-30 683.5	-32 430.6	-32 786.3	-31 703.6	-30 872.5	-31 949.5	Transf. courants : débit
Capital Acct.,nie: Credit	1 163.1	1 883.4	2 412.6	2 098.5	1 885.7	1 923.2	1 154.2	Compte de cap.,nia : crédit
Capital Account: Debit	-655.7	-648.9	-933.9	-632.4	-313.5	-528.3	-1 275.1	Compte de capital : débit
Financial Account, nie	-7 325.3	-22 344.5	-37 598.2	-29 289.9	-36 133.7	-30 282.3	-31 565.5	Compte d'op. fin., nia
Net Errors and Omissions	-3 310.1	788.7	4 258.7	9 939.5	-1 869.6	6 026.6	4 861.0	Erreurs et omissions nettes
Reserves & Related Items	-712.4	-239.3	-5 940.0	-19 815.1	1 392.3	2 432.6	5 466.3	Rés. et postes appareutés
Gabon								**Gabon**
Goods: Exports fob	2 727.8	3 334.2	3 032.7	1 907.6	2 498.8	...	...	Biens : exportations, fab
Goods: Imports fob	-880.9	-961.6	-1 030.6	-1 163.2	-910.5	...	...	Biens : importations, fab
Serv. & Income: Credit	252.1	276.7	271.9	277.1	365.1	...	...	Serv. & revenu : crédit
Serv. & Income: Debit	-1 592.1	-1 723.6	-1 708.2	-1 563.5	-1 520.1	...	...	Serv & revenu : débit
Current Trans.,nie: Credit	58.0	65.2	62.7	36.6	42.6	...	...	Transf. cour.,nia : crédit
Current Transfers: Debit	-100.3	-102.1	-97.1	-90.0	-85.6	...	...	Transf. courants : débit
Capital Acct.,nie: Credit	5.6	9.6	7.5	3.6	5.7	...	...	Compte de cap.,nia : crédit
Capital Account: Debit	-0.8	-4.5	-1.7	-1.8	-0.3	...	...	Compte de capital : débit
Financial Account, nie	-724.7	-1 047.6	-626.2	-165.8	-686.8	...	...	Compte d'op. fin., nia
Net Errors and Omissions	-181.1	-97.4	-108.4	92.5	-106.7	...	...	Erreurs et omissions nettes
Reserves & Related Items	436.3	251.2	197.4	667.0	397.8	...	...	Rés. et postes appareutés
Gambia								**Gambie**
Goods: Exports fob	123.0	118.7	119.6	...	...	...	...	Biens : exportations, fab
Goods: Imports fob	-162.5	-217.1	-207.1	...	...	...	...	Biens : importations, fab
Serv. & Income: Credit	58.1	107.2	113.1	...	...	...	...	Serv. & revenu : crédit
Serv. & Income: Debit	-78.8	-86.3	-86.0	...	...	...	...	Serv & revenu : débit
Current Trans.,nie: Credit	55.8	35.1	45.0	...	...	...	...	Transf. cour.,nia : crédit
Current Transfers: Debit	-3.7	-5.4	-8.2	...	...	...	...	Transf. courants : débit
Capital Acct.,nie: Credit	0.0	8.5	5.7	...	...	...	...	Compte de cap.,nia : crédit
Capital Account: Debit	0.0	0.0	0.0	...	...	...	...	Compte de capital : débit
Financial Account, nie	24.8	58.6	39.4	...	...	...	...	Compte d'op. fin., nia
Net Errors and Omissions	-15.6	-4.9	-14.2	...	...	...	...	Erreurs et omissions nettes
Reserves & Related Items	-0.9	-14.5	-7.4	...	...	...	...	Rés. et postes appareutés
Georgia								**Géorgie**
Goods: Exports fob	...	...	376.5	299.9	329.5	459.0	...	Biens : exportations, fab
Goods: Imports fob	...	...	-1 162.9	-994.5	-863.4	-970.5	...	Biens : importations, fab
Serv. & Income: Credit	...	...	384.6	608.7	428.3	385.0	...	Serv. & revenu : crédit
Serv. & Income: Debit	...	...	-308.9	-397.9	-288.5	-277.4	...	Serv & revenu : débit
Current Trans.,nie: Credit	...	...	205.5	219.9	228.7	163.2	...	Transf. cour.,nia : crédit
Current Transfers: Debit	...	...	-9.0	-11.8	-33.0	-28.3	...	Transf. courants : débit
Capital Acct.,nie: Credit	...	...	0.0	0.0	0.0	0.0	...	Compte de cap.,nia : crédit
Capital Account: Debit	...	...	-6.5	-6.1	-7.1	-4.8	...	Compte de capital : débit
Financial Account, nie	...	...	322.7	348.8	135.5	92.8	...	Compte d'op. fin., nia
Net Errors and Omissions	...	...	136.0	-170.5	55.7	187.4	...	Erreurs et omissions nettes
Reserves & Related Items	...	...	62.0	103.5	14.3	-6.4	...	Rés. et postes appareutés
Germany								**Allemagne**
Goods: Exports fob	523 584.0	522 579.0	510 022.0	542 620.0	542 726.0	549 841.0	569 951.0	Biens : exportations, fab
Goods: Imports fob	-458477.0	-453199.0	-439903.0	-465707.0	-472692.0	-492331.0	-481439.0	Biens : importations, fab
Serv. & Income: Credit	166 727.2	166 916.6	164 823.5	169 351.6	173 052.3	185 468.1	192 842.5	Serv. & revenu : crédit
Serv. & Income: Debit	-211791.1	-210239.7	-207398.4	-222040.1	-234852.8	-238468.0	-255089.0	Serv & revenu : débit
Current Trans.,nie: Credit	16 866.2	17 890.1	16 470.5	15 964.1	16 958.5	15 771.2	15 153.2	Transf. cour.,nia : crédit
Current Transfers: Debit	-55 841.0	-51 915.2	-46 850.6	-46 302.6	-44 261.1	-40 671.2	-38 976.6	Transf. courants : débit
Capital Acct.,nie: Credit	1 676.0	2 760.6	2 826.0	3 310.8	3 004.8	9 407.2	1 869.0	Compte de cap.,nia : crédit
Capital Account: Debit	-4 409.4	-4 938.9	-2 824.5	-2 591.8	-3 161.2	-3 216.2	-2 702.8	Compte de capital : débit
Financial Account, nie	43 979.7	16 126.0	1 132.9	8 360.2	-30 248.2	35 712.1	-26 282.8	Compte d'op. fin., nia

78

Summary of balance of payments
Millions of US dollars *[cont.]*

Résumé des balances des paiements
Millions de dollars des E.-U. *[suite]*

Country or area	1995	1996	1997	1998	1999	2000	2001	Pays ou zone
Net Errors and Omissions	-15 090.5	-7 174.1	-2 048.9	1 049.9	35 358.6	-26 734.9	19 208.6	Erreurs et omissions nettes
Reserves & Related Items	-7 223.9	1 195.0	3 751.2	-4 015.4	14 114.8	5 222.2	5 466.1	Rés. et postes appareutés
Ghana								**Ghana**
Goods: Exports fob	1 431.2	1 570.1	1 489.9	2 090.8	2 005.5	1 898.4	...	Biens : exportations, fab
Goods: Imports fob	-1 687.8	-1 937.0	-2 128.2	-2 896.5	-3 228.1	-2 741.3	...	Biens : importations, fab
Serv. & Income: Credit	164.3	180.3	191.6	465.3	482.8	519.9	...	Serv. & revenu : crédit
Serv. & Income: Debit	-575.6	-619.8	-663.1	-836.6	-812.7	-720.5	...	Serv & revenu : débit
Current Trans.,nie: Credit	538.9	497.9	576.5	751.0	637.8	649.3	...	Transf. cour.,nia : crédit
Current Transfers: Debit	-15.7	-16.2	-16.4	-17.1	-17.8	-18.4	...	Transf. courants : débit
Capital Acct.,nie: Credit	0.0	0.0	0.0	0.0	0.0	0.0	...	Compte de cap.,nia : crédit
Capital Account: Debit	-1.0	-1.0	-1.0	-1.0	-1.0	0.0	...	Compte de capital : débit
Financial Account, nie	462.1	285.1	493.8	449.9	554.5	265.8	...	Compte d'op. fin., nia
Net Errors and Omissions	-65.6	20.2	83.6	102.1	289.4	-111.7	...	Erreurs et omissions nettes
Reserves & Related Items	-250.8	20.4	-26.7	-107.9	89.6	258.5	...	Rés. et postes appareutés
Greece								**Grèce**
Goods: Exports fob	5 918.0	5 890.0	5 576.0	...	8 544.7	10 201.5	10 615.0	Biens : exportations, fab
Goods: Imports fob	-20 343.0	-21 395.0	-20 951.0	...	-26 495.6	-30 440.4	-29 702.0	Biens : importations, fab
Serv. & Income: Credit	10 917.0	10 504.0	10 495.0	...	19 082.3	22 046.1	21 340.7	Serv. & revenu : crédit
Serv. & Income: Debit	-7 364.0	-7 575.0	-7 490.0	...	-12 498.8	-14 978.5	-15 240.6	Serv & revenu : débit
Current Trans.,nie: Credit	8 039.0	8 053.0	7 538.0	...	4 956.5	4 115.8	4 592.0	Transf. cour.,nia : crédit
Current Transfers: Debit	-31.0	-31.0	-28.0	...	-884.0	-764.2	-1 005.0	Transf. courants : débit
Capital Acct.,nie: Credit	0.0	0.0	0.0	...	2 318.2	2 243.5	2 320.0	Compte de cap.,nia : crédit
Capital Account: Debit	0.0	0.0	0.0	...	-107.0	-131.2	-167.0	Compte de capital : débit
Financial Account, nie	3 162.0	8 658.0	119.0	...	7 477.5	10 830.0	536.7	Compte d'op. fin., nia
Net Errors and Omissions	-321.3	110.6	225.8	...	41.6	-549.8	1 010.9	Erreurs et omissions nettes
Reserves & Related Items	23.3	-4 214.6	4 515.2	...	-2 435.5	-2 572.8	5 699.4	Rés. et postes appareutés
Grenada								**Grenada**
Goods: Exports fob	24.6	24.9	32.8	45.9	74.3	84.5	...	Biens : exportations, fab
Goods: Imports fob	-129.8	-147.4	-154.9	-183.0	-184.6	-220.9	...	Biens : importations, fab
Serv. & Income: Credit	104.1	111.4	110.8	123.9	152.8	156.4	...	Serv. & revenu : crédit
Serv. & Income: Debit	-56.8	-65.9	-77.4	-96.5	-108.3	-119.2	...	Serv & revenu : débit
Current Trans.,nie: Credit	21.6	25.5	25.5	34.2	26.8	30.4	...	Transf. cour.,nia : crédit
Current Transfers: Debit	-4.5	-4.1	-4.0	-5.0	-7.6	-10.2	...	Transf. courants : débit
Capital Acct.,nie: Credit	27.3	31.4	33.4	30.4	33.1	31.7	...	Compte de cap.,nia : crédit
Capital Account: Debit	-1.4	0.0	-1.6	-1.8	-1.9	-2.1	...	Compte de capital : débit
Financial Account, nie	3.1	26.2	55.1	57.1	33.6	68.7	...	Compte d'op. fin., nia
Net Errors and Omissions	17.9	-1.6	-12.8	-1.1	-13.6	-12.6	...	Erreurs et omissions nettes
Reserves & Related Items	-6.0	-0.4	-6.9	-4.2	-4.6	-6.6	...	Rés. et postes appareutés
Guatemala								**Guatemala**
Goods: Exports fob	2 157.5	2 236.9	2 602.9	2 846.9	2 780.6	3 085.1	2 864.6	Biens : exportations, fab
Goods: Imports fob	-3 032.6	-2 880.3	-3 542.7	-4 255.7	-4 225.7	-4 742.0	-5 142.1	Biens : importations, fab
Serv. & Income: Credit	712.5	599.2	661.2	731.3	775.7	991.4	1 348.5	Serv. & revenu : crédit
Serv. & Income: Debit	-900.6	-929.8	-961.6	-1 066.9	-1 071.4	-1 249.4	-1 305.6	Serv & revenu : débit
Current Trans.,nie: Credit	508.2	537.1	628.8	742.9	754.4	908.2	1 031.8	Transf. cour.,nia : crédit
Current Transfers: Debit	-17.0	-14.6	-22.1	-37.6	-39.5	-42.9	-35.1	Transf. courants : débit
Capital Acct.,nie: Credit	61.6	65.0	85.0	71.0	68.4	85.5	93.3	Compte de cap.,nia : crédit
Capital Account: Debit	0.0	0.0	0.0	0.0	0.0	0.0	0.0	Compte de capital : débit
Financial Account, nie	494.8	672.3	737.4	1 136.7	637.5	1 520.7	1 520.8	Compte d'op. fin., nia
Net Errors and Omissions	-136.2	-71.7	40.7	66.8	195.0	86.1	98.1	Erreurs et omissions nettes
Reserves & Related Items	151.8	-214.1	-229.6	-235.4	125.0	-642.7	-474.3	Rés. et postes appareutés
Guinea								**Guinée**
Goods: Exports fob	582.8	636.5	630.1	693.0	635.7	666.4	731.0	Biens : exportations, fab
Goods: Imports fob	-621.7	-525.3	-512.5	-572.0	-581.8	-587.1	-561.8	Biens : importations, fab
Serv. & Income: Credit	130.4	136.9	118.4	119.7	137.8	91.5	114.2	Serv. & revenu : crédit
Serv. & Income: Debit	-486.8	-527.9	-442.9	-516.3	-471.5	-386.0	-432.8	Serv & revenu : débit
Current Trans.,nie: Credit	258.3	137.8	131.4	116.2	80.0	88.6	91.5	Transf. cour.,nia : crédit
Current Transfers: Debit	-79.3	-35.3	-15.6	-24.3	-15.1	-28.5	-44.5	Transf. courants : débit
Capital Acct.,nie: Credit	0.0	0.0	0.0	0.0	0.0	0.0	0.0	Compte de cap.,nia : crédit
Capital Account: Debit	0.0	0.0	0.0	0.0	0.0	0.0	0.0	Compte de capital : débit
Financial Account, nie	109.2	47.5	-89.3	8.0	116.5	8.3	-12.2	Compte d'op. fin., nia
Net Errors and Omissions	34.8	69.9	49.8	17.8	22.4	82.1	-1.9	Erreurs et omissions nettes
Reserves & Related Items	72.5	59.9	130.6	157.8	76.0	64.7	116.5	Rés. et postes appareutés

78

Summary of balance of payments
Millions of US dollars *[cont.]*

Résumé des balances des paiements
Millions de dollars des E.-U. *[suite]*

Country or area	1995	1996	1997	1998	1999	2000	2001	Pays ou zone
Guinea-Bissau								**Guinée-Bissau**
Goods: Exports fob	23.9	21.6	48.9	...	...	...	...	Biens : exportations, fab
Goods: Imports fob	-59.3	-56.8	-62.5	...	...	...	...	Biens : importations, fab
Serv. & Income: Credit [2]	5.7	7.0	8.0	...	...	...	...	Serv. & revenu : crédit [2]
Serv. & Income: Debit	-51.0	-47.9	-40.5	...	...	...	...	Serv & revenu : débit
Current Trans.,nie: Credit	31.4	15.7	15.8	...	...	...	...	Transf. cour.,nia : crédit
Current Transfers: Debit	-1.3	0.0	0.0	...	...	...	...	Transf. courants : débit
Capital Acct.,nie: Credit	49.2	40.7	32.2	...	...	...	...	Compte de cap.,nia : crédit
Capital Account: Debit	0.0	0.0	0.0	...	...	...	...	Compte de capital : débit
Financial Account, nie	-28.3	-12.3	2.0	...	...	...	...	Compte d'op. fin., nia
Net Errors and Omissions	-10.9	-11.5	-19.2	...	...	...	...	Erreurs et omissions nettes
Reserves & Related Items	40.6	43.5	15.2	...	...	...	...	Rés. et postes appareutés
Guyana								**Guyana**
Goods: Exports fob	495.7	...	...	...	...	...	...	Biens : exportations, fab
Goods: Imports fob	-536.5	...	...	...	...	...	...	Biens : importations, fab
Serv. & Income: Credit	145.7	...	...	...	...	...	...	Serv. & revenu : crédit
Serv. & Income: Debit	-301.7	...	...	...	...	...	...	Serv & revenu : débit
Current Trans.,nie: Credit	67.4	...	...	...	...	...	...	Transf. cour.,nia : crédit
Current Transfers: Debit	-5.3	...	...	...	...	...	...	Transf. courants : débit
Capital Acct.,nie: Credit	12.5	...	...	...	...	...	...	Compte de cap.,nia : crédit
Capital Account: Debit	-3.0	...	...	...	...	...	...	Compte de capital : débit
Financial Account, nie	71.1	...	...	...	...	...	...	Compte d'op. fin., nia
Net Errors and Omissions	11.2	...	...	...	...	...	...	Erreurs et omissions nettes
Reserves & Related Items	43.0	...	...	...	...	...	...	Rés. et postes appareutés
Haiti								**Haïti**
Goods: Exports fob	88.3	82.5	205.4	299.3	...	...	...	Biens : exportations, fab
Goods: Imports fob	-517.2	-498.6	-559.6	-640.7	...	...	...	Biens : importations, fab
Serv. & Income: Credit	0.0	0.0	0.0	0.0	...	...	...	Serv. & revenu : crédit
Serv. & Income: Debit	-315.2	-293.2	-345.1	-392.3	...	...	...	Serv & revenu : débit
Current Trans.,nie: Credit	552.9	462.5	477.9	515.6	...	...	...	Transf. cour.,nia : crédit
Current Transfers: Debit	0.0	0.0	0.0	0.0	...	...	...	Transf. courants : débit
Capital Account: Debit	0.0	0.0	0.0	0.0	...	...	...	Compte de capital : débit
Financial Account, nie	99.2	67.9	61.5	193.1	...	...	...	Compte d'op. fin., nia
Net Errors and Omissions	125.0	19.4	16.0	-120.5	...	...	...	Erreurs et omissions nettes
Reserves & Related Items	-137.1	50.4	-29.8	-34.5	...	...	...	Rés. et postes appareutés
Honduras								**Honduras**
Goods: Exports fob	1 377.2	1 638.4	1 856.5	2 047.9	1 756.3	2 001.2	1 930.9	Biens : exportations, fab
Goods: Imports fob	-1 518.6	-1 925.8	-2 150.4	-2 370.5	-2 509.6	-2 669.6	-2 807.4	Biens : importations, fab
Serv. & Income: Credit	289.9	344.5	404.9	436.6	554.6	588.9	568.8	Serv. & revenu : crédit
Serv. & Income: Debit	-591.9	-619.8	-642.7	-710.4	-738.1	-879.7	-888.6	Serv & revenu : débit
Current Trans.,nie: Credit	243.7	271.7	306.8	241.7	354.6	447.4	573.7	Transf. cour.,nia : crédit
Current Transfers: Debit	-1.2	-44.4	-47.3	-40.1	-42.4	-44.9	-47.2	Transf. courants : débit
Capital Acct.,nie: Credit	0.0	29.2	15.3	29.4	110.9	98.9	95.0	Compte de cap.,nia : crédit
Capital Account: Debit	0.0	-0.7	-0.7	0.0	0.0	0.0	0.0	Compte de capital : débit
Financial Account, nie	114.6	70.2	243.3	113.9	203.4	-29.5	154.9	Compte d'op. fin., nia
Net Errors and Omissions	45.0	157.9	196.5	96.1	122.0	129.9	87.7	Erreurs et omissions nettes
Reserves & Related Items	41.3	78.8	-182.2	155.4	188.3	357.4	332.2	Rés. et postes appareutés
Hungary								**Hongrie**
Goods: Exports fob	12 864.1	14 183.8	19 639.9	20 746.6	21 848.1	25 746.7	28 071.2	Biens : exportations, fab
Goods: Imports fob	-15 297.2	-16 835.5	-21 601.7	-23 100.9	-24 036.8	-27 506.5	-30 088.7	Biens : importations, fab
Serv. & Income: Credit	5 980.1	7 181.8	7 115.2	7 032.2	6 423.8	7 192.8	8 818.7	Serv. & revenu : crédit
Serv. & Income: Debit	-6 217.6	-6 164.2	-6 273.7	-7 130.5	-6 680.8	-6 992.3	-8 143.3	Serv & revenu : débit
Current Trans.,nie: Credit	363.6	159.8	334.9	379.4	582.0	520.1	589.3	Transf. cour.,nia : crédit
Current Transfers: Debit	-222.5	-214.5	-196.6	-230.9	-242.7	-288.9	-343.8	Transf. courants : débit
Capital Acct.,nie: Credit	79.5	266.2	266.5	408.0	509.0	458.2	417.5	Compte de cap.,nia : crédit
Capital Account: Debit	-20.5	-110.3	-149.4	-219.3	-479.5	-188.0	-100.6	Compte de capital : débit
Financial Account, nie	7 080.3	-686.7	658.4	3 017.5	4 693.5	2 219.3	617.3	Compte d'op. fin., nia
Net Errors and Omissions	789.1	975.6	31.7	48.6	-281.5	-109.2	78.5	Erreurs et omissions nettes
Reserves & Related Items	-5 399.0	1 244.0	174.9	-950.7	-2 335.0	-1 052.2	83.9	Rés. et postes appareutés
Iceland								**Islande**
Goods: Exports fob	1 804.0	1 890.0	1 855.0	1 927.0	2 009.0	1 901.9	...	Biens : exportations, fab
Goods: Imports fob	-1 598.0	-1 871.0	-1 850.0	-2 279.0	-2 316.9	-2 376.0	...	Biens : importations, fab

78

Summary of balance of payments
Millions of US dollars *[cont.]*

Résumé des balances des paiements
Millions de dollars des E.-U. *[suite]*

Country or area	1995	1996	1997	1998	1999	2000	2001	Pays ou zone
Serv. & Income: Credit	780.0	881.0	948.0	1 070.0	1 060.5	1 202.6	...	Serv. & revenu : crédit
Serv. & Income: Debit	-927.0	-1 011.0	-1 073.0	-1 262.0	-1 333.0	-1 567.2	...	Serv & revenu : débit
Current Trans.,nie: Credit	15.0	10.0	17.0	4.0	4.8	6.1	...	Transf. cour.,nia : crédit
Current Transfers: Debit	-20.0	-16.0	-22.0	-20.0	-14.9	-15.6	...	Transf. courants : débit
Capital Acct.,nie: Credit	13.0	10.0	11.0	9.0	17.3	17.5	...	Compte de cap.,nia : crédit
Capital Account: Debit	-16.0	-11.0	-10.0	-14.0	-18.1	-20.7	...	Compte de capital : débit
Financial Account, nie	-17.0	303.0	195.0	679.0	907.5	853.3	...	Compte d'op. fin., nia
Net Errors and Omissions	-30.1	-32.1	-115.0	-82.0	-230.6	-70.6	...	Erreurs et omissions nettes
Reserves & Related Items	-3.9	-152.9	44.0	-32.0	-85.6	68.7	...	Rés. et postes appareutés
India								**Inde**
Goods: Exports fob	31 238.5	33 737.3	35 702.1	34 075.7	36 877.3	43 131.7	...	Biens : exportations, fab
Goods: Imports fob	-37 957.3	-43 789.0	-45 730.1	-44 828.0	-45 556.2	-55 324.6	...	Biens : importations, fab
Serv. & Income: Credit	8 260.3	8 649.4	10 594.3	13 497.2	16 428.5	20 610.7	...	Serv. & revenu : crédit
Serv. & Income: Debit	-15 487.0	-15 837.6	-17 444.4	-19 982.5	-22 900.6	-26 068.4	...	Serv & revenu : débit
Current Trans.,nie: Credit	8 409.6	11 349.5	13 975.4	10 401.8	11 957.9	13 503.6	...	Transf. cour.,nia : crédit
Current Transfers: Debit	-27.3	-65.8	-62.4	-67.4	-34.9	-51.3	...	Transf. courants : débit
Capital Acct.,nie: Credit	0.0	0.0	0.0	0.0	0.0	0.0	...	Compte de cap.,nia : crédit
Capital Account: Debit	0.0	0.0	0.0	0.0	0.0	0.0	...	Compte de capital : débit
Financial Account, nie	3 860.9	11 847.8	9 634.7	8 583.9	9 578.6	9 615.7	...	Compte d'op. fin., nia
Net Errors and Omissions	969.7	-1 934.1	-1 348.4	1 389.9	313.2	669.5	...	Erreurs et omissions nettes
Reserves & Related Items	732.6	-3 957.6	-5 321.1	-3 070.7	-6 663.7	-6 086.9	...	Rés. et postes appareutés
Indonesia								**Indonésie**
Goods: Exports fob	47 454.0	50 188.0	56 298.0	50 371.0	51 242.0	65 406.0	57 364.0	Biens : exportations, fab
Goods: Imports fob	-40 921.0	-44 240.0	-46 223.0	-31 942.0	-30 598.0	-40 366.0	-34 669.0	Biens : importations, fab
Serv. & Income: Credit	6 775.0	7 809.0	8 796.0	6 389.0	6 490.0	7 669.0	7 504.0	Serv. & revenu : crédit
Serv. & Income: Debit	-20 720.0	-22 357.0	-24 794.0	-22 060.0	-23 263.0	-26 540.0	-24 820.0	Serv & revenu : débit
Current Trans.,nie: Credit	981.0	937.0	1 034.0	1 338.0	1 914.0	1 816.0	1 520.0	Transf. cour.,nia : crédit
Current Transfers: Debit	0.0	0.0	0.0	0.0	0.0	0.0	0.0	Transf. courants : débit
Capital Acct.,nie: Credit	0.0	0.0	0.0	0.0	0.0	0.0	0.0	Compte de cap.,nia : crédit
Capital Account: Debit	0.0	0.0	0.0	0.0	0.0	0.0	0.0	Compte de capital : débit
Financial Account, nie	10 259.0	10 847.0	-603.0	-9 638.0	-5 941.0	-7 896.0	-7 616.0	Compte d'op. fin., nia
Net Errors and Omissions	-2 254.6	1 318.7	-2 645.4	1 849.5	2 127.5	3 637.1	702.2	Erreurs et omissions nettes
Reserves & Related Items	-1 573.4	-4 502.7	8 137.4	3 692.5	-1 971.5	-3 726.1	14.8	Rés. et postes appareutés
Iran (Islamic Rep. of)								**Iran (Rép. islamique d')**
Goods: Exports fob	18 360.0	22 391.0	18 381.0	13 118.0	21 030.0	28 345.0	...	Biens : exportations, fab
Goods: Imports fob	-12 774.0	-14 989.0	-14 123.0	-14 286.0	-13 433.0	-15 207.0	...	Biens : importations, fab
Serv. & Income: Credit	909.0	1 348.0	1 658.0	2 023.0	1 397.0	1 786.0	...	Serv. & revenu : crédit
Serv. & Income: Debit	-3 133.0	-3 981.0	-4 096.0	-3 491.0	-2 930.0	-2 900.0	...	Serv & revenu : débit
Current Trans.,nie: Credit	0.0	471.0	400.0	500.0	508.0	539.0	...	Transf. cour.,nia : crédit
Current Transfers: Debit	-4.0	-8.0	-7.0	-3.0	17.0	82.0	...	Transf. courants : débit
Capital Acct.,nie: Credit	0.0	0.0	0.0	0.0	0.0	0.0	...	Compte de cap.,nia : crédit
Capital Account: Debit	0.0	0.0	0.0	0.0	0.0	0.0	...	Compte de capital : débit
Financial Account, nie	-774.0	-5 508.0	-4 822.0	2 270.0	-5 894.0	-10 189.0	...	Compte d'op. fin., nia
Net Errors and Omissions	201.8	2 717.3	-1 088.2	-1 121.7	-243.5	-1 372.5	...	Erreurs et omissions nettes
Reserves & Related Items	-2 785.8	-2 441.3	3 697.2	990.7	-451.5	-1 083.5	...	Rés. et postes appareutés
Ireland								**Irlande**
Goods: Exports fob	44 422.5	49 183.9	55 292.7	78 562.0	68 539.8	73 432.9	78 371.5	Biens : exportations, fab
Goods: Imports fob	-30 865.9	-33 429.7	-36 667.7	-53 172.1	-44 283.6	-48 016.9	-48 368.5	Biens : importations, fab
Serv. & Income: Credit	10 126.6	11 325.4	13 538.9	42 165.6	39 964.6	46 760.8	48 891.9	Serv. & revenu : crédit
Serv. & Income: Debit	-23 738.1	-27 220.2	-32 254.0	-68 425.3	-65 120.1	-73 719.3	-80 414.5	Serv & revenu : débit
Current Trans.,nie: Credit	3 009.0	3 538.2	3 083.4	7 428.5	5 308.1	4 303.7	4 294.5	Transf. cour.,nia : crédit
Current Transfers: Debit	-1 233.1	-1 349.0	-1 127.7	-5 542.6	-4 054.9	-3 354.6	-3 817.6	Transf. courants : débit
Capital Acct.,nie: Credit	913.6	880.8	961.7	1 326.7	674.4	1 167.1	667.1	Compte de cap.,nia : crédit
Capital Account: Debit	-96.2	-96.0	-91.0	-108.3	-81.0	-70.2	-68.9	Compte de capital : débit
Financial Account, nie	-33.0	-2 779.7	-7 484.3	4 686.1	-3 892.6	8 901.2	36.5	Compte d'op. fin., nia
Net Errors and Omissions	-166.6	-106.0	3 639.4	-3 708.0	971.8	-9 283.6	803.1	Erreurs et omissions nettes
Reserves & Related Items	-2 338.8	52.3	1 108.7	-3 212.4	1 973.5	-121.2	-395.2	Rés. et postes appareutés
Israel								**Israël**
Goods: Exports fob	19 662.5	21 332.6	22 698.1	22 974.2	25 576.5	30 947.1	27 678.4	Biens : exportations, fab
Goods: Imports fob	-26 889.6	-28 468.7	-27 875.4	-26 241.0	-30 040.8	-34 035.8	-30 942.2	Biens : importations, fab
Serv. & Income: Credit	9 515.9	9 876.6	10 624.2	12 201.8	13 999.6	18 534.2	15 535.3	Serv. & revenu : crédit
Serv. & Income: Debit	-12 934.0	-14 375.4	-15 341.0	-16 339.8	-19 127.7	-23 888.4	-20 522.5	Serv & revenu : débit

78

Summary of balance of payments
Millions of US dollars *[cont.]*

Résumé des balances des paiements
Millions de dollars des E.-U. *[suite]*

Country or area	1995	1996	1997	1998	1999	2000	2001	Pays ou zone
Current Trans.,nie: Credit	5 941.1	6 441.4	6 373.6	6 686.1	7 125.0	7 483.4	7 530.7	Transf. cour.,nia : crédit
Current Transfers: Debit	-267.9	-304.3	-324.6	-606.4	-809.4	-1 014.5	-1 132.0	Transf. courants : débit
Capital Acct.,nie: Credit	809.2	773.7	723.1	577.0	568.7	455.2	681.2	*Compte de cap.,nia : crédit*
Capital Account: Debit	0.0	0.0	0.0	0.0	0.0	0.0	0.0	Compte de capital : débit
Financial Account, nie	4 216.8	4 534.6	7 238.4	-649.9	2 040.1	2 981.8	-109.6	Compte d'op. fin., nia
Net Errors and Omissions	425.7	1 395.6	2 960.1	1 305.0	677.2	-1 591.5	1 476.7	Erreurs et omissions nettes
Reserves & Related Items	-479.7	-1 206.1	-7 076.5	93.0	-9.2	128.4	-196.0	Rés. et postes appareutés
Italy								**Italie**
Goods: Exports fob	233 998.0	252 039.0	240 404.0	242 572.0	235 856.0	240 473.0	242 430.0	Biens : exportations, fab
Goods: Imports fob	-195269.0	-197921.0	-200527.0	-206941.0	-212420.0	-230925.0	-226568.0	Biens : importations, fab
Serv. & Income: Credit	95 787.2	105 801.3	112 725.1	118 867.5	105 148.5	95 226.8	96 196.8	Serv. & revenu : crédit
Serv. & Income: Debit	-104861.3	-112706.0	-116163.1	-127015.2	-115118.3	-106281.1	-106274.0	Serv & revenu : débit
Current Trans.,nie: Credit	14 287.1	14 320.3	15 551.5	14 402.3	16 776.2	15 797.4	16 176.5	Transf. cour.,nia : crédit
Current Transfers: Debit	-18 866.1	-21 534.8	-19 587.9	-21 887.4	-22 132.3	-20 073.0	-22 124.6	*Transf. courants : débit*
Capital Acct.,nie: Credit	2 796.6	1 414.0	4 582.4	3 359.4	4 571.9	4 172.1	2 098.0	Compte de cap.,nia : crédit
Capital Account: Debit	-1 125.5	-1 348.0	-1 147.9	-1 001.5	-1 608.0	-1 293.0	-1 251.8	Compte de capital : débit
Financial Account, nie	-2 889.1	-7 982.2	-6 878.3	-18 074.0	-17 414.7	7 504.3	-3 211.3	Compte d'op. fin., nia
Net Errors and Omissions	-21 054.2	-20 176.2	-15 809.8	-25 753.7	-1 710.8	-1 355.2	1 940.4	Erreurs et omissions nettes
Reserves & Related Items	-2 803.6	-11 906.7	-13 149.7	21 471.9	8 051.1	-3 247.0	587.9	Rés. et postes appareutés
Jamaica								**Jamaïque**
Goods: Exports fob	1 796.0	1 721.0	1 700.3	1 613.4	1 499.1	1 562.8	1 454.4	Biens : exportations, fab
Goods: Imports fob	-2 625.3	-2 715.2	-2 832.6	-2 743.9	-2 685.6	-3 004.3	-3 072.6	Biens : importations, fab
Serv. & Income: Credit	1 744.5	1 743.7	1 846.2	1 926.7	2 144.2	2 218.8	2 118.9	Serv. & revenu : crédit
Serv. & Income: Debit	-1 621.1	-1 515.7	-1 670.9	-1 758.0	-1 821.3	-1 985.1	-2 175.2	Serv & revenu : débit
Current Trans.,nie: Credit	669.6	709.3	705.7	733.5	757.9	969.4	1 062.7	Transf. cour.,nia : crédit
Current Transfers: Debit	-62.6	-85.7	-80.9	-99.6	-110.6	-148.6	-176.6	Transf. courants : débit
Capital Acct.,nie: Credit	34.5	42.5	21.7	20.3	19.1	29.6	15.2	Compte de cap.,nia : crédit
Capital Account: Debit	-24.0	-25.9	-33.3	-29.0	-30.0	-27.4	-37.5	Compte de capital : débit
Financial Account, nie	108.3	388.6	163.5	337.3	94.8	854.0	1 660.5	Compte d'op. fin., nia
Net Errors and Omissions	7.1	8.8	9.9	43.2	-4.0	49.2	15.2	Erreurs et omissions nettes
Reserves & Related Items	-27.0	-271.4	170.4	-43.9	136.4	-518.4	-865.0	Rés. et postes appareutés
Japan								**Japon**
Goods: Exports fob	428 717.0	400 287.0	409 240.0	374 044.0	403 694.0	459 513.0	383 592.0	Biens : exportations, fab
Goods: Imports fob	-296931.0	-316702.0	-307640.0	-251655.0	-280369.0	-342797.0	-313378.0	Biens : importations, fab
Serv. & Income: Credit	257 720.0	180 150.2	181 128.5	162 747.0	153 046.8	166 437.3	167 610.4	Serv. & revenu : crédit
Serv. & Income: Debit	-270786.0	-188936.3	-177081.0	-157544.9	-149628.7	-153662.7	-142122.7	Serv & revenu : débit
Current Trans.,nie: Credit	1 983.2	6 023.4	6 010.6	5 531.1	6 211.5	7 380.4	6 151.7	Transf. cour.,nia : crédit
Current Transfers: Debit	-9 659.3	-15 030.2	-14 844.7	-14 373.3	-18 350.3	-17 211.1	-14 056.0	Transf. courants : débit
Capital Acct.,nie: Credit	6.2	1 224.8	1 516.7	1 568.7	745.9	780.9	994.7	Compte de cap.,nia : crédit
Capital Account: Debit	-2 235.2	-4 512.4	-5 566.0	-16 022.9	-17 213.4	-10 039.5	-3 863.5	Compte de capital : débit
Financial Account, nie	-63 979.5	-28 016.8	-120509.0	-114816.0	-38 845.4	-78 312.7	-48 160.0	Compte d'op. fin., nia
Net Errors and Omissions	13 775.6	652.7	34 311.3	4 357.0	16 965.2	16 865.9	3 718.7	Erreurs et omissions nettes
Reserves & Related Items	-58 611.3	-35 140.5	-6 567.2	6 164.4	-76 256.3	-48 955.0	-40 487.0	Rés. et postes appareutés
Jordan								**Jordanie**
Goods: Exports fob	1 769.6	1 816.9	1 835.5	1 802.4	1 831.9	1 899.3	2 294.4	Biens : exportations, fab
Goods: Imports fob	-3 287.8	-3 818.1	-3 648.5	-3 404.0	-3 292.0	-4 073.6	-4 301.4	Biens : importations, fab
Serv. & Income: Credit	1 824.9	1 958.0	1 985.0	2 132.0	2 169.3	2 306.8	2 130.2	Serv. & revenu : crédit
Serv. & Income: Debit	-2 009.5	-2 010.4	-1 994.2	-2 228.8	-2 177.7	-2 258.0	-2 186.4	Serv & revenu : débit
Current Trans.,nie: Credit	1 591.8	1 970.2	2 096.1	1 984.3	2 154.9	2 461.5	2 361.8	Transf. cour.,nia : crédit
Current Transfers: Debit	-147.6	-138.5	-244.6	-271.9	-281.4	-277.4	-302.8	Transf. courants : débit
Capital Acct.,nie: Credit	197.2	157.7	163.8	81.1	90.3	64.9	21.6	Compte de cap.,nia : crédit
Capital Account: Debit	0.0	0.0	0.0	0.0	0.0	0.0	0.0	Compte de capital : débit
Financial Account, nie	230.0	233.9	242.3	-177.3	725.1	1 387.6	527.8	Compte d'op. fin., nia
Net Errors and Omissions	-339.9	-357.9	-160.8	-454.0	28.7	315.6	80.0	Erreurs et omissions nettes
Reserves & Related Items	171.3	188.2	-274.6	536.1	-1 249.0	-1 826.6	-625.3	Rés. et postes appareutés
Kazakhstan								**Kazakhstan**
Goods: Exports fob	5 440.0	6 291.6	6 899.3	5 870.5	5 988.7	9 288.1	9 024.8	Biens : exportations, fab
Goods: Imports fob	-5 325.9	-6 626.7	-7 175.7	-6 671.7	-5 645.0	-6 848.2	-7 849.8	Biens : importations, fab
Serv. & Income: Credit	579.7	731.1	915.7	999.8	1 041.1	1 272.1	1 512.8	Serv. & revenu : crédit
Serv. & Income: Debit	-965.9	-1 205.4	-1 513.2	-1 545.9	-1 712.5	-3 285.5	-4 157.8	Serv & revenu : débit
Current Trans.,nie: Credit	79.9	83.4	104.7	141.4	174.7	352.2	392.7	Transf. cour.,nia : crédit
Current Transfers: Debit	-20.9	-25.0	-30.1	-19.0	-18.0	-103.2	-163.0	Transf. courants : débit

78

Summary of balance of payments
Millions of US dollars *[cont.]*
Résumé des balances des paiements
Millions de dollars des E.-U. *[suite]*

Country or area	1995	1996	1997	1998	1999	2000	2001	Pays ou zone
Capital Acct.,nie: Credit	116.1	87.9	58.3	65.9	61.1	66.3	89.2	Compte de cap.,nia : crédit
Capital Account: Debit	-496.7	-403.4	-498.1	-435.0	-295.1	-356.9	-286.5	Compte de capital : débit
Financial Account, nie	1 162.5	2 005.1	2 901.6	2 229.1	1 299.2	1 308.1	2 717.4	*Compte d'op. fin., nia*
Net Errors and Omissions	-270.1	-780.0	-1 114.1	-1 078.4	-641.6	-1 122.7	-894.9	Erreurs et omissions nettes
Reserves & Related Items	-298.7	-158.6	-548.4	443.3	-252.6	-570.3	-384.9	Rés. et postes appareutés
Kenya								**Kenya**
Goods: Exports fob	1 923.8	2 083.3	2 062.6	2 017.0	1 756.7	1 782.2	1 894.0	Biens : exportations, fab
Goods: Imports fob	-2 673.9	-2 598.2	-2 948.4	-3 028.7	-2 731.8	-3 044.0	-3 176.1	Biens : importations, fab
Serv. & Income: Credit	1 050.1	957.6	937.4	871.7	966.2	1 038.3	1 130.0	Serv. & revenu : crédit
Serv. & Income: Debit	-1 218.6	-1 096.2	-1 080.9	-909.4	-761.3	-902.6	-1 015.7	Serv & revenu : débit
Current Trans.,nie: Credit	563.6	585.4	572.5	578.6	685.3	926.6	850.0	Transf. cour.,nia : crédit
Current Transfers: Debit	-45.5	-5.4	0.0	-4.5	-4.7	-4.2	0.0	Transf. courants : débit
Capital Acct.,nie: Credit	0.0	0.0	76.8	84.3	55.4	49.6	69.0	Compte de cap.,nia : crédit
Capital Account: Debit	-0.4	-0.4	0.0	0.0	0.0	0.0	0.0	Compte de capital : débit
Financial Account, nie	247.9	589.1	362.6	562.1	165.7	157.4	84.3	Compte d'op. fin., nia
Net Errors and Omissions	11.4	-128.2	32.8	-88.6	-165.5	-10.0	117.0	Erreurs et omissions nettes
Reserves & Related Items	141.6	-387.0	-15.5	-82.6	34.0	6.8	47.5	Rés. et postes appareutés
Korea, Republic of								**Corée, République de**
Goods: Exports fob	124 632.0	129 968.0	138 619.0	132 122.0	145 164.0	175 948.0	151 370.0	Biens : exportations, fab
Goods: Imports fob	-129076.0	-144933.0	-141798.0	-90 494.8	-116793.0	-159076.0	-137979.0	Biens : importations, fab
Serv. & Income: Credit	26 313.1	27 078.5	30 179.5	28 239.5	29 773.4	36 909.0	36 642.5	Serv. & revenu : crédit
Serv. & Income: Debit	-30 593.5	-35 073.4	-35 834.6	-32 853.7	-35 583.4	-42 219.5	-41 054.5	Serv & revenu : débit
Current Trans.,nie: Credit	4 104.0	4 279.0	5 287.9	6 736.6	6 421.3	6 500.1	6 548.4	Transf. cour.,nia : crédit
Current Transfers: Debit	-3 885.9	-4 325.1	-4 620.9	-3 384.3	-4 505.5	-5 820.0	-6 911.2	Transf. courants : débit
Capital Acct.,nie: Credit	14.5	18.9	16.6	463.6	95.1	97.8	28.8	Compte de cap.,nia : crédit
Capital Account: Debit	-502.1	-616.5	-624.2	-292.5	-484.4	-713.0	-471.3	Compte de capital : débit
Financial Account, nie	17 273.2	23 924.4	-9 195.0	-8 381.0	12 708.8	12 725.2	2 543.3	Compte d'op. fin., nia
Net Errors and Omissions	-1 239.9	1 094.6	-5 009.6	-6 224.9	-3 536.0	-561.2	2 698.4	Erreurs et omissions nettes
Reserves & Related Items	-7 039.2	-1 415.7	22 979.4	-25 930.1	-33 260.2	-23 790.0	-13 416.0	Rés. et postes appareutés
Kuwait								**Koweït**
Goods: Exports fob	12 833.1	14 946.1	14 280.6	9 617.5	12 276.0	19 478.3	16 166.6	Biens : exportations, fab
Goods: Imports fob	-7 254.2	-7 949.0	-7 747.2	-7 714.7	-6 708.0	-6 451.5	-6 929.0	Biens : importations, fab
Serv. & Income: Credit	7 525.6	7 929.0	9 503.9	8 925.2	7 654.0	9 137.7	7 268.1	Serv. & revenu : crédit
Serv. & Income: Debit	-6 624.3	-6 329.1	-6 596.4	-6 838.3	-6 156.1	-5 539.0	-5 863.1	Serv & revenu : débit
Current Trans.,nie: Credit	53.6	53.4	79.1	98.4	98.5	84.8	52.2	Transf. cour.,nia : crédit
Current Transfers: Debit	-1 517.9	-1 543.0	-1 585.6	-1 873.6	-2 102.4	-2 040.7	-2 132.5	Transf. courants : débit
Capital Acct.,nie: Credit	0.0	3.3	115.4	288.8	716.1	2 236.3	2 950.9	Compte de cap.,nia : crédit
Capital Account: Debit	-194.3	-207.1	-211.0	-210.0	-13.1	-19.6	-19.6	Compte de capital : débit
Financial Account, nie	157.5	-7 631.7	-6 210.7	-2 920.4	-5 706.0	-13 307.2	-6 035.6	Compte d'op. fin., nia
Net Errors and Omissions	-5 120.3	703.5	-1 622.1	885.1	859.0	-1 311.0	-2 553.3	Erreurs et omissions nettes
Reserves & Related Items	141.2	24.6	-6.1	-258.0	-918.1	-2 268.2	-2 904.8	Rés. et postes appareutés
Kyrgyzstan								**Kirghizistan**
Goods: Exports fob	408.9	531.2	630.8	535.1	462.6	510.9	480.3	Biens : exportations, fab
Goods: Imports fob	-531.0	-782.9	-646.1	-755.7	-551.1	-506.4	-441.2	Biens : importations, fab
Serv. & Income: Credit	42.9	35.9	51.8	75.4	75.9	78.8	92.4	Serv. & revenu : crédit
Serv. & Income: Debit	-234.3	-292.9	-242.6	-267.4	-239.8	-249.7	-202.5	Serv & revenu : débit
Current Trans.,nie: Credit	80.4	85.9	69.8	2.2	1.2	43.0	21.6	Transf. cour.,nia : crédit
Current Transfers: Debit	-1.7	-1.9	-2.2	-2.0	-1.2	-2.4	-3.2	Transf. courants : débit
Capital Acct.,nie: Credit	2.2	9.0	6.2	3.9	14.6	22.8	9.2	Compte de cap.,nia : crédit
Capital Account: Debit	-31.3	-25.0	-14.6	-12.0	-29.8	-34.2	-41.2	Compte de capital : débit
Financial Account, nie	259.9	362.5	250.7	284.6	220.8	56.9	31.4	Compte d'op. fin., nia
Net Errors and Omissions	-76.9	58.4	-57.7	63.4	-3.0	9.8	21.3	Erreurs et omissions nettes
Reserves & Related Items	80.7	19.8	-46.2	72.7	49.7	70.4	32.0	Rés. et postes appareutés
Lao People's Dem. Rep.								**Rép. dém. pop. lao**
Goods: Exports fob	310.9	322.8	318.3	342.1	338.2	330.3	311.1	Biens : exportations, fab
Goods: Imports fob	-626.8	-643.7	-601.3	-506.8	-527.7	-535.3	-527.9	Biens : importations, fab
Serv. & Income: Credit	104.2	113.6	116.9	151.9	140.5	183.0	171.9	Serv. & revenu : crédit
Serv. & Income: Debit	-134.5	-139.5	-139.4	-137.3	-101.7	-102.7	-71.3	Serv & revenu : débit
Current Trans.,nie: Credit	0.0	0.0	0.0	0.0	80.2	116.3	33.7	*Transf. cour.,nia : crédit*
Current Transfers: Debit	0.0	0.0	0.0	0.0	-50.6	0.0	0.0	Transf. courants : débit
Capital Acct.,nie: Credit	21.7	44.9	40.3	49.4	0.0	0.0	0.0	Compte de cap.,nia : crédit
Capital Account: Debit	-8.5	-9.9	-6.9	-6.3	0.0	0.0	0.0	Compte de capital : débit

78

Summary of balance of payments
Millions of US dollars *[cont.]*

Résumé des balances des paiements
Millions de dollars des E.-U. *[suite]*

Country or area	1995	1996	1997	1998	1999	2000	2001	Pays ou zone
Financial Account, nie	90.0	135.7	3.5	-43.4	-46.9	126.1	135.7	Compte d'op. fin., nia
Net Errors and Omissions	92.4	17.7	-100.5	-103.8	-165.1	-74.2	-57.2	Erreurs et omissions nettes
Reserves & Related Items	150.6	158.4	369.1	254.2	333.1	-43.4	3.9	Rés. et postes appareutés
Latvia								**Lettonie**
Goods: Exports fob	1 367.6	1 487.6	1 838.1	2 011.2	1 889.1	2 058.1	2 215.9	Biens : exportations, fab
Goods: Imports fob	-1 947.2	-2 285.9	-2 686.0	-3 141.4	-2 916.1	-3 116.3	-3 566.4	Biens : importations, fab
Serv. & Income: Credit	791.2	1 266.0	1 210.0	1 315.8	1 182.0	1 427.4	1 464.9	Serv. & revenu : crédit
Serv. & Income: Debit	-298.5	-841.0	-784.5	-959.6	-902.1	-961.0	-926.9	Serv & revenu : débit
Current Trans.,nie: Credit	75.4	98.1	90.9	137.3	113.8	202.8	220.9	Transf. cour.,nia : crédit
Current Transfers: Debit	-4.6	-4.6	-13.6	-12.8	-21.0	-105.4	-142.7	Transf. courants : débit
Capital Acct.,nie: Credit	0.0	0.0	13.7	14.1	12.6	38.5	55.8	Compte de cap.,nia : crédit
Capital Account: Debit	0.0	0.0	0.0	0.0	0.0	-8.9	-12.0	Compte de capital : débit
Financial Account, nie	635.6	537.1	346.9	601.1	768.4	518.9	956.0	Compte d'op. fin., nia
Net Errors and Omissions	-652.6	-46.3	86.5	96.9	38.3	-26.3	48.9	Erreurs et omissions nettes
Reserves & Related Items	33.2	-211.1	-102.2	-62.6	-165.0	-27.8	-314.3	Rés. et postes appareutés
Lesotho								**Lesotho**
Goods: Exports fob	160.0	186.9	196.1	193.4	172.5	211.1	278.6	Biens : exportations, fab
Goods: Imports fob	-985.2	-998.6	-1 024.4	-866.0	-779.2	-727.6	-678.6	Biens : importations, fab
Serv. & Income: Credit	510.6	495.6	534.3	411.2	368.7	331.4	275.8	Serv. & revenu : crédit
Serv. & Income: Debit	-218.5	-175.4	-177.6	-175.8	-130.7	-105.2	-105.5	Serv & revenu : débit
Current Trans.,nie: Credit	211.3	190.2	202.9	158.0	149.4	139.8	137.2	Transf. cour.,nia : crédit
Current Transfers: Debit	-1.2	-1.1	-0.5	-1.2	-1.6	-1.0	-2.5	Transf. courants : débit
Capital Acct.,nie: Credit	43.7	45.5	44.5	22.9	15.2	22.0	16.8	Compte de cap.,nia : crédit
Capital Account: Debit	0.0	0.0	0.0	0.0	0.0	0.0	0.0	Compte de capital : débit
Financial Account, nie	349.1	350.6	323.7	316.1	135.8	85.2	89.1	Compte d'op. fin., nia
Net Errors and Omissions	28.1	23.3	42.1	56.8	29.0	62.1	154.7	Erreurs et omissions nettes
Reserves & Related Items	-97.8	-116.9	-141.0	-115.6	40.8	-17.8	-165.7	Rés. et postes appareutés
Libyan Arab Jamah.								**Jamah. arabe libyenne**
Goods: Exports fob	9 037.9	9 577.9	9 876.1	6 328.0	6 757.8	...	...	Biens : exportations, fab
Goods: Imports fob	-6 257.1	-7 059.2	-7 159.8	-5 857.1	-3 995.7	...	...	Biens : importations, fab
Serv. & Income: Credit	563.0	603.9	673.3	680.0	561.9	...	...	Serv. & revenu : crédit
Serv. & Income: Debit	-1 080.9	-1 306.8	-1 274.2	-1 274.5	-1 136.7	...	...	Serv & revenu : débit
Current Trans.,nie: Credit	4.9	3.0	3.9	5.1	6.4	...	...	Transf. cour.,nia : crédit
Current Transfers: Debit	-270.1	-342.0	-244.0	-271.9	-209.9	...	...	Transf. courants : débit
Capital Acct.,nie: Credit	0.0	0.0	0.0	0.0	0.0	...	...	Compte de cap.,nia : crédit
Capital Account: Debit	0.0	0.0	0.0	0.0	0.0	...	...	Compte de capital : débit
Financial Account, nie	-250.1	224.2	-884.0	-554.7	-970.8	...	...	Compte d'op. fin., nia
Net Errors and Omissions	299.1	-234.1	877.7	432.1	-371.8	...	...	Erreurs et omissions nettes
Reserves & Related Items	-2 046.7	-1 467.0	-1 868.9	513.2	-641.3	...	...	Rés. et postes appareutés
Lithuania								**Lituanie**
Goods: Exports fob	2 706.1	3 413.2	4 192.4	3 961.6	3 146.7	4 050.4	4 889.0	Biens : exportations, fab
Goods: Imports fob	-3 404.0	-4 309.3	-5 339.9	-5 479.9	-4 551.3	-5 154.1	-5 997.0	Biens : importations, fab
Serv. & Income: Credit	536.1	849.5	1 112.3	1 233.5	1 206.4	1 244.3	1 362.7	Serv. & revenu : crédit
Serv. & Income: Debit	-561.8	-819.7	-1 176.1	-1 248.4	-1 158.6	-1 058.0	-1 085.8	Serv & revenu : débit
Current Trans.,nie: Credit	112.3	149.4	237.0	240.4	167.4	246.8	262.0	Transf. cour.,nia : crédit
Current Transfers: Debit	-3.0	-5.6	-7.0	-5.4	-4.6	-4.3	-4.5	Transf. courants : débit
Capital Acct.,nie: Credit	3.3	5.5	4.5	0.9	2.7	2.6	1.5	Compte de cap.,nia : crédit
Capital Account: Debit	-42.3	0.0	-0.4	-2.6	-6.0	-0.4	-0.1	Compte de capital : débit
Financial Account, nie	534.4	645.6	1 005.6	1 443.9	1 060.7	702.4	777.6	Compte d'op. fin., nia
Net Errors and Omissions	287.2	66.7	195.8	282.9	-42.1	128.3	153.6	Erreurs et omissions nettes
Reserves & Related Items	-168.3	4.8	-224.2	-426.8	178.7	-158.0	-359.0	Rés. et postes appareutés
Luxembourg								**Luxembourg**
Goods: Exports fob	8 578.5	7 944.4	7 744.7	8 557.1	8 565.1	8 635.4	8 995.7	Biens : exportations, fab
Goods: Imports fob	-10 268.5	-9 871.9	-9 769.6	-10 881.4	-11 151.3	-11 055.6	-11 394.8	Biens : importations, fab
Serv. & Income: Credit	59 417.3	52 405.1	51 021.8	60 897.8	65 065.6	70 701.0	72 246.9	Serv. & revenu : crédit
Serv. & Income: Debit	-54 728.2	-47 703.2	-46 654.8	-56 524.5	-60 252.7	-65 258.4	-67 649.0	Serv & revenu : débit
Current Trans.,nie: Credit	1 791.3	2 186.5	1 984.9	2 185.2	2 281.7	2 750.0	2 268.5	Transf. cour.,nia : crédit
Current Transfers: Debit	-2 364.1	-2 741.3	-2 493.3	-2 608.3	-2 858.7	-3 210.8	-2 793.5	Transf. courants : débit
Madagascar								**Madagascar**
Goods: Exports fob	506.6	509.3	516.1	538.2	584.0	823.7	110.7	Biens : exportations, fab
Goods: Imports fob	-628.1	-629.0	-694.1	-692.7	-742.5	-997.5	-113.9	Biens : importations, fab
Serv. & Income: Credit	249.6	299.5	292.0	315.6	346.7	386.5	44.7	Serv. & revenu : crédit

78
Summary of balance of payments
Millions of US dollars *[cont.]*
Résumé des balances des paiements
Millions de dollars des E.-U. *[suite]*

Country or area	1995	1996	1997	1998	1999	2000	2001	Pays ou zone
Serv. & Income: Debit	-532.7	-542.4	-500.9	-538.6	-519.3	-586.2	-73.6	Serv & revenu : débit
Current Trans.,nie: Credit	141.1	94.4	156.3	109.5	110.9	121.9	13.6	Transf. cour.,nia : crédit
Current Transfers: Debit	-12.4	-22.6	-35.3	-32.7	-31.8	-31.3	-1.8	Transf. courants : débit
Capital Acct.,nie: Credit	45.1	5.1	115.4	102.7	128.8	115.0	13.4	Compte de cap.,nia : crédit
Capital Account: Debit	0.0	0.0	0.0	0.0	0.0	0.0	0.0	Compte de capital : débit
Financial Account, nie	-197.5	133.3	109.7	-76.3	-13.6	-30.7	-16.5	Compte d'op. fin., nia
Net Errors and Omissions	98.5	58.8	24.6	-25.0	32.4	38.6	-30.7	Erreurs et omissions nettes
Reserves & Related Items	330.0	93.7	16.1	299.2	104.3	160.0	54.0	Rés. et postes appareutés
Malaysia								**Malaisie**
Goods: Exports fob	71 767.2	76 985.1	77 538.3	71 882.8	84 096.8	98 429.1	87 980.5	Biens : exportations, fab
Goods: Imports fob	-71 870.6	-73 136.8	-74 028.7	-54 377.8	-61 452.6	-77 602.4	-69 597.4	Biens : importations, fab
Serv. & Income: Credit	14 225.0	17 828.3	18 212.0	13 058.9	13 922.5	15 926.6	16 301.8	Serv. & revenu : crédit
Serv. & Income: Debit	-21 747.7	-24 956.0	-26 147.6	-18 572.7	-22 234.8	-26 341.1	-25 246.3	Serv & revenu : débit
Current Trans.,nie: Credit	700.0	765.9	944.1	727.8	800.8	756.2	536.8	Transf. cour.,nia : crédit
Current Transfers: Debit	-1 717.4	-1 948.4	-2 453.4	-3 190.3	-2 529.1	-2 680.5	-2 688.7	Transf. courants : débit
Capital Acct.,nie: Credit	0.0	0.0	0.0	0.0	0.0	0.0	0.0	Compte de cap.,nia : crédit
Capital Account: Debit	0.0	0.0	0.0	0.0	0.0	0.0	0.0	Compte de capital : débit
Financial Account, nie	7 642.5	9 476.8	2 197.5	-2 549.7	-6 619.4	-6 275.5	-3 894.0	Compte d'op. fin., nia
Net Errors and Omissions	-761.6	-2 501.6	-136.9	3 038.8	-1 272.8	-3 220.9	-2 394.2	Erreurs et omissions nettes
Reserves & Related Items	1 762.7	-2 513.3	3 874.7	-10 017.7	-4 711.9	1 008.8	-1 000.3	Rés. et postes appareutés
Maldives								**Maldives**
Goods: Exports fob	85.0	80.0	93.0	95.6	91.4	108.7	110.2	Biens : exportations, fab
Goods: Imports fob	-235.8	-265.5	-307.0	-311.5	-353.9	-342.0	-348.0	Biens : importations, fab
Serv. & Income: Credit	237.3	294.9	319.6	339.9	351.8	358.8	361.0	Serv. & revenu : crédit
Serv. & Income: Debit	-101.2	-115.6	-129.1	-135.6	-148.2	-150.1	-154.7	Serv & revenu : débit
Current Trans.,nie: Credit	23.0	26.2	17.2	18.9	17.7	17.7	20.1	Transf. cour.,nia : crédit
Current Transfers: Debit	-26.6	-27.3	-27.9	-30.6	-40.5	-46.2	-49.6	Transf. courants : débit
Capital Acct.,nie: Credit	0.0	0.0	0.0	0.0	0.0	0.0	0.0	Compte de cap.,nia : crédit
Capital Account: Debit	0.0	0.0	0.0	0.0	0.0	0.0	0.0	Compte de capital : débit
Financial Account, nie	67.6	52.2	71.0	60.3	76.1	40.0	35.1	Compte d'op. fin., nia
Net Errors and Omissions	-32.2	-16.6	-14.6	-16.9	14.2	8.8	-3.8	Erreurs et omissions nettes
Reserves & Related Items	-17.1	-28.3	-22.2	-20.1	-8.6	4.3	29.7	Rés. et postes appareutés
Mali								**Mali**
Goods: Exports fob	441.8	433.5	561.6	...	...	...	...	Biens : exportations, fab
Goods: Imports fob	-556.8	-551.5	-551.9	...	...	...	...	Biens : importations, fab
Serv. & Income: Credit	95.8	98.5	92.7	...	...	...	...	Serv. & revenu : crédit
Serv. & Income: Debit	-483.5	-449.8	-407.3	...	...	...	...	Serv & revenu : débit
Current Trans.,nie: Credit	266.8	246.1	170.0	...	...	...	...	Transf. cour.,nia : crédit
Current Transfers: Debit	-48.0	-50.0	-43.5	...	...	...	...	Transf. courants : débit
Capital Acct.,nie: Credit	126.2	136.4	108.6	...	...	...	...	Compte de cap.,nia : crédit
Capital Account: Debit	0.0	0.0	0.0	...	...	...	...	Compte de capital : débit
Financial Account, nie	118.6	174.6	52.7	...	...	...	...	Compte d'op. fin., nia
Net Errors and Omissions	-13.0	-8.8	7.9	...	...	...	...	Erreurs et omissions nettes
Reserves & Related Items	52.0	-29.0	9.2	...	...	...	...	Rés. et postes appareutés
Malta								**Malte**
Goods: Exports fob	1 949.4	1 772.8	1 663.2	1 824.3	2 017.0	2 478.3	2 002.8	Biens : exportations, fab
Goods: Imports fob	-2 673.1	-2 536.2	-2 320.7	-2 417.0	-2 588.4	-3 096.2	-2 492.4	Biens : importations, fab
Serv. & Income: Credit	1 335.3	1 380.5	1 471.9	1 692.0	2 453.8	2 004.2	1 922.0	Serv. & revenu : crédit
Serv. & Income: Debit	-998.5	-1 052.1	-1 070.8	-1 378.8	-2 046.3	-1 882.3	-1 612.3	Serv & revenu : débit
Current Trans.,nie: Credit	80.5	87.1	122.4	114.9	120.1	101.7	190.2	Transf. cour.,nia : crédit
Current Transfers: Debit	-54.3	-56.1	-66.9	-56.9	-77.8	-76.1	-182.7	Transf. courants : débit
Capital Acct.,nie: Credit	16.8	64.2	32.9	33.1	31.0	23.8	4.4	Compte de cap.,nia : crédit
Capital Account: Debit	-4.3	-6.1	-24.5	-4.6	-5.5	-5.6	-2.9	Compte de capital : débit
Financial Account, nie	25.0	205.9	107.5	294.8	401.9	157.0	252.0	Compte d'op. fin., nia
Net Errors and Omissions	16.3	55.1	91.8	89.1	-67.3	73.7	174.0	Erreurs et omissions nettes
Reserves & Related Items	307.1	84.9	-6.8	-190.9	-238.4	221.6	-255.1	Rés. et postes appareutés
Mauritania								**Mauritanie**
Goods: Exports fob	476.4	480.0	423.6	358.6	...	...	...	Biens : exportations, fab
Goods: Imports fob	-292.6	-346.1	-316.5	-318.7	...	...	...	Biens : importations, fab
Serv. & Income: Credit	29.2	32.5	36.3	36.4	...	...	...	Serv. & revenu : crédit
Serv. & Income: Debit	-266.5	-277.2	-240.2	-186.6	...	...	...	Serv & revenu : débit
Current Trans.,nie: Credit	94.7	217.5	157.9	198.3	...	...	...	Transf. cour.,nia : crédit

78

Summary of balance of payments
Millions of US dollars *[cont.]*

Résumé des balances des paiements
Millions de dollars des E.-U. *[suite]*

Country or area	1995	1996	1997	1998	1999	2000	2001	Pays ou zone
Current Transfers: Debit	-19.2	-15.5	-13.3	-10.8	...	...	...	Transf. courants : débit
Capital Acct.,nie: Credit	0.0	0.0	0.0	0.0	...	...	...	Compte de cap.,nia : crédit
Capital Account: Debit	0.0	0.0	0.0	0.0	...	...	...	Compte de capital : débit
Financial Account, nie	-10.2	-86.1	-17.3	-25.9	...	...	...	Compte d'op. fin., nia
Net Errors and Omissions	-18.1	-1.0	-3.0	-8.1	...	...	...	Erreurs et omissions nettes
Reserves & Related Items	6.2	-4.2	-27.6	-43.2	...	...	...	Rés. et postes appareutés
Mauritius								**Maurice**
Goods: Exports fob	1 571.7	1 810.6	1 600.1	1 669.3	1 589.2	1 552.2	1 615.4	Biens : exportations, fab
Goods: Imports fob	-1 812.2	-2 136.3	-2 036.1	-1 933.3	-2 107.9	-1 944.4	-1 871.2	Biens : importations, fab
Serv. & Income: Credit	829.9	991.9	940.6	964.8	1 070.7	1 118.8	1 297.2	Serv. & revenu : crédit
Serv. & Income: Debit	-712.6	-748.0	-720.9	-792.4	-786.8	-827.4	-864.2	Serv & revenu : débit
Current Trans.,nie: Credit	146.8	182.8	206.4	186.8	196.4	167.6	195.5	Transf. cour.,nia : crédit
Current Transfers: Debit	-45.4	-67.0	-79.0	-91.8	-92.7	-103.8	-126.0	Transf. courants : débit
Capital Acct.,nie: Credit	0.0	0.0	0.0	0.0	0.0	0.0	0.0	Compte de cap.,nia : crédit
Capital Account: Debit	-1.1	-0.8	-0.5	-0.8	-0.5	-0.6	-1.4	Compte de capital : débit
Financial Account, nie	25.1	91.9	-18.6	-26.0	134.0	118.6	-375.3	Compte d'op. fin., nia
Net Errors and Omissions	106.7	-76.8	73.4	-41.9	187.3	6.6	-15.9	Erreurs et omissions nettes
Reserves & Related Items	-108.8	-48.3	34.6	65.4	-189.7	-87.6	146.0	Rés. et postes appareutés
Mexico								**Mexique**
Goods: Exports fob	79 541.6	96 002.0	110 431.0	117 459.0	136 392.0	166 456.0	158 443.0	Biens : exportations, fab
Goods: Imports fob	-72 453.0	-89 469.0	-109808.0	-125374.0	-141975.0	-174457.0	-168398.0	Biens : importations, fab
Serv. & Income: Credit	13 492.8	14 756.0	15 613.0	16 573.0	16 213.0	19 801.0	17 797.0	Serv. & revenu : crédit
Serv. & Income: Debit	-26 117.7	-28 323.0	-29 152.0	-30 743.0	-30 935.0	-36 536.0	-34 866.0	Serv & revenu : débit
Current Trans.,nie: Credit	3 995.0	4 535.0	5 245.0	6 016.0	6 315.0	7 001.0	9 338.0	Transf. cour.,nia : crédit
Current Transfers: Debit	-35.0	-30.0	-25.0	-28.0	-27.0	-29.0	-22.0	Transf. courants : débit
Capital Acct.,nie: Credit	0.0	0.0	0.0	0.0	0.0	0.0	0.0	Compte de cap.,nia : crédit
Capital Account: Debit	0.0	0.0	0.0	0.0	0.0	0.0	0.0	Compte de capital : débit
Financial Account, nie	-10 487.3	4 248.0	25 745.0	12 194.0	14 445.0	25 547.0	22 267.0	Compte d'op. fin., nia
Net Errors and Omissions	-4 247.8	229.4	2 411.4	401.6	735.4	3 673.1	2 317.0	Erreurs et omissions nettes
Reserves & Related Items	16 311.5	-1 948.4	-20 460.4	3 501.4	-1 163.4	-11 456.1	-6 876.0	Rés. et postes appareutés
Mongolia								**Mongolie**
Goods: Exports fob	451.0	423.4	568.5	462.4	454.3	535.8	460.0	Biens : exportations, fab
Goods: Imports fob	-425.7	-459.7	-453.1	-524.2	-510.7	-608.4	-549.3	Biens : importations, fab
Serv. & Income: Credit	60.3	69.1	58.8	87.9	82.5	90.7	107.2	Serv. & revenu : crédit
Serv. & Income: Debit	-123.8	-139.5	-123.2	-156.5	-152.3	-182.3	-190.3	Serv & revenu : débit
Current Trans.,nie: Credit	77.1	6.2	4.2	5.5	17.6	25.0	41.2	Transf. cour.,nia : crédit
Current Transfers: Debit	0.0	0.0	0.0	-3.6	-3.6	-16.9	-19.4	Transf. courants : débit
Capital Acct.,nie: Credit	0.0	0.0	0.0	0.0	0.0	0.0	0.0	Compte de cap.,nia : crédit
Capital Account: Debit	0.0	0.0	0.0	0.0	0.0	0.0	0.0	Compte de capital : débit
Financial Account, nie	-15.9	41.3	27.0	126.2	69.6	89.9	121.3	Compte d'op. fin., nia
Net Errors and Omissions	9.1	-28.1	-75.6	-50.2	23.6	-19.3	-53.9	Erreurs et omissions nettes
Reserves & Related Items	-32.1	87.3	-6.6	52.5	19.0	85.5	83.2	Rés. et postes appareutés
Montserrat								**Montserrat**
Goods: Exports fob	12.1	41.3	8.2	1.2	1.3	1.1	...	Biens : exportations, fab
Goods: Imports fob	-33.9	-36.0	-28.1	-19.4	-19.3	-19.0	...	Biens : importations, fab
Serv. & Income: Credit	25.3	16.1	14.8	13.8	21.5	17.2	...	Serv. & revenu : crédit
Serv. & Income: Debit	-17.7	-19.4	-16.2	-24.8	-28.8	-22.8	...	Serv & revenu : débit
Current Trans.,nie: Credit	13.6	14.9	20.4	33.2	26.5	18.9	...	Transf. cour.,nia : crédit
Current Transfers: Debit	-1.3	-1.3	-1.1	-2.2	-2.7	-4.3	...	Transf. courants : débit
Capital Acct.,nie: Credit	6.7	2.3	7.2	7.2	5.0	5.3	...	Compte de cap.,nia : crédit
Capital Account: Debit	-1.5	-14.8	-3.6	-3.6	-3.6	-2.9	...	Compte de capital : débit
Financial Account, nie	1.9	-5.9	-8.9	4.0	-5.9	3.5	...	Compte d'op. fin., nia
Net Errors and Omissions	-3.9	2.5	10.0	4.1	-4.6	-0.5	...	Erreurs et omissions nettes
Reserves & Related Items	-1.2	0.1	-2.6	-13.5	10.6	3.6	...	Rés. et postes appareutés
Morocco								**Maroc**
Goods: Exports fob	6 871.0	6 886.2	7 039.1	7 143.7	7 509.0	7 418.6	7 141.8	Biens : exportations, fab
Goods: Imports fob	-9 353.1	-9 079.6	-8 903.0	-9 462.6	-9 956.6	-10 653.6	-10 163.8	Biens : importations, fab
Serv. & Income: Credit	2 424.5	2 932.0	2 643.4	3 020.3	3 301.7	3 310.1	4 355.1	Serv. & revenu : crédit
Serv. & Income: Debit	-3 458.7	-3 279.9	-3 071.8	-3 189.9	-3 174.9	-3 032.8	-3 277.3	Serv & revenu : débit
Current Trans.,nie: Credit	2 298.0	2 565.4	2 204.2	2 437.7	2 246.1	2 574.2	3 670.3	Transf. cour.,nia : crédit
Current Transfers: Debit	-78.0	-82.5	-80.6	-95.0	-96.0	-117.6	-120.1	Transf. courants : débit
Capital Acct.,nie: Credit	0.0	78.1	0.5	0.1	0.2	0.1	0.0	Compte de cap.,nia : crédit

78

Summary of balance of payments
Millions of US dollars *[cont.]*

Résumé des balances des paiements
Millions de dollars des E.-U. *[suite]*

Country or area	1995	1996	1997	1998	1999	2000	2001	Pays ou zone
Capital Account: Debit	-5.7	-4.8	-5.0	-10.2	-8.8	-6.0	-8.9	Compte de capital : débit
Financial Account, nie	-984.4	-896.6	-989.8	-644.1	-13.0	-774.3	-966.8	Compte d'op. fin., nia
Net Errors and Omissions	391.1	208.7	174.8	160.4	123.5	114.2	229.7	Erreurs et omissions nettes
Reserves & Related Items	1 895.4	673.1	988.2	639.5	68.8	1 167.2	-859.9	Rés. et postes appareutés
Mozambique								**Mozambique**
Goods: Exports fob	168.9	226.1	230.0	244.6	283.8	364.0	1 713.6	Biens : exportations, fab
Goods: Imports fob	-705.2	-704.4	-684.0	-735.6	-1 090.0	-1 046.0	-2 438.3	Biens : importations, fab
Serv. & Income: Credit	301.5	314.2	342.3	332.5	353.0	404.7	720.0	Serv. & revenu : crédit
Serv. & Income: Debit	-549.1	-481.1	-496.8	-584.0	-620.5	-717.2	-2 170.5	Serv & revenu : débit
Current Trans.,nie: Credit	339.2	224.7	312.9	313.2	256.3	337.3	657.5	Transf. cour.,nia : crédit
Current Transfers: Debit	0.0	0.0	0.0	0.0	-94.6	-106.4	-86.2	Transf. courants : débit
Capital Acct.,nie: Credit	0.0	0.0	0.0	0.0	180.3	226.8	584.6	Compte de cap.,nia : crédit
Capital Account: Debit	0.0	0.0	0.0	0.0	0.0	0.0	0.0	Compte de capital : débit
Financial Account, nie	366.7	235.0	182.2	300.4	403.9	83.2	-271.6	Compte d'op. fin., nia
Net Errors and Omissions	-308.6	-238.3	-364.8	-263.8	1.5	37.5	-134.5	Erreurs et omissions nettes
Reserves & Related Items	386.6	423.8	478.2	392.7	326.3	416.1	1 425.4	Rés. et postes appareutés
Myanmar								**Myanmar**
Goods: Exports fob	933.2	937.9	974.5	1 065.2	1 281.1	1 638.4	2 294.5	Biens : exportations, fab
Goods: Imports fob	-1 756.3	-1 869.1	-2 106.6	-2 451.2	-2 159.6	-2 136.9	-2 563.0	Biens : importations, fab
Serv. & Income: Credit	376.3	436.8	528.2	637.0	558.2	506.3	455.2	Serv. & revenu : crédit
Serv. & Income: Debit	-368.0	-355.0	-463.6	-376.1	-342.2	-489.9	-775.3	Serv & revenu : débit
Current Trans.,nie: Credit	564.2	598.4	685.1	631.2	381.0	285.8	295.7	Transf. cour.,nia : crédit
Current Transfers: Debit	-8.0	-28.8	-29.7	-0.3	-0.3	-13.9	-12.6	Transf. courants : débit
Capital Acct.,nie: Credit	0.0	0.0	0.0	0.0	0.0	0.0	0.0	Compte de cap.,nia : crédit
Capital Account: Debit	0.0	0.0	0.0	0.0	0.0	0.0	0.0	Compte de capital : débit
Financial Account, nie	242.8	266.8	469.1	535.1	248.8	210.2	395.1	Compte d'op. fin., nia
Net Errors and Omissions	-16.2	-11.7	-26.0	18.8	-12.3	-23.4	88.4	Erreurs et omissions nettes
Reserves & Related Items	31.8	24.7	-31.0	-59.7	45.4	23.3	-178.0	Rés. et postes appareutés
Namibia								**Namibie**
Goods: Exports fob	1 418.4	1 403.7	1 343.3	1 278.3	...	...	...	Biens : exportations, fab
Goods: Imports fob	-1 548.2	-1 530.9	-1 615.0	-1 450.9	...	...	...	Biens : importations, fab
Serv. & Income: Credit	689.3	656.5	632.1	553.8	...	...	...	Serv. & revenu : crédit
Serv. & Income: Debit	-786.6	-829.9	-714.3	-622.8	...	...	...	Serv & revenu : débit
Current Trans.,nie: Credit	426.9	437.3	462.2	418.2	...	...	...	Transf. cour.,nia : crédit
Current Transfers: Debit	-23.9	-21.0	-18.0	-14.7	...	...	...	Transf. courants : débit
Capital Acct.,nie: Credit	40.7	42.5	33.9	24.2	...	...	...	Compte de cap.,nia : crédit
Capital Account: Debit	-0.6	-0.5	-0.4	-0.4	...	...	...	Compte de capital : débit
Financial Account, nie	-205.3	-174.0	-71.4	-145.6	...	...	...	Compte d'op. fin., nia
Net Errors and Omissions	13.4	39.1	15.3	15.7	...	...	...	Erreurs et omissions nettes
Reserves & Related Items	-24.2	-22.9	-67.8	-55.8		...	...	Rés. et postes appareutés
Nepal								**Népal**
Goods: Exports fob	349.9	388.7	413.8	482.0	612.3	776.1	720.5	Biens : exportations, fab
Goods: Imports fob	-1 310.8	-1 494.7	-1 691.9	-1 239.1	-1 494.2	-1 590.1	-1 485.7	Biens : importations, fab
Serv. & Income: Credit	722.6	790.6	897.6	610.6	710.9	578.1	483.6	Serv. & revenu : crédit
Serv. & Income: Debit	-348.1	-274.8	-253.1	-222.7	-240.9	-235.1	-273.5	Serv & revenu : débit
Current Trans.,nie: Credit	239.2	281.6	267.4	326.0	182.3	189.0	240.2	Transf. cour.,nia : crédit
Current Transfers: Debit	-9.1	-18.0	-21.8	-24.1	-26.9	-16.7	-24.3	Transf. courants : débit
Capital Acct.,nie: Credit	0.0	0.0	0.0	0.0	0.0	0.0	0.0	Compte de cap.,nia : crédit
Capital Account: Debit	0.0	0.0	0.0	0.0	0.0	0.0	0.0	Compte de capital : débit
Financial Account, nie	368.5	275.2	340.3	212.9	-24.5	76.1	-216.9	Compte d'op. fin., nia
Net Errors and Omissions	2.8	82.3	216.6	134.0	58.3	145.7	256.5	Erreurs et omissions nettes
Reserves & Related Items	-15.0	-30.9	-168.8	-279.7	222.7	77.0	299.6	Rés. et postes appareutés
Netherlands								**Pays-Bas**
Goods: Exports fob	195 600.0	195 079.0	188 988.0	196 041.0	195 691.0	204 411.0	202 947.0	Biens : exportations, fab
Goods: Imports fob	-171788.0	-172312.0	-168051.0	-175611.0	-179657.0	-186848.0	-183082.0	Biens : importations, fab
Serv. & Income: Credit	82 468.6	84 521.2	88 884.0	87 358.1	97 457.6	95 070.8	90 911.0	Serv. & revenu : crédit
Serv. & Income: Debit	-74 294.9	-79 290.4	-79 107.3	-87 157.4	-91 600.1	-98 924.6	-100406.8	Serv & revenu : débit
Current Trans.,nie: Credit	4 725.0	4 319.3	4 345.5	3 798.7	4 565.8	4 365.8	4 586.0	Transf. cour.,nia : crédit
Current Transfers: Debit	-11 158.7	-11 089.3	-10 465.2	-10 980.6	-10 917.8	-10 616.8	-11 212.5	Transf. courants : débit
Capital Acct.,nie: Credit	855.8	1 266.7	1 099.2	1 037.4	1 688.0	2 855.8	1 117.7	Compte de cap.,nia : crédit
Capital Account: Debit	-1 954.9	-3 290.7	-2 396.3	-1 457.2	-1 902.1	-2 249.5	-1 683.5	Compte de capital : débit
Financial Account, nie	-18 613.8	-5 198.4	-13 839.0	-14 536.5	-12 421.7	-8 023.3	-11 179.7	Compte d'op. fin., nia

78

Summary of balance of payments
Millions of US dollars *[cont.]*

Résumé des balances des paiements
Millions de dollars des E.-U. *[suite]*

Country or area	1995	1996	1997	1998	1999	2000	2001	Pays ou zone
Net Errors and Omissions	-7 752.2	-19 696.0	-12 165.4	-831.7	-7 514.8	179.1	7 652.9	Erreurs et omissions nettes
Reserves & Related Items	1 912.9	5 690.7	2 707.9	2 338.8	4 611.0	-220.5	349.8	Rés. et postes appareutés
Netherlands Antilles								**Antilles néerlandaises**
Goods: Exports fob	586.5	614.6	501.4	465.6	467.0	614.7	548.9	Biens : exportations, fab
Goods: Imports fob	-1 621.5	-1 743.7	-1 476.7	-1 513.2	-1 584.3	-1 619.2	-1 548.4	Biens : importations, fab
Serv. & Income: Credit	1 609.1	1 541.3	1 525.8	1 655.1	1 565.9	1 749.0	1 771.7	Serv. & revenu : crédit
Serv. & Income: Debit	-662.7	-695.7	-628.8	-720.6	-783.4	-895.9	-911.6	Serv & revenu : débit
Current Trans.,nie: Credit	365.8	174.7	165.3	137.2	179.6	242.5	219.1	Transf. cour.,nia : crédit
Current Transfers: Debit	-149.6	-145.0	-152.1	-161.0	-175.8	-204.6	-199.6	Transf. courants : débit
Capital Acct.,nie: Credit	66.8	71.9	76.9	91.3	109.8	31.3	37.8	Compte de cap.,nia : crédit
Capital Account: Debit	-4.9	-0.6	-1.7	-4.4	-1.5	-1.5	-0.6	Compte de capital : débit
Financial Account, nie	-142.5	95.8	-31.2	58.0	123.2	-72.4	298.4	Compte d'op. fin., nia
Net Errors and Omissions	13.4	14.8	14.9	17.4	24.6	38.7	15.0	Erreurs et omissions nettes
Reserves & Related Items	-60.4	71.9	6.3	-25.5	74.7	117.5	-230.8	Rés. et postes appareutés
New Zealand								**Nouvelle-Zélande**
Goods: Exports fob	13 554.1	14 337.5	14 282.4	12 245.6	12 656.8	13 529.7	13 919.7	Biens : exportations, fab
Goods: Imports fob	-12 583.5	-13 814.5	-13 379.6	-11 333.5	-13 028.0	-12 848.3	-12 445.5	Biens : importations, fab
Serv. & Income: Credit	5 420.5	4 891.1	4 465.3	4 452.1	5 112.9	4 959.8	4 913.0	Serv. & revenu : crédit
Serv. & Income: Debit	-9 589.3	-9 840.0	-9 967.0	-7 815.9	-8 424.4	-8 540.9	-7 931.3	Serv & revenu : débit
Current Trans.,nie: Credit	557.6	896.7	680.5	680.9	609.5	634.1	576.0	Transf. cour.,nia : crédit
Current Transfers: Debit	-362.6	-354.0	-383.0	-339.2	-415.2	-409.4	-435.4	Transf. courants : débit
Capital Acct.,nie: Credit	1 651.6	1 837.5	777.4	260.5	258.6	236.4	818.1	Compte de cap.,nia : crédit
Capital Account: Debit	-427.2	-502.4	-541.1	-443.7	-476.8	-418.0	-378.7	Compte de capital : débit
Financial Account, nie	4 664.9	3 571.4	4 045.4	1 580.3	1 973.6	3 274.0	1 926.7	Compte d'op. fin., nia
Net Errors and Omissions	-2 502.1	748.8	-1 422.5	227.0	1 921.4	-560.2	-1 150.0	Erreurs et omissions nettes
Reserves & Related Items	-384.0	-1 772.2	1 442.3	486.0	-188.4	142.8	187.2	Rés. et postes appareutés
Nicaragua								**Nicaragua**
Goods: Exports fob	470.5	470.2	581.6	580.1	552.4	652.8	601.9	Biens : exportations, fab
Goods: Imports fob	-882.3	-1 044.3	-1 371.2	-1 397.1	-1 698.2	-1 647.3	-1 629.5	Biens : importations, fab
Serv. & Income: Credit	149.4	183.7	230.4	276.9	317.6	334.2	346.5	Serv. & revenu : crédit
Serv. & Income: Debit	-599.7	-587.6	-518.8	-479.0	-562.2	-575.9	-616.7	Serv & revenu : débit
Current Trans.,nie: Credit	285.5	350.2	407.4	518.0	696.5	749.9	736.7	Transf. cour.,nia : crédit
Current Transfers: Debit	0.0	0.0	0.0	0.0	0.0	0.0	0.0	Transf. courants : débit
Capital Acct.,nie: Credit	0.0	0.0	0.0	0.0	0.0	0.0	0.0	Compte de cap.,nia : crédit
Capital Account: Debit	0.0	0.0	0.0	0.0	0.0	0.0	0.0	Compte de capital : débit
Financial Account, nie	-625.0	-355.0	3.2	197.1	488.2	60.8	40.4	Compte d'op. fin., nia
Net Errors and Omissions	157.8	172.7	352.8	-105.6	-254.6	-42.2	-13.3	Erreurs et omissions nettes
Reserves & Related Items	1 043.8	810.1	314.6	409.6	460.3	467.7	534.0	Rés. et postes appareutés
Niger								**Niger**
Goods: Exports fob	288.1	...	...	...	...	...	...	Biens : exportations, fab
Goods: Imports fob	-305.6	...	...	...	...	...	...	Biens : importations, fab
Serv. & Income: Credit	39.1	...	...	...	...	...	...	Serv. & revenu : crédit
Serv. & Income: Debit	-204.7	...	...	...	...	...	...	Serv & revenu : débit
Current Trans.,nie: Credit	60.6	...	...	...	...	...	...	Transf. cour.,nia : crédit
Current Transfers: Debit	-29.1	...	...	...	...	...	...	Transf. courants : débit
Capital Acct.,nie: Credit	65.3	...	...	...	...	...	...	Compte de cap.,nia : crédit
Capital Account: Debit	0.0	...	...	...	...	...	...	Compte de capital : débit
Financial Account, nie	-46.1	...	...	...	...	...	...	Compte d'op. fin., nia
Net Errors and Omissions	114.4	...	...	...	...	...	...	Erreurs et omissions nettes
Reserves & Related Items	18.1	...	...	...	...	...	...	Rés. et postes appareutés
Nigeria								**Nigéria**
Goods: Exports fob	11 734.4	16 117.0	15 207.3	8 971.2	12 875.7	...	...	Biens : exportations, fab
Goods: Imports fob	-8 221.5	-6 438.4	-9 501.4	-9 211.3	-8 587.6	...	...	Biens : importations, fab
Serv. & Income: Credit	708.3	847.5	1 044.9	1 216.6	1 219.3	...	...	Serv. & revenu : crédit
Serv. & Income: Debit	-7 598.4	-7 964.1	-8 115.7	-6 789.5	-6 293.3	...	...	Serv & revenu : débit
Current Trans.,nie: Credit	803.5	946.6	1 920.3	1 574.2	1 301.1	...	...	Transf. cour.,nia : crédit
Current Transfers: Debit	-4.7	-1.7	-3.8	-4.7	-9.4	...	...	Transf. courants : débit
Capital Acct.,nie: Credit	0.0	0.0	0.0	0.0	0.0	...	...	Compte de cap.,nia : crédit
Capital Account: Debit	-66.2	-68.1	-49.4	-54.3	-47.7	...	...	Compte de capital : débit
Financial Account, nie	-46.2	-4 155.0	-424.9	1 502.5	-4 002.4	...	...	Compte d'op. fin., nia
Net Errors and Omissions	-82.9	-44.8	-62.1	-77.5	6.8	...	...	Erreurs et omissions nettes
Reserves & Related Items	2 773.7	761.0	-15.1	2 872.8	3 537.6	...	...	Rés. et postes appareutés

78

Summary of balance of payments
Millions of US dollars *[cont.]*

Résumé des balances des paiements
Millions de dollars des E.-U. *[suite]*

Country or area	1995	1996	1997	1998	1999	2000	2001	Pays ou zone
Norway								**Norvège**
Goods: Exports fob	42 385.4	50 080.6	49 375.4	40 887.8	46 224.3	60 462.7	59 698.6	Biens : exportations, fab
Goods: Imports fob	-33 700.6	-37 108.8	-37 727.0	-38 826.6	-35 501.5	-34 520.2	-33 680.6	Biens : importations, fab
Serv. & Income: Credit	18 262.9	19 983.4	21 297.4	22 350.9	21 978.4	23 972.1	25 547.9	Serv. & revenu : crédit
Serv. & Income: Debit	-19 656.5	-20 480.4	-21 516.8	-22 872.7	-22 879.9	-23 717.4	-23 922.0	Serv & revenu : débit
Current Trans.,nie: Credit	1 280.2	1 329.2	1 468.1	1 500.5	1 680.7	1 321.1	1 472.9	Transf. cour.,nia : crédit
Current Transfers: Debit	-3 338.9	-2 835.2	-2 861.2	-3 033.7	-3 124.3	-2 711.6	-3 156.6	Transf. courants : débit
Capital Acct.,nie: Credit	85.8	64.5	30.2	43.7	40.5	33.5	104.7	Compte de cap.,nia : crédit
Capital Account: Debit	-255.1	-191.9	-214.1	-159.9	-156.4	-219.8	-197.5	Compte de capital : débit
Financial Account, nie	-541.5	-1 461.6	-6 607.3	60.7	431.4	-13 154.6	-23 877.5	Compte d'op. fin., nia
Net Errors and Omissions	-3 946.6	-2 910.0	-4 442.6	-6 334.6	-2 709.5	-7 780.1	-4 104.4	Erreurs et omissions nettes
Reserves & Related Items	-574.8	-6 469.9	1 197.9	6 384.0	-5 983.7	-3 685.8	2 114.4	Rés. et postes appareutés
Oman								**Oman**
Goods: Exports fob	6 065.0	7 373.2	7 656.7	5 521.5	7 238.8	11 318.6	11 074.1	Biens : exportations, fab
Goods: Imports fob	-4 049.9	-4 231.5	-4 645.0	-5 214.6	-4 299.6	-4 593.0	-5 310.8	Biens : importations, fab
Serv. & Income: Credit	338.1	494.1	652.8	707.4	587.8	715.2	658.0	Serv. & revenu : crédit
Serv. & Income: Debit	-1 684.3	-1 927.2	-2 241.6	-2 497.0	-2 380.0	-2 567.0	-2 574.8	Serv & revenu : débit
Current Trans.,nie: Credit	67.6	0.0	0.0	0.0	0.0	0.0	0.0	Transf. cour.,nia : crédit
Current Transfers: Debit	-1 537.1	-1 370.6	-1 500.7	-1 466.8	-1 438.4	-1 451.2	-1 531.9	Transf. courants : débit
Capital Acct.,nie: Credit	0.0	28.6	54.6	20.8	15.6	33.8	7.8	Compte de cap.,nia : crédit
Capital Account: Debit	0.0	-18.2	-23.4	-26.0	-18.2	-26.0	-18.2	Compte de capital : débit
Financial Account, nie	-18.7	260.1	52.0	1 487.7	109.2	-494.1	-886.9	Compte d'op. fin., nia
Net Errors and Omissions	387.7	-420.1	525.5	701.7	399.3	-673.9	-383.4	Erreurs et omissions nettes
Reserves & Related Items	431.6	-188.5	-531.0	765.4	-214.6	-2 262.4	-1 033.6	Rés. et postes appareutés
Pakistan								**Pakistan**
Goods: Exports fob	8 356.4	8 507.3	8 350.7	7 850.0	7 673.0	8 739.0	9 131.0	Biens : exportations, fab
Goods: Imports fob	-11 247.8	-12 163.7	-10 750.2	-9 834.0	-9 520.0	-9 896.0	-9 739.0	Biens : importations, fab
Serv. & Income: Credit	2 043.9	2 191.7	1 771.8	1 487.0	1 492.0	1 498.0	1 572.0	Serv. & revenu : crédit
Serv. & Income: Debit	-5 062.9	-5 656.6	-5 024.6	-4 524.0	-4 105.0	-4 588.0	-4 522.0	Serv & revenu : débit
Current Trans.,nie: Credit	2 610.7	2 739.5	3 980.6	2 801.0	3 582.0	4 200.0	5 499.0	Transf. cour.,nia : crédit
Current Transfers: Debit	-49.0	-54.1	-39.9	-28.0	-42.0	-38.0	-61.0	Transf. courants : débit
Capital Acct.,nie: Credit	0.0	0.0	0.0	0.0	0.0	0.0	0.0	Compte de cap.,nia : crédit
Capital Account: Debit	0.0	0.0	0.0	0.0	0.0	0.0	0.0	Compte de capital : débit
Financial Account, nie	2 449.4	3 496.2	2 321.1	-1 873.0	-2 364.0	-3 099.0	-399.0	Compte d'op. fin., nia
Net Errors and Omissions	-304.2	159.6	-71.8	1 011.2	768.1	556.9	715.7	Erreurs et omissions nettes
Reserves & Related Items	1 203.6	780.3	-537.7	3 109.8	2 515.9	2 627.1	-2 196.7	Rés. et postes appareutés
Panama								**Panama**
Goods: Exports fob	6 090.9	5 822.9	6 669.7	6 350.1	5 303.3	5 836.7	5 883.7	Biens : exportations, fab
Goods: Imports fob	-6 679.8	-6 467.0	-7 354.9	-7 714.6	-6 689.4	-7 026.6	-6 709.5	Biens : importations, fab
Serv. & Income: Credit	3 163.5	3 014.1	3 156.7	3 516.5	3 296.5	3 410.0	3 215.6	Serv. & revenu : crédit
Serv. & Income: Debit	-3 197.8	-2 705.3	-3 128.8	-3 492.9	-3 401.7	-3 330.2	-3 088.0	Serv & revenu : débit
Current Trans.,nie: Credit	184.1	167.7	185.2	195.2	202.7	208.6	226.8	Transf. cour.,nia : crédit
Current Transfers: Debit	-31.5	-33.0	-34.6	-36.6	-31.6	-31.7	-28.1	Transf. courants : débit
Capital Acct.,nie: Credit	8.5	2.5	72.7	50.9	3.0	1.7	1.6	Compte de cap.,nia : crédit
Capital Account: Debit	0.0	0.0	0.0	0.0	0.0	0.0	0.0	Compte de capital : débit
Financial Account, nie	115.6	561.2	972.3	1 076.8	1 398.2	2.1	587.1	Compte d'op. fin., nia
Net Errors and Omissions	15.2	-96.3	-195.0	-325.1	-228.7	602.4	-387.7	Erreurs et omissions nettes
Reserves & Related Items	331.3	-266.8	-343.3	379.7	147.7	327.0	298.5	Rés. et postes appareutés
Papua New Guinea								**Papouasie-Nvl-Guinée**
Goods: Exports fob	2 670.4	2 529.8	2 160.1	1 773.3	1 927.4	2 094.1	1 812.9	Biens : exportations, fab
Goods: Imports fob	-1 262.4	-1 513.3	-1 483.3	-1 078.3	-1 071.4	-998.8	-932.4	Biens : importations, fab
Serv. & Income: Credit	343.9	464.3	432.1	339.0	266.1	274.7	305.1	Serv. & revenu : crédit
Serv. & Income: Debit	-1 152.8	-1 239.7	-1 268.4	-1 073.6	-1 019.0	-1 014.4	-912.2	Serv & revenu : débit
Current Trans.,nie: Credit	66.7	252.1	69.9	82.4	60.3	62.4	75.9	Transf. cour.,nia : crédit
Current Transfers: Debit	-173.9	-304.2	-102.6	-71.6	-68.7	-72.7	-67.3	Transf. courants : débit
Capital Acct.,nie: Credit	15.7	15.2	13.9	9.7	7.8	7.2	5.9	Compte de cap.,nia : crédit
Capital Account: Debit	-15.7	-15.2	-13.9	-9.7	-7.8	-7.2	-5.9	Compte de capital : débit
Financial Account, nie	-444.7	46.6	8.0	-179.7	16.0	-254.1	-151.9	Compte d'op. fin., nia
Net Errors and Omissions	-86.6	-33.1	7.3	-12.5	14.3	13.1	-1.6	*Erreurs et omissions nettes*
Reserves & Related Items	39.5	-202.5	177.0	221.0	-125.0	-104.5	-128.6	Rés. et postes appareutés
Paraguay								**Paraguay**
Goods: Exports fob	4 218.6	3 796.9	3 327.5	3 548.6	2 312.4	2 225.8	2 408.5	Biens : exportations, fab

78

Summary of balance of payments
Millions of US dollars *[cont.]*
Résumé des balances des paiements
Millions de dollars des E.-U. *[suite]*

Country or area	1995	1996	1997	1998	1999	2000	2001	Pays ou zone
Goods: Imports fob	-4 489.0	-4 383.4	-4 192.4	-3 941.5	-2 752.9	-2 904.0	-2 954.2	Biens : importations, fab
Serv. & Income: Credit	856.4	881.4	933.1	891.8	787.9	866.4	798.3	Serv. & revenu : crédit
Serv. & Income: Debit	-873.6	-830.0	-899.5	-836.2	-688.0	-655.5	-626.0	Serv & revenu : débit
Current Trans.,nie: Credit	199.7	183.0	182.2	178.3	176.7	178.3	168.0	Transf. cour.,nia : crédit
Current Transfers: Debit	-4.4	-0.8	-1.3	-1.0	-1.5	-1.5	-1.6	Transf. courants : débit
Capital Acct.,nie: Credit	10.6	14.2	7.5	5.4	19.6	3.0	15.2	Compte de cap.,nia : crédit
Capital Acct.: Debit	0.0	0.0	0.0	0.0	0.0	0.0	0.0	Compte de capital : débit
Financial Account, nie	232.5	152.4	421.3	312.9	89.2	27.4	278.0	Compte d'op. fin., nia
Net Errors and Omissions	-106.0	139.8	5.8	-141.6	-244.3	-79.3	-136.4	Erreurs et omissions nettes
Reserves & Related Items	-44.8	46.5	215.8	-16.7	300.9	339.4	50.2	Rés. et postes appareutés
Peru								**Pérou**
Goods: Exports fob	5 587.0	5 898.0	6 831.0	5 757.0	6 116.0	7 033.0	7 106.0	Biens : exportations, fab
Goods: Imports fob	-7 755.0	-7 884.0	-8 554.0	-8 219.0	-6 748.0	-7 350.0	-7 198.0	Biens : importations, fab
Serv. & Income: Credit	1 705.0	2 025.0	2 281.0	2 558.0	2 239.0	2 317.0	2 125.0	Serv. & revenu : crédit
Serv. & Income: Debit	-4 964.0	-4 610.0	-4 892.0	-4 431.0	-4 056.0	-4 564.0	-4 128.0	Serv & revenu : débit
Current Trans.,nie: Credit	814.0	898.0	929.0	989.0	993.0	1 004.0	1 006.0	Transf. cour.,nia : crédit
Current Transfers: Debit	-5.0	-8.0	-8.0	-11.0	-27.0	-8.0	-9.0	Transf. courants : débit
Capital Acct.,nie: Credit	66.0	52.0	25.0	21.0	25.0	24.0	32.0	Compte de cap.,nia : crédit
Capital Account: Debit	-33.0	-29.0	-74.0	-78.0	-79.0	-92.0	-99.0	Compte de capital : débit
Financial Account, nie	3 510.0	3 640.0	5 867.0	1 832.0	532.0	879.0	1 031.0	Compte d'op. fin., nia
Net Errors and Omissions	483.4	714.6	-350.4	340.9	138.1	627.9	532.8	Erreurs et omissions nettes
Reserves & Related Items	591.6	-696.6	-2 054.6	1 241.1	866.9	129.1	-398.8	Rés. et postes appareutés
Philippines								**Philippines**
Goods: Exports fob	17 447.0	20 543.0	25 228.0	29 496.0	34 209.6	37 295.0	31 242.0	Biens : exportations, fab
Goods: Imports fob	-26 391.0	-31 885.0	-36 355.0	-29 524.0	-29 252.0	-30 377.0	-28 496.0	Biens : importations, fab
Serv. & Income: Credit	15 415.0	19 006.0	22 835.0	13 917.0	12 883.0	11 776.0	10 499.0	Serv. & revenu : crédit
Serv. & Income: Debit	-9 331.0	-12 206.0	-17 139.0	-12 778.0	-10 425.0	-10 672.0	-9 186.0	Serv & revenu : débit
Current Trans.,nie: Credit	1 147.0	1 185.0	1 670.0	758.0	610.0	552.0	515.0	Transf. cour.,nia : crédit
Current Transfers: Debit	-267.0	-596.0	-590.0	-323.0	-116.0	-115.0	-71.0	Transf. courants : débit
Capital Acct.,nie: Credit	0.0	0.0	0.0	0.0	44.0	74.0	12.0	Compte de cap.,nia : crédit
Capital Account: Debit	0.0	0.0	0.0	0.0	-53.0	-36.0	-24.0	Compte de capital : débit
Financial Account, nie	5 309.0	11 277.0	6 498.0	483.0	-935.0	-6 497.0	-4 317.0	Compte d'op. fin., nia
Net Errors and Omissions	-2 093.6	-2 986.0	-5 241.4	-749.9	-3 306.5	-2 480.6	-854.5	Erreurs et omissions nettes
Reserves & Related Items	-1 235.4	-4 338.0	3 094.4	-1 279.1	-3 659.1	480.5	680.5	Rés. et postes appareutés
Poland								**Pologne**
Goods: Exports fob	25 041.0	27 557.0	30 731.0	32 467.0	30 060.0	35 902.0	41 664.0	Biens : exportations, fab
Goods: Imports fob	-26 687.0	-34 844.0	-40 553.0	-45 303.0	-45 132.0	-48 210.0	-49 324.0	Biens : importations, fab
Serv. & Income: Credit	11 764.0	11 274.0	10 382.0	13 066.0	10 200.0	12 637.0	12 380.0	Serv. & revenu : crédit
Serv. & Income: Debit	-10 222.0	-8 945.0	-8 339.0	-10 028.0	-9 829.0	-12 707.0	-12 966.0	Serv & revenu : débit
Current Trans.,nie: Credit	2 459.0	2 825.0	2 700.0	3 520.0	2 898.0	3 008.0	3 737.0	Transf. cour.,nia : crédit
Current Transfers: Debit	-1 501.0	-1 131.0	-665.0	-623.0	-684.0	-628.0	-848.0	Transf. courants : débit
Capital Acct.,nie: Credit	285.0	5 833.0	91.0	117.0	95.0	109.0	112.0	Compte de cap.,nia : crédit
Capital Account: Debit	0.0	-5 739.0	-25.0	-54.0	-40.0	-77.0	-37.0	Compte de capital : débit
Financial Account, nie	9 260.0	6 673.0	7 410.0	13 282.0	10 462.0	10 204.0	3 172.0	Compte d'op. fin., nia
Net Errors and Omissions	-563.6	321.3	1 309.3	-519.6	2 125.6	387.2	1 681.7	Erreurs et omissions nettes
Reserves & Related Items	-9 835.4	-3 824.3	-3 041.3	-5 924.4	-155.6	-625.2	428.3	Rés. et postes appareutés
Portugal								**Portugal**
Goods: Exports fob	24 024.3	25 623.0	25 379.2	25 617.9	25 468.4	25 219.1	25 794.9	Biens : exportations, fab
Goods: Imports fob	-32 934.4	-35 344.8	-35 721.2	-37 828.9	-39 226.6	-39 154.8	-38 773.8	Biens : importations, fab
Serv. & Income: Credit	12 331.2	12 289.6	12 239.9	13 325.4	12 919.5	13 264.7	13 915.2	Serv. & revenu : crédit
Serv. & Income: Debit	-10 685.1	-12 055.4	-12 316.3	-13 037.9	-12 830.0	-13 694.3	-14 375.5	Serv & revenu : débit
Current Trans.,nie: Credit	9 045.9	6 514.8	5 985.1	6 169.6	6 047.6	5 386.0	5 625.8	Transf. cour.,nia : crédit
Current Transfers: Debit	-1 913.6	-2 243.2	-2 031.3	-2 079.5	-2 143.2	-1 983.1	-2 145.5	Transf. courants : débit
Capital Acct.,nie: Credit	0.0	2 836.4	2 892.7	2 724.2	2 641.9	1 680.6	1 276.1	Compte de cap.,nia : crédit
Capital Account: Debit	0.0	-141.4	-188.9	-178.7	-183.1	-168.7	-209.3	Compte de capital : débit
Financial Account, nie	3 024.7	3 835.2	6 662.3	5 980.3	9 098.2	11 184.2	10 385.8	Compte d'op. fin., nia
Net Errors and Omissions	-3 192.8	-766.7	-1 927.7	-184.5	-1 577.0	-1 363.0	-641.9	Erreurs et omissions nettes
Reserves & Related Items	299.8	-547.5	-973.7	-507.9	-215.6	-370.7	-851.8	Rés. et postes appareutés
Republic of Moldova								**République de Moldova**
Goods: Exports fob	739.0	822.9	889.6	643.6	474.1	476.5	569.5	Biens : exportations, fab
Goods: Imports fob	-809.2	-1 082.5	-1 237.6	-1 031.7	-609.8	-768.3	-882.3	Biens : importations, fab
Serv. & Income: Credit	158.7	205.3	300.5	288.8	261.3	335.2	403.9	Serv. & revenu : crédit

78

Summary of balance of payments
Millions of US dollars *[cont.]*
Résumé des balances des paiements
Millions de dollars des E.-U. *[suite]*

Country or area	1995	1996	1997	1998	1999	2000	2001	Pays ou zone
Serv. & Income: Debit	-228.7	-210.6	-281.4	-300.9	-266.2	-307.3	-342.8	Serv & revenu : débit
Current Trans.,nie: Credit	66.6	72.9	104.1	110.9	114.7	162.9	160.9	Transf. cour.,nia : crédit
Current Transfers: Debit	-14.1	-2.8	-50.0	-45.5	-39.6	-15.2	-18.0	Transf. courants : débit
Capital Acct.,nie: Credit	0.0	0.1	0.1	2.1	1.5	2.8	1.1	Compte de cap.,nia : crédit
Capital Account: Debit	-0.4	-0.1	-0.3	-2.5	-0.4	-0.9	-3.0	Compte de capital : débit
Financial Account, nie	-68.8	76.6	95.2	5.2	-35.9	144.9	31.3	Compte d'op. fin., nia
Net Errors and Omissions	-18.4	15.5	-7.9	-22.8	-20.1	-4.8	44.6	Erreurs et omissions nettes
Reserves & Related Items	175.4	102.7	187.8	352.8	120.4	-25.8	34.8	Rés. et postes appareutés
Romania								**Roumanie**
Goods: Exports fob	7 910.0	8 085.0	8 431.0	8 302.0	8 503.0	10 366.0	11 385.0	Biens : exportations, fab
Goods: Imports fob	-9 487.0	-10 555.0	-10 411.0	-10 927.0	-9 595.0	-12 050.0	-14 354.0	Biens : importations, fab
Serv. & Income: Credit	1 575.0	1 641.0	1 728.0	1 530.0	1 517.0	2 092.0	2 449.0	Serv. & revenu : crédit
Serv. & Income: Debit	-2 141.0	-2 335.0	-2 464.0	-2 576.0	-2 348.0	-2 627.0	-2 940.0	Serv & revenu : débit
Current Trans.,nie: Credit	473.0	667.0	731.0	886.0	804.0	1 079.0	1 417.0	Transf. cour.,nia : crédit
Current Transfers: Debit	-110.0	-82.0	-152.0	-133.0	-178.0	-219.0	-274.0	Transf. courants : débit
Capital Acct.,nie: Credit	32.0	152.0	43.0	39.0	46.0	37.0	108.0	Compte de cap.,nia : crédit
Capital Account: Debit	0.0	0.0	0.0	0.0	-1.0	-1.0	-13.0	Compte de capital : débit
Financial Account, nie	812.0	1 486.0	2 458.0	2 042.0	697.0	1 943.0	2 938.0	Compte d'op. fin., nia
Net Errors and Omissions	456.4	358.6	1 094.9	194.4	794.5	286.0	818.6	Erreurs et omissions nettes
Reserves & Related Items	479.6	582.4	-1 458.9	642.6	-239.5	-906.0	-1 534.6	Rés. et postes appareutés
Russian Federation								**Fédération de Russie**
Goods: Exports fob	82 913.4	90 562.9	89 007.8	74 884.2	75 665.6	105 565.0	101 603.0	Biens : exportations, fab
Goods: Imports fob	-62 603.5	-68 092.3	-71 983.0	-58 015.3	-39 536.9	-44 861.7	-53 763.5	Biens : importations, fab
Serv. & Income: Credit	14 845.5	17 614.8	18 446.4	16 673.8	12 948.6	14 727.7	17 703.5	Serv. & revenu : crédit
Serv. & Income: Debit	-27 855.4	-28 432.4	-33 083.1	-32 546.9	-24 948.3	-28 207.0	-30 163.5	Serv & revenu : débit
Current Trans.,nie: Credit	894.2	772.5	410.1	307.6	1 182.8	807.4	381.4	Transf. cour.,nia : crédit
Current Transfers: Debit	-737.7	-700.4	-766.4	-644.4	-581.7	-738.2	-1 140.1	Transf. courants : débit
Capital Acct.,nie: Credit	3 122.0	3 065.5	2 136.8	1 704.3	885.0	11 543.0	2 124.9	Compte de cap.,nia : crédit
Capital Account: Debit	-3 469.1	-3 528.8	-2 933.5	-2 086.5	-1 213.0	-867.3	-11 502.9	Compte de capital : débit
Financial Account, nie	-7 468.1	-23 580.8	-2 901.6	-12 582.2	-19 073.3	-34 290.2	-4 737.5	Compte d'op. fin., nia
Net Errors and Omissions	-7 966.9	-4 897.8	-4 852.0	-9 072.9	-7 032.4	-9 755.8	-9 239.2	Erreurs et omissions nettes
Reserves & Related Items	8 325.6	17 216.8	6 518.5	21 378.3	1 703.6	-13 923.0	-11 266.0	Rés. et postes appareutés
Rwanda								Rwanda
Goods: Exports fob	56.7	61.7	93.2	64.5	62.3	69.1	93.3	Biens : exportations, fab
Goods: Imports fob	-219.1	-218.5	-278.2	-234.0	-249.7	-225.3	-245.1	Biens : importations, fab
Serv. & Income: Credit	42.2	27.0	59.2	57.2	59.2	54.5	64.2	Serv. & revenu : crédit
Serv. & Income: Debit	-172.2	-168.5	-223.1	-206.5	-214.2	-230.7	-223.1	Serv & revenu : débit
Current Trans.,nie: Credit	354.9	293.9	311.6	252.6	212.3	235.1	210.4	Transf. cour.,nia : crédit
Current Transfers: Debit	-4.9	-4.1	-24.9	-16.9	-12.8	-17.2	-17.9	Transf. courants : débit
Capital Acct.,nie: Credit	0.0	0.0	0.0	0.0	71.0	62.7	50.2	Compte de cap.,nia : crédit
Capital Account: Debit	0.0	0.0	0.0	0.0	0.0	0.0	0.0	Compte de capital : débit
Financial Account, nie	-10.7	24.8	46.8	-16.8	-33.6	10.8	-44.0	Compte d'op. fin., nia
Net Errors and Omissions	5.8	4.1	46.0	92.8	33.0	-91.1	41.7	Erreurs et omissions nettes
Reserves & Related Items	-52.6	-20.3	-30.5	7.0	72.6	132.1	70.3	Rés. et postes appareutés
Saint Kitts and Nevis								**Saint-Kitts-et-Nevis**
Goods: Exports fob	36.6	39.1	51.4	44.8	44.9	54.6	...	Biens : exportations, fab
Goods: Imports fob	-117.1	-131.5	-129.7	-131.1	-135.2	-172.6	...	Biens : importations, fab
Serv. & Income: Credit	88.7	90.4	98.4	110.1	106.0	102.2	...	Serv. & revenu : crédit
Serv. & Income: Debit	-72.8	-80.1	-89.1	-92.4	-119.2	-109.2	...	Serv & revenu : débit
Current Trans.,nie: Credit	23.3	20.8	21.8	33.7	24.1	69.9	...	Transf. cour.,nia : crédit
Current Transfers: Debit	-4.1	-4.6	-6.7	-6.6	-3.6	-7.3	...	Transf. courants : débit
Capital Acct.,nie: Credit	7.4	5.6	4.4	8.4	6.0	12.4	...	Compte de cap.,nia : crédit
Capital Account: Debit	-0.2	-0.2	-0.2	-0.2	-0.2	-0.2	...	Compte de capital : débit
Financial Account, nie	24.8	48.4	43.4	35.8	94.8	66.6	...	Compte d'op. fin., nia
Net Errors and Omissions	15.7	11.2	9.5	8.4	-14.9	-20.8	...	Erreurs et omissions nettes
Reserves & Related Items	-2.3	0.9	-3.0	-11.0	-2.7	4.3	...	Rés. et postes appareutés
Saint Lucia								Sainte-Lucie
Goods: Exports fob	114.6	86.3	70.3	70.4	60.9	54.8	...	Biens : exportations, fab
Goods: Imports fob	-269.4	-267.4	-292.4	-295.1	-312.0	-308.0	...	Biens : importations, fab
Serv. & Income: Credit	270.8	270.2	291.7	317.2	323.5	312.4	...	Serv. & revenu : crédit
Serv. & Income: Debit	-168.1	-156.7	-161.0	-178.0	-173.6	-159.6	...	Serv & revenu : débit
Current Trans.,nie: Credit	28.4	28.5	24.6	29.6	31.6	29.4	...	Transf. cour.,nia : crédit

78

Summary of balance of payments
Millions of US dollars *[cont.]*

Résumé des balances des paiements
Millions de dollars des E.-U. *[suite]*

Country or area	1995	1996	1997	1998	1999	2000	2001	Pays ou zone
Current Transfers: Debit	-9.5	-15.4	-11.6	-10.1	-9.6	-11.4	...	Transf. courants : débit
Capital Acct.,nie: Credit	13.6	11.1	10.4	23.3	26.8	20.1	...	Compte de cap.,nia : crédit
Capital Account: Debit	-0.4	-0.7	-0.8	-0.8	-0.7	-2.3	...	Compte de capital : débit
Financial Account, nie	27.6	41.4	86.6	55.8	57.4	66.1	...	Compte d'op. fin., nia
Net Errors and Omissions	-2.0	-3.7	-12.9	2.8	3.6	6.7	...	Erreurs et omissions nettes
Reserves & Related Items	-5.7	6.3	-5.0	-15.1	-7.8	-8.1	...	Rés. et postes appareutés
St. Vincent-Grenadines								**St. Vincent-Grenadines**
Goods: Exports fob	61.9	52.6	47.3	50.2	49.6	51.8	...	Biens : exportations, fab
Goods: Imports fob	-119.4	-128.1	-152.6	-170.0	-177.1	-142.9	...	Biens : importations, fab
Serv. & Income: Credit	78.4	100.7	102.1	110.2	128.9	129.4	...	Serv. & revenu : crédit
Serv. & Income: Debit	-70.8	-71.4	-91.7	-95.7	-89.3	-83.3	...	Serv & revenu : débit
Current Trans.,nie: Credit	16.8	19.7	20.8	21.6	23.4	25.4	...	Transf. cour.,nia : crédit
Current Transfers: Debit	-7.6	-9.3	-10.1	-10.6	-8.0	-6.7	...	Transf. courants : débit
Capital Acct.,nie: Credit	6.9	4.9	7.0	14.6	9.1	13.4	...	Compte de cap.,nia : crédit
Capital Account: Debit	-1.1	-1.1	-1.1	-1.3	-1.3	-1.3	...	Compte de capital : débit
Financial Account, nie	35.1	35.9	81.8	91.2	55.5	14.3	...	Compte d'op. fin., nia
Net Errors and Omissions	-1.7	-3.7	-2.5	-1.6	12.3	11.9	...	Erreurs et omissions nettes
Reserves & Related Items	1.4	-0.4	-1.1	-8.7	-3.2	-12.1	...	Rés. et postes appareutés
Samoa								**Samoa**
Goods: Exports fob	8.8	10.1	14.6	20.4	18.2	...	...	Biens : exportations, fab
Goods: Imports fob	-80.3	-90.8	-100.1	-96.9	-115.7	...	...	Biens : importations, fab
Serv. & Income: Credit	60.4	70.6	70.8	68.5	64.1	...	...	Serv. & revenu : crédit
Serv. & Income: Debit	-39.6	-36.8	-44.2	-31.5	-26.9	...	...	Serv & revenu : débit
Current Trans.,nie: Credit	66.7	66.9	73.7	64.1	44.7	...	...	Transf. cour.,nia : crédit
Current Transfers: Debit	-6.6	-7.8	-5.6	-4.6	-3.1	...	...	Transf. courants : débit
Capital Acct.,nie: Credit	0.0	0.0	0.0	0.0	27.1	...	...	Compte de cap.,nia : crédit
Capital Account: Debit	0.0	0.0	0.0	0.0	-2.7	...	...	Compte de capital : débit
Financial Account, nie	-5.6	-3.6	-5.9	-5.0	-0.7	...	...	Compte d'op. fin., nia
Net Errors and Omissions	-1.7	-1.3	7.9	-9.6	2.1	...	...	Erreurs et omissions nettes
Reserves & Related Items	-2.0	-7.4	-11.1	-5.5	-7.0	...	...	Rés. et postes appareutés
Sao Tome and Principe								**Sao Tomé-et-Principe**
Goods: Exports fob	...	...	...	...	...	...	3.3	Biens : exportations, fab
Goods: Imports fob	...	...	...	...	...	...	-24.4	Biens : importations, fab
Serv. & Income: Credit	...	...	...	...	...	...	0.0	Serv. & revenu : crédit
Serv. & Income: Debit	...	...	...	...	...	...	-18.9	Serv & revenu : débit
Current Trans.,nie: Credit	...	...	...	...	...	...	5.1	Transf. cour.,nia : crédit
Current Transfers: Debit	...	...	...	...	...	...	0.0	Transf. courants : débit
Capital Acct.,nie: Credit	...	...	...	...	...	...	11.4	Compte de cap.,nia : crédit
Capital Account: Debit	...	...	...	...	...	...	0.0	Compte de capital : débit
Financial Account, nie	...	...	...	...	...	...	8.9	Compte d'op. fin., nia
Net Errors and Omissions	...	...	...	...	...	...	3.7	Erreurs et omissions nettes
Reserves & Related Items	...	...	...	...	...	...	-2.6	Rés. et postes appareutés
Saudi Arabia								**Arabie saoudite**
Goods: Exports fob	50 040.9	60 728.7	60 731.4	38 821.9	50 756.7	77 584.0	73 032.0	Biens : exportations, fab
Goods: Imports fob	-25 650.5	-25 358.3	-26 369.8	-27 534.6	-25 717.5	-27 741.0	-28 645.1	Biens : importations, fab
Serv. & Income: Credit	8 467.6	7 899.1	10 012.3	10 539.1	11 191.2	8 134.6	9 312.4	Serv. & revenu : crédit
Serv. & Income: Debit	-21 267.2	-26 975.7	-28 934.0	-19 923.1	-21 741.5	-28 130.9	-23 957.0	Serv & revenu : débit
Current Trans.,nie: Credit	0.0	0.0	0.0	0.0	0.0	0.0	0.0	Transf. cour.,nia : crédit
Current Transfers: Debit	-16 916.0	-15 613.2	-15 134.4	-15 052.9	-14 076.9	-15 510.8	-15 240.1	Transf. courants : débit
Capital Acct.,nie: Credit	0.0	0.0	0.0	0.0	0.0	0.0	0.0	Compte de cap.,nia : crédit
Capital Account: Debit	0.0	0.0	0.0	0.0	0.0	0.0	0.0	Compte de capital : débit
Financial Account, nie	6 542.1	5 068.6	343.1	12 430.7	2 402.9	-11 671.6	-16 410.9	Compte d'op. fin., nia
Net Errors and Omissions	0.0	-0.1	-0.5	-0.1	-0.4	0.5	-0.1	Erreurs et omissions nettes
Reserves & Related Items	-1 216.9	-5 749.0	-648.1	718.9	-2 814.6	-2 664.8	1 908.8	Rés. et postes appareutés
Senegal								**Sénégal**
Goods: Exports fob	993.3	988.0	904.6	967.7	1 027.1	...	...	Biens : exportations, fab
Goods: Imports fob	-1 242.9	-1 264.0	-1 176.0	-1 280.6	-1 372.8	...	...	Biens : importations, fab
Serv. & Income: Credit	599.7	459.9	439.6	501.8	499.4	...	...	Serv. & revenu : crédit
Serv. & Income: Debit	-789.7	-550.0	-531.5	-607.5	-632.9	...	...	Serv & revenu : débit
Current Trans.,nie: Credit	284.7	244.3	258.8	254.7	225.4	...	...	Transf. cour.,nia : crédit
Current Transfers: Debit	-89.6	-77.8	-80.3	-83.6	-66.3	...	...	Transf. courants : débit
Capital Acct.,nie: Credit	201.2	169.3	96.3	98.8	99.0	...	...	Compte de cap.,nia : crédit

78

Summary of balance of payments
Millions of US dollars *[cont.]*
Résumé des balances des paiements
Millions de dollars des E.-U. *[suite]*

Country or area	1995	1996	1997	1998	1999	2000	2001	Pays ou zone
Capital Account: Debit	-14.2	-0.1	-0.3	-0.4	-0.5	...	...	Compte de capital : débit
Financial Account, nie	44.2	-179.1	3.5	-109.7	-54.8	...	...	Compte d'op. fin., nia
Net Errors and Omissions	-19.6	7.6	-9.3	10.7	8.2	...	...	Erreurs et omissions nettes
Reserves & Related Items	32.9	201.9	94.7	248.1	268.2	...	...	Rés. et postes appareutés
Seychelles								**Seychelles**
Goods: Exports fob	53.5	96.7	113.6	122.8	145.7	194.8	215.3	Biens : exportations, fab
Goods: Imports fob	-214.3	-267.0	-303.5	-334.6	-374.6	-304.1	-386.9	Biens : importations, fab
Serv. & Income: Credit	237.2	247.5	265.5	252.9	284.3	279.8	292.1	Serv. & revenu : crédit
Serv. & Income: Debit	-132.5	-139.6	-149.6	-158.6	-190.0	-220.6	-220.9	Serv & revenu : débit
Current Trans.,nie: Credit	13.5	15.2	14.2	9.8	10.1	8.1	10.5	Transf. cour.,nia : crédit
Current Transfers: Debit	-11.3	-12.1	-13.1	-11.4	-10.8	-10.0	-10.2	Transf. courants : débit
Capital Acct.,nie: Credit	1.1	5.7	6.8	21.7	16.5	8.8	9.4	Compte de cap.,nia : crédit
Capital Account: Debit	0.0	0.0	0.0	0.0	0.0	0.0	0.0	Compte de capital : débit
Financial Account, nie	30.9	21.3	48.7	56.1	50.2	-0.7	125.2	Compte d'op. fin., nia
Net Errors and Omissions	10.0	7.1	11.6	-2.8	11.4	-18.8	-12.6	Erreurs et omissions nettes
Reserves & Related Items	11.8	25.3	5.7	44.2	57.4	62.7	-21.9	Rés. et postes appareutés
Sierra Leone								**Sierra Leone**
Goods: Exports fob	41.5	...	...	...	...	...	...	Biens : exportations, fab
Goods: Imports fob	-168.1	...	...	...	...	...	...	Biens : importations, fab
Serv. & Income: Credit	87.6	...	...	...	...	...	...	Serv. & revenu : crédit
Serv. & Income: Debit	-113.2	...	...	...	...	...	...	Serv & revenu : débit
Current Trans.,nie: Credit	35.3	...	...	...	...	...	...	Transf. cour.,nia : crédit
Current Transfers: Debit	-9.5	...	...	...	...	...	...	Transf. courants : débit
Capital Acct.,nie: Credit	0.0	...	...	...	...	...	...	Compte de cap.,nia : crédit
Capital Account: Debit	0.0	...	...	...	...	...	...	Compte de capital : débit
Financial Account, nie	61.6	...	...	...	...	...	...	Compte d'op. fin., nia
Net Errors and Omissions	19.3	...	...	...	...	...	...	Erreurs et omissions nettes
Reserves & Related Items	45.6	...	...	...	...	...	...	Rés. et postes appareutés
Singapore								**Singapour**
Goods: Exports fob	118 456.0	126 012.0	125 732.0	110 591.0	115 514.0	139 054.0	122 478.0	Biens : exportations, fab
Goods: Imports fob	-117480.0	-123819.0	-124701.0	-95 684.5	-104287.0	-127483.0	-109605.0	Biens : importations, fab
Serv. & Income: Credit	42 606.4	42 217.6	44 445.6	30 789.6	39 874.0	43 056.1	41 088.6	Serv. & revenu : crédit
Serv. & Income: Debit	-27 797.0	-30 767.7	-26 146.4	-24 803.7	-33 391.0	-37 393.7	-34 699.4	Serv & revenu : débit
Current Trans.,nie: Credit	155.9	160.9	152.5	130.1	134.3	127.4	123.3	Transf. cour.,nia : crédit
Current Transfers: Debit	-1 041.5	-1 232.4	-1 360.5	-1 316.7	-1 317.1	-1 440.6	-1 500.5	Transf. courants : débit
Capital Acct.,nie: Credit	0.0	0.0	0.0	0.0	0.0	0.0	0.0	Compte de cap.,nia : crédit
Capital Account: Debit	-71.3	-138.7	-173.2	-225.7	-191.2	-162.7	-161.2	Compte de capital : débit
Financial Account, nie	-878.0	-8 771.0	-13 641.7	-21 008.8	-11 359.2	-10 836.4	-18 768.0	Compte d'op. fin., nia
Net Errors and Omissions	-5 351.6	3 734.4	3 632.2	4 493.8	-782.6	1 884.3	184.0	Erreurs et omissions nettes
Reserves & Related Items	-8 599.1	-7 395.6	-7 939.8	-2 965.4	-4 193.9	-6 806.0	860.9	Rés. et postes appareutés
Slovakia								**Slovaquie**
Goods: Exports fob	8 590.8	8 823.8	9 640.7	10 720.2	10 201.3	11 896.1	...	Biens : exportations, fab
Goods: Imports fob	-8 820.1	-11 106.5	-11 725.2	-13 070.9	-11 310.3	-12 790.6	...	Biens : importations, fab
Serv. & Income: Credit	2 628.1	2 289.1	2 482.5	2 729.4	2 167.7	2 508.9	...	Serv. & revenu : crédit
Serv. & Income: Debit	-2 101.5	-2 297.8	-2 532.7	-2 870.8	-2 411.8	-2 428.5	...	Serv & revenu : débit
Current Trans.,nie: Credit	242.5	482.9	540.4	645.0	466.0	343.8	...	Transf. cour.,nia : crédit
Current Transfers: Debit	-149.9	-282.0	-367.1	-279.3	-268.1	-224.0	...	Transf. courants : débit
Capital Acct.,nie: Credit	45.6	30.3	0.0	82.8	171.0	105.7	...	Compte de cap.,nia : crédit
Capital Account: Debit	0.0	0.0	0.0	-12.4	-13.4	-14.8	...	Compte de capital : débit
Financial Account, nie	1 211.2	2 267.9	1 780.1	1 911.5	1 788.8	1 472.4	...	Compte d'op. fin., nia
Net Errors and Omissions	144.4	162.2	280.1	-333.1	-14.3	50.7	...	Erreurs et omissions nettes
Reserves & Related Items	-1 791.3	-370.0	-98.9	477.6	-777.0	-919.7	...	Rés. et postes appareutés
Slovenia								**Slovénie**
Goods: Exports fob	8 350.2	8 352.6	8 405.9	9 090.9	8 623.2	8 807.9	9 342.8	Biens : exportations, fab
Goods: Imports fob	-9 304.2	-9 178.7	-9 180.7	-9 882.9	-9 858.3	-9 946.9	-9 962.3	Biens : importations, fab
Serv. & Income: Credit	2 432.5	2 547.8	2 432.2	2 437.5	2 302.3	2 321.7	2 422.2	Serv. & revenu : crédit
Serv. & Income: Debit	-1 648.5	-1 754.1	-1 721.2	-1 880.9	-1 885.0	-1 845.8	-1 901.0	Serv & revenu : débit
Current Trans.,nie: Credit	247.7	250.9	259.5	299.8	334.9	340.8	390.0	Transf. cour.,nia : crédit
Current Transfers: Debit	-152.4	-163.1	-145.3	-182.4	-215.3	-225.4	-260.8	Transf. courants : débit
Capital Acct.,nie: Credit	3.1	5.5	5.0	3.5	3.3	6.8	3.3	Compte de cap.,nia : crédit
Capital Account: Debit	-10.1	-7.4	-3.9	-5.0	-4.0	-3.3	-6.9	Compte de capital : débit
Financial Account, nie	516.3	534.5	1 162.9	215.8	576.1	680.4	1 204.3	Compte d'op. fin., nia

78

Summary of balance of payments
Millions of US dollars *[cont.]*
Résumé des balances des paiements
Millions de dollars des E.-U. *[suite]*

Country or area	1995	1996	1997	1998	1999	2000	2001	Pays ou zone
Net Errors and Omissions	-194.6	2.0	74.0	61.4	41.5	42.1	53.0	Erreurs et omissions nettes
Reserves & Related Items	-240.0	-590.0	-1 288.4	-157.8	81.4	-178.3	-1 284.6	Rés. et postes appareutés
Solomon Islands								***Iles Salomon***
Goods: Exports fob	168.3	161.5	156.4	141.8	164.6	...	...	Biens : exportations, fab
Goods: Imports fob	-154.5	-150.5	-184.5	-159.9	-110.0	...	...	Biens : importations, fab
Serv. & Income: Credit	43.0	55.5	73.0	57.2	61.8	...	...	Serv. & revenu : crédit
Serv. & Income: Debit	-84.9	-94.9	-118.4	-64.5	-109.9	...	...	Serv & revenu : débit
Current Trans.,nie: Credit	53.2	57.5	52.6	56.4	41.5	...	...	Transf. cour.,nia : crédit
Current Transfers: Debit	-16.7	-14.5	-17.1	-22.9	-26.5	...	...	Transf. courants : débit
Capital Acct.,nie: Credit	1.5	0.5	0.3	6.9	9.2	...	...	Compte de cap.,nia : crédit
Capital Account: Debit	-0.9	-2.7	-1.3	-0.3	0.0	...	...	Compte de capital : débit
Financial Account, nie	-8.3	-1.4	45.7	16.9	-33.8	...	...	Compte d'op. fin., nia
Net Errors and Omissions	-1.4	7.0	2.3	-14.4	-1.6	...	...	Erreurs et omissions nettes
Reserves & Related Items	0.8	-18.0	-9.1	-17.2	4.7	...	...	Rés. et postes appareutés
South Africa								***Afrique du Sud***
Goods: Exports fob	30 071.1	30 262.8	31 171.3	29 263.7	28 626.6	31 636.1	30 642.5	Biens : exportations, fab
Goods: Imports fob	-27 404.2	-27 567.7	-28 847.5	-27 207.6	-24 553.7	-27 320.2	-25 676.7	Biens : importations, fab
Serv. & Income: Credit	5 753.5	6 104.4	6 631.4	6 588.0	6 641.8	7 155.5	6 829.3	Serv. & revenu : crédit
Serv. & Income: Debit	-9 980.0	-9 926.7	-10 504.4	-10 057.8	-10 427.9	-11 120.0	-11 222.1	Serv & revenu : débit
Current Trans.,nie: Credit	195.6	54.3	138.4	60.3	66.2	106.4	126.1	Transf. cour.,nia : crédit
Current Transfers: Debit	-841.1	-807.5	-862.5	-803.8	-992.7	-1 032.9	-864.6	Transf. courants : débit
Capital Acct.,nie: Credit	22.1	25.0	29.5	24.4	20.5	19.0	15.1	Compte de cap.,nia : crédit
Capital Account: Debit	-62.0	-72.0	-222.1	-80.4	-82.2	-71.0	-47.1	Compte de capital : débit
Financial Account, nie	4 003.5	3 018.0	8 131.1	4 851.9	5 305.4	98.6	500.5	Compte d'op. fin., nia
Net Errors and Omissions	-851.9	-2 362.7	-1 069.8	-1 718.5	-388.7	928.2	1 855.0	Erreurs et omissions nettes
Reserves & Related Items	-906.6	1 272.0	-4 595.4	-920.2	-4 215.2	-399.8	-2 158.1	Rés. et postes appareutés
Spain								***Espagne***
Goods: Exports fob	93 439.2	102 735.0	106 926.0	111 986.0	112 664.0	116 205.0	117 561.0	Biens : exportations, fab
Goods: Imports fob	-111854.0	-119017.0	-120333.0	-132744.0	-143002.0	-151025.0	-149061.0	Biens : importations, fab
Serv. & Income: Credit	53 897.8	58 482.4	57 322.2	63 928.4	66 053.9	68 556.1	77 570.8	Serv. & revenu : crédit
Serv. & Income: Debit	-39 326.0	-44 185.9	-44 225.9	-49 555.1	-52 618.8	-54 551.2	-62 857.9	Serv & revenu : débit
Current Trans.,nie: Credit	12 055.0	11 111.8	11 738.0	12 690.5	13 434.6	11 628.7	12 566.9	Transf. cour.,nia : crédit
Current Transfers: Debit	-7 419.6	-8 718.4	-8 915.9	-9 441.2	-10 291.7	-10 050.3	-10 862.0	Transf. courants : débit
Capital Acct.,nie: Credit	7 374.1	7 713.0	7 274.6	7 159.8	8 060.4	5 806.0	5 832.5	Compte de cap.,nia : crédit
Capital Account: Debit	-1 370.0	-1 123.8	-837.2	-829.5	-1 093.8	-1 013.6	-872.4	Compte de capital : débit
Financial Account, nie	-7 950.5	20 138.2	8 547.4	-14 155.7	-10 997.2	16 942.2	15 885.9	Compte d'op. fin., nia
Net Errors and Omissions	-5 259.8	-2 856.1	-5 740.9	-3 394.6	-5 059.2	-5 378.7	-7 104.0	Erreurs et omissions nettes
Reserves & Related Items	6 413.9	-24 278.8	-11 755.7	14 355.5	22 850.3	2 880.9	1 340.3	Rés. et postes appareutés
Sri Lanka								***Sri Lanka***
Goods: Exports fob	3 797.9	4 095.2	4 638.7	4 808.0	4 596.2	5 439.6	4 821.1	Biens : exportations, fab
Goods: Imports fob	-4 782.6	-4 895.0	-5 278.3	-5 313.4	-5 365.5	-6 483.6	-5 374.6	Biens : importations, fab
Serv. & Income: Credit	1 042.5	940.6	1 108.6	1 130.8	1 131.1	1 087.7	1 459.3	Serv. & revenu : crédit
Serv. & Income: Debit	-1 559.7	-1 582.5	-1 695.5	-1 756.2	-1 833.0	-2 070.3	-2 129.5	Serv & revenu : débit
Current Trans.,nie: Credit	846.7	881.4	966.5	1 054.5	1 078.1	1 165.7	1 145.7	Transf. cour.,nia : crédit
Current Transfers: Debit	-114.7	-122.4	-134.7	-151.3	-168.2	-182.7	-186.8	Transf. courants : débit
Capital Acct.,nie: Credit	124.2	99.7	91.3	84.6	85.2	55.0	54.9	Compte de cap.,nia : crédit
Capital Account: Debit	-3.5	-3.8	-4.2	-4.7	-5.2	-5.7	-5.8	Compte de capital : débit
Financial Account, nie	730.1	452.2	466.7	345.1	413.4	447.2	380.2	*Compte d'op. fin., nia*
Net Errors and Omissions	157.9	143.6	148.0	26.3	-27.3	186.2	164.7	Erreurs et omissions nettes
Reserves & Related Items	-238.7	-9.0	-307.2	-223.6	95.2	360.8	-329.3	Rés. et postes appareutés
Sudan								***Soudan***
Goods: Exports fob	555.7	620.3	594.2	595.7	780.1	1 806.7	1 698.7	Biens : exportations, fab
Goods: Imports fob	-1 066.0	-1 339.5	-1 421.9	-1 732.2	-1 256.0	-1 366.3	-1 395.1	Biens : importations, fab
Serv. & Income: Credit	127.2	57.0	48.4	29.5	100.7	32.0	32.4	Serv. & revenu : crédit
Serv. & Income: Debit	-177.2	-201.5	-178.1	-214.6	-398.1	-1 227.2	-1 232.2	Serv & revenu : débit
Current Trans.,nie: Credit	346.2	236.3	439.1	731.8	702.2	651.3	730.4	Transf. cour.,nia : crédit
Current Transfers: Debit	-285.8	-199.4	-309.8	-366.7	-393.7	-453.3	-452.5	Transf. courants : débit
Capital Acct.,nie: Credit	0.0	0.0	0.0	13.0	45.8	16.5	11.9	Compte de cap.,nia : crédit
Capital Account: Debit	0.0	0.0	0.0	-67.2	-68.7	-135.8	-105.2	Compte de capital : débit
Financial Account, nie	473.7	136.8	195.0	333.4	435.3	431.6	561.2	Compte d'op. fin., nia
Net Errors and Omissions	89.3	727.5	651.2	750.5	167.2	368.4	-0.5	Erreurs et omissions nettes
Reserves & Related Items	-63.1	-37.5	-18.1	-73.2	-114.8	-123.9	150.9	Rés. et postes appareutés

78

Summary of balance of payments
Millions of US dollars *[cont.]*

Résumé des balances des paiements
Millions de dollars des E.-U. *[suite]*

Country or area	1995	1996	1997	1998	1999	2000	2001	Pays ou zone
Suriname								**Suriname**
Goods: Exports fob	415.6	397.2	401.6	349.7	342.0	399.1	437.0	Biens : exportations, fab
Goods: Imports fob	-292.6	-398.8	-365.5	-376.9	-297.9	-246.1	-297.2	Biens : importations, fab
Serv. & Income: Credit	106.8	110.8	99.0	78.5	87.0	104.1	64.8	Serv. & revenu : crédit
Serv. & Income: Debit	-166.7	-173.8	-203.8	-203.9	-158.7	-222.7	-287.7	Serv & revenu : débit
Current Trans.,nie: Credit	2.0	3.6	4.0	1.3	1.8	1.2	2.1	Transf. cour.,nia : crédit
Current Transfers: Debit	-2.3	-2.5	-3.0	-3.6	-3.3	-3.3	-3.0	Transf. courants : débit
Capital Acct.,nie: Credit	22.1	41.6	14.6	6.6	3.5	2.3	1.5	Compte de cap.,nia : crédit
Capital Account: Debit	0.0	0.0	0.0	0.0	0.0	0.0	0.0	Compte de capital : débit
Financial Account, nie	-6.7	27.7	26.9	30.5	-21.6	-139.1	104.5	Compte d'op. fin., nia
Net Errors and Omissions	41.6	-7.5	45.3	125.9	42.8	114.3	56.1	Erreurs et omissions nettes
Reserves & Related Items	-119.8	1.7	-19.1	-8.1	4.4	-9.8	-78.1	Rés. et postes appareutés
Swaziland								**Swaziland**
Goods: Exports fob	867.8	850.5	961.3	967.8	936.7	905.0	809.3	Biens : exportations, fab
Goods: Imports fob	-1 064.4	-1 054.4	-1 065.5	-1 073.8	-1 067.9	-1 040.9	-882.0	Biens : importations, fab
Serv. & Income: Credit	314.4	301.5	274.6	259.3	259.3	232.6	203.8	Serv. & revenu : crédit
Serv. & Income: Debit	-291.5	-309.4	-289.5	-379.1	-280.8	-271.4	-263.4	Serv & revenu : débit
Current Trans.,nie: Credit	257.2	268.7	226.8	242.7	241.4	234.1	186.1	Transf. cour.,nia : crédit
Current Transfers: Debit	-113.3	-108.9	-110.5	-110.3	-110.2	-110.9	-106.5	Transf. courants : débit
Capital Acct.,nie: Credit	0.3	0.1	0.1	0.0	0.0	0.1	0.2	Compte de cap.,nia : crédit
Capital Account: Debit	-0.3	0.0	0.0	0.0	0.0	0.0	0.4	Compte de capital : débit
Financial Account, nie	-47.3	-8.6	31.4	117.0	37.7	36.1	-43.2	Compte d'op. fin., nia
Net Errors and Omissions	78.9	36.9	-16.8	4.1	10.0	9.5	12.1	Erreurs et omissions nettes
Reserves & Related Items	-1.8	23.5	-11.9	-27.8	-26.0	5.7	83.3	Rés. et postes appareutés
Sweden								**Suède**
Goods: Exports fob	79 903.4	84 689.6	83 193.7	85 179.0	87 568.0	87 431.0	76 200.0	Biens : exportations, fab
Goods: Imports fob	-63 925.6	-66 053.4	-65 194.8	-67 547.3	-71 854.2	-72 215.7	-62 368.4	Biens : importations, fab
Serv. & Income: Credit	30 527.6	31 268.4	32 173.3	34 515.3	39 774.8	40 325.8	39 931.0	Serv. & revenu : crédit
Serv. & Income: Debit	-38 595.1	-41 396.3	-40 037.1	-44 069.9	-45 907.3	-45 577.0	-43 805.3	Serv & revenu : débit
Current Trans.,nie: Credit	1 554.6	2 524.0	2 318.6	2 266.0	2 340.6	2 602.5	2 577.6	Transf. cour.,nia : crédit
Current Transfers: Debit	-4 524.6	-5 140.0	-5 048.1	-5 703.7	-5 939.6	-5 950.1	-5 838.8	Transf. courants : débit
Capital Acct.,nie: Credit	32.3	31.3	210.9	1 502.2	1 288.6	1 225.7	1 110.7	Compte de cap.,nia : crédit
Capital Account: Debit	-18.3	-22.4	-438.6	-634.0	-3 431.9	-841.2	-601.2	Compte de capital : débit
Financial Account, nie	-5 052.5	-10 046.2	-10 121.2	5 960.7	-1 412.9	-3 296.6	1 824.2	Compte d'op. fin., nia
Net Errors and Omissions	-1 566.0	-2 240.6	-3 768.9	-8 214.5	-544.6	-3 533.9	-10 077.8	Erreurs et omissions nettes
Reserves & Related Items	1 664.1	6 385.6	6 712.1	-3 253.8	-1 881.4	-170.5	1 048.2	Rés. et postes appareutés
Switzerland								**Suisse**
Goods: Exports fob	97 139.1	95 543.7	95 039.5	93 781.7	91 823.4	94 841.9	95 825.8	Biens : exportations, fab
Goods: Imports fob	-93 879.8	-93 675.6	-92 302.0	-92 849.2	-90 980.6	-92 738.1	-94 262.0	Biens : importations, fab
Serv. & Income: Credit	57 600.5	59 247.3	60 366.5	72 658.2	78 569.8	89 913.7	77 476.8	Serv. & revenu : crédit
Serv. & Income: Debit	-34 814.4	-36 073.3	-33 023.9	-43 135.2	-45 687.7	-55 455.7	-52 343.1	Serv & revenu : débit
Current Trans.,nie: Credit	2 995.4	2 961.1	2 625.9	2 785.9	7 637.7	6 852.6	9 681.7	Transf. cour.,nia : crédit
Current Transfers: Debit	-7 236.6	-6 949.0	-6 027.7	-6 467.0	-11 751.8	-9 776.5	-13 754.9	Transf. courants : débit
Capital Acct.,nie: Credit	-121.8	-104.4	-42.7	664.2	-35.3	406.2	1 922.2	Compte de cap.,nia : crédit
Capital Account: Debit	-472.7	-233.0	-202.6	-406.3	-267.0	-3 478.7	-1 733.2	Compte de capital : débit
Financial Account, nie	-8 643.8	-24 252.2	-22 758.7	-22 988.5	-34 077.0	-28 163.1	-30 691.2	Compte d'op. fin., nia
Net Errors and Omissions	-12 536.8	6 056.8	-1 520.5	-2 864.6	2 284.0	-6 406.9	8 516.3	Erreurs et omissions nettes
Reserves & Related Items	-29.1	-2 521.5	-2 153.9	-1 179.2	2 484.5	4 004.6	-638.3	Rés. et postes appareutés
Syrian Arab Republic								**Rép. arabe syrienne**
Goods: Exports fob	3 858.0	4 178.0	4 057.0	3 142.0	3 806.0	5 146.0	...	Biens : exportations, fab
Goods: Imports fob	-4 004.0	-4 516.0	-3 603.0	-3 320.0	-3 590.0	-3 723.0	...	Biens : importations, fab
Serv. & Income: Credit	2 343.0	2 326.0	2 003.0	2 035.0	2 007.0	2 045.0	...	Serv. & revenu : crédit
Serv. & Income: Debit	-2 541.0	-2 572.0	-2 495.0	-2 330.0	-2 511.0	-2 891.0	...	Serv & revenu : débit
Current Trans.,nie: Credit	610.0	630.0	504.0	533.0	491.0	495.0	...	Transf. cour.,nia : crédit
Current Transfers: Debit	-3.0	-6.0	-5.0	-2.0	-2.0	-10.0	...	Transf. courants : débit
Capital Acct.,nie: Credit	20.0	26.0	18.0	27.0	80.0	63.0	...	Compte de cap.,nia : crédit
Capital Account: Debit	0.0	0.0	0.0	0.0	0.0	0.0	...	Compte de capital : débit
Financial Account, nie	521.0	782.0	65.0	196.0	173.0	-392.0	...	Compte d'op. fin., nia
Net Errors and Omissions	35.0	139.0	-95.0	153.1	-195.0	-192.0	...	Erreurs et omissions nettes
Reserves & Related Items	-839.0	-987.0	-449.0	-434.1	-259.0	-541.0	...	Rés. et postes appareutés
Thailand								**Thaïlande**
Goods: Exports fob	55 446.6	54 408.4	56 655.9	52 752.9	56 775.1	67 893.6	63 201.8	Biens : exportations, fab

78

Summary of balance of payments
Millions of US dollars *[cont.]*

Résumé des balances des paiements
Millions de dollars des E.-U. *[suite]*

Country or area	1995	1996	1997	1998	1999	2000	2001	Pays ou zone
Goods: Imports fob	-63 414.9	-63 896.6	-55 084.3	-36 514.9	-42 761.8	-56 193.0	-54 619.7	Biens : importations, fab
Serv. & Income: Credit	18 646.1	20 976.3	19 505.6	16 479.3	17 726.9	18 103.1	16 863.2	Serv. & revenu : crédit
Serv. & Income: Debit	-24 718.3	-26 939.3	-24 577.0	-18 889.1	-19 665.6	-21 076.5	-19 819.1	Serv & revenu : débit
Current Trans.,nie: Credit	1 190.2	1 651.0	1 392.1	819.8	805.6	951.6	990.0	Transf. cour.,nia : crédit
Current Transfers: Debit	-703.7	-891.3	-913.3	-405.4	-452.5	-365.7	-389.2	Transf. courants : débit
Capital Acct.,nie: Credit	0.0	0.0	0.0	0.0	0.0	0.0	0.0	Compte de cap.,nia : crédit
Capital Account: Debit	0.0	0.0	0.0	0.0	0.0	0.0	0.0	Compte de capital : débit
Financial Account, nie	21 908.6	19 486.0	-12 055.7	-14 110.3	-11 073.0	-10 434.3	-3 907.8	Compte d'op. fin., nia
Net Errors and Omissions	-1 196.0	-2 627.3	-3 173.0	-2 828.1	33.4	-685.2	155.5	Erreurs et omissions nettes
Reserves & Related Items	-7 158.7	-2 167.3	18 249.8	2 696.0	-1 388.3	1 806.4	-2 474.6	Rés. et postes appareutés
TFYR of Macedonia								**L'ex-R.y. Macédoine**
Goods: Exports fob	...	1 147.4	1 201.4	1 292.9	1 192.1	1 317.1	1 153.5	Biens : exportations, fab
Goods: Imports fob	...	-1 464.0	-1 589.1	-1 713.2	-1 602.2	-1 875.2	-1 574.9	Biens : importations, fab
Serv. & Income: Credit	...	199.6	167.3	154.9	270.9	345.2	281.9	Serv. & revenu : crédit
Serv. & Income: Debit	...	-384.3	-345.4	-372.7	-390.1	-445.0	-425.3	Serv & revenu : débit
Current Trans.,nie: Credit	...	475.4	535.0	692.6	750.3	923.1	872.5	Transf. cour.,nia : crédit
Current Transfers: Debit	...	-262.3	-244.8	-366.2	-330.2	-372.4	-632.0	Transf. courants : débit
Capital Acct.,nie: Credit	...	0.0	0.0	11.2	4.4	0.3	3.6	Compte de cap.,nia : crédit
Capital Account: Debit	...	0.0	0.0	-1.8	0.0	0.0	-2.3	Compte de capital : débit
Financial Account, nie	...	174.3	186.8	449.2	189.6	385.2	388.2	Compte d'op. fin., nia
Net Errors and Omissions	...	18.8	-29.9	-114.8	34.5	-46.0	25.9	Erreurs et omissions nettes
Reserves & Related Items	...	95.1	118.6	-32.1	-119.2	-232.3	-91.1	Rés. et postes appareutés
Togo								**Togo**
Goods: Exports fob	377.4	440.6	422.5	420.3	391.5	361.8	...	Biens : exportations, fab
Goods: Imports fob	-506.5	-567.8	-530.6	-553.5	-489.4	-484.6	...	Biens : importations, fab
Serv. & Income: Credit	96.1	161.8	123.5	120.4	108.6	94.7	...	Serv. & revenu : crédit
Serv. & Income: Debit	-206.6	-273.4	-231.7	-217.0	-209.1	-179.5	...	Serv & revenu : débit
Current Trans.,nie: Credit	129.7	106.8	120.2	101.8	73.6	73.3	...	Transf. cour.,nia : crédit
Current Transfers: Debit	-12.1	-21.9	-20.8	-12.2	-2.2	-5.4	...	Transf. courants : débit
Capital Acct.,nie: Credit	0.0	5.6	5.8	6.1	6.9	8.7	...	Compte de cap.,nia : crédit
Capital Account: Debit	0.0	0.0	0.0	0.0	0.0	0.0	...	Compte de capital : débit
Financial Account, nie	-52.8	151.3	126.9	114.1	155.5	162.8	...	Compte d'op. fin., nia
Net Errors and Omissions	-19.3	-27.9	-2.7	2.7	-3.7	5.0	...	Erreurs et omissions nettes
Reserves & Related Items	194.0	24.9	-13.1	17.2	-31.6	-36.8	...	Rés. et postes appareutés
Tonga								**Tonga**
Goods: Exports fob	...	...	...	...	...	...	6.7	Biens : exportations, fab
Goods: Imports fob	...	...	...	...	...	...	-63.7	Biens : importations, fab
Serv. & Income: Credit	...	...	...	...	...	...	22.8	Serv. & revenu : crédit
Serv. & Income: Debit	...	...	...	...	...	...	-29.4	Serv & revenu : débit
Current Trans.,nie: Credit	...	...	...	...	...	...	62.5	Transf. cour.,nia : crédit
Current Transfers: Debit	...	...	...	...	...	...	-11.7	Transf. courants : débit
Capital Acct.,nie: Credit	...	...	...	...	...	...	11.7	Compte de cap.,nia : crédit
Capital Account: Debit	...	...	...	...	...	...	-2.6	Compte de capital : débit
Financial Account, nie	...	...	...	...	...	...	1.0	Compte d'op. fin., nia
Net Errors and Omissions	...	...	...	...	...	...	4.3	Erreurs et omissions nettes
Reserves & Related Items	...	...	...	...	...	...	-1.6	Rés. et postes appareutés
Trinidad and Tobago								**Trinité-et-Tobago**
Goods: Exports fob	2 456.1	2 354.1	2 448.0	2 258.0	...	...	...	Biens : exportations, fab
Goods: Imports fob	-1 868.5	-1 971.6	-2 976.6	-2 998.9	...	...	...	Biens : importations, fab
Serv. & Income: Credit	419.2	500.3	610.3	735.8	...	...	...	Serv. & revenu : crédit
Serv. & Income: Debit	-708.6	-770.6	-699.0	-660.7	...	...	...	Serv & revenu : débit
Current Trans.,nie: Credit	34.0	34.2	37.0	58.4	...	...	...	Transf. cour.,nia : crédit
Current Transfers: Debit	-38.5	-41.3	-33.2	-36.2	...	...	...	Transf. courants : débit
Capital Acct.,nie: Credit	1.1	0.0	0.0	0.0	...	...	...	Compte de cap.,nia : crédit
Capital Account: Debit	-13.0	0.0	0.0	0.0	...	...	...	Compte de capital : débit
Financial Account, nie	-214.7	43.0	697.2	471.5	...	...	...	Compte d'op. fin., nia
Net Errors and Omissions	16.5	90.0	110.1	252.2	...	...	...	Erreurs et omissions nettes
Reserves & Related Items	-83.7	-238.1	-193.6	-80.2	...	...	...	Rés. et postes appareutés
Tunisia								**Tunisie**
Goods: Exports fob	5 469.7	5 518.8	5 559.2	5 724.0	5 873.3	5 840.2	6 605.9	Biens : exportations, fab
Goods: Imports fob	-7 458.6	-7 279.6	-7 514.2	-7 875.5	-8 014.5	-8 093.0	-8 996.9	Biens : importations, fab
Serv. & Income: Credit	2 628.6	2 697.7	2 690.1	2 847.9	3 009.5	2 860.6	3 006.9	Serv. & revenu : crédit

78

Summary of balance of payments
Millions of US dollars [cont.]
Résumé des balances des paiements
Millions de dollars des E.-U. [suite]

Country or area	1995	1996	1997	1998	1999	2000	2001	Pays ou zone
Serv. & Income: Debit	-2 187.7	-2 274.5	-2 121.3	-2 203.3	-2 212.1	-2 254.4	-2 460.5	Serv & revenu : débit
Current Trans.,nie: Credit	804.7	879.4	821.0	851.8	919.7	825.1	958.5	Transf. cour.,nia : crédit
Current Transfers: Debit	-30.7	-19.5	-29.8	-20.2	-17.7	0.0	23.6	Transf. courants : débit
Capital Acct.,nie: Credit	46.5	46.2	94.9	82.5	72.5	8.8	55.6	Compte de cap.,nia : crédit
Capital Account: Debit	-14.8	-9.2	-18.1	-22.0	-13.5	-5.8	-2.8	Compte de capital : débit
Financial Account, nie	958.0	815.7	699.0	489.1	1 083.3	646.4	1 125.3	Compte d'op. fin., nia
Net Errors and Omissions	-118.9	67.0	205.6	-12.0	37.6	-32.8	-27.2	Erreurs et omissions nettes
Reserves & Related Items	-96.8	-442.0	-386.5	137.6	-738.1	205.0	-288.4	Rés. et postes appareutés
Turkey								**Turquie**
Goods: Exports fob	21 975.0	32 067.0	32 110.0	30 662.0	28 842.0	30 721.0	34 379.0	Biens : exportations, fab
Goods: Imports fob	-35 187.0	-42 681.0	-47 513.0	-44 926.0	-39 326.0	-53 131.0	-38 916.0	Biens : importations, fab
Serv. & Income: Credit	16 095.0	15 007.0	21 810.0	26 360.0	19 231.0	23 265.0	18 812.0	Serv. & revenu : crédit
Serv. & Income: Debit	-9 717.0	-11 277.0	-13 911.0	-15 839.0	-15 282.0	-15 899.0	-14 682.0	Serv & revenu : débit
Current Trans.,nie: Credit	4 512.0	4 466.0	4 909.0	5 861.0	5 295.0	5 317.0	3 861.0	Transf. cour.,nia : crédit
Current Transfers: Debit	-16.0	-19.0	-43.0	-134.0	-120.0	-92.0	-58.0	Transf. courants : débit
Capital Acct.,nie: Credit	0.0	0.0	0.0	0.0	0.0	0.0	0.0	Compte de cap.,nia : crédit
Capital Account: Debit	0.0	0.0	0.0	0.0	0.0	0.0	0.0	Compte de capital : débit
Financial Account, nie	4 643.0	5 483.0	6 969.0	-840.0	5 085.0	8 610.0	-14 198.0	Compte d'op. fin., nia
Net Errors and Omissions	2 355.3	1 497.5	-987.8	-703.1	1 629.5	-2 724.5	-2 085.5	Erreurs et omissions nettes
Reserves & Related Items	-4 660.3	-4 543.5	-3 343.2	-440.9	-5 354.5	3 933.5	12 887.5	Rés. et postes appareutés
Turkmenistan								**Turkménistan**
Goods: Exports fob	...	1 692.0	774.2	...	...	...	...	Biens : exportations, fab
Goods: Imports fob	...	-1 388.3	-1 005.1	...	...	...	...	Biens : importations, fab
Serv. & Income: Credit	...	209.6	428.7	...	...	...	...	Serv. & revenu : crédit
Serv. & Income: Debit	...	-518.4	-746.6	...	...	...	...	Serv & revenu : débit
Current Trans.,nie: Credit	...	4.8	49.9	...	...	...	...	Transf. cour.,nia : crédit
Current Transfers: Debit	...	0.0	-81.2	...	...	...	...	Transf. courants : débit
Capital Acct.,nie: Credit	...	2.8	14.0	...	...	...	...	Compte de cap.,nia : crédit
Capital Account: Debit	...	-159.7	-22.9	...	...	...	...	Compte de capital : débit
Financial Account, nie	...	113.4	1 060.0	...	...	...	...	Compte d'op. fin., nia
Net Errors and Omissions	...	51.6	-72.9	...	...	...	...	Erreurs et omissions nettes
Reserves & Related Items	...	-7.9	-398.0	...	...	...	...	Rés. et postes appareutés
Uganda								**Ouganda**
Goods: Exports fob	560.3	639.3	592.6	510.2	483.5	449.9	451.8	Biens : exportations, fab
Goods: Imports fob	-926.8	-986.9	-1 042.6	-1 166.3	-989.1	-949.7	-1 026.6	Biens : importations, fab
Serv. & Income: Credit	121.7	174.4	205.1	227.0	218.7	237.4	219.9	Serv. & revenu : crédit
Serv. & Income: Debit	-676.0	-753.8	-724.6	-788.0	-581.7	-620.6	-669.5	Serv & revenu : débit
Current Trans.,nie: Credit	581.9	674.7	602.6	714.6	329.7	340.0	583.0	Transf. cour.,nia : crédit
Current Transfers: Debit	0.0	0.0	0.0	0.0	-184.2	-307.6	-367.9	Transf. courants : débit
Capital Acct.,nie: Credit	48.3	61.4	31.9	49.5	0.0	0.0	0.0	Compte de cap.,nia : crédit
Capital Account: Debit	0.0	0.0	0.0	0.0	0.0	0.0	0.0	Compte de capital : débit
Financial Account, nie	210.7	140.5	298.8	372.8	253.3	320.5	499.7	Compte d'op. fin., nia
Net Errors and Omissions	28.8	41.3	-4.8	39.7	14.4	65.8	70.9	Erreurs et omissions nettes
Reserves & Related Items	51.2	9.1	40.9	40.6	455.4	464.3	238.9	Rés. et postes appareutés
Ukraine								**Ukraine**
Goods: Exports fob	14 244.0	15 547.0	15 418.0	13 699.0	13 189.0	15 722.0	17 091.0	Biens : exportations, fab
Goods: Imports fob	-16 946.0	-19 843.0	-19 623.0	-16 283.0	-12 945.0	-14 943.0	-16 893.0	Biens : importations, fab
Serv. & Income: Credit	3 093.0	4 901.0	5 095.0	4 044.0	3 967.0	3 943.0	4 162.0	Serv. & revenu : crédit
Serv. & Income: Debit	-2 015.0	-2 298.0	-3 070.0	-3 538.0	-3 259.0	-4 089.0	-4 414.0	Serv & revenu : débit
Current Trans.,nie: Credit	557.0	619.0	942.0	868.0	754.0	967.0	1 516.0	Transf. cour.,nia : crédit
Current Transfers: Debit	-85.0	-110.0	-97.0	-86.0	-48.0	-119.0	-60.0	Transf. courants : débit
Capital Acct.,nie: Credit	6.0	5.0	0.0	0.0	0.0	0.0	8.0	Compte de cap.,nia : crédit
Capital Account: Debit	0.0	0.0	0.0	-3.0	-10.0	-8.0	-5.0	Compte de capital : débit
Financial Account, nie	-726.0	317.0	1 413.0	-1 340.0	-879.0	-752.0	-191.0	Compte d'op. fin., nia
Net Errors and Omissions	248.2	259.3	-780.7	-817.9	-953.1	-148.2	-220.8	Erreurs et omissions nettes
Reserves & Related Items	1 623.8	602.8	702.7	3 456.9	184.1	-572.8	-993.2	Rés. et postes appareutés
United Kingdom								**Royaume-Uni**
Goods: Exports fob	242 318.0	261 247.0	281 537.0	271 723.0	268 884.0	284 378.0	276 108.0	Biens : exportations, fab
Goods: Imports fob	-261324.0	-282475.0	-301739.0	-307851.0	-313179.0	-330269.0	-324367.0	Biens : importations, fab
Serv. & Income: Credit	217 657.1	231 834.2	255 456.7	279 154.0	277 039.0	321 174.0	311 179.0	Serv. & revenu : crédit
Serv. & Income: Debit	-201000.6	-214997.0	-228595.7	-237348.0	-253874.8	-288962.1	-282915.1	Serv & revenu : débit
Current Trans.,nie: Credit	19 697.8	29 456.4	21 443.0	20 589.5	22 699.1	18 656.7	23 574.2	Transf. cour.,nia : crédit

78

Summary of balance of payments
Millions of US dollars *[cont.]*
Résumé des balances des paiements
Millions de dollars des E.-U. *[suite]*

Country or area	1995	1996	1997	1998	1999	2000	2001	Pays ou zone
Current Transfers: Debit	-31 640.7	-38 506.2	-30 952.4	-34 233.0	-33 512.3	-33 796.0	-33 857.5	Transf. courants : débit
Capital Acct.,nie: Credit	1 835.4	2 182.8	2 771.4	2 435.5	2 906.5	4 361.8	3 859.3	Compte de cap.,nia : crédit
Capital Account: Debit	-994.4	-1 039.8	-1 452.0	-1 647.2	-1 385.0	-1 604.2	-2 144.3	Compte de capital : débit
Financial Account, nie	7 470.4	7 983.0	-12 157.5	234.8	30 968.1	26 165.6	16 225.6	Compte d'op. fin., nia
Net Errors and Omissions	5 127.0	3 663.2	9 786.8	6 684.3	-1 582.0	5 193.8	7 879.6	Erreurs et omissions nettes
Reserves & Related Items	853.0	651.0	3 902.5	257.0	1 035.9	-5 298.4	4 456.5	Rés. et postes appareutés
United Rep. of Tanzania								**Rép.-Unie de Tanzanie**
Goods: Exports fob	682.5	764.1	715.3	589.5	542.9	665.7	...	Biens : exportations, fab
Goods: Imports fob	-1 340.0	-1 213.1	-1 164.5	-1 365.3	-1 368.3	-1 339.8	...	Biens : importations, fab
Serv. & Income: Credit	614.4	658.4	539.0	590.0	679.3	674.1	...	Serv. & revenu : crédit
Serv. & Income: Debit	-941.4	-1 058.7	-965.5	-1 161.8	-889.9	-809.4	...	Serv & revenu : débit
Current Trans.,nie: Credit	370.5	370.9	313.6	426.4	413.4	406.0	...	Transf. cour.,nia : crédit
Current Transfers: Debit	-32.3	-32.3	-67.7	-35.5	-123.3	-77.0	...	Transf. courants : débit
Capital Acct.,nie: Credit	190.9	191.0	360.6	422.9	322.5	331.7	...	Compte de cap.,nia : crédit
Capital Account: Debit	0.0	0.0	0.0	0.0	0.0	0.0	...	Compte de capital : débit
Financial Account, nie	66.7	-92.8	3.6	77.6	80.8	-123.8	...	Compte d'op. fin., nia
Net Errors and Omissions	30.0	158.6	-31.9	-53.5	269.3	137.7	...	Erreurs et omissions nettes
Reserves & Related Items	358.7	254.0	297.5	509.4	73.4	134.8	...	Rés. et postes appareutés
United States								**Etats-Unis**
Goods: Exports fob	577 050.0	614 020.0	680 330.0	672 380.0	686 280.0	774 640.0	721 750.0	Biens : exportations, fab
Goods: Imports fob	-749380.0	-803120.0	-876510.0	-917120.0	-1029980.0	-1224430.0	-1145980.0	Biens : importations, fab
Serv. & Income: Credit	429 000.0	464 030.0	515 280.0	519 680.0	561 460.0	642 660.0	560 040.0	Serv. & revenu : crédit
Serv. & Income: Debit	-328420.0	-352680.0	-406670.0	-434290.0	-461 860.0	-549 740.0	-479 730.0	Serv & revenu : débit
Current Trans.,nie: Credit	7 680.0	8 890.0	8 490.0	9 190.0	9 570.0	10 650.0	10 470.0	Transf. cour.,nia : crédit
Current Transfers: Debit	-41 750.0	-48 980.0	-49 280.0	-53 690.0	-58 330.0	-64 080.0	-59 940.0	Transf. courants : débit
Capital Acct.,nie: Credit	671.0	693.0	350.0	704.0	598.0	837.0	826.0	Compte de cap.,nia : crédit
Capital Account: Debit	-300.0	0.0	0.0	0.0	-3 990.0	0.0	0.0	Compte de capital : débit
Financial Account, nie	95 938.0	130 517.0	220 160.0	70 604.0	256 113.0	409 813.0	386 786.0	Compte d'op. fin., nia
Net Errors and Omissions	19 260.3	-20 038.8	-91 133.0	139 286.0	31 405.0	-51.1	10 703.7	Erreurs et omissions nettes
Reserves & Related Items	-9 749.3	6 668.8	-1 017.0	-6 744.3	8 734.0	-298.9	-4 925.7	Rés. et postes appareutés
Uruguay								**Uruguay**
Goods: Exports fob	2 147.6	2 448.5	2 793.1	2 829.3	2 290.6	2 383.8	2 143.6	Biens : exportations, fab
Goods: Imports fob	-2 710.6	-3 135.4	-3 497.5	-3 601.4	-3 187.2	-3 311.1	-2 914.5	Biens : importations, fab
Serv. & Income: Credit	1 763.5	1 859.2	1 971.4	1 927.1	1 997.1	2 057.2	1 959.5	Serv. & revenu : crédit
Serv. & Income: Debit	-1 489.0	-1 488.2	-1 628.6	-1 689.5	-1 681.6	-1 723.6	-1 744.3	Serv & revenu : débit
Current Trans.,nie: Credit	84.0	90.7	83.0	75.0	78.4	48.0	48.0	Transf. cour.,nia : crédit
Current Transfers: Debit	-8.0	-8.2	-8.8	-16.0	-4.9	-20.5	-4.8	Transf. courants : débit
Capital Acct.,nie: Credit	0.0	0.0	0.0	0.0	0.0	0.0	0.0	Compte de cap.,nia : crédit
Capital Account: Debit	0.0	0.0	0.0	0.0	0.0	0.0	0.0	Compte de capital : débit
Financial Account, nie	421.7	233.6	608.7	545.1	147.1	779.3	799.6	Compte d'op. fin., nia
Net Errors and Omissions	18.6	152.2	78.8	285.5	250.9	-46.6	16.5	Erreurs et omissions nettes
Reserves & Related Items	-227.8	-152.4	-400.1	-355.1	109.6	-166.5	-303.6	Rés. et postes appareutés
Vanuatu								**Vanuatu**
Goods: Exports fob	28.3	30.2	35.3	33.8	25.7	27.2	19.9	Biens : exportations, fab
Goods: Imports fob	-79.4	-81.1	-79.0	-76.2	-84.5	-76.9	-78.0	Biens : importations, fab
Serv. & Income: Credit	94.7	108.6	103.2	134.9	135.8	148.5	136.5	Serv. & revenu : crédit
Serv. & Income: Debit	-85.1	-84.0	-81.6	-86.2	-98.2	-101.9	-94.2	Serv & revenu : débit
Current Trans.,nie: Credit	23.8	22.4	21.8	15.6	18.7	27.4	39.5	Transf. cour.,nia : crédit
Current Transfers: Debit	-0.6	-22.9	-19.0	-31.2	-30.8	-38.0	-38.3	Transf. courants : débit
Capital Acct.,nie: Credit	38.3	43.4	23.8	25.4	23.9	31.9	46.1	Compte de cap.,nia : crédit
Capital Account: Debit	-6.7	-38.5	-29.2	-46.3	-73.7	-55.5	-62.1	Compte de capital : débit
Financial Account, nie	25.3	20.9	-16.7	17.4	56.2	19.3	12.8	Compte d'op. fin., nia
Net Errors and Omissions	-33.4	-4.1	39.4	6.0	3.6	-0.9	7.5	Erreurs et omissions nettes
Reserves & Related Items	-5.3	5.3	2.2	6.9	23.2	18.8	10.3	Rés. et postes appareutés
Venezuela								**Venezuela**
Goods: Exports fob	19 082.0	23 707.0	23 703.0	17 576.0	20 819.0	32 998.0	26 726.0	Biens : exportations, fab
Goods: Imports fob	-12 069.0	-9 937.0	-13 678.0	-15 105.0	-13 213.0	-15 491.0	-17 391.0	Biens : importations, fab
Serv. & Income: Credit	3 538.0	3 152.0	3 628.0	3 747.0	3 469.0	4 136.0	3 775.0	Serv. & revenu : crédit
Serv. & Income: Debit	-8 646.0	-8 146.0	-10 042.0	-9 363.0	-7 456.0	-8 391.0	-8 562.0	Serv & revenu : débit
Current Trans.,nie: Credit	413.0	526.0	221.0	275.0	191.0	222.0	196.0	Transf. cour.,nia : crédit
Current Transfers: Debit	-304.0	-388.0	-365.0	-383.0	-251.0	-444.0	-813.0	Transf. courants : débit
Capital Acct.,nie: Credit	0.0	0.0	0.0	0.0	0.0	0.0	0.0	Compte de cap.,nia : crédit

78

Summary of balance of payments
Millions of US dollars *[cont.]*

Résumé des balances des paiements
Millions de dollars des E.-U. *[suite]*

Country or area	1995	1996	1997	1998	1999	2000	2001	Pays ou zone
Capital Account: Debit	0.0	0.0	0.0	0.0	0.0	0.0	0.0	Compte de capital : débit
Financial Account, nie	-2 964.0	-1 784.0	1 069.0	1 764.0	-1 010.0	-2 955.0	-811.0	Compte d'op. fin., nia
Net Errors and Omissions	-494.2	-891.8	-1 460.6	-1 442.3	-1 510.0	-4 250.2	-5 183.4	Erreurs et omissions nettes
Reserves & Related Items	1 444.2	-6 238.2	-3 075.4	2 931.3	-1 039.0	-5 824.8	2 063.4	Rés. et postes appareutés
Viet Nam								**Viet Nam**
Goods: Exports fob	...	7 255.0	9 185.0	9 361.0	11 540.0	14 448.0	15 027.0	Biens : exportations, fab
Goods: Imports fob	...	-10 030.0	-10 432.0	-10 350.0	-10 568.0	-14 073.0	-14 546.0	Biens : importations, fab
Serv. & Income: Credit	...	2 383.0	2 666.0	2 743.0	2 635.0	3 033.0	3 128.0	Serv. & revenu : crédit
Serv. & Income: Debit	...	-2 828.0	-3 832.0	-3 950.0	-3 611.0	-4 034.0	-4 177.0	Serv & revenu : débit
Current Trans.,nie: Credit	...	1 200.0	885.0	1 122.0	1 181.0	1 732.0	1 250.0	Transf. cour.,nia : crédit
Current Transfers: Debit	...	0.0	0.0	0.0	0.0	0.0	0.0	Transf. courants : débit
Capital Acct.,nie: Credit	...	0.0	0.0	0.0	0.0	0.0	0.0	Compte de cap.,nia : crédit
Capital Account: Debit	...	0.0	0.0	0.0	0.0	0.0	0.0	Compte de capital : débit
Financial Account, nie	...	2 909.0	2 125.0	1 646.0	1 058.0	-316.0	371.0	Compte d'op. fin., nia
Net Errors and Omissions	...	-611.3	-269.2	-534.9	-925.0	-680.1	-846.7	Erreurs et omissions nettes
Reserves & Related Items	...	-277.7	-327.8	-37.1	-1 310.0	-109.9	-206.3	Rés. et postes appareutés
Yemen								**Yémen**
Goods: Exports fob	1 980.1	2 262.7	2 274.0	1 503.7	2 478.3	4 093.8	...	Biens : exportations, fab
Goods: Imports fob	-1 831.5	-2 293.5	-2 406.5	-2 288.8	-2 120.4	-2 484.4	...	Biens : importations, fab
Serv. & Income: Credit	216.8	232.5	277.2	275.5	277.3	508.2	...	Serv. & revenu : crédit
Serv. & Income: Debit	-1 237.7	-1 236.1	-1 348.0	-969.5	-1 289.5	-1 654.7	...	Serv & revenu : débit
Current Trans.,nie: Credit	1 080.5	1 140.1	1 177.6	1 223.5	1 262.1	1 471.9	...	Transf. cour.,nia : crédit
Current Transfers: Debit	-64.5	-66.9	-43.1	-47.7	-30.7	-72.4	...	Transf. courants : débit
Capital Acct.,nie: Credit	0.0	0.0	4 236.2	2.2	1.5	391.8	...	Compte de cap.,nia : crédit
Capital Account: Debit	0.0	0.0	0.0	0.0	0.0	-80.0	...	Compte de capital : débit
Financial Account, nie	-858.4	-367.8	-197.6	-468.0	-549.8	-913.1	...	Compte d'op. fin., nia
Net Errors and Omissions	186.5	-107.0	48.4	188.2	45.2	333.3	...	Erreurs et omissions nettes
Reserves & Related Items	528.2	436.0	-4 018.2	580.9	-74.0	-1 594.4	...	Rés. et postes appareutés
Zambia								**Zambie**
Goods: Exports fob	...	...	1 110.4	818.0	772.0	757.0	...	Biens : exportations, fab
Goods: Imports fob	...	...	-1 056.0	-971.0	-870.0	-978.0	...	Biens : importations, fab
Serv. & Income: Credit	...	...	188.6	146.3	150.5	160.6	...	Serv. & revenu : crédit
Serv. & Income: Debit	...	...	-577.2	-539.7	-483.4	-505.9	...	Serv & revenu : débit
Current Trans.,nie: Credit	...	...	0.0	0.0	0.0	0.0	...	Transf. cour.,nia : crédit
Current Transfers: Debit	...	...	-19.0	-27.0	-16.0	-18.0	...	Transf. courants : débit
Capital Acct.,nie: Credit	...	...	0.0	203.0	196.0	153.0	...	Compte de cap.,nia : crédit
Capital Account: Debit	...	...	0.0	0.0	0.0	0.0	...	Compte de capital : débit
Financial Account, nie	...	...	-323.8	-263.7	-173.9	-273.6	...	Compte d'op. fin., nia
Net Errors and Omissions	...	...	-255.4	-37.4	-229.4	184.8	...	Erreurs et omissions nettes
Reserves & Related Items	...	...	932.4	671.4	654.2	520.2	...	Rés. et postes appareutés

Source:
International Monetary Fund (IMF), Washington, D.C., "International Financial Statistics," January 2003 and the IMF database.

Source:
Fonds monétaire international (FMI), Washington, D.C.,"Statistiques Financières Internationales," janvier 2003 et la base de données du FMI.

1 BLEU trade data refer to the Belgium-Luxembourg Economic Union and exclude transactions between the two countries. Beginning in 1997, trade data are for Belgium only, which includes trade between Belgium and Luxembourg.

2 Services only.

1 Les données sur le commerce extérieur se rapportent à l'Union économique belgo-luxembourgeoise (UEBL) et ne couvrent pas les transactions entre les deux pays. A compter de 1997, les données sur le commerce extérieur ne se rapportent qu'à la Belgique, et recouvrent les échanges entre la Belgique et le Luxembourg.

2 Service seulement.

Technical notes, table 78

A balance of payments can be broadly described as the record of an economy's international economic transactions. It shows (a) transactions in goods, services and income between an economy and the rest of the world, (b) changes of ownership and other changes in that economy's monetary gold, special drawing rights (SDRs) and claims on and liabilities to the rest of the world, and (c) unrequited transfers and counterpart entries needed to balance in the accounting sense any entries for the foregoing transactions and changes which are not mutually offsetting.

The balance of payments are presented on the basis of the methodology and presentation of the fifth edition of the *Balance of Payments Manual* (BPM5) [41], published by the International Monetary Fund in September 1993. The BPM5 incorporates several major changes to take account of developments in international trade and finance over the past decade, and to better harmonize the Fund's balance of payments methodology with the methodology of the 1993 *System of National Accounts* (SNA) [59]. The Fund's balance of payments has been converted for all periods from the BPM4 basis to the BPM5 basis; thus the time series conform to the BPM5 methodology with no methodological breaks.

The detailed definitions concerning the content of the basic categories of the balance of payments are given in the *Balance of Payments Manual (fifth edition)* [41]. Brief explanatory notes are given below to clarify the scope of the major items.

Goods: Exports f.o.b. and *Goods: Imports f.o.b.* are both measured on the "free-on-board" (f.o.b.) basis—that is, by the value of the goods at the border of the exporting country; in the case of imports, this excludes the cost of freight and insurance incurred beyond the border of the exporting country.

Services and income covers transactions in real resources between residents and non-residents other than those classified as merchandise, including (a) shipment and other transportation services, including freight, insurance and other distributive services in connection with the movement of commodities, (b) travel, i.e. goods and services acquired by non-resident travellers in a given country and similar acquisitions by resident travellers abroad, and (c) investment income which covers income of non-residents from their financial assets invested in the compiling economy (debit) and similar income of residents from their financial assets invested abroad (credit).

Current Transfers, n.i.e.: Credit comprises all current transfers received by the reporting country, except those made to the country to finance its "overall bal-

Notes techniques, tableau 78

La balance des paiements peut se définir d'une façon générale comme le relevé des transactions économiques internationales d'une économie. Elle indique (a) les transactions sur biens, services et revenus entre une économie et le reste du monde, (b) les transferts de propriété et autres variations intervenues dans les avoirs en or monétaire de cette économie, dans ses avoirs en droits de tirages spéciaux (DTS) ainsi que dans ses créances financières sur le reste du monde ou dans ses engagements financiers envers lui et (c) les "inscriptions de transferts sans contrepartie" et de "contrepartie" destinées à équilibrer, d'un point de vue comptable, les transactions et changements précités qui ne se compensent pas réciproquement.

Les données de balance des paiements sont présentées conformément à la méthodologie et à la classification recommandées dans la cinquième édition du *Manuel de la balance des paiements* [41], publiée en septembre 1993 par le Fonds monétaire international. La cinquième édition fait état de plusieurs changements importants qui ont été opérés de manière à rendre compte de l'évolution des finances et des changes internationaux pendant la décennie écoulée et à harmoniser davantage la méthodologie de la balance des paiements du FMI avec celle du *Système de comptabilité nationale* (SCN) [59] de 1993. Les statistiques incluses dans la balance des paiements du FMI ont été converties et sont désormais établies, pour toutes les périodes, sur la base de la cinquième et non plus de la quatrième édition; en conséquence, les séries chronologiques sont conformes aux principes de la cinquième édition, sans rupture due à des différences d'ordre méthodologique.

Les définitions détaillées relatives au contenu des postes fondamentaux de la balance des paiements figurent dans le *Manuel de la balance des paiements (cinquième édition)* [41]. De brèves notes explicatives sont présentées ci-après pour clarifier la portée de ces principales rubriques.

Les Biens: exportations, f.à.b. et *Biens: importations, f.à.b.* sont évalués sur la base f.à.b. (franco à bord)—c'est-à-dire à la frontière du pays exportateur; dans le cas des importations, cette valeur exclut le coût du fret et de l'assurance au-delà de la frontière du pays exportateur.

Services et revenus: transactions en ressources effectuées entre résidents et non résidents, autres que celles qui sont considérées comme des marchandises, notamment: (a) expéditions et autres services de transport, y compris le fret, l'assurance et les autres services de distribution liés aux mouvements de marchandises; (b) voyages, à savoir les biens et services acquis par des

ance", hence, the label "n.i.e." (not included elsewhere). (Note: some of the capital and financial accounts labeled "n.i.e." denote that *Exceptional Financing items* and *Liabilities Constituting Foreign Authorities' Reserves* (LCFARs) have been excluded.)

Capital Account, n.i.e.: *Credit* refers mainly to capital transfers linked to the acquisition of a fixed asset other than transactions relating to debt forgiveness plus the disposal of nonproduced, nonfinancial assets. *Capital Account*: *Debit* refers mainly to capital transfers linked to the disposal of fixed assets by the donor or to the financing of capital formation by the recipient, plus the acquisition of nonproduced, nonfinancial assets.

Financial Account, n.i.e. is the net sum of the balance of direct investment, portfolio investment, and other investment transactions.

Net Errors and Omissions is a residual category needed to ensure that all debit and credit entries in the balance of payments statement sum to zero and reflects statistical inconsistencies in the recording of the credit and debit entries.

Reserves and Related Items is the sum of transactions in reserve assets, LCFARs, exceptional financing, and use of Fund credit and loans.

For further information see *International Financial Statistics* [15] and <www.imf.org>.

voyageurs non résidents dans un pays donné et achats similaires faits par des résidents voyageant à l'étranger; et (c) revenus des investissements, qui correspondent aux revenus que les non résidents tirent de leurs avoirs financiers placés dans l'économie déclarante (débit) et les revenus similaires que les résidents tirent de leurs avoirs financiers placés à l'étranger (crédit).

Les transferts courants, n.i.a: *Crédit* englobent tous les transferts courants reçus par l'économie qui établit sa balance des paiements, à l'exception de ceux qui sont destinés à financer sa "balance globale"—c'est ce qui explique la mention "n.i.a." (non inclus ailleurs). (Note: comptes de capital et d'opérations financières portent la mention "n.i.a.", ce qui signifie que les postes de *Financement exceptionnel* et les *Engagements constituant des réserves pour les autorités étrangères* ont été exclus de ces composantes du compte de capital et d'opérations financières.

Le Compte de capital, n.i.a.: *crédit* retrace principalement les transferts de capital liés à l'acquisition d'un actif fixe autres que les transactions ayant trait à des remises de dettes plus les cessions d'actifs non financiers non produits. Le *Compte de capital*: *débit* retrace principalement les transferts de capital liés à la cession d'actifs fixes par le donateur ou au financement de la formation de capital par le bénéficiaire, plus les acquisitions d'actifs non financiers non produits.

Le solde du *Compte d'op. Fin., n.i.a.* (compte d'opérations financières, n.i.a.) est la somme des soldes des investissements directs, des investissements de portefeuille et des autres investissements.

Le poste des *Erreurs et omissions* nettes est une catégorie résiduelle qui est nécessaire pour assurer que la somme de toutes les inscriptions effectuées au débit et au crédit est égal à zéro et qui laisse apparaître les écarts entre les montants portés au débit et ceux qui sont inscrits au crédit.

Le montant de *Réserves et postes apparentés* est égal à la somme de transactions afférentes aux avoirs de réserve, aux engagements constituant des réserves pour les autorités étrangères, au financement exceptionnel et à l'utilisation des crédits et des prêts du FMI.

Pour plus de renseignements, voir *Statistiques financières internationales* [15] et <www.imf.org>.

79

Exchange rates
National currency per US dollar

Cours des changes
Valeur du dollar des États-Unis en monnaie nationale

Country or area Pays ou zone	1992	1993	1994	1995	1996	1997	1998	1999	2000	2001
Afghanistan[1]: afghani Afghanistan[1]: afghani										
End of period										
Fin de période	50.600	50.600	500.000	1 000.000	3 000.000	3 000.000	3 000.000	3 000.000	3 000.000	3 000.000
Period average										
Moyenne sur période	50.600	50.600	425.100	833.333	2 333.330	3 000.000	3 000.000	3 000.000	3 000.000	3 000.000
Albania: lek Albanie: lek										
End of period										
Fin de période	102.900	98.700	95.590	94.240	103.070	149.140	140.580	135.120	142.640	136.550
Period average										
Moyenne sur période	75.033	102.062	94.623	92.698	104.499	148.933	150.633	137.691	143.709	143.485
Algeria: Algerian dinar Algérie: dinar algérien										
End of period										
Fin de période	22.781	24.123	42.893	52.175	56.186	58.414	60.353	69.314	75.343	77.820
Period average										
Moyenne sur période	21.836	23.345	35.059	47.663	54.749	57.707	58.739	66.574	75.260	77.215
Angola: readjusted kwanza Angola: réajusté kwanza										
End of period										
Fin de période	0.000	0.000	0.001	0.006	0.202	0.262	0.697	5.580	16.818	31.949
Period average										
Moyenne sur période	0.000	0.000	0.000	0.003	0.128	0.229	0.393	2.791	10.041	22.058
Antigua and Barbuda: EC dollar Antigua-et-Barbuda: dollar des Caraïbes orientales										
End of period										
Fin de période	2.700	2.700	2.700	2.700	2.700	2.700	2.700	2.700	2.700	2.700
Argentina[2]: Argentine peso Argentine[2]: peso argentin										
End of period										
Fin de période	0.991	0.999	1.000	1.000	1.000	1.000	1.000	1.000	1.000	1.000
Period average										
Moyenne sur période	0.991	0.999	0.999	1.000	1.000	1.000	1.000	1.000	1.000	1.000
Armenia: dram Arménie: dram										
End of period										
Fin de période	2.070	75.000	405.510	402.000	435.070	494.980	522.030	523.770	552.180	561.810
Period average										
Moyenne sur période	...	9.105	288.651	405.908	414.041	490.847	504.915	535.062	539.526	555.078
Aruba: Aruban florin Aruba: florin de Aruba										
End of period										
Fin de période	1.790	1.790	1.790	1.790	1.790	1.790	1.790	1.790	1.790	1.790
Australia: Australian dollar Australie: dollar australien										
End of period										
Fin de période	1.452	1.477	1.287	1.342	1.256	1.532	1.629	1.530	1.805	1.959
Period average										
Moyenne sur période	1.362	1.471	1.368	1.349	1.278	1.347	1.592	1.550	1.725	1.933
Austria[3]: Austrian schilling Autriche[3]: schilling autrichien										
End of period										
Fin de période	11.354	12.143	10.969	10.088	10.954	12.633	11.747	...	...	...
Period average										
Moyenne sur période	10.989	11.632	11.422	10.082	10.587	12.204	12.379	...	...	...
Azerbaijan: manat Azerbaïdjan: manat										
End of period										
Fin de période	48.600	118.000	4 182.000	4 440.000	4 098.000	3 888.000	3 890.000	4 378.000	4 565.000	4 775.000
Period average										
Moyenne sur période	54.200	99.975	1 570.220	4 413.540	4 301.260	3 985.370	3 869.000	4 120.170	4 474.150	4 656.580
Bahamas[1]: Bahamian dollar Bahamas[1]: dollar des Bahamas										
End of period										
Fin de période	1.000	1.000	1.000	1.000	1.000	1.000	1.000	1.000	1.000	1.000
Bahrain: Bahrain dinar Bahreïn: dinar de Bahreïn										
End of period										
Fin de période	0.376	0.376	0.376	0.376	0.376	0.376	0.376	0.376	0.376	0.376
Bangladesh[1]: taka Bangladesh[1]: taka										
End of period										
Fin de période	39.000	39.850	40.250	40.750	42.450	45.450	48.500	51.000	54.000	57.000

79

Exchange rates
National currency per US dollar [cont.]

Cours des changes
Valeur du dollar des Etats-Unis en monnaie nationale [suite]

Country or area Pays ou zone	1992	1993	1994	1995	1996	1997	1998	1999	2000	2001
Period average										
Moyenne sur période	38.951	39.567	40.212	40.278	41.794	43.892	46.906	49.085	52.142	55.807
Barbados: Barbados dollar Barbade: dollar de la Barbade										
End of period										
Fin de période	2.000	2.000	2.000	2.000	2.000	2.000	2.000	2.000	2.000	2.000
Belarus: Belarussian rouble Bélarus: rouble bélarussien										
End of period										
Fin de période	0.015	0.699	10.600	11.500	15.500	30.740	106.000	320.000	1 180.000	1 580.000
Period average										
Moyenne sur période	...	...	...	11.521	13.230	26.020	46.127	248.795	876.750	1 390.000
Belgium[3]: Belgian franc Belgique[3]: franc belge										
End of period										
Fin de période	33.180	36.110	31.838	29.415	32.005	36.920	34.575	...	...	...
Period average										
Moyenne sur période	32.150	34.597	33.457	29.480	30.962	35.774	36.299	...	...	...
Belize: Belize dollar Belize: dollar du Belize										
End of period										
Fin de période	2.000	2.000	2.000	2.000	2.000	2.000	2.000	2.000	2.000	2.000
Benin[4]: CFA franc Bénin[4]: franc CFA										
End of period										
Fin de période	275.325	294.775	534.600	490.000	523.700	598.810	562.210	652.953	704.951	744.306
Period average										
Moyenne sur période	264.692	283.163	555.205	499.148	511.552	583.669	589.952	615.699	711.976	733.039
Bhutan: ngultrum Bhoutan: ngultrum										
End of period										
Fin de période	26.200	31.380	31.380	35.180	35.930	39.280	42.480	43.490	46.750	48.180
Period average										
Moyenne sur période	25.918	30.493	31.374	32.427	35.433	36.313	41.259	43.055	44.942	47.186
Bolivia[5]: boliviano Bolivie[5]: boliviano										
End of period										
Fin de période	4.095	4.475	4.695	4.935	5.185	5.365	5.645	5.990	6.390	6.820
Period average										
Moyenne sur période	3.901	4.265	4.621	4.800	5.075	5.254	5.510	5.812	6.184	6.607
Bosnia and Herzegovina: convertible mark Bosnie-Herzégovine: mark convertible										
End of period										
Fin de période	...	...	...	...	...	1.792	1.673	1.947	2.102	2.219
Period average										
Moyenne sur période	...	...	...	...	...	1.734	1.760	1.837	2.124	2.187
Botswana: pula Botswana: pula										
End of period										
Fin de période	2.257	2.565	2.717	2.822	3.644	3.810	4.458	4.632	5.362	6.983
Period average										
Moyenne sur période	2.110	2.423	2.685	2.772	3.324	3.651	4.226	4.624	5.102	5.841
Brazil[1,6]: real Brésil[1,6]: real										
End of period										
Fin de période	4 504.550	# 0.119	0.846	0.973	1.039	1.116	1.209	1.789	1.955	2.320
Period average										
Moyenne sur période	1 641.090	# 0.032	0.639	0.918	1.005	1.078	1.161	1.815	1.830	2.358
Brunei Darussalam: Brunei dollar Brunéi Darussalam: dollar du Brunéi										
End of period										
Fin de période	1.645	1.608	1.461	1.414	1.400	1.676	1.661	1.666	1.732	1.851
Period average										
Moyenne sur période	1.629	1.616	1.527	1.417	1.410	1.485	1.674	1.695	1.724	1.792
Bulgaria: lev Bulgarie: lev										
End of period										
Fin de période	0.025	0.033	0.066	0.071	0.487	1.777	1.675	1.947	2.102	2.219
Period average										
Moyenne sur période	0.023	0.028	0.054	0.067	0.178	1.682	1.760	1.836	2.123	2.185
Burkina Faso[4]: CFA franc Burkina Faso[4]: franc CFA										
End of period										
Fin de période	275.325	294.775	534.600	490.000	523.700	598.810	562.210	652.953	704.951	744.306

79

Exchange rates
National currency per US dollar [cont.]

Cours des changes
Valeur du dollar des Etats-Unis en monnaie nationale [suite]

Country or area Pays ou zone	1992	1993	1994	1995	1996	1997	1998	1999	2000	2001
Period average Moyenne sur période	264.692	283.163	555.205	499.148	511.552	583.669	589.952	615.699	711.976	733.039
Burundi: Burundi franc Burundi: franc burundais										
End of period Fin de période	236.550	264.380	246.940	277.920	322.350	408.380	505.160	628.580	778.200	864.200
Period average Moyenne sur période	208.303	242.780	252.662	249.757	302.747	352.351	447.766	563.562	720.673	830.353
Cambodia: riel Cambodge: riel										
End of period Fin de période	2 000.000	2 305.000	2 575.000	2 526.000	2 713.000	3 452.000	3 770.000	3 770.000	3 905.000	3 895.000
Period average Moyenne sur période	1 266.580	2 689.000	2 545.250	2 450.830	2 624.080	2 946.250	3 744.420	3 807.830	3 840.750	3 916.330
Cameroon[4]: CFA franc Cameroun[4]: franc CFA										
End of period Fin de période	275.325	294.775	534.600	490.000	523.700	598.810	562.210	652.953	704.951	744.306
Period average Moyenne sur période	264.692	283.163	555.205	499.148	511.552	583.669	589.952	615.699	711.976	733.039
Canada: Canadian dollar Canada: dollar canadien										
End of period Fin de période	1.271	1.324	1.403	1.365	1.370	1.429	1.531	1.443	1.500	1.593
Period average Moyenne sur période	1.209	1.290	1.366	1.372	1.364	1.385	1.484	1.486	1.485	1.549
Cape Verde: Cape Verde escudo Cap-Vert: escudo du Cap-Vert										
End of period Fin de période	73.089	85.992	81.140	77.455	85.165	96.235	94.255	107.575	118.760	124.974
Period average Moyenne sur période	68.018	80.427	81.891	76.853	82.592	93.177	98.158	102.700	115.877	123.213
Central African Rep.[4]: CFA franc Rép. centrafricaine[4]: franc CFA										
End of period Fin de période	275.325	294.775	534.600	490.000	523.700	598.810	562.210	652.953	704.951	744.306
Period average Moyenne sur période	264.692	283.163	555.205	499.148	511.552	583.669	589.952	615.699	711.976	733.039
Chad[4]: CFA franc Tchad[4]: franc CFA										
End of period Fin de période	275.325	294.775	534.600	490.000	523.700	598.810	562.210	652.953	704.951	744.306
Period average Moyenne sur période	264.692	283.163	555.205	499.148	511.552	583.669	589.952	615.699	711.976	733.039
Chile[1]: Chilean peso Chili[1]: peso chilien										
End of period Fin de période	382.330	431.040	404.090	407.130	424.970	439.810	473.770	530.070	572.680	656.200
Period average Moyenne sur période	362.576	404.166	420.177	396.773	412.267	419.295	460.287	508.777	535.466	634.938
China[1]: yuan Chine[1]: yuan										
End of period Fin de période	5.752	5.800	8.446	8.317	8.298	8.280	8.279	8.280	8.277	8.277
Period average Moyenne sur période	5.515	5.762	8.619	8.351	8.314	8.290	8.279	8.278	8.279	8.277
China, Hong Kong SAR: Hong Kong dollar Chine, Hong Kong RAS: dollar de Hong Kong										
End of period Fin de période	7.743	7.726	7.738	7.732	7.736	7.746	7.746	7.771	7.796	7.797
Period average Moyenne sur période	7.741	7.736	7.728	7.736	7.734	7.742	7.745	7.758	7.791	7.799
China, Macao SAR: Macao pataca Chine, Macao RAS: pataca de Macao										
End of period Fin de période	7.972	7.956	7.970	7.965	7.968	7.982	7.980	8.005	8.034	8.031
Period average Moyenne sur période	7.972	7.968	7.960	7.968	7.966	7.975	7.979	7.992	8.026	8.034
Colombia: Colombian peso Colombie: peso colombien										
End of period Fin de période	811.770	917.330	831.270	987.650	1 005.330	1 293.580	1 507.520	1 873.770	2 187.020	2 301.330

79

Exchange rates
National currency per US dollar [cont.]

Cours des changes
Valeur du dollar des Etats-Unis en monnaie nationale [suite]

Country or area Pays ou zone	1992	1993	1994	1995	1996	1997	1998	1999	2000	2001
Period average Moyenne sur période	759.282	863.065	844.836	912.826	1 036.690	1 140.960	1 426.040	1 756.230	2 087.900	2 299.630
Comoros[7]: Comorian franc Comores[7]: franc comorien										
End of period Fin de période	275.322	294.772	400.948	367.498	392.773	449.105	421.655	489.715	528.714	558.230
Period average Moyenne sur période	264.690	283.160	416.399	374.357	383.660	437.747	442.459	461.775	533.982	549.779
Congo[4]: CFA franc Congo[4]: franc CFA										
End of period Fin de période	275.325	294.775	534.600	490.000	523.700	598.810	562.210	652.953	704.951	744.306
Period average Moyenne sur période	264.692	283.163	555.205	499.148	511.552	583.669	589.952	615.699	711.976	733.039
Costa Rica: Costa Rican colón Costa Rica: colón costa-ricien										
End of period Fin de période	137.430	151.440	165.070	194.900	220.110	244.290	271.420	298.190	318.020	341.670
Period average Moyenne sur période	134.506	142.172	157.067	179.729	207.689	232.597	257.229	285.685	308.187	328.871
Côte d'Ivoire[4]: CFA franc Côte d'Ivoire[4]: franc CFA										
End of period Fin de période	275.325	294.775	534.600	490.000	523.700	598.810	562.210	652.953	704.951	744.306
Period average Moyenne sur période	264.692	283.163	555.205	499.148	511.552	583.669	589.952	615.699	711.976	733.039
Croatia: kuna Croatie: kuna										
End of period Fin de période	0.798	6.562	5.629	5.316	5.540	6.303	6.248	7.648	8.155	8.356
Period average Moyenne sur période	...	3.577	5.996	5.230	5.434	6.101	6.362	7.112	8.277	8.340
Cyprus: Cyprus pound Chypre: livre chypriote										
End of period Fin de période	0.483	0.520	0.476	0.457	0.470	0.526	0.498	0.575	0.617	0.650
Period average Moyenne sur période	0.450	0.497	0.492	0.452	0.466	0.514	0.518	0.543	0.622	0.643
Czech Republic: Czech koruna République tchèque: couronne tchèque										
End of period Fin de période	...	29.955	28.049	26.602	27.332	34.636	29.855	35.979	37.813	36.259
Period average[1] Moyenne sur période[1]	...	29.153	28.785	26.541	27.145	31.698	32.281	34.569	38.598	38.035
Dem. Rep. of the Congo[8]: Congo franc Rép. dém. du Congo[8]: franc congolais										
End of period Fin de période	6.633	350.000	# 32.500	148.310	1 156.000	1 060.000	# 2.450	4.500	50.000	...
Period average Moyenne sur période	2.151	25.144	# 11.941	70.245	501.849	1 313.450	# 1.607	4.018	21.818	...
Denmark: Danish krone Danemark: couronne danoise										
End of period Fin de période	6.256	6.773	6.083	5.546	5.945	6.826	6.387	7.399	8.021	8.410
Period average Moyenne sur période	6.036	6.484	6.361	5.602	5.799	6.605	6.701	6.976	8.083	8.323
Djibouti: Djibouti franc Djibouti: franc djiboutien										
End of period Fin de période	177.721	177.721	177.721	177.721	177.721	177.721	177.721	177.721	177.721	177.721
Dominica: EC dollar Dominique: dollar des Caraïbes orientales										
End of period Fin de période	2.700	2.700	2.700	2.700	2.700	2.700	2.700	2.700	2.700	2.700
Dominican Republic[1]: Dominican peso Rép. dominicaine[1]: peso dominicain										
End of period Fin de période	12.575	12.767	13.064	13.465	14.062	14.366	15.788	16.039	16.674	17.149
Period average Moyenne sur période	12.774	12.676	13.160	13.597	13.775	14.266	15.267	16.033	16.415	16.952
Ecuador[1]: sucre Equateur[1]: sucre										
End of period Fin de période	1 844.250	2 043.780	2 269.000	2 923.500	3 635.000	4 428.000	6 825.000	20 243.000	25 000.000	25 000.000

79

Exchange rates
National currency per US dollar [cont.]

Cours des changes
Valeur du dollar des Etats-Unis en monnaie nationale [suite]

Country or area Pays ou zone	1992	1993	1994	1995	1996	1997	1998	1999	2000	2001
Period average Moyenne sur période	1 533.960	1 919.100	2 196.730	2 564.490	3 189.470	3 998.270	5 446.570	11 786.800	24 988.400	25 000.000
Egypt[1]: Egyptian pound Egypte[1]: livre égyptienne										
End of period Fin de période	3.339	3.372	3.391	3.390	3.388	3.388	3.388	3.405	3.690	4.490
Period average Moyenne sur période	3.322	3.353	3.385	3.392	3.392	3.389	3.388	3.395	3.472	3.973
El Salvador[1]: El Salvadoran colón El Salvador[1]: cólon salvadorien										
End of period Fin de période	9.170	8.670	8.750	8.755	8.755	8.755	8.755	8.755	8.755	8.750
Period average Moyenne sur période	8.361	8.703	8.729	8.755	8.755	8.756	8.755	8.755	8.755	8.750
Equatorial Guinea[4]: CFA franc Guinée équatoriale[4]: franc CFA										
End of period Fin de période	275.325	294.775	534.600	490.000	523.700	598.810	562.210	652.953	704.951	744.306
Period average Moyenne sur période	264.692	283.163	555.205	499.148	511.552	583.669	589.952	615.699	711.976	733.039
Estonia: Estonian kroon Estonie: couronne estonienne										
End of period Fin de période	12.912	13.878	12.390	11.462	12.440	14.336	13.410	15.562	16.820	17.692
Period average Moyenne sur période	...	13.223	12.991	11.465	12.034	13.882	14.075	14.678	16.969	17.564
Ethiopia: Ethiopian birr Ethiopie: birr éthiopien										
End of period Fin de période	5.000	5.000	5.950	6.320	6.426	6.864	7.503	8.134	8.314	8.558
Period average Moyenne sur période	2.803	5.000	5.465	6.158	6.352	6.709	7.116	7.942	8.217	8.458
Euro Area[9]: euro Zone euro[9]: euro										
End of period Fin de période	...	...	...	...	...	...	...	0.995	1.075	1.135
Period average Moyenne sur période	...	...	...	...	...	...	...	0.939	1.085	1.118
Fiji: Fiji dollar Fidji: dollar des Fidji										
End of period Fin de période	1.565	1.541	1.409	1.429	1.384	1.549	1.986	1.966	2.186	2.309
Period average Moyenne sur période	1.503	1.542	1.464	1.406	1.403	1.444	1.987	1.970	2.129	2.277
Finland[3]: Finnish markka Finlande[3]: markka finlandais										
End of period Fin de période	5.245	5.785	4.743	4.359	4.644	5.421	5.096	...	...	...
Period average Moyenne sur période	4.479	5.712	5.224	4.367	4.594	5.191	5.344	...	...	...
France[3]: French franc France[3]: franc français										
End of period Fin de période	5.507	5.896	5.346	4.900	5.237	5.988	5.622	...	...	...
Period average Moyenne sur période	5.294	5.663	5.552	4.992	5.116	5.837	5.900	...	...	...
Gabon[4]: CFA franc Gabon[4]: franc CFA										
End of period Fin de période	275.325	294.775	534.600	490.000	523.700	598.810	562.210	652.953	704.951	744.306
Period average Moyenne sur période	264.692	283.163	555.205	499.148	511.552	583.669	589.952	615.699	711.976	733.039
Gambia: dalasi Gambie: dalasi										
End of period Fin de période	9.217	9.535	9.579	9.640	9.892	10.530	10.991	11.547	14.888	16.932
Period average Moyenne sur période	8.888	9.129	9.576	9.546	9.789	10.200	10.643	11.395	12.788	15.687
Georgia: lari Géorgie: lari										
End of period Fin de période	...	...	...	1.230	1.276	1.304	1.800	1.930	1.975	2.060

79

Exchange rates
National currency per US dollar [cont.]

Cours des changes
Valeur du dollar des Etats-Unis en monnaie nationale [suite]

Country or area Pays ou zone	1992	1993	1994	1995	1996	1997	1998	1999	2000	2001
Period average Moyenne sur période	...	...	...	...	1.263	1.298	1.390	2.025	1.976	2.073
Germany[3]: deutsche mark Allemagne[3]: deutsche mark										
End of period Fin de période	1.614	1.726	1.549	1.434	1.555	1.792	1.673	...	...	...
Period average Moyenne sur période	1.562	1.653	1.623	1.433	1.505	1.734	1.760	...	...	...
Ghana[1]: cedi Ghana[1]: cedi										
End of period Fin de période	* 520.833	819.672	1 052.630	1 449.280	1 754.390	2 272.730	2 325.580	3 535.140	7 047.650	7 321.940
Period average Moyenne sur période	* 437.087	649.061	956.711	1 200.430	1 637.230	2 050.170	2 314.150	2 669.300	5 455.060	7 170.760
Greece[10]: drachma Grèce[10]: drachme										
End of period Fin de période	214.580	249.220	240.100	237.040	247.020	282.610	282.570	328.440	365.620	...
Period average Moyenne sur période	190.624	229.250	242.603	231.663	240.712	273.058	295.529	305.647	365.399	...
Grenada: EC dollar Grenade: dollar des Caraïbes orientales										
End of period Fin de période	2.700	2.700	2.700	2.700	2.700	2.700	2.700	2.700	2.700	2.700
Guatemala: quetzal Guatemala: quetzal										
End of period Fin de période	5.274	5.815	5.649	6.042	5.966	6.177	6.848	7.821	7.731	8.001
Period average Moyenne sur période	5.171	5.635	5.751	5.810	6.050	6.065	6.395	7.386	7.763	7.859
Guinea: Guinean franc Guinée: franc guinéen										
End of period Fin de période	922.410	972.414	981.024	997.984	1 039.130	1 144.950	1 298.030	1 736.000	1 882.270	1 988.330
Period average Moyenne sur période	902.001	955.490	976.636	991.411	1 004.020	1 095.330	1 236.830	1 387.400	1 746.870	1 950.560
Guinea-Bissau[11]: CFA franc Guinée-Bissau[11]: franc CFA										
End of period Fin de période	133.162	176.366	236.451	337.366	537.482	598.810	562.210	652.953	704.951	744.306
Period average Moyenne sur période	106.676	155.106	198.341	278.039	405.745	583.669	589.952	615.699	711.976	733.039
Guyana[1]: Guyana dollar Guyana[1]: dollar guyanais										
End of period Fin de période	126.000	130.750	142.500	140.500	141.250	144.000	162.250	180.500	184.750	189.500
Period average Moyenne sur période	125.002	126.730	138.290	141.989	140.375	142.401	150.519	177.995	182.430	187.321
Haiti[1]: gourde Haïti[1]: gourde										
End of period Fin de période	10.953	12.805	12.947	16.160	15.093	17.311	16.505	17.965	22.524	26.339
Period average Moyenne sur période	9.802	12.823	15.040	15.110	15.701	16.655	16.766	16.938	21.171	24.429
Honduras[1]: lempira Honduras[1]: lempira										
End of period Fin de période	5.830	7.260	9.400	10.343	12.869	13.094	13.808	14.504	15.141	15.920
Period average Moyenne sur période	5.498	6.472	8.409	9.471	11.705	13.004	13.385	14.213	14.839	15.474
Hungary: forint Hongrie: forint										
End of period Fin de période	83.970	100.700	110.690	139.470	164.930	203.500	219.030	252.520	284.730	279.030
Period average Moyenne sur période	78.988	91.933	105.160	125.681	152.647	186.789	214.402	237.146	282.179	286.490
Iceland: Icelandic króna Islande: couronne islandaise										
End of period Fin de période	63.920	72.730	68.300	65.230	66.890	72.180	69.320	72.550	84.700	102.950
Period average Moyenne sur période	57.546	67.603	69.944	64.692	66.500	70.904	70.958	72.335	78.616	97.425

79

Exchange rates
National currency per US dollar [cont.]

Cours des changes
Valeur du dollar des Etats-Unis en monnaie nationale [suite]

Country or area Pays ou zone	1992	1993	1994	1995	1996	1997	1998	1999	2000	2001
India: Indian rupee Inde: roupie indienne										
End of period										
Fin de période	26.200	31.380	31.380	35.180	35.930	39.280	42.480	43.490	46.750	48.180
Period average										
Moyenne sur période	25.918	30.493	31.374	32.427	35.433	36.313	41.259	43.055	44.942	47.186
Indonesia: Indonesian rupiah Indonésie: roupie indonésien										
End of period										
Fin de période	2 062.000	2 110.000	2 200.000	2 308.000	2 383.000	4 650.000	8 025.000	7 085.000	9 595.000	10 400.000
Period average										
Moyenne sur période	2 029.920	2 087.100	2 160.750	2 248.610	2 342.300	2 909.380	10 013.600	7 855.150	8 421.770	10 260.800
Iran (Islamic Rep. of)[1]: Iranian rial Iran (Rép. islamique d')[1]: rial iranien										
End of period										
Fin de période	67.039	1 758.560	1 735.970	1 747.500	1 749.140	1 754.260	1 750.930	1 752.290	2 262.930	1 750.950
Period average										
Moyenne sur période	65.552	1 267.770	1 748.750	1 747.930	1 750.760	1 752.920	1 751.860	1 752.930	1 764.430	1 753.560
Iraq[1]: Iraqi dinar Iraq[1]: dinar iraquien										
End of period										
Fin de période	0.311	0.311	0.311	0.311	0.311	0.311	0.311	0.311	0.311	0.311
Ireland[3]: Irish pound Irlande[3]: livre irlandaise										
End of period										
Fin de période	0.614	0.709	0.646	0.623	0.595	0.699	0.672	...	...	...
Period average										
Moyenne sur période	0.588	0.677	0.669	0.624	0.625	0.660	0.702	...	...	...
Israel: new sheqel Israël: nouveau sheqel										
End of period										
Fin de période	2.764	2.986	3.018	3.135	3.251	3.536	4.161	4.153	4.041	4.416
Period average										
Moyenne sur période	2.459	2.830	3.011	3.011	3.192	3.449	3.800	4.140	4.077	4.206
Italy[3]: Italian lira Italie[3]: lire italienne										
End of period										
Fin de période	1 470.860	1 703.970	1 629.740	1 584.720	1 530.570	1 759.190	1 653.100	...	...	...
Period average										
Moyenne sur période	1 232.410	1 573.670	1 612.440	1 628.930	1 542.950	1 703.100	1 736.210	...	...	...
Jamaica: Jamaican dollar Jamaïque: dollar jamaïcain										
End of period										
Fin de période	22.185	32.475	33.202	39.616	34.865	36.341	37.055	41.291	45.415	47.286
Period average										
Moyenne sur période	22.960	24.949	33.086	35.142	37.120	35.405	36.550	39.044	42.701	45.996
Japan: yen Japon: yen										
End of period										
Fin de période	124.750	111.850	99.740	102.830	116.000	129.950	115.600	102.200	114.900	131.800
Period average										
Moyenne sur période	126.651	111.198	102.208	94.060	108.779	120.991	130.905	113.907	107.765	121.529
Jordan: Jordan dinar Jordanie: dinar jordanien										
End of period										
Fin de période	0.691	0.704	0.701	0.709	0.709	0.709	0.709	0.709	0.709	0.709
Period average										
Moyenne sur période	0.680	0.693	0.699	0.700	0.709	0.709	0.709	0.709	0.709	0.709
Kazakhstan: tenge Kazakhstan: tenge										
End of period										
Fin de période	...	6.310	54.260	63.950	73.300	75.550	83.800	138.200	144.500	150.200
Period average										
Moyenne sur période	...	...	35.538	60.950	67.303	75.438	78.303	119.523	142.133	146.736
Kenya: Kenya shilling Kenya: shilling du Kenya										
End of period										
Fin de période	36.216	68.163	44.839	55.939	55.021	62.678	61.906	72.931	78.036	78.600
Period average										
Moyenne sur période	32.217	58.001	56.051	51.430	57.115	58.732	60.367	70.326	76.176	78.563
Kiribati: Australian dollar Kiribati: dollar australien										
End of period										
Fin de période	1.452	1.477	1.287	1.342	1.256	1.532	1.629	1.530	1.805	1.959

79

Exchange rates
National currency per US dollar [cont.]

Cours des changes
Valeur du dollar des Etats-Unis en monnaie nationale [suite]

Country or area Pays ou zone	1992	1993	1994	1995	1996	1997	1998	1999	2000	2001
Period average Moyenne sur période	1.362	1.471	1.368	1.349	1.278	1.347	1.592	1.550	1.725	1.933
Korea, Republic of: Korean won Corée, République de: won coréen										
End of period Fin de période	788.400	808.100	788.700	774.700	844.200	1 695.000	1 204.000	1 138.000	1 264.500	1 313.500
Period average Moyenne sur période	780.651	802.671	803.446	771.273	804.453	951.289	1 401.440	1 188.820	1 130.960	1 290.990
Kuwait: Kuwaiti dinar Koweït: dinar koweïtien										
End of period Fin de période	0.303	0.298	0.300	0.299	0.300	0.305	0.302	0.304	0.305	0.308
Period average Moyenne sur période	0.293	0.302	0.297	0.298	0.299	0.303	0.305	0.304	0.307	0.307
Kyrgyzstan: Kyrgyz som Kirghizistan: som kirghize										
End of period Fin de période	...	8.030	10.650	11.200	16.700	17.375	29.376	45.429	48.304	47.719
Period average Moyenne sur période	...	...	10.842	10.822	12.810	17.363	20.838	39.008	47.704	48.378
Lao People's Dem. Rep.: kip Rép. dém. pop. lao: kip										
End of period Fin de période	717.000	718.000	719.000	# 923.000	935.000	2 634.500	4 274.000	7 600.000	8 218.000	9 490.000
Period average Moyenne sur période	716.083	716.250	717.667	# 804.691	921.022	1 259.980	3 298.330	7 102.020	7 887.640	8 954.580
Latvia: lats Lettonie: lats										
End of period Fin de période	0.835	0.595	0.548	0.537	0.556	0.590	0.569	0.583	0.613	0.638
Period average Moyenne sur période	0.737	0.675	0.560	0.528	0.551	0.581	0.590	0.585	0.607	0.628
Lebanon: Lebanese pound Liban: livre libanaise										
End of period Fin de période	1 838.000	1 711.000	1 647.000	1 596.000	1 552.000	1 527.000	1 508.000	1 507.500	1 507.500	1 507.500
Period average Moyenne sur période	1 712.790	1 741.360	1 680.070	1 621.410	1 571.440	1 539.450	1 516.130	1 507.840	1 507.500	1 507.500
Lesotho[1]: loti Lesotho[1]: loti										
End of period Fin de période	3.053	3.398	3.544	3.648	4.683	4.868	5.860	6.155	7.569	12.127
Period average Moyenne sur période	2.852	3.268	3.551	3.627	4.299	4.608	5.528	6.110	6.940	8.609
Liberia[1]: Liberian dollar Libéria[1]: dollar libérien										
End of period Fin de période	1.000	1.000	1.000	1.000	1.000	1.000	43.250	39.500	42.750	49.500
Period average Moyenne sur période	1.000	1.000	1.000	1.000	1.000	1.000	41.508	41.903	40.953	48.583
Libyan Arab Jamah.: Libyan dinar Jamah. arabe libyenne: dinar libyen										
End of period Fin de période	0.301	0.325	0.360	0.353	0.365	0.389	0.379	0.540	0.540	0.652
Period average Moyenne sur période	0.285	0.305	0.321	0.346	0.362	0.382	0.394	0.499	0.510	0.597
Lithuania: litas Lituanie: litas										
End of period Fin de période	3.790	3.900	4.000	4.000	4.000	4.000	4.000	4.000	4.000	4.000
Period average Moyenne sur période	1.773	4.344	3.978	4.000	4.000	4.000	4.000	4.000	4.000	4.000
Luxembourg[3]: Luxembourg franc Luxembourg[3]: franc luxembourgeois										
End of period Fin de période	33.180	36.110	31.838	29.415	32.005	36.920	34.575	...	...	...
Period average Moyenne sur période	32.150	34.597	33.457	29.480	30.962	35.774	36.299	...	...	...
Madagascar: Malagasy franc Madagascar: franc malgache										
End of period Fin de période	1 910.170	1 962.670	3 871.080	3 422.970	4 328.470	5 284.670	5 402.210	6 543.200	6 550.440	6 631.190

79

Exchange rates
National currency per US dollar [cont.]

Cours des changes
Valeur du dollar des Etats-Unis en monnaie nationale [suite]

Country or area Pays ou zone	1992	1993	1994	1995	1996	1997	1998	1999	2000	2001
Period average Moyenne sur période	1 863.970	1 913.780	3 067.340	4 265.630	4 061.250	5 090.890	5 441.400	6 283.770	6 767.480	6 588.490
Malawi: Malawi kwacha Malawi: kwacha malawien										
End of period Fin de période	4.396	4.494	15.299	15.303	15.323	21.228	43.884	46.438	80.076	67.294
Period average Moyenne sur période	3.603	4.403	8.736	15.284	15.309	16.444	31.073	44.088	59.544	72.197
Malaysia: ringgit Malaisie: ringgit										
End of period Fin de période	2.612	2.702	2.560	2.542	2.529	3.892	3.800	3.800	3.800	3.800
Period average Moyenne sur période	2.547	2.574	2.624	2.504	2.516	2.813	3.924	3.800	3.800	3.800
Maldives: rufiyaa Maldives: rufiyaa										
End of period Fin de période	10.535	11.105	11.770	11.770	11.770	11.770	11.770	11.770	11.770	12.800
Period average Moyenne sur période	10.569	10.957	11.586	11.770	11.770	11.770	11.770	11.770	11.770	12.242
Mali[4]: CFA franc Mali[4]: franc CFA										
End of period Fin de période	275.325	294.775	534.600	490.000	523.700	598.810	562.210	652.953	704.951	744.306
Period average Moyenne sur période	264.692	283.163	555.205	499.148	511.552	583.669	589.952	615.699	711.976	733.039
Malta: Maltese lira Malte: lire maltaise										
End of period Fin de période	0.374	0.395	0.368	0.352	0.360	0.391	0.377	0.412	0.438	0.452
Period average Moyenne sur période	0.319	0.382	0.378	0.353	0.361	0.386	0.389	0.399	0.438	0.450
Mauritania: ouguiya Mauritanie: ouguiya										
End of period Fin de période	115.100	124.160	128.370	137.110	142.450	168.350	205.780	225.000	252.300	264.120
Period average Moyenne sur période	87.027	120.806	123.575	129.768	137.222	151.853	188.476	209.514	238.923	255.629
Mauritius: Mauritian rupee Maurice: roupie mauricienne										
End of period Fin de période	16.998	18.656	17.863	17.664	17.972	22.265	24.784	25.468	27.882	30.394
Period average Moyenne sur période	15.563	17.648	17.960	17.386	17.948	21.057	23.993	25.186	26.250	29.129
Mexico[1]: Mexican peso Mexique[1]: peso mexicain										
End of period Fin de période	3.115	3.106	5.325	7.643	7.851	8.083	9.865	9.514	9.572	9.142
Period average Moyenne sur période	3.095	3.116	3.375	6.419	7.600	7.919	9.136	9.560	9.456	9.342
Micronesia (Fed. States): US dollar Micronésie (Etats féd. de): dollar des Etats-Unis										
End of period Fin de période	1.000	1.000	1.000	1.000	1.000	1.000	1.000	1.000	1.000	1.000
Mongolia: togrog Mongolie: togrog										
End of period Fin de période	105.067	# 396.510	414.090	473.620	693.510	813.160	902.000	1 072.370	1 097.000	1 102.000
Period average Moyenne sur période	42.559	...	# 412.721	448.613	548.403	789.992	840.828	1 021.870	1 076.670	1 097.700
Morocco: Moroccan dirham Maroc: dirham marocain										
End of period Fin de période	9.049	9.651	8.960	8.469	8.800	9.714	9.255	10.087	10.619	11.560
Period average Moyenne sur période	8.538	9.299	9.203	8.540	8.716	9.527	9.604	9.804	10.626	11.303
Mozambique[1]: metical Mozambique[1]: metical										
End of period Fin de période	2 940.950	5 324.240	6 627.450	10 851.400	11 336.700	11 502.100	12 322.200	13 252.900	17 140.500	23 320.400
Period average Moyenne sur période	2 566.480	3 951.110	6 158.400	9 203.390	11 517.800	11 772.600	12 110.200	13 028.600	15 447.100	20 703.600

79

Exchange rates
National currency per US dollar [cont.]

Cours des changes
Valeur du dollar des Etats-Unis en monnaie nationale [suite]

Country or area Pays ou zone	1992	1993	1994	1995	1996	1997	1998	1999	2000	2001
Myanmar: kyat Myanmar: kyat										
End of period										
Fin de période	6.241	6.246	5.903	5.781	5.988	6.363	6.109	6.268	6.599	6.850
Period average										
Moyenne sur période	6.105	6.157	5.975	5.667	5.918	6.242	6.343	6.286	6.517	6.749
Namibia: Namibia dollar Namibie: dollar namibia										
End of period										
Fin de période	3.053	3.398	3.544	3.648	4.683	4.868	5.860	6.155	7.569	12.127
Period average										
Moyenne sur période	2.852	3.268	3.551	3.627	4.299	4.608	5.528	6.110	6.940	8.609
Nepal: Nepalese rupee Népal: roupie népalaise										
End of period										
Fin de période	43.200	49.240	49.880	56.000	57.030	63.300	67.675	68.725	74.300	76.475
Period average										
Moyenne sur période	42.718	48.607	49.398	51.890	56.692	58.010	65.976	68.239	71.094	74.949
Netherlands[3]: Netherlands guilder Pays-Bas[3]: florin néerlandais										
End of period										
Fin de période	1.814	1.941	1.735	1.604	1.744	2.017	1.889	...	...	...
Period average										
Moyenne sur période	1.759	1.857	1.820	1.606	1.686	1.951	1.984	...	...	...
Netherlands Antilles: Netherlands Antillean guilder Antilles néerlandaises: florin des Antilles néerlandaises										
End of period										
Fin de période	1.790	1.790	1.790	1.790	1.790	1.790	1.790	1.790	1.790	1.790
New Zealand: New Zealand dollar Nouvelle-Zélande: dollar néo-zélandais										
End of period										
Fin de période	1.944	1.790	1.556	1.531	1.416	1.719	1.898	1.921	2.272	2.407
Period average										
Moyenne sur période	1.862	1.851	1.687	1.524	1.455	1.512	1.868	1.890	2.201	2.379
Nicaragua[1,12]: córdoba Nicaragua[1,12]: córdoba										
End of period										
Fin de période	5.000	6.350	7.112	7.965	8.924	9.995	11.194	12.318	13.057	13.841
Period average										
Moyenne sur période	5.000	5.620	6.723	7.546	8.436	9.448	10.582	11.809	12.684	13.372
Niger[4]: CFA franc Niger[4]: franc CFA										
End of period										
Fin de période	275.325	294.775	534.600	490.000	523.700	598.810	562.210	652.953	704.951	744.306
Period average										
Moyenne sur période	264.692	283.163	555.205	499.148	511.552	583.669	589.952	615.699	711.976	733.039
Nigeria[1]: naira Nigéria[1]: naira										
End of period										
Fin de période	19.646	21.882	21.997	21.887	21.886	21.886	21.886	97.950	109.550	112.950
Period average										
Moyenne sur période	17.298	22.065	21.996	21.895	21.884	21.886	21.886	92.338	101.697	111.231
Norway: Norwegian krone Norvège: couronne norvégienne										
End of period										
Fin de période	6.925	7.518	6.762	6.319	6.443	7.316	7.600	8.040	8.849	9.012
Period average										
Moyenne sur période	6.215	7.094	7.058	6.335	6.450	7.073	7.545	7.799	8.802	8.992
Oman: rial Omani Oman: rial omani										
End of period										
Fin de période	0.385	0.385	0.385	0.385	0.385	0.385	0.385	0.385	0.385	0.385
Pakistan: Pakistan rupee Pakistan: roupie pakistanaise										
End of period										
Fin de période	25.636	30.045	30.723	34.165	40.020	43.940	45.885	# 51.785	58.029	60.864
Period average										
Moyenne sur période	24.965	27.975	30.423	31.494	35.909	40.918	44.943	49.118	53.648	61.927
Panama: balboa Panama: balboa										
End of period										
Fin de période	1.000	1.000	1.000	1.000	1.000	1.000	1.000	1.000	1.000	1.000

79

Exchange rates
National currency per US dollar [cont.]

Cours des changes
Valeur du dollar des Etats-Unis en monnaie nationale [suite]

Country or area Pays ou zone	1992	1993	1994	1995	1996	1997	1998	1999	2000	2001
Papua New Guinea: kina Papouasie-Nvl-Guinée: kina										
End of period										
Fin de période	0.988	0.981	1.179	1.335	1.347	1.751	2.096	2.695	3.072	3.762
Period average										
Moyenne sur période	0.965	0.978	1.011	1.280	1.319	1.438	2.074	2.571	2.782	3.389
Paraguay: guaraní Paraguay: guaraní										
End of period										
Fin de période	1 630.000	1 880.000	1 924.700	1 979.660	2 109.670	2 360.000	2 840.190	3 328.860	3 526.900	4 682.000
Period average										
Moyenne sur période	1 500.260	1 744.350	1 904.760	1 963.020	2 056.810	2 177.860	2 726.490	3 119.070	3 486.350	4 105.920
Peru[13]: new sol Pérou[13]: nouveau sol										
End of period										
Fin de période	1.630	2.160	2.180	2.310	2.600	2.730	3.160	3.510	3.527	3.444
Period average										
Moyenne sur période	1.246	1.988	2.195	2.253	2.453	2.664	2.930	3.383	3.490	3.507
Philippines: Philippine peso Philippines: peso philippin										
End of period										
Fin de période	25.096	27.699	24.418	26.214	26.288	39.975	39.059	40.313	49.998	51.404
Period average										
Moyenne sur période	25.513	27.120	26.417	25.715	26.216	29.471	40.893	39.089	44.192	50.993
Poland: new zloty Pologne: nouveau zloty										
End of period										
Fin de période	1.577	2.134	2.437	2.468	2.876	3.518	3.504	4.148	4.143	3.986
Period average										
Moyenne sur période	1.363	1.812	2.272	2.425	2.696	3.279	3.475	3.967	4.346	4.094
Portugal[3]: Portuguese escudo Portugal[3]: escudo portugais										
End of period										
Fin de période	146.758	176.812	159.093	149.413	156.385	183.326	171.829	...	...	...
Period average										
Moyenne sur période	134.998	160.800	165.993	151.106	154.244	175.312	180.104	...	...	...
Qatar: Qatar riyal Qatar: riyal qatarien										
End of period										
Fin de période	3.640	3.640	3.640	3.640	3.640	3.640	3.640	3.640	3.640	3.640
Republic of Moldova: Moldovan leu République de Moldova: leu moldove										
End of period										
Fin de période	0.414	# 3.640	4.270	4.499	4.674	4.661	8.323	11.590	12.383	13.091
Period average										
Moyenne sur période	...	...	...	4.496	4.605	4.624	5.371	10.516	12.434	12.865
Romania[1]: Romanian leu Roumanie[1]: leu roumain										
End of period										
Fin de période	460.000	1 276.000	1 767.000	2 578.000	4 035.000	8 023.000	10 951.000	18 255.000	25 926.000	31 597.000
Period average										
Moyenne sur période	# 307.953	760.051	1 655.090	2 033.280	3 084.220	7 167.940	8 875.580	15 332.800	21 708.700	29 060.800
Russian Federation[14]: ruble Fédération de Russie[14]: ruble										
End of period										
Fin de période	0.415	1.247	3.550	4.640	5.560	5.960	20.650	27.000	28.160	30.140
Period average										
Moyenne sur période	...	0.992	2.191	4.559	5.121	5.785	9.705	24.620	28.129	29.169
Rwanda: Rwanda franc Rwanda: franc rwandais										
End of period										
Fin de période	146.270	146.370	138.330	299.811	304.164	304.672	320.338	349.530	430.486	457.900
Period average										
Moyenne sur période	133.350	144.307	220.000	262.197	306.820	301.530	312.314	333.942	389.696	442.992
Saint Kitts and Nevis: EC dollar Saint-Kitts-et-Nevis: dollar des Caraïbes orientales										
End of period										
Fin de période	2.700	2.700	2.700	2.700	2.700	2.700	2.700	2.700	2.700	2.700
Saint Lucia: EC dollar Sainte-Lucie: dollar des Caraïbes orientales										
End of period										
Fin de période	2.700	2.700	2.700	2.700	2.700	2.700	2.700	2.700	2.700	2.700

79

Exchange rates
National currency per US dollar [cont.]

Cours des changes
Valeur du dollar des Etats-Unis en monnaie nationale [suite]

Country or area Pays ou zone	1992	1993	1994	1995	1996	1997	1998	1999	2000	2001
St. Vincent-Grenadines: EC dollar St. Vincent-Grenadines: dollar des Caraïbes orientales										
End of period										
Fin de période	2.700	2.700	2.700	2.700	2.700	2.700	2.700	2.700	2.700	2.700
Samoa: tala Samoa: tala										
End of period										
Fin de période	2.558	2.608	2.452	2.527	2.434	2.766	3.010	3.018	3.341	3.551
Period average										
Moyenne sur période	2.466	2.569	2.535	2.473	2.462	2.559	2.948	3.013	3.286	3.478
San Marino[3]: Italian lira Saint-Marin[3]: lire italienne										
End of period										
Fin de période	1 470.860	1 703.970	1 629.740	1 584.720	1 530.570	1 759.190	1 653.100	...	...	...
Period average										
Moyenne sur période	1 232.410	1 573.670	1 612.440	1 628.930	1 542.950	1 703.100	1 736.210	...	...	...
Sao Tome and Principe: dobra Sao Tomé-et-Principe: dobra										
End of period										
Fin de période	375.540	516.700	1 185.310	1 756.870	2 833.210	6 969.730	6 885.000	7 300.000	8 610.650	9 019.710
Period average										
Moyenne sur période	321.337	429.854	732.628	1 420.340	2 203.160	4 552.510	6 883.240	7 118.960	7 978.170	8 842.110
Saudi Arabia: Saudi Arabian riyal Arabie saoudite: riyal saoudien										
End of period										
Fin de période	3.745	3.745	3.745	3.745	3.745	3.745	3.745	3.745	3.745	3.745
Senegal[4]: CFA franc Sénégal[4]: franc CFA										
End of period										
Fin de période	275.325	294.775	534.600	490.000	523.700	598.810	562.210	652.953	704.951	744.306
Period average										
Moyenne sur période	264.692	283.163	555.205	499.148	511.552	583.669	589.952	615.699	711.976	733.039
Seychelles: Seychelles rupee Seychelles: roupie seychelloises										
End of period										
Fin de période	5.255	5.258	4.970	4.864	4.995	5.125	5.452	5.368	6.269	5.752
Period average										
Moyenne sur période	5.122	5.182	5.056	4.762	4.970	5.026	5.262	5.343	5.714	5.858
Sierra Leone: leone Sierra Leone: leone										
End of period										
Fin de période	526.316	577.634	613.008	943.396	909.091	1 333.330	1 590.760	2 276.050	1 666.670	2 161.270
Period average										
Moyenne sur période	499.442	567.459	586.740	755.216	920.732	981.482	1 563.620	1 804.190	2 092.120	1 986.150
Singapore: Singapore dollar Singapour: dollar singapourien										
End of period										
Fin de période	1.645	1.608	1.461	1.414	1.400	1.676	1.661	1.666	1.732	1.851
Period average										
Moyenne sur période	1.629	1.616	1.527	1.417	1.410	1.485	1.674	1.695	1.724	1.792
Slovakia: Slovak koruna Slovaquie: couronne slovaque										
End of period										
Fin de période	...	33.202	31.277	29.569	31.895	34.782	36.913	42.266	47.389	48.467
Period average[1]										
Moyenne sur période[1]	...	30.770	32.045	29.713	30.654	33.616	35.233	41.363	46.035	48.355
Slovenia: tolar Slovénie: tolar										
End of period										
Fin de période	98.701	131.842	126.458	125.990	141.480	169.180	161.200	196.770	227.377	250.946
Period average										
Moyenne sur période	81.287	113.242	128.809	118.518	135.364	159.688	166.134	181.769	222.656	242.749
Solomon Islands: Solomon Islands dollar Iles Salomon: dollar des Iles Salomon										
End of period										
Fin de période	3.100	3.248	3.329	3.476	3.622	4.748	4.859	5.076	5.099	...
Period average										
Moyenne sur période	2.928	3.188	3.291	3.406	3.566	3.717	4.816	4.838	5.089	...
South Africa[1]: rand Afrique du Sud[1]: rand										
End of period										
Fin de période	3.053	3.398	3.544	3.648	4.683	4.868	5.860	6.155	7.569	12.127
Period average										
Moyenne sur période	2.852	3.268	3.551	3.627	4.299	4.608	5.528	6.110	6.940	8.609

79

Exchange rates
National currency per US dollar [cont.]
Cours des changes
Valeur du dollar des Etats-Unis en monnaie nationale [suite]

Country or area Pays ou zone	1992	1993	1994	1995	1996	1997	1998	1999	2000	2001
Spain[3]: peseta Espagne[3]: peseta										
End of period										
Fin de période	114.623	142.214	131.739	121.409	131.275	151.702	142.607	...	...	...
Period average										
Moyenne sur période	102.379	127.260	133.958	124.689	126.662	146.414	149.395	...	...	...
Sri Lanka: Sri Lanka rupee Sri Lanka: roupie sri-lankaise										
End of period										
Fin de période	46.000	49.562	49.980	54.048	56.705	61.285	68.297	72.170	82.580	93.159
Period average										
Moyenne sur période	43.830	48.322	49.415	51.252	55.271	58.995	64.450	70.635	77.005	89.383
Sudan[1]: Sudanese pound Soudan[1]: livre soudanaise										
End of period										
Fin de période	13.514	21.739	40.000	52.632	144.928	172.200	237.800	257.700	257.350	261.430
Period average										
Moyenne sur période	9.743	15.931	28.961	58.087	125.079	157.574	200.802	252.550	257.122	258.702
Suriname: Suriname guilder Suriname: florin surinamais										
End of period										
Fin de période	1.785	1.785	# 409.500	407.000	401.000	401.000	401.000	987.500	2 178.500	2 178.500
Period average										
Moyenne sur période	1.785	1.785	# 134.117	442.228	401.258	401.000	401.000	859.437	1 322.470	2 178.500
Swaziland: lilangeni Swaziland: lilangeni										
End of period										
Fin de période	3.053	3.398	3.544	3.648	4.683	4.868	5.860	6.155	7.569	12.127
Period average										
Moyenne sur période	2.852	3.268	3.551	3.627	4.299	4.608	5.528	6.110	6.940	8.609
Sweden: Swedish krona Suède: couronne suédoise										
End of period										
Fin de période	7.043	8.304	7.462	6.658	6.871	7.877	8.061	8.525	9.535	10.668
Period average										
Moyenne sur période	5.824	7.783	7.716	7.133	6.706	7.635	7.950	8.262	9.162	10.329
Switzerland: Swiss franc Suisse: franc suisse										
End of period										
Fin de période	1.456	1.480	1.312	1.151	1.346	1.455	1.377	1.600	1.637	1.677
Period average										
Moyenne sur période	1.406	1.478	1.368	1.183	1.236	1.451	1.450	1.502	1.689	1.688
Syrian Arab Republic[1]: Syrian pound Rép. arabe syrienne[1]: livre syrienne										
End of period										
Fin de période	11.225	11.225	11.225	11.225	11.225	11.225	11.225	11.225	11.225	11.225
Tajikistan: somoni Tadjikistan: somoni										
End of period										
Fin de période	0.005	0.014	0.039	0.294	0.328	0.747	0.978	1.436	2.200	2.550
Period average										
Moyenne sur période	0.003	0.010	0.025	0.123	0.296	0.562	0.777	1.238	2.076	2.372
Thailand: baht Thaïlande: baht										
End of period										
Fin de période	25.520	25.540	25.090	25.190	25.610	# 47.247	36.691	37.470	43.268	44.222
Period average										
Moyenne sur période	25.400	25.320	25.150	24.915	25.343	31.364	41.359	37.814	40.112	44.432
TFYR of Macedonia: TFYR Macedonian denar L'ex-R.y. Macédoine: denar de l'ex-R.Y. Macédoine										
End of period										
Fin de période	...	44.456	40.596	37.980	41.411	55.421	51.836	60.339	66.328	69.172
Period average										
Moyenne sur période	...	...	43.263	37.882	39.981	50.004	54.462	56.902	65.904	68.037
Togo[4]: CFA franc Togo[4]: franc CFA										
End of period										
Fin de période	275.325	294.775	534.600	490.000	523.700	598.810	562.210	652.953	704.951	744.306
Period average										
Moyenne sur période	264.692	283.163	555.205	499.148	511.552	583.669	589.952	615.699	711.976	733.039
Tonga: pa'anga Tonga: pa'anga										
End of period										
Fin de période	1.385	1.375	1.254	1.266	1.209	1.357	1.610	1.608	1.977	2.207

79

Exchange rates
National currency per US dollar [cont.]
Cours des changes
Valeur du dollar des Etats-Unis en monnaie nationale [suite]

Country or area Pays ou zone	1992	1993	1994	1995	1996	1997	1998	1999	2000	2001
Period average Moyenne sur période	1.347	1.384	1.320	1.271	1.232	1.264	1.492	1.599	1.759	2.124
Trinidad and Tobago: Trinidad and Tobago dollar Trinité-et-Tobago: dollar de la Trinité-et-Tobago										
End of period Fin de période	4.250	5.814	5.933	5.997	6.195	6.300	6.597	6.300	6.300	6.290
Period average Moyenne sur période	4.250	5.351	5.925	5.948	6.005	6.252	6.298	6.299	6.300	6.233
Tunisia: Tunisian dinar Tunisie: dinar tunisien										
End of period Fin de période	0.951	1.047	0.991	0.951	0.999	1.148	1.101	1.253	1.385	1.468
Period average Moyenne sur période	0.884	1.004	1.012	0.946	0.973	1.106	1.139	1.186	1.371	1.439
Turkey: Turkish lira Turquie: livre turque										
End of period Fin de période	8 564.430	14 472.500	38 726.000	59 650.000	107 775.00	205 605.00	314 464.00	541 400.00	673 385.00	1 450 130. 0
Period average Moyenne sur période	6 872.420	10 984.600	29 608.700	45 845.100	81 404.900	151 865.00	260 724.00	418 783.00	625 218.00	1 225 590.0
Turkmenistan: Turkmen manat Turkménistan: manat turkmene										
End of period Fin de période	...	1.990	75.000	200.000	4 070.000	4 165.000	5 200.000	5 200.000	5 200.000	5 200.000
Period average Moyenne sur période	...	...	19.198	110.917	3 257.670	4 143.420	4 890.170	5 200.000	5 200.000	5 200.000
Uganda[1]: Uganda shilling Ouganda[1]: shilling ougandais										
End of period Fin de période	1 217.150	1 130.150	926.770	1 009.450	1 029.590	1 140.110	1 362.690	1 506.040	1 766.680	1 727.400
Period average Moyenne sur période	1 133.830	1 195.020	979.445	968.917	1 046.080	1 083.010	1 240.310	1 454.830	1 644.480	1 755.660
Ukraine: hryvnia Ukraine: hryvnia										
End of period Fin de période	0.006	0.126	1.042	1.794	# 1.889	1.899	3.427	5.216	5.435	5.299
Period average Moyenne sur période	...	0.045	0.328	1.473	1.830	1.862	2.450	4.130	5.440	5.372
United Arab Emirates: UAE dirham Emirats arabes unis: dirham des EAU										
End of period Fin de période	3.671	3.671	3.671	3.671	3.671	3.673	3.673	3.673	3.673	3.673
United Kingdom: pound sterling Royaume-Uni: livre sterling										
End of period Fin de période	0.661	0.675	0.640	0.645	0.589	0.605	0.601	0.619	0.670	0.690
Period average Moyenne sur période	0.570	0.667	0.653	0.634	0.641	0.611	0.604	0.618	0.661	0.695
United Rep. of Tanzania: Tanzania shilling Rép.-Unie de Tanzanie: shilling tanzanien										
End of period Fin de période	335.000	479.871	523.453	550.360	595.640	624.570	681.000	797.330	803.260	916.300
Period average Moyenne sur période	297.708	405.274	509.631	574.762	579.977	612.122	664.671	744.759	800.409	876.412
Uruguay: Uruguayan peso Uruguay: peso uruguayen										
End of period Fin de période	3.480	# 4.416	5.601	7.111	8.713	10.040	10.817	11.615	12.515	14.768
Period average Moyenne sur période	3.025	# 3.941	5.044	6.349	7.972	9.442	10.472	11.339	12.100	13.319
Uzbekistan: Uzbek som Ouzbékistan: som ouzbek										
End of period Fin de période	...	...	...	...	...	...	...	140.000	...	...
Period average Moyenne sur période	...	...	...	29.775	40.067	62.917	94.492	124.625	236.608	...
Vanuatu: vatu Vanuatu: vatu										
End of period Fin de période	119.000	120.800	112.080	113.740	110.770	124.310	129.780	128.890	142.810	146.740
Period average Moyenne sur période	113.392	121.581	116.405	112.112	111.719	115.873	127.517	129.075	137.643	145.312

79

Exchange rates
National currency per US dollar [cont.]

Cours des changes
Valeur du dollar des Etats-Unis en monnaie nationale [suite]

Country or area Pays ou zone	1992	1993	1994	1995	1996	1997	1998	1999	2000	2001
Venezuela: bolívar Venezuela: bolívar										
End of period										
Fin de période	79.450	105.640	# 170.000	290.000	476.500	504.250	564.500	648.250	699.750	763.000
Period average										
Moyenne sur période	68.376	90.826	148.503	# 176.842	417.332	488.635	547.556	605.717	679.960	723.666
Viet Nam: dong Viet Nam: dong										
End of period										
Fin de période	10 565.000	10 842.500	11 051.000	11 015.000	11 149.000	12 292.000	13 890.000	14 028.000	14 514.000	15 084.000
Period average										
Moyenne sur période	11 202.200	10 641.000	10 965.700	11 038.200	11 032.600	11 683.300	13 268.000	13 943.200	14 167.700	14 725.200
Yemen: Yemeni rial Yémen: rial yéménite										
End of period										
Fin de période	12.010	12.010	12.010	# 50.040	# 126.910	130.460	141.650	159.100	165.590	173.270
Period average										
Moyenne sur période	12.010	12.010	12.010	# 40.839	# 94.160	129.281	135.882	155.718	161.718	168.672
Zambia: Zambia kwacha Zambie: kwacha zambie										
End of period										
Fin de période	359.712	500.000	680.272	956.130	1 282.690	1 414.840	2 298.920	2 632.190	4 157.830	3 830.400
Period average										
Moyenne sur période	172.214	452.763	669.371	864.119	1 207.900	1 314.500	1 862.070	2 388.020	3 110.840	3 610.930
Zimbabwe: Zimbabwe dollar Zimbabwe: dollar zimbabwéen										
End of period										
Fin de période	5.483	6.935	8.387	9.311	10.839	18.608	37.369	38.139	55.066	55.036
Period average										
Moyenne sur période	5.099	6.483	8.152	8.665	10.002	12.111	23.679	38.301	44.418	55.052

Source:
International Monetary Fund (IMF), Washington, D.C., "International Financial Statistics," January 2003 and the IMF database.

Source:
Fonds monétaire international (FMI), Washington, D.C.,"Statistiques Financières Internationales," janvier 2003 et la base de données du FMI.

1 Principal rate.
2 Pesos per million US dollars through 1983, per thousand US dollars through 1988 and per US dollar thereafter.

3 Beginning 1999, Euros per US dollar. See Euro Area.

4 Prior to January 1999, the official rate was pegged to the French franc. On 12 January 1994, the CFA franc was devalued to CFAF 100 per French franc from CFAF 50 at which it had been fixed since 1948. From 1 January 1 1999, the CFAF is pegged to the euro at a rate of CFA francs 655.957 per euro.

5 Bolivianos per million US dollars through 1983, per thousand US dollars for 1984, and per US dollar thereafter.

6 Reals per trillion US dollars through 1983, per billion US dollars 1984-1988, per million US dollars 1989-1992, and per US dollar thereafter.

7 The official rate is pegged to the French franc. Beginning January 12, 1994, the CFA franc was devalued to CFAF 75 per French franc from CFAF 50 at which it had been fixed since 1948.
8 New Zaires per million US dollars through 1990, per thousand US dollars for 1991-1995, and per US dollar thereafter.

9 "Euro Area" is an official descriptor for the European Economic and Monetary Union (EMU). The participating member states of the EMU are Austria, Belgium, Finland, France, Germany,

1 Taux principal.
2 Pesos par million de dollars des États-Unis jusqu'en 1983, par millier de dollars des États-Unis jusqu'en 1988 et par dollar des États-Unis après cette date.
3 A partir de 1999, euros pour un dollar des États-Unis. Voir la Zone euro.

4 Avant janvier 1999, le taux officiel était établi par référence au franc français. Le 12 janvier 1994, le franc CFA a été dévalué; son taux par rapport au franc français, auquel il est rattaché depuis 1948, est passé de 50 à 100 francs CFA pour 1 franc français. A compter du 1er janvier 1999, le taux officiel est établi par référence à l'euro à un taux de 655 957 francs CFA pour un euro.

5 Bolivianos par million de dollars des États-Unis jusqu'en 1983, par millier de dollars des États-Unis en 1984, et par dollar des États-Unis après cette date.
6 Reals par trillion de dollars des États-Unis jusqu'en 1983, par millard de dollars des États-Unis 1984-1988, par million de dollars des États-Unis 1989-1992, et par dollar des État-Unis après cette date.
7 Le taux de change officiel est raccroché au taux de change du franc français. Le 12 janvier 1994, le CFA a été dévalué de 50 par franc français, valeur qu'il avait conservée depuis 1948, à 75 par franc français.
8 Nouveaux zaïres par million de dollars des États-Unis jusqu'en 1990, par millier de dollars des États-Unis en 1991 et 1995, et par dollar des États-Unis après cette date.
9 L'expression "zone euro" est un intitulé officiel pour l'Union économique et monétaire (UEM) européene. L'UEM est composée des pays membres suivants : Allemagne, Autriche,

79

Exchange rates
National currency per US dollar [cont.]

Cours des changes
Valeur du dollar des États-Unis en monnaie nationale [suite]

Greece (beginning 2001), Ireland, Italy, Luxembourg, Netherlands, Portugal, and Spain.

10 Beginning 2001, Euros per US dollar. See Euro Area.

11 Prior to January 1999, the official rate was pegged to the French franc at CFAF 100 per French franc. The CFA franc was adopted as national currency as of May 2, 1997. The Guinean peso and the CFA franc were set at PG65 per CFA franc. From January 1, 1999, the CFAF is pegged to the euro at a rate of CFA franc 655.957 per euro.

12 Gold córdoba per billion US dollars through 1987, per million US dollars for 1988, per thousand US dollars for 1989-1990 and per US dollar thereafter.

13 New soles per billion US dollars through 1987, per million US dollars for 1988-1989, and per US dollar thereafter.

14 The post-1 January 1998 ruble is equal to 1,000 of the pre-January 1998 rubles.

Belgique, Espagne, Finlande, France, Grèce (à partir de 2001), Irlande, Italie, Luxembourg, Pays-Bas et Portugal.

10 A partir de 2001, euros pour un dollar des État-Unis. Voir la Zone euro.

11 Le taux de change officiel est raccroché au taux de change du franc français à CFA 100 pour franc français. Le franc CFA été adopté comme monnaie nationale au 2 mai 1997. Le peso guinéen et le franc CFA été établi à 65 pesos guinéen pour 1 franc CFA. A compter du 1er janvier 1999, le taux officiel est établi par référence à l'euro à un taux de 655 957 francs CFA pour un euro.

12 Cordobas or par milliard de dollars des États-Unis jusqu'en 1987, par million de dollars en 1988, par millier de dollars des États-Unis en 1989-1990 et par dollar des États Unis après cette date.

13 Nouveaux soles par milliard de dollars des États-Unis jusqu'en 1987, par million de dollars des États-Unis en 1988-1989 et par dollar des États-Unis après cette date.

14 Le rouble ayant cours après le 1er janvier 1998 vaut 1 000 roubles de la période antérieure à cette date.

80
Total external and public/publicly guaranteed long-term debt of developing countries
Million US dollars
Total de la dette extérieure et dette publique extérieure à long terme garantie par l'Etat des pays en développement
Millions de dollars E.-U.

A. Total external debt [1] • Total de la dette extérieure [1]

	1993	1994	1995	1996	1997	1998	1999	2000	
Total long-term debt (LDOD)	1411171	1565539	1669043	1721723	1798897	2044467	2093021	2046392	**Total de la dette à long terme (LDOD)**
Public and publicly guaranteed	1283176	1373919	1431464	1421366	1409743	1513793	1542035	1489140	**Dette publique ou garantie par l'Etat**
Official creditors	760220	831010	863227	829457	791908	841757	865525	842538	Créanciers publics
Multilateral	248238	274215	289902	285850	289499	328505	345681	345246	Multilatéraux
IBRD	102669	110089	113849	107145	106022	115907	119608	120150	BIRD
IDA	58306	66505	71631	75219	77473	84159	86672	87025	IDA
Bilateral	511983	556795	573325	543607	502409	513252	519844	497293	Bilatéraux
Private creditors	522956	542909	568237	591909	617834	672036	676518	646602	Créanciers privés
Bonds	161480	234692	256985	292878	308453	346084	366945	392401	Obligations
Commercial banks	221303	167445	172939	173182	206864	235983	227587	178238	Banques commerciales
Other private	140173	140771	138312	125849	102517	89969	81986	75963	Autres institutions privées
Private non-guaranteed	127995	191620	237579	300357	389154	530674	550986	557251	**Dette privée non garantie**
Undisbursed debt	252779	256786	258657	245878	237849	259919	301257	212095	**Dette (montants non versés)**
Official creditors	191206	201365	205895	191913	185509	208444	257792	173824	Créanciers publics
Private creditors	61572	55421	52762	53965	52341	51475	43466	38271	Créanciers privés
Commitments	140551	120871	153984	171719	190062	194649	152369	124924	**Engagements**
Official creditors	62974	61934	80705	60601	73054	88402	69995	36609	Créanciers publics
Private creditors	77578	58937	73279	111118	117008	106293	82374	88315	Créanciers privés
Disbursements	176332	177307	213595	267475	305720	303273	271395	264686	**Versements**
Public and publicly guaranteed	127361	116480	144750	163706	180015	178048	156830	143582	**Dette publique ou garantie par l'Etat**
Official creditors	54032	50046	66291	55972	65938	68963	62632	54166	Créanciers publics
Multilateral	31314	29404	32356	33682	41003	46432	38000	33626	Multilatéraux
IBRD	13140	11578	13234	13357	17657	17514	15141	13448	BIRD
IDA	4862	6051	5476	6315	5937	5556	5397	5218	IDA
Bilateral	22719	20642	33934	22290	24934	22531	24633	20540	Bilatéraux
Private creditors	73329	66434	78460	107733	114077	109085	94198	89416	Créanciers privés
Bonds	26012	24126	29862	58465	61576	57955	53446	55440	Obligations
Commercial banks	18498	18112	26982	29049	33124	36683	26801	23196	Banques commerciales
Other private	28818	24196	21616	20219	19377	14447	13952	10780	Autres institutions privées
Private non-guaranteed	48970	60827	68844	103770	125705	125225	114565	121104	**Dette privée non garantie**
Principal repayments	101302	112802	129058	168689	193498	188419	248604	251052	**Remboursements du principal**
Public and publicly guaranteed	75053	83476	97676	122554	129792	111741	132613	141125	**Dette publique ou garantie par l'Etat**
Official creditors	29005	36723	45016	53717	51801	43532	45524	48820	Créanciers publics
Multilateral	16428	19172	21296	20989	19796	18713	19267	23100	Multilatéraux
IBRD	10376	11881	12129	11995	10942	10712	10050	10054	BIRD
IDA	397	458	546	593	650	742	887	1014	IDA
Bilateral	12577	17551	23720	32728	32004	24818	26258	25720	Bilatéraux
Private creditors	46049	46753	52659	68837	77991	68209	87089	92305	Créanciers privés
Bonds	8901	7160	12994	21767	35165	24765	25707	40809	Obligations
Commercial banks	17555	19108	19745	28926	26335	25633	46903	38197	Banques commerciales
Other private	19593	20485	19920	18144	16491	17811	14478	13299	Autres institutions privées
Private non-guaranteed	26248	29326	31382	46135	63706	76678	115991	109927	**Dette privée non garantie**

80
Total external and public/publicly guaranteed long-term debt of developing countries
Million US dollars [cont.]
Total de la dette extérieure et dette publique extérieure à long terme garantie par l'Etat des pays en développement
Millions de dollars E.-U. [suite]

A. Total external debt [1] · Total de la dette extérieure [1]

	1993	1994	1995	1996	1997	1998	1999	2000	
Net flows	**75030**	**64504**	**84537**	**98787**	**112222**	**114854**	**22791**	**13634**	**Apports nets**
Public and publicly									**Dette publique ou**
guaranteed	**52308**	**33004**	**47075**	**41152**	**50223**	**66308**	**24218**	**2457**	**garantie par l'Etat**
Official creditors	25028	13323	21274	2255	14137	25431	17108	5347	Créanciers publics
Multilateral	14886	10232	11060	12693	21207	27719	18733	10526	Multilatéraux
IBRD	2764	−303	1104	1362	6715	6803	5091	3394	BIRD
IDA	4465	5593	4930	5723	5287	4814	4510	4204	IDA
Bilateral	10142	3091	10214	−10438	−7070	−2287	−1625	−5179	Bilatéraux
Private creditors	27280	19681	25800	38897	36086	40876	7110	−2889	Créanciers privés
Bonds	17111	16966	16867	36698	26411	33190	27738	14631	Obligations
Commercial banks	944	−996	7236	123	6789	11050	−20102	−15002	Banques commerciales
Other private	9225	3711	1697	2076	2886	−3364	−527	−2519	Autres institutions privées
Private non-guaranteed	**22722**	**31501**	**37462**	**57635**	**61999**	**48546**	**−1426**	**11177**	**Dette privée non garantie**
Interest payments (LINT)	**51855**	**60263**	**77195**	**81046**	**87687**	**95017**	**99535**	**104104**	**Paiements d'intêrcts (LINT)**
Public and publicly									**Dette publique ou**
guaranteed	**44912**	**50783**	**63766**	**64882**	**65669**	**67258**	**70927**	**73337**	**garantie par l'Etat**
Official creditors	23347	25130	30234	30747	28354	27880	28624	28868	Créanciers publics
Multilateral	12933	13571	13965	13760	12841	13257	15570	16003	Multilatéraux
IBRD	8003	8000	8137	7806	6892	7028	7724	8249	BIRD
IDA	395	432	504	512	532	554	600	605	IDA
Bilateral	10414	11558	16270	16986	15513	14623	13054	12865	Bilatéraux
Private creditors	21564	25654	33532	34136	37315	39378	42303	44469	Créanciers privés
Bonds	8521	11163	16914	16776	19623	21398	25111	28624	Obligations
Commercial banks	7630	7671	9340	10656	11652	12510	12392	11485	Banques commerciales
Other private	5414	6820	7278	6704	6040	5470	4759	4360	Autres institutions privées
Private non-guaranteed	**6943**	**9480**	**13428**	**16163**	**22017**	**27759**	**28731**	**30966**	**Dette privée non garantie**
Net transfers	**23175**	**4241**	**7343**	**17741**	**24535**	**19837**	**−76866**	**−90668**	**Transferts nets**
Public and publicly									**Dette publique ou**
guaranteed	**7396**	**−17780**	**−16692**	**−23731**	**−15446**	**−951**	**−46709**	**−70879**	**garantie par l'Etat**
Official creditors	1681	−11807	−8960	−28492	−14217	−2449	−11516	−23521	Créanciers publics
Multilateral	1953	−3340	−2905	−1067	8366	14462	3163	−5477	Multilatéraux
IBRD	−5238	−8303	−7033	−6444	−177	−226	−2633	−4855	BIRD
IDA	4070	5162	4426	5210	4756	4260	3909	3600	IDA
Bilateral	−272	−8468	−6055	−27425	−22583	−16910	−14679	−18044	Bilatéraux
Private creditors	5716	−5972	−7732	4761	−1229	1498	−35193	−47358	Créanciers privés
Bonds	8591	5804	−47	19922	6789	11792	2587	−13993	Obligations
Commercial banks	−6687	−8668	−2104	−10532	−4863	−1460	−32494	−26487	Banques commerciales
Other private	3812	−3108	−5581	−4628	−3154	−8834	−5286	−6879	Autres institutions privées
Private non-guaranteed	**15779**	**22021**	**24034**	**41472**	**39981**	**20787**	**−30157**	**−19789**	**Dette privée non garantie**
Total debt service									**Total du service de la**
(LTDS)	**153157**	**173065**	**206252**	**249734**	**281185**	**283436**	**348138**	**355355**	**dette (LTDS)**
Public and publicly									**Dette publique ou**
guaranteed	**119965**	**134259**	**161442**	**187436**	**195461**	**178999**	**203540**	**214462**	**garantie par l'Etat**
Official creditors	52352	61853	75251	84464	80155	71412	74148	77688	Créanciers publics
Multilateral	29361	32743	35261	34749	32637	31970	34836	39103	Multilatéraux
IBRD	18378	19881	20267	19801	17834	17740	17775	18303	BIRD
IDA	792	890	1050	1105	1181	1296	1487	1618	IDA
Bilateral	22991	29110	39990	49715	47518	39441	39312	38584	Bilatéraux
Private creditors	67613	72406	86191	102972	115306	107587	129392	136774	Créanciers privés
Bonds	17421	18322	29908	38544	54788	46163	50858	69433	Obligations
Commercial banks	25185	26779	29086	39581	37988	38144	59296	49682	Banques commerciales
Other private	25006	27304	27198	24847	22531	23281	19238	17659	Autres institutions privées
Private non-guaranteed	**33192**	**38806**	**44810**	**62298**	**85724**	**104437**	**144722**	**140893**	**Dette privée non garantie**

80
Total external and public/publicly guaranteed long-term debt of developing countries
Million US dollars [*cont.*]
Total de la dette extérieure et dette publique extérieure à long terme garantie par l'Etat des pays en développement
Millions de dollars E.-U. [*suite*]

B. Public and publicly guaranteed long-term debt • Dette publique extérieure à long terme garantie par l'Etat

Country or area Pays ou zone	1991	1992	1993	1994	1995	1996	1997	1998	1999	2000
Albania Albanie	86.2	126.9	179.0	247.6	329.6	405.1	412.1	506.1	580.7	644.2
Algeria Algérie	25969.0	25494.6	24852.7	28163.5	31032.8	31059.5	28714.5	28479.7	25903.0	23061.9
Angola Angola	7705.6	8139.6	8704.1	9001.2	9421.7	9256.5	8571.6	9361.8	9397.6	8757.6
Argentina Argentine	47574.1	47611.0	46176.4	50634.0	55250.0	62560.3	67143.9	77285.4	84081.5	86598.9
Armenia Arménie	...	...	133.9	188.6	298.3	402.7	484.4	563.6	632.5	658.1
Azerbaijan Azerbaïdjan	...	...	35.5	103.2	206.1	247.9	235.9	313.1	493.3	593.5
Bangladesh Bangladesh	12195.6	12595.4	13420.7	14758.0	15103.0	14657.9	13874.0	15099.6	15961.2	15098.1
Belarus Bélarus	...	...	865.1	1123.8	1301.1	728.9	681.4	796.4	708.2	692.0
Belize Belize	151.0	170.0	175.6	182.4	219.4	250.4	268.1	282.9	295.6	449.0
Benin Bénin	1239.9	1324.1	1371.4	1487.3	1483.0	1446.4	1395.8	1471.4	1472.3	1442.8
Bhutan Bhoutan	84.8	88.3	94.9	103.8	105.2	112.9	117.6	171.0	181.8	197.3
Bolivia Bolivie	3529.5	3669.4	3694.8	4122.4	4461.5	4259.4	4133.0	4295.8	4245.7	4119.5
Bosnia and Herzegovina Bosnie–Herzégovine	...	...	...	...	...	...	...	...	2766.0	2568.6
Botswana Botswana	613.2	605.5	651.8	677.5	693.2	607.5	522.0	508.2	454.7	397.6
Brazil Brésil	85632.5	90991.4	91560.8	95367.4	98295.2	96351.7	87304.8	98174.6	92057.2	92589.8
Bulgaria Bulgarie	9761.1	9654.7	9693.3	8371.1	8688.5	8096.2	7617.1	7653.9	7497.3	7513.2
Burkina Faso Burkina Faso	882.6	978.9	1066.0	1039.9	1135.9	1159.5	1139.0	1234.0	1298.2	1135.4
Burundi Burundi	901.2	947.0	998.0	1061.9	1095.1	1081.0	1022.1	1078.9	1049.6	1028.0
Cambodia Cambodge	1688.6	1679.8	1685.4	1745.2	1946.3	2012.5	2031.0	2101.7	2135.8	2180.3
Cameroon Cameroun	5600.6	6279.5	6166.3	7247.6	8009.7	7950.7	7729.5	8188.9	7615.5	7356.6
Cape Verde Cap–Vert	129.5	136.1	140.8	166.4	185.0	196.0	199.5	240.9	308.0	314.6
Central African Rep. Rép. centrafricaine	716.9	729.6	773.2	802.4	853.9	850.4	801.5	841.0	826.1	810.1
Chad Tchad	559.6	671.1	713.4	758.5	833.4	914.2	938.5	1004.9	1045.0	1009.3
Chile Chili	10070.5	9577.5	8867.3	8995.0	7178.3	4883.3	4367.3	5005.0	5654.7	5210.1
China Chine	49479.2	58462.6	70076.2	82391.2	94674.5	102260.2	112821.4	99424.1	108162.9	104709.4
Colombia Colombie	14468.7	13476.1	13242.9	14357.6	13949.6	14854.1	15294.7	17003.9	20473.9	20950.5
Comoros Comores	168.2	177.3	174.0	188.4	200.1	205.0	202.7	211.6	206.2	201.9
Congo Congo	4041.3	3875.6	4114.2	4774.0	4955.4	4665.7	4283.8	4250.5	3933.7	3757.5
Costa Rica Costa Rica	3291.9	3175.7	3130.8	3218.4	3133.4	2923.2	2766.8	3026.1	3186.3	3274.1

80
Total external and public/publicly guaranteed long–term debt of developing countries
Million US dollars [*cont.*]
Total de la dette extérieure et dette publique extérieure à long terme garantie par l'Etat des pays en développement
Millions de dollars E.–U. [*suite*]

B. Public and publicly guaranteed long–term debt • Dette publique extérieure à long terme garantie par l'Etat

Country or area Pays ou zone	1991	1992	1993	1994	1995	1996	1997	1998	1999	2000
Côte d'Ivoire Côte d'Ivoire	11264.6	11243.9	11110.6	11241.0	11902.1	11366.7	10427.1	10799.7	9699.1	9063.4
Croatia Croatie	...	...	601.2	643.4	1860.1	4811.3	5728.7	6388.7	6881.6	7685.5
Czech Republic République tchèque	4807.6	4539.8	5869.8	7023.7	9688.1	12218.1	12837.2	12557.2	9912.4	8131.6
Dem. Rep. of the Congo Rép. dém. du Congo	9285.0	8960.7	8780.9	9293.9	9635.8	9275.2	8628.3	9214.3	8221.0	7841.9
Djibouti Djibouti	204.7	219.3	230.9	254.9	268.9	279.3	253.0	263.8	248.4	237.9
Dominica Dominique	87.8	88.6	92.4	88.7	94.1	97.8	90.6	90.9	88.7	89.2
Dominican Republic Rép. dominicaine	3756.6	3736.4	3791.5	3619.3	3652.6	3523.4	3467.1	3533.2	3657.2	3368.0
Ecuador Equateur	9946.2	9826.7	9966.8	10544.5	12067.7	12443.8	12876.2	13089.0	13555.8	11366.3
Egypt Egypte	28531.8	27809.3	27860.6	29878.1	30548.3	28875.0	26804.3	27622.1	26026.4	24279.4
El Salvador El Salvador	2058.3	2148.0	1916.1	2014.2	2079.8	2316.6	2397.1	2443.2	2649.2	2774.9
Equatorial Guinea Guinée équatoriale	215.5	214.4	214.8	219.3	229.6	222.2	208.6	216.5	207.9	198.9
Eritrea Erythrée	...	...	...	29.1	36.7	44.3	75.5	146.1	252.6	298.0
Estonia Estonie	...	33.8	84.9	108.6	159.3	216.5	197.5	234.4	205.5	206.3
Ethiopia Ethiopie	8842.9	9003.2	9286.6	9567.0	9773.6	9483.7	9423.4	9613.8	5361.9	5324.9
Fiji Fidji	270.6	226.9	199.4	180.7	168.3	147.2	129.9	140.1	120.6	101.2
Gabon Gabon	3224.5	3048.8	2933.3	3694.4	3976.4	3971.6	3664.8	3832.8	3290.2	3511.5
Gambia Gambie	322.5	346.2	350.2	368.1	386.5	412.8	402.0	433.5	430.7	425.2
Georgia Géorgie	...	79.3	558.8	924.1	1039.4	1106.3	1189.5	1301.0	1307.1	1270.8
Ghana Ghana	3118.6	3319.2	3637.8	4156.9	4639.1	4975.7	5056.2	5651.0	5729.2	5529.1
Grenada Grenade	131.6	125.7	125.4	133.1	131.4	137.7	143.6	141.7	144.8	180.9
Guatemala Guatemala	2483.7	2376.4	2493.7	2739.2	2823.6	2755.4	2871.9	2992.1	3125.6	3145.7
Guinea Guinée	2399.2	2450.2	2659.2	2886.4	2987.1	2980.6	3008.7	3126.4	3061.0	2940.4
Guinea–Bissau Guinée–Bissau	676.4	692.3	712.5	761.6	797.7	856.2	838.4	874.3	834.2	818.3
Guyana Guyana	1784.2	1697.1	1755.5	1811.0	1805.8	1394.2	1370.3	1229.4	1225.7	1209.3
Haiti Haïti	639.6	655.0	662.2	646.8	760.8	843.2	902.1	982.4	1049.2	1039.5
Honduras Honduras	3095.8	3510.0	3929.3	4156.1	4187.4	4020.9	4058.5	4042.9	4216.0	4336.9
Hungary Hongrie	18937.9	17896.2	19949.6	22378.5	23973.1	18710.8	15116.7	15889.5	16828.3	14250.7
India Inde	73355.3	77920.8	83905.9	87480.2	80427.6	78049.1	79401.5	84613.1	86255.5	86293.0
Indonesia Indonésie	51891.4	53664.1	57155.9	63926.0	65308.8	60011.9	55856.7	67304.7	73301.7	69160.7
Iran (Islamic Rep. of) Iran (Rép. islamique d')	2064.5	1780.1	5898.7	15529.7	15115.6	11712.0	8262.7	7583.8	6183.6	3812.3

80
Total external and public/publicly guaranteed long-term debt of developing countries
Million US dollars [*cont.*]
Total de la dette extérieure et dette publique extérieure à long terme garantie par l'Etat des pays en développement
Millions de dollars E.–U. [*suite*]

B. Public and publicly guaranteed long-term debt · Dette publique extérieure à long terme garantie par l'Etat

Country or area Pays ou zone	1991	1992	1993	1994	1995	1996	1997	1998	1999	2000
Jamaica Jamaïque	3712.5	3563.6	3452.7	3438.0	3409.2	3134.2	2929.0	3109.3	2909.9	3372.8
Jordan Jordanie	7457.5	6922.2	6770.0	6883.4	7022.9	7091.4	6936.2	7354.2	7536.9	7054.9
Kazakhstan Kazakhstan	...	25.7	1621.1	2227.0	2833.8	1946.5	2621.6	3037.8	3335.9	3601.6
Kenya Kenya	5265.0	5149.0	5245.6	5588.5	5959.9	5684.6	5224.5	5560.7	5323.2	5180.3
Korea, Republic of Corée, République de	22480.5	24049.9	24565.6	19252.6	22123.4	25423.1	33852.4	57956.0	57763.3	46940.7
Kyrgyzstan Kirghizistan	...	5.5	231.7	356.1	478.2	632.3	756.6	939.9	1140.5	1223.6
Lao People's Dem. Rep. Rép. dém. pop. lao	1849.6	1886.7	1948.2	2022.0	2091.2	2185.8	2246.8	2373.1	2471.3	2449.4
Latvia Lettonie	...	30.0	123.6	207.5	271.1	300.4	313.7	404.2	864.8	827.1
Lebanon Liban	336.2	300.5	368.0	778.2	1550.5	1933.4	2356.7	4055.9	5361.7	7033.9
Lesotho Lesotho	425.7	464.7	503.2	577.4	641.4	663.0	667.2	717.1	707.2	697.8
Liberia Libéria	1106.3	1081.2	1101.9	1137.0	1161.4	1110.0	1061.3	1092.3	1062.2	1040.1
Lithuania Lituanie	...	27.4	205.2	277.3	429.9	736.2	1053.4	1220.6	2122.6	2188.2
Madagascar Madagascar	3518.8	3469.0	3316.2	3536.6	3705.7	3552.0	3875.0	4106.4	4368.9	4295.3
Malawi Malawi	1517.6	1568.0	1729.5	1900.4	2083.0	2095.6	2099.2	2309.9	2595.7	2555.2
Malaysia Malaisie	12538.7	12370.5	13460.3	14692.9	16022.7	15702.0	16807.5	18154.5	18929.1	19089.7
Maldives Maldives	78.0	90.5	109.3	122.5	151.9	163.5	164.3	183.4	194.1	185.3
Mali Mali	2461.4	2777.0	2784.9	2544.7	2738.7	2762.2	2691.8	2827.4	2798.5	2644.6
Mauritania Mauritanie	1819.0	1825.3	1903.4	1989.5	2080.8	2125.0	2039.8	2009.9	2137.7	2150.1
Mauritius Maurice	816.8	747.9	733.0	852.2	1147.9	1152.5	1186.6	1151.6	1155.3	889.1
Mexico Mexique	77824.7	71155.1	75143.2	79521.8	95157.6	94038.3	84372.1	88472.1	89197.6	81549.5
Mongolia Mongolie	...	272.2	338.5	400.5	464.9	481.0	532.6	631.7	816.3	794.8
Morocco Maroc	20791.7	21030.1	20680.2	21529.5	22084.6	21172.2	19011.7	19164.0	17313.7	15792.5
Mozambique Mozambique	4337.5	4701.1	4841.1	5219.0	5208.7	5357.8	5211.0	5972.6	4644.9	4598.5
Myanmar Myanmar	4579.7	5003.0	5389.8	6153.8	5377.7	4803.5	5068.7	5052.7	5337.1	5359.9
Nepal Népal	1712.5	1757.6	1939.6	2209.9	2346.5	2345.7	2332.3	2590.6	2909.9	2784.3
Nicaragua Nicaragua	9194.2	9351.0	9343.7	9666.1	8578.2	5160.9	5376.8	5648.1	5899.2	5602.2
Niger Niger	1137.6	1166.0	1209.9	1268.2	1330.0	1329.7	1322.4	1442.6	1423.3	1413.3
Nigeria Nigéria	32325.0	26477.8	26420.6	27954.5	28140.0	25430.5	22631.2	23455.0	22422.6	32735.4
Oman Oman	2473.5	2340.3	2314.7	2607.5	2637.3	2645.8	2567.1	2235.0	2595.8	2672.7
Pakistan Pakistan	17736.6	18562.7	20421.6	22709.4	23787.5	23627.8	23979.4	26150.3	28144.0	27140.2

80
Total external and public/publicly guaranteed long-term debt of developing countries
Million US dollars [*cont.*]
Total de la dette extérieure et dette publique extérieure à long terme garantie par l'Etat des pays en développement
Millions de dollars E.-U. [*suite*]

B. Public and publicly guaranteed long-term debt · Dette publique extérieure à long terme garantie par l'Etat

Country or area Pays ou zone	1991	1992	1993	1994	1995	1996	1997	1998	1999	2000
Panama Panama	3859.5	3618.6	3646.7	3798.5	3781.7	5135.6	5073.8	5418.6	5677.9	5722.6
Papua New Guinea Papouasie−Nvl−Guinée	1631.1	1592.1	1616.1	1732.1	1668.2	1546.0	1340.4	1435.8	1529.4	1501.8
Paraguay Paraguay	1684.6	1364.4	1282.6	1358.7	1440.7	1402.8	1451.5	1578.2	2071.8	2061.3
Peru Pérou	15442.2	15579.9	16384.8	17680.6	18927.4	20224.3	19225.2	19319.2	19500.2	19204.7
Philippines Philippines	25058.3	25618.1	27481.9	29687.0	28291.9	26868.4	26199.9	28637.4	34565.9	33429.4
Poland Pologne	44866.7	42740.8	41296.5	39503.4	41073.4	39208.4	34177.5	35136.2	33150.6	30784.5
Republic of Moldova République de Moldova	...	38.5	190.2	326.4	449.5	554.5	801.4	801.4	722.5	854.4
Romania Roumanie	218.0	1286.7	2069.9	2925.3	3908.9	5523.0	6212.5	6428.1	5752.9	6430.3
Russian Federation Fédération de Russie	55154.7	64551.3	101681.1	108281.7	101762.8	102057.6	106493.6	121233.1	120793.9	111418.7
Rwanda Rwanda	747.1	789.9	837.6	905.3	970.1	984.5	993.5	1119.8	1161.7	1146.6
Saint Kitts and Nevis Saint−Kitts−et−Nevis	48.6	47.4	49.7	55.2	54.1	62.7	112.3	125.0	135.7	135.8
Saint Lucia Sainte−Lucie	76.1	89.8	96.5	103.6	111.3	121.4	119.9	133.5	143.2	169.2
St. Vincent−Grenadines St. Vincent−Grenadines	65.6	74.4	78.4	92.3	92.3	93.9	92.8	108.1	162.6	161.0
Samoa Samoa	113.4	117.8	140.4	156.7	168.1	162.8	148.3	154.3	156.6	147.0
Sao Tome and Principe Sao Tomé−et−Principe	149.8	168.5	181.3	200.7	231.6	226.4	226.7	243.5	291.3	294.4
Senegal Sénégal	2879.6	2992.3	3046.5	3048.5	3190.5	3115.7	3102.6	3270.5	3114.8	2958.3
Serbia and Montenegro Serbie−et−Monténégro	11640.5	11116.9	8231.4	6613.4	6827.4	6565.6	6147.9	6500.1	6233.6	6073.9
Seychelles Seychelles	125.5	130.5	132.1	147.8	145.8	138.1	131.3	145.0	132.2	124.4
Sierra Leone Sierra Leone	616.3	677.1	763.8	848.9	905.8	903.0	890.0	958.8	940.6	969.2
Slovakia Slovaquie	1764.0	1709.7	2120.3	2866.2	3487.5	3962.8	4443.1	4363.1	4424.3	4883.2
Solomon Islands Iles Salomon	98.4	92.5	94.3	98.4	100.3	100.5	96.5	113.7	125.3	120.7
Somalia Somalie	1945.2	1897.8	1897.0	1934.8	1960.8	1918.2	1852.5	1886.4	1859.4	1825.1
South Africa Afrique du Sud	...	...	...	7789.0	9836.7	10347.5	11516.9	10667.8	8173.0	9088.1
Sri Lanka Sri Lanka	5670.7	5661.5	6029.6	6721.9	7149.5	7066.2	6986.5	7950.7	8506.2	8035.1
Sudan Soudan	9220.1	8983.6	8993.8	9399.9	9779.4	9369.2	8998.2	9225.9	8852.0	8646.5
Swaziland Swaziland	240.5	215.7	200.0	210.2	223.0	219.6	210.1	222.5	204.8	198.2
Syrian Arab Republic Rép. arabe syrienne	16561.4	16111.8	16437.1	16628.9	16853.3	16762.2	16326.4	16352.6	16142.4	15930.0
Tajikistan Tadjikistan	...	9.7	384.9	562.0	590.4	656.8	669.0	709.1	611.7	625.6
Thailand Thaïlande	13240.1	13282.5	14696.7	16202.7	16826.4	16887.1	22292.0	28086.4	31304.7	29417.8
TFYR of Macedonia L'ex−R.y. Macédoine	...	...	703.9	708.9	788.4	856.3	941.7	1053.8	1138.3	1164.8

80

Total external and public/publicly guaranteed long-term debt of developing countries
Million US dollars [cont.]

Total de la dette extérieure et dette publique extérieure à long terme garantie par l'Etat des pays en développement
Millions de dollars E.-U. [suite]

B. Public and publicly guaranteed long-term debt · Dette publique extérieure à long terme garantie par l'Etat

Country or area Pays ou zone	1991	1992	1993	1994	1995	1996	1997	1998	1999	2000
Togo Togo	1139.6	1135.3	1127.8	1229.2	1286.2	1310.2	1215.3	1329.1	1289.8	1232.2
Tonga Tonga	44.2	42.6	43.7	57.6	62.8	62.5	56.3	60.8	63.5	58.0
Trinidad and Tobago Trinité-et-Tobago	1764.8	1802.7	1820.3	1972.2	1949.8	1876.2	1532.8	1477.9	1485.4	1496.2
Tunisia Tunisie	7110.6	7201.9	7417.0	8007.2	9023.7	9377.8	9334.3	9499.5	9494.6	8869.3
Turkey Turquie	39828.8	40462.7	44066.7	48442.8	50326.0	48215.8	47498.9	50216.5	50581.0	55292.8
Turkmenistan Turkménistan	...	...	276.4	346.3	384.9	464.2	1242.4	1731.2	...	...
Uganda Ouganda	2283.3	2433.2	2599.2	2869.1	3062.4	3151.5	3405.3	3471.9	2979.7	2996.6
Ukraine Ukraine	...	453.6	3682.1	4809.6	6580.5	6647.5	7015.2	8966.3	9581.0	8139.2
United Rep. of Tanzania Rép.-Unie de Tanzanie	5793.6	5852.9	5814.5	6135.2	6211.1	6089.0	6020.7	6431.8	6686.5	6325.4
Uruguay Uruguay	2897.3	3140.2	3369.0	3749.9	3833.2	4096.9	4585.7	5142.0	5109.7	5596.9
Uzbekistan Ouzbékistan	...	59.7	939.5	952.8	1417.6	1995.8	2032.6	2590.6	3444.9	3577.6
Vanuatu Vanuatu	38.1	39.6	39.4	41.5	43.2	42.2	38.9	54.2	63.4	67.2
Venezuela Venezuela	24938.6	25829.5	26855.3	28040.0	28222.5	27790.8	27085.1	28111.2	27761.1	27628.1
Viet Nam Viet Nam	21360.5	21648.5	21599.0	21854.5	21777.3	21964.3	18985.5	19918.0	20528.7	11546.0
Yemen Yémen	6512.3	6372.6	6179.1	5874.7	5915.5	5678.1	3433.7	4356.5	4501.3	4524.5
Zambia Zambie	4703.6	4513.5	4397.4	5174.2	5285.1	5362.8	5244.8	5319.9	4497.7	4448.3
Zimbabwe Zimbabwe	2612.6	2841.5	3097.4	3407.8	3479.5	3309.3	3103.4	3331.8	3222.0	2947.7

Source:
World Bank, Washington, D.C., "Global Development
Finance 2002", volumes 1 and 2.

Source:
Banque mondiale, Washington, D.C., "Global Development
Finance 2002", volumes 1 et 2.

1   The following abbreviations have been used in the table:
    LDOD: Long-term debt outstanding and disbursed
    IBRD: International Bank for Reconstruction and Development
    IDA: International Development Association
    LINT: Loan interest
    LTDS: Long-term debt service

1 Les abbréviations ci-après ont été utilisées dans le tableau:
    LDOD: Dette à long terme
    BIRD: Banque internationale pour la réconstruction et le
    développement
    IDA: Association internationale de développement
    LINT: Paiement d'intérêts
    LTDS: Service de la dette à long terme

Technical notes, tables 79 and 80

Table 79: Foreign exchange rates are shown in units of national currency per US dollar. The exchange rates are classified into three broad categories, reflecting both the role of the authorities in the determination of the exchange and/or the multiplicity of exchange rates in a country. The *market rate* is used to describe exchange rates determined largely by market forces; the *official rate* is an exchange rate determined by the authorities, sometimes in a flexible manner. For countries maintaining multiple exchange arrangements, the rates are labeled *principal rate*, *secondary rate*, and *tertiary rate*. Unless otherwise stated, the table refers to end of period and period averages of market exchange rates or official exchange rates. For further information see *International Financial Statistics* [15] and <www.imf.org>.

Table 80: Data were extracted from *Global Development Finance 2002* [35], published by the World Bank.

Long term external debt is defined as debt that has an original or extended maturity of more than one year and is owed to non-residents and repayable in foreign currency, goods, or services. A distinction is made between:

— Public debt which is an external obligation of a public debtor, which could be a national government, a political sub-division, an agency of either of the above or, in fact, any autonomous public body;

— Publicly guaranteed debt, which is an external obligation of a private debtor that is guaranteed for repayment by a public entity;

— Private non-guaranteed external debt, which is an external obligation of a private debtor that is not guaranteed for repayment by a public entity.

The data referring to public and publicly guaranteed debt do not include data for (a) transactions with the International Monetary Fund, (b) debt repayable in local currency, (c) direct investment and (d) short-term debt (that is, debt with an original maturity of less than a year).

The data referring to private non-guaranteed debt also exclude the above items but include contractual obligations on loans to direct-investment enterprises by foreign parent companies or their affiliates.

Data are aggregated by type of creditor. The breakdown is as follows:

Official creditors:

(a) Loans from international organizations (multilateral loans), excluding loans from funds administered by an international organization on behalf of a single donor government. The latter are classified as loans from governments;

(b) Loans from governments (bilateral loans) and

Notes techniques, tableaux 79 et 80

Tableau 79: Les taux des changes sont exprimés par nombre d'unités de monnaie nationale pour un dollar des Etats-Unis. Les taux de change sont classés en trois catégories, qui dénotent le rôle des autorités dans l'établissement des taux de change et/ou la multiplicité des taux de change dans un pays. Par *taux du marché*, on entend les taux de change déterminés essentiellement par les forces du marché; le *taux officiel* est un taux de change établi par les autorités, parfois selon des dispositions souples. Pour les pays qui continuent de mettre en œuvre des régimes de taux de change multiples, les taux sont désignés par les appellations suivantes: "taux principal", "taux secondaire" et "taux tertiaire". Sauf indication contraire, le tableau indique des taux de fin de période et les moyennes sur la période, des taux de change du marché ou des taux de change officiels. Pour plus de renseignements, voir *Statistiques financières internationales* [15] et <www.imf.org>.

Tableau 80: Les données sont extraites de *Global Development Finance 2002* [35] publié par la Banque mondiale.

La dette extérieure à long terme désigne la dette dont l'échéance initiale ou reportée est de plus d'un an, due à des non résidents et remboursable en devises, biens ou services. On établit les distinctions suivantes:

— La dette publique, qui est une obligation extérieure d'un débiteur public, pouvant être un gouvernement, un organe politique, une institution de l'un ou l'autre ou, en fait, tout organisme public autonome.

— La dette garantie par l'Etat, qui est une obligation extérieure d'un débiteur privé, dont le remboursement est garanti par un organisme public.

— La dette extérieure privée non garantie, qui est une obligation extérieure d'un débiteur privé, dont le remboursement n'est pas garanti par un organisme public.

Les statistiques relatives à la dette publique ou à la dette garantie par l'Etat ne comprennent pas les données concernant: (a) les transactions avec le Fonds monétaire international; (b) la dette remboursable en monnaie nationale; (c) les investissements directs; et (d) la dette à court terme (c'est-à-dire la dette dont l'échéance initiale est inférieure à un an).

Les statistiques relatives à la dette privée non garantie ne comprennent pas non plus les éléments précités, mais comprennent les obligations contractuelles au titre des prêts consentis par des sociétés mères étrangères ou leurs filiales à des entreprises créées dans le cadre d'investissements directs.

Les données sont groupées par type de créancier, comme suit:

Créanciers publics:

(a) Les prêts obtenus auprès d'organisations interna-

from autonomous public bodies;

Private creditors:

(a) Suppliers: Credits from manufacturers, exporters, or other suppliers of goods;

(b) Financial markets: Loans from private banks and other private financial institutions as well as publicly issued and privately placed bonds;

(c) Other: External liabilities on account of nationalized properties and unclassified debts to private creditors.

A distinction is made between the following categories of external public debt:

— Debt outstanding (including undisbursed) is the sum of disbursed and undisbursed debt and represents the total outstanding external obligations of the borrower at year-end;

— Debt outstanding (disbursed only) is total outstanding debt drawn by the borrower at year end;

— Commitments are the total of loans for which contracts are signed in the year specified;

— Disbursements are drawings on outstanding loan commitments during the year specified;

— Service payments are actual repayments of principal amortization and interest payments made in foreign currencies, goods or services in the year specified;

— Net flows (or net lending) are disbursements minus principal repayments;

— Net transfers are net flows minus interest payments or disbursements minus total debt-service payments.

The countries included in the table are those for which data are sufficiently reliable to provide a meaningful presentation of debt outstanding and future service payments.

tionales (prêts multilatéraux), à l'exclusion des prêts au titre de fonds administrés par une organisation internationale pour le compte d'un gouvernement donateur précis, qui sont classés comme prêts consentis par des gouvernements;

(b) Les prêts consentis par des gouvernements (prêts bilatéraux) et par des organisations publiques autonomes.

Créanciers privés:

(a) Fournisseurs: Crédits consentis par des fabricants exportateurs et autre fournisseurs de biens;

(b) Marchés financiers: prêts consentis par des banques privées et autres institutions financières privées, et émissions publiques d'obligations placées auprès d'investisseurs privés;

(c) Autres créanciers: engagements vis-à-vis de l'extérieur au titre des biens nationalisés et dettes diverses à l'égard de créanciers privés.

On fait une distinction entre les catégories suivantes de dette publique extérieure:

— L'encours de la dette (y compris les fonds non décaissés) est la somme des fonds décaissés et non décaissés et représente le total des obligations extérieures en cours de l'emprunteur à la fin de l'année;

— L'encours de la dette (fonds décaissés seulement) est le montant total des tirages effectués par l'emprunteur sur sa dette en cours à la fin de l'année;

— Les engagements représentent le total des prêts dont les contrats ont été signés au cours de l'année considérée;

— Les décaissements sont les sommes tirées sur l'encours des prêts pendant l'année considérée;

— Les paiements au titre du service de la dette sont les remboursements effectifs du principal et les paiements d'intérêts effectués en devises, biens ou services pendant l'année considérée;

— Les flux nets (ou prêts nets) sont les décaissements moins les remboursements de principal;

— Les transferts nets désignent les flux nets moins les paiements d'intérêts, ou les décaissements moins le total des paiements au titre du service de la dette.

Les pays figurant sur ce tableau sont ceux pour lesquels les données sont suffisamment fiables pour permettre une présentation significative de l'encours de la dette et des paiements futurs au titre du service de la dette.

81
Disbursements of bilateral and multilateral official development assistance and official aid to individual recipients
Versements d'aide publique au développement et d'aide publique bilatérales et multilatérales aux bénéficiares

Region, country or area Région, pays ou zone	Year Année	Net disbursements (US $) — Versements nets ($ E.−U.)			
		Bilateral Bilatérale (millions)	Multilateral[1] Multilatérale[1] (millions)	Total (millions)	Per capita[2] Par habitant[2]
Total Total	**1998** 1999 2000	**39 724.1** 42 717.0 40 923.2	**17 501.4** 17 249.6 16 447.3	**57 225.5** 60 146.6 57 370.5	... ...
Africa Afrique	**1998** 1999 2000	**11 218.7** 10 291.2 10 353.8	**6 034.7** 5 483.4 5 076.2	**17 253.4** 15 774.6 15 430.0	... ...
Algeria Algérie	1998 1999 2000	121.9 37.1 27.1	253.3 21.0 64.1	375.2 58.1 91.2	12.7 1.9 3.0
Angola Angola	1998 1999 2000	214.5 251.8 189.1	120.7 135.7 111.5	335.2 387.5 300.6	27.0 30.4 22.9
Benin Bénin	1998 1999 2000	143.9 119.3 190.5	68.1 93.2 49.2	212.0 212.5 239.7	36.5 35.5 38.9
Botswana Botswana	1998 1999 2000	73.1 41.1 23.5	35.9 20.6 8.1	109.0 61.7 31.6	69.3 38.3 19.1
Burkina Faso Burkina Faso	1998 1999 2000	226.6 232.0 227.8	167.4 156.8 104.5	394.0 388.8 332.3	36.9 34.6 28.8
Burundi Burundi	1998 1999 2000	44.4 52.0 40.9	32.8 22.2 51.7	77.2 74.2 92.6	12.3 11.4 14.6
Cameroon Cameroun	1998 1999 2000	303.0 254.3 213.5	124.8 183.3 169.1	427.8 437.6 382.6	29.6 30.1 25.7
Cape Verde Cap−Vert	1998 1999 2000	85.2 88.7 69.7	44.8 48.3 24.7	130.0 137.0 94.4	311.8 320.1 221.1
Central African Republic République centrafricaine	1998 1999 2000	56.5 59.1 53.0	63.4 58.1 23.0	119.9 117.2 76.0	33.5 32.1 20.4
Chad Tchad	1998 1999 2000	74.5 64.5 53.3	88.2 116.5 77.1	162.7 181.0 130.4	22.0 23.7 16.5
Comoros Comores	1998 1999 2000	18.6 13.2 10.8	16.6 8.3 7.7	35.2 21.5 18.5	52.9 31.4 26.2
Congo Congo	1998 1999 2000	59.7 121.4 22.2	6.0 20.2 10.2	65.7 141.6 32.4	23.1 48.3 10.7
Côte d'Ivoire Côte d'Ivoire	1998 1999 2000	489.5 365.6 250.1	309.1 81.0 101.2	798.6 446.6 351.3	52.0 28.5 21.4
Dem. Republic of the Congo République dém. du Congo	1998 1999 2000	79.7 87.0 102.7	43.5 45.3 80.7	123.2 132.3 183.4	2.5 2.7 3.6
Djibouti Djibouti	1998 1999 2000	62.3 55.4 42.1	16.9 18.7 19.7	79.2 74.1 61.8	132.4 120.1 97.8
Egypt Egypte	1998 1999 2000	1 472.3 1 298.1 1 138.9	268.4 210.8 135.6	1 740.7 1 508.9 1 274.5	28.4 24.1 19.9
Equatorial Guinea Guinée équatoriale	1998 1999 2000	18.3 14.6 18.2	6.5 5.6 3.3	24.8 20.2 21.5	57.4 45.5 47.0
Eritrea Erythrée	1998 1999 2000	97.7 80.5 111.9	38.1 49.7 54.9	135.8 130.2 166.8	39.8 36.9 45.6

81
**Disbursements of bilateral and multilateral official development assistance
and official aid to individual recipients [cont.]
Versements d'aide publique au développement et d'aide publique
bilatérales et multilatérales aux bénéficiares [suite]**

Region, country or area Région, pays ou zone	Year Année	Net disbursements (US $) — Versements nets ($ E.—U.)			
		Bilateral Bilatérale (millions)	Multilateral [1] Multilatérale [1] (millions)	Total (millions)	Per capita [2] Par habitant [2]
Ethiopia	1998	365.1	282.2	647.3	11.5
Ethiopie	1999	325.0	303.1	628.1	10.8
	2000	379.5	298.4	677.9	11.3
Gabon	1998	37.4	8.6	46.0	40.1
Gabon	1999	34.5	13.1	47.6	40.4
	2000	− 11.7	23.4	11.7	9.7
Gambia	1998	13.5	24.6	38.1	31.0
Gambie	1999	13.2	19.0	32.2	23.2
	2000	14.6	32.0	46.6	33.5
Ghana	1998	374.5	325.1	699.6	37.8
Ghana	1999	355.6	249.9	605.5	32.0
	2000	385.0	222.1	607.1	33.0
Guinea	1998	148.5	187.1	335.6	42.6
Guinée	1999	111.1	108.7	219.8	27.4
	2000	92.8	57.3	150.1	18.4
Guinea−Bissau	1998	64.8	31.0	95.8	83.4
Guinée−Bissau	1999	32.1	20.3	52.4	44.7
	2000	41.6	38.8	80.4	67.1
Kenya	1998	275.8	200.8	476.6	16.2
Kenya	1999	253.7	53.5	307.2	10.2
	2000	293.0	214.5	507.5	16.5
Lesotho	1998	32.5	34.9	67.4	34.1
Lesotho	1999	25.6	6.6	32.2	15.3
	2000	21.8	20.9	42.7	19.9
Liberia	1998	31.3	41.3	72.6	29.0
Libéria	1999	44.6	49.4	94.0	34.7
	2000	23.8	44.0	67.8	23.3
Libyan Arab Jamahiriya	1998	3.6	3.4	7.0	1.4
Jamahiriya arabe libyenne	1999	3.3	3.9	7.2	1.4
	2000	11.9	3.1	15.0	2.8
Madagascar	1998	333.7	161.5	495.2	32.9
Madagascar	1999	192.4	166.1	358.5	23.1
	2000	138.7	184.6	323.3	20.2
Malawi	1998	203.6	230.2	433.8	40.4
Malawi	1999	227.7	214.3	442.0	40.1
	2000	269.2	170.8	440.0	38.9
Mali	1998	236.2	116.7	352.9	32.9
Mali	1999	237.3	117.4	354.7	32.1
	2000	299.8	61.3	361.1	31.8
Mauritania	1998	63.5	115.1	178.6	71.4
Mauritanie	1999	88.7	124.8	213.5	82.7
	2000	82.5	129.3	211.8	79.5
Mauritius	1998	19.9	22.6	42.5	36.6
Maurice	1999	5.1	36.7	41.8	35.6
	2000	12.4	7.5	19.9	16.8
Mayotte	1998	104.4	0.0	104.4	...
Mayotte	1999	109.3	2.5	111.8	...
	2000	103.0	0.2	103.2	...
Morocco	1998	250.7	249.1	499.8	18.0
Maroc	1999	333.5	316.0	649.5	23.0
	2000	293.1	130.3	423.4	14.8
Mozambique	1998	712.6	329.6	1 042.2	61.6
Mozambique	1999	593.2	213.2	806.4	46.6
	2000	623.5	253.8	877.3	49.6
Namibia	1998	128.7	51.5	180.2	106.6
Namibie	1999	117.2	60.4	177.6	103.0
	2000	96.8	54.8	151.6	83.4
Niger	1998	144.6	145.9	290.5	28.8
Niger	1999	120.2	66.3	186.5	17.8
	2000	105.8	105.1	210.9	19.5
Nigeria	1998	34.3	169.8	204.1	1.9
Nigéria	1999	52.9	96.3	149.2	1.3
	2000	84.3	100.2	184.5	1.6

81
Disbursements of bilateral and multilateral official development assistance
and official aid to individual recipients [*cont.*]
Versements d'aide publique au développement et d'aide publique
bilatérales et multilatérales aux bénéficiares [*suite*]

Region, country or area Région, pays ou zone	Year Année	Net disbursements (US $) — Versements nets ($ E.—U.)			
		Bilateral Bilatérale (millions)	Multilateral[1] Multilatérale[1] (millions)	Total (millions)	Per capita[2] Par habitant[2]
Rwanda Rwanda	1998 1999 2000	209.0 180.5 175.4	140.9 192.4 146.5	349.9 372.9 321.9	54.5 52.6 42.3
Saint Helena Sainte—Hélène	1998 1999 2000	14.4 13.5 18.4	1.4 0.3 0.3	15.8 13.8 18.7	3 160.0 2 760.0 3 740.0
Sao Tome and Principe Sao Tomé—et—Principe	1998 1999 2000	18.1 19.1 17.7	10.1 8.4 17.3	28.2 27.5 35.0	212.0 203.7 253.6
Senegal Sénégal	1998 1999 2000	289.0 416.2 288.4	211.2 115.3 139.7	500.2 531.5 428.1	55.3 57.3 44.9
Seychelles Seychelles	1998 1999 2000	17.2 4.8 3.3	6.1 6.2 8.4	23.3 11.0 11.7	294.9 137.5 144.4
Sierra Leone Sierra Leone	1998 1999 2000	53.2 59.9 115.6	50.5 13.3 66.8	103.7 73.2 182.4	24.8 17.1 41.4
Somalia Somalie	1998 1999 2000	41.7 75.9 56.4	38.3 38.7 47.3	80.0 114.6 103.7	9.9 13.6 11.8
South Africa Afrique du Sud	1998 1999 2000	420.7 386.1 353.6	92.4 153.4 131.9	513.1 539.5 485.5	12.2 12.5 11.1
Sudan Soudan	1998 1999 2000	150.2 158.5 90.3	58.5 58.2 35.7	208.7 216.7 126.0	7.0 7.1 4.1
Swaziland Swaziland	1998 1999 2000	16.8 14.9 2.8	13.6 14.1 10.3	30.4 29.0 13.1	34.1 31.9 14.2
Togo Togo	1998 1999 2000	66.1 47.0 51.9	61.2 21.2 16.4	127.3 68.2 68.3	30.0 15.5 15.1
Tunisia Tunisie	1998 1999 2000	102.3 102.0 150.3	78.3 161.2 71.9	180.6 263.2 222.2	19.4 27.8 23.2
Uganda Ouganda	1998 1999 2000	383.9 357.5 578.2	263.4 232.4 235.6	647.3 589.9 813.8	30.8 27.3 36.6
United Republic of Tanzania Rép.—Unie de Tanzanie	1998 1999 2000	769.1 613.4 778.7	228.3 375.8 268.5	997.4 989.2 1 047.2	29.8 28.9 29.8
Zambia Zambie	1998 1999 2000	256.5 340.0 486.2	93.2 283.4 308.6	349.7 623.4 794.8	34.6 59.9 74.1
Zimbabwe Zimbabwe	1998 1999 2000	216.3 219.2 192.6	64.7 25.5 − 13.9	281.0 244.7 178.7	22.2 18.7 14.2
Other and unallocated Autres et non—ventilés	1998 1999 2000	973.1 770.7 847.5	187.3 247.1 336.4	1 160.4 1 017.8 1 183.9	... ...
Americas **Amériques**	**1998** **1999** **2000**	**4 015.5** **4 242.2** **4 034.1**	**1 637.8** **1 792.0** **1 079.1**	**5 630.0** **6 019.4** **4 918.2**	... ...
Anguilla Anguilla	1998 1999 2000	3.2 2.7 3.8	− 0.2 − 0.3 − 0.3	3.0 2.4 3.5	375.0 300.0 437.5
Antigua and Barbuda Antigua—et—Barbuda	1998 1999 2000	5.0 8.2 3.7	2.1 0.8 1.1	7.1 9.0 4.8	110.9 138.5 73.8
Argentina Argentine	1998 1999 2000	28.9 31.3 43.5	51.0 64.1 25.3	79.9 95.4 68.8	2.2 2.6 1.9

81
Disbursements of bilateral and multilateral official development assistance
and official aid to individual recipients [*cont.*]
Versements d'aide publique au développement et d'aide publique
bilatérales et multilatérales aux bénéficiares [*suite*]

Region, country or area Région, pays ou zone	Year Année	Net disbursements (US $) — Versements nets ($ E.—U.)			
		Bilateral Bilatérale [1] (millions)	Multilateral Multilatérale [1] (millions)	Total (millions)	Per capita [2] Par habitant [2]
Aruba Aruba	1998	10.7	0.6	11.3	122.8
	1999	− 7.1	− 0.3	− 7.4	− 78.7
	2000	10.7	0.8	11.5	113.9
Bahamas Bahamas	1998	0.2	22.4	22.6	77.1
	1999	0.9	10.7	11.6	38.9
	2000	5.2	0.3	5.5	18.2
Barbados Barbade	1998	0.5	15.2	15.7	59.0
	1999	1.4	− 3.5	− 2.1	− 7.9
	2000	1.0	− 0.8	0.2	0.7
Belize Belize	1998	2.6	8.8	11.4	47.9
	1999	37.5	8.8	46.3	208.6
	2000	2.9	11.2	14.1	56.4
Bermuda Bermudes	1998	1.0	0.0	1.0	16.1
	1999	0.0	0.0	0.0	0.0
	2000	0.1	0.0	0.1	1.6
Bolivia Bolivie	1998	416.2	212.3	628.5	79.1
	1999	397.3	171.4	568.7	69.9
	2000	336.1	140.2	476.3	57.2
Brazil Brésil	1998	218.9	114.9	333.8	2.1
	1999	98.4	87.5	185.9	1.1
	2000	222.5	98.4	320.9	1.9
British Virgin Islands Iles Vierges britanniques	1998	1.5	− 0.3	1.2	54.5
	1999	2.8	− 0.2	2.6	113.0
	2000	1.2	3.6	4.8	200.0
Cayman Islands Iles Caïmanes	1998	− 1.5	1.7	0.2	− 5.6
	1999	0.5	2.6	3.1	83.8
	2000	− 3.1	− 0.5	− 3.6	− 94.7
Chile Chili	1998	95.1	10.9	106.0	7.2
	1999	63.5	6.0	69.5	4.6
	2000	41.0	7.7	48.7	3.2
Colombia Colombie	1998	160.8	7.2	168.0	4.1
	1999	292.3	9.3	301.6	7.3
	2000	178.5	7.8	186.3	4.4
Costa Rica Costa Rica	1998	21.9	6.9	28.8	8.2
	1999	− 4.3	− 4.9	− 9.2	− 2.6
	2000	17.2	− 6.2	11.0	2.9
Cuba Cuba	1998	56.8	23.0	79.8	7.2
	1999	35.5	22.7	58.2	5.2
	2000	30.8	12.9	43.7	3.9
Dominica Dominique	1998	5.7	13.7	19.4	255.3
	1999	6.9	3.0	9.9	139.4
	2000	5.9	6.7	12.6	175.0
Dominican Republic République dominicaine	1998	60.4	60.0	120.4	14.9
	1999	151.9	42.8	194.7	23.4
	2000	44.6	17.8	62.4	7.3
Ecuador Equateur	1998	155.2	23.5	178.7	14.7
	1999	128.9	17.1	146.0	11.8
	2000	137.4	8.6	146.0	11.5
El Salvador El Salvador	1998	154.4	25.4	179.8	29.8
	1999	173.7	9.3	183.0	29.7
	2000	172.3	7.1	179.4	28.6
Falkland Islands Iles Falkland	1998	0.0	0.0	0.0	0.0
	1999	0.0	0.0	0.0	0.0
	2000	0.0	− 0.2	− 0.2	− 100.0
Grenada Grenade	1998	3.4	2.6	6.0	64.5
	1999	2.4	3.0	5.4	53.5
	2000	9.9	3.2	13.1	129.7
Guatemala Guatemala	1998	181.7	50.9	232.6	21.5
	1999	230.7	62.3	293.0	26.4
	2000	230.3	32.8	263.1	23.1
Guyana Guyana	1998	51.8	41.2	93.0	123.3
	1999	39.6	39.9	79.5	103.1
	2000	51.9	56.4	108.3	140.3

81

Disbursements of bilateral and multilateral official development assistance
and official aid to individual recipients [*cont.*]
Versements d'aide publique au développement et d'aide publique
bilatérales et multilatérales aux bénéficiares [*suite*]

Net disbursements (US $)   –   Versements nets ($ E.–U.)

Region, country or area Région, pays ou zone	Year Année	Bilateral Bilatérale (millions)	Multilatéral[1] Multilatérale[1] (millions)	Total (millions)	Per capita[2] Par habitant[2]
Haiti	1998	250.9	156.2	407.1	53.2
Haïti	1999	157.2	105.7	262.9	33.7
	2000	153.9	54.4	208.3	26.2
Honduras	1998	192.9	125.0	317.9	51.4
Honduras	1999	355.1	460.2	815.3	127.7
	2000	310.6	133.9	444.5	69.3
Jamaica	1998	3.5	15.8	19.3	7.5
Jamaïque	1999	− 22.7	0.0	− 22.7	− 8.8
	2000	− 26.4	29.9	3.5	1.3
Mexico	1998	3.9	39.6	43.5	0.5
Mexique	1999	21.9	14.8	36.7	0.4
	2000	− 68.4	13.7	− 54.7	− 0.6
Montserrat	1998	65.1	0.5	65.6	10 933.3
Montserrat	1999	40.5	0.4	40.9	8 180.0
	2000	30.9	0.1	31.0	6 200.0
Netherlands Antilles	1998	125.7	3.4	129.1	620.7
Antilles néerlandaises	1999	126.2	0.8	127.0	619.5
	2000	173.8	3.1	176.9	822.8
Nicaragua	1998	323.5	249.2	572.7	119.2
Nicaragua	1999	323.4	351.7	675.1	136.8
	2000	325.9	235.5	561.4	110.7
Panama	1998	22.4	− 0.3	22.1	8.0
Panama	1999	15.2	− 0.8	14.4	5.1
	2000	11.7	− 3.3	8.4	2.9
Paraguay	1998	55.7	20.3	76.0	14.6
Paraguay	1999	65.5	12.1	77.6	14.5
	2000	72.8	8.4	81.2	14.8
Peru	1998	381.6	120.0	501.6	20.2
Pérou	1999	407.3	45.0	452.3	17.9
	2000	372.7	26.0	398.7	15.5
Saint Kitts and Nevis	1998	1.3	2.6	3.9	100.0
Saint−Kitts−et−Nevis	1999	0.3	4.3	4.6	109.5
	2000	0.1	4.1	4.2	105.0
Saint Lucia	1998	0.4	4.8	5.2	34.2
Sainte−Lucie	1999	9.9	14.1	24.0	164.4
	2000	7.1	4.4	11.5	77.7
Saint Vincent & Grenadines	1998	3.3	16.4	19.7	177.5
St. Vincent−et−Grenadines	1999	6.0	8.6	14.6	130.4
	2000	3.8	1.2	5.0	44.2
Suriname	1998	52.2	6.6	58.8	138.4
Suriname	1999	30.1	5.8	35.9	83.5
	2000	29.1	5.2	34.3	78.7
Trinidad and Tobago	1998	− 2.3	16.0	13.7	10.7
Trinité−et−Tobago	1999	0.2	26.1	26.3	20.4
	2000	4.3	− 5.9	− 1.6	− 1.2
Turks and Caicos Islands	1998	4.9	1.1	6.0	375.0
Iles Turques et Caiques	1999	5.4	2.0	7.4	462.5
	2000	5.6	1.1	6.7	394.1
Uruguay	1998	19.4	5.3	24.7	7.5
Uruguay	1999	19.0	2.7	21.7	6.5
	2000	15.3	1.4	16.7	5.0
Venezuela	1998	21.4	20.7	42.1	1.8
Venezuela	1999	34.1	9.8	43.9	1.9
	2000	61.3	14.6	75.9	3.1
Other and unallocated	1998	855.8	140.7	996.5	...
Autres et non−ventilés	1999	952.9	176.6	1 129.5	...
	2000	1 002.8	117.3	1 120.1	...
Asia	**1998**	**11 515.2**	**5 439.8**	**16 955.0**	**...**
Asie	**1999**	**13 578.7**	**4 741.2**	**18 319.9**	**...**
	2000	**11 623.9**	**4 620.6**	**16 244.5**	**...**
Afghanistan	1998	88.2	65.7	153.9	7.4
Afghanistan	1999	104.1	38.3	142.4	6.7
	2000	87.5	52.7	140.2	6.4

81
Disbursements of bilateral and multilateral official development assistance
and official aid to individual recipients [*cont.*]
Versements d'aide publique au développement et d'aide publique
bilatérales et multilatérales aux bénéficiares [*suite*]

Region, country or area Région, pays ou zone	Year Année	Net disbursements (US $) − Versements nets ($ E.−U.)			
		Bilateral Bilatérale (millions)	Multilateral[1] Multilatérale[1] (millions)	Total (millions)	Per capita[2] Par habitant[2]
Armenia	1998	66.9	75.6	142.5	37.5
Arménie	1999	75.3	133.2	208.5	54.9
	2000	139.3	75.6	214.9	56.5
Azerbaijan	1998	35.6	52.8	88.4	11.3
Azerbaïdjan	1999	52.4	109.3	161.7	20.4
	2000	70.7	60.5	131.2	16.4
Bahrain	1998	1.1	0.7	1.8	2.8
Bahreïn	1999	1.6	0.6	2.2	3.3
	2000	1.6	0.0	1.6	2.3
Bangladesh	1998	623.9	630.1	1 254.0	9.5
Bangladesh	1999	607.3	588.2	1 195.5	8.9
	2000	616.5	519.6	1 136.1	8.3
Bhutan	1998	41.0	16.0	57.0	28.9
Bhoutan	1999	53.0	14.7	67.7	33.4
	2000	33.7	20.0	53.7	25.8
Brunei Darussalam	1998	0.3	0.0	0.3	1.0
Brunéi Darussalam	1999	1.4	0.0	1.0	3.0
	2000	0.6	0.0	0.6	1.8
Cambodia	1998	230.6	106.5	337.1	29.5
Cambodge	1999	167.1	111.8	278.9	21.8
	2000	248.0	149.8	397.8	30.4
China	1998	1 731.7	707.8	2 439.5	1.9
Chine	1999	1 821.6	548.3	2 369.9	1.9
	2000	1 257.5	462.2	1 719.7	1.3
China, Hong Kong SAR	1998	6.7	0.1	6.8	1.0
Chine, Hong Kong RAS	1999	3.8	− 0.1	3.7	0.6
	2000	4.2	0.1	4.3	0.6
China, Macao SAR	1998	0.1	0.4	0.5	1.2
Chine, Macao RAS	1999	0.3	0.0	0.3	0.7
	2000	0.2	0.5	0.7	1.6
Georgia	1998	78.5	87.9	166.4	31.4
Géorgie	1999	77.7	161.2	238.9	44.2
	2000	120.3	43.2	163.5	31.1
India	1998	915.1	713.1	1 628.2	1.7
Inde	1999	838.3	664.6	1 502.9	1.5
	2000	650.3	848.5	1 498.8	1.5
Indonesia	1998	1 243.3	27.1	1 270.4	6.2
Indonésie	1999	2 169.4	40.2	2 209.6	10.7
	2000	1 617.2	109.5	1 726.7	8.2
Iran (Islamic Rep. of)	1998	142.4	22.2	164.6	2.7
Iran (Rép. islamique d')	1999	138.4	23.0	161.4	2.6
	2000	112.8	17.2	130.0	2.0
Iraq	1998	74.7	40.9	115.6	5.3
Iraq	1999	79.0	− 3.1	75.9	3.4
	2000	84.1	16.6	100.7	4.4
Israel	1998	1 055.0	10.6	1 065.6	178.5
Israël	1999	902.0	4.1	905.6	147.9
	2000	800.4	− 0.4	800.0	132.5
Jordan	1998	277.0	133.6	410.6	88.0
Jordanie	1999	325.3	105.8	431.1	90.1
	2000	385.3	168.0	553.3	112.6
Kazakhstan	1998	176.6	30.7	207.3	13.8
Kazakhstan	1999	133.6	27.1	160.7	10.8
	2000	159.3	14.8	174.1	11.7
Korea, Dem. People's Republic	1998	23.5	83.4	106.9	4.9
Corée, Rép. populaire dém. de	1999	165.1	35.6	200.7	9.1
	2000	26.9	48.3	75.2	3.4
Korea, Republic of	1998	− 49.1	− 1.3	− 50.4	− 1.1
Corée, République de	1999	− 53.8	− 1.4	− 55.2	− 1.2
	2000	− 196.6	− 1.5	− 198.1	− 4.2

81

**Disbursements of bilateral and multilateral official development assistance
and official aid to individual recipients [cont.]
Versements d'aide publique au développement et d'aide publique
bilatérales et multilatérales aux bénéficiares [suite]**

Region, country or area Région, pays ou zone	Year Année	Net disbursements (US $) – Versements nets ($ E.–U.)			
		Bilateral Bilatérale (millions)	Multilateral[1] Multilatérale[1] (millions)	Total (millions)	Per capita[2] Par habitant[2]
Kuwait	1998	4.9	1.0	5.9	3.3
Koweït	1999	5.6	1.7	7.3	3.9
	2000	2.0	0.9	2.9	1.5
Kyrgyzstan	1998	79.8	136.0	215.8	45.3
Kirghizistan	1999	115.6	151.1	266.7	55.2
	2000	91.3	111.9	203.2	41.5
Lao People's Dem. Rep.	1998	165.7	116.5	282.2	56.0
République dém. pop. lao	1999	210.5	84.5	295.0	57.2
	2000	194.3	86.1	280.4	53.7
Lebanon	1998	73.9	125.3	199.2	58.9
Liban	1999	80.3	67.6	147.9	43.0
	2000	90.5	91.3	181.8	52.0
Malaysia	1998	198.1	9.8	207.9	9.4
Malaisie	1999	140.1	6.8	146.9	6.5
	2000	43.3	3.3	46.6	2.0
Maldives	1998	16.6	9.1	25.7	96.3
Maldives	1999	25.5	6.5	32.0	115.1
	2000	13.3	7.2	20.5	75.6
Mongolia	1998	141.4	60.2	201.6	83.9
Mongolie	1999	138.2	79.4	217.6	92.2
	2000	150.8	60.6	211.4	88.5
Myanmar	1998	27.4	31.3	58.7	1.3
Myanmar	1999	44.7	28.6	73.3	1.6
	2000	68.1	37.8	105.9	2.2
Nepal	1998	212.7	189.4	402.1	18.4
Népal	1999	204.8	138.8	343.6	15.4
	2000	231.2	155.1	386.3	16.9
Occupied Palestinian Terr.	1998	336.4	245.2	581.6	561.4
Territoire palestinien occupé	1999	326.6	168.6	495.2	459.8
	2000	305.2	226.1	531.3	493.3
Oman	1998	19.8	2.7	22.5	9.8
Oman	1999	8.8	2.3	11.1	4.8
	2000	9.2	2.3	11.5	4.8
Pakistan	1998	534.8	522.0	1 056.8	8.0
Pakistan	1999	435.2	297.2	732.4	5.4
	2000	475.1	226.8	701.9	5.1
Philippines	1998	528.0	92.3	620.3	8.3
Philippines	1999	616.0	79.1	695.1	9.3
	2000	502.3	72.2	574.5	7.5
Qatar	1998	1.1	0.2	1.3	2.4
Qatar	1999	4.7	0.2	4.9	8.8
	2000	1.1	− 0.6	0.5	0.9
Saudi Arabia	1998	14.7	10.7	25.4	1.3
Arabie saoudite	1999	19.1	9.7	28.8	1.4
	2000	18.0	11.2	29.2	1.4
Singapore	1998	1.3	0.3	1.6	0.4
Singapour	1999	− 1.5	0.4	− 1.1	0.3
	2000	0.7	0.4	1.1	0.3
Sri Lanka	1998	282.3	210.3	492.6	26.2
Sri Lanka	1999	207.7	43.7	251.4	13.2
	2000	240.2	25.2	265.4	13.7
Syrian Arab Republic	1998	83.3	43.8	127.1	8.1
Rép. arabe syrienne	1999	172.3	34.6	206.9	12.8
	2000	97.3	38.6	135.9	8.3
Tajikistan	1998	40.0	65.1	105.1	17.2
Tadjikistan	1999	35.1	87.0	122.1	19.6
	2000	38.1	103.5	141.6	22.9
Thailand	1998	675.7	27.7	703.4	11.5
Thaïlande	1999	994.8	16.4	1 011.2	16.4
	2000	625.2	17.7	642.9	10.3
Timor−Leste	1998	1.7	0.0	1.7	2.2
Timor−Leste	1999	147.2	5.6	152.8	205.4
	2000	212.3	20.6	232.9	316.0
Turkmenistan	1998	8.2	8.4	16.6	3.4
Turkménistan	1999	11.5	9.0	20.5	4.4
	2000	9.8	5.7	15.5	3.3

81
Disbursements of bilateral and multilateral official development assistance
and official aid to individual recipients [cont.]
Versements d'aide publique au développement et d'aide publique
bilatérales et multilatérales aux bénéficiares [suite]

Region, country or area Région, pays ou zone	Year Année	Net disbursements (US $) — Versements nets ($ E.—U.)			
		Bilateral Bilatérale (millions)	Multilateral[1] Multilatérale[1] (millions)	Total (millions)	Per capita[2] Par habitant[2]
United Arab Emirates	1998	3.5	0.5	4.0	1.5
Emirats arabes unis	1999	2.9	1.2	4.1	1.4
	2000	2.7	1.3	4.0	1.5
Uzbekistan	1998	123.6	19.6	143.2	6.0
Ouzbékistan	1999	112.8	20.9	133.7	5.6
	2000	133.8	17.0	150.8	6.1
Viet Nam	1998	712.6	451.9	1 164.5	15.3
Viet Nam	1999	1 017.7	407.1	1 424.8	18.5
	2000	1 247.6	435.9	1 683.5	21.7
Yemen	1998	166.8	143.4	310.2	36.4
Yémen	1999	177.3	278.9	456.2	51.5
	2000	159.6	104.1	263.7	28.7
Other and unallocated	1998	220.6	113.2	333.8	...
Autres et non−ventilés	1999	650.0	113.0	763.0	...
	2000	431.4	153.1	584.5	...
Europe	**1998**	**4 499.0**	**3 277.7**	**7 776.7**	...
Europe	**1999**	**6 395.4**	**4 029.6**	**10 425.0**	...
	2000	**5 335.7**	**4 458.3**	**9 794.0**	...
Albania	1998	93.8	162.9	256.7	67.7
Albanie	1999	254.1	224.9	479.0	153.0
	2000	141.4	176.6	318.0	101.5
Belarus	1998	20.9	7.6	28.5	2.8
Bélarus	1999	15.5	9.6	25.1	2.5
	2000	14.9	8.6	23.5	2.4
Bosnia and Herzegovina	1998	599.1	284.5	883.6	241.9
Bosnie − Herzégovine	1999	734.5	325.2	1 059.7	275.5
	2000	452.2	266.5	718.7	180.7
Bulgaria	1998	137.7	98.6	236.3	28.6
Bulgarie	1999	137.1	131.0	268.1	32.7
	2000	207.0	101.8	308.8	38.9
Croatia	1998	26.3	12.9	39.2	8.7
Croatie	1999	27.8	20.3	48.1	10.6
	2000	42.5	22.8	65.3	14.9
Cyprus	1998	13.0	18.7	31.7	42.3
Chypre	1999	4.9	50.3	55.2	73.3
	2000	11.9	45.8	57.7	76.2
Czech Republic	1998	48.9	399.1	448.0	43.5
République tchèque	1999	29.8	293.7	323.5	31.5
	2000	25.3	411.9	437.2	42.6
Estonia	1998	35.9	54.1	90.0	62.1
Estonie	1999	28.6	54.1	82.7	57.4
	2000	23.7	39.4	63.1	46.1
Gibraltar	1998	0.2	0.0	0.2	7.4
Gibraltar	1999	0.0	0.0	0.0	0.0
	2000	0.0	0.0	0.0	0.0
Hungary	1998	111.1	130.6	241.7	23.9
Hongrie	1999	29.2	219.0	248.2	24.7
	2000	53.5	197.1	250.6	25.0
Latvia	1998	47.0	49.9	96.9	39.6
Lettonie	1999	44.1	52.9	97.0	39.9
	2000	34.3	53.7	88.0	36.2
Lithuania	1998	66.7	57.7	124.4	33.6
Lituanie	1999	61.3	68.8	130.1	35.2
	2000	46.1	48.0	94.1	25.5
Malta	1998	23.8	1.6	25.4	67.4
Malte	1999	23.8	3.2	27.0	71.2
	2000	21.2	0.9	22.1	56.5
Poland	1998	471.4	431.6	903.0	23.4
Pologne	1999	580.1	605.3	1 185.4	30.7
	2000	552.5	843.0	1 395.5	36.1
Republic of Moldova	1998	21.7	12.6	34.3	9.4
République de Moldova	1999	51.2	51.0	102.2	28.0
	2000	61.5	51.2	112.7	31.0

81
Disbursements of bilateral and multilateral official development assistance
and official aid to individual recipients [cont.]
Versements d'aide publique au développement et d'aide publique
bilatérales et multilatérales aux bénéficiares [suite]

Region, country or area Région, pays ou zone	Year Année	Net disbursements (US $) — Versements nets ($ E.−U.)			
		Bilateral Bilatérale (millions)	Multilateral[1] Multilatérale[1] (millions)	Total (millions)	Per capita[2] Par habitant[2]
Romania Roumanie	1998	176.1	181.8	357.9	15.9
	1999	122.5	251.3	373.8	16.6
	2000	157.7	271.5	429.2	19.1
Russian Federation Fédération de Russie	1998	871.4	148.9	1 020.3	7.0
	1999	1 599.9	224.9	1 824.8	12.5
	2000	1 344.2	121.4	1 465.6	10.1
Serbia and Montenegro Serbie−et−Monténégro	1998	94.6	12.6	107.2	10.1
	1999	635.1	3.1	638.2	60.0
	2000	592.9	541.3	1 134.2	106.6
Slovakia Slovaquie	1998	39.0	115.9	154.9	28.7
	1999	35.0	283.6	318.6	59.1
	2000	25.3	87.2	112.5	20.8
Slovenia Slovenie	1998	5.6	36.3	41.9	21.1
	1999	1.3	29.7	31.0	15.6
	2000	0.6	60.2	60.8	30.6
TFYR of Macedonia l'ex−République y. Macédoine	1998	32.1	60.2	92.3	46.0
	1999	136.5	134.3	270.8	134.3
	2000	110.9	139.5	250.4	123.1
Turkey Turquie	1998	− 80.5	96.0	15.5	0.2
	1999	− 66.4	27.3	− 39.1	− 0.6
	2000	97.5	190.7	288.2	4.4
Ukraine Ukraine	1998	273.6	109.1	382.7	7.7
	1999	401.7	78.3	480.0	9.6
	2000	352.1	79.4	431.5	8.7
Yugoslavia SFR[3] Yougoslavie, Rfs[3]	1998	53.3	52.9	106.2	...
	1999	161.6	272.6	434.2	...
	2000	223.4	81.3	304.7	...
Other and unallocated Autres et non−ventilés	1998	1 316.2	741.6	2 057.8	...
	1999	1 346.2	615.1	1 961.3	...
	2000	743.0	618.5	1 361.5	...
Oceania **Océanie**	**1998**	**1 525.8**	**124.4**	**1 650.2**	...
	1999	**1 371.8**	**51.5**	**1 423.3**	...
	2000	**1 459.1**	**106.9**	**1 566.0**	...
Cook Islands Iles Cook	1998	5.9	2.1	8.0	470.6
	1999	4.5	1.4	5.9	368.8
	2000	3.4	0.9	4.3	238.9
Fiji Fidji	1998	35.8	0.6	36.4	45.7
	1999	38.0	− 3.6	34.4	42.7
	2000	28.7	0.2	28.9	35.5
French Polynesia Polynésie française	1998	368.7	1.7	370.4	1 653.6
	1999	353.2	− 1.7	351.5	1 541.7
	2000	400.1	2.4	402.5	1 727.5
Kiribati Kiribati	1998	16.2	1.1	17.3	213.6
	1999	19.6	1.3	20.9	254.9
	2000	14.8	3.1	17.9	215.7
Marshall Islands Iles Marshall	1998	42.1	8.2	50.3	838.3
	1999	58.7	4.2	62.9	1 014.5
	2000	47.1	10.1	57.2	922.6
Micronesia (Fed. States of) Micronésie (Etats fédérés de)	1998	73.8	6.3	80.1	702.6
	1999	102.3	5.6	107.9	930.2
	2000	96.6	5.0	101.6	875.9
Nauru Nauru	1998	2.0	0.1	2.1	175.0
	1999	6.5	0.1	6.6	550.0
	2000	3.9	0.1	4.0	333.3
New Caledonia Nouvelle−Calédonie	1998	336.3	2.1	338.4	1 658.8
	1999	314.9	− 0.4	314.5	1 526.7
	2000	348.7	1.4	350.1	1 659.2
Niue Nioué	1998	3.9	0.2	4.1	2 050.0
	1999	3.9	0.2	4.1	2 050.0
	2000	3.0	0.2	3.2	1 600.0
Northern Mariana Islands Iles Mariannes du Nord	1998	0.0	0.2	0.2	2.9
	1999	0.0	0.1	0.1	1.4
	2000	0.0	0.2	0.2	2.7

81
Disbursements of bilateral and multilateral official development assistance
and official aid to individual recipients [cont.]
Versements d'aide publique au développement et d'aide publique
bilatérales et multilatérales aux bénéficiares [suite]

Region, country or area Région, pays ou zone	Year Année	Net disbursements (US $) – Versements nets ($ E.–U.)			
		Bilateral Bilatérale (millions)	Multilateral[1] Multilatérale[1] (millions)	Total (millions)	Per capita[2] Par habitant[2]
Palau	1998	89.0	0.1	89.1	4 689.5
Palaos	1999	28.7	0.1	28.8	1 515.8
	2000	38.9	0.1	39.0	2 052.6
Papua New Guinea	1998	311.9	49.6	361.5	78.6
Papouasie–Nvl–Guinée	1999	212.3	3.9	216.2	46.0
	2000	268.6	5.2	273.8	56.9
Samoa	1998	29.7	6.5	36.2	215.5
Samoa	1999	22.4	0.5	22.9	135.5
	2000	18.1	9.2	27.3	159.6
Solomon Islands	1998	23.6	19.2	42.8	102.4
Iles Salomon	1999	20.5	16.5	37.0	85.6
	2000	20.8	46.3	67.1	150.1
Tokelau	1998	3.5	0.1	3.6	3 600.0
Tokélaou	1999	4.6	0.1	4.7	4 700.0
	2000	3.4	0.1	3.5	3 500.0
Tonga	1998	16.3	8.4	24.7	252.0
Tonga	1999	15.2	5.9	21.1	213.1
	2000	14.8	4.0	18.8	189.9
Tuvalu	1998	4.9	0.3	5.2	472.7
Tuvalu	1999	3.5	3.2	6.7	609.1
	2000	3.8	0.2	4.0	363.6
Vanuatu	1998	26.1	14.6	40.7	217.6
Vanuatu	1999	28.9	8.3	37.2	193.8
	2000	28.3	17.5	45.8	232.5
Wallis and Futuna Islands	1998	46.5	0.8	47.3	3 378.6
Iles Wallis et Futuna	1999	50.1	0.3	50.4	3 600.0
	2000	52.1	0.0	52.1	3 721.4
Other and unallocated	1998	89.7	2.2	91.9	...
Autres et non–ventilés	1999	83.8	5.5	89.3	...
	2000	64.0	0.7	64.7	...
Unspecified	**1998**	**6 949.9**	**987.0**	**7 936.9**	...
Non–specifiés	**1999**	**6 837.7**	**1 151.9**	**7 989.6**	...
	2000	**8 116.6**	**1 106.2**	**9 222.8**	...

Source:
Organisation for Economic Co–operation and Development (OECD),
Paris, "Geographical Distribution of Financial Flows to Aid Recipients,
1996 – 2000" and the OECD Development Assistance Database. Per
capita calculated by the UN Statistics Division.

1   As reported by OECD/DAC, covers agencies of the United Nations
    family, the European Union, IDA and the concessional lending
    facilities of regional development banks. Excludes non – concessional
    flows (i.e., less than 25% grant elements).

2   Population based on estimates of mid–year population.

3   Data refer to Yugoslavia, SFR unspecified.

Source:
Organisation de coopération et de développement économiques
(OCDE), Paris, "Répartition géographique des ressources financières
allouées aux pays bénéficiaires de l'aide, 1996 – 2000" et la base de
données de l'OCDE sur l'aide au développement. Les données par
habitant ont été calculées par la Division de statistique de l'ONU.

1   Communiqué par le Comité d'aide au développement de l'OCDE.
    Comprend les institutions et organismes du système des Nations
    Unies, l'Union européene, l'Association internationale de
    développement, et les mécanismes de prêt à des conditions
    privilégiées des banques régionales de développement. Les apports
    aux conditions du marché (élément de libéralité inférieur à 25%)
    en sont exclus.

2   Population d'après des estimations de la population au milieu
    de l'année.

3   Les données concernent Yougoslavie, Rfs non spécifié.

82
Net official development assistance from DAC countries to developing countries and multilateral organizations
Net disbursements: millions of US dollars and as a percentage of gross national income (GNI)
Aide publique au développement nette de pays du CAD aux pays en développement et aux organisations multilatérales
Versements nets: millions de dollars E.-U. et en pourcentage du revenu national brut (RNB)

Country or area Pays ou zone	1995 US $ $ E.-U. (millions)	As % of GNI En % du RNB	1996 US $ $ E.-U. (millions)	As % of GNI En % du RNB	1997 US $ $ E.-U. (millions)	As % of GNI En % du RNB	1998 US $ $ E.-U. (millions)	As % of GNI En % du RNB	1999 US $ $ E.-U. (millions)	As % of GNI En % du RNB	2000 US $ $ E.-U. (millions)	As % of GNI En % du RNB
Total	**58 926**	**0.27**	**55 622**	**0.25**	**48 497**	**0.22**	**52 084**	**0.23**	**56 428**	**0.24**	**53 737**	**0.22**
Australia Australie	1 194	0.36	1 074	0.28	1 061	0.28	960	0.27	982	0.26	987	0.27
Austria Autriche	767	0.33	557	0.24	527	0.26	456	0.22	527	0.26	423	0.23
Belgium Belgique	1 034	0.38	913	0.34	764	0.31	883	0.35	760	0.30	820	0.36
Canada Canada	2 067	0.38	1 795	0.32	2 045	0.34	1 707	0.30	1 706	0.28	1 744	0.25
Denmark Danemark	1 623	0.96	1 772	1.04	1 637	0.97	1 704	0.99	1 733	1.01	1 664	1.06
Finland Finlande	388	0.32	408	0.34	379	0.33	396	0.32	416	0.33	371	0.31
France France	8 443	0.55	7 451	0.48	6 307	0.45	5 742	0.40	5 639	0.39	4 105	0.32
Germany Allemagne	7 524	0.31	7 601	0.32	5 857	0.28	5 581	0.26	5 515	0.26	5 030	0.27
Greece Grèce	...	...	184	0.15	173	0.14	179	0.15	194	0.15	226	0.20
Ireland Irlande	153	0.29	179	0.31	187	0.31	199	0.30	245	0.31	235	0.30
Italy Italie	1 623	0.15	2 416	0.20	1 266	0.11	2 278	0.20	1 806	0.15	1 376	0.13
Japan Japon	14 489	0.28	9 439	0.20	9 358	0.22	10 640	0.28	15 323	0.34	13 508	0.28
Luxembourg Luxembourg	65	0.36	82	0.44	95	0.55	112	0.65	119	0.66	127	0.71
Netherlands Pays-Bas	3 226	0.81	3 246	0.81	2 947	0.81	3 042	0.80	3 134	0.79	3 135	0.84
New Zealand Nouvelle-Zélande	123	0.23	122	0.21	154	0.26	130	0.27	134	0.27	113	0.25
Norway Norvège	1 244	0.87	1 311	0.85	1 306	0.86	1 321	0.91	1 370	0.90	1 264	0.80
Portugal Portugal	258	0.25	218	0.21	250	0.25	259	0.24	276	0.26	271	0.26
Spain Espagne	1 348	0.24	1 251	0.22	1 234	0.24	1 376	0.24	1 363	0.23	1 195	0.22
Sweden Suède	1 704	0.77	1 999	0.84	1 731	0.79	1 573	0.72	1 630	0.70	1 799	0.80
Switzerland Suisse	1 084	0.34	1 026	0.34	911	0.34	898	0.32	984	0.35	890	0.34
United Kingdom Royaume-Uni	3 202	0.29	3 199	0.27	3 433	0.26	3 864	0.27	3 426	0.24	4 501	0.32
United States Etats-Unis	7 367	0.10	9 377	0.12	6 878	0.09	8 786	0.10	9 145	0.10	9 955	0.10

Source:
Organisation for Economic Co-operation and Development (OECD), Paris, "Development Co-operation, 2001 Report" and previous issues.

Source:
Organisation de Coopération et de Développement Economiques (OCDE), Paris, "Coopération pour le développement, Rapport 2001" et éditions précédentes.

83
Socio-economic development assistance through the United Nations system
Thousand US dollars
Assistance en matière de développement socioéconomique fournie par le système des Nations Unies
Milliers de dollars E.−U.

Development grant expenditures [1] • Aide au développement [1]

Country or area Pays ou zone	Year Année	UNDP PNUD Central resources Ressources centrales	Special funds Fonds gérés	UNFPA FNUAP	UNICEF	WFP PAM	Other UN system Autres organis. −ONU Regular budget Budget ordinaire	Extra−budgetary Extra−budgétaire	Total	Gov't self−supporting Auto−assistance gouverne−mentale
Total	**2000**	**1457911**	**459788**	**134132**	**884984**	**1491035**	**469575**	**1553320**	**6450745**	**589022**
Total	**2001**	**1526176**	**500432**	**313625**	**1011923**	**1744073**	**423991**	**1612681**	**7132902**	**570871**
Regional programmes	**2000**	**99186**	**73780**	**17653**	**35947**	**0**	**195373**	**865210**	**1287149**	**287868**
Totaux régionaux	**2001**	**79966**	**95201**	**124522**	**46059**	**59475**	**187601**	**894020**	**1486843**	**232468**
Africa	2000	22346	12191	2897	5233	0	41093	203534	287394	164559
Afrique	2001	24147	13233	2787	7745	12653	32275	165917	258758	134735
Asia and the Pacific	2000	15094	8214	1085	2909	0	33268	57134	117704	17911
Asie et le Pacifique	2001	12692	13615	8900	4211	41376	26560	47978	155332	20291
Europe	2000	2680	4939	566	586	0	22454	23752	54977	15966
Europe	2001	3142	6853	810	1915	4929	21612	22166	61427	12866
Latin America	2000	4176	6204	1159	1353	0	30844	23233	66970	2559
Amérique latine	2001	10291	7509	1503	1665	517	21108	24580	67173	4942
Western Asia	2000	3281	2647	666	852	0	25177	302403	335026	8513
Asie occidentale	2001	4318	3401	694	1421	0	21655	365808	397297	8770
Interregional	2000	11928	10426	11281	0	0	11235	102318	147188	346
Interrégional	2001	15954	34982	0	29102	0	8979	145290	234307	50730
Global	2000	39681	29159	0	25014	0	31301	152835	277991	78014
Global	2001	9422	15608	109828	0	0	55411	122280	312550	133
Country programmes	**2000**	**1351401**	**353539**	**113615**	**783001**	**1457918**	**268069**	**666593**	**4994136**	**283500**
Programmes, pays	**2001**	**1414879**	**365092**	**183451**	**890646**	**1587026**	**221354**	**692272**	**5354720**	**329055**
Afghanistan	2000	8475	2631	755	13544	62491	3361	5468	96725	4912
Afghanistan	2001	7746	1364	771	29870	119050	3600	6255	168656	3600
Albania	2000	4260	761	220	5759	1	445	2309	13755	1556
Albanie	2001	3196	730	449	5866	1663	416	1353	13673	508
Algeria	2000	912	280	425	878	4312	2167	984	9959	144
Algérie	2001	1193	68	1168	1252	6738	1318	973	12709	96
Andorra	2000	0	0	0	0	0	87	0	87	0
Andorre	2001	0	0	0	0	0	92	0	92	0
Angola	2000	2763	3543	1313	13762	108493	1979	6766	138619	4457
Angola	2001	2519	793	1726	15884	94033	1451	8100	124506	5871
Anguilla	2000	10	7	0	0	0	0	7	24	0
Anguilla	2001	14	0	0	0	0	0	0	14	0
Antigua and Barbuda	2000	76	242	0	0	0	172	0	490	0
Antigua−et−Barbuda	2001	49	66	0	0	0	419	0	534	0
Argentina	2000	179021	1919	0	2815	0	2126	26615	212496	23516
Argentine	2001	135634	1289	6	3367	0	1927	8798	151022	5450
Aruba	2000	179	0	0	0	0	88	0	267	0
Aruba	2001	175	0	0	0	0	90	0	265	0
Azerbaijan	2000	3983	500	620	1680	3515	370	448	11116	287
Azerbaïdjan	2001	3610	468	778	1548	5653	388	152	12597	165
Bahamas	2000	0	76	0	0	0	329	41	446	41
Bahamas	2001	−15	−20	0	0	0	430	56	451	56
Bahrain	2000	1029	288	1	0	0	127	79	1523	22
Bahreïn	2001	1190	46	9	0	0	390	61	1695	55
Bangladesh	2000	19601	335	3680	34771	23135	5483	5332	92336	3569
Bangladesh	2001	13738	500	13718	31155	45922	6619	10408	122060	5198
Barbados	2000	14	14	0	0	0	354	11	393	11
Barbade	2001	4	341	0	0	0	690	1	1036	1
Belize	2000	33	1156	22	629	45	571	10	2466	0
Belize	2001	4	2247	0	996	204	643	23	4116	3
Benin	2000	3327	1200	715	2769	1978	1873	752	12615	147
Bénin	2001	1262	577	1867	3613	1287	1044	1888	11538	1549
Bermuda	2000	0	0	0	0	0	0	0	0	0
Bermudes	2001	0	0	0	0	0	0	0	0	0
Bhutan	2000	3407	1542	1431	2077	1623	1775	392	12247	173
Bhoutan	2001	1987	1459	626	2203	1990	949	109	9322	44

83

Socio−economic development assistance through the United Nations system
Thousand US dollars [*cont.*]

Assistance en matière de développement socioéconomique fournie par le système des Nations Unies
Milliers de dollars E.−U. [*suite*]

Development grant expenditures [1] • Aide au développement [1]

Country or area Pays ou zone	Year Année	UNDP PNUD Central resources Ressources centrales	Special funds Fonds gérés	UNFPA FNUAP	UNICEF	WFP PAM	Other UN system Autres organis. −ONU Regular budget Budget ordinaire	Extra− budgetary Extra− budgétaire	Total	Gov't self− supporting Auto− assistance gouverne− mentale
Bolivia	2000	9366	2111	1108	7748	6255	1674	5159	33421	2591
Bolivie	2001	23929	1711	2722	7532	6001	2315	5330	49539	1269
Botswana	2000	3555	485	350	1066	0	1745	238	7439	90
Botswana	2001	3864	443	1006	1341	0	487	380	7521	303
Brazil	2000	186244	8132	847	8048	0	3131	96169	302573	90154
Brésil	2001	209477	10329	1222	7401	4714	3816	125743	362703	120119
British Virgin Islands	2000	−7	0	0	0	0	98	0	91	0
Iles Vierges britanniques	2001	0	0	0	0	0	113	0	113	0
Brunei Darussalam	2000	0	0	0	0	0	14	0	14	0
Brunéi Darussalam	2001	0	0	0	0	0	55	0	55	0
Bulgaria	2000	14178	373	74	0	0	743	365	15734	19
Bulgarie	2001	18235	452	133	0	0	794	328	19943	26
Burkina Faso	2000	4226	1357	1129	5975	1000	2624	1981	18292	1087
Burkina Faso	2001	4434	1108	1415	7996	1805	1575	3289	21621	2653
Burundi	2000	6400	1413	674	6598	4186	2897	2618	24786	69
Burundi	2001	5795	5551	784	11262	24222	518	313	48444	222
Cambodia	2000	4598	16053	3231	12380	23679	2628	8329	70898	2543
Cambodge	2001	6973	13231	3054	13206	25206	2134	8738	72541	2036
Cameroon	2000	1098	−22	1510	2591	406	1826	1402	8811	614
Cameroun	2001	2438	150	1336	4357	1086	1668	1283	12318	906
Cape Verde	2000	583	760	329	767	893	1782	1484	6598	173
Cap−Vert	2001	338	997	846	868	649	1107	698	5503	35
Cayman Islands	2000	73	0	0	0	0	0	0	73	0
Iles Caïmanes	2001	0	0	0	0	0	0	0	0	0
Central African Rep.	2000	1961	1717	740	1716	1635	1951	202	9921	112
Rép. centrafricaine	2001	1315	1308	746	2714	710	1113	605	8510	587
Chad	2000	5236	878	1029	4016	3896	2215	753	18022	587
Tchad	2001	3478	34	933	4107	10339	1800	2063	22755	1990
Chile	2000	18598	726	62	1002	0	1438	1374	23200	389
Chili	2001	20083	756	61	891	0	1362	1050	24203	232
China	2000	22875	17641	3497	23796	13938	5461	16776	103985	4323
Chine	2001	28728	22415	3630	16242	12495	7042	21588	112140	2477
China, Hong Kong SAR	2000	0	0	0	0	0	106	0	106	0
Chine, Hong Kong RAS	2001	32	0	0	0	0	10	0	42	0
China, Macao SAR	2000	0	0	0	0	0	10	0	10	0
Chine, Macao RAS	2001	0	0	0	0	0	41	9	50	9
Colombia	2000	83981	1248	340	3223	4146	2647	1507	97091	397
Colombie	2001	130466	844	703	3863	0	1668	1316	138859	386
Comoros	2000	557	328	86	659	7	1469	41	3148	40
Comores	2001	1101	1311	490	740	0	631	125	4398	93
Congo	2000	1001	178	235	3199	5361	2510	922	13407	95
Congo	2001	3879	1158	271	3110	2608	960	1976	13963	1015
Cook Islands	2000	140	47	55	0	0	360	0	602	0
Iles Cook	2001	83	90	50	0	0	332	0	555	0
Costa Rica	2000	3495	1537	160	692	0	1501	1217	8602	416
Costa Rica	2001	4172	1818	237	1070	0	1017	1834	10148	446
Côte d'Ivoire	2000	1502	4035	1071	3203	1485	1704	1848	14848	1076
Côte d'Ivoire	2001	2820	845	991	4605	3988	1191	3252	17692	988
Cuba	2000	1110	1752	269	1439	2868	1622	1194	10255	17
Cuba	2001	2207	3541	567	1804	2961	1708	993	13781	94
Cyprus	2000	6610	0	0	0	0	169	90	6869	76
Chypre	2001	12019	41	0	0	0	338	121	12520	10
Czech Republic	2000	346	304	0	0	0	476	108	1234	113
République tchèque	2001	138	294	0	0	0	306	201	939	174
Dem. Rep. of the Congo	2000	3242	173	646	29143	22685	3171	8648	67708	6413
Rép. dém. du Congo	2001	5242	242	1740	35844	31571	2320	23303	100262	19490
Djibouti	2000	764	75	277	940	5979	1221	33	9289	8
Djibouti	2001	568	201	539	893	7685	839	43	10768	2

83
Socio — economic development assistance through the United Nations system
Thousand US dollars [*cont.*]
Assistance en matière de développement socioéconomique fournie par le système des Nations Unies
Milliers de dollars E. — U. [*suite*]

Development grant expenditures [1] • Aide au développement [1]

Country or area Pays ou zone	Year Année	UNDP PNUD Central resources Ressources centrales	Special funds Fonds gérés	UNFPA FNUAP	UNICEF	WFP PAM	Other UN system Autres organis. — ONU Regular budget Budget ordinaire	Extra — budgetary Extra — budgétaire	Total	Gov't self — supporting Auto — assistance gouverne — mentale
Dominica	2000	81	68	0	0	0	277	99	525	37
Dominique	2001	48	197	0	0	0	380	42	667	42
Dominican Republic	2000	10581	774	580	1610	1108	1549	6562	22764	6325
Rép. dominicaine	2001	8309	765	979	4886	2924	1078	1213	20154	797
Ecuador	2000	16001	1301	622	3604	2628	2052	2812	29020	324
Equateur	2001	30235	1004	953	3011	2275	1073	2215	40767	314
Egypt	2000	16148	2729	1899	6585	9131	2083	2148	40723	727
Egypte	2001	19374	3679	3169	6963	1548	3371	2973	41078	1031
El Salvador	2000	17077	2976	561	2762	874	1334	1181	26765	28
El Salvador	2001	17106	3796	952	4992	8233	1375	1639	38093	174
Equatorial Guinea	2000	924	62	508	979	0	1363	48	3884	9
Guinée équatoriale	2001	1138	−85	522	646	0	454	12	2686	12
Eritrea	2000	2455	1861	637	10357	41434	2317	1478	60538	163
Erythrée	2001	6374	6775	2705	10841	46046	550	1894	75184	325
Ethiopia	2000	20326	2226	2956	33108	236953	4443	9912	309923	6830
Ethiopia	2001	18833	2173	3328	42614	168377	2271	18342	255938	12067
Fiji	2000	274	108	109	0	0	1653	231	2375	1
Fidji	2001	629	125	115	0	0	900	52	1821	33
French Guiana	2000	0	0	0	0	0	19	0	19	0
Guyane française	2001	0	0	0	0	0	106	0	106	0
French Polynesia	2000	0	0	0	0	0	0	0	0	0
Polynésie française	2001	0	0	0	0	0	27	0	27	0
Gabon	2000	804	245	161	721	588	1434	182	4136	104
Gabon	2001	448	216	181	1370	259	588	753	3816	237
Gambia	2000	1702	1265	371	1232	1562	2054	856	9042	103
Gambie	2001	2311	571	409	1739	1967	1119	789	8905	95
Ghana	2000	5388	855	1800	6699	1549	2573	2234	21098	736
Ghana	2001	4293	2416	2795	8936	1109	1509	4348	25406	2687
Greece	2000	0	0	0	0	0	221	142	363	142
Grèce	2001	0	0	0	0	0	133	619	753	619
Grenada	2000	62	124	0	0	0	164	44	394	13
Grenade	2001	60	93	0	0	0	204	0	357	0
Guam	2000	0	0	0	0	0	5	0	5	0
Guam	2001	0	0	0	0	0	110	873	983	0
Guatemala	2000	29847	5182	267	3757	3076	1160	3822	47112	176
Guatemala	2001	36897	3106	612	5234	2265	637	3837	52588	130
Guinea	2000	1680	763	565	4104	996	2200	280	10588	144
Guinée	2001	1492	837	799	7278	8995	1433	949	21783	734
Guinea — Bissau	2000	1147	−264	195	2300	1181	1697	1184	7440	131
Guinée — Bissau	2001	1174	1330	501	1444	1251	1468	1806	8974	204
Guyana	2000	1866	410	282	956	46	727	82	4369	13
Guyana	2001	1906	874	66	859	0	563	2	4270	0
Haiti	2000	4434	1597	1198	4519	6068	620	1494	19932	90
Haïti	2001	3016	2476	2872	3806	5165	1322	1677	20333	57
Honduras	2000	36671	7832	759	2385	978	781	5248	54654	997
Honduras	2001	38530	8897	1345	2300	7296	454	3555	62376	575
Hungary	2000	131	0	0	0	0	379	250	760	0
Hongrie	2001	389	19	0	0	0	548	137	1093	0
India	2000	22028	9206	8974	85507	29968	9024	27468	192174	22548
Inde	2001	20568	17002	11090	103221	21546	7744	27011	208181	22468
Indonesia	2000	4658	6799	2505	19346	57899	6633	5716	103556	3389
Indonésie	2001	9542	8641	6777	10284	15830	6412	6189	63676	3792
Iran (Islamic Rep. of)	2000	1536	2141	1135	2309	1043	2222	1989	12376	184
Iran (Rép. islamique d')	2001	1502	6304	2132	4440	3373	3186	6577	27513	2749
Iraq	2000	926	87837	326	6886	20078	1565	200144	317763	1274
Iraq	2001	1121	95368	255	7499	26587	1881	158964	291674	1278
Jamaica	2000	921	192	197	1052	0	2003	72	4437	0
Jamaïque	2001	297	202	−11	1235	0	1338	37	3099	0

83
Socio—economic development assistance through the United Nations system
Thousand US dollars [cont.]
Assistance en matière de développement socioéconomique fournie par le système des Nations Unies
Milliers de dollars E.—U. [suite]

Development grant expenditures [1] • Aide au développement [1]

Country or area Pays ou zone	Year Année	UNDP PNUD Central resources Ressources centrales	Special funds Fonds gérés	UNFPA FNUAP	UNICEF	WFP PAM	Other UN system Autres organis. —ONU Regular budget Budget ordinaire	Extra— budgetary Extra— budgétaire	Total	Gov't self— supporting Auto— assistance gouverne— mentale
Jordan	2000	1604	2217	438	1158	3728	1103	1478	11725	4
Jordanie	2001	2984	937	846	1454	1579	1783	2214	11796	45
Kazakhstan	2000	1735	656	785	761	0	784	747	5469	366
Kazakhstan	2001	1639	4190	676	14309	0	821	723	22358	322
Kenya	2000	5337	1542	1855	8407	115714	2260	3071	138187	2200
Kenya	2001	7219	1652	2108	12254	122255	1490	3233	150212	1907
Kiribati	2000	402	121	72	0	0	565	−1	1160	0
Kiribati	2001	18	129	11	0	0	285	0	443	0
Korea, Dem. P. R.	2000	1783	310	354	4126	123069	2233	5329	137205	1886
Corée, Rep. dém. de	2001	1051	464	722	6663	230859	2600	4200	246558	2242
Korea, Republic of	2000	864	0	0	0	0	1621	169	2654	125
Corée, République de	2001	370	27	0	0	0	781	187	1365	187
Kuwait	2000	2328	0	0	95	0	205	47	2675	47
Koweït	2001	2998	0	0	0	0	181	45	3223	45
Kyrgyzstan	2000	2111	827	434	907	0	308	283	4870	85
Kirghizistan	2001	1429	1105	455	2453	0	362	577	6380	490
Lao People's Dem. Rep.	2000	6436	10905	1432	4866	1369	1741	1403	28151	183
Rép. dém. pop. lao	2001	3930	1815	1869	4571	2623	1651	1361	17820	648
Lebanon	2000	5501	1525	261	1905	0	1991	2056	13239	424
Liban	2001	6531	1046	1071	1355	0	1191	1561	12755	355
Lesotho	2000	1194	300	183	849	1192	1334	439	5491	27
Lesotho	2001	748	435	245	1219	872	811	39	4370	7
Liberia	2000	4325	105	740	4529	37711	2390	376	50175	376
Libéria	2001	3233	12	823	5303	12721	1341	926	24359	814
Libyan Arab Jamahiriya	2000	2493	16	0	0	0	895	1709	5113	1666
Jamah. arabe libyenne	2001	3219	326	0	0	0	1102	3318	7966	3111
Madagascar	2000	6053	2066	1395	10187	6251	2468	2010	30431	518
Madagascar	2001	6519	3358	1769	6290	5058	1749	2915	27658	298
Malawi	2000	3493	1734	1130	6474	2543	1959	663	17997	117
Malawi	2001	3943	3753	2482	11207	7050	1727	570	30732	309
Malaysia	2000	374	2592	154	435	0	1270	352	5177	0
Malaisie	2001	1098	3327	143	678	0	1187	202	6636	59
Maldives	2000	1048	214	576	599	0	1671	133	4241	120
Maldives	2001	1046	575	733	654	0	828	177	4013	177
Mali	2000	2323	5271	810	8001	3295	2408	1884	23992	512
Mali	2001	5016	3326	2074	9305	4135	1397	3359	28611	2176
Malta	2000	53	0	0	0	0	111	21	185	1
Malte	2001	0	10	0	0	0	213	26	249	15
Marshall Islands	2000	95	30	105	0	0	144	212	585	0
Iles Marshall	2001	93	0	50	0	0	201	−7	338	0
Mauritania	2000	2042	3513	722	3041	2260	2482	1166	15226	508
Mauritanie	2001	1682	1993	1292	2437	3472	911	786	12572	225
Mauritius	2000	531	98	88	631	0	862	163	2372	87
Maurice	2001	202	246	193	561	0	659	493	2354	351
Mexico	2000	8251	3095	1190	1768	0	2425	2201	18931	1415
Mexique	2001	3189	2373	1560	2513	0	2520	2353	14508	1607
Micronesia (Fed. States of)	2000	257	100	58	0	0	268	83	766	77
Micronésie (Etats féd. de)	2001	55	387	66	0	0	304	43	854	39
Mongolia	2000	3882	661	1494	1831	0	1844	908	10620	66
Mongolie	2001	3256	1165	2166	2443	0	3093	1992	14114	318
Montserrat	2000	38	2	0	0	0	1	4	45	3
Montserrat	2001	128	6	0	0	0	0	15	148	15
Morocco	2000	3465	512	1268	1517	2189	1994	3007	13952	464
Maroc	2001	2908	686	827	2295	2045	2927	3533	15221	428
Mozambique	2000	18600	8743	3408	21877	31024	2212	8088	93952	943
Mozambique	2001	23891	7864	5784	23070	17889	1315	12642	92454	1605
Myanmar	2000	14938	0	821	11217	1865	5435	1641	35918	1173
Myanmar	2001	15949	0	1464	14534	1337	3335	2733	39353	1534

83

Socio—economic development assistance through the United Nations system
Thousand US dollars [*cont.*]

Assistance en matière de développement socioéconomique fournie par le système des Nations Unies
Milliers de dollars E.−U. [*suite*]

Development grant expenditures [1] • Aide au développement [1]

Country or area Pays ou zone	Year Année	UNDP PNUD		UNFPA FNUAP	UNICEF	WFP PAM	Other UN system Autres organis. −ONU		Total	Gov't self− supporting Auto− assistance gouverne− mentale
		Central resources Ressources centrales	Special funds Fonds gérés				Regular budget Budget ordinaire	Extra− budgetary Extra− budgétaire		
Namibia	2000	1246	136	439	1994	730	1752	918	7215	378
Namibie	2001	515	87	550	1941	1094	1666	881	6734	612
Nauru	2000	0	0	0	0	0	91	0	91	0
Nauru	2001	0	0	0	0	0	126	0	126	0
Nepal	2000	8577	3010	2478	10647	9961	4135	4124	42933	2339
Népal	2001	9365	1501	4888	13140	16543	3260	5166	53864	3442
Netherlands Antilles	2000	395	0	0	0	0	114	0	509	0
Antilles néerlandaises	2001	163	0	0	0	0	152	0	315	0
New Caledonia	2000	...	...	...	...	...	...	...	...	...
Nouvelle−Calédonie	2001	0	0	0	0	0	20	0	20	0
Nicaragua	2000	8260	3962	1198	3032	12657	1162	2162	32434	341
Nicaragua	2001	5148	4271	2433	3175	11736	1115	2636	30514	702
Niger	2000	5889	1141	985	7860	3302	2583	3524	25283	2510
Niger	2001	5439	1321	2341	8184	6468	2148	2989	28891	1613
Nigeria	2000	6542	1701	3684	31556	0	3269	12645	59397	11131
Nigéria	2001	9799	3841	5628	46319	0	3280	18691	87557	16995
Niue	2000	123	84	0	0	0	102	21	330	0
Nioué	2001	37	51	0	0	0	59	11	158	0
Oman	2000	0	0	10	805	0	947	667	2429	595
Oman	2001	0	0	27	521	0	687	547	1782	517
Pakistan	2000	5231	1670	652	22268	5112	3790	12505	51228	10340
Pakistan	2001	10229	5173	3277	33070	10390	3769	8320	74228	6182
Palau	2000	0	0	0	0	0	152	0	152	0
Palaos	2001	0	0	0	0	0	175	0	175	0
Panama	2000	94849	976	213	904	0	1000	527	98468	487
Panama	2001	117768	553	399	1533	0	628	529	121410	529
Papua New Guinea	2000	2132	525	686	1547	0	2416	74	7379	27
Papouasie−Nvl−Guinée	2001	2317	377	543	1112	0	1282	330	5961	263
Paraguay	2000	28936	415	546	1057	0	971	424	32349	226
Paraguay	2001	28320	939	649	1047	0	539	148	31642	4
Peru	2000	54678	1144	1394	4819	3841	1949	4526	72352	3468
Pérou	2001	43761	3250	1590	4360	3153	2090	4873	63077	3510
Philippines	2000	4170	2228	997	8115	0	1029	5620	22159	2298
Philippines	2001	4681	1683	2915	8995	0	4084	4615	26973	1437
Poland	2000	1864	431	113	0	0	1668	91	4167	0
Pologne	2001	1371	740	109	0	0	565	23	2807	20
Portugal	2000	0	0	0	0	0	155	6	161	0
Portugal	2001	0	0	0	0	0	118	26	143	24
Qatar	2000	29	0	0	0	0	146	297	472	0
Qatar	2001	0	72	0	0	0	216	353	640	1
Réunion	2000	0	0	0	0	0	35	0	35	0
Réunion	2001	0	0	0	0	0	80	0	80	0
Romania	2000	1052	49	280	1446	0	510	1957	5294	143
Roumanie	2001	1451	129	483	1824	0	1143	684	5714	−10
Rwanda	2000	5474	20905	724	5900	73263	2877	2278	111420	564
Rwanda	2001	3173	8649	1556	5792	20806	1487	1037	42501	−428
Saint Helena	2000	259	0	0	0	0	0	0	259	0
Sainte−Hélène	2001	385	0	0	0	0	46	0	431	0
Saint Kitts and Nevis	2000	0	27	0	0	0	336	13	376	13
Saint−Kitts−et−Nevis	2001	0	78	0	0	0	311	0	389	0
Saint Lucia	2000	1	60	0	0	0	354	67	482	9
Sainte−Lucie	2001	0	52	0	0	0	289	26	367	25
Saint Vincent−Grenadines	2000	38	58	0	0	0	163	9	268	0
Saint Vincent−Grenadines	2001	13	4	0	0	0	260	0	277	0
Samoa	2000	665	49	24	0	0	1021	138	1897	0
Samoa	2001	382	88	50	0	0	771	6	1297	0
Sao Tome and Principe	2000	572	366	278	404	1166	1672	89	4547	81
Sao Tomé−et−Principe	2001	427	56	581	946	499	484	99	3092	58

83
Socio—economic development assistance through the United Nations system
Thousand US dollars [*cont.*]
Assistance en matière de développement socioéconomique fournie par le système des Nations Unies
Milliers de dollars E.—U. [*suite*]

Development grant expenditures [1] • Aide au développement [1]

Country or area Pays ou zone	Year Année	UNDP PNUD Central resources Ressources centrales	Special funds Fonds gérés	UNFPA FNUAP	UNICEF	WFP PAM	Other UN system Autres organis. —ONU Regular budget Budget ordinaire	Extra— budgetary Extra— budgétaire	Total	Gov't self— supporting Auto— assistance gouverne— mentale
Saudi Arabia	2000	3033	0	0	0	0	840	9205	13079	9086
Arabie saoudite	2001	3591	0	4	0	0	565	14071	18231	14040
Senegal	2000	3368	1489	1037	4527	12741	3195	4869	31225	292
Sénégal	2001	2593	1918	2191	4768	2470	1553	3912	19405	131
Serbia and Montenegro	2000	3856	6098	69	11610	67551	386	10778	100348	1136
Serbie—et—Monténégro	2001	15902	4095	1563	11883	68126	132	8950	110651	1953
Seychelles	2000	32	24	52	0	0	874	-2	980	-2
Seychelles	2001	27	18	59	0	0	715	42	861	42
Sierra Leone	2000	890	1	225	10424	4007	2342	2420	20309	1768
Sierra Leone	2001	3542	190	500	11198	16714	1462	5170	38776	1685
Singapore	2000	0	0	0	0	0	316	17	333	17
Singapour	2001	0	0	0	0	0	75	123	198	123
Solomon Islands	2000	570	0	58	0	0	637	144	1409	150
Iles Salomon	2001	1092	153	77	0	0	820	65	2208	72
Somalia	2000	9424	779	365	16782	14732	3707	4667	50456	2822
Somalie	2001	11920	1684	147	18572	6202	2388	7010	47924	1983
South Africa	2000	3476	567	334	3210	0	2754	1336	11677	222
Afrique du Sud	2001	1978	186	1576	4390	0	2631	1451	12212	622
Sri Lanka	2000	6488	1251	554	3848	3925	3348	1771	21186	545
Sri Lanka	2001	3534	590	1385	5086	3548	3586	1813	19542	201
Sudan	2000	6622	204	1567	15821	102923	3928	6084	137149	5008
Soudan	2001	2652	1392	2467	22401	118808	5945	9634	163299	4858
Suriname	2000	293	2627	573	179	0	539	256	4467	34
Suriname	2001	106	6334	39	0	0	371	265	7114	1
Swaziland	2000	929	207	199	732	0	1557	73	3697	64
Swaziland	2001	540	183	201	778	0	1080	110	2892	110
Syrian Arab Republic	2000	1273	1873	944	1064	5952	2408	3580	17095	508
Rép. arabe syrienne	2001	1135	1608	2491	940	2416	2787	4361	15738	2367
Tajikistan	2000	5519	868	369	1801	11860	380	1845	22642	1187
Tajikistan	2001	4737	614	631	1773	37869	427	1335	47386	553
Thailand	2000	2019	1378	570	3059	289	5091	1660	14066	151
Thaïlande	2001	1271	389	707	4109	0	2692	1391	10558	-10
TFYR of Macedonia	2000	1875	399	-11	5079	0	431	1317	9090	779
L'ex—R.y. Macédoine	2001	1132	409	0	6352	829	500	3069	12290	799
Timor—Leste	2000	...	...	...	...	...	...	...	...	...
Timor—Leste	2001	3794	586	281	5763	6488	571	2339	19822	781
Togo	2000	2829	1241	493	1629	0	1503	376	8072	203
Togo	2001	2424	97	1239	3533	0	1276	2361	10929	593
Tokelau	2000	76	0	0	0	0	57	0	133	0
Tokélaou	2001	98	0	0	0	0	2	0	100	0
Tonga	2000	124	0	46	0	0	794	6	970	0
Tonga	2001	11	31	24	0	0	741	0	807	0
Trinidad and Tobago	2000	107	248	0	0	0	838	138	1331	32
Trinité—et—Tobago	2001	113	407	0	0	0	473	94	1087	0
Tunisia	2000	743	485	361	1045	0	1125	1156	4916	406
Tunisie	2001	493	465	765	1058	0	1377	2696	6855	736
Turkey	2000	2327	2404	502	11156	0	864	1842	19094	331
Turquie	2001	2981	859	724	3631	0	759	1830	10784	608
Turkmenistan	2000	1231	88	426	943	0	110	27	2826	27
Turkménistan	2001	1056	202	693	1262	1973	141	67	5395	67
Turks and Caicos Islands	2000	363	42	0	0	0	39	42	486	0
Iles Turques et Caïques	2001	380	0	0	0	0	12	0	392	0
Tuvalu	2000	165	1	35	0	0	21	1	223	0
Tuvalu	2001	157	0	0	0	0	58	0	215	0
Uganda	2000	5174	5586	2619	22549	20463	2678	5711	64779	2352
Ouganda	2001	4436	4746	4831	14858	27344	2200	5669	64084	2954
United Arab Emirates	2000	3954	10	8	0	0	98	755	4825	755
Emirats arabes unis	2001	3879	0	0	0	0	256	611	4746	611

83
Socio−economic development assistance through the United Nations system
Thousand US dollars [*cont.*]

Assistance en matière de développement socioéconomique fournie par le système des Nations Unies
Milliers de dollars E.−U. [*suite*]

Development grant expenditures [1] • Aide au développement [1]

Country or area Pays ou zone	Year Année	UNDP PNUD Central resources Ressources centrales	Special funds Fonds gérés	UNFPA FNUAP	UNICEF	WFP PAM	Other UN system Autres organis. −ONU Regular budget Budget ordinaire	Extra− budgetary Extra− budgétaire	Total	Gov't self− supporting Auto− assistance gouverne− mentale
United Rep. of Tanzania	2000	10305	3209	2388	22443	4598	3021	5461	51424	2676
Rép.− Unie de Tanzanie	2001	6667	3785	4095	15085	55201	2173	5282	92290	2723
Uruguay	2000	26232	1145	107	676	0	526	320	29005	23
Uruguay	2001	21172	748	134	942	0	767	475	24238	219
Uzbekistan	2000	9669	1478	553	1549	0	732	466	14447	159
Ouzbékistan	2001	13370	342	719	1899	0	522	353	17205	77
Vanuatu	2000	111	0	79	0	0	1049	13	1251	1
Vanuatu	2001	136	14	71	0	0	502	13	736	4
Venezuela	2000	38659	3814	322	4070	635	2017	1083	50601	180
Venezuela	2001	32677	1735	640	1842	10	1131	1610	39644	399
Viet Nam	2000	15325	2936	4202	10799	10125	3353	3945	50686	387
Viet Nam	2001	12208	6564	3903	10653	193	6000	4196	43718	973
Yemen	2000	9827	1976	1824	5063	7197	2406	3436	31729	2076
Yémen	2001	7760	1731	4002	6714	4597	3000	4482	32286	2944
Zambia	2000	3402	2150	3421	10864	7447	2831	1652	31767	458
Zambie	2001	4030	1316	1078	9747	12788	2077	1843	32878	437
Zimbabwe	2000	3607	602	451	5160	13	2446	4014	16293	2231
Zimbabwe	2001	2485	2001	1623	4694	1240	2012	4110	18164	2002
Other countries	2000	28476	10183	894	11717	20043	8394	16456	96164	4367
Autres pays	2001	25788	8713	2224	8345	92418	12301	37692	187481	22332
Not elsewhere classified	**2000**	**7324**	**32469**	**2969**	**66036**	**33116**	**6134**	**21518**	**169566**	**17654**
Non−classé ailleurs	**2001**	**5543**	**31426**	**3428**	**66873**	**5154**	**2736**	**−11302**	**103858**	**−12983**

Source: United Nations, "Operational activities of the United Nations
for international development cooperation, Report of the Secretary−
General, Addendum, Comprehensive statistical data on operational
activities for development for the year 2000" and
"Operational activities of the United Nations for international
development cooperation, Report of the Secretary−General, Addendum,
Comprehensive statistical data on operational activities for development
for the year 2001" (advanced version).

Source: Nations Unies, "Activités opérationnelles du système des
Nations Unies au service de la coopération internationale pour
le développement, Rapport du Secrétaire général, Additif,
Données statistiques globales sur les activités opérationnelles
au service du développement pour 2000" et
"Activités opérationnelles du système des Nations Unies au service
de la coopération internationale pour le développement, Rapport du
Secrétaire général, Additif, Données statistiques globales sur les
activités opérationnelles au service du développement pour 2001"
(version préliminaire).

1   The following abbreviations have been used in the table:
    UNDP: United Nations Development Programme
    UNFPA: United Nations Population Fund
    UNICEF: United Nations Children's Fund
    WFP: World Food Programme

1   Les abbréviations ci−après ont été utilisées dans le tableau:
    PNUD : Programme des Nations Unies pour le développement
    FNUAP : Fonds des Nations Unies pour la population
    UNICEF : Fonds des Nations Unies pour l'enfance
    PAM : Programme alimentaire mondial.

Technical notes, tables 81-83

Table 81 presents estimates of flows of financial resources to individual recipients either directly (bilaterally) or through multilateral institutions (multilaterally).

The multilateral institutions include the World Bank Group, regional banks, financial institutions of the European Union and a number of United Nations institutions, programmes and trust funds.

The main source of data is the Development Assistance Committee of OECD to which member countries reported data on their flow of resources to developing countries and territories and countries and territories in transition, and multilateral institutions.

Additional information on definitions, methods and sources can be found in OECD's *Geographical Distribution of Financial Flows to Aid Recipients* [21] and <www.oecd.org>.

Table 82 presents the development assistance expenditures of donor countries. This table includes donors' contributions to multilateral agencies, so the overall totals differ from those in table 81, which include disbursements by multilateral agencies.

Table 83 includes data on expenditures on operational activities for development undertaken by the organizations of the United Nations system. Operational activities encompass, in general, those activities of a development cooperation character that seek to mobilize or increase the potential and capacity of countries to promote economic and social development and welfare, including the transfer of resources to developing countries or regions in a tangible or intangible form. The table also covers, as a memo item, expenditures on activities of an emergency character, the purpose of which is immediate relief in crisis situations, such as assistance to refugees, humanitarian work and activities in respect of disasters.

Expenditures on operational activities for development are financed from contributions from governments and other official and non-official sources to a variety of funding channels in the United Nations system. These include United Nations funds and programmes such as contributions to the United Nations Development Programme, contributions to funds administered by the United Nations Development Programme, and regular (assessed) and other extrabudgetary contributions to specialized agencies.

Data are taken from the 2000 and 2001 reports of the Secretary-General to the General Assembly on operational activities for development [28].

Notes techniques, tableaux 81 à 83

Le *Tableau 81* présente les estimations des flux de ressources financières mises à la disposition des pays soit directement (aide bilatérale) soit par l'intermédiaire d'institutions multilatérales (aide multilatérale).

Les institutions multilatérales comprennent le Groupe de la Banque mondiale, les banques régionales, les institutions financières de l'Union européenne et un certain nombre d'institutions, de programmes et de fonds d'affectation spéciale des Nations Unies.

La principale source de données est le Comité d'aide au développement de l'OCDE, auquel les pays membres ont communiqué des données sur les flux de ressources qu'ils mettent à la disposition des pays et territoires en développement et en transition et des institutions multilatérales.

Pour plus de renseignements sur les définitions, méthodes et sources, se reporter à la publication de l'OCDE, la *Répartition géographique des ressources financières de aux pays bénéficiaires de l'Aide* [21] et <www.oecd.org>.

Le *Tableau 82* présente les dépenses que les pays donateurs consacrent à l'aide publique au développement (APD). Ces chiffres incluent les contributions des donateurs à des agences multilatérales, de sorte que les totaux diffèrent de ceux du tableau 81, qui incluent les dépenses des agences multilatérales.

Le *Tableau 83* présente des données sur les dépenses consacrées à des activités opérationnelles pour le développement par les organisations du système des Nations Unies. Par "activités opérationnelles", on entend en général les activités ayant trait à la coopération au développement, qui visent à mobiliser ou à accroître les potentialités et aptitudes que présentent les pays pour promouvoir le développement et le bien-être économiques et sociaux, y compris les transferts de ressources vers les pays ou régions en développement sous forme tangible ou non. Ce tableau indique également, pour mémoire, les dépenses liées à des activités revêtant un caractère d'urgence, qui ont pour but d'apporter un secours immédiat dans les situations de crise, telles que l'aide aux réfugiés, l'assistance humanitaire et les secours en cas de catastrophe.

Les dépenses consacrées aux activités opérationnelles pour le développement sont financées au moyen de contributions que les gouvernements et d'autres sources officielles et non officielles apportent à divers organes de financement, tels que fonds et programmes du système des Nations Unies. On peut citer notamment les contributions au Programme des Nations Unies pour le développement, les contributions aux fonds gérés par le Programme des Nations Unies pour le développement, les contributions régulières (budgétaires) et les contributions extrabudgétaires aux institutions spécialisées.

Les données sont extraites des rapports annuels de 2000 et de 2001 du Secrétaire général à la session de l'Assemblée générale sur les activités opérationnelles pour le développement [28].

Annex I

Country and area nomenclature, regional and other groupings

A.   Changes in country or area names
In the periods covered by the statistics in the *Statistical Yearbook*, the following changes in designation have taken place:

Brunei Darussalam was formerly listed as Brunei;
Burkina Faso was formerly listed as Upper Volta;
Cambodia was formerly listed as Democratic Kampuchea;
Cameroon was formerly listed as United Republic of Cameroon;
Côte d'Ivoire was formerly listed as Ivory Coast;
Czech Republic, Slovakia: Since 1 January 1993, data for the Czech Republic and Slovakia, where available, are shown separately under the appropriate country name. For periods prior to 1 January 1993, where no separate data are available for the Czech Republic and Slovakia, unless otherwise indicated, data for the former Czechoslovakia are shown under the country name "former Czechoslovakia";
Democratic Republic of the Congo was formerly listed as Zaire;
Germany: Through the accession of the German Democratic Republic to the Federal Republic of Germany with effect from 3 October 1990, the two German States have united to form one sovereign State. As from the date of unification, the Federal Republic of Germany acts in the United Nations under the designation "Germany". All data shown which pertain to Germany prior to 3 October 1990 are indicated separately for the Federal Republic of Germany and the former German Democratic Republic based on their respective territories at the time indicated;
Hong Kong Special Administrative Region of China: Pursuant to a Joint Declaration signed on 19 December 1984, the United Kingdom restored Hong Kong to the People's Republic of China with effect from 1 July 1997; the People's Republic of China resumed the exercise of sovereignty over the territory with effect from that date;
Macao Special Administrative Region of China: Pursuant to the joint declaration signed on 13 April 1987, Portugal restored Macao to the People's Republic of China with effect from 20 December 1999; the People's Republic of China resumed the exercise of sovereignty over the territory with effect from that date;
Myanmar was formerly listed as Burma;
Palau was formerly listed as Pacific Islands and includes data for Federated States of Micronesia, Marshall Islands and Northern Mariana Islands;
Saint Kitts and Nevis was formerly listed as Saint Christopher and Nevis;
Serbia and Montenegro: As of 4 February 2003, the official name of the "Federal Republic of Yugoslavia" has been changed to "Serbia and Montenegro". Unless otherwise indicated, data provided for Yugoslavia prior to 1 January 1992 refer to the Socialist Federal

Annexe I

Nomenclature des pays ou zones, groupements régionaux et autres groupements

A.   Changements dans le nom des pays ou zones
Au cours des périodes sur lesquelles portent les statistiques, dans l'*Annuaire Statistique* les changements de désignation suivants ont eu lieu:

Le *Brunéi Darussalam* apparaissait antérieurement sous le nom de Brunéi;
Le *Burkino Faso* apparaissait antérieurement sous le nom de la Haute-Volta;
Le *Cambodge* apparaissait antérieurement sous le nom de la Kampuchea démocratique;
Le *Cameroun* apparaissait antérieurement sous le nom de République-Unie du Cameroun;
République tchèque, Slovaquie: Depuis le 1er janvier 1993, les données relatives à la République tchèque, et à la Slovaquie, lorsqu'elles sont disponibles, sont présentées séparément sous le nom de chacun des pays. En ce qui concerne la période précédant le 1er janvier 1993, pour laquelle on ne possède pas de données séparées pour les deux Républiques, les données relatives à l'ex-Tchécoslovaquie sont, sauf indication contraire, présentées sous le titre "l'ex-Tchécoslovaquie";
La *République démocratique du Congo* apparaissait antérieurement sous le nom de Zaïre;
Allemagne: En vertu de l'adhésion de la République démocratique allemande à la République fédérale d'Allemagne, prenant effet le 3 octobre 1990, les deux Etats allemands se sont unis pour former un seul Etat souverain. A compter de la date de l'unification, la République fédérale d'Allemagne est désigné à l'ONU sous le nom d'"Allemagne". Toutes les données se rapportant à l'Allemagne avant le 3 octobre figurent dans deux rubriques séparées basées sur les territoires respectifs de la République fédérale d'Allemagne et l'ex-République démocratique allemande selon la période indiquée;
Hong Kong, région administrative spéciale de Chine: Conformément à une Déclaration commune signée le 19 décembre 1984, le Royaume-Uni a rétrocédé Hong Kong à la République populaire de Chine, avec effet au 1er juillet 1997; la souveraineté de la République populaire de Chine s'exerce à nouveau sur le territoire à compter de cette date;
Macao, région administrative spéciale de Chine: Conformément à une Déclaration commune signée le 13 avril 1987, le Portugal a rétrocédé Macao à la République populaire de Chine, avec effet au 20 décembre 1999; la souveraineté de la République populaire de Chine s'exerce à nouveau sur le territoire à compter de cette date;
Le *Myanmar* apparaissait antérieurement sous le nom de Birmanie;
Les *Palaos* apparaissait antérieurement sous le nom de Iles du Pacifique y compris les données pour les Etats fédérés de Micronésie, les îles Marshall et îles Mariannes du Nord;
Saint-Kitts-et-Nevis apparaissait antérieurement sous le nom de Saint-Christophe-et-Nevis;
Serbie-et-Monténégro: A compter de février 2003, la "République fédérale de Yougoslavie" ayant changé de nom officiel, est devenue la "Serbie-et-Monténégro". Sauf indication contraire, les données fournies pour la Yougoslavie avant le 1er janvier 1992 se rapportent à la République fédé-

Republic of Yugoslavia which was composed of six republics. Data provided for Yugoslavia after that date
refer to the Federal Republic of Yugoslavia which is
composed of two republics (Serbia and Montenegro);

Timor-Leste: Formerly East Timor;

Former *USSR*: In 1991, the Union of Soviet Socialist Republics formally dissolved into fifteen independent countries (Armenia, Azerbaijan, Belarus, Esto-
nia, Georgia, Kazakhstan, Kyrgyzstan, Latvia, Lithua-
nia, Republic of Moldova, Russian Federation, Tajikistan, Turkmenistan, Ukraine and Uzbekistan). Whenever
possible, data are shown for the individual countries.
Otherwise, data are shown for the former USSR;

Yemen: On 22 May 1990 Democratic Yemen and
Yemen merged to form a single State. Since that date
they have been represented as one Member with the
name 'Yemen'.

Data relating to the People's Republic of China
generally include those for Taiwan Province in the field
of statistics relating to population, area, natural resources and natural conditions such as climate. In other
fields of statistics, they do not include Taiwan Province
unless otherwise stated.

B.   *Regional groupings*

The scheme of regional groupings given below
presents seven regions based mainly on continents. Five
of the seven continental regions are further subdivided
into 21 regions that are so drawn as to obtain greater
homogeneity in sizes of population, demographic circumstances and accuracy of demographic statistics [22,
59]. This nomenclature is widely used in international
statistics and is followed to the greatest extent possible
in the present *Yearbook* in order to promote consistency
and facilitate comparability and analysis. However, it is
by no means universal in international statistical compilation, even at the level of continental regions, and
variations in international statistical sources and methods dictate many unavoidable differences in particular
fields in the present *Yearbook*. General differences are
indicated in the footnotes to the classification presented
below. More detailed differences are given in the footnotes and technical notes to individual tables.

Neither is there international standardization in the
use of the terms "developed" and "developing" countries, areas or regions. These terms are used in the present publication to refer to regional groupings generally
considered as "developed": these are Europe and the
former USSR, the United States of America and Canada
in Northern America, and Australia, Japan and New
Zealand in Asia and Oceania. These designations are
intended for statistical convenience and do not necessarily express a judgement about the stage reached by a
particular country or area in the development process.
Differences from this usage are indicated in the notes to
individual tables.

rative socialiste de Yougoslavie, qui était composée de six
républiques. Les données fournies pour la Yougoslavie après
cette date se rapportent à la République fédérative de Yougoslavie, qui est composée de deux républiques (Serbie et
Monténégro);

Timor-Leste: Ex Timor oriental;

L'ex-*URSS*: En 1991, l'Union des républiques socia-
listes soviétiques s'est séparé en 15 pays distincts (Arménie,
Azerbaïdjan, Bélarus, Estonie, Géorgie, Kazakhstan, Kirghizistan, Lettonie, Lituanie, République de Moldova, Fédération de Russie, Tadjikistan, Turkménistan, Ukraine, Ouzbékistan). Les données sont présentées pour ces pays pris séparément quand cela est possible. Autrement, les données sont
présentées pour l'ex-URSS;

Yémen: Le Yémen et le Yémen démocratique ont fu-
sionné le 22 mai 1990 pour ne plus former qu'un seul Etat,
qui est depuis lors représenté comme tel à l'Organisation,
sous le nom 'Yémen'.

Les données relatives à la République populaire de
Chine comprennent en général les données relatives à la
province de Taïwan lorsqu'il s'agit de statistiques concernant la population, la superficie, les ressources naturelles, et
les conditions naturelles telles que le climat, etc. Dans les
statistiques relatives à d'autres domaines, la province de
Taïwan n'est pas comprise, sauf indication contraire.

B.   *Groupements régionaux*

Le système de groupements régionaux présenté ci-
dessous comporte sept régions basés principalement sur les
continents. Cinq des sept régions continentales sont elles-
mêmes subdivisées, formant ainsi 21 régions délimitées de
manière à obtenir une homogénéité accrue dans les effectifs
de population, les situations démographiques et la précision
des statistiques démographiques [22, 59]. Cette nomenclature est couramment utilisée aux fins des statistiques internationales et a été appliquée autant qu'il a été possible dans
le présent *Annuaire* en vue de renforcer la cohérence et de
faciliter la comparaison et l'analyse. Son utilisation pour
l'établissement des statistiques internationales n'est cependant rien moins qu'universelle, même au niveau des régions
continentales, et les variations que présentent les sources et
méthodes statistiques internationales entraînent inévitablement de nombreuses différences dans certains domaines de
cet *Annuaire*. Les différences d'ordre général sont indiquées
dans les notes figurant au bas de la classification présentée
ci-dessous. Les différences plus spécifiques sont mention-
nées dans les notes techniques et notes infrapaginales accompagnant les divers tableaux.

L'application des expressions "développés" et "en développement" aux pays, zones ou régions n'est pas non plus
normalisée à l'échelle internationale. Ces expressions sont
utilisées dans la présente publication en référence aux groupements régionaux généralement considérés comme "développés", à savoir l'Europe et l'ex-URSS, les Etats-Unis
d'Amérique et le Canada en Amérique septentrionale, et
l'Australie, le Japon et la Nouvelle-Zélande dans la région
de l'Asie et du Pacifique. Ces appellations sont employées
pour des raisons de commodité statistique et n'expriment
pas nécessairement un jugement sur le stade de développement atteint par tel ou tel pays ou zone. Les cas différant de
cet usage sont signalés dans les notes accompagnant les tableaux concernés.

Africa

Eastern Africa

Burundi	Réunion
Comoros	Rwanda
Djibouti	Seychelles
Eritrea	Somalia
Ethiopia	Uganda
Kenya	United Republic of
Madagascar	Tanzania
Malawi	Zambia
Mauritius	Zimbabwe
Mozambique	

Middle Africa

Angola	Democratic Republic of
Cameroon	the Congo
Central African Republic	Equatorial Guinea
Chad	Gabon
Congo	Sao Tome and Principe

Northern Africa

Algeria	Sudan
Egypt	Tunisia
Libyan Arab Jamahiriya	Western Sahara
Morocco	

Southern Africa

Botswana	South Africa
Lesotho	Swaziland
Namibia	

Western Africa

Benin	Mali
Burkina Faso	Mauritania
Cape Verde	Niger
Côte d'Ivoire	Nigeria
Gambia	Saint Helena
Ghana	Senegal
Guinea	Sierra Leone
Guinea-Bissau	Togo
Liberia	

Americas

Latin America and the Caribbean
Caribbean

Anguilla	Jamaica
Antigua and Barbuda	Martinique
Aruba	Montserrat
Bahamas	Netherlands Antilles
Barbados	Puerto Rico
British Virgin Islands	Saint Kitts and Nevis
Cayman Islands	Saint Lucia
Cuba	Saint Vincent and the
Dominica	Grenadines
Dominican Republic	Trinidad and Tobago
Grenada	Turks and Caicos Islands

Afrique

Afrique orientale

Burundi	Ouganda
Comores	République-Unie de
Djibouti	Tanzanie
Erythrée	Réunion
Ethiopie	Rwanda
Kenya	Seychelles
Madagascar	Somalie
Malawi	Zambie
Maurice	Zimbabwe
Mozambique	

Afrique centrale

Angola	République centrafricaine
Cameroun	République démocratique
Congo	du Congo
Gabon	Sao Tomé-et-Principe
Guinée équatoriale	Tchad

Afrique septentrionale

Algérie	Sahara occidental
Egypte	Soudan
Jamahiriya arabe libyenne	Tunisie
Maroc	

Afrique australe

Afrique du Sud	Namibie
Botswana	Swaziland
Lesotho	

Afrique occidentale

Bénin	Mali
Burkina Faso	Mauritanie
Cap-Vert	Niger
Côte d'Ivoire	Nigéria
Gambie	Sainte-Hélène
Ghana	Sénégal
Guinée	Sierra Leone
Guinée-Bissau	Togo
Libéria	

Amériques

Amérique latine et Caraïbes
Caraïbes

Anguilla	Iles Turques et Caïques
Antigua-et-Barbuda	Iles Vierges américaines
Antilles néerlandaises	Iles Vierges britanniques
Aruba	Jamaïque
Bahamas	Martinique
Barbade	Montserrat
Cuba	Porto Rico
Dominique	République dominicaine
Grenade	Sainte-Lucie
Guadeloupe	Saint-Kitts-et-Nevis
Haïti	Saint-Vincent-et-les Grenadines

Guadeloupe
Haiti

| | United States Virgin Islands | Iles Caïmanes | Trinité-et-Tobago |

Central America

Belize	Honduras
Costa Rica	Mexico
El Salvador	Nicaragua
Guatemala	Panama

South America

Argentina	French Guiana
Bolivia	Guyana
Brazil	Paraguay
Chile	Peru
Colombia	Suriname
Ecuador	Uruguay
Falkland Islands (Malvinas)	Venezuela

Northern America [a]

Bermuda	Saint Pierre and Miquelon
Canada	United States of America
Greenland	

Asia

Eastern Asia

China	Democratic People's
China, Hong Kong Special	Republic of Korea
Administrative Region	Japan
China, Macao Special	Mongolia
Administrative Region	Republic of Korea

South-central Asia

Afghanistan	Maldives
Bangladesh	Nepal
Bhutan	Pakistan
India	Sri Lanka
Iran (Islamic Republic of)	Tajikistan
Kazakhstan	Turkmenistan
Kyrgyzstan	Uzbekistan

South-eastern Asia

Brunei Darussalam	Myanmar
Cambodia	Philippines
Indonesia	Singapore
Lao People's Democratic	Thailand
Republic	Timor-Leste
Malaysia	Viet Nam

Western Asia

Armenia	Occupied Palestinian
Azerbaijan	Territory
Bahrain	Oman
Cyprus	Qatar
Georgia	Saudi Arabia
Iraq	Syrian Arab Republic
Israel	Turkey

Amérique centrale

Belize	Honduras
Costa Rica	Mexique
El Salvador	Nicaragua
Guatemala	Panama

Amérique du Sud

Argentine	Guyane française
Bolivie	Iles Falkland (Malvinas)
Brésil	Paraguay
Chili	Pérou
Colombie	Suriname
Equateur	Uruguay
Guyana	Venezuela

Amérique septentrionale [a]

Bermudes	Groenland
Canada	Saint-Pierre-et-Miquelon
Etats-Unis d'Amérique	

Asie

Asie orientale

Chine	Japon
Chine, Hong Kong, région	Mongolie
administrative spéciale	République de Corée
Chine, Macao, région	République populaire
administrative spéciale	démocratique de Corée

Asie centrale et du Sud

Afghanistan	Maldives
Bangladesh	Népal
Bhoutan	Ouzbékistan
Inde	Pakistan
Iran (République	Sri Lanka
islamique d')	Tadjikistan
Kazakhstan	Turkménistan
Kirghizistan	

Asie du Sud-Est

Brunéi Darussalam	République démocratique
Cambodge	populaire lao
Indonésie	Singapour
Malaisie	Thaïlande
Myanmar	Timor-Leste
Philippines	Viet Nam

Asie occidentale

Arabie saoudite	Jordanie
Arménie	Koweït
Azerbaïdjan	Liban
Bahreïn	Oman
Chypre	Qatar
Emirats arabes unis	République arabe syrienne
Géorgie	Territoire palestinien occupé

Jordan	United Arab Emirates	Iraq	Turquie
Kuwait	Yemen	Israël	Yémen
Lebanon			

Europe

Eastern Europe

Belarus	Republic of Moldova
Bulgaria	Romania
Czech Republic	Russian Federation
Hungary	Slovakia
Poland	Ukraine

Northern Europe

Channel Islands	Latvia
Denmark	Lithuania
Estonia	Norway
Faeroe Islands	Svalbard and Jan Mayen
Finland	Islands
Iceland	Sweden
Ireland	United Kingdom
Isle of Man	

Southern Europe

Albania	Malta
Andorra	Portugal
Bosnia and Herzegovina	San Marino
Croatia	Serbia and Montenegro
Gibraltar	Slovenia
Greece	Spain
Holy See	The former Yugoslav Re-
Italy	public of Macedonia

Western Europe

Austria	Luxembourg
Belgium	Monaco
France	Netherlands
Germany	Switzerland
Liechtenstein	

Oceania

Australia and New Zealand

Australia	Norfolk Island
New Zealand	

Melanesia

Fiji	Solomon Islands
New Caledonia	Vanuatu
Papua New Guinea	

Micronesia-Polynesia
Micronesia

Guam	Nauru
Kiribati	Northern Mariana
Marshall Islands	Islands
Micronesia (Federated	Palau
States of)	

Europe

Europe orientale

Bélarus	République de Moldova
Bulgarie	République tchèque
Fédération de Russie	Roumanie
Hongrie	Slovaquie
Pologne	Ukraine

Europe septentrionale

Danemark	Irlande
Estonie	Islande
Finlande	Lettonie
Ile de Man	Lituanie
Iles Anglo-Normandes	Norvège
Iles Féroé	Royaume-Uni
Iles Svalbard et Jan	Suède
Mayen	

Europe méridionale

Albanie	Grèce
Andorre	Italie
Bosnie-Herzégovine	Malte
Croatie	Portugal
Espagne	Saint-Marin
Ex-République yougoslave	Saint-Siège
de Macédoine	Serbie-et-Monténégro
Gibraltar	Slovénie

Europe occidentale

Allemagne	Luxembourg
Autriche	Monaco
Belgique	Pays-Bas
France	Suisse
Liechtenstein	

Océanie

Australie et Nouvelle-Zélande

Australie	Nouvelle-Zélande
Ile Norfolk	

Mélanésie

Fidji	Papouasie-Nouvelle-Guinée
Iles Salomon	Vanuatu
Nouvelle-Calédonie	

Micronésie-Polynésie
Micronésie

Guam	Kiribati
Iles Mariannes	Micronésie (Etats fédérés de)
septentrionales	Nauru
Iles Marshall	Palaos

Polynesia	
American Samoa	Samoa
Cook Islands	Tokelau
French Polynesia	Tonga
Niue	Tuvalu
Pitcairn	Wallis and Futuna Islands

Polynésie	
Iles Cook	Samoa
Iles Wallis-et-Futuna	Samoa américaines
Nioué	Tokélaou
Pitcairn	Tonga
Polynésie française	Tuvalu

C. Other groupings

Following is a list of other groupings and their compositions presented in the *Yearbook*. These groupings are organized mainly around economic and trade interests in regional associations.

Andean Common Market (ANCOM)
   Bolivia
   Colombia
   Ecuador
   Peru
   Venezuela

Asia-Pacific Economic Cooperation (APEC)
   Australia
   Brunei Darussalam
   Canada
   Chile
   China
   China, Hong Kong Special Administrative Region
   Indonesia
   Japan
   Malaysia
   Mexico
   New Zealand
   Papua New Guinea
   Peru
   Philippines
   Republic of Korea
   Russian Federation
   Singapore
   Taiwan Province of China
   Thailand
   United States of America
   Viet Nam

Association of Southeast Asian Nations (ASEAN)
   Brunei Darussalam
   Cambodia
   Indonesia
   Lao People's Democratic Republic
   Malaysia
   Myanmar
   Philippines
   Singapore
   Thailand
   Viet Nam

Caribbean Community and Common Market (CARICOM)
   Antigua and Barbuda
   Bahamas (member of the Community only)
   Barbados

C. Autres groupements

On trouvera ci-après une liste des autres groupements et de leur composition, présentée dans l'*Annuaire*. Ces groupements correspondent essentiellement à des intérêts économiques et commerciaux d'après les associations régionales.

Marché commun andin (ANCOM)
   Bolivie
   Colombie
   Equateur
   Pérou
   Vénézuela

Coopération économique Asie-Pacifique (CEAP)
   Australie
   Brunéi Darussalam
   Canada
   Chili
   Chine
   Chine, Hong Kong, région administrative spéciale
   Etats-Unis d'Amérique
   Fédération de Russie
   Indonésie
   Japon
   Malaisie
   Mexique
   Nouvelle-Zélande
   Papouasie-Nouvelle-Guinée
   Pérou
   Philippines
   Province chinoise de Taiwan
   République de Corée
   Singapour
   Thaïlande
   Viet Nam

Association des nations de l'Asie du Sud-Est (ANASE)
   Brunéi Darussalam
   Cambodge
   Indonésie
   Malaisie
   Myanmar
   Philippines
   République démocratique populaire lao
   Singapour
   Thaïlande
   Viet Nam

Communauté des Caraïbes et Marché commun des Caraïbes (CARICOM)
   Antigua-et-Barbuda
   Bahamas (membre de la communauté seulement)
   Barbade

Belize	Belize
Dominica	Dominique
Grenada	Grenade
Guyana	Guyana
Haiti	Haïti
Jamaica	Jamaïque
Montserrat	Montserrat
Saint Kitts and Nevis	Sainte-Lucie
Saint Lucia	Saint-Kitts-et-Nevis
Saint Vincent and the Grenadines	Saint-Vincent-et-les Grenadines
Suriname	Suriname
Trinidad and Tobago	Trinité-et-Tobago

Central American Common Market (CACM) / **Marché commun centraméricain** (MCC)

Costa Rica	Costa Rica
El Salvador	El Salvador
Guatemala	Guatemala
Honduras	Honduras
Nicaragua	Nicaragua

Common Market for Eastern and Southern Africa (COMESA) / **Marché commun de l'Afrique de l'Est et de l'Afrique australe** (COMESA)

Angola	Angola
Burundi	Burundi
Comoros	Comores
Democratic Republic of the Congo	Djibouti
Djibouti	Egypte
Egypt	Erythrée
Eritrea	Ethiopie
Ethiopia	Kenya
Kenya	Madagascar
Madagascar	Malawi
Malawi	Maurice
Mauritius	Namibie
Namibia	Ouganda
Rwanda	République démocratique du Congo
Seychelles	Rwanda
Sudan	Seychelles
Swaziland	Soudan
Uganda	Swaziland
Zambia	Zambie
Zimbabwe	Zimbabwe

Commonwealth of Independent States (CIS) / **Communauté d'Etats indépendants** (CEI)

Armenia	Arménie
Azerbaijan	Azerbaïdjan
Belarus	Bélarus
Georgia	Fédération de Russie
Kazakhstan	Géorgie
Kyrgyzstan	Kazakhstan
Republic of Moldova	Kirghizistan
Russian Federation	Ouzbékistan
Tajikistan	République de Moldova
Turkmenistan	Tadjikistan
Ukraine	Turkménistan
Uzbekistan	Ukraine

Economic and Monetary Community of Central Africa (EMCCA) / **Communauté économique et monétaire de l'Afrique centrale** (CEMAC)

Cameroon	Cameroun
Central African Republic	Congo

Chad	Gabon
Congo	Guinée équatoriale
Equatorial Guinea	République centrafricaine
Gabon	Tchad

Economic Community of West African States (ECOWAS)	*Communauté économique des Etats de l'Afrique de l'Ouest* (CEDEAO)
Benin	Bénin
Burkina Faso	Burkina Faso
Cape Verde	Cap-Vert
Côte d'Ivoire	Côte d'Ivoire
Gambia	Gambie
Ghana	Ghana
Guinea	Guinée
Guinea-Bissau	Guinée-Bissau
Liberia	Libéria
Mali	Mali
Niger	Niger
Nigeria	Nigéria
Senegal	Sénégal
Sierra Leone	Sierra Leone
Togo	Togo

European Free Trade Association (EFTA)	*Association européenne de libre-échange* (AELE)
Iceland	Islande
Liechtenstein	Liechtenstein
Norway	Norvège
Switzerland	Suisse

European Union (EU)	*Union européenne* (UE)
Austria	Allemagne
Belgium	Autriche
Denmark	Belgique
Finland	Danemark
France	Espagne
Germany	Finlande
Greece	France
Ireland	Grèce
Italy	Irlande
Luxembourg	Italie
Netherlands	Luxembourg
Portugal	Pays-Bas
Spain	Portugal
Sweden	Royaume-Uni
United Kingdom	Suède

Latin American Integration Association (LAIA)	*Association latino-américaine pour l'intégration* (ALAI)
Argentina	Argentine
Bolivia	Bolivie
Brazil	Brésil
Chile	Chili
Colombia	Colombie
Ecuador	Equateur
Mexico	Mexique
Paraguay	Paraguay
Peru	Pérou
Uruguay	Uruguay
Venezuela	Venezuela

Least developed countries (LDCs) [b]	*Pays les moins avançés* (PMA) [b]
Afghanistan	Afghanistan
Angola	Angola

Bangladesh
Benin
Bhutan
Burkina Faso
Burundi
Cambodia
Cape Verde
Central African Republic
Chad
Comoros
Democratic Republic of the Congo
Djibouti
Equatorial Guinea
Eritrea
Ethiopia
Gambia
Guinea
Guinea-Bissau
Haiti
Kiribati
Lao People's Democratic Republic
Lesotho
Liberia
Madagascar
Malawi
Maldives
Mali
Mauritania
Mozambique
Myanmar
Nepal
Niger
Rwanda
Samoa
Sao Tome and Principe
Senegal
Sierra Leone
Solomon Islands
Somalia
Sudan
Togo
Tuvalu
Uganda
United Republic of Tanzania
Vanuatu
Yemen
Zambia

Bangladesh
Bénin
Bhoutan
Burkina Faso
Burundi
Cambodge
Cap-Vert
Comores
Djibouti
Erythrée
Ethiopie
Gambie
Guinée
Guinée équatoriale
Guinée-Bissau
Haïti
Iles Salomon
Kiribati
Lesotho
Libéria
Madagascar
Malawi
Maldives
Mali
Mauritanie
Mozambique
Myanmar
Népal
Niger
Ouganda
République centrafricaine
République démocratique du Congo
République démocratique populaire lao
République-Unie de Tanzanie
Rwanda
Samoa
Sao Tomé-et-Principe
Sénégal
Sierra Leone
Somalie
Soudan
Tchad
Togo
Tuvalu
Vanuatu
Yémen
Zambie

Mercado Común Sudamericano (MERCOSUR)
  Argentina
  Brazil
  Paraguay
  Uruguay

Marché commun sud-américain (Mercosur)
  Argentine
  Brésil
  Paraguay
  Uruguay

North American Free Trade Agreement (NAFTA)
  Canada
  Mexico
  United States of America

Accord de libre-échange nord-américain (ALENA)
  Canada
  Etats-Unis d'Amérique
  Mexique

Organisation for Economic Cooperation and Development (OECD)
>   Australia
>   Austria
>   Belgium
>   Canada
>   Czech Republic
>   Denmark
>   Finland
>   France
>   Germany
>   Greece
>   Hungary
>   Iceland
>   Ireland
>   Italy
>   Japan
>   Luxembourg
>   Mexico
>   Netherlands
>   New Zealand
>   Norway
>   Poland
>   Portugal
>   Republic of Korea
>   Slovakia
>   Spain
>   Sweden
>   Switzerland
>   Turkey
>   United Kingdom
>   United States of America

Organization of Petroleum Exporting Countries (OPEC)
>   Algeria
>   Indonesia
>   Iran (Islamic Republic of)
>   Iraq
>   Kuwait
>   Libyan Arab Jamahiriya
>   Nigeria
>   Qatar
>   Saudi Arabia
>   United Arab Emirates
>   Venezuela

Southern African Customs Union (SACU)
>   Botswana
>   Lesotho
>   Namibia
>   South Africa
>   Swaziland

Organisation de coopération et de développement économiques (OCDE)
>   Allemagne
>   Australie
>   Autriche
>   Belgique
>   Canada
>   Danemark
>   Espagne
>   Etats-Unis d'Amérique
>   Finlande
>   France
>   Grèce
>   Hongrie
>   Irlande
>   Islande
>   Italie
>   Japon
>   Luxembourg
>   Mexique
>   Norvège
>   Nouvelle-Zélande
>   Pays-Bas
>   Pologne
>   Portugal
>   République de Corée
>   République tchèque
>   Royaume-Uni
>   Slovaquie
>   Suède
>   Suisse
>   Turquie

Organisation des pays exportateurs de pétrole (OPEP)
>   Algérie
>   Arabie saoudite
>   Emirats arabes unis
>   Indonésie
>   Iran (République islamique d')
>   Iraq
>   Jamahiriya arabe libyenne
>   Koweït
>   Nigéria
>   Qatar
>   Venezuela

Union douanière d'Afrique australe
>   Afrique du Sud
>   Botswana
>   Lesotho
>   Namibie
>   Swaziland

a   The continent of North America comprises Northern America, Caribbean and Central America.
b   As determined by the General Assembly in its resolution 49/133.

a   Le continent de l'Amérique du Nord comprend l'Amérique septentrionale, les Caraïbes et l'Amérique centrale.
b   Comme déterminé par l'Assemblée générale dans sa résolution 49/133.

Annex II

Conversion coefficients and factors

The metric system of weights and measures is employed in the *Statistical Yearbook*. In this system, the relationship between units of volume and capacity is: 1 litre = 1 cubic decimetre (dm^3) exactly (as decided by the 12th International Conference of Weights and Measures, New Delhi, November 1964).

Section A shows the equivalents of the basic metric, British imperial and United States units of measurements. According to an agreement between the national standards institutions of English-speaking nations, the British and United States units of length, area and volume are now identical, and based on the yard = 0.9144 metre exactly. The weight measures in both systems are based on the pound = 0.45359237 kilogram exactly (Weights and Measures Act 1963 (London), and *Federal Register* announcement of 1 July 1959: *Refinement of Values for the Yard and Pound* (Washington D.C.)).

Section B shows various derived or conventional conversion coefficients and equivalents.

Section C shows other conversion coefficients or factors which have been utilized in the compilation of certain tables in the *Statistical Yearbook*. Some of these are only of an approximate character and have been employed solely to obtain a reasonable measure of international comparability in the tables.

For a comprehensive survey of international and national systems of weights and measures and of units weights for a large number of commodities in different countries, see *World Weights and Measures* [61].

Annexe II

Coefficients et facteurs de conversion

L'*Annuaire statistique* utilise le système métrique pour les poids et mesures. La relation entre unités métriques de volume et de capacité est: 1 litre = 1 décimètre cube (dm^3) exactement (comme fut décidé à la Conférence internationale des poids et mesures, New Delhi, novembre 1964).

La section A fournit les équivalents principaux des systèmes de mesure métrique, britannique et américain. Suivant un accord entre les institutions de normalisation nationales des pays de langue anglaise, les mesures britanniques et américaines de longueur, superficie et volume sont désormais identiques, et sont basées sur le yard = 0:9144 mètre exactement. Les mesures de poids se rapportent, dans les deux systèmes, à la livre (pound) = 0.45359237 kilogramme exactement ("Weights and Measures Act 1963" (Londres), et "Federal Register Announcement of 1 July 1959: Refinement of Values for the Yard and Pound" (Washington, D.C.)).

La section B fournit divers coefficients et facteurs de conversion conventionnels ou dérivés.

La section C fournit d'autres coefficients ou facteurs de conversion utilisés dans l'élaboration de certains tableaux de l'*Annuaire statistique*. D'aucuns ne sont que des approximations et n'ont été utilisés que pour obtenir un degré raisonnable de comparabilité sur le plan international.

Pour une étude d'ensemble des systèmes internationaux et nationaux de poids et mesures, et d'unités de poids pour un grand nombre de produits dans différents pays, voir "*World Weights and Measures*" [61].

A. Equivalents of metric, British imperial and United States units of measure
A. Equivalents des unités métriques, britanniques et des Etats-Unis

Metric units / Unités métriques	British imperial and US equivalents / Equivalents en mesures britanniques et des Etats-Unis	British imperial and US units / Unités britanniques et des Etats-Unis	Metric equivalents / Equivalents en mesures métriques	
Length — Longueur				
1 centimetre – centimètre (cm)	0.3937008 inch	1 inch	2.540	cm
1 metre – mètre (m)	3.280840 feet	1 foot	30.480	cm
	1.093613 yard	1 yard	0.9144	m
1 kilometre – kilomètre (km)	0.6213712 mile	1 mile	1609.344	m
	0.5399568 int. naut. mile	1 international nautical mile	1852.000	m
Area — Superficie				
1 square centimetre – (cm²)	0.1550003 square inch	1 square inch	6.45160	cm²
1 square metre – (m²)	10.763910 square feet	1 square foot	9.290304	dm²
	1.195990 square yards	1 square yard	0.83612736	m²
1 hectare – (ha)	2.471054 acres	1 acre	0.4046856	ha
1 square kilometre – (km²)	0.3861022 square mile	1 square mile	2.589988	km²
Volume				
1 cubic centimetre – (cm³)	0.06102374 cubic inch	1 cubic inch	16.38706	cm³
1 cubic metre – (m³)	35.31467 cubic feet	1 cubic foot	28.316847	dm³
	1.307951 cubic yards	1 cubic yard	0.76455486	m³
Capacity — Capacité				
1 litre (l)	0.8798766 imp. quart	1 British imperial quart	1.136523	l
	1.056688 U.S. liq. quart	1 U.S. liquid quart	0.9463529	l
	0.908083 U.S. dry quart	1 U.S. dry quart	1.1012208	l
1 hectolitre (hl)	21.99692 imp. gallons	1 imperial gallon	4.546092	l
	26.417200 U.S. gallons	1 U.S. gallon	3.785412	l
	2.749614 imp. bushels	1 imperial bushel	36.368735	l
	2.837760 U.S. bushels	1 U.S. bushel	35.239067	l
Weight or mass — Poids				
1 kilogram (kg)	35.27396 av. ounces	1 av. ounce	28.349523	g
	32.15075 troy ounces	1 troy ounce	31.10348	g
	2.204623 av. pounds	1 av. pound	453.59237	g
		1 cental (100 lb.)	45.359237	kg
		1 hundredweight (112 lb.)	50.802345	kg
1 ton – tonne (t)	1.1023113 short tons	1 short ton (2 000 lb.)	0.9071847	t
	0.9842065 long tons	1 long ton (2 240 lb.)	1.0160469	t

B.   Various conventional or derived coefficients

Railway and air transport

1 passenger-mile = 1.609344 voyageur (passager) - kilomètre

1 short ton-mile = 1.459972 tonne-kilomètre

1 long ton-mile = 1.635169 tonne kilomètre

Ship tonnage

1 register ton (100 cubic feet) — tonne de jauge = 2.83m^3

1 British shipping ton (42 cubic feet) = 1.19m^3

1 U.S. shipping ton (40 cubic feet) = 1.13m^3

1 deadweight ton (dwt ton = long ton) = 1.016047 metric ton — tonne métrique

Electric energy

1 Kilowatt (kW) =   1.34102 British horsepower (hp)

1.35962 cheval vapeur (cv)

C.   Other coefficients or conversion factors employed in *Statistical Yearbook* tables

Roundwood

Equivalent in solid volume without bark.

Sugar

1 metric ton raw sugar = 0.9 metric ton refined sugar.

For the United States and its possessions:

1 metric ton refined sugar = 1.07 metric tons raw sugar.

B.   Divers coefficients conventionnels ou dérivés

Transport ferroviaire et aérien

1 voyageur (passager) - kilomètre = 0.621371) passenger-mile

1 tonne-kilomètre =   0.684945 short ton-mile

0.611558 long ton-mile

Tonnage de navire

1 cubic metre – m^3 = 0.353 register ton - tonne de jauge

0.841 British shipping ton

0.885 US shipping ton

1 metric ton — tonne métrique — 0.984 dwt ton

Energie électrique

1 British horsepower (hp) = 0.7457 kW

1 cheval vapeur (cv) = 0.735499 kW

C.   Autres coefficients ou facteurs de conversion utilisés dans les tableaux de l'*Annuaire statistique*

Bois rond

Equivalences en volume solide sans écorce.

Sucre

1 tonne métrique de sucre brut = 0.9 tonne métrique de sucre raffiné.

Pour les Etats-Unis et leurs possessions:

1 tonne métrique de sucre raffiné = 1.07 t.m. de sucre brut.

Annex III

Tables added and omitted

A. Tables added

The present issue of the *Statistical Yearbook* (2000) includes the following five tables which were not presented in the previous issue:

Table 9: Education at the primary, secondary and tertiary levels;

Table 24: Government final consumption expenditure by function at current prices;

Table 25: Household consumption expenditure by purpose in current prices;

Table 68: Ozone-depleting chlorofluorocarbons;

Table 70: Gross domestic expenditure on R&D by source of funds.

B.

The following six tables which were presented in the previous issues (45th and 46th) are not presented in the present issue. They will be updated in future issues of the *Yearbook* when new data become available:

Table 9: Population in urban and rural areas, rates of growth and largest urban agglomeration population (46th issue);

Table 10: Public expenditure on education: total and current (45th issue);

Table 11: Selected indicators of life expectancy, childbearing and mortality (46th issue);

Table 17: Television and radio receivers (46th issue);

Table 66: Water supply and sanitation coverage (45th issue);

Table 67: Threatened species (45th issue).

Annexe III

Tableaux ajoutés et supprimés

A. Tableaux ajoutés

Dans ce numéro de l'*Annuaire statistique* (2000), les cinq tableaux suivants qui n'ont pas été présentés dans le numéro antérieur, ont été ajoutés:

Tableau 9: Enseignement primaire, secondaire et supérieur;

Tableau 24: Consommation finale des administrations publiques par fonction aux prix courants;

Tableau 25: Dépenses de consommation des ménages par fonction aux prix courants;

Tableau 68: Chlorofluorocarbones qui appauvrissent la couche d'ozone;

Tableau 70: Dépenses intérieures brutes de recherche et développement par source de fonds.

B.

Les six tableaux suivants qui ont été repris dans les éditions antérieures (la 45ème et la 46ème éditions) n'ont pas été repris dans la présente édition. Ils seront actualisés dans les futures livraisons de l'*Annuaire* à mesure que des données nouvelles deviendront disponibles:

Tableau 9: Population urbaine, population rurale, taux d'accroissement et population de l'agglomération urbaine la plus peuplée (46ème édition);

Tableau 10: Dépenses publiques afférentes à l'éducation: totales et ordinaires (45ème édition);

Tableau 11: Choix d'indicateurs de l'espérance de vie, de maternité et de la mortalité (46ème édition);

Tableau 17: Récepteurs de télévision et de radiodiffusion sonore (46ème édition);

Tableau 66: Accès à l'eau et à l'assainissement (45ème édition);

Tableau 67: Espèces menacées (45ème édition).

Statistical sources and references

A.   Statistical sources

1.   American Automobile Manufacturers Association, *Motor Vehicle Facts and Figures 1997* (Detroit, USA).

2.   Auto and Truck International, *2001-2002 World Automotive Market Report* (Illinois, USA).

3.   Carbon Dioxide Information Analysis Center, *Global, Regional, and National CO$_2$ Emissions Estimates from Fossil-Fuel Burning, Hydraulic Cement Production, and Gas Flaring* (Oak Ridge, Tennessee, USA).

4.   Food and Agriculture Organization of the United Nations, *FAO Fertilizer Yearbook 2001* (Rome).

5.   _____, *FAO Food balance sheets, 1998-2000 average,* (Rome).

6.   _____, *FAO Production Yearbook 2001* (Rome).

7.   _____, *FAO Yearbook of Fishery Statistics 2000, Aquaculture production* (Rome).

8.   _____, *FAO Yearbook of Fishery Statistics 2000, Capture production* (Rome).

9.   _____, *FAO Yearbook of Forest Products 2001* (Rome).

10.   _____, *Global Forest Resources Assessment 2000* (Rome).

11.   International Civil Aviation Organization, *Civil Aviation Statistics of the World 1998* (Montreal).

12.   _____, *Digest of statistics — Traffic 1996-2000* (Montreal).

13.   International Labour Office, *Yearbook of Labour Statistics 2001* (Geneva).

14.   International Monetary Fund, *Balance of Payments Statistics Yearbook 2001* (Washington, D.C.).

15.   _____, *International Financial Statistics,* January 2003 (Washington, D.C.).

16.   International Sugar Organization, *Sugar Yearbook 2001* (London).

17.   International Telecommunication Union, *World Telecommunication Development Report 2002* (Geneva).

18.   _____, *Yearbook of Statistics, Telecommunication Services, Chronological Time Series 1991-2000* (Geneva).

19.   Lloyd's Register of Shipping, *World Fleet Statistics 2001* (London).

20.   Organisation for Economic Cooperation and Development, *Development Cooperation, 2001 Report* (Paris).

21.   _____, *Geographical Distribution of Financial Flows to Aid Recipients, 1996-2000* (Paris).

22.   United Nations, *Demographic Yearbook 2000* (United Nations publication, Sales No. E/F.02.XIII.1.

Sources statistiques et références

A.   Sources statistiques

1.   "American Automobile Manufacturers Association, *Motor Vehicle Facts and Figures 1997*" (Detroit, USA).

2.   "Auto and Truck International, *2001-2002 World Automotive Market Report*" (Illinois, USA).

3.   "Carbon Dioxide Information Analysis Center, "*Global, Regional, and National CO$_2$ Emissions Estimates from Fossil-Fuel Burning, Hydraulic Cement Production, and Gas Flaring*" (Oak Ridge, Tennessee, USA).

4.   Organisation des Nations Unies pour l'alimentation et l'agriculture, *Annuaire FAO des engrais 2001* (Rome).

5.   _____, *Bilans alimentaires de la FAO, moyenne 1998-2000* (Rome).

6.   _____, *Annuaire FAO de la production 2001* (Rome).

7.   _____, *Annuaire statistique des pêches 2000, production de l'aquaculture* (Rome).

8.   _____, *Annuaire statistique des pêches 2000, captures* (Rome).

9.   _____, *Annuaire FAO des produits forestiers 2001* (Rome).

10.   _____, *Evaluation des ressources forestières mondiales 2000* (Rome).

11.   Organisation de l'aviation civile internationale, *Statistiques de l'aviation civile dans le monde 1998* (Montréal).

12.   _____, *Recueil de statistiques — trafic 1996-2000* (Montréal).

13.   Bureau international du Travail, *Annuaire des statistiques du Travail 2001* (Genève).

14.   Fonds monétaire international, "*Balance of Payments Statistics Yearbook 2001*", (Washington, D.C.).

15.   _____, *Statistiques financières internationales,* janvier 2003 (Washington, D.C.).

16.   Organisation internationale du sucre, *Annuaire du sucre 2001* (Londres).

17.   Union internationale des télécommunications, "*World Telecommunication Development Report 2002*" (Genève).

18.   _____, "*Yearbook of Statistics, Telecommunication Services, Chronological Time Series 1991-2000*" (Genève).

19.   "Lloyd's Register of Shipping, *World Fleet Statistics 2001*" (Londres).

20.   Organisation de Coopération et de Développement Economiques, *Coopération pour le développement, Rapport 2001* (Paris).

21.   _____, *Répartition géographique des ressources financières allouées aux pays bénéficiaires de l'aide, 1996-2000* (Paris).

23. _____, *Energy Statistics Yearbook 1999* (United Nations publication, Sales No. E/F.02.XVII.7).

24. _____, *Industrial Commodity Statistics Yearbook 2000* (United Nations publications, Sales No. E/F.02.XVII.16).

25. _____, *International Trade Statistics Yearbook 2000*, vols. I and II (United Nations publication, Sales No. E/F.02.XVII.4).

26. _____, *Monthly Bulletin of Statistics*, various issues up to January 2003 (United Nations publication, Series Q).

27. _____, *National Accounts Statistics: Main Aggregates and Detailed Tables, 2000* (United Nations publication, Sales No. E.02.XVII.14).

28. _____, *Operational activities of the United Nations for international development cooperation , Report of the Secretary-General, Addendum, Comprehensive statistical data on operational activities for development for the year 2000* (A/56/320/Add2) and *Operational activities ... for the year 2001* (advanced version).

29. _____, *World Population Prospects: The 2000 Revision*, vols. I and II (United Nations publication, Sales No. E.01.XIII.8 and E.01.XIII.9).

30. _____, *World Urbanization Prospects: The 2001 Revision, Data Tables and Highlights* (ESA/P/WP.173, 20 March 2002).

31. United Nations Educational, Scientific and Cultural Organization Institute for Statistics, *Statistical Yearbook 1999* (Paris).

32. United Nations Environment Programme, Ozone Secretariat, *Production and Consumption of Ozone-Depleting Substances, 1986-1998* (Nairobi).

33. _____, World Conservation Monitoring Centre, *United Nations List of Protected Areas* (Nairobi).

34. United Nations Programme on HIV/AIDS and the World Health Organization, *Aids epidemic update: December 2002* (Geneva).

35. World Bank, *Global Development Finance*, vols. I and II, 2002 (Washington, D.C.).

36. World Health Organization and United Nations Children's Fund, *Revised 1990 Estimates of Maternal Mortality, A New Approach by WHO and UNICEF"* (Geneva).

37. World Intellectual Property Organization, *Industrial Property Statistics 2000, Publication A* (Geneva).

38. World Tourism Organization, *Yearbook of Tourism Statistics 2002* (Madrid).

22. Nations Unies, *Annuaire démographique 2000* (publication des Nations Unies, No de vente E/F.02.XIII.1).

23. _____, *Annuaire des statistiques de l'énergie 1999* (publication des Nations Unies, No de vente E/F.02.XVII.7).

24. _____, *Annuaire des statistiques industrielles par produit 2000* (publications des Nations Unies, No de vente E/F.02.XVII.16).

25. _____, *Annuaire statistique du commerce international 2000*, Vols. I et II (publication des Nations Unies, No de vente E/F.02.XVII.4).

26. _____, *Bulletin mensuel de statistique*, différentes éditions, jusqu'à janvier 2003 (publication des Nations Unies, Série Q).

27. _____, *"National Accounts Statistics: Main Aggregates and Detailed Tables 2000"* (publication des Nations Unies, No de vente E.02.XVII.14).

28. _____, *Activités opérationnelles du système des Nations Unies au service de la coopération internationale pour le développement, Rapport du Secrétaire général, Additif, Données statistiques globales sur les activités opérationnelles au service du développement pour 2000* (A/56/320/Add.2) et *Activités ... pour 2001* (version préliminaire).

29. _____, *"World Population Prospects: The 2000 Revision"*, Vols. I et II (publication des Nations Unies, No de vente E.01.XIII.8 et E.01.XIII.9).

30. _____, *World Urbanization Prospects: The 2001 Revision, Data Tables and Highlights* (ESA/P/WP.173, 20 mars 2002).

31. Institut de statististique de l'Organisation des Nations Unies pour l'éducation, la science et la culture, *Annuaire statistique 1999* (Paris).

32. Programme des Nations Unies pour l'environnement, Secrétariat de l'ozone, *"Production et consommation des substances qui appauvrissent la couche d'ozone, 1986-1998"* (Nairobi).

33. _____,, Centre mondial de surveillance pour la conservation, *"United Nations List of Protected Areas"* (Nairobi).

34. Programme des Nations Unies sur le VIH/SIDA et l'Organisation mondiale de la santé, *Le point sur l'épidémie de SIDA: décembre 2002* (Genève)

35. Banque mondiale, *"Global Development Finance, Vols. I et II, 2002"* (Washington, D.C.).

36. Organisation mondiale de la santé et Fonds des Nations Unies pour l'enfance, *"Revised 1990 Estimates of Maternal Mortality, A New Approach by WHO and UNICEF"* (Genève).

37. Organisation mondiale de la propriété intellectuelle, *Statistiques de propriété industrielle 2000, Publication A* (Genève).

38. Organisation mondiale du tourisme, *Annuaire des statistiques du tourisme 2002* (Madrid).

B.   References

39.   Food and Agriculture Organization of the United Nations, *The Fifth World Food Survey 1985* (Rome 1985).

40.   International Labour Office, *International Standard Classification of Occupations, Revised Edition 1968* (Geneva, 1969); revised edition, 1988, *ISCO-88* (Geneva, 1990).

41.   International Monetary Fund, *Balance of Payments Manual, Fifth Edition* (Washington, D.C., 1993).

42.   Stanton, C. et al, *Modelling maternal mortality in the developing world*, mimeo, November 1995 (Geneva and New York, WHO, UNICEF).

43.   United Nations, *Basic Methodological Principles Governing the Compilation of the System of Statistical Balances of the National Economy*, Studies in Methods, Series F, No. 17, Rev. 1, vols. 1 and 2 (United Nations publications, Sales No. E.89.XVII.5 and E.89.XVII.3).

44.   _____, *Classifications of Expenditure According to Purpose: Classification of the Functions of Government (COFOG), Classification of Individual Consumption According to Purpose (COICOP), Classification of the Purposes of Non-Profit Institutions Serving Households (COPNI), Classification of the Outlays of Producers According to Purpose (COPP)*, Series M, No. 84 (United Nations publication, Sales No. E.00.XVII.6).

45.   _____, *Energy Statistics: Definitions, Units of Measure and Conversion Factors*, Series F, No. 44 (United Nations publication, Sales No. E.86.XVII.21).

46.   _____, *Energy Statistics: Manual for Developing Countries*, Series F, No. 56 (United Nations publication, Sales No. E.91.XVII.10).

47.   _____, *Handbook of Vital Statistics Systems and Methods*, vol. I, *Legal, Organization and Technical Aspects*, Series F, No. 35, vol. I (United Nations publication, Sales No. E.91.XVII.5).

48.   _____, *Handbook on Social Indicators*, Studies in Methods, Series F, No. 49 (United Nations publication, Sales No. E.89.XVII.6).

49.   _____, *International Recommendations for Industrial Statistics*, Series M, No. 48, Rev. 1 (United Nations publication, Sales No. E.83.XVII.8).

50.   _____, *International Standard Industrial Classification of All Economic Activities*, Statistical Papers, Series M, No. 4, Rev. 2 (United Nations publication, Sales No. E.68.XVII.8); Rev. 3 (United Nations publication, Sales No. E.90.XVII.11).

51.   _____, *International Trade Statistics: Concepts and Definitions*, Series M, No. 52, Rev. 1 (United Nations publication, Sales No. E.82.XVII.14).

52.   _____, *Methods Used in Compiling the United Nations Price Indexes for External Trade*, volume 1, Statistical Papers, Series M, No. 82 (United Nations Publication, Sales No. E.87.XVII.4).

B.   Références

39.   Organisation des Nations Unies pour l'alimentation et l'agriculture, *Cinquième enquête mondiale sur l'alimentation 1985* (Rome, 1985).

40.   Organisation internationale du Travail, *Classification internationale type des professions, édition révisée* 1968 (Genève, 1969); édition révisée 1988, *CITP-88* (Genève, 1990).

41.   Fonds monétaire international, *Manuel de la balance des paiements, cinquième édition* (Washington, D.C., 1993).

42.   Stanton, C, et al, "*Modelling maternal mortality in the developing world*", novembre 1995 (Genève et New York, WHO, UNICEF).

43.   Organisation des Nations Unies, *Principes méthodologiques de base régissant l'établissement des balances statistiques de l'économie nationale*, Série F, No 17, Rev.1 Vol. 1 et Vol. 2 (publication des Nations Unies, No de vente F.89.XVII.5 et F.89.XVII.3).

44.   _____, "*Classifications of Expenditure According to Purpose: Classification of the Functions of Government (COFOG), Classification of Individual Consumption According to Purpose (COICOP), Classification of the Purposes of Non-Profit Institutions Serving Households (COPNI), Classification of the Outlays of Producers According to Purpose (COPP)*", Série M, No 84 (publication des Nations Unies, No de vente E. 00.XVII.6).

45.   _____, *Statistiques de l'énergie: définitions, unités de mesures et facteurs de conversion*, Série F, No 44 (publication des Nations Unies, No de vente F.86.XVII.21).

46.   _____, *Statistiques de l'énergie: Manuel pour les pays en développement*, Série F, No 56 (publication des Nations Unies, No de vente F.91.XVII.10).

47.   _____, "*Handbook of Vital Statistics System and Methods*, Vol. 1, *Legal, Organization and Technical Aspects*", Série F, No 35, Vol. 1 (publication des Nations Unies, No de vente E.91.XVII.5).

48.   _____, *Manuel des indicateurs sociaux*, Série F, No 49 (publication des Nations Unies, No de vente F.89.XVII.6).

49.   _____, *Recommandations internationales concernant les statistiques industrielles*, Série M, No 48, Rev. 1 (publication des Nations Unies, No de vente F.83.XVII.8).

50.   _____, *Classification internationale type, par industrie, de toutes les branches d'activité économique*, Série M, No 4, Rev. 2 (publication des Nations Unies, No de vente F.68.XVII.8); Rev. 3 (publication des Nations Unies, No de vente F.90.XVII.11).

51.   _____, *Statistiques du commerce international: Concepts et définitions*, Série M, No 52, Rev. 1 (publication des Nations Unies, No de vente F.82.XVII.14).

53.   _____, *Principles and Recommendations for Population and Housing Censuses*, Statistical Papers, Series M, No. 67 (United Nations publication, Sales No. E.80.XVII.8).

54.   _____, *Provisional Guidelines on Statistics of International Tourism*, Statistical Papers, Series M, No. 62 (United Nations publication, Sales No. E.78.XVII.6).

55.   _____ and World Tourism Organization, *Recommendations on Tourism Statistics*, Statistical Papers, Series M, No. 83 (United Nations publication, Sales No. E.94.XVII.6).

56.   _____, *Standard International Trade Classification, Revision 3*, Statistical Papers, Series M, No. 34, Rev. 3 (United Nations publication, Sales No. E.86.XVII.12), *Revision 2*, Series M, No. 34, Rev. 2 (United Nations publication), *Revision*, Series M, No. 34, Revision (United Nations publication, Sales No. E.61.XVII.6).

57.   _____, *Supplement to the Statistical Yearbook and the Monthly Bulletin of Statistics, 1977,* Series S and Series Q, Supplement 2 (United Nations publication, Sales No. E.78.XVII.10).

58.   _____, *System of National Accounts, Studies in Methods*, Series F, No. 2, Rev. 3 (United Nations publication, Sales No. E.69.XVII.3).

59.   _____, *System of National Accounts 1993*, Studies in Methods, Series F, No. 2, Rev. 4 (United Nations publication, Sales No. E.94.XVII.4).

60.   _____, *Towards a System of Social and Demographic Statistics, Studies in Methods*, Series F, No. 18 (United Nations publication, Sales No. E.74.XVII.8).

61.   _____, World Weights and Measures (United Nations publication, Sales No. E.66.XVII.3).

62.   World Health Organization, *Manual of the International Statistical Classification of Diseases, Injuries and Causes of Death*, vol. 1 (Geneva, 1977).

63.   World Tourism Organization, *Methodological Supplement to World Travel and Tourism Statistics* (Madrid, 1985).

52.   _____, *Méthodes utilisées par les Nations Unies pour établir les indices des prix des produits de base entrant dans le commerce international*, Série M, No 82, Vol. 1 (publication des Nations Unies, No de vente F.87.XVII.4).

53.   _____, *Principes et recommandations concernant les recensements de la population et de l'habitation*, Série M, No 67 (publication des Nations Unies, No de vente F.80.XVII.8).

54.   _____, *Directives provisoires pour l'établissement des statistiques du tourisme international*, Série M, No 62 (publication des Nations Unies, No de vente 78.XVII.6).

55.   _____ et l'Organisation mondiale du tourisme, "*Recommendations on Tourism Statistics*, Statistical Papers", Série M, No. 83 (publication des Nations Unies, No. de vente E.94.XVII.6).

56.   _____, *Classification type pour le commerce international (troisième version révisée)*, Série M, No 34, Rev. 3 (publication des Nations Unies, No de vente F.86.XVII.12), *Révision 2*, Série M, No 34, Rev. 2 (publication des Nations Unies), *Révision*, Série M, No. 34, Révision (publication des Nations Unies, No de vente F.61.XVII.6).

57.   _____, *Supplément à l'Annuaire statistique et au bulletin mensuel de statistique, 1977,* Série S et Série Q, supplément 2 (publication des Nations Unies, No de vente F.78.XVII.10).

58.   _____, *Système de comptabilité nationale*, Série F, No 2, Rev. 3 (publication des Nations Unies, No de vente F.69.XVII.3).

59.   _____, *Système de comptabilité nationale 1993*, Série F, No 2, Rev. 4 (publication des Nations Unies, No de vente F.94.XVII.4).

60.   _____, *Vers un système de statistiques démographiques et sociales, Etudes méthodologiques,* Série F, No 18 (publication des Nations Unies, No. de vente F.74.XVII.8).

61.   _____, "*World Weights and Measures*" (publication des Nations Unies, No. de vente E.66.XVII.3).

62.   Organisation mondiale de la santé, *Manuel de la classification statistique internationale des maladies, traumatismes et causes de décès*, Vol. 1 (Genève, 1977).

63.   Organisation mondiale du tourisme, *Supplément méthodologique aux statistiques des voyages et du tourisme mondiaux* (Madrid, 1985).

Index

Note: References to tables are indicated by **boldface** type. For citations of organizations, see the Index of Organizations.

Index of Organizations